Gerontologic Nursing

9,30,27,29,11,13,10

Gerontologic Nursing

ANNETTE G. LUECKENOTTE, MS, RN, CS

Gerontological Nurse Practitioner
Alexian Brothers Senior Health Center
St. Louis, Missouri

WITH 227 ILLUSTRATONS

Mosby

St. Louis Baltimore Boston Carlsbad Chicago Naples New York Philadelphia Portland
London Madrid Mexico City Singapore Sydney Tokyo Toronto Wiesbaden

Mosby
Dedicated to Publishing Excellence

A Times Mirror
Company

Publisher: Nancy L. Coon
Editor: Michael S. Ledbetter
Associate Developmental Editor: Cecily S. Barolak
Project Manager: Deborah L. Vogel
Production Editor: Mamata Reddy
Manufacturing Supervisor: Linda Ierardi
Designer: Elizabeth Fett
Original Illustrations: Jack Reuter
Unit Opener Photographs: Loy W. Ledbetter, Jr., Ursula Ruhl, Rod Schmall

A Note to the Reader:
The author and publisher have made every attempt to check dosages and nursing content for accuracy. Because the science of pharmacology is continually advancing, our knowledge base continues to expand. Therefore we recommend that the reader always check product information for changes in dosage or administration before administering any medication. This is particularly important with new or rarely used drugs.

Printed in the United States of America
Composition by Graphic World, Inc.
Printing/binding by Courier Companies, Inc.

Mosby-Year Book, Inc.
11830 Westline Industrial Drive
St. Louis, Missouri 63146

Library of Congress Cataloging-in-Publication Data

Gerontologic nursing / [edited by] Annette G. Lueckenotte.
p. cm.
Includes bibliographical references and index.
ISBN 0-8016-7414-X (alk. paper)
1. Geriatric nursing. I. Lueckenotte, Annette Giesler.
[DNLM: 1. Geriatric Nursing. 2. Aged—psychology. 3. Long-Term Care—in old age. WY 152 G37705 1995]
RC954.G4735 1995
610.73'65—dc20
DNLM/DLC
for Library of Congress 95-38025
CIP

95 96 97 98 99 / 9 8 7 6 5 4 3 2 1

Contributors

Karen Baker, MSN, RN,C
Clinical Nurse Specialist
Clinical Center
National Institutes of Health
Bethesda, Maryland

Diana C. Ballard, JD, MBA, RN
President
Ballard Management Group
Cheshire, Connecticut
of counsel
Susman, Duffy & Segaloff, PC
ATTORNEYS AT LAW
New Haven, Connecticut

Martha Hains Bramlett, PhD, RN
Research Scientist
Gerontology Center
University of Georgia
Athens, Georgia

Gina M. Bufe, MSN(R), RN, CS
Psychiatric Clinical Nurse Specialist
Barnes-Jewish Psychiatric Services
Barnes Hospital
St. Louis, Missouri

Patricia M. Burbank, DNSc, RN
Associate Professor
College of Nursing
University of Rhode Island
White Hall, Kingston, Rhode Island

Kathryn E. Christiansen, DNSc, MA, BSN
Assistant Professor
Department of Community Health
Rush University College of Nursing
Administrator
Rush Home Care Network
Chicago, Illinois

Brenda S. Gregory Dawes, MSN, RN, CNOR
Director
Surgical Services
St. Anthony's Hospital
St. Petersburg, Florida

Donna Deane, PhD, RN
Professor Emeritus of Nursing
Wright State University
Dayton, Ohio

Mary Ellen Dellefield, MS, RN
Instructor
University of Phoenix
San Diego, California

Sharon Dudley-Brown, PhD, MS, RN,C, FNP
Assistant Professor
Department of Nursing
The Chinese University of Hong Kong
Hong Kong

Janet Dugan, MS, RN
Coordinator
Continuing Education
Good Samaritan Hospital
Dayton, Ohio

Sandra Joyce Hayes Engberg, PhD, CRNP
School of Nursing
University of Pittsburgh
Pittsburgh, Pennsylvania

Betty R. Ferrell, PhD, RN, FAAN
Associate Research Scientist
City of Hope National Medical Center
Duarte, California

Teresa Morris Garrison, BSN, RN,C
Clinical Nurse Manager
Vencor-St. Louis Hospital
St. Louis, Missouri

Sarah H. Gueldner, DNSc, FAAN
Professor and Director of Doctoral Studies
College of Nursing
Medical University of South Carolina
Charleston, South Carolina

Joyce A. Guillory, PhD, RN
Assistant Professor and Director
Cancer Prevention Awareness Program
Department of Community Health/Preventive Medicine
Morehouse School of Medicine
Atlanta, Georgia

Sandra L. Hensel, MSN(R), RN
Inservice/Quality Improvement Coordinator
Barnes Extended Care
Clayton, Missouri

Mildred O. Hogstel, PhD, RN,C
Professor Emeritus
Harris College of Nursing
Texas Christian University
Fort Worth, Texas

June F. Johnson, PhD
Pharmacotherapy Specialist
Fellow of the American Society of Health-System Pharmacists
Assistant Professor of Pharmacy
Department of Pharmacy Practice
Drake University
Des Moines, Iowa

Rhonda Kirk-Gardner, MSN, RN, BSN, BAd
Associate Professor
School of Nursing
Lakehead University
Thunder Bay, Ontario
Canada

Karen Van Dyke Lamb, ND, RN, CS
Practitioner-Teacher and Assistant Professor
Rush University College of Nursing
Chicago, Illinois

Marjorie A. Maddox, EdD, MSN, ARNP, ANP-C
Associate Professor and Coordinator
Adult Nurse Practitioner Option
School of Nursing
University of Louisville
Louisville, Kentucky

Judith J. McCann, DNSc, RN
Assistant Professor in Gerontological Nursing
Rush University College of Nursing
Research Faculty
Rush Institute on Aging
Rush-Presbyterian—St. Luke's Medical Center
Chicago, Illinois

B. Joan McDowell, PhD, CRNP, FAAN
School of Nursing
University of Pittsburgh
Pittsburgh, Pennsylvania

Deanna Lynn Gray Miceli, MSN, RN, CS
Gerontological Nurse Practitioner
Center for Aging
School of Osteopathic Medicine
University of Medicine and Dentistry of New Jersey
Stratford, New Jersey

Jean R. Miller, PhD, RN
Professor
College of Nursing
University of Rhode Island
White Hall, Kingston, Rhode Island

Linda K. Mosel, MSN, RN, CS
Gerontology Clinical Nurse Specialist
Good Samaritan Hospital
Dayton, Ohio

Catherine E. O'Connor, DNSc, RN, CS
Former Associate Chief
Nursing Service for Long-Term Care
Veterans Administration
Miami, Florida

Ann Peterson, MSN, RN, CDE
Clinical Nurse Specialist
Clinical Center
National Institutes of Health
Bethesda, Maryland

Lynne M. Rivera, MSN, RN
Research Specialist
City of Hope National Medical Center
Duarte, California

Susan L. Sanders, MSN, RN,C, GNP
Nurse Practitioner
Midland Community Clinics
Midland, Texas

Vicki L. Schmall, PhD
Professor Emeritus
Oregon State University
Former Gerontology Specialist
Oregon State University Extension Service
Corvallis, Oregon

Darlene Steven, PhD, MHSA, BSN, BA, RN
Associate Professor
School of Nursing
Lakehead University
Thunder Bay, Ontario
Canada

Tamara Reavis Tripp, MSN, RN, CS
Gerontological Nurse Practitioner
Nalle Clinic
Charlotte, North Carolina

Meredith Wallace, MSN, RN, CS
Geriatric Nurse Specialist
Senior Services
Hospital of Saint Raphael
Lecturer
Department of Nursing
Southern Connecticut State University
New Haven, Connecticut

Susan Mace Weeks, MS, RN
Instructor of Nursing
Harris College of Nursing
Texas Christian University
Fort Worth, Texas

Ruth B. Weg, PhD, MS, BA
Professor Emeritus in Gerontology and Biology
Andrus Gerontology Center
University of Southern California
Los Angeles, California

Pamela Becker Weilitz, MSN(R), RN, CS
Manager, Nursing Care Delivery
Barnes-Jewish Hospitals
BJC Health System
Pulmonary Clinical Nurse Specialist
Adult Nurse Practitioner
Assistant Clinical Professor
Saint Louis University
St. Louis, Missouri

Alice Welch, PhD, RN, CTN
Nursing Consultant
Associate Professor
School of Nursing
Indiana State University
Terre Haute, Indiana

Gail Wilkerson, MSN, RN, CS
Quality Practice Manager
Gerontological Clinical Specialist
Deaconess Home Health Services
St. Louis, Missouri

Carol Will, MA, RN,C
Nurse Gerontologist
Consultant to Health Care Facilities, Educational Institutions, and Businesses
Private Care Manager
Will's Consulting
Keokuk, Iowa

Clinical Consultants

June N. Allen, MSN, RN,C
Associate Professor and Certified Gerontology Nurse
Lorain County Community College
Elyria, Ohio

Judith A. Anderson, MSN, RN
Assistant Professor
Medical College of Ohio
Toledo, Ohio

Doris Almoney, BS, GDH
Quality of Life, Inc.
St. Louis, Missouri

Margaret M. Andrews, PhD, RN, CTN
Chairperson and Professor, Department of Nursing
Nazareth College
Rochester, New York

Linda M.E. Auton, JD, RN
Law Office of Linda M.E. Auton
Abington, Massachusettes

Elizabeth Burch, MSN, BSN, RN
Douglas, Georgia

MaryBeth Tank Buschmann, PhD, MS, BSN, RN
Professor Medical-Surgical Nursing
University of Illinois at Chicago
Chicago, Illinois

Carol J. Chancey, MS, RN
Nursing Department
St. Petersburg Junior College
St. Petersburg, Florida

Nancy Ciasulli, MA, RN, CS
Instructor
Ann May School of Nursing
Neptune, New Jersey

Renee Clermont, RN, CS-P
The Kennedy Krieger Institute
Baltimore, Maryland

Mary Ann Cosgarea, BSN, RN
Portage Lakes Career Center
W. Howard Nicol School of Practical Nursing
Green, Ohio

Charlene M. Courbet, BA, RN
Director of Needs Assessment and Referral
Charter Behavioral Health Systems-Palm Springs
Cathedral City, California

Dorothy Crews, MA, RN
Instructor
Modesto Junior College A.S.D.N.
Modesto, California

Pamela D. Dennison, MSN, RN
Charlottesville, Virginia

Kristen L. Easton, MS, RN, CRRN
Assistant Professor of Nursing
Valparaiso University
Valparaiso, Indiana

Janet N. Franck, MBA, RN, CIC
President
Consulting Practitioners, Inc.
St. Louis, Missouri

Eleanor Sidor Garrison, MS, RN
College of Nursing
Arizona State University
Tempe, Arizona

Judith W. Harmer, MS, RN
Golden West College
Huntington Beach, California

Sandra Hirst, MSC(nEd), RN, THD(c)
University of Calgary
Calgary, Alberta
Canada

Linda M. Hollinger-Smith, PhD, RN
Rush University College of Nursing
Rush-Presbyterian—St. Luke's Medical Center
Chicago, Illinois

Katherine Purgatorio Howard, MSN, RN,C
Newark Beth Israel Medical Center
Newark, New Jersey

Barbara B. Hutchinson
Professor
Associate Degree Nursing Program
Mt. San Antonio College
Walnut, California

Joan M. Iannone, MSN, RN,C, GNP
WAKE-AHEC Internal Medicine
Raleigh, North Carolina

Mary L. Killeen, PhD, RN
College of Nursing
Arizona State University
Tempe, Arizona

Janet C. Lundstrom, MS, RSN
Blackhawk Technical College
Janesville, Wisconsin

Janet L. McDaniel, PhD, RN
Associate Professor and Graduate Program Coordinator
School of Nursing
Radford University
Radford, Virginia

Andrew T. McPhee
Former LPN Instructor
Windham Regional Technical School
Wilmantic, Connecticut

Helen Monea, MS, RN
Lecturer
School of Nursing
San Francisco State University
San Francisco, California

Sheila A. Niles, MSN, RN,C
Director
Community Projects and Elder Health
Visiting Nurse Association of Cleveland
Cleveland, Ohio

Doris Price-Nealy, MSN, RN
Director
Associate Degree Nursing Program
Department of Nursing
Lamar University
Beaumont, Texas

Claire H. Raymond, Pharm D
Medical Services Manager
Bristol-Meyers Squibb
Cincinnati, Ohio

Susan Ruzicka, MSN(R), CNS
Doctoral Student
University of Texas Health Science Center at San Antonio
San Antonio, Texas

Mary Ellen Simmons, MS, RN,C, BSN
Assistant Professor of Nursing
Oakton Community College
Des Plaines, Illinois

Marlene Smith, MSN, RN, CS, FNP
Clinical Faculty
College of Nursing
University of Illinois at Chicago
Chicago, Illinois

Yvonne N. Stock, MS, RN
Professor of Nursing
Iowa Western Community College
Council Bluffs, Iowa

Barbara Swanson, DNSc, RN
University of Illinois
Chicago, Illinois

Anna M. Tichy, PhD, MS, BS
Professor
Department of Public Health, Mental Health, and Administrative Nursing
University of Illinois at Chicago
Chicago, Illinois

Golden Tradewell, MA, MSN, RN
Assistant Professor
McNeese State University
Lake Charles, Louisiana

Ralph W. Trottier, PhD, JD
Department of Pharmacology and Toxicology
Morehouse School of Medicine
Atlanta, Georgia

Barbara Redding Weaver, MS, RN,C
Professor Emeritus
School of Nursing
Capital University
Columbus, Ohio

Darline J. Wilke, EdD, RN
North Park College
Chicago, Illinois

Arlene Witman, GNP, MSN, RN
Ocean County College
Toms Rivers, New Jersey

IN LOVING MEMORY OF MY PARENTS, *TURK* AND *BERNICE,*

MY GRANDPARENTS,

AND ALL OF THE OLDER PEOPLE IN MY CIRCLE OF FAMILY AND FRIENDS

WHO INSTILLED IN ME A HEALTHY OUTLOOK

ON OLD AGE AND AGING.

THEIR SPIRITS CONTINUE TO GUIDE ME.

Preface

Throughout history, nursing has evolved to meet the continually changing needs and demands of the populations being served. The many, varied clients nurses have cared for and the nature of their problems have largely defined the knowledge and skills required for practice. So it is that the nearly 13 million people in the United States today who are 65 and older have shaped the practice of nursing in a most profound manner. As the fastest-growing segment of the entire population, the multiple complex issues concerning older adult's health have become a determining force in the national health care scene. Medical advances and technologic achievements have resulted in longer, healthier lives with fewer diseases and more treatable conditions. Consequently, nurses in a wide variety of settings and roles are finding themselves challenged to provide care to an increasing number of older people, all in the face of the great demands being placed on human and material resources in today's cost-conscious environment. To effectively meet this challenge, nurses must be knowledgeable and caring professionals committed to providing quality, age-appropriate nursing care to this special group of people.

Gerontologic Nursing has been developed to provide students a sound foundation to meet the challenges of gerontologic nursing practice. This textbook provides comprehensive theoretical and practical information about basic and complex concepts and issues relevant to the care of older people in a variety of settings. The extensive coverage provides the student with information necessary to make sound clinical judgments, while emphasizing the concepts, skills, and techniques of gerontologic nursing practice. Psychologic and sociocultural issues and aspects of older adult care are given special emphasis, while at the same time, are integrated throughout the textbook. Care of both well and sick older people and their families/caregivers is included.

Intended for use by undergraduate nursing students in all levels of professional nursing programs, *Gerontologic Nursing* may be used in gerontologic nursing or medical-surgical nursing courses, or within programs that integrate gerontologic content throughout the educational program. Graduate students beginning their course of gerontologic nursing study will find this textbook to be comprehensive and complete in its coverage of essential content.

ORGANIZATION

The 33 chapters of *Gerontologic Nursing* are divided into seven parts. Part One, Introduction to Gerontologic Nursing, includes four chapters that serve as the foundation for the remainder of the textbook. Chapter 1 introduces the student to the specialty by addressing historical developments, educational preparation and practice roles, future trends, and demographic factors relevant to the health and well-being of older people. Basic tenets of selected biologic, sociologic, and psychologic theories of aging, and their relevance to nursing practice are presented in Chapter 2. Chapter 3 presents an overview of practice standards, relevant laws affecting care of older adults in a variety of settings, and principles of values, ethics, and legal issues as related to care of older people. The fourth chapter discusses the importance of a nursing-focused assessment, special considerations affecting assessment of the older person, and strategies and techniques for collecting a comprehensive health assessment. Functional, mental status, affective, and social assessment tools and techniques are included.

Part Two, Influences on Health and Illness, includes three chapters on cultural, family, and socioeconomic and environmental influences. Chapter 5 presents cultural concepts within the contexts of aging, and the health and illness experiences of older people. Roles and functions of families, common family issues and decisions in later life, and family caregiving are described in Chapter 6. Techniques and considerations for working with aging families, including crisis intervention, are also explained. Chapter 7 presents an overview of socioeconomic and environmental factors that affect health and illness, including issues associated with resource availability.

Part Three, Special Issues, details the needs and nursing care of older adults in the areas of nutrition, sleep and activity, intimacy and sexuality, safety, and mental health. Chapter 8 explores the role of nutrition in health and illness and its impact on the aging process. Age-related factors in maintaining a balance between sleep and activity and their impact on the older person's lifestyle are discussed in Chapter 9. Chapter 10 sensitively addresses the intimacy and sexuality needs of older adults, offering practical management strategies. Chapter 11 stresses the importance of a safe environment within the context of maintaining the older person's autonomy. In Chapter 12, the commonly occurring mental, emotional, and behavioral problems experienced by older people are discussed, including availability of resources and trends in treatment and care. Each chapter presents the normal physiologic structure, alterations, or changes related to the aging process, and nursing interventions to promote healthy adaptation to the identified changes.

Part Four, Common Psychophysiologic Stressors, focuses on the special needs of older adults with pain, infection, cancer, chronic illness, and substance abuse, as well as nursing measures related to loss, death, and dying. Chapter 13 provides an overview of pain and the special issues surrounding pain management in older people. The importance and significance of immunity and factors affecting immunocompetence in aging, as well as associated common problems and conditions, are explored in Chapter 14. The nursing management of older adults with the most commonly occurring cancers is addressed in Chapter 15. Chapter 16 examines the concepts of chronic illness and rehabilitation in aging, as well as the related concepts of compliance, self-care, functional ability, psychosocial and physiologic needs, and the impact on family and caregiver. Chapter 17 discusses perceptions, meanings, responses, and nursing care of the older adult experiencing loss, dying, and death. The problem of substance abuse in older adults is presented in Chapter 18, including risk factors, assessment tools and techniques, and nursing interventions for the most commonly abused substances. All of these chapters emphasize the nurse's role in effectively managing the nursing care of clients with these problems.

Part Five, Special Interventions, includes Chapter 19, Laboratory and Diagnostic Tests, and Chapter 20, Pharmacologic Management. Principles of laboratory testing in older adults, including values for hematologic, blood, and urine chemistry as well as other important screening tests for this population, are presented in Chapter 19. Chapter 20 contains current and comprehensive information on the critical issue of medications and the myriad of issues pertinent to drug use in this population.

Part Six, Nursing Care of Clients with Physiologic and Psychologic Disorders, contains nine chapters that detail nursing management of older adults with diseases or conditions of cardiovascular, respiratory, endocrine, liver, gastrointestinal, renal and urinary, neurologic and cognitive, integumentary, sensory, and musculoskeletal function.

Part Seven, Special Care Settings, includes the final three chapters in which the critical issues surrounding care of older people in acute, home, and long-term care settings are discussed.

An attempt was made to organize *Gerontologic Nursing* in a logical sequence, and by grouping related topics. However, it is not necessary to read the text in sequence. Material is cross-referenced throughout the text, and an extensive index is included.

FEATURES

Each chapter begins with **Learning Objectives** to help the student focus on the important subject matter. **Emergency Treatment** boxes alert students to emergency situations and provide immediate interventions. **Client/Family Teaching** boxes are included where appropriate to provide guidelines for instructing the client and family for continued quality care. **Research** boxes are presented to emphasize the application of relevant study findings to current nursing practice. **Insights** are integrated throughout that present an idea, concept or notion aimed at challenging traditional thought related to gerontologic nursing care. **Cultural Awareness** boxes are included where applicable to develop the student's cultural sensitivity to assuring effective care.

Each chapter concludes with a brief **Summary,** followed by **Key Points** that highlight important principles discussed in the chapter. **Critical Thinking Exercises** at the end of every chapter stimulate the student to reflect on the material learned and to guide the students to apply their knowledge. In addition, at the conclusion of the body system and clinical chapters, **Home Care Tips** provide pragmatic suggestions for care of the home care client and family.

FORMAT

The information in *Gerontologic Nursing* has been formatted for ease of use and reference. The clinical examples depict nurses practicing in many different roles from a wide variety of care settings. An attempt has been made to delete sexist language when referring to both clients and nurses.

All body system chapters include an overview of **normal structure and function,** followed by **age-related changes in structure and function.** Common problems and conditions are presented in a format that includes the definition, etiology, pathophysiology, and typical clinical presentation for each. **Medical Management** boxes provide a brief summary of the diagnosis, treatment, and prognosis of common problems and conditions. The **Nursing Management** of the problems/conditions is central to each of these chapters and follows the five-step nursing process format of assessment, diagnosis, planning, intervention, and evaluation. **Nursing Care Plans** for selected problems/conditions begin with a realistic clinical situation and emphasize the nursing diagnoses pertinent to the situation, expected outcomes, and interventions, all within an easy-to-reference, three-column format.

An *Instructor's Resource Manual,* the first for a gerontologic nursing textbook, has been developed in response to great demand for such an item. This ancillary follows the textbook chapter by chapter, and includes chapter outlines and overviews, as well as teaching suggestions to aid lecture preparation. Classroom and practice applications focus on teaching strategies to help students apply what they have learned in the classroom and in clinical settings. The Instructor's Resource Manual also includes a 350-question test bank in NCLEX format, with an answer key including textbook page references.

ACKNOWLEDGMENTS

I am sincerely grateful for the many contributions made by the following people, without whom the creation and development of this textbook would not have been possible:

To the original editor at the beginning of this project, Linda Duncan, for her publishing knowledge and experience that guided the development of the concept of this textbook. And to the original developmental editor, Kathy Sartori, for her incredible energy, enthusiasm, and commitment to getting this project off the ground.

To my editor, Michael Ledbetter, whose support, encouragement, and good humor from the beginning of our relationship have served to guide me through some difficult times in creating this textbook.

To Cecily Barolak, my developmental editor, who came on board in the middle of this project with her quiet determination and tenacity. Her commitment to tracking the progress of contributors and manuscripts, attention to every detail, and patience with the many people and problems associated with this undertaking have meant the difference between success and failure in many instances. Her assistance and support have sustained me.

To my production editor, Mamata Reddy, for her enthusiasm, attention to detail, and sincere interest in creating a quality finished product. It has been my pleasure to work with such an energetic and dedicated woman.

To the many talented experts who have contributed to *Gerontologic Nursing,* I am genuinely grateful to each of you for the commitment of time and effort to making this work possible. You have provided current, comprehensive, and essential concepts and principles related to the care of older people that will add to the growing body of gerontologic nursing literature.

To Carol J. Green and Penny L. Marshall, for their work in developing the Instructor's Resource Manual.

To Margaret Andrews, for developing the Cultural Awareness boxes, and to Golden Tradewell, for developing the Home Care Tips boxes.

To the reviewers, who have provided valuable feedback and recommendations, enabling me to develop a quality textbook that meets the needs of students.

To illustrators Jack Reuter and Nadine Sokol of St. Louis, and to photographers Loy Ledbetter and Ursula Ruhl of St. Louis and Rod Schmall of West Linn, Oregon, all of whose work has reinforced the textbook's visual appeal.

To my loving family and friends, for their patience, understanding, and support during these several years of sacrifice. The words of encouragement and emotional support each of you so generously gave made all of this worthwhile. I treasure ALL of you in my heart.

Annette Giesler Lueckenotte

Contents

Part Six

Nursing Care of Physiologic and Psychologic Disorders

Part Seven
Special Care Settings

Part One

Introduction to Gerontologic Nursing

CHAPTER 1

Overview of Gerontologic Nursing

LEARNING OBJECTIVES

On completion of this chapter, the reader will be able to:

1. Trace the historic development of gerontologic nursing as a specialty.
2. Distinguish the educational preparation, practice roles, and certification requirements of the gerontologic nurse generalist, practitioner, and clinical nurse specialist.
3. Discuss the major demographic trends in the United States in relation to the older adult population.
4. Identify the factors responsible for the rapidly growing older adult population.
5. Describe the effects of each of the following demographic factors on the health, well-being, and life expectancy of older people:
   - Sex and marital status
   - Race
   - Housing/living situation
   - Educational status
   - Financial status
6. Explain why old age is considered a woman's problem.
7. Describe the effect of functional ability on the overall health status of an older person.
8. Discuss how the "aging of the aged" will affect health care delivery.
9. Explore future trends in gerontologic nursing care in the acute, long-term, and home care settings.
10. Explore the concept of ageism as related to the care of older people in various settings.
11. Discuss the development of gerontologic nursing content in curricula at all levels of nursing education.
12. Analyze the issues affecting the development and future of gerontologic nursing research.

FOUNDATIONS OF THE SPECIALTY OF GERONTOLOGIC NURSING

The rich, diverse history of nursing has always been shaped by the population it serves. From the early beginnings of Florence Nightingale's experiences during the Crimean War to the present, when nurses are caring for growing immigrant and prison populations, the mentally ill, substance abusers, teenage mothers, the homeless, and those infected with the human immunodeficiency virus (HIV), nurses are reminded that these clients and the nature of their problems define the knowledge and skills required for practice.

The nearly 13 million people in the United States today who are age 65 and older are another steadfast group that has gradually shaped the practice of nursing; but only in recent decades has the impact been realized. The number of older adults has grown steadily since 1900, and they are now the fastest growing segment of the population. With the "gerontology boom" less than 20 years away, gerontologic nursing is finally being recognized as a legitimate specialty. The struggle for recognition can be traced back to the beginning of this century.

History and Evolution

Burnside (1988) conducted an extensive review of the *American Journal of Nursing (AJN)* for historic materials related to gerontologic nursing. Between 1900 and 1940 she found 23 writings with a focus on older adults, including works by Lavinia Dock, covering such topics as rural nursing, almshouse and private duty nursing, as well as early case studies and clinical issues addressing home care for a fractured femur, dementia, and delirium. Burnside discovered an anonymous column in *AJN* entitled "Care of the Aged," written in 1925, that appears to be one of the earliest references to the need for a specialty in older adult care:

> The modern health movement is constantly increasing the span of life expectancy by its steady onslaught against preventable disease . . . The nursing profession therefore must expect to care for relatively larger and larger numbers of patients suffering from degenerative conditions. Is it perhaps time for nurses to consider yet another specialty?

During World War II and the postwar years (1940 to 1960), the population of older persons steadily increased, but articles about the care of older adults were general in nature and not particularly comprehensive (Burnside, 1988). It was not until 1962, when the geriatric nursing conference group was established during the American Nurses Association (ANA) convention, that the question posed by that anonymous *AJN* columnist was finally addressed.

Professional Origins

In 1966 the ANA established the Division of Geriatric Nursing Practice and defined geriatric nursing as "... concerned with the assessment of nursing needs of older people; planning and implementing nursing care to meet those needs; and evaluating the effectiveness of such care . . ." In 1976 the Division of Geriatric Nursing Practice was changed to the Division of Gerontological Nursing Practice, to reflect the nursing roles of providing care to healthy, ill, and frail older people. It became the Council of Gerontological Nursing in 1984, to reflect the emphasis on issues beyond clinical practice. In September 1993 the ANA Board of Directors approved and adopted a new council "substructure," the purpose of which is to position "... the councils as a resource to the Congress of Nursing Practice for addressing the policy and interpretation needs of the association and for advancing Nursing's Agenda for Health Care Reform" (ANA, 1993). The new substructure consists of the following six councils:

- Council for Acute Care Nursing Practice
- Council for Advanced Nursing Practice
- Council for Community, Primary and Long Term Care Nursing Practice
- Council for Nursing Research
- Council for Nursing Systems and Administration
- Council for Professional Nursing Education and Development

At the December 1993 meeting of the ANA Board of Directors, the transition plan for the above ANA councils was approved. Several activities occurred in 1994 to end the current council structure and to implement the new councils. It remains to be seen what effect this new council structure will have on the specialty of gerontologic nursing as the specialty expands to meet increased societal demands. Clearly, council members will be challenged to assure that gerontologic nursing practice issues continue to be proactively addressed, with the goal of improving the quality of care and life of older persons in all settings.

Standards of Practice

The years 1960 to 1970 can be characterized by many "firsts," as the specialty devoted to care of older adults began its exciting development (Table 1-1). Journals, textbooks, workshops and seminars, formal education programs, professional certification, and research have since developed with a focus on gerontologic nursing. However, the singular event that truly legitimized the specialty occurred in 1969, when a committee appointed by the ANA Division of Geriatric Nursing Practice completed the first *Standards of Practice for Geriatric Nursing* (ANA, 1991). These standards were widely circulated over the next several years; in 1976 they were revised and the title changed to *Standards of Gerontological*

TABLE 1-1

Development of Gerontologic Nursing, 1960-1970

Year	Event
1961	ANA recommended formation of specialty group for geriatric nurses
1962	First national meeting of ANA Conference on Geriatric Nursing Practice in Detroit, Michigan
1962	American Nurses' Foundation received grant workshop on aged
1962	First research in geriatric nursing published in England (Norton D et al: *An investigation of geriatric nursing problems in hospital,* National Corporation for the Care of Old People, 1962)
1966	First gerontologic clinical specialist nursing program, Duke University, developed by Virginia Stone
1966	Formation of Geriatric Nursing Division of ANA; monograph published: *Exploring Progress in Geriatric Nursing Practice*
1968	Laurie Gunter is the first nurse to present a paper at the International Congress of Gerontology in Washington, D.C.
1968	First gerontologic nursing interest group formed, named Geriatric Nursing
1968	Barbara Davis is the first nurse to speak before the American Geriatric Society
1969	First article on nursing curriculum regarding gerontologic nursing is published (Delora JR, Moses DV: Specialty preferences and characteristics of nursing students in baccalaureate programs, *Nurs Res* March/April 1969)
1969	Development of the nine standards for geriatric nursing practice
1970	First publication of *Standards of Geriatric Nursing Practice*
1970	First gerontologic clinical nurse specialists graduated from Duke University

Modified from Burnside IM: *Nursing and the aged: a self care approach,* ed 3, New York, 1988, McGraw-Hill.

Nursing Practice. In 1981 *A Statement on the Scope of Gerontological Nursing Practice* was published. The revised *Standards and Scope of Gerontological Nursing Practice* were published in 1987, reflecting the comprehensive concepts and dimensions of practice for the nurse working with older adults (Box 1-1). The recommendation of the ANA Board of Directors is to reassign the revision of the *Scope of Practice and Standards of Gerontological Nursing* to the Council for Community, Primary and Long Term Care Nursing Practice, based on the new council structure.

Another hallmark in the continued growth of the specialty of gerontologic nursing was in 1973, when the first gerontologic nurses were certified through the ANA. Certification is an additional credential granted by the ANA, providing a means for recognizing excellence in a clinical or functional area (ANA, 1994). Certification is usually voluntary, enabling the nurse to demonstrate to peers and others that a distinct degree of knowledge and expertise has been achieved. In some cases, certification can mean eligibility for third-party reimbursement for nursing services rendered. From that initial certification offering as a generalist in gerontologic nursing, to the first gerontologic nurse practitioner (GNP) examination offering in 1979, to the most recent gerontologic clinical nurse specialist examination first administered in 1989, this specialty continues to grow and to attract a high level of interest (Box 1-2).

Roles

The growth of the nursing profession as a whole, increasing educational opportunities, demographic changes, and changes in health care delivery systems have all influenced the development of the generalist role in gerontologic nursing, as well as the advanced practice roles of gerontologic clinical nurse specialist and gerontologic nurse practitioner. The generalist in gerontologic nursing has completed a basic entry-level educational program. As of 1998, however, the baccalaureate degree requires the generalist certification examination (ANA, 1994). This generalist nurse may practice in a wide variety of institutions, including the home and community, providing care to older adults and their families within the nursing process framework. The gerontologic nurse generalist is challenged to identify the older client's strengths and assist the client in maximizing independence. Clients participate as much as possible in any decision making about their care. The generalist consults with the advanced practice nurse for assistance in meeting complex care needs of older adults.

The gerontologic clinical nurse specialist (CNS) is prepared at the master's degree level. The first program of its kind was launched in 1966 at Duke University. The gerontologic master's program typically focuses on the advanced knowledge and skills required to care for older adults in a wide variety of settings, and the graduate is prepared to assume a leadership role in the delivery of that care. The CNS functions as a clinician, educator, consultant, administrator or researcher to plan or to improve the quality of nursing care for older adults and their families. Specialists provide comprehensive care based on theory and research. Today CNSs can be found practicing in an acute hospital, long-term care, or home care setting, or in independent practice.

The GNP may be educationally prepared in a num-

BOX 1-1

ANA Standards of Gerontological Nursing Practice

Standard I: Organization of gerontological nursing services

All gerontological nursing services are planned, organized, and directed by a nurse executive. The nurse executive has baccalaureate or master's preparation and has experience in gerontological nursing and administration of long-term or acute care services for older clients.

Standard II: Theory

The nurse participates in the generation and testing of theory as a basis for clinical decisions. The nurse uses theoretical concepts to guide the effective practice of gerontological nursing.

Standard III: Data collection

The health status of the older person is regularly assessed in a comprehensive, accurate, and systematic manner. The information obtained during the health assessment is accessible to and shared with appropriate members of the interdisciplinary health care team, including the older person and the family.

Standard IV: Nursing diagnosis

The nurse uses health assessment data to determine nursing diagnoses.

Standard V: Planning and continuity of care

The nurse develops the plan of care in conjunction with the older person and appropriate others. Mutual goals, priorities, nursing approaches, and measures in the care plan address the therapeutic, preventive, restorative, and rehabilitative needs of the older person. The care plan helps the older person attain and maintain the highest level of health, well-being and quality of life achievable, as well as a peaceful death. The plan of care facilitates continuity of care over time as the client moves to various care settings, and is revised as necessary.

Standard VI: Intervention

The nurse, guided by the plan of care, intervenes to provide care to restore the older person's functional capabilities and to prevent complications and excess disability. Nursing interventions are derived from nursing diagnoses and are based on gerontologic nursing theory.

Standard VII: Evaluation

The nurse continually evaluates the client's and family's responses to interventions in order to determine progress toward goal attainment and to revise the data base, nursing diagnoses, and plan of care.

Standard VIII: Interdisciplinary collaboration

The nurse collaborates with other members of the health care team in the various settings in which care is given to the older person. The team meets regularly to evaluate the effectiveness of the care plan for the client and family and to adjust the plan of care to accommodate changing needs.

Standard IX: Research

The nurse participates in research designed to generate an organized body of gerontological nursing knowledge, disseminates research findings, and uses them in practice.

Standard X: Ethics

The nurse uses the code for nurses established by the ANA as a guide for ethical decision making in practice.

Standard XI: Professional development

The nurse assumes responsibility for professional development and contributes to the professional growth of interdisciplinary team members. The nurse participates in peer review and other means of evaluation to assure the quality of nursing practice.

Reprinted with permission from American Nurses Association: *Standards of gerontological nursing practice,* Kansas City, Mo., 1987, The Association.

ber of different ways. In the early 1970s, the first GNPs were prepared primarily through continuing education programs. Another early group of GNPs received their training and clinical supervision from physicians. Only since the late 1980s has master's-level education been available with a focus on primary care nursing. As a provider of primary care and a case manager, the GNP conducts health assessments, identifies nursing diagnoses, and plans, implements, and evaluates nursing care for older clients. A GNP has the knowledge and skills to detect and to manage limited acute and chronic stable conditions; coordination and collaboration with other health care providers is a related essential function. The GNP's activities include interventions for health promotion, maintenance, and restoration. GNPs usually provide primary ambulatory care and inpatient care in the acute care hospital or long-term care care setting, or in private practice. As of 1992 a nurse must have completed a master's degree or higher in nursing to be eligible to take the GNP certification examination (ANA, 1990).

Since the initial gerontologic certification offering in the early 1970s through 1992, 9,437 nurses have become certified (Box 1-3). Certification can elevate the status of the nurse practicing with older adults in any setting. More importantly, it enables the nurse to meet the professional responsibility of assuring the delivery of quality care to older adult clients.

BOX 1-2

American Nurses Credentialing Center Eligibility Requirements for Certification in Gerontological Nursing

Gerontological Nurse

1. Currently hold an active RN license in the United States or its territories; AND
2. Have a *minimum* of 4,000 hours of practice as a licensed registered nurse in gerontological nursing practice (51% of the patient population must be over the age of 65); 2,000 of the 4,000 hours must have occurred within the past 2 years. (Time spent in a formal program of advanced nursing study may count toward 300 hours of this requirement.) This requirement can be met if you are engaged in direct patient care or direct clinical management, supervision, education, or direction of other persons to help achieve patient/client goals; AND
3. Have had 30 contact hours of continuing education applicable to gerontology/gerontological nursing within the past 2 years; documentation of continuing education must be submitted. (Independent study which has been approved for continuing education credit or academic credit may not constitute more than 20% of this requirement.)

Gerontological Nurse Practitioner (GNP)

1. Currently hold an active RN license in the United States or its territories; AND
2. Hold a master's degree in nursing; AND
3. Have been prepared as a nurse practitioner in either:
   A. A gerontological nurse practitioner master's degree in nursing program; OR
   B. A formal postgraduate GNP track or program within a school of nursing granting graduate-level academic credit (e.g., graduate, nonmatriculating program). Evidence of successful completion will be either a certificate or a letter from the program director.*

Clinical Specialist in Gerontological Nursing

1. Currently hold an active RN license in the United States or its territories; AND
2. Hold a master's or higher degree in nursing, preferably in gerontological nursing†; AND
3. Have practiced a minimum of 12 months following completion of a master's degree; AND
4. Meet the following in your current practice:
   A. If you are a clinical specialist, you must have provided a *minimum* of 800 hours (post-master's) of direct patient care or clinical management in gerontological nursing within the past 24 months; OR
   B. If you are a consultant, researcher, educator, or administrator, you must have provided a *minimum* of 400 hours (post-master's) of direct patient care or clinical management in gerontological nursing within the past 24 months.‡

Reprinted with permission from *American Nurses Credentialing Center Certification Catalog,*§ 1995, Washington D.C., 1994, The Center.

*If you do not meet 3a or 3b, the following options will be acceptable through the 1995 test administration:
- completion of an adult or family nurse practitioner master's degree in nursing program;

OR
- completion of a gerontological, family, or adult nurse practitioner certificate program that was at least 9 months or 1 academic year of full-time study or its equivalent **before completing a master's degree in nursing.**

†Effective with the 1998 test administration, Criterion 2 of the eligibility requirements will be:
2a. Hold a master's or higher degree in gerontologic nursing
OR
2b. Hold a master's or higher degree in nursing with a specialization in gerontologic nursing.

‡Supervision of student's patient care fulfills the requirement for direct patient care or clinical management only when the supervisor intervenes with the patient/client and is personally responsible and accountable for the outcome of that intervention.

§To keep current with the changing scope, standards, and education requirement, the eligibility criteria are reviewed yearly and are subject to change. Therefore, if applying to sit for a ceritification examination, a current catalog must be requested from the Center, and compliance with the current eligibility criteria is required.

Terminology

Any discussion of older adult nursing is complicated by the existence of a wide variety of terms used interchangeably to describe this relatively new specialty. Some terms are used because of personal preference or because they suggest a certain perspective. Still others are avoided because of the negative inferences they evoke. As can be seen in the preceding overview of the evolution of the specialty, the terminology has changed over the years. The following are the most commonly used terms and definitions:

- **Geriatrics**—from the Greek *geras* meaning "old age," it is the branch of medicine that deals with the diseases and problems of old age. Viewed by many nurses as having limited application to nursing because of its medical and disease orientation, the term geriatrics is generally not used when describing the nursing of older adults.

BOX 1-3

ANCC Gerontologic Certified Nurses as of 1994

Gerontologic nurse	10,651
Gerontologic nurse practitioner	1,760
Clinical specialist in gerontologic nursing	631

Reprinted with permission from American Nurses Credentialing Center (ANCC), Washington, DC.

- **Gerontology**—from the Greek *geron* meaning "old man," it means the scientific study of the process of aging and the problems of aged people; it includes the biologic, sociologic, psychologic, and economic aspects.
- **Gerontologic nursing**—the specialty of nursing concerned with assessment of the health and functional status of older adults, planning and implementing health care and services to meet the identified needs, and evaluating the effectiveness of such care. This is the term most often used by nurses specializing in this field.
- **Gerontic nursing**—a term developed by Gunter and Estes (1979) meant to be more inclusive than geriatric or gerontologic nursing by not being limited to diseases or scientific principles. Gerontic nursing connotes nursing of older people: the art and practice of nurturing, caring, and comforting. This term has not gained wide acceptance, but it is viewed by some as a more appropriate description of the specialty.

These terms and their usages spark a great deal of interest and controversy among nurses practicing with older adults. As the specialty continues to grow and develop, it is likely the terminology will do so as well.

DEMOGRAPHIC PROFILE OF THE OLDER POPULATION

Since the early beginnings of gerontologic nursing practice in almshouses and nursing homes, nurses today find themselves caring for many more older adults in a wider variety of settings. Emergency rooms, medical-surgical and critical care units in hospitals, outpatient surgical centers, home care agencies, and rehabilitation centers are some of the sites where nurses are caring for a rapidly growing older population. Nurses in any of these settings need only count the number of clients 65 and older to know first-hand what demographers have termed the "graying of America." This trend has only recently begun to attract attention, but it is clearly one that promises to shape the future practice of nursing in profound and dramatic ways.

Demography is the statistical science dealing with the distribution, density, and vital statistics of human populations. In the following review of basic demographic facts about older people, the reader is cautioned against believing that age 65 automatically places a person in the category of "old." The rate and intensity of aging is highly variable and individual. It occurs gradually and in no predictable sequence.

Butler (1975) in his classic book, *Why survive? Being old in America,* cautions against using chronologic age as a measure of old, and offers the following on why age 65 is the discretionary cutoff for defining old:

> Society has arbitrarily chosen ages 60-65 as the beginning of late life (borrowing the idea from Bismarck's social legislation in Germany in the 1880's) primarily for the purpose of determining a point for retirement and eligibility for services and financial entitlements for the elderly.

When the social security program was established in 1935, it was believed that age 65 would be a reasonable age for the purpose of allocating benefits and services. Today, with so many older people living productive, highly functional lives well beyond age 65, this age may be an inappropriate one for determining old. However, demographic and other forms of data are still reported using age 65 as the defining standard for old.

The Older Population

Since 1900 the percentage of Americans age 65 and older has tripled, from 4.1% in 1900 to 12.6% in 1991, and the number has increased more than 10 times, from 3.1 million to 31.8 million (American Association of Retired Persons [AARP], 1992). Not only has the *number* of over-65 people increased but also the *proportion* of this group to the total population. By 1992 the total number of older Americans had increased 24% since 1980, compared with an increase of only 9% for the under-65 population during that same period. The relatively high birth rate during the late nineteenth and early twentieth centuries accounts in part for the large number of older people today (Burnside, 1988). Reduced infant and child mortality as a result of improved sanitation, advances in vaccination, and the development of antibiotics have also contributed. The large influx of immigrants before World War I is an additional important factor. The net effect, associated with a reduction in mortality for all ages with fertility rates at a replacement level, has been an increase in the older adult population.

Not only are large numbers of people living to reach age 65, but they are also living longer. A child born in 1990 could expect to live 75.4 years, or about 28 years longer than a child born in 1900. Life expectancy at age 65 increased by only 2.4 years between 1900 and 1960,

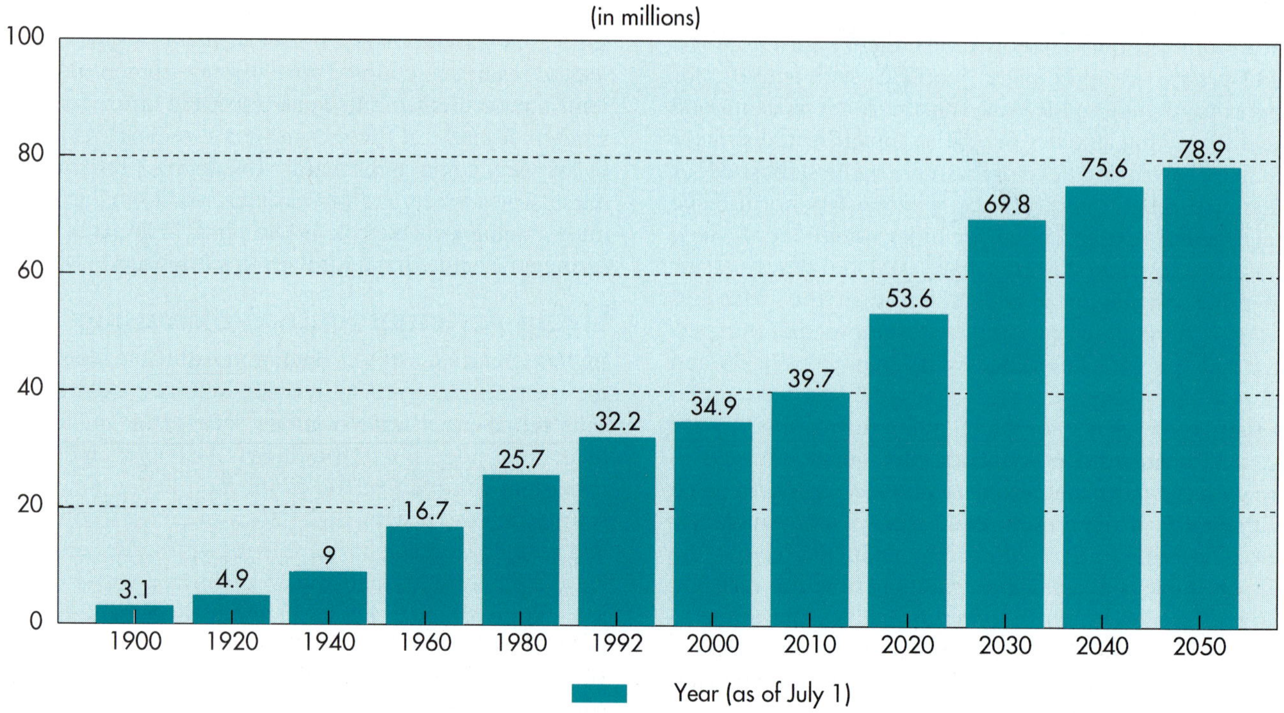

Fig. 1-1 Population trends of people 65 and older: 1990-2050. (From US Bureau of the Census: Statistical abstracts of the United States: 1993, Washington, D.C., 1993, US Government Printing Office.)

but it has increased by 3 years for the period 1960 to 1992. In 1991 the 65 to 74 age group was 8 times larger than in 1900, but the 75 to 84 age group was 13 times larger and the 85 and older group was 25 times larger (AARP, 1992). The approximately 3 million people 85 and older represent the fastest growing subset, with a growth rate of nearly three times that of the overall older population. Sometimes termed the "aging of the aged," this phenomenon represents one of the greatest concerns and challenges for society and the health care system.

This is primarily because people in advanced age are more vulnerable to the multiple losses typically associated with aging, thus making them more frail. These frail older adults have higher intensity care needs in all the health care settings in which they are found. Coupled with the growth of life-extending therapies and the continuous development of additional treatment measures, the structure, services, and financing of the health care delivery system are currently not equipped to effectively manage the needs of this population segment.

As will be discussed throughout the remaining chapters of this text, the population of older people may be more physically frail as a result of diminished physical functioning, susceptibility to injuries and acute illness, chronic illness, and cognitive impairment. In addition to these physical aspects of frailty, there are psychologic, social, and financial components. The combination of these factors distinguishes the care of older adults as unique and different, and will continue to influence the future practice of gerontologic nursing. Prevention and reduction of such frailty will provide challenges to nursing this special population.

Projected Growth

It is expected that the older population will continue to grow, with those over age 65 expected to number 34 million people, or about 13% of the total population by the year 2000. The most dramatic and rapid growth will occur between the years 2010 and 2030, when the "baby boom" generation reaches 65 years of age. Estimates for the year 2010 are for 39 million people over age 65; by 2030 this number could increase to over 65 million (Fig. 1-1).

In 1990, minority populations represented 14% of the total older adult population; by 2030 this percentage is expected to climb to 25%. The greatest increases will be in the Hispanic and Asian/Pacific Islander races. The white older adult population is projected to have a moderate decline; the black population will increase slightly. According to the U.S. Census Bureau, the over-85 segment of the population will double from 1980 to 2000 and redouble from 2000 to 2040. The number of centenarians will continue to grow at a steady rate. Currently, there are approximately 46,000 people age 100 and older (US Bureau of the Census, 1989). By 2080 the number is expected to increase to approximately 1,440,000.

The previous discussion of "older" people does not mean to imply that all people over age 65 are a homogenous group. Grouping older people as such is useful for reporting demographic data, but the nurse is cautioned against viewing all older people as similar. Landmarks for human growth and development are well established for infancy through middlescence, whereas few norms have been as discreetly defined for older adulthood. In fact, most developmental norms that have been described for later life categorize all older people in the "over 65" group. One could argue from a developmental perspective that as great a difference exists among 65, 75, 85, and 95 year olds as does among 2, 3, 4, and 5 year olds. Yet no definitive standards for older adult development have been established. Consequently, the nurse is urged to view each *older* client as one would *any* client—a being with a richly diverse and unique array of internal and external variables that ultimately influence how the person thinks and acts. Understanding how the variables interact and affect an older adult enables the nurse to provide individualized care. Additionally, the nurse is encouraged to use the individual client as the standard, comparing a client's previous level and pattern of health and function with the current status.

Marital Status

In 1991, 77% of men over age 65 were married, compared with 41% of women (AARP, 1992). Widowhood for females also increases with advancing age—nearly half of all women over age 65 were widows in 1991, and there were five times as many widows (8.5 million) as widowers (1.8 million). Only 5% of all persons over age 65 were divorced. Blacks have higher divorce rates than whites and other minorities. Marital status is an important determinant of health and well-being, since it influences income, mobility, housing, intimacy, and social interaction.

Gender

Since 1930, women began living longer than men as a result of reduced maternal mortality, decreased death rate from infectious disease, and an increased rate of death in men from chronic disease. Prior to that time, the number of older men and women was nearly equal. In 1991 there were 19 million older women and 12.8 million older men, which translates into a gender ratio of 148 women for every 100 men (AARP, 1992). The discrepancy between proportions of older women and men is expected to continue to increase as the over-85 age group increases, a group in which women represent the clear majority.

This demographic fact has important health care and policy implications, since the majority of older women are likely to be poor, live alone, and have a greater degree of functional impairment and chronic disease. The resulting increased reliance on social, financial, and health-related resources, coupled with the emerging health care reform movement, points to an uncertain future for older women. Because of these considerations, many gerontologists view aging as primarily a woman's problem. The nursing profession, and gerontologic nurses in particular, must assume a visible role in the political arena by advocating an agenda that addresses this important issue.

Living Arrangements and Housing

In 1991 the majority of older, noninstitutionalized people over age 65 lived in a family setting (AARP, 1992). This represented approximately 81% (10.3 million) of older men, and 56% (9.8 million) of older women. It is important to note that the proportion living in a family setting decreases with age. A total of 23% of both men and women over age 65 were living with other relatives; another 2% of both men and women lived with nonrelatives. Approximately 42% of all noninstitutionalized older women and 16% of older men lived alone. Older, noninstitutionalized people living alone increased by 33% between 1980 and 1991, compared with 22% for the balance of the older population. In 1991 approximately 81% of older men and 56% of older women lived with families (Fig. 1-2).

About 1.4 million (5%) of people over age 65 lived in nursing homes in 1987 (AARP, 1992). Of significance is that the percentage increased dramatically with age: 1% for people age 65 to 74 to 5% for people age 75 to 84 and 25% for people age 85 and older. Every person reaching age 65 has a 36% to 63% chance of entering a nursing home at some time during their lifetime (Cassetta, 1993).

Of the 20.5 million households headed by older people in 1991, 77% were owners and 23% were renters (AARP, 1992). More than one-fourth of older renters lived in publicly owned or subsidized housing in 1989, compared with 12% for younger renters. The owners of homes were more likely to be male, couples, and of the young-old population segment. The housing of older people is typically older and less adequate than that of the rest of the country. Roughly 40% of homes owned by older adults in 1989 were built prior to 1950, compared with 24% for younger owners. In 1989 the median value of homes owned by older people was $65,900. A full 82% owned their homes free and clear; however, there is an increased possibility of losing a home at this age as a result of property taxes and maintenance costs that are difficult to pay on a fixed, limited income.

A person's overall degree of health and well-being greatly influences the selection of housing in old age. Ideally, housing should be selected to promote functional independence while emphasizing safety and social interaction needs.

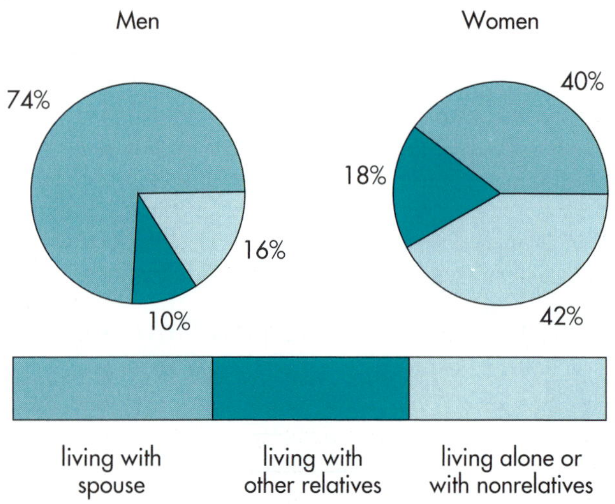

Fig. 1-2 Living arrangements of people 65 and older: 1992. (From US Bureau of the Census: *Statistical abstracts of the United States: 1993,* Washington, D.C., 1993, US Government Printing Office.)

Race

Of the approximately 31 million Americans over age 65 in 1990, 89% were white, 8% were black, and the remaining 3% represented other races, including American Indian, Eskimo, Aleut, Asian, and Pacific Islander. People of Hispanic origin represented 4% of the older population (AARP, 1992).* The higher proportion of older whites is expected to remain stable and to continue as such into the early part of the next century, at which time the nonwhite segment of the population is expected to increase at a higher rate.

The impact of such changing demographic characteristics must be considered by the nursing profession. Because people become more diverse as they age, it must be recognized that the increasing longevity of the nonwhite segment of the population will present unique challenges for care.

Geographic Distribution

In 1991 more than half (52%) of the population of people 65 years of age and older lived in nine states: California, Florida, New York, Pennsylvania, Texas, Illinois, Ohio, Michigan, and New Jersey (AARP, 1992). People age 65 and older constituted 14% or more of the total population in 10 states: North Dakota, South Dakota, Nebraska, Iowa, Missouri, Arkansas, Pennsylvania, West Virginia, Rhode Island, and Florida (Fig. 1-3) (US Bureau of the Census, 1992). An impressive population statistic is depicted in Fig. 1-4: a total of 13 states and the District of Columbia experienced a population increase of 30% or more between 1980 and 1990 in the 65 years and older age group. These states include Alaska, Washington, Nevada, Utah, Arizona, Colorado, New Mexico, Delaware, Maryland, Virginia, North Carolina, South Carolina, and Florida (US Bureau of the Census, 1992). People 65 years of age and older were less likely to live in metropolitan areas in 1992 than younger people, but only by 5%. About 30% of older persons lived in central cities; 44% lived in the suburbs (AARP, 1992).

Older adults as a group are less likely to change residence than other age groups. A variety of factors can influence the decision to move. Dependency and health status may require an older person to move to be near a caregiver(s). Countermigration describes the move some older adults make back to their home states, after an earlier migration to the sunbelt states for retirement. Dwindling financial resources may necessitate a move to a more economical location; conversely, economic stability or affluence may afford the opportunity to move to a retirement community or a location with a temperate climate and recreational offerings. Aging-in-place has been an important factor in the 65 years of age and older population growth of both metropolitan and nonmetropolitan areas since 1950 (Yurick et al, 1989). People simply grow older wherever they reside, without moving. Overall, however, older adults are less likely to change residence than other age groups. In fact, in 1990 only 5% of people 65 years of age and older had moved since 1989 (compared with 20% of people under 65). The majority (78%) had moved to another home in the same state.

Education

Although less well-educated than younger people overall, the educational level of the older adult population has been steadily increasing. Between 1970 and 1991, the median level of education increased from 8.7 years to 12.2 years, and the percentage who had completed high school increased from 28% to 58%. About 12% in 1991 had 4 or more years of college (AARP, 1992). Educational levels are significantly different between whites and nonwhites. In 1992 61% of whites completed high school, whereas only 28% of blacks and 26% of Hispanics completed the same level of education.

Low levels of education can impair an older person's ability to live a healthy lifestyle, to access service and benefit programs, to recognize health problems and to seek appropriate care, or to follow recommendations for care. The educational level of the older adult client also affects the nurse-client health teaching process.

*Hispanics may be of any race, but they have their origins in the Spanish-speaking countries of Central or South America. They are counted in the census by racial groups, usually as white, black, or other.

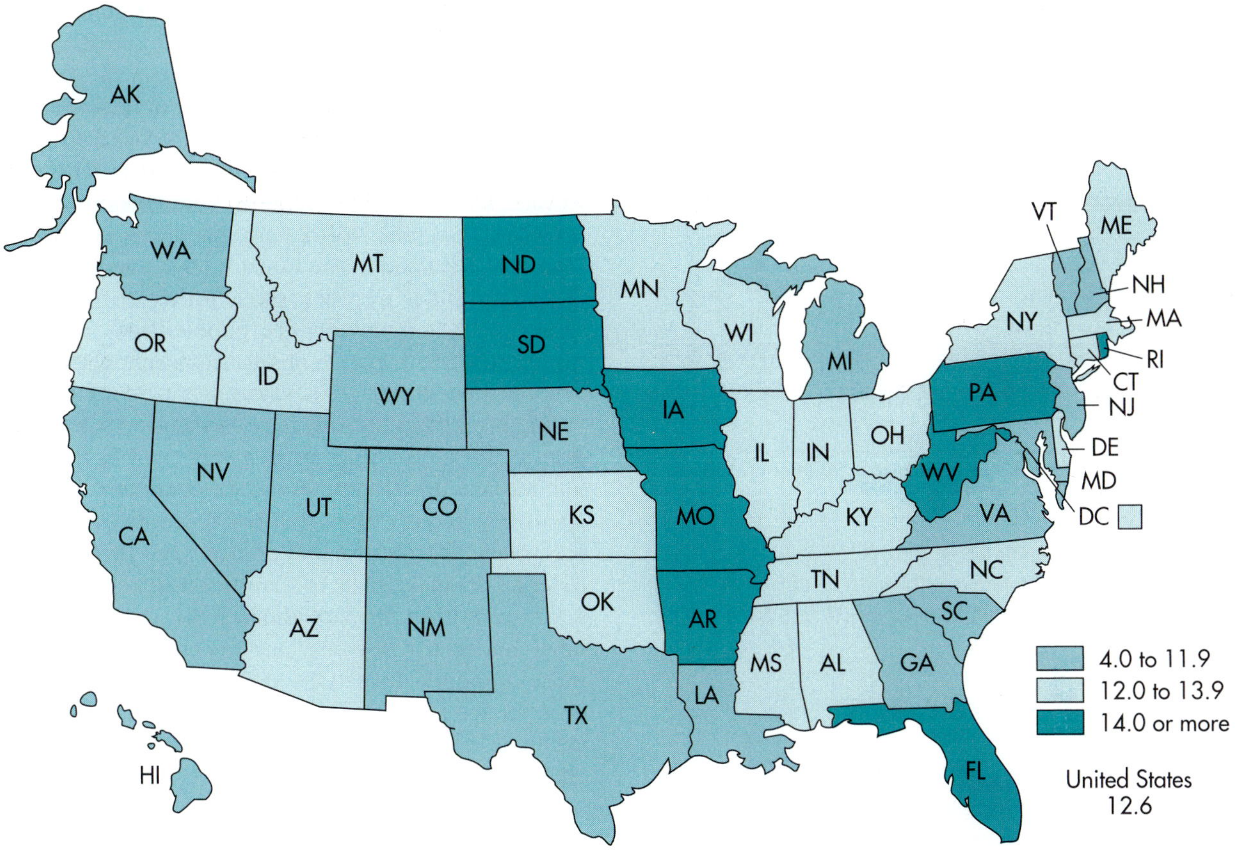

Fig. 1-3 Percentage of total state population 65 years and older: 1990. (From US Bureau of the Census: *1990 census of population and housing,* Summary Tape File 1A.)

Income and Poverty

Based on data from the U.S. Bureau of the Census (1991), the median income of older people was $14,357 for men and $8,189 for women. However, after adjusting for a 1990 to 1991 inflation rate of 4%, these figures actually represented a 3% *decrease* in real income since 1990 for men and a 2% decrease for women. The major source of income for both older individuals and couples in 1990 was Social Security (37%), a plan that was originally developed to be a supplemental source of income in old age. Clearly, as people age, they have come to depend more and more on Social Security as the major source of income. Other income sources in rank order were: asset income (25%), earnings (18%), public and private pensions (18%), and all other sources (3%) (AARP, 1992).

Family households headed by people 65 years of age and older had a median income in 1991 of $24,865. Nonwhites continue to have substantially lower incomes than their white counterparts. Blacks had a median income of $15,977 and Hispanics $19,633 versus $25,741 for whites. Almost 45% of all family households headed by an older adult had annual median incomes of less than $15,000: 32% had incomes of $30,000 or more (Fig. 1-5).

Approximately 3.8 million older adults were below the poverty level in 1991 (by the official 1991 definition of $8,241 for an older couple household or $6,532 for an older individual living alone). The poverty rate for people 65 years of age and older continues to be higher (12.4%) than the rate for people 18 to 64 years of age (11.4%). Another 2.3 million older people were classified as "near poor," with incomes between the poverty level and 125% of this level. In 1991 a full 20% of the older, noninstitutionalized population was poor or near-poor (AARP, 1992).

Gender and race are significant indicators of poverty. Older women had a poverty rate twice as high as older men in 1991. Only 10% of older whites were poor in 1991, compared to about 34% of older blacks and 21% of older Hispanics.

The most important relationship between income and health is the lifestyle changes imposed by reduced or dwindling financial resources. People unable to meet

basic needs typically reduce the amount of, or even avoid spending any, health-related dollars to stretch their limited resources and to try to meet those basic needs.

Employment

About 3.5 million older adults (12%) were classified as labor force participants (employed or actively seeking employment) in 1991, of which about 7% were men, and 5% women. A little more than half of the workers 65 years of age and older worked part-time. Approximately 24% of older workers were self-employed, a rate of three times as great as their younger counterparts. Nearly three-fourths of older, self-employed workers were men. The labor force participation of older men has remained fairly constant since 1900, with only minor increases and decreases. The rate in 1991 was 15.8%

The number of older women in the labor force showed a steady participation rate from 1900 to the 1950s, at which time the rate was 10.8% of the total labor force. There was a slight fall in 1985 to 7.3%, but it rose again in 1991 to 8.6% (AARP, 1992).

HEALTH STATUS OF OLDER ADULTS

Before beginning a discussion of the health status of older adults, it is necessary to offer a word of caution: *old age is not synonymous with disease!* Although selected portions of this text address disease and disability in old age by emphasizing the provision of age-appropriate nursing care of people with a variety of conditions, this does not mean to imply that disease is a normal, expected outcome of aging. Clearly, the risk of health problems and disability increases with age, but older adults are not necessarily incapacitated by these problems. They may also have health problems that are multiple and complex in nature, resulting in sickness and institutionalization, but again the nurse should not view this as the norm for this population. The nurse is advised to remember that even an older person with disease and/or disability is healthy and well to some degree. In fact, most older adults tend to view their personal health positively.

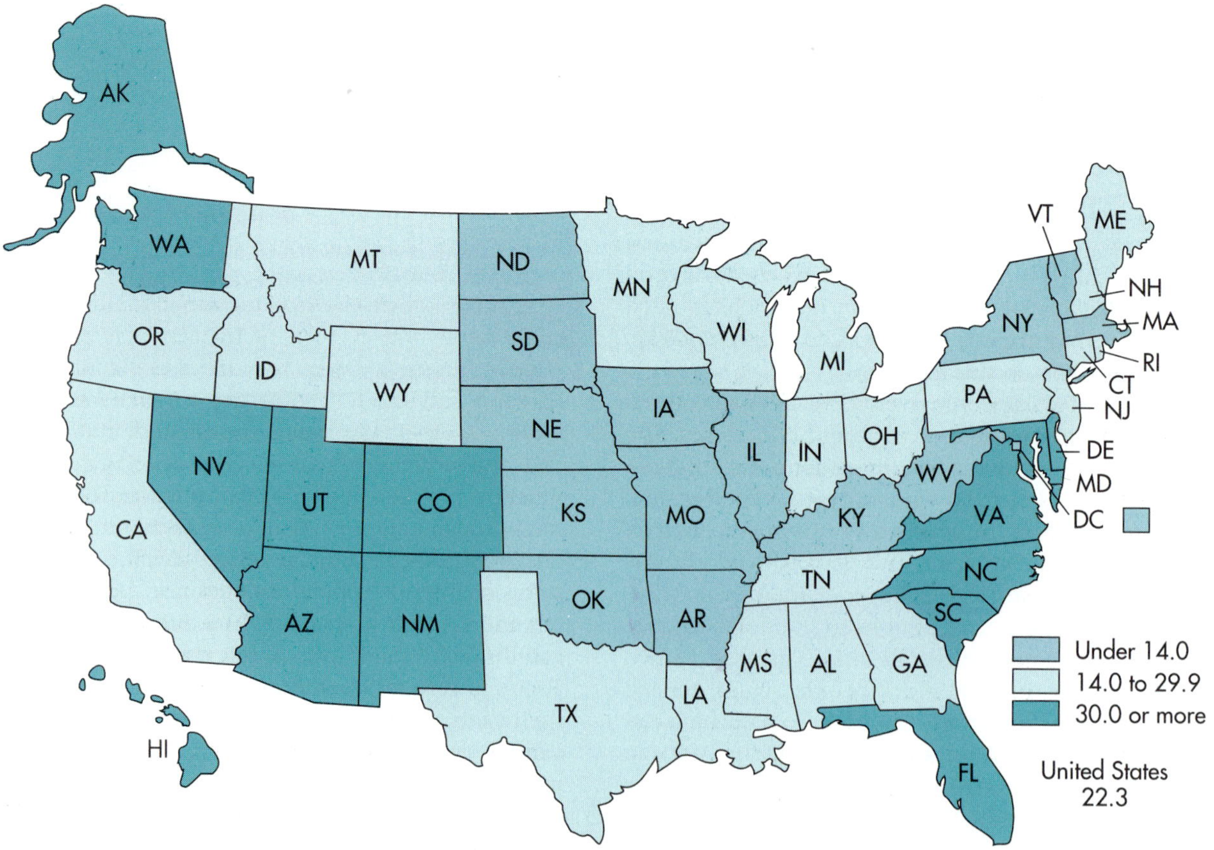

Fig. 1-4 Percent change in population 65 years and older, by state: 1980-1990. (From US Bureau of the Census, 1980 and 1990: *Censuses of population—for 1980,* General population characteristics, PC80-1-B1, Table 67; for 1990, Summary Tape File 1A.)

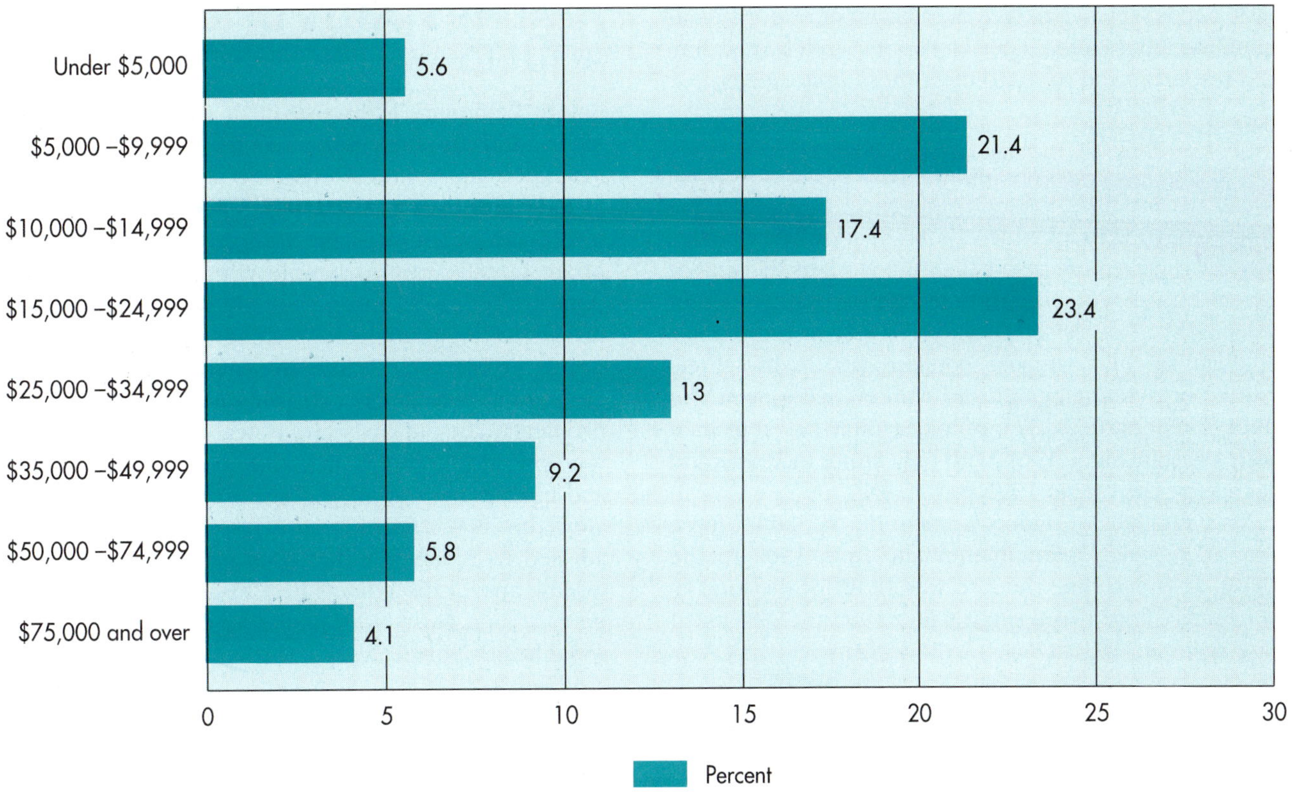

Fig. 1-5 Percent distribution by income in households headed by people 65 and older, 1991. (From US Bureau of the Census: *Statistical abstract of the United States: 1993,* Washington, D.C., 1993, US Government Printing Office.)

Self-Assessed Health and Chronic Disease

In 1990, 28% of older people assessed their health as fair or poor; 72% rated their own health as excellent or good (AARP, 1992). More older blacks than older whites rated their health as fair or poor. There was little difference between the genders on this measure.

More than 80% of people over 65 years of age are estimated to have one or more chronic conditions. The most commonly occurring conditions for noninstitutionalized older adults in 1990 were arthritis, hypertension, hearing impairments, heart disease, orthopedic impairments, cataracts and sinusitis, and diabetes and tinnitus (Fig. 1-6). The three leading causes of death for older people in 1990 (in rank order) were heart conditions, malignant neoplasms, and cerebrovascular diseases (AARP, 1992). More than 108,000 older people are in nursing homes because of limitations resulting from chronic cardiovascular diseases. Another 177,000 are in nursing homes as because of strokes and associated physical disabilities (National Institutes of Health [NIH], 1991).

Functional Status

The degree of functional ability is of greater concern to both older adults and nurses than incidence and prevalence of chronic disease. Functional ability is classified by activities of daily living (ADLs), such as bathing, dressing, eating, transferring, and toileting (Katz, 1963), and instrumental activities of daily living (IADLs), which include home management activities such as shopping, cooking, housekeeping, laundry, and handling money (Lawton and Brody, 1969). Use of such measurement tools or scales to determine the effect of chronic disease and normal aging on physical, psychologic, and social function provides objective information about the person's overall degree of health. Assessment of the impact of chronic disease and age-related decline on functional status enables the nurse to determine needs, to plan interventions, and to evaluate outcomes. Chronic disease and disability can impair physical and emotional health, ability to care for oneself, and independence. Improving the health and functional status of older adults and preventing complications of chronic disease and disability may help to avert the onset of physical frailty and cognitive impairment, two conditions that increase the likelihood of institutionalization (NIH, 1991).

In 1984 about 6 million (23%) older people living in the community had health-related difficulties with one or more personal care activities, and 7.1 million (27%)

had difficulty with one or more home management activities. All required some degree of personal help; the percentages needing and receiving help increased sharply with age. The number of days in which usual activities are restricted because of illness or injury increases with age. In 1990 older people averaged 31 such days and spent all or most of 14 of these days in bed (AARP, 1992).

Data from the 1987 National Medical Expenditure Study showed that about 21% of older people in the population had at least some degree of ADL, IADL, or walking difficulty (Leon and Lair, 1990). Of those 65 years of age and older, about 13% had difficulties with at least one ADL or with walking. Nearly 18% had difficulties with at least one IADL task; the most common problems were getting around the community and being able to shop. Age and gender were closely correlated with increased functional dependence in both ADLs and IADLs. The rate of problems increased overall after age 65, and increased sharply at age 80 and again at age 85. Women had higher rates of difficulties than men in all age categories; difficulties increased progressively with advancing age. Given that the number of older people will increase in the coming decades, the clear implication is for even more institutional and community-based services.

Health Care Expenditure and Use

The majority of health care in the United States is funded by the federal government. Benefits from Medicare ($72 billion), Medicaid ($20 billion), and others ($10 billion) accounted for 63% of the health expenditures of older people in 1987, compared to only 26% for persons less than 65 years of age (AARP, 1992). In that same year, people age 65 years and older represented 12% of the total U.S. population, but accounted for 36% of the total personal health care expenditures. These expenditures were a little over four times that spent for younger people. The projected increases in the older adult population, coupled with the current national concern over rising costs of government programs and health care, will force tough decisions by this country's leaders and policy makers alike. The question of whether the outcomes of reform will be appropriate to meet the needs of the elderly is still largely unanswered. As the debate continues, nurses may find themselves facing a number of different dilemmas surrounding the delivery of health care to older people.

In 1987 hospital expenses accounted for 42% of health-related dollars spent by older persons, followed by physicians at 21%, and nursing home care at 20%. Older people accounted for 34% of all hospital stays and 45% of all days of care in hospitals in 1990. Although Di-

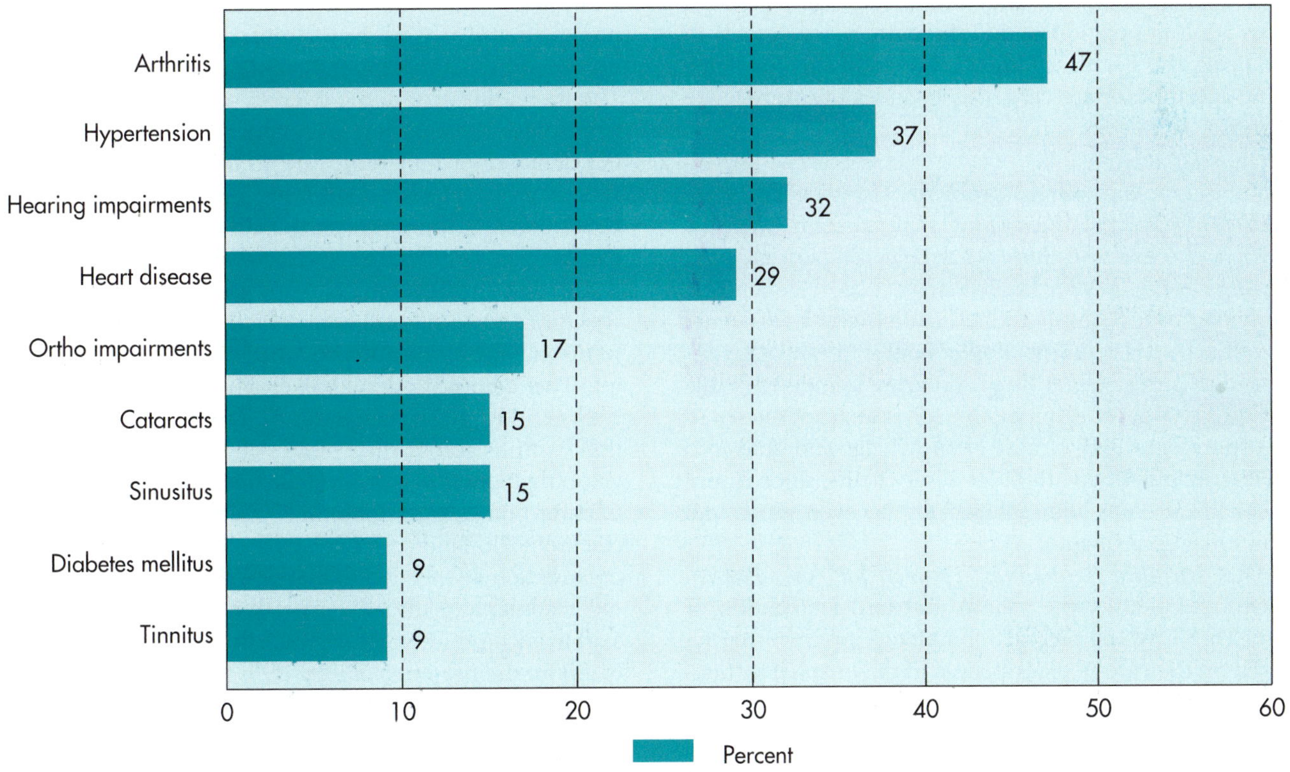

Fig. 1-6 Most commonly occurring conditions in people 65 and older, 1990. (From US Bureau of the Census: *Statistical abstract of the United States: 1993,* Washington, D.C., 1993, US Government Printing Office.)

agnostic Related Groups (DRGs) have contributed to a decrease in the overall length of stay for older people, the average length of a hospital stay in 1990 was 8.7 days for older people, compared with only 5.3 days for people less than 65 years of age (AARP, 1992).

Implications for Health Care Delivery

Although the future direction of health care is uncertain, it can confidently be surmised from the demographic profile presented above that nurses in a wide variety of settings and roles will be challenged to provide care to an increasingly divergent, complex group of older people. An urgent need exists for gerontologic nurses to: (1) create roles that meet the needs of the older population across the continuum of care; (2) develop models of care delivery directed at all levels of prevention, with special emphasis on primary prevention and health promotion services in community-based settings; and (3) assume positions of leadership and influence in institutions and settings where care is currently provided to older people. The overriding fact to be remembered while carrying out these activities is that the majority of problems experienced by older adults fall within the scope of *nursing* practice.

Acute Care

The immediate need is for nurses in the acute care work force to recognize that they are already caring for an older adult population, and to therefore move quickly in acquiring the necessary knowledge and skills for delivering age-appropriate care. This includes (1) knowledge of what is normal aging versus abnormal aging; (2) strong assessment skills to detect subtle changes that indicate impending, serious problems; (3) excellent communication skills for interacting with not only "normal" older people but also those with delirium, dementia, and depression; (4) a keen understanding of rehabilitation principles as they apply to the maintenance and promotion of functional ability in older adults; (5) and sensitivity and patience so that older adults are treated with dignity and respect. It is imperative for acute care nurses to incorporate the above cadre of knowledge and skills into their daily practice with older adult clients, since future hospitalized older adults will likely be even more frail than today (see Chapter 31).

The *Hospital Outcomes Project for the Elderly* (HOPE), funded by the John A. Hartford Foundation of New York City, is a recently completed program that focused on the care of older people in the hospital setting. The project resulted in five models of nursing care that acute care hospitals can implement to improve geriatric health (Box 1-4).

The *Nurses Improving Care to the Hospitalized Elderly* (NICHE) is a related project in that it attempts to share the nursing care models developed in the HOPE program with other hospitals around the country. Dr. Terry Fulmer of Columbia University School of Nursing is the principal investigator, and Dr. Mathy Mezey of New York University School of Nursing is the coinvestigator of the NICHE project. As of this writing, four participating hospitals will be selected to (1) implement a nursing care model for care of older adults; (2) implement one or more practice protocols on care for clients with urinary incontinence, sleep disorders, pressure ulcers, and mechanical restraints; and (3) develop a database from which to monitor progress in achieving the hospital's goals for care of older adult patients. This project is clearly a timely one, given the number of older adults in the acute care setting today, and the great need for nurses to acquire the appropriate knowledge and skills for providing quality care to this population.

Long-Term Care

The emphasis on reducing costs in the hospital setting through earlier discharge has led to the shift of more acutely ill residents to long-term care facilities. Unfortunately, some facilities do not have an adequate number of qualified, professional nursing staff to provide the complex care these residents require; or the staff does not have up-to-date knowledge and skill. Also, the nursing staff mix may not be sufficient to meet the needs of this more acutely ill population. Finally, the physical environment and systems for delivering care in the traditional nursing home may not be the most appropriate for meeting the needs of this more ill, more unstable population. The increasing size of the over-85 segment of the population with their decline in function has already caused the demand for long-term care to dramatically increase, with a promise for a continuing demand well into the next century. Economics, particularly as driven by health care reform, will determine the future of these facilities.

In 1982, the Teaching Nursing Home Project (TNHP) was initiated with funding provided by the Robert Wood Johnson Foundation and the American Academy of Nursing. This demonstration project consisted of affiliations between 11 university schools of nursing and 12 nursing homes from across the country for the purpose of developing models of gerontologic nursing care delivery in nursing homes that combined practice, education, and research. This landmark endeavor exemplifies the kind of creative activity needed to improve the long-term care of older adults and the education and training of nursing staff in such facilities. Efforts such as these must continue to assure the presence of long-term facilities that provide quality nursing care that meets the needs of the population being served. The reader is referred to the text *Teaching nursing homes: the nursing perspective* (1988), edited by Small and Walsh, for a complete report of the project.

Nurses practicing in long-term care need to gain new

BOX 1-4

The Hope Project: Models of Nursing Care For the Hospitalized Older Adults

Unit-Based Geriatric Care at Yale-New Haven Hospital

A unit-based, nurse-centered Geriatric Care Program (GCP) integrated geriatric resource nurses (GRNs), gerontologic nurse specialists (GNSs), primary nurses, and a geriatrician on the geriatric care team (GCT). Four target conditions, referred to as "geriatric vital signs," were selected to serve as markers of general functional decline in the hospitalized elderly: delirium, decline in physical functioning, incontinence, and pressure ulcers. It was hypothesized that through improved recognition, prevention, and effective remedial therapy, the target conditions would be reduced in the intervention group as compared to the nonintervention group.

Acute Care of the Elderly (ACE) Medical-Surgical Nursing Unit at University Hospitals of Cleveland in Conjunction with the Frances Payne Bolton School of Nursing at Case Western Reserve University

A 29-bed medical-surgical specialty unit was renovated and dedicated as an Acute Care of the Elderly (ACE) unit to prevent functional decline in this targeted group of patients. The unit was designed with special attention to the physical environment, collaborative team building, and development of nurse-initiated clinical protocols of care. Clinicians worked with designers to adapt the environment to enhance patient function. In this model the geriatric medical director and clinical nurse specialist held dual roles.

Improving Nurses' Accuracy and Speed in Detecting and Managing Delirium at the University of Chicago Hospitals

This model provided consultation and education by a doctorate level GNS to improve nurse's accuracy and speed in detecting and managing delirium in hospitalized elderly patients. Nurses were taught (1) the use and interpretation of simple bedside tests for assessing cognition, (2) the clinical features that distinguish delirium, dementia, and depression, (3) when and how to communicate patient's symptoms to physicians, (4) common causes of delirium in this patient population, (5) independent, interdependent, and dependent strategies for preventing and managing delirium, and (6) how to document findings in the medical record. The model attempted to measure the effect of the GNS in alleviating one discrete clinical problem.

Comprehensive Discharge Planning for the Elderly at the University of Pennsylvania

The objectives of this model were to (1) use a comprehensive discharge planning protocol developed specifically for the hospitalized elderly and implemented by GNSs and (2) evaluate the effectiveness of this model as compared to the hospital's general discharge planning procedures. The intervention, which targeted elderly at high risk for postdischarge outcomes, included direct care by a clinical nurse specialist from the time of admission, up to 4 weeks through the post discharge period. Preliminary findings from the first 3 years of implementation of this model showed that the clinical intervention lengthened the time between rehospitalizations for subjects in the experimental group.

Managed Care

The objectives of the managed care model include (1) providing outcome oriented patient care, (2) using appropriate resources based on specific case type, (3) promoting the integration and coordination of clinical services, (4) monitoring the use of patient care resources, (5) supporting collaborative practice and continuity of care, and (6) enhancing patient and provider satisfaction. Nurses as case managers serve as coordinators and facilitators of resources to the patients assigned to their caseload from [the time of] admission through discharge. Multidisciplinary action plans (MAPs), the time-lined plan of care designed to guide all disciplines toward the achievement of high quality and cost-effective care, is an integral part of this model.

Reprinted with permission from Fulmer T: *Program announcement,* 1993, New York, John A. Hartford Foundation.

knowledge to care for the more acutely ill resident. In some cases, the overall caliber of nurses needs to be raised. Directors of nursing must alter environmental design elements and systems to accommodate this type of resident and to support the safe delivery of nursing care. As the role of advanced practice nurse takes shape within the health care reform movement, gerontologic nurse practitioners can serve as case managers and coordinators of care in this setting. CNSs can provide staff education and training and serve as consultants to the nursing staff in assessing and planning nursing care for complex residents. Innovative models of care delivery that go beyond the task or functional approach are needed to improve the quality of care. An even stronger focus is needed on the functional status of the resident, as well as an emphasis on prevention and health promotion, to assure that dependency is minimized and functional ability maximized.

Home Care

Corresponding to the increasing demand for long-term care is a significant demand for community-based services, especially home care. In 1990 about 7% of the population resided in nursing homes (*McKnight's Long Term Care News,* 1993). The need for such institutional care will always exist for this small segment of the population, but the greater number of older people are in need of long-term supportive services to maintain their independence in their community of residence. The desire and preference of most older people to stay in their own home for as long as possible is a major driving force influencing the need for increasing home care services. An additional factor is the earlier hospital discharge that has become a financial necessity.

The older home care client today has multiple complex problems. In addition to possessing the knowledge and skills of acute care nurses previously noted, home care nurses must be self-directed and capable of functioning with a multidisciplinary team that is widely dispersed throughout the community. Keen clinical judgment skills are essential, since the home care nurse is often called on to make decisions about whether a client's condition requires physician referral. In addition to individual client assessment, the home care nurse is responsible for determining the older client's functional status, and assessing home safety considerations and family and other caregiver support. Excellent coordination and collaboration skills are necessary, since it is the nurse who is the primary resource of the older client, calling in other resources as warranted. Finally, a genuine respect for the older client's desires and rights as related to living at home is key.

Nurses caring for homebound older adults need to become increasingly more involved in conducting community assessments that focus specifically on the aged population. This data obtained from this type of assessment can be used to plan age-specific programs and services aimed at all levels of prevention, however, the demographic forecasts specifically call for refinement of health screening, promotion, and maintenance activities. Linking these activities to community-based programs and organizations already used by older persons can begin now. Community-based clinics that are operated and served by nurses will become more prevalent as the movement toward keeping frail and impaired older persons at home gains momentum (see Chapter 32).

Continuum of Care

President Bill Clinton introduced the American Health Security Act of 1993 in September of that year. This proposed blueprint for health care reform represented as sweeping a social change as the introduction of social security in 1935. The recommendations for change were massive and complex, and it ultimately failed to gain bipartisan support.

Future efforts to restructure of the health care system for the older adult population must consider the widely ranging levels of care needed by this group. From services that promote wellness among older adults, who are maintaining their health and independence, to the acute care setting, where care is provided to treat conditions that are short-term or episodic in nature, to nursing homes or the home, where the focus is the provision of health, personal, and social services, to people who lack some degree of functional capacity, there must be initiatives that consider the need for ease of movement along this continuum. As so eloquently stated by Ebersole and Hess (1990): "Fragmented or superficial care is particularly dangerous to the elderly. Their functions become more and more interdependent as they age. A small disturbance is like a pebble in a still lake. The ripples extend outward in all directions." The future is uncertain, but older adults and the people who care for them are anxiously awaiting the new choices that will be presented, in hopes of making new decisions that will more effectively meet the needs of a growing and demographically changing population.

IMPACT OF AN AGING ADULT POPULATION ON GERONTOLOGIC NURSING

The information and facts presented previously about the development of this specialty and the changing demographics emphasize the growing interest in and development of gerontologic nursing as an emerging force in the health care arena. The time is now for gerontologic nurses to consider what the future will be in terms of practice, education, and research.

Ageism

Ageism is a term coined by Butler (1969) that describes the deep and profound prejudice in American society against older adults: "Ageism reflects a deep-seated uneasiness on the part of young and middle-aged—a personal revulsion and distaste for growing old, disease, disability; and fear of powerlessness, 'uselessness,' and death." In a society that highly values and has great regard for youth and vitality, it is of no surprise that ageism exists. Butler also likens ageism with bigotry: "Ageism can be seen as a process of systematic stereotyping of and discrimination against people because they are old, just as racism and sexism accomplish this with skin color and gender. Ageism allows the younger generation to see older people as different from themselves; thus they subtly ceases to identify with their elders as human beings" (Butler, 1977).

Negative attitudes are a component of ageism. Since generally negative attitudes about older people are held by society at large, and nurses are a subset of society, it follows that nurses may hold ageist views. Insofar as such attitudes might be held by the recruits to nursing, there are significant implications for practice, education, and research.

Nursing Practice

Gerontologic nursing practice is evolving as new issues concerning the health care of older adults demand attention. One of those issues relates to the treatment of an ill older adult. The traditional, medical model of care focuses on the presenting signs and/or symptoms. The older adult, however, seldom seeks care for a single symptom or disorder. Furthermore, even if an older adult does have a singular problem, it is likely to be intertwined with other variables. Consequently, an even greater emphasis must be placed on the impact of many intervening variables on the health status of the older adult. The psychologic, social, and financial needs must be considered commensurate with the presenting physical needs. The ability to comprehensively assess all of these areas will require the nurse to possess refined and highly discriminating assessment skills. This will become increasingly more important as nurses take on more responsibility for the care and treatment of older adults in all settings.

Skills required by nurses to support the care of older adults in their own homes and through community-based services include teaching families and other caregivers about safe and effective caregiving techniques, as well as services available to support them in their efforts. Since most of these older clients will have varying degrees of functional impairment, the nurse must have a comprehensive knowledge of functional assessment as well as intervention and management strategies from a rehabilitative perspective.

Medical advances have resulted in longer life spans with fewer diseases. Alzheimer's disease, the incidence of which increases with advancing age, will require gerontologic nurses to have not only a wide range of assessment skills but also an extensive knowledge of treatment modalities and therapeutic interventions for these seriously impaired older adults. HIV-related dementia, a growing concern in the aged population, requires the nurse to possess these same skills.

The prevalence of Alzheimer's disease and related dementias in the older adult population, coupled with the increased risk of depression secondary to sustained, multiple losses, chronic physical conditions, and loneliness substantiates the need for nurses prepared as geropsychiatric specialists. With their broad experience and advanced education, these nurses will be needed to provide mental and behavioral assessments, advocacy, therapy, crisis intervention, and case management.

Nursing Education

The need for adequately prepared nurses to care for the growing population of older adults continues to intensify. According to Alford (1987), between 1980 and 2030 the estimated number of registered nurses needed to care for older adults will increase by 466%. These figures, coupled with demographic forecasts, should prompt nurse faculty to no longer view gerontologic nursing content as a luxury; it is clearly a necessary component of the curriculum.

The pioneering work of Gunter and Estes (1979) defined an educational program specific to five levels of nursing: nursing assistant/technician, licensed practical/vocational nurse, registered nurse, graduate education at the master's degree level, and graduate education at the doctoral level. Although there are no reports in the nursing literature of the use of this framework for curriculum development, this work has been an invaluable reference to nurse educators and in-service education staff in a variety of settings, since it represented the first attempt to provide a conceptual framework, delineation, and definition for the specialty. Since the publication of this work 15 years ago, the published literature has cited some agreement among nurse educators as to what constitutes essential gerontologic content in the baccalaureate program. And through the Community College-Nursing Home Partnership Project, ideas about essential gerontologic nursing content in the associate degree program have been offered (Waters, 1991). Despite the many recommendations made, however, unanimous agreement still does not exist as to what constitutes "core" gerontologic nursing content at any level of nursing education. Without established consensus on this matter of "core" content at all levels, nurse faculty will continue to struggle with the many issues surrounding gerontologic nursing curriculum development. The specialty cannot afford to continue leaving this matter undecided.

Despite this lack of agreement, there are programs that provide gerontologic nursing content. However, the direction of these programs is dependent on the preparation and expertise of the nurse faculty. A study conducted by Edel (1986) to determine the gerontology/gerontologic nursing educational preparation of faculty in baccalaureate nursing programs accredited by the National League for Nursing revealed a paucity of adequately prepared faculty; only 4.41% of 4,762 faculty had completed course work in gerontology or gerontologic nursing. Findings of a recent study conducted by Yurchuck and Brower (1994) indicated only 12% of faculty have gerontologic nursing preparation; only 5% have master's preparation in gerontology/gerontologic nurs-

BOX 1-5

Issues Influencing the Inclusion of Gerontologic Nursing Content in Nursing Curricula

- Reluctance to recognize gerontologic nursing as a legitimate academic and practice specialty
- Perceived low status compared with other areas of nursing practice
- Lack of adequate academic preparation of nurse faculty in gerontologic nursing
- Questionable clinical competence of nongerontologic prepared nurse faculty
- Ageist attitudes of nongerontologic prepared nurse faculty
- Little gerontologic nursing content on NCLEX-RN
- Lack of requirement of a gerontologic nursing text

ing. The survey sample consisted of 211 undergraduate associate and baccalaureate nursing programs in the 15-state Southern Regional Education Board (SREB). Of the programs, 128 (61%) were associate degree programs, and 83 (39%) represented baccalaureate programs. As long as there continues to be such a limited number of gerontologic nursing prepared faculty, curriculum development, appropriate clinical site selection with faculty role models, student interest in the specialty, and the conduct of research will continue to be hindered (Yurchuck, Brower, 1994). Related issues often cited in the literature that adversely influence the inclusion of gerontologic nursing content in the curriculum are found in Box 1-5.

The American Association of Colleges of Nursing (AACN) developed a position statement, *Nursing Education's Agenda for the 21st Century* in 1993 that "... delineates a suggested role for nursing education in the context of *Nursing's Agenda for Health Care Reform,* the goals of *Healthy People 2000,* and evolutions in health care delivery." The statement charges nursing education with anticipating and preparing for the changes indicated in the above named documents (both of which address issues related to care of older persons) to educate its students at the baccalaureate, master's, and doctoral levels for this new environment. In addition, the position statement identifies the need for curricular content that prepares nurses for roles in future health care systems, which includes acute care *and* health promotion and maintenance in relation to chronic conditions and geriatric health. In terms of program evaluation and outcomes, the statement maintains that to meet the challenges of these documents and the evolutions in health care, "... nursing curricula, instructional strategies, and clinical practice models should respond to major trends in health care." Nurse educators ought to examine their programs to assure agreement with current professional standards and health care trends; programs should include clinical practice opportunities in acute *and* long-term care (AACN, 1993). A consistent theme that emerges from this statement is that schools and colleges of nursing are being challenged to use approaches that prepare nurses at the baccalaureate, master's, and doctoral levels to meet the health care system's future needs as related to older people.

Assuring nursing students that they will be sufficiently prepared to practice in the future, a future that will undeniably include care of older adults in a wide variety of settings, necessitates answering many questions concerning nursing education. The primary question is *not* whether to include gerontologic nursing content, but to what degree it should be included. Until a sufficient number of nurse faculty are prepared in the specialty, this question will remain unanswered.

Nursing Research

Over a 22-year period, a total of nine reviews of gerontologic nursing research were found in the literature: Basson (1967), Gunter and Miller (1977), Brimmer (1979), Kayser-Jones (1981), Robinson (1981), Wolanin (1983), Burnside (1985), Cora and Lapierre (1986), and Haight (1989). The reader is referred to each original source for a detailed discussion of the contents of the review and findings. Although the methods of review were different, there were similarities in the findings that have implications for a future agenda for gerontologic nursing research.

The lack or inconsistent use of a theoretic or conceptual framework, a lack of longitudinal and descriptive studies, few replication studies, imprecise descriptions of the age of subjects, the study of mostly institutionalized older people, a high degree of interest in psychosocial-related issues, a fair number of attitude studies, and a lack of focus on clinical problems or outcomes of care represent the common conclusions of the earlier-named reviews. In recent years, there has been an increase in reports of results of the scientific study of clinical problems such as acute confusion, incontinence, restraint use, and falls. More studies such as these are needed to provide a broader data base of information and generate new knowledge so that solutions can be found to the ongoing clinical problems of older people.

The leading gerontologic nursing research questions for the future should be framed within larger issues such as patient-centered outcomes, health promotion and maintenance, prevention of disease and disability, and early detection of disease and illness—all within traditional and alternative health care delivery systems. Knowledge built through research is imperative for the development of a safe and sound knowledge base that guides clinical practice as well as for the promotion of the specialty.

Summary

This chapter discussed the historical development of the specialty of gerontologic nursing and presented demographic data about the older adult population. Implications of this growing population for health care delivery and the specialty were considered. Despite the slow progress that has been made, nursing care of older adults is now recognized as a legitimate specialty. The important groundwork that has been laid now serves as the basis from which the specialty will forge into the future. Gerontologic nurses at all levels of educational preparation and in all settings of care must now venture into that future with pride and determination as they meet their professional responsibility of providing quality care to older people everywhere. The time is now for seizing the opportunity to spearhead health care reform efforts as they affect the care of older people.

The remaining chapters in Part I focus on topics that are the foundation of gerontologic nursing care. Part II addresses influences on health and illness. Special issues related to nursing care of older people are covered in Part III. Part IV describes the special interventions of laboratory and diagnostic testing and pharmacology. Nursing care of older persons with a variety of physiologic and psychologic disorders is detailed in Part VI, with the settings of care delivery described in Part VII.

Key Points

- The growth of the nursing profession as a whole, increasing educational opportunities, demographic changes, and changes in health care delivery systems have all influenced the development of a variety of gerontologic nursing roles.
- Age 65 and older is widely accepted and used for reporting demographic statistics about older people; the number "65," however, does not automatically place one in the category of "old."
- The nurse is cautioned against viewing all older people as similar, despite the fact that most demographic data place all people over age 65 into a single reporting group.
- People 65 years of age and older currently represent about 13% of the total population.
- The most rapid and dramatic growth of the older adult segment of the total U.S. population will occur between the years 2010 and 2030, when the "baby boom" generation reaches 65 years of age.
- Based on 1991 data, there were five times as many widows as widowers in the United States.
- There are nearly three women for every man age 65 years and older.
- About 5% of people over age 65 reside in nursing homes.
- More than half of all people over age 65 live in only nine states: California, Florida, New York, Pennsylvania, Texas, Illinois, Ohio, Michigan, and New Jersey.
- Gender and race are significant indicators of poverty: older women have a poverty rate twice as high as older men, and a significant percent of blacks and Hispanics are poor in comparison to whites.
- Estimates indicate that over 80% of people over 65 years of age have one or more chronic health conditions.
- The three leading causes of death for older people in rank order are: heart conditions, malignant neoplasms, and cerebrovascular diseases.
- Nurses in a wide variety of settings and roles are challenged to provide age-appropriate and age-specific care based on a comprehensive and scientific knowledge base.
- Ageism is prejudice against the old just because they are old.
- Gerontologic nursing content should be included in all basic nursing education programs.

Critical Thinking Exercises

1. Care of the older person today is considerably different than it was 50 years ago. Cite examples of how and why care of older people is different today than in the past.
2. On reporting for work, you note that you have been assigned to two 72-year-old women for the evening. Is it safe to assume that the care of these two women will be similar, since they are the same age? Why or why not? How would their care be enhanced or be compromised if they were treated similarly?
3. As a student, you are often assigned to care for older people. At what point in your education do you feel care of the older person should be included? Early, late, or throughout your nursing program. Support your position.

REFERENCES

Alford D: Gerontological nursing: trends and transitions. In Pettengill MM, editor: *Society in transition: impact on nursing. Proceedings of the eighth annual meeting and program, midwest alliance in nursing, St. Louis, Mo,* Indianapolis, 1987, Midwest Alliance in Nursing.

American Association of Colleges of Nursing: *Position statement: nursing education's agenda for the 21st century,* Washington, D.C., 1993, The Association.

American Association of Retired Persons: *A profile of older Americans: 1992,* Washington, D.C., 1992, The Association.

American Nurses Association: Board approves new substructure, *Coun Perspect* 2(3):12, 1993.

American Nurses Association: Nursing practice standards and guidelines, *Oasis: Council on Gerontological Nursing Practice* 8(4):2, 1991.

American Nurses Association: *Professional certification: 1990 certification catalogue,* Kansas City, Mo., 1990, The Association.

American Nurses Association: *Standards and scope of gerontological nursing practice,* Kansas City, Mo., 1987, The Association.

American Nurses Credentialing Center Certification Catalogue: 1994, Washington, D.C., 1994, The Center.

Basson P: The gerontological nursing literature search: study and results, *Nurs Res* 16:267-272, 1967.

Brimmer P: The past, present and future in gerontological nursing research, *J Gerontol Nurs* 5(1):27-34, 1979.

Burnside IM: *Nursing and the aged: a self care approach,* ed 3, New York, 1988, McGraw-Hill.

Burnside IM: Gerontological nursing research: 1975-1984. In National League for Nursing, editor: *Overcoming the bias of ageism in long-term care,* New York, 1985, The League.

Butler RN, Lewis MI: *Aging and mental health,* ed 2, St. Louis, 1977, Mosby.

Butler RN: *Why survive? Being old in America,* New York, 1975, Harper & Row.

Butler RN: Age-ism: another form of bigotry, *Gerontologist* 9:243, 1969.

Cassetta RA: Opportunities on the rise in long-term care, *Am Nurse* 25(7):13-14, July/August 1993.

Columbia University School of Nursing, New York University School of Nursing, and Education Development Center, Inc.: *Dissemination of the hospital outcomes project for the elderly: Request for proposals,* December 1993.

Cora V, Lapierre E: ANA speaks out (Current research and ANA's statement on the Scope of Gerontological Nursing Practice), *J Gerontolog Nurs* 12(6):21-26, 1986.

Ebersole P, Hess P: *Toward healthy aging: human needs and nursing response,* ed 3, St. Louis, 1990, Mosby.

Edel MK: Recognizing gerontological content, *J Gerontol Nurs* 12(10):28-32, 1986.

Gunter L, Estes C: *Education for gerontic nursing,* New York, 1979, Springer.

Gunter L, Miller J: Toward a nursing gerontology, *Nurs Res* 26:208-221, 1977.

Haight BK: Update on research in long-term care: 1984-1988. In National League for Nursing, editor: *Indices for quality in long-term care: research and practice,* New York, 1989, The League.

Katz L, et al: Studies of illness in the aged. The index of ADL: a standardized measure of biological and psychosocial function, *JAMA* 185:94-98, 1963.

Kayser-Jones J: Gerontological nursing research revisited, *J Gerontol Nurs* 7:217-233, 1981.

Lawton MP, Brody EM: Assessment of older people: self maintaining and instrumental activities of daily living, *Gerontologist* 9:179, 1969.

Leon J, Lair T: *Functional status of the noninstitutionalized elderly: estimates of ADL and IADL difficulties,* DHHS Pub No (PHS) 90-3462, National Medical Expenditure Survey Research Findings 4, Agency for Health Care Policy and Research, Rockville, Md., 1990, Public Health Service.

McKnight's long term care news 14(1):1, January 1993.

National Institutes of Health: *Physical frailty: a reducible barrier to independence for older americans,* NIH Publication No 91-397, 1991, National Institute on Aging.

Robinson L: Gerontological nursing research. In Burnside IM, editor: *Nursing and the aged,* ed 2, New York, 1981, McGraw-Hill.

Small NR, Walsh MB, editors: *Teaching nursing homes: the nursing perspective,* Owings Mills, Md., 1988, National Health Publishing.

US Bureau of the Census: *Statistical abstract of the United States: 1993,* Washington, D.C., 1993, US Government Printing Office.

US Bureau of the Census: Current population reports. Special Studies, P23-178RV, *Sixty-Five Plus in America,* Washington, D.C., 1992, US Government Printing Office.

US Bureau of the Census: *Population report series, p 25, no 1018. Projections of the population of the US by age, sex and race 1988-2080,* Washington, D.C., 1989, US Government Printing Office.

Waters V, editor: *Teaching gerontology: the curriculum imperative,* New York, 1991, National League for Nursing Press.

Wolanin, MO: Clinical geriatric: Clinical geriatric research. In Werley H, Fitzpatrick J, editors: *Annual review of nursing research,* New York, 1983, Springer.

Yurchuck ER, Brower HT: Faculty preparation for gerontological nursing, *J Gerontol Nurs* 20(1):17-24, 1994.

Yurick AG et al: *The aged person and the nursing process,* ed 3, Norwalk, 1989, Appleton & Lange.

CHAPTER 2

Theories of Aging

LEARNING OBJECTIVES

On completion of this chapter, the reader will be able to:

1. Identify the basic assumptions guiding research and clinical practice related to aging theory.
2. Define aging from a biologic, sociologic, and psychologic framework.
3. Discuss the rationale for using an eclectic approach in the development of aging theories.
4. Analyze the prominent biologic, sociologic, and psychologic theories of aging.
5. Compare and contrast five sociologic theories of aging.
6. Develop nursing interventions based on the psychosocial changes associated with older adulthood.
7. Discuss several nursing implications for each of the major biologic, sociologic, and psychologic theories of aging.

For many years, American society has been searching for a concise definition of aging and the "one" theory that can explain this phenomenon. Recently, however, many scholars have concluded this quest to be vain and that no such "one" definition or theory exists that explains all aspects of aging. Perhaps future generations will be better able to understand the aging phenomenon, for which several definitions currently exist, complemented by theories. Theories function to help make sense of a particular phenomenon; they provide a sense of order and give a perspective from which to view the facts.

Because *aging* means so many things to so many individuals, it is only natural that several definitions have been proposed. Aging can be viewed as incorporating aspects of the biologic, social, psychologic, functional, and spiritual domains. Biologic, social, and psychologic theories of aging have been proposed as an attempt to explain and to support these various definitions. This chapter explores the *prominent theories* of aging in an effort to help guide the nurse in developing a gerontologic nursing theory from which to practice. Because no single gerontologic nursing theory has been identified and accepted by all individuals in this speciality, nurses often glean information from a variety of sources from which

BOX 2-1

Definitions of Aging

Biologic aging
Refers to the changes in structure and functions of the body that occur over the lifespan (Zarit, 1980).

Functional aging
Refers to the capacities of individuals for functioning in society, as compared with that of others of the same age (Birren, Renner, 1977).

Psychologic aging
Refers to behavioral changes, changes in self-perception, and reactions to the biologic changes (Gress, Bahr, 1984).

Sociologic aging
Refers to the roles and social habits of individuals in society (Birren, Renner, 1977).

Spiritual aging
Refers to changes in self and perceptions of self, of relationships of self to others, of the place of self in the world, and of the self's world view (Stallwood, Stoll, 1975).

to base their clinical decision making. Another term often used when discussing issues related to aging theories is **senescence.** Senescence has been defined as a change in behavior of the organism with age, leading to a decreased power of survival and adjustment (Comfort, 1970) (Box 2-1).

By incorporating a multidisciplinary approach to the care of older adults, nurses can view this ever-increasing portion of the population more globally. Interacting with adults is not limited to a specific disease or physiologic process, absolute developmental tasks, or psychosocial changes. Nurses have the ability to synthesize various aspects of the different aging theories, and they visualize older adults interfacing with their total environment, including physical, mental/emotional, and social aspects. Therefore an eclectic approach provides an excellent foundation when planning quality care for the older adult.

Through the years, theories have been proposed in an attempt to "explain" aging, and as more scholars continue to study this phenomenon in greater detail, even more theories are being presented. To assist the novice in understanding aging theories, several basic assumptions and concepts have been accepted over the years as guiding research and clinical practice related to the phenomena of aging (Rockstein, Chesky, Sussman, 1977; Rockstein, Sussman, 1979; Sinex, 1977). Human aging is viewed as a total process and one that begins at conception. Although aging is a continuous process, no one dies just from old age. Because individuals have uniquely different genetic, social, psychologic, and economic factors intertwined in their lives, the course of aging varies from individual to individual. Throughout a person's life, various traumatic experiences, either physical and/or emotional, may actually weaken the individual's ability to repair or maintain himself or herself. And lastly, the final period of life called senescence occurs when the biologic organism cannot balance the "breaking down and repairing" mechanisms in the body.

BIOLOGIC THEORIES OF AGING

Biologic theories are concerned with answering basic questions regarding the physiologic processes that occur in all living organisms as they chronologically age. These age-related changes occur independently of any external or pathologic influence. The primary question being addressed relates to the factors that trigger the actual aging process in organisms.

The foci of biologic theories in relation to age-related changes include explanations of the following: certain deleterious effects leading to decreasing function of the organism, which ultimately leads to a complete failure of either an organ or an entire system; gradually occurring age-related changes that are progressive over time; and intrinsic changes that can affect all members of a species because of chronologic age (Hayflick, 1977). In addition, according to these theories, all organs in any one organism do not age at the same rate, and any one organ does not necessarily age at the same rate in different individuals of the same species (Table 2-1).

Hayflick Limit Theory

One of the first proposed biologic theories is based on a study completed in 1961 by Hayflick and Moorehead. This particular study included an experiment on fetal fibroblastic cells and their reproductive capabilities. The results of this landmark study changed the way scientists viewed the biologic aging process.

Hayflick and Moorehead's study showed that there are functional changes that do occur within cells and are responsible for the aging of the cells and organism. The study further supported the hypothesis that a cumulative effect of improper functioning of cells and eventual loss of cells in organs and tissues is therefore responsible for the "aging phenomenon." This study contradicted earlier studies by Carrel and Ebeling in which chick embryo cells were able to be kept alive indefinitely in a laboratory setting; the conclusion from this 1912 experiment was that cells do not wear out but continue to function normally forever. An interesting aspect of the 1961 study was that freezing was found to halt the biologic cellular clock (Hayflick, Moorehead, 1961).

TABLE 2-1

Summary of Biologic Theories of Aging

Theory	Dynamics	Retardants
Molecular theories		
Error	Faulty synthesis of DNA and/or RNA	
Somatic	Alteration in RNA/DNA; protein or enzyme synthesis causes defective structure or function	
Transcription	Failure of transcription or translation between cells; malfunctions of RNA or related enzymes	
Programmed	Biologic clock triggers specific cell behavior at specific time	Hypothermia and diet can delay cell division but not number of divisions
Run-out-of-program	Organism capable of specific number of cell divisions and specific life span	
System level theories		
Immunologic/autoimmune	Alteration of B- and T-cells lead to loss of capacity for self-regulation; normal or age-altered cells recognized as foreign matter; system reacts by forming antibodies to destroy these cells	Immunoengineering, selective alteration, and replacement or rejuvenation of immune system
Cellular theories		
Free radical	Oxidation of fats, proteins, carbohydrates, and elements creates free electrons, which attach to other molecules, altering cellular structure	Improve environmental monitoring; decrease intake of free radical–stimulating foods; increase vitamin A and C intake (mercaptans); increase vitamin E intake; use of Coenyzme Q10
Cross-link	Lipids, proteins, carbohydrates, and nucleic acid react with chemicals or radiation to form bonds that cause an increase in cell rigidity and instability	Caloric restrictions, lathyrogen-antilink agents
Clinker	Mix of somatic, cross-link, and free radical theories	
Wear-and-tear	Repeated injury or overuse of cells, tissues, organs, or systems	

From Ebersole P, Hess P: *Toward healthy aging: human needs and nursing response,* ed 4, St. Louis, 1994, Mosby.

Based on this 1961 study, unlimited cell-division was not found to occur; the immortality of individual cells was found to be more abnormal than a normal occurrence. Therefore this study seemed to support the Hayflick Limit Theory. Life expectancy was generally seen as being preprogrammed, within a species-specific range; this biologic clock for humans was estimated as being 110 to 120 years (Stanley, Pye, MacGregor, 1975). Based on the conclusions of this experiment, the Hayflick Limit Theory is sometimes called the "Biological Clock," "Cellular Aging," or "Genetic Theory," as well as the "Program Theory of Aging" (Fig. 2-1).

The Error Theory

As a cell ages, various changes do occur naturally in its DNA and RNA, the building blocks of the cell. There tends to be an increase in the size of the cell's nucleus without substantial increase in DNA substance. This is not true of RNA. RNA does increase with the expansion of the nucleus but without a corresponding increase in RNA synthesis; in actuality, there is a decrease in RNA synthesis. Other age-related nucleus changes include clumping, shrinking, fragmentation, and a dissolution of the nondividing or chromatic chromosomes. Aging DNA/RNA also have a decreased ability to divide and reproduce.

In 1963 Orgel proposed the Error Theory, sometimes called the Error Catastrophe Theory. The hypothesis of this theory is based on the idea that errors can occur in the transcription in any step of protein synthesis and this eventually leads to either the aging or the actual death of a cell. The error would cause the reproduction of an enzyme or protein that was not an exact copy of the original. The next transcription would again contain an error. As the effect continued through several generations of proteins, the end product would not even resemble the original cell (Sonneborn, 1979).

In recent years, the theory has not been supported by research. Although changes do occur in the activity of various enzymes with aging, studies have not found that

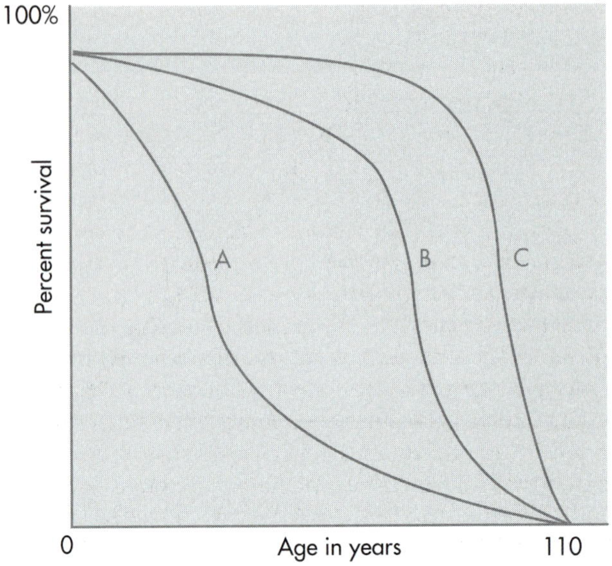

Fig. 2-1 Increase in human life span toward the longevity curve. When deaths are primarily the result of many random events (disease, accidents, etc.), a curve noting the progressive loss of individuals from a population resembles curve *A*. This curve has such a shape because individual deaths are occurring at any time with little regard to age. As deaths occurring in the early years are eliminated, a curve like *B* is seen. However, when accident and disease become less and less common, curve *C* shows that the mean life span is closer to the maximum life span. The latter is the same regardless of the mean life span, since it is more fully representative of death associated with aging phenomena. (From Hampton J: *The biology of human aging,* Dubuque, Ia., 1991, Wm C Brown.)

all aged cells contain altered or misspecified proteins, nor is aging automatically or necessarily accelerated if misspecified proteins or enzymes are introduced to a cell (Hayflick, 1983).

Wear and Tear Theory

This theory has much physiologic support for its hypothesis that cells wear out over time because of continued use. When this theory was first proposed in 1891 by Weisman, death was seen as a result of tissues being worn out because they could not rejuvenate themselves in an endless manner (Hayflick, 1988). Essentially, the theory reflects a belief that organs/tissues have a preprogrammed amount of energy available to them and eventually wear out when the allotted energy is expended. Eventually, this leads to the death of the entire organism.

Under this theory, aging is viewed as almost a preprogrammed process—a process thought to be vulnerable to stress, or an accumulation of injuries or trauma, which may actually accelerate it. Aging then can be seen as "a physiological process determined by the amount of wear and tear to which a person has been exposed" (Matteson, McConnell, 1988).

Proponents of this theory cite microscopic signs of wear and tear that have been found in striated and smooth muscle tissue, and in nerve cells. Researchers are once again questioning this theory with the additional emphasis on daily exercise and increasing activity patterns even in persons with chronic limiting states such as rheumatoid arthritis. If exercising has been found to increase a person's level of functioning rather than decreasing it, how can the wear and tear hypothesis be true?

Free-Radical Theory

In 1956 D. Harman proposed the concept of free radical molecules being normally present in the body and being predictive of chronologic age. These unstable molecules have a high affinity for reacting with other molecules but with the oxygen molecule in particular. Although naturally occurring as a byproduct of normal metabolism, free radicals can be produced: (1) by the oxygenation process involved with various environmental pollutants such as ozone or pesticides; (2) as a reaction to exposure to radiation; or (3) simply as a chain reaction with other free radical molecules in a self-propagating manner.

The highly reactive free radicals tend to attach themselves to cell membranes, in particular, membranes composed of unsaturated lipids such as the mitochrondria, lysosomes, and nuclear membranes. This action monopolizes the receptor sites on the membrane, thereby inhibiting the interaction with other substances that normally use the sites; this chemical reaction is called lipid perioxidation (Harman, 1956). Therefore the mitochrondria, for example, can no longer function as efficiently, and its cell membrane may become damaged resulting in increased permeability. If excessive fluid is either lost or gained, the internal homeostasis is disrupted and cell death may result.

There are other deleterious results related to free radical molecules in the body. Although these molecules do not contain DNA themselves, they can cause mutations to occur in the DNA-RNA transcription, thereby producing mutations of the original protein. In nervous and muscle tissue, to which free radicals have a high affinity, a substance called lipofuscin has been found and is thought to be indicative of chronologic age.

Lipofuscin, a lipid- and protein-enriched pigmented material, has been found to accumulate in older adults' tissues, and is commonly referred to as "age spots." As the lipofuscin's presence increases, healthy tissue is slowly being deprived of its oxygen and nutrient supply. Further degeneration of surrounding tissue eventually leads to the actual death of the tissue. The body does have naturally occurring antioxidants or protective mechanisms. Vitamins C and E are two of these substances that can inhibit the functioning of the free radicals or possibly decrease the production of them in the body.

According to Rockstein and Sussman (1979), butylated hydroxytoluene, a common food preservative, has been shown to be an antioxidant when fed to mice. It has not been proven that the substance has the same effect in humans. Further research is continuing in the area of free radicals and their role in cell damage. The role of lipofuscin as a chronologic age marker remains unquestioned (Brody, 1987).

Immunity Theory

As a person ages, the immune system functions less effectively; the term *immunosenescence* has been given to this age-related decrease in function. The changes are most apparent in the T-lymphocytes, although changes also occur in the functioning capabilities of B-lymphocyte. Accompanying these changes is a decrease in the body's defense against foreign pathogens, and an increase in the production of autoantibodies leading to an increase in the development of autoimmune-related diseases in older age (Figs. 2-2 through 2-4, pp. 28-29).

The changes occurring in the immune system cannot precisely be explained by an exact cause-and-effect relationship, but they do seem to increase with advancing age. The majority of the changes relate to the changes seen in T-lymphocytes. These changes include a decrease in humoral immune response, often predisposing the older adult to (1) decreased resistance to a tumor cell challenge and the development of cancer, (2) decreased ability to initiate the immune process and mobilize the body's defenses in aggressively attacking pathogens, and (3) heightened production of autoantigens, often leading to an increase in autoimmune-related diseases.

Because the immune theory closely relates to the concept of autoimmunity, some scholars combine this concept with the broader theory. The autoimmune theory states that aging is directly related to the changes occurring because of an increase in the production of autoantibodies. Therefore these two theories are interrelated and are often regarded as being combined into the broader concept of the immune theory.

Cross-linkage Theory

A theory closely intertwined with the immune theory is the cross-linkage theory first introduced by J. Bjorksten in 1942 (1976). According to this theory, normally separated molecular structures are bound together through chemical reactions. Primarily this involves collagen, which is a relatively inert long-chain macromolecule produced by fibroblasts. As new fibers are created, they become enmeshed with old fibers and form an actual chemical cross link. The end result of this cross-linkage process is an increase in density of the collagen molecule but a decrease in the capacity to transport nutrients to, and to remove waste products from, the cells. Eventually, this results in a decrease in the function of the structure (see Figs. 2-5 and 2-6, p. 30).

Cross-linkage agents have been found in unsaturated fats, polyvalent metal ions like aluminum, zinc, and magnesium, and in association with excessive radiation exposure. Many of the medications ingested by the older population contain aluminum (antacids and coagulants), as well as the common cooking ingredient baking powder. Some research supports a combination of exercise and dietary restrictions in helping to inhibit the cross-linkage process as well as the use of vitamin C prophylactically as an antioxidant agent (Bjorksten, 1976).

As a person ages and the immune system begins to decrease in its efficiency, the body's defense mechanism cannot remove the cross-linking agent before it becomes securely established. After the agent has attached itself to the second DNA strand, normal mitosis cannot occur, and incomplete cell division and even death can result. The elastin in the collagen molecule becomes fragmented and calcification becomes more prominent. The end result is a brittle quality of cartilage, predisposing the site to being damaged by minimal trauma. Cross linkage is proposed as a primary cause of arteriosclerosis, a decrease in efficiency of the immune system with age, and the loss of elasticity often seen in older adult skin.

Implications for Nursing

When interacting with the older population, it is important to relate the key concepts of the biologic theories to the care being provided. Although these theories do not provide *the answer,* they certainly can provide an explanation for some of the changes seen in the aging individual. Aging and disease do not necessarily go together, and the person involved in providing care for an older adult needs to have a clear understanding of the difference between age-related changes and those that may actually be pathologic.

Activity continues to play an important role in the lives of older adults. Daily routines need to incorporate opportunities to capitalize on existing abilities, to strengthen potential weakened muscles, and to prevent further atrophy of muscles related to disuse. Encouraging the older adult to participate in activities, especially new ones or ones resulting in frustration, may prove a real challenge to nurses interacting with these clients.

The ability to perform the activities of daily living (ADLs) require functional use of extremities. Daily exercises enhancing upper-arm strength and hand dexterity contribute to the older adult's ability to successfully perform dressing and grooming activities. Even chair-based activities like deep breathing increase the oxygen flow to the brain, thereby promoting clear mental cognition, minimizing dizziness, and promoting stamina with activity.

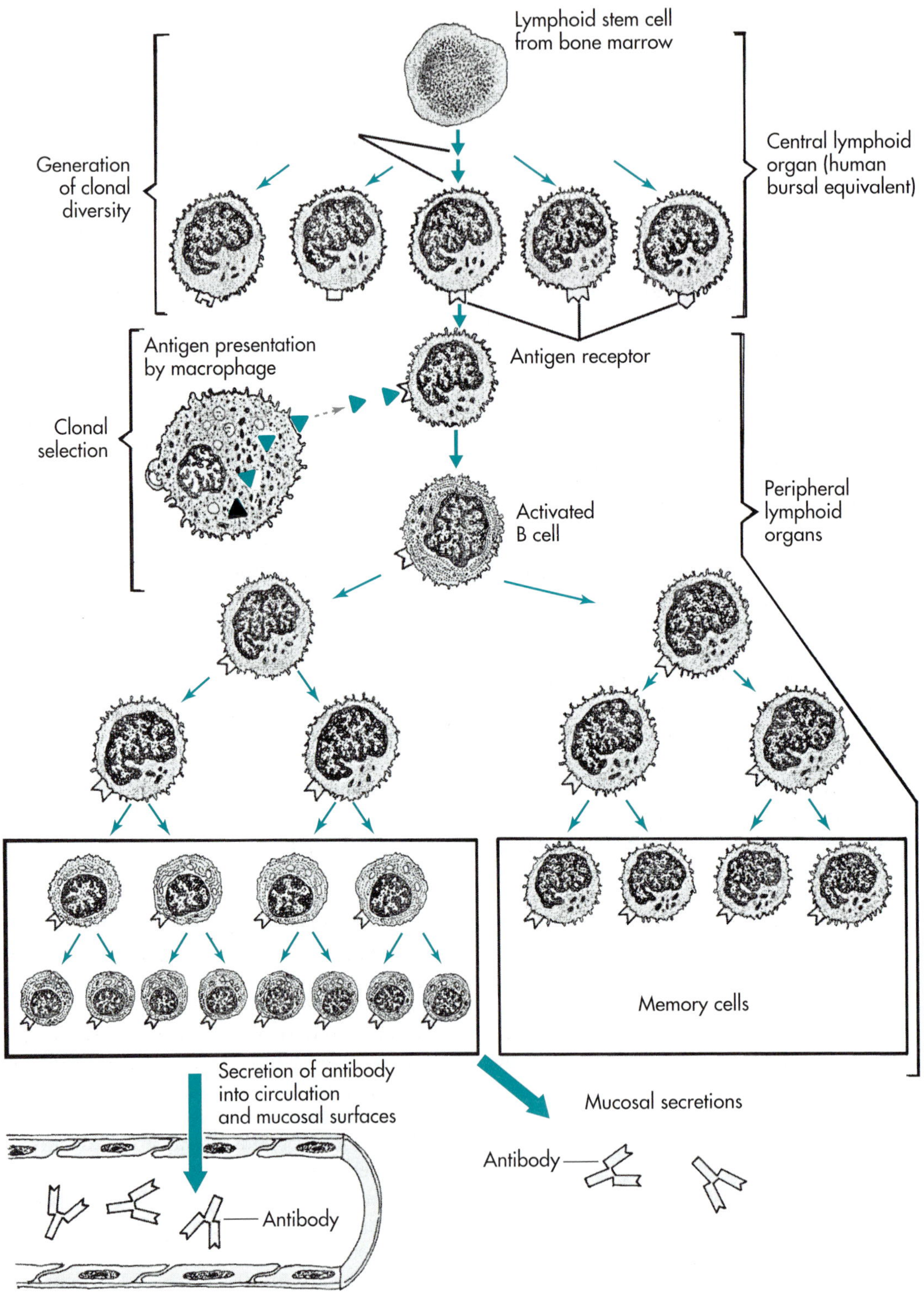

Fig. 2-2 The process involved in the concept of immunity in the body. Antigen-specific B-lymphocytes are under the control of hormones and are directly involved in providing a defense against foreign sources. Antigens originating in macrophages interact with specific receptor sites on the lymphocytes and initiate the process of antibody production. (From McCance KL, Huether SE: *Pathophysiology: the biological basis for disease in adults and children,* ed 2, St. Louis, 1994, Mosby.)

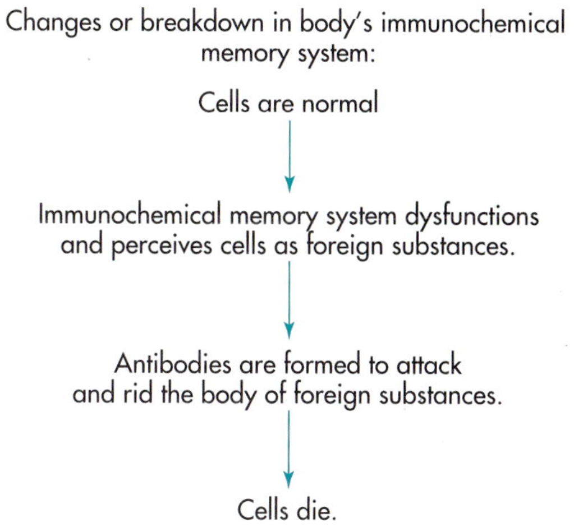

Fig. 2-3 Changes or breakdowns in body's immunochemical memory system. (From Eliopoulos C: *Gerontological nursing,* ed 3, Philadelphia, 1993, JB Lippincott.)

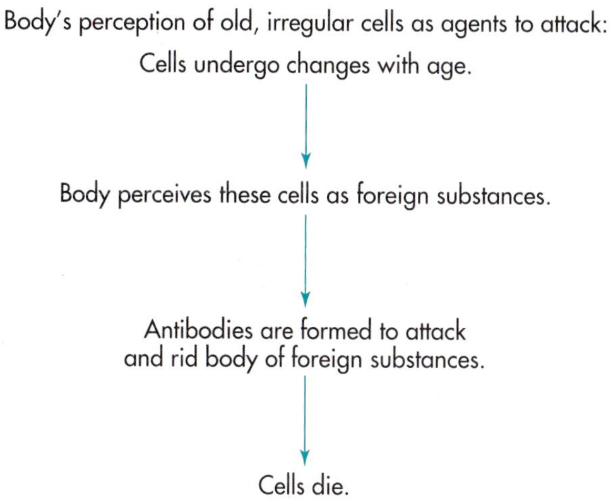

Fig. 2-4 Body's perception of old, irregular cells as agents to attack. (From Eliopoulos C: *Gerontological nursing,* ed 3, Philadelphia, 1993, JB Lippincott.)

Encouraging the older adult to participate in daily walking, even on a limited basis, facilitates peripheral circulation and promotes the development of collateral circulation. Walking can also be helpful with weight control, which often becomes a problem in the older adult. Additional benefits of walking include (1) replacement of fat with muscle tissue, (2) prevention of muscle atrophy, and (3) a generalized increase in the person's sense of well-being.

The health care delivery system is turning its focus toward disease prevention and health promotion. The older adult must be included in this focus. Stereotypic views related to older adults being "too old to learn new things" must be replaced with factual knowledge about the cognitive abilities of older adults. It is necessary for client teaching to stress the concept that certain conditions or diseases are not inevitable just because of advancing years. A high level of wellness is needed to help minimize the potential damage caused by disease in later years. Although aging brings with it a decrease in the normal functioning of the immune system, older adults should not suffer needlessly from infections and/or disease. Encouraging preventive measures like an annual influenza vaccine or a one-time innoculation with the pneumococcal vaccine are essential to providing a quality life experience for the older population.

Other applications of biologic theories to practice include the recognition that life stresses, both physical and psychologic, have an impact on the aging process. In planning interventions, attention should be paid to the various stress factors in an older person's life. Activities to minimize stress and to promote healthy coping mechanisms must be included in the client teaching plan for the older adult.

Teaching the basic techniques of relaxation, guided imagery, visualization, distraction, and music therapy facilitates a sense of control over potential stress-producing situations. Additional options involving the application of hot or cold therapeutic touch and massage therapy might be explored. Being aware of individual cultural preferences and sharing these among other health care professionals will further help promote positive interactions with older adults in all settings.

SOCIOLOGIC THEORIES OF AGING

Sociologic theories differ from biologic theories in that they tend to focus on roles and relationships in which each individual participates in later life. In some respects, sociologic theories relate to various social adaptations in the life of the older adult. One of the easiest ways to view the sociologic theories is to view them in context of the societal values of the time frame in which they were written.

During the 1960s, sociologists focused on the losses related to older age and the manner in which individuals adjust to these losses in the context of their roles and reference groups. A decade later, society began to have a broader view of aging as reflected in the aging theories proposed during this period. These theories focused on more global, societal, and structural factors that influenced the lives of the aging person. The 1980s and 1990s again brought another change in focus from society. At this point, sociologists began to explore interrelationships—interrelationships between older adults and the physical, political, and even socioeconomic milieu in which they lived.

Disengagement Theory

When the disengagement theory was introduced by Cumming and Henry in 1961, the theory sparked immediate controversy. These two theorists viewed aging as a developmental task in and of itself, with its own norms and appropriate patterns of behavior. These appropriate patterns of behavior were conceptualized as a mutual agreement between the older adult and society on a reciprocal withdrawal. The individual would change from being centered on society and interacting in the community, to a self-centered person withdrawing from society, by virtue of becoming "old." Therefore social equilibrium would be achieved as the end result (Cumming, Henry, 1961).

The idea that older adults preferred to withdraw from society and to voluntarily decrease their interactions with others was not readily accepted by the general public, much less the older population. Although the theory oversimplified the aging process, the lasting benefit of the theory relates to the controversy it created. The theory itself is no longer supported, but the discussion stemming from its premise continues today.

Activity Theory

With one group of theorists proposing the concept that older adults need to disengage from society, other sociologists proposed that people need to stay active if they are to age successfully. In 1953 Havighurst and Albrecht first proposed the idea that aging successfully meant staying active. It wasn't until 10 years later that the phrase "activity theory" was actually coined by Havighurst and his associates (Havighurst, Neugarten, Tobin, 1963).

Activity is viewed by this theory as being necessary to maintain a person's life satisfaction and a positive self-concept. By remaining active, the older person stays young and alive and does not withdraw from society because of an age parameter. Essentially, the person actively participates in a continuous struggle to remain "middle-aged."

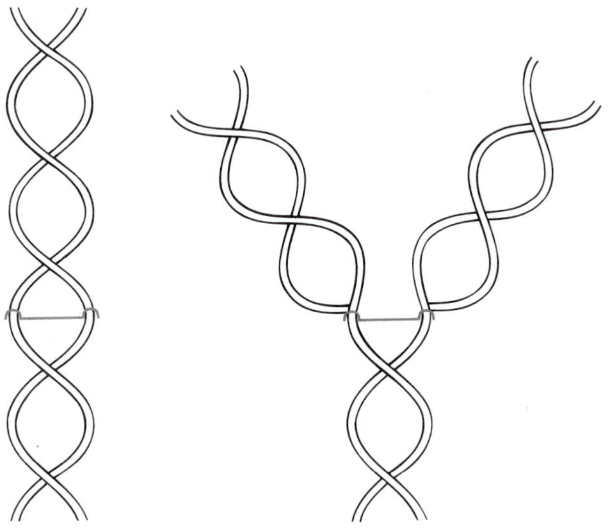

Fig. 2-5 Here the cross-linking agent has become attached to the second strand of DNA before the defense mechanism could excise it. When this happens, the cell is doomed. If the cross-linker is excised, there will be no template for repair as both strands are involved at the same point. If the cross-linker remains, it will block the normal parting of strands in mitosis at a stage where the resultant DNA can neither return to normal nor complete the division. (Bjorkstein J: Cross-linkage and the aging process. In Rockstein M, et al, editors: *Theoretical aspects of aging,* New York, 1974, Academic Press. Cited in Matteson MA, McConnell ES: *Gerontological nursing,* Philadelphia, 1988, WB Saunders.)

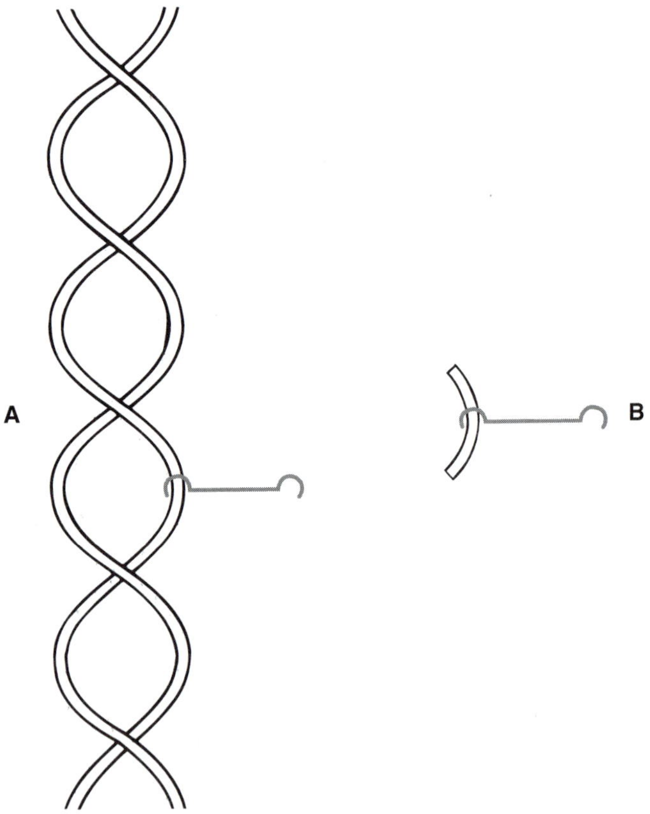

Fig. 2-6 **A** A cross-linking agent attaches itself at one point of a DNA molecule, involving one strand only. **B** The agent is excised by defense mechanisms, together with a piece of the DNA affected. The damage is then repaired; the unaffected strand is the template. (Bjorkstein J: Cross-linkage and the aging process. In Rockstein M et al, editors: *Theoretical aspects of aging,* New York, 1974, Academic Press. Cited in Matteson MA, McConnell ES: *Gerontological nursing,* Philadelphia, 1988, WB Saunders.)

The theory is based on three assumptions: it is better to be active than inactive; it is better to be happy than unhappy; and that an older individual is the best judge of his or her own success in achieving the first two assumptions (Havighurst, 1972). Within the context of this theory, activity can be viewed very broadly as being physical or intellectual. Therefore even with illness or advancing age, the older person can remain "active" and achieve a sense of life satisfaction (Havighurst, Neugarten, Tobin, 1963).

Continuity Theory

The continuity theory dispels the premise of both the disengagement and activity theories. According to this theory, being active, trying to maintain a sense of being middle-aged, or willingly withdrawing from society does not necessarily bring happiness. Instead, the continuity theory proposes that how a person has been throughout life is how that person will *continue* through the remainder of life (Havighurst, Neugarten, Tobin, 1963).

Old age is not viewed as a terminal or final part of life separated from the rest of life. According to this theory, the latter part of life is a continuation of the earlier part and therefore an integral component of the entire life cycle. When viewed from this perspective, the theory can be seen as a developmental theory. Simply stated, the theory proposes that, as people age, they try to maintain or continue previous habits, preferences, commitments, values, beliefs, and all the factors that have contributed to their personalities (Havighurst, Neugarten, Tobin, 1963).

Age Stratification Theory

Beginning in the 1970s, aging theories began to focus more broadly on societal and structural factors, which influenced how the older population was being viewed. The age stratification theory is only one example of a theory addressing societal values. The key societal issue being addressed in this theory is the concept of interdependence between the aging person and society at large (Riley, Johnson, Foner, 1972).

According to this theory, the aging person is viewed as an individual element of society and also as a member with peers as a social process. The theory attempts to explain the interdependence between the older adult and society and how they are constantly influencing each other in a variety of ways.

Riley (1985) discusses the five major concepts of this theory: each individual progresses through society in groups of cohorts that are collectively aging socially, biologically, and psychologically; new cohorts are continually being born, and each of them experiences their own unique sense of history; society itself can be divided into various strata according to the parameters of age and roles; not only are people and roles within each strata continuously changing, but so is society at large; and finally, the interaction between individual aging people and the entire society is not stagnant but remains dynamic.

Person-Environment Fit Theory

One of the newer aging theories relates the individual's personal competence within the environment in which he or she interacts. This theory was proposed by Lawton (1982) and examines the concept of interrelationships between the competencies of a group of people, older adults, and their society or environment.

Everyone, including the older person, has certain personal competencies that help mold and shape the person throughout life. Lawton (1982) identified these personal competencies as including: ego strength, level of motor skills, individual biologic health, and cognitive and sensory-perceptual capacities. All of these help a person deal with the environment in which one lives.

As a person ages, there may be changes or even decreases in some of these personal competencies. These changes influence the individual's abilities to interrelate with the environment. If a person develops one or more chronic diseases such as rheumatoid arthritis or cardiovascular disease, then competencies may be impaired and the level of interrelatedness may be limited.

The theory further proposes that, as a person ages, the environment becomes more threatening and one may feel incompetent in dealing with it. In a society constantly making rapid technologic advances, this theory helps explain why an older person might feel inhibited and might even retreat from society (Box 2-2).

Implications for Nursing

Because society is becoming older, it is important to remember that the aging population cannot be grouped collectively as just *one* segment of the population. These individuals are just that, individuals. They represent different cohorts, each with their own unique view of history. Older adults do not represent a sociologic and homogeneous group, and care needs to be taken not to treat them as if they do.

Older adults respond to current experiences based on their past life encounters, beliefs, and expectations. If their "normal" reaction to stress, challenges, or fear is to disengage from interactions, then current situations often produce the same responses. Because older adults are individuals, their responses must be respected. Conversely, encouraging participation in group activities may facilitate the individual's ability to cope with a particular life situation.

Withdrawal may be a manifestation of a deeper problem such as depression. Using assessment abilities and specific tools, nurses can further investigate the situation and plan appropriate interventions to help resolve a potentially adverse situation. The older adult may refuse to

BOX 2-2

Sociologic Theories of Aging

Activity

The more active older adults are, the greater the life satisfaction. Self-concept is related to roles, and previous roles must be replaced with new ones to remain active (Cavin, 1949; Havighurst, Albrecht, 1953).

Disengagement

Society withdraws from the aging person to the same extent that the person withdraws from society. Mutual withdrawal (Cumming, Henry, 1961).

Continuity

In the process of becoming an adult, the individual develops habits, commitments, preferences, and a host of other dispositions that become part of his or her personality. As the person ages, these are maintained. In the life cycle, these predispositions constantly evolve from interactions among personal preferences and experiences and biologic and psychologic capacities (Atchley, 1972).

Age stratification

Society consists of groups of cohorts that age collectively. The people and roles in these cohorts change and influence each other, as does society at large. A high degree of interdependence therefore exists between the older adult and society (Riley, Johnson, Foner, 1972).

Person-environment fit

Personal competencies mold and shape all people which in turn, assist them in dealing with environments. Changes occur in competencies with age, thus affecting the older person's ability to interrelate with the environment (Lawton, 1982).

Modified from Patrick M: Characteristics of older people and introduction to theories of aging. In Carnevali D, Patrick M: *Nursing management for the elderly*, ed 3, Philadelphia, 1993, JB Lipponcott.

engage in a particular activity because of "fear of failure" or frustration in not being able to perform the activity. Planning realistic activities for particular client groups is crucial to successful group interactions. The successful completion of a group activity provides an opportunity for increasing an older person's self-confidence, whereas frustration over an impossible task further promotes feelings of inadequacy and uselessness.

By looking at the past and being aware of significant events or even beliefs about health and illness, the health care provider can develop a deeper understanding of *why* these particular older adults act or believe the way they do. This knowledge can certainly assist in helping to plan not only activities but also meaningful client teaching. The health care provider will gain insight into how a particular group of older adults responds to illness and views *healthy aging.*

Another application of the sociologic theories relates to assisting older adults in adapting to various limitations and in securing appropriate living arrangements. Following the passage of the 1990 Americans with Disabilities Act in a majority of buildings are now easily accessible to individuals with special needs. These special needs may include doorways that are wide enough for wheelchairs, ramps instead of stairs, handrails in hallways, and working elevators. While these changes assist younger members of society with limited physical capabilities, they also benefit the older adult. In addition, older adults might consider the installation of medical alert devices, preprogrammed and/or large-numbered phones, and even special security systems.

Helping older adults adjust to limitations, while accentuating positive attributes, may aid older people in remaining independent and may perpetuate a high quality of life during later years. These adaptations may encourage the older adult to remain in the community, perhaps even in the family home, instead of being prematurely institutionalized. The older adult continues to feel valued and viewed as an active member of society when allowed to maintain a sense of control over the living environment.

In some cities, multigenerational communities are developing, and a sharing of different cultures as well as generations is being fostered. Schools are promoting "adopt a grandparent" programs, day care centers are combining services for children and older adults, and older volunteers visit hospitalized children or phone "latch key" children after school. All of these are examples of sociologic aging theories in place in society today. Older adults are continuing to be active, engaging or disengaging as they wish, and continuing to be valued members of the population.

PSYCHOLOGIC THEORIES OF AGING

The psychologic theories of aging are much broader in scope than the previous theories, because they are influenced by both biology and sociology. Therefore it is safe to say that psychologic aging cannot readily be separated from biologic and sociologic influences.

As a person ages psychologically, various adaptive changes occur that assist the person to cope with or accept some of the biologic changes. Some of the adaptive mechanisms include memory, learning capacity, feelings, intellectual functioning, and motivations to do or not to do particular activities (Birren, Cunningham, 1985). Psychologic aging therefore includes not only behavioral changes but also developmental aspects related to the life of an older adult. How does behavior change in relation to advancing age? Are these behavioral changes consistent in pattern from one individual to another? Theorists are searching for answers to questions such as these.

Maslow's Hierarchy of Human Needs Theory

According to this theory, each individual has an innate internal hierarchy of needs that motivates all human behaviors (Maslow, 1954). These human needs have different orders of priorities. When people achieve fulfillment of elemental needs, they strive to meet those on the next level until the highest order of needs is reached. These human needs are often depicted as a triangle with the most elemental needs at the base.

The initial human needs each person must meet relate to physiologic needs, or needs for basic survival. Initially, a starving person worries about obtaining food to survive. Once this need is met, the next concern is about safety and security. These needs must be met, at least to some extent, before the need for being loved and accepted, and feeling of belonging become a concern. According to Maslow (1968), as each succeeding layer of needs is addressed, the individual is motivated to look to the needs at the next higher step.

Maslow's fully developed, self-actualized person displays high levels of all of the following characteristics: perception of reality; acceptance of self, others, and nature; spontaneity; problem-solving ability; self-direction; detachment and the desire for privacy; freshness of peak experiences; identification with other human beings; satisfying and changing relationships with other people; a democratic character structure; creativity; and a sense of values (Maslow, 1968). Maslow's ideal "self-actualized person" is probably only attained by about 1% of the population (Thomas, Chess, 1977). Although limited actual achievement of this final level may be true, the person developing in a healthy way is always moving to more self-fulfilling levels (Fig. 2-7).

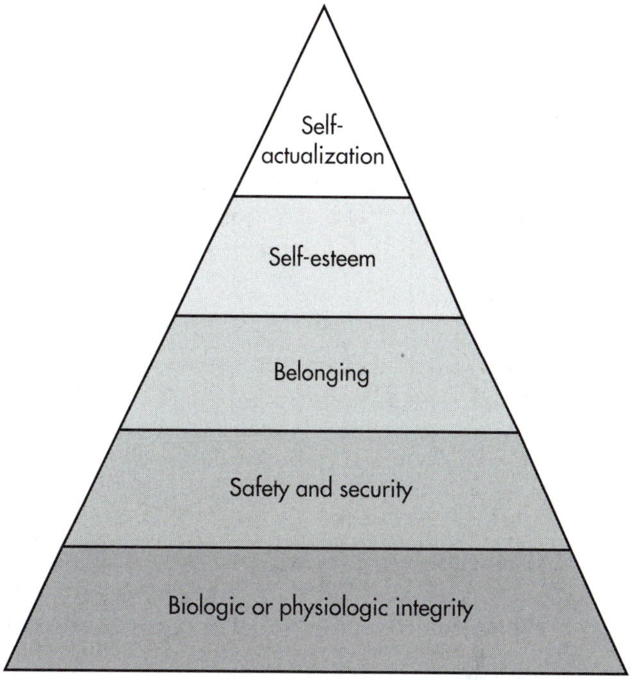

Fig. 2-7 Maslow's hierarchy of needs. (From Ebersole P, Hess P: *Toward healthy aging: human needs and nursing response,* ed 4, St. Louis, 1994, Mosby.)

Jung's Theory of Individualism

The Swiss psychologist Carl Jung (1960) proposed a theory of personality development throughout life: childhood, youth and young adulthood, middle age, and old age. An individual's personality is composed of the ego, the personal unconsciousness, and the collective unconsciousness. According to this theory, a person's personality is visualized to be either oriented toward the external world (extroverted) or toward subjective, inner experiences (introverted). A balance between these two forces, which are present in every individual, is essential for mental health.

Applying Jung's theory to individuals as they progress through life, it is at the onset of middle age that the person begins to question values, beliefs, and possible dreams left undone. The phrase "midlife crisis" became popular based on this theory and refers to a period of emotional, and sometimes behavioral, turmoil that heralds the onset of middle age. This period may last for several years, with the exact time and duration varying from person to person.

During this period, the individual often searches for answers about reaching goals—whether a part of their personality or "true self" has been neglected and whether time is running out for the completion of these quests. This may be the first time that the individual becomes aware of the effects of the aging process and that the first part of the adult life is over. This realization does not necessarily signal a time of trauma. For many people, it is just another "rite of passage."

As the person ages chronologically, the personality often begins to change from being outwardly focused and concerned about establishing oneself in society, to becoming more inward, as the individual begins to search for answers from within. Successful aging, when viewed from Jung's theory, is when a person looks inward and values oneself for more than just current physical limitations or losses. The individual accepts past accomplishments and limitations.

Course of Human Life Theory

Charlotte Buhler (1968) proposed a theory describing human development based on an extensive study of bio-

TABLE 2-2

Summary of Erikson's Theory: Middle and Older Adulthood

Stages and ages	Characteristics of stages	Theory addendum
Generativity versus self-absorption or stagnation (40 to 65 years) (middle adulthood) Mode: nurturing Virtue: care	Mature adult is concerned with establishing and guiding next generation. Adult looks beyond self and expresses concern for future of world in general.	Self-absorbed adult will be preoccupied with personal well-being and material gains. Preoccupation with self leads to stagnation of life.
Ego integrity versus despair (65 years to death) (older adulthood) Mode: acceptance Virtue: wisdom	Older adult can look back with sense of satisfaction and acceptance of life and death.	Unsuccessful resolution of this crisis may result in sense of despair in which individual views life as series of misfortunes, disappointments, and failures.

Modified from Potter PA, Perry AG: *Fundamentals of nursing,* ed 3, St. Louis, 1993, Mosby.

graphic materials and personal interviews. The focus of this theory is on identifying and attaining personal life goals throughout five phases of development. She proposed that self-fulfillment was the key to healthy development and that unhappy or maladjusted people are unfulfilled in some way.

In 1968 Buhler expanded her earlier thoughts to clearly identify five separate phases in the attainment of personal life goals through which a person passes. During childhood, the person has not really formalized specific life goals and the future is viewed in vague terms. Once adolescence and young adulthood is reached, a person begins to conceptualize specific life goals and gains an understanding of individual potential. By age 25, a person becomes more concrete about life goals and actively works toward achieving them. It is during the middle years, or years of mature adulthood, that the individual begins the process of "life review:" looking back over life, evaluating what has or has not been accomplished, and often beginning to revise life goals, or simply plan for the future. Buhler saw the final phase of old age (age 65 or 70) as being a time to rest from aspiring to achieve life goals.

Eight Stages of Life Theory

Erikson (1950) proposed a theory of psychologic development that reflects cultural and societal influences. The major focus of development in this theory is with an individual's ego structure, or sense of self, especially in response to the ways in which society shapes its development. In each of the eight stages identified by Erikson, a "crisis" occurs that impacts the development of the person's ego. The manner in which a person masters any particular stage influences future success or lack of success in mastering the next stage of development.

When considering the older adult, attention needs to be focused on the developmental tasks of both middle and older adulthood. The task of middle adulthood is resolving the conflict between generativity and self-absorption. During older adulthood, the developmental task needing resolution is balancing the search for integrity and wholeness with a sense of despair (Table 2-2).

In 1968 Peck expanded Erikson's original theory regarding the eighth stage of the older adult. Erikson grouped all individuals together into "old age" beginning at age 65 years and did not anticipate that a person may potentially live for another 30 to 40 years beyond this identified milestone. Since people were living longer, there became an obvious need to identify additional stages for older adults. Peck (1968) expanded the eighth stage of ego integrity versus despair into three stages: ego differentiation versus work role preoccupation, body transcendence versus body preoccupation, and ego transcendence versus ego preoccupation.

During the stage of ego differentiation versus work role preoccupation, the task for the older adult is to achieve identity and feelings of worth from sources other than the work role. The onset of retirement and termination of the work role may reduce feelings of self-worth. In contrast, a person with a well-differentiated ego, who is defined by many dimensions, can replace the work role as the major defining source for self-esteem.

The second stage of body transcendence versus body preoccupation refers to the older person's view of the physical changes that occur as a result of the aging process. The task is to adjust to or transcend the declines that may occur in order to maintain feelings of well-being. This task can be successfully resolved by focusing on the satisfaction obtained from interpersonal interactions and psychosocial-related activities.

The third and final task of ego transcendence versus ego preoccupation involves acceptance of the individual's eventual death without dwelling on the prospect of it. Remaining actively involved with a future that extends beyond a person's morality is the adjustment that must be made to achieve ego transcendence.

Developmental Task Theory

According to Havighurst (1972), each individual must learn specific developmental tasks at various stages of life; the successful achievement of these tasks contribute to the individual's happiness and feelings of success. The specific developmental tasks arise from several sources: (1) physical maturation; (2) cultural expectations of society; and (3) the individual's personal values and aspirations. The developmental tasks of the older adult include: adjusting to decreasing physical strength and health; adjusting to retirement and reduced income; adjusting to the death of a spouse or a significant other; establishing an explicit association with one's age group; adopting and adapting social roles in a flexible way; and establishing satisfactory physical living arrangements (Havighurst, 1972).

Implications for Nursing

Integrating the psychologic aging theories into nursing practice becomes increasingly important as the population continues to age. Present and future generations can learn from the past. Older adults should be encouraged to engage in a "life review" process; this can be accomplished using a variety of techniques like reminiscence, oral histories, and story telling. Looking back over life's accomplishments or failures is crucial in assisting the older adult to accomplish developmental tasks, to promote a positive self-esteem, and to acknowledge that one "did not live in vain."

As nurses apply the psychologic theories to the care of older adults in any setting, they help to dispel many of the myths about "being old." If an older person is talking about retirement, worrying about physical living space, or even planning funeral arrangements, these are all part of the developmental tasks appropriate for this age group. Instead of trying to change the topic or attempting to help the person not be so "morbid," the nurse must understand that each stage of life has specific developmental tasks to achieve. Instead of hampering, the nurse should attempt to facilitate their achievement.

Only about 5% of older adults actually reside in nursing homes. The remainder are living in the community. Many are living on very limited incomes and are trying to remain "independent." As the community nurse attempts to meet an individual's health care needs, Maslow's hierarchy of needs can assist in keeping the client's needs in perspective. Most individuals try to maintain basic human needs like food and water before they consider their safety (e.g., location of housing and home security measures). As health care shifts to a prevention mode, older adults must also be included. But the nurse must remember that preventive health care needs fall within the self-esteem level of Maslow's hierarchy and that the other levels must be at least partially met before individuals will worry about valuing themselves enough to seek preventive care.

Nurses also need to keep in mind that intellectual functioning continues to remain intact in the majority of older adults. The older adult can share life experiences and wisdom gained by living, as well as information about a time in history that the nurse may not have experienced. A younger person can certainly gain a lot by observing older people, listening to how they have coped with life experiences, and discussing their plans for the future.

In planning activities for the older adult, nurses need to remember that all individuals enjoy feeling needed and respected, and being considered a contributing member of society. Perhaps activities like collecting an oral history, or creating a mural or quilt depicting a particular event or even an individual's lifetime could be included. Not only would this activity be valuing the individual, but it would also serve to pass on information from one generation to the next; this is an important task that is often forgotten.

Programs promoting interaction between older adults and younger children might prove beneficial to all concerned. For some older adults, having small children represented a happy time in their lives. Rocking, cuddling and playing with children might bring back feelings of being valued and needed. The touching aspects of this activity are also important in relieving stress; many older adults no longer enjoy any type of physical contact with others, and all individuals need physical contact with others.

As eyesight and manual dexterity diminish, many older adults enjoy the opportunity to cook or to work in a garden. Often the touch of dirt between the fingers is relaxing and brings back memories of beautiful flowers and prize vegetables. For the older woman in particular, preparing a meal may be an activity she has not been allowed to do for several years, and with assistance, she may find baking cookies a pleasant activity filled with memories of holidays and loved ones, or prizes at the county fair. Older men may also enjoy cooking and should not be ruled out of this activity. Preparing muffins for the morning snack would be an activity in which everyone could participate (see Research boxes, p. 36).

Summary

When interacting with the older adult, the nurse often functions in the role of "case manager." Nurses have the background to incorporate information from a variety of sources when planning care for the older adult. By using an eclectic approach to aging theories, the nurse will have a broad background from which to draw specific

RESEARCH

Modified from Young C: Spirituality and the chronically ill Christian elderly, *Ger Nurs* 14(6):298-303, 1993.

Sample, setting

The sample included 12 older adults ages 65 to 89, with at least one chronic illness living in nursing homes or individual homes located in Gainesville, Florida.

Methodology

One-hour, in-depth, semistructured interviews were conducted with the subjects. Each interview consisted of open-ended questions, were tape-recorded, and transcribed for data analysis.

Findings

Spiritual concepts were identified and categorized during the data analysis. The recurrent themes of hope, comfort, strength, and well-being became evident as spirituality was discussed. Spirituality increased in importance as subjects aged. The belief in a superior being helped promote a positive feeling of well-being.

Implications

If spiritual well-being in older adults is characterized by an inner harmony and manifested by being content with life, then the concept of spirituality merits consideration in nursing care plans and interventions. Nurses are in an ideal position to assist older clients in attaining spiritual comfort by allowing them an opportunity to share their spiritual feelings or by referring them to an appropriate religious representative.

details to provide clarity, explanations, or additional insight into a particular situation.

Biologic theories help the nurse to understand how the physical body may change with advancing years, and what factors may increase the older adult's vulnerability to stress or disease. Understanding sociologic theories broadens the nurses view of older adults and their interactions with society. Psychologic theories provide an understanding of the values and beliefs an older person may have. By integrating the various components of these theories, quality care can be planned for older adults. As the population continues to age, nurses with the capability to understand and apply aging theories from several disciplines will be the leaders of gerontologic nursing in the future.

RESEARCH

Modified from Taylor HA: Geriatric nurses and models of help orientation, *Ger Nurs* 13(4):197-200, 1992.

Sample, setting

The sample consisted of 68 female nurse subjects with a median age of 43 years. The education level of the subjects ranged from less than a high school education to more than a master's degree. The number of years employed in nursing for the sample averaged 14.5 years; the number of years employed in the present position averaged 4.7 years. The subjects worked with geriatric patients in nursing homes and home health care.

Methodology

The help orientation of the 68 nurse subjects was measured using the Help Orientation Test. The test measures four models of helping: moral, enlightenment, compensatory and medical. Each of these help orientations included perceptions of the help recipient, the helper, and the help to be given.

Findings

The mean scores for the total sample of subjects indicated that the medical model was the help orientation model rated highest by the subjects. This model is defined by attributions to the help recipient of low-level responsibility for both the cause and the solution of problems. Help recipients are seen as ill or victims of social forces; they are passive, expected to accept this view of themselves, and freed of any social obligations other than to accept the treatments of the expert. The helper is the expert, the primary agent of change, and is responsible for finding solutions to the problems by providing service or treatment.

Implications

Caregivers of older adults whose help orientations are consistent with the medical model, would seem to support dependence rather than independence, helplessness rather than responsibility for solutions. Caregivers may then inadvertently facilitate the lessening of competency and the associated low ratings of satisfaction that older adults may experience within their life satisfaction.

Key Points

- There is no one theory or definition of aging.
- An eclectic approach incorporating concepts from biology, sociology, and psychology was used in developing aging theories.
- Biologic theories must address what factors actually trigger the aging process in organisms.
- Organisms are thought to have a biologic clock of 110 to 120 years.
- A change in efficiency of immune processes may predispose individuals to disease with advancing age.
- Biologic theories alone *do not* provide a comprehensive explanation of the aging process.
- Reminiscence is supported by sociologic theories and assists the older adult in appreciating past memories.

- Each individual is unique, no matter what age. Older adults are not a homogenous population.
- The activity theory remains popular because it reflects current societal beliefs about aging.
- As a person ages psychologically, various adaptive changes occur, which assist the person in coping with or accepting some of the biologic changes.
- There is no convincing evidence of any one universal developmental process associated with aging.

Critical Thinking Exercises

1. Project how sociologic theories of aging may be influenced by changing societal values (e.g., advanced technology or community health care focus) in the next decade.
2. A 62-year-old woman believes that heart disease and poor circulation are inevitable consequences of growing older and is resistant to altering her ADLs and dietary regimen. How would you respond?
3. Think of various programs and institutions in your community for the care of older people. Identify two and discuss the sociologic aging theories exemplified in each example.
4. A 74-year-old man repeatedly talks about how he wishes he were as strong and energetic as he was when he was younger. His family consistently changes the topic or scolds him for being so grim. How would you intervene in this situation?

REFERENCES

Atchley RC: *The forces of later life,* Florence, Ky., 1972, Wadsworth.

Birren JE, Cunningham WR: Research on the psychology of aging. In Birren JE, Schaie KW, editors: *Handbook of the psychology of aging,* New York, 1985, Van Nostrand Reinhold.

Birren JE, Renner JV: Research on psychology of aging. In Birren JE, Schaie KW, editors: *Handbook of the principles and experimentation, psychology of aging,* New York, 1977, Van Nostrand Reinhold.

Bjorkstein J: Cross-linkage and the aging process. In Rockstein M et al, editors: *Theoretical aspects of aging,* New York, 1971, Academic Press.

Bjorkstein J: The crosslinkage theory of aging: clinical implications, *Comp Therapy* 11:65, 1976.

Brody H: Lipofuscin. In Maddox GL, editor: *The encyclopedia of aging,* New York, 1987, Springer.

Buhler C: The development structure of goal setting in group and individual studies. In Buhler C, Massarek F, editors: *The course of human life,* New York, 1968, Springer.

Cavin RS: Self and role in adjustment during old age. In Rose A, editor: *Human behavior and social processes,* Boston, 1949, Houghton Mifflin.

Comfort A: Biological theories of aging, *Hum Dev* 13:127-139, 1970.

Cumming E, Henry W: *Growing old: the process of disengagement,* New York, 1961, Basic Books.

Erikson E: *Childhood and society,* New York, 1950, WW Norton.

Gress LD, Bahr RT: *The aging person: a holistic perspective,* St. Louis, 1984, Mosby.

Harman D: Aging: A theory based on free radical and radiation chemistry, *J Gerontol* 11:298-300, 1956.

Havighurst RJ: *Developmental tasks and education,* ed 3, New York, 1972, David McKay.

Havighurst RJ, Albrecht R: *Older people,* New York, 1953, Longmans, Green.

Havighurst RJ, Neugarten BL, Tobin SS: Disengagement, personality and life satisfaction in the later years. In Hansen P, editor: *Age with a future,* Copenhagen, 1963, Munksgoasrd.

Hayflick L: Why do we live so long? *Geriatrics* 43(10):77-87, 1988.

Hayflick L: Theories of aging. In Cape R, Coe R, Rodstein M, editors: *Fundamentals of geriatric medicine,* New York, 1983, Raven Press.

Hayflick L: The cellular basis for biological aging. In Finch CE, Hayflick L, editors: *Handbook of the biology of aging,* New York, 1977, Von Nostrand Reinhold.

Hayflick L, Moorehead PS: The serial cultivation of human diploid all strains, *Exp Cell Res* 25:585, 1961.

Lawton MP: Competence, environmental press, and the adaptation of older people. In Lawton MP, Windley PG, Byerts TO, editors: *Aging and the environment: theoretical approaches,* New York, 1982, Springer.

Maslow A: *Motivation and personality,* New York, 1954, Harper & Row.

Maslow A: *Toward a psychology of being,* ed 2, Princeton, N.J., 1968, Van Nostrand Reinhold.

Matteson MA, McConnell ES: *Gerontological nursing: concepts and practice,* Philadelphia, 1988, WB Saunders.

Peck R: Psychological development in the second half of life. In Neugarten B, editor: *Middle and aging,* Chicago, 1968, University of Chicago Press.

Riley MW: Age strata in social systems. In Binstock RH, Shanas E, editors: *Handbook of aging and social sciences,* New York, 1985, Van Nostrand Reinhold.

Riley MW, Johnson M, Foner A: *Aging and society: volume 3, a sociology of age stratification,* New York, 1972, Russel Stage Foundation.

Rockstein M, Chesky J, Sussman M: *Comparative biology and evaluation of aging: handbook of the biology of aging,* New York, 1977, Van Nostrand Reinhold.

Rockstein M, Sussman M: *Biology of aging,* Belmont, Calif., 1979, Wadsworth.

Sinex L: The molecular genetics of aging. In Finch CE, Hayflick L, editors: *Handbook of biology of aging,* New York, 1977, Van Nostrand Reinhold.

Sonneborn T: The origin, evolution, nature and causes of aging. In Behnke J., Finch CE, Moment C, editors: *The biology of aging,* New York, 1979, Plenum Press.

Stallwood J, Stoll R: Spiritual dimensions of nursing. In Beland IL, Parsos JY, editors: *Clinical nursing,* ed 3, New York, 1975, Macmillan.

Stanley JF, Pye D, MacGregor A: Comparison of double numbers attained by cultural animal cells with life span of species, *Nature* 255:158, 1975.

Thomas A, Chess S: *Temperament and development,* New York, 1977, Brunner/Masel.

Zarit SH: *Aging and mental disorders: psychological approaches and assessment and treatment,* New York, 1980, The Free Press.

BIBLIOGRAPHY

Blatter B: *Holistic nursing,* Englewood Cliffs, N.J., 1981, Prentice Hall.

Blumer H: *Symbolic interactionism,* Englewood Cliffs, N.J., 1969, Prentice Hall.

Butler R, Lewis M: *Aging and mental health: positive psychosocial approaches,* ed 2, St. Louis, 1977, Mosby.

Dowd J: Aging as exchange: a preface to theory, *Gerontologist* 30:584, 1975.

Jung C: The stages of life. In *Collected works: volume 8, the structure and dynamics of the psyche,* New York, 1960, Pantheon Books.

Lemon BW, Bengston VL, Peterson JA: An exploration of the activity theory of aging: activity types and life satisfaction among in-movers to a retirement community, *J Gerontol* 27:511-523, 1972.

Mead GH: *Mind, self and society,* Chicago, 1934, University of Chicago Press.

Newman BM, Newman PR: *Development through life: a psychological approach,* ed 3, Homewood, Ill., 1984, Dorsey Press.

Walford RL: *Maximum life span,* New York, 1983, WW Norton.

CHAPTER 3

Legal and Ethical Issues

LEARNING OBJECTIVES

On completion of this chapter, the reader will be able to:

1. Identify sources of professional standards, and understand how they are used to measure the degree to which the duty of nursing care of the client is met.
2. Know the sources and definitions of laws such as statutes, regulations, and case law and the levels of laws, such as federal, state and local.
3. Explore why older adults are considered a vulnerable population, why this is legally significant, and the legal implications that such a designation connotes.
4. Discuss the reasons behind the sweeping nursing home reform legislation known as OBRA '87 and understand the significance of its provisions to residents and caregivers in nursing homes.
5. Identify OBRA's three major parts and describe the key areas addressed in each.
6. Discuss the legal history of autonomy and self-determination, and cite major laws that have influenced contemporary thought and practice.
7. Name and state the purpose of the legal tools known as "advance directives," and list the major points that should be addressed in a Do Not Resuscitate policy.
8. Explain the requirements of the four major provisions of the Patient Self Determination Act and the nurse's responsibility with respect to advance directives.
9. Describe the values history, and state how it can be helpful for clients and health care professionals in preparing for end of life decisions.
10. State the function and role, as well as recommended membership composition of an institutional ethics committee.
11. Relate at least three major reasons why the skillful practice of professional nursing can improve the quality of life for older adults in health care settings.

Never before has so much attention been focused on the needs of older adults. Changing demographics are responsible for much of this interest (see Chapter 1).

According to the Social Security Administration, there will be between 64 and 74 million older adults in the United States by the year 2030, when the baby boomer generation enters its 70s and 80s—more than twice the older adult population of 1980 *(Long Term Care Standards Manual,* 1990*)*. According to the U.S. Bureau of the Census, this will amount to about 21% of the total U.S. population. For most purposes discussed in this chapter, older adults are defined as those age 65 and older.

During the Social Security "crisis" of 1982, certain implications of this aging population in the United States became apparent *(The Milbank Quarterly,* 1991*)*. It was realized that the projections of life span used to forecast the use of the Social Security Trust Fund had significantly underestimated the size of the older adult population in future years.

The conclusion that there would be many more older Americans in future years raised major concerns for the economic effects on Social Security and Medicare. Health changes occur more often as we age. According to the U.S. Department of Health and Human Services (DHHS), 80% of those over age 65 have at least one chronic medical condition, and 20% have at least a mild degree of functional disability *(Long Term Care Standards Manual,* 1990*)*.

Furthermore, more than half of both nursing home care and home care in the United States is financed through public funds—primarily the Medicare and Medicaid programs *(Marion Merrill Dow Inc., Managed Care Digest,* 1994*)*. The government's concerns over whether there will be enough money available to continue to provide service to the older adult populations, who consume the largest percentage of these services, have led to measures designed to improve efficiency and to reduce the cost of services.

An important example is the **Prospective Payment System (PPS).** PPS was initially designed to control Medicare hospitalization costs by establishing reimbursement through Diagnosis Related Groups (DRGs). Medicare payment under a prospective system began in 1983. DRGs group and classify diseases, and establish in advance what the reimbursement level will be for a person receiving treatment for that specific condition. As a result of this program, a reported $18 billion was saved by 1990 (Manton, 1991). Similar systems are and will continue to be implemented and expanded into other areas of government-reimbursed services to older adults, such as home care and nursing home care.

Simply stated, programs such as PPS save money by changing reimbursement principals and reconfiguring the manner in which services are provided. We have seen some of the results—shorter hospital stays, older people discharged sooner to the home or long-term institutional care, and the enactment of strict rules governing the use of resources in providing their care.

The implications for nurses are significant. Older, more sick clients leave hospitals more rapidly than before. They return home or to institutional settings more sick than before. And quality care must be provided according to restrictions in reimbursement that can limit resource availability.

Thus there is good reason to be concerned about how the health needs of older adults will be met. Their unique characteristics and needs present meaningful questions of legal and ethical significance. As their functional independence is compromised and they become more reliant on health care that is paid for through public funds, the policies that accompany the flow of money can interfere in many ways with their personal autonomy (Kane, Kane, 1990).

Older adults depend more on the health care system to deliver the care that optimizes their health status and functional capabilities. Thus their quality of life is often dependent on the type and quality of nursing care they receive (Northrop, Kelly, 1987). This chapter focuses on the issues and legal concerns of nurses who care for older adults.

PROFESSIONAL STANDARDS: THEIR ORIGIN AND LEGAL SIGNIFICANCE

Health care providers have a general obligation to live up to accepted or customary **standards** of care, which may be determined either on a regional or on a national basis *(Health Care Facility Management,* 1990*)*. Nurses are responsible for providing care to the degree, skill, and diligence as measured by recognized and applicable standards of care. The **duty** of care rises as the patient's physical and mental conditions, and ability for self-care declines (Strauss et al, 1990).

Nursing standards of practice are measured according to the expected level of professional practice of those in similar roles and clinical fields. For example, the standards of practice of a gerontologic nurse practicing at the generalist level would be measured against the practice of other nurse generalists practicing in the area of gerontology. The advanced practice gerontologic nurse, who has at least a master's degree in an applicable field, would be expected to conform to standards established for similarly situated advanced practice nurses.

A standard of care is a measure with which conduct is compared to ascertain **negligence** *(Nursing-legal survival: a risk management guide for nurses,* 1992*)*. It is used to evaluate whether care administered to a client meets the appropriate level of skill and diligence as can reasonably be expected, given the nurse's level of skill, education, and experience.

Standards originate from many sources. Both state and federal statutes may help to establish standards, although a state's minimum standards do not necessarily prove due care. Conformity with local standards or comparison with similar facilities in the region may be considered evidence of proper care (Strauss et al, 1990).

The published standards of professional organizations representing the opinion of "experts in the field," are important in establishing the proper standard of care. The Standards and Scope of Gerontologic Nursing Practice published by the American Nurses Association (ANA) in 1987 are such an example. It contains the rationale and other explanatory information that pertain to each standard, as well as information specific to the gerontologic nurse generalist and specialist (see Box 1-1, p. 6). Nurses who care for older clients should be familiar with these standards and those from all relevant sources. The nursing student should also refer to these standards when reading other sections of this chapter, since many points covered here have direct relevance to these statements.

Accreditation organizations such as the Joint Commission on Accreditation of Healthcare Organizations (JCAHO) are often referred to in court cases to ascertain standards. The JCAHO, for example, is often considered the "industry standard," even for facilities that are not accredited (Schreiber, 1990).

U.S. federal and state statutes require nursing facilities to have written health care and safety policies, which have been used successfully to establish a standard of care in court cases. Bylaws and internal rules and policies also help to establish the standard of care in an organization, although, depending on the circumstances of a situation, their importance may vary. In any event, it is important for nurses to be aware of their organization's policies; failure to follow "your own rules" clearly poses a liability risk—both to yourself and the organization.

OVERVIEW OF RELEVANT LAWS

Sources of Law

Statutes are laws created by legislation and can be enacted at the federal and state level. Common laws are principles and rules of action, which derive authority from judgments and decrees of the court, and are also known as case law (Black, 1979). Regulations are rules of action and conduct often developed to explain and interpret statutes and to prescribe methods for carrying out statutory mandates. Regulations are also promulgated at the federal and state levels.

> **Insight** • *Standards are the ""scale" against which professional conduct is measured to determine whether nurses have met their duty of care to a client. Bylaws and internal rules and policies* may *help to establish the standard of care in an organization. . .thus it is important for nurses to be aware of their organization's policies.* ***Failure to follow "your own rules" clearly poses a liability risk—both to yourself and to the organization.***

Federal and State Laws

The U.S. federal government, under the Social Security Act, has the primary responsibility of providing medical services to certain aged and indigent Americans. The government fulfills this obligation through the **Medicare** and **Medicaid** programs (Schabes, 1991). These programs were enacted as part of the Social Security Amendments of 1965 (P.L. No. 89-97, July 30, 1965).[1]

DHHS promulgates regulations for the Medicare and Medicaid programs. The Health Care Financing Administration (HCFA) is the federal agency that administers the Medicare and Medicaid programs.

Medicare pays only for skilled care, which includes nursing, physical therapy, occupational therapy, and speech therapy, and for Medicare-insured people in long-term care facilities; Medicaid pays for both intermediate and skilled care for indigent people. See the introduction of this chapter for a related discussion on Medicare and Medicaid reimbursement of home care and hospital services.

The **Omnibus Budget Reconciliation Act of 1987**, or **OBRA '87**, (see Nursing Home Reform, p. 42), refers to *skilled nursing facilities (SNFs)* only in relation to Medicare facilities, and has merged the distinctions "skilled" and "intermediate" into the single term *nursing facility (NF)* for Medicaid purposes. SNFs provide more technical and complex care, and offer more skilled levels of professional staff. For survey purposes, however, a single set of survey requirements is used.

Survey and certification procedures, and the process by which HCFA validates provider compliance with the Medicare and Medicaid requirements, are the responsibilities of the Health Standards and Quality Bureau, a division of HCFA.

Continued public policy interest in the welfare and quality of life of older adults in the United States is expressed in other legislation such as the Older Americans Act (OAA), which requires states to maintain a minimal bureaucratic system to perform various services for older adults. The objectives of the OAA are to secure basic rights for all older adults in the United States. It defines older adults as those over age 60.

The OAA amendments (1988) increase the states' responsibilities for maintaining an effective long-term care ombudsman program. Ombudsmen are usually trained volunteers. Their role is to receive and resolve health and human services complaints affecting residents in nursing home facilities. NFs must cooperate with and must provide access for the ombudsman to meet with residents.

Older Adult Abuse and Protective Services

The need to protect older adults from abuse is a subject of great public policy interest. It has already been stated that the incidence of illness and disability increases with age. Frail older adults, or those over age 85, comprise the fastest growing group (Zedlewski, 1989) and their health status often leads to changes in living arrangements both in homes and in institutions (see Chapter 1).

Some problems of aging may go beyond those caused by societal issues or the normal process of aging. They may also be caused by neglect, deliberate abuse, or exploitation. Life changes may compromise an older adult's ability to manage affairs. The necessity of turning over to others the management of certain activities may open the door to mistreatment. The legal recognition of this "vulnerability" is reflected in laws enacted specifically to protect older adults.

Elderly Protective Services refers to the range of laws and regulations enacted to deal with abusive situations. They include: protective orders issued to shield an older adult from an abusive member of their household; elder abuse statues, which outlaw harmful acts that victimize older adults; and laws enacted to protect older residents of nursing homes from abuse (Strauss et al, 1990).

Elder abuse laws levy criminal penalties against those who commit harmful acts against older adults. Many states' laws enhance the penalties for criminal offenses against older people, such as violent or property offenses, and some outlaw any acts that victimize older adults.* These laws typically apply to the abuse of older adults in the community.

States may also penalize acts of elder abuse that are committed by those who are responsible for care of older adults in nursing homes or other facilities (Strauss et al, 1990). These laws are in addition to those already in effect to protect the rights of clients in facilities governed by federal regulation. In most states, there are mandatory reporting requirements for nurses, other health care workers, and facility employees who have a reasonable suspicion of elder abuse.

The definition of what constitutes elder abuse under these statutes varies. For example, emotional abuse can be acts such as "ridiculing or demeaning . . . or making derogatory remarks to a . . . resident"[2]; any non-accidental infliction of physical injury, sexual abuse, or mental injury . . . [3]; and unauthorized use of physical or chemical restraint, medication, or isolation . . . .[4]

For the purposes of these types of statutes, some states define older adults as age 60 and older. It is important to know the legal requirements relating to abuse of older adults for the state in which a nurse practices. It should be noted that a report of suspected abuse may be required on a "reasonable suspicion." This implies that actual knowledge or certainty is not necessary. Furthermore, there may be penalties for failure to enter a mandatory report.

A nurse should determine where reports and complaints are received. Most states provide immunity from civil liability for any report of older adult abuse that is made on reasonable suspicion and in good faith, even if it is later shown that they were mistaken.

Nurses must be aware at all times of the responsibility to respect and to preserve the autonomy and individual right of older adults (see Box 1-1, p. 6, Standards of Gerontological Nursing Practice Standard X, Ethics, *Process Criterion 2).* All people, including older adults have the right to decide what is to be done to them, as well as the right to exercise maximum control of their personal environments and living conditions. The nurse's responsibility in this regard emanates from both legal and professional standards.

The fact of ongoing legislative responses to the identification and preservation of these rights underscores this point. The nurse is often the health professional closest to older clients and therefore may be in the best position to communicate and understand their wishes. This presents both an unequaled opportunity, and a legally recognizable and indisputable responsibility to advocate on their behalf. Thus the need to be legally informed and professionally conscientious is greater than ever.

NURSING HOME REFORM

In 1985, 5% of the older adult population resided in nursing homes (1.5 million people) (Collier, 1990). The HCFA estimated that by the year 2000, 8.8 % of the older adult population will reside in nursing homes. One half of people over age 85 require long-term care.

During the 1970s disturbing evidence emerged from studies, reports, and books suggesting widespread abuse of residents in the nation's nursing homes, and that state and federal officials were lax in overseeing their regulation (Hamme, 1991). In 1983 the DHHS contracted with the Institute of Medicine of the National Academy of Sciences to conduct a comprehensive study of U.S. federal and state regulations and policies for nursing home cer-

* E.g., *see* Conn. Gen. Statutes Ann.§46a-15.

tification, and to formulate recommendations for legislative and agency action (Hamme, 1991). That study served as the impetus for nursing home reform (*Long Term Care Management,* 1993), and many of the recommendations of the study were adopted by the U.S. Congress when it enacted OBRA '87 (Hamme, 1991).

Coupled with the increasing challenges of meeting the needs of the aging population, Congress passed the Omnibus Budget Reconciliation Act of 1987 (OBRA '87) a sweeping new form of legislation that brought about dramatic changes in the way nursing homes in this country are run.

OBRA '87 applies to all Medicare- and Medicaid-certified nursing homes, including (1) beds in acute care hospitals certified to be used as long-term nursing care beds at times when they are not needed for acute care purposes and are called "swing beds," and (2) beds in acute care hospitals certified as separate units for Medicare-approved services and are called "distinct part" units* (Collier, 1990). It is the most sweeping reform affecting Medicare and Medicaid nursing facilities since the programs began.

Since OBRA '87 was enacted, there have been amendments and new regulations. In this chapter, OBRA '87 encompasses any changes made as of the printing of this text, including OBRA '90 and any subsequent modifications.

OBRA's Three Major Parts

OBRA '87 provisions are divided into three parts: (1) provision of service requirements for nursing facilities, (2) survey and certification process, and (3) enforcement mechanisms and sanctions.

The *provision of service* requirements for nursing facilities include resident assessments, preadmission and annual screening of residents, maintenance of minimal nurse staffing levels, required and approved nurse aide training programs and competency levels, professional social worker services in facilities with 120 or more beds, and the important focus on specifying and assuring resident rights.

The *survey and certification* process was substantially revised with the enactment of OBRA. New types of surveys were established to evaluate facilities. In brief, each facility is subject to a standard annual survey. Any change in facility management or ownership is further evaluated by a "special" survey. If any survey suggests that care may be substandard, it may be subject to a more detailed "extended" survey. States are also evaluated for the effectiveness of their survey process through a "validation" survey. Furthermore, the federal authorities may make an independent and binding determination of a facility's compliance through a "special compliance" survey.

OBRA also brought a new range of *enforcement mechanisms* and **sanctions.** Thus there are a number of corrective measures that can be applied to repair deficiencies, and they are applied based on the severity of the risk to residents. More on these three parts of OBRA provisions are discussed in the following sections.

Overall, it can be seen that the regulations focus on the quality of life of nursing home residents and emphasize their individual rights. OBRA has created a new regulatory environment by empowering nursing home residents, giving them a greater say in these quality of life issues (Salkin, 1991).

*On the effective date of OBRA '87, October 1, 1990, the distinction between skilled and intermediate nursing facilities was eliminated for Medicaid-certified facilities; thus Medicare-certified facilities are known as SNFs, whereas Medicaid-certified facilities are known an NFs.

"Provision of Service" Requirements

Quality of Care

Nursing facility residents must be assessed to identify medical problems, to describe their capacity to perform daily life functions, and to note any significant impairments in their functional capacity. A state-specified instrument must be used to conduct the assessment, which is based on a uniform data set, referred to as the minimum data set, or MDS, established by the DHHS. Residents must be reassessed if there is any change in their condition, at least annually.

The assessment is used to develop a written and comprehensive plan of care for each resident. The plan must quantify expected levels of functioning and must be reviewed quarterly.

The assessment and planning for the care of nursing home residents is a most important role for the professional nurse. As can be seen from this discussion of nursing home reform, it is a center point for determining the care and services that a particular resident will need. Careful assessment and planning are time-consuming activities and also require the professional nurse to be skilled and knowledgeable in carrying out these functions.

Because of the complexity of the rules and regulations governing nursing homes, the current trend is to employ better qualified administrators and nursing directors. However, since most nursing homes rely to a great degree on reimbursement from the Medicare and Medicaid programs, which may not pay for some of their services, the numbers of nursing home staff have been reduced to keep expenses at an acceptable level (Conely, Campbell, 1991).

The advent of OBRA and nursing home reform has ushered in a new phase of professional accountability. It has increased the demands on nursing time and performance, has forced nursing homes to change the very structure of their operation, and has resulted in a very different image of what nursing homes are and how they care for their residents.

Medicare SNFs and Medicaid NFs must have 24-hour-per-day and 7-day-per-week licensed nursing services available. A registered professional nurse must be on duty at least eight hours per day, seven days per week.

Nursing assistants must be trained according to regulatory specifications and meet state-approved competency evaluations. They must receive classroom training before any contact with residents and must receive training in such areas as interpersonal skills, infection control, safety procedures, and resident rights (Hamme, 1991).

Nursing assistants often comprise the largest number of employees in nursing facilities. In addition, they have the greatest turnover rate of any employee group. In 1993 the turnover rate of nursing assistants (or nurse aides), was 43.7% *(Marion Merrell Dow, Inc., Managed care digest,* 1994*).* Since they provide most of the direct care for nursing homes residents, it is not surprising that stringent requirements for their training and evaluation have been enacted.

Resident Rights

A primary thrust of the nursing home reform provisions of OBRA '87 is to protect and to promote the rights of nursing home residents to enhance the quality of life. Thus the legislation contains numerous requirements to assure the preservation of a resident's rights.[5]

New disclosure obligations were imposed on nursing facilities to apprise residents of their rights, requiring that residents be notified, both orally and in writing, of their rights and responsibilities, and of all rules governing resident conduct. This notification and disclosure must take place before or up to the time of admission and must be updated and reviewed during the course of a resident's stay. See Box 3-1 for a sample of OBRA's resident bill of rights statements, as adapted from the Code of Federal Regulations.

Most facilities have developed a contract for new residents (or a family member or other responsible person) to sign at the time of admission. This is usually called the admission agreement. This agreement sets forth the rights, obligations, and expectations of each party. It is a good way to inform residents of a facility's rules, regulation, and philosophy of care. Thus it is a practical way to meet OBRA's notification and disclosure requirements.

As with any agreement, it can only be a valid contract if the parties entering into the agreement are capable of understanding its provisions. If the resident is not capable of doing this, then a family member or other responsible person may sign on the resident's behalf. The laws of the particular state should be explored to determine who has "standing" to contract on behalf of the resident.

OBRA limits a facility's ability to transfer or discharge residents to the following conditions: if the needs of the resident cannot be met in the facility; if their stay is no longer required for their medical condition; if they fail to pay for their care as agreed to; or if the facility ceases to operate. These provisions are designed to establish the basic right of a resident to remain in a facility and to not be transferred involuntarily unless one of the above conditions exists, and the resident has been given proper notice with the opportunity to appeal the decision.

This was, in part, a response to situations where older residents of nursing homes were "ousted" without notice, and perhaps without regard to the detrimental effects (both physical and emotional) that they would suffer by being uprooted from familiar surroundings.

The requirement for a bill of rights for residents is not an entirely new item on the landscape. Many states have had such provisions in their facility licensure statutes for many years. Medicare and Medicaid regulations have included resident rights requirements for some time as well. OBRA '87 strengthened and enhanced the importance of these requirements by enforcing them as part of the facility survey process.

Although the specific contents of resident's rights laws vary considerably from state to state, both the state and federal contents have some similarities. In particular, participation in medical decision making, privacy, dig-

BOX 3-1

Resident Bill of Rights:

A facility must protect and must promote the exercise of rights for all residents.

The following are some of those rights:

1. The right to select a personal attending physician and to receive complete information about one's care and treatment, including access to all records pertaining to the resident
2. Freedom from physical or mental abuse, corporal punishment, involuntary seclusion, and any unwarranted physical or chemical restraints
3. Privacy with regard to accommodations, medical treatment, mail and telephone communication, visits, and meetings of family and resident groups
4. Confidentiality regarding personal and clinical records
5. Residing and receiving services with reasonable accommodations of individual needs and preferences
6. Protesting one's treatment or care without discrimination or reprisal including refusal to participate in experimental research
7. Participation in resident and family groups
8. Participation in social, religious, and community activities
9. The right to examine the federal or state authorities' survey of a nursing home

Modified from 42 CFR§483.10.

nity, access to visitors and services, ability to pursue grievances, selection of a physician, and transfer and discharge rights have been mutual areas of concern (Johnson, 1991).

Unnecessary Drug Use, and Chemical and Physical Restraints

OBRA '87 requires that nursing home residents be free from unnecessary drugs of all types; from chemical restraints, commonly thought of as psychotropic drugs; and from physical restraints. Chemical restraints are drugs that are used to limit or inhibit specific behavior or movement.

Physical restraints are appliances that inhibit free physical movement, such as limbs restraints, vests, jackets, and waist belts. Wheelchairs, geriatric chairs, and side rails can, in some circumstances, also be forms of physical restraint (Conely, Campbell, 1991).

Unnecessary Drugs

OBRA's guidelines for unnecessary drug use pertain to the use of antipsychotics, benzodiazepines, and other anxiolytic/sedative drugs and hypnotics. As of this writing, HCFA has not developed guidelines concerning antidepressant use, since it is believed that depression is undertreated and underrecognized in nursing homes (see Chapter 12).

The drug use guidelines are based on the general principles that certain problems can be handled with nondrug interventions and that such forms of treatment must be ruled out before drug therapy is initiated. Furthermore, when used, drugs must maintain or must improve a resident's functional status.

OBRA's guidelines detail doses but do not set maximum dosage limitations. The dosage detailing is a way to draw attention to the need for comprehensive assessment and review of drug use. Surveyors review duration of drug therapy regimens and look for documentation of indications for use of the drug therapy. Nurses should also carefully document observed effects of drug therapy.

This is an area where the nurse should exercise skill and leadership, by working with others on the resident's care team to assure that the resident is not overmedicated or unnecessarily medicated. For example, the nurse can work with the interdisciplinary care team to plan nondrug interventions. The nurse is also in a position to inform the resident's physician about OBRA's unnecessary drug use guidelines. Not only may this be new information for the physician, but it may also provide a sound explanation for the physician to use with a resident's family members who may be requesting drug interventions. In fact, the nurse is in the best position to work with the resident *and* the family to provide information and reinforcement about this important approach to care.

Chemical and Physical Restraints

Research has shown that many psychoactive drugs have been misused (Cooper, 1990). They have been administered based on a patient's symptoms rather than the underlying condition. Psychoactive drugs are rarely beneficial as chemical restraints and are often harmful to the patient (Cooper, 1990).

Drug toxicities have been underestimated, and at time, drugs have been used to meet the desires of nursing or other facility staff for "environmental control," such as to settle patients down for "sleep time." The need to manage the environment can pose a genuine dilemma for the nurse, since certain resident behaviors such as yelling or wandering into other resident's rooms can be disruptive. They may cause family members to "pressure" the nurse to quiet another client or take other steps to stop the "bothersome" behavior. Nursing facility clients can be challenging, in spite of a nursing staff's intent to provide good care and to identify causes of resident's disturbing behavior (Cooper, 1990). However, drug therapy may not be used for environmental control.

Physical restraints may be used only where there are specific medical indications and when a physician has written a specific order for their use. The order must include the type of restraint, the condition or specific behavior for which it is to be applied, and a specified time or duration for its use. Orders for restraints must be reevaluated and if appropriate, renewed at least every 30 days.

The nurse must carefully document the behavior or condition that led to the order for restraints, and monitor the resident's ongoing condition, noting responses to the application of restraints and changes in condition. When physical restraints are used, the resident must be observed and the restraints must be released at regular intervals. Records documenting these activities must be kept.

OBRA guidelines require that antipsychotic drugs be used in the minimal dose necessary. This minimalization must be assured through careful monitoring and documentation by the staff to identify why a behavioral problem may exist and whether the antipsychotic treatment is actually effecting a change in the target symptom.

A client receiving an antipsychotic drug must have an indication for use of the drug based on one of 12 conditions. The conditions include schizophrenia or schizo-affective disorder; delusional disorder; acute psychosis or mania with psychotic mood; brief reactive psychosis; atypical psychosis; Tourette's syndrome; Huntington's chorea; short-term symptomatic treatment of nausea, vomiting, hiccups or itching; or dementia associated with psychotic or violent features that represent a danger to the client or others.

Reasons for the use of antipsychotic drugs must be documented in the physician's orders and in the resident care plan. They should not be used for behaviors such as restlessness, insomnia, yelling or screaming, "inability to manage patient," or wandering.

OBRA '87 mandates a 25% reduction in dose trial, unless it has been tried previously and resulted in decompensation of the client or the resident has one of the 12 conditions listed above. A "reduction in dose trial" consists of a reduction in the dose of the drug, coupled with observations targeted toward observing return of symptoms or adverse side effects. The dose is gradually increased until optimum effectiveness in treatment response and minimum necessary dose is achieved.

The physician's order must include specific information as to (1) the reasons for use of antipsychotic drugs, including medical indications; (2) the target behaviors that the drug therapy is intended to treat; (3) the goals of the therapy; and (4) common side effects. These notations must also be entered in the client's care plan. The observations and charting made by the nurse must address these specific points as well.

Insight • *OBRA's mandates for dose reduction trials, as well as the prohibition against unnecessary restraints, should be of considerable interest to the nurse for at least a couple of reasons. First, the nurse may be the most informed caregiver with respect to these issues. The physician may not, in some cases, be aware of the rule's importance or, in some cases even the rule's existence. Furthermore, professional nurses have an obligation to challenge questionable orders and to advocate on behalf of their patients. Remember, the nurse is not free of liability just because "the doctor ordered it."*

A facility is not absolved from regulatory liability by the mere presence of a physician's written order for restraints of any kind. The professional responsibility of the nursing staff is to challenge questionable orders (Johnson, 1991). For example, statement three and its interpretation in the Code For Nurses identify the nurses' responsibility to "safeguard the client," and to act on any "questionable practice in the provision of health care." Nurses should participate in the development of problem-solving procedures, established to help provide constructive and effective ways to resolve disputes involving patient care issues. Such procedures generally provide an avenue of communication that can be used to resolve questions or disagreements that arise between health care professionals. When a question or issue does arise, the nurse must institute the procedure promptly.

Dramatic reductions in the use of physical restraints and almost universal use of HCFA's resident assessment system are indications that nursing home reform is working (*Long Term Care Management,* 1993). Recent studies indicate that antipsychotic drug use is down, resulting in economic benefits and improving the quality of life to nursing home residents (Starr, 1992).

Nurses have been very successful in employing practices directed toward avoiding the use of chemical or physical restraints. Some of these techniques are: companionship; increased patient supervision; meeting physical needs such as toileting, exercise, or hunger; modifying staff attitudes; and other psychosocial approaches. Again, it can be seen that nurses are in a unique position to positively affect the quality of life of institutionalized older adults. Nurses should continue to educate others about these behavior management techniques. According to Wayne Ray, a Vanderbilt University researcher, "When the nursing staff had the knowledge and techniques to deal with maladaptive behavior that comes from dementia, they didn't have to use physical or chemical restraints" (Starr, 1992).

Urinary Incontinence

Urinary incontinence (UI) is one of three key reasons older adults enter nursing homes *(Long Term Care Management,* 1993*)*. In fact, more than one half of nursing home residents are incontinent. Left untreated, the condition can lead to other physical problems such as infections and skin breakdown.

Since this is therefore a prevalent condition and one that has implications for the quality and enjoyment of life, it can be expected that it will continue to be a major area of regulatory scrutiny. Under OBRA '87, nursing homes are required to include incontinence in the comprehensive assessment of a resident's functions and to provide the necessary treatment.

Furthermore, HCFA surveyors are being instructed to focus on this problem by evaluating the problem's occurrence in the nursing homes they survey and assessing the extent to which nursing home residents are in bladder training programs.

Nurses should be familiar with guidelines and procedures for management of incontinence, such as the Agency for Health Care Policy and Research (AHCPR) Guidelines. Refer to Chapter 26 for more information on this subject. Charting should be specific to reflect the presence and extent of the problem of incontinence, and note the treatment plan that has been established and the effects of the treatment. From the OBRA perspective, behavioral approaches are preferable to more intense mechanical or chemical therapies.

Facility Survey and Certification

HCFA is determined that every nursing facility implement and comply with the letter and spirit of OBRA's requirements. This is enforced through a process of surveying facilities and is based on the results of the survey, which certifies their compliance with OBRA laws and regulations.

The enactment of OBRA created a new survey process. In general, the standard survey is conducted to review the quality of care as indicated by an evaluation of criteria such as medical, nursing and rehabilitative care, dietary services, infection control, and the physical environment.

Written care plans and resident assessments are evaluated for their adequacy and accuracy, and the surveyors look for compliance with residents' rights (Hamme, 1991). OBRA long-term care survey processes have a renewed emphasis on the outcome of resident care, rather than mere paper compliance with regulatory requirements (Schabes, 1991).

By contractual arrangement with DHHS, state survey agencies are authorized to certify the compliance of facilities (see "Provisions of Service" Requirements, p. 43, for description of types of surveys). States are also required to educate facility staff as to the survey process, and are further authorized to investigate complaints of all types.

Surveys are conducted by a multidisciplinary survey team of professionals including at least one registered professional nurse. Survey participants include facility personnel, residents and their families, and the state's long-term care ombudsman. Surveyors interview residents and ask them about facility policies and procedures. They observe staff in the performance of their duties, and staff may be asked to complete forms required by the survey team.

Enforcement Mechanisms and Sanctions

DHHS and the states may apply sanctions or penalties against a facility for failure to meet requirements and standards. Such sanctions can include civil money penalties, appointment of a temporary manager to run a facility while deficiencies are remedied, or even closure of a facility or transfer of residents to another facility, or both.

The sanctions applied must be appropriate to the facility deficiency. This often depends on whether an immediate threat to the health and safety of residents exists. Sanctions may also be increased if there are repeat or uncorrected deficiencies.

It is important for the nurse to understand that officials authorized by the state or federal agencies who oversee the operation of nursing homes (or any licensed healthcare institution or setting) may enter and may review activities at any time. They are not required to announce the visit in advance (in fact, OBRA regulations specifically prohibit this for the annual standard survey), and the nurse must respond to their questions and requests for information and records.

The director of nursing has an important role in the survey process. If requested to do so by the surveyor, the director may be asked to participate in rounds or other activities of the surveyor—and most certainly is present at a closing conference, where the overall results of the survey are discussed. Often, the surveyors follow up the visit by telephone or may return for additional visits to a facility if further information is needed.

A written report of the survey is ultimately sent to the facility, and if there are deficiencies or violations, the director of nursing and other members of the nursing staff may participate in formulating a plan of correction to submit to the regulatory officials.

In the course of an inspection, a surveyor may find information suggesting that the practice of a licensed nurse may have been improper or may not have met the proper standard of care. For example, a particular nurse may have a high incidence of medication errors or may not have taken proper action when a client experienced a change in condition. In such an instance, the surveyor may forward the record showing the relevant findings to the appropriate state agency or board for review of the nurse's practice, requesting a determination as to whether the nurse may have violated the state's nurse practice act. The board may find no basis for further action and may not proceed, or it may require a hearing or other measures that could lead to disciplinary action. Disciplinary action could range from reprimand, to required educational remediation, or to suspension or revocation of the nurse's license. This again underscores the need for nurses to be diligent and conscientious in their professional practice and to remember that they will be held accountable for their individual performance.

AUTONOMY AND SELF-DETERMINATION

The right to self-determination has its basis in the doctrine of informed consent. **Informed consent** is the process by which competent individuals are provided with information that enables them to make a reasoned decision about any treatment or intervention in which they are to take part.

A great deal of legal analysis has been put to the question, "What is enough information for a person to make a reasonable decision?" It is generally accepted that for a consent to be valid, a standard of disclosure must be met which includes the diagnosis, the nature and purpose of the treatment, the risks of the treatment, the probability of success of the treatment, available treatment alternatives, and the consequences of not receiving the treatment.

Informed consent has developed out of strong judicial deference toward individual autonomy, reflecting a belief that an individual has a right to be free from nonconsensual interference with his or her person, and a basic moral principle that it is wrong to force another to act against his or her will (Furrow, 1987). The judicial system's strong deference toward individual autonomy *in the medical context* was long ago articulated by Justice Benjamin Cardozo in the following:

> Every human being of adult years and sound mind has a right to determine what be done with his own body....
>
> **Schloendorf v. Society of New York Hospital 211 N.Y. 125, 129 (1914)**

As this sections explains, the right to self-determination includes the removal of life support or life-sustaining treatments and life-prolonging or life-saving measures. These issues are particularly relevant to the older adult. Although individuals of all ages are concerned with these matters and young people do die, the fact is that the incidence of disease increases with age. Incapacity and infirmity are more common in old age. Therefore it is just a "fact of life" that more frequent discussion of the need to preserve the right to self-determination occurs among older adults.

The doctrine and standards of informed consent are intended to apply to the decision-making capability of one who is "competent" to make such a decision. In this context, competent means one who is able to understand the proposed treatment or procedure and thereby make an informed decision.

Where a person is not competent, the decision may be made by a surrogate. This is known as "substituted" judgment. More discussion on this point appears later in the chapter.

Do Not Resuscitate Orders

A **Do Not Resuscitate (DNR)** order is a specific order from a physician and entered on the physician order sheet, which instructs health care providers not to use or order specific methods of therapy, which are referred to as cardiopulmonary resuscitation (CPR) (Lieberson, 1992).

CPR generally includes those measures and therapies used to restore cardiac function or to support ventilation in the event of a cardiac or respiratory arrest,[6] and to handle emergencies caused by sudden loss of oxygen supply to the brain as a result of lung or heart failure.

DNR orders have been used for many years. In 1974 the American Medical Association (AMA) recommended that decisions not to resuscitate a client be formally entered into the medical record, a practice that had already become widespread (Lieberson, 1992). The concept of withholding resuscitation in appropriate circumstances is widely accepted (Schreiber, 1990).

New York is one of only a few states that have passed specific **codified** procedures covering DNR orders, and their statute is useful to look to for guidelines.[7] The law applies to patients in general hospitals and in nursing homes.[8] In New York, consent to CPR is presumed unless a DNR order has been issued.[9] As is customary, there is also a presumption of competency to make such a decision.[10] Competent individuals may choose to forego any treatment or care, even if it means that the choice will result in death.

To determine whether a person can choose to accept or reject medical care, a determination must be made of whether the person is **competent.** The reluctance of courts to articulate a standard for competence has resulted in very few reported opinions that state any formal opinion of competency. Rather, courts prefer to involve physicians, often psychiatrists, and other caregivers, in testifying about the mental state of a person and base the determination of competency on that information (Furrow, 1987).

In a court determination of competency, the nurse may be called on to testify and will be asked to offer information relative to the patient's behavior or verbalizations that may offer evidence as to the person's state of mind. The medical record is extremely important in this type of proceeding, and the nurse will want to use it to back up any testimony given.

It has been noted that older adults are more often faced with issues concerning the right to self-determination and that in such matters, the resident's statements and other indications of their wishes, as well as their state of mind, are critical. Nurses should keep these points in mind when responsible for the care of older adults, and should assure that records and notations, assessments, and other ongoing observations are carefully, objectively, and accurately documented.

If a time comes when a nurse needs to refer to them to testify in a court proceeding, the information provided will be used to help determine how an individual's basic rights are being addressed. A nurse can be secure in knowing that everything has been done to see that the resident's rights are respected.

Guidelines for DNR Policies in Nursing Homes

Nurses often raise questions and are faced with dilemmas about DNR policies because there is inconsistency or uncertainty either in the existing policy or in the application of procedures that may not have been well thought out. Since the nurse may be the only health professional present in the nursing facility at any given time, it is imperative for nurses to request that the facility have a detailed and specific policy that will provide the necessary guidance.

If a facility does develop a DNR policy, the following guidelines should be considered. The variation in state laws makes it imperative to examine the requirements of the jurisdiction. Whatever policies are adopted should be well communicated to the staff and should be adhered to scrupulously. The policy should indicate:

- That a facility must have competently trained staff available 24 hours per day to provide CPR (Schrieber, 1990).
- Whether CPR will be performed unless there is a DNR order.
- The conditions under which the facility will issue DNR orders. These factors should be in compliance with applicable state law, thus it is necessary to examine the DNR provisions of the jurisdiction. Considerations include required physician consultations as to medical condition, and discussions with the client and family members with documentation.
- That competency is established, again with proper documentation or medical consultation, as may be indicated by applicable state law.
- The origin of consent for the order: via the client, while competent; by an advance medical directive (AMD); or by a substitute or surrogate decision maker.
- Provide for renewal of DNR orders at appropriate time intervals with ongoing documentation of condition to note changes.

As required by the JCAHO standards, the policy should address the roles of the various staff members, and it should be approved through all appropriate channels.*

Advance Medical Directives

AMDs are documents that permit people to set forth in writing their wishes and preferences regarding health care, which are to be used to make such decisions if the time should come when they are unable to speak for themselves. Some advance directives also permit people to designate someone to convey their wishes in the event that they are rendered unable to do so. AMDs are helpful to professionals, since they provide information and guidance when treatment decisions must be made.

Sometimes, the policy of the provider or the judgment of the treating physician may not be in accord with the wishes of the client. In such cases, it is necessary to advise the client of this. For example, if a nursing home does not offer CPR, and this is desired by the client, then the facility must advise the client and offer the option of transfer. In the same way, a physician who does not agree with or cannot carry out the wishes of a client must advise the client of this and must then transfer the care of the client to another physician as soon as is practicable.

*See Standard CP 1.5.18 and its subsections, *The Joint Commission 1990 LTC: Long Term Care Standards Manual*, Chicago, 1989, JCAHO.

It is important to remember that the right to self-determination is well grounded in the common law and is interpreted in the U.S. Constitution under the right of liberty. The statutory developments and codification of these principles promote communication and make it easier for individuals to exercise their right to autonomy. For more information on the role of the nurse regarding advance directives, see Nurses' Responsibilities, p. 53.

The Legal Tools

Living Wills or Designation of Health Care Agents

Living wills are intended to provide written expressions of a client's wishes regarding the use of medical treatments in the event of a terminal illness or condition (Doukas, 1991). **Health care agent** designations are made to appoint a trusted person to express the client's wishes regarding the withholding or withdrawal of life support.

Allowing for variations among states, in general living wills are not effective until (1) the attending physician has the document and the client has been determined to be incompetent, (2) the physician has determined the client has a terminal condition or a condition such that any therapy provided would only have the effect of prolonging dying, and (3) the physician has written the appropriate orders in the medical record (Lieberson, 1992).

States vary in the instruments used for these purposes. For example, New York does not have a living will statute but does have a health care proxy provision, which combines the elements of the living will and designation of a health care agent.

Durable or General Power of Attorney: Differences and Indications

The **durable* power of attorney** is a legal instrument by which a person can designate someone else to make health care decisions at a time in the future when he or she may be rendered incompetent. This is called a springing power, one that comes into effect in the future on occurrence of a specific event, in this case, the incompetence of the client.

The person delegating the power of attorney is called the *principal*, whereas the person to whom the power is granted is known as the *agent.* A durable power of attorney is different from a *general* power of attorney, in that a general power of attorney would become invalid on incompetence of the principal.

Thus the durable power of attorney allows the designation of a legally enforceable surrogate decision maker. The role of the designated surrogate in this situation is to make the decisions that most closely align with the wishes, desires, and values of the clients.

*The word *durable* is important here. A simple power of attorney becomes invalid on the incompetency of the principal, whereas a durable power survives the principal's incapacity.

BOX 3-2

End-of-Life Decision Diagram

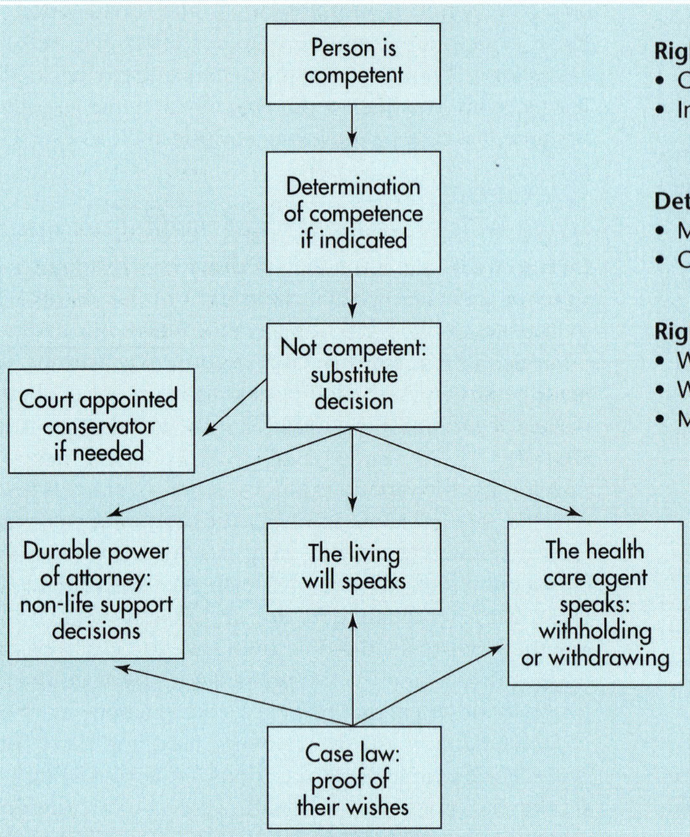

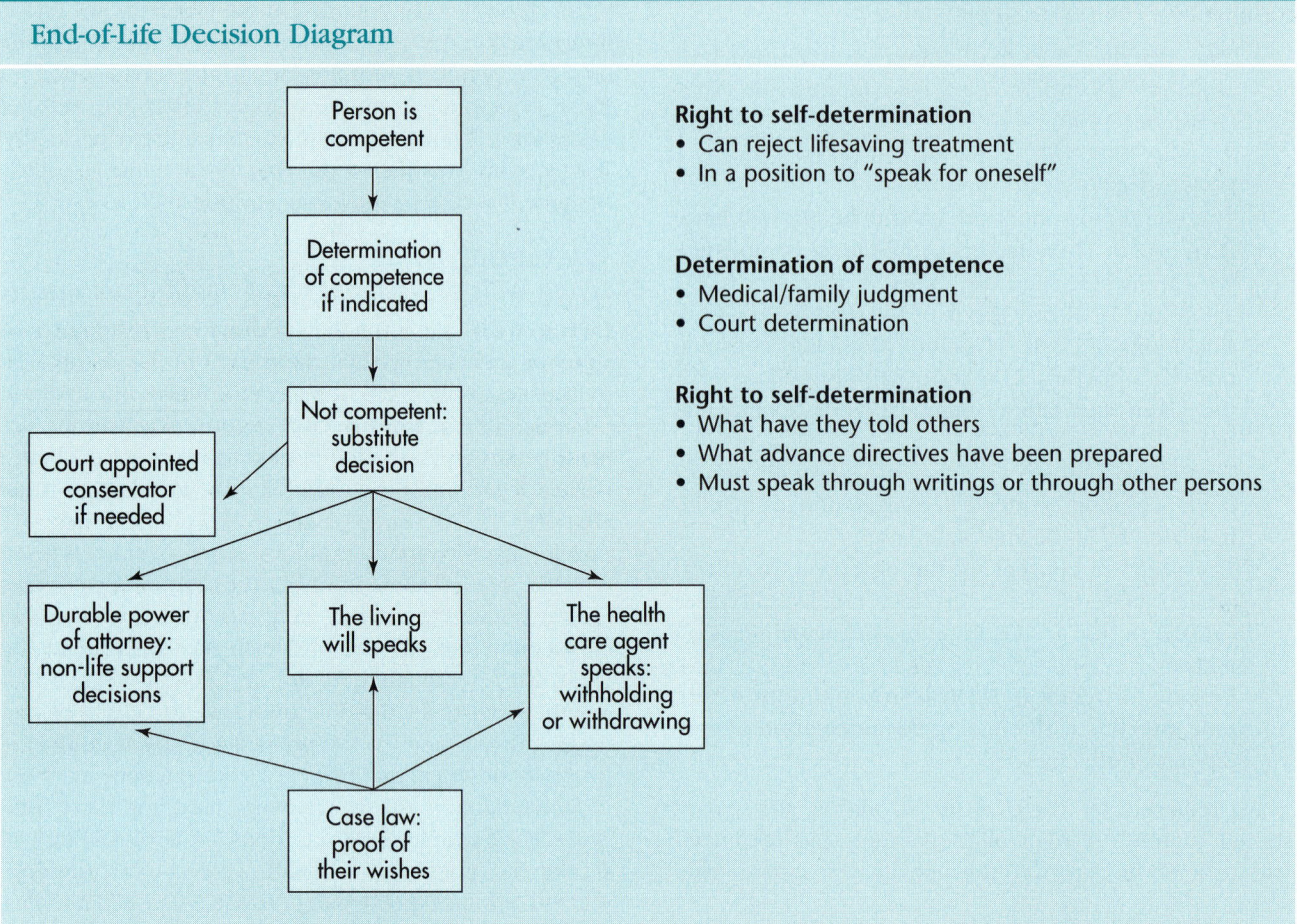

Right to self-determination
- Can reject lifesaving treatment
- In a position to "speak for oneself"

Determination of competence
- Medical/family judgment
- Court determination

Right to self-determination
- What have they told others
- What advance directives have been prepared
- Must speak through writings or through other persons

The durable power of attorney has an advantage over the living will, in that the designated agent can assess the current situation, ask questions and gather other information to assist in determining the wishes of the client (Peters, 1987). The living will, on the other hand, speaks for clients who cannot themselves speak, and obviously, cannot ask questions.

All states now have laws providing for living wills, durable powers of attorney, or both. Since specifics of the laws vary from state to state, it is important for the nurse to be knowledgeable of the laws in the state in which the nurse practices. Furthermore, since this is a developing area of the law, the nurse should keep abreast of the changes. Depending on a nurse's work environment, resources for this information may be facility administration, risk management staff, legal counsel, or another appropriate source.

General Provisions in Living Wills

Living wills may be executed by any competent adult. Most statutes contain specific language excluding **euthanasia** and declaring that withholding care in compliance with the document does not constitute suicide.

Most statutes require that the signature of the client be witnessed. The witness usually does not have to *attest* as to the mental competence of the client; however, many forms require that the witness indicate that the principal "appeared" to be of sound mind.

In general, it is also prohibited for an owner or employee of a facility in which a client resides to serve as a witness to a signature, unless the owner is a relative. In some states, a person who has an interest in the estate of the client may not serve as witness or be designated as the health care agent.

Pain and comfort measures may not be withheld. A living will may be revoked at any time and *by any means.*

Decision Diagram

The decision diagram assists in understanding the thought process that should be followed when trying to analyze end-of-life decision-making situations (Box 3-2).

If clients are competent, then they are capable of making their own decisions. While competent, a person can prepare for possible future incompetence by executing AMDs and by discussing personal wishes with health professionals and family members so that the nature of that person's specific preferences for future care and treatment are fully understood.

When the time comes for AMDs to be used, a verification of incompetence will be made. This can normally be accomplished by medical judgment and family discussion. Laws of any jurisdiction should be evaluated to see what types of documentation and procedures may be required.

Once deemed incompetent, substituted decision-making alternatives must be chosen. If a person has not executed AMDs, other people are looked to for their knowledge about the client's wishes. If all are in agreement as to the client's medical condition, then the statutory order of priority for surrogates can be looked to for designation of the decision maker. In New York, for example, decision makers are selected in this order (also considered is their willingness): spouse, son or daughter over age 18, parent, brother or sister over age 18, or a close friend.

If there are executed AMDs, and there is agreement among health professionals and family, then the wishes may be carried out according to the directives. There is comprehensive immunity from civil liability for physicians who, in good faith, rely on AMDs in carrying out treatment directives.

Where there is lack of agreement or confusion, it may be necessary to seek a court-ordered **conservator.** (This is sometimes referred to as a **guardian;** the word *conservator* is used here, but it should be noted that jurisdictions may assign varied meanings to these terms.) The conservator then acts as the surrogate and decides according to the wishes of the client as can best be determined by available information. The conservator also makes such decisions in the best interest of the client. This is in reference to a conservator of the *person*, as contrasted with a conservator of the *property*, who deals with matters related to the property and belongings of an individual and thus is not a subject of this discussion.

The court-appointed conservator has priority over other decision makers. The conservator may be a spouse, parent, or other family member. It may also be any other person, as the court determines to best serve the interests of the client. For a paradigm of end-of-life decision making, see Box 3-2.

An example of a typical living will document is presented in Box 3-3 and an example of the document concerning appointment of a health care agent is presented in Box 3-4. States usually provide forms for these purposes, but may not require that the specific form be used. Rather, most require that the executed documents

BOX 3-3

Connecticut General Statutes § 19a-575. Form of Document

Any person 18 years of age or older may execute a document which shall contain directions as to specific life support systems which such person chooses to have administered. Such document shall be signed and dated by the maker with at least two witnesses and may be substantially in the following form:

DOCUMENT CONCERNING WITHHOLDING OR WITHDRAWAL OF LIFE SUPPORT SYSTEMS

If the time comes when I am incapacitated to the point where I can no longer actively take part in decisions for my own life, and am unable to direct my physician as to my own medical care, I wish this statement to stand as a testament of my wishes.

"I....(NAME) request that, if my condition is deemed terminal or if it is determined that I will be permanently unconscious, I be allowed to die and not be kept alive through life support systems. By terminal condition, I mean that I have an incurable or irreversible medical condition which, without the administration of life support systems, will, in the opinion of my attending physician, result in death within a relatively short time. By permanently unconscious I mean that I am in a permanent coma or persistent vegetative state which is an irreversible condition in which I am at no time aware of myself or the environment and show no behavioral response to the environment. The life support systems which I do not want include, but are not limited to the following:

Artificial respiration
Cardiopulmonary resuscitation
Artificial means of providing nutrition and hydration
(Cross out any initial life support systems you want administered.)
I do not intend any direct taking of my life, but only that my dying not be unreasonably prolonged.
Other specific requests:

This request is made, after careful reflection, while I am of sound mind.

.....(Signature)
.....(Date)

This document was signed in our presence, by the above-named . . .(NAME) who appeared to be 18 years of age or older, of sound mind, and able to understand the nature and consequences of health care decisions at the time the document was signed.

.....(Witness)
.....(Address)
.....(Witness)
.....(Address)

Modified from: 1985, P.A. 85-606, §6;1991, P.A. 91-283,§5; 1992, May SpSess., P.A. 92-11, §2. effective June 1, 1992.

BOX 3-4

Connecticut Health Care Agent (C.G.S. §19a-577)

(a) Any person 18 years of age or older may execute a document that may, but need not be in substantially the following form:

DOCUMENT CONCERNING THE APPOINMENT OF HEALTH CARE AGENT

I appoint ....(NAME) to be my health care agent. If my attending physician determines that I am unable to understand and appreciate the nature and consequences of health care decisions and to reach and communicate an informed decision regarding treatment, my health care agent is authorized to:

(1) convey to my physician my wishes concerning the withholding or removal of life support systems.
(2) take whatever actions are necessary to ensure that my wishes are given effect.

If this person is unwilling or unable to serve as my health care agent, I appoint .....(Name) to be my alternative health care agent.

This request is made, after careful reflection, while I am of sound mind.

.....(Signature)
.....(Date)

This document was signed in our presence, by the above-named .....(Name) who appeared to be 18 years of age or older, of sound mind, and able to understand the nature and consequences of health care decisions at the time the document was signed.

.....(Witness)
.....(Address)
.....(Witness)
.....(Address)

Modified from: 1991, P.A. 91-283, §6.

be only in *substantially* the same form. In any event, the laws of the jurisdiction should be reviewed to see if a specific form or document is required.

THE PATIENT SELF DETERMINATION ACT

The Patient Self Determination Act[11] (PSDA) became effective December 1, 1991. The intent of this law is to assure that clients are given information about the extent to which their rights already exist under state law. The PSDA itself does not create any new substantive legal right for individuals regarding their decision making. Rather, its focus is one of education and communication.

The PSDA requires hospitals, nursing homes, and other health care providers who receive federal funds such as Medicare or Medicaid, to give clients written information explaining their legal options for refusing or accepting treatment should they become incapacitated.

Background: the Cruzan Case

On January 11, 1983, Nancy Cruzan, a healthy 25-year-old woman, was seriously injured in an automobile accident and rendered comatose and in a "persistent vegetative state." Seven years later, the U.S. Supreme Court considered whether her life support could be withdrawn. Her parents, who had also been designated her coguardians by a judgment of the court, sought a court order to withdraw the artificial feeding and hydration equipment after it became apparent that she had virtually no chance of regaining her cognitive facilities.[12]

In June 1990 in a 5-4 decision, the court held that because there was no clear and convincing evidence of Nancy's desire to have life-sustaining treatment withdrawn under such circumstances, her parents lacked the authority to effectuate such a request.[12] The court affirmed that the Missouri Supreme Court was within its rights to request more evidence to indicate what Nancy's decision would be if she were in a position to make that decision herself. It was in this decision that the court permitted the state of Missouri [and thus made it constitutionally permissible] to require "clear and convincing proof" as the standard of proof needed to determine a person's wishes regarding the withdrawal of life support.

Most states have not adopted this rigorous standard of proof for such decisions. In fact, as of this writing, only two states, Missouri and New York, use the "clear and convincing" standard. In most jurisdictions, family members, those close to the individual, or other surrogate decision makers may make decisions for a client who has not left specific oral or written instructions (Coleman, 1994).

Clear and Convincing Proof

It is difficult if not impossible to come up with a precise meaning of this term. Although not applied in most states, this discussion is presented here to provide insight into the Cruzan case, to understand the significance of the court's decision to initiate AMD legislation nationwide and to enact the PSDA, and to provide some clarification that helps in understanding a lesser standard of proof.

The clear and convincing standard is an intermediate standard of evidence, higher than a "preponderance of the evidence," but below certainty beyond a reasonable doubt." A clear and convincing presentation should provide enough facts that produce in the mind of the trier a "firm belief or conviction" regarding the events to be established (Black, 1979).

An AMD may help to meet this standard. However, in the absence of an AMD, the evidence required to meet this standard may be somewhat cloudy. Writings such as the living will would be accorded more weight than oral statements.

In *re Westchester County Medical Center on Behalf of O'Connor*[13] the clear and convincing standard was described as a "a firm and settled commitment. . .under circumstances like those presented" and must be "more than immediate reactions to the unsettling experience of seeing or hearing another's unnecessarily prolonged death.[14]

The Cruzan decision must be examined for the areas of clarification it provided. While it did not declare a "right to die" as such, it did provide much stimulus for the development of legislation in states that would clarify the existing rights to self-determination. In addition, it also served as the catalyst for the enactment of the PSDA:

> A competent person has a constitutionally protected right under the Fourteenth Amendment to refuse medical treatment, even life saving nutrition and hydration; an incompetent or incapacitated person may have that right exercised by a surrogate.
>
> **Cruzan v. Director,**
> **Missouri Department of Health,**
> **111 L Ed 2d 224, 110 S Ct 2841 (1990).**

In her concurring opinion, U.S. Supreme Court Justice Sandra Day O'Connor made the following points*:

- Artificial provision of nutrition and hydration involves intrusion and restraint and invokes the same due process concerns as any other medical treatment.
- One does not by incompetence lose one's due process liberty interests.
- The U.S. Constitution may require the states to implement the decision of a client's duly appointed surrogate.

The PSDA's Four Significant Provisions:

1. Requires hospitals, skilled nursing facilities, home health agencies, hospice programs, and HMOs, which participate in Medicare and Medicaid programs, to maintain written policies and procedures guaranteeing that every adult receiving medical care be given written information regarding their involvement in treatment decisions. This information must include: individual rights under state law, either statutory or case law; and written policies of the provider or organization regarding the implementation of such rights.

   The information must be provided in hospitals at time of admission, in nursing facilities at the time of admission as a resident; for a hospice program at the time of initial receipt of hospice care; for HMOs at time of enrollment of the individual, and for a home health agency in advance of the individual coming under the care of the agency.

   The PSDA further requires that written information be distributed that describes each facility's policy for implementing the rights of the clients. *Each client's medical record must document whether the client has executed an AMD (emphasis added).*

   The PSDA also provides protection against discrimination or refusal to provide care based on whether an individual has executed an AMD.
2. The provider must provide for education of staff and community on issues concerning AMDs.
3. States are required to develop a written description of the law concerning AMDs in their respective jurisdictions, and to distribute the material to providers who provide it to clients according to the requirements of the PSDA.
4. The Secretary of DHHS was also required, no later than 6 months after the enactment date, to develop and implement a national campaign to inform the public of the option to execute AMDs and of the client's right to participate and direct their health care decisions.

*Interpretation is the author's analysis of points taken from the concurring opinion of Justice O'Connor. (Modified from: Cruzan V. Director, Missouri Dept of Health (1990, US) 111 L Ed 2d 224,247-251, 110 S Ct 2841.)

Nurses' Responsibilities

The ANA published the following statement made by their Board of Trustees, articulating the nurse's important role in implementation of the PSDA:

> Nurses should know the laws of the state in which [they] practice . . . and should be familiar with the strengths and limitations of the various forms of advance directive.
>
> The nurse has a responsibility to facilitate informed decision making, including but not limited to advance directives.
>
> The ANA recommends that the following questions be part of the nursing admission assessment:
>
> - Do you have basic information about advance care directives, including living wills and durable power of attorney?
> - Do you wish to initiate an advance care directive?
> - If you have already prepared an advance care directive, can you provide it now?
> - Have you discussed your end-of-life choices with your

family or designated surrogate and health care team workers?*

Problems and Ethical Dilemmas Associated with Implementation of the PSDA

Although public and medical professionals overwhelmingly support AMDs, clients have historically been reluctant to complete them. Even distribution of forms and information in the past has failed to increase the participation rate.

There may be indications, however, of some increase in the execution of living wills. A survey by the *Boston Globe* in November 1991, showed that 24% of respondents had living wills as compared with 20% in November 1990 and 14% in May 1990 (*Choice in Dying Newsletter,* 1992). Further evidence of acceptance is reported—80% of doctors would disconnect life support at a dying patient's request—up from 62% a year ago . . . (*Hartford Courant,* 1993).

Other research indicates that the care of dying clients may not be keeping pace with national guidelines or legal decisions upholding clients' rights to accept or refuse treatment. Based on a survey of 1,400 health care providers at five hospitals in several states, some 47% of nurses and physicians and 70% of medical and surgical residents said they acted against their conscience in providing care to the terminally ill. Only a third said they were satisfied that clients receive the information and help they need to make treatment decisions (*Modern Healthcare,* 1993).

Questions arise about the effectiveness of AMDs in situations where, for example, the person is away from home, a person changes his or her mind, or a situation arises that is not anticipated. Some approaches have been advised regarding these issues.

For example, some states have included in the language of living will provisions that a validly executed living will from another jurisdiction will be honored. However, it is probably wise if there is any uncertainty to have people from another state execute a new document as soon as possible.

AMD provisions appropriately provide that people can change their minds at any time and by any means. Nurses need to be alert to any indications they may receive from a client. Based on the person's medical condition, subtle signs such as a gesture or a nod of the head may be easily overlooked.

The protocols established by facilities to comply with the PSDA may turn the "tangible indicators of extremely important and personal decisions into just another piece of paper." AMDs must be part of a clinical process, not an administrative one (LaPuma, Orrentlicher, Moss, 1991). At least one nurse has reported that questioning about AMDs is done in the admitting office, where "they already ask very invasive questions about finances and next-of-kin" (*American Journal of Nursing,* 1992). The meaning and importance of these issues may be undermined if it becomes a mere familiar administrative procedure.

Many have questioned whether the time of admission to a hospital or a nursing home is the best time to enter into discussions about advance directives. At such times, client may be fearful, uncomfortable or in pain, and anxious. These emotional states may affect a client's understanding and level of competence. It is important for the nurse to facilitate this process using the professional skills and understanding necessary to comply with the PSDA in such circumstances.

Conflicts between medical judgment and client choices are bound to become more common. It will be necessary to take steps to assure that the directives of clients are accorded the compliance that is appropriate and that the judgment of health professionals is respected.

As discussed previously, both the PSDA and OBRA require a facility or a physician that is unable to comply with the wishes of the client, to notify the client of when it is appropriate to be transferred to another facility or the care of another physician so that the client's wishes can be respected. This assures that the client's wishes are met and preserves the integrity of the medical practitioner and provider. The medical record should reflect only the facts of such a situation. It is neither necessary or appropriate to "make a case" in the record as to which party was right or wrong. It is appropriate only to show that proper procedures were followed and that all relevant matters were fully explained.

There are still many questions that are unanswered in the PSDA that will have to be sorted out over time. For example, the exact time of admission may be unclear. How is the matter handled with minors or those who are illiterate? What would the nurse do if clients refuse to produce their AMDs?

In the case of surrogate decision makers, what about the response of a designated agent who is then called on to decide about the removal of life support? If and when the time comes, will the person be able to carry out the principal's wishes? Will the instructions left be clear enough to assure that those wishes are carried out (Ballard, 1993)?

It must be noted that the responsibility to make these truly awesome decisions may arise at times of great personal difficulty and may in fact be more demanding than the agent ever thought possible. A realistic approach to these points at the time such instruments are executed will help to resolve such dilemmas. The nurse should be

*ANA Board of Directors Task Force on the nurse's role in end of life decisions.

alert for opportunities to gain information from both clients and their families or health agents to gauge their level of understanding. The nurse's role in helping to clarify matters and explaining information that has been received may help to alleviate the emotional dilemma associated with carrying out end-of-life decisions.

THE VALUES HISTORY

AMDs such as living wills and durable powers of attorney are helping to ease some of the difficult situations faced by health care professionals and families when making treatment decisions used to prolong life. However, one criticism of such documents is that they may not offer insight into the person's own values or underlying beliefs regarding such directives (Doukas, 1991).

A **values history** may help to add this dimension to the matter of advanced health care decision making. The values history is an instrument that asks questions related to quality versus length of life, and tries to determine what values a person sees as important to maintain during terminal care. The instrument asks people to specify their wishes regarding several types of medical situations. It presents the types of treatment that may be available in each situation, and describes with whom these matters have been discussed in the past and who should be involved in the actual decision making.

As a practical matter, its use may be limited by the time required for discussion with the physician, or the physician's reluctance or discomfort to directly address the issues. But this should not serve as a reason for abandonment of this potentially useful tool.

The values history has important implications for the nurse. The values history, although a document with questions and answers, is really more than that. It is a process of "reflection and communication that can take place over a lifetime" (Lieberson, 1992). Nurses' close interpersonal relationships with clients and families and high degree of communication skills speak to the critical role they can play in this process. As the life and death situations become more complex and demanding of real knowledge of the client's wishes, the values history may serve a useful purpose in preserving the autonomy of the individual.

The values history forces extended conversation between individuals and their physicians and other health professionals. This type of instrument may increase autonomy by providing a better basis for representing the desires of a client when they can no longer express their wishes. A copy of the values history developed at the University of New Mexico is included in Appendix 3A, p. 61.

Insight • *Nurses should be careful to avoid the "administrative task trap," which results when important communications and interactions between clients and their nurses are reduced to nothing more significant than assuring that a task has been marked off a checklist. Many of these checklists have been developed to assure implementation of some of life's most emotional decisions—those associated with end-of-life decision making.*

Because of their close personal relationship and high degree of communication skill, nurses occupy a unique and treasured role with clients and families. As the life and death situations become more complex and demanding, the need to interact with clients on these sensitive matters often falls to the nurse. Nurses can help clients navigate these intricate and complex situations and use their professional skills to affect the quality of life of their clients.

NURSES' ETHICAL CODE

Ethics relate to the moral actions, behavior, and character of an individual. Nurses occupy a most trusted place in society, and conforming to a code of ethics gives evidence of acceptance of that responsibility and trust. A code of ethical conduct offers general principles to guide and to evaluate nursing actions (ANA, 1985).

The previously mentioned Standards and Scope of Gerontological Nursing Practice, Number X, state that a nurse uses the Code for Nurses (Box 3-5), established by the ANA as the guide for ethical decision making in the practice of nursing (ANA, 1987). A violation of ethical code may not itself be a violation of law. The state's nursing association may take action against a nurse in violation of the ethical code. More importantly, the ethical code serves to regulate professional practice from within the profession and assure ethical conduct in the professional setting. Maintaining mutual respect among practitioners in the field is arguably one of the best ways to bring respect to a profession and to oneself.

ETHICAL DILEMMAS AND CONSIDERATIONS

Euthanasia, Suicide, and Assisted Suicide

Even with Michigan's Dr. Jack Kevorkian,* there are actually few reported cases of assisted suicide or euthanasia,

*The debate on euthanasia was renewed nationally with the high publicity case of Dr. Jack Kevorkian, who invented a "suicide machine," first used by client Janet Adkins to take her own life in June 1990.

BOX 3-5

Code for Nurses

1. The nurse provides services with respect for human dignity and the uniqueness of the client, unrestricted by considerations of social or economic status, personal attributes, or the nature of health problems.
2. The nurse safeguards the client's right to privacy by judiciously protecting information of a confidential nature.
3. The nurse acts to safeguard the client and the public when health care and safety are affected by the incompetent, unethical, or illegal practice of any person.
4. The nurse assumes responsibility and accountability for individual nursing judgments and actions.
5. The nurse maintains competence in nursing.
6. The nurse exercises informed judgment and uses individual competence and qualifications as criteria in seeking consultation, accepting responsibilities, and delegating nursing activities to others.
7. The nurse participates in activities that contribute to the ongoing development of the profession's body of knowledge.
8. The nurse participates in the profession's efforts to implement and improve standards of nursing.
9. The nurse participates in the profession's efforts to protect the public from misinformation and misrepresentation and to maintain the integrity of nursing.
10. The nurse collaborates with members of the health professions and other citizens in promoting community and national efforts to meet the health needs of the public.

and no data on the number of assisted suicides in the United States are available. There are, however, suggestions of considerable interest on the part of many citizens, some physicians, and other health professionals that doctors should be allowed to help a severely ill person take their own life (Lieberson, 1992). In some states, assisted suicide is considered an illegal act. However, an act of affirmative euthanasia (actual administration of the instrumentality that causes death) would constitute an illegal criminal offense in all 50 states.

If such acts occur, they may be handled with subtlety and thus may be unlikely to be recognized or even detected as affirmative euthanasia. Actions such as failure to take steps to prevent a suicide, deliberate administration of a medication in a dosage that will suppress respiration and cause death, or the heavy doses of pain medications needed to comfort a terminally ill client may be intentional or inadvertent acts of assisting suicide or euthanasia. The nurse in particular may be in the middle of the conflict between the therapeutic necessity of treatment and the likely outcomes. Unlike an act of affirmative euthanasia, where the nurse's actions are clear, in situations where there are competing interests, (e.g. therapeutic necessity and likely outcomes), the nurse must rely on the client's needs and his or her own professional judgment. The nurse should not hesitate to request assistance from the institutional ethics committee to help cope with such dilemmas.

What about the person who, although not terminally ill or in a persistent vegetative state, is in her 80s and wishes to stop eating or drinking with the intent of causing her own death? In *re Application of Brooks* (NY Sup CT, Albany County, June 10, 1987), the court denied the petition of a nursing home administrator to authorize force feeding. Although there was disagreement among physicians regarding her competence, the court decided that she was competent and thus had a right to determine what was to be done with her body. It found that failing to force feed is not abetting suicide.

There may be signs of increased public support for aid-in-dying. The report of a study released in 1992 (Blendon et al, 1992) shows an increase of approval for physician aid-in-dying on request of the client and family, which is up from 34% to 63% between 1950 to 1991. They conclude that efforts to change and shape public policy on this issue will continue in the future.

Experimentation and Research

As previously discussed, nursing home residents are accorded specific rights with respect to their treatment. The patient/resident bill of rights entitles them to choose a primary physician if desired. Furthermore, they have the right to be informed about their medical condition and proposed plan of treatment.

Nursing home residents, or any client, may refuse to participate in experimental research,* or to be examined, observed, or treated by students or other staff without jeopardizing their access to care.†

The goals of research are different from the goals of care. Research seeks to acquire knowledge with no intended benefit to the subjects, because much of clinical research is conducted to determine effective treatments or potential benefits of new drugs and medical

*E.g., *see Annotated code of Maryland,* 1957, § 19-344(f): and *Vermont statutes annotated,* Title 18 § 1852(a)(10) and Title 33 § 3781(3), as redesignated by Act 219, L. 1990, effective July 1, 1990.

†E.g., *see* 1990 edition, *General laws of Massachusetts,* supplemented by the 1991 Supplement, Chapter 111:70E9h.

devices. The goal of client care, on the other hand, is to provide benefit only to a specific client (Brett et al, 1991). This is a complex and controversial subject. Key points to consider in such issues are the goals and value of the research, conflicts between institutional interests and researchers, and the medical interests of the individual.

DHHS regulations may permit waiving the right to informed consent under the following specific circumstances where: the research poses only a minimal risk; there will be no adverse effects on the rights and welfare of the subjects; the research could not effectively be carried out without the waiver; and whenever possible, the participants are provided with pertinent information during or after participation.

Only a full review of the research that includes legal analysis determines whether a waiver of informed consent can be justified. It may be that the right to informed consent cannot be waived even when the research poses minimal risk.

Research involving humans should be examined by an appropriate review board (Brett et al, 1991). All aspects of the proposed study must be evaluated to assure that the research is justified and is of benefit, and that the individual rights of all people, including volunteer participants, are not sacrificed. Nurses, as a professional group closely involved with the clinical aspects of human research, should be represented on the review board.

There are both state and federal regulatory provisions governing human research investigations. The diligent efforts of the research review board considers not only these laws and regulations but also their application to the particular benefits of the proposed research. A nurse involved in any aspect of human research should ask to see the details of the proposed study, and the deliberations and decision of the institutional review board. It is not improper for a nurse to ask to attend a meeting of the review board, if the nurse is involved in carrying out any aspect of the research or has any information that is of importance to the board as it considers a proposal. Furthermore, the nurse should report to the board at any time issues that may arise with respect to the research, if it appears that individual rights are in question.

Ethics Committees

Biomedical ethics committees can play a pivotal role in dealing with the sensitive conflicts about treatment decisions. They can help to resolve conflicts that might otherwise force treatment decisions "from the bedside to the courtroom" (McCormick, 1991). Their objective is to carefully evaluate differing positions to achieve a consensus that is ethically and legally acceptable to all parties (Houge, 1993).

Ethics committees do not have any legal authority. Their main service is to create a forum where clients, client representatives, and providers can express and consider different points of view.

Two thirds of general hospitals with more than 200 beds have such panels. Their presence in nursing homes is not as widespread. Membership on ethics committees should be diverse to minimize a group's tendency to view the task as technical, to help maintain a "balanced view" among professionals and special interest groups, and to offer variety of perspectives to those seeking guidance (Hollerman, 1991).

The nurse's role is crucial. Representation should be diverse, and include administrative and staff nurses, as well as nurses practicing in specialty areas. It is recommended that nurses comprise approximately one third of committee members (Hollerman, 1991).

Ethics committees' primary purposes are (1) to provide education and help guide policy making regarding ethical issues, (2) to facilitate and aid in the resolution of ethical dilemmas, and (3) to take an activist role in involving all interested parties in promoting the best care for patients (*Brown University Long Term Care Letter,* 1990).

Issues and topics that might be discussed by an ethics committee include euthanasia, patient competency and decision-making capacities, guardianship issues, DNR orders and policies, patient refusal of treatment, starting, continuing, or stopping treatment, informed consent, use of feeding tubes, use of restraints—the list could be almost endless.

An organization considering the establishment of an ethics committee should be prepared to make the necessary commitment of time and resources. A committee should be visible and available, and should publish clear notice of means to obtain access. It is important to note that ethics committees provide a process, not a decision.

Summary

This chapter presented the legal and ethical issues associated with nursing care of older adults. Professional standards of practice were identified as the legal measure against which nursing practice is judged, and sources of such standards were identified. Laws applicable to older adults generally were presented, and since older adults who reside in nursing homes are particularly vulnerable, comprehensive coverage of nursing home regulations was included.

Issues associated with autonomy and self-determination were described, including do not resuscitate orders, advance directives, and end of life decision making. Ethical considerations were discussed, including issues associated with euthanasia and human research investigation. Nurses have an important role in helping to meet the health care needs of older adults, whose unique char-

HOME CARE TIPS

- Home care agencies' standards are based on the Standards and Scope of Gerontological Nursing Practice as published by the ANA.
- Assess for older adult abuse and notify the proper authorities (e.g., local Elderly Protective Services or Ombudsmen Program).
- On initial assessment, inform the homebound older adult and caregiver of home care client rights. Have them sign a copy that validates that they have been informed of their rights.
- Inform caregivers and homebound older adults of their right to self-determination. Validate with a signature from the caregiver or the homebound older adult that they have been informed. Advance directives must be part of a clinical assessment.
- Obtain a copy of homebound older adult's advance directives and keep on file in older adult's chart. Send a copy to physician to file.
- A Do Not Resuscitate Order must be signed by the physician within 48 hours, as specified by Medicare regulations.
- To assist caregivers and homebound older adults to make treatment decisions used to prolong life, the home care nurse may use a values history. The values history is an instrument that asks questions related to quality versus length of life and the values that the person sees as important to maintain during terminal care.

acteristics and needs present new challenges. The older person's quality of life will be affected to a great extent by the quality of nursing care they receive.

Key Points

- The nurse's duty to the client is to provide care according to a measurable standard. When a client's physical and mental conditions, and their ability to care for themselves decline, the duty of care rises.
- Older adults, and in particular infirm older adults are considered a vulnerable population, and therefore their treatment in licensed health care institutions and other settings is carefully regulated.
- Evidence provided to the U.S. Congress in 1983 suggested widespread abuse of residents in nursing homes and resulted in the enactment of OBRA '87, the most sweeping reform affecting Medicare and Medicaid nursing facilities since the programs began.
- OBRA '87 focuses on the quality of life of residents of nursing facilities and assurance of the preservation of their human rights and due process interests. The new regulations address virtually every element of life in a nursing facility. OBRA's regulations are enforced through a survey process that focuses on the outcomes of residential care and includes sanctions designed to force compliance.
- There is a strong judicial deference toward individual autonomy. This assures every human being the right to determine what shall be done with his own body. These rights are guaranteed in the U.S. Constitution and have been additionally interpreted in case laws and state laws.
- Legal tools and instruments such as advance directives, DNR orders, designation of health care agents, and durable powers of attorney help plan for future decision making so that a person's wishes can be carried out even when they are no longer able to speak for themselves.
- The right to self-determination was given even more emphasis with the passage of the U.S. federal Patient Self Determination Act, which went into effect December 1991. This law requires health care providers to inform and to educate clients about their rights as they exist under the laws of each state.
- The technologic advancements that help us to live longer also contribute to the complicated ethical dilemmas that emerge in the care of older adults. Ethics committees can help in these matters by responding to the need for the education of and communication between caregivers and clients.
- It is preferable to resolve client care dilemmas at the bedside rather than in the courtroom. The courts prefer such matters to be handled by clients, their families, and health professionals. With careful guidance and discussion, this can often be achieved.
- The aging of the population brings a new phenomenon to this country. Never before have so many people lived so long. Likewise, nursing care of the population poses challenges that have never before been faced. Knowledge and understanding will help nurses to meet these challenges.

Critical Thinking Exercises

1. An 80-year-old man has been able to care for himself with minimum assistance until recently. Should he and his family decide that it is time for him to move to a long-term care facility? How will his rights as an individual be protected, since he will be giving up his independence? Explain.
2. A 94-year-old man resides in a long-term care facility. He has signed an AMD in case he becomes seriously ill. A 72-year-old woman is being treated in the hospital for a recent cerebral vascular accident (CVA) that has left her severely incapacitated. Her family has requested a DNR order. How do these two instruments differ? In what ways do they protect each person's rights?

REFERENCES

American Nurses Association: *Standards and scope of gerontological nursing practice,* Washington, D.C., 1987, The Association.

American Nurses Association: *Code for nurses with interpretive statements,* Washington, D.C., 1985, The Association.

American Nurses Association: *Position Statement on Nursing and the Patient Self-Determination Act,* published compendium of position statements on the nurse's role in End-of-Life Decisions, Washington, D.C., 1992, American Nurses Publishing, The Association.

Ballard D: Don't leave final decisions to doctors, *Hartford Courant* May 17, 1993.

Black HC: *Black's law dictionary,* ed 5, St. Paul, Minn., 1979, West Publishing.

Blendon RI, et al: Should physicians aid their patients in dying? *JAMA* 267 (19):2658-2662, 1992.

Brett A et al: Ethical aspects of human experimentation in health services research, *JAMA*, 265(14):1854, 1991.

Coleman CH: Surrogate decision-making in New York: the legislative proposal of the New York state task force on life and the law. In American Bar Association: *Newsletter of the medicine and law committee,* Chicago, 1994, The Association.

Collier HG: Current issues in federal regulation of long-term care. In Gosfield AG, editor: *Health law handbook,* New York, 1990, Clark Boardman.

Conely GC, Campbell LA: The use of restraints in caring for the elderly: realities, consequences and alternatives, *Nurse Prac* 16(12):51, 1991.

Cooper JW: OBRA regulations and chemical restraints, *Nurs Homes Sen Cit Care* 39(5-6), 1990.

Doukas DJ et al: The values history: the evaluation of the patient's values and advance directives, *Fam Prac* 32(2):145, 1991.

Furrow BR et al: *Health law: cases, materials and problems,* Minnesota, 1987, West Publishing.

Hamme JM: An overview of OBRA '87 and '90. In the National Health Lawyers Association: *Long term care handbook,* Washington, D.C., 1991, The Association.

Health care facility management, Chicago, 1990, Commerce Clearing House, 1060.

Hollerman CE: Membership of institutional ethics committees, *Phys Exec* 17(3):34, 1991.

Houge EE: Ethics committees help facilities to cope with the PSDA, *Brown University Long Term Care Qual Newslet* 5(3):5, 1993.

Johnson SH: Residents' rights under OBRA of 1987. In the National Health Lawyers Association: *Long term care handbook,* Washington, D.C., 1991, The Association.

Kane RL, Kane RA: The impact of long-term-care financing on personal autonomy, *Generations* 14(SUP):86, Annual 1990.

LaPuma J, Orrentlicher D, Moss RJ: Advance directives on admission: clinical implications and analysis of the Patient Self-Determination Act, *JAMA*, 266:402, 1991.

Law enlarges caregiver role in end-of-life decisions, *AJN* 92(1), 1992.

Learn from others when forming ethics committees, *Brown Univ Long Term Care Newslet* 2(24):1, 1990.

Lieberson AD: *Advance medical directives,* New York, 1992, Clark Boardman Callaghan.

Long term care standards manual 1990, Chicago, 1989, Joint Commission of Accreditation of Healthcare Organizations, December 23, 1990.

Manton KG: The dynamics of population aging: demography and policy analysis, *Milbank Q* 69(2):309, Summer 1991.

Marion Merrell Dow Inc., Managed care digest, Long Term Care edition, Kansas City, Mo., 1994, SMG Marketing Group.

McCormick B: Right to die dilemma: are ethics committees equipped to fill their roles? *Am Med News* 34(42):3, 1991.

Manton, KG: *Milbank Q* 69(2):309(30), Summer 1991.

Northrop CE, Kelly ME: *Legal issues in nursing,* St. Louis, 1987, Mosby.

Nursing-legal survival: a risk management guide for nurses, Illinois, 1992, University Hospital Consortium.

Older Americans Act Amendments of 1988, Public Law 100-175.

Peters: Advance medical directives: the case for the durable power of attorney for health care, *8J Legal Med* 437, 451, 1987.

Reported in *Choice in Dying Newsletter,* 1:1:2, 1992.

Reported in *Modern Healthcare,* February 15, 1993, p 22. Results of study in *Pub Health Iss,* January 1993.

Salkin S: Do you know about OBRA? It could affect your sales to nursing homes, *Institut Distrib* 27(7):78, 1991.

Schabes AE: LTC surveys. In the National Health Lawyers Association: *Long term care handbook,* Washington, D.C., 1991, The Association.

Schreiber JC. Decision-making in treatment issues. In Gosfield AG, editor: *Health law handbook,* New York, 1990, Clark Boardman.

Special Report: Bruce Vladeck takes HCFA's helm, *Long Term Care Manag* 22(13), 1993.

Starr C: Consultants and OBRA regs: an Rx for better care, *Drug Top* 136(23), 1992.

Starr C: Consultants and OBRA regs: an Rx for better care, *Drug Top* 136(23):18, 1992.

Strauss PJ et al: *Aging and the law,* Chicago, 1990, Commerce Clearing House.

Suffering in silence, *Long Term Care Manag,* June 2, 1993.

Twenty-eight percent would aid suicide, *Hartford Courant* "Advances," April 15, 1993, .

Vladeck sees improvement in nursing home quality, *Long Term Care Manag* 22(15), 1993.

Zedlewski SR et al: *Needs of the elderly in the 21st century,* Washington, D.C., 1989, Urban Institute.

FOOTNOTES

[1]42 U.S.C. § 3001 (1965).

[2]Delaware Title 16 § § 1132 and 1135.

[3]Illinois Chapter 111½¶ 4161-176.

[4]California Welfare and Institutions § § 15600-15637.

[5]OBRA '87 at § 4211(a), 42 U.S.C.A. § 139r(c) (West Supp 1989).

[6]*McKinney's consolidated laws of New York annotated,* Public Health Law § § 2961.(4).

[7]*McKinney's consolidated laws of New York annotated,* Pub-

lic Health Law § § 2960 to 2979, as amended by Ch. 370, L. 1991, effective July 15, 1991. *See also* Florida Statutes § 765.101(2) and Colorado Revised Statutes § 15-18.6-101(1).

[8]*McKinney's consolidates laws of New York annotated,* Public Health Law § § 2800(1) and (3). (McKinney 1993).

[9]*McKinney's consolidated laws of New York annotated,* Public Health Law § 2962.(1). (McKinney 1993).

[10]*McKinney's consolidated laws of New York annotated,* Public Health Law §2963.(1). (McKinney 1993).

[11]42 U.S.C. §§ 1395 and 1396 (1990).

[12]*Cruzan versus Director, Missouri Dept. of Health* (1990, US) 111 L Ed 2D 224, 234, 110 S Ct 2841.

[13]72 NY2d 517, 534 NYS2d 886, 531 NE2d 607 (1988).

[14]72 NY2d 517, 534 NYS2d 886, 531 NE2d 607 (1988) at 903.

APPENDIX 3A

VALUES HISTORY FORM

Name: ______________________________

Date: ______________________________

If someone assisted you in completing this form, please fill in his or her name, address, and relationship to you.

Name: ______________________________

Address: ______________________________

____

Relationship: ______________________________

The purpose of this form is to assist you in thinking about and writing down what is important to you about your health. If you should at some time become unable to make health care decisions for yourself, your thoughts as expressed on this form may help others make a decision for you in accordance with what you would have chosen.

The first section of this form asks whether you have already expressed your wishes concerning medical treatment through either written or oral communications and if not, whether you would like to do so now. The second section of this form provides an opportunity for you to discuss your values, wishes, and preferences in a number of different areas, such as your personal relationships, your overall attitude toward life, and your thoughts about illness.

From: Center for Health and Law Ethics, Institute of Public Law, University of New Mexico, Albuquerque, N.M.

SECTION 1

A. Written Legal Documents

Have you written any of the following legal documents?

___

If so, please complete the requested information.

Living Will

Date written:___

Document location:___

Comments: (e.g., any limitations, special requests, etc.)___

___

___

___

___

Durable Power of Attorney

Date written: ___

Document location: ___

Comments: (e.g., whom have you named to be your decision maker?) ___

___

___

Durable Power of Attorney for Health Care Decisions

Date written: ___

Document location: ___

Comments: (e.g., whom have you named to be your decision maker?) ___

___

___

Organ Donations

Date written: ___

Document location: ___

Comments: (e.g., and limitations on which organs you would like to donate?)___

___

___

___

B. Wishes Concerning Specific Medical Procedures

If you have ever expressed your wishes, either written or orally, concerning any of the following medical procedures, please complete the requested information. If you have not previously indicated your wishes on these procedures and would like to do so now, please complete this information.

Organ Donation

To whom expressed: ___

If oral, when? ___

If written, when? ___

Document location:___

Comments:___

___

___

___

___

Kidney Dialysis

To whom expressed:___

If oral, when? ___

If written, when? ___

Document location: ___

Comments:___

___

___

___

___

___

Cardiopulmonary Resuscitation (CPR)

To whom expressed:___

If oral, when? ___

If written, when?___

Document location: ___

Comments:___

___

___

___

Respirators

To whom expressed:______________________________

If oral, when?______________________________

If written, when?______________________________

Document location: ______________________________

Comments:______________________________

____

____

____

____

Artificial Nutrition

To whom expressed:______________________________

If oral, when?______________________________

If written, when?______________________________

Document location: ______________________________

Comments:______________________________

____

____

____

____

Artificial Hydration

To whom expressed:______________________________

If oral, when?______________________________

If written, when?______________________________

Document location: ______________________________

Comments:______________________________

____

____

____

C. General Comments

Do you wish to make any general comments about the information you provided in this section?

____

____

____

____

SECTION 2

A. Your Overall Attitude Toward Your Health

1. How would you describe your current health status? If you currently have any medical problems, how would you describe them?______________________________

   ____

   ____

   ____

2. If you have current medical problems, in what ways, if any, do they affect your ability to function?______________________________

   ____

   ____

   ____

3. How do you feel about your current health status?

   ____

   ____

   ____

   ____

4. How well are you able to meet the basic necessities of life—eating, food preparation, sleeping, personal hygiene, etc.?______________________________

   ____

   ____

5. Do you wish to make any general comments about your overall health?______________________________

   ____

   ____

   ____

B. Your Perception of the Role of Your Doctor and Other Health Caregivers

1. Do you like your doctors?______________________________

   ____

2. Do you trust your doctors?______________________________

   ____

   ____

3. Do you think your doctors should make the final decision concerning any treatment you might need? ______________________________

   ____

   ____

4. How do you relate to your caregivers, including nurses, therapists, chaplains, social workers, etc.?

5. Do you wish to make any general comments about your doctor and other health caregivers?

C. Your Thoughts About Independence and Control

1. How important is independence and self-sufficiency in your life?

2. If you were to experience decreased physical and mental abilities, how would that affect your attitude toward independence and self-sufficiency?

3. Do you wish to make any general comments about the value of independence and control in your life?

D. Your Personal Relationships

1. Do you expect that your friends, family and/or others will support your decisions regarding medical treatment you may need now or in the future?

2. Have you made any arrangements for your family or friends to make medical treatment decisions on your behalf? If so, who has agreed to make decisions for you and in what circumstances?

3. What, if any, unfinished business from the past are you concerned about (e.g., personal and family relationships, business and legal matters)?

4. What role do your friends and family play in your life?

5. Do you wish to make any general comments about the personal relationships in your life?

E. Your Overall Attitude Toward Life

1. What activities do you enjoy (e.g., hobbies, watching TV, etc.)?

2. Are you happy to be alive?

3. Do you feel that life is worth living?

4. How satisfied are you with what you have achieved in your life?

5. What makes you laugh/cry?

6. What do you fear most? What frightens or upsets you?

7. What goals do you have for the future?

8. Do you wish to make any general comments about your attitude toward life?

F. Your Attitude Toward Illness, Dying, and Death

1. What will be important to you when you are dying (e.g., physical comfort, no pain, family members present, etc.)?

2. Where would you prefer to die?

3. What is your attitude toward death?

4. How do you feel about the use of life-sustaining measures in the face of:

Terminal illness:

Permanent coma:

Irreversible chronic illness (e.g., Alzheimer's disease)?

5. Do you wish to make any general comments about your attitude toward illness, dying, and death?

G. Your Religious Background and Beliefs

1. What is your religious background?

2. How do your religious beliefs affect your attitude toward serious or terminal illness?

3. Does your attitude toward death find support in your religion?

4. How does your faith community, church or synagogue view the role of prayer or religious sacraments in an illness?

5. Do you wish to make any general comments about your religious background and beliefs?

H. Your Living Environment

1. What has been your living situation over the last 10 years (e.g., lived alone, lived with others, etc.)

2. How difficult is it for you to maintain the kind of environment for yourself that you find comfortable? Does any illness or medical problem you have now mean that it will be harder in the future?

3. Do you wish to make any general comments about your living environment?

I. Your Attitude Concerning Finances

1. How much do you worry about having enough money to provide for your care?
2. Would you prefer to spend less money on your care so that more money can be saved for the benefit of your relatives and/or friends?
3. Do you wish to make any general comments concerning your finances and the cost of health care?

J. Your Wishes Concerning Your Funeral

1. What are your wishes concerning your funeral and burial or cremation?
2. Have you made your funeral arrangements? If so, with whom?
3. Do you wish to make any general comments about how you would like your funeral and burial or cremation to be arranged or conducted?

Optional Questions

1. How would you like your obituary (announcement of your death) to read?
2. Write yourself a brief eulogy (a statement about yourself to be read at your funeral).

Suggestions for Use

After you have completed this form, you may wish to provide copies to your doctors and other health caregivers, your family, your friends, and your attorney. If you have a Living Will or Durable Power of Attorney for Health Care Decisions, you may wish to attach a copy of this form to those documents.

CHAPTER 4

Gerontologic Assessment

LEARNING OBJECTIVES

On completion of this chapter, the reader will be able to:

1. Explain the interrelationship between the physical and psychosocial aspects of aging as it affects the assessment process.
2. Describe how the nature of disease, homeostatic mechanisms, and diversity in the older adult affect the assessment process.
3. Compare and contrast the clinical presentation of delirium and dementia.
4. Describe the assessment modifications that may be necessary when conducting an assessment on an older adult.
5. Describe strategies and techniques to assure collection of a relevant and comprehensive health history on an older adult.
6. Identify the basic components of a health history.
7. List the principles to observe when conducting a physical examination of an older adult.
8. Explain the rationale for conducting an assessment of functional status in an older adult.
9. Describe the elements of a functional assessment.
10. Describe the basic components of a mental status assessment.
11. Discuss the rationale for conducting effective assessment in the older adult.
12. Explain the rationale for assessing social function in the older adult.
13. Conduct a comprehensive health assessment on an older adult client.

The nursing process is a problem-solving process that provides the organizational framework for the provision of nursing care. Assessment, the crucial foundation on which the remaining steps of the process are built, includes the collection and analysis of data and results in a nursing diagnosis. A nursing-focused assessment is crucial in determining nursing diagnoses that are amenable to nursing intervention. Unless the approach to assessment maintains a nursing focus, the sequential steps of the nursing process, diagnosis, planning, implementation, and evaluation cannot be carried out.

A nursing focus evolves from an awareness and understanding of the purpose of nursing. This purpose, as defined in the American Nurses' Association's (ANA) publication, *Nursing: A Social Policy Statement,* ". . . is the diagnosis and treatment of human responses to actual or potential health problems"(ANA, 1980). This definition directs the nurse to gather data that assists in determining the client's response to actual or potential health problems. A comprehensive, nursing-focused assessment should yield responses that reflect the degree to which the client is meeting physical and psychosocial needs. An analysis of client responses that reveals an inability to satisfactorily meet these needs is cause for nursing intervention.

Nursing-focused assessment of older people occurs in the traditional settings of the hospital, home, or long-term care facility, as well as in nontraditional settings such as senior centers, congregate living units, or independent or group nursing practices. The setting dictates the way data collection and analysis occur to serve clients best. Although the approach to nursing-focused assessment of older adult clients may vary with regard to the setting, the purpose remains to determine the older person's response to actual or potential health problems. Specifically, the purpose of older adult assessment is to identify client strengths and limitations so that effective and appropriate interventions can be delivered to promote optimum functioning and to prevent disability and dependence.

Gerontologic nurses recognize that assessing older adult clients involves the application of a broad range of skills and abilities, as well as consideration of many complex and varied issues. Nursing-focused assessment based on a sound, gerontologic knowledge base, coupled with repeated practice to acquire the *art* of assessment, is essential for the nurse to recognize client responses that reflect unmet needs. Many frameworks and tools are available to guide the nurse in assessing the older adult. Regardless of the framework or tool used, the nurse should collect the data while observing the following key principles: (1) using an individual, person-centered approach; (2) viewing the client as a participant in health monitoring and treatment; and (3) emphasizing the client's functional ability.

SPECIAL CONSIDERATIONS AFFECTING ASSESSMENT

Nursing assessment of an older adult is a complex and challenging process that must take into account the following points to ensure an age-specific approach.

Interrelationship Between Physical and Psychosocial Aspects of Aging

The health of people of all ages is subject to the influence of any number and kind of physical and psychosocial factors within the environment. The balance that is achieved within that environment of many factors greatly influences a person's health status. For the older person, factors such as the reduced ability to respond to stress, the increased frequency and multiplicity of loss, and the physical changes associated with normal aging can combine to place the older adult at high risk for loss of functional ability. Consider the following case, which illustrates how the interaction of select physical and psychosocial factors can seriously compromise function.

Mrs. L., age 81, arrived in the emergency room after being found in her home by a neighbor. The neighbor had become concerned because he noticed Mrs. L. had not picked up her newspapers for the past 3 days. She was found in her bed, weak and lethargic. She stated that she had the flu for the past week, so she was unable to eat or drink much because of the associated nausea and vomiting. Except for her

TABLE 4-1

Effect of Selected Variables on Functional Status

Variable	Effect
Visual and auditory loss	Apathy Confusion, disorientation Dependency, loss of control
Multiple strange and unfamiliar environments	Confusion Dependency, loss of control Sleep disturbance Relocation stress
Acute medical illness	Mobility impairment Dependency, loss of control Sleep disturbance
Altered pharmacokinetics and pharmacodynamics	Persistent confusion Drug toxicity Potential for further mobility impairment, loss of function, and altered patterns of bowel and bladder elimination Loss of appetite, in turn affecting wound healing, bowel function, and energy level; dehydration Sleep disturbance (oversedation)

From Lueckenotte AG: *Pocket guide to gerontologic assessment,* ed 2, St. Louis, 1994, Mosby.

mild hypertension, which is medically managed with an antihypertensive agent, she has enjoyed relatively good health prior to this acute illness. She is admitted to the hospital with pneumonia.

Because of the emergent nature of the admission, Mrs. L. did not have any personal belongings with her, including her hearing aid, glasses, and dentures. She develops congestive heart failure after treatment of her dehydration with intravenous (IV) fluids. She then becomes confused and agitated, and begins receiving haloperidol (Haldol) as needed. Her impaired mobility resulting from the chemical restraint has caused her to become incontinent of urine and stool, and she has developed a stage 2 pressure ulcer. She needs to be fed because of her confusion and eats very little. She is sleeping at intervals throughout the day and night, and when she is awake, she is usually crying.

Table 4-1 depicts the many serious consequences of the interacting physical and psychosocial factors in this case. Undue emphasis should not be placed on individual decrements. In fact, it is imperative that the gerontologic nurse search for the client's strengths and abilities, and build the plan of care on these. However, in a situation such as this, the nurse should be aware of the potential for the consequences illustrated here. A single problem is not likely, since multiple conditions are often superimposed on one another. In addition, the cause of one problem is often best understood in view of the accompanying problems. Careful consideration, then, of the interrelationships between physical and psychosocial factors in every client situation is essential.

Effects of Disease and Disability on Functional Status

Aging does not necessarily result in disease and disability. Most older people remain functionally independent despite the increasing prevalence of chronic disease with advancing age. However, what cannot be ignored is that chronic disease increases the older adult's vulnerability to functional decline. Comprehensive assessment of physical and psychosocial function is important because it can provide valuable clues to a disease's effect on functional status. Also, the self-report of vague signs and symptoms such as lethargy, incontinence, decreased appetite, and weight loss can be indicators of functional impairment. Ignoring the older adult's vague symptomatology exposes the client to an increased risk of physical frailty. Physical frailty, or the impairments in the physical abilities that are needed to live independently, is a major contributor to the need for long-term care. Therefore it is essential to comprehensively investigate the report of nonspecific signs and symptoms to determine whether there are any possible underlying conditions that may contribute to the older person's frailty (National Institutes of Health, 1991).

Declining organ and system function, and diminishing physiologic reserve with advancing age are well-documented in the literature. Such normal changes of aging may make the body more susceptible to disease and disability, the risk of which increases exponentially with advancing age. It can be difficult for the nurse to differentiate normal age-related findings from indicators of disease or disability. In fact, it is not uncommon for nurses and older adults alike to mistakenly attribute vague signs and symptoms to normal aging changes or just "growing old." However, it is essential for the nurse to determine what is "normal" versus what may be an indicator of disease or disability so that treatable conditions are not disregarded.

Decreased Efficiency of Homeostatic Mechanisms

Declining physiologic function and increased prevalence of disease, particularly in the oldest old (age 85 and older), are in part a result of a reduction in the body's ability to respond to stress through all of its homeostatic mechanisms. The older person's adaptive reserves are reduced and their homeostatic mechanisms weakened; these factors result in a decreased ability to respond to physical or emotional stress. The return to prestress levels of functioning is also slowed with age. The older adult client may be less able than a younger person to cope with infection, blood loss, a high-tech environment, or loss of a significant person (see Chapters 17 and 31). The nurse should therefore assess older adults for the presence of stressors, and their physical and emotional manifestations.

Lack of Standards for Health and Illness Norms

Determining an older adult's physical and psychosocial health status is not easy, because norms for health and illness are always being redefined. Established standards for what is normal versus abnormal are changing as more scientific studies are conducted and the knowledge base is expanded.

One area where recent study is changing how health care providers interpret normal versus abnormal is with laboratory values. Relying on established norms for laboratory values when analyzing an older adult's assessment data could lead to incorrect conclusions. A fasting blood glucose of 70 mg/100 ml may be within the normal range for a young adult, but an older person with that same level may experience symptoms of hypoglycemia. Polypharmacy and the multiplicity of illness and disease are only two variables that may affect laboratory data interpretation in the older adult (see Chapters 19 and 20).

In addition, there are no definitive aging norms for many pathologic conditions. For example, controversy has existed over what constitutes "normal" blood pressure for older people. Is a high systolic pressure simply a function of age, or does it require treatment? Recent studies have shown that cardiovascular morbidity and mortality in older people have been reduced with therapy. As more studies are conducted in this area and others, norms will continue to be redefined.

Landmarks for human growth and development are well established for infancy through middlescence, whereas few norms are defined for older adulthood. Developmental norms that have been described for later life categorize all older people in the "over-65" group. However, it could easily be argued from a developmental perspective that as great a difference exists among adults ages 65, 75, 85, and 95 as it does among children ages 2, 3, 4, and 5. In fact, given the demographic facts and predictions, there exists a very pressing need to know the developmental characteristics of older people for each decade of life.

To compensate for the lack of definitive standards, the nurse should first assume heterogeneity rather than homogeneity when caring for older people. It is crucial to respect the uniqueness of each person's life experiences and to preserve the individuality created by those experiences. The older person's experiences represent a rich and vast background that the nurse can use to develop an individualized plan of care. Secondly, the nurse can compare the older person's own previous patterns of physical and psychosocial health and function with the current status, using the individual as the standard (Matteson, McConnell, 1988). Finally, the nurse must have a complete and current knowledge base and skills in gerontologic nursing to apply to each individual older adult client situation.

Altered Presentation of and Response to Specific Diseases

With advanced age, the body does not respond as vigorously to illness or disease because of diminished physiologic reserve. It is important to note that the diminished reserve poses no particular problems for most older people as they carry out their daily routines. However, in times of physical and emotional stress, it causes older people to not always exhibit the expected, or "classic" signs and symptoms. The characteristic presentation of illness in older adults is more commonly one of blunted or atypical signs and symptoms.

The atypical presentation of illness can be displayed in various ways. For example, the signs and symptoms may be modified in some way, as in the case of pneumonia, when an older adult may exhibit a dry cough instead of the classic productive cough. Also, the presenting signs and symptoms may be totally unrelated to the actual problem, such as the confusion that may accompany a urinary tract infection. Finally, the expected signs and symptoms may not be present at all, as in the case of a myocardial infarction that includes no chest pain. All of these atypical presentations challenge the nurse to conduct careful and thorough assessments and analyses of symptoms to ensure appropriate treatment. Again, a simple and safe strategy is to compare the presenting signs

TABLE 4-2

How Illness Changes With Age

Problem	Classic presentation in younger client	Presentation in older adult
Urinary tract infection	Dysuria, frequency, urgency, nocturia	Dysuria often *absent,* frequency, urgency, nocturia sometimes present. Incontinence, confusion, anorexia are other signs.
Myocardial infarction	Severe substernal chest pain, diaphoresis, nausea, shortness of breath	Sometimes no chest pain, or atypical pain location such as in jaw, neck, shoulder. Shortness of breath may be present. Other signs are tachypnea, arrhythmia, hypotension, restlessness, syncope.
Pneumonia (bacterial)	Cough productive of purulent sputum, chills and fever, pleuritic chest pain, elevated white blood count	Cough may be productive, dry, or absent; chills and fever and/or elevated white count also may be absent. Tachypnea, slight cyanosis, confusion, anorexia, nausea and vomiting, tachycardia may be present.
Congestive heart failure	Increased dyspnea (orthopnea, paroxysmal nocturnal dyspnea), fatigue, weight gain, pedal edema, night cough and nocturia, bibasilar rales	All of the manifestations of young adult and/or anorexia, restlessness, confusion, cyanosis, falls.
Hyperthyroidism	Heat intolerance, fast pace, exophthalmos, increased pulse, hyperreflexia, tremor	Slowing down (apathetic hyperthyroidism), lethargy, weakness, depression, atrial fibrillation, and congestive heart failure.
Depression	Sad mood and thoughts, withdrawal, crying, weight loss, constipation, insomnia	Any of classic symptoms, plus memory and concentration problems, weight gain, increased sleep.

From Henderson ML: Altered presentations, *AJN* 15:1104-1106, 1986.

BOX 4-1

Physiologic, Psychologic, and Environmental Causes of Acute Confusional States in the Hospitalized Older Adult

Physiologic

A. Primary cerebral disease

1. Nonstructural factors
   a. Vascular insufficiency—transient ischemic attacks, cerebral vascular accidents, thrombosis
   b. Central nervous system infection—acute and chronic meningitis, neurosyphillis, brain abscess
2. Structural factors
   a. Trauma—subdural hematoma, concussion, contusion, intracranial hemorrhage
   b. Tumors—primary and metastatic
   c. Normal pressure hydrocephalus

B. Extracranial disease

1. Cardiovascular abnormalities
   a. Decreased cardiac output state—myocardial infarction, arrhythmias, congestive heart failure, cardiogenic shock
   b. Alterations in peripheral vascular resistance—increased and decreased states
   c. Vascular occlusion—disseminated intravascular coagulopathy, emboli
2. Pulmonary abnormalities
   a. Inadequate gas exchange states—pulmonary disease, alveolar hypoventilation
   b. Infection—pneumonias
3. Systemic infective processes—acute and chronic
   a. Viral
   b. Bacterial—endocarditis, pyelonephritis, cystitis, mycotic
4. Metabolic disturbances
   a. Electrolyte abnormalities—hypercalcemia, hypo- and hypernatremia, hypo- and hyperkalemia, hypo- and hyperchloremia, hyperphosphatemia
   b. Acidosis/alkalosis
   c. Hypo- and hyperglycemia
   d. Acute and chronic renal failure
   e. Volume depletion—hemorrhage, inadequate fluid intake, diuretics
   f. Hepatic failure
   g. Porphyria
5. Drug intoxications—therapeutic and substance abuse
   a. Misuse of prescribed medications
   b. Side effects of therapeutic medications
   c. Drug-drug interactions
   d. Improper use of over-the-counter medications
   e. Ingestion of heavy metals and industrial poisons
6. Endocrine disturbance
   a. Hypo-and hyperthyroidism
   b. Diabete mellitus
   c. Hypopituitarism
   d. Hypo- and hyperparathyroidism
7. Nutritional deficiencies
   a. B vitamins
   b. Vitamin C
   c. Protein
8. Physiologic stress—pain, surgery
9. Alterations in temperature regulation—hypo- and hyperthermia
10. Unknown physiologic abnormality—sometimes defined as pseudodelirium

Psychologic

1. Severe emotional stress—postoperative states, relocation, hospitalization
2. Depression
3. Anxiety
4. Pain—acute and chronic
5. Fatigue
6. Grief
7. Sensory/perceptual deficits—noise, alteration in functioning of senses
8. Mania
9. Paranoia
10. Situational disturbances

Environmental

1. Unfamiliar environment creating a lack of meaning in the environment
2. Sensory deprivation/environmental monotony creating a lack of meaning in the environment
3. Sensory overload
4. Immobilization—therapeutic, physical, pharmacologic
5. Sleep deprivation
6. Lack of temporospatial reference points

Modified from Foreman MD: Acute confusional states in hospitalized elderly: a research dilemma, *Nurs Res* 35:34-37, 1986.

and symptoms with the older adult's normal baseline (Table 4-2).

Cognitive Impairment

As can be seen from Table 4-2, p. 70, confusion is one of the most common, atypical presentations of illness in the older adult, representing a wide variety of potential problems. Confusion, mental status changes, cognitive changes, and delirium are some of the terms used to describe one of the most common manifestations of illness in old age. Foreman (1986) advocates use of the term *acute confusional state* (ACS) to describe "... an organic brain syndrome characterized by transient, global cognitive impairment of abrupt onset and relatively brief duration, accompanied by diurnal fluctuation of simultaneous disturbances of the sleep-wake cycle, psychomotor behavior, attention, and affect." Unfortunately, the ageist views of many health care providers cause them to believe that an ACS is a normal, expected outcome of aging, thus robbing the older adult of a complete and thorough workup of this syndrome. The nurse as the advocate for the older person may need to remind other team members that a sudden change in cognitive function is often the result of illness, *not* aging. Knowing the older adult's baseline mental status is key to avoid overlooking a serious illness manifesting itself as an ACS. Box 4-1 outlines the multivariate causes associated with an ACS that the nurse must consider during assessment.

One of the more challenging aspects of older adult assessment is distinguishing a reversible ACS from irreversible cognitive changes such as those seen in dementia and other related disorders. In contrast to the characteristics of an ACS noted previously, dementia is a global, sustained deterioration of cognitive function in an alert client. Other diagnostic features of dementia include impairment in abstract thinking, impaired judgment, aphasia, apraxia, agnosia, "constructional difficulty" (e.g., inability to copy three-dimensional figures, to assemble blocks, or to arrange sticks in specific designs), and personality change (DSM-IV, 1987). Primary dementias include senile dementia of the Alzheimer's type (SDAT), Pick's disease, Creutzfeldt-Jakob's disease, and multiinfarct dementia (MID). Secondary dementias that have the same presenting symptoms but are often reversible with

TABLE 4-3

Differentiating Dementia and ACS

Feature	ACS	Dementia
Essential feature	A clouded state of consciousness	Not based on disordered consciousness; based on loss of intellectual functions of sufficient severity to interfere with social and occupational functioning
Associated features	Variable affective changes with fear, apprehension, and bewilderment predominating	Affect tends to be superficial, inappropriate, and labile, and includes apathy, depression, and euphoria with some degree of personality change
	Symptoms of autonomic hyperarousal	Attempts to conceal deficits in intellect
	Some degree of disorientation	
Onset	Acute/subacute, depends on cause	Chronic, generally insidious, depends on cause
Course	Short, diurnal fluctuations in symptoms, worse at night, dark, and on awakening	Long, no diurnal effects, symptoms progressive yet relatively stable over time
Duration	Hours to less than 1 month	Months to years
Awareness	Fluctuates, generally impaired	Generally normal
Alertness	Fluctuates, reduced or increased	Generally normal
Orientation	Fluctuates in severity, generally impaired	May be impaired
Memory	Recent and immediate impaired, unable to register new information or recall recent events	Recent and remote impaired, loss of recent first sign, some loss of common knowledge
Thinking	Disorganized, distorted, fragmented, slow, or accelerated	Difficulty with abstraction
Perception	Distorted, based on state of arousal or mood, illusions, delusions, or hallucinations	Misperceptions often absent
Sleep-wake cycle	Disturbed, cycle reversed	Fragmented
EEG	Predominance of slow or fast cycles related to state of arousal	Normal or slow

From Foreman MD: Acute confusional states in hospitalized elderly: a research dilemma, *Nurs Res* 35:34-37, 1987.

early diagnosis include normal pressure hydrocephalus (NPH), intracranial masses or lesions, pseudodementia, and Parkinson's dementia. Table 4-3 depicts the distinguishing features of an ACS and dementia. See Chapter 27 for a complete description of these primary and secondary dementing diseases.

Assessment can be complex because of the multiple associated characteristics of an ACS and dementia. In fact, it is not uncommon for an ACS to be superimposed on dementia. In this case, the symptoms of a new illness may be accentuated or may be masked, thus confounding assessment (Hall, 1991). Therefore the nurse must have a clear understanding of the differences between an ACS and dementia, and must recognize that only very subtle evidence may be present to indicate the existence of a problem. Also, it may not be possible or desirable to complete the total assessment during the first encounter with the client. In conducting the initial review of the clinical course of the presenting symptoms, the nurse should remember that families and friends of the client can be valuable sources of data regarding the onset, duration, and associated symptoms. Specific components of a nursing assessment related to cognitive changes are discussed in detail on p. 93).

TAILORING THE NURSING ASSESSMENT TO THE OLDER PERSON

The health assessment may be collected in a variety of physical settings, including hospital, home, office, day care center, and long-term facility. Any of these settings can be adapted to be conducive to the free exchange of information between the nurse and older adult. The overall atmosphere established by the nurse should be one that conveys trust, caring, and confidentiality. The following general suggestions related to preparation of the environment and consideration of individual client need fosters the collection of meaningful data (see Cultural Awareness box below).

Environmental modifications made during the assessment should take into account sensory and musculoskeletal changes. The following points should be considered in preparation of the environment:

- Provide adequate space, particularly if the client uses a mobility aid.
- Minimize noise and distraction such as that generated from television, radio, intercom, or other nearby activity.
- Set a comfortable, sufficiently warm temperature with no drafts.
- Use diffuse lighting with increased illumination; avoid directional or localized light.
- Avoid glossy or highly polished surfaces, including floors, walls, ceilings, or furnishings.
- Place in comfortable seating position that facilitates information exchange.
- Maintain proximity to a bathroom.
- Keep water or other preferred fluids available.
- Provide a place to hang or store garments and belongings.
- Maintain absolute privacy.
- Plan the assessment, taking into account the older adult's energy level, pace, and adaptability. More than one session may be necessary to complete the assessment.
- Be patient, relaxed, and unhurried.
- Allow the client plenty of time to respond to questions and directions.
- Maximize the use of silence to allow the client time to collect thoughts before responding.
- Be alert to signs of increasing fatigue such as sighing, grimacing, irritability, leaning against objects for support, dropping of head and shoulders, and progressive slowing.
- Conduct assessment during client's peak energy time.

Regardless of the degree of decrement and decline an older adult client may exhibit, there are assets and capabilities that allow the client to function within the limitations imposed by that decline. During the assessment, the nurse must provide an environment that gives the older adult the opportunity to demonstrate those abilities. Failure to do so could result in incorrect conclusions about the client's functional ability, which may lead to inappropriate care and treatment:

CULTURAL AWARENESS

Cultural Assessment

Cultural or **culturologic** nursing assessment refers to a systematic appraisal or examination of older adult individuals, groups, and communities in relation to their cultural beliefs, values, and practices to determine explicit nursing needs and interventions within the cultural context of the people being evaluated. Because they deal with cultural values, belief systems, and lifeways, cultural assessments tend to be broad and comprehensive, though it is possible to focus on a smaller segment. Cultural assessment consists of both *process* and *content*. The process aspect concerns the nurse's approach to the client, consideration of verbal and nonverbal communication, and the sequence or order in which data are gathered. The content of the cultural assessment consists of the actual data categories in which information about clients is gathered.

- Assess more than once and at different times of day.
- Measure performance under the most favorable of conditions.
- Take advantage of natural opportunities that would elicit assets and capabilities; collect data during bathing, grooming, and mealtime.
- Ensure that assistive sensory devices (glasses, hearing aid) and mobility devices (walker, cane, prosthesis) are in place and functioning correctly.
- Interview family, friends, and significant others who are involved in the client's care to validate assessment data.
- Use body language, touch, eye contact, and speech to promote the client's maximum degree of participation.
- Be aware of the client's emotional state and concerns; fear, anxiety, and boredom can lead to inaccurate assessment conclusions regarding functional ability.

THE HEALTH HISTORY

The nursing health history and interview, as the first phase of a comprehensive health assessment, provides a subjective account of the older adult's current and past health status. The interview forms the basis of a therapeutic nurse-client relationship, in which the client's well-being is the mutual concern. The establishment of this relationship with the older adult is essential to gathering useful, significant data. The data obtained from the health history alert the nurse to focus on key areas of the physical examination that require further investigation. By talking with the nurse about health concerns, the older adult's awareness of health is increased, and topics for health teaching can be identified. Finally, the process of recounting a client's history in a purposeful, systematic way can have the therapeutic effect of serving as a life review.

Although a number of formats exist for the nursing health history, all have similar, basic components (Box 4-2). In addition, the nursing health history for the older adult should include assessment of functional, cognitive, affective, and social well-being. Specific tools for the collection of this data are addressed later in this chapter.

The physical, psychosocial, cultural, and functional aspects of the older adult client, coupled with a life history filled with people, places, and events, demand adaptations in interviewing styles and techniques. Making adaptations that reflect a genuine sensitivity toward the older adult and a sound, theoretic knowledge base of aging enhances the interview process.

The Interviewer

The ability of the interviewer to elicit meaningful data from the client depends on the interviewer's attitudes and stereotypes about aging and older people. The nurse must be aware of these factors because they affect nurse-client communication during the assessment (see Cultural Awareness boxes below and on p. 79, at left).

Attitude as a feeling, value, or belief about something determines behavior. If the nurse has an attitude that characterizes older people as less healthy and alert and more dependent, then the interview structure reflects this attitude. For example, if the nurse believes that dependence in self-care normally accompanies advanced age, the client will not be questioned about strengths and abilities. The resulting inaccurate functional assessment does little to promote client independence. Myths and stereotypes about older adults also can affect the nurse's questioning. For example, believing that older people do not participate in sexual relationships can result in the nurse's failure to interview the client about sexual health matters. The nurse's own anxiety and fear of personal aging, as well as a lack of knowledge regarding older people, contribute to commonly held negative attitudes, myths, and stereotypes about older people. Gerontologic nurses have a responsibility to themselves and to their older adult clients to improve their understanding of the aging process and aging people.

To ensure a successful interview, the nurse should explain to the client the reason for the interview and should give a brief overview of the format to be followed. This alleviates anxiety and uncertainty, and the client can then focus on telling the story. Another strategy that can be employed in some settings is to give the client selected portions of the interview form to com-

CULTURAL AWARENESS

Cultural Considerations during the Interview: Introductions and Names

Because initial impressions are so important in all human relationships, cross-cultural considerations concerning introductions warrant a few brief remarks. To ensure that a mutually respectful relationship is established, nurses should introduce themselves and should indicate to the client how they prefer to be called (i.e., by first name, last name, or title). They should elicit the same information from the client, because this enables nurses to address the person in a manner that is culturally appropriate and could actually spare considerable embarrassment. For example, it is the custom among some Asian and European cultures to write the last name first so that the nurse is sure to have the client's name correct. Avoid the use of nicknames (e.g., Grandma, Pop, Dear, and others) that may be offensive to the older adult client. Regardless of the nurse's good intentions, the older adult may construe the use of such terms as overly familiar, ill-mannered, or inappropriate.

BOX 4-2

Sample Older Adult Health History Format

1. Client Profile/Biographic Data
Name ________ Address ________
Telephone ______ Date and place of birth/age ______
Sex ___ Race _____ Religion _____ Marital status ____
Education _______ Nearest contact person _________
Address/Telephone ______________________

2. Family Profile
Spouse(s) ____________ Children ____________
  Living ____________ Living ____________
  Health status _________ Names and addresses
  Age _______ ______________
  Occupation _________ ______________
  ____
  Deceased ___________ Deceased ___________
    Year of death _______ Year of death _______
    Cause of death _____ Cause of death ______

3. Occupational Profile
Current work status ______________________
Previous occupations ______________________
Source(s) of income and adequacy for needs _________
____
____
____
____

4. Living Environment Profile
Type of dwelling ______________________
Number of rooms _______ Number of levels _______
Number of people living in dwelling ______________
Degree of privacy ________ Nearest neighbor _______
Address/telephone ______________________
____

5. Recreation/Leisure Profile
Hobbies/interests ______________________
Organizational memberships ______________________
Vacations/travel ______________________

6. Resources/Support Systems Used
Physician(s) ______________________
____
Hospital ______________________
Clinic ______________________
Home health agency ______________________
Meals on Wheels ______________________
Adult day care ______________________
Other ______________________
____

7. Description of Typical Day (include usual bedtime ritual)
____
____
____

8. Present Health Status
General health status during past year ____________
____
____
General health status during past 5 years __________
____

____
Chief complaint ______________________
____
Knowledge/understanding and management of health problems (e.g., special diet, dressing changes) ________
____
____
Overall degree of function relative to health problems and medical diagnoses ______________________
____

Medications
Name(s) ______________________
____
____
Dosage ______________________
____
How/when taken ______________________
____
Prescribing physician ______________________
Date of prescription ______________________
Problems with adherence (complicated regimen with large number and variety of drugs, visual deficits, unpleasant side effects, perception of effectiveness, difficulty obtaining, affordability)

Immunization status (note date of most recent immunization)
Tetanus, diphtheria ____________
PPD ___________
Influenza ___________
Pneumovax _____________

Allergies (note specific agent and reaction)
Drugs ______________________
Foods ______________________
Contact substances ______________________
Environmental factors ______________________

Nutrition
24-hour diet recall (include fluid intake)
Special diet, food restrictions, or preferences _________
____
____
History of weight gain/loss ______________________
Food consumption patterns (e.g., frequency, alone or with others) ______________________
____
____
Problems affecting food intake (e.g., inadequate income, lack of transportation, chewing/swallowing problems, emotional stress) ______________________
____
Habits ______________________
____
____

From Lueckenotte, AG: *Pocket Guide to gerontologic assessment,* ed 2, St. Louis, 1994, Mosby.

Continued.

BOX 4-2

Sample Older Adult Health History Format—cont'd

9. Past Health Status

Childhood illnesses ______________________________

Serious or chronic illnesses ______________________________

Trauma ______________________________

Hospitalizations (note reason, date, place, duration, physician[s]) ______________________________

Operations (note type, date, place, reason, physician[s]) ______________________________

Obstetric history ______________________________

10. Family History

Draw pedigree (identify grandparents, parents, aunts, uncles, siblings, spouse[s], children)

Survey the following: cancer, diabetes mellitus, heart disease, hypertension, seizure disorder, renal disease, arthritis, alcoholism, mental health problems, anemia

11. Review of Systems

Check yes or no for each symptom and include full symptom analysis on positive responses at end of each system.

General	Yes	No
Fatigue		
Weight change in past year		
Appetite change		
Fever		
Night sweats		
Sleeping difficulty		
Frequent colds, infections		

Self-rating of overall health status ______________________________

Ability to carry out Activities of Daily Living (ADL) ______________________________

Integument	Yes	No
Lesions/wounds		
Pruritus		
Pigmentation changes		
Texture changes		
Nevi changes		
Frequent bruising		
Hair changes		
Nail changes		
Corns, bunions, calluses		

Integument, cont'd	Yes	No
Chronic sun exposure		

Healing pattern of lesions, bruises ______________________________

Hematopoietic	Yes	No
Abnormal bleeding/bruising		
Lymph node swelling		
Anemia		

Blood transfusion history ______________________________

Head	Yes	No
Headache		
Past significant trauma		
Dizziness		
Scalp itching		

Eyes	Yes	No
Vision changes		
Glasses/contact lenses		
Pain		
Excessive tearing		
Pruritus		
Swelling around eyes		
Floaters		
Diplopia		
Blurring		
Photophobia		
Scotomata		
History of infections		

Date of most recent vision examination ______________________________

Date of most recent glaucoma check ______________________________

Impact on ADL performance ______________________________

Ears	Yes	No
Hearing changes		
Discharge		
Tinnitus		
Vertigo		
Hearing sensitivity		
Prosthetic device(s)		
History of infection		

Date of most recent auditory examination ______________________________

Usual ear care habits ______________________________

Impact on ADL performance ______________________________

Nose and sinuses	Yes	No
Rhinorrhea		
Discharge		

BOX 4-2

Sample Older Adult Health History Format—cont'd

Nose and sinuses, cont'd	Yes	No
Epistaxis		
Obstruction		
Snoring		
Pain over sinuses		
Postnasal drip		
Allergies		
History of infections		

Self-rating of olfactory ability ____________

____

Mouth and throat	Yes	No
Sore throat		
Lesions/ulcers		
Hoarseness		
Voice changes		
Difficulty swallowing		
Bleeding gums		
Caries		
Altered taste		
Difficulty chewing		
Prosthetic device(s)		
History of infections		

Date of most recent dental examination ____________

Brushing pattern ____________

____

Flossing pattern ____________

____

Denture cleaning routine and problems ____________

____

____

Neck	Yes	No
Stiffness		
Pain/tenderness		
Lumps/masses		
Limited movement		

Breasts	Yes	No
Lumps/masses		
Pain/tenderness		
Swelling		
Nipple discharge		
Nipple changes		

Breast self-examination pattern ____________

____

Date and results of most recent mammogram ____________

____

Respiratory	Yes	No
Cough		
Shortness of breath		
Hemoptysis		
Sputum		

Respiratory	Yes	No
Wheezing		
Asthma/respiratory allergy		

Date and results of most recent chest x-ray examination

____

Cardiovascular	Yes	No
Chest pain/discomfort		
Palpitations		
Shortness of breath		
Dyspnea on exertion		
Paroxysmal nocturnal dyspnea		
Orthopnea		
Murmur		
Edema		
Varicosities		
Claudication		
Paresthesias		
Leg color changes		

Gastrointestinal	Yes	No
Dysphagia		
Indigestion		
Heartburn		
Nausea/vomiting		
Hematemesis		
Appetite changes		
Food intolerances		
Ulcers		
Pain		
Jaundice		
Lumps/masses		
Change in bowel habits		
Diarrhea		
Constipation		
Melena		
Hemorrhoids		
Rectal bleeding		

Usual bowel pattern ____________

____

Urinary	Yes	No
Dysuria		
Frequency		
Dribbling		
Hesitancy		
Urgency		
Hematuria		
Polyuria		
Oliguria		
Nocturia		
Incontinence		
Painful urination		
Stones		

Continued.

BOX 4-2

Sample Older Adult Health History Format—cont'd

Urinary, cont'd	**Yes**	**No**
Infections		

Genitoreproductive—male	**Yes**	**No**
Lesions		
Discharge		
Testicular pain		
Testicular mass(es)		
Prostate problems		
Venereal disease(s)		
Change in sex drive		
Impotence		
Concerns re: sexual activity		

Genitoreproductive—female	**Yes**	**No**
Lesions		
Discharge		
Dyspareunia		
Postcoital bleeding		
Pelvic pain		
Cystocele/rectocele/prolapse		
Venereal disease(s)		
Infections		
Concerns re: sexual activity		

Menstrual history (age of onset, date of last menstrual period) ____________

Menopausal history (age, symptoms, postmenopausal problems) ____________

Date and result of most recent Pap test ____________

Gr _____ P _____ A _____

Musculoskeletal	**Yes**	**No**
Joint pain		
Stiffness		
Joint swelling		
Deformity		
Spasm		
Cramping		
Muscle weakness		
Gait problems		
Back pain		
Prosthesis(es)		

Musculoskeletal, cont'd

Usual exercise pattern ____________

Impact on ADL performance ____________

Central nervous system	**Yes**	**No**
Headache		
Seizures		
Syncope/drop attacks		
Paralysis		
Paresis		
Coordination problems		
Tic/tremor/spasm		
Paresthesias		
Head injury		
Memory problems		

Endocrine system	**Yes**	**No**
Heat intolerance		
Cold intolerance		
Goiter		
Skin pigmentation/texture changes		
Hair changes		
Polyphagia		
Polydipsia		
Polyuria		

Psychosocial	**Yes**	**No**
Anxious		
Depressed		
Insomnia		
Crying spells		
Nervous		
Fearful		
Trouble with decision making		
Difficulty concentrating		

Statement of general feelings of satisfaction/frustration ____________

Usual coping mechanisms ____________

Current stresses ____________

Concerns about death ____________

Impact on ADL performance ____________

plete *before* meeting with the nurse. This allows clients sufficient time to recall their long life histories, thus enabling the collection of important health-related data.

Because of their long lives, older people have lengthy and often complicated histories. A goal-directed interviewing process helps the client share the pertinent information, but the tendency to reminisce may make it difficult for the client to stay focused on the topic. *Guided reminiscence,* however, can elicit valuable data and can promote a supportive therapeutic relationship.

CULTURAL AWARENESS

Cultural Considerations and the Interviewer

Be respectful of, interested in, and understanding of other cultures without being judgmental.

Avoid stereotypes by gender, age, ethnicity, religion, sexual orientation, socioeconomic status, and other social categories.

Know the traditional health-related beliefs and practices prevalent among members of the cultural group with which the client identifies, and encourage the client to discuss his or her cultural beliefs and practices.

Learn about the traditional or folk illnesses and remedies common to the cultural group with which the client identifies.

Try to understand the client's perceptions of appropriate sick role behaviors and expectations of health care providers in times of health and illness.

Study the cultural expressions and manifestations of caring and noncaring behaviors expected by the client.

Avoid stereotypic associations with danger, violence, poverty, crime, limited ability, irresponsibility, low level of education, "noncompliant" behaviors, and other stereotypes that may adversely affect the nurse-client relationship.

Learn to value the richness of cultural diversity as an asset rather than a hindrance to communication and effective intervention.

Using such a technique helps the nurse balance the need to collect the required information with the client's need to relate what is personally important. For example, the client may relate a story about a social outing that seems irrelevant, but it may elicit important information about available resources and support systems. The interplay of the previously noted factors may necessitate more than one encounter with the client to complete the data base. Setting a time limit in advance helps the client focus on the interview and aids with the problem of decreased time perception. Keeping a clock that is easy to read within view of the client may be helpful.

Because of the need to structure the interview, there is a tendency for the nurse to exhibit controlling behavior with the client. To promote client comfort and sharing of data, the nurse and client should mutually establish the organization of the interview. In addition, the nurse should seek the client's permission to take notes during the interview. The client should feel that the nurse is a caring person who treats others with respect. Self-esteem is enhanced if the client feels included in the decision-making process.

At the beginning of the interview, the nurse and client need to determine the most effective and comfortable distance and position for the session. The ability to see and hear within a comfortable territory is critical to the communication process (see Cultural Awareness box above, at right) (Figs. 4-1 to 4-3).

CULTURAL AWARENESS

Space and Distance

Both the older adult's and the nurse's sense of spatial distance are significant in cross-cultural communication with the perception of appropriate distance zones varying widely among cultural groups. Although there are individual variations in spatial requirements, people of the same culture tend to act similarly. For example, white nurses may find themselves backing away from clients of Hispanic, East Indian, or Middle Eastern origins who seemingly invade the nurse's personal space with regularity in an attempt to bring the nurse into the space that is comfortable to them. Although nurses may be uncomfortable with the close physical proximity of these clients, the clients are perplexed by the nurse's distancing behaviors and may perceive the nurse as aloof and unfriendly.

Because individuals are not usually consciously aware of their personal space requirements, they often have difficulty understanding a different cultural pattern. For example, sitting closely may be perceived by one client as an expression of warmth and friendliness but by another as a threatening invasion of personal space. Research reveals that Americans, Canadians, and British require the most personal space, whereas Latin American, Japanese, and Middle Eastern clients need the least.

The appropriate use of touch during the interview can reduce the anxiety associated with the initial encounter. The importance of and comfort with touch is highly individual, but most older people need and appreciate it. Burnside (1988) advises that the nurse does not have to be overly professional and cautious about the use of touch with the older adult client. However, a word of caution about the use of touch with the older adult—do not use touch in a condescending manner (see Cultural Awareness box, p. 81). Touch should always convey respect, caring, and sensitivity. Do not be surprised if the older person reciprocates because of an unmet need for intimacy.

Finally, the nurse does not have to obtain the entire history in the traditional manner of a seated, face-to-face interview. In fact, this technique may be inappropriate with the older adult, depending on the situation. The nurse should not overlook the natural opportunities available in the setting for gathering information. Interviewing the client during the bath, at mealtime, or even while participating in a game, hobby, or other social activity often provides much more meaningful data about a variety of areas.

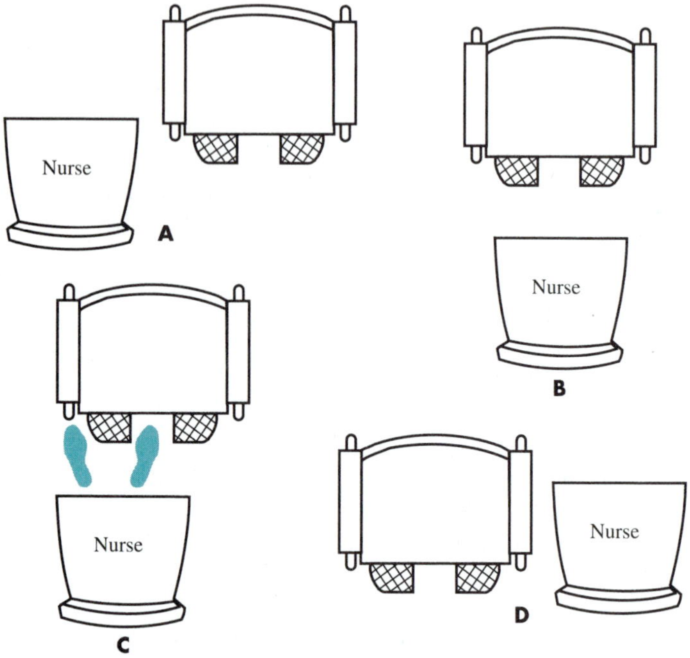

Fig. 4-1 Interview positions with wheelchair-bound client. **A,** One common placement of the interviewer when the client is in a wheelchair. **B,** A position for the interviewer who wants to ensure that eye contact is maintained. **C,** The best position to use with older people in wheelchairs who are visually impaired, hearing-impaired, or sensor-deprived. **D,** The best placement for the nurse when interviewing clients in wheelchairs, or even in conventional chairs, if the client has better hearing in one ear than in the other. (From Burnside IM: *Psychosocial care of the aged,* ed 2, 1980, McGraw-Hill, by permission of Mosby.)

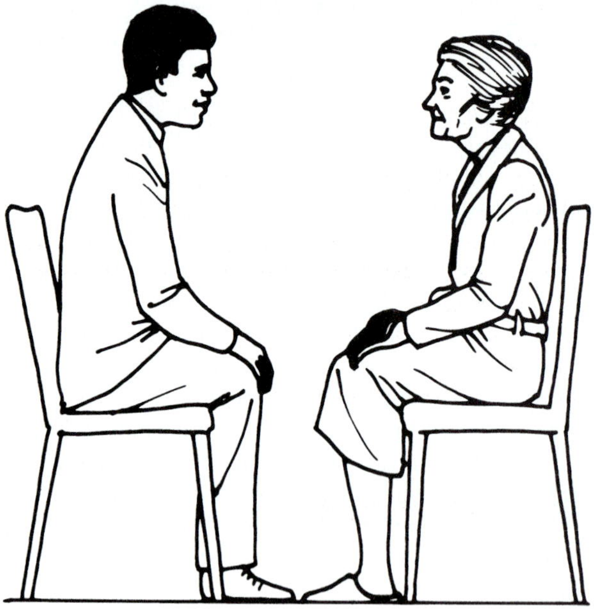

Fig. 4-2 Interview position with seated client. Ordinarily the interviewer should sit very close to and facing an older adult client. Sitting as close as 1 to 2 feet away is acceptable when there is loss of vision or hearing. If the individual seems guarded or frightened, the distance can be greater at the beginning of the interview and then lessened as the interview progresses. The interviewer should be seated, with head as near to client's eye level as possible. (From Burnside IM: *Psychosocial care of the aged,* ed 2, 1980, McGraw-Hill, by permission of Mosby.)

The Client

Several factors influence the ability of the client to participate meaningfully in the interview. The nurse must be aware of these factors because they affect the older adult's ability to communicate all of the information necessary for determining appropriate, comprehensive interventions. Sensory-perceptual deficits, anxiety, reduced energy level, pain, the multiplicity and interrelatedness of health problems, and the tendency to reminisce are the major client factors requiring special consideration while the nurse elicits the health history (see Cultural Awareness boxes, pp. 82-83). Table 4-4, p. 84, contains recommendations for managing these factors.

The Health History Format

The components of the sample format for collecting a health history (see Box 4-2, pp. 75-78) are extensive, and they focus on the special needs and concerns of the older adult client. Although the entire format may seem overwhelming and repetitive in places, remember that for this population there are many physical and psychosocial conditions that may be present, some of which may overlap. Depending on the setting and purpose, not every client needs to be asked every question. The suggested format can be used as a reference from which to proceed in collecting data from each client. The order of the components enables the nurse to begin with the less threatening, "get-acquainted" type of questioning that eases the tension and anxiety and builds trust. The nurse then gradually moves to the more personal and sensitive

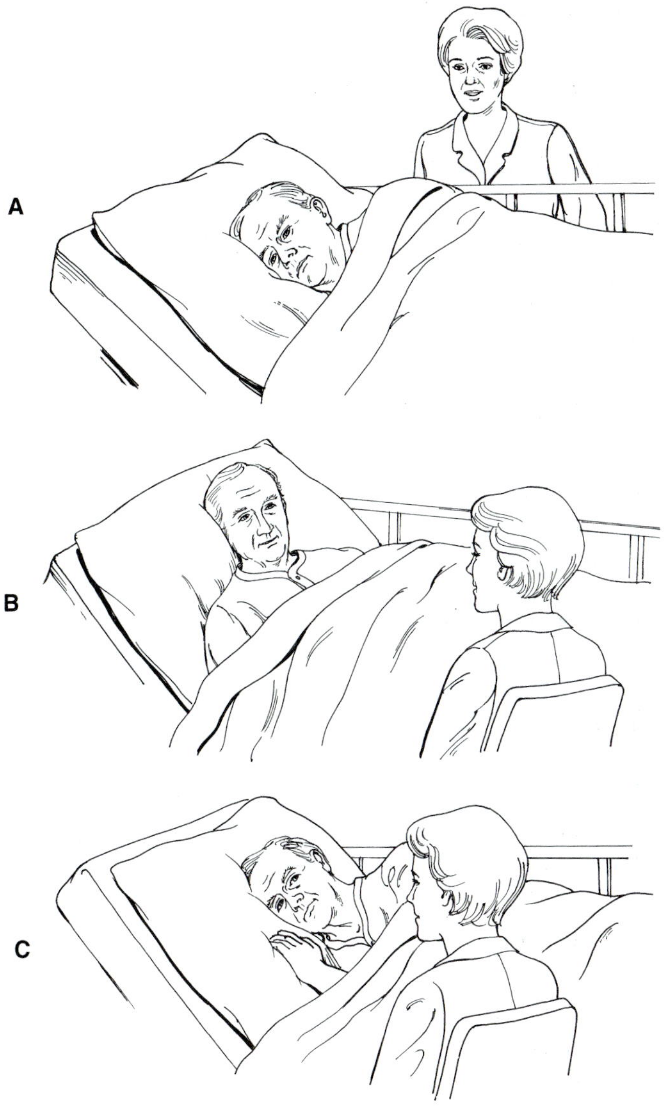

Fig. 4-3 Interview positions with bedridden client. **A,** An awkward, ineffective position to use with bedridden older clients. **B,** A better position, but the nurse is still not close enough for frail, visually impaired, or hearing-impaired clients. **C,** The best position, because the nurse is close to the client.
(From Burnside IM: Psychosocial care of the aged, ed 2, 1980, McGraw-Hill, by permission of Mosby.)

CULTURAL AWARENESS

Culture and Touch

Although recognizing the many reported benefits to establishing rapport with clients through touch (including the promotion of healing through therapeutic touch), physical contact with clients conveys various meanings cross-culturally. In many cultures, (e.g., Middle Eastern and Hispanic) male health care providers may be prohibited from touching or examining either all or certain parts of the female body. Older women, for example those having a gynecologic examination, may prefer female health care providers or may actually refuse to be examined by a male. The nurse should be aware that the client's significant others may also exert pressure on nurses by enforcing these culturally meaningful norms in the health care setting.

The following beliefs concerning touch are stereotypes that should be validated with clients to ascertain individual beliefs, practices, and preferences.

Hispanics
Highly tactile
Very modest (men and women)
May request health care provider of same gender
Women may refuse to be examined by male health care providers

Asian/Pacific Islanders
Avoid touching (patting the head is strictly taboo)
Touching during an argument equals loss of control (shame)
Putting feet on furniture is both impolite and disrespectful
Public displays of affection toward members of same gender is permissible, but not toward members of the opposite gender.

Blacks
Do not touch without permission

American Indians
Usually shake hands lightly
Do not touch without permission

questions. Box 4-3 is a discussion of each of the components.

Client Profile/Biographic Data

This profile is basic, factual data about the older adult. In this section, it is often useful to include a comment regarding the reliability of the information source. For example, if the client's cognitive ability prevents giving accurate information, secondary sources such as family, friends, or other medical records should be consulted. Knowledge of the source(s) of the data alerts the reader or user to the context within which he or she must consider the information.

Family Profile

This information about immediate family members gives a quick overview of who may be living in the client's home or who may represent important support systems

CULTURAL AWARENESS

Overcoming Language Barriers

What to do when there is no interpreter

1. Be polite and formal.
2. Greet the person using the appropriate title (Mr., Mrs., Ms., Dr., Rev., Col., etc.) and last or complete name.
   Gesture to yourself, and say your name.
   Offer a handshake or nod. Smile.
3. Proceed in an unhurried manner. Pay attention to any effort by the client or family to communicate.
4. Speak in a low, moderate voice. Avoid talking loudly. Remember that there is a tendency to raise the volume and pitch of your voice when the listener appears to not understand. The listener may perceive that the nurse is shouting or is angry.
5. Use any words known in the client's language. This indicates that the nurse is aware of and respects the client's culture.
6. Use simple words such as "pain" instead of "discomfort." Avoid medical jargon, idioms, and slang. Avoid using contractions (e.g., don't, can't, won't, etc.).
   Use nouns repeatedly instead of pronouns.
   EXAMPLE:
   Do not say: "He has been taking his medicine, hasn't he?"
   Say: "Does Juan take medicine?"
7. Pantomime words and simple actions while verbalizing them.
8. Give instructions in the proper sequence.
   EXAMPLE:
   Do not say: "Before you rinse the bottle, sterilize it."
   Say: "First wash the bottle. Second, rinse the bottle."
9. Discuss one topic at a time. Avoid using conjunctions.
   EXAMPLE:
   Do not say: "Are you cold and in pain?"
   Say: "Are you cold (while pantomiming)? Are you in pain?"
10. Validate if the client understands by having him or her repeat instructions, demonstrate the procedure, or act out the meaning.
11. Write out several short sentences in English and determine the person's ability to read them.
12. Try a third language. Many Southeast Asians speak French. Europeans often know three or four languages. Try Latin words or phrases, if you are familiar with the language.
13. Ask if anyone among the client's family and friends could serve as an interpreter.
14. Obtain phrase books from a library or bookstore, make or purchase flash cards with commonly used words.

Modified from: Andrews M: Transcultural considerations: crosscultural communication. In Jarvis C: *Physical examination and health assessment,* Philadelphia, 1992, WB Saunders, p 75.

BOX 4-3

Basic Components of a Nursing Health History

Client Profile/Biographic Data: Address and telephone number, date and place of birth/age, gender, race, religion, marital status, education, name, address, and telephone number of nearest contact person

Family Profile: Family members' names and addresses, year and cause of death of deceased spouse and children

Occupational Profile: Current work or retirement status, previous jobs, source(s) of income, and perceived adequacy for needs

Living Environment Profile: Type of dwelling, number of rooms, levels, and people residing, degree of privacy, name, address, and telephone number of nearest neighbor

Recreation/Leisure Profile: Hobbies or interests, organization memberships, vacations or travel

Resources/Support Systems Used: Names of physician(s), hospital, clinic, and other community services

Description of Typical Day: Type and amount of time spent in each activity

Present Health Status: Description of perception of health in past 1 and 5 years, chief complaint and full symptom analysis, prescribed and self-prescribed medications, immunizations, allergies, eating and nutritional patterns

Past Health Status: Previous illnesses throughout life, traumatic injuries, hospitalizations, operations, and obstetric history

Family History: Health status of immediate and living relatives, causes of death of immediate relatives, and survey for risk of specific diseases and disorders

Review of Systems: Head-to-toe review of all body systems and review of health promotion habits for same

CULTURAL AWARENESS

Overcoming Language Barriers: Use of an Interpreter

- Before locating an interpreter, be sure that the language the client speaks at home is known, since it may be different from the language spoken publicly (e.g., French is sometimes spoken at home by well-educated and upper-class members of certain Asian or Middle Eastern cultures).
- Avoid interpreters from a rival tribe, state, region, or nation (e.g., a Palestinian who knows Hebrew may not be the best interpreter for a Jewish client).
- Be aware of gender differences between interpreter and client. In general, same gender is preferred.
- Be aware of age differences between interpreter and client. In general, an older, more mature interpreter is preferred to a younger, less experienced one.
- Be aware of socioeconomic differences between interpreter and client.
- Ask the interpreter to translate as closely to verbatim as possible.
- An interpreter who is a nonrelative may seek compensation for services rendered.
- An interpreter who is a relative can change the meaning of what is said out of concern for the older family member's well-being.

Recommendations: For institutions

- Maintain a computerized list of interpreters who may be contacted as needed.
- Network with area hospitals, colleges, universities, and other organizations, which may serve as resources.
- Use the translation services provided by telephone companies (e.g., AT&T).

Modified from: Andrews MM: Transcultural considerations: cross-cultural communication. In Jarvis C: *Physical examination and health assessment*, Philadelphia, 1992, WB Saunders, p. 75.

for the client. These data also establish a basis for a later description of family health history.

Occupational Profile

Information about work history and experiences can alert the nurse to possible health risks or exposures, lifestyle or social patterns, activity level, and intellectual performance. Retirement concerns may also be identified. Obtaining the client's perception of the adequacy of income for meeting daily living needs can have implications for designing nursing interventions. Financial resources and health have an interdependent relationship.

Living Environment Profile

Any nursing interventions planned for the client must be done with consideration of the living environment. Degree of function, safety, and security, and feelings of well-being are a few of the areas that are affected by a client's living environment.

Recreation/Leisure Profile

Identifying what the client does to relax and to have fun, and how the client uses free time can provide clues to some of the social and emotional dimensions of the client.

Resources/Support Systems Used

Obtaining information about the various health care providers and agencies used by the client can alert the nurse to patterns of use of health care and related services, perceptions of such resources, and attitudes about the importance of health maintenance.

Description of a Typical Day

Identifying the activities of a client during a full 24-hour period provides data about practices that either support or hinder healthy living. Analysis of the usual activities carried out by the client can serve to explain symptoms that may be described later in the Review of Systems, p. 87. Clues about relationships, lifestyle practices, and spiritual dimensions of the client may also be uncovered.

Present Health Status

The client's perception of health in both the past year and past 5 years, coupled with information about health habits, reveals much about the physical integrity of the person. Based on how the client responds, the nurse may be able to ascertain whether the client needs health maintenance, promotion, or restoration.

The chief complaint, stated in the client's own words, enables the nurse to identify specifically why the client is seeking health care. If a symptom is the reason, usually its duration is included as well. A complete and careful symptom analysis can be carried out for the chief complaint by collecting information on the factors identified in Box 4-4, p. 85. When the client does not display specific symptomatology but instead has broader health concerns, the nurse should identify those concerns to begin establishing potential nursing interventions.

Information about the client's knowledge and understanding of current health state, including treatments and management strategies, helps the nurse to focus on possible areas of health teaching and reinforcement, to identify a client's access to and use of resources, to discover coping styles and strategies, and to determine health behavior patterns. Data about the client's perception of functional ability in light of perceived health

TABLE 4-4

Client Factors Affecting History Taking and Recommendations

Factor	Recommendations
Visual disturbance	Position self in full view of client
	Provide diffused, bright light; avoid glare
	Make sure client's glasses are worn and in good working order
	Face client when speaking; do not cover mouth
Hearing deficit	Speak directly to client in clear, low tones at a moderate rate; do not cover mouth
	Articulate consonants with special care
	Restate if client does not understand question initially
	Speak toward "good" ear
	Reduce background noises
	Make sure client's hearing aid is worn and is working properly
Anxiety	Give sufficient time to respond to questions
	Establish rapport and trust by acknowledging expressed concerns
	Determine mutual expectations of interview
	Use open-ended questions that indicate an interest in learning about the client
	Explain why information is needed
	Use a conversational style
	Allow for some degree of life review
	Offer a cup of coffee, tea, or soup
	Call the client often by name
Reduced energy level	Position comfortably to promote alertness
	Allow for more than one assessment encounter; vary the meeting times
	Be alert to subtle signs of fatigue, inability to concentrate, reduced attention span, restlessness, posture
	Be patient; establish a slow pace for the interview
Pain	Position comfortably to reduce pain
	Ask client about degree of pain; intervene before interview or reschedule
	Comfort and communicate through touch
	Use distraction techniques
	Provide a relaxed, "warm" environment
Multiplicity and interrelatedness of health problems	Be alert to subjective and objective cues about body systems, and emotional and cognitive function
	Give client opportunity to prioritize physical and psychosocial health concerns
	Be supportive and reassuring about deficits created by multiple diseases
	Complete full analysis on all reported symptoms
	Be alert to reporting of new or changing symptoms
	Allow for more than one interview time
	Compare and validate data with old records, family, friends, or confidants
Tendency to reminisce	Structure reminiscence to gather necessary data
	Express interest and concern for issues raised by reminiscing
	Put memories into chronologic perspective to appreciate the significance and span of client's life

From Lueckenotte AG: *Pocket guide to gerontologic assessment,* ed 2, St. Louis, 1988, Mosby.

problems and medical diagnoses provide valuable insight into the individual's overall sense of physical, social, emotional, and cognitive well-being.

Medications Assessment of the older adult's current medications is usually accomplished by having the client bring *all* prescription and over-the-counter (OTC) drugs, as well as regularly and occasionally used home remedies. Obtaining the medications in this manner allows the nurse to examine medication labels, which may show the use of multiple physicians and pharmacies. Also, the nurse can determine the client's pattern of drug taking (including compliance), knowledge of medications, expiration dates of medications, and potential risk for drug interaction(s).

Immunization status The older adult's immunization status for these specific diseases and illnesses is particularly important because of the degree of risk for this age group. More attention is increasingly being paid to the immunization status of the older adult population, primarily because of inappropriate use and underuse of

BOX 4-4

Symptom Analysis Factors

Dimensions of a symptom	Questions to ask
1. Location	"Where do you feel it? Does it move around? Does it radiate? Show me where it hurts."
2. Quality or character	"What does it feel like?"
3. Quantity or severity	"On a scale of 1 to 10, with 10 being the worst pain you could have, how would you rate the discomfort you have now?" "How does this interfere with your usual activities?" "How bad is it?"
4. Timing	"When did you first notice it? How long does it last? How often does it happen?"
5. Setting	"Does this occur in a particular place or under certain circumstances? Is it associated with any specific activity?"
6. Aggravating or alleviating factors	"What makes it better? What makes it worse?"
7. Associated symptoms	"Have you noticed other changes that occur with this symptom?"

From Barkauskas VH et al: *Health and physical assessment,* St. Louis, 1994, Mosby.

CULTURAL AWARENESS

Cultural Assessment of Nutritional Needs

- What is the meaning of food and eating to the client?
- What does the client eat during:
  - A typical day?
  - Special events such as secular or religious holidays? (E.g., Muslims fast during the month of Ramadan; some blacks eat moderately during the week but consume very large, heavy meals on weekends.)
- How does the client define food? (E.g., unless rice is served, many from India do not consider the ingestion of food to be a meal; some Vietnamese clients consume large quantities of calcium-rich pork bones and shells, which offsets their lower intake of milk products.)
- What is the timing and sequencing of meals?
- With whom does the client usually eat (alone, with others of the same gender, with spouse, etc.)?
- What does the client believe comprises a "healthy" versus "unhealthy" diet? Any hot/cold or yin/yang beliefs? (See Chapter 5.)
- From what source(s) does the client obtain food items (ethnic grocery store, home garden, restaurant, etc.)? Who usually does the grocery shopping?
- How are foods prepared (type of preparation; cooking oil(s) used, length of time foods are cooked; amount and type of seasoning added before, during, and after preparation)?
- Has the client chosen a particular nutritional practice such as vegetarianism or abstinence from alcoholic beverages?
- Do religious beliefs and practices influence the client's diet or eating habits (e.g., amount, type, preparations or designation of acceptable food items or combinations)? Ask the client to explain the religious calendar and guidelines that govern these dietary practices, including exemptions for older adults and the sick.

vaccines in the past, especially the influenza and pneumococcal vaccines (Abrams, Berkow, 1990). (See Chapter 22 for a more complete discussion of influenza and pneumonia.) Tetanus and diphtheria toxoids (Td) are recommended as a booster at 10-year intervals for adults who have been previously immunized in adult life or as children. Tuberculosis, a disease that was once fairly well-controlled, is now exhibiting a resurgence in this country. Older adults who may have had a tubercular lesion at a young age can experience a reactivation as a result of age-related immune system changes, chronic illness, and poor nutrition.

Allergies Determining the older adult's drug, food, and other contact and environmental allergies is essential to planning nursing interventions. It is particularly important to note their reactions and usual treatments.

Nutrition A 24-hour diet recall is a useful screening tool that provides information about the intake of daily requirements, including the intake of "empty" calories, the adherence to prescribed dietary therapies, and the practice of unusual or "fad" diets. The nurse should also assess the time meals and snacks are taken. If a 24-hour recall cannot be obtained or the information gleaned raises more questions, having the client keep a food diary may be indicated. The diets of older adults may be nutritionally inadequate due to advanced age, multiple chronic illnesses, lack of financial resources, mobility impairments, dental health problems, and loneliness. The diet recall and diary provide nutritional assessment data that reflects the client's overall health and well-being (see Cultural Awareness box above).

Past Health Status

Since the present health status of a person can depend on past health conditions, it is essential to gather data about common childhood illnesses, serious or chronic illnesses, trauma, hospitalizations, operations, and obstetric history. The client's history of measles, mumps, rubella, chicken pox, diphtheria, pertussis, tetanus, rheumatic fever, and poliomyelitis should be obtained to identify potential risk factors for future health problems.

An older adult client may not be aware what diseases are considered as major or may not fully appreciate why it is important to screen for the presence of certain diseases. In such cases, the nurse should ask the client directly about the presence of specific diseases. It is also important to note the dates of onset or occurrence, and the treatment measures prescribed for each disease.

For the older adult, the history of traumatic injuries should be completely described, noting date, time, place, the circumstances surrounding the incident, and the impact of the incident on the client's overall degree of function. Based on the information gathered about previous hospitalizations, operations, and obstetric history, additional data may be needed to gain a complete picture of the older client's health status. The client may need to be guided through this process because of forgetfulness or because of a lengthy, complicated personal history.

Family History

Collecting a family health history provides valuable information about inherited diseases and familial tendencies, whether environmental or genetic, for the purposes of identifying risk and determining need for preventive services. In surveying the health of blood relatives, note the degree of overall health, the presence of disease or illness, and age; if deceased, note the cause of death. By collecting this data the nurse may also be able to identify the existence and degree of family support systems. Data are usually recorded in a family tree format (Box 4-5).

BOX 4-5

Sample Family Tree

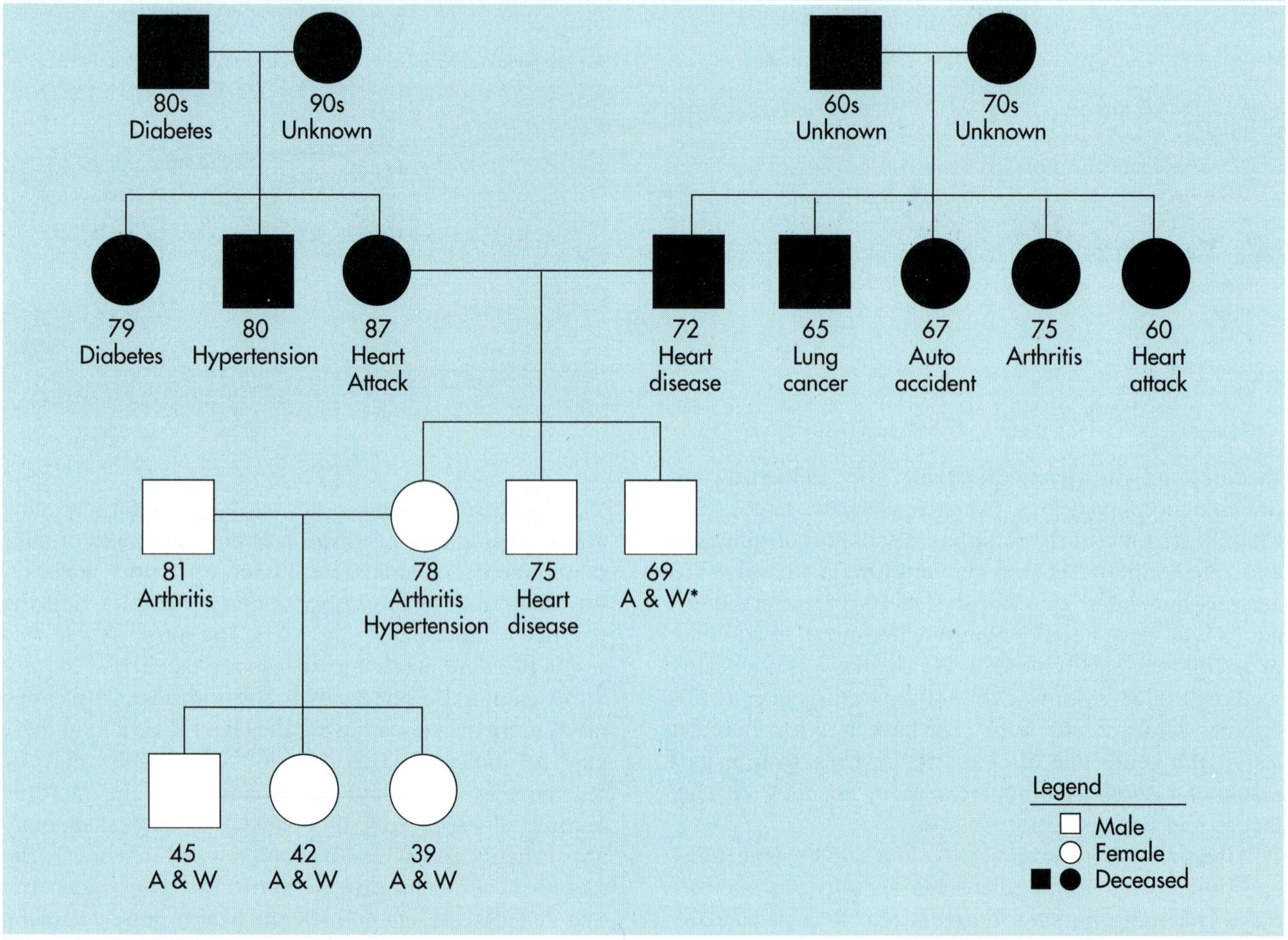

*A&W—Alive and well client

Review of Systems

The review is generally a head-to-toe screening to ascertain the presence or absence of key symptoms within each of the body systems. It is important to question the client in lay terminology, and if a positive response is elicited, conduct a complete symptom analysis to clarify the course of the symptomatology (Box 4-4). To reduce confusion and to ensure the collection of accurate data, the nurse should ask the client for only one piece of information at a time. Information obtained here serves to alert the nurse about what to focus on during the physical examination.

THE PHYSICAL EXAMINATION

Examination Approach and Sequence

The objective information acquired in the physical examination adds to the subjective data base already gathered. Together, these components serve as the basis for establishing nursing diagnoses and planning, developing interventions, and evaluating nursing care.

Physical examination is typically performed after the health history. The approach should be a systematic and deliberate one that allows the nurse to (1) determine client strengths and capabilities, as well as disabilities and limitations; (2) verify and gain objective support for subjective findings; and (3) gather objective data not previously known (see Cultural Awareness box below).

There is no single right way to put together the parts of the physical examination, but a head-to-toe approach is generally the most efficient. The sequence used to conduct the physical examination within this approach is a highly individual one, depending on the individual older adult client. In all cases, however, a side-to-side comparison of findings is made using the client as the control. To promote mastery in conducting an integrated and comprehensive physical examination, the nurse should develop a method of organization and should use it consistently.

Ultimately, the practice setting and client condition together determine the type and method of examination to be performed. For example, an older adult admitted to an acute care hospital with a medical diagnosis of congestive heart failure initially requires respiratory and cardiovascular system assessments to plan appropriate interventions for improving activity tolerance. In the home care setting, assessment of the client's musculoskeletal system is a priority for determining potential for fall-related injury and ability to perform basic self-care tasks. The frail, immobile client in a long-term care setting requires an initial skin assessment to determine risk for pressure ulcer development and preventive measures required. Regular examination of the skin thereafter is necessary to assess effectiveness of the prevention measures instituted.

In all of the above situations, complete physical examinations are important and should eventually be carried out, but client and setting dictate priorities. Con-

CULTURAL AWARENESS

Culture-Congruent Care for Older Adults: Clinical Decision Making and Nursing Actions

After comprehensive cultural assessment and physical examination have been completed, the nurse is ready for clinical decision making and nursing actions. Leininger (1991) suggests three major modalities to guide nursing judgments, decisions, and actions for the purpose of providing cultural congruent care that is beneficial, satisfying, and meaningful to the people nurses serve. The three modes are *cultural preservation* and *maintenance, cultural care accommodation* and *negotiation,* and *cultural care repatterning* or *restructuring.*

Cultural preservation and *maintenance* refers to "those assistive, supporting, facilitative, or enabling professional actions and decisions that help people of a particular culture retain and/or preserve relevant care values so that they can maintain their well being, recover from illness, or face handicaps and/or death" (Leininger, 1991, p. 48).

Cultural care accommodation and *negotiation* refers to "those assistive, supporting, facilitative, or enabling creative professional actions and decisions that help people of a designated culture to adapt to, or to negotiate with, others for beneficial or satisfying health outcome with professional careproviders" (Leininger, 1991, p. 48). Cultural negotiation is sometimes referred to as *culture brokering.*

Cultural care repatterning or *restructuring* refers to "those assistive, supporting, facilitative, or enabling professional actions and decisions that help a client(s) reorder, change, or greatly modify their lifeways for new, different, and beneficial health care patterns while respecting the client(s) cultural values and beliefs and still providing a beneficial or healthier lifeway than before the changes were co-established with the client(s)" (Leininger, 1991, p. 49).

These models are care-centered and are based on the use of the client's care knowledge. Negotiation increases understanding between the client and the nurse and promotes culture-congruent nursing care.

From Leininger MM: *Culture care diversity and universality: a theory of nursing,* New York, 1991, National League for Nursing Press.

sider the subjective client data already obtained in terms of the urgency of the situation, the acute or chronic nature of the problem, the extent of the problem on the basis of body systems affected, and the interrelatedness of physical and psychosocial factors in determining where to begin.

General Guidelines

Regardless of the approach and sequence used, the following principles should be considered while conducting the physical examination:

- Recognize that the older adult may have no previous experience with a nurse conducting a physical examination, so an explanation may be warranted. Project warmth, sincerity, and interest in attempting to allay any anxiety or fear.
- Be alert to the older client's energy level. If the situation warrants it, complete the most important parts of the examination first, and complete the other parts of the examination at another time. Generally, it should take approximately 45 to 60 minutes to conduct the examination.
- Respect the client's modesty. Allow privacy for changing into a gown; if assistance is needed, do so in such a way as not to expose the client's body or cause embarrassment.
- Keep the client comfortably draped. Do not unnecessarily expose a body part; expose only the part to be examined.
- Sequence the examination to keep position changes to a minimum. Clients with limited range of motion and strength may require assistance. Be prepared to use alternative positions if the client is unable to assume the usual position for examination of a body part.
- Develop an efficient sequence for examination that minimizes both nurse and client movement. Variations that may be necessary will not be disruptive if the sequence is consistently followed. Working from one side of the patient, generally the right side, promotes efficiency.
- Ensure comfort for the client. Offer a blanket for added warmth, or a pillow or alternative position for comfortable positioning.
- Explain each step in simple terms. Give clear, concise directions and instructions for performing required movements.
- Warn of any discomfort that might occur. Be gentle.
- Share findings with the client to reassure when possible. Encourage client to ask questions.
- Take advantage of "teachable moments" that may occur while conducting the examination, for example, breast self-examination.
- Develop a standard format on which to note selected findings. Not all data need to be recorded, but the goal is to reduce the potential for forgetting certain data, particularly measurements.

Equipment and Skills

Because the older adult client may become easily fatigued during the physical examination, the nurse should ensure proper functioning and readiness of all equipment before the examination begins to avoid unnecessary delays. Place the equipment within easy reach and in the order in which it will be used (Box 4-6).

The traditional techniques of inspection, palpation, percussion, and auscultation are used with older adults, with age-specific variations for some areas. See the body systems Chapters 21-30 for these variations.

BOX 4-6

Equipment for Physical Examination

Sphygmomanometer
Stethoscope with diaphragm and bell
Thermometer
Tuning fork with frequencies of 500 to 1000 cps
Otoscope
Ear and nasal specula
Ophthalmoscope
Percussion hammer
Penlight
Measuring tape (180 to 200 cm)
10 cm transparent, flexible pocket ruler
Sharp and dull testing implements
Marking pen
Tongue depressors
Cerumen spoon
Olfactory testing substances
Taste testing substances
Examination gloves
Cotton-tipped applicators
Cotton balls
Lubricant
Visual acuity screening chart
Scale with height measurement rod
Tissues

Specimen gathering materials
Culture media
Occult blood testing materials
Vaginal speculum
Pap smear spatula
Sterile cotton-tipped applicator
Glass slides
Fixative

From Lueckenotte AG: *Pocket guide to gerontologic assessment,* ed 2, St. Louis, 1994, Mosby.

BOX 4-7

Katz Index of ADL

Index of Independence in Activities of Daily Living

The Index of Independence in Activities of Daily Living is based on an evaluation of the functional independence or dependence of clients in bathing, dressing, going to toilet, transferring, continence, and feeding. Specific definitions of functional independence and dependence appear below the index.

A—Independent in feeding, continence, transferring, going to toilet, dressing, and bathing
B—Independent in all but one of these functions
C—Independent in all but bathing and one additional function
D—Independent in all but bathing, dressing, and one additional function
E—Independent in all but bathing, dressing, going to toilet, and one additional function
F—Independent in all but bathing, dressing, going to toilet, transferring, and one additional function
G—Dependent in all six functions
Other-Dependent in at least two functions, but not classifiable as C, D, E, or F

Independence means without supervision, direction, or active personal assistance, except as specifically noted below. This is based on actual status and not on ability. A client who refuses to perform a function is considered as not performing the function, even though he or she is deemed able.

Bathing (sponge, shower or tub)
Independent: assistance only in bathing a single part (such as back or disabled extremity) or bathes self completely
Dependent: assistance in bathing more than one part or body, assistance in getting in or out of tub, or does not bathe self

Dressing
Independent: gets clothes from closets and drawers; puts on clothes, outer garments, braces; manages fasteners; act of tying shoes is excluded
Dependent: does not dress self or remains partly undressed

Going to toilet
Independent: gets to toilet; gets on and off toilet; arranges clothes; cleans organs of excretion; (may manage own bedpan used at night only and may or may not be using mechanical supports)
Dependent: uses bedpan or commode or receives assistance in getting to and using toilet

Transfer
Independent: moves in and out of bed independently and moves in and out of chair independently (may or may not be using mechanical supports)
Dependent: assistance in moving in or out of bed and/or chair; does not perform one or more transfers

Continence
Independent: urination and defecation entirely self-controlled
Dependent: partial or total incontinence in urination or defecation; partial or total control by enemas, catheters, or regulated use of urinals and/or bedpans

Feeding
Independent: gets food from plate or its equivalent into mouth; (precutting of meat and preparation of food, as buttering bread, are excluded from evaluation)
Dependent: assistance in act of feeding (see above); does not eat at all, or parenteral feeding

Evaluation form
Name ________________ Date of evaluation _______
For each area of functioning listed below, check the description that applies. (The word "assistance" means supervision, direction of personal assistance.)

Bathing—either sponge bath, tub bath, or shower
- Receives no assistance (gets in and out of tub by self if tub is usual means of bathing)
- Receives assistance in bathing only one part of the body (such as back or a leg)
- Receives assistance in bathing more than one part of the body (or not bathed)

Dressing—gets clothes from closets and drawers—including underclothes, outer garments and using fasteners (including braces if worn)
- Gets clothes and gets completely dressed without assistance
- Gets clothes and gets dressed without assistance except for assistance in tying shoes
- Receives assistance in getting clothes or in getting dressed, or stays partly or completely undressed

Toileting—going to the "toilet room" for bowel and urine eliminations; cleaning self after elimination, and arranging clothes
- Goes to "toilet room," cleans self, and arranges clothes with assistance (may use object for support such as cane, walker, or wheelchair, and may manage night bedpan or commode, emptying same in morning)
- Receives assistance in going to "toilet room," in cleansing self, or in arranging clothes after elimination, or in use of night bedpan or commode
- Does not go to "toilet room" for the elimination process

From Katz S, et al: Studies of illness in the aged. The index of ADL: a standardized measure of biological and pschological function, *JAMA* 185:914-919, ©1963, American Medical Association.

BOX 4-7

Katz Index of ADL—cont'd

Transfer
- •Moves in and out of bed as well as in and out of chair without assistance (may be using object for support such as cane or walker)
- •Moves in or out of bed or chair with assistance
- •Does not get out of bed

Continence
- •Controls urination and bowel movement completely by self
- •Has occasional "accidents"
- •Supervision helps keep urine or bowel control; catheter is used, or is incontinent

Feeding
- •Feeds self without assistance
- •Feeds self except for cutting meat or buttering bread
- •Receives assistance in feeding or is fed partly or completely by using tubes or intravenous fluids

Additional Assessment Measures

Obtaining the health history as described above does not always provide sufficient data for planning nursing care for the older adult. Assessment of *all* the dimensions of the older adult is essential to establishing baseline functional ability and providing good care.

The extremely delicate balance of homeostatic mechanisms the older adult is able to achieve is vulnerable to assault from a variety of sources, thus increasing the risk of impairment or disability. The primary reason for such a precarious situation is that the physical, mental/emotional, and social well-being of the older adult are all closely interrelated. Medical diagnoses alone do not provide a reliable measure of functional ability. In fact, a lengthy medical problem list may not correlate at all with any degree of functional loss. Therefore what is crucial for the nurse to know is how the older person has adapted to manage all dimensions of life with the diagnosed medical problem(s). Standardized tools and measures of functional status that enable health care providers to objectively determine the older person's ability to function independently *despite* disease, mental/emotional, and social disability are important adjuncts to traditional assessment. These assessments include determination of the client's ability to perform activities of daily living (ADLs) and instrumental activities of daily living (IADLs), as well as the client's cognitive, affective, and social level of function. Obtaining this additional data provides a more comprehensive view of the impact of all of the interrelated variables on the older adult's total functioning.

Functional Status Assessment

Functional status assessment is a measurement of the older adult's ability to perform basic self-care tasks, or ADLs, and those that require more complex activities for independent living, referred to as IADLs (Kane, Kane, 1981). Determination of the degree of functional independence in these areas can identify client abilities and limitations, leading to the selection of appropriate interventions. The client situation determines the time of day when any of the scales or tools should be administered, as well as the number of times the client may need to be tested to ensure accurate results. Many tools are available, but the nurse should use only those that are valid, reliable, and relevant to the practice setting. The following is a description of tools that are appropriate for use with older adults in most settings.

The Katz Index of ADL (Katz et al, 1963) is a tool widely used to determine the results of treatment and prognosis in older and chronically ill people (Box 4-7). The index ranks adequacy of performance in the six functions of bathing, dressing, toileting, transferring, continence, and feeding. A dichotomous rating of independence or dependence is made for each of the functions. One point is given for each dependent item. Only people who can perform the function without any help at all are rated as independent; the actual evaluation form merely shows the rater how a dependent item is determined. The order of items reflects the natural progression in loss *and* restoration of function, based on studies conducted by Katz and his colleagues (Kane, Kane, 1981). The Katz Index is a useful tool for the nurse because it describes the client's functional level at a specific point in time and objectively measures the effects of treatment intended to restore function. The tool only takes about 5 minutes to administer and can be used in most settings.

The Barthel Index (Mahoney, Barthel, 1965), another tool used for measuring functional status, rates self-care abilities in the areas of feeding, moving, toileting, bathing, walking, propelling a wheelchair, using stairs, dressing, and bowel and bladder control (Box 4-8). For each item the individual is rated based on ability to perform the task independently or with help; more points are scored for independence, with a maximum score of 100 indicating independence on all items. However, the instrument developers note that a score of 100 does not not necessarily mean one could live alone or with out assisstance, The Barthel index is most appropriate for use in rehabilitation settings for documenting improvement in performance and abilitiy.

IADLs represent a range of activities more complex

BOX 4-8

Barthel Index

Action	With help	Independent
1. Feeding (if food needs to be cut up=help)	5	10
2. Moving from wheelchair to bed and return (includes sitting up in bed)	5-10	15
3. Personal toilet (wash face, comb hair, shave, clean teeth)	0	5
4. Getting on and off toilet (handling clothes, wipe, flush)	5	10
5. Bathing self	0	5
6. Walking on level surface (of if unable to walk, propel wheelchair)	0*	5*
7. Ascend and descend stairs	5	10
8. Dressing (includes tying shoes, fastening fasteners)	5	10
9. Controlling bowels	5	10
10. Controlling bladder	5	10

A client scoring 100 BDI is continent, feeds himself, dresses himself, gets up out of bed and chairs, bathes himself, walks at least a block, and can ascend and descend stairs. This does not mean that the client is able to live alone: the client may not be able to cook, keep house, and meet the public but may be able to get along without attendant care.

Definition and discussion of scoring

1. Feeding
   - 10 = Independent. The client can feed himself a meal from a tray or table when someone puts the food within his reach. He must put on an assistive device if this is needed, cut up the food, use salt and pepper, spread butter, etc. He must accomplish this in a reasonable time.
   - 5 = Some help is necessary (with cutting up food, etc., as listed above)
2. Moving from wheelchair to bed and return
   - 15 = Independent in all phases of this activity. Client can safely approach the bed in her wheelchair, lock brakes, lift footrests, move safely from bed, lie down, come to a sitting position on the side of the bed, change the position of the wheelchair, if necessary, to transfer back into it safely and return to the wheelchair.
   - 10 = Either some minimal help is needed in some step of this activity or the client needs to be reminded or supervised for safety of one or more parts of this activity.
   - 5 = Client can come to a sitting position without the help of a second person but needs to be lifted out of bed, or if she transfers, with a great deal of help.
3. Doing personal toilet
   - 5 = Client can wash hands and face, comb hair, clean teeth, and shave. He may use any kind of razor but he must put in blade or plug in razor without help as well as get it from the drawer or cabinet. Female clients must put on own makeup, if used, but need not braid or style hair.
4. Getting on and off toilet
   - 10 = Client is able to get on and off toilet, fasten and unfasten clothes, prevent soiling of clothes, and use toilet paper without help. She may use a wall bar or other stable object for support if needed. If it is necessary to use a bed pan instead of toilet, he must be able to place it on a chair, empty it, and clean it.
   - 5 = Client needs help because of imbalance, in handling clothes, or in using toilet paper.
5. Bathing self
   - 5 = Client may use a bathtub, a shower, or take a complete sponge bath. He must be able to do all the steps involved in whichever method is employed without another person being present.
6. Walking on a level surface
   - 15 = Client can walk at least 50 yards without help or supervision. She may wear braces or prostheses and use crutches, canes, or a walkerette but not a rolling walker. She must be able to lock and unlock braces if used, assume the standing position and sit down, get the necessary mechanical aids into position for use, and dispose of them when she sits. (Putting on and taking off braces is scored under Dressing).

6a. Propelling a wheelchair
   - 5 = If a client cannot ambulate but can propel a wheelchair independently, he must be able to go around corners, turn around, maneuver the chair to a table, bed, toilet, etc. He must be able to push a chair at least 50 yards. Do not score this item if the client gets a score for walking.

7. Ascending and descending stairs
   - 10 = Client is able to go up and down a flight of stairs safely without help or supervision. She may and should use handrails, canes, or crutches when needed. She must be able to carry canes or crutches as she ascends or descends stair.
   - 5 = Client needs help with or supervision of any one of the above items.

*Score if only unable to walk.

Modified from Mahoney FI, Barthel DW: Functional evaluation: the Barthel index, *Maryland State Med J* 14:61-65, 1965.

Continued.

BOX 4-8

Barthel Index—cont'd

8. Dressing and undressing
   10 = Client is able to put on and remove and fasten all clothing, and tie shoe laces (unless it is necessary to use adaptations for this). This activity includes putting on and removing and fastening corset or braces when these are prescribed. Such special clothing as suspenders, loafer shoes, dresses that open down the front may be used when necessary.
   5 = Client needs help in putting on and removing or fastening any clothing. He must do at least half the work himself. He must accomplish this in a reasonable time.

Women need not be scored on use of a brassiere or girdle unless these are prescribed garments.

9. Continence of bowels
   10 = Client is able to control her bowels and have no accidents. She can use a suppository or take an enema when necessary (as for spinal cord injury clients who have had bowel training).
   5 = Client needs help in using a suppository or taking an enema or has occasional accidents.
10. Controlling bladder
    10 = Client is able to control his bladder day and night. Spinal cord injury clients who wear an external device and leg bag must put them on independently, clean and empty bag, and stay dry day and night.
    5 = Client has occasional accidents, cannot wait for the bed pan, cannot get to the toilet in time, or needs help with an external device.

The total score is not as significant or meaningful as the breakdown into individual items, since these indicate where the deficiencies are.

Any applicant to a chronic care setting who scores 100 BDI should be evaluated carefully before admission to see whether such hospitalization is indicated. Discharged clients with 100 BDI should not require further physical therapy but may benefit from a home visit to see whether any environmental adjustments are indicated.

than the self-care tasks described in the above tools (Kane, Kane, 1981). Lawton and Brody (1969) described the Philadelphia Geriatric Center Instrumental Activities of Daily Living Scale as one that measures complex activities such as using a telephone, shopping, food preparation, housekeeping, laundry, transportation, taking medication, and handling finances (Box 4-9). Limitations of the scale include no instructions for summing up the items, as well as an emphasis on tasks traditionally performed by women, especially for today's cohort of older people (Kane, Kane, 1981). Its usefulness is that it may identify people living in the community who need help, which enables the nurse to match services and other sources of support for clients.

Nurses practicing in all settings should begin incorporating the tools noted previously into routine assessments, as well as others described in the comprehensive text by Kane and Kane (1981), to determine a client's baseline functional ability. However, with all of the previously mentioned tools, the nurse should remember the following points:

- Scores will be affected by the environment in which the tool is administered.
- The client's affective and cognitive state will affect performance.
- The result represents but one piece of the total assessment.

Cognitive/Affective Assessment

The purpose of mental status assessment in the older adult is to determine the client's thoughts and mental processes, and the effect on functioning. This assessment is usually integrated into the interview and physical examination, with testing conducted in a natural, nonthreatening manner with consideration of ethnicity. Table 4-5 identifies typical areas to assess in a mental status assessment. Note that this mental status assessment provides a baseline that identifies the need for the administration of one of the standardized mental status examinations.

There are multiple physiologic, phsycologic, and environmental causes of cognitive impairment in older adults. Coupled with the commonly held view by many health care providers that mental impairment is a normal, age-related process, it is not surprising that assessment of this problem is often incomplete. Standardized examinations test a variety of cognitive functions, aiding identification of deficits that impact overall functional ability. Formal, systematic testing of mental status can help the nurse determine which behaviors are impaired and warrant intervention.

The Short Portable Mental Status Questionaire (SPMSQ) (Box 4-10), used to detect the presence and degree of intellectual impairment, consists of 10 items that test orientation, memory in relation to self-care ability, re-

TABLE 4-5

Mental Status Assessment

Exam component	Area to assess
General appearance	Observe physical appearance, coordination of movements, grooming and hygiene, facial expression, and posture as measures of mental function
Behavior	Note level of consciousness; observe gait, coordination, and movement
Mood or affect	Note verbal and nonverbal behaviors for appropriateness, degree, and range of affect
Speech	Evaluate comprehension of and ability to use the spoken language; note volume, pace, amount, and degree of spontaneity
Orientation	Note awareness of person, place, and time
Attention and concentration	Note clarity and logic of responses, and ability to maintain interest
Judgment	Note ability to evaluate a situation and determine appropriate reaction/response
Memory	Note ability to accurately recall data or events (may need to verify with collateral sources)
Thought content and processes	Observe for rational, logical, and realistic thinking; note ability to relate history in a clear, sequential, and logical manner

BOX 4-9

Instrumental Activities of Daily Living Scale

	Score
1. Ability to use telephone	
A. Operates telephone on own initiative—looks up and dials numbers, etc.	1
B. Dials a few well-known numbers	1
C. Answers telephone but does not dial	1
D. Does not use telephone at all	0
2. Shopping	
A. Takes care of all shopping needs independently	1
B. Shops independently for small purchases	0
C. Needs to be accompanied on any shopping trip	0
D. Completely unable to shop	0
3. Food preparation	
A. Plans, prepares and serves adequate meals independently	1
B. Prepares adequate meals if supplied with ingredients	0
C. Heats and serves prepared meals, or prepares meals but does not maintain adequate diet	0
D. Needs to have meals prepared and served	0
4. Housekeeping	
A. Maintains house alone or with occasional assistance (e.g.,"heavy work—domestic help")	1
B. Performs light daily tasks such as dishwashing and bedmaking	1
C. Performs light daily tasks but cannot maintain acceptable level of cleanliness	1
D. Needs help with all home maintenance tasks	1
E. Does not participate in any housekeeping tasks	0
5. Laundry	
A. Does personal laundry completely	1
B. Launders small items—rinses socks, stockings, etc.	1
C. All laundry must be done by others	0
6. Mode of transportation	
A. Travels independently on public transportation or drives own car	1
B. Arranges own travel via taxi but does not otherwise use public transportation	1
C. Travels on public transportation when assisted or accompanied by another	1
D. Travel limited to taxi or automobile with assistance of another	0
E. Does not travel at all	0
7. Responsibility for own medications	
A. Is responsible for taking medication in correct dosages at correct time	1
B. Takes responsibility if medication is prepared in advance in separate dosages	0
C. Is not capable of dispensing own medication	0
8. Ability to handle finances	
A. Manages financial matters independently (budgets, writes checks, pays rent, bills, goes to bank), collects and keeps track of income	1
B. Manages day-to-day purchases but needs help with banking, major purchases, etc.	1
C. Incapable of handling money	0

From Lawton HP, Brody EM: Assessment of older people: self maintaining and instrumental activities of daily living, *Gerontologist* 9:179-186, 1969.

BOX 4-10

Short Portable Mental Status Questionnaire (SPMSQ)

Instructions: Ask questions 1-10 in this list, and record all answers. Ask question 4A only if patient does not have a telephone. Record total number of errors based on 10 questions.

+	−	
___	___	1. What is the date today? ___________ Month Day Year
___	___	2. What day of the week is it? _________
	___	3. What is the name of this place? ______ ___________________
___	___	4. What is your telephone number? ____
___	___	4a. What is your street address ________ ___________________ (Ask only if patient does not have a telephone)
___	___	5. How old are you? _______________
___	___	6. When were you born? ____________
___	___	7. Who is the President of the U.S. now? ___________________
___	___	8. Who was the President just before him? ___________________
___	___	9. What was your mother's maiden name? ___________________
		10. Subtract 3 from 20 and keep subtracting 3 from each new number, all the way down.
	___	Total Number of Errors

To be completed by interviewer

Patient's name: __________________ Date _________

Sex: _____ Male Race: ____ White
_____ Female ____ Black
____ Other

Years of education: ____ ____ Grade School
____ High School
____ Beyond High School

Interviewer's name: ___________________________

Instructions for Completion of the Short Portable Mental Status Questionnaire (SPMSQ)

All responses to be scored as correct must be given by subject without reference to calendar, newspaper, birth certificate, or other aid to memory.

Question 1 is to be scored as correct only when the exact month, exact date, and the exact year are given correctly.

Question 2 is self-explanatory.

Question 3 should be scored as correct if any correct description of the location is given. "My home," correct name of the town or city of residence, or the name of hospital or institution if subject is institutionalized are all acceptable.

Question 4 should be scored as correct when the correct telephone number can be verified, or when the subject can repeat the same number at another point in the questioning.

Question 5 is scored as correct when stated age corresponds to date of birth.

Question 6 is to be scored as correct only when the month, exact date, and year are all given.

Question 7 requires only the last name of the President.

Question 8 requires only the last name of the previous President.

Question 9 does not need to be verified. It is scored as correct if a female first name plus a last name other than subject's last name is given.

Question 10 requires that the entire series must be performed correctly in order to be scored as correct. Any error in the series or unwillingness to attempt the series is scored as incorrect.

Scoring of the Short Portable Mental Status Questionnaire (SPMSQ)

The data suggest that both education and race influence performance on the Mental Status Questionnaire and they must accordingly be taken into account in evaluating the score attained by an individual.

For the purposes of scoring, three educational levels have been established: (1) persons who have had only a grade school education; (2) persons who have had any high school education or who have completed high school; (3) persons who have had any education beyond the high school level, including college, graduate school, or business school.

For white subjects with at least some high school education, but not more than high school education, the following criteria have been established:

0-2 errors	Intact intellectual functioning
3-4 errors	Mild intellectual impairment
5-7 errors	Moderate intellectual impairment
8-10 errors	Severe intellectual impairment

Allow one more error if subject has had only a grade school education.

Allow one less error if subject has had education beyond high school.

Allow one more error for black subjects, using identical education criteria.

From Pfeiffer E: A short portable questionnaire for the assessment of organic brain deficit in elderly patients, *J Am Geriatr Soc* 23:433-441, 1975.

BOX 4-11

Mini-Mental State Examination (MMSE)

Score Maximum	Patient	
Orientation		
5	______	What is the year) (season) (date) (day) (month)?
5	______	Where are we: (state) (county) (town) (hospital) (floor)?
Registration		
3	______	Name 3 objects: 1 second to say each. Then ask the client all 3 after you have said them. Give 1 point for each correct answer. Then repeat them until he learns all 3. Count trials and record. Trials ______
Attention and calculation		
5	______	Serial 7's. 1 point for each correct. Stop after 5 answers. Alternatively spell "world" backwards.
Recall		
3	______	Ask for the 3 objects repeated above. Give 1 point for each correct.
Language		
9	______	Name a pencil, and watch (2 points). Repeat the following: "No ifs, ands, or buts" (1 point).

Follow a 3-stage command: "Take a paper in your right hand, fold it in half, and put it on the floor" (3 points).
Read and obey the following:
"Close your eyes" (1 point).
Write a sentence (1 point).
Copy design (1 point).
Total score ______

Assess level of consciousness along a continuum like the following one:

Alert Drowsy Stupor Coma

Instructions of Administration of Mini-Mental State Examination (MMSE)

Orientation

1. Ask for the date. Then ask specifically for parts omitted, e.g., "Can you also tell me what season it is?" One point for each correct answer.
2. Ask in turn "Can you tell me the name of this hospital, town, county, etc.?" One point for each correct answer.

Registration

Ask the client if you may test his or her memory. Then say the names of three unrelated objects, clearly and slowly, allowing about one second for each. After you have said all three, ask him or her to repeat them. This first repetition determines his or her score (0-3) but keep saying them until he or she can repeat all three, up to 6 trials. If he or she does not eventually learn all three, recall cannot be meaningfully tested.

Attention and calculation

Ask the patient to begin with 100 and count backwards by 7. Stop after five subtractions (93, 86, 79, 72, 65). Score the total number of correct answers.

If the patient cannot or will not perform this task, ask him or her to spell the word "world" backwards. The score is the number of letters in correct order, e.g., dlrow − 5, dlorw − 3.

Recall

Ask the patient if he or she can recall the three words you previously asked him or her to remember. Score 0-3.

Language

Naming: Show the patient a wrist watch and ask him or her what it is. Repeat for pencil. Score 0-2.
Repetition: Ask the patient to repeat the sentence after you. Allow only one trial. Score 0 or 1.
Three-stage command: Give the patient a piece of plain blank paper and repeat the command. Score 1 point for each part correctly executed.

From Folstein MF, Folstein SE, McHugh PR: Mini-mental state: a practical method for grading the cognitive state of patients for the clinician, *J Psychiatr Res* 12:189-198, Elsevier Science Ltd, Pergamon Imprint, Oxford, England, 1975.

BOX 4-12

Beck Depression Inventory, Short Form

Instructions: This is a questionnaire. On the questionnaire are groups of statements. Please read the entire group of statements in each category. Then pick out the one statement in that group which best describes the way you feel today, that is, *right now!* Circle the number beside the statement you have chosen. If several statements in the group seem to apply equally well, circle each one.

Be sure to read all the statements in each group before making your choice.

A. (Sadness)
- **3** I am so sad or unhappy that I can't stand it.
- **2** I am blue or sad all the time and I can't snap out of it.
- **1** I feel sad or blue.
- **0** I do not feel sad.

B. (Pessimism)
- **3** I feel that the future is hopeless and that things cannot improve.
- **2** I feel I have nothing to look forward to.
- **1** I feel discouraged about the future.
- **0** I am not particularly pessimistic or discouraged about the future.

C. (Sense of failure)
- **3** I feel I am a complete failure as a person (parent, husband, wife).
- **2** As I look back on my life, all I can see is a lot of failures.
- **1** I feel I have failed more than the average person.
- **0** I do not feel like a failure.

D. (Dissatisfaction)
- **3** I am dissatisfied with everything.
- **2** I don't get satisfaction out of anything anymore.
- **1** I don't enjoy things the way I used to.
- **0** I am not particularly dissatisfied.

E. (Guilt)
- **3** I feel as though I am very bad or worthless.
- **2** I feel quite guilty.
- **1** I feel bad or unworthy a good part of the time.
- **0** I don't feel particularly guilty.

F. (Self-dislike)
- **3** I hate myself.
- **2** I am disgusted with myself.
- **1** I am disappointed in myself.
- **0** I don't feel disappointed in myself.

G. (Self-harm)
- **3** I would kill myself if I had the chance.
- **2** I have definite plans about committing suicide.
- **1** I feel I would be better off dead.
- **0** I don't have any thoughts of harming myself.

H. (Social withdrawal)
- **3** I have lost all of my interest in other people and don't care about them at all.
- **2** I have lost most of my interest in other people and have little feeling for them.
- **1** I am less interested in other people than I used to be.
- **0** I have not lost interest in other people.

I. (Indecisiveness)
- **3** I can't make any decisions at all anymore.
- **2** I have great difficulty in making decisions.
- **1** I try to put off making decisions.
- **0** I make decisions about as well as ever.

J. (Self-image change)
- **3** I feel that I am ugly or repulsive-looking.
- **2** I feel that there are permanent changes in my appearance and they make me look unattractive.
- **1** I am worried that I am looking old or unattractive.
- **0** I don't feel that I look any worse than I used to.

K. (Work difficulty)
- **3** I can't do any work at all.
- **2** I have to push myself very hard to do anything.
- **1** It takes extra effort to get started at doing something.
- **0** I can work about as well as before.

L. (Fatigability)
- **3** I get too tired to do anything.
- **2** I get tired from doing anything.
- **1** I get tired more easily than I used to
- **0** I don't get any more tired than usual.

M. (Anorexia)
- **3** I have no appetite at all anymore.
- **2** My appetite is much worse now.
- **1** My appetite is not as good as it used to be.
- **0** My appetite is no worse than usual.

Scoring

0-4 None or minimal depression
5-7 Mild depression
8-15 Moderate depression
16+ Severe depression

From Beck AT, Beck RW: Screening depressed patients in family practice: a rapid technique, *Postgrad Med* 52(6):81-85, 1972.

mote memory, and mathematical ability (Pfeiffer, 1975). The simple scoring method rates the level of intellectual functioning, which aids in making clinical decisions regarding self-care capacity.

Since the SPSMQ is given orally, it is easy to memorize. It can be administered as a screening assessment to older people in acute, community-based, and long-term care settings. Based on the score, a more complete mental status assessment and psychiatric evaluation may be warranted.

The Mini-Mental State Examination (MMSE) (Box 4-11) tests the cognitive aspects of mental functions:

orientation, registration, attention and calculation, recall, and language (Folstein et al, 1975). The highest possible score is 30, with a score of 21 or less generally indicative of cognitive impairment requiring further investigation. The examination takes only a few minutes to complete and is easily scored, but it cannot be used alone for diagnostic purposes. Because the MMSE quantifies the severity of cognitive impairment and demonstrates cognitive changes over time and with treatment, it is a useful tool for assessing client progress in relation to interventions. As with the SPMSQ, if the MMSE score demonstrates the client is impaired, additional diagnostic testing and mental status examination is indicated.

Affective status measurement tools are used to differentiate the type of serious depression that affects many domains of function from the low mood common to many people. Depression is common in older adults and is often associated with confusion and disorientation, so depressed older people are often mistakenly labeled demented. It is important to note here that people who are depressed usually respond to items on mental status exams by saying: "I don't know," which leads to poor performance. Since mental status exams are not able to distinguish between dementia and depression, a response of "I don't know" should be interpreted as a sign that further affective assessment is warranted. Mental status examinations do not clearly distinguish between depression and dementia, so affective assessment is an important additional tool.

The Beck Depression Inventory (Box 4-12) contains 13 items describing a variety of symptoms and attitudes associated with depression (Beck, Beck, 1972). Each item is rated using a 4-point scale to designate the intensity of the symptom. The tool is easily scored and can be self-administered or given by the nurse in about 5 minutes. Depending on the degree of impairment, the number of responses for each item could be confusing or could create difficulty for the older client. The nurse may need to assist clients experiencing this problem with the tool. The scoring cutoff points aid in estimating the severity of the depression (Beck, Beck, 1972).

The short form Geriatric Depression Scale (Box 4-13), derived from the original 30-question Geriatric Depression Scale, is a convenient instrument designed specifically for use with older people to screen for depression (Yesavage, Brink, 1983). Questions answered as indicated score one point. A score of 5 or more may indicate depression.

The instruments described above for assessing cognitive and affective status are valuable screening tools the nurse can use to supplement other assessments. They may also be used to monitor a client's condition over time. The results of any screening mental or affective status examination should never be accepted as conclusive; they are subject to change based on further workup or after treatment interventions have been implemented.

BOX 4-13

Yesavage Geriatric Depression Scale, Short Form

1. Are you basically satisfied with your life? (no)
2. Have you dropped many of your activities and interests? (yes)
3. Do you feel that your life is empty? (yes)
4. Do you often get bored? (yes)
5. Are you in good spirits most of the time? (no)
6. Are you afraid that something bad is going to happen to you? (yes)
7. Do you feel happy most of the time? (no)
8. Do you often feel helpless? (yes)
9. Do you prefer to stay home at night, rather than go out and do new things? (yes)
10. Do you feel that you have more problems with memory than most? (yes)
11. Do you think it is wonderful to be alive now? (no)
12. Do you feel pretty worthless the way you are now? (yes)
13. Do you feel full of energy? (no)
14. Do you feel that your situation is hopeless? (yes)
15. Do you think that most persons are better off than you are? (yes)

Score 1 point for each response that matches the yes or no answer after the question.

From Yesavage JA, Brink TL: Development and validation of a geriatric depression screening scale: a preliminary report, *J Psychiatr Res* 17:37-49, Elsevier Science Ltd, Pergamon Imprint, Oxford, England, 1983.

BOX 4-14

Family APGAR

1. I am satisfied that I can turn to my family (friends) for help when something is troubling me. *(adaptation)*
2. I am satisfied with the way my family (friends) talks over things with me and shares problems with me. *(partnership)*
3. I am satisfied that my family (friends) accepts and supports my wishes to take on new activities or directions. *(growth)*
4. I am satisfied with the way my family (friends) expresses affection and responds to my emotions, such as anger, sorrow, or love. *(affection)*
5. I am satisfied with the way my family (friends) and I share time together. *(resolve)*

Scoring:

Statements are answered *always* (2 points), *some of the time* (1 point), *hardly ever* (0 points).

Reprinted with permission from Appleton & Lange. From Smilkstein G, Ashworth C, Montano MA: Validity and reliability of the Family APGAR as a test of family function, *J Fam Prac* 15:303-311, 1982.

BOX 4-15

OARS Social Resource Scale

Now I'd like to ask you some questions about your family and friends.

Are you single, married, widowed, divorced, or separated?

1 Single   3 Widowed   5 Separated
2 Married   4 Divorced   __ Not answered

If "2" ask following
Does your spouse live here also?
1 yes
0 no
__ Not answered

Who lives with you?
(Check "yes" or "no" for each of the following.)

Yes	No	
______	______	No one
______	______	Husband or wife
______	______	Children
______	______	Grandchildren
______	______	Parents
______	______	Grandparents
______	______	Brothers and sisters
______	______	Other relatives (does not include inlaws covered in the above categories)
______	______	Friends
______	______	Nonrelated paid help (includes free room)
______	______	Others (specify)________

In the past year about how often did you leave here to visit your family and/or friends for weekends or holidays or to go on shopping trips or outings?
1 Once a week or more
2 1-3 times a month
3 Less than once a month or only on holidays
4 Never
__ Not answered

How many people do you know well enough to visit with in their homes?
3 Five or more
2 Three to four
1 One to two
0 None
__ Not answered

About how many times did you talk to someone—friends, relatives or others—on the telephone in the past week (either you called them or they called you)? (If subject has no phone, question still applies.)
3 Once a day or more
2 Twice
1 Once
0 Not at all
__ Not answered

How many times during the past week did you spend some time with someone who does not live with you, that is, you went to see them, or they came to visit you, or you went out to do things together?
How many times in the past week did you visit with someone, either with people who live here or people who visited you here?
3 Once a day or more
2 Two to six
1 Once
0 Not at all
__ Not answered

Do you have someone you can trust and confide in?
1 Yes
0 No
__ Not answered

Do you find yourself feeling lonely quite often, sometimes, or almost never?
0 Quite often
1 Sometimes
2 Almost never
__ Not answered

Do you see your relatives and friends as often as you want to, or not?
1 As often as wants to
0 Not as often as wants to
__ Not answered

Is there someone *(outside this place)* who would give you any help at all if you were sick or disabled, for example, your husband/wife, a member of your family, or a friend?
1 Yes
0 No one willing and able to help
__ Not answered
If "yes" ask a and b.

A. Is there someone *(outside this place)* who would take care of you as long as needed, or only for a short time, or only someone who would help you now and then (for example, taking you to the doctor, or fixing lunch occasionally, etc.)?
3 Someone who would take care of subject indefinitely (as long as needed)
2 Someone who would take care of subject for a short time (a few weeks to six months)
1 Someone who would help subject now and then (taking him to the doctor or fixing lunch, etc.)
__ Not answered

B. Who is this person?
Name ______________________
Relationship ______________________

From Duke University Center for the Study of Aging and Human Developments: *OARS multidimensional functional assessment: questionnaire,* Durham, N.C., 1988, Duke University.

BOX 4-15

OARS Social Resource Scale—cont'd

Rating scale

Rate the current social resources of the person being evaluated along the 6-point scale presented below. Circle the *one* number that best describes the person's present circumstances.

1. *Excellent Social Resources:* Social relationships are very satisfying and extensive; at least one person would take care of him (her) indefinitely.
2. *Good Social Resources:* Social relationships are fairly satisfying and adequate and at least one person would take care of him (her) indefinitely, *or*
   Social relationships are very satisfying and extensive, and only short-term help is available.
3. *Mildly Socially Impaired:* Social relationships are unsatisfactory, of poor quality, few; but as least one person would take care of him (her) indefinitely, *or*
   Social relationships are fairly satisfactory and adequate, and only short-term help is available.
4. *Moderately Socially Impaired:* Social relationships are unsatisfactory, of poor quality, few; and only short-term care is available, *or*
   Social relationships are at least adequate or satisfactory, but help would only be available now and then.
5. *Severely Socially Impaired:* Social relationships are unsatisfactory, of poor quality, few; and help would be available only now and then, *or*
   Social relationships are at least satisfactory or adequate, but help is not available even now and then.
6. *Totally Socially Impaired:* Social relationships are unsatisfactory, of poor quality, few; and help is not available even now and then.

Social Assessment

The broad concept of social functioning is a vague one, so much so that there remains disagreement as to what aspects of it are important, as well as what represents adequate performance (Kane, Kane, 1981). Therefore a wide range of instruments is available, claiming to ascertain the social well-being of older adults.

It is agreed that there are several, legitimate reasons why health care providers should screen for social functioning in older people, despite the diverse concepts of what constitutes social functioning (Kane, Kane, 1981). First, social functioning is correlated with physical and mental functioning. Alterations in activity patterns can negatively impact physical and mental health and vice versa. Second, an individual's social well-being can positively impact coping with physical impairments and the ability to remain independent. Third, a satisfactory level of social functioning is a significant outcome in and of itself. The degree of the quality of life an older person experiences is closely linked to social functioning dimensions such as self-esteem, life satisfaction, socioeconomic status, and physical health and functional status.

The relationship the older adult has with family plays a central role in the overall level of health and well-being the older adult experiences. The assessment of this aspect of the client's social system can yield vital information about an important part of the total support network. Despite popular belief, families provide substantial help to their older members. Consequently, the level of family involvement and support cannot be disregarded when collecting data.

A short screening tool that can be used to assess the older person's social functioning is the Family APGAR (Smilkstein et al, 1982). Adaptation, partnership, growth, affection, and resolve (APGAR) are the aspects of family functioning that the tool assesses (Box 4-14, p. 97). The tool can be easily adapted for use with clients who have more intimate social relationships with friends than family by simply substituting the term "friends" for "family" in the statements. A score of less than 3 suggests a highly dysfunctional family; a score of 4-6 a moderately dysfunctional family. The use of this screening instrument with a new client, of following a serious, stressful life event is appropriate.

One of the components of the Older Adults Resources and Services (OARS) Multidimensional Functional Assessment Questionnaire developed at Duke University is the Social Resource Scale (Duke University Center for the Study of Aging and Human Development, 1978) (Box 4-15). This scale is one of the better known measures of general social functioning for older adults. The questions extract data about family structure, patterns of friendship and visiting, availability of a confidant, satisfaction with degree of social interaction, and availability of a helper in the event of illness or disability. Different questions (noted in italics in Box 4-15) are used for clients residing in institutions. The interviewer rates the client using a 6-point scale ranging from "excellent social resources" to "totally socially impaired" based on the responses to the questions.

Many other measures of social functioning can be found in the literature, but a lack of consensus by experts as to which are most suitable for use with older adults makes it difficult to recommend any one with certainty. The nurse should therefore use these tools with caution and care, remembering that it is crucial to attempt to screen for those older people at social risk.

For all of the additional assessment measures discussed above, the nurse should bear in mind that these are meant to augment the traditional health assessment, not replace it. Care needs to be taken to assure the tools are used appropriately with regard to purpose, setting, timing, and safety. Doing so can lead to a more accurate appraisal on which to base nursing diagnostic statements and to plan suitable and effective interventions.

LABORATORY DATA

The last component of a comprehensive assessment is evaluation of laboratory tests. The results of laboratory tests can validate history and physical examination findings, and can also identify potential health problems not pointed out by the client or the nurse. Data are considered with regard to established norms based on age and gender. See Chapter 19 for a comprehensive discussion of age-related changes in laboratory tests.

Summary

This chapter presented the components of a comprehensive nursing-focused assessment with an older adult, including special considerations to ensure an age-specific approach, as well as pragmatic modifications for conducting the assessment with this unique age group. Components of the health history and physical examination were discussed, with consideration given to additional functional status assessment measures that can be used with older adults. Compiling an accurate and thorough assessment of an older adult client, which serves as the foundation for application of the remaining steps of the nursing process, involves the blending of many skills, and is an art not easily mastered.

HOME CARE TIPS

1. Include social support systems, as well as environmental and safety needs in the assessment of the older adult.
2. Assessing and intervening when an older adult has vague signs and symptoms can reduce the risk of hospitalization.
3. Laboratory data are important indicators of the older adult's compliance to the medication regimen.
4. Obtain data from family members if the older adult has an ACS or dementia to ensure collection of reliable information.

Key Points

- The less vigorous response to illness and disease in older adults, coupled with the diminished stress response, causes an atypical presentation of and response to illness and disease.
- Cognitive change is one of the most common manifestations of illness in old age.
- An abrupt onset ACS in the older adult is not a normal expected outcome of aging.
- Conducting a health assessment with an older adult requires modification of the environment, consideration of the client's energy level and adaptability, and opportunity for demonstrating assets and capabilities.
- Sensory-perceptual deficits, anxiety, reduced energy level, pain, the multiplicity and interrelatedness of health problems, and the tendency to reminisce are the major factors requiring special consideration by the nurse while conducting the health history with the older adult.
- The older adult's physical health alone does not provide a reliable measure of functional ability; assessment of physical, cognitive, affective, and social function provides a comprehensive view of the older adult's total degree of functioning.
- The purpose of older adult assessment is to identify client strengths and limitations so that effective and appropriate interventions can be delivered to promote optimum functioning and to prevent disability and dependence.
- The older adult's reduced ability to respond to stress, the increased frequency and multiplicity of loss, and the physical changes associated with normal aging combine to place the older adult at high risk for loss of functional ability.
- A comprehensive assessment of an older adult's report of unspecific signs and symptoms is essential to determine the presence of underlying conditions that may lead to functional decline.
- To compensate for the lack of definitive standards for what constitutes "normal" in older adults, the nurse can compare the older client's own previous patterns of physical and psychosocial health and function with the client's current status.

Critical Thinking Exercises

1. You are interviewing a 78-year-old man just admitted to the hospital. He states he is hard of hearing; you note that he is restless and apprehensive. How would you revise your history-taking interview based on these initial observations?
2. Three individuals, ages 65, 81, and 98, have blood pres-

sure readings of 152/88, 168/90, and 170/92 respectively. The nurse infers that all older people are hypertensive. Analyze the nurse's conclusion. Is faulty logic being used in this situation? What assumption(s) did the nurse make with regard to older people in general?

REFERENCES

Abrams WB, Berkow R, editors: *The Merck manual of geriatrics,* Rahway, NJ, 1990, Merck.

American Nurses Association: *Nursing: a social policy statement,* Kansas City, Mo.,1980, The Association.

American Psychiatric Association: *Diagnostic and statistical manual of mental disorders (DSM-III-R), third edition revised,* Washington, DC, 1987, The Association.

Barkouskas VH et al: *Health and physical assessment,* St. Louis, 1994, Mosby.

Beck AT, Beck RW: Screening depressed patients in family practice: a rapid technique, *Postgrad Med* 52:81-85, 1972.

Burnside IM: *Nursing and the aged: a self-care approach,* ed 3, New York, 1988, McGraw-Hill.

Duke University Center for the Study of Aging and Human Development: *Multidimensional functional assessment: the OARS methodology,* Durham, NC, 1978, Duke University.

Folstein MF, Folstein SE, McHugh PR: Mini-mental state: practical method for grading the cognitive state of patients for the clinician, *J Psychiatr Res* 12:189-198, 1975.

Foreman, MD: Acute confusional states in hospitalized elderly: a research dilemma, *Nurs Res* 35:34-37, 1986.

Hall GR: This hospitalized patient has Alzheimer's, *AJN,* 10:44-50, 1991

Kane RA, Kane RL: *Assessing the elderly: a practical guide to measurement,* Lexington, MA, 1981, Lexington Books.

Katz S, et al: Studies of illness in the aged. The index of ADL: a standardized measure of biological and psychosocial function, *JAMA* 185:94-99, 1963.

Lawton HP, Brody EM: Assessment of older people: self maintaining and instrumental activities of daily living, *Gerontologist* 9:179-186, 1969.

Mahoney FI, Barthel DW: Functional evaluation: the Barthel index, *Maryland State Med J* 14:61-65, 1965.

Matteson MA, McConnell, EJ: *Gerontological nursing: concepts and practice,* Philadelphia, 1988, WB Saunders.

Pfeiffer E: A short portable mental status questionnaire for the assessment of organic brain deficit in elderly patients, *J Am Geriatr Soc* 23:433-441, 1975.

Physical frailty: a reducible barrier to independence for older Americans, Bethesda, MD, 1991, National Institute on Aging, NIH Pub No 91-397.

Smilkstein G, Ashworth C, Montano MA: Validity and reliability of the Family APGAR as a test of family function, *J Fam Prac* 15:303-311, 1982.

Yesavage JA, Brink TL: Development and validation of a geriatric depression screening scale: a preliminary report, *J Psychiatr Res* 17:37-49, 1983.

Part Two

Influences on Health and Illness

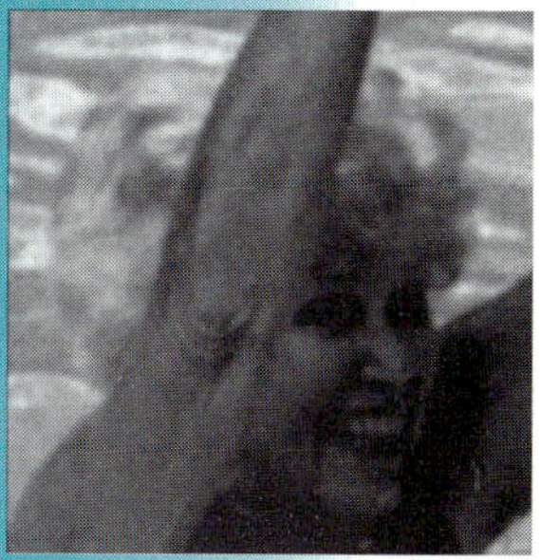

CHAPTER 5

Cultural Influences

LEARNING OBJECTIVES

On completion of this chapter, the reader will be able to:

1. Discuss the major demographic trends in the United States in relation to the various older adult ethnic populations.
2. Discuss the nursing implications of ethnic demographic changes.
3. Define culture and transcultural nursing care.
4. Discuss the dominant values of the African-American, Mexican-American, Filipino-American, and Native-American subcultures.
5. Explore cultural stumbling blocks and building blocks as related to care of older adults.
6. Discuss cultural variations in health and illness.
7. Apply culturally appropriate verbal and nonverbal communication techniques with older adult clients.
8. Explain the need for a nurse's cultural self-assessment when providing care to older adults from other ethnic groups.
9. Perform a cultural assessment using the Welch Culturologic Assessment Guide.
10. Discuss ways in which planning and implementation of nursing interventions can be adapted to an older adult's ethnicity.

DEMOGRAPHICS

Diversity of the Older Adult Population in the United States

The older adult population in the United States is larger and more diverse than it has ever been in its history. This population represents the broadest range of races; cultures; languages and ethnic groups; and political, educational, socioeconomic, religious, immigration, and historical experiences ever witnessed in this country (Burton, Dilworth-Anderson, 1991).

There is a larger percentage of racially, ethnically, and culturally diverse older people than ever before. There are currently 28 million Caucasian; 2.5 million African-American; 1.1 million Hispanic; 450,000 Asian/Pacific Islanders; and 116,000 Native American, Eskimo, and Aleut older adults in this country (US Bureau of the Census, 1993) (Table 5-1).

In the year 2,000 and beyond, the United States is expected to experience a "gerontologic explosion" of older adults age 65 and older from racially and ethnically di-

TABLE 5-1

Resident Population: White, Black, Asian/Pacific Islander, Native American, and Hispanic Origin Population, by Single Years of Age: 1991 (in thousands, except as indicated, as of July 1, resident population)

Age	White	Black	Native American, Eskimo, Aleut	Asian/ Pacific Islander	Hispanic origin*
55-59 years	9,037	2,050	65	271	656
55 years	1,825	229	14	60	140
56 years	1,909	217	14	55	143
57 years	1,789	212	13	55	130
58 years	1,697	188	12	49	120
59 years	1,816	204	12	52	123
60-64 years	9,312	979	54	237	580
60 years	1,858	203	12	51	126
61 years	1,847	194	11	48	120
62 years	1,822	196	11	47	115
63 years	1,900	189	10	45	113
64 years	1,884	198	10	45	107
65-69 years	8,926	873	44	194	458
65 years	1,820	198	10	44	102
66 years	1,838	182	9	40	97
67 years	1,806	173	9	38	92
68 years	1,703	161	8	37	85
69 years	1,758	159	8	35	81
70-74 years	7,412	663	32	135	312
70 years	1,688	157	8	34	77
71 years	1,551	144	7	30	68
72 years	1,484	130	7	28	61
73 years	1,372	118	6	23	54
74 years	1,317	114	5	22	51
75-79 years	5,679	489	23	88	223
75 years	1,271	108	5	21	49
76 years	1,211	99	5	19	47
77 years	1,125	97	5	18	44
78 years	1,086	97	4	16	44
79 years	985	87	4	15	39
80-84 years	3,677	297	13	47	141
80 years	881	73	3	12	35
81 years	802	67	3	10	31
82 years	732	56	3	9	27
83 years	676	51	2	8	25
84 years	585	49	2	8	22
85-89 years	1,915	147	7	21	72
90-94 years	741	60	3	8	26
95-99 years	194	17	1	2	7
100 years	36	7	†	1	2

*People of Hispanic origin may be of any race.
†Represents or rounds to zero.
From US Bureau of the Census: *Current population report* P25-1095, 1992.

verse populations (Angel, Hogan, 1991). It is projected by 2050 the older adult population will be even more diverse than in 1990. The African-American older adult population will more than quadruple (10 million) and their proportion of the total older adult population will increase from 8% to 12%. The largest growth in the older adult population will occur in the Hispanic groups—from 1.1 million to 8 million. Asian/Pacific Islanders, Native Americans, and Alaskans will increase by 5 million each (American Society of Retired Persons [AARP], 1991; US Bureau of the Census, 1993).

Immigrants from Other Countries

According to the Immigration and Naturalization Service (1994), 904,292 immigrants entered this country during 1993. Of these individuals, 39,869 were age 65 and older (Table 5-2). The largest number of immigrant older adults came from Vietnam, the former Soviet Union, the Philip-

TABLE 5-2

Immigrants Admitted By Age and Gender Fiscal Years 1983-93

Age and gender	1983	1984	1985	1986	1987	1988	1989	1990	1991	1992	1993
55-59 years	14,383	14,787	15,826	18,028	18,515	20,887	30,042	39,776	41,330	28,368	28,246
60-64 years	12,070	12,456	13,801	15,905	15,931	17,549	22,700	30,329	30,856	24,537	24,758
65-69 years	8,404	8,624	9,503	11,226	11,348	12,359	16,786	21,338	21,616	18,604	19,400
70-74 years	5,249	5,406	6,069	7,012	6,542	6,827	8,824	11,021	11,109	10,202	11,131
75-79 years	2,595	2,650	3,083	3,689	3,363	3,836	4,904	6,369	5,938	5,222	5,347
80 years and over	1,632	1,451	1,847	2,276	2,006	2,497	2,841	4,082	3,680	3,586	3,888
Unknown	*	*	*	*	70	25	150	190	373	135	103
Male											
55-59 years	5,494	5,903	6,442	7,329	7,738	9,245	13,583	18,904	23,893	12,496	11,916
60-64 years	4,835	5,257	5,696	6,627	6,691	7,482	9,917	13,275	15,741	10,767	10,318
65-69 years	3,523	3,692	4,159	4,800	5,148	5,665	7,445	9,180	10,331	8,150	8,110
70-74 years	2,214	2,316	2,607	3,003	2,888	2,956	3,826	4,639	5,047	4,559	4,841
75-79 years	1,038	1,126	1,290	1,549	1,434	1,608	2,019	2,518	2,611	2,206	2,284
80 years and over	623	606	688	949	873	1,027	1,095	1,467	1,507	1,451	1,565
Unknown	*	*	*	*	42	12	76	110	279	92	58
Female											
55-59 years	8,299	8,884	9,384	10,699	10,777	11,642	16,455	20,867	17,432	15,867	16,330
60-64 years	6,745	7,199	8,105	9,278	9,240	10,067	12,783	17,042	15,109	13,764	14,438
65-69 years	4,599	4,932	5,344	6,426	6,200	6,694	9,340	12,149	11,278	10,449	11,290
70-74 years	2,825	3,090	3,462	4,009	3,654	3,871	4,997	6,375	6,053	5,639	6,289
75-79 years	1,457	1,524	1,793	2,140	1,929	2,228	2,883	3,846	3,325	3,016	3,063
80 years and over	946	845	1,159	1,327	1,133	1,470	1,746	2,614	2,172	2,132	2,323
Unknown	*	*	*	*	28	13	74	80	94	43	45

*Represents zero; rounds to less than 0.05%

From US Department of Justice, Immigration and Naturalization Services: *1993 statistical yearbook of the immigration and naturalization services,* September 1994, The Department.

pines, mainland China, Mexico, and India. Table 5-3 depicts the 15 countries with the largest number of older adults emigrating to this country during the fiscal year 1993.

Increased immigration from countries once discriminated against by U.S. immigration policy is also adding to the growing diversity of the older adult population of America. In the early 1900s, most of the immigrants came to the United States from Europe. Changes in the immigration policy from the "quota system" to the "preference system" in 1965 increased the number of older adults entering from Asian countries such as the Philippines, Korea, India, China, and Hong Kong (Gelfand, Yee, 1991). The preference system permits the reunification of families. Most of these older adults have come to join their adult offspring, to be watched over and to be cared for, and reciprocally, to assist with housekeeping and child care of their grandchildren (Welch, 1982; 1987).

The Refugee Act of 1980 has dramatically increased the number of Cubans, Vietnamese, Laotians, Cambodians, and Soviet Jews in the United States. The number of older adults in the refugee and **asylee** group tends to be

TABLE 5-3

Top 15 Countries with the Largest Number of Older Adults Age 55 and Older Emigrating to the United States in 1993

Countries	Number of older adults
1. Vietnam	14,740
2. Soviet Union	12,878
3. Philippines	10,457
4. Mainland China	9,310
5. Mexico	6,180
6. India	5,820
7. Iran	3,877
8. Cuba	3,392
9. Dominican Republic	2,633
10. Korea	1,886
11. Poland	1,795
12. Peru	1,594
13. Haiti	1,245
14. El Salvador	1,170
15. Guyana	1,156

From US Department of Justice, Immigration and Naturalization Service: *1993 statistical yearbook of immigration and naturalization service,* September 1994, The Department.

small at this time. Of the refugee and **asylee** older adults age 55 and older, 19,531 were granted permanent resident status during 1993 (US Department of Justice, Immigration and Naturalization Service, 1994). The exact number of older adults age 55 and older from each country is not readily available at this time.

Geographic Areas of the United States with the Largest Racial Ethnic Populations

More than 50% of African-American older adults resided in the South in 1990. The states with 100,000 or more African-American older adults who are age 65 and older are California, Texas, Florida, Alabama, Louisiana, Georgia, North Carolina, Virginia, New York, Illinois, Michigan, Ohio, and Pennsylvania. The oldest old (age 85 years and older) African Americans were more widely dispersed across the country than other ethnic or racial groups. Older adults of all races age 85 and older resided in 20 states (US Bureau of the Census, 1993) (Fig. 5-1).

In 1990, 22 cities in the United States had 1,000 or more African-American older adults age 85 and older (Table 5-4).

In 1990 the largest percentage of Native American/Eskimo, and Aleut older adults age 65 and older were located in Oklahoma, California, Arizona, New Mexico, and New York. The cities with the largest number of Native--

TABLE 5-4

U.S. Cities with 1,000 or More Black Older Adults Age 85 Years and Older

New York City	13,828
Chicago	8,174
Detroit	7,005
Philadelphia	5,822
Los Angeles	4,535
Washington, D.C.	4,253
Baltimore	3,267
Memphis	2,843
Houston	2,840
St. Louis	2,515
New Orleans	2,346
Cleveland	2,272
Atlanta	2,157
Birmingham, Ala.	1,988
Dallas	1,643
Indianapolis	1,551
Cincinnati	1,269
Pittsburgh	1,249
Oakland, Calif.	1,243
Jacksonville, Fla.	1,199
Kansas City, Mo.	1,119
Nashville-Davidson, Tenn.	1,008

From US Bureau of the Census: Current Population Report, Special Studies, P 3-178 RV *Sixty-five plus in America,* Washington D.C., revised May 1993, US Government Printing Office.

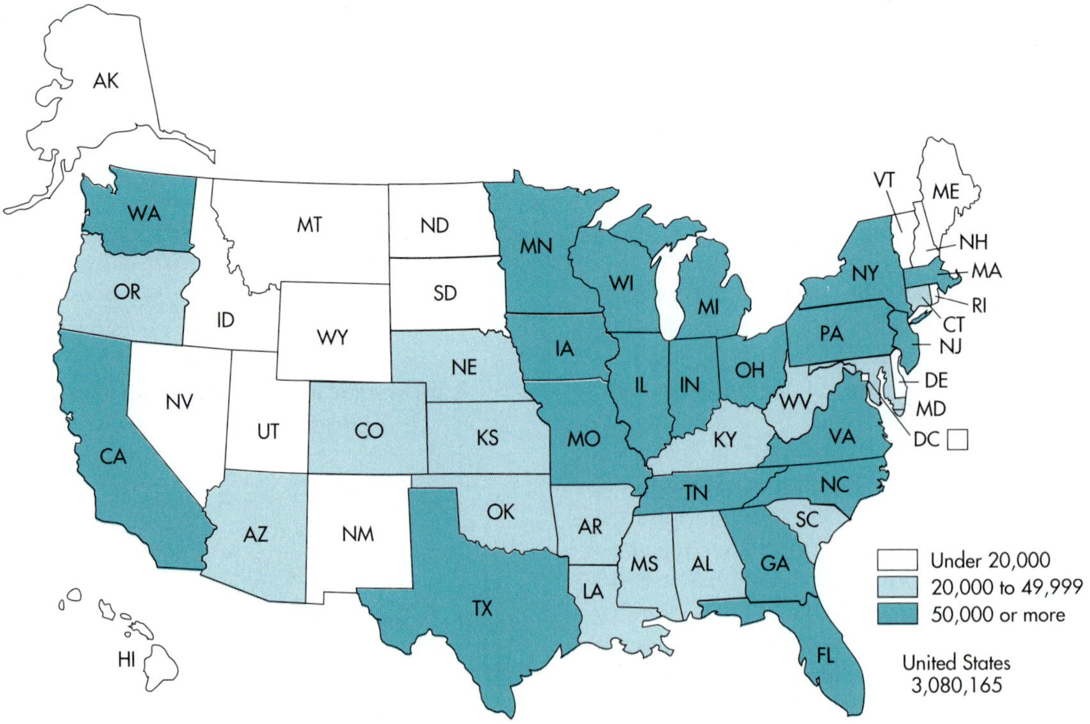

Fig. 5-1 Total population 85 years and over by state: 1990. (From US Bureau of the Census: *Census population and housing,* 1990 Summary Tape File 1A, The Bureau.)

TABLE 5-5

U.S. Cities with 1,000 or More Hispanic Older Adults Age 85 and Older

New York City	8,480
Los Angeles	4,365
Miami	4,254
San Antonio	3,272
El Paso, Tex.	2,055
Hialeah, Fla.	1,912
Chicago	1,262
Houston	1,091
San Francisco	1,013

American, Eskimo and Aleut older adults age 85 and older are New York City (148), Tulsa, OK (111), Oklahoma City (86), and Los Angeles (84).

The states with 5,000 or more Asian/Pacific Islanders age 65 and older in 1990 were Hawaii, California, Washington, Texas, Michigan, Pennsylvania, New York, Massachusetts, New Jersey, Delaware, Maryland, Virginia, and Florida. The majority of the oldest of these ethnic groups resided in California, Hawaii, Washington, Michigan, New York, and New Jersey (US Bureau of the Census, 1993).

The four cities with 1,000 or more Asian/Pacific Islanders age 85 and older in 1990 were Honolulu (3,922), Los Angeles (2,374), San Francisco (2,163), and New York City (2,112). Hispanic older adults are widely distributed along the Pacific, Gulf, North-Atlantic, and Mid-Atlantic coasts, as well as the Great Lakes.

Those states with 5,000 or more Hispanic older adults age 65 and older are Washington, California, Nevada, Arizona, Idaho, Colorado, Texas, Louisiana, Florida, Michigan, Indiana, Ohio, New York, Pennsylvania, Massachusetts, Connecticut, New Jersey, Delaware, Maryland, and Virginia (US Bureau of the Census, 1993). See Table 5-5 for the nine cities with the largest Hispanic older adult population age 85 and older in 1990.

Implications of Ethnic Demographic Changes for the Growth of Gerontologic Nursing

The explosion of older adult ethnic and cultural groups in the United States has implications for nursing as present and future practitioners are educated. The diversity of the older adult population by ethnicity, immigration, language, historic experience, social and economic status, and culture requires a nursing model that is broad and inclusive enough to provide a framework for delivering care that is culturally sensitive. Leininger's Theoretical Cultural Care Sunrise Model provides such a framework and is discussed on p. 128 of this chapter.

The continued growth in the immigrant populations from the Pacific Rim countries, Eastern Europe, the Soviet Union, the Middle East, and Africa may necessitate a broader, more culturally sensitive curriculum. Courses in anthropology (political, economic, and cultural), world religions, intercultural communication, scientific health and folk care systems, cross-cultural nutrition, and languages are relevant for nursing students. Consider that more than 1,000 languages are spoken by the Pacific Rim countries alone. Many immigrant older adults have difficulty learning English because of the unavailability of classes targeted for this population, or because of their own beliefs that they are too old to learn (Welch, 1987). This creates a need for nurses who are bilingual or multilingual. Nurses need formal preparation in transcultural nursing concepts to have the awareness, knowledge, skills, and attitudes to meet the health needs of a culturally diverse older adult population.

Today nurses may provide nursing care to clients from at least five ethnic groups in the course of 1 day. Nurses practicing in areas of the country with large ethnic, immigrant, and refugee older adult populations such as New York, California, Chicago, Minnesota, Florida, and Texas may have an even more diverse daily population. Table 5-6 depicts the ethnic mix of U.S. cities and states. Such information can lead schools of nursing, students, practitioners, and health care institutions to become more culturally sensitive to the diversity of their present and potential client population.

Another implication of the demographic data emanates from the diversity within groups. The Asian/Pacific Islander category includes Chinese, Filipinos, Japanese, Koreans, Asian Indians, Vietnamese, Hawaiians, Samoans, Guamanians, and others. The "other" category includes individuals from Burma, Malaysia, Singapore, Thailand, Laos, Cambodia, and Afghanistan. However, it is a misnomer to use the Asian category in an all-inclusive manner to teach cultural knowledge or to give care. Older adults in this category represent many countries, ethnic groups, languages, religions, etc. The same implication exists for Native Americans since this category includes more than 500 tribal groups.

A final important implication for the nurse providing culturally sensitive care is to ascertain whether the ethnic older adult came to this country as a child, a young adult, an older adult, or was born in the United States. This impacts their level of acculturation, eligibility for benefits and services, as well as nursing decisions and actions regarding care.

Providing nursing care for older adults is a transcultural experience. The context and process of nursing often involve individuals from very different cultures and lifeways. Transcultural knowledge of the various cultural groups in the practice setting can minimize frustration and cultural conflict between the older adult client, nurses, and other health care providers.

Text continued on p. 114

TABLE 5-6

Population of People Age 65 and Older in Cities with Populations of 100,000 or More, by Age, Race, and Hispanic Origin: 1990 (rank based on total, all races, all ages)

			Total, all races			Black		Native American, Eskimo and Aleut		Asian and Pacific Islander		Hispanic origin*	
Rank	State	City	All ages	65 years and over	85 years and over	65 years and over	85 years and over	65 years and over	85 years and over	65 years and over	85 years and over	65 years and over	85 years and over
1	NY	New York	7,322,564	953,317	102,554	174,798	13,828	1,771	148	33,214	2,112	108,702	8,480
2	CA	Los Angeles	3,485,398	347,713	35,419	51,893	4,535	958	84	31,891	2,374	50,058	4,365
3	IL	Chicago	2,783,726	330,182	30,522	98,181	8,174	414	36	8,361	499	19,283	1,262
4	TX	Houston	1,630,553	135,077	12,129	32,586	2,840	236	15	2,848	118	15,303	1,091
5	PA	Philadelphia	1,585,577	240,714	22,801	70,253	5,822	361	29	2,225	128	4,076	273
6	CA	San Diego	1,110,549	113,495	10,203	5,368	384	351	27	7,246	281	10,388	826
7	MI	Detroit	1,027,974	124,933	12,506	77,444	7,005	295	24	498	31	1,897	168
8	TX	Dallas	1,006,877	97,891	10,131	18,565	1,643	263	21	636	31	6,470	513
9	AZ	Phoenix	983,403	95,226	7,832	3,379	343	469	31	864	64	7,856	576
10	TX	San Antonio	935,933	98,365	9,421	6,895	667	235	17	513	31	38,524	3,272
11	CA	San Jose	782,248	56,358	5,022	1,105	83	180	11	8,810	451	7,894	639
12	MD	Baltimore	736,014	100,916	9,695	41,981	3,267	160	20	439	38	698	51
13	IN	Indianapolis	731,327	83,628	8,505	15,330	1,551	125	12	248	16	366	28
14	CA	San Francisco	723,959	105,380	12,148	9,932	763	196	16	27,168	2,163	9,094	1,013
15	FL	Jacksonville (remainder)	635,230	67,343	5,792	14,182	1,199	94	5	517	21	996	78
16	OH	Columbus	632,910	57,939	5,961	10,761	911	92	11	369	14	294	17
17	WI	Milwaukee	628,088	78,145	8,781	8,578	611	197	12	410	15	1,375	103
18	TN	Memphis	610,337	74,597	7,341	27,969	2,843	72	4	193	8	243	21
19	DC	Washington	606,900	77,847	7,847	52,263	4,253	184	14	785	69	1,585	149
20	MA	Boston	574,283	65,950	8,219	9,864	806	136	13	2,191	201	2,380	184
21	WA	Seattle	516,259	78,400	9,271	4,577	311	391	20	6,062	505	988	83
22	TX	El Paso	515,342	45,016	3,770	768	52	130	8	283	11	23,938	2,055
23	OH	Cleveland	505,616	70,753	6,612	27,266	2,272	119	9	297	23	1,029	65
24	LA	New Orleans	496,938	64,658	6,656	27,279	2,346	64	7	478	41	2,244	230
25	TN	Nashville-Davidson (remainder)	488,374	55,826	5,747	10,087	1,008	64	6	175	8	205	15
26	CO	Denver	467,610	64,805	7,648	5,207	486	267	25	912	63	6,547	537
27	TX	Austin	465,622	34,577	3,709	3,858	420	66	6	251	14	3,966	309
28	TX	Fort Worth	447,619	50,225	5,133	8,195	791	120	7	201	13	2,979	234
29	OK	Oklahoma City	444,719	52,779	5,310	5,653	570	1,277	86	317	20	768	65
30	OR	Portland	437,319	63,657	7,551	2,730	164	270	16	1,640	121	674	69
31	MO	Kansas City	435,146	56,166	6,393	11,910	1,119	139	10	247	17	1,143	109
32	CA	Long Beach	429,433	46,463	5,426	2,087	162	165	12	3,130	142	2,741	201
33	AZ	Tucson	405,390	51,198	5,228	1,360	120	315	38	325	16	7,350	635
34	MO	St. Louis	396,685	66,001	8,389	23,236	2,515	98	11	125	18	525	75
35	NC	Charlotte	395,934	38,802	3,603	8,188	642	56	3	175	6	272	17
36	GA	Atlanta	394,017	44,432	5,071	24,039	2,157	43	4	143	9	442	40
37	VA	Virginia Beach	393,069	23,214	1,846	2,062	164	31	1	724	13	261	20
38	NM	Albuquerque	384,736	42,767	3,761	668	58	445	28	250	10	9,066	746
39	CA	Oakland	372,242	44,855	5,303	16,038	1,243	154	13	5,555	395	2,692	276
40	PA	Pittsburgh	369,879	66,336	6,624	12,155	1,249	67	7	143	12	330	36
41	CA	Sacramento	369,365	44,619	4,464	3,748	272	260	14	5,144	400	3,453	284
42	MN	Minneapolis	368,383	47,718	7,475	2,006	171	285	11	508	32	319	38
43	OK	Tulsa	367,302	46,684	4,828	4,196	479	1,344	111	156	4	431	30
44	HI	Honolulu	365,272	58,279	5,312	169	17	49	2	43,075	3,922	1,318	107
45	OH	Cincinnati	364,040	50,726	6,230	14,220	1,269	51	7	186	13	132	19
46	FL	Miami	358,548	59,347	6,284	7,084	527	42	5	171	27	43,710	4,254
47	CA	Fresno	354,202	35,804	3,989	2,453	212	193	12	2,003	130	4,664	389

*Hispanic origin may be of any race.

From US Bureau of the Census: 1990 Census of Population and Housing, Summary Tape File 1-A, 1990.

TABLE 5-6

Population of People Age 65 and Older in Cities with Populations of 100,000 or More, by Age, Race, and Hispanic Origin: 1990 (rank based on total, all races, all ages)—cont'd

			Total, all races			Black		Native American, Eskimo and Aleut		Asian and Pacific Islander		Hispanic origin*	
Rank	State	City	All ages	65 years and over	85 years and over	65 years and over	85 years and over	65 years and over	85 years and over	65 years and over	85 years and over	65 years and over	85 years and over
48	NE	Omaha	335,795	43,297	4,980	3,284	328	114	4	107	10	580	45
49	OH	Toledo	332,943	45,201	4,421	5,507	472	51	2	140	12	613	52
50	NY	Buffalo	328,123	48,703	5,083	9,191	709	144	9	80	4	723	65
51	KS	Wichita	304,011	37,655	3,894	2,393	193	205	12	199	16	666	45
52	CA	Santa Ana	293,742	16,522	1,776	379	24	85	7	1,424	65	4,216	320
53	AZ	Mesa	288,091	35,713	2,933	241	31	88	5	112	4	992	78
54	CO	Colorado Springs	281,140	25,781	2,545	605	39	109	12	292	8	1,115	85
55	FL	Tampa	280,015	40,934	4,104	6,130	600	80	7	130	4	7,916	818
56	NJ	Newark	275,221	25,547	2,139	12,882	943	54	6	138	10	3,421	259
57	MN	St. Paul	272,235	37,412	5,309	1,112	111	120	12	556	22	540	55
58	KY	Louisville	269,063	44,641	5,064	9,750	970	45	5	75	5	172	18
59	CA	Anaheim	266,406	22,292	2,266	104	5	69	7	1,257	77	2,123	165
60	AL	Birmingham	265,968	39,480	4,552	19,254	1,988	29	3	31	3	95	8
61	TX	Arlington	261,721	13,012	1,038	171	7	57	7	188	11	330	18
62	VA	Norfolk	261,229	27,458	2,313	8,970	660	43	1	321	11	245	18
63	NV	Las Vegas	258,295	26,532	1,566	1,761	119	114	5	525	20	1,406	71
64	TX	Corpus Christi	257,453	25,933	2,186	1,439	116	71	5	119	2	9,035	680
65	FL	St. Petersburg	238,629	52,945	7,975	4,034	340	49	8	143	12	828	89
66	NY	Rochester	231,636	28,135	4,036	3,542	265	73	6	112	4	770	49
67	NJ	Jersey City	228,537	25,287	2,384	4,145	292	46	1	1,307	53	2,384	154
68	CA	Riverside	226,505	20,266	2,116	975	85	101	3	411	14	2,143	173
69	AK	Anchorage	226,338	8,258	374	328	14	420	24	538	17	141	10
70	KY	Lexington-Fayette	225,366	22,312	2,308	2,778	285	17	2	66	3	81	6
71	OH	Akron	223,019	33,171	3,470	5,179	401	42	6	62	2	124	17
72	CO	Aurora	222,103	15,044	1,135	445	26	45	2	424	19	414	31
73	LA	Baton Rouge	219,531	25,161	2,356	7,685	662	26	4	92	5	281	19
74	CA	Stockton	210,943	22,107	2,213	1,741	124	131	5	3,346	295	2,873	204
75	NC	Raleigh	207,951	18,332	1,814	3,814	358	20	2	102	8	110	7
76	VA	Richmond	203,056	31,181	3,435	12,345	934	44	2	91	4	141	16
77	LA	Shreveport	198,525	27,206	3,105	8,203	947	34	9	31	3	151	15
78	MS	Jackson	196,637	22,851	2,247	8,080	815	12	2	31	3	86	7
79	AL	Mobile	196,278	26,900	2,618	7,718	672	31	3	59	3	199	18
80	IA	Des Moines	193,187	25,884	3,053	1,325	123	40	5	167	11	251	22
81	NE	Lincoln	191,972	21,005	2,674	198	13	29	2	92	2	148	8
82	WI	Madison	191,262	17,831	2,211	210	15	14	0	155	5	104	5
83	MI	Grand Rapids	189,126	24,711	3,508	2,077	159	48	2	65	7	281	27
84	NY	Yonkers	188,082	30,935	2,979	1,684	158	13	2	256	9	1,410	118
85	FL	Hialeah	188,004	26,338	2,362	292	20	14	0	52	8	22,747	1,912
86	AL	Montgomery	187,106	21,884	2,185	6,574	680	21	0	33	1	87	10
87	TX	Lubbock	186,206	18,299	1,842	1,143	98	32	3	40	1	1,580	91
88	NC	Greensboro	183,521	21,591	2,239	4,736	442	43	4	71	2	96	7
89	OH	Dayton	182,044	23,929	2,060	7,931	568	28	0	56	6	71	5
90	CA	Huntington Beach	181,519	15,088	1,211	24	2	33	4	825	46	660	74
91	TX	Garland	180,650	9,970	715	381	33	30	2	263	4	416	24
92	CA	Glendale	180,038	23,977	3,208	78	10	32	7	1,306	59	2,075	221
93	GA	Columbus (remainder)	178,681	19,254	1,570	5,138	442	15	0	67	2	191	8

Continued.

TABLE 5-6

Population of People Age 65 and Older in Cities with Populations of 100,000 or More, by Age, Race, and Hispanic Origin: 1990 (rank based on total, all races, all ages)—cont'd

			Total, all races			Black		Native American, Eskimo and Aleut		Asian and Pacific Islander		Hispanic origin*	
Rank	State	City	All ages	65 years and over	85 years and over	65 years and over	85 years and over	65 years and over	85 years and over	65 years and over	85 years and over	65 years and over	85 years and over
94	WA	Spokane	177,196	28,788	3,539	296	17	160	8	344	24	195	16
95	WA	Tacoma	176,664	24,658	3,235	1,118	72	178	13	553	24	278	18
96	AR	Little Rock	175,795	22,071	2,497	4,461	545	32	2	62	3	58	6
97	CA	Bakersfield	174,820	15,998	1,696	1,323	144	115	14	368	25	1,160	94
98	CA	Fremont	173,339	11,541	951	123	4	42	3	1,705	67	1,023	71
99	IN	Fort Wayne	173,072	23,091	2,807	1,637	117	19	0	47	5	200	11
100	VA	Arlington	170,936	19,409	1,738	1,357	106	27	3	542	29	700	61
101	VA	Newport News	170,045	15,804	1,192	4,400	254	17	1	123	5	140	7
102	MA	Worcester	169,759	27,287	3,466	301	27	37	3	96	4	508	35
103	TN	Knoxville	165,121	25,441	2,708	2,979	271	40	5	29	3	58	4
104	CA	Modesto	164,730	17,268	1,769	260	22	99	4	441	24	1,001	70
105	FL	Orlando	164,693	18,755	2,180	3,101	262	15	0	98	10	1,111	88
106	CA	San Bernardino	164,164	16,396	1,616	1,658	153	99	9	266	11	2,754	228
107	NY	Syracuse	163,860	24,394	3,327	1,784	189	86	7	81	2	175	16
108	RI	Providence	160,728	21,802	2,659	1,379	111	90	17	263	19	839	55
109	UT	Salt Lake City	159,936	23,192	2,832	228	13	43	3	468	45	878	63
110	AL	Huntsville	159,789	15,982	1,351	2,137	240	30	1	85	0	79	4
111	TX	Amarillo	157,615	18,974	1,876	771	73	77	5	77	4	745	57
112	MA	Springfield	156,983	21,568	2,384	2,024	166	22	3	64	1	744	52
113	TX	Irving	155,037	8,413	645	122	10	22	1	172	11	412	24
114	TN	Chattanooga	152,466	23,269	2,584	5,713	577	29	6	44	2	67	4
115	VA	Chesapeake	151,976	12,844	991	3,223	230	24	0	73	5	95	7
116	KS	Kansas City	149,767	19,489	2,022	4,163	503	67	8	73	1	614	52
117	LA	Metairie CDP	149,428	21,013	1,474	537	35	11	0	129	6	903	79
118	FL	Fort Lauderdale	149,377	26,562	3,351	2,156	142	21	2	60	2	991	89
119	AZ	Glendale	148,134	11,675	1,154	143	7	42	1	194	16	882	77
120	MI	Warren	144,864	21,555	1,677	35	2	30	1	98	6	172	8
121	NC	Winston-Salem	143,485	20,331	2,355	5,497	531	21	0	37	0	55	4
122	CA	Garden Grove	143,050	12,512	1,083	60	5	53	1	1,400	71	917	72
123	CA	Oxnard	142,216	11,003	876	445	21	61	2	925	45	2,924	200
124	AZ	Tempe	141,865	9,305	850	90	4	25	2	136	13	506	41
125	CT	Bridgeport	141,686	19,245	2,064	2,190	133	16	0	90	3	1,592	117
126	NJ	Paterson	140,891	13,551	1,197	2,706	170	24	0	57	2	2,245	129
127	MI	Flint	140,761	15,100	1,619	4,294	300	55	7	28	3	199	27
128	MO	Springfield	140,494	21,329	2,696	301	30	77	4	45	4	60	9
129	CT	Hartford	139,739	13,809	1,536	3,453	240	32	4	72	8	1,475	108
130	IL	Rockford	139,426	20,535	2,644	1,167	80	14	1	68	5	213	18
131	GA	Savannah	137,560	18,957	1,576	7,758	635	16	2	79	6	98	12
132	NC	Durham	136,611	15,443	1,677	5,405	522	17	2	60	0	52	3
133	CA	Chula Vista	135,163	15,767	1,417	199	13	50	3	833	55	2,903	197
134	NV	Reno	133,850	15,802	1,264	251	16	80	3	334	13	556	39
135	VA	Hampton	133,793	12,801	898	3,985	290	32	2	75	6	106	5
136	CA	Ontario	133,179	8,489	706	267	13	47	0	188	7	1,459	111
137	CA	Torrance	133,107	15,900	1,546	56	7	28	2	1,620	97	831	69
138	CA	Pomona	131,723	9,191	1,036	883	68	43	1	409	12	1,777	125
139	CA	Pasadena	131,591	17,338	2,500	2,372	289	43	7	974	58	1,522	128
140	CT	New Haven	130,474	16,067	1,965	2,925	225	40	7	53	6	546	50

*Hispanic origin may be of any race.

TABLE 5-6

Population of People Age 65 and Older in Cities with Populations of 100,000 or More, by Age, Race, and Hispanic Origin: 1990 (rank based on total, all races, all ages)—cont'd

			Total, all races			Black		Native American, Eskimo and Aleut		Asian and Pacific Islander		Hispanic origin*	
Rank	State	City	All ages	65 years and over	85 years and over	65 years and over	85 years and over	65 years and over	85 years and over	65 years and over	85 years and over	65 years and over	85 years and over
141	AZ	Scottsdale	130,069	21,199	1,901	42	1	54	6	82	1	302	23
142	TX	Plano	128,713	4,577	437	152	15	11	1	142	1	123	8
143	CA	Oceanside	128,398	18,010	1,193	186	8	43	3	377	15	1,072	78
144	MI	Lansing	127,321	12,171	1,205	1,131	90	45	1	68	2	351	18
145	CO	Lakewood	126,481	13,343	1,448	66	5	24	3	155	9	493	68
146	CA	East Los Angeles	126,379	9,617	1,017	25	3	38	2	417	32	8,255	879
147	IN	Evansville	126,272	21,661	2,464	1,369	142	33	2	18	2	67	7
148	ID	Boise City	125,738	14,970	1,627	25	5	30	4	63	5	188	23
149	FL	Tallahassee	124,773	10,946	1,035	2,546	245	9	1	59	3	119	16
150	NV	Paradise	124,682	15,864	692	373	13	47	1	279	9	716	35
151	TX	Laredo	122,899	10,020	1,019	4	0	9	2	14	1	9,253	943
152	FL	Hollywood	121,697	28,101	3,817	557	55	15	0	88	5	1,287	122
153	KS	Topeka	119,883	17,681	2,100	1,236	153	90	3	59	3	515	37
154	TX	Pasadena	119,363	9,142	677	25	3	27	2	46	1	952	56
155	CA	Moreno Valley	118,779	4,734	211	369	18	27	4	338	10	616	27
156	MI	Sterling Heights	117,810	10,872	856	16	0	10	2	163	8	76	3
157	CA	Sunnyvale	117,229	12,191	1,015	81	4	17	0	1,374	59	1,047	85
158	IN	Gary	116,646	13,261	992	9,059	663	17	2	13	0	571	38
159	TX	Beaumont	114,323	15,737	1,668	4,405	430	21	1	80	5	349	26
160	CA	Fullerton	114,144	11,668	1,251	68	5	36	2	604	28	878	85
161	IL	Peoria	113,504	16,381	1,756	1,359	93	12	2	53	4	116	11
162	CA	Santa Rosa	113,313	18,472	1,960	64	5	72	1	184	12	453	43
163	OR	Eugene	112,669	14,276	1,710	43	2	31	3	61	5	116	8
164	MO	Indepenence	112,301	16,148	1,547	92	17	45	2	42	2	75	7
165	KS	Overland Park	111,790	11,068	950	43	3	23	1	82	3	77	8
166	CA	Hayward	111,498	11,910	1,076	296	29	57	4	1,901	74	1,572	128
167	CA	Concord	111,348	10,543	1,009	63	3	41	5	524	27	563	53
168	VA	Alexandria	111,183	11,406	1,380	1,615	133	7	2	262	6	236	12
169	CA	Orange	110,658	9,631	1,070	33	2	33	2	436	27	759	76
170	CA	Santa Clarita	110,642	6,916	563	42	6	48	3	202	4	390	18
171	CA	Irvine	110,330	6,357	527	30	1	8	1	671	27	210	10
172	NJ	Elizabeth	110,002	13,270	1,289	1,278	111	17	2	136	9	2,524	164
173	CA	Inglewood	109,602	7,494	778	3,291	265	27	1	194	14	1,050	72
174	MI	Ann Arbor	109,592	7,881	990	620	58	8	1	139	11	74	13
175	CA	Vallejo	109,199	11,851	978	1,725	97	48	6	1,802	95	684	57
176	CT	Waterbury	108,961	17,925	1,864	1,037	87	23	0	22	0	565	49
177	CA	Salinas	108,777	9,048	853	129	10	68	4	894	69	1,667	111
178	IA	Cedar Rapids	108,751	14,324	1,732	157	14	11	0	25	0	72	6
179	PA	Erie	108,718	17,488	1,638	789	56	14	1	24	1	86	4
180	CA	Escondido	108,635	14,074	1,778	23	3	58	7	189	15	774	70
181	CT	Stamford	108,056	14,333	1,521	1,244	96	12	1	141	9	476	39
182	OR	Salem	107,786	15,679	1,862	26	3	80	10	100	5	167	16
183	CA	Citrus Heights	107,439	10,326	708	75	4	54	3	140	3	287	11
184	TX	Abilene	106,654	12,568	1,533	527	59	19	1	34	3	647	43
185	GA	Macon	106,612	15,521	1,401	5,416	491	17	4	12	2	51	1
186	CA	El Monte	106,209	6,824	620	26	4	30	3	828	34	2,404	186
187	IN	South Bend	105,511	17,740	1,932	2,067	161	20	1	40	1	127	9
188	IL	Springfield	105,227	15,632	1,878	986	94	23	5	38	4	81	6

Continued.

TABLE 5-6

Population of People Age 65 and Older in Cities with Populations of 100,000 or More, by Age, Race, and Hispanic Origin: 1990 (rank based on total, all races, all ages)—cont'd

			Total, all races			Black		Native American, Eskimo and Aleut		Asian and Pacific Islander		Hispanic origin*	
Rank	State	City	All ages	65 years and over	85 years and over	65 years and over	85 years and over	65 years and over	85 years and over	65 years and over	85 years and over	65 years and over	85 years and over
189	PA	Allentown	105,090	17,767	1,950	186	6	9	0	53	3	323	14
190	CA	Thousand Oaks	104,352	9,427	958	34	2	24	0	247	14	327	36
191	VA	Portsmouth	103,907	14,399	1,083	5,687	415	21	1	45	4	74	8
192	TX	Waco	103,590	15,450	1,854	2,424	273	20	0	19	1	965	79
193	MA	Lowell	103,439	12,510	1,449	80	8	7	0	218	13	290	21
194	CA	Berkeley	102,724	11,252	1,459	3,313	325	30	1	1,239	119	344	38
195	TX	Mesquite	101,484	5,365	568	39	3	15	2	102	2	202	10
196	CA	Rancho Cucamonga	101,409	5,125	332	138	9	20	3	224	9	644	41
197	NY	Albany	101,082	15,495	2,338	1,267	104	19	2	64	3	139	17
198	MI	Livonia	100,850	13,180	1,395	17	4	17	1	81	7	96	9
199	SD	Sioux Falls	100,814	11,775	1,520	32	3	36	0	12	0	32	3
200	CA	Simi Valley	100,217	5,273	389	38	0	18	0	226	11	380	28

*Hispanic origin may be of any race.

TERMS GERMANE TO CULTURE

The terms *race, ethnicity,* and *culture* are often used interchangeably and incorrectly by health professionals and nonprofessionals alike in general discussions and in the literature. These and other terms are defined in the following as they are used in the subfield of transcultural nursing.

Race is defined as "a division of the species which differs from other divisions by the frequency with which certain hereditary traits appear among its members" (Bruce, 1977). Hereditary traits include skin and eye color; facial structure; shape of the eyes, nose, and lips; texture of the hair; and shape and proportions of the body. The racial differences have developed in response to earlier environmental conditions and continue to evolve. There are four major racial groups world wide: Caucasoid, Mongoloid, Negroid, and Australoid. Native Americans are descendants of the Mongoloid race (Overfield, 1985).

Ethnicity differs from race in that it is based on socialization and not on hereditary traits. Ethnicity is defined as a social differentiation of people based on group membership, shared history, common place of origin, shared values, perceptions, feelings, assumptions, and physical characteristics (Matteson, McConnell, 1988).

Ethnic identity is the willingness of an individual to identify and embrace the rules, customs, values, history, and perceptions of the group. The nurse needs to understand that with ethnic identity, the individual chooses to be identified with the group.

Culture is "learned and transmitted knowledge about a particular culture with its values, beliefs, rules of behavior, and lifestyle practices that guides a designated group in their thinking and actions in patterned ways" (Leininger, 1995).

Subculture is a "fairly large aggregation of people who are members of a larger cultural group, that have shared characteristics which are not common to all members of the culture, and which enable them to be thought of as a distinguishable subgroup" (Saunders, 1954).

Acculturation is "a process of cultural change in individuals leading them to adopt elements of one or more cultural groups distinct from their own" (Werner, 1979).

Enculturation is the process of acquiring knowledge, and internalizing values, ways of thinking and acting as transmitted by previous generations, to become a competent adult in the culture of their community. A simple way of defining enculturation is to say it is the process of learning a person's culture. This process is also known as as socialization in sociology and psychology.

Assimilation involves:

> ...two distinct processes: (1) The disappearance of outward behavior traits that distinguish a minority population or an individual from the host culture; and (2) The disappearance of exclusive and discriminatory behavior on the

part of the members of the host culture which permits the minority group or individual to join the host society (Keifer, 1974).

"**Cultural adaptation** is the process by which a cultural or subcultural group learns to adjust, to cope, or to struggle with modes of behavior and attributes of other cultures to meet cultural expectations, live by desired norms, and/or to survive" (Leininger, 1995).

Transcultural nursing is:

> ...the subfield of nursing which focuses upon a comparative study and analysis of different cultures and subcultures in the world with respect to their caring behavior; nursing care; and health-illness, values, beliefs and patterns of behavior with the goal of developing a scientific and humanistic body of knowledge in order to provide culture-specific and culture-universal nurse care practices (Leininger, 1995).

CULTURE CONCEPTS

This section explores the nature and characteristics of culture, human value orientation, common U.S. values, as well as the dominant values of four ethnic older adult populations, and ends by describing cultural stumbling and building blocks.

Three scientific postulates were formulated by Herskovits in 1955 concerning the nature of culture:

1. Culture is universal in [human] experience, yet each local or regional manifestation of it is unique.
2. Culture is stable, yet is also dynamic, and manifests constant change.
3. Culture fills and largely determines the course of [people's] lives, yet rarely intrudes into conscious thought.

Out of these postulates the following basic characteristics of culture have evolved.

Characteristics of Culture

Culture is learned and transmitted from one generation to another through the process of enculturation, socialization, and language acquisition from birth through old age. It provides individuals with a blueprint for interacting within the family, community, and country. White (1959) states that "the purpose and function of culture is to make life secure and enduring to the human species." Therefore culture provides security for the individual and group. It allows members of the culture to predict each other's behavior and respond appropriately.

Culture is universal. It is a phenomenon found in all parts of the world where people reside. It is unique. No two cultures are exactly alike; there are similarities, but there are distinct differences that make them unique. Culture is stable in that it has been present through many generations.

Culture is dynamic, continuously evolving. All aspects of culture do not change simultaneously. Dominant values change less rapidly than superficial ones. This can be illustrated by the following example. Immigrants coming to America may immediately change their style of dress because of the climate or their desire to be less conspicuous, but their food habits, religion, values, beliefs, family roles and relationship, and communication styles remain the same.

Variability is another characteristic of culture. Factors such as age, education, social and educational status, use of language of the dominant culture, and whether the individual resided in the urban or rural area in the country of origin all affect the degree of adherence to cultural values, beliefs, and lifeways (Clark, 1992; Samovar, Porter, 1991).

Culture is adaptive. It is responsive to changes in the conditions of the environment, availability of resources, cultural contact with other cultures, and technologic development.

Another characteristic of culture is that it is integrated. All components of culture are interrelated and function as a whole. Universal components of culture include religion, kinship, food, dress, language, styles of communication, education, economics, politics, social systems, roles and relationships, health and healing practices, technology, and art. All of these components together provide the cultural context. When nurses conduct cultural research on the various subcultures, they must include the cultural context because the components are interrelated.

The final characteristic is that culture is **ethnocentric** (Samovar, Porter, 1991). "Each culture places its own culture and society in a central position of priority and worth" (Keesing, 1965). One's culture is the lens through which others are viewed and judged.

Cultural behavior is both ideal and manifest. In all societies, there are discrepancies between what people say they believe and do in specific situations and what they actually do. **Culture manifest** represents the behaviors, beliefs, and feelings of a group that outsiders can readily observe. **Cultural ideals** are the behaviors members of the society say should occur. Cultures make allowances for behaviors that differ from the ideal.

The following example illustrates culture ideals and manifest. The immigrant older adult Filipino women stated that they ate very healthy diets—fresh fish with many fresh fruits and vegetables. During participant observations at family meals and senior citizen gatherings, it was observed that the fish was served with patis or bagoong (commercial fish sauces) both of which are extremely high in sodium. Also, dried fish was often consumed. Salt was often sprinkled on fresh fruit, and Accént seasoning was used on vegetables during cooking. It was very helpful to watch food being prepared and consumed to observe the differ-

ences between what the participants said and believed they were doing versus what actually occurred.

Values

Values are a universal feature of all cultures. They provide the framework for beliefs, attitudes, and behavior. Values are learned early in childhood, during the process of enculturation. Samovar and Porter (1991) defined values "as a standard or criterion for guiding action, for developing and maintaining attitudes toward relevant objects and situations, for justifying one's own and others' actions and attitudes, for morally judging self and others, and for comparing self with others." Individuals are often unaware of their values, but are able to describe their beliefs and customs.

There are three levels of values: (1) primary, (2) secondary, and (3) tertiary. Primary values are those for which one would go to war and sacrifice human life. Secondary values are important but are not strong enough to sacrifice human life. These values are important enough to cause people to provide aid and other humanitarian measures. For example, the people of the United States were recently concerned enough about people dying of starvation in Somalia and Ethiopia to send food, but generally were not supportive when the armed forces were deployed to Somalia with a possibility that human life would be lost.

Tertiary values are at the bottom of the hierarchy of values. The level of classification a value is given is culturally determined.

Cultural examples of the classification of values may further clarify the system. In the African-American, Filipino-American, and Mexican-American cultures, the extended family is primary, whereas it is tertiary in the white, middle- and upper-class Protestant culture in the United States. Universal health care is a primary value in Canada, but it is a secondary value in the United States and a tertiary value in Mexico, Africa, and many Third World countries. Punctuality is a primary value in the white middle- and upper-class cultures of the United States, but it is secondary in the African-American culture and tertiary in the Native-American and Eastern cultures.

The classic work completed on value orientation was done by Kluckhohn and Strodtbeck (1961). They developed a tool whereby cultures could be compared and contrasted to identify their basic value orientation. They defined value orientation as "complex but definitely patterned (rank ordered) principles...which give order and direction to the ever flowing stream of human acts and thoughts as these relate to the solution of 'common human problems.'" Five basic questions were considered by the authors as basic to any culture's value system:

1. What is man's innate human nature? (human nature orientation)
2. What is man's relationship to nature? (man-nature orientation)
3. What is man's significant time dimension? (time orientation)
4. What is the purpose of man's being? (activity orientation)
5. What is man's relationship with his fellow man? (social orientation)

These five key questions became the framework of the model for comparing cultures' value orientations. They were able to show that a dominant value orientation can be identified for all culture groups, even though there are some variances among the individual members. Table 5-7 describes various ethnic groups' views on these key notions from Kluckhohn and Strodtbeck's framework

Dominant American Values

People generally are not conscious of their values because they are stored on the unconscious level. The assistance of a social scientist, ethicist, or transcultural nurse is often needed to assess cultural values. It is imperative that nurses be aware of the dominant values of the middle-class, white American culture, as well as their own personal values and the impact of those values on their thoughts and actions. Knowledge of value differences and similarities of the client, institution, and professional nurse can minimize tension, cultural conflict, avoidance, and ineffective nursing actions.

The dominant middle-class, white American values are individuality, achievement and success, democracy, money, freedom, punctuality, independence, competition, privacy, cleanliness, health, equality, rationality, material wealth, comfort, humanitarianism, science, automation and technology, education, and respectability. (Leininger, 1989; Samovar, Porter, 1991). The following is a brief discussion of some of these values with specific relevance to nursing.

Individuality

The middle-class, white American value of rugged individualism has its roots in the founding of the nation. Many of our early leaders, presidents, pioneers, and heroes were self-made individuals. The American culture emphasizes the importance of the individual over the group. Childbearing practices focus on the development of a strong sense of self and individual identity. Individuality is a primary value in America and a tertiary value in Eastern cultures.

The Eastern perspective is the opposite—the group is more important than the individual. People of Eastern cultures obtain their identity from affiliation with and participation in the social context. They develop a strong social ego, self is minimized, and group awareness is maximized.

TABLE 5-7

Comparative Chart of Various Cultures

Ethnic group	Basic human nature	Relationship to nature	Relationship to other people	Activity orientation	Time orientation
Anglo-American Middle and Upper Class	Basically evil	Mastery over nature	Individual	Doing	Future
Southern Appalachian	Evil	Subjugated	Lineal-collateral	Being	Present
African-American	Basically evil	Subjugated	Collateral-lineal	Being	Present
Mexican-American	Good	Subjugated	Collateral-lineal	Being	Present
Navajo/Native-American	Neutral	Harmony	Collateral-lineal	Being	Present
Arab-American Muslim	Neutral	Subjugated	Lineal	Being	Present
Filipino-American	Good	Subjugated	Lineal	Being	Present
Cambodian-American	Neutral	Harmony	Lineal	Being	Present
East Indians Hindu	Neutral	Subjugated	Lineal	Being	
Korean-American	Neutral	Harmony	Lineal	Being	Past

When a Caucasian nurse who values individuality provides care for an Asian client who has a group orientation, there is the potential for cultural conflict, illustrated by the following scenario.

> An older Filipino woman is seen in her home by a public health nurse and found to have a blood pressure of 210/100 mm Hg, and a blood sugar of 380 mg/110 ml. The nurse insists on calling the client's physician and arranging immediate transportation to the health facility of the physician's choice. The older Filipina insists that she must wait until her son-in-law and daughter get off work to tell them of her condition. The daughter and her husband must decide where and when the client will go for treatment. She is concerned about the welfare of the family and wants to ensure that income is not lost by leaving work early. The family also jointly decides if they can afford a doctor's visit and a possible hospitalization, since the client does not have health insurance. The nurse's main concern is the health of the individual older adult Filipina, and the client's concern is the family. The nurse is operating from the American value that says an individual is independent and responsible for personal health care decisions (Welch, 1987).

Punctuality

Punctuality is a primary value in middle-class, white American culture. Schedules, appointments, and the rhythms of the clock organize the business and personal lives of Americans. Time is considered money. Individuals are expected to arrive for appointments on time.

This value is not shared by many of the subcultures in America. African Americans, Mexican Americans, Filipino Americans, and Native Americans believe in completing the activity in which they are presently involved rather than interrupting it to keep an appointment. Being on times means arriving a half hour to an hour late for most of their business and social interactions. In some Asian cultures, it is considered impolite to arrive early or at the designated time (Herberg, 1995).

In African-American health care facilities, several clients are given the same appointment time, and the first appointments are given a couple of hours before the physician is scheduled to arrive. This scheduling regimen assures that clients will be present and staff will complete the examination in a timely manner. Clients are placed at somewhat of an inconvenience. Punctuality is a secondary value in the African-American culture and a tertiary value in Eastern cultures.

Competition

Competition is highly valued in the middle-class, white American culture. It is reflected in all phases of American life: employment, entertainment, education, and politics. In Native-American, Asian, and Appalachian cultures it is considered impolite to compete with others. Cooperation is the valued behavior in preference to competition. In the 1990s, a shift appears to be emerging in the nursing education and nursing service value for competitive employees. Employment ads are beginning to appear for the "team player." Before 1990 employees who were aggressive and competitive were sought after, promoted, and valued. More recently, there appears to be a change to team players and cooperation becoming the value.

Cleanliness

Cleanliness is a primary middle-class, white American and nursing value. Americans are overzealous about personal cleanliness and clean environments, for example, in the office, home, public buildings, parks, and streets.

A clean mind, body, and spirit are tenets of the Judeo-Christian ethic. "Cleanliness is next to godliness" is an American proverb that illustrates this value. In fact, Americans consider themselves the cleanest people in the world, taking great pride in bathing daily. Americans soak, wash, and rinse in the same bath water, but wash clothes and dishes using different water for each step. According to Japanese standard, American bodies are dirty at the end of the bathing process. The Japanese bathe before entering the tub, soak, then rinse; all three steps use fresh water.

In the hospital setting, nursing staff spend significant amounts of time bathing clients and changing bed linens. Clients are often admitted to the hospital in the afternoon or evening, their bodies are bathed, and their bed linen is changed the next morning, even when it is not indicated. Beds with clean white linen and tidy, organized rooms are the norm for American hospitals and nursing homes. These examples illustrate Americans' obsession with cleanliness.

Independence

The value of independence is a primary middle-class, white American value. This was illustrated in how the 13

BOX 5-1

Anglo-American Culture (Mainly U.S. Middle and Upper Class)

Cultural values are:
Individualism—focus on a self-reliant person
Independence and freedom
Competition and achievement
Materialism (things and money)
Technology dependent
Instant time and actions
Youth and beauty
Equal sex rights
Leisure time highly valued
Reliance on scientific facts and numbers
Less respect for authority and older adults
Generosity in time of crisis

Culture care meanings and action modes are:
Alleviate stress
- Physical means
- Emotional means

Personalized acts
- Doing special things
- Giving individual attention

Self-reliance (individualism) by:
- Reliance on self
- Reliance on self (self-care)
- Becoming as independent as [possible]
- Reliance on technology

Health instruction
- Explain how "to do" this care for self
- Give the "medical" facts

From Miklininger M, editor: Culture care diversity and universality: a theory of nursing, New York, 1991, National League of Nursing.

BOX 5-2

Appalachian Culture*

Cultural values are:	Culture care meanings and action modes are:
Keep ties with kin from the "hollows"	Knowing and trusting "true friends"
Personalized religion	Being kind to others
Folk practices as "the best lifeways"	Being watchful of strangers or outsiders
Guard against "strangers"	Do for others; less for self
Be frugal: always use home remedies	Keep with kin and local folks
Stay near home for protection	Use of home remedies "first and last"
Mother is decision maker	Help from kin as needed (primary care)
Community interdependency	Help people stay away from hospitals—"the place where people die"

From Miklininger M, editor: Culture care diversity and universality: a theory of nursing, New York, 1991, National League of Nursing.

BOX 5-3

African-American Culture*

Cultural values are:	Culture care meanings and action modes are:
Extended family networks	Concern for my "brothers and sisters"
Religion valued (many are Baptists)	Being involved
Interdependence with "Blacks"	Giving presence (physical)
Daily survival	Family support and "get togethers"
Technology valued, e.g., radio, car, etc.	Touching appropriately
Folk (soul) foods	Reliance on folk home remedies
Folk healing modes	Rely on "Jesus to save us" with prayers and songs
Music and physical activities	

From Miklininger M, editor: Culture care diversity and universality: a theory of nursing, New York, 1991, National League of Nursing.

original U.S. colonies emphasized independence early in the nation's development. Over the course of history, Americans have also been willing to assist other countries to fight for their independence. Independence is manifested in white middle-class Protestant families when children 18 years of age are expected to move out of their parents' homes. In other American subcultures where family is a primary value, adult offspring are expected to live with the family until marriage.

The value of independence is also manifested in the health care system through the concept of self-care. Health teaching tends to focus on the individual instead of the family. It is assumed by many health care providers that all cultures value self-care, resulting in the neglect of individual cultural group values during health and illness.

Privacy

Privacy is another dominant middle-class, white American value. This is manifested in the erection of privacy fences around our public buildings and private dwellings. In the health care setting it is evidenced by building institutions with mostly private and semiprivate rooms and in restricting family members from remaining with clients overnight. Parents must give permission for their names and their newborn's gender to be published in the birth announcements of local newspapers. The above measures are illustrations of how privacy is implemented in the American culture (Boxes 5-1 through 5-4).

BOX 5-4

Arab-American Muslim Culture*

Culture care meanings and action modes are:

1. Providing family care and support—a responsibility
2. Offering respect and privacy time for religious beliefs and prayers (5 times each day)
3. Respecting and protecting gender culturally role differences
4. Knowing cultural taboos and norms (e.g., no pork, alcohol, smoking, etc.)
5. Recognizing honor with obligation
6. Helping to "save face" and preserve cultural values
7. Obligation and responsibility to visit the sick
8. Following the teaching of the Koran
9. Helping especially children and elderly when ill

From Miklininger M, editor: Culture care diversity and universality: a theory of nursing, New York, 1991, National League of Nursing.

Cultural Stumbling Blocks

Cultural stumbling blocks are those negative responses individuals and groups display when they encounter people from other ethnic groups. These responses include cultural blindness, cultural shock, cultural conflict, cultural imposition, ethnocentrism, discrimination, prejudice, racism, and stereotyping (Clark, 1992; Herberg, 1995).

According to Herberg, prejudice, racism, stereotyping, and discrimination are results of a combination of the following factors:

1. Lack of understanding of ethnic groups other than a person's own
2. Stereotyping of members of ethnic groups without consideration of individual differences within the group
3. Judging other ethnic groups according to the standards and values of a person's own group
4. Assigning negative attributes to the members of other ethnic groups
5. Viewing the quality and experiences of other groups as inferior to those of a person's own group

Prejudice as a stumbling block is a hostile attitude toward individuals simply because they belong to a particular group assumed to have objectionable qualities (Dibble, 1983). Earlier knowledge or stereotyping of people may be involved in this process.

Discrimination is the differential treatment of individuals because they belong to a specific racial, ethnic, religious, or social group. The results of differential treatment are inequitable experiences and opportunities for the disadvantaged group and advantages for the perpetrator. Discrimination is really the behavioral expression of prejudice (Ritzer, Kammeyer, Yetman, 1982).

Racism is a combination of the hostile attitude of prejudice, and the differential treatment and behavior of discrimination that is directed at a specific ethnic or minority group. The discrimination is usually based on the belief that some races are by nature superior to others.

Another stumbling block is **stereotyping,** a rigid, preconceived idea, opinion, attitude, or belief about a cultural group that is applied indiscriminately to all of its members. An example of stereotyping can be gleaned from the following situation.

A young immigrant Filipino nurse successfully completed an advanced cardiac assessment course for coronary care nurses and an assertiveness training class for foreign nurses at a large university in the intermountain western area of the United States. She relocated to the northeastern area of the country the following year. She was employed as a charge nurse on the 3 PM-to-11 PM shift in a coronary care unit of a large metropolitan general hospital.

She called the physician because the arrhythmia she observed on the monitor indicated the prescribed medication was contraindicated. The physician reported her to the nursing director after a lengthy discussion. When she was called to the office, the nursing director stated, "You do not act like other Filipino nurses; they would have given the medication and not tried to defend their nursing judgment."

The stereotype illustrated here is that all Filipino nurses are docile, seek harmony, and do not disagree with a person in authority. The physician believed that all the Filipino nurses were not licensed and had not completed an advanced course in coronary care nursing, and consequently, were incapable of making such a judgment. The physician was surprised to learn that the Filipino nurse had advanced training and a B.S.N. from a prominent U.S. university.

Stereotypes can be both positive and negative. Positive stereotypes often can provide a barrier to needed care, as illustrated in the following example.

The African-American church provides financial assistance for its eldest members, and its congregation assists with home care in the absence of immediate family. This may be true in some small communities, but with so many African-American women in the work place in urban areas, there are fewer people available to provide this needed service today. It is important to assess each older adult for social and financial services required as a result of their health status.

Ethnocentrism is defined as believing that one culture's lifeways and practices are superior to all others. Other cultures are judged using the value system of a person's own group. **Cultural imposition** as a stumbling block is imposing personal values, beliefs, and practices on another individual or group. This usually is an extension of ethnocentrism. Cultural imposition can be illustrated by an American Caucasian nurse conducting a diabetic diet management class for older adult Filipino Americans and Mexican Americans using a standard American diet sheet, and insisting that only those foods be consumed. The nurse in this example is guilty of cultural imposition by impressing American food choices on them without considering that these older adults probably consume ethnic foods that are not included on the standard diet sheet.

Cultural blindness is seeing all cultures as the same. An example of this is a nurse addressing a multicultural audience and saying "I only see human beings in my practice; I don't see clients as Native-Americans, African-Americans, Mexican-Americans, and Asian Indians. I treat them all the same." The nurse in this example is unable to recognize the differences of values, beliefs, and lifeways of other ethnic groups, and in essence, is denying their presence.

Cultural conflict is the anxiety experienced when people interact with individuals who have different beliefs, values, customs, languages, and lifeways than their own. The response is often a ridiculing of the client's lifeways in an attempt to bolster their own security in their cultural lifeways:

An immigrant Korean nurse is instructed to ambulate an 80-year-old African-American client. The client says that he is tired and wants to remain in bed this morning. The nurse does not insist, because the client is an older adult. The Caucasian head nurse reprimands the immigrant Korean nurse for not ambulating the client as ordered. The immigrant Korean nurse says to another Korean nurse: "Those Americans do not respect their elders; they talk to them as if they were children." The white American nurse tells the physician that "those Asian nurses allow men to run all over them."

In the Korean culture, men are the decision makers, and older adults are revered. Middle-class, white Americans do not consider age or gender in these circumstances. In the responses of both nurses, each denigrated the other's culturally prescribed behavior to underscore that their own cultural response was "correct."

Cultural shock is the final stumbling block. This is a state of disorientation, confusion, frustration, and a feeling of helplessness produced by being in a culture markedly different from one's own. This emotional stress is caused by not recognizing familiar cultural clues, signs, symbols, sounds, odors or fragrances, cultural values, beliefs, and practices. This response can become very intense, triggering anger, bitterness, homesickness, somatic complaints, and depression.

Patronization is often listed as a cultural stumbling block, but if the nurse talks with members of various ethnic groups, they explain that to be shown favoritism or kindness in a condescending manner causes posturing, anger, and hostility, which blocks communication and meaningful interactions.

The negative responses described earlier as stumbling blocks interfere with the nurse's ability to promote health, to negotiate, to preserve beneficial health practices prescribed by the culture, and most importantly, to restructure or to repattern harmful practices used by the diverse older adult population of this country and the world.

Cultural Building Blocks

Attitudes, behaviors, and interventions, which affirm and promote diversity of the older adult population, are known as cultural building blocks. Positive responses to older adults from cultures different from the caregiver's include cultural sensitivity, cultural relativism, and cultural accommodation.

Cultural sensitivity occurs when an individual becomes aware, recognizes, acknowledges, and values that behavior patterns vary between and within ethnic groups. The caregiver recognizes the significance of culture in health and illness. Sensitivity also implies that the caregiver realizes the significance of ascertaining the meaning of a situation from the older adult's perspective, which is known as the insider's view, or emic perspective (Pelto, Pelto, 1978).

Cultural relativism strives to understand the clients' behavior within their own cultural system. It is the attitude that other approaches (e.g., preventing illness), though different, have merit and may be equally valid.

Cultural negotiation or accommodation is modifying the health care system to permit inclusion into the health care plan of those folk health practices that are harmless but that promote the client's well-being. The following example illustrates cultural negotiation and accommodation.

> An 80-year-old African-American woman was scheduled for emergency surgery for a ruptured peptic ulcer. Her granddaughter refused to sign the operative permit until the minister came, prayed, and rubbed the abdomen with a special oil. The nurse was concerned about contamination of the abdominal area, which had been prepared for surgery. A nurse specialist in medical/surgical and transcultural nursing was able to help the surgeon and nurses understand the client's and family's needs, and perspectives. The nurse specialist talked with the minister, family, and members of the health team. The surgeon agreed that the oil could be applied. The abdomen would be cleansed with soap and an antiseptic in the operative suite. The minister confirmed that the removal of the oil in the operative suite would not negate the effectiveness of the prayer intervention.

Was the application of the oil and prayer effective in the uneventful recovery of this woman? The client went to the operating room in a positive frame of mind believing that God would guide the hand of the surgeon. The minister remained with the family in the waiting room and was a source of support. The staff attributed the client's recovery to the skill of the surgeon, the client attributed her recovery to God's healing power and guidance of the surgeon.

It is important that the caregivers recognize, affirm, and promote the diversity of the various older adult ethnic population in their practices. Cultural knowledge and transcultural skills in communication and modes of intervention are needed to promote diversity and provide culturally congruent care that is acceptable, meaningful, and satisfying to the client.

CULTURE VARIATION IN HEALTH AND ILLNESS

Health and Culture

The concept of health is embedded within the values, beliefs, and practices of the culture. Regardless of the educational background of caregivers, it is imperative that they first identify their own concepts of health and illness before attempting to elicit those of their older adult clients. As caregivers are socialized and progress through the educational programs of their professions, it is expected that folk definitions of health will be replaced by scientific ones. However, self-assessment reveals that some cultures' folk health beliefs are still embraced and practiced.

Health is often perceived differently by older adult clients than by caregivers. Caregivers often embrace the World Health Organization's (WHO) definition of health, which states "health is the complete physical, mental, and social well-being and not merely the absence of disease (WHO, 1947)."

Transcultural research studies have been conducted to ascertain the meaning of health in many ethnic groups. Common components that have been identified include the ability to think, work, and carry out prescribed social roles. Few ethnic participants defined health as the absence of disease, pain, or minor complaints associated with aging. Examples of definitions of health from selected ethnic groups are illustrated in the following.

Bailey's study (1990) of African-American older adults residing in Michigan defined health in terms of survival. Examples of this definition include these statements:

- "Health means being able to live day by day."
- "Health means doing whatever it takes to stay alive."

A black older adult woman residing in a rural coastal area of Virginia in Roberson's study (1983) described health as:

- "Feeling good, good appetite—do what you want, go where you want. I used to work all day, come home, fix dinner, do chores, and go to the oyster house at midnight to shuck oysters all night—that's healthy."

In Mitchell's study of Jamaicans (1983), health was "having a good appetite, feeling strong and energetic, performing activities of daily living without difficulty, and being sexually active and fertile."

Older adult immigrant Filipino women representing various islands defined good health in terms of physical, mental, and social activity; absence of pain; fortune and appearance (Welch, 1987). Most of the older adults' definitions contained three or more of these components.

- "Good health means the body is able to do everything. You are physically and mentally healthy if you can think, read, [and] work in the house, yard, and on the job."
- "Good health means having lots of friends mingling with people, not being lonely, enjoying oneself and being with other people" (Welch, 1987).

Tom-Orme's study of Native American older adults (1988) found that health was defined also in terms of physical, emotional, and spiritual well-being, as well as having family support. Harmony is a key concept in the Navajo world view. Health is impossible without a balance between mind, body, and spirit. Examples of each are included in the following:

- "Health is remaining actively involved in herding, weaving, [and] gardening; freedom from pain."
- "Health is harmonious balance between mind, body, and spirit; relationship with family and kin."
- "Health is respect for supernatural; good dreams."
- "Health is expression of keh' to and by others and visits by family members."

In a study (Hautman, Harrison, 1982) of middle-class white Americans residing in California, half of the participants defined good health as the absence of illness, and 5% defined it as being able to work.

In summary, most of the ethnic older adults of color defined health in terms of being able to work, to perform self-care activities, and to maintain prescribed roles with family and friends, whereas many Caucasians defined health in terms of the absence of pain, symptoms, and disease (see Cultural Awareness box below).

Illness and Culture

Culture plays an important role in the meaning older adults attach to symptoms and illness-related behaviors. As long as the behaviors do not interfere with a person's ability to work, to engage in daily activities, and to fulfill role obligations, very little importance is attached to it (O'Brien, 1982; Welch, 1987; Bailey, 1990). The individual's perception of illness is often influenced by others within the family and culture. Older adults have long life experiences with illness of self, family, and others within their ethnic groups. The significance they attach to illness symptoms and their reactions are related to the outcomes they have experienced or observed in the past.

Theories of Illness Causation

Human beings throughout history have attempted to understand illness and disease. Anthropologists have identified three major ways in which disease causation may be viewed—from magico-religious, naturalistic/holistic, or biomedical/scientific perspectives.

In the magico-religious theory of illness/disease causation, disease is caused by the action of God, gods, or supernatural forces or agents. Health is viewed as a blessing or reward of God and illness as a punishment. Illness/disease causation attributed to the wrath of God is prevalent among members of the Holiness, Pentecostal, and Fundamental Baptist churches. Examples of magical causes of illness are voodoo, especially among blacks in the Caribbean, root work among southern African-Americans; hexing among Mexican-Americans and African-Americans, and Gaba among Filipino-American older adults (Box 5-5).

CULTURAL AWARENESS

Health Care Needs of Older Adult Mexican Americans

In an analysis of the social factors and values of older adult Mexican Americans residing in an urban area, McKenna (1989) reports that this population is at high risk for chronic conditions associated with age and for health problems related to migrant status, poverty-level incomes, and low levels of education and nutrition. Their care needs include assistance, succorance, nurturance, stress alleviation, and support in a stressful urban environment in which they encounter barriers of language, transportation, eligibility requirements for health and welfare services, and self-perceptions of inferior ethnic identity.

In research by Leininger (1991), the following cultural values, culture care meanings, and action modes pertaining to nursing care of Mexican-American clients were identified.

Cultural values	Culture care meanings and action modes
Extended family (la familia) highly valued Interdependence with kin and social activities	Succorance (direct family aid) Involvement with extended family (e.g., being cared for by others during illness)
Patriarchal (machismo) Exact time less valued	Filial love/loving Protective (external) male care Mother as care decision maker
High respect for authority and older adults Religion valued (many Roman Catholics) Traditional Mexican foods for well being Belief in hot/cold theory	Respect for authority Acceptance of God's will Healing with foods
Traditional folk-care healers for folk illnesses	Touching

From McKenna MA: Elderly Mexican Americans' health care needs, *J Transcult Nurs* 1(1), 46-52, 1989; Leininger MM *Culture care diversity and universality: a theory of nursing,* New York, 1991, National League for Nursing Press.

BOX 5-5

Religious Beliefs That Affect Nursing Care

Beliefs Regarding Medical Care

Adventist (Seventh-Day Adventist; Church of God)
Some believe in divine healing and practice anointing with oil and use of prayer
May desire communion or baptism when ill
Believe in man's choice and God's sovereignty
Some oppose hypnosis as therapy

Baptist (27 groups)
"Laying on of hands" (some)
May encounter some resistance to some therapies, such as abortion
Believe God functions through physician
Some believe in predestination; may respond passively to care

Black Muslim
Faith healing unacceptable
Always maintain personal habits of cleanliness

Buddhist Churches of America
Illness believed to be a trial to aid development of soul; illness due to Karmic causes
May be reluctant to have surgery or certain treatments on holy days
Cleanliness believed to be of great importance
Family may request Buddhist priest for counseling

Church of Christ Scientist (Christian Science)
Deny the existence of health crisis; see sickness and sin as errors of mind that can be altered by prayer
Oppose human intervention with drugs or other therapies; however, accept legally required immunizations
Many adhere to belief that disease is a human mental concept that can be dispelled by "spiritual truth" to extent that they refuse all medical treatment

Church of Jesus Christ of Latter Day Saints (Mormon)
Devout adherents believe in divine healing through anointment with oil and "laying on of hands" by church officials (appointed church members)
Medical therapy not prohibited

Eastern Orthodox (Turkey, Egypt, Syria, Rumania, Bulgaria, Cyprus, Albania, etc.)
Anointment of the sick
No conflict with medical science

Episcopal (Anglican)
Some believe in spiritual healing
Rite for anointing sick available but not mandatory

Friends (Quakers)
No special rites or restrictions

Greek Orthodox
Each health crisis handled by ordained priest; deacon may also serve in some cases
Holy Communion administered in hospital
Some may desire Sacrament of the Holy Unction performed by priest

Hindu
Illness or injury believed to represent sins committed in previous life
Accept most modern medical practices

Islam (Muslim/Moslem)
Faith healing not acceptable unless psychologic condition of patient is deteriorating; performed for morale
Ritual washing after prayer; prayer takes place five times daily (on rising, midday, afternoon, early evening, and before bed); during prayer, face Mecca and kneel on prayer rug

Jehovah's Witness
Adherents are generally absolutely opposed to transfusions of whole blood, packed red blood cells, platelets, and fresh or frozen plasma, including banking of own blood; individuals can sometimes be persuaded in emergencies
May be opposed to use of albumin, globulin, factor replacement (hemophilia), vaccines
Not opposed to nonblood plasma expanders

Judaism (Orthodox and Conservative)
May resist surgical procedures during Sabbath, which extends from sundown Friday until sundown Saturday
Seriously ill and pregnant women are exempt from fasting
Illness is grounds for violating dietary laws (e.g., patient with congestive heart failure does not have to use kosher meats, which are high in sodium)

Lutheran
Church or pastor notified of hospitalization
Communion may be given before or after surgery or similar crisis

Mennonite (similar to Amish)
No illness rituals
Deep concern for dignity and self-determination of individual that would conflict with shock treatment or medical treatment affecting personality or will

From Whaley LF, Wong DL: *Nursing care of infants and children,* ed 4, St. Louis, 1991, Mosby; Beliefs that can affect therapy, *Ped Nurs* 5(3):40-43, 1979; and Spector RE: Cultural diversity in health and illness, ed 2, New York, 1985, Appleton-Century-Croft.

Continued.

BOX 5-5

Religious Beliefs That Affect Nursing Care—cont'd

Methodist
Communion may be requested before surgery or similar crisis

Nazarene
Church official administers communion and laying on of hands
Adherents believe in divine healing but not exclusive of medical treatment

Pentecostal (Assembly of God, Four-Square)
No restrictions regarding medical care
Deliverance from sickness is provided for in atonement; may pray for divine intervention in health matters and seek God in prayer for themselves and others when ill

Orthodox Presbyterian
Communion administered when appropriate and convenient
Blood transfusion accepted when advisable
Pastor or elder should be called for ill person
Believe science should be used for relief of suffering

Roman Catholic
Encourage anointing of sick, although this may be interpreted by older members of church as equivalent to old terminology "extreme unction" or "last rites"; they may require careful explanation if reluctance is associated with fear of imminent death
Traditional church teaching does not approve of contraceptives or abortion

Russian Orthodox
Cross necklace is important and should be removed only when necessary and replaced as soon as possible
Adherents believe in divine healing, but not exclusive of medical treatment

Unitarian Universalist
Most believe in general goodness of their fellow humans and appreciate expression of that goodness by visits from clergy and fellow parishioners during times of illness

The second way people view illness and disease causation is that an imbalance or disharmony occurs among the geophysical and metaphysical forces of the universe. Balance and harmony in the universe and person results in health. Native-American and many Filipino-American older adults attribute illness/disease causation to disharmony and imbalance in the body, nature, and interpersonal relationships.

The yin/yang theory is an ancient Chinese theory of disease causation. It has been used continuously for the past 5,000 years. The theory posits that all organisms and things in the universe consist of yin and yang energy forces. The seat of the energy forces are within the autonomic nervous system. Health is a state of perfect balance between the yin and the yang. When one is in balance, a feeling of inner and outer peace is experienced. Illness represents an imbalance of yin and yang. Balance may be restored by herbs, acupuncture (insertion of the needles into points along the body's meridians), acupressure (application of pressure or massage to the same meridian points), or controlled deep breathing exercises.

Yin forces represent the negative forces of the moon, such as cold, darkness, and emptiness. Yang forces are positive, warm forces of the sun energy and represent fullness. The sympathetic nervous system represents yang forces. Too much yang causes rapid heartbeat, tenseness, irritability, increased blood pressure, fever, and dehydration. The parasympathetic nervous system represents yin forces. Yin forces conserve energy and control body functions. Too much yin results in colds and gastrointestinal illness.

The yin/yang theory is used throughout Asia and is gaining acceptance in the United States. Chinese and other Asian groups apply it along with practices of western medicine. The yin/yang theory is often referred to as Chinese medicine.

Foods are classified as hot (yang) and cold (yin) under this theory. Foods are believed to be transformed to yin and yang energy when they are metabolized by the body. Hot foods are eaten during cold illnesses and cold foods are eaten during hot illnesses.

The biomedical theory of disease is based on the assumption that all events in life have a cause and effect. The human body is seen as a machine, consisting of many parts. The body is believed to be divided into the mind, body, and spirit. The germ theory is an example of a biomedical/scientific explanation of disease. Microorganisms such as bacteria or viruses enter the body and overpower the natural resistance, causing an inflammatory response. Treatment is directed at removal of the damaged part or use of drugs to kill or to retard the growth of the causative organism. Most physicians, nurses, and other health workers subscribe to this theory of disease causation.

Use of Both Folk and Biomedical Health Systems

In most cultures, older adults are likely to treat themselves for familiar or chronic conditions they have successfully treated in the past. When self-treatment fails, then the older adult consults with the folk healer or professional within the health care system. Many of the rural disadvantaged Anglo-Americans, immigrants, and ethnic older adults use the folk health system. Older adults often choose the folk health system to treat and to prevent disease or illness, because these people speak their languages and reside near them. There is a minimum cost and it may take the form of exchange of services, goods, or food.

Older adults from the ethnic groups will not attend public clinics and other health facilities if they do not see personnel and other older adults from their ethnic group. They are fearful that the personnel may not understand how their bodies react to disease and may give them too much medication. The older adults in this author's study said immigrant Filipinos cannot take the same dosage of drugs that whites can, which explains why they take only half the dose of medication prescribed by a Caucasian physician. They also dislike the impersonality of the members of the health team, which is interpreted as prejudice on the part of the personnel, and not being welcomed by the health facility.

Immigrant older adults often establish the same type of folk health care services found in their native land (Aroian, 1990; DeSantis, Thomas, 1990; Lipson, 1992; Meleis, Lipson, Paul, 1992; Welch, 1987). Preparation of medications for self-care is a part of those folk health care systems. Immigrant older adults are accustomed to brewing certain herbs, grasses, plants, and leaves to make herbal teas, drinks, solutions, poultices, decoctions, and medicines to prevent and treat illness. In fact, in many countries such as the Philippines, herbal medicine is a part of the curriculum from grade school through college. The department of health makes available posters and books with pictures of plants, trees, bark, buds, leaves, grasses, fruits, vegetables, and herbs, providing explicit directions for preparation of home remedies to keep the people healthy (Welch, 1987). This practice is especially prevalent in remote rural areas where biomedical services may be a day or more away in travel from the older adult's residence.

Many of the same drugs prescribed by physicians are prepared by the older adult immigrants at a cheaper cost than buying the drug at the pharmacy. When these people come to America many of these same plants, leaves, buds, and grasses can be obtained in Asian stores in dried form. The Filipino older adult women in Welch's study (1987) had potted plants in their homes, and herb and vegetable gardens in their backyards for medicinal and nutritional purposes. Older adults with gardens often shared herbs and vegetables with those who lived in apartments. In rural southwest Virginia, Appalachian older adult Anglo-Americans had stores that specialized in dried herbs, plants, and other folk remedies used to maintain and to restore health. Religious practices such as praying, meditating, fasting, wearing amulets, burning candles, and establishing a family alter are activities in which older adults participate on a regular basis to promote health and treat disease in the folk health system.

During health assessment, health professionals should ascertain which over-the-counter drugs, herbal medicines, and folk remedies the older adult is taking before new medicines are given to prevent overdosage and drug interactions. It should also be ascertained if the older adult is seeing a folk health healer in conjunction with the professional health practitioner. Research has shown that many ethnic older adults continue to use the folk and professional system simultaneously (see Cultural Awareness box, p. 126).

CONCEPTS OF INTERCULTURAL COMMUNICATION WITH OLDER ADULTS

Nurse-Client Relationship

Nurses caring for older adults from diverse ethnic and cultural backgrounds should understand that the nurse-client relationship is based on a different orientation to communication than in the West. Those older adults from Southeast Asia, the Philippines, Korea, China, and Japan have a social relationship and communication orientation that is based on Confucianism.

Confucianism stresses strong social relationships. This type of relationship promotes a warm, relaxed atmosphere that is conducive to cooperation, group harmony, and consideration of others. The main function of communication under Confucian philosophy is to initiate, to develop, and to maintain a strong social relationship over time. The emphasis is on process and not outcomes. In this framework, it is important to engage in small talk to ascertain personal information concerning the individual and family so as to place that person in the proper context before conducting business.

Communication in the West is based on the strong values of individualism, autonomy, and self-actualization. The discipline of nursing in the United States has identified the professional relationship as its preferred mode of interaction within the nurse-client relationship. Small talk is usually discouraged and limited to a greeting, name, and title of the caregiver. The outcome of communication is more important than the process. Communication is usually short-term, and generally terminated once the goals of care are achieved. Table 5-8 displays a comparison of east and west orientation to communication.

CULTURAL AWARENESS

Traditional, Folk, or Indigenous Healers

Older adults from culturally diverse backgrounds may seek the assistance of traditional, folk, or indigenous healers. The following is a partial listing of healers used by selected cultural groups.

Group	Healer	Scope of practice
African American	Voodoo priest(ess) or Hougan	Recommends herbal remedies for voodoo illnesses Also treats Mexican Americans and Native Americans
	Spiritualist	Treatment of physical, mental, and spiritual problems Most prevalent in urban communities
	"Old Lady"	Older adult woman who gives advice on childrearing and common illnesses in children and adults Practices in both urban and rural settings
Chinese American	Herbalist	Diagnoses illnesses after interviewing, palpating pulses, auscultating, and inspecting Prescribes herbal remedies; sometimes owns a small store in Chinatown area
	Acupuncturist	Treats painful conditions and provides regional anesthesia by passing long thin needles through the skin to specific points; free end of needle is twirled and used to conduct a weak electric current, or transmit heat (called moxibustion)
	Acupressurist	Same as above only pressure is used instead of needle
	Bone setter	Specializes in setting fractures; sometimes skillful as an herbalist as well
Hispanic	Curandero (male) Curandera (female)	Treatment of traditional illnesses using herbs, diet, massage, and rituals; trained in an apprenticeship; usually enjoys respect from community members
	Espiritualista	Emphasis on prevention of illness or bewitchment with use of religious medals, amulets, and prayers; can analyze dreams and foretell future events; born with special gifts, which may be developed through apprenticeship with an older practitioner
	Sabador	Treats musculoskeletal conditions using massage and manipulation of bones and muscles
	Santero	Diagnoses and treats mental disorders, which are caused by spirits outside the body; client may be taken to a psychiatrist to be "calmed down" in preparation for treatment by a santero
	Yerbo	Consulted for preventive and curative use of herbs for both traditional and Western illnesses; no formal training
Native American	Medicine Man Medicine Woman Shaman Herbalist	With 510 federally recognized tribes, wide variation exists; three major categories: (1) preventive measures; (2) treatment regimens; (3) health maintenance.

Nonverbal Communication

Handshake

A handshake, the customary greeting in the business world in the United States, consists of a warm smile, extending of the hand, and the grasping of another's. The quality of the handshake is open to varied interpretation. A firm handshake in dominant American culture is a sign of good character and strength. Many Native-American older adults interpret a vigorous handshake as a sign of aggression. They may offer their hand, but it is more of a passing of the hand with light touch. Caregivers often interpret this as a sign of not being welcome or of weakness.

To the Soviet older adult immigrant, a handshake may be interpreted as insolent and frivolous (Tripp-Reimer, Lauer, 1987). Handshakes also raise gender issues with

TABLE 5-8

Comparison Between the North American and the East Asian Orientations to Communication Patterns

East Asian orientations	North American orientations
1. Process orientation Communication is perceived as a process of infinite interpretation	1. Outcome orientation Communication is perceived as the transference of messages
2. Differentiated linguistic codes Different linguistics codes are used depending on people involved and situations	2. Less differentiated linguistic codes Linguistic codes are not as extensively differentiated as East Asia
3. Indirect communication emphasis The use of indirect communication is prevalent and accepted as normative	3. Direct communication emphasis Direct communication is a norm despite the extensive use of indirect communication
4. Receiver centered Meaning is in the interpretation Emphasis is on listening, sensitivity, and removal of preconception	4. Sender centered Meaning is in the messages created by the sender Emphasis is on how to formulate the best messages, how to improve source credibility, and how to improve delivery skills

From Yum JO: The impact of Confucianism on interpersonal relationships and communication pattern in East Asia. In Samovar L, Porter R: *Intercultural communication: a reader,* ed 7, Belmont, CA, 1994, Wadsworth.

older adults from the Middle East. Same-gender individuals may shake hands, but touch outside of marriage is forbidden by individuals of the opposite gender. If the nurse is of the same gender as the older adult, then a handshake will be received.

Silence

The value, use, and interpretation of silence also varies markedly from one culture to another. Generally speaking, Eastern cultures value silence over the use of words; in Western cultures, the opposite is true. For older adults of many Eastern cultural groups, especially those in which the Confucian philosophy is embraced, silence is a sign of respect for the wisdom and expertise of others. Silence is expected by young family members and also of family members who have less authority. In traditional Japanese and Chinese families, silence during a conversation may indicate the speaker is giving the listener time to ponder what has been said, before moving on to another idea. Silence in Native-American cultures is highly valued because it builds character. It is believed that one learns self-control, courage, patience, and dignity from remaining silent (Johannesen, 1974). Silence during a conversation may signify that the listener is reflecting on what the speaker has just verbalized. French, Spanish, and Soviet older adult immigrants may interpret silence as a sign of agreement (Tripp-Reimer, Lauer, 1987; Andrews, Boyl, 1995).

Eye Contact

In the United States, direct eye contact is a sign of being honest, trustworthy, straightforward, and truthful. Nursing students are taught to establish and to maintain eye contact when interacting with clients, but this behavior may be misinterpreted by older adults of different ethnic groups. This behavior may also lead to erroneous conclusions on the part of the caregiver.

Native-American older adults do not allow the nurse to lock gaze with them. Generally, their eyes are constantly, slowly moving, from the floor to the ceiling and around the room. The eyes are believed to be the window to the soul. Staring into the eyes of another is viewed as an invasion of that person's privacy, is considered disrespectful, and can endanger the spirits of both parties (Primeaux, 1977).

In many Asian cultures, looking one directly into the eyes implies equality. An older adult may avoid eye contact with doctors and nurses, because the health professionals are authority figures. Generally, direct eye contact is considered disrespectful in Asian cultures.

There are gender issues in maintaining eye contact. In the Middle Eastern culture, direct eye contact between the sexes is forbidden, except between husband and wife. It is interpreted as a sexual invitation. Nurses should avoid direct eye contact with clients and physicians of the opposite gender.

Verbal Communication

First Names

People of the dominant culture in the United States today generally refer to each other on a first name basis. Using a person's first name denotes a sign of equality and friendliness. During the slavery and segregation era, Caucasians referred to African-Americans by their first names as a sign of disrespect. For example, during that period, the race of an individual could be learned simply by listening to the physician-nurse and nurse-client communication. An African-American nurse was called Nurse Jones, whereas her Causasian counterpart would be addressed as Miss Jones. African-American clients were called by their first names and Caucasians were addressed as Mrs. Smith. Today's African-American older adults grew up and worked during the segregation era. To be called today by their first name by a Caucasian person of any age is interpreted as a form of racism and considered disrespectful. African-American older adults therefore may not respond when Caucasians call them by their first names. In fact, African-Americans do not refer to their own parents, relatives, or other adults by their first name, since it is considered disrespectful. In addition, calling older adults grandmother, grandpa, auntie, or uncle is culturally inappropriate and is viewed as racist and disrespectful, especially if said by a Caucasian person.

Confucian guidelines prescribe that older adults be called by honorific titles. Asian-Americans, Hispanics, Native Americans, and most ethnic groups do not call older adults by their first names. A safe rule of thumb for nurses is to call older adults and any adult client by their last names unless instructed otherwise by the client.

Girl and Boy

Use of the word "boy" or "girl" when addressing African-American men and women is very inflammatory and insulting, especially when used by Caucasians or other ethnic groups. This was the way slave owners referred to their slaves. Using this term today with African-Americans of any age group can elicit rage and unpredictable behavior. Making this mistake can be a terrifying, unforgettable experience, whether it occurs between coworkers or between the nurse and client.

"Yes" at Face Value

Immigrant older adults who speak and understand little English often smile, nod, and say "yes" when they really do not understand what is being said or explained to them. In the Asian cultures, it is disrespectful and embarrassing to tell a person of authority or one who has more education than the older adult, that the authority figure did not properly teach, explain, or demonstrate something. A hesitant "yes" usually means "no." It is always best to ask the older adult or family member to demonstrate the instructions given to them. Filipino-Americans use others to tell nurses and physicians that they do not understand. These other individuals are known as the "go between," and are the culturally approved method to clarify the misunderstanding.

Pronouns and Calendar Dates

The pronouns "he" and "she" do not exist in many Asian languages, and consequently, many older adults interchange these terms, creating confusion for the listener. For example, Filipino-American older adults often say last year when they mean last month. Once the date has past, they consider it the last year. A Filipino client may have been seen in the clinic on May 1, 1995, and today's date may be May 15, 1995. If questioned today about when last seen in the clinic, he or she may say "last year, the 1st of May."

These and other cultural variables can affect the nurse's ability to communicate effectively with the older adult of a different culture. The nurse must modify common communication approaches to meet the individual client's cultural needs, since communication is central to the development of a therapeutic relationship based on trust. Sometimes, the use of a culturally sensitive interpreter can improve communication. In this situation, the interpreter must translate not only the words but the message as well (see Cultural Awareness box, Chapter 4, p. 83). If the nurse experiences difficulty in overcoming language barriers and no interpreter is available, there are a number of alternative means of communicating that can be used (see Cultural Awareness box, Chapter 4, p. 82).

CULTURAL THEORY AND FRAMEWORK

It can be gleaned from the demographic data presented earlier in this chapter that the older adult population of the United States is more diverse than it has been in its history (see Demographics, p. 105). This population consists of people from many countries, representing many cultures, ethnic groups, religions, and languages, as well as diverse socioeconomic, political, educational, historical, and immigration experiences. This diversity underscores the relevance and necessity for a theory that addresses the care and caring needs of this group.

Leininger's Theory

Leininger's theory of Cultural Care Diversity and Universality (1991) is unique and appropriate for use with the older adult population because it was designed primarily to assist nurses in discovering ways to provide culturally congruent care to people with different lifeways than those of the professional nurse.

Leininger's theory uses worldview, social structure, language, ethnohistory, environmental context, folk systems, and professional systems as the framework for looking at the influences on cultural care and well being. The components of cultural and social structure dimensions are technologic, religious, philosophic, kinship, social, political, legal, economic, and educational factors, as well as cultural values and lifeways.

The theory identifies three modes of action for the

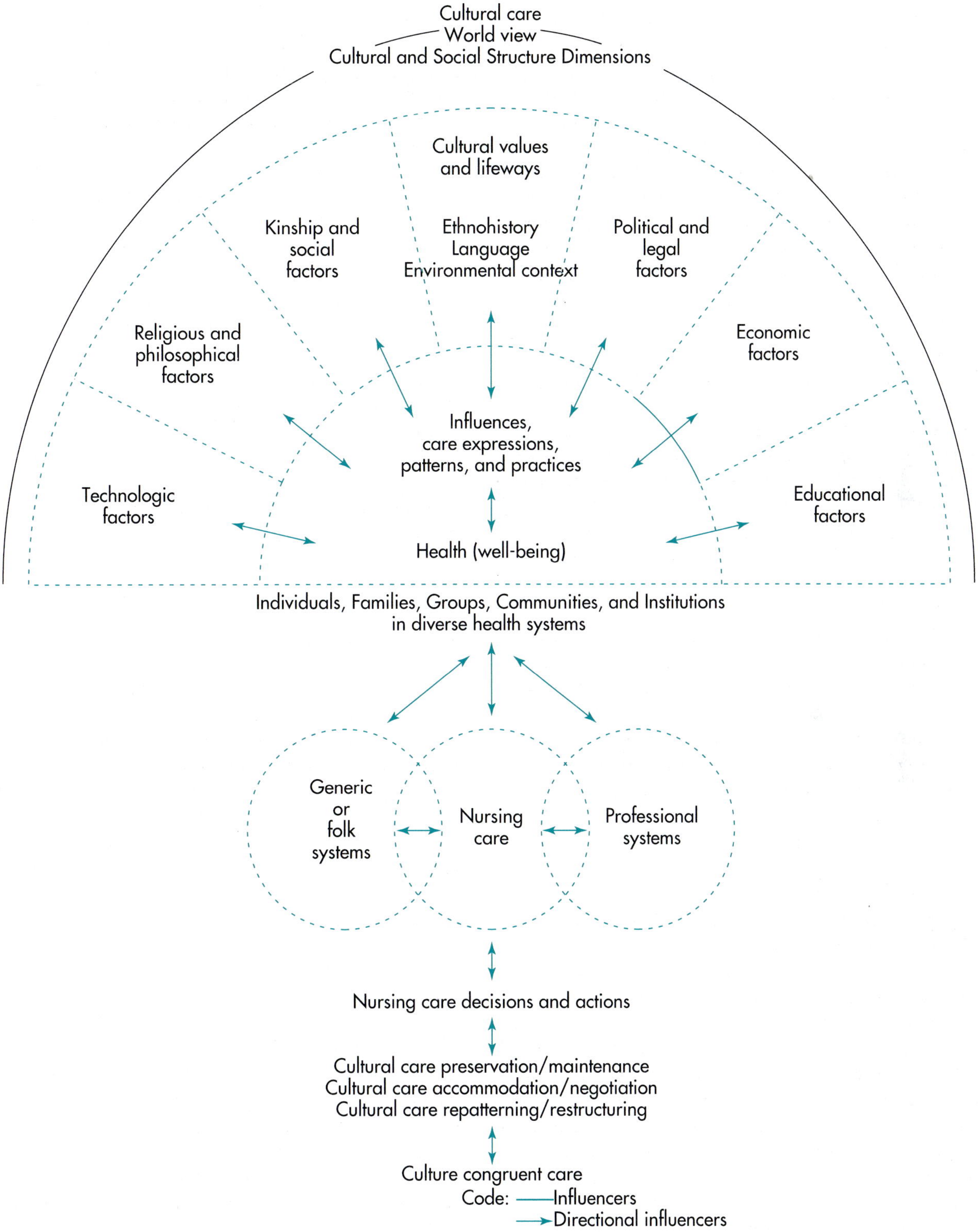

Fig. 5-2 Leininger's model to discover transcultural nursing care and do cultural assessments. (From Leininger M: *Culture care: diversity and universality,* New York, 1991, National League for Nursing.)

BOX 5-6

Welch Culturologic Assessment Guide

Race and ethnicity
- What race does the older adult affirm?
- Which ethnic group does the older adult embrace?

Communication
- Does the older adult have a speech or hearing impairment?
- Which language(s) and or dialect(s) does the older adult speak?
- Which language or dialect does the older adult prefer nurses and other health care providers to use when conversing with them?
- Is the older adult able to speak, to read, and to understand English, and to what degree?
- Are bilingual interpreters required?
- Are there ethnic, gender, or age restrictions for individuals serving as interpreters for the older adult?
- Is there a relative, friend, or member of the ethnic group who the older adult would prefer to serve as an interpreter?
- How does the older adult prefer to be addressed (i.e., by first name only, last name with appropriate title, or honorific prefix)?
- Are there cultural restrictions regarding the discussion of certain topics in groups or with individuals of the opposite gender, regardless of whether they may be health professionals?
- Are there certain communication styles or situations that may cause the older adult to "lose face" or feel shame (e.g., direct confrontation, open disagreement, or the raising of a younger person's voice)?
- Are there certain gestures with the hands, feet, eyes, or other body parts that cause the older adult to feel uncomfortable during conversation (e.g., direct eye contact, beckoning with the hand, a thumbs up, or sign of a "V"-held palm)?
- How are silence, smiles, nods of the head, and yes and no used in the culture when communicating with strangers, superiors, and others?
- Does the older adult use the pronoun "he" and "she" appropriately? (NOTE: Many Asian immigrants interchange these personal pronouns because there are no such pronouns in their native languages.)
- Are there cultural restrictions regarding individuals who share with health professionals the health history of living or dead family members?

Place of birth and countries where older adult has resided
- In what country, state, city was the older adult born?
- In what country, state, city, or province did the older adult reside during childhood?
- What countries has the older adult resided in during his or her adult years?

Historical and immigrant experience
- To which category does the older adult belong: (1) native-born, (2) emigrated to the United States as a child or young adult, (3) immigrated to the United States as an older adult, or (4) arrived in the United States "yesterday" (number of days or months)?
- What year did the older adult arrive in the United States, and what age was he or she?
- Is the older adult an immigrant or refugee?
- Is residence in the United States temporary or permanent?
- Is the older adult in the United States alone and without family?
- What is the history of the ethnic group of the older adult? (I.e., was he or she a migrant worker; a survivor of concentration or refugee camps, or a war-torn country; a descendant of slaves; or an individual brought to this country against free will?)

Current residence and seasonal relocation pattern
- In what urban or rural area does the older adult reside?
- Does the older adult reside alone or with spouse, adult children, or relatives?
- Does the older adult reside with different adult children or extended family on a rotational or seasonal basis?
- If residence is rotated, identify seasonal location, country, state, and city.

Spring__________________Summer__________________
Fall__________________Winter__________________

(NOTE: Filipino immigrants and Asian Indians often rotate between home country, Canada, Europe, and the United States. Weather is often a determining factor. Winter and Fall are often spent in California, Florida, Virginia, and Texas. Summer and Spring are spent in colder climates such as Michigan, New York, Minnesota, and Illinois.)

- If older adult is a recent immigrant, who is legally responsible for the older adult? I.e., which adult offspring, spouse, or relative?

Philosophy and religion
- What is the dominant philosophy or religion that permeated all aspects of life of the older adult's home country (e.g., Confucionism, Islam, Mennonite, Christianity, Judaism, and Buddhism)?
- Which world religion does the older adult embrace?
- Which denomination, if Christian, does the older adult hold membership?
- Are there special healing practices that the older adult believes hasten healing and recovery?
- Are there special rituals and healing practices that the older adult's religion mandates during illness, disease, death, or special occasions?
- If special rituals or healing practices are to be carried out, then will special accommodations be required?

BOX 5-6

Welch Culturologic Assessment Guide—cont'd

Philosophy and religion—cont'd

- Who are the special religious representatives or healers that may visit the older adult during illness and perform certain functions (e.g., priests, ministers, older adults, deacons, Buddhist monks, etc.)?

Values orientation

- How are strangers seen, as people who can be trusted or who should be checked out, because they can be good or bad?
- Does the older adult focus on the past or present events and ways of doing things or does he or she look forward to tomorrow's new technology?
- How is old age determined and viewed by the older adult? (I.e., is it revered, dreaded, a milestone, or an accomplishment?)

Cultural sanctions and restrictions

- Are there cultural restrictions regarding discussion of sexuality issues surrounding sterilization, spinal cord injuries, cerebrovascular accident (CVA), diabetes, and participation in alternative practices?
- Are there restrictions regarding discussion of dead relatives and handling of the dead bodies?
- Are there culturally prescribed rules regarding modesty, and relationships between men and women within home, society, and specifically health care?
- Are there cultural rules regarding amputated parts being buried with the body?

Health-related beliefs and practices

- How is good health defined? Is good health related to the ability to work, to fulfill roles and to survive?
- What does the older adult believe caused the present illness or disease? (I.e., wrath of God, an imbalance, a hex, the germ theory, etc.?)
- What kinds of foods, activities, rituals, and amulet does the older adult believe promotes good health?
- Who determines when and if an older adult is ill or healthy? What symptoms indicate health, sickness, or illness? Who decides the older adult is no longer ill? Does the older adult use the services of cultural healers such as root doctors, curanderos, herbalists, etc.? What herbal medicines, potions, remedies, massages, amulets, talisman, charms, healing ceremonies, or rituals is the older adult currently using or anticipating to use during this illness?
- Is the older adult wearing certain metals, charms, objects, or garments that should not be removed during illness or hospitalization?

Care and caring

- What are the older adult's values and beliefs concerning life, health, illness, assisted suicide, suicide, and death?
- How does the older adult view placement in long-term care facilities such as nursing homes, extended care, etc.?
- Who is the key family member responsible for health-related decisions? (E.g., it may be the grandmother, if all relatives are deceased; the minister in an African-American family; or the eldest offspring in certain cultures)?
- What is appropriate "sick role" behavior? Who cares for the older adult in the home during this period?
- What is the role expectation of nurses during hospitalization of an older adult?
- What are the older adult's expectations of family, friends, and neighbors during an illness or a hospitalization? Are these individuals expected to participate in bathing, feeding, comfort measures, and sitting with the client during illness?
- What is the older adult's preference of gender and ethnic background of health care workers, especially if they are new arrivals in this country?
- Are there specific tribes, classes, castes, genders, or ethnic groups from which the older adult would refuse to accept services or to share accommodations?
- Are there special restrictions regarding gender, touching, bathing, and exposure of body parts during treatments and daily hygiene?
- What caring behaviors does the older adult desire of nurses, physicians, and other health professionals?
- List those behaviors which the older adult considers noncaring on the part of nurses, physicians, and other health care providers.

Nutrition

- What kind of foods does the older adult believe are necessary to maintain good health?
- What are the cultural meanings of food? What about preferences, preparation, and serving?
- Does the older adult eat predominantly ethnic foods? What is the dominant flavor, principal, or seasoning used in preparation of meals (e.g., salt, garlic, onions, soy sauce, cultural-specific fish sauce, monosodium glutamate, pork, vinegar, etc.)? How are foods generally prepared? (I.e., are they baked, fried, or broiled and what type of cooking oil is used?)
- Are there religious restrictions pertaining to the older adult's diet (e.g., Kosher foods only or avoidance of pork and shellfish)?
- How many meals are usually consumed during the day? Which meal is the largest?
- Does the older adult's religion or culture prescribe certain periods for fasting? What is the older adult's meaning of fasting—absolutely no food or drink, water only, or in moderation? What is the time frame for the prescribed fast?

Continued.

BOX 5-6

Welch Culturologic Assessment Guide—cont'd

Nutrition—cont'd

- Are exceptions permitted to the fast during illness? If so, who grants the permission?
- How does the older adult feel about abstaining?

Cultural expressions of pain, grief, and grieving

- How does the older adult's culture expect individuals to express emotions, feelings, and pain?
- Does the older adult expect to experience pain during this illness? How does the older adult expect the pain to be managed? Can health professionals expect the older adult to ask for pain medications or is the professional expected to offer the medication?
- How are family members to be told if death is anticipated or has occurred? Who should be told first?
- Should spiritual leaders be contacted when death is imminent? Are special rites to be performed with the body before it is removed from the room? (I.e., should it be washed by family, and applied with special oils and cloths, or should prayers, last rites be conducted?)

Economic factors

- Are there cultural, immigration, and legal factors that would prevent older adults from discussing financial problems with health care providers?
- What are the main sources of income—social security, Supplemental Security Income, pension or family sources?
- Is the older adult eligible to receive social entitlement programs such as Medicaid, Medicare, veterans benefits, food stamps, or rent and utilities assistance? Does the older adult have private health insurance?
- What impact does the economic status of the older adult have on his or her health-maintenance, health-seeking, and health-promotion behaviors? Does the older adult have money to purchase medication?
- What impact do economic factors have on living arrangements, need for assistance with home or personal care, and other discharge planning issues?

Political and legal factors

- How do recent revisions of immigration, refugee, and illegal alien laws impact the older adult's health-seeking, health-maintenance, and health-promotion behaviors?
- How does the political climate of the country, geographic regions, and immediate community impact these behaviors? (E.g., if the older adult is an immigrant, refugee, or illegal alien, political upheaval in his or her homeland can cause worry and depression.)
- If the older adult is a new immigrant (in the United States less than 2 years), what are the legal implications if the relative that sponsored the older adult is unable to pay the medical bills, and Medicaid funding is initiated?
- What influence do cultural and ethnic political organizations have on older adults receiving care (e.g., NAACP, National Black and Hispanic Caucus, Organization of Migrant Workers, National Illocano Association, and community-based health care programs and clinics)?

Kinship and social factors

- Who comprises the family of the older adults? What is the role of godchildren? Who is the head of the family and decision maker?
- What is the role of the older adult in the family?
- What is the older adult's social network (i.e., church, monoethnic senior citizen group, family, clubs, etc.)? Is the older adult isolated from the traditional cultural social network and immersed in the offspring's network due to rotation of residence on a seasonal basis?
- How does the social network impact upon the older adult's transportation, recreation, shopping, and health- or illness-seeking, health maintenance behaviors?

Educational factors

- What is the highest educational level attained by an older adult? Is the older adult able to read the newspaper in his or her language and in English?
- In which language does the older adult prefer health teaching and written materials?
- With which learning styles do the older adults feel most comfortable—one-on-one, in group settings, using printed materials, participating in audio-visual demonstrations, or listening to oral explanations?
- What other members of the family or social network should be included in the teaching sessions?

Biologic variations in disease incidence and laboratory values

- Does the older adult have a disease or condition that is genetic or more prevalent in a special cultural group (e.g., diabetes, Tay-Sachs disease, hypertension, gout, lactose intolerance)?
- Are there diseases or conditions in which the cultural group has increased resistance (e.g., skin cancer in dark-pigmented individuals)?
- Are the older adult's laboratory findings lower or higher than is expected for Caucasians (E.g., African Americans have lower hemoglobin and hematocrit levels; Japanese and Pima Indians have lower cholesterol levels than whites; and pulmonary function values are lower in African Americans, Asians, and Native Americans than in Caucasians)?
- Has the older adult experienced increased frequency of side effects with prescription drugs? Does the older adult reduce the dose of prescribed medications? (I.e., there are pharmacokinetic differences in varying cultural groups.)

professional nurse to provide culturally congruent care: (1) cultural care preservation or maintenance, (2) cultural care accommodation or negotiation, and (3) cultural care repatterning or restructuring. Leininger defines the three modes of nurse decisions and actions as follows:

1. Cultural care preservation or maintenance refers to those assistive, supporting, facilitative, or enabling professional actions and decisions that help people of a particular culture to retain and to maintain their well-being, to recover from illness, or to face handicaps or death.
2. Cultural care accommodation or negotiation refers to those assistive, supporting, facilitative, or enabling creative professional actions and decisions that help people of a designated culture to adapt to, or to negotiate with, others for a beneficial or satisfying health outcome with professional care providers.
3. Cultural care repatterning or restructuring refers to those assistive, supporting, facilitative, or enabling professional actions and decisions that help a client(s) reorder, change, or greatly modify their lifeways for new, different, and beneficial health care patterns while respecting the client(s)' cultural values and beliefs and still providing a beneficial or healthier lifeway than before the changes were coestablished with the client(s) (Leininger, 1991).

This theory can be used with individuals, families, groups, communities, and institutions in diverse health care delivery systems. Leininger has developed the Sunrise Model to depict the components of the theory and the interrelationship of its components. This model can be used as a visual and cognitive map to guide the nurse in teasing out the essential data from all the dimensions of the influencers so as to gain clues to providing culturally congruent care. (Fig. 5-2)

A culturologic assessment tool has been developed by the author to assist the novice nurse in teasing out the essential data from the cultural and social structure, environmental context, language, and ethnohistory dimensions of the model. This tool is an adaptation of Leininger's Acculturation Health Assessment and the method developed by Andrews and Boyle and is specific to the older adult population (Box 5-6).

Cultural Self-Assessment

Conducting a cultural self-assessment before assessing clients can be a useful exercise to identify a person's beliefs about aging and immigrant populations coming to this country as older adults. For example, how do your parents, grandparents, friends, and significant others feel about immigrants and other ethnic older adults? What

BOX 5-7

Cultural Self-Assessment

1. What are my personal beliefs about older adults from different cultures?
2. What past experiences have influenced my values, biases, ideas, and attitudes toward older adults from different cultures?
3. What are my values as related to health, illness, and health-related practices?
4. How do my values and attitudes affect my clinical judgments?
5. How do my values influence my thinking and behaving?
6. What are my personal habits and typical communication patterns when interacting with others? How would these be perceived by older adults of different cultures?

CULTURAL AWARENESS

Cultural Care of Older Greek Canadian Widows

Nurses interact with widowed women of different cultural groups during the time of their husbands' deaths and in subsequent years. Grieving widows are a population at risk for health problems and mortality, and are of special interest to nurses who could provide relevant cultural care (Rigdon, Clayton, Dimond, 1987). Research by Rosenbaum (1990) reveals that, for older Greek Canadian widows, the care constructs of responsibility for reciprocation, concern, love, companionship, family protection, hospitality, and helping are embedded in the Greek Canadian social structure features of kinship, religion, cultural beliefs and values, and environmental context. Cultural care continuity diminishes the spousal care void and contributes to the health of Greek Canadian widows.

Grown children and other relatives help to meet the widow's care needs without requesting assistance from sources outside the Greek community. The centrality of the Orthodox church and religion is manifested in several ways. Prayer, along with the organizational and social activities of the Greek Orthodox church, provides meaningful community care.

From Rigdon I, Clayton B, Dimond M: (1987). Toward a theory of helpfulness for the elderly bereaved: an invitation to a new life. *Adv Nurs Sci* 9(2):32-43, 1987; Rosenbaum JN: Cultural care of older Greek Canadian widows within Leininger's theory of culture care, *Transcult Nurs* 2(1):37-47, 1990.

are your own health-related beliefs, attitudes, values, and practices? Answers to such questions require self-honesty, sincerity, and reflection. Interviews with parents and grandparents may prove to be very enlightening. Everyone has ethnocentric tendencies, and they must be brought to consciousness before they can be modified. Being aware of your own cultural baggage is an important prerequisite to becoming sensitive to providing culturally relevant care (Box 5-7) (see Cultural Awareness box, p. 133).

Summary

Gerontologic nurses need to develop an awareness and sensitivity to the cultural needs of a variety of ethnic groups. Conducting a cultural self-assessment can be a useful exercise in enabling the nurse to provide culturally sensitive and relevant nursing care. In addition, the body of knowledge related to transcultural nursing is continuing to grow and develop, making it possible for nurses to provide culturally competent nursing care.

Members of minority cultures across the country are demanding health care that meets their cultural needs. Delivery of comprehensive gerontologic nursing care makes it imperative for nurses from all cultural backgrounds to identify and meet the cultural needs of the diverse groups encountered in the practice setting.

Key Points

- The current older adult population is more culturally diverse than it has ever been in history.
- Broader, more culturally sensitive curricula need to be developed to prepare nurses to meet the needs of a growing culturally diverse older adult population.
- Culture is a universal phenomena that is learned and transmitted from one generation to another, providing the blueprint for a person's beliefs, behaviors, attitudes, and values.
- Culture affects all dimensions of a person's health and well-being, so the nurse must consider a client's culture when planning and delivering nursing care.
- Ethnocentrism can hinder the delivery of care to older adults of any given culture.
- A dominant value orientation can be identified for all cultures, even though some variances exist among the individual members of a given culture.
- The cultural stumbling blocks of cultural blindness, cultural shock, cultural conflict, cultural imposition, ethnocentrism, discrimination, prejudice, racism, and stereotyping displayed by nurses when they encounter older adults from other ethnic groups interfere with the nurse's ability to promote health, to negotiate and to preserve beneficial health practices prescribed by the culture, and to restructure or to repattern harmful practices.

HOME CARE TIPS

1. Ascertain whether the older adult came to the United States as a child, young adult, during old age, or was born in America, because this impacts their level of acculturation and eligibility of benefits and services. Refer to the appropriate agency or social worker for assistance if necessary.
2. Knowledge of the differences and similarities of values of the homebound client can minimize tension and cultural conflict within the home care setting. Adapt communication styles as needed to reduce the potential for conflict.
3. Assess caregiver's and client's own concepts of health and illness.
4. Communication between culturally different clients and nurses must be ethnically appropriate.
5. Assess the home environment for evidence of cultural values, and determine views on health-illness concepts. Incorporate this data into the plan of care to meet the cultural needs of the client and family.

- The cultural building blocks of sensitivity, relativism, and accommodation reflect the attitudes, behaviors, and interventions that affirm and promote diversity of the older adult population.
- The nurse should be knowledgeable of the predominant characteristics of the cultural groups for which care is provided but should still individualize the care rather than generalize about all clients in any given group.
- Nurses caring for older adults from diverse ethnic and cultural backgrounds should be aware that the nurse-client relationship is based on a different orientation to communication than the typical Western mode.
- Nurses should conduct a cultural self-assessment to determine how they are influenced by their own cultures, and how their cultures affect their interactions with people of different cultures.
- Nursing interventions should be adapted to meet the cultural needs of the individual older adult client.

Critical Thinking Exercise

- Why is it essential for the nurse to understand the importance of how race, ethnicity, and social factors may affect illness when encountered by the older person?

REFERENCES

American Society of Retired Persons: *Healthy aging: making health promotion work for minority elders,* Washington, DC, 1991.

Andrews M, Boyl J: *Transcultural concepts in nursing care, Philadelphia,* 1995, JB Lippincott.

Angel JL, Hogan DP: *The demography of minority aging populations. Minority elders: longevity, economics, and health,* Washington, D.C., 1991, Gerontological Society of America.

Aroian K: A model of psychological adaptation to migration, and resettlement, *Nurs Res* 39(1):5-10, 1990.

Bailey EJ: *Hypertension and African-American ethnocare therapy,* Washington, D.C., 1990, paper presented at the 88th American Anthropological Association Meeting.

Bruce AM: *People and races,* New York, 1977, Macmillian.

Burton LM, Dilworth-Anderson P: Creating culturally ways of thinking about relevant diversity and aging, *Generations: J Am Soc Aging* 15:67-72, 1991.

Clark M: *Nursing in the community,* Norwalk, 1992, Appleton & Lange.

Department of Justice, Immigration and Naturalization Service: *1993 statistical yearbook of immigration and naturalization service,* September 1994, The Department.

DeSantis L, Thomas J: The immigrant Haitian mother: transcultural nursing perspective on preventive health care for children, *J Transcult Nurs* 2:1990.

Dibble C: *Epilogue,* unpublished handout from educational Psychology 636: Cross-Cultural Counseling, 1983, University of Utah, Educational Psychology Department, Salt Lake City, Utah, 84112.

Gelfand D, Yee BW: Trends and forces: influence of immigration, migration, and acculturation on the fabric of aging in America, *Generations: J Am Soc Aging* 15(4):7-10, 1991.

Hautman M, Harrison JK: Health beliefs and practices in a middle-income Anglo-American neighborhood, *Adv Nurs Sci* 4(3):49-64, 1982.

Herberg P: Theoretical foundations of transcultural nursing. In Andrews M, Boyl J: *Transcultural concepts in nursing care,* Philadelphia, 1995, JB Lippincott.

Herskovits MJ: *Cultural anthropology,* New York, 1955, Alfred A Knopf Inc.

Johannesen R: The function of silence: a plea for communication research, *West Speech* 38:27, 1974.

Keesing F: *Cultural anthropology: the science of custom,* New York, 1965, Holt Rinehart & Winston.

Keifer CW: *Changing cultures changing lives: an ethnographic study of three generations of Japanese-Americans,* San Francisco, 1974, Jossey-Bass.

Kluckhohn, Strodtbeck: *Variation in value orientation,* 1961, Row Peterson, now published by Greenwood Press, Emsford, NY.

Leininger M: Significance of cultural concepts in nursing, *J Transcult Nurs* 2(1):22-26, Summer 1989.

Leininger M: The theory of culture care diversity and universality. In Leininger M, editor: *Culture care diversity and universality: a theory of nursing,* New York, 1991, National League for Nursing Press, Pub No 15-2402, 3-68.

Leininger M: *Transcultural nursing: concepts, theories and practice,* ed 2, New York, 1995, McGraw-Hill.

Lipson J: Afghan refugee health: some findings and suggestions, *Qualitat Health Res* 1(3):349-369, 1991.

Lipson J: Iranian immigrants: health and adjustment, *West J Nurs Res* 14(1):10-24, 1992.

Matteson M, McConnell E: *Gerontological nursing: concepts and practice,* Philadelphia, 1988, WB Saunders.

Meleis A, Lipson J, Paul S: Ethnicity and health among five Middle Eastern immigrant groups, *Nurs Res* 41(2):98-103, 1992.

Mitchell M: Popular medical concepts in Jamaica and their impact on drug use, *West J Med* 139:841-847, 1983.

O'Brien M: Pragmatic survivalism: behavior patterns affecting low-level wellness among minority group members, *Adv Nurs Sci* 4(3):13-26, 1982.

Overfield T: *Biological variation in health and illness,* Menlo Park, Calif., 1985, Addison-Wesley.

Pelto PJ, Pelto GH: Anthropological research: the structure of inquiry, ed 2, Cambridge, UK, 1978, Cambridge University Press.

Primeaux M: Caring for the American Indian patient, *AJN* 77:91-94, 1977.

Ritzer G, Kammeyer K, Yetman R: *Sociology: experiencing a changing society,* Boston, 1982, Allyn & Bacon.

Roberson M: *Folk health beliefs and practice of rural black Virginians,* doctoral dissertation, Salt Lake City, 1983, College of Nursing, University of Utah.

Samovar L, Porter R: *Communication between cultures,* Belmont, 1991, Wadsworth.

Saunders L: *Cultural differences and medical care,* New York, 1954, Russell Sage Foundation.

Social Security Administration: *Retirement,* Pub No 05=10035, January 1991.

Tom-Orme L: Diabetes in a Navajo community: a qualitative study of health, illness beliefs and practices, doctoral dissertation, Salt Lake City, 1988, College of Nursing, University of Utah.

Tripp-Reimer T, Lauer GM: Ethnicity and families with chronic illness. In Wright LM, Leahy M, editors: *Families and chronic illness,* Springhouse, Penn., 1987, Springhouse.

US Bureau of the Census, Current Population Report, Special Studies, P 3-178, RV *Sixty-five plus in America,* Washington D.C., revised May 1993, US Government Printing Office.

Welch AZ: Mini-ethnography: caring behaviors of Filipino and Korean elders, unpublished manuscript, 1982.

Welch AZ: *Concepts of health, illness, caring, aging and problems of adjustment among elderly Filipinas residing in Hampton Roads, Virginia,* doctoral dissertation, Salt Lake City, 1987, College of Nursing, University of Utah.

Werner E: *Cross-cultural child development: a view from planet earth,* Monterey, Calif., 1979, Brook Cole.

White L: *The evolution of culture,* New York, 1959, McGraw-Hill.

World Health Organization: *Chronicle of WHO* 1:1-2, 1947, New York, The Organization.

CHAPTER 6

Family Influences

LEARNING OBJECTIVES

On completion of this chapter, the reader will be able to:

1. Gain an understanding of the role of families in the lives of older people.
2. Examine and dispel common myths about families in later life.
3. Understand common dilemmas and decisions older adults and their families face in later life.
4. Develop approaches that can be suggested to families faced with aging-related concerns.
5. Identify common stresses family members experience when providing caregiving to frail older relatives.
6. Identify interventions to support families.
7. Plan strategies for working more effectively one-on-one with families of older adult clients.

You have been married 45 years. Your husband recently had a severe stroke and cannot communicate. He managed the family finances and made the family decisions. Now, you do not know anything about your financial affairs or where important papers are located.

- Your mother, 86, is mentally competent, but her physical condition means she cannot manage alone in her home. She refuses all offers of help and rejects any other living situation.
- Your father is dying. You promised him that no heroic measures would be taken to prolong his life; he did "not want to die with tubes hooked up to his body." Your brother, however, demands the doctor use all possible measures to keep your father alive.
- Your father's reactions and eyesight are poor. You don't want your children with him when he is driving. He always takes the grandchildren for rides to get ice cream and will be hurt if you say he cannot take the children. A vacation at Grandpa's begins today.

Situations like these are difficult for families (Schmall, Staton, Weaver, 1984). What would you do if you were faced with these situations? Although each situation involves medical considerations, family members face tough issues and decisions that extend beyond the medical ones:

- How independent and risk-taking do I allow my family member to be?
- Is my family member fully capable of making his or her decisions?
- When should I, if I even should, step in and take control of the situation?
- What do I do if my family member refuses help or to change a situation that I feel needs to be changed?
- What do I do if my family member's actions are putting others at risk?

In working with families of older adults, the nurse needs to be aware of the role families play in the lives of their older family members, to be sensitive to the family needs as well as the needs of the older person for whom care is being provided, and to recognize and to accept that some families are limited in the level of support and caregiving they can provide to older relatives.

ROLE AND FUNCTIONS OF FAMILIES

Families play a significant role in the lives of nearly all older people. When family is not a part of an older person's life, it is generally because the older person has no living relatives nearby or there has been long-standing relationship problems and estrangement. Contrary to popular belief, when older people need assistance, families provide at least 80% of the support. Compared with "the good old days," families today provide more extensive caregiving for longer periods (Schmall, Pratt, 1993).

Although adult children are a major source of support to older parents, several demographic and social trends have a significant impact on the ability of family members to provide support. These trends include:

- **Increase in the oldest of the old.** The age-85-and-over population is the fastest growing segment of the older population and has tripled as a percentage of the total population in the last 40 years (US Bureau of Census, 1992). Although this age group is still relatively small as a percentage of the total population, people over age 85 are most likely to be frail, to have multiple health problems, and to be dependent on others for care. At the time support is needed, their adult children may also be older—in their 60s, 70s, or even early 80s—and adjusting to age-related changes. Of the older people in the United States, 15% have adult children who are also over age 65. Sometimes the "old" parent is providing assistance to his or her "old" child.
- **Decrease in fertility.** A declining birth rate means fewer adult children are available to share in the support of aging parents (Himes, 1992).
- **Increased employment of women.** Traditionally, women have been the primary caregivers. However, women are increasingly employed, working out of necessity or pursuing careers. Although research shows that employed women provide as much support as their nonemployed counterparts, they often sacrifice personal time. A national study (National Survey, 1982) found that 1 out of 10 caregivers leaves the work force to provide care for older family members. Among those who continue to work, many rearrange work schedules, reduce work hours, or take time off without pay. Change in employment status can have implications for the financial security of these women in their own later years.

CULTURAL AWARENESS

Cultural Attitudes Toward Older Adults

Blacks	Greater respect for older adults and their role in the family compared with Anglos Value placed on kinship and extended family bonds
Whites	Less respect for older adults and their role in the family Tendency for men and women to share more equally in family and for democratic family structure Aging parents expected to be self-sufficient and not overly dependent on adult children
East Asians	Very high level of respect for older adults Hierarchic family roles, ascribed status (age, gender) Oldest son assumes responsibility for aging parents as part of filial duty
Hispanics	More overt respect for older adults than whites Tendency toward a more patriarchal family structure Aging parents invited to live in household that consists of extended family members
American Indian (510 federally recognized tribes)	High level of respect for older adults and the years of accumulated wisdom and knowledge; sought after for advice

- **Increase in mobility of families.** Families today may live not only in a different city from their older relative but also in another state, region, or country. Geographic distance makes it more difficult to provide directly the ongoing assistance an older family member may need. Decisions often must be made on the basis of telephone calls and letters.
- **Increase in divorce and remarriage.** Marital changes—divorce, separation or widowhood—affect intergenerational helping patterns (Johnson, 1992) and are associated with giving fewer types of care to older adult parents (Cicerelli, 1983). Divorce and remarriage of a person's parents also can increase the complexity of relationships and decision-making. It can be difficult for children of divorced parents to provide the care needed because of family conflicts and the logistics of caring for two people who do not live together. In some situations, remarriage increases the potential pool of family members available to provide care. In other situations, it may create more disputes because of the different perspectives of stepchildren and birth children (see Cultural Awareness box on p. 137).

COMMON LATE-LIFE FAMILY ISSUES AND DECISIONS

Families play a significant role in the lives of most older people, especially when changes occur in an older person's physical or mental functioning. Family members are generally involved in making decisions about an

Insight •

MYTH *In the past, three-generation households were the most common living arrangement.*

REALITY *Co-residence of three generations has never been the dominant living arrangement in the United States (Hareven, 1992). Most households consisted of nuclear, not extended, families.*

MYTH *Most older people want to live with their children.*

REALITY *As long as older people can manage independently, they prefer to live in households separate from their children. "Intimacy at a distance" is preferred both by older people and by their adult children.*

MYTH *Older people often are abandoned by their families.*

REALITY *For almost all older people, families are important. The family is still the number-one provider of support and caregiving to older people, providing at least 80% of the needed support. Even when bedridden or homebound, older people are twice as likely to be cared for at home than in an institution, with care being provided by a spouse, adult child, or other relative. Extended family members—for example, a niece, nephew, or grandchild—often help when an older person does not have a spouse or adult children. Brothers and sisters often play an important role in the lives of older people who are widowed or have never married.*

MYTH *Families use nursing homes as a "dumping ground" for frail older family members.*

REALITY *Most people in care facilities are greatly impaired and need comprehensive care. Older people who do not have children and live alone are the most vulnerable to nursing home placement. Approximately half of all nursing home residents are single women or widows without close family.*

Families do not suddenly "dump" and abandon their older family members in care facilities. The reality is that most families use nursing homes as "a last resort," only after they have exhausted other alternatives. Families often endure tremendous hardship and stress to maintain older family members in the community.

MYTH *If family-oriented services are made readily available, families will be less likely to provide caregiving.*

REALITY *Policymakers sometimes fear that requests for services will be overwhelming if respite and adult day care programs are subsidized; yet, studies show that caregivers, in general, are willing to pay for what they can afford and are modest in their use of services (Brody, Saperstein, Lawton, 1989; Henry, 1992; Meltzer, 1982). Fear of the "woodwork effect"—that is, that people will come out of the woodwork to use a service and overload the system if a service is made readily available—is not supported by research on respite and day care.*

older person's living situation, arranging for social services and health care, and caregiving (Noelker, 1994). They also can facilitate, obstruct, or prohibit the care or access to services of older family members.

Caregiving is also an activity involving not only the caregiver and care receiver; other family members also influence, and are affected by, caregiving decisions (Schmall, 1994). The stress and burden experienced by family caregivers also has an influence on the use of community services by older adults (Noelker, 1994).

Although the issues and decisions families face in later life vary from family to family, some of the most common and difficult issues include changes in living arrangements, making decisions about a nursing home, financial and legal concerns, end-of-life health care decisions, vehicle driving issues, and family caregiving.

Changes in Living Arrangements

Many families face the question of "What should we do?" when an older family member begins to have difficulty living alone. Common scenarios heard from families include the following (Schmall, Stiehl, 1989):

- "Dad is so unsteady on his feet. I don't know how he can continue to live alone. He has already fallen twice this month. I'm scared he will fall again and really injure himself the next time. He refuses help, and he won't move. I don't know what to do."
- "Mom had a stroke and the doctor says she cannot return home. It looks like she'll have to live with us or go to a nursing home. We have never really gotten along but she will be very angry if we place her in a nursing home."
- "Grandmother has become increasingly depressed and isolated in her home. She refuses to cook, and she hardly eats. She has outlived most of her friends. Wouldn't she be better off living in a group setting where meals, activities, and social contact are provided?"

Family members often feel emotionally torn between whether to allow their parent to be as independent as possible or to create a more secure environment. They may wonder if they should force a change, particularly if they feel a parent's choice is not in his or her best interest. A family member may be focused on the advantages a group living situation provides for an increasingly frail family member—for example, good nutrition, socialization, and security. For the older person, however, a move may represent a loss of independence or "stepping one foot closer into the grave."

In addition to providing an objective assessment of an older person's functional ability, the nurse plays an important role in exploring with families ways to maintain an older relative in his or her home, alternative living arrangements, and the advantages and disadvantages of options. It is also important to help families understand the older person's perspective of the meaning of home, significance of accepting help, or moving to a new environment.

It can be particularly frustrating for families when they know an older family member has difficulty functioning independently yet refuses help in the home. As long as the older person has mental capacity, he or she cannot be forced to accept help. To have any success in dealing with resistance, a family must first understand the reason(s) underlying the resistance. Encourage the family to ask themselves questions (Schmall, Stiehl, 1989):

- Is my family member concerned about the cost of the service and its impact on personal financial resources?
- Does my relative feel he or she does not have a problem?
- Does my family member view agency assistance as "welfare," "charity," or "going on the dole?"
- Does my family member fear having a stranger in the house or having possessions stolen?
- Does my relative feel that the tasks I want to hire someone to do are ones that he or she can do, or that family should do?
- Does my family member view accepting outside help as a loss of control and independence?
- Are the requirements of community agencies—financial disclosure, application process, interviews—overwhelming to my family member?

Depending on the answers to the above questions, one or more of the following suggestions may be helpful to a family (Schmall, Stiehl, 1989):

- **Deal with your relative's perceptions and feelings.** For example, if your older mother feels she does not have any problems, be objective and specific in describing your observations. Indicate that you know it must be hard to experience change. If your father views government-supported services as "welfare," emphasize that he has paid for the service in past years through taxes.
- **Approach your family member in such a way that he or she does not feel helpless.** Many people, regardless of age, do not find it easy to ask for or accept help. Try to present the need for assistance in a positive way, emphasizing how it enables the person to live more independently. Emphasizing only ways in which the person is dependent and that "you can't do that anymore" generally only increases resistance.
- **Suggest only one change or service at a time.** And, if possible, begin with a small change. People generally need time to think about and accept changes. Introducing ideas slowly rather than push-

ing for immediate action increases the chances of acceptance.

- **Suggest a trial period.** Some people are more willing to try a service or program when they initially see it as a short-term arrangement, rather than a long-term commitment. Some families have found that giving a service as a gift works.
- **Focus on your needs.** If an older person persists in asserting, "I'm okay. I don't need help," it can be helpful for family members to focus on their own needs rather than the older person's needs. For example, saying, "I would feel better if . . .," or "I care about you and I worry about . . . will you consider doing this for me so I will worry less?" sometimes makes it easier for a person to try a service.
- **Consider who has "listening leverage."** For example, an adult child may not be the best person to raise a particular issue with an older parent. Sometimes an older person's willingness to listen to a concern, consider a service, or think about moving from one's home is strongly influenced by who opens the discussion. It may be that an older person "hears" the information better when it is shared by a certain family member, a close friend, or a doctor (Box 6-1).

Making A Decision About a Nursing Home

The decision to move an older family member into a nursing home is very difficult for most families. It's often a decision filled with guilt, sadness, anxiety, doubt, and anger, even when it is the older person who makes the decision. The difficulty of the decision is reflected in the following comments of family members:

- "It was easier to bury my first husband than to place my second husband in a nursing home."
- "On a scale of 1 to 10, the difficulty of the decision was a 10-plus for me, even though the doctor said my mother needed the care a nursing home provides."

Although today there are more community services that enable older people to live longer in their own homes, the following statistics indicate that more people will face decisions about a long-term care facility (Schmall, 1993):

- A married couple with four parents who each live to age 65 has a 90% chance that at least one parent eventually will be cared for in a nursing home.
- If a married couple both live over age 65, there is a 70% chance that one of them will spend some time in a nursing home.

BOX 6-1

When Older Adults and Families are Considering Living Together

Sharing a household with an older family member requires major adjustments by everyone. For some families it works well, enriching the lives of everyone (Fig. 6-1). For others, it does not work at all. Before joining households, it's important for everyone to carefully weigh the advantages and disadvantages and to consider the possible consequences for everyone involved. Thoughtful decision-making reduces feelings of guilt and resentment. Although each family has unique concerns to deal with, the following questions point to areas that should be considered and discussed before making a final decision. Honestly answering these questions can help families decide whether joining households is a good option. If they do decide to live together, the answers may help families identify potential "trouble spots" and deal with them before problems develop (Schmall, Stiehl, 1989):

- Can you honestly expect to get along together day-to-day?
- How do other members of the household feel about joining households?
- Can the home physically accommodate everyone comfortably?
- How will common living spaces be shared?
- Are family members willing and able to communicate with each other?
- Is there agreement about who will do what in the household?
- Does your relative(s) have personal habits that irritate family members?
- Can everyone agree on financial arrangements?
- Can you and your relative accept differences in each other's way of living or would these differences be too distressing?
- Will children be a source of conflict?
- What changes will family members have to make in activities, daily routine or lifestyle?
- Will your relative be dependent on you and the family?

Since no one can predict the outcome of joint residence, the nurse should suggest that families consider, if possible, a trial period before making a long-term commitment, and options if living together proves not to be satisfactory or if situations change. This provides a dignified way out for everyone.

- More than 40% of people who live over age 65 will need nursing home care at some point. More than half of that 40% will be in a nursing home for a year or longer.

In working with families, it is as important to deal with their feelings about nursing homes and placement as it is to focus on the objective need for nursing home care. For many people, their view of nursing homes is only negative and comes primarily from what they have seen in the media—pictures of neglect, abuse, and abandonment.

One of the most common feelings people express when placing a person in a nursing home is guilt. Guilt may come from several sources including: (1) pressures and comments from others (e.g., "I would never place my mother in a nursing home," or "If you really loved me, you wouldn't put me in a nursing home"); (2) family tradition and values (e.g., "My family has always believed in taking care of its own—and that means you provide care to family members at home"); (3) the meaning of nursing home placement (e.g., "I am abandoning my husband," "I should be able to take care of my mother. She took care of me when I needed care," or "You do not put someone you love in a nursing home"); (4) and promises (e.g., "I promised Mother I would always take care of Dad," or "When I married, I promised 'til death do us part").

Studies show that a nursing home can be a positive experience for an older person and that family relationships are often strengthened following an older person's move into a care facility (Smith, Bengston, 1979). The time the family spends with the older person can be more focused on social interaction and recreational activities rather than on caregiving tasks (Fig. 6-1). Talking with family members about the potential benefits of nursing home care can be helpful.

Fig. 6-1 Grandfather helping with responsibilities of feeding baby. (Courtesy Rod Schmall, West Linn, Ore.)

For many people, it is not easy walking into a nursing home for the first time. It is helpful to prepare families about what to expect and to give guidelines for evaluating facilities, moving an older family member into a care facility, and helping an older family member adjust to the changes.

Financial and Legal Concerns

Major financial issues some families face in later life include: (1) paying for long-term care, (2) helping an older person who has problems managing money, (3) knowing about and accessing resources for the older family member whose income is not sufficient, (4) responding when an older family member is depleting financial resources on "prize contests" and scams, and (5) planning for and talking about potential incapacity (Schmall, Stiehl, 1992).

In working with families, one of the most important things the nurse can do is to become knowledgeable about the resources in the community that are available to help families who are faced with financial and legal concerns, as well as eligibility requirements for programs, program access issues, and options for older people who need assistance in managing their finances. If a family and an older relative have not already discussed potential financial concerns, the nurse should encourage them to do so.

Many families have not discussed finances before crisis—and then it is often too late to do so. However, talking about finances is not easy for many families (Goetting, Schmall, 1993). Sometimes adult children hesitate to discuss financial concerns for fear of appearing overly interested in inheritance. After all, talking about passing on Mom and Dad's money usually means talking about the circumstances under which it will be transferred. Few people feel comfortable starting a conversation with, "Dad, when you die . . .," or "Mom, if you become unable to make decisions . . . ."

When a person has been diagnosed with Alzheimer's disease or a related disorder, it is critical that the family makes financial and legal plans while the older person is able to participate in the planning (Nay et al, 1989). Once the older person becomes incapacitated, and if advance plans have not been made, the available options are fewer, more complex, and more intrusive (Goetting, Schmall, 1993). It may require a family to seek a conservatorship, which requires court action (see Chapter 3).

Seeking a conservatorship (or a guardian of the estate) is usually emotionally painful for both the family and the older person (Schmall, Stiehl, 1992). The older person, if present, must listen to the allegations and evidence concerning his or her own mental decline. The family must publicly declare the loss of capacity experienced by their older relative. The older person's situation and intimate family matters are exposed, particularly if a court trial is held. The conservatorship process is also expensive, involving attorney and court filing fees.

Older people with limited mobility, low vision, or loss of hand dexterity may need only minimal assistance with finances—for example, help with reading fine print, balancing a checkbook, preparing checks for signature, or dealing with Medicare or other benefit programs (Schmall, Nay, 1993). Others who are homebound because of poor health, but still are able to direct their finances, may need someone to direct their financial affairs. In such situations, a family's intent should be to assist, not to take away control. The goal is to choose the least intrusive intervention that will enable the older person to remain as independent as possible.

End-of-life Health Care Decisions

The use of life-sustaining procedures is another difficult decision for many families, especially when they are uncertain about the older person's wishes or there is disagreement among siblings about "What Mom (or Dad) would want" (Hare, 1992). Yet, when an older person is ill and unable to make health care decisions, the family is generally asked about what the client would want.

The nurse can be most helpful in encouraging older adults to complete an advance directive or a power of attorney for health care (see Chapter 3). However, in addition to completing such forms, it is important to encourage people to discuss their values, beliefs, and wishes in regard to medical care with family members (especially with the person who is being considered as the surrogate decision-maker). A person should always be asked if whether he or she is willing to act as a surrogate decision-maker.

Tangible expressions of a person's wishes are often comforting to families during times of crisis (Hare, 1992). The nurse may suggest that older clients write a personal letter or make a video or audio tape in which they discuss their feelings concerning end-of-life health care.

Adult children, who may be approaching a parent about end-of-life decisions, need to remember that mental incapacity is not always related to aging and illness. A debilitating accident can happen to anyone, regardless of age. Parents may be more resistant to discuss or more likely to question the motives of adult children who have not prepared their own wills, power of attorney for health care, or advance medical directive for health care, and yet are expecting the parent to do so (Goetting, Schmall, 1993).

The Issue of Driving

The ability to drive a vehicle is one of the most important instrumental activities of daily living for maintaining independence (Perrson, 1993). A car means much more than transportation. For many people, driving symbolizes autonomy, control, competence, self-reliance, freedom, and belonging to the mainstream of society.

Most older people alter their driving when they experience a decline in their abilities (Oriol, 1993). They may drive only during daylight hours, avoid heavy traffic times, limit the geographic area in which they drive, or limit driving to roadways that are less complicated. Some couples begin to drive in tandem with the passenger acting as copilot (Perrson, 1993). Sometimes following the death of a spouse, other family members begin to notice that "For the first time, Dad is having problems with driving." What family members may not realize is that Dad had problems with driving for at least 2 years before his wife died, but she had served as his eyes and ears when he was behind the wheel of the car.

Families face a difficult time when an older relative shows signs of unsafe driving. A special concern for many is the safety of their children who ride in their grandparent's car. It is not unusual for family members to be worried about safety and yet, at the same time, to be reluctant to raise concerns with their family member about driving or to take action. The issue of driving is even more complicated when the older person is cognitively impaired and does not perceive the deterioration he or she has experienced and does not appreciate his or her potential driving risk (Gillins, 1990; Kaszniak et al, 1991). Studies show, for example, that people with Alzheimer's disease are likely to rate themselves as highly capable of driving when they are not.

Sometimes, families also have difficulty accepting that an older family member may need to give up driving. A family member may rationalize, "Mom only drives short distances in the neighborhood," or may feel, "I just can't ask Dad not to drive. The car is too important to him." Some families are continually faced with dealing with a cognitively impaired person who cannot remember from day to day that he or she cannot drive and insists on driving.

Families may need assistance in assessing a person's driving ability and how to best carry out a recommendation that an older family member should limit or discontinue driving. Health care professionals can play a critical role in discussing the issue of driving with an older person. Some older people view a health care professional as more objective than the family, and thus are more willing to listen to advice and recommendations from a health care professional than from family. When asked in focus groups who should talk to an older person about driving, older people reported the physician should, since "when the doctor says you can't drive anymore, that's definite" (Perrson, 1993). Many participants in the focus groups indicated that family advice alone would not influence their decision to quit driving. This is clearly reflected in the following statement of one person (Perrson, 1993):

> I know of their [family] concern, but they knew I wouldn't take their advice if they told me to quit driving. I might have resented it because I thought I was still a good driver.

A written prescription from a doctor or other health care professional that simply states "no driving" may remind the cognitively impaired person and divert blame from the family (Schmall, Cleland, 1984). Families also may need information about how to make a car inoperable for the cognitively impaired person.

If a family member will be addressing the issue of driving with an older relative, the nurse could suggest they first read the booklet *Concerned about an Older Driver? A Guide for Families and Friends* (Malfetti, Winter, 1991). The nurse could also share the following recommendations with the family, emphasizing that the usefulness of the recommendations depends on the situation and the relationship between the family and the older driver:

- **Carefully choose your words and your attitude.** An attitude of "getting the person off the road" or accusations of unsafe driving are likely to meet with anger and denial. Concerns about a person's driving need to be approached with sensitivity. In focus groups, researchers found that the words used may make a difference. For example, older drivers did not respond well to the word "restriction"; they preferred the use of "requirements" or "conditions" for safe driving (Oriol, 1993).
- **Acknowledge the losses (or potential losses).** Although family may view a change in a person's driving as "for the best," the older person generally feels a sense of loss, a loss that needs to be acknowledged by others. The older person should be given an opportunity to talk about and to grieve the losses.
- **Do not equate giving up the license with giving up the car.** All too often when a person must give up driving, family and friends encourage the selling of the car. Because of the symbolic meaning of the automobile, for some people, it is still important to keep the car in the driveway or garage. Furthermore, on a practical level, some people also feel less dependent if they can offer their car when they must depend on others to drive them.

FAMILY CAREGIVING

Providing care to frail, dependent older adults is increasingly a common experience for individuals and families (Brody, 1985), and "may be one of life's most formidable challenges" (Zarit, 1994). Studies show that 75% of family caregiving is provided by women. Nearly one fourth of caregivers are spouses. More than one third of spouses and adult children who are caregivers are age 65 and over (Stone, Kemper, 1990).

Caregiving can evolve as a family member gradually becomes frail and needs more assistance, or it can occur

RESEARCH

Beach DL: Gerontological caregiving: analysis of family experience, *J Gerontolog Nurs* 19(12):35-41, 1993.

Sample, setting

The convenience sample consisted of 10 family caregivers, eight white and two black, living in a large southern California metropolitan area. Caregivers had to be the spouse or child of an older adult and to have provided the majority of care within the past 5 years.

Methodology

This nonexperimental descriptive study used a grounded theory methodology to examine the experiences of family caregivers. Data were collected by conducting a 30-minute semistructured interview at the caregiver's home or at a neutral site selected by the caregiver. Caregivers were asked to describe their experiences with specific reference to the following:

- Inevitability of the client's death
- Patient's preferred courses of action
- Family roles and interactional experiences
- Patient denial
- Previous patterns of caregiving
- Personal activity
- Employment problems associated with caregiving
- Thoughts about institutionalizing the patient
- Coping with patient personality changes
- Bereavement

Responses were audiotaped, transcribed verbatim, and analyzed using grounded theory methodology.

Findings

Caregiver experiences fell into the three categories of: (1) role strain, (2) sense of self, and (3) problem solving/coping. Caregivers reported a strong sense of caregiving responsibility, with married couples identifying caring for an impaired spouse as a normal part of life. Although most caregivers reported having a family support system in place, they rarely used it. Women caregivers reported more social limitations as a result of caregiving when compared with men. Informants also reported significant changes in work schedules, including a complete end to employment. Both men and women caregivers reported consideration of institutionalization of their care recipient only when they could no longer handle the responsibility themselves. Caregivers also reported difficulty coping with personality changes caused by illness or medications.

Implications

Nurses in institutional and community settings who are working with caregiving families should identify and should acknowledge the caregiving experiences of their clients, and the effect of those experiences on the caregivers' subjective feelings of stress. Interventions aimed at assisting caregivers with: (1) balancing workloads and responsibilities, (2) identifying when they are doing more than they can effectively handle, (3) coping with the physical and behavioral changes that can occur in the care recipient, and (4) identifying alternative options for caregiving can be provided on a one-to-one or group basis.

suddenly as the result of a stroke or accident. A family may adjust better to the demands of caregiving when a relative's need for support gradually increases rather than when there is a sudden drop in the person's functional ability as a result of an acute health crisis (Harkins, 1985). Although short-term caregiving can be stressful, stress tends to be highest when caregiving is prolonged over months or years, the person's care needs are increasing, and the caregiver feels he or she receives little or no support (Schmall, Stiehl, 1987) (see Research box above).

Providing caregiving to a family member who has a dementing illness such as Alzheimer's disease can be particularly stressful. The person not only requires increasing assistance and supervision as the disease progresses but also becomes increasingly impaired in language, reasoning ability, memory and social behavior (Gwyther, 1987). As the dementia progresses, clients lose insight into their condition. Although a person who is physically ill but mentally intact can show appreciation to the caregiver, "thank yous" are generally absent from the cognitively impaired person.

Losing the person that family members have always known is one of the most difficult aspects of coping with a progressive, dementing illness. As one woman said, "I've already watched the death of my husband. Now I'm watching the death of the disease." Another stated, "The personality that was my husband's is no longer present. I feel as though I am tending the shell of who he was—that is, his body. That is all that remains."

More and more families are faced with long-distance caregiving. They may find themselves driving or flying back and forth to repeated crises or spending long weekends "getting things in order" or "checking on Mom and Dad." Such long-distance managing takes not only time and money but can also be emotionally and physically exhausting as well. Trying to connect with and to coordinate services from a distance can be quite frustrating, especially when the arrangements the family has made are cancelled by the older person once the family has returned home. **Care managers** can be particularly helpful for long-distance caregivers. A private care manager can: (1) evaluate an older person's situation and needs, (2) establish an interface with health care providers and arrange for needed services, (3) monitor the older person's status and compliance with treatment plans, (4) provide on-the-spot crisis management, and (5) keep the family informed about progress and changes in the older person's condition and situation.

Contrary to popular belief, nursing home placement does not necessarily relieve a caregiver's feelings of stress. Studies show that caregivers of institutionalized older adults experience the same feelings of burden as caregivers of community-dwelling older adults, although the sources of burden shift (Pratt, Schmall, Wright, 1987). Many injunctions exist about placement, and as a result, a caregiver may feel a sense of failure, even when placement is the best decision. Stress may also result from difficult visits, traveling to and from the care facility, worrying about the quality of the care, family conflicts regarding placement, and paying for nursing home care.

Stresses of Caregiving

Caregiving involves many changes for both the caregiver and the care receiver. The direction, amount, and nature of aid patterns between parent and child generally change from being mutual or reciprocal to a one-way pattern of aid (Archbold, 1980). Previous ways of interacting with each other may change. An adult son or daughter or the healthy spouse of the frail person may need to become more assertive. This can be particularly uncomfortable and difficult if the caregiver was the passive person in the relationship (Schmall, Isbell, 1982).

The older person receiving care may resent being a burden, may feel anger and frustration in relinquishing roles, or may become demanding in an attempt to regain some control (Schmall, Isbell, 1982). If the care receiver suffers from dementia or other chronic mental illness, and exhibits behavior problems and emotional disturbances, caregiver stress tends to be higher than if the care receiver had only physical disabilities (Zarit, 1994).

A poor relationship between the care receiver and the caregiver before caregiving is related to increased emotional distress in caregiving (Williamson, Schulz, 1990). The need for caregiving can threaten a previously established relationship. For example, if a spousal or parent-child relationship primarily survived on the "distancing" that was created in the relationship, caregiving may be stressful if increased contact is required. Some older people may have been difficult all of their lives and may be even more so when they need the support of others. As one woman said:

> The hardest thing for me is not being able to please Mom. No matter what I do, she criticizes how I do it or makes me feel I never do enough. When I've mentioned this to my brother, he reminds me that Mom's behavior is not new. The truth is it seems I have never been able to please her—only it's worse now.

Tobin and Kulys (1979) found that aged parents were more likely to label themselves as being "closest to" their child before caregiving but not afterwards.

Readjusting the caregiver's expectations of the ill family member can be difficult, particularly if the person was once a strong, independent person, exercised control, or made the family decisions. Readjusting expectations can be particularly difficult if the caregiver's own identity is strongly tied to who the ill family member was. However, hanging on to who the person was and what the person could do but now no longer can leaves a caregiver open to a continual, prolonged grieving (Schmall, Stiehl, 1987; Eisdorfer and Cohen, 1987).

Restriction of personal activities and social life is one of the most commonly cited problems among caregivers to moderately and severely impaired older adults (Zarit, 1987). The healthy spouse may lose a companion, sex partner, and someone with whom to share life's joys and problems (Schmall, Cleland, 1984). Feeling "trapped in one's own home" or being a "prisoner of love" is not uncommon. Maintaining contact with family and friends, and involvement in outside activities is critical for caregiver well-being.

Financial concerns also can be a major source of stress. One spouse said, "The greatest worry I have is I have used up the last of the money we received from the sale of the house. Now we will be using up our small store of stocks and bonds . . . then, who will look after me." A daughter stated, "I interrupted my career for 8 years to care for my mother. Not only did I lose a salary during that time . . . my retirement income is considerably smaller than it would have been had I continued

> **Insight** • *Care managers are health care professionals who can help locate and coordinate services for families when they live at a distance from an older relative. Care manager services are offered by local Area Agencies on Aging, hospitals, and private practitioners. Area Agencies on Aging can connect families with publicly funded care or case management services.*
> *Information about private care managers within an area can be obtained from:*
> *National Association*
> *of Private Geriatric Care Managers*
> *655 N. Alvernon Way, Suite 108*
> *Tucson, AZ 86711*
> *(602) 881-8088*

working." Competent financial and legal advice can make the difference between economic survival and destitution (Pratt et al, 1989).

Caregivers often experience role overload, finding themselves pulled by the many roles they play—parent, spouse, employee, and adult child. There simply may not be enough time to meet all demands. The potential for role conflict is particularly high for middle-age women who provide child and older adult care simultaneously. Marital and family problems can arise if time spent providing care to older adult relatives means a couple's or family's time together is severely curtailed. Caregivers often struggle with the ethical question of, "Where should I put my primary obligations and responsibilities?" Health professionals can be important in helping a caregiver answer this question.

Caregivers often struggle to balance their expectations for themselves with what they can actually achieve. Women caregivers seem to be particularly vulnerable to the "shoulds" and believe they should be able to do everything themselves (Pratt et al, 1987b). When unable to do so, they often feel guilty or become depressed.

Research shows that family caregivers are at high-risk for developing stress-related problems (Zarit, 1994). Several studies have documented high rates of depression among caregivers (Gallagher et al, 1989; Friss, Whitlatch, 1991), high levels of anxiety (Anthony-Bergstone, Zarit, Gatz, 1988), and an increased vulnerability to physical health problems (George, Gwyther, 1986; Moritz, Kasl, Ostfeld, 1992).

A caregiver's perception of the caregiving situation, however, may be more important in determining the degree of stress than the amount of actual change or disruption created by caregiving. For example, Archbold (1980) found that families who did not perceive their relative's stroke as disruptive reported less stress than families who did. Also, while some people find being employed and providing caregiving at the same time to be stressful, others view work as a respite from caregiving and find that working enhances the ability to give care (Zarit, 1994). This means that when evaluating a caregiver's stress, it is important to assess the meaning a caregiver ascribes to an event or stressor (see Research box below).

RESEARCH

Pratt C, Schmall V, Wright S: Burden, coping and health status: a comparison of family caregivers to community dwelling and institutionalized Alzheimer's patients. *J Gerontolog Social Work* 10(1-2):99-112, 1987.

Sample, setting

Of 240 family caregivers of older adults with dementia: 61% were members of Alzheimer's support groups; mean age of caregivers was 61.3 years; mean length of caregiving 49.1 months; 22% were male and 78% female; 62% provided care to relatives who resided in the community and 28% had relatives who resided in institutions.

Methodology

Zarit's Caregiver Burden Scale, Lawton's 7-item morale scale, and the Family Crisis Oriented Personal Evaluation Scales (F-COPES) were used to measure caregiver burden, morale and coping strategies. An investigator-designed instrument was used to measure self-assessed health before and after caregiving began and to gather selected descriptive information about the caregivers and clients.

Findings

Caregiver burden scores, morale scores, and coping strategies were not significantly different between caregivers of institutionalized or community dwelling clients. However, sources of burden did vary. Caregivers of institutionalized clients gave significantly higher ratings to burden scale items that assessed concerns about not having enough money to provide care, being unable to continue providing care, wishing they could leave the care to someone else, and feeling they should do more. Burden scores were significantly related to caregivers' morale levels for both caregiver groups.

When the effect of age was controlled, caregiver burden scores were significantly higher for caregivers who rated their own health as fair or poor, for both caregivers of community-dwelling and institutionalized relatives. Caregivers' ratings of their own health before caregiving began were not significantly related to the relatives' residence. However, caregivers' ratings of their current health were significantly related to relative residence, with caregivers of institutionalized relatives significantly more likely to rate their current health status as fair or poor.

For caregivers of institutionalized relatives, burden and morale were significantly related to confidence in problem solving. Greater burden and lower morale were significantly related to passivity as a coping strategy.

Implications

The common belief that institutionalization abates the stresses of caregiving is not well-founded for relatives of people with dementia. Although institutionalization may ease some problems, caregivers often confront new problems or concerns. It is important for health professionals to recognize and to assess family needs, and to give support to family members whose relatives are in care facilities. Such support may be particularly critical for older spouses or other family members whose physical and emotional health have declined as a result of caregiving.

Coping style and social support are important mediators of stress. A direct style of coping with problems is more effective than avoidance or expression of emotions (Zarit, 1994). Therefore in evaluating a caregiver's situation and ability to provide caregiving, it is important to consider the caregiver's coping style and how it impacts on caregiving and to assess the extent and quality of the support system. Disagreements among family members about care arrangements, and negative and conflicted social relationships can contribute to caregiver stress (Zarit, 1994; Schmall, Stiehl, 1987).

Long-distance Versus Nearby Family

People who provide daily support to an older family member often feel unappreciated. The person receiving care sometimes takes out feelings of frustration and loss on those providing day-to-day support and talks in glowing terms about sons and daughters who live at a distance.

Conflict can also arise between family members who live near the older person and those who live at a distance because of their different perspectives (Schmall, Stiehl, 1987). To the family member who lives at a distance and sees the older person only for a few days, the care needs may not seem as great as they do to the family member who has daily responsibility. Sometimes, also, the older person may "perk up" in response to a visit by a rarely seen family member and may not display the symptoms and difficult behavior that he or she exhibited before the visit. Some older people also "dump" on one family member and show a cheerful side to another. This behavior may be related to distance or past relationships.

Family members who are unable to visit regularly sometimes are shocked at the deterioration in their older relative. Sometimes they become upset because they have not been told "just how bad Mom or Dad is." The problem is that they may have only two points of reference—the last time they saw the older person (which may have been several months or a year earlier) and now. On the other hand, when changes have occurred gradually, family members who have regular contact with the older person often are not aware of the degree of change because they have gradually adjusted to the changes.

Family conflict can occur simply because of these different experiences. The nurse working with the family can often help family members to understand the reasons for different perceptions. Family members at a distance may need to be reminded not to let apparent differences in behavior between what they see and what the local caregiver has said necessarily discredit the caregiver. It helps too if family members will remember that local caregivers often have to compromise with the older person and accept imperfect solutions to problems.

INTERVENTIONS TO SUPPORT FAMILY CAREGIVERS

Education

The number one need of many families is for information and referral (Friss, 1990; Lorenson, 1992). One advantage of education—whether provided one-on-one or in group settings—over other intervention strategies is its nonintrusive nature. Many people who would not attend a support group or would not seek counseling may attend a program labeled "education." An educational program, however, can be a springboard for a person to seek out other needed intervention programs. As one woman said:

> I avoided going to a support group because I didn't want to air my 'dirty laundry.' It was not until after I attended an educational program that I realized my concerns and fears were not abnormal. It was then I felt more comfortable talking to others and joining the support group.

For family members providing care to people with dementia, disruptive behaviors, or personal care dependencies, the need for information may be even more critical because of the higher stress involved in these caregiving situations (Office of Technology Assessment, 1987) (see Research box on p. 148). For example, caregivers need information early on about the nature of a dementing illness, the limitations caused by it, and how it may affect the relationship between the caregiver and the care receiver, and strategies for coping. Fortinsky and Hathaway (1990) found that the most important need of family caregivers at the time of diagnosis of Alzheimer's disease was for education specific to Alzheimer's disease. Moreover, the need for education continued even after caregivers were no longer providing care.

Although a caregiver's needs for information are diverse, they fall into six general categories (Schmall, 1994):

1. **Understanding the family member's medical condition.** This is of fundamental importance. Caregivers need information about the progression, signs, symptoms, and outcomes; common medical treatments; impact on the older adult's functional abilities; and implications for the caregiver and family. It is important to dispel any myths and misinformation. Unrealistic expectations and misunderstandings often occur when caregivers are not informed about the limitations caused by a medical condition. For example, when caregivers of a person with dementia do not understand behavior caused by brain damage, they often view the person's behavior as intentional.
2. **Improving coping skills.** Coping skills may include stress management, social network-building skills, behavioral management skills, problem-solv-

RESEARCH

Schmall V, Pratt C: Community education on mental health in later life: findings from an evaluation of a series of three model programs, *J Ment Health Administr* 20(3):190-200, 1993.

Sample, setting

Of the 389 people who attended one of three 3-hour multimedia community education workshops focused on a specific mental health concern in later life—loss and grief *(The Second Story)*, depression and suicide *(The Final Course)*, or alcohol abuse *(Winter Comforts)*, about 80% of the subjects were white, non-Hispanic.

Methodology

Pre/post data were collected for control groups and people attending 14 community education workshops. The measures used were developed to reflect the specific objectives established for each program. A true-false test of knowledge (19 to 12 items) was developed for each of the three multimedia educational programs, using the methodology described by Diekman et al. (1988). A behavioral intention scale (6 to 7 items), developed for each program, asked participants to rate the likelihood that they would take specific actions in response to an older person who exhibited the specific mental health problem that was the focus of the workshop. On the posttest, participants also were asked to assess the impact of the workshop in their skills. Data analysis included cross tabulations, t-tests, and analysis of covariance.

Findings

Participants' knowledge, skills, and behavioral intentions increased significantly ($P \leqq 0.05$) as a result of the workshops. Significant increases were reported in participants' ability to recognize the signs of mental health problems and to take appropriate actions, including identifying community and professional resources. There were no significant findings related to age, gender, or level of education.

Implications

Family members and others who have knowledge and skills are more likely to intervene earlier with an older person who is at risk for, or exhibiting symptoms of, a mental health problem and to seek precrisis advice and mental health services. All too often, people who are in key roles for recognizing a mental health problem, intervening and getting treatment for older people do not do so. Sometimes family members assume symptoms are signs of "normal aging" or the result of dementia or an existing chronic illness. At other times when a problem is recognized, action is not taken because family members believe nothing can be done or that treatment will not be successful because of the person's age, or they simply do not know what to do. Beliefs and misconceptions such as "It has been 3 months since Dad died," "Mom should be getting on with her life," "To be old is to be depressed," "She's too old to stop drinking," and "Drinking is Dad's only remaining pleasure" are major barriers in getting treatment for the older person. Denial, fear of alienation, or not wanting to offend the person also keep people from taking action.

Evaluation data show that the three multimedia educational programs evaluated in this study—*The Second Story, The Final Course,* and *Winter Comforts*—were highly effective in increasing knowledge and encouraging individuals to take appropriate actions when an older person is exhibiting signs of grieving, depression, or alcohol abuse.

From Diekman L et al: The Alzheimer's disease knowledge tests, *Gerontologist* 28:402-407, 1988.

ing skills, and the ability to perform specific tasks of caregiving—such as managing incontinence, feeding a person with swallowing difficulties, or meeting an older adult's emotional needs.

3. **Dealing with family issues.** Family issues often involve how to get support from other family members, identifying how much and what type of help family members can give, and dealing with conflictual feelings toward family members who do not help. Decisions about older adult care and caregiving generally affect not only the caregiver and care receiver but also other family members. Family members who are not actively involved in caregiving may be, or perceive that they should be, a part of the decision making regarding changes in an older family member's life situation and care arrangements (Townsend, Poulshock, 1986). Anger and family dissension can occur when caregivers do not attend to these relationships, the thoughts and feelings of other family members, or the family's perceptions of the meaning of a potential change.
4. **Communicating effectively with elders.** Family members often need to know how to communicate effectively their concerns to older people who are competent, as well as to communicate with those who suffer from an inability to understand or to communicate. Communicating effectively with brain-impaired people often requires learning communication skills contrary to those learned over a lifetime; yet, using appropriate techniques can reduce stress for everyone. Niederehe

and Funk (1987), for example, found that family caregivers who interacted in encouraging and supportive ways with their family member with dementia had lower levels of stress than family caregivers who used an authoritarian or reasoning style. The benefits of such information are reflected in the following adult son's comments:

> The hardest thing about dealing with Alzheimer's disease is learning to relate in new ways and accepting my Dad as he is today. What a difference it made for me when I learned in the caregiver class to 'step into my Dad's world,' rather than keep asking him questions about things he simply could not remember. Our times together are now much more enjoyable for the both of us.

5. **Using community services.** Many caregivers do not know about the range of community services, type of help, and the care alternatives available, and how to access services.
6. **Long-term planning.** This includes making legal and financial plans and considering changes in the current caregiving situation, including possible nursing home placement.

Two major goals of caregiver education should be to: (1) empower caregivers and (2) increase caregiver confidence and competence (Schmall, 1994). Caregivers often experience feelings of powerlessness, a sense that they have no control over events (Davidhizar, 1992). Feeling powerless has a significant impact on a caregiver's physical and emotional health. Although the factors that affect powerlessness in caregiving are complex and vary from person to person (Davidhizar, 1992; Miller, 1986), it is generally helpful to use educational approaches that do the following (Schmall, 1994):

- **Help caregivers set realistic goals and expectations.** Never reaching goals reinforces feelings of powerlessness. Achieving goals helps to decrease those feelings and increase morale. A caregiver whose goal is to "make mother happy" is less likely to experience "success" than a caregiver whose goal is to plan one enjoyable activity each week with her mother.
- **Provide caregivers with needed skills.** Being able to do the tasks that need to be done, to get needed support, or to access community resources enhances feelings of being in control.
- **Enhance a caregiver's decision making skills.** This includes sharing information about options and considering the potential consequences of various options for the older person, the caregiver, and other family members.
- **Help caregivers solve problems.** The ability to solve problems in managing care reduces feelings of powerlessness and stress. Since personal perceptions affect a person's approach to problem solving, it is important to address caregiver perceptions of problems and explore reframing as a coping technique.

People are more likely to do something if they believe they will be able to perform successfully. They also have to believe that a skill or action will make a positive difference; otherwise, it probably will not be adopted (Stiehl, Bessey, 1993). Therefore one of the goals of education should be to provide caregivers with the confidence that they can do a task or take an action. This means it is critical to give caregivers an opportunity to practice skills in a learning environment that is nonthreatening and psychologically safe.

Skill-building is enhanced when a caregiver has the opportunity to practice the skill in an educational setting and to receive feedback; to apply the skill in the home environment; and then to return to discuss how well the technique worked, the problems that were encountered, and what they might do differently the next time in applying the skill (Fig. 6-2).

It is also important to address the barriers a caregiver may confront in the real world and discuss and practice methods for overcoming these barriers. For example, professionals often talk about the importance of caregivers setting limits but do not always prepare caregivers for the possible consequences of doing so. For instance, the manipulative behavior of a family member may worsen for a time after a caregiver begins setting limits, particularly if in the past, such behavior generally resulted in the family member getting what he or she wanted.

Family members also need to know that there may be times when they have to step back and wait until a crisis occurs before they can act (e.g., when a mentally intact older family member refuses to go to a doctor or refuses to stop drinking despite attempts at intervention). In such situations, however, family members many times feel as though they have failed. Families may need help to recognize when "failures" are the result of a challenging situation and not their performance.

Sharing printed information—handouts the nurse has prepared, pamphlets, and articles—and videotapes are other important ways to provide education. The value of **bibliotherapy** (literally translated, this means healing through books, but it refers to materials in many media, including pamphlets, audiotapes, and videotapes) is recognized in chemical dependency treatment. In an evaluation of the effectiveness of various treatment activities at Hazelden Treatment Center, reading assignments were rated highly, second in value only to formal peer interaction (Toft, 1993). According to Toft (1993), "a book or tape carries the voice of a human being; reading, listening or watching is a form of meeting. Bibliotherapy is

Fig. 6-2 Family caregiver putting wheelchair in trunk of car to take receiver to the health care provider. (Courtesy Rod Schmall, West Linn, Ore.)

valuable for people learning new behaviors. It gives them the opportunity to reflect and the tools to turn that reflection into action."

Evidence indicates that bibliotherapy may be equally valuable for some caregivers. Fortinsky and Hathaway (1990), for example, found that active and former caregivers of family members with Alzheimer's disease rated written materials about the disease process as their most important need at the time of diagnosis. The comments of some caregivers also indicate the value of printed materials:

> The *36-Hour Day* is my 'Bible' in dealing with my husband's illness. When I am at a loss about what to do, I turn to it. It has gotten me through many tough times.
>
> In reading the Extension publication, *Depression in Later Life,* my brother and I realized we should not consider it normal for Dad to be depressed just because he is 73. We followed the advice about talking with Dad about the physical changes we saw in him rather than talking with him about 'being depressed.' It worked . . . I thought we'd never get him to see a doctor.
>
> I learned a lot of crucial material through the materials the Alzheimer's Association sent to me.

Adults also learn independently. Workbooks can provide caregivers with a step-by-step guide for taking action. *The Carebook: A Workbook for Caregiver Peace of Mind* (Beedle, 1991) gives caregivers a step-by-step guide for preparing substitute caregivers. Information and forms in *Organizing Your Family Records* (Gregerson, 1991) and *Do You Know Your Valuable Papers?* (1993) can help families talk with aging parents about financial records and the organization and storage of important documents.

Because the time that people have is often limited,

Toft (1993) suggests that educational materials be short and to the point, solution-focused, and designed to empower people. Print materials provided to caregivers, when shared with other family members, can help create a common base of information and understanding (Schmall, 1994). Sometimes other family members "listen" more readily to information in a handout developed by a professional than to the same information shared verbally by the caregiver. Print materials are beneficial for another reason. It is difficult for people who are anxious or in crisis to hear everything that is said or to remember all the details about a newly learned skill or procedure. Written information gives the person a reference for later use.

Respite Programs

Studies suggest that family members are better able to tolerate long-term caregiving if they obtain **respite,** that is, "relief" or "time off" from caregiving responsibilities (Anthony-Bergstone, Zarit, Gatz, 1988; Zarit, Teri, 1991). Without breaks, the stresses inherent to caregiving can jeopardize the physical and mental health of the caregiver (Sharlach, Frenzel, 1986) and can even lead to neglect or abuse of the care recipient (Schmall, Webb, 1993).

Although the primary intended beneficiary of respite services is the caregiver, the care receiver also benefits (Crozier, 1982). In many cases, a respite care provider may be the only outside-the-family socialization for the care receiver. A care receiver also benefits from a caregiver being more "refreshed" following a break in caregiving (Evidence mounts, 1990).

Respite services may be provided in-home or out-of-home and for a few hours, a day, overnight, a weekend, or longer (Schmall, Webb, 1993). In-home respite care can include companion sitter programs or the temporary use of homemaker or home health services. Out-of-home respite services include adult day care or short stays in adult foster care homes, nursing homes, or hospitals.

Respite services are often underused by caregivers. Barriers to access and use of services include (Schmall, Webb, 1993):

- **Lack of awareness.** Often families are not aware of the availability of respite services or program eligibility, or they are not familiar with the provider agency.
- **Apprehension.** With in-home respite services a caregiver can be apprehensive about leaving a family member with a "stranger" or nonprofessional.
- **Caregiver attitudes.** Some caregivers feel, "I can care (or should be able to care) for my family member myself," or "No one can care for my family member like I can." Others feel guilty and that it is selfish to leave an ill family member in the care of someone else to meet their own needs.
- **Timing.** Caregivers often view respite services as " a last resort." They seek help much too late—when they are in crisis, or a family member is severely debilitated and requires care beyond what respite workers or an adult day program can provide.
- **Finances.** The cost of respite care, or the anticipation of future expenditures, is another reason some caregivers are unwilling to use or to delay the use of such programs. Others are unwilling to pay for a program they may view as a "babysitting service."
- **A care receiver's resistance.** Negative reactions by the care receiver, such as resentment toward someone coming into the house or the caregiver's leaving, may be the reasons why a caregiver does not use a respite program.
- **Energy required to use the program.** The time and energy required to prepare and to transport the care receiver can limit some caregivers' use of adult day care. In their study of caregiver activity on respite and nonrespite program days, Berry, Zarit, and Rabatkin (1991) found that caregivers who used day care services actually spent more time performing caregiving activities on respite care days.
- **Program inflexibility and bureaucracy.** Program inflexibility may also contribute to caregivers' lower usage of respite care. System barriers reported by caregivers include (Malone-Beach et al, 1992; Meltzer, 1982): (1) services not available when most wanted or needed, such as weekends or in the evenings; (2) services accommodated only older people with a narrow band of need; (3) lack of responsiveness of the service system to changing conditions of the care receiver; (4) system not allowing caregivers to have one respite worker with whom they could relate to over time; and (5) having to make several calls to arrange for respite care.

These may be issues the nurse needs to address when working with a caregiver in regard to the use of community respite and adult day care services.

Caregivers who delay using respite care until a crisis or until they are "burnt out" are less likely to benefit from it because it is "too little . . . too late" (Deimling, 1989). Respite care is most beneficial when a caregiver begins to use it early in caregiving to prevent physical and mental exhaustion rather than to treat it. Dunn (1987) suggests that one reason respite may be viewed as a "service of last resort" is that often the message given to caregivers is that "respite is a service when you are having trouble coping or the condition of your loved one is progressing to the point where placement may be necessary.

In general, women caregivers appear to have more difficulty using respite and day care. Bader (1985) suggests that women may buy into the view that "caregiving is women's work." Because they have been socialized to be nurturers and caregivers, women may feel caregiving is something they *should do.* As a result, they may be more reluctant to let go of the caregiver role and to accept outside help. Men, on the other hand, may feel less secure in the caregiver role and may perceive that they do not have the needed skills to "take care of someone else." Thus they tend to be more willing to use services.

The nurse should help caregivers recognize that caregiving is a job. Just as employees benefit from regular breaks and vacations, a caregiver benefits from a "break" in the job. The nurse should emphasize that the need for respite care begins with the onset of caregiving.

The message presented to a caregiver also may be important. Although respite programs are designed primarily to benefit the caregiver, some caregivers are reluctant to take advantage of services for themselves. One study (Beisecker, Wright, 1991), found that caregivers who perceived adult day care as primarily benefiting themselves were less likely to use the service than caregivers who perceived adult day care as primarily benefiting the care receiver. Malone-Beach et al. (1992) found that:

> Caregivers generally had more difficulty accepting assistance if the focus was on their needs or if the service was perceived as merely 'babysitting' . . . Some caregivers indicated they could more readily accept a service if it focused on the client and not them. Many caregivers did not see a connection between their own physical and psychological well-being and being able to continue with caregiving.

Therefore for some caregivers, resistance to respite and day care programs may decrease if the nurse emphasizes how a program can benefit the care receiver. Lawton, Brody, and Saperstein (1989) suggested additional ways to increase the appeal of respite care to caregivers: (1) portray respite as a program that is helpful to anyone, even the most successful of caregivers; (2) emphasize how respite helps to maintain the positive aspects of caregiving; and (3) provide reassurance that caregivers deserve time away from caregiving and that they are not deserting their family members by taking such breaks in caregiving. They state that, "these appeals affirm the basic strengths of the caregiver, yet they will not be lost on the overworked or depressed caregiver" (Lawton et al, 1989).

It is generally assumed that respite is inherently beneficial to the caregiver. However, how caregivers spend their time while using respite and day care may have an impact on how effective it is in alleviating stress (Lawton et al, 1989; Montgomery, Borgatta, 1989; Wright, Lund, Caserta, 1990). Ehrlich and White (1991) report that some caregivers may interpret respite as primarily providing assistance with ongoing daily tasks rather than time away from the care recipient. In a study of caregivers, Wright, Lund, and Caserta (1990) found that differential uses of respite time may lead to differential outcomes. Their findings showed that caregivers who primarily use respite time for discretionary activities such as social activities, rest, and exercise experience more favorable outcomes than caregivers who spend the time primarily in obligatory activities such as housework, other domestic chores, or providing care to another person. These studies indicate that it may be worthwhile to pursue with caregivers how they plan to use the respite time.

Even when formal respite services are not available, the nurse plays a vital role in encouraging caregivers to take breaks in caregiving and in helping caregivers to identify and to overcome barriers to obtaining respite. Members of the caregiver's informal support system may be able to provide respite when formal respite services do not exist or are not accessible. However, some caregivers need help to reach out and to ask for assistance, particularly those who view asking for help as a sign of weakness, helplessness, inadequacy or failure. A written "prescription for respite" by a health care provider for certain hours of respite per week or month may provide the authority a caregiver needs to begin taking breaks from the demands of caregiving (Dunn, 1987) (Box 6-2).

Support Groups

Many caregivers benefit from sharing their feelings with someone who is supportive and who listens nonjudgmentally. Such sharing with a confidant often relieves tension, helps to give a new perspective on the situation, increases mutual understanding, and builds support (Schmall, Stiehl, 1987). In many communities, caregiver support groups have developed for this particular kind of sharing.

Some support groups are oriented to specific diseases like cancer, Parkinson's disease, lung disease, stroke, or Alzheimer's disease and related dementias. Others are for family caregivers in general.

A support group can be a place where caregivers get advice, gain knowledge about their older relatives' medical conditions and problems, share experiences, develop new coping strategies, learn about community resources and care alternatives, and let off steam. Participation in a support group may help to normalize a caregiver's experience (Rzetelny, Mellor, 1981). Discovering that they are not alone can provide much-needed emotional relief to some caregivers. For the isolated caregiver deprived of intimacy and support from the care receiver, a support group may also provide an acceptable outlet for socializing (Gwyther, 1987).

Research on caregiver support groups has several limitations; however, findings to date suggest the following (Gallagher-Thompson, 1994; Zarit, 1994):

- Levels of caregiver burden may be more influenced by chan ges in a person's caregiving situation than by support group participation.

BOX 6-2

Video Respite: An Innovative Caregiver Resource

- "I can't seem to find any time for myself. I'm suffocating."
- "I never have time alone, not even in my own home. I can't even take a bath, fix dinner, or make a phone call without interruption. I have no privacy."
- "I'm tired of my mother following me around and asking questions constantly, like a broken record. I need some time and space to breathe."

Such comments are common from caregivers of people with dementia. One of their greatest needs is for regular breaks from caregiving. Although adult day and respite programs provide caregivers with much needed time away from the demands of caregiving, caregivers often need 15-minute or half-hour breaks to take a short rest, to have time alone, to attend to personal matters, to make telephone calls, or to do household chores without interruption. *Video Respite,* developed by researchers at the University of Utah Gerontology Center after 10 years of research on caregiving, is a unique, innovative approach to making it possible for caregivers to get these brief "breaks" in caregiving without leaving home.

Video Respite consists of a series of videotapes simulating a personal and friendly visit. Each video actively engages people who have memory/cognitive impairments in an enjoyable and meaningful interaction. As the memory-impaired individual interacts with the person on the videotape, a caregiver can take some time for himself or herself.

Video Respite currently includes two video programs: *Favorite Things* and *Gonna Do a Little Music. Favorite Things,* designed for people with moderate to advanced memory-impairment, is a 33-minute simulated visit with Marilyn. Marilyn talks with the person who has Alzheimer's disease about a variety of familiar things such as babies, vegetable gardens, animals, and holidays. She introduces a 1-year-old baby, a dog, and objects to prompt conversation. Marilyn invites the viewer to join her in singing favorite old songs such as "Let Me Call You Sweetheart" and "Daisy," and in doing simple hand and arm exercises.

Gonna Do a Little Music, a 50-minute visit with Marianne, is designed for use with people who have slight to moderate memory impairment. As she plays the guitar and autoharp, Marianne engages viewers in singing familiar songs and discussing memories related to subjects such as love, music lessons, family gatherings, and childhood friends. Marianne also leads the viewer in simple hand, arm, and leg movements. Although some people may not be able to do all of the physical exercises, the tape holds the attention of memory-impaired people as evidenced by their participatory actions such as toe-tapping.

It is exciting to observe a person with Alzheimer's disease "converse" with Marilyn or Marianne, and even more importantly feel good about his or her "visit." Strengths of these videos for the person with Alzheimer's disease include:

- **A personalized approach.** The people on the videos are friendly and present themselves and the content in such a way that it feels as though the viewer is being talked with directly.
- **An opportunity for positive interaction.** Questions, pauses, and feedback from Marilyn and Marianne encourage involvement and conversation from the memory-impaired person.
- **A focus on long-term memory.** Through familiar images and childhood songs, the videos capture the attention and trigger long-term memories of people with dementia. The objects, people, events, and early life experiences that are discussed are familiar to most of today's older people.
- **A slow pacing and visually uncluttered screen.** The slower pace gives people with memory impairment the necessary time to understand and to respond to information. The visual simplicity helps to keep the viewer focused and reduces distraction. The faster pace and content of most television programs are not optimum for sustaining the attention of most people with Alzheimer's disease.

Studies conducted by University of Utah researchers also show that the videos can be useful in calming the person who is agitated. One caregiver stated:

> When Herb is agitated and I'm at my wit's end is when I need the tape the most, and I forget to use it. And then I'll call my son, and he'll say, 'Put the tape in first, if that doesn't work then I'll be over,' but it always works. He's not attentive to TV, but he is to the tape.

Because of the loss of recent memory in Alzheimer's disease, the *Video Respite* tapes can be used again and again. Another caregiver reported:

> This kept Mother entertained like nothing else has for years. I could use it every day or back-to-back because it's like a new tape each time. If she is depressed or irritable it will get her out of it. She won't watch TV, but she is glued to the tape.

Because *Video Respite* tapes engage the person with Alzheimer's disease, caregivers can get short breaks in caregiving whenever needed. For a caregiver, 30 to 50 minutes of uninterrupted time can be significant. The tapes are also: (1) quick, convenient and easy for a caregiver to incorporate into the daily routine; (2) portable, so that they can be used in many different settings or places; and (3) appropriate for repeated use. The videos also may help to give caregivers who feel helpless a greater sense

(From Innovative Caregiving Resources, Salt Lake City, UT)

Continued.

BOX 6-2

Video Respite: An Innovative Caregiver Resource—cont'd

of control. As one caregiver said, "The videos help me to feel as though I am doing something positive for Mother."

Considerable research and evaluation, including a 2-year grant from the national Alzheimer's Association, went into the development of these *Video Respite* tapes. *Video Respite* is also being tested in nursing homes, special care units, adult daycare centers, and a state mental hospital. Early findings show favorable results.

Video Respite is not a panacea or a substitute for a caregiver or other services; however, it does offer considerable promise in providing caregivers with an opportunity for respite time.

- A support group with a focused agenda such as dealing with feelings of anger or depression may have more measurable benefits than a support group with a broader focus.
- Some caregivers may benefit most from an initial period of counseling in which their specific concerns are addressed, followed by participation in a support group.
- Support groups may be most fruitful when they are tailored for specific groups of caregivers. The needs of male caregivers may be different from those of female caregivers; the needs of spouses may be different from adult children who are caregivers; and the needs of newly diagnosed families may be different from families dealing with late-stage chronic illness.

Support groups are not for everyone. However, research shows that participants find support groups helpful even when research findings are not positive (Zarit, 1994).

Family Conference

Although one family member is generally responsible for caregiving, other family members are important in providing support. However, each family member may have a different idea about what is the problem or how to handle a situation. For example, one brother might not want a parent's resources—his potential inheritance—spent for in-home care. He may prefer that the family provide the needed care, whereas another brother may feel, "Mom's money is there to spend on her," and prefers to purchase services. Beliefs about "what is best" often differ, creating family dissension. One person may be adamant that the older person should be kept at home at all costs; another may feel that a care facility is the best care setting. Intense conflicts often result when one person insists that the older person be maintained at home and another is advocating for nursing home placement.

Unless differences are discussed and resolved, disagreements among family members usually only magnify. The family conference is one strategy for deciding how to share caregiving responsibilities and to reach consensus about needs, problems, and decisions (Schmall, Isbell, 1982; Schmall, Stiehl, 1987).

A family conference should be held as early as possible after the need for caregiving arises. Everyone who is concerned or may be affected by decisions should be involved, including the older person (if at all possible) for whom plans are being made. Calling distant family members to get their input and keeping them informed can help them feel as if they are a part of the decision making. A family member should not be excluded because of distance, personality, family history, or limited resources. It is just as important to invite the difficult, argumentative family member or the one who seldom visits as it is to involve those who are supportive. Such involvement ensures greater success and support for any plans that are developed and can help prevent later undermining of decisions.

Sometimes, families find it helpful to hold a two-step conference. The first meeting is held without the older person for the purpose of discussing ideas and feelings, raising concerns, and identifying information that is needed. The purpose is not to make the decision or to "gang up" on the older person. A second meeting is then held with the older person, who is actively involved in evaluating options and making decisions.

A family conference is not always easy. It is most difficult for family members who have never discussed emotion-laden concerns, hold differing values and outlooks in regard to the situation, or have a history of poor relationships and conflict. A family in conflict may easily become angry, and get sidetracked from current issues and the decisions that need to be made. Old resentments and conflicts, which may have been dormant since child-

hood, can reemerge with regard to relationships, family roles, expectations, the authority to make decisions, and even inheritance. A family conference is often even more important in these situations.

If family conflicts or hidden resentments prevent rational discussion, it often helps to have a health care professional skilled in working with older adults and their families facilitate the family conference. Most importantly, the professional—whether a nurse, social worker, clergy, or counselor—should be well versed in aging-related issues and family dynamics, and have group facilitation skills. The mere presence of an "outsider" often keeps the atmosphere calm, and the discussion focused and objective. An objective third party also can help move the family past emotions to common interests and can handle many difficult situations. Some practitioners and agencies offer family consultation services that include facilitation of family conferences (Herr, Weakland, 1979).

A family conference is more likely to be successful if the following are considered (Schmall, Stiehl, 1987; Silverstone, Hyman, 1982):

- Hold the family conference in a neutral setting. A family conference in the older person's home may help to give him or her a greater sense of control, especially if the person is feeling a loss of control over his or her life.
- Create a feeling of support and confidentiality.
- Give recognition to the fact that everyone has a different relationship with each other and that current life circumstances vary. These factors need to be respected and considered as decisions are discussed and made.
- Have each family member address the problem from his or her perspective. This increases commitment to the process and contributes to defining and reaching agreement on "the problem" and possible solutions.
- Give everyone the opportunity to express feelings, voice preferences, and offer suggestions without being criticized.
- Keep the conference focused on current concerns rather than on other issues, past conflicts, personalities, or resentments.
- Focus on the positive things family members do, or are willing and able to do, and encourage everyone to be honest about their limitations. Sharing information about other responsibilities can help others understand the reasons support might be limited.
- Prepare a written plan about decisions made, and what each person will do and by when. A written plan can prevent later disagreements.

WORKING WITH AGING FAMILIES: CONSIDERATIONS AND STRATEGIES

The following are considerations in working with families.

Identify Who is the Client and Who is the Family

Critical questions to ask when working with older adults includes: (1) Who is the client? (2) Is it just the older person? Or (3) should the older person's family also be considered the "client?"

Although the older person is generally identified as the client, there are times when it is most appropriate to consider the family as the client as well. Family members are often intimately involved in the decisions to be made, are affected by potential decisions, or are actively involved in caregiving to the older person. If only the needs of the older person are considered and not the needs and situation of the family, a plan of care may have less chance for success, particularly if family members are to be responsible for carrying out a care plan.

Genevay (1994) points out that taking a family perspective is also:

> . . . an extremely useful way for professionals to merge family caregiving functions with their own . . . The rewards for the older person and the family are often multiple when the family is included, but is sometimes hard for paid care providers to include a group of 'outsiders' who have differing values about care.

Another significant question for professionals to ask is, "Who is family, as defined by the older person?" The definition of *family* needs to be broadened beyond blood relatives to include other people who are significant in the life of the older person. As Kimmel (1992) points out, blood is not always "thicker than water." Many older people are connected to others by love and friendship and function as a family to each other. These relationships often extend into caregiving. Examples of such "families" include the following (Schmall, 1994):

- Red, who divorced in his early 70s, never had children. His only blood relatives were his nieces, nephews, and older adult sisters, each of whom lived hundreds of miles away. During the last 12 years of his life, nearly all support was provided by a person Red referred to as "my adopted granddaughter." When medical crises occurred and care arrangements were needed, Red looked to his "granddaughter" to make the necessary arrangements.
- Florence's son divorced his first wife, Jane, and remarried. The divorce, however, did not end the re-

lationship between Florence and Jane. Florence continued to view Jane as "the daughter I never had," not as her "ex-daughter-in-law." When Florence became frail, she did not turn to her sons or the current daughters-in-law for help—it was Jane she turned to for both day-to-day assistance and emotional support.

- Elizabeth and Mary had lived together as a couple for 30 years when Elizabeth developed cancer. Although Elizabeth's "blood relatives" were supportive during the downhill course of the disease, Mary was the primary caregiver, the person with whom Elizabeth consulted when she faced medical decisions, and the one who made decisions when Elizabeth was no longer able to do so.

In "created, but not legally recognized families," it may be important to help individuals take steps—such as completing an AMD, or power of attorney for health care or durable power of attorney for financial decisions—to ensure that the relationship can continue into caregiving, especially if one person loses the capacity to make decisions. As Mary stated, "Elizabeth's giving me power of attorney for health care ensured that our relationship could continue as it had been for 30 years. We knew another couple who were in a similar situation, and the [blood] relatives stepped in and took over control, disregarding the relationship Jim and Bill had for 20 years."

In the health care setting, it may also be important to reevaluate the definition of family. If "blood relatives only allowed in intensive care" and other rules are followed, some older people may be deprived of their most significant sources of support.

Other important questions for the nurse to ask are, "Who is the decision-maker? Or who owns the care plan?" The primary role of the nurse is to empower older people and their families. This means giving the information, guidelines, options, and skills that will enable older people and their families to make the best decisions possible and to better manage a medical condition or their situation. However, it is easy to become frustrated and angry—and eventually experience burnout—if older people or families choose a course of action that the nurse feels is not the best. It is important for nurses to remember that they have not failed when an older person or family selects an option different from the nurse's recommendation. Depending on the situation, the primary responsibility for implementation lies with the older person or the family.

Assess the Family

There are no easy answers when an older person's life situation or physical or mental status changes. What may be the best answer for one older person and his or her family may be inappropriate for another family whose situation seems exactly the same.

Each older person and family system is different. It can be just as important to understand the family's history, current circumstances, and needs as it is to know about an older person's needs and level of functioning. A family's willingness to provide care, for example, says nothing about their actual ability to do so. Sometimes the care an older person needs exceeds that which an individual or family can provide, and the caregiver becomes the "hidden client." As one adult daughter stated, "My father was the person with Alzheimer's disease, but his illness also killed my mother." To not evaluate the ability of family members to provide caregiving is a disservice to older clients (Gallo, Reichel, Anderson, 1988).

Information from a family assessment can result in more effective older adult care planning and decision making. Gallo, Reichel, and Anderson (1988) point out that another benefit of assessing how well a caregiver is doing is that it validates a person's caregiving effort and sends a message that the nurse is concerned about the caregiver's well-being, as well as the older adult's health.

There are many tools for conducting assessments of family functioning and the level of caregiving burden (Berkey, Hanson, 1991; Gallo, Reichel, Anderson, 1988; Vitaliano, Young, Russo, 1991). Depending on the family, older adult, and the decisions to be made, the following may be among the important factors to consider in conducting a family assessment.

Past Relationship

Lifetime relationships with each other can influence the family members' abilities to plan and to make decisions together, and to provide support to the older person. It is important to remember that every adult child has a different history with an aging parent, even though all children may have shared the same family events. Families who have a history of alcoholism, or poor or abusive relationships cannot always be expected to provide the assistance an older person needs.

Consider the *degree of emotional intensity*—the closeness, affection, and openness—that has existed in the relationships of family members. Parental/spousal disability sometimes can threaten a person's identity or the level of emotional relationship that has been established. For example, some married couples, parents, and children have had an emotionally distant relationship for many years. Spouses may have shared the same household but lived separate lives. Some adult children have maintained emotional distance from a parent by choosing to live and to work at a geographic distance. People for whom these kinds of situations are true may be reluctant to enter the care system or may have more difficulty with caregiving. It may be unrealistic to expect such family members to meet the emotional needs of the older person; they may feel more comfortable with meeting a person's instrumental needs, that is, doing tasks.

Family Dynamics

Family dynamics are the ways family members interact with each other, including the communication patterns, family alliances, and symbiotic relationships. Exploring the beliefs of the older people and their family members about autonomy in decision making is critical (Noelker, 1994). What are family members' views about how decisions should be made, particularly in regard to the role of the older adult in decisions about his or her life? To what degree are family members paternalistic, that is, think that the older person should submit to their decisions or a provider's recommendations?

Roles

It can be useful to know if there are distinctive roles assigned to individual family members. If so, what role(s) does each person have? What are the expectations held by the person fulfilling the role and by other family members? Do any of the roles generate conflict for the people who bear them? For example, family members may have always assumed that if a parent needed care, a particular daughter would provide the care because she "is the oldest, lives the closest, is a nurse, or has always taken care of everyone who needed help." The daughter may also have always viewed caregiving as her role. However, this "assigned" role may or may not be realistic given the daughter's current life situation or the needs of the parent. Sometimes, the older person or family member may not make a decision until the "decision maker" in the family is consulted. The importance of considering who plays which roles is exemplified by this daughter's comments:

> I lived in the same town as my Dad, so when he needed help, I was the one who provided it on a daily basis. Dad expected me to help because I was his daughter. But, when it came to making decisions, my opinions never counted with him. His son's opinions, however, mattered, and he would listen to them. I think his basic view throughout his life was, 'women are there to serve men,' and 'men are by far more knowledgeable than women.' It didn't matter that I had a college education, and my brother didn't.

A survey conducted by the Benjamin Rose Institute also found that it is not unusual for an older person and his or her case manager to have different perceptions about who is the primary informal caregiver to the older person (Noelker, 1994). Knowing who does what for the older person makes for more effective planning.

Old family roles also can come to the foreground when brothers and sisters are brought together to address the care needs of a parent. Marla stated:

> I lived in the same community as my parents, so when they became ill, I did everything that needed to be done and arranged for support services. Both of my sisters lived hundreds of miles away. Although I am a competent business woman, it seemed that when both of my sisters, who are older, came home, I immediately became the 'baby of the family' again.

The roles family members may play can be varied. Examples of potential roles include the prime mover—the person who gets things done in the family; the scapegoat—when problems arise, this person often becomes the focus of attention; the decision maker—this role may vary depending on whether the decision to be made regards finances, living arrangements, or health care; the peacemaker—the person who always tries to create peace when there is family dissension; the "pot-stirrer"—the person who seems to keep things "stirred up" in the family; the black sheep; the burden bearer; the favorite child; the model child; and the escapee—the person who disappears when there are tough decisions to be made or work to be done.

It can be helpful to identify how family roles are affected, especially that of the older person, as a result of the older adult's increased frailty. What are the perceptions of family member's regarding the role of the older person? Do any adult children perceive that their role now is to "parent their parent?" Sometimes people talk about "role reversal." Although a family member may take on "parent-like" responsibilities, a parent is still a parent and a spouse is still a spouse emotionally no matter how dependent that person has become. Decades of adult experiences cannot be repressed. If family members think of an older family member as a child, they are more likely to treat that person in child-like ways and, in return, get child-like behavior.

Consider the older adult's view of his or her role with respect to the rest of the family. For example, does the older person feel she is still a contributing family member or that she has no role? Does the person feel he is entitled to care from family members just because "I am your father?"

Loyalties and Obligations

This refers to interpersonal allegiances. Family members are often struggling with two questions:

1. What should be my primary priority—meeting the needs of my aging family member? My spouse and children? My career?
2. How much do I owe to whom?

Caregivers who have not been able to deal with these questions may find themselves stressed by trying to do too much. They may also feel guilty because they feel they are not doing enough.

Sometimes family members, in looking at older adult care issues, are also weighing how much various family members "owe" to the person who needs assistance. Is any particular member viewed as being more obligated or more indebted to providing care because of how much the older person has given to him or her in the past? In other words, which family members are viewed as "creditors" and which as "debtors," and to whom do they owe? For example:

> Sue did not feel obligated to provide hands-on care to her mother. She felt, 'Mother never did anything to help me. All I got from her was criticism—about everything!' On the other hand, Louise (Sue's younger sister) felt, 'Mother has always been there for me. I don't know what I would have done after my divorce if Mom hadn't opened her doors to me and my three children for those 2 years.' Sue also felt Louise 'owed' their mother more than she did.

Levels of stress are generally higher for the person who provides caregiving only out of a sense of obligation.

Dependence/Independence

Some families accept and adjust easier than other families to the increased dependence of a family member. Answers to the following questions can be helpful in determining how well family members are dealing with or will deal with increased frailty in an older family member.

- What are the attitudes and expectations of family members, including the older person, about dependency?
- Has the family experienced a shift in who is dependent? If so, what is the response of individual family members to this shift?
- Are any family members threatened by the increased dependence of the older person?
- Is the older person giving family members mixed messages about how independent or dependent he or she is?
- Do family members perceive the dependency needs of the person realistically? Is anyone denying, minimizing, or overexaggerating the dependence? Is anyone overprotecting or forcing dependency?

Providing caregiving to a family member can be more difficult if the caregiver had been the dependent person in the relationship. The care receiver also may resent the caregiver exercising more control.

Caregiver Stress

Caregiver stress and **burden** impact the caregiver's health and his or her ability to continue to provide caregiving; therefore it is critical to assess the nature and extent of caregiver stress. It is important not only to identify actual stressors—which may or may not be a direct result of caregiving—but also to assess their significance to the caregiver. The meaning a caregiver gives to a stressor is a stronger predictor of its impact than the actual stressor (Zarit, 1994). Other useful areas to assess are a caregiver's style of coping; the caregiver's support system; the caregiver's evaluation of the adequacy of his or her support system; the care needs of the older person, including behavioral and emotional problems, and the caregiver's perception of those care needs; and financial resources.

Just as an older adult's situation can change and can require reassessment, so can a family's situation and the ability of a caregiver to provide care. As Gallo, Reichel, and Anderson state (1988) in the following:

> The assessment of family functioning is not a static determination. The strength of the support for the elder needs to be periodically reevaluated. Change in the elder's condition may compel a fresh look at caregiving roles and stresses. The spouse may be able to manage a demented elder until the tasks of caregiving become too physically demanding because of the development of incontinence by the patient. Changes within the family may necessitate a restructuring of social support. A new job may take a child away from an elderly parent. The death or illness of a spouse may leave an elder stranded. New sources of assistance may need to be rallied in order to provide adequate care for the family member.

Encourage Families to Plan in Advance of Need

Age-related issues tend not to be discussed by families until faced with a crisis (Cicerelli, 1992; Noelker, 1994). As a result, many adult children are often unaware of parental preferences, views about care arrangements, or the existence and location of important documents.

Planning ahead requires anticipating negative situations—dependency, disability, incapacity, and death—and exploring solutions to uncertain, hard-to-face problems (Goetting, Schmall, 1993). Discussing such subjects can be uncomfortable to all family members. For some people, talking about potential incapacity and inability to manage is more difficult than talking about death.

A critical time for discussion is when a family member shows signs of deterioration or has been diagnosed with a degenerative disease like Alzheimer's. To wait for the situation to worsen reduces the options. Although planning ahead does not prevent all problems, it does prepare families to act more effectively if a crisis does occur. Planning ahead also can:

- Help avoid crisis decision making and make decisions easier in difficult times.
- Reduce emotional and financial upheaval later.
- Ensure that the older person's lifestyle, personal philosophies, and choices are known if a time should come when the person is not able to actively participate in making decisions.
- Decrease the possibility that the family will have to take more intrusive, restrictive actions such as petitioning the court for a guardianship or conservator-

ship if their older family member becomes incapacitated.
- Reduce disagreements and misunderstandings among family members.

Families may find the following suggestions helpful in opening up discussion with a reluctant older family member (Schmall, Isbell, 1982; Goetting, Schmall, 1993).

Look for Natural Opportunities to Talk

A natural opportunity might be a life event such as when a friend or another family member experiences a health crisis, is diagnosed with Alzheimer's disease, or moves into a care facility; a situation reported in the media, such as a person dying without a will; or when the older person is recovering from an illness. If a parent says, "When I die . . ., family members should listen and encourage expression of feelings. Too often, families discourage discussion by saying things such as, "Don't be so morbid," "You'll probably outlive all of us," or "We have lots of time to talk about such things."

Talk About "What If's"

A person might say, "If a time came when you could no longer make decisions about your own health care, who would you want to make decisions for you?" Or " If you could no longer care for yourself at home, even with the help of community services, what would you want to happen?" Some families who play board games have found the educational game *Families and Aging: Dilemmas and Decisions* (Schmall, Staton, Weaver, 1984) is a nonthreatening way to raise and discuss potential decisions.

Share Personal Preferences and Plans in the Event of One's Own Illness or Death

Incapacity is not always a function of getting older; a debilitating accident can happen to anyone regardless of age. Some parents question the motives of adult children who express concern about parental finances, but have not made plans themselves, for example, prepared a will, an AMD, or a durable power of attorney.

Express Good Intentions and a Willingness to Listen

The objective is to set the right tone for discussion. A loving, caring approach moves a discussion farther than an, "I know what's best for you" attitude. Adult children who take a paternalistic approach—that is, believe that older parents should submit to their decisions—are likely to encounter resistance.

An appropriate role for the nurse is to educate older clients about the benefits of advance planning and the importance of making plans while their capacities are intact. A positive approach can be to emphasize how making plans in advance of need can give the person greater control and provide greater assurance that his or her preferences will be known and honored.

Help Family Members to Communicate Their Concerns to Older Relatives Honestly and in Positive Ways

Open, honest communication helps build and maintain relationships; yet, such communication is not easy if family communication has been one of "game playing." An adult son or daughter may say only what they think a parent wants to hear or what they think will not upset a parent. However, this tends to create mistrust and wastes energy as family members "walk on ice" with each other.

Family members often express concerns about an older relative's situation, with "you" messages, that is, telling the person what to do or not to do. An example of such a message is "Mother, you are no longer safe living in your home. It's time for you to move into a retirement facility." The worst "you" message is the threat of "If you don't . . . then I will . . . ." "You" messages sound dictatorial, tend to create defensiveness and resistance, and close off communication.

An older person is more likely to listen to family members who present issues in terms of being concerned, rather than family members who talk as if it is the older person who has the problem. An example is to use "I" messages. With a good "I" message, a person states his or her feeling, describes the specific behavior or situation of concern, and gives a concrete reason for the concern. "I" messages are specific rather than general, and attention is focused on problems, not personalities. An example of an "I" message is: "Mom, because of your recent fall, I'm concerned about your safety living in this house. I'm afraid you might fall again and the next time, you might not be found for several hours or longer. Can we talk about my concern?"

The words, "I am concerned about . . ." sound quite different to a person than, "You should . . . ." When done correctly, "I" messages come across to another person as "speaking from the heart." "I" messages also communicate that the person bringing up the issue or concern recognizes that what is being said is his or her belief, and this leaves room for other perceptions. With an "I" message, it is also more difficult for another person to argue with what has been said because it is the speaker's feelings that were shared.

Adequately expressing one's concerns to an older family member is only one part of effective communication. Family members also may need help to actively listen and to empathize, that is, to understand the feelings and emotional needs of the older person. Sometimes, when family members think an older person needs to make a change—for example, move to a group-living situation or give up driving—they focus only on the change as being "for the best" and fail to acknowledge the older person's losses and feelings (Schmall, 1993b). The older person may experience a wide range of feelings—fear, anger, grief, helplessness, frustration, and relief. It is easier for many older people to talk openly about their situations, concerns, and feelings if they have an adult son or daughter who listens, acknowledges, and accepts these feelings.

It is helpful if family members try to imagine how a situation looks and feels from the perspective of the older person. The nurse should encourage adult children to ask themselves, "How would I feel if I were in Dad's shoes?" Older people who sense empathy and understanding are more willing to listen to concerns expressed by family members.

Involve the Older Person in Decision Making

Too often, the older person, especially if he or she is frail, is excluded from decisions being made about his or her own life (Schmall, 1982; Cicerelli, 1992). Family members may fail to tell the person what is happening or about the decisions under consideration. A person who is excluded from decision making is more likely to become angry, demanding, helpless, or withdrawn. Plans also are more likely to backfire.

Involvement in decision making provides greater assurance that a person will accept and will adapt to a change, even if the change is not the person's preferred choice. A person who is railroaded into a new situation usually makes a poor adjustment. For example, studies find that nursing home residents who are involved in the entry decision feel more in control of their lives, report higher levels of well-being, and are more likely to adjust than those who are forced into a nursing home (Schmall, 1993a; Noelker, 1994).

Change is anxiety-producing, but not being involved in decisions about a potential change creates even more anxiety and an atmosphere of distrust. Even if an older person cannot actively participate in making or carrying out decisions, he or she should still be informed about alternatives and plans that are being made.

Only in a few extreme cases such as advanced Alzheimer's disease or a massive stroke are people unable to make decisions. It is also critical for a family to understand that an older family member with a memory impairment may not be able to remember discussions or agreements made. Yet the person often feels a sense of being involved in what is happening. One son stated (Schmall, 1993a):

> Talking to a parent about a potential move is good advice even if it does not always work out. I talked to my mother many times concerning her condition (in response to her own concerns) and we agreed on the appropriate plan. She could not remember even 30 minutes .... It is well to understand that even when everything has been done with love and careful consideration, the loved one may not understand and may be unhappy. However, it is still a good idea to discuss the plan so that the family will have a feeling of doing what is right.

Families usually must take greater control in making and carrying out decisions regarding older relatives with Alzheimer's disease or other dementia. It is unrealistic to expect the older person to be able to do so. However, family members may experience anger, hostility, and rejection from their older relative. It is important to prepare family members for such reactions and to help them understand that even though these feelings may be directed toward them, these feelings are really the result of the "pain of the situation." One person wrote about her difficult situation:

> My grandmother and I had always been close. As a result of a series of small strokes, changes occurred, which included her driving down streets in the wrong lanes. We tried talking with my grandmother about her unsafe driving, but to no avail. Finally, I had to remove her car from the premises. We talked with her about the reasons she could no longer drive and made plans for meeting her transportation needs. For weeks, my grandmother was angry and accused me of stealing her car. Of course, it hurt, but I also realized that it probably felt to my grandmother as though her car had been stolen, and because of the disease process (and her life-long personality), it was unrealistic for me to expect her to fully comprehend the true situation.

Health care providers also need to avoid taking a paternalistic approach with older clients. Haug and Ory (1987) point out that sometimes providers communicate primarily with the family about an older person's condition, care plans, and the decisions to be made even when the older person is present and capable of participating in and making decisions. As Noelker (1994) adeptly stated, "Regardless of whether the intent is to avoid fatiguing or troubling the older person, [to] obtain the most complete and accurate information, or [to] complete the process as quickly as possible, this approach serves to undermine the older person's sense of control and esteem."

Validate Feelings

Families often experience a myriad of emotions when faced with difficult decisions and caregiving. These emotions may include grief, frustration, anger, resentment, embarrassment or guilt. At times a caregiver may have wished that the care receiver would die. The increasing frailty of an older family member also can become a daily reminder of that person's mortality—and a family member's own mortality.

Family members also may need to adjust their perception of the ill person, and this can be emotionally painful (Schmall, Stiehl, 1987). It may not be easy to accept that "my husband is no longer the strong and powerful man he once was," or "my mother who crocheted beautifully now no longer recognizes what to do with a crochet hook." It is particularly painful when a family member is no longer recognized by the person with Alzheimer's disease or a related disorder. In *Loss of Self,* Eisdorfer and Cohen (1987) discuss the importance of caregivers "setting emotional distance," that is, creating some detachment by viewing the family member as a person with a disease over which neither has any control and maintaining at the same time, a closeness to the person.

Because feelings, beliefs, and attitudes influence behavior, it is important to address the belief systems and feelings of family members. When feelings are not dealt with, decisions are more likely to be made on the basis of guilt, promises, and "shoulds" and "should nots" rather than on the circumstances and what is best for everyone.

Feelings are validated by bringing them up for discussion and acknowledging their commonality. It is particularly important to emphasize that feelings are neither good nor bad; it is how family members act on them that makes a difference.

Address Feelings of Guilt

It is important to deal with feelings of guilt family members may have. Guilt reduces objectivity and the ability to make decisions that are best for everyone. In addition, decisions made on the basis of guilt are likely to create feelings of resentment. For example, family members who feel guilty about moving a relative into a care facility are more likely to be critical of staff or overprotective of their older relative, or to not visit.

Underlying guilt feelings is generally a "rule" that a person feels he or she has broken. Most guilt "rules" are black and white, inflexible, and impossible to conform to completely. Examples of rules include:

- "A good daughter provides care to an ailing parent."
- "You should always keep a promise."
- "I vowed we would be together for better or for worse."
- "A son doesn't tell his father what to do."
- "A loving person would never put a family member in a nursing home."

Telling people they have no reason to feel guilty generally does not lessen the feelings of guilt. It is more helpful to assist people to: (1) identify and examine the rules that are causing the guilt feelings; (2) evaluate the impact of that rule (a critical question is "Does the rule work to the detriment of anyone—yourself, the person receiving care, or other family members?"); and (3) rewrite the rule, often with qualifiers, to make it more realistic and appropriate to the current situation.

If a promise is the source of guilt feelings, explore with the person the conditions under which the promise was made and the current situation. Usually the conditions are quite different. Comparing "what was" with "what is" can often help a family member to look more objectively at the current situation.

Emphasize Goodness of Intent of Actions

Sometimes, a family member says, "I wish I had known this information earlier. I would have done things differently." In most cases, families are trying to make good decisions and to do what is best. Actions are generally based on good intentions. For example, following a workshop, one woman wrote:

> A year ago, we moved mother from Texas to Oregon. She had lived in the small Texan community all of her life, and of course, everyone knew Mom. I now realize why the move has been so difficult for Mom and that she probably would have been less lonely living in Texas, even though it would have meant moving her into a care facility. I came to the workshop feeling guilty, and I could have left the workshop feeling an even heavier load of guilt except that [the nurse] emphasized the goodness of intent behind actions. For me, this was to give Mom the help she needed, to keep Mom out of a nursing facility and in a home environment, and to add the 'pleasure of family' to her life.

In working with families, it is important to start with the premise that most families are doing their best, and to discuss and to reinforce the "goodness of intent" underlying their actions when the actual action taken may turn out not to be the best choice.

Recognize Your Role as Permission Giver

Because health care professionals are often looked on as "experts," their messages can carry a lot of power and authority with families. **Care managers,** like these 16 health care professionals who work with family caregivers, identified 10 important messages caregivers often need to hear (Schmall, 1987; Schmall, Stiehl, 1987):

1. **Take care of yourself.** Providing care to an older family member at the expense of your own health or relationships with your spouse or children does not benefit anyone, including the person who needs care. Although a caregiver may not be able to stop the impact an illness has on the older person, it is critical that a caregiver does not allow a family member's illness to destroy them or other family members.
2. **Maintain contact with friends and involvement in outside activities.** This is critical to caregiver well-being. Studies show that sacrificing yourself in the care of another and removing pleasurable events from your life can lead to emo-

tional exhaustion, depression, and physical illness in caregivers. Ask yourself, "What happens if my family member enters a care facility or dies? Will I have been so wrapped up in caregiving that I will be 'used up' and without a life separate from caregiving?"

3. **Caregiving to adults is more stressful than childrearing.** With a baby, a person looks forward to a child's increasing independence. With older adult caregiving, the prognosis is generally for decline and increasing dependence, not recovery. In addition, it is generally difficult to predict how long caregiving will be needed.
4. **It is all right not to love (or like) the older person who needs care.** Not all older family members have been lovable or likable. It is important to take into consideration personalities and your past relationship as you consider your level of involvement in caregiving.
5. **Asking for help is not a sign of weakness, inadequacy, or failure.** Knowing your limits and reaching out for assistance before you are beyond your limits is characteristic of a strong individual and family. It also helps to ensure quality care for your relative.
6. **You have a right to set limits and to say "no."** Trying "to do it all" or "to do it alone" only makes you physically and emotionally exhausted.
7. **Begin taking regular breaks early in caregiving—it is not selfish.** Breaks from the demands of caregiving are a must. They are as important to health as diet, rest, and exercise. Respite benefits the care receiver as well—you are likely to be a more loving and less exhausted caregiver. Ask yourself, "If my health deteriorates, or I die, what will happen to my family member?" If you wait until you are "burnt out," these breaks will not be enough.
8. **Make caregiving decisions based on the needs of everyone involved.** Decisions should not be made only on the basis of the needs and desires of the older person.
9. **Moving a family member in a care facility can be the most loving step to take.** It does not mean an end to your caring relationship. Being a manager and coordinator of a family member's care is just as important as providing hands-on care. When you are no longer devoting your time to meeting physical and safety needs, you will be better able to meet your relative's emotional and social needs. Meeting these needs add immensely to a person's quality of life.
10. **Focus on what you have done well—and forgive yourself.** Too often, caregivers focus only on what they have not done. Remind yourself of the many things you have done well. Ask yourself: "What are my personal strengths?" "How have I made a difference for my family member?" "What have I done that I feel good about?" Not everything will be as you would like. There will be times when you wish you had done things differently. You are only human. If you make a mistake, admit it, learn from it, and then go on.

Although family members and friends may have given these messages to a caregiver, many caregivers do not take such messages to heart until they are stated by a health care professional. It is also helpful for nurses to pursue specifics with caregivers.

Recommend a Decision-making Model to Families

Many times families find it helpful to have a model to follow as they make decisions or solve problems. Fig. 6-3 depicts one six-step model (Schmall, Stiehl, 1984).

Gather Information

The goal is for the family to make an informed decision; therefore, the first step is for them to clearly identify the issue and to gather pertinent information. Families are often so concerned about making a decision or solving a difficult situation that questions, which could provide a better base for decision making, go unasked and unanswered. A professional assessment of the older person's health and level of functioning also may be needed.

Formulate Options

Once the issue has been identified, the nurse should help the family formulate all possible options in resolving it. This involves considering the resources of the older person, family, and community. Health care and social service professionals can be important in helping families to identify options.

This should be the brainstorming portion of decision

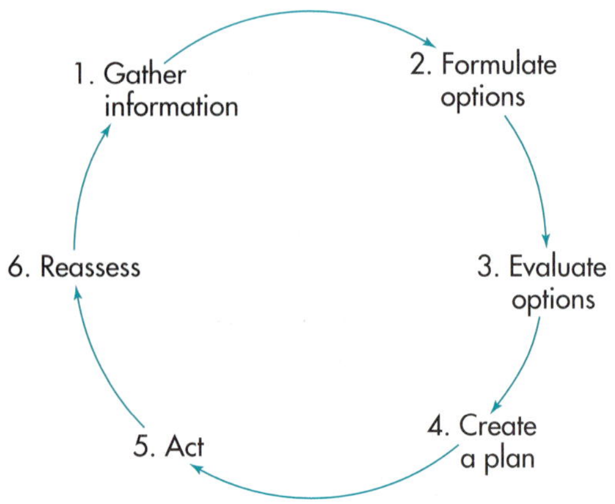

Fig. 6-3 Making a decision.

making. By generating a variety of possible options, families increase the chances of a successful outcome. In addition, keeping the decision separate from the possible options or solutions tends to take pressure away from people defending positions.

Evaluate Options

After all options have been identified, the next step is for the family to assess the advantages and limitations of each option. First identifying the criteria or standards by which potential options will be evaluated is helpful. These can include financial constraints and personal preferences. Getting agreement on the criteria makes it easier to identify the best of the options. A good guideline to follow is "Be easy on people; be tough on issues." Keeping the focus on the issue, not the positions people may take, increases effective decision making. Again, professionals can be helpful to families as they evaluate potential consequences of various options.

It is critical that family members are open and honest about their abilities to fulfill any responsibilities associated with an identified alternative. Honest communication helps to prevent unrealistic expectations and keeps people from feeling overwhelmed or burdened.

Create a Plan

Sometimes, this is the most difficult aspect of decision making, especially if there does not seem to be a single best choice. However, identifying and evaluating all possible alternatives helps ensure against making unsatisfactory decisions that may be regretted later. At times, also, families may feel that there simply is no good choice and that they must select "the best of the worst." It is important for the professional to recognize that a plan developed by one family may be quite different from a plan developed by another family whose "problem" appears to be the same.

Some families find that putting a plan in writing and indicating who has agreed to do which tasks by when can be helpful and can reduce disagreements about the plan. A written plan can also be useful later when it is reevaluated.

Act on the Plan

The fifth step in decision making is to put the plan into action. As with any decision, a plan should not be considered as "final and forever," because situations do change. If possible, it can be helpful to establish a trial period, approaching the decision from the perspective of "This seems like the best decision for now. Let's give it a try for one month, then evaluate the situation and how well our plan is working." This can be difficult to do, especially if the family wants closure to a difficult situation; however, flexibility is a key to quality decision making.

Reassess

It is important for the family to make plans for assessing the outcomes of the decision by asking, "How well is the plan working?" and then by making adjustments, as necessary, in the plan.

Decision making is seldom easy. It is influenced by many factors, such as the specific decision being faced, the personalities of family members, the quality of family relationships and communication, whether the older person is mentally intact and capable of full participation in making the decision or is cognitively impaired, whether decisions are being made in advance of need or at a time of crisis, and whether family members are living nearby or at a great distance. However, a model for decision making can provide families with a method for approaching decisions.

Summary

Providing quality care to older adults requires recognizing the role of the family and evaluating and responding to the needs of family members, particularly those who are the caregivers. Family members should be considered as a part of the care team, not as outsiders. The nurse should invite families to share the knowledge they have gained in caregiving, particularly when placing an older relative in a care setting.

It is also important to be nonjudgmental and to remember that each family has its history and values. Nurses need to be aware of their own values regarding

HOME CARE TIPS

1. Collaborate with the social worker to identify community resources for assisting caregivers and the homebound older adult.
2. Assist family members in discussing AMDs with homebound older adult.
3. Communicate homebound older adult's needs and progress to long-distance family members.
4. Refer caregivers to support groups to help ease burden of caring for a homebound older adult with a chronic illness.
5. Refer to a respite program so caregivers can obtain "time out" from caregiving responsibilities.
6. Collaborate with the social worker when conducting family conferences aimed at reducing conflict that may occur from the stress of caring for a homebound older adult.
7. Validate family members' and homebound older adults' feelings by bringing them up for discussion and acknowledging them.

what constitutes a family and their feelings about family behavior and relationships. It is important for nurses to not allow personal values to prevent them from working effectively with families whose values or relationships with each other may be different. Nurses should not label such families as "dysfunctional." It is necessary for nurses to try to identify the strengths within each family and to build on those strengths while at the same time, to recognize the family's limitations in providing support and caregiving.

Key Points

- Families are significant in the lives of older people and provide 80% of the support to older adults.
- Common dilemmas and decisions families face in later life involve changes in living arrangements, nursing home placement, financial and legal issues, end-of-life medical treatments, the safety of an older family member's driving, and caregiving.
- Moving an older family member to a nursing home is a difficult decision for most families.
- When working with older adults it is as important to address the needs of the family as to focus on the older person's needs. If only the older person's needs are considered, a care plan is less likely to be successful, particularly if the family is responsible for implementing it.
- Caregiving tends to be more stressful if the care receiver has a dementing illness, behavior problems, or emotional disturbance than if a care receiver is physically disabled only.
- The meaning a caregiver ascribes to a stressor is a stronger predictor of its impact than the actual stressor.
- Family caregivers often experience restriction of personal activities and social life, emotional strain, competing demands, role conflict, and financial stress. They may need to readjust their expectations in regard to their ill family member, themselves as caregivers, and their stage of life.
- Caregiving for frail older adults differs from providing care to children.
- Education—whether provided one-on-one or in a group setting—should be designed to empower caregivers and to increase their confidence and competence in problem-solving, decision making, and applying skills.
- Respite is most effective when a caregiver begins to use it early to prevent physical and emotional exhaustion rather than to treat it.
- The family conference is one strategy for a family to use to decide how to share caregiving responsibilities and to reach consensus about problems, needs, and decisions.
- *Family* is more than relationships determined by blood and marital ties.
- Factors to consider in conducting a family assessment include a history of relationships, family dynamics, family roles, the impact of increased dependence of an older person on all family members, the family's ability to provide the needed care, and the nature and degree of caregiver stress.
- Strategies and considerations for nurses in working with families of older adults include:
  - Identify who is the client and who is family.
  - Conduct an assessment of the family as well as of the older person.
  - Encourage families to plan in advance of need.
  - Help families to communicate their concerns to older relatives honestly and in positive ways.
  - Involve the older person in decisions to be made about his or her life.
  - Validate the feelings and experiences of family members.
  - Address feelings of guilt.
  - Emphasize the goodness of intent of actions.
  - Recognize the nurse's role as "permission-giver."
  - Recommend a decision making model.
- The nurse should try to "step into the shoes" of family members. Nurses who look at the situation from the perspective of a family member can increase their understanding of "where that person is coming from," and their insight and sensitivity.

Critical Thinking Exercises

1. Think about your own family relationships. What individual and family values might influence the care of the older adult family members? How might your current perceptions change over the next decade?
2. An 82-year-old woman is recovering from pneumonia. She has Alzheimer's disease, and has become increasingly hostile and unmanageable in the home setting. Her 65-year-old daughter is distraught with the idea of placing her mother in a long-term care facility but feels less able to care for her. What is your role as nurse in this situation?

REFERENCES

Anthony-Bergstone CR, Zarit SH, Gatz M: Symptoms of psychological distress among caregivers of dementia patients, *Psychol Aging* 3:245-248, 1988.

Archbold P: Impact of parent-caring on middle-aged offspring, *J Gerontolog Nurs* 6(2):78-84, 1980.

Bader J: Respite care: temporary relief for caregivers, *Women Health* 10(2-3):39-52, 1985.

Beedle J: *The carebook—a workbook for caregiver peace of mind.* Portland, Ore., eg. Ladybug Press, 1991.

Beisecker A, Wright L: *Benefits and barriers to use of ADC: perceptions of family caregivers of individuals with Alzheimer's disease,* paper presented at the annual meeting of the Gerontological Society of America, San Francisco, November 1991.

Berkey KM, Hanson SM: *Pocket guide to family assessment and intervention,* St. Louis, 1991, Mosby.

Berry GL, Zarit SH, Rabatin VX: Caregiver activity on respite and nonrespite days: a comparison of two service approaches, *Gerontologist* 31(6):830-835, 1991.

Brody E: Parent care as a normative family stress, *Gerontologist* 25(1):19-29, 1985.

Brody E, Saperstein A, Lawton MP: A multiservice respite program for caregivers of Alzheimer's patients. *Gerontolog Soc Work* 14(1/2):41-74, 1989.

Cicerelli V: A comparison of helping behavior to elderly parents of adult children with intact and disrupted marriages, *Gerontologist* 23:619-625, 1983.

Cicerelli V: Family caregiving: autonomous and paternalistic decision making, Newbury Park, Calif., 1992, Sage.

Crozier M: Respite care keeps elders at home longer, *Perspect Aging* 11(5), September/October, 1982.

Davidhizar R: Understanding powerlessness in family member caregivers of the chronically ill, *Geriatr Nurs* 34(1):66-69, 1992.

Deimling GT: The respite experience, *Benjamin Rose Inst Bul* Third Quarter, 1989, p 1.

Do you know your valuable papers?, EC 1234, Corvallis, Ore., 1993, Oregon State University Extension Service.

Dunn L: Respite: preventing burnout, *Advice Adults Aging Parents* 2(6):2-4, 1987.

Ehrlich P, White J: Tops: A consumer approach to Alzheimer's respite programs, *Gerontologist* 31(5):686-691, 1991.

Eisdorfer C, Cohen D: *The loss of self,* New York, 1987, Penguin.

Evidence mounts on effectiveness of respite services, *Aging Connect* February/March, 1990, p 6.

Fortinsky RH, Hathaway TJ: Information and service needs among active and former family caregivers of persons with Alzheimer's disease, *Gerontologist* 30(5):604-609, 1990.

Friss L: A model state-level approach to family survival for caregivers of brain-impaired adults, *Gerontologist* 31(1):7-8, 1990.

Friss LR, Whitlatch CJ: Who's taking care? A statewide study of family caregivers, *Am J Alzheimer's Care Rel Disord Res* September/October, 1991.

Gallagher D: Prevalence of depression in family caregivers, *Gerontolog* 29(4):449-456, 1989.

Gallagher-Thompson D: Direct services and interventions for caregivers. In Cantor MH, editor: *Family caregiving: an agenda for the future,* San Francisco, 1994, American Society on Aging, pp 102-122.

Gallo JJ, Reichel W, and Anderson L: *Handbook of geriatric assessment,* Rockville, Md., 1988, Aspen Publishers.

Genevay B: Family issues/family dynamics. In Cantor MH, editor: *Family caregiving: an agenda for the future,* San Francisco, 1994, American Society on Aging, pp 89-101.

George L, Gwyther L: Caregiver well-being: a multidimensional examination of family caregivers of demented adults, *Gerontologist* 26:253-259, 1986.

Gillins L: Yielding to age: when the elderly can no longer drive, *J Gerontolog Nurs* 16(11):12-15, 1990.

Goetting MA, Schmall VL: Talking with aging parents about finances, *J Home Econ* 85(1):42-46, 1993.

Gregerson D: *Organizing your family records,* EC 1302, Corvallis, Ore., 1991, Oregon State University Extension Service.

Gwyther L: The Duke aging center family support program: a grassroots outreach program generates principles and guidelines, *Cent Rep Adv Res* 11(2), 1987.

Hare J: *Talking to your family and doctor about difficult health care decisions,* EC 1386, Corvallis, Ore., 1992, Oregon State University Extension Service.

Hareven TK: Family and generational relations in the later years: a historical perspective, *Generations* 27(3):7-12, 1992.

Harkins E: *Family support and costs of services for the frail elderly: final report,* HCFA grant, Richmond, Va., 1985, Virginia Commonwealth University.

Haug MR, Ory MG: Issues in elderly patient-provider interactions, *Res Aging* 9:3-44, 1987.

Henry RS: Financial lessons to be applied to new program, *Respite Rep* Winter, 1992, p 3.

Herr J, Weakland J: *Counseling elders and their families; practical techniques for applied gerontology,* New York, 1979, Springer.

Himes CL: Social demography of contemporary families and aging, *Generations* 23(3):13-16, 1992.

Johnson CL: Divorced and reconstituted families: effects on the older generation, *Generations* 22(3):17-20, 1992.

Kaszniak AW, Keyl PM, Albert MS: Dementia and the older driver, *Hum Fact* 33(5):527-537, 1991.

Kimmel D: The families of older gay men and lesbians, *Generations* 17(3):37-38, 1992.

Lawton MP, Brody EM, Saperstein A: Respite care for Alzheimer's families: research findings and their relevance to providers, *Am J Alzheimer's Care Rel Disord Res* November/December, 1989, pp 31-38.

Lorensen M: Health and social support of elderly families in developed countries, *J Gerontolog Nurs* 18(6):25-32, 1992.

Malfetti JL, Winter DJ: *Concerned about an older driver? A guide for families and friends,* Washington, D.C., 1991, American Automobile Association Foundation for Traffic Safety.

Malone-Beach EE, Zarit SH, Spore DL: Caregivers' perceptions of case management and community-based services: barriers to service use, *J Appl Gerontol* 11(2):145-149, 1992.

Miller JF:, *Coping with chronic illness: overcoming powerlessness,* Philadelphia, 1986, FA Davis.

Meltzer JW: *Respite care: an emerging family support service,* Washington, D.C., 1982, Center for Study of Social Policy.

Montgomery RJ, Borgatta E: The effects of alternative support strategies on family caregiving, *Gerontologist* 29:457-464, 1989.

Moritz DJ, Kasl SV, Ostfeld AM: The health impact of living with a cognitively elderly spouse, *J Aging Health* 4(2):244-267, 1992.

National survey describes caregivers, *Parent Care* 2(3):1-2. March/April, 1987.

Niederehe G, Funk J: *Family interaction with dementia patients: caregiver styles and their correlates,* paper presented at the 95th annual convention of the American Psychological Association, New York, 1987.

Noelker LS: The interface between health and social services and family caregivers. In Cantor MH, editor: *Family caregiving: an agenda for the future,* San Francisco, 1994, American Society on Aging, pp 77-88.

Office of Technology Assessment: *Losing a million minds: confronting the tragedy of Alzheimer's disease and other dementias,* OTA-BA-323, Washington, D.C., 1987, US Government Printing Office.

Oriol W: Older drivers: keep 'em rolling (safely), *Perspect Aging* 22(3):4-11, July-September, 1993.

Persson D: The elderly driver: deciding when to stop, *Gerontologist* 33(1):88-91, 1993.

Pratt C et al: A model legal-financial education workshop for families caring for neurologically impaired elders, *Gerontologist* 29(2):258-262, 1989.

Pratt C et al: Ethical concerns of family caregivers to dementia patients, *Gerontologist* 27(5):632-638, 1987.

Pratt C et al: Burden and coping strategies of caregivers to Alzheimer's patients, *Fam Rel* 34(1):27-34, 1985.

Pratt C, Schmall V, Wright S: Burden, coping and health status: a comparison of family caregivers to community dwelling and institutionalized dementia patients, *J Gerontolog Soc Work* 10(1&2):99-112, 1987a.

Rzetelny H, Mellor J: *Support groups for caregivers of the aged,* New York, 1981, Natural Supports Program, Community Services Agency.

Schmall V: Family caregiving: a training and education perspective, In Cantor MH, editor: *Family caregiving: an agenda for the future,* San Francisco, 1994, American Society on Aging.

Schmall V: *Choosing when there is no choice: the nursing home decision,* Alexandria, Va., 1993a, American College of Health Care Administrators.

Schmall V: *Loss and grief in later life,* Pacific Northwest Extension Publication, PNW 439, Corvallis, Ore., 1993b, Oregon State University Extension Service.

Schmall V: *The dollmaker: a workshop guide on caregiving,* Corvallis, Ore., 1987, Oregon State University Extension Service.

Schmall V, Cleland: *Helping Memory-Impaired Elders,* Pacific Northwest Extension Publication, PNW 314, Corvallis, Ore., 1984, Oregon State University Extension Service.

Schmall V, Isbell L: *Aging parents: helping when health fails,* Pacific Northwest Extension Publication, PNE 246, Corvallis, Ore., 1982, Oregon State University Extension Service.

Schmall V, Nay T: Helping your older family member handle finances, Corvallis, Ore., 1993, Oregon State University Extension Service.

Schmall V, Pratt R: *What do you know about aging? Facts and fallacies,* Pacific Northwest Extension Publication, PNW 453, Corvallis, Ore., 1993, Oregon State University Extension Service.

Schmall V, Staton M, Weaver D: *Families and aging: dilemmas and decisions,* Corvallis, Ore., 1984, Oregon State University Extension Service.

Schmall V, Stiehl R: *Due upon receipt: a workshop guide on how the family can help a parent prepare for financial uncertainties,* Corvallis, Ore., 1992, Oregon State University Extension Service.

Schmall V, Stiehl R: *Living arrangements in later life,* Pacific Northwest Extension Publication, PNN 318, Corvallis, Ore., 1989, Oregon State University Extension Service.

Schmall V, Stiehl R: *Coping with caregiving: how to manage stress when caring for elderly relatives,* Pacific Northwest Extension Publication, PNW 315, Corvallis, Ore., 1987, Oregon State University Extension Service.

Schmall V, Webb LC: Respite and adult day care for rural elders. In Krout JA, editor: *Providing community based services to the rural elderly: research and practice,* Thousand Oaks, Calif., 1993, Sage Publications.

Sharlach A, Frenzel C: An evaluation of institution-based respite care, *Gerontologist* 26(1):77-82, 1986.

Silverstone B, Hyman HK: *You and your aging parent,* New York, 1982, Pantheon Books.

Smith KF, Bengston VL: Positive consequences of institutionalization: solidarity between elderly parents and their middle-aged children, *Gerontologist* 19(2):438-447, 1979.

Stiehl R, Bessey B: *Managing learning in high performance organizations,* Corvallis, Ore., 1993, The Learning Organization.

Stone RI, Kemper P: Spouses and children of disabled elders: how large a constituency for long-term care reform? *Milbank Q* 67(3-4):485-506, 1990.

Tobin S, Kulys R: The family and services. In Eisdorfer C, editor: *Annual Review of Gerontology and Geriatrics,* New York, 1979, Springer, pp 370-399.

Toft D: Bibliotherapy: always a key component of recovery, *Hazelden News and Professional Update* January:1-3, 1993.

Townsend AL, Poulshock SW: Intergenerational perspectives on impaired elders' support networks, *J Gerontol* 41(2):101-109, 1986.

US Bureau of the Census: Growth of America's oldest old population, *Prof America's Elder* No 2, Washington, D.C., 1992, US Department of Commerce.

Vitaliano PP, Young HM, Russo J: Burden: a review of measures used among caregivers of individuals with dementia, *Gerontologist* 31(1):67-75, 1991.

Williamson GM, Schulz R: Relationship orientation, quality of prior relationship, and distress among caregivers of Alzheimer's patients, *Psychol Aging* 5(4):502-509, 1990.

Wright AD, Lund DA, Caserta M: *The use of respite services by caregivers of dementia patients: an analysis of time-use strategies,* poster presentation, National Council on Family Relations, Seattle, November 13, 1990.

Zarit S: Research perspectives on family caregiving. In Cantor MH: *Family caregiving: an agenda for the future,* San Francisco, 1994, American Society on Aging.

Zarit S: In Kalicki AC: The burden of caregiving: confronting Alzheimer's disease, Washington, D.C., 1987, The American Association of Homes for the Aging.

CHAPTER 7

Socioeconomic and Environmental Influences

LEARNING OBJECTIVES

On completion of this chapter, the reader will be able to:

1. Identify the major socioeconomic and environmental factors that influence the health of the older adult.
2. Explain the importance of age cohorts in understanding the older adult.
3. Describe the economic factors that influence the lives of older people.
4. Distinguish between the Medicare and Medicaid programs.
5. Discuss the influence of support systems on the health and well-being of older adults.
6. Distinguish between a conservator, guardian, and durable power of attorney.
7. Discuss environmental factors that affect the safety and security of the older adult.
8. Compare and contrast the major features of the housing options available for older adults.
9. Compare the influence of income, education, and health status on quality of life.
10. Analyze the effect of criminal victimization on the lives of older adults.
11. Relate strategies for protecting older people in the community from criminal victimization.
12. Assess the ability of older adults to advocate for themselves.

We are all products not only of our genetic inheritance but also of our environment and our life experiences. Social status, economic conditions, and environment influence our health and our response to illness. This chapter discusses the socioeconomic and environmental conditions that influence the way older adults respond to the health care system.

Socioeconomic factors such as income, level of education, present health status, and availability of support systems all affect the way the older adult perceives the health care system. Benefits and entitlements may influence the availability of quality health care. A small number of older adults may not be competent to manage their own health care, hence they need the protection of a conservator or guardian (see Chapter 3). Environmental factors such as geographic area, housing, perceived criminal victimization, and community resources make a difference in the older adult's need for health care.

In 1989 older adults accounted for 33% of all hospital stays. They also averaged more doctor contacts than people under age 65, with nine contacts versus five contacts (AARP, 1991; US Bureau of the Census, 1992). One of the strongest and most consistent predictors of illness and death is socioeconomic status (Winkleby et al, 1992). The environment also influences safety and well-being. Therefore it is imperative that health care professionals understand the older adult's socioeconomic and environmental status.

Older adult health care consumers often depend on the health care professional for advocacy. To be an effective advocate, the nurse must understand the factors that shape the older consumer's perceptions of environment, socioeconomic status, and access to health care.

SOCIOECONOMIC FACTORS

Age Cohorts

People who share a particular event or time in history are grouped together in what is called a **cohort.** They have some shared experiences at similar stages of physical, psychologic, and social development that influence the way they perceive the world. Therefore they develop attitudes and values that are similar (Cox, 1986). By understanding cohorts, the nurse develops a greater understanding of the older adult's value system. For example, the person who reached maturity in the Depression learned the value of having a job and working hard to keep it. Generally, people in this cohort have been loyal workers. They feel better if they are "doing their jobs." The nurse might increase compliance for a treatment regimen by referring to the need for compliance as the older adult's "job."

Ways to classify cohorts include by age, historical events, or geographic area of residence. Today's older Americans have shared many momentous experiences. The "Roaring Twenties," the Depression, and World War II made impressions on everyone who lived through these events, but especially on those who were young at the time these events occurred. Values and pace of life, which vary between communities and regions of the country, influence the perceptions of the residents of these areas.

The age cohort that reached young adulthood in the post-World War II era benefited from a very productive time in American history. The late 1940s, 1950s, and 1960s were times of rapidly increasing earnings and heavy spending. Strong unions negotiated for better pension plans and medical benefits. This cohort became accustomed to contacting professionals for services, thereby becoming more conscious of preventive health care than previous generations. This group has become aware of wellness techniques and self-care strategies that improve health. Members of this cohort usually have at least a high school education and often have some form of higher education. Many pursued further educational opportunities. As a group, however, they experience a less cohesive family life. Many have moved from their home communities, and may have experienced divorce, remarriage, or other circumstances that complicate family support (Johnson, 1992).

The age cohort that matured just before and during World War II was strongly influenced by the war. Many people gained identity and status through some mode of participation in the war. Those who served in the armed forces were shaped by their direct involvement, whereas most of those at home worked in the defense industry; experienced the rationing of food, clothing, and fuel; and waited for the men and women of the service to come home. Life revolved around the war. Movies and music featured war themes and rationing was a reminder that all resources were needed primarily for the war effort. Signs and billboards urged people to sign up or to purchase war bonds. Windows of houses displayed stars to indicate members of families who were serving or who had died in the war.

The work force was expanded to include more women, many of whom continued to work after the war. In 1940, 12 million women were working and by 1945, 19 million women were working (Wapner, Demick, Redondo, 1990). Men and women serving in the armed forces became accustomed to regular physical and dental checkups, and extended these practices to their families after the war. Many veterans took advantage of the GI Bill to pursue a college education, which would not have been available to them otherwise. With the help of veterans benefits, they purchased houses for little or no money down. Having experienced the trauma of war, this group developed an appetite for the good things in life and willingly paid for them.

Today the oldest Americans are strongly influenced by having lived through the Great Depression of the 1930s. At the time, today's oldest older adults (age 85 and older) were struggling to keep families together, and today's younger older adults (age 70 and older) were attempting to find work and start families. The struggles of those times have shaped the lives of older Americans over age 70.

People of this era are generally frugal and often do not spend money, even if they have it. The oldest old fear they will outlive their money, since they remember what it is like to have nothing. In addition, this age cohort did not have the experience of receiving regular health care. Visits to the doctor or dentist occurred only when absolutely necessary, with home remedies used as the first line of defense. Education often ended with the eighth grade so children could help support the family. Receiving a college education was rare.

During this era, families were close and supportive. However, the family was a closed unit, and personal matters remained within the family. Unhappy family situations, mental illness, family finances, and abusive situations were not usually discussed outside the family. Gender roles were well-defined.

Many of today's conveniences, including antibiotics, were not available during the 1930s. The technology now used in health care settings, ranging from electronic thermometers to **computed tomography (CT)** and **positron emission topography (PET)** scanners, represent a true technologic explosion to people who have witnessed its development. Today's older adult cohort has survived many significant changes.

Income Sources

Income and income sources for older adults differ according to age (Table 7-1). Although income generally decreases with age, net worth peaks among householders age 65 to 69. However, as net worth decreases with advancing age, it remains substantial in older age groups (Table 7-2). For those with property and money to invest, this is primarily as a result of home equity increases and investments bringing a higher yield.

Social security is the primary income source for Americans over age 65. Social security is a federal government package of protection that provides benefits for individuals at retirement, survivors of participants, and the disabled. Funds for social security are derived from payroll taxes and benefits are earned by accumulating credits based on annual income. A person can earn up to four credits per year by working and paying social security taxes. In 1991 a person received one credit for each $540 in earnings. The number of credits needed to receive retirement benefits depends on the date of birth. Those born in 1929 or later need 40 credits (10 years of work). Those born before 1929 need fewer than 40 credits (39 credits if born in 1928, 38 credits if born in 1927, etc.) (*Retirement,* 1991).

Retirement age in the United States is age 70. However, a person can begin receiving social security retirement benefits as early as age 62. However, if a person be-

TABLE 7-1

Income and Income Sources for People Age 55 and Older

INSIDE the NEST EGG

As householders age, they depend more on social security and less on wages and salaries.
Percent of households headed by someone age 55 and older, by percent receiving each source of income and by age of householder

	AGE OF HOUSEHOLDER				
Type of income	55 and older By percent	55 to 64 By percent	65 to 74 By percent	75 to 84 By percent	85 and older By percent
Interest	71.1	69.8	72.7	71.1	70.5
Social Security	69.3	30.2	91.3	96.4	94.2
Wage and salary	45.8	76.0	36.7	15.9	8.4
Pensions	34.3	23.8	45.1	36.7	26.7
Dividends	20.3	21.4	21.0	18.6	14.2
Rentals, royalties, estates, or trust	11.3	12.9	11.0	9.5	9.4
Nonfarm self-employment	7.9	12.8	6.3	3.3	2.1
Survivors' benefits	7.4	4.4	8.7	9.9	10.5
Supplemental Security Income	6.2	5.3	6.4	7.1	8.6
Veterans' benefits	5.1	4.4	6.9	4.0	2.2
Unemployment compensation	4.0	7.7	2.2	1.2	0.5
Disability benefits	2.6	4.1	2.1	1.0	1.0
Educational assistance	2.2	4.0	1.4	0.7	0.4
Public assistance	2.1	3.5	1.3	1.1	1.6
Farm self-employment	1.6	2.8	1.2	0.4	0.2
Worker's compensation	1.3	2.7	0.7	0.3	0.2
Child support	0.8	1.4	0.5	0.4	0.1
Financial assistance*	0.7	0.8	0.5	0.7	1.2
Alimony	0.4	0.7	0.3	0.1	0.1
Other income	2.2	2.1	2.5	1.9	2.5

*Includes regular voluntary contributions from female members and other sources
From Current US Population Survey, March 1991.

TABLE 7-2

Family Net Worth—Mean and Median of Net Worth, by Selected Characteristics: 1989

Characteristic	Percent of families	Net worth (in thousands) Mean	Median
All families	100%	$183.7	$47.2
White	87	203.8	58.5
Nonwhite and Hispanic	13	45.9	4.0
Under 35 years old	26	46.9	6.8
35 to 44 years old	23	148.3	52.8
45 to 54 years old	14	286.4	86.7
55 to 64 years old	15	292.5	91.3
65 to 74 years old	13	278.3	77.6
75 years old and over	9	194.5	66.1

From US Bureau of the Census: *Statistical abstract of the United States,* ed 112, Washington, D.C., 1992, US Government Printing Office.

Insight • *Social security is the nation's basic method of assuring a continuing income when earnings stop or are reduced by retirement, disability, or death. However, social security was never intended to replace all lost earnings. The plan aimed to supplement savings, pensions, insurance, and investments accumulated during working years.*

Benefits replace a proportion of preretirement earnings, and the exact amount depends on the level of earnings. For example, a retired worker who had always earned the maximum that applies toward social security can receive about 26% of preretirement earnings, whereas a retired minimum-wage worker can receive about 60% of preretirement earnings. For individuals who had average earnings, 42% of preretirement earnings are replaced.

gins receiving benefits earlier, monthly payments will be lower. Social security earnings must be limited, since the purpose of the program is to provide continuing income to a retired worker when traditional work income is cut off or reduced. Benefits are reduced if a person earns more than the exempt amount. After age 70, there is no reduction in benefits. Only earnings from employment or self-employment are included. Income from savings, pensions, and investments are not applied to reduce benefits (US Department of Health and Human Services).

Very poor older adults depend on another federal government program. **Supplemental Security Income (SSI)** pays monthly checks to people who are aged, disabled, or sight-impaired, and who have few assets and minimum income. This program is also regulated by the Social Security Administration, but the money to provide benefits is from income tax sources rather than social security payroll taxes. Eligibility depends on income and assets. A single person received $446 per month and a couple received $669 per month in 1994.

Age 55 to 64

Those who are in the preretirement age cohort of 55 to 64 are generally in their peak earning years. Most are married, but few have children under age 18 still residing in the family home. The heavy expenses of child-rearing are over, and homeowners have completely or nearly paid for their homes. This age cohort tends to have an increased **disposable income** yet is acutely aware of impending retirement, so saving and investing are priorities.

Income sources for this age group are diverse. Most members of the group are still working, and wage and salary earnings are substantial. Households often have two incomes, since more women in this age group work. However, the number of men in this age group participating in the labor force has reduced dramatically since 1970. Many retire early (between age 60 and 65), and those who do so tend to have strong **pension** packages. For those over age 62 social security provides part of the income. Interest and investment dividends contribute to income, but the income from interest and investment dividends is usually insignificant (Wapner, Demick, Redondo, 1990).

People in this age group are generally healthy and have resources to maintain housing. Of this age cohort, 22% rate their health as excellent, 24% rate it as very good, and 31% rate it as good (Van Nostrand, Furner, Suzman, 1993). In 1990 the average annual income of households headed by someone age 55 to 64 was $32,365. This group has been vested in pension plans most of their working lives, and because of higher earnings, they have contributed more to social security than older age groups. Many held jobs with disability benefits, which now may be contributing to income. Those who served in the armed forces may be eligible for veterans benefits.

Age 65 to 74

Retirement ordinarily causes income to reduce by about 30% or more. The median income before taxes for households age 65 to 74 is $21,501, which is $13,808 less than the median income of households in the 55 to 64 age bracket (US Bureau of the Census, 1990). This reduction in income is often offset by reduced expenditures associated with working, such as transportation, clothing, and

TABLE 7-3

Average Annual Income and Expenditures of All Consumer Units (in dollars): 1990

	All consumer units	55 to 64 years old	65 to 74 years old	75 years and older
Characteristic				
Income before taxes	31,889	35,309	21,501	15,435
Total expenditures	28,369	29,244	20,895	15,448
Food-TOTAL	4,296	4,430	3,305	2,406
At home				
Total	2,485	2,601	2,106	1,654
Cereal, bakery products	368	378	324	268
Meats, poultry, fish, eggs	668	747	598	405
Dairy products	295	291	247	201
Fruits and vegetables	408	447	392	347
Away from home	1,811	1,830	1,190	752
Alcoholic beverages	293	254	166	71
Housing-TOTAL	8,886	8,610	6,591	5,527
Shelter	5,032	4,390	3,339	2,857
Fuel, utilities, public services	1,890	2,160	1,838	1,515
Household operations and furnishings	1,557	1,572	1,051	882
Housekeeping supplies	406	488	362	273
Apparel and services	1,617	1,557	972	489
Transportation				
Vehicle purchases	2,129	2,014	1,163	921
Gasoline and oil	1,047	1,134	792	396
All other	1,946	2,151	1,511	815
Health care	1,480	1,791	2,197	2,223
Insurance and pensions	2,592	2,958	1,071	261
Other expenditures	4,080	4,345	3,127	2,338
Personal taxes	2,952	3,507	1,378	829

From US Bureau of the Census: *Statistical abstracts of the United States,* ed 112, Washington, D.C., 1992, US Government Printing Office.

meals (Table 7-3). In this age group, 19% of household heads continue to work. Only half of those wage earners, however, bring home more than $12,500 per year (Wapner, Demick, Redondo, 1990). The work is generally part-time work, so the portion of household income from wages and salary is reduced.

Of the people in this age group, 91% receive social security income. Almost half of the households in this group have income from pensions. For those who have investments, earnings from this source are about twice the investment earnings for younger retirees or preretirees. Only 2% receive disability payments because jobs offering disability benefits were rare until recently (Wapner, Demick, Redondo, 1990). The use of SSI increases as household members age.

Today this age group includes many veterans from World War II. Veterans benefits are important to this age group because of the increased risk of chronic disease and other acute health problems. Eligibility for veterans benefits is based on military service, service-related disability, and income. Benefits are considered on an individual basis (*Federal Benefits for Veterans and Dependents,* 1993) (Box 7-1). Although benefits such as Medicare, food stamps, or housing assistance are not often thought of as income, they are factors used when assessing the poverty status of older adults in the United States.

Age 75 to 84

After age 75, women outnumber men in American society. Many older people in this age group live alone, which affects the household income of those age 75 and older. Most women in this age group did not work outside the home, so their incomes are dependent on their spouses' pensions or social security benefits. Surviving spouses with no work experience receive about two thirds of the

BOX 7-1

Veterans Benefits

Benefits for eligible veterans include:

- Disability compensation
- Pension
- Education and training
- Home loan guaranties
- Life insurance
- Burial benefits
- Health care benefits

TABLE 7-4

Population 65 Years Old and Older by Age Group and Gender 1970 TO 1991

	Percent distribution		
Age group and gender	1970	1980	1991
People 65 years and older	100.0	100.0	100.0
65 to 69 years old	35.0	34.3	31.6
70 to 74 years old	27.3	26.6	26.0
75 to 79 years old	19.2	18.8	19.8
80 to 84 years old	11.4	11.5	12.7
85 years old and older	7.1	8.8	10.0
Men, 65 years and over	100.0	100.0	100.0
65 to 69 years old	37.3	37.8	35.1
70 to 74 years old	27.7	27.7	27.6
75 to 79 years old	18.7	18.0	19.4
80 to 84 years old	10.5	9.9	11.0
85 years old and older	5.8	6.6	6.9
Women 65 years and over	100.0	100.0	100.0
65 to 69 years old	33.4	31.9	29.2
70 to 74 years old	27.0	25.9	24.8
75 to 79 years old	19.6	19.3	20.0
80 to 84 years old	12.1	12.6	13.9
85 years old and older	7.9	10.3	12.0

From US Bureau of the Census: *Statistical abstract of the United States,* ed 112, Washington, D.C., 1992, US Government Printing Office.

overall income earned before the death of their spouses (Wapner, Demick, Redondo, 1990).

When people in this age group were working, salaries and wages were much lower, hence they contributed less to social security. Pensions were less generous or nonexistent. These factors combine to reduce the income range of most older people.

Since few people in this age group are employed and most who still work are self-employed, wages and salaries are a small income factor. Social security is the most important factor. Pensions are available to fewer people, and those who receive pensions receive less than younger age groups. Income from investments increases slightly (Wapner, Demick, Redondo, 1990).

As health problems increase with age, so do expenses for prescriptions and assistive devices such as eyeglasses, hearing aids, and dentures. The quality of housing deteriorates as the house ages and less money is available for maintenance. Decreased strength and endurance reduce the ability to conduct household chores. Income is reduced as expenses increase.

Age 85 and Older

The over age 85 group is the fastest growing segment of our population (Table 7-4). Although the lifespan of Americans has been prolonged by medical and social advances, this age cohort is at risk for an increase in chronic disease, resulting in decreased ability to perform **activities of daily living (ADLs)** and increased expenses for assistance, assistive devices, and medication (Van Nostrand, Furner, Suzman, 1993).

This group has the lowest average annual income level (under $15,000) of all older Americans (US Bureau of the Census, 1992). Social security is the primary income source, although fewer members of this oldest-old group are covered by social security. Pension and investment income is less than for younger groups, whereas SSI is increased. More members of this age group receive assistance from family, but the amount is small and often sporadic. Few receive wages or salary.

The age 85 and older group is more likely to need assistance with ADLs. They are also more likely to need institutional care (US Bureau of the Census, 1992; Van Nostrand, Furner, Suzman, 1993). Dependence on medication and assistive devices increases.

If people in this age group live independently, their housing is likely to be old, and in need of repairs and maintenance (Pynoos, 1992). Adaptations to compensate for decreasing abilities help older adults remain in their homes but these changes can be costly. Some older adults chose to move in with family or to facilities that offer assistance (see Housing, pp. 181-186).

The political climate or financial stability of the nation can affect the sources of income of older adults at any time. Decreased interest earnings, for example, affect those with money market investments, or certificates of deposit, whereas the political climate affects the type and amount of taxes paid. Social security and SSI are indexed for inflation. As Atchley (1992) states, "Ironically, while low income people often have inadequate funds, the amount they do receive is more secure against economic shifts than the incomes of those in higher earning brackets" (see Cultural Awareness box, p. 173).

CULTURAL AWARENESS

Cultural Differences in the Health Practices of Economically Disadvantaged Older Adults

Gender and ethnic differences in personal health practices were examined with a sample of 1,021 Medicaid recipients age 65 years and older. Six health practices were studied including never smoking cigarettes, not currently smoking cigarettes, limiting consumption of alcoholic beverages, exercising regularly, maintaining desirable weight for height, and maintaining adequate social networks.

Although gender differences were noted with respect to all of the health practices examined, neither men nor women were consistently favored in adhering to desired health practices. Women were more apt than men to refrain from smoking and drinking, risk factors that have been linked to major health consequences. Ethnicity was also a factor in all of the health practices examined. Hispanic and black older adults were very similar to whites, whereas Asian/Pacific Islander older adults generally adhered to more desired health practices than did whites, blacks, or Hispanics. Hispanics age 75 and older were twice as likely as whites to engage in physical exercise. Older blacks were only half as likely to maintain recommended body weights as whites. Generally, Asian/Pacific Islander older adults age 65 to 74 engaged in more desirable health practices than did whites—not smoking, limiting drinking, and getting regular exercise. The implications of these findings could benefit health promotion programs for low-income older adults.

Modified from Lubben JE, Weiler PG, Chi I: Gender and ethnic differences in the health practices of the elderly poor, *J Clin Epidemiol* 42(8), 725-733, 1989.

TABLE 7-5

Number and Percent of Older Adults Below Poverty by Race, Hispanic Origin, and Gender, 1990

Race and Hispanic origin	Number (thousands)	Percent
White:		
Male	634	5.6
Female	2,073	13.2
TOTAL	2,707	10.1
Black:		
Male	286	27.8
Female	574	37.9
TOTAL	860	33.8
Hispanic*:		
Male	86	18.6
Female	159	25.3
TOTAL	245	22.5
All races:		
Male	959	7.6
Female	2,699	15.4
TOTAL	3,658	12.2

*Hispanic people may be of any race.

From US Bureau of the Census: "Poverty in the United States: 1990," *Cur Pop Rep* Series P-60, No 175, August 1991.

TABLE 7-6

Selected Measures of Educational Attainment by Age Group, Gender, Race, and Hispanic Origin: 1990

	Mean years of school completed	
Gender	25 and older	65 and older
Total	12.6	11.8
Male	13.0	11.0
Female	12.4	10.9
Race and Hispanic origin		
White	12.6	11.1
Black	11.1	8.2
Hispanic origin	10.0	7.4

From US Bureau of the Census: Money Income of Households, Families, and Persons in the United States, 1990, *Cur Pop Rep*, Series P-60, No 174, September 1991.

Poverty

In 1990 almost one fifth of those age 65 and older were classified as poor or near-poor, with income between the **poverty level** and 125% of this level (American Association of Retired Persons [AARP], 1991). One tenth of older adult whites are poor compared with one third of older adult blacks and one fifth of older adult Hispanics (Table 7-5). The poverty rate for older women is 15%, whereas the rate for older men is 8%. Seven of ten black women age 75 and older who live alone are poor. The poverty rate is also high for those who live in metropolitan areas or the South, have not completed high school, or are too ill or disabled to work (AARP, 1991; Freeman, 1992; Mor-Barak, Miller, Syme, 1991; US Bureau of the Census, 1992).

Older blacks and hispanics are more vulnerable to poverty. Many were more likely to have held low-paying jobs with few or no benefits. They are less-educated (Table 7-6) than whites, and have less access to organizations such as unions that advocated for them as workers. Black and Hispanic women had even fewer employment opportunities (Freeman, 1992). Dr. Manuel Miranda,

Ph.D., of the National Institute on Aging states, "Many elderly minorities are unable to find employment due to age and race discrimination in the work place, or they are encumbered with a greater degree of physical disability—the result of a lifetime of physical labor—that prevents them from working" (1992).

When considering income for older adults, government benefits such as Medicare, food stamps, and subsidized housing are considered part of the income. Cynthia Tauber, chief of the Sex and Age Statistics Branch of the U.S. Bureau of the Census states, "... in 1990, before taxes and without government transfers, 46.8% of elderly would have had incomes below poverty" (Kleyman, 1992).

Inadequate income may affect the quality of life for the older adult. For example, basics such as housing and diet may be inadequate. An aging wardrobe and lack of transportation may cause the older adult to avoid social contact, leading to isolation. The older adult may delay seeking medical help, or may not follow through with prescribed treatment or medications because of limited income. Eyeglasses, hearing aids, and dental work may become unaffordable luxuries. Identifying an older client's income level enables the nurse to direct the client to agencies and services that are available to those with limited resources.

RESEARCH

Crystal S, Shea D, Krishnaswami S: Educational attainment, occupational history, and stratification: determinants of later-life economic outcomes, *Gerontol* 47(2):S213-S221, 1992.

Sample, setting

The U.S. Census Bureau's 1984 Survey of Income and Program Participation had a data base of 12,757 men—6,289 men in younger working years, 4,249 in the midlife years, and 2,219 in the retirement years (65 and older).

Methodology

The effects of education on occupational status, employment status, and self-employment were studied along with ethnic minority status.

Findings

The results suggest that education, directly and through its effects on occupational status, has strong effects on economic well-being at all ages. This effect persists in the later years. Respondents with more education had access to higher-status jobs, were able to continue working longer, and were more likely to be self-employed. These factors tend to increase income.

Implications

As the educational level of older adults increases, retirement income level should also increase. Future income levels are important, since maintaining economic well-being among older adults is an important public policy and results in a significant impact on the US budget.

Education

Education has been shown to have a strong relationship to health risk factors (Winkleby, 1992). Education level influences earning ability, information absorption, problem-solving ability, value system, and lifestyle behaviors. The better-educated person often has more access to wellness programs and preventive health options (see Research box below).

The education of the older population has been steadily increasing, reflecting increased mandatory education and better educational opportunities in the last 50 years (Table 7-7). The percentage of individuals who completed high school varies by race and ethnic origin. In 1990, 58% of older whites had completed high school, compared with 27% of blacks and 27% of Hispanics (AARP, 1991; US Bureau of the Census).

Many older adults are continuing their education in their later years. Some are completing high school or taking college courses. High-school equivalency programs and reduced college tuitions encourage this trend. Others take advantage of continuing education programs such as Elderhostel to explore subjects of interest. The Elderhostel program offers opportunities for people over age 60 and their spouses to attend courses on specific topics, often held in 1-week segments, on college campuses all over the world. The students usually reside on campus during the program. The low cost makes the program available to many.

Seeking educational opportunities in later life has many benefits for the older adult. Life-long learning promotes intellectual growth, increases self-esteem, and enhances socialization. The older adult has an opportunity to stimulate creativity and to remain alert and involved with the world (Clough, 1992; Penning, Wasyliw, 1992). Erickson's seventh stage of development stresses the importance of generativity versus stagnation to the individual's sense of achievement and fulfillment in life (Cox, 1986). Education provides an opportunity to avoid stagnation and isolation, and adds to the enjoyment of later life.

Health Status

The health status of the older adult influences socioeconomic status. People over age 65 have an average of two chronic conditions (Lorig, 1993). The most common chronic problems in 1989 were arthritis (48%), followed by hypertension (38%), hearing impairments (32%), and

TABLE 7-7

People age 65 and Older—Characteristics by Gender: 1970 to 1990

	Total (percent)				Male (percent)				Female (percent)			
Characteristic	1970	1980	1985	1990	1970	1980	1985	1990	1970	1980	1985	1990
Years of school completed												
8 years or less	58.3	43.1	35.4	28.5	61.5	45.3	37.2	30.0	56.1	41.6	34.1	27.5
1 to 3 years of high school	13.4	16.2	16.5	16.1	12.6	15.5	15.7	15.7	13.9	16.7	17.0	16.4
4 years of high school	15.7	24.0	29.0	32.9	12.5	21.4	26.4	29.0	18.1	25.8	30.7	35.6
1 to 3 years of college	6.2	8.2	9.8	10.9	5.6	7.5	9.1	10.8	6.7	8.6	10.3	11.0
4 or more years of college	6.3	8.6	9.4	11.6	7.9	10.3	11.5	14.5	5.2	7.4	8.0	9.5

From US Bureau of the Census: *Statistical abstract of the United States,* ed 112, Washington, D.C., 1992, US Government Printing Office.

TABLE 7-8

Prevalence of Selected Reported Chronic Conditions by Age 1989:

Chronic Condition	Rate per 1000 people	
Age	**65 to 74**	**75 and older**
Heart condition	231.6	353.0
Hypertension	383.8	375.6
Varicose veins of lower extremities	72.6	86.6
Hemorrhoids	77.4	57.5
Chronic bronchitis	54.2	57.6
Asthma	57.3	42.3
Chronic sinusitis	151.8	155.8
Hay fever, allergic rhinitis without asthma	69.4	65.5
Dermatitis, including eczema	33.5	32.9
Disease of sebaceous glands	9.3	5.7
Arthritis	437.3	554.5
Trouble with:		
Ingrown nails	36.1	64.8
Corns and calluses	41.0	54.3
Dry (itching) skin	23.4	35.5
Diabetes	89.7	85.7
Migraine	29.8	11.8
Diseases of urinary system	57.4	62.2
Visual impairments	69.3	101.7
Cataracts	107.4	234.3
Hearing impairment	239.4	360.3
Tinnitus	76.4	68.9
Deformities or orthopedic impairments	141.4	177.0
Hernia of abdominal cavity	57.3	52.0
Frequent indigestion	34.9	42.8
Frequent constipation	42.2	92.2

From US Bureau of the Census: *Statistical abstract of the United States,* ed 112, Washington, D.C., 1992, US Government Printing Office.

heart disease (28%) (US Bureau of the Census, 1992) (Table 7-8). The influence health problems exert often depends on the older person's perception of the problem. Some approach health problems with an attitude of acceptance, whereas others find that chronic problems require a considerable amount of energy, spending extensive time and resources to find ways to cope or to adapt (Burke, Flaherty, 1993).

Functional status is affected by chronic conditions. The Centers for Disease Control and Prevention reports in *Health Data on Older Americans* that functional status is important, because it serves as an indicator of an older adult's ability to remain independent in the community. Functional ability is measured by the individual's ability to perform ADLs and instrumental activities of daily living (IADLs). ADLs include seven personal care activities—eating, toileting, bathing, transferring, walking, and going outside. IADLs refer to six home-management activities—meal preparation, shopping, money management, telephone use, light housework, and heavy housework. Data concerning ability to perform ADLs and IADLs were gathered through the National Health Interview Survey. Table 7-9 shows the percentage of people reporting difficulties in performing ADLs and IADLs by sex and age. Almost 67% of those surveyed reported no difficulties with either ADLs or IADLs. The percentage reporting difficulty increases with age (Van Nostrand, Furner, Suzman, 1993).

Nurses can work with older adults to prolong independence by encouraging self-management of chronic conditions. Self-management is defined as learning and practicing the skills necessary to carry on an active and emotionally satisfying life in the face of a chronic condition (Lorig, 1993). Education and support help the older adult make informed choices, practice good health behaviors, and take responsibility for the care of a chronic condition.

The amount of money available for food, shelter, clothing, and recreation can be greatly affected by the need to pay for medication, health care equipment, glasses, hear-

TABLE 7-9

Percent distribution of people with difficulty in ADLs and IADLs, by gender and age

Gender and age	Difficulties in ADLs and IADLs			
	None	ADL difficulty only	IADL difficulty only	Both
Total	66.6	5.2	10.9	17.3
Gender				
Male	74.7	6.6	7.4	11.3
Female	60.9	4.3	13.4	21.5
Age				
65-74 years	74.1	4.7	9.2	12.0
75-84 years	58.7	6.5	12.5	22.4
85 years or over	37.1	4.8	18.3	39.8

From Van Nostrand JF, Furner SE, Suzman R, editors: *Health data on older Americans: United States, 1992,* National Center for Health Statistics, *Vital Health Stat* 3(27), 1993.

ing aids, dental care, medical care, home care assistance, and nursing home care, some of which may not be covered by insurance programs. In addition, the insurance premiums themselves may cause financial distress. Restricted finances can affect the safety of the environment, nutritional status, and social opportunities that in turn can result in an altered quality of life.

By making the older adult aware of programs such as equipment loan programs, as well as optical, auditory, and dental assistance programs, the nurse can help the older adult receive services necessary to maintain health status and thus to maximize quality of life even though finances are restricted.

Insurance Coverage

Older Americans should review their insurance coverage often to see if the coverage they have is necessary, appropriate, and adequate. Residential insurance purchased several years ago may be inadequate today. For example, home insurance should cover at least 80% of the replacement cost; however, many older adult home owners are insured for the assessed value of the home when it was purchased. Content and liability coverage may also be inadequate. The older home owner may be unaware that policies are outdated or may not be able to afford the premiums updating would require. An insurance checkup would reveal inadequacies. The older adult may wish to investigate several insurance companies to find the best coverage for the least cost. The AARP publishes the booklet, *Insurance Checklist,* which is helpful in reviewing insurance status.

Many older people have automobiles that have reached maximum depreciation. These automobile owners may still be carrying full coverage when all they need is liability insurance. They may also be able to save money by investigating senior discounts, choosing higher deductibles, and comparing premiums from several companies. Completion of a defensive driving course such as the AARP's *55 Alive* program may help an older adult qualify for lower insurance rates.

Life insurance is valuable when providing for dependents. In old age, the primary reason for life insurance is to cover burial expenses. A single-term policy would accomplish this purpose. Many older people can substantially reduce life insurance coverage. Proceeds from those policies and premium payments that are no longer due can be invested for greater yield.

Health insurance is a necessity for older adults, because medical problems, and therefore medical expenses, increase with age. As people age, they visit the doctor more often (Van Nostrand, Furner, Suzman, 1993). Older adults spend more time in the hospital—an average of 8.9 days—compared with the average of 5.3 days spent by those under age 65 (US Bureau of the Census, 1992) (Table 7-10). They also require more long-term care. The age 65 to 74 cohort represents only 1.25% of the long-term care population, whereas older adults age 75 to 84 comprise 5.77% of the population, and those over age 85 are 22% of the population (Van Nostrand, Furner, Suzman, 1992).

Medicare is a federal health insurance program for people over age 65 or people of any age with chronic kidney disease. Medicare has two parts—hospital insurance and medical insurance.

Part A, the hospital insurance, *helps* pay for inpatient hospital care and some follow-up care such as a skilled nursing facility, home health services, and hospice care. A person is eligible for Medicare Hospital Insurance if they are age 65 and older and (1) are eligible for any type of monthly social security benefit or railroad retirement system benefit, or (2) are retired from or the spouse of a person who was employed in a Medicare-covered government position (*The Medicare 1993 Handbook,* 1993).

Part A is financed through part of the social security tax. Most medicare recipients pay a supplemental premium that is deduced from monthly social security payments. In addition, they pay an annual deductible on hospital and skilled nursing care benefits.

Part B, the medical insurance, *helps* pay for the following:

- Physician services
- Vision services provided by a qualified optometrist (excluding the cost of glasses)
- Physical therapy
- Inpatient treatment of mental illness
- Outpatient rehabilitation

TABLE 7-10

Hospital Utilization by Age

	Days of care (per 1000 people)			Average stay (days)		
	Total	Male	Female	Total	Male	Female
Age 65 to 74	2,116	2,232	2,022	8.2	7.9	8.5
Age 75 and over	4,087	4,507	3,861	9.4	7.3	9.5

From US Bureau of the Census: *Statistical abstract of the United States,* ed 112, Washington, D.C., 1992, US Government Printing Office.

- Diagnostic x-ray, laboratory, and other tests
- Blood for transfusions
- X-ray therapy
- Surgical dressings, splints, casts, etc.
- Necessary ambulance services
- Rental or purchase of durable medical equipment used in the home
- Colostomy bags and supplies
- Braces for limbs, back, or neck
- Artificial limbs or eyes
- Pneumonia vaccine (*The Medicare 1993 Handbook,* 1993).

Part B is financed by monthly premiums. In 1993 the monthly premium was $36.60 for most beneficiaries with an annual deductible of $100 and a patient coinsurance payment of 20% of the Medicare-approved amount (*The Medicare 1993 Handbook,* 1993).

Medicare covers long-term care *only* in skilled care facilities and *only* under specific situations. Long-term care, which is not covered by Medicare can deplete a person's savings in a very short time. Therefore some people are purchasing long-term care insurance. Most policies offer a specific coverage amount per day for a specific time (e.g., $60 per day for 3 years). Some also cover in-home care. Premiums depend on the extent of the benefits and the age of the purchaser.

Medicare rules and benefits change often. Many older people do not understand Medicare and are often confused by the paperwork, billing, and notices they receive regarding claims. They are encouraged to contact the Social Security Administration or the insurance departments of their local medical facilities if they have questions.

Those older adults who are still working may continue to be covered by their employers' health insurance plans. A retiree is sometimes covered by a former employer's health plan. In that case the employer's insurance supplements the Medicare insurance. Many insurance companies offer supplemental insurance for those not covered by present or former employers. These are referred to as "Medigap" policies. People shopping for Medigap insurance should look for insurance that meets their specific needs at the most reasonable cost.

Medicaid is a state-administered program designed for people with very low incomes. It uses federal funds and covers certain medical expenses not covered by Medicare. Each state has different coverage and requirements.

Some insurance companies offer policies that cover one specific disease such as cancer. These policies might be appropriate for someone who is at high risk for that specific disease.

The AARP has several publications that explain insurance policies in a language that most people can understand. Some of the publications are free; others are available at a minimum cost. The Social Security Administration publishes free updated pamphlets annually that explain Medicare. Insurance trade associations such as the Health Insurance Association of America, The Insurance Information Institute, and the American Council of Life Insurance publish a variety of free educational materials to help people understand insurance.

Support Systems

Throughout life, new acquaintances are made, friendships are developed, and family circles are formed. People identify with schools, churches or synagogues, clubs, neighborhoods, and towns. These are the places and people a person turns to when he or she needs advice or help, wants to celebrate, or is grieving. With age, a person can lose some of these support systems. Family and friends move away or die, and organizations and neighborhoods change. Changing work roles and financial status may require changes in the groups with whom a person associates. To cope with losses such as family members, friends, health, and independence, individuals need a large social network. In a study of poor, frail older adults, Mor-Barak, Miller, and Syme (1991) found that social networks act as buffers against the harmful effects of major life events on the health of the older adult. "Social networks can ameliorate the harmful effects of life events on health (1991)."

Marital status affects the older person in several ways. A married person is likely to live in a household with more income than the older adult who lives alone. Nutritional status is likely to be better for the married person than for the person living alone (Frongillo et al,

TABLE 7-11

Living Arrangements of People age 55 and Older by Selected Characteristics

Age and gender	Total in thousands	All races percent living: Alone	With spouse	With other relatives	With non-relatives	White people percent living: Alone	With spouse	With other relatives	Black people percent living: Alone	With spouse	With other relatives
Total	193,519	12	55	26	6	12	58	23	13	33	48
55 to 64	21,345	14	73	10	3	13	76	8	20	45	26
65 and over	30,093	31	54	13	2	31	56	11	33	38	26
65 to 74	18,238	25	64	10	2	24	66	9	31	44	21
75 and over	11,855	41	39	17	3	42	41	15	36	28	34
Male	92,840	10	57	25	8	10	60	22	13	37	41
55 to 64	10,161	11	79	6	4	10	82	5	19	52	14
65 and over	12,547	16	74	7	2	16	76	6	23	55	16
65 to 74	8,156	13	79	6	2	13	81	5	23	57	13
75 and over	4,391	21	66	11	3	21	67	9	23	51	22
Female	100,680	14	53	28	5	15	56	24	13	30	54
55 to 64	11,184	17	67	14	2	16	71	11	22	40	36
65 and over	17,546	42	40	16	2	43	41	14	39	27	33
65 to 74	10,081	34	51	10	2	34	53	12	36	34	28
75 and over	7,464	53	24	20	3	55	25	18	43	16	40

From US Bureau of the Census: *Statistical abstract of the United States,* ed 112, Washington, D.C., 1992, US Government Printing Office.

1992). Men benefit most from marriage. They do not cultivate the close friendships that women do outside the marriage, so the spouse is a vital friend and supporter. Traditionally, men do not engage in cooking, cleaning house, mending clothes, and doing the laundry, and thus miss these services when they lose their spouses. There are also more older women than older men, so many men marry again. In 1990 about 73% of men over age 65 were living with their spouses (Himes 1991; U.S. Bureau of the Census, 1992). Because there is a greater chance of a woman outliving her spouse, more older women live alone. In 1990 only about 38% of women over age 65 lived with their spouse (Table 7-11).

An older adult man sees his role in marriage as the provider and protector. A woman feels responsible for her family's comfort and happiness (Quirouette, 1992). These roles may be blurred in the older marriage as disease and disability increase, forcing role changes. When the older adult loses his or her traditional role, self-esteem and hence, satisfaction with life may be affected.

Children continue to provide support to their older parents. About two thirds of older people in the United States live within 30 minutes of a child. Many visit at least weekly with children and most talk on the phone at least once a week with a child. Female children are more likely to assist with hands-on care, whereas male children are more likely to provide business and financial support (Miller, Montgomery, 1990; U.S. Government Printing Office, 1990). Although many families are separated by miles, the children are concerned about their parents and attempt to arrange needed services for them. Area Agencies on Aging, local social service organizations, and private care managers are some of the resources available.

Often older adult siblings draw closer and may live together, providing support for each other as they grow older. Many older adults develop extended families of younger neighbors or fellow church members. These extended families provide emotional as well as practical support.

The financial status of the older adult can affect the support system. Older adults tend to feel an obligation to return favors. If someone does something for them they want to be able to reciprocate. If they are financially unable to do this, they might withdraw so as not to be put in an embarrassing position. In addition, the inability to afford adequate clothing or to maintain clean clothing can cause others to avoid the older person.

The emotional status of the older adult can also affect the support system. It may be difficult for friends and family of the depressed or negative older person to maintain contact with the person because of the behaviors exhibited. A complete health history and physical examination should be conducted to rule out physical causes of emotional problems. Peer counseling, support groups, or professional assistance such as mental health professionals, clergy, or a community nursing service may help the older adult express feelings and concerns. Close friends may be able to help the person find the positive aspects of life.

Benefits and Entitlements

In addition to social security, SSI, Medicare, and Medicaid, older Americans are eligible for a variety of other benefits and **entitlements** that help socioeconomic status. Entitlement programs require that the beneficiary meet certain guidelines such as income or disability, whereas other benefits may be enjoyed by all older Americans.

Subsidized housing is available in almost every community in the nation. Most are supervised by the U.S. Department of Housing and Urban Development with one major program under the authority of the Farmers Home Administration of the U.S. Department of Agriculture. Once the person establishes eligibility, suitable housing may be located in existing rental buildings, or a unit in a public housing development may be chosen. The housing authority then contracts with the building owner for rent on the unit, or the renter pays a portion of the rent and the housing authority pays the rest. Eligibility standards differ for each program. Income, assets, and expenses are all considered in determining eligibility.

Another entitlement program available to older adults is food stamps. Food stamp programs are usually administered by a state's Department of Health and Human Services. Eligibility and the amount of food stamps a family may receive are based on family size, available income, and other resources. Nutritious meals are available at congregate meal sites throughout the country. A small donation is requested for each meal. If the older adult is homebound, arrangements can usually be made to have the meal delivered.

Energy assistance is also available. This program is administered differently in each community. Information on the program can be obtained at the local senior center. Again, income requirements must be met.

In 1991 there were 7,646 veterans over age 65 in the United States (U.S. Bureau of the Census, 1992) (Table 7-12). Many of these veterans are eligible for veterans benefits. The benefit used most often is access to Veterans Administration (VA) health care. As the population has aged, the large number of veterans from World War II has put a strain on the VA health care facilities. As a result, the VA has tightened the rules, making it more difficult to qualify for care. Veterans who require health care because of a war-related injury or disease are given priority. Those needing long-term care are now being referred back to their communities for that care (*Federal Benefits for Veterans and Dependents,* 1993).

Local Area Agencies on Aging provide several services for older people. Area Agencies on Aging were created in 1973 as an amendment to the **Older Americans Act.**

TABLE 7-12

Veterans Living In the United States and Puerto Rico, by Age and Service: 1991

	Age 60 to 64	Age 65 and over
Total veterans	3,194	7,646
Wartime veterans:		
TOTAL	3,027	7,458
Vietnam era		
TOTAL	228	192
No prior wartime service	30	10
Korean conflict		
TOTAL	2,023	730
No prior wartime service	1,792	126
World War II	1,204	7,257
World War I		65
Peacetime veterans		
TOTAL	167	187
Post-Vietnam era	3	less than 500

From US Bureau of the Census: *Statistical abstract of the United States,* ed 112, Washington, D.C., 1992, US Government Printing Office.

The purpose of the agencies is to plan and implement social service programs at the local level. Benefits available through Area Agencies on Aging include:

- Nutrition services through congregate meal sites and home-delivered meals
- Recreational opportunities
- Chore service
- Legal assistance
- Transportation
- Information and referral

It is not the purpose of the Area Agency on Aging to duplicate services. In fact, these agencies try to encourage community-based services. However, if a service is not available, the Area Agency on Aging attempts to provide it.

Conservators and Guardians

When older adults are unable to handle their own financial affairs, a conservator may be appointed. This does not necessarily indicate that the older person is incompetent. For example, the person may be visually impaired. In such a case, the conservator may be selected voluntarily by the older adult. However, if the older person is incompetent the court selects the conservator. In either case, the conservator is legally appointed and court supervised (see Chapter 3).

A guardian may be appointed to handle decisions not related to financial matters. The guardian makes decisions about housing, health care, and other similar mat-

BOX 7-2

Definitions

Conservator–A *conservator* manages the older person's financial resources. An annual report must be filed with the court detailing how the funds were spent on the disabled person's behalf.

Guardian–A *guardian* is appointed to make personal care decisions for the disabled individual. Personal care includes medical treatment and other decisions promoting comfort, safety, and health. The guardian must file an annual report with the court on the individual's condition.

Durable power of attorney–A *durable power of attorney* is a document by which one person (the principal) gives legal authority to another (the agent or attorney-in-fact) to act on behalf of the principal. It is called *durable* because it continues to be effective even after the principal has lost capacity as a result of illness or injury. The two types of durable power of attorney are:

- **Durable power of attorney for financial matters**—This authority to handle financial affairs can be as broad or limited as the parties agree upon.
- **Durable power of attorney for health care decisions**—The agent or attorney-in-fact is not required to report actions on behalf of the principal to the court.

From American Association of Retired Persons: *A matter of choice,* Washington, D.C., The Association; In Hamilton A, editor: *Legal guide for senior citizens,* Topeka, Kan., 1991, Kansas Department on Aging.

BOX 7-3

The Older Body's Response to Temperature Extremes

Older adults are susceptible to hypothermia and hyperthermia because:

The ability to perceive heat or cold diminishes with age.

Body water acts as a thermal buffer and heat reservoir, but in older adults, total body water is decreased.

The sweat threshold increases, and the volume of perspiration is decreased.

The ability to shiver, which helps to retain heat, is compromised in the older adult.

Decreased metabolic rate alters the ability to maintain normal core temperature.

Circulation may be compromised.

Abrams W, Berkow R, editors: *Merck manual of geriatrics,* Rahway, NJ, 1990, Merck.

ters. This may be the same person as the conservator or a different person.

A guardian or conservator may affect the person's socioeconomic status. By wisely handling the assets, the conservator may help the older person remain at least financially independent for longer than he or she could have independently. By supervising housing and health matters, the knowledgeable guardian may assist the older person to function at the highest possible level (Box 7-2).

ENVIRONMENTAL INFLUENCES

The environment contributes to a person's perception of life. Although the environment might not be noticeable unless it is uncomfortable, it does significantly affect emotional as well as physical health and well-being. Environment can be described as hot or cold, dark or light, hard or soft, safe or dangerous. The environmental factors of adequate shelter, safety, and comfort contribute to a person's ability to function well. These factors take on added importance to older adults in the presence of decreased functional ability. Geographic location, transportation, housing, and safety issues as related to the environment of the older person are discussed in the following sections.

Geographic Location of Residence

Geographic factors influence individuals differently. Climate is important to older adults because they are very susceptible to temperature extremes (Box 7-3). Those who live in cold climates need adequate heat and clothing. Those in temperate areas need cooling systems available during very warm seasons. Because older adults are concerned about accidental injuries, weather extremes such as snow and ice can contribute to isolation.

Whether a person lives in an urban or rural location can affect access to services, availability of support systems, and safety perceptions. Urban neighborhoods tend to be older and subject to change because of suburban migration. The notion of a friendly and convenient neighborhood in larger urban areas is rapidly declining. Such changing neighborhoods may affect the socialization of older adults because of the foreign and frightening atmosphere created. The majority of older Americans, however, have lived in the same geographic area for more than 30 years and are not planning to move (Figs. 7-1 and 7-2).

Older people residing in rural areas have different problems. Geographic isolation may result from long distances between contacts and services, and inadequate transportation services. However, the social supports obtained through churches, friends, and neighbors can be strong and reliable. Although a larger percentage of rural older adults own their own homes than those in metro-

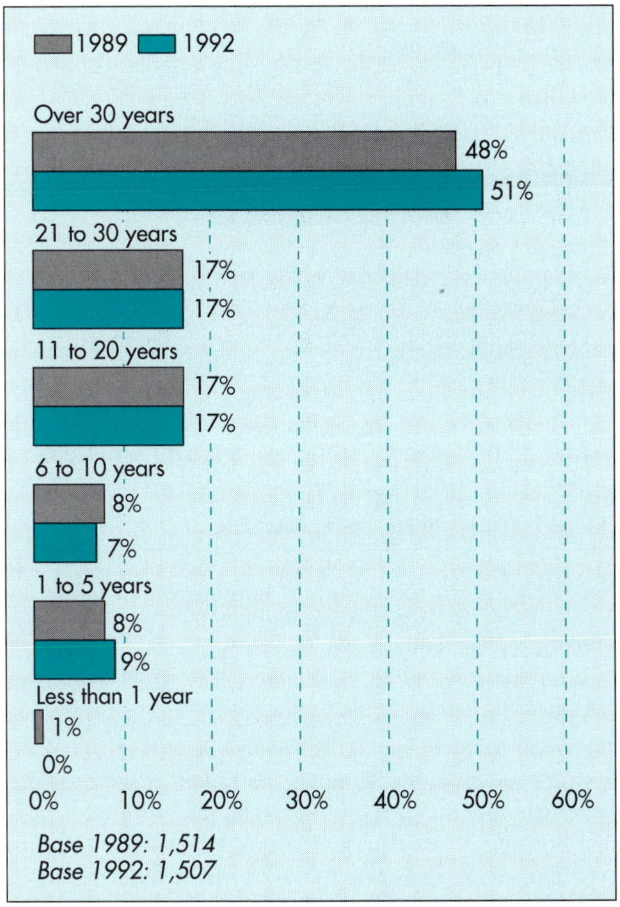

Fig. 7-1 Length of residence in geographic area (From American Association of Retired Persons: *Understanding senior housing for the 1990's,* Washington, D.C., 1993, The Association.)

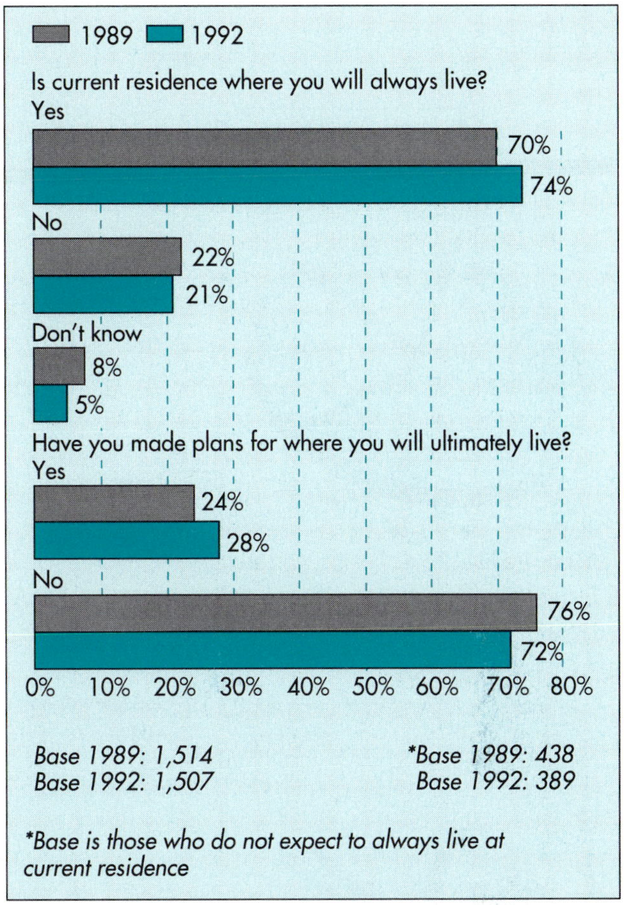

Fig. 7-2 Plans for future residence (From American Association of Retired Persons: *Understanding senior housing for the 1990's,* Washington, D.C., 1993, The Association.)

politan areas, they occupy a disproportionate share of the nation's substandard housing. There are fewer formal services available for the rural older adult (Coward, 1993).

Transportation

To many older adults an automobile is the symbol of independence. In some areas, an automobile is necessary for transportation to shopping areas, medical facilities, and social centers. Using data from the Public Use Microdata Sample, Cutler and Coward (1992) found that 76% of older adults live in households where personal transportation was available. However, the data do not indicate whether the older adults actually use available vehicles. Advancing age, being female, and residing in inner cities were associated with a greater likelihood of lack of transportation (Cutler, Coward, 1992).

Low-cost transportation is an objective of the Older Americans Act and is the responsibility of the Administration on Aging. Each Area Agency on Aging is charged with the responsibility of assuring that transportation is available in the area. Obstacles preventing public transportation use include cost, scheduling, distance from home, coverage of rural areas, lack of awareness of the service, and reluctance of some older adults to use public transportation.

Housing

As the saying goes, "a person's home is his castle." Home is a true reflection of the individual and for the older person, it signifies independence. Emotional and physical health are affected by where a person lives.

After World War II, home ownership was encouraged by the offering of insured mortgages, and deductions of property taxes and mortgage interest to stimulate the postwar economy. Therefore for the older generation, striving for home ownership was a goal many sought to achieve (Burke, Flaherty, 1993). A 1992 housing survey conducted for the AARP found that 62% of older Americans own their home outright, whereas another 21% are

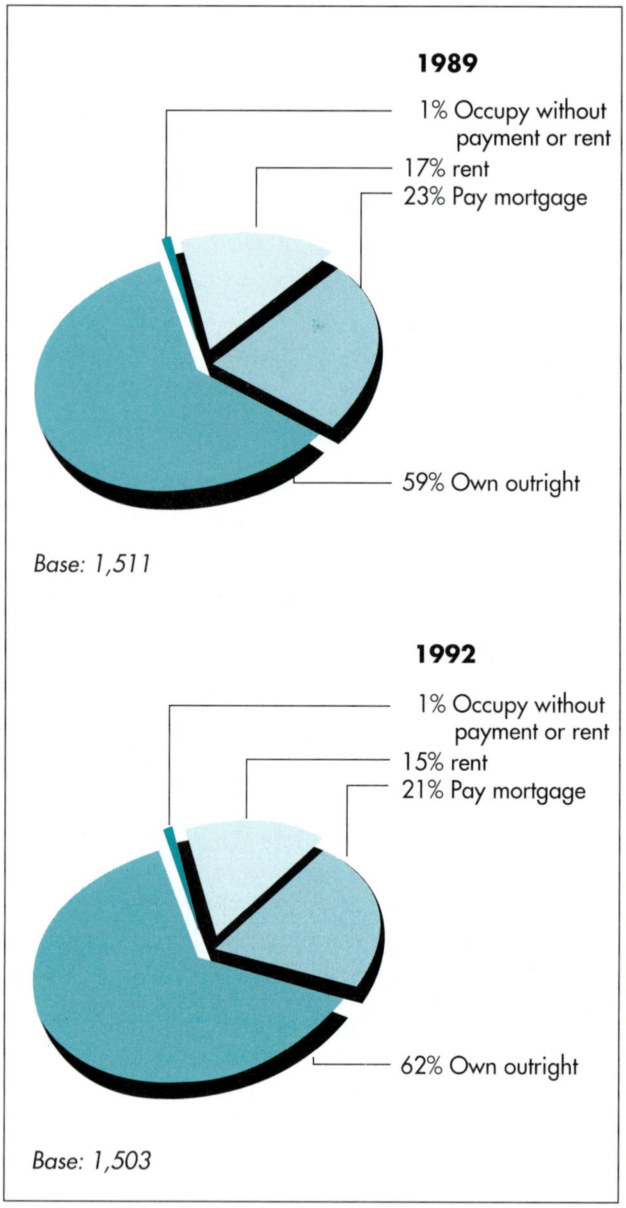

Fig. 7-3 Ownership status of home (From American Association of Retired Persons: *Understanding senior housing for the 1990's,* Washington, D.C., 1993, The Association.)

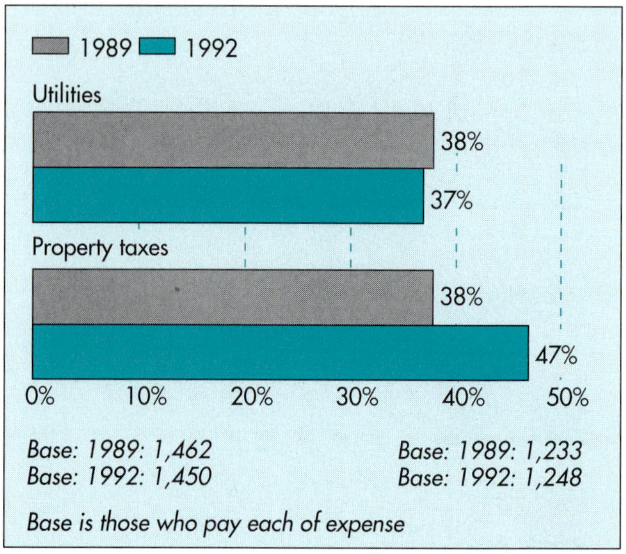

Fig. 7-4 Concern about current housing-related payments (percent who believe they pay too much). (From American Association of Retired Persons: *Understanding senior housing for the 1990's,* Washington, D.C., 1993, The Association.)

still paying on mortgages (AARP, 1993) (Fig. 7-3). The home is often the major asset and in fact, may be the only asset. It may be the house in which the older person was born and reared, then raised his or her own children. More often, a young married couple bought the house, raised the family in that same house, then continued to live there as a couple or after the death of a spouse.

The house may be old, poorly insulated with inefficient heating and cooling systems, and in need of repair. Of the white older adults who own houses, 4% live in moderately to severely inadequate housing, compared with 23% of older blacks and 13% of older Hispanics. The lower the income of the older adult, the more likely it is that housing is inadequate (Pynoos, 1992). In 1992 property taxes were of concern to 42% of the older adults in the AARP survey, whereas utility costs were of concern to 37% (Fig. 7-4).

Another concern is the availability of features that support an older adult's ability to function in the home. Most homes occupied by older adults were designed for younger, active individuals. The AARP survey (1993) found that 71% of older Americans have performed a home modification (Fig. 7-5). An estimated 20% of older adults' homes are in need of modification (Pynoos, 1992).

For those who wish to remain in their homes but need funds for maintenance, repairs, or even extra income, home equity conversion, which is also known as reverse mortgage, might be an alternative. The home owner arranges regular payments with a bank in exchange for future transfer of the property. The home owner then receives regular payments while remaining in the home.

Older adults who rent face the problem of locating affordable rental property. Once located, however, rental cost increases can outpace the older adult's fixed income. The tenant/property manager relationship can be altered as the property management changes hands. As with home owners, the structure itself and appliances may be inadequate to support independent functioning.

In urban areas, some older people live in single-room occupancy (SRO) hotels. SRO hotels offer single, sparsely

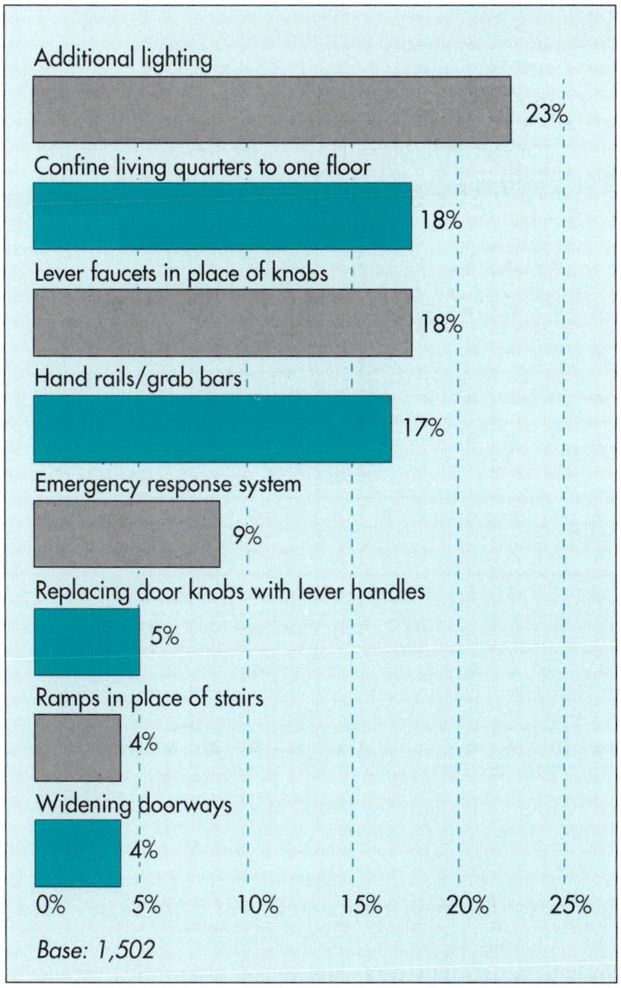

Fig. 7-5 Home modifications (From American Association of Retired Persons: *Understanding senior housing for the 1990's*, Washington, D.C., 1993, The Association.)

furnished rooms with limited cooking facilities and communal bathrooms. Tenants are traditionally single people with limited incomes, mental illness, or substance abuse problems. Typically, they have few contacts with other tenants and no other family to provide support. An increasing incidence of chronic disease or disability can keep an individual from leaving his or her room and can further restrict the person's living environment. This can affect a tenant's physical and mental health by isolating him or her and preventing access to services (Rollinson 1991) (see Research box at right).

Safety can be a problem in all of these living arrangements. Aging furnaces and appliances; worn linoleum or carpeting; poor lighting; unprotected stairs; lack of smoke alarms and assistive **grab bars;** and aging, sagging, or broken furniture all pose hazards for older adults (see Chapter 11).

Insight • *Few older adults plan ahead for housing needs in their later years. Those who do the least planning are the most vulnerable groups (e.g., the oldest old—age 85 and older, women, those with lower income, widows, renters, and minorities). These subgroups tend to have the fewest resources and therefore experience restrictive housing choices and housing crises. As a result they may find themselves in unsuitable housing.*

From American Association of Retired Persons: *Understanding senior housing for 1990s,* Washington, D.C., 1993, The Association.

RESEARCH

Rollinson P: Elderly single room occupancy (SRO) hotel tenants: still alone, *Soc Work* 36(4):303-308, 1991.

Sample, setting

Data were collected from 53 older adult tenants of four hotels in an inner-city neighborhood of Chicago.

Methodology

The subjects were studied through observation and interviews.

Findings

The older adults studied had few resources or alternatives and were highly dependent on the SRO hotels in which they lived. They suffered from a variety of untreated chronic ailments and were reluctant to seek help because of perceived independence issues. Lack of support systems and services, as well as danger of attack and robbery outside of the hotels, lead to increased isolation and withdrawal from society.

Implications

Health and social services must be brought to SRO hotels to help the tenants remain independent without isolation. The community health nurse is in a unique position to advocate for the appropriate health services for this population.

For those who decide to give up their homes, there are several options (Fig. 7-6). Independent housing options may include mobile homes, condominiums, or cooperatives.

Increasingly, older adults are sharing houses. They may move in with family into a single room, or into an accessory apartment or a portable housing unit on the family property. Others team up with a group of older people to buy or rent a house. Typically, in this situation,

Usually=●
Sometimes=■
Rarely=▲
Blank areas=not applicable

	Financing			Amenities										Restrictions				
	Own	Rent	Extra fees/dues	Home health care	Housekeeping services	Laundry services	Meals provided	Nursing care	Property maintenance	Recreational facilities	Resident governance	Social activities	Transportation	Age	Waiting list	Rules/regulations	Children allowed	Pets allowed
1 Acessory apartment	■	■												▲				
2 Apartment		●	▲		▲	▲			●	■	■	■		▲	■	■	■	■
3 & 4 Assisted-living facility/board-and-care home		●		●	●	●	●	■	●	■	■	■	●	■	■	●		■
5 Congregate housing		●	●	■	●	●	●	▲	●	●	■	●	●	●	■	●	▲	■
6 Continuing-care retirement community	■	■	●	●	●	●	●	●	●	●	●	●	●	●	■	●	▲	■
7 Cooperative housing			●	▲	▲	▲	▲	▲	●	■	●	■	▲	■	■	●	■	■
8 ECHO housing	■	●												■				
9 Foster-care home		●		●	●	●	●	▲	●	■	▲	■	●	■	■	●	■	■
10 Manufactured (mobile) home	●	■	●	▲	▲	▲	▲	▲	●	■	■	■	▲	■	■	●	■	■
11 Retirement community	■	■	●	■	■	■	■	■	■	●	●	●	■	●	■	●		■
12 Retirement hotel		●	■	▲	●	■	■	▲	●	■	▲	■	▲	●	■	●	▲	▲
13 Shared housing	■	■	■	▲	■	■	■	▲	■	▲	●	■	■	■	■	●	■	■
14 Single-family residence	●	■																
15 Townhouse/condominium	●	■	●	▲	▲	▲	▲	▲	■	■	●	■		▲	▲	●	■	■

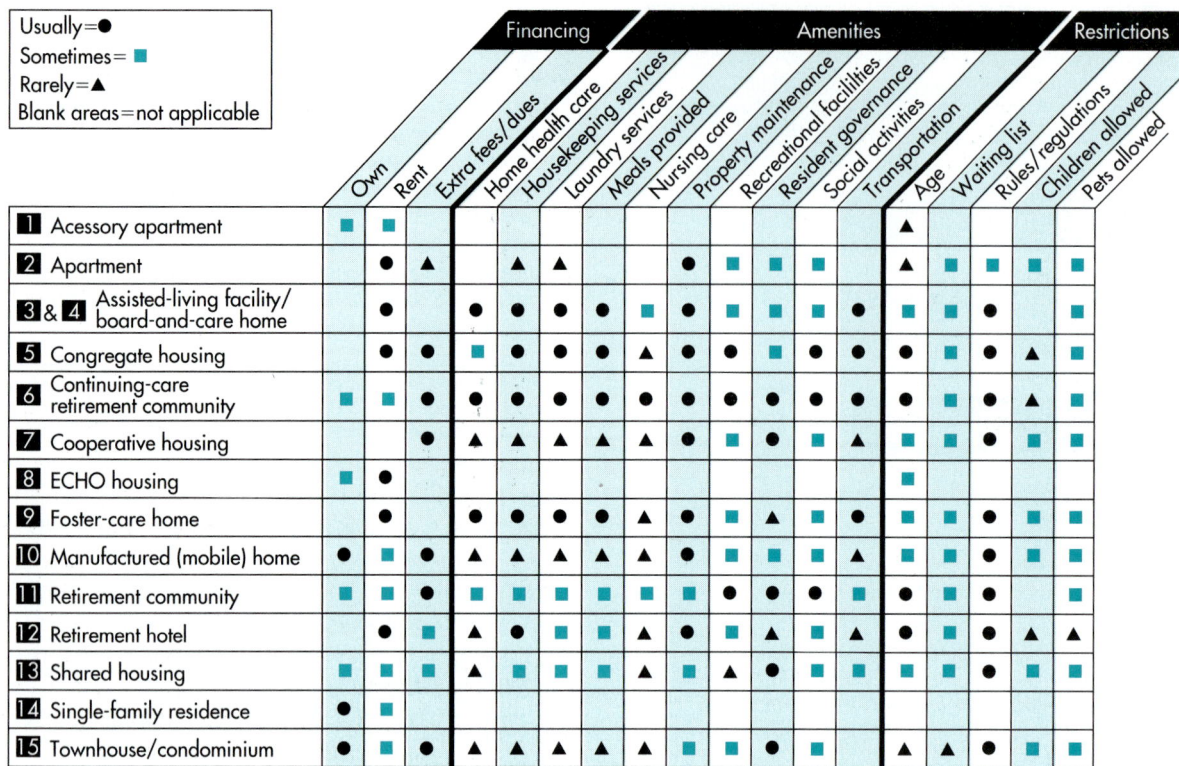

Fig. 7-6 Which living arrangement is for you? (From Porcino J: Designs for living, *Modern Maturity* April-May 36(2):32-33, 1993, American Association of Retired Persons.)

each person has a private room, sharing the living, dining, and kitchen areas. Chores are also shared, and in some instances, a housekeeper or manager for the house is hired. Some older people take in boarders to help with expenses and household chores. The boarder is often a younger person who can do the "heavy" housework.

Home matching programs are gaining in popularity. These agencies locate and match people who can share a home. Through interviews and screening conducted by the agency, applicants are able to locate a compatible housemate.

A growing number of older people are living a mobile life. These are usually the younger old who live in warmer climates in the winter and cooler climates in the summer. They may own a home in one area and rent in another, or they may use a recreational vehicle as a second home. The real nomads are those who travel all year from place to place in recreational vehicles. As these older adults age and begin to have health problems, they often return to their home communities where long-established support systems of family and friends are available.

Retirement communities appeal to some. Of the older Americans surveyed by the AARP, 6% live in retirement housing (US Bureau of the Census, 1992) (Fig. 7-7). These communities may have facilities only for independent people, or they may include a variety of housing alternatives for those with various levels of dependency. Separate housing units for the independent residents, congregate apartment units for those who need meals or housekeeping help, and nursing facilities for those who need more care may be found in a continuing care community. Residents may move from one level to another as their needs change. Most require a substantial entrance fee in addition to monthly charges. Benefits include activity programs, and assistance with housekeeping and chores. Transportation is often included.

For those who require increasing assistance but are still able to function independently, assisted living facilities are a viable option. These facilities have separate units with common dining facilities and social rooms. Meals, transportation, housekeeping, and some laundry services are provided. Most have activity programs and encourage residents to socialize. Staff are present around the clock should a resident need help.

Board and care homes, also known as sheltered housing, provide a home to a small number of older adults. Services provided vary widely. Basic rent usually includes room, board, laundry, and housekeeping. Some offer other services such as assistance with personal care for an additional fee. Board and care homes try to create a home-like atmosphere by remaining small and friendly (Wolinsky et al, 1992).

A nursing care facility or nursing home are other

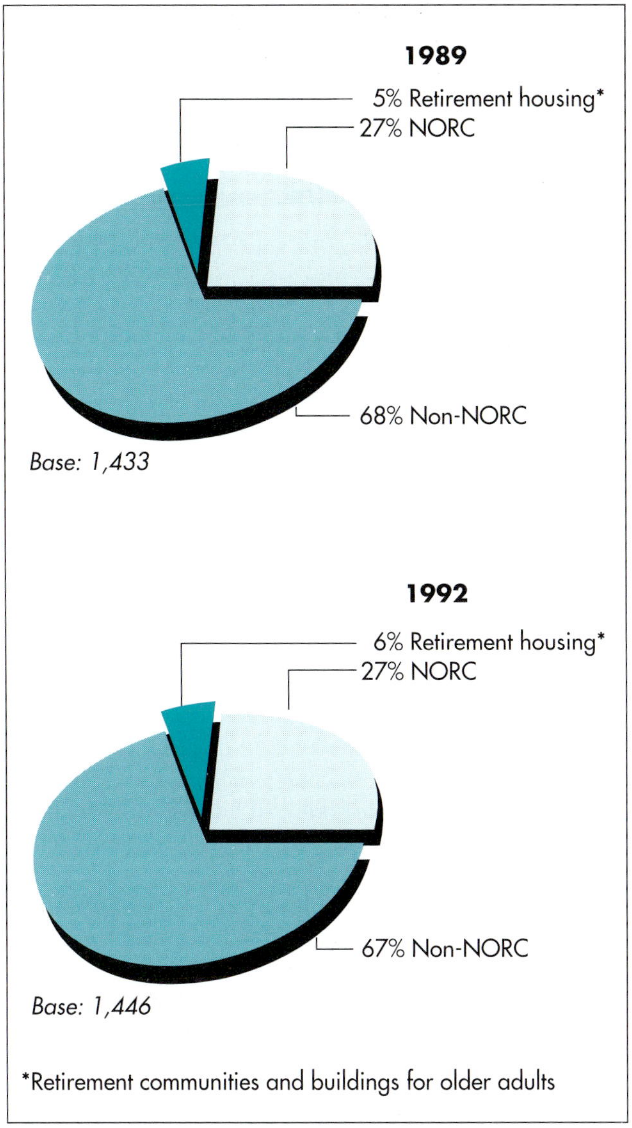

Fig. 7-7 Retirement and older adult housing (From American Association of Retired Persons: *Understanding senior housing for the 1990's,* Washington, D.C., 1993, The Association.)

housing options for the person who is no longer able to function independently. Residents of nursing care facilities depend on assistance with ADLs for survival. The resident occupies a single room or shares a room with one or more people. The facility is staffed 24 hours a day with nursing professionals and trained personnel who can provide needed assistance. The services on the premises generally include meals, personal laundry services, and a hair salon. Activity programming is provided to meet the needs of individual residents. Rehabilitation services are available as required by the residents.

In any assistive facility, it should be noted that the resident is renting the room or part of the room, and to him or her, that is home. It should be arranged as the resident wishes and furnished with as many personal possessions as possible to provide a sense of historic continuity and belonging, identity, and comfort (Grant, Skinkle, Lipps, 1992; Kruzich, Clinton, Kelber, 1992; Waldrop, 1992). Staff should be encouraged to act and to respond to a resident in a courteous and respectful manner, as if they are visitors. For example, a person would not go to a friend's house, and turn on the television or rearrange the furniture without permission. By recognizing the importance of the older adult's personal space, staff members reaffirm the older adult's rights and enhance his or her sense of dignity.

> ***Insight*** • *Older adults living in apartments or nursing care facilities benefit from easy access to nature. Sitting, observing, and enjoying flower gardens and other outdoor settings contribute to satisfaction with their housing and lives. Window views displaying nature are also important. Designing space so that older adults have access to nature allows opportunities for reflection and appreciation for life's changes.*

When older people change environments there are dangers of **translocation** crises resulting from relocation stress. Moving to any setting is often associated with loss. Older people may move because of a loss of spouse, health, home, or functional independence. Depression, withdrawal, confusion, increased dependency, lowered life satisfaction, and increased health problems may result from a move, especially if the older adult is not prepared or when the move is abrupt. If older people make the decision to move after careful consideration over a period of time, they are familiar with the new environment, and they are able to take cherished possessions with them, they can make the move with minimal stress. When the move is precipitous, with little or no input from the older adult, the move may have negative effects on health and possibly increase mortality (Grant, Skinkle, Lipps, 1992; Kennedy et al, 1992; Waldrop, 1992).

There is a segment of the older population that is homeless. Data about homelessness are difficult to quantify because of the very nature of the problem. Estimates of the percentage of older adults among the homeless range from one in every 16 to one in four. Women are among an increasing number of homeless older adults. Most have some source of income (social security or SSI), however it is usually insufficient to obtain adequate housing. Approximately 30% of homeless older adults have mental illness or dementia. Many may also suffer from chronic illness, and visual and hearing problems. In 1986 the Aging Health Policy Center survey of homeless individuals indicated that 66% of the older men and 74% of older women were in poor health. An older adult's impaired judgment may lead to financial mismanagement, eviction, or exploitation of his or her property by others, leading to loss of residence. Locating a new residence is difficult because of limited income, mental, and physical health problems, and a lack of information about affordable housing (Keigher, Greenblatt, 1992; Kutza, Keigher, 1991).

Homeless older adults require interventions that can connect them with needed services. Medical and mental assessments, emergency shelter, and long-term supervision may be required. In a study by Harris and Williams (1991), homeless men identified needs such as clean water, healthful food, adequate rest and exercise, obtaining medications and health care, adequate clothing, a safe place to stay at night, as well as money and facilities for bathing and washing clothing.

Whatever the housing status of the older person, it must be remembered that each person has a right to determine where to live unless proven incompetent. Nurses, as health care professionals, must respect that right and work with the person to maintain as much independence and dignity as possible.

BOX 7-4

Types of Crimes Committed Against Older Adults

The kinds of crime most often committed against older adults include:

- **Larceny or theft**—Noncontact crime resulting in loss of property
- **Robbery**—Taking of property by force or threat of force
- **Burglary**—Taking of property by being in the victim's residence, place of business, or automobile without authorization
- **Auto theft**—Taking of vehicle with intent to keep it
- **Assault**—Verbal communication (such as a threat) that puts the victim in reasonable apprehension of physical harm
- **Battery**—Physically harming the victim
- **Fraud**—Intentional deception to cause a person to give up property or some lawful right
- **Abuse** or neglect—Willful or negligent acts of caregivers resulting in physical or emotional harm to the older adult

Ferraro K, LaGrange R: Are older people most afraid of crime? Reconsidering age differences in fear of victimization, *J Gerontol* 47(5):S233-244, 1992.

AARP provides many books on housing options, adaptations, and safety. Many are free and others are available at a minimum cost. The federal government also provides materials on housing options through the Consumer Information Center.

Criminal Victimization

Data sources such as the U.S. Department of Justice, the Law Enforcement Assistance Administration, and the findings of "victim surveys" over the last 15 years show that there is a lower victimization rate among older adults in connection with assault, robbery, rape, theft and burglary than in the younger population (Cox, 1986; Fattah, Sacco, 1989) (Box 7-4). Older adults are least at risk for homicide. However, they are actually at greater risk for homicide committed during a robbery (Cox, 1986; Fattah, Sacco, 1989). Whatever the risk, it is the perception of risk by the older adult that affects his or her lifestyle (Fattah, Sacco, 1989). Ferraro and LaGrange conducted a survey in 1990, which found that older adults do not perceive their risk of victimization as high (Ferraro, LaGrange, 1992). Most older adults cite concerns relating to health and finances as a priority, whereas a few are genuinely afraid of becoming victims of crime (Table 7-13). Declining health and limited finances are factors contributing to feelings of vulnerability. As a result, older people may withdraw behind locked doors, becoming isolated. They may rarely leave home and may even refuse to permit services within the home. Such imposed social isolation has a negative effect on the older adult's overall health and well-being.

Older adults are often victims of fraud and scams. Just how often is not known because the older adult may not realize they have been victimized or may be too embarrassed to admit to victimization. In a 1991 special report on fraud by *Modern Maturity* magazine, the staff direc-

TABLE 7-13

Current and Future Concern About Crime

	1989 Percent total	1992 Percent total
Current		
Very secure	58	58
Somewhat secure	38	38
Not at all secure	5	4
(Base)	(1,509)	(1,499)
Future		
Very concerned	29	32
Somewhat concerned	38	44
Not at all concerned	33	24
(Base)	(1,483)	(1,471)

From American Association of Retired Persons: *Understanding senior housing for the 1990's*, Washington, D.C., 1993, The Association.

tor of the U.S. House of Representatives Subcommittee on Health and Long-Term Care stated that people over age 65 probably make up 30% of scam victims (Bekey, 1991) (Box 7-5).

The older adult becomes a victim for several unique reasons (Box 7-6). They are perceived as vulnerable. The ageist views of society often portray the older adult as weak and gullible; older adults may even see themselves this way.

The older adult is highly visible. Appearance advertises age. Older adults follow the same routines daily, which makes their movements predictable. They tend to rely on public transportation, and if they live in undesirable urban areas, they are vulnerable when walking to and from that transportation.

The level of dependency is an indicator for victimization. The more dependent an individual, the greater the risk of victimization (Douglass, 1987; Gailbraith, 1986). Some older adults have a diminished sense of sight or hearing. They are unable to see well enough to recognize danger in the immediate area or to read contracts. They cannot hear well enough to understand what is being said and may not ask for clarification.

Loss of physical strength reduces the ability to fight back. If there is a loss of cognitive ability, the older adult has less ability to reason rationally and therefore is vulnerable to fraud and abuse.

Con artists commonly prey on older adults. Loneliness and a life of trusting others leave older adults vulnerable. Door-to-door con artists use friendliness to gain the trust of the older person. They will visit for as long as it takes to accomplish their goal. They rely on the older adult's fears related to safety and health to sell their products. They convince the older adult that the roof needs repair, the driveway needs sealcoating, or a burglar alarm system should be installed. Other older adults respond to appeals and advertising seen on the television, in the Sunday supplements of newspapers, or in the mail. They may order products that turn out to be different than advertised, for example, a "solar clothes dryer" for $39.99 that ended up being a clothes line and clothespins (Bekey, 1991).

The older adult who has been victimized is likely to be confused, disoriented, fearful, or angry. When trying to assist the older adult victim the nurse should give the impression of nonhostile authority. Firm direction should be tempered with empathy. It is important to listen carefully to the victim. This conveys an attitude of empathy and respect and helps the victim sort out the facts. The nurse must exhibit an attitude of calmness and reassure the person that help will be provided throughout this crisis.

At times, the nurse may need to allow time for the victim to regain composure. One way to accomplish this is to distract the person by asking for demographic information. Inquire about address, phone number, family, and other support systems to help calm the older adult.

Follow-up procedures such as referral to a social service agency or victim support group, or a phone call to let the victim know how the case is progressing helps

BOX 7-5

Consumer Frauds Most Perpetrated Against Older Adults

Health and medical frauds—these include quackery or merchandising of drugs, health aids, or insurance.
Mail order frauds—merchandising through the mail that includes false or misleading information about the product.
Income creation and investment frauds—Get-rich-quick schemes such as pyramid selling, work at home scams, selling fraudulent franchises, and real estate investment opportunities.
Social psychologic frauds—Merchandising of products and services that exploit fears by promising solutions to problems and loneliness.
Con games—Schemes such as the "pigeon drop," the vacation lure, the bank swindle, or the oil well investment. Con games are usually perpetrated by professional con operators.

From Bekey M: Dial S-W-I-N-D-L-E, *Modern Maturity* 34(2):31-44, 88-89, 1991; Fattah E, Sacco V: *Crime and victimization of the elderly,* New York, 1989, Springer-Verlag.

BOX 7-6

Reasons Older Adults Are Fraud Victims

1. Older adults are often lonely and isolated. They are more likely to be at home and therefore available to both door-to-door and phone scams. They welcome con artists who are willing to spend time visiting.
2. The older adult has fewer resources to turn to for advice. They may be reluctant to "bother" friends, family or professionals.
3. The older adult may be more susceptible to con artists who are polite, who appear knowledgeable, or who represent authority.
4. Older adults often have concerns about maintaining a comfortable lifestyle on a fixed income, affording good medical and long-term care, or providing for spouse and children.
5. Chronic illness leads many older adults to consider medical remedies offered by health fraud promoters.

the victim know that the professional cares. However, precautions must be taken to avoid encouraging excessive dependency.

Community resources for crime victims vary from one area to another. In some communities, victim and witness assistance programs can offer short-term immediate help. Support groups may help a victim work through feelings of anger and fear. Volunteer action programs such as a neighborhood watch aid in prevention and also help the older adult feel safer. The Area Agency on Aging is a good resource for information about assistance programs for older people. Local law enforcement agencies are also available for help.

Every state has an older adult abuse law that includes methods for reporting suspected abuse. Most state laws define the abuse and provide a system of investigation. Many states maintain a registry of reports on suspected abuse. Some states mandate professionals working with older adults to report suspected abuse. In other states, reporting is voluntary. The local Department of Social Service or Area Agency on Aging can provide information on reporting requirements.

It is important for the older adult to feel control over his or her environment and to have a voice in the community. Educational programs help older adults to identify potential crime situations and ways to protect themselves. Law enforcement organizations and the AARP are establishing local senior advisory groups to assist sheriffs and police chiefs in understanding senior community needs. Such groups are also identifying and recommending programs, as well as assisting in planning and in integrating law enforcement concerns with other social service needs throughout the community (Miller, 1992). Older adults who take responsibility for their own environment feel in control, and that attitude is recognized by those who would victimize older adults.

ADVOCACY

Older adults as a group are good advocates for their own special needs and interests. They write to legislators, consumer protection groups, government agencies, and other groups that control issues affecting older adults. They vote. By advocating for themselves, older adults are taking charge of their environment, their resources, their mental and physical health, and the future of all older adults. Older adults know from experience that they *can* make a difference.

However, there are some older adults who are not able to plead their cause. Older women were not taught to be assertive and to stand up for themselves. The physically or mentally disabled, the undereducated, minority groups, those who do not speak the language, and the financially disadvantaged all need assistance to find and to take advantage of services and programs that may benefit them.

The nurse is often the best person to initiate and provide that assistance. The nurse is trained to listen and to assess, is aware of aging physiology and psychology, is familiar with community resources, and is motivated to serve the older adult. The nurse may be the one member of the formal support group with the most complete information about the older adult.

By listening to and consulting with the older adult, the nurse develops an understanding of the values and perceptions that guide the older adult's thoughts and feelings about life. The nurse forms a partnership with the older adult to defend and promote those rights.

The nurse advocate determines what the older adult wants then helps to find ways to satisfy those desires. If staying at home is important to the older adult the nurse can assist in enabling the person to stay home. By involving the older person in the planning from the start, the nurse establishes a partnership that strengthens the older adult's self-esteem, promotes dignity, and enhances satisfaction with life.

Within the hospital or nursing facility the nurse can advocate for the older adult by clearly documenting his or her concerns and problems, and any nursing care approaches. The nurse is in a key position to advocate for the older adult by bringing problems to the attention of the physician, social services department, or administra-

Insight • *America has a growing population of older prisoners. There are two types of older offenders—chronic offenders, who may cycle through the prison system many times during their lives, and those who commit a first offense after a lifetime of obeying the law.*

Older first offenders usually have committed crimes against people, which tend to be violent crimes such as murders of wives, neighbors, or relatives. Alcohol consumption is a factor in more than half of all incidences of criminal behavior. Sexual offenses involving children are also common criminal acts.

Concerns about the growing population of older prisoners include the high cost of special health care, special diets, and decreasing ability to perform ADLs.

Both federal and state prison systems are exploring policy options for handling older offenders, such as separate housing, appropriate heating, lighting, and accessibility to bathrooms, relaxation of some rules, and training of prison staffs in the aging process and its effects.

BOX 7-7

Advocate Organizations for Older Adults*

- American Association of Retired Persons
- Gray Panthers
- Older Women's League
- Organizations of professionals working in the field of aging
- Gerontological Society of America
- American Health Care Association (Nursing Homes)
- National Gerontological Nursing Association
- National Association of Social Workers
- National Association of Professional Geriatric Care Managers
- Hispanic Council on Aging
- National Council on Aging
- American Society on Aging
- Alzheimer's Disease and Related Disorders Association

*For addresses and phone numbers, see Appendix 7A, p. 192 and Appendix A, pp. A-1 to A-6.

tor as appropriate. In cases where client competency is questioned, it may be appropriate for the nurse to encourage legal counsel or to insist on comprehensive evaluation by a qualified geriatric specialist to determine the cause of symptoms.

Whatever the setting, the nurse's advocacy for the older adult is important to assure the older adult of continuing to control his or her life. There are many organizations in the United States that advocate for the older adult (Box 7-7).

Local and regional organizations also advocate for older adults, including state Departments of Aging and the local Area Agency on Aging.

Summary

The older adult's perception of the health care system in its entirety is influenced by experience. The nurse needs a sound understanding of the major historic events that have influenced the perceptions of today's older adult client so as to understand their response to health care issues.

Recent and present socioeconomic issues, including income sources, prosperity or poverty, education level, health status, and formal and informal support systems all affect the ability of the older adult to comprehend and comply with health care regimens.

Older adults and their families may not be aware of community resources. The nurse should be aware of housing options, nutrition programs, transportation opportunities, respite programs, and legal assistance programs that are available in the community.

By understanding the eligibility requirements for benefits and entitlements, the nurse can assist the older adult in receiving optimum services. By understanding the necessity for and the availability of durable power of attorney, conservator or guardian, the nurse can help the older adult and family cope with diminishing abilities.

The sensitive nurse understands the concerns of the older adult, and supports and reassures. The nurse can also encourage the older adult's informal support system of friends and family. Often, the nurse can coordinate the formal and informal support systems for maximum positive effect on the health and well-being of the older adult.

Advocates for older people, whether they are older adults or professionals in the field of aging, can help make socioeconomic and environmental factors a positive rather than a negative influence on the older adult.

To provide maximum benefits to aging health care consumers, the nurse must understand the factors that influence their perceptions of their health. To work with older adults successfully, the nurse must understand not only where they are but also where they have been.

HOME CARE TIPS

For socioeconomic influences:

- Assess the older adult's outside sources of income. Many supplemental policies cover excess costs that Medicare does not cover, thus ensuring more equipment and supplies for the older adult.
- The goal of home care is to restore the older adult to independence by teaching self-management of chronic conditions.
- Use social workers to identify community resources for financial assistance for the homebound older adult.
- Arrange for Meals-on-Wheels to be delivered to the homebound older adult if necessary.

For environmental influences

- Many meal delivery services deliver food that has been prepared and frozen. Assess the older adult's functional ability and environment to ensure that they can complete preparation of the food that has been delivered (such as having a stove, electricity, or a microwave).
- Use a social worker to identify community resources for housing options for the homebound older adult with multiple problems.
- Assess for signs of older adult abuse which may be manifested by consumer frauds. Report any suspicions of consumer frauds.
- Consumer frauds can be reduced by decreasing social isolation in the homebound older adult.

Key Points

- Socioeconomic factors such as income level, income sources, insurance coverage, benefits and entitlements, and education level influence the older adult's perception of his or her health and approach to health care.
- Environmental factors such as geographic location, housing, transportation, and perception of safety influence the availability of services as well as the older adult's knowledge and use of those services.
- The strength of the formal and informal support systems including community services, medical care, spiritual resources, and family and friends may influence the maintenance of independence for the older adult.
- Experience has a strong influence on shaping value systems, coping skills, and perceptions. It is important to understand the events that occurred early in the older adult's life to understand their values and perceptions.
- Education has a strong positive influence on economic well-being and on health status. Education prepares a person to make positive decisions that contribute to a higher perceived quality of life.
- Medicare is a federal program that provides health insurance for older adults. It consists of two parts—part A, hospital insurance that helps pay for inpatient care and some follow-up care, and part B, medical insurance that helps pay for physician services and some outpatient services.
- Medicaid is a state-administered program that uses federal funds to provide some medical expenses not covered by Medicare. Each state has different coverage and requirements. Medicaid is designed for people with very low incomes and minimal assets.
- Older adults who are no longer able to handle their affairs or make decisions about their lives may benefit from a conservator, guardian, or durable power of attorney. A conservator manages financial resources, a guardian makes personal decisions, and a durable power of attorney is a document that names an agent to act on behalf of the person for a specific function such as financial or health care decisions.
- The condition of the home and furnishings, the composition of the neighborhood, and the availability and type of transportation affect the security and safety of the older adult. Aging and outdated homes and appliances, worn furniture, and unreliable transportation can lead to accidents and injury. Deteriorating neighborhoods with changing populations may foster a feeling of insecurity in the older adult.
- Most communities in America have a variety of housing options to meet the needs of the older adult including single family residences, apartments, congregate housing, shared housing, retirement communities, assisted-living facilities and nursing homes. Each option provides a different level of service to help the older adult realize maximum independence.
- Perceived victimization in the older adult may result in decreased trust, increased suspicion, and eventual withdrawal and isolation that can create a resulting negative effect on health and well-being.
- A strong support system helps to protect the older adult from criminal victimization. Professional service providers, friends, and family may monitor the older adult's environment and offer guidance when necessary. Community programs such as neighborhood watch programs and educational programs on victimization help the older adult actively participate in crime prevention.
- Through advocacy, nurses can protect the dignity of older adults and improve their quality of life.

Critical Thinking Exercises

1. A 65-year-old chronically ill woman has few financial resources, no formal education, and only one child who can assist her. Her son is married with five children and has a job that barely manages to support him and his family. Speculate how the woman's situation may affect her perception of her health care. In what ways can the nurse intervene to assist her?
2. A 73-year-old man is a retired banker whose wife died several years ago. He is able to perform all ADLs but needs help with meal preparation and transportation. He lives in a deteriorating neighborhood and no longer feels safe. He does not want to live with family members or completely give up his independence. What housing options would be appropriate for him? What advantages would such housing options offer over living alone?

REFERENCES

American Association of Retired Persons: *Understanding senior housing for the 1990's,* Washington, D.C., 1993, The Association.

American Association of Retired Persons: *A profile of older Americans,* Washington, D.C., 1991, The Association.

American Association of Retired Persons: *A matter of choice,* Washington, D.C., The Association.

Abrams W, Berkow R, editors: *Merck manual of geriatrics,* Rahway, N.J., 1990, Merck.

Atchley RC: The myth of fixed income, *Aging Today* September/October 13(5):10, 1992.

Bekey M: Dial S-W-I-N-D-L-E, *Mod Matur* 34(2):31-44, 88-89, 1991.

Burke M, Flaherty MJ: Coping strategies and health status of elderly arthritic women, *J Adv Nurs* 18:7-13, 1993.

Clough B: Broadening perspectives on learning activities in later life, *Educ Gerontol* 18(5):447-459, 1992.

Coward R: Double jeopardy—aging beyond the country myth, *Aging Today* September/October 14(5):7-9, 1993.

Cox H: *Later life,* Englewood Cliffs, N.J., 1986, Prentice Hall.

Cutler S, Coward R: Availability of personal transportation in households of elders: age, gender, and residence differences, *Gerontologist* 32(1):77-81, 1992.

Douglass R: *Domestic mistreatment of the elderly—towards prevention,* Washington, D.C.,1987, American Association of Retired Persons.

Fattah E, Sacco V: *Crime and victimization of the elderly,* New York, 1989, Springer-Verlag.

Federal Benefits for Veterans and Dependents, Washington, D.C., 1993, Office of Public Affairs.

Ferraro K, LaGrange R: Are older people most afraid of crime? Reconsidering age differences in fear of victimization, *J Gerontol* 47(5):S233-S244, 1992.

Fox JA, Levin J: Homicide against the elderly: a research note, *Criminol* 29(2):317-326, 1991.

Freeman F: Minority elder growth: impetus for reform, *In Touch AOA,* Washington, D.C., 1992, US Administration on Aging.

Frongillo EA et al: Characteristics related to elderly persons' not eating for 1 or more days: implications for meal programs, *Am J Pub Health* 82:600-602, 1992.

Gailbraith M: Elder abuse: an overview. Elder abuse: perspectives on an emerging crisis, Kansas City, Mo., 1986, Mid-America Congress on Aging.

Grant PR, Skinkle RR, Lipps G: The impact of an interinstitutional relocation on nursing home residents requiring a high level of care, *Gerontologist* 32(6):834-842, 1992.

Hamilton A, editor: *Legal guide for senior citizens,* Topeka, Kan., 1991, Kansas Department on Aging.

Harris JL, Williams LK: Universal self-care requisites as identified by homeless elderly men, *J Gerontolog Nurs* 17(6):39-43, 1991.

Himes C: Social demography of contemporary families and aging, *Generations* 17(3):13-16, 1992.

Johnson C: Divorced and reconstituted families: effects on the older generation, *Generations* 17(3):17-20, 1992:

Keigher S, Greenblatt S: Housing emergencies and the etiology of homelessness among the urban elderly, *Gerontologist* 32(4):457-465, 1992.

Kennedy S et al: Responses of nursing home residents to intrainstitutional relocation, *Geriat Nurs* 13(4):192-200, 1992.

Kleyman P, editor: The illusion of affluence, *Aging Today* September/October 13(5):7, 1992.

Kruzich J, Clinton J, Kelber S: Personal and environmental influences on nursing home satisfaction, *Gerontologist* 32(3):342-350, 1992.

Kutza EA, Keigher SM: The elderly "new homeless:" an emerging population at risk, *Soc Work* 36(4):288-293, 1991.

Lorig K: Self-management of chronic illness: a model for the future, *Generations* 17(3):11-14, 1993.

Miller B, Montgomery A: Family caregivers and limitations in social activities, *Res Aging* 12(1):72-93, 1990.

Miller W: The graying of America and its implications for policing, *Police Chief* October 59:56-57, 1992.

Miranda M: Quality of life in the later years: why we must challenge the continuing disparity between whites and minorities, *Perspect Aging* 21(1):4-10, 1992.

Mor-Barak ME, Miller LS, Syme LS: Social networks, life events, and health of the poor, frail elderly: a longitudinal study of the buffering versus the direct effect, *Fam Commun Health* 14(2):1-13, 1991.

Older women's league: failing America's caregivers: a status report on women who care. Sharing the caring: options for the 90s and beyond, Washington, D.C., 1990, US Government Printing Office.

Penning M, Wasyliw D: Homebound learning opportunities: reaching out to older shut-ins and their caregivers, *Gerontologist* 32(5):704-707, 1992.

Pynoos J: Strategies for home modification and repair, *Generations* 16(2):21-25, 1992.

Porcino J: Designs for living, *Mod Matur* 36(2):24-33, 1993.

Quirouette C, Gold DP: Spousal characteristics as predictors of well-being in older couples, *Int J Aging Hum Dev* 34(4):257-269, 1992.

Rollinson PA: Elderly single room occupancy (SRO) hotel tenants: still alone, *Soc Work* 36(4):303-308, 1991.

Retirement, Baltimore, MD, 1990, US Department of Health and Human Services, Social Security Administration.

SSI, Baltimore, MD, 1993, US Department of Health and Human Services, Social Security Administration.

The Medicare 1993 Handbook, Baltimore, MD, 1993, US Department of Health and Human Services, Health Care Financing Administration.

US Bureau of the Census, *Statistical Abstract of the United States: 1992,* ed 112, Washington, D.C., 1992.

Van Nostrand JF, Furner SE, Suzman R, editors: *Health data on older Americans: United States, 1992,* National Center for Health Statistics, *Vital Health Stat* 3(27):26, 27, 144, 1993.

Waldrop J: Old money, *Am Demograph* 14:24-26, 1992.

Wapner S, Demick J, Redondo JP: Cherished possessions and adaptation of older people to nursing homes, *Int J Aging Hum Dev* 31(3):219-235, 1990.

Winkleby MA et al: Socioeconomic status and health: how education, income, and occupation contribute to risk factors for cardiovascular disease, *Am J Pub Health* 82:816-820, 1992.

Wolinsky F et al: The risk of nursing home placement and subsequent death among older adults, *J Gerontol* 47(4):S173-S182, 1992.

BIBLIOGRAPHY

Davis MA et al: Living arrangements and impact on survival, *Am J Pub Health* 82:401-406, 1992.

Gollup JO: *The decade matrix,* Reading, Mass., 1991, Addison-Wesley.

Stevenson C, Capezuti E: Guardianship: protection versus peril, *Geriatr Nurs* 12(1), 1991.

Talbot J, Kaplan R: The benefits of nearly nature for elderly apartment residents, *Int J Aging Hum Dev* 33(2):119-130, 1991.

Understanding social security, US Department of Health and Human Services, Social Security Administration, 1993.

US Department of Health and Human Services: *Understanding social security,* Social Security Administration, 1993.

Weatherford D: *American women and World War II,* New York, 1990, Facts on File.

Zevitz R, Gurnack A: Factors related to elderly crime victims' satisfaction with police service: the impact of Milwaukee's "Gray Squad," *Gerontologist* 31(1):92-101, 1991.

APPENDIX 7A*

Resources

ORGANIZATIONS OF OLDER ADULTS

American Association of Retired Persons (AARP)
601 E Street NW
Washington, DC 20049
(202) 434-2277

Gray Panthers
2025 Pennsylvania Ave. NW
Suite 821
Washington, DC 20006
(202) 466-3132

Older Women's League (OWL)
666 11th Street NW
Washington, DC 20001
(202) 783-6686

ORGANIZATIONS OF PROFESSIONALS WORKING IN THE FIELD OF AGING

American Health Care Association
1201 L Street NW
Washington, DC 20005-4014
(202) 842-4444

Gerontological Society of America
1275 K Street NW
Suite 350
Washington, DC 20005-4006
(202) 842-1275

Hispanic Council on Aging
2713 Ontario Rd NW
Washington, DC 20009
(202) 265-1288

National Association of Professional Geriatric Care Managers
National Association of Social Workers
750 First Street NE
Washington, DC 20002
(202) 408-8600

National Gerontological Nursing Association
c/o Mosby-Year Book, Inc.
Suite 510
7250 Parkway Dr.
Hanover, MD 21076
(800) 723-0560

*For a more complete listing of gerontologic resources, see Appendix A, pp. A-1 to A-6.

ORGANIZATIONS OF BOTH PROFESSIONALS AND OLDER ADULTS

Alzheimer's Disease and Related Disorders Association
919 North Michigan Avenue
Chicago, IL 60611-1676
(312) 335-8700

American Society on Aging
833 Market Street
Suite 511
San Francisco, CA 94103-1824
(415) 882-2910

National Council on the Aging
(Includes National Institute of Senior Citizens and National Institute on Adult Day Care)
409 3rd Street SW
Suite 200
Washington, DC 20024
(202) 479-1200

Part Three

Special Issues

CHAPTER 8

Nutrition

LEARNING OBJECTIVES

On completion of this chapter, the reader will be able to:

1. Understand data, particularly from longitudinal studies, about aging processes and older people in relation to nutrition and wellness.
2. Diffuse the stereotypes of older people with recent, positive information.
3. Recognize that age alone is the poorest predictor of capacities, needs, performance, and health status.
4. Appreciate the long history of food as magic and nurturance.
5. Identify the role of nutrition adequacy in promoting wellness during the life span as it relates to the prevention and therapy of terminal chronic diseases that are regarded as inevitable with age.
6. Identify the highest risk for disease among older people as it relates to controllable lifestyle factors.
7. Describe the nutritional requirements of older people.

Seneca (4 BC–65 AD) said, "Man does not die, he kills himself" (Lorand, 1928).

Furthermore, Lorand, a Czech physician, was convinced so very long ago that people should eat to live and not live to eat. He also believed that more people die prematurely from overeating and that "foundations of many diseases are laid by excessive eating" (Lorand, 1928).

EARLY PEOPLE AND FOOD

Food has played changing and magical roles throughout human history and prehistory. Over the millennia, certain foods have alternated as poisons, potions, or panaceas for health, potency, long life, and love. The most respected physician of ancient days, Hippocrates (460-377 BC), the Father of Medicine, reflected his commitment to the importance of diet in a statement from the Hippocratic Oath: "I will apply dietetic measures for the benefit of the sick according to my ability and judgement; I will keep them from harm and injustice," (Lyons et al, 1978). Cato the Elder (234-149 BC), a Roman statesman, ate large amounts of cabbage in the belief it had special healing properties. A later Roman scholar, Pliny (23-79 AD), ate the foot and snout of the hippopotamus to enhance sexual potency. A Chinese physician of the sixth century BC prescribed certain foods for clients to stimulate the yin (female principle) and the yang (male principle) to keep a person healthy (Tannahill, 1988).

As a physician, Hippocrates' methodology was to assist nature by noninvasive, gentle approaches such as diet, rest, and exercise. He preceded contemporary medical practice by centuries in emphasizing prevention of illness with particular hygienic regimens. An eleventh-century Chinese physician said, "Experts at curing disease are inferior to those specialists who warn against disease. Experts in the use of medicines are inferior to those who recommended proper diet," (Tannahill, 1973). He, like Hippocrates, adhered to the principle and practice of observing and caring for the *whole* person. Both of these scholars came so close to today's "wellness" perspective that modern medicine will soon incorporate this notion into American practice. Another Hippocratic principle—to assist nature—is also becoming apparent. It modifies conditions to the point that "the natural forces in the body [reach] harmony and therefore health," (Lyons et al, 1978).

In the beginning, early human families were vagabond hunters. Their hunting behavior was controlled by the weather. They gathered fruits, berries, and roots during the rainy seasons. When it was dry, they ate small game and whatever the predators left behind. By approximately 10,000 BC, bows and arrows, hooks, traps, and nets expanded the human diet to include other animals and fish. Over time, domestic herds of sheep, goats, and cattle appeared, so primitive people had a captive population to provide food. Although various human groups remained wanderers for thousands of years, there were those who added a very special food source at around 8,000-7,000 BC. They were not only food gatherers but also producers, sowing seeds for crops. Anthropologists and archaeologists have identified this as the "Agricultural Revolution" or "Great Transition."

In the beginning, the primary concern of the human family was the quantity of food. Little attention was given to variety, balance, or contamination. Today the focus is on quality, nutrient density, appropriate calories, and food that is free of toxins or disease-causing organisms. Food excesses or deficiencies require specific nutrient information and attention to nutritional adequacy for wellness promotion and disease prevention. Dietary intake is perceived by allied health researchers and practitioners to be one of the most significant, controllable tools for wellness, disease prevention, rehabilitation, and treatment or therapy for a wide range of disorders.

Demographic Imperative

What is so important about the consideration of nutrition, aging, and wellness? Since 1900 the average life expectancy has increased by 28 years. By 2030 life expectancy is projected to be 34 years more than it was at the dawn of the twentieth century. The reality of demographics (see Chapter 1) in the United States suggests that certain factors need to be emphasized that can enhance these additional later years so that they are the healthiest possible. Currently, the "graying of America" is not the unusual phenomenon it was in the early twentieth century. What has been unexpected is the more than 33 million (12.7%) Americans age 65 and older who are living longer and experiencing fewer of the so-called inevitable, age-related diseases. There are reliable indications that a number of the major chronic disorders (e.g., cardiovascular disease, cancer, stroke, osteoporosis, and diabetes) become symptomatic later and are repeatedly correlated with dietary intake, exercise, stress management, and locus of control. More often, the diagnoses of such diseases occur among the oldest old (age 85 and older) and closer to the periods of dying and death in the ninth and tenth decades of life. By the year 2000, 35 million people (about 17%) will be 65 and older, and in 2030 there will be about 70 million. The age cohort of 85 and older, which was 3.4 million of the total population in 1993, is the fastest growing segment and is 10% of the older population. America is growing older. Life expectancy has increased, but life span has not, with today's average life expectancy at birth at about 75.7 years. Life span is still considered to be 115 years, although a record of 120 years was set in March 1995 by a woman in France. The oldest old will continue to be the fastest growing group and is predicted by the U.S. Bureau of Census to be 8.6 million by 2030. By 2050 this group may be 25% of the 65 and older population (American Association of Retired Persons Administration on Aging [AARP/AOA], 1994; Manton, Stallord, Tolley, 1991; Metropolitan Life Insurance, 1991).

There will be social, economic, and affective consequences of an America growing older in the face of lowered birth and mortality rates among young and old. Promotion of wellness and disease prevention into the later years are therefore of even greater significance for the happiness and productivity of individuals of all ages, families, communities, and societies (Campanelli, 1990).

GROWING OLDER: WHAT IS AGING?

"Our culture is not much interested in *why* we grow old, *how* we ought to grow old, or *what* it means to grow old" (Cole, 1992).

Aging is an individually unique, human, lifetime experience. Indeed, it is the summation of change over the lifetime, whether positive, negative, or neutral, in all human dimensions. It is a result of unique genetics interacting with many environments and lifestyles. Older adults are not a single group; rather they are the most heterogeneous of all age cohorts. They represent ethnic, racial, and cultural diversity. Some are well, active, and at work; some need medical or social care; others live within a family, some with a partner, and still others live alone. A considerable percentage of those over age 75 are retired, others work part time for income, and many more volunteer time and energy. Finances can be a major concern for at least 20% of the older adults who are poor or near poor, according to the government evaluation of poverty. There is no group called "the old," yet the media continue to refer to older people as such. Every older adult requires individual evaluation and deserves to be regarded as a complete older person with unique needs, capacities, and desires. At best, older adults will be invited to share life experiences and to contribute to the society.

However, aging is not a disease nor a series of catastrophes leading inevitably to invalidism. The much-used stereotypes of older people in this century have pervaded the opinions of most of society, including those of older adults. The images of nonproductive, incompetent, and dependent wrinkled people with halting gaits and speech, diminished mental capacities, and often in need of medical attention have contributed to the extant ageism in American communities and institutions. These stereotypes and practices isolate, discriminate, and segregate older people solely on the basis of age. The "less-than" aging adult persona is thus reinforced (Butler, 1975).

Normative, Successful Aging

Aging does slowly leave its message of time in individuals and populations, with wrinkles, perhaps a diminution in speed of response, and some minimal systemic changes; but age alone does not herald massive systemic decline, worthlessness, and living sexless and loveless for years with a bitter end of life.

Recent data from research studies and long-term longitudinal studies of the National Institute on Aging (NIA) have finally provided information on **successful aging.** It is now appropriate to develop a different reality of aging based on the accumulation of new knowledge. What was considered **normative aging** (i.e., usual or functional aging) in the early decades of this century included some treated and controlled disorders and diseases with continued function. There is now wide consensus that a growing cohort of older people, who are aware of and in control of varied risk factors, experiences successful aging, or a more efficient state of wellness that is free of chronic disease (NIA, 1993; Roff, Atherton, 1989; Rowe, Kahn, 1987). It is this subgroup

> **Insight** • *On the contrary, age alone is the poorest predictor of capabilities, performance, interests, health or wellness, other human attributes, and what is happening in the person's life.*

that has increased markedly during the last 10 to 15 years and will be even larger in the twenty-first century. Baby boomers and their progeny will be the beneficiaries of health promotion and disease prevention, the only reasonable allied health care of the near and far future.

New Knowledge

Among the most valuable resources for information are the major longitudinal studies such as the Baltimore Longitudinal Study on Aging (BLSA), Duke University Studies (Palmore et al, 1985), and Framingham Studies (Kannel, Larson, 1993). These inquiries have provided an increasingly positive picture of good-to-excellent systemic function (i.e., with kidney and cardiovascular functions), and ability to remember and to problem-solve. Corroborating data are available from animal studies, as well as biochemic and anatomic evidence from cell suspension investigations (Hayflick, 1994; Walford, 1994). The BLSA, begun in 1958 by Nathan Shock of the Gerontology Research Center and now part of the NIA, demonstrates that the decremental changes that may occur can be a result of (1) unattended time-dependent processes, (2) disuse or misuse, and (3) pathology.

This multidisciplinary investigation (Shock et al, 1984) followed healthy men age 17 to 96. This study measured physiologic, psychologic, and social variables in the same individuals every 18 months, 2 years, or 6 years. In 1978, women were included as subjects (Ss) to this all-male study that continues to collect and assess data. Aging can no longer be considered a "unicausal," singular process; it is rather a pattern of *complex, interacting processes* that result in the changes and stabilities that can now be associated with the passage of time. Such processes are characterized by a gradual nature and a susceptibility to interventions such as dietary modification, exercise, stress management, and social, psychologic, and affective factors that are environmentally induced and integrated within the individual.

These studies enable clear, documented data that contradict earlier cross-sectional comparisons between young and old in physiologic and behavioral perspectives. Patterns that have emerged, including examples of each, are as follows:

1. Stabilities
    - There is an absence of significant change in important functions (e.g., resting heart rate, kid ney activity).

- Personality remains fairly constant but continues to develop and to adapt.

2. Decrements with age that are not supportable in longitudinal investigations include the following:
   - Cross-sectional studies indicated diminution in kidney efficiency. The longitudinal inquiry following the same healthy individual failed to support this decline.
   - Testosterone cross-sectional studies found a decline with age. Healthy men carefully screened for disease in longitudinal investigations showed no such significant difference.
3. Precipitous changes in old age
   - More often than not, sudden changes are an expression of disease or factors related to disease (e.g., pseudodementia or dementia).
4. Change related to cultural shifts
   - Change is essential to the correct interpretation of research data on the aging. For example, nutritional data demonstrate a reduction of dietary cholesterol intake since the BLSA has been established.

Distinguishing Between Aging and Disease

These longitudinal studies have also indicated that decrements and disease do not inevitably accompany growing older; rather, there is a widespread, specific systemic stability or improvement contrary to the cross-sectional data that consistently found older adults wanting and failing (BLSA, 1989; Shock et al, 1984).

1. Brain and behavior (Tucker et al, 1990)
   - No decline occurred in brain glucose metabolism with age.
   - Little, if any, decline occurred in performance on various intelligence tests.
   - Young and middle-age subjects performed equally well on vigilance tasks; some individuals age 70 and older did show a decline over a 6-year period.
   - Reaction time to infrequent auditory stimuli did not slow progressively over entire life span; the slowing that was measured occurred among people in the over age 70 group.
   - Problem-solving age decrements were not demonstrable in subjects until over age 70; *some Ss group members did not decline at all* from measurement at age 70.
   - Memory for visual design in the Ss group members age 20 to 70 showed only slight impairment.

   In every age group, even among the oldest individuals, performance on mental tasks did not diminish with age. It was most significantly indistinguishable from younger adults. *It is now generally agreed that people can maintain mental activity into their 80s and longer.*
   - Personality characteristics among older people often thought to connote inflexibility are now considered to be stable during adult years; there is no evidence to support the notion that the old are hypochondriacal.
   - Nerve cells are lost early on in maturity between ages 40 and 50; with use, those that do remain increase their intercellular connectivity, maximizing maintenance of function.
     -Transplanted embryonic nerve cells can survive and restore function in damaged, aging brain.
     -Serious dementia in older people is not simply a result of age, but it is in large part because of certain disease processes.

   It is possible to attain and to sustain improved mental function in older subjects with mild cognitive impairment using carefully designed training sessions (Schaie, Willis, 1986).
2. Cardiovascular function
   - Healthy volunteers studied in the BLSA inquiry showed no downward trend in cardiac output with age; studies before 1984, which stated an inevitable decrease in cardiac output in advancing years, appear to be incorrect.
   - Atherosclerotic vascular disease incidence and severity increases with age; it is another disorder that is not an inevitable concomitant of age. Current data demonstrate that this disease responds to intervention with appropriate dietary intake, exercise, stress management, and for women, sex hormone replacement therapy. Atherosclerosis has been minimized, reversed, and is potentially preventable (Lakatta, 1990).
3. Renal function
   - Cross-sectional information pointed to decrements with age in globular filtration rate and other renal functions. Among BLSA volunteers:
     -30% No change with age in creatinine clearance
     -5% Showed some increase
     -65% Showed variable decline
   - It is important to consider that since decline in renal function is not inevitable with age, drug dosage based on earlier cross-sectional expectations can be wrong. Therefore decisions need to be based on individual clinical information.
4. Endocrine activity
   - Many endocrine regulatory systems (with the exception of the female reproductive system) maintain stability throughout the mature life span of most people.
   - A recent inquiry into growth hormone respon-

sivity to the hypothalamic stimulating hormone in "normal" Ss group members at yearly intervals across their life spans found the highest responses from individuals in their 20s and 30s. There was some decline at age 40 and relatively no change at least into the 70s.

5. Muscle function and vigor (disease, misuse, disuse)
   - Cross-sectional studies indicated many losses in muscle, bone mass, and strength.
   - Recent investigations suggest a different reality (Paffenbarger et al, 1994). A group of sedentary older people in their 60s to 80s and in good health made "essentially the same gains in a fitness program" as did younger subjects (Grimby et al, 1994; Makrides, Simpson, Officer, 1995).
   - It appears that much of the expected common decline in strength and vigor among older people is a result of disuse, misuse, and illness rather than age. A significant percentage can be regained with exercise and dietary regimens.
6. Immune system
   - It is probably the best-documented age-related diminution.
   - There is an increase in autoimmune disorders.
   - The ability to maintain surveillance against cancer may diminish.

There is mounting correlational evidence that alteration in exercise, nutrition, and stress response can improve the immune response (Hill, Castle, Makinodan, 1990). Depression and grief have a measurable negative effect on the immune system response (Zisook et al, 1994). Fitness and wellness help maintain an effective immune function (Chandra, 1990).

WELLNESS: HEALTH PROMOTION AND DISEASE PREVENTION

There are moral and financial imperatives relative to demographic and recent health data which demand a significant change in behavior on the part of middle-age and older adults, health professionals, government, policy makers and society at large. Consensus on these imperatives was formed among the different groups involved and convincingly indicates that there is no alternative to health promotion, disease prevention, and wellness at any age (McGinnis, 1989; Zeman, 1990). Most importantly, the medical "disease model" and professionals must strike a new path that moves away from the disease/cure to a therapy/care model. Not only can the runaway costs of present so-called health care be reduced, but human suffering can be minimized. The chronic disorders mistakenly perceived as part of aging for so long can be delayed, prevented, and at a minimum, treated appropriately with early risk identification. The time is *now* for the practice of medical science and healing arts to work toward keeping people well, especially the more vulnerable members of the middle-age and old groups, and to screen for risks with proven intervention in *preventing* disorder and disease (Abdellah, Moore, 1988; Campanelli, 1990; Zeman, 1990).

> **Insight** • *Protein-calorie deficiencies, sedentary states, nutrient undernutrition, and unresolved stress response can severely diminish appropriate immune activity.*

Wellness is a dynamic series of processes, and is perceived as an active state of becoming and continually working to create harmony among spiritual, affective, physiologic, psychologic, and social well-being. The individual is a participant and decides on the commitment to active, vital living. Dependence on health professionals to maintain health for clients delays the partnership and inhibits motivation, self-determination, and other steps that must be initiated and managed by the individual.

Key Factors

Key factors in wellness include the following:

- Prevent isolation and stay involved.
- Develop friendships, intimate relationships, affective ties.
- Practice strategies to remain "in control."
- Maintain self-responsibility.
- Maintain reasonable body weight.
- Practice physical fitness—exercise in a range determined suitable.
- Develop the ability to relax and to energize.
- Carry out stress management.
- Be motivated to learn and to grow as a personality.
- Maintain nutritional awareness and prudent eating.
- Partner with a primary care clinician who acknowledges distinction between typical, successful aging and pathology, and who is prepared to discuss and to practice health promotion and disease prevention.

The four major areas of activity that together make wellness probable include the following:

1. Maintaining control of one's life adds to the sense of self (self-esteem), promotes wellness by stimulating immune response, and triggers motivation for personal interactions and participation in community activities.

2. Regular exercise improves a wide variety of physiologic functions; tends to slow down physical trends typically associated with aging (i.e., improves muscle strength and stamina, increases bone density, lowers cholesterol level, stabilizes glucose tolerance, and increases energy and oxygen use).
3. Stress management (e.g., relaxation and meditation techniques) has been demonstrated to produce sustained reductions in negative symptoms of stress response in older adults (i.e., it maintains adequate immune response and heart function, and reduces risk of depression).
4. Adequate and appropriate dietary intake contributes to low incidence of certain chronic disease and resistance to disease. It maximizes energy and resistance to symptoms that were considered part of aging, prolongs maintenance of viable cell function, and significantly improves the nutrient concentration available to cells.

Health: One Facet of Wellness

We have lived for such a long time according to a "great myth" that medical care always equals *health*. It is difficult to believe this could be in error. There are estimates that the medical care system itself affects about 10% to 15% of the common indices for measuring health (i.e., whether you live, how well you live, and how long you live). It has been suggested that the remaining 85% to 90% of the indices may be mostly determined by variables over which medical practice has little or no control—lifestyle, social conditions, and the physical environment. Rehabilitation perspectives for older adults are not yet integral to the practice of medicine (Nadelson, 1993; Teague, 1987; Weg, 1989, 1990).

There is now an increasing consensus that people are killing themselves by careless, personal lifestyle habits such as sedentary lifestyle, smoking, excessive drinking, overeating, or undernutrition. Furthermore, social and political realities are reducing the effectiveness of the individual's efforts with air, soil, and water pollution, as well as poverty, hunger, and ignorance, which all increase health risks, especially for infants, children, and older people.

Joseph A. Califano, the former director of Health, Education and Welfare (HEW), said before he resigned, "You, the individual, can do more for your own health and well-being than any doctor, hospital, any drug, any exotic medical advice" (Richmond, 1979).

Health is dependent on many variables, only some of which individuals can control. Health status at any point is one facet of wellness and is a result of the interaction and interdependence of three major areas: genetics, public health environmental issues, and lifestyle factors.

1. Genetics (relatively uncontrollable by individual, until genetic counseling, and genetic surgery enters significant practice)
2. Public health environmental issues—air, water, and soil pollution, as well as radiation
3. Lifestyle factors within personal province and management:
   - Nutrition and diet
   - Exercise
   - Stress response and stress management
   - Drugs, drug abuse, smoking, and alcoholism
   - Involvement with family, community, and purposeful activities
   - Challenging of the intellect; excitement of growing, learning, and giving
   - Expansion of spiritual, emotional, intellectual, and physical capabilities
   - Maintenance or expansion of personal relationships in friendship, companionship, and loving
   - Autonomy and validation of self
   - Control of one's life decisions
   - Flexibility as an important aspect of living in a micro- and macroenvironment of change
   - Partnership with health professionals concerning strategies working towards achieving on-going wellness.

These lifestyle variables are the behaviors most susceptible to modification and growth toward wellness.

A visual representation (Fig. 8-1) helps to see all aspects of the health continuum in motion.

NUTRITION: AN ALLY IN AGING AND WELLNESS

Widespread Acknowledgement

There is a growing consensus that older adults have the same or even greater nutrient requirements as the ones they had earlier in their lives (Munro, 1992; Scrimshaw, 1990; Vellas, 1992; Young, 1990). However, since many older people reduce their daily nutrient and caloric in-

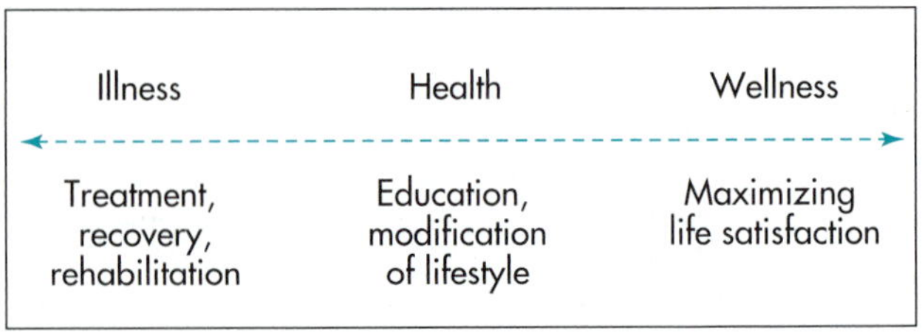

Fig. 8-1 Health continuum.

take, it is essential that foods eaten are high in nutrient density. If density is lacking, inadequate nutrition can first develop into subclinical malnutrition (Weg, 1978), and then, if intake is not corrected, frank malnutritional deficiencies and subsequent illness follow (Chernoff, 1991; Manson and Shea, 1991).

In identifying more than 50 nutrients that humans require each day, both macronutrients and micronutrients are included. The four macronutrients include (1) proteins, (2) fats, (3) carbohydrates, and (4) water. The micronutrients required by all ages in much smaller amounts include certain minerals, vitamins, essential fatty acids, and essential amino acids, the building blocks for protein. These are "essential," since the body generally does not synthesize all of these substances. Therefore they must be in foods of the daily dietary intake. Digestion provides the smaller amino acids from protein breakdown and glucose from the digestive breakdown of more complex carbohydrates. The micronutrients, minerals, and vitamins are commonly found as necessary cofactors in enzymatic reactions that enable all cell and body functions. As noted in Tables 8-1 and 8-2, a considerable number of these have been correlated with prevention and therapy for the disorders discussed on pp. 200-201. Deficiencies of micronutrients over any extended period contribute to or exacerbate these same diseases.

Nutritional sciences are breaking ground in medical, nursing, and allied health education. Heightened public interest and awareness is also evident. Nutritional food labels on products, magazine articles, and radio and television programs draw attention to the potential hazards of the westernized diet and the value of modifying dietary intake to more closely resemble the prudent diet (Table 8-3). The westernized diet is characterized by high lipids, cholesterol, and salt; low fiber, vitamin, and mineral di-

TABLE 8-1

Nutrition as Preventive and Therapeutic

The following information underscores the importance of nutrition, particularly to the aging population, by listing the general associations that research has identified between adequate amounts of specific nutrients and the prevention or treatment of disorders and diseases.

Dietary Factors Associated With Prevention and Therapy

Nutrient	Disorder
Fiber Adequate fluid intake or rehydration	Diabetes, diverticulosis, constipation, electrolyte imbalance, cancer, coronary heart disease (CHD)/atherosclerosis
Vitamins, minerals, amino acids, neurotransmitter precursors	Confusion, memory, depression, pseudodementia, wound repair, immune response
Complex carbohydrates	Atherosclerosis, obesity, diabetes, hypertension, CHD, cerebrovascular disease (CVD)
Low salt, low refined sugar, adequate/increased calcium intake	Hypertension, diabetes, atherosclerosis
Low chromium, zinc	Maturity-onset diabetes
Proteins, C and B vitamins (e.g., folic acid), zinc	Wound repair, immune response
Low total lipid (low saturated), complex carbohydrates , fiber, vitamins A and C, selenium	Malignancies (breast, bladder, colon, prostate), atherosclerosis
Calcium, vitamins D and K, fluoride, magnesium	Osteoporosis, periodontitis, hypertension
Protein, calorie adequacy	Immune response, energy level, wound repair, confusion, dementia
Low zinc, low calcium	Eye problems, functional efficiency, cataracts, macular degeneration
High selenium, high levels of vitamin E and C, carotenoids (e.g., beta carotene)	Appear to reduce risk for cataracts and malignancies, cardiovascular disease
Low omega-3 fatty acids in fish oils, high lipids and cholesterol	Atherosclerosis, coronary heart disease, coronary artery disease

In this table, adequate amounts of the itemized nutrients (that are found readily in the prudent diet) may prevent, may delay, or may treat the disorders or disease indicated. Some researchers rush to identify a single nutrient as capable of acting alone in these roles. There is increasing evidence that it is more reasonable to suggest that in vegetables and fruits, groups of antioxidants such as vitamin A, C, and B-complex, as well as minerals such as zinc and selenium together with still unknown substances have joint metabolic effects. Increased double-blind longitudinal studies are the primary techniques in the provision of data that will permit more definitive conclusions.

TABLE 8-2

Disorders and Disease Lifestyle

Disorders/disease	Lifestyle factors
Arteriosclerosis, atherosclerosis, coronary artery disease (CAD) hypertension	High fat/high simple carbohydrate diet; high salt; obesity; sedentary lifestyle; cigarette smoking; heavy drinking, alcoholism; unresolved, continual stress response and personality type; low calcium; inadequate protein/calories with consequences for immune response
Cerebrovascular accident	Sedentary lifestyle; low fiber/high fat/high salt diet; heavy drinking or alcoholism, which contributes to atherosclerosis/arteriosclerosis, and hypertension, which are risk factors for cerebrovascular accidents
Osteoporosis, periodontitis	Malnutrition; inadequate calcium, protein, vitamin K, fluoride, magnesium, and vitamin D metabolite; lack of exercise; bed rest, sedentary lifestyle; immobility; for women, sex steroid starvation
Chronic pulmonary disorders	Cigarette smoking; air pollution; excessive stress response; sedentary habits; westernized diet leading to weight gain, excess fat storage, and increased heart load
Obesity	Low chronic caloric output (sedentary), high caloric intake; high stress levels; heavy drinking or alcoholism; low self-esteem
Cancer	Possible correlation with personality type; unabated stressors; exposure to environmental carcinogens over a long period of time; nutritional deficiencies (especially antioxidants and protein/calories) and excesses; radiation, sex hormones; nutritional additives; cigarette smoking; occupational carcinogens (e.g., asbestos); occult viruses; diminution of immune capacity response (immune surveillance)
Dementia, pseudodementia	Malnutrition; long illness and bed rest; drug abuse (polypharmacy, iatrogenesis); anemia; other organ system disease; bereavement; social isolation
Depression	Malnutrition; sedentary habits; isolation; little opportunity for decision making; low self-esteem
Sexual dysfunction, concerns	Ignorance (i.e., the older individual and society at large); societal, stereotypic attitudes; early socialization; inappropriate partner or lack of one; drug effects (e.g., antihypertensive drugs); psychogenic origin; long periods of abstinence; serious systemic disease

etary intake; and health risks (Gaby et al, 1991; Posner et al, 1991).

Nutrition and more specifically, the nutrients of daily dietary intake, make a significant difference in reaching human wellness beyond the magic and symbolism of prehistory (Carper, 1993). Nutrition, as an area of study, has been restored to academic curricula and is now perceived as basic and necessary to raising the wellness level of all age groups. This is an important technique for decreasing the skyrocketing costs of so-called health care, which, for decades, has been practiced as disease care. Governmental agencies are also seriously committed to finding controllable factors that can assist the U.S. population in working toward wellness in the face of what former Surgeon Generals J. Richmond and C. Everett Koop considered "a very sick health care system" (Koop, 1988; McGinnis, 1989; Richmond, 1979). Efforts to embark on health promotion and disease prevention include adequate nutrition, exercise, stress management, public education, and changing attitudes, as well as information regarding responsibility of individuals and health care professionals in this change of perspective and practice.

Many dimensions of the whole person are needed to understand the particular mechanisms and milieux in which nutrition functions in its interactions with other variables. Recent investigations, especially the longitudinal studies noted in the foregoing comments, are enlightening and encouraging. It is never too late to change dietary intake patterns. BLSA participants demonstrate that being age 75 and older does not mean it is difficult to change earlier eating habits when there is adequate information that different eating patterns enhance health (Barnes, Terry, 1991; Hallfrish et al, 1990; Popkin, Haines, Patterson, 1992).

Correlations With Chronic Disease

It is apparent that the implementation of new information now available from longitudinal studies (that "successful aging" is increasingly probable for older adults) has unfortunately been delayed. In the launching of health promotion and disease prevention, investigations

TABLE 8-3

Prudent Versus Average Westernized Diet

	Prudent diet (Health promoting) Daily caloric intake (1,800 to 2,400 calories)	American westernized diet Daily caloric intake (2,800 to 3,000 calories)
Carbohydrates (CHO)	45% to 55% Complex carbohydrates: whole grain cereal, breads, fruits, vegetables	35% to 40% Refined carbohydrates, simple sugars
Refined/Processed sugars	10% or less of total CHO	Sugar, honey: 15% to 25% to 35% (greater than 100 gm/day)
Fats Saturated Unsaturated	30% to 25% to 20% 1:1 ratio or slightly in favor of unsaturated	40% to 50% High saturated fats
Cholesterol	Maximum 200 mG Less than 180 mg preferable	High intake 700 to 800 mg/day
Proteins	12% to 15% Mixed sources*: planr products, animal products	12% to 15% Majority of animal origin, (meat and whole milk products, egg yolk)
Salt	Maximum 2 to 3 gm No added salt	10 to 12 gm

*Lean beef, veal, lamb, poultry, fish; nuts, legumes, seeds, nonfat milk, yogurt, or cheese.

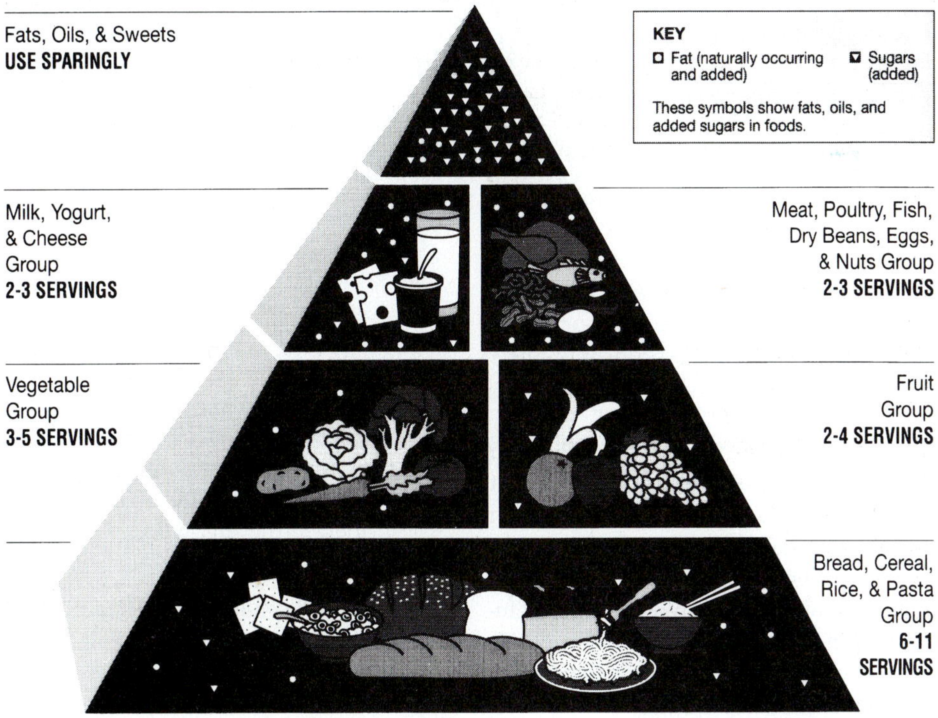

Fig. 8-2 Food guide pyramid. It is important to note that in each group (e.g., meat, poultry, fish, dry beans, eggs) there are some foods considered by research and the Center for Science in Public Interest (publisher of *Nutrition Action Healthletter*) to be better than others for maximum achievement of wellness. Two to three servings of that group does not mean two to three servings of eggs and meat. In general, the consensus continues to escalate that foods of plant origin (beans), fish, and poultry are preferable to the meat and eggs, both high in cholesterol and/or saturated fats. (Adapted from *Nutrition Action Healthletter* 19(10):8-9, December 1992.)

support the positive effect of a particular nutrient density in relation to chronic disorders (see Table 8-1). "Successful aging" is relatively free of disease and marked by eating patterns more characteristic of the Food Guide Pyramid (Fig. 8-2) and the prudent diet rather than the westernized diet. However, a current group of older people who have not benefited from health screening or knowledge of new risk factors for chronic disease experience distressing symptoms. The positive relationships between certain nutrients and chronic disease prevention or therapy are noted in Tables 8-1 and 8-2. Although some differences of opinion and controversy remain, the correlations addressed result from a considerable number of investigations reported in a variety of refereed scientific journals (Arnaud, Sanchez, 1990; Bales, 1990; Fontham et al, 1988; Guillem, Matsui, O'Brien, 1987; Hendersen et al, 1990; Katan, 1990; Johnson et al, 1992; La Vecchia et al, 1991; Pauling, 1986; Preuss, 1993).

Malnutrition: Undernutrition

Despite growing awareness and early research reports of undernutrition among middle-age and older adults in the 1980s, a survey from May 1992 to August 1992 still found inadequate energy and nutrient intake among a sizable percentage of the 474 individuals age 65 to 98 years (Ryan, Craig, Finn, 1992). These individuals represented 355 households, and the data were collected by interview and 24-hour dietary recall. Men and women differed in their inadequacies. More than 40% of the men had dietary intakes of vitamins A and E, whereas their intakes of calcium and zinc fell below two thirds of the Recommended Dietary Allowances (RDAs). More than 40% of the women had intakes of two thirds of RDA of vitamin E, calcium, and zinc. Moreover, more than 20% of both genders skipped lunch. It is noteworthy that in almost 15 years, little has changed—"a large proportion of noninstitutionalized elderly Americans consume diets that fail to meet dietary standards" (Ryan, Craig, Finn, 1992) (see Research box, above).

Older people are at greater risk for malnutrition than other age groups. However, it is important to note that aging in and of itself is not a cause for malnutrition in healthy older people. A number of epidemiologic studies have demonstrated nutritional deficiencies do exist in older adult populations. Surveys of independent community older people found that consumption of minerals and vitamins are below the RDA, and blood levels are subnormal in 10% to 30%. In addition, a summary of nursing homes surveyed indicated that 30% to 50% of the residents are substandard in body weight, midarm muscle circumference, and serum albumin concentration, all of which suggest widespread protein-calorie malnutrition. **Supplementation** may be not only useful but also necessary among middle-age and older adults. With a daily dietary intake determined to be less than two thirds of the RDA and stressful life situations that remain relatively unabated, supplementation can make the difference between intensified malnutrition and possible resulting illness, and nutrition adequacy (Mares-Perlman et al, 1993; Read et al, 1991; Wilson, Barry, 1993). Malnutrition, a multidimensional state, includes both undernutrition and overnutrition. Table 8-1, p. 203, indicates specific nutrient deficiencies that correlate with disorders or disease. Risk factors for malnutrition include physiologic, psychologic, affective, and social (Unosson et al, 1991) and are described in the following:

1. Physiologic
   - Body changes that occur in some older adults *decrease appetite* (e.g., sense of smell, taste, and clouded vision).
   - *Less efficient absorption* of nutrients in the small intestine (i.e., a smaller percentage of calcium is absorbed) so less is available for optimum systemic function.
   - *Slower peristalsis* results in food that contains potential carcinogens or toxins to remain in the digestive system longer.
   - The normally acidic nature of the stomach may

RESEARCH

Ryan AS, Craig D, Finn SC: Nutrient intake and dietary patterns of older Americans: a national study, *J Gerontol Med Sci* 47:145, 150, 1992.

Sample, setting

The subjects included 474 noninstitutionalized men and women age 65-98, surveyed in May to August 1992.

Methodology

Undernutrition was measured by determination of nutrient percentages that fail to meet RDA standards. Data were collected by interview and 24-hour dietary recall.

Findings

There was inadequate energy and nutrient intake among sizable percentage of those surveyed with men and women having different inadequacies. More than 40% of men had below two thirds of RDA in vitamins A and E, as well as calcium and zinc. More than 40% of the women had below two thirds of RDA in vitamin E, calcium, and zinc. More than 20% of both genders skipped lunch.

Implications

Epidemiologic studies along with this information confirm the significant undernutrition of older people in communities and nursing homes. It is therefore reasonable for the nurse and other allied health professionals to assess nutritional status and to plan intervention when necessary.

TABLE 8-4

Common Drug Groups and Drugs that May Cause Nutrient Depletion and Nutritional Deficiencies*

Drug Group	Drug	Deficiency
Antacids	Sodium bicarbonate	Folate, phosphate, calcium, copper
	Aluminum hydroxide	
Anticonvulsants	Phenytoin	Vitamins D and K
	Phenobarbital	
	Primidone	
Antibiotics	Valproic acid	Carnitine
	Tetracycline	Calcium
	Gentamicin	Potassium, magnesium
Antibacterial agents	Neomycin	Fat, nitrogen
	Boric acid	Riboflavin
	Trimethoprim	Folate
	Isoniazid	Vitamin B_6, niacin, vitamin D
Antiinflammatory agents	Sulfasalazine	Folate
	Aspirin	Vitamin C, folate, iron
Anticancer drugs	Colchicine	Fat, vitamin B_{12}
	Prednisone	Calcium
	Methotrexate	Folate, calcium
	Cisplatin	Magnesium
Anticoagulants	Warfarin	Vitamin K
Antihypertensive agents	Hydralazine	Vitamin B_6
Antimalarials	Pyrimethamine	Folate
Diuretics	Thiazides	Potassium
	Furosemide	Potassium, calcium, magnesium
H^2 receptor antagonists	Triamterene	Folate
	Cimetidine	Vitamin B_{12}
	Ranitidine	
Hypocholesterolemic agents	Cholestyramine	Fat
	Colestipol	Vitamin K, vitamin A, folate, vitamin B_{12}
Laxatives	Mineral Oil	Caryotene, retinol, vitamins D, K
	Phenolphthalein	Potassium
	Senna	Fat, calcium
Oral contraceptives		Vitamin B_6, folate, vitamin C
Tranquilizers	Chlorpromazine	Riboflavin

Reprinted with permission from Van Nostrand Reinhold. From Roe DA: *Diet and drug interactions,* New York, 1989, Van Nostrand Reinhold.

be reduced to the degree that the *stomach develops an essentially alkaline environment* (e.g., hypochlorhydria and achlorhydria, both of which create difficulty with protein digestion).

- *Chronic disease* may escalate in the later years unless older adults and allied health practitioners have committed to health promotion or disease prevention. Nutrient deficiencies and excesses contribute to disease initiation and development. Correction of such malnutrition is an intervention that can slow the progress of the disease (O'Keefe, Hahn, Betts, 1991). This effectively reduces the dysfunction caused by the disorder. One or more of the chronic disorders may have different or synergistic effects on nutrition needed for energy and maintenance.
- *Coronary heart disease, hypertension, diabetes, osteoporosis, and diminished cognition* may also present problems in shopping and cooking so that inadequate nutrition becomes more likely.
- A number of conditions and situations may find some older adults ages 70 to 80 using *alcohol as a "relaxer."* If alcohol is abused, fatigue, confusion, and self-neglect often result in poor eating.
- *Oral difficulties* (e.g., canker sores, missing teeth, inflammation of gums, periodontitis, or ill-fitting dentures) can make eating a task rather than a pleasure.
- *Polypharmacy* is all too common in malnutri-

tion. Medical practitioners prescribe multiple drugs that are now known to seriously affect appetite and nutrient absorption, and may also introduce confusion and a tendency for falling (Table 8-4). In addition, over-the-counter (OTC) medication and the resulting synergy or contrary action to prescribed medication can compound the barrier to balanced nutrition (Roe, 1989; Carr, Carr, 1994).

- *Hospitalization* may be necessary for a period of acute illness, but a stay contributes significantly to malnutrition. It is also true that a percentage of older adult admits are already malnourished, and unfortunately, malnutrition is even more acute at their discharge (McWhirter, Pennington, 1994).

2. Psychologic/social
   - *Depression* is widespread among older adults and often minimizes interest in eating and especially healthful eating. A number of physical, situational, or affective changes in older adulthood may be responsible, hence making positive attitudes problematic. New, adaptive coping strategies should be developed.
   - *Loneliness* may be a destructive partner in the lives of some older people. For most of the life span, eating is a shared activity. Widows and widowers may not bother cooking for one (Adams, Blieszner, 1989).
   - As noted previously, *societal stereotypes* about older adults and aging have been adopted by older people. Such beliefs exacerbate isolation, diminish self-esteem, and promote a sense of inevitability in becoming "less than."
   - At this time, of adults over age 65, *20% are in poverty or near poverty.* It is helpful to know

Insight • *Malnutrition is multifaceted, but some generalizations are possible. Protein-calorie malnutrition is often a function of acute or chronic disease; avitaminosis is a common consequence of deficient dietary intake, particularly deficient in fruits and vegetables; drugs exacerbate this low, unbalanced intake by interfering most with essential minerals (Roe, 1992).*

TABLE 8-5

A New Weight Table for Older Adults

This age-adjusted weight chart, devised by Johns Hopkins University gerontologist Dr. Reubin Andres, indicates medically sound weight ranges for people in their 50s and 60s. The ideal weight for most people is around the midpoint for each person's age and height. Those in the lower ranges are probably heavy enough to maintain good health, as long as there is no sudden or unexplained weight loss. Weights in the upper ranges may also be acceptable, but if a client finds himself or herself on the high side, he or she should talk with a physician about the possibility of losing weight. A physician makes recommendations based on where the client tends to store fat and his or her general health.

Height	Weight ages 50 to 59	Weight ages 60 to 69*
4′10″	107-135 lbs	115-142 lbs
4′11″	111-139	119-147
5′0″	114-142	123-152
5′1″	118-148	127-157
5′2″	122-153	131-163
5′3″	126-158	135-168
5′4″	130-163	140-173
5′5″	134-168	144-179
5′6″	138-174	148-184
5′7″	143-179	153-190
5′8″	147-184	158-196
5′9″	151-190	162-201
5′10″	156-195	167-207
5′11″	160-201	172-213
6′0″	165-207	177-219
6′1″	169-213	182-225
6′2″	174-219	187-232
6′3″	179-225	192-238
6′4″	184-231	197-244

*Those over age 69 should use the ranges for individuals in their 60s.
Reprinted with permission from The Johns Hopkins Medical Letter: *Health after 50,* 7(1):5, March 1995.

that some older adults, ambulatory or institutionalized, may not be in a position economically to live in the housing they prefer or may not be able to maintain the balanced diet suggested in the Food Guide Pyramid (see Fig. 8-2).

Malnutrition: Overnutrition, Obesity

Undernutrition is involved in the complex natural history of many chronic illnesses and diseases (see Table 8-1). Equally destructive to functional, physiologic, psychologic, affective, spiritual, and social health is contrasting overnutrition and its common consequence of obesity (Benotti et al, 1992).

Food excesses can involve any of the macronutrients (e.g., proteins and carbohydrates), but typically fats and simple sugars present serious risks for the same chronic diseases with which nutrient deficiencies correlate, such as coronary artery disease, atherosclerosis, hypercholesterolemia, colorectal and breast cancer, diabetes, hernias, peptic ulcers, colitis, kidney disease, and arthritis. Surveys of weight changes with age reveal that the younger old are more likely to be overweight, whereas the oldest old tend to be underweight (Andres et al, 1985). With age, there is a loss of lean body mass and an increase of body fat, therefore body weight alone can be misleading. Older adults should be cautioned against extreme leanness. Andres et al. (1985) report an increased mortality risk as compared with those older people with 10% to 15% more body weight. With this new information, Andres created a new table of heights and weights (Table 8-5). To overcome this dysfunctional situation, strength and exercise training can reduce some body fat and recover a percentage of muscle mass and strength, even among people in their 70s, 80s and 90s (Charette et al, 1991; Pyka, Lindenberger et al, 1994). Mild exercise and weight training, in addition to decreasing dietary fats, cholesterol, and sweets, are interacting interventions that complement one another (Brown, McCartney, Sale, 1990; Grimby et al, 1992). For most Americans, dietary fat represents 40% to 50% or more of daily caloric intake. A daily diet of 20% fat can supply an adequate concentration of fat-soluble vitamins and essential fatty acids (Fiatorone, 1990).

Recommended Dietary Allowances

Even the most recent RDAs (Tables 8-6 to 8-8) are barely applicable for older Americans. In fact, RDAs are described by their creators, the Food and Nutrition Board and National Research Council, as average nutrient allowances for healthy people. Despite the known differences established in important longitudinal data on the heterogeneity of the older population, the tenth edition lists those age 51 and older as a reference group for all adults 51 and older (Table 8-6). Some of today's older adults are at risk for malnutrition as a function of a num-

TABLE 8-6

Recommended Dietary Allowances for Persons Ages 51 and Over (Revised 1989)

	Males	Females
Weight*		
(kg)	77	65
(lb)	170	143
Height*		
(cm)	173	160
(in)	68	63
Protein (g)	63	50
Vitamin A (μg RE)†	1000	800
Vitamin D (μg)‡	5	5
Vitamin E (mg α-TE)§	10	8
Vitamin K (μg)	80	65
Vitamin C (mg)	60	60
Thiamin (mg)	1.2	1.0
Riboflavin (mg)	1.4	1.2
Niacin (mg NE)‖	15	13
Vitamin B_6 (mg)	2.0	1.6
Folate (μg)	200	180
Vitamin B_{12} (μg)	2.0	2.0
Calcium (mg)	800	800
Phosphorous (mg)	800	800
Magnesium (mg)	350	280
Iron (mg)	10	10
Zinc (mg)	15	12
Iodine (μg)	150	150
Selenium (μg)	70	55

*Weights and heights given are actual median values for the U.S. population ages 51 and over as reported by National Health and Nutrition Examination Survey II. These height-to-weight ratios may not be ideal.
†Retinol equivalents: 1 retinol equivalent = 1 μg retinol or 6 μg β-carotene.
‡As cholecalciferol: 10 μg cholecalciferol = 400 IU of vitamin D.
§α-Tocopherol equivalents: 1 mg d-α tocopherol = 1 α-TE.
‖1NE (niacin equivalent) = 1 mg niacin or 60 mg dietary tryptophan.

TABLE 8-7

Estimated Safe and Adequate Daily Dietary Intakes of Selected Vitamins and Minerals for Adults

Vitamin/mineral	Intake*
Biotin	30-100 μg
Pantothenic acid	4.0-7.0 mg
Copper	1.5-3.0 mg†
Manganese	2.0-5.0 mg†
Fluoride	1.5-4.0 mg†
Chromium	50-200 μg†
Molybdenum	75-250 μg†

*Because there is less information on which to base allowances, these figures are provided in the form of ranges of recommended intakes.
†Because the toxic levels for many trace minerals may be only several times the usual intakes, the upper levels given in this table should not be habitually exceeded.

ber of factors noted earlier. The Food and Nutrition Board does attempt to address the differential in energy requirements (Table 8-9) and estimated minimum requirements of additional vitamins and minerals. However, these much-needed modifications still do not adequately consider the diversity of the older adult population.

However, the Recommended Nutrient Intake for Canadians (Tables 8-10 to 8-11) is more realistic. Noted in Table 8-10 are the varied nutrients and energy requirements within the older population, ranging in age from 25 to 49, 50 to 74, and 75 and older (National Academy of Sciences, 1989; Whitney, Hamilton, Rolfes, 1990).

TABLE 8-8

Estimated Sodium, Chloride, and Potassium Minimum Requirements of Healthy Adults

Mineral	Intake*
Sodium*	500 mg
Chloride*	750 mg
Potassium†	2000 mg

Modified from Food and Nutrition Board: *Recommended dietary allowances*, ed 10, Washington, D.C., 1989, National Academy Press.

*No evidence suggests that higher intakes confer any health benefit.

†Desirable intake may considerably exceed this value (about 3500 mg for adults).

NUTRITION, EXERCISE, AND WELLNESS

Emphasis on dietary intake and age appears to ignore other interactive variables that are significant to the maintenance of active, vital, and healthful living in older adulthood. Two of these variables are exercise and stress management.

Sedentary Habits and Immobility

No statistical data have yet shown that exercise prolongs life or delays aging, but there is supportive evidence that with certain disorders, exercise and nutrition enable wellness (Grimby et al, 1994). *Inactivity can produce many of the changes traditionally identified with aging.* Some decline in function is inevitable, but inactivity makes matters worse (e.g., dyspnea after exertion, diminished muscle strength, lean muscle mass, general stiffening of joints, and loss of bone mass.

Sustained Exercise

Sustained exercise may encourage the following:

- Lower blood pressure of hypertension (by 10 points)
- Generally lower total serum cholesterol while raising level of desirable high-density lipoproteins (HDLs)

TABLE 8-9

Median Heights and Weights and Recommended Energy Intake

Category	Age (years) or condition	Weight kg	Weight lb	Height cm	Height in	REE* kcal/day	Average energy allowance (kcal): Multiples of REE	Per kg body weight	Per day†
Infants	0.0-0.5	6	13	60	24	320		108	650
	0.5-1.0	9	20	71	28	500		98	850
Children	1-3	13	29	90	35	740		102	1,300
	4-6	20	44	112	44	950		90	1,800
	7-10	28	62	132	52	1,130		70	2,000
Men	11-14	45	99	157	62	1,440	1.70	55	2,500
	15-18	66	145	176	69	1,760	1.67	45	3,000
	19-24	72	160	177	70	1,780	1.67	40	2,900
	25-50	79	174	176	70	1,800	1.60	37	2,900
	51 and older	77	170	173	68	1,530	1.50	30	2,300
Women	11-14	46	101	157	62	1,310	1.67	47	2,200
	15-18	55	120	163	64	1,370	1.60	40	2,200
	19-24	58	128	164	65	1,350	1.60	38	2,200
	25-50	63	138	163	64	1,380	1.55	36	2,200
	51 and older	65	143	160	63	1,280	1.50	30	1,900
Pregnant	1st trimester								+0
	2nd trimester								+300
	3rd trimester								+300
Lactating	1st 6 months								+500
	2nd 6 months								+500

*Resting energy expenditure (REE); calculation based on Food and Agriculture Organization (FAO) equations, then rounded. This is the same as resting metabolic rate (RMR).

†Figure is rounded.

TABLE 8-10

Recommended Nutrient Intakes for Canadians

Age	Gender	Energy (kcal)	Thiamin (mg)	Riboflavin (mg)	Niacin NE*	n-3 PUFA (gm)	n-6 PUFA (gm)
0-4 months	Both	600	0.3	0.3	4	0.5	3
5-12 months	Both	900	0.4	0.5	7	0.5	3
1 year	Both	1,100	0.5	0.6	8	0.6	4
2-3 years	Both	1,300	0.6	0.7	9	0.7	4
4-6 years	Both	1,800	0.7	0.9	13	1.0	6
7-9 years	M	2,200	0.9	1.1	16	1.2	7
	F	1,900	0.8	1.0	14	1.0	6
10-12 years	M	2,500	1.0	1.3	18	1.4	8
	F	2,200	0.9	1.1	16	1.2	7
13-15 years	M	2,800	1.1	1.4	20	1.5	9
	F	2,200	0.9	1.1	16	1.2	7
16-18 years	M	3,200	1.3	1.6	23	1.8	11
	F	2,100	0.8	1.1	15	1.2	7
19-24 years	M	3,000	1.2	1.5	22	1.6	10
	F	2,100	0.8	1.1	15	1.2	7
25-49 years	M	2,700	1.1	1.4	19	1.5	9
	F	1,900	0.8	1.0	14	1.1	7
50-74 years	M	2,300	0.9	1.2	16	1.3	8
	F	1,800	0.8†	1.0†	14†	1.1†	7†
75 + years	M	2,000	0.8	1.0	14	1.1	7
	F‡	1,700	0.8†	1.0†	14†	1.1†	7†
Pregnancy (additional)							
1st trimester		100	0.1	0.1	0.11	0.05	0.3
2nd trimester		300	0.1	0.3	0.22	0.16	0.9
3rd trimester		300	0.1	0.3	0.22	0.16	0.9
Lactation (additional)		450	0.2	0.4	0.33	0.25	1.5

*Ne, niacin equivalents; PUFA, polyunsaturated fatty acids.
†Level below which intake should not fall.
‡Assumes moderate physical activity.
From Scientific Review Committee: *Nutrition recommendations,* Ottawa, 1990, Health and Welfare.

- Reduce excess weight—walking or running 1 mile, or swimming ¼ mile daily can reduce weight by more than 10 lbs/year
- Support healthy cardiovascular function
  - -Minimize chest pain in clients with angina and those recovering from heart attacks, helping to increase the amount of activity that can be performed pain-free
  - -Contribute to the prevention of myocardial infarction or atherosclerosis
  - -Increase cardiac efficiency; improve blood circulation
- Lower blood sugar and insulin requirement in diabetics
- Free overweight adults, who have developed mature-onset diabetes, of any indication of disease when normal weight is achieved through diet and exercise or lowering of body fat
- Contribute to bone health and function
  - -Maintain bone flexibility and relative freedom from joint pain (arthritis) for a longer period in life span
  - -Help in prevention or deceleration of osteoporosis (i.e., with nutritional or drug therapy)
- Increase size and strength of muscles
- Improve aerobic ventilation (lung capacity) and usable O_2
- Enhance feeling of well-being

Interactions

Exercise interacts with diet and stress. Stress effects are relieved and nutrient metabolism is enhanced. On average, reaching fitness takes about 3 months. If exercise ceases, the same time is required to return to original physical condition.

> 1 lb of fat = 3,500 calories; walking 20 min = 100 cal, therefore a 20-minute walk daily eliminates 10 lbs of fat/year; walk briskly = 300 cal/hr; tennis = 400 to 500 cal/hr; row a short distance = 1,000 cal

Regular, vigorous exercise was found to decrease risk of heart disease independently of other risk factors such as cigarette smoking or high blood pressure. The kinds of physical activity probably most beneficial to the cardiovascular system are:

TABLE 8-11

Summary Examples of Recommended Nutrient Intake Based on Age and Body Weight Expressed as Daily Rates

Age	Gender	Weight (kg)	Protein (gm)	Vitamin A RE*	Vitamin D (μg)	Vitamin E (mg)	Vitamin C (mg)	Folate (μg)	Vitamin B_{12} (μg)	Calcium (mg)	Phosphorus (mg)	Magnesium (mg)	Iron (mg)	Iodine (μg)	Zinc (mg)
0-4 months	Both	6.0	12†	400	10	3	20	25	0.3	250‡	150	20	0.3§	30	2§
5-12 months	Both	9.0	12	400	10	3	20	40	0.4	400	200	32	7	40	3
1 year	Both	11	13	400	10	3	20	40	0.5	500	300	40	6	55	4
2-3 years	Both	14	16	400	5	4	20	50	0.6	550	350	50	6	65	4
4-6 years	Both	18	19	500	5	5	25	70	0.8	600	400	65	8	85	5
7-9 years	M	25	26	700	2.5	7	25	90	1.0	700	500	100	8	110	7
	F	25	26	700	2.5	6	25	90	1.0	700	500	100	8	95	7
10-12 years	M	34	34	800	2.5	8	25	120	1.0	900	700	130	8	125	9
	F	36	36	800	2.5	7	25	130	1.0	1,100	800	135	8	110	9
13-15 years	M	50	49	900	2.5	9	30	175	1.0	1,100	900	185	10	160	12
	F	48	46	800	2.5	7	30	170	1.0	1,000	850	180	13	160	9
16-18 years	M	62	58	1,000	2.5	10	40**	220	1.0	900	1,000	230	10	160	12
	F	53	47	800	2.5	7	30**	190	1.0	700	850	200	12	160	9
19-24 years	M	71	61	1,000	2.5	10	40**	220	1.0	800	1,000	240	9	160	12
	F	58	50	800	2.5	7	30**	180	1.0	700	850	200	13	160	9
25-49 years	M	74	64	1,000	2.5	9	40**	230	1.0	800	1,000	250	9	160	12
	F	59	51	800	2.5	6	30**	185	1.0	700	850	200	13	160	9
50-74 years	M	73	63	1,000	5	7	40**	230	1.0	800	1,000	250	9	160	12
	F	63	54	800	5	6	30**	195	1.0	800	850	210	8	160	9
75 + years	M	69	59	1,000	5	6	40**	215	1.0	800	1,000	230	9	160	12
	F	64	55	800	5	5	30**	200	1.0	800	850	210	8	160	9
Pregnancy (additional)															
1st trimester			5	0	2.5	2	0	200	1.2	500	200	15	0	25	6
2nd trimester			20	0	2.5	2	10	200	1.2	500	200	45	5	25	6
3rd trimester			24	0	2.5	2	10	200	1.2	500	200	45	10	25	6
Lactation (additional)			20	400	2.5	3	25	100	0.2	500	200	65	0	50	6

*RE: retinol equivalents.
†Protein is assumed to be from breast milk and must be adjusted for infant formula.
‡Infant formula with high phosphorus should contain 375 mg of calcium.
§Breast milk is assumed to be the source of the mineral.
**Smokers should increase vitamin C by 50%.
From Scientific Review Committee: *Nutrition recommendations,* Ottawa, 1990, Health and Welfare.

- Aerobic exercise, which requires large amounts of O_2 for energy production
- Brisk walking
- Stair climbing
- Running
- Cross-country skiing and swimming

A reasonable goal is often described as 15 to 30 minutes of exercise three times/week. Recently, the benefits of mild, regular activity to systemic function have earned more support than aerobics alone (Makrides, Simpson, Officer, 1995; O'Brien, Vertinsky, 1990).

WELLNESS AND STRESS RESPONSE

Body-Mind Interaction

Thoughts and feelings affect the way and how well the body functions, just as what is happening in the body affects feelings, thoughts, and spirit. They all interact, generally to keep a desirable level of efficiency, adapting to each shift of internal and external environments. For example:

- A stomachache or headache can interfere with thinking about or making love.
- If someone moves to threaten an individual menacingly, the person may lose control over voice projection and may fail to call out.
- When an occasion is anticipated, such as a wedding, a race, a swim meet, or marathon, sweat droplets appear, the heart beats faster, blood pressure increases, and secretions of many hormones increase.

Stressors, anxiety, frustration, anger, rage, pain, and fear can influence health and can alter the kind of quality of hormones, enzymes, sugars, and fatty acids secreted into the blood stream. All of these products are part of the body's response to emotional and cognitive messages from the brain. Appropriate, timely stress management may determine outcomes of illness or disease under therapy (Cooper, 1984; Trzcieniecka-Green, Steptoe, 1994).

The contrary may also be true. It is reasonable to assume that positive messages, happy emotions, and good spirits can create a more supportive, biochemic environment for body cells and organs. This assumption has become integral to the cancer support movement and the value of positive attitudes and humor in recovery from illness to regain the pre-illness state (Cousins, 1989; Peterson, Bossio, 1991). Stressors and stress response alone are known to cause vertigo, blindness, certain types of body aches, ulcers, circulatory ailments, and temporary paralysis. Unmitigated stress response and mortality is often implicated in a number of serious diseases.

Extremely stressful situations that are deliberately created have been used in ritual executions in places such as Australia, Borneo, Central Africa, and islands of the Caribbean. Death is an extreme result of the stress response, and an exceptional extreme, but the body-mind responses of everyday life are more obvious. They include the following:

- Displeasure—Muscles of face in a scowl
- Boredom—Yawn
- Humorous joke—Muscles of diaphragm contract to produce laughter
- Oppressed by sadness—Sighs or tears

Each is part of the response to a stimulus (stressor) that disturbs the inner balance and initiates physiologic reactions in an attempt to relieve the tension (or lack of balance) and to restore equilibrium. Even if the individual successfully hides emotions, at a deeper level, the inner signs of the stress response are still there. In ancient China, police separated the innocent from the guilty by forcing all suspects to fill their mouths with dry cooked rice. According to their lore, the culprit cannot moisten his mouth with saliva and swallow the rice. Today technology provides the polygraph and lie detector to measure involuntary reactions to stress and stressors. Telltale signs of failure include the rise and fall in pulse rate, blood pressure, breathing, and electrical skin response when particular words or thoughts are introduced into a conversation.

Stress and Disease Connection

Temporary conditions such as a "tension headache" or an "upset stomach" can also be directly related to stressful situations. But what about more chronic and serious states of disease, especially cardiovascular disease and cancer? Although less clear, recent work is suggestive, encouraging, and in some instances, definitive (Anderson, Kiecoltglaser, Glaser, 1994).

Laboratory studies with animals demonstrate a clear connection between isolated stimuli (e.g., electrical shocks or separation from mates) and the development of heart disease. Greater complexity creates difficulty with human studies, since the environment may have many potentially stressful variables. An example, usually with some difference of opinion, is the Type-A personality (Delistraty et al, 1992). A Type-A personality is the achieving, competitive, time-conscious person who is prone to coronary artery disease. Behavioral scientists who use various meditation techniques to moderately lower blood pressure point to the connection between emotions and elevated blood pressure. Nevertheless, it is misleading to suggest that being "high-strung" can be equated with hypertension or that an apparently placid person is immune to high blood pressure.

A theory exists that destructive emotions can contribute to or can cause cancer. It is currently unwarranted to suggest that any cancer is caused by faulty emotions, but there are persuasive studies that indicate how positive emotions improve the quality of life with cancer. One study suggests that destructive emotions can weaken the body's surveillance of the immune system. Research continues that encourages clients with cancer to fight disease with positive attitudes and medication therapy.

Stress-induced disorders include the following: asthma, peptic ulcers, migraine headaches, allergies, colitis, and malnutrition. Many physicians believe that stress response is an important contributing factor to the exacerbation of any problem in which symptoms and total impact on a client's life are concerned. To minimize the impact of an unabated stress response, effective suggestions such as exercise, meditation or relaxation exercises or techniques, and reevaluation of priorities can be made. In general, this kind of stress management reduces the probability of persistent discomfort becoming a disease (Benson, 1976). What can be done about the damaging role stress can play?

An important first consideration is to avoid equating "pace" with "damaging stress." Many stress researchers suggest, for example, that the person who works long hours and leads a busy life may be far less frustrated than a person trapped in a limited, demeaning position with no sense of release or accomplishment. Most significant to neutralizing loss of identity and ego strength is **locus of control,** or being in charge of one's life (Rodin, 1986). Although many feel trapped in circumstances over which there is little control, the need remains to identify areas that can be changed. Time must be used to recognize what is well done and enjoyable. Hope for a useful strategy is in the realization that the stress response is potentially manageable.

Stress Response and Nutrition

Demands on the body during stressful periods such as a variety of life changes may lead not only to nutritional imbalance but also to illness and finally to affecting the rate of age changes (Rahe, Mahan, Holmes, 1967; Holmes, Masuda, 1972; Schapira et al, 1991). The reality of multiple changes (psychologic, social, and physiologic) during the middle and later years in American contemporary society can be described as increasingly stressful; such unrelieved hormonal and nutritional highs and lows tax homeostatic and coping capacities. This breakdown in adaptability, with nutrient imbalance as one factor, increases vulnerability to illness, disease, and death.

Relief of Stress Response Effects in the Individual

The individual, even as a partner with allied health professionals, has opportunities and responsibilities in diminishing serious consequences of unabated stress response. Constructive reactions and strategies range from philosophic, intellectual, physical, and affective behavior (Degeus, Vandoornen, Orlebeke, 1993) and can include the following:

- The individual's changing perceptions control physical and mental wellness, and achieve a more philosophic or positive attitude toward the pressures and urgencies of everyday life. Such behavior seems to help significantly in counteracting internal, physiologic responses to stressors.
- Diet changes
- Program of regular exercise
- Reordering of daily priorities
- Deliberate slowing of pace
- At times, even a complete change of lifestyle
- Meditation or biofeedback (visceral learning)
- Identification of new interests or resurrection of earlier activities such as new skills, new kinds of recreation or play

For some older people, positive adaptation to the results of the stress response needs to be consciously learned. Some choose not to make that effort and seek comfort in negative stress relievers such as overeating, alcoholism, drug use and abuse (tranquilizers, mood elevators, or sleeping pills), and smoking. The consequences of these choices may be diseases (cancer or emphysema); an increase in release of stress hormones, heightened blood pressure, or diminished fat metabolism. Temporary, short-lived soothing effects take place with tragic, long-term penalties (King, Campbell, Edwards, 1993). Without intervention, a number of the diseases discussed throughout this chapter finally progress to full-blown, disabling symptoms. Before more extreme decisions must be made, nutrition, exercise therapy, and effective strategies for stress response management may stabilize the disease, and even improve the state of function.

ALLIED HEALTH PROFESSIONALS: OPPORTUNITIES AND RESPONSIBILITIES

> In the health field we are no longer content to treat illness, we seek to prevent it. Health is not merely the absence of disease, it is a dynamic, positive state of physical and mental well-being (Feamon, 1948).

Feamon, a medical and social consultant with the Social Security Administration at the time the article was written for the *American Journal of Nursing,* also noted that in the health field, the client should be treated as a "whole person." Feamon's thoughts and words were prophetic in the best tradition of her profession—nursing. The perspective she espoused fits the wellness approach that is now receiving deserved support and application.

Gerontologic care is finding its niche as a team practice. New gerontologic and biomedical data are calling for different objectives in seeking wellness for older adults (Hazzard et al, 1990; Pathy, 1990). Men and women grow older differently and have been treated differently by the health care establishment with negative consequences for women (Sharpe, Clark, Janz, 1991; Steingart et al, 1991). Medical schools are attempting to include these changes in curricula, albeit slowly. Effective prevention, therapy and rehabilitation are no longer based singularly on the medical model but on health promotion and disease prevention. Still necessary is the treatment of some members of the older population who experience one or more of the chronic disorders. Methodology in these instances remains as "after the fact" disease care, or the medical model. Older clients have been socialized for years to see a physician or clinic only when ill. Until recently, the treatment invariably was to effect a cure. If that was not possible, then palliation with drug therapy followed. There was little inquiry concerning general affects, diet, exercise, living conditions, or any other complaints outside of the immediate discomfort that triggered the visit. Nevertheless, opportunities are growing for wellness teaching and therapy for clients as partners in their own care and decision making.

TABLE 8-12

Checklist to Determine Your Nutritional Health

The warning signs of poor nutritional health are often overlooked. To see whether you (or people you know) are at nutritional risk, take this simple quiz. Read the statements below. Circle the number in the "yes" column for those that apply. To find your total score, add the numbers you circled. The greater the score, the higher your nutritional risk.

	Yes
I have an illness or condition that made me change the kind or amount of food I eat.	2
I eat fewer than two meals/day.	3
I eat few fruits or vegetables, or milk products.	2
I have three or more drinks of beer, liquor, or wine almost every day.	2
I have tooth or mouth problems that make it hard for me to eat.	2
I don't always have enough money to buy the food I need.	4
I eat alone most of the time.	1
I take three or more different prescribed or OTC drugs a day.	1
Without wanting to, I have lost or gained 10 pounds in the last six months.	2
I am not always physically able to shop, cook, or feed myself.	2
TOTAL NUTRITIONAL SCORE ______	

These materials were developed and are distributed by the Nutrition Screening Initiative, a joint project of the American Academy of Family Physicians, the American Dietetic Association, and the National Council on the Aging, Inc.

Modified and reprinted with permission from the Johns Hopkins Medical Letter: *Health after 50*, 10:3, 4, September 1992.

Nurses and nurse practitioners, as members of the interdisciplinary gerontologic team, have the most direct contact hours in the care of the client. Nurses are therefore in a unique position to actively participate in overall wellness assessment and therapy in terms of adequate and appropriate nutrition. The nurse can determine the level of nutritional adequacy and risks to recommend any modifications to the team and client.

Home care is on the rise, and the home care nurse can observe the lifestyle and can be knowledgeable about the nutrient requirements and therapy of the homebound older adult. Use of the brief nutrition assessment questionnaire provides nurse and client with a sense of the state of nutrition adequacy (Table 8-12). What factors are present that require observation, attention, and potential intervention?

Nutrition Screening Initiative

The Nutrition Screening Initiative (NSI), (Dwyer, 1991), a 5-year, multifaceted national effort to promote routine nutrition screening, began in 1990 under the direction of the American Academy of Family Physicians, the American Dietetic Association, and the National Council on the Aging. A nutritional health checklist was developed as part of the initiative to be used by older adults or caregivers to determine risk factors associated with nutrition and health (see Table 8-12). The administration of additional, in-depth screening tools and assessments may be indicated by the score on the checklist. These assessments are administered by health care professionals and include a number of questions, tests, and measures to gain information to be used in developing nutritional support interventions for older adults in various settings. The assessments are both broad and specific and include the following:

1. Physiologic/physical
   - Protein-caloric malnutrition
   - Fluid intake
   - Skin condition
   - Lips, oral mucosa, and dentition
   - Review of medications, alcohol, and other OTC or addictive drugs
   - Evaluation of vision, hearing, and mobility
   - Complaints or comments regarding food, digestive system, appetite, likes and dislikes, taste, and smell

CULTURAL AWARENESS

Selected Examples of Cultural Meanings of Food

Critical life force for survival
Relief of hunger
Peaceful coexistence
Promotion of disease or illness
Prevention of disease or illness
Expression of caring for another
Interpersonal closeness or distance
Promotion of kinship and familial alliances
Solidification of social ties
Celebration of life events (e.g., birthday or marriage)
Expression of gratitude or appreciation
Recognition of achievement or accomplishment
Business negotiations
Information exchange
Validation of social, cultural, or religious ceremonial functions
Way to generate income
Expression of affluence, wealth, or social status

Modified from Leininger M: Transcultural eating patterns and nutrition, *Holist Nurs Pract* 3(1):19, 1988.

- Meal "timing" (i.e., skipping meals, or having more than three meals/day or one large meal/day, or snacking)
- Individual's standard daily dietary intake (over a minimum 3 days)
- A diary of food eaten daily is more useful than memory recall alone

2. Psychosocial/affective
   - Social nature of meals (i.e., if eaten alone, with television, in a congregate nutrition site, through Meals on Wheels programs)
   - Living situation, capacity for food preparation, cooking, and food storage
   - Eating in anticipation or dread
   - Consider cultural and ethnic attributes, influence on nutrition intake and elimination patterns (see Cultural Awareness boxes, above and on p. 217)
   - Assess presence of depression
   - Fleeting and situational depression can be evaluated and treated more readily.
   - Clinical depression suggests need for expert opinion—anyone who can be a team member.
   - Depression can result in confusion or memory loss, can lower appetite severely, and can affect digestion, absorption, and function of immune system

Additional Specific Evaluations

In addition to the rather long list of physiologic/physical and psychosocial/affective variables identified above, certain evaluations are recommended by the Nutrition Screening Initiative. These variables range from a medical history and a careful physical examination, to serum proteins and creatinine.

- Blood analysis
  -Creatinine – An index of body muscle mass
  -Serum proteins – Essential for syntheses of antibodies and lymphocytes (T cells) in cellular immunity, enzymes, hormones, other widespread structural cellular, and tissue structures
  -Immune status – Includes a variety of tests and history of possible autoimmune disorders and response to infections
- Body weight
  -Current weight as compared with "ideal" weight
  -Unintentional weight loss suggestive of disorder not readily observable or otherwise symptomatic
- Anthropometry
  -Measurements of midarm muscle, triceps and subscapular skinfold thickness
- Discriminant analysis
  -Uses a traditional physical examination and detailed history

These variables impinge on overall health status and specifically on nutritional status. The complete data from the foregoing items with the brief nutrition inventory in Table 8-12 provide information to suggest plans for intervention, such as whether it is needed, what kind, and when and who will be part of the team to achieve nutritional adequacy and to optimize function.

Teacher/Client Rapport

Health promotion and disease prevention (wellness) education is a significant responsibility, since the information and understanding enables the client to share in the responsibility for health care and wellness behavior. The nurse accepts that role of the educator. It is important for the nurse to use cultural and ethnic differences as advantages. A client cannot be required to eat a certain way, nor can the nurse expect the client to reject a lifetime of familiar foods and eating patterns. Nutrition education must accommodate such differences to succeed.

If the nurse is in an ongoing, close relationship with the client, use of home remedies can be shared. The nurse is often asked questions about what kind of vitamins and minerals are needed, as well as how much they cost and where to purchase them. Nurses should have an answer readily available (Wilt, Hubbard, Thomas, 1990). Additional help from a nutritionist or dietician can be arranged. Dieticians are often a part of the interdiscipli-

CULTURAL AWARENESS

Dietary Practices of Selected Religious Groups

Prohibited Foods and Beverages

Hinduism
- All meats

Islam
- Pork and pork products
- Animal shortenings
- Alcoholic products (including extracts such as vanilla or lemon)
- Marshmallows, as well as gelatin and other confections made with pork

NOTE: Fasting is common. Mandatory fasting in the daylight hours during month of Ramadan

Judaism
- Pork
- Predatory fowl
- Shellfish or scavenger fish (e.g., catfish, shrimp, escargot, or lobster); fish with fins and scales are permissible
- Mixing milk and meat dishes at same meal
- Blood by ingestion (e.g., blood sausage or raw meat); blood by transfusion is acceptable

NOTES:
1. Only meat from cloven-hoofed animals that chew cud (e.g., cattle, sheep, goat, or deer) is allowed. The animals must have been slaughtered observing rigid rules that result in minimum pain to the animal and maximum blood drainage.
   Foods should be *kosher* (meaning "proper" or "fitting"), which is accomplished in one of two methods:
   A. Meat is soaked in cold water for 1 half hour with coarse salt, and drained to deplete blood content. It is then thoroughly washed under cold, running water and drained again before cooking.
   B. Meat is first prepared by quick searing or cooking over an open flame, which permits liver to be eaten, since it cannot be prepared by the above method.
2. Meat and dairy products cannot be served at the same meal nor can they be cooked or served in the same set of dishes. Milk or milk products may be consumed just before a meal but not until 6 hours after eating a meal with meat products. Fish or eggs can be eaten with dairy products or meat meals.

Mormonism (Church of Jesus Christ of Latter-Day Saints)
- Alcohol
- Tobacco
- Stimulants (including beverages containing caffeine such as coffee, nonherbal teas, colas, and selected carbonated soft drinks)

Seventh-Day Adventism
- Pork
- Certain seafood including shellfish
- Fermented beverages

NOTES:
1. Optional vegetarianism includes (1) strict vegetarianism, (2) ovolactovegetarianism, or (3) no pork or pork products, shellfish, or blood.
2. Snacking between meals is discouraged.

nary team. In addition, the nurse becomes a personal resource for the client in search of meal sites, home-delivered meals, food stamps, and other nutritional information. The nurse is perhaps the only member of the team who uses the opportunities to "care" in multiple ways. This behavior develops confidence and compliance. The resulting positive attitudes contribute to every aspect of the nurse-client relationship in fulfilling the goals of wellness.

CONTROVERSIES AND WORKS IN PROGRESS

Considerable ongoing nutrition research seeking correlations with disease and wellness is being conducted. Study results do not invariably lead to widespread agreement. Health food stores, the media, and a public hungry for understandable information relating foods and wellness may attempt application of some published comments that appear promising. However, dieticians, physicians, and researchers continue their inquiries and dialogue (see Research box, p. 206). A few of the more significant and frequently discussed issues are noted in this section. Definitive conclusions concerning these works in progress may be premature. Keeping a watch on the current literature is both stimulating and advisable:

- Dietary restriction
  -Since 1935 and early work with dietary restriction and laboratory rats (McKay et al, 1935), the interest in life extension has waxed and waned. Only recently, the studies have more carefully examined the connections between health, longevity, and diet quantity. Rodents and other species have demonstrated an increase in longevity and a marked decrease in age-re-

lated disease, primarily because of caloric restriction. Can such benefits accrue to humans (Walford, 1990; McKay, Cromwell, Maynar, 1935)?

- Antioxidants provide the most recent promise. The nutrients of vitamins A, B-complex, C, E, and carotenoids, as well as trace elements selenium, zinc, copper, and iron appear to correlate with a reduction in cancer, age-related macular degeneration (AMD), cataracts, heart disease, and immune dysfunction.
  -Work reported from five major eye research centers found that carrots appear to prevent AMD but that leafy green vegetables may be better. Women and men who consumed the most carotenoids had a 43% lower risk of AMD than those who ate less *(Harvard women's health watch, 1995)*.
  -Vitamin E is particularly regarded as an antioxidant that lowers the risk of heart disease and reduces the level of oxidized low-density lipoprotein (LDL) cholesterol, which has been implicated in atherogenesis. Recent studies *suggest* that it takes at least 100 IUs a day to reduce the risk of heart disease. To prevent heart disease, much larger doses may be necessary, such as 800 to 1000 IUs. Clinical trials are in progress *(Nutritional action health letter,* 1994; Rimm et al, 1993; *Environmental nutrition,* 1993).
  -Dr. Stanley N. Gershoff of the Human Nutrition Research Center on Aging at Tufts University reported that 800 IUs/per day of vitamin E enhance the immune response in older people. The university researchers continue to experiment with other antioxidants (Center for Science in the Public Interest [CSPI], 1992).
  -Beta carotene is metabolized to vitamin A by the body as needed. A Harvard University Medical School research study, following 22,000 male physicians as part of a 10-year health study, found that men with a history of chronic disease who were given beta carotene supplements had half as many heart attacks, strokes, and incidences of death as those taking placebo pills (*Johns Hopkins medical letter*, 1994; University of California at Berkeley *Wellness Letter,* 1994).
- Exercise increases need for antioxidant supplementation.
  -Dr. Kenneth Cooper, editor of the University of California at Berkeley *Wellness Letter*, suggests that exercise increases the production of cell-damaging free radicals. Free radicals are natural byproducts of digestion and processing of oxygen. Cooper claims (but no research has indicated) that free radicals may affect the immune system and increase risk for cancer, heart disease, and other disorders.
  -Eat at least five antioxidant-rich fruits and vegetables, add *supplements* of the following:

Vitamin C	250 to 500 mg
Vitamin E	200 to 800 mg
Beta carotene	6 to 15 mg

  (*University of California at Berkeley Wellness Letter*, 1991; Freeman, 1991)
- Cholesterol and aging
  -Most research has focused on middle-aged men.
  -Yale University researchers tracked nearly 1000 men and women age 70 and older for 4 years. Those with a low level of high-density lipoprotein (HDL) were not at greater risk than those with a high level of HDL.
  -Other studies have shown correlation between elevated LDL cholesterol and heart disease, and that HDL reduces risk.
  Dr. Simon Margolis, editor of Johns Hopkins' *Health After 50* newsletter, states that there is no cutoff age at which time there is no longer reason for concern about cholesterol (University of California at Berkeley Wellness Letter, 1995).
- Omega-3 fatty acids in reduction of heart disease risk
  -Seafood, and primarily seafood, contains longer chains of omega-3 fatty acids
  -These fish oils reduce tendency for blood to clot. The fatty acids in question include eicosapentaenoic acid (EPA) and docosahexaenoic acid (DHA). Many heart attacks and strokes occur if blood clots in arteries that are already narrowed.
  -Another omega-3 fatty acid, alpha-linoleic acid, can be found in plant oils such as linseed, canola, and walnut, as well as in oils of some leafy vegetables (Liebman, 1992).
- Cancer risk reduced by eating a low-fat diet.
  -Diet has been linked to 30% of all cancers.
  -The American Cancer Society recommends maintaining a desirable weight, eating a varied diet with five or more servings of fruits and vegetables daily, eating high-fiber foods, and cutting total fat intake.
  -Most cases of colorectal cancer relate to a high-fat, low-fiber diet.
  -Food choices may lower the risk for ovarian cancer, that is the more saturated fats in a diet, the higher the risk for ovarian cancer (John Hopkins Medical Letter, 1994).
- Margarine-butter controversy
  -When Dr. Lichtenstein of Tufts University's studies on heart disease learned that Harvard researchers were suggesting butter, and not margarine, as the spread of choice to avoid heart disease, she considered their statements to be misrepresented facts that could confuse consumers.
  -In an opinion paper published in a scientific journal, two Harvard epidemiologists stated that the trans-fatty acids in margarines represent a major

risk in heart disease, to a greater degree than the saturated fat in butter and other animal products. They noted that the trans-fatty acids, like saturated fats, raise levels of LDL cholesterol. Moreover, they added that these acids lower HDL cholesterol as well.

Lichtenstein and others note that the number of studies on this subject right now is very small, and the inquiries concerning trans-fatty acids are not unanimous. They may not have the "double whammy" of raising LDL and lowering HDL cholesterol.

The epidemiologists report that trans-fatty acids are about 2% of American caloric intake. However, saturated fats are currently about 15% of caloric intake. Lichtenstein and the epidemiologists agree the major effort should be directed to cutting down all fats (Tufts University Diet and Nutrition Letters, 1994).

-Another researcher still maintains margarine as the healthier option over butter. It contains less saturated fat and no cholesterol. Other alternatives to margarine and butter include olive oil, which contains monosaturated fat and less cholesterol, or even jam or jelly. Emphasis is on the reduction of total fat intake (Johns Hopkins Medical Letter, 1994).

- Garlic/cardiovascular disease

-During ancient times, garlic was used as a nonspecific medicinal food for a multitude of illnesses to enhance strength and stamina. It is thought to have been used by the workers building pyramids. Currently, it is being suggested as a potential beneficial food remedy in treatment for cardiovascular disease.

One study conducted by New York Medical College researchers, worked with pooled data (meta-analysis) from similar earlier published trials from 1987 to 1990 and had mildly favorable results.

At least 75% of 365 subjects had cholesterol higher than 200 mg/100 ml. One half took a garlic supplement for 12 to 24 weeks, 600 to 1000 mg daily (about two thirds of one garlic clove); others were given a placebo. Cholesterol levels decreased by an average of 9% in the supplement group.

No data existed on subjects' body weights, how the subjects were selected, whether garlic was in their dietary intakes (and how much), or what, if any, effort was made to make the placebo look like the experimental garlic dose. Furthermore, data on triglyceride levels or what effect garlic appeared to have on HDL and LDL cholesterol are not available (John Hopkins Medical Letter, 1994).

The previously listed examples are not all of the controversial opinions and study results that propose the latest panacea in the fight to limit and to finally overwhelm nutrient- and age-related diseases. In addition, there are mounting suggestions to apply new nutrient and other lifestyle changes to the prevention of disease and promotion of health during the later years of older people experiencing healthy, active, and successful aging.

Summary

The literature that demonstrates the correlation between nutrients and chronic disease is persuasive. In journals of medicine, biology and gerontology, such connections between food and health have grown into a critical mass.

Nutrition awareness and dietary changes are already in place and growing steadily in North America and Europe. Changing attitudes, knowledge, and practice are not evenly distributed across this country, in the allied health professions, or in the society at large. Surveys, small group studies, food manufacturers, restaurants, and the media show a commitment to better health through diet. In fact, the prudent diet may be used as a model of dietary intake for the growing middle-age and older population—to lower fat, especially saturated fat, cholesterol, and salt; and to increase consumption of fruits and vegetables, as well as whole grain cereals and breads. This changed diet is expected to contribute to increasingly lower morbidity and mortality from cardiovascular disease, cancer, stroke, and diabetes, and to minimize other disorders such as cataracts and AMD.

Investigations of dietary intake and effects on diet-related chronic disease have only recently included sufficient numbers of older people. Moreover, there are even fewer controlled inquiries completed to provide any more than suggested correlations, or clues for additional research and some application. Epidemiologic studies emphasize the health benefits for people eating a prudent diet over the frequent illnesses characteristic of those on the westernized diet.

Older people are willing to change harmful habits so that they can remain active during later years. It is never too late for change. The Food Guide Pyramid applies nutritional information to the entire life span. Scientists and lay people alike would appreciate having scientifically sound data that supports the wisdom of eliminating the last 75 years of westernized dietary practices proven to be hazardous to health and wellness. Until such data are definitive, "educated guesses" about necessary changes in the dietary intake are being made, and thousands of middle-age and older people are benefiting. Not only has there been a delay in the symptoms of major chronic diseases, but reversals in existing disorders also have been achieved.

For so long, many diseases were considered inevitable with advancing years, often equated with "aging."

Information from longitudinal studies breaks down the myths and distinguishes clearly between healthy, successful aging, and disease. Appropriate, adequate nutrition provides energy and raw materials for the essential syntheses of substances and structures enabling improved systemic function (e.g., brain power, cardiac health, immune response, kidney function, muscle and joint activity, vision, and hearing). The nurse should recall that nutrition is not alone in prevention of therapy for development of wellness. Exercise, stress response management, locus of control, personal relationships, intellectual challenges, and physical environments all reinforce the potential of the prudent diet.

Life expectancy and successful aging are on the rise, which suggests that future cohorts of middle-age and older people will depart markedly from the present stereotypic characterizations. Ageism will diminish, and further regard and opportunities for the 70 million or more people in 2030 will develop. This segment of the population will be active participants in society, accepted as whole people who are making the contributions that are possible only from long, varied experiences.

In April 1993 the National Institute on Aging published a newsletter reviewing recent studies by university researchers and other aging research centers headlined "Older Population Healthier than Expected." It attempted to prove that aging is not a disease, greater numbers of older people are relatively free of disease and highly functional, and genes have a share of responsibility in how aging proceeds. Most importantly, it was indicated that the lifestyle factors, over which people have considerable control, may be even more significant for the overall health and well-being of the older person.

HOME CARE TIPS

1. Instruct caregivers and homebound older adults to keep a nutritional log for a defined period to enable the home care nurse to compare it with the Food Guide Pyramid.
2. Instruct caregivers and homebound older adults on nutrients and selected food sources that supply required vitamins and minerals.
3. Geographic location, culture, and religion play a part in food patterns, preferences, and the meaning of food for the homebound older adult.
4. Assess physiologic conditions and psychosocial issues that may place the homebound older adult at risk for nutritional deficiencies.
5. Assess the homebound older adult's medications for any that predispose to nutritional deficiencies.
6. Instruct the caregiver and homebound older adult on assistive devices that promote independence in eating (e.g., strong plastic plates and bowls with suction cups or padded utensils).
7. Instruct the caregiver and homebound older adult on any treatments that provide nutritional support (e.g., enteral nutrition).

Key Points

- Appropriate food intake for health maintenance was recognized by the likes of Hippocrates (460-377 BC) and other early scholars.
- Explosion of the older population to more than 33 million calls for controlling lifestyle factors such as adequate nutrition.
- Among the middle-age and old, age alone is the poorest predictor of capacities, interests, performance, and health status.
- Wellness, as contrasted to health, is an ongoing dynamic process in the state of becoming, and the prime objective of health promotion and disease prevention.
- Longitudinal investigations find that the 65 and older population is becoming healthier than expected, resulting in a group of "successful agers."
- Recent literature has determined a correlation between nutrients and chronic disease.
- Studies demonstrate the wisdom of the prudent diet: high in fiber and low in fat, cholesterol, and salt. Whole grain cereals and bread, as well as fruits and vegetables promote health and prevent disease.
- Epidemiologic inquiries indicate that populations around the world characterized by the westernized diet have chronic diseases such as coronary artery disease, cancer, stroke, diabetes, and osteoporosis.
- Older people are nutritional "label readers" and are ready to change poor eating habits.
- Malnutrition, deficiencies, and excesses exist among middle-age and older subpopulations.
- A balanced dietary intake, using the prudent diet and the Food Guide Pyramid as guides, can eliminate subclinical and frank malnutrition.
- Promotion of health, stamina, and strength, as well as prevention of illness and disease involve other lifestyle factors, including exercise, stress management, autonomy, positive psychosocial variables, and appropriate dietary intake.
- As a result of long contact hours with clients, nurses have the opportunity and responsibility to assess nutritional status.
- Nurses and other members of the interdisciplinary team recommend necessary changes in daily dietary intake.
- The future will find older people with longer active life expectancies into their eighth, ninth, and tenth decades of life.

Critical Thinking Exercises

1. A 67-year-old woman has been referred to your home health agency for follow-up care related to her diabetes. She has numerous leg ulcers that must be cleaned and dressed. While visiting her, you note that she has soup cans, doughnut boxes, and macaroni and cheese boxes on the counter tops. On further investigation into her dietary habits, you learn that she has no interest in cooking and prefers convenience foods. Speculate about the best way to approach your client regarding her eating habits. What suggestions can you make that would meet her need for convenience without sacrificing her need for adequate nutrition?
2. An 81-year-old woman who is 5'4" tall, weighs 152 lbs., and is in generally good health records the following 24-hour intake:

   Breakfast: 1 glass orange juice; 2 slices whole wheat toast; 1 tablespoon butter

   Lunch: 1/2 cup cottage cheese; 1 bag cheese curls; 1/2 peanut butter and jelly sandwich; 1 cup tea

   Dinner: 1 cup wheat flakes cereal; 1/2 cup skim milk

   Snack: 1 candy bar; 1 cup ice cream

   Analyze your client's diet. What conclusions, if any, can be made about her dietary status based on this 24-hour recall?

REFERENCES

Abdellah FG, Moore SR, editors: *Health promotion and aging* (Surgeon General's Workshop). Washington, D.C., 1988, US Department of Health and Human Services.

Adams RG, Blieszner R: *Older adult friendship: structure and process,* Newbury Park, Calif., 1989, Sage Publications.

American Association of Retired Persons Fulfillment, Administration On Aging: *A profile of older Americans,* Washington, D.C., 1994, US Department of Health and Human Services.

Anderson BL, Kiecoltglaser JK, Glaser R: A biobehavioral model of cancer stress and disease, *Am Psychol* 49:389-404, 1994.

Andres R et al: Impact of age on weight and goals, *Ann Int Med* 103:1030-1033, 1985.

Arnaud CD, Sanchez SD: The role of calcium in osteoporosis, *Ann Rev Nutr* 10:397-414, 1990.

Bales CW: Nutritional aspects of osteoporosis: recommendations for the elderly at risk, *Ann Rev Gerontol Geriatr* 10:7-34, 1990.

Barnes MS, Terry RD: Adherence to the cardiac diet: attitudes of patients after myocardial infarction, *J Am Diet Assoc* 91:53-58, 1991.

Benotti PN et al: Heart disease and hypertension in severe obesity: the benefits of weight reduction, *Am J Clin Nutr* 55(2 suppl):536S-590S, 1992.

Benson H: *The relaxation response,* New York, 1976, William and Morrow and Co.

Brown AB, McCartney N, Sale DG: Positive adaptations to weight-lifting training in the elderly, *J Appl Physiol* 69:1725-1733, 1990.

Butler RN: *Why survive: being old in America,* New York, 1975, Harper & Row.

Campanelli LC: Health promotion and geriatric screenings: appendix, summary tables of objectives to maintain the vitality and independence of older people, *Top Geriatr Rehab* 6:3-5, 1990.

Carper J: *Food, your miracle medicine,* New York, 1993, Harper Collins.

Carr M, Carr M: Dangerous brew, *Canad Nurse,* 1994.

Chandra RK: The relation between immunology, nutrition and disease in elderly people, *Age Aging* 19:S25-31, 1990.

Charette SL et al: Muscle hypertrophy response to resistance training in older women, *J Appl Physiol* 70:1912-1916, 1991.

Chernoff R, editor: *Geriatric nutrition: the health professional handbook,* Gaithersburg, Md., 1991, Aspen.

Cole TR: *The journey of life,* Cambridge, 1992, Cambridge University Press.

Cooper EL, editor: *Stress, intimacy, and aging,* New York, 1984, Marcel Dekker.

Cousins N: *Head first: the biology of hope,* New York, 1989, EP Dutton.

Degeus EJC, Vandoormen LJP, Orlebeke JF: Regular exercise and aerobic fitness in relation to psychological make up and physiological reactivity, *Psychosom Med* 55:347-363, 1993.

Delistraty DA et al: Cardiovascular reactivity in type A and B males to mental arithmetic and aerobic exercise at equivalent oxygen uptake. *Psychophysiol* 29(3):264-271, 1992.

Dwyer JT: *Screening older Americans nutritional health: current practices and future responsibilities,* Washington D.C., 1991, Nutrition Screening Institute.

Environmental nutrition 16(4):8, April 1993.

Feamon G: Better care for our older patients, *Am J Nurs* 48:702-705, 1948.

Fiatorone M: Nutrition in the geriatric patient, *Hosp Pract* 25(9A):38-40, 45, 49-54, 1990.

Fontham ETH et al: Dietary vitamins A and C and lung cancer risk in Louisiana, *Cancer* 62:2267-2273, 1988.

Food and Nutrition Board: recommended dietary allowances, ed 10, Washington, D.C., 1989, National Academy Press.

Freedman ML: Nutritional supplements in the ambulatory geriatric population: should they be recommended? *Drugs Aging* 1:168-175, 1991.

Gaby SK et al: *Vitamin intake and health,* New York, 1991, Marcel Dekker.

Grimby G et al: Training can improve muscle strength and endurance in 78- to 84-yr-old men, *J Gerontol* 49:M22-M28, 1994.

Guillem JG, Matsui MS, O'Brien CA: Nutrition in the prevention of neoplastic disease in the elderly, *Clinics Geriatr Med* 3(2):373-387, 1987.

Hallfrisch J et al: Continuing diet trends in men: the Baltimore longitudinal study of aging, *J Gerontol Med Sci* 45:M186-191, 1990.

Hayflick L: *How and why we age,* New York, 1994, Ballatine Books.

Hazzard WR et al: *Principles of geriatric medicine and gerontology,* ed 2, New York, 1990, McGraw-Hill.

Henderson MM et al: Feasibility of a randomized trial of a low-fat diet for the prevention of breast cancer: dietary compliance in the woman's health trial vanguard study, *Prevent Med* 19(2):115-133, 1990.

Hill JS, Castle SC, Makinodan T: Modulation of age-associated immune dysfunction by nutritional intervention. In Morley JE, Glick A, Rubenstein LZ: *Geriatric nutrition,* New York, 1990, Raven Press.

Holmes T, Masuda M: Psychosomatic syndrome, *Psychol Today* 106:71-72, 1972.

Johnson MA et al: Nutritional patterns of centenarians, *Intl J Aging Hum Dev* 34:57-76, 1992.

Kannel W, Larson M: Long term epidemiologic prediction of coronary disease: the Framingham experience, *Cardiol* 82(2-3):137-152, 1993.

Katan MB: Effect of cholesterol-lowering treatment on coronary heart disease morbidity and mortality: the evidence from trials and beyond, *Cardiol* 77:8-13, 1990.

King JA, Campbell D, Edwards E: Differential development of the stress response in congenital learned helplessness, *Intl J Dev Neurosci* 11:435-442, 1993.

Koop CE: *The Surgeon General's report on nutrition and health: summary and recommendations,* Washington, D.C., 1988, US Department of Health and Human Services, Pub. No 88-50211.

Lakatta E: Heart and circulation. In Schneider EL, Rowe JW, editors: *Handbook of the biology of aging,* ed 3, San Diego, 1990, Academic Press.

La Vecchia AB et al: Dietary indicators of oral and pharyngeal cancer, *Intl J Epidemiol* 20:39-44, 1991.

Liebman B: Seafood, fishing for omega-3's, *Nutrition Action Health Letter* 19(9):10-11, November 1992.

Lorand A: *Old age deferred,* ed 6, Philadelphia, 1928, FA Davis.

Lyons AS et al: *Medicine: an illustrated history,* New York, 1978, Harry N Abrams.

Makrides L, Simpson C, Officer S: Exercise training in the older person with coronary heart disease, *Top Geriatr Rehab* 10:23-32, 1995.

Manson A, Shea S: Malnutrition in elderly ambulatory medical patients, *Am J Pub Health* 81:1195-1197, 1991.

Manton KG, Stallord E, Tolley HD: Limits to human life expectancy: evidence, prospects, and implications, *Pop Dev Rev* 17:603-636, 1991.

Mares-Perlman JA et al: Nutrient supplements contribute to the dietary intake of middle-and older-aged residents of Beaver Dam, Wis., *J Nutr* 123(2):176-188, 1993.

McGinnis M: *Promoting health/preventing disease: year 2000 objectives for the nation,* Office of Disease Prevention and Health Promotion, Washington, D.C., 1989, US Government Printing Office.

McKay CM, Cromwell MF, Maynar LA: The effect of retarded growth upon length of lifespan and upon the ultimate body size, *J Nutrition* 10: 63, 1935.

McWhirter JB, Pennington CR: Incidence and recognition of malnutrition in hospital, *BMJ Med J* 308:945-948, 1994.

Metropolitan Life Insurance Company: Longevity gains continue, *Stat Bull* 71:19-26, 1991.

Munro HM: Introduction in nutrition of the elderly. In Munro H, Schlierf, editors: *Nutrition of the elderly,* New York, 1992, Nestec Ltd, Vevy/Raven Press.

National Institutes on Aging: *Older population healthier than expected,* Washington, D.C., April 1993.

Nadelson CC: Ethics, empathy, and gender in health care, *Am J Psychiatr* 150(9):1309-1314, 1993.

O'Brien SJ, Vertinsky PA: Elderly women, exercise and healthy aging, *J Women Aging* 2:41-65, 1990.

O'Keefe CE, Hahn DF, Betts NM: Physician's perspectives on cholesterol and heart disease, *J Am Diet Assoc* 91(2):189-192, 1991.

Paffenbarger RS et al: Some interrelations of physical activity, physiological fitness, health, and longevity. In Bouchard C, Shepard RJ, Stephen T, editors: *Physical activity, fitness, and health: international proceedings and consensus statement,* Champaign, Ill., 1994, Human Kinetics.

Palmore E et al, editors: *Normal aging III: reports from the Duke longitudinal studies, 1975-1984,* Durham, N.C., 1985, Duke University Press.

Pathy MSJ, editor: *Principles and practice of geriatric medicine,* ed 2, New York, 1990, John Wiley & Sons.

Pauling L: *How to liver longer and feel better,* New York, 1986, WH Freeman.

Peterson C, Bossio LM: *Health and optimism,* New York, 1991, Free Press.

Popkin BM, Haines PS, Patterson RE: Dietary changes in older Americans: 1977-1987, *Am J Clin Med* 55(4):823-830, 1992.

Posner BM et al: Dietary lipid predictors of coronary heart disease in men: the Framingham study, *Arch Int Med* 151(6):1181-1187, 1991.

Preuss HG: Nutrition and disease of women: cardiovascular disorders, *J Am Coll Nutr* 12:417-425, 1993.

Rahe H, Mahan J, Arthur RJ: Predictions of near and future health: change from subjects preceding life change, *J Psychosom Res* 14:401-406, 1970.

Read MA et al: Relationship of vitamin/mineral supplementation to certain psychological factors, *J Am Diet Assoc* 91:1429-1431, 1991.

Recommended Dietary Allowances, ed 10, Washington, D.C., 1989, National Academy Press.

Richmond JB: *Healthy people (Surgeon General's report on health promotion and disease prevention),* Washington, D.C., 1979, Department Of Health Education and Welfare (Public Health Service) Pub No 79-55071.

Rimm EB et al: Vitamin E consumption and risk of coronary heart disease in men, *New Eng J Med* 328(20):1450-1455, 1993.

Rodin J: Aging and health: effects of the sense of control, *Science* 233:1271-1276, 1986.

Roe DA: *Diet and drug interactions,* New York, 1989, Van Nostrand Reinhold.

Roe DA: *Geriatric nutrition,* ed 3, New York, 1992, Prentice Hall.

Roff LL, Atherton CR: *Promoting successful aging,* Chicago, 1989, Nelson-Hall.

Rowe JW, Kahn RL: Human aging: usual and successful, *Science* 237:143-149, 1987.

Ryan AS, Craig D, Finn SC: Nutrient intakes and dietary patterns of older Americans: a national study, *J Gerontol Med Sci* 47(5):M145-150, 1992.

Schaie KW, Willis SL: Learning and memory: acquiring and retaining information. In Schaie KW, Willis SL, editors: *Adult development and aging,* ed 2, Boston, 1986, Little, Brown.

Schapira DV et al: The effect of duration of intervention and locus of control on dietary change, *Am J Prevent Med* 7:341-347, 1991.

Scrimshaw NS: Nutrition: prospects of the 1990's, *Ann Rev Pub Health* 11:53-68, 1990.

Sharpe PA, Clark NM, Janz NK: Differences in the impact and management of heart disease between older women and men, *Women Health* 17(2):25-43, 1991.

Shock et al: *Normal human aging; The baltimore longitudinal study on aging,* Washington, D.C., 1984, US Department of Health and Human Services, National Institute of Health Pub No 84-2450.

Steingart RM et al: Sex differences in the management of coronary artery disease, *New Engl J Med* 325(4):226-230, 1991.

Tannahill R, *Food in history,* New York, 1973, Stein & Day.

Tannahill R: *Food in history,* New York, 1988, Crown Publishers.

Teague ML: *Health promotion: achieving high-level wellness in the later years.* Indianapolis, Ind., 1987, Benchmark Press.

Trzcieniecka-Green A, Steptoe A: Stress management in cardiac patients-a preliminary study of the predictors of improvements in quality of life, *J Psychosom Res* 38:267-280, 1994.

Tucker DM et al: Nutrition status and brain function in aging, *Am J Clin Nutr* 52(1):93-102, 1990.

Unosson M et al: Demographical, sociomedical and physical characteristics in relation to malnutrition in geriatric patients, *J Adv Nurs* 16:1406-1412, 1991.

Vellas B: Effects of aging process on nutritional status of elderly persons. In Munro H, Schlierf G, editors: *Nestle nutrition workshop series 29,* New York, 1992, Vevy Raven Press, 75-78.

Walford RL: The clinical promise of diet restriction, *Geriatrics* 45: 81-87, 1990.

Walford RL, Walford L: *The anti-aging plan,* New York, 1994, Four Walls Eight Windows.

Weg RB: *Nutrition and the later years,* Los Angeles, 1978, University of Southern California Press.

Weg RB: Nutrition: a crucial given in rehabilitation, *Top Geri Rehab* 5:1-26, 1989.

Weg RB: Preventative and therapeutic nutrition. In Brody SJ, Paulson LG, editors: *Aging and rehabilitation II,* New York, 1990, Springer.

Whiteney EN, Hamilton EMN, Rolfes SR: *Understanding nutrition,* ed 5, Los Angeles, 1990, West Publishing.

Wilson S, Barry J: Serve Our Seniors, Inc.—a demonstration program for proposed California menu guidelines for senior nutrition, *J Nutr Elder* 13:37-59, 1993.

Wilt S, Hubbard A, Thomas A, Knowledge, attitudes, treatment practices, and health behaviors of nurses regarding blood cholesterol and cardiovascular disease, *Prevent Med* 19(4):466-475, 1990.

Young VR: Amino acids and proteins in relation to the nutrition of elderly people, *Age Aging* 19:S10-24, 1990.

Zeman S: Screening and health promotion in the older adult, *Top Geri Rehab* 6:6-18, 1990.

Zisook S et al: Bereavement, depression, and immune function, *Psychiatr Res* 52:1-10, 1994.

NEWSLETTERS

Centers for Science in the Public Interest, *Nutrition Action Health Letter,* 1875 Connecticut Avenue, N.W. Suite 300, Washington, DC 20009-5728

Harvard Medical School Health Letter, P.O. Box 10943, Des Moines, IA 50340

Harvard Women's Health Letter, 164 Longwood Avenue, Boston, MA 02115

Johns Hopkins Medical Letter, Health After 50, P.O. Box 420235, Palm Coast, FL 32142-0235.

Public Citizen Health Research Group, *Health Letter,* Health Letter, Circulation Department, 2000 P Street, N.W., Washington, DC 20036

Tufts University, *Diet and Nutrition Letter,* 53 Park Place, New York, NY 10007

University of California at Berkley, *Wellness Letter* (Newletter of nutrition, fitness, stress management), P.O. Box 420148, Palm Coast, FL 32142

BIBLIOGRAPHY

Baltimore Longitudinal Study of Aging: Older and wider, NIH Pub No 89-2797, Washington, D.C., September 1989, US Government Printing Office.

George LK, Clipp EC, editors: Aging well, *Generations* XV, 1991 (entire issue).

Hoffman NB: Dehydration in the elderly: insidious and manageable, *Geriatrics* 46(6):35-38, 1991.

Chapter 9

Sleep and Activity

LEARNING OBJECTIVES

On completion of this chapter, the reader will be able to:

1. Discuss ways in which older people define sleep.
2. Explain the progression of normal sleep, from non-REM to REM.
3. Name two normal changes in sleep patterns in older adults.
4. Discuss the major factors that influence the older adult's quality of sleep.
5. Identify three myths related to common sleep patterns among older adults.
6. Describe three environmental conditions that can adversely affect sleep among institutionalized older adults.
7. Discuss three common medical problems that can adversely affect an older adult's ability to sleep.
8. Differentiate among the effects that caffeine, alcohol, sedative-hypnotics, and antianxiety drugs can have on sleep.
9. Discuss the major sleep disorders that can lead to insomnia among older adults, including pharmacologic and nonpharmacologic remedies.
10. Conduct a complete sleep history of an older adult.
11. Develop a care plan for an older adult with a sleep pattern disturbance.
12. Develop nursing interventions for the older adult that promote adaptation to the normal age-related changes in activity and sleep.

Sleep and activity are two universal, dichotomous functions of all human beings. Sleep is a term derived from the Latin word *somnus* meaning a natural, periodically recurring, physiologic state of rest for the body and mind. Activity can be defined as "natural or normal function" (*Webster's Ninth New Collegiate Dictionary,* 1991). Sleep is a state of inactivity or repose that is required to remain active. William Shakespeare said of sleep, ". . . our foster-nurse of nature is repose." The amount and frequency of sleep and activity are life-long patterns determined by several biologic factors and influenced by age, disease, lifestyle, and extraneous factors such as medication, diet, and environmental conditions. Some important aspects of normal and abnormal sleep among older adults are discussed in this chapter.

BIOLOGIC BRAIN FUNCTIONS RESPONSIBLE FOR SLEEP

Regulation of sleep and wakefulness occurs primarily in the hypothalamus, which contains both a sleep center and a wakefulness center. The thalamus, limbic system, and reticular activating system are controlled by the hypothalamus and also influence sleep and wakefulness. The hypothalamus consists of several masses of nuclei, interconnected with other parts of the nervous system, and is located below the thalamus, where it forms the floor and part of the lateral walls of the third ventricle. Sleep is a changed state of consciousness, where the physiologic changes of reduced blood pressure, pulse rate, and respiratory rate occur along with decreased response to external stimuli.

STAGES OF SLEEP

There are two major types of normal sleep that have been subdivided into **REM** (rapid eye movement) and **non-REM** sleep (Table 9-1). Non-REM sleep is characterized by slow wave sleep. The first stage of non-REM sleep, or Stage I, is referred to as descending sleep—a transitional phase between wakefulness and sleep lasting a few seconds to several minutes. Responses to external stimuli diminish and bodily functions slow as a person passes from Stage I to Stage IV. Slow, regular breathing results from chemoreceptor control of ventilation. Ventilation rate is slow, because metabolic rate is slow (Fox, 1984). The electroencephalogram (EEG) shows a regular synchronized wave pattern. During Stage II, or unequivocal sleep, delta waves appear on the electroencephalogram (EEG). The delta waves reflect restorative sleep, which continues into Stages III (deep sleep) and IV (cerebral sleep). By the end of Stage IV, there are few eye movements and other processes have slowed considerably. In approximately 1 to 2 hours, REM sleep begins with the cycle repeating roughly every 90 minutes (Gorbien, 1993).

REM sleep consists of the eyes moving rapidly, body movements increasing, and a generalized state of stressfulness with increased respiration, heart rate, blood pressure, and gastric juice secretion. Breathing during REM sleep is less sensitive to chemoreceptor stimulation, so that arterial P_{CO_2} can increase to between 40 mm Hg and 46 mm Hg (Fox, 1984). Dreaming typically occurs several times during REM sleep. Brain waves appearing on the EEG are irregular and desynchronized during this stage. The REM periods lengthen and alternate with nonREM Stages II or III. Approximately four to six REM periods occur nightly, accounting for 20% to 25% of all sleep (Gorbien, 1993).

NORMAL AGE-RELATED CHANGES IN SLEEP

Research on sleep in older adults has revealed a decrease in the average number of hours of sleep (Monk et al, 1992). This is caused by an increase in the number of nocturnal awakenings and an overall decrease in nocturnal sleep efficiency (Bliwise, 1993). Sleep becomes fragmented as brief or complete awakenings occur, causing the older person to spend more time in bed awake. It is a myth that older people reduce their total sleep time or need less sleep as they age.

Most noteworthy is the decrease in slow wave (Stages III and IV) sleep (Gorbien, 1993; Bliwise, 1993), which, according to one study, may be worse in older men. For those over age 90, Stages III and IV sleep may even dis-

TABLE 9-1

Normal Stages of Sleep

Stage of sleep	Terminology	Ventilation
Non-REM		
Stage 0	Wakefulness	
Stage I	Descending	Decreased
Stage II	Unequivocal	
Stage III	Deep wave	
Stage IV	Cerebral	
REM		
	Slow wave	Increased

Insight • *Teach the older adult that it is a myth to expect to require less total sleep as he or she gets older. The average number of hours a person sleeps decreases because of an increased frequency of nocturnal awakenings in older adults. Ensuring an understanding of this important aging change informs the older adult. The older adult can then experience less anxiety about perceived sleep problems, less reliance on medications, and ultimately, improved sleep.*

appear entirely (Bliwise, 1993). It appears that more time is spent in Stage I sleep and that the older adult is more likely to return to Stage I in a typical night's cycle (Bliwise, 1993).

In addition, daytime napping is more common in older adults and can influence nocturnal sleep. It is essential to observe the application of these age-related sleep changes to the clinical practice setting. Educating older adults about expected sleep changes improves insight into sleep behavior and thus allays anxiety in some cases. For example, a client complaining of not sleeping well may be observed by the nurse to have achieved an adequate amount of sleep but may be experiencing more frequent interruptions in sleep. Once older adults are aware of normal age-related changes, expectations about sleep may change and changes in lifestyle may also occur. Counseling may be appropriate for older people who fail to adjust their lifestyles accordingly or who have unrealistic expectations about sleep.

Nursing interventions include first determining the older person's self-perception of sleep, cultural beliefs about sleep (see Cultural Awareness box below) or age-related biases about sleep. For those older people experiencing difficulty with sleep, keeping a sleep diary, which accounts for both daytime and nighttime sleep patterns (including frequency and amount of sleep, symptomatology, agents used to promote sleep, and beverages consumed before sleep and activity) can be helpful in determining the cause of a sleep problem. Direct nursing intervention also includes following a sleep regimen in which the older adult is taught to retire and to awaken at the same time each day. Setting an alarm clock can help with this plan. Daytime napping should be discouraged to allow for more continuity in nighttime sleep patterns. Older people should be taught to avoid beverages that cause insomnia, such as cola products, hot chocolate, coffee, or tea. The older adult should be encouraged to drink beverages such as hot water, warm milk, or juice.

CULTURAL AWARENESS

Sleep and Activity: Cultural Considerations

Sleep

What is the client's normal sleep pattern? Does the client sleep alone or with others (e.g., grandchildren or other members of the extended family)?

Are there bedtime routines that help the client fall asleep (e.g., ingestion of herbs, recitation of prayers, etc.)?

On what does the client normally sleep—futon, mat, mattress and box springs, floor, etc.?

Activity

What are culturally acceptable activities for older adults? Are there any cultural restrictions on activities? Are there any gender-related considerations (e.g., same-gender social support networks or organizations)? Are there culturally determined expectations concerning the age of retirement?* How does the person spend time? Does the older adult have any hobbies or participate in any recreational activities? Does he or she have any limitations in activity level?

*Transculturally, there is wide variation in expectations.

Circadian Rhythm

Normal physiologic events, like the sleep-wake cycle, follow a **circadian rhythm,** which is roughly a 24-hour period. The hypothalamus controls many circadian rhythms, which include the release of certain hormones during sleep. Numerous influences can gradually strengthen or weaken the sleep and wake aspect of circadian rhythm, including the perception of time, travel across time zones, light exposure, seasonal changes, living habits, stress, illness, and medication (Allen, 1994).

One study hypothesized that the decrease in nighttime sleep and the increase in daytime napping that accompanies normal aging may result from changes in the circadian aspect of sleep regulation. These researchers have observed weaker rhythmic circadian trends among older adult men as compared with older adult women (Buysse et al, 1991).

GETTING A GOOD NIGHT'S SLEEP

Defining Sleep

Proper sleep is essential for a person's sense of well-being and health. **Sleep** is often defined subjectively and correlated with the symptomatology of how a person feels when awakening. When describing how well they sleep, people of all ages often describe feelings of fatigue and inadequate sleep. Often, productiveness in daily activities is reflected in discussion about sleep quality. For example, feeling tired and less alert after a poor night's sleep often gives rise to being less active and productive during the day. Many more factors influence sleep quality in older adults than in younger adults because of any one or a combination of the following changes: advancing age, environment, pain, disease, diet, medication use, and the psychosocial issues or events that can alter a person's lifestyle. The following is a more detailed discussion of these issues.

Environment

Environment can positively or negatively influence the quality and amount of sleep a person receives. For the older adult, environments conducive to relaxation are likely to be soporific. Such environments include low levels of stimuli, dimmed lights, silence and comfortable furniture. Hospitalization or institutionalization can have serious deleterious effects on sleep. Not only are these environments unfamiliar, but they typically have bright lights, noisy people and machines, limited privacy and space, and uncomfortable mattresses. Physical discomfort or pain may be caused by invasive procedures such as Foley catheterization, intravenous lines, venipuncture, oxygen masks, casts or traction devices, mechanical ventilation and other equipment. Fear of the unexpected or unknown may also be a factor that keeps older adults awake, especially those in acute care. In this setting, the client is often awakened to receive medications or treatments, or is assessed for vital signs and condition. Although all of these factors are likely to interrupt sleep, in some individuals, sleep remains uninterrupted.

The consequences of environmental noise include (1) potential for sleep deprivation, (2) alteration in comfort, (3) potential for pain, and (4) stress or difficulty concentrating, which can interfere with the enjoyment of pleasurable activities. Nursing interventions are aimed at reducing environmental noise and bright lights, and improving client comfort through body positioning and other soporific modalities.

In the institutional setting, environmental changes become more challenging as there are more obstacles to overcome. Dimming the lights in the hallway at night darkens the environment and promotes relaxation. However, this may pose danger for individuals with visual impairment, who may wander the hallways at night. Therefore people are more likely to sustain falls, which places a greater emphasis on using night-lights, hall lights, and bathroom lights. The nurse should assess environmental lighting in the institutional setting for glare, brightness, and uneven levels of illumination.

Nursing interventions that minimize glare can improve concentration and can aid the older person in maintaining independence in tasks of daily living. Reducing glare by closing the blinds, drawing the curtains, or placing a plant in front of a window emitting bright light scatters the light. Bright light is the most troublesome, therefore indirect lighting such as broad-spectrum, fluorescent lighting is recommended (Kolanowski, 1992). Research findings have also suggested that the majority of individuals are more relaxed under the broad-spectrum lighting than other types of lighting (Kolanowski, 1992). An outdoor walk or a visit to the solarium daily as part of the care plan can expose the client to natural light. For clients in long-term care facilities, both indoor and outdoor walking facilities should be provided.

Other environmental problems such as a noisy roommate can contribute to sleeplessness. Because of limited occupancy, a room change may not be a viable option. Therefore roommates should be evaluated to determine appropriate measures for reducing agitation and/or noise.

Pain

One of the most discomforting causes of sleeplessness for an older person may be related to pain. Although pain threshold increases with age, pain does occur and can cause significant distress and discomfort. One of the most important aspects of caring for older adults is to meet their basic physiologic needs, among which is providing comfort. If unrelieved, pain can result in sleeplessness. If overtreated, such as with narcotic analgesia, it can cause excessive sleep or changes in the level of alertness, and thereby alter functional ability. Other factors contributing to pain include illness, disease, and improper body positioning.

Common rheumatologic and neurologic diseases capable of causing pain in older adults include rheumatoid arthritis, polymyalgia rheumatica, degenerative joint disease, osteoporosis, fractures, cerebrovascular accident (CVA) with thalamic involvement, headaches, and peripheral neuropathies. Pleuritic pain may result from pneumonia and bronchitis, whereas herpes zoster, partial- and full-thickness burns, and pressure sores can cause focal pain of the skin. Abdominal pain may result from fecal impaction or bowel obstruction, and joint contractures can cause pain particularly among the immobilized. An older person's symptoms often include atypical types of pain associated with the presentation of an atypical disease. A classic example of this is abdominal pain as a result of a urinary tract infection. Chronic pain may also coexist with depression in older adults. Older adults with depression often have multiple body aches and pains.

Physical restraint can cause pain, especially if circulatory compromise to the chest or extremity occurs or when the body is positioned improperly. Institutionalized older people with dementia are particularly vulnerable to poor body positionings, because they are unable to maintain proper positioning to achieve comfort. Care must be taken to find the appropriately sized chair, bed, or assistive device for these individuals.

In addition, boredom and loneliness can have a significant effect on the older person's perception of and report of pain (Herr, Mobily, 1991). Cultural beliefs about pain also influence perception of pain and subsequent reporting of pain. Different ethnic groups may either over- or underrate pain perception because of lifelong patterns, previous experiences, personality, and family support. Likewise, the older person may have ageist beliefs and expect pain as a normal part of aging.

If pain is poorly managed, several events are likely to develop. The nurse may notice the older adult experiencing distress signs such as restlessness, agitation, moaning, crying, listlessness, or despondency. Clients may wince when touched or move away from the examiner thereby limiting the accuracy of assessment of the pain origin. Compounded by this is the observation that pain in the older person may be referred to another area, and pain response may not be as keen as expected. Nutritional changes caused by pain include eating less than the necessary body requirements, resulting in a potential for weight loss and inefffective coping, and resulting in a potential for depression. Pain can also result in high blood pressure, thus increasing the chance for problems in people with hypertension.

Nursing interventions to reduce pain must first include observation of the older adult and an assessment of the location, severity and type of pain, aggravating or alleviating factors, and the impact that the pain has on the older person's functional ability. Pain may preclude independence in basic activities of daily living such as ambulation, feeding oneself with painful, arthritic joints, or getting comfortable in bed. Pain may also result in significant psychosocial changes such as less socialization or other pleasurable activities.

Several measurement tools designed to assess pain are available (see Chapter 13). Older adults can self-administer tools that ask to rate the pain on a scale of 0 to 10 with 0 indicating no pain and 10 as the most severe pain. A diagram of the client's body can illustrate the location of the pain for a person who is unable to rate the pain. A facial expression scale, which depicts various levels of pain, can also be administered.

The most important nursing intervention after pain has been reported or detected is to reduce or to eliminate pain. Pain can be reduced both physically and psychologically. Nonpharmacologic measures include touch, stress-reduction techniques, and certain positioning aids or devices. One study shows progressive relaxation to have significantly improved certain sleep parameters among noninstitutionalized older women, particularly those who reported disturbed sleep patterns and sleep dissatisfaction (Johnson, 1991). This intervention involves focusing attention on a muscle group, followed by contracting and relaxing that muscle. In the long-term care setting, this activity can be instituted using a group format and can even be part of an exercise program. Guided imagery has been described in the literature to help with stress reduction. This involves the use of imagination to visualize pleasant images or scenes and may have a role along with other measures in the management of chronic pain. Forms of touch such as a back rub and warm baths can promote muscle relaxation and sleep in some individuals.

An individual who cannot assume a supine position may find comfort in using a rocking chair on a stationary platform. The constant motion is rhythmic and soothing to some individuals, and can reduce pain and can promote sleep. Reclining chairs with soft cushions may be advantageous over a high Fowler's position in bed for individuals with chronic congestive heart failure or severe chronic obstructive pulmonary disease. Such individuals are often unable to maintain a supine position as a result of impaired respiratory excursion. Extra pillows should be used to support painful limbs and help in body positioning. Down-filled comforters, elbow and heel protectors, as well as water mattresses also provide comfort. Nighttime garments should be made of a soft material such as cotton and should not be restrictive to allow freedom of movement. Headphones provide relaxing music for the older adult seeking sleep and reduce background noise.

Pharmacologic interventions can also reduce pain if nonpharmacologic ones fail. Such interventions include acetaminophen (Tylenol) to promote sleep, or warm milk and aspirin (unless medically contraindicated) to stimulate the body to naturally produce L-tryptophane, a chemical that can promote sleep. See Drugs Influencing Sleep, p. 230, for medications that specifically promote sleep.

Depression

Puzzling patterns or distributions of pain problems can indicate depression (Herr and Mobily, 1991). Depression among older adults is a treatable condition that often manifests itself with insomnia as the chief complaint. Clients awaken in the early morning and are unable to return to sleep. Symptoms of older adults may also include anxiety or agitation as a prominent feature of depression, or listlessness and difficulty engaging in activities. Evaluation and treatment is essential once depression is suspected. Declining participation in pleasurable activities, reduced motivation or interest to participate in previous activities, memory deficits, guilt feelings, vegetative signs such as a change in appetite, and constipation or sleep disturbances are symptoms that can confirm the diagnosis. Screening measurement tools that question the older client about depression symptomatology can be used in making a clinical diagnosis.

Treatment involves both pharmacologic and nonpharmacologic interventions. Clients should be informed that sleep disorders as a result of depression may take several days or weeks to abate. Antidepressants with sedative properties can often be used when insomnia or motor restlessness is troublesome to the older client. The nurse should emphasize that changes may occur slowly. As pharmacologic aids are introduced, nursing interventions should be implemented adjunctively, to encourage self-esteem and optimum functioning in a client's environment through promotion of independence. Encouraging independence in activities and offering praise for successful accomplishments can improve self-esteem. Older adults will feel valued if their autonomy is recognized. This can be accomplished by including older adults in decisions that affect their lifestyles, such as the overall care plan. The nurse should include the institutionalized older person in routine tasks around the unit or within the facility, which are in keeping with the person's interests. This may also foster positive attitudes in the older person about himself or herself.

Social Changes With Age Influencing Sleep

In the United States, widowhood is a common life event in the older adult population. For women, the possibility of widowhood is much more common than it is for older men. Most women over age 75 are widowed, whereas most older men tend to be married.

Widowhood is often a tragic event that leaves the older person without a "touch partner." Loss of a bed partner can make sleep psychologically less comforting and can therefore alter it. In the long-term care setting, feelings of loneliness and depression may be voiced by residents or may be observed by the nurse when older people withdraw from daily activities or remain in their rooms. For previously married individuals, whose lifelong pattern has been to sleep with another individual, loss of a spouse can also result in feelings of loneliness. In the institutional setting where widowhood is common, residents may seek fellow residents to provide companionship and a "sleep partner." In this situation, nursing staff concerns are less common among consenting adults than they are when the resident is incapable of making these decisions. For regressed residents and those with severe dementia, who are demonstrating loneliness or depression and difficulty sleeping, the nurse can provide a soft, stuffed animal or doll to cuddle. Using a rocking chair, the nurse can gently rock the client in bed. In short, a basic human need is the need for love and belonging. Companionship is an extension of this need and a lack thereof may result in loneliness, depression, and sleep difficulties.

Nursing interventions to reduce loneliness and to provide companionship revolve around a careful assessment of the older person's psychosocial needs. Questions about satisfying relationships, close confidants and friends, and the ability to seek these types of relationships need to be explored. For the widowed, the degree of socialization can be explored by asking open-ended questions such as, "How do you spend your time?" or "Are you able to maintain the same relationships with friends and family as you once did?" These questions are important to ask any institutionalized older adult. In this setting, older adults capable of communicating their interest should be part of the roommate selection process. Many sleep-related problems often occur in this setting, as roommates do not get along with one another because of different interests or lifestyles. For example, one older adult may watch television to fall asleep and the other may find this disruptive to sleep. Every effort must be made by the nursing staff to review significant psychosocial interests with residents and to match roommates accordingly. Ideally, residents should be allowed to select individuals with whom they share common interests.

In older couples, the bed partner who snores loudly, sleep walks, talks in his or her sleep, or has an annoying tick or restless leg syndrome can create sleeplessness for his or her bed partner. Treatment must be directed toward resolving the bed partner's problem or disease.

Diet

The link between certain food substances and sleeplessness has been most strongly associated with the xanthine derivatives. Diets high in xanthine substances cause sleeplessness, since they are central nervous system stimulants. Beverages with xanthine and **caffeine,** such as coffee, tea, and cola, tend to be consumed often throughout the day by young and older adults alike. Coffee comprises nearly 90% of the U.S. population's caffeine intake (Rall, 1980).

Caffeine, theophylline, and theobromine are methylated xanthines and are naturally occurring substances found in plants throughout the world. Tea is derived from the *thea sinesis* leaves and contains mostly caffeine, and smaller amounts of theophylline and theobromine. Cocoa and chocolate come from seeds of *theobroma cacao* and contain theobromine and caffeine. Coffee is extracted from the fruit of *coffea arabica.* Cola-flavored drinks contain considerable amounts of caffeine because they are partially extracted from the nuts of *cola acuminato* and caffeine is also often added in the production. The average 8-ounce cup of coffee contains 85 mg of caffeine, one 8-ounce cup of tea contains 50 mg of caffeine, and a 12-ounce cola beverage contains about 50 mg of caffeine (Rall, 1980).

Although caffeine is the most customary beverage consumed for breakfast, and sometimes for lunch and dinner among older adults, theophylline is a much more potent central nervous system stimulant. Central nervous system (CNS) effects from caffeine and theophylline include less drowsiness and fatigue, and more clear thought. Excessive caffeine results in restlessness, nervousness, insomnia, tremors, decrease in peripheral vascular resistance, increase in heart rate, and relaxation of bronchial smooth muscle. It appears that the methylxanthines excite the medullary respiratory centers and stimulatory actions of CO_2, resulting in sleep alteration.

The nurse should obtain a health history, noting the amount and type of caffeinated beverages consumed during a 24-hour period and most importantly, before bedtime. Older adults should be educated about the effects of caffeinated beverages on sleep. Clients should be instructed to gradually substitute decaffeinated bever-

Insight • *Older individuals with restlessness or agitation leading to insomnia should avoid chocolates and caffeinated beverages such as coffee, tea, and cola products, all of which contain methylxanthine derivatives. In older adults with dementia, the nurse must use keen observation skills to detect subtle changes in behavior or sleep-wake disturbances. As the dementia progresses, these individuals are unable to communicate their needs, therefore observation of behavior in relation to comfort, pain, and sleep becomes essential.*

ages by first combining decaffeinated coffee with smaller amounts of caffeinated coffee and gradually reducing the total intake of caffeine. In the institutionalized setting, nurses can review with the dietician the number of servings per day and then discuss it with the client if appropriate.

DRUGS INFLUENCING SLEEP

Drugs that inhibit sleep are called **antisoporific;** those that promote sleep are called **soporific.** Both prescription drugs and over-the-counter drugs can contribute to sleep disturbances. The following discussion includes sleep disturbances and the mechanisms for inhibiting or promoting sleep. Table 9-2 illustrates both prescription and nonprescription drugs that affect the sleep-wake cycle by promoting or inhibiting sleep.

Antihistamines

Antihistamines are a class of drugs that cause drowsiness. These drugs are found in many nonprescription products such as cold remedies. Occasionally, antihistamines can cause nervousness, restlessness, or insomnia. In the older adult, antihistamines can cause changes in mental status, acute or increasing confusion, or agitation. The active ingredients in many antihistamine products are chlorpheniramine hydroxyzine, diphenhydramine HCL, chlorpheniramine maleate, brompheniramine maleate, and pheniramine maleate. Potential for anxiety, fatigue, altered thought processes, and sleep pattern disturbance are some of the nursing diagnoses that may be applicable to older adults using these agents.

In clinical practice, the **anticholinergic** effect of antihistamines can cause dry mouth, (xerostomia) blurred vision, constipation, and urinary retention. Older people with glaucoma, constipation, xerostomia, or prostatic enlargement are particularly at risk for these problems. Of critical significance is the older adult who is sensitive to the anticholinergic effects of these medications and who has acute confusion. An acute confusional state (ACS) may result from these types of medications or may be secondary to an acute medical illness. Nurses must recognize these symptoms and signs and then investigate possible origins, always evaluating the drug regimen and recommending elimination of unnecessary medications. Older people with ACS that developed after the initiation of an antihistamine should discontinue its use. A period of close observation for resolution of the symptoms and detection of other medical problems should follow. If the antihistamine was used for symptomatic relief of a common cold, then other interventions should be attempted instead, including increasing fluids and offering analgesia for myalgia. Clients should be advised that the common cold runs a course from 7 to 10 days.

TABLE 9-2

Prescription and Nonprescription Drugs that Influence the Sleep-Wake Cycle

	Prescription	Nonprescription
Antihistamines		
Allerdryl		x
Atarax	x	
Benadryl		x
Chlor-Trimeton		x
Dimetane		x
Periactin	x	
Seldane	x	x
Vistaril	x	
Nasal decongestants		
Afrinol		x
Sudafed		x
Combination Drugs		
Actifed		x
Allarest		x
Chlor-Trimeton-decongestant		x
Dimetapp		x
Drixoral		x
Entex	x	
Naldecon	x	x
Novafed	x	x
Ornade	x	
Sudafed Plus		x
Tavist-D	x	x

Nasal Decongestants

Nasal decongestants contain pseudoephedrine hydrochloride (HCL), a drug that has amphetamine-like properties and typically causes nervousness or sleepless ness. Most over-the-counter cold remedies contain both an antihistamine and a nasal decongestant, making this type of drug improper to use with older adults. Some of these agents can have adverse effects on the cardiovascular system, causing arrhythmias or alterations in the conduction system. Older people with a history of cardiovascular problems such as myocardial infarction or arrhythmia should not use these agents. Pseudoephedrine HCL causes cardiovascular stimulation and use in older people with coronary artery disease is strictly contraindicated. Older people with hypertension are also at risk for high blood pressure as a result of the long-term effects of pseudoephedrine HCL.

Older people with nasal congestion should be encouraged first to try remedies such as nasal humidification using a bedside vaporizer or normal saline nasal spray, which can aid in humidification and shrink inflamed nasal mucosa. Low-dose nasal steroids are often used to reduce nasal inflammation and subsequent congestion. These measures should be attempted first, before the use of oral nasal decongestants. In addition, clients can be taught how to clear a blocked eustacian tube, by pinching the tip of the nares and gently blowing the nose. This exercise is usually beneficial for certain types of sinus problems when repeated several times daily.

Psychoactive Drugs

Although people over age 60 make up only 16% (slightly less than one sixth) of the population, they use almost 40% of all prescription drugs (*Statistical Abstract of the United States,* 1985). Drugs with psychoactive properties are the third leading type of drug use among this age group. Older adults are prescribed well over one third of the tranquilizers, antipsychotics, and antidepressants, as well as more than one half of the sleeping pills in the United States (*Drug Utilization in the United States,* 1985). As health care providers, nurses encounter widespread use of this class of drugs as they care for older adults at home, in the hospital, or in long-term care institutions. Nurses must be aware of the widespread use of these drugs, and the significant adverse side effects that are observed among older adults and that can go unrecognized or even attributed to advancing age.

Tranquilizers and Sedative-Hypnotics

The most commonly used drugs of minor tranquilizers or **anxiolytics** are the benzodiazepines. The use of these drugs in the older adult population, especially ones with a long half-life, is potentially dangerous because of the altered **pharmacokinetics** associated with age. The drug half-life is the length of time the drug remains active in the body. Pharmacokinetics is the process by which drugs are absorbed, distributed, metabolized, and excreted. As a result of age-related changes, disease, or medication use, the dosages of benzodiazepines must be calculated quite carefully and at very low dosages. In general, the use of benzodiazepines with older adults is avoided and replaced by nonpharmacologic interventions.

TABLE 9-3

Prescription Sedatives-Hypnotics

Drug	Dosage*	Frequency
Librium*†	5-20 mg	TID-QID
Valium*†	2-10 mg	BID-QID
Dalmane*†	15-30 mg	Once at bedtime
Ativan*†	0.5-1.0 mg	BID-TID
Serax*‡	10-15 mg	TID-QID
Xanax*‡	0.25-0.5 mg	BID-TID
Halcion*§	0.25-0.5 mg	BID-TID

*The rule of thumb when prescribing any of these drugs is to start at the lowest possible dose to achieve the desired effect.

†Because of the long half-life, these drugs are generally avoided in older adults.

‡Drugs with shorter half-life.

§Significant adverse effects in the elderly including amnesia.

Many of the longer-acting benzodiazepines also contain active metabolites that remain active in the body for several hours or even days, which means the drug can potentially interact with other agents. The benzodiazepines possess **sedative** properties in that they decrease activity, moderate excitement, and calm the recipient. A **hypnotic** drug produces drowsiness, and facilitates the onset and maintenance of a state of sleep that resembles natural sleep with EEG characteristics, from which the recipient can be easily aroused (Harvey, 1980).

Table 9-3 lists some of the sedative-hypnotic agents available with ranges of dosage and frequency. If used, the nurse should promote beginning with the lowest possible dose to achieve the desired effects. The nurse and the older person should carefully monitor significant adverse effects. If these drugs are taken at bedtime, adverse reactions may occur, including daytime drowsiness, somnolence, or lethargy. Reduced activity can foster daytime napping, increased difficulty with sleeping at night, and subsequent weight gain. People should be cautioned about driving and cooking if daytime sedation occurs. Changes in mental status may cause falls. Memory deficits may occur as a result of the psychoactive properties of these drugs. In general, alcohol can intensify the effects of these drugs and should be carefully avoided. Information fact sheets can be given to older people and periodically reviewed by the nurse.

Pharmacologic Properties of Benzodiazepines in Relation to Sleep

Benzodiazepines alter both nonREM and REM sleep, each to a different degree, depending on their exact chemical composition. Overall, changes occur to increase total sleep time. Stage I (descending sleep) is usually decreased, whereas Stage II sleep (unequivocal nonREM sleep) is increased. Time spent in slow wave sleep or deep sleep (Stage III) and especially cerebral sleep (Stage IV) is decreased. REM sleep is altered, as indicated by an increase in REM latency, since the time spent in REM sleep is usually shortened and the number of cycles of REM sleep is often increased.

The benzodiazepines have been observed to have some effect on respiration but more so in hypnotic doses as they depress the response to CO_2. Sleep apnea can occur at longer intervals, whereas CO_2 narcosis can occur among individuals with chronic obstructive pulmonary disease.

In addition, although the benzodiazepines are used for their sedative and anxiolytic effects, in certain individuals, they have been shown to cause a paradoxic increase in agitation with accompanying restlessness, anxiety, and insomnia. Nursing implications include the potential for discomforting behavioral problems and insomnia that alters daytime functioning. Both of these problems can be attributed to the adverse side effects of medication. Nursing interventions include frequent monitoring for adverse side effects, among which include changes in memory, as well as pattern and level of daytime activity, including daytime napping; behavioral problems such as an increase in agitation or restlessness; and a new onset insomnia.

Pharmacologic Properties of Hypnotics in Relation to Sleep

The hypnotics cause depression of the CNS ranging from mild sedation to general anesthesia. Hypnotics generally decrease sleep latency and the number of stage shifts from falling asleep to Stage I. Hence, the number of nocturnal awakenings and amount of body movement decrease. Deep sleep (Stages III and IV) is typically reduced. This type of medication is often used by the primary care providers of older adults with frequent nocturnal awakenings. Older people may not understand expected age-related changes in sleep and therefore may take "a sleeping pill" in hopes of restoring their previous sleeping patterns. Health care providers must use caution in prescribing these drugs and must educate the older adult about normal, expected changes in sleep.

Antidepressants

Major depression is a disease affecting older adults that results in alteration in the sleep-wake cycle. The classic symptomatology is insomnia with early morning awakening. In older adults, however, excessive sleep may occur, as well as inability to fall asleep or stay asleep. Anxiety may be a predominant feature.

The most commonly prescribed antidepressants are included in the class of drugs called tricyclic antidepressants. These drugs exert some degree of sedation, ranging from mild to moderate to strong, depending on their chemical structures. As with other medication prescribed for older people, the degree of sedation is dose-dependent and also varies based on individual pharmacokinetic activity. Table 9-4 lists commonly used agents, sedative profiles, and dosages.

Like sedative-hypnotics, the effects of tricyclic and antidepressants on sleep include (1) reduction in the number of nocturnal awakenings, (2) increase in Stage IV sleep, and (3) markedly decreased time in REM sleep. Nursing implications for older clients who are prescribed a **tricyclic antidepressant** include the potential for orthostatic hypotension, falls, and constipation. Nursing interventions include monitoring for orthostatic hypotension and if it occurs, recommending discontinuation of the medication. Some tricyclic antidepressants are more potent than others in producing orthostasis. The older person's bowel habits must be carefully reviewed, since unrelieved constipation can lead to fecal impaction, ileus or bowel obstruction, sepsis, and even death. Typically, older people on tricyclic antidepressants are also given a prescription for an osmotic-type laxative for daily use. Bowel problems may progress quickly for

TABLE 9-4

Antidepressant Drugs*

Drug name	Class	Selected side effects
Asendin	Tricyclic	Drowsiness, TD, CNS Stimulant
Desyrel	Triazolopyridine	Drowsiness, dizziness EPS, CNS stimulant
Elavil	Tricyclic	Drowsiness, EPS Anticholinergic
Norpramin	Tricyclic	Drowsiness Anticholinergic
Pamelor	Tricyclic	Drowsiness, Anticholinergic Orthostatic hypotension
Paxil	SSRI	Drowsiness, dizziness Orthostatic hypotension
Prozac	SSRI	CNS stimulation Insomnia
Sinequan	Tricyclic	Drowsiness, EPS Anticholinergic
Zoloft	SSRI, insomnia	Anxiety, Somnolence

TD–Tardive dyskinesia
CNS–Central nervous system
EPS–Extrapyridimal side effects
SSRI–Selective Serotonin Reuptake Inhibitor
*This is only a partial listing of possible side effects for each drug

the older person who has a history of constipation, is on other medications that can cause constipation, or has a sedentary lifestyle with little physical mobility. Nursing interventions include forcing fluids, encouraging a high-fiber diet, promoting exercise or activity, evaluating with the physician the possibility of discontinuing other constipating agents, and establishing a regular toileting regimen. Other nursing interventions include monitoring of serum blood levels of these drugs for a therapeutic range. In older people, a relatively low dose may produce the desired therapeutic range. Nurses should reassess the client's progress on the antidepressant. If clinical observations, including client statements or professional observation of improved function, suggest that the client is feeling better, then the current dosage may not need to be adjusted.

Monoamine oxide inhibitors (MAOIs) are a class of antidepressants that have demonstrated the most profound effects on sleep. These drugs suppress REM sleep and have been used for the treatment of narcolepsy. The **Selective serotonin reuptake inhibitors (SSRI)** are a new class of antidepressants that seem to have infrequent adverse effects such as postural hypotension and falls. These drugs can, however, cause significant adverse effects among which include gastrointestinal disturbances (e.g., loss of appetite), insomnia, somnolence, agitation, and nervousness. Nursing interventions are directed at monitoring for adverse side effects, weight, and oral intake (when appropriate) as well as assessing for improvement in depression. If sleep disturbances occur from a nighttime dosing regimen, the physician should be notified; these drugs can be given during the daytime, which may help the older adult sleep better at night.

Antipsychotics

Psychosis may occur from a variety of diseases. Among older people, these most notably include dementing illnesses (e.g., Alzheimer's disease [AD]) with associated psychotic features and psychiatric illnesses such as chronic schizophrenia, obsessive-compulsive disorder, and paraphrenia. Among older adults, AD is the fourth leading cause of death in the United States. It has been estimated that nearly 50% to 60% of nursing home populations have dementia. Federal and state regulations have sought to curtail the previously wide-spread use of antipsychotics, which may be disruptive to the older adult or may cause treatment interference that can be life-threatening for behaviors other than psychosis. Antipsychotic drugs alleviate symptoms of hallucinations, delusions, agitation, and paranoia. They cause significant side effects such as parkinsonism and irreversible side effects such as **akathesia** (motor restlessness), **tardive dyskinesia (TD),** and **dystonia** (spasm of muscles), all of which can be debilitating. Because of such effects, these drugs are usually the last option chosen in behavioral management. Antipsychotics normalize sleep disturbances associated with psychotic states.

The nurse needs to monitor the client receiving antipsychotics for gait abnormalities, ranging from a parkinsonian gait to inability to initiate motion; swallowing difficulties; increased agitation; postural hypotension; and falls. Once any of these adverse effects occur, the drug must be discontinued. Nursing interventions include close monitoring of mobility for any changes, even mild ones, which may include the inability to stand from a seated position or to walk; slowness of movement, which alters functional ability (e.g., basic self-care skills like grooming, toileting, feeding, transferring or continence); dizziness with standing up; or falls. Tremors may also occur, which can affect the person's lifestyle in relation to basic self-care skills, as well as cooking, driving, shopping or writing. Increased drooling, as well as dysphagia and other swallowing difficulties, may develop. Dysphagia can interfere with adequate hydration and nutrition and can also be implicated in asphyxiation. Careful monitoring of weight, dietary intake, and ability to drink liquids should commence once dysphagia is reported. On physical examination, the nurse should assess the older client for tremors, gait, balance, rigidity of muscles, and the presence or absence of a gag reflex. Significant findings should be reported to the physician. A geropsychiatrist can evaluate the older client for possible use of other agents with less adverse side effects.

> ***Insight* • *Some antipsychotics and many anticholinergic medications should be avoided in older adults whenever possible, since the medications can worsen confusion, can increase agitation, and can alter the sleep-wake cycle.***

Alcohol

Alcoholic beverages, perhaps the most well-known CNS depressants, have been used for centuries to cloud consciousness and to promote sleep. Alcohol in moderate amounts causes respiratory depression and produces slowing of the alpha waves of the brain. Sleep apnea has also been associated with alcohol ingestion.

Alcoholism continues to be a poorly recognized disease among older adults. Alcohol abuse and dependency in people over age 65 occurs in 2% to 5% of men and about 1% of women (Blazer, 1990). Many adults include alcohol as a part of their normal lifestyle and continue to do so in advancing age. They continue to enjoy a glass of wine or sherry with an evening meal, or an occasional beer or mixed drink. Using alcohol with other prescription or over-the-counter (OTC) medications can increase the effects of the medication. The sedative-hypnotics, antidepressants and antipsychotics are all drugs that contraindicate the concomitant use of alcohol. Chronic, excessive use of alcohol causes memory loss, sleep disturbances, and psychoses. Nursing assessment includes quantifying the amount, frequency, and pattern of alcohol use; the use of prescription and OTC medications; and sleeping habits, including amount and quality of sleep. During an environmental assessment of the home, the nurse should determine the presence and type of alcohol available to the client at home.

SLEEP DISORDERS AND CONDITIONS INFLUENCING SLEEP

Sleep disorders occur more commonly among older people than younger adults, especially among institutionalized older adults. Sleep disorders are disruptive to the individual and family. Older people with insomnia may get out of bed to engage in an activity that they may believe promotes sleep, or they may engage in an activity until they develop a sense of fatigue. These activities may interrupt other family members' sleep and may result in insomnia. In addition, sleep disorders are often underdiagnosed or haphazardly treated with a prescription drug that is inappropriate for the older adult's use. Sleep disorders in older people have treatable causes and therefore care must be taken with establishing a diagnosis. Many sleep disorders in older people are transitional and reflect significant events such as stress, diagnosis of disease, loss of a loved one (including a pet), or inappropriate medication use.

Sleep disorders that can lead to insomnia among older adults include sleep apnea, restless leg syndrome, periodic limb movement, motor restlessness, sundown syndrome associated with dementia, circadian rhythm disorders, narcolepsy, and drug-induced disorders. Differential diagnoses of insomnia seek to determine if the difficulty in sleeping is (1) falling asleep or sleep onset insomnia, (2) sleep maintenance insomnia, or (3) early morning awakenings. Causes of insomnia include medications, alcohol, disease, psychologic problems, environmental issues, or travel across time zones. Pollack (1991) and colleagues have found impressive implications of sleep disorders among community-dwelling older adults. In older adult men, insomnia was found to be predictive of both institutionalization and death. In older adult women, however, insomnia had less of an impact and was viewed as a common occurrence.

Sleep Apnea

Apnea is a term describing "cessation of breathing." Individuals with **sleep apnea** do not breathe properly during sleep and therefore may not get enough oxygen when sleeping. There are characteristically recurrent episodes of apnea or hypoventilation during sleep. The degree of sleep apnea may vary from mild to severe forms in which depression, congestive heart failure, cardiac arrhythmia, cardiac arrest, or high blood pressure may develop. It is common for normal individuals to have apnea during sleep, especially if they are heavy snorers.

There are two major types of sleep apnea. Central apnea occurs when both airflow and respiratory efforts are absent. Although central apnea occurs more often, the more dangerous type is obstructive sleep apnea. In this condition, there are repetitive episodes of upper airway obstruction in which respiratory efforts persist, although airflow through the nose and mouth is absent. Complete cessation of breathing for more than 10 seconds during sleep occurs, while diaphragmatic efforts persist to overcome the obstruction. As a result, profound oxygen desaturation occurs, leading to sudden death, cardiac arrhythmia, and other life-threatening sequelae. The Pickwickian syndrome is a type of obstructive apnea that is accompanied by obesity and classically leads to heart failure if not treated. Approximately 80% of individuals with obstructive sleep apnea have hypertension and a higher amount of body fat.

In older adults, sleep apnea is a well-established sleep disorder with a high morbidity and mortality, ranging from 18% to 73%. It occurs more often among middle-aged men (Fleury, 1992). Fleury (1992) also found that a high apnea and hypopnea index are ominous predictors of mortality in the older adult population and that a very high level of sleep-disordered breathing is an extremely significant risk factor for mortality during the sleep

EMERGENCY TREATMENT

Sleep Apnea

If obstructive sleep apnea is suspected:

Assess client for the following:

- Level of consciousness
- Rate and regularity of breathing
- Loud snoring
- Position in bed
- History of obesity
- History of hypertension

If apnea occurs for prolonged periods:

- Awaken the client and turn to his or her side (if supine) or onto the stomach.
- Monitor blood pressure.
- Monitor heart rate and regularity.
- Encourage weight loss.
- Encourage elimination of alcohol, sedative-hypnotic agents.
- If CPAP is applied, ensure correct application.

phase of these clients (see Emergency Treatment box, p. 234).

Because of the differences in respiratory control during REM sleep, problems with sleep apnea are more likely to occur during REM sleep. Physiologic changes during apnea include a decrease in oxygen saturation and an increase in carbon dioxide levels. Symptomatology includes loud snoring, morning fatigue, excessive daytime sleepiness, grogginess or a dull feeling in the morning, headaches, depression, and cognitive impairment on awakening. Evaluation includes overnight polysomnography, oximetry, or sleep latency testing. Treatment includes conventional measures of cessation of sedative-hypnotic agents and alcohol, weight loss, sleeping on one's side or in prone position, continuous positive airway pressure (CPAP), tongue retaining devices, tracheostomy, or medications (see nursing Care Plan, p. 236-237).

Sleep-related Respiratory Disturbance

Sleep-disordered breathing has been observed to occur among healthy older adults in the absence of disease. It has been found to increase with advancing age, at least to age 60 (Rosenthal et al, 1992). Roughly 35% of asymptomatic people over age 65 have more than five periods of apnea (mostly central apnea) per hour. Hoch et al. (1990) noted the incidence of apnea-hypopnea to be highest among 80-year-olds (39.9%), versus 33.3% among 70-year-olds and 2.9% among 60-year-olds. Apnea (as defined by five or more apneic episodes per hour of sleep) was 18.9% among those in their 80s, 12.1% among those in their 70s and 0% among those in their 60s. These findings underscore the increased frequency of sleep-disordered breathing among healthy older people. In addition to sleep-disordered breathing, snoring has been shown to increase with age. Snoring may be disruptive to family members' sleep, and if significant, can impair gaseous exchange in the respiratory tree.

Family members may be the only ones reporting a history of snoring, because the snoring person may be unaware of his or her disruption.

Restless Leg Syndrome and Periodic Leg Movements In Sleep

Research has shown that periodic leg movements are much more common in older adults than are sleep-related respiratory disorders. In one study, about 45% of the independently living over-65 population met the criteria for periodic leg movement, among which included nocturnal myoclonus (Ancoli-Israel, 1991). Medical problems that may be possible causes of periodic leg movements include diseases of the spine, degenerative joint disease of the disks with narrowing of the lumbar-sacral region, peripheral vascular disease, and iron deficiency anemia. Nurses should question older adults about the presence of pain in the legs when sleeping. The administration of analgesia may have little effect on nocturnal myoclonus.

Restless leg syndrome, a type of periodic leg movement, also appears to be more common with advancing age (Phoha et al, 1990). This is a condition in which the client has leg twitching or discomfort that is exacerbated with rest and relieved with movement. Diagnosis is made by history and polysomnogram. Drugs used to treat this disorder include the benzodiazepines, particularly clonazepam, and more recently, L-Dopa. Horiguchi (1992) and colleagues found a significant decrease in the total number of leg movements and the number of leg movements per hour with the administered dosage of clonazepam as 0.5 to 1.5 mg PO. In addition, all clients given this treatment had improved subjective complaints. Nursing interventions include obtaining a sleep history from the client's bed partner when appropriate to detect this problem. Typically, clients have restless leg syndrome as they fall asleep and are aware of the problem, but sometimes, it may occur while they are sleeping and may go unnoticed by the client. Once treatment has been initiated, nurses need to monitor the effects of the medication used.

CHANGES IN SLEEP AMONG THOSE WITH DEMENTIA

In AD, loss of intellectual function occurs as a result of neurofibrillary tangles, plaques and cell loss, as well as reductions in neurotransmitter substances such as choline acetyltransferase. Relationships between neurotransmitter substances and REM sleep have been documented in both animal and human studies. In some studies, REM sleep has been suggested to be decreased in dementia. Most research has found a diffuse slowing of EEG activity, especially of the delta and theta waves (Bliwise, 1993). One study has found a correlation between diffuse EEG slowing in AD, and pathology-verified amyloid plaques and neurofibrillary tangles (Mueller, 1978).

Sundown Syndrome

Dementia-related behavioral problems typically occur as a result of neuronal damage, making it difficult for the person to make sense of the environment. One of the classic behavioral problems, which usually indicates the diagnosis of dementia is **sundowning** or **sundown syndrome.** Sundowning has been observed among clients with dementia who developed increasing confusion as the "sun went down," as there was less light and environmental stimuli. As darkness ensues, changes occur in the clients and their interactions with the environment. Clients who have difficulty functioning in their environments are observed to have even greater difficulty with less light, people, and familiar sounds. Previ-

CARE PLAN

SLEEP PATTERN DISTURBANCE

Clinical situation Mr. B is a 78-year-old single white male who is admitted to the nursing home for convalescence following a tracheotomy for obstructive sleep apnea. He was living alone before hospitalization on the third floor of an apartment complex for older adults. He describes himself as limited in activities such as driving, traveling, and cooking because of respiratory distress. He reports daytime fatigue associated with grooming, dressing, feeding, and toileting. He admits to sleeping poorly with several nighttime awakenings and general fatigue all day long, which prompts him to take a daytime nap.

Past medical history includes hypertension, obesity, chronic obstructive pulmonary disease, severe peripheral vascular disease with a Stage II venous stasis ulcer of the lower leg, and recent tracheotomy for obstructive sleep apnea.

While at the nursing home, Mr. B tells you that he plans on discharging himself home in 1 to 2 weeks. He is observed to need assistance in mobility and uses a wheelchair to wheel himself around his room. He refuses to go to the dining room but requests to have a refrigerator in his room. He eats all of his meals in his room and rarely socializes with any resident or staff member. His pasttimes include playing solitaire in his room and watching television. He is a retired salesman, having worked in the business for more than 40 years.

Nursing diagnosis	Outcomes	Interventions
Sleep pattern disturbance related to obesity and reduced activity level	Client will identify personal lifestyle habits contributing to sleep pattern disturbance. Client will achieve weight loss of 1 lb/week. Client will eat a well-balanced diet, as evidenced by food diary. Client will participate in one group activity/day. Client will walk 100 feet twice daily, increasing distance to tolerance. Client will report increased length of uninterrupted periods of sleep.	Teach relationship between weight and sleep pattern, and importance of losing weight to improve sleep pattern. Explore motivators with client to lose weight; reinforce as needed. Conduct total caloric intake and expenditure of calories using the basal energy expenditure (BEE) formula then discuss with client ideal body weight and goals of weight reduction Teach food pyramid and assist in identifying nutritious foods. Teach use of food diary for self-monitoring. Offer nutritious foods as snacks. Encourage client to increase level of activity on the unit by increasing mobility and engaging in nonsedentary activities; review list of available activities with client. Offer to accompany client on a walk on the unit to his tolerance at least twice a day to help with wound healing and weight reduction. Introduce client to fellow residents in the unit who share common interests. Encourage client to join other residents in activities to tolerance. Explore with client his likes or dislikes, previous hobbies, and level of activity during middle adulthood. Schedule an activity with the client that will be part of his daily routine. Discourage daytime napping; instead, replace it with a stimulating activity. Teach client to monitor pulse, to watch for symptoms of respiratory distress when engaging in activities on the unit, and to stop if respiratory distress occurs or increase in heart rate causes adverse symptoms.

CARE PLAN

SLEEP PATTERN DISTURBANCE—cont'd

Nursing diagnosis	Outcomes	Interventions
		Offer praise and positive reinforcement when he performs a non-sedentary activity and when weight loss is achieved. Observe client during sleep for signs of obstructive apnea such as loud snoring or periods of apnea. Observe for daytime fatigue and somnolence. Encourage client to assume a side-lying position for sleep. Discuss with client plans for discharge and explore alternative living arrangements, which can include residence on a first floor apartment, especially if mobility is impaired.

ous research by Evans (1987) notes that institutionalized clients with sundowning have experienced recent room transfers and incontinence.

Sundowning has been defined as the differential nocturnal exacerbation of disruptive behaviors and agitation (Bliwise, 1993). Some have described sundowning as a nocturnal form of delirium. Delirium is hallmarked by changes in the sleep-wake cycle, level of alertness, and other psychotic features such as delusions, hallucinations, and paranoia. Indeed, anecdotal observations reveal that people with sundowning do take on delirium-like features, but unlike delirium, which is viewed as a treatable medical emergency, sundowning tends to follow a daily chronic pattern that has no "treatable," or reversible, characteristics.

Sundowning can be modified by behavioral interventions that include redirecting the person, providing companionship and empathy, improving sensory conditions such as lighting, reducing noise, and attending to the client's basic physiologic needs. It is still unclear, however, if sundowning can be prevented unless basic needs are met. According to Maslow, the basic physiologic needs include comfort, elimination, hunger or thirst, oxygenation, and sexuality. Following a step-wise progression, clients should be assessed for any of these potential alterations and then offered remedies. For example, those who are restless, pacing, and possibly exhausted may be sundowning as a result of thirst, hunger, or the need to eliminate. Because of dementia, it does not occur to clients to seek basic necessities or to report discomfort. Offering the client food or fluids may be the only step necessary to reduce sundowning. Keeping clients dry and free from urine and fecal matter can aid in comfort. Likewise, clients in pain may be in need of analgesia or other soothing devices (see Emergency Treatment box, below).

Unfortunately, the exact cause of sundowning is unclear, and the treatment rests on an individualized "trial-and-error" approach. Medications should be avoided unless psychosis accompanies the sundowning. Medications that can be applied include anxiolytic agents such as the benzodiazepines, antidepressants, antipsychotics

EMERGENCY TREATMENT

Sundowning

If sundowning occurs among older people with dementia, assess the client for the following:

- Hunger
- Thirst
- Pain
- Discomfort
- Need to eliminate
- Safety/security needs
- Love/belonging needs

Nursing interventions include the following:

- Maintain continence
- Maintain comfort
- Control pain with nonpharmacologic measures (back rub, moist heat, touch) and nonnarcotic analgesia such as Tylenol or aspirin
- Ensure privacy
- Promote individuality
- Provide diversion and distraction through the use of touch or music

and antiseizure drugs. However, most of these have significant side effects in older adults, which can worsen confusion, increase agitation, alter the sleep-wake cycle or cause undesirable side effects like akathesia and TD.

MANAGEMENT OF SLEEP DISORDERS

Successful management of sleep disorders is contingent on accurate diagnosis, which begins with history taking, observation, administration of measurement tools to assess quality and quantity of sleep, and diagnostic studies such as EEG monitoring and sleep study evaluation. Basic sleep hygiene can aid in improving sleep (Box 9-1.)

Components of the Sleep History

A complete sleep history begins with the client's self-report of sleep pattern and sleep-related problems encountered. The quality of sleep is usually described along a continuum of poor, fair, good, or excellent. The quantity of sleep refers to the amount of sleep in a 24-hour period, including daytime naps. Quantity may be difficult to calculate, especially in the client with frequent nocturnal awakenings who cannot recall if sleep occurred after the awakening. The nurse should elicit when the client retires for bed, falls asleep, and usually awakens. The number of nocturnal awakenings and length of time awake at night are important to review with the client. If a client retires at 9 PM, does not fall asleep until 11 PM, arises at 4 AM, and takes a daytime nap from 4 PM to 5 PM daily, then this individual has slept a total of 6 hours. Information about a person's typical bedtime rituals or practices should be obtained as well.

The older adult is likely to seek additional help in achieving satisfaction with sleeping habits. If the older adult is too tired or fatigued to perform normal activities, then the sleep problem may be viewed as disruptive to the daily routine and may require further evaluation. The nurse should ascertain if the older adult experiences daytime sleepiness or has a strong desire to take a nap.

A client's activities before bedtime and exercise or activity pattern provide additional information about sleep habits. In general, strenuous activity should be avoided at least 2 hours before bedtime. The nurse should identify what type of activities the client does to relax before bedtime. This may include reading or drinking a warm beverage. The nurse should question the client having difficulty with sleep about the consumption of alcohol, caffeinated beverages, sedative-hypnotics, sleeping pills, and other practices before bedtime.

Questions about the type of bed in which the person sleeps are also important. Does the client sleep in the same bed every night? Is it comfortable? Is the mattress soft or unsupportive? Some individuals who are unable to sleep in a recumbent position because of medical problems may actually sleep semirecumbent in a lounge chair. Clients who are unable to fall asleep supine and who need several pillows or cushions in bed require further medical evaluation for heart failure, pulmonary disease, or musculoskeletal problems. Chronic obstructive pulmonary disease, rheumatologic problems such as osteoporosis; degenerative joint disease of the spine, hips, or neck; and rheumatoid arthritis are common problems that cause pain and discomfort in bed. Older men with prostatic enlargement need to urinate in the middle of the night (nocturia). Nocturia often occurs several times in the course of one night and therefore must be further evaluated. People with congestive heart failure or urinary tract infections may also have nocturia.

BOX 9-1

Nursing Interventions to Promote Sleep

- Darken the environment
- Promote a noise-free environment
- Play soft music
- Avoid alcohol, sleeping pills, and other soporific drugs in older adults

Administer the following:

- Warm beverages
- Warm bath
- Rocking chair
- Use of touch
- Stress-reduction techniques
- Back rub
- Activity 2 to 3 hours before sleep

Evaluation of Sleep Disorders

In evaluating sleep disorders, a client must recall the amount of sleep, habits, and possible symptoms over a 24-hour period. Information entered into a sleep diary can be quantifiable. The client keeps a diary detailing events of his or her sleep, including type and quantity of activity during a 24-hour period. The nurse should assist the older person in completing the sleep diary or should enlist the assistance of a family member if necessary. The nurse can suggest measures such as tape recording entries to help clients with visual impairment enter diary information. Calendars help individuals with memory impairment as well.

Sleep laboratories specialize in treating clients with primary sleep disorders. Clients are asked to spend the night so that a sleep study can be administered. This often includes a polysomnogram, which provides data about the stages of sleep and ventilation, and an EEG for graphic tracing of the variations in the brain's electric force. Physicians specially trained in sleep disorders evaluate the history and objective findings to arrive at a diagnosis and treatment plan, which will include a review of basic sleep hygienic measures.

Sleep Hygiene

Basic sleep hygiene refers to activities that foster normal sleep and that individuals can practice on a routine basis to achieve normal sleep. Retiring the same time every night and waking at the same time every morning help establish a routine. A client can condition himself or herself to such a routine over time. Likewise, limiting the amount of time spent in bed to only the time spent sleeping establishes a routine for sleep. Retiring in the same location such as the bedroom and not a couch or chair on some nights, also helps solidify the routine.

Eliminating noise and creating a darkened environment promotes sleep. Avoiding caffeinated beverages, sleeping pills, and alcohol can reduce the chances of sleep-related breathing disorders. The basic measures to help reduce episodes of sleep apnea include losing weight, sleeping on one's side or stomach, avoiding CNS depressants such as sedative-hypnotics and alcohol, and treating any obvious nasal or upper airway diseases (see Client/Family Teaching box below).

CLIENT/FAMILY TEACHING

Basic Sleep Hygiene Practices

- Retire at the same time each night, and arise at the same time each morning.
- Conduct typical bedtime rituals, and do what naturally helps you unwind.
- Retire to your bed; do not fall asleep on the couch or in a recliner and then go to bed.
- Do not nap during the daytime.
- Incorporate a daily exercise routine, but perform any exercise at least 3 hours before bedtime.
- Use your bedroom and bed only for sleep; if unable to sleep, get up and move to another area to perform other activities.
- Create an atmosphere that promotes relaxation and comfort; this is highly individualized. In general, eliminate loud noise and bright light. If reading or listening to soft music helps you relax, do so for only a brief period.
- Avoid eating a heavy meal, drinking caffeinated beverages, taking sleeping pills, and drinking alcohol before bedtime.
- A warm beverage sometimes promotes sleep, especially warm milk. Warm milk contains tryptophan, an amino acid that is a precursor of serotonin, which is believed to promote sleep.

Nursing Interventions

Nursing interventions include educating clients about lifestyle modifications, diet, measures to promote sleep hygiene, normal age-related changes in sleep, changes as a result of disease, and side effects of medications that may be soporific. Environmental changes in the home may be easier to accomplish than in a nursing care facility. The nurse should first determine the cause of sleep problems and then follow a systematic approach for intervention. Many sleep disorders and significant lifestyle changes can be managed so that older adults need not suffer.

ACTIVITY IN OLDER ADULTS

Activity is a function of all human beings that may decline with advancing age as a direct result of physiologic age-related changes, and functional changes from lifestyle, disease, medications, and environmental conditions. Although research is not conclusive, age-related changes in activity may be attributed to changes in basal metabolic rate (BMR). BMR has been shown to decrease linearly with age and is related to a decline in skeletal muscle mass (Shimokata, Kuzuya, 1993). However, there are marathon runners who are in their ninth or tenth decade of life.

Among institutionalized older adults, constraints on activity are more commonplace as a result of many iatrogenic conditions that result in immobility. Physical or cognitive impairments can limit the older resident's participation in activities. For example, an older individual with moderate dementia of the Alzheimer's type would have difficulty participating in a current events discussion. Activities in long-term care settings must therefore be developed for individuals with various diseases and at various stages. Assessment of cognition is essential to make an appropriate selection of a particular group activity. Box 9-2 suggests some common activities for institutionalized older adults.

Nursing implications include reducing the incidence of immobility; preventing iatrogenic problems, and if they do occur, detecting them early; unnecessary use of medications; promoting independence; reducing the incidence of learned helplessness; offering hope and reassurance; and becoming an effective advocate. Improvement in all of these areas can help the older resident participate more often and more appropriately in different types of activities.

Among healthy older adults, activity patterns clearly change over the decades, although interest usually remains unchanged. How an older adult views his or her activity level may be determined subjectively according to the older adult's perception of health and well-being. For example, a sedentary older woman who spends most

BOX 9-2

Activities for Institutionalized Older Adults

Group activities	Games	Crafts	Individual activities
Dancing*	Cards†	Woodworking†	Reading†
Singing*	Playing the piano/instruments†	Painting†	Writing†
Cooking/baking	Checkers†	Stenciling†	Walking*
Gardening	Chess†	Knitting/crochet†	Listening to music‡
Shopping	Bingo†	Needlework†	
Day trips			
Exercise in a group*			
Caring for a pet			
Reminiscent groups†			
Current event discussion groups†			
Swimming (if facilities are available)			
Ball toss‡			
Sensory stimulation groups‡			
Movies†			

*Activities appropriate for older adults with moderate-to-severe dementia
†Sedentary activities
‡Sedentary activities appropriate for older adults with moderate-to-severe dementia

of her time in her room at home because of poor vision and an immobilizing degenerative joint disease may truly view herself as "active," since she is still able to attend to her basic needs. She may not view herself as limited in activity, since she can no longer drive; instead, she views herself as active, since she can still focus on her remaining capabilities. However, asking her to compare her activity level today with how active she was 5 years ago may reveal some substantial differences.

Observation of activity is therefore the most likely objective determinant of a person's degree of activity. Many measurement tools exist to help quantify an older adult's participation in physical and social activity. Table 9-5 provides a partial list of common activities and energy expenditures among noninstitutionalized older adults.

Exercise is a universal activity that has beneficial effects for older adults. Research has proven that exercise can affect the psychologic well-being of older adults and can increase bone mineral density. Additional studies show that exercise may have a role in improving a number of sensorimotor systems and contribute to stability, balance, reaction time, and muscular strength and may help prevent falls in older women (Lord, Caplan, Ward, 1993). Tai Chi, a martial art, is practiced daily in the People's Republic of China as an energizing and relaxing activity for older adults. It involves dance-like, opposing body movements (McNeely, Clements, Wolf, 1992). Table 9-6 provides an estimation of energy needs based on calculation of **basal energy expenditure (BEE).**

Activity is determined by a person's state of health—both physical and mental. Individuals with chronic diseases that influence their functional abilities are likely to have limited activity (Table 9-7). Likewise, those with dementia, depression, or mental illness may be limited in activity performance.

TABLE 9-5

Activities and Amount of Energy Expended

Activity	Metabolism (ratio to basal)
Brisk walking (3.5 mph)	5.2
Sewing	1.6
Playing piano	2.5 to 3.5
Bicycling (slowly)	3.0
Running	7.4
Mowing lawn	9.0

From Kottke FJ: *Therapeutic exercises to maintain mobility.* In Kottke FJ, Stillwell GK, Lehmann JF, editors, *Krusen's handbook of phyical medicine and rehabilitation,* 3, 1982, WB Saunders.

The role of the gerontologic nurse in educating older adults about appropriate activities is an essential one. The prevention of iatrogenic problems such as falls is also a part of health promotion and disease prevention. Activity history taking should focus on any changes in activity and the client's perception of such changes affecting his or her lifestyle. The amount, duration and frequency of activity, including the client's baseline and current level of activity, type of activity, and any support such as a visual aid or other assistive device are important for the nurse to determine about each client.

Activities need not involve physical mobility. Activities may be sedentary, such as those that are psychologically stimulating—reading, writing, drawing, painting, or play-

TABLE 9-6

Estimation of Energy Needs

Basal energy expenditure (BEE)

Women

BEE = 655 + (9.6 × weight in kg) + (1.7 × height in cm) − (4.7 × age in years)

Men

BEE = 66 + (13.7 × weight in kg) + (5 × height in cm) − (6.8 × age in years)

Add to BEE for activity:
- 20% Sedentary
- 35% Moderately active
- 50% Active

Add to BEE for stress:
- 10% to 15% Uncomplicated elective surgery
- 20% to 40% Complicated surgery or fractures
- 50% to 100% Major burns

Add to BEE for fever:
- 13% degree centigrade over 37°C (98.6°F)

Add to BEE for growth:
- 5% Moderate weight loss
- 10% to 15% Severe weight loss

From Harris JA, Benedict FG: *A biometric study of basal metabolism in man,* Washington DC, 1919, Carnegie Institution of Washington.

A

B

Fig. 9-1 Recreational activities, performed individually or in a group, are important for older adults. (**A,** Courtesy Loy Ledbetter, St. Louis, Mo; **B,** From Sorrentino SA: *Mosby's textbook for nursing assistants,* ed 3, St. Louis, 1992, Mosby.)

TABLE 9-7

Common Conditions Among Older Adults that Can Influence Functional Ability

Disease	Presenting Problem
Emphysema	Dyspnea on exertion
Diabetes mellitus	Decreased vision or sensation in lower extremities; orthostatic hypotension
Congestive heart failure	Shortness of breath
Aortic stenosis	Falls, light-headedness or angina
Carotid stenosis	Light-headedness with quick movement
Cerebrovascular accident	Unilateral weakness or neglect
Degenerative joints	Pain in joints with motion
Hip fracture	Pain with mobility
Cataract	Visual distortions
Dementia	Visual-spatial deficits
Urinary Incontinence	Embarrassment during activity and or accident

Gray-Miceli D: Evaluating the older patient's ability to function, *J Am Acad Nurs Pract* 5:4, 167-174, 1993.

ing a musical instrument. Activities may be performed in private or with larger groups (Fig. 9-1). The individual may need transportation to those activities outside the home. For those residing in the community, older people may need to be informed about the location of community activities. Nursing intervention includes informing the older person about local community agencies. The Area Agency on Aging and other national organizations such as the American Association for Retired Persons (AARP) host many community activities from trips, elderhostels, and educational seminars, to dances and other types of social get-togethers (see Research box, p. 242).

Summary

Activities are a normal part of a person's lifestyle, whether they are sedentary or nonsedentary. Amount of

RESEARCH

Gueldner SH, Spradley J: Outdoor walking lowers fatigue, *J Gerontol Nurs* 14(10):6-12, 1988.

Sample, setting

Of 32 ambulatory, mentally alert residents, 16 resided in an urban nursing home and 16 resided in a retirement village.

Methodology

A modified Solomon-Four design was used with a secondary control group that was posttested only. Subjects asked to complete questionnaires about self-perceived fatigue, information about sleep, activity, and appetite.

Findings

Nursing home residents who participated in a 3-week walking regimen felt significantly less fatigued than both their counterparts in the retirement village and in the control group, who did not walk. Nursing home residents also slept better and had better appetites than retirement home residents.

Implications

Outdoor walking is an inexpensive, readily accessible activity, perceived by nursing home residents to lower fatigue. Less fatigue means the potential for higher levels of activity, which can improve sleep. Outdoor walking also increases socialization and sunlight exposure, which can help treat osteoporosis.

HOME CARE TIPS

- Assess high risk factors (e.g., environment, pain, or equipment such as a foley catheter) that would predispose a homebound older adult to sleep disturbances.
- Identify medications such as nasal decongestants or theophylline that may interfere with the homebound older adult's sleep pattern.
- Instruct caregivers and homebound older adults on activities that would foster normal sleep, such as avoidance of caffeinated beverages and alcohol.
- Assist caregivers and homebound older adults with environmental changes that would foster normal sleep, such as using a rocking chair or giving a warm bath.

activity often depends on sleep. To achieve relaxation and comfort, activities should be pleasurable for the individual. The types of activities in which a person engages during older adulthood is determined by many factors such as likes or dislikes, previous hobbies, occupation, education, personality, family responsibilities, financial resources, and accessibility. The nurse's role is to facilitate appropriate activity whenever possible.

Key Points

- Breathing during REM sleep is less sensitive to chemoreceptor stimuli so that arterial P_{CO_2} can rise between 40 mm Hg to 46 mm Hg.
- More frequent nocturnal awakenings and a decrease in sleep efficiency are normal age-related changes requiring client education.
- Daytime napping occurs more often with older adults, which can influence the quality and quantity of nocturnal sleep.
- Diets high in xanthine derivatives cause sleeplessness, since they are CNS stimulants.
- Excessive caffeine results in restlessness, nervousness, insomnia, an increase in heart rate, and a decrease in peripheral vascular resistance.
- Older adults are often prescribed medications for sleep, which can actually compound the underlying sleep problem.
- Sleep disorders have been estimated to occur in more than 50% of older adults. Common causes include sleep apnea, restless leg syndrome, and sundowning as a result of dementia.
- Sleep apnea in older adult men causes a high rate of morbidity and mortality. It results in profound desaturation of oxygen, which can lead to cardiac arrhythmia or sudden death.
- Soporific environments are those with low levels of stimuli such as dimmed lights, soft music, or quiet, comfortable furniture.
- Pain in the older adult is an important risk factor for sleeplessness.
- Social changes such as widowhood can significantly alter an older person's sleep pattern.
- Medical problems are often the cause of periodic leg movements in older adults.
- Sundowning is a behavioral manifestation of dementia, especially in AD, which can lead to sleeplessness. It can be modified by meeting the client's basic needs, providing companionship, reducing noise, and providing comfort.
- Activity is a normal part of daily living. Disturbances in maintaining activity occur in the older adult and typically are a result of functional limitations, medications, disease, and lack of accessibility to resources.

Critical Thinking Exercises

1. While making rounds on your assigned clients during the middle of the night, you note that your 74-year-old female client is awake and restless. What information should you obtain from your client regarding her inability to sleep? How could offering her a sedative actually compound her inability to sleep? What alternatives to medication can you suggest to her?
2. Sedatives, hypnotics, and antidepressants are often prescribed for adult clients. How do the effects of these drugs differ when given to older adult clients? What concerns should the nurse have when administering such drugs to older adult clients?

REFERENCES

Allen T: Sleepless in Seattle . . . and San Francisco . . ., *Adv Nurse Practition* 2:4, 26-31, 1994.

Ancoli-Israel S et al: Periodic limb movements in sleep in community dwelling elderly, *Sleep* 14:486-495, 1991.

Blazer DG: Alcohol abuse and dependence. In *The Merck manual of geriatrics,* 1990, Merck Sharp & Dohme Research Laboratories.

Bliwise DL: Sleep in normal aging and dementia, *Sleep* 16(1):40-81, 1993.

Buysse DJ et al: Quantification of subjective sleep quality in healthy elderly men and women using the Pittsburgh sleep quality index, *Sleep* 14:331-338, 1991.

Department of Health and Human Services, Food and Drug Administration: *Drug utilization in the United States,* 1985, The Department.

Evans LK: Sundown syndrome in institutionalized elderly, *J Am Geriatr Soc* 35:101-108, 1987.

Fleury B: Sleep apnea syndrome in the elderly, *Sleep* 15:S39-S41, 1992.

Fox SI: *Human physiology,* Dubuque, Ia., 1984, Wm C Brown.

Gorbien MJ: When your older patient can't sleep: how to put insomnia to rest, *Geriatrics* 48(9):65-75, 1993.

Harvey SC: Hypnotics and sedatives. In *Goodman and Gilman's the pharmacological basis of therapeutics,* ed 6, New York, 1980, Macmillan.

Herr KA, Mobily PR: Complexities of pain assessment in the elderly clinical considerations, *J Gerontolog Nurs* 17:4, 12–19, 1991.

Hoch CC et al: Comparison of sleep-disordered breathing among healthy elderly in the seventh, eighth, and ninth decades of life, *Sleep* 13(6):502-511, 1990.

Horiguchi J et al: Periodic leg movements in sleep with restless legs syndrome: Effect of Clonazepam Treatment, *Jpn J Psychiatry Neurol* 46(3):727-732, 1992.

Johnson JE: Progressive relaxation and the sleep of older noninstitutionalized women, *Appl Nurs Res* 4(4):165-170, 1991.

Kolanowski AM: The clinical importance of environmental lighting to the elderly, *J Gerontolog Nurs* 18:1, 10-14, 1992.

Lord SR, Caplan GA, Ward JA: Balance, reaction time, and muscular strength in exercising and nonexercising older women: a pilot study, *Arch Phys Med Rehab* 74(8):837-839, 1993.

McNeely E, Clements SD, Wolf S: A program to reduce frailty in the elderly. In Funk SG et al, editors: *Key aspects of elder care,* New York, 1992, Springer.

Monk TH et al: Rhythmic versus homeostatic influences on mood, activation and performance in the elderly, *J Gerontol* 47:221-227, 1992.

Mueller HF, Schwartz G: Electroencephalograms and autopsy findings in geropsychiatry, *J Gerontol* 33:504-513, 1978.

Phoha RL, Dickel MJ, Mosko SS: Preliminary longitudinal sleep in the elderly, *Sleep* 13(5):425-429, 1990.

Pollack CP, Perlick D: Sleep problems and institutionalization of the elderly, *J Geriatr Psychiatry Neurol* 4:204-210, 1991.

Rall TW: Central nervous system stimulants: the xanthines. In *Goodman and Gilman's the pharmacological basis of therapeutics,* ed 6, New York, 1980, Macmillan.

Rosenthal LD, Roehrs TA, Roth T: Nature of sleep disorders in the elderly. In Kuna ST, Suratt PM, Remmers JE, editors: *Sleep and respiration in aging adults,* New York, 1992, Elsevier Science Publishing.

Shimokata H, Kuzuya F: Aging, basal metabolic rate, and nutrition, *Jpn J Geriatr* 30(7):572-576, 1993.

US Bureau of the Census: *Statistical abstract of the United States,* 1985, The Bureau.

Webster's Ninth New Collegiate Dictionary, 1991, Merriam Webster.

CHAPTER 10

Intimacy and Sexuality

LEARNING OBJECTIVES

On completion of this chapter, the reader will be able to:

1. Identify the myths surrounding sexual practice in older adults.
2. Explore the possible reasons for a nurse's hesitancy in assisting older adults with fulfilling their sexual desires.
3. Describe the normal changes of the aging male and female sexual systems.
4. Describe the pathologic problems of the aging male and female sexual systems.
5. Explain the influence of dementia on an older adult's sexual desire and practice.
6. Discuss the environmental barriers to an older adult's sexual practice and the ways to manipulate these barriers.
7. Conduct an assessment interview related to an older adult's sexuality and intimacy.
8. State two nursing diagnoses applicable to an older adult's sexual practice.
9. Plan nursing interventions for assisting older adults in fulfilling their sexual desires.
10. State one alternative to an older adult's sexual practice other than sexual intercourse.

THE OLDER ADULT'S NEED FOR SEXUALITY AND INTIMACY

Although it is commonly believed that sexual desires diminish with age, Whipple and Scura, along with other researchers, have identified that sexual patterns persist throughout the lifespan (1989). The Consumer's Union studied the sexual life of 4,246 older adults and found that 16% of women and 46% of men over age 70 were sexually active (Brecker, 1984). The landmark study by Masters and Johnson (1986) indicated that older adults continue to enjoy sexual relationships throughout each decade of their lives (see Cultural Awareness box at right).

In addition to the older adult's ongoing need to express his or her sexuality through traditional sexual methods, the older adult also must fulfill the human need to touch and to be touched. Touch is an overt expression

Insight • *Although the literature indicates that individual differences persist, sexual interest among older adults exists and is active. There may be a decline in sexual activity with advancing age, but sexuality remains important to most older adults.*

of closeness, intimacy, and sexuality and is an integral part of sexuality. In fact, Colton (1983) states that touch is such a basic human need, that when human beings experience lack of touch, it is equivalent to the experience of malnutrition and may possibly cause psychotic breakdown. Furthermore, Thayer (1982) states that touch can be used to relieve stress, to cleanse, to show joy and beautification, and to express sexual pleasure. The importance of touch is often undervalued by society. However, touch may be both a welcome addition to traditional sexual methods or an alternative sexual expression when intercourse is not desired or possible.

The expression of sexuality among older adults results in a higher quality of life achieved by fulfilling a natural desire. Butler and Lewis (1976) suggest that sexual orgasm relieves anxiety and contributes to the general well-being of older adults. Kassell (1983) states that "sex is an opportunity for good clean entertainment that provides laughter and joy in the heart and the intimate giving of one person to the other." Sexual relationships could provide love, intimacy, and closeness, as well as physical stimulation, all of which could serve as motivating factors for continued or improved quality of life.

Although the need to express sexuality continues among older adults, they are more susceptible to many disabling medical conditions such as cardiac problems and arthritis, as well as normal aging changes that may make the expression of sexuality difficult or impossible. In addition, the treatments used for these medical conditions may also hinder the older adult's sexual response. Nurses are in an ideal position to assess these normal aging changes, as well as disabling medical conditions and medications, and to intervene at an early point to prevent or to correct sexual problems.

NURSING'S RELUCTANCE TO MANAGE THE SEXUALITY OF OLDER ADULTS

Despite the fact that literature supports the existence of sexual interest and practice in older adults, few interventions are being carried out by health care professionals to facilitate the older adults' expression of their sexuality. Several reasons account for this lack of information and implementation. The most obvious is society's distaste for and lack of insight into the sexual behavior of older adults. Kain, Reilly, and Schultz (1990) report that society's views on sexual behavior of older individuals are primarily negative and that such views inhibit the expression of sexuality among older adults. Smedley (1991) reports that sexual intercourse is mainly considered to be a younger person's activity for the purpose of procreation. The thought of older, often disabled people engaging in sexual intercourse is not appealing to society. Nurses are also susceptible to society's myths and anxieties toward the sexual expressions of older adults. A nurse's basic discomfort with sexuality issues may actually distort his or her perceptions of clients' needs (Kaas, 1978). Opposing moral values may also add to the nursing staff's reluctance to intervene and to facilitate the sexual satisfaction of older adults.

Quinn-Krach and Van Hoozer (1988) report that another reason why nurses do not intervene and facilitate the expression of sexuality among older adults is because they lack the knowledge and training to do so. Furthermore, they report that nursing programs generally do not provide adequate gerontologic nursing theory or sufficient realistic clinical training in the area of older adults' sexual desires and functionings. Without such training and experience, nurses are not confident enough to venture into such a sensitive area.

In long-term care facilities, there is an increased need

CULTURAL AWARENESS

Intimacy and Sexuality: Cultural Considerations

Although the need for intimacy is culture-universal, the manner in which this need is satisfied varies among cultures. The relationship between husband and wife, degree of physical and emotional closeness, expectations of marriage, relationship with in-laws and extended family members, as well as financial, religious, and social obligations differs greatly.

Although marital fidelity and heterosexuality are the norm transculturally, acceptance of extramarital sexual relationships, same-gender relationships, and bisexual relationships in married couples—as well as the unmarried—differs. Assumptions about older adults' sexual attitudes, beliefs, and practices should be validated with data gathered from the health interview and physical examination.

to address the sexual needs of older adults because of the prevalence of older adults' disabilities within these residences. Yet Kaas (1978) found that the staffs of nursing homes were more accepting of the sexual needs of various groups such as the physically and cognitively disabled, than they were of the sexual needs of older adults.

Acute care nurses are in an ideal position to address new onset or potential sexual dysfunctions before discharge to a community setting or long-term care environment. However, because of the discomfort, myths, and lack of training in the area of sexuality, these problems are often ignored. The end result is that older adults are discharged to another setting with a new onset or old sexual dysfunction that prevents them from functioning sexually.

In the community setting, nurses have access to the client's entire family unit in his or her natural surroundings. The information needed to make a sexual assessment is therefore readily accessible. Yet nurses may feel intimidated or uncomfortable questioning older adults about their sexual desires and needs. Consequently, the information needed to intervene so that older adults can experience satisfying sexual function is not obtained.

As a result of the reasons discussed above, nursing has recoiled from venturing into such unchartered territory. The end result is that sexually interested older adults are in a situation in which they may have multiple disabilities, no privacy, no support, and no appropriate way in which to express their sexual feelings.

NORMAL CHANGES OF THE AGING SEXUAL RESPONSE

To assist older adults in fulfilling their sexual desires most effectively, it is of paramount importance that the nurse understand the normal changes of the aging sexual system. Knowledge about these normal changes enables the nurse to work more confidently with the client to compensate for these changes, to assist the client in understanding these changes and to become aware of possible pathologic problems within the aging sexual system.

In both genders, reduced availability of **sex hormones** in the older adult results in less rapid and less extreme vascular responses to sexual arousal (Masters,

TABLE 10-1

Normal Age-Related Changes in Sexual Arousal and Orgasm

Women	Men
Arousal	
Foreshortening of vagina	Delayed and less firm erection
Delayed and less voluminous vaginal secretion	Longer interval to ejaculation
Little or no Bartholin gland secretion	Poorly defined sense of impending orgasm
Delayed and reduced vaginal expansion	Shorter period of ejaculatory inevitability (sometimes longer, as a result of painful prostatic spasms)
Less constriction of introitus	
No enlargement and poor elevation of uterus during arousal	
Orgasm	
Fewer orgasmic contractions	Shorter ejaculatory event
Occasional painful uterine spasms	Fewer expulsive contractions of urethra
	Less forceful expulsion of seminal fluid
	Reduced volume of seminal fluid
Postorgasm	
No dilatation of external cervical orifice	Rapid loss of erection
Vaginal irritation and clitoral pain as a result of mechanical trauma	Longer refractory period
Extragenital	
Waning of maculopapular flush	Less discernible swelling and erection of nipples
Reduced increase in breast volume during arousal	Absence of maculopapular flush
Less areolar enlargement	Absence of extragenital muscle spasms at climax
Longer postorgasmic retention of nipple erection	Infrequent rectal sphincter contractions
Infrequent rectal sphincter contractions	Reduced testicular elevation
No gaping of urinary meatus during intense orgasm	
Variant of "honeymoon cystitis"	
Bladder and urethral irritability	
Immediate postcoital need to urinate	

Masters WH: Sex and aging-expectations and reality, *Hosp Pract* August 15, 1986.

1986). The lack of circulating hormones in both men and women results in changes in four areas of the sexual system: (1) arousal, (2) **orgasm,** (3) postorgasm, and (4) extragenital changes (Master, 1986) (Table 10-1).

Some of the common physiologic changes associated with the aging man is the increased length of time needed for erections and **ejaculation** to be achieved. Semen volume is decreased and the **refractory period** between ejaculations is long. Pubic hair becomes thinner and the testicles atrophy (Kain, Reilly, Schultz, 1990).

The aging woman experiences **follicular depletion** in the ovaries as a result of a decrease in circulating hormones. This also leads to a lowered secretion of estrogen and progesterone (Masters, 1986). The strength of the orgasmic contraction decreases and the orgasmic phase is shortened. The labia atrophies and sometimes hangs in folds because of lack of subcutaneous fat tissue. The vulva takes on a dry, pale appearance without rugations, and the introitus shrinks. The breast tissue is replaced by fatty tissue, changing the external appearance of the older woman (Morrison-Beedy, Robbins, 1989).

The normal changes of the older man and woman may result in some common problems with sexual function. **Impotence** is not commonly considered to be a problem resulting from normal changes of the older man's sexual system (Kain, Reilly, Schultz, 1990). In fact, with an understanding of the normal changes of the aging sexual system and a lack of pathologic conditions, the older adult man is generally free to pursue his sexuality without difficulty.

The main consequences of these normal physiologic changes experienced by older adult women during intercourse are an increase in response time and **dyspareunia** (painful intercourse). This generally results from a decrease in vaginal lubrications (Kain, Reilly, Schultz, 1990; Morrison-Beedy, Robbins, 1989) and shortening and narrowing of the vagina (Morrison-Beedy, Robbins, 1989). Morrison-Beedy (1989) also states that a woman may experience an inhibited sexual desire, orgasmic dysfunction, and **vaginismus** as a result of a decrease in the amount of circulating hormones or a behaviorally rooted problem.

> **Insight** • *Impotence is not a normal aging change. Impotence in the aging man is generally related to chronic illness or the use of medications. The medical conditions that most often accompany impotence are endocrine, hormonal, or vascular in origin (Kain, Reilly, Schultz, 1990). The medications that most commonly cause impotence include tranquilizers, antidepressants, antihypertensives, and phenothiazines (Wallace, 1992). Treatment of the medical condition or removal of the causative medication generally results in the resolution of the problem. However, if identification and elimination of the causative agent is not possible, surgical and nonsurgical treatments are available to treat impotence in the aging man.*

Important consequences of the normal changes associated with the aging sexual system may be experienced behaviorally. It is common for older adults to be uncomfortable with the changes in their internal and external sexual systems. It is important to note that older adult clients may experience fear of rejection or failure, as well as some boredom or hostility surrounding their sexual performance. Such feelings need to be addressed immediately to prevent the development of depression (Morrison-Beedy, Robbins, 1989).

ALTERNATIVE SEXUAL PRACTICE AMONG OLDER ADULTS

In addition to the burden experienced by society's lack of understanding of the sexuality of older adults, aging homosexuals have the additional burden of society's lack of understanding of homosexuality. Very little information is available regarding the homosexual practices of older adults. Kelly (1977) conducted a limited study and found that the homosexual activity of aging men was low-to-moderate. In a study of 100 lesbians, age 60 to 86, many women found themselves lonely, presently celibate, and desiring a relationship with women within 10 years of their own ages (Kehoe, 1988). Interestingly, nearly one third of the lesbians studied came out after the age of 50 (Robertson, 1979).

The nurse needs to assure that their own personal beliefs about alternative sexual practices do not prevent the older homosexual client from fulfilling his or her sexual desires. It is important to consider the individual needs and desires of each older client and to intervene appropriately to ensure that these special needs are met (see Cultural Awareness box on p. 248). Nurses may best assist the homosexual older client by first assessing their own attitudes and prejudices regarding homosexuality (Hogan, 1980). Examination of the nurse's own feelings toward this alternative sexual practice may allow the nurse to recognize the depth, variety, and meaning of the homosexual lifestyle to the client (Hogan, 1980). This allows the nurse to enter into a therapeutic relationship with the older adult without the interference of personal feelings. The homosexual client's partner should be encouraged to participate in the sexual assessment and planning when appropriate (Hogan, 1980). Nurses should also remember that no information about the sexual orientation of the client should be shared with the client's family unless permission has been given to do so (Hogan, 1980).

CULTURAL AWARENESS

Cultural Considerations in the Care of Lesbian, Gay, or Bisexual Older Adults

Cultures and subcultures reflect a learned set of values, attitudes, beliefs, and practices about intimacy and sexuality. These values are conveyed from one generation to the next through the complex process of socialization. In the majority of cultures, socialization is heavily influenced by gender, and compulsory heterosexuality is the norm. Heterosexual relationships are promoted throughout socialization and most health care systems are heterosexually biased.

For example, nearly every health history form asks, "Are you married?" Although many same gender couples are in committed, long-term relationships, there is no category that acknowledges the relationship. An option for "partnered" should be included in health history forms. Nurses are usually not interested in marital status itself but in whether there is a partner who is involved in the client's care. Thus the following question may provide more relevant information: "Is there anyone you want to include in our discussions or in your care?" When eliciting information about the client's sexual activity, it is suggested that the following question be asked: "Are you sexually active with men, women, or both?" rather than merely, "Are you sexually active?" (Eliason, 1993).

Additional cultural and linguistic modification may be appropriate for older adults from certain cultural groups. For example, Marshall (1990) reports that, when translating a quality of life questionnaire for Chinese-speaking clients, the question "How satisfied are you with your sex life?" became "How satisfied are you with your intimacy with your spouse?"

Because oppression related to being gay, lesbian, and bisexual is stressful, assessment should include data that uncover stress-related disorders such as drug and alcohol abuse, depression and suicidal tendencies, as well as conditions that are transmitted sexually. Be aware that the client may have experienced harassment and discrimination when seeking health care or may have avoided telling health care providers about his or her sexual preferences. Some urban communities have treatment and support groups specifically for gay, lesbian, and bisexual people.

From Eliason MJ: Cultural diversity in nursing care: the lesbian, gay, or bisexual client, *J Transcult Nurs* 5(1):14-20, 1993; Marshall PA: Cultural influences on perceived quality of life, *Sem Oncol Nurs* 6(4):278-284, 1990.

PATHOLOGIC CONDITIONS AFFECTING OLDER ADULT'S SEXUAL RESPONSE

Illness and Medication

Sexual dysfunction is not a normal process of aging. However, the prevalence of chronic illness and medication use is higher among older adults than it is in the younger population. Such illnesses and medications can interfere with the normal sexual function of the older man and woman (Box 10-1).

Because of associated neuropathies and vascular deficiencies, the incidence of erectile impotence in men with diabetes is about 50% and rises with age (Korenman, 1990). Other decreases in vascularization to the genital area, such as those occurring with atherosclerosis, may also result in impotence in the older man (Korenman, 1990). Decreases in human chorionic gonadotropin (HCG) and testosterone, resulting from decreased hypothalamic and testicular secretion, may also result in erectile impotence (Korenman, 1990). Impotence is not a common problem of aging and is generally associated with one or more of these medical conditions or classes of medications. Treatment of the condition or removal of the causative medication generally results in the resolution of such problems (Kain, Reilly, Schultz, 1990).

Human Immunodeficiency Virus

The number of clients with acquired immune deficiency syndrome (AIDS) over age 60 has risen steadily in the past decade, with more than 1,400 cases reported in 1991. In the next decade, the proportion of clients with AIDS who are age 60 and older is expected to rise from 3% to approximately 10%. In comparison to younger clients with AIDS, a higher proportion of older clients with AIDS are Caucasians and women. Homosexual activity accounts for only about 20% of AIDS cases in clients over age 70. Nevertheless, homosexual behavior remains the predominant risk factor of AIDS until age 70 (McCormick, Wood, 1992).

Heterosexual activity should not preclude assessing for the presence of human immunodeficiency virus (HIV) in the older population. For example, age-related thinning of the vaginal mucosa and the subsequent vaginal tissue disruption, less frequent use of condoms, and possibly other age-related diminutions in immune function place older adult female partners of HIV-infected men at a greater risk than their younger counterparts (McCormick, Wood, 1992).

Signs and symptoms of AIDS in older clients are often more vague than in younger clients, including fatigue, weight loss, and decreased physical and cognitive functions (Wallace, Paauw, Spach, 1993). However, the opportunistic infections are common to all age groups (Annon,

BOX 10-1

Related Factors for Sexual Dysfunction

Biopsychosocial alteration of sexuality
- Ineffectual or absent role models
- Physical abuse
- Psychosocial abuse (e.g. harmful relationships)
- Vulnerability
- Misinformation or lack or knowledge
- Values conflict
- Lack of privacy
- Lack of significant other
- Altered body structure or function: pregnancy, recent childbirth, drugs, surgery, anomalies, disease process, trauma, radiation

Kim MJ et al: *Pocket guide to nursing diagnoses,* ed 6, 1995, St. Louis, Mosby.

1976). The disease progresses more rapidly in the older client, and there appears to be a shorter survival time than in younger clients (Wallace, Paauw, Spach, 1993). Research has shown that as a result of the presence of concomitant chronic illness, the diagnosis of HIV may be overlooked (McCormick, Wood, 1992).

Dementia

Dementia has been defined as a clinical syndrome involving the loss of intellectual functions and memory which can be of sufficient severity to cause dysfunction in daily living (see Chapter 27). Older adults are at greater risk for developing specific types of dementia than younger populations. Dementia may have a slow or sudden onset and may have a mild or more pronounced influence on the older client's ability to make independent decisions.

Clients with dementia should be given special attention to ensure their safety when deciding to engage in sexual relationships. It is important to accurately assess the level of dementia and to determine whether the older adult can make competent decisions regarding entering a sexual relationship. See Nursing Management, p. 249, for tips on assessing clients with dementia. If the client is unable to make competent decisions, then a spouse or partner should be prevented from taking advantage of the client. The nurse should contact the appropriate administrators of the facility, social services, and the client's family to develop a plan to ensure the client's safety.

One behavior that may be manifested by the client with dementia is **sexual deviance.** The older adult with dementia may masturbate in public, strip himself or herself of clothing, expose himself or herself, or make overt gestures to other clients or staff. Although there may be no apparent explanation for such behavior, it may indicate that the sexual needs of the older adult are not being met.

ENVIRONMENTAL BARRIERS TO SEXUAL PRACTICE

One of the most difficult problems encountered when intervening to assist older adults with meeting sexual needs is overcoming environmental barriers. In the community setting, the older couple may be hindered by a lack of assistive equipment needed to safely fulfill their sexual desires. In long-term and acute care facilities, privacy is an issue that often prevents older clients from pursuing sexual relationships. Interventions used to manipulate these environmental barriers are discussed on p. 250 of this chapter.

NURSING MANAGEMENT

ASSESSMENT

The PLISSIT model has been used to assess and to manage the sexuality of adults (Annon, 1976). The model includes obtaining permission from the client to initiate sexual discussion *(P)*, providing the limited information needed to function sexually *(LI)*, giving specific suggestions for the individual to proceed with sexual relations *(SS)*, and providing intensive therapy surrounding the issues of sexuality for that client *(IT)*. The goal of the assessment, regardless of the model used, is to gather information that allows the client to express his or her sexuality safely and to feel uninhibited by normal or pathologic problems.

It is common for nurses and nursing students to feel uncomfortable with assessing the sexual desires and functions of older clients. Regardless, a sexual assessment should be performed as a routine part of the nursing assessment. Knowledge, skill, and a sense of comfort is necessary for the nurse to assess the sexuality of older adults. The nurse should review the literature and should gather appropriate information on the subject of sexuality in older clients. Skill and a sense of comfort in assessing sexuality comes with practice (Hogan, 1980) (see Research box, p. 250).

Creating a nonthreatening environment conducive to communication is the first step toward assessing the sexuality of the older client (Hogan, 1980). The assessment should be performed in a manner that conveys an understanding of how sexuality is a continuing human need that can be addressed openly (Smedley, 1991; Talashek, Tichy, Epping, 1990). The nurse should be an objective, accepting, and sympathetic sexual counselor (Morrison-Beedy, Robbins, 1989). The nurse should not

RESEARCH

Quinn-Krach P, Van Hoozer H: Sexuality of the aged and the attitudes and knowledge of nursing students, *J Nurs Educ* 27(8):359-363, 1988.

Sample, setting

Of 158 female nursing students enrolled in a university nursing school, 79 were Caucasian and 79 were Asian/Pacific Islanders.

Methodology

All students completed the 1982 White Aging Sexuality Knowledge and Attitude Scale (ASKAS) and a cover sheet eliciting demographic data.

Findings

The results suggested that there is a weak yet positive relationship between attitude and knowledge. Older nursing students have more positive attitudes and are more knowledgeable about sexuality of older adults. Life experience and type of experience in health care did not predict student attitude or knowledge.

Implications

The results of the study suggest that increased knowledge regarding older adult sexuality, desire, and function may result in a more positive attitude toward sexual behavior in older adults. The nurse should review the literature to obtain current and accurate information on the subject of older adult sexuality to promote a positive view of aging and sexuality.

allow personal feelings about the sexuality, including homosexuality of older adults, to be imposed on the older client. Listening to and perceiving nonverbal clues regarding the sexual needs of the client are essential components of the sexual assessment. Maintaining silence is an important technique that may be used if the client is struggling to express his or her needs during the interview (Hogan, 1980).

The assessment should include a history of past sexual experiences, perceptions, and difficulties (Morrison-Beedy, Robbins, 1989), as well as the presence of any sexually transmitted diseases (STDs) and HIV (Talashek, Tichy, Epping, 1990). Information gathered during the client's initial assessment regarding medical conditions, disabilities, surgical conditions and medications should be reviewed by the nurse for potential risk factors for sexual dysfunction (Kain, Reilly, Schultz, 1990).

Information on alternative sexual preferences should also be obtained. An assessment of the environment in which the client lives should follow. It should be determined where the client plans to participate in sexual activity. In the acute and long-term care settings, the environment should be assessed for privacy and safety. This enables the older adult to proceed with sexual activity safely and comfortably. In the community setting, the environment should be assessed for safety and the availability of adaptive equipment such as siderails, trapezes, and specialized beds that are needed to allow older adults to practice sexual activity safely within the home.

The nursing staff should be alert for indications of sexual interest in the older adult. Although a therapeutic relationship should be established between the nurse and the client during the sexual assessment, the client may not feel comfortable approaching the nurse to discuss sexual intentions (Smedley, 1991). Overt gestures of sexuality in public areas or hints of sexual interest during conversations with the client should not be ignored or punished; they should be brought to the attention of the nurse as an indication of sexual interest between two older adults.

Older adults should not thoughtlessly enter into sexual relationships. Among older adults, there is the added risk factor of a potential cognitive impairment, which may hinder the client's decision-making ability. Before the sexual relationship commences, it may be appropriate for the nurse to meet with both clients individually and then together to discuss their intentions and expectations regarding the sexual relationship. In so doing, the clients' fears and apprehensions regarding the relationship can be expressed and their questions can be answered (Morrison-Beedy, Robbins, 1989). In addition, such a discussion could reveal whether one client is being coerced into the relationship or is not mentally competent to decide to enter into such a relationship.

A Mini-Mental Status Examination (MMSE) (Folstein, Folstein, McHugh, 1975) or other cognitive assessment (see Chapter 1) should be performed as part of the assessment of an older adult. The information gained from this assessment is useful if the nurse suspects the client is cognitively impaired and unable to make the decision to participate in the sexual relationship. If the MMSE does not provide sufficiently clear information regarding the client's decision-making ability, a more thorough assessment by a psychologic team may be necessary to prevent anyone from taking advantage of the client.

✣ DIAGNOSIS

After the assessment of the older adult's sexuality, the nurse is prepared to make a nursing diagnosis. Two nursing diagnoses are appropriate for the older adult experiencing actual or potential sexual problems. The first, ***Altered Sexuality Patterns***, is defined as the state in which a client expresses concern about sexuality (Kim et al, 1995). This diagnosis is appropriate when the older adult has experienced a life change causing a new impediment to sexual functioning. Examples of this in-

CARE PLAN

ALTERED SEXUALITY PATTERNS

Clinical situation Mr. B, a 76-year-old retired brick layer, came to the clinic complaining of headaches that have been increasing in severity over the past several months. His initial assessment showed severe hypertension. During the nursing assessment, it was revealed that Mr. B was a widower who lived alone. However, he had a female friend who visited him often, and they had sexual intercourse every 1 to 2 weeks. To date, he has not experienced any problems with his sexual performance. He was placed on a beta-blocker to control his hypertension.

Nursing diagnosis	Outcome	Interventions
Potential altered sexuality patterns related to risk of side effects from antihypertensive medication.	Client will not experience a disruption in his sexual patterns.	Instruct client on the normal changes of the male and female aging sexual systems. Instruct client that impotence is not a normal aging change and may be a side effect of his antihypertensive medication. Instruct client to notify his physician if impotence or any other sexual problems arise. Suggest that client's partner meet with the nurse and client to discuss current medical condition, normal changes of aging, and the precautions outlined by the Centers for Disease Control and Prevention (CDC).

clude the onset of an acute medical problem or the loss of a loved one. The related factors for this diagnosis are listed in Box 10-2 (see nursing Care Plan, above).

The second diagnosis that may be appropriate for the older adult experiencing a sexual problem is **sexual dysfunction,** defined as the state in which an individual's sexual health or function is viewed as unsatisfying, unrewarding, or inadequate (Kim et al, 1995). This diagnosis would be appropriate if the older client were exhibiting unacceptable sexual activity such as exposure. This diagnosis might also be applicable if the aging female client was experiencing dyspareunia, or decreased or absent sexual desire (see nursing Care Plan, p. 252).

PLANNING

An individualized plan of care, which includes the information elicited during the client's history, and discussion about specific sexual relationships should be developed. This plan should (1) compensate for the physical disabilities of the older adult, (2) prevent the spread of infection, (3) provide for the emotional well-being of the older adult, (4) keep the peace among family members, and (5) ensure the client's safety.

INTERVENTION

Client teaching regarding the normal changes of the aging sexual system should be the first intervention taken

BOX 10-2

Related Factors for Altered Sexuality Patterns

Related factors

Knowledge/skill deficit about alternative responses to health-related transitions, altered body function or structure, illness, or medical treatment
Lack of privacy
Lack of significant other
Ineffective or absent role model
Conflicts with sexual orientation or variant preferences
Fear of pregnancy or of acquiring sexually transmitted disease
Impaired relationship with significant other

Defining characteristics

Reported difficulties, limitations, or changes in sexual behaviors or activities

Kim Mj et al: *Pocket guide to nursing diagnoses*, ed 6, 1995, St. Louis, Mosby.

CARE PLAN

SEXUAL DYSFUNCTION

Clinical situation Mr. J is a 74-year-old retired boxer who has resided at Happy Trails nursing home for 3 years. He has Parkinson's disease and ambulates with a walker. He is generally happy and pleasant. Ms. H is an alert 75-year-old widow who was admitted to Happy Trails 1 month ago after a stroke left her wheelchair-bound and unable to perform her activities of daily living independently. She was very upset when she arrived at the nursing home and had some difficulty adjusting to her new home.

Over the past 2 weeks a close relationship has developed between the two residents. Mrs. H has been happier than she was on admission, and both residents appear to have a new sense of energy and enthusiasm for life. Recently, the nursing staff has noticed that they display sexual expression and signs of intimacy to each other in public areas.

Nursing diagnosis	Outcome	Interventions
Sexual dysfunction related to lack of privacy	Clients will be free to pursue their sexual relationship in private.	Perform sexual assessment of both clients. Provide climate in which both can openly discuss and respond with trust and confidence. Pay close attention to verbal and nonverbal cues while listening. Provide reassurance as needed. Meet with both clients individually to assess each one's desire regarding sexual activity and degree of competence. Assess level of comfort in discussing topic and issues alone or with each other present; provide opportunity for both. Provide teaching on normal changes of the aging sexual system (see Table 10-1, p. 246; and Client/Family Teaching boxes, p. 253). Compensate for any physical disabilities assessed. Implement precautions against spread of sexually transmitted diseases. Find a safe, private location for the couple to pursue their sexuality interests.

with all aging adults (Quinn-Krach, Van Hoozer, 1988; Morrison-Beedy, Robbins, 1989). The changes listed in Table 10-1 are often unknown by the client. Sexuality and sexual expression were not formally or informally taught during the development years of today's cohort of older adults. The client may view the normal changes of aging as embarrassing or indicative of illness. Teaching and reassurance by the nurse that these changes are a normal part of aging allows clients to understand their bodies and feel comfortable learning how to compensate for these changes (see Client/Family Teaching boxes, p. 253).

As discussed previously, cognitively impaired clients often display sexual behavior. The behaviors they exhibit may take the form of exposure or advances toward other clients and staff. It is important for the nurse to manage these difficult behaviors while maintaining the dignity of the older adult. Ignoring the behavior or punishing the older adult does not curtail the behavior. A thorough assessment of the older adult's mental status and sexuality is necessary to isolate the cause of the behavior.

Inappropriate behaviors can best be managed by redirecting the cognitively impaired older adult's sexual interest toward socially acceptable behaviors such as directing the older adult to a private location to masturbate.

When sexual intercourse is not the preferred method of intimacy or is not possible for the older couple, the couple may be taught alternative methods of intimacy in the form of touch. As mentioned previously in this chap-

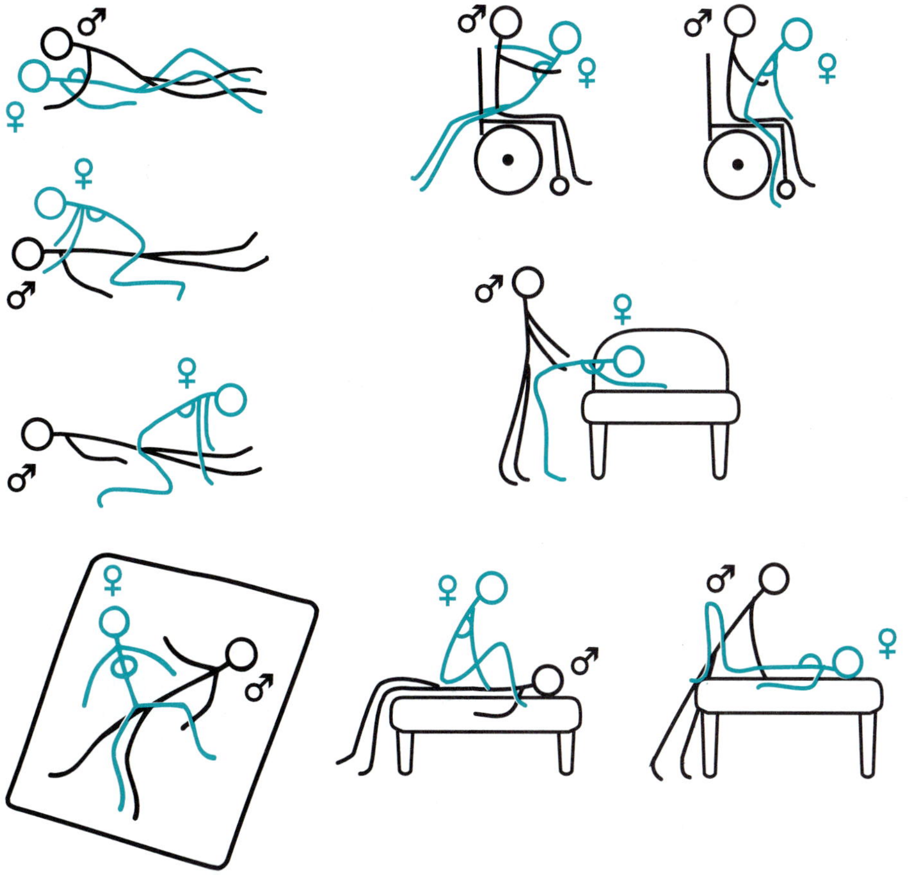

Fig. 10-1 Coital positioning for couples.

CLIENT/FAMILY TEACHING

Normal Changes of the Aging Female Sexual System

Instruct the female client that:

- Vaginal secretions diminish, so use of an artificial water-based lubricant helps to decrease discomfort.
- The vagina becomes shorter and does not expand as well to accommodate the penis. Some discomfort may be experienced, so alternative positions for intercourse (Fig. 10-1) may help to decrease discomfort.
- Orgasmic contractions are fewer and may be accompanied by painful uterine contractions. However, these generally do not indicate pathologic problems.
- Vaginal irritation and clitoral pain are common and do not signify illness.
- The breasts lose tone, and the areolar area does not enlarge as considerably.
- Infrequent rectal sphincter contractions that do not interfere with orgasm and the postcoital need to void may be experienced.

CLIENT/FAMILY TEACHING

Normal Changes of the Aging Male Sexual System

Instruct the male client that:

- The penis may take longer to become firm and may not be as firm as at a younger age; therefore a longer period of foreplay should be planned.
- Ejaculation may take longer to achieve, may be less expulsive, and may be shorter in duration; conserve strength, and do not work hard at the beginning of intercourse, which could result in tiring before climax.
- The erection diminishes more quickly after climax so if condoms are being used, plan to withdraw immediately following climax.
- It takes longer to achieve a second orgasm, so plan to resume foreplay, or use this time to touch or talk.
- Rectal sphincter contractions may be experienced, but these do not interfere with orgasm.

ter, touch is a means of expressing intimacy and closeness that may fulfill the sexual needs and desires of older clients. Touch can best be fulfilled by acquiring a comfortable environment in which the older adult couple can expose parts of their bodies to each other as they feel comfortable. A shower or bath may be enjoyable. The couple should be taught to slowly or lightly move their fingertips over each other's skin while enjoying the closeness of the other person. Soft music may add to creating a conducive environment for the older couple.

Proper precautions need to be implemented to prevent the spread of disease from one client to another. All clients should be considered as potentially infected with HIV and other blood-borne pathogens (Whipple, Scura, 1989). Therefore all older adults should follow the safe sex guidelines recommended by the CDC (1987) (Box 10-3).

If the client is concerned about his or her family's feelings regarding the sexual relationship, further counseling should be provided and should include the family. At this time, the family members can bring forth their concerns regarding the relationship, and the client can answer them with a nurse present. It is very important for the client's family to understand and to accept the older adult's decisions about his or her relationships. However, if no agreement can be reached that is amenable to both the client and family, the client's needs must be the nurse's primary consideration.

Acute and long-term care facilities should make proper arrangements for privacy during the older client's sexual experience. The physical facilities within each setting vary. The ideal situation is to set up a pleasant room that can be used for a variety of activities but may also be reserved by the older adult for private visits with his or her spouse or sexual partner. In most settings, this may not be possible and a client's room may be used while the nursing staff gains permission from and plans alternate activities for the client's roommate.

In any setting, the clients' safety should be maintained. The call lights should be easily accessible to the clients. Siderails on the bed should be used if necessary, and the room should be situated so that the nursing staff is aware of when it is in use. Although the privacy of the clients is very important, the clients should not be allowed to be alone in any situation in which they may injure themselves.

In the community setting, adaptive equipment such as hospital beds, siderails, or trapezes may be needed to allow clients to function safely. Based on the information gathered from the assessment, the nurse should assist the client in ordering the necessary devices. The nurse may also need to demonstrate the transfer process with the

BOX 10-3

Safe Sex Practices for Prevention of Sexually Transmitted Diseases

- Avoid multiple or anonymous sexual partners, prostitutes, and other people with multiple sex partners.
- Avoid sexual contact with a person who has a genital discharge, genital warts, herpes, other suspicious lesions, or a medical diagnosis of HIV or hepatitis B.
- Avoid oral/anal sex.
- Avoid genital contact with oral sores.
- Use latex condoms and diaphragms in combination with spermicides.

Centers for Disease Control: Recommendations for prevention of HIV transmission in health-care settings: Leads from Morbidity and Mortality Weekly Report, *JAMA* 258:1441-1452, November 1987.

RESEARCH

Kaas MJ: Sexual expression of the elderly in nursing homes, *Gerontologist* 18(4):372-377, 1978.

Sample, setting

Of those chosen, 85 were residents and 207 were staff members from three different Detroit city nursing homes and two Detroit suburban nursing homes.

Methodology

A client interview schedule and a parallel staff questionnaire developed by the researcher were administered to the subject groups. Each questionnaire consisted of 32 statements related to attitudes toward sexual expression and sexual needs. Demographic data were also obtained on each subject.

Findings

The staffs of the nursing homes were significantly more accepting of the sexual needs of the various other groups than the residents. Staff attitudes were more accepting of the sexual expression of older adults than they were of older adult behavior. Residents and staff stated that masturbation was not an acceptable means of sexual expression, but staff felt less strongly about this. Both staff and residents agreed that sex was normal in that sexual attractiveness was an important part of sexuality, and that lack of privacy was a barrier to sexual practice.

Implications

The results of this study indicate that both staff and residents lacked knowledge regarding older adult sexual practice and that the lack of knowledge resulted in barriers to sexual practice. It appears likely that increased knowledge and training for both residents and staff regarding the sexual practice of older adults can result in fulfillment of older adult's sexual desires.

client to ensure that the client is able to transfer and to function independently, or with the help of his or her partner.

In any setting, staff training and discussion of sexuality among older adults is essential (Morrison-Beedy, Robbins, 1989). The training should begin by discussing and expelling the myths surrounding older adult sexual desires and sexual activity. The training should include normal changes associated with older men and women, and how to compensate for specific physical disabilities. A more positive attitude toward the sexual expression of the older adult may develop with increased knowledge and may allow such expression to become a natural part of the aging process (see Research box on p. 254).

Training should conclude by implementing discussion groups to allow the staff members to discuss their own feelings about sexuality and its role in the life of the older adult. Role-playing may be an effective technique to gain understanding of the impact of the nursing staff's personal values on the older adult. It should be emphasized that although it is acceptable to have different or even opposing moral values, it is of paramount importance that the staff members realize that their own personal sexual standards must not be imposed on older adults (Morrison-Beedy, Robbins, 1989). Nursing education and discussion allows the staff to become more comfortable and knowledgeable about the sexuality of older adults.

✣ EVALUATION

Evaluation of the older adult with sexual health-related concerns is based on the client's achievement of the established expected outcomes. The older adult can attain a satisfying level of sexual activity that is compatible with functional capacity with the help of sound, sensitive nursing interventions.

Summary

It has been established that the need and desire to function sexually continues throughout the life span. It is the role of the nurse to disregard the myths of society toward the sexual practices of homosexual, heterosexual, and bisexual older adults, and to assist older adults in reaching sexual potential. Many normal and pathologic changes are common in older men and women. However, most of these changes can be compensated for so that the older adult can continue to practice sexually.

With a thorough nursing assessment and management of the normal and pathologic changes of the aging sexual system, the older adult is free to pursue sexuality as desired. The end result can be an older adult who is able to pursue the highest quality of life attainable.

HOME CARE TIPS

- Assess sexual patterns in the homebound older adult who has a chronic condition.
- Provide information regarding sexual positions or sexual function to accommodate environmental barriers (e.g., a Foley catheter) to both the homebound older adult and the significant other.
- Foster a supportive environment for the homebound older adult and the partner to discuss sexual-related fears, concerns, and feelings.
- Explain pathologic conditions that may affect an older adult's sexual response, such as types of medications and chronic illnesses.
- Teach safe sex practices to homebound older adults and their partners.
- Teach alternate methods of intimacy to both the homebound older adult and the significant other, based on the identified sexual dysfunction or alteration.

Key Points

- Sexual desire and interest persist throughout the life span of older adults.
- Nurses are often subject to the myths surrounding the sexual practices of older adults and often lack the knowledge and training on how to assist older adults in fulfilling their sexual desires.
- Older adults may experience normal, age-related changes in their sexual systems, which may hinder their sexual response.
- Pathologic problems with the aging sexual response are often related to medical illnesses and medications.
- Older adults with dementia may display sexual behavior and may not be competent to participate in sexual relationships.
- Environmental barriers in the home, as well as acute and long-term care settings may prevent older adults from fulfilling their sexual desires.
- It is imperative that all older adults receive a sexual assessment so that normal and pathologic changes in the older adult can be identified.
- Normal changes of aging can be compensated for by teaching the older adult about the changes.
- Interventions used to assist the older adult in adapting to age-related changes include manipulation of the environment, and procurement of assistive equipment and devices needed to continue to function sexually.
- Touch can be an alternative to sexual intercourse and can provide the intimacy needed by some older adults.

Critical Thinking Exercises

1. A 73-year-old female client confides in you that she is really embarrassed because her 75-year-old male friend wants to know why he is having difficulty getting an erection. She confesses that she is very uncomfortable and does not know how to help her friend. What suggestions can you offer in dealing with this sensitive but important matter?
2. A married couple reside in the long-term care facility where you are employed. The husband is ambulatory, but his wife needs a great deal of assistance with her daily care. One afternoon as you enter their room with medication, you find the couple in bed together, and it is obvious they are attempting to have sex. How should you respond? Discuss your feelings about this situation.

REFERENCES

Annon J: The PLISSIT model: a proposed conceptual scheme for behavioral treatment of sexual problems, *J Sex Educ Ther* January 2, 1976.

Brecker E: *Love, sex and aging,* Boston, 1984, Little, Brown.

Butler R, Lewis M: *Sex after sixty,* New York, 1976, Harper & Row.

Centers for Disease Control: Recommendations for prevention of HIV transmission in health-care settings. Leads from Morbidity and Mortality Weekly Report, *JAMA* 258:1441-1452, November 1987.

Colton H: *The gift of touch,* New York, 1983, Seaview & Putnam.

Folstein MF, Folstein SE, McHugh PR: Mini-mental state: a practical method of grading the cognitive state of patients for the clinician, *J Psychiatr Res* 12:189-198, 1975.

Hogan R: *Human sexuality: a nursing perspective,* New York, 1980, Appleton-Century-Crofts.

Kaas MJ: Sexual expression of the elderly in nursing homes, *Gerontologist* 18:372-377, April 1978.

Kain CD, Reilly N, Schultz ED: The older adult: a comparative assessment, *Nurs Clinics North Am* 25:833-848, December 1990.

Kassell C: Long-term care institutions. In Weg R, editor: *Sexuality in later years,* New York, 1983, Academic Press.

Kehoe M: Have you ever seen a lesbian over 60? *Aging Connect* 4(4):4, 1988.

Kelly J: The aging male homosexual—myth and reality, *Gerontologist* 17:328, 1977.

Kim MJ et al: *Pocket guide to nursing diagnoses,* ed 6, St. Louis, 1995, Mosby.

Korenman SG: Impotence. In Hazzard WR et al: *Principles of geriatric medicine and gerontology,* New York, 1990, McGraw-Hill.

Masters WH: Sex and aging—expectations and reality, *Hosp Pract* August 15, 1986.

McCormick WC, Wood RW: Clinical decisions in the care of the elderly persons with AIDS, *J Am Geriatr Society* 40:917-921, 1992.

Morrison-Beedy S, Robbins L: Sexual assessment and the aging female, *Nurse Practition* 14:35-45, December 1989.

Quinn-Krach P, Van Hoozer H: Sexuality of the aged and the attitudes and knowledge of nursing students, *J Nurs Educ* 27:359-363, October 1988.

Robertson M: *The older lesbian,* Masters thesis, Carson, Calif, 1979, California State University-Dominguez Hills.

Smedley G: Addressing sexuality in the elderly, *Rehab Nurs* 16:9-11, January-February 1991.

Talashek ML, Tichy AM, Epping H: Sexually transmitted diseases in the elderly: issues and recommendations, *J Gerontolog Nurs* 16:33-39, April 1990.

Thayer S: Social touching. In Schiff W, Foulke E: *Tactile perception: a source book,* Cambridge, 1982, Cambridge University Press.

Wallace JI, Paauw DS, Spach DH: HIV infection in older patients: when to suspect the unexpected, *Geriatrics* 48(6):61-67, 1993.

Wallace M: Management of sexual relationships among elderly residents of long-term care facilities, *Geriatr Nurs,* November-December 1992.

Whipple B, Scura KW: HIV and the older adult: taking the necessary precautions, *J Gerontolog Nursing* 15:15-18, September 1989.

CHAPTER 11

Safety

LEARNING OBJECTIVES

On completion of this chapter, the reader will be able to:

1. Discuss the relationship between safety and autonomy.
2. Identify at least five risk factors contributing to falls in the older adult.
3. Discuss methods for the prevention of falls.
4. Identify nursing diagnoses associated with age-related risks to safety.
5. Using a case study, develop a nursing care plan for fall prevention.
6. Describe three causes of unintentional injuries in older adults that are not fall-related.
7. List two factors that contribute to motor vehicle accidents in older adults.
8. Describe risk factors for suicide in the older adult.
9. Describe several risk factors associated with burns in the older adult population.
10. Name three risk factors that contribute to abuse of the older adult.
11. Describe three mechanisms for prevention of assaults with the older adult.
12. Describe nursing interventions for reducing risk of burns and motor vehicle accidents.

Safety is a concept not often well-defined in nursing research, rather it is stated in terms of what is *described.* Ebersole and Hess (1994) state that safety and security coexist with biologic integrity at a basic level. At a higher level, safety is the feeling and perception of one's surroundings, which include environmental security (Ebersole, Hess, 1994). Maslow (1962) placed safety on a hierarchy of needs. Maslow (1954) lists several aspects of safety as the following: security; stability; protection; and freedom from fear, anxiety, and chaos. Butler and Lewis (1977) describe a safe environment as essential to the mental health of older people, that is, to be living without the threat of physical harm. In addition, they state that older adults need protection when encountering forgetfulness or getting lost. Older adults may experience an increased number of home accidents and feelings of isolation and self-neglect. Wolanin (1981) describes another form of safety in relation to confused older people.

This form is behavioral and corresponds with a person's mental abilities. Thus ethical concerns evolve for clinical gerontologic nurses between safety and autonomy. There is a delicate balance between a person's individual freedom to act and society's ability to protect older people in any setting (Hogstel, Gaul, 1991).

Mroz (1978) defines safety as the "prevention of accidents and the mitigation of personal injury or property damage which may result from accidents," or rather, preventive safety and accident mitigation.

Preventive safety implies the interruption of a sequence of events that results in an accident. Removing or anchoring area rugs in the home, or installing side rails along hallways in institutions to assist ambulation are measures intended to avoid accidents.

Accident mitigation occurs after an accident-producing sequence. In institutional populations, an example of mitigation would be to lower beds near floor level to reduce the impact of a fall (Mroz, 1978). Therefore safety is closely related to activities of daily living (ADLs). The nurse should consider the inherent age-related risks of falling and the prevention of injuries when assessing and planning an older adult's care.

Another concept closely related to safety is autonomy. Beauchamp and Childress (1979) defined autonomy as:

> ...[a] form of personal liberty of action where the individual determines his or her own course of action in accordance with a plan chosen by himself or herself ... The autonomous person is one who not only deliberates about and chooses such plans but who is capable of acting on the basis of such deliberations ... A person of diminished autonomy, by contrast, is highly dependent on others and in at least some respect incapable of deliberating or acting on the basis of such deliberations.

Autonomy is also closely related to ADLs and personal choices. Hogstel and Gaul (1991) cite decreased energy and balance as factors in falling. Decreased hearing and vision also make driving hazardous. Sensory changes such as inability to detect spoiled food or gas leaks in the home may prove dangerous to the individual's health. In addition, handling financial affairs such as balancing a checkbook or driving to the bank can affect the autonomy of a person with visual deficits.

It is not clearly defined when another person should take over the decision-making process. When planning care with the individual, the positive aspects of accident prevention or mitigation should be considered. Basic knowledge about age-related risk factors in falling is necessary to provide proper nursing care.

AGE-RELATED RISK FACTORS IN FALLING

Falls are a common event for older adults. It is essential to identify some of the more common risk factors before planning nursing interventions or preventive measures (Box 11-1).

BOX 11-1

Risk Factors in Falling

- History of Falls
- Sensory impairment
  - Impaired vision
  - Vestibular changes
- Neuromuscular dysfunction
  - Gait
- Increased age
- Cognitive impairment
  - Dementia
- Recent admission to institution
- Polypharmacy
- Living alone
- Use of restraints
- Substance abuse
- Dim lighting
- Unstable furniture
- Scatter rugs
- Decreased energy
- Fatigue
- Osteoporosis
- Generalized weakness
- Postural hypotension
- Cerebrovascular accident (CVA)
- Incontinence
- Mood disturbance
  - Depression
- Multiple medical diagnoses
  - Congestive heart failure (CHF)
  - Diabetes
  - Osteoarthritis
  - Hypertension
- Amputation
- Unsafe footwear
- Waxed floor with glare
- Elevated bed positions

Neuromuscular Dysfunction

A major function of the central nervous system is the regulation of posture and simple reflexes, and the translation of drives, thoughts, and emotions into purposeful action or behavior and movement. Generally, specific areas of the brain receive sensory input from tactile, proprioceptive, visual, and vestibular sources. In normal individuals, these inputs translate into adjustments that plan, initiate, and guide movements. Output is a smooth, highly coordinated performance. Sensory and motor functions may be altered by disease, aging processes, or both (Sorock, Labiner, 1992) (see Research box on p. 259).

Numerous studies include the relationship between sensory and motor functions (Hornbrook, Stevens, Wingfield, 1993; Tinetti et al, 1993; Roberts, Wykle, 1993). A history of increased number of falls was associated with decreased sense of positioning in the toes and ankles. The risk of falling increases in people with weak, distal lower extremities (Tinetti, Speechley, Ginter, 1988). Moreover, recurrent falls are associated with difficulty standing up from a chair (Tinetti, Speechley, Ginter, 1988; Corbett, Pennypacker, 1992). Therefore having two or three

RESEARCH

Sorock G, Labiner DM: Peripheral neuromuscular dysfunction and falls in an elderly cohort, *Am J Epidemiol* 136(5): 584-591, 1992.

Sample, setting

Subjects included 169 tenants of senior citizen housing in New Jersey.

Methodology

Baseline interviews and physical assessments were performed. A neuromuscular assessment was conducted to determine nine sensory tests of the lower extemities, one test of muscle strength, and gait assessment.

Findings

Peripheral neuromuscular dysfunction was associated with first falls Neuromuscular dysfunction was defined as the presence of one or more of the following three factors: (1) a reduced toe position sense, (2) reduced sharp-dull discrimination on physical examination and to a lesser extent, (3) reduced ankle strength.

Implications

These findings suggest that impaired sensory and motor functions of the lower extremities play important roles with falls in older adults. The nurse should incorporate neuromuscular assessment findings into the older adult's care plan with the goal of reducing falls and fall-related injuries.

sensory or motor deficits may increase the risk of falling (Sorock, Labiner, 1992).

Osteoporosis

Osteoporosis of the spine is a second risk factor cited in research (see Chapter 30). Ali and Bennett (1992) encourage an admission assessment for osteoporosis, especially if cortisol or antacid medications are consumed. These drugs may interfere with calcium maintenance in the body. Women are particularly vulnerable to loss of bone mass. Decreased bone mass at appendicular sites (e.g., radius and calcaneus) place older women at risk for fractures. A number of factors influence the bone mass of older adult women. Older age, low weight, decreased muscle strength, and low estrogen values may be the most important of these factors (Bauer, et al, 1993). Furthermore, Haldeman and Rubenstein (1992) stated that older adults are increasingly seeking chiropractic adjustments. They concluded that adjustments of the spine carry a risk of compression fractures. They recommend that an older adult with a history of a fall receive an x-ray before manipulation of the spine and that special care be taken with people with osteoporosis (1992).

Stroke

A third risk factor is the prevalence of stroke in the older adult population. Sackley (1991) has found no gender differences in subjects having right-side or left-side hemiplegia. However, asymmetry and favoring of the unaffected side, both in left- and right-side brain injury, were common in people recovering from a stroke. It was speculated that impairments of a perceptual or sensory nature as a result of a stroke caused falls, although it was not studied. In addition, Byers, Arrington, and Finstuen (1990) have found that clients with stroke, histories of falls, impaired decision-making, generalized weakness, restlessness, quick fatigue, and abnormally high or low hematocrits should be identified as being at high risk for falling. Hematocrit can influence anemia, whole blood viscosity, and fluid and nutritional status. High hematocrit is a possible, but weak risk factor for stroke.

Sensory Impairment

Visual acuity is another age-related risk factor that impinges on safety. Jantti (1993) studied nursing home residents and discovered that visual acuity was important in maintaining balance. Furthermore, dementia contributed to falling. Lord, Clark, and Webster (1991) concurred that impaired vision may predispose older adults to postural imbalance and falls. Moreover, impaired or altered adaptation to darkness may temporarily blind an older person (McMurdo, Gaskell, 1991). As a result, this can lead to an increased number of falls, especially at night. Night lights may offset the influence of variations in visual acuity. Tobis, et al. (1990) studied visual-perceptual feedback as a major contributor to falling. They hypothesized that the hearing- and sight-impaired older adult would show an increased frequency in falling. This was supported in their study. They concluded that nursing interventions with the hearing-impaired should focus on **visual feedback training.** Exercise may increase musculoskeletal strength and reduce the frequency of falls in sight-impaired older adults.

Nursing Implications

Assessment Kane (1993) discussed the implications of assessment in relation to physical frailty and subsequent dependence in old age. Assessments are performed for better clinical decision making. Although a plethora of assessment instruments exists, he indicated that new assessment instruments do not necessarily improve care. Nonetheless, a relationship exists between biologic, psychologic, social, and environmental factors, as well as safety. It is important to define the meanings of the findings of the assessment.

Gait assessment has been conducted in several studies (Kane, 1993; Roberts, Wykle, 1993; Fried et al, 1990; Wolfson et al, 1990; Fleming, Wilson, Pendergast, 1991). Roberts and Wykle (1993) use the Roberts Balance Scale in which subjects performed eight stances to determine the danger of falling. Balance measures can be conducted safely with frail, institutionalized older adults. People at risk for falling may be identified. Fried, et al. (1990) has discussed gait assessment parameters that included step length, walking speed, initial style of walking, ability to turn head while walking, and **static balance.** A slow-walking speed was associated with depression. This function-based instrument detected early risk factors for falls and mobility problems. Wolfson, et al. (1990) evaluates 16 facets of gait. Arm swing amplitude, upper-lower extremity synchrony, and guardedness of gait were the most common impairments among the study sample. Fleming, Wilson, and Pendergast (1991) describe an easily performed muscle test. Subjects sat in chairs, with hips and knees at 90-degree angles, over a force transducer. They stood as quickly as possible and after five seconds of standing, they sat as quickly as possible. The subjects who fell had a significantly lower rate of change in force. Nurses then might assess the older adult's muscle strength for walking by asking clients to perform certain physical tasks. If enough strength is present to safely sustain these movements, then it can be assumed that the older adult has the strength to ambulate without falling.

Performance Studenski (1993) describes several tasks that indicate levels of performance. The ultimate goal for the gerontologic nurse is to identify reversible conditions that adversely affect performance and to institute measures that maximize independent functioning. Table 11-1 illustrates a scale with which gerontologic nurses can assess performance.

TABLE 11-1

Physical Performance Tasks

Performance level/rating	Task
Low level	Sits on a firm-surface chair for 60 seconds, without touching the chair back or using arms for support
Moderate level	Rises from a chair with arms folded
	Walks and turns with no more than three, smooth continuous steps
High level	Stands on one foot for 30 seconds with the other leg flexed at the knee
	Tandem walks (one foot placed directly in front of the other) for six continuous steps

RISK FACTORS IN REHABILITATION SETTINGS

Additional key factors that place older adults at a greater risk for falls include the following: increased age, amputation of a lower extremity, neurologic impairment, and history of previous falls (Eliopoulos, 1993). Personal characteristics that increase the risk for falls include the following: urinary and bladder dysfunction; medical diagnoses such as transient ischemic attacks (TIAs), orthostatic syncope, cardiac abnormalities, and hypoglycemia; polypharmacy, and substance abuse (Brady et al, 1993).

Environmental Factors

Wheelchair usage, unstable furniture, elevated bed positions, waxed floors with glare, dim lighting, and unsafe footwear also contribute to falls (Brody et al, 1993). For example, studies (Robbins, Gouw, McClaran, 1992; Chaffin, Wolstad, Trujillo, 1992) have compared soft-sole with hard-sole shoes and found that when hard neolite shoes come into contact with smooth, wet walking surfaces there is less chance for hazards to occur. Poorly fitting slippers and shoes should be eliminated (Eliopoulos, 1993).

Client Factors

Fall-prone Clients

Calvani and Douris (1991) state that the most important physical task for clients is transferring in and out of a bed, chair, or toilet. Those who are unable to transfer cannot be left alone for long periods without increasing the risk of falling.

Despite new research on the fall-prone client, little attention has been paid to clients who fall repeatedly (O'Connor, 1990; Tinetti, Speechley, Ginter, 1988; Morse, Tylko, Dixon, 1985). Wright, et al. (1990) examines psychologic factors in frequently falling residents. According to their studies, older adults valued their lifelong independence and often denied the fall, describing what happened as a slip or trip. These clients disclaimed fear, and denied falling or feeling any anxiety as a result of falling. Tinetti, et al. (1986) has found that a mobility test is the best predictor of recurrent falling. More recently, Lipsitz, et al. (1991) studied correlates of recurrent falls. The subjects who fell were functionally more impaired and were taking more medications. In addition, they took more steps to turn 360 degrees and could not stand up from a chair without pushing off, and their senses of position were impaired.

Fear of Falling

Tinetti, et al. (1991) has developed the Falls Efficacy Scale (FES) that measures the fear of falling. The instrument has high validity and reliability. Subjects who report avoiding activities for fear of falling score higher on the FES. The higher score represents lower self-confidence. Other predictors are typical walking pace (a measure of physical ability), anxiety, and depression. The FES may be useful in addition to measures of functional decline.

Maki, et al. (1991) also examined the fear of falling and postural performance. Subjects who expressed a fear of falling had significantly poorer performance in ADLs with eyes open or closed. The incidence of hip fracture and other injuries contributes to fear of falling. Cummings and Nevitt (1989) stated that hip fractures are common, disabling, and perhaps fatal in older adults. The incidence of hip fracture rises exponentially with age. See Chapter 30 for further evaluation of this concept.

Other Risk Factors

Medications significantly contribute to falls. According to Poster, et al. (1991), side effects of medications for older psychiatric clients contribute to increased numbers of falls or greater risks of falling. Campbell (1991) states that medications increase the risk of falling through sedation, increased reaction time, and impaired balance. Evidence has shown that psychoactive drugs are clinically associated with the risk of falling. Myers, et al. (1991) states that vasodilators, diuretics, age, and a history of falls places older people at high risks for falling. Diuretic use or a diagnosis of dementia was positively correlated with injury. Furthermore, Cumming, et al. (1991) relates depression, cognitive impairment, and the use of alcohol and other medications as important risk factors in frequent falling. Such medications include diazepam, diltiazem, diuretics, and laxatives. Caution is urged before prescribing diuretics or psychotherapeutic agents for older adults.

Insight • *Falls are* preventable. *Regardless of the setting, the nurse is responsible for conducting an ongoing assessment to identify those older adults at risk for falling. It is essential to identify a history of previous falls and the presence of risk factors for falling. Likewise, it is important to conduct a full, careful body system review focusing on the neuromuscular and sensory systems, and the older adult's ability to negotiate the everyday (home) and present (hospital, rehabilitation, or long-term care setting) environments. A physical examination that includes assessment of functional ability must also be performed.*

The nurse faces a challenge in balancing the need to promote the older adult's independence and functional ability with the needs to promote safety and to prevent injury. It may be helpful to remember that life has inherent risks, and people of all *ages are faced with multiple risks on a daily basis. To reduce risk, the nurse should not place greater restriction on the older adult than what is absolutely necessary. Risks associated with immobility are often greater than the risk of falling. The nurse should encourage* safe *activity or mobility rather than immobility in the name of protecting an older adult from harm. (Fig. 11-1).*

PREVENTION

As the nurse examines the risk factors that affect safety (see Box 11-1, p. 258) in older adults, it becomes apparent that few older people are excluded from being at risk (Kilpack et al, 1991). Costa (1991) states that regular physical examinations provide the opportunity to promote a healthy lifestyle and offer information for functional improvement. The gerontologic nurse in any setting should take advantage of the assessment opportunities that arise to determine client-specific, fall-related risk factors. Based on the assessment findings, the nurse develops specific, individualized interventions aimed at reducing the risk of fall and injury. Recommendations often require interdisciplinary collaboration with the goal of helping the older adult foster the highest degree of functional independence. As always, the client and any family or significant others are included in the planning process.

For example, exercise programs that include aerobic conditioning, muscle strengthening, and gait or balance training can be recommended to people at risk for falling. In addition, Fiatarone, et al. (1993) states that nutritional supplementation not only is effective for people who are undernourished but also may be helpful in older frail people undergoing fitness training.

A critical assessment of risk factors regardless of setting is needed in fall prevention. Nelson (1990) observed the results of falls in a medical emergency room. He stated that most falls result from the interaction of intrinsic *and* extrinsic factors. The nurse should also conduct a thorough assessment of the older adult's *external* environment to identify any additional factors that may contribute to an increased risk of falling and injury. General factors in the client's environment, such as lighting, room color, signs/signage, noise, and texture should be used in such a way that not only promotes safety but also enriches living there as well. This assessment can and should be done in any setting. To illustrate, the acute care environment may be conducive to health care providers delivering care, but it is confusing and frightening to an older adult and can increase the risk of injury. The number and variety of caregivers with whom the client must interact; the unusual, and often noisy, hazardous equipment used to assess, to monitor, and to deliver care; and the designer-perfect but functionally inadequate rooms and furnishings are only a few examples of external hazards that can increase the risk of falls and injuries for the older adult in this setting.

Risk Assessment Tools

Although extensive research exists that assesses risk for falling, little is based on the effectiveness of using re-

A

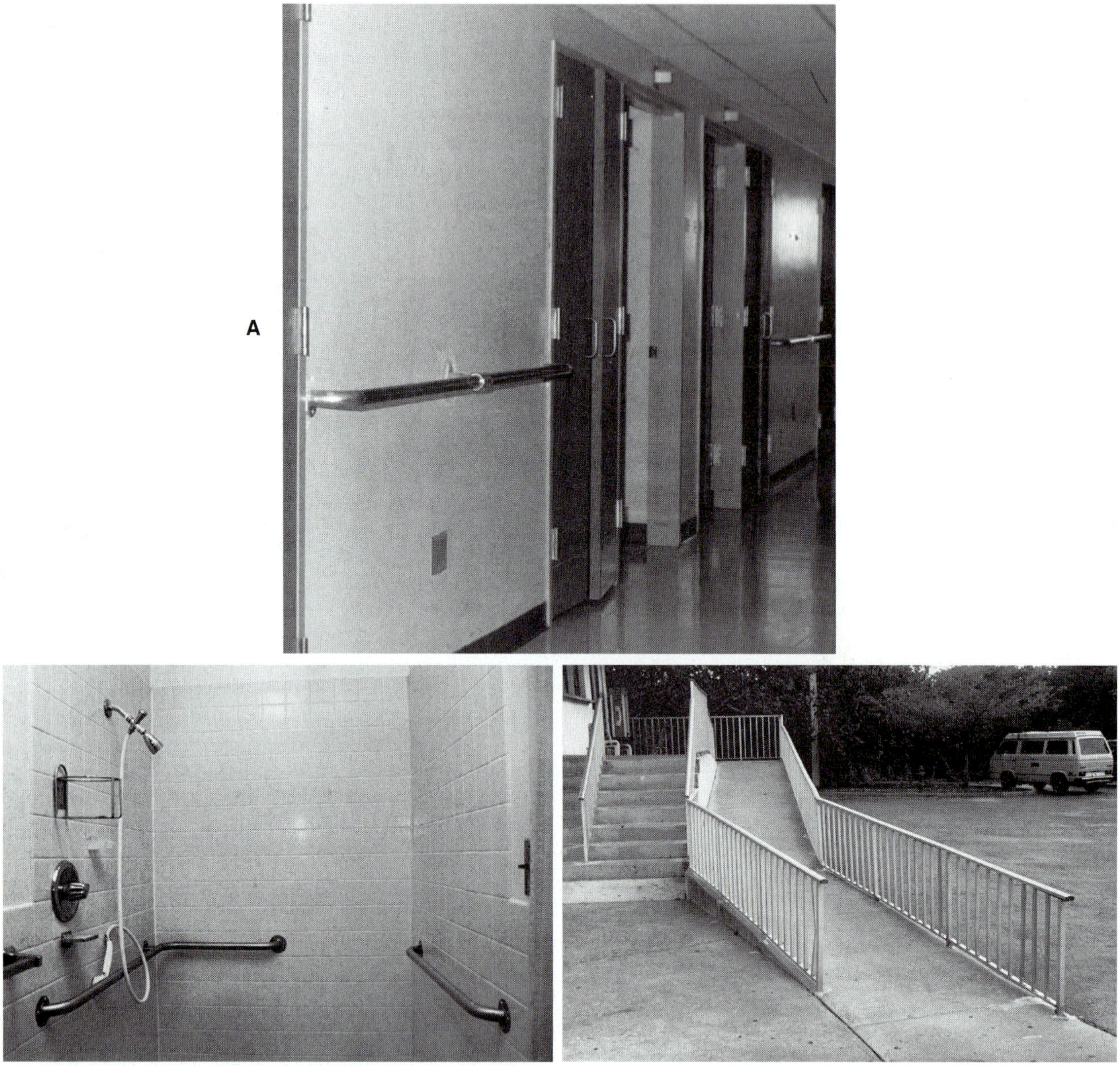

B

C

Fig. 11-1 Safety measures such as handrails or access ramps for the wheelchair-bound older adult aid in fall and injury prevention. (**A** and **C** courtesy Loy Ledbetter, St. Louis, Mo ; **B** courtesy Ursula Ruhl, St. Louis, Mo.)

search-based interventions (Campbell, 1991). Signs at the bedside and information in charts encourage staff awareness (Campbell, 1991; Zepp, 1991) of people at risk for falling. Other interventions include moving clients closer to the nurses' station and the use of sitters.

A variety of nursing measures to promote safety and to reduce injury, such as those noted previously, provide general guidance and direction for care planning. Ultimately, the nurse selects highly individualized interventions based on the assessment of a particular older adult client and thus enhances the likelihood of achieving the expected outcomes.

Alarms

In the past, as an attempt to guard against the risk of falls and physical injury, most long-term care facilities resorted to the use of side rails, vest or waist restraints, or trays on chairs (Jagella et al, 1992). These measures were

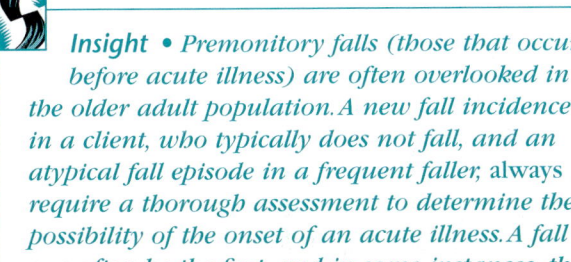

> *Insight* • *Premonitory falls (those that occur before acute illness) are often overlooked in the older adult population. A new fall incidence in a client, who typically does not fall, and an atypical fall episode in a frequent faller,* always *require a thorough assessment to determine the possibility of the onset of an acute illness. A fall can often be the first, and in some instances, the* only *presenting symptom of illness. Infection, cardiovascular abnormalities, and fluid volume alterations are the most commonly presenting acute health problems of this population.*

implemented to restrict transferring out of beds and chairs, which was the most common source of falls (Robbins, Gouw, McClaran, 1992). With the onset of the Omnibus Budget Reconciliation Act of 1987 (OBRA), health care providers in long-term care settings have been re quired to develop alternatives to restraints. An alarm device (Strumpf et al, 1992) provides one alternative. The device, which attaches to the bed or chair, allows a zone of free movement. When that safe zone is exceeded, an alarm sounds to alert the staff. Morton (1989) employed a bed alarm system. Bed alarms not only identified the person at high risk, they also reduced the falls to 60% in 2 years. Recurring falls dropped an additional 29%. Jagella, et al. (1992) cautioned that more precise research is needed.

CARE PLAN

FALL PREVENTION

Clinical situation: Mrs. T is an 80-year-old, newly admitted resident of the extended care facility. She has exhibited some mental status changes as a result of her recent relocation from the hospital, where she was treated for pneumonia. Her vision is poor as a result of the irreversible effects of glaucoma and cataracts. She is weak and unsteady as a result of the hospitalization and osteoarthritis; her hips and knees are especially affected. She has fallen three times since her admission to the facility 2 days ago, but has sustained no injury. Medications include a sedative at night for insomnia and a nonsteroidal antiinflammatory for joint pain and stiffness.

Nursing diagnoses	Outcomes	Interventions
High risk for injury related to mental status changes, relocation	Client will remain free of personal injury during stay.	Orient to surroundings, and introduce self when status changes, relocation entering room. Keep immediate environment free of obstacles, and place call light within reach to encourage client to call for assistance. Keep bed in low position with side rails up as needed. Provide well-fitting, nonskid footwear, and involve family in planning to promote meaningful and significant interaction with environment. Encourage autonomy and participation in decision making affecting care. Provide opportunities to talk about feelings associated with changes and losses related to relocation.
Impaired physical mobility related to hip and/or knee pain and stiffness and decreased visual acuity	Client will safely perform self-care within limitations imposed by disease.	Administer analgesics and antiinflammatory medication on consistent, regular basis. Apply warm, moist heat as needed to affected joints, and provide range of motion to affected joints TID. Ambulate with assistance or walker. Refer to physical therapy for muscle strengthening program. Encourage use of eyewear during waking hours, and provide ample, nonglare lighting.

Another safety mechanism developed for use with confused or wandering clients is the Electronic Security System. This device avoids the "locked door" concept. Such devices allow complete freedom of movement until a designated threshold is crossed. Audio and visual alarms are then activated. Staff can quickly come to the safety of clients who may be at risk for injury when unescorted or unsupervised (Negley, Molla, Obenchain, 1990) (see nursing Care Plan, p. 263).

Ethics of Restraint

Ethical principles abound when considering safety with older adults. Nonmaleficence, or "to at least do no harm," is a basic requirement in caring for older adults. Tammelleo (1993) describes a case in which a nurse left a client medicated for nausea alone in the shower. The client was drowsy from the medication, a known side effect of trimethobenzamide hydrochloride (Tigan). The client slipped and fell, sustaining injuries. The nurse was found to be negligent because she failed to provide ordinary precautions and care.

However, a balance is sought between autonomy and paternalism. Many staff, in a task-oriented manner, perform ADLs for clients. Older adults are particularly vulnerable to coercion. Labels such as noncompliant, uncooperative, unmotivated, and difficult are often used when clients are expected to do what they are told. Coercion and vulnerability further decrease individual autonomy (MacPherson et al, 1990). The use of restraints has been associated with greater mortality, longer stays during hospitalization, increased pressure ulcers, higher incidence of nosocomial infections, incontinence, immobility, and continued falls and injuries (Tinetti, Liu, Ginter, 1992; Mitchell, 1991). The nurse must give careful thought and consideration to these issues when attempting to determine the most appropriate measures for preventing falls and injuries (see Chapter 3).

MAJOR NON–FALL-RELATED INJURIES

Motor Vehicle

One of the most relevant activities for maintaining independence in aging is the ability to drive (Kline et al, 1992). For newly retired people between age 65 and 75, comfort and safety in automobiles need to be considered. Accident rates per driven mile rise at this time (Evans, 1993). Self-reported driving distances may decline dramatically. The decline in safe use of motor vehicles may be a result of presbyopia, decreased dark adaptation, decreased depth perception, susceptibility to glare, and the general slowing of reflexes and cognitive processing. Evidence suggests that the physical capabilities needed for safe driving begin to decline at age 55 and decline precipitously after age 75 (Persson, 1993). Skills required are visual acuity and peripheral vision. A decline in either of these skills may account for the most common types of accidents such as right-of-way accidents and turning accidents (Persson, 1993). Vision accounts for 90% of the information used in driving. Motor vehicle accidents are the leading causes of accidental death in adults age 65 to 74 and the second leading cause for those over age 75 (falls are first). Even when driving shorter distances or in daylight hours only, and avoiding rush-hour traffic, drivers 69 and older are twice as likely to be involved in a fatal accident as middle age drivers (National Research Council, 1988). See the Research box below for recently published data regarding the older adult driver and the physician's influence on the decision to stop driving (Persson, 1993; Miller, Morley, 1993)(see Research box below).

Another dilemma that presents itself is the older driver who is developing or already has dementia (Hunt et al, 1993). Hunt, et al. (1993) concluded that some people with dementia retain "safe" driving skills, but the stronger the dementia, the more apparent poor driving skills become. At present, it remains uncertain how current road tests of "safe" driving correlate with accidents and violations that cause accidents.

RESEARCH

Persson D: The elderly driver: deciding when to stop, *Gerontologist* 33(1):88-91, 1993.

Sample, setting

Of the 56 participants ages 66 to 96, 63% were women, 68% were widowed, 98% were Caucasian, ex-drivers who lived in retirement communities.

Methodology

Discussion and questionnaires were coded.

Findings

The decision to stop driving was made with reluctance for several reasons (Table 11-2). Only 32% of physicians seldom raised the issue, and even fewer health care professionals (9%) discussed driving. Families (33%) and friends (11%) influenced the decision to stop driving.

Implications

Health care professionals should develop specific clinical guide-lines to evaluate the ability of the older adult driver. Driver improvement courses may be helpful. Edu cating older adults about the physiologic and cognitive changes associated with aging and how they impact driving is necessary.

Prevention

Little information is available on safe older adult driving patterns and the cessation of driving. Campbell, et al. (1993) discuss the six medical conditions responsible for having to give up driving: (1) macular degeneration, (2) any activity limitation, (3) syncope, (4) Parkinson's disease, (5) retinal hemorrhage, and (6) stroke sequelae. However, half of all people with these conditions continue to drive. Thus the decision not to drive is clearly a complex one. At present, medical diagnosis is an incomplete reason for cessation of driving; clear guidelines for prevention require far more research as the nation's population ages.

Ebersole and Hess (1994) advise that if the older person continues to drive, then nurses should instruct them to: avoid night driving; wear hearing aids and glasses to augment sensory awareness; avoid driving under the influence of medications or alcohol; avoid driving in fog, heavy rain, snow, and ice; plan relief for drivers on long distance trips; and keep vehicles in good repair (Ebersole, Hess, 1994).

Pedestrians

The Automobile Association of America (AAA) (1993) states that older adults are particularly vulnerable as pedestrians. More than half of the unsafe incidents occur at intersections with or without traffic signals (Box 11-2).

Suicide

Suicide is one leading cause of death in older adults and is often associated with alcohol or drug dependence. In fact, in addition to advancing age in men, alcohol and drug dependence are among the greatest risk factors Curtis, Geller, Stokes, 1989). Marital status is also a significant factor. Married people throughout life have the lowest rate of suicide. Widowed and divorced older men and women have rates of suicide that are two or three times greater than their married counterparts (Wolf, Rivara, 1992).

Additional risk factors for suicide in older adults include the following:

- Poor physical health
- Past history of suicide attempts
- Family history of suicide attempts or completion
- Alcohol abuse
- Depression
- Social isolation

Sad or depressed older people require a careful review of suicidal ideation and intent. The nurse should address passive death wishes. Specific intent, methods, and plans need to be explored (Sadavoy, Lazarus, Jarvik, 1991) (see Chapter 12).

Burns

Burns are the fourth leading cause of death from injury in the United States, with approximately 500 deaths per year (Stephen, Murray, 1991). Almost 90% of these deaths occur in residential fires. In all geographic locations, the death rate is much higher for adults over age 65 than it is for younger people. Scald burns, often caused by hot food or drink, are the most common nonfatal cause of injury in older adults (Stephen, Murray, 1991; Josephson,

TABLE 11-2

Reasons Given for Older Adults to Stop Driving (N = 56)

Reason	N	Percent
Advice from doctor	15	27
Increased nervousness behind wheel	11	20
Trouble seeing pedestrians and cars	11	20
Medical conditions	10	18
Advice from family or friends	9	16
Difficulty in coordinating hand or foot movement	5	9
Transportation provided by retirement center	5	9
Cost of upkeep or age of vehicle	4	7
Involvement in minor accidents	3	5
License revoked	2	4

BOX 11-2

Most Commonly Cited Reasons for Pedestrian Accidents

- Left-turning vehicles are more dangerous than right-turning vehicles. Pedestrians step off the curb before sighted by left-turning vehicles.
- Pedestrians are most vulnerable when first stepping off the curb, because there is less time for driver or pedestrian to react or to respond.
- Vehicles leaving an intersection are more dangerous, because they are picking up speed.
- Pedestrians or vehicles may initially be hidden from each others' view by visual screens.
- Immediate action by pedestrians occurs as signal turns green or changes to WALK, often while the vehicle is still in the intersection.
- WALK/green signal does not give sufficient time to allow older people to cross safely.

AAA: Pedestrian safety for the older (65+) adult, *Motorist* May/June 1993, The Association.

Fabacher, Rubenstein, 1991). A household survey found that 71% of the hot water heater installations are at temperatures of 60°C (140°F) or greater (National Center for Health Statistics, 1990); this is alarmingly high. Many of these scalds occurred during bathing or showering, or while cooking with hot liquids because of high water temperature (National Center for Health Statistics, 1990). To reduce scald injuries, water heater temperatures should be set below 60°C (140°F).

Risk Factors

Risk factors for burns in older adults are likely to be the same as in other groups. Poverty is one of the most common risk factors. Substandard housing is often seen in poor neighborhoods. Economic conditions and fire occurrences are related to substandard housing (Campbell, 1991); medical risk factors include sensory impairment, dementia, muscle weakness, impaired mobility, and poor balance. Alcoholism and cigarette smoking, often in combination, are widely known risk factors for house fires and deaths (Wolf, Rivara, 1992; Josephson, Fabacher, Rubenstein, 1991).

Prevention of Burns and Scalds

Smoke detectors are perhaps the least costly deterrent. The majority of fire deaths result from smoke inhalation rather than burns. Sprinkler systems enhance the effectiveness of smoke detectors and markedly reduce the spread of the fire. Ebersole (1994) suggests the following measures to promote a fire safe environment:

- Use of noncombustible building materials
- Sprinkler systems
- Smoke detectors
- Closed air spaces
- Flame-retardant fabrics
- Fire prevention procedures
- Inspection by safety personnel

Nurses need to assure older adult clients that the personnel are familiar with fire policy and procedures in institutions. Staff should also report and correct any fire hazards (1994). In addition, the practice of regular fire drills, with planned routes of evacuation, ensure that appropriate actions are taken in the event of an emergency.

Assaults and Abuse

In 1990 the National Center for Health Statistics reported 1,330 deaths from assaults on people over age 65. It is felt that this figure far underestimates the true nature of the problem. Unfortunately, domestic violence against older people is also a common problem. There are few national research studies, therefore data are limited to local studies. Busse and Blazer (1989) describe the existence of caregiver physical, psychosocial, and financial abuse of older adults. It is a serious concern for dependent, debilitated older adults. **Abuse** is defined as an act or omission that results in harm or threatened harm to the welfare of an older adult. Abuse includes intentional infliction of verbal, physical, or mental injury; sexual abuse; and withholding of necessary food, clothing, and medical care. Since the abuser is often someone close to the person, both parties tend to deny its existence.

Adult Abusers

In about 86% of the reported cases (Pillemer, Moore, 1990), the abuser is a relative. Approximately 50% of these are adult children or grandchildren. Spouses account for about 40%. Pillemer, et al. (1990), reported that about 10% of nursing assistants stated they had committed at least one act of physical abuse within 1 year, with 40% reporting having committed psychologic abuse at least once. Abuse is thought to be widespread in nursing homes.

Risk Factors for Abuse

It has been reported that men are more likely to be physically abused than women (Wolf, Rivara, 1992). Those with declining health are more likely to be abused. Women are more seriously injured when abused and thus receive official attention. Physical or mental dependency increases the risk of abuse. Advanced age plays a role. Alcohol abuse intensifies domestic violence (Wolf, Rivara, 1992; Busse, Blazer, 1989; Pillemer, Hudson, 1993). Key elements for risk assessments include the client history and physical findings. Gerontologic nurses should observe the client and the individual accompanying him or her. There should also be a comparison of the severity of an injury with an explanation of the events. If any doubts arise, then separate interviews should be held to achieve identification of the problem.

Prevention of Abuse

Psychotherapy may be useful in helping (1) to identify the cause of the frustration that provokes abuse, (2) to develop coping strategies, and (3) to prevent loss of control. Community resources need to be explored to provide social, medical, psychiatric, legal, or other services for the distressed family (Busse, Blazer, 1989). Pillemer and Hudson (1993) have developed a curriculum for an abuse prevention program with eight training modules for nursing assistants. Role playing allows the participants to test various interventions in dealing with difficult situations. The success of the program rests with providing a safe, comfortable environment in which discussion takes place.

Other preventive measures are community education campaigns that arouse community awareness. Community projects such as visitation, respite, and adult day care are creative ways to prevent abuse of older people.

HOME CARE TIPS

1. Assess the home environment for the presence of hazards and risk factors that predispose a homebound older adult to falls.
2. Carefully assess the homebound older adult's physical status for risk factors that predispose to falls (i.e., examine feet, gait, vision, posture, muscle control, and memory).
3. Instruct caregivers and homebound older adults on tools and techniques to maximize independent functioning.
4. Assist caregivers and homebound older adults in planning a safe environment for the homebound older adult based on the identified risks and hazards.
5. Physical therapy can be valuable in assessing the home setting, to determine what environmental adaptations should be made to make it safer and easier for the homebound older adult.

Summary

The concept of safety encompasses many aspects of the older person's internal and external environment. The challenge for the nurse caring for any older client is to conduct individualized safety assessments, to identify age-related risk factors that impact safety, and to develop interventions aimed at prevention of harm and injury.

Non–fall-related injuries such as burns and motor vehicle accidents have been described, and preventive approaches have been discussed. Currently, more attention is being placed on the assessment and prevention of older adult abuse in both home settings and institutions. Gerontologic nurses can be on the cutting edge for the enhanced nursing care and research opportunities that safety issues warrant. The most challenging step is prevention.

Key Points

- Safety and freedom from harm are essential to an older adult's sense of well-being.
- A direct correlation exists between an older person's sense of autonomy and personal safety.
- Some risk factors contributing to falls in older adults include sensory impairment, cognitive impairment, unsafe living environments (e.g., poor lighting, scatter rugs, and unstable furniture), substance abuse, neuromuscular dysfunction, and a history of previous falls.
- An integral part of fall prevention is thorough and accurate assessment of the risk factors related to falls.
- Methods for preventing falls in older adults might include exercise programs, alarms, and safer environmental conditions. The nurse must keep the older client's sense of autonomy in mind when implementing fall prevention methods.
- Operating a motor vehicle is often a basic ingredient in an older adult's independence. Yet with this independence comes increased risk for accidents, mainly as a result of decreased visual acuity and peripheral vision.
- Suicide is a leading cause of death in older adults, often contributed to by poor physical or psychological health, alcohol or drug abuse, past history of suicide attempts, and social isolation.
- Burns are another leading cause of injury in older adults. Risk factors include poverty, sensory impairment, dementia, muscle weakness, poor balance, alcoholism, and cigarette smoking.
- Many older adults are victims of abuse, usually from a relative. Risk factors include poor health, physical or mental dependency, advanced age, and alcohol abuse.
- Nurses must be aware of the risk factors associated with safety and injury in older adults, and they must implement the necessary methods to prevent harm.

Critical Thinking Exercises

1. You are a home care nurse visiting a 69-year-old man at home following his recent CVA. During your intial visit, you note that he lives in a small, poorly lighted basement apartment. His rooms are not carpeted; consequently, he has numerous small rugs lying about. His bathroom has a tub but no shower. The kitchen area is small, and the cabinets extend to the ceiling. He is unable to reach food in the upper cabinets. He is able to move about the apartment with a walker, cook for himself, and care for his daily hygienic needs. Assess your client's potential for accidents or injury. What actions can you take to assure he has a safe living environment?
2. A 92-year-old woman is admitted to the hospital for urinary sepsis. She is very concerned about having to urinate so often and fears she will soil her bed. She is alert and oriented. What precaution should you take to ensure her safety without compromising her control and independence.

REFERENCES

Ali NS, Bennett SJ: Postmenopausal women: factors in osteoporosis preventive behaviors, *J Gerontolog Nurs* 18(12): 23-32, 1992.

Automobile Association of America: Pedestrian safety for the older (65+) adult, *Motorist* May/June:14, 1993, The Association.

Bauer DC, et al: Factors associated with appendicular bone mass in older women, *Ann Intern Med* 118(9):657-665, 1993.

Beauchamp TL, Childress JF: *Principles of biomedical ethics,* New York, 1979, Oxford University Press.

Brady R et al: Geriatric falls: prevention strategies for the staff, *J Gerontolog Nurs* 19(9):26-32, 1993.

Busse EW, Blazer DG: *Geriatric psychiatry,* Washington, DC, 1989, American Geriatric Press.

Butler R, Lewis M: *Aging and mental health,* ed 2, St. Louis, 1977, Mosby.

Byers V, Arrington ME, Finstuen K: Predictive risk factors associated with stroke patient falls in acute care settings, *J Neurosci Nurs* 22(3):147-154, 1990.

Calvani DL, Douris KR: Functional assessment: a holistic approach to rehabilitation of the geriatric client, *Rehab Nurs* 16(6):330-336, 1991.

Campbell AJ: Drug treatment as a cause of falls in old age, *Drugs-Aging* 1(4):289-302, 1991.

Campbell MK, Bush TL, Hale WE: Medical conditions associated with driving cessation in community-dwelling, ambulatory elders, *J Gerontol* 48(4):S230-S234, 1993.

Chaffin DB, Wolstad JC, Trujillo A: Floor/shoe slip resistance measurement, *Am Indust Hyg Assoc J* 53(5):283-289, 1992.

Corbett C, Pennypacker B: Using a quality improvement team to reduce patient falls, *JHO* 14(5):38-54, 1992.

Costa AJ: Preventing falls in your elderly patients, *Postgrad Med* 89(1):139-142, 1991.

Cumming RG et al: Medications and multiple falls in elderly people: the St. Louis OASIS study, *Age-Ageing* 20(6):455-461, 1991.

Cummings SR, Nevitt MC: A hypothesis: the cause of hip fracture, *J Gerontol* 44(4):M107-M111, 1989.

Curtis JR, Geller G, Stokes EG: Characteristics, diagnosis, and treatment of alcoholism in elderly patients, *J Am Geriatr Soc* 37:310-316, 1989.

Ebersole P, Hess P: *Toward healthy aging: human needs and nursing response,* ed 4, St. Louis, 1994, Mosby.

Eliopoulos C: *Gerontological nursing,* ed 3, Philadelphia, 1993, JB Lippincott.

Evans L: Focus on comfort and safety, *Gerontology News* April:2, 1993.

Fiatarone MA et al: The Boston FICSIT study: the effects of resistance training and nutritional supplementation on physical frailty in the oldest old, *J Am Geriatr Soc* 41(3):333-337, 1993.

Fleming BE, Wilson DR, Pendergast DR: A portable, easily performed muscle power test and its association with falls by elderly persons, *Arch Phys Med Rehab* 72(11):886-889, 1991.

Fried AV et al: *International disabilities studies* 12(4): 161-164, 1990.

Haldeman S, Rubenstein SM:Compression fractures in patients undergoing spinal manipulative therapy, *J Manipulative Physiol Ther* 15(7):450-454, 1992.

Hogstel MO, Gaul AL: Safety or autonomy, *J Gerontol Nurs* 17(3):6-11, 1991.

Hornbrook MC, Stevens VJ, Wingfield DJ: Seniors' program for injury control and education, *J Am Geriatr Soc* 41(3):309-314, 1993.

Hunt L et al: Driving performance in persons with mild senile dementia of the Alzheimer Type, *J Am Geriatr Soc* 41(7):747-753, 1993.

Jagella E et al: Alarm devices instead of restraints? *J Am Geriatr Soc* 40(2):191, 1992.

Jantti PO, Pyykko VI, Hervonen A: Falls among elderly nursing home residents, *Pub Health* 107:89-96, 1993.

Josephson KR, Fabacher DA, Rubenstein LZ: Home safety and fall prevention, *Geriatr Home Care,* 7(4):707-731, 1991.

Kane RL: The implications of assessment, *Gerontology* 48(special issue):27-31, 1993.

Kilpack V et al: Using research-based interventions to decrease patient falls, *App Nurs Res* 4(2):50-56, 1991.

Kline D et al: Vision, aging, and driving: the problems of older drivers, *J Gerontol* 47:P27-P34, 1992.

Lipsitz LA et al: Causes and correlates of recurrent falls in ambulatory frail elderly, *J Gerontol* 46(4):M114-M122, 1991.

Lord SR, Clark RD, Webster IW: Visual acuity and contrast sensitivity in relation to falls in an elderly population, *Age-Ageing* 20(3):175-181, 1991.

MacPherson DS et al: Deciding to restrain medical patients, *J Am Geriat Soc* 38:516-520, 1990.

Maki BE, Holliday PJ, Topper AK: Fear of falling and postural performance in the elderly, *J Gerontol* July:46(4):M123-M131, 1991.

Maslow A: *Toward a psychology of being,* Princeton, NJ, 1962, Van Nostrand.

Maslow A: *Motivation and personality,* ed 2, New York, 1954, Harper & Row.

McMurdo ME, Gaskell A: Dark adaptation and falls in the elderly, *Gerontology* 37(4):221-224, 1991.

Miller DJ, Morley JE: Attitudes of physicians toward elderly drivers and driving policy, *J Am Geriatr Soc* 41(7):722-724, 1993.

Mitchell GJ: Nursing diagnosis: an ethical analysis, *Image* 23(2):99-103, 1991.

Morse J, Tylko S, Dixon H: The patient who falls and falls again, *J Gerontolog Nurs* 11(11):15-18, 1985.

Morton D: Five years of fewer falls, *AJN* February:204-205, 1989.

Mroz J: *Safety in everyday living,* Dubuque, Ia., 1978, Wm C Brown.

Myers AH, et al: Risk factors associated with falls among elderly institutionalized persons, *Am J Epidemiol* 133(11): 1179-1190, 1991.

National Center for Health Statistics: *Vital statistics of the United States 2,* Part B: Mortality, Hyattsville, MD, 1990, Department of Health and Human Services, Public Health Service.

National Research Council: *Transportation in an aging society,* Washington, DC, 1988, Transportation Research Board.

Negley EN, Molla PM, Obenchain J: No exit, *J Gerontolog Nurs* 16(8):21-25, 1990.

Nelson RC, Amin MA: Falls in the elderly, *Emerg Med Clin North Am* 8(2):309-324, 1990.

O'Connor CE: *Selected variables associated with falling in a male geriatric rehabilitation and long term care setting,* doctoral dissertation, Washington, D.C., 1990, Catholic University of America.

Persson D: The elderly driver: deciding when to stop, *Gerontologist* 33(1):88-91, 1993.

Pillemer K, Moore DW: Highlights from a study of abuse of patients in nursing homes, *J Elder Abuse Neglect* 2:5-29, 1990.

Pillemer K, Hudson B: A model abuse prevention program for nursing assistants, *Gerontologist* 33(1):128-131, 1993.

Poster EC, Pelletier LR, Kay K: A retrospective cohort study of falls in a psychiatric setting, *Hosp Community Psychiatry* 42(7):714-720, 1991.

Robbins S, Gouw GJ, McClaran J: Which shoes are best for older adults? *J Am Geriatr Soc* 40(11):1089, 1992.

Roberts BL, Wykle ML: Pilot study results: falls among institutionalized elderly, *J Gerontolog Nurs* 19(5):21-27, 1993.

Sackley CM: Falls, sway and symmetry of weight-bearing after stroke, *Int Disabil Stud* 13(1):1-4, 1991.

Sadavoy J, Lazarus LW, Jarvik L: *Comprehensive review of geriatric psychiatry,* Washington, DC, 1991, American Geriatric Press.

Sorock GS, Labiner DM: Peripheral neuromuscular dysfunction and falls, *Am J Epidemiol* 136(5):584-591, 1992.

Stephen FR, Murray JP: The prevention of hot tap water burns, *Burns* 17(5):417-422, 1991.

Strumpf N et al: *Reducing restraints: individualized approaches to behavior,* Huntingdon Valley, Pa., 1992, Whitman.

Studenski S: Physical performance tasks. In Calkins E, editor: *The practice of geriatrics,* ed 2, Philadelphia, 1993, WB Saunders.

Tammelleo AD: Legal case briefs for nurses. [OKay:] Slip and fall of "medicated patient," *Regan Rep Nurs Law* 33(12):3, 1993.

Tinetti ME, Williams F, Mayewski R: Fall risk index for elderly patients based on number of chronic disabilities, *Am J Med* 80(March):429-434, 1986.

Tinetti ME, Speechley M, Ginter SF: Risk factors for falls among elderly persons living in the community, *New Engl J Med* 319:1701-1707, 1988.

Tinetti ME, Richman D, Powell L: Falls efficacy as a measure of fear of falling, *J Gerontol* 45(6):P239-P243, 1991.

Tinetti ME, Liu WL, Ginter SF: Mechanical restraints use, *Ann Intern Med* 116(5):369-374, 1992.

Tinetti ME et al: Yale FICSIT: Risk factor abatement strategy for fall prevention, *J Am Geriatr Soc* 41(3):315-320, 1993.

Tobis JS et al: Falling among the sensorially impaired elderly, *Arch Phys Med Rehab* 71(2):144-147, 1990.

Wolanin MO, Phillips LR: *Confusion,* St Louis, 1981, Mosby.

Wolf ME, Rivara FP: Nonfall injuries in older adults, *Annu Rev Pub Health* 13:509-528, 1992.

Wolfson L et al: Gait assessment in the elderly: a gait abnormality rating scale and its relation to falls, *J Gerontol* 45(1):M12-M19, 1990.

Wright BA et al: Frequent fallers, *Gerontolog Nurs* 16(4):15-19, 1990.

Zepp S: Ban "A" fall: a nursing innovation to reduce patient falls, *Kan Nurs* 66(7):13, 1991.

CHAPTER 12

Mental Health

LEARNING OBJECTIVES

On completion of this chapter, the reader will be able to:

1. Discuss why many older people with mental and behavioral symptoms often are not diagnosed and treated.
2. Relate the concept of ageism to psychiatric diagnosis in older adults.
3. State the prevalence of mental morbidity among nursing facility residents.
4. Explore major factors that contribute to mental health wellness.
5. Recognize the prevalence and significance of mental health problems in the older adult.
6. Describe the range of mental health problems experienced by older adults.
7. Distinguish between the identified mental health problems.
8. Apply the nursing process to older adult clients experiencing mental health distress.
9. Identify appropriate nursing interventions when caring for older adults using psychotropic medications.
10. Evaluate the extent of mental health resources available in the care of older people.
11. Describe trends in the mental health treatment and care of older clients.
12. Identify needs for research in geropsychiatric nursing.

Older people experience mental health problems just like any other age group. These problems can be divided into two broad categories: functional (e.g., depression) and organic (e.g., Alzheimer's disease [AD]). However, many functional disorders have an organic or chemical component and organic diseases certainly affect behavior and functional status. Hippocrates even described many mental disorders in early times that included some pertinent to old age, such as phobias; mania; melancholia; paranoia; hysteria; memory disturbances; and delirium, claiming that the brain was the sole cause of mental disease (Koenig, 1994). This chapter focuses primarily on depression, the most common functional psychiatric disorder in older people; dementia of the Alzheimer's type (DAT), particularly in later stages; anxiety disorders; schizophrenia and paranoid disorders, especially paraphrenia; mental retardation, an increasing problem as mentally retarded people reach old age; and other psychiatric disorders in old age commonly caused by medical conditions. Substance abuse disorders, particularly those caused by alcohol abuse and misuse of medications, are also major problems in old age and are discussed in Chapter 18.

DIFFICULTY IN DIAGNOSIS

One of the major problems in the care of older people with mental disorders is the difficulty with diagnosis. Several chronic, physical health problems often take precedence in the minds of the older person, family members, *and* the primary care physician. However, multiple physical health problems may be the cause of depression or an anxiety disorder. Paranoid beliefs may be caused by a decreasing ability to perceive the environment correctly because of declining vision or hearing. Both physical and mental problems may be caused by **polypharmacy**—taking multiple prescription and **over-the-counter (OTC)** medications that together cause adverse side effects and complications. Two of the most common side effects of many medications taken by older people are mental confusion and disorientation, because some medications cross the blood-brain barrier more easily in this age group than in younger people. Therefore the question becomes are early signs of memory loss and confusion caused by a reversible physical condition such as an infection, an adverse effect of a medication taken for a chronic physical condition, or the beginning symptoms of depression or irreversible dementia?

Older people often are reluctant to seek care from a mental health professional, especially a psychiatrist, because they grew up during a period when there was a strong stigma about mental illness, mental hospitals, and mental treatment. Many older people are very independent and self-reliant and may still believe that a mental or emotional problem is a sign of a "weakness of character." They do not want family or friends to know that they are having a mental problem of some kind and are seeking treatment for it, because they think that it might reflect negatively on other family members. A geriatric care manager, geriatric mental health specialist, home health care nurse, or social worker can perform a screening mental health assessment in the home and, if a mental health problem is suspected, can convince the older person to see a mental health specialist such as a psychiatrist or psychologist for further evaluation and treatment.

Effect of Ageism on Diagnosis and Treatment

Older individuals usually seek care from their primary care physician for a physical problem, although the underlying cause can be a mental or emotional problem. When the older person visits a primary care physician, in family practice or in internal medicine, the physician may not see that the real cause is a mental or emotional problem, because he or she may lack special education or experience with the needs of older clients. The physician may not order the appropriate number and type of diagnostic tests needed to make an accurate diagnosis because of the additional expense or false beliefs that the observed behavior is "part of the normal aging process," or mental health treatment is "not effective in older clients." All of these reasons are examples of ageism, a negative, prejudiced view of aging and older people. In addition, the physician may note vague symptoms of a cognitive disorder and give the client an outdated diagnosis such as senile dementia or a meaningless diagnosis such as organic brain syndrome, without the benefit of specific diagnosis or treatment.

Prescription medications may be ordered for anxiety or depression without determining the cause of the anxiety or depression. Medications may be ordered for aggressive, disruptive, paranoid-type behavior without assessing the reasons for the behavior. Thus symptoms may be suppressed without determining the cause and possible cure. This type of action is similar to giving medication for pain without knowing what is causing the pain, which results in severe complications later, such as a ruptured appendix or gallbladder.

Preventing Premature Institutionalization

Adequate, accurate diagnosis is essential. There may be no specific *cure* (e.g., AD), but it is essential to know if the symptoms and behavior are reversible or not. Even those irreversible disorders *can* and *should* be treated with appropriate medications if useful, and effective communication techniques and environmental strategies as needed.

In one study of 868 residents in long-term care facilities, Parmelee, Katz, and Lawton (1992) identified 44.8% of the people with possible major or minor depression using a number of reliable instruments. Parmelee, et al. (1992) noted that residents with minor depressive symptoms are at risk for major depression and that people with major depression are at risk for mortality. The percentage of residents in nursing facilities with mental illness who are not diagnosed is probably much larger. In one study, German, et al. (1992) reported that 80% of nursing facility residents had some type of mental morbidity, with 60% of these having some degree of dementia (see Research box, p. 272).

RESEARCH

German PS et al: The mental morbidity in the nursing home experience, *Gerontologist* 32(2):152-158, 1992.

Sample, setting

The subjects included 454 residents age 65 and older (77% women, 23% men) newly admitted to eight nursing homes located in the Baltimore metropolitan area.

Methodology

Data on mental status were collected within 2 weeks after admission, at 2 months, and at end of 1 year from residents and staff. Data were collected on resident status and behavior, and events leading to admission from a family member or friend within 1 month of admission. Methods included a full psychiatric evaluation of each resident including history, neurologic examination, the modified Present State Examination, the Mini-Mental State Examination, the Hamilton Depression Scale, the DSM-III-R assessment form, and questions related to satisfaction with life, friendships, and routines. Staff data included interviews related to the Katz Index ADLs, social activities, and the Psychogeriatric Dependency Rating Scale. Data were also abstracted from various medical records.

Findings

On admission, 80% had a diagnosed mental illness, 60% of which had dementia. There was a slightly higher rate at the end of 1 year. About one half of the 60% with dementia had complicating and tentially treatable other mental morbidity.

Implications

Physical and chemical restraints increase maladaptive behavior and increase staff time. Nursing home residents need assessment for and treatment of mental illness to improve their care and quality of life.

If individuals with symptoms of depression or dementia are diagnosed and treated early, institutionalization may be prevented or at least delayed, especially in the case of AD. For example, one person who has had a diagnosis of AD for 10 years is still living at home with family, although there is periodic respite care for the family when the person goes to an adult day care center. Unfortunately, there are many nursing home residents with major mental, emotional, and behavioral problems who have never had the benefit of thorough diagnostic evaluation or mental health treatment. It has been reported that "as many as two thirds of nursing home residents in the United States have serious mental health problems, but few have access to mental health professionals" (*Finding mental health care,* 1995). Brower (1993) noted that estimates of mental illness among residents in nursing facilities are underestimated, because the figures are self-reported by the facilities and "not the results of professional diagnostic activity."

MENTAL HEALTH WELLNESS

Mental health wellness is one of the major components of successful aging, together with physical health, adequate income, and a strong support system (e.g., family, friends, church, neighbors). However, Koenig (1994), a geriatric psychiatrist, has defined successful aging as "how an older person feels, thinks, and acts in whatever circumstances he or she finds themselves." This definition is more broad than the traditional concepts of physical health, financial security, a strong support system, or family or occupational successes.

Many aspects of aging are difficult. The well-known phrase, "old age is not for sissies" is probably true. Examples of losses in old age abound in the literature on gerontology, and especially depression. Much of the depression in older people is caused by situational factors in the environment, for example, loss of family, the stresses of physical illness, or the loneliness of a nursing home. Therefore "where symptoms are mild or antidepressants are contraindicated or unsafe (the majority of cases), then, treatment should be directed at relieving the situation" (Koenig, 1994). However, medications are too often considered the first part of treatment rather than the last.

Losses of physical health, employment and income, family and friends, as well as house and comfortable environment are difficult to accept, especially if they all occur within a relatively short period. Retirement can be difficult and depressing for many, especially those who formerly were involved in interesting, rewarding work. Comorbidity, or the presence of multiple chronic health problems, may prevent older people from enjoying life and may lead to depression.

One of the keys to successful aging is adjusting, or perhaps more accurately, adapting, but not necessarily accepting changes that occur in one's life. Some people adapt to change better than others, depending on their personal feelings of self-concept and self-worth. For example, a man who has always been very independent in decisions about personal financial matters may find it difficult to accept suggestions if his physical condition prevents him from performing all of the activities he has in the past. Alternatives and substitutions should be evaluated carefully and used slowly. A woman whose self-concept and feelings of self-worth have primarily been based on her perception of personal beauty may develop insecure feelings or self-hatred and may consider self-destruction when changes with age occur. She may seek all kinds of artificial beauty aids such as breast implants, eye tucks, and face lifts. These are substitutions that may be essential to her feelings of self-worth. Another woman who was never beautiful in her younger years may not even be aware of, or at least concerned about, physical changes in appearance. A French woman whose age was documented to be 120 in 1995 stated, "I was never very pretty, or ugly either and aging actually suits me rather well." She also said, "I see badly, I hear badly, I can't feel anything, but everything's fine" (Whitney, 1995). She evidently has adapted well to many losses and years of aging.

Prevention of Mental Illness

The focus on prevention of physical illnesses among older people has increased in recent years. However, there has been less focus on the prevention of mental illness, especially among older adults. As previously mentioned, part of this problem may be as a result of ageism. Another reason may be the lack of specific, well-thought-out, and planned programs and activities for older people with the primary focus on prevention of mental and emotional problems.

Retirement planning seminars and workshops have been provided by some employers for many years. However, the primary focus of these sessions often concentrates on financial planning, with some time spent on living arrangements, physical health, and leisure activities. Perhaps it can be concluded that all of these factors are related to mental health wellness. However, specific discussion of mental health wellness, issues, and prevention of mental health problems during retirement is usually not stressed. With the many losses that may accompany retirement, such as the loss of challenging and stimulating work, the loss of relationships with colleagues, and the reduction in income, these issues should be considered and plans should be made.

Physical Wellness

Physical wellness is obviously important to mental health wellness. The young-old, those age 65 to 74, are increasingly interested in health promotion activities such as good nutrition, mild aerobic exercise, and routine health assessments by a qualified health care professional. They attend health education classes at wellness centers, senior centers, American Association of Retired Persons (AARP) chapter meetings, and church meetings, where they learn about good health practices and the dangers of polypharmacy, thus contributing to their mental health wellness. They learn that continued physical *and* mental activity are essential to good health.

Activities that contribute to mental health wellness may be volunteer activities based on experience and expertise, part-time employment, continuing education to seek a degree (an increasing number of people in their 70s and 80s are completing baccalaureate, master's, and doctoral degrees), attending local or regional workshops or seminars, as well as participating in political organizations and activities and hostel programs on university campuses while traveling.

Older adults who experience acute physical illnesses and recover rather quickly are probably not as high-risk for mental health problems as those who develop chronic, long-lasting, incurable diseases that cause them to become frustrated, depressed, and sometimes suicidal.

Support Systems

Another important factor that is essential in maintaining mental health wellness in old age is a strong support system of some kind. Support may be provided by family members, the church, friends, neighbors, and others. A person needs someone to turn to, confide in, and have available during times of wellness *and* illness. This type of support is especially important when people reach the older ages, especially the late 80s, 90s, and 100s, because they are more likely to develop physical and dependency needs.

The family continues to be the first source of support for older people. This support may be regular contact through visiting or telephoning; participation with them in recreational activities; social and psychologic support; assistance with transportation, shopping, and financial matters such as paying bills; or more direct physical caregiving.

The church is the second source of support for many older people. In fact, the church or congregation is often the first source of support for many older people, especially those in their late 80s, 90s, and 100s. They may have lost their spouses, siblings, and adult children to death. Or, in our mobile society, adult children may live thousands of miles away and not be readily available in times of need.

People age 65 and older tend to have been more active in church activities during their lifetime than younger age groups and often continue or even increase these activities when they retire. "Most studies demonstrate that the current generation of elderly Americans are more religiously oriented than are their younger peers" (Koenig, 1994). Religious beliefs and practices, as well as a more broad concept of spirituality (simply defined as belief in something beyond self) contribute to feelings of security, hope, love, and self-worth, all of which strengthen mental health. According to Koenig (1994), "all persons have spiritual needs, whether they recognize them as such or not."

In a period of decreased federal and state funding for social services for older people, many believe that the organized church should return to more of their original goals and activities by providing increased support and social services to those in need. "Given the current and future health needs of aging Americans, and the limited governmental resources being made available, there is great opportunity (and responsibility) for the religious community to demonstrate their own faith and trust by supporting and ministering to the emotional, spiritual, and sometimes physical needs of this population" (Koenig, 1994). The church can be a major factor in improving the quality of life of older people and preventing premature institutionalization.

The expanding role of the parish nurse is important in helping older people to maintain both physical and mental health. The primary roles of the parish nurse are health education, personal counseling, referral to community resources, and coordinating volunteers (Beal, 1994). By training church lay volunteer visitors how to make quality one-on-one visits to older people, their feelings of loneliness and depression are often reduced (Hogstel, Smith, 1994). Some studies have shown "that religion either protects against or helps to relieve depressive symptoms in medical inpatients" (Koenig, 1994).

Role of the Nurse in Mental Health Wellness

Nurses need to be aware of their personal attitudes and opinions about aging and the care of older people. Ageism is usually the result of inaccurate information and inadequate knowledge. "Age also influences how health care professionals respond to [clients]. Adverse incidents in older [clients] often lead to interventions such as administering psychotropic medications, applying physical restraints, and inserting urinary catheters—interventions that carry their own intrinsic risks" (*Geriatric models of care: which one's right for your institution?*, 1994). The nurse who understands the aging process and conditions that may accompany the aging process does not label an acutely ill hospitalized older adult as *demented* when the client's behavior is most likely a symptom of *delirium,* a reversible, temporary condition brought on by a change in environment, anesthesia, medication, or other physical factors. The nurse should communicate with and should attentively listen to the older person, taking into consideration any sensory deficits assessed during the admission history and physical examination. The nurse should involve the older client and his or her family in the care plan. The nurse should do everything possible to maintain or to enhance the older client's feelings of self-concept and self-worth by providing privacy, seeking his or her opinion in matters of care, treating the older client with respect and if needed, seeking referrals for specific diagnosis and treatment of possible mental health problems.

> **Insight** • *An alert, independent 91-year-old woman was admitted to a general hospital for repair of a fractured hip. Because of sudden relocation, anesthesia, and medications for pain, she was labeled "uncooperative" in her confusion (and possibly the staff's lack of communication), which was caused by temporary reversible delirium. She was given haloperidol (Haldol), which caused her to exhibit more erratic behaviors that were also labeled "uncooperative." She was then restrained, which caused her to become incontinent (iatrogenesis), because she could not signal for a bedpan. She then became hostile and would not eat, so a urinary catheter and nasogastric feeding tube were inserted. Her recovery was hindered, her hospitalization lengthened, and the hospital bill increased. All of these complications probably could have been prevented if she had an understanding nurse who recognized the reasons for her delirium and communicated with her in an effective manner (Ball, 1989).*

MAJOR MENTAL HEALTH PROBLEMS

It is estimated that 15% to 25% of individuals age 65 and over are experiencing mental disorders. This represents 2.4 million individuals each year in the United States (Keltner, 1995). The most common psychiatric diagnoses seen in older adults are depression (42%), schizophrenia (22%), and bipolar disorders (13%) (Krach, Yang, 1992). These statistics represent a significant impact on American society and also present a challenge for nurses as the role of nursing in interdisciplinary care of older adults and their family members increases (Abraham, Smullen, Thompson-Heisterman, 1992).

To adequately perform the nursing role, a comprehensive body of knowledge that includes theories of aging, health and illness, mental health, biopsychosocial interplay, and clinical skills must be identified (Abraham, Smullen, Thompson-Heisterman, 1992). Nurses must also understand the relevant neurobehavioral theories, the use of psychotherapeutic medications, and the potential adverse reactions or drug interactions that can be seen when these drugs are used (Abraham, Buckwalter, 1994).

The goals for which nurses strive when working with older adults experiencing major mental health problems include maximizing the individual's functioning, independence, and quality of life; providing support for clients and their families; adapting interventions to multiple settings such as the home, community, and long-term care institutions; lowering morbidity; decreasing suffering; improving the older adult's self-esteem and integrity; enhancing the client's daily life experience; and ensuring continuity of care with smooth transitions between the various levels of care (Abraham, Buckwalter, 1994).

Depression

Depression is the most common functional mental illness seen in older adults. Current estimates indicate that 15% to 20% of older adults experience depression (Stuart, Sundeen, 1995). The prevalence of depression increases among older adults in long-term care facilities. The incidence of depression in this population may range from 30% to 50% (Matthiesen, 1995). The increased dependency that older adults may experience can lead to hopelessness, helplessness, a lowered sense of self-control, and decreased self-esteem and self-worth. These changes can interfere with the older adult's daily functioning and therefore may lead to depression (Hogstel, 1995). Unfortunately, depression in older adults is often overlooked and is therefore left untreated. When left untreated, depression can lead to an increase in both morbidity and mortality among older adults (Kurlowicz, 1993). Equally problematic is the fact that depressive disorders are often misdiagnosed as a result of the unique types of symptoms that depression in older adults may manifest. Symptoms that may appear to be representative of a cognitive disorder are often in reality symptoms of depression (Kah, Kupper, 1993).

A number of theories attempt to explain the cause of depression. As each theory asserts its own stance, the depression that clinicians see in older adults seems to represent an interplay of biologic, psychologic, and social factors. Older adults at highest risk for depressive symptoms are women over age 85, who are unmarried, in an urban area, living in a long-term care setting, experiencing physical illness or disability, lacking adequate social support, of a lower socioeconomic status, and are likely to be experiencing a significant loss (Kurlowicz, 1993). Factors that seem to protect older adults from depression include hardiness (defined as a personal characteristic of commitment, control, and challenge) and development of healthy attitudes toward death (Cataldo, 1994).

Depression in older adults may be divided into the two broad categories of *depressive disorder* and *bipolar disorder.* Depressive disorders can range from an acute major depression to dysthymia, which is a chronic (2 years or longer) range of depressive symptoms. In bipolar disorders the depressive symptoms alternate with manic symptoms, which are seen as an abnormal elevation of mood. The swings between depression and mania can be drastic, as seen in Bipolar Type I disorder; they can alternate between major depression and less severe manic behavior (hypomanic), as seen in Bipolar Type II disorder; or the client may exhibit signs of dysthymia alternating with hypomanic symptoms and thus be referred to as cyclothymic (American Psychiatric Association [APA], 1994.)

Although the course of depressive symptoms varies from individual to individual, there are some common elements in the development of depression in older adults. The change in the older adult's self-concept, combined with a sense of loneliness and isolation, often leads to a feeling of increased dependence on family members or other caregivers. This sense of dependency can lead to a progressive decline as the depression begins. Also contributing to the development of depression can be factors such as preexisting mental illness and the loss of loved ones, especially if multiple losses occur in a short period. A number of physical disorders are associated with the development of depression in older adults. These include disorders such as congestive heart failure, diabetes mellitus, infectious diseases, changes in gastrointestinal function, cancer, seizure disorders, anemia, and sleep disorders. A number of medications used by older adults are associated with depressive symptoms. In particular, cardiovascular agents, antianxiety drugs, amphetamines, narcotics, and hormone medications may all play a role in the development of depression. Substance abuse of alcohol, illegal drugs, prescription medications, or OTC medications can pose a significant risk for depression (Browning, 1995).

Symptoms of depression in older adults can include distressful feelings, cognitive changes, behavioral changes, and physical symptoms. Feelings that older adults may experience when they are depressed include malaise, fatigue, lack of interest, inability to experience pleasure, sense of uselessness, hopelessness, helplessness, decreased sexual interest, increased dependency, and anxiety. Cognitive changes that may signal depression in an older adult include a slowing or unreliability of the individual's memory, paranoia, agitation, a focus on the past, thoughts of death, and thoughts of suicide as a potential option. The older adult with depression may show behavioral changes such as difficulty completing activities of daily living (ADLs), change in appetite (most commonly, a decrease), changes in sleeping patterns (usually insomnia), lowered energy level, poor grooming, and withdrawal from people and interests they have enjoyed in the past. Physical symptoms that are commonly seen in older adults experiencing depression include muscle aches, abdominal pain or tightness, flatulence, nausea and vomiting, dry mouth, and headaches (Browning, 1995).

Nursing Management

✣ ASSESSMENT

Assessing depression in an older adult can be accomplished with standardized rating scales or with a comprehensive nursing assessment that includes an evaluation of several key components of depression. A number of instruments have been developed to screen older adults for depression, and other instruments provide a standardized approach to rating its severity. One of the most commonly used scales in assessing the presence or absence of depression in older adults is the Geriatric Depression Scale (see Chapter 4). The simplicity and versatility that it allows the clinician make it particularly useful (Baldwin, Stevens, Friedman, 1995).

When the nursing assessment indicates the possibility of depression, the nurse can further assess the symptoms of depression previously mentioned. The comprehensive assessment includes a health history, physical assessment, medication history, mental status examination, nutritional history, family assessment, and an assessment of the client's ADLs. Diagnostic tests that may be useful in ascertaining the presence of depression versus another illness include certain laboratory tests (complete blood count [CBC], thyroid function studies, urinalysis, dexamethasone suppression test), electrocardiogram (ECG), electroencephalogram (EEG), magnetic resonance image (MRI), or computed tomography (CT) scans.

✣ DIAGNOSIS

See Box 12-1.

BOX 12-1

NANDA Nursing Diagnoses Appropriate for Older Adults with Depression

- Ineffective individual coping
- Altered family processes
- Dysfunctional grieving
- High risk for self-directed violence
- Hopelessness
- Impaired social interaction
- Powerlessness
- Risk for loneliness
- Self-care deficit
- Self-esteem disturbance
- Spiritual distress

✣ PLANNING

In planning the care for older adults with depression, the nurse should set both short- and long-term goals that are appropriate for the nursing diagnoses identified for the client.

✣ INTERVENTION

Nurses have a unique role in the interdisciplinary team approach that is most often used in the treatment of depression. The focus of nursing care is to intervene with the human responses that occur as a result of the depression. Nursing intervention can occur at numerous points along the continuum of care and in settings ranging from the client's home to an outpatient clinic to a partial hospitalization program or in an inpatient unit (see nursing Care Plan, p. 277).

Regardless of the setting in which nursing care is provided, safety is the primary goal. Older adults who are depressed are often at risk because of their inability to care for themselves and may also be at risk as a result of self-destructive behavior or suicidal ideation or plans. The nurse must constantly assess the level of risk for the clients with whom they work and must take appropriate steps to ensure their clients' safety (see Research box, p. 278). The issue of suicide in older adults is further addressed on p. 278.

Physical needs are also a priority for frequent intervention in depressed older adults. They may be unable to perform their own ADLs and need assistance or motivation to do so. They may also have numerous somatic concerns such as insomnia, decreased appetite, pain, gastrointestinal distress, and headaches with which the nurse should intervene.

The cornerstone of the nurse's ability to positively affect change in the older adult's response to depression lies in the development of a therapeutic relationship. The nurse must model unconditional positive regard and empathy in a professional manner so that trust can be developed. Once trust has been established, the client becomes far more open to the nurse's intervention steps.

In an inpatient setting, the professional nurse is most often considered the milieu manager and as such, must provide an optimum environment for the client's treatment. Nursing has considered the role that the environment plays in a client's recovery as far back as the experiences of Florence Nightingale. These factors include color, light, art, movement, level of activity, and the interpersonal environment. Recent research has shown a role for exposure to sunlight in the treatment of clients with depression (Loving, Kripke, 1992).

A number of psychotherapeutic modalities are used to respond to depression in the older adult. These include milieu, individual, family, and group therapy. Group therapy is particularly effective with older adults, since it

CARE PLAN

MAJOR DEPRESSION

Clinical situation Mrs. S is an 81-year-old widow whose husband died suddenly 4 years ago after a massive myocardial infarction. She has one daughter who lives 800 miles away and visits once a year. Her major source of support and friendship since her husband's death had been a neighbor, Mrs. J, who died 1 month ago after suffering a stroke. Mrs. S tells the nurse practitioner at a recent office visit, "I just don't know how to deal with this. I handled things well after my husband died but when my neighbor died last month, I just fell apart. I don't feel like eating, I can't fall asleep at night, and my daughter tells me I sound like I'm going to pieces." On assessment, the nurse practitioner finds Mrs. S with symptoms that include slow motor movements and thought processes. Her grooming is poor, and she appears to be sleep-deprived. She has lost 12 pounds since her last visit 5 weeks ago. She is tearful with frequent sobbing.

Nursing diagnosis	Outcomes	Interventions
Ineffective, individual coping related to death of husband 4 years ago and recent death of neighbor	*Short term:* Client will verbalize two coping strategies that have been effective for her in the past at the time of the next appointment (3 days). *Long term:* Client will develop a prioritized list of issues that she plans to address with the identified coping strategies within 1 month of the initial assessment.	Assess client's risk for injury as a result of self-directed violence by completing an assessment of suicidal risk. If client is suicidal, arrange for a higher level of care, such as partial hospitalization or inpatient care. Develop a therapeutic relationship with client based on trust and empathy. Assist client to identify coping strategies that she has successfully used in the past. Assist client to develop list of individuals (with phone numbers) who have been or could be supportive. Help client outline a daily schedule that can guide her completion of ADLs. Assist client in developing a list of problems from most to least urgent. Assess need for initiation for antidepressant medication. Educate client and family of need for ongoing support. Refer client to local grief support group.

allows them to self-express and to receive support (Clark, Vorst, 1994). A specific type of group therapy that seems to be useful with older adults is reminiscence therapy in which they are encouraged to discuss past events to identify problem-solving skills that have worked for them in the past. Older adults who are displaying unhealthy behavioral changes in response to their depression may also benefit from behavior therapy (Gomez, Gomez, 1993). The key to behavior therapy in older adults is to use a direct and structured approach that also maintains the client's integrity and autonomy. Allowing the client to have choices and options that clearly delineated consequences for their choices enables them to maintain a sense of control.

Nurses also play a significant role in the biologic interventions that are used to treat depression. A thorough understanding of the appropriate use of psychotherapeutic medications, drug-drug interactions, drug-food interactions, potential adverse reactions, and legal and ethical implications of these medications is necessary for the nurse to intervene appropriately with depressed older adults. Electroconvulsive therapy (ECT) is sometimes used for depression in older adults. The nurse who intervenes with clients receiving ECT must have a comprehensive understanding of the indications, benefits, and risks inherent in this therapeutic intervention.

Nursing intervention with older adults who are depressed occurs on three levels: primary, secondary, and tertiary. Primary intervention involves actions that promote health and decrease the likelihood of depression. Secondary intervention includes the nurse's response when the client is experiencing the acute symptoms of depression. Tertiary intervention is the restorative or rehabilitative functions that the nurse performs to assist a client in his or her recovery process. An important aspect of tertiary intervention involving clients with depression is teaching new coping skills to lessen the likelihood of recurring depression.

✣ EVALUATION

In evaluating the care a nurse has provided to an older adult experiencing depression, the nurse should initially compare the client outcomes with the short- and long-term goals that were outlined in the planning phase of the nursing process. Appropriate alterations should then be made to the continuing treatment plan to ensure optimum client response. It is helpful to assess the level of satisfaction that clients and their families feel toward the nursing care that has been provided. It is also important for nurses to assess their own reactions to the client and the care that has been provided to ascertain the impact (positive or negative) that the client has had on the nurse (see Research box, below).

RESEARCH

Cataldo J: Hardiness and death attitudes: predictors of depression in the institutionalized elderly, *Arch Psychiatr Nurs* 8(5):326-332, 1994.

Sample, setting

The subjects included 90 men and women age 65 to 92 in a long-term care setting in a large municipal hospital system in New York City.

Methodology

Depressive symptoms were measured using the Zung Self-rating Depression Scale (SDS). Hardiness (defined as commitment, challenge, and control) was measured using the Health-Related Hardiness Scale (HRHS). Death attitudes were measured using the Death Attitude profile (DAP).

Findings

The absence of hardiness was positively correlated with depression. Healthy death attitudes were negatively correlated with depression. The combination of nonhardiness and health-limiting death attitudes can predict a likelihood of depression in older adults who are institutionalized.

Implications

Nurses in long-term care settings can predict an increased incidence of depression in clients who lack hardiness and in clients who have negative death atti-tudes. This highlights the impor-tance of psychosocial nursing as-sessment of older clients who are institutionalized and adds to the body of knowledge with which gerontologic nurses should be familiar.

Suicide

Suicide among older adults is a growing problem in our society. Older adults account for 12% of the U.S. population (*A profile of older Americans,* 1994), but 39% of suicide deaths are in individuals over age 65 (Stuart, Sundeen, 1995). The rate of suicide by older adults has increased by 25% in the last 20 years. The highest suicide rate is seen in older adults, particularly those between 75 and 85 years of age (Stuart, Sundeen, 1995). It is believed that by the year 2000, suicide by older adults will occur 10,500 times each year (Keltner, 1995). Suicide attempts by older adults also tend to be fatal more often than when seen in other age groups. Suicide attempts by individuals over age 60 are five times more likely to result in a completed suicide than are those attempts made by individuals in other age groups (Schmid, Manjee, Shah, 1994). Older adults attempt suicide less often than individuals in other age groups, but one out of every two suicide attempts by an older adult results in death (Keltner, 1995).

Despite these rather sobering statistics, American society continues to ignore suicide in older adults. Older adults are less likely to communicate their intent to commit suicide and as a result many health care professionals have assumed erroneously that suicide is not a significant issue among older adults (Mellick, Buckwalter, Stolley, 1992).

Some older adult suicides are attempts to remain in control by deciding the appropriate time to die (Courage et al, 1993). Such an attempt is sometimes called **benign suicide** or **rational suicide.** These terms refer to suicides planned by individuals as a result of perceiving life to have no remaining quality. These types of suicide pose an ethical dilemma for nurses regarding client autonomy versus the value of life and often also pose a legal issue because of the recent publicity resulting from a reexamination of laws in several states (Courage et al, 1993). Despite the inherent uncertainty in these cases, several nursing scholars have supported a nursing perspective that affirms life by enhancing the individual's quality of life rather than assuring them of their right to die (Moore, 1993).

Another issue that nurses deal with in caring for older adults is that of passive suicide. This is also called subintentioned suicide (Varcarolis, 1994) and is a passive attempt to hasten one's death. This type of self-destructive behavior often goes unrecognized (Brady, 1993) and can range from noncompliance with one's health care regimen (e.g., refusing safe and appropriate use of needed medication) to behaviors that harm the individual in a more active manner (e.g., continued smoking, alcohol

BOX 12-2

Risk Factors for Suicide in Older Adults

- Age (especially those between ages 75 and 85)
- Lower socioeconomic status
- Male
- Caucasian
- Living alone
- Physical illness
- Chronic pain
- Recent personal loss (especially within 1 year of death of spouse)
- Other losses such as economic, social, prestige, or cumulative losses
- Substance abuse (alcohol, prescription medication, OTC medications, or illegal substances)
- Familial history of suicide
- Prior suicide attempts
- Fear of institutionalization or fear of increasing dependence
- Recent retirement
- Social isolation
- Chronic sleep problems
- Symptoms of depression (related to 50% to 70% of suicides by older adults)
- Impulsivity

Data compiled from Browning MA: Depression, suicide and bereavement. In Hogstel MO, editor: *Geropsychiatric nursing,* ed 2, St Louis, 1995, Mosby; Courage M et al: Suicide in the elderly: staying in control, *J Psychosocial Nurs* 31(7):25-31, 1993; Holzapfel SK: The elderly. In Varcarolis EM, editor: *Foundations of psychiatric mental health nursing,* ed 2, Philadelphia, 1994, WB Saunders; Varcarolis EM: People who contemplate suicide: aggression toward self. In Varcarolis EM, editor: *Foundations of psychiatric mental health nursing,* ed 2, Philadelphia, 1994, WB Saunders.

abuse, or an eating disorder) to participating in dangerous situations (e.g., reckless driving).

Risk Factors

The risk factors for suicide in older adults are presented in Box 12-2. At highest risk for suicide are Protestant white males who are living alone in their homes. They often demonstrate a neat appearance and calm behavior and are often taking either antianxiety or antipsychotic medications (Schmid, Manjee, Shah, 1994).

NURSING MANAGEMENT

Many of the steps outlined in the nursing process of older adults with depression are also appropriate for an older adult who is at risk for suicide. The following are steps that are more specific to suicidal clients.

BOX 12-3

Questions to Ask a Client for the Potential for Suicide

- What has been the most difficult moment for you in the recent past?
- Have things been so bad that you have thought about escaping?
- If so, how?
- Are there times when death seems like an attractive option to you?
- Have you thought of harming yourself?
- Have you thought about killing yourself?
- If you were to harm yourself, how would you do so?
- Do you have access to the items you would need to carry out your plan? (This includes a gun, quantities of medication, a rope, an enclosed garage.)
- Have you thought about or attempted to harm yourself in the past?
- What has kept you from harming yourself thus far?
- What might keep you from harming yourself in the future?

✣ ASSESSMENT

In assessing a client for the potential for suicide, it is helpful to have a series of questions for interviewing the client (Box 12-3).

Although not all questions are needed or appropriate for all clients, it is helpful to have a progressive series of assessment items in mind that can be adapted to the situation in which the nurse is functioning. The basic components of suicide assessment include evaluating suicidal ideation (thoughts), prior attempts, the client's suicide plan, the lethality of the plan, the availability of the implements of the plan, coexisting substance abuse, and the pervasiveness of the despair that he or she is experiencing.

✣ DIAGNOSIS

Nursing diagnoses for the older adult at risk for suicide include but are not limited to the following: (1) ineffective individual coping, (2) dysfunctional grieving, (3) hopelessness, (4) high risk for violence, and (5) spiritual distress.

Insight • *It is essential that nurses assess the perception of the future in all older adult clients with whom they work because of the prevalence of suicide among this age group. When appropriate, a more thorough and systematic assessment can then be made.*

PLANNING

Planning care for the suicidal older adult client requires a strong interpersonal connectedness with the client. Expected outcomes include but are not limited to the following: (1) client identifies and verbalizes thoughts and feelings related to emotional state, (2) client reports absence of suicidal ideation, (3) client demonstrates effective coping skills in managing stress and frustration, (4) client experiences behavior control with assistance of others, and (5) client expresses satisfaction with spiritual well-being.

INTERVENTION

When a risk of suicide is identified in an older adult client, the appropriate safety measures must be taken. These safety measures can be tailored to the specifics of the client's suicide plan, the setting in which the nurse is intervening (i.e., in the client's home versus an inpatient setting), as well as the extent of human connectedness that the client has. It may be necessary for the nurse to arrange with the local mental health authorities for inpatient hospitalization (voluntary or involuntary), if the client's safety cannot be assured in an outpatient setting. The client's significant others can often be helpful in assisting the client to develop a plan of safety. *It is essential for nurses to remember that no extent of environmental precautions can take the place of a strong interpersonal connection with the client.* Clients who are suicidal are able to be creative and adaptive in finding alternative methods of suicide. Without a strong therapeutic relationship to assist the client, the nurse's best effort to keep a client safe may prove to be fruitless. Asking the client about potential suicidal thoughts does not plant the idea in the client's mind. If the nurse has reason to believe that the client may be suicidal, it is quite likely that the client has already considered this option.

A useful tool with suicidal individuals is a "no-suicide contract." This is an agreement (ideally written and signed) between the client and the health care provider that the client will not harm himself or herself. The specific wording of the agreement may differ based on the client's risk factors and the setting in which the care is occurring. For example, on an inpatient unit an agreement might state, "I commit that I will not harm myself while in the hospital, and if I have thoughts of harming myself, I will immediately inform a staff member."

Insight • *Nurses who deal with older adults experiencing suicidal ideation should encourage these clients to express and to process their suicidal thoughts rather than to attempt to avoid the topic.*

Once clients are past the immediate danger of suicidal behavior, it is helpful to assist them to develop a suicide prevention plan. Such a plan can include alternatives to consider other than suicide and may also include specific steps that clients can take if they are to again experience suicidal thoughts. This plan encourages clients to take a problem-solving (active) approach to the potential for self-harm and therefore increases their sense of control.

Nurses have the ability to play a significant role in suicide prevention in older adults. Essential components in such preventive intervention include assessing all older adults for potential self-harm issues, proactively identifying and treating depression in older adults, developing community programs focused on prevention of older adult suicide, and teaching health care professionals who work with older adults in different settings about the risk for suicide.

EVALUATION

Unfortunately, despite excellent nursing assessment and intervention, older adults do continue to commit suicide at a distressingly high rate. When an older adult has committed suicide the nurse's focus may be to assist the survivors of the suicide to cope with the resulting grief and trauma. A **psychologic autopsy,** or the processing of events and behaviors surrounding the client's suicide, may be useful both to the health care professionals as well as to the surviving family and friends. It is also helpful to encourage the survivors to obtain assistance from a support group for survivors of suicide.

Delirium, Dementia, and Related Disorders

Many individuals accept a decline in intellectual functioning as a normal part of aging. Although there may be changes in the older adult's intellectual functioning, a recognizable impairment such as confusion, hallucination, or delusion is not a normal aspect of aging and may represent an active disease process. Accurate diagnosis of these impairments becomes essential to successfully treat or cure some processes or to provide optimum intervention in those which cannot be cured (Lind, 1995).

Delirium, dementia, and related disorders comprise a group of disorders known as cognitive disorders. These disorders may have multiple causes and show wide variations in clinical presentation. Delirium and dementia are the foci in this section, especially the later stages of these processes, the chronic long-term care needs, and the related nursing management. Early and acute stages of diagnosis, treatment, and nursing management are covered in Chapter 27.

The APA Diagnostic Statistic Manual (DSM-IV) (1994) divides the cognitive disorders into four categories: *delirium, dementia, amnestic disorders,* and *other cognitive disorders.* The delirium disorders may be related to a general medical condition or substance withdrawal, may be substance-induced, may have multiple causes, or may fit into a broad category labeled "not otherwise specified" (APA, 1994). The dementia disorders may be of the Alzheimer's type; vascular type; or related to a general medical condition, persistent and substance-induced as a result of multiple causes; or may fit into the "not otherwise specified" category.

Delirium disorders are organic brain disorders that are evidenced by a change in the individual's level of consciousness and cognition. Delirium develops rapidly over a short period. Dementia is a disorder of multiple cognitive deficits and memory impairment. It is important to differentiate between delirium and dementia. Symptoms from both include memory impairment, but delirium disorders also show a change in the client's level of consciousness. In delirium disorders the symptoms may fluctuate over time, whereas in dementia, the symptoms are more stable over time. Delirium may occur in an older adult who has experienced symptoms or a diagnosis of dementia before (APA, 1994). When delirium symptoms are superimposed on dementia symptoms, it becomes vital to sort out the difference and the illness process that the delirium symptoms may represent. Essentially, delirium is a disorder with an acute onset and a reversible cause, whereas dementia is a disorder with a chronic onset and an often irreversible cause (Lind, 1995).

Dementia

Dementia is a broad category that includes disorders manifested by a decrease in the older adult's intellectual ability, which interferes with ADLs. Vocational and interpersonal functioning is often altered. The cardinal signs that are seen in dementia disorders are alterations in memory, abstract thinking, judgment, and perception (Keltner, 1995). Of dementia disorders, 25% to 35% are the result of a treatable cause (Lind, 1995). In other dementia disorders, no specific cause can be identified and the disorders may be permanent.

Early recognition of dementia disorders can be helpful to allow the development of the optimum plan of care for the client, as well as to allow clients to help plan their own future care. There is no single, specific diagnostic test for dementia, therefore observations by the health care team and the client's family members and friends are used to develop a case history. A thorough health and medication history, physical assessment, laboratory studies, neurologic examination, and other diagnostic studies are used to rule out other causes of the dementia. There are a number of rating scales that have been developed to assess cognitive functioning (see Chapter 27). Jutagir (1994) discusses the differences between the common cognitive decline that may be seen in aging versus the symptoms of dementia.

The early and acute stages of dementia are addressed in Chapter 27. Briefly, the diagnostic criteria that identify a dementia are memory impairment and cognitive disturbances such as aphasia (disturbed language), apraxia (impaired motor activity), agnosia (inability to recognize objects), and disturbed planning and organizing functions (APA, 1994).

Dementia of the Alzheimer's Type

Alzheimer's disease is a progressive dementia that usually ends in death, often about 5 to 8 years after the onset of the disease (Lind, 1995). Diagnosis of Alzheimer's is made by excluding other possible causes of the client's symptoms. A definite diagnosis can only be made by biopsy (which is rare) or during autopsy.

Brady (1993) divides the progression of Alzheimer's disease into three stages. In the early stage, the primary symptom is memory loss. In the middle stage, the client's language skills become impaired, as do motor activity and ability to recognize objects. The most rapid cognitive deterioration is seen in the middle stage (Stern et al, 1994). In the final or terminal stage of the disease, the client may become incontinent, unable to ambulate, and may show a complete loss of language skills.

NURSING MANAGEMENT

ASSESSMENT

Most of the assessment phase can be completed before the client reaches the later stage of DAT. The nurse should review the client's records and obtain information from available sources to assure that comprehensive health and medication histories, as well as physical and mental status assessments have been completed recently. An assessment of current func-tioning and behavior should be compared with the information available about the functioning before the development of dementia, as well as functioning in the early and middle stages of the disease's progression. It is also useful to assess when the symptoms are most and least noticeable, what seems to help or worsen the symptoms, and what impact the symptoms are having on the client's daily functioning. The nurse should acquire information about the client's previous coping skills and support systems so that these can be used to the greatest extent possible in planning for the nursing interventions.

It is also necessary to differentiate the symptoms of dementia from symptoms that may represent a primary psychiatric disorder such as a depression, anxiety, or psychosis. Sleep deprivation, sensory deprivation, pain, stress, and grief reactions may all contribute to the development of a primary mental disorder that can coexist with DAT (Detwiler, 1993).

BOX 12-4

NANDA Nursing Diagnoses Appropriate for a Client with Dementia

Altered thought processes
High risk for injury
High risk for violence, directed at self or others
Impaired social interaction
Ineffective individual coping
Ineffective family coping
Powerlessness
Self-care deficit
Self-concept disturbance
Sleep pattern disturbance

From Detwiler CS: Organic mental disorders. In Johnson B, editor: *Psychiatric mental health nursing: adaptation and growth,* ed 3, Philadelphia, 1993, JB Lippincott.

DIAGNOSIS

See Box 12-4.

PLANNING

Detwiler (1993) outlines four broad goals to be used in planning nursing care for clients with DAT: (1) to prevent the acceleration of symptoms; (2) to preserve the clients' dignity; (3) to promote health, socialization, and independent functioning to the greatest extent possible; and (4) to preserve the family's unity. Other factors that are useful to remember in planning clients' care are the goals of providing safety, decreasing clients' stressors, providing a structured environment for clients, and developing a therapeutic interpersonal relationship with clients. It is also imperative to involve clients and their identified support systems as much as possible.

INTERVENTION

The interventions used in caring for an older adult with DAT should be custom-designed to fit the setting in which the client is receiving care. In the home setting, extensive support may be needed by the family and caregivers who also may have their own health problems. The nurse can assist the caregivers in the development of problem-solving skills that transcend the course of the illness. Depression and grief reactions are human responses often seen in the caregivers of individuals with AD (Hall et al, 1995). Information about the availability of support services such as community support groups and respite care are essential to the AD caregiver (McCabe et al, 1995). The nurse is the ideal person to collect and disseminate this information because of nursing's holistic and comprehensive focus.

Day care programs designed especially for the older adult with DAT may give the caregivers the flexibility they need to continue their own occupations or other

> **Insight** • *Nurses should involve the client's family in the care and should be prepared to deal with the behavior the family members may demonstrate in response to their loved one's progressive decline.*

ADLs. The use of AD day care services has been shown to have a positive effect both on clients with dementia and their caregivers (Suwa-Kobayashi, Yuasa, Noguchi, 1995).

The severe cognitive decline characteristic of the later stages of AD may necessitate the admission of the client into a long-term care setting. This is especially true for clients who demonstrate potentially dangerous behaviors such as wandering outside, aggression, and paranoid-type behaviors.

Nurses have the opportunity to play a significant role in the planning of care provided to older adults in long-term care settings. Nurses can provide education and training for the long-term care staff, and can serve as supervisors, role models, and supporters for the other staff members. The nurse with advanced education and experience can serve as a consultant, expert caregiver, researcher, and educator. There is a need for creative and innovative nursing interventions when caring for clients with AD (Perlaky, 1994).

Lind (1995) outlines nursing interventions that may be appropriate in providing care to an older adult client with DAT. These interventions address safety issues, health promotion, rest/wake cycles, the environment of care, and the nurse's interactions with the client.

Safety Issues

Providing a safe care setting is the highest priority for nurses functioning in a long-term care setting. It is often the inability to ensure the client's safety in other settings that causes the client to be admitted into a long-term care facility. Basic precautions should be taken to prevent the client from falling. It is also necessary to assess the objects that clients use in ADLs such as razors, electrical appliances, and walkers. These items should be modified or stored in different ways to keep the client from using them in dangerous ways. Attention should be given to temperature control of foods, beverages, and bath water, because the client may not be able to make safe judgments about the use of heat. Cleaning or personal hygiene products should be kept in locked areas to prevent the client's ingestion of these substances.

Special nursing interventions may be necessary for the client who demonstrates wandering behavior. *Wandering* is a term used when a client leaves a designated area without the permission or knowledge of the caregiver. This often proves to be dangerous for the client and may lead to the client's elopement from the care facility. The client who demonstrates wandering behavior should be closely supervised and alarm systems should be installed on exterior doors to alert the staff of clients who may be attempting to elope. The client's clothing should be labeled with his or her name and the phone number of the facility so that the client may be identified and returned to the care facility if elopement occurs. Wandering behavior can be decreased by providing clients with a large secure area in which they can safely pace and have freedom of movement, such as a circular hallway. When staff members observe the client wandering, they may intervene by politely asking the client to take a walk with them or by gently leading the client by the hand back to a safe area.

At times, the client with AD may demonstrate aggressive behavior. Agitation rating scales have been developed to provide guidelines for intervention with these clients (Rosen et al, 1994). Calming and soothing techniques can often be used to calm the agitated or aggressive client. Individualized music therapy has shown positive results with confused, agitated older adult clients (Gerdner, Swanson, 1993). When clients demonstrate extreme aggressive behavior that threatens their own safety or the safety of others, chemical or physical restraints may be necessary. However, these interventions induce a new set of physical and emotional challenges on the client and also have ethical and legal ramifications for the health care providers (see Chapter 3).

Two safety issues that may need to be addressed in caring for older adults with late-stage AD are seizures and yelling behavior. Seizures are seen in 10% to 20% of clients with AD in the final stages (Ugarriza, Gray, 1993). The nurse must assess the client for the development of seizures and when appropriate, take seizure precautions. The client may also need anticonvulsant medications in the final stages of DAT. Spontaneous yelling may occur in the late stages, which should not be ignored by the staff of caregivers. The nurse should first assess the client to determine any other cause for the yelling, such as pain, fear, or infection. If no other reason for the yelling can be found, attempts to calm and soothe the client should be instituted.

Health Promotion

A daily physical assessment should be included in the care of clients with AD, because they may be unable to communicate physical complaints or changes (Kah, Kupper, 1993). Attention should also be given to their daily hygiene needs, nutrition and hydration, bowel and bladder routines, and skin care. Timely turning, proper positioning, and the use of pillows to decrease the occurrence of pressure ulcers are necessary to prevent skin breakdown (Ugarriza, Gray, 1993).

Rest/wake Cycle

The sleep/wake cycle in older adults with dementia often becomes disrupted. The client may become easily fatigued and may also experience periods of insomnia. Activities and visits may need to be shortened to allow the client to maintain an adequate energy level. The use of brief naps at consistent times may be helpful, but long naps or naps at irregular times may lead to decreased sleep at night. Daytime naps may be less problematic if provided in an environment other than the client's bed. This promotes the use of their bed as a safe place for longer sleep activity at night. Some facilities report success with the use of rolling recliners that allow clients to nap in a quiet place away from their room. At night, the client's room should allow an optimum environment for sleep. If nightlights are used for safety or orientation, they should be at a low enough level to not interfere with sleep. If the client awakens at night, keeping the lights at a low level and using soothing techniques such as quiet music or a back rub promote sleep (see Chapter 9).

Environment of Care

The ideal care environment for an older adult with AD is one that is safe and provides stimulation that promotes orientation without overwhelming the client. It is important to maintain a balance between providing adequate sensory stimuli versus inducing sensory overload (Brady, 1993). A consistent daily schedule and a routine process of grooming, hygiene, eating, sleeping, and interacting helps maintain the client's highest possible level of orientation. Activities that provide stimulation such as visitors, pets, children, or entertainment may be best held in areas outside of the client's room. A common room may be an appropriate place for these interventions. This plan helps the client associate their room as the place for relaxation and rest.

Interaction

When interacting with clients with AD, it is helpful to speak in a slow and deliberate manner. It is also helpful to limit the introduction of new stimuli such as new topics of conversation because the client may be unable to integrate new cognitive patterns with the remaining cognitive skills. The nurse should speak slowly and clearly to promote the client's understanding of the verbal message. Providing limited choices gives the client a sense of control without overly frustrating the client. For example, the nurse may ask, "Would you like to wear your blue outfit or your green outfit today?" instead of "Which outfit would you like to pick from your closet?" Self-contained units that provide all activities and services in a stable environment prove to be particularly useful in the long-term care of clients with late-stage AD.

Attempts to orient such a client to reality may lead the client to frustration, anxiety, and diminished trust. Although cognitive nursing group interventions may lead to improved cognitive status in some clients with AD, the technique is more useful in clients with mild to moderate cognitive impairment rather than those in the later stages of the disease's progression (Abraham, Reel, 1992). The nurse can use a routine orientation to person, place, and time, and beyond those aspects, can simply answer the client's questions. Kah and Kupper (1993) describe the nurse's ability to integrate orientation into conversation with the client. Statements such as, "Since it's 11:30, would you like to eat your lunch?" can provide the client with orientation information without a sense that they must cognitively hold onto the information. Reminiscence is also helpful to give the client a sense of orientation that belongs to them, thereby providing them with a sense of control (Mills, Walker, 1994).

✣ EVALUATION

Nurses can evaluate the care that has been provided to a client with DAT by comparing client outcome data to the identified client goals and then modifying the plan of care accordingly. Nurses with advanced education and experience can also work toward the development of a nursing paradigm of cognitive function or impairment in older adults that can help advance nursing research and evaluation efforts in this area (McDougall, 1995).

Anxiety

Anxiety is one of the most common symptoms seen in older adults (Keltner, 1995). The most common anxiety disorder seen in older people is obsessive-compulsive disorder (OCD) (Riley, 1995). OCD is composed of obsessive symptoms (e.g., persistent, intrusive thoughts) as well as compulsive symptoms (e.g., repetitive behavior that is performed in an attempt to reduce anxiety). For example, older adults may manifest OCD in morning routines so ritualistic that they miss both their breakfast and their lunch. Other anxiety disorders seen in older adults may be generalized anxiety disorder (GAD) and phobic disorders. GAD is known as worry that is beyond the individual's control (APA, 1994) and may be evidenced by symptoms such as restlessness, fatigue, decreased concentration, irritability, muscle tension, or disturbed sleep. A phobic disorder is manifested by a persistent, irrational fear that is provoked by the feared object or situation.

Anxiety disorders in older adults may develop as a result of a specific event or a general pattern of change experienced by the client as threatening. Such changes can include a decline in health, illness, financial strain, an actual or potential change in living situation, the death of a significant other, or loss of independence. Retirement is a change that often is associated with the development of an anxiety disorder in older adults (Brady, 1993).

BOX 12-5

Factors to Assess in Older Adults With an Anxiety Disorder

- Precipitating events or factors
- Recent changes
- Degree of anxiety
- Interference of the anxiety with ADLs
- Physical symptoms (vital signs, gastrointestinal (GI) function, headaches, tremor)

Nursing Management

✣ ASSESSMENT

Older adult clients with anxiety disorders are usually able to describe their anxieties without the nurse needing to probe extensively. They may also exhibit behavioral clues such as pacing, irritability, and fidgeting (Brady, 1993). The nurse should also assess associated changes that may accompany the anxiety, such as the client's sleeping habits and appetite, the presence or absence of depression, and any physical pain of which the client complains. Box 12-5 lists factors that should be addressed when assessing the older adult with an anxiety disorder.

✣ DIAGNOSIS

The nursing diagnoses for the older adult with an anxiety disorder usually include anxiety and ineffective individual coping.

✣ PLANNING

Expected outcomes include but are not limited to the following: (1) client identifies own anxiety and coping patterns, (2) client reports an increase in psychologic and physiologic comfort, (3) client demonstrates effective coping skills as evidenced by ability to problem-solve and to meet self-care needs, and (4) client demonstrates use of appropriate relaxation techniques.

✣ INTERVENTION

The nurse can intervene with the older adult experiencing anxiety in a number of ways. Clients can be provided with a person and place to process their anxiety. It may be helpful to assist clients in examining their own "worst case scenario." By developing strategies that could be used to cope with the worst possible situation, clients may feel an increased ability to cope with their current situation. Relaxation strategies such as progressive muscle relaxation, breathing techniques, therapeutic use of music, and exercise are useful in helping the client alleviate the acute anxiety states that are most distressing to them. The nurse should help clients learn to identify increasing anxiety early in the anxiety cycle so that they can take steps to reduce it to a lower level. Family education may also be beneficial to obtain support systems for the client. Clients who are experiencing moderate to panic-level anxiety may need a referral for antianxiety medications. Clients who continue to experience distress as a result of anxiety may benefit from psychotherapy. Behavior modification techniques are especially effective with phobic disorders.

✣ EVALUATION

The nurse can evaluate the care that has been provided to a client experiencing anxiety by monitoring progress toward achievement of the expected outcomes. Effectiveness of any health teaching is evident in the client's ability to conduct relaxation techniques and to use constructive problem-solving.

Schizophrenia

Schizophrenia is a thought disorder characterized by an altered perception of reality, alterations in thought processes (both form and content), and a decline in the client's ADLs, as well as occupational and social functioning. The onset of schizophrenia usually occurs between the late teens and the mid-30s. However, there have been rare cases of schizophrenia with onset occurring after age 45 (APA, 1994).

Typically, the older adult client with schizophrenia has been dealing with the disorder for a long time but may experience exacerbations of the schizophrenic symptoms with the stress of the aging process. In older adults with schizophrenia the nurse is less likely to see symptoms such as hallucinations and delusions and more likely to see the symptoms such as a **flat affect** and **poverty of speech** (Keltner, 1995).

Schizophrenia is divided into five types: paranoid, disorganized, catatonic, undifferentiated, and residual (APA, 1994) (Table 12-1).

TABLE 12-1

Types of Schizophrenia

Type	Characteristics
Paranoid	Preoccupied with delusions and/or hallucinations Mistrustful of others May be hostile at times
Disorganized	Disorganized speech and behavior Flat or inappropriate affect (feeling state)
Catatonic	Motor dysfunction ranging from near stuporous to excessive activity Resistance to interaction Peculiar movements or speech patterns
Undifferentiated	Schizophrenia that does not meet the criteria for paranoid, disorganized, or catatonic type
Residual	Continued evidence of schizophrenia without prominent symptoms such as hallucination or delusions

Nursing Management

✣ ASSESSMENT

The reader is referred to a general psychiatric nursing textbook for a complete review of the assessment process in individuals with a diagnosis of schizophrenia.

✣ DIAGNOSIS

Nursing diagnoses appropriate to the older adult with schizophrenia include, but are not limited to, the following: (1) social isolation, (2) altered thought processes, (3) sensory/perceptual alterations, and (4) sleep pattern disturbance.

✣ PLANNING

Schizophrenia is an illness that shows periods of exacerbation and remission. The goal of nursing intervention in individuals with schizophrenia is safe, effective treatment rather than a cure. A reduction in symptoms and an improved quality of life are goals that the nurse should work toward. Other goals include a reduction in the client's anxiety (anxiety usually exacerbates the schizophrenic symptoms), building of a therapeutic relationship with the client, providing continuity of care, and eliciting the support of the family and friends to enhance the client's function and experience.

✣ INTERVENTION

Nursing interventions with an older adult with schizophrenia should provide a compre-hensive approach to the maintenance of ADLs, nutrition, hygiene, health promotion, and reality orientation. The reader is referred to a general psychiatric nursing text for a thorough review of nursing interventions with clients with schizophrenia. Interventions that may be most essential in dealing with older adults with schizophrenia include providing adequate family or social support, responding to the client's symptoms,the appropriate use of touch, and dealing with aggressive behavior.

If the client gives evidence (verbal or nonverbal) of hallucinations or delusions, the nurse should focus on responding to the client's feelings without arguing the reality or unreality of his or her perceptual experience. For example, if the client states that the television is broadcasting the client's thoughts, the nurse could respond by saying, "That must be frightening," rather than saying, "Now Mr. D, you know that the television can't do that!" Attempting to argue the perception with the client only escalates his or her anxiety. It may, however, be helpful to reorient the client without being confrontational.

Clients with schizophrenia may easily misinterpret touch by the nurse as being harmful or threatening to them. Therefore the nurse should only touch the client when there is a purpose and then only after asking the client's permission.

Older adults with schizophrenia may at times present a danger to themselves or others. The nurse should assess the level of danger with each client. If the nurse's assessment shows that the client has a potential for aggression, steps should be taken to de-escalate the client's anger and to provide safety for the client and others.

✣ EVALUATION

Evaluation is based on achievement of the identified expected outcomes. The nature of the disorder may make it difficult for the nurse to establish a relationship with the client, and thus the nurse may feel hopeless, frustrated, and inadequate while attempting to provide care. It is often helpful to establish short-term goals with the client with schizophrenia that are easily achievable and very specific. Examples of achievable expected outcomes include the following; (1) client spends less alone time and enjoys participating in activities with others; (2) client is oriented to person, place, and time; (3) client begins using problem-solving methods; (4) client no longer hears voices, and (5) client verbalizes a feeling of being refreshed and well-rested on awakening.

Paranoid Disorders/Paraphrenia

Some older adults develop the human response of fear or paranoia during the aging process (Baldwin, Stevens, Friedman, 1995). The older adult experiencing paranoia may exhibit general or specific symptoms that can help the nurse recognize the distress that the client feels.

Paraphrenia is a term used to describe a late-onset delusion of persecution (Riley, 1995). Symptoms of paraphrenia may appear that are similar to symptoms seen in paranoid schizophrenia or the paranoia that may be seen in delirium or dementia. However, the client experiencing paraphrenia does not have the accompanying signs of schizophrenia, delirium, or dementia. Paraphrenia appears more often in women than in men. Its cause remains unknown, however sensory impairment such as vision or hearing impairment is believed to play a role (Buckwalter, 1992). Older adults experiencing paraphrenia tend to isolate themselves both physically and socially. They begin to believe that others are stealing from them or poisoning them. They may exhibit violence in more extreme episodes.

Nurses dealing with older adult clients may also observe **paranoid personality disorders.** An increased incidence of paranoid thoughts is not uncommon in older adults as a result of the decreased feelings of independence and the social isolation that may accompany that dependence (Riley, 1995). If the individual experienced paranoia before the aging process, that individual may show an increased level of suspicion as the aging process occurs.

Individuals with a paranoid personality disorder differ from those with paranoid schizophrenia in that their delusions are less bizarre. They may be withdrawn, reserved, fearful, and secretive. Isolation and mistrust mark their day-to-day functioning and interactions. Stressful situations may promote paranoid behaviors in older adults who have not experienced previous paranoid thoughts. Factors that may play a role in the development of the paranoia seen in older adults include medications, sensory impairment, powerlessness, helplessness, and increased dependence.

Nursing Management

✣ ASSESSMENT

Individuals with paranoia rarely seek help for themselves because of their mistrust of others, including health care professionals. When they are evaluated by a nurse, they may be angry and even verbally or physically abusive. If older adult clients do begin to trust the nurse enough to discuss their paranoid thoughts and beliefs, the nurse should show respect in a politely disinterested manner. If the nurse shows extreme interest in the paranoid client, the client can become suspicious of the nurse's motive for being so interested. It can be difficult to build a therapeutic relationship with older adults with paranoia, because trust is so difficult for them. The nurse can use a slow, reliable, and consistent approach to building the relationship. Compliance is likely to be poor in all phases of the nursing process with the client with paranoia, and the nurse may therefore need to rely on data provided by family members and friends to obtain a thorough assessment. In the assessment phase, the content and degree of intrusiveness of the paranoid thoughts may be assessed to identify potential safety concerns. Individuals with paranoia, who are also experiencing dementia, often demonstrate paranoid thoughts that are less organized and change over time.

✣ DIAGNOSIS

Nursing diagnoses appropriate to the older adult with paranoia include, but are not limited to, the following: (1) anxiety, (2) altered thought processes, (3) sensory/perceptual alterations, and (4) impaired social interaction.

✣ PLANNING

An important goal in planning the care of an older adult with paranoia is the reduction of the anxiety level. The degree of paranoia is often directly related to the anxiety level. If clients can be assisted to reduce their anxiety, there may be an accompanying benefit of reduced paranoia. Another benefit to focusing the plan on anxiety is that clients are often more receptive to interventions targeting their anxiety rather than interventions that target their paranoia.

✣ INTERVENTION

There is a delicate balance between providing adequate intervention for an older adult's paranoid thoughts or behavior versus respecting the client's resistance to changing thought patterns. The nurse and the client can become quickly frustrated if an attempt is made to challenge, argue, or disprove the delusion. This approach merely escalates the client's anxiety. The nurse can attempt to reduce the client's anxiety by responding to the client's feelings without acknowledging the delusion. The use of silence may often be helpful if the nurse is uncertain how to respond. This plan also maintains the pattern of polite disinterest. The client should be allowed to set the parameters for the interpersonal relationship between the client and the nurse to the greatest extent possible. The nurse should show respect for the client's personal space and belongings. The client's participation in activities, especially group activities, should not be forced. The individual with paranoia may become easily overwhelmed by sensory stimuli and need frequent moments of privacy and retreat. Family education and support are vital, because the family members may be puzzled, hurt, and distressed by the changes they observe in their loved one.

✣ EVALUATION

Evaluation is based on achievement of the identified expected outcomes. The immediate outcome of reducing the anxiety that leads to the formation of paranoid ideas can only be achieved by careful, slow assessment and intervention so as to not result in rejection by the client. Achievement of any of the expected outcomes depends on the relationship established between the nurse and client, the parameters of which must be established by the client with paranoia.

Mental Retardation

Mental retardation is characterized by below-average intellectual functioning. The onset occurs before age 18 and is accompanied by an alteration in the individual's ability to cope with life's demands and function independently (APA, 1994). The individual's functioning such as communication, self-care ability, ADLs, interpersonal relationships, occupational functioning, as well as health and safety behaviors may all be affected by the mental retardation. There are multiple causes related to mental retardation. The functioning of clients with mental retardation is affected throughout their life span, including their later years. These individuals are also more susceptible to alterations in emotional states.

BOX 12-6

Factors to Assess in the Older Adult With Mental Retardation

- Sociocultural factors
- Community setting
- Family support
- Functional status
- Education
- Personal characteristics
- Occupational opportunities
- Social setting

NURSING MANAGEMENT

✣ ASSESSMENT

Variables that may determine the client's level of functioning should be assessed to determine the extent to which they enhance or detract from the client's well-being (Box 12-6).

✣ DIAGNOSIS

The most common nursing diagnosis seen in older adults with mental retardation is an altered thought processes. This may be evidenced by delusions, a decreased attention span, or impaired problem solving. This diagnosis represents the ongoing challenge with which older adults with mental retardation are living. Other common nursing diagnoses for older adults with mental retardation include self-care deficit and a potential for violence directed at self or others.

✣ PLANNING

In planning the client's short- and long-term goals, care should be taken to customize the plan of care to the client's intellectual abilities. Adaptations to routine interventions may need to be made to assist clients in comprehending their care and thereby being able to participate in the care. It may be useful to know the client's intellectual functioning in terms of age level. Interventions can then be adapted to an age-appropriate level.

✣ INTERVENTION

Nursing interventions that are specifically useful in dealing with older adults with mental retardation primarily involve customizing the care routine to their level of intellectual functioning. When communicating with the client, the nurse should use clear, simple instructions. Caregivers may be assigned a parental role by the client with mental retardation. This may represent a challenge for these clients because of continued dependence throughout their life span. This is especially true if parents or other family members who have cared for the client throughout his or her life have become disabled or are now deceased (Hochberger, 1993). Therefore many mentally retarded older adults with physical problems are being admitted to nursing facilities for care.

✣ EVALUATION

In evaluating the care provided to older adult clients with mental retardation, the nurse should also become aware of the need for an expanded nursing focus in this population. The opportunities for nursing research and service, especially in community settings, are varied and abundant.

Conditions Associated with Physical Problems

This category includes mental health symptoms that result from a physiologic process or a general medical condition, as well as the somatoform disorders. An example of a mental health symptom that may be a result of a physiologic process would be a catatonic disorder resulting from head trauma. An example of a mental health symptom that may be a result of a general medical condition can be personality changes that are a result of hypothyroidism (APA, 1994). Somatoform disorders are seen in a higher incidence among older adults. They are described as complaints of physical symptoms without the medical condition(s) that would explain the existence of the symptom (Riley, 1995). Table 12-2 outlines the various types of somatoform disorders.

TABLE 12-2

Types of Somatoform Disorders

Type	Characteristics
Somatization disorder	Multiple symptoms, usually a combination of symptoms and/or pain, often GI or sexual symptoms
Conversion disorder	Unexplained neurologic motor or sensory deficits
Pain disorder	Pain of unexplained onset, severity, or duration
Hypochondriasis	Preoccupation with or fear of serious disease that leads to an inordinate focus on body functions or symptoms, most common somatoform disorder seen in older adults
Body dysmorphic disorder	Preoccupation with an exaggerated or imaginary physical appearance deficit

Health care professionals often minimize the physical complaints exhibited by older adults with somatoform disorders, but this can be a fatal mistake. Diagnoses can be missed and clients who have true somatoform disorders may develop physical illnesses that are unrelated to their somatoform disorder. Failure to diagnose and to appropriately treat such an illness can be disastrous. In addition to assessing the physical and mental status of the client, an attempt should be made to understand the secondary gain that the client may be receiving from the somatoform disorder. Often, this information is best elicited by assessing the impact of the somatoform disorder on the client's family members and friends.

NURSING MANAGEMENT

✣ ASSESSMENT

The initial priority when assessing these clients is their physical status, which determines the interplay that is occurring between their physical and mental status. Therefore a thorough health history, medication history, physical assessment, and mental status examination should be completed. Physical symptoms should not be ignored. Their presence should either be explained by a physical illness or their possible causes should be ruled out.

✣ DIAGNOSIS AND PLANNING

The care of the older adult with a somatoform disorder is often planned around the nursing diagnosis of ineffective individual coping. The short- and long-term goals are then centered around enhancing the client's coping skills.

✣ INTERVENTION

The nurse should reinforce positive, healthy *well-role* behaviors and attitudes that the client may demonstrate. At the same time the nurse can encourage and reward the client's discussion of non–symptom-related topics. When clients attempt to focus on their physical symptoms, the nurse can respond with a caring but neutral attitude that does not encourage the focus on the physical symptom. The nurse should not try to convince clients that they are not ill or that they are not really experiencing the physical symptoms. Such efforts can be futile and frustrating for the client and the nurse. The nurse should respond to the client's emotional feelings rather than focusing on the symptom. The nurse should be alert to the possibility of the client using multiple physicians who are unaware of one another as well as the possibility of the client overusing both prescription and OTC medications.

✣ EVALUATION

The nurse may become easily frustrated if all evaluation criteria center around the client's somatoform symptoms. These are not symptoms that are easily treated or readily relinquished. It may be helpful to use markers such as the consistency of the care the client received, any decrease seen in the clients' levels of anxiety, or the clients' improved awareness of their emotions.

MEDICATION MANAGEMENT

Psychotropic Medications

The second most common type of medication used by older adults are **psychotropic agents.** These drugs affect the client's brain function, behavior, or experience (Luke, 1995). Older adults exhibit changes in the absorption, distribution, metabolism, and excretion of medications, as well as in the central nervous system neurotransmitters and receptor sites that these drugs impact. Therefore there is a corresponding change in the indications and contraindications for appropriate use of these medications (see Chapter 20).

In the past, psychotropics have been commonly used among long-term care residents. This use was often inappropriate and/or excessive. In 1987, federal regulations were developed (Omnibus Budget Reconciliation Act, or OBRA-87) that were designed to decrease the inappropriate use of antipsychotic medications (Keltner, 1995). There has been a corresponding decline in the frequency of use of antipsychotic agents in long-term care residents. Psychotropic medications *are* appropriate when used in long-term care settings for what Drinka (1993) terms the "3 Ds": "Danger, to the resident or others; distress for the resident; dysfunction of the resident including interference with basic nursing care" (p. 466).

A primary goal in medication management with the older adult client is to find the lowest effective dose with the least adverse effects (Gomez, Gomez, 1992). It is also essential to remain aware of drug-drug interactions, drug-food interactions, nonadherence issues, substance abuse and dependency issues when psychotropic medications are used in older adults. Nursing implications of antianxiety medications, antidepressants, antimanic agents, antipsychotics and other psychoactive medications used in older adults are discussed in this section.

Antianxiety Agents

Antianxiety medications are also called anxiolytics. In the past, barbiturates were the main types of drugs used for anxiety, however, benzodiazepines are now used because of their improved safety over barbiturates. Long-term use (usually defined as longer than 1 to 2 months) of benzodiazepines does put the client at risk for the development of dependence, and they do have potential adverse interactions, especially with sedative agents and alcohol. There are two broad categories of benzodiazepines: short-acting (e.g., alprazolam [Xanax], lorazepam [Ativan], and oxazepam [Serax]) and long-acting (e.g., diazepam [Valium], chlordiazepoxide [Librium], and clonazepam [Klonopin]). The short-acting agents are preferred in older adults because of their lower potential for buildup leading to sedation and depression.

When used for anxiety, the lowest possible dose of a benzodiazepine should be used for the shortest possible time. Therefore the precipitating cause of the client's anxiety needs to be evaluated and addressed while the benzodiazepine is being used. Although alprazolam may be used on a long-term basis for panic in older adults, most benzodiazepines should be used for less than 30 days. When used for longer periods, the client may experience withdrawal symptoms that can be as severe as seizures. When discontinuing the drug, it should be tapered slowly to prevent withdrawal symptoms or to rebound anxiety symptoms. Of particular concern in older adults is the potential for benzodiazepines to exacerbate sleep apnea. Therefore older adults should be assessed for alterations in sleep patterns (especially snoring) before using a benzodiazepine.

There are other options in addition to benzodiazepines in older adults who need an anxiolytic. Buspirone (Buspar) is a chemically unique antianxiety agent that does not produce dependence or interaction with benzodiazepines or alcohol. Its drawback lies in its slow onset of action (often up to 2 weeks) that tends to limit client compliance. Nurses can play an important role in educating clients about the slow action onset of buspirone, thereby improving the clients' adherence to their medication regimens and *giving older adults a safer option for reducing anxiety.* Other medications that are used to manage anxiety in older adults include antidepressants and beta blockers such as propranolol or Inderal.

Antidepressants

Antidepressant medications include monoamine oxidase inhibitors (MAOIs), tricyclics, and selective serotonin reuptake inhibitors (SSRIs). The MAOIs (e.g., phenelzine [Nardil] and tranylcypromine [Parnate]) affect the monoamine neurotransmitter system but are rarely used because of their potential drug-food interaction with tyramine that can precipitate a hypertensive crisis. They are used for refractory depression and in older adults with cardiac arrhythmias, because they do not produce the cardiovascular side effects of other antidepressants.

When clients are taking MAOIs, they must adhere to a tyramine-free diet and must be warned of the potential for a hypertensive crisis from drug-drug interactions with a number of other medications. Their physicians and pharmacist should monitor any new prescription or OTC medications.

The tricyclic antidepressants such as amitriptyline (Elavil), imipramine (Tofranil), desipramine (Norpramin), and nortriptyline (Pamelor) block the reuptake of norepinephrine and serotonin. Older adults are usually started on a dose half of that used in younger adults. The dose is gradually titrated upward to a therapeutic level. It may take 10 days to 3 weeks for the client to experience the antidepressant benefits, and in the meantime, the side effects are present. This is a factor in nonadherence with antidepressant medications in older adults. Client education regarding the time of onset of action can help improve compliance. The side effects tend to diminish as the therapeutic benefit of these drugs begins to be seen. The side effects include anticholinergic effects, sedation, hypotension, dry mouth, tachycardia, blurred vision, constipation, and urinary retention. These medications are contraindicated in clients with recent myocardial infarctions or cardiac arrhythmias.

The most recent addition to the antidepressant category are the SSRIs such as fluoxetine (Prozac), sertraline (Zoloft), paroxetene (Paxil), and venlafaxine (Effexor). These medications increase the client's serotonin levels and have rare side-effect profiles, which may include GI upset, decreased appetite, insomnia, anxiety, and headaches. The SSRIs have a lower risk of overdose effects than do other antidepressants and are also used in the treatment of OCD.

Additional helpful information about antidepressants includes the course of treatment. Antidepressants are commonly used until the client has been free of symptoms of depression for 6 months to 2 years. They are then gradually tapered off the medication to prevent the development of a rebound depression. Some clients with recurrent major depression may continue to use antidepressants indefinitely. Electroconvulsive therapy (ECT) may be used in clients with life-threatening depression if antidepressants have not been effective. The usual course of ECT would be 10 to 14 treatments every other day. ECT is now considered a humane and effective treatment for depression because of the use of anesthesia and muscle relaxants during the procedure.

Antimanic Medications

Antimanic medications are used for bipolar mood disorders (formerly called manic-depression). See Depression, p. 275, for the symptoms seen in bipolar mood disorders. Lithium carbonate (Lithium) is the most common drug used for bipolar disorders, although some anticonvulsant agents, calcium channel blockers, and beta blockers are also used for rapid cycling (occurs more than three times per year) bipolar disorders.

Before beginning Lithium use, the client should have baseline ECG, CBC, renal, thyroid, and liver function studies. In the older adult, Lithium begins at a low dose (e.g., 300 mg/day) and a blood level is obtained in 3 to 4 days. This level should be drawn 12 hours after the last dose of Lithium. The dose is then titrated until the client reaches a therapeutic blood level (usually 0.4 to 1.5 mEQ/L). Blood levels are drawn every 3 to 4 days until the therapeutic level is attained. The frequency of levels can then be decreased to once per month for the first 6 months, then every 2 to 3 months indefinitely. Renal, liver, and thyroid studies should be evaluated every 6 months because of potential toxicity (Luke, 1995).

Side effects seen in older adults who are taking Lithium include GI distress, fine hand tremors, ataxia, and weight gain. Cardiovascular side effects may also occur, therefore periodic ECGs may be obtained as needed. Lithium toxicity can be evident in blood levels greater than 1.5 mEQ/L, moderate to severe toxicity can be seen in levels greater than 2.0 mEQ/L, and death may occur with blood levels greater than 2.5 mEQ/L. Clients should inform all physicians and pharmacists involved in their care of any Lithium use because of the potential for drug-drug interactions. The client's blood pressure should be measured on a routine basis especially in clients taking calcium channel blockers or beta blockers. Older adults who have used Lithium over time may require a reduced dosage as they age (Luke, 1995).

Antipsychotic Medications

Antipsychotic medications are also called **neuroleptics.** They work by blocking the action of dopamine. Neuroleptics are used in schizophrenia, acute psychosis, delirium, and may be used to treat the agitation and aggression sometimes seen in dementia. The specific choice of a neuroleptic agent is made both by the client's clinical symptoms and the side-effect profiles of the various neuroleptic agents. Older adults are usually started on lower doses (one half to one third of normal dose) of the high-potency neuroleptics such as haloperidol (Haldol), thiothixene (Navane), or thifluoperazine (Stelazine). The high-potency neuroleptics have a lower frequency of anticholinergic, cardiovascular, and sedation side effects than do the lower-potency neuroleptics such as chlorpromazine (Thorazine) and thioridazine (Mellaril). However, the high-potency neuroleptics have an increased rate of **extrapyramidal symptoms (EPS)** in comparison with the low-potency neuroleptics. Therefore it is essential to monitor all clients on neuroleptics for EPS, which is discussed later in this chapter. Haloperidol and fluphenazine (Prolixin) are neuroleptics that are available in long-acting deconate forms for nonadhering clients and may be administered weekly to monthly.

However, the deconates are rarely used in older adults because of their long half-life of 1 to 4 weeks. This treatment could be dangerous should side effects become problematic.

Clozapine (Clozaril) is a newer, atypical antipsychotic with a decreased incidence of side effects and EPS. Unfortunately, it carries with it a potentially dangerous side effect of agranulocytosis, therefore weekly CBCs must be obtained on all clients receiving Clozapine. Its safety is uncertain in older adults, so it is not considered a first choice medication (Luke, 1995).

Side Effects

Extrapyramidal Symptoms

Nurses play a vital role in the monitoring, education, and evaluation of EPS in clients who are receiving neuroleptic medications. The EPS are described in Table 12-3.

The EPS are treated with anticholinergic or antiparkinson agents such as diphenhydramine (Benadryl), benztropine (Cogentin), or trihexyphenidyl (Artane). Amantadine (Symmetrel, a dopamine agonist) may be used, especially in older clients and those with cardiovascular dysfunction, because of its reduced anticholinergic effects.

Tardive Dyskinesia

Tardive dyskinesia (TD) is a potential permanent, neurologic side effect of neuroleptic medications. Clients and their families must be informed of the risk of TD before initiating neuroleptic therapy. TD is characterized by involuntary movements especially of the face, lips, and tongue. The trunk and extremities may also be involved. TD is most likely to develop in clients who have used neuroleptics longer than 2 years. Clients should be evaluated for TD at each appointment. Unfortunately, no effective treatment for TD exists. The best prevention is using the lowest possible dose of a neuroleptic for the shortest time necessary.

TABLE 12-3

EPS

Symptom	Characteristic
Acute dystonic reaction	Muscle rigidity, eyes fixed in deviated position, arched posture; treated on an emergent basis with an anticholinergic agent such as diphenhydramine
Akathisia	Inability to sit still
Akinesia	Decreased psychomotor movements, shuffle gait
Pseudoparkinsonism	Tremor of extremities that resembles Parkinson's disease
Perioral tremor (Rabbit syndrome)	Fine rapid lip movements

Neuroleptic Malignant Syndrome

Neuroleptic malignant syndrome (NMS) is a rare but serious side effect that may lead to death. Its frequency increases with the high potency antipsychotics. The initial symptoms include a decreased temperature, the development of EPS, and delirium. If untreated, it then progresses to hyperthermia, stupor, severe EPS, and coma. It is treated by immediately discontinuing any neuroleptic medication. Dantroline sodium, which can cause liver toxicity, or bromocriptine may also be used. Because of the potential for death from NMS, all clients receiving neuroleptic medications in an inpatient or long-term care setting should have their vital signs measured daily. Clients who take neuroleptics on an outpatient basis should be educated on the signs of NMS, particularly the cardinal sign of a temperature change.

EPS, TD, and NMS all present significant risks for clients taking neuroleptic medications. It is therefore essential that nurses educate clients and their caregivers of the need for routine monitoring for the development of these side effects.

Other Psychoactive Medications Used in Older Adults

Alzheimer's Agents

Although a number of medications have been tested for the treatment of dementia, especially DAT, the drug that is the most promising is tacrine hydrochloride (Cognex). Cognex acts by increasing acetylcholine concentrations in the cerebral cortex (Saul, Keltner, 1995). Potential side effects from Cognex include bradycardia, increased gastric acid secretion leading to ulcers, nausea or vomiting (occurs in 20% of clients), and loose stools (Keltner, 1994). The most serious adverse effect is liver toxicity that occurs in 30% of clients receiving Cognex. Therefore alanine aminotransferase and serum glutamic-pyruvic transaminase (ALT/SGPT) levels are monitored every other week for the first 16 weeks of therapy for those clients without significant ALT elevations. Monitoring may then be decreased to monthly for 2 months and every 3 months thereafter. Cognex also has a potential drug-drug interaction with Theophylline. It is ideally taken between meals but can be taken with meals if GI upset occurs. Unfortunately, taking Cognex with meals decreases the plasma levels by 30% to 40%. The current maximum dose is 120 mg/day (Saul, Keltner, 1995). However, a recent study found significantly superior results when the dosage was pushed to 160 mg/day (Knapp, 1994).

Anafranil

Clomipramine (Anafranil) is a tricyclic antidepressant that is specifically helpful for obsessive-compulsive disorder. Its side-effect profile is consistent with that of other tricyclics.

Antiparkinson Agents

As discussed earlier, the antiparkinson agents such as benzotropine (Cogentin) and trihexyphenidyl (Artane) are used to treat side effects elicited by antipsychotic medications.

Sedative-Hypnotics

Sleep patterns change with age and older adults may experience a decrease both in the quantity and quality of sleep. Delayed onset of sleep and nighttime wakings are not uncommon in older adults. Sedative-hypnotic agents can be dangerous when used in older adults, therefore they are only used if the client is unable to function on a daily basis as a result of insomnia. Long-term use of sedative-hypnotics can produce a disturbed sleep/wake cycle and can lead to dependence and a decrease in restedness, even after an adequate amount of sleep. In older adults whose symptoms include insomnia, other causes should first be ruled out. Early insomnia may be indicative of anxiety or pain (e.g., arthritis) and middle to late insomnia may be seen with depression. Additional information on the nursing management of sleep disorders in older adults may be found in Chapter 9.

MENTAL HEALTH RESOURCES

The number and quality of resources for the care of mental illness in older people are minimal, because geropsychiatric care is a relatively new specialty within gerontology. These resources include human resources (mental health professionals [e.g., physicians and nurses]); physical resources (e.g., hospitals, clinics, nursing facilities, and dementia units); and financial resources needed to pay for mental health care (e.g., Medicare, Medicaid, and health insurance coverage).

Human Resources

Geriatric psychiatrists are those physicians trained as psychiatrists with special preparation in the care of older people with mental and behavioral problems. They may be nationally certified in general psychiatry with additional qualifications in geriatric psychiatry. They work with older individuals and their families in private practice, group practice, clinics, and hospitals, using a wide variety of treatment modalities. Psychiatrists trained in geriatrics are more likely to meet the needs and satisfaction of older clients.

However, according to Koenig (1994), "few health professionals . . . choose geriatrics as their primary specialty," especially psychiatrists who receive such low reimbursement from Medicare. Physicians just completing a residency receive even less. For example, for performing a comprehensive assessment taking about 2 hours, Medicare pays about $56, whereas the fee for the same service for another client would be about $180. Therefore few young physicians are motivated for a career in geriatric psychiatry (Koenig, 1994).

Geropsychiatric nurses and *geriatric mental health nurses* are trained at the master's level, usually in programs that offer some combination of psychiatric or mental health nursing and gerontologic nursing course work (Hoeffer, 1994). The primary major is usually psychiatric/mental health nursing with some courses in gerontologic nursing. These nurses may be certified by the American Nurses Credentialing Center as a Clinical Nurse Specialist in Adult Psychiatric and Mental Health Nursing and/or Gerontologic Nursing if they have master's preparation in one or both specialties. These specialists should be prepared to assess and to care for individuals who often have multiple, complex, physical, *and* mental or emotional problems.

More geropsychiatric nurses are needed to work as staff or consultants in hospitals, nursing facilities, outpatient clinics, day treatment centers, adult day care centers, dementia centers, and home health agencies. As previously mentioned, many older people are never adequately diagnosed and treated for underlying psychopathologic problems. Nurses in these settings can help to prevent that problem from occurring. These nurses are also greatly needed to teach technical nursing staff members, who have close contact with these clients, how to communicate with and relate to older people with mental and emotional disturbances.

Because an interdisciplinary approach is very important in the health care of older adults, psychiatrists, social workers, dietitians, clergy, speech pathologists, and physical and occupational therapists with some formal preparation in geriatrics and gerontology are also essential to quality care for geropsychiatric clients.

Physical Resources

Older clients with mental and emotional problems are increasingly being treated on an outpatient basis primarily because of available methods of payment in a partial hospitalization program (where the client goes home at night and on weekends), mental health clinic, or physician's office. Perhaps these programs are better for older clients than residential treatment in hospitals, which can cause relocation confusion, loss of familiar environment and sensory stimulation, or functional decline associated with the hospitalization. On the other hand, individuals without family members or an adequate support system may have problems managing difficult medication regimens alone at home. Those people with major depression especially are at greater risk for potential suicide.

Some general hospitals have geropsychiatric units that are staffed and equipped to care for the mental *and* physical needs of older clients. These units provide thorough assessments and an interdisciplinary approach to total care and rehabilitation on a relatively short-term basis for older clients with *primarily* mental and emotional problems (Wagner, 1995). Unless the general psychiatric hospital has a specific unit planned for older clients, such a facility may have difficulty meeting their needs. In fact, many general psychiatric hospitals do not even admit clients who also have physical problems and needs. Most geropsychiatric units are usually located in psychiatric facilities associated with medical schools, where fellowships are available to psychiatrists specializing in this area. Some psychiatric hospitals have well-developed day hospitalization programs that provide treatment, care, and supervision on a daily basis. However, adequate transportation to and from the hospital each day can be a problem for the older person. Some hospitals and community agencies provide this type of medical transportation when the individual or family cannot provide it. However, escort services from the van to the area of treatment may not be available so that the older person cannot make the trip alone for safety reasons.

The large majority of older people who have some type of chronic mental health problem are found in long-term care nursing facilities with some type of dementia or depression related to physical or environmental factors. In fact, Brower (1993) has stated that nursing facilities "are in reality mini-geropsychiatric facilities—but without the trained psychiatric staff." As previously mentioned, many of these residents have not had the benefit of a thorough mental status assessment and diagnosis and therefore proper treatment and care. In addition to ageism, another reason for this problem is the lack of adequate financial resources for this assessment and treatment.

Some nursing facilities have **dementia special care units (DSCUs)** or **Alzheimer's units (AUs),** that provide more intensive care for residents with DAT. In 1991 Hyde and Mace (1992) estimated that 10% of nursing facilities had such a unit and predicted that the number would increase. These units should provide specially prepared staff to care for residents with mental, behavioral, and psychosocial problems; a safe, secure, and comfortable environment, where wandering can be therapeutic; and special programs that provide just the right amount of exercise, stimulation, and rest. Some states have instituted specific regulations for the licensure and regulation of these units (Brower, 1993). There is a need to determine if the higher cost for care on these units is worth the extra expense.

There are also a few special care centers that are devoted exclusively to the care of residents with dementia and related disorders (Hogstel, Nichols, 1995). Residents are thoroughly assessed on admission by a geriatrician and placed according to their required level of care. These centers may also provide adult day care for people with dementia and family support groups.

Financial Resources

One of the greatest issues in the care of mental health problems in older adults is the lack of adequate financial resources to provide for needed care. For people age 65 and older, Medicare coverage is limited, as shown in Table 12-4.

Medicare Medigap policies purchased from private health insurance companies generally pay for what Medicare does not pay based on the approved amount less the deductibles (some plans also pay for the Part B excess [15% allowed] that is charged by the physician). However, because Medicare does not pay anything after the lifetime limit of 190 days of inpatient care in a psychiatric hospital, neither does the Medigap policy. Also, all Medigap health insurance policies pay "50% of approved charges for outpatient mental health services" (*Guide to health insurance for people with Medicare* 1995) rather than 20% as for other medical care.

Medicaid is a federal-state program that differs somewhat from state to state. Services for mental health care for both inpatient and outpatient care are very limited for Medicaid recipients (Hogstel, Nichols, 1995). There is a current trend in many states to place people on Medicaid in coordinated (managed) care plans to save money. States must receive a waiver from the federal government for this plan, because partial federal funds are used. How this proposal works will be of interest to many individuals, especially for those with dementia in nursing facilities. If nursing facilities bid on Medicaid-

TABLE 12-4

Medicare Coverage for Mental Health Care

Medicare	Coverage
Part A (Hospital)	Lifetime limit of 190 days in a participating psychiatric hospital Inpatient psychiatric care in a general hospital the same as any other Medicare inpatient hospital care
Part B (Outpatient) after initial $100 deductible	Partial hospitalization (day treatment) for approved care in a Medicare participating hospital Pays 50% of approved amount of mental health care by physicians, clinical psychologists, clinical social workers and other nonphysician practitioners in a mental health care center, skilled nursing facility, or physician's office

From *Your Medicare 1995 Handbook,* Baltimore, Md., 1995, US Department of Health and Human Services, Pub No HCFA 10050; Social Security Administration.

coordinated (managed) care contracts for their residents on Medicaid, there is fear that there will be less money available for total care and even less for mental health care.

TRENDS AND NEEDS

The need to focus more on the mental and emotional health care needs of older people will continue to increase (Box 12-7). Nurses and family members must advocate for older people who have mental health problems and who are not being adequately diagnosed and treated. State and local **ombudsmen** programs are expanding with plans to have at least one or two certified trained volunteer ombudsmen in all long-term care facilities, including nursing facilities, hospital skilled nursing units (SNUs), and personal (assisted) care homes.

Long periods of hospitalization in a psychiatric hospital will be rare. More people will be treated in the home setting and in partial hospitalization and outpatient settings. Other community organizations such as churches and congregations, senior citizens' groups, and other social organizations are developing programs to help older people maintain their mental health by preventing loneliness and depression. There will be increased emphasis on improving the quality of care in long-term care facilities, which is important considering that it has been estimated that there is an 80% mental morbidity in such facilities (German et al, 1992). The primary need will be to focus more on mental health problems, psychosocial issues, and communication skills, for example, in inservice training for *all* personnel. Perhaps this goal will be accomplished through state legislation or regulatory agencies. There will also be more emphasis on increasing gerontologic, geriatric, and geropsychiatric content in the curricula of medical, nursing, and social work educational programs. Advocacy groups should work toward including more of such content in state licensing examinations.

Family members will also need to learn more about the aging process, especially the *normal, common,* and *abnormal* changes in behavior as one ages so that they will know more about how to relate to and care for their older family members if needed. Although respite care is available to some extent (e.g., adult day care programs and nursing facilities) for those family members who care for an older person with mental and behavioral problems, there is a great need for additional short-term respite care. Family members who are caring for an older person in the home need a couple of hours of relief now and then, perhaps by a volunteer from a church, so that he or she can take a walk, can go to a movie, or can go shopping. Trained volunteers can easily provide this kind of short-term respite care that assists the caregiver and ultimately, the older family member.

BOX 12-7

Trends and Needs in Mental Health Care of Older People

- Strong advocacy
- Increased outpatient care
- Expanded community resources
- Improved quality of long-term care
- Additional legislation/regulations related to psychosocial training for staff in long-term care facilities
- More emphasis on gerontology, geriatrics, and geropsychiatry education for health care providers
- More educational programs for family members
- Short-term respite care for family members

NEEDS FOR RESEARCH

There is much need for research in the nursing care of older people with mental, emotional, and behavioral problems. Some questions and needs to consider include the following:

- Are DSCUs cost-effective? Is the quality of care better than the care for a resident with dementia on a regular unit? At what stage of the illness should residents with dementia be placed on a DSCU?
- Should some type of mental status screening tool be used in the assessment of *all* older people admitted to general hospitals and nursing facilities to detect possible problems for earlier treatment? If so, which ones?
- What is the *actual* prevalence of mental morbidity in long-term care facilities?
- To what extent are licensed nurses in nursing facilities knowledgeable about the diagnosis, treatment, and nursing care of residents with depression and dementia?
- What can nurses do to decrease loneliness and depression in older people, especially in home health care and nursing facilities?
- Is group psychotherapy effective in decreasing depression in nursing facility residents? Who should lead these groups?
- To what extent do home health care nurses assess mental status in their clients?
- What will be the effect of decreasing Medicare and Medicaid funding on the mental health treatment and care of older people?
- To what extent do coordinated (managed) care plans (e.g., Medicare Health Maintenance Organiza-

tions and Medicaid) provide mental health care for seniors? What is the quality of that care? Is there a focus on prevention of mental health problems?

Summary

Many older people experience mental, emotional, and behavioral problems. One of the major problems is that they are often not diagnosed or treated. Some of the reasons for this problem is a false belief that mental symptoms are a part of the normal aging process; that these symptoms are not treatable or curable—a reflection of ageism, or because older people themselves are reluctant to admit the need and seek treatment and care from mental health professionals because of a stigma about mental illness.

Important factors in maintaining mental health wellness among older adults are physical wellness, especially good nutrition, exercise, and limited prescription medications; physical *and* mental activity and stimulation; and a strong support system comprised of family, church, friends, and neighbors.

Nurses play important and varied roles in the management of mental health alterations that are experienced by older adults. The nurse has the opportunity to enhance the quality of life in older adult clients by maintaining an awareness of the alterations that may be seen in this population and appropriately intervening when alterations are recognized. The establishment of effective communication, a therapeutic relationship, and health promotion activities are functions that are integral in the treatment of mental health alterations. These are also functions that nurses have the education, skills and ex-

CULTURAL AWARENESS

Selected Culture-Bound Syndromes

Group	Disorder	Remarks
African American/ Haitian	Blackout	Collapse, dizziness, inability to move
	Low blood	Not enough blood or weakness of the blood that is often treated with diet
	High blood	Blood that is too rich is a result of ingestion of too much red meat or rich foods
	Thin blood	Occurs in women, children and old people; renders the individual more susceptible to illness in general
	Diseases of hex, witch-craft, or conjuring	Sense of being doomed by spell; gastrointestinal symptoms such as vomiting, hallucinations, part of voodoo beliefs
Chinese/ Southeast Asian	Koro	Intense anxiety that penis is retracting into body
Eskimos	Pibloktoq	Traumatic anxiety state, bizarre, over dramatized behavior such as running naked through the snow.
Greeks	Hysteria	Bizarre complaints and behavior because the uterus leaves the pelvis for another part of the body
Hispanics	Empacho	Food forms into a ball and clings to the stomach or intestines causing pain and cramping
	Fatigue	Asthma-like symptoms
	Pasmo	Paralysis-like symptoms of face or limbs, often prevented or relieved by massage
	Susto	Anxiety, trembling, phobias from sudden fright
American Indians	Ghost	Terror, hallucinations, sense of danger
	Trance disassociation Soul loss	Caused by the loss of one's soul or the invasion of a benign or evil spirit, it is viewed as a mystical state; some vision quests result in altered states of consciousness similar to this
Japanese	Wagamama	Apathetic childish behavior with emotional outbursts
Korean	Hwa-Byung	Multiple somatic and psychologic symptoms, "pushing up sensation of chest, palpitations, flushing, headache"; epigastric mass, dysphoria, anxiety, irritability, and difficulty concentrating; mostly afflicts married women

CULTURAL AWARENESS

Cultural Influences on Mental Health and Mental Illness

- Regardless of whether they are understood, people of all cultures have reasons for their behavior.
- Normal and abnormal behaviors are cultural phenomena.
- Culture influences the expression, presentation, recognition, labeling, explanations for and distribution of mental illness, as well as its treatments and healers.
- Mental health and mental illness are more difficult to delineate than physical disorders, for example, visions and dream states, hallucinations, trances, delusions, belief in spirits, speaking in "tongues," drug or alcohol intoxication, or suicide may be judged normal or abnormal according to the cultural context.
- At times, cultural groups encourage altered states of consciousness that may be viewed as mental disturbances to outsiders.
- Although mental disorders occur in every society, cultural tolerance for variations in human behavior vary markedly from one cultural group to the next.

perience to implement in an expert manner. The nursing focus on promoting a biopsychosocial approach, encouraging family involvement and developing an effective continuity of care also allows nursing to play a unique and vital role in the treatment of mental health alterations seen in older adults.

The major mental health problems experienced by older adults include depression, suicide, delirium, dementia, anxiety, schizophrenia, paranoid disorders, mental retardation, and somatoform disorders. The major psychotropic medication groups were summarized with a focus on their nursing implications.

Resources for the treatment and care of mental illness in older adults are limited. These resources include geriatric psychiatrists, geropsychiatric nurses, and other mental health professionals prepared in geropsychiatry; geropsychiatric units in general and psychiatric hospitals; dementia special care units in nursing facilities; and special stand-alone dementia care facilities. Medicare, Medicaid, and private health insurance companies provide only limited coverage and care for mental health illnesses, in part because these illnesses often are chronic long-term problems and the benefits of diagnosis, treatment, and care are less predictive than for physical illness.

More geropsychiatric diagnoses and treatments are being done on partial hospitalization or outpatient bases for community-dwelling older adults. However, there continues to be a great need to provide more mental health care and support to older residents in the 23,000 nursing facilities in the United States. Nurses need to be strong advocates for their older clients by helping them to maintain their independence, self-respect, and self-worth; by referring them for specific diagnosis and treatment when mental or emotional problems are noted; and by improving the quality of psychosocial communication and care of older people in all health care settings (see Cultural Awareness boxes, p. 295, and above).

HOME CARE TIPS

1. Two of the most common side effects of many medications taken by older people are mental confusion and disorientation, which makes diagnosing mental disorders difficult in the homebound client.
2. Ageism, a negative, prejudiced view of aging and older people, may prevent the physician from ordering diagnostic tests needed to make an accurate diagnosis.
3. Assess situational factors in the environment that may predispose the homebound client to depression.
4. Chronic, long-lasting incurable diseases predispose homebound clients to feelings of frustration and depression, and may even lead to suicide.
5. In assessing the older adult, behavioral changes such as difficulty completing ADLs, decrease in appetite, changes in sleep patterns, lowered energy levels, poor grooming, and withdrawal from people and interests may be indicative of depression.
6. Physiologic symptoms that may be seen in the homebound client experiencing depression include muscle aches, abdominal pain or tightness, flatulence, nausea and vomiting, dry mouth, and headaches.
7. The Geriatric Depression Scale is an effective screening tool that can be used to assess depression in an older homebound client.
8. Assess the perception of the future in all homebound clients, since there is an increased incidence of suicide in this population.
9. Use psychiatric/mental health specialists to provide counseling to homebound clients or caregivers.
10. Early recognition of dementia disorders can be helpful in planning the care for the homebound client.

Key Points

- Health care providers and older people themselves often blame mental and emotional problems on the aging process.
- Many older people with mental health problems are never diagnosed and treated.
- It is estimated that 80% of nursing facility residents have some type of mental morbidity, 60% of which can be classified as dementia.
- Physical wellness, mental and physical activity, adaptation to the changes of aging, and a strong support system contribute to mental health wellness.

- To positively affect an older adult client who is experiencing an alteration in mental health, the nurse must first develop a therapeutic relationship based on trust.
- Nurses who care for older adult clients must be aware of the clients' significant risk for suicide.
- Delirium is a disorder with an acute onset and a reversible cause, whereas dementia is a disorder with a chronic onset and an often irreversible cause.
- The reduction of anxiety is a central focus of nursing intervention in caring for an older adult experiencing paranoia.
- A central goal in psychotropic medication use in older adults is finding the lowest effective dose with the least adverse effects.
- There are very few geropsychiatrists and geropsychiatric nurses in the United States.
- Most acute mental health problems in older people are treated on a partial hospitalization or outpatient basis.
- There is a lifetime limit of 190 days of inpatient care in a psychiatric hospital that is provided payment by Medicare.
- Medicare pays only 50% (not 80%) for outpatient psychiatric care.
- Nurses need to be strong advocates for their older clients in obtaining accurate diagnosis and treatment of mental health problems.

Critical Thinking Exercises

1. The wife of a 68-year-old man died 1 year ago. During a routine blood pressure screening, he admits to the nurse that he is depressed. What additional data should the nurse obtain?
2. On admission to the hospital of an older woman with long-standing chronic emphysema, the nurse performs a thorough physical assessment but overlooks the psychologic assessment. Should this oversight be called to the nurse's attention? Why is a psychologic assessment of particular importance in the older adult?
3. Analyze sociocultural, economic, and technologic trends of the next decade, into the early 21st century. How might future trends affect the mental and emotional health care needs of older people? What role will the nurse play in addressing the mental health needs of this population?

REFERENCES

Abraham I, Buckwalter K: Geropsychiatric nursing: a clinical knowledge base in community and institutional settings, *J Psychosocial Nurs* 32(4):27-30, 1994.

Abraham I, Reel S: Cognitive nursing interventions with long-term care residents: effects on neurocognitive dimensions, *Arch Psychatr Nurs* VI(6):356-365, 1992.

Abraham I, Smullen D, Thompson-Heisterman A: Geriatric mental health: assessing geropsychiatric patients, *J Psychosocial Nurs* 30(9):13-19, 1992.

American Psychiatric Association: *Diagnostic and statistical manual of mental disorders: DSM-IV,* ed 4, Washington, D.C., 1994, The Association.

American Assiciation of Retired Persons: *A profile of older Americans,* Washington, D.C., 1994, The Association.

Baldwin B, Stevens G, Friedman S: Geriatric psychiatric nursing. In Stuart S, Sundeen W, editors: *Principles and practice of psychiatric nursing,* ed 5, St. Louis, 1995, Mosby.

Ball BL: When the care is care, *AJN* 89(11):1466-1467, 1989.

Beal G: The parish as a healing place, *Lutheran Brotherhood Bond* 17(1):4-6, 1994.

Brady PF: Mental health of the aging. In Johnson B, editor: *Psychiatric-mental health nursing: adaptation and growth,* ed 3, Philadelphia, 1993, JB Lippincott.

Brower HT: Special care units for dementia, *J Gerontolog Nurs* 19(2):3, 6, 1993.

Browning MA: Depression, suicide and bereavement. In Hogstel MO, editor: *Geropsychiatric nursing,* ed 2, St. Louis, 1995, Mosby.

Buckwalter K: Phantom of the nursing home, *J Gerontolog Nurs* 18(9):46-47, 1992.

Cataldo J: Hardiness and death attitudes: predictors of depression in the institutionalized elderly, *Arch Psychiatr Nurs* 8(5):326-332, 1994.

Clark W, Vorst V: Group therapy with chronically depressed geriatric patients, *J Psychosocial Nurs* 32(5):9-13, 1994.

Courage M et al: Suicide in the elderly: staying in control, *J Psychosocial Nurs* 31(7):25-31, 1993.

Detwiler CS: Organic mental disorders. In Johnson B, editor: *Psychiatric-mental health nursing: adaptation and growth,* ed 3, Philadelphia, 1993, JB Lippincott.

Drinka D: OBRA-1987 Nursing home regulations, *J Amer Geriatr Soc* 41(4):466, 1993.

Finding mental health care for nursing home residents, *Horizons* 5(1):6, 1995.

Gerdner L, Swanson E: Effects of individualized music on confused and agitated elderly patient, *Arch Psychiatr Nurs* 8(5):284-291, 1993.

Geriatric models of care: which one's right for your institution? *AJN* 94(7):21-23, 1994.

German PS et al: The role of mental morbidity in the nursing home experience, *Gerontologist* 32(2):152-158, 1992.

Gomez G, Gomez E: The use of anti-depressants with elderly patients, *J Psychosocial Nurs* 30(11):21-26, 1992.

Gomez G, Gomez E: Depression in the elderly, *J Psychosocial Nurs* 31(5):28-33, 1993.

Guide to health insurance for people with Medicare, Baltimore, MD, 1995, National Association of Insurance Commissioners and the Health Care Financing Administration, US Department of Health and Human Services.

Hall G et al: Standardized care plan: Managing Alzheimer's patients at home, *J Gerontologic Nurs* 21(1):37-47, 1995.

Hochberger J: A special population: Nursing diagnoses for the psychiatric client with mental retardation, *Arch Psychiatr Nurs* 8(5):308-310, 1993.

Hoeffer B: Essential curriculum content, *J Psychosocial Nurs* 32(4):33-38, 1994.

Hogstel MO: Mental and behavioral problems in the nursing home. In Hogstel MO, editor: *Geropsychiatric nursing,* ed 2, St. Louis, 1995, Mosby.

Hogstel MO, Nichols MK: Resources. In Hogstel MO, editor: *Geropsychiatric nursing,* ed 2, St. Louis, 1995, Mosby.

Hogstel MO, Smith H: *Eldercare and support in the church,* Fort Worth, 1994, Tarrant Area Community of Churches.

Jutagir R: Psychological aspects of aging: when does memory loss signal dementia? *Geriatrics* 49(3):45-53, 1994.

Kah S, Kupper NS: Mood disorders: Depression and bipolar disorders. In Johnson B, editor: *Psychiatric-mental health nursing: adaptation and growth,* ed 3, Philadelphia, 1993, JB Lippincott.

Keltner N: Tacrine: A pharmacological approach to Alzheimer's disease, *J Psychosocial Nurs* 32(3):37-39, 1994.

Keltner N: Working with the elderly mentally ill. In Keltner N, Schwecke L, Bostrom C, editors: *Psychiatric nursing,* ed 2, St. Louis, 1995, Mosby.

Knapp M: A 30-week randomized controlled trial of high-dose Tacrine in patients with Alzheimer's disease, *JAMA* 271:985-991, 1994.

Koenig HG: *Aging and God,* New York, 1994, Haworth.

Krach P, Yang J: Functional status of older persons with chronic mental illness living in a home setting, *Arch Psychiatr Nurs* 8(2):90-97, 1992.

Kurlowicz L: Social factors and depression in late life, *Arch of Psychiatr Nurs* 8(1):30-36, 1993.

Lind AL: Delirium, dementia, and other cognitive disorders. In Hogstel MO, editor: *Geropsychiatric nursing,* ed 2, St. Louis, 1995, Mosby.

Loving R, Kripke D: Daily light exposure among psychiatric inpatients, *J Psychosocial Nurs* 30(11):15-19, 1992.

Luke EA: Psychotropic drugs. In Hogstel MO, editors: *Geropsychiatric nursing,* ed 2, St. Louis, 1995, Mosby.

Matthiesen V: Disorders of older adults. In Fontaine K, Fletcher J, editors: *Essentials of mental health nursing,* ed 3, pp 430-443, Redwood City, Calif., 1995, Addison-Wesley.

McCabe B et al: Availability and utilization of services by Alzheimer's disease caregivers, *J Gerontologic Nurs* 21(1):14-22, 1995.

McDougall G: A critical review of research on cognitive function/impairment in older adults, *Arch Psychiatr Nurs* 8(1):22-23, 1995.

Mellick E, Buckwalter K, Stolley J: Suicide among elderly white men: Development of a profile, *J Psychosocial Nurs* 30(2):29-34, 1992.

Mills M, Walker J: Memory, mood, and dementia: a case study, *J Aging Stud* 8:17-27, 1994.

Moore S: Rational suicide among older adults: a cause of concern? *Arch Psychiatr Nurs* 8(2):106-110, 1993.

Perlaky D: Responding creatively to dementia, *Nursing 94* 24(1):60-62, 1994.

Parmelee PA, Katz IR, Lawton MP: Incidence of depression in long-term care settings, *J Gerontol* 47(6):M189-M196, 1992.

Riley B, Schizophrenia, paranoid, anxiety, and somatoform disorders. In Hogstel MO, editor: *Geropsychiatric nursing,* ed 2, St. Louis, 1995, Mosby.

Rosen J et al: The Pittsburgh agitation scale: a user-friendly instrument for rating agitation in dementia patients, *Am J Geriatr Psychiatr* 2:52-59, 1994.

Saul RW, Keltner NL: Cognitive disorders. In Keltner N, Schwecke L, Bostrom C, editors: *Psychiatric nursing,* ed 2, St. Louis, 1995, Mosby.

Schmid H, Manjee K, Shah T: On the distinction of suicidal ideation versus attempt in elderly psychiatric inpatients, *Gerontologist* 34:332-339, 1994.

Stern R et al: A longitudinal study of Alzheimer's disease: measurement, rate, and predictors of cognitive deterioration, *Am J Psychiatr* 151:390-396, 1994.

Stuart GW, Sundeen SJ: Self-protective responses and suicidal behavior, In Stuart S, Sundeen W, editors: *Principles and practice of psychiatric nursing,* ed 5, St. Louis, 1995, Mosby.

Suwa-Kobayashi S, Yuasa M, Noguchi M: Nursing in Japan caregivers in elderly family members with dementia, *J Gerontolog Nurs* 21(1):23-30, 1995.

Ugarriza D, Gray T: Alzheimer's disease: nursing interventions for clients and caretakers, *J Psychosocial Nurs* 31(10):7-10, 1993.

Varcarolis EM: People who contemplate suicide: Aggression toward self. In Varcarolis EM, editor: *Foundations of psychiatric-mental health nursing,* ed 2, Philadelphia, 1994, WB Saunders.

Wagner J: Inpatient geropsychiatric nursing in a general hospital, In Hogstel MO, editor: *Geropsychiatric nursing,* ed 2, St. Louis, 1995, Mosby.

Whitney CR: Oldest person in the world turns 120, *Fort Worth Star Telegram,* February 22, 1995, Sec A:1, 11.

BIBLIOGRAPHY

American Association of Retired Persons: *A profile of older Americans,* Washington, D.C., 1994, The Association.

Graham M: Subacute psychiatric care: Strategies for survival in health care reform, *J Subacute Care* 1(3):30-32, 1995.

Holzapfel SK: The elderly. In Varcarolis EM, editor: *Foundations of psychiatric mental health nursing,* ed 2, Philadelphia, 1994, WB Saunders.

Hyde J, Mace N: Special care unit for people with Alzheimer's and other dementia: consumer education, research, regulatory, and reimbursement issues, Washington, D.C., 1992, Office of Technology Assessment.

National Association of Insurance Commissioners and the Health Care Financing Administration, US Department of Health and Human Services: *Guide to health insurance for people with Medicare,* Baltimore, MD., 1995, The Association.

Part Four

AEROBIC & LOWER BODY WORKOUT
IN ONLY TWENTY MINUTES
1. WARM-UP
2. WORKOUT
3. COOL-DOWN
StairMaster

Common Psychophysiologic Stressors

CHAPTER 13

Pain

LEARNING OBJECTIVES

On completion of this chapter, the reader will be able to:

1. Define the concept of pain.
2. Discuss the goals of pain management in the older adult.
3. Identify barriers that affect pain assessment or its management in the older adult client.
4. Describe the impact of pain on quality of life in the older adult client.
5. Identify factors that may affect the older adult's pain experience.
6. Describe the use of pharmacologic or nondrug therapies that can be used in the older adult with pain.
7. Identify the nurse's role in pain management for the older adult client.
8. Use a pain assessment tool to rate the client's pain intensity.
9. Differentiate between pain intensity and pain distress.
10. Discuss the role of family caregivers in pain management for the older adult.

OVERVIEW OF PAIN IN THE OLDER ADULT

In the last decade, many advances in pain management have occurred. Despite these advances, pain remains underrecognized and undertreated in the older adult. This situation has occurred, because the study of pain has generally been limited to the young and to clients with cancer-related pain in acute care settings. More recently, studies have focused on the special needs of older adults in other care settings such as nursing homes (Ferrell, Ferrell, Osterweil, 1990), home or community (Crook, Rideout, Browne, 1984; Ferrell, Rubenstein, 1991; Ferrell et al, 1991a; Ferrell, Schneider, 1988; Roy, Michael, 1988), and hospice (Morris et al, 1987).

The older adult offers unique challenges to health care professionals in the diagnosis and treatment of pain. The nurse caring for the older adult with pain should have an understanding of the special needs of this diverse population. Although older adults are at risk for chronic disease and the often painful conditions accompanying those ailments, their pain is often underrecognized and undertreated. Therefore accurate and ongoing assessment is essential to effective pain management in the older adult. Goals for pain management in older adults include control of chronic disease conditions causing pain, maintenance of mobility and functional status, promotion of maximum independence, and improved quality of life. These goals can be achieved through education of the client, family, and health care professionals, and with good nursing care.

Epidemiology of Pain

Pain is a personal experience that can consume the individual. Although the prevalence of pain in the geriatric population is not accurately known, pain has been reported to occur in up to 70% of noninstitutionalized older adults (Crook, Rideout, Browne, 1984) and in 45% to 83% of nursing home residents (Ferrell, Ferrell, Osterweil, 1990; Roy, Michael, 1988). Many painful diseases are more common in older adults. Arthritis may affect up to 80% of individuals over age 65, causing significant pain for most of these individuals (Davis, 1988). Cancer is more predominant in older adults. Pain is more prevalent in those clients with advanced disease and those clients being treated in hospice or other specialty units (McGuire, Scheidler, 1993). Other pain problems affecting older people include postherpetic neuralgia, polymyalgia rheumatica, atherosclerotic peripheral vascular disease, and temporal arteritis. Thus nurses working with older adults encounter pain assessment and pain management issues in this population.

A relationship between pain, functional status, and overall quality of life has been documented (Ferrell, Wisdom, Wenzl, 1989). Ferrell (in press) has reported that, in older adult nursing home residents, pain can influence participation in recreational and social events, ambulation, posture, appetite, memory, dressing, grooming, and sleep patterns. The pain experience may also cause or exacerbate depression and anxiety. In fact, older individuals with pain may choose to dine alone in their room rather than participate in community dining, may refuse to participate in community or family activities, or may be unable to continue with usual activities of daily living (ADLs) (Ferrell, Ferrell, Osterweil, 1990).

This chapter focuses on the issues of pain management related to the provision of nursing care for the older adult. The chapter is not intended to provide a comprehensive overview of pain management in older people. Instead, it builds on basic knowledge related to pain management to promote appropriate and individualized care of the older adult client with pain and to increase the nurse's awareness about pain management issues of older individuals with pain.

Barriers to Effective Pain Management in the Older Adult

Many barriers exist making pain assessment and pain management difficult in the older adult (Table 13-1). Although reports on age-associated changes in pain perception are controversial, many health care professionals, as well as older clients and their family members have the belief that pain is a natural occurrence of aging and chronic disease (Ferrell, in press). This belief can lead to underreporting of pain and can prevent accurate pain assessment and appropriate use of pain relief measures.

Laboratory study findings suggesting an age-related decline in pain sensitivity and perception are questionable (Ferrell, Rhiner, Ferrell, 1993; Tucker et al, 1989; Woodrow et al, 1972). The nurse should realize that experimentally induced pain may not be comparable to

TABLE 13-1

Barriers to Pain Assessment and Management in Older Adults

Physiologic barriers	Education and attitude barriers	Regulatory and policy barriers
Multiple medical problems	Inadequate knowledge and skills of health care professionals related to pain management	Nursing home policies regarding use of heating pads and other non-drug therapies
Visual spatial skills impairment (inability to use pain rating scales)	Ageism	Regulatory restraints regarding opioids
Memory impairment	Pain is expected	Client and family fears of controlled substances
Visual impairment	Stoicism	Limited diagnostic and treatment facilities for nursing home residents and frail older adults
Hearing impairment	Religiosity (pain is deserved)	Restrictive reimbursement schedules
Impaired abstraction	Hopelessness	
Limited ability to complete written surveys	Fear of addiction and tolerance	
High prevalence of neuropathies		
Increased sensitivity to side effects		
Altered pharmacokinetics and pharmacodynamics		

Modified from Ferrell BR, Ferrell BA: Pain in the elderly. In McGuire DB, Yarbro CH, Ferrell BR, editors: *Cancer pain management,* Boston, 1995, Jones and Bartlett.

clinically experienced pain (Harkins, Kwentus, Price, 1984). Pain sensitivity and perception should be examined in relation to analgesic use, coexisting disease, and comorbid conditions. Therefore the nurse must question whether a physiologic decline in pain perception is related to the normal aging process, coexisting disease, or comorbid conditions.

Another barrier to accurate assessment and pain management occurs when older clients underreport their pain. A recent study reported that the older adult may not complain of pain to avoid undergoing painful diagnostic procedures (Ferrell, Ferrell, Osterweil, 1990). In addition, older clients may underreport pain, because they believe that stoicism and refusal to "give in" to the pain are appropriate behaviors or attitudes (Foley, 1985). Pain assessment may also be hindered by older clients who do not report pain, because they "don't want to bother anyone" or they believe that their report of pain will not be believed (Ferrell, Ferrell, Osterweil, 1990).

Research has also documented that the older adult with cancer may fear the meaning of pain and its implications for worsening disease and possible death (Ferrell et al, 1991b). Clients experiencing cancer-related pain have also expressed a belief that their pain cannot be relieved or that it is a natural outcome of cancer. These clients and their family members needlessly suffer from the clients' experiences of pain.

Accessing diagnostic services is another barrier influencing appropriate pain assessment for older residents of nursing homes and frail older adults in the community. This situation occurs when scheduling appointments and arranging transportation so that a family member or health care professional can accompany the client for diagnostic testing. This barrier can prevent thorough evaluation of the client's complaint of pain (Ouslander, 1989). In addition, nursing home rules and lack of resources may prohibit the use of nondrug pain relief measures such as heating pads or ice packs.

Accurate pain assessment and effective pain control may also be restricted by the older adult's functional decline, including hearing, visual, and motor impairments; mood disturbances; and behavioral changes (Ferrell, Ferrell, 1989). Cognitive and functional impairments may restrict the nurse's ability to obtain an accurate pain history, as well as prevent an accurate pain assessment and evaluation of the effectiveness of pain relief methods used by the client. The older client's report of pain also may differ from that of a younger client as a result of physiologic, psychologic, and cultural changes associated with aging (Fordyce, 1978). These factors should be considered when assessing and managing pain in the older adult.

Pain assessment tools such as visual analogue scales, word descriptor scales, and numeric scales have not been validated in the older adult population. Cognitive, visual, hearing, and motor impairments may prevent accurate use of these pain assessment methods. Researchers in pediatric pain are assessing the use of adapted pain assessment instruments with children (Hester, Barcus, 1986; Wong, Baker, 1988). Similar work is needed in the older adult population. When using any pain assessment tool, the nurse must evaluate each client's ability to use that tool.

An additional barrier to effective pain management arises from the extensive use of pain behaviors to identify and to validate the presence of pain in older adults with dementia. Researchers have attempted to verify pain behaviors such as facial grimacing, agitation, restlessness, and groaning as valid signs indicating pain. However, the assessment of pain with behavior indicators should be used with caution, because clients in pain may not portray any visible signs of pain or distress, or may be unable to communicate their pain.

Research has identified that nurses often interpret behaviors incorrectly and then medicate their clients based on their observations rather than on the client's self-report of pain (McCaffery, Ferrell, 1991a). This research also identified that nurses were unaware that their personal biases influenced their documentation of the client's report of pain and their medication choices. In another study, McCaffery and Ferrell (1991b) identified that nurses' biases regarding client age also influenced

Insight • *Pain is always subjective (American Pain Society, 1992). Only the client knows how much pain he or she is experiencing. A client's evaluation of his pain (the intensity rating) should be accepted and should be documented in the medical record. However, research has shown that nurses are influenced by the age of the client. They are more willing to accept the pain rating of an older adult than the rating of a younger individual (McCaffery, Ferrell, 1991b). Age also influences nurses' administration of analgesic medications. Research shows that nurses are less likely to increase an opioid analgesic dose for an older adult in pain than for a younger individual. This practice occurs despite stable vital signs and in the absence of opioid side effects. The nurse must be aware that older adults may exhibit unpredictable sensitivity or side effects from analgesic medications (Kaiko et al, 1982). This must be taken into consideration when administering analgesic medications. As with all medications, the nurse must assess each client, whether young or old, to determine the effectiveness of the analgesic and the absence or presence of side effects.*

pain assessment and medication choices. The undertreatment of pain because of age is more likely to occur in adults 65 years or older than in younger adults. These practices cause unnecessary suffering for the older adult with pain. Nurses must always be aware of the negative influence ageism has on pain management in older adults.

In the minds of health care professionals, clients, and their family members, fear of addiction is a barrier to effective pain management. Although evidence strongly suggests that the risk of addiction is not an issue in clients who require opioids for pain relief, many health care professionals continue to overestimate the risk (Edgar, Hamilton, 1992; McCaffery, Ferrell, 1992; McCaffery et al, 1990; Weissman, Dahl, 1990). Studies report that clients and their family caregivers use less medication at home than in the hospital, because they fear drug addiction, tolerance, or respiratory depression (Ferrell, Schneider, 1988; Lavsky-Shulan et al, 1985; McCaffery, Ferrell, 1991a). Addiction should not be a consideration in the appropriate use of pain-relieving medications.

Inadequacies in the pain education provided to nursing and medical students are also barriers affecting pain management. In a survey of the curriculum content in 305 baccalaureate programs accredited by the National League of Nursing, it was determined that 48% of these nursing programs have 4 hours or less devoted to the topic of pain (Graffam, 1990). This situation is compounded by the fact that inaccurate information is often provided to health care professionals. Ferrell et al. (1992) reviewed 14 nursing textbooks published after 1985, encompassing over 10,000 pages of text. The texts contained inaccurate or confusing information about addiction and excluded content on general pain. Accurate information is needed by students and nurses to form the basis for nursing practice. These findings indicate that students may unknowingly receive inaccurate information. Unfortunately, this misinformation tends to encourage the fears of addiction held by many clients, family caregivers, and health care professionals, which can result in inadequate pain management.

The pharmacodynamics and the pharmacokinetics of commonly prescribed medications differ in older adults compared with individuals in other age groups. Yet research on the pharmacologic approaches of pain management has generally been limited to single-dose studies in young or middle-age adults (Agency for Health Care Policy and Research [AHCPR], 1992). In addition, information on actual frequency of complications associated with analgesic use in older adults is not available (AHCPR, 1992). Although opioids have been accepted as a treatment for acute pain and cancer-related pain, they have not been widely accepted as a treatment modality for chronic, nonmalignant pain. Physicians' reluctance to prescribe opioids for chronic, nonmalignant pain may have a negative influence on pain management in older adults experiencing this type of pain.

Many factors influence the management of pain in the older adult population. Ineffective pain management has unhealthy implications for mood, sleep, functional status, social well-being, and quality of life (Ferrell, Ferrell, Osterweil, 1990; Lavsky-Shulan et al, 1985; Parmelee, Katz, Lawton, 1991; Spross, 1985). Nurses should accept the challenge to advocate for appropriate and effective pain management in their older adult clients.

Pathophysiology of Pain in the Older Adult

Pain is a universal sensation and a personal experience that should always be assessed from the viewpoint of the person experiencing it (American Pain Society, 1992). Although older adults develop more chronic diseases as they age (Office of Technology Assessment, 1985), the occurrence of pain does not need to be an expectation of normal aging. An understanding of pain physiology and pain theories is essential to effective pain management in older adults. Although a discussion of these topics is beyond the scope of this chapter, several excellent resources are available including a text by McCaffery and Beebe (1989), as well as articles by McGuire and Scheidler (1993), and Paice (1991).

Pain Assessment

Accurate pain assessment begins with the nurse accepting the client's self-report of pain and taking that report of pain seriously. Assessment is essential in differentiating acute, life-threatening pain from longstanding, chronic pain. Disease progression and acute injuries may go unrecognized and be attributed to preexisting disease or illness. Table 13-2 identifies components of the clinical assessment process for pain in the older adult.

Pain assessment should include a thorough history and physical examination. This is especially important in older clients, because effective pain management is often dependent on the appropriate treatment of underlying disease or illness.

Family members can provide nurses and other health care professionals with information useful in assessing the older adult client with pain. Family members can provide information about the client's functional status, pain history, as well as use of analgesic medications and nonpharmacologic pain relief methods. The family's assistance is particularly helpful with the client who is unable or unwilling to provide accurate information, or with the client who does not speak the same language as the nurse or physician. The nurse should also assess the family's role in pain management (see Research boxes, p. 308).

Pain assessment should include an evaluation of the impact of pain on the client's **quality of life (QOL).** The

TABLE 13-2

The Clinical Assessment of Pain in Older Adults

History	Physical examination	Assessment of other variables
Medical history Chronic illnesses Acute illnesses Previous surgeries	**Routine examination**	**Depression scales** Hamilton Yesavage Beck
Pain history Location Frequency Duration Severity Interventions Exacerbations Alleviating factors	**Signs of trauma** Bruises Discoloration Tenderness	**Activities of daily living scales** Katz Lawton
History of trauma Recent falls Other injuries	**Musculoskeletal examination** Trigger points Swelling Masses Tender spots Inflammation	**Mood or quality of life scales** Profile of Mood States Pain/Quality of Life scale
Medications Drug Dose Route Frequency Efficacy Side effects	**Range of motion** Painful movement	**Observation** Facial grimace Posture
Previous pain experiences	**Functional impairment**	

From Ferrell BR, Ferrell BA: Pain in the elderly. In McGuire DB, Yarbro CH, Ferrell BR, editors: *Cancer pain management,* Boston, 1995, Jones and Bartlett.

QOL model developed by Ferrell and colleagues (1991) portrays the relationship between pain and quality of life (Fig. 13-1). The model illustrates the multidimensional viewpoint of the pain experience, showing the impact of pain on the entire individual. The QOL model identifies four domains affected by pain, including physical well-being, psychologic well-being, social concerns, and spiritual well-being.

Clinical experience and research findings identified the relationship between pain and QOL (Ferrell, Wisdom, Wenzl, 1989).

- Pain is associated with physical symptoms such as decreased functional ability, fatigue, nausea, constipation, and appetite and sleep disturbances.
- Pain is also associated with psychologic symptoms, including anxiety, depression, pain distress, happiness, and fear.
- Pain affects the client's social well-being, including roles and relationships, sexual function, and appearance.
- Pain also affects the client's spiritual well-being, including the meaning of pain, suffering, religiosity, and transcendence.

Pain is not an isolated phenomenon but an experience that influences all dimensions of an individual's QOL.

The client's description of the pain should be recorded in the medical record using the client's own words. The client's rating of the pain should be identified using a standard pain assessment tool. The analgesic medication and the amount taken should also be identified and recorded, as should other nondrug therapies used by the client such as distraction, heat, or cold. The nurse should assess and document the impact of the pain on the client's daily activities, including activi-

RESEARCH

Ferrell BR et al: Pain as a metaphor for illness. Part I: Impact of cancer pain on family caregivers, *Oncol Nurs Forum* 18(8):1303-1309, 1991.

Sample, setting

Subjects participating in this study included 85 cancer clients and their family caregivers (N = 85) from three southern California settings. The sites included a community hospital, a national cancer center, and a home-based community hospice program.

Methodology

This qualitative study used interview data to provide an understanding of the family perspective of pain. A demographic tool and the Family Pain Survey (FPS), both developed by the researchers, were used to gather data. The FPS included six open-ended questions.

Findings

The mean client age was 62 years. Of the clients, 85% were women. The average time since diagnosis was 35 months, and the onset of pain was at 14 months. The mean family caregiver age was 54 years. Of the caregivers, 72% of the caregivers were women. Clients were primarily receiving oral and intravenous analgesics. The clients' mean rating of pain (on a scale of 0 to 100 with 0 = no pain and 100 = extreme pain) was 45.5. The caregivers' mean rating of the pain was 69.9. Caregivers used 43 different descriptors to describe the clients' pain, including agonizing, debilitating, intense, overwhelming, terrible, and unbearable. Pain was viewed as an indicator of the clients' status and a sign of progressive disease. Many caregivers viewed death as an awaited relief from the pain.

Implications

Nurses can provide supportive care to the family dealing with the burdens of coping with the illness and hiding emotions about the pain. Nurses can also help families address the guilt they may feel about their wishes for death. Nurses can also plan interventions that assist family caregivers with pain control.

RESEARCH

Ferrell BR et al: Pain as a metaphor for illness. Part II: Family caregivers' management of pain, *Oncol Nurs Forum* 18(8):1315-1321, 1991.

Sample, setting

The subjects participating in this study included 85 cancer clients and their family caregivers (N = 85) from three southern California settings. The sites included a community hospital, a national cancer center, and a home-based community hospice program.

Methodology

This qualitative study used interview data to provide an understanding of the family perspective of pain. A demographic tool and the FPS, both developed by the researchers, were used to gather data. The FPS included six open-ended questions.

Findings

Family caregivers identified seven themes that described their roles in pharmacologic pain management: (1) deciding what medication to give; (2) deciding when to give the medication; (3) performing night duty, which included medication administration and pain assessment; (4) reminding or encouraging the client to take medications; (5) maintaining records to keep track of the medications for themselves and to communicate with the physician; (6) guarding the medication because of their own or the client's fears of addiction; and (7) doing everything—taking total responsibility for pain medications.

Family caregivers identified eight themes regarding their roles in nonpharmacologic pain management: (1) positioning the client using pillows and assisting with ambulation, (2) performing massage, (3) using ointments or lotions, (4) using heat, (5) using cold, (6) using touch, (7) avoiding touch when the client did not want to be touched or when touch caused pain, and (8) using talk and other distraction techniques to divert attention from the pain.

Family caregivers identified five themes on what doctors and nurses can do to help relieve the pain: (1) be supportive and offer hope, (2) explain symptoms and treatments, (3) be honest and listen, (4) overcome addiction concerns that prevented adequate pain control for the client, and (5) give medication that provides adequate pain control while balancing the side effects.

Family caregivers identified five themes that outlined their questions and concerns about the pain experience: (1) concern for the future (Would the pain get worse? Would they be able to handle it? Would the pain cause death?), (2) understanding why (Is there a meaning to the pain and suffering?), (3) death (The pain was linked to worsening disease and approaching death. They avoided death and yet welcomed it as a relief from the pain), (4) concern about medications (They expressed fears that the medications would not control the pain, that tolerance to analgesics would develop, and that side effects of the medications would cause more discomfort), and (5) fear about what to do at home and their abilities to manage care at home.

Implications

Nurses can provide family caregivers with education on pharmacologic and nondrug interventions and support to assume their roles. Nurses can be instrumental in developing family-related pain education materials.

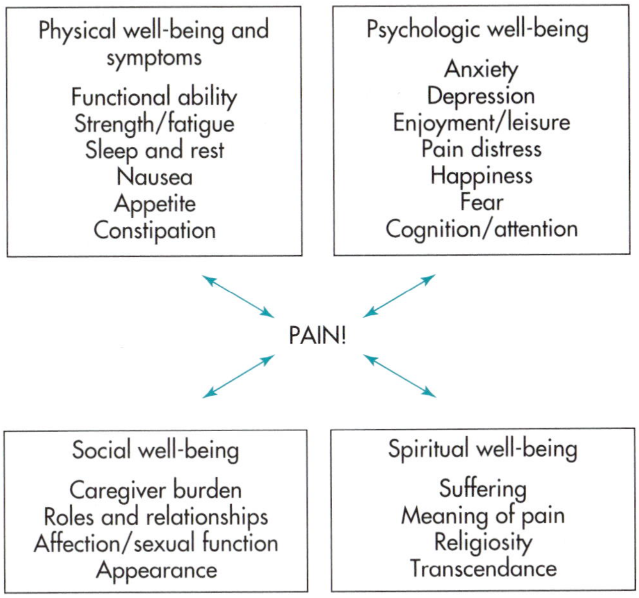

Fig. 13-1 Pain-quality of life model. (From Ferrell BR et al: Pain as a metaphor for illness. Part I: Impact of cancer pain on family caregivers, *Oncol Nurs Forum* 18(8):1303-1309, 1991.)

Daily Pain Diary

Name ____________________ Date __________

Hour	Pain-rating scale = 0-__	Medication taken, dose	Other pain relief measures tried or anything that helps your pain	Major activity: lying, sitting, standing/walking
12 Midnight				
1 a.m.				
2				
3				
4				
5				
6				
7				
8				
9				
10				
11				
12 Noon				
1 p.m.				
2				
3				
4				
5				
6				
7				
8				
9				
10				
11				

Comments: ____________________

Fig. 13-2 Daily pain diary. (From McCaffery M, Beebe A: *Pain: clinical manual for nursing practice,* St. Louis, 1989, Mosby.)

ties that the client can or cannot accomplish, the presence or absence of physical limitations, and the distress associated with the pain. In the home, the client or family members can record this same information using a daily pain diary (Fig. 13-2) or a pain management log (Fig. 13-3).

The client's report of pain should also be evaluated for **pain intensity** and **pain distress.** Pain intensity is a measure of the amount of pain that the client is experiencing (Ferrell, Ferrell, 1995). Pain intensity is identified by the client through the use of a numeric pain rating scale such as a 0 to 10 scale with 0 = no pain to 10 = the worst pain. Use of a numeric pain rating scale translates the client's report of pain into a number that provides the health care professional with an objective description of the client's pain.

Pain intensity, as reported by the client, and the parameters of the scale used should be documented in the client's medical record. For example the nurse should record, "The client rates his abdominal pain as '3' on a scale of 0 to 10 with 0 = no pain to 10 = the worst pain." The client's pain should be treated based on the client's report of pain.

The nurse should also establish what level of pain intensity is acceptable for the client. The client should be asked, "At what number is the pain at an acceptable level for you?" This question acknowledges that the client's pain experience is an individual one as is tolerance of that pain. On a 0 to 10 scale, "3" may be an acceptable level of pain control for one individual, whereas "0 to 1" may be acceptable for another. The number identified by the client becomes the goal that the client and the health care professionals work toward. The goal is to relieve as much pain as possible.

Clinical experience also reveals that many clients do not have an understanding of pain management techniques and are often unaware that pain can be controlled. Thus older clients who rate their acute or chronic pain as "8" on a scale of 0 to 10 when 0 = no pain to 10 = the worst pain may express satisfaction with the level of pain relief they are receiving, not realizing that a better level of pain management is possible. The nurse should advise clients of the right to receive the best level of pain relief that can be safely provided and should then follow through with appropriate pain management activities.

Consistent use of a pain assessment tool assists both the clients and health care professionals to evaluate the effectiveness of an intervention. Accurate record keeping promotes effective pain management activities.

Pain distress measures the extent to which pain affects the client (Ferrell, Ferrell, 1995). The distress asso-

Please use this pain assessment scale to fill out your self care log:

0 1 2 3 4 5 6 7 8 9 10

No pain Worst pain

Date	Time	How severe is the pain?	How distressing is the pain to you?	Describe action or medicine taken	How severe is the pain after 1 hour?

Fig. 13-3 Self-care pain management log. (From Ferrell BR, Ferrell BA: Pain in the elderly. In McGuire DB, Yarbro CH, Ferrell BR, editors: *Cancer pain management,* Boston, 1995, Bartlett and Jones.)

ciated with pain is dynamic and may change depending on other factors present in the client's life. Clinical experience has demonstrated that a client reporting a mild to moderate pain intensity may report a great deal of pain distress (Ferrell et al, 1991). For example, an older adult woman may rate the pain intensity in her hip as "4" on a 0 to 10 scale with 0 = no pain to 10 = the worst pain and rate the pain distress as "8" on a 0 to 10 scale with 0 = no distress to 10 = unbearable distress, because she believes that her pain will prevent her from playing softball with her grandchildren who are visiting. On another day when the same client plans to spend her day reading, she may rate her hip pain as "4" but may rate the pain distress as "0."

Pain is an individual experience. Therefore clients evaluate their pain intensity and the pain distress associated with their pain based on several factors such as culture, past pain experience, individual attributes, and pain threshold. The nurse should regularly evaluate pain intensity and pain distress with every client.

Pain Assessment Tools

Pain assessment tools assist health care professionals to objectively and accurately measure the client's report of pain. Pain assessment tools include numeric pain rating scales such as a 0 to 10 scale when 0 = no pain to 10 = the worst pain; visual analog scales; and descriptive pain intensity scales such as no pain, a little pain, a lot of pain, too much pain; pain diaries; and pain logs. Examples of pain assessment tools are illustrated in Fig. 13-4.

It should be remembered that some older adult clients may have difficulty completing or using these tools as a result of cognitive or functional impairments, or the impact of their diseases or treatments, such as fatigue or inability to concentrate. Therefore each client must be evaluated individually for ability to use the pain assessment tool. For example, if the older client is unable to use a numeric rating scale, the nurse should identify another assessment tool such as a descriptive pain intensity scale to objectively measure the intensity of the client's pain.

Pain assessment tools that have been developed for use in younger populations must be evaluated for appropriate use in older adults, especially in frail older adults and in those individuals with cognitive or functional impairment. These clients may be unable to use a numeric scale to rate their pain, because the numbers do not make sense to them. In such cases, a group of descriptive words may be helpful, such as no pain, mild pain, moderate pain, severe pain, or excruciating pain.

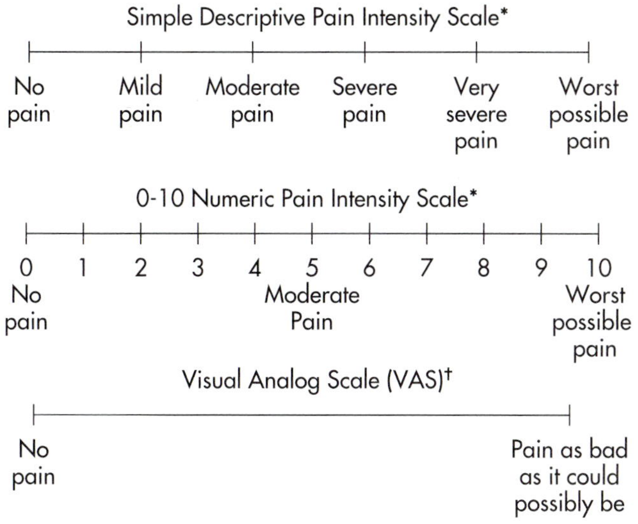

* If used as a graphic rating scale, a 10-cm baseline is recommended.
† A 10-cm baseline is recommended for VAS scales.

Fig. 13-4 Examples of pain assessment tools. (From Acute Pain Management Guideline Panel: *Acute pain management: operative or medical procedures and trauma,* "Clinical Practice Guideline," AHCPR Pub No 92-0032. Rockville, MD, 1992, Agency for Health Care Policy and Research, Public Health Service, US Department of Health and Human Services.)

Which pain rating scale or the phrases used to rate the client's pain intensity is not as important as it is for the nurse to apply the following guidelines (McCaffery, Ferrell, 1992):

- Use the assessment tool that makes sense to the client.
- Be consistent. Use the same assessment tool every time the client's pain is assessed.
- Each time that an assessment tool is used, specify the parameters of that tool so that the meaning of the client's pain rating is clear.

A self-care pain management log (see Fig. 13-3, p. 310) has been successfully used, on which older adult clients and family members record pain intensity, pain distress, the action (pharmacologic or nonpharmacologic methods) taken to relieve the pain, and the outcome of that action (Rhiner et al, 1993). The self-care pain management log is an important tool that furnishes clients, family members, and clinicians with the information needed to provide effective pain assessment and management.

Psychologic Evaluation

Pain assessment in the older adult also includes a psychologic evaluation. At one time or another, most clients experiencing chronic pain have significant depressive symptoms. These clients may benefit from psychologic or psychiatric intervention. A persistent depression affects the person's ability to cope with the pain, so it must be treated. In addition, anxiety may be a significant psychologic factor influencing the effective management of chronic pain. Treatment of anxiety and depressive symptoms are important components to effectively managing pain in the older adult. However, clinicians must not attribute all pain to depression or psychogenic causes (Parmelee, Katz, Lawton, 1991).

History

Careful questioning and thorough assessment of the older adult client's report of pain should be performed. This is especially important in the older adult because of the tendency for multiple sources of pain (Ferrell, [in press]; Ferrell, Ferrell, Osterweil, 1990). Acute pain is often attributed to chronic illness but should be evaluated with the knowledge that older adults often demonstrate altered presentation of common acute illnesses, including "silent" myocardial infarctions and "painless" intra-abdominal emergencies (Bayer et al, 1986; Bender, 1989). On the other hand, chronic pain is characterized by variable intensity and character, and thus is often overlooked.

Physical Examination

Pain assessment for the older adult also includes a comprehensive physical examination of the musculoskeletal and nervous systems. This is an important aspect of pain assessment in this population, because many older adults experience painful traumatic and degenerative musculoskeletal problems. A thorough neurologic assessment includes an evaluation for autonomic, sensory, or motor deficits, which may be indicative of neuropathic conditions or nerve injuries.

Functional impairment Impaired functional status is a major problem for older adults. An evaluation of the older adult's level of function is important so that mobility and independence can be maximized. Evaluation of functional status includes the assessment of ADLs, ambulation, psychosocial well-being, and overall quality of life. Functional activities may be restricted by the presence and intensity of pain (Ferrell, 1991). Functional evaluation includes an assessment of factors that contribute to or help to alleviate pain. Functional status can be significantly improved through aggressive pain management.

Nursing Care of Older Adult Clients with Pain

Older people often respond with unpredictable sensitivity and frequent side effects to many classes of drugs, including analgesics (Kaiko et al, 1982). The aging process probably affects drug absorption, distribution, metabolism, and excretion (Morgan, Furst, 1986).

Among the changes that require ongoing assessment of the client's response to a medication with subsequent adjustments in dose and dosing intervals, or drug prescribed are the following: changes in physiologic factors such as decreased gastric acid production and gastrointestinal motility (Geokas, Haverbeck, 1969); changes in body composition such as decreased total body water, lean body mass, serum protein, and increased body fat (Kaiko et al, 1982); changes in organ function such as decreased hepatic blood flow (Tucker et al, 1989); and reduced glomerular filtration rates (Kaiko et al, 1982).

It is important to remember that the drug selected should depend on the type of pain and its intensity. For example, the client who reports mild-to-moderate pain that is not responsive to a nonopioid analgesic or is poorly tolerated may require a weak opioid analgesic such as oxycodone. Therapy must always be individualized for the client. Effective pain management requires ongoing assessment of the medication used in relation to its analgesic effect and side effects.

Analgesic drugs can be classified into three broad categories: (1) mild analgesics, including nonopioid analgesics and some weak opioid analgesics such as codeine, oxycodone, and propoxyphene; (2) strong opioid analgesics, including morphine; and (3) **adjuvant drugs,** including those agents that enhance the analgesic effects of opioids and those that have intrinsic analgesic activity.

Mild Analgesics

The mild analgesics are used as a first-line approach to pain management. Aspirin, acetaminophen (Tylenol), ibuprofen (Motrin, Advil), naproxen (Naprosyn) and fenprofen (Feldene) are examples of mild analgesics. These drugs block pain by inhibiting pain reception at the local level. As with all medications, usage must be continuously monitored in the older adult.

Nonsteroidal antiinflammatory drugs (NSAIDs) are especially effective for treating mild to moderate arthritic pain and bone pain as a result of malignant metastases. The NSAIDs have been associated with a variety of adverse side effects in older adults including stomach ulcers, renal insufficiency, and a tendency for bleeding. The most common complaint associated with NSAIDs is indigestion. Indigestion may be reduced with antacid use or food consumption timed to coincide with analgesic intake. However, the health care professional must remember that gastroduodenal irritation may occur in the absence of any symptoms. Severe ulceration can result in extensive bleeding or perforation. Although previously considered the safest form of analgesic, recent studies are beginning to question the overall safety of NSAIDs for frail older adults (Butt, Barthel, Moore, 1988; Roth, 1989). The older adult's response to the medication must be followed and evaluated closely.

Acetaminophen is as effective as aspirin for its analgesic and antipyretic properties but less effective than aspirin for its antiinflammatory properties. Although acetaminophen has not been associated with renal or gastric problems, it can result in hepatic toxicity in clients with a history of alcohol abuse or following ingestion of very high doses.

Ketorolac (Toredol) is a new NSAID that has similar side effects of other NSAIDs. There is a high risk of gastric problems with continued use beyond 5 to 7 days parenterally; or 10 to 14 days orally. Ketorolac is intended for short-term use, generally in the postoperative period.

The analgesic effect of NSAIDs and acetaminophen is also limited by a ceiling effect. In other words, raising the drug's dose beyond a given dose does not result in added analgesia.

Opioid Analgesics

For the client with mild-to-moderate pain that cannot be adequately managed with a mild analgesic or that is poorly tolerated, the clinician should consider using an opioid analgesic. Clinical experience suggests that older adults are particularly sensitive to the effects of opioid analgesics, because they experience a higher peak and longer duration of pain relief (Bellville et al, 1971; Kaiko, 1980; Kaiko et al, 1982). Common side effects include nausea, vomiting, constipation, and urinary retention, especially in the individual with prostatic hypertrophy. Probably as a result of altered distribution and excretion of medications, older adults are more sensitive to sedation and respiratory depression. This is especially true in the opioid-naïve client. **Opioid-naïve** refers to the client who has not had earlier exposure to opioids (see nursing Care Plan, p. 313-314).

Side effects Constipation is a common side effect of opioid use and of particular concern in older clients, since many of them may have preexisting bowel problems. Careful assessment of bowel habits, including the use of stool softeners, laxatives, and dietary intake of high-fiber foods, is essential when using opioids. It is the rare adult client who does not require a program of bowel management. The health care professional must stress to the client and family the importance of being proactive, that is, preventing the occurrence of constipation rather than waiting for it to occur (see Client/Family Teaching box p. 314). McCaffery and Beebe (1989) provide a useful bowel regimen for preventing constipation in clients using opioids.

Although nausea and vomiting caused by opioid use usually disappear after a few days of taking the medication, it is critical that clinicians take a preventive approach in treating these side effects (McCaffery, Beebe, 1989). As with all medications, antiemetics must be evaluated in the older adult for their effectiveness in controlling nausea and vomiting, as well as for side effects such as sedation. The nurse should advise clients and

CARE PLAN

PAIN: PROSTATE CANCER WITH BONE METASTASES

Clinical situation: Mr. V is a 79-year-old retired telephone company executive who has been admitted into the local hospital-based home care program. Mr. V has always been in good health until his diagnosis of prostate cancer 2 years ago. He and his wife have enjoyed an active social life. Her four adult children live in cities throughout the United States. They do not have any church affiliation. Mr. and Mrs. V have been married for 10 years and live in a mobile home park in the desert. They also own a condominium in the city but do not have any resources for support in that neighborhood. Three years ago, they acquired a puppy whom they named Max. Until the last 2 to 2-1/2 months, Mr. V has taken morning and evening walks with Max throughout the neighborhood and local park.

In the last 2 months, Mr. V has complained about a great deal of pain in his legs and back. He has lost 35 lbs. in the last month. He tires easily and is unable to walk outside his home or for distances longer than 25 feet without resting. Mr. V's first wife died 20 years ago from breast cancer. Mr. V relates how she suffered intensely from the effects of chemotherapy and severe pain. He has refused all treatment for his cancer until 6 months ago when he started receiving hormone therapy. He has refused to take the long-acting opioid prescribed by his physician, because he does not "want to get hooked." Mr. V rates his pain as "9" on a scale of 0 to 10 with 0 = no pain to 10 = the worst pain. Mrs. V is having difficulty caring for him and dealing with his impending death.

Nursing diagnoses	Outcomes	Interventions
Chronic pain related to inadequate knowledge of pain management	Client will report decreased pain (between 0 and 3) at rest and with activity as evidenced by self-report.	Discuss general pain content information with Mr. and Mrs. V. Identify Mr. V's description of his pain, including the quality of the pain, its location, and its precipitating and relieving factors. Identify the intensity of Mr. V's pain using a pain assessment tool. Identify the distress Mr. V experiences in relation to his pain. Evaluate Mr. V's current use of pharmacologic and non-drug pain relief methods. Discuss with Mr. V his fear of addiction, and his need to maintain control of his life and remain alert and functional. Implement use of a self-care pain management log, including the use of a pain rating scale. Instruct Mr. and Mrs. V about around-the-clock scheduling for analgesics. Discuss current pain management regimen and plans for further treatment with Mr. V's physician.
Potential for alteration in bowel elimination related to analgesic use	Client will continue his usual bowel elimination pattern—a soft, formed stool every day.	Identify Mr. V's current bowel elimination pattern. Explain physician's prescription for a stool softener. Discuss use of a mild laxative if there is no bowel movement after 2 days. Encourage fluid intake of at least eight glasses of water each day. Modify diet to increase intake of high-fiber foods. Discuss the effect of analgesics on bowel elimination. Reinforce the fact that although constipation is an expected side effect of opioids, it can be prevented.

Continued.

CARE PLAN

PAIN: PROSTATE CANCER WITH BONE METASTASES—cont'd

Nursing diagnoses	Outcome	Interventions
Impaired physical mobility related to pain.	Mr. V will maintain ADLs and other physical activities as he is able.	Instruct Mr. V to take analgesic medications on a regular basis. Identify activities that are important to Mr. V and that he would like to maintain. Encourage short walks with his dog and sitting in the dining room for his meals. Encourage use of the self-care log. Instruct Mr. V about energy conservation and about the need to space activities with periods of rest. Evaluate environment to determine need for ambulatory or other activity equipment.

family members that sedation may occur as a result of the antiemetic. McCaffery and Beebe (1989) provide useful information for treating opioid-induced nausea, and for client and family teaching.

Sedation is another opioid-related side effect. Sedation may occur when an opioid is first started or when there is a significant dosage increase (AHCPR, 1992). The sedation usually decreases in 1 to 3 days. If it does not, the physician should be notified. Sedation may also be related to sleep deprivation resulting from unrelieved pain. The nurse must not forget that sedation can occur without adequate pain relief. McCaffery and Beebe (1989) provide useful information for managing opioid-related sedation.

Although the older adult may be more sensitive to opioids, this does not justify withholding opioids (Melzack, 1990). Therefore choosing an appropriate opioid drug for use in the older adult client with pain requires special consideration. Problems arise with opioids having long half-lives, such as methadone (Dolophine) or levorphanol (Levo-Dromoran). The **half-life** of an opioid refers to the time it takes for the drug to decrease to half its initial plasma concentration. Plasma levels of drugs having long half-lives rise slowly over several days after initiating a dosing schedule. Thus the risk of delayed toxicity is much greater in these drugs than with drugs having shorter half-lives. Codeine, hydromorphone (Dilaudid), and morphine, in appropriate doses, can safely be used in the older adult with pain. Table 13-3 identifies analgesics that should be avoided in older adults.

Data have shown that adult clients experience enhanced pain relief from opioids as compared with younger clients (Kaiko et al, 1982). Interestingly, this effect has been demonstrated for postoperative pain and chronic cancer pain, possibly as a result of altered pharmacokinetics and excretion of drugs in older clients. The effects of analgesic drugs vary widely among individuals. Therefore health care professionals cannot generalize or cannot predict responses in older adults. Smaller doses of opioids can be used in the older adult as a result of

CLIENT/FAMILY TEACHING

What Can You Do For Constipation?

Opioid analgesics cause constipation in most people. By following the information below, you should be able to prevent constipation from becoming a problem and causing you discomfort.

- Eat foods high in fiber, such as uncooked fruits and vegetables, and whole-grain breads and cereals.
- Add 1 or 2 tablespoons of unprocessed bran to your foods.
- Drink plenty of liquids—eight to ten glasses per day.
- Eat foods that have helped you to relieve constipation in the past.
- Plan your bowel movement for the same time each day, if possible.
- Use the toilet or bedside commode when you have your bowel movement.
- Have a hot drink about 30 minutes before your planned time for a bowel movement.
- Consult with your physician about using a bulk laxative such as Metamucil or any other laxative or stool softener.

Modified from American Cancer Society/National Cancer Institute: *Questions and answers about pain control: a guide for people with cancer and their families,* Atlanta, 1992, The Society.

TABLE 13-3

Analgesic Drugs to Avoid in Older Adults

Drug	Precautions	Potential solutions
Meperidine (Demerol)	Extremely low oral potency; metabolite, normeperidine may accumulate and may cause confusion, agitation, and seizure activity, especially among clients with renal impairment	Choose a drug with higher oral potency; there are no advantages of either oral or parenteral meperidine over other opioid drugs
Pentazocine (Talwin)	Mixed opioid agonist/antagonist activity often leads to central nervous system excitement, confusion, and agitation	Avoid all use in frail older adults
Propoxyphene (Darvon)	Potency no better than aspirin; significant abuse potential and potential for renal injury	Choose NSAID or weak opioid
Methadone (Dolophine)	Plasma half-life may be extremely prolonged in older adults; analgesic half-life relatively short	Short-acting or long-acting morphine is a better alternative
Transdermal fentanyl (Duragesic)	Extremely potent; drug retention in tissue reservoir may result in extremely prolonged half-life	Decreased drug clearance in older adults; avoid in opioid-naïve; or cachectic or debilitated clients who have altered pharmacokinetics because of poor fat stores, muscle wasting, or altered clearance

From Ferrell BR, Ferrell BA: Pain in the elderly. In McGuire DB, Yarbro CH, Ferrell BR, editors; *Cancer pain management,* Boston, 1995, Jones and Bartlett.

prolonged half-life and altered pharmacokinetics of these drugs. Opioid analgesics can be safely used in older adult clients, but their use in this population requires careful monitoring and recognition of opioid pharmacokinetics (Portenoy, 1987). This is especially important in opioid-naïve clients.

The literature reveals that the risk of addiction to opioids is less than 1% in clients treated for pain without a prior history of addiction (Foley, Rogers, 1981; Marks, Sacher, 1973; Porter, Jick, 1980; Twycross, 1974; Vallerand, 1991). Vallerand (1991) identifies three situations in which opioids can be considered appropriate for the treatment of nonmalignant pain: (1) to provide pain relief during procedures and those times when other treatment regimens are being incorporated into the client's care, (2) to provide pain control during times of exacerbation, and (3) to control the discomfort and suffering associated with severe chronic pain. Nurses and other health care professionals must remember that the majority of individuals using opioids for pain relief stop taking opioids when the pain stops (McCaffery, Beebe, 1989).

Adjuvant Medications

Adjuvant medications, defined as medications without intrinsic analgesic properties, are helpful in treating certain types of chronic pain. For example, treatment of underlying depression or mood disorders may enhance other pain management strategies. Adjuvant medications include antidepressants, anticonvulsants, and some sedatives. Anticonvulsants, or other drugs usually used to treat seizures, are often helpful in controlling painful conditions such as postherpetic neuralgia, diabetic neuropathies, and phantom limb pain. However, in the older adult, some sedatives or tranquilizers may cause side effects such as increased confusion and constipation, whereas anticonvulsants may cause blood dyscrasias. Thus the use of these medications in older adults must be continuously monitored. The nurse plays a vital role in this process, as well as in educating the client and family members about the appropriate use of these adjuvant medications. The nurse should always explain the rationale for concurrent use of an analgesic and adjuvant medication.

It is also important that the nurse identify for clients and their family members when these adjuvant medications are being used to treat the client's pain. Clinical experience has shown that a client may discontinue the analgesic when an adjuvant medication is added. The client may also take an adjuvant medication such as an antidepressant without realizing that it is being used in conjunction with the analgesic for pain itself. As with all analgesics, the nurse must continue to assess the client's report of pain, and the effectiveness and side effects of the adjuvant medication used to treat the client's pain.

Routes of Administration

It is important to remember that the majority of clients can be effectively treated with oral analgesics. Oral medications are the preferred route of administration (American Pain Society, 1992). The use of "high-tech" routes such as intravenous or epidural analgesic administration must be evaluated from the perspectives of cost, comfort, risk for complications, and caregiver burden. A conservative approach to high-tech pain management is advised.

Placebos

The nurse must recognize that placebos do not play any role in pain management nor should they ever be used to assess the nature of a client's pain (American Pain Society, 1992). McCaffery and Beebe (1989) define a **placebo** "as any medical treatment or nursing care that produces an effect in a client because of its implicit or explicit intent and not because of its specific nature or therapeutic properties." The American Pain Society (1992) contends that the deceptive use of placebos and misinterpretation of the placebo response is unethical. McCaffery and Beebe (1989) provide excellent suggestions for the nurse who is faced with having to deal with placebo prescriptions.

The primary consideration in selecting pain relief methods is individual planning. Clients vary greatly in their medication requirements, choices of nondrug interventions, and prior pain experiences. Clients should be involved in choosing pain management methods and should share responsibility for implementing pain relief measures. Active involvement of clients and family caregivers is essential in successfully implementing pain management regimens. This applies to both pharmacologic and nondrug pain relief measures.

Research

Research in pain management supports the combined use of drug and nondrug pain management therapies. Nondrug methods include the use of heat, cold, relaxation or distraction, imagery, massage, transcutaneous nerve stimulation (TENS), biofeedback, and hypnosis. Clinical experience suggests that many of these techniques are quite effective in individual cases. As with all treatment modalities, individual response must be evaluated.

Physical methods, including heat, cold, and massage, are important pain relief methods for use in older adults (McCaffery, Beebe, 1989). These physical methods relax tense muscles and are effective in treating a variety of painful problems. Generally, a heating pad or ice pack can be easily managed by the older client. However, clients and their caregivers must be cautioned to avoid thermal burns, which can occur in older adult clients during prolonged use.

Insight • *In the past, health care professionals were responsible for providing pain relief measures. In a changing health care system, clients and families are increasingly expected to manage pain at home with little experience and minimal support. Pain is best treated using a combination of pharmacologic and nonpharmacologic interventions. Nurses can provide family members with informa-tion on general pain content as well as information on the effective use of pharmacologic and nondrug pain relief measures (Rhiner M et al, 1993). To get the best pain relief, the client, family, physician, and nurse must work together as a team.*

In a study conducted by Ferrell, et al. (1993), clients with chronic cancer pain tended to choose nondrug methods based on personal preference. These older clients preferred physical methods for pain relief such as heat and vibration over cognitive methods. In this study, clients and their family caregivers were very receptive to learning how to use nondrug pain relief methods as adjuncts to their analgesic medications. They were taught to use heat, cold, massage or vibration, distraction, and relaxation. Learning how to appropriately and effectively use nondrug methods often provided clients and their caregivers with a sense of control in an otherwise uncontrollable situation. The nondrug methods used in this study are readily available in local retail stores such as Target, Osco, K-Mart, Thrifty's, and Wal-Mart.

In this same study, preliminary analysis of client outcomes indicated that the structured pain education program was effective in decreasing pain intensity, perception of pain severity, fear of addiction, and anxiety, as well as increasing the use of pain medications (Ferrell, Rhiner, Ferrell, 1993). Clients also reported improved sleep and increased knowledge of pain content.

Other Modalities

TENS has been used successfully in older adults for a variety of chronic pain conditions. Pain associated with diabetic neuropathies, shoulder pain or bursitis, and fractured ribs respond to TENS therapy (Thorsteinsson, 1987). An important issue in the successful use of TENS therapy is appropriate placement of the electrodes and adjustment of the electrical current amplitude and pulse pattern. This requires careful and diligent work to find the optimum settings to provide effective pain relief. It may take several weeks of continuous TENS before optimum pain control is reached or before one should consider abandoning treatment (Carbelli, Kellerman, 1985). TENS therapy requires a physician's prescription.

CULTURAL AWARENESS

Alternative Practices in Pain Management

Culture often influences the older adult's choice of interventions for dealing with pain. The following is an illustrative, but not exhaustive, list of alternative or complementary practices sometimes used by clients from culturally diverse backgrounds for pain management.

- Herbal remedies
- Meditation
- Progressive relaxation
- Hypnosis
- Yoga
- Imagery
- Therapeutic touch
- Acupuncture or acupressure
- Application of heat or cold
- Music
- Humor

CLIENT/FAMILY TEACHING

Controlling Pain Through a Team Approach

The best way to control your pain is through a team approach involving you (the client), your family, and your nurse and physician. In addition to telling them how much pain you have, you should also give them the following information.

- Where is your pain located?
- When did the pain start?
- Describe the pain. Is it sharp? Dull? Throbbing? Burning?
- Does the pain come and go, or is it constant?
- What makes the pain worse?
- What makes the pain better?
- What medications are you taking for your pain?
- Are there any other methods that you are using to relieve your pain such as relaxation, the heating pad, or a cold pack? Do they seem to help?

Modified from Supportive Care Services Committee: *City of Hope patient handbook for cancer pain management,* Duarte, Calif., 1994, City of Hope National Medical Center.

Physical therapy, focusing on stretching and strengthening exercises, may also be useful in relieving muscle spasm and improving functional activity. However, intense, vigorous stretching and exercise can lead to injury in the older adult client with pain. Referral to a physical therapist should be obtained before using these techniques for painful conditions in older clients.

Although psychologic interventions such as biofeedback, relaxation, and hypnosis may be very effective in controlling pain in the older person, it is important to remember that these methods usually require higher levels of cognitive function and therefore may not be appropriate for use in clients with significant cognitive impairment. A psychologist or therapist should be consulted for these techniques. Clinical experience has indicated that some older adult clients may be reluctant to try these pain relief methods. However, clients should be offered these treatment options.

Distraction may be effective in decreasing the perception of pain. Many clients find comfort in prayer, meditation, television, reminiscence, or music (see Cultural Awareness box above). Others find pain relief through activities such as exercise and recreation. These clients should be encouraged to participate in distraction activities as tolerated, with care given to avoid overexertion.

Other Considerations

When selecting any pain relief method the clinician should consider its financial impact on the client. Pain medications are costly and the financial burden to clients and their family caregivers, who may have already assumed the high costs of surgery, other treatments, or hospitalization, can be overwhelming. Financial considerations are particularly problematic for older people because of fixed incomes and third-party reimbursement schedules that may be restrictive. Cost/benefit in pain treatment can best be achieved by using the least invasive, least costly pain treatment method. All pharmacologic and nondrug interventions should be carefully evaluated for cost and benefit.

When selecting or implementing analgesic treatments, nurses should consider the following guidelines:

- Use a ladder approach as defined by the World Health Organization (World Health Organization, 1990).
- Provide adequate analgesia consistent with the intensity of the client's pain.
- Aggressively treat side effects such as constipation and nausea.
- Continuously reevaluate the client's status to determine the optimum treatment approach.
- Develop expertise in the use of high-dose morphine; learn current pain content.
- Assist with the development of hospital-wide guidelines on treatment modalities and procedures.
- Consider the impact of psychosocial influences on the effectiveness of a pain relief method.
- Use a multidisciplinary approach to pain management, including nursing, medicine, pharmacy, social services, and pastoral care (see Client/Family Teaching box above).

Summary

Pain assessment and management for older adult clients with pain should be based on comprehensive and appropriate use of current pain knowledge and technology. For older clients, frequent and systematic evaluation of pain is critical in achieving effective outcomes. Pain management in the older adult should include the use of appropriate medications and nondrug therapies. The clinician should have an awareness of the multiple and complex illnesses experienced in the older adult population. In addition, the clinician should have an appreciation for the increased sensitivity to drug side effects; potential for cognitive, sensory, and functional impairment; the impact of the pain experience on the client and family; and the regulatory issues affecting pain management in the older adult population.

HOME CARE TIPS

1. Nurses caring for the older homebound adult should know the impact that pain has on functional status and quality of life
2. The home care nurse should evaluate pain at each home visit.
3. Assess factors (e.g., motor impairments, cognitive, and functional impairments) that may influence effective pain control in the homebound older adult.
4. When using a pain assessment tool, the home care nurse must evaluate the homebound older adult's ability to use the tool.
5. Caregivers are an important source of information in assessing the homebound older adult with pain.
6. Instruct caregivers and homebound older adults on adjunctive therapies that can be used in conjunction with analgesic to medication pain therapy.
7. Assess and identify barriers held by caregivers and homebound older adults related to pain and its management.

Key Points

- Pain often remains underrecognized and undertreated in older adults, mainly because of limited research. Therefore nurses must have special understanding, coupled with accurate and ongoing assessment, of the pain needs of this population.
- Goals for pain management in older adults include control of chronic disease conditions that cause pain, maintenance of mobility and functional status, promotion of maximum independence, and improved quality of life.
- Barriers to effective pain management in older adults include the misconception that intolerance to pain is age-related, underreporting of pain, accessing diagnostic services, cognitive and functional impairment, the inability to communicate pain effectively through pain behavior scales, fear of addiction, and inadequacies in pain education.
- Accurate and ongoing assessment, as well as a thorough understanding of pain physiology, is essential for effective pain management in the older adult.
- The nurse's clinical assessment of older adults' pain includes a number of important components: medical history; pain history; history of trauma, medications, and previous pain experiences; physical examination focusing on signs of trauma; musculoskeletal examination; assessment of range of motion; and any functional impairments. A variety of tools and scales can be used to augment the above-named assessments.
- The quality of life (QOL) model is one method used to assess pain. This model identifies how pain impacts spiritual, physical, and psychologic well-being, as well as social concerns.
- Pharmacologic pain management includes the use of analgesics, opioid analgesics, and adjuvant medications. Nondrug therapies include physical methods using cold, heat, and massage; relaxation or distraction; imagery; transcutaneous nerve stimulation (TENS); biofeedback; and hypnosis. For the pain management to be effective, the nurse must continually assess the client's response to pain when employing any of these methods.
- A standard assessment scale that differentiates between pain intensity and pain distress in the older adult client is a useful tool for nurses when planning successful pain interventions. Consistent use of this tool, coupled with accurate record keeping, helps to promote effective pain management.
- Family members often play an integral role in pain management for the older adult. Family members can often provide insight to the older adult client's pain experience by offering the nurse information that the client may not be willing or able to accurately share.

Critical Thinking Exercises

1. A 90-year-old woman is admitted to the hospital from a long-term care facility with a small bowel obstruction. She also has a history of dementia and is incoherent. Discuss how you would revise your assessment and evaluation techniques in managing her pain.
2. What criteria would you use to determine if the older adult client requires an adjustment in dose or dosing intervals, or a drug prescribed for pain management?

3. In caring for a 77-year-old man following a prostatectomy, you have an option of administering Demerol 50 mg IM, Morphine Sulfate 10 mg IV, Toredol 30 mg IM, and Talwin 50 mg IM. Which of these drugs would you choose to give and why? Is there any additional data that you would need to know before making your choice?

REFERENCES

Acute Pain Management Guideline Pain: *Acute pain management: operative or medical procedures and trauma.* In Clinical practice guideline, AHCPR Pub No 92-0032. Rockville, Md., 1992, Agency for Health Care Policy and Research, Public Health Service, US Department of Health and Human Services.

American Pain Society: *Principles of analgesic use in the treatment of acute pain and cancer pain,* Skokie, Ill., 1992, The Society.

Bayer AJ et al: Changing presentations of myocardial infarctions with increasing old age, *J Am Geriatr Soc* 34:263-266, 1986.

Bellville WJ, et al: Influence of age on pain relief from analgesics. a study of postoperative patients, *JAMA* 217:1835-1841, 1971.

Bender JS: Approach to the acute abdomen, *Medical Clinics of North America* 73:1413-1422, 1989.

Butt JH, Barthel JS, Moore RA: Clinical spectrum of the upper gastrointestinal effects of non steroidal antiinflammatory drugs: natural history, symptomatology and significance, *Am J Med* 84(2A):5-14, 1988.

Carbelli RA, Kellerman WC: Phantom limb pain: relief by application of TENS to contralateral extremity, *Arch Phys Med Rehab* 66:466-467, 1985.

Crook J, Rideout E, Browne G: The prevalence of pain complaints in a general population, *Pain* 18:299-314, 1984.

Davis MA: Epidemiology of osteoarthritis, *Clin Geriatr Med* 4:241-255, 1988.

Edgar L, Hamilton J: A survey examining nurses' knowledge of pain control, *J Pain Symptom Manage* 7:18-26, 1992.

Ferrell BA: Pain evaluation and management in the nursing home, *Ann Intern Med* (in press).

Ferrell BA: Pain management in elderly people, *J Am Geriatr Soc* 39:63-73, 1991.

Ferrell BA, Ferrell BR: Assessment of chronic pain in the elderly, *Geriatr Med Today* 8(5):123-134, 1989.

Ferrell BA, Ferrell BR, Osterweil D: Pain in the nursing home, *J Am Geriatr Soc* 38(4):9-14, 1990.

Ferrell BR, Ferrell BA: Pain in elderly persons. In McGuire DB, Yarbro CH, Ferrell BR: *Cancer pain management,* Boston, 1995, Jones and Bartlett.

Ferrell BA, Rubenstein LZ, editors: *Clinics in geriatric medicine: geriatric home care.* Philadelphia, 1991, WB Saunders.

Ferrell BR et al: Pain as a metaphor for illness. Part II: Family caregivers' management of pain, *Oncol Nurs Forum* 18(8):1315-1321, 1991a.

Ferrell BR et al: Family factors influencing cancer pain, *Post Grad Med J* 67(Suppl 2):S64-S69, 1991b.

Ferrell BR et al: Pain as a metaphor for illness. Part I: Impact of cancer pain on family caregivers, *Oncol Nurs Forum* 18(8):1303-1309, 1991c.

Ferrell BR, McCaffery M, Rhiner M: Pain and addiction: an urgent need for change in nursing education, *J Pain Sympt Manage* 7(2):117-124, 1992.

Ferrell BR, Rhiner M, Ferrell BA: Development and implementation of a pain education program, *Cancer* 72:3426-3432, 1993.

Ferrell BR, Schneider C: Experience and management of cancer home, *Cancer Nurs* 11(2):84-90, 1988.

Ferrell BR, Wisdom C, Wenzl C: Quality of life as an outcome variable in the management of cancer pain, *Cancer* 63(11):2321-2327, 1989.

Foley KM: The treatment of cancer pain, *N Engl J Med* 313:84-95, 1985.

Foley KM, Rogers A: The management of cancer pain. In Nutley NJ: *The rationale use of analgesics in the management of cancer pain,* vol 2, Hoffman-LaRoche, 1981.

Fordyce WE: Evaluating and managing chronic pain, *Geriatrics* 33:59-62, 1978.

Geokas MC, Haverbeck BJ: The aging gastrointestinal tract, *Am J Surgery* 117:881-889, 1969.

Graffam S: Pain content in the curriculum: a survey, *Nurse Educ* 15:20-23, 1990.

Harkins SW, Kwentus J, Price DD: Pain and the elderly, In Beneditti C, Chapman C, Moricca G, editors: *Advances in pain research and therapy,* vol 7, New York, 1984, Raven Press.

Hester NO, Barcus C: Assessment and management of pain in children, *Pediatr Nurs Update* 1:2-7, 1986.

Kaiko RF: Age and morphine analgesia in cancer patients with post-operative pain, *Clin Pharmacol Ther* 28:823-826, 1980.

Kaiko RF, et al: Narcotics in the elderly, *Med Clin North Am* 66(5):1079-1089, 1982.

Lavsky-Shulan M et al: Prevalence and functional correlates of low back pain in the elderly: the Iowa + 65 Rural Health Survey, *J Am Geriatr Soc* 33(1):23-28, 1985.

Marks RM, Sachar EJ: Undertreatment of medical inpatients with narcotic analgesics, *Ann Intern Med* 78:173-181, 1973.

McCaffery M, Beebe A: *Pain: clinical manual for nursing practice,* St. Louis, 1989, Mosby.

McCaffery M, Ferrell B: How would you respond to these patients in pain? *Nurs 91* 34-37, June 1991a.

McCaffery M, Ferrell BR: Patient age: Does it affect your pain-control decisions? *Nurs 91* 44-48, September 1991b.

McCaffery M, Ferrell BR: Opioid analgesics: Nurses' knowledge of doses and psychological dependence, *J Nurs Staff Devel* 8(2):77-84, 1992.

McCaffery M et al: Nurses' knowledge of opioid analgesic drugs and psychological dependence, *Cancer Nurs* 13(1):21-27, 1990.

McGuire D, Sheidler V: Pain. In Groenwald SL et al, editors: *Cancer nursing: principles and practice,* Boston, 1993, Jones and Bartlett.

Melzack R: The tragedy of needless pain. *Sci Am* 262(2):27-33, 1990.

Morgan J, Furst DE: Implications of drug therapy in the elderly, *Clin Rheumatol Dis* 12:227-244, 1986.

Morris JN et al: The effect of treatment setting and patient characteristics on terminal cancer patients: report from the national hospice study, *J Chron Dis* 39(1):27-37, 1987.

Office of Technology Assessment: *Technology and aging in America,* Pub No OTA-BA-264, Washington, DC, 1985, The Office.

Ouslander JG: Medical care in the nursing home, *JAMA* 262(18):2582-2590, 1989.

Paice JA: Unraveling the mystery of pain, *Oncol Nurs Forum* 18(5):843-849, 1991.

Parmelee PA, Katz IR, Lawton MP: The relation of pain to depression among institutionalized aged, *J Gerontol* 64(1):P15-P21, 1991.

Portenoy RK: Optimal pain control in elderly cancer patients, *Geratrics* 42:33-44, 1987.

Porter J, Jick H: Addiction reare in patients treated with narcotics, *New Engl J Med* 302:123, 1980.

Rhiner M, et al: A structured nondrug intervention program for cancer pain, *Cancer Prac* 1(2):137-143, 1993.

Roth SH: Merits and liabilities of NSAID therapy, *Clin Rheumat Dis* 15(3):479-498, 1989.

Roy R, Michael T: A survey of chronic pain in an elderly population, *Can Fam Phys* 32:513-516, 1988.

Spross J: Cancer pain and suffering: Clinical lessons from life, literature, and legend, *Oncol Nurs Forum* 12(4):23-31, 1985.

Thorsteinsson G: Chronic pain: Use of TENS in the elderly, *Geriatrics* 43(5):29-47, 1987.

Tucker MA et al: Age-associated change in pain threshold measured by neuronal electrical stimulation, *Age Aging* 18:241-24, 1989.

Twycross RG: Clinical experience with diamorphine in advanced malignant disease. *Int J Clin Pharmacol* 9:184-198, 1974.

Vallerand AH: The use of narcotic analgesics in chronic nonmalignant pain, *J Holistic Nurs Pract* 6(1):17-23, 1991.

Weissman DE, Dahl JL: Attitudes about cancer pain: a survey of Wisconsin's first-year medical students, *J Pain Sympt Manage* 5:345-349, 1990.

Wong D, Baker C: Pain in children, *Pediatr Nurs* 14(1):9, 1988.

Woodrow KM, et al: Pain tolerance: Differences according to age, sex, and race, *Psychosom Med* 34:548-556, 1972.

World Health Organization: Cancer pain relief and palliative care. Geneva, Switzerland, 1990, The Organization.

CHAPTER 14

Infection

LEARNING OBJECTIVES

On completion of this chapter, the reader will be able to:

1. Express a basic understanding of the primary lymphoid organs of the immune system.
2. Express a basic understanding of the secondary lymphoid organs of the immune system.
3. Express a basic understanding of the cellular and protein elements of the immune system.
4. Briefly describe the normal primary immune response.
5. Briefly describe the normal secondary immune response.
6. Describe alterations occurring in the immune system with aging.
7. Describe nutritional factors that influence immune status.
8. Describe psychosocial factors that influence immune status.
9. Describe the effect of exercise on immune status.
10. Describe the effect of lifestyle factors on immune status.
11. Describe the effect of medications and drugs on immune status.
12. Incorporate nutritional, psychosocial, and lifestyle factors in a nursing care plan.

The immune system, which provides the body's ability to defend itself against outside infections and altered cells such as neoplasms within the body, is vital to human survival. Yet with aging, this system exhibits a diminished ability to provide such protection (Chandra, 1992b). In a system with which there is such fundamental importance to maintain health, a clear understanding of the changes in the immune system that accompany aging is crucial.

The immune system has two primary functions: (1) to discriminate between that which is self and nonself and (2) to remove from the body that which is recognized as nonself. The system accomplishing this is composed of several organs, cells, and proteins (Flannery, 1992).

Furthermore, this system interacts with the neurologic and endocrine systems in a highly complex manner to modulate functioning of the human immune response. Therefore immunologic functioning can be mediated by psychologic and behavioral factors. There is an increasing awareness of the impact of mood, activity level, stress, and nutrition on the capacity of this system to provide optimum protection.

This chapter examines the normal physiologic functioning of the immune system and how the immune system normally functions to protect the individual from disease. The influences of other factors on immune status of older adults, such as psychosocial influences and nutrition, are also discussed. Changes that normally occur in the immune system with aging and the care of the older adult with altered immunologic functioning (e.g., infection, cancer, and autoimmunity) are presented.

NORMAL STRUCTURE AND FUNCTION OF THE IMMUNE SYSTEM

Anatomy

The skin provides a nonspecific first line of defense against infection by serving as a mechanical barrier to infectious organisms. Cilia and mucus such as those found in the respiratory tract also provide a nonspecific defense. Mucus, in addition to carrying antibodies, provides a barrier, whereas cilia constantly move, pushing contaminants out of the body.

Three types of organs comprise the immune system: (1) primary lymphoid organs, (2) secondary lymphoid organs, and (3) the immune cells which include lymphocytes and mononuclear phagocytes. Primary lymphoid organs include the thymus gland, bone marrow, gut-associated lymphoepithelial tissue (GALT), and Peyer's patches. Secondary lymphoid organs include peripheral lymph nodes, peripheral lymphoid tissue such as the tonsils and appendix, and the spleen. Immune cells include lymphocytes, mononuclear phagocytes, and killer cells (Flannery, 1992; Sahai, Louie, 1993).

Primary Lymphoid Organs

Primary lymphoid organs, the thymus gland, bone marrow, GALT, and Peyer's patches are responsible for the maturation and differentiation of T- and B-stem cells (lymphocytes), and functional cells. More specifically, the thymus gland is responsible for the differentiation and maturation of cells that develop into T-lymphocytes. It is in the thymus gland where T-lymphocytes, as they mature, develop specificity for foreign antigens and also learn recognition of self. This process occurs most markedly during fetal development and early infancy. T-lymphocytes are then carried by peripheral circulation to the secondary lymphoid organs for exposure to antigens (Flannery, 1992; Sahai, Louie, 1993). The thymus gland atrophies with age so that by age 60, no thymic hormones are detectable (Fretwell, 1993).

B-lymphocytes differentiate and mature in islands of hematopoietic cells located in the bone marrow, the fetal liver, Peyer's patches, and GALT cells. Like T-lymphocytes, B-lymphocytes develop specificity for antigens and are then transported to secondary lymphoid organs. Similarly, during maturation, B-lymphocytes learn recognition and tolerance of self. This self-recognition in both T- and B-cells is essential for survival. Without it, individuals would be attacked and destroyed by their own immune system (Flannery, 1992; Sahai, Louie, 1993).

Secondary Lymphoid Organs

The spleen filters and concentrates foreign protein for presentation to lymphocytes. Lymph nodes, found throughout the body and connected to lymphatic channels, also facilitate exposure of lymphocytes to antigens. Within these secondary lymphoid tissues, aggregates of immune cells reside, thus facilitating their early exposure to pathogens. Antigenic material is filtered by lymph nodes and exposed to macrophages, leading to phagocytosis of foreign cells or pathogens. On antigenic exposure, T-lymphocytes and B-lymphocytes are stimulated by antigens to proliferate and differentiate. Activated lymphocytes are then disseminated, yielding an immune response. This exposure stimulates B-lymphocytes to produce antibodies. This response is antigen-specific with each lymphocyte proliferating only in response to a specific antigen (Flannery, 1992; Hatfield, 1993a).

Cells

Three major types of cells contribute to immunity. These three categories are lymphocytes, phagocytic cells, and killer cells.

Lymphocytes Lymphocytes play a crucial role in immune responses. Within both T- and B-lymphocyte populations, certain cells are designated as memory cells. These memory cells develop after exposure to an antigen. They "remember" the specific antigen to which they are sensitized and become activated when that specific antigen is presented again (Flannery, 1992; Hatfield, 1993a).

T-lymphocytes T-cells further differentiate into effector cells or cytotoxic cells (killer T-cells) and regulator cells (helper T-cells and supressor T-cells). Helper T-cells (T_h) identify specific foreign antigens and then release a variety of proteins called cytokines that stimulate the production of antibodies by B-cells. Cytokines produced by T_h-cells include interleukins (ILs), B-cell growth factor (BCGF), B-cell differentiation factor (BCDF), and gamma interferon. Interleukin-2 (IL-2) and gamma interferon produced by T_h-cells stimulate killer (T_k) cells to differentiate and grow. T_k-cells destroy cells that have been invaded by viruses by binding to infected cells and lysing or dissolving the cell walls. The actual role of suppressor T-cells, the third kind of T-cell, is a source of some controversy. However, suppressor T-cells are thought to be activated by IL-2 to suppress growth and differentiation of both T_h-cells and B-cells. This suppression may be crucial in preventing overreaction of the immune system and subsequent destruction of normal cells. Various types of T-cells can be identified by receptors on the cell surfaces. T_h-cells carry a receptor designated as CD4. Similarly, T_k-cells and suppressor T-cells carry the CD8 receptor. These receptors are often used in research to identify specific cell types. T-cells are responsible for mediating and affecting cellular or cell-mediated immunity. Cell-mediated immunity is the immune response mounted by sensitized T-cells. Cell-mediated immunity includes delayed sensitivity responses such as graft rejection, response to malignant cells, and response to some bacteria and viruses (Flannery, 1992; Hatfield, 1993a).

B-lymphocytes B-cells are responsible for production of antibodies. On encountering an antigen, B-lymphocytes reproduce and differentiate into plasma cells. This differentiation and cell growth is mediated by cytokines secreted by T_h-cells. Plasma cells are responsible for antibody production with plasma cell descendants of a single B-cell–producing antibodies or immunoglobulins for the same specific antigen (Flannery, 1992; Hatfield, 1993a). This immune response involving antibodies is called the humoral immune response.

B- and T-lymphocytes are responsible for primary and secondary immune responses. The primary immune response is the response mounted by the immune system the first time it sees a specific antigen. Since neither B- nor T-cells have seen the antigen before, memory cells have not yet developed. Therefore B-cells begin to differentiate into memory B-cells and cells capable of producing antibodies. Circulating antibodies can usually be seen in circulation within 1 to 30 days following exposure to a new antigen. Antibodies combine with a group of proteins, collectively referred to as **complement,** to become activated. T-cells also differentiate into memory cells and helper cells during this time, although the immune response is mounted by B-cells (Flannery, 1992; Hatfield, 1993a).

The secondary immune response occurs on subsequent exposure to an antigen. In addition, if an antigen is closely related to one to which the immune system has been previously exposed, a secondary immune response may be elicited. For example, the original vaccine for smallpox was derived from people exposed to the cowpox virus. Since the virus responsible for smallpox is similar to the one responsible for cowpox, exposure to the cowpox antigen also provides immunity against smallpox. Because memory B- and T-cells are present, less time is required for cells to divide and to become active, giving a faster immune response. Individuals may retain the ability to mount a secondary immune response for years (Flannery, 1992; Hatfield, 1993a).

Phagocytic cells The immune system uses phagocytic cells as well as lymphocytes. Phagocytic cells destroy foreign pathogens in several ways. Sometimes these cells engulf or surround foreign material, breaking it down so that the antigen can be excreted and can be presented to T-lymphocytes to facilitate the immune response. Alternatively, phagocytic cells bind to the foreign material, either breaking down the material or making it more accessible to T- and B-cells for antibody production. Phagocytic cells include monocytes, macrophages and neutrophils. Monocytes develop in the bone marrow and then migrate into tissues, where they further develop into a variety of macrophages. It is believed that these macrophages live many months in the tissues. Macrophages produce interleukin-1 (IL-1), a protein that mediates the activation of T-cells. Macrophages are, in turn, stimulated by the IL-2, which is produced by activated T_h-cells. These monocyte-derived macrophages are the most important antigen-presenting cells in the body (Benjamin, Leskowitz, 1988; Hatfield, 1993a; Riott, Brostoff, Male, 1989).

Neutrophils, like monocytes, develop in the bone marrow and then enter the circulation. After circulating for several hours, neutrophils enter the tissues, where they survive for 1 to 2 days. Neutrophils are attracted by the bacterial products, damaged tissue, and activated components of complement. They engulf and digest the bacterium or antigen. This attraction is known as **chemotaxis.** Neutrophils are important in protecting the body against bacterial infection (Flannery, 1992; Hatfield, 1993a).

NK cells and LAK cells Natural killer cells (NK cells) and Lymphokine Activated Killer cells (LAK cells) are both significant in nonspecific, natural immunity. (Lymphokines are a subcategory of cytokines.) Nonspecific means that NK and LAK cells attack any foreign material rather than being specific for a particular foreign protein or antigen as are T- and B-cells. A subpopulation of lymphocytes, NK cells regulate natural cell-mediated cytotoxicity by recognizing and lysing specific tumor cells and virally infected cells, which are independent of immunoglobulin (Shar, Golub, 1985). Lacking antigen specificity, NK cells have the ability to lyse a variety of types of target cells. They therefore have an important role in the prevention and spread of tumors, comprising part of the body's antitumor surveillance system (Kiecolt-Glaser et al, 1985), and are key to the control of infectious diseases, particularly those of viral origin. LAK cells develop following exposure of peripheral blood lymphocytes in vitro to IL-2, a cytokine, for at least 48 hours. LAK cells have been noted for their broad specificity for freshly isolated tumor cells and their lack of cytotoxicity for normal tissue cells (Kiecolt-Glaser, Glaser, 1991).

Proteins

A variety of proteins are critical to immunity. These include complement, antibodies or immunoglobulins, cytokines, and interferons.

Complement

Antibodies combine with antigens to form antigen-antibody complex, which is then exposed to the first of a group of proteins called complement. These complement proteins, when combined with the antigen-antibody complex, go through a chain of reactions called the complement cascade. This cascade activates the complement, yielding one of three possible outcomes: (1) opsonization, (2) chemotaxis, and (3) lysis. In **opsonization,** the antigen is coated by antibodies, thus making the antigen more susceptible to phagocytosis. In chemotaxis, fragments split off from complement proteins and attract macrophages. Lysis of infected cells is accomplished by altering the permeability of the cell membrane, resulting in osmotic loss of cells' contents (Flannery, 1992; Schindler, 1990).

Antibodies/immunoglobulins The five major classes of antibodies produced by the B-cells include: IgG, IgA, IgM, IgD, and IgE. Different antibodies are found in different parts of the body and in differing concentration. Thus although IgG is found primarily in serum, IgA is more prevalent in body secretions. Hence each provides a slightly differing immune function. See Table 14-1 for normal adult serum immunoglobulin levels.

IgG is the prominent immunoglobulin in serum composing approximately 80% to 85% (12 mg/ml) of the immunoglobulins; it is found in plasma, interstitial fluid, cerebrospinal fluid, and closed cavities. Some IgG subclasses have relatively long half-lives (approximately 23 days), thus making IgG a suitable medium for passive immunization through transfer of the immunoglobulin. This passive immunity occurs naturally during fetal development and can also be accomplished by injection. IgG has the capacity for opsonization as well as the ability to activate the complement cascade, which is discussed later. Opsonization is a process in which antibodies and complement coat the surface of antigens, making them more vulnerable to phagocytosis (Flannery, 1992; Schindler, 1990).

IgA composes only about 15% of the immunoglobulins in plasma. Predominantly in body secretions such as tears, sweat, and mucous, this immunoglobulin plays a key role in protecting body surfaces and mucous membranes by preventing attachment and colonization of organisms. It is therefore important as a first line of defense. IgA provides protection against localized infections, as well as respiratory and gastrointestinal infections (Flannery, 1992; Schindler, 1990).

IgM is present primarily in intravascular spaces with serum levels of only 1 mg/ml. IgM is responsible for increased primary immune response and is also the first immunoglobulin produced in primary immune responses. This immunoglobulin is highly efficient in complement activation and in agglutination of antigens. IgM also carries the antibodies responsible for ABO blood type antibody reactions (Flannery, 1992; Schindler, 1990).

IgD is present only in trace levels in serum and is most often found on B-lymphocyte surfaces, where it is involved in the differentiation of these cells. *IgE,* also present in trace levels in serum, is primarily in interstitial fluid, exocrine secretions, and on skin. It is the only immunoglobulin to bind to basophils and skin mast cells.

IgE induces histamine release by inflammatory cells, and thus is responsible for hypersensitivity reactions ranging from the wheal following a mosquito bite to systemic anaphylaxis (Flannery, 1992; Schindler, 1990).

TABLE 14-1

Normal Adult Serum Immunoglobulin Values

Ig	Amount in serum	Percent of total
IgG	639 to 1,349 mg/100ml	75
IgA	70 to 312 mg/100ml	10-15
IgM	86 to 352 mg/100ml	7-10
IgD	0.5 to 3 mg/100ml	<1
IgE	0.01 to 0.04 mg/100ml	<1

From Corbett JV: *Laboratory tests and diagnostic procedures,* ed 3, Norwalk, Conn., 1992, Appleton & Lange.

Cytokines

Cytokines are a class of molecules that play a crucial role in signaling between cells of the immune system. Interleukins constitute a major group of cytokines with 7 different interleukins identified (IL-1-7). Interleukins are crucial in the activation of both T-cells and B-cells, promoting cell division. They also potentiate monocyte activation, and natural killer cell activation (Hatfield, 1993a; Schindler, 1990).

Interferons, a group of chemicals that are active in viral infections, are produced by viral-infected cells, as well as by certain types of activated T-cells and NK cells. Interferons induce viral resistance in uninfected cells, promote differentiation of B-cells, and stimulate additional NK cell activity (Hatfield, 1993a).

Normal Immune Response

The normal immune response is illustrated in Fig. 14-1. The immune response begins with exposure to an antigen. Macrophages present in the tissues bind with the antigen and process the antigen for presentation to T_h-cells. They then travel through lymphatic vessels to appropriate lymphoid tissue and present antigen to T- and B-cells until the cells specific for that antigen are found. The T_h-cells are activated and begin to grow and to divide. With activation, the T_h-cells produce interleukins,

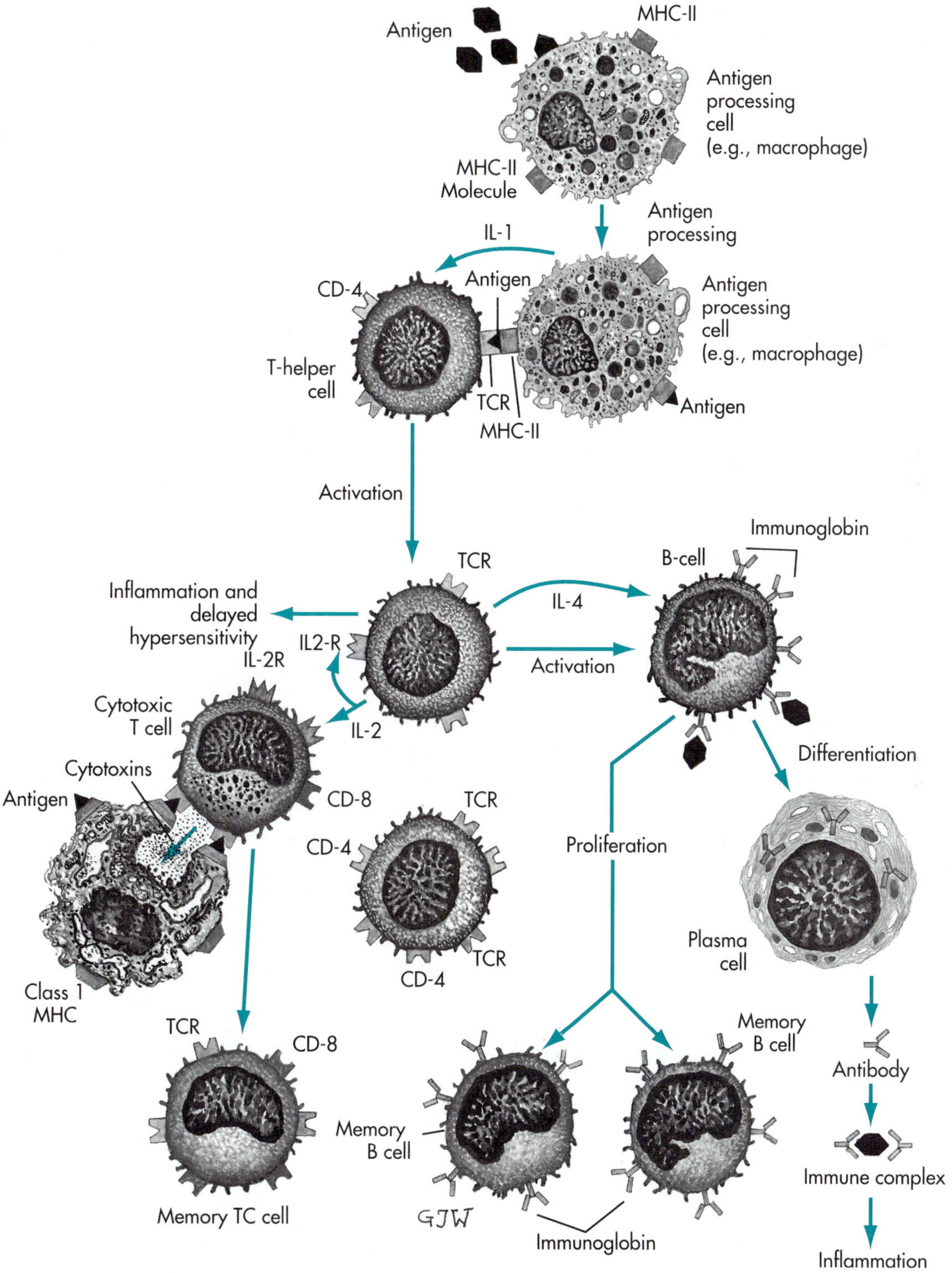

Fig. 14-1 Normal immune response. (From Mudge-Grout C: *Mosby's clinical nursing series: immunologic disorders,* St. Louis, 1993, Mosby.)

which stimulate T_h- and T_k-cell growth and activation. The cytokines also facilitate B-cell differentiation and maintain the inflammatory response by keeping macrophages at the site of infection. Activated T_k-cells attack and lyse the cell walls of viral-infected cells. Activated B-cells differentiate into plasma cells that produce antibodies. Antibodies then bind with the antigen to form antigen-antibody complex. The antigen-antibody complex can activate complement (Flannery, 1992; Hatfield, 1993a).

Simultaneously, an attack on the antigen is waged by NK cells. NK cells, on exposure to the antigen, attack and lyse cells infected with the antigen. NK cells are especially sensitive to tumor cells and cells infected by virus (Flannery, 1992; Hatfield, 1993a).

As the infection is resolved, suppressor T-cells function to dampen the immune response. Specifically, the suppressor cells limit cell growth and differentiation of both T_h-cells and B-cells. This suppression limits the immune response, thereby preventing attack on normal tissues (Flannery, 1992; Hatfield, 1993a).

Primary Immune Response

An individual's first exposure to a specific antigen elicits the primary or humoral immune response. This is a response primarily by B-cells. Antibodies produced by the B-cells against the antigen can be detected in the blood between 1 and 30 days after exposure. During the primary immune response, memory cells for both T- and B-cells develop (Flannery, 1992).

Secondary Immune Response

On subsequent exposures to the antigen, the secondary or cellular immune response is elicited. Because of the previous exposure, T- and B-memory cells, formed during the primary immune response, quickly mobilize to stimulate the antibody production, leading to rapid increases in antibody levels (Flannery, 1992).

Measures of Immune Status

Numerous diagnostic tests are used as indicators of immune function. One of the most common measures of immunologic status is a simple count of the total number of white blood cells (WBCs). Although a WBC count determines the presence of elevated numbers of WBCs and hence the likelihood that an infection may be present, additional information is generally required. Therefore for evaluating immune status, a WBC differential is generally indicated. In the differential, the subsets of WBCs are reported as percentages. A variety of WBCs are reported in the differential count, including neutrophils and lymphocytes. Sometimes there is a need to determine the number of B-cells versus the number of T-cells. In addition, the percentage of lymphocytes that are T_h-cells as opposed to suppressor T-cells must sometimes be determined. One situation where such phenotyping may be useful is in people seropositive for human immunodeficiency virus (HIV). Both adrenocorticosteroid and severe malnutrition also cause alterations in this ratio (Corbett, 1992).

Lymphocyte Counts

Lymphocyte counts are normally conducted as part of WBC count differentials but can also be conducted independently. Normal values (660 to 4,600/ml total WBC) (Ford, 1987) do not change with age. However, this value may have limited significance in older adults, since it reflects neither the subpopulations of lymphocytes nor the functional capacity of the lymphocytes. Thus the older adult may have a normal overall number of lymphocytes, whereas the individual may have a surplus of T_h-cells and a deficit of B-cells. Alternatively, the older adult may have normal numbers of all cell subpopulations; however, these cells do not differentiate and do not multiply when exposed to an antigen (Fox, 1984).

Lymphocyte Transformation Tests

Lymphocyte transformation tests include nitrogen assay, antigen assay, and mixed lymphocyte culture (MLC) assay. These tests provide indicators of the responsiveness of lymphocytes to antigens (Ford, 1987; Houldin et al., 1991).

TABLE 14-2

Normal Values for Immune Tests

Cells	Normal values
Total WBC	4,300 to 10,800/ml
Bands or stabs (young neutrophils)	3% to 5%
Neutrophils	51% to 67%
Eosinophils	1% to 4%
Basophils	0% to 1%
Lymphocytes	25% to 33%
Lymphocyte counts	0.66 to 4.60 (in thousands)/ml
Monocytes	2% to 6%
T-cells	60.1% to 88.1%
T_h(CD4)-cells	34% to 67%
T-cell count	644 to 2201 cells/ml
T_h cell count (CD4)	493 to 1191 cells/ml
Suppressor T-cell (CD8)	10% to 41.9%
Suppressor T-cell count (CD8)	182 to 785 cells/ml
CD4-CD8 ratio:	0.6:2.8
B-cells	3% to 20.8%
B-cell count	82-392 cells/μl
Mitogen assay stimulation index	>10
Antigen assay stimulation index	>3

Lymphocyte Marker Assays

Lymphocyte marker assays facilitate the determination of the relative amounts of various subsets of lymphocytes. In addition to differentiation between B- and T-lymphocytes, this method can differentiate between T_h-cells (CD4) and suppressor T-/cytotoxic cells (CD8). See Table 14-2 for normal values.

Measurement of Antibodies

Measurement of antibodies that are specific to latent herpes viruses such as Epstein-Barr virus (EBV), cytomegalovirus (CMV), and herpes simplex virus (HSV) also provides a measure of immunocompetence. Elevated levels of these antibodies indicate suppressed cellular immune control that has resulted in viral replication.

Skin Test

Skin tests provide a means of evaluating the cellular immune response. Antigens are injected intradermally or applied topically to elicit a delayed hypersensitivity reaction, which is the hallmark of the cell-mediated immune response. New antigens such as dinitrochlorobenzene (DNCB), to which the individual has not been previously exposed, can be used to evaluate the primary immune response. Recall antigens such as purified protein derivative (PPD), mumps, candida, or mixed respiratory vaccine, to which the individual is likely to have a previous exposure, can be used to evaluate the secondary immune response (Flannery, 1992; Houldin et al, 1991).

Immunoglobulin Assay

Immunoglobulin assay involves the determination of the presence and amount of various immunoglobulins in serum. Immunoelectrophoresis is a common method used to accomplish this. Levels of immunoglobulin can also be determined using radial immunodiffusion. See See Table 14-1, p. 324, for normal adult serum immunoglobulin levels.

AGE-RELATED CHANGES IN THE IMMUNE SYSTEM

It is believed that much of the illness seen in older adults may be the direct consequence of declining immunocompetence (Chandra, 1992b). Alterations in immune status can be held accountable for infections, cancer, and autoimmune processes, all of which can be life-threatening (Nossal, 1993; Paul, 1993; Steinman, 1993). Scientists have tried to determine whether the diminished immunocompetence noted with age is a result of decreased numbers of immune cells or decreased functioning of cells. However, since immunocompetence is affected by numerous other factors, it has been difficult to isolate changes that are related to age alone. Thymic atrophy, which occurs naturally with aging, is believed to account for the major age-related changes in the immune system (Fretwell, 1993). Both diminished cellular (T-cell–mediated) and humoral (B-cell–mediated) immunity have been associated with aging. See Box 14-1 for a summary of age-related changes in the immune system.

Changes in Cell-Mediated Immunity

Diminished cell-mediated immunity in older adults is generally associated with declining T-cell function (Adler, Nagel, 1981; Fretwell, 1993; Miller, 1990). Although the total number of T-cells remains within normal parameters, T-cells seem to have a decreased ability to produce the cytokines needed to facilitate growth and maturation of B-cells. Furthermore, T-cells exhibit a diminished ability to proliferate when exposed to an antigen (Miller, 1990).

BOX 14-1

Age-Related Changes in the Immune System

Lymphocytes
No change in total number of lymphocytes
No change in number of B-cells
No change or increase in T_h-cells
Decrease in suppressor T-cells
Decreased T-cell responsiveness

Polymorphonuclear leukocytes
Reduced migration ability

Antibody
Decrease of T-cell–dependent antibody responsivity
Decreased primary response to new antigens
Secondary response to antigens maintained
Increased globulins associated with secondary response and autoimmunity
Increased incidence of antibodies to self-antigens

Lymphoid tissue
Involution of thymus
Atrophy of thymic cortex
Atrophy, hypertrophy of some lymph nodes

Mechanical barriers
Changes in skin and mucous membranes result in reduced effectiveness of physical barriers.

Modified from Gueldner SH, Bramlett MH, Guillory J: Immune function and aging. Unpublished book chapter: accepted for publication in Dye C, editor: *Gerontological nursing,* 1992.

Changes in Humoral Immunity

The effect of aging on B-lymphocytes is less clear. With aging, B-cells exhibit a decreased production of immunoglobulin (Kiecolt-Glaser, Glaser, 1991). It is unclear whether this decrease should be attributed to altered B-cell functioning or whether the decrease is a result of decreased cytokine stimulation from T-cells. Like T-cells, B-cells retain their normal numbers with aging (Kiecolt-Glaser, Glaser, 1991). However, with the decreased Ig production, there is a concurrent decrease in hypersensitivity or allergic reactions. The primary immune response is decreased, whereas the secondary immune response is maintained. There are increases in immunoglobulins associated with autoimmunity, although these increases are not necessarily associated with actual autoimmune processes, since the incidence of autoimmune disease actually decreases after middle age (Miller, 1990).

Changes in NK Cell Activity

Although a decrease in NK cell activity has been documented by some researchers in older adult populations, most human research has failed to confirm an age-related loss of NK function (Miller, 1990).

Changes in Barrier Protection

Another area of age-associated change has significant influence on immune status. With aging, the skin, the body's first line of defense, becomes more fragile and prone to breakdown or abrasion. Simultaneously, the amount of oils and mucous secretions decreases, leaving the skin physically more fragile and decreasing the amount of available IgA to protect against infection (Magnussen, 1989; Miller, 1990).

FACTORS AFFECTING IMMUNOCOMPETENCE

Nutritional Aspects of Immunocompetence

Nutritional and dietary status is of critical importance to immune function. This is especially true in the older adult population. It has been noted that older adults are at high risk for nutritional deficits, with at least one third of individuals over age 65 having nutritional deficiencies (Chandra, 1985a; Meydani, 1993; Penn et al, 1991). (See Chapter 8 for more information on nutritional status of older adults.) Numerous factors may contribute to this tendency toward inadequate nutrition, including altered taste, social isolation, physical inability to prepare food, altered absorption, and poverty. Individuals with nutritional deficiency have been shown to have significant reductions in delayed cutaneous hypersensitivity. In addition, they have demonstrated lower numbers of T-cells and less responsive T-cells. Research studies have shown that by correcting nutritional deficits, the immune status of older individuals can be improved (Chandra, 1992b; Chandra, 1985b; Chandra et al, 1992; Meydani, 1993). These improvements include improved antibody response to influenza vaccines (Chandra, 1985b). The importance of such improvement cannot be underestimated, since influenza presents a substantive threat to older adults. Some nutrients have been especially noted for their effect on immunocompetence.

Protein-Energy (Caloric) Malnutrition

Significant deprivation of protein and energy (caloric) nutrients has been shown to result in major alterations in immune function (Chandra, 1992b; Lipschitz, 1986). Maturation of T-cells is impaired, and serum IgG and IgM levels are decreased. There is reduced microbicidal activity, perhaps because phagocytic cells are functioning abnormally (Chandra, 1985b; Zeman, 1990). These changes result in increased susceptibility to infectious disease. In a sample of hospitalized older adults with protein deprivation, it was confirmed that immune status can be improved by restoring these older adults to a state of nutritional balance, especially protein balance (Lipschitz, Mitchell, 1982).

Iron and Trace Element Deficiency

Although the effects of iron deficiency on immunocompetence and susceptibility to infection have not yet been fully determined, it has been established that lymphocyte and granulocyte function is compromised in the presence of iron deficiency (Chandra, 1985a; Sherman, 1992), and that there is a decrease in circulating T-cells. Three trace metals, zinc, selenium and copper, are thought to be associated with immune function (Chandra, 1992a; Chandra, 1985a; Lipschitz, 1986; Meydani, 1993; Miller, 1990).

A prolonged zinc deficiency leads to impaired cell-mediated immunity (Chandra, 1992a; Chandra, 1985a; Good, Lorenz, 1992; Lipschitz, 1986; Miller, 1990). Improved immune function following the administration of moderate amounts of zinc to older adults has been reported. These improvements include increases in circulating T-cells and appropriate delayed cutaneous hypersensitivity to a variety of antigens (Chandra, 1992a).

There is also evidence to suggest that other trace metals such as selenium and copper enhance humoral immunity (Chandra, 1992a; Sherman, 1992). Trace metals, especially zinc, are thought to be particularly important in maintaining resistance to malignancy. These trace metals are readily available in the diet, provided foods rich in these minerals are normally eaten. Selenium is present in fish and in grain, depending on the selenium content of the soil in which the grain was grown. Good dietary sources of copper include organ meats, nuts, seeds and legumes. The best sources of zinc are meats (especially beef), seafood (especially oysters), eggs, and poultry. Although present in legumes and whole-grain foods, these sources are less readily available for use by the body. Thus since meats are the better source, people with vegetarian diets may be at increased risk for zinc deficiency (Schlenker, 1993).

Vitamin Deficiencies

Numerous vitamins have been shown to have impact on immune function. These include vitamins A, B_6 (pyridoxine), B_{12}, C, D, and E. The impact of other vitamins on immune function is under review. Vitamins influencing cell-mediated immunity include vitamins A, C, D, E, and B_6 (pyridoxine) (Bendich, 1992; Chandra, 1992a; Penn et al, 1991). Vitamin C (ascorbic acid) supplements (500 mg/day) have been demonstrated to enhance lymphocyte responsiveness and to enhance skin reactivity to PPD (Kennes et al, 1983). Dietary supplements of vitamins A, C, and E have also been shown to enhance cellular immunity in institutionalized older adults (Chandra, 1992a; Penn et al, 1991).

Fat Intake

Both the amount and type of fat consumed may affect immune function. Unsaturated fat, especially in excessive amounts, may depress immune function and increase the likelihood of autoimmune disease (Maki, Newberne, 1992). Polyunsaturated fats have been associated with diminished T-cell function. However, saturated fats have been associated with increased responsiveness of T-cells. Furthermore, diets deficient in essential fatty acids may result in deficient antibody responses involving both IgM and IgG (Zeman, 1990).

Psychosocial Factors Affecting Immunocompetence

There is a growing awareness of the potential impact of psychosocial factors on immune status. These factors include chronic and acute stress, depression, bereavement, and social relationships. Recognition that such factors influence immune status is relatively recent, so the level of understanding of the nature of these relationships is constantly changing. Therefore the clinical relevance of these changes remains a source of investigation and controversy (Hillhouse, Adler, 1991; Houldin et al, 1991). However, since older adults endure so many psychosocial assaults, the potential impact on immune status must be considered. Older adults often have to deal with bereavement as they lose family and friends. They also often endure a shrinking sphere of social relationships and exhibit a high incidence of depression. Such factors may be particularly relevant for older individuals.

Stress

There is a growing awareness of the impact of stress on the immune system (Kiecolt-Glaser, Glaser, 1991). Some of this influence may be accounted for by stress hormones such as cortisol. Cortisol, which is secreted in increased amounts during times of stress, can suppress certain aspects of cellular immunity, including NK and T-cell functioning (Houldin et al, 1991; Johnson et al, 1982).

Chronic stress depresses the immune system, causing diminished numbers and activity of NK cells, inhibition of lymphocyte proliferation, and decreased production of interferon (Houldin et al, 1991; Kiecolt-Glaser, Glaser, 1991). Acute stress can also negatively affect the immune system. Individuals undergoing acute stress have been shown to demonstrate diminished NK cell activity and changes in the total number of T-cells. Furthermore, as in chronic stress, the responsiveness of T-cells seems to be diminished (Houldin et al, 1991; Kiecolt-Glaser, Glaser, 1991).

Depression

Depression has also been associated with decreased immune capacity. This is significant, since approximately 15% of community-dwelling older adults have symptoms of depression. Furthermore, suicide is more common in older adults than in any other age group (Cohen, 1990). Individuals with depression generally have fewer T_h-cells and fewer suppressor T-cells. Furthermore, their T-cells seem to be less responsive to antigen stimulation (Denney et al, 1988; Hillhouse, Adler, 1991; Kiecolt-Glaser, Glaser, 1991). There is some evidence that the negative impact of depression on the immune system increases with age (Schleifer, 1989). Thus older adults who are depressed may be at risk for greater immune deficiencies than younger depressed individuals.

Bereavement

It has long been noted that bereaved spouses are at higher risk for illness or death than the general population (Irwin et al, 1987; Kiecolt-Glaser, Glaser, 1991). Diminished immune function may account for this higher risk. Studies have consistently shown that the lymphocytes of bereaved spouses are less responsive, thus weakening both cellular and humoral immunity (Kiecolt-Glaser, Glaser, 1991). Admittedly, bereavement and depression may go hand in hand. Yet in the population of older adults where so many individuals are surviving the death of a spouse, the high impact this event may have on immune status must be noted (Houldin et al, 1991).

Social Relationships

Social relationships, either by their presence or absence, can have a substantive impact on immune status. Loneliness has been strongly associated with a diminished immune response (Kiecolt-Glaser et al, 1984). On the other hand, the presence of interpersonal relationships may have a positive impact on immune status (Kennedy, Kiecolt-Glaser, Glaser, 1988; Kiecolt-Glaser, Glaser, 1991). The quality of the relationships has been found to be an important factor in the effect on the immune response

(Houldin et al, 1991; Kiecolt-Glaser et al, 1987). Social relationships cannot be merely counted. It is the closeness of the relationship that contributes positively to immune status.

Lifestyle Factors

Activity Level

Activity level has also been shown to affect immune status (Gueldner et al, 1994; Targan, Britvan, Dorey, 1981). Physical exercise has been shown to induce increased cellular-medicated tumor cytotoxicity and NK cell activity in older adult women (Crist et al, 1989). Improvements in NK cell activity have been shown with as little as 5 minutes of moderate physical activity in healthy adults (Denney et al, 1988; Houldin et al, 1991; Kiecolt-Glaser et al, 1987).

Smoking

Smoking may also have a detrimental effect on the immune system. Research has linked smoking with changes in lymphocyte populations, decreased IgA secretion, and increased IgE secretion (Shirakawa, Morimoto, 1991; Kumar, Ankathil, Devi, 1993; Fischer, Konig, 1994; Mustonen, Hemminki, 1992). In addition, Langerhans' cells, cells in the mucosa that manufacture immunoglobulins, are decreased in number in people who smoke (*Smoking and immunity,* 1990). IgA is especially active in the mucous membranes and thus may be related to the individual's vulnerability to respiratory infections. IgE is the antibody associated with allergies. Research indicates that individuals who smoke and who are seropositive for HIV progress to acquired immunodeficiency syndrome (AIDS) more quickly than their nonsmoking counterparts. Specifically, the smokers developed *Pneumocystis carinii* pneumonia sooner than nonsmokers (Nieman et al, 1993). Thus smoking, in addition to its carcinogenic effects, may also suppress immune function.

Medications

Drug exposures can also have immune impact. A variety of medications are known for affecting the immune system. These include immunosuppressants and immunoenhancers. Many drugs given for therapeutic purposes have an immunosuppressant effect. Some of these drugs include corticosteroids, cyclosporine, and chemotherapeutics for cancer. Corticosteroids such as prednisone are given for a variety of reasons, including treatment of autoimmune processes such as rheumatoid arthritis (Hatfield, 1993b). However, this category of drugs suppresses lymphoid tissue, resulting in decreased numbers of circulating lymphocytes (Clark, Queener, Karb, 1993). Thus individuals receiving corticosteroids have a diminished inflammatory process and decreased immunity. People taking high doses or taking these drugs over prolonged periods probably have greater levels of immunosuppression than those individuals taking lower doses for shorter periods. Similarly, individuals taking cyclosporine, which is given after transplants to diminish the chance of organ rejection, or individuals taking certain anticancer drugs are at higher risk for infection (Hatfield, 1993b).

Other drugs with potential impact on the immune system are usually taken for less therapeutic reasons. These include alcohol and marijuana. Chronic alcohol use has long been associated with higher incidence of diseases such as tuberculosis and cancer. Alcohol is thought to inhibit cell-mediated immunity (Spinozzi et al, 1991). This effect is both direct in its suppression of immune function, and indirect through the alcohol-associated nutritional deficits that also compromise immune status. In addition to alcohol, marijuana is suspected of having a negative impact on the immune system. Marijuana is thought to inhibit the growth and activity of phagocytic cells (Tang et al, 1992). The amounts of marijuana needed to elicit this inhibition are still unknown. Thus individuals using either alcohol or marijuana must be evaluated for their immune status.

COMMON PROBLEMS AND CONDITIONS

The immune deficits seen so often in older adults make this population more vulnerable to both infection and cancer, thus contributing to increased rates of infections such as pneumonia and influenza, as well as a wide variety of malignancies. With aging, there is an increased likelihood that autoimmune antibodies be found in serum, suggesting an increased likelihood of autoimmune processes. However, there is controversy on whether such autoimmune processes are actually age-related (Miller, 1990).

Numerous infections are possible for any individual with diminished immune capacity, with some infections more common in older adults. Infections in older adults may be viral, bacterial, or fungal in origin. These include, but are not limited to, influenza, pneumonia, urinary tract infections (especially in women), and shingles (herpes zoster) (Levin et al, 1992; Miller, 1990). (See Chapter 22 for additional information about specific respiratory diseases.) With diminished IgA production, the barriers of skin and mucous membranes are less effective. Furthermore, as these barriers become more fragile with aging, entry of infectants is more easily achieved. Medical management of infections consists primarily of determining the source of the infection and prescribing the appropriate antibiotic or antiviral medication (see Medical Management box, p. 331). In addition, some vaccinations may be appropriate as preventive measures. Older adults are generally at higher risk for contracting influenza and pneumoccoccal pneumonia. Vaccines are available for

MEDICAL MANAGEMENT

Care of the Older Adult With Infection

Diagnostic tests
Culture and sensitivity
WBC with differential

Treatment
Antibiotic, antiviral, or antifungal agent
Nutrition supplement as needed
Medications for symptoms (Tylenol, expectorants)
Rest
Fluids
Careful monitoring for progression of illness

Preventive care
Vaccinations

Prognosis (varies with the following):
Severity of infection
Virulence of pathogens
Timing of intervention
Immune status of individual
General health of individual
Of influenza-related deaths, 80% to 90% occur in older adults.
Pneumonia is the most common cause of death in older adults.

both and are recommended for individuals over age 65. The influenza vaccine is administered annually to prevent viral influenza. The target virus for the vaccine varies yearly according to the types of viral infection expected. The pneumonia vaccine is administered once in a lifetime (see Chapter 22). Precautions recommended to individuals throughout life also take on added importance. For example, older adults need to maintain tetanus immunization every 10 years, since their immune response may be diminished. These older adults also become more vulnerable to tuberculosis, which has increased in prevalence in recent years. These older adults, who may have been exposed earlier in their life, may now be less able to defend themselves against the *tuberculosis bacillus.* The older adult is also more likely to contract the bacillus in environments where tuberculosis is prevalent.

Cancer

Neoplasms also occur with greater frequency in older adults. The weakened immune system evidently loses some of its ability to maintain surveillance for aberrant cell growth (Miller, 1990). Thus cells within the body that would normally be eliminated by the immune system are now able to grow uncontrolled. Again a wide variety of types of cancer are possible in older adults.

Insight • *Malignant neoplasms are the second most common cause of death among older adults. Detection is not easy, because presenting signs and symptoms may be mistakenly identified as part of the normal aging process. Physicians who have not received adequate education and training in geriatric medicine may unwittingly ignore or postpone work-up of an older adult's signs and symptoms of cancer. The nurse must advocate for older adults in such situations to promote timely diagnosis and potentially more effective treatments. The nurse is also in a key position to develop programs to educate older adult clients about early detection of cancer.*

Common types of cancer in older adults include lung cancer, breast cancer and prostate cancer. However, the potential for numerous other forms of cancer should not be overlooked. The presence of the cancer itself reveals the presence of an immune deficiency. Cancer cells are normally detected by the immune system and eliminated after being recognized as nonnormal cells. It is only when the immune system fails to carry out this function that cancer occurs. However, the cancer itself and the cancer treatment can induce additional immune deficits. For example, cancer is often accompanied by a decrease in appetite, thus increasing the possibility of malnutrition. Furthermore, anticancer drugs often deplete immune cells, causing further debilitation of the immune system. Since many of these drugs have their greatest impact on rapidly dividing cells, the rapidly dividing immune system cells are attacked concurrently with the cancer cells. The prognosis for cancer is highly variable depending on the time of diagnosis, the general health of the client, and the type of cancer. However, even with the worst prognosis, unexplained recoveries have occurred (Burrell, 1992) (see Medical Management box, p. 332, at top). For specific information on management of older adults with cancer, see Chapter 15.

Autoimmunity

There is an increase in autoimmune antibodies with aging as well as a decrease in suppressor T-cells, whereas there is no firm evidence that these findings result in an increase in autoimmune diseases (Miller, 1990). Therefore, although older adults may have autoimmune diseases such as rheumatoid arthritis, these cannot necessarily be considered age-associated. Yet older adults with autoimmune diseases are more likely to take immuno-

MEDICAL MANAGEMENT

Immune Status in Individuals With Cancer

Diagnostic tests
WBC with differential
Tests of immune status as indicated
Culture of suspect infections

Treatment
Chemotherapy, radiation, and/or surgery
Antibiotic, antiviral, or antifungal agents for secondary infection
Nutrition supplement as needed
Medications for symptoms as needed

Preventive care
Screening for early cancer detection
Screening for secondary infection

Prognosis (varies with the following):
Staging of cancer at diagnosis
Type of cancer
General health of individual

MEDICAL MANAGEMENT

Care of the Older Adult With Autoimmune Diseases

Diagnostic tests and procedures
Tests for antinuclear antibodies (ANA)
WBC with differential
Tests of immune status as indicated

Treatment
Antibiotic, antiviral, or antifungal
Antiinflammatory medications
Immunosuppressants
Medications for symptoms

Preventive care
Avoid unnecessary exposure to pathogens

Prognosis (varies with the following):
Severity of autoimmune process
Timing of intervention
Immune status of individual
General health of individual

suppressant drugs as treatment for their disease process, and they still risk the immune deficits that accompany aging. Therefore these older adults carry higher risks for infection than other older adults without autoimmune disease (Flannery, 1992) (see Medical Management box above).

NURSING MANAGEMENT

ASSESSMENT

Obviously, with such a variety of possible infections, the clinical assessment varies widely. However, there are some crucial aspects to assessing older adults for the presence of infection. Older adults with possible immune deficits may not exhibit classic symptoms of infection. For example, diminished inflammatory responses may lead to false negatives for skin tests used in the diagnosis of disease. Thus an individual who previously exhibited a positive response to PPD tests for tuberculosis may respond with no response or with a very reduced response (Magnussen, 1989). Similarly, redness, swelling, or inflammation may be reduced with infections. These reduced responses are even more likely to occur in people with diseases or drug treatments that further suppress the immune system, such as people with cancer or taking immunosuppressants.

Another classic example of a reduced response to infection is the absence of fever. With an infection, local or systemic fever is provoked by the immune response. In healthy adults, an elevated temperature provides an indicator of the presence of infection. However, individuals such as older adults who have immune deficits may experience only a limited temperature increase or no increase at all (Magnussen, 1989). Symptoms of pain may also be reduced or absent. Thus before detection, infection in these older adults can progress to life-threatening stages.

Because of this reduced immune response, small symptoms such as a low-grade fever must be taken seriously. Close observation is needed to observe for subtle symptoms. Changes in behavior of the client, such as increased malaise or fatigue, especially combined with other symptoms, may indicate the onset of infection. Fever and inflammation may be reduced, whereas the WBC count can still reflect an increased value (Magnussen, 1989). Yet if immunosuppression is present from drug treatment for diseases such as cancer or AIDS, elevations in WBC counts may not be seen, even with severe infection.

Insight • *Older adults with possible immune deficits may exhibit diminished inflammatory responses, including only minimal redness, swelling, inflammation or fever, even in the presence of severe infection. Even slight symptoms should be taken seriously.*

In addition to observed data, subjective and historic data are valuable when evaluating the older adult with infection. A history of previous episodes of infection, including the timing, nature, and severity of the infection are important. Infections in older adults can often be recurrent. Although the individual can normally develop immunity following the first infection, older adults may be unable to develop an adequate immune response and are therefore more likely to be susceptible to succumbing to the same infection again. Information regarding exposure to others with infections may also be helpful. Older adults are more susceptible to infection, especially if they are living in environments conducive to the spread of pathogens. Such environments include nursing homes, hospitals, and crowded environments, where hygiene standards are difficult to maintain. Immunization records also provide important information that needs to be kept on file.

It is also important to determine other disease processes for which the client may currently be receiving treatment. People with cancer may be experiencing assaults on their immune systems from the disease and from cancer treatments. Older adults with autoimmune diseases may be receiving antiinflammatory immunosuppressant drugs. Individuals with HIV infection are obviously experiencing an extreme assault on their immune system. All of these make the older adult more prone to a variety of infections. In such situations, the most likely infections are often those resulting from the individual's own normal flora, such as candida. Respiratory infections are also very likely (Magnussen, 1989).

A thorough record of medications is necessary to detect the potential for drug-related immunosuppression. This record should include both prescription and over-the-counter (OTC) drugs. Clients receiving drugs with immunosuppressant qualities are obviously more prone to contract infections. In addition, information on the use of alcohol, tobacco, or other drugs, as well as exposure to toxic substances should be obtained (Magnussen, 1989).

Information about the client's lifestyle can provide invaluable information in developing a plan of care. This should include a thorough nutritional history, as well as an indication of activity and exercise. An understanding of the individual's social support system should be gained and indicators of life stressors should be elicited. A classic life stressor is bereavement, especially of a spouse. However, loss of friends and other family members should not be overlooked. Even the loss of one's home or relocation can yield a sense of bereavement (Magnussen, 1989) (Box 14-2).

BOX 14-2

Assessment of the Individual at High Risk for Infection

Subjective

History

- Previous infections
- Predisposing illnesses
- Medications
- Vaccinations
- Living environment
- Lifestyle (e.g., smoking, activity level, chemical exposures)
- Social support system

Objective

Assess for signs and symptoms of infection

- Fever—high- or low-grade
- Inflammation—pronounced or slight
- Pain—slight or severe
- Malaise, fatigue

Alterations in body fluids:

- Turbidity, odor, amount

Laboratory work

- WBC count
- Differential cell count

✣ DIAGNOSIS

Several nursing diagnoses may be applicable to the older client either with an infection or at high risk for developing an infection. The individual's risk factors, determined during assessment, indicate some potential nursing diagnoses. For example, many older adults are either inadequately or inappropriately nourished. Thus a diagnosis of "altered nutrition: less than body requirements," is likely. People with cancer may be malnourished because of lack of appetite or side effects resulting from medications. Poor nutrition may also be attributed to a self-care deficit in preparing and eating food. Older adults sometimes have difficulty preparing their own meals. These difficulties may be related to a variety of problems such as visual deficits, arthritis, or depression. Regardless of cause, if these self-care deficits result in poor nutrition, the older adults are then at higher risk for infection. The diagnosis, high risk for infection, is applicable to those at high risk and those with existing infections. The presence of an infection indicates that the immune system is already challenged. This increases the likelihood of a secondary infection. For instance, it is not unusual for an individual with viral influenza to later develop a secondary infection of pneumoccocal pneumonia.

A diagnosis of knowledge deficit is also a possibility. Knowledge deficits may refer to: (1) nutrition, (2) vaccinations, or (3) protection against infection from oneself or from others. Clients may be unaware of nutritional needs or the relationship between nutritional and

BOX 14-3

NANDA Nursing Diagnoses Appropriate for Older Adults With Autoimmune Diseases

Infection: high risk for
Altered nutrition: less than body requirements
Self-care deficit: feeding
Knowledge deficit: immunizations, nutrition, protection from infection
Health-seeking behavior deficit: exercise
Social isolation

immune status. With such knowledge, older adults may be more likely to consume appropriate nutrition. Similarly, older adults may be unaware of available vaccinations or the benefit such vaccinations may hold for them. Older individuals need information on ways to protect themselves from contracting infections to reduce risk.

Individuals at risk for infection who do not exercise either in a formal program or incidentally, through activities of daily living (ADLs) may be diagnosed with health-seeking behavior deficit, since exercise has been shown to enhance immune status as well as other health parameters. Finally, social isolation may be a relevant diagnosis associated with the individual at risk for infection, since social support has also been associated with immune status (Box 14-3).

✣ PLANNING

In planning care for the older client, goals of care must be mutually set with the client and the health care team. Goals must be congruent with realistic expectations and with the client's desired outcome. For the individual at increased risk for infection, goals include: (1) avoiding primary or secondary infection and (2) maintaining or improving immune status. A careful assessment of the client's knowledge in areas related to infection prevention, maintenance of immune status, and health practices determines the goals for client teaching. In setting nutritional goals, a consultation with a registered dietitian may be appropriate. The client's dietary preferences, as well as financial ability to afford food if not in an institutional setting, must be considered. An outcome might be that the client consumes a well-balanced, high-caloric diet. A client with cancer may have even more extreme nutritional needs. An outcome for this individual might be that the client stabilize body weight, then gradually increase at a rate of one pound every 3 weeks. Another outcome may be that the client perform self-care activities with minimal energy expenditure and risk of injury. For the client with an activity deficit, an appropriate goal might be to participate in 15 minutes of moderate exercise three times per week. The exact delineation of the target goal for exercise should be established in consultation with the primary care provider and possibly physical therapy.

✣ INTERVENTION

Nursing management of the older adult with alterations in immunity focuses on the prevention of infections. Interventions addressing this goal are targeted at (1) preventing exposure to infections, and (2) enhancing the immune system to enable the client to better resist infections. Totally preventing exposure to pathogens is impossible, especially since one source of pathogens is the body's own natural flora. However, exposure can be minimized for the individual with diminished immune capacity. During times of epidemic, such as influenza season, crowds of people can be avoided. In an institutional or home setting, visitors can be screened for respiratory infections. If contact by an infected visitor is unavoidable, despite the chance for spread of infection, the visitor can be given a mask to wear to minimize potential contamination of the client. Any catheters, intravenous (IV) fluids, or similar therapeutic devices should be carefully assessed for pathogen growth. Finally, hygiene standards should be rigorously maintained, especially for clients experiencing treatment-induced immune suppression, as seen with some anticancer drugs. In addition to normal bathing, careful attention should be paid to oral care and perineal care. Both client and caregiver should be alert for changes in color, consistency, and odor of body fluids to detect the onset of infections.

Nutrition Interventions

Other measures can be taken to strengthen the immune system to better enable the client to resist infection. As previously mentioned, optimum nutrition status is important. To achieve this status, the client must receive adequate energy and protein through nutrition, as well as sufficient vitamins, iron, and trace minerals, with special emphasis on zinc, selenium, and copper. Although all of the nutritional needs can be met for the healthy older adult through normal dietary intake, many older adults have dietary deficiencies. For clients with cancer, the nutritional deficits can be quite extreme. Following assessment, efforts should be made to resolve detected deficiencies. In institutional settings dietary supplements and frequent meals can be supplied. Food can be prepared specifically to suit the tastes and needs of the client. For older adults in the community, social services such as Meals on Wheels, assistance with food preparation, or attendance at nutrition sites is helpful. Liquid food supplements or OTC vitamins are also possible alternatives. However, these may be beyond the financial resources of some clients.

The inability to feed oneself is another barrier to proper nutrition. The individual feeding the client, either in the home or institutional setting, must ensure that the client receives a balanced nutritional diet. Family members or nonprofessional care providers may need special instruction on how best to accomplish this with the client.

Psychosocial Interventions

Based on the relationships between psychosocial factors and immunity, a variety of modalities are available that may enhance immunocompetence. These include (1) relaxation and visualization, (2) exercise, and (3) social support.

Relaxation training, either alone or in conjunction with imagery, has been associated with increased levels of salivary IgA (Green, Green, Santoro, 1988). Since IgA is an important aspect of the body's defenses against gastrointestinal and respiratory infections, both common in older adults, this could have significant impact for older adults' health. In addition, visualization and guided imagery, used in combination with relaxation has been shown to increase NK cell activity (Kiecolt-Glaser, Glaser, 1991; Nguyen, 1991).

As previously discussed, exercise even in moderate amounts may have an immunoenhancing impact. Therefore implementation of an exercise program may be beneficial. Exercise programs should be created to fit the abilities of the individual. For those with physical debilities, exercise programs can be tailored to meet the specific needs and interests of the client. Possible exercises include walking, dancing or dance-like movement, water exercises, or swimming. It is important to develop exercise programs that are moderately difficult rather than strenuous for the older individual.

Since social support has been associated with immune status, facilitating the maintenance or development of a system of social support may have immune benefit. This may be accomplished by mobilizing a group of existing friends and relatives, or introducing the client to new groups (Hillhouse, Adler, 1991). One possibility might be to establish a network of people who check on each other, either by phone or letters, or in person. Another possibility is to get people with similar interests together for activity or discussion groups. For example, one group might get together to discuss politics, another to discuss literature, or a third to do quilting or woodcarving. Many of these groups may already be active in senior centers or churches.

As the relationship between immune status and numerous variables are explored, new modalities are developed. Modalities currently being explored include biofeedback, therapeutic touch, and hypnosis (Hillhouse, Adler, 1991; Quinn, Strelkauskas, 1993) (see Research box at right).

✣ EVALUATION

Monitoring success of interventions is based on the client's response in meeting their goals or outcomes. One standard for evaluation is whether or not the client

RESEARCH

Quinn JF, Strelkauskas AJ: Psychoimmunological effects of therapeutic touch on practitioners and recently bereaved recipients-a pilot study, *Adv Nurs Sci* 15(4):13-26, 1993.

Sample, setting

Subjects included four recently bereaved clients and two therapeutic touch (TT) practitioners.

Methodology

Measures

State-trait anxiety inventory
Affect balance scale
Effectiveness of therapeutic touch (visual analog scale)
Lymphocyte subset composition
Mixed lymphocyte reactivity (MLC)
Cell-mediated toxicity (CML)
Lymphocyte stimulation
NK cell assays

Protocol

Subjects were tested before first treatment, after first TT treatment, and again before and after last treatment of the 2-week course of treatment. The duration of the course of TT treatments for each subject was determined by the therapists.

For therapists, questionnaires and repeat blood samples were drawn after all their treatments for each day were completed.

Findings

Significant decreases in anxiety of the recipients were demonstrated. Significant increases in positive affect and significant decreases in negative affect were seen in all TT recipients. Decreases in the number of suppressor T-cells were found in all clients.

One practitioner exhibited low suppressor T-cell counts at onset of study which remained low. The remaining practitioner showed decreases similar to the subjects.

Implications

Because of the pilot nature of this study, and the small sample size, it is premature to draw conclusions about the impact of TT on immune status.

However, the results of this study do confirm the findings of other studies demonstrating the relaxing effect of TT. Therefore TT may be an alternative means to facilitate relaxation and to decrease the impact of stress.

CARE PLAN

PNEUMOCOCCAL PNEUMONIA

Clinical situation Mrs. T is a 78-year-old woman, admitted to the hospital for treatment of pneumococcal pneumonia, which she developed while she had influenza. She lives alone in a low-rent housing development in a large city, having moved there 2 years ago after the death of her husband. Without his income, she was unable to afford the rent on her previous home. Her nearest family member, a niece, lives 75 miles away and rarely visits. Her former neighbors, who live across town, are unable to visit because of the distance and because of their own debilities. Mrs. T is 20% underweight for her height and is anemic. Her WBC count is high. Her blood values are listed below:

Laboratory values

RBC	3.7/ml
Hct	34%
Hgb	10.8
WBC	18,200/ml
Serum albumin	2.6 gm/100ml

Nursing diagnoses	Outcomes	Interventions
High risk for infection related to compromised immune status.	Mrs. T will not experience additional infections as evidenced by (1) WBC count returns to normal limits, (2) afebrile state, and (3) other vital signs within normal limits. Client will verbalize an understanding of knowledge of infection prevention strategies.	Screen all visitors with infection who may come into direct contact with client. Provide family and visitors with information on transmission of infection. Teach Mrs. T that she is at high risk for additional infections because of her depressed immune status, and should limit her exposure to additional pathogens. Observe for slight increases in temperature every 4 hours or more often as needed. Be aware that Mrs. T may develop subtle or undetected signs and symptoms of infection and that slight changes in temperature may be highly significant. Observe for increased respiratory difficulty. Auscultate lungs every shift. Have client report sore throat.
Altered nutrition: less than body requirements related to low income, transportation difficulties, and social isolation.	Mrs. T will have adequate nutrition as demonstrated by (1) weight gain of one half pound per week, (2) increased hemoglobin, and (3) increased serum protein. Consumes a well-balanced, sufficient caloric diet, as evidenced by (1) calorie counts show intake of at least 1,800 calories per day; and (2) consumes food from all food groups, including protein sources, breads, fruits and vegetables, and dairy products.	Monitor dietary intake using calorie counts. Teach what constitutes a well-balanced diet, high in protein. Assure adequate intake of vitamin and trace minerals through diet or through supplements. Encourage using foods that include vitamins and minerals, as well as trace minerals such as zinc and magnesium. Mrs. T may need vitamin and mineral supplements in addition to the high protein diet. Acquire Meals on Wheels on discharge, or facilitate attendance at a nutrition site to provide better nutrition after discharge. Refer to churches or other organizations to include Mrs. T in their social gatherings to reestablish a social support system.

CARE PLAN

PNEUMOCOCCAL PNEUMONIA—cont'd

Nursing diagnoses	Outcomes	Interventions
		Assess Mrs. T's level of stress to determine if an easily accessible, low-exertion relaxation program is indicated. A relaxation program may provide an easily accessible, low-exertion intervention with immune benefit. Plan a program of graduated exercise designed to fit Mrs. T's tolerance.
Social isolation related to loss of friends and limited contact with family	Mrs. T will acquire social contacts desirable to her as evidenced by (1) spending time each week with others, (2) voicing satisfaction with social contacts.	Contact social services or local senior citizen center to identify center activities and transportation. Contact area organizations or churches for information about activities. Provide information to Mrs. T and develop a plan of action with her.
Knowledge deficit (influenza and pneumococcal vaccine) related to new experience.	Mrs. T will identify the advantages of the influenza and pneumococcal vaccine.	Provide information for Mrs. T regarding the influenza vaccine: that (1) influenza can be a serious, life-threatening condition in older people; (2) yearly immunization (in early fall) is important to protect herself from getting influenza; (3) signs and symptoms of influenza—weakness, cough, headache, sudden increase in temperature, aches, chills, and occasional vomiting—can occur; (4) pneumonia is a common complication of influenza. Refer to primary care provider for specific advice regarding recuperation time before taking vaccine. Provide information for Mrs. T on pneumococcal vaccine—primarily that she should be immunized once in her lifetime. Inform her that the vaccine should not be administered soon after having pneumonia. Refer to care provider for the specific timing of administration following her illness.

contracts an infection either through contact from others or from their own flora. Another goal is to improve or at least maintain immune status. This second goal may be more difficult to reach for some clients, since the understanding of the immune system and the concomitant changes that occur with aging are incomplete. Furthermore, many individuals are enduring severe assaults on their immune systems. People with cancer receive anticancer drugs that can literally destroy the immune response. In people with AIDS, the immune system is directly targeted by viral attack. Interventions such as diet, exercise, and psychosocial enhancement are rarely sufficient in overcoming such odds, although unexplained recoveries have been known to occur. For the majority of situations, it may be unreasonable to expect a return to normal status for the immunocompromised individual. However, any improvement in immune status or even maintenance may allow the older client to live a better life than one without such interventions (see nursing Care Plans, pp. 336-338).

CARE PLAN

EFFECTS OF CHEMOTHERAPY

Clinical situation Ms. A is a 69-year-old woman who is receiving chemotherapy following a modified radical mastectomy for breast cancer. Although previously well-nourished, with chemotherapy her appetite has declined and stomatitis has made eating painful. In addition, the chemotherapy has decreased her WBC count to 2,000. Ms. A lives with her husband in their home. She receives her chemotherapy on an outpatient basis but is visited daily by a home health nurse to maintain her Hickman catheter.

Nursing diagnoses	Outcomes	Interventions
High risk for infection related to suppressed immune system.	Client will not develop an infection, as evidenced by (1) no temperature elevation; (2) no elevation in WBC count; (3) no sore throat or mouth; (4) no redness or irritation around wounds, IV fluids, or catheters.	Teach Ms. A to minimize exposure to pathogens, and to screen visitors with contagious infections. Explain the need to maintain careful hygiene (e.g., daily shower, proper oral, foot, and perineal care). Use sterile technique when working with Hickman catheter. Monitor mouth and throat for signs of infection such as white patches or redness; teach Ms. A to report same to nurse. Auscultate lungs at each visit. Teach her to monitor body fluid for alterations in color, odor, or consistency. Encourage fluid intake of at least 2,000 cc per day unless otherwise indicated.
Altered nutrition: less than body requirements related to inability to eat secondary to side effects of chemotherapy.	Client will have adequate intake of proteins, vitamins, and minerals, as evidenced by (1) calorie counts of at least 2,000 calories per day, and (2) maintenance of body weight.	Teach client to eat small, frequent meals, rich in protein, vitamins, and minerals. Teach client food sources high in calories, protein, vitamins and minerals. Use food supplements to increase intake if needed. Encourage small, frequent meals to increase intake, if necessary. Teach importance of eating nutrient dense foods, that is, those with high nutritional content in small volumes. Acquire oral anesthetic for stomatitis. Teach client how to prepare bland foods of moderate temperature.

Summary

This chapter explored the normal physiologic functioning of the immune system, including how the system normally functions to protect the individual from disease. The influences of other factors on the immune status of the older adult, such as psychosocial influences and nutrition, were also discussed. Normally occurring, age-related changes in the immune system and nursing care of older adults with infection, cancer, and autoimmune disorders were presented.

A key role of the nurse in caring for older adults in all settings is to recognize the potential for infection in this population and to develop plans of care to prevent as well as at the very least, to promote early detection of infection. Because of the increased risk of morbidity and mortality associated with infection in this age group, immunizations and interventions specific to various body systems should be implemented for those identified as susceptible to infection.

HOME CARE TIPS

1. Assess nutritional and dietary status to ensure proper immune function in the homebound older adult.
2. Instruct the older adult and caregiver about the need to receive a balanced nutritional diet and the role of vitamin supplements in promoting proper immune function.
3. An altered emotional state may lead to a decreased immune function in the homebound older adult.
4. Vaccinations are imperative for the homebound older adult (e.g., annual influenza vaccine).
5. Assess and report any signs of impaired immunity (e.g., fever, changes in WBCs).
6. Bedbound older adults and immunocompromised older adults are at high risk for infections. Instruct older adult and caregiver(s) ways to protect the older adult against infection from oneself and from others.
7. Tailor an exercise program that can be done by the homebound or bedbound older adult to enhance their immune system and to prevent infection.

Key Points

- With aging, the immune response diminishes.
- The diminished immune response reduces the normal responses to infection, such as fever, making infection in older adults more difficult to detect.
- Nutrition, especially protein energy, vitamins, and trace minerals, have a substantial impact on immune status.
- Activity has a substantive impact on immune status. Even moderate amounts of daily exercise can enhance immune status.
- Mood can influence immune status. Depression is associated with a decreased immune response.
- Stress, both chronic and acute, is associated with decreased immune responses.
- Interventions dealing with infection and decreased immune response must address nutrition, exercise, mood state, and stress, as well as physical protection.

Critical Thinking Exercises

1. Compare and contrast the immune response of an older adult with an infection with that of an adult in his or her mid-40s. How is the immune response of the older adult similar to that of an infant or young child?
2. Your neighbor is a 68-year-old woman whose husband died last year. Since his death, she has become sedentary and withdrawn. Concerned, you decide to stop by to see her. She explains that she has been ill off and on for the past few weeks and does not understand why she keeps getting sick. She says she is losing faith in her doctor. Recognizing that her depression and sedentary lifestyle can alter her immune response, how might you intervene to help her?

REFERENCES

Adler WH, Nagel JE: Studies of immune function in a human population. In Segre D, Smith L, editors: *Immunological aspects of aging,* New York, 1981, Dekker.

Bendich A: Vitamins and immunity, *J Nutr* 122:601-603, 1992.

Benjamin E, Leskowitz S: *Immunology: a short course,* New York, 1988, Alan R. Liss.

Burrell N: Nursing management of patients with cancer. In Burrell L, editor: *Adult nursing,* Norwalk, Conn., 1992, Appleton & Lange.

Chandra RK: Effect of vitamin and trace-element supplementation on immune responses and infection in elderly subjects, *Lancet* 340:1124-1127, 1992a.

Chandra RK: Protein-energy malnutrition and immunological responses, *J Nutr* 122:597-600, 1992b.

Chandra RK: *Nutrition, immunity and illness in the elderly,* New York, 1985a, Pergamon Press.

Chandra RK: Nutritional regulation of immunocompetence and risk of disease in the elderly. In WHO Scientific Group: *Nutrition of the elderly,* Washington, DC, 1985b, Pan American Health Organization.

Chandra RK, et al: Nutrition and immunocompetence of the elderly. Effect of short-term supplementation on cell-mediated immunity and lymphocyte subsets, *Nutrition Res* 2:223-232, 1982.

Clark JB, Queener SF, Karb VB, editor: *Pharmacologic basis of nursing practice,* ed 4, St. Louis, 1993, Mosby.

Cohen GD: Psychopathology and mental health in the mature and elderly adult. In Birren JE, Schaie KW, editors: *Handbook of the psychology of aging,* ed 3, New York, 1990, Academic Press.

Corbett JV: *Laboratory tests and diagnostic procedures,* ed 3, Norwalk, Conn., 1992, Appleton & Lange.

Crist DM et al: Physical exercise increases natural cellular-mediated tumor cytotoxicity in elderly women, *Gerontology* 35u:66-71, 1989.

Denney DR et al: Lymphocyte subclasses and depression, *J Abnorm Psychol* 97:499-502, 1988.

Edwards AK et al: Changes in the populations of lymphoid cells in human peripheral blood following physical exercise, *Clin Exp Immunol* 58:420-427, 1984.

Fischer A, Konig W: Modulation of in-vitro immunoglobulin-synthesis of human peripheral-blood mononuclear-cells by nicotine and cotinine, *Clin Investigat* 72(3):225-232, 1994.

Flannery JC: Immunologic disorders. In Burrell L, editor: *Adult nursing,* Norwalk, Conn., 1992, Appleton & Lange.

Ford RD, editor: *Diagnostic tests handbook,* Springhouse, Penn., 1987, Springhouse.

Fox RA: The effect of aging on the immune response. In Fox RA, editor: *Immunology and infection in the elderly,* New York, 1984, Churchill Livingstone.

Fretwell MD: Age changes in structure and function. In Carnevali DL, Patrick M, editor: *Nursing management for the elderly,* ed 3, Philadelphia, 1993, JB Lippincott.

Good RA, Lorenz E: Nutrition and cellular immunity, *J Immunopharmacol* 14(3):361-366, 1992.

Green ML, Green RG, Santoro W: Daily relaxation modifies serum and salivary immunoglobulins and psychophysiologic symptom severity, *Biofeedback Self Reg* 13(3):187-199, 1988.

Gueldner SH et al: *The relationship between exercise and immune function in a sample of healthy older females.* Paper presented at the 7th International Research Congress or Sigma Theta Tau International in Sydney, Australia, July 11-13, 1994.

Hatfield S: Basic function of the immune system. In Clark JB, Queener SF, Karb VB, editor: *Pharmacologic basis of nursing practice,* ed 4, St. Louis, 1993a, Mosby.

Hatfield S: Immunomodulators. In Clark JB, Queener SF, Karb VB, editor: *Pharmacologic basis of nursing practice,* ed 4, St. Louis, 1993b, Mosby.

Hillhouse J, Adler C: Stress, health and immunity: a review of the literature and implications for the nursing profession, *Holistic Nurs Pract* 5(4):22-31, 1991.

Houldin AD et al: Psychoneuroimmunology: a review of literature, *Holistic Nurs Pract* 5(4):10-21, 1991.

Irwin M et al: Impaired natural killer cell activity during bereavement, *Brain Behavior Immun* 1:98-104, 1987.

Johnson HM et al: Neuroendocrine hormone regulation of in vitro antibody production, *Proc Nat Acad Sci (USA)* 79:4171-4174, 1982.

Kennedy S, Kiecolt-Glaser JK, Glaser R: Immunological consequences of acute and chronic stressors: mediating role of interpersonal relationships, *Brit J Med Psychol* 61:77-85, 1988.

Kennes B et al: Effect of vitamin C supplements on cell-mediated immunity in old people, *Gerontol* 29:305-311, 1983.

Kiecolt-Glaser J, Glaser R: Stress and immune function in humans. In Ader R, Felten D, Cohen N, editors: *Psychoneuroimmunol* New York, 1991, Academic Press.

Kiecolt-Glaser JK et al: Marital quality, marital disruption, and immune function, *Psychosom Med* 49:13-35, 1987.

Kiecolt-Glaser J et al: Psychosocial enhancement of immunocompetence in a geriatric population, *Health Psychol* 4(1):25-41, 1985.

Kiecolt-Glaser JK et al: Psychosocial modifiers of immunocompetence in medical students, *Psychom Med* 46:7-14, 1984.

Kumar KBS, Ankathil R, Devi KS: Chromosomal aberrations induced by methyl parathion in human peripheral lymphocytes of alcoholics and smokers, *Humso Exp Toxicol* 12(4):285-288, 1993.

Levin MJ et al: Immune response of elderly individuals to live attenuated varicella vaccine, *J Infect Dis* 166:253-259, 1992.

Lipschitz DA: The role of nutrition in age-related changes in hematopoiesis and immunocompetence. In Young EA, editor: *Nutrition, aging, and health,* New York, 1986, Alan R Liss.

Lipschitz DA, Mitchell CO: The correctability of the nutritional, immune and hematopoietic manifestations of protein calorie malnutrition in the elderly, *J Am Coll Nutr* 1:17-25, 1982.

Magnussen MH: Body protection in the aged and the nursing process. In Yurick AG et al, editors: *The aged person and the nursing process,* Norwalk, Conn., 1989, Appleton & Lange.

Maki PA, Newberne PM: Dietary lipids and immune function, *J Nutr* 122:610-614, 1992.

Meydani SM: Vitamin/mineral supplementation, the aging immune response, and risk of infection, *Nutr Rev* 51(4):106-115, 1993.

Miller RA: Aging and the immune response. In Schneider EL, Rowe JW, editors: *Handbook of the biology of aging,* ed 3, New York, 1990, Academic Press.

Mustonen R, Hemminki K: 7 methylguanine levels in DNA of smokers' and non-smokers' total white blood cells granulocytes and lymphocytes, *Carcinogenesis* 13(11):1951-1955, 1992.

Nguyen TV: Mind, brain, and immunity: a critical review, *Holistic Nurs Pract* 5(4):1-9, 1991.

Nieman RB et al: The effect of cigarette-smoking on the development of AIDS in HIV-1 seropositive individuals, *AIDS* 7(5):705-710, 1993.

Nossal GJ: Life, death and the immune system, *Sci Am* 269(3):52-62, 1993.

Paul WE: Infectious diseases and the immune system, *Sci Am* 269(3):90-105, 1993.

Penn ND et al: The effect of dietary supplementation of vitamins A, C and E on cell-mediated immune function in elderly long-stay patients: a randomized controlled trial, *Age Aging* 20(3):169-174, 1991.

Quinn JF, Strelkauskas AJ: Psychoimmunological effects of therapeutic touch on practitioners and recently bereaved recipients—a pilot study, *Adv Nurs Sci* 15(4):13-26, 1993.

Riott IM, Brostoff J, Male D: *Immunology,* New York, 1989, Gower Medical Publishing.

Sahai J, Louie SG: Overview of the immune and hematopoietic systems, *Am J Hosp Pharm* 50(*Suppl* 3):s4-s9, 1993.

Schindler LW: Understanding the immune system, *NIH Pub* 90:529, March 1990.

Schleifer S, et al: Major depressive disorder and immunity: role of age, sex, severity and hospitalization, *Arch Gen Psychiatr* 46:81-87, 1989.

Schlenker ED: *Nutrition in aging,* ed 2, St. Louis, 1993, Mosby.

Shar H, Golub SH: Signals for activation of natural killer and natural killer-like activity, *Nat Immune Cell Growth Reg* 4:113-119, 1985.

Sherman AR: Zinc, copper and iron nutrition and immunity, *J Nutr* 122:604-609, 1992.

Shirakawa T, Morimoto K: Life-style effect on total IGE—lifestyles have a cumulative impact on controlling total IGE levels, *Allergy* 46(8):561-569, 1991.

Smoking and immunity (editorial), *Lancet* 335:8705, 1561, 1990.

Spinozzi F et al: T-lymphocyte activation pathways in alcoholic liver disease, *Immunol* 72:140-146, 1991.

Steinman L: Autoimmune disease, *Sci Am* 269(3):106-115, 1993.

Tang J et al: Marijuana and immunity: tetrahydrocannabinol-mediated inhibition of growth and phagocytic activity of the murine macrophage cell line, P388D1, *J Immunopharmacol* 14(2):253-262, 1992.

Targan S, Britvan L, Dorey F: Activation of human NKCC by moderate exercise: increased frequency of NK cells and enhanced capability of effector-target lytic interactions, *Clin Exp Immunol* 45:352-360, 1981.

Zeman FJ: *Clinical nutrition and dietetics,* Lexington, Mass., 1990, Collamore Press.

Chapter 15

Cancer

LEARNING OBJECTIVES

On completion of this chapter, the reader will be able to:

1. Describe the pathophysiology of malignant tumors, focusing on the concepts of tumor growth and metastasis.
2. Describe the nurse's role in cancer prevention and health education.
3. Explain the rationale for the categories of cancer therapy and discuss nursing interventions for clients receiving those therapies.
4. Compare and contrast intrinsic and extrinsic factors related to carcinogenesis.
5. Describe the tumor, node, metastasis (TNM) system for cancer staging and grading.
6. Discuss the cause, incidence, and prevention of cancer.
7. Describe the management of the client in pain.
8. Discuss common psychosocial and spiritual problems encountered by the client with cancer.

Cancer is a group of diseases characterized by uncontrolled growth and spread of abnormal cells. It is one of the most feared diseases of this century. The term cancer was associated with death until this past decade. Today, with modern technology and advances in research, society has gained some hope for the future after a diagnosis of cancer.

Cancer is an opportunistic group of diseases. It does not discriminate against race, creed, ethnic origin, or age. Cancer can occur at any age but is predominantly a disease of middle and old age (Baird, McCorkle, Grant, 1991). It is the second leading cause of death after heart disease, and 50% of all documented cancers occur in the 12% of the population over age 65 (Cox, 1987). The risk of developing cancer doubles every 5 years after age 25, establishing age as the single, most important risk factor in the development of cancer. Thus as the numbers of older adults grow, so does the demand on health care sources (Office of Technology Assessment, 1987) (Tables 15-1 and 15-2).

TABLE 15-1

Mortality for the Five Leading Cancer Sites for Males by Age Group, United States, 1991

Age (in years) 35 to 54	55 to 74	75 and older
All cancer 27,529	All cancer 142,089	All cancer 98,067
Lung 8,741	Lung 55,890	Lung 26,896
Colon and rectum 2,393	Colon and rectum 13,888	Prostate 20,909
Non-Hodgkin's lymphomas 1,726	Prostate 12,306	Colon and rectum 11,686
Brain and Central nervous system (CNS) 1,577	Pancreas 6,730	Pancreas 4,299
Pancreas 1,298	Non-Hodgkin's lymphomas 4,600	Bladder 3,698

From Wingo PA, Tong T, Bolden S: Cancer statistics, 1995, *CA: Cancer J Clinicians* 45 (1), Jan/Feb, 1995.

TABLE 15-2

Mortality for the Five Leading Cancer Sites for Females by Age Group, United States, 1991

Age (in years) 35 to 54	55 to 74	75 and older
All cancer 29,302	All cancer 111,419	All cancer 97,388
Breast 9,188	Lung 30,154	Colon and rectum 15,727
Lung 5,372	Breast 19,900	Lung 16,400
Uterus 1,779	Colon and rectum 11,117	Breast 13,834
Colon and rectum 1,999	Ovary 6,720	Pancreas 6,637
Ovary 1,799	Pancreas 5,669	Ovary 4,601

From Wingo PA, Tong T, Bolden S: Cancer statistics, 1995, *CA: Cancer J Clinicians* 45 (1), Jan/Feb, 1995.

The incidence for the majority of cancers increases continually after the first decade of life; the older the person becomes, the more likely he or she is to develop cancer. After 85 to 90 years of age, both incidence and mortality from all forms of cancer decline for both white men and women (Paige, Asire, 1985).

Incidence

The incidence for all sites of cancer combined rises steadily throughout life until it peaks at 2,308 per 100,000 in people age 85 years and older (American Cancer Society, 1994). Data from the National Cancer Institute's Surveillance, Epidemiology, and End Results (SEER) Program show that although the absolute cancer incidence rates rise progressively through the middle-age years and level off in the later years, the age-specific rates rise progressively throughout the age range (Belcher, 1992; Boring, Squires, Tong, 1994).

The incidence of some cancers (Table 15-3) is increasing in older adults. The mortality rates also continue to rise, especially in the socioeconomically disadvantaged.

CANCER PREVENTION AND CONTROL

Risk Factors

Risk factors may be classified as both intrinsic and extrinsic. Intrinsic risk factors include age, the function of the immune system, and genetic predisposition. Extrinsic factors include environmental issues such as radiation, chemicals, pollution, and personal lifestyle.

Intrinsic Factors

Age The advanced age of the person is probably the single, most significant risk factor related to the development of cancer (Baird, McCorkle, Grant, 1991). Of all cancers, 50% occur in individuals older than age 65 (Baranovsky, Myers, 1986). The higher incidence in this age group may reflect lifelong accumulation of DNA alterations or cell mutation, which result in cell transformation and neoplasia. The body may no longer be able to repair these mutations, as it did in earlier years. The effectiveness of the immune system is also reduced in older adults (see Chapter 14). The thymus, which is the site of maturation of T-lymphocytes (cells), begins a process of involution at the time of sexual maturity and by age 50, only 10% of the thymus remains (McCance, Huether, 1990). The result is a loss of thymic capacity of differentiated T-cells, a subsequent increase in immature T-cells in the circulation, and a reduced response of the immune system to altered cells (McCance, Huether, 1990; Schneider, Hogan, 1993).

Manifestation of a malignancy in the older adult may

TABLE 15-3

Percentage of Population (Probability) Developing Invasive Cancers at Certain Ages (in years)

		Birth to 39	40 to 59	60 to 79	Ever (birth to death)
All sites	Male	1.68 (1 in 60)	7.51 (1 in 13)	32.27 (1 in 3)	42.52 (1 in 2)
	Female	1.91 (1 in 52)	9.29 (1 in 11)	23.06 (1 in 4)	38.88 (1 in 3)
Breast	Female	0.45 (1 in 222)	3.78 (1 in 26)	6.78 (1 in 15)	12.20 (1 in 8)
Colon & rectum	Male	0.06 (1 in 1,667)	0.91 (1 in 110)	4.45 (1 in 22)	6.12 (1 in 16)
	Female	0.05 (1 in 2,000)	0.73 (1 in 137)	3.34 (1 in 30)	5.96 (1 in 17)
Prostate	Male	Less than 1 in 10,000	0.78 (1 in 128)	10.71 (1 in 9)	13.05 (1 in 8)
Lung	Male	0.04 (1 in 2,500)	1.60 (1 in 63)	6.69 (1 in 15)	8.43 (1 in 12)
	Female	0.03 (1 in 3,333)	1.07 (1 in 93)	3.49 (1 in 29)	5.02 (1 in 20)

NOTE: This chart shows the risks of being diagnosed with the most common cancers over certain age intervals. These risks are calculated for people free of the specified cancer at the beginning of the age interval. Risk estimates do not assume all people live to the end of the age interval or to any fixed age. Risk estimates are presented to give an approximate measure of the burden of cancer to society. Measures are based on population level rates and do not take into account individual behaviors and risk factors. For example, lung cancer is rare among nonsmokers or people not heavily exposed to environmental tobacco smoke, so the risk for a nonsmoking man getting lung cancer in his lifetime is much lower than 8.4%, and it is much higher for a smoker. It is clear that the risk of developing cancer increases with age. For prostate cancer, the risk before age 60 is very low, but between age 60 and 80, one in nine men will be diagnosed with prostate cancer.

From Applied Research Branch, National Cancer Institute.

be overlooked and attributed to changes that coincide with normal aging (Baranovsky, Myers, 1986). It is essential that the older adult be aware of and report to health care providers symptoms associated with the seven warning signs. Nurses should take into consideration the need to teach older adults so that they may be empowered to make adequate self assessments. The nurse can point out common problems confronting older adults, especially those areas closely associated with malignancy.

Immune surveillance The functions of the immune system are (1) to protect the body against injury from foreign substances (antigens), (2) to distinguish self from nonself and destroy nonself substances, (3) to establish homeostasis, and (4) to provide surveillance or prevention of growth and development of aberrant cells that might otherwise develop into neoplasms (Alkire, Groenwald, 1990; McCance, Huether, 1990; Schneider, Hogan, 1993).

Nonself cells include cells that are made in the body but are altered (e.g., cancer cells). The portion of the immune system that is most responsible for protecting against cancer is cell-mediated immunity. Of the cells that are involved in cell-mediated immunity, natural killer (NK) cells are most important for immune surveillance. When an NK cell recognizes a nonself cell, it binds to the membrane of that cell and releases a series of lysosomal enzymes into the nonself cell. The cell immediately destructs after enzymes inside the target cell digest critical components of the cell. NK cells also release a substance called natural killer cytotoxic factor that acts directly on the target cell (Alkire, Groenwald, 1990; McCance, Huether, 1990). See Chapter 14 for a detailed discussion of age-related immune system changes and their effect on the development of neoplasms.

Genetic predisposition The development of cancer depends on more than the presence of photo-oncogenes. **Photo-oncogenes** are precursors of **oncogenes** that are passed on from generation to generation. When cancer develops, the photo-oncogene has been altered or damaged to allow expression of the oncogene. Other genetic predispositions for specific cancers have also been identified. These include inherited conditions associated with malignancies, and familial clustering and predispositions for certain cancers (Alkire, Groenwald, 1990; Schneider, Hogan, 1993).

Several cancers, such as breast cancer, are thought to occur because a defective gene is inherited from one parent. In this instance, the person who receives the dominant defective gene is initiated at the time of conception. Malignancy develops at a later time when the gene is exposed to a promoting agent (McCance, Huether, 1990; Schneider, Hogan, 1993).

Colon cancer is associated with familial polyps. Both colon and breast cancers are seen more often in older adults.

Race Race or ethnicity and culture should not be considered in their entirety in the development of cancer. Other factors such as lifestyle issues, access to care, genetic structure, and socioeconomic status must be taken into consideration (see Cultural Awareness box, p. 344). Data from the American Cancer Society (1995) revealed that African Americans have an overall higher incidence of cancer and a higher mortality than whites.

CULTURAL AWARENESS

Cultural Considerations in Cancer

Patterns of cancer distribution among U.S. population groups vary according to racial and ethnic background. These patterns challenge nurses and other health care providers to provide explanations for the large differences in cancer incidence, mortality, and survival among the federally defined minority groups when compared with the white population.

African Americans have the highest overall rates of cancer incidence and cancer mortality of any U.S. population group. The overall 5-year relative survival for cancer for African Americans is 12% below whites. Of the 25 primary cancer sites for which survival data are available, African Americans have lower survival rates for all but three cancer sites (ovary, brain, and multiple myeloma).

Differences in survival status seem to be substantially based on socioeconomic status and the overrepresentation of an ethnic group in the lower categories of socioeconomic status. Socioeconomic status affects access to health services, nutritional status, immune status and function, educational level, employment status, cancer prevention attitudes, awarenesses and practices, and acceptance of cancer as a real and potential threat. In turn, all of these affect survival and ultimately mortality.

HIGHER INCIDENCE RATES ACCORDING TO LOCATION OF CANCER

Blacks	Hispanics	Asian/Pacific Islander (varies by group)
Esophagus	Stomach	Stomach (Japanese Americans)
Pancreas	Prostate	Cervix and nasopharynx (Chinese Americans)
Stomach	Esophagus	Breast and lung (Hawaiians)
Cervix	Pancreas	
Prostate	Uterus	
Larynx		

Native Americans (highly variable among the greater than 500 tribes)
Lung (Oklahoma Indians)
Gall bladder (Southwest Indians)
Liver (Alaskan Natives)

NOTE: Overall cancer incidence is lower for Native-American groups compared with the general population because of younger average age, biocultural variations, and environmental factors.

From United States Department of Health and Human Services, Indian Health Service: *Trends in Indian Health—1992,* Washington, DC, 1992, US Government Printing Office; US Department of Health and Human Services: *Healthy people 2000,* Washington, DC, 1992, US Government Printing Office.

Extrinsic Factors

It is estimated that 80% of all cancers in the United States may be the result of environmental or extrinsic factors. Many of the cancers caused by extrinsic factors are lifestyle-related. Therefore environmental factors can and should be controlled in an effort to reduce the development and risk of cancer. Environmental carcinogens are physical, chemical, or biologic agents. A major problem with associating carcinogenic agents with the actual diagnosis is a delay (many times for years) between exposure to the carcinogen and the diagnosis of cancer (Kupchell, 1991; Schneider, Hogan, 1993).

Chemical There are more than 20 identified organic and inorganic industrial chemicals and other products known to be carcinogenic. Many chemical exposures are unintentional and are occupational-related. Occupational hazards are a major health concern in the older adult population, since the actual exposure could have been years earlier. An example is soot, a carcinogenic agent that causes scrotal cancer in chimney sweeps (Schneider, Hogan, 1993).

Tobacco use is responsible for more than one in six deaths in the United States (American Cancer Society, 1994; Baird, McCorkle, Grant, 1991). Cancer of the lip and tongue are associated with the use of dipping snuff, chewing tobacco and smoking a pipe, all common practices among the current cohort of older Americans. Cancer of the lung, pharynx, larynx, esophagus, bladder, kidneys, mouth, uterus, cervix, and pancreas also are associated with smoking cigarettes. Tobacco use is quite common among older adults in some regions of the country. Based on data from the American Cancer Society's Cancer Prevention Study II, it is estimated that smoking is related to more than 400,000 U.S. deaths each year (Baird, McCorkle, Grant, 1991; Boring, Squires, Tong, 1994).

Radiation Sources of ionizing radiation are capable of causing carcinogenesis. Ingestion of contaminated food and water is an easy route for radiation to enter the body. Other sources of radiation include the sun, diagnostic and therapeutic x-rays, and radioisotopes (Strohl, 1988; Alkire, Groenwald, 1990). Cancers associated with radiation are breast, thyroid, and leukemia.

Diet The relationship between dietary practices and carcinogenesis is highly considered in cancer prevention. The American Cancer Society (1995) indicates that people may reduce their cancer risk by maintaining desirable weight, decreasing intake of fat content, and eating in moderation. Foods such as vegetables, fruits, and fiber also are encouraged. Consumption of vegetables and fruits are associated with decreased cancer of the lungs, prostate, bladder, esophagus, and stomach. A high-fiber intake has been shown to decrease colon cancer. Decreased consumption of alcohol, salt-cured, smoked, and nitrite-cured foods is also recommended (American Cancer Society, 1995).

Lifestyle choices over which an older adult has some control, such as the previously named dietary practices, play a role in exacerbating or reducing the risk of developing cancer. The nurse should remember that among community-dwelling older adults, people who live alone and have incomes below the poverty level are at greatest risk for poor nutritional status. Thus the challenge is to improve their nutritional health, thereby reducing their risk and improving their quality of life.

OVERVIEW OF CANCER

Characteristics of Cancer Cells

Cancer cells have abnormally rapid cell division and unusually large nuclei. They do not respect tissue borders, and they become uninhibited in their movement. Normal tissue on the other hand is composed of mature cells of uniform size and shape. Within each cell is a nucleus that contains the chromosomes, a specific number for every species, and within each chromosome is deoxyribonucleic acid (DNA). DNA is a large molecule, the chemical composition of which controls the characteristics of ribonucleic acid (RNA), which is found both in the nucleoli and cytoplasm of the cell itself; DNA also regulates cell growth and function (McCance, Huether, 1990; Schneider, Hogan, 1993). In the development of various organs and parts of the body, cells undergo differentiation in size, appearance, and arrangement; thus the histologist or the pathologist can examine a piece of prepared tissue through a microscope and can identify the portion of the body from which it has come. Cancerous cells lose their ability to differentiate (Alkire, Groenwald, 1990; Baird, McCorkle, Grant, 1991; McCance, Huether, 1990).

Classification of Tumors

Benign Neoplasms

Alteration in cell growth may produce tumors, or neoplasms, that are benign or malignant (Table 15-4). Benign neoplasms involve cellular proliferation of adult or mature cells growing slowly in an orderly manner in a capsule (Schneider, Hogan, 1993). These tumors do not invade surrounding tissue but may cause harm through pressure on vital structures. Benign tumors remain localized, do not metastasize (spread), and do not recur after they are completely removed.

TABLE 15-4

Characteristics of Benign and Malignant Neoplasms

Benign	Malignant
Encapsulated	Nonencapsulated
Noninvasive	Invasive
Highly differentiated	Poorly differentiated
Mitosis is rare	Mitosis is common
Slow growth	Rapid growth
Little anaplasia	Anaplasia varies
No metastases	Metastases

Malignant Neoplasms

The production of malignant cells is poorly understood. It is believed that the basic process involves a disturbance in the regulatory functions of DNA. Any minute alteration or DNA mutation produces a distortion in biologic information resulting in abnormal cells. The malignant neoplasm occurs as a result of a defect in the nucleus of the cell. Regardless of cause, the malignant cell loses its specialized function and may take on new characteristics (McCance, Huether, 1990; Schneider, Hogan, 1993).

A characteristic of malignant cells is loss of differentiation. This loss of differentiation is called **anaplasia,** and its extent is a determining factor in the degree of malignancy of the tumor.

Anaplasia is characterized by alterations in intracellular macromolecular synthesis and intercellular relationships and associations. Two types of anaplasia have been identified. In positional or organizational anaplasia, the usual distinct histologic patterns in tissues are altered. In cytologic anaplasia, there is increased or altered nucleic acid synthesis in growing tissues. Anaplasia is one of the most reliable indicators of malignancy, is seen only in malignancies, and does not appear in benign tumors (Baird, McCorkle, Grant, 1991; Kart, Metress, Metress, 1992; Schneider, Hogan, 1993).

The nuclei of malignant cells vary in size, many of which contain unusually large amounts of **chromatin**. The proportion of cells actively proliferating in malignant tumors is generally greater than that of normal cells. Malignant neoplasms are not encapsulated; therefore they invade adjacent tissue, including lymph and blood vessels, through which they metastasize to distant parts of the body to set up new tumors. Malignant neoplasms may recur after extensive treatment (Kupchell, 1991; McCance, Huether, 1990; Schneider, Hogan, 1993).

Cancer Metastasis

Metastasis refers to the spread of cancer from the primary tumor to distant parts of the body. Cancer cells metastasize through several different routes (Box 15-1). Metastasis of the cancer is the major cause of cancer deaths. Metastasis may occur by several different routes; direct extension, penetration, release of tumor into body cavity and lymph system, implantation, and local seeding.

Direct extension into neighboring tissue produces the typical local effects of ulcerating, bulky, hemorrhagic masses or indurative, fibrotic lesions with tissue fixation, distortion of the structure, and pitting of the skin as seen in some breast cancers. A tumor may penetrate the wall of the ovaries and its cells implant on the surface of the peritoneal cavity. Cancer cells can also be implanted by the surgeon into the operative area, causing metastatic lesions (mechanical transplantation) (Kupchell, 1991; Schneider, Hogan, 1993).

Metastatic spread occurs when cancer cells invade vascular or lymphatic channels and travel to distant parts of the body where implantation occurs. Lymph node metastasis is present in approximately half of all fatal cancers. In lymph vessels, cells may detach and may become emboli, which lodge in the regional lymph nodes that receive their drainage from the tumor site. Spread continues to the next group of nodes and into the other organs. Cells also may gain access to the bloodstream by way of the thoracic duct (Kupchell, 1991; Olson, Frank-Stromberg, 1991).

Vascular embolism of malignant cells may occur through the veins or arteries to various parts of the body, depending on the vascular drainage of the organs involved. The liver is a common metastatic site for cancers originating in the gastrointestinal tract, pancreas, and spleen because of routing through the portal vein before entering the general circulation. Because venous blood travels through the lungs, this is another common site for secondary growth through the venous system. Cancer cells in the arterial system often form secondary neoplasm in the bone and the brain, especially if the primary site is in the lungs, where cancer cells can gain direct access to the left heart and systemic circulation (Schneider, Hogan, 1993).

BOX 15-1

Metastasis of Cancer Cells

Direct extension of the primary tumor into surrounding tissues
Penetration of the tumor into body cavities and vessels
Release into blood and lymph system
Implantation into secondary sites
Local seeding

Classifying Neoplasms

Tumors derive their names from the tissue of origin. Some tumors carry the suffix -oma following the name of the tissue of origin, for example, neuroma or fibroma (Baird, McCorkle, Grant, 1991; Schneider and Hogan, 1993). Malignant tumors generally are of two types, epithelial and connective tissue. The term **carcinoma** denotes a malignant tumor of epithelial cells, and the term **sarcoma** denotes a malignant tumor of connective tissue cells (Alkire, Groenwald, 1990; McCance, Huether, 1990; Schneider, Hogan, 1993). Hematopoietic or blood-forming tissues are involved in malignant processes that are disseminated from the onset, in contrast to solid tumors that initially are confined to a specific tissue or organ.

Tumors containing embryonic elements of all three primary germ layers such as hair and teeth are called teratomas. These are usually benign and often found in the ovaries (Baird, McCorkle, and Grant, 1991).

Some tumors are known by the names of the scientists who first described them, such as Hodgkin's disease and Wilm's tumor. Other types of malignant neoplasms occur with a wide variety of seemingly unrelated names. The diversity in naming malignant neoplasms reflects the complexities involved in identifying and classifying the many forms of cancer (Baird, McCorkle, Grant, 1991; Schneider, Hogan, 1993). There are two major methods for classifying cancers: (1) grading, according to histologic criteria and (2) staging, according to the extent of the spread of the disease. Tumors are staged and graded to determine accurate treatment. Tumors may be graded by roman or arabic numerals into four grades; the higher the grade, the worse the prognosis (Table 15-5).

Adding a number to the letters (e.g., T1, T2, N1, N2) indicates the extent of the malignancy (Alkire, Groenwald, 1990; Baird, McCorkle, Grant, 1991). The purpose of the TNM system is to describe the extent of disease at the time of diagnosis to aid in treatment planning. A TNM classification has been identified for major cancer sites, and the choice of treatment depends on the clinical TNM stage, both for the primary tumor and the lymph nodes (Alkire, Groenwald, 1990; Schneider, Hogan, 1993).

Different staging systems exist for some specific types of cancer. An example of this is the Dukes classification system for adenocarcinoma of the colon. However, the American Joint Committee for Cancer Staging and End-Result Reporting advocates use of the TNM system, because it can be easily understood and applied to all tumor types. The consistent terminology of the TNM system facilitates communication among health care providers.

Common Malignancies in Older Adults

Breast Cancer

Breast cancer is the most common invasive malignant cancer in women, and it increases in incidence with advancing age (Alkire, Groenwald, 1990; Baird, McCorkle, Grant, 1991; Schneider, Hogan, 1993). About 50,000

TABLE 15-5

Stage of Breast Cancer Using TNM Classifications

T (Tumor)	
T O	No evidence of tumor
TIS	In situ carcinoma
T 1	Tumor is 2 cm or less at greatest dimension
T 2	Tumor is more than 2 cm but not greater than 5 cm at greatest dimension
T 3	Tumor is greater than 5 cm at greatest dimension
T 4	Any size tumor with extension to chest wall or skin
N (Node)	
N 0	No palpable homolateral axillary nodes
N 1	Moveable homolateral axillary nodes
N 2	Homolateral axillary nodes that are considered to contain cancer and are fixed
N 3	Homolateral axillary supraclavicular or infraclavicular nodes
M (Metastasis)	
M 0	No evidence of distant metastases
M 1	Distant Metastases

Modified from: American Cancer Society: *A cancer source book for nurses,* The Society, 1991.

BOX 15-2

Breast Cancer Risk Factors

Advanced age
Family history of breast cancer (mother or sister)
History of previous breast cancer
History of endometrial cancer
Obesity
Nulliparity
First pregnancy after age 30 years
Late menopause
Caucasian
European-Jewish descent
History of high-fat diet
History of cystic breast disease
Oral contraception
Estrogen replacement therapy
High socioeconomic status

Possible risks
Excessive alcohol intake
Cigarette smoking

Modified from American Cancer Society: *Cancer facts and figures,* Atlanta, 1995, The Society; Baird SB, McCorkle R, Grant M: *Cancer nursing: a comprehensive textbook,* 1991, Philadelphia, WB Saunders.

women in the United States age 65 and older are diagnosed annually with breast cancer, making it one of the most common serious health problems for women in this age group (Cox, 1987). Of breast cancer cases, 80% occur in women older than age 50, and it is the leading cause of death in women 55 to 74 years of age. It is the second leading cause of cancer deaths after lung cancer in women (Alkire, Groenwald, 1990; Cox, 1987; American Cancer Society, 1995; 1994). Late-stage diagnosis is a serious concern in older adults. Approximately 10% of women show symptoms of metastasis as the first indication of malignant disease (Baquet, Ringer, Young, 1986; Breiele et al, 1986; Cox, 1987). Although breast cancer is more common in white women, African-American women die more often.

Risk factors Certain factors (Box 15-2) may increase or decrease the "average" risk of breast cancer. However, it is important to note that 70% to 80% of all women with breast cancer have no known risk factors.

Hormones, both endogenous and exogenous, have been identified as a major causal factor in the development of breast cancer (Alkire, Groenwald, 1990). The highest incidence of breast cancer is in women age 50 to 59. There is, however, a first-peak occurrence in premenopausal women or menopausal women between the ages of 45 and 49. The high incidence in this age group is thought to be related to ovarian estrogens. The second-peak incidence occurs in women between the ages of 65 and 69 and appears to be related to an imbalance of adrenal estrogens (Baird, McCorkle, Grant, 1991; Goodman, Harte, 1991). Owing to these findings, breast cancer is now thought of as two separate diseases based on menopausal status (Goodman, Harte, 1991).

Obesity, a high-fat diet, and oral contraceptives are other risk factors that may play a role in the incidence of mortality of breast cancer in African-American and poor women. In particular, many African-American diets are high in fat content because of traditional ways of seasoning "soul food." Dietary habits of the poor have been of concern for many years. Some diets consist of fried and other fatty foods, vegetables seasoned with high-fat products, and diets that are high in carbohydrates, all of which may lead to high cholesterol, obesity, and other life-threatening illnesses. African-Americans are known for consuming "soul foods," many of which (green leafy vegetables and the cruciferious) are recommended by the American Cancer Society and other nutritional groups. However, much of the time this food is cooked for long periods, which destroys the nutrients, and is seasoned with high-fat products, salt, and sugar (Guillory, 1994).

Since breast cancer is a disease of older women, breast screening is a life-long process. Boxes 15-3 and 15-4 present the American Cancer Society guidelines for breast screening. Older women who may have poor tac-

BOX 15-3

Mammogram Guidelines

- Mammogram every 1 to 2 years for asymptomatic women
- Annual mammogram for asymptomatic women ages 50 and older

Modified from: American Cancer Society: *Cancer facts and figures,* Atlanta, 1995, The Society.

BOX 15-4

Breast Screening and Detection Guidelines

- Breast self-examination (BSE) monthly
- Mammogram
- Clinical physical examination every 3 years for women age 20 to 40 and annually after age 40

Modified from: American Cancer Society: *Cancer facts and figures,* Atlanta, 1995, The Society.

RESEARCH

Williams RD: Factors affecting the practice of breast self-examination of older women, *Oncol Nurs Forum* 15(5):611-616, 1988.

Sample, setting

The sample for this study included 253 women age 62 to 93, who reside in senior housing.

Methodology

Research questions explored the relationships between frequency of BSE and health beliefs, health history, and knowledge. Health beliefs were measured with the Champion's Health Beliefs Scale and BSE knowledge was measured with the Williams Breast Inventory.

Findings

Those subjects taught BSE by nurses and those examined by doctors evidenced greater frequency of BSE. Of the older women, 23% reported performing BSE as recommended. Barriers, the second most important concept, accounted for 8% of the variance. Knowledge of breast cancer was significantly related to frequency of BSE.

Implications

The fact that health motivation provided a positive relationship with BSE should offer direction for nursing practice. Women already engaged in health motivation activities need to be assessed for BSE practice. Also, BSE practices should be adapted to older women's special needs. Nurses having extended contact with their clients are in a good position to encourage continued practice of BSE and listen to women's concerns about findings.

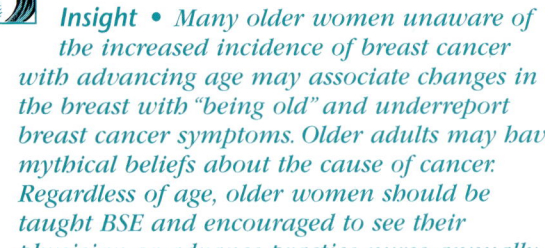

Insight • Many older women unaware of the increased incidence of breast cancer with advancing age may associate changes in the breast with "being old" and underreport breast cancer symptoms. Older adults may have mythical beliefs about the cause of cancer. Regardless of age, older women should be taught BSE and encouraged to see their physician or advance practice nurse annually for clinical breast examination and mammography.

tile stimulation and vision, as well as decreased range of motion should also be encouraged to conduct a BSE (Guillory, 1994). Guillory (1994) modified the American Cancer Society guidelines for older women. With this technique, the woman is encouraged to use the palm of her hand and with a sweeping motion, move from the chest wall towards the nipple (see Research box above, Cultural Awareness box, p. 349, and nursing Care Plan, pp. 350-351).

Stomach Cancer

Although the incidence of stomach cancer is declining, it still remains one of the common cancers among older adults. Cancer of the stomach is more common in men with type-A blood, and in individuals over age 60. It usually reaches its peak incidence in the eighth or ninth decades of life. The most common sites of stomach cancer are the antrum and pylorus. Those individuals who have suffered pernicious anemia and atrophy of the gastric mucosa have been observed to have a higher incidence (Kart, Metress, Metress, 1992; Kupchell, 1991; Schneider, Hogan, 1993).

The classic symptoms of stomach cancer are nausea, hematemesis, indigestion, difficulty swallowing, and tarry stools. However, symptoms of stomach cancer in the older adult are insidious and often nonspecific. Some of the more common symptoms include weight loss, loss of appetite, malaise, anemia, and possibly epigastric discomfort, most of which are associated with other types of cancer as well. In addition to a lesion, achlorhydria (absence of hydrochloric acid) may also be a symptom of stomach cancer (Schneider, Hogan, 1993).

CULTURAL AWARENESS

Cultural Considerations in Breast Cancer Screening

Although screening mammography for early detection of breast cancer has been shown to be an effective method for reducing mortality in older women, those from culturally diverse backgrounds have low prevalence rates. In a study by Caplan, Wells, and Haynes (1992) using national data, among women age 75 and older, 83.5% of African-American women, 93.2% of Hispanic women, and 75% of white women have never had a mammogram.

Among women age 75 and older, African-American and Hispanic women had markedly lower rates of clinical breast examination in the last year (23.4% and 20.5% respectively) as compared with white women (35.2%). The most common reasons for not having a mammogram among African-American women age 65 and older was that the physician or nurse practitioner did not recommend one. For Hispanic and white women in this age group, the most common reason was that a mammogram was not needed or not necessary.

Barriers to early detection of breast cancer among women from culturally diverse backgrounds were identified as the following: inaccurate knowledge of breast cancer and early screening, low awareness of the necessity for early detection, lack of health insurance to cover screening mammograms, lack of reimbursement to health care providers for clinical breast examinations and health teaching for early detection, and virtually no data on knowledge and attitudes for older adult Asian-American and Native-American women.

The researchers identified the following strategies to reduce barriers to early detection of breast cancer among older African-American and Hispanic women:

- Educate health care providers about the necessity of early breast cancer detection and their role in recommending it to clients.
- Conduct research to identify culturally appropriate messages and intervention strategies for each of the at-risk groups to influence their early detection behaviors.
- Use the media to increase knowledge and promote positive early detection practices among older women from culturally diverse backgrounds.
- Use prompt systems for health care providers to increase the use of screening mammography.

Caplan LS, Wells BL, and Haynes S: Breast cancer screening among older racial/ethnic minorities and whites: Barriers to early detection, *J Gerontol* 47:101-110, 1992.

A wide variety of diseases and illnesses in the older adult tend to include many of these same symptoms. In addition, the increased number of chronic problems of older people can confuse or can mask the symptoms of a true malignancy. The nurse must exercise caution when the older adult client reports such symptoms so that a potentially serious problem is not overlooked.

Diagnosis is usually confirmed by cytologic sample, which is accurate in 85% to 90% of the cases. Radical surgery is often contraindicated in older adults as the risks outweigh the benefits. The survival rate for those who have undergone surgery is 5% to 10%. Radiation therapy and chemotherapy are of minimum benefit. The prognosis for stomach cancer remains poor.

Gallbladder Cancer

Cancer of the gallbladder, although rare, occurs with advancing age. It is more common in women than men and usually occurs after age 70. It is difficult to diagnose and is often diagnosed after metastasis has occurred. The symptoms are vague and often associated with liver disease or calculous cholecystitis. Traditional cancer treatments are found to provide little to no promise. Prognosis is exceptionally poor with a short life expectancy once diagnosis is made (Allen, Britt, 1983; Guillory, 1993).

Pancreatic Cancer

Cancer of the pancreas is more common in men than women with a 3:1 ratio. The peak incidence is during the sixth decade of life. The incidence has been rare but steadily increasing, and is now the fourth leading cause of cancer deaths in the United States. Diagnosis may involve the use of radioactive protoscan; pancreatic angiography; and serologic analysis of serum lipase, amylase, and alkaline phosphatase levels. Pancreatic cancer is difficult to diagnose early. Its symptoms are associated with chronic pancreatitis, liver disease, or peptic ulcer disease. The head of the pancreas is involved in 60% of cases. This cancer usually metastasizes to liver, lungs, and bones. In most cases, metastasis has occurred when the differential diagnosis is confirmed (Kart, Metress, Metress, 1992).

The major symptom of pancreatic cancer is epigastric pain that radiates to the back and is relieved by bending forward. Indigestion characterized by belching, heartburn, and nausea is common, along with constipation, diarrhea, and painless jaundice. Anemia is rare, however, blood may appear in the stool.

Treatment is usually palliative for pain relief and discomfort. Surgery and chemotherapy have not proven effective in the management of pancreatic cancer, and the prognosis is poor.

CARE PLAN

BREAST CANCER

Clinical situation Mrs. G, a 65-year-old woman, found a lump in her right breast while doing her monthly BSE. Since she had not been taught how to examine her breasts, she was not sure of what she was feeling. Mrs. G was examined by her daughter's physician, who ordered a mammogram and later scheduled Mrs. G for a tissue biopsy. Both tests were positive and a diagnosis of breast cancer was confirmed. Mrs. G underwent a modified radical mastectomy.

Nursing diagnoses	Outcomes	Interventions
Body image disturbance related to loss of breast	Client will freely verbalize grief about loss of breast and changes in body image as evidenced by (1) making honest statements regarding her feelings and perceptions about mastectomy and perceived image, (2) making positive statements about body image, (3) personalizing loss of breast, (4) looking at or touching operative site.	Provide opportunities for exploring feelings, and assist to express these. Observe for signs of her touching dressing, and use this as an opening to discuss her thoughts and feelings about the surgery. Help identify personal meaning of loss of breast to clarify fears, concerns, and needs. Respect need for a period of withdrawal or denial, and assure that it is normal to experience these feelings. Encourage visits by spouse, family members, and friends.
	Client will identify available community resources or support groups to assist with adjustment and lifestyle changes.	Provide information about resources for cosmetic aids and breast prostheses. Refer to American Cancer Society's Reach to Recovery program for volunteer peer support. Discuss the use of prosthesis options and clothing style adjustments.
Fear related to nature of cancer	Client will experience reduction in fear as evidenced by verbalization of decreased fear.	Encourage to express feelings she is experiencing, especially regarding perception of danger, coping ability and skills, and needs for assistance. Help clarify what fears actually are of and about. Dispel misconceptions; provide factual information to reduce distortions. Encourage to be specific in describing fears; discourage broad generalizations. For fear of disfigurement, arrange visit by Reach to Recovery volunteer who has had same experience and has adjusted well to the situation. Encourage use of measures such as visits from friends and family, religious practices, reading, and music as distraction from fears. Include family and significant others in any interactions or discussions.
	Client will engage in adaptive coping as evidenced by (1) verbalizing repertoire of effective coping skills used in past, (2) incorporating those skills into current situation, and (3) identifying and using alternative coping skills and strategies to assist in current situation.	Assist in identifying past stressful and difficult situations, and skills used to successfully manage them. Help verbalize own perceptions of coping styles. Teach new coping styles to add to repertoire. Encourage use of support systems to assist with coping and promote comfort and relaxation.

CARE PLAN

BREAST CANCER—cont'd

Nursing diagnoses	Outcomes	Interventions
Pain related to tissue trauma from surgical incision	Verbalizes comfort after administration of analgesic Able to participate in self-care activities with comfort	Administer analgesic as prescribed. Monitor pain character, intensity, and frequency to assess effectiveness of analgesic, and make changes as indicated. Use proper body positioning to promote comfort and to enhance effectiveness of analgesic, such as semi-Fowler's position or elevation of affected arm. Promote passive and active exercises of affected arm, shoulder, and hand. Offer additional strategies to augment pain relief (e.g., relaxation, guided imagery, or diversional activities).

RESEARCH

Weinrich S et al: Knowledge of colorectal cancer among older persons, *Cancer Nurs* 15(5):322-330, 1992.

Sample, setting

The sample was randomly selected from congregate meal sites and was comprised of 12 sites with 211 older study participants.

Methodology

A quasiexperimental pre-posttest two-by-two factorial design was used to measure the effects of knowledge on fecal occult blood testing. Knowledge was measured with the Colorectal Cancer Knowledge Questionnaire.

Findings

Education, race, and income were predictors of colorectal cancer knowledge. Undereducated poor are at greatest risk of failing to participate in screening and consequently having cancer detected.

Implications

An outreach program can be started within local hospitals and colorectal cancer support groups that include each person or family member with colorectal cancer, making an effort to tell someone else at risk on a monthly basis. A speakers bureau may be a possibility from within such groups.

Cancer of the Colon and Rectum

Cancer of the colon is one of the most common malignancies in people over age 70. It is more common in women, whereas cancer of the rectum is more common in men. The signs and symptoms vary with the section of the bowel affected. Any signs of change in bowel habits along with loss of appetite, weakness, weight loss, and anemia should be thoroughly investigated. Colon cancer is often confused with a fecal impaction in the rectosigmoid because of the hard mass that is often found; however, the mass resulting from cancer is usually fixed (Goodman, Harte, 1991; Kart, Metress, Metress, 1992). Colon or rectal cancer may go undiagnosed until late, because older individuals often complain of bowel problems (see Research box above and nursing Care Plan, p. 352).

Prostate Cancer

Cancer of the prostate is the most commonly occurring cancer in men. The peak incidence age is between the sixth and seventh decades of life. More than 80% of all prostate cancers are diagnosed in men over age 65. This cancer is more common in North America and northwestern Europe (Baird, McCorkle, Grant, 1991). For reasons not clearly understood, African-American men have the highest incidence in the world. There is some familial association, but it is unclear whether this results from genetic or environmental factors. Dietary fat has been shown to be a factor. According to the American Cancer Society (1993) one of every 11 men develops prostate cancer. Overall, it is the second most common malignancy in American men and the third most common

CARE PLAN

COLON CANCER

Clinical situation Mrs. E is an 80-year-old African-American woman with colon cancer who has been treated with chemotherapy. She is now experiencing nausea and vomiting, which have persisted for several days.

Nursing diagnosis	Outcome	Interventions
Fluid volume deficit related to nausea and vomiting	Client will maintain adequate fluid and electrolyte balance as evidenced by (1) blood pressure (BP) and pulse (P) within normal limits (WNL), (2) skin turgor WNL, (3) balanced intake and output, and (4) electrolyte levels WNL.	Assess for nausea and vomiting. Assess skin turgor and vital signs at regular intervals. Administer antiemetics as prescribed. Plan rest periods before and after meals. Provide small bland meals, avoiding fatty foods. Offer frequent mouth care. Provide an odorless, clean environment for meals. Avoid foods with strong odors. Avoid sights, sounds, and odors that stimulate nausea. Monitor intake and output. Identify food preferences, and provide them. Promote increased fluid intake by mouth to 2,000 ml per day. Use relaxation and distracting techniques.

cause of cancer deaths in men over the age of 55 (Baird, McCorkle, Grant, 1991; Goodman, Harte, 1991; Kart, Metress, Metress, 1992).

Symptoms of prostate cancer include weak and interrupted urine flow; inability to urinate, or difficulty starting or stopping the urine flow; urgency; frequency, especially at night; hematuria; and pain or burning on urination. Symptoms such as pain in the lower back, pelvis and upper thighs often indicate advanced disease. In many cases, diagnosis is made late (Baird, McCorkle, Grant, 1991), because many symptoms are associated with the aging process.

A blood test for prostate-specific antigen (PSA) is currently being used for early detection of prostate cancer. PSA is a glycoprotein secreted only by the prostate gland. However, since it is produced by both normal and malignant cells, elevations can occur in nonmalignant conditions. Consequently, an elevated PSA level may be a false positive result. Transrectal ultrasound with biopsy remains the screening procedure of choice.

Prostate cancer is treated surgically, alone, or in combination with radiation and/or hormone or chemotherapy. Hormone therapy and chemotherapy may control prostate cancer for long periods by shrinking the size of the tumor and greatly relieving pain. In men over the age of 70, surgery is rarely recommended, because the individual's life expectancy is relatively unaffected by the condition. At advanced ages, individuals often die of other causes before the cancer takes its toll (Baird, McCorkle, Grant, 1991; Schneider, Hogan, 1993).

Prognosis is good if diagnosed while the tumor is localized. The 5-year survival rate for clients whose tumors are diagnosed at this stage is 88%. Survival rates for all stages combined have steadily improved and have increased from 50% to 74% in the past 30 years (Goodman, Harte, 1991; Kart, Metress, Metress, 1992).

Skin Cancer

Skin cancer is the most common of all malignant cancers. Skin cancers are quite common in older adults, especially those who have worked outside over the years. Cancers of the skin consist of basal cell carcinoma (BCC), squamous cell carcinoma (SCC) and malignant melanoma. BCC and SCC are often grouped together and classified as nonmelanoma skin cancers. Malignant melanoma has a low incidence but is the most serious form of skin cancer (Ferrell, Schneider, 1989; Schneider, Hogan, 1993). It arises from the epidermis and is noted for its metastasizing ability. Nonmelanoma skin cancers have a higher incidence, but they have a low metastatic potential and mortality. They are associated with an overall 5-year survival rate of 95% but account for an estimated 2,000 deaths annually (Schneider, Hogan, 1993). Nonmelanoma skin cancers often require costly, extensive, and repeated treatment, which can result in cosmetic deformities.

More than 500,000 new cases of skin cancers are reported annually. The incidence of skin cancer increases with advancing age, usually occurring in adults between the ages of 50 and 60 years (Kart, Metress, Metress, 1992). The most common incidence of skin cancer among older adults is related to, among other things, the cumulative sun exposure they have experienced over a lifetime. There are various causes of skin cancer. A minute number of the lesions may be present at birth, whereas others develop over the life span. Any change in pigmentation can be indicative of skin cancer (Averette, Boike, Jarrell, 1990).

Consequently, client education regarding use of sunscreen products, self-examination of all skin areas on a regular basis, and the type of changes to observe are important for this population. Depending on the older adult's degree of functional ability, assistance may be needed in conducting the skin self-examination.

Basal cell carcinoma BCC is the most common of the skin cancers, comprising at least 75% of cases in the southern United States and more than 90% in the northern United States. BCC occurs twice as often in men than women and is the least aggressive type of skin cancer.

BCC usually appears as small, translucent pearly nodules on sun-exposed areas of the skin, such as the head, ear lobes, face, and neck. Ulceration often occurs, forming a crust on the surface. BCC usually grows slowly by direct extension and has the capacity to cause major local destruction. Although metastasis is rare, the most common metastatic site is to the lymph nodes. Other sites of metastasis are bones, lungs, liver, brain, dura, kidneys, and even less commonly, the skin (Baird, McCorkle, Grant, 1991; McCance, Huether, 1990; Schneider, Hogan, 1993).

Squamous cell carcinoma SCC arises from the epidermal cells and may appear on any part of the body that is exposed to the sun. The most highly exposed areas of the skin, such as the top of the nose, the forehead, helices of the ears, back of the hands, and lower lip are commonly affected. SCC can also arise in old scars that are the result of ultraviolet, thermal, or chemical burns. Tumors that originate in these areas are more aggressive and have a high frequency of metastasis. The lesions are usually firm, slightly red or pearly nodules. SCC appears as a flesh-colored or erythematous, raised, firm papule. It may be crusted with keratin products or in its early or late stages may ulcerate and bleed, becoming tender and painful (Baird, McCorkle, Grant, 1991; Goodman, Harte, 1991). Treatment for nonmelanoma skin cancers includes surgical excision (90% of cases), radiation therapy, electrodesiccation (tissue destruction by heat) and cryotherapy (tissue destruction by freezing). For nonmelanoma skin cancer, cure is highly likely if detected and treated early.

Malignant melanoma Malignant melanoma is the most lethal form of skin cancer. It arises from the melanocyte, which is a cell that specializes in the biosynthesis and transport of melanin. This cancer usually begins as a small mole and is noted for its metastasizing ability. It changes color, enlarges, and bleeds easily from minor trauma. Lesions may be flat or raised but with irregular margins. Melanoma is generally well-pigmented with shades of the tumor ranging in color from brown to black to red to blue (Baird, McCorkle, Grant, 1991; Schneider, Hogan, 1993).

The older adult client needs to be taught the risk factors for development of melanoma—fair, sandy-complexion, a lifetime of excessive sun exposure, and a history of serious sunburn. The previously noted characteristics of melanoma should also be taught.

Lung

The incidence of lung cancer has been increasing steadily in both men and women for several decades, however, the increase for women is higher than for men. Since 1987 more women have died of lung cancer than breast cancer, which for more than 40 years was the major cause of cancer deaths in women (American Cancer Society, 1995). There is a sharp increase in incidence starting between the ages of 45 and 50 with the peak incidence between ages 70 and 74 for women and 75 and 79 for men.

Early detection of lung cancer is extremely difficult; signs and symptoms may not become bothersome until the disease is advanced. Signs and symptoms of lung cancer may include persistent cough, blood-tinged sputum, chest pain, recurring pneumonia or other upper respiratory infections. Risk factors include exposure to cigarette smoke and several industrial substances such as arsenic, asbestos, radiation exposure, and radon exposure (Schneider, Hogan, 1993).

The 5-year survival rate is only 13% in all clients, regardless of stage at diagnosis. The rate is 47% for cases detected when the disease is still localized (American Cancer Society, 1995; 1992).

Treatment of lung cancer includes surgery, radiation therapy, and chemotherapy. Surgery is usually the treatment of choice, however, because of the typically advanced stage of disease at the time of diagnosis, radiation and/or chemotherapy are often used (Baird, McCorkle, Grant, 1991).

Ovarian Cancer

Ovarian cancer is the leading cause of death from gynecologic cancers in the United States (ACS, 1995). More deaths occur from ovarian cancer than cervical and endometrial cancer combined. Two thirds of ovarian cancers occur between the ages of 40 and 70 years of age, whereas more than 90% occur between the ages of 20 and 65. In 1994 there will be approximately 24,000 new cases and 13,600 deaths from ovarian cancer (Baird, McCorkle, Grant, 1991; Otto, 1991).

Ovarian cancer is often "silent," showing no obvious signs or symptoms until late in its development (American Cancer Society, 1995). The most common sign is enlargement of the abdomen, which is caused by the accumulation of fluid. There is rarely any abnormal vaginal bleeding. In women over 40, vague digestive distubances (stomach discomfort, gas, or distention) that persist and cannot be explained by any other cause may indicate the need for a thorough evaluation for ovarian cancer (American Cancer Society, 1995). Symptoms such as nausea, dyspepsia, frequent urination, gradual change in bowel habits, and vague abdominal and pelvic discomfort indicate advanced disease.

An exploratory laparotomy is performed to confirm and stage the ovarian cancer. Several biopsies are obtained, including diaphragmatic washings for cytology. CA-125, a possible "tumor marker" for ovarian cancer, is currently used in diagnostic evaluation. CA-125 is a cancer antigen that is detectable in blood serum levels and peritoneal ascites (Otto, Fraser, Kellerstrass, 1991; Otto, 1991).

In many cases, surgery is the only treatment for stages I and II ovarian cancer. Chemotherapy is often administered for 12 months, followed by a second exploratory laparotomy, called a "second look." This second surgery is used to assess or to reevaluate the effectiveness of the previous treatment. Most ovarian disease recurrence develops within a period of 18 to 24 months following the first occurrence (American Cancer Society, 1994; Baird, McCorkle, Grant, 1991). For cancer prevention and early detection tips, see the Client/Family Teaching box below.

CLIENT/FAMILY TEACHING

Cancer Risk and Detection

As a group, older people generally require more individualized health teaching about cancer risk and detection. The reasons for this vary but can include (1) a lack of awareness of the risks of cancer with advanced age or even the warning signs of cancer, (2) reluctance to report physical complaints that could be indicative of a malignancy, and (3) concern or fear about a possible diagnosis of cancer and its overall impact on life and well-being. The nurse should teach older people the following early detection and cancer-related guidelines:

- Annual oral examination
- Annual screening mammogram, with breast examination by physician or advance practice nurse
- Monthly BSE
- Screening proctosigmoidoscopy every three to five years
- Annual screening for fecal occult blood
- Annual digital rectal examination (DRE) of the prostate
- Annual skin inspection by physician/advance practice nurse
- Avoid sun exposure between 11:00 AM and 2:30 PM
- Use broad-spectrum sunscreen when going out into the sun
- Report any new, slow-growing nodular or papular lesions that are flesh-colored or translucent; report if bleeding or ulceration occurs
- Stop smoking; eliminate tobacco use from all sources
- Eat high-fiber foods
- Decrease or eliminate alcohol consumption

Common Physiologic Complications

There are various physiologic aspects of cancer. Symptoms usually manifest late when metastasis has already begun. Other symptoms associated with cancer are actually related to either the side effects of therapy or complications from advanced disease at the time of diagnosis.

Pain

Pain is the most dreaded effect of cancer (other than death), although it is often the last symptom to appear. Even in terminal stages, 60% of people with cancer experience mild or no pain (Schneider, Hogan, 1993; Ferrell, Schneider, 1989). The cause of cancer pain is complex, because it has physical, psychologic, social, and spiritual aspects.

The three stages of cancer pain include (1) early, (2) intermediate, and (3) late. Early pain usually occurs after initial surgery for diagnosis or treatment and usually subsides after the third day; thus this pain is acute and short-term (Ferrell, Schneider, 1989; Schneider, Hogan, 1993; Vannicola, 1988).

Intermediate-stage pain results from postoperative contraction of scars and nerve entrapment, or from cancer recurrence or metastasis. This pain may subside or may be controlled by palliative therapy such as radiation, chemotherapy, neurosurgery, and analgesics (Ferrell, Schneider, 1989).

Late-stage pain is chronic and occurs in terminal cancer when therapy no longer controls the disease. Its intensity may gradually increase or this pain may be considered intractable. Severe chronic pain occurs in about 25% of clients who die from cancer (Ferrell and Schneider, 1989; Schneider, Hogan, 1993).

Pathophysiology of pain Malignant neoplasms cause pain by five physiologic changes: (1) bone destruction; (2) obstruction of lumens (viscera of vessels); (3) peripheral nerve involvement; (4) pressure of growing tumors causing ischemia or distention; and (5) inflammation, infection, or necrosis of the tissue.

Bone destruction with infraction (fractures without displacement) is the most common cause of pain, usually resulting from metastatic lesions (Schneider, Hogan, 1993). Bone destruction may cause increased sensitivity over the area or sharp, continuous pain. Obstruction of a viscus such as in the gastrointestinal or genitourinary tract causes severe, colicky, cramp-type pain. Visceral pain is dull, diffuse, and poorly localized. Obstruction of an artery, vein, or lymphatic vessel may initiate arterial ischemia, venous engorgement, or edema. This pain is dull, diffuse, and aching (Ferrell, Schneider, 1989; Schneider, Hogan, 1993).

Infiltration or compression of peripheral nerves or nerve plexuses causes continuous, sharp, or stabbing pain, sometimes accompanied by hyperesthesia or paresthesia (Schneider, Hogan, 1993). Infiltration or distention of the integument, fascia, or tissue initiates a severe localized, dull, aching pain that increases in intensity as tumor size increases. An example of this is the pain resulting from distention of the abdomen by ascites or the stretching of the skin by carcinoma of the neck.

Finally, inflammation, infection, and necrosis of the tissue itself may cause pain by producing either pressure or ischemia. Chemical mediators of pain are present during inflammation and necrosis.

Side effects of cancer pain include fatigue, sleeplessness, anorexia, and decreased movement, followed by the complications of immobility, namely muscle weakness, pressure sores, contracture, and respiratory dysfunction.

Medical therapy in early stage pain is directed at the cancer. Chronic or late-stage pain is treated symptomatically by analgesia, neurosurgery, and nerve blocks. Cancer pain, like other types of severe pain, may consume the client's entire attention, and unless treated vigorously, may demoralize the client and interfere with eating, resting, or sleeping. Interventions are directed toward helping the client live as normal a life as possible and cope with the pain. Pain tolerance is increased when the client's energy is preserved for enjoyable activities (Vannicola, 1988).

General comfort measures to promote rest and sleep, proper body positioning, and nutrition can increase the client's pain tolerance. Teaching clients conscious muscle relaxation during which they systematically contract and relax muscle groups throughout the body may decrease pain from muscle tenseness, as well as anxiety associated with the pain.

CLIENT/FAMILY TEACHING

Pain

- Teach clients what to anticipate about the pain experience associated with their specific form of cancer to reduce anxiety, to promote feelings of control, to prevent misinterpretation of the painful event, and to promote understanding of what to expect. If possible, explain the cause of the pain, times of occurrence, duration, quality, and measures available for relief.
- Describe any procedures and associated discomfort to promote more effective pain tolerance.
- Assure clients that there are many different types of pain-relief measures available, and that modalities and therapies can be changed to provide adequate relief.
- Let clients know that they are the experts on their pain experience and that they should suggest to the nurse any measures they feel can make their pain therapy successful.
- Teach strategies to augment medication, such as distraction, relaxation, and guided imagery.
- Teach family members and significant others to use other comfort-inducing measures such as a back rub, massage, clean sheets, moist heat, and body positioning.
- Explain that it is acceptable to use pain medication and that effectiveness of medication is greater if taken or used early in the pain experience.
- Teach the use of a pain log to record type of pain, measures used to control pain, and pain relief obtained to increase perception of control.

Diversionary activities help decrease the perception of pain by distraction. These activities may be physical (work, walking, rocking, or swimming), social, or mental (watching television, reading, or crafts). Some clients find imagery (waking-imagined analgesia) helpful. Others may try to separate the pain from their bodies thereby "quieting the mind by letting the body drop away" (Ferrell, Schneider, 1989; Schneider, Hogan, 1993) (see Client/Family Teaching box above). See Chapter 13 for pain management in the older adult.

Cachexia

Cachexia is almost universal at some point in the development of malignant disease and is usually a sign of advanced cancer. It is characterized by anorexia, hypermetabolism, excess energy consumption over nutritional supply, and wasting as a result of negative protein and fat balance in the body. Weight loss may be gradual or rapid (Goodman, Harte, 1991; Schneider, Hogan, 1993).

Anorexia

Anorexia may also accompany the cancer therapy, and the increased protein needs of the body resulting from tumor growth may be difficult to meet. A variety of nursing actions should be implemented to assist the older person to eat. Mealtimes should be incorporated with family visiting, or clients can eat together if possible (Schneider, Hogan, 1993). A high-protein diet enhances the response to therapy, and an adequate intake of calories spares protein for cell building. Because chewing may be difficult, food should be cut in small pieces and creamed or combined with cooked vegetables, rice, or noodles. Meat may also be ground or used as a base for soups or stews. Fish, cottage cheese, and eggs are also good sources of protein.

Therapy for the cachectic state is rarely successful unless the underlying cancer is treated. Total parenteral nutrition (TPN) may be used as an adjunct to therapy. TPN has not been found to stimulate tumor growth, and it may result in a return of immune system competence, a decrease in sepsis and wound healing, and an increase in response to chemotherapy (Otto, 1991; Schneider, Hogan, 1993).

Treatment Modalities

Treatment of cancer is based on the stage, biophysiologic characteristics of the tumor, age, and biopsychosocial condition of the client. The histologic type of the tumor is important in prescribing the treatment regimen.

Therapy may be administered for curative or palliative (i.e., directed only toward relieving symptoms) purposes. Presently, there are four major forms of treatment: (1) surgery, (2) radiotherapy, (3) chemotherapy, and (4) immunotherapy. Immunotherapy has become a major therapy over the past two decades. Each form of treatment may be used alone or in combination (Otto, 1991; Schneider, Hogan, 1993).

Surgery

Surgery, the oldest method of treating cancer, may be either curative or palliative. The best treatment for cancer at present is complete surgical removal of all malignant tissues before metastasis occurs (Goodman, Harte, 1991). Operative procedures are individualized and have been discussed under specific types of cancers.

The preoperative older adult who is scheduled to undergo a major surgical resection or reconstruction as a result of cancer needs psychosocial care and support because of the lifestyle and body image changes that may occur. A relationship of trust that is characterized by open and honest dialogue encourages open and frank discussion of the client's fears, hopes, and goals. The nurse should advise the client to talk about these issues with the family members or other significant people with whom such a relationship is established. If there are no such people available, the nurse should help the client explore feelings regarding the impending surgery and its effects. Alternatively, the nurse should remember that it may be necessary to provide explanations and support to family members, since they also may be anxious and fearful about the outcome of their older family member. The losses the older adult may have already incurred, coupled with any potential losses of function, independence, or body parts that may result from the surgery, have the potential to seriously stress the client's coping skills and emotional reserves. Nursing interventions should be aimed at providing the appropriate emotional support and counseling.

Because of the normal, age-related changes that occur in most of the body systems, the older adult is at greater risk of postoperative complications. This does not mean that age should be considered a contraindication to a major surgical procedure for cancer. However, it does mean that the older adult surgical candidate requires a careful preoperative evaluation by the physician.

Postoperative nursing care priorities should focus on preventing respiratory complications and promoting cardiac and renal function. See Chapters 21, 22, and 26 for a more complete discussion of the age-related changes in these systems. Because of the overall reduced compensatory reserves in these systems, older adults are susceptible to a number of serious complications such as hemorrhage, shock, congestive heart failure, electrolyte imbalances, hypoxia, and dehydration. Pulmonary embolism is a common cause of death postoperatively in this age group. In addition, compromised immune function predisposes them to sepsis from a variety of invasive lines and catheters that may be in place. The overall stress of surgery, including the use of anesthesia and other centrally acting medications, predisposes the older adult to the development of delirium. Paralytic ileus, constipation, and pressure ulcers are additional risks the older adult faces during this period. Careful, complete, ongoing assessment of all of the body systems that can be adversely affected by curative or palliative surgery for cancer enables the nurse to accurately diagnose, plan, implement, and evaluate nursing care during the post operative period.

Radiotherapy

Radiation has been used as a treatment of cancer for most of this century. The most common sources of radiation for external beam therapy are the linear accelerator and cobalt 60 teletherapy machines. These machines produce radiation of varying types of energy, which control the depth of penetration of the x-rays into tissues.

Radiotherapy is used for its curative effects and to control the growth of cancer cells when a cure is considered impossible. Because it may deter the growth of cancer cells, it may also relieve pain, even when extension of the disease is such that a cure is impossible (Strohl, 1988).

Therapeutic doses of radiotherapy are calculated to destroy or to delay the growth of malignant cells without destroying normal tissue. Rotation of either the target site in the client or the radiation beam makes it possible to deliver a high dose to the tumor, whereas at the same time only part of the dose reaches the noncancerous tissue surrounding it.

Internal radiation may be delivered by sealed or unsealed methods. In either type, special precautions may be necessary, depending on the amount of radioactive material used, its location, and the kind of rays being emitted. Special precautions should be taken if more than a trace diagnostic dose has been given. Personnel should be fully acquainted with all precautions and should be supervised in carrying them out. Generally, the client is placed in a single room or a double room with another client who is also receiving radiation therapy. A radiation precaution sign should be placed on the door to the client's room, and visitors should be restricted (Averett, Boike, Jarrell, 1990; Baird, McCorkle, Grant, 1991). Time, distance, and shielding are major principles in the management of the client with radium implants (see Research box below).

Chemotherapy

Chemotherapy is the use of drugs to destroy cancer cells with minimal toxicity to healthy cells. The goal of therapy may be curative or palliative. At this time, chemotherapy is administered in combination, since there is no drug that can effectively destroy cancerous cells.

Knowledge of the cell cycle is important in understanding tumor growth and the principles of chemotherapy. The reader is referred to a physiology textbook for review of the concept of cell cycle.

Chemotherapeutic agents may be classified as alkylating agents, antimetabolites, plant (vinca) alkaloids, antibiotics, and hormones. These agents act on cells at various stages of the cell cycle.

Alkylating agents The alkylating agents are highly reactive compounds. They are cell cycle-nonspecific and act against already formed nucleic acids by cross-linking DNA strands, thereby preventing DNA replication and RNA transcription (Kart, Metress, Metress, 1992; Schneider, Hogan, 1993).

Antimetabolites The antimetabolites act by interfering with the synthesis of chromosomal nucleic acid. Antimetabolites are analogs of normal metabolites and block the enzyme necessary for synthesis of essential factors, or are incorporated into the DNA or RNA and thus prevent replication (Baird, McCorkle, Grant, 1991). Most antimetabolites are pyrimidine analogs, purine analogs, or folic acid antagonists and are, in general, cell cycle-specific.

RESEARCH

Larson P et al: Influence of age on problems experienced by patients with lung cancer undergoing radiation therapy, *Oncol Nurs Forum,* 20(3):473-480, 1993.

Sample, setting

The sample included 33 newly diagnosed clients with lung cancer in the greater San Francisco bay area who were to receive radiation therapy. Middle age was considered less than age 65, and old age was classified as greater than 65.

Methodology

The purpose of this prospective, longitudinal study was to determine if clients with lung cancer who are 65 years of age or older experience problems differently than do clients younger than 65 during and following radiation treatment. The moderator and outcome variables selected for study were recognized attendant problems that may develop during lung cancer treatment and that may influence the treatment regimen and response. Social support was measured with Norbeck's Social Support Scale. Dodd's Self-Care Behavior Log was used to record side effects.

Findings

No statistically significant differences were found between clients age 65 or older and those younger than age 65 on caloric intake, adequacy of energy intake, total radiation dose, concurrent illnesses, and social support at any of the four data collection periods. Similarly, there were no significant differences on weight, body mass index, and multidimensional functional status. The relationship between social support subscales and functional status measures for the 65-or-older group suggested that those subjects with lower social support perceived themselves to have better functional status.

Implications

The results suggest that chronologic age alone may not be a sufficient criterion to determine therapeutic regimen or that unique problems may occur as a result of advanced age.

Vinca alkaloids The vinca alkaloids are derived from the periwinkle plant. They act as mitotic inhibitors and exert their cytotoxic effect by binding to proteins within the cells. The vinca alkaloids are cell cycle-specific (Baird, McCorkle, Grant, 1991; Schneider, Hogan, 1993).

Antibiotics The cytotoxic antibiotics are cell cycle-nonspecific agents. Antibiotics appear to be active in all phases of the cell cycle. They are natural products of various strains of the soil fungus. The antitumor antibiotics bind to DNA, and prevent DNA and RNA synthesis (Alkire, Groenwald, 1990; Schneider, Hogan, 1993).

Steroids The corticosteroids are produced by the adrenal cortex and include mineralcorticoid and glucocorticoid. It is the glucocorticoids that, in addition to their use in numerous nonmalignant diseases, are effective in the treatment of many neoplastic disorders. Steroids are also able to reduce edema and inflammation around a tumor, and therefore are useful for symptom relief. Many side effects are associated with long-term steroid use. Steroids in cancer treatment regimens are often given intermittently and for short periods of time, so clients do not experience the debilitating side effects associated with chronic, long-term use (Alkire, Groenwald, 1990; McCance, Huether, 1990; Schneider, Hogan, 1993).

Hormones Hormonal alteration may be a desired therapeutic goal when tumor growth is directly influenced by certain hormones. The mechanism whereby the steroid hormones stimulate or inhibit cellular growth is not clear, but an important mechanism may be interference or alteration in the cell membrane (Baird, McCorkle, Grant, 1991).

Immunotherapy

The role of biologic response modifier (BRM) therapy in the prevention and treatment of cancer is presently being studied. The term BRM actually applies to the broad category of biologic agents that have the potential to control the growth and metastasis of neoplasms (Schneider, Hogan, 1993). Immunotherapy has numerous limitations as a cancer therapy in older adults.

Combination Chemotherapy

Combination chemotherapy is administered to enhance the therapy. It is also given in repeated short courses to reduce the immunosuppressive effects. Drugs considered for combination chemotherapy are those that (1) are active when used alone, (2) have different mechanisms of action, (3) have a biochemical basis for possible synergism, (4) do not produce toxicity in the same organs, and (5) produce toxicity at different times after administration (Averette, Boike, Jarrell, 1990).

Side Effects of Chemotherapy

There are numerous side effects associated with the available chemotherapeutic agents. The older adult is especially vulnerable to the side effects of these toxic drugs (Table 15-6). Treatment regimens need to be planned in view of these age-related changes to avoid excessive toxicity.

Some degree of injury to normal cells often occurs with treatment by chemotherapeutic agents. The basis for normal cells being affected is their rate of proliferation (Baird, McCorkle, Grant, 1991). Many normal tissues have a high proliferation capacity, in some instances exceeding that of malignant disease. It is these rapidly proliferating tissues (e.g., bone marrow, gastrointestinal epithelium, and hair follicles) that bear the brunt of the toxic effects of many of the cytotoxic drugs (Averette, Boike, Jarrell, 1990; Schneider, Hogan, 1993).

Before initiating treatment, it is the nurse's responsibility to inform the older adult client of the common side effects. As always, parenteral chemotherapy should be administered with caution in this age group to assess tolerance and to monitor for toxic effects. Since the skin is flaccid and the blood vessels more fragile in older adults, infiltration can easily occur.

Bone marrow suppression Bone marrow suppression is the major life-threatening toxicity associated with chemotherapy. It is very important to monitor blood counts in older adults, considering bone marrow does not reproduce rapidly. Frequent blood counts are taken to monitor this toxicity, and astute attention must be given to the results of the white blood count, platelet count, and hemoglobin with appropriate modification of

TABLE 15-6

Physiologic and Metabolic Changes of Aging
Body composition
Increased adipose tissue
Decreased protein and water
Liver
Decreased hepatic blood flow
Decreased ability to activate carcinogens and drugs
Decreased ability to conjugate drugs
Increased ability to deactivate carcinogens
Kidney
Decreased glomerular filtration rate
Decreased renal blood flow
Hematopoietic system
Decreased hematopoietic stem cell reserve

From Balducci L, et al: Cancer chemotherapy in the elderly, *Am Fam Phys* 35:135, 1987.

> **Insight** • *The major limiting factor for the use of most chemotherapeutic agents in older adults is hematologic toxicity. Older and younger people alike demonstrate toxicities to chemotherapy; however, it has been shown that older people develop more hematologic toxicities than younger people. A major nursing function in the care of older adults receiving chemotherapy is to maintain close observations for signs and symptoms of hemotoxicity.*

drug dosage (Schneider, Hogan, 1993; Vannicola, 1988). Clients who have received previous chemotherapy or radiation therapy, particularly to areas of bone marrow reserve (e.g., sternum, hips, or pelvis), may have an increased sensitivity to myelosuppression. Blood counts are done before the administration of chemotherapy and at regular intervals to assess the predictable lowest point, which varies with the drugs used (Averette, Boike, Jarrell, 1990; Schneider, Hogan, 1993).

Infection Infections are quite prevalent in older adult clients that are myelosuppressed (see Chapter 14). Every effort should be made to prevent the client from acquiring nosocomial infections. Health care providers should wear masks if they have colds or other upper respiratory infections. In addition, families of clients are instructed not to visit if they have colds or other infections (Baird, McCorkle, Grant, 1991; Goodman, Harte, 1991; Schneider, Hogan, 1993).

Injections are usually avoided if at all possible. Aseptic technique must be scrupulously maintained during intravenous infusions and dressing changes. In preventing all types of infections good medical asepsis, especially careful handwashing, is important (Kupchell, 1991; Schneider, Hogan, 1993).

Gastrointestinal effects Gastrointestinal distress is a concern for the healthy older adult, therefore, special attention must be given and frequent assessments performed with older adults undergoing chemotherapy. Clients may experience nausea, vomiting, diarrhea, or constipation as side effects of chemotherapy. Changes in bowel habits commonly occur but may or may not require intervention. If diarrhea becomes marked or persists, an antidiarrheal medication such as diphenoxylate with atropine (Lomotil) may be prescribed. Metamucil is also recommended to increase bulk. Clients receiving vincristine are assessed for signs of paralytic ileus and instructed to report constipation (Schneider, Hogan, 1993).

Nausea and vomiting Nausea and vomiting are among the most uncomfortable and distressing side effects of chemotherapy. The onset and duration vary greatly among clients and with the drug given (Otto, Fraser, Kellerstrass, 1991; Otto, 1991; Schneider, Hogan, 1993). For the ambulatory client, nausea may interfere with all aspects of activities of daily living (ADLs). Persistent vomiting may result in fluid and electrolyte imbalance, generalized weakness, and weight loss. It is important to observe older adults closely, because they are prone to dehydration. The nurse should be alert to the fact that in some cases, it is difficult to assess hydration status by skin turgor alone. Decline of nutritional status as a result of the nausea and vomiting renders the client more susceptible to infection and perhaps less able to tolerate therapy. Some physiologic symptoms can accompany or can precipitate psychologic responses that might include depression and withdrawal.

Stomatitis **Stomatitis** is a major discomfort for the client undergoing chemotherapy. Stomatitis, an inflammation of the mucous membranes of the oral cavity, may range from an erythema of the oral mucosa to mild or severe ulceration. Methotrexate, 5-fluorouracil, doxorubicin, dactinomycin, and bleomycin are the chemotherapeutic drugs that most commonly cause stomatitis. Clients may also develop a superimposed candida infection of the mouth and esophagus, for which oral nystatin is usually prescribed (Otto, Fraser, Kellerstrass, 1991; Schneider, Hogan, 1993). Meticulous mouth care is important. If the client wears dentures, the nurse should be certain that the dentures fit well and are cleaned frequently.

Alopecia Alopecia, (loss of hair) may occur by two mechanisms. If the hair roots are atrophied, alopecia occurs readily. The hair either falls out spontaneously or by hair combing, often in large clumps. If the hair shaft is constricted because of atrophy or necrosis, the hair will break off very near the scalp (Belcher, 1992; Schneider, Hogan, 1993). The root remains in the scalp and a patchy, thinning pattern of hair loss occurs. Hair loss may occur on other parts of the body in addition to the scalp.

When the treatment is given with a drug known to cause alopecia, the client should be informed that severe loss can begin within a few days or weeks of treatment and that partial or complete baldness can quickly ensue. The client should also be told that drug-induced alopecia is never permanent. The client may experience a change in hair color or texture when regrowth occurs.

Effects on skin Vesicant drugs may cause severe tissue necrosis if infiltration occurs. Chemotherapy should be administered with caution in older adults because of age-related skin changes. Also, the venous network is often difficult to access, since the veins may be tiny or may roll. Other skin reactions to vesicant drugs that might occur are hyperpigmentation, nail changes, and an increased sensitivity to the sun (photosensitivity) (Schneider, Hogan, 1993; Strohl, 1988).

Urinary effects Hemorrhagic cystitis occurs in about 10% of clients being treated with cyclophosphamide but rarely occurs with other agents. Clients receiving cyclophosphamide are encouraged to drink a large amount of fluid to minimize this effect, unless contraindicated by congestive heart failure. Taking the cyclophosphamide early in the day may also be of some benefit. Renal toxicity is associated with several drugs but most notably with cisplatin and streptozotocin (Schneider, Hogan, 1993).

PSYCHOSOCIAL IMPACT OF CANCER

Because of its catastrophic nature, the diagnosis of cancer is a disease that almost universally generates feelings of stress in the individual on confirmation of the diagnosis. Patterns of cancer threat are as follows: (1) fear of dying, (2) changes in body integrity and comfort, (3) changes in self-concept and disruption of future plans, (4) inability to maintain emotional equilibrium, (5) lack of fulfillment of social roles and activities, and (6) inability to adapt to new physical and social environments. Other negative feelings associated with its diagnosis include loss of control, hopelessness, uncertainty, and lifestyle issues that emerge as a person lives over time with the disease. In addition, cancer and its treatment are known to cause marked and other debilitating changes in a person's spiritual and physiologic ability to function on a daily basis (Baird, McCorkle, Grant, 1991; Welch-McCaffrey et al, 1990).

There is a general consensus that the discovery of cancer is a stressful and traumatic event generating responses ranging from anger to guilt, anxiety to disbelief, and self-pity to bitterness and hostility (Baranovsky, Myers, 1986). It has been documented that feelings change somewhat as the individual moves beyond the diagnosis phase. New challenges and problems, such that the client's emotions change from those initial feelings of shock to those of sheer determination to survive the series of events, are to follow. The nurse must be alert for subtle cues that may indicate that intervention is needed (Guillory, 1992).

During the grieving process, the client and family may go through a period of denial. Anxiety, depression, regressive behavior, and anger may all be manifested and should be anticipated by the health care team. To many, the diagnosis of cancer signifies the end of life itself, the ultimate loss. Nurses must be careful not to communicate any negative reactions to cancer (Welch-McCaffrey et al, 1990). This is an opportune time for the new nurse to assess personal feelings and attitudes toward working with clients diagnosed with cancer.

Insight • *The older person's struggle with cancer can be as much an emotional battle as a physical one. The effects of the disease extend far beyond the physical changes that occur. Older people identify fear, abandonment, dependency, disfigurement, suffering, as well as death and dying as the major sources of emotional distress when dealing with cancer. In addition, the older person with cancer is often angry as a result of the loss of health, self-esteem, independence, or privacy. Changes in body image are also a common problem that pose unique challenges to the older adult with cancer. Therefore psychosocial-related nursing interventions are crucial to the overall care of these clients.*

Cancer, its treatment, and resulting changes in appearance, disabilities, and loss of function often cause a change in body image and can negatively affect a person's self-esteem. Emphasis on physical attractiveness places an additional burden on individuals who must sustain disfigurement or dysfunction from cancer. Changes in body image that are not realistically integrated into the client's self-concept hinder adaptation and adjustment (Baird, McCorkle, Grant, 1991; Schneider, Hogan, 1993; Welch-McCaffrey et al, 1990).

Self-Blame and Guilt

Self-blame is very common with the person who has recently been diagnosed with cancer. Perhaps lifestyle issues have been in conflict with societal rules, or the client may have neglected seeking medical advice. Guilt is a common psychologic response to the cancer diagnosis. Often, the client diagnosed with cancer feels that the disease is a punishment from God. Family members often feel guilty, because they or other family members were not stricken with the disease (Schneider, Hogan, 1993; Welch-McCaffrey et al, 1990).

Sense of Isolation

Perhaps one of the most prevalent reactions described by clients with cancer is a sense of isolation (McCance, Huether, 1990), of being cut off from those people and things of importance. Clients with cancer may report that there is a gradual break in relationships. In some cases, the isolation is client-initiated; in others, it may result from actions of significant others because of their negative attitudes toward the disease. Perhaps the most profound isolation is psychologic isolation, an inability to relate to and derive comfort from others—the feeling of being alone in a crowd (Schneider, Hogan, 1993; Welch-McCaffrey et al, 1990).

> ***Insight*** • *Lack of knowledge places the family in a precarious situation. The family may be on the periphery of the cancer experience, and so may not understand the care and may have difficulty interpreting information from health care providers. Family members of the older client may be old themselves, limiting their abilities to serve as the family advocates. Therefore nursing home placement may become an issue. Refer family members to the social worker early in the client's illness for additional support, information, and resource referral.*

Family Responses to the Cancer Diagnosis

Family members are often distraught and in disbelief when informed of a cancer diagnosis of a loved one. Many times, they need the assistance of a nurse, social worker, or an unbiased person so that they can make immediate and long-term plans.

A diagnosis of cancer in an older person often leads family members to make decisions about treatment and other long-term decisions. Often family members of older people may decide treatment strictly on age rather than disease state. Family members may be encouraged to base decisions about treatment on the client's previous health status and usefulness, and by all means, to take into consideration the desires of the client.

The Nurse's Response to a Cancer Diagnosis of Older Adults

A diagnosis of cancer can also be overwhelming to the inexperienced nurse. When the nurse is confronted with an older client who has recently been diagnosed with cancer, it gives the nurse ample opportunity to confront personal feelings. The care given depends on the nurse's personal philosophy for working with not only the older person but also the older client with cancer.

Many nurses have negative attitudes about working with older adults. Because they are old, many nurses believe that the diagnosis is acceptable, since the older person is "nearing death anyway." Others may feel that the older adult has completed life by the mere fact that they are old. Such feelings may lead the older adult to feel that health providers do not value them.

SPIRITUALITY AND CANCER

Humans, who are three-dimensional (spirit, soul, and body), have sought a oneness with God/divine being/higher power since the beginning of time. Spirituality centers on the belief that people can make contact with a superior power and call on that power for solutions. It encompasses questions about the meaning of life, illness, and death and guides the energy and strength that is present in all human beings (Amenta, 1988; Amenta, Bohnet, 1986; Soeken, Carson, 1987).

Each dimension of spirit, soul, and body affects and is affected by the others. These parts cannot be separated but rather can function as an integrated unit with the whole person being more than the sum of the parts. When illness such as cancer occurs at one level (the physical), it reverberates throughout the other two (Soeken, Carson, 1987).

Often, guilt, fear, anxiety, and resentment are emotions experienced by the person with cancer. Faith in God, a major component of spirituality, is important to overcome these emotions. Faith helps to reaffirm the value of life and gives meaning to it. Faith is the absolute trust in the grace of God. It is the love of God that is believed to remove all guilt, fear, anxiety, and resentment.

Nurses play a major role in spiritual care (Highfield, 1989). Many institutions provide clergy visits; however, it is the nurse who is with the client for 24 hours every day. Since nursing ascribes to the fact that individuals should be cared for in a manner that preserves their uniqueness, then the religious beliefs, rituals, and prayers of clients should be included in comprehensive care.

The minister, priest, or other religious advisors should be included in the client's plan of care. When these religious people visit the client, privacy should be respected, since many people wish to discuss or to confess confidential matters. If the client wishes communion, the nurse may assist the minister by providing any necessary articles for this ceremony (Amenta, Bohnet, 1986).

Older adults may have religious articles such as the Bible, the Koran, or other items at the bedside. The nurse should be aware that articles such as a crucifix, religious medals, prayer shawls, handkerchiefs, small bottles with oil, or other items may be found at the bedside and should not be tampered with or thrown away.

Privacy should be maintained if the client wishes to meditate. If religious services are available, every effort should be made to assist the client to attend.

Often, clients who are experiencing distress of the human spirit may request the nurse to pray with them. This request should be honored to the extent that the nurse is comfortable. If the nurse is uncomfortable praying, another health care provider should be called, or the nurse may wish to read to the client from one of the religious books available. A complete spiritual assessment should be conducted on admission to the health care facility from which a plan of care can be developed that addresses the client's spirituality.

In providing spiritual care, the nurses may need some assistance in assessing their own spirituality. If the nurse is anxious or uncomfortable about spiritual care, perhaps a reassignment is necessary. The concept of spirituality has grown significantly over the past several decades and is believed to be the integral dimension of cancer survivorship.

Summary

For many people, cancer remains a mysterious disease. The incidence of most cancers increases with advancing age. Yet is has only been in recent years that attention has been given to the special needs of the older adult in relation to cancer screening and early awareness. Recent studies also indicate that older people have little knowledge of their risk for cancer.

Nursing must play an integral role in decreasing the mortality of cancer. Cancer mortality cannot be decreased without the efforts of society in general. Although the public is overloaded with information about prevention, cause, and treatment, still more can be done. Nurses can identify high risk people and can teach them that they can incorporate lifestyle practices to decrease their chance of cancer. Because the incidence of cancer increases with age, nurses can assist older people to differentiate between the warning signals of cancer and the symptoms of the normal aging process. In addition to teaching and identifying high-risk people, nurses can have a significant impact in the fight against cancer by being positive role models.

HOME CARE TIPS

1. Instruct caregivers and homebound older adults to be aware of and to report symptoms associated with the seven warning signs of cancer.
2. Breast cancer is a disease of older women, thus breast screening is a lifelong process. Instruct homebound older women on the American Cancer Society's modified guidelines for BSE.
3. Assess nonspecific symptoms such as indigestion, loss of appetite, and weight loss in both older men and women. These warning signs are seen in cancer of the stomach, colon, or rectum.
4. Instruct caregivers and homebound older adults with cancer on general comfort measures to promote rest and sleep, with the goal of increasing pain tolerance in older adults.
5. Assess for side effects of cancer treatment therapies (e.g., radiation therapy, chemotherapy), and report to physician as needed for treatment recommendations.
6. Instruct caregivers and homebound older adults on measures to reduce side effects of cancer treatment therapies.
7. Refer to hospice during last 6 months of terminal illness.

Key Points

- The three most prevalent malignancies and leading cause of death in women between ages 55 and 74 are lung, breast, and colorectal cancer; in men, between these same ages, the most deaths occur from lung, colorectal, and prostate cancer.
- Clinical manifestation of a malignancy in older people may be mistakenly attributed to normal, age-related changes. Therefore it is essential that older people be aware of and report symptoms associated with the seven warning signs of cancer to health care providers.
- Alterations in cell-mediated immunity with increasing age contributes to the increased incidence of cancer in older people.
- The incidence of skin cancer increases with advancing age, usually occurring in people between the ages of 50 and 60, as a result of the cumulative lifetime sun exposure.
- The nurse caring for older people has a major responsibility to recommend select strategies aimed at the prevention and early detection of cancer in this age group.
- The clinical manifestations of cancer in older people (pain, cachexia, and anorexia) may be diverse and affect a variety of body systems. The nurse must be aware of the signs and symptoms associated with these manifestations to aid in early detection and to monitor the side effects of therapy.
- The major treatment modalities for cancer include surgery, radiotherapy, chemotherapy, and immunotherapy. Therapy with any of these modalities may be curative or palliative.
- The older person undergoing a major surgical resection or reconstruction as a result of cancer is at greater risk for postoperative complications. Although age is not necessarily a contraindication to a surgical procedure, it does mean the older surgical candidate requires nursing care aimed at preventing respiratory complications, and promoting cardiac and renal function.
- The older adult is especially vulnerable to the hematologic toxic side effects of chemotherapeutic agents.
- Nursing care of the older adult with cancer includes interventions aimed at managing the psychosocial impact of the disease and spiritual care.

Critical Thinking Exercises

1. Of the risk factors that can be generalized to all age groups, identify those that place the older adult at greater risk for cancer.
2. You are caring for two women ages 32 and 74. Each has breast cancer and is schelduled for a modified radical mastectomy. Discuss how these two women are likely to differ with regard to their psychologic reaction to the diagnosis and surgery.
3. A 74-year-old woman has severe rheumatoid arthritis. Discuss how you would assist her in adjusting her technique for a BSE.

REFERENCES

Alkire K, Groenwald SL: Relation of the immune system to cancer. In Groenwald S et al, editors: *Cancer nursing: principles and practice,* Boston, 1990, Jones and Bartlett.

Allen L, Britt DW: Black women in American society: a resource development perspective, *Iss Ment Health Nurs* 5(4):61-79, 1983.

Amenta M: Nurses as primary spiritual care workers, *Hospice J* 4(3):47-55, 1988.

Amenta M, Bohnet E: *Nursing care of the terminally ill,* Boston, 1986, Little, Brown.

American Cancer Society: *Cancer facts and figures,* Atlanta, 1995, The Society.

American Cancer Society: *Cancer facts and figures,* Atlanta, 1994, The Society.

American Cancer Society: *Cancer facts and figures,* Atlanta, 1993, The Society.

Averette H, Boike, Jarrell M: Effects of cancer chemotherapy on gonadal function and reproductive capacity, *CA* 40(40):199-209, 1990.

Baird SB, McCorkle R, Grant M, editors: *Cancer nursing: a comprehensive textbook,* Philadelphia, 1991, WB Saunders.

Baquet C, Ringer K, Young J: *Cancer among Blacks and other minorities statistical profiles,* NIH Pub. No. 86-2785, 1986, Bethesda, Md., National Cancer Institute.

Baranovsky A, Myers MH: Cancer incidence and survival in patients 65 years of age and older, *CA* 36(1):26-41, 1986.

Belcher A: *Cancer nursing,* St. Louis, 1992, Mosby.

Boring C, Squires T, Tong T: Cancer statistics, *CA* 44(1):7-26, 1994.

Breiele H, Walker M, Wild L, Wood F: Results of treatment of stage I-III breast cancer in Black Americans: the Cook County hospital experience, 1973-1987, *Cancer* 65(5):1062-1071, 1986.

Cox EB: Breast Cancer in the elderly, *Clin Geriatr Med* 3(4):695-713, 1987.

Ferrell B, Schneider C: Effects of controlled released morphine on quality of life for cancer patients, *Oncol Nurs Forum* 16(4):521-526, 1989.

Goodman M, Harte N: Breast cancer. In Groenwald S et al, editors: *Cancer nursing: principles and practice,* Boston, 1991, Jones and Bartlett.

Guillory J: *Relationships of selected physiological, psychosocial and spiritual variables associated with survivorship in African American women breast cancer,* dissertation, Augusta, Ga., 1992, Medical College of Georgia.

Guillory J: Breast Cancer: a serious threat to elderly women, *J women aging* 6(1-2):151-164, 1994.

Guillory J: Cancer of the breast in socioeconomically disadvantaged African American and elderly women, *Innov Oncol* 9(1):1, 15-18, 1993.

Highfield M: *The spiritual health of oncology patients: a comparison of nurse and patient perception,* Unpublished doctoral dissertation, Denton, Tex., 1989, Texas Woman's University.

Kart C, Metress E, Metress S: *Human aging and chronic disease,* Boston, 1992, Jones and Bartlett.

Kupchell C: The spread of cancer: Invasion and metastasis. In Groenwald S, Frogg M, Goodman M, Yarbro C, editors: *Cancer nursing: principles and practice,* Boston, 1991, Jones and Bartlett.

Larson P et al: Influence of age on problems experienced by patients with lung cancer undergoing radiation therapy, *Oncol Nurs Forum,* 20(3): 473-480, 1993.

McCance K, Huether S: Pathophysiology: *The biologic basis for disease in adults and children,* St. Louis, 1990, Mosby.

Office of Technology Assessment: *Life sustaining technologies and the elderly,* Washington, D.C., 1987, US Government Printing Office.

Olson SJ, Frank-Stromberg M: Cancer screening and early detection. In Baird S, McCorkle R, Grant M, editors: *Cancer nursing: a comprehensive textbook,* Philadelphia, 1991, WB Saunders.

Otto S, editor: *Oncology nursing,* St. Louis, 1991, Mosby.

Otto S, Fraser G, Kellerstrass B: Gynecologic Cancer. In Otto S, editor: *Oncology nursing,* St. Louis, 1991, Mosby.

Paige H, Asire A: *Cancer rates and risk,* ed 3, NIH Pub. No. 85-691, Washington, D.C., 1985, US Government Printing Office.

Schneider S M, Hogan R: Cancer. In Long BC, Phipps WJ, Cassmeyer VL, editors: *Medical-surgical nursing: a nursing approach,* ed 3, St. Louis, 1993, Mosby.

Soeken KL, Carson VJ: Responding to the spiritual needs of the chronically ill, *Nurs Clin North Am* 22(3):603-609, 1987.

Strohl R: The nursing role in radiation oncology: symptom management of acute and chronic reactions, *Oncol Nurs Forum* 15(4):429-434, 1988.

Vannicola P: *An overview of the physiologic changes of aging and their effects on cancer,* Atlanta, 1988, American Cancer Society.

Welch-McCaffrey D et al: Psychosocial dimensions: issues in survivorship. In Groenwald S, Frogge M, Goodman M, Yarbro C, editors: *Cancer nursing: principles and practice,* ed 3, Boston, 1990, Jones and Bartlett.

Weinrich S et al: Knowledge of colorectal cancer among older persons, *Cancer Nurs* (15): 322-330, 1992.

Williams RD: Factors affecting the practice of breast self-examination of older women, *Oncol Nurs Forum* 15(5): 611-616, 1988.

Wirgo PA, Tong T, Bolden S: Cancer statistics, 1995, *CA: Cancer J Clinicians* 45(1), Jan/Feb, 1995.

CHAPTER 16

Chronic Illness and Rehabilitation

LEARNING OBJECTIVES

On completion of this chapter, the reader will be able to:

1. Explain reasons for the expansion of chronic conditions.
2. Define chronic illness and rehabilitation.
3. Apply the trajectory concept to a chronic condition.
4. Identify nursing goals in chronic care and rehabilitation.
5. Plan interventions that support an older adult's adaptation to a chronic illness or disability.
6. Analyze the nurse's role in assisting clients to manage a chronic condition.
7. Develop ways in which the nurse can assist families to manage caregiver stress.
8. Identify opportunities for change in the health care system to improve care for the disabled older adult.

CHRONICITY

Chronic illness is a biopsychosocial phenomenon. Chron-ic conditions occur more often in the adult age 65 or older, and these conditions persist for longer periods. The nurse's concern for the whole person is central to the care of the older adult with a chronic condition. In assessing the older adult, the nurse should be aware of age-related changes and pathologic alterations. How do multiple diseases affect one another? Living with a chronic disease affects interactions with others and lifestyle. Many chronically ill older adults become homebound, and this decreased contact with the community leads to social isolation. Isolation can be compounded by changes in personal relationships, leading to problems with marriage and family. The chronically ill may perceive themselves as burdens, and families often experience caregiver stress. By nature, chronic illnesses are long-term and expensive. Funding the treatments necessary for survival is another challenge for the older adult. The nurse should be aware of the socioeconomic losses the older adult may sustain. It is necessary for the nurse to understand the payment systems that are regulated by state and federal governments so that reimbursement issues can be addressed when planning care with the older adult.

Chronic conditions are increasing in proportion to life-saving technologies, an expanding population of older adults, and increasing life expectancy (Ebersole, Hess, 1994). Older adults who in the past would have succumbed to an acute illness now recover to live with chronic conditions. In addition to the health and medical contexts of life, chronic illness spans the political, economic, social, and cultural contexts. In 1993 nearly half of all adults age 65 and older reported some limitation of activity as a result of a chronic condition (Table 16-1). Approximately 47% of women age 75 and older experienced total limitation of activity. The black population age 75 or older had the greatest percentage (53.6%) of activity limitation.

Even though the prevalence of chronic conditions has created additional complex issues for the health care industry, most health care services remain oriented to acute, episodic illness. The result is often a conflict between expectations of the person with a chronic illness and those of health care providers. The conflict may result in dissatisfaction and a diminished level of care.

The acute care model is based on diagnosis, treatment, and interventions designed to cure illness. In contrast, the care of a client with a chronic condition is based on the fact that recovery will not occur. Consequently, nursing care activities are focused on goals aimed at increasing functional ability, delaying deterioration, promoting the highest quality of life, and providing comfort and dignity in dying. A key role for the nurse caring for an older adult with a chronic condition is to facilitate the client's coping skills and strategies.

Health care providers typically view an ill older person within a disease framework, whereas people with chronic conditions identify their situation in much broader terms. The older adult may see the medical or illness aspect of the condition as only one part of the life changes required. More important may be economic, work life, and role changes within the family. The older adult may face problems accessing community resources, or may confront legislative barriers or the social stigma of the disabled.

Defining Chronic Illness

The Commission of Chronic Illness (1951) defined **chronic illness** as the following:

> All impairments or deviations from normal which have one or more of the following characteristics: (a) are permanent, (b) leave residual disability, (c) are caused by nonreversible pathological alteration, (d) require special training of the client for rehabilitation and (e) may be expected to require a long period of supervision, observation or care.

This definition is still widely used. Lubkin (1990) defined chronic illness as the following:

> ... the irreversible presence, accumulation, or latency of disease states or impairments that involve the total human environment for supportive care and self-care, maintenance of function and prevention of further disability.

Chronic illness may be differentiated from acute illness by duration. Therefore a chronic illness is an impairment lasting 3 months or longer, that has ongoing psychosocial and economic complications, and requires involvement of health care professionals for support and maintenance of the client's self-care capacity.

Prevalence of Chronic Illness

The incidence of chronic illness triples in adults over age 45 (Ebersole, Hess, 1994). Table 16-2 depicts the estimated number of people in the United States with chronic conditions. Coronary artery disease, hypertension, and arthritis affect the largest groups of people. The most prevalent chronic conditions for men 65 and older include hearing impairment, arthritis, heart disease, hypertension, vision impairment, and orthopedic

TABLE 16-1

Limitation of Activity Caused by Chronic Conditions (1991)

	Percent of population			
	Total loss	Limited but not in major activity	Limited in amount or kind of major activity	Unable to carry on major activity
Men age 65 to 74	36.1	14.3	9.8	12.1
Men age 75 and older	42.5	22.1	10.9	9.4
Women age 65 to 74	33.1	13.1	11	9
Women age 75 and older	46.9	16.4	18.5	12
White age 65 to 74	34	13.8	10.4	9.8
White age 75 and older	44.6	18.8	15.3	10.4
Black age 65 to 74	41.4	13.3	11.4	16.6
Black age 75 and older	53.6	16.9	18.7	18

Modified from National Center for Health Statistics, US Department of Health and Human Services, May 1994.

TABLE 16-2

Estimated Number of People in United States with Selected Chronic Conditions

Condition	Number
Coronary artery disease	66,000,000
Hypertension	58,000,000
Arthritis all types	37,000,000
Hearing impairment	13,000,000
Diabetes	11,000,000
Asthma	9,600,000
Mental retardation	6,700,000
Cancer	5,000,000
Alzheimer's disease	3,000,000
Blindness	1,000,000
Spinal cord injury	500,000
Stroke	500,000

From US Department of Health and Human Services: *Prevalence of selected chronic conditions,* 1993.

TABLE 16-3

Rank Order Prevalence of Chronic Conditions by Gender per 1,000 People Age 65 or Older (1990)

Men	
Condition	**Rate**
Hearing impairment	830
Arthritis	750
Heart disease	680
Hypertension	589
Vision impairment	382
Orthopedic impairment	273
Women	
Condition	**Rate**
Arthritis	1,100
Hypertension	853
Hearing impairment	564
Vision impairment	546
Heart disease	534
Orthopedic impairment	501

From US Bureau of Census: *Statistical abstract of the United States,* ed 113, 1993, Washington, D.C., The Bureau.

TABLE 16-4

Hospital Discharges and Days of Care by Age, Gender and Diagnoses (1991) per 1,000 People

	Number of discharges	Days of care	Days of stay
Men age 65 and older	4,708	3,056.5	8.3
Heart disease	1,107	611.2	7.1
Malignant neoplasm	455	369.9	10.4
Pneumonia	286	215.4	9.6
Cerebrovascular	263	195.5	9.5
Prostate	180	67	4.8
Women age 65 and older	6,098	2,839.6	8.8
Heart disease	1,254	480	7.3
Malignant neoplasm	428	221.8	9.8
Cerebrovascular	377	196	9.9
Fractures	346	208.5	11.4
Pneumonia	303	171.3	10.7

From US Bureau of Census: *Statistical abstract of the United States,* ed 113, 1993, Washington, D.C., The Bureau.

impairment. For women 65 and older the rank order changes. Arthritis is first, followed by hypertension, hearing impairment, vision impairment, heart disease, and orthopedic impairment (Table 16-3).

People with chronic conditions typically have repeated hospitalizations to treat exacerbations of their illness. For men over age 65, the most common diagnoses for hospitalization are heart disease, malignant neoplasm, pneumonia, and cerebrovascular disease (Table 16-4). For women over age 65, the most common reasons for hospitalization are heart disease, malignant neo-plasm, cerebrovascular disease, fractures, and pneumonia. The average hospital stay for a male older adult was 8.3 days, whereas female older adults stayed 8.8 days.

The picture of chronic conditions broadens when leading causes of death for people over age 65 are added.

Chronic conditions are not only the leading cause of disability and activity restriction but are also the leading cause of death. Each of the leading causes of death noted in Table 16-5, with the exceptions of accidents and suicide, has a chronic condition or component.

TABLE 16-5

Leading Causes of Death for Persons Age 65 or Older 1991

Cause of death	Rate per 100,000 population
Heart disease	597.3
Malignant neoplasm	354.7
Cerebrovascular disease	125.1
Chronic obstructive pulmonary disease (COPD)	76.4
Pneumonia and influenza	68.9
Diabetes	36.5
Unintentional injury	26.4
Septicemia	15.8
Suicide	12.7

From National Center for Heatlh Statistics, US Department of Health and Human Services, May 1994.

BOX 16-1

Trajectory of Diabetes Mellitus

Pretrajectory - Risk factors for diabetes: hypertension, atherosclerosis, smoking, obesity, hyperlipidemia, and family history of diabetes.

Trajectory - Disruption of metabolism (glucose), increased appetite, increased thirst, increased urine volume, pruritus vulvae, weight loss, weakness, and fatigue.

Crisis - Increased risk of cardiovascular, renal, and neurologic sensory problems; uncontrollable blood glucose levels; and possible ketoacidosis.

Acute - Rehabilitation and recovery; learn skin care, medications, actions to take with signs and symptoms, blood glucose monitoring, diet, and exercise.

Stable - Blood glucose levels stable; free from infection; adaptating to lifestyle changes.

Unstable - Disruption of metabolism that may be a result of infection, poor compliance with methods to control or to monitor, illness, or stress.

Downward - Cardiovascular, renal, and neurologic complications; blindness, dementia, or amputations as a result of vascular changes.

Dying - Multisystem organ failure resulting from degenerative changes, diabetic ketoacidosis, myocardial infarction (MI), gastroparesis, end-stage renal failure, and stroke.

Chronic Illness Trajectory

The trajectory model of chronic illness was created by Anselm Strauss in 1975. This model charts the course of illness through eight phases. Movement through these phases may be in any direction or may be plateaued. In chronic illness, the trajectory model includes a pretrajectory phase, or preventive phase, in which the course of illness has not yet begun. The trajectory onset includes the diagnostic period showing signs and symptoms of the illness. The crisis phase can be a life-threatening period unless treatment begins. In the acute phase, hospitalization is required for management of the active illness or its complications. When a regimen is developed to control the course of the illness or symptoms, the older adult enters the stable phase. The unstable phase is defined by the illness or symptoms becoming uncontrollable. The downward phase is characterized by progressive deterioration and increasing disability or symptoms. The trajectory model ends with the dying phase.

The trajectory of chronic illness varies with the individual and the illness. It may progress slowly or unpredictably with exacerbations and remissions, or it may be influenced by other disorders and treatments. Box 16-1 depicts the trajectory of diabetes mellitus.

The trajectory model of chronic illness facilitates the comprehensive, holistic view of the client, which is the focus of nursing. Its use encourages plans of care that go beyond the physical aspects of the condition to encompass social, emotional, psychologic, economic, cultural, and technologic considerations. One nursing goal for chronic conditions, using trajectory concepts, can be to maintain a plateau over a long period of time. Another goal can be clarifying and resolving differences in how the course of the condition is perceived by the older adult and provider. Older individuals in an unstable phase may have the goal of gaining greater control over their symptoms that are interfering with quality of life or impeding activities of daily living (ADLs).

Maslow's model of the five levels of need that affect function and self-perception complement the trajectory model. The older adult's perception of needs and biologic functional limitations can predict movement within the illness trajectory. For example, an older adult with chronic obstructive pulmonary disease may be malnourished because of increased energy expenditure to breathe. Malnutrition and inadequate oxygen exchange threaten this older person's biologic integrity. Weakened by malnutrition and unable to breathe, the older adult is not interested in exploring productive, sedentary activities to increase self-esteem, until treatment meets these basic survival needs. If such survival needs are not met, the trajectory of the illness proceeds downward. Wellness in chronic illness is a continuum, from treatment to maximizing life satisfaction (Ebersole, Hess, 1994). The nurse's approach to wellness with an older adult who has a chronic condition should include interventions to assist the older adult in meeting as many of Maslow's de-

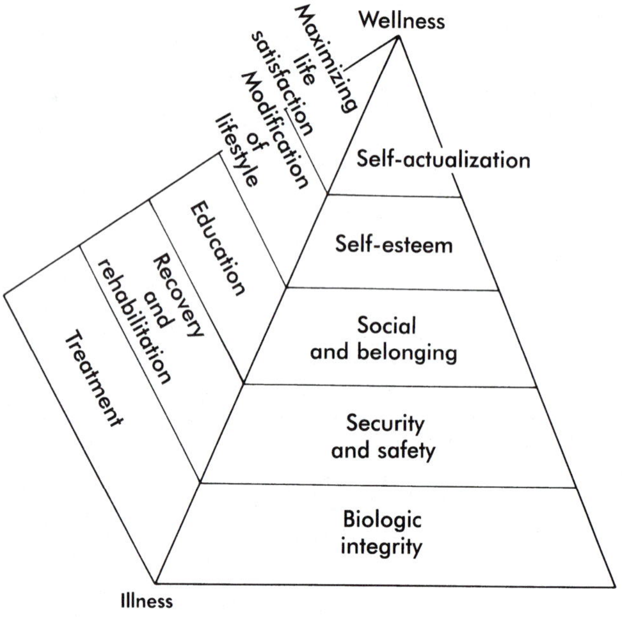

Fig. 16-1 Correlation between illness-wellness continuum and Maslow's hierarchy of needs. (From Ebersole P, Hess P: *Toward healthy aging: human needs and nursing response*, ed 4, St. Louis, 1994, Mosby.)

fined needs as possible. Fig. 16-1 shows the correlation between the illness-wellness continuum and Maslow's hierarchy of needs.

For example, to achieve maximum life satisfaction and optimum wellness, diabetics must change their lifestyle. The initial priorities include (1) restoring fluid and electrolyte balance, which may be associated with osmotic diuresis from hyperglycemia; and (2) correcting metabolic abnormalities related to insulin deficiency. This causes decreased uptake and use of glucose by the tissues, which results in increased protein and fat metabolism. After homeostasis is achieved, the nurse can teach the older adult diabetic about the disease process, management of the disease, self-care needs, and the therapeutic regimen. The nurse and the older adult can work together to identify food preferences, incorporating these with ethnic and cultural choices into the meal plan. The nurse can teach the older adult how to perform finger stick glucose testing and how to administer insulin (Fig. 16-2). By incorporating older adults' preferences into their therapeutic regimens, the nurse promotes their feelings of involvement. As the older adult learns how to control diabetes, he or she can make the necessary adaptations to achieve wellness and control over the chronic illness. These adaptations include dietary modifications, glucose monitoring, use of medications, ways to prevent or to reduce risk of infection, establishment of an exercise regimen, and smoking cessation. Continued support is usually necessary to sustain lifestyle changes and to promote well-being. The nurse can provide the older adult information on community resources such as the American Diabetes Association, home health nursing, weight loss, or smoking-cessation clinics. Without lifestyle adaptation, the older adult's diabetes can enter an unstable trajectory.

Features of chronic illness must be understood by the nurse to effectively assist the older adult in influencing or changing the trajectory of the illness. Strauss and Corbin (1988) identified the features of chronic illness to be the following:

- Long-term
- Uncertain
- Requiring great efforts for palliation
- Requiring a variety of ancillary services
- Expensive
- Intrusive
- The goal of which is to maintain a stable phase of trajectory

The following case study demonstrates how these features of chronic illness and how trajectory of one illness are influenced by the superimposition of other disorders.

Case Study

Mr. A, a 67-year-old African-American man, was hospitalized for a unilateral below-knee (BK) amputation. He also had end-stage renal disease (ESRD), for which he has been receiving hemodialysis 3 times a week for 2 years. His length of hospital stay and rehabilitation was 54 days, compared with the average of 36 days. On discharge he was prosthetically restored and independent in ambulation. The factors that affected the trajectory of his illness were ESRD, anemia, deconditioning, and depression. These factors imposed exercise and endurance limitations, which lengthened his stay, recovery, and rehabilitation.

Depression in the older adult also contributes to a lack of psychic energy that can further impede physical recovery. The addition of the amputation further interfered with his level of function because of the high-energy cost of using a prosthesis. Energy requirements increase at least 25% in unilateral BK amputees (Sioson, Kerfoot, Ziat, 1993).

In addition to nursing care, Mr. A required a variety of ancillary services, including physical and occupational therapy, hemodialysis, a prosthetist, a psychiatrist, and social services. His stay was more expensive because of the comorbidity of ESRD. Medical and nursing efforts were also directed at maintaining his ESRD in the stable phase of its trajectory.

A paradigm shift is needed when deciding what con-

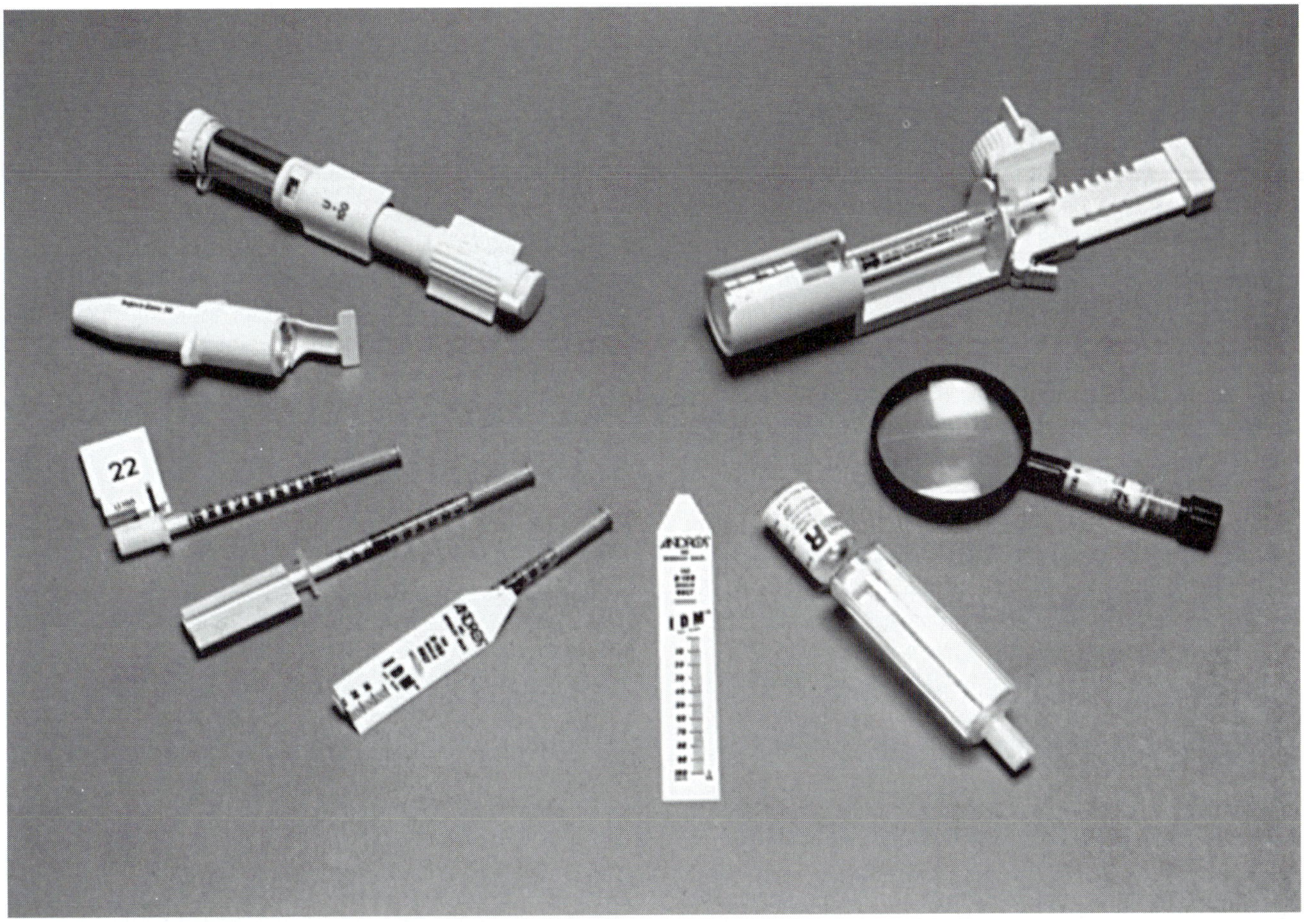

Fig. 16-2 Insulin injection devices. These are particularly well-suited for visually impaired people but the jet injector and Inject-Ease can be used by persons who have trouble injecting themselves. *Left to right:* Jet Injector, Inject-Ease, BD chip, generic syringe chip, Andros IDM on syringe, Andros IDM, BD Magnifier, generic magnifier, Insul-ease device. (From Phipps WJ et al: *Medical-surgical nursing: concepts and clinical practice,* ed 5, St. Louis, 1995, Mosby.)

stitutes wellness in a chronic illness. Health care providers see the older adult in a disease framework, whereas the individual may see the medical or illness aspect of the condition as only one part of life. Once the physical care requirements imposed by the condition are learned and mastered, older adults may view themselves as "well." The greatest factor in achieving wellness is adaptation (Ebersole, Hess, 1994). The physical traits of chronic illness should not determine the older adult's state of wellness. Many older adults are now more involved in their health care and are accepting responsibility for their wellness. They are seeking education about health promotion and management of their illness. The nurse can support older adults by working with them to identify areas that may be hindering progress along the wellness continuum and providing health teaching for self-care management in these areas.

Case Study

Mrs. B, a 70-year-old insulin-dependent woman who has had diabetes for 10 years, is able to self-monitor her blood glucose and to administer her insulin. She confides in her nurse that when she cheats on her diet, she "ups the insulin a little and that fixes it." The nurse also discovers that Mrs. B trims her corns with a razor blade. Mrs. B expresses great pride in taking care of herself and being independent.

How can the nurse in this case channel Mrs. B's desire for independence into safer actions that are health-promoting? The goal is to assist and to support Mrs. B in making attitude and lifestyle changes to maintain the stable phase of her diabetes and to prevent complications. To achieve these goals, the nurse emphasized Mrs. B's abilities rather than limitations. For example, the nurse reviewed the relationship between insulin and diet, as well as proper foot care. The nurse and Mrs. B reviewed her dietary program, usual eating pattern, and recent intake to identify deficits and deviations from her therapeutic needs. The nurse reinforced with Mrs. B that with correct insulin dosage, glucose can enter the cells and be used for energy. Complex carbohydrates such as corn, peas, carrots, and broccoli can decrease glucose levels and insulin needs, and can promote satiation.

The nurse also reminded Mrs. B that her peripheral circulation may be impaired, which places her at risk for skin breakdown and infection. The nurse taught Mrs. B to inspect her feet daily for signs of infection and inflammation, including redness, flushed appearance, and open sores or drainage. Mrs. B learned to dry her feet thoroughly after bathing and to keep her skin dry. She was instructed to keep her feet warm but to avoid hot water or the use of a heating pad. Sudden development of cold hands or feet may reflect hypoglycemia and her blood glucose level should be tested. Mrs. B came to the understanding that receiving foot care from the podiatrist was not being dependent but was a responsible decision. Mrs. B also accepted the referral to the dietician, and together they created a diet plan that included more of her favorite foods but remained within her caloric limitations.

Quality of Life and Perceived Health

Quality of life is an issue of both importance and frustration in gerontologic nursing. Advancement of knowledge in gerontologic nursing requires integration of theory and research (Moore et al, 1993). Researchers continue to struggle with a variety of definitions and techniques to measure the quality of life. A single definition of quality of life and a reliable method of measurement are yet to be developed. A review of gerontologic nursing research (1980-1990) revealed that terminology regarding the quality of life and perceived health were inconsistent (Moore et al, 1993). Current nursing research indicates a strong positive relationship between perception of health and quality of life in the older adult (Lang et al, 1990; Moore et al, 1993).

The importance of self-perceived health in the older adult must be recognized by nurses and reflected in their practice. Many historic non-nursing studies have demonstrated that self-perceived health is significantly related to quality of life for older adults (Edwards, 1973; Spreitzer, 1974; Harris, 1976). These studies are the foundation from which nurse researchers examine the relationship between quality of life and self-perceived health. Lang's (1990) review of 476 nursing studies on the quality of life for the older adult found that life satisfaction was related to better health perception and internal locus of control. Additional research is needed to develop and to test interventions. There is also a paucity of nursing theories to use as a framework for such research. See the Research box above for the relationship of stress and perceived health in rural older adults.

RESEARCH

Johnson J, Waldo M, Johnson R: Research considerations: stress and perceived health status in the rural elderly, *J Gerontolog Nurs* 19(10):24-29, 1993.

Sample, setting

Subjects included 50 women and 32 men, ages 64 to 98 from rural areas in western United States who were noninstitutionalized.

Methodology

Stress was measured using the Stokes-Gordon Stress Scale. Perceived health was measured by the Perceived Health Status Questionnaire.

Findings

Results of this study must be interpreted cautiously because of the small sample. The findings suggest that rural older adults experience a high level of stress and a fair-to-poor level of health. The most common stressful life events were sleep changes (64%), decreasing number of friends (63%), and loneliness (61%). Married people reported better health and less stress. There was no significant relationship between gender and stress level, or gender and perceived health.

Implications

Nurses who care for older adults in rural areas need to be aware that there is a direct relationship between stress levels and perceived health. The nurse should assess the amount of stress a client is experiencing and be alert to its impact on health. Nurses need to be aware that some events are more stressful for the rural adult. Loss, changes in financial status, and decreased self-care activities may be a greater stress because of the isolation of living in a rural area. The nurse can then develop strategies to mediate the stress experienced and to enhance coping skills.

Health Belief and Compliance in Chronic Illness

Compliance occurs when older adults change their behavior to follow medical or health-related instructions. Noncompliance to therapeutic regimens is a major problem for older adults living with a chronic illness (Ebersole, Hess, 1994). Nonadherance in long-term health programs is very high. More than 50% fail to maintain compliance with instructions provided at discharge (Rhodes, Morrissey, Ward, 1992). Therapeutic regimens require adherence to certain behaviors and perseverance in these behaviors is necessary for success.

Many complex issues surround noncompliance. Self-motivation has been linked to compliance (Rhodes, Morrissey, Ward, 1992). Self-motivation is "socially learned, and dependent on the ability to delay gratification and on the capacity for self-reinforcement" (Rhodes, Morrissey, Ward, 1992).

In addition to self-motivation, another issue affecting compliance is self-destructive behaviors. The older adult may have engaged in a lifetime habit of self-destructive behaviors. What does the individual gain from these behaviors? Does the older adult with congestive heart failure receive more attention from his family if he does not comply with his sodium restriction? Does he equate scolding from his family as love? What is his definition of quality of life? Is quality of life related to a long life dependent on a program of lifestyle changes or a shortened life of doing exactly as he wants? If his chronic illness becomes stable does his role in the family change? How do we, as members of society, contribute to noncompliance through regulations and policies? These are just a few of the issues that surround noncompliance for the older adult.

Because of increased life expectancy, the older adult population has grown at a rate of 3.5 times that of the overall U.S. population since 1900 (Gershkoff, Cifu, Means, 1993). Butler (1991) calls this "the century of old age." Since 1980 there has been a 9% increase in chronic disorders (Ebersole, Hess, 1994). These changes in the U.S. population have increased the rehabilitative needs of older adults. For example, each year, 5.4 million people are diagnosed with coronary artery disease with an estimated annual direct health cost of $8 billion (Rhodes, Morrissey, Ward, 1992). Within the older adult population, this disease affects one of every two people (Rhodes, Morrissey, Ward, 1992). In spite of highly technical and advanced acute care, many chronically ill people are readmitted to the hospital with the same problem. This self-defeating process may be offset by the present-day emphasis on rehabilitation. However, the success of any therapeutic regimen depends on compliance. The nurse plays an important role in facilitating the older adult's adherence to the regimen.

The nurse must first assess the older adult's belief in the mutually established outcomes and the energy required for compliance (Ebersole, Hess, 1994). The assessment should include identification of strengths such as self-motivation. Studies suggest that self-motivation does not change with age, therefore the older adult has every promise of complying as any other age group (Rhodes, Morrissey, Ward, 1992).

An environmental assessment aids in the reduction of risk factors for the older adult. In assessing the older adult's home, the nurse should observe for safety hazards such as throw rugs that increase the chance of tripping and falling, which can possibly cause a hip fracture. Safety handrails can be installed by the toilet, tub, and shower. A tub bench can be used to prevent falls and fatigue during bathing. If the toilet is too low, a raised toilet seat can be installed. For some older adults, the access to the bathroom may be difficult. The bathroom may be upstairs and the older adult may have difficulty climbing the stairs in time or at all. The assessment should include heating and cooling of the home. Many older adults live at or below the poverty level and are on fixed incomes. They may be forced to choose between heat, medications, and food. Interventions include referrals to appropriate resources, health-promotion teaching, lifestyle modifications, and means of improving function.

The cost of today's health care requires that nurses be aware of specific needs of older adults in structuring their therapeutic regimens. Regimens should place emphasis on activities that build endurance and self-reliance to facilitate self-care and quality of life. Compliance is directly related to hope (Ebersole, Hess, 1994). Older adults must believe that a therapeutic regimen aids in recovery or maintenance of their functional level.

Positive Coping

Personal perceptions and coping strategies can be the most important aspect of dealing with a chronic illness (Davidhizar, 1992). The way older people view their situations and their personality strengths are often more crucial than how a situation is handled. Older adults may perceive chronic illness in terms of loss (i.e., loss of money, love, or independence). Each older adult may view his or her situation as one more adaptation in a changing life. An older adult's interest in life may undermine his or her ability to deal with a chronic illness. Personal coping strategies include the ability to solve problems in managing care, including environmental changes and adaptation to untoward events in the illness. An older adult must also maintain his or her self-image, including social relationships.

Case Study

Mrs. D is a 65-year-old woman who has been married for 40 years. She is receiving home health services following a cerebrovascular accident (CVA) with left hemiparesis. On the nurse's first visit to Mrs. D's home, she noticed that Mrs. D appeared depressed and withdrawn. She established eye contact only when discussing her role as a wife and homemaker. Mrs. D felt significant loss regarding these roles, which were crucial to her self-image. Her husband did not understand her feelings. He felt she should appreciate everything he was doing for her. The nurse assisted Mr. and Mrs. D in confronting the loss of identity Mrs. D felt and Mr. D's response to his wife's disability. The nurse focused on homemaking tasks that Mrs. D could perform from her wheelchair, such as meal prep and laundry. The nurse referred Mr. and Mrs. D to a community agency that provided homemaker assistance. Mrs. D planned the meals and the homemaker did the grocery shopping. Mrs. D made decisions about how her house should be run, and she regained her sense of purpose. The nurse identified the stresses Mr. and Mrs. D were experiencing as a result of their role reversals and helped them to cope with Mrs. D's disability.

Changes in positions within the family affect family duties and responsibilities. Successful coping requires a positive attitude toward new roles and the ability to obtain a feeling of independence and security (Miller, 1992). Traditional roles are often masked in the hospital, and on returning home, the client feels that everything will be fine. However, the transition from hospital to home is often difficult for the client and family. They discover how much has changed, and they begin to face their losses. Roles may need to be renegotiated, and those no longer applicable must be acknowledged and mourned (Miller, 1992).

The nurse can guide, educate, and support the older adult and family in developing positive coping strategies. Understanding the illness and what to expect is directly related to the ability to cope (Davidhizar, 1992). In providing support to the older adult and family, the nurse assists them in identifying their feelings.

One of the most difficult tasks in adjustment is balancing hope and realism (Miller, 1992). The client and family may need to express frustration and anger with the course of the illness and rehabilitation. By setting mutually agreed on goals in small increments, the nurse and the older adult can note achievements. Personal coping also involves problem solving. The nurse serves as a resource for the older adult and family in solving care management problems.

A supportive social network also has been found to have significant impact on stress (Davidhizar, 1992). Referrals for day care, home health nursing, temporary long-term care, or respite care may be needed.

Another obstacle is understanding and coping with role reversals. The nurse can guide the older adult in finding tasks and responsibilities within the new role and can assist in conflict resolution as old roles are redefined.

Chronic illness requires long-term adaptation on the part of the older adult and family. Ongoing support by health care professionals is crucial for the older adult and family to feel enough power to continue coping (Davidhizar, 1992).

Orem's Self-Care Model

A nursing system is a helping system (Metha, 1993). Orem (1995) identified three basic variations in nursing systems based on the belief that the client can perform

RESEARCH

Smits M, Kee C: Correlates of self-care among the independent elderly. Self concept affects well being, *J Gerontolog Nurs* 18(9):13-17, 1992.

Sample, setting

Subjects included 48 independently living people age 65 or older, half of whom were living in independent retirement complexes and half of whom were participants in senior citizen centers.

Methodology

Self-concept was measured by the Tennessee Self-Concept Scale (TSCS) and self-care was measured through the Exercise of Self-care Agency Scale (ESCA). Functional health was measured by Roscow and Breslau's Guttman Health Scale for the Aged.

Findings

A strong, significant relationship was found between self-care and total self-concept. Self-care was also related to social self, physical self, and self-satisfaction. No differences on self-care scores were noted according to age, income, gender, or employment. There was a significant correlation between functional health status and self-care.

Implications

With knowledge that self-care is significantly related to self-concept, the nurse can attempt to maximize self-care agency for the older adult. Psychosocial intervention to enhance self-concept may be necessary before an adequate level of self-care can be achieved. The nurse can use the following strategies to enhance the well-being of the older adult:

- Reinforce positive health behavior so that the moral-ethical component of self-concept is strengthened.
- Avoid emphasis on self-care deficits.
- Teach health-promoting self-care activities.
- Encourage the older adult to engage in ADLs that contribute to achieving independent functioning through self-care.
- Maintain professional behavior in interacting with the older adult to communicate care and respect.

self-care, the nurse can provide care, or the care can be provided in combination. The basic nursing systems indicate (1) wholly compensatory, (2) partly compensatory, and (3) supportive-educative (Orem, 1995).

It is the condition of the client that determines which nursing system applies. Clients move from system to system as their care needs change. A wholly compensatory system is required when the client is entirely dependent on others for sustenance and well-being. A partly compensatory system is used when the client can and should perform some self-care. A supportive-educative system is needed when the client is able to perform or to learn to perform self-care, but requires professional assistance. In this system, the areas for help are confined to decision making, behavior control, or gaining new knowledge or skills.

Orem's conceptual framework of self-care is useful in planning care for the older adult, because maintaining independence and adapting to aging are concerns of most older adults. Orem's framework allows older adults to retain control and physical functioning, both of which are usually lost when the nurse does not involve the older adult in the caregiving process (Metha, 1993). The framework provides a method to assess clients for variables that could affect their ability to care for themselves. The framework also directs the nurse in developing an individual and realistic plan of care. Nurses can assist older adults to exercise self-care agency and to successfully meet therapeutic self-care demands by focusing on psychosocial needs, as well as physical interventions (Smits, Kee, 1992). Smits' study (see Research box on p. 372) applies Orem's framework by demonstrating the relationship between self-concept and self-care.

Case Study

Mrs. F, a 75-year-old African-American woman, was admitted to the emergency department after her son found her on the floor of her home. An x-ray confirms an intertrochanteric fracture; a prosthetic device is used to repair the fracture.

Postoperatively, using Orem's self-care model, the nurse assesses Mrs. F's universal self-care requisites: air, water, food, elimination, activity and rest, solitude and social balance, safety, and promotion of normalcy. The nurse plans the appropriate level of care for Mrs. F based on her capacity to care for herself. For the first few days postoperatively, Mrs. F requires a wholly compensatory nursing system because of her immobility. The nurse plans interventions that assist Mrs. F in progressing to a partially compensatory system before discharge. After discharge, a supportive-educative system can be provided by home health. The goals for Mrs. F focus on retaining control and dignity, and gradually assuming self-care as her condition progresses. By moving Mrs. F toward the supportive-educative system, the nurse is preparing her for discharge. Orem's theory also allows the nurse to use roles such as teacher, change agent, and referral agent (Metha, 1993).

Functional Assessment

Regular, comprehensive assessment of the older adult is considered a central principle of geriatric care (Calvani, Douris, 1991). As early as 1959, a World Health Organization advisory group stated, "Health in the elderly is best measured in terms of function." Improved function rather than cure is a therapeutic goal for the chronically ill person (Calvani, Douris, 1991). Function is a useful measure in the diagnosis of illness and self-care deficits. The functional assessment can assist older adults and their families in identifying problem areas and planning appropriate interventions to assist in treatment or provision of support measures. See Chapter 4 for a discussion of various tools and instruments.

The functional assessment can be a part of the initial nursing assessment. It can be used to determine pre-illness or disability level of functioning, and rehabilitation potential (Calvani, Douris, 1991). In long-term care and rehabilitation settings, the functional assessment data can be used in the resident's plan of care to correct deficits that are amenable to treatment. Such tools can periodically measure progress and can aid in determining discharge readiness. Some deficits in ADLs and independent activities of daily living (IADLs) may be compensated through the use of adaptive equipment, home aid assistance, and additional social supports. Once compensated, the older adult may function well enough to be discharged home. In the community, a functional assessment may help prevent unnecessary hospitalization or premature institutionalization.

Case Study

Mr. G is 80 years old and has been referred to home health because of his poorly controlled insulin-dependent diabetes and his noncompliance with diet and medications. On initial assessment, the nurse found that although he could see the numbers on the syringe, he lacked the fine motor control needed to withdraw the insulin and inject himself. His 70-year-old wife with dementia is dependent on Mr. G for care. They rely on neighbors and their son for grocery shopping. They have no reliable transportation and often miss medical appointments.

The nurse identified several factors contributing to Mr. G's noncompliance: Mr. G's inability to administer his insulin, difficulty obtaining groceries, lack of transportation, and caregiving demands on Mr. G. Had the nurse not personally observed his home setting, important information needed for a realistic plan of care would have been missed.

Keys for Completing the Functional Assessment

1. The nurse should have an understanding of the client's mental status before assessment. For example, some people with cognitive impairment deny any problems, or people with depression may just respond with "I don't know."
2. Assessment approach should be adapted to the degree of potential or actual disability. Healthy older adults may only need to be assessed in areas of social function, ADLs and IADLs. The old er adult with complex problems needs specific assessments to define their needs and abilities.
3. When selecting a tool, both self-reporting and observational tools may be needed. Some older adults may deny any functional difficulty or may minimize the amount of assistance needed. Ask older adults what they have done rather than what they can do.
4. Screen for the factors that limit older adults in their self-care or ability to remain in their home: (1) confusion, (2) safety awareness, (3) toileting, (4) continence, (5) depression or poor motivation, (6) falls, and (7) transfer ability. The most important physical task for the older adult is the ability to transfer in and out of a bed or chair. A person who cannot transfer from bed to chair or chair to toilet cannot be left alone for long periods of time (Calvani, Douris, 1991).

Geriatric assessment and interventions must consider the older adult's values and beliefs. The older client's cultural and spiritual beliefs, feelings regarding health practices, and thoughts on quality of life issues should be incorporated into the plan of care.

Psychosocial Needs of the Chronically Ill Older Adult

The nurse needs to understand the relationship between social, psychologic and biologic factors of aging to assist the older adult in preserving independence. Although many studies on aging have emphasized the losses of aging, researchers contend that the beneficial effects on aging of diet, exercise, personal habits, and psychosocial factors have been underestimated. "It is not merely a matter of what aging does to people but also of what people do with aging" (Smits, Kee, 1992). Understanding the interplay of these factors can help the nurse assist older adults in adapting to aging and maintaining independence.

The older adult's concept of self plays an important role in adaptation to aging and chronic illness. Morris (1985) defined self-concept as the person's appraisal of appearance, background, origins, abilities, resources, attitudes, and feelings that culminate as a directing force for behavior. Past research has found that physical alterations, whether from illness or normal aging, can be integrated into self-concept with both positive and negative results. The capacity for self-concept to change in response to new demands is consistent with Holtzclaw's (1985) statement that self-concept is "permanent yet permeable." See Research Box on p. 372 for Smits' study regarding nursing interventions to enhance self-concept in the older adult.

Powerlessness

Older adults' self-concept can also be affected if they feel unable to control their illness or disability, or feel that their self-care patterns have contributed to the present disorder. Powerlessness can be a result of normal aging changes, an altered body image, or numerous losses. Older people grieve the loss of function or the loss of their former self. How they grieve is individual, and the significance of the loss also influences the grieving process. The result of powerlessness is loss of hope. In addition, older adults who feel powerless may also lose their independence to family members or health professionals who take over and make decisions for them. This cycle of powerlessness, loss of locus of control, and dependence may be perpetuated by well-meaning caregivers.

Case Study

Mr. J is a 62-year-old small store owner with a recent mild CVA. He told his wife and the nurse that he would never return to work. He would have to give up everything now. His wife cannot understand his sudden decision to abandon his store. She told the nurse that his store was his life. Mr. J worked two jobs as a young man to save money to start his business. At last, with considerable embarrassment, he revealed to the nurse that he experienced episodes of fecal incontinence: "Losing this control means losing everything. I can't work like this. I'll never be independent again." A long history of constipation led him to frequent laxative use and the CVA had damaged rectal enervation. Mr. J was not always aware of the sensations of a full bowel.

After an assessment, the nurse developed a short-term plan with Mr. J to use incontinence pads and take a change of clothes to work. The nurse developed a midrange plan with Mr. J to increase his daily exercise and intake of water and other noncaffeinated fluids. He gradually added high-fiber foods, established a consistent daily toileting time, and avoided using laxatives. Several weeks later, Mr. J reported a more regular bowel pattern with decreased incontinent episodes. He stated his morale had improved, and he felt in control of his life. Assisting Mr. J with his fecal incontinence returned his feeling of control and enabled him to then focus on other rehabilitation goals.

Meaning of Life in Adjustment

Adaptation and adjustment to chronic illness or disability is also affected by the meaning the older adult attaches to life. According to Frankl (1962), a person's search for meaning in life is the primary source of motivation. The older adult with a disability or illness faces a variety of losses, including loss of former self, changes in body image, loss of control over a disease process, and possibly loss of work and changes in residence. In addition, the older adult may experience other losses associated with age-related changes, such as death of significant others, retirement, and declining health status.

Research has suggested that loss of meaning is a serious threat to older adults because of the multiple changes and losses they encounter. Researchers have found a significant correlation between purpose in life and physical health status. Although meaning of life has been linked to health, further exploration with the older adult population is needed (Burbank, 1992). Clients feeling a loss of meaning need to be identified, and interventions need to be planned to help them increase their level of fulfillment. A question the nurse may ask in the psychosocial assessment to ascertain the older adult's meaning of life can be: "Is there one thing or things so important to you in your life that they give your life meaning?" By asking clients to describe things that are meaningful, the nurse can gain insight into their needs and behaviors based on what is meaningful to them (Burbank, 1992).

As the nurse learns what is meaningful, interventions can be planned to support or strengthen these areas, such as supporting an existing relationship, finding ways to continue an enjoyable hobby, or arranging transportation to church. Through the interaction of the assessment, the nurse assists older adults in redefining their situation and rediscovering meaning. These discussions lead to descriptions of situations that are important, and as these situations are defined, the meaning emerges. Through interactions with others, the older adult can define and discover meaning in all aspects of life situations (Burbank, 1992).

Nursing Interventions to Assist Psychosocial Adjustment

The ability of the older adult to cope with the issues and problems encountered in the course of living with and managing a chronic illness determines the nurse's role and the type of interventions needed. A collaborative relationship may be most effective in facilitating psychosocial adjustment (Strauss, Corbin, 1988). This type of relationship allows older adults to participate in their care planning and to retain control and dignity (Metha, 1993), since independence is a major concern for older people, especially in the American culture, where it is highly valued. In addition, the nurse often uses the supportive-educative nursing system. Teaching older adult clients the trajectory model may actually help them cope with acute exacerbations (Strauss, Corbin, 1988).

> **Insight** • *How and why do older adults lose their driver's licenses? A survey of physicians found the majority felt driving was a privilege, but more than 60% had never referred a client for evaluation of driving status. Less than 10% of the physicians used loss of vision or loss of mental status as a criterion for recommending driving restrictions. They rarely referred clients to refresher driving courses such as the 55 Alive/Mature Driving program, which is sponsored by American Association of Retired Persons (AARP), (Miller, Morley, 1993).*
>
> *The nurse should be alert for any changes in the older adult's mental status. An assessment tool such as the Folstein Mini-Mental State Exam can be a useful screening instrument. The nurse can refer the older adult to a driving training program or an occupational therapist trained in the assessment of older adult drivers. Nurses can participate in research to gain greater understanding of driving deficiencies in the older adult and the development of cost-effective ways to compensate for these deficiencies.*

Adjustment is an individual process and depends on the circumstances of the disability. Developmental changes, life transitions, and meaning placed on the disability or illness influences this ongoing process (Miller, 1992). Interventions may include supporting existing relationships or referring older adults who have lost significant relationships to a senior center where new relationships may be established (Burbank, 1992). The nurse may also explore with the client interventions that meet spiritual needs. The nurse can refer and encourage the older adult to participate in formal or informal learning opportunities available in the community.

The group process is one way to assist clients in their psychosocial adjustment. Self-help groups provide a support system in which older adults redefine themselves, focus on issues, adjust to new roles, or learn about their disease processes and how others manage (Ebersole, Hess, 1994).

Physiologic Needs of the Chronically Ill Older Adult

A thorough nursing health history includes a comprehensive review of body systems, as well as medication and treatment review (see Chapter 4). The medication review should include both prescription drugs and over the counter (OTC) medications (see Chapter 20). The older adult may have more than one physician prescribing drugs in addition to using nonprescribed remedies.

Pain

A major issue with chronic disorders is the management of pain. In evaluating pain, the nurse should note its characteristics, location, and intensity (1 to 10 scale). An assessment of causes of possible discomfort other than the chronic illness should be made. In addition to analgesia, the nurse can teach the client relaxation techniques, deep breathing exercises, guided imagery, and visualization. These techniques can relieve muscle and emotional tension, enhance the sense of control, and may improve coping abilities. See Chapter 13 for a more detailed discussion of pain management and treatment strategies.

Fatigue

Older adults living with a chronic disorder often experience fatigue. Fatigue can be unpredictable, making it difficult to manage or to alleviate. The nurse can help the older adult identify causes and patterns of fatigue. Older people may need to be taught how to conserve energy to enjoy meaningful activities. Reassuring that periodic rest periods, a slower pace of activity, and more time to complete tasks may be needed helps the older client cope and feel in control. The nurse should encourage the older adult to choose where to expend energy and should respect the priorities established.

Immobility and Activity Intolerance

Older adults commonly perceive health in relation to their level of activity (Butler, 1991). Physical activity and psychosocial interaction is important in maintaining the chronically ill older adult on the continuum of wellness. Inactivity results in further functional loss and as activity levels decline, this vicious cycle is repeated. Problems as a result of inactivity are compounded when clients, families, and health care professionals display reduced expectations of the debilitated older adult (Butler, 1991). In the United States, people age 75 years and older can expect to live an additional 10 to 11 years, and therefore care based on preserving or restoring functional ability is essential (Butler, 1991). One possible nursing goal may be to prevent complications of prolonged inactivity during an acute exacerbation of illness.

Sexual Activity

Changes in the client's sexual life, imposed by the chronic condition, may cause psychologic distress. Effects of the condition, medications, treatments, fatigue, changes in body image, and the feeling that one is no longer attractive may present difficult emotional barriers. Open communication between partners with frank discussion of needs and feelings may result in helpful adjustments in sexual practices and deeper commitments to the relationship. Counseling the partners or the individual client may smooth over these transitions. In addition to a medication review, a sexual history provides the nurse with insight into the client's needs. The nurse should create an open, accepting atmosphere to facilitate discussion of sexuality and to provide information in a nonjudgmental manner. Only when concerns are identified and discussed can problem solving occur (see Chapter 10).

Impact of Chronic Illness on Family or Caregiver

Increasingly greater numbers of families are faced with providing care for chronically ill older family members because of the rapidly aging population and the present management of chronic illness. Nearly 80% of all inhome care is given by spouses, parents, and children (Beach, 1993) (Fig. 16-3). Studies have enhanced our awareness of family caregiver stress and the difficulty of balancing caregiving with other activities such as personal time or social activities. The primary family caregiver receives little help from siblings or children and considers institutionalization only when physically or emotionally exhausted (Beach, 1993).

Situational factors in caring for a chronically ill older adult contribute to caregiver stress. As noted previously, chronic illnesses are long-term and uncertain. Periods of improvement, stability and exacerbations in the trajectory of the illness cause uncertainty. The degree of anticipation of these phases can also be stress-producing. Some chronic conditions develop slowly, and advance planning for crisis periods is possible (Davidhizar, 1992). Advance notice of impending stress can allow the caregiver to activate coping strategies and can reduce the stress experienced. However, anticipation can also be related to fear of the worst possible outcome.

The characteristics of the chronic illness can contribute to stress of caregivers. When the client does not recognize family caregivers or does not remember the previously shared relationship because of cognitive changes, caregivers report stress (Davidhizar, 1992). Behavioral problems resulting from the illness also contribute to stress. Functional ability of the client and the type and amount of care needed affect caregiver stress. Ongoing care or the perception that ongoing care is needed can be physically and psychologically draining (Davidhizar, 1992).

Studies have shown, for example, that the degree of burden and stress in caregivers is increased as symptoms of dementia worsen (Kobayashi, Masaki, Noguchi, 1993). Kobayashi, Masaki, and Noguchi also found that in Japan, however, family caregivers of older adults with Alzheimer's who became aware of nonverbal communication, also became more sympathetic and considerate in their care. Once they learned about interacting with

Fig. 16-3 Daughter caregiver assisting her mother down hallway of her home. (Courtesy Rod Schmall, West Linn, Ore.)

the family member with dementia and actively tried to communicate feelings and relations nonverbally, their care became more warm. This use of nonverbal communication allows the caregiver to recognize qualities of the older adult that transcend any disabilities caused by dementia. Kobayashi suggests stimulating the expressions, movements, and behavior (nonverbal signs) of the person with dementia, and teaching the caregiver how to become aware of these signs to prompt changes in the perceptions and attitudes of the caregivers.

Role strains are problematic features inherent to balancing the role as primary caregiver with other roles within the family network (Beach, 1993). Most caregivers feel a strong sense of responsibility to caregiving and although most have a family system in place, it is rarely used as a source of support. Maintaining a healthy sense of self and successful coping with role strain require balancing caregiving with caring for one's self. Personal activity may include work outside the home. As many as 67% of caregivers experience work conflict, resulting in changes in work schedules or performance (Beach, 1993). However, caregivers often cease employment completely.

Powerlessness is defined as thinking one has no control over events, and it can be related to a lifestyle of helplessness or a current situation in which the person perceives stressors as unalterable (Davidhizar, 1992). Fewer than 15% of all "helper days of care" for people needing help with ADLs are provided by paid caregivers or sources outside the family (Davidhizar, 1992). Factors that influence coping with caregiver stress and powerlessness are personal characteristics (e.g., age, sex, marital status, health, and social roles), knowledge of the illness, knowledge of available resources, as well as personal perceptions and coping strategies. Assumption of a role previously assigned to the chronically ill older adult can significantly affect stress levels. A family caregiver who perceives the chronic illness in terms of loss (i.e., loss of time, loss of money, or loss of love) can be overwhelmed with powerlessness.

Nursing Implications of Caregiver Stress

Effective nursing care of a client with chronic illness requires providing care not only to the identified client but also to the family member caregiver. The caregiver's personal characteristics, socioemotional support, financial resources, and the perception of the caregiving situation should be assessed in relation to risk for feelings of powerlessness. Personal coping strategies that include the ability to solve problems in managing care need to be explored by the nurse. Questions such as, "Many family member caregivers have trouble with... Have you found that to be true for you?" can help the nurse determine stressors and problem-solving abilities in a nonthreatening manner.

Support from other resources such as community social service agencies, local church members, visiting nurse organizations and other family members can be used. Support groups for caregivers also are becoming more prevalent. Group participation decreases the sense of isolation and may help the caregiver cope with each situation. The nurse can provide information about the illness and reassurance that feelings of frustration or helplessness are not unusual reactions. Referrals to a social worker may be necessary to provide detailed information regarding Medicare coverage and Medicaid eligibility, as well as other means of accessing assistance in the health care system. Stress may be reduced by the use of adult day care or home health nursing. Temporary placement in long-term care provides the caregiver a much-needed respite.

Caring for the older adult with a chronic disorder requires long-term adaptation on the part of family members. The family member caregiver, to continue in the

Insight • *Do family caregivers recognize malnutrition in the frail older adult? Family caregivers often make strong claims. They keep their parent alive, and they know the client better than the doctor. Hence, the client can do more because of their care. Albert (1993) found that caregivers do recognize signs of malnutrition and increase nutritional care in response. He concludes that caregivers deserve some measure of support for their claims of health expertise.*

In assessing the older adult's nutrition and hydration, the nurse should pay close attention to the caregiver's assessment and to actions that the caregiver has taken in response to the assessment. The nurse can support the caregiver's interventions and provide teaching to enhance the caregiver's skill in caring for the older adult. For example, how to monitor intake, how much fluid the older client should drink, what foods can be modified, how to encourage the older adult to eat, as well as types of nutritional supplement and when to use them.

caregiving role, needs ongoing support by all involved health care professionals (see Chapter 6).

REHABILITATION

A range of definitions of rehabilitation is available. Rehabilitation has traditionally been defined as the restoration of the person with a disability to the fullest physical, mental, social, vocational, and economic usefulness of which he or she is capable. **Rehabilitation** is a process that is flexible and led by ability to enable the individual to pursue an independent existence (Williams, 1993). Hyams (1969) describes rehabilitation as planned withdrawal of support.

A definition of rehabilitation specifically for the older adult needs to reflect the view that any improvement in functional ability should be seen as an achievement. Williams' (1993) definition of rehabilitation, applicable to the older adult, states that:

> Rehabilitation seeks to improve the individual's quality of life in any way, no matter how small, in relation to physical, emotional or spiritual well-being and ultimately return that individual to a residence of his choice and at minimal personal risk. This implies integration into society plus support in and by the community.

The nurse needs to be aware of the following definitions related to rehabilitation. **Impairment** is a pathophysiologic condition that does not always result in a secondary disability. **Handicap** follows impairment and is a burden the person must overcome to maintain functional ability. **Disability** is a failure to function at an expected level. Impairment produces a handicap that may or may not result in a degree of disability (Matteson, McConnell, 1988). A primary handicap is a disability that is part of the illness. A secondary handicap is the nonadaptive reaction to the illness. For example, the older adult may suffer a CVA (impairment), which produces hemiplegia (primary handicap). If the older adult cannot achieve independent ambulation because of the extent of the hemiplegia, then dependent mobility is the disability. The older adult may then have difficulty working through the grieving process, which is the secondary handicap.

The highest percentage of people with disabilities is in the very old age group, those over age 75 years (Mayer, 1991). By the year 2001, the number of people in this age group will form almost half of the older adult population. People 75 and older represent half the inpatient acute care administered in the United States (Butler, 1991). More strokes occur after age 65, as do most amputations. Hip fractures peak in the eighth decade of life (Butler, 1991). Car drivers age 60 or older have approximately twice as many car accidents per 1 million miles as people age 30 to 49 years (Miller, Morley, 1993). These data suggest an increasing need for rehabilitation with a gerontologic focus. Rehabilitation planning should begin at the time the older adult is first seen or hospitalized (Butler, 1991).

The growth of the older population has specific implications for disability, and it affects the nurses who provide preventive, restorative, and rehabilitation services to this population. Age-related physiologic changes can slow recovery and can increase residual debilitation from an acute illness or injury. Age-related changes also increase the likelihood of physical limitations from a chronic illness (Gershkoff, Cifu, Means, 1993). Studies agree that older adults are more likely to be functionally impaired in ADLs and mobility. People age 85 and older account for about one third of the disabilities in the older adult population.

Treatment Environments

Rehabilitation services are offered in a variety of settings. Bedside therapy on acute medical-surgical units can assist the client in maintaining strength when on bed rest. However, the acute medical environment offers little opportunity for generalization of skills learned in therapy and often emphasizes bed rest and inactivity (Gershkoff, Cifu, Means, 1993). Rehabilitation services lasting 1 to 2 hours per day are available in intermediate rehabilitation facilities and skilled care facilities (Fig. 16-4). This environment is suitable for the older adult with the goal of returning home, who is unable to tolerate more therapy or who only requires one therapy discipline. Intensive re-

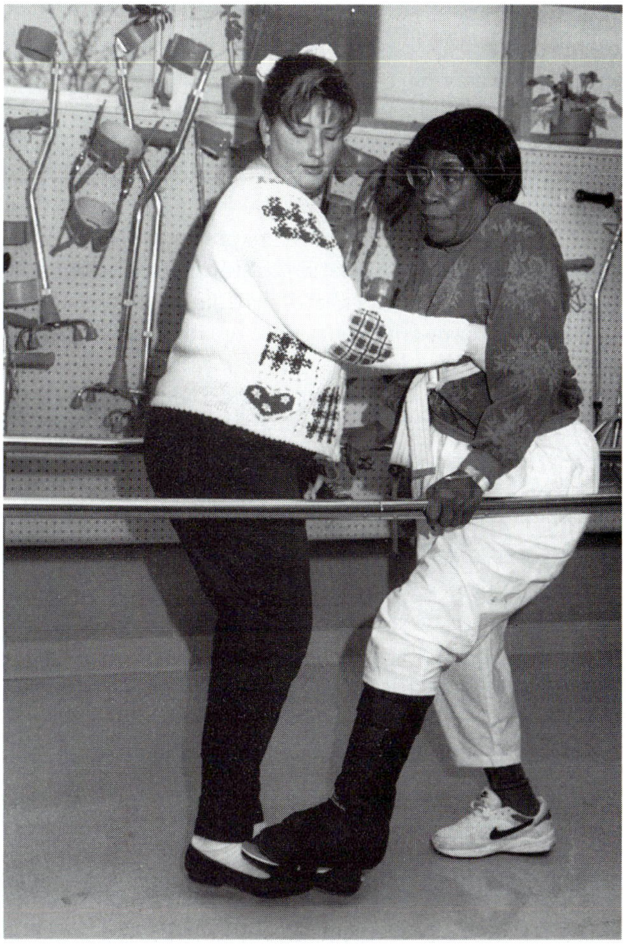

Fig. 16-4 Client receiving therapy in a rehab setting. (Courtesy Loy Ledbetter, St. Louis, Mo.)

habilitation, 3 hours or more of therapy, is available in the rehabilitation units of acute care hospitals, freestanding rehabilitation hospitals, and some geriatric assessment units. Outpatient rehabilitation therapy services are available to the older adult in his or her home, day hospitals, and adult day care programs.

Reimbursement Issues

Medicare provides nationwide health insurance to 98% of all older adults (Gerhskoff, 1993). In 1994, social security and Medicare paid about $490 billion in benefits, about $170 billion of which was in Medicare benefits (Detlefs, Myers, 1993). Medicare becomes available at age 65 whether or not the older adult remains working. Part A, or basic coverage (inpatient hospital coverage), is without cost to those who qualify. Part B (more comprehensive coverage) is available for a monthly premium with deductibles. A variety of private insurance plans are available to cover the "Medigap" or the 20% of service costs not reimbursed under Medicare guidelines. Box 16-2 outlines those items Medicare does not cover.

BOX 16-2

What Medicare Does Not Cover

- Services not reasonable or medically necessary
- Items or services that individuals are not legally obligated to pay
- Services paid by the government or worker's compensation
- Services performed by a relative
- Services outside the United States (some Canadian and Mexican exceptions)
- Routine physical examinations
- Routine eye examinations and glasses
- Hearing aids
- Dental services (except surgery on or reduction of jaw or facial bones)
- Routine foot care or orthopedic shoes (except cases of diabetes)
- Custodial care
- Cosmetic surgery (except after an accident)
- Most prescription drugs taken at home
- Acupuncture
- Most immunizations
- First three pints of blood per year
- Meals delivered to your home
- Private nurses
- Private hospital room (unless medically necessary)
- Homemaker services (except under hospice)

From Detlefs D, Myers R: *1994 Medicare,* December 1993. Reprinted with permission of William M. Mercer, Inc., Louisville, Ky.

Medicaid is a state-specific medical care funding source for people of low income. It varies from state to state, but generally inpatient, outpatient, home health, and nursing home rehablitation is partially reimbursed. Medicaid is responsible for over 85% of publicly funded nursing home care (Gershkoff, Cifu, Means, 1993). Increasing fiscal constraints in local, state, and federal agencies will affect rehabilitation reimbursement and may further decrease resources available to the older adult (Gershkoff, Cifu, Means, 1993).

Public Policy and Legislation

Nurses have the power to influence public policy and legislation by advocating the needs of the older adult with disabilities, and supporting and conducting relevant nursing research. The process of national public policy making started in 1951 when the first White House Conference on Aging was held. This conference made the problems of the older adult visible and since then, has been held each decade. The Older Americans Act of 1965 introduced the concept of a focal point for services for the older adult. Also in 1965, Medicare and Medicaid were established and have been revised through the years. In 1982 the Tax Equity and Fiscal Responsibility Act (TEFRA) introduced prospective reimbursement for hospitals under Medicare Diagnostic Related Groups (DRGs).

The Americans with Disabilities Act (ADA) of 1990, however, did not eliminate discrimination inherent to the current system of risk-based health insurance (DeJong, 1993). Insurers may continue to discriminate on the basis of risk, provided that risk classifications are based on sound actuarial data. The World Institute on Disability (WID), a policy analysis and advocacy organization, has proposed a "Personal Assistance for Independent Living Act" (PAIL), that would require each state to greatly expand personal assistant services that are consistent with consumer-based values of autonomy, self-management, and choice (DeJong, 1993).

The most definitive position on health care reform to date is the statement issued by the Health Task Force of the Consortium for Citizens with Disabilities. The statement includes the following principles: (1) nondiscrimination; (2) comprehensiveness of services; (3) appropriateness to individual need, preference and choice; (4) equity; and (5) efficiency. These principles have also been affirmed by the American Congress of Rehabilitation Medicine (ACRM) and acknowledged by the National Council on Disability (NCD).

Rehabilitation in the United States and United Kingdom

Cross-cultural perspectives offer unique and helpful insights on rehabilitative care for the older adult. The United States and United Kingdom share a common heritage and language, but terms such as "welfare," "physician," and "nursing home" differ in connotation. In the United Kingdom, to be a recipient of welfare is a privilege of being a citizen, and physicians are always internists by specialty. The United Kingdom emphasizes primary health care, expanded social services, and overall lower costs. Nursing homes refer to for-profit institutions, which are few (Strasser, 1992). Americans emphasize improvement of an individual's functional ability, whereas the United Kingdom places more importance on adaptation to the disability and necessary environmental changes to foster that adaptation. Table 16-6 compares and contrasts the geriatric rehabilitation in these two countries.

Rationing health services has a profound influence on rehabilitation services in both countries. In the United States, rationing of health services is usually an economic issue. In the United Kingdom, renal dialysis is not routinely considered for people older than 65 years. Older adults in the the United Kingdom routinely receive rehabilitation as part of comprehensive geriatric medical care. In the United Kingdom, "geriatrics" and "geriatric rehabilitation" are synonymous. The different systems of care developed, because they responded to the perceived needs of each society (Strasser, 1992).

What insights can be gained? The United Kingdom has comprehensive geriatric services in which the boundaries of medical care, social services, and rehabilitation are less distinct. There is also greater cooperative effort across inpatient, outpatient, day treatment, home health, and social services. This is promoted by the National Health Service (NHS), the agency that organizes all health care services in the United Kingdom. The NHS has demonstrated the ability to produce outcomes for the older adult at a significantly lower cost and with less

TABLE 16-6

Geriatric Rehabilitation

	United States	United Kingdom
Health Care Funding	Individual, private and government sources	National Health Service (NHS) funded by government revenue
Life expectancy	Men-70.8 years Women-78.2 years	Men-70.4 years Women-76.6 years
Percent of population 65 and older by the year 2000	11.3%	15.3%
Percent of population 65 and older in nursing homes and institutions	5.3%	3.9%
Percent of population 65 and older in group living quarters	0.5%	5.4%
Percent of health care spent on primary care	18%	25%
Percent of population unable to receive care for financial reasons	7.5%	0.1%
Establishment of certification in geriatric rehabilitation	1988	1940

From Strasser D: Geriatric rehabilitation: perspectives from the United Kingdom, *Arch Phys Med Rehab* 73(6):582-585, 1992.

administrative overhead. The United Kingdom has responded to a fixed budget on health care and public policy with a centralized coordination of services for the older adult that has enhanced the continuum of care. This centralized coordination of services can decrease cost without affecting outcomes (Strasser, 1992).

The sense of individualism in the United States contrasts with the United Kingdom's sense of collectivism. High cost of health care, diverse funding sources, and service provisions have set the stage for health care reform in the United States.

The strengths and weaknesses of each society's system of care must be examined. Perhaps health care reformers in the United States can incorporate the strengths of other health care systems into their plan for the United States.

Enhancement of Fitness and Function

In rehabilitation, the functional assessment provides baseline data and thus a means to quantify the impact of therapy. It can be used periodically to monitor progress and discharge readiness (Calvani, Douris, 1991).

Case Study

Mr. L was admitted to the rehabilitation unit of a skilled nursing facility following a left CVA. On admission, his Barthel Index was 50 (see Chapter 4). Through intensive rehabilitation, he learned how to transfer, to bathe, and to dress himself independently. His Barthel Index was 75 on discharge. The ongoing use of the Barthel scale throughout his rehabilitation gave Mr. L positive reinforcement for his efforts in therapy. Areas not included in the index are health or physical condition, socioemotional support, and availability of financial resources (Calvani, Douris, 1991).

Deconditioning

The effects of deconditioning can be reversible to the extent of the age-related decline in physiologic systems (Means, Currie, Gershkoff, 1993). The cardiac changes include a decrease in maximum aerobic capacity, cardiac output, left ventricular function, and stroke volume. Associated changes in other body systems include lower extremity venous stasis; decreased vital capacity; negative nitrogen balance; and progressive loss of strength, endurance, and coordination (Means, Currie, Gershkoff, 1993). Deconditioning in the older adult appears earlier and is more severe, taking longer to reverse than deconditioning in younger people.

Exercise training and endurance training can be used to reverse the effects of disuse and to maintain the health status of the older adult. Strength training improves muscle strength in the older adult and muscle building can be achieved through the tenth decade (Means, Currie, Gershkoff, 1993). Endurance training is beneficial and circuit training is a safe method of exercise to improve strength and endurance in the older adult (Means, Currie, Gershkoff, 1993).

The goal in caring for disabled older adults is maintaining or improving function. Maintaining mobility, even when hospitalized, can prevent or can decrease the effects of deconditioning. A referral to physical therapy assists the nurse in developing and implementing an exercise plan. Many activities that older adults enjoy such as walking, swimming, cycling, rowing and even dancing can be incorporated into exercise and endurance training. In teaching older adults that deconditioning can be reversed, the nurse should stress that activity and exercise not only increase muscle strength and endurance but also help reduce diastolic blood pressure, body fat, and the risk of coronary artery disease. Other benefits include increased mineral bone density, improved joint flexibility, and improved mental health (Means, Currie, Gershkoff, 1993).

Health Promotion

Rehabilitation includes the health promotion activities of making changes, using resources, and carrying out whatever activities are required to develop, to sustain, and to increase healthy functioning (Pascucci, 1992). Even though health promotion activities enhance function, what motivates older adults to health promotion? In 1951 B.F. Skinner stated that all activity is motivated behavior. Motives are desires, intentions, and goal sets, whereas incentives are praise, rewards, and punishments (Pascucci, 1992). Although chronic disease and disability cannot be eliminated, health promotion in rehabilitation allows the older adult to achieve a maximum level of functioning and increase longevity. Determining reasons why an older adult participates in rehabilitation may provide the nurse insights to further promote health in the client. Pascucci (1992) found that fitness, health, independence, and socialization are important incentives to the older adult (Fig. 16-5). Motivational assessment tools can be used in rehabilitation programs to facilitate planning of interventions to enhance participation and compliance.

The nurse can use King's theory of goal attainment in the older adult's rehabilitation. King (1981) states the goal of nursing is to "help individuals maintain their health so they can function in their roles." Nurses assist clients through purposeful interaction to set goals and to agree on actions to achieve those goals. As a result of interactions, transactions occur. Transactions involve bargaining, negotiating, and social exchange. Such role performance and role expectations of the nurse and client influence the transactions. Therefore any misunderstanding of roles or distortions in perception may influence the outcome of care (Temple, Fawdry, 1992).

Fig. 16-5 Older adults in exercise class: practicing health promotion. (Courtesy Ursula Ruhl, St. Louis, Mo.)

Case Study

Mr. P is a 76-year-old man who has been married for 50 years and has three children. Mr. P had been diagnosed and treated for prostate cancer. He developed bladder incontinence, which he has had a great deal of difficulty accepting. Mrs. P called his home health nurse for assistance. Using King's theory, the nurse suggested to Mr. P that they talk about the situation. Mr. P agreed, only because he wanted to enjoy his grandchildren with a minimum of embarrassment and disruption. The nurse agreed with this goal, and they planned a course of action. The nurse showed Mr. P how to use a Texas catheter and how to use an incontinence pad. Mr. P practiced application and developed a comfortable means of wearing the protection. This bargaining allowed the nurse to function in her role and Mr. P in his role as client. By assisting Mr. P to maintain his role of man and grandfather, the nurse protected his self-esteem and his ability to function with comfort.

Had Mr. P's incontinence not been managed to his satisfaction, his embarrassment would have hindered continued role performances (Temple, Fawdry, 1992). Further interaction and consequently goal attainment would have been impeded. By supporting Mr. P in roles that had satisfied him, the nurse facilitated continued interaction between herself and Mr. P. This led to the action plan and short-term goal. King's theory provides the nurse with a means of coping with the potentially debilitating effect of conflict between two roles or two perceptions of a role (Temple, Fawdry, 1992).

Insight • *Incontinence affects an estimated one half of all long-term care residents. Diapers and incontinent pads/pants are no longer the only treatment option for nursing home residents because of state and federal emphasis on the resident's quality of life. Incontinence is not an inevitable result of aging and can be effectively treated or eliminated with surgery or behavioral intervention (Hegland, 1993).*

In assessing the resident for causal factors leading to incontinence, the nurse should review the resident's history and medications, should examine the resident, and should evaluate the resident's postvoid residual volume. Treatment might include biofeedback, bowel and bladder retraining/electrical stimulation, or fluid and fiber management.

Some geriatric nurse practitioners are responding to long-term care regulations by serving as consultants to nursing homes and creating nurse-managed continence programs. The Borun Gerontological Institute at the University of California-Los Angeles (UCLA) has created a computer system that manages and monitors a prompted voiding program. The certified nursing assistants input data such as the volume of urine voided and patterns in the ability to initiate voiding. The computer analyzes this and other data such as cognitive responsiveness and the ability to store urine, and then identifies residents who are candidates for the prompted-voiding program. If a resident is not a candidate for a continence restoration program, a regimen of scheduled toileting or a bowel routine may keep the resident dry and can eliminate the use of diapers and incontinent pads/pants.

Management of Acquired Disabling Disorders

It is important for the nurse to understand the normal, physiologic effects of aging and their impact on rehabilitation. For example, there is no evidence that age can be used as a predictor in the efficacy of a cardiac, peripheral vascular, amputation, or a pulmonary rehabilitation program (Cifu et al, 1993). A cardiac rehabilitation program should focus on exercise training, education, secondary prevention, and vocational couseling. Modifications in exercise training may be needed for older adults with other physical impairments. Walking raises the heart rate (70% to 80% of predicted maximum) and may be used to provide aerobic training (Cifu et al, 1993).

Peripheral vascular disease frequently limits activities of endurance. A graded reconditioning program to the limit of claudication or endurance is most successful. If amputation is required, premorbid function, postoperative mobility, condition of the residual limb, and goals of the amputee should determine rehabilitation goals and prosthetic candidacy.

An older adult who is incapacitated with pulmonary disease can improve his or her quality of life and can ease functional tasks through pulmonary rehabilitation. Success depends on a motivated older adult, because there may be improvement in symptom management but a lack of improvement in pulmonary function testing.

Acute presentation of neurologic disorders in older clients is confounded by comorbid conditions. The morbidity and mortality following acute brain injury is higher in older adults (Cifu et al, 1993). With pharmacologic reduction of blood pressure, the older adult stroke client is at greater risk for compromised cerebral perfusion. Functionally, the older adult who survives a brain injury needs more personal assistance and is more likely to require institutional care for some period of time.

Older adults with spinal cord injuries have earlier mortality than younger people primarily as a result of preexisting heart and lung diseases. In this age group, a higher proportion of injuries involves the cervical spine, usually resulting from falls (Cifu et al, 1993). Although the rate of medical complications in older and younger clients with spinal-cord injury is similar, function is more severely impaired in the older adult. The chance of ambulation for older adults with central cord lesions is less than 50% for younger people.

Older adults with Parkinson's disease experience postural problems and contracture of hips and shoulders. As many as half experience depression. Essential elements of rehabilitation are stretching, coordination, and gait training. Depression also needs to be assessed as part of the overall management (see Chapter 12).

Late Life Effects of Early Life Disabilities

There is a small body of literature, most of it descriptive, on later-life complications of congenital or early-onset acquired disabilities. There is little research directed at how to prevent or treat later-life complications. As more becomes known about aging with disabilities, it may be possible to prevent some causes of functional loss (Currie, Gershkoff, Cifu, 1993).

Aging with cerebral palsy is a prototype for aging with a neuromuscular disorder, since it has been studied extensively. Nutritional problems of these older adults range from obesity (overeating and inactivity) to malnutrition (dysphagia). The musculoskeletal system displays changes in young adulthood that are usually seen much later in life, such as degenerative joint disease and osteoporosis with pathologic fractures. Therefore aggressive range-of-motion exercises should be avoided. Destructive behavioral factors in young adulthood, such as restricting or witholding fluids and voluntary retention of urine and feces leads to urinary tract dysfunction, constipation, diverticula, and hemorrhoids in the older adult.

Post-polio syndrome (PPS) is new weakness, fatigue, joint and muscle pain, and loss of function decades after acquisition of the original disability of poliomyelitis (Currie, Gershkoff, Cifu, 1993). Longitudinal studies of older adults with PPS show a loss of strength of about 1% per year until a functional loss occurs. Other problems contributing to weakness include arthritis, deconditioning from disuse, obesity and coronary artery disease. Rehabilitation programs include the use of lightweight splints and braces to reduce muscular overuse, adaptive equipment and techniques for energy conservation, weight reduction, postural training, and stress reduction (Currie, Gershkoff, Cifu, 1993). Introduction of assistive devices is often difficult for the older adult with PPS to accept in light of the efforts expended over many years to avoid such devices.

Currie, Gershkoff, and Cifu (1993) give the following generalizations about older adults with childhood onset disabilities:

- Many have a limited social life.
- Few live independently.
- Few are or were competitively employed.
- Intellectual potential has more influence on vocational outcome than does physical disability.
- Many lose access to the health care system after age 21.

Life Issues

Complications and continued deterioration of function may go unrecognized as a result of the inadequate transition to adult health services. People with disabilities treated by rehabilitation are usually not "sick," yet it is known that a person with a disability has a narrower margin of health. Many people with disabilities state that they must constantly educate health professionals about the idiosyncracies of their impairment and how it needs to be considered when prescribing treatment (*ACRM White Paper*, 1993).

There is a wide range of response to disability. The individual who has had arthritis for many years may attach little significance to the condition. The individual faced with a long rehabilitation after a stroke may respond with shock, fear, and disbelief. The human spirit is remarkably resilient, adjusting to seemingly unbearable circumstances. Most people in their own time and way accept the reality of their condition.

The person with a chronic illness or disability finds that taking health or ability for granted is no longer possible. Symptoms may spoil plans for the day, week, or month. Side effects from medications may present a variety of problems from dry mouth to ataxia. A short trip to the store may be impossible if the day is windy or sidewalks are wet or icy. As discussed previously, fatigue is a constant companion for many older adults with chronic disabilities.

Older adults must also reorganize their lives to enhance their functional ability and rehabilitation. The nurse can assist the older adult in the organization. For example, calendars, schedules, and lists can assist with organizing self-care activities. Home blood glucose and blood pressure monitoring, weight, self-assessments of physical condition based on specific illness, and record keeping of findings are examples. Organizing medication and treatments might include establishing a schedule for medications or treatments such as catheterization, toileting, or home dialysis. Organizing to work with professionals might include establishing a means to make and keep appointments, preparing for the visit, obtaining the information needed to improve self-care, and collaborating with professionals.

The nurse can help the older adult client to maximize financial resources by interpreting insurance coverage and making referrals to community agencies. For example, more than 250,000 adults age 75 and older need assistive devices but cannot afford them (Ebersole, Hess, 1994). Most assistive devices, handrails, canes, walkers, and hearing aids are paid for out of pocket. The nurse should encourage the client to shop around, ask questions, try the equipment, and inquire about service and cost of repairs. Used equipment may be purchased at medical supply stores or privately from individuals. Nurses need to influence legislators regarding the insurance industry's coverage of monitoring equipment, adaptive equipment, and supplies needed to maintain health. In addition, the American Health Security Act of 1993, introduced in September of that same year by President Bill Clinton, included coverage of preexisting conditions, prescription drugs, and medical supplies. Although this bill was not passed by Congress, universal health insurance is still a priority for millions of Americans as well as some politicians.

Nursing Strategies

In addition to helping the older adult to cope with rehabilitation, the nurse can assist in setting and achieving goals to facilitate reintegration to the former environment. Goals the older adult needs to achieve in rehabilitation include the following.

- Prevention of secondary complications
- Maintenance of existing ability
- Restoration to an acceptable level of functional ability

The nurse should clarify role expectations with the client. Drawing up a contract with the older adult to direct the progress can achieve clarification of these expectations. The strategy of providing home-like routines is consistent with teaching clients how to live with their illnesses and disabilities (Kirk, 1993). Incorporating normal routine into teaching content can provide a sense of security that facilitates learning. Showing interest by listening to older adult clients and involving them in all decision making increases their confidence in their ability to achieve the care outcomes. Norman's (1991) study suggests that clients who believed in their internal locus of control progressed further in rehabilitation than those who believed in powerful others, or chance locus of control. Rehabilitation is a process, not an end unto itself, in which the greatest steps are usually small ones (Williams, 1993).

Case Study

Mrs. W is a 73-year-old woman, admitted to a skilled nursing facility for rehabilitation following a CVA with right hemiparesis. She has a history of hypertension. In addition to the hemiparesis, she displays fatigue and emotional lability. She receives physical and occupational therapy twice a day. Her goal is to return home with her husband. The priorities in her care are (1) to prevent complications and permanent disabilities; (2) to achieve independence in daily living activities; (3) to support the coping process and integration of changes into self-concept; and (4) to provide information about the CVA, prognosis, and treatment.

Nursing staff assisted Mrs. W in turning and repositioning until she mastered bed mobility in physical therapy. Mrs. W became tearful and frustrated with her attempts at self-care. She was upset with the length of time and effort needed to complete tasks. The nurse supported Mrs. W by anticipating the time required for the self-care and getting her started. The nurse provided assistance only as necessary, maintaining a supportive but firm attitude. The nurse praised Mrs. W's efforts, and slowly Mrs. W gained a sense of self-worth that encouraged her continued endeavors. She loudly expressed her feelings about her body. She referred to the affected side as "it." The nurse acknowledged Mrs. W's feeling about betrayal of her body but remained matter-of-fact that Mrs. W could still use the unaffected side and learn to control the affected side. The staff used words such as weak, affected, right, and left to incorporate that side as a part of her body. Small gains in function were celebrated. Mrs. W was also referred to social services for additional support.

After 60 days, Mrs. W was independent in ambulation with a quad cane and independent in self-care. She could assist in meal preparation while sitting. She was discharged home with her husband. Follow-up home care included an assessment of the home environment by the occupational therapist and additional physical therapy in the home. Homemaker assistance was not necessary because of family support.

Rehabilitation and the Future

At present there is no system of postrehabilitation primary care, and once a person is discharged, the older adult has an "orphaned condition" that is not the province of any one medical discipline (*ACRM White Paper,* 1993). Preparing people with disabilities to live independently or productively is undermined when they face recurring health problems that limit their ability to participate fully in life. The ACRM identified the following five health care service issues that dominate the lives of most people following rehabilitation: (1) high rate of unscheduled rehospitalizations, (2) lack of access to primary care, (3) development of new health problems as a person ages with a disability, (4) lack of access to long-term services such as home care and personal assistance services, and (5) lack of access to appropriate health insurance coverage and its impact on willingness to accept gainful work.

These five health care service issues have many implications for nursing. Nursing can help reduce rehospitalization of older adults with disabilities through assessment, early detection, and treatment of changes in their medical conditions. Acting as an advocate for older adults with disabilities, the nurse can arrange a continuum of health care before discharge from the rehabilitation program to ensure a plan for primary care. In each interaction with chronically ill older adults or older adults with disabilities, the nurse should focus on maintenance and restoration of function. Rehabilitation health care professionals must take leadership in addressing the ongoing needs of clients with disabilities through education, advocacy, and direct provision of primary care.

Summary

This past decade has seen a shift from reduction of mortality in the older adult to prevention of morbidity. Williams (1993) lists these five factors affecting the future of rehabilitation: (1) multidisciplinary and multiagency collaboration and cooperation, (2) raising awareness of efficacy of rehabilitation, (3) research and evaluation of rehabilitation methods, (4) adequate community and caregiver support, and (5) access to rehabilitation in a variety of settings.

One major shortcoming in the health care system in the United States is the manner in which it pays for health care. The current system offers no incentive for providers and payors to make up-front investments to avert medical problems later. The health care system is quickly changing in the face of competition, rapid growth of costs, and health care reform. These changes offer a window of opportunity to address the health care needs of older adults with disabilities.

HOME CARE TIPS

1. Arthritis, the number one chronic illness, is commonly found in homebound older adults.
2. A homebound older adult with a chronic condition most likely has a functional limitation that has the potential to affect independence.
3. Use caregivers as sources for data about a homebound older adult's ability to cope with diagnosed chronic conditions.
4. Refer caregivers and homebound older adults to equipment vendors for assistive devices (e.g., canes, walkers, shower chairs, grab bars, and glucose monitoring machines) that promote independence at home.
5. Use social workers as sources for identifying community resources for financial assistance for the homebound older adult.
6. Assist caregivers and homebound older adults in adjusting to the necessary lifestyle changes to promote coping with the chronic illness.
7. Encourage caregivers to attend support groups to help ease the burden of caring for a homebound older adult with a chronic illness.

Key Points

- The trajectory of chronic illness varies with the individual and the illness.
- Orem's model of self-care provides the nurse with a framework to assess for variables that affect the older adult's ability to care for himself or herself.
- Regular, comprehensive assessment is the central principle of care of the older adult.
- Assessing what is meaningful to the older adult helps the nurse plan interventions to support psychosocial adjustment to a chronic condition or illness.
- Rehabilitation of the older adult focuses on improving functional ability.
- Health promotion incentives that are important to the older adult are fitness, health, independence, and socialization.

Critical Thinking Exercise

- A 75-year-old-woman, independent and in relatively good health, has had a nagging cough for the past several months. She is concerned that the cough may indicate a serious illness. She is reluctant to seek help, because she does not want to prolong her life if it means loss of quality. Make a judgment about where she fits within the illness trajectory, and explain how the nurse can be of assistance.

REFERENCES

ACRM White Paper: Addressing the post-rehabilitation health care needs of persons with disabilities, *Arch Phys Med Rehab* 14(12):8-14, 1993.

Beach D: Gerontological nursing: analysis of family experience, *J Gerontolog Nurs* 19(12):35-41, 1993.

Burbank P: Assessing meaning in life among older adult clients, *J Gerontolog Nurs* 18(9):19-28, 1992.

Butler M: Geriatric rehabilitation nursing, *Rehab Nurs* 16(6):318-321, 1991.

Calvani D, Douris K: Functional assessment: a holistic approach to rehabilitation of the geriatric client, *Rehab Nurs* 16(6):330-333, 1991.

Cifu D et al: Geriatric rehabilitation. 2. Diagnosis and management of acquired disabling disorders, *Arch Phys Med Rehab* 75(5):406-411, 1993.

Currie D, Gershkoff A, Cifu D: Geriatric rehabilitation. 3. Mid- and late-life effects of early life disabilities, *Arch Phys Med Rehab* 74(5):413-415, 1993.

Davidhizar R: Understanding powerlessness in family member caregivers of the chronically ill, *Geriatr Nurs* 13(2):66-69, 1992.

De Jong G: Post rehabilitation health care for people with disabilities, *Arch Phys Med Rehab* 74(12):2-7, 1993.

Detlefs D, Myers R: *1994 Medicare*, Louisville, Ky., December 1993, William M. Mercer.

Ebersole P, Hess P: *Toward healthy aging: human needs and nursing response,* ed 4, St. Louis, 1994, Mosby.

Edwards JN, Klemmack DL: Correlates of life satisfaction: a reexamination, *J Gerontol* 28:497-502, 1973.

Frankl V: *Man's search for meaning,* New York, 1962, Simon & Schuster.

Gershkoff A, Cifu D, Means K: Geriatric rehabilitation. 1. Social, attitudinal, economic factors, *Arch Phys Med Rehab* 74(5):402-405, 1993.

Harris I: *The myth and reality of dying in America,* Washington D.C., 1976, National Council on Dying.

Holtzclaw LR: The importance of self-concept for the older adult, *J Religion Aging,* 1(3):23-29, 1985.

Hyams DE: Psychological factors in the rehabilitation of the elderly, *Gerontologica Clinica,* 11:129-136, 1969.

King I: *A theory of nursing,* New York, 1981, Wiley and Sons.

Kirk K: Chronically ill patient's perceptions of nursing care, *Rehab Nurs* 13(2):99-104, 1993.

Kobayashi S, Masaki H, Noguchi M: Family caregivers of demented Japanese, *J Gerontolog Nurs* 19(10):7-13, 1993.

Lang NM et al: *Quality of health care for older people in America: a review of nursing studies,* Kansas City, Mo. 1990, American Nurses Association.

Lubkin IM: *Chronic illness: impact and interventions,* Boston, 1990, Jones and Bartlett.

Matteson M, McConnell E: *Gerontological nursing concepts and practice,* Philadelphia, 1988, WB Saunders.

Mayer A: Rehabilitation around the clock, *Nurs Times* 87(6):65-68, 1991.

Means K, Currie D, Gershkoff A: Geriatric rehabilitation. 4. Assessment, preservation and enhancement of fitness and function. *Arch Phys Med Rehab* 74(5):417-419, 1993.

Metha S: Applying Orem's self-care framework, *Geriatr Nurs* 14(4):182-185, 1993.

Miller D, Morley J: Attitudes of physicians toward elderly drivers and driving policy, *J Am Geriatr Soc* 41(7):722-724, 1993.

Miller J: The psychosocial aspects of rehabilitation, *Caring* August 4:20-26, 1992.

Moore B et al: Nursing research: quality of life and perceived health in the elderly, *J Gerontolog Nurs* 19(11):7-15, 1993.

Norman EJ, Norman VI: Relationship of patient's health locus of control beliefs to progress in rehabilitation, *J Rehab* 27-31, January 1991.

Orem D: *Nursing: concepts of practice,* ed 5, St. Louis, 1995, Mosby.

Pascucci M: Measuring incentives to health promotion in older adults, *J Geronotolog Nurs* 18(3):16-23, 1992.

Rhodes R, Morrissey M, Ward A: Self-motivation: a driving force for elders in cardiac rehabilitation, *Geriatr Nurs* 13(2):94-98, 1992.

Sioson ER, Kerfoot S, Ziat LM: Rehabilitation outcome of older patients with end stage renal disease and lower extremity amputation, *J Am Geriatr* 41(6):667-688, June 1993.

Smits M, Kee C: Correlates of self-care among the independent elderly, *J Gerontolog Nurs* 18(9):13-17, 1992.

Strauss A, Corbin J: *Shaping a new health care system,* San Francisco, 1988, Jossey-Bass.

Temple A, Fawdry K: King's theory of goal attainment, *J Gerontolog Nurs* 18(3):11-15, 1992.

Williams J: Rehabilitation challenge, *Nurs Times* 18(31):66-70, 1993.

BIBLIOGRAPHY

Albert S: Do family caregivers recognize malnutrition in the frail elderly? *J Am Geriatr Soc* 41(6):617-622, June 1993.

Hegland A: Customizing Continence, *Contemp Long Term Care* 71-73, 1993.

Johnson J, Waldo M, Johnson R: Stress and perceived health status in the rural elderly, *J Gerontolog Nurs* 19(10):24-29, 1993.

National Center for Health Statistics, Hyattsville, Md., 1994, Public Health Service.

Strasser DC: Geriatric rehabilitation: perspectives from the United Kingdom, *Arch Phys Med Rehab* 73(6):582-585, 1992.

US Bureau of Census: *Statistical abstract of the United States,* ed 113, Washington D.C., 1993.

US Department of Health and Human Services: *Prevalence of selected chronic conditions.* 1993.

APPENDIX 16A

RESOURCES

Alzheimer's Disease Education and Referral Center
P.O. Box 8250
Silver Spring, MD 20907

American Academy of Physical Medicine and Rehabilitation
1225 Michigan Avenue, Suite 1300
Chicago, IL 60603
(312) 922-9366

American Parkinson's Disease Association
60 Bay Street, Suite 401
Staten Island, NY 10301
(800) 825-2732

Arthritis Foundation
P.O. Box 19000
Atlanta, GA 30326
(404) 872-7100

House Select Committee on Aging
House Office Building
Annex 1, Room 712
Washington, DC 20515

National Rehabilitation Information Center
4407 Eight Street NE
Washington, DC 20017-2277
(202) 635-5822

National Stroke Association
8480 East Orchard Road, Suite 1000
Englewood, CO 80111-5015
(303) 771-1700

National Caucus and Center on Black Aged
1424 K Street NW, Suite 500
Washington, DC 20005
(202) 637-8400

Senate Special Committee on Aging
Dirkson Senate Office Building, Room 623
Washington, DC 20510

CHAPTER 17

Loss, Dying, and Death

LEARNING OBJECTIVES

On completion of this chapter, the reader will be able to:

1. Distinguish between grief, mourning, and bereavement.
2. Discuss characteristics of grief.
3. State Worden's four tasks of mourning.
4. Identify psychologic, physical, social, and spiritual aspects of normal grief responses.
5. Describe four ways that complicated grief reactions may be manifested.
6. Provide nursing care activities to assist the grieving older adult.
7. Discuss physical, psychologic, social, and spiritual aspects of dying for older people.
8. Explain age-related changes affecting older people who are dying.
9. Describe nursing strategies for assisting dying older people and their families.
10. Discuss the philosophy and characteristics of hospice programs.

The experience of aging may include transitions—employment to retirement; lifelong home to another, often smaller home; activity to less activity; health to chronic illness; marriage to widowhood; and extensive social networks to smaller circles of family and friends. These transitions are defined as losses within American society and are often viewed negatively. *Successful aging* requires coping with these losses; grieving, or mourning appropriately; and accepting one's new status positively.

The purpose of this chapter is to provide basic knowledge regarding loss and grief and the experience of dying so that nurses can assist the grieving, the dying, and their families during this process. The nature of life transitions, especially those focused around death and dying; the meaning that these changes may have for older people and their families; and typical ways in which people respond to such changes are discussed. A holistic approach, incorporating physiologic, psychosocial, and spiritual aspects, is applied with discussion of nursing care of older people and their families throughout this process.

American culture typically defines aging in a negative way, and death and dying is often considered a "taboo" issue. Only recently has research shown that life transitions such as dying can act as catalysts for personal growth. Such intense times of crisis in people's lives have the potential to stimulate spiritual and psychologic growth if the crisis can be successfully managed. A **healthy death** is the goal. This has been defined as a death "that has positive benefits for the dying person, the dying person's family, and the dying person's caregivers" (Smith, Maher, 1991). Nurses often act as guides to accompany the older person and their family members through this final life transition.

LOSS, GRIEF, AND MOURNING

Most of the literature and research on bereavement among older people focuses on the death of a spouse with less attention on responses to loss of parents, siblings, adult children, and friends. Other gradual and abrupt life transitions such as retirement, changing residence, ill health, loss of pets, and inability to drive are also viewed as losses evoking varying degrees of bereavement responses. For all types of transitions, from moving to a new home to the death of a loved one, people's responses to these transitions depend on their perceptions of the event, and the meaning it has for them within the context of their lives and their physical, psychosocial, and spiritual life patterns.

Demographics

Although American society values preserving and prolonging life, the death of an older person is often viewed as acceptable and timely (Kowalski, 1986). Death has become associated with aging since more than 70% of all deaths in the United States occur among those over age 65 (Fulton, 1987). In one study, 22% of the sample over age 60 knew eight or more people who had died within the past 2 years. An additional 33% knew between four and seven people who had died during that same period (Kalish, Reynolds, 1981). These statistics show that dealing with the deaths of those close to them as well as confronting their own impending mortality are common experiences for many older adults.

Loss of Relationships

Death of one's spouse is usually the most significant loss that the older person may experience. It involves loss of a companion who is often one's best friend, sexual partner, partner in decision making and household management, and a source for one's definition of self or identity. Among today's older couples, there is often a sharp division of labor with regard to many of the tasks of daily living. This makes living alone even more difficult, since surviving spouses must learn new roles and tasks during a time when they are experiencing extreme emotional loss (Osterweis, 1985).

Although bereavement following the death of a spouse has been found to be a highly stressful process, Lund's summary (1989) of studies on widowed people concludes that many older surviving spouses are quite resilient. Of those studied, 72% reported that the spouse's death was the most stressful event that they had ever experienced, although they also reported high coping abilities. The overall effects of bereavement on the physical and mental health of many older widows was not as severe as expected, with both positive and negative feelings experienced simultaneously. Loneliness and problems associated with tasks of daily living were two of the most common difficulties reported. Although many differences existed among the ways older bereaved adults adjusted to the deaths of their spouses, the most difficult period occurred in the first several months, improving gradually but unsteadily over time (Lund, 1989).

Another factor that influenced bereavement adjustments, based on Lund's review (1989) were that older men and women were more similar than dissimilar in their bereavement experiences and adjustment. Age, income, education, and anticipation or forewarning of death did not seem to have much impact on future adjustment processes. Religion-related variables also did not contribute much to the explanation of adjustment. Social support was moderately helpful in the adjustment process, as were internal types of coping resources such as independence, self-efficacy, self-esteem and competency in performing tasks of daily living.

Older adults' normal grief responses to the losses of their spouses have been summarized by Lund (1989). The following conclusions were drawn from his work and speak specifically to the bereavement experiences of older people:

1. Bereavement adjustments are multidimensional, in that nearly every aspect of a person's life can be affected by the loss.
2. Bereavement is a highly stressful process, but many older surviving spouses are quite resilient.
3. The overall impact of bereavement on the physical and mental health of many older spouses is not as devastating as expected.
4. Older bereaved spouses commonly experience both positive and negative feelings simultaneously.
5. Loneliness and problems associated with the tasks of daily living are two of the most common and difficult adjustments for older bereaved spouses.
6. The course of spousal bereavement in later life might be best described as a process that is most difficult in the first several months but improves gradually, if unsteadily, over time. (The improve-

ment may continue for many years or for some, it may never end.)

7. There is a great deal of diversity in how older bereaved adults adjust to the death of the spouse (Lund, 1989).

The deaths of loved ones remind those left behind of their own mortality and evokes significant meanings for those who are grieving (see Research box below). To an adult child, the death of a parent often has many conflicting meanings, depending on the nature of the parent-child relationship. Meanings of parental death range from being orphaned, becoming the oldest generation next in line for death, coming into one's own, changing roles, becoming a role model for one's own aging process, experiencing relief, or ending the opportunity to complete unfinished business (Kowalski, 1986). Often, death of a parent is preceded by an extended period of caregiving, usually by a daughter. Inherent in this caregiving role are a multitude of potential problems. Feelings of guilt, anger, ambivalence, role reversal, burden, and problems among siblings can all influence the bereavement process and adjustment following the death of a parent.

RESEARCH

Faletti MV et al: Longitudinal course of bereavement in older adults. In Lund D, editor: *Older bereaved spouses,* New York, 1989, Hemisphere.

Sample, setting

The subjects included 251 bereaved spouses age 55 to 93 living in the community (68% female and 32% male).

Methodology

Interview protocols over 18 months following the death through use of the Beck Depression Inventory, the Hopkins Symptom Check Lists, and other checklists.

Implications

Depression and other psychosocial indicators were relatively low throughout the 18 months, with the highest levels at 2 months following the death. Only 5% of the sample was severely depressed, and this was related to perceived health status regardless of the time of the interview. Couples who shared social and recreational tasks had lower mean levels of depression.

Findings

Nurses need to encourage health promotion and healthy relationships throughout all stages of life. Support for the surviving spouse is particularly important 2 months following the death. Situational factors should be taken into consideration when assessing and planning interventions with the bereaved.

When siblings die, it is an even more powerful reminder of one's own mortality for they are of the same generation. The death of a sibling may trigger realignment of family responsibilities or increased feelings of vulnerability when the death is a result of an inheritable disease. Bereavement adjustment may depend on the emotional closeness of the siblings' relationship, which is often complicated by ambivalent feelings common among siblings (Osterweis, 1985).

The death of an adult child has received relatively little attention in the literature. Parents usually expect their children to outlive them, so the untimely death of a child, even an adult child, is especially difficult. Feelings of anger and guilt often complicate the grieving process. An adult child's death may leave the older person without a caretaker, making lifestyle changes necessary as well (Osterweis, 1985).

In death-attitude research among older people, O'Laughlin (1983) reported a theme of strong emotional reactions toward learning about the death of friends and neighbors. Friends are especially important in old age and contact with close friends is often associated with life satisfaction and mental health. Age-segregated housing for older adults increases the frequency and visibility of deaths of neighbors, often reducing interaction and initiating negative stereotyping of other older adults within the building (O'Laughlin, 1983). As more friends are lost, one's sense of abandonment may intensify.

Definitions

Although some authors such as Gonad and Ruark (1984) differentiate among the terms grief, mourning, and bereavement, these terms are often used interchangeably in the literature. **Grief** is defined here as the acute reaction to one's perception of loss, incorporating physical, psychologic, social, and spiritual aspects. Other characteristics of grief are that (1) it involves many changes over time; (2) it is a natural reaction to all kinds of losses, not just death; and (3) it is based on one's unique perception of the loss (Rando, 1988). Grief responses are characterized in two ways—normal and uncomplicated, or complicated grief reactions.

Mourning refers to the longer range process of resolving acute grief reactions and enables mourning people to resume living a satisfying life. Mourning involves both unconscious and conscious processes that gradually loosen ties to the loved one, that help in adapting to the loss, and that assist in the process of learning to live a healthy life in the world without the loved one (Rando, 1988). **Bereavement** signifies the state of having experienced a significant loss.

Perceptions and Meanings

Loss and death are interwoven in the fabric of life. The longer people live, the more losses and separations become a part of their lives. It is through the experiences of attachment and loss that people learn to cope and to draw on their internal and external resources. The culture transmits meanings and values through rites and rituals that help people cope with loss and death.

The meaning of loss has been perceived in a variety of ways. Some of the more common meanings attached to illness and loss are punishment by a supreme being, suffering that must be overcome or must be endured, a normal part of the life experience, and opportunities for personal growth and transcendence.

Personal beliefs and attitudes, including cultural and religious ones, influence how losses are perceived. A person who views homosexuality as a sin may perceive acquired immunodeficiency syndrome (AIDS) as a punishment by God for homosexual individuals. Losses are often viewed as stressful events that must be overcome to get on with life. For others, suffering may be viewed as a virtue, something that may bring a person closer to God. Still others may seek to find meaning in the loss and in life after the loss, transcend the suffering associated with it, and experience personal growth as a result of it. The meaning of the loss to bereaved people has a significant impact on their responses to the loss. For this reason, it is important that caregivers explore the perceptions of the bereaved to better understand and to assist them through the grieving process.

Responses to Loss

Responses to loss have been labeled as grief. Lindemann's (1944) early work studying survivors of the 1942 Coconut Grove fire of Boston resulted in identification of physical and psychologic symptoms associated with acute grief. However, the ages of the mourners were not known. Since then, several other researchers have identified stages or phases of grief experienced by those who have lost loved ones (Gorer, 1965; Kavanaugh, 1972; Parkes, 1970; Raphael, 1983; Weizman, Kamm, 1985). Although there are important differences in content, these stage models can be characterized by time—an early, middle, and last phase of grief reaction. In the early phase, shock, disbelief, and denial are common. This phase commonly ends as people begin to accept the reality of the loss following the funeral. The middle phase is a time of intense emotional pain and separation, and may be accompanied by physical symptoms and volatile emotions. Lastly, there is a reintegration and relief as the pain gradually subsides and a degree of physical and mental balance returns (DeSpelder, Strickland, 1992).

In a different approach, Worden (1991) views the grief process as an active one rather than as something that normally happens over time to the bereaved. He identified tasks rather than stages and described the following four tasks of mourning: (1) accept the reality of the loss, (2) work through the pain of grief, (3) adjust to an environment in which the deceased is missing, and (4) emotionally relocate the deceased and move on with life. Accepting the reality of the loss involves coming to the realization that the person is dead, that he or she will not return, and that reunion, at least in life as it is known, is impossible. The second task—to experience the pain of grief—is necessary or the pain can manifest itself in some other symptom or problematic behavior. Sociocultural customs that discourage open expression of grief often contribute to unresolved grief work. Adjusting to an environment in which the deceased is missing, the third task, involves developing new skills and learning roles for which the deceased was responsible. Lastly, the withdrawal of emotional energy and the reinvestment in another relationship entails withdrawing emotional attachment to the lost person and loving another living person in a similar way. For many, this task is the most difficult to accomplish.

Worden's tasks of mourning are often a more useful way to think of grief work among older people than going through stages of grief. Stage models of grief imply a progression of stages beginning with shock and disbelief, but many older adults do not go through the first stage. They may have expected the death or may be beyond shock and disbelief after having experienced multiple losses in their lifetime. They also may undergo several of the stages at the same time, so looking at the tasks of grieving may be more helpful for the older person than expecting to progress through stages of grief. Regardless of whether shock or anticipation occurs, the task of accepting the reality of the loss is relevant for all.

It is critically important that older people who have lost loved ones acknowledge that pain is associated with grief and loss and that they must adjust to an environment where the loved one is absent. The expression of pain is in part culturally determined and also depends on the quality of the relationship with the lost loved one. Guilt often accompanies the pain of grief.

Adjustment to one's environment after the loss of a loved one involves learning new roles such as those previously assumed by the deceased, and new ways of interacting with others in one's social environment. This can be especially difficult if a spouse is the loved one lost and the social network consisted primarily of other couples.

The final task of emotionally relocating the deceased and moving on with life gives the bereaved person permission to emotionally invest in others without being disloyal to the lost loved one. Although Worden points out that, in one sense, mourning is never over, he also states that the process takes at least 1 full year before the wrenching pain subsides in losses involving a great deal of emotional attachment. Some older spouses have reported that they feel as though they will never "get over" their loss; instead, they have learned to live with it (Lund, 1989).

Anticipatory grief refers to grieving that occurs before the actual loss. It includes the processes of mourning, coping, and planning that are initiated when the impending loss of a loved one becomes apparent (Rando, 1986). Anticipatory grief may account for the apparent lack of overt grief reactions following the death of a loved one who has experienced a long terminal illness. There is some evidence that among the people for whom anticipatory grief work was possible, adjustment following the actual death may have occurred more rapidly (Parkes, 1975; Carey, 1977). However, Lund concluded in his summarization of research with older bereaved spouses that anticipation of bereavement did not have much effect on subsequent adjustment for older spouses. Nonetheless, anticipatory grief did help to reduce early shock, confusion, and depression.

Normal Grief Responses

Human beings respond as whole people, manifesting grief physically, psychologically, socially, and spiritually. These different aspects of the whole are discussed specifically to aid in better understanding their nature. The nurse should remember that each aspect is integrated within the whole person. Also, interventions directed at one of these areas affects the other areas. Thus an approach that separates the mind, body, and spirit is not advocated.

Psychologic Responses

Studies of grief responses have consistently identified common psychologic responses. Feelings of sadness are the emotions most often stated (Worden, 1991). Other common feelings include guilt, anxiety, anger, depression, helplessness, and loneliness. Shock and disbelief may be present immediately following the death or loss. The bereaved person may also display diminished self-concern, a preoccupation with the deceased, and a yearning for his or her presence. Some older people become confused and unable to concentrate following the death of someone significant to them. *Grief spasms,* periods of acute grief that come on when least expected, may occur (Rando, 1988). How the grief response manifests itself is individual and determined by many factors, including sociocultural factors, and the quality of the relationship between the deceased and the mourner. For some older people, the grief experience may include feelings of relief and emancipation, especially following prolonged suffering or a difficult relationship.

Physical Symptoms

Physical symptoms associated with the acute grief response are quite common. Tearfulness, crying, loss of appetite, feelings of hollowness in the stomach, decreased energy, fatigue, apathy, lethargy, and sleep difficulties are common symptoms of grief. Other physical sensations may include tension, weight loss or gain, sighing, feeling something stuck in the throat, tightness in the chest or throat, heart palpitations, restlessness, shortness of breath, dry mouth, and dreams of the deceased.

A sense of "interiority" or a turning inward with increased awareness of bodily sensations, is believed to be associated with old age (Neugarten, 1968). This increased sense of "interiority" may be related to intensified experiences of physical symptoms during mourning among older people; however, more research is needed in this area.

Social Changes

Social changes following the loss of a loved one depends on the type of relationship and the definition of social roles within the relationship. Widowhood is the loss that generally brings with it the greatest impact on social role change, but any loss of a person within one's household is especially difficult. In addition to deep psychologic pain, the bereaved person must often learn new skills and roles to manage tasks of daily living. All of this occurs at a time when withdrawal, a lack of interest in activities, and a lack of energy make decision making and action very difficult. Socialization and interaction patterns also change. If an older couple often socialized together with other couples, widowhood may bring dramatic changes in the type and style of interaction. For others who have strong social support and established patterns of independent interaction outside of the lost relationship, the adjustment process to new social roles and interactions may occur more quickly.

Spiritual Aspects

Lastly, the death of a loved one inevitably causes bereaved people to ponder the existential issues of life and to examine the meaning of not only the lost loved one's life but also their own. Spiritual issues may surface as the person searches for meaning. Anger at God, sometimes followed by a crisis of faith and meaning, may accompany bereavement. It may be very important for the bereaved to view the death of their loved one as a transition to a life with God in the spirit. Meaning in life is highly individualized, but the importance of finding meaning in life is well documented (Reker, Peacock, Wong, 1987; Burbank, 1988). What the person finds meaningful is not as important as the ability to look back on life and see that it has been meaningful, and that life can continue to be meaningful even in its last stages.

O'Laughlin (1983) reviewed studies of older people's attitudes toward death and mourning. Lund's (1989) work supported O'Laughlin's findings that death and mourning initiate a variety of feelings and responses. Conflicting results are found in studies exploring death anxiety, gender differences, and responses to losses. This may be because responses to loss are so ambiguous, con-

CULTURAL AWARENESS

Cultural Considerations in Loss, Dying, and Death

In some cultures, people believe that particular omens may warn of approaching death (e.g., the appearance of an owl and messages in dreams that foreshadow death, prevalent among some Native-American and Mexican-American groups). Research indicates that the desire to be told of one's impending death varies according to culture, with 71% of Caucasians, 60% of African Americans, 49% of Japanese Americans, and 37% of Mexican Americans in favor of having health care providers tell the individual that he or she is dying. Each of the previously mentioned groups indicated that the physician is the most appropriate person to communicate the information, whereas a family member is the second most appropriate choice.

Although death is a universal human experience, there are culture-specific considerations concerning attitudes toward the loss of a loved one according to *age* (i.e., child versus older adult) and *cause* of death. In many Asian-American cultures, the loss of an older adult who is perceived as having accumulated years of wisdom and knowledge may be mourned more than the loss of an infant or child who is viewed as being able to make a lesser contribution to society because of fewer years of life experiences. For many Caucasians, the reverse may be true, with relatively greater sorrow expressed over the loss of a younger person who is perceived to have been cheated out of achieving his or her fullest potential than that shown toward an older individual who has lived a full and productive life. It should be noted that, regardless of age, human life is valued by all cultures and loss of life is mourned by those who knew and loved the deceased.

Among the Tohono O'odham (Papago Indians of Arizona), the concept of "good" and "bad" death prevails. A good death comes at the end of a full life, when a person is prepared for death, whereas a bad death occurs unexpectedly and violently (e.g., accidents, homicides, suicides), leaving the victim without a chance to settle affairs or say goodbye. Some cultural and religious groups consider suicide to be taboo and may impose sanctions even after death (e.g., some Catholics may be denied burial in church cemeteries).

Both culture and religion influence postmortem rituals. Muslims have specific rituals for washing, dressing, and positioning the body, whereas some Jewish groups discourage cosmetic restoration or attempts to hasten or to retard decomposition by artificial means. Among some Asian-American groups, it is customary for family and friends of the same gender to wash and to prepare the body for burial or cremation. As part of their lifelong preparation for death, Amish women sew white burial garments for themselves and their family members. Deceased members of the Church of Jesus Christ of Latter-Day Saints (Mormons) are dressed in white temple clothing before being viewed by family and friends. Some Native Americans believe that the spirit of the deceased person is contaminated and refuse to touch the body after death. With traditional Navajo, the body is dressed in fine apparel, adorned with expensive jewelry, and money, and wrapped in new blankets. Some Navajo believe that the structure in which the person died must be burned.

Often interrelated with religious beliefs and practices, culture influences funeral and burial or cremation practices as well as what is expected of bereaved family members (e.g., who grieves, for how long, culturally appropriate behaviors during mourning, etc.). Among Chinese-Americans, five degrees of kinship *(wu-fu)* are recognized and these determine the severity of mourning that is expected according to closeness and importance of the deceased to the mourner.

Lastly, the nurse should be aware that culture may influence the final resting place for the deceased person. For example, the bodies of older Jewish clients may be flown to Jerusalem for burial, Catholics may prefer to be buried in ground blessed by a priest, and those who have been cremated may express various preferences for the disposition of the ashes. Traditional Chinese Americans may follow a system of double burial. The initial burial in a coffin lasts for 7 years, and the remains are then exhumed and stored in an urn.

From Andrews MM, Hanson PA: Religion, culture and nursing. In Andrews MM, Boyle JS, editors: *Transcultural concepts in nursing care,* ed 2, Philadelphia, 1995, JB Lippincott; Kozak DL: Dying badly: violent death and religious change among the Tohono O'odham, *Omega* 23(3):207-216, 1991; Mahoney MC: Fatal motor vehicle accidents among Native Americans, *Am J Prev Med* 7(2):112-116, 1991.

taining negative, positive, and variable dimensions (see Cultural Awareness box, above).

Complicated Grief Reactions

What has been described above is the range of responses generally considered to be "normal" or uncomplicated grief reactions. When grief progresses in an unhealthy way and does not move toward resolution, it is called complicated mourning or abnormal grief. In this situation, the person is overwhelmed and resorts to maladaptive behavior (Horowitz, 1980). The nursing diagnosis that deals with this syndrome is called **dysfunctional grieving** and includes many of the defining characteristics discussed as part of the normal grief process; however, they occur to an abnormal degree or for an extended length of time (Gordon, 1991). Nurses need to be familiar with dysfunctional grieving and should refer clients to advanced practice nurses or other health professionals skilled in working with complicated grieving (see Client/Family Teaching box, p. 394).

CLIENT/FAMILY TEACHING

Common Symptoms of Normal Grief Responses

Grief responses have physical, psychologic, social, and spiritual aspects. The duration and intensity of these symptoms is highly variable. Most of the more intense symptoms subside in 6 to 12 months; however, the duration of mourning may continue for several years.

Physical symptoms commonly include crying, loss of appetite, decreased energy and fatigue, and sleep difficulties.

Psychologic responses most commonly include feelings of sadness, guilt, anxiety, anger, depression, helplessness, and loneliness.

Social changes following the loss of a loved one are dependent on the role of the deceased. With widowhood, there is a loss of social support, often a change to living alone, and sometimes the inability to manage tasks of daily living, unless new skills are learned.

Spiritual aspects often lead the bereaved to search for meaning in life and to reexamine one's own faith and belief system.

Complicated grief reactions may manifest themselves in one of four ways: (1) chronic, (2) delayed, (3) exaggerated, or (4) masked grief reactions. Chronic grief is a prolonged grief reaction that never comes to a satisfactory conclusion. Since bereaved individuals are aware of their continuing grief, this type of reaction is fairly easy to recognize. The help of a therapist is needed to assess which task of grieving is not being resolved and why. The goal of the intervention is to resolve these tasks (Worden, 1991).

In delayed or postponed grief reactions, the response at the time of the loss is either absent or not sufficient to deal with the loss. At some future time, the person may experience an intense grief reaction triggered by a subsequent, smaller loss, or by any other event that triggers sadness. This usually occurs when there are feelings of hostility or ambivalence toward the deceased (Burnside, 1988).

Exaggerated grief reactions occur when the normal feelings of anxiety, depression, or hopelessness grow to unmanageable proportions. These people may feel overwhelmed and may feel that they are unable to live without the deceased person. They may lose the sense that the acute grief reaction is transient and may continue in this intense despair over a long period of time (Worden, 1991).

Lastly, masked grief reactions occur when bereaved people experience feelings related to the loss, but they do not express or do not recognize these feelings as related to the loss. It has been suggested that this may occur as a self-protective mechanism, because these people may not be able to bear the stress of mourning. Repression of grief responses in this way usually manifests in other ways, as either a physical symptom, often in medical symptoms similar to those that the deceased experienced, or through some type of maladaptive behavior (Worden, 1991).

Factors Affecting Grief Response

Rando (1988) has outlined factors that influence how people experience and express their grief reactions. Categories of psychologic factors include the characteristics and meaning of the lost relationship, personal characteristics of the bereaved, and specific circumstances surrounding the death (Table 17-1). Social factors include one's support system, sociocultural and religious background, education and economic status, and funerary rituals. An individual's physical state also influences the grief response. Important physical factors are drugs and sedatives, nutritional state, adequacy of rest and sleep, exercise, and general physical health. Nurses need to be aware of how all these factors affect dying people and their families so that they can provide the best care possible under the circumstances.

Nursing Care

The goal of nursing care for older people who are grieving is not to "make them feel better" quickly, as nurses are often tempted to do. The goal is to assist and support bereaved people through the grieving process, recognizing that pain is a normal and healthy response to loss and allowing bereaved people to accomplish the tasks of mourning in their own way.

Grief counseling is used to facilitate successful progression through the grief response, whereas grief therapy is intended for those who are experiencing complicated mourning. Nurses, other health professionals, and specially trained volunteers can provide grief counseling, whereas therapy should be under the guidance of a skilled therapist (Worden, 1991). The following is a discussion on grief counseling.

Worden (1991) suggested four ways that grief counselors can assist grieving people with the tasks of mourning. They include (1) increasing the reality of the loss, (2) helping the counselee deal with both expressed and latent affect, (3) assisting the counselee to deal with various impediments to readjustment after the loss, and (4) encouraging the counselee to make a healthy emotional withdrawal from the deceased and to feel comfortable reinvesting that emotion in another relationship.

Nurses working in hospitals encounter clients who are dealing with many different kinds of losses and who are experiencing intense grief reactions on a routine ba-

TABLE 17-1

Psychologic Factors Influencing Grief Responses

Characteristics and meaning of lost relationship	Personal characteristics of bereaved	Specific circumstances of the death
Nature and meaning of loss Qualities of lost relationship Role and function filled by deceased Characteristics of deceased Amount of unfinished business between bereaved and loved one Perception of deceased's fulfillment in life Number, type, and quality of secondary losses the death brings	Coping behaviors, personality and mental health Level of maturity and intelligence Past experiences with loss and death Social, cultural, ethnic and religious background Sex-role conditioning Presence of concurrent stress or crises in life	Immediate circumstances of death Timeliness of death Perception of preventability Sudden versus expected death Length of illness before death Anticipatory grief and involvement

sis. Despite the fact that nurses often have limited time to interact with bereaved clients and family members in the hospital setting, there are many ways that nurses can intervene. In nursing homes or community health settings, the staff or visiting nurses have repeated encounters with clients and families over a much longer period than hospital-based nurses. Regardless of setting, nurses have contact with at least some of a bereaved person's support systems, which can assist in the mourning process. This requires that nurses recognize grief responses, identify the primary task of mourning for the bereaved person, and intervene by using grief counseling principles. Worden's (1991) counseling principles can be useful in this process:

1. **Help the survivor actualize the loss.** Nurses are often the first to initiate this process, especially following the death of a client in a health care institution. Nurses are usually the professionals who are present to offer details and descriptions of the death event or explanations of puzzling situations that may not be understood by family members. Having information about the death and the events preceding and following it are important in helping to actualize the loss. Survivors may need to be encouraged to talk about the loss, to tell the story of events surrounding the death, and to relate memories of the deceased. This process takes time. Worden (1991) found that many of the widows studied took up to 3 months before they began to believe and to accept the reality that their spouse was dead and not going to return.
2. **Help the survivor to identify and express feelings.** Because of the unpleasantness of the feelings accompanying bereavement, these feelings may not be expressed or recognized by the bereaved person. Nurses need to assess the bereaved person's feelings and to ask specific questions that encourage expression of feelings. Feelings that often go unexpressed include anger, guilt, anxiety, and helplessness (Worden, 1991).

   Sometimes these emotions are displaced. For example, anger may be directed at the deceased for leaving or at God, but the anger may also be expressed toward the physician or the nurse who helped the family care for the loved one. Such anger is difficult to understand, but it is helpful for targets of the anger to detach themselves and not respond defensively. Sociocultural and gender differences influence expression of emotions and need to be taken into account by the nurse. Older people may also express their emotions differently than younger people, especially after having dealt with multiple losses. For example, crying may be a less common indicator of sadness among older people.
3. **Assist living without the deceased.** To accomplish this, the nurse needs to assess the survivor's daily living situation and identify any actual or potential problems. The roles played by the deceased must now be assumed by the survivor or someone else if tasks of daily living are to be accomplished. Knowledge of community resources and teaching of practical skills are necessary to meet this need. In general, survivors should be

counseled to postpone making major decisions that involve life changes, such as selling property or moving. Calling on the survivor's social support system is also useful in this area.

4. **Facilitate emotional withdrawal from the deceased.** The nurse needs to be especially sensitive to when the bereaved should emotionally withdraw from the deceased and should begin developing new relationships. This is especially difficult if the relationship lost was that of spouse. Research has shown, however, that older people who lose a confidant are less likely to replace the confidant than younger people. Perhaps they are unwilling to invest emotionally in another intimate relationship with the risk of repeated loss being so high. Other types of relationships such as close friendships may be encouraged to help meet the older person's needs for intimacy.
5. **Provide time to grieve.** It was formerly believed that after the first anniversary following the death, grief should be resolved. This has been shown to be inaccurate, with many factors influencing the length of time for adjustment, as discussed earlier. Two points in time seem to be especially critical: 3 months and 1 year after the death (Worden, 1991). For older people with multiple losses, more time may be needed. For some, the loss may never be resolved; the person may simply learn to live with the feelings of grief.
6. **Interpret "normal" behavior.** It is important that nurses, with a clear understanding of the range of normal grief responses, communicate acceptance and reassurance of the normalcy of the grieving person's responses. Grieving individuals can be reassured with the knowledge that they are not going crazy, that their physical and psychologic responses are normal in the face of significant loss, and that they will feel better in time.
7. **Allow for individual differences.** Just as nurses must be sensitive to individual differences in styles of grieving, family and friends need to be accepting of differences among themselves in their grief responses. Nurses may need to explain the wide range of responses and to assist the mourners with allowing one another to grieve in their own unique ways.
8. **Provide continuing support.** Although nurses' interactions with bereaved people may be brief or intermittent, referrals can be made for outside support. This may include referrals to community resources and support groups. Nurses can also encourage the bereaved to mobilize their own support system of family and friends.
9. **Examine defenses and coping styles.** Certain coping behaviors are healthy, whereas others are not. The older person has a lifetime of experience coping with stressful situations, and usually has well-established patterns of coping. Under normal circumstances, these defenses and coping mechanisms can often be used successfully; however, they may not be effective in dealing with monumental or accumulated losses. When the coping mechanisms are unhealthy they may lead to destructive behaviors such as alcoholism. Nurses can help the bereaved identify their coping mechanisms, evaluate their effectiveness, and either encourage their continued use or explore other ways of coping more positively.
10. **Identify pathology and refer.** When assistance through grief counseling and professional guidance is not sufficient, additional problems may arise, which require more intensive help. Nurses need to be particularly alert to serious depressive illness and refer accordingly. Loss of a spouse and living alone put the older person at risk for depression. Older white males have the highest suicide rate of any group, which may suggest that depression is a significant problem for this age group. For example, 71.9 white men per 100,000 resident population age 85 and older die each year from suicide, in comparison with 22.2 black men, 6.2 white women, and 22.8 for all races (Health United States, 1991). Discussion of meaning in life with older men may give the nurse clues to problems in this area.

In general, medications are overused in treating the symptoms of grief reactions and have been called the most inappropriate therapeutic tool for dealing with grief (Gonda, Ruark, 1984). This causes special problems among Americans over the age of 65 who on the average take about 15 prescriptions per year, three times as many prescriptions as younger people (U.S. Printing Service, 1992). With each added drug, the risk of drug interactions increases. Also, the risk for side effects and toxic reactions is greater among older adults than for younger people (see Chapter 20).

In summary, nurses in all types of settings are in a position to assist the bereaved at various levels of grief. Nurses are the most effective, however, when they examine their own losses, grief expectations, and patterns of coping with loss. Personal experiences with loss inevitably influence the effectiveness of the help that nurses can give to others who are mourning. The nurse who has successfully worked through a loss, big or small, and who has reflected on the experience has gained valuable insight into the grieving process. On the other hand, the nurse who is grieving may be unable to invest emotional energy to care for a client experiencing an acute grief response.

THE PROCESS OF DYING: OLDER PEOPLE'S PERSPECTIVES

The following addresses the nature of dying among older people, including stages of dying; attitudes toward death; and physical, psychosocial, and spiritual responses. Nursing strategies for working with older people who are dying, environmental considerations, and family and caregiver perspectives are among other important aspects to understanding the nature of dying.

Kübler-Ross (1969) in her classic work on death and dying, identified five stages that have become a basis for practice with dying clients. Kübler-Ross' model purports that dying individuals progress through the stages of denial, anger, bargaining, depression, and finally, acceptance of death. All clients may not move through these stages in a sequential and orderly fashion, with some even moving back and forth between the stages, but this stage theory has become very popular in interpreting the behavior and feelings of dying people sometimes to their detriment.

Kübler-Ross' (1969) stage theory may be irrelevant and detrimental for older people who are dying, since some may be accepting death and may be ready to die. Retsinas (1988) argues for a model of death in older people that takes into account several factors: (1) that very old people see themselves as confronting impending death; (2) that they are used to the "sick role" and gradual decrease of vitality; (3) that roles have already been redefined; and (4) that death may truly be timely for them.

Kastenbaum (1978) attributes such assumptions about older people being ready for a timely death as evidence of our society's ageist attitudes. Although the literature demonstrates that older people have a variety of attitudes toward death, fear of their own death is relatively rare. Research has generally proven that there is less fear of death among older people than among younger ones, with older adults also more concerned about being in control and life after death (Thorson, Powell, 1988). Major concerns about dying among older people are fears of being a burden, suffering, and use of life-prolonging technology (Kowalski, 1986; Matthews, 1979; Kohn, Menon, 1988). The person who has had positive experiences of coping and is relatively well-adjusted usually approaches the stress of being close to death with adaptation and acceptance. Individual assessments, however, still need to be conducted, since older adults have widely varied experiences and attitudes.

Psychologic Aspects

Factors other than age are important in determining the older person's feelings toward his or her own death. Sociocultural and religious background, physical and functional status (especially degree of pain and dependency on others), social isolation and loneliness (usually resulting from death of more than one significant other), and the meaningfulness of everyday life are all important factors determining one's approach to impending death. These, more than age alone, must be considered in assessing and understanding the older person's attitudes toward dying and death.

Once people have identified themselves as nearing the end of their lives, they commonly engage in a process called life review (Butler, 1963), where they try to make sense of life as a whole. Erikson (1963) identified the psychosocial crisis of integrity versus despair as characteristic of the last stage of life. In this theory, older people nearing the end of their lives are expected to review their lives and draw some conclusions about the positive and negative aspects of their lives. If they can generally say that their life was meaningful and worth living, then a sense of ego integrity emerges. If, however, their lives are negatively evaluated, a sense of regret or meaninglessness and despair may be experienced.

Spiritual Aspects

Religious beliefs and spiritual experiences play an important part in older people making sense of their lives. Faith in a supreme power can give life a transcendent meaning and help people view their lives within the context of a greater purpose or meaning. Sometimes dying or threat of loss can trigger a crisis of faith where people question their previous beliefs in an effort to make sense of the present experience. It is in life transitions such as dying and death that one's most deeply held beliefs are challenged and opportunities for growth (or regression and despair) are presented.

Three spiritual needs of dying people have been identified by Doka (1993): (1) to search for meaning of life, (2) to die appropriately, and (3) to find hope that extends beyond the grave. These three needs reflect Erickson's developmental task for the last stage of life, as well as other research findings regarding fears associated with dying for older people. Religious or spiritual beliefs and experiences can be instrumental in helping the older person to meet these fears. Some nurses are comfortable discussing spiritual concerns with clients, whereas other nurses prefer to make referrals to the client's religious leader or the hospital chaplain. When asked, the client or family usually feels free to indicate how they would like spiritual assistance.

Social Aspects

Once the term "dying" is applied to an individual, role changes are often initiated or reinforced by family and friends. The adopted sick role may be accompanied by an acceptance of one's fate. Alternately, dying individuals may adopt a fighting stance, determined to do all they can to outwit or to forestall approaching death. Some move ahead with the resolve to define themselves as "still living" and refuse to accept the label of "dying," thus living each day as fully as possible. The stance people take toward dying is affected by sociocultural, psychologic, and life history factors. Some of these attitudes toward dying are positive and growth-promoting, whereas others are negative and difficult to endure, not only for dying people but also for those around them. For example, it is troublesome when family members want to resolve issues while the client denies that he or she is dying and refuses to discuss matters that need resolution.

Because death and dying have been regarded as taboo topics for discussion in American society, most people are uncomfortable, at least initially, in talking about death with someone who is dying. This is partly because of having to confront one's own mortality when death is faced in others. It is fairly easy to live in an illusion of stability and immortality when around young, healthy people. When a loved one is "dying," thoughts turn to one's own mortality and what life will be like without this person. Since these thoughts are uncomfortable for most, one way of relieving this discomfort is by avoiding the dying person. Social isolation often results as friends and sometimes family seemingly abandon the dying person. A special concern for older people results from society's attitudes that old people are ready to die and therefore have less need to interact with others. It is seen as normal and natural for them to disengage and to die quietly as expected. This attitude also fosters social isolation. Thus social isolation, loneliness, and role changes are common concomitants of dying for older people.

Physical Aspects

An obvious and sometimes puzzling question for those working with older people is when to consider a person to be dying? Is a diagnosis of terminal illness necessary? Are there certain physical signs that must be present? In one respect, all human beings are in the process of dying. The length of time, however, before death occurs or the certainty of a fatal illness determine whether one is defined as dying. Life expectancy also enters into people's attitudes about when dying occurs. There is generally a greater expectation of impending death for a spry 100-year old than for an energetic 75-year-old. Mortality statistics support this expectancy with 71% of the deaths in the United States occurring in those age 65 and older, with the over-85-year-old group having the highest death rate (National Center for Health Statistics, 1990). Because there is no clear definition of the stage of "dying" for older people not diagnosed with a terminal illness, this must also be individually explored.

Cause of death among older people usually results from complications from one or more chronic illnessess rather than from a sudden, unexpected incident or illness. Corbin and Strauss (1988) described the chronic illness trajectory and the adjustments necessary by the dying person and family members. Dealing with a long-term illness with its many ups and downs can put tremendous strain on both the older person and his or her family. Adjustments include, among others, preparation for death and bringing closure to life.

General Health Care Needs

Regardless of needs arising from specific diseases and functional problems, there are general health care needs of the dying individual. According to Walborn (1980), these general needs revolve around (1) stabilizing and supporting vital functions, and facilitating integrated functioning; (2) determining the functional deviation and adjusting treatment; (3) relieving distressing symptoms and suffering; (4) assisting client and family interaction; and (5) supporting client and family coping with the realities of death.

Impact of Age-Related Changes

Nursing care aimed at meeting the physical needs of older people who are dying is not different than the meticulous care needed by any other client with a debilitated condition. Age-related changes, however, and the effects of long-term chronic illnesses predispose the older person to greater potential for problems in hygiene and skin care, nutrition, elimination, mobility and transfers, rest and sleep, pain management, respiration, and cognitive and behavioral functioning (Sanker, 1991). Only the areas that pose special problems for older people are discussed here.

Age-related changes in the integumentary and vascular systems, coupled with alterations in nutrition, elimination, and mobility, quickly lead to skin breakdown. Loss of the subcutaneous fat layer and a decrease in sebaceous gland activity cause the skin to become thin and dry, thus making it more susceptible to the hazards of immobility. Pressure ulcers are a difficult problem for older, debilitated clients, often quick to form and slow to heal. Sometimes even the best skin care and positioning cannot prevent the formation of pressure ulcers (see Chapter 28).

Rigidity of the chest wall, and decreased ciliary activity, cough, and gag reflex all predispose the older person to respiratory problems, especially pneumonia (see Chapter 22). Aspiration pneumonia is a common problem for older clients who are unable to feed themselves and who have difficulty maintaining an upright position. Decreased effectiveness of the immune system and presentation of uncommon symptoms for pneumonia can make the diagnosis and treatment of pneumonia in the older person more complicated. Shortness of breath and altered respiratory patterns in sleep, such as Cheyne-Stokes respirations or sleep apnea, are more prevalent

> ***Insight*** • *Immobility has been known to cause many physical and psychosocial problems. Alteration in skin integrity, in the form of pressure ulcers, often causes difficulty for older people. The process by which pressure ulcers occur is further accentuated by the multisystem deterioration that often accompanies the dying process. Traditional nursing care suggests turning and careful respositioning every 2 hours to prevent pressure ulcers. For the immobilized older person with a decreased layer of subcutaneous fat, increased bony prominences, and compromised cardiovascular status, more frequent repositioning is necessary. Repeated assessment and meticulous attention to pressure areas are necessary. The nurse or caregiver needs to gauge the frequency of repositioning to the client's needs based on the ongoing assessment of skin conditions.*

> ***Insight*** • *Typically, environmental stimuli such as light and sound are reduced in the room of a person who is close to death. Visitors speak in subdued tones, shades are drawn, and the lights are dimmed. Although individual preferences must be assessed and requests must be followed as much as possible, older people who are dying may benefit from maintenance of an everyday level of environmental stimulation, or even increased stimuli to compensate for decreased sensory acuity. For many dying older people, being surrounded by loved ones and cherished possessions in a familiar environment is especially comforting. Environmental stimulation should be arranged to provide for adequate lighting, and family and visitors should speak in tones loud enough to be easily heard. This decreases anxiety and provides the dying person with the potential of interacting with their loved ones in a comfortable environment.*

among older people and can become problematic for the older person who is seriously ill or dying.

Digestive changes associated with age include decreased amount of saliva and digestive fluids and enzymes, decreased peristaltic activity, and decreased absorption through the intestinal wall. These changes predispose the older person who is dying to additional problems with maintaining adequate nutritional status and bowel function. These changes are exacerbated by the hazards of immobility and often contribute to constipation, fecal impaction, and sometimes diarrhea. Although health care professionals often downplay the seriousness of constipation, this problem can cause major discomfort for the dying person and contribute to other life-threatening complications (see Chapter 24).

Changes in vision and hearing that commonly accompany advanced age result in the older person receiving less stimulation from the environment. This is complicated by the usual practice of removing eyeglasses and hearing aids from clients who are ill, as well as providing a quiet, darkened, and peaceful environment. Sensory deprivation has been shown to lead to mental confusion among healthy individuals and is of even greater importance among older adults who are dying (see Chapter 28).

Environmental change and unfamiliar people and settings also contribute to cognitive impairment among older people. Because hospitalization or a move to a nursing home often accompanies the dying experience for older people, the acute confusion that may result from such a move may be permanent. Institutionalization, even if temporary, may be experienced as a rite of passage for the older person and may serve as an external indicator that their illness is progressing and death is becoming more imminent.

Although it is believed that the superficial pain experience of older people is unchanged, many older adults seem to experience less deep pain, such as the deep organ pain associated with terminal illnesses like cancer. On the other hand, older people reportedly have an increased sense of introspection, which means they have heightened experiences of their internal bodily functions and feelings (Neugarten, 1968). This increased introspect may give rise to more reports (often perceived as complaints) of pain and discomfort that need to be heeded and validated by the nurse (see Chapter 13). Nonmedication interventions for pain relief such as therapeutic touch, massage, accupressure, relaxation, and visualization need to be used whenever possible.

Age-related changes in pharmacokinetics and pharmacodynamics lead to atypical drug responses (see Chapter 20). Because drugs are so widely used as an essential part of medical treatment, their effectiveness, side effects and reactions need to be closely monitored. Physiologic changes associated with dying, such as circulatory changes, increase the probability of difficulty managing drug regimens.

Sleep patterns are also disturbed by physiologic changes, pain, and changes in the environment. Medications are the most common answer to complaints of inability to sleep by those who are dying. Although these may be appropriate in some instances, they need to be prescribed with caution and monitored carefully. For the older person who is dying, sleep medications may cause new problems such as incontinence or acute confusion. Again, nondrug therapies should be used first. Psychologic causes of sleeplessness should also be explored. For example, if older people fear dying alone in their sleep and they have unfinished business to resolve with their families, sleep medications are not the answer. Instead, a careful assessment of the cause of sleeplessness must be followed by treatment appropriate for the cause (see Chapter 9).

Nursing Care

Excellent nursing care of dying older people begins with examination of the nurse's own value system regarding older people in American society. In such a youth-oriented culture, old age is not highly esteemed or valued. With a growing problem of overpopulation, death in old age greatly benefits society. An overworked nurse in a hospital has to prioritize efficiently so that younger clients with greater probability for survival usually receive more attention than older dying clients with physician orders for "do not resuscitate, comfort measures only." Sedating medications may be administered to make that task easier. The realities of the U.S. health care system and ageist societal values often force nurses to compromise the quality of care they deliver to dying older clients. Death often comes quietly, and the nurse cannot always be present to care for the dying persons' physical and emotional needs and to share in the wisdom and knowledge that only a lifetime of experiences can bring.

Assessment

As with any other nursing care, careful and ongoing assessments must be made of physical, psychosocial, and spiritual needs. Assessment tools for physical needs are described in an earlier chapter and are relevant for ill and dying older adults. Special attention, however, needs to be given to potential problem areas such as skin integrity, respiratory status, nutrition, elimination, sensory abilities, cognitive functioning, comfort, and rest.

Psychosocial needs of the dying person, family, and caregivers must also be carefully assessed. This can be a difficult area to approach, especially when time is limited, or when the client's or family's feelings about the dying process are unknown. Spiritual needs are often discussed with psychosocial needs, since these needs are interrelated and affect each other. Areas for careful assessment of spiritual needs include the search for meaning in life, dying appropriately, and finding hope that extends beyond the grave (Doka, 1993).

Meaning in life often emerges as a theme among those who are grieving, as well as those who are dying or nearing the end of their lives. Leading a meaningful life has been found to be associated with both physical health and a lack of depressive symptoms among a group of community-living older adults (Burbank, 1988). A series of questions that are useful in assessing the degree of meaningfulness in life can be found in Box 17-1.

A hierarchy of the dying person's needs, based on Maslow's hierarchy of needs framework, can assist

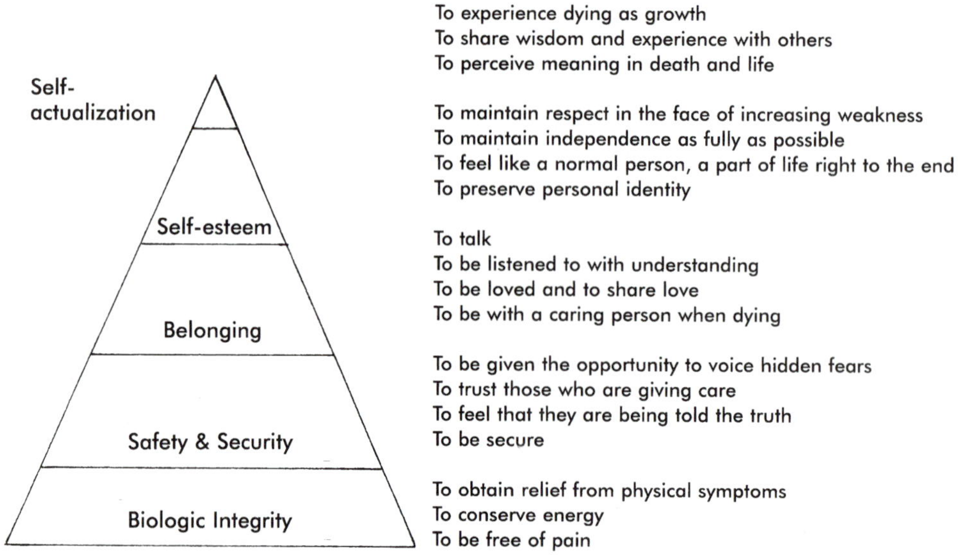

Fig. 17-1 Hierarchy of the dying person's needs. (Modified from Ebersole P, Hess P: *Toward healthy aging*, ed 4, St. Louis, 1994, Mosby).

BOX 17-1

Fullfillment of Meaning Scale

For each of the following statements, circle the response that is most nearly true for you at this time.

1. I feel that I have found a significant meaning or meanings for leading my life.
   Strongly disagree — Disagree — Uncertain — Agree — Strongly agree
2. Even though there may be a purpose in my life, I do not try to do much about it.
   Strongly disagree — Disagree — Uncertain — Agree — Strongly agree
3. I have a belief or beliefs about life that gives my living significance.
   Strongly disagree — Disagree — Uncertain — Agree — Strongly agree
4. Something seems to stop me from doing what I really want to do.
   Strongly disagree — Disagree — Uncertain — Agree — Strongly agree
5. I do not value what I am doing in my life.
   Strongly disagree — Disagree — Uncertain — Agree — Strongly agree
6. The things that are the most important to me dominate my activities.
   Strongly disagree — Disagree — Uncertain — Agree — Strongly agree
7. In thinking of my life, it is hard for me to see a reason for my being here.
   Strongly disagree — Disagree — Uncertain — Agree — Strongly agree
8. Basically, I am living the kind of life I want to live.
   Strongly disagree — Disagree — Uncertain — Agree — Strongly agree
9. In life, I have no goals or aims at all.
   Strongly disagree — Disagree — Uncertain — Agree — Strongly agree
10. My personal existence is purposeful and meaningful.
    Strongly disagree — Disagree — Uncertain — Agree — Strongly agree
11. Life seems to be completely routine.
    Strongly disagree — Disagree — Uncertain — Agree — Strongly agree
12. Facing my daily tasks is a source of pleasure and satisfaction.
    Strongly disagree — Disagree — Uncertain — Agree — Strongly agree

Meaning Framework Question

Is there something or things so important to you in your life that they give your life meaning?
Yes No

If no, please describe your life situation at this time.
If yes, please list those things that are currently important to you and that give your life meaning.

Adapted from Sankar A: *Dying at home: a family guide for caregiving,* Baltimore, 1991. Reprinted by permission of the Johns Hopkins University Press.

nurses in identifying the older dying person's specific needs at each level (Fig. 17-1). By careful assessment at the level of need that the dying person is experiencing, the nurse can then design specific individualized strategies to help meet these needs.

Strategies

There is little difference between nursing strategies for meeting the physical needs of younger people who are ill or for older dying people. In general, the same strategies may be applied, but more frequent assessment, application, and evaluation of the effectiveness of the strategies is necessary. For instance, a debilitated, immobile younger person may require repositioning less often than an older person who is also debilitated and immobile. Older people who are dying may suffer from more severe dry mouths than younger people with the same condition. The nurse needs to assure that care is not delivered less often because of personal biases and devaluation of old people. Pacing of care is especially important, with time and patience being given to encourage as much independent functioning as possible.

Good communication skills are essential in dealing with dying people and their families. Maintaining eye contact, using touch sensitively, and clarifying statements by using reflection (i.e., restating the message as you have understood it and asking for verification of meaning) are important. Awareness of one's own limitations and strengths is critical because of the level of involvement that can result from interactions with people confronting death. Once a nurse becomes committed to working with a client and family through the dying process, it is important to follow through on that commitment if at all possible.

Life review is a useful intervention for assisting older dying people with their psychologic and spiritual tasks. Although this intervention includes reminiscence, the nurse assists the dying person to go farther by facilitating ego integrity instead of despair. The nurse acts as a therapeutic listener and assists older people to critically analyze their lives by helping them reframe events in an accepting and empathetic environment (Haight, Burnside, 1993). Life review and reminiscence may not be appropriate for all older people, however. Those with a history of psychologic or social dysfunction, or few interpersonal resources may not benefit from the process (Sherwood, Mor, 1980; Peterson, 1980).

Another important role of the nurse in assisting dying people is in education and support of their families and caregivers. Caregivers experience a multitude of problems that include decreasing energy levels, health problems, deep grief, and fears associated with life without their loved one. Nurses need to be sensitive to caregiver needs and to provide education, psychologic support, and referrals for additional services.

Social support has been found to help reduce the negative impact of bereavement on mental health. Social support received early in the bereavement process has proven most beneficial (Schuster, Butler, 1989) as has stable social support over time (Duran, Turner, Lund, 1989). As a result, it is important that the nurse assess social support networks and help mobilize support for clients and caregivers, if necessary.

Nurses as caregivers are not immune to intense feelings of grief following the death of a person for whom they have cared. This can occur when close relationships develop between the nurse and client, especially in long-term care and hospice settings. This may occur when the dying person has certain characteristics that invoke memories of previous unresolved losses that the nurse has experienced. Such grief needs to be recognized, accepted, and evaluated, just as any other experience of loss and grief needs resolution. The first step is recognition of unresolved grief. The nurse's next steps may include expressing his or her thoughts and feelings with a coworker, friend, or family member. If additional help is needed, more sources such as the Employee Assistance Program, the clergy, or other counselors can be contacted.

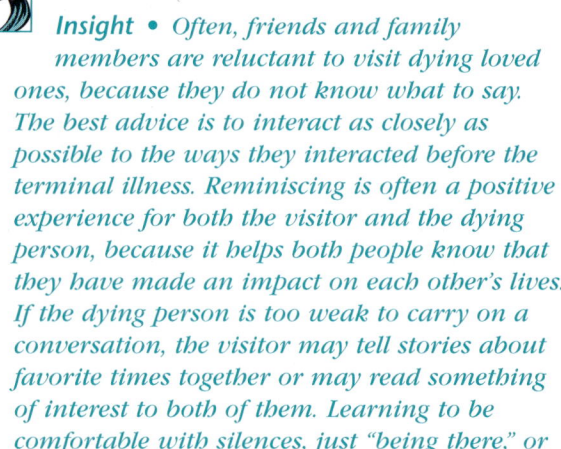

Insight • *Often, friends and family members are reluctant to visit dying loved ones, because they do not know what to say. The best advice is to interact as closely as possible to the ways they interacted before the terminal illness. Reminiscing is often a positive experience for both the visitor and the dying person, because it helps both people know that they have made an impact on each other's lives. If the dying person is too weak to carry on a conversation, the visitor may tell stories about favorite times together or may read something of interest to both of them. Learning to be comfortable with silences, just "being there," or praying with each other (if that is acceptable to both parties) can also be helpful.*

Environment

Of deaths that occur in the United States, 80% take place in an institutional setting, either in a hospital or nursing home setting. This reflects a significant change from the turn of the century, when approximately 75% to 80% of Americans died at home (DeSpelder, Strickland, 1992). Often, an older person who is dying moves back and forth, as his or her condition changes, between acute care (hospitalization) and any number and kind of long-term care settings.

The hospital setting is particularly problematic for older dying people, since the primary goal in this setting is restoration of health. Since the implementation of **diagnosis related groups (DRGs),** economic constraints on hospitals force clients to be discharged if active treatment (treatment that cannot be provided in the home) is not provided (Csordas, Kleinman, 1990). Since hospitals are not reimbursed for custodial care (Daigneault, 1993), a healthy death is a rare occurrence in the hospital setting. Too many times, life-supporting technology is applied and death becomes even more impersonal. Isolation of the old in hospitals when they are dying is the final indignity (Butler, 1975).

Nursing homes and long-term care institutions have different goals and different reimbursement systems. The goal of a nursing home is to provide a caring environment for those who are unable to care for themselves because of illness, disability, or old age. The emphasis is on care, not cure. Approximately 20% of older adults are residents of a nursing home at some time in their lives, although only 5% of the over-65 population live in nursing homes at any one time (Eliopoulos, 1993). Approximately 30% of all nursing home residents die each year (Davidson, 1988). These statistics show that clearly, nursing home settings can foster healthy dying through their primary goal of caring; however, the reality of the situation is that care in many nursing homes is sorely lacking, with estimates that 50% of nursing homes do not meet federal standards (Stephenson, 1985). Thus compassionate care of the dying is not assured in either the hospital or the nursing home setting.

Hospice care was founded on the philosophy of compassionate humane care of the dying and their families. Although hospice may be a place where dying people go, hospice in the United States usually refers to a caring ideology that can be implemented wherever the client may be dying—home, hospital, or nursing home. A basic goal for hospice care is to help the dying live as fully as possible on a day-to-day basis. This requires that a person be given as much control as possible over all that affects him or her. Hospices are organized (1) to provide symptom control, especially pain management; (2) to address the psychologic needs of clients; (3) to support and to assist families in their caregiving role; (4) to help address environmental problems; and (5) to relieve spiritual distress (Gonda, Ruark, 1984). With hospice care, the goal is that a dying person should not be distracted by suffering or fear of suffering, but still be able to think clearly, maintain significant relationships, and have a sense of trust and security in his or her environment (Mor, Greer, 1988).

For admission into a hospice program, a person must have a diagnosis of a terminal illness with a prognosis usually of less than 6 months. Although each hospice program may be slightly different, a general consensus of characteristics that a well-rounded hospice program should provide include the following:

1. The client and family comprise the unit of care.
2. Home care services in collaboration with inpatient backup facilities are available and are coordinated by a central agency.
3. Care is provided by a multidisciplinary team, comprised of a physician, nurse, social worker, chaplain, and volunteer, with special expertise in symptom control.
4. Skills of the multidisciplinary group are available on a 24-hour-per-day/7-day-per-week basis with provisions for on-call coverage.
5. Follow-up care for key loved ones extends through the mourning period.
6. Ongoing emotional support is provided for all hospice personnel on a systematic basis (Gonda, Ruark, 1984).

Home care does not necessarily include hospice care. Many older people die at home, cared for only by their family, or sometimes they have the assistance of visiting nurses or home health aides who help with personal care. In these instances, the goals are much the same as hospice goals; however, the dying person and family is without the benefit of a multidisciplinary team and organized approach to follow-up care.

Other topics relevant to dying and death within the health care system include ethical decisions, advance directives, euthanasia, and suicide; however, these topics are so complex that they preclude a cursory treatment of them here (see Chapter 3).

Summary

This chapter has covered two major topics, that of loss and grief in response to loss, and the process of dying. Characteristics of older people who are grieving or who are dying were presented, focusing on the differences between the experiences of older people and younger adults. Lastly, ways of assessing the needs of those who are mourning or who are dying have been described along with strategies for the nurse to use to help meet these identified needs. Examination of the nurse's own value system and prior experience with loss are emphasized. Health care system approaches to care of the dying have also been described. With increased knowledge and positive attitudes, it is hoped that care and support for older people who are grieving and who are dying will improve. This should be to the advantage of both the older adult and the nurse, who has much knowledge and wisdom to gain from those who have the most experience in life.

Key Points

- Grief is the acute reaction to one's perception of loss, whereas mourning refers to the longer range process of resolving acute grief reactions, and bereavement is the state of having experienced a significant loss.
- Grief involves many changes over time, is a natural response to all kinds of losses (not just death), and is based on one's unique perception of the loss.
- Worden viewed the grief process as an active one involving the following four tasks of mourning: (1) accept the reality of the loss, (2) work through the pain of grief, (3) adjust to an environment in which the deceased is missing, and (4) emotionally relocate the deceased and move on with life.
- Human beings respond as whole people, with grief manifested in physical symptoms, psychologic responses, changes in socialization patterns, and spiritually with issues around meaning in life.
- Complicated grief reactions may manifest themselves in one of four ways (1) chronic, (2) delayed, (3) exaggerated, or (4) masked grief reactions.
- Nursing care activities to assist in the grieving process include helping the survivor express feelings, providing time to grieve, explaining "normal" grieving behaviors, examining defenses and coping styles, and

HOME CARE TIPS

1. Homebound older adults who have lost a spouse or significant other may manifest grief with physical symptoms.
2. A homebound older adult may develop a crisis of faith and express anger at God. It is important for the homecare nurse to avoid being judgmental and to allow the older adult to verbalize anger and/or grief.
3. Refer to an advanced practice nurse or other health professionals skilled in working with complicated grieving if a homebound older adult experiences dysfunctional grieving.
4. Loss of a spouse or significant other, coupled with living alone, place the homebound older adult at risk for depression.
5. Assess the terminally ill homebound older adult's feelings toward his or her own death.
6. Instruct family members and caregivers on the stages of dying and the physiologic changes that accompany dying.
7. Use hospice care to help the dying homebound older adult live as fully as possible on a day-to-day basis.
8. If hospice care is not available, the home care nurse can assist the homebound older adult in completing the dying phase.

identifying pathology and making appropriate referrals.

- Sociocultural and religious background, physical and functional status, social isolation and loneliness, and the meaningfulness of everyday life are all important factors determining one's approach to impending death.
- Age-related changes predispose the older person to greater potential problems in areas such as hygiene and skin care, nutrition, elimination, mobility, transfers, rest, sleep, pain, respiratory management, and cognitive and behavior functioning.
- Nursing strategies for assisting dying older people include delivering excellent physical care, using good communication skills, conducting life review, and educating and supporting family caregivers.
- Hospice programs help dying people to live as fully as possible on a day-to-day basis by providing symptom control, addressing psychologic needs of clients, supporting family caregivers, dealing with environmental problems, and assisting with spiritual concerns.

Critical Thinking Exercises

1. You are attending to a 58-year-old female during the terminal phases of breast cancer. The family asks you to participate in a bedside prayer. How would you feel about this request? Identify factors or beliefs that would influence your decision to participate or not. How would you respond if you were uncomfortable in this situation?
2. A 68-year-old Jewish man is admitted to the emergency room following a car crash in which he sustained severe trauma. Despite emergency efforts, he dies. Because he resides in another state, his family has not been located. Discuss how you would manage nursing care during this postmortem period, taking into account cultural considerations. Describe how you would help the family members actualize the loss.

REFERENCES

Accessibility and affordability of prescription drugs for older Americans, Staff report, US Senate, US Printing Service, 1992.

Burbank PM: An exploratory study: assessing the meaning in life among older adult clients, *J Gerontolog Nurs* 18(4):19-28, 1992.

Burbank PM: Meaning in life among older persons. Unpublished doctoral dissertation, Boston, 1988, Boston University.

Burnside IM: *Nursing and the aged: a self-care approach,* New York, 1988, McGraw-Hill.

Butler R: The life review: an interpretation of reminiscences in the aged, *Psychiatry* 26(1):65-76, 1963.

Butler RN: *Why survive? Being old in America,* New York, 1975, Harper and Row.

Carey RG: The widowed: a year later, *J Counsel Psych* 24, 125-131, 1977.

Corbin JM, Strauss L: *Unending work and care: managing chronic illness at home,* San Francisco, 1988, Jossey-Bass.

Csordas TJ, Kleinman A: The therapeutic process. In Johnson T, Sargent C, editors: *Medical anthropology: contemporary theory and method,* New York, 1990, Praeger.

Daigneault C: *Now and at the hour of death,* unpublished manuscript, 1993.

Davidson GW: Hospice care for the dying. In Wass H, Bernardo F, Neimeyer R, editors: *Dying: facing the facts,* ed 2, Washington, 1988, Hemisphere.

DeSpelder LA, Strickland AL: *The last dance: encouraging death and dying,* ed 3, Mountain View, Calif., 1992, Mayfield.

Doka KY: The spiritual needs of the dying. In Doka KJ, editor: *Death and spirituality,* Amityville, N.Y., 1993, Baywood Publishing.

Duran A, Turner CW, Lund DA: Social support, perceived stress, and depression following the death of a spouse in later life. In Lund DH, editor: *Older bereaved spouses and research with practical applications,* New York, 1989, Hemisphere Publishing.

Ebersole P, Hess P: *Toward healthy aging,* ed 4, St. Louis, 1994, Mosby.

Eliopoulos C: *Gerontological nursing,* ed 3, Philadelphia, 1993, JB Lippincott.

Erikson E: *Childhood and society,* New York, 1963, WW Norton.

Fulton R: The many faces of grief, *Death Studies,* 11:243-256, 1987.

Gonda TA, Ruark JE: *Dying dignified: the health professional's guide to care,* Reading, Mass., 1984, Addison-Wesley.

Gordon M: *Manual of nursing diagnosis,* St Louis, 1991, Mosby.

Gorer G: *Death, grief, and mourning in contemporary Britain,* London, 1965, Cresset Press.

Haight BK, Burnside I: Reminiscence and life review: explaining the differences, *Arch Psychiatr Nurs* 7(2), 91-98, 1993.

Health United States, 1991: National Center for Health Statistics, Hyattsville, Md., 1992, Public Health Service.

Horowitz MJ et al: Pathological grief and the activation of latent self-images, *Am J Psychol* 137, 1157-1162, 1980.

Kalish RH, Reynolds DK: *Death and ethnicity: a psychocultural study,* Farmingdale, N.Y,. 1981, Baywood Publishing.

Kastenbaum R: Death, dying and bereavement in older age, *Aged Care Serv Rev* 1(3), 1-10, 1978.

Kavenaugh RE: *Facing death,* Los Angeles, 1972, Nash.

Kohn M, Menon G: Life prolongation: views of elderly outpatients and health care professionals, *J Am Geriatr Soc* 36, 840-844, 1988.

Kowalski NC: The older person's anticipation of her own death. In Rando TA, Fulton R, editors: *Loss and anticipatory grief,* Lexington, Mass., 1986, Lexington Books.

Kübler-Ross E: *On death and dying,* New York, 1969, Macmillan.

Lindemann E: Symptoms and management of acute grief, *Am J Psychol* 101:141, 1944.

Lund DA: Conclusions about bereavement in later life and implications for interventions and future research. In Lund DA, editor: *Older bereaved spouses: research with practical applications,* New York, 1989, Hemisphere.

Matthews SH: *The social world of old women,* Beverly Hills, Calif., 1979, Sage.

Mor V, Greer DS, Kastenbaum R: *The hospice experiment,* Baltimore, 1988, Johns Hopkins University Press.

National Center for Health Statistics: Births, marriages, divorces, and deaths for 1989, *Monthly Vital Stat Rep* 38(12), 1990.

Neugarten BL: Adult personality: toward a psychology of the life cycle. In Neugarten BL, editor: *Middle age and aging,* Chicago, 1968, University of Chicago Press.

O'Laughlin K: The final challenge: facing death. In Markson EW, editor: *Older women,* Lexington, Mass., 1983, Lexington Books.

Osterweis M: Bereavement and the elderly, *Aging* 348:8-13, 1985.

Parkes CM: Determinants of outcome following bereavement, *Omega* 6, 303-323, 1975.

Parkes CM: The first year of bereavement: a longitudinal study of the reaction of London widows to the death of their husbands, *Psychiatry* 33, 444-467, 1970.

Peterson J: Social-psychological aspects of death and dying and mental health. In Bliven J, Sloane R, editors: *Handbook of mental health and aging,* Englewood Cliffs, N.J., 1980, Prentice Hall.

Rando TA: *Grieving: how to go on living when someone you love dies.* Lexington, Mass., 1988, DC Heath.

Rando TA: *Loss and anticipatory grief,* Lexington, Mass., 1986, Lexington Books.

Raphael B: *The anatomy of bereavement,* New York, 1983, Basic Books.

Reker G, Peacock E, Wong P: Meaning and purpose in life and well-being: a life span perspective, *J Gerontol* 42, 44, 1987.

Retsinas J: The theoretical reassessment of the applicability of Kübler-Ross' stages of dying, *Death Stud* 12, 207-216, 1988.

Sankar A: *Dying at home: a family guide for caregiving,* Baltimore, 1991, Johns Hopkins University Press.

Schuster TL, Butler EW: Bereavement social networks, social support and mental health. In Lund DH, editor: *Older bereaved spouses and research with practical applications,* New York, 1989, Hemisphere.

Sherwood S, Mor V: Mental health institutions and the elderly. In Bliven J, Sloane R eds: *Handbook of mental health and aging,* Englewood Cliffs, N.J., 1980, Prentice Hall.

Smith DC, Maher MF: Healthy death, *Counsel Val* 36(1):42-48, 1991.

Stephenson JS: *Death, grief, and mourning: individual and social realities,* New York, 1985, Free Press.

Thorson JA, Powell FC: Elements of death anxiety and meanings of death, *J Clinical Psychol* 44, 691-701, 1988.

Walborn K: A nursing model for the hospice: primary and self-care nursing, *Nurs Clin North Am* 15(1), 205-217, 1980.

Weizman SG, Kamm P: *About mourning: support and guidance for the bereaved,* New York, 1985, Human Sciences Press.

Worden JW: *Grief counseling and grief therapy,* ed 2, New York, 1991, Springer.

Chapter 18

Substance Abuse

LEARNING OBJECTIVES

On completion of this chapter, the reader will be able to:

1. Identify key physiologic, psychologic, and sociologic changes associated with aging that make the identification and treatment of substance abuse in the older adult client difficult.
2. List the key components of assessing the older adult for substance abuse.
3. Identify the key independent and collaborative nursing interventions for the older adult client who abuses substances.
4. Identify the signs and symptoms of alcohol abuse and withdrawal in the older adult client, and describe the corresponding nursing interventions.
5. Identify the signs and symptoms of prescription medication abuse and withdrawal in the older adult client, and describe the corresponding nursing interventions.
6. Identify the signs and symptoms of nonprescription medication abuse and withdrawal in the older adult client, and describe the corresponding nursing interventions.
7. Identify the signs and symptoms of nicotine abuse and withdrawal in the older adult client, and describe the corresponding nursing interventions.
8. Identify the signs and symptoms of caffeine abuse and withdrawal in the older adult client and describe the corresponding nursing interventions.

Older adults are often described as having increased opportunities to participate in leisure activities as a result of decreased work responsibility. However, many older adults are unable to enjoy leisure activities because of the emotional, physical, and social changes associated with aging. This generation has experienced the pharmacologic revolution in medicine and has been socialized to the belief that a pill can take care of most physical and emotional aches and pains. This belief contributes to 1,148,000 to 2,324,000 current cases of substance abuse of older adults in the United States (Thibault, Maly, 1993). Less than 1% of these cases is a result of illicit substance abuse (Miller, Belkin, Gold, 1991). In fact, the major substances abused by older adults are alcohol, prescription drugs, nonprescription drugs, nicotine, and caffeine (Miller, Belkin, Gold, 1991; Thibault, Maly, 1993). This chapter addresses the risk factors associated with substance abuse in the older adult. In addition, the assessment and nursing interventions associated with the abuse of alcohol, prescription medications, nonprescription medications, nicotine, an caffeine in older adults is also addressed.

DEFINITIONS

Nurses must understand definitions associated with substance abuse to correctly assess substance abuse in the older adult and plan appropriate interventions for this population. The Diagnostic and Statistical Manual of Mental Disorders, fourth edition (DSM-IV) is used by physicians to aid in diagnosing clients. The DSM-IV distinguishes between substance abuse and substance dependence. **Substance abuse** is defined as "a maladaptive pattern of substance use manifested by recurrent and significant adverse consequences related to the repeated use of substances (American Psychiatric Association (APA), 1994). **Substance dependence** is defined as "a cluster of cognitive, behavioral, and physiologic symptoms indicating that the individual continues use of the substance despite significant substance-related problems (APA, 1994). Substance dependence also has the distinct phases of tolerance, withdrawal, and compulsive drug-taking and drug-seeking behavior. Box 18-1 demonstrates the DSM-IV diagnostic criteria for substance abuse and substance dependence.

RISK FACTORS

The physiologic, psychologic, and sociologic changes associated with aging make the identification and treatment of substance abuse in the older adult client difficult. The age-related physiologic changes in absorption,

BOX 18-1

DSM-IV Diagnostic Criteria

Substance abuse

A. A maladaptive pattern of substance use leading to clinically significant impairment or distress, as manifested by one (or more) of the following, occurring within a 12-month period:
   1. Recurrent substance use resulting in a failure to fulfill major role obligations at work, school, or home (e.g., repeated absences or poor work performance associated with substance use; substance-related absences, suspensions, or expulsions from school; or neglect of children or household)
   2. Recurrent substance use in situations in which it is physically hazardous (e.g., driving an automobile or operating a machine when impaired by substance use)
   3. Recurrent substance-related legal problems (e.g., arrests for substance-related disorderly conduct)
   4. Continued substance use despite having persistent or recurrent social or interpersonal problems caused or exacerbated by the effects of the substance (e.g., arguments with spouse about consequences of intoxication, physical fights)

B. The symptoms have never met the criteria for substance dependence for this class of substance.

Substance dependence

A. A maladaptive pattern of substance use, leading to clinically significant impairment or distress, as manifested by three (or more) of the following, occurring at any time in the same 12-month period:
   1. Tolerance, as defined by either of the following:
      a. A need for markedly increased amounts of the substance to achieve intoxication or desired effect
      b. Markedly diminished effect with continued use of the same amount of the substance
   2. Withdrawal, as manifested by either of the following:
      a. The characteristic withdrawal syndrome for the substance
      b. The same (or a closely related) substance is taken to relieve or avoid withdrawal symptoms
   3. The substance is often taken in larger amounts or over a longer period than was intended
   4. There is a persistent desire or unsuccessful efforts to cut down or control substance use
   5. A great deal of time is spent in activities necessary to obtain the substance (e.g., visiting multiple doctors or driving long distances), use the substance (e.g., chain-smoking), or recover from its effects
   6. Important social, occupational, or recreational activities are given up or reduced because of substance use
   7. The substance use is continued despite knowledge of having a persistent or recurrent physical or psychologic problem that is likely to have been caused or exacerbated by the substance (e.g., current cocaine use despite recognition of cocaine-induced depression, or continued drinking despite recognition that an ulcer was made worse by alcohol consumption)

distribution, metabolism, and excretion affect drug usage (Ahronheim, 1992; Thibault, Maly, 1993). Furthermore, some of the age-related psychologic changes mimic the cardinal manifestations of alcohol and drug abuse (Miller, Belkin, Gold, 1991; Thibault, Maly, 1993). In addition, several sociocultural changes place the older adult client at risk for substance abuse and misuse (McDonald, Abrahams, 1990).

Physiologic Changes

Some of the age-related physiologic changes that affect drug usage are altered absorption, distribution, metabolism, and excretion (Ahronheim, 1992; Thibault, Maly, 1993). The absorption rate and length of time a drug remains in the body is affected by the physiologic changes of increased body fat and decreased muscle (Walker, 1992). Absorption rate is also affected by the age-related physiologic change of decreased cells in the intestine, resulting in decreased absorptive surface (Walker, 1992). Furthermore, decreased volume of intestinal fluids may result in higher concentrations of water-soluble substances in the older adult (Thibault, Maly, 1993). As a result of decreased absorption, the older adult accumulates substances more rapidly than the younger adult, indicating the need for lower medication dosages in the older adult population (Solomon et al, 1993). However, the standard dosages for new medications are typically set to serve 90% of the target population. Thus the standard dosage is usually too high for older adults and places this population at risk for possible misuse and abuse of medications (Lipman, 1993).

The nurse should also know that the distribution of substances in the older adult may be impaired as a result of the physiologic change of decreased blood flow. Decreased blood flow and decreased total body water content in the older adult changes distribution volume, resulting in alteration in blood levels of substances used (Thibault, Maly, 1993).

A significant decline in renal excretion occurs with aging. Glomerular filtration rate decreases an average of 50% between the ages of 20 to 90. Therefore the nurse should be cautious when administering substances to the older adult that depend on renal function for their clearance, since the risk for multiple drug reactions and unpredictable drug activity is more common than in younger adults (Ahronheim, 1992; Thibault, Maly, 1993).

Fig. 18-1 Loneliness and hopelessness can be manifestations of alcohol abuse. (Courtesy Ursula Ruhl, St. Louis, Mo.)

Metabolism is also altered in the older adult and places the older adult at risk for substance abuse and misuse. A decrease in liver mass and cardiac output tends to impair liver function. As a result of impaired function, the risk for drug toxicity increases (Ahronheim, 1992; Thibault, Maly, 1993).

Nurses should be aware of these physiologic changes of absorption, distribution, excretion, and metabolism of substances in the older adult population. The assessment of these changes in relation to substance use is essential in planning interventions to prevent or to halt substance abuse and misuse in the older adult population. (see Chapter 20).

Psychologic Changes

Psychologic changes in the older adult result primarily from the numerous losses this age group may incur in a relatively short period of time. Some common losses that older adults experience are bereavement of family and friends, retirement, physical health, and ability to participate in previous social activities. These losses often contribute to feelings of isolation, sadness, hopelessness, helplessness, and anxiousness (Miller, Belkin, Gold, 1991; Thibault, Maly, 1993) (Fig. 18-1). Such feelings are also the cardinal manifestations of alcohol and drug dependence and abuse (Miller, Belkin, Gold, 1991). The nurse should avoid automatically attributing these feelings to aging, and should use this information to carefully assess the possibility of substance abuse in clients who express these feelings.

In addition, nurses should be aware of the misconception that select prescribed or over the counter (OTC) substances can help the client meet unmet psychologic needs. For example, an older adult may become anxious if sleep has decreased to less than 8 hours. As a result of this misconception, older adults may "seek sedatives because of the mistaken notion that these drugs will allow them to have the 8 hours of sleep that they believe is normal" (Tilbault, Maly, 1993). In addition, some older adults tend to use certain substances to mask negative feelings about themselves and may eventually attribute some of their positive personality characteristics to the substances (Thibault, Maly, 1993). Examples of such substances include alcohol and benzodiazepines (Diazepam). Clients who are given a benzodiazepine by a physician for a limited period may become dependent on the medication and may find another physician to prescribe the medication when their original physician discontinues it (Thibault, Maly, 1993).

The nurse must also assess the older adult client who demonstrates feelings for suicidal ideations. Clients should be asked whether they have had thoughts of wanting to harm themselves and if they have a plan to carry out these thoughts. Advancing age and substance abuse are among the greatest risk factors for suicide (Miller, Belkin, Gold, 1991). Suicide rates tend to increase with age in Caucasian men (Carethers, 1992). The APA (1988) states that the highest suicide rate in the United States is among older adults. In addition, it is estimated that approximately 6,000 older adults commit suicide each year (APA, 1988) (see Chapter 12).

Sociologic Changes

The social changes of decreased finances, transportation, and social support tend to place the older adult client at risk for substance abuse and misuse (McDonald, Abrahams, 1990). As a result of decreased finances and transportation, many older adults fill prescriptions through mail-order pharmacies (Leary, Donehew, Swanson, 1992). However, mail-order pharmacies tend to increase the potential for drug abuse and misuse as a result of prescription error, late arrival, and the large quantities of the drug received (Leary, Donehew, Swanson, 1992). The social conditions of income, access, and socialization tend to affect the nutrition of the older adult client. The nurse should educate the older adult client about the dual effects of nutritional status and drug metabolism. For instance, caffeine reduces the effectiveness of many benzodiazepines and may contribute to the increased use of benzodiazepines in the older adult (Ahronheim, 1992).

Sociocultural factors of gender and race are also risk factors of substance abuse in the older adult. The older woman is at risk for substance abuse as a result of living alone, decreased social relationships, prior dependency on a significant other who is deceased, and inadequate financial support (Szwabo, 1993). As a result of these stressors, the older woman may self-medicate (Szwabo, 1993). Furthermore, minorities tend to self-medicate and to purchase OTC medications more often than nonminorities (Hess, 1986; Lile, 1991; Szwabo, 1993). Some of the contributing factors to this behavior are lack of finances, poor access to health care, language barriers, and cultural differences associated with health and illness (Hess,1986; Lile, 1991; Szwabo, 1993). The nurse should assess the social and cultural aspects of older adults to identify potential risk factors for substance abuse in this population (see Chapter 5). Early identification of substance abuse in the older adult population is imperative to successful treatment of this population (Solomon et al, 1993).

ASSESSMENT

The following is a general overview of the key concepts in assessing and planning nursing interventions for substance abuse in the older adult population. Nurses should be aware of the specific assessment and nursing intervention strategies for alcohol abuse, prescription medications abuse, nonprescription medication abuse, nicotine abuse, and caffeine abuse.

Substance Abuse History

The DSM-IV criteria for substance abuse are developed for the general population and not specifically for the older adult population (see Box 18-1, p. 407). Therefore it is also essential for the nurse to take a client's medical and psychologic history. After the history is complete, the nurse should identify whether the key medical and psychologic manifestations of substance abuse are present (Boxes 18-2 and 18-3).

Screening Tools

Another important aspect in assessing for substance abuse in the older adult is to obtain a history of substance use (Lindblom et al, 1992; Szwabo, 1993). The history should specifically address what type of substance the client uses, how much the client uses, and how often the client uses it (Solomon, et al, 1993; Szwabo, 1993). Several screening tools are available to assess alcohol use. The two most commonly used tools are the CAGE (Mayfield, McLeod, Hall, 1974), and the

BOX 18-2

Medical Manifestations of Substance Abuse in the Older Adult

Peripheral neuropathy
Diminished proprioception
Alcoholic liver disease (hepatitis or cirrhosis)
Alcoholic pancreatitis
Gastrointestinal bleeding
Esophageal varices
Peptic ulcer or gastritis
Malignancies
Cardiomyopathy
Protein-calorie malnutrition
Hypovitaminosis (particularly B vitamins)
Anemia
Osteopenia
Susceptibility to infections
Electrolyte disturbances
Hypercortisolemia
Delirium tremens (occurs after recent cessation or reduction of alcohol intake; is marked by signs of delirium with autonomic hyperactivity-tachycardia, sweating, hallucinations, delusions, agitation, tremor, fever, and seizures.)
Seizures
Hypertension
Acquired immunodeficiency syndrome (AIDS)
Peripheral muscle weakness
Falls
Orthostatic hypotension

Reprinted with permission from Solomon K et al: Alcoholism and prescription drug abuse in the elderly. St. Louis University Grand Rounds, *J Am Geriatr Soc* 41, 1993.

BOX 18-3

Psychologic Manifestations of Substance Abuse in the Older Adult

Manic (expansively elevated) mood or behavior
Depressed mood
Social withdrawal
Vegetative symptoms of depression
Apathy or poor motivation
Suicidal ideation, plans, or behavior
Violent threats or behavior
Paranoid or nonparanoid delusions
Auditory, visual, olfactory, or gustatory hallucinations
Anxiety
Panic attacks
Phobias
Poor personal hygiene
Poor activity of daily living (ADL) skills
Personality change
Irritability
Sleep disturbances
Memory loss (immediate, recent, or remote)
Delirium (intoxication or withdrawal)
"Flashbacks"
Marital, social, or legal difficulties
Noncompliance with medical care
Hallucinations
Alcoholic dementia (Wernicke-Korsakoff's syndrome)

Reprinted with permission from Solomon K et al: Alcoholism and prescription drug abuse in the elderly: St. Louis University Grand Rounds, *J Am Geriatr Soc* 41, 1993.

BOX 18-4

CAGE

1. Have you ever felt the need to **C**ut down on drinking?
2. Have you ever felt **A**nnoyed by the criticism of drinking?
3. Have you ever had **G**uilty feelings about drinking?
4. Have you ever taken a morning **E**ye opener?

NOTE: If the client answers "yes" to any of the above questions, further assessment for alcohol abuse is warranted.

Reprinted with permission from Mayfield D, McLeod G, Hall P: The CAGE questionnaire: validation of a new alcoholism screening instrument, *Am J Psychiatry* 131:1121-1123, 1974.

BOX 18-5

Michigan Alcoholism Screening Test (MAST)*

	Yes	No
1. Do you enjoy having a drink now and then?	0	
2. Do you feel you are a normal drinker? (By normal, we mean do you drink less than or as much as most other people and you have not gotten into any recurring trouble while drinking.)		2
3. Have you ever awakened the morning after some drinking the night before and found that you could not remember a part of the evening?	2	
4. Does either of your parents, or any other near relative, or your spouse, or any girlfriend or boyfriend ever worry or complain about your drinking?	1	
5. Can you stop drinking without a struggle after one or two drinks?		2
6. Do you feel guilty about your drinking?	1	
7. Do friends or relatives think you are a normal drinker?		2
8. Are you able to stop drinking when you want to?		2
9. Have you ever attended a meeting of Alcoholics Anonymous (AA)?	5	
10. Have you gotten into physical fights when you have been drinking?	1	
11. Has your drinking ever created problems between you and either of your parents, another relative, your spouse, or girlfriend or boyfriend?	2	
12. Have any of your family members ever gone to anyone for help about your drinking?	2	
13. Have you ever lost friends because of your drinking?	2	
14. Have you ever gotten into trouble at work or at school because of drinking?	2	
15. Have you ever lost a job because of drinking?	2	
16. Have you ever neglected your obligations, school work, your family, or your job for 2 or more days in a row because you were drinking?	2	
17. Do you drink before noon fairly often?	1	
18. Have you ever been told you have liver trouble? Cirrhosis?	2	
19. After heavy drinking have you ever had severe shaking, heard voices, or seen things that really weren't there [e.g., delirium tremens (DTs)]?	2 (5 DTs)	
20. Have you ever gone to anyone for help about your drinking?	5	
21. Have you ever been a patient in a psychiatric hospital or on a psychiatric ward of a general hospital where drinking was part of the problem that resulted in hospitalization?	2	
22. Have you ever been seen at a psychiatric or mental health clinic, or gone to any doctor, social worker, or clergy for help with any emotional problem, where drinking was part of the problem?	2	
23. Have you ever been arrested for drunk driving, driving while intoxicated, or driving under the influence of alcoholic beverages or any other drug? (If YES, how many times? _______)	2 each	
24. Have you ever been arrested, or taken into custody, even for a few hours, because of other drunk behavior, whether as a result of alcohol or another drug? (If YES, how many times? _______)	2 each	

*Interpretation: Standard MAST-0 to 3 points = probable normal drinker; 4 points = borderline score; 5 to 9 points = 80% associated with alcoholism/chemical dependence; 10 or more = 100% associated with alcoholism.

Modified from Selzer ML: The Michigan Alcoholism Screening Test: the quest for a new diagnostic instrument, *Am J Psychiatry* 127:1653-1658, 1971. Reprinted with permission.

BOX 18-6

BMAST*

	Yes	No
1. Do you feel that you are a normal drinker?		2
2. Do friends think that you are a normal drinker?		2
3. Have you ever attended an AA meeting?	5	
4. Have you ever lost friends, girlfriend or boyfriend because of drinking?	2	
5. Have you ever gotten into trouble at work because of drinking?	2	
6. Have you neglected your obligations, family, or work for 2 or more days in a row because you were drinking?	2	
7. Have you ever had DTs, heard voices, or seen things that were not there after heavy drinking?	2	
8. Have you ever gone to anyone to help stop your drinking?	5	
9. Have you ever been in a hospital because of drinking?	5	
10. Have you ever been arrested for drunk driving or driving after drinking?	2	

*Alcoholism is indicated by a score of greater than 5. Test scores are determined by tallying values for answers that are on a progressive scale of 0, 2, and 5. Modified from Pokorny AD, Miller BA, Kaplan HB: The brief MAST: a shortened version of the Michigan Alcoholism Screening Test, *Am J Psychiatry* 129:342-345, 1972. Reprinted with permission.

Michigan Alcoholism Screening Test (MAST) (Selzer, 1971). The Brief Michigan Alcoholism Screening Test (BMAST) is the modified form of the MAST (Lindblom et al, 1992). It should also be noted that Dr. Frederick Blow is presently developing the geriatric version of the MAST (Solomon et al, 1993). Even though further research is indicated to validate the use of these tools with other substance abuse besides alcohol, good clinical results have been identified by the use of these tools with the substitution of the word "substance" or "prescription medication" for the word "drinker." These tools are presented in Boxes 18-4, 18-5, and 18-6.

A final key concept in assessing the older adult for substance abuse is that the nurse must be aware of his or her own perceptions and attitudes regarding substance abuse in the older adult population. Many health care providers overlook the possibility that the cause of presenting symptoms in an older adult may be related to substance abuse (McDonald, Abrahams, 1990; Szwabo, 1993; Thibault, Maly, 1993). Many health care providers also forget that physiologic changes in the older adult increase the risk of intoxication in this population (Thibault, Maly, 1993). Solomon, et al. (1993) emphasize that health care providers must change cognitive sets when assessing the older adult for substance abuse by not implicitly trusting the client's statements about abuse, and making sure statements are confirmed before believed. The researchers also emphasize that because of the high incidence of denial in this population, a drug-use history must be obtained in a detailed, nonjudgmental manner (see Research box, p. 413).

Insight • *The nurse should be aware of any attitudes about the older substance abuse client that cause an emotional reaction in the nurse based on the nurse's past experience (countertransference). These attitudes prevent the nurse from being able to accurately assess the older adult client for substance abuse. Nurses need to be able to answer the following questions to handle their attitudes appropriately:*

- *How do I feel about substance abusers?*
- *How do I feel about the older adult who abuses substances?*
- *What behaviors about the older adult substance abuser do I dislike or like?*

INTERVENTIONS

The nursing interventions with the older substance abuse client vary depending on which phase of treatment the client is undergoing. The four phases of treatment include (1) abstinence and detoxification, (2) admission, (3) acceptance, and (4) surrender (Solomon et al, 1993). The core of treatment for the older client with substance abuse is based on the 12-Step Alcoholic Anonymous (AA) model (1976).

Independent Interventions

Independent nursing interventions for the first phase of abstinence and detoxification are to observe for signs and symptoms of withdrawal and to administer the appropriate precautions for the individual experiencing withdrawal. The most common sign of severe with-

RESEARCH

Moos R, Mertens J, Brennan P: Patterns of diagnosis and treatment among late–middle-aged older substance abuse patients, *J Stud Alcohol*, 54(4):479-487, 1993.

Sample, setting

The subjects included 22,678 substance abuse clients who were inpatients at Department of Veterans Affairs (VA) Medical Centers with 23% age 55 and older, and 80% having a coexisting medical disorder.

Methodology

Retrospective survey design of substance abuse clients admitted to Department of Veterans Affairs Medical Centers.

Findings

Older substance abusers were less likely to receive specialized treatment for their substance abuse problem. Generally, the older clients tended to receive services oriented toward their medical problems.

Implications

The findings indicate the need for health care professionals to stop denying the existence of substance abuse in the older adult client. Furthermore, there exists a need to develop treatment programs tailored to the characteristics and substance abuse problems of older adults.

EMERGENCY TREATMENT

Delirium Tremens

The following nursing interventions should be implemented with the client who experiences DTs:

1. Vital signs
2. Safe environment (padded side rails, decreased stimulation)
3. Close observation
4. Administer medications as ordered such as chlordiazepoxide, lorazepam, or diazepam for symptoms such as agitation, tremors, or increased temperature, blood pressure, or pulse.

drawal is **delirium tremens (DTs).** DTs can be fatal and usually consist of frightening visual hallucinations, diaphoresis, and seizures (Solomon et al, 1993). Other signs of withdrawal may include tactile hallucinations, attention deficit, altered speech, apraxia, agitation, hypertension, tachycardia, tachypnea, hypoglycemia, dehydration, aspiration, arrhythmias, and fever. These symptoms usually begin 48 to 96 hours after the last use of the substance. But, symptoms may occur 6 hours after last usage or as late as 1 week after the last usage (Solomon et al, 1993; Szwabo, 1993). The most important nursing interventions during this stage are to observe and document signs of withdrawal, provide an environment of low stimulation (dim lights, quiet atmosphere), seizure precautions (padded side rails), and one-to-one supervision (see Emergency Treatment box, above).

Collaborative Interventions

Dependent nursing interventions during the first phase of abstinence and detoxification consist primarily of pharmacotherapy. The older adult client may require 8 to 10 weeks to detoxify (Szwabo, 1993). During withdrawal, the older adult client requires a gradual reduction of the abused substance over time to minimize the symptoms associated with withdrawal (Solomon et al, 1993; Szwabo, 1993). The client who has been abusing alcohol is withdrawn by the administration of chloridiazepoxide (Librium), lorazepam (Ativan), or diazepam (Valium). Most physicians prefer chlordiazepoxide (Librium), because the intermediate half-life produces a smoother withdrawal with less sedation (Miller, Belkin, Gold, 1991). The aforementioned medications are also used to withdraw the older adult who abuses benzodiazepines (Solomon et al, 1993). Phenobarbital is used for clients who abuse barbiturates, clonidine for oral narcotic abuse, and desipramine for cocaine abuse (Solomon et al, 1993). In addition, nutritional support, thiamine, multivitamins, and intravenous fluids may be indicated (Miller, Belkin, Gold, 1991; Solomon et al, 1993; Szwabo, 1993).

Independent and dependent nursing interventions in the stage of admission include continued administration of medications, group therapy, individual therapy, family therapy, and introduction to the 12-Step program (Solomon et al, 1993; Szwabo, 1993). It should be noted that group, individual, and family therapy are conducted by a trained therapist and the nurse may be asked to assist the therapist with therapy sessions. During this stage of treatment, the individual and family learn the concept of addiction as an illness.

The next stage is compliance. The nursing interventions used in the stage of admission are also used in this stage. The goal of the compliance stage is to help the client identify the effects that the substance abuse has had on the client's life. During the phases of acceptance and surrender, the client begins integration back to the community and continues treatment on an outpatient basis. The nurse supports the client in these phases by helping the client to establish a plan (1) to maintain sobriety in the community and (2) overcome potential future triggers for future substance use/abuse (Solomon et al, 1993; Szwabo, 1993).

Evaluation

The evaluation of the treatment for the older adult substance abuser consists of a safe detoxification, the adherence to sobriety treatment plan, and outpatient support (Solomon et al, 1993). Safe detoxification consists of the client weaning from the abused substance without seizures, DTs, changes in vital signs, or other complications of withdrawal. Adherence is measured by noting if the client is abstaining from substance use, attending meetings (AA or Narcotics Anonymous [NA]) and individual or family group sessions. Finally, outpatient support is indicated by noting if the client is maintaining the relationship with the sponsor. A sponsor is someone who can be a mentor and can support the client during abstinence.

COMMONLY ABUSED SUBSTANCES IN THE OLDER ADULT

Alcohol

Prevalence

Alcohol abuse can be difficult to assess as a result of the legal status of this drug. In addition, the socialization of this drug as recreational in the United States has confounded the difficulty in identifying abuse (Twadell, 1991). Regardless of the difficult nature of identifying alcohol abuse, the fact remains that the incidence of identified older adults who abuse alcohol is less than 10% of the older adult population (Carethers, 1992; Cutezo, Dellasega, 1992; Solomon et al, 1993). The number of older adults who abuse alcohol may appear low, but the current cohort of older adults grew up during Prohibition and the Great Depression, when alcohol was considered illegal or was too expensive (Thibault, Maly, 1993). The prevalence rate of alcohol abuse is projected to increase as the current middle-aged generation reaches older adulthood, since this generation is much more accustomed to alcohol use (Thibault, Maly, 1993). Factors such as a lack of knowledge about alcohol abuse throughout the life span and lack of knowledge about normal aging also contribute to the health care provider's inability to recognize alcohol abuse in the older adult (Thibault, Maly, 1993).

Assessment

The older adult who abuses alcohol usually displays the symptoms of anxiety, nervousness, memory impairment, depression, blackouts, confusion, weight loss, and falls (Solomon et al, 1993; Szwabo, 1993). In addition, physical examination may indicate the effects of alcohol on the body system of the older adult. Table 18-1 demonstrates the age and alcohol-related changes in select body systems of the older adult. The nurse should carefully assess for the following signs and symptoms: impaired sensations in the extremities, poor coordination, confusion, facial edema, alcohol on the breath, liver enlargement, jaundice, ascites, trembling or fidgeting, lack of attention to personal hygiene, and poor eating habits (Miller, Belkin, Gold, 1991; Solomon et al 1993; Szwabo, 1993). Secondary problems may include malnutrition, cirrhosis, compromised hepatic function, osteomalacia as a result of compromised metabolism of vitamin D, cardiomyopathies, atropic gastritis, and decline in cognitive status, especially in memory and information processing (Solomon et al, 1993). Laboratory evaluation should include liver function studies, electrolytes, glucose, magnesium, and electrocardiogram (Solomon et al, 1993). Alcohol abuse may not be accurately assessed in the older adult, because many symptoms such as falls, bruises, cardiovascular problems, hypertension, and memory problems may resemble other medical disease processes (Carethers, 1992). Therefore it is imperative, if the older adult displays these symptoms, that the nurse assess for the possibility of alcohol abuse. See Boxes 18-2 and

TABLE 18-1

Age- and Alcohol-Related Changes in the Body Systems of Older Adults

Age-related change	Corresponding alcohol-related change
Decline in liver function	Hepatotoxicity
Delayed neurologic conduction	Increase of Parkinson's symptoms, altered balance
Idiopathic tremors	Tremors related to withdrawal
Prone to falls	Prone to falls
Loss of short-term memory	Impairment of short-term memory
Decreased glucose tolerance	Inhibition of glucogenesis
Decreased secretion of hydrocholoric acid	Impaired absorption of nutrients
Slowed peristalsis	
Decreased saliva production	
Increase in cholesterol levels and cardiovascular disease	Increased plasma triglycerides
Less efficient cardiovascular function	Risk of congestive heart failure
Increased incidence of arthritis and gout	Increased uric acid levels
Decline in immunologic competence	Increased susceptibility to infection

*Developed from Cutezo EA, Dellasega C: Substance abuse in the homebound elderly, *Home Healthcare Nurse* 10(1):19-23, 1992.

BOX 18-7

DSM-IV Diagnostic Criteria for Alcohol Intoxication

A. Recent ingestion of alcohol
B. Clinically significant maladaptive behavioral or psychologic changes (e.g., inappropriate sexual or aggressive behavior, mood lability, impaired judgment, impaired social or occupational functioning) that developed during or shortly after alcohol ingestion.
C. One (or more) of the following signs, developing during or shortly after alcohol use:
   1. Slurred speech
   2. Incoordination
   3. Unsteady gait
   4. Nystagmus
   5. Impairment in attention or memory
   6. Stupor or coma
D. The symptoms are not a result of a general medical condition and are not better accounted for by another mental disorder.

BOX 18-8

DSM-IV Diagnostic Criteria for Alcohol Withdrawal

A. Cessation of (or reduction in) alcohol use that has been heavy and prolonged
B. Two (or more) of the following, developing within several hours to a few days after Criterion A:
   1. Autonomic hyperactivity (e.g., sweating or pulse rate greater than 100)
   2. Increased hand tremor
   3. Insomnia
   4. Nausea or vomiting
   5. Transient visual, tactile, or auditory hallucinations or illusions
   6. Psychomotor agitation
   7. Anxiety
   8. Grand mal seizures
C. The symptoms in Criterion B cause clinically significant distress or impairment in social, occupational, or other important areas of functioning.
D. The symptoms are not a result of a general medical condition and are not better accounted for by another mental disorder.

18-3, p. 410, for information regarding the medical and psychologic manifestations of substance abuse in the older adult.

After obtaining the health history and physical examination, the nurse should begin to assess specifically for alcohol abuse. The CAGE, MAST, and BMAST screening tools should be used to help the nurse identify the amount of alcohol the client uses and how often the client uses alcohol. Input from family and friends should also be obtained. Family and friends may deny the problem, therefore it is imperative that the nurse obtain the alcohol use history in a detailed, nonjudgmental manner (Solomon et al, 1993).

The nurse should be able to distinguish alcohol intoxication from alcohol withdrawal to apply the appropriate nursing interventions. Signs associated with alcohol intoxication include the scent of alcohol on the breath, slurred speech, uncoordination, unsteady gait, nystagmus, impairment in attention or memory, and stupor or coma (APA, 1994). The DSM-IV criteria for alcohol intoxication can be found in Box 18-7. Assessment of the signs and symptoms of alcohol withdrawal is essential in providing the appropriate treatment and preventing DTs and seizures. Indications of alcohol withdrawal are elevated blood pressure, pulse, and autonomic hyperactivity. In addition, fever, increased hand tremors, insomnia, nausea, vomiting, transient visual, tactile, or auditory hallucinations or illusions, psychomotor agitation, anxiety, and grand mal seizures may occur (APA, 1994). Withdrawal symptoms begin 4 to 12 hours after alcohol use has been stopped or reduced. Symptoms tend to peak 48 to 72 hours after the client's last drink (APA, 1994). It is important to assess the older client for the possibility of alcohol withdrawal if agitation, hallucinations, anxiety, or seizures develop 2 to 3 days after hospitalization (Box 18-8).

Interventions

Nursing interventions for the older alcohol abuse client vary according to whether the client is in detoxification or rehabilitation. Nurses should observe and document signs of withdrawal, should provide an environment of low stimulation (dim lights, quiet atmosphere), and should initiate seizure precautions (padded side rails) during the detoxification process (Szwabo, 1993). In addition, the nurse should administer prescribed medications that are cross-tolerant to alcohol to minimize the symptoms associated with withdrawal and minimize the potential for seizures (Solomon et al, 1993; Szwabo, 1993). The alcohol-abusing client is withdrawn by the administration of chlordiazepoxide (Librium), lorazepam (Ativan), or diazepam (Valium). Chlordiazepoxide (Librium) is usually the medication of choice by physicians, since the intermediate half-life produces a smooth with-

TABLE 18-2

Effects of Alcohol on Selected Prescription Medications

Classification	Effects
Antiarrhythmics	
Flecainide (Tambocor)	Individuals who have impaired liver function as a result of alcohol abuse require a lower dosage
Antianginal	
Nitroglycerin (Nitrostat)	Can cause rapid lowering of blood pressure, resulting in weakness, dizziness, and fainting
Tricyclic antidepressants	
Nortriptyline (Pamelor) Amitriptyline (Elavil) Imipramine (Tofranil)	Increases the effects of sedation, confusion, and tremors
Antidiabetics	
Oral (Diabinese)	Flushing of the face and body, as well as breathlessness, throbbing head and neck pain, difficulty breathing, nausea, vomiting, sweating, hypotension, weakness, dizziness, blurred vision, and confusion.
Insulin	Can lower blood sugar; reduced dosage may be indicated
Benzodiazepines	
Chlordiazepoxide (Librium) Diazepam (Valium) Lorazepam (Ativan)	If client is using these medications as antianxiety medications, alcohol may cause excessive depression, drowsiness, and difficulty breathing.
Anticoagulants	
Warfarin (Coumadin)	Decreases the effect of Warfarin
Narcotic analgesic	
Propoxyphene (Darvon)	Causes drowsiness and sedation
Non-narcotic analgesic	
Acetaminophen (Tylenol)	Increases the chances of liver toxicity
Bronchodilator	
Theophylline (Bronkodyl)	May decrease theophylline levels
Antihistamines	
Diphenhydramine Hydrochloride (Benadryl)	Excessive drowsiness and decreased concentration

From Silverman HM: *The pill book,* ed 6, New York, 1994, Bantam Books.

drawal with less sedation (Miller, Belkin, Gold, 1991). The nutritionally compromised older adult may require nutritional support, thiamine, multivitamins, and intravenous fluids (Miller, Belkin, Gold, 1991; Solomon et al, 1993; Szwabo, 1993).

During the rehabilitation stage, nursing interventions of education, continued administration of medications, group therapy, individual therapy, family therapy, and an introduction to the 12-Step program are advocated (Solomon et al, 1993; Szwabo, 1993). The nurse supports the client by educating him or her about the harmful effects that alcohol has on the body, the effects alcohol has on prescription and nonprescription medications (Table 18-2), various methods to overcome potential triggers for future substance abuse, and various plans to maintain sobriety in the community (Solomon et al, 1993; Szwabo, 1993). The nurse should also educate family members to the potential changes in family dynamics that may result from the client's sobriety. For example, nurses need to educate family members to avoid

Fig. 18-2 Older adults' concurrent use of many prescription medications can lead to polypharmacy. (Courtesy Loy Ledbetter, St. Louis, Mo.)

enabling the abuser by covering up, protecting, shielding, or in some way minimizing the problems created by alcohol abuse (Lindblom et al, 1992). Home health nurses should visit the older adult client after discharge to determine progress and encourage participation in community activities (Lindblom et al, 1992). Recall that individual, group, and family therapy sessions are conducted by a trained therapist and the nurse may assist the therapist as indicated.

Evaluation

The evaluation of the treatment of the older alcohol abuse client consists of safe detoxification, adherence to a treatment plan for sobriety, and outpatient support (Lindblom et al, 1992; Szwabo, 1993). Safe detoxification consists of the weaning from alcohol without seizures, DTs, or other withdrawal complications. The nurse also assesses whether the client is adhering to the sobriety protocol of abstinence, attendance at AA meetings, and individual or family therapy. In addition, continued relationship with the client's sponsor and progress as stated by home health nurses evaluates the client's transition back into the community (Lindblom, 1992; Szwabo, 1993).

Prescription Medications

Prevalence

The prevalence of chronic conditions in 80% of older Americans contributes to the many medications prescribed for older adults. As a result, concurrent use of multiple medications is common among the older adult population (Montamat, Cusack, 1992). Furthermore, the greater the number of medications prescribed correlates with the increased risk of inadvertent misuse of medications. As a result, the possibility of polypharmacy can occur (Montamat, Cusack, 1992) (Fig. 18-2). **Polypharmacy** is the prescription, use, or administration of more medications than indicated clinically (Montamat, Cusack, 1992). Prescription drugs commonly used by independent older people are cardiovascular medications, benzodiazepines, diuretics, cathartics, antacids, thyroidals, and anticoagulants (Lewis, Ellis, Wagner, 1992). It should be noted that benzodiazepines have a high incidence of abuse and because of the cross-tolerance with alcohol, there is an increased potential for cross-addiction (Juergens, 1993; Thibault, Maly, 1993) (see Chapter 20). The nurse most likely is the professional who identifies the possibility of prescription medication abuse by taking the client's health history. In addition, the rapport

RESEARCH

Desai T, Rajput A, Desai H: Use and abuse of drugs in the elderly. In *Progress in neuro-psychopharmacology & biological psychiatry,* 14(5):779-84, 1990.

Sample, setting

Subjects included 100 men and women age 65 and older admitted to the Geriatric Assessment Unit.

Methodology

Retrospective chart review was used to examine drug therapy in older adults.

Findings

Average took 5.15 drugs on admission. In addition, 14% of the sample indicated inaccurate dosages, 31% found drug interactions, 23% were noted to have drug contraindications, and 39% had at least one unnecessary drug prescribed. Furthermore, 8% of the sample had potential drug interactions that could result from the medications prescribed at discharge.

Implications

The knowledge of the relatively high percentage of clients who received inappropriate drug therapy can be used to stress the importance of nursing assessment of inappropriate polypharmacy in the older adult. If inappropriate polypharmacy is identified early, misdiagnosis and ineffective treatments may be prevented.

that is established with the nurse allows the client to feel comfortable discussing medications with this health professional. Therefore it is imperative that the nurse assess for the possibility of prescription medication abuse in the older adult population (see Research box, above).

Assessment

Nursing assessment for prescription drug abuse in the older adult client is very similar to the assessment used for alcohol abuse. The nurse should begin the assessment by taking a careful history, using the screening tools of the CAGE, MAST, and BMAST (Szwabo, 1993). The nurse should remember to substitute the term "prescription medications" in place of "alcohol." In addition, the nurse should assess the client for repeated loss of prescriptions or pills (e.g., "I threw it away by accident," or "I didn't think I would use them, so I flushed them down the toilet."), prescriptions from multiple physicians, frequent emergency room visits, strong preference for particular medications (e.g., "Only X medication works for pain for me" or "I'm allergic to Y, so I can only take X."), above-average knowledge about medications, and if the verbalization of the severity of the complaint does not match the clinical presentation (Finch, 1993). Finally, assess the client for signs associated with withdrawal such as anxiety, irritability, insomnia, fatigue, headache, tremors, sweating, dizziness, decreased concentration, nausea, depression, and visual or tactile hallucinations (Juergens, 1993).

Interventions

The interventions for prescription drug abuse are similar to the interventions associated with alcohol abuse. First, if prescription drug abuse is suspected, ask the client or a family member to bring in all medications that the client is presently using and inform the physician so a plan for safe detoxification can be established (Finch, 1993). Inform the client that, by bringing in all medications presently being used, the health care team can develop a comprehensive plan of care that addresses the client's physical needs. In addition, the physician can try to prevent any untoward drug interactions as a result of prescribing a new medication that is countraindicated to an existing medication that the client is using (Finch, 1993). The nurse should then document any signs of withdrawal, should provide an environment of low stimulation, and should implement seizure precautions (Solomon et al, 1993). In addition, the nurse should administer in a planned reduction schedule any medications ordered to minimize withdrawal symptoms (Solomon et al, 1993; Szwabo). Nutritional support interventions should also be implemented for clients with a compromised nutritional status (Miller, Belkin, Gold, 1991). Finally, the concern about prescription drug abuse along with treatment options such as an AA or NA, group, and individual therapy should be presented to the client and family members in a client care conference after discussion with the multidisciplinary team (Solomon et al, 1993).

Evaluation

The evaluation of nursing interventions for the prescription medication abuser includes safe detoxification, participation in a rehabilitation treatment plan, and decreased drug-seeking behaviors (Solomon et al, 1993). The nurse should also observe and document the client's response to any teaching done by the nurse regarding appropriate medication use and the effects of medication misuse on the body.

Nonprescription Medications

Prevalence

Nonprescription medications are consumed by 60% to 70% of older adults (Palmieri, 1991). Older adults often use nonprescription medications to alleviate ailments as a result of the costs associated with physician visits and

TABLE 18-3

Reactions and Interactions of Nonprescription Medications in Older Adults

Medication	Adverse effect
Aspirin	Large doses can alter blood coagulation time and cause irritation and bleeding in the gastrointestinal system. Laboratory values may be altered. Sodium and chloride excretion can be altered leading to toxicity. Alone or in combination with other drugs, it can lead to hypothermia. In older adults, lower doses may produce toxic effects exhibited by confusion, irritability, diarrhea, hearing and vision disturbances.
Laxatives	Interfere with the absorption of nutrients and fluids and with habitual use, create bowel dependency, diarrhea, weight loss, weakness, fluid, and electrolyte imbalances.
Antacids	May increase antibiotic absorption and decrease the absorption of digitalis, psychoactive drugs, and nutrients. Interact with iron salts, Inderal, and Kayexalate to affect bone mineral metabolism and to cause bone weakening. May also cause constipation or diarrhea and may delay gastric emptying, which prolongs the absorption of medications.
Vitamins	Vitamins containing iron may contribute to constipation. Large amounts of vitamins A and D can cause toxicity. Large amounts of thiamine can adversely affect the cardiovascular and nervous systems. Excessive niacin may result in abnormal liver function. Large quantities of vitamin C may cause kidney stones.
Sleeping medications	May contain bromides, which contribute to confusion, and may lead to dependence. Overuse may lead to depression and other neurologic symptoms. Many preparations have scopolamine and should not be taken by people with glaucoma.
Cough mixtures	May contain phenylpropanolamine, which may alter blood pressure or may precipitate psychiatric-type symptoms.
Antihistamines	May cause agitation and excitement.

Developed from Trainor PA: Over-the-counter drugs: count them in, *Geriatric Nurs* September/October: 228-229, 1988.

prescription medications (Palmieri, 1991). Furthermore, older adult clients may not tell their physicians about the nonprescription medications that they are taking, and physicians may prescribe medications that the client is already taking (Montamat, Cusack, 1992). The addition of nonprescription medications to an existing drug regimen may create serious adverse drug interactions. The most commonly used nonprescription medications by the older adult are analgesics, laxatives, antacids, cough preparations, milk of magnesia, Pepto-Bismol, eye washes, and vitamins (Miller, Belkin, Gold, 1991).

Assessment, Interventions, and Evaluation

The nurse should begin with assessing the client's nonprescription medication history. Clients should be asked how often they "pick something up at the grocery or drug store" for an ailment. Clients should also be asked about what specific nonprescription medications they buy, for what ailment, and how much they use (Montamat, Cusack 1992). Furthermore, the nurse should observe during the physical assessment for any signs of reactions and interactions of nonprescription medications (Trainor, 1988) (Table 18-3).

Nursing interventions include educating clients about the adverse effects of nonprescription medications. Additional education regarding the importance of contacting the physician or pharmacist before taking nonprescription medication is an essential step in reducing the number of unintentional medication interactions in the older adult (Montamat, Cusack, et al, 1992). Evaluation of the nursing interventions include the decreased number of nonprescription medications used and the understanding of the effects of nonprescription medications (Miller, Belkin, Gold, 1991; Solomon, 1993) (see Client/Family Teaching box on p. 420).

Nicotine

Prevalence

Tobacco use is the single greatest cause of preventable disease and disability in the United States (Carethers, 1992). Tobacco use is a risk factor in six of the 13 leading causes of death in older adults (Carethers, 1992). Of

CLIENT/FAMILY TEACHING

Safe Use of Medications

Know the name, amount, type, frequency, purpose, and side effects of both the prescription and nonprescription drugs that you are taking.

If you see more than one provider of care, always bring all of your medications to every provider visit you make.

Never "borrow" medication from anyone else or share your medications with anyone else.

Make sure your family members can safely self-administer medications; adequate vision, memory, judgment, and coordination are all essential.

Supervise medication administration for those people who cannot safely self-administer. Talk to the doctor or advanced practice nurse about simplifying the medication regimen by using once or twice daily dosing.

Never mix alcohol with *any* medication.

Encourage using a single pharmacy for filling all prescriptions to reduce potential for interactions as well as abuse and misuse.

Be suspicious of people who repeatedly lose medications, have a strong preference for particular medications, have seemingly above-average knowledge about medications, or have complaints that do not seem to match how they look.

BOX 18-9

Fagerstorm Nicotine Tolerance Quiz

Answer the following questions, and then add up the points:

1. How many cigarettes do you smoke a day?
   ____ 15 or less (0 points)
   ____ 16 to 25 (1 point)
   ____ 26 or more (2 points)
2. How much nicotine is in each cigarette you smoke? (See package.)
   ____ 0.9 mg or less (0 points)
   ____ 1.0 mg to 1.2 mg (1 point)
   ____ 1.3 mg or more (2 points)
3. How often do you inhale?
   ____ Never (0 points)
   ____ Sometimes (1 point)
   ____ Always (2 points)
4. Do you smoke more during the first 2 hours of the day than during the rest of the day?
   ____ No (0 points)
   ____ Yes (1 point)
5. How soon after you wake up do you smoke your first cigarette?
   ____ More than 30 minutes (0 points)
   ____ Less than 30 minutes (1 point)
6. Which cigarette would you most hate to give up?
   ____ The first one in the morning (1 point)
   ____ Any other (0 points)
7. Do you find it difficult not to smoke when it's forbidden?
   ____ No (0 points)
   ____ Yes (1 point)
8. Do you smoke even if you are so ill that you are in bed most of the day?
   ____ No (0 points)
   ____ Yes (1 point)

NOTE Individuals who score 7 or more probably suffer from a physical addiction to nicotine and can expect severe withdrawal symptoms.

Nicotine patches: a better way to quit smoking? © Consumer Union of U.S., Inc., Yonkers, NY 10703-1057. Reprinted by permission from *Consumer Reports on Health,* September 1992.

the tobacco users 50 years and older, 57% would like to quit (Salive et al, 1992). However, only those older adults with chronic illness tend to have the motivation to follow through with their plan to quit (American Cancer Society, 1990). Furthermore, the older adult who stops tobacco usage can increase life expectancy (Carethers, 1992).

Assessment

The nurse should thoroughly assess the client's tobacco use pattern and for signs of nicotine withdrawal. A helpful assessment tool is the Fagerstorm Nicotine Tolerance Quiz in Box 18-9. The client's responses allow the nurse to plan appropriate interventions for the client. The older adult should also be observed for signs of nicotine withdrawal such as depressed mood, insomnia, irritability, frustration, anger, anxiety, difficulty concentrating, restlessness, decreased heart rate, and increased appetite (APA, 1994). The DSM-IV criteria for nicotine withdrawal can be found in Box 18-10.

Interventions and Evaluation

Nursing interventions for the client who abuses tobacco include observing for signs of withdrawal, administering nicotine replacement, behavior modification, and education. The type of nicotine replacement used is determined by the physician, and typically consists of nicotine gum or nicotine transdermal patches (Hughes, 1993). The treatment period lasts from 6 weeks to several months and reduces the craving for cigarettes by weaning the client from nicotine and preventing withdrawal symptoms (Hughes, 1993). Clients who do not tolerate nicotine replacement patches may respond bet-

BOX 18-10

DSM-IV Diagnostic Criteria for Nicotine Withdrawal

A. Daily use of nicotine for at least several weeks.
B. Abrupt cessation of nicotine use, or reduction in the amount of nicotine used, followed by four (or more) of the following signs:
   1. Dysphoric or depressed mood
   2. Insomnia
   3. Irritability, frustration, or anger
   4. Anxiety
   5. Difficulty concentrating
   6. Restlessness
   7. Decreased heart rate
   8. Increased appetite or weight gain
C. The symptoms in Criterion B cause clinically significant distress or impairment in social, occupational, or other important areas of functioning.
D. The symptoms are not results of a general medical condition and are not better accounted for by another mental disorder.

Reprinted with permission from *Diagnostic and statistical manual of mental disorders,* ed 4 © 1994, American Psychiatric Association.

ter to Clonidine patches (*Consumers reports on health,* 1992). Clonidine is an antihypertensive that blocks the neurologic symptoms that produce nicotine withdrawal. Older adults should be treated with lower dosages as a result of the increased susceptibility to this medication's effects (Silverman, 1994).

Blum (1993) reports a behavior modification technique that is useful in decreasing tobacco use. The technique is called Postpone/Inhale/Reconsider and has been successful with clients in coping with stress (Blum, 1993). The technique requires the client to take a cigarette from a pack, replace it, and wait for 5 minutes. During the 5-minute interval, the client places two fingers to the mouth as if smoking and inhales slowly. After 5 minutes, the entire process is repeated. Clients have reduced smoking by 50% after using this technique (Blum, 1993). Box 18-11 outlines some additional nursing interventions that can be used to help clients quit tobacco use.

The older adult client should also be educated on the effects tobacco has on prescription medications (Table 18-4). Evaluation of nursing interventions includes assessing for decreased use of tobacco, the adherence to a plan to reduce tobacco use, and verbalization of the understanding of the effects tobacco or nicotine has on the body.

BOX 18-11

Intervention Plan for Clients Who Smoke

Ask all clients about smoking.
Encourage and support physicians who advise clients to quit smoking.
Educate your clients about the health risks associated with smoking.
Assist the client who wants to quit smoking now:
- Help the client select a stop date.
- Provide self-help materials.
- Administer any physician-prescribed nicotine replacement therapies.

Arrange follow-up visits or calls.

Modified from Manley M et al: Clinical interventions in tobacco control, *JAMA* 266:3172-3173, 1991.

Caffeine

Prevalence

Little literature exists that indicates the prevalence of caffeine misuse and abuse among older adults. However, the effects of caffeine on the major body systems have important implications for older adults. Caffeine stimulates the sympathetic nervous system, producing an increase in motor activity, muscle capacity, and alertness; a decrease in fatigue; rapid pulse; and slightly decreased basal metabolism (Ochs, Holmes, Karst, 1992). Therefore the nurse must be aware of signs of caffeine intoxication and caffeine withdrawal so that appropriate nursing interventions are implemented and symptoms of other physical illnesses are not masked.

Assessment

Caffeine adds to the complexity of assessment of the older adult client. Many symptoms associated with feine intoxication mimic gastrointestinal, urinary, cardiovascular, and psychiatric disorders (Ochs, Holmes, Karst, 1992). The DSM-IV criteria for caffeine intoxication is displayed in Box 18-12, p. 423. The assessment of the amount and type of caffeine consumed each day is beneficial in determining the possibility of caffeine abuse in the older adult. Table 18-5 indicates the amount of caffeine in various products.

The effects of caffeine withdrawal must also be addressed by the nurse. The onset of withdrawal occurs 12 to 24 hours after discontinuation of caffeine, peaks at 20 to 48 hours, and may last up to 1 week (Work, 1991). Symptoms include headache, fatigue, depression, anxi-

TABLE 18-4

Effects of Tobacco Use on Selected Prescription Medications

Classification	Effects
Antiarrhythmics	
Flecainide (Tambocor)	Reduces flecainide serum concentrations Smokers may require increased doses
Lidocaine (Xylocaine)	May occasionally alter lidocaine metabolism
Tricyclic antidepressants	
Nortriptyline (Pamelor) Imipramine (Tofranil) Amitriptyline (Elavil)	May not be as responsive to usual dosages
Antidiabetics	
Insulin	May increase glucose concentrations Change in tobacco usage may change insulin dosage
Benzodiazepines	
Chlordiazepoxide (Librium) Diazepam (Valium)	May be resistant to effects of benzodiazepines; may require larger doses to achieve sedative effects
Anticoagulant	
Heparin	May require higher dosages
Narcotic analgesic antagonist	
Pentazocine (Talwin)	May require higher dosages
Narcotic analgesic	
Propoxyphene (Darvon)	May require higher dosages
Bronchodilator	
Theophylline (Bronkodyl)	May require higher dosages to achieve adequate serum levels since elimination is increased with tobacco use

From Hansten PD, Horn JR: *Drug interactions & updates.* Pennsylvania, 1990, Lea & Febiger.

TABLE 18-5

Caffeine-Containing Products

Product	Mg of caffeine
Drip-brewed coffee (6 oz)	130-180
Instant coffee	50-130
Decaffeinated coffee	2-6
Tea (6 oz)	36
Cola (12 oz)	46
Hot cocoa (6 oz)	4
Chocolate milk (8 oz)	6
Cadbury milk chocolate (1 oz)	15
Dannon coffee-flavored yogurt (8 oz)	45
Excedrin (2 Tablets)	130
Anacin (2 Tablets)	64

Reprinted with permission from Tufts University Diet and Nutrition Letter: *Light coffee drinkers are hooked too,* 10(10):1-2, 1992, Editorial Board.

ety, nausea, vomiting, muscle pain and stiffness (APA, 1994). APA studies indicate that caffeine withdrawal can be classified as diagnostic criteria. Box 18-13, p. 423, provides Research Criteria for Caffeine Withdrawal for the DSM-IV (1994).

Interventions and Evaluation

Nurses should document signs of caffeine withdrawal or intoxication and should provide appropriate comfort measures, based on the symptoms exhibited by the client. Some physicians may advocate the gradual reduction of the use of Excedrine as the client withdraws from caffeine (Ochs, Holmes, Karst, 1992). The nurse may also instruct the older adult to switch from caffeinated to noncaffeinated products. In addition, the nurse should educate the client on the effects of caffeine on medications and should document client's understanding of the teaching (Table 18-6).

BOX 18-12

DSM-IV Diagnostic Criteria for Caffeine Intoxication

A. Recent consumption of caffeine, usually in excess of 250 mg (e.g., more than 2-3 cups of brewed coffee).
B. Five (or more) of the following signs, developing during, or shortly after, caffeine use:
   1. Restlessness
   2. Nervousness
   3. Excitement
   4. Insomnia
   5. Flushed face
   6. Diuresis
   7. Gastrointestinal disturbance
   8. Muscle twitching
   9. Rambling flow of thought and speech
   10. Tachycardia or cardiac arrhythmia
   11. Periods of inexhaustibility
   12. Psychomotor agitation
C. The symptoms in Criterion B cause clinically significant distress or impairment in social, occupational, or other important areas of functioning.
D. The symptoms are not results of a general medical condition and are not better accounted for by another mental disorder (e.g., an anxiety disorder).

Reprinted with permission from *Diagnostic and statistical manual of mental disorders,* ed 4 © 1994, American Psychiatric Association.

BOX 18-13

DSM-IV Research Criteria for Caffeine Withdrawal

A. Prolonged daily use of caffeine
B. Abrupt cessation of caffeine use, or reduction in the amount of caffeine used, closely followed by headache and one (or more) of the following symptoms:
   1. Marked fatigue or drowsiness
   2. Marked anxiety or depression
   3. Nausea or vomiting
C. The symptoms in Criterion B cause clinically significant distress or impairment in social, occupational, or other important areas of functioning.
D. The symptoms are not a result of the direct physiologic effects of a general medical condition (e.g., migraine, viral illness) and are not better accounted for by another mental disorder.

Reprinted with permission from *Diagnostic and statistical manual of mental disorders,* ed 4 © 1994, The American Psychiatric Association.

TABLE 18-6

The Effect of Caffeine on Medications

Classification	Effect
Antiarrhythmic	
Adenocard (Adenocine)	Reduces adenocine's effect, increases heart rate and systolic pressure; higher dosage may be indicated
Alcohol	Does *not* reverse side effects of alcohol intoxication
Benzodiazepines	Counteracts the effects of benzodiazepines
Calcium channel blockers	
Nifedipine (Procardia) Verapamil (Calan)	Does not appear to affect; hypertensive clients should limit caffeine intake
Aspirin	May slightly increase the absorption of aspirin.

Modified from Hansten PD, Horn JR: *Drug interactions & updates* Pennsylvania, 1990, Lea & Febiger.

FUTURE TRENDS

There is presently little research identifying the prevalence of illicit drug use and abuse in the older adult population of such drugs as cannabis, cocaine, and phencyclidine (Miller, Belkin, Gold, 1991). However, as the current middle-age generation reaches the older adult age group, the prevalence of illicit drug use is likely to be on the rise (Thibault, Maly, 1993). Therefore research regarding prevention and intervention of illicit drug use and abuse in the older adult must be developed now.

Summary

The prognosis for untreated alcohol and substance abuse in older adults is poor (Miller, Belkin, Gold, 1991). Nurses must identify substance abuse in older adults and must examine their own attitudes about substance abuse in this population. Early identification and intervention are essential in preventing misdiagnosis, ineffective, and costly treatments. Nurses should recognize that effective treatment for the older adult substance abuser does exist. The first step in effective treatment is identification. After identification of the problem, cost-effective treatment can be initiated to help the older adult return to a healthy lifestyle.

HOME CARE TIPS

1. Obtain a prescription medication inventory, including the physician sources of all prescriptions.
2. Mail-order prescription suppliers send large quantities of drugs to homebound older adults, which predisposes to drug wasting, overdosing, or other misuse.
3. Assess the number of caregivers involved with medication administration to prevent overdosing or other administration errors.
4. Drug use patterns by homebound older adults, which include prescription drugs, over-the-counter drugs, and home remedies, are influenced by cultural and ethnic health practices.
5. During assessment of the homebound older adult, an inventory of use of caffeine, nicotine, and/or alcohol should be included.
6. Assess high risk factors (e.g., social isolation, depression) that may predispose a homebound older adult to substance abuse.
7. Assess for signs of substance abuse in the homebound older adult.
8. Encourage caregivers to attend support groups such as AA to help ease the burden of caring for a homebound older adult with a substance abuse problem.

Key Points

- The age-related physiologic changes of altered absorption, distribution, metabolism, and excretion affect drug usage and place the older adult at an increased risk for substance abuse.
- The psychologic changes in the older adult result primarily because of the numerous losses this age group may incur in a relatively short period of time and place the older adult at an increased risk for substance abuse.
- The social changes of decreased finances, transportation, and social support as well as the cultural factors of gender and race place the older adult client at risk for substance abuse and misuse.
- The substances most often abused by the older adult population are alcohol, prescription medications, nonprescription medications, nicotine, and caffeine.
- The nurse should assess the older adult client for key medical and psychologic manifestations of substance abuse when taking the client's health history. Some of these key manifestations are falls, hypertension, memory loss, depressed mood, and social withdrawal.
- Screening tools such as the CAGE, MAST, and BMAST should be used to obtain a history of substance use in older adult clients.
- Key nursing interventions for substance abuse in the older adult client include assessing for signs of withdrawal, administering appropriate medications to provide a safe detoxification, providing a safe environment, educating the client regarding the harmful effects of the abused substance on the body, and encouraging the client to participate in AA or NA, individual, family, and group therapy.

Critical Thinking Exercises

1. Compare and contrast nursing assessment and interventions for prescription drug, nonprescription drug, and alcohol abuse. How are they similar and/or different? How might assessment techniques be revised for the older population?
2. Analyze your own perceptions and attitudes regarding substance abuse in general. How do these perceptions and attitudes differ with regard to substance abuse in the older adult population? What factors and/or assumptions contribute to these perceptions?
3. How might the DSM-IV criteria for substance abuse be revised to specifically address the older adult population?

REFERENCES

Ahronheim JC: *Handbook of prescribing medications for geriatric patients,* Boston, 1992, Little, Brown.

Alcoholics Anonymous: *Alcoholics Anonymous,* ed 3, New York, 1976, Alcoholics Anonymous World Services.

American Cancer Society: *The most often asked questions about smoking tobacco and health and ... the answers,* Georgia, 1990, American Cancer Society.

American Psychiatric Association: *Diagnostic and statistical manual of mental disorders,* Fourth Edition. Washington, D.C., 1994, The Association.

American Psychiatric Association: *Let's talk facts about mental health of the elderly,* [pamphlet], Washington, D.C., 1988, The Association.

Blum A: Consumer advocacy: An approach to counseling, *Patient Care* February, 80-83, 1993.

Carethers M: Health promotion in the elderly, *Am Fam Phys* 45(5):2253-2259, 1992.

Consumer Reports on Health: Nicotine patches: a better way to quit smoking?, September:70-71, 1992.

Cutezo EA, Dellasega C: Substance abuse in the homebound elderly, *Home Healthcare Nurse,* 10(1):19-23, 1992.

Finch J: Prescription drug abuse, *Prim Care* 20(1):231-239, 1993.

Hess P: Chinese and Hispanic elders and OTC drugs, *Geriat Nurs* November/December, 314-318, 1986.

Hughes JR: Is the Nicotine patch the answer?, *Patient Care,* February, 68-79, 1993.

Juergens SM: Problems with benzodiazepines in elderly patients, *Mayo Clin Proceed* 68:818-820, 1993.

Leary BW, Donehew GR, Swanson L: Does mail-order pharmacy satisfy the needs of the elderly? *Pharm Times* August, 82-89, 1992.

Lewis CB, Ellis A, Wagner M: Drugs and the elderly patient, *Clin Manag* 12(2):54-63, 1992.

Lile JL: Medications-taking by the frail elderly in two ethnic groups, *Nurs Forum* 26(4):19-24, 1991.

Lindblom L, et al: Chemical abuse: An intervention program for the elderly, *J Gerontolog Nurs* 18(4):6-14, 1992.

Lipman MM: Are you taking higher drug dosages than you need? *Cons Rep Health* May 5, 1993.

Mayfield D, McLeod G, Hall P: The CAGE questionnaire: validation of a new alcoholism screening instrument, *Am J Psychiatry,* 131:1121-1123, 1974.

McDonald AJ, Abrahams ST: Social emergencies in the elderly, *Emerg Med Clin North Am* 8(2):443-459, 1990.

Miller NS, Belkin, BM, Gold MS: Alcohol and drug dependence among the elderly: epidemiology, diagnosis, and treatment, *Comprehens Psychiatry,* 32(2):153-165, 1991.

Montamat SC, Cusack B: Overcoming problems with polypharmacy and drug misuse in the elderly, *Clin Geriatr Med* 8(1):143-158, 1992.

Ochs LA, Holmes GE, Karst RH: Caffeine consumption and disability: Chemical issues in rehabilitation, *J Rehab* July/August/September:44-50, 1992.

Palmieri DT: Adverse effects of medications in the elderly, *J Gerontolog Nurs,* 17(10):32-35, 1991.

Salive ME et al: Predictors of smoking cessation and relapse in older adults, *Am J Pub Health,* 82(9):1268-1271, 1992.

Selzer ML: The Michigan Alcoholism Screening Test: the quest for a new diagnostic instrument, *Am J Psychiatry* 127:89-94, 1971.

Silverman HM: *The pill book,* ed 6, New York, 1994, Bantam Books.

Solomon K et al: Alcoholism and prescription drug abuse in the elderly: St. Louis University Grand Rounds, *J Am Geriatr Soc* 41:57-69, 1993.

Szwabo PA: Substance abuse in older women, *Clin Geriatr Med* 9(1):197-208, 1993.

Thibault JM, Maly RC: Recognition and treatment of substance abuse in the elderly, *Prim Care,* 20(1):155-165, 1993.

Trainor PA: Over-the-counter drugs: count them in, *Geriatr Nurs* September/October:228-229, 1988.

Twadell PAS: Recreational drugs: societal and professional issues, *Nurs Clin North Am* 26(2), 499-509, 1991.

Walker MK: Pharmacology and drug therapy in critically ill elderly patients. In *Critical care nursing of the elderly,* New York, 1992, Springer.

Work JA: Are java junkies poor sports? *J Rehab* January: 31-34;86-88, 1991.

Part Five

Special Interventions

CHAPTER 19

Laboratory and Diagnostic Tests

LEARNING OBJECTIVES

On completion of this chapter, the reader will be able to:

1. Identify key lab values that increase or decrease with aging.
2. Describe the effect of aging on the erythrocyte sedimentation rate (ESR).
3. Name two medications that can interfere with potassium excretion and affect serum potassium levels.
4. Explain the relationship between serum sodium levels and pseudohyponatremia.
5. Name the two body systems the function of which can be reflected in the blood urea nitrogen level.
6. Explain the difference between serum creatinine concentrations in younger adults and older adults.
7. Relate the relationship between bacteria in the urine and urinary infections in older adults.
8. List the current recommendations for mammography, sigmoidoscopy, and prostate-specific antigen screening in older adults.
9. Discuss the role of laboratory tests in determining thyroid function in the older adult.
10. Describe the nurse's role in interpreting lab values in older adults.

Diagnostic testing in the older adult takes on a different meaning than testing in younger adults. The nurse must realize that laboratory values in aging can be classified into three general groups: (1) those that change with aging; (2) those that do not change; (3) and those where it is unclear whether aging, disease, or both create change in the values. Cavalieri, Chopra, and Bryman (1992) identify additional factors that contribute to this confusing equation, such as the following: (1) the atypical presentation of disease in the older adult; (2) the realization that older adults rarely have just one chronic illness; and (3) the frequent polypharmacy in older adults, including prescription and over-the-counter (OTC) medicines.

The gerontologic nurse must consider the effect of laboratory and diagnostic testing on the older adult's overall health and well-being. For example, with aging, subcutaneous tissue is decreased, and the fragility of veins increases. Consequently, the frail older adult is more likely to have increased bruising and discomfort after a venous blood drawing than a younger adult. It is also important for the nurse to know what tests have been ordered so that an explanation can be given to the sometimes anxious older adult. This anxiety may range from concerns about the cost of tests to a concern for privacy (e.g., with sigmoidoscopy and mammography testing), to cultural concerns (see Cultural Awareness box, below). For example, the Chinese and Vietnamese believe that drawn blood is irreplaceable and thus may become upset with repeated blood testing (Burnside, 1988).

The intent of this chapter is to give the gerontologic nurse a basic understanding of the purpose of commonly ordered laboratory and diagnostic tests, the importance of selected hematologic and blood and urine chemistry components in the body's overall function, and the relative "normal" ranges for younger and older adults. These normal ranges may vary from institution to institution, as well as among sources (Table 19-1). Because of the scant research conducted on the older adult, geriatricians and gerontologists also may disagree as to whether changes are related to aging or disease (Abrams, Berkow, 1990). However, most of these aging experts do agree that older adults should be treated as individuals and viewed in terms of symptoms, test results, and overall condition when deciding the best course of treatment.

COMPONENTS OF HEMATOLOGIC TESTING

Blood is a complex connective tissue composed of cells (erythrocytes and leukocytes), specialized cell fragments (platelets), and a fluid matrix called plasma. These cells and cell fragments are suspended in the plasma, which is one of the body's three major body fluids (Thibodeau, Patton, 1993).

Red Blood Cells (Erythrocytes)

Red blood cells, or erythrocytes, are disk-shaped cells that carry molecules of hemoglobin. The hemoglobin allows the transport and exchange of oxygen and carbon dioxide. Erythrocytes lack a nuclei and other internal cell structures. This not only allows for a greater surface area to carry hemoglobin but also prevents erythrocytes from reproducing themselves or maintaining function indefinitely. The average life span of an erythrocyte is about 120 days. Although aging does not affect the life span of the erythrocyte, replenishment after bleeding occurs may be delayed (McCance, Huether, 1994).

CULTURAL AWARENESS

Cultural Influences on Diagnostic and Laboratory Tests

The nurse should be aware that biocultural variations in older adults occur with some diagnostic and laboratory tests, such as measurement of *blood glucose* and blood analysis of *hemoglobin/hematocrit, glucose* and *serum cholesterol.*

African Americans have an average blood pressure reading 5 mm Hg higher than whites, which can be less at younger ages but more at older ages. African-American women over age 45 have a reading as much as 16 mm Hg higher than white women in the same age group.

Although healthy older people have hemogloblin and hematocrit values within the range of younger people, gender difference in these blood values (men have higher readings than women) decreases with aging. Women experience a rise in the measures up to age 60 and then a slight decline, whereas men show a constant decline from the age of 30 to the end of life. By age 60, men and women have similar blood measures. The racial difference in hemoglobin levels continues into old age. African Americans have lower hemoglobin levels than whites, but they follow the same gender pattern of increasingly similar hemoglobin levels with age.

Whether measured by the glucose tolerance test or by glycosylated hemoglobin determination, the blood glucose level rises with age. The mean blood glucose level, after a challenge, rises from 99.7 mg/100 ml at ages 18 to 24 to 166.3 mg/100 ml at ages 75 to 79. Mean glycosylated hemoglobin determinations are 6.9% at ages 50 to 69 and rise to 8.6% at ages 80 to 89. Women have higher blood levels than men. This gender difference widens with age, being 9.5 mg/100 ml at ages 18 to 24 and 24.1 mg/100 ml at 75 to 79 years. African Americans have slightly higher levels than whites, but the difference is not apparent between individuals of similar socioeconomic status.

Cholesterol levels rise with age in both men and women, but their patterns of increase differ. In men, peak levels occur in the 45 to 54 age group, and then decline slightly thereafter. In women, levels continue to rise steadily until age 65 and over, when the rise decelerates slightly. African Americans and whites have similar cholesterol levels, but other groups differ substantially. Pima Indians from the Southwest and the Japanese have lower cholesterol levels than African Americans or whites. The mean value for Pima Indians is 189 mg/100 ml and for the Japanese is 152 mg/100 ml, whereas African Americans and whites have a mean of 223 mg/100 ml.

Overfield T: *Biologic variation in health and illness,* Menlo Park, Calif, 1985, Addison-Wesley.

TABLE 19-1

Hematology

Test name	Adult normals	Older adult normals	Significance of deviations*
Erythrocytes	4.05-5.64 million/unit[†]	Unchanged with aging[‡]	*Low:* hemorrhage, anemias, chronic infections, chronic renal failure *High:* high altitude, polycythemia, advanced chronic obstructive pulmonary disease (COPD), dehydration
Hemoglobin	12.5-17.0 gm/100 ml[†]	Unchanged with aging[§]	*Low:* anemia, hemorrhage, cancer, kidney disease, fluid overload *High:* COPD, congestive heart failure (CHF), dehydration, high altitude
Hematocrit	36.9% to 52.0%[†]	Unchanged with aging[§]	*Low:* anemia, cirrhosis, malnutrition, rheumatoid arthritis (RA) *High:* dehydration, severe diarrhea, burns, late stage emphysema
White blood cells (Total)	5.1-10.8 thousand/μl[†]	Unchanged with aging[§] number same but decreased function[‡]	*Low:* Viral infections, alcoholism, systemic lupus erythematosus (SLE), RA, drug toxicity, dietary deficiency *High:* acute infections, inflammatory diseases, trauma, stress, tissue necrosis
Neutrophils	55% to 70%: Segmental cells 50% to 65%[†] Bands 0% to 8%[†]	Unchanged with aging[§]	*Low:* overwhelming bacterial infections, viral infections, radiation therapy *High:* trauma, RA, gout, physical and emotional stress
Eosinophils	0.0-0.5 thousand/μl[†]	Unchanged with aging[§]	*Low:* increased adrenosteroid production *High:* parasitic infections, allergic reactions, eczema, autoimmune diseases
Basophils	0.0-0.2 thousand/μl[†]	Unchanged with aging[§]	*Low:* allergic reactions, hyperthyroidism *High:* myeloproliferative leukemia
Monocytes	0.1-0.8 thousand/μl[†]	Unchanged with aging[§]	*Low:* prednisone therapy *High:* chronic inflammatory disorders, tuberculosis, chronic ulcerative colitis
Lymphocytes	1.0-4.5 thousand/μl[†]	Unchanged with aging[§]	*Low:* leukemia, sepsis, chemotherapy, radiation *High:* chronic bacterial infection, viral infection, radiation, infectious hepatitis
Folate	2.2-17.3[†] μgm/ml	Unchanged with aging[‡]	*Low:* malnutrition, folic acid or B_6 deficiency, hemolytic anemia, liver disease *High:* pernicious anemia
B_{12}	240-1240 picogm/ml	Decrease to 60% to 80% young adult value by age 70 years[‡]	*Low:* inadequate intake, pernicious anemia, gastrectomy *High:* acute hepatitis, myelocytic leukemia, polycythemia

*This is a representation of deviations and not an inclusive listing.
†From Presbyterian Hospital Normal Reference Values, 1993, Charlotte, NC.
‡From Mezey MD Rauckhorst LH, Stokes SA: *Health assessment of the older adult,* New York, 1993, Springer.
§From Kane RI, Ouslander JG, Abrass IB: *Essentials of clinical geriatrics,* ed 3, New York, 1994, McGraw-Hill.

Continued.

TABLE 19-1

Hematology—cont'd

Test name	Adult normals	Older adult normals	Significance of deviations*
Total iron binding capacity (TIBC)	250-450 μgm/100 ml 2-3x serum Fe level[‡]	Unchanged with aging	Evaluate for malnutrition or gastrointestinal blood loss if decreased
Iron (Fe)	M: 76-198 μgm/100 ml W: 26-170 μgm/100 ml	Decreases progressively in both genders with aging[‖]	Same as for TIBC
Uric acid	M: 3.9-7.8 mg/100 ml[†] W: 2.4-5.1 mg/100 ml[†]	Men slightly higher; women increase at 40 to 50 years[‡]	*Low:* folic acid anemia, burns *High:* gout, alcoholism, metastatic cancer (CA), CHF, renal failure, leukemias
Prothrombin time (PT)	11-12.5 seconds; 85% to 100%	Unchanged with aging[¶]	*High:* cirrhosis, hepatitis, coumadin therapy/ingestion, vitamin K deficiency, bile duct obstruction
Partial thromboplastin time (PTT)	60-70 seconds; patients receiving anticoagulant therapy 1.5-2.5 times control value seconds	Unchanged with aging[¶]	*Low:* extensive cancer, early stages disseminated intravascular coagulation (DIC) *High:* cirrhosis, vitamin K deficiency, DIC, acquired or congenital clotting factor deficiency
	M: 0-10 mm/hr[‡] W: 0-20 mm/hr[‡]	Mild increase (10-20 mm) may be considered an age-related change	*Low:* polycythemia, CHF, degenerative arthritis *High:* Acute MI, SLE +RA, gout, surgery, burns, malignancy, bacterial infections
Platelets	140-450 thousand/l[†]	Unchanged with aging	*Low:* hemorrhage, leukemias, liver disease, SLE, pernicious anemia, chemotherapy *High:* leukemia, polycythemia, cirrhosis, RA, trauma

‖ From Baime MJ, Nelson JB, Castell DO: Aging of the gastrointestinal system. In Hazard WR et al, editors: *Principles of geriatric medicine and gerontology,* ed 3, New York, 1994, McGraw-Hill.

¶From Cavalier TA, Chopra A, Bryman PN: When outside the norm is normal: interpreting lab data in the aged, *Geriatrics,* 47:66-70, May 1992.

Red blood cells are necessary to maintain oxygen and carbon dioxide transport. A reduction in the number of red blood cells, or a decrease in quality or quantity of hemoglobin is classified as **anemia.** Causes of anemia may be attributed to (1) impaired erythrocyte production; (2) blood loss; (3) increased erythrocyte destruction; or (4) a combination of the above (McCance, Huether, 1994). Common signs and symptoms of anemia include fatigue, confusion, and depression (Ebersole, Hess, 1994). In addition, clinicians can miss signs of anemia even in markedly anemic people (Ham, Sloane, 1992). This combination of vague symptomatology and clinical presentation may lead the health provider to attribute the older adult's complaints to "old age" and fail to investigate adequately. Other conditions involving erythrocytes are related to increased and decreased cell numbers. Increases in red blood cell count in people living in higher altitudes is known as secondary polycythemia. This occurs as an essential physiologic response to hypoxia encountered at high altitudes and is an example of one of the body's compensatory mechanisms. Abnormally high numbers of red blood cells can lead to thrombosis and bleeding (Thibodeau, Patton, 1993). In sickle cell anemia, the red blood cells become abnormal in shape and surface composition as a result of a genetic defect in the hemoglobin.

Hemoglobin

Hemoglobin is an important iron-containing protein that is carried on red blood cells and comprises about one third of the weight of the red blood cell. Hemoglobin is necessary for the transport of oxygen. A reduction in hemoglobin can result in a decrease in oxygen content and an increase in fatigue, possibly indicating anemia. Abnormal hemoglobin from mutant genes can cause abnormalities of the red blood cell, such as with sickle cell anemia.

Hematocrit

The **hematocrit** is the percentage of total blood volume that represents erythrocytes. This is determined in the laboratory by spinning (centrifuging) a sample of blood, causing the heavier red cells to sink to the bottom of the tube while the less dense plasma rises to the top. The percentage of cells to liquid is calculated, giving the hematocrit reading. An increase in the hematocrit can signal volume depletion (Melillo, 1993). Decreases in hematocrit may be a result of diseases or dietary deficiencies (Pagana, Pagana, 1992).

Effects of aging on the hemoglobin and hematocrit vary among references. Hemoglobin has been reported to remain unchanged (Mezey, Rauckhorst, Stokes, 1993) or change slightly, possibly from extrinsic factors rather than as a result of normal aging (Lipschitz, 1994). The hematocrit level remains unchanged across the life span for women (Helman, Rubenstein, 1975; Kelly, Munan, 1977; Htoo, Kofkoff, Freedman, 1979). However, studies have shown that for men, hematocrit values decline with age (Htoo, Kofkoff, Freedman, 1979; Dybkaer, Lauritzen, Krakauer, 1981).

Insight • *Many experts in the field of gerontology agree that anemia is not a consequence of normal aging. Anemia in the older adult can be caused by a variety of disorders, including blood loss, inflammation, chronic disease, and protein-energy malnutrition. Anemia from protein-energy malnutrition is a common form seen in older adults who are hospitalized (Lipschitz, 1994). Older adults with a hemoglobin below 12 gm/100 ml should have the cause investigated. Initial evaluation of this client should include a complete history, physical and nutritional assessment, and a complete blood count (Lipschitz, 1994). These studies can confirm the presence of anemia. Additional studies such as lactate dehydrogenase (LDH), mean corpuscular volume (MCV), and stools for occult blood help determine the type of anemia.*

White Blood Cells

White blood cells, or leukocytes, are another type of cell present in the blood. Their major function is defense against foreign substances. The site of function of the white blood cell is mainly in the interstitial fluid. Leukocytes consist of neutrophils, lymphocytes, monocytes, eosinophils, and basophils.

Insight • *Immune system function in the older adult tends to decline with age. The response of the older adult with an infection also varies from younger adults. Adler and Nagle (1994) state that in the initial stages of sepsis, 25% of older adults are hypothermic or have a temperature less than 100°F. Other common signs of impending sepsis are the sudden onset of confusion and disorientation. Although infections can usually be linked to a specific site or organism, older clients who are immunocompromised account for 30% of the sepsis cases where no readily identifiable organism or site can be determined.*

A decrease in leukocytes in the older adult may be related to drugs or sepsis (Cavalieri, Chopra, Bryman, 1992). An example of drugs that can cause a decrease in leukocytes include antimetabolites, cytotoxic agents, analgesics, phenothiazines, and gold salts (Rothstein, 1994). An increase in leukocytes is generally seen in infections. However, a white cell count may be only moderately elevated in the older adult when infection is present, such as pneumonia. Consequently, the nurse must be alert to other signs and symptoms of impending infection, such as the sudden onset of confusion. Other typical symptoms of infection such as fever, pain, and enlarged lymph glands (lymphadenopathy) may be at a minimum or absent in the older adult with an infection (Dever, Rothkopf, 1994).

Neutrophils, eosinophils, and basophils are produced in the bone marrow and possess similar structures of lobulated nuclei and many membrane-bound granules. Their primary function is phagocytosis (ingestion and destruction of particulate material). In addition, the basophil's cytoplasmic granules contain powerful chemicals such as histamine, which contribute to tissue damage and allergy (Thibodeau, Patton, 1993).

The monocyte, the largest of the leukocytes, is produced in bone marrow and differs in appearance from neutrophils, eosinophils, and basophils. The monocyte has a single nucleus and is capable of destroying large bacterial organisms and viral-infected cells by phagocytosis (Thibodeau, Patton, 1993).

Lymphocytes, the smallest of the leukocytes, are classified into two types—B and T. The lymphocytes have a large nucleus and relatively little cytoplasm. Originating in the bone marrow and thymus, lymphocytes are housed in the lymph nodes, spleen, and tonsils. Lymphocytes do not act as phagocytes, but rather produce antibodies and "other specific defenses" against antibodies (Thibodeau, Patton, 1993) (see Chapter 14).

Aging does not appear to affect the function of neutrophils, though there is a reduced effect on the bone marrow to release and store these cells. Lymphocytes of older adults have shown impaired function in vitro and are suspected to be the cause of a reduction in the antibody response in later life (Rothstein, 1994). The number of monocytes increases in older men and women (Rochman, 1988). Regarding monocyte function, however, Rothstein (1994) reports monocytes in older rodents decline in function; however, these results have not been replicable in older humans. There is suspicion that a decline in monocyte function exists when reviewing the increase of susceptibility to infections and increased incidence of malignancies in older adults. The last of the leukocytes, eosinophils and basophils, have not been shown to be affected by aging.

The presence and function of leukocytes is necessary for the body's resistance and response to infections, cancers, and other foreign substances. The implications related to infections and malignancies include recognizing subtle and sometimes altered responses to infections and diseases in the older adults. In addition, educating the older adult about the importance of participating in cancer screenings and maintaining immunizations throughout the life span is warranted.

Folic Acid

Folic acid is one of the eight B vitamins that comprise the B-complex group. Folic acid is a water soluble vitamin that functions as a coenzyme, which means it is inactive unless linked to an enzyme. Aging does not appear to have an effect on folic acid levels (Mezey, Rauckhorst, Stokes, 1993). A decrease in folic acid can indicate protein-energy malnutrition, chronic renal failure, macrocytic anemia, and excessive alcohol consumption. Alcohol and various other drugs are known to interfere with the absorption of folate (Lipschitz, 1994). Folic acid is necessary for normal functioning of red and white blood cells. Because of the relationship of nutrition and alcohol consumption to folic acid levels, it is important for the gerontologic nurse to assess clients for nutritional intake, including habits regarding alcohol consumption (see Chapters 8 and 18).

Vitamin B_{12}

Another of the water soluble vitamins that makes up the B-complex group and acts as a coenzyme is vitamin B_{12} or cobalamine. Although changes in B_{12} levels are seen in many older adults, some scientists do not feel that aging affects the ileal absorption of B_{12} (Baime, Nelson, Castell, 1994). They cite that problems with B_{12} tend to be the result of diseases and other conditions such as gastric achlorhydria, pernicious anemia, pancreatic insufficiency, and ileal disease, each of which has much greater impact on B_{12} absorption than aging by itself (Baime, Nelson, Castell, 1994). Some references report that B_{12} decreases by 60% to 80% that of younger adult values by the age of 70 and older (Garner, 1989).

Malabsorption of B_{12} can be caused by the effect of antibodies against gastric parietal cells and a decrease in the intrinsic factor, the factor underlying pernicious anemia. The prevalence of pernicious anemia increases significantly with aging (Lipschitz, 1994).

B_{12} is important for normal erythrocyte maturation (McCance, Huether, 1994), and acts as a coenzyme with folic acid. The synthesis of nucleic acids and hence, deoxyribonucleic acid (DNA), depend on B_{12}-containing enzymes (Davis, Sherer, 1993). Vitamin B_{12} deficiency can lead to degeneration of dorsal and lateral spinal columns, which in turn can lead to paresthesia of the feet and fingers and can progress to spastic ataxia (Gaspard, 1994).

Total Iron Binding Capacity

Transferrin is a protein in the plasma that collects iron and transports it to the bone marrow for incorporation into hemoglobin. Total iron binding capacity (TIBC) measures the amount of iron in the serum and the amount of transferrin available in the serum (McCance, Huether, 1994). Transferrin is a major transport protein responsible for the transport of iron in the body.

Iron

Iron is found in the hemoglobin of the red blood cells. When iron-containing foods are ingested, the iron is absorbed by the small intestine and transported to the plasma (Pagana, Pagana, 1992). Iron is necessary for "conversion of betacarotene to vitamin A, synthesis of collagen, formation of purines as part of nucleic acid, and production of antibodies" (Davis, Sherer, 1993). Serum iron levels reflect progressive decreases in both genders with advancing age, though iron absorption appears to remain intact (Baime, Nelson, Castell, 1994).

Iron-deficiency anemia is the most common form of anemia seen in older adults. However, in spite of the decreases in serum iron levels seen in aging, anemia in older adults is not a normal consequence of aging. Gerontologic nurses should assess older adults for lack of iron-containing foods in their diet, occult and/or chronic blood loss, and poor absorption of iron.

Uric Acid

Uric acid is a product of metabolism, specifically purine catabolism. Uric acid is excreted by the kidney. Changes in aging related to uric acid levels are more significant between the genders. Since estrogen is thought to promote the excretion of uric acid, elevated levels are rarely seen in women before the onset of menopause (McCance, Huether, 1994).

Problems with uric acid may be because of faulty excretion (kidney failure), overproduction of uric acid, or the presence of other substances that compete for excretion sites (i.e., ketoacids) (Pagana, Pagana, 1992). Elevated uric acid levels are seen in clients experiencing gout. Gout is a common condition in older adults in which a disturbance in the body's control of uric acid production or excretion occurs. Excess uric acid accumulates in the body's fluids, especially the blood and synovial fluids, forming crystals at high concentrations. These crystals deposit in the connective tissue of the body causing painful, inflamed joints. Thiazide diuretics are a common cause of increases in uric acid levels in older adults (Jeppesen, 1993).

Prothrombin Time

Prothrombin is a plasma protein that is converted to thrombin in the first step of the clotting process. Clotting is necessary to prevent loss of vital body fluids that occurs when blood vessels rupture (Thibodeau, Patton, 1993). The presence of thromboplastin and calcium are required for this conversion (Pagana, Pagana, 1992). In addition to measuring the prothrombin time (PT), the effectiveness of the activity of fibrinogen, and clotting factors V, VII, and X are also measured. The results of the prothrombin time laboratory test also reveals how effective the vitamin K-dependent coagulation factors of the extrinsic and common pathways of the coagulation cascade are performing (McCance, Cipriano, 1994). Increased levels are seen in the presence of deficiencies of vitamin K and in chronic liver disease such as cirrhosis (Huether, 1994). Older adults often are prescribed the drug coumadin after open-heart surgery and in cases of chronic atrial fibrillation. Coumadin interferes with the production of vitamin K-dependent clotting factors, thereby decreasing the chances of thrombus formation. Coumadin can interact with many medications, especially those often consumed by older adults, such as aspirin, quinidine, sulfa, and indomethacin (Pagana, Pagana, 1990). Gerontologic nurses should help clients understand the importance of keeping their appointments for PT checks and consulting their health providers before taking medications not prescribed (see Emergency Treatment box, above). The adequacy of coumadin therapy can be guided by following the client's PT level. Traditional reporting of the patient's PT value is in seconds, which is compared with a control value. Newer reporting methods include a value called the international normalized ratio (INR). INR is a mathematical "correction" of the results of the one-stage PT and was created to standardize results due to the variation in reagents. The Committee on Antithrombotic Therapy of the American College of Chest Physicians recommends that the therapeutic range for PT be maintained between 2.0 and 3.0 for most thrombosis and embolus conditions, and 2.5 and 3.5 for people with mechanical prosthetic valves (DuPont Pharma, 1994).

EMERGENCY TREATM

Abnormal Laboratory Values: Inc Prothrombin Time

Coumadin ingestion

If greatly prolonged, observe for bleeding tendencies such as blood in urine and stool; assess for bruises, petechiae, and lower back pain.

In cases of severe bleeding, apply slow intravenous administration of vitamin K (phytonadione) (Pagana, Pagana, 1992).

Partial Thromboplastin Time

Partial thromboplastin time (PTT) refers to the measurement of the common pathway of clot formation. Heparin can inactivate prothrombin, so the PTT is a good indicator of whether the client is receiving adequate anticoagulation therapy. Considerations for maintenance of homeostasis are the same as for PT.

Erythrocyte Sedimentation Rate

The erythrocyte sedimentation rate (ESR) test measures the time that red blood cells take to settle in normal saline over 1 hour. The measurement values are reported in millimeters. The test does not relate to one specific condition or disorder, but indicates the presence of inflammation, so it is useful in monitoring the course of inflammatory activity in rheumatic diseases. In addition,

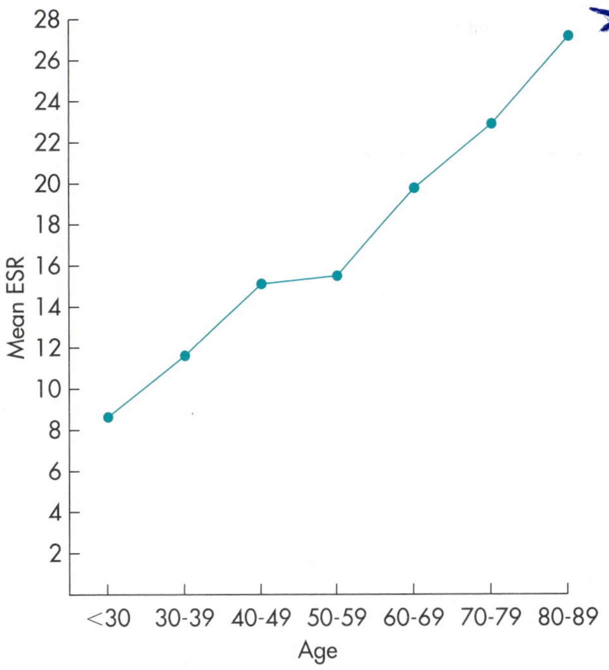

Fig. 19-1 Mean erythrocyte sedimentation rate by age. (From Hayes GS, Stinson IN; Erythrocyte sedimentation rate and age. *Arch Ophthalmol* 94:939, 1976.

when the test is performed with a white cell count, an elevation can indicate infection. Kane, Ouslander, and Abrass (1994) state that mild elevations in the ESR of 10 to 20 mm may be an age-related change. Other scientists report elevations may be seen as high as 30 to 35 mm/hr above normal adult values, even though no evidence of inflammatory disorders are present. This makes interpretation of the results of this test in older adults difficult without other clinical data, particularly in making differential diagnoses (Caulkins, Reinhard, Vladutiu, 1994) (Fig. 19-1).

Platelets

Platelets are small, irregular bodies, also known as thrombocytes, that are essential for clotting (Pagana, Pagana, 1992). They are formed in the red bone marrow, the lungs, and the spleen. When platelets are damaged, they can release thromboplastin, which is necessary for the conversion of prothrombin to thrombin (see Partial Thromboplastin Time, p. 435) (Thibodeau, Patton, 1993). In aging, evidence has shown that platelet adhesiveness increases, though no changes in platelet numbers or structure have been reported (Adams, Meyet, 1966). Owen (1994) states that the effects of "age on disorders of hemostasis is at best poorly understood."

Platelets are important for normal body functioning because of their essential nature for normal blood clotting to occur. Decreases in platelet counts (less than 100,000) require investigation. At platelet levels below 20,000, the nurse should observe for spontaneous bleeding. If the client's levels are 40,000 or below, prolonged bleeding after procedures can occur (Pagana, Pagana, 1992).

In assessing clients for a potential or hidden blood loss, nurses traditionally have questioned clients about color and consistency of their bowel movements. The gerontologic nurse, however, must recognize that older adults who take iron supplements have changes in bowel habits and stool color that may not necessarily indicate the passage of occult blood.

COMPONENTS OF BLOOD CHEMISTRY TESTING

Blood chemistry testing involves electrolytes, glucose, and various other levels of blood components. Although many of these are done in groups, others may be ordered individually to determine the presence or absence of a particular disorder. Many institutions "package" these chemistries into groups that are only specific within that particular institution, such as "Chem-7," "SMA-16," or "Profile Package." The nurse should learn the terminology specific to the workplace and be able to identify the individual tests contained in these packages.

Electrolytes

Electrolytes are inorganic substances that include acids, bases, and salts. In solutions, electrolytes break up to form charged particles, known as ions, which are positive or negative. Positively charged ions are known as cations, and negatively charged ions are called anions. Compounds that are formed from acids and bases are known as salts. Blood testing measures the amount of an electrolyte in the circulating blood (extracellular fluid). Although there are many types of electrolytes that can be tested, only the most common are discussed here.

Older adults particularly may have serious problems with electrolyte imbalances. Dehydration is the most common form of electrolyte disorder that occurs in older adults, and it can usually be attributed to excess loss of water and/or impaired water ingestion. Excess water loss can occur from infections, such as pneumonia and urinary tract infections, or environmental conditions. Impaired water ingestion may be a result of the normal decrease in the thirst sensation in older adults or as a result of decreased function that limits the intake of water (Davis, Minaker, 1994).

Sodium

The test for sodium (Na^+) measures the amount of sodium in the circulating blood but actually is an index of water deficit or excess in the body (Davis, Sherer, 1993). Although sodium is also present in the intracellular fluid, the majority resides in the extracellular fluid, making it the major cation of the extracellular fluid. The result of sodium testing describes the balance between sodium, which is ingested, and that which is excreted by the kidney (Pagana, Pagana, 1992). In the older adult, kidney changes such as a decrease in the glomerular filtration rate and in the number of nephrons, do not lead to disability or disease (Beck, 1994) (see Chapter 25). However, these changes could mean that in the presence of crises such as sodium depletion or overload, the older adult may have difficulty in maintaining homeostasis (Table 19-2).

For example, when volume depletion occurs, the younger individual's kidney adjusts for a decrease in sodium by limiting excretion of this electrolyte. In the older adult, however, the kidney, because of sluggish renin-angiotension and aldosterone response, may not respond as appropriately, and further sodium loss may continue to occur (Beck, 1994).

A normal sodium is necessary for maintaining the extracellular fluid balance (osmolarity). As noted previously, the sodium level relates more to the balance of water in the body, than the index of sodium in the blood. Sodium, along with potassium and calcium, is necessary for the proper function of muscles and nerves (Thibodeau, Patton, 1993).

TABLE 19-2

Blood Chemistry

Test name	Adult normals	Older adult normals	Significance of deviations*
Sodium	136-145 mmoles/l[†]	Unchanged with aging[‡]	*Low:* decreased intake, diarrhea, vomiting or nasogastric (NG) suctioning, excessive oral water intake, CHF, peripheral edema, ascites *High:* increased intake, Cushing's syndrome, thermal burns, osmotic diuresis
Potassium	3.5-5.1 mmoles/l[†];	Unchanged with aging;[‡] slight age-related increase after age 60[§]	*Low:* vomiting, diarrhea, laxative abuse, dehydration, starvation, stress, burns, trauma, surgery *High:* renal failure, metabolic acidosis, hyperadrenalism
Chloride	98-107 mmoles/l[†]	Unchanged with aging[‡]	*Low:* overhydration, CHF, vomiting/NG suctioning, burns, diuretic therapy, chronic respiratory acidosis *High:* dehydration, kidney dysfunction, anemia, excessive IV normal saline
Calcium	8.2-10.5 mg/100 ml[†]	Values slightly decreased[‖]	*Low:* renal failure, malabsorption, pancreatitis *High:* Paget's disease, metastatic disease
Phosphorus	2.6-4.9 mg/100 ml[†]	Values slightly lower[‖]	*Low:* chronic antacid ingestion, inadequate intake of phosphorus, alcoholism, osteomalacia *High:* hypoparathyroidism, renal failure, bone metastasis, liver disease
Magnesium	1.6-2.4 mg/100 ml[†]	Decreases by 15% between ages 30 and 80 years[¶]	*Low:* GI disturbances with diarrhea, renal disease, delirium tremens in chronic alcoholism
Fasting glucose	70-108 mg/100 ml[†]	70-120 mg/100 ml or increase 2 mg/100 ml after age 35[§]	*Low:* malnutrition, alcoholism *High:* uncontrolled diabetes mellitus (DM)
Postprandial glucose	< 140 mg/100 ml 2 hrs postmeal[‡]	< 160 mg/100 ml 2 hours postmeal[§]	*Low:* cancer of stomach, liver, or lung; cirrhosis, stress, infection, thiazides
Glucose tolerance testing (GTT)	1 hr: < 170 mg/100 ml 2 hrs: < 125 mg/100 ml 3 hrs: fasting level or below	Fasting plasma glucose increases faster in first 2 hours, then returns to baseline slowly[§]	*Low:* hyperinsulinism, malabsorption, protein malnutrition *High:* decrease glucose tolerance, DM, CA of pancreas, sedentary lifestyle with high-fat diet

*This is a representation of deviations and is not an inclusive listing.
†From Presbyterian Hospital Normal Reference Values, 1993, Charlotte, N.C.
‡From Kane RI, Ouslander JG, Abrass IB: *Essentials of clinical geriatrics,* ed 3, New York, 1994, McGraw-Hill.
§From Mezey MD, Rauckhorst LH, Stokes SA: *Health assessment of the older adult,* New York, 1993, Springer.
‖From Pagana KD, Pagana TJ: *Mosby's diagnostic and lab test reference,* St. Louis, 1992, Mosby.
¶ From Cavalieri TA, Chopra A, Bryman PN: When outside the norm is normal: interpreting lab data in the aged, *Geriatrics* 47:66-70, May 1992.
# From Mulkerrin JD et al: Glycosylated haemoglobin in the diagnosis of diabetes mellitus in elderly people, *Age Ageing* 21:175-177, 1992.

Continued.

TABLE 19-2

Blood Chemistry—cont'd

Test name	Adult normals	Older adult normals	Significance of deviations*
Amylase	34-122 units/l†	May be slightly increased‖	*High:* acute pancreatitis, perforated bowel, pulmonary infarction, necrotic bowel
HbA_{1c}	5-8%#	5-8%§	*High:* may indicate DM
Total protein	6.1-8.0 gm/100 ml†	6.1-8.0 gm/100 ml†	*Low:* liver disease, malnutrition, malabsorption syndromes, burns, ascites *High:* hemoconcentration
Albumin	3.5-4.8 gm/100 ml†	Slightly decreased§	*Low:* ulcerative colitis, renal disease, malabsorption
Blood urea nitrogen (BUN)	7-22 mg/100 ml†	Increases with age in both genders though average values in women are lower than men§	*Low:* overhydration, low protein diet, liver damage *High:* dehydration, renal disease, DM, acute MI, excessive protein intake
Creatinine	0.5-1.2 mg/100 ml†	Minimal changes noted though decreased in renal function and muscle mass§	*High:* renal failure, acute MI, cancer, systemic lupus erythematosis (SLE), diabetic neuropathy
Creatinine clearance	85-135 ml/min‡	Progressive decline§	*Low:* hyperthyroidism, renal dysfunction, amyotrophic lateral sclerosis (ALS) *High:* hypothyroidism, exercise, hypertension
Cholesterol (total)	120-200 mg/100 ml†	Increased in men to age 50; decreased in women to age 50; increased to age 70; decreased after age 70§	*Low:* hyperthyroidism, starvation, malabsorption *High:* dietary increase, hypothyroidism, cirrhosis, hyperlipoproteinemia, nephrotic syndrome
High-density lipoprotein	> 45 mg/100 ml = low risk§	Slightly higher in men until 7th decade§	*Low:* low cardiac risk *High:* high cardiac risk
Low-density lipoprotein	60-180 mg/100 ml†		*Low:* malnutrition, malabsorption *High:* hyperlipidemia, increased ingestion of fat containing foods
Alkaline phosphatase	37-107 units/l†	Slightly increased in both genders, especially women§	*Low:* hypothyroidism, malnutrition, pernicious anemia *High:* CA of bone, breast; Paget's disease, leukemia
Acid phosphatase	0-0.8 units/l†	0.11-0.60 units/l‖	*High:* prostatic and other cancers, Paget's disease, renal impairment, hyperparathyroidism
Serum glutamic-oxaloacetic transaminase (SGOT)	8-42 units/l†	Slightly higher‖	*Low:* diabetic ketoacidosis (DKA) *High:* acute MI, hepatitis, pancreatitis, severe burns, acute renal disease, multiple trauma, primary muscle diseases
Creatinine kinase (CK)	M: 61-224† W: 38-173†	Elevation may not be seen in acute MI's as in younger adults§	*High:* acute MI, skeletal disease

In the older adult, the presence of hyponatremia (low sodium levels) increases with age. The majority of cases are related to the kidney's inability to excrete free water. Symptoms can be vague, such as malaise, confusion, headache, and nausea, but can progress to coma and seizures (Davis, Minaker, 1994). It is important, though, to distinguish if the older adult has low sodium levels but normal osmolarity. This is known as **pseudohyponatremia.** In these cases, the osmolarity remains normal or high as a result of the presence of other osmolites in excess in the blood, such as glucose, triglycerides, or plasma proteins. By discovering the underlying cause and providing appropriate treatment, the sodium levels should return to normal (Davis, Minaker, 1994). The role of the gerontologic nurse in clients with fluid and sodium disorders is to understand the goal of treatment. In clients with fluid deficiencies, the nurse can help identify reasons for the condition, such as restrictions in mobility, visual disturbances, prevention of incontinence, and swallowing disorders. Hypernatremia (high sodium levels) can occur from infusion of high sodium solute fluids, excess water loss, and excessive diarrhea. Hypernatremia is often seen in older hospitalized adults; some cases are present on admission, whereas some are the consequence of hospitalization. Symptoms are similar to hyponatremia, with the neurologic signs of obtundation, lethargy, and coma being the most common. The pathophysiology behind the neurologic signs is thought to be a result of neuronal cell dehydration and brain shrinkage (Beck, 1994). Laxative abuse, usually unreported but often present in older adults, can also lead to hypernatremia (Davis, Minaker, 1994).

Potassium

Potassium (K^+) is another electrolyte that is present in both the intracellular and extracellular fluid. Its presence, however, is opposite from sodium. The majority of potassium is found within the cell, with minute amounts in extracellular fluid. This extracellular amount is measured by serum testing. Potassium levels are widely thought to be affected by aging, but conclusive studies have not confirmed this theorem (Beck, 1994) (see Table 19-2, pp. 437-438). However, potassium imbalances in the older adult can occur from the same changes in the renal system mentioned in the sodium discussion. Salt-substitutes, used by many older adults with hypertension or congestive heart failure, are high in potassium and should be used with caution. Many medications, such as potassium-sparing diuretics used in conjunction with potassium supplements, can cause hyperkalemia (high potassium levels) in older adults. Also, nonsteroidal antiinflammatory drugs (NSAIDs) such as ibuprofen interfere with potassium excretion (Beck, 1994). Hypokalemia (low potassium levels) can be caused by gastrointestinal loss and diuretic use. Hypokalemia can predispose older adults to tachyarrhythmias and potentiate digitalis toxicity in older adults (Beck, 1994). Since OTC medication use has increased, it is important for the gerontologic nurse to carefully assess the older client's prescription and OTC medication history (see Emergency Treatment box above).

> **EMERGENCY TREATMENT**
>
> **Abnormal Laboratory Values: Potassium**
>
> **Hypokalemia**
>
> If asymptomatic, may repeat test before treatment.
>
> Monitor for possible cardiac dysrhythmias (e.g., sinus bradycardia, A-V block, paroxysmal atrial tachycardia [PAT])
>
> Observe for signs of digitalis toxicity
>
> Maximum replacement of oral replacement is 40-80 mEq/day if renal function normal
>
> Maximum safe rate for IV replacement is 20 mEq/hr; maximum concentration of 40 mEq/L should be used.
>
> Repeat after replacement therapy (McCance, Huether, 1994)

Potassium, like sodium, maintains cell osmolarity, muscle function, and nerve impulse transmission, and regulates acid-base balance (Davis, Sherer, 1994). The cardiac muscles are especially important. Hyperkalemia can cause muscle twitching, arrhythmias, and gastrointestinal symptoms (Davis, Sherer, 1994). Hypokalemia can occur because of excess loss of potassium through the gastrointestinal tract, usually vomiting. Symptoms include muscle weakness, confusion, and absence of bowel sounds. As noted previously, drugs such as diuretics are also a major source of potassium loss in older adults. When replacing potassium in older adults, caution must be taken not to cross the thin line to hyperkalemia.

Chloride

Chloride (Cl^-) is mostly present in the fluid outside the cell, which makes it the major anion in the extracellular fluid. Chloride is closely tied to sodium. Sodium (Na^+) and chloride (Cl^-) combine to make the salt compound sodium chloride (NaCl). A neutralization reaction occurs when positive and negative ions are allowed to mix, forming a salt and water. For example, when hydrochloric acid (HCl) and sodium hydroxide (NaOH) combine, a neutralization reaction occurs that results in sodium chloride (NaCl) and H_2O being formed (Thibodeau, Patton, 1993). Chloride levels have not been shown to change with aging (Table 19-2, pp. 437-438). Since losses and excesses in sodium are closely related to chloride, waterbalance is also affected (Pagana, Pagana, 1992).

Calcium

The serum calcium level measures only the amount of calcium in the blood, which is about 1% of the body's total calcium. Approximately 99% of the body's calcium is found in the bones and teeth (Davis, Sherer, 1994). There is no age-related increase or decrease in the calcium level even though there are changes in calcium metabolism with aging (see Table 19-2, pp. 437-438). The loss of calcium from the bone maintains the normal blood level, though this resulting bone loss can lead to osteoporosis (Baylink, Jennings, 1994). The circulating calcium in the blood is important in blood clotting, conduction of nerve impulses, enzyme activity, and especially in muscle contraction and relaxation (Davis, Sherer, 1994). The calcium levels measure both free calcium and calcium that is protein-bound with albumin. Therefore when calcium levels fall, albumin levels also decrease (Pagana, Pagana, 1992).

Calcium metabolism is one of the factors that determines phosphorus levels as they are inversely related. A decrease in calcium can cause an increase in the phosphorus, as well as the reverse. The parathyroid hormone (PTH) also affects phosphorus levels by affecting the reabsorption of phosphorus in the kidney (Pagana, Pagana, 1992). The parathyroid hormone acts on its plasma membrane receptor of the nephron of the kidney to increase the reabsorption of calcium and to decrease the reabsorption of phosphorus (McCance, Huether, 1994).

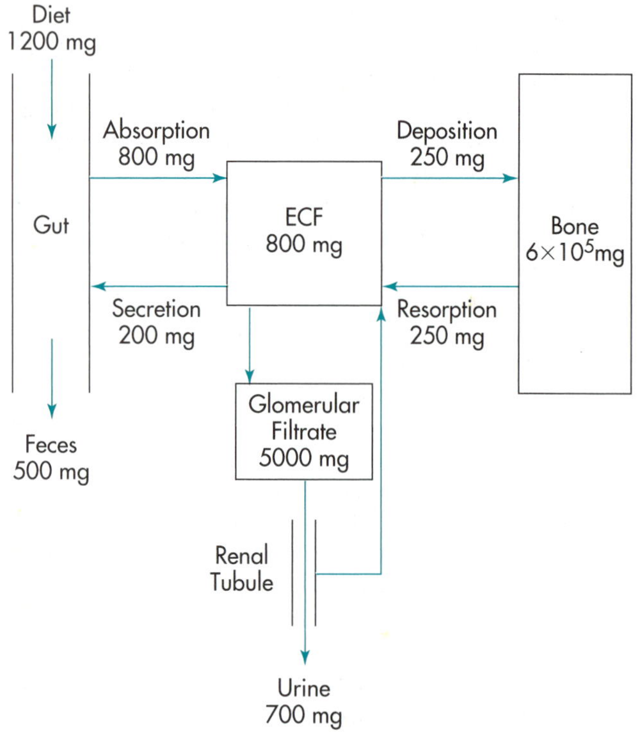

Fig. 19-2 Schema of normal phosphate metabolism. All values associated with fluxes are in milligrams per day. For example, dietary phosphorus intake is 1200 mg/day. The values for ECF and bone represent phosphate content in milligrams. (Reproduced with permission from Hazzard WR et al, editors: *Principles of geriatric medicine and gerontology,* ed 3, New York, 1994, McGraw-Hill.)

Phosphorus

Phosphorus (phosphate) is a mineral found mostly in the bone, in combination with calcium (Pagana, Pagana, 1992). Phosphorus is well-absorbed, so if malfunctions with absorption occur, it is generally related to decreases in kidney function or the long-term use of antacids, which bind to the phosphorus (Baylink, 1994) (Fig. 19-2). Phosphorus plays important roles in maintaining homeostasis as a component in DNA and ribonucleic acid (RNA), the metabolism of fats, carbohydrates, and proteins, and the transfer of energy stored as adenosine triphosphate (ATP) (Davis, Sherer, 1993). In older adults, phosphorus levels are slighly decreased in comparison with younger adults (see Table 19-2, pp. 437-438). This data represent the normal phosphate metabolism expressed in milligrams per day, using an example of 1,200 mg/day intake of dietary phosphorus. Phosphate is normally well-absorbed, and the bone, kidney, and gut are involved in the transfer of phosphate through the body. Deficiencies of phosphate may occur when binders such as antacids are introduced into the gut, resulting in hypophosphatemia and osteomalacia (Baylink, Jennings, 1994).

Magnesium

Magnesium is a mineral important to enzyme action for the production of energy. The most important sites of function are the muscles (especially heart) and nerves. Approximately two thirds of the body's magnesium is contained in the bones (Davis, Sherer, 1993). Magnesium levels have been reported to decrease by 15% between the third and eighth decades (Cavalieri, Chopra, Bryman, 1992) (see Table 19-2, pp. 437-438). Magnesium is vital for muscle (especially the heart muscle) and nerve function. Enzyme action related to the production of ATP is another function of magnesium (Davis, Sherer, 1994).

Glucose

The most common circulating sugar in the blood, glucose, is used for energy by the cells (Davis, Sherer, 1994). The results of blood testing for glucose must be evaluated as to the time and circumstance the sample was drawn. Glucose levels normally rise after a meal and peak at 30 to 60 minutes. Glucose levels in healthy individuals should return to normal within 3 hours (Davis, Sherer, 1993).

A fasting blood sugar (FBS) is usually drawn in the early morning, after the client has been fasting for at least 8 hours. Fasting longer than 16 hours can cause an artificial rise in glucose levels (Pagana, Pagana, 1992).

Postprandial blood sugars are those samples drawn approximately 2 hours after a meal. The purpose is to determine if insulin is being secreted to bring the glucose level within pre-meal range. Usually this test is done as a screening for diabetes (Pagana and Pagana, 1992). For older adults, a postprandial blood sugar should be less than 160 mg/100 ml 2 hours postmeal (Mezey, Rauckhorst, Stokes, 1993) (see Table 19-2, pp. 437-438).

Glucose tolerance testing is a more definitive test of insulin efficiency. The client has baseline blood and urine tests for glucose obtained and is then given glucose orally (if client is unable to tolerate oral, intravenous (IV) glucose may be given). Subsequent blood samples are drawn at predetermined intervals to monitor the rise and fall of the serum glucose.

In the older adult, however, there are special concerns regarding glucose testing. Fasting glucose testing is recommended in older clients exhibiting signs and symptoms of diabetes (Kane, Ouslander, Abrass, 1994). The fasting time should be 10 to 16 hours, with no smoking during fasting hours, since nicotine can stimulate glucose (Goldberg, Coon, 1994; Pagana, Pagana, 1992). Some older adults have the signs and symptoms of diabetes, but have normal fasting glucose testing. In these individuals, Goldberg and Coon state that oral glucose tolerance testing (GTT) is indicated. Others, such as Kane, Ouslander, and Abrass (1994) feel it is not indicated because of the prevalence of glucose intolerance in the older adult. Urine testing for glucose is considered unreliable in the older adult in view of age-related changes in the renal system.

Another laboratory test used in managing the course of diabetes in the older adult is the **HbA_{1c}**. This test is a measurement of glycosylated hemoglobin, that "theoretically reflects the time-integrated blood glucose level of the 120-day life span of the erythrocyte" (Goldberg, Coon, 1994). This test allows the health provider a view of the stability of the client's glucose levels over time. It can be particularly useful to the health provider to evaluate if the prescribed treatment for individual clients is effective. The gerontologic nurse can assist in assessing whether the older adult is taking medications as prescribed to control diabetes. The higher the HbA_{1c} level, the greater the fluctuation in glucose levels over a 100 to 120-day period *before* the test (see Table 19-2, pp. 437-438). The HbA_{1c} is also sometimes used as a diagnostic test to screen for diabetes, in those individuals with other symptoms of the disease. However, because of the presence of false-positive results noted in some normal individuals, its use as a primary diagnostic tool of diabetes in the older adult has not been proven conclusively (Goldberg, Coon, 1994; Mulkerrin, 1992).

The principal blood sugar used for energy by the cells is glucose. Glucose must be maintained within a narrow range between 70 mg/100 ml and 108 mg/100 ml for the body to function in balance. States of low blood sugar (hypoglycemia) cause central nervous system (CNS) changes such as confusion, which is related to brain cell starvation. In the older diabetic client, the effect of hypoglycemia is more profound, and has been called the "most frequent acute emergency that may precipitate cerebrovascular accidents, myocardial infarctions, coma, and death" (Goldberg, Coon, 1994). Diagnosing and treating hypoglycemia in the older adult can be difficult, because determining whether low glucose levels are as a result of a decrease in glucose metabolism in aging or the result of noninsulin-dependent diabetes (Type II), affects the treatment of choice. High blood sugar (hyperglycemia) causes symptoms that include extreme thirst, drowsiness, and frequent urination. More common in older adults than ketoacidosis is hyperosmolar hyperglycemic nonketonic coma (HHNC), which has a 40% to 70% mortality rate (Goldberg, Coon, 1994).

Amylase

Amylase is an important enzyme in catabolism of carbohydrates. It is produced by the acinar units of the pancreas and is also secreted by the salivary glands (Thibodeau, Patton, 1993). Amylase levels are primarily tested in ruling out pancreatitis. Abnormal levels may be increased or decreased, though are generally elevated when reported as abnormal. This may be because of damage or disease of the pancreas or interference in the flow of amylase from the pancreas. Elevated amylase levels also may be seen in nonpancreatic disorders such as perforated ulcers and perforated and/or necrotic bowels. With aging, amylase may be seen as slightly increased (Pagana, Pagana, 1992) (see Table 19-2, pp. 437-438).

In acute pancreatitis, an obstruction causes pancreatic enzymes, including amylase, to "back up" into the pancreas, causing self-digestion of the pancreas. Since amylase plays an important part in the digestion of starches, decreases can effect digestion. Amylase is needed to convert disaccharides to monosaccharides, and diarrhea can occur when this conversion does not happen as a result of decreased amylase. Amylase is also present in the saliva, where it initiates carbohydrate digestion in the mouth and stomach (McCance, Huether, 1994). Although most older adults experience some decrease in saliva production, others develop a severe dryness of the mouth called xerostomia. Causes range from salivary gland dysfunction to one of the 400 medications known to cause dry mouth (Ebersole, Hess, 1994). The role of the gerontologic nurse is to assist the older adult with recognizing the causes of dry mouth and to help identify solutions to cope with the problem, such as eating moist foods, providing adequate liquids during meals, and using saliva substitutes.

Total Protein

Total protein testing measures the amount of albumin and globulin within the body. Albumin constitutes approximately 60% of the total protein. Globulins are important in the function of antibodies, and to a lesser degree than albumin, in the maintenance of osmotic pressure.

Albumin

Serum albumin is an indicator of protein nutrition. In older adults with impaired skin integrity such as pressure sores, the assessment of the albumin level helps determine if the balance is correct for proper wound healing to occur. Clients with low albumin levels need nutritional support to promote healing of wounds. Albumin decreases slightly with age (see Table 19-2, pp. 437-438). As albumin levels fall, the chances of morbidity in the older adult increase.

Blood Urea Nitrogen

Measurement of the urea in the blood is known as the blood urea nitrogen (BUN). Urea is a major waste product of protein catabolism, and is a result of ammonia conversion in the liver. Urea is excreted from the body by the kidneys. BUN levels are indicative of both liver and kidney function. In older men, values are slightly higher than the adult normal levels of 7 mg/100 ml to 22 mg/100 ml. In older women, BUN levels are also increased, but at lower levels than older men (Mezey, Rauckhorst, Stokes, 1993) (see Table 19-2, pp. 437-438).

Creatinine

Creatinine is another end product of protein metabolism. A rise in a client's BUN and creatinine is indicative of kidney failure (Davis, Sherer, 1994). The physiologic decline in the glomerular filtration rate (GFR) in older adults does not generally cause a subsequent rise in the creatinine level (Burkhart, 1994). The expected rise in the creatinine level does not occur because with aging there is a parallel decrease in mean muscle mass and actual creatinine production (Kane, Ouslander, Abrass, 1994). An 80 year old and a 30 year old who have the same creatinine concentrations do not have comparable GFR rates. In this example, the older adult has approximately 40% to 50% *less* GFR than the younger adult (Beck, 1994). Therefore a creatinine level in an older adult should not be considered an independent indicator of renal function as it is in a younger individual. It should be used instead to calculate the creatinine clearance for a more realistic indication of renal function in older adults.

Creatinine Clearance

Creatinine clearance is the measure of the GFR, estimated from serum creatinine and urine creatinine levels. A 24-hour urine is required along with a serum level within the same 24-hour period. To allow for changes with aging that are not reflected in the creatinine level, many primary care providers use the Cockcroft and Gault formula to estimate creatinine clearance:

$$\text{Creatinine clearance (ml/min)} = \frac{140 - \text{age in years} \times \text{weight in kg}}{72 \times \text{serum creatinine (\% mg/100 ml)}}$$

(For women, multiply final result by 0.85)

Kane, Ouslander, and Abrass (1994) recommend that this formula be used for initial estimates of creatinine clearance for drug dosing in older adults while also considering other factors such as cardiac output and hydration status. The gerontologic nurse should recognize the importance of the creatinine clearance on the older adult's overall health status. The older adult's responses to medications, especially newly prescribed drugs, should be monitored, since impaired renal function can precipitate side effects that may be overlooked.

Triglycerides

Triglycerides are the principal lipids (fats) found in circulating blood bound to a protein; they form high- and low-density lipoproteins (HDLs and LDLs). Triglycerides are produced in the liver from glycerol and fatty acids found in the blood. When the triglyceride level in the blood reaches its peak, the excess is deposited in the fatty tissue (Pagana, Pagana, 1992). The triglyceride level increases with age to about middle age, then decreases thereafter (Hazzard, 1994). However, the increase in triglycerides that occurs in women until middle age occurs at a slower rate than in men. Moreover, further changes in triglycerol levels occur in women after age 50 when an abrupt increase has been noted related to the decrease in estrogen (Hazzard, 1994).

Total Cholesterol

Cholesterol is a steroid compound that helps stabilize the membranes of the body's cells (Thibodeau, Patton, 1993). It is also the major lipid associated with cardiovascular disease. The liver metabolizes cholesterol and binds it to LDLs and HDLs for transport in the bloodstream (Pagana, Pagana, 1992). Total cholesterol levels are a combination of LDL and HDL levels in the blood stream. Changes in cholesterol levels with aging mirror changes in triglyceride levels, except that the peak that occurs after age 50 in women is thought to be mediated by changes in relative body weight (Hazzard, 1994) (see Table 19-2, pp. 437-438).

High-Density Lipoprotein

HDL, referred to as the "good cholesterol," carries more amounts of protein and less amounts of lipids, hence the term high-density. Approximately 25% of cholesterol is bound to HDLs. HDLs are thought to have a protective effect on heart disease, but their levels are not affected by diet. Low levels of HDLs are related to medications, obesity, lack of exercise, and genetic factors (Thibodeau, Patton, 1993). Oral estrogen has been shown to increase HDL levels in postmenopausal women, but further stud ies are needed to determine if this is the only variable in the relationship (Hazzard, 1994).

Low-Density Lipoprotein

The remaining 75% of cholesterol in the blood stream is bound to LDL (Pagana, Pagana, 1992). LDL can be calculated from total cholesterol levels, HDL levels, and fasting triglycerides by using the following equation (Davis, Sherer, 1994):

$$\text{LDL cholesterol} = \text{Total cholesterol} - \text{HDL cholesterol} - (\text{Triglyceride level} \div 5)$$

With aging, changes in the HDL and LDL levels differ between the genders. LDL mean levels rise in both genders between puberty and menopause, with LDL levels in women rising sharply after menopause, exceeding the levels of men at comparable ages (Hazzard, 1994). As noted previously, the increase in LDL after menopause is related to decreasing estrogen levels in women. HDL levels in men and women remain similar until puberty, when HDL is noted to decrease in boys. Average levels of HDL in men remain lower than women throughout advancing age after puberty (Hazzard, 1994).

> **Insight** • *There is some concern that underweight older adults are being told to restrict cholesterol, when in fact, they need a less restricted diet to maintain adequate weight status. The client's weight history, cholesterol level, and overall health status should be considered in the decision to restrict cholesterol.*

Alkaline Phosphatase

Alkaline phosphatase is an enzyme found in many tissues but has its highest concentrations in the liver and bone. Testing for alkaline phosphatase is used to determine liver and bone disorders (Pagana, Pagana, 1992). Testing of the alkaline phosphatase levels in older adults is often used in the biochemical assessment of Paget's disease (Singer, 1994) and other bone diseases. Slight increases in the alkaline phosphatase level are seen in aging of both sexes (Mezey, Rauckhorst, Stokes, 1993) (see Table 19-2, pp. 437-438).

Acid Phosphatase

Acid phosphatase is also an enzyme, but it is primarily located in the prostate gland. Acid phosphatase levels are used to diagnose prostate cancer and to estimate the extent of the disease. The incidence of prostate cancer increases substantially after age 50 and is the second most common malignancy in men in the United States (Brendler, 1994) (see Chapter 15). The acid phosphatase level, in addition to assisting with diagnosing, is also helpful in determining if treatment for prostatic cancer has been effective (Pagana, Pagana, 1992). The role of the gerontologic nurse in working with older men is to educate them about the incidence of this disease and to encourage prostate examinations every 2 years after age 50 (Ebersole, Hess, 1994).

Serum Glutamic-Oxaloacetic Transaminase

Serum glutamic-oxaloacetic transaminase (SGOT), now called aspartate aminotransferase (AST), measures the enzyme of the same name which is found in heart muscle, skeletal muscles, liver, kidney, and pancreas. Since the AST is found in several organs, it may be used to diagnose hepatitis, liver necrosis, and skeletal muscle damage. AST/SGOT levels may be helpful in diagnosing MI but are not as specific as other tests such as the creatinine phosphokinase and creatinine phosphokinase-MB (Pagana, Pagana, 1992). In treating TB in older adults, a three- to five-fold increase in the SGOT can be indicative of hepatoxicity from drugs such as Isoniazid, Rifampin, Ethambutol, and Pyrazinamide (Stead, Dutt, 1994). A rise in the AST/SGOT is also seen in renal arterial occlusion, with the increase being noted within 24 hours and decreasing by the fourth day (Burkart, Canzanello, 1994).

Creatinine Phosphokinase

Creatinine phosphokinase (CPK), which is also known as creatinine kinase, is present in various parts of the body and can be isolated into three isoenzymes to pinpoint the area of the body affected. The CPK_1 is primarily found in the lungs and brain, whereas CPK_2 is associated with cardiac muscle cells. CPK_3 is found normally in the circulation and rises when there is damage to the skeletal muscles. CPK rises and peaks at specific intervals during MI and is used with lactate dehydrogenase (LDH) and AST/SGOT testing in determining the amount and prognosis of myocardial damage (Pagana, Pagana, 1992). In older adults, an elevated CPK_2 level may be seen in hypothyroidism (Kane, Ouslander, Abrass, 1994). The nurse should also expect an elevated CPK if the older adult has experienced recent falls or other skeletal muscle trauma.

Lactic Dehydrogenase

Lactic dehydrogenase (LDH), an enzyme found throughout the body, is used in conjunction with the CPK and AST/SGOT in assessing myocardial damage. As with the

CPK, LDH can be fractionalized into five isoenzymes (CPK has three). These isoenzymes can clarify the site of release of the LDH and assist the nurse in targeting assessment and monitoring of specific complications related to the site of injury. The older adult's condition is monitored by peaks and duration of elevated levels.

LDH-2 is normally the higher of the five isoenzymes, originating mainly from the reticuloendothelial system. The origin of LDH-1 lies mainly in the heart and red blood vessels, and its levels are monitored for degree of myocardial activity and damage (Pagana, Pagana, 1992). In the older adult, an elevated LDH may be seen in atheroembolic renal disease (Burkart, Canzanello, 1994). In this case, with labs that are able to fractionalize the LDH into isoenzymes, the LDH-4 is the more likely elevated portion, since it is found in the kidney.

Thyroid

The thyroid gland has been the focus of many studies in aging. Testing of function includes the assessment of two hormones secreted by the thyroid gland: thyroxine (T_4), and triiodothyronine (T_3). A hormone secreted by the antipituitary gland, the thyroid-stimulating hormone (TSH), is also usually tested when investigating thyroid function. In fact, serum TSH determination has become an excellent means of screening for hyperthyroidism. Its measurement also aids in differentiating primary from secondary hypothyroidism.

T_4 and T_3 are both secreted by the thyroid gland and are responsible for the increase in the rate of metabolism. Although T_4 is secreted in larger amounts, scientists now believe that T_3 is the primary thyroid hormone. The rationale is that most of the T_4 in the blood stream is converted to T_3, and that T_3 binds more easily to target cells than T_4 (Thibodeau, Patton, 1993).

TSH promotes the growth and development of the thyroid gland, as well as the secretion of T_3 and T_4 from the thyroid gland. With normal aging, the secretion of thyroid hormones remains unchanged, though the metabolic clearance rate of these hormones is decreased. Decreased T_4 levels (specifically, free T_4) and an elevated TSH are indicative of primary hypothyroidism (Kane, Ouslander, Abrass, 1994). The CPK may also be elevated. The T_4, T_3, and radioactive iodine uptake are used in diagnosing hyperthyroidism (Kane, Ouslander, Abrass, 1994).

The presence of thyroid disease in the older adult can be difficult to determine. Classic signs of thyroid disorders seen in younger adults are often absent or clouded because of concomitant illnesses in the older adult. Similar to other complaints common among many older adults are some symptoms of thyroid disorders, such as anorexia, constipation, lack of energy, mental clouding, cold intolerance, fatigue, and skin dryness and scaling. The older adult may have a feeling that something is not right but may be unable to articulate this feeling. For these reasons, health care professionals may not take the older adult's complaints seriously and may attribute these complaints to the aging process. The gerontologic nurse should be aware that thyroid disease can be present in the older adult without overt symptoms. Assessment of thyroid function should be undertaken in those adults with vague, but persistent, symptoms.

Hypothyroidism results from decreased secretion of thyroid hormones. The decrease in hormone secretion may be as a result of an autoimmune response and is often idiopathic (Gregerman, Katz, 1994). Symptoms of hypothyroidism in the older adult may be manifested as confusion, dementia, depression, syncope, seizures, and mild psychotic disturbances. Clients being screened for dementia should have thyroid testing included in the panel of laboratory tests. Thyroid testing in the older adult with hypothyroidism usually reveals a combination of a low T_4 and an elevated TSH. The T_3 level is decreased in normal aging (Table 19-3), and may be seen as "normal" in hypothyroidism. For this reason, T_3 levels are not useful in diagnosing hypothyroidism.

Hyperthyroidism in the older adult is more prevalent than scientists originally believed (Gregerman, Katz, 1994). Most symptoms of hyperthyroidism are nonspecific and vague. Younger clients may complain of fatigue, lack of energy, and nervousness, but the older adult may not have these symptoms. However, apathy, weight loss and palpitations are symptoms that commonly appear in both the young and the old with hyperthyroidism. More than 50% of older adults with hyperthyroidism have CHF, which may be initially seen as acute pulmonary edema. Laboratory assessment reveals an elevated T_4 and free T_4 index in most older adults with hyperthyroidism. However, approximately 2% of older adults with the disease have normal T_4 levels and an elevated T_3. But since T_3 is often reported as normal in 30% to 40% of the older adults, it is more useful in differentiating the origin of elevated T_4 levels, rather than primary diagnosing of hyperthyroidism (Gregerman, Katz, 1994).

URINE CHEMISTRY

Urine chemistry testing includes testing for the presence of protein, glucose, bacteria, blood, ketones, and leukocytes. It also involves studying the sample for properties of specific gravity and pH. Urine is a waste product that is formed by the kidneys and consists of 95% water. The composition of urine can inform the health professional of the status of many systems in the body. When blood passes through the kidney, water, nitrogen compounds, toxins, and electrolytes are filtered, reabsorbed, and secreted (Thibodeau, Patton, 1993). The amounts retained or excreted affect the body's homeostasis.

TABLE 19-3

Thyroid Testing

Test name	Adult normals	Older adult normals	Significance of deviations*
T_4	Free T_4 1.0-2.3 mg/100 ml‡	Slight decrease‡	*Low:* hypothyroidism, protein malnutrition, renal failure *High:* hyperthyroidism, viral hepatitis
T_3	T_3RIA 80-200 mg/100 ml‡	M: decreased after 60 years W: decreased after 70-80 years‡	*Low:* severe illness or trauma malnutrition *High:* hyperthyroidism
TSH	0.40-4.9 UIU/ml†	Increased in men and women after 60 years‡	*Low:* hyperthyroidism *High:* hypothyroidism, antithyroid drugs

*This is a representation of deviations and not an inclusive listing.
†From Presbyterian Hospital Normal Reference Values, 1993, Charlotte, NC.
‡From Mezey MD, Rauckhorst LH, Stokes SA: Health assessment of the older adult, New York, 1993, Springer.

Protein

Protein in the urine (**proteinuria**) is usually considered an abnormal finding and its presence indicates a disruption in normal kidney function. Excessive loss of protein from the body can lead to nephrotic syndrome, the result of proteinuria and edema (Pagana, Pagana, 1992). In the older adult, however, proteinuria is commonly found and may not be of any clinical significance (Ebersole, Hess, 1994). Its presence does warrant investigation to rule out urinary tract infections and kidney disease.

Glucose

When glucose appears in the urine (**glycosuria**), it may be an indicator of diabetes, although it may also be seen in cases of normal serum glucose levels. In diabetes, the amount of glucose in the filtrate formed by the kidney exceeds the maximum capacity of the transport system that removes it. In cases of normal serum blood glucose levels, elevated urine glucose levels may be the result of a congenital defect called renal diabetes (Thibodeau, Patton, 1993). Glucose in the urine of older adults may or may not be a sign of diabetes or disease. The reabsorption of glucose diminishes as a normal process of aging, therefore more glucose may be seen in the urine of older adults in the absence of disease (McCance, Huether, 1994).

Bacteria and Leukocytes

Although occasional trace amounts of bacteria (**bacteriuria**) may appear normally in the urine, significant amounts, defined as greater than 10^5 colony-forming units (CFU) per ml of urine, indicate infection within the body. If the infection is in the renal system, it must be determined if the site is the kidney, bladder, or urethra. The gerontologic nurse should assess and document the older adult for symptoms of recent onset of incontinence, flank pain, fever, or frequency of suprapubic pain. However, since these symptoms may be absent in most older adults, urinalysis remains an important screening test. Women are more prone to lower urinary tract infections than men because of the shorter urethra and its close proximity to the anus. In adults over age 65, bacteria in the urine is found in approximately 20% of women and 10% of men (Tunkel, Kaye, 1994). Significant numbers of older adults are asymptomatic even when bacteria is found in the urine. Pus in the urine (pyuria) is more indicative of a symptomatic urinary tract infection and is defined as having greater than 10 leukocytes per mm^3 of urine on microscopic exam (see Research box on p. 446).

Insight • *The decision to treat asymptomatic urinary tract infections (UTIs) in older adults in the absence of renal obstruction is still debatable. The effects of nontreatment on mortality and morbidity need more scientific study. Primary care providers must weigh the client's possible adverse response to antimicrobial therapy and the potential for development of resistant organisms. Most geriatricians, however, agree that indwelling urinary catheters lead to an increased incidence of UTIs, and will advocate for the use of intermittent catheterization and/or external urinary collection devices (Tunkel, Kaye, 1994).*

RESEARCH

Whippo CC, Creason NS: Bacteriuria and urinary incontinence in aged female nursing home residents, *J Adv Nurs* 14:217-225, 1989.

Sample, setting

Subjects included 65 female nursing home residents in midwestern United States who were incontinent for at least 2 weeks, according to nursing home administrators.

Methodology

Data on bacteriuria were examined, including the following variables: physical symptoms, physical examination findings, mental status, and functional abilities.

Findings

Escherichia coli was the type of bacteria identified in 67% of the subjects (n = 18), with *Klebsiella pneumonae* as the next most common bacteria at 20% (n = 5). The subjects were separated into three groups: (1) negative (those with negative cultures), (2) over (those with bacteria counts over 100,000/ml of urine), and (3) under (those with bacterial count under 100,000/ml of urine). The majority of subjects who were incontinent 76%-100% of the time were from the "over" group (47%), with 35% from the "under" group, and 18% from the "negative" group. Nocturia was a common complaint in all three groups with a total of 89% voiding two to four times a night. Cognition, as measured by the Mini-Mental Status Examination, showed that 59% of the "over" group scored 0-20, which indicated dementia, with 36% of the "negative" group scoring in the normal range of 27-30. This suggests a relationship between mental status functioning and the presence of bacteriuria. Subjects with higher mental functioning were less likely to have a urinary tract infection.

Implications

Assessment of incontinence should include urinalysis, physical symptoms, physical examination, cognitive functioning, and functional status to identify older adults

Ketones

The presence of ketones, the result of fatty acid breakdown, is another abnormal finding in the urine. When overaccumulation occurs in the blood, the excess is excreted in the urine. Causes of ketones in the urine include a high-protein diet, starvation/fasting, and ingestion of isoprophyl alcohol (Pagana, Pagana, 1992).

pH

The pH of the urine sample indicates the acid or base of the urine, which reflects the body's homeostatic state. The normal range for urine pH is 4.6 to 8.0 (Table 19-4). Some drugs can cause the urine to be alkaline or acid. Renal calculi are acid or base in origin, depending on the underlying substances that form the stones. Prevention and treatment is aimed at changing the urine to the reverse pH of the stone's composition (Pagana, Pagana, 1992). When collecting the urine specimens, it is important to cover the sample, as urine left open can change its pH.

Blood

The presence of blood in the urine (hematuria) is always an abnormal finding. The cause may be renal obstruction from calculi, trauma to the kidney, or inflammation/infection or malignancy. The blood may be grossly apparent, or occult, giving the urine a cloudy and/or pink color on visual inspection.

COMPONENTS OF ARTERIAL BLOOD GAS TESTING

Arterial blood gas (ABG) testing involves drawing a sample of blood from an artery, usually from the radial or brachial artery. Components of ABG testing are pH, oxygen, and carbon dioxide content, oxygen saturation, and bicarbonate level (Table 19-5). It is important that the primary care provider and lab personnel are aware of the oxygenation conditions of the client under which the blood was drawn (i.e., client on room air, amount of oxygen support, and type of oxygen delivery device). Pulse oximetry has been shown to be a reliable alternative to ABG testing when desiring the oxygen saturation percentage of the blood. Using pulse oximetry is less painful, less expensive, and results are immediately available (Ogburn-Russell, Johnson, 1990; Pagana, Pagana, 1992).

Oxygen

Oxygen (PO_2) levels have been shown to decline significantly with age (Cavalieri, Chopra, Bryman, 1992). Age-related changes such as a decrease in chest wall recoil, decrease in alveolar surface area, and less effective O_2 to CO_2 exchange all contribute to this change in the oxygen level. However, in the absence of disease, the older adult's respiratory function remains adequate. Changes in PO_2, however, should be considered in view of the client's age. The PO_2 decreases approximately 25% between ages 30 and 80 years of age (Cavalieri, Chopra, Bryman, 1992). The following formula for arterial oxygen may be used in calculating age-appropriate PO_2 levels (Cavalieri, Chopra, Bryman, 1992):

$$PaO_2 \text{ (mm Hg)} = 100.1 - (0.325)\text{ (age)}$$

TABLE 19-4

Urine Chemistry

Test name	Adult normals	Older adult normals	Significance of deviations*
Color	Yellow; amber		Cloudy urine may indicate presence of pus, casts, blood, bacteria; straw-colored urine indicates dilution
Appearance	Clear		See color
Specific gravity	1.005-1.030†	Decreased with advancing age†	*Low:* overhydration, renal failure, diuresis, hypothermia *High:* dehydration, water restriction, vomiting, diarrhea, decreased renal flow
pH	4.6-8.0†		*Acidic urine:* diarrhea, metabolic acidosis, DM, respiratory acidosis, emphysema, pyrexia *Alkaline urine:* respiratory alkalosis, metabolic acidosis, vomiting, gastric suctioning, diuretic therapy, urinary tract infection (UTI)
Protein	None or up to 8 mg/100 ml†	Same†	*Positive:* DM, CHF, malignant hypertension, lupus, nephrotic syndrome
Glucose	Negative	Negative†	*Positive:* DM, Cushing's syndrome, severe stress, infection, drug therapy
Ketones	Negative	Negative†	*Positive:* uncontrolled DM, starvation, excessive aspirin ingestion, high-protein diets, dehydration, isopropanol ingestion
Blood	Negative	Negative†	*Positive:* renal trauma, renal stones, cystitis, glomerulonephritis, prostatitis
Leukocyte esterase (tested with urine dipstick)	Negative	Negative†	Possible urinary tract infection; follow through with microscopic exam of urine
Bacteria	Negative	May be seen in older adult without symptoms; evaluate for pyuria and symptoms	UTI

*This is a representation of deviations and not an inclusive listing.
†Pagana KD, Pagana TJ: *Mosby's diagnostic and lab test reference,* St. Louis, 1992, Mosby.

pH of the Blood

The pH of the blood triggers an increase or decrease in the respiratory rate to adjust for blood carbon dioxide content (Thibodeau, Patton, 1993). No significant changes in the pH of the arterial blood are seen with aging (Cavalieri, Chopra, Bryman, 1992). The normal adult values for blood pH are 7.35 to 7.45 (see Table 19-5, p. 448).

Carbon Dioxide

No significant changes in the carbon dioxide (PCO_2) level is seen in aging (Cavalieri, Chopra, Bryman, 1992). The normal adult range for PCO_2 is 35 to 45 mm Hg.

Oxygen Saturation

Oxygen saturation (O_2 Sat %) refers to the binding of oxygen onto molecules of hemoglobin. The saturation of venous blood is approximately 75% with a PaO_2 of 40 mm Hg. In the arterial blood, the saturation is approximately 97%, with a PaO_2 of 100 mm Hg. The normal adult value for O_2 saturation is greater than 97%. There are some researchers, however, who believe that the normal value of the older adult O_2 saturation is slightly lower than the younger adult, at 95% O_2 saturation (Ogburn-Russell, Johnson, 1990; Pagana, Pagana, 1992) (see Emergency Treatment box, p. 448).

TABLE 19-5

Arterial Blood Gases

Test name	Adult normals	Older adult normals	Significance of deviations*
pH	7.35-7.45†	Unchanged with aging†	*Low:* respiratory or metabolic acidosis *High:* respiratory or metabolic alkalosis
PaO_2	80-100 mm Hg†	Decreased by 25‡	*Low:* cardiac or respiratory disease
$PaCO_2$	35-45 mm Hg†	Unchanged with aging Unchanged or slightly increased with age§	*Low:* respiratory alkalosis *High:* respiratory acidosis
O_2 Saturation	Less than 97%†	Questionable, may be slightly lower in well older adults (approximately 95%)‖	*Low:* impaired respiratory function and/or abnormal gas exchange
HCO_3	24-26 MEG/l†	Unchanged with aging¶	*Low:* metabolic acidosis *High:* metabolic alkalosis

*This is a representation of deviations and not an inclusive listing.
†From Presbyterian Hospital Normal Reference Values, 1993, Charlotte, N.C.
‡From Cavalieri TA, Chopra A, Bryman PN: When outside the norm is normal: Interpreting lab data in the aged, *Geriatrics* 47:66-70, May 1992.
§From Mezey MD, Rauckhorst LH, Stokes SA: *Health assessment of the older adult,* New York, 1993, Springer.
‖From Ogburn-Russel L, Johnson JE: Oxygen saturation levels in the well elderly: altitude makes a difference, *J Gerontolog Nurs* 16:10, 26-30, 1990.
¶From Pagana KD, Pagana TJ: *Mosby's diagnostic and lab test reference,* St. Louis, 1992, Mosby.

EMERGENCY TREATMENT

Abnormal Laboratory Values: PaO_2

Hypoxemia

Assess airway and reason for impaired oxygen exchange.
Administer oxygen as prescribed.
Position client to allow for maximum lung expansion.
Reassure client, and keep calm.

Bicarbonate

Bicarbonate (HCO_3) is a buffer present in the blood that plays an important role in acid-base balance. When there is an increase in acidity of the blood, the kidneys conserve bicarbonate in an effort to regain proper acid-base balance. When the blood is alkalotic, the kidney increases its excretion of bicarbonate. In aging, bicarbonate levels in the blood are unchanged (Pagana, Pagana, 1992).

Additional Tests

There are other specific tests that should be part of the health care team's recommendation for the early detection of cancer in older adults (Table 19-6). These tests, include mammography, sigmoidoscopy, and prostate-specific antigen testing.

Mammography

A mammogram is a radiologic procedure performed to detect the presence of tumors and abnormalities of breast tissue. Used as an early detection procedure, it does not replace monthly breast self-examinations that women should be encouraged to perform. Rather, the mammogram serves as a screening and diagnostic tool for detecting abnormalities of breast tissue on an interval basis, or when lumps are discovered on self-examination. Although mammography is not recommended for men, breast self-examination for men is encouraged, since 900 new breast cancer cases in men are diagnosed yearly (Kinne, Hakes, 1994). The American Cancer Society (1993) recommends a screening mammography for women by age 40. This screening serves as a baseline reading on which subsequent readings are compared. After the baseline screening, women age 40 to 49 should have a mammogram every 1 to 2 years. After age 50, mammography screening should be done yearly.

Sigmoidoscopy

A sigmoidoscopy involves the insertion of a sigmoidoscope through the rectum for the detection of precancerous lesions. It may also be done for the investigation of chronic diarrhea, rectal bleeding, or mucus in the stool. Screening sigmoidoscopy, preferably done with a flexible sigmoidoscope, is recommended by the American Cancer Society (1993) for men and women age 50 and over every 3 to 5 years.

TABLE 19-6

Health Maintenance Studies

Test name	Gender/Age	Frequency	Normals
Mammography	*W*: 50 and older	Every year	Absence of abnormal tissue densities
Sigmoidoscopy	*M* and W: 50 and older	Every 3 to 5 years	Absence of polyps, abnormal tissue areas
Prostate-specific antigen (PSA)	*M*: 50 years and older	Annually with digital examination; may be appropriate at younger age if member of high-risk group (e.g., African-American, family history)	Abnormal levels may be associated with benign prostatic hyperplasia or prostatitis, the absence of cancer; normal levels: less than 4.0 ng/ml (monoclonal) or 7.0 ng/ml (polyclonal)

From American Cancer Society: *Guidelines for the cancer-related checkup,* Atlanta, 1993, The Society.

Prostate Specific Antigen

The American Cancer Society (1993) recommends an annual examination for early detection of prostate cancer in men from age fifty. This examination should include digital rectal examination (DRE) and possibly serum **prostate-specific antigen** (PSA) testing. PSA is a glycoprotein produced by both benign and malignant prostate epithelial tissue. Although its measurement can improve the early detection of prostate cancer, its specificity at this time is approximately 33%, too low to warrant its use as a screening test. Until the benefits of early detection have been more clearly established, widespread screening cannot be recommended.

The role of the gerontologic nurse in health screening for older adults includes educating them about recommendations for health maintenance activities, providing information about where these services are available, and emphasizing early detection and treatment of conditions. Older adults may need the nurse's help in taking responsibility for their own health. In addition, the gerontologic nurse must recognize that some older adults may base their health practices on incorrect or incomplete information, obtained from the health experiences of friends and family members. If after presenting adequate information on health maintenance practices, the older adult decides not to participate in health maintenance activities, the gerontologic nurse must accept and support this decision as one based in the right to self-determination.

Summary

Aging today is vastly different from the aging of our parents and grandparents. Health care researchers and scientists have traditionally used young or middle-age men for studies, generalizing findings and results to both genders and a variety of age groups. Researchers are now beginning to realize that older adults have different "normals" than younger adults, as well as complex health histories that can affect the overall response of the body to stressors and disease.

In providing age-specific and appropriate health care, providers must recognize that individuals do not respond the same to similar experiences. Although many laboratory values are being rewritten to compensate for age-related changes in the older adult, there are still many unanswered questions. The older adult must be considered within the total context of a person with unique responses to disease. Laboratory tests and their results should be considered as an adjunct to detection and treatment of illness, not in isolation of the presenting clinical picture.

HOME CARE TIPS

1. The home care nurse must know the purpose of the tests ordered and must explain the reasoning for the tests to both the caregiver and the homebound older adult.
2. Assess cultural values regarding diagnostic testing in a homebound older adult.
3. Homecare nurses must realize that laboratory values in homebound older adults may be altered because of aging or medication regimens.
4. Homecare nurses must be able to differentiate normal versus abnormal laboratory results in the homebound older adult, and must know when to notify the physician.
5. Instruct caregiver and homebound older adult on activities required before laboratory testing (i.e., NPO from midnight).

The gerontologic nurse plays an important role in promoting the well-being of older adults through review and reporting of laboratory values. Awareness of the changes in laboratory and diagnostic test values as a result of age can augment the management of the older adult's health problems. The gerontologic nurse may need to serve as an advocate for the older adult when repeated symptoms and concerns are not addressed by their primary care provider but are attributed to complaints of "old age." As always, appropriate assessments are carried out, supplemented by laboratory testing, before establishing nursing interventions.

Key Points

- The ESR rises approximately 10 mm to 20 mm in older adults and is considered a normal age-related change.
- Potassium-sparing diuretics and NSAIDs can interfere with potassium excretion.
- The older adult may have hyponatremia in the presence of normal osmolarity, indicating the presence of other osmolarities in excess in the blood.
- Renal and hepatic system functioning can be reflected in the BUN level.
- Hypokalemia can potentiate digitalis toxicity in older adults.
- Comparable serum creatinine levels in the younger adult and the older adult are not indicators of comparable kidney function.
- Urine testing for glucose in the older adult is considered unreliable in view of age-related changes in renal function.
- Thyroid disease can be present in the older adult without the overt symptoms typically seen in younger adults with thyroid disorders.
- Older adults may be asymptomatic in the presence of bacteriuria.
- Pyuria is more indicative of a symptomatic urinary tract infection than the presence of bacteria in the urine of an older adult.
- The "normal" oxygen saturation in older adults may be 95% or greater in the arterial blood.
- The American Cancer Society recommends that women over 50 years of age receive a yearly screening mammography.

Critical Thinking Exercises

1. When evaluating the laboratory data for a 74-year-old male client, you note that his ESR and serum creatinine are slightly elevated and his serum magnesium is decreased. What conclusion, if any, can be drawn from these findings? Should the data be reported to the physican?
2. You are making home visits to an 81-year-old female client who is recovering from a fractured femur. During your last three visits you have noted that she consistently complains of being cold, even though it is summer and her house is very warm. In addition, she has had frequent complaints of constipation, not feeling like eating, and being tired. She also has a bottle of hand lotion next to her chair for her dry skin. What is your assessment of her, and is any action warranted on your part?

REFERENCES

Abrams WB, Berkow R: *The Merck manual of geriatrics,* Rahway, NJ, 1990, Merck.

Adams EB, Meyet FG: Hypochromic anaemia in chronic infections, *South African Med J* 40, 1966.

American Cancer Society: *Guidelines for the cancer-related checkup,* Atlanta, 1993, American Cancer Society.

Baime MJ, Nelson JB, Castell DO: Aging of the gastrointestinal system. In Hazzard WR et al, editors: *Principles of geriatric medicine and gerontology,* ed 3, New York, 1994, McGraw-Hill.

Baylink DJ: Osteomalacia. In Hazzard WR et al, editors: *Principles of geriatric medicine and gerontology,* ed 3, New York, 1994, McGraw-Hill.

Baylink DJ, Jennings JC: Calcium and bone homeostasis changes with aging. In Hazzard WR et al, editors: *Principles of geriatric medicine and gerontology,* ed 3, New York, 1994, McGraw-Hill.

Beck LH: The renal system and urinary tract. In Hazzard WR et al, editors: *Principles of geriatric medicine and gerontology,* ed 3, New York, 1994, McGraw-Hill.

Brendler CB: Disorders of the prostate. In Hazzard WR et al, editors: *Principles of geriatric medicine and gerontology,* ed 3, New York, 1994, McGraw-Hill.

Burkart JM, Canzanello VJ: Renal disease. In Hazzard WR et al, editors: *Principles of geriatric medicine and gerontology,* ed 3, New York, 1994, McGraw-Hill.

Burnside IM: *Nursing and the aged,* ed 3, New York, McGraw-Hill, 1988.

Calkins E, Reinhard HD, Vladutiu AO: Rheumatoid arthritis and the autoimmune rheumatic diseases in the older patient. In Hazzard WR et al, editors: *Principles of geriatric medicine and gerontology,* ed 3, New York, 1994, McGraw-Hill.

Cavalieri TA, Chopra A, Bryman PN: When outside the norm is normal: interpreting lab data in the aged, *Geriatrics* 47:66-70, May 1992.

Davis J, Sherer K: *Applied nutrition and diet therapy for nurses,* ed 2, Philadelphia, 1993, WB Saunders.

Davis KM, Minaker KL: Disorders of fluid balance: dehydration and hyponatremia. In Hazzard WR et al, editors: *Principles of geriatric medicine and gerontology,* ed 3, New York, 1994, McGraw-Hill.

Dever AM, Rothkopf RM: Laboratory values and implications for the aged. In Ebersole P, Hess P: *Toward healthy aging: human needs and nursing response,* ed 4, St. Louis, 1994, Mosby.

DuPont Pharma: *INR questions and answers,* Wilmington, Del. 1994, DuPont Pharma.

Dybkaer R, Lauritzen M, Krakauer R: Relative reference values for clinical chemical and haematological quantities in "healthy" elderly people, *Acta Med Scand* 209:1, 1981.

Ebersole P, Hess P: *Toward healthy aging: human needs and nursing response,* ed 4, St. Louis, 1994, Mosby.

Garner B: Guide to changing lab values in elders, *Geriatr Nurs* May/June, 144-145, 1989.

Gaspard KJ: The red blood cell and alterations in oxygen transport. In Porth CM: *Pathophysiology: concepts of altered health states,* ed 4, Philadelphia, 1994, JB Lippincott.

Goldberg AP, Coon PJ: Diabetes mellitus and glucose metabolism in the elderly. In Hazzard WR et al, editors: *Principles of geriatric medicine and gerontology,* ed 3, New York, 1994, McGraw-Hill.

Gregerman RI, Katz MS: In Hazzard WR et al, editors: *Principles of geriatric medicine and gerontology,* ed 3, New York, 1994, McGraw-Hill.

Ham RJ, Sloane PD: *Primary care geriatrics,* ed 2, St Louis, 1992, Mosby. Hazzard WR: The sex differential in longevity. In Hazzard WR et al, editors: *Principles of geriatric medicine and gerontology,* ed 3, New York, 1994, McGraw-Hill.

Helman N, Rubenstein L: The effects of age, sex, and smoking on erythrocytes and leukocytes, *Am J Clin Pathol* 63:35, 1975.

Htoo MSH, Kofkoff R, Freedman M: Erythrocyte parameters in the elderly: an argument against new geriatric normal values, *J Am Geriatr Soc* 27:547, 1979.

Huether SE: Structure and function of the digestive system. In McCance KL, Huether SE: *Pathophysiology: the biologic basis for disease in adults and children,* ed 2, St Louis, 1994, Mosby.

Jeppesen M: Laboratory values for the elderly. In Carnevali D, Patrick M, editors: *Nursing management for the elderly,* ed 2, Philadelphia, JB Lippincott.

Kane RL, Ouslander JG, Abrass IB: *Essentials of clinical geriatrics,* ed 3, New York, 1994, McGraw-Hill.

Kelly A, Munan L: Haematologic profile of natural populations: red cell parameters, *Brit J Haematol* 35:153, 1977.

Kinne DW, Hakes TB: Male breast cancer. In Harris JR et al, editors: *Breast diseases,* ed 2, Philadelphia, 1992, JB Lippincott.

Lipschitz DA: Anemia. In Hazzard WR et al, editors: *Principles of geriatric medicine and gerontology,* ed 3, New York, 1994, McGraw-Hill.

McCance KL, Cipriano PF: Structure and function of the hematologic system. In McCance KL, Huether SE: *Pathophysiology: the biologic basis for disease in adults and children,* ed 2, St. Louis, 1994, Mosby.

McCance KL, Huether SE: *Pathophysiology: the biologic basis for disease in adults and children,* ed 2, St. Louis, 1994, Mosby.

Melillo KD: Interpretation of abnormal laboratory values in older adults, *J Gerontolog Nurs* January:39-35, 1993.

Mezey MD, Rauckhorst LH, Stokes SA: *Health assessment of the older adult,* ed 2, New York, 1993, Springer.

Mourad LA, Hoare K, Donohoe KM: Alterations of musculoskeletal function. In McCance KL, Huether SE: *Pathophysiology: the biologic basis for disease in adults and children,* ed 2, St. Louis, 1994, Mosby.

Mulkerrin JD et al: Glycosylated haemoglobin in the diagnosis of diabetes mellitus in elderly people, *Age Ageing,* 21:175-177, 1992.

Ogburn-Russell L, Johnson JE: Oxygen saturation levels in the well elderly: altitude makes a difference, *J Gerontolog Nurs* 16:10, 26-30, 1990.

Owen J: Thrombotic and hemorrhagic disorders in the elderly. In Hazzard WR et al, editors: *Principles of geriatric medicine and gerontology,* ed 3, New York, 1994, McGraw-Hill.

Pagana KD, Pagana TJ: *Mosby's diagnostic and lab test reference,* St. Louis, 1992, Mosby.

Pagana KD, Pagana TJ: *Diagnostic testing and nursing implications,* St. Louis, 1990, Mosby.

Rochman H: *Clinical pathology in the elderly,* New York, 1988, Karger.

Rothstein G: White cell disorders. In Hazzard WR et al, editors: *Principles of geriatric medicine and gerontology,* ed 3, New York, 1994, McGraw-Hill.

Singer FR: Paget's disease of bone. In Hazzard WR et al, editors: *Principles of geriatric medicine and gerontology,* ed 3, New York, 1994, McGraw-Hill.

Stead WW, Dutt AK: Tuberculosis: A special problem in the elderly. In Hazzard WR et al, editors: *Principles of geriatric medicine and gerontology,* ed 3, New York, 1994, McGraw-Hill.

Thibodeau GA, Patton KT: *Anatomy and physiology,* ed 2, St. Louis, 1993, Mosby.

Tunkel AR, Kaye D: Urinary tract infections. In Hazzard WR et al, editors: *Principles of geriatric medicine and gerontology,* ed 3, New York, 1994, McGraw-Hill.

CHAPTER 20

Pharmacologic Management

LEARNING OBJECTIVES

On completion of this chapter, the reader will be able to:

1. Describe medication use patterns among older clients.
2. Give examples of medication overuse, underuse, and misuse.
3. Identify potential risk factors for adverse drug reactions.
4. Recall the effects of physiologic changes with aging on drug disposition and give examples.
5. Describe significant drug interactions, their mechanism and time course, and alternative strategies.
6. Recognize drugs that may cause problems with function, including cognition, mobility, continence, and balance.
7. Describe advantages and disadvantages of various psychotropic agents prescribed for older clients.
8. Describe advantages and disadvantages of the angiotension converting enzyme inhibitors (ACEIs), beta-blockers, and calcium channel antagonists when prescribed for an older client.
9. Recognize risk factors for noncompliance and suggest strategies to improve compliance.
10. Recall general principles of prescribing for the older client.

The use of medications as modern tools for improving the health of the older population constitutes a delicate balancing act. Health care professionals are challenged to provide optimum cure or management of a condition while minimizing the negative effects on a client's quality of life from an adverse drug event. Although researchers have repeatedly cited overuse of medications in older adults, the benefits of medication use are emphasized in a recent report in New Hampshire that observed a two-fold increase in the rate of admissions to nursing homes and an increase in hospitalization rates after a cap of three prescriptions per month was imposed on Medicaid recipients (*Wall Street Journal,* 1990).

This chapter provides insights into problem areas of medication use in older adults, the nurse's role in assessing the client for risk factors associated with adverse drug events, and key principles to use when evaluating a client's medication regimen.

Overview of Medication Use and Problems

Demographics of Medication Use

The pharmaceutical needs of the aging population continue to grow dramatically. One half of the pharmaceutical industry's $7.3 billion research budget for 1990 was devoted to developing medications to treat conditions commonly affecting older adults (Contemporary Senior Health, 1990). Diseases of the cardiovascular system, including stroke and hypertension, cancer, Alzheimer's, arthritis and osteoporosis are promising areas for new drug development.

The older adult segment of the U.S. population consumes 25% to 30% of all prescription and 40% of all nonprescription medications, spending a total of about $3 billion annually (Vestal, 1990). Of ambulatory older adults, 80% have at least one chronic condition requiring medications, although multiple medical diagnoses are often present (Delafuente, 1991).

In the hospital, older adults with chronic conditions comprise a significant proportion of admissions and readmissions as well as the longest lengths of stay (Lamy, 1992b). In addition, the number of medications prescribed in the hospital increases in proportion to the client's age and length of stay (Vestal, 1990). Nursing home clients receive an average of seven medications, one half of which are prescribed on an as-needed basis (Delafuente, 1990). Regardless of the health care setting, excessive medication use increases the risk of adverse drug events and drug interactions that have negative influences on health care costs and client morbidity.

Medication Overuse, Misuse, and Underuse

A number of studies have cited the overuse of certain medication categories in the elderly. **Psychotropic agents** have long been scrutinized in the nursing home setting. A recent survey of 12 nursing homes in California found inappropriate prescribing of long-acting benzodiazepines in one in five residents (Beers, 1992). Overuse of the H2 antagonists (cimetidine [Tagamet], ranitidine [Zantac], famotidine [Pepcid], nizatidine [Axid]) was observed in 70% of nursing home residents in one study and 41% in another (Beers, 1992; Gurwitz, Noonan, Soumerai, 1992). Not only does overuse expose the client to the risk of short-term and long-term adverse effects, but it also increases the cost of medical management.

Misuse of metoclopramide (Reglan) for simple heartburn was cited in 13% of clients in an ambulatory Veterans Administration (VA) clinic (Mason, 1989). This may be problematic, since metoclopramide has been associated with sometimes irreversible movement disorders, such as tardive dyskinesia, with chronic use.

Alternatively, undertreatment of certain conditions continues to occur. According to a recent National Institutes of Health (NIH) consensus panel, up to 90% of older adults with depression may receive inadequate psychiatric treatment (*NIH Consensus Development Conference Consensus Statement,* 1991). Although this lack of treatment may be as a result of valid concerns for adverse drug effects such as hypotension or conduction abnormalities in clients with coexisting cardiac disease, the negative attitudes of health care practitioners toward depression (e.g., "It's a normal part of the aging process.") may cause only minimal value to be placed on treatment. The consequences of untreated depression include increased use of health services, longer hospital stays, poor treatment compliance, and increased morbidity and mortality from medical illness and suicide (Depression Guideline Panel, 1993).

Difficulties in detection and undertreatment of pain in older clients has been observed in nursing home populations (Sengstaken, King, 1993; Marzinski, 1991) (see Research box above).

Recognition of pain is especially difficult in noncommunicative clients and warrants the use of better assessment tools in this population. Marzinski (1991) suggests different ways to assess pain in confused clients (Table 20-1).

Adverse drug reactions: assessing risk factors Adverse drug reactions (ADRs) exact a toll on older clients. ADRs directly or indirectly account for 10% to

RESEARCH

Sengstaken EA, King SA: The problems of pain and its detection among geriatric nursing home residents, *J Am Geriatr Soc* 41(5):541-544, 1993.

Sample, setting

Subjects included 100 nursing home residents age 65 or older.

Methodology

Chart review and client interview were used to determine presence and duration of pain and use of analgesics.

Findings

Although 66% of communicative clients had chronic pain, physicians did not detect this problem in 34% of the residents. In addition, fewer noncommunicative than communicative residents were receiving regularly scheduled acetaminophen (4% versus 21%) and antidepressants (4% versus 22%).

Implications

Pain may be underdiagnosed in older nursing home clients and result in inadequate treatment. Standard methods of assessment may not be appropriate in the noncommunicative population.

TABLE 20-1

Differences Between Normal Behaviors and Pain Behaviors in Confused Patients*

Normal behavior	Pain behavior
Moaning and rocking	Withdrawn and quiet
Disjointed verbalization	Accurate description of location of pain
Quiet and nonverbal	Rapid blinking with slight facial grimace
Friendly and outgoing	Agitated and combative
Outgoing and easily involved in activities	Cries easily and withdraws from activities

*N = 5; clients had clear differences between normal behavior and pain.
From Marzinski L: The tragedy of dementia: clinically assessing pain in the confused, nonverbal elderly, *J Gerontol Nurs* 17:25-28, 1991.

TABLE 20-2

Risk Factors Associated With ADRs

Population	Risk factors associated with ADRs
Hospital (age ≥65)	Greater than four medications Length of stay > 14 days > 4 active medical problems Admission to medical vs geriatric ward Alcohol
Hospital and outpatient (age ≥65)	Living alone Recent (≥ 3 months) change in nutritional status > 4 medications Documented compliance problems before admission Recent (≤ 3 months) medication changes
Outpatient (age ≥70)	Presence of potential drug interactions Use of drugs with narrow therapeutic ranges

Data compiled from Schneider JK, Mion LC, Frengley JD: Adverse drug reactions in an elderly outpatient population, *Am J Hosp Pharm* 49(1):90-96, 1992.

31% of hospital admissions (Delafuente, 1991; Bero, Lipton, Bird, 1991). In addition, one study found 20% of readmissions to be associated with drug-related problems including ADRs, noncompliance, overdose, lack of necessary drug therapy, and underdosage (Bero, Lipton, Bird, 1991). In the outpatient population, an ADR incidence of 21% has been reported (Schneider, Mion, Frengley, 1992). Lipton et al (1992) published a disturbing report, which found 88% of a sample of older clients discharged from a community hospital with at least one significant drug problem, and 22% having a potentially serious or life-threatening consequence. The severity of ADRs appears to increase with age. In one report, serious or fatal ADRs occurred in 41.9% of clients 85 and older compared with 30.1% of those 75 to 84 and 18.5% of those age 55 to 64 (Delafuente, 1991).

Multiple risk factors may contribute to ADRs in older adults. A number of studies have suggested that the incidence of ADRs increases with the number of medications prescribed (Carbonin et al, 1991; Johnson, Cappuccio, 1992; Gurwitz, Avorn, 1991). However, it is not always an easy task to reduce the number of medications prescribed, since 80% of the elderly population have at least one chronic condition requiring treatment with medication (Delafuente, 1991). Clients may expect a prescription after an office or clinic visit to validate their complaints and feel that they have gotten their "money's worth." Alternatively, prescribers may "give in" to a client because of frequent complaints, client demands to prescribe a medication that has been directly marketed and promoted to the general public, or to maintain a relationship with the client, despite questionable benefits.

Both over- and undercompliance may contribute to ADRs. For example, overcompliance with analgesics in clients with back pain from compression fractures may result in undesirable side effects such as mental confusion or falls, whereas undercompliance with antihypertensive regimens may result in stroke or heart attack.

Fragmentation of health care, evidenced by the continued interest in subspecialization by the majority of medical school graduates, increases the likelihood that older adults may not always have their care coordinated by a single health care professional. Current managed care strategies are reversing this trend by focusing more on primary and preventive care. "Pharmacy shopping" for best price because of expensive medication regimens contributes to the possibility of an adverse drug event or interaction as a result of inability of pharmacists to maintain a complete, up-to-date medication profile for screening a client's regimen. In addition, medication expense is often a major deterrent to compliance in older clients. Generic equivalents may not be available for recently marketed medications. It is not unusual for a client taking multiple cardiac medications along with an **H2 antagonist** or a new **nonsteroidal anti-inflammatory drug (NSAID)** to be faced with a monthly prescription cost of $150 or more. Cost must be considered in discharge planning and counseling to ensure the desired

TABLE 20-3

Drug Categories Associated With ADRs

Population	Drug categories associated with ADRs* (by percent)
Hospital and outpatient (Age ≥65)	Cardiovascular (37) Psychotropics (35) Antiinfectives (9) Theophylline (5)
Hospital compared clients ≤60 with those >60	Narcotic analgesics (31) Antiinfectives (23.3) Cardiovascular agents (19.4)
Outpatient Age ≥70	Anticoagulants (9.3) ACEIs (17) Diuretics (14) Antidepressants (10)
Varied	NSAIDs (10) Benzodiazepines(†) Antihypertensives NSAIDs Anticoagulants

*Only categories with ≥ 5% incidence are listed.
†No percentage available.
Data compiled from Johnson JF, Cappuccio J: Risk factors associated with adverse drug reactions in elderly patients, *Pharmacother* 12(3):265, 1992 (abstract); Schneider JK, Mion LC, Frengley JD: Adverse drug reactions in an elderly outpatient population, *Am J Hosp Pharm* 49(1):90-96, 1992; Classen DC et al: Computerized surveillance of adverse drug events in hospital patients, *JAMA* 266:2847-2851, 1991; Gurwitz JH, Avorn J: The ambiguous relation between aging and adverse drug reactions, *Ann Intern Med* 114(11):956-966, 1991.

TABLE 20-4

Risk of Hospitalization for Hemorrhagic Peptic Ulcer Disease by Oral Anticoagulation and NSAID Use

Client category	Relative risk (95% confidence interval)
NSAID nonuser	
Oral anticoagulant nonuser	1.0 (reference)
Noncurrent oral anticoagulant user	1.2
Current oral anticoagulant user*	4.3
Current NSAID user	
Oral anticoagulant nonuser†	4.0
Noncurrent oral anticoagulant user†	4.5
Current oral anticoagulant user	12.7

*Current user: Includes the day the prescription was filled, usually at discharge, through day 60, after the end of the days' supply.
†Noncurrent user: Includes days 1 through 365 after the last day of current use.
From Shorr RI et al: Concurrent use of nonsteroidal antiinflammatory drugs and oral anticoagulants places elderly people at high risk for hemorrhagic peptic ulcer disease, *Arch Intern Med,* 153(14):1665-1670, 1993.

outcome. Dysfunctional prescribing and lack of knowledge regarding changes in drug disposition (pharmacokinetics) or end organ response (pharmacodynamics) may lead to apparently increased rates of ADRs in older adults (Gurwitz, Avorn, 1991).

Various authors have reported other risk factors and medication categories associated with ADRs (Tables 20-2 and 20-3).

The nonsteroidal antiinflammatory drugs are of particular concern because of their frequent use in older adults and increasing nonprescription availability. Griffin et al. (1991) found a four-fold increase in the likelihood of developing peptic ulcer disease in older NSAID users when compared with nonusers. This risk also increased with increasing dosage and was greatest during the first month of use (Fig. 20-1).

In addition, use of NSAIDs along with oral anticoagulants has been shown to significantly increase the likelihood of hospitalization as a result of hemorrhagic ulcer (Shorr et al, 1993) (Table 20-4).

Some authors have suggested a method of calculating the statistical risk of developing a serious NSAID-induced gastrointestinal (GI) hemorrhage (Fries et al, 1991; *Reducing the costs of NSAID-induced gastropathy,* 1993)

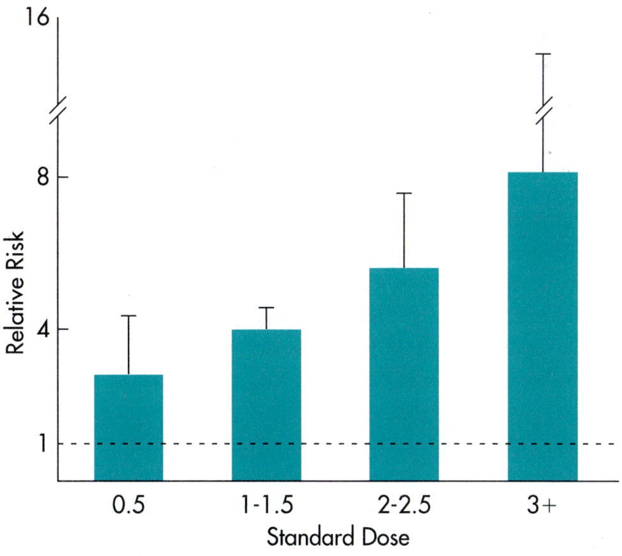

Fig. 20-1 Relative risk for the development of peptic ulcer disease by standard dose among current users of nonaspirin NSAIDs. Case clients and control people were enrollees in the Tennessee Medicaid program from 1984 through 1986. (From Griffin MR et al: Nonsteroidal anti-inflammatory drug use and increased risk for peptic ulcer disease in elderly persons, *Ann Intern Med* 114(4):257-263, 1991.)

TABLE 20-5

Suggested Method for Calculating the Risk of Serious NSAID-Induced GI Hemorrhage over a 12-Month Period (Moderately High Risk = 2 to 3%; High Risk ≥ 3%)

Risk factor	Scoring system
Age > 50 years	For each 5 years > 50, 0.3*
Concomitant prednisone use	If yes, add 1.2
Previous NSAID-induced GI adverse effect	If yes, add 1.4
Disability (American Rheumatism Association [ARA] functional class III or IV)	If yes, add 0.5
Overall percent risk for next 12-month period	Total score (by percent)

*e.g., age 65 years: 3 × 0.3 = 0.9.
From Reducing the costs of NSAID-induced gastropathy, *Drugs and Therapy Perspectives* 1(12):July 5, 1993.

(Table 20-5). This may serve as a useful screen to better recognize and to reduce the risk of NSAID-induced gastropathy. To reduce these NSAID-related problems, health care professionals must be sure that there is a valid indication for prescribing an NSAID. Concurrent use of misoprostol (Cytotec) should be considered as primary prevention of NSAID-induced gastropathy in clients at high risk (Graham et al, 1993). Another alternative should be avoidance of the NSAIDs for osteoarthritis unaccompanied by inflammation. Bradley et al. (1991) compared short-term (4-week) pain relief in a group of clients with osteoarthritis of the knee randomized to either 1,200 mg (analgesic dose) or 2,400 mg (antiinflammatory dose) daily of ibuprofen (Motrin) or 4,000 mg daily of acetaminophen. The efficacy of acetaminophen was comparable to either the analgesic or antiinflammatory dose of ibuprofen.

Detection of an ADR in the older client may be easily missed, especially if only subtle changes occur or in the absence of toxic serum drug levels. Confusion, falls, depression, sedation, deterioration of function, urinary retention, and incontinence are commonly manifested as drug toxicity but may also be discounted as a normal part of aging.

Beers and Ouslander (1989) have listed those medications that should be prescribed cautiously in older adults (Table 20-6).

Agencies and Regulations Affecting Drug Use

The first federal legislation to provide rules for prescribing in nursing homes was the Omnibus Budget Reconciliation Act or OBRA, passed in 1987. In response to a 25% to 50% prevalence in the use of major tranquilizers (antipsychotics), this law prohibited prescription of antipsychotics simply for behavioral control. Approved indications that warrant their use and must be documented in the client's chart include (1) hallucinations, delusions, or paranoia; (2) psychomotor agitation interfering with the provision of basic care and activities of daily living (ADLs); and (3) hiccups, nausea, vomiting, or pruritus. These regulations have resulted in prescribing changes as evidenced by a recent survey of Baltimore nursing homes, which showed a decrease in neuroleptic and benzodiazepine use and an increase in antidepressant prescriptions (Rovner et al, 1992).

The development of clinical practice guidelines (CPGs) has become a major focus for the federal Agency for Health Care Policy and Research (AHCPR). The purpose of these guidelines is to improve the quality of health care by having panels of experts design strategies to improve appropriateness, effectiveness, and efficiency of health care. The Joint Commission on Accreditation of Health Care Organizations (JCAHO) uses CPGs as sources of comparative data for quality assessment and improvement processes. These CPGs are an excellent starting point for nurses caring for older clients to compare with current practice in their particular setting (Depression Guideline Panel, 1993; Urinary Incontinence Panel, 1992).

Physiologic Changes of Aging: Effects on Drug Response

Pharmacokinetic Changes in Drug Disposition

One of the reasons previously cited as a risk factor for ADRs was changes in pharmacokinetics or drug disposition (drug absorption, distribution, metabolism, or excretion) with age. However, the *degree* of change may vary greatly among older adult clients, for example, the "young-old" (65 to 74 years) versus the "old-old" (greater than 85 years), or healthy older adults versus those with multiple chronic illnesses or multiorgan failure. Other influences on drug disposition include interacting medications; nutritional status; intake of caffeine, tobacco, and alcohol; and exposure to environmental substances (see Cultural Awareness box, p. 458). These variables must be kept in mind when extrapolating study results to a specific population of older adults.

Alterations in drug absorption as a result of age-related changes in GI physiology with age may influence drug dissolution, rate, and extent of absorption (Table 20-7).

Although information is available on alterations in absorption of oral medications with age, there is a need for studies examining the influences of age on absorption of medications given by rectal, pulmonary, intramuscular, or dermal routes.

TABLE 20-6

Drugs Posing Special Risks in Older Adults

Drug	Special considerations
Amitriptyline	Most anticholinergic of all tricyclics. It can lead to confusion, orthostatic hypotension, dry mouth, blurred vision, urinary retention. Also the most sedating of all the tricyclics and so can lead to confusion and unstable gait
Antiemetics	These are phenothiazines and are therefore both anticholinergic and sedating. They may lead to confusion, orthostatic hypotension, blurred vision, falls, dry mouth, and urinary retention
Antipsychotics	There is no evidence that antipsychotics have any significant effect in treating the behavior problems associated with dementia. Their contribution may be through sedation. Only thioridazine and mesoridazine are FDA approved for this use. All are anticholinergic, although haloperidol is the least anticholinergic. Cause movement disorders with high incidence. TD and tardive akathisia may not be reversible on stopping the drug. Also cause Parkinson's syndrome
Barbiturates	Are addictive; safer alternatives are available. Are fat-soluble and have prolonged duration in older adults. Induce hepatic enzymes and thus may affect the concentrations of other medications used concurrently
β-Blockers	May be less effective in the older adults. There is evidence [that] they exacerbate depression
Chlorpropamide	Prolonged half-life and can therefore lead to prolonged hypoglycemia. Only oral hypoglycemic agent that induces SIADH with significant incidence
Digoxin	Role in the treatment of congestive heart failure is controversial and as many as 50% of clients can be withdrawn from therapy without adverse effects. Toxicity is common and may be subtle and can occur at normal serum concentrations. Toxic reactions include anorexia, visual disturbances, syncope, and weakness
Diphenhydramine	Of all the medications used to induce sleep, diphenhydramine is the only one with anticholinergic side effects. It is rarely the drug of choice for older clients, because it can lead to dry mouth, confusion, orthostatic hypotension, falls, and urinary retention
Disopyramide	Highly anticholinergic and a negative inotrope; may exacerbate congestive heart failure
GI antispasmodics	Effectiveness of all [of] these is in doubt; all are anticholinergic
H_2-Blockers	Require dose reduction in older adults. The appropriate dose in most older adults is ranitidine 150 mg once daily, cimetidine 300 mg twice daily
Long acting benzodiazepines: diazepam, flurazepam, chlordiazepoxide	Half-lives are prolonged in older adults up to as much as 4 days. They can lead to CNS toxicity such as confusion, oversedation, falls and fractures
Narcotics	Older adults are more sensitive to all narcotics. Doses should be started low. Older adults are prone to constipation, and all narcotics tend to constipate. Stimulant laxatives should be given routinely when narcotics are used
OTC cold remedies	Most contain antihistamines that are highly anticholinergic. They can lead to dry mouth, confusion, urinary retention, blurred vision, falls
Propoxyphene	Can lead to sedation and confusion and offers no benefit over paracetamol (acetaminophen) or salicylates
Reserpine	Very dangerous in older adults via its effect on the autonomic nervous system
Timolol	Systemically absorbed and can cause manifestations of β-blocker use
Xanthenes	Significant dose reduction is required

Abbreviations: CNS = central nervous system; FDA = Food and Drug Administration (US); OTC-over-the-counter SIADH = syndrome of inappropriate antidiuretic hormone secretion; TD= tardive dyskinesia. (From Beers MH, Ouslander JG: Risk factors in geriatric drug prescribing. A practical guide to avoiding problems, *Drugs* 37(1):105-112, 1989.)

Drug distribution into peripheral circulation and tissues is altered as a function of age. A decrease in plasma albumin levels with age may result in decreased binding of drugs that are mainly bound to serum albumin, such as acidic drugs. Since it is the unbound fraction of a drug that is available to cause the desired pharmacologic effect or toxicity, an increase of unbound drug with age may result in exaggerated pharmacologic effects or side effects. Not only aging itself but also disease states, gender, coadministration of other drugs, acute illness and nutritional status may influence serum protein binding. Alternatively, some authors have observed an increase in alpha 1-acid glycoprotein with age, resulting in an *increased* binding of basic drugs normally bound to this

CULTURAL AWARENESS

Ethnopharmacology

Metabolic, genetic, and environmental factors

Cultural differences in drug response and metabolism have been identified by numerous researchers. The majority of studies providing evidence for transcultural differences in pharmacokinetic and pharmacodynamic properties of various drugs have compared individuals of Asian, African-American, Hispanic, and Native-American descent to whites.

Differences in pharmacokinetics may be genetic or may be a result of environmental influences. Among African-American and white individuals, only about 9% are considered to be slow metabolizers whereas 32% of Asian Americans are. There also is evidence of variability in protein binding based on ethnicity. Habits such as smoking and drinking alcohol are known to speed drug metabolism, whereas a low-protein, high carbohydrate diet is known to slow metabolism. The fact that whites and African-Americans drink significantly more alcohol than Asians and eat differently, may provide an environmental explanation for the greater drug impact experienced by Asian-American clients.

Misdiagnosis

African-American older adults are significantly misdiagnosed as psychotic, viewed as more violent by staff, and spend more time in seclusion than whites, Hispanics or Asian Americans. Thus the actual dose of medication prescribed for African-Americans may be more of a function of staff perception than a decision based on serum levels or clinical observations. Asian Americans in general, and Chinese-American clients in particular, require significantly smaller doses of neuroleptics, tricyclic antidepressants (TCAs), and lithium than do whites, sometimes one half the dose. Similar differences have been reported between Asian Indian or Pakistani clients, and white older adults.

Perception of side effects

Research indicates that Asian Americans are more sensitive to neuroleptics than whites. In one study, Asian-American clients began experiencing extrapyramidal effects at dosages approximately one half that for whites. At equivalent doses, 95% of Asians experienced extrapyramidal effects, whereas only 67% of whites and African Americans experienced those side effects. Hispanic clients taking tricyclic antidepressants experienced side effects at half the dosage observed in whites. African-Americans are more susceptible to TCA delirium than whites.

Culture and level of "compliance"

Comparing three subgroups from Southeast Asia (Hmong, Cambodian, and Laotian), the client's failure to take the medication as prescribed accounted for changes in plasma levels in approximately one half of the subjects in a study by Kroll et al. (1990). Thus cultural influences were concluded to account for a significant degree of "noncompliance." Members of some cultural groups may perceive that medication should have a short-term effect and are not culturally conditioned to continue medication that does not produce an immediate response.

A less empirical but real consideration is the issue of the client's confidence and trust in the health care provider. Based on a combination of historic fact and myth, some Hispanic clients do not have confidence nor trust in white health care providers. Other cultural considerations such as traditional beliefs and practices, advice of traditional, folk, or indigenous healers, religious beliefs, and other factures undoubtedly influence "compliance" with drug regimens prescribed by physicians and nurse practitioners.

Keltner NL, Folks DG: Psychopharmacology update: culture as a variable in drug therapy, *Perspec Psychiatr Care* 28(1):33-36, 1992; Kroll J et al.: Medication compliance, antidepressant blood levels, and side effects in Southeast Asian patients, *J Clin Pharmacol* 10(4):27-9282, 1990; Lefley H: Culture and chronic mental illness, *Hosp Commun Psychiatry* 41:277-286, 1990; Lin T: Multiculturalism and Canadian psychiatry: opportunities and challenges, *Canad J Psychiatry,* 31(7):681-690; Mendoza R et al: Ethnic psychopharmacology: the Hispanic and Native American perspective, *Psychopharmacol Bullet* 27(4):449-461; Wood AJ, Zhou HH: Ethnic differences in drug disposition and responsiveness, *Clin Pharmacokinetics* 20:1-24.

protein. Examples of drugs with increased or decreased binding are listed in Box 20-1.

The half-life of a drug may be altered by changes in protein binding, although this depends on renal and nonrenal clearance and volume of distribution. For drugs where serum concentration monitoring is not used, the practitioner must adjust based on clinical observations of pharmacologic and toxicologic effects. The nurse needs to be aware of side effects that may be related to high serum drug concentrations and discuss concerns with the prescriber. For drugs where serum concentration monitoring is available, dose adjustments may depend on drug levels. However, assays for certain drugs such as phenytoin (Dilantin) may only report *total* drug concentrations, which may be misleading. For example, a client may have a serum phenytoin concentration of 12 mcg/ml, which is within the normal range of 10 to 20 mcg/ml. However, if this client had a low serum albumin because of protein wasting or malnutrition, their *free* phenytoin concentration, normally 10% to 20% of total, may be elevated. It is this free concentration that relates to clinical toxicity. Free drug concentrations may need to

TABLE 20-7

Changes in Gastrointestinal Function

Feature	Implications
Reduction in number of acinar cells of salivary glands	• Increased susceptibility to mucosal drying effects of anticholinergics (e.g., *diphenhydramine* [Benadryl], *amitriptyline* [Elavil], *thioridazine [Mellaril]*)
Slowed gastric emptying, reduced gastric and intestinal blood flow (further reduced in congestive heart failure [CHF])	• Delayed onset of drug effect • Alteration in absorption of poorly dissolving dosage forms more pronounced compared with liquids or rapidly dissolving dosage forms
Decreased gastric acid secretion, high prevalence of atrophic gastritis*	• Increased absorption of *digoxin* as a result of a decrease in formation of metabolites‡ • Decreased secretion of intrinsic factor; *vitamin B_{12}* malabsorption if severe† • Decreased degradation of drugs unstable in acidic pH (i.e., *penicillin G, erythromycin*) • Decreased *calcium* absorption as a result of decreased dissociation from food particles and decreased dissolution with high gastric pH • Decreased absorption of drugs dependent on acidic pH for dissolution (i.e., *chlorazepate* [Tranxene]) • Decreased absorption of *ferric iron*
Decreased activity of small intestine brush border enzymes; reduced mucosal surface area	• Decreased rate of absorption

*The H2 antagonists prescribed long-term may cause vitamin B_{12} malabsorption by inhibiting release of intrinsic factor or decreasing stomach acid.
†Neurologic changes which accompany vitamin B_{12} deficiency include weakness, ataxia, impaired sensation, and altered mental state.
‡Coadministration of omeprazole (Prilosec) or H2 antagonists may also increase digoxin absorption.
From Russell RM: Changes in gastrointestinal function attributed to aging, *Am J Clin Nutr* 55(6):1203S-1207S, 1992; Mayersohn MB: Special pharmocokinetic considerations in the elderly. In Evans WE, Schentag JJ, Jusko WJ, editors: *Applied pharmacokinetics: principles of therapeutic drug monitoring,* ed 3, Vancouver, Wash., 1992, Applied Therapeutics; Cohen AF et al: Influence of gastric acidity on the bioavailability of digoxin, *Ann Intern Med* 115(7):540-545, 1991; Force RW, Nahata MC: Effect of histamine H2-receptor antagonists on vitamin B12 absorption, *Ann Pharmacotherap* 26:1283-1286, 1992.

BOX 20-1

Drugs with Altered Protein Binding as a Function of Age

Decreased binding as a result of decreased albumin

Carbenoxolone	Phenytoin (Dilantin)
Ceftriaxone (Rocephin)	Temazepam (Restoril)
Diazepam (Valium)	Tolbutamide (Orinase)
Fluphenazine (Prolixin)	Triazolam (Halcion) (men only)
Lorazepam (Ativan)	Valproic acid (Depakene)
Meperidine (Demerol)	Warfarin (Coumadin)
Naproxen (Naprosyn)	

Increased binding as a result of increased alpha 1-acid glycoprotein

Lidocaine

From Mayersohn MB: Special pharmocokinetic considerations in the elderly. In Evans WE, Schentag JJ, Jusko WJ, editors: *Applied pharmacokinetics: principles of therapeutic drug monitoring,* ed 3, Vancouver, Wash., 1992, Applied Therapeutics.

be monitored in cases where alterations in protein binding may be significant and may cause changes in the toxicity or pharmacologic profile for a drug.

Changes in body composition, which differ in magnitude between men and women, may influence drug distribution. A decrease in total body and intracellular water volumes may lead to increased serum concentrations of water-soluble drugs such as lithium. Fat mass generally increases with age, although a recent study suggested a significantly lower percent of body fat in the age group 85 or older (Silver et al, 1993) (Figs. 20-2 and 20-3).

The volume of distribution *increases* for drugs highly distributed into fatty tissues. This may lead to prolonged half lives and accumulation of fat-soluble drugs such as thiopental and the long-acting benzodiazepines, such as diazepam (Valium) and chlordiazepoxide (Librium). Lean body mass declines in men and women. The serum concentration of drugs that are distributed mainly to lean body mass (e.g., alcohol or digoxin) may increase as a consequence of a decreased volume of distribution.

Changes in hepatic drug metabolism with age are not easily measured. Although a reduction in liver size and hepatic blood flow has been observed with age, results of liver function tests are not useful in predicting the ex-

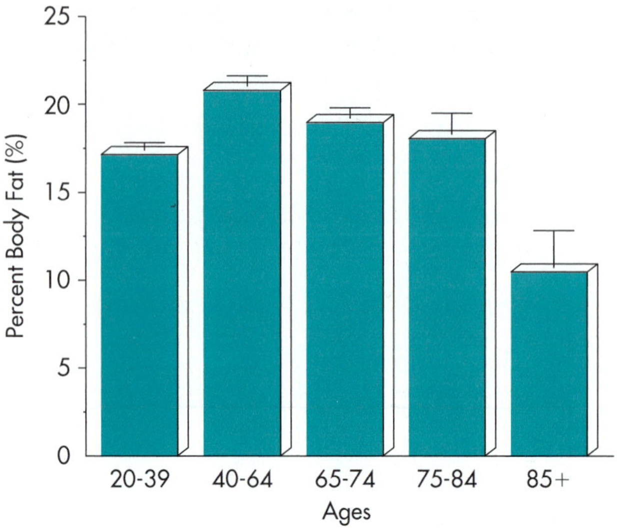

Fig. 20-2 The effect of aging on percentage body fat in males. Data are shown as mean ± standard error of the mean. Significance at the P < 0.05 level was noted between the 20-to-39 and 40-to-64 age groups, the 40-to-64 and 85-and-older age groups, and the 65-to-74 and 85-and-older age groups.
(From Silver AJ et al: Effect of aging on body fat, *J Am Geriatr Soc* 41(3):211-213, 1993.)

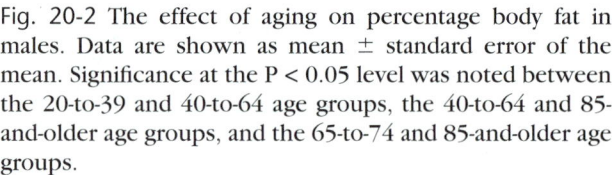

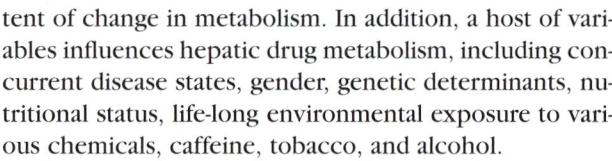

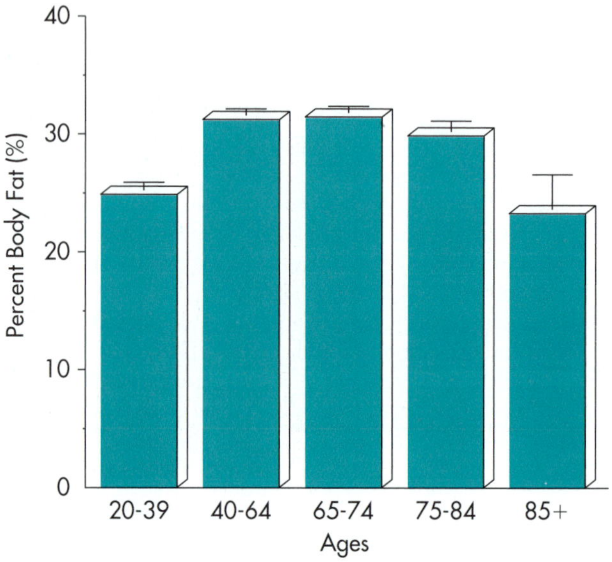

Fig. 20-3 The effect of aging on percentage body fat in females. Data are shown as mean ± standard error of the mean. There was a significant difference (P < 0.05) between the 20-to-39 age group and all other age groups. There was also a significant difference between the 85-and-older age group and all other age groups.
(From Silver AJ et al: Effect of aging on body fat, *J Am Geriatr Soc* 41(3):211-213, 1993.)

tent of change in metabolism. In addition, a host of variables influences hepatic drug metabolism, including concurrent disease states, gender, genetic determinants, nutritional status, life-long environmental exposure to various chemicals, caffeine, tobacco, and alcohol.

It has been observed that drugs that undergo Phase I metabolism (oxidation, reduction, or hydrolysis to more polar compounds), such as long-acting benzodiazepines, are more likely to have reduced hepatic clearance and an increased half-life. Alternatively, those drugs undergoing Phase II metabolism (conjugation to a more water-soluble molecule), such as intermediate- to short-acting benzodiazepines, are more likely to be cleared similarly to younger clients. Unfortunately, since no general conclusions can be drawn, nurses must again rely on knowledge and assessment of pharmacologic or toxicologic effects in a given client, alerting the prescriber if problems are suspected.

Changes in renal excretion of drugs as a function of age are better understood than hepatic metabolism and may result in significant decreases in renal elimination for drugs primarily eliminated by the renal route. This may require a decreased dose or increase in the dosing interval for certain drugs.

Serum creatinine may be used to estimate renal function by calculating creatinine clearance:

$$\text{Creatinine clearance (ml/min)} = \frac{140 - \text{age in years} \times \text{weight in kg}}{72 \times \text{serum creatinine (\% mg/100 ml)}}$$

(For women, multiply final result by 0.85)

Creatinine clearance is an estimate of glomerular filtration rate and decreases by 30% to 40% at an average age of 80. It is important to realize that even though an older adult client may have a serum creatinine value that is "within normal limits" by laboratory standards, this does NOT mean that creatinine clearance is normal. This is because of decreased muscle mass and muscle metabolism, which is normally responsible for decomposition of creatine to creatinine. A number of medications, including allopurinol (Zyloprim), amantadine (Symmetrel), cimetidine (Tagamet), digoxin (Lanoxin), ranitidine (Zantac) and many antibiotics, may need to be given at a lower dose or less frequently. The reader is referred to a comprehensive pocket reference for adjustments of drug dosing in varying degrees of renal function (Bennett et al, 1994).

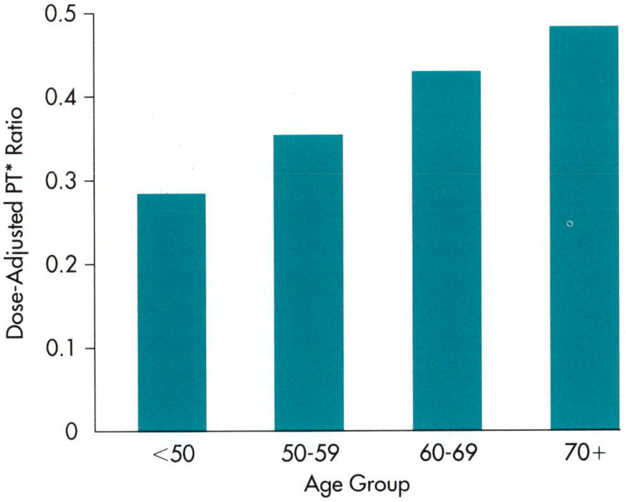

Fig. 20-4 The relationship between dose-adjusted prothrombin time ratio and age group (P < 0.001). (From Gurwitz JH et al: Aging and the anticoagulant response to warfarin therapy, *Ann Intern Med* 116(11):901-904, 1992.)
*PT = prothrombin time

BOX 20-2

Commonly Used Medications Having Anticholinergic Properties

Cardiovascular
Disopyramide (Norpace)

Psychotropic
Tricyclic antidepressants
Neuroleptics
Antihistamines (e.g., Benadryl)

Gastrointestinal
Oxybutinin (Ditropan)
Propantheline (Probanthine)
Diphenoxylate with atropine (Lomotil)

Antiparkinson
Amantadine (Symmetrel)
Benztropine (Cogentin)
Trihexyphenidyl (Artane)

Other
Scopolamine

Pharmacodynamic Changes: Altered Receptor Response

There are a few studies that have observed an exaggerated response in older adults in the face of serum concentrations similar to those in a younger population. It has been demonstrated that a lower blood concentration of diazepam (Valium) in older clients is adequate to provide a given degree of central nervous system depression (Roberts, Turner, 1988). Early studies with warfarin (Coumadin) suggested a greater anticoagulant effect in older adults despite unaltered pharmacokinetics. More recent studies have supported this increased response based on the need for a decreased dosage of warfarin to achieve the desired anticoagulant response (Gurwitz et al, 1992) (Fig. 20-4). A number of studies have found reductions in beta-receptor concentrations or receptor affinity with age. This may explain a more blunted response to sympathomimetic agents. Decreases in baroreceptor sensitivity and other homeostatic mechanisms may increase the likelihood of hypotension from cardiovascular medications.

A decrease in the concentration of neurotransmitters, such as acetylcholine, may increase the likelihood of sensitivity to anticholinergic drugs and their attendant toxicities, including delirium (Box 20-2). This is especially important in clients with Alzheimer's disease who may already have cholinergic deficiency. More research is needed in the area of pharmacodynamic changes to assist the practitioner in making appropriate alterations in medication regimens.

Polypharmacy and Drug Interactions: Assessment of Significance and Preventive Strategies

Drug interactions are commonly encountered in the older client as a result of concurrent prescribing of multiple medications (polypharmacy). These interactions are often considered great "masqueraders," since they may be mistaken as drug toxicity, an increase in disease severity or suboptimal treatment, or an apparently unrelated event. The consequences of an unrecognized drug interaction include client injury, additional office or emergency department visits, unnecessary invasive testing, weakening of the client/prescriber relationship, and inappropriate medication or dose changes.

Assessing the clinical significance of a drug interaction depends on the following (McInnes, Brodie, 1988; Tatro, 1993):

1. **The therapeutic index of the affected (object) drug** Medications such as phenytoin (Dilantin), digoxin (Lanoxin), theophylline (Theodur), or lithium, which have a narrow therapeutic index or margin of safety, may place a client at high risk for experiencing a significant adverse event from a drug interaction.

2. **Magnitude of hepatic enzyme induction or inhibition** The degree to which the serum concentration of an object drug may increase as a result of an interacting (precipitant) drug inhibiting its hepatic metabolism, or decrease as a result of an interacting drug inducing its metabolism, is variable and often unpredictable. Monitoring of serum concentrations may be required to assess the magnitude of these changes.
3. **The client's clinical status** The same interaction may have different effects on a young and healthy client with intact homeostatic mechanisms, compared with the older frail client with multiple medical problems who is acutely ill and exposed to multiple physiologic or pharmacologic "stressors."
4. **The order of administration** The timing of medication administration for drugs, which may, for example, alter drug absorption, may be important in determining the magnitude of changes in serum concentrations and therapeutic effect.
5. **Interclient variability in response** As is true with the variability in hepatic clearance with age, genetic factors, environmental influences such as exposure to various environmental chemicals, alcohol, caffeine, and tobacco may affect a client's clinical response to a drug interaction.

Tables 20-8 through 20-12* review drug interactions occurring as a result of changes in pharmacokinetics or pharmacodynamics. Examples are included.

Drug Interactions: Absorption

Changes in drug absorption from the GI tract may result from alterations in gastric pH, formation of drug complexes, or altered motility or emptying. Most often this results in a decrease in serum concentration of the object drug. The effect is observed as soon as the two interacting drugs are given together. Modifying the time of administration by a minimum of 2 hours or using alternate drugs should minimize changes in drug absorption.

Drug Interactions: Distribution

Many drugs are highly bound to plasma proteins. Concurrent administration of more than one drug capable of binding to the same protein site may cause a transient increase in the free (unbound) concentration of the dis-

*These tables are NOT exhaustive, but include many common interactions of clinical significance.

TABLE 20-8

Significant Drug Interactions Involving Drug Absorption

Precipitant drugs	Object drugs	Possible result
Iron salts, antacids, calcium, magnesium, or aluminum salts, zinc, sucralfate (Carafate)	Ciprofloxacin (Cipro)	Decreased ciprofloxacin levels and efficacy
Psyllium (Metamucil), antacids, kaolin/pectin (Kaopectate), cholestyramine (Questran)	Digoxin (Lanoxin)	Decreased digoxin levels and efficacy
Antacids, H2 antagonists (Tagamet, Zantac, Pepcid, Axid), omeprazole (Prilosec)	Ketoconazole (Nizoral)	Decreased ketoconazole levels and efficacy
Cholestyramine (Questran)	Warfarin (Coumadin)	Decreased prothrombin time (PT), decreased international normalized ratio (INR)*, and decreased anticoagulation effect
Antacids, iron salts, calcium	Tetracyclines	Decreased tetracycline levels and efficacy

*INR = observed prothrombin ratio^{ISI}

ISI = index of sensitivity for thromboplastin reagent used for the test

TABLE 20-9

Significant Drug Interactions Involving Protein Displacement

Precipitant drugs	Object drugs	Possible result
Salicylates (aspirin, Trilisate)	Oral hypoglycemics	Hypoglycemia
Sulfa antibiotics (Bactrim or Septra)	Warfarin	Increased PTs and INRs, increased anticoagulant effect

TABLE 20-10

Significant Drug Interactions Involving Inhibition of Liver Metabolism

Precipitant drugs	Object drugs	Possible result
Fluoxetine (Prozac)	Tricyclic antidepressants	Increased antidepressant levels and toxicity
Fluconazole (Diflucan), ketoconazole (Nizoral), itraconazole (Sporanox), fluoxetine, omeprazole, cimetidine, ranitidine, sulfa antibiotics, phenylbutazone (Butazolidin)	Anticonvulsants (phenytoin [Dilantin]), Barbiturates, carbamazepine (Tegretol)	Increased anticonvulsant levels and toxicity
Erythromycin, fluconazole, itraconazole, ketoconazole	Nonsedating Antihistamines: astimazole (Hismanal), terfenadine (Seldane)	*Concurrent use contraindicated;* Increased antihistamine levels and cardiotoxicity; (Ventricular tachycardia, torsades de pointes, potentially *fatal*)
Quinidine, verapamil (Calan, Isoptin), amiodarone (Cordarone)	Digoxin (Lanoxin)	Increased digoxin levels and toxicity
Sulfa antibiotics, metronidazole (Flagyl), chloramphenicol, fluoxetine, fluconazole, ketoconazole, itraconazole	Oral hypoglycemics	Increased incidence of hypoglycemia
Ciprofloxacin (Cipro), clarithromycin (Biaxin), cimetidine, ranitidine, erythromcyin	Theophylline (Theodur)	Increased theophylline levels and toxicity
Metronidazole, fluconazole, cimetidine, ranitidine, sulfa antibiotics, erythromycin, amiodarone, chloramphenicol, phenylbutazone, omeprazole	Warfarin (Coumadin)	Increased PTs and anticoagulation effect

TABLE 20-11

Significant Drug Interactions Involving Induction of Liver Metabolism

Precipitant drugs	Object drugs	Possible result
Anticonvulsants, cigarette smoke	Theophylline	Decreased theophylline levels and efficacy
Rifampin, anticonvulsants	Coumadin	Decreased PTs and INRs, and decreased anticoagulation effect
Rifampin, anticonvulsants	Anticonvulsants	Decreased anticonvulsant levels and efficacy
Rifampin, anticonvulsants	Oral hypoglycemics	Decreased efficacy of the oral agent; hyperglycemia

TABLE 20-12

Significant Drug Interactions Involving Decreased Renal Excretion

Precipitant drugs	Object drugs	Possible result
Quinidine	Digoxin (Lanoxin)	Increased digoxin levels and toxicity
Probenecid (Benemid)	Penicillins/cephalosporins	Increased antibiotic levels
Nonsteroidal antiinflammatory agents (e.g., ibuprofen [Motrin], naproxen [Naprosyn])	Lithium	Increased lithium levels and toxicity
Thiazide and loop diuretics	Lithium	Increased lithium levels and toxicity

placed drug. Although this effect is usually immediate, it is not usually clinically significant. The serum concentration of the displaced drug usually reequilibrates with time since more free drug is available for metabolism, excretion, and redistribution into tissues.

Drug Interactions: Metabolism

The most common type of drug interaction involves inhibition of drug metabolism as a result of competitive binding of an inhibitor drug (precipitant) to hepatic cytochrome P-450, an enzyme in the microsomal enzyme oxidation system of the hepatocyte needed for drug metabolism. Since this same enzyme site is necessary for the metabolism of the object drug, the result is an increased serum concentration of the object drug. The onset of this effect usually occurs within the first one or two doses of the inhibitor drug, whereas peak effect may not be seen until a new steady state concentration is achieved. This depends on the half-life of both the object and precipitant drug. The magnitude of this effect is *dose-dependent.* However, influences on hepatic metabolism cannot always be extrapolated across a similar class of drugs. For example, among the H2 antagonists, cimetidine (Tagamet) has the highest affinity for hepatic cytochrome P-450, ranitidine (Zantac) is intermediate, and both famotidine (Pepcid) and nizatidine (Axid) have negligible binding. Awareness of these differences should guide the prescriber in drug or dose selection when attempting to minimize drug interactions in clients at risk. A potentially life-threatening interaction may occur when the nonsedating antihistamines astimazole (Hismanol) and terfenadine (Seldane) are used concurrently with erythromycin or with triazole or imidazole antifungals. Alternative antihistamines, antibiotics or antifungals should be chosen to avoid serious cardiac toxicity. The nurse should be aware of these interactions, monitor clients for adverse effects as a result of increased drug concentrations, and notify the prescriber if adjustments are needed.

Hepatic enzyme induction also influences drug metabolism. This involves a precipitant drug *increasing* the rate of metabolism of an object drug by increasing the synthesis of hepatic enzymes. The result is a decrease in serum concentration and desired effect of the object drug. Although this effect has a gradual onset, maximal effect may be delayed for up to 3 weeks. Reversal of this effect after discontinuation of the precipitant drug may be more prolonged, especially with drugs having long half-lives. Careful attention to dose adjustments, guided by serum drug concentrations if available, are needed during this period. The nurse should monitor the client for expected therapeutic effects and notify the prescriber if client response is diminished because of this interaction.

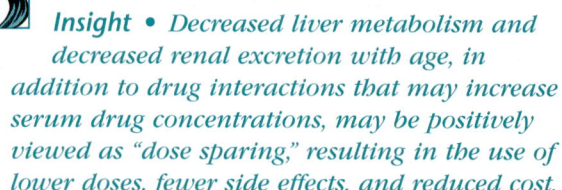

Insight • *Decreased liver metabolism and decreased renal excretion with age, in addition to drug interactions that may increase serum drug concentrations, may be positively viewed as "dose sparing," resulting in the use of lower doses, fewer side effects, and reduced cost.*

Drug Interactions: Renal Excretion

One drug may increase or decrease the renal elimination of another by affecting renal tubular transport or inhibiting renal prostaglandin synthesis. This may result in increased serum concentrations. This effect occurs rapidly by the time maximum serum concentrations of the precipitant drug are attained. The nurse should monitor clients for adverse effects as a result of increased drug concentrations and notify the prescriber if adjustments are needed.

Pharmacodynamic Drug Interactions

Medications often interact by antagonizing or augmenting the pharmacologic or toxic effects of either drug. For example, drugs with anticholinergic or sedative activity, such as tricyclic antidepressants and antihistamines, would expect to have additive adverse effects, such as lethargy, urinary retention, or dry mouth. Alternatively, antagonism of the desired anticoagulation response occurs if vitamin K is administered to a client on warfarin.

To assist the practitioner in screening for drug interactions, a number of excellent references is available. *Drug Interaction Facts* has the advantage of quarterly updates, affordability, and user-friendly monographs that include significance ratings, proposed mechanism for the interactions, management and discussion sections, an evaluation of the quality of published literature on the interaction, and references (Tatro, 1993). A variety of computer software programs are also available that can quickly automate the task of identifying multiple drug interactions (Fox, 1991). Pharmacists use computer programs to screen a client's medications before filling a prescription and can offer alternatives if a significant drug interaction is detected. The nurse should consult the pharmacist, a valuable team member, to avoid drug interactions when new medications are started or if adverse effects from a drug interaction are suspected. The nurse should also consult the pharmacist in screening clients started on potentially interacting medications.

MEDICATIONS AND QUALITY OF LIFE

Traditionally, outcomes such as disease cure or reduction in surrogate endpoints, such as blood pressure, have been viewed as measurements of success when prescribing medications. However, these outcomes may not reflect influences of pharmacotherapy on a client's quality of life. Increasing emphasis is being placed on achieving client-centered goals as indicators of success. However, enabling clients to achieve a more "effective" life and preserve functioning and well-being has been difficult to measure because of the lack of reliable data collection tools. One recently developed for use in clinical practice and research is the Medical Outcome Study (MOS) 36-Item Health Survey (SF-36) (Ware, Sherbourne, 1992) (Box 20-3). This survey can be completed by the

BOX 20-3

SF-36 Questions*

1. In general, would you say your health is:
2. *Compared to 1 year ago,* how would you rate your health in general *now?*
3. The following items are about activities you might do during a typical day. Does *your health now limit you* in these activities? If so, how much?
   A. *Vigorous activities* such as running, lifting heavy objects, participating in strenuous sports
   B. *Moderate activities* such as moving a table, pushing a vacuum cleaner, bowling, or playing golf
   C. Lifting or carrying groceries
   D. Climbing *several* flights of stairs
   E. Climbing *one* flight of stairs
   F. Bending, kneeling, or stooping
   G. Walking *more than a mile*
   H. Walking *several blocks*
   I. Walking *one block*
   J. Bathing or dressing yourself
4. During the *past 4 weeks,* have you had any of the following problems with your work or other regular daily activities *as a result of your physical health?*
   A. Cut down the *amount of time* you spent on work or other activities.
   B. *Accomplished less* than you would like
   C. Were limited in the *kind* of work or other activities
   D. Had *difficulty* performing the work or other activities (e.g., it took extra effort)
5. During the *past 4 weeks,* have you had any of the following problems with your work or other regular daily activities *as a result of any emotional problems* (e.g., feeling depressed or anxious)?
   A. Cut down the *amount of time* you spent on work or other activities
   B. *Accomplished less* than you would like
   C. Didn't do work or other activities as *carefully* as usual
6. During the *past 4 weeks,* to what extent has your physical health or emotional problems interfered with your normal social activities with family, friends, neighbors, or groups?
7. How much *bodily* pain have you had during the *past 4 weeks?*
8. During the *past 4 weeks,* how much did *pain* interfere with your normal work (including both work outside the home and housework)?
9. These questions are about how you feel and how things have been with you *during the past 4 weeks.* For each question, please give the one answer that comes closest to the way you have been feeling. How much of the time during the *past 4 weeks:*
   A. Did you feel full of pep?
   B. Have you been a very nervous person?
   C. Have you felt so down in the dumps that nothing could cheer you up?
   D. Have you felt calm and peaceful?
   E. Did you have a lot of energy?
   F. Have you felt downhearted and blue?
   G. Did you feel worn out?
   H. Have you been a happy person?
   I. Did you feel tired?
10. During the *past 4 weeks,* how much of the time has your *physical health or emotional problems* interfered with your social activities (like visiting with friends, relatives, etc.)?
11. How TRUE or FALSE is *each* of the following statements for you?
   A. I seem to get sick a little easier than other people
   B. I am as healthy as anybody I know
   C. I expect my health to get worse
   D. My health is excellent

SF-36 response choices*

1. Excellent, Very Good, Good, Fair, Poor
2. Much better now than 1 year ago, Somewhat better now than one year ago, About the same as 1 year ago. Somewhat worse now than 1 year ago, Much worse than 1 year ago
3. Yes, Limited a lot; Yes, Limited a little; No, Not limited at all
4. A-D. Yes, No
5. A-C. Yes, No
6. Not at all, slightly, moderately, quite a bit, extremely
7. None, very mild, mild, moderate, severe, very severe
8. Not at all, a little bit, moderately, quite a bit, extremely
9. All of the time, most of the time, a good bit of the time, some of the time, a little of the time, none of the time
10. All of the time, most of the time, some of the time, a little of the time, none of the time
11. Definitely true, mostly true, do not know, mostly false, definitely false

From Ware JE Jr, Sherbourne CD: The MOS 36-item short-form health survey (SF-36), *Med Care* 30(6):473-483, 1992.

TABLE 20-13

Effect of Antihypertensive Therapy on Well-being*

Domain	Placebo	Hydrochlorothiazide	Propranolol†	Enalapril†
Pain	32.7 (1)	33.1 (1)	32.7 (1)	33.1 (1)
Physical mobility	33.0 (3)	31.7 (3)	42.9 (4)	33.6 (3)
Sleep	127.9 (6)	193.0 (5)	244.0 (7)	167.8 (4)
Emotional reaction	20.2 (1)	27.3 (2)	101.2 (4)	9.8 (1)
Social isolation	0	0	16.0 (1)	0
Energy	100.0 (1)	24.0 (1)	239.2 (3)	24.0 (1)

*Data reported as the total aggregated score (number of clients with complaints) in each domain on part I of the Nottingham health profile. Scores were determined at the end of each treatment period. Maximum possible score for 17 clients in each category is 1700.

†Propranolol and enalapril were significantly different ($p < 0.05$).

From McCorvey E et al: Effect of hydrochlorothiazide, enalapril, and propranolol on quality of life and cognitive and motor function in hypertensive patients, *Clin Pharm* 12(4):300-305, 1993, American Society of Hospital Pharmacists.

TABLE 20-14

Drug-Induced Impairment in Mental State

Type of impairment	Drugs
Metabolic alterations hyper- or hypoglycemia, electrolyte disturbances	Beta-blockers, corticosteroids, diuretics, sulfonylureas, diuretics
Cognitive impairment dementia, memory loss	Methyldopa, propranolol, hydrochlorothiazide, reserpine, neuroleptics, opiate narcotics, cimetidine, amantadine, benzodiazepines, anticonvulsants
Behavioral toxicity insomnia, nightmares, sedation, agitation, irritability, restlessness leading to: delirium, psychosis, hallucinations	Anticholinergics, cimetidine, ranitidine, digoxin, bromocriptine, amantadine, baclofen, levodopa, opiate narcotics, sympathomimetics, corticosteroids
Depression	Reserpine, methyldopa, beta-blockers, corticosteroids

From Owens NJ, Silliman RA, Fretwell MD: The relationship between comprehensive functional assessment and optimal pharmacotherapy in the older patient, *DICP* 23:847-854, 1989.

client or administered by a trained interviewer in person or by telephone. Information obtained from the client can help explain how pharmacologic management of certain conditions affects an older client's functional capacity. Activities of daily living (ADLs) functional scores provide a record of feeding, bathing, dressing, toileting, transfer ability, mobility, and continence (Abrams, Berkow, 1990). The Folstein Mini-Mental State Examination (MMSE) may provide clues for assessing the effect of pharmacotherapy on cognition, orientation, and memory (Abrams, Berkow, 1990) (see Chapter 4).

The antihypertensives are one class of drugs which have been studied for their effects on quality of life. McCorvey et al. (1993) examined the effects of hydrochlorothiazide, propranolol (Inderal) and enalapril (Vasotec) on cognitive and motor function and quality of life. The results suggest that effects on sleep and energy are more pronounced with propranolol than with enalapril (Table 20-13).

Medications from diverse categories may have detrimental effects on cognition, emotional status, ability to ambulate, continence, and maintenance of posture (Tables 20-14 through 20-17). Medications prescribed in certain settings, such as intensive care units, may cause or contribute to delirium (Box 20-4). Drug-induced pseudoparkinsonism or extrapyramidal side effects caused by dopamine-blocking drugs such as the antipsychotics, the promotility agent metoclopramide (Reglan), or the antiemetic prochlorperazine (Compazine) can significantly affect a client's functional status. These negative affects on the older client's quality of life must be carefully considered when selecting certain medications and dosages. In assessing the client, the nurse must consider whether or not functional or cognitive deficits or changes are related to drug therapy and discuss these concerns with the prescriber.

Commonly Used Medications: Comparative Issues

Psychotropics

Psychotropic medications, which include antipsychotics (neuroleptics or major tranquilizers), antidepressants,

TABLE 20-15

Medications Reportedly Associated With Depression

Cardiovascular drugs	Hormones	Psychotropics
Alpha-methyldopa Reserpine Propranolol Guanethidine Clonidine Thiazide diuretics Digitalis	Oral contraceptives ACTH (corticotropin) and glucocorticoids Anabolic steroids	Benzodiazepines Neuroleptics
Anticancer agents	**Antiinflammatory/antiinfective agents**	**Others**
Cycloserine	Nonsteroidal anti-inflammatory agents Ethambutol Disulfiram Sulfonamides Baclofen Metaclopramide	Cocaine (withdrawal) Amphetamines (withdrawal) L-dopa Cimetidine Ranitidine

NOTE: These medications have been reported to induce depression in some cases. Not everyone receiving one of these will necessarily be depressed. The cause of depression in a depressed person receiving treatment is not necessarily the medication. This list indicates some medications that should be evaluated as possible causes in depression in particular clients. The degree of certainty of a causal relationship is shown in parentheses for selected drugs.

Developed from Popkin MK: "Secondary" syndromes in DSM-IV: a review of the literature. In Frances AJ, Widiger T, editors: DSM-IV sourcebook. Washington, D.C., American Psychiatric Press; in press, Depression Guideline Panel: Depression in Primary Care, vols 1 and 2, *Clin Pract Guide* No 5, Rockville, Md., US Department of Health and Human Services, Public Health Service, Agency for Health Care Policy and Research, April 1993.

TABLE 20-16

Drug-Induced Impairments in Mobility

Type of impairment	Drugs
Supporting structure	
Arthralgias, myopathies	Corticosteroids, lithium
Osteoporosis, osteomalacia	Corticosteroids, phenytoin, heparin
Movement disorders	
Extrapyramidal symptoms (EPSs) tardive dyskinesia (TD)	Neuroleptics, metoclopramide, amoxapine, methyldopa
Balance	
Neuritis, neuropathies	Metronidazole, phenytoin
Tinnitus, vertigo	Aspirin, aminoglycosides, furosemide, ethacrynic acid
Hypotension	Beta-blockers, calcium channel blockers, neuroleptics, antidepressants, diuretics, vasodilators, benzodiazepines, levodopa, metoclopramide
Psychomotor retardation	Neuroleptics, benzodiazepines, antihistamines, antidepressants

From Owens NJ, Silliman RA, Fretwell MD: The relationship between comprehensive functional assessment and optimal pharmacotherapy in the older patient, *DICP* 23:847-854, 1989.

and sedative-hypnotics (anxiolytics) are the most commonly prescribed class of medications in older adult population (Cadieux, 1993). Psychotropics are likely to be prescribed for nursing home populations, since as many as 80% may be psychiatrically impaired. Estimates of the frequency of psychotropic use are as high as 92% of institutionalized older adults. Major psychiatric symptoms or disorders may affect 15% to 25% of clients age 65 or older. Some general problems observed in older adults include (1) overprescribing of anxiolytics and hypnotics, often at doses that are too high and for extended, rather than short-term periods; (2) underprescribing of antide-

TABLE 20-17

Drug-Induced Urinary Incontinence

Type of incontinence	Drugs
Overflow	
Urinary retention	Anticholinergic agents: benztropine Agents with anticholinergic effects: amitriptyline, imipramine, thioridazine, antihistamines, disopyramide Smooth muscle relaxants: nifedipine Alpha-agonists: phenylpropanolamine
Stress	Alpha-antagonists: prazosin
Urge	
Polyuria	Diuretics, lithium
Central inhibition	Neuroleptics
Secondary	
Oversedation	Benzodiazepines, sedatives, or hypnotics

From Owens NJ, Silliman RA, Fretwell MD: The relationship between comprehensive functional assessment and optimal pharmacotherapy in the older patient, *DICP* 23:847-854, 1989.

BOX 20-4

Drugs Commonly Used in the Intensive Care Unit That Have Been Reported to Cause Psychosis and Delirium

Acyclovir	Ketamine
Aminocaproic acid	Ketoconazole
Amphotericin B	Lidocaine
Anticonvulsants	Methyldopa
Anticholinergic agents	Metoclopramide
	Metronidazole
Antihistamines	Narcotic analgesics
Benzodiazepines	Nifedipine
Captopril	Nitroprusside sodium
Cephalosporins	NSAIDs
Cimetidine	Penicillin
Ciprofloxacin	Procainamide
Clonidine	Propranolol
Corticosteroids	Quinidine sulfate
Digitalis	Ranitidine
Imipenem-cilastatin	Theophylline
	Trimethoprim-sulfamethoxazole

From Fish DN: Treatment of delirium in the critically ill patient, *Clin Pharm* 10(6):456-466, 1991, American Society of Hospital Pharmacists.

pressants and maintenance of subtherapeutic doses that may cause side effects but may not provide maximum therapeutic benefit; and (3) both underprescribing and overprescribing of antipsychotics, potentially denying benefit to some and causing side effects without therapeutic benefit in others. Certainly these medications should only be prescribed after nonpharmacologic means have been tried, including behavioral modification, psychotherapy, relaxation therapy, supportive counseling, and lifestyle changes.

If psychotropics are considered, a few principles should be kept in mind. Anxiolytics or hypnotics should be prescribed only if symptoms are frequent or intense, aggravate underlying physical disorders, or significantly interfere with sleep, work, or interpersonal relationships.

In selecting an agent, it is preferred that benzodiazepine anxiolytics with long half-lives be avoided because of the likelihood of accumulation of the parent and active metabolite, and an association with an increased risk of falling and hip fracture (Ray, Griffin, Downey, 1989). The lowest dosage should be selected at the beginning of treatment, since older adults may be more sensitive to the effects of hypnotics such as triazolam (Halcion) on postural sway (Greenblatt et al, 1991; Robin et al, 1991). Clients' needs for anxiolytics or hypnotics should be periodically reevaluated, since only a small subset of clients are appropriate for chronic treatment. Table 20-18 compares the usual doses and likelihood of accumulation with sedative hypnotics.

The benzodiazepines offer the advantage of a wide margin of safety and few serious drug interactions. However, because they may impair memory, psychomotor performance, and balance, they should be used with great caution in older adults. Barbiturates are not recommended with older adults because of their narrow margin of safety, potential for significant drug interactions, and dependence liability. Although the antihistamines may be used at low doses as alternatives to the benzodiazepines, there are no adequately controlled long-term studies of their efficacy, and anticholinergic side effects such as dry mouth, blurred vision, urinary retention, and delirium may occur. Relatively new additions are the nonbenzodiazepines: the anxiolytic buspirone (Buspar) and the hypnotic zolpidem (Ambien). They may be pre-

TABLE 20-18

Anxiolytics and Hypnotics in Older Adults Comparative Table

Class	Age-related change in clearance	Onset (hrs)	Half-life (hrs)	Initial daily dose in older adults (mg)	Maximum daily dose (mg)
Benzodiazepines					
Long-acting	Yes (decrease)				
Diazepam (Valium)		0.5-2 (F)	20-80*	2-5	20
Chlorazepate (Tranxene)		1-2 (F)	30-100*	7.5-15	30
Chlordiazepoxide (Librium)		0.5-4 (I)	5-30*	5-20	30
Estazolam (Prosom) **H**†		2 (S)	10-24	1	2
Flurazepam (Dalmane) **H***		0.5-1 (metabolite) 1-3) (S)	0.5-3*	15	30
Halazepam (Paxipam)		1-3	14*	60	160
Prazepam (Centrax)		6 (S)	30-100*	20	60
Quazepam (Doral) **H**†		2 (S)	39*	7.5	15
Active desalkylated metabolite			40-280		
Intermediate	No				
Alprazolam (Xanax)		1-2 (I)	12-15	0.25-0.75	4
Lorazepam (Ativan)		1-6 (I)	10-20	0.5-2	10
Oxazepam (Serax)		2-4 (S)	5-20	10-30	60
Temazepam (Restoril) **H**†		2-4 (S)	9-12	15	30
Short-acting	Yes (decrease)				
Triazolam (Halcion) **H**†		0.5-2 (F)	2-6	0.125	0.25
Nonbenzodiazepines	No				
Buspirone (Buspar)		0.5-1.5 (F)	2-11	5-15	60
Zolpidem (Ambien) **H**†		0.5-1 (F)	1.7-2.5	2.5-5	20
Antihistamines					
Diphenhydramine (Benadryl)		2-3 (S)	3-9	25	100
Hydroxyzine (Vistaril; Atarax)		2-3 (S)	7-20	10-40	50-100
Others					
Chloral hydrate **H***		0.5 (F)	4-14	250-500	1000

F = Fast; I = Intermediate; S = Slow
*Has active desalkylated metabolite
†Hypnotic use only

ferred in older adults, since they are well tolerated; have a wide margin of safety; do not produce dependence or withdrawal; and are less likely to impair memory, cognition, or psychomotor performance.

Antidepressants should be considered for older clients having at least four of the following symptoms consistent with depression: (1) sleep disturbance, (2) appetite disturbance, (3) weight loss, (4) psychomotor retardation, (5) suicidal ideation, (6) poor concentration, (7) feelings of guilt, and (8) lack of interest in usual activities (Abrams, Berkow, 1990).

Selection of a particular agent is based on side effects profiles that differ among available agents (Table 20-19).

Antidepressants having a low anticholinergic and sedative profile and minimal potential for orthostatic hypotension are preferred in older clients. Nortriptyline is often the tricyclic of choice among traditional antidepressants, since it has shown less orthostatic hypotension and has a well-defined "therapeutic window" of desirable therapeutic serum concentrations that can guide the prescriber in dose adjustments. However, the traditional or first generation agents are often problematic because of their lack of receptor site specificity and resultant side effects. The newer serotonin selective reuptake inhibitors (SSRIs) are being considered as antidepressants of first choice in older adults because of their lack

TABLE 20-19

Considerations in Choice of Antidepressants in Older Adults

Medication	Daily dose range	Maximum daily dose	Side effects profile: Antimuscarinic	Sedative	Postural hypotension	Comments
Tertiary						
Amitriptyline (Elavil)	10-100	200	H	H	I-H	
Imipramine (Tofranil)	10-100	200	H	I	I-H	
Doxepin (Sinequan)	10-100	200	I	H	I-H	
Secondary						
Desipramine (Norpramin)	10-100	200	L	L	H	
Nortriptyline (Pamelor)	10-100	100	L-I	L	L-I	Therapeutic window
Protriptyline (Vivactil)	5-30	40	I-H	L	I	
Dibenzoxazepine						
Amoxapine (Asendin)	25-150	200	L-I	L-I	H	Antipsychotic properties
Tetracyclic						
Maprotiline (Ludiomil)	10-150	200	L-I	I-H	I	Caution in seizure clients
Triazolopyridine						
Trazodone (Desyrel)	25-300	300	L	I-H	L-I	Priapism
Bicyclic						
Fluoxetine (Prozac)	20-40	60	L	L	L	Dose-related effects: GI, nervousness, insomnia; concurrent monoamine oxidase inhibitors (MAOIs) contraindicated; half-life of active metabolite 6-15 days
Paroxetine (Paxil)	20-40	40	L	L	L	Similar to fluoxetine, no active metabolites, half-life 24 hrs
Setraline (Zoloft)	50-200	200	L	L	L	Similar to fluoxetine, half-life of metabolite: 2-4 days
Monocyclic						
Bupropion (Wellbutrin)	100-300	300	L	L	L	High doses cause decreased response; questionable increased seizure risk

Abbreviations: H = High; I = Intermediate; L = Low

of tricyclic-associated side effects. However, their profiles are more prominent for gastrointestinal disturbances and CNS arousal effects, although these are dose-related.

Antipsychotics should only be prescribed where valid and clear documentation of need exists. Nursing interventions to modify behavior and assessment of reversible or treatable causes of psychotic symptoms should *always* be initiated before adding antipsychotics with known toxicities. Appropriate indications for an-

TABLE 20-20

Recommendations for Use of Antipsychotics in Older Clients

		Side effects profile			
Medication	Geriatric dose range* (mg/day)	Orthostasis	Sedation	Antimuscarinic	Extrapyramidal
Phenothiazines					
Chlorpromazine (Thorazine)	20-200	H	H	I	I
Thioridazine (Mellaril)	20-200	I-H	H	H	L
Mesoridazine (Serentil)	10-100	I-H	H	I	L
Trifluoperazine (Stelazine)	1-20	L	L	L	H
Fluphenazine (Prolixin)	1-4	L	L	L	H
Other					
Haloperidol (Haldol)	0.5-4	L	L	L	H
Thiothixene (Navane)	1-10	L	L	L	H
Molindone (Moban)	5-20	L	L	L	H
Loxitane (Loxapine)	5-20	I	I	L	H

Abbreviations: H = high; I = intermediate; L = low
*May be exceeded for severe symptoms (short-term) and/or on an acute basis. Doses are generally one third to one half the dose recommended in younger clients.

tipsychotic prescription include schizophrenia, paranoid states, and symptoms of psychosis such as hallucinations and delusions. One author has suggested that, in accordance with OBRA guidelines, the presence of the following "3Ds" may justify antipsychotic use (Drinka, 1993): (1) Danger to the resident or others; (2) distress for the resident; and (3) dysfunction of the resident, including interference with basic nursing care.

Generally, the high-potency, low-dose drugs such as haloperidol (Haldol) are chosen because of their safer cardiovascular profile, lower adverse sedative and anticholinergic effects, and minimum orthostasis. However, even small doses of these drugs may cause excess sedation, which may impair function for days in sensitive older clients (Table 20-20).

These higher potency agents are more frequently associated with extrapyramidal side effects such as tremors, akinesia, akathisia, and rigidity. All the antipsychotics have been reported to cause TDs with chronic use of even small doses. The Abnormal Involuntary Movement Scale (AIMS) is useful for monitoring the presence of movement disorders in clients treated with antipsychotics (Box 20-5).

Cardiovascular Medications

The most commonly prescribed class of medications for older adults are the cardiovascular agents. Although the familiar diuretics or centrally-acting agents such as methyldopa (Aldomet) still have a place in treatment of cardiac conditions, a wide variety of new agents may provide beneficial alternatives to older medications. The three main categories of newer agents—the **angiotensin-converting enzyme inhibitors (ACEIs), beta-blockers,** and **calcium channel antagonists**—have properties that may offer some advantages to the older client.

The ACEIs are prescribed for hypertension or congestive heart failure (CHF). Two ACEIs—enalapril (Vasotec) and captopril (Capoten)—have recently been approved for use in post-myocardial infarction (MI) clients to prevent ventricular dilatation. They are a significant advance in the treatment of CHF, demonstrating an increase in quality of life, decrease in hospitalization rates, regression of left ventricular hypertrophy and improved life expectancy. As a class, the ACEIs are generally well tolerated in older adults and have few adverse metabolic effects on uric acid, glucose, lipids, and electrolytes when compared with diuretics. The ACEIs work by blocking the enzyme that converts angiotensin I to angiotensin II, a potent vasoconstrictor and stimulus for adrenal cortical aldosterone release. As a result, blood pressure, sodium retention, and plasma volume are all decreased. Comparative information is listed in Table 20-21.

The beta-blockers are indicated for treatment of hypertension, coronary artery disease, and arrhythmias. These drugs work by decreasing contractility, myocardial oxygen demand, arterial pressure, and heart rate. However, the variety of beta-blockers available have differential effects on blockade of β_{-1} (heart) and β_{-2} (lungs, peripheral vascular and other noncardiac sites) receptors, partial beta-agonist activity (intrinsic sympathomimetic activity [ISA]), lipid solubility, metabolic clearance, route of excretion, and ability to also block alpha-receptors (Table 20-22).

Although the fifth report of the Joint National Committee in Detection, Evaluation and Treatment of Hyper-

BOX 20-5

Modified Abnormal Involuntary Movement Scale (AIMS)

Instructions	Complete examination procedure before making ratings. For movement ratings, rate highest severity observed.	Code: 0 = None 1 = Minimal, may be extreme normal 2 = Mild 3 = Moderate 4 = Severe					
		(Circle one)					
Facial and oral movements	1. Muscles of facial expression (e.g., movements of forehead, eyebrows, periorbital area); include frowning, blinking, grimacing of upper face	0	1	2	3	4	
	2. Lips and perioral area (e.g., puckering, pouting, smacking)	0	1	2	3	4	
	3. Jaw (e.g., biting, clenching, chewing, mouth opening, lateral movement)	0	1	2	3	4	
	4. Tongue (Rate only increase in movement both in and out of mouth, *not* inability to sustain movement.)	0	1	2	3	4	
Extremity movements	5. Upper (arms, wrists, hands, fingers) (Include choreic movements [rapid, objectively purposeless, irregular, spontaneous] and athetoid movements [slow, irregular, complex, serpentine]. *Do not* include tremor [repetitive, regular, rhythmic].)	0	1	2	3	4	
	6. Lower (legs, knees, ankles, toes) (e.g., lateral knee movement, foot tapping, heel dropping, foot squirming, inversion, and eversion of foot)	0	1	2	3	4	
Trunk movements	7. Neck, shoulders, hips (e.g., rocking, twisting, squirming, pelvic gyrations). Include diaphragmatic movements.	0	1	2	3	4	
Global judgments	8. Severity of abnormal movements (Score based on highest single score on items 1-7 above.)	None, Normal					0
		Minimal					1
		Mild					2
		Moderate					3
		Severe					4
	9. Incapacitation as a result of abnormal movements	None, Normal					0
		Minimal					1
		Mild					2
		Moderate					3
		Severe					4
	10. Client's awareness of abnormal movements	No awareness					0
		Aware, no distress					1
		Aware, mild distress					2
		Aware, moderate distress					3
		Aware, severe distress					4
Dental status	11. Current problems with teeth and/or dentures	No					0
		Yes					1
	12. Does client usually wear dentures?	No					0
		Yes					1

From Munetz MR, Benjamin SB: How to examine patients using the abnormal involuntary movement scale, *Hosp Commun Psychiatry* 39(1):1172-1177, 1988.

TABLE 20-21

Comparative Table: ACEIs

Medication name	Advantages	Disadvantages	Cautions/side effects	Drug interactions	Administration issues
Benazepril (Lotensin); Enalapril (Vasotec); Lisinopril (Prinivil, Zestril); Ramipril (Altace); Quinapril (Accupril)	Once daily, long duration of action. No reflex tachycardia. Increase renal blood flow, may improve glomerular filtration rate (GFR) in client with mild renal impairment. Sexual dysfunction not prominent. Depression not prominent.	Decreased dose needed in renal impairment (Creatinine > 2.5-3); Enalapril is a **pro-drug,** requiring normal liver function for conversion to active enalaprilat, which has delayed peak effect (4-8 hrs).	*Hyperkalemia:* clients at risk—renal insufficiency, diabetic, dehydrated, receiving K+- sparing diuretics or K+ supplements; longer-acting agents. *Excessive hypotension:* dose-related; clients with volume or salt depletion are at high risk; sustained with long-acting agents. *Cough:* Dry, nonproductive (5%-20% of clients); may have to switch to different class. *Angioneurotic edema* (0.1%-0.2%): occurs within hours to 1 week; if laryngeal edema and shock, can be *fatal.* *Renal failure:* Clients with bilateral renal artery stenosis. *Skin rash:* dose dependent. *Taste disturbances*	*Diuretics, other antihypertensives;* additive hypotensive effects. *K+ sparing or K+ supplements.* *Benemid:* Can decrease tubular secretion and increase levels of ACEIs. *NSAIDs:* may decrease hypotensive response to ACEIs. Antacids	Best to take on *empty* stomach; Capoten, Accupril. May take with or without meals: Lotensin, Vasotec, Monopril, Prinivil/Zestril, Altace.
Fosinopril (Monopril)	No dose adjustment needed in renal failure; see 1-5 above	Slow onset	See above	See above	
Captopril (Capoten)	Onset 0.5-1 hour; see 2-5 above.	TID dosing	See above	See above	

Data compiled from Raia JJ et al: Angiotensin-converting enzyme inhibitors: a comparative review, *DICP Ann Pharmacother* 24:506-525, 1990; Little to choose between ACE inhibitors, *Drug Therap Perspect* 1(9):May 24, 1993; *Drug facts and comparisons,* St Louis, 1993, Facts and Comparisons, Inc.; Burris JF: Management of complicated hypertension, *Geriatr Med Today* 10(5):31-44, 1991; Lam YWF, Shephard AMM: Drug interactions in hypertensive patients: pharmacokinetic, pharmacodynamic and genetic considerations, *Clin Pharmacokin* 18(4):295-317, 1990.

TABLE 20-22

Comparative Table: Beta-blockers

Medication name	Advantages	Disadvantages	Cautions/side effects	Administration issues
Intrinsic Sympathomimetic Agents (ISA): Pindolol (Visken)*† Acebutolol (Sectral)* Penbutolol (Levatol) Carteolol (Cartrol)†	May be preferred in clients with peripheral vascular disease (PVD), left ventricular (LV) dysfunction, bradycardia, exercise intolerance, diabetes, pulmonary disease	Loss of antihypertensive efficacy at higher doses because of increased β_1 stimulation	Similar to other beta-blockers but to lesser degree	May take without regard to meals
β_1 selective: Atenolol (Tenormin)† Metoprolol (Lopressor) Acebutolol (Sectral)* Betaxolol (Kerlone)*	May be preferred in clients with cold extremities who are receiving nonselective agents, clients with lipid disorders, or PVD	Must keep dose of atenolol or metoprolol < 100 mg daily to retain β_1 selectivity Caution in clients with asthma, chronic obstructive pulmonary disease (COPD), diabetes Avoid atenolol if preexisting renal failure	Bradycardia Conduction abnormalities LV failure/CHF Shortness of breath, fatigue	May take without regard to meals
Nonselective for β_1: Nadolol (Corgard)† Propranolol (Inderal)* Timolol (Blocadren) Labetolol (Normodyne/Trandate) Carteolol (Cartrol)† Penbutolol (Levatol) Pindolol (Visken)*† Sotalol (Betapace)†	Propranolol and timolol: improve survival in post MI clients	May worsen PVD, LV dysfunction Central nervous system side effects (depression) Decreases GFR Avoid nadolol if preexisting renal function	As above; in addition: cold extremities, bronchospasm; Propranolol: drowsiness, fatigue, depression.	May take without regard to meals
Concomitant alpha-blockers: Labetolol (Normodyne/Trandate)	Useful for hypertensive emergencies The only beta-blocker found effective as monotherapy in older adults No effects on GFR, effective in concomitant renal disease May speed left ventricular hypertrophy (LVH) regression Preferred if PVD, pulmonary disease, bradycardia, lipid disorder No change in cardiac output		Orthostatic hypotension (dose-related); others as above, but to lesser degree	May take without regard to meals

*Membrane stabilizing.

†May need dose adjustment if renal failure.

Modified from *Drug facts and comparisons,* St Louis, 1993, Facts and Comparisons, Inc.; Schulman SP et al: The effects of antihypertensive therapy on left ventricular mass in elderly patients, *N Engl J Med* 322(19):1350-1356, 1990; Wallin JD, Shah SV: Beta-adrenergic blocking agents in the treatment of hypertension. Choices based on pharmacologic properties and patient characteristics, *Arch Intern Med* 147(4):654-659, 1987.

tension advocates the use of beta-blockers and diuretics as first-line monotherapy, beta-blockers, which may increase peripheral vascular resistance, increase bronchoconstriction, decrease cardiac output and reduce renal blood flow are not generally preferred in older clients with peripheral vascular disease, CHF, renal dysfunction, or lung disease.

Alternatively, beta-blockers with ISA cause less marked changes in cardiac output, pulse rate, and peripheral vascular resistance. Beta-blockers, which also block α receptors (labetolol) lessen the effects of peripheral blockade on many organ systems.

The calcium channel antagonists are used for treatment of hypertension, coronary artery disease, and arrhythmias. These agents block calcium influx into cardiac and vascular smooth muscle, thereby reducing contractile force and causing vasodilation. In addition, by blocking calcium influx into the sinoatrial (SA) or atrioventricular (AV) nodes of the heart, they decrease heart rate.

Older clients generally tolerate these agents well, since they are spared the metabolic abnormalities commonly seen with diuretics. Lower doses are often effective in older adults because of a decrease in first-pass hepatic metabolism, which results in increased serum concentrations. The Type 1 agents are more prominent on slowing AV conduction, whereas the Type 2 agents are potent vasodilators, resulting in different side effects profiles (Table 20-23).

Nonprescription Agents

The rate of growth in OTC or nonprescription medications is accelerating and is expected to grow by $4 to $5 billion in annual sales by 1997 (Covington, 1993). From

TABLE 20-23

Comparative Table: Calcium Channel Antagonists

Medication name	Advantages	Disadvantages	Cautions/side effects	Administration issues
Type 1 agents (Slow AV conduction, relax vascular smooth muscle) Diltiazem (Cardizem) Verapamil (Calan)	Better tolerated than Type 2 agents; useful for atrial and supraventricular arrhythmias	May worsen bradycardia, heart block, CHF	Combination with beta-blocker can worsen LV dysfunction, bradycardia Combination with digoxin causes increased digoxin levels Verapamil: may cause constipation Combination with beta-blockers may cause conduction disturbance, CHF	Diltiazem: plain tabs (best on empty stomach); Cardizem SR: best on emtpy stomach; Cardizem controlled delivery (CD) caps: with or without food; Verapamil: plain tabs with or without food; Verapamil SR: *with* food.
Type 2 agents *Potent vasodilators:* Nifedipine (Procardia) Nicardipine (Cardene) Amlodipine (Norvasc) Felodipine (Plendil) Isradipine (Dynacirc)	Preferred with conduction disturbances or severe LV dysfunction; Amlodipine has long duration of action	May worsen angina with reflex tachycardia	Reflex tachycardia, weight gain, peripheral edema, headache, dizziness, flushing; use of sustained release (SR) dosage or administration with food can decrease these side effects†	May take without regard to meals
Type 4 agents Bepridil (Vascor)	Long duration of action	*Proarrythmic potential:* reserve for clients with refractory angina	Older adults at highest risk for Torsade de Pointes, use *low* doses; Bepridil can increase digoxin levels.	May take without regard to meals

Data compiled from *Drug facts and comparisons*, St. Louis, 1993, Facts and Comparisons, Inc.; Burris JF: Management of complicated hypertension, *Geriatr Med Tod* 10(5) : 31-44, 1991; Lam YWF, Shephard AMN: Drug interactions in hypertensive patients: pharmacokinetic, pharmacodynamic and genetic considerations, *Clin Pharmacokin* 18(4): 295-317, 1990.

a health economics perspective, this is viewed as a positive trend. The switch of prescription drugs to OTC status proposes to save on physician visits and expenditures by the managed care industry, since OTCs are not usually a covered benefit. For example, the switch of 0.25% and 0.5% hydrocortisone ointment and cream from prescription to OTC status was estimated to save $300 million per year. In addition, these changes are consistent with the trend toward "lifestyle medicine" as a result of an increasingly informed public that wants more control and ownership over its health care. A wide variety of agents, including the H2 antagonists and many of the NSAIDs, are likely to be switched from prescription to OTC status (Covington, 1993; McCarthy, 1993).

Although consumers may look forward to these changes, health care practitioners may have to assume an increased educational role if clients are to avoid adverse effects or drug interactions from unmonitored access. The American Pharmaceutical Association has been encouraging the development of a "transition class" of drugs that would only be available from a pharmacist for a limited time (McCarthy, 1993). However, the FDA has not yet authorized this class of drugs.

CLIENT EDUCATION AND COMPLIANCE

Assessing Risk Factors for Noncompliance

Noncompliance may contribute significantly to increased morbidity in older clients. It is estimated that 125,000 deaths and 300,000 hospitalizations each year are results of noncompliance with cardiovascular drugs alone. Noncompliance with chronic disease management is evidenced by the fact that only 55% of tuberculosis clients, 48% of diabetics, 46% of asthmatics, and 42% of glaucoma clients use their medications properly (Lamy, 1992a).

Many factors may place older clients at risk for noncompliance. Living alone without social supports, especially if depression or cognitive impairment is present, may lead clients into a declining pattern of self-care. Visual or auditory impairments may distort the older client's perception of information given by a health care professional or may simply make the medication label itself hard to read and interpret.

The use of multiple health care providers and multiple pharmacies along with a large medication burden or complex medication regimens is a recipe for trouble. The increasing use of alcohol with advancing age may lead to noncompliance. Lack of knowledge about the purpose of a client's medications, instruction for use, and management of side effects contribute to compliance problems. Socioeconomic factors, such as inadequate insurance or high deductibles or copayments, may force clients to choose between housing, food, or medication. Certain dosage forms such as unpalatable bulk powders or large tablets may act as barriers to client compliance. The presence of arthritis may be painful and reduce dexterity necessary to open child-proof caps.

The interchangeability of trade and generic names is a common cause of client confusion. A pharmacy's substitution of one generic brand with another that is identical chemically but different in shape or color may increase the likelihood of medication error. The presence of learning barriers such as low literacy limits a client's ability to organize thoughts and perceptions concerning medication instructions (Hussey, 1991).

Strategies for Improving Compliance

A complete client assessment during an intake interview by the nurse is essential in determining the risk factors present in a particular client. The following key questions should be asked:

1. In the client's (or caregiver's) own words, what were the prescription and nonprescription medications and regimens used just before the office or hospital visit? Can office records, prescription vials, a written list from home, or pharmacy files be used to help verify this information?
2. Who prescribed the medications? When were they started? Were there any recent changes and why were these made?
3. Does the client understand the purpose of each medication and benefits to be gained?
4. Does the client know what side effects to expect? What would they do if they experienced one?
5. What should the client do if they miss a dose?
6. Does the client have any memory aids to assist them, for example, written list, medication calendar, pill box, etc.?
7. Does the client have any psychiatric diagnosis or symptoms that may affect learning and memory (obtained from client's chart)?
8. What is the client's living situation? Is the client taking the medications on their own or does someone assist?
9. How do they pay for their medication? If necessary, how much do they have to pay out of pocket per month? Do they sometimes need to stretch their medications because of expense?
10. What is their perception (for example, on a scale of one to five) of the value of medication? Do they feel better or worse, since it was started?

Once this assessment is completed, a number of approaches can be taken to improve compliance based on a client's unique risk profile. If information deficits are a problem, provide verbal education reinforced with writ-

TABLE 20-24

Your SAFE LIST for OTC Medicines

Your name: ______________________ Your doctor's name: ______________________

If you have:	Generally avoid OTC medicines containing:	Examples:	Because:	Safer alternatives:
Asthma/lung disease	Ephedrine Epinephrine Extra Theophylline Pseudoephedrine Caffeine	Bronkaid Primatene Bronkaid Sudafed NoDoz, Dewitt's Pills	May cause insomnia, nervousness, irregular heart beats, especially when taking prescsription asthma medicines	Ask your doctor
	Aspirin/salicylates (if you have aspirin allergy) NSAIDs (if you have aspirin allergy)	Ecotrin Nuprin	May have allergic reaction (wheezing, itching, hives, etc.)	Acetaminophen (Tylenol)
Blood clots (and are taking blood thinners)	Aspirin/salicylates	Ecotrin, Vanquish, Alka Seltzer, Pepto-Bismol	May cause bleeding	Acetaminophen Kaopectate
	NSAIDs	Nuprin	May cause bleeding	
Heart problems (high blood pressure, heart failure, abnormal heart beats)	Sodium/salt Phenylpropranolamine Ephedrine Epinephrine Pseudoephedrine Caffeine	Alka-Seltzer, antacids Dexatrim Bronkaid Primatene Sudafed No-Doz	May worsen your condition	Acetaminophen, nasal sprays, nonmedicated throat lozenges
Diabetes	Liquid/syrups containing alcohol or sugar	Emetrol, many cough/cold syrups	May alter blood sugar	Sugar-free, sugarless, or alcohol-free liquids
	Phenylpropanolamine Ephedrine Epinephrine	Dexatrim Acutrim Bronkaid, Primatene	May increase blood sugar	Nonmedicated nose sprays, throat lozenges
	Aspirin/salicylates	Ecotrin, Pepto-Bismol	May decrease blood sugar if taking oral diabetes pills to lower sugar	Kaopectate, acetaminophen

These are general suggestions and should be discussed with your doctor. He or she may want to change this list or may add suggestions to fit your individual needs. *Always* read the label on nonprescription (OTC) medicines before purchasing and have a pharmacist assist you if you're not sure what choice to make.

Continued.

TABLE 20-24

Your SAFE LIST for OTC Medicines—cont'd

If you have:	Generally avoid OTC medicines containing:	Examples:	Because:	Safer alternatives:
Seizures	Aspirin/salicylates		May change levels of prescription seizure medicines	Acetaminophen
	Antihistamines (depressant medicine)	Benadryl, Unisom	May add to drowsiness caused by prescription seizure medicines	Ask your doctor
	Theophylline	Bronkaid	May change levels of prescription seizure medicine	
Stomach ulcers	Aspirin/salicylates	Ecotrin	May worsen your ulcers	Acetaminophen
	Non-steroidal antiinflammatory drugs	Nuprin		
	Theophylline	Bronkaid	May have more side effects from theophylline if on certain prescription ulcer medicines	Ask your doctor

ten instructions and allow time for client feedback. Maintain a log of these sessions along with current medications prescribed in an easily accessible part of the client's medical record. Reinforcement and review at subsequent visits strengthens the client's understanding and allow opportunity for clarification if needed. Encourage clients who "pharmacy shop" to have their prescriptions filled at the same pharmacy each time. Provide clients with cues to assist them in remembering to take medications, for example, when brushing teeth, removing glasses, or cleaning dentures. Tailor the medication regimen around the client's home schedule to cause the least disruption in their daily life and give them a sense of control over their medications. Simplify the regimen as much as possible, avoiding multiple daily doses where appropriate.

Test the client's functional ability to take the medication by ensuring that the client can actually read the prescription label, open and close the cap, remove a specified number of pills, recognize the color of the dosage form, and correctly interpret instructions (e.g., "If your doctor told you to take this three times a day, when would you take it?") Although this process may be time consuming initially, the investment should return itself in improved client understanding and compliance.

The "safe" OTC list Clients should be just as informed about their OTC medication selections as they are with their prescribed medications. Unfortunately, they often find themselves surrounded by a confusing array of nonprescription choices in the pharmacy. Even if the client requests help, the pharmacist may be unaware of certain aspects of a client's medical history that could significantly affect their recommendation. The ideal time to assist clients is while they are in the office and a health care provider familiar with their unique medical history can help make the best choice for them. A "safe list" for OTC product selection should be reviewed with the client before the office visit is completed (Table 20-24).

Strategies to Improve Prescribing of Medication

Success Stories

There are a number of recent examples of successful efforts to improve psychotropic prescribing in nursing homes. Rovner et al. (1992) had a pharmacy department conduct inservice educational programs for nurses and physicians to review proper indications for drug use, recognition of drug side effects and appropriate documentation. As a result, prescribing of neuroleptics decreased, prescribing of antidepressant increased, prescribing of benzodiazepine decreased, and the use of physical restraints decreased. Another group of investigators arranged interactive visits by clinical pharmacists with physicians whose prescribing of psychoactive drugs exceeded established threshold levels as determined by a geriatrician. In addition, since "academic detailing" to physicians alone was not felt to be completely effective, four training sessions were held at the nursing home with nurses and nursing assistants. Use of antipsychotics, long-acting benzodiazepines, and antihistamine hypnotics were significantly reduced without adverse effects on the functional level or overall behavior of the residents (Avon et al, 1992). Ray et al. (1993) took an even more comprehensive approach by not only actively educating physicians and nursing staff on prescribing of antipsychotics but also by developing a structured behavior management program and providing guidelines for gradual antipsychotic withdrawal. Antipsychotic use decreased by 72% versus 13% in control nursing homes, and days of physical restraint use decreased 36% in the education homes versus 5% in control homes (see Research box below). The common themes for these studies include active interpersonal educational sessions with both physicians and nursing staff, the use of guidelines to reinforce appropriate use, and education on alternatives to psychotropic use. These principles should provide a broad basis for attempts to improve prescribing in other classes of medications as well.

RESEARCH

Ray WA et al: Reducing antipsychotic drug use in nursing homes. A controlled trial of provider education, *Arch Intern Med* 153:713-21, 1993.

Sample, setting

The subjects included 194 older residents in two study (education) community nursing homes and 184 residents in two control nursing homes in Tennessee.

Methodology

A geropsychiatrist visited physicians caring for clients in the education nursing homes to provide education on the risks and benefits of antipsychotics and other psychotropics. A trained nurse educator conducted a series of inservices and follow-up sessions to nursing home staff to provide background on a comprehensive behavior management program, using case examples, role-playing, and problem-solving.

Findings

Provision of structured guidelines and active education in the study nursing homes resulted in a 72% reduction in antipsychotic use compared with a 13% decrease in the control nursing homes. Days of physical restraint decreased by 36% in study nursing homes compared with 5% in control nursing homes.

Implications

A comprehensive educational program in the nursing home can significantly reduce the inappropriate use of antipsychotics and restraints. Nurses can play a key educational role in use of psychotropics in the nursing home.

Questions to Ask in Assessing the Regimen

Nurses confronted with a complex medication regimen in an older client should determine the answers to the following questions:

1. Is there a documented and appropriate indication for the medication? For example, is an H2 antagonist prescribed in a client without peptic ulcer disease?
2. Is the dose appropriate for the client's age, weight, renal or liver function, etc? For example, is digoxin 0.25 mg daily acceptable in a cachectic 92-year-old woman with renal insufficiency?
3. Does the client have a documented drug allergy to a medication? For example, is a client allergic to penicillin and receiving ampicillin?
4. Is the dose being scheduled appropriately? For example, is furosemide (Lasix) being taken at 10 P.M. instead of 10 A.M.?
5. Is the duration of treatment appropriate? For example, is an antibiotic for an uncomplicated condition being prescribed for more than two weeks?
6. Is the medication chosen the best one (most effective with least side effects) for the client? For example, is amitriptyline (Elavil) initially prescribed for a depressed client with urinary retention?
7. Are two or more similar drugs prescribed (therapeutic duplication)? For example, an H2 antagonist with omeprazole (Prilosec)?
8. Is the client experiencing an adverse drug reaction? For example, is there a dramatic increase in blood urea nitrogen and creatinine in a client with congestive heart failure who is started on an NSAID?
9. Is there a drug-drug interaction? For example, is the client receiving both theophylline and full doses of cimetidine (Tagamet)?
10. Is there a medical indication for use of a medication but none is prescribed? For example, does the client have a vitamin B_{12} deficiency anemia but is not receiving B_{12}?
11. Is the client using over the counter medications inappropriately? For example, is the client on warfarin (Coumadin) and also taking a cough/cold combination containing aspirin?

Insight • Achieving a "perfect" medical outcome may not be in the best interest of older clients if their quality of life and function decline as a result of overly zealous pharmacologic management.

12. Is the client compliant? For example, are blood levels subtherapeutic at doses appropriate for the client's condition?

GENERAL PRESCRIBING PRINCIPLES

The MASTER Rules for Rational Drug Therapy

It may be helpful to remember this mnemonic when using medications in the older client:

- **M**inimize number of drugs used. Use the fewest number of drugs possible.
- **A**lternatives should be considered. Alternative therapy, drugs, and dosage forms should be considered for older adult clients.
- **S**tart low, and go slow. Start with lowest dosage and increase gradually.
- **T**itrate therapy. Adjust initial dosage according to individual characteristics and readjust dosage to optimize the monitored plasma levels and/or clinical response.
- **E**ducate the client. To increase compliance and to decrease side effects, instruct client or family about the need for and potential problems of therapy.
- **R**eview regularly. Monitor response regularly, and reevaluate need periodically.

HOME CARE TIPS

1. Assess during each home visit both the prescription and nonprescription medications being taken by the homebound older adult.
2. Document and notify primary physician of homebound older adult's medication regimen and of multiple physician sources.
3. Teach complications and interactions of all prescribed OTC medications to both the homebound older adult and caregiver.
4. Use social workers to identify community resources for financial assistance with pharmaceutical needs.
5. Use laboratory parameters to monitor overuse and underuse of medications, as well as interactive states of medications.
6. Monitor urinary output status, since changes in renal excretion may require a decrease or increase in drug dosage.
7. Assist the homebound older adult by setting up a daily or weekly supply of medications, using a method or tool that fosters safe, independent administration.
8. Reduce the chance of medication error by labeling and/or color coding medication bottles.
9. Keep an accurate record of the homebound older adult's weight, since many medication dosages are calculated by body weight.
10. Teach drug safety in the home environment:
    - Keep drugs in original, labeled container.
    - Dispose of outdated medications in a sink or toilet only, never in the trash within reach of children.
    - Never "share" drugs with a friend or family member.
    - Always finish a prescribed medication; do not save for a future illness.
    - Read labels carefully and follow all instructions.

Summary

A reduction in adverse events as a result of medications requires a knowledge of changes in drug distribution and response in normal and frail, chronically ill older adults. Health care professionals must accept this responsibility if improved client outcomes are to be realized.

Key Points

- The older adult consumes a large portion of pharmaceutical products: 25% to 30% of all prescription and 40% of all nonprescription medications.
- Antipsychotic agents and H2 antagonists are often overused in older adults, whereas antidepressants and pain medications are often underused.
- Older clients may be at risk for adverse drug reactions because of changes in drug disposition with age, multiple chronic illnesses, polypharmacy, dysfunctional prescribing, client demands and expectations, deficits in compliance and education, fragmentation of health care, as well as medication expense.
- Reduction of drug dosage is often required in the older client where renal or hepatic function and ability to eliminate medications is reduced.
- Knowledge of clinically important drug interactions is essential in planning alternate medication regimens and preventing potentially serious adverse drug events.
- Medications should always be suspects in clients experiencing overt or subtle changes in cognitive or physical function.

- Psychotropics should be used judiciously in older adults and agents with the lowest side effects profiles should be preferred.
- Newer cardiac medications may offer opportunities for an improved quality of life for older clients.
- The nurse can play a key role in assessing clients for risk factors that may reduce compliance and developing strategies to reduce or to eliminate these risks.
- Start low, go slow, and periodically review medication regimens!

Critical Thinking Exercises

1. An 82-year-old man with a history of CHF is taking a number of prescription medications including Metamucil, Lanoxin, Dilantin and Cimetidine. He is 5'9" tall and weighs 139 lbs. Based on potential drug interactions, identify relevant assessment priorities. What factors place this client at risk for drug toxicity?
2. A home care nurse is seeing an 81-year-old man who is on a complex medication regimen. He cannot remember when he last took several of his medications, and his wife states she is confused by the recent switch of several drugs to another generic brand. What questions should the nurse ask to establish the client's risk for noncompliance?

REFERENCES

Abrams WB, Berkow R: *The Merck manual of geriatrics,* Rahway, N.J., 1990, Merck.

Avon J et al: A randomized trial of a program to reduce the use of psychoactive drugs in nursing home, *N Engl J Med* 327:168-173, 1992.

Beers MH et al: Inappropriate medication prescribing in skilled nursing facilities, *Ann Intern Med* 117(8):684-689, 1992.

Beers MH, Ouslander JG: Risk factors in geriatric drug prescribing. A practical guide to avoiding problems, *Drugs* 37(1):105-112, 1989.

Bennett WM et al: *Drug prescribing in renal failure: dosing guidelines for adults,* ed 2, Philadelphia, Penn., 1991, American College of Physicians.

Bero LA, Lipton HL, Bird JA: Characterization of geriatric drug-related hospital readmissions, *Med Care* 29(10):989-1003, 1991.

Bradley JD et al: Comparison of an anti-inflammatory dose of ibuprofen, an analgesic dose of ibuprofen, and acetaminophen in the treatment of patients with osteoarthritis of the knee, *N Engl J Med* 325(2):87-91, 1991.

Cadieux RJ: Geriatric psychopharmacology, *Postgrad Med* 93(4):281-301, 1993.

Carbonin P et al: Is age an independent risk factor of adverse drug reactions in hospitalized medical patients? *J Am Geriatr Soc* 39:1093-1099, 1991.

Contemporary Senior Health, Spring 1990.

Covington TR: Trends in self-care: The Rx to OTC switch movement, *Drug Newslet* 12(2):15-16, February 1993.

Delafuente JC: Perspectives on geriatric pharmacotherapy, *Pharmacotherap* 11(3):222-224, 1991.

Depression Guideline Panel: Depression in Primary Care, vols 1 and 2, *Clin Pract Guide* No 5, Rockville, Md., US Department of Health and Human Services (DHHS), Public Health Service (PHS), Agency for Health Care Policy and Research (AHCPR), April 1993.

Diagnosis and treatment of depression in late life, *NIH Consensus Development Conference Consensus Statement* 9(3), Nov. 4-6, 1991.

Drinka P: OBRA-1987 nursing home regulations (letter), *J Am Geriatr Soc* 41(4):466, 1993.

Fox GN: Drug interactions software programs, *J Fam Pract* 33(3):273-280, 1991.

Fries JF et al: Nonsteroidal antiinflammatory drug-associated gastropathy: incidence and risk factor models, *Am J Med* 91(3):213-222, 1991.

Graham DY et al: Duodenal and gastric ulcer prevention with misoprostol in arthritis patients taking NSAIDs, *Ann Intern Med* 119(4):257-262, 1993.

Greenblatt DJ et al: Sensitivity to triazolam in the elderly, *N Engl J Med* 324(24):1691-1698, 1991.

Griffin MR et al: Nonsteroidal anti-inflammatory drug use and increased risk for peptic ulcer disease in elderly persons, *Ann Intern Med* 114(4):257-263, 1991.

Gurwitz JH, Avorn J: The ambiguous relation between aging and adverse drug reactions, *Ann Intern Med* 114(11):956-966, 1991.

Gurwitz JH, Noonan JP, Soumerai SB: Reducing the use of H2-receptor antagonists in the long-term-care setting, *J Am Geriatr Soc* 40(4):359-364, 1992.

Gurwitz JH et al: Aging and the anticoagulant response to warfarin therapy, *Ann Intern Med* 116(11):901-904, 1992.

Hussey LC: Overcoming the clinical barriers of low literacy and medication noncompliance among the elderly, *J Gerontolog Nurs* 17(3):27-29, 1991.

Jankel CA, Speedie SM: Detecting drug interactions: a review of the literature, *DICP Ann Pharmacotherap* 24:982-989, 1990.

Johnson JF, Cappuccio J: Risk factors associated with adverse drug reactions in elderly patients, *Pharmacotherp* 12(3):265, 1992 (abstract).

Lamy PP: The elderly, communications, and compliance, *Pharm Times* 33-49, August 1992a.

Lamy PP: Issues in geriatric research, *Welcome Trends Hosp Pharm* 2-4, September 1992b.

Lipton HL et al: The impact of clinical pharmacists consultations on physicians' geriatric drug prescribing, *Med Care* 30(7):646-658, 1992.

Marzinski L: The tragedy of dementia: Clinically assessing pain in the confused, nonverbal elderly, *J Gerontolog Nurs* 17:25-28, 1991.

Mason BJ: Metoclopramide utilization review, *Q Rev Bul* 15(4):114-16, April 1989.

McCarthy R: Impact of OTC H2 antagonists on retail pharmacy, *Pharm Times* 62-71, May 1993.

McCorvey E et al: Effect of hydrochlorothiazide, enalapril, and propranolol on quality of life and cognitive and motor function in hypertensive patients, *Clin Pharm* 12(4):300-305, 1993.

McInnes GT, Brodie MJ: Drug interactions that matter: a critical reappraisal, *Drugs* 36:83-110, 1988.

Ray WA, Taylor JA, Meador KG: Reducing antipsychotic drug use in nursing homes. A controlled trial of provider education, *Arch Intern Med* 153:713-721, 1993.

Ray WA, Griffin MR, Downey W: Benzodiazepines of long and short elimination half-life and the risk of hip fracture, *JAMA* 262:3303-3307, 1989.

Reducing the costs of NSAID-induced gastropathy, *Drugs Therap Perspect* 1(12), July 5, 1993.

Roberts J, Turner N: Pharmacodynamic basis for altered drug action in the elderly, *Clin Geriatr Med* 4(1):127-149, 1988.

Robin DW et al: Dose-related effect of triazolam on postural sway, *Clin Pharmacol Ther* 49(5):581-588, 1991.

Rovner B et al: The impact of antipsychotic drug regulations on psychotropic prescribing practices in nursing homes, *Am J Psychiatry* 149(10):1390-1392, 1992.

Schneider JK, Mion LC, Frengley JD: Adverse drug reactions in an elderly outpatient population, *Am J Hosp Pharm* 49(1):90-96, 1992.

Sengstaken EA, King SA: The problems of pain and its detection among geriatric nursing home residents, *J Am Geriatr Soc* 41(5):541-544, 1993.

Shorr RI et al: Concurrent use of nonsteroidal anti-inflammatory drugs and oral anticoagulants places elderly persons at high risk for hemorrhagic peptic ulcer disease, *Arch Intern Med* 153(14):1665-1670, 1993.

Silver AJ et al: Effect of aging on body fat, *J Am Geriatr Soc* 41(3):211-213, 1993.

Tatro DS, editor: *Drug interaction facts,* St. Louis, 1993, Facts and Comparisons, Inc.

Urinary Incontinence Guideline Panel: Urinary incontinence in adults: quick reference guide for clinicians, *AHCPR,* Pub No 92-0041, Rockville, Md., US DHHS, PHS, AHCPR, March 1992.

Vestal RE: Clinical pharmacology. In Hazzard WR et al, editors: *Principles of geriatric medicine and gerontology,* ed 2, New York, 1990, McGraw-Hill.

Wall Street Journal, June 27, 1990.

Ware JE Jr, Sherbourne CD: The MOS 36-item short-form health survey (SF-36), *Med Care* 30(6):473-483, 1992.

Ware JE, Fries JF, Williams CA, Bloch DA: Nonsteroidal anti-inflammatory drug associated gastropathy: Incidence and risk factor models, *Am J Med* 91(3):213-222, 1991.

BIBLIOGRAPHY

Burris JF: Management of complicated hypertension, *Geriatr Med Tod* 10(5):31-44, 1991.

Classen DC et al: Computerized surveillance of adverse drug events in hospital patients, *JAMA* 266:2847-2851, 1991.

Cohen AF et al: Influence of gastric acidity on the bioavailability of digoxin, *Ann Intern Med* 115(7):540-545, 1991.

Fish DN: Treatment of delirium in the critically ill patient, *Clin Pharm* 10(6):456-466, 1991.

Force RW, Nahata MC: Effect of histamine H2-receptor antagonists on vitamin B12 absorption, *Ann Pharmacotherap* 26:1283-1286, 1992.

Lam YWF, Shephard AMM: Drug interactions in hypertensive patients: Pharmacokinetic, pharmacodynamic and genetic considerations, *Clin Pharmacokin* 18(4):295-317, 1990.

Little to choose between ACE inhibitors, *Drug Therap Perspect* 1(9):May 24, 1993.

Mayersohn MB: Special pharmacokinetic considerations in the elderly. In Evans WE, Schentag JJ, Jusko WJ, editors: *Applied pharmacokinetics: principles of therapeutic drug monitoring,* ed 3, Vancouver, Wash., 1992, Applied Therapeutics.

Munetz MR, Benjamin SB: How to examine patients using the abnormal involuntary movement scale, *Hosp Commun Psychiatry* 39(1):1172-1177, 1988.

Olin BR, editor: Drug facts and comparisons, St. Louis, 1993, Facts and Comparisons, Inc.

Owens NJ, Silliman RA, Fretwell MD: The relationship between comprehensive functional assessment and optimal pharmacotherapy in the older patient, *DICP* 23:847-854, 1989.

Raia JJ et al: Angiotensin-converting enzyme inhibitors: A comparative review, *DICP Ann Pharmacotherap* 24(5):506-525, 1990.

Russell RM: Changes in gastrointestinal function attributed to aging, *Am J Clin Nutr* 55(6):1203S-1207S, 1992.

Schulman SP et al: The effects of antihypertensive therapy on left ventricular mass in elderly patients, *N Eng J Med* 322(19):1350-1356, 1990.

Wallin JD, Shah SV: Beta-adrenergic blocking agents in the treatment of hypertension. Choices based on pharmacologic properties and patient characteristics, *Arch Intern Med* 147(4):654-659, 1987.

APPENDIX 20A
Additional Resources

List of Older Adult Resource Organizations

American Association of Retired Persons (AARP)
601 E Street
Washington, DC 20049
(202) 434-2277 or (703) 684-0244

Elder Health Program
University of Maryland School of Pharmacy
20 N. Pine St.
Baltimore, MD 21201
(410) 328-3243

National Council of Patient Information and Education
Washington, DC 20001
(202) 347-6711

National Institute on Aging
Building 31, Room 5C-3S
9000 Rockville Pike
Bethesda, MD 20892
(800) 992-0841

National Institute on Drug Abuse
National Clearinghouse for Alcohol and Drug Information
P.O. Box 2345
Rockville, MD 20852
(800) 729-6686

USP-Patient Drug Education
Order Processing Department 842
12601 Twinbrook Parkway
Rockville, MD 20852
(800) 227-8772

Agency for Health Care Policy and Research
For copies of clinical practice guidelines, call (800) 358-9295

This chapter is dedicated to my nursing colleagues who continue to teach me how to care for and about our older clients.

Part Six

Nursing Care of Physiologic and Psychologic Disorders

CHAPTER 21

Cardiovascular Function

LEARNING OBJECTIVES

On completion of this chapter, the reader will be able to:

1. Discuss the structure and function of the cardiovascular system.
2. Explain the age-related changes in the structure and function of the cardiovascular system.
3. Identify contributing risk factors for cardiovascular disease.
4. Explain pathophysiology and treatment regimen for cardiovascular conditions common in older adults.
5. List nursing interventions for the older client with cardiovascular conditions.
6. Implement the nursing process for older adults with cardiovascular conditions.

Cardiovascular disease (CVD) is the leading cause of mortality for both men and women in the United States and Canada. For those over age 65, 70% of all deaths are attributed to CVD (Canada Year Book, 1992; Gawlinski, Jensen, 1991; US Department of Commerce, 1992). CVD continues to be a major cause of illness, disability, and death despite the decline in mortality rates over recent decades (Canada Year Book, 1992; Heart & Stroke Foundation, 1991; US Department of Commerce, 1992); it is estimated that one in two adults over 65 years have heart disease (Gawlinski, Jensen, 1991). For men and women over the age of 65, mortality rates for CVD sharply increase, and it is anticipated that the actual number of deaths resulting from CVD will escalate as the proportion of the older population increases.

This chapter examines normal structure and function of the cardiovascular system, age-related changes, and common problems and conditions that affect older adults.

NORMAL STRUCTURE AND FUNCTION

The heart is a hollow, muscular organ, approximately the size of an adult fist, and is located in the mediastinal space of the thoracic cavity between the lungs. A pericardial sac surrounds the heart to protect the organ from trauma and infection. The visceral pericardium, or inner layer, adheres to the heart muscles, whereas the parietal pericardium, or outer layer, is attached to surrounding structures. The two pericardial layers are separated by a small amount of lubricating fluid to reduce friction between the pericardial surfaces during the pumping activities of the heart. The heart itself consists of three layers: (1) the endocardium (inner endothelial layer that lines the inner chambers of the heart and the four valves), (2) the myocardium (middle muscular layer), and (3) the epicardium (outer layer) of the heart. The myocardium is composed of striated muscle fibers and is responsible for the contractile force of the heart.

Within the heart are four chambers. The upper chambers, or atria, are separated from the bottom chambers, or ventricles, by a fibrous ring. Within this ring are the four heart valves. The interatrial septum divides the two ventricles. The right atria and ventricle propel venous blood into the pulmonic system. The left atria and ventricle pump oxygenated blood into the systemic circulation. Venous blood enters the right atrium via the superior and inferior vena cavae and the coronary sinus and flows into the right ventricle (mainly by gravity) when the tricuspid valve is open. The right ventricle pumps blood into the pulmonary system through the pulmonary artery. Oxygenated blood returns from the lungs into the left atrium via four pulmonary veins and enters the left ventricle (mainly by gravity) when the mitral valve is open. The left ventricle pumps its contents into the systemic circulation via the aorta. Both atria are thin-walled structures that serve as blood reservoirs for venous (right) and oxygenated (left) blood (Fig. 21-1).

With advancing age, the left atria enlarges to enhance ventricular filling. In most healthy older adults, a fourth audible heart sound can be heard as a result of atrial enlargement (Lakatta, 1993).

Both ventricles serve as pumping chambers and have thicker walls than the atria. The wall thickness of the right ventricle is one third the thickness of the left ventricle as the right side pumps blood into an area of low pressure, whereas the left side pumps blood into the systemic system, which is a high pressure system. Consequently, the workload of the right ventricle is less than that of the left ventricle.

The normal aging process affects the size and muscle layers of the heart. The overall size of the heart increases in mass with some estimates of 1 gm per year in men and 1.5 gms in women after the age of 30. There is also a corresponding increase in the ratio of heart weight to body weight (Lakatta, 1993). The increase in heart mass may be significantly higher in older adults with coronary heart disease or hypertension. In addition to the presence of disease, heart mass may be substantially altered by lifestyle behaviors.

In both genders, the intraventricular septal thickness increases with aging, and a moderate increase in left ventricular wall thickness appears to occur. These changes are as a result of an increase in the size of cardiac myocytes. These changes in structure create a stiffness in the ventricular walls, which impedes the heart's ability to contract and relax. In those individuals age 80 and over, the left ventricular mass may actually decrease; however, research in this age group is limited.

Valves

Four cardiac valves maintain the forward propulsion of blood through the chambers of the heart. The valves open and close passively in response to volume and pressure changes within the cardiac chambers. These valves consist of two types: atrioventricular (AV) valves and the semilunar valves.

The AV valves separate the atria from the ventricles. The tricuspid valve is composed of three delicate leaflets (cusps) and is located between the right atrium and right ventricle. The mitral or bicuspid valve consists of two leaflets and is located between the left atrium and left ventricle. The leaflets of both valves are attached to tough fibrous strands called **chordae tendineae,** which are extensions of the papillary muscle on the ventricular walls. The chordae tendineae support the valves during contraction of the ventricles to cause closure of the valves and prevent backflow (regurgitation) of blood into the atria from the ventricle when it contracts.

Both semilunar valves consist of three symmetrical cup-like cusps secured to a fibrous ring. The pulmonic valve is situated between the right ventricle and pulmonary artery, whereas the aortic valve is located between the left ventricle and aorta. Both valves prevent backflow from the pulmonary artery or aorta into the ventricle when it is relaxed.

Heart valves in the older adult may be thicker and stiffer as a result of lipid accumulation, collagen degeneration, and fibrosis. Systolic ejection murmurs may be a normal finding in the older adult.

Coronary Circulation

The sinuses of Valsalva are located immediately above the aortic valve and contain the openings to the coronary arteries. The coronary arteries supply blood to the heart muscle itself and fill during ventricular diastole when the aortic valve is closed. The diastolic blood pressure must be 60 mm Hg to maintain adequate blood flow through the coronary arteries or autoregulatory mechanism are activated to maintain blood flow to the myocardium.

Coronary circulation consists of the right coronary artery (RCA) and the left coronary artery (LCA). The LCA branches into the left anterior descending artery (LAD) and the left circumflex coronary artery (CCA). These ar-

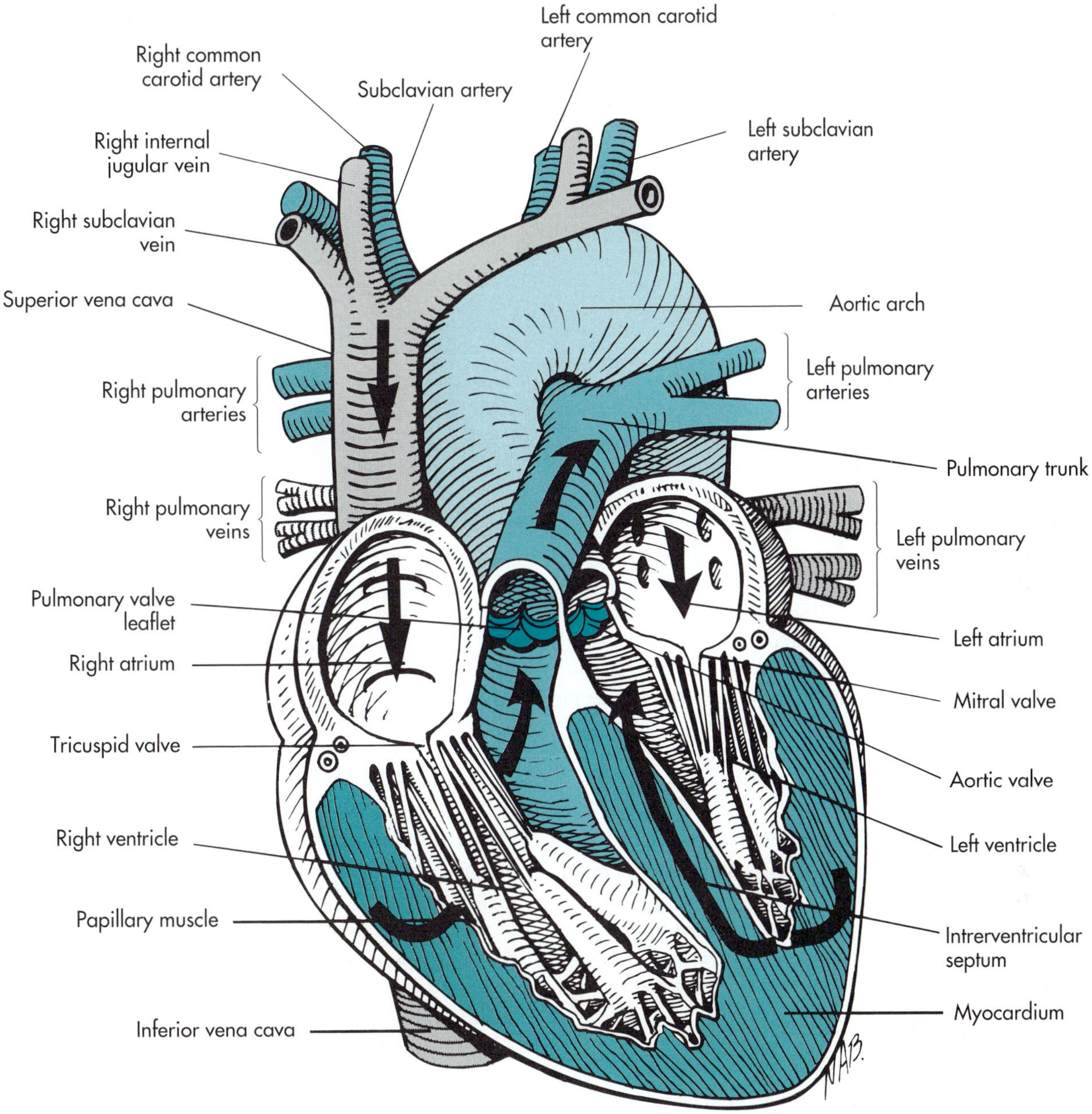

Fig. 21-1 Heart in frontal section; course of blood flow through the chambers. (From Phipps WJ et al: *Medical-surgical nursing: concepts and clinical practice,* ed 5, St. Louis, 1995, Mosby.)

teries flow around the heart and meet on the posterior surface of the heart known as the crux of the heart (Fig. 21-2).

The CCA supplies the left atrium and the lateral and posterior surfaces of the left ventricle. The RCA supplies the right atrium and ventricle as well as the inferior portion of the left ventricle. In most individuals, the sinoatrial (SA) node and AV node are supplied by the RCA; however, in some situations the CCA may be the supplier.

As a result of the anatomic and functional properties of the coronary arteries, injury to these vessels, such as ischemia or blockage, have significant clinical implications. Injury to the RCA is associated with conduction disturbances, whereas damage to the LAD impedes the pumping action of the left ventricle. Throughout the myocardium, peripheral branches of the coronary arteries anastomose. The smaller vessels can provide collateral circulation to deprived areas of myocardium if a major vessel becomes blocked.

The venous system of the heart has three subdivisions: (1) the thesbian veins, (2) the anterior cardiac veins, and (3) the coronary sinus on the posterior sur-

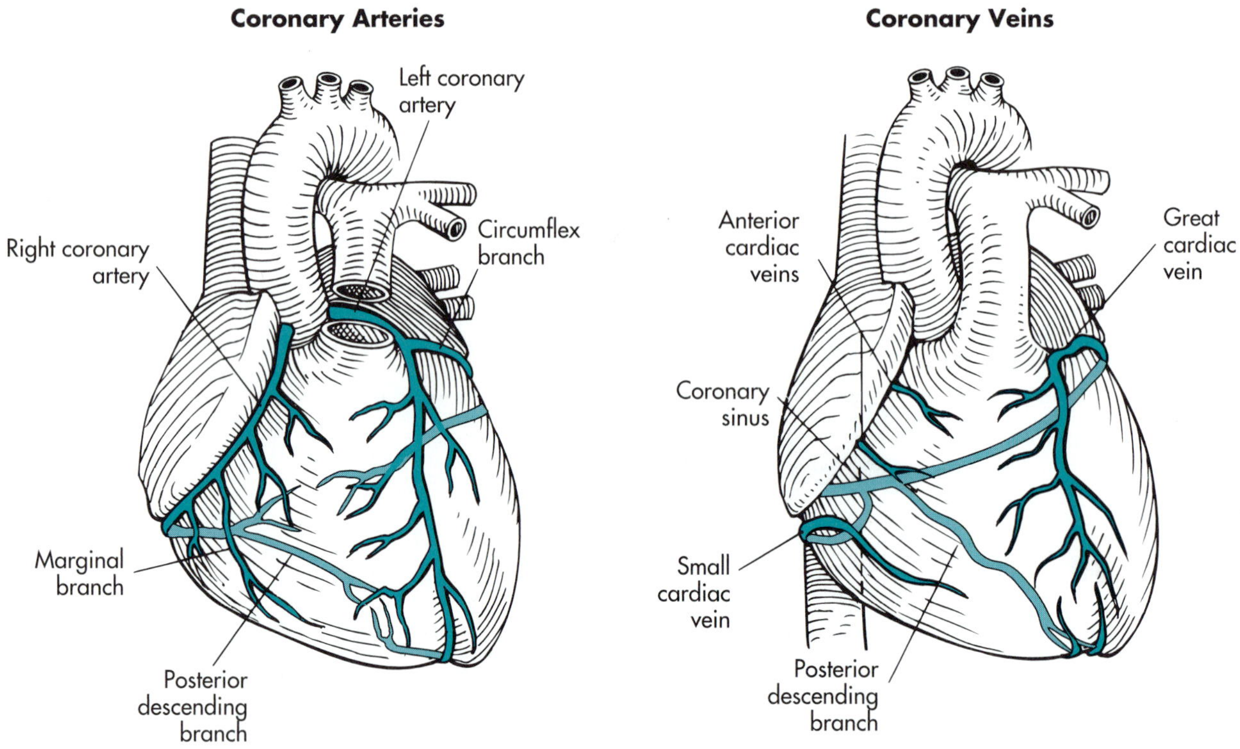

Fig. 21-2 Coronary blood vessels. (From Phipps WJ et al: *Medical-surgical nursing: concepts and clinical practice,* ed 5, St. Louis, 1995, Mosby.)

face of the heart where deoxygenated blood drains into the right atrium.

With advancing age, coronary arteries lose their elastic qualities and become thicker, which affects the distribution of coronary blood flow. More blood flows to venous vessels and sinusoids, and less blood flows to the coronary arteries. These arteries are smaller in size and are prone to the development of arteriosclerotic plaques in individuals with adverse lifestyle behaviors. Consequently, the heart of an older adult may be less able to meet body demands for increased oxygen. This generalized stiffness of the coronary arteries can be a result of natural aging or the high prevalence of atherosclerosis in older individuals; it is difficult to differentiate between the two causes.

Conduction System

Each cardiac cycle consists of a sequence of interdependent electrical and mechanical events. When electrical excitation (depolarization) spreads from the SA node through the conduction system to the myocardium, muscular contraction is stimulated. Depolarization is followed by repolarization or electrical recovery. The mechanical responses are systole (muscular contraction) and diastole (muscular relaxation).

Electrophysiologic Properties

Myocardial working cells (excitatory cells), which are located throughout the myocardium, and pacemaker cells in specialized tissue known as the cardiac conduction system, are two types of cardiac muscle cells. Pacemaker cells activate spontaneously, whereas myocardial working cells need a stimulus to start depolarization. The cardiac muscle cells that make up the conduction system are unique when compared with other cells of the body, because they possess the following properties:

1. **Automaticity**—The ability to spontaneously initiate impulses
2. **Excitability**—The ability to respond to a stimulus by generating a cardiac impulse (depolarization)
3. **Conductivity**—The ability to transmit an electrical impulse along cell membranes
4. **Contractility**—The ability of cardiac cells to respond to an impulse by contracting

These properties allow the heart to initiate spontaneous rhythmic impulses that are transmitted throughout the conduction system to excite the myocardium and stimulate muscular contraction.

The electrical activity of the heart is the result of changes in the permeability of cell membranes which

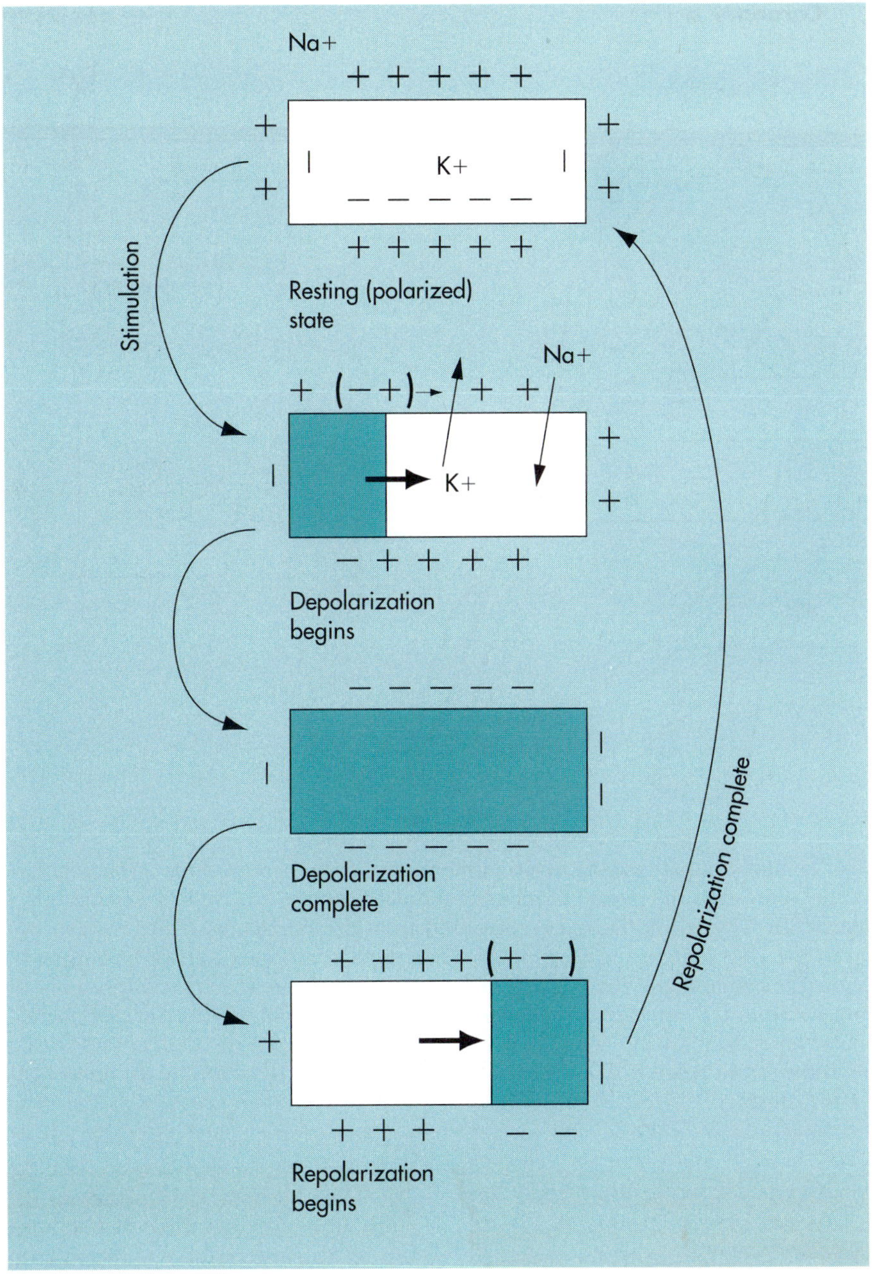

Fig. 21-3 Schematic diagram illustrating process of depolarization and repolarization. (From Phipps WJ et al: *Medical-surgical nursing: concepts and clinical practice,* ed 5, St. Louis, 1995, Mosby.)

allows movement of ions across the cell membrane, causing an alteration in the electrical charge. Potassium, sodium, and calcium ions are the chief ions that influence the electrophysiology of cardiac muscle. Potassium is the predominant intracellular ion, and sodium and calcium concentrations are highest extracellularly (Fig. 21-3).

Calcium, chloride, and magnesium ions also play a role in the action potential. The electrical current stimulates the release of calcium ions, which catalyze the reaction of myocardial contraction.

The electrical activity of myocardial cells can be recorded on an electrocardiogram.

Conduction Pathway

Specialized conduction pathways are found within the myocardium to ensure rhythmic and synchronized excitation and contraction of heart muscle (Fig. 21-4).

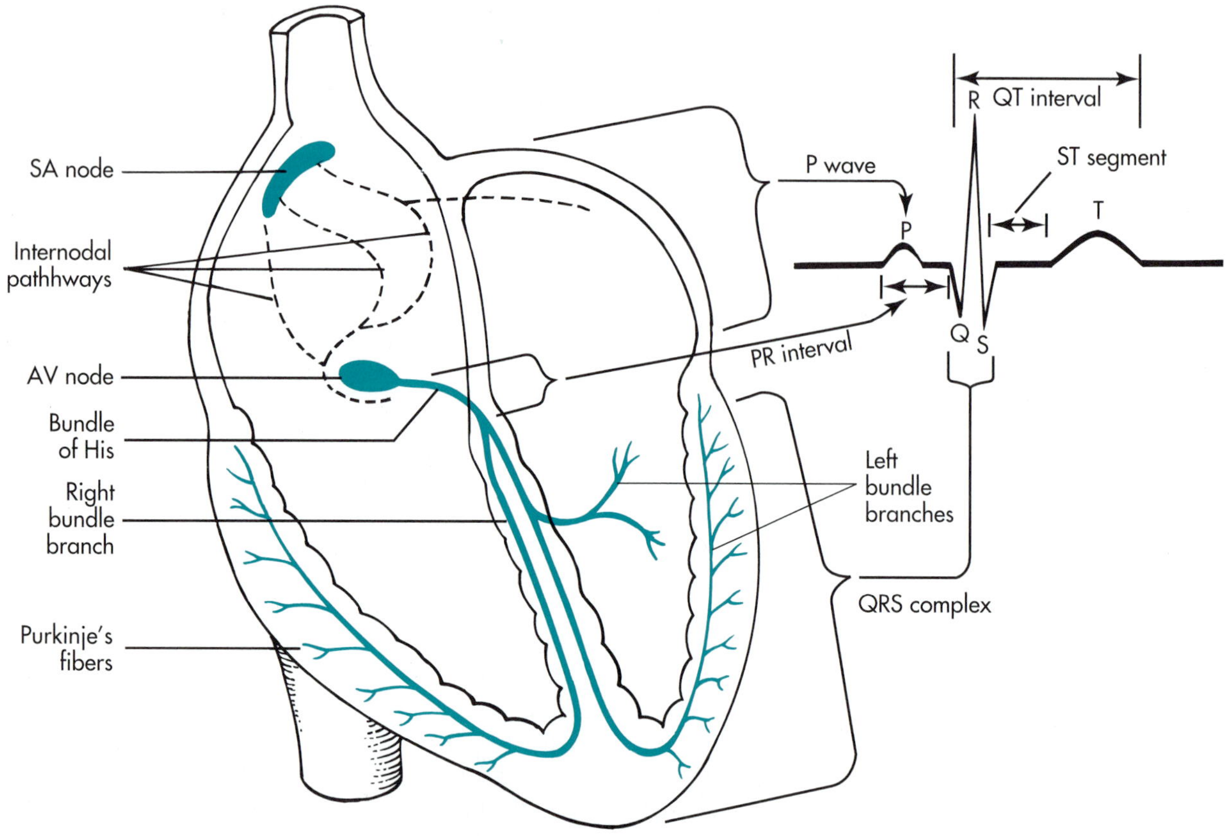

Fig. 21-4 Conduction pathway and ECG components. *P wave* represents atrial depolarization; *PR interval* represents the period from atrial depolarization to atrioventricular holding, just before ventricular depolarization, and is measured from the beginning of the P wave to the beginning of the QRS complex; *QRS complex* represents ventricular depolarization and is measured from the beginning of the *Q wave* to the end of the *S wave; T wave* represents ventricular repolarization; *QT interval* represents the total time from ventricular depolarization to ventricular repolarization and is measured from the beginning of the QRS complex to the end of the T wave. (From Beare P, Myers J: *Principles and practice of adult health nursing,* ed 2, St. Louis, 1994, Mosby.)

The SA node is the natural pacemaker of the heart and is located at the junction of the right atrium and the superior vena cava. A cardiac impulse normally originates in the SA node, at a rate of 60 to 100 beats per minute, and travels to the AV node via specialized atrial conduction pathways.

Beginning at age 60, the number of pacemaker cells in the SA node decreases and by age 75, less then 10% of the cell number remains when compared with a young adult. An accumulation of fat around the SA node and increased elastic and collagenous tissue throughout the conduction system occur during the natural aging process. The older adult may have a prolonged transmission time from the SA to AV node (within normal limits) and a higher frequency of supraventricular and ventricular premature beats, which are not deemed to be clinically significant (Lakatta, 1993).

The electrical impulse then reaches the AV node, which is located on the right side of the interatrial septum near the opening of the coronary sinus. The AV node, also referred to as the junctional or nodal area, is the normal route of transmission between the atria and ventricles. If the SA node fails to stimulate an impulse, cells in the junctional area are capable of generating an electrical impulse at a rate of 40 to 60 beats per minute. The AV node performs two critical functions: (1) it delays impulse conduction for approximately one tenth of a second before reaching the ventricles to permit ventricular filling during atrial contraction, and (2) it controls the number of atrial impulses reaching the ventricles to protect the ventricles from certain abnormal cardiac rhythms.

Electrical excitation spreads from the AV node to the bundle of histidine (His), which is a continuation of the AV node. This bundle of His is a thick bundle of fibers that extends down the right side of the interventricular septum. The bundle separates into the right bundle branch and left bundle branch, of which the left bundle branch then further divides into anterior and posterior divisions. These branches descend on opposite sides of the interventricular septum to the terminal branches of the conduction system known as the Purkinje fibers. The Purkinje fibers rapidly spread the wave of depolarization throughout the inner surface of both ventricles. If the SA node and AV node are unable to generate impulses at an adequate rate, the Purkinje fibers can function as a pacemaker at a rate of 20 to 40 beats per minute.

Mechanical Events

The mechanical responses to electrical events (depolarization) are diastole and systole. Relaxation and filling of the chambers occur during diastole, whereas contraction and emptying take place during systole. Calcium ions play a focal role in the relaxation and contraction of heart muscle.

Cardiac Output

The result of the cardiac electrical and mechanical events is the ejection of blood into the pulmonic and systemic circulations. The volume of blood ejected by each ventricle per minute is known as the cardiac output. An average cardiac output is 5 l/min; however, cardiac output varies as a result of body size and requirements of the peripheral tissues for oxygen and nutrients (i.e., strenuous exercise, infection, stress). Cardiac output is dependent on the relationship between heart rate and stroke volume as indicated by the following equation:

$$\text{Cardiac output} = \text{Heart rate} \times \text{stroke volume}$$

Heart rate refers to the frequency of ventricular contractions per minute. The rate is primarily controlled by the autonomic nervous system (ANS) and its branches. The sympathetic branch of the ANS exerts an excitatory effect, whereas the parasympathetic branch has an inhibitory effect on heart rate. In the normal resting heart, the rate is controlled by the vagus nerve (parasympathetic branch). Both of these nervous systems along with circulating catecholamines (e.g., norepinephrine, epinephrine, and dopamine) control and mediate the heart rate. In addition, the central nervous system (CNS) and baroreceptor reflexes can alter the effects of the sympathetic and parasympathetic nervous systems.

As a result of the aging process, heart rate decreases in both men and women in the sitting position, although there does not appear to be a difference between younger and older adults in the supine position. These findings suggest that there may be a reduction in the parasympathetic and sympathetic modulation (Lakatta, 1993), which is an important aspect to consider during the nursing assessment.

The volume of blood ejected during each ventricular contraction is referred to as stroke volume. Essentially, stroke volume is the difference between the blood volume in the ventricle at the end of diastole and the residual ventricular volume at the end of systole. Stroke volume can be affected by the following three factors:

1. **Preload**—the degree of stretch of myocardial fibers before contraction,
2. **Contractility**—change in the inotropic state of heart muscle (force of contraction) without a change in the length of muscle fiber or preload, and
3. **Afterload**—amount of tension created by the ventricles during contraction to eject blood against pressure in the aortic valve and in the pulmonic and circulatory systems.

Cardiac output steadily declines between the ages of 20 to 80 years. Stiffness of the ventricular walls impedes the ability of the heart to contract and to relax so the older heart is less able to meet the demands for increased oxygen. The older heart attempts to compensate for decreased contractility by developing a longer ejection phase and delaying early diastolic filling to enhance complete emptying of the ventricle during systole. The nurse should assess the electrocardiogram (ECG) of an older adult for longer pulmonic regulation (PR) and QT intervals; however, these findings should still be within normal limits. The heart of an older adult contracts less frequently and with less force, which affects the response to exertion.

Vascular System

The vascular system consists of arteries, veins, and capillaries (the functional unit). Blood flow is assisted by the lymphatic system. Arteries and veins consist of three tissue layers: (1) an outer layer of connective tissue (adventitia); (2) a middle layer of connective tissue, smooth muscle, or elastic fibers (media); and (3) an inner layer of endothelium (intima) (Fig. 21-5).

Arteries

The arteries serve as a conduit and distribute oxygenated blood flow to peripheral tissues. Arterial walls are thick and elastic to permit stretching during ventricular systole and recoil during diastole. These stretching and recoil movements propel blood forward through the vascular system.

Arteries branch into smaller arterioles as they near the capillaries. As the arteries become smaller, the diameter decreases and the velocity of blood flow is reduced. The smaller arteries and arterioles can dilate or constrict through nervous, hormonal, and chemical factors, to control the flow of blood to the capillaries and to facilitate the exchange of nutrients and waste products. The arterial system is a low-volume, high-pressure circuit, since it contains approximately 15% of total blood volume. Arteries assist with temperature regulation of the

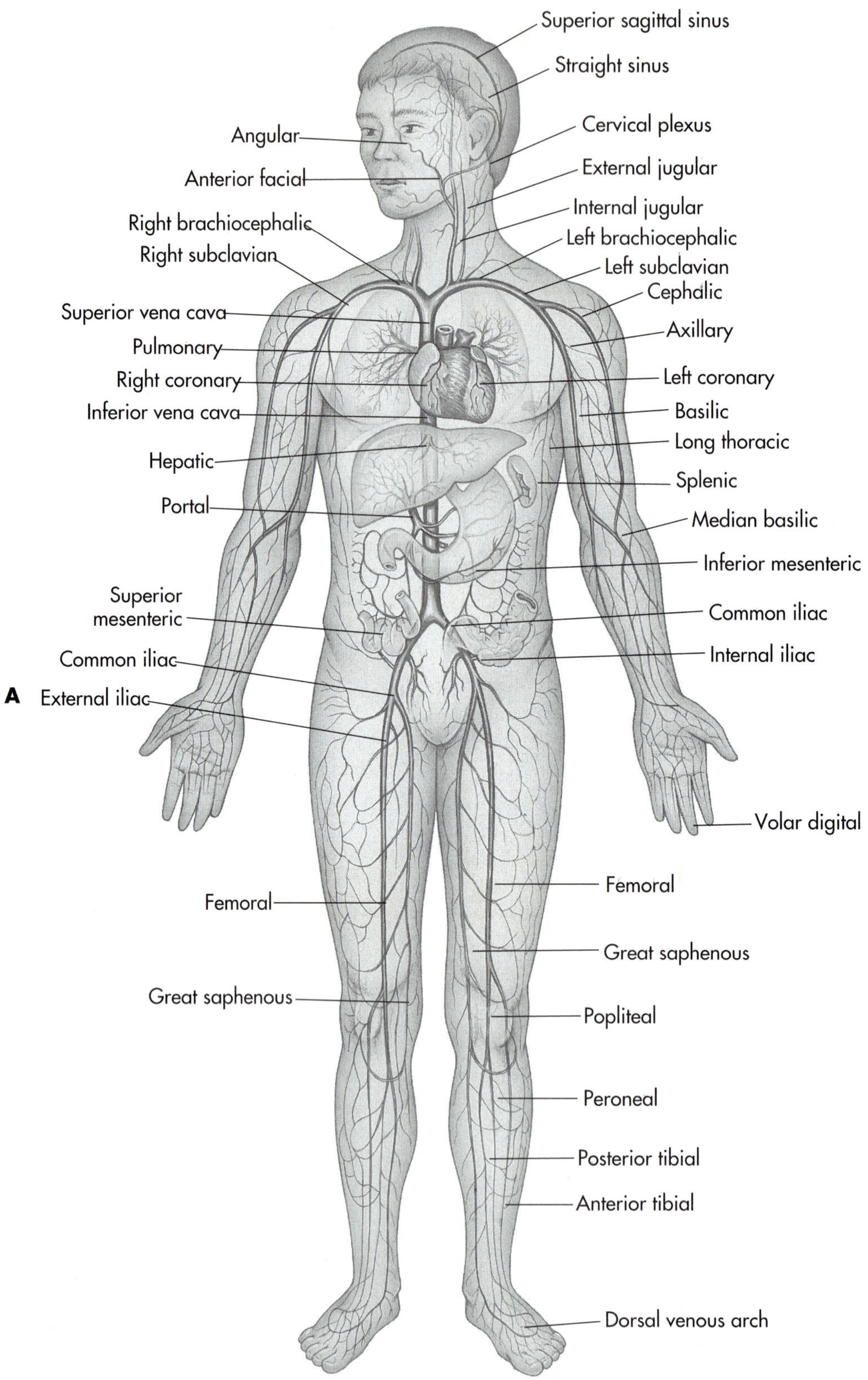

Fig. 21-5 Anatomy of arterial and venous systems. **A,** Arterial circulation. (From Canobbio MM: *Mosby's clinical nursing series: cardiovascular disorders,* St. Louis, 1990, Mosby.)

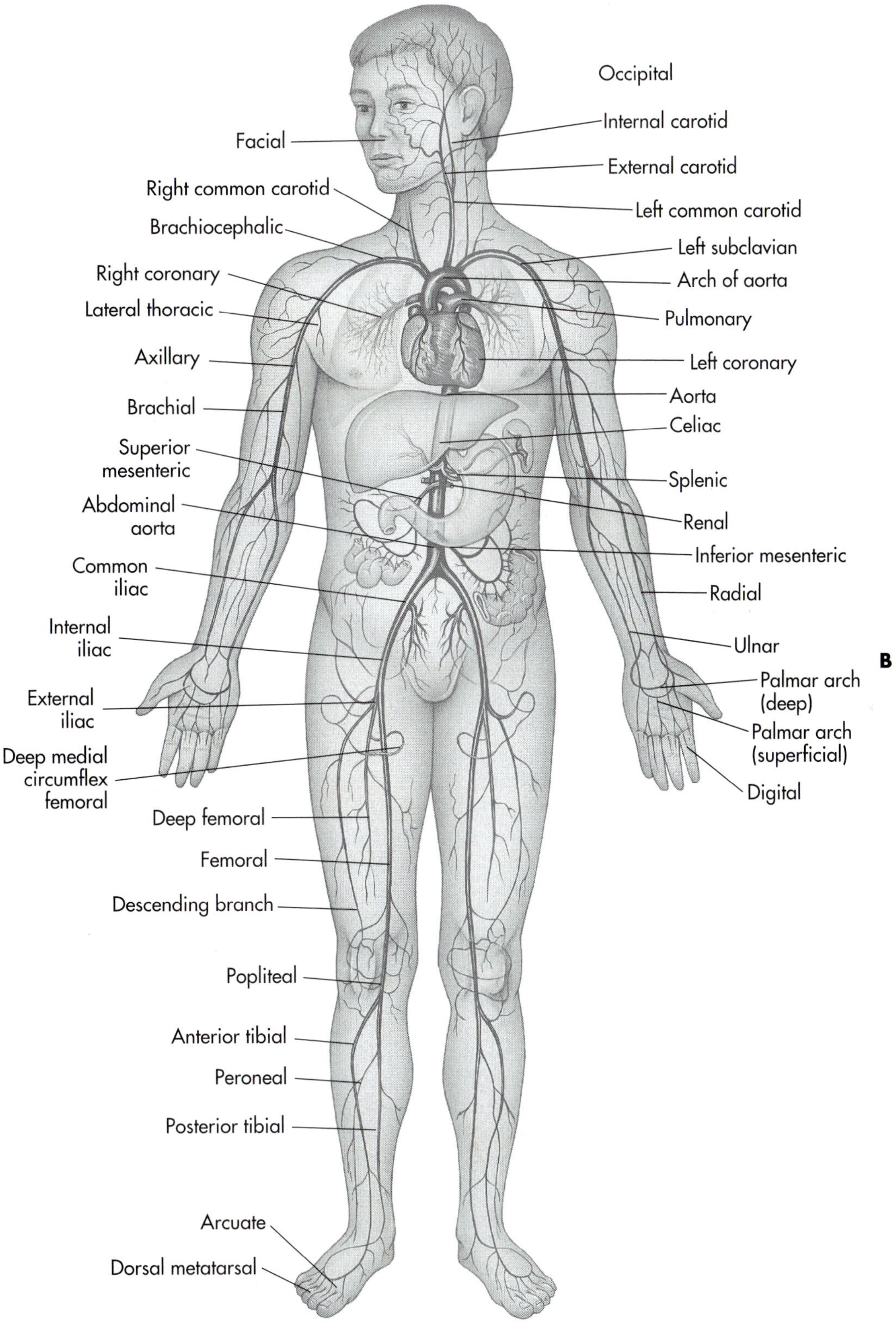
Occipital
Facial
Internal carotid
External carotid
Right common carotid
Left common carotid
Brachiocephalic
Left subclavian
Right coronary
Arch of aorta
Lateral thoracic
Pulmonary
Axillary
Left coronary
Aorta
Brachial
Celiac
Superior mesenteric
Splenic
Abdominal aorta
Renal
Inferior mesenteric
Common iliac
Radial
Internal iliac
Ulnar
B
Palmar arch (deep)
External iliac
Palmar arch (superficial)
Deep medial circumflex femoral
Digital
Deep femoral
Femoral
Descending branch
Popliteal
Anterior tibial
Peroneal
Posterior tibial
Arcuate
Dorsal metatarsal

Fig. 21-5, cont'd **B,** Venous circulation.

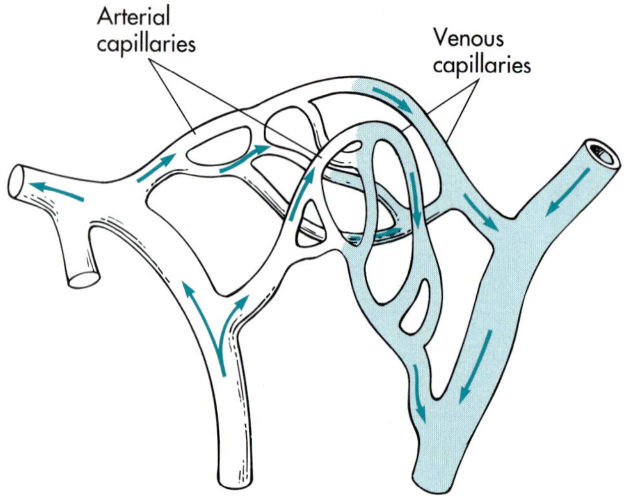

Fig. 21-6 Capillary bed.

body by diverting blood away from the skin (warming effect) or toward the skin (cooling effect).

With aging, the proportion of collagen increases and elastin decreases in the arterial walls, resulting in thicker and stiffer arteries with larger diameters. The reduced elasticity, evident after age 60, limits the ability of the arteries to stretch and to recoil in response to blood volumes ejected during systole and reduces the proportion of blood volume that can be stored in the arterial system. The degree of arterial distensibility can be modified by diet (salt reduction) and exercise (Lakatta, 1993). Although peripheral vascular resistance increases, the increase is not as dramatic in healthy older adults. Damage to the endothelium during a lifetime limits the protective ability of the vascular system, and atherosclerotic plaques may form. Plaque formation is accelerated by disease or unhealthy lifestyles, and is not a normal process associated with aging. Reduced distensibility of arteries can lead to left ventricular hypertrophy as the heart attempts to overcome peripheral resistance.

Capillaries

Capillaries bridge the arterial and venous systems. As blood flows through the capillaries, the velocity slows to allow adequate exchange time across the capillary membranes. The exchange of substances across the semipermeable membranes in both directions occurs by diffusion, osmosis, and filtration. The movement of fluid between the blood vessels and the interstitial spaces is dependent on hydrostatic and osmotic pressures of the capillary bed. Some fluid enters the circulatory system through lymphatic circulation.

In the older adult, tissue perfusion is reduced and capillary tissue diffusion gradients increase as a result of changes in the density and thickness of capillary membranes. Tissue damage is not evident unless the older adult has an increased demand for oxygen or if trauma or disease impedes blood delivery (Beare, Myers, 1994).

Veins

The venous system transports deoxygenated blood from the capillaries and terminal arterioles to the right atrium for circulation. Blood from these distal sites flows into numerous thin-walled venules that merge into large vessels called veins. The inner layer of distant veins have valves that prevent the retrograde movement of blood. Blood flows toward the heart as a result of venous compression caused by movement of skeletal muscles and by alterations in thoracic and abdominal pressures during respiration. Venous walls have less muscle than arteries, which allows more expansion to accommodate large blood volumes with minimum change in venous pressure. Of the total blood volume, 50% to 60% is located within the venous system, so it is regarded as a high-volume, low-pressure system.

In older adults, venous elasticity also declines and veins become more tortuous. The ability to store blood volume is reduced and the efficiency of peripheral valves decreases. In areas of high venous pressure, the older adult is at risk for the development of varicosities (Beare, Myers, 1994). In older adults with reduced skeletal muscle movement, blood may not return to the heart as readily as in younger individuals (Fig. 21-6).

Lymphatic System

The lymphatic system begins in the interstitial spaces of tissue. The system consists of miniature capillary networks that merge into larger vessels that eventually empty into subclavian veins. Lymph nodes (small bodies of lymphoid tissue) are situated at intervals within the vessels and act as filters for the lymph fluid (similar to plasma). The lymphatic system lies adjacent to blood vessels throughout the body (except the CNS).

Blood Pressure

In addition to the structure of the arterial system, capillaries, and venous system, blood flow through this closed circuit is dependent on the pressure propelling the blood and by the resistance to flow. Pressure gradients (differences in pressure) between the arterial and venous system exist to move the blood forward. Pressure in the large arteries is approximately 100 mm Hg and decreases to 25 mm Hg in the capillaries. When blood reaches the right atrium the pressure is close to 0 mm Hg. Hence pressure gradually declines throughout the systemic circulation.

Arterial blood pressure is determined by cardiac output and resistance in the arterioles (radius of the blood vessels). An increase in one of these factors causes a rise in blood pressure. Generally, blood pressure remains constant so that an alteration in one of these factors (e.g., cardiac output) induces an opposite response by the other factor (e.g., peripheral vascular resistance).

In the older adult, the loss of arterial distensibility causes an increase in systolic blood pressure. The diastolic pressure remains the same or may elevate slightly resulting in a wider pulse pressure.

Summary of Normal Function

The purpose of the cardiovascular system is to transport and to distribute oxygen and other essential substances to body tissues, and to remove carbon dioxide and other waste products. The system is a closed circuit and consists of the systemic and pulmonic circulation. After blood is ejected from the left ventricle, it flows into the arterial system to the capillaries, where nutrients and waste products are exchanged, returns through the venous system to the right atrium, and then progresses through the pulmonary system. This circuitous flow of blood is assisted by the lymph system.

The cardiovascular system adapts to internal and external factors by the ANS, which stimulates either the parasympathetic or sympathetic nervous systems. Circulatory information is relayed to the ANS through sensory receptors located within the cardiovascular system.

Baroreceptors in the aorta and internal carotid arteries become stimulated when the arterial walls are stretched with blood, causing inhibition of the vasomotor center within the brainstem and a reflex lowering of blood pressure. With advancing age, the baroreceptors become less sensitive and adults over age 70 are more prone to feelings of dizziness and episodes of syncope with orthostatic changes (Lakatta, 1993).

Stretch receptors in the venae cavae and right atrium sense volume and pressure changes and stimulate the ANS to increase the heart rate and to constrict peripheral vessels. Structural changes within the heart and arteries, as well as delayed vasculature adjustment by the ANS that occurs with aging may impair the response to volume and pressure changes (Lakatta, 1993).

Chemoreceptors in the carotid arteries and aorta sense hypoxemia and stimulate vasoconstriction. Again, these responses might be impaired in the older adult.

The renal systems also contribute to the function of the cardiovascular system by sensing low blood pressure and reduced blood flow. The renal system stimulates the renin-angiotension-aldosterone mechanism, retains water and sodium, and stimulates the release of antidiuretic hormone from the posterior pituitary gland to maintain cardiac output. Reduced blood flow to the kidneys and high systolic pressure in an older adult may adversely affect responses from the renal system. See Box 21-1 for a summary of structural and functional changes in the older adult. All of the changes are interdependent and affect the overall functioning of the cardiovascular system.

BOX 21-1

A Summary of Cardiovascular Changes in Older Adults

Structural

Left atrial enlargement
Increase in heart mass/weight
Increase in ventricular septal thickness
Calcification of cardiac valves
Decreased elasticity of coronary arteries and veins
Reduction of the number of pacemaker cells in SA node
Increase in the thickness of aorta and peripheral arteries
Increase in fat accumulation around the SA node

Functional

Decreased contractility of ventricular walls
Decreased elasticity of coronary arteries
Prolonged PR and QT intervals of ECG
Decreased heart rate at rest
Decreased cardiac output at rest (sitting) and during exercise
Increased peripheral vascular resistance
Decreased reserve pumping capacity
Increased systolic pressure
Wider pulse pressure
Decreased sensitivity of baroreceptors
Increased stroke volume with exercise

Modified from Blair K: Aging: physiological aspects and clinical implications, *Nurse Pract* 15(2):14-16, 18, 26-28, 1990; Gawlinski A, Jensen G: The complications of cardiovascular aging, *AJN* 91(11):26-32, 1991; Lakatta E: Cardiovasculatory regulatory mechanisms in advanced age, *Physiolog Rev* 73(2):413-467, 1993; Lakatta E: The aging heart. In Geokas M, moderator: The aging process, *Ann Intern Med* 113:455-466, 1990.

Decreased elasticity of arteries and stiffness of the ventricular walls affect the contractility and afterload factors, thus impairing cardiac output in the older adult. To compensate for decreased cardiac output, the arteries increase in diameter, atrial enlargement occurs, and ventricular filling time is longer. These structural and functional changes appear to be a normal part of the aging process to maintain cardiac output. At rest, differences in cardiac output are not apparent between healthy older adults and younger individuals; however, the cardiovascular system may not meet metabolic demands during periods of exertion. With exertion, healthy older adults tend to experience cardiac dysrhythmias, but they are not deemed to be clinically significant. Structural changes in the cardiovascular system and the limited reserve pumping capacity predispose older adults to activity intolerance during exertion.

COMMON CARDIOVASCULAR PROBLEMS

CVD is the leading cause of death in Canada and the United States and accounts for 41% to 50% of all deaths (Heart & Stroke Foundation of Canada, 1991; US Department of Commerce, Economics and Statistics, 1992). In addition, cardiovascular diseases account for the most hospital admissions. Changes in the cardiovascular system from advancing age predispose the older adult to a variety of problems and conditions such as coronary heart disease (ischemic heart disease), hypertension, pump failure, dysrhythmias (particularly heart block), valvular conditions, and peripheral vascular disease.

The normal aging process varies among individuals, which may be attributed to factors of heredity. In addition, the effects of advancing age on cardiovascular structure and function is influenced by the presence of noncardiovascular diseases and variations in lifestyle. Research endeavors to date encounter difficulty separating *true* aging from these contributing conditions (Lakatta, 1993). Many forms of cardiovascular disease can be accelerated by unhealthy lifestyle choices such as smoking, physical inactivity, high-risk dietary behaviors, obesity, stress, and hormonal use by females.

Contributing Factors in Heart Disease

Risk factors have been classified as nonmodifiable and modifiable. Risk factors of age, gender, and family history are factors that cannot be modified. Risk factors of smoking, high blood pressure, diet (cholesterol), obesity, physical activity, and stress are amenable to change, and research has demonstrated that the adoption of a healthier lifestyle has the potential to reduce or to prevent the incidence of morbidity and death from ischemic heart disease and stroke (Box 21-2).

BOX 21-2

Risk Factors for CVD

Nonmodifiable
Age
Gender
Family history

Modifiable
Blood pressure/hypertension
Smoking
Elevated blood cholesterol levels
Diabetes
Physical activity
Obesity
Stress
Hormonal use
Alcohol intake

The factors to be discussed in this section include blood pressure, diet, smoking, physical activity, diabetes, stress, alcohol use, oral contraceptives, and supplemental female hormones.

Blood Pressure

High blood pressure is a major risk factor that contributes to the more than 500,000 strokes and the 150,000 deaths from stroke that occur annually in the United States. It is also one of the major risk factors in the approximately 1 million heart attacks and 500,000 deaths from heart attacks that occur annually (National High Blood Pressure Education Program Working Group, 1994). The relative risk of cardiovascular disease is greater among older adults compared with middle-aged individuals at every level. Furthermore, the likelihood that an older individual will have a cardiovascular event is substantially greater than for someone of a younger age, reflecting the effect of age as a cardiovascular risk factor. Thus blood pressure reduction is likely to produce a greater benefit in older adults. There is some evidence that increased diastolic blood pressure is associated with increased survival in those age 85 and older (National High Blood Pressure Education Program Working Group, 1994).

The goal of therapy is to reduce blood pressure cautiously in older adults. The National High Blood Pressure Education Program Working Group suggests the following measures:

- Lifestyle modification, including weight reduction, physical activity, and restriction of dietary calories for those who weigh approximately 10% above their ideal body weight
- Restriction of salt intake to less than 6 gms sodium chloride per day, since older adults are likely to be salt-sensitive
- Limiting alcohol intake to two glasses of wine, two beers, or 2 oz. of liquor daily
- Reduction of dietary saturated fat and cholesterol
- Adequate intake of potassium, calcium, and mag-nesium
- Smoking cessation

Diet

An elevated serum level of low-density lipoprotein (LDL) cholesterol has been recognized for many years as a major risk factor for coronary heart disease (Frick et al, 1987). Three epidemiologic studies—the Framingham Heart Study, the Pooling project, and a study conducted in Israel—suggest that coronary heart disease rates are essentially constant for cholesterol levels up to 200 to 220 mg/100 ml; above this "threshold" range, increased levels of cholesterol are associated with increased coronary risk. However, the findings are controversial. In the Multiple Risk Factor Intervention Trial, 331,666 men were screened. This larger study did not show the threshold relation between coronary heart disease mortality and cholesterol level suggested by a previous survey; instead, the relation was continuous over a broad range of cholesterol levels. For example, above 200 mg/100 ml, coronary risk essentially doubled for every 50 mg/100 ml increment of plasma cholesterol (Ernst et al, 1988; 1987; Frick et al, 1987; Grundy et al, 1987; Johansen et al, 1987; Kris-Etherton et al, 1988; Murray et al, 1990).

The association of high blood cholesterol with coronary artery disease (CAD) in older adults is uncertain (Rubin et al, 1990). There appears to be limited evidence as to whether older clients benefit from intervention, since the strength of association between LDL cholesterol and coronary heart disease diminishes with age. It has been suggested by experts in the field that dietary intervention in older adults has potential benefits. A diet low in fat is recommended. In considering diet therapy for older adults classified at high risk, the value of diet modification for prevention of atherosclerotic disease must be balanced against the possibility of inadequate nutrition (Expert Panel, 1988).

Smoking

Smoking continues to be a major risk factor in the development of heart disease. Although there has been a tremendous decrease in the use of tobacco in the last 25 years, largely as a result of health promotion campaigns, clean air environments, and peer pressure, smoking is still attributed to 20% of all deaths. In 1987 the prevalence of smoking declined among men age 20 and older in the United States, from 43% in 1974 to 32%. Among adult women, smoking prevalence declined at a slower rate, from 32% in 1974 to 27%. The prevalence of smoking among adults age 65 and older showed a modest decline among older men, from 24.8% in 1974 to 17.2% but a slight increase among older women, from 12% to 13.7%. The Surgeon General's report concluded that one in six deaths in the United States is attributable to smoking (LaCroix, Omenn, 1992).

The effects of smoking on older adults has received considerable attention in the literature. The questions posed in a recent study relate to whether continued smoking after age 65 alters the risk of cardiovascular and cancer mortality, chronic health problems such as chronic obstructive pulmonary disease (COPD), and pneumonia, or overall physical ability. The review suggests the following:

1. Older smokers who quit have a reduced risk of death compared with current smokers within 1 to 2 years after quitting. Their overall risk of death approaches that of those who never smoked after 15 to 20 years of abstinence.
2. Smoking cessation in older adults markedly reduces the risks of coronary events and of cardiac deaths within 1 year of quitting, and risk continues to decline gradually for many years. This is true for older adults both with and without a previous history of coronary disease and symptoms.
3. Risks of dying from several smoking-related cancers are reduced by quitting. Although the decline in risk may be more gradual for older rather than middle-age adults, the benefits of cessation are apparent within 10 to 15 years of quitting.
4. Smoking cessation reduces the risk of COPD mortality after 10 to 15 years of abstinence in women. Within a shorter period, quitting reduces functional impairments and the prevalence of respiratory symptoms, slows the rate of decline in pulmonary function, and improves tolerance for exercise.
5. Smoking cessation may help slow osteoporosis and may reduce the risk of hip fractures, but effects on rates of bone loss or subsequent risk of fracture have not yet been studied adequately.
6. Continued smoking in late life is associated with the development and progression of several major chronic conditions, loss of mobility, and poorer physical function. Former smokers appear to have higher levels of physical function and better quality of life than continuing smokers. (LaCroix, Omenn, 1992).

The question of whether a relationship exists between environmental tobacco smoke (ETS) and heart disease has received considerable attention by researchers. This relationship has recently been confirmed (Research box on p. 500).

Physical Activity

Exercise has been shown to reduce the risk for heart disease and to control other risk factors of high blood pressure, obesity, and diabetes (Braun, 1991; Kasch et al, 1993; Grundy et al, 1987). Prevalence data on physical activity is difficult to compare because of the variety of definitions used in the surveys. Acceptable physical activity levels are continuous, rhythmic activity performed at least three times per week for a minimum of 15 minutes. The capacity for the older client to perform exercise is affected by changes in cardiac output, skeletal muscle and joint function, and decreasing overall muscle power and coordination. In addition, older adults may hesitate to engage in outdoor physical activities such as walking because of climactic factors. Kasch et al. (1993) conducted a longitudinal study over a period of 25 years on 12 men age 44 to 79 on the effect of exercise on cardiovascular aging. The authors found that the group's

RESEARCH

Glantz S, Parmley W: Passive smoking and heart disease: Epidemiology, physiology and biochemistry, *Circulation* 83(1):1-12, 1991.

Sample, setting

Studies reviewed included a wide variety of smoking and nonsmoking adult men and women in the United States and abroad. Four studies presented data on men, eight on women, and one on both genders combined.

Methodology

A review of epidemiologic studies that included examination of environmental tobacco smoke (ETS) and coronary heart disease in the United States, United Kingdom, Japan, Scotland, and China was employed. The number of deaths and relative risk in the population were reviewed.

Findings

Ten epidemiologic studies confirm that there is a 30% increase in risk of death from ischemic heart disease or myocardial infarction (MI) among nonsmokers living with smokers. The larger studies also demonstrate a significant dose-response effect with greater exposure to ETS associated with greater risk of death.

These epidemiologic studies are complemented by a variety of physiologic and biochemical data that show how ETS adversely affects platelet function and damages arterial endothelium, increasing risk of heart disease.

These results suggest that heart disease is an important consequence of exposure to ETS. The combination of epidemiologic studies, demonstration of physiologic changes with exposure to ETS, and biochemical evidence proving that elements of ETS have significant adverse effects on the cardiovascular system leads to the conclusion that ETS causes heart disease. This increase in risk translates into about 10 times as many deaths from ETS-induced heart disease as lung cancer.

Implications

The findings have implications for enhanced smoking cessation programs, legislation of clean air environments in shopping malls, homes for older adults, residential settings, restaurants, and other settings as applicable.

cardiovascular function remained 60% greater than the average of 10 other investigations. Blair et al. (1989) conducted a prospective study of 13,344 healthy men and women who were followed for an average of 8 years to assess the association between physical fitness and mortality from all causes, CVD, and cancer. The major findings include the following:

- Death rates from all causes for the least-fit men were 3.4 times higher.
- Higher levels of physical fitness were beneficial even in those with other risk factors such as high blood pressure, elevated cholesterol, cigarette smoking, and a family history of heart disease.
- Cancer death rates were much lower in physically fit men and women.
- Moderate levels of exercise result in a fitness level that can be associated with a reduced risk of death.

Obesity

The relation between body weight and CVD is the subject of continuing debate. The terms overweight and obesity need to be outlined. Being overweight can be defined as exceeding an arbitrary standard, based on weight and height. Obesity normally refers to an abnormally high percentage of total body fat. A number of epidemiologic studies confirm that being overweight is an independent risk factor for coronary heart disease, although the results from particular populations may not be generalized (Grundy et al, 1987). One group of researchers found that obesity is a risk factor for coronary heart disease only when the waist-to-hip measurement ratio is greater than average.

Diabetes

Cholesterol, blood pressure, and smoking are strong independent predictors of CVD. In a recent study of 345,978 men between the ages of 35 to 57, it was found that during an average follow-up of 12 years, the death rate was five times higher in individuals with diabetes than in those without the disease (Stamler et al, 1993). The presence of one or more factors was associated with a significant increase in mortality. Increased risk has been reported for individuals with both insulin-dependent and noninsulin-dependent diabetes. Abnormalities in the metabolism of lipoproteins are common among people with diabetes and may accelerate atherosclerosis (Grundy et al, 1987).

The study by Stamler et al. (1993) confirms the importance of enhanced efforts to lower blood pressure, lower cholesterol intake, and to convince diabetics of smoking cessation. It further supports the need to prevent diabetes on a massive scale by exercise and a low-fat diet. It is important to note that women and older adults age 65 and older were not included in this study.

Stress

At one particular time, stress was thought to be associated with Type A behavior—the goal- and task-oriented high achiever. This belief is now being modified, and researchers are now examining the individual's adaptation to stress from other perspectives such as anger control, support by family, friends, or significant others, and the means by which individuals cope with stress.

There are several methods to decrease stress and

much literature is available on the topic. Yoga, meditation, relaxation tapes, visualization, and physical activity are a few of the methods used. It is imperative that research continues to examine the effects of stress on those age 65 and older and that nurses examine those factors in the client's environment that are amenable to change. For example, an older client may not be able to prepare meals because of physical limitations or safety reasons. Referral to a Meals on Wheels program or a community-based program in which individuals share meals is just one example of a simple modification. Older individuals living in an apartment; sharing their meals; and dividing tasks of shopping, meal preparation, and clean-up activities are other popular concepts. In this way, the older client receives a balanced diet.

Hormonal Usage

The effects of estrogen on the development of heart disease are still being debated in the literature.

One of the most convincing studies that showed estrogen's effect was conducted in the United States and tracked 47,470 nurses by mail for 10 years. Estrogen-treated women had only half the risk of coronary heart disease compared with that of untreated women. It is important to note that this study, like most other studies, included few women over age 65 (Stampfer et al, 1991).

The risk of cardiovascular factors warrants further investigation by practitioners regarding the overall relationship of all risk factors to heart disease. Nurses have an essential role to play in assisting clients through education regarding risk factors and lifestyle changes.

> **Insight** • *Because heart disease is rare in women before menopause and because the risk of heart disease seems to increase in women who had an early oophorectomy, the female advantage had been attributed to estrogen. By the early 1950s, Stamler et al. (1953) found that estrogen reduced atherosclerosis in an animal model and Barr et al. (1952) discovered that estrogen lowered LDL cholesterol and raised HDL cholesterol in humans. These studies supported the postulate that estrogen was protective. Then a strange thing happened—estrogen was studied in men but not women.*
>
> *In the Coronary Drug Project, vascular complications and death rates were higher in men who were given estrogen than in men who were given the placebo, and the estrogen treatment arms were discontinued. Whether the untoward findings resulted from the very high doses of estrogen used or reflected the possibility that estrogen is good for women but not men is not known. In any event, no randomized clinical trial designed to determine whether estrogen prevents fatal or nonfatal heart disease in healthy women has begun as of yet, and any primary prevention trials begun now would not provide answers until the next century (Barrett-Connor, Miller, 1993).*

COMMON CARDIOVASCULAR PROBLEMS AND CONDITIONS IN THE OLDER CLIENT

Hypertension

Hypertension has been termed the "silent killer," since it is estimated that approximately one half of the population with high blood pressure is unaware of having this condition, despite the availability of advanced screening programs. The importance of the relationship between high blood pressure and the incidence and mortality from coronary heart disease, including MI, stroke, congestive heart failure, peripheral vascular disease, and other cardiac abnormalities, has been well-documented (Stamler, Stamler, Neaton, 1993):

> When the National High Blood Pressure Education Program (NHBPEP) was launched in the United States 20 years ago, one of its main [foci] on solving the large problem of undetected, untreated, and uncontrolled high blood pressure (HBP) was limited on how this disease could be prevented. There was also at that time little or no understanding in the medical community that the blood pressure problem actually involved the large majority of the population with blood pressures at levels carrying excess risks.
>
> Today the knowledge is in hand to deal with the total blood pressure problem. Prevention of hypertension is now a realistic goal, a goal based on improving the level of blood pressure in the general population . . . The tools available to accomplish this lifesaving goal are contained in the large body of evidence, increased greatly in the last two decades, implicating key aspects of modern lifestyle as the causes of the epidemic of hypertension and the population-wide BP problem. Through use of all scientific methods at our disposal—animal experimentation, clinical investigation, intervention trial, and epidemiologic research, several key factors underlying the modern blood pressure pattern have been identified: (1) salt intake 10 or more times physiologic need, (2) low intake of potassium and a consequent high ratio of dietary sodium to potassium, (3) overweight as a mass phenomenon, and (4) excess alcohol intake among a significant proportion of the population.
>
> These are features of modern life . . . adoption of healthier lifestyles, particularly of healthier eating patterns, starting in childhood and youth, can prevent and reverse blood pressure patterns.

TABLE 21-1

Stages of Hypertension

Stage	Systolic pressure/mm Hg	Diastolic pressure/mm Hg
Stage 1	140-159	90-99
Stage 2	160-179	100-109
Stage 3	180-209	110-119
Stage 4	210 or higher	120 or higher

From the Joint National Committee: Report of the Joint National Committee on detection, evaluation and treatment of high blood pressure, Washington, D.C., 1992, US Department of Health and Human Services.

It is important to note that the studies addressing hypertension and related cardiovascular risks have been limited in the aging population, especially in women. Barry (1993) found that nearly all randomized controlled studies on risk factors, treatment, and outcomes of cardiovascular disease have exclusively involved men, and extrapolation of those findings to women has resulted in misinterpretations. Of importance is the fact that numerous studies have failed to take into consideration the contributing factors of smoking, alcohol consumption, hormonal intake, stress, and other dietary factors in this population.

Hypertension is defined as sustained systolic blood pressure, greater than 160 mm Hg, or diastolic blood pressure greater than 90 mm Hg. The Joint National Committee (1992) has recently adopted hypertension guidelines and reclassified the disease into four stages (Table 21-1).

The diagnosis is made on at least two subsequent visits and the blood pressure is measured with the client supine or sitting, and then standing (except for those clients whose systolic pressure is greater than 210 and diastolic pressure is greater than 120; these individuals are deemed to have high blood pressure on one visit).

The Joint National Committee (1992) recommends that blood pressure be monitored as follows:

- In 1 week, if client is in Stage 3
- In 1 month, if the client is in Stage 2
- In 1 year, if the systolic pressure is 130-139 and the diastolic pressure is 85-89
- In 2 years, if the systolic pressure is below 130 and the diastolic pressure is below 85.

Blood pressure and pulse pressure progressively increase with age in industrialized societies, and hypertension occurs often in older adults. It is estimated that more than 45% to 50% of the population age 65 and over have high blood pressure. The consequences of hypertension are the most common causes of morbidity and mortality in this population, including MI, stroke, congestive heart failure (CHF), and peripheral vascular disease (Elnicki Kotchen, 1993).

Isolated systolic hypertension is more common in older adults, as systolic blood pressure rises disproportionately to diastolic pressure, owing to increased arterial stiffness and rigidity. In the past, it was argued that hypertension was a normal process of aging and did not require therapy. Data from the Framingham Heart Study confirms that cardiovascular risk escalates dramatically in older adults. The addition of risk factors such as smoking, glucose intolerance, hypercholesterolemia, and left ventricular hypertrophy elevate the risk remarkedly.

The phenomenon of pseudohypertension has been described in the literature. It has been estimated that approximately 7.1% of outpatient older clients have this condition (Elnicki, Kotchen, 1993). Pseudohypertension is a result of the calcification of the arterial wall; sclerotic changes result in rigidity in the brachial artery, leading to ineffective compression of the brachial artery with a sphygmomanometer. Pseudohypertension may be suspected when (1) the blood pressure is elevated without evidence of organ damage, (2) there is a discrepancy in blood pressure of different extremities, or (3) if hypotensive symptoms develop with therapy. Osler's maneuver is a screening test for pseudohypertension, although the results have been questioned. It is performed by palpating the brachial or radial artery after inflating the cuff above the systolic pressure. A normal artery can collapse, and one that is still palpable requires that readings be correlated with an intra-arterial reading (Elnicki, Kotchen, 1993).

Hypertension has been classified into two types: primary and secondary. Primary hypertension is the most common form and although the exact cause is unknown, the contributing factors are family history, age, race, diet (e.g., high in saturated fats and salt; decreased potassium, magnesium, and calcium intake), smoking, stress, alcohol and drug consumption, physical activity, and hormonal intake.

Secondary hypertension refers to elevated blood pressure as a result of underlying disease such as renal artery disease, renal parenchymal disorders, endocrine and metabolic disorders, CNS disorders, coarctation of the aorta, and increased intravascular volume.

A positive correlation exists between weight (obesity) and high blood pressure. Advancing age is associated with a loss of lean body mass and an increase in adipose tissue. Recent epidemiologic studies suggest that there may be an association between centripetal fat (greater proportion of adipose tissue is distributed on the trunk compared with the extremities) and hypertension, heart disease, and stroke. Although the exact mechanisms are not clear, some plausible reasons include that (1) the fat in abdominal adipocytes is more labile than fat in femoral and gluteal adipocytes and (2) since abdominal adipocytes drain into the portal vein and liver, it has been theorized that an excess flow of fatty acids into the liver may reduce hepatic clearance of insulin, resulting in hyperinsulinism. The resulting hyperinsulinemia may lead to hypertension by promoting sodium retension, inducing cellular membrane transport abnormalities of sodium and potassium, stimulating the sympathetic nervous system, or directly altering vascular tone (Carethers, Blanchette, 1989). This factor has significance, since it underlies the importance of weight reduction in the older adult population.

The pathophysiology of hypertension is complex, since various environmental, structural, renal, hormonal, and homeostatic mechanisms contribute to blood pressure maintenance, especially in the aging population. A detailed description of the mechanisms involved is outside the scope of this review.

Hypertension has been associated with arteriolar thickening, vascular smooth muscle constriction, and elevated vascular resistance. With advancing age, the peripheral vascular resistance elevates significantly. It is also possible that functional changes in the vascular smooth muscle contribute to these changes. Alpha-adrenergic responsiveness of the vascular smooth muscle does not change with age; however, the beta-adrenergic responsiveness of vascular smooth muscle declines with age with a consequent decrease in the relaxation of vascular smooth muscle. There also appears to be increased renovascular resistance and lower renal blood flow. Left ventricular hypertrophy occurs as an adaptation to long-standing hypertension and may lead to CHF. Once this occurs, there is a significant increase in cardiovascular risk, particularly from ventricular arrhythmias and sudden death.

Older adults with hypertension have lower renin levels and plasma volume, and this factor is important when considering the selection of drug therapy for this population. Baroreflex sensitivity declines with age, which predisposes the older client to hypotension (Applegate, 1992; Lakatta, 1993).

Signs and Symptoms

In mild-to-moderate hypertension, the client may be asymptomatic. As the disease progresses the client may experience fatigue, dizziness, headache, vertigo, and palpitations. In severe hypertension the client may experience throbbing occipital headache, confusion, visual loss, focal deficits, epistaxis, and coma.

It is imperative that the practitioner observe for other target organ damage and symptoms (see Medical Management box, pp. 504-505). Hypertension may lead to damage in various organs, resulting in the following:

1. Heart—CHF, ventricular hypertrophy, angina, MI, and sudden death
2. CNS—Transient ischemic attack or stroke
3. Peripheral vessels—Peripheral vascular disease, aneurysm
4. Renal—Serum creatine > 133 mmol/L (1.5 mg/100 ml), proteinuria, microalbuminuria
5. Eye—Hemorrhage or exudates, with or without papilledema.

NURSING MANAGEMENT

✣ ASSESSMENT

The majority of clients are asymptomatic. Symptoms that do occur are variable depending on the progression of the disease on target organs. Vague discomfort, fatigue, headache, epistaxis, and dizziness may be early indicators. Severe hypertension may result in a throbbing occipital headache, particularly prevalent in the morning and disappearing several hours later, as well as confusion, visual loss, focal deficits, and coma. Symptoms of heart failure such as dyspnea may be present. If the kidneys are affected, hematuria or nocturia may be noted.

Objective data include a thorough assessment of blood pressure on three separate occasions (observe carefully for pseudohypertension).

The following case study is based on a client who attended the Hearts for Life program and was unaware that she had high blood pressure.

Mrs. S is 64 years old, 290 lbs., and 5 ft. 4 in. tall. She completed a Coronary Risk Profile, which questions participants regarding age, gender, family history of heart disease, smoking patterns, diet, exercise, and cholesterol levels. The data were then analyzed through the use of a computer program and an individualized risk profile obtained. The researcher noted that the client's weight was high compared with her height and that her blood pressure was 220/110. The researcher contacted Mrs. S at home to advise her about contacting her physician as soon as possible. Mrs. S started crying and said:

> This is the first time that anyone has ever cared enough about me to call me. I am so very lonely since my husband died. I work as a homemaker, and when I come home at night, I just sit in front of the television and eat potato chips or cookies and have a couple of drinks. I smoke too much as well. The lovely young lady at the program told me that my blood pressure was high but I just haven't got around to seeing the doctor. As a homemaker, I am too busy caring for others, rather than myself. I will have to make some very serious lifestyle changes if I want to live—I think I know what to do—I just have to do it, but I am so confused about what to do. It is funny that I did not notice any signs or symptoms—I work very hard as a homemaker. Occasionally I get a headache in the morning but it only lasts for 1 hour or so. I will see my doctor as soon as possible.

✣ DIAGNOSIS

Nursing diagnoses for the older adult client in this case include knowledge deficit and impaired social interac-

MEDICAL MANAGEMENT

Hypertension

Diagnostic tests and procedures

The evaluation of older adults with suspected hypertension differs from that of younger clients. The overall goals include the following:

- To determine if the client has a sustained systolic pressure of >160 mm Hg or a diastolic pressure of >90 mm Hg
- To search for secondary causes
- To assess end-organ damage
- To assess comorbidity as older clients are likely to have coexisting cardiac, vascular, and renal disease, as well as atherosclerosis.
- Obtain history regarding lifestyle factors and conduct an in-depth physical examination. Generally, the following tests are conducted:
  - Hemoglobin and hematocrit to exclude anemia or polycythemia
  - Urinalysis to investigate for proteinuria or other signs of renal disease
  - Serum sodium, potassium, creatinine, and calcium, uric acid, and glucose to screen for secondary hypertension caused by hyperparathyroidism, hyperaldosteronism, or renal insufficiency
  - Serum uric acid, since an acute gout attack may be precipitated by diuretic therapy
  - Fasting serum glucose as diabetes is an independent cardiac risk factor that may be affected by antihypertensive therapy
  - Nonfasting serum total cholesterol and HDL to assess for hyperlipidemia
  - ECG, chest x-ray, and echocardiogram to assess for left ventricle hypertrophy (Elnicki, Kotchen, 1993)

If renal artery stenosis is suspected, a renal arteriography, ultrasonography, nuclear renogram or intravenous (IV) pyelogram may be performed.

Treatment

Nonpharmacologic

Lifestyle modification is the foundation of hypertension control and has implications for physicians and nurses. The Joint National Committee on Detection, Evaluation and Treatment of High Blood Pressure (1992) suggests the following guidelines for lifestyle modifications:

- Reduce weight if more than 10% above ideal weight.
- Limit alcohol intake to no more than 1 ounce of ethanol (e.g., 2 ounces of liquor, 8 ounces wine, 24 ounces of beer) per day.
- Participate in regular aerobic exercise (e.g., a 30 to 45 minute brisk walk) three to five times per week.
- Limit sodium intake to 2 gm daily (5 gm sodium chloride).
- Include the recommended daily allowances (RDAs) of potassium, calcium, and magnesium in diet.
- Participate in a smoking cessation program.
- Reduce dietary saturated fat and cholesterol (Tables 21-2 and 21-3, pp. 506-508).

If the blood pressure remains above 140/90 mm Hg over 3 to 6 months following the nonpharmacologic regimen, then consider drug therapy.

Pharmacologic

One of the most important considerations in drug therapy in older individuals is that blood pressure should be lowered gradually, beginning with low doses of a single agent.

The various steps involved in treatment of blood pressure include the following:

- **Step 1**: Nonpharmacologic intervention, lifestyle interventions
- **Step 2**: Select an appropriate agent with consideration for comorbidity
- **Step 3**: Increase dose of first drug, and then add a second drug of different class or substitute a drug from a different class
- **Step 4**: Add a third drug, or substitute a second drug
- **Step 5**: Further evaluation and referral or the addition of a fourth drug

The general principles for managing high blood pressure in older clients include the following:

1. Systolic-diastolic hypertension (SDH) should be treated with medication if the average blood pressure on at least two visits (three measurements per visit) is >140 to 160 mm Hg systolic and >100 mm Hg diastolic.
2. Mild systolic-diastolic hypertension should be treated conservatively with nonpharmacologic interventions. If the diastolic blood pressure remains >95 mm Hg, pharmacologic intervention should be initiated.
3. Isolated systolic hypertension (SBP >160 mm Hg and DBP <90 mm Hg) should be treated.
4. For older clients with mild systolic-diastolic hypertension, the absolute benefit of drug treatment in terms of mortal and morbid events reduced per 1,000 person-years of treatment is significant, but possibly not *so* great that individual clients need always be treated in the face of disabling side effects from hypertensive medications.
5. In using pharmacologic therapy, the initial daily dose should be half that recommended as the starting dose for middle-age clients.
6. A diuretic is the first choice of drug for the treatment of hypertension in older clients. Diuretic dosages equivalent to 12.5 to 25 mg per day of hydrochlorothiazide appear to be most effective.
7. The choice of an alternative first-step drug or a sec-

MEDICAL MANAGEMENT

Hypertension—cont'd

ond-step drug should be based on individual client characteristics.

8. Pharmacologic therapy should not be continued for older clients with mild or isolated systolic hypertension in whom significant side effects persist, despite therapy with a variety of pharmacologic agents.
9. After blood pressure has been controlled for 6 months, the dosage of the drug should be stepped down if possible (Applegate, 1992). The initial drug selection should be based on comorbidity (Table 21-4, p. 508).

Diuretics

The thiazide diueretics (hydrochlorothiazide or chlorthalidone, which are generally preferred in clinical trials) continue to be the most commonly prescribed antihypertensive agents for older adults. The initial dosage should be 12.5 to 25 mg once daily. Loop diuretics (bumetanide, ethacrynic acid, and furosemide) are not used unless the client has renal impairment or CHF.

The primary concern related to diuretic therapy is hypotension or hypokalemia. At low doses, the chance of developing hypokalemia is approximately 20%, therefore it is not necessary to initiate treatment with potassium or a potassium-sparing agent (amiloride, spironolactone, or triamterene). Clients should be carefully monitored for hypokalemia for 2 to 4 weeks after therapy commences. If hypokalemia becomes difficult to manage, an alternate antihypertensive agent is considered.

Hypomagnesemia and hyperglycemia may also occur. Increases in blood sugar are generally minor and are associated with hypokalemia.

The effect of thiazides on plasma lipids is inconclusive, and it has been argued that the elevation in serum cholesterol may be sufficient to negate the beneficial effects on blood pressure reduction.

Beta-blockers

Beta-blockers (acebutolol, atenolol, betaxolol, carteolol, metroprolol, nadolol, propranolol, timolol) are not as effective in older adults, since these drugs may lower cardiac output and may initially increase peripheral vascular resistance. These hemodynamic factors have a detrimental effect on the older adult. Older clients often have conditions that contraindicate use of beta-blockers, including CHF, asthma or COPD, insulin-dependent diabetes, bradycardia, or peripheral vascular insufficiency. Clients with a history of asthma, impaired circulation, or diabetes may be able to tolerate a subgroup of beta-blockers—those that are cardioselective (acebutolol, atenolol, betaxolol, and metroprolol). The precaution with alpha-beta–blockers (labetalol) and alpha l-receptor–blockers (doxazosin, prazosin, and terazosin) is that they may cause orthostatic hypotension in older adults.

Angiotensin-converting enzyme inhibitors

ACEIs (captopril, enalapril, and lisinopril) inhibit the converting enzyme that is responsible for the formation of angiotensin II, a potent vasoconstrictor that stimulates the release of aldosterone. This drug appears to improve the survival rate of older adults with hypertension and CHF.

Side effects of this drug include cough, rash, taste disturbance, neutropenia, and protenuria. If clients are taking aspirin with ACE inhibitors, blood pressure control may decrease, and this is an important factor, since many older clients believe that aspirin is effective in decreasing risks from cardiovascular disease.

ACE inhibitors should not be used if acute renal failure or bilateral artery stenosis is suspected.

Calcium channel blockers

Calcium channel blockers (dilitiazem, nicardipine, nifedipine, verapamil) inhibit the inward movement of calcium across the cell membrane of vascular smooth muscle, and this results in vasodilation of peripheral, coronary, and renal arteries. It has been shown that dilitiazem and verapamil may aggravate CHF. For those clients who require a calcium channel blocker and who have CHF, or are taking a beta blocker, the most appropriate drug choice is nifedipine.

These drugs typically have vasodilator effects such as headache, flushing, dizziness, and weakness. Constipation may also occur. The calcium channel blockers are very useful agents in the treatment of older adults and can be used when diuretics are not tolerated or contraindicated.

The use of antihypertensive drugs (diuretics, beta-blockers, ACE inhibitors and calcium channel blockers) has been shown to be effective and well-tolerated by older adults, although it may be necessary to combine two or more drugs. The prescription is "to proceed slowly and with caution" and to monitor for adverse reactions. If this principle is observed, the older client can be treated with minimal side effects. See Table 21-5, p. 509-510, for the classification of antihypertensive drugs, adverse effects, and nursing considerations.

Prognosis

Hypertension, if unrecognized and untreated, significantly increases the risk of coronary disease, heart and renal failure, and stroke. Risk increases with smoking, glucose intolerance, hyperlipidemia, left ventricular hypertrophy, male gender, African-American race, or increasing age. With an individual pharmacologic and nonpharmacologic treatment program based on assessment of total cardiovascular risk, the risk of cardiovascular-related death from stroke and heart attack can be reduced. The degree of end-organ damage affects overall morbidity and mortality.

TABLE 21-2

Low-Cholesterol Diet

Foods to avoid	Foods to substitute
Butter, lard, coconut oil, salt pork, suet, bacon and meat drippings, gravies and sauces unless made with the allowed fat	Safflower oil, corn oil, and margarine made from these polyunsaturated oils
Whole milk, cream	1% milk, skim milk, dried nonfat milk
Most cheese	Small quantities of cheese made with skim milk
Egg yolk (limited to three per week)	Egg white
Cold cuts, hot dogs, sausages, bacon, goose, duck, poultry skin, organ meats, hamburger, spareribs, canned or frozen meats in sauces or gravies (especially frozen meals)	Lean beef, lamb, pork, veal, chicken, turkey, dried or chopped beef
Shellfish (shrimp, crab, lobster)	Fresh or frozen fish (no sauces added)
Biscuits, muffins, sweet rolls, corn bread, pancakes, waffles, French toast, hot rolls	Bran, whole wheat, rye or white bread, graham crackers, unsalted crackers, baked goods containing no whole milk
Buttered, creamed, or fried vegetables prepared with excluded fats	Any fresh or frozen vegetables cooked with allowed fats
Commercial soups except those indicated for salt-free diets (check labels carefully)	Bouillon, clear broth, cream soups made with skim milk
Avocado, except in small quantities	Fresh, frozen, or canned fruits (check labels carefully)
Pies, cakes, cookies, or other desserts containing whole milk, fat, or egg yolks; ice cream, whipped toppings, chocolate	Angel food cake, puddings or frozen desserts made with skim milk, gelatin desserts, fruit ices, ice milk, sherbets

tion. Other nursing diagnoses that may be appropriate for an older adult client with hypertension include, but are not limited to ineffective individual coping, ineffective management of therapeutic regimen, and altered nutrition—more than body requirements.

✤ PLANNING

Expected outcomes for an older client with hypertension include, but are not limited to the following: (1) client identifies personal risk factors, (2) client explains the disease process and its effects on health and well-being, (3) client incorporates nonpharmacologic treatment measures into daily living, (4) client verbalizes purpose, dose, action, and significant and reportable side effects of medications prescribed for hypertension, (5) client increases social interaction as evidenced by participation in activities outside the home with others two to three times per week, (6) client eats a low-fat and low-cholesterol, reduced-calorie diet as evidenced by 1-to-2 lbs.-per-week weight loss.

✤ INTERVENTION

Knowledge levels of hypertension clients vary among individuals. Although Mrs. S is employed as a homemaker, it is obvious that she requires specific information regarding risk factors associated with heart disease. The content of the teaching plan should incorporate an explanation of the disease process and therapeutic (nonpharmacologic and pharmacologic) interventions.

An explanation of the physical examination and appropriate tests should be given to allay anxiety. Anxiety, depression, denial, and fear are often involved with a chronic condition. Although these emotions diminish as the condition is controlled, the client's ability to absorb this information and make the required changes is difficult during the initial phase, because the client may still be in denial. For the older adult, participation in a Hearts for Life program using videotapes and handouts with large print may be beneficial.

Content of a teaching plan is presented in the Client Family Teaching box on p. 511. It is obvious that Mrs. S is very lonely and leads an isolated existence apart from work. Although she is a very warm, compassionate and caring individual, she has not attempted to make friends outside of work. Refer client to *55 Plus,* a recreational activity center for those age 55 and older, so that she can socialize with others and decrease her loneliness. Mrs. S may also wish to consider volunteer activities. She will be retiring next year and will need to involve herself in other interests. A new program is being developed in the community in which she can volunteer to be a "grand" friend to younger children, assisting in their social development.

Client education includes providing information re-

Text continued on p. 511

TABLE 21-3

Fat Finder

0-5 Grams of fat/serving	6-10 Grams of fat/serving	11-20 Grams of fat/serving	More than 20 Grams of fat/serving
Milk and milk products			
1 serving 5 250 ml(1 cup) or 45 gm (1 1/2 oz) cheese or equivalent as indicated.			
All milk except whole	Milkshake	Cheese (except those listed)	
2% or dry cottage cheese	Mozzarella cheese	Eggnog	
Skim processed cheddar	Feta cheese	Goat's milk	
125 ml (1/2 cup) ice milk	Ricotta cheese	125 ml (1/2 cup) premium ice cream	
Low-fat yogurt	Whole milk		
Part-skim ricotta cheese	Creamed cottage cheese		
	125 ml (1/2 cup) regular ice cream		
	Frozen yogurt		
Meat, fish, poultry and alternates			
1 serving = 90 gm (3 oz) cooked lean meat, fish, poultry (visible fat and/or skin removed) or 250 ml (1 cup) cooked dried peas, beans, lentils or equivalent as indicated			
Cooked sliced deli ham or beef	Lamb roast or chop	Salami	125 ml (1/2 cup) nuts or seeds
Beef top round steak	Pork leg	Corned beef, ground beef	60 ml (4 tbsp) peanut butter
Pork tenderloin	Pork picnic shoulder	Beef blade, cross rib	
Lobster, scallops, shrimp	Pork loin (center cut)	Pork loin-rib end	
Water-packed tuna	Pork loin (tenderloin end)	Fried chicken or nuggets	
Sole, clams, crab	Beef rump, sirloin tip	Herring	
Cod, halibut, haddock	Beef rib, sirloin, loin	Mackerel	
Beans, peas, lentils	Beef flank, round	Canned salmon	
Pastrami	Back bacon	Beans and weiners	
	Chicken or turkey (dark meat)	Chicken or turkey breast	
	Roast chicken	Chili	
	Salmon or oil-packed tuna	1 wiener	
	Fish sticks	2 eggs	
	Montreal smoked meat	4 slices side bacon	
	Veal	3 sausages	
Breads and cereals			
1 serving = 1 slice of bread or 125 ml (1/2 cup) cooked cereal, pasta, rice, or 175 ml (3/4 cup) ready-to-eat cereal or equivalent as indicated			
All types bread or rolls	1 brownie	Granola	
English muffin	2 shortbread cookies	1 croissant	
Cereals (except granola)	2 sugar cookies	1 piece pie (125 gm/4 oz)	
Pasta	2 peanut butter cookies	1 piece carrot cake (125 gm/4 oz)	
Rice	1 cake doughnut	1 piece cheesecake (125 gm/4 oz)	
1 pancake or small waffle	1 piece fruit cake	1 Danish	
4 crackers	1 piece pound cake	1 yeast doughnut	
2 cookies (except as indicated)	1 piece coffee cake		
1 small muffin	1 piece iced cake		

From the Canadian Nutrient File: Health and Welfare Canada, 1989. Reprinted with permission from the minister of Supply and Services Canada, 1995.

Continued.

TABLE 21-3

Fat Finder—cont'd

0-5 Grams of fat/serving	6-10 Grams of fat/serving	11-20 Grams of fat/serving	More than 20 Grams of fat/serving
Fruit and vegetables			
1 serving = 125 ml (1/2 cup) or equivalent as indicated			
All fruits and vegetables (except for those listed)	Mashed potatoes	Potato salad	
	Scalloped potatoes	Hash brown potatoes	
	10 french fries	5 onion rings	
		1/2 avocado	
Fats and oils			
1 serving = 15 ml (1 tbsp) or equivalent as indicated			
Sour cream	Regular salad dressing	Mayonnaise	
Table cream		Lard	
Reduced calorie salad dressing		Shortening	
Whipping cream		Oil	
Cream cheese			
5 olives			
5 ml (1 tsp) butter			
5 ml (1 tsp) margarine			
Combination dishes/other			
1 serving = 250 ml (1 cup) or equivalent as indicated			
Plain popcorn	Stew	Cream soups	Chicken a la king
Water-based soups	10 potato chips	Chop suey	Fish sandwich (fast food)
6 hard candies	Meatloaf (90 gm/3 oz)	1 regular hamburger (60 gm/2 oz)	Macaroni and cheese
Beans with pork	Cheese pizza (90 gm/3 oz)	1 taco	1 large cheeseburger (120 gm/4 oz)
		1 chocolate bar (45 gm/1 1/2 oz)	Quiche (150 gm/5 oz)
			Meat pie (210 gm/7 oz)

TABLE 21-4

Influence of Comorbidity on Selection of an Initial Antihypertensive

Comorbid condition	Preferred drug class	Not recommended for initial therapy
Coronary heart disease	Beta-blocker Calcium channel blocker	Vasodilator
Congestive heart failure	ACE inhibitor Diuretic	Beta-blocker Verapamil
Left ventricular hypertrophy	ACE inhibitor Calcium Channel Blocker Central alpha 2 agonist	Vasodilator Beta-blocker
Diabetes/hyperlipidemia	As above plus peripheral alpha antagonist	Beta-blocker Diuretic
Renal insufficiency	Diuretic (loop diuretic may be required), beta-blocker, vasodilator, calcium channel blocker	Central alpha-agonist (in uremia)
Stroke	Calcium channel blocker	Vasodilator
Subarachnoid hemorrhage	Nimodipine	Central agent

From Elnicki M, Kotchen T: Hypertension: patient evaluation, indications for treatment, *Geriatrics* 48(4):60, 1993.

TABLE 21-5

Classification of Antihypertensive Drugs, Adverse Effects, and Nursing Considerations

Antihypertensive drug	Adverse effects	Nursing considerations
Diuretics		
Thiazides		
Bendroflumethiazide (Naturetin) Benzthiazide (Aquatag, Exna) Chlorothiazide (Diuril) Chlorthalidone (Hygroton) Cyclothiazide (Anhydron) Hydrochlorthiazide (Esidrix, HydroDIURIL) Hydrofluemethiazide (Diucardin, Saluron) Indapamide (Lozol) Methychlothiazide (Enduron, Aquatensen) Metolazone (Diulo, Zaroxolyn) Polythiazide (Renese) Quinethazone (Hydromox) Trichlormethiazide (Metahydrin, Naqua)	Hypokalemia Hypomagnesemia Hyponatremia Hyperuricemia, acute gout attack Hyperglycemia Hypercholesterolemia and hypertriglyceridemia, possible increased risk of heart attack Fluid and electrolyte imbalance Hypersensitivity to sulfonamides Sexual dysfunction	Encourage clients to restrict sodium intake and to eat foods high in potassium. Diabetics may require an increase in insulin. Check baseline and later levels of LDL cholesterol and triglycerides. Report mouth dryness, muscle weakness, cramps, drowsiness and loss of appetite which may be indicative of electrolyte imbalance. Check for any signs of rash. NOTE: High doses of aspirin may reduce the antihypertensive effects of diuretics.
Loop diuretics		
Bumetanide (Bumex) Ethacrynic acid (Edecrin) Furosemide (Lasix)	Fluid electrolyte imbalance Diuresis may lead to hypovolemia, hypotension and shock Older clients may suffer thromboembolism Ethacrynic acid may cause watery stools	Observe for signs of dehydration and acid base imbalance. Monitor blood pressure to detect signs and symptoms of hypotension and shock. Observe for signs and symptoms of thromboembolism.
Potassium-sparing diuretics		
Amiloride (Midamor) Spironolactone (Aldactone) Triamterene (Dyrenium)	Hyperkalemia May cause breast pain and amenorrhea in women May cause renal calculi Impotence, sexual dysfunction	Monitor serum potassium levels. Potassium supplements should be discontinued when these drugs are added to the sulfonamide diuretic regimen. Triameterene should be given cautiously to clients taking indomethacin.
Beta-blockers		
Acebutolol (Sectral) Atenolol (Tenormin) Betaxolol (Kerlone) Carteolol (Cartrol) Labetalol (Normodyne, Trandate) Metoprolol (Lopressor) Nadolol (Corgard) Penbutolol (Levatol)	Cardiac effects, including bradycardia, atrioventricular conduction block, and decreased strength of myocardial contractions Marked slowing of the heart rate leading to dizziness and fainting Fatigue, weakness, lethargy, mental depression, disorientation and hallucinations	Report any changes in cardiac rate and rhythm (especially in regard to slowing of heart rate). Do not administer drugs to clients in heart failure or with advanced degrees of heart block. Observe client for any changes in physical and mental status.

Modified from Joint National Committee on Detection: *Report of the Joint National Committee on detection, evaluation, and treatment of high blood pressure,* Washington, D.C., 1992, US Department of Health and Human Services; Johannsen: Update: guidelines for treating hypertension, *AJN* 93(3):42-49, 51-53, 1993; Rodman, 1991a.

Continued.

TABLE 21-5

Classification of Antihypertensive Drugs, Adverse Effects, and Nursing Considerations—cont'd

Antihypertensive drug	Adverse effects	Nursing considerations
Pindolol (Visken) Propranolol (Inderal) Propranolol, long acting (Inderal LA) Timolol (Blocadren)	Gastrointestinal effects—nausea, vomiting, abdominal cramps, diarrhea or constipation Bronchospasm in patients with asthma May mask hypoglycemia May aggravate peripheral vascular insufficiency and exacerbate CHF Impotence, sexual dysfunction	Warn clients of possible side effects and to report to physician. Check lab reports for any changes in HDL and triglyceride levels. Warn clients to never abruptly discontinue the drug.
ACEIs		
Captopril (Capoten) Enalapril maleate (Vasotec) Lisinopril (Prinivil, Zestril)	Drug-induced tickle in the throat, hacking cough, bronchospasm Hyperkalemia in older clients taking a potassium supplement or a potassium-sparing diuretic Hypersensitivity reaction with rash and swelling of the skin and mucous membranes Hypotension has been observed in clients with high plasma renin activity or in those receiving diuretic therapy May cause reversible, acute renal failure in clients with renal-artery stenosis, cardiac failure or proteinuria Dizziness, headache, diarrhea and fatigue Impaired sense of taste and sexual dysfunction rare	Observe clients for cough. Check electrolytes for rise in potassium. Observe for any signs of rash or swelling. Check lab reports for a rise in blood urea nitrogen (BUN) or serum creatinine which may signal renal failure. Observe for signs of dizziness, headache and diarrhea.
Calcium antagonists		
Diltiazem (Cardizem) Nicardipine (Cardene) Nifedipine, sustained release, (Procardia XL) Verapamil, sustained release (Calan SR, Isoptin SR)	Headache Dizziness Weakness Flushing Edema Nausea Constipation (especially with verapamil) Atrioventricular block Bradycardia	Monitor heart rate closely. Monitor blood pressure during dose adjustment. Check lab results of liver and kidney function tests and report abnormalities. Use cautiously in clients in second or third degree heart block, CHF, or those taking digitalis or beta-adrenergic blocking drugs. Use cautiously when these drugs are given in combination with other antihypertensive agents to avoid an excess reduction in blood pressure.

CLIENT/FAMILY TEACHING

Hypertension

Disease and healing process

Signs and symptoms of hypertension

Medication

Explain the purpose, dosage, side effects, and special considerations, including signs and symptoms of side effects from diuretics.

Emotions

Anxiety, depression, and denial are normal and subside with appropriate treatment and lifestyle changes. It is imperative that the individual be cautioned regarding side effects of selected antihypertensive agents, since these cause physical and mental changes, as well as sexual impotence, which may further aggravate anxiety and depression.

Modifiable risk factors

Smoking	Reduce or eliminate intake, join a smoking cessation program, discuss therapeutic aids with physician (e.g., Habitrol), hypnotism or behavior modification
Hypertension	Stress the importance of regular blood pressure measurements and physician visits, maintain a low-sodium, high-potassium and low-fat, low-cholesterol diet, a regular exercise program (e.g., walking), and medication regimen; lose weight if indicated
Weight loss	Refer to a dietician or a weight-loss program; set realistic goals (1 to 2 pounds per week); become more active; read labels to avoid sodium, sugar content, and hydrogenated products; suggest to bake/boil/steam food and to eat plenty of fresh fruits and vegetables, especially broccoli
Exercise	Walk for 10 to 15 minutes and gradually increase to 1 hour three to four times per week; suggest a mall-walking program or aquaerobics with other women
Diet	Follow reduced cholesterol and saturated fat diet, and eat three to four small meals daily; limit alcohol intake
Stress	Identify stressful situations at work and home and modify reactions; meditation, relaxation, visualization, relaxation tapes, or a program in the community for stress management may be indicated

garding disease process, treatment regimen, and the need for frequent monitoring of blood pressure and risk factors. Explain the importance of a low-sodium, high-potassium, low-fat, reduced-calorie diet. Discuss the importance of alcohol restriction and smoking cessation. Explain the relationship between stress, anxiety, anger, and hypertension, and teach relaxation techniques.

✜ EVALUATION

Evaluation includes determining the client's achievement of the expected outcomes. Regular, ongoing assessment of blood pressure and screening for signs and symptoms of hypertension are necessary to assess effectiveness of the pharmacologic and nonpharmacologic treatment measures instituted.

Coronary Artery Disease

CAD or ischemic heart disease refers to a broad group of conditions that partially or completely obstruct blood flow to the heart muscle. Obstruction of coronary arteries can result in ischemia (an imbalance between the oxygen supply and demands of the heart) or infarction (death or necrosis) of the myocardium, when the oxygen supply is unable to meet the demands of the heart. Atherosclerosis is the usual cause of coronary artery disease; angina, MI, and sudden death may be the final outcomes.

Atherosclerosis usually begins in childhood and is characterized by a local accumulation of lipid and fibrous tissue along the intimal layer of the artery. Lipids accumulate and infiltrate the area forming a raised fibrous plaque over the site. Eventually, the plaque becomes calcified causing the vessel to lose its elasticity and dilatory qualities. Progressive narrowing of the artery occurs resulting in compromised blood flow to the area of myocardium supplied by that vessel. In advanced stages of the disease, hemorrhage into the atheromatous plaque, thrombus formation, embolization of a thrombus or plaque fragment, and coronary arterial spasm can cause additional insult to the body (Fig. 21-7). Although the development of atherosclerosis appears to be a normal process of aging, the severity of this process can be accelerated with the adverse lifestyle behaviors of smoking, sedentary lifestyle and obesity, as well as elevated serum cholesterol levels, hypertension, and diabetes. Promoting healthy lifestyles in younger and older individuals is an important aspect of care in the prevention of CAD. The adoption of healthier lifestyles by an older adult may be difficult as a result of long-term habits; however, healthy behavior changes can slow or halt the progression of the disease.

The risk of CAD increases with age. Although the rate of progression varies, clinical manifestations in men tend to appear in the fourth, fifth, and sixth decades, and 10

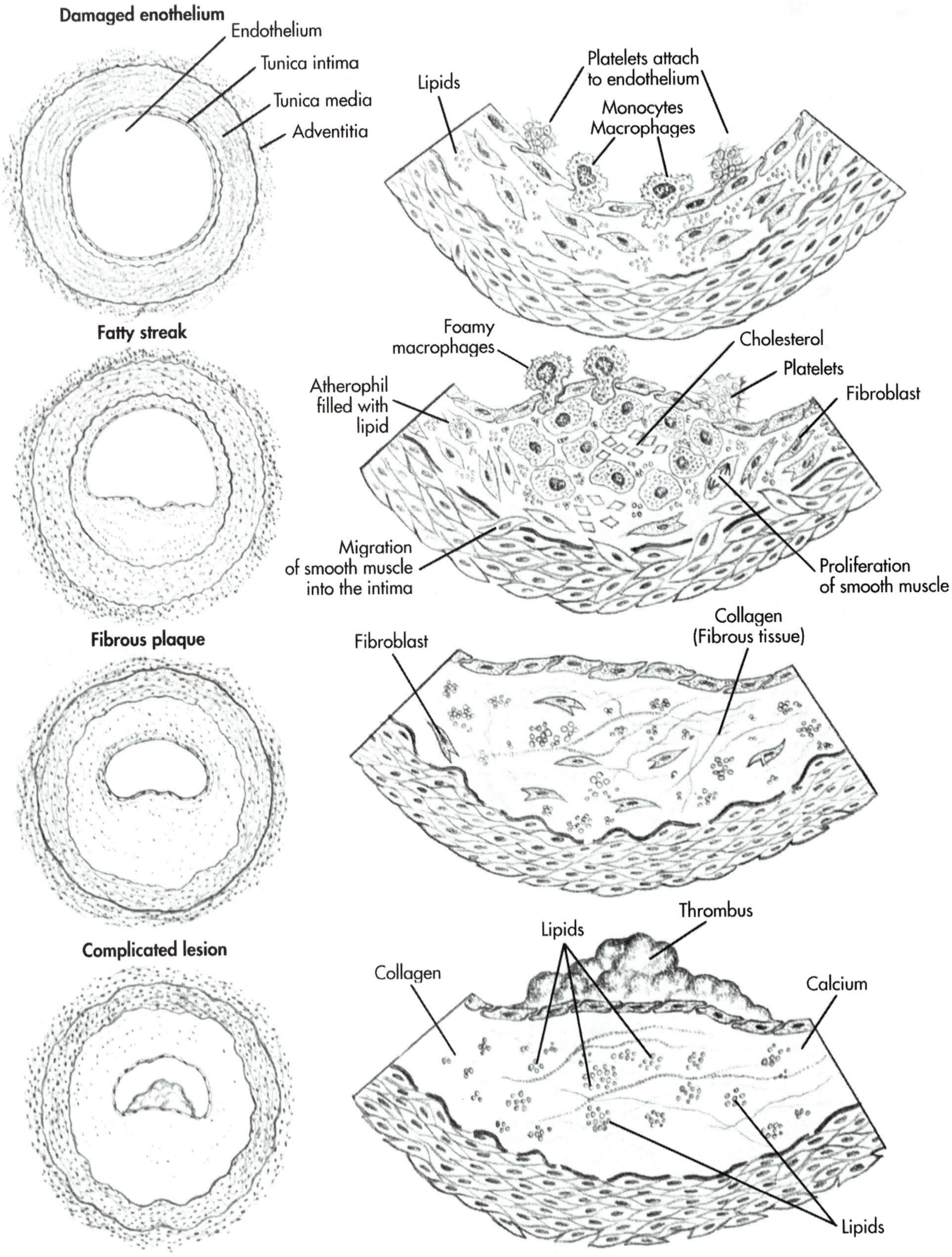

Fig. 21-7 Progression of artherosclerosis. (From McCance KL, Huether SE: *Pathophysiology: the biological basis for disease in adults and children,* ed 2, St. Louis, 1994, Mosby.)

BOX 21-3

Symptoms of Angina or MI

- Chest pain (heavy, squeezing, crushing sensation in the sternal area that may radiate to the neck, jaw, and/or external aspects of the left arm)
- Nausea
- Vomiting
- Diaphoresis
- Dizziness
- Weakness
- Dyspnea
- Palpitations
- Indigestion

EMERGENCY TREATMENT

Chest Pain

- Take charge of situation (anticipate denial)
- Remain calm
- Assist to sitting position
- Loosen restrictive clothing
- Determine presence of heart disease by asking and/or checking medical alert bracelet
- Assist with medication
- Direct someone to call 911 or call yourself if alone
- Stay with individual until help arrives
- Institute cardiopulmonary resuscitation (CPR) if indicated

years later in women (Barry, 1993; Heart and Stroke Foundation, 1991).

CAD is the most common cause of death in people over age 65. Although this age group constitutes about 12% of the population, 80% of all deaths attributed to MI occur in this age group, and 60% of deaths occur in adults 75 years and older (Gurwitz et al, 1991). The prevalence of coronary artery disease in the older adult is estimated to be 50% to 70%, and more than half of all individuals hospitalized for acute MI are older than age 65 (Ambepitiya, Iyengar, Roberts, 1993; House, 1992b). Statistics suggest that 60,000 Canadians and 1.5 million Americans are diagnosed with MI annually (Long, Long, 1992). Older adults with CAD are more likely to have multivessel disease (Forman, Wei, 1993).

Presenting symptoms of MI depend on the location, site, and depth of myocardial damage. Typical symptoms of MI are listed in Box 21-3. Complaints of radiating chest pain (angina) are the most common symptoms experienced, lasting 3 to 5 minutes (or as long as 30 minutes), whereas chest discomfort with MI can last longer than 30 minutes. In the older adult, MI is the most common symptom of CAD (Giordaro, 1992). Women tend to have anginal symptoms more than men; however, after age 80, angina for both genders progressively decreases. Clinical manifestations of MI in older adults tend to have atypical symptoms (Box 21-3). Complaints of pain may be scattered and less severe than in younger individuals, and up to 30% of older adults may not feel pain in the early stages of MI (Gawlinski, Jensen, 1991; Giordano, 1992). Treadmill testing suggests that older adults take three times longer than younger adults to experience the onset of electrical ischemia, and these findings could be attributed to dysfunction of the ANS, perceptual alteration, or chronic pain suppression (Giordano, 1992). Older adults may not recognize the onset of ischemia, and initial symptoms may consist of sudden dyspnea, confusion, fatigue, weakness, vertigo, syncope, vomiting, and exacerbation of heart failure (Gawlinski, Jensen, 1991; Giordano, 1992). Diagnosis is based on client history and alterations in ECGs and serum cardiac enzyme tests (see Medical Management box pp. 514-517).

NURSING MANAGEMENT

ASSESSMENT

Chest pain is the usual symptom that motivates individuals to seek medical attention during episodes of myocardial ischemia. Of older adults, 50% may not experience chest pain, and delay seeking assistance if symptoms are vague or not intense (Gawlinski, Jensen, 1993; Giordano, 1992; Hartford et al, 1993).

Emergency treatment of clients with chest pain is presented in the Emergency Treatment box above. Chest pain attributed to angina or MI is difficult to differentiate, and ECGs and serum cardiac enzymes are usually required to rule out or confirm the diagnosis of infarction.

Assessment of the older adult with CAD begins with a complete health history and physical examination (Box 21-4). Complaints of dyspnea, fatigue, syncope, vertigo, and confusion warrant further investigation as older adults tend to present with these symptoms rather than chest pain (Gawlinski, Jensen, 1993; Giordano, 1992). Subjective data may have to be collected when vital signs are stable and discomfort is relieved. Older adults are prone to auditory disturbances, and if evident, the nurse should face the client and speak slowly and clearly with a lower-pitched voice (Foreman, 1992).

Details that are significant to the nurse may not be significant to the older client, so specific health questions

Text continued on p. 518

MEDICAL MANAGEMENT

CAD

Diagnostic tests and procedures

- Serum cardiac enzymes of creatinine phosphokinase (CPK) and lactic dehydrogenase (LDH); Serum CPK values rise shortly after the infarction as a result of myocardial damage, peak at 24 hours, and return to normal levels within 72 to 96 hours; Serum LDH values increase after infarction, peak within 48 to 72 hours and return to baseline levels in 7 to 14 days
- Cardiac-specific isoenzymes of CPK-MB, LDH and LDH_2; elevations of these isoenzymes confirm a diagnosis of MI
- ECG to obtain information on rate, rhythm, hypertrophy, myocardial injury (ischemia or infarction), and the cardiac effects of electrolytes and medication
- Complete blood count (CBC) to determine if angina is caused by anemia
- White blood cell count to assess the typical inflammatory process associated with infarction (Kain, Reilly, Schultz, 1990)
- Serum electrolytes, particularly sodium, potassium, and calcium, as elevated or reduced concentrations of these electrolytes can lead to fluid imbalance, ventricular dysrhythmias, or asystole.
- Chest x-ray to determine overall size, shape, and position of the heart; however, in an older adult an echocardiogram may be superior in assessing cardiac chamber size, and left ventricular wall mass and thickness (House, 1992b)
- Arterial blood gases and coagulation studies may also be performed; reference values for serum testing vary and may not reflect changes associated with aging (Giordano, 1992); serum values from older clients should be compared with findings from the physical assessment
- Myocardial imaging (using thallium or pyrophosphate), multiple-gated acquisition cardiac blood pool imaging (MUGA scan), and/or digital subtraction angiography (DS) to evaluate myocardial perfusion or ventricular abnormalities
- Cardiac catheterization to detect the presence, location, and extent of lesions in coronary arteries; catheterization performed during an acute stage usually includes treatment to eliminate the coronary obstruction; with this procedure, older adults carry a higher risk for complications (Esberger, Hughes, 1989) (Fig. 21-8).
- Exercise stress test to determine activity tolerance; stress tests can be combined with myocardial imaging to identify changes in myocardial perfusion during exercise
- Holter monitors or echocardiograms for older clients who may not tolerate the demands for test completion because of debilitating conditions such as musculoskeletal or CNS system impairments (Kaplan, Pratley, Hawkins, 1991)

Treatment

Pharmacologic

Treatment is directed toward restoring the balance between myocardial oxygen demand and oxygen supply and for the prevention of CAD. Pharmaceutical agents play a major role in therapy and include the use of nitrates, beta-blockers, calcium channel blockers, anticoagulants, antidysrhythmics, and antihyperlipidemics. CAD is usually more extensive in older adults and multiple cardiac drugs are often prescribed. Normal changes with aging (alterations in body mass, water composition, liver size, renal system, and plasma protein concentration) tend to increase the concentration and prolong the excretion of standard drug doses, so smaller doses are generally prescribed for the older adult (Herbert, 1992).

Nitrates

These agents are used for the prevention and termination of anginal attacks and for reducing the pain associated with myocardial ischemia. These agents decrease the preload and afterload of the circulatory system, which reduces the myocardial demand for oxygen via its vasodilating effects on coronary arteries and peripheral vessels. Intravenous, sublingual (Nitrostat, Isordil), and aerosol (Nitrolingual) preparations have a rapid onset of action (1 to 3 minutes) and are used to prevent or to terminate an anginal attack. Daily doses of oral (Nitrogard, Isordil, and Cardilate) or dermal (Nitro-Bid, Nitrong, Nitrol, and Nitrodisc) preparations have a prolonged and continual onset of action and are used to prevent anginal attacks; however, tolerance by blood vessels to these preparations reduce drug effectiveness and periods of discontinuation are recommended. Headache, flushing, dizziness, hypotension, syncope, and tachycardia are side effects attributed to the vasodilating effects (Anderson, 1991). Nitrates are effective in older adults; however, aggressive therapy to reduce the preload and afterload may trigger reflex tachycardia and severe orthostatic hypotension because of age-related changes (e.g., ventricular distensibility, delayed ventricular filling times). Older adults should take rapid-acting nitrates in the sitting or lying position to prevent fainting or falls (Forman, Wei, 1993; Stanley, 1992).

Beta-blockers

These agents are used to prevent attacks in clients with stable angina or to reduce the size of infarction and complications with MI. Reduced heart rate, stroke volume, contractility, and decreased myocardial requirements are attributable to decreased sympathetic nervous stimulation through blockage of the beta adrenergic receptors in the heart. Side effects include bradycardia,

Continued.

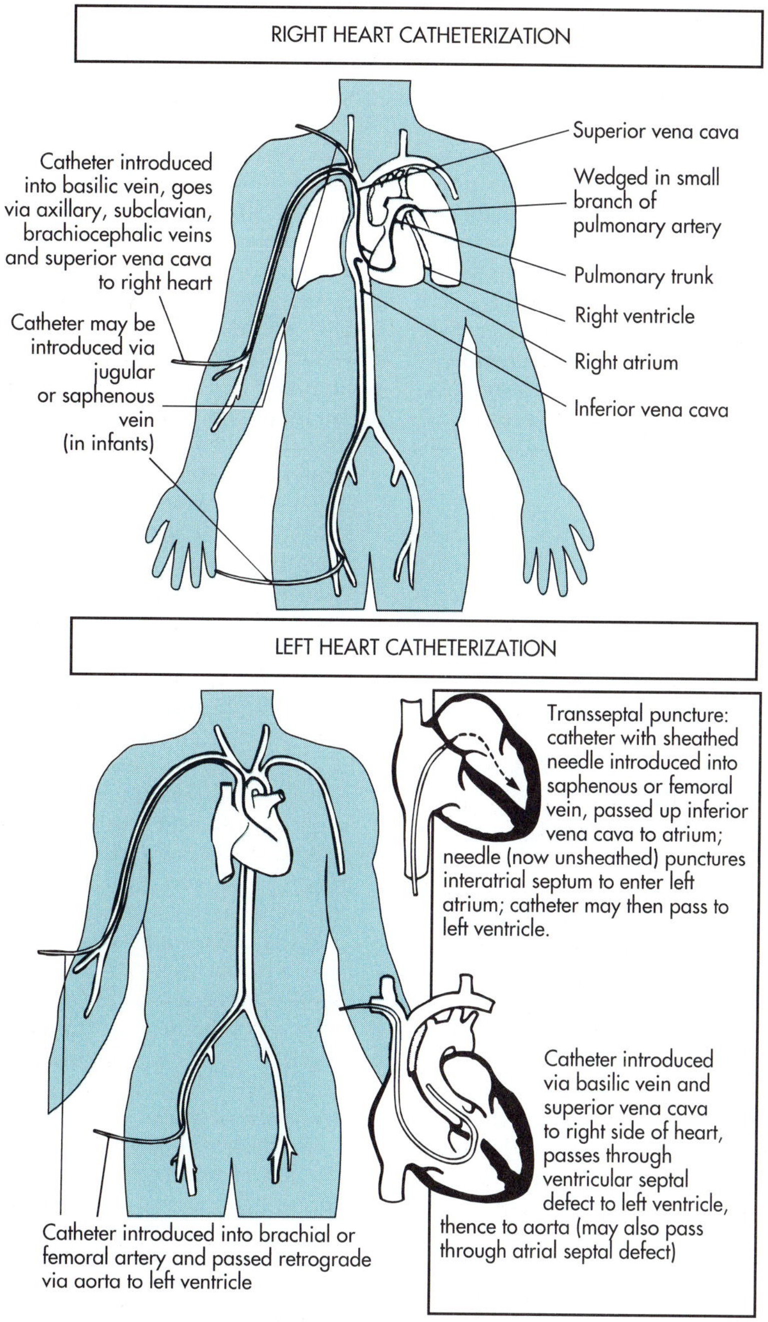
RIGHT HEART CATHETERIZATION
Catheter introduced into basilic vein, goes via axillary, subclavian, brachiocephalic veins and superior vena cava to right heart
Catheter may be introduced via jugular or saphenous vein (in infants)
Superior vena cava
Wedged in small branch of pulmonary artery
Pulmonary trunk
Right ventricle
Right atrium
Inferior vena cava
LEFT HEART CATHETERIZATION
Transseptal puncture: catheter with sheathed needle introduced into saphenous or femoral vein, passed up inferior vena cava to atrium; needle (now unsheathed) punctures interatrial septum to enter left atrium; catheter may then pass to left ventricle.
Catheter introduced via basilic vein and superior vena cava to right side of heart, passes through ventricular septal defect to left ventricle, thence to aorta (may also pass through atrial septal defect)
Catheter introduced into brachial or femoral artery and passed retrograde via aorta to left ventricle

Fig. 21-8 Right and left heart catheterization from the brachial and femoral approaches. (From Kern MF: *The Cardiac catheterization handbook,* ed 2, St. Louis, 1994, Mosby.)

MEDICAL MANAGEMENT

CAD—cont'd

hypotension, dyspnea, dizziness, syncope, gait difficulties, impaired vision, impotence, CHF, heart block, bronchoconstriction and depression (Forman, Wei, 1993; Newbern, 1991). Examples of beta-blockers are propranolol (Inderol), metoprolol (Lopressor), atenolol (Tenormin), timolol (Blocadren), nadolol (Corgard), and pindolol (Visken). For clients with lung disease, metoprolol and atenolol are safer to administer. Sudden cessation of therapy can induce myocardial ischemia. Older adults are more susceptible to adverse effects causing physicians to avoid prescribing beta-blocker therapy. Research suggests that older adults benefit from beta blockage during the early stages of MI. Effective therapy during the late stages of MI is evident in adults from age 60 to 75. Side effects may be mistaken for the normal consequences of aging. Older adults may need to test various beta-blockers to obtain a drug that is suitable to their needs (Newbern, 1991).

Calcium channel blockers

These agents are used in the prophylactic treatment of stable and variant angina and to increase coronary perfusion, reduce blood pressure, and decrease myocardial contractility in individuals with myocardial infarction (Forman, Wei, 1993). These drugs decrease the myocardial oxygen demand and increase coronary perfusion by blocking the entry of calcium ions into vascular muscle cells. Nifedipine (Adalat, Procardia), diltiazem (Cardizem), and verapamil (Isoptin) are commonly prescribed for angina as simple agents, or selectively combined with beta-blockers or nitrates. Adverse reactions are bradycardia, hypotension, flushing, dizziness, syncope, headaches, dyspnea, palpitations, peripheral edema, and dysrythmias. Research has not concentrated on the effects of calcium channel bockers in older adults; however, older adults may benefit from these agents with monitoring for vasodilating effects (Forman, Wei, 1993). Nicotine and alcohol reduce the effectiveness of these drugs and induce hypotensive episodes.

Anticoagulants

Fibrinolytic, anticoagulant, and antiplatelet agents are used to prevent, to reduce, and to dissolve thrombi around atherosclerotic plaques by altering blood-clotting mechanisms. Fibrinolytic or thrombolytic agents given by intravenous or intracardiac routes within 6 to 8 hours after the onset of symptoms of MI can dissolve obstructive thrombi and can restore coronary blood flow to damaged myocardial tissue. Examples of these agents are alteplase (Activase or TPA), anistreplase (Eminase), streptokinase (Streptase, Kabikinase) and urokinase (intravenous route only). Clients must be observed for dysrhythmias, myocardial ischemia from emboli obstructing smaller vessels, allergic reactions, and hemorrhage (Cronin, 1993). Aminocaproic acid (Amicar), an antidote, should be available. Heparin followed by oral anticoagulation should be administered after cessation of fibrinolytic effects to prevent secondary clot formation. Criteria for fibrinolytic therapy are well-defined, and older adults may be excluded from therapy as a result of age, delay in seeking treatment, presence of contraindicated conditions, and their risk for serious hemorrhagic complications (Arino, Bayer, 1993; Cronin, 1993). Few studies have specifically examined the effects of fibrinolytic therapy on older adults; however, research suggests that older adults may benefit more from therapy than younger adults, and should not be denied treatment (Forman, Wei, 1993).

Parenteral (intravenous or subcutaneous heparin) and oral (Warfarin, Coumadin) anticoagulants are used to prevent the enlargement of existing thrombi and new clot formation following MI. Therapeutic effects of heparin are monitored via partial thromboplastin times, or PTT (the antidote is Protamine Sulphate), and oral therapy is monitored by prothrombin time, or PT (the antidote is vitamin K in Phytonadione or Synkavite). Clients who are initially anticoagulated with heparin and need oral anticoagulation for maintenance, usually take both forms of medication for 3 to 5 days to develop a prolonged PT value within the therapeutic range. Internal or external hemorrhage is a major complication.

Antiplatelets inhibit adherence and aggregation of platelets along damaged vessels and are used in clients with unstable angina, MI, and following cardiac surgery to prevent thrombus formation and vessel occlusion (Long, Long, 1992). Examples of antiplatelets include acetylsalicylic acid (Aspirin), sulfinopyrazone (Anturan), and dipyridamole (Persantine); side effects are bruising, melena, and epistaxis (Dalen, Goldberg, 1992). Aspirin is the most common prophylactic drug prescribed; however, its use in older adults is unclear and older adults have a higher incidence of side effects. Older adults may benefit from aspirin in lower doses of 80 to 325 mg daily, every second day, or a few times per week (Long, Long, 1992).

Antidysrhythmics

Dysrhythmias are frequent complications following MI, and antidysrhythmics may be prescribed to modify impulse conduction and restore normal sinus rhythm. These drug classifications are presented in Table 21-6. Side effects include hypotension, dizziness, syncope, nausea, vomiting, diarrhea, confusion, parasthesia, slurring of speech, seizure activity, heart failure, and dysrhythmias. Aggressive treatment of dysrhythmias (intravenous) with lidocaine in the older client should be of limited duration and at a lower dose than younger individuals (Forman, Wei, 1993).

Antihyperlipidemics

These agents are used to lower serum lipid levels by preventing absorption of cholesterol and promoting fecal se-

MEDICAL MANAGEMENT

CAD—cont'd

cretion of the substance by inhibiting biosynthesis of cholesterol (or low density lipoprotein), or by reducing the synthesis of lipids to lower triglyceride levels. Examples of these agents are cholestyramine (Questran), colestipol (Colestid), clofibrate (Atromid-S), gemfibrozil (Lopid), lovastatin (Mevacor), and probucol (Lorelco). Common side effects are gastrointestinal upset, and older adults are prone to constipation. Antihyperlipidemics are given prophylactically to prevent CAD and should be prescribed if dietary and activity measures are ineffective. Older adults can benefit from cholesterol lowering treatment.

Nonpharmacologic

Elimination/reduction of risk factors

Older adults with risk factors of inactivity, obesity, and smoking should be encouraged to eliminate or reduce these factors and to control conditions of diabetes and hypertension. Elimination of these risk factors has the potential to half or reduce the progression of CAD.

Invasive and surgical procedures

- **Percutaneous transluminal coronary angioplasty (PTCA)** - PTCA involves the insertion of a specially designed balloon-tipped catheter (under fluroscopy) through advancement from the femoral or brachial artery. When situated over the stenotic or occluded area, the balloon is inflated to compress the obstructing plaque resulting in a larger vessel lumen and improved blood flow to the myocardium. Clients with persistent angina that is unresponsive to medical treatment, single lesions that are not calcified, and/or atheromatous plaques in proximal/accessible vessels may benefit from PTCA (Fig. 21-9).
- **Coronary artery bypass grafts (CABGs)** - CABG is a surgical procedure that grafts portions of the saphenous vein or internal mammary artery to sites above and below the occluded coronary artery to bypass the stenotic vessel and supply blood to the ischemic myocardium.

CABG is performed on clients with severe myocardial ischemia that is unresponsive to medical treatment and not amenable to PTCA (Fig. 21-10).

Older adults who are healthy, active, and independent with few associated diseases and cardiac risk factors, as well as adequate support systems, are appropriate candidates (Brown, 1992; Costello 1993; Foreman, 1992).

Research suggests that the risk of morbidity and mortality increases with emergency CABG, so elective surgery should be scheduled following stabilization with medication, intraortic balloon pumps, and other temporary measures (Foreman, 1992).

Prognosis

Infarct-related mortality before hospital discharge in older adults (ages 70 to 99 years) is estimated to be 32%. Cardiac mortality within 1 year following infarction is approximately 12% for adults between age 65 to 75 years and 17.6% for adults over age 75 (House, 1992b). Age-related physiologic changes, long duration of adverse lifestyle behaviors, and the presence of other disease conditions in older adults can complicate the progress and treatment of CAD; however, advances in the medical and surgical treatment and the adoption of healthier lifestyles has the potential to influence the course and outcome of this disease in older adults.

TABLE 21-6

Antidysrhythmic Drug Classification

Class	Action	Antiarrythmic drugs
I	Depresses depolarization rate and conduction velocity by retarding sodium flow into cell during depolarization	Quinidine Procainamide (Pronestyl) Disopryramide (Rhythmodan) Lidocaine (Xylocaine) Mexiletine (Mexitil) Tocainide (Tonocard) Phenytoin (Dilantin)
II	Depresses sympathetic stimulation by blocking beta-adrenergic receptors	Propranolol (Inderal) Metoprolol (Lopressor) Timolol (Blocadren) Atenolol (Tenormin) Nadolol (Corgard)
III	Prolongs absolute refractory periods and action potentials by antifibrillatory effects	Bretylium (Bretylol) Amiodarone (Cordarone)
IV	Depresses SA and AV node activity, prolongs AV node conduction, increases refractoriness at AV node by blocking calcium channels	Verapamil (Isoptin) Diltiazem (Cardizem) Nifedipine (Adalat)

during the assessment (e.g., "Are you able to shop for groceries?") may elicit more detailed responses than open-ended questions (e.g., "Do you have any difficulties with activities at home?"). When gathering objective data, older adults may have slower heart rates, irregular rhythms, the presence of a third or fourth sound, systolic ejection murmurs, higher systolic blood pressures, and wider pulse pressures as a result of the normal aging process, not the current ischemic episode (Lakatta, 1993).

✣ DIAGNOSIS

Nursing diagnoses common for the older client with CAD include, but are not limited to (1) pain, (2) decreased cardiac output, (3) activity intolerance, (4) constipation, and (5) knowledge deficit.

✣ PLANNING

As with all clients, the older adult with CAD should be included in the planning of care. Family should also be included in the planning process; however, older adults should be consulted to determine the extent of the family involvement. Discharge planning should begin on admission to the hospital with special attention given to the necessary support services in the home.

Expected outcomes for the older client with CAD include, but are not limited to the following: (1) client verbalizes pain relief; (2) client maintains adequate circulation as evidenced by stable vital signs, mental alertness, urine output greater than 30 ml/hr, and clear breath sounds; (3) client tolerates activity as evidenced by stable vital signs; (4) client maintains normal bowel elimination pattern, (5) client explains the disease process and therapeutic plan; and (6) client identifies cardiac risk factors and methods to reduce these factors.

✣ INTERVENTION

Chest Pain Related to Alternation in Cardiopulmonary Tissue Perfusion and Anxiety

Chest pain is caused by myocardial ischemia and can be intensified if the client is anxious. Pain caused by angina is usually precipitated by activities that increase myocardial demand for oxygen and is relieved by rest and nitroglycerine. Severe ischemia and infarction are not relieved by rest. Nursing interventions include the administration of nitrates, either sublingually or intravenously, and morphine sulphate intravenously. Sufficient medication should be given to alleviate discomfort regardless of age; however, older adults may require more intensive monitoring of blood pressure and respiratory rate to prevent severe hypotension and respiratory depression. Supplemental oxygen and bed rest can improve circulating oxygen levels while decreasing myocardial workload. Older adults may be hesitant to complain about pain so

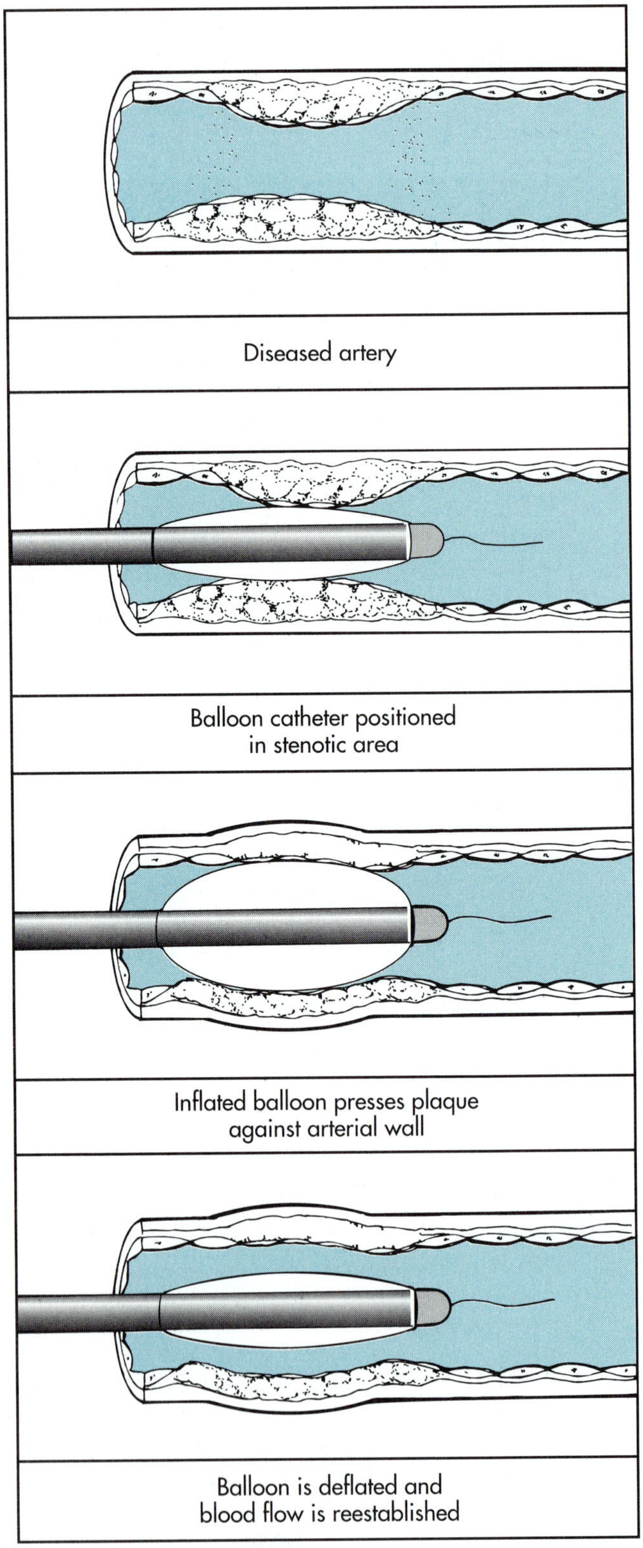
Diseased artery
Balloon catheter positioned in stenotic area
Inflated balloon presses plaque against arterial wall
Balloon is deflated and blood flow is reestablished

Fig. 21-9 Coronary angioplasty procedure. (From Canobbio MM: *Mosby's clinical nursing series: cardiovascular disorders,* St. Louis, 1990, Mosby.)

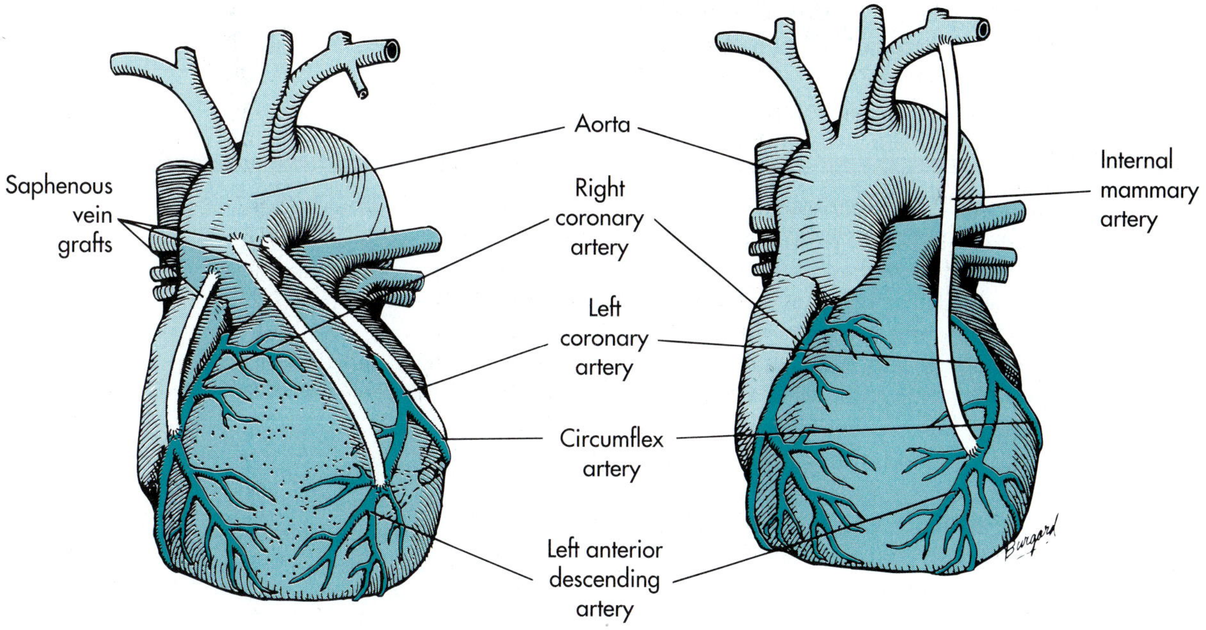

Fig. 21-10 Two methods of coronary artery bypass grafting. Saphenous vein revascularization is more common, but results appear to be longer lasting with internal mammary artery revascularization. The procedure used depends on the nature of the CAD and the condition of the vessels available for grafting. (From Phipps WJ et al: *Medical-surgical nursing: concepts and clinical practice,* ed 5, St. Louis, 1995, Mosby.)

BOX 21-4

Assessment of Clients with Chest Pain

Subjective data

- Chest pain (location, intensity, radiation, onset, duration)
- Precipitating factors (activity, emotions, rest, hot/cold exposure, and eating)
- Associated symptoms (diaphoresis, dyspnea, vomiting, weakness, palpitations, and indigestion)
- Relieving factors (rest, nitrates)
- Prior hospitalization (for angina, MI and other disorders)
- Medications
- Family history (parents or siblings with CAD onset before age 50)
- Modifiable cardiac risk factors (smoking, high cholesterol levels, hypertension, diabetes, obesity, physical inactivity)
- Psychosocial state (denial, anxiety, fear, anger)
- Activity levels (to perform activities of daily living [ADLs])
- Support systems

Objective data

- Behaviors (nervous, lethargic, rubbing chest, grimacing)
- Changes in vital signs (increased or decreased pulse and blood pressure)
- Changes in rhythm
- Associated symptoms (diaphoresis; pallor; cold, clammy skin)
- Peripheral pulses (radial, femoral, pedal)
- Apical heart sounds and murmurs
- Respiratory rate and breath sounds (diminished, clear, crackles, wheezes)
- Jugular venous distention
- Diagnostic test results (elevated serum cardiac enzymes, ECG changes of ST elevation, inverted T waves, abnormal Q waves, abnormal chest x-ray, elevated or depressed hemoglobin, hematocrit, white cell count, and electrolytes)

the nurse should encourage the client to relay sensations when they occur and often ask the client if chest pain is present. Depending on the symptoms, additional vasodilators (e.g., beta-blockers and/or calcium channel blockers) may be prescribed. Fluid diets and assistance with ADLs (e.g., bathing, toileting, and feeding) can be provided during initial stages to decrease myocardial workload and avoid discomfort. For clients with CABG, chest pain needs to be differentiated from incisional pain. Nitrates or other vasodilating agents may be used to treat chest pain resulting from ischemia. Analgesics, splinting devices, positioning, and balancing activities with rest help alleviate incisional pain.

Interventions to reduce anxiety include explanations of equipment, procedures, and unit routines to the client and family or significant others. Explanations with reinforcements are helpful to older clients. Expression of feelings and questions about treatment should be encouraged. The presence of supportive family members or friends, personal belongings (e.g., blanket, sleepwear), and pastoral care may help relieve anxiety. Older clients and family may express concern about emergency measures such as rescusitation or life support. The nurse should be sensitive to these needs and initiate discussion with the client, family, and physician to establish a plan of action.

Decreased Cardiac Output Related to Electrical and Mechanical Dysfunction

Disturbances in electrical conduction or pumping mechanisms of the heart are attributed to myocardial ischemia. Initially, vital signs need frequent monitoring (every 15 to 60 minutes) and when stabilized, every few hours. Heart rate and rhythm patterns should be observed often on a bedside monitor or telemetry unit. Several dysrhythmias are not life-threatening, but are transient and disappear with improved coronary circulation. Any dysrhythmia requires monitoring to prevent deterioration into severe or life-threatening situations. Healthy older adults tend to have supraventricular rhythm disturbances and occasional premature ventricular beats; these normal disturbances need to be differentiated because of ischemic episodes (Lakatta, 1993). Antidysrhythmics or temporary pacemakers need to be used to restore regular rhythms and conduction deficits.

Cardiovascular, respiratory, renal, and neurologic assessments should be conducted on a regular basis to detect progress and to prevent complications. Older adults with MI or with CABG have an increased risk for complications and require close supervision (Forman, Bernal, Wei 1992; House, 1992b). See Box 21-5 for signs and symptoms of common cardiac complications. Accurate intake and output measurements are important nursing functions. Diagnostic tests (especially potassium, as older clients are prone to hyperkalemia) should be evaluated daily and any adverse changes in client status should be reported to the physician. Critically low levels of cardiac output require hemodynamic monitoring by Swan Ganz catheter insertion; inotropic medications such as dopamine, dobutamine, or amrinone (Inacor); or insertion of an intraortic balloon pump.

Pulmonary embolism and reinfarction or extension are complications caused by thromboemboli and affect cardiac output. Clients with current or previous infarctions are prone to thrombus formation as a result of the presence of atherosclerosis. These clients require anticoagulation therapy. Interventions to promote venous return and to prevent thromboemboli formation consist of active and passive range-of-motion exercises for clients on bed rest, early ambulation, and the use of antiembolitic stockings. Antiplatelet drugs may be prescribed for prophylaxis.

Pharmacologic therapy comprises the main treatment for alterations in cardiac output and older adults are more susceptible to side effects with single and multiple medications (Carr, 1994; Forman, Wei, 1993). Nursing in-

BOX 21-5

Signs and Symptoms of MI Complications

Cardiogenic shock
Low blood pressure (systolic less than 90 mm Hg)
Tachycardia
Oliguria (less than 30 ml/hr)
Pallor, cyanosis
Cool, clammy skin
Mental confusion

Heart failure
Stable blood pressure (drops when compensatory mechanisms fail)
Presence of S_3 heart sounds
Elevated JVD (if progresses to right side)
Dyspnea, orthopnea, tachypnea
Wheezes, crackles, pink frothy sputum
Pallor, cyanosis
Weight gain
Peripheral edema
Restlessness

Thromboemboli
Sudden pain in chest or legs
Tachycardia
Dyspnea
Pallor

terventions involve monitoring therapeutic and adverse effects of medication and being observant for drug interactions. New symptoms in older adults should be investigated as possible adverse reactions to pharmacologic therapy (Forman, Wei, 1993).

Activity Intolerance Related to Imbalance of Myocardial Oxygen Supply and Demand

When the myocardium is damaged from infarction or surgery, rest and activity must be balanced to avoid stressing the healing heart. During the acute phase of recovery (24 to 48 hours), activity is restricted to bedrest with supplemental oxygen and bedside commode privileges. Cardiovascular fitness deteriorates more rapidly in older individuals than in younger adults and extensive deterioration can occur within 2 days (Herbert, 1992). Early mobilization is encouraged to prevent deterioration and enhance independence. When restricted to bedrest, older adults need active and passive range-of-motion exercises to maintain muscle strength and tone, and to prevent stasis. The client should be reminded every hour when awake to wiggle the toes and to flex and to extend the muscles of the foot and leg to enhance circulation. Older adults may benefit from a trapeze apparatus to maintain strength in the upper limbs. If tolerated, clients can perform their ADLs with the nurse providing assistance when needed (Herbert, 1992). Personal articles should be within reach.

Structural cardiovascular changes (e.g., reduced sensitivity of baroreceptors, slower ANS response, delayed early diastolic filling), and the limited reserve pumping capacity predispose healthy older adults to activity intolerance during exertion (Lakatta, 1993). The added stressors of infarction or surgery, medication, and immobility compound responses to exertion and stress, so the nurse should allow longer time intervals for activity completion with close supervision (Gawlinski, Jensen, 1993).

Resumption of activity begins on the second or third day following admission with activities increasing from simple to complex as tolerated. Progressive activities begin with dangling feet at the bedside for 5 to 10 minutes (using a footstool and bedside table for support), and advance to sitting in a chair with armrests and ambulating short distances, with each activity increasing in duration and frequency. Balance and activity may be affected by musculoskeletal alterations in the older adult (e.g., arthritis, corns and bunions), and soft slippers or shoes with good support and hand rails may enhance mobility. Some clients may benefit from supplemental oxygen and nitrates before and during activity. Older adults are prone to feelings of dizziness and syncope as a result of decreased sensitivity of baroreceptors to position changes and vasodilating agents, so clients should be encouraged to alter position changes slowly (i.e., sit for 3 to 5 minutes before walking) with assistance to prevent falls and injury. After each activity, fatigue, blood pressure, heart rate and rhythm, and respiratory rate should be evaluated to determine tolerance. The absence of chest pain, dyspnea, dysrhythmias, and systolic blood pressure changes, as well as a heart rate increase of less than 20 beats per minute suggest cardiac tolerance (Beare, Myers, 1994). Clients should be encouraged to recognize adverse sensations and cease activity when such conditions appear.

Activity levels can be measured by the amount of energy used per activity or metabolic equivalent (MET) units, where one MET is equal to a person at rest using 3.5 ml of oxygen/kg/min. Older clients are often restricted to very light activities during hospitalization with the exception of commode privileges (Beare, Myers, 1994). Clients can use the MET system to guide activity levels during each phase of recovery in combination with cardiac tolerance criteria. Before discharge or within a month following discharge, exercise stress tests or heart catheterization may be performed to determine activity levels and to assess myocardial damage. The nurse should prepare clients for these diagnostic tests.

Constipation Related to Activity Intolerance, Therapeutic Regimen

Older adults are susceptible to constipation as a result of the aging process, activity restrictions, and side effects of medication. Elimination patterns vary among individuals, so the nurse should assess the client's particular pattern and remedies for prevention. Straining during defecation should be avoided to prevent an increase in myocardial workload. During the acute phase, dietary intake is usually restricted to fluids to ease myocardial workload and unless contraindicated, 1,500 to 2,500 ml of water should be consumed daily by the older adult. Range-of-motion exercises and early ambulation help prevent constipation. With dietary increases, foods high in fiber such as carrots, potatoes, bran, fruit (especially prunes), and whole grains may provide bulk for the stool without roughage. As a last resort, laxatives or stool softeners may be prescribed (de Leon, 1989; Vander Horst, Sykula, Lingley, 1994). Some older adults prefer a cup of hot water in the morning to promote defecation.

Knowledge Deficit (Disease Process, Treatment Plan, Modification of Risk Factors) Related to Lack of Exposure or Recall

Knowledge levels of CAD and treatment vary among individuals and teaching plans are developed following a thorough assessment of knowledge levels. Recovery from MI or bypass surgery is completed within 6 to 8 weeks; however, recovery may be delayed in older adults as a result of a higher incidence of complications with longer stays in hospital (Costello 1993; House, 1992b).

Content of a teaching plan for clients with CAD is presented in the Client/Family Teaching Box, at right. Although all clients benefit from teaching before discharge, older adults may prefer to focus on symptom management, medications, risk factors, and home activity rather than physiologic details (Duryee, 1992). Standard teaching plans provide direction for content; however, older adults exhibit special needs. A large percentage of older adults experience atypical symptoms with angina and myocardial infarction and the nurse should focus on sensations experienced with the current hospitalization to help clients recognize symptoms other than chest pain (Hicks, 1994). A diary to record symptoms, duration, intensity, location, activity, mood, and treatment may help older clients to identify patterns (Basilicato et al, 1992).

Multiple drugs are often prescribed for clients with CAD. An older adult who has difficulty with compliance may benefit from a designated support person who can contact the client about treatment effects and can remind to refill medications (Morrison, 1993). Clients should carry a record of all medications and be encouraged to bring all medications for review with the physician during appointments (Carr, 1994). Older clients should also be instructed on limiting alcohol content and use of over-the-counter (OTC) medications that can adversely affect the treatment regimen.

Discharge medications vary; however, most clients with CAD are prescribed sublingual or aerosol nitroglycerine. Older clients, especially those individuals using other vasodilating agents, are prone to hypotensive episodes and should use nitrates in the sitting or lying position. With the onset of chest pain, the client should use a nitroglycerine tablet, and if the pain is not relieved within 5 minutes, another tablet should be used. Nitroglycerine should be repeated every 5 minutes until a maximum dose of three tablets. Pain persisting after three doses requires emergency medical attention. Tablets should be stored in the original container in a cool, dark location. When opened, the date should be written on the container, since tablets are potent for 3 to 6 months. The cotton should then be removed to prevent absorption of the drug. Nitroglycerine should be with the individual at all times. Canisters of lingual spray are stable for approximately 3 years (Yakabowich, 1992).

The nurse should explain that anxiety, depression, and denial are common emotional responses to MI. Although these emotions subside as recovery progresses, older adults with complications, additional medical disorders, and some medications such as beta-blockers may experience prolonged depression (Foreman, 1992). These emotions may affect motivation for learning and knowledge retention during hospitalization, so family and significant others should be included in teaching sessions to assist with the reinforcement of learning material during hospital and home recovery. Research suggests that family members (particularly spouses) tend to neglect their own needs and become exhausted with their roles as caregivers (McCrae, 1991). The nurse should encourage verbalization of these emotional responses and perceptions of role changes, and provide both client and caregiver with assistance and direction for coping.

Identification and reduction of risk factors can reduce the risk of early cardiac death and enhance long-term

CLIENT/FAMILY TEACHING

CAD

Disease and healing process

Signs and symptoms of angina and MI

Medication

Explain the purpose, dosage, side effects and special considerations.

Emotions

Anxiety, depression, and denial are normal feelings, which subside with recovery.

Modifiable cardiac risk factors

Smoking	Reduce or eliminate intake, join a cessation program, discuss therapeutic aids with physician.
Hypertension	Regular blood pressure measurements and maintainence of diet, activity, and medication regimen.
Diabetes	Regular glucose measurements and maintainence of diet, activity, and medication regimen.
Weight loss	Join a weight-loss program, set realistic goals, reduce caloric intake, remain active, read labels to avoid hydrogenated foods and items with high sugar content, bake/boil/steam food, eat plenty of fruits and vegetables.
Exercise	Progressive activity plan (walking), join a cardiac rehabilitation program, learn to monitor pulse, space activities with rest periods, stop activities if tired or chest pain develops, avoid heavy lifting, resume sexual activity within 4 to 8 weeks.
Diet	Follow reduced cholesterol and saturated fat diet and 3 to 4 small meals daily, rest after eating, limit alcohol and caffeine products.
Stress	Identify stressful situations and avoid them or modify reactions, walk to relieve anger, develop relaxation techniques, join a stress management group.

survival in older clients (Hicks, 1994). Restricted cholesterol or saturated fat, low sodium, and/or calorie-reducing diets may be prescribed by the physician in consultation with a dietician. The nurse can assist with client learning by reinforcing content of restricted diets, encouraging food label reading, and developing sample meal plans based on food preferences. Clients with CAD tend to be older women on fixed incomes, so creative meal plans may be needed (Eaker et al, 1992).

Exercise and ADLs should be gradually resumed during the first 6 weeks of recovery. Clients should be taught to monitor pulse and respiratory rate to evaluate tolerance to activity. Walking, with a progressive increase in duration and frequency, is recommended during the first 6 weeks after discharge, and clients are advised to avoid strenuous lifting. Clients should be reminded to space activities (e.g., housecleaning, gardening) throughout the day or week rather than performing all activities at once. Research suggests that women merit special attention with planning of household and family roles, since they are reluctant to relinquish the tasks and to accept help (MacKenzie, 1993). Older adults may benefit from a written plan of progressive activities following discharge.

Sexual relations can be resumed within 4 to 6 weeks, or when recommended by the physician. Nurses should assess the older client and partner's perception of the sexual role, and knowledge of the relationship between CAD and sexual ability (Panchal, Kmetz, 1991). Impotence is not a characteristic of aging, and the inability to achieve sexual relations may be attributed to CAD or adverse effects of medication (Kain, Reilly, Schultz, 1990; Panchal, Kmetz, 1991). Tolerance to this activity can be measured by climbing two flights of stairs. Anticipated strenuous activity, emotions, and sexual intercourse can be treated prophylactically with nitrates (see Chapter 10).

After 6 weeks, aerobic activities can be instituted with physician approval and guided by exercise, stress testing and the MET system. Jogging may not appeal to older adults, but activities such as dancing, bowling, cycling, swimming, and water aerobics may be preferable to promote cardiovascular fitness. Activities should be performed with supervision. Older adults require longer warm-up periods and longer rest periods between activities. Exercising in extreme temperatures should be avoided. Older clients should exercise for 30 minutes at least three times per week (House, Griego, 1992). Activity tolerance may be affected by older clients on beta-blockers as heart rate is depressed (Foreman, 1992).

Discharge Planning

Discharge planning involves teaching the client and family appropriate self-care activities during recovery at home. Cardiac rehabilitation programs are recommended for individuals recovering from MI and bypass surgery. These programs offer education, support, and supervised activity and are usually affiliated with local hospitals or major recreational centers. Most cardiac programs offer graduate follow-up for long-term recovery. Older adults who are unable to tolerate stress testing may be denied access to these programs, and the nurse can assist the client to locate alternate programs if required.

Visiting nurse programs can provide education, support, and supervised activities in the home environment if older clients are unable to attend outpatient services. Homecare services are usually available to assist the older client with ADLs. Both programs may require physician referral.

Local heart associations are excellent sources for learning materials and community programs on CAD. Some heart associations offer educational and support programs for clients recovering from CAD (e.g., Heart to Heart) or surgery (e.g., Mended Hearts), and can usually provide direction for community programs on risk factor reduction, cardiopulmonary resuscitation, and mall-walking.

Older clients often live alone and should be encouraged to wear medical-alert bracelets and assistive "help" devices that are available at local pharmacies. For those homebound clients who have difficulty with meal preparation, *Meals on Wheels* programs deliver one nutritious meal daily to the home.

✣ EVALUATION

Evaluation of the older client with CAD focuses on achievement of goals outlined in the planning process. Older adults should demonstrate adequate circulation, ability to return to ADLs, and control of symptoms before discharge from the hospital (see Nursing Care Plan, pp. 524-525).

Dysrhythmias

Dysrhythmias are abnormal heart rates or rhythms caused by a disturbance in automaticity, conductivity, or both. Dysrhythmias can originate in the atria, ventricles, or AV junctions, and can result in decreased cardiac output and impaired perfusion of coronary arteries.

Older adults can develop any type of arryhthmia; however, atrial fibrillation, sick sinus syndrome, and heart block appear more often in the older population as a result of fewer pacemaker cells and extensive deposits of fat and fibrous tissue throughout the conduction system (Gawlinski, Jensen, 1991; Lakatta, 1993; Stanley, 1992). Atrial fibrillation is the most common dysrhythmia of older adults, with estimated incidence of 2% to 4% in those individuals over age 65 (Repique, Shah, Marais, 1992; Sneed, Hollerback, 1992; Stanley, 1992). Atrial fibrillation is characterized by chaotic depolarization within the atria (greater than 350 beats per minute) with an irregular ventricular response. Older adults need increased diastolic filling pressures to compensate for structural

CARE PLAN

MI

Clinical situation Mrs. S is an 83-year old widow who was admitted to the hospital from a nursing home with complaints of fatigue, weakness, and vertigo. Staff at the nursing home became concerned after two episodes of syncope. Mrs. S suffered a stroke 4 years ago that left her with severe weakness in her left arm and left leg. She was unable to care for herself at home; her daughter encouraged her to enter the nursing home. She has been following a diet low in saturated fat and cholesterol and takes enteric-coated aspirin daily, as well as synthroid for hypothyroidism. Mrs. S is mobile with the use of a walker.

A routine ECG showed pathologic Q-waves and cardiac enzymes were tested. CPK levels were normal but LDH was elevated. She was diagnosed with an inferior MI. Since she did not meet the time criteria for fibrinolytic therapy, the physician instituted prophylactic measures with oral anticoagulants on a daily basis. Mrs. S developed occasional premature contractions and periodic bouts of atrial fibrillation. Digoxin and nitroglycerin were added to her regimen. She became very agitated in the coronary care unit about being a burden to her family and declined invasive treatment procedures. The nurse organized a meeting with the physician, daughter, and client to discuss her anxiety and a "no resuscitation" order was written. Lorazepam 1 mg PRN TID was added to the protocol.

Currently, Mrs. S denies having chest pain and can ambulate short distances with her walker. She follows a low-cholesterol/low-saturated fat diet and she is scheduled for an echocardiogram later in the week. Her blood pressure is in the low to normal range and her pulse is irregular at 102 beats per minute. Propranolol has been added to the regimen schedule to reduce the heart rate.

Nursing diagnoses	Outcomes	Interventions
Anxiety related to threat of death, change in health status	Client will verbalize reduced anxiety as evidenced by slower heart rate, reduced apprehension, and participation in self-care.	Explain equipment, procedures, and unit routine. Encourage verbalization of feelings. Teach relaxation techniques and guided imagery to alleviate anxiety. Supervise tolerance to visitation. Offer Lorazepam as needed. Encourage participation in care, and emphasize improvements in health status.
High risk for chest pain related to alteration in cardiopulmonary perfusion	Client will obtain pain relief as evidenced by verbal statements.	Encourage to relay pain sensations to nurse. Explain how sensations of fatigue, weakness, and vertigo may be symptoms of ischemia and need to be related to nurse. Encourage to take nitroglycerin at onset of chest pain or at sensations of ischemia. Obtain vital signs during episodes and contact physician if medication is ineffective. Offer oxygen if needed. Monitor therapeutic effects of nitrates and Propranolol, observing for hypotensive effects.
Decreased cardiac output related to electrical dysfunction	Client will maintain adequate circulation as evidence by stable vital signs, mental alertness, urine output >30 ml/hr, clear breath sounds.	Measure BP, apical pulse and rhythm every 4 hours. Auscultate heart/lungs every 8 hours. Monitor ECG for reversion to normal sinus rhythm, PT, digoxin levels, and electrolytes. Administer and evaluate the effects of Coumadin, Digoxin and Propranolol. Observe for signs of hemorrhage, shock, heart failure, and emboli.

CARE PLAN

MI—cont'd

Nursing diagnoses	Outcomes	Interventions
Activity intolerance related to imbalance of myocardial oxygen supply and demand, left peripheral limb weakness	Client will tolerate activity as evidenced by stable vital signs, absence of pain/weakness/fatigue/vertigo, participation in activity.	Assist with ADLs as needed. Remind to perform leg exercises every hour and range of motion exercises. Apply antiembolic stockings. Before ambulation, encourage leg exercises and sit at bedside for 3 to 5 minutes before standing. Gradually increase distance and frequency of walking.
Knowledge deficit (disease process, treatment plan) related to lack of exposure	Client will demonstrate knowledge of disease process and symptoms of ischemia with appropriate response and treatment plan, as evidenced by explanation and participation with plan.	Monitor vital signs before and after activity. Offer nitroglycerin and oxygen if needed. Keep call bell and walker within reach. Use shoes with good support and ambulate in lighted areas. Balance activity with rest. Teach to count own pulse. Encourage recognition of sensations of ischemia and cease activity when they occur. Include daughter in teaching sessions. Describe the disease and healing process of MI using pictures, models, and large printed material. Describe the client's sensations of ischemia, and teach appropriate use of nitrates and rest. Discuss and provide written information for medication dosage, purpose, side effects, and special precautions for Coumadin, Digoxin and Propranolol. Encourage progressive increase in activity. Assess emotions and reassure depression is common.
	Client demonstrates accurate pulse-taking method.	Teach to take radial pulse and to monitor before activity, during, and after activity.

changes within the heart and to maintain cardiac output, so chaotic or quivering depolarization within the atria diminishes this atrial kick needed for adequate ventricular filling (Lakatta, 1993). A sudden onset of atrial fibrillation can be precipitated by MI, sick sinus syndrome, fever, infection, or thyrotoxicosis, and can lead to angina, CHF or hypotension (Stanley, 1992). Chronic atrial fibrillation tends to occur in clients with hypertension, CAD, rheumatic heart disease, cardiac valve disease, and cardiomyopathy, and increases the risk for pulmonary, peripheral, and cerebral thromboembolization. Atrial fibrillation can be idiopathic in normal hearts (Repique, Shah, Marais, 1992; Stanley, 1992).

Sick sinus syndrome is characterized by alternating episodes of bradycardia (less than 60 beats per minute), normal sinus rhythm (60 to 100 beats per minute), tachycardia (greater than 100 beats per minute) and periods of long sinus pause that fail to stimulate the atria or ventricles. Sick sinus syndrome tends to occur in clients with CAD, rheumatic heart disease, and hypertension.

Heart block is characterized by delayed or blocked impulses between the atria and ventricles and are classified as first-, second-, or third-degree heart block, with each classification increasing in severity. First-degree block is common in older adults with or without CAD and is a common complication of MI. First-degree block attributed to MI is more likely to progress to a more severe form of block. Second- and third-degree block can also be caused by degeneration within the conduction system, ischemia, enhanced vagal tone, electrolytes, and effects of drugs (e.g., digoxin, beta-blockers, and calcium channel blockers), which are common conditions and treatments associated with aging (Cooke, 1992).

Symptoms of these dysrhythmias are weakness, fa-

MEDICAL MANAGEMENT

Dysrhythmias

Diagnostic tests and procedures

Dysrhythmias are diagnosed by ECG evaluation. When a dysrhythmia is diagnosed, a variety of tests may be performed to determine a causative factor. Continuous ECG monitoring provides the most efficient and reliable method of detection. A Holter monitor is often employed.

Treatment

Treatment is directed toward relief of symptoms, restoring normal rhythm, improving cardiac performance and preventing complications (Repique, Shah, Marais, 1992).

Atrial fibrillation

Aggressive therapy is required for a sudden onset of atrial fibrillation or uncontrolled fibrillation (ventricular response >100 beats per minute). Digoxin is the main therapy for this dysrhythmia, but it must be administered with caution to older adults, since they are susceptible to Digoxin toxicity (Cooke, 1992; Stanley, 1992). Beta-blockers or calcium channel blockers may be added to the regimen to suppress ectopic impulses.

Elective cardioversion may be instituted for sudden onset of atrial fibrillation if pharmacologic treatment is not effective.

Controlled (ventricular response < 100 beats per minute) and chronic atrial fibrillation is not life-threatening, so aggressive therapy is not indicated (Stanley, 1992). Clients may be treated with Digoxin and/or other antidysrhythmics to enhance cardiac performance. Oral anticoagulants are usually prescribed to reduce the risk for thromboembolic events (Repique, Shah, Marais, 1992). If the dysrhythmia is severe, a pacemaker may be inserted to control ventricular response.

Sick sinus syndrome

Treatment may include the administration of vagolytic agents such as atropine to block vagal impulses resulting in increased heart rate, or sympathomimetic agents (Isoproterenol, Isuprel) to stimulate beta receptors in the heart, resulting in an increased heart rate and force of contraction. Generally, sick sinus syndrome is corrected with the insertion of a pacemaker.

Heart block

Treatment for first-degree block includes observation to prevent deterioration into severe blocks, coupled with correcting the causative factor (e.g., electrolyte imbalance, drug toxicity). With second- and third-degree block, vagolytic and sympathomimetic agents are usually employed to increase heart rate and conduction. Pacemakers may also be inserted to correct the dysrhythmia.

Prognosis

Older adults with the dysrhythmias of sick sinus syndrome and heart block have an excellent prognosis when these dysrhythmias are corrected by pacemaker insertion. For clients with atrial fibrillation, benefits from aggressive pharmacologic treatment are not as great in older adults when compared with younger individuals (Stanley, 1992). Approximately 15% of all strokes are attributed to thromboembolic events associated with atrial fibrillation (Repique, Shah, Marais, 1992).

tigue, forgetfulness, palpitations, dizziness, hypotension, and syncope, all of which predispose the older client to falls and injuries (Snowberger, 1993a; 1993b; Stanley, 1992). Clients with first-degree block and fibrillation may have no symptoms, and clients with atrial fibrillation have an irregular pulse (see Medical Management box above).

NURSING MANAGEMENT

✣ ASSESSMENT

Assessment begins with a complete health history and physical examination. Older adults should be assessed for history of CAD, pump failure, rheumatic heart disease, hypertension, cardiac valve disease, and current medications (e.g., cardiac, diuretic, and electrolyte supplements) that may be causative factors of dysrhythmias. Symptoms of weakness, forgetfulness, palpitations, dizziness, and syncope should be investigated for frequency, length, precipitating factors and home treatment remedies (Snowberger, 1993; Stanley, 1992).

Objective data should focus on the circulatory response to the dysrhythmia and include heart rate, rhythm, blood pressure, peripheral pulses, urine output, and sensorium. Measuring the apical pulse for 60 seconds yields the most accurate measurement of heart rate. Apical and radial rates should be compared to assess peripheral perfusion (Sneed, Hollerbach, 1992). Electrolyte, hemoglobin, and hematocrit values should be assessed as older adults have a higher incidence of hyperkalemia and anemia that may trigger dysrhythmias (Kee, 1992).

✣ DIAGNOSIS

Nursing diagnoses common for the older client with dysrhythmias include, but are not limited to (1) decreased cardiac output, (2) activity intolerance, (3) high risk for injury, and (4) knowledge deficit.

✣ PLANNING

The client, family, spouse, and any other caregivers should be included in the planning process. The overall goals for the client with dysrhythmias are to maintain ADLs and adequate heart rate, to sustain cardiac output, and to prevent complications. Expected outcomes include, but are not limited to the following: (1) client will maintain adequate circulation as evidenced by natural or paced cardiac rate and rhythm within normal range, stable blood pressure, peripheral pulsations, mental alertness, urine output > 30 ml/hr and clear breath sounds; (2) client will tolerate activity as evidenced by stable vital signs and no complaints of dizziness, fatigue, or syncope; (3) client will remain free from injury; (4) client will explain the disease process and therapeutic plan; and (5) client will demonstrate procedure to measure radial pulse.

✣ INTERVENTION

Decreased Cardiac Output Related to Dysrhythmia, Loss of Atrial Kick With or Without Pacemaker

Vital signs should be monitored every 15 to 60 minutes if the client's condition is acute and every 4 hours if stable. Heart rate and rhythm should be continuously monitored through a telemetry unit or Holter monitor. The client should be encouraged to promptly relay symptoms of weakness, dizziness, and palpitations to the nurse for comparison with electrical cardiac activity. Showers and baths should be avoided if monitor electrodes are in place. Cardiovascular, respiratory, and neurologic systems, as well as intake and output measurements, should be assessed on a regular basis. Nursing interventions include the administration of antidysrhythmic agents with frequent evaluation of therapeutic and adverse effects as toxicity levels of these agents are more apparent in older adults (Foreman, 1992; Kee, 1992). Older clients with slow or fast ventricular responses to atrial fibrillation, long periods of sinus arrest with sick sinus syndrome, and second- or third-degree heart block are at risk for asystole and sudden death, so the nurse should be prepared to administer cardiopulmonary resuscitation measures.

Clients needing pacemakers require an explanation of the procedure and preoperative preparation. Following pacemaker insertion, nursing interventions include monitoring vital signs and performing incisional care. The monitor should be observed for normal and paced configurations, and electrical activity of the heart should be compared with peripheral perfusion parameters. Disturbances in pacemaker functioning (sensing, firing, capturing, or pacemaker syndrome) produce abnormal configurations on the monitor and symptoms of fatigue, weakness, dizziness, lack of energy, exhaustion, and hypotension. Changes in client status should be reported to the physician. Although VVI models are the most common pacemakers inserted, sensing and firing occur in the right ventricle without regard to atrial activity, and older adults who lose the atrial kick are prone to lower ventricular filling volumes and decreased cardiac output on exertion.

Activity Intolerance Related to Decreased Cardiac Output, Immobility

Sensations of weakness, fatigue, dizziness, or dyspnea affect a client's tolerance of activity. The nurse can assist clients with the identification of factors that increase or decrease activity tolerance. Activity patterns spaced with adequate rest can be developed. Physiologic responses to activity should be monitored.

For clients with pacemaker insertion, movement is restricted to bedrest for 24 hours following surgery, with limited shoulder movement on the operative side (i.e., the arm should not be raised higher than shoulder for 48 hours). Activity is restricted to promote attachment of

BOX 21-6

Educational Information for Clients with Pacemakers

- Maintain follow-up care with a physician, because it is important to check the pacemaker site; begin regular pacemaker function checks with magnet and ECG evaluation.
- Watch for signs of infection at the incision site (e.g., redness, swelling, and drainage).
- Keep incision dry for 1 week after discharge.
- With activity, avoid direct blows to generator site (i.e., avoid contact sports and use of rifles).
- Avoid close proximity to high output electrical generators or to large magnets such as magnetic resonance imaging (MRI) scanner. These devices can reprogram the pacemaker.
- Microwave ovens are safe to use and do not threaten pacemaker function.
- Travel without restrictions is allowed. The metal case of a small implanted pacemaker rarely sets off an airport security alarm.
- Learn how to take pulse rate.
- Carry pacemaker information card at all times.

From Johns C: Nursing role in management dysrhythmias. In Lewis S, Collier I: *Medical-surgical nursing: assessment and management of clinical problems,* ed 3, St Louis, 1992, Mosby.

pacing catheters to cardiac tissue during healing (Beare, Myers, 1994). Cardiovascular fitness can be lost within a few days, so early mobilization of the older client is encouraged. Active or passive range-of-motion exercises should be implemented every hour when awake (Herbert, 1992). Older adults can flex and extend the affected arm, and can squeeze a rubber ball or similar item to maintain upper limb strength. Regular activities can be resumed within 24 hours, and the nurse should monitor the client's response to activity for potential pacemaker malfunction.

High Risk for Injury Related to Decreased Cardiac Output

Tachycardias, bradycardias, and long periods of sinus pause reduce cardiac output and place these clients at a higher risk for fainting and falls. Older adults are also at risk for falls with orthostatic position changes. Interventions to prevent injury include (1) sitting for 3 to 5 minutes before an activity and (2) protecting the client from objects with sharp or protruding edges by rearranging or padding objects in the room or hallway. Safety helmets during activity may protect the client from head injuries. Older clients should be monitored closely when active, and episodes of falls should be correlated with electrical activity of the heart.

Knowledge Deficit (Disease Process and Treatment Plan With or Without a Pacemaker) Related to Lack of Exposure

Family, significant others, and caregivers should be included during teaching sessions to assist with reinforcement of learned material during hospital and home recovery. The disease process and the dosage and side effects of all medications should be reviewed with the client. Older adults have a higher incidence of toxicity and adverse reactions with Digoxin, beta-blockers, and calcium channel blockers; written materials on these medications may be beneficial (Cooke, 1992; Foreman, 1992). For clients on anticoagulants, special consideration to prevent injury should be explained.

Educational information for older clients with pacemakers is presented in Box 21-6. Every pacemaker has an accompanying card with information relevant to that particular pacemaker. Information should be reviewed with the client. Clients are often concerned about how the pacemaker works and how long the device lasts. Clients should be taught to take their radial pulse at the same time each day and to evaluate their rate and regularity of the rhythm. Radial rates greater than 100 beats per minute, rates below the predetermined setting, and increases in irregularities should be reported to the physician. Older clients may benefit from recording the pulse and other data in a log book. Clients need to be aware of symptoms of decreased cardiac output.

Discharge Planning

Discharge planning involves teaching the client appropriate self-care during recovery at home. Following pacemaker insertion, clients are able to resume ADLs. If older clients anticipate difficulty with home recovery, visiting nurse organizations may be consulted. Heart associations are excellent sources for information and community programs, and family or significant others of clients with dysrhythmias should be encouraged to attend cardiopulmonary resuscitation programs. All clients should be encouraged to wear medical-alert bracelets to identify the dysrhythmia or pacemaker, as well as medication used.

✣ EVALUATION

Older clients with dysrhythmias or pacemakers should demonstrate a cardiac rhythm that supports adequate cardiac output. An ability to resume ADLs, knowledge of the therapeutic plan, and achievement of expected outcomes from the nursing care plan suggest that the client is ready for discharge (see nursing Care Plan, pp. 529-530).

Valvular Disease

Valvular disease occurs when the cardiac valves do not completely open (stenosis) or close (regurgitation insufficiency), which prevents efficient circulation of blood through the heart and increases myocardial workload. Valvular disease is more common in the mitral and aortic valves on the left side of the heart.

Stenosis of the mitral valve impedes blood flow from the left atrium to the ventricle during diastole. With time, the left atrium becomes accustomed to increasing volumes and pressure, causing dilation and hypertrophy. Stenosis of the aortic valve obstructs blood flow from the left ventricle to the aortic arch during systole. With time, hypertrophy of the left ventricle occurs as a result of increased pressures and volumes. Both stenotic conditions can eventually lead to hypertrophy of pulmonary vessels and decreased cardiac output.

Mitral regurgitation allows ejected blood to flow back into the left atrium from the ventricle during systole, resulting in dilation and hypertrophy of the left atrium and ventricle. Aortic regurgitation allows ejected blood to flow back into the left ventricle from the aorta during diastole, leading to volume overloads in dilation and hypertrophy of the left ventricle. Mitral valve prolapse (a form of valvular insufficiency) occurs when one or both cusps prolapse into the left atrium during ventricular systole. The prolapse is normally benign but can progress to severe regurgitation with ventricular dilation.

Rheumatic fever is the most common cause of valvu-

CARE PLAN

THE CLIENT WITH A PACEMAKER

Clinical situation Mr. G, 81, was admitted to the hospital with complaints of frequent falls and periods of confusion. He lives in a senior citizen apartment complex that provides minor home care services. He was brought to the emergency room by the health care worker in his apartment complex, and she stressed concern about alcohol abuse. Mr. G had bruises to his face and upper limbs and stated that he consumes two beers daily before his evening meal. His previous medical history includes hypertension and osteoarthritis of the lumbar area and both knees, but he ambulated slowly and without difficulty with the use of a cane. His apartment was equipped with hand rails and a communication system for contacting the health care worker. He has several friends living in the complex with whom he plays cards three times a week. He was attending an organized swimming program twice a week within his complex, but he quit the program a few weeks ago because of concern about his increasing falls and memory lapses. Mr. G has no living relatives and refers to his friends in the complex as his family. Current medications are supervised by the health care worker and include aspirin and aldactone.

On admission, Mr. G was alert and appeared healthy for his age. Vital signs, serum electrolytes, hemoglobin and hematocrit, chest x-ray, and ECG were within normal range. He continued to deny alcohol abuse and wished to return to his apartment before the owners leased it to someone else. Mr. G was sent home with a Holter monitor for a 24-hour period. Evaluation of the recording showed numerous periods of sinus arrest and bradycardic episodes, which coincided with feelings of dizziness, weakness, and one fainting spell. He was diagnosed with sick sinus syndrome, and he was hospitalized for insertion of a permanent pacemaker.

Nursing diagnoses	Outcomes	Interventions
Anxiety related to change in health status and change in environment	Client will demonstrate effective coping skills as evidenced by abilities to meet self-care needs and to problem solve.	Explain equipment, procedures, and unit routine. Encourage verbalization of feelings. Explore coping methods and identify methods that are successful in reducing anxiety. Encourage self-care with supervision. If necessary, arrange meeting with physician and apartment complex health care worker to address concerns.
Decreased cardiac output related to dysrhythmia	Client will maintain normal cardiac output as evidenced by normal heart rate and rhythm, blood pressure, peripheral pulses, adequate urine output, intact sensorium, and the absence of dizziness, fatigue, palpitations, and fainting spells.	Measure apical and radial pulse for 60 seconds, blood pressure, and cardiac rhythm every 1 to 4 hours. Encourage client to relate symptoms of decreased cardiac output promptly and compare with ECG rhythms. Encourage self-care at bedside (i.e., avoid baths or showers). Assess intake/output, cardiovascular, respiratory and neurologic systems every shift. Observe client and monitor for signs of pacemaker malfunction.
Activity intolerance related to immobility from surgery	Client will resume preoperative activity levels as evidenced by stable vital signs and absence of dizziness, fatigue, palpitations, and fainting spells.	Restrict activities to bedrest for 24 hours following pacemaker insertion. Limit operative shoulder movement for 48 hours. Encourage range of motion exercises every 1 hour when awake. Encourage flexion and extension of operative arm every 1 hour and hand pumping with a ball.

Continued.

CARE PLAN

THE CLIENT WITH A PACEMAKER—cont'd

Nursing diagnosis	Outcomes	Interventions
		Before activity, encourage to sit for 3 to 5 minutes to adjust for postural changes. Encourage activity resumption after 24 hours while observing client, and monitor for symptoms of decreased cardiac output and evidence of pacemaker malfunction.
Knowledge deficit (disease process and treatment plan with pacemaker) related to lack of exposure	Client will explain disease process and therapeutic plan.	Include health care worker in teaching sessions. Explain sick sinus syndrome and purpose of pacemaker. Review information card that accompanies pacemaker. Explain home care activities associated with pacemaker (i.e., physician follow-up, signs and symptoms of incisional infection, avoidance of objects containing large magnets or electrical generators). Provide educational information in written format. Encourage purchase of medical-alert bracelet. Encourage resumption of activities (especially swimming), after first visit with physician.
	Client will explain symptoms of decreased cardiac output. Client will demonstrate procedure to measure and record radial pulse.	Explain avoidance of vigorous arm and shoulder movement and lifting objects more than 10 pounds for 6 weeks after surgery. Review symptoms of decreased cardiac output associated with pacemaker malfunction (e.g., weakness, fatigue, exhaustion, palpitations, forgetfulness, dizziness, syncope and pulse rates $>$ 100 beats per minute, rates $<$ predetermined rate, increases in irregularities). Demonstrate procedure to measure radial pulse for 60 seconds. Observe client measuring pulse. Assist with the development of a daily diary to record pulse rate and adverse sensations.

lar disease, although the incidence of rheumatic fever has declined with the introduction of antibiotics. Inflammatory, infective connective tissue disorders and atherosclerosis are other causes. Mitral regurgitation and aortic stenosis can also be attributed to degeneration or calcification of the valves.

Aortic insufficiency, mitral stenosis, and mitral valve prolapse are more common in younger individuals. Pulmonary and tricuspid valvular disorders do not often occur in individuals. In older adults, aortic stenosis and mitral regurgitation are more common as a result of the degenerative process. Cardiac valve degeneration is evident in one third of individuals over age 75 (Gawlinski, Jensen, 1991; Leibovitch, 1989).

Individuals with valvular disease may be asymptomatic for many years, but with deterioration of the valves and hypertrophic changes in the atria or ventricles, symptoms become evident (Table 21-7). Of older adults, 40% initially experience dyspnea, 15% to 20% complain of dizziness, fatigue, weakness, and palpitations, 20% with heart failure (pulmonary congestion, distended neck veins, and pitting edema), and 15% initially present with syncope (Leibovitch, 1989). Atrial fibrillation is often associated with mitral disorders and symptoms of angina

MEDICAL MANAGEMENT

Valvular Disease

Diagnostic tests and procedures

A chest x-ray and ECG are initial diagnostic tests that may suggest valvular problems or evaluate damage to the heart from valvular problems. An echocardiogram (two dimensional or M-mode) with Doppler and ultrasound provide the most detailed information on structure of the valves, function (abnormal cusp movement), and chamber enlargement. The most definitive test is cardiac catheterization, which may be done to assess the severity of the valve disorder (valve size, pressure changes within the chamber, pressure gradients across valves) and additional effects on the heart (O'Sullivan, 1992). Exercise tests may also be conducted to evaluate the client's symptomatic response to exertion and capacity of the heart to function.

Treatment

Treatment is directed toward management of presenting symptoms and correcting the cause of the valvular disorder. Treatment for symptoms of heart failure consists of digoxin therapy, diuretics, vasodilating agents, restricted sodium intake, and oxygen therapy. Symptoms of decreased cardiac output related to atrial fibrillation (resulting from loss of atrial kick) are treated with digoxin therapy, beta-blockers, calcium channel blockers, cardioversion, or anticoagulation therapy. Symptoms of decreased cardiac output related to ischemia are treated with vasodilating agents. Prophylactic antibiotics before invasive procedures (e.g., surgery, invasive tests, and dental tests) are recommended for all clients with valvular disease to prevent the incidence of infective endocarditis. For clients with valvular disorders resulting from degenerative processes, medical treatment of symptoms tends to be unsuccessful over time and surgical repair or replacement of diseased valves may be necessary.

Prognosis

Mortality and morbidity rates are higher for older adults with valvular replacement or repair when compared with younger individuals. Older adults tend to have more advanced heart disease, experience more cardiac damage before diagnosis, have more coexisting ailments, and are more likely to experience complications following surgery (Brown, 1992; Gortner et al, 1994; Leibovitch, 1989). Mortality rates of 9.5% for adults in the seventh decade of life and 10% to 11% for adults in the eighth decade of life have been reported for cardiac surgeries, in comparison with 2.2% for those under age 70 (Gortner et al, 1994). Mortality rates are higher in older adults who undergo emergency surgery or if combined with other surgeries such as CABG (O'Sullivan, 1992). Mortality rates with valve repair are lower when compared with valve replacement; however, clients with surgical repair often require replacement at a later date. Valvular surgery on older adults has steadily increased during the past decade with survivors reporting symptomatic improvement and enhanced quality of life (Gortner et al, 1994).

TABLE 21-7

Clinical Manifestations of Valvular Heart Disease

Mitral stenosis	Mitral regurgitation	Aortic stenosis	Aortic regurgitation
Dyspnea, hemoptysis, fatigue, palpitations, loud accentuated S_1, opening snap, low-pitched rumbling diastolic murmur	Weakness, fatigue, dyspnea, peripheral edema, soft S_1, widely split S_2, S_3, high pitched pansystolic murmur	Angina pectoris, syncope, heart failure, normal or soft S_1, prominent S_4, crescendo-decrescendo systolic murmur	Exertional dyspnea, orthopnea, nocturnal angina, Corrigan's pulse, soft or absent S_2, S_3, or S_4, soft decrescendo high-pitched diastolic murmur, low frequency diastolic murmur (Austin-Flint murmur), especially in acute cases

From Kupper N, Duke E: Nursing role in management of inflammatory and valvular heart disease. In Lewis S, Collier I: *Medical-surgical nursing: assessment and management of clinical problems,* ed 3, St Louis, 1992, Mosby.

are more common with aortic disorders because of decreased cardiac output. Symptoms of valvular disease may be difficult to recognize in older adults as a result of nonspecific symptoms and a higher incidence of CAD in this population (Brown, 1992; Leibovitch, 1989) (see Medical Management box above).

NURSING MANAGEMENT

ASSESSMENT

Assessment of the older client with valvular disease begins with a complete health history and physical examination. Prior episodes of rheumatic fever, infective endocarditis, staphylococcal and streptococcal infections, as well as a family history of cardiac disease should be explored. Symptoms of valvular disease (fatigue, dyspnea, palpitations, dizziness, weakness, syncope, peripheral edema, distended neck veins, periods of memory loss or confusion, or chest pain) or related complications (dysrhythmias, angina, and heart failure) require further investigation. The older client's level of fatigue, toleration of activity, and current medications should be assessed. Older clients should be asked specific health questions to elicit an accurate health history.

Objective data should be obtained from the cardiovascular, respiratory, and neurologic assessment. Cardiovascular data include blood pressure (pulse pressure), heart rate and rhythm, weight loss or gain, peripheral pulses, presence of peripheral edema, neck vein distention, and heart sounds. Different heart sounds can be heard with each valvular disorder, and these sounds should be ausculated for abnormalities or changes (see Table 21-7). Respiratory data include rate, depth, and breath sounds. Diagnostic tests should be assessed for abnormalities.

Aortic stenosis is the most common valvular disorder among older adults because of calcification of the valve with aging. Stenosis of this valve tends to occur without fusion of the cusps, resulting in a spray of blood through the valve rather than forceful propulsion. Physical examination may reveal softer and more musical heart murmurs that can be confused with the normal aging process rather than a valvular disorder (Leibovitch, 1989). Older adults may require diagnostic testing to support a diagnosis of valvular disease.

✣ DIAGNOSIS

Nursing diagnoses common for the older client with valvular disease include but are not limited to (1) decreased cardiac output, (2) activity intolerance, (3) pain, (4) high risk for injury, and (5) knowledge deficit.

✣ PLANNING

As with all clients, the older adult with valvular disease and family should be included in the planning process. Discharge planning should begin on admission to the hospital with special attention given to necessary support services in the home.

Expected outcomes for the older client with valvular disease include but are not limited to the following: (1) client maintains adequate cardiac output as evidenced by stable vital signs, mental alertness, urine output > 30 ml/hr and clear breath sounds; (2) client tolerates activity as evidenced by stable vital signs; (3) client verbalizes reduction in or relief from pain; (4) client remains free from injury and complications; and (5) client explains the disease process, therapeutic plan, and preventive precautions.

✣ INTERVENTION

Decreased Cardiac Output Related to Narrowed Valves (Obstruction of Blood Flow) and/or Incompetent Valves (Backflow of Blood), Dysrhythmias, and/or Heart Failure

Cardiovascular, respiratory, and neurologic assessments should be conducted on a regular basis to detect progress and to prevent complications. Nursing responsibilities will vary with different symptoms. For clients with symptoms of dysrhythmias, particularly atrial fibrillation, therapy may include digoxin, beta-blockers, calcium channel blockers, anticoagulants, or cardioversion. For clients with symptoms of heart failure, therapy may include digoxin, diuretics, vasodilating agents, oxygen, and sodium/fluid restrictions. For clients with symptoms of myocardial ischemia, vasodilating agents may be prescribed. The nurse should monitor the client for therapeutic and adverse reactions to the above-named treatments. Bed rest is often prescribed to reduce myocardial activity and older clients need frequent range-of-motion exercises to prevent deterioration of cardiovascular fitness (Herbert, 1992).

For clients who do not respond to medical treatment, valvular surgery may be necessary to improve cardiac performance. Older clients benefit more from surgery when their condition is stabilized and performed on an elective basis. With older adults, the tendency is to repair valvular disorders rather than replacement interventions (Brown, 1992). Clients scheduled for valvular surgery are subjected to extensive diagnostic tests (e.g., ECG, nuclear scanning, heart catheterization and coronary arteriography, echocardiograms, ultrasounds, and chest x-ray) and serum studies (e.g., complete blood counts, electrolytes, blood urea nitrogen, creatinine, cardiac enzymes, coagulation profiles, and typing/crossing of blood). All procedures should be explained to the client and family to alleviate anxiety. Before surgery, prophylactic antibiotics are administered and certain drugs (e.g., digoxin, propranolol, diuretics, and anticoagulants) are weaned or discontinued. The client should be oriented to the intensive or coronary care unit and to the equipment used postoperatively (e.g., ventilator, ECG monitor, chest tubes, arterial lines, and drainage systems). The frequency of vital sign assessment postoperatively should be explained as should routine activities of deep breathing and coughing, incentive spirometry, and early mobilization. Research suggests that older clients with presurgical goals derive more benefits from cardiac surgery (Gortner et al, 1994).

Postoperatively older clients should be monitored closely for complications of MI, heart failure, thromboemboli, hemorrhage, dysrhythmias, and infection. Older clients have a greater risk for complications than younger individuals (Brown, 1992). Older adults are also prone to confusion following surgery because of the aging process, drug therapy, environmental alterations, and reduced cerebral perfusion during the procedure. The presence of family, familiar belongings, and use of personal hearing or visual devices may alleviate episodes of confusion (see Chapter 27 and 31).

Vital signs should be monitored often and when stable, every 4 hours. The client should be monitored for signs and symptoms of infection of the sternal incision and fluid imbalance.

Activity Intolerance Related to Decreased Cardiac Output, Heart Failure

For clients with severe symptoms of valvular disease or following surgical intervention, bed rest is recommended to reduce the workload of the myocardium. Older adults need active and passive range-of-motion exercises every hour when awake to maintain muscle strength and tone (Herbert, 1992). Early ambulation is encouraged and older adults may progress to chair sitting on the first day following surgery. Older adults are prone to feelings of dizziness and syncope with position changes resulting from decreased sensitivity of the baroreceptors (Lakatta, 1993). Position changes should be altered slowly (i.e., sit for 3 to 5 minutes before standing) with close supervision by the nurse. Ambulation can generally increase in distance and frequency. Older adults require secure footwear, and hand rails should be used for support. See Table 21-8 for additional nursing interventions.

Pain Related to Myocardial Ischemia, Impaired Skin Integrity

Complaints of chest pain need to be differentiated between angina type pain and incisional pain. Older adults are prone to silent ischemia, so dyspnea, fatigue, syncope, vertigo, and confusion may be evident rather than classical chest pain (Gawlinski, Jensen, 1991; Hicks, 1994). The nurse should encourage the older client to describe the pain (i.e., pattern, quality, intensity, duration, and precipitating events) or sensation. Nitrates may be prescribed for the ischemic pain. Analgesics, splinting devices, positioning, and balancing activity with rest may help to alleviate incisional pain. The incisional site should be observed every 4 to 8 hours for infection.

Risk for Injury Related to Valvular Disease, Alteration in Tissue Perfusion (Cardiopulmonary, Cerebral, and Peripheral)

Clients with valvular disease are at a high risk for development of infective endocarditis. Prophylactic antibiotics should be given before surgery or invasive procedures. Following surgery, antibiotic administration should continue for several days.

Older adults are prone to thrombus formation along the diseased valve and if dislodged, thromboemboli can affect any system. The risk is compounded in older adults with atrial fibrillation. Oral anticoagulants are usually prescribed as a prophylactic measure. Following valvular surgery, cardiovascular, neurologic, respiratory and peripheral assessments should be performed every 4 to 8 hours (when stabilized). Range-of-motion exercises, deep breathing and coughing, repositioning in bed, antiembolic stockings, and early ambulation are prophylactic interventions that reduce this risk for injury. For clients with prosthetic valves, oral anticoagulation therapy is prescribed for the duration of the valve.

CLIENT/FAMILY TEACHING

Valvular Disease

Disease process, surgical interventions

Signs and symptoms of valvular disease

Myocardial ischemia, atrial fibrillation, heart failure, infective endocarditis

Medication

Explain the purpose, dosage, side effects, and special considerations (anticoagulants, antibiotics)

Activity

Space activities with rest periods, avoid fatigue, and record and avoid precipitating factors that induce symptoms. Learn to take pulse. With surgery, avoid lifting heavy objects (greater than 10 pounds), and exercise caution with driving to permit healing of incision.

Diet

Review content, plan menus, and read labels if low sodium/saturated fat/cholesterol diet prescribed. With surgery, plan high-protein/calorie diets to enhance healing.

Incisional

Monitor for redness, drainage, and fever. Avoid showers and baths until sutures removed.

Preventive precautions

Report all invasive, surgical, and dental work to physician for prophylactic antibiotic therapy to prevent bacteremia. Inform dentist and gynecologist of valvular disease and have frequent checkups with dentist. Avoid dental surgery for 6 months following surgery. Perform thorough oral hygiene twice daily with manual toothbrush followed by oral rinses. Avoid electric and irrigation devices to prevent damage and possible bacteriemia. Obtain medical-alert bracelet for condition and medications.

TABLE 21-8

Nursing Interventions for the Older Client Following Open-Heart Surgery

Potential problems	Rationale	Interventions
Cardiovascular dysrhythmias, heart failure, postural hypotension	Older adult has inappropriate clearance of drugs, shifts in electrolyte levels, reduced vascular elasticity, decreased cardiac reserve, reduced vasomotor response.	Assess for signs and symptoms of dysrhythmias and heart failure. Monitor ECGs, electrolyte levels. Observe for drug effects and interactions. Monitor heart sounds, blood pressure, and heart rate regularly (pulse rate changes before blood pressure). Move and turn slowly, and exercise legs in bed before sitting. Recognize that heart rate takes longer to return to normal, and tachycardia may not indicate fatigue or activity intolerance. Observe for fatigue, activity intolerance, and altered breathing pattern. Balance activity with rest, and help pace activities.
Respiratory (pneumonia, atelectasis, ventilator dependency)	Older adults have weakened, atrophied respiratory muscles; diminished immunity; and higher incidence of respiratory diseases.	Deep breathing, coughing and incentive spirometry every 1 to 2 hours. Turn every 2 hours. Elevate head of bed. Splint incision with hand or pillow. Perform more frequent lung assessment (i.e., for sputum or abnormal breath sounds). Recognize that temperature does not elevate much with fever because of aging effects on temperature control (hypothalamus). Wean from ventilator when alert, able to cough, and has strength to breathe spontaneously.
Fluid and electrolye imbalances (dehydration)	Aging cells store less water, and kidneys concentrate urine less effectively.	Closely monitor intake and output, electrolyte levels, creatinine, BUN, and daily weight. Monitor intravenous fluids, since older adults are prone to overload. Inspect mucous membranes (skin turgor test not reliable in older adults). Remind to drink fluids at regular intervals.
Skin (impaired wound healing, infection)	Older adults heal slower because of decreased capillary perfusion, diminished immunity, osteoporosis of sternum.	Assess incision regularly and provide adequate nutrition (may need enteral or parenteral nutrition).
Elimination (paralytic ileus, constipation, urinary tract infection)	Older adults have decreased peristalsis and intestinal motility, diminished immunity, and reduced clearance of anesthetics and narcotics.	Encourage early ambulation, fluid intake, high-fiber diet (if able), and document bowel activity. Record urine output, perform perineal care, offer bedpan and urinal every 2 hours, and provide privacy and positioning for urination and defecation.

From Brown C: Cardiac surgery in the elderly: the critical care phase, *AACN Clin Iss Crit Care Nurs* 3(1):57-63, 1992.

TABLE 21-8

Nursing Interventions for the Older Client Following Open-Heart Surgery—cont'd

Potential problems	Rationale	Interventions
Musculoskeletal (pain, immobility, falls, and fractures)	Joints are less mobile and cartilage erodes in older adults. Reaction times are slower. Alterations occur in cerebellum affecting gravity center and balance.	Support and protect joints on movement. With range-of-motion exercises, support and move joints without force. Use supportive shoes. Canes or walkers may help until fully mobile. Ambulate in lighted areas with hand rails.
Neurologic (cerebrovascular accident [CVA], confusion).	Reactions occur more frequently in older adults than in younger individuals; chronic pain may be evident.	Combine analgesics with other pain relief measures (e.g., guided imagery, distraction, positioning, and touch). Nonnarcotics may be needed for chronic pain conditions. Prevent conditions/circumstances that predipose to the development of acute confusion.

Knowledge Deficit (Disease Process, Treatment Plan, Preventive Precautions) Related to Lack of Exposure

Teaching sessions should include the client, family members, or caregiver to assist with reinforcement of learning material during hospital and home recovery (see Client/Family Teaching box, p. 533). Although all clients benefit from teaching before discharge, older adults may prefer to focus on symptom management, medications, and home activity rather than physiologic details (Duryee, 1992).

Older clients with valvular disease may receive treatment to alleviate symptoms. Before discharge, signs and symptoms of deteriorating valve disease should be reviewed with the client, since surgery may be required at a later date to correct the disorder (Brown, 1992). The nurse can assist the client with dietary restrictions and the planning of activity schedules to avoid fatigue. Depending on the symptoms and underlying cause of valvular disorders, a variety of medications may be prescribed and should be reviewed with the client. Anticoagulants and prophylactic use of antibiotics before invasive procedures, surgery, and dental work are usually prescribed. Special considerations associated with these medications should be emphasized with the client.

Appropriate oral hygiene should be explained to the older client to prevent trauma and the incidence of infective endocarditis.

Recovery from valvular surgery is completed within 6 to 8 weeks; however, recovery may be delayed in older adults as a result of a higher incidence of complications with longer stays in hospital (Brown, 1992). Exercise and ADLs should be gradually resumed during the first 6 weeks of recovery. Clients should be taught to monitor their pulse and respiratory rate to evaluate tolerance to activity. Walking with a progressive increase in duration and frequency is recommended and clients should avoid lifting heavy objects. Driving a car may impede healing of the sternal incision. Prophylactic use of antibiotics should be explained to the client. Anticoagulants can be prescribed for clients with prosthetic valves and special precautions should be elaborated. Signs and symptoms of valvular disease and complications should be reviewed with the client, since clients with surgical repair may develop deteriorating symptoms necessitating valve replacement, and clients with valve replacement may need new valves inserted over time (Brown, 1992).

✣ EVALUATION

Evaluation of the older client with valvular disease focuses on achievement of goals outlined in the planning process. Older adults should demonstrate adequate cardiac output, ability to perform ADLs within limitations, and control of symptoms before discharge from hospital. The incidence of valvular surgery on older adults has steadily increased in recent years and research suggests that survival and quality of life are improved following surgical intervention (Brown, 1992; Gortner et al, 1994).

Congestive Heart Failure

In the last two decades, mortality from CAD disease and stroke have declined by more than 10%; whereas the death rate from CHF has increased by approximately 33% in those 45 and older. Approximately 500,000 individuals are diagnosed annually with this condition. CHF incidence rises dramatically for those individuals age 65 and over (Jessup et al, 1992a). It is estimated that approximately 2.3 million people have CHF, accounting for 1.8 million office visits and 1.5 million hospital visits per year (Nagelhout, 1991). Congestive heart failure is a:

> . . . clinical syndrome in which abnormal cardiac function is responsible for the heart's inability to pump sufficient blood to meet the body's metabolic needs and is characterized by a pattern of hemodynamic, renal, neural and hormonal responses (Congestive heart failure, 1989; Wright, 1990).

Several disorders are associated with CHF, including hypertension (75% of cases), CAD (39% of cases), hypertension and CAD (29%), rheumatic heart disease (21%), and diabetes mellitus (DM) (25%). The 5-year survival rate of individuals with CHF is approximately 50% (Nagelhout, 1991).

The factors which have been associated as contributing to CHF include age; hypertension; CAD; rheumatic heart disease; valvular heart disease; arrhythmias; renal disease; inadequate diet; DM; thyrotoxicosis; MI; cardiomyopathy; pulmonary embolism; infection; anemia; liver disease; emotional stress; and other factors related to biologic, iatrogenic, socioeconomic, and lifestyle considerations (Table 21-9).

Age-associated cardiovascular and renal changes affecting the clinical course of CHF and the responses to treatment include decreased renal and systemic blood flow, increased arterial stiffness and peripheral resistance, reduced ventricular compliance, and reduced maximal aerobic capacity.

TABLE 21-9

Factors Precipitating Heart Failure in the Older Adult

Cause	Example
Primary muscle disease	Cardiomyopathy Myocarditis
Secondary myocardial dysfunction	CAD with ischemia/infarction Low calcium, magnesium Bradyarrhythmias, tachyarrhythmias, especially atrial fibrillation and atrioventricular block.
Congenital, rheumatic, or acquired valvular disease	Aortic, mitral, pulmonic, or tricuspid insufficiency or stenosis
Obstructive disorders	Idiopathic hypertrophic subaortic stenosis Coarctation of the aorta Hypertension
Restrictive disorders	Cardiac tamponade Restrictive pericarditis
Endocrine/metabolic and system disorders	Thyrotoxicosis Anemia Infection and fever DM Liver disease Hyperthyroidism Hypothyroidism Renal insufficiency
Biologic, lifestyle, socioeconomic and iatrogenic considerations	Age Inadequate diet Emotional stress Excess dietary sodium Fluid overload Medications that depress myocardial function (beta-blockers or calcium channel blockers) Medications that promote sodium retention (nonsteroidal antiinflammatory drugs) The client's inability to follow prescribed therapy because of economic constraints

Modified from Jessup M et al: CHF in the elderly. Is it different? *Patient Care* 26(14): 40-43, 46, 49, 1992 a; Nagelhout J: Pharmacologic treatment of heart failure, *Nurs Clin North Am* 26 (2) 401-415, 1991; Wright S: Pathophysiology of congestive heart failure, *J Cardiovasc Nurs* 4(3):1-16, 1990.

In the elderly person, myocardial fibrosis is not the only cause of depressed ventricular compliance; prolonged calcium activation of the contractile machinery from the prior heartbeat may also make the heart stiffer when it must fill the next time (Jessup et al, 1992a) (Fig. 21-11).

The most important differences in clients 65 and over arise from the loss of ventricular compliance (shortness of breath and accumulation of fluid). As a result, any disease that affects the normal aging heart tends to cause cardiovascular symptoms earlier than it would in a younger person, and the finding of CHF in an older person warrants its own etiologic and pathologic consideration (Jessup et al, 1992a).

The pathophysiology of CHF may be characterized as an overload or by a myocardial deficiency, leading to inadequate contractility, or filling. Inadequate contractility may be as a result of MI, CAD, cardiomyopathy, or infection. Improper filling results from conditions that hinder myocardial relaxation during diastole, such as infection, tamponade, or ischemia. An increased load on the heart can be caused by either pressure or volume overload. Pressure overload is usually associated with hyperten-

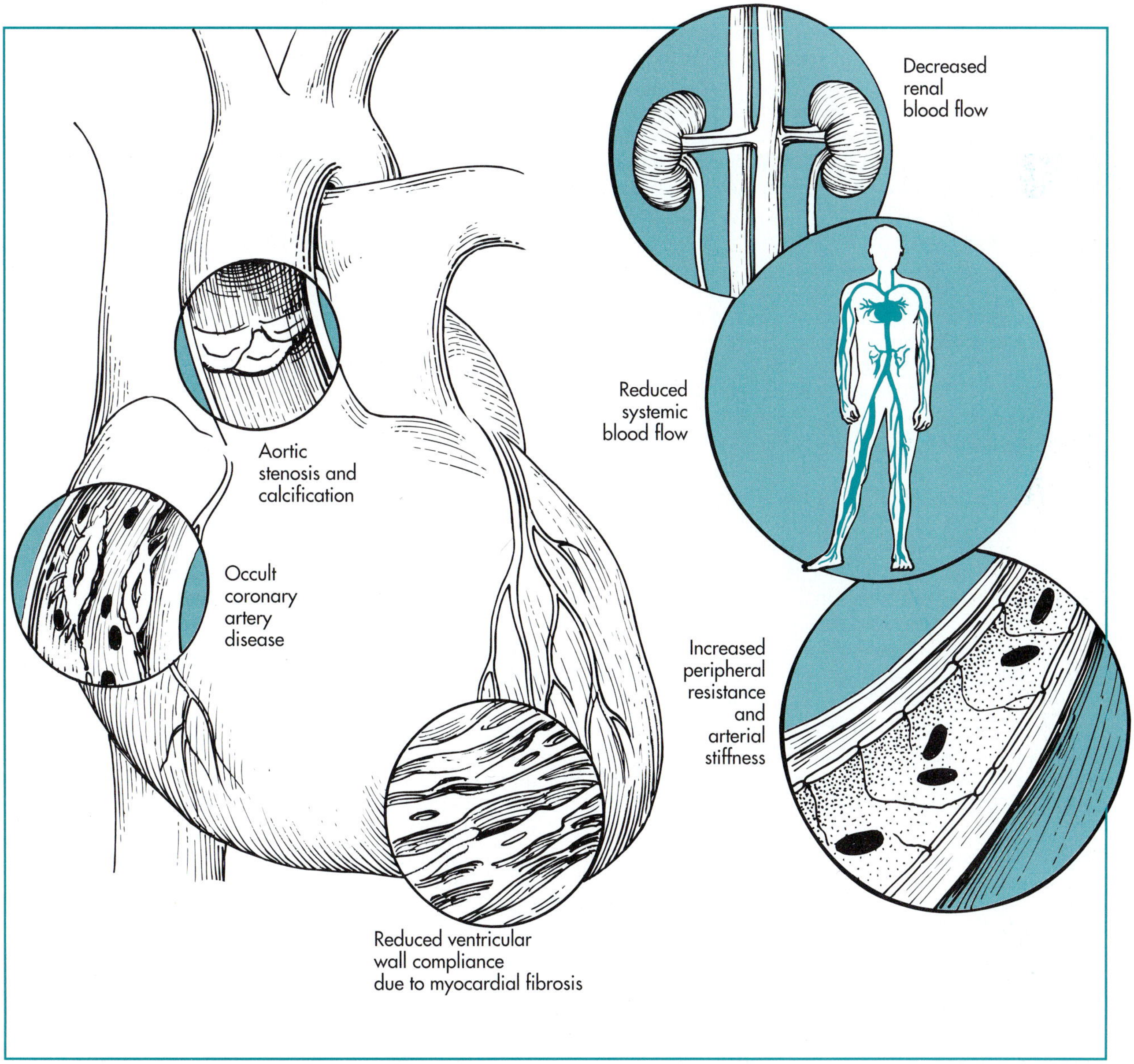

Fig. 21-11 Age-related cardiovascular and renal changes affecting congestive heart failure. (From Jessup M et al: CHF in the elderly. Is it different? *Pat Care* 26(14);40-43, 46, 49, 1992a)

MEDICAL MANAGEMENT

CHF

Diagnostic tests and procedures

- Measurement of blood pressure, evaluation for pitting edema of the legs and ankles, assessment of jugular venous pressure, heart and lung auscultation, and percussion of the lung for effusions
- Assessment for dyspnea, edema, cough, orthopnea, fatigue at rest, paroxysmal nocturnal dyspnea, frequent nocturnal urination, and dependent edema
- ECG monitoring (12 lead), chest x-ray, CBC, standard blood chemistries and electrolytes, aspartate aminotransferase, lactate dehydrogenase, creatinine kinase, and digitalis level, if the client is taking the drug; arterial blood gases may also be performed, depending on the status of the client

Cardiologists advise that left ventricular function be measured at least once noninvasively by echocardiography (ideally with Doppler techniques) or multigated blood-pool radionuclide ventriculography (MUGA scan) in older clients with CHF to determine if diastolic or systolic dysfunction is present.

Treatment

Management of CHF in the older client requires careful control of precipitating factors, pharmacologic therapy, a low-sodium diet, restriction of fluids (8 glasses per day, or 2,000 ml), and appropriate rest and exercise. The commonly used therapeutic agents for the treatment of CHF are diuretics, vasodilators, and digitalis glycosides.

Pharmacologic treatment for the older client questions whether clients should first be treated with diuretics or ACEIs. As of yet, there are no firm guidelines for the population in general, and to identify them for older adults is particularly difficult. Dr. Carl Leier, Director of Cardiology at Ohio State University, states that "one of the most significant changes of the past decade in the approach to heart failure is the recognition that therapy need not begin with a diuretic for every patient. . . . " There is growing evidence that low-level ACEI therapy may be a good first choice when heart failure is very mild, there is no evidence of renal insufficiency, and the client is comfortable enough to allow weeks rather than days for diuresis (Jessup et al, 1992b).

Cardiac glycosides (inotropic)

Systolic dysfunction and atrial fibrillation are the principal indications for digitalis in the older client with CHF. Usually, digitalis is added to a regimen of diuretics and an ACEI. The usual dosage of digoxin is 0.125 mg/per day, and the therapeutic serum level is about 1.0 ng/ml, but symptoms should be the main guide to efficacy and toxicity.

Diuretics

Diuretics reduce the symptoms associated with pulmonary and systemic vascular congestion. There are three types of diuretics commonly employed in practice: (1) potassium-sparing (spironolactone, triamterene and amiloride), (2) thiazides, and (3) loop diuretics. The older client with early, mild CHF, characterized by normal renal function and only minimum ankle edema, might do well with a thiazide diuretic, possibly in combination with a potassium-sparing agent. For more severe heart failure, predictable and controllable diuresis can be achieved with a loop diuretic.

Vasodilators and ACEIs

Vasodilators act to decrease arterial and venous vasoconstriction, resulting in the reduction of preload, afterload, or both. They are classified as arterial, venous, or balanced (i.e., affecting both arterioles and veins). Generally, administration of arterial dilators reduces afterload, which leads to increased cardiac output and stroke volume, whereas venodilators decrease left ventricular filling pressures (preload) with little or no change in cardiac output or stroke volume. Commonly used vasodilators include nitroprusside (Nipride), glyderal ternitate (Nitroglycerin), captopril (Capoten), hydralazine (Apresoline), prazosin (Minipress).

Nonspecific vasodilators include hydralazine and organic nitrates. Hydralazine is an arterial vasodilator, and nitrates are primarily venous dilators. Thus their combination results in arterial and venous vasodilation. This balanced effect is similar in nature to the ACEIs.

ACEIs (captopril, enalapril, and lisinopril) inhibit the converting enzyme that is responsible for the formation of angiotensin II, a potent vasoconstrictor that stimulates the release of aldosterone. This drug appears to improve the survival rate of older adults with hypertension and CHF.

Inotropes

A positive inotropic agent enhances, whereas a negative inotropic agent reduces myocardial contractility. Glycoside agents (digoxin and digitoxin) increase the force of myocardial contraction and thus are considered inotropic agents.

Adrenergic agents (adrenaline, noradrenaline, dopamine, dopexamine, and isoprenaline) are the most widely used drugs in the treatment of heart failure and have been used in emergency treatment since the early 1990s.

Calcium channel blockers

All calcium channel blockers have negative inotropic effects when used in the treatment of CHF. Little improvement in clients has been seen with long-term therapy. In addition, up to 40% of clients experi-

MEDICAL MANAGEMENT

CHF—cont'd

ence hemodynamic or clinical deterioration while receiving these agents. Therefore the use of calcium channel blockers in advanced CHF is not recommended (Stanley, 1990). See Table 21-11 for selected drugs used in CHF.

Beta-blockers

Beta adrenergic receptor antagonists are well-tolerated by some clients with heart failure because of the role that sympathetic nervous activity plays in the pathogenesis of sustained ventricular arrhythmias and because of the influence of beta-blockers on myocardial oxygen. Results of trials suggest inconclusive evidence regarding whether these particular drugs should be used in treatment of CHF in older adults. Until these studies are comp therapy cannot be recommended.

Prognosis

There are relatively few studies of long-term survival o individuals with CHF that begin surveillance with the onset of symptoms. All are characterized by high mortality within the first 1 to 5 years, regardless of age. A recent study by Taffet et al. (1992), which followed veterans age 75 and older, found that at the end of 1 year, 28% of the clients had died. This study confirms one conducted in 1956, that found that "if a patient survives the first year after coming under treatment (for CHF), his expectation of life will be at least equal to the normal."

sion or an outflow obstruction, whereas volume overload may be secondary to hypervolemia, anemia, or thyroid disease (Nagelhout, 1991).

The categories of heart failure are as follows:

1. **Backward heart failure**—Backward failure results when the ventricle (left or right) fails to eject its contents, resulting in the accumulation of blood in the atria, pulmonary, and venous system; vital organs; and the entire systemic circulation.
2. **Forward heart failure**—Forward failure results when low cardiac ejection in the arterial system leads to poor perfusion and congestion of vital organs, which is evidenced by mental confusion; muscle weakness; renal, mesenteric or hepatic insufficiency; and shock.
3. Right or left failure—Although left ventricle failure is more prevalent, a number of individuals experience failure in both ventricles, especially those with chronic disease. In left ventricle failure, pulmonary symptoms predominate, whereas in right-sided failure, generalized systemic symptoms appear.
4. Acute versus chronic heart failure—Acute heart failure results from a sudden reduction in cardiac output and inadequate organ perfusion, and may lead to pulmonary edema and circulatory collapse. Chronic heart failure occurs slowly, often as a result of hypertension, valvular or ischemic heart disease, or chronic lung disease (see Medical Management box pp. 538-539). The heart may have time for compensatory mechanisms to minimize clinical symptoms. CHF is associated with decreased cardiac output, renal conservation of salt and water, and systemic congestion (Wright, 1990). See Table 21-10 for the clinical symptoms for right and left CHF.

NURSING MANAGEMENT

✣ ASSESSMENT

Assessment begins with a complete health history and physical examination. Older adults should be assessed for history of CAD, pump failure, rheumatic heart disease, hypertension, cardiac valve disease, infection, and current medications. The initial physical evaluation of the older adult suspected to have CHF includes measurement of blood pressure, evaluation for pitting edema of the legs and ankles, assessment of jugular venous pressure, heart and lung auscultation, and percussion of the lung for effusions. It should be noted that although dyspnea, edema, cough, and fatigue are the hallmark of CHF in the older client, orthopnea, fatigue at rest, paroxysmal nocturnal dyspnea, nocturnal urination, and edema are also important.

Normally, ECG monitoring, chest x-ray, blood tests (CBC, electrolyte, hemoglobin and hematocrit, aspartate aminotransferase, lactate dehydrogenase, and creatinine kinase) and digitalis level (if the client is taking the drug) are ordered.

✣ DIAGNOSIS

Potential nursing diagnoses for the client with CHF include, but are not limited to the following: (1) decreased cardiac output R/T ineffective ventricular pump, decreased stroke volume, hypoxia, electrolyte disturbances, digitalis toxicity, and origin of pump failure; (2) impaired gas exchange R/T pulmonary venous congestion: (3) fluid volume excess R/T increased sodium and water reabsorption; and (4) anxiety R/T dyspnea, lack of knowledge regarding treatment and diagnosis, and fear.

Congestive

	art failure
	vein distention
	l
	abdominal dis-
	gular reflex
Hoarseness	Hepatomegaly
Rales, crackles, wheezes	Splenomegaly
Pleural effusion	Peripheral edema
Hemoptysis	Weight gain
Cyanosis	Elevated central venous pressure and right atrial pressure
Cheyne-Stokes breathing	
Palpitations	
Tachycardia	Cyanosis
Dysrhythmia	Nocturia
S_3 gallop	
Cardiomegaly	
Elevated pulmonary artery wedge pressure and left atrial pressure	
Nocturia	
Decreased urine output	
Diaphoresis	
Acidosis	

Modified from Solomon J: Managing a failing heart, *RN,* 54(8): 46-51, © 1991, reprinted with permission from *Medical Economics,* Montvale, N.J.; Wright S: Pathophysiology of congestive heart failure, *J Cardiovas Nurs* 4(3): 1-16, 1990. © Aspen Publishers.

✣ PLANNING

The client, family, and significant others, or caregivers, should be included in all aspects of the planning process, whether the client is in the acute stage of CHF, awaiting a CABG, or is in the chronic stage. The course of CHF varies from client to client and the most important factor to keep in mind is that each situation demands individualized planning and treatment goals. In general, the medical treatment goals include (1) eliminating or minimizing the underlying cause of CHF, (2) reducing the heart's workload by decreasing preload and afterload, and (3) increasing cardiac contractility. To plan nursing care for the client with CHF is a challenge, since factors such as physical condition; medical regimen; age; occupation; personality; motivation; desire to cooperate with treatment; and psychosocial aspects, including the client, family, and their understanding of the condition, must be taken into consideration. The importance of client education and self-care activities in both the hospital and home settings should be emphasized in the planning of care. A recent study by Hagenhoff et al. (1994) found that client education needs of CHF clients included the following:

- Clients valued education highly during their hospitalization for CHF, and this should continue as an important focus of nursing care.
- Clients rated medication content as the most important aspect, including side effects of medication and appropriate care if problems occurred.
- Knowledge of anatomy and physiology, risk factors, and diet was important.
- Information about psychologic factors was best received in the home setting.

In another related study on self-care teaching for clients with CHF, the author found that (1) older clients with CHF have a high incidence of mortality, morbidity, and hospital readmission; (2) of the 41 clients with CHF, almost all clients could not correctly define CHF, less than half could correctly define their medications, and almost three fourths of the clients did not weigh themselves daily; (3) the clients who followed self-care intervention during their hospital stay (e.g., daily weigh-ins, taking medications at the bedside, and identifying symptoms of CHF) were older, less-educated, widowed, and lived alone (Bushnell, 1992).

These findings have implications for the planning of client care in all settings. Nurses play an important role in teaching risk factors, preventive measures and treatment regimens. Nursing interventions can enhance the quality of life of clients, reduce hospitalizations, and affect the cost-effectiveness and efficiency of cardiovascular programs.

✣ INTERVENTION

Decreased Cardiac Output Related to Mechanical Factors (Preload, Afterload and Contractility)

It is essential that the nurse assess blood pressure, apical pulse, heart rate, and heart and lung sounds to detect early signs and symptoms of decreased cardiac output. In the acute phase, the client should be on bed rest to conserve energy and decrease oxygen demand (elevate head of bed 30 to 60 degrees—high-Fowler's position). An assessment for edema should be done every 2 hours, especially in older clients, since their condition changes rapidly. The hemodynamic parameters (blood pressure, arterial pressure, pulmonary artery pressure [PAP], pulmonary capillary wedge pressure [PCWP] and cardiac output [CO] reflect left ventricular end diastolic pressure (LVEDP) and myocardial contractility. The intake and output should be monitored hourly and IV fluids restricted as ordered to prevent circulatory overload. Drugs (vasodilators and inotropes) should be administered as or-

TABLE 21-11

Selected Drugs Used in CHF

Drug classification	Adverse reactions	Precautions
Cardiac glycosides Digoxin	Altered color perception, visual disturbances, confusion, headache, fatigue, muscle weakness, paresthesia, malaise, nausea, vomiting, anorexia, abdominal pain, arrhythmias, AV block, slow or irregular pulse	Use with caution in older clients or clients with hypokalemia, hypercalcemia, hypomagnesia, and hyperthyroidism. Use with caution in clients with idiopathic hypertrophic subaortic stenosis (IHSS).
Diuretics		
Potassium-sparing		
Spironolactone (Aldactone)	Hyperkalemia and sodium depletion, cramping, diarrhea, rashes, drug fever, ataxia	Avoid excess potassium. Aspirin can negate the action of spironolactone.
Triamterene (Dyrenium)	Gastrointestinal disturbances, dizziness, hypotension, weakness, muscle cramps, dry mouth, rash	Avoid potassium products.
Amiloride (MIdamor)	Gastrointestinal disturbances, skin rashes.	Avoid potassium.
Thiazides		
Hydrochlorothiazide (Hydrodiuril) **Chlorothiazide** (Diuril) **Chlorthalidone** (Hygroton)	Hypokalemia, hypomagnesia, hyponatremia, acid/base imbalance, hypovolemia, hyperglycemia, anorexia, gastric irritation, nausea, vomiting, cramping, diarrhea, constipation.	Monitor for signs of hyperglycemia. In diabetics, need for hypoglycemic agents or insulin may increase.
Loop diuretics		
Furosemide (Lasix) **Ethacrynic acid** (Edecrin)	Electrolyte depletion, anorexia, vomiting, nausea, diarrhea, abdominal discomfort, malaise, dysphagia, rash, chills, fever, fatigue, apprehension, and mental confusion	Dramatic increase occurs in urine output. Encourage potassium supplements (drugs or diet).
Vasodilators and ACEIs		
Nitroprusside (Nipride)	Nausea, vomiting, palpitations, muscle twitching, and restlessness	Drug is light-sensitive—after mixing wrap in foil to prevent deterioration.
Nitroglycerin	Increased heart rate, postural hypotension, and headache	Application site may relate to symptoms. Apply to chest or abdomen. Abdominal application may reduce dizziness. Application before retiring may reduce paroxysmal dyspnea.
Captopril (Capoten)	Mouth sores, skin rash, nausea/vomiting, diarrhea, postural hypotension, taste disturbances, diaphoresis, hyperkalemia, and false-positive urine test for acetone	Monitor renal function. Take at least 1 hour before meals. Avoid sudden changes in posture.
Hydralazine (Apresoline)	Headache, tachycardia, and fluid retention	Monitor heart rate and weight.
Prazosin (Minipress)	First dose effect may include postural hypotension, faintness, dizziness, and palpitations	Give first dose in safe environment with close observation. Warn client about hypotensive effects.

Continued.

TABLE 21-11

Selected Drugs Used in CHF—cont'd

Drug classification	Adverse reactions	Precautions
Inotropes		
Epineprine (Adrenalin)	Anxiety, insomnia, nervousness, headache, sweating, pallor, tremor, nausea, vomiting, urinary retention, hyperglycemia, lactic acidosis, palpitations, tachycardia, and arrhythmia	Contraindicated in clients with IHSS, severe hypertension, glaucoma, or hypersensitivity to metabisulphite.
Dopamine (Dopastat, Intropin, Revimine)	Nausea, vomiting, headache, tachycardia, arrhythmias, hypertension, hypotension, and vasoconstriction	Contraindicated in clients with IHSS, uncorrected tachyarrhythmias. Use with caution in clients with history of occlusive vascular disease. Contraindicated in clients with hypersensitivity to any sulfite.
Dobutamine (Dobutrex)	Headache, nausea, vomiting, chest pain, palpitations, tachycardia, arrhythmias, hypotension, and minor increase in systolic pressure	Contraindicated in clients with IHSS, or hypersensitivity to metabisulphite. Use with caution in clients with hypertension and hypotension.
Isoproterenol (Isoprenaline)	Headache, flushing, mild tremor, nausea, vomiting, cardiac ischemia, tachycardia, palpitations, arrhythmias, angina, hypertension and hypotension	Contraindicated in clients with IHSS or hypersensitivity to metabisulphite Use with caution in clients with CAD, recent MI, severe hypertension, hyperthyroidism, or history of occlusive vascular disease.
Amrinone (Inocor)	Headache, anorexia, nausea, vomiting, hepatotoxicity, thrombocytopenia, hypotension, and arrhythmias	Contraindicated in clients with metabisulphite hypersensitivity. Use with caution in clients with CAD or recent MI.
Milrinone (Corotrope)	Ventricular and supraventricular arrhythmias, hypotension, chest pain, and headache	Contraindicated in clients with IHSS or sensitivity to amrinone. Use with caution in clients with CAD or recent MI. The dose should be reduced in clients with renal insufficiency.

dered, and the nurse should monitor for signs and symptoms of drug toxicity. The client should be assessed continually for signs and symptoms of decreased perfusion to vital organs (e.g., diaphoresis, restlessness, cool skin, decreased urine output and confusion). The expected outcome will be that the hemodynamic stability is restored with an effective cardiac output as evidenced by normal laboratory values for the older client, reduction in edema, improvement in breath sounds, orientation to time and place, and urinary output > 30 ml/hr.

Impaired Gas Exchange Related to Altered Oxygen Supply

Assess respiratory status (rate, rhythm, and auscultation for presence of adventitious sounds to detect increases in congestion) every hour and PRN. Observe skin color, presence of dyspnea, orthopnea and paroxysmal nocturnal dyspnea. The client should be on bed rest and maintained in a semi- or high-Fowler's position. Administer oxygen (through nasal prongs or mask) as ordered, or maintain on mechanical ventilator. Monitor arterial blood gases as ordered (no significant alterations of pH or PCO_2 occur as a function of age, but as a result of age-related changes, PO_2 of a 75-year-old person would be approximately 75 mm Hg.). Administer diuretics as ordered, and monitor intake and output every hour. Observe for signs and symptoms of dehydration related to the administration of diuretics. A chest x-ray should be ordered on a daily basis. The older client experiencing difficulty breathing, as well as the family members, may become frightened and anxious during episodes of dyspnea. The nurse should encourage the client to take slow deep breaths during the episode and maintain a calm environment in the room. The expected outcome is that pulmonary congestion will be restored as evidenced by normal respiratory rate and rhythm, clear breath sounds, absence of shortness of breath, dyspnea, orthopnea, and cough.

Fluid Volume Excess Related to Increased Systemic Venous Congestion

It is imperative that intake and output be recorded every hour. The client should be on a restricted sodium and fluid intake to control for sodium absorption. Diuretics are administered as ordered. Monitor the client closely for signs and symptoms of electrolyte imbalance. For example, with sodium deficit, the client exhibits abdominal cramps, apprehension, convulsions, oliguria or anuria; with sodium excess, dry, sticky mucous membranes, flushed skin, oliguria or anuria, thirst, and rough, dry tongue. The client should be weighed daily at the same time to monitor for fluid loss or retention. In the older adult, this factor is of importance, since a prolonged weight gain, even 1 or 2 pounds per week, is a danger sign (Jessup et al, 1992b). The expected outcomes are that normal fluid and electrolyte balance will be restored, as evidenced by decrease in weight and edema; diuresis will occur in response to pharmacologic therapy; and electrolytes, blood urea nitrogen (BUN), creatinine, and chest x-ray will be within normal limits.

Anxiety Related to Dyspnea and Lack of Knowledge Regarding Treatment and Prognosis

The emotional status of any individual influences one's desire and ability to focus on change, learning, and factors outside of oneself. In assessing anxiety, it is important to consider whether the individual is experiencing moderate anxiety (e.g., fear of procedures, routines, or people) or depression (e.g., feelings of anxiety, helplessness, and powerlessness). Older adults need to be given instructions on their condition, procedures, diet, and risk factors in a clear, simple manner, using proper language, reading level, and cultural considerations. Researchers recently found that older adults are willing to change behaviors if instructions are given in clear, simple terms (Ferrini, Edelstein, Barrett-Connor, 1994). To assist the older client, the nurse should maintain an environment as relaxed and quiet as possible, explain all procedures before beginning, and answer questions clearly and concisely. The nurse should also provide opportunities for the older client and family members to verbalize their concerns (see nursing Care Plan, p. 544-545).

Discharge planning is directed toward long-term management of the therapeutic program. The nurse should discuss the anatomy and physiology of the heart, precipitating factors, medication regimen, especially in regard to dose and side effects, exercise tolerance, daily weight, dietary factors (e.g., low sodium, fluid restriction), and the importance of weighing and recording the weight at the same period every day. The importance of ensuring that clients are given this information in simple, clear, concise, and understandable language cannot be emphasized enough, especially in the older client. Referral to a home visiting agency to assist with ADLs, and referral to "Meals on Wheels" may be necessary for some individuals. The client may wish to enter a cardiac rehabilitation program to monitor activity tolerance in a secure environment. A dietician can provide excellent information about meal preparation for a low-sodium diet. Caution the older client to avoid prepared foods in the frozen food section and to use salt substitutes. A weight gain of 2 lbs. in 24 hours and a return of any symptoms should be reported to the physician immediately.

✣ EVALUATION

Older clients should demonstrate that ventricular function is improved, fluid overload is decreased, gas exchange is improved and anxiety level is decreased. In addition, the older client demonstrates ability to return to usual ADLs.

Peripheral Artery Disease

Peripheral artery disease (PAD) is any disturbance in the systemic arteries that impairs tissue perfusion. Arteriosclerosis (hardening or thickening of arterial wall) and atherosclerosis (usual cause of arteriosclerosis involving plaque formation within the arterial wall) are common disturbances affecting the arterial vasculature. Atherosclerosis is the most common cause of **arteriosclerosis obliterans,** the narrowing or obstruction of arterial walls. Although the exact cause of atherosclerosis is unknown, several risk factors have been identified. These include smoking, elevated serum cholesterol, hypertension, DM, physical inactivity, obesity, and family history.

Atherosclerosis involves the development of atheromatous plaques on the intimal layer of arterial vessels. These lesions progressively narrow the artery lumen and lead to the formation of thrombi and aneurysms.

Arteriosclerosis obliterans is a chronic occlusive disease of the arteries caused by plaque formation. As the lumen narrows, partial or complete obstruction can occur leading to inadequate tissue perfusion beyond the lesion and ischemia. Common sites for atherosclerotic lesions are the aortoileac vessels, femoral-popliteal vessels, and popliteal-tibial arteries. Symptoms appear when the artery is unable to supply the tissues with adequate oxygenated blood flow.

Thrombi that develop at the site of the atherosclerotic lesion or within arterial aneurysms can break loose and circulate through the arterial system. Thromboemboli also originate in the heart as a result of atrial fibrillation, MI, or mitral stenosis. Thromboemboli tend to block ar-

CARE PLAN

CHF

Clinical situation Mr. N is a 67-year-old retired businessman who is married and lives with his wife in a single-dwelling home. He is experiencing breathlessness, dyspnea on exertion, nocturnal dyspnea and orthopnea. He went to the emergency room when his breathing difficulty became intolerable. On admission to the hospital, it was noted that Mr. N weighed 240 lbs. and his height was 5 ft 8 in. The initial assessment:

- Blood pressure 110/170
- Pulse 86 beats/min, irregular
- Respiratory rate 36/min
- Temperature 36.7° C (98° F)
- Dyspnea on exertion
- Paroxysmal nocturnal dyspnea
- Cough
- Hoarseness
- Crackles and wheezes
- S_3 gallop
- Nocturia
- Diaphoresis
- Pitting edema of ankles and feet bilaterally
- Bloating, abdominal distention
- Jugular vein distention

Mr. N kept repeating to the nurse, "There is nothing wrong with me ... I just have pneumonia."

An ECG (12 lead) was applied, and an IV was started with normal saline (client is diabetic). Stat blood work, arterial blood gases, and a portable chest x-ray were conducted. Oxygen was administered through an oxygen mask. Digoxin and furosemide were given per physician's orders. The client was transferred to the intensive care unit (ICU).

Nursing diagnoses	Outcomes	Interventions
Decreased cardiac output related to an ineffective ventricular pump	Hemodynamic stability will be restored as evidenced by vital signs within normal limits, reduction in edema, improvement in breath sounds, activity tolerance, and urine output >30 ml/hr.	Assess cardiovascular status every hour and PRN, including vital signs and auscultation of heart and lung sounds. Assess respiratory status every hour and PRN. Assess for edema every 2 to 4 hours. Monitor intake and output every hour. Administer cardiac glycosides and diuretics as ordered. Administer IV inotropic drugs and vasodilators as ordered. Assess client for signs and symptoms of decreased perfusion to vital organs (e.g., diaphoresis, restlessness, cool skin, decreased urine output, confusion). Elevate head of bed to a semi- or high-Fowler's position.
Impaired gas exchange related to altered oxygen supply	Pulmonary venous congestion will decrease and normal gas exchange will be restored as evidenced by normal respiratory rate and rhythm, clear breath sounds, absence of shortness of breath, normal skin color and temperature, chest x-ray within normal limits, activity tolerance	Assess respiratory status every hour and PRN (e.g., rate, rhythm, use of accessory muscles, and auscultation for presence of adventitious sounds). Observe skin color, presence of dyspnea, orthopnea, and paroxysmal nocturnal dyspnea. Administer oxygen as ordered. Monitor arterial blood gases as ordered. Maintain client in a semi- or high-Fowler's posi-

CARE PLAN

CHF—cont'd

Nursing diagnoses	Outcomes	Interventions
		tion. Assist with ADLs as required.
Fluid volume excess related to sodium and water reabsorption	Normal fluid and electrolyte balance will be restored as evidenced by decrease in weight and decrease in dependent edema. Diuresis will occur in response to pharmacologic therapy; electrolytes, BUN, creatinine and chest x-ray will be within normal limits; and pulmonary congeston will decrease.	Monitor chest x-ray on a daily basis. Monitor and record accurate intake and output every hour. Administer diuretics as ordered and monitor client's response. Assess for signs/symptoms of electrolyte imbalance. Consult with dietician regarding sodium and fluid restrictions and monitor for compliance. Monitor and record weight at the same time of day. Auscultate heart sounds and note presence of S_3. Evaluate changes in venous pressure, neck vein distention, hepatojugular reflux, peripheral edema.
Anxiety related to dyspnea, lack of knowledge regarding treatment, diagnosis, fear of death	Anxiety will be reduced and the client and family will verbalize an understanding of treatment measures.	Assess client's level of anxiety. Display a calm, reassuring attitude. Explain measures and procedures in a simple manner with consideration for the client's educational level and cultural background. Maintain as quiet and relaxed an environment as possible. Answer client's and family's questions as clearly as possible.

From Bousquet G: Congestive heart failure: a review of nonpharmacological therapies, *J Cardiovas Nurs* 4(3):35-46, 1990; Thompson J et al: *Mosby's clinical nursing,* ed 3, Toronto, 1993, Mosby.

teries at bifurcation points of the femoral and popliteal arteries. Impaired blood flow and ischemia occur at sites distal to the occlusion.

As the atheromatous plaque progresses, the medial layer of the wall calcifies and loses elasticity, which weakens the arterial wall. As the vessel wall weakens, pouches or aneurysms form. Pressure within the arteries, especially in the presence of hypertension, can further dilate the aneurysm until it ruptures. Aneurysms commonly occur in large arteries such as the abdominal aorta. Multiple aneurysms can develop in the popliteal artery. Thrombi can form within the aneurysm and circulate to smaller distal vessels in the arterial system.

Signs and symptoms of arterial insufficiency depend on the site, extent of occlusion, and degree of collateral circulation. Collateral circulation often develops with the gradual elevation of plaque formation.

Intermittent claudication (muscle ischemia) is one of the initial symptoms with atherosclerotic obliterans. Pain in the foot or calf is experienced with exercise and subsides with rest. As the disease progresses, the distance walked becomes shorter before pain is felt. Burning pain in the foot at rest or during sleep indicates a severe form of the disease. Cold, numbness, and tingling may accompany the pain. The foot appears pale when elevated and red in dependent positions. Dry skin, thickened toenails, loss of pedal hair, and cool skin can result from poor circulation. Advanced stages of ischemia lead to necrosis, ulceration, and gangrene of the toes.

The pain with arterial emboli is sudden and severe. The affected extremity appears pale and cool and distal pulses are absent. Impaired motor and sensory function is evident. Shock can develop if large arteries are occluded.

With abdominal and peripheral aneurysms, there are usually no overt signs and symptoms until rupture or acute thrombosis. A pulsating mass may be palpated in the abdominal area with aortic aneurysms, and clients may sense abdominal or back pain.

MEDICAL MANAGEMENT

PAD

Diagnostic tests and procedures

Doppler ultrasonography detects and measures the velocity of blood flow through arterial segments and grafts. Reduced or blocked sounds distal to the damaged site suggest the presence of arterial occlusion.

Segmental limb pressures measure the systolic blood pressure from the thigh, upper calf, and above the ankle. Pneumatic pressure cuffs are applied to these sites and Dopplers are used to determine pressure readings. Pressures are compared with the brachial blood pressure measurement. Readings from the thigh and calf are normally higher than upper extremities so decreased pressures (20 to 30 mmHg) in lower limbs indicate the presence of arterial disease.

Plethysmography depicts graphic tracing of arterial flow during cuff inflation and deflation. Depressed wave forms are indicative of arterial occlusion. This test is particularly useful for assessment of the foot and toes.

Exercise stress testing uses segmental plethysmography and pressure measurements during rest and exercise (treadmill walking). In the presence of PAD, exercise induces abnormalities in blood flow, depressed waveforms, decreasing ankle pressures, and a reduction or disappearance of distal pulses in the affected limb.

Radionuclide scans involve the injection of dye with scanning at intervals to determine radionuclide accumulation in the damaged vessel. Blood flow through arteries and grafts can be assessed, perfusion pressures can be calculated, and the vascular system can be visualized.

Digital subtraction angiography (DSA) involves the injection of contrast material into the venous system to create an image, which is then converted into numbers, indicating the presence and extent of arterial occlusion.

Arteriography is performed to determine the exact location and extent of arterial obstruction. Contrast material is injected into the arterial system through a specialized catheter inserted into the brachial or femoral artery and a series of x-rays traces the dye through the arterial system.

Treatment

Cyclandelate (Cyclospasmol) and Isoxsuprine (Vasodilan) may be prescribed to relax the smooth muscle of arteries and improve blood flow.

Pentoxifylline (Trental) reduces blood viscosity, enhances flexibility of red blood cells, and improves tissueperfusion. Use of this drug with intermittent claudication has been more effective than vasodilators in clients with segmental limb pressures of 0.8 or greater. Drug effectiveness occurs within 4 months.

Antiplatelet drugs such as acetylsalicyclic acid (Aspirin) and dipyridamole (Persantine) inhibit the adherence and aggregation of platelets along damaged arterial walls. These prophylactic drugs may help to reduce blood viscosity.

A variety of surgical procedures can be performed to reduce the effects of PAD. Procedure selection varies with the extent and location of damage within the artery.

Arteriosclerosis obliterans

Percutaneous transluminal angioplasty (PTA) involves gaining access to the arterial system with a specialized balloon-tipped catheter. The catheter is advanced under fluoroscopy to the atherosclerotic lesion and inflated over the site to compress the plaque and to improve blood flow. Arterial bypass surgery and reconstruction may be performed.

Advanced cases of atherosclerosis and gangrene of the extremities necessitates amputation of the limb. The goal of surgery is to amputate the least amount of tissue while maintaining sufficient stump for prosthetic application.

Arterial emboli

Fibrinolytic and anticoagulation therapy are initiated to dissolve the thrombus and prevent further clot formation. Occlusive thrombi can be surgically treated with bypass grafts.

Aneurysm

Medical treatment involves controlling hypertension; surgical treatment consists of removing the aneurysm.

Prognosis

Pharmaceutic agents are not particularly effective in the treatment of PAD; however, surgical interventions have been more successful. Death seldom results from PAD. Frequent surgery, amputation, or exacerbations of symptoms, as well as progressive disability are common outcomes endured by the older adult with PAD. The key to preventing or halting the progress of PAD and subsequent complications appears to rely on controlling the risk factors for atherosclerosis.

Nursing Management

ASSESSMENT

Assessment of the older adult with PAD begins with a complete history and physical examination. Subjective and objective assessment of a client with PAD is outlined in Box 21-7. Care should be taken to examine both extremities for comparison purposes. Data should reflect the presence of acute or chronic arterial insufficiency. Painful arterial ulcers may be noticed on the toes, between the toes, or on the upper aspect of the foot. Cold extremities with mottling, delayed filling of capillaries, and absent pedal pulses are indicative of acute arterial insufficiency and should be treated immediately.

BOX 21-7

Assessment of Clients with PAD

Subjective data

Pain in extremity (location, intensity, onset, duration)
Precipitating factors (activity, rest)
Relieving factors (activity, rest, position)
Presence of intermittent claudication (frequency, distance)
Modifiable risk factors (smoking, high cholesterol levels, hypertension, diabetes, obesity, physical inactivity)
Personal and family history (coronary artery disease, PAD)
Psychosocial state (anxiety, fear, depression)
Sexual function in males

Objective data

Skin changes (color, temperature, appearance, sensations)
Condition of nailbeds
Circulation (peripheral pulses, bruits, capillary filling)
Muscle tone

DIAGNOSIS

Nursing diagnoses for older adults with PAD include but are not limited to (1) altered tissue perfusion (peripheral), (2) activity intolerance, (3) impaired skin integrity, and (4) knowledge deficit.

PLANNING

Older clients with PAD and their family members should be included in the planning of care. Discharge planning should begin as soon as the older client is admitted to the hospital, since this client typically needs additional support services during home recovery.

Expected outcomes for the older client with PAD include but are not limited to the following: (1) client will manifest reduced signs and symptoms of arterial insufficiency as evidenced by warm temperatures, presence of pedal pulses, and decreased claudication in affected extremities; (2) client will participate in activities that improve collateral circulation and reduce pain; (3) client will demonstrate protective behavior to prevent injury to skin or measures to promote healing of impaired skin; (4) client will describe disease process and treatment plan; (5) client will identify personal risk factors and methods to reduce these factors.

INTERVENTION

Altered Tissue Perfusion Related to Interruption of Arterial Flow

Nursing interventions include the administration of vasodilators, antiplatelet agents or anticoagulants to older adults with chronic arterial insufficiency. The effectiveness and adverse reactions need to be evaluated.

Nurses can initiate a graduated, regular exercise program to enhance collateral circulation, which improves blood supply to the ischemic extremity. Clients should be encouraged to balance activities with rest and may need assistance to develop a schedule of paced activities. During rest, the legs should be placed in a slightly dependent position to improve blood flow. Older adults may benefit from raising the head of the bed on blocks. Pressure points should be padded as older adults are prone to skin breakdown and should be encouraged to change positions often. Clients should avoid long periods of sitting or standing.

Warm environments (21° C, or 70 to 72° F) enhance vasodilation. During winter, thermal underwear, heavy socks, and gloves are recommended to provide warmth. Constrictive clothing (e.g., garters, knee socks, tight waistbands), leg crossing, and direct heat application such as hot water bottles, heating pads, and hot compresses should be avoided.

If applicable, clients should be encouraged to stop smoking and lose weight. For older clients with surgical intervention, vital signs and peripheral perfusion should be assessed regularly. Marking an *X* over the site is a helpful gesture and a Doppler reading may help to detect arterial flow. Segmental limb pressures may be conducted to ensure adequate perfusion. Color, temperature, and motor and sensory function need to be monitored and compared with baseline assessment. Deterioration in status should be reported to the physician. Clients are usually restricted to bed rest for 24 hours postoperatively. When clients progress to sitting positions, the affected limb should be elevated to prevent edema.

Following amputation, the operative site should be assessed for blood loss and warmth (i.e., should not be hot). The closest proximal pulse should be palpated to evaluate circulation.

Activity Intolerance Related to Immobility, Pain, Knowledge Deficit

Exercise enhances collateral circulation to ischemic areas, improves muscle tone, and reduces pain. For older clients with chronic arterial insufficiency, individual exercise plans should be developed. The nurse should assess the distance walked before intermittent claudication develops and assist the client to set reasonable goals that progressively increase the distance. Flat areas are recommended; hills and stairs should be avoided. Older adults may benefit from recording distances in a daily diary. When discomfort is experienced in the affected limb during walking, the client should be encouraged to rest. Swimming and biking are alternate exercises that promote activity tolerance.

Pain associated with atherosclerosis obliterans is chronic and difficult to relieve. Pain can range from discomfort with activity to severe pain at rest. Elevation of the head of the bed on blocks and use of a bed cradle or board may reduce the pain sensations at rest. After activity, the client should rest until the discomfort is relieved. Analgesics may relieve the pain but relaxation techniques and guided imagery should also be incorporated into the daily routine. Warm clothing may also reduce pain by enhancing vasodilation. Relaxation techniques, positioning, and narcotic analgesics are interventions that reduce pain following surgery.

Clients with surgery are usually restricted to bed rest for 24 hours. The older client should be encouraged to participate in active and passive range-of-motion exercises to maintain muscle strength and tone, and to prevent complications. Crutches or walkers may be used to enhance mobilization of an older adult during the early phase of recovery.

Older adults with amputation encounter difficulty with mobility because of the loss of a limb. If possible, before surgery, exercises to strengthen muscles in the upper extremities should be initiated in preparation for ambulation with crutches or walker. A trapeze and overbed frame help develop muscle strength and promote independence in bed. To maintain extension of the hip and knee joints, clients should be placed in the prone position for 30 minutes every 4 hours following surgery. For older adults, the prone position may be uncomfortable and may cause disorientation, especially at night, so nurses should monitor the client closely and exercise judgment if adverse effects (e.g., confusion) occur that compromise safety. With below knee amputation pillows should be used under the knee to avoid flexion contractures. With amputations, clients should be mobilized slowly from lying to sitting to standing positions to prevent orthostatic hypotension. Older clients need assistance and close supervision with mobilization following surgery. Physiotherapy consults are beneficial. In preparation for discharge, clients should be encouraged to install hand rails in strategic areas of the home, such as the bathroom, and to sit on a chair when showering or performing ADLs.

Ambulating with chronic forms of arterial insufficiency or following surgery can be frustrating for the older client. Nursing intervention involves listening to their concerns, providing assistance with ambulation, and identifying areas of improvement.

Impaired Skin Integrity Related to Altered Circulation, Immobility

Older adults with arterial insufficiency are prone to ulcer formation and infection as a result of skin changes associated with the aging process and altered peripheral circulation. Arterial ulcers tend to form on the tips of the toes, heels and over the phalangeal and metatarsal heads (Beare, Myers, 1994). Foot soaks, topical antibiotics, and dry dressings enhance healing. Debriding agents with wet to dry saline dressings may be used for ulcers without granulation tissue or surgical debridement can be performed. Amputation of the extremity may be necessary for serious ulcers that do not respond to medical therapy.

Prevention of ulcer formation (especially with diabetic clients) is of prime importance. The nurse should encourage ambulation to enhance collateral circulation and should instruct the client on foot care. The skin should be inspected daily. The extremity should be washed gently in tepid water with a neutral pH soap. Each toe should be dried gently followed by liberal application of lubricant with moisturizing properties. Older clients who complain of dry, itchy skin should take fewer baths and increase the application of lubricants. Nails should be clipped straight across. Clients should avoid walking barefoot and should wear shoes that are large enough to prevent pressure on the affected foot and to avoid injury. Shoes should be removed several times during the day and aired after use. Older adult clients may benefit from the placement of cotton or lambswool between all toes or protective booties.

Clients with bypass grafts or aneurysm repair require routine incisional care. With amputations, pressure dressings and drains remain in place for 48 to 72 hours after surgery. The site should be inspected for healing. Prosthetic devices can be applied immediately after amputation; however, older adults with above-knee amputations are usually fitted for prosthetic devices 3 to 6 months after surgery. For these clients, proper bandaging shapes the stump for future prosthetic fitting. Following surgery, a compression elastic bandage is applied to reduce edema, to provide support, to hasten shrinkage, and to mold the stump. The elastic bandage requires

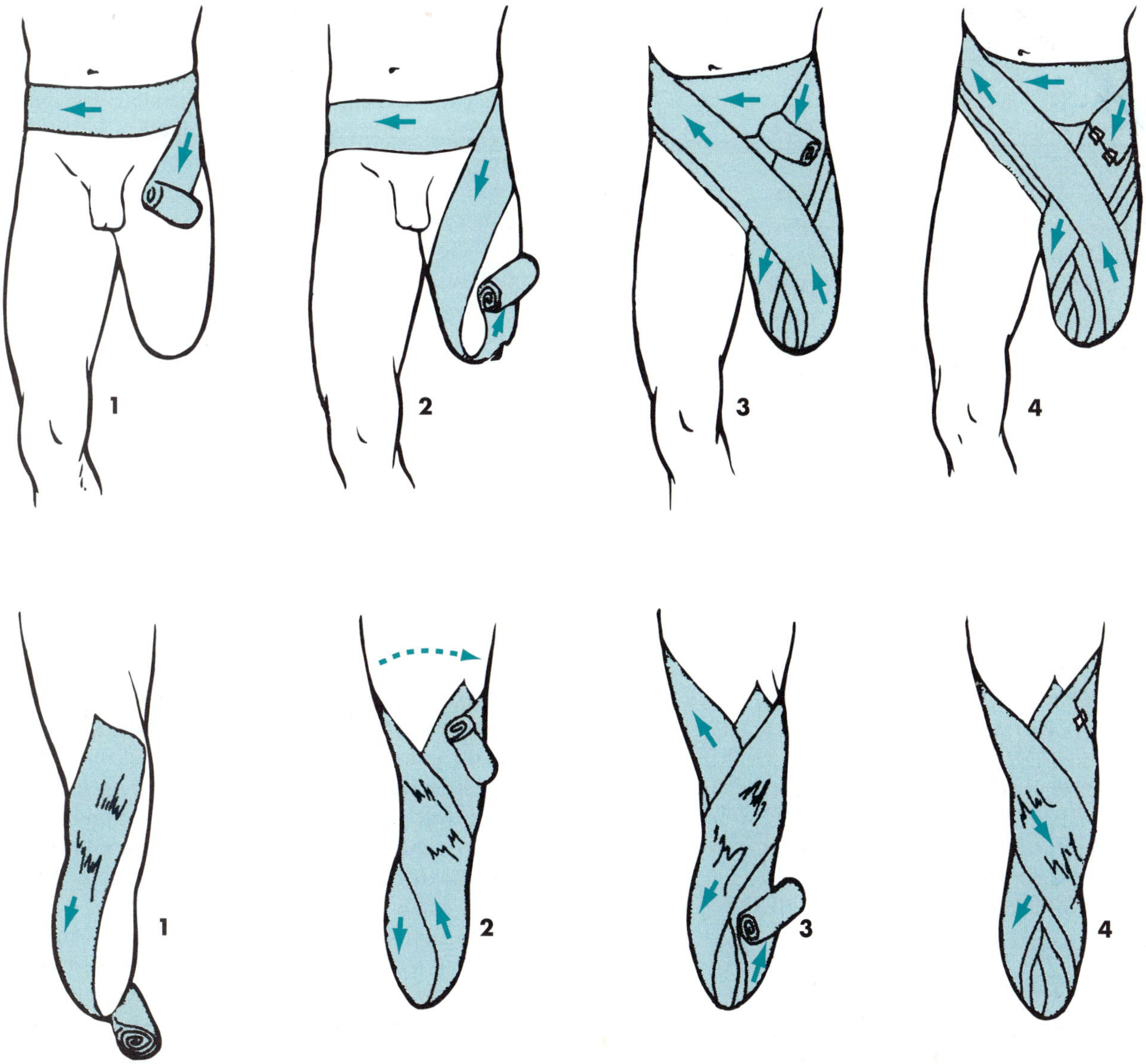

Fig. 21-12 *Top,* Correct method for bandaging through midthigh amputation stump. Note that bandage must be anchored around patient's waist. *Bottom,* Correct method for bandaging midcalf amputation stump. NOTE: The bandage need not be anchored around the waist. (From Phipps WJ et al: *Medical-surgical nursing: concepts and clinical practice,* ed 5, St. Louis, 1995, Mosby.)

removal and reapplication during the day (Fig. 21-12). Some older clients with associated illnesses may not respond to aggressive therapy and may opt for amputation without prosthesis. Clients need assistance with initial transfers to and from bed and chair. Physiotherapy plays an integral role with the rehabilitation, and nurses should understand all facets of the ambulation regimen to reinforce and to monitor the client's progress (Ruda, 1992). Before discharge, care of the stump should be reviewed with both the client and family (see Client/Family Teaching box, p. 550).

Knowledge Deficit (Modification of Risk Factors) Related to Lack of Exposure

Nursing intervention includes assisting the older client to recognize risk factors affecting arterial insufficiency (smoking, elevated serum cholesterol, hypertension, DM, physical inactivity, and obesity) and encouraging clients to modify their behaviors or to control their conditions. Important education topics for the nurse to include in the teaching plan are as follows: (1) explain to the older adult the need to avoid the use of nicotine; (2) teach about a low-cholesterol and low-fat diet; (3) provide weight counseling; (4) discuss a daily progressive

CLIENT/FAMILY TEACHING

Stump Care

- Inspect the stump daily for signs of skin irritation, especially redness.
- Discontinue use of prothesis if an irritation develops. Have the area checked by the physician or nurse before resuming use of the prosthesis.
- Wash thoroughly each night with warm water and a bacteriostatic soap. Rinse thoroughly and dry gently. Expose the stump to air for 20 minutes.
- Do not use any substance such as lotions, alcohol, powders, or oil unless prescribed by the physician.
- If a stump sock is worn, wear only the one supplied by the prosthetist, and change daily. Launder in a mild soap, squeeze, and lay flat to dry.

walking program; and (5) teach appropriate self-care practices related to chronic disease management of hypertension and diabetes.

✤ EVALUATION

Evaluation of the older client with PAD focuses on goals outlined in the planning process. Older adults should demonstrate improved peripheral circulation, a reduction in pain, and the ability to perform ADLs within limitations or with support before discharge from hospital.

Peripheral Vascular Disease: Venous Disorders

Peripheral vascular disease (PVD) is any disturbance that impairs tissue perfusion. The most common underlying causes of peripheral venous disease are (1) varicose veins, (2) deep vein thrombosis and pulmonary embolism, (3) venous ulceration, and (4) lymphatic disorders.

Varicose veins of the leg occur particularly in women and may be divided into primary and secondary varicose veins. Primary varicose veins are more common, and the varicosity, which occurs in the wall of the vein, may be related to weakness of the wall or to incompetent valves of the saphenofemoral junction or the perforating veins. Underlying causes include, but are not limited to, obesity, estrogenic hormones, and in older adults, a previous occupation that required long periods of standing. Secondary varicose veins are the result of thrombosis in the deep system, which may subsequently occur with obstruction of the valves. The signs and symptoms of varicose veins are protrusion of veins on the legs, aching, ankle swelling, night cramps; skin changes, including itching, varicose eczema; and in extreme cases, a hemorrhage. The majority of cases may be treated with conservative therapy, including the use of elastic support bandages, regular exercise, and reduction of weight. In more severe cases, surgical intervention such as sclerotherapy and ligation may be required.

Deep vein thrombosis is a common and serious disorder and has been associated with 300,000 to 600,000 hospitalizations each year. Approximately 140,000 individuals die each year as a result of pulmonary embolism. Immobility (prolonged bed rest), advancing age (over age 45), obesity, hormonal usage, and cigarette smoking are contributing factors. Medical conditions predisposing individuals to deep vein thrombosis include blood dyscrasia, cancer, systemic infection, dehydration, heart disease, stroke, inflammatory bowel disease, and incompetent venous valve. General surgical clients over age 40 have a 19% incidence. Surgical clients at highest risk are those undergoing hip surgery and knee reconstruction. The older adult after surgery is at a particularly high risk (Bright, Georgi, 1992).

Venous or gravitational ulcer occurs in clients who have chronic venous insufficiency. The superficial system is subjected to high pressure, which results in poor tissue oxygenation of the lower limb. Venous ulcers occur on the medial side of the lower half of the leg. The ulcer is usually painful, may be easily infected, and if left untreated, may involve the circumference of the leg. The management of venous ulceration is dependent on relieving the hypertension occurring in the superficial system through bed rest, elevation of the limb, and compression bandaging.

The lymphatic system is often overlooked during discussion of the circulatory system. Failure of the lymphatic system to move fluid from the extracellular space is often a result of obstruction. Lymphedema, or swelling, results from stasis of lymph because of impediment of flow. As with veins, the lymph vessels dilate and the valves become incompetent. The fluid seeks new pathways through the tissues, causing inflammation, lymphatic thrombosis, and eventually fibrosis. The causes of secondary lymphedema include radiation, trauma, or excision of lymph pathways; or malignant disease and its treatment. Conservative treatment is aimed at decreasing edema by improving lymph drainage (e.g., elevating the foot of the bed), elastic stockings, and bed rest with the affected leg elevated on pillows (see Medical Management box on p. 551).

NURSING MANAGEMENT

✤ ASSESSMENT

Assessment of the older adult with PVD begins with a complete history and physical examination. Subjective

MEDICAL MANAGEMENT

PVD

Diagnostic tests and treatment

The diagnosis of PVD is based on presenting symptoms, physical assessment of the peripheral vascular system and various noninvasive tests.

Indirect methods to detect obstruction include Doppler ultrasonography, plethysmography, ambulatory venous pressure measurement, manual compression, retrograde filling test, magnetic resonance imaging (MRI), venography, and B/mode venous imaging. Doppler ultrasonography measures venous obstruction and reflux of blood by changes in the frequency of sound waves.

Treatment

The therapeutic aim in peripheral vascular disease is to preserve not only the limb, but also its function. Interventions range from palliative measures to ease symptoms to the use of pharmalogic and surgical strategies to enhance blood flow and prevent clot formation.

Palliative measures are important for maintaining comfort. Preservation of skin integrity in both arterial and venous disease is of prime importance in maintaining the overall health of the limb.

Pharmacologic intervention is directed at increasing blood flow and preventing clot formation. Vasodilation appears to have a limited effect in peripheral vascular disease.

Anticoagulant therapy (heparin) prevents thrombosis by activating antithrombin III, a naturally occurring inhibitor of several blood-clotting factors. The effect of heparin is immediate but short-lived; the half-life is only 90 minutes.

Warfarin (Coumadin) alters coagulation by interfering with the participation of vitamin K in the synthesis of prothrombin and clotting factors VII, IX, and X. Effective coagulation does not begin until the drug has been taken orally for 4 to 5 days.

Dextran 40 alters platelet function, interferes with fibrin formation, and enhances clot lysis. It is given intravenously in daily doses of 500 ml over 4 to 6 hours.

Antiplatelet drugs such as acetylsalicylic acid (aspirin) and dipyridamole (Persantine) inhibit the adherence and aggregation of platelets. Aspirin eliminates the "stickiness" of platelets, and decreases their affinity for one another. Dipyridamole inhibits collagen and adenosine diphosphate (ADP) induced platelet aggregation in whole blood.

Thrombolytic drugs (streptokinase, urokinase) have been used in lysis of pulmonary emboli, for extensive thrombi of deep veins, or for clearing of occluded arteriovenous cannulas as an alternative to surgery.

A variety of surgical procedures can be performed to reduce the effects of PVD. Surgical procedures involve the superficial venous system or the deep venous system, or surgery for venous obstruction.

Prognosis

The prevalence, risk factors, and mortality rate for PVD in the older adult population has received limited attention in the literature. Varicose veins are one of the most prevalent conditions in industrial societies. The prevalence of varicose veins in those age 70 and older in the United States is 50%, and in a recent study conducted in Turkey, the total prevalence was 36.7% in men and 22.1% in women (Komsuolglu et al, 1994).

Deep vein thrombosis has been associated with 300,000 to 600,000 hospitalizations and approximately 140,000 deaths in the United States. Surgical clients at higher risk include those with hip and knee construction.

data include pain in the extremity, precipitating factors, relieving factors, modifiable risk factors (e.g., smoking, hypertension, diabetes, obesity, and physical inactivity), and personal and family history. Objective assessment includes skin color, hair distribution (i.e., lack of hair growth may indicate inadequate circulation), atrophy, edema, varicosities, petechiae, lesions, and ulcerations. See Table 21-12 for the assessment for peripheral and venous disease.

✜ DIAGNOSIS

Nursing diagnoses for older adults with PVD include, but are not limited to (1) risk for impaired skin integrity related to venous stasis and fragility of small blood vessels, (2) altered tissue perfusion related to interruption of venous flow, (3) pain related to inflammatory process and (4) risk for impaired gas exchange related to altered circulation.

✜ PLANNING

Older clients with PVD and their family members should be included in the planning of care. Discharge planning should begin as soon as the older client is admitted to the hospital.

Expected outcomes for the older client include the following: (1) skin integrity is maintained or improved, (2) client exhibits no ulceration or signs of the inflammatory process, (3) tissue perfusion is improved, and (4) client exhibits no signs of respiratory distress.

✜ INTERVENTION

Risk for Impaired Skin Integrity Related to Venous Stasis and Fragility of Small Blood Vessels

Nursing interventions include assessment of skin integrity, elevation of affected extremity, elastic compres-

TABLE 21-12

Physical Assessment for PVD

Assess	Arterial disease	Venous disease
Pain	**Acute**—Sudden, severe pain that peaks rapidly	**Acute**—Little or no pain, tenderness along course of inflamed vein
	Chronic—Intermittent claudication, rest pain	**Chronic**—Heaviness, fullness
Impotence	May be present with aorto-iliac femoral disease	Not associated
Hair	Hair loss distal to occlusion	No hair loss
Nails	Thick, brittle	Normal
Skeletal muscle	Atrophy may be present; may have restricted limb movement	Normal
Sensation	Possible paresthesia	Normal
Skin color	Pallor or reactive hyperemia (pallor when limb is elevated; rubor [red] when limb is dependent)	Brawny (reddish-brown); cyanotic if dependent
Skin texture	Thin, shiny, dry	Stasis dermatitis; veins may be visible; skin mottling
Skin temperature	Cool	Warm
Skin breakdown (ulcers)	Severely painful; usually on or between toes or on upper surface of foot over metatarsal heads or other bony prominences	Mildly painful, with pain relieved by leg elevation; usually in ankle area
Edema	None or mild, usually unilateral	Typically present—usually foot to calf; may be unilateral or bilateral
Pulses	Diminished, weak, or absent	Normal
Blood flow	Bruit may be present; pressure readings are lower below stenosis	Normal

From Bright L, Georgi S: Peripheral vascular disease: is it arterial or venous? *AJN* 92(9):34-43, 45-47, 1992.

sion and administration of daily hygiene. The skin is assessed for any signs of redness, skin breakdown, and ulcerations. The affected extremity should be elevated on pillows to eliminate venous hypertension. Older adults are prone to ulcer formation and altered circulation as a result of the aging process. Managing venous stasis ulcers that do occur involves healing the ulcer and preventing recurrence. Two types of occlusive dressings can be used: oxygen permeable (e.g., Op Site) and oxygen impermeable (e.g., DuoDerm). The dressing site should be observed often and changed to keep the ulcer clean.

Prevention of ulcer formation (especially in diabetic clients) is of prime importance. The nurse should encourage ambulation to enhance collateral circulation and instruct the client on foot care. The skin should be inspected daily. The extremity should be washed gently in tepid water with a neutral soap. Older clients who complain of dry, itchy skin should take fewer baths and increase the application of lubricants. Nails should be clipped straight across. Shoes should be well-fitting, and ladies should avoid pointed-toe shoes. Shoes should be removed several times during the day and aired after use. The use of bedcradles may relieve pressure on the affected extremity.

Altered Tissue Perfusion Related to Interruption of Venous Flow

Nursing interventions include assessment of circulation of affected extremity (i.e., for pain, color, skin texture, skin temperature, skin breakdown, and edema) and check pulses in all extremities. Use Doppler sensor if pulses seem absent. Measure and record size of affected limb every day. If the client is in the acute phase, elevate affected extremity to facilitate venous circulation. The client should be instructed to avoid wearing garters and knee-high stockings with tight elastic, crossing legs, and nicotine, since all of these practices increase vasoconstriction. A progressive exercise program should be commenced, and clients should be instructed to wear support stockings before ambulating and to avoid standing for prolonged periods.

Pain Related to Inflammatory Process

Nursing interventions include assessment of the quality, frequency, and location of pain. Pain assessment tools may be used to assess the continuum of pain. The client should be placed on bed rest. The affected limb should be elevated on pillows. Bed cradles should be used to decrease pressure of linen on the affected limb. Administer analgesics as ordered. Nursing measures should be implemented that prevent the hazards of immobility, depending on the degree of bed rest required.

Risk for Impaired Gas Exchange (High Risk for) Related to Altered Circulation

Nursing interventions include observing for signs and symptoms of pulmonary embolism (chest pain, dyspnea, tachypnea). The client and family should be taught signs and symptoms of pulmonary embolism and to seek medical assistance immediately. The lung sounds should be auscultated every 8 hours or as indicated. The client should be instructed to avoid exercising and massaging affected extremity. Anticoagulants are administered as ordered.

✣ EVALUATION

Evaluation focuses on goals related to improved skin integrity, improved venous circulation, a reduction in pain, and the ability to perform ADLs within limitations or with support before discharge from the hospital.

Cardiomyopathy

Cardiomyopathy refers to diseases of the heart muscle; the particular muscle involved is the ventricular myocardium. The exact cause of cardiomyopathy is unknown; however, two etiologic categories have been proposed. Primary cardiomyopathy is ideopathic in origin (unknown cause). Secondary causes are attributed to suspected or known precipitating conditions such as viral, autoimmune, toxic (alcohol), metabolic, and peripartal conditions. Secondary causes are the typical causation factors in the older adult.

Cardiomyopathies are classified by structural and functional abnormalities, including hypertrophic, congestive (dilated), and restrictive.

Symptoms of hypertrophic cardiomyopathy are evident in younger adults. Increased muscle mass (especially along the septum), rigid walls, and small heart chambers are characteristic findings. During systole, anterior leaflets of the mitral valve press against the enlarged septum, obstructing the amount of blood ejected. Heart failure can develop (Table 21-13).

Fibrosis of the myocardial and endocardial layers of the heart is the underlying feature of congestive cardiomyopathy. Cardiac output is reduced as a result of the impaired contractile force of the ventricle and heart failure results. As volumes and pressures increase within the cardiac cavity, all four heart chambers dilate. Thrombi formation is prevalent because of the pooling and stasis of blood. Congestive cardiomyopathy is more prevalent in the older population.

Fibrosis of myocardial and endocardial fibers also occurs with restrictive cardiomyopathy; however, with this type of condition the fibrosed walls cannot expand or contract. The ventricular chambers decrease in size and impaired ventricular filling occurs (similar to constrictive pericarditis). Emboli are common with restrictive cardiomyopathy.

Congestive cardiomyopathy is more prevalent in left-sided heart failure; however, biventricular failure can develop. Fatigue, weakness, and dyspnea on exertion are common initial symptoms. If right-sided failure develops, dyspnea at rest, fluid retention, and abdominal swelling may occur. Moderate to severe cardiomegaly may be evident and S_3 and S_4 heart sounds can be heard. Dysrhythmias, heart block, and systemic or pulmonary emboli may develop.

Symptoms of right sided failure are more apt to appear with restrictive cardiomyopathy. Decreased cardiac output resulting from fixed ventricular volumes usually causes fatigue and dyspnea on exertion. Mild to moderate cardiomegaly may be evident and heart block or emboli can develop (see Medical Management box, above).

MEDICAL MANAGEMENT

Cardiomyopathy

Diagnostic tests and procedures

Chest x-rays, echocardiography, radionuclide imaging, and cardiac catheterization are used to diagnose and classify cardiomyopathies. Chest x-ray may detect ventricular dilation or narrowing before the presence of symptoms. In later stages of the disease process, x-ray depicts cardiac and pulmonary changes associated with heart failure.

Echocardiography and ultrasound are used to assess the size of the cardiac chambers, ejection fraction, and the motion of the cardiac walls.

Radionuclide imaging assesses ventricular functioning, and cardiac catheterization provides information on cardiac structural components, oxygenation, cardiac pressures and output, and coronary circulation.

Treatment

Medical care is palliative in nature and involves treatment of the symptoms.

Pharmaceutic agents used to treat congestive and restrictive, cardiomyopathies are drugs prescribed for heart failure: cardiac glycosides and diuretics, vasodilators, and antidysrhythmics.

Prognosis

The prognosis is poor for clients with cardiomyopathy. The damage to heart muscle cannot be repaired so treatment is palliative, not curative, and most clients die within 5 years after symptom onset. When severe or end-stage failure is imminent, heart transplantation may be considered; however, older clients do not meet age criteria for this option.

TABLE 21-13

Pathophysiology of Cardiomyopathy

	Hypertrophic cardiomyopathy		
Dilated cardiomyopathy	**Nonobstructed**	**Obstructed**	**Restrictive cardiomyopathy**
Pathophysiology			
Fibrosis of myocardium and endocardium Dilated chambers Mural wall thrombi prevalent	Hypertrophy of all walls Hypertrophied septum Relatively small chamber size	Same as nonobstructed, except for obstruction of left ventricular outflow tract associated with the hypertrophied septum and mitral valve incompetence	Mimics constrictive pericarditis Fibrosed walls cannot expand or contract Chambers narrowed; emboli common
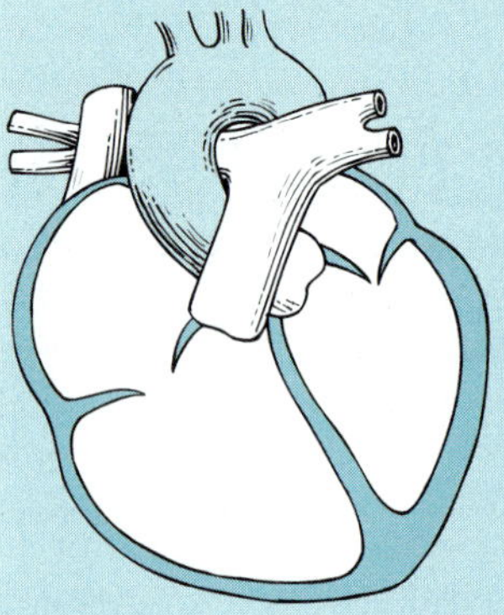	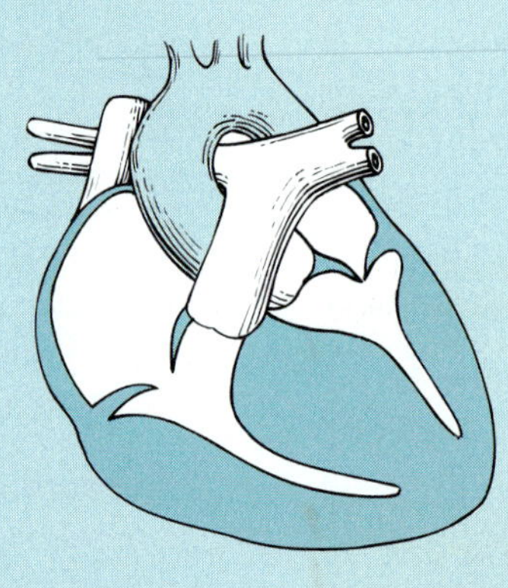		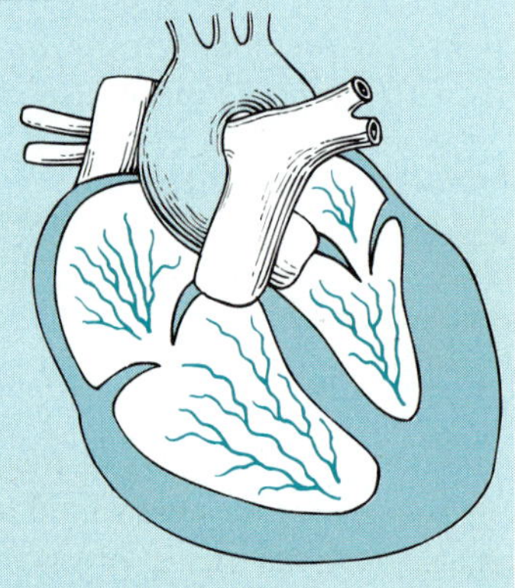
Signs and symptoms			
Fatigue and weakness Heart failure (left sided) Dysrhythmias or heart block Systemic or pulmonary emboli S_3 and S_4 gallops Moderate to severe cardiomegaly	Dyspnea Angina Fatigue, syncope, palpitations Mild cardiomegaly S_4 gallop Ventricular dysrhythmias Sudden death common Heart failure	Same as for nonobstructed, except with mitral regurgitation murmur Atrial fibrillation	Dyspnea and fatigue Heart failure (right sided) Mild to moderate cardiomegaly S_3 and S_4 gallops Heart block Emboli
Treament			
Symptomatic treatment of heart failure Vasodilators Control of dysrhythmias Surgery: heart transplant	*For both:* Symptomatic treatment Beta-blockers Conversion of atrial fibrillation Surgery: ventriculomyotomy or muscle resection with mitral valve replacement Digitalis, nitrates, and other vasodilators contraindicated with the obstructed form		Supportive treatment of symptoms Treatment of hypertension Conversation from dysrhythmias Exercise restrictions Emergency treatment of acute pulmonary edema

From Wynne J, Braunwald E: The cardiomyopathies and myocarditis. In Braunwald E, editors: *Heart disease: a textbook of cardiovascular medicine,* ed 3, Philadelphia, WB Saunders.

NURSING MANAGEMENT

ASSESSMENT

Assessment of the cardiovascular and respiratory systems take precedence when examining a client with cardiomyopathy, as heart failure is the usual cause for hospital admission. Abnormal heart sounds (S_3 and S_4), crackles, and dyspnea at rest or on exertion are suggestive of left-sided failure. Jugular distention and edema of the limbs and torso indicate right-sided failure. Results of electrocardiogram and chest x-ray provide additional data on dysrhythmias and pulmonary or cardiac involvement.

DIAGNOSIS, PLANNING, AND INTERVENTION

Nursing diagnoses, expected outcomes, and interventions are identical to those described under heart failure. The poor prognosis for cardiomyopathy may enhance feelings of fear. For older clients, death is inevitable, but many fear the *process* of dying. The nurse can provide guidance and support as the client encounters the various phases of the dying process. Caring and listening skills assist the client to cope with the inevitable. Pastoral care services designed to meet the emotional needs of the dying may be summoned to complement nursing activities. Clients need physical assistance to complete ADLs and should be encouraged to participate in all aspects of their care to tolerance.

Discharge preparation on dietary, activity, and medication treatments are similar to those described with heart failure. For clients encountering difficulty with ADLs visiting nurses and home care services may be an available option. Depending on community availability, older adults may benefit from hospice programs.

Endocarditis

Endocarditis may be defined as "an infection of the smooth lining of the heart" (Handerhan, 1991). The incidence of infective endocarditis appears to be increasing, with approximately 10,000 to 20,000 new cases diagnosed annually. This is in various measure because of the number of individuals undergoing prosthetic valve replacement and the greater number of older clients with degenerative valve disease or pacemakers.

Approximately 15% to 25% of cases of endocarditis are associated with invasive dental, gastrointestinal, or genitourinary procedures in clients with underlying valvular heart disease. There are several underlying causes of endocarditis, including the following:

1. **Septicemia**—Endocardial tissue may be infected by bacterial or fungal contaminants in the blood.
2. Blood turbulence—Endocardial damage may result from blood turbulence created by a malfunctioning valve. A dense network of platelets and fibrin mesh forms at the site of the malfunction, providing a safe environment for microorganisms while resisting penetration by phagocytes.
3. Microbial adherence—The surface of some microbes permits them to adhere to valvular endothelium, triggering infection.
4. Autoimmune response—Antibodies may overreact to offending organisms, forming immunologic complexes that can be deposited on the heart (Handerhan, 1991).

The American Heart Association recommends prophylaxis of bacterial endocarditis for clients with valvular abnormalities and other defects during certain procedures (Table 21-14).

The signs and symptoms of this disease vary, especially in the older client, but can include fever, fatigue, weight loss, joint pain, back pain, and headache. Petechiae, splinter hemorrhages, glomerulonephritis, and hematuria may be present. The mean age of endocarditis in clients is approximately age 55, and 40% to 50% of the clients are over 50. Older clients may not exhibit typical signs and symptoms such as fever and heart murmurs but may instead be confused, or show signs of seizure or stroke (Bayer, Hutter, Wilson, 1991) (see Medical Management box, p. 557).

NURSING MANAGEMENT

ASSESSMENT

Assessment of the individual for general complaints including low-grade fever, weakness, malaise, weight loss, anorexia, night sweats, headache, and syncope is essential.

The nurse should also assess for signs of embolization, including petechiae, splinter hemorrhage (linear dark red streaks on nail beds), Osler's nodes (small, tender raised nodules often found on finger and toe pads), Janeway lesions (nontender, flat, erythematous macules on palms and soles); splenomegaly, Roth's spots (retinal hemorrhages with white centers), and neurologic changes (confusion, behavioral changes). The nurse also should assess the client for any changes in murmurs.

DIAGNOSIS

Diagnoses for older adults with endocarditis include, but are not limited to (1) altered nutrition related to biologic factors (fever, infection), (2) high risk for altered tissue perfusion, and (3) fear related to knowledge deficit regarding significance of condition.

TABLE 21-14

Conditions Warranting Prophylactic Treatment for Endocarditis

Cardiac conditions	Dental and surgical procedures
Prosthetic cardiac valves, including bioprosthetic and homograft valves	Dental procedures known to induce gingival or mucosal bleeding, including professional cleaning
Previous bacterial endocarditis	Surgical operations that involve intestinal or respiratory mucosa
Rheumatic and other acquired valvular dysfunctions	Bronchoscopy
Hypertrophic cardiomyopathy	Esophageal dilation
Mitral valve prolapse with valvular regurgitation	Gallbladder surgery
	Cystoscopy
	Urethral catheterization if urinary infection is present
	Urinary tract surgery if infection is present
	Prostatic surgery
	Incision and drainage of infected tissue

Modified from Bayer A, Hutter A, Wilson W: Current management of infective endocarditis, *Patient Care* 25(2):15-18, 21-23, 28, 1991.

✣ PLANNING

The older client and family should be included in the planning of care. Discharge planning should begin as soon as the older client is admitted to the hospital. A number of clients are now treated with antibiotic therapy in the home setting via use of IV pumps, and therefore it is essential that clients be aware of the condition, complications, and treatment modalities. Psychologic support should be provided to the client and family with regard to the anxiety associated with this condition and the ultimate prognosis and complications.

Expected outcomes include the following: (1) client demonstrates improved nutritional status as well-being improves with the absence of infection and fever, (2) tissue perfusion is maintained, and (3) client and family acquire skills for managing their fears.

✣ INTERVENTION

Altered Nutrition Related to Biologic Factors (Fever, Infection)

The client should be monitored for dehydration, diaphoresis, poor skin turgor, and weight loss. Every effort should be made to provide a high-caloric, high-protein diet during the acute phase of the illness. The older client must be provided a calm, quiet atmosphere during mealtime and encouraged to eat as tolerated (with dietary considerations for preference and culture). Intake and output should be monitored and the client should be weighed daily. The vital signs should be taken every 4 hours. Antibiotic therapy and analgesics are to be given as ordered.

High Risk for Altered Tissue Perfusion

Nursing interventions include observing for signs and symptoms of pulmonary embolism (chest pain, dyspnea, tachypnea). The client and family should be taught symptoms of pulmonary embolism and to seek assistance immediately. The lung sounds should be auscultated every 8 hours or as indicated. Anticoagulants are administered as ordered.

Fear Related to Knowledge Deficit Regarding Significance of Condition and Complications

It is imperative that a calm, quiet and nonthreatening environment be created either in the hospital or the home setting. The nurse should be prepared to answer all questions in a clear, concise manner that is understandable at the client's level of education and cultural background. Allow time for the client and family to express their concerns.

Teach the client and family the nature of the condition, presenting signs and symptoms, medical intervention, surgical intervention (if warranted), medication regimen, and complications. The precipitating factors related to bacteremia and reinfection and the importance of prophylactic treatment before cardiac procedures, dental work, gastrointestinal, and genitourinary procedures should be explained. Also, the client should be encouraged to maintain good oral hygiene and regular dental care, as well as to see the physician on a regular basis.

✣ EVALUATION

Evaluation focuses on the absence of signs and symptoms related to the inflammatory process. The nutritional status improves, tissue perfusion is maintained, and the client and family openly discuss concerns.

Summary

Age-related changes in structure and function of the cardiovascular system were addressed and major clinical problems and conditions discussed. In the older adult population, it is often difficult to clearly distinguish differences between cardiovascular disease and "normal" aging. The presentation as well as effects of cardiovascular disease can vary widely from person to person. The signs of cardiovascular problems can be at a minimum, and in some cases even undetectable, yet the degree of functional impairment can be profound.

MEDICAL MANAGEMENT

Endocarditis

Diagnostic tests and procedures

Physical health history and assessment, laboratory findings, electrocardiography, blood cultures, and echocardiography are used to diagnose infective endocarditis. The physical assessment should include information related to an antecedent event such as a cardiac or dental procedure, or a cystoscopy, as well as the presenting signs and symptoms.

Regurgitant aortic or mitral valves produce signs and symptoms of left-sided heart failure (tachycardia, gallop rhythm, dyspnea, crackles and hypotension). If the tricuspid valve is affected, the presenting signs and symptoms include peripheral edema, neck vein distension, hepatomegaly, ascites, and atrial arrhythmias.

Extracardiac signs and symptoms of endocarditis include fever, chills, night sweats, weight loss, weakness, and petechiae on the trunk or on the buccal, pharyngeal, or conjunctival mucosa (Handerhan, 1991). The initial laboratory workup includes a CBC with differential as well as erythrocyte sedimentation rate (ESR) (the ESR is also a good indicator to follow the course of therapy, since it will drop with successful treatment).

Initial electrocardiography findings may reveal premature ventricular contractions, T-wave abnormalities and intraventricular conduction defects. New conduction defects, especially heart blocks, may represent an abscess or an infection spreading from the valve tissue into the conduction system.

Electrocardiography is useful for documenting the presence of vegetation, valvular regurgitation, stenosis, stability of the prosthetic valve, and left ventricular function.

Blood cultures are positive in approximately 95% of the cases.

Treatment

The antibiotic therapy is based on identification of the infecting organism. In most instances, the infective agent is a group of organisms called *viridans streptococci.* Three regimens are used: (1) penicillin for 4 weeks alone, (2) penicillin in combination with streptomycin sulfate or gentamicin sulfate (Garamycin) for 2 weeks, or for streptococcal endocarditis, a combination of penicillin with streptomycin and gentamicin for 2 weeks (Table 21-15).

Surgical management

Most authorities consider moderate to severe heart failure related to valve dysfunction to be an indication for surgical intervention in endocarditis. Surgery is also indicated for clients who have sudden hemodynamic compromise and acute valvular insufficiency. There is no consensus regarding the appropriateness of surgery if prosthetic valve endocarditis occurs within 1 to 2 months of implantation. Consensus is also lacking when there is late prosthetic valve endocarditis from nonstreptococcal organisms (Bayer, Hutter, Wilson, 1991).

Prognosis

Although short-term outcome is good for uncomplicated endocarditis, authorities offer a cautionary note for the long-term prognosis of endocarditis clients. Even in uncomplicated viridans streptococcal endocarditis, particularly in older clients, the 5-year survival rate at this time is only 50% to 60% (Bayer, Hutter, Wilson, 1991).

Among the complications of infective endocarditis, the most serious is CHF. Other complications include the following: development of infective endocarditis, myocardial abscess, intracardiac fistulae, or mycotic aneurysm. Extracardiac complications of endocarditis include emboli leading to acute stroke for mycotic aneurysms that result in subarachnoid hemorrhage. Mycotic aneurysms in the large arteries such as splenic, celiac, and hepatic have been reported. Aneurysms may rupture, leading to massive intraabdominal bleeding.

The challenge for the nurse is to obtain an accurate and complete assessment of the older adult with a cardiovascular problem so that appropriate physical and psychosocial care can be planned with the client and family.

Key Points

- CVD is the leading cause of mortality for both men and women.
- For those over age 65, mortality rates for CVD sharply rise, and it is anticipated that the actual number of deaths resulting from CVD will escalate as the proportion of the older population increases.
- Risk factors of age, gender, and family history are factors that cannot be modified.
- Risk factors of smoking, high blood pressure, diet (cholesterol), obesity, physical activity, and stress are amenable to change, and research has demonstrated that the adoption of a healthier lifestyle has the potential to reduce or to prevent the incidence of morbidity and death from ischemic heart disease and stroke.
- Smoking cessation in older adults markedly reduces the risks of coronary events and of cardiac death within 1 year of quitting, and the risk continues to decline gradually for many years thereafter.
- An increased risk for CVD was found among insulin and noninsulin-dependent individuals with diabetes. The death rate for CVD was five times higher in individuals with diabetes.

TABLE 21-15

Treatment Regimen for Adults with Endocarditis Caused by Penicillin-Susceptible Streptococcal Pathogens

Antibiotic	Adult regimen	Duration (by week)
Aqueous penicillin G*	10 to 20 million Units/24 hr IV either continuously or in six equally divided doses	4
Aqueous penicillin G*	10 to 20 million Units/24 hr IV either continuously or in six equally divided doses	2
With streptomycin sulfate† or	7.5 mg/kg intramuscularly (IM) (not to exceed 500 mg) every 12 hrs.	2
with gentamicin sulfate (Garamycin)†	1.0 mg/kg IM or IV (not to exceed 80 mg) every 8 hrs.	2
Aqueous penicillin G*	10 to 20 million Units/24 hr IV either continuously or in six equally divided doses	4
With streptomycin sulfate† or	7.5 mg/kg IM (not to exceed 500 mg) every 12 hrs.	2
with gentamicin†	1.0 mg/kg IM or IV (not to exceed 80 mg) every 8 hrs.	2
In penicillin-allergic clients:		
Cephalothin sodium (Keflin)‡	2 gm IV every 4 hrs.	4
or Cefazolin sodium (Ancef, Kefzol, Zolicef)‡	1 gm IM or IV every 4 hrs.	4
Vancomycin HCl (Vancocin, Vancoled)§	30 mg/kg every 24 hrs. IV in two or four equally divided doses (not to exceed 2 gm/24 hrs unless serum levels are moni-	4

*Procaine penicillin G, 1.2 million Units IM every 6 hrs. may be given instead.

†Peak streptomycin levels of approximately 20 μg/ml and peak gentamicin levels of approximately 3 μg/ml are desirable. Dosing of aminoglycosides on a milligram-per-kilogram basis produces higher serum concentrations in obese than in lean clients. Relative contraindications to use of aminoglycosides are age > 65 or renal or eighth nerve impairment. Aminoglycoside dosages must be modified for clients with renal dysfunction.

‡There is potential cross-allergenicity between penicillins and cephalosporins. Cephalosporins should be avoided in clients with immediate-type hypersensitivity to penicillin.

§Peak serum concentrations of vancomycin should be obtained 1 hour after infusion and should be in the range of 30 to 45 μg/ml for bid dosing and 20 to 35 μg/ml for qid dosing. Vancomycin given on a milligram-per-kilogram basis produces higher serum concentrations in obese than in lean clients. Each dose of vancomycin should be infused over 1 hour. Vancomycin dosages must be modified for clients with renal dysfunction.

Modified with permission from Bisno AL, Dismukes WE, Durack DT et al: Antimicrobial treatment of infective endocarditis due to viridans streptococci, enterococci, and staphylococci, *JAMA* 1989:261:1471-1477. © 1989, American Medical Association; and Bayer A, Hutter A, Wilson W,: Current management of infective endocarditis, *Pat Care,* 25 (2), 15-18, 21-23, 28, 1991.

- It is estimated that more than 45% to 50% of the population over age 65 has high blood pressure, and the consequences are the most common causes of morbidity and mortality including MI, CHF and PVD.
- Thiazide diuretics are the most commonly prescribed antihypertensive agent in older adults.
- CAD is the most common cause of death in people over age 65. It is estimated that 1.5 million Americans are diagnosed with MI annually. Older adults with CAD are more likely to have multivessel disease.
- Older women tend to have anginal symptoms more than men; however, after age 80, angina for both genders progressively decreases.
- Older adults may not recognize the onset of ischemia, and initial symptoms may consist of sudden dyspnea, confusion, fatigue, weakness, vertigo, syncope, vomiting, and exacerbation of heart failure.
- Atrial fibrillation is the most common dysrhythmia (abnormal heart rate or rhythm) in the older adult, with an estimated incidence of 2% to 4% in individuals over age 65.
- Atrial fibrillation, sick sinus syndrome, and heart block appear more often in the older population as a result of fewer pacemaker cells and extensive deposits of fat and fibrous tissue throughout the conduction system.
- Older adults have a higher incidence of toxicity and adverse reactions with digoxin, beta-blockers, and calcium channel blockers; therefore, it is imperative that the nurse monitor carefully for any untoward effects.
- The death rate for CHF has increased by approximately 33% in those age 45 and older. It is estimated that 2.3 million people have CHF, accounting for 1.8 million office visits and 1.5 million hospital visits per year.
- Age-associated cardiovascular and renal changes affecting the clinical course of CHF and the responses to treatment include decreased renal and systemic blood flow, increased arterial stiffness and peripheral resistance, reduced ventricular compliance, and reduced maximum aerobic capacity. Any disease that affects the normal aging heart tends to cause cardiovascular symptoms earlier than it would in a younger person.
- Recent research confirms that individuals valued education during their hospitalization, with medication

HOME CARE TIPS

1. The homebound older adult client, spouse, family, significant others, and/or caregivers should be included in all aspects of the care planning process in the home setting.
2. Clients value education in the home care setting, and this should continue after hospitalization as an important focus of care.
3. Clients dealing with chronic disease management in the home setting often experience anxiety, frustration and depression. This factor should be taken into consideration when providing home care services, initiating appropriate interagency referrals as indicated.
4. The fear of dying is often a major factor for homebound older adults with cardiovascular disease, and in particular congestive heart failure. Counseling and referral to agencies should be provided.
5. The nurse should direct teaching of the homebound older adult to the anatomy and physiology of the heart, modifiable risk factors, medication regimen (especially in regard to dose and side effects), exercise tolerance, daily weight monitoring, and dietary factors (low sodium, low fat, and fluid restriction).
6. Assistance with ADLs may be required, especially for those homebound older adults who live alone or are responsible for household tasks. Often these clients do not request assistance, so the nurse should offer these services where appropriate.
7. Participation in a cardiac rehabilitation program or activities such as walking or swimming should be encouraged by the home care nurse.
8. Homebound older adult clients should be encouraged to wear medical-alert bracelets that identify their condition and medications.

content as the most important aspect, followed by anatomy and physiology, risk factors, and diet. These findings have implications for the planning of client care.

- Nursing interventions (role of risk factors, preventive measures, and treatment regimen) can enhance the quality of life of older clients, reduce hospitalization, and affect the cost-effectiveness and efficiency of cardiovascular programs.
- Discharge planning involves teaching the client appropriate self-care during recovery at home. All teaching materials should be easily read by the older person with consideration for visual, literacy level and cultural aspects. All material presented should be in large print.
- All clients should be encouraged to visit their physician on a regular basis, follow treatment regimens and be encouraged to wear medical-alert bracelets specifying the condition and medications.

Critical Thinking Exercises

1. You are preparing to teach an 83-year-old woman about the actions and side effects of Isordil for the treatment of angina. What aspects of teaching would you emphasize given the client's age?
2. A 76-year-old woman has a long standing history of atrial fibrillation. She takes Lanoxin 0.125 mg and Coumadin 2.0 mg daily. She recently read of the advantages of taking aspirin and started taking four tablets daily. How would you intervene in this situation and why?
3. What specific assessment findings indicate that an older adult client being treated for CHF is not responding to Digoxin, Lasix, and vasodilator therapy? How would you differentiate between expected, adverse, and toxic side effects?

REFERENCES

Ambepitiya G, Iyengar E, Roberts M: Review: silent exertional myocardial ischaemia and perception of angina in elderly people, *Age and Ageing* 22(4):302-307, 1993.

Anderson K: A practical guide to nitrate use, *Postgrad Med* 89(1):67-70, 75-76, 78, 1991.

Applegate W: High blood pressure treatment in the elderly, *Clin Geriatr Med* 8(1):103-117, 1992.

Arino S, Bayer A: Potential influence of previous medical pathology on use of thrombolysis in the elderly with suspected acute myocardial infarction, *Gerontology* 39(1):33-37, 1993.

Barbiere C: PTCA: Treating the tough cases . . . percutaneous transluminal coronary angioplasty, *RN* 54(2):38-43, 1991.

Barrett-Connor E, Miller V: Estrogens, lipids and heart disease, *Clin Geriatr Med* 9(1):57-67, 1993.

Barry P: Coronary artery disease in older women, *Geriatrics* 48(1):4-8, 1993.

Basilicato S et al: Effect of concurrent chest pain assessment on retrospective reports by cardiac patients, *J Cardiovasc Nurs* 7(1):56-67, 1992.

Bayer A, Hutter A, Wilson W: Current management of infective endocarditis, *Patient Care* 25(2):15-18, 21-23, 28, 1991.

Beare P, Myers J: *Principles and practice of adult health nursing,* ed 2, St. Louis, 1994, Mosby.

Bisno A, Dismukes W, Durack D et al: Antimicrobial treatment of infective endocarditis due to viridens streptococci, enterococci, and staphylococci. *JAMA* 261, 1471-1477, 1991.

Blair S et al: Physical fitness and all-cause mortality, *J Am Med Assoc* 262(17):2395-2401, 1989.

Blank C, Irwin G: Peripheral vascular disorders: assessment and intervention, *Nurs Clin North Am* 25(4):777-794, 1990.

Bloomfield R, Pearce K, Cross H: Hypertension: choosing therapy when coexisting disease confounds the choice, *Consultant* 33(7):69-72, 77-79, 1993a.

Bloomfield R, Pearce K, Cross H: Practical recommendations for evaluation and nonpharmacologic intervention . . . hypertension, *Consultant* 33(3):47-52, 54-60, 1993b.

Bousquet G: Congestive heart failure: a review of nonpharmacological therapies. *J Cardiovas Nurs*, 4(3):35-46, 1990.

Braun L: Exercise physiology and cardiovascular fitness, *Nurs Clin North Am* 26(1):135-147, 1991.

Bresler M: Acute pericarditis and myocarditis, *Emerg Med Clin North Am* 24(8):34-36, 39-42, 51, 1992.

Bright L, Georgi S: Peripheral vascular disease: is it arterial or venous? *Am J Nurs* 92(9):34-43, 45-47, 1992.

Brown C: Cardiac surgery in the elderly: the critical care phase, *AACN Clin Iss Crit Care Nurs* 3(1):57-63, 1992.

Bushnell F: Self-care teaching for congestive heart failure patients, *J Gerontol Nurs* 18(10):27-32, 1992.

Canada Year Book 1992: *Statistics Canada,* Ottawa, 1991, Job Deyell.

Canadian Nutrient File: Health and Welfare Canada, 1989.

Carethers M, Blanchette P: Pathophysiology of hypertension, *Clin Geriatr Med* 5(4):657-674, 1989.

Carr M: Dangerous brew, *Can Nurse* 90(1):34-36, 1994.

Congestive heart failure, *Med times* 117(4):87-88, 1989.

Cooke D: Shielding your patient from digitalis toxicity, *Nursing 92* 22(7):44-47, 1992.

Costello J: Is your patient too old for cardiac surgery? *Can J Cardiovasc Nurs* 4(2):24-25, 1993.

Criado E, Johnson G: Surgery for chronic vein insufficiency, *Today's OR Nurse* 13(7):12-17, 1991.

Cronin L: Beat the clock: saving the heart with thrombolytic drugs, *Nursing 93* 23(8):34-43, 1993.

Dalen J, Goldberg R: Prophylactoic aspirin and the elderly population, *Clin Geriat Med* 8(1):119-126, 1992.

de Leon A: Improve your skills in physical diagnosis: fine tuning the examination of the heart, *Consultant* 29(4):51-54, 59-61, 1989.

Duryee R: The efficacy of inpatient education after myocardia infarction, *Heart Lung J Crit Care* 21(3):217-227, 1992.

Eaker E et al: Heart disease in women: how different? *Patient Care* 26(3):191-194, 197-202, 204, 1992.

Elnicki M, Kotchen T: Hypertension: Patient evaluation, indications for treatment, *Geriatrics* 48(4):47-50, 59-62, April 1993.

Ernst, N et al: The national cholesterol education program: implications for dietetic practitioners from the adult treatment panel recommendations, *J Am Diet Assoc* 88(11):1401-1408, 1411, 1988.

Esberger K, Hughes S: *Nursing care of the aged,* Norwalk, Conn., 1989, Appleton & Lange.

Expert Panel: Report of the National Cholesterol Education Program expert panel on detection, evaluation, and treatment of high blood cholesterol in adults, *Arch Intern Med* 148(1):36-69, 1988.

Ferrini R, Edelstein S, Barrett-Connor E: The association between health beliefs and health behavior in older adults, *Prev Med* 23:1-5, 1994.

Forman D, Bernal J, Wei J: Management of acute myocardial infarction in the very elderly, *Am J Nurs* 93(3):315-326, 1992.

Forman D, Wei J: MI: Making therapeutic choices when the options are unclear, *Geriatrics* 48(7):32-38, 43-45, 1993.

Foreman M: Adverse psychological responses of the elderly to critical illness, *AACN Clin Iss Crit Care Nurs* 3(1):64-72, 1992.

Frick M et al: Helsinki heart study, *N Engl J Med* 317(20):1237-1245, 1987.

Gawlinski A, Jensen G: The complications of cardiovascular aging, *Am J Nurs* 91(11):26-32, 1991.

Giordano M: Clinical assessment of the geriatric patient, *CINAHL* 16(12):42-45, 1992.

Glantz S, Parmley W: Passive smoking and heart disease, *Circulation* 83(1):1-12, 1991.

Gortner S, Dirks J, Wolfe M: The road to recovery after CABG, *Am J Nurs* 92(8):44-49, 1992.

Gortner S et al: Elders expected and realized benefits from cardiac surgery, *Cardiovasc Nurs* 30(2):9-14, 1994.

Greenberg M, Mueller H: Why the excess mortality in women after PCTA? *Circulation* 87(3):1030-1032, 1993.

Grundy S et al: Cardiovascular and risk factor evaluation of healthy American adults, *Circulation* 75(6):1340A-1362A, 1987.

Gurwitz J et al: Diagnostic testing in acute myocardial infarction: does patient age influence utilization patterns, *Am J Epidemiol* 134:948-957, 1991.

Hagenhoff B et al: Patient education needs as reported by congestive heart failure patients and their nurses, *J Adv Nurs* 19:685-690, 1994.

Handerhan B: Staying alert for endocarditis, *Nursing 91* 21(7):14-15, 1991.

Hartford M et al: Symptoms, thoughts, and environmental factors in suspected acute myocardial infarction, *Heart Lung J Crit Care* 22(1):64-70, 1993.

Health and Welfare Canada: Canadian nutrient file: *Fat finder,* Ottawa, 1989, Author.

Heart and Stroke Foundation of Canada, Health & Welfare Canada: *Statistics Canada: cardiovasculare disease in Canada,* Ottawa, 1991, The Foundation.

Herbert R: The normal aging process reviewed, *Int Nurs Rev* 39(3):93-96, 1992.

Hicks S: Standing guard against silent ischemia and infarction, *Nursing 94* 24(1):34-38, 1994.

Hochrein M, Sohl L: Heart smart: a guide to cardiac tests, *Am J Nurs* 92(12):22-25, 1992.

House M: Thrombolytic therapy for acute myocardial infarction: the elderly population, *AACN Clin Iss Crit Care Nurs* 3(1):106-113, 1992b.

House M, Griego L: Nursing role in management of coronary artery disease. In Lewis S, Collier I, editors: *Medical surgical nursing: assessment and management of clinical problems,* ed 3, St. Louis, 1992, Mosby.

Iniguez A et al: Percutaneous transluminal coronary angioplasty for post infarction angina in elderly patients, *Age and Ageing* 22(1):31-36, 1993.

Jessup M et al: CHF in the elderly. Is it different? *Patient Care* 26(14):40-43, 46, 49, 1992a.

Jessup M et al: Managing CHF in the older patient, *Patient Care* 26(14):65-68, 73-80, 85-88, 1992b.

Johansen H et al: Important risk factors for death in adults: a 10 year follow up of the Nutrition Canada survey cohort, *Can Med Assoc J* 136(8):823-828, 1987.

Johannsen J: Update: guidelines for treating hypertension, AJN 93(3):42-49, 51-53, 1993.

Joint National Committee: *Report of the Joint National Committee on detection, evaluation, and treatment of high blood pressure,* Washington, D.C., 1992, US Department of Health and Human Services.

Kain C, Reilly N, Schultz E: The older adult: a comparative assessment, *Nurs Clin North Am* 25(4):833-848, 1990.

Kaplan M, Pratley R, Hawkins W: Silent myocardial ischemia during rehabilitation for cerebrovascular disease, *Arch Phys Med Rehabil* 72(1):59-61, 1991.

Kasch F et al: Effect of exercise on cardiovascular ageing, *Age and Ageing* 22(1):5-10, 1993.

Kee C: Age-related changes in the renal system: causes, consequences, and nursing implications, *Geriatr Nurs 13(2):*80-83, 1992.

Komsuolglu B et al: Prevalence and risk factors of varicose veins in an elderly population, *Gerontology* 40:25-31, 1994.

Kris-Etherton P et al: The effect of diet on plasma lipids, lipoproteins, and coronary artery disease, *J Am Diet Assoc* 88(11):1373-1400, 1988.

LaCroix A, Omenn G: Older adults and smoking, *Clin Geriatr Med* 8(1):69-87, 1992.

Lakatta E: Cardiovasculatory regulatory mechanisms in advanced age, *Physiol Rev* 73(2):413-467, 1993.

Leibovitch E: Cardiac valve disorders: growing significance in the elderly, *Geriatrics* 44(3):91-100, 1989.

Long K, Long R: The role of aspirin in the prevention of cardiovascular and cerebrovascular disease, *Nurse Pract* 3(2):58-59, 1992.

Luchi R, Taffet G, Teasdale T: Congestive heart failure in the elderly, *J Am Geriatr Soc* 39(8):810-825, 1991.

MacKenzie G: Role patterns and emotional responses of women with IHD 4-6 weeks after discharge from hospital, *Can J Cardiovasc Nurs* 4(2):9-15, 1993.

McCrae M: Holding death at bay: the experience of the spouses of patients undergoing cardiovascular surgery, *Can J Cardiovasc Nurs* 2(2):14-20, 1991.

Meyers A, Branch L, Lederman R: Alcohol, tobacco, and cannabis used by independently living adults with major disabling conditions, *Int J Addict* 23(7):671-685, 1988.

Morrison R: Medication non-compliance, *Can Nurse* 89(4):15-18, 1993.

Murray D et al: Cholesterol reduction through low-intensity interventions: results from the Minnesota heart health program, *Prev Med* 19(2):181-189, 1990.

Nagelhout J: Pharmacologic treatment of heart failure, *Nurs Clin North Am* 26(2):401-415, 1991.

National High Blood Pressure Education Program Working Group: national high blood pressure education program working group report on hypertension in the elderly, *Hypertension* 23(3):275-285, 1994.

Naylor C et al: Placing patients in the queue for coronary surgery: does age and work status alter Canadian specialists decisions? *J Gen Intern Med* 7:492-498, 1992.

Newbern V: Cautionary tales on using beta blockers, *Geriatr Nurs* 12(3):119-122, 1991.

O'Sullivan C: Mitral regurgitation as a complication of MI: pathophysiology and nursing implications, *J Cardiovasc Nurs* 6(4):26-37, 1992.

Panchal J, Kmetz L: The puzzle of educating the client with a cardiovascular disorder: making all the pieces fit, *J Home Health Care Pract* 4(1):1-12, 1991.

Pierce C: Acute post MI pericarditis, *J Cardiovasc Nurs* 6(4):46-56, 1992.

Powers E, Bergin J: Congestive heart failure: how to tailor therapy from a variety of therapeutic options, *Consultant* 33(4):154-156, 158-159, 1993.

Radack K, Deck C, Huster G: The effects of low doses of n-3 fatty acid supplementation on blood pressure in hypertensive subjects: a randomized controlled trial, *Arch Intern Med* 151(6):1173-1180, 1991.

Repique L, Shah S, Marais G: Atrial fibrillation 1992: management strategies in flux, *Chest Cardiopulmon J* 10(4):1095-1103, 1992.

Rodman M. Hypertension: first line drug therapy. *RN* 54(1):32-39, 1991a.

Rubin S et al: High blood cholesterol in elderly men and the excess risk for coronary heart disease, *Ann Intern Med* 113(12):917-920, 1990.

Ruda S, Nursing role in management of musculoskeletal problems. In Lewis S, Collier I, editors: *Medical surgical nursing: assessment and management of clinical problems,* St. Louis, 1992, Mosby.

Sneed N, Hollerbach A: Accuracy of heart rate assessment in atrial fibrillation, *Heart Lung J Crit Care* 21(5):427-433, 1992.

Snowberger P: Third degree heart block, *RN* 56(6):52-54, 1993a.

Snowberger P: Second degree AV block, *RN* 56(2):43-45, 1993b.

Solomon J: Managing a failing heart, *RN* 54(8):46-51, 1991.

Stamler J, Stamler R, Neaton J: Blood pressure, systolic and diastolic, and cardiovascular risks, *Arch Intern Med* 153(5):598-615, 1993.

Stamler J et al: Diabetes, other risk factors, and 12 year cardiovascular mortality for men screened in the multiple risk factor intervention trial, *Diabetes Care* 16(2):434-444, 1993.

Stampfer M et al: Postmenopausal estogen therapy and cardiovascular disease: ten year follow up from the Nurses' Health Study, *N Engl J Med* 325(11):756-762, 1991.

Stanley M: Elderly patients in critical care: an overview, *AACN Clin Iss Crit Care Nurs* 3(1):120-128, 1992.

Stanley R: Drug therapy of heart failure, *J Cardiovasc Nurs* 4(3):17-34, 1990.

Taffet G et al: Survival of elderly men with congestive heart failure, *Age and Ageing* 21(1):49-55, 1992.

Thompson J et al: *Mosby's clinical nursing,* Toronto, 1993, Mosby.

US Department of Commerce, Economics, and Statistics, Bureau of the Census: *Statistical abstract of the United States,* Washington, D.C., 1992, US Government Printing Office.

Vander Horst M, Sykula J, Lingley K: The constipation quandry, *Can Nurse* 90(1):25-30, 1994.

Wright S: Pathophysiology of congestive heart failure, *J Cardiovasc Nurs* 4(3):1-16, 1990.

Yakabowich M: What you should know about administering nitrates, *Nursing* 92 22(9):52-55, 1992.

BIBLIOGRAPHY

Abelmann W, Fowler M, Gilbert E: Heart failure with no apparent cause, *Patient Care* 24(2):24-31, 35-36, 38-39, 1990.

Adams H, Gordon D: Epidemiology of and stroke-preventive strategies for atherothromboembolic brain infarction in the elderly, *Clin Geriatr Med* 7(3):401-416, 1991.

Allen J: Impact of the cholesterol education program for nurses: a pilot project evaluation, *Cardiovasc Nurs* 29(1):1-5, 1993.

American Geriatric Society: Older women's health: task force on older women's health, *J Am Geriatr Soc* 41(6):680-683, 1993.

Ames R: Incorporating cholesterol control into the hypertension treatment plan, *Physician Assist* 15(5):74-80, 99-101, 1991.

Apple S, Thurkauf G: Preparing for and understanding transesophageal echocardiography, *Crit Care Nurse* 12(6):29-34, 1992.

Auld G et al: Gender differences in adults' knowledge about fat and cholesterol, *J Am Diet Assoc* 91(11):1391-1397, 1991.

Bach J, Bolton E, Cook D: the failing heart, *Patient Care* 23(1):132-137, 141, 144, 1989.

Barbiere C, Liberatore K: from emergent transvenous pacemaker to permanent implant and follow-up, *Crit Care Nurse* 13(2):39-44, 1993.

Barr D, Russ E, Eder H: Influence of estrogens on lipoproteins in atherosclerosis, *Trans Assoc Am Physicians* 65:102-113, 1952.

Beckingham G, DuGas B: *Promoting healthy aging: a nursing and community perspective,* Toronto, 1993, Mosby.

Benfante R, Reed D, Frank J: Does cigarette smoking have an independent effect on coronary heart disease incidence in the elderly? *Am J Public Health* 81(7):897-899, 1991.

Berger C et al: Prognosis after first myocardial infarction: comparison of Q-wave and non Q-wave myocardial infarction the Framingham heart study, *J Am Med Assoc* 268(12):1545-1551, 1992.

Blackenhorn D, Hodis H: Treating serum lipid abnormalities in high-priority patients, *Postgrad Med* 89(1):81-82, 87-90, 93-96, 1991.

Blair K: Aging: physiologic aspects and clinical implications, *Nurse Pract* 15(2):14-16, 18, 26-28, 1990.

Borgini L, Almgren C: Peripheral vascular angioscopy, *AORN J* 52(3):543-550, 1990.

Brown K: Boosting the failing heart with inotropic drugs, *Nursing 93* 23(4):34-44, 1993.

Buchanan L et al: Measurement of recovery from myocardial infarction using heart rate variability and psychological outcomes, *Nurs Res* 42(2):74-78, 1993.

Burke L, Rodgers B, Jenkins L: Living with recurrent ventricular dysrhythmias, *AACN Focus Crit Care* 19(1):60-62, 64-66, 68, 1992.

Carter B: Antihypertensive therapy in the elderly, *Prim Care* 16(2):395-410, 1989.

Cavalieri T, Chopra A, Bryman P: When outside the norm is normal: interpretating lab data in the aged, *Geriatrics* 47(5):66-70, 1992.

Christ M, Hohlock F: *Gerontologic nursing,* Springhouse, 1993, Springhouse.

Chronic heart failure: Early diagnosis and treatment saves lives, *Univ Texas Lifetime Healthlet* 4(4):1, 5, 1992.

Cohen L: Managing patients after myocardial infarction, *Hosp Pract* 25(3):49-60, 1990.

Congestive heart failure: Intensive research is leading to earlier more effective care, *Mayo Clin Health Letter* 9(3):1-3, 1991.

Coombs V, Black L, Townsend S: Myocardial reperfusion injury, *Crit Care Clin North Am* 4(2):339-346, 1992.

Costello J: Heart valve surgery: nursing issues, *Can J Cardiovasc Nurs* 3(2):32-33, 1992.

Currie P: Valvular heart disease, *Postgrad Med* 89(6):123-126, 131-134, 136, 1991.

Cushman W et al: Treatment of hypertension in the elderly III: response of isolated systolic hypertension to various doses of hydrochlorothiazide, *Arch Intern Med* 151(10):1954-1960, 1991.

Cvach M, Durran J: Cocaine induced cardiovascular dysfunction: a case study, *J Cardiovasc Nurs* 6(2):31-35, 1992.

Dahlof B et al: Morbidity and mortality in the Swedish trial of older patients with hypertension, *Lancet* 338(8778):1281-1285, 1991.

Davis W, Hart R: Cardiogenic stroke in the elderly, *Clin Geriatr Med* 7(3):429-442, 1991.

Dennison R: Understanding the four determinants of cardiac output . . . heart rate, preload, afterload, and contactility, *Nursing 90* 20(7):34-42, 1990.

DeTurk W: Exercise and the intolerant heart, *Clin Manage* 12 (1):67-73, 1992a.

DeTurk W: The intolerant heart, *Clin Manage* 12(2):32-39, 1992b.

Dice J: Cellular molecular mechanisms of aging, *Physiol Rev* 73(1):149-159, 1993.

DiLucente L, Gorcscan J: Transesophageal echocardiography: application to the postoperative cardiac surgery patient, *Dimens Crit Care Nurs* 10(2):74-80, 1991.

Dodge J et al: Nonparticipation of older adults in heart disease self-management project: factors influencing involvement, *Res Aging* 15(2):220-237, 1993.

Dubin S: The physiologic changes of aging, *Orthop Nurs* 11(3):45-50, 1992.

Duetsche J, Green D: Deep vein thrombosis in the critically ill patient, *Crit Care Nurs Quart* 13(2):29-39, 1990.

Ekelund L et al: Physical fitness as a predictor of cardiovascular mortality in asymptomatic North American men, *N Engl J Med* 319(21):1379-1384, 1988.

Eliopoulos C: *Gerontological nursing,* Philadelphia, 1993, JB Lippincott.

Elizabeth J et al: Arterial oxygen saturation and posture in acute stroke, *Age and Ageing* 22(4):269-272, 1993.

Fallen E et al: Report of the Canadian Cardiovascular Society's consensus conference on the management of the postmyocardial infarction patient, *Can Med Assoc J* (Suppl) 144(8):1015-1025, 1991.

Farnsworth T, Heseltine D: Treatment of elderly hypertensives: some questions remain unanswered, *Age and Ageing* 22(1):1-4, 1993.

Farrar D, Woodward J, Chow E: Pacing-induced dilated cardiomyopathy increases left to right ventricular systolic interaction, *Circulation* 88(2):720-725, 1993.

Feagins C, Daniel D: Management of congestive heart failure in the home setting: a guide to clinical management and patient education, *J Home Health Care Prac* 4(1):31-37, 1991.

Ferri R: *Care planning for the older adult: nursing diagnosis in long term care,* Philadelphia, 1994, WB Saunders.

Fletcher A, Bulpitt C: How far should blood pressure be lowered? *N Engl J Med* 326(4):251-254, 1992.

Fleury J: Long term management of the patient with stable angina, *Nurs Clin North Am* 27(1):205-230, 1992.

Fournet K: Support for significant others of elderly cardiac patients, *AACN Clin Iss Crit Care Nurs* 3(1):73-78, 1992.

French J et al: Association of angiographically detected coronary artery disease with low levels of high-density lipoprotein, cholesterol, and systemic hypertension, *Am J Cardiol* 71(7):505-510, 1993.

Geokas M et al: The aging process, *Ann Intern Med* 113(6):455-466, 1990.

Gilliss C et al: A randomized clinical trial of nursing care for recovery from cardiac surgery, *Heart Lung J Crit Care* 22(2):125-133, 1993.

Gilliss C: The family dimension of cardiovascular care, *Can J Cardiovasc Nurs* 2(1):3-8, 1991.

Grady D et al: Hormone therapy to prevent disease and prolong life in postmenopausal women, *Ann Intern Med* 117(12):1016-1037, 1992.

Graver J: Inotropes: an overview, *Intensive Crit Care Nurs* 8(3):169-179, 1992.

Greatbatch W: Cardiovascular technology: origins of the implantable cardiac pacemaker, *J Cardiovasc Nurs* 5(3):80-85, 1991.

Green D, Miller V: The role of dipyridamole in the therapy of vascular disease, *Geriatrics* 48(1):46, 51-53, 57-58, 1993.

Gullickson C: Client centered drug choice: an alternative approach in managing hypertension, *Nurse Pract* 18(3):30-32, 37, 41, 1993.

Haddad A: The risks and benefits of intravenous amrinone therapy, *Home Healthcare Nurse* 10(5):17-18, 70, 1992.

Hale M: Use of antidepressants and anxiolytics in patients with heart disease, *Physician Assist* 15(4):41, 43-45, 47-50, 1991.

Hancock E: Acute myocardial infarction or pericarditis, *Hosp Pract* 27(11):25-26, 1992.

Hancock E: Myelodysplasia, pericarditis, and an irregular tachycardia, *Hosp Pract* 28(1):133-134, 1993.

Hartzler G et al: What to expect from PTCA today, *Patient Care* 26(3):36-40, 45, 48-50, 1992.

Healthy Aging, *Phillipp J Nurs* 62(2):2-9, 1992.

Heart infection: Prevention is the best treatment, *Mayo Clin Health Let* 9(11):1-12, 1991.

Hecht G et al: Coexistence of sudden cardiac death and end-stage heart failure in familial hypertrophic cardiomyopathy, *J Am Coll Cardiol* 22(2):489-497, 1993.

Herzog J: Deep vein thrombosis in the rehabilitation client: diagnostic tools, prevention and treatment modalities, *Rehabil Nurs* 18(1):8-11, 1993.

Hiatt W, Regensteiner J: Nonsurgical management of peripheral arterial disease, *Hosp Pract* 28(2):59-63, 67-68, 70, 76-77, 81-82, 1993.

Hockenberry B: Multiple drug therapy in the treatment of essential hypertension, *Nurs Clin North Am* 26(2):417-436, 1991.

Holzum D: Interventions to support the failing right ventricle, *J Cardiovasc Nurs* 6(1):70-79, 1991.

House M: Cardiovascular effects of cocaine, *J Cardiovasc Nurs* 6(2):1-11, 1992a.

Hussar D: New drugs, *Nursing 93* 23(5):57-64, 1993.

Isaksson H, Konarski K, Theorell T: The psychological and social condition of hypertensives resistant to pharmacologic treatment, *Soc Sci Med* 35(7):869-875, 1992.

Itskovitz H: Alpha 1 blockers: safe, effective treatment for hypertension, *Postgrad Med* 89(8):89-92, 95-98, 103-106, 1991.

Jessup M et al: Managing CHF in the older patient, *Patient Care* 24(5):55-58, 61-62, 65, 1990.

Johannsen J: Update: guidelines for treating hypertension, *Am J Nurs* 93(3):42-49, 51-53, 1993.

Johns C: Nursing role in management dysrhythmias. In Lewis S, Collier I, editors: *Medical surgical nursing: assessment and management of clinical problems,* St. Louis, 1992, Mosby.

Johnston D et al: Effect of stress management on blood pressure in mild primary hypertension, *BMJ* 306(6883):963-966, 1993.

Kahn J: Progressive congestive heart failure: ways to approach office management, *Postgrad Med* 89(6):102-107, 205-207, 1991.

Kar S, Norlander R: Coronary veins: an alternate route to ischemic heart disease, *Heart Lung J Crit Care* 21(2):148-157, 1992.

Kater K, Kuhrik N, Kuhrik M: Corralling atrial fibrillation with maze surgery, *Am J Nurs* 92(7):34-38, 1992.

Kawachi I et al: Smoking cessation and decreased risk of stroke in women, *JAMA* 269(2):232-236, 1993.

Kellick K: Diuretics, *AACN Clin Iss Crit Care Nurs* 3(2):472-482, 1992.

Kelso L: Dysrythmias associate with digoxin toxicity, *AACN Clin Iss Crit Care Nurs* 3(1):220-225, 1992.

Kennedy G: Acute congestive heart failure: pharmacological intervention, *Crit Care Nurs Clin North Am* 4(2):365-375, 1992.

Kennedy J: Health education and heart disease, *Nurs Stand* 7(4):50-51, 1992.

Keresztes P, Dan A: Estrogen and cardiovascular disease, *Cardiovasc Nurs* 28(1):1-6, 1992.

Kern, L: The elderly heart surgery patient, *Crit Care Nurs Clin North Am* 3(4):749-756, 1991.

Khanna P, Geller J: Clinical implications in the elderly, *Top Emerg Med* 14(3):1-9, 1992.

Khosla S, Somberg J: Mild heart failure: why the switch to ACE inhibitors, *Geriatrics* 48(11):47-54, 1992.

Khosla S, Somberg J: Mild heart failure: why the switch to ACE inhibitors? *Geriatrics* 48(11):47-48, 51-54, 1993.

Kirk-Gardner R, Crossman J, Eyjolfsson K: Modifiable cardiac risk factors of obesity, inactivity, and stress: a community survey, *Can J Cardiovasc Nurs* 3(2):25-29, 1992.

Kirk-Gardner R, Steven D: *Hearts for life: a community program on heart disease,* report prepared for the Ontario Ministry of Health, Thunder Bay, Ontario, 1994.

Kirk-Gardner R, Crossman J: Cardiac risk factors of smoking, hypertension, obesity, and family history: a review of the literature, *Can J Cardiovasc Nurs* 2(1):9-14, 1991.

Kirk-Gardner R, Steven D: *An analysis of the Ontario Health Survey from a cardiovascular perspective,* Toronto, 1992, Ontario Ministry of Health.

Kuhn M: Angiotensin-converting enzyme inhibitors, *AACN Clin Iss Crit Care Nurs* 3(2):461-471, 1992.

Kupper N, Duke E: Nursing role in management of inflammatory and valvular heart disease. In Lewis S, Collier I, editors: *Medical surgical nursing: assessment and management of clinical problems,* ed 3, St. Louis, 1992, Mosby.

Lakatta E: The aging heart. In Geokas, M, moderator: The aging process, *Ann Intern Med* 113:455-466, 1990.

Lavie C et al: Exercise and the heart: good, benign, or evil? *Postgrad Med* 91(2);130-134, 143-150, 1992.

Lefkowitz D: Asymptomatic carotid artery disease in the elderly: diagnosis and management strategies, *Clin Geriatr Med* 7(3):417-428, 1991.

Lehav M et al: Intermittent administration of furosemide vs. continuous infusion preceded by a loading dose for congestive heart failure, *Chest* 102(3):725-731, 1992.

Letterer R et al: Learning to live with congestive heart failure, *Nursing 92* 22(5):34-41, 1992.

Lueckenotte A: *A pocket guide to geriatric assessment,* ed 2, St. Louis, 1994, Mosby.

Ligeti R: Prevention of deep vein thrombosis, *J Am Acad Physician's Assist* 3(5):319-328, 1990.

Lombess P: Taking the mystery out of rhythm interpretation: atrial electrograms, *Heart Lung J Crit Care* 21(5):415-426, 1992.

Lynam M: Taking culture into account: a challenging prospect for cardiovascular nursing, *Can J Cardiovasc Nurs* 2(3):10-16, 1991.

MacLennan W et al: Hydroxyethylrutosides in elderly patients with chronic venous insufficiency, *Gerontology* 40:45-52, 1994.

Marcus F: Digitalis: how well are you using it, *Patient Care* 25(17):21-28, 31, 34, 1991.

McKenna M: Management of the patient undergoing myocardial revascularization: percutaneous transluminal coronary angioplasty, *Nurs Clin North Am* 27(1):231-242, 1992.

Melillo K: Interpretation of abnormal laboratory values in older adults: part 1, *J Gerontol Nurs* 19(1):39-45, 1993a.

Melillo K: Interpretation of abnormal laboratory values in older adults: part 2, *J Gerontol Nurs* 19(2):35-40, 1993b.

Merz R: Healthy aging: Why we get old, *Harvard Health Let* 10(9):9-12, 1992.

Miers L, Arnold R: The cardiovascular response to exercise in the patient with congestive heart failure, *J Cardiovasc Nurs* 4(3):47-58, 1990.

Milander M, Kuhn M: Lipid-lowering drugs, *AACN Clin Iss Crit Care Nurs* 3(2):494-506, 1992.

Miller D, Kaiser F: Assessment of the older woman, *Clin Geriatr Med* 9(1):1-31, 1993.

Ministry of Supply Services: *Statistics Canada: mortality summary list of causes,* (Cat No 84-206) Ottawa, 1988, The Ministry.

Moy J, Realin J: Guidelines for counseling postmenopausal women about preventive hormone therapy: a policy review, *J Am Board Fam Pract* 6(2):153-162, 1993.

MRC Working Party: Medical research council trial of treatment of hypertension in older adults: principal results, *BMJ* 304:405-412, 1992.

Naylor C et al: Assigning priority to patients requiring coronary revascularization: consensus principles from a panel of cardiologist and cardiac surgeons, *Can J Cardiol* 7(5):207-213, 1991.

Nyman I, Larsson N, Wallantin L: Prevention of serious cardiac events by low-dose aspirin in patients with silent myocardial ischaemia: the research group on instability in coronary artery disease in southeast Sweden, *Lancet* 340(8818):497-501, 1992.

Ontario Ministry of Health: *Ontario health survey 1990,* Toronto, 1992, The Ministry.

Owen P et al: Reading, readability and patient education materials, *Cardiovasc Nurs* 29(2);9-13, 1993.

Pagley P et al: Gender differences in the treatment of patients with acute myocardial infarction: a multihospital, community based perspective, *Arch Intern Med* 153(5):625-629, 1993.

Pearson M et al: Differences in quality of care for hospitalized elderly men and women, *JAMA* 268(14):1883-1889, 1992.

Prissant M, Carr A, Hawkins D: Treating hypertensive emergencies, *Postgrad Med* 93(2):92-96, 101-104, 108-110, 1993.

Rashid A et al: An audit of cardiac pacing in the elderly: effect of myocardial infarction on outcome, *J Am Geriatr Soc* 41(5):488-90, 1993.

Rideout E: Chronic heart failure and quality of life: the impact of nursing, *Can J Cardiovasc Nurs* 3(1):4-7, 1992.

Rieger T: The heart: guilty until proven innocent, *Prof Med Assist* 26(1):8-10, 1993.

Rodman M: Hypertension: first line drug therapy, *RN* 54(1);32-39, 1991a.

Rodman M: Hypertension: step care management, *RN* 54(2):24-31, 1991b.

Ronayne R: Uncertainty in peripheral valvular disease, *Can J Cardiovasc Nurs* 1(2):26-30, 1989.

Rose M: Evaluation of a peer-education program on heart disease prevention with older adults, *Public Health Nurs* 9(4):242-247, 1992.

Rouleau J et al: A comparison of management patterns after acute myocardial infarction in Canada and the United States, *N Engl J Med* 328(11):779-784, 1993.

Rubin S et al: High blood cholesterol in elderly men and the excess risk for coronary heart disease, *Ann Intern Med* 113(12):917-920, 1990.

Schaefer K, Potlycki M: Fatigue associated with congestive heart failure: use of Levine's conservation model, *J Adv Nurs* 18(2):260-268, 1993.

Shabetai R: Diseases of the pericardium. In Hurst J, editor: *The heart,* vol 2, ed 7, New York, 1990, McGraw-Hill.

Sharpe P, Clark N, Janz N: Differences in the impact and management of heart disease between older women and men, *Women's Health* 17(2):25-43, 1991.

Shopland D, Brown C: Toward the 1990 objectives for smoking: measuring the progress with 1985 NHIS data, *Public Health Rep* 102(1):68-73, 1987.

Sifri-Steele C, Meyer L: Implementing changes in standards of care for patients with unstable angina: Wellens' syndrome, *Crit Care Nurse* 13(2):23-28, 1993.

Solomon J: Hypertension: new drug therapies, *RN* 57(1):26-32, 1994.

Solomon J: Hypertension: new guidelines, new roles, *RN* 56(12):54-59, 1993.

Speroff L: Menopause and hormone replacement therapy, *Clin Geriatr Med* 9(1):33-55, 1993.

Stamler J, Pick R, Katz L: Prevention of coronary atherosclerosis by estrogen-androgen administration in the cholesterol-fed chick, *Circ Res* 1:94-98, 1953.

Steptoe A, Johnston D: Clinical applications of cardiovascular assessment, *Psychol Assess* 3(3):337-349, 1991.

Stier F: Antidysrhythmic agents, *AACN Clin Iss Crit Care Nurs* 3(2):483-493, 1992.

Stilwell R: Assessing elderly people, *Nurs Stand* 6(35):9-14, 16, 1992.

Stillwell S, Randall E: *Pocket guide to cardiovascular care,* St. Louis, 1990, Mosby.

Suter E et al: Effects of self-monitored jogging on physical fitness, blood pressure and serum lipids: A controlled study in sedentary middle aged-men, *Int J Sports Med* 11:425-432, 1990.

Taigman M, Canan S: Cardiology practicum: precursors to complete heart block, *J Emerg Med Serv* 16(9):87-89, 1991.

Teplitz L: Classification of cardiac pacemakers: the pacemaker code, *J Cardiovasc Nurs* 5(3):1-8, 1991.

Thibonnier M: Ambulatory blood pressure monitoring, *Postgrad Med* 91(1):263-264, 267-270, 272, 1992.

Vaitkus P et al: Stroke complicating acute myocardial infarction: a meta-analysis of risk modification by anticoagulation and thrombolytic therapy, *Arch Intern Med* 152(10):2020-2024, 1992.

Van Buskirk M, Gradman A: Monitoring blood pressure in ambulatory patients, *Am J Nurs* 93(6):44-47, 1993.

Vander Horst M, Sykula J, Lingley K: The constipation quandry, *Can Nurse* 90(1):25-30, 1994.

Verderher A, Fitzsimmons L, Shively M: Research connection: cocaine abuse, *J Cardiovasc Nurs* 6(2):43-45, 1992.

Viscoli C, Horwitz R, Singer B: Beta-blockers after myocardial infarction: influence of first year clinical course on long term effectiveness, *Ann Intern Med* 118(2):99-105, 1993.

Weishrod R et al: Current status of health promotion activities in four midwest cities, *Pub Health Rep* 106(3):310-317, 1991.

Woo M: Clinical management of the patient with an acute myocardial infarction, *Nurs Clin North Am* 27(1):189-203, 1992.

Wynne J, Braunwald E: The cardiomyopathies and myocarditis. In Braunwald E, editor: *Heart disease: a textbook of cardiovascular medicine,* ed 3, Philadelphia, 1988, WB Saunders.

Yancy C: Severe congestive heart failure: how successful are drug and transplant therapies? *Postgrad Med* 89(6):111-115, 118, 205-207, 1991.

Young H: Peripheral vascular disease: venous disorders of the lower limb, *Br J Occup Ther* 52(4):130-134, 1989.

Younis L, Chaitman R: The prognostic value of exercise testing, *Cardiol Clin* 11(2):229-240, 1993.

CHAPTER 22

Respiratory Function

LEARNING OBJECTIVES

On completion of this chapter, the reader will be able to:

1. State the normal anatomy of the respiratory system.
2. Identify changes in the anatomy of the respiratory system that are related to the normal aging process.
3. Describe the alterations in ventilation as a result of normal aging.
4. Conduct a respiratory assessment for the older client.
5. List the most commonly used nursing diagnoses for the older client with respiratory diseases.
6. Develop nursing interventions for the older client with various respiratory alterations.
7. Demonstrate breathing techniques used in the older client with chronic obstructive pulmonary disease (COPD).
8. Demonstrate coughing techniques.

The respiratory system is responsible for gas exchange between the environment and the lung parenchyma and respiration at the cellular level between the oxygen molecule and the cell. The process of respiration is achieved through the coordination of the neural chemical control and the muscles of respiration.

The respiratory system is divided into two portions: the upper airway, consisting of the nose, mouth, pharynx and larynx; and the lower airway, consisting of the trachea, the lungs, and the lung parenchyma. Both extrapulmonary and intrapulmonary factors affect the respiratory system. The extrapulmonary factors are the thoracic cage and muscles of the thorax and upper torso. The intrapulmonary factor is the lung parenchyma.

LUNG STRUCTURE

Upper Airway

Air enters the respiratory system through the nose and mouth. The nasal cavity is lined with a mucous membrane that contains serous glands and goblet cells, responsible for secreting a thin layer of watery mucous. The entire surface of the nasal mucous membrane is lined with tiny hairlike projections, called **cilia**, that fil-

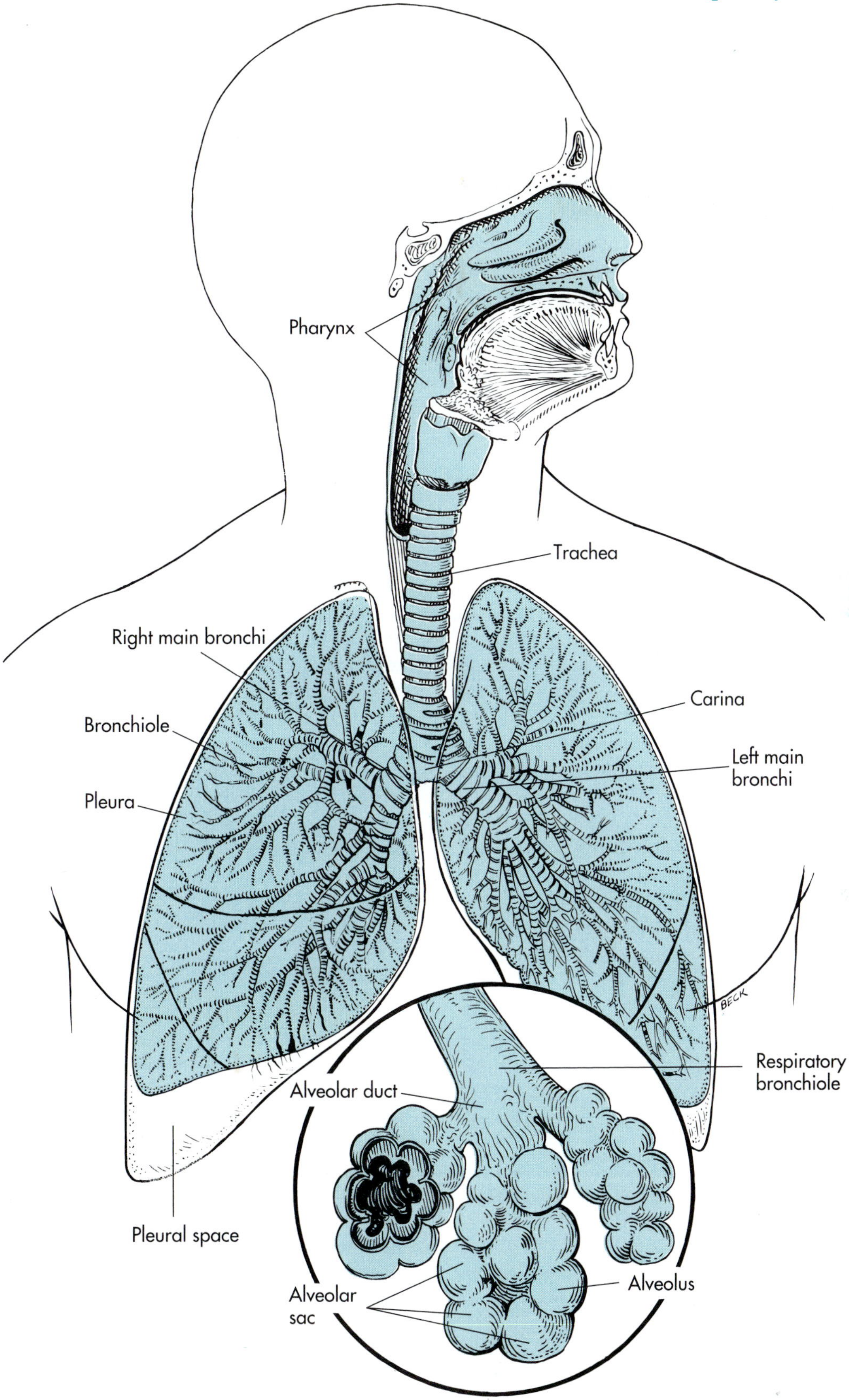

Fig. 22-1 Structures of the pulmonary system. The circle denotes the acinus, in which oxygen and carbon dioxide are exchanged. (From Thibodeau G: *Anthony's textbook of anatomy and physiology,* ed 13, St. Louis, 1990, Mosby.)

ter inhaled particles trapping them in the watery mucous. The primary function of the nose and mouth is to warm, filter, and humidify the inspired air.

Lower Airway

The lower airway consists of the trachea, right and left main stem bronchus, bronchioles, and **alveoli** (Fig. 22-1). The tracheobronchial tree is a conducting system to get air to the gas-exchanging units, the alveoli. The left main stem bronchus divides into two lobar branches that further subdivide into four segments each. The right main stem bronchus divides into three lobar branches, one for each lobe of the right lung; the right upper, middle, and lower lobe. The bronchi subdivide 20 or more times into subsegmental bronchi, terminal bronchi, **bronchioles**, terminal bronchioles, and respiratory bronchioles. The terminal bronchioles end in the alveolar duct, alveolar sacs, and the alveoli, which are the gas-exchanging unit of the lung. Each subdivision of the tracheal bronchial tree is referred to as a generation (Fig. 22-2).

The bronchi are surrounded by muscle and cartilage. At the level of the bronchioles, no cartilage is found, and the airway is supported by the elastic recoil property of the smooth muscle surrounding the airway. Destruction of peripheral airways results in collapse of distal airways and alveoli (Dettenmeier, 1992).

The bronchi are lined with a pseudostratified ciliated columnar epithelium. Goblet cells within the epithelium are responsible for producing a mucous blanket that coats the airways. The cilia beat in a wave-like fashion to move the mucous blanket upward to the trachea and mouth. The effectiveness of the cilia is diminished by infection and nicotine. Repeated infections result in loss of the cilia and replacement with nonciliated epithelium. Nicotine paralyzes ciliary action, allowing for buildup of mucus and possible infection.

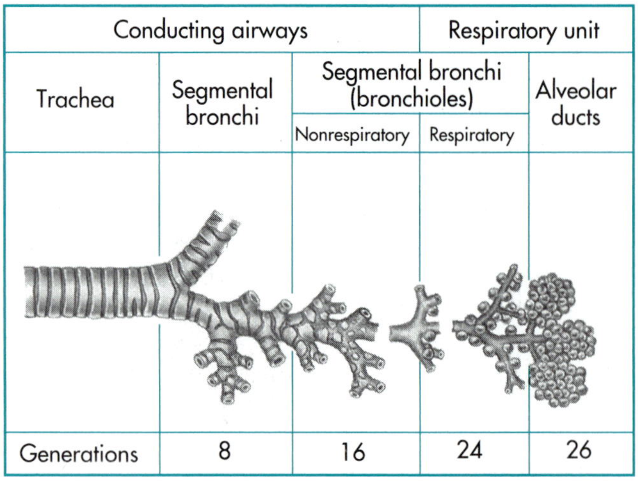

Fig. 22-2 Structure of the lower airway.

The older adult has a decrease in the number and effectiveness of cilia in the tracheobronchial tree. If there is a history of repeated respiratory infections or smoking, the effectiveness of the ciliary action as well as the number of cilia present will be markedly decreased, resulting in an ineffective mucociliary escalator. The older adult experiences an increased difficulty in clearing secretions and is at risk for increased respiratory tract infections.

Extrapulmonary Structures

Thoracic Cage

The thoracic cage is the structural component of the respiratory system that functions to protect the lungs, heart, and great vessels. It consists of 12 ribs anteriorly and 12 thoracic vertebrae posteriorly. In the normal adult, the thorax has a conical appearance because of the C-shaped structure of the ribs. The first seven ribs are attached directly to the sternum by the costal cartilage. The lower five ribs are not directly attached, and ribs 11 and 12 are only attached posteriorly at the vertebrae.

Normal aging results in changes to the ribs and vertebrae. Osteoporosis and calcification of the costal cartilages lead to increased rigidity and stiffness of the thoracic cage. The ribs are less mobile, and the compliance of the chest wall decreases. If the older adult has kyphosis or scoliosis, degeneration of the intervertebral disks is seen, resulting in a shorter thorax with an increased anteroposterior diameter. Advanced cases may result in marked limitation of thoracic movement because the rib cage rests on the pelvic bones (Burke, Walsh, 1992). In addition, a reduction in maximal inspiratory and expiratory force occurs as a result of a decrease in the breathing efficiency.

Airway Structure

Calcification of cartilage structures in the airways themselves results in enlarging of the tracheal and large bronchi diameters. These structures are normally dead space. Dead space ventilation is the amount of air in each breath that does not participate in gas exchange. The trachea, right and left mainstem bronchi, and tracheobronchial tree subdivisions down to the terminal bronchioles, cannot exchange oxygen and carbon dioxide; they are conducting channels to get the air to the alveoli where gas exchange does take place. In the older client, the functional dead space ventilation is increased from one third to as much as one half of each breath. The net result is a decrease in the volume of air that can participate in gas exchange.

Muscular Structure

The primary muscles of respiration include the **diaphragm** and the interal and external intracostal muscles. The diaphragm lies at the base of the thorax, and is the major muscle of respiration. As the dome-shaped diaphragm contracts, it pulls the central tendon downward, increasing the volume of the thoracic cage and initiating inspiration. Simultaneously, the external intercostal and scalene muscles contract, increasing the anteroposterior and lateral chest size. Expiration, a passive process, occurs when the respiratory muscles relax and allow the air to move out of the lung. The normal elastic recoil of the lung and chest wall allow the chest to return to its normal resting position.

The respiratory muscles weaken with aging, as do all other muscles in the body. Inspiratory and expiratory efforts are decreased by the less forceful contractions. The older adult's breathing is less efficient because of the increased stiffness of the chest wall and the decreased muscle strength. Because of this, the older adult uses the accessory muscles of respiration, such as the abdominal, sternocleidomastoid, and trapezius muscles, for respiration. These muscles are less efficient and result in an increased effort to breathe. The diaphragm does not lose mass with aging; however, it may flatten and become less efficient with advancing COPD as the chest takes on the barrel-shaped configuration.

Intrapulmonary Structures

Lung Parenchyma

The lung parenchyma is composed of the terminal bronchioles, alveolar ducts, and the approximately 300 million alveoli responsible for the exchange of carbon dioxide (CO_2) and oxygen (O_2). Surrounding each alveoli is a capillary network. Gas exchange occurs at the alveolar capillary membrane (Fig. 22-3).

In the healthy aging adult, the number of alveoli changes little; however, the structure is altered. As the alveoli age, the number of functional alveoli decreases. The changes are similar to those seen in emphysema. The supporting structures of the alveoli deteriorate, leading to a progressive loss of the intraalveolar septum. In addition, the walls of the alveoli become thinner, contributing to a loss of alveolar septal tissue and fewer capillaries available for gas exchange. The alveoli become larger with dilatation of the proximal bronchioles. The net result is a decrease in the surface area available for gas exchange. It is reduced to 65 to 70 m^2 by the age of 70, compared with the normal of 80 m^2 at the age of 20.

A progressive loss of the elastic recoil of the lung parenchyma and conducting airways occurs with age. The elastic recoil of the lung is reduced as are the opposing forces of the chest wall. It is believed that the lung becomes less elastic as a result of stiffening of the collagen substances surrounding the alveoli and alveolar ducts. The collagen stiffens and forms cross-linkages that interfere with the lungs' elastic properties. This results in an increase in the lung tissue compliance. The increased compliance of the lung partially compensates

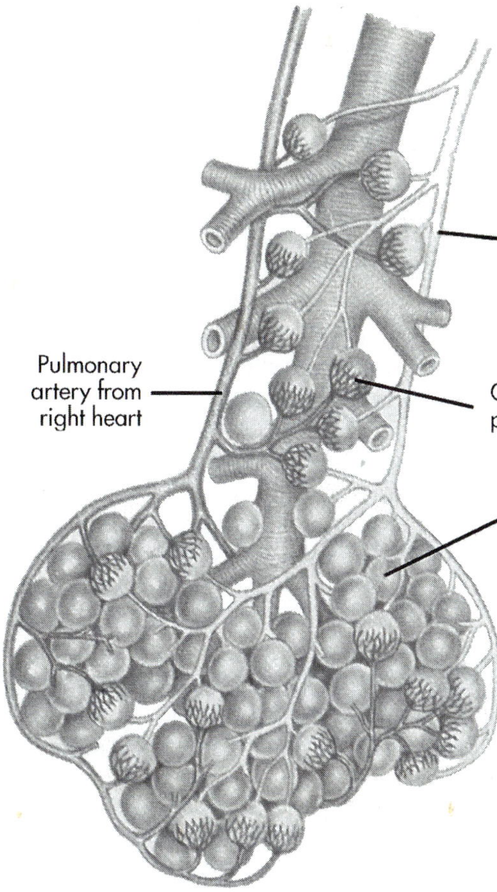

Fig. 22-3 Terminal respiratory unit. (From Thompson JM et al: *Mosby's manual of clinical nursing,* ed 3, St Louis, 1993, Mosby.)

for the decrease in the chest wall compliance, thereby reducing the work required of the weakened respiratory muscles to move the stiffened chest wall. Overall, the compliance of the respiratory system decreases with advanced age.

Pulmonary Vessels and Circulation

The lung receives blood from the pulmonary and bronchial circulation. The pulmonary circulation consists of the blood returned to the right side of the heart, where it is sent to the lung through the pulmonary artery. The poorly oxygenated blood travels through a series of progressively smaller arteries and arterioles until the blood reaches the pulmonary capillary, where gas exchange takes place. Blood rich in O_2 then leaves the lung, returning to the left side of the heart through the pulmonary veins, where it is propelled forward through the body. The bronchial circulation originates from the aorta or subclavian artery and supplies blood to the perihilar region. Blood returns from the bronchial circulation through the azygos vein to the left atrium.

In the normal adult, the pulmonary vascular circulation is a relatively low pressure system with high distensibility and low resistance. As the adult ages, the vessels become less distensible and more fibrous. The pulmonary artery increases in diameter as does the thickness of the vessel wall. This results in an increased pulmonary vascular resistance and increased pulmonary artery pressure.

The alveolar-capillary structure is affected by aging. The alveolar capillary membrane thickens, affecting the surface area available for gas exchange. The number of functional capillaries declines, resulting in decreased alveolar vascularity. Combined with a diminished cardiac output, there is a decrease in the pulmonary capillary blood volume.

Production of surfactant in the lung does not appear to decrease with the aging process. However, production of Type II alveolar cells, the cells responsible for surfactant production, has been shown to decrease with aging.

LUNG FUNCTION

Control of Ventilation

Breathing is coordinated by the medullary respiratory center and the apneustic and pneumotaxic centers in the brain stem. The medullary center is responsible for the rhythm of inspiration and expiration. The apneustic and pneumotaxic centers are located in the pons directly anterior to the medulla. The apneustic center stimulates inspiration and is inhibited by the vagus nerve and the pneumotaxic center or the expiratory center in the medulla. The pneumotaxic center is thought to inhibit inspiration by inhibiting the apneustic center and possibly the medullary center, thereby regulating respiratory rate (Kersten, 1989).

Mechanical receptors in the lungs, airways and the chest wall trigger reflexes responsible for the control of the rate and depth of respiration. In the bronchial smooth muscle, pulmonary stretch receptors are stimulated by lung distensibility, causing inhibition of inspiration through the medullary center. This is known as the Hering-Breuer reflex. The depth of respiration is decreased by prolonging the expiratory component of the medullary center. In adults, this reflex is largely inactive unless tidal volume exceeds 1 l, as in exercise. Chest wall receptors, located in the chest wall of the thorax, are believed to be responsible for the feeling of dyspnea. The breathing pattern is modified through receptor input about chest wall position. This leads to changes in intercostal muscle activity and alteration in the breathing pattern.

The breathing patterns of the older adult are more dependent on intraabdominal pressure changes. Positioning and increased abdominal pressure can greatly affect their breathing patterns. Respiratory rates are generally higher in the older adult with normal 16 to 25 breaths per minute (Pierson, 1992). The increase in the respiratory rate does not alter the arterial carbon dioxide (CO_2) because of a decrease in the tidal volume (V_T).

The chemical control of breathing is regulated through the central and peripheral chemoreceptors. These receptors respond to changes in the surrounding body fluid. The central chemoreceptors are located near the ventral surface of the medulla near the exit of the ninth and tenth cranial nerves (Kersten, 1989). The receptors respond to alterations in the hydrogen ion concentration of the cerebrospinal fluid (CSF). The main stimulus is the amount of CO_2 in the CSF. This regulator of breathing allows for the minute to minute control of the breathing pattern.

The peripheral chemoreceptors are the carotid and aortic bodies located at the bifurcation of the common carotid artery and above and below the arch of the aorta respectively. These receptors respond to changes in the arterial blood. A decrease in the partial pressure of arterial oxygen (PaO_2) and pH, and an increase in the partial pressure of arterial carbon dioxide ($PaCO_2$) result in stimulation of breathing. The greater the drop in PaO_2 the greater the increase in the respiratory rate (Kersten, 1989). The peripheral chemoreceptors account for only 20% of the ventilatory response with the majority of the ventilatory response attributed to the central chemoreceptor activity. Chemical changes sensed by peripheral chemoreceptors act synergistically (Kersten, 1989).

The response of the older adult to **hypoxemia** or **hypercapnia** appears to be blunted. The normal clinical response to hypoxemia is an increase in the rate and depth of respiration, as well as an increase in the heart rate and blood pressure. Older clients show less increase in heart rate and a lower response to increasing CO_2. Ventilatory responses to hypoxia and hypercapnia may be diminished by as much as 50% in comparison with adults in their 20s (Pierson, 1992). The blunted response in the older client is the result of reduced sympathetic nervous system response. Therefore the circulatory response to hypoxemia may be inadequate. The most sensitive clinical indicator for hypoxia and hypercapnia in the older client is mental status changes and complaints of occipital headache or forgetfulness that are not otherwise explained. The response to hypoxemia and treatment are both blunted. A minor increase in O_2 demand can result more quickly in hypoxic symptoms in the older adult.

Lung Defense Mechanisms

Lungs have a number of defense mechanisms that help protect them from harm. The upper airway defense mechanisms include the filtering, warming, and humidification of inspired air and the sneeze. The nasal hairs filter inhaled particles larger than 10 microns. The watery mucus that lines the nasal cavity, pharynx, and larynx helps trap particles that may get past the nasal hairs before they can reach the lungs.

The lower airways are protected by the mucociliary escalator, the cough reflex, the **alveolar macrophage**, and the lymphatics. The mucociliary escalator traps particles in the mucous blanket, whereas the cilia beat in a wave-like motion, moving the debris toward the carina, where it is coughed out. Since the older client has a reduction in the number of functional cilia and reduced ciliary action, the mucociliary escalator is less effective in removing particles from the lower airways. The cough mechanism in the older client is also less efficient in its volume, force, and flow rate, most likely because of the weakened respiratory muscles.

The alveolar macrophage is responsible for keeping the alveoli free of particles that reach the acinus. The alveolar macrophage protects the alveoli by phagocytosis of bacteria and foreign materials that reach the acinus. Alveolar macrophage activity is defective in older clients, especially smokers.

Lymph nodes are found throughout the lung at the level of the respiratory and terminal bronchioles. The lymphatic system drains particles or microorganisms that have reached the alveoli. The older client has a decrease in IgA, an immunoglobulin found in the nasal respiratory mucosal surfaces that neutralizes viruses.

AGE-RELATED CHANGES IN STRUCTURE AND FUNCTION

See Table 22-1 for a summary of changes in the aging respiratory system.

TABLE 22-1

Age-Related Changes in the Respiratory System

Respiratory function	Pathophysiologic change	Clinical presentation
Mechanics of breathing	Increased chest wall compliance Loss of elastic recoil Decreased respiratory muscle mass and strength	Decreased vital capacity Increased reserve volume Decreased expiratory flow rates
Oxygenation	Increased ventilation/perfusion mismatch Decreased cardiac output Decreased mixed venous O_2 Increased physiologic dead space Decreased alveolar surface area available for gas exchange Reduced CO_2 diffusion capacity	Decreased PaO_2 Increased alveolar-arterial O_2 gradient
Control of ventilation	Decreased responsiveness of central and peripheral chemoreceptors to hypoxemia and hypercapnia	Decreased tidal volume Increased respiratory rate Increased minute ventilation
Lung defense mechanisms	Decreased number of cilia Decreased effectiveness of the mucociliary clearance Decreased cough reflex Decreased humoral and cellular immunity Decreased IgA production	Decreased ability to clear secretions Increased susceptibility to infection Increased risk of aspiration
Sleep and breathing	Decreased ventilatory drive Decreased upper airway muscle tone Decreased arousal	Increased frequency of apnea, hypopnea, and arterial oxygen desaturation during sleep Increased risk of aspiration Snoring Obstructive sleep apnea
Exercise capacity	Muscle deconditioning Decreased muscle mass Decreased efficiency of respiratory muscles Decreased reserves	Decreased maximum oxygen consumption Breathlessness at low exercise levels
Breathing pattern	Decreased responsiveness to hypoxemia and hypercapnia Change in respiratory mechanics	Increased respiratory rate Decreased tidal volume Increased minute ventilation

Modified from Pierson DJ, Kacmarek RM, editors: *Foundations of respiratory care,* New York, 1992, Churchill Livingstone.

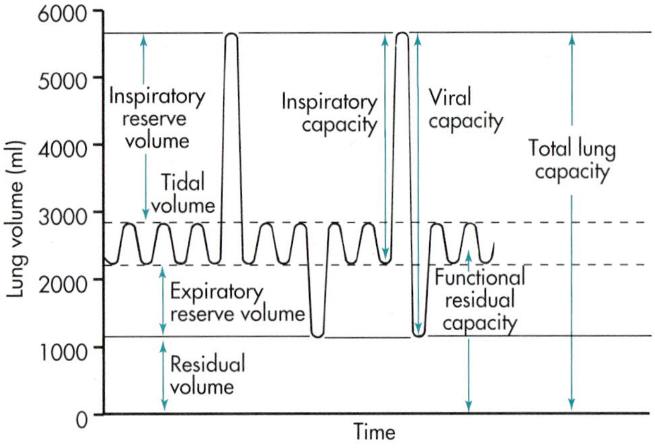

Fig. 22-4 Pulmonary function volumes. (From Perry A, Potter P: *Shock,* St Louis, 1983, Mosby.)

Ventilation

Pulmonary Functions

Pulmonary function testing (PFT) is used to determine the functionality of the respiratory system, to measure the lung volumes, and to assess health and illness (Fig. 22-4). Obstructive and restrictive diseases can be differentiated by PFTs. The information is used to assess level of functioning and determine disability. The ability to determine accurate pulmonary function test results relies on the complete cooperation of the client. The older client may not be able to perform an accurate test due to musculoskeletal changes and may require an extended period of time to complete the testing (see Cultural Awareness box at right).

The changes in pulmonary function tests are related to the changes in elastic recoil and musculoskeletal changes of the chest wall in the older client. Table 22-2 lists the lung volumes measured, the normal findings, and alterations related to aging. The total lung capacity is affected little; however, the components of the total lung capacity (TLC) are changed dramatically.

Decreased **compliance** of the thorax accounts for the increase in the residual volume and expiratory reserve volume. Vital capacity, the volume of air that can be exhaled after a maximum inhalation, decreases as a result of the decreased mobility of the chest wall, and altered inspiratory and expiratory capabilities.

The tidal volume, the amount of air inhaled or exhaled with each breath, is decreased in the older adult. The rate of reduction of vital capacity is greater in older male adults than in older female adults. The inspiratory capacity is affected by the decreased ability to take a deep breath with age. The reduction in muscle strength and more shallow breathing patterns contribute to the increase in the residual volume.

CULTURAL AWARENESS

Biocultural Variations in Chest Size and Pulmonary Function

Pulmonary function, as determined by vital capacity and forced expiratory volume, has significant cultural variation, presumably because of differences in the size of the thoracic cavity. Whites have the largest chest volumes, followed by African Americans, then Asian Americans and Native Americans. Although African Americans and whites are similar in height, chest volume is smaller in African Americans. When the shorter overall height of Asian Americans is taken into consideration, their chest volume is still significantly lower than either African Americans or whites. These biocultural variations affect the following pulmonary function tests: forced expiratory volume (FEV_1), forced vital capacity (FVC), and the derived function FEV_1/FVC.

The following pulmonary function results are based on mean values for white, African-American, Asian-American, and Native-American male subjects ages 38 to 70.

	FEV (in liters)	FVC (in liters)	FEV/FVC (by percent)
White	3.22	4.3	74.4
African American	2.85	3.7	76.7
Asian American	2.53	3.27	77.0
Native American	2.53	3.27	77.0

Data from Overfield T: *Biologic variation in health and illness,* Menlo Park, Calif., 1985, Addison-Wesley.

Airflow Rates

Airflow in the tracheobronchial tree is affected by four factors: (1) the size of the airway, (2) the resistance in the airway, (3) the muscle strength, and (4) the elastic recoil. Forced vital capacity (FVC), forced expiratory flow rate in 1 second (FEV_1), and the forced expiratory flow (FEF) are all measures of air flow in the airway. When measured in the older client, these indices are decreased. The maximum voluntary ventilation (MVV) is a measure of the individual's reserve. It is accomplished by asking the client to breath in and out as rapidly as possible for 15 seconds, which is then multiplied by four. The older client can demonstrate as much as a 50% reduction in the MVV and forced expiratory volume (FEV) between ages 30 and 90. The FEV_1 is reported to drop between 25 to 30 ml/year after age 30. The changes in the airflow measures are related to the stiffness of the chest wall and the loss of elastic recoil of the lung. The decrease in thoracic muscular strength contributes to the decreased force of the air moved.

TABLE 22-2

Pulmonary Function Changes in the Older Adult

	Description	Average value	
		Adult male	Older client
Lung volume			
Tidal volume (V_T)	Volume of air inhaled or exhaled per breath	5 to 10 ml/kg	Decreased
Inspiratory reserve volume (IRV)	Volume of air inhaled in addition to normal V_T	3,000 ml	Decreased
Expiratory reserve volume (ERV)	Maximum volume of air that can be exhaled in addition to normal V_T	1,200 ml	Decreased
Residual volume (RV)	Volume of air left in the lungs after maximum exhalation	1,200 ml	Increased by as much as 25%
Lung capacity			
Functional residual capacity (FRC)	Volume of air left in the lung after a normal exhalation (RV + ERV)	2,400 ml	Increased
Residual volume/total lung capacity (RV/TLC)	Ratio of reserve volume to total lung capacity expressed as a percentage	33%	Increased
Vital capacity (VC)	Volume of air exhaled after a maximal inhalation (IRV + V_T + ERV)	4,800 ml	Decreased by as much as 25%
Total lung capacity (TLC)	Total volume of air in the lungs following a maximal inhalation (IRV + V_T + ERC + RV)	6,000 ml	Unchanged

Airway Closure

Early airway closure is seen in the older client as a result of the increased compliance of the lung. At low tidal volumes, the small airways tend to close early because of the loss of elastic recoil, trapping air in the alveoli. The increased resistance of the airway decreases the flow rate contributing to the early airway closure. In addition, the closing capacity (CC), the lung volume at which smaller airways close during forced exhalation, contributes to the early airway closure at low lung volumes. The CC is defined as the closing volume plus the reserve volume. The CC increases with age and by age 65, exceeds the functional residual capacity when in the upright position (Pierson, 1992). This contributes to early airway closure and increased ventilation/perfusion mismatch. Other factors contributing to early airway closure include supine positioning, advanced age and shallow breathing. Upright positioning and encouraging deep breathing help diminish airway collapse in the older adult.

Distribution of Ventilation

The distribution of ventilation is affected by positioning. In the healthy upright adult, ventilation is in excess of perfusion in the upper lobes of the lung. Perfusion, conversely, is greater in the base of the lung because of the influence of gravity. Positioning shifts the balance between ventilation and perfusion, with the down side at the advantage for perfusion. The shallow breathing pattern of the older client may result in hypoxemia and hypercapnia as the alveoli at the base of the lung are underventilated. The result is a decrease in the ventilation/perfusion ratio and ineffective alveolar gas exchange. The reduction in cardiac output and mixed venous oxygen content that are associated with aging compounds the effect of ventilation perfusion imbalance in the older adult. The less uniform ventilation perfusion matching leads to an increase in the physiologic dead space and a compensatory increase in resting minute ventilation, which is of no clinical significance (Pierson, 1992).

Oxygenation

Arterial Oxygen

One of the primary functions of the respiratory system is gas exchange: CO_2 and O_2. PaO_2 falls at a rate of 4 mm Hg per decade of life. A normal PaO_2 for a 70 year old is between 75 to 80 mm Hg; a normal PaO_2 for a 20 year old is 90 to 100 mm Hg. The mnemonic "70 at 70" is for the absolute lower limit of normal PaO_2 in the older adult. Most healthy older adults have arterial oxygen levels well above 70 mm Hg at sea level (Pierson, 1992). The falling PaO_2 is most likely caused by the increased closing volume seen during tidal breathing.

The changes in the alveoli result in less surface area for gas exchange to take place, contributing to the overall reduction in the PaO_2. The increase in dead space is seen as the capillary structures surrounding the alveoli diminish.

Oxygen-Carrying Capacity

The oxygen-carrying capacity (Hgb × 1.34) of the blood is reduced with age. Hemoglobin, responsible for the transport of oxygen from the lung to the peripheral tissue, is diminished in the older client.

Alveolar-Arterial Oxygen Gradient

The **alveolar-arterial (A-a) oxygen gradient** is one measure of lung function. It describes the difference between the amount of oxygen in the alveoli and that actually reaching the arterial blood. The alveolar air value is determined by calculation using the alveolar air equation ($[P_B - P_{H_2O}] \times FiO_2 - PaO_2/0.8$), where the arterial O_2 value is obtained from the arterial blood gas report, the barometric pressure (PB) is 760 mm Hg, and the water vapor pressure is 47 mm Hg (or can be obtained from a barometer), and the FiO_2 is the amount of oxygen delivered to the client. After calculating the alveolar air, the PaO_2 is subtracted from the alveolar air. The normal A-a O_2 gradient is 10 mm Hg in the 20-year-old adult and 25 mm Hg in the octogenarian. Age-related mean values for room air $P(A\text{-}a)O_2$ are predicted from the following equation: $P(A\text{-}a)O_2 = 2.5 = +/- (0.21)$ (age in years) (Pierson, 1992).

The A-a O_2 gradient widens with advancing age, most likely because of ventilation perfusion inequalities. An increase in right to left shunt of blood occurs, most likely as a result of a reduction in mixed venous O_2 content, related to a decreased cardiac output and an increase in postpulmonary shunting through thebesian or bronchial veins.

Arterial pH and $PaCO_2$

The arterial pH of the older adult remains within its normal range of 7.35 to 7.45 unless influenced by acute illness. The $PaCO_2$ remains unchanged with advanced age. Despite the increase in **physiologic dead space** seen in the older adult, the $PaCO_2$ does not increase because of the increased ventilation (Kinzel, 1991).

Lifestyle Factors Affecting Lung Function

Exercise and Immobility

Exercise has been shown to have a positive effect on the respiratory and cardiovascular system (Karper, Boschen, 1993) (see Research box at right). However, the capacity for the older client to perform exercise is affected by the changes in cardiac output, skeletal muscle, and joint function, as well as decreasing overall muscle power and coordination. In addition, the older client may have cardiovascular and respiratory illness. The increased oxygen demands needed in the exercise period may exceed the ability of the older client to meet metabolic demands. This is also related to the decrease in maximum O_2 consumption associated with age. Yerg et al. (1985) compared 14 master athletes, age 63, with 14 healthy 63-year-old men. They found that maximum oxygen consumption was greater in the aged athletes, and they displayed less hyperventilation than the control group. Yerg et al. (1985) also found that endurance training can decrease the maximum oxygen consumption and ventilatory response to exercise.

Breathlessness associated with exercise and increased ventilation is a direct result of the increase in physiologic dead space as heart rate and respiratory rate increases. Yerg (1985) noted a significant increase in the ventilatory cost of submaximum exercise between the age of 64 and 70 years.

RESEARCH

Karper WB, Boschen MB: Effects of exercise on acute respiratory tract infections and related symptoms, *Geriatr Nurs* 14(1):15-18, 1993.

Sample, setting

The sample included 16 volunteer subjects aged 60 to 72, who were not habitual exercisers. They were selected on the basis of absence of coronary artery disease (CAD), COPD, diabetes mellitus (DM), renal disease, bone marrow depression, steroid use, cytotoxic drug use, and a smoking habit.

Methodology

At the beginning and end of the study, subjects completed a walking test of 440 yards (400 meters) in which they walked as fast as they felt comfortable. The time was recorded. Each subject then completed four written forms about self-perceived frustration, tension, and coping ability related to stress. Medical information about diagnosis, treated illness, and prescribed medications for the period of the study and 1 year before the study was obtained from the subject's private physician.

Findings

Pretest and nursing data indicated that all of the subjects increased their walking capacity. Of the 14 subjects who completed the study, 12 showed a reduction in the incidence of upper and lower respiratory infections (ULRI) and related symptoms. All but one of the 12 subjects improved their scores on the stress forms, reporting less self-perceived stress.

Implications

An important factor is the lowering of stress through exercise. Aerobic activity may produce a buffering effect against stress in certain people under certain conditions. The side effects of appropriate exercise include improved cardiovascular-respiratory function, improved musculoskeletal strength and endurance, and improved joint flexibility. Recommended exercise for the older client is 30 minutes 3 to 5 days per week, with a 10-minute warm up and a 10-minute cool down period of light calisthenics and stretching.

In a study of Johnson et al. (1992) it was noted that activity intolerance was the most common cause of immobility in the older client. For the older client with COPD, this will be exacerbated. The older client's strength and endurance may be reduced, leading to increased immobility, which in turn leads to increased breathlessness when activity is attempted. The older client with COPD and immobility may benefit from a program of regular exercise to increase strength and endurance and decrease breathlessness as the respiratory muscles are trained.

Smoking

Smoking has long been known to damage the lung. Most recently, the effects of prolonged exposure to secondhand smoke have been shown to cause damage in the lungs of nonsmokers (American Thoracic Society, 1985; Kuhn, McGovern, 1992). Heavy smokers may demonstrate a nine-fold increase in the reduction of the FEV_1 over normal expected reductions. Cilia are paralyzed by the nicotine, preventing them from cleaning the lung. The tobacco smoke increases the goblet cell's production of mucus. Cigarette smoke has been shown to cause bronchoconstriction, increase airway resistance and increase closing volumes. Older clients who did not smoke but were exposed to prolonged inhalation of secondhand smoke may show similar changes in the lung.

Smoking interferes with gas exchange because the carbon monoxide by-product competes with oxygen for the hemoglobin molecule (Foyt, 1992). Bed rest compounds gas exchange in the older smoker.

Many medications are affected by smoking. Smoking can decrease the drug clearance and cause an increase in serum drug levels. Some drugs altered by smoking include propranolol, lidocaine, antidepressants, theophylline, aminophylline, insulin, and lidocaine (Foyt, 1992; Karb et al, 1989).

Obesity

Obesity results in a decrease in chest wall compliance and reduction in functional residual capacity (FRC), vital capacity (VC), and expiratory reserve volume (ERV). In the older client with already decreased chest wall mobility and stiffening of the chest, the added weight markedly reduces pulmonary functions and increases the feeling of breathlessness. Ventilation at the bases of the lungs may be diminished because of the client's inability to take a deep breath. Coupled with immobility, the risk of the older obese client developing atelectasis and upper and lower respiratory infections is increased. Early airway closure may also be associated with under ventilation of the lower lobes of the lungs.

Sleep

The increased sleep time in the older adult increases the risk of aspiration and oxygen desaturation during sleep (Bachman, 1992). The older adult has a diminished ventilatory drive and loss of upper airway tone that predisposes to apnea, **hypopnea**, and nocturnal oxygen desaturation. The diminished cough reflex and arousal reflex increase the likelihood of aspiration during sleep (Pierson, 1992).

RESPIRATORY CHANGES ASSOCIATED WITH ANESTHESIA AND SURGERY

The older client undergoing surgery has an increased risk for aspiration as a result of loss of laryngeal reflexes (Foyt, 1992). If the surgery is an emergency, the risk in-

Insight • *Nursing care measures for the older client undergoing surgery include encouraging deep breathing and the use of an incentive spirometer postoperatively. The older client should be instructed preoperatively in the use of the incentive spirometer, the importance of getting out of bed often postoperatively, how to splint the incision site, the importance of hydration, coughing techniques and the plan for pain management. It is imperative to promote good pulmonary hygiene in the postoperative period to prevent atelectasis and subsequent pneumonia. Many older clients may benefit from a pulmonary rehabilitation program preoperatively to increase their muscle strength, help clear airways and promote a sense of well-being. If this is not covered by the client's health care plan, a plan for walking can be established preoperatively. Walking provides overall body conditioning. The client is encouraged to walk daily starting at 10 to 15 minutes as tolerated and increase to 30 to 45 minutes as tolerated. The physician should be consulted and a collaborative plan for preoperative exercise developed. As soon as possible, the older client needs to be encouraged to get out of bed and sit up in the chair several times a day. Have the older client get out of bed more often, 6 to 8 or more times per day, and sit in the chair for shorter periods of 30-45 minutes. This promotes deep breathing, reduces skin integrity problems, and improves overall conditioning. It is important to provide adequate hydration to prevent secretions from becoming thickened and from increasing the risk of airway plugging.*

BOX 22-1

Lung Changes Related to Anesthesia and Surgery

Decreased vital capacity
Decreased tidal volume
Decreased inspiratory reserve volume
Decreased expiratory reserve volume
Decreased alveolar volume
Atelectasis

creases as a result of the older client's delayed gastric emptying and the potential for a full stomach.

Incisions, pain, and decreased deep breathing postoperatively increases the older client's chance of developing postoperative atelectasis (Box 22-1). The subsequent immobility decreases ventilation and effective airway clearance. Hypovolemia contributes to thickened secretions. Because the older client has a decreased effective cough, a painful incision further diminishes the likelihood of effective airway clearance (Foyt, 1992). Promotion of deep breathing, adequate hydration, frequent position changes, and early mobility will decrease the risk of developing atelectasis.

COMMON RESPIRATORY PROBLEMS AND CONDITIONS IN THE OLDER CLIENT

Respiratory disease in the older client accounts for approximately 200,000 deaths per year in people age 65 and older. COPD and pneumonia are the fourth and fifth leading cause of death in clients over the age of 65 years (Gail, Lenfant, 1992). COPD and asthma affect approximately 14% of clients over the age of 65 years, an estimated 4 million older adults in the United States. In addition, respiratory disease in the older client accounts for over 8.5 million hospital days (Gail, Lenfant, 1992).

Prevention of respiratory illness is an important part of care. The promotion of smoking cessation, decreasing the number of individuals who start smoking, early detection of lung disease in high-risk populations, and immunization for influenza and pneumonia are a few preventive measures. Populations at risk for development of lung disease and those exposed to environmental pollutants need education about decreasing their risks. Older clients with existing lung disease benefit from education about how to prevent exacerbation of their illness and maintain a level of wellness.

Respiratory illness is a chronic disease that affects not only the older client, but also the family. Many clients with respiratory illness feel a loss of control over their lives because of the breathlessness they experience on exertion and often at rest. The behavior of the older client may become demanding and controlling in dealing with their families and friends. This is related to the lack of control older adults have over their lung disease, so they try to control their environments. It is well-documented that the quality of the older client's life is dependent on their feelings about the disease and control of the disease (Dettenmeier, 1992; Kersten, 1989). There are support groups available for clients with respiratory disease and their families. Usually they are sponsored by the American Lung Association or the local hospital. These groups are designed to help the client and family deal with the anger, loss of control, and hopelessness many clients with a chronic respiratory disease experience.

The family or a significant other needs to be included in all aspects of planning and care for the older client with respiratory illness. The success of the older client to comply with the medical recommendations may depend on getting to the physician's office, getting to the pharmacy for medications, assistance with administering medications, and assistance with activities of daily living (ADLs). The older client with respiratory disease needs a good family support system as well as a team of caregivers to support both the older client and the family.

Classification of Respiratory Disease

Pulmonary disease is often divided into two categories: (1) **obstructive lung disease** and (2) **restrictive lung disease**. Obstructive lung diseases are characterized by changes in expiratory airflow rates and obstruction of the airway. The lumen of the airway can be decreased by mucus, edema of the lining of the airway, or constriction of the muscles surrounding the airway causing bronchoconstriction.

Restrictive lung disease decreases the ability to expand the chest and impairs inhalation resulting in decreased lung volumes. The chest wall, lung parenchyma, pleural space, and extrapulmonary factors such as body mass can result in restrictive lung disease. Examples of these diseases include bronchogenic carcinoma and tuberculosis.

Other respiratory diseases seen in the older client include bronchopulmonary infections, pulmonary edema, and pulmonary emboli. To begin the discussion of respiratory disease, it is important to understand some of the respiratory symptoms common to the older client.

Respiratory Symptoms

Respiratory symptoms common to the older client include alterations in breathing patterns, dyspnea, and cough.

Breathing Pattern

The normal older client has an increased respiratory rate of 16 to 25 breaths per minute with a decreased tidal

Insight • *One of the first signs that the older client is having respiratory problems is a change in mental status. The older client's response to hypoxemia and hypercapnia is blunted. Changes in heart rate, respiratory rate, and blood pressure may be delayed. Mental status changes may be subtle, such as forgetfulness and increased irritability. The older client may complain of an occipital headache or confusion when awakening from sleep. If these signs persist, a more in-depth evaluation of the client's respiratory status is indicated.*

volume and minute ventilation. Abnormal breathing patterns in the older client can be indicative of other metabolic and respiratory illnesses.

Cough

The cough mechanism in the older client is altered because of the loss of elastic recoil, decreased respiratory muscle strength (King, 1990) and decreased tidal volume. Causes of cough in the older client include postnasal drip, chronic bronchitis, acute respiratory tract infections, aspiration, gastroesophageal reflux, congestive heart failure (CHF), interstitial lung disease, and cancers.

Insight • *Because of the age-related changes affecting the older client's cough mechanism, it is important to recommend cough suppressants with caution. Suppression of the cough and depression of any respiratory function could lead to retained pulmonary secretions, plugged airways, and atelectasis.*

Dyspnea

Complaints of **dyspnea** or breathlessness in the older client are often associated with respiratory and cardiac disease. Because dyspnea is a perception of breathlessness, it is difficult for the older client to quantify and therefore may be dismissed, especially when no clinical evidence can be attributed to the complaint (Morris, 1990). King (1990) reports that older clients most often describe the sensation as an inability to get enough air, difficulty taking a deep breath, breathing rapidly, a choking feeling, or smothering.

The normal age-related changes in the lung, in addition to the changes related to the acute or chronic illness, further decrease the respiratory reserve. Dyspnea

Insight • *Dyspnea is a common complaint in the older client with pulmonary disease. However, older clients usually do not complain of dyspnea until it begins to interfere with their ADLs, and then only if those activities are important to them. For example, it may become difficult to use the stairs. The older client may simply choose the elevator or escalator, and not consider reporting the shortness of breath associated with stairclimbing. It is an important assessment parameter to determine what ADLs the older client no longer participates in and why.*

at rest is most often associated with an acute respiratory or cardiac illness, whereas dyspnea on exertion may be related to immobility and respiratory muscle deconditioning. Older clients with COPD may experience dyspnea on exertion initially and dyspnea at rest as the disease progresses.

OBSTRUCTIVE PULMONARY DISEASE

Chronic Obstructive Pulmonary Disease

Chronic obstructive pulmonary disease (COPD) is characterized by airway obstruction and decreased expiratory flow rates (Weilitz, 1991). The two reversible components in COPD are airway diameter and expiratory flow rates. Emphysema, chronic bronchitis and bronchiectasis are most often referred to as COPD. Asthma may also be included in COPD, especially if there is a component of airway hyperreactivity (Dettenmeier, 1992).

COPD is a progressive and ultimately fatal disease and is the fifth leading cause of death in the United States (O'Donnell et al, 1993). Gail and Lenfant (1992) report the fatality rate for COPD is more than two times as high in men than in women between ages 65 and 74, and three times as high between the ages of 75 to 84. Although more common in men than in women, the male to female ratio has dropped from 6:1 in 1981 to 2.5:1 in 1991 (Webster, Kadah, 1991). This is most likely a result of the increased number of women who smoke. Risk factors for COPD include age, male gender, reduced lung function, air pollution, exposure to secondhand smoke, familial allergies, poor nutrition, and alcohol intake. COPD is often a comorbid factor in deaths from pneumonia and influenza, accounting for increased physician visits (Webster, Kadah, 1991).

Symptoms of COPD vary depending on whether

MEDICAL MANAGEMENT

COPD

Diagnostic tests and procedures

The diagnosis of COPD is made based on a history of progressive dyspnea, cough, wheezing, and sputum production, usually in the morning. (Listello, Glauser, 1992). Pulmonary function testing (PFT) or simple spirometry is used for the initial diagnosis of airflow obstruction. An FEV_1 of less than 70% of the total forced vital capacity (FVC) or a maximum midexpiratory flow (MMEF) rate of less than 65% of predicted is evidence of significant airway obstruction (Morris, 1990). A resting arterial blood gas measurement and a standard baseline posterior-anterior (PA) chest x-ray are also obtained. A blood hemoglobin level is obtained to assess the presence of polycythemia, which is an indicator of prolonged hypoxemia (Listello, Glauser, 1992).

Treatment

Treatment is directed toward management of the symptoms. Other goals include increased physical activity, independent self-care, and reduction in need for hospitalization (Morris, 1990). Medications include the use of bronchodilators, beta-adrenergic drugs, anticholinergic drugs, corticosteroids, and oxygen therapy. Both inhaled and oral bronchodilators are used to improve air flow.

Beta agonists

These sympathomimetic drugs work by stimulating the $beta_2$ receptors in the lung. This results in bronchial dilatation, increased mucociliary clearance, and possibly increased diaphragmatic function (Listello, Glauser, 1992). The drugs may be administered by metered dose inhalers (MDIs) with a spacer or aerosolized therapy (Fig. 22-5). Oral sympathomimetics are available but are associated with more systemic side effects, tremors, and cardiac dysrhythmias. Beta agonists should be used with caution in the older client with ischemic heart disease (Listello, Glauser, 1992). Examples of beta agonists include albuterol (Proventil, Ventolin), metaproterenol sulfate (Alupent, Metaprel), Bitolterol mesylate (Tornalate), and pirbuterol acetate (Maxair).

Anticholinergics

Inhaled anticholinergic, atropine sulfate (Dey-Dose), or ipratropium bromide (Atrovent) are used to treat chronic bronchitis. They work by inhibiting vagal stimulation of the lung, preventing contraction of the smooth muscle and decreasing mucous production.

Theophylline

Theophylline increases diaphragmatic muscle strength, resulting in a decrease in dyspnea. It also enhances mucociliary clearance, reduces mast cell mediator release and stimulates the release of catecholamine from the adrenal medulla (Poe, Utell, 1991). Management of theophylline is accomplished through the use of blood levels. The therapeutic range is narrow, from 5 to 15 μgm/L (Kuhn, McGovern, 1992) to 10 to 20 μgm/ml (Poe, Utell, 1991). Theophylline toxicity is manifested by nausea, nervousness, diarrhea, palpitations, insomnia, dysrhythmias and seizures (Bloom, Barreuther, 1993; Listello, Glauser, 1992; Poe, Utell, 1991).

Steroids

Oral steroids may be used in clients who have a reversible component (Listello, Glauser, 1992). The dosage is guided by improvement in spirometry and client symptoms. Steroid therapy may not be well tolerated in the older client.

Oxygen therapy

Supplemental oxygen therapy is indicated for clients with a resting $PaO_2 < 55$ mm Hg or a saturation $< 85\%$ by pulse oximetry (Fig. 22-6). O_2 therapy may also be indicated if the PaO_2 is between 56 to 59 mm Hg and there is evidence of right heart failure or secondary polycythemia, hematocrit $> 56\%$ (Listello, Glauser, 1992). O_2 desaturation associated with sleep or exercise is also an indication for supplemental O_2 therapy. These criteria are used by third party payors for determining whether O_2 therapy will be covered.

Antibiotics

Antibiotics are used when there is a concommitant bacterial infection. The choice of antibiotic is based on the infecting organism, with therapy lasting from 7 to 14 days.

Smoking cessation

If the older client with COPD is a smoker, it is critical to stop smoking. Benefits to smoking cessation include reduction in number of respiratory infections, improvement in the function of the mucociliary clearance of the lung, decreased cough and dyspnea, increased appetite and decreased sputum production. Secondhand smoke should also be avoided by the older client with COPD, since it can cause bronchospasm and coughing.

Nutrition

Proper nutrition is essential to promote efficient respiratory muscle work. Adequate nutrition maintains muscle mass, muscle function, and immunologic competence (Webster, Kadah, 1991).

Immunization

Pneumococcal vaccine is recommended. The influenza vaccine is recommended annually for the older client, especially if there is underlying lung disease. During peak influenza season, the older client with COPD should avoid crowds to decrease the risk of contracting influenza.

Prognosis

Clients with an FEV_1 of < 1 L per second have a poor prognosis (Listello, Glauser, 1992). The usual time from diagnosis to death is approximately 10 years. When a reversible airway component is present the survival rate of COPD increases from 76% at 5 years to 92% at 5 years (Listello, Glauser, 1992).

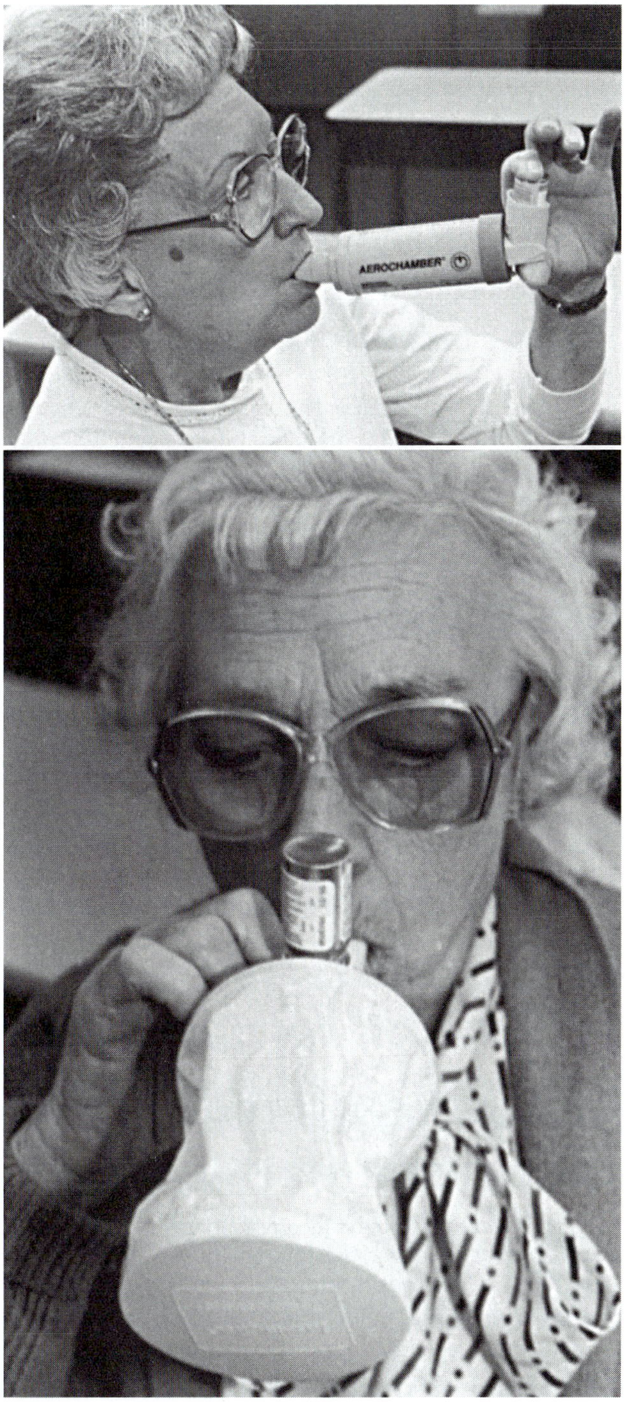

Fig. 22-5 Commercial spacers for MDIs: *Top,* AeroChamber; *bottom,* InspirEase. (From Dettenmeier P: *Pulomonary nursing care,* St Louis, 1992, Mosby-Year Book.)

Fig. 22-6 Nasal cannula oxygen delivery device. (From Dettenmeier P: *Pulmonary nursing care,* St Louis, 1992, Mosby.)

emphysema or chronic bronchitis is the predominant factor. Symptoms include dyspnea, especially on exertion, cough, sputum production, weight loss, and complaints of fatigue. Diagnosis is based on client history and alterations in the pulmonary function tests (see Medical Management box, p. 578).

Asthma

Asthma is characterized by reversible airway obstruction either spontaneously or by treatment, airway inflammation and increased airway responsiveness to a variety of stimuli (US Department of Health and Human Services, 1991). The airway becomes narrowed as a result of inflammation and edema of the mucosal wall. There is an increase in mucous production, coughing, and wheezing.

The incidence of asthma is approximately 40 cases in 100 persons (Gail, Lenfant, 1992). Asthma causes few deaths in older clients; however, epidemiologic studies have detected an increasing number of deaths over the past 10 years in clients age 75 and older (Gail, Lenfant, 1992).

An asthmatic attack can be precipitated by exposure to allergens or irritants such as change in weather, odors, or stress. In the older client, asthma is often associated with a viral respiratory infection (Gail, Lenfant, 1992). Signs and symptoms include dyspnea, audible wheezing, palpitations, increased respiratory rate, use of accessory muscles of respiration, tachycardia, pulsus paradoxus, diaphoresis, and chest hyperinflation. Initially the client will hyperventilate and effectively blow off the increasing CO_2. A falling $Paco_2$ and pH with a rising $Paco_2$ is indicative of imminent respiratory failure. The increasing $Paco_2$ is a result of the client's tiring and inability to hyperventilate.

Chronic Bronchitis

The American Thoracic Society (1987) defines chronic bronchitis as a clinical syndrome characterized by excessive mucous production with chronic or recurring cough on most days for a minimum of 3 months of the year for at least 2 consecutive years. There is hypertrophy of the bronchial mucous gland, increase in the number of goblet cells and a decrease in the effectiveness of the mucociliary escalator, usually as a result of repeated respiratory infections. Cigarette smoking is the single factor that contributes to the exacerbation of chronic bronchitis.

Chronic bronchitis is associated with right-sided heart failure (cor pulmonale), polycythemia, hypoxemia, and respiratory insufficiency. Clinical presentation includes persistent cough, dyspnea on exertion, purulent sputum, cyanosis, crackles on auscultation, tachycardia, pedal edema, unexplained weight gain, and a decreased $Paco_2$ with a normal or elevated $Paco_2$.

Emphysema

Emphysema occurs between ages 60 and 70. Emphysema resulting from a deficiency of $alpha_1$ antitrypsin enzyme occurs in young-to-middle-age adults rather than the older adult. Emphysema is characterized by progressive destruction of the alveoli and their supporting structures. The alveoli distal to the terminal bronchioles become enlarged. Loss of connective tissue supporting the alveoli lead to permanent obliteration of the peripheral airways (Webster, Kadah, 1991). Physical signs include the classic barrel chest appearance with use of accessory muscles of respiration. Emphysema is often associated with clients with a history of smoking.

Clinical presentation includes dyspnea on exertion or at rest, decreased weight, chronic cough with little sputum production, digital clubbing, hyperresonant chest to percussion, elevated hemoglobin, crackles and wheezes on auscultation, and abnormal pulmonary function tests, with decreased VC, increased TLC, increased FRC, and decreased FEV_1.

Nursing Management

✣ ASSESSMENT

Assessment of the older client with COPD begins with a complete health history and physical examination (see Box 22-8, p. 597).

✣ DIAGNOSIS

Nursing diagnoses common with the older client with COPD include, but are not limited to: (1) ineffective airway clearance (2) impaired gas exchange, (3) altered health maintenance, (4) risk for infection, (5) knowledge deficit (specify), (6) altered nutrition—less than body requirements, (7) altered role performance, (8) ineffective breathing pattern, and (9) inability to sustain spontaneous ventilation (Boxes 22-2 and 22-3).

✣ PLANNING

As with all clients, the older client with COPD should be included in the planning of care. It is important to include the spouse, significant other, family and any other caregivers in the planning process. Discharge planning should begin as soon as the older client is admitted to the hospital. If the older client requires special equipment for home care, such as supplemental oxygen therapy or aerosolized therapy, the client and family can benefit from learning the new skills in the acute care setting.

Expected outcomes for the older client with COPD include, but are not limited to, the following:

1. Client will maintain a patent airway.
2. Client will maintain a stable weight.

BOX 22-2

Nursing Diagnoses for Clients with Respiratory Alterations

Ineffective airway clearance

Definition

The state in which an individual is unable to clear secretions or obstructions from the respiratory tract to maintain airway patency

Related factors

Decreased energy and fatigue, tracheobronchial infection, obstruction or secretion, and perceptual and/or cognitive impairment

Defining characteristics

Abnormal breath sounds such as crackles, wheezes, rhonchus, changes in respiratory rate or depth, tachypnea, effective/ineffective cough, with or without sputum, cyanosis, dyspnea at rest or on exertion, and fever

Ineffective breathing pattern

Definition

The state in which an individual's inhalation and/or exhalation pattern does not enable adequate ventilation

Related factors

Neuromuscular impairment, pain, musculoskeletal impairment, perceptual or cognitive impairment, anxiety, decreased energy and fatigue, inflammatory process, decreased lung expansion, and tracheobronchial obstruction

Defining characteristics

Dyspnea, shortness of breath, tachypnea, fremitus, abnormal arterial blood gases, cyanosis, cough, nasal flaring, respiratory depth changes, assumption of the three-point position (i.e., orthopneic position, pursed-lip breathing, and prolonged expiratory phase), increased anteroposterior diameter, use of accessory muscles, altered chest expansion

Impaired gas exchange

Definition

The state in which the individual experiences an imbalance between O_2 uptake and CO_2 elimination at the alveolar-capillary gas exchange area

Related factors

Altered oxygen supply, alveolar-capillary membrane changes, altered blood flow, altered oxygen-carrying capacity of the blood

Defining characteristics

Confusion, somnolence, irritability, inability to move secretions, hypercapnia, and hypoxia

Inability to sustain spontaneous ventilation

Definition

A state in which the response pattern of decreased energy reserves results in an individual's ability to maintain breathing adequate to support life (Kim et al, 1993)

Related factors

Metabolic factors and respiratory muscle fatigue

Defining characteristics

Major: Dyspnea and increased metabolic rate

Minor: Increased restlessness, apprehension, increased use of accessory muscles, heart rate, and $Paco_2$; and decreased tidal volume, Pao_2 level, cooperation and Pao_2 saturation.

3. Client will maintain arterial blood gas values at baseline.
4. Client will maintain a balanced intake and output.
5. Client will be able to effectively clear secretions.
6. Client will be able to demonstrate diaphragmatic and pursed lip breathing.
7. Client will be able to demonstrate relaxation techniques to control breathing.
8. Client will maintain a respiratory rate between 16 and 25 breaths per minute.
9. Client will be able to list the signs and symptoms to report to the physician.

✣ INTERVENTION

Interventions for clients with COPD include maximizing the effects of bronchodilator therapy, administering medications at the designated time intervals, and promoting hydration, good nutrition, and increasing mobility.

The majority of nursing care for the client with COPD includes extensive education. Topics to be taught include normal respiratory anatomy and changes associated with the disease; medical intervention, including tests and medications; and lifestyle changes such as smoking cessation, weight gain or loss, exercise requirements, and breathing retraining.

Client Education for COPD

Smoking cessation Older clients with COPD who continue to smoke increase their risk of repeated respiratory infections and progression of the underlying disease process (American Thoracic Society, 1985). Older

BOX 22-3

Associated Nursing Diagnoses for the Older Client With Respiratory Alterations

The following nursing diagnoses are nursing care problems often associated with clients with respiratory alterations.

Activity intolerance

A state in which an individual has insufficient physiologic or psychologic energy to endure or complete required or desired daily activities.

Related factors	Defining characteristics
Generalized weakness	Verbal report of fatigue or weakness
Sedentary lifestyle	Abnormal heart rate or blood pressure response to activity
Imbalance between oxygen supply and demand	Exertional discomfort or dyspnea
Bedrest	ECG changes reflecting arrhythmias or ischemia
Immobility	

Ineffective individual coping

Impairment of adaptive behaviors and problem-solving abilities of a person in meeting life's demands and roles.

Related factors	Defining characteristics
Situational crisis	Verbalization of inability to cope or inability to ask for help
Maturational crisis	Inability to meet role expectations
Personal vulnerability	Inability to problem solve
Multiple life changes	Alteration in societal participation
No vacations	Destructive behavior toward self or others
Inadequate relaxation	Inappropriate use of defense mechanisms
Inadequate support systems	Change in usual communication patterns
Little or no exercise	Verbal manipulation
Poor nutrition	High illness rate
Unmet expectations	High rate of accidents
Work overload	Overeating
Too many deadlines	Lack of appetite
Unrealistic perceptions	Excessive smoking
	Excessive drinking
	Overuse of prescribed tranquilizers
	Alcohol
	Chronic fatigue
	Insomnia
	Muscular tension
	Ulcers
	Frequent headaches
	Frequent neckaches
	Irritable bowel
	Chronic worry
	General irritability
	Poor self-esteem
	Chronic anxiety
	Emotional tension
	Chronic depression

From Weilitz PB: *Pocket guide to respiratory care,* St. Louis, 1991, Mosby.

BOX 22-3

Associated Nursing Diagnoses for the Older Client With Respiratory Alterations—cont'd

Knowledge deficit (Specify)

A state in which specific information is lacking

Related factors

Lack of exposure
Lack of recall
Information misinterpretation
Cognitive limitation
Lack of interest in learning
Unfamiliarity with information resources
Client's request for no information

Defining characteristics

Verbalization of the problem
Inaccurate follow-through of instruction
Inadequate performance of test
Inappropriate or exaggerated behaviors: anger, hostility, apathy, hysteria
Statement of misconception
Request for information

Altered nutrition: less than body requirements

The state in which an individual experiences an intake of nutrients insufficient to meet metabolic needs

Related factors

Inability to ingest food, digest food, or absorb nutrients because of biologic, psychologic, or economic factors

Defining characteristics

Loss of weight with adequate food intake
Body weight 20% or more under ideal for height and frame
Reported inadequate food intake less than recommended daily allowances (RDA)
Weakness of muscles required for swallowing or mastication
Reported evidence of lack of food
Lack of interest in food
Perceived inability to ingest food
Aversion to eating
Reported altered taste sensation
Satiety immediately after ingesting food
Abdominal pain with or without pathologic conditions
Sore, inflamed buccal cavity

Altered health maintenance

Inability to identify, manage, and/or seek help to maintain health

Related factors

Lack of or significant alteration in communication skills
Inability to make deliberate and thoughtful judgments
Perceptual or cognitive impairment
Alteration in fine and/or gross motor skills
Ineffective individual coping
Dysfunctional grieving
Lack of material resources
Unachieved developmental tasks
Ineffective family coping
Disabling spiritual distress

Defining characteristics

Demonstrated lack of knowledge regarding basic health practices
Demonstrated lack of adaptive behaviors to internal or external environmental changes
Reported or observed inability to take responsibility for meeting basic health practices in any or all functional pattern areas
History of lack of health-seeking behavior
Reported or observed lack of equipment, financial and/or other resources
Reported or observed impairment of personal support system

clients should be encouraged to stop smoking. Programs are available through the American Lung Association, the American Cancer Society, and many community hospitals. It is important to provide support for the older client attempting to quit smoking. The success of the individual is in part dependent on the support of family and friends. Many older clients find it impossible to stop smoking completely. Encourage them to decrease the amount and frequency they smoke. Although not ideal, it may help to decrease some of the symptoms associated with the respiratory illness.

Nutrition The older client needs to be instructed on the benefits of eating nutritious meals. Adequate nutrition is often difficult to maintain in the older client (see Chapter 8). The client with COPD has the additional problem of breathlessness which makes eating difficult. Instruct the client to eat frequent small meals, avoid gas-producing foods, reduce carbohydrates to only 50% of their diet (the breakdown of carbohydrates has been shown to increase the CO_2 load, thereby increasing the work of breathing, especially in the CO_2 retainer), eat high-protein foods, and reduce the intake of fat.

Breathing retraining Clients with COPD needs to be taught how to breathe effectively. The goals of breathing retraining include decreasing the work of breathing, improving oxygenation, increasing the efficiency of breathing patterns, and client control of breathing. Two of the most commonly taught techniques include di-

BOX 22-4

Diaphragmatic Breathing

- Have the client lie in a supine or semi-Fowler's position.
- Place one hand on the middle of the stomach below the sternum.
- Place other hand on the upper chest.
- Inhale slowly through the nose. The stomach should expand. (Note the movement of the hand over the stomach.)
- Exhale slowly through pursed lips. The stomach should contract.
- Rest.
- Repeat.

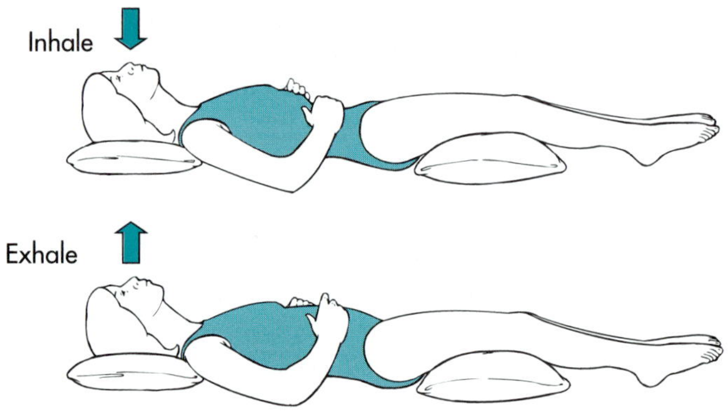

Fig. 22-7 Diaphragmatic breathing. (From Weilitz PB: *Pocket guide to respiratory care,* St. Louis, 1991, Mosby.)

BOX 22-5

Pursed Lip Breathing

- Assume a comfortable position.
- Inhale slowly through the nose, keeping the mouth closed.
- Remember to use the diaphragmatic breathing technique.
- Pucker the lips as if blowing out a candle, kissing, or whistling.
- Exhale slowly, blowing through the pursed lips.
- Exhalation should be at least twice as long as inhalation.
- Rest.
- Repeat.

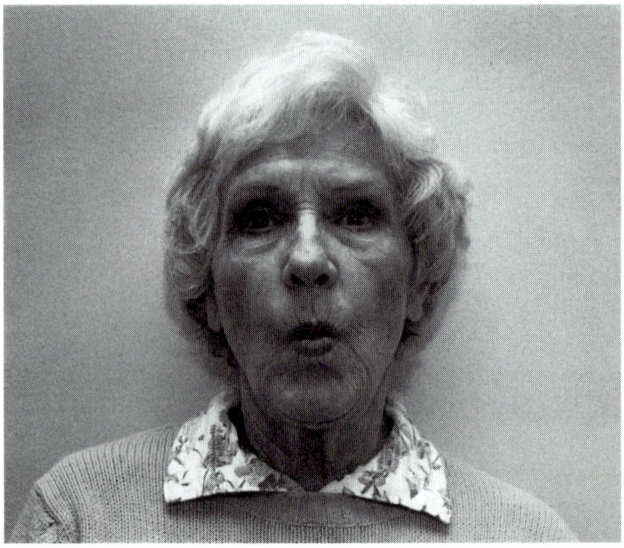

Fig. 22-8 Pursed-lip breathing. (Courtesy Ursula Ruhl, St. Louis, Mo.)

aphragmatic breathing and pursed-lip breathing (Boxes 22-4 and 22-5) (Figs. 22-7 and 22-8). Diaphragmatic breathing increases client awareness of the breathing pattern and improves the efficiency of breathing. Pursed-lip breathing increases expiratory pressure, improves oxygenation, helps prevent early airway closure, increases exhalation time, reduces the respiratory rate and allows clients to slow their breathing (Weilitz, 1991).

Chest physiotherapy Chest physiotherapy (CPT) includes chest percussion, postural drainage (PD), and vibration and rib shaking. CPT is used for clients who have difficulty clearing their own secretions. Contraindications include hemoptysis, pulmonary emboli, osteoporosis and bleeding disorders. Postural drainage is the positioning of the client in a head down position after CPT to facilitate drainage of pulmonary secretions. The older client may not tolerate the head down position of PD or the percussion of CPT. Explain to clients that they may experience increased breathlessness as a result of the mobilization of secretions and increased coughing as they try to clear their airways. To help decrease discomfort associated with chest percussion, place a bath towel over the area being percussed.

Pulmonary hygiene Pulmonary hygiene includes hydration, deep breathing exercises and cough techniques (Box 22-6). Older clients are prone to dehydration, and therefore are at risk for airway plugging. Encourage oral fluids of 4 to 6 quarts per day, if not contraindicated by CVD. Instruct the older client to sip fluids all day to decrease feeling full by drinking a large amount at one time.

The older client is instructed in the signs and symptoms that are associated with a respiratory infection. These include sputum color changes, fever, chills, and a change in the breathing pattern.

Medications Client education regarding medications includes the purpose of the medication, dosage, side effects and schedule of administration. Medications are administered PO, by metered-dose inhaler (MDI), or by nebulizer (Box 22-7) (Figs. 22-9 and 22-10).

BOX 22-6

Effective Cough Techniques

Cascade cough

1. Take a deep breath and hold it for 1 to 3 seconds.
2. Cough out forcefully several times until all air is exhaled (usually two to six coughs).
3. Inhale slowly through the nose.
4. Repeat once, if necessary.
5. Rest.
6. Repeat as needed.

Huff cough

1. Take a deep breath and hold it for 1 to 3 seconds.
2. Keeping glottis open, cough out several times until all air is exhaled (usually two to six huff coughs). Sometimes it helps to say the word "huff" while coughing.
3. Inhale slowly through the nose.
4. Repeat as necessary.

End-expiratory cough

1. Take a deep breath and hold it for 1 to 3 seconds.
2. Exhale slowly.
3. At the end of the exhalation, cough once.
4. Inhale slowly through the nose.
5. Repeat as necessary.
6. Follow with a cascade or huff cough, in which secretions are moved from small to larger airways.

Augmented cough

1. Take a deep breath and hold it for 1 to 3 seconds.
2. Perform one or more of the following maneuvers:
   a. Tighten knees and buttocks to increase intraabdominal pressure
   b. Bend forward at the waist to increase intraabdominal pressure
   c. Place the hand flat on the upper abdomen just under the xiphoid process and press in and up abruptly during the cough or exhalation, *or* place hands on the lateral rib cage and quickly press in and release with each cough (called rib springing).
   d. Keep hands on the chest wall and press inward with each cough.
3. Inhale slowly through the nose.
4. Rest, if necessary.
5. Repeat as needed.

From Dettenmeier P: *Pulmonary nursing care,* St Louis, 1992, Mosby.

Home O_2 Therapy

Oxygen therapy has been shown to decrease morbidity and mortality for clients with COPD when used more than 18 hours per day. The client's acceptance of O_2 therapy and attitude about the disease determines compliance with treatment. O_2 therapy is considered a medication and should be treated as such. The client and family need to be taught the proper liter flow, the time the O_2 is to be used, and how to properly use the equipment.

Home O_2 therapy is available in E-cylinder, concentrators and liquid systems. The liquid oxygen system with portability is the most easily transported and may provide the older client with more mobility, however it is the most expensive. The concentrator is a machine, about the size of small bedside table. It is stationary and is usually accompanied by an E-cylinder for a small amount of portability. The E-cylinder, a small green tank that can be pulled on a cart similar to a luggage rack, is economical although a little less portable because of its size.

BOX 22-7

Using a Metered-Dose Inhaler (MDI)

1. Select the appropriate canister of medication.
2. Shake the inhaler 15 to 20 times.
3. Hold the inhaler directly in front of the mouth about 2 to 3 inches from the mouth. *When a spacer is used, place the inhaler in the spacer and place the mouth piece directly into the mouth.*
4. Take a deep breath and exhale completely.
5. Open your mouth wide. *If you are using a spacer, seal your lips around the mouth piece.*
6. Activate the inhaler.
7. Inhale slowly and deeply.
8. Hold your breath for a count of 10.
9. Exhale slowly.
10. Wait 1 to 5 minutes between puffs. Repeat the steps for each puff ordered.

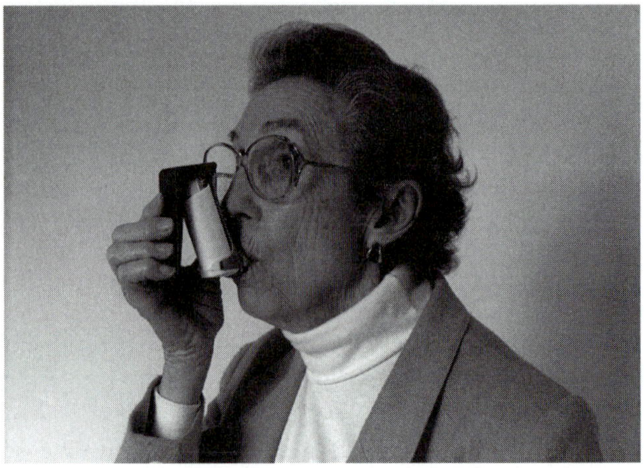

Fig. 22-9 Glaxo MDI adaptor for older client who has difficult using the standard cannister. (Adaptor and inhaler provided by Glaxo Inc., Research Triangle Park, North Carolina; photo courtesy Loy Ledbetter, St. Louis, Mo.)

The older client, the family, the physician, and the nurse should discuss the client's level of activity and select the right system to support the older client's lifestyle. The social services representative is helpful in determining the amount and type of insurance coverage the client has available for O_2 therapy in the home. Many third-party payors do not cover the liquid O_2 system unless the client is active and spends a good portion of the day out of the home. If the older client is homebound, only leaving the home for medical appointments, the most economical system is the concentrator with an E cylinder for those trips to the physician's office.

✣ EVALUATION

Evaluation of the older client with COPD will focus on ability to return to ADLs, control of symptoms and achievement of the expected outcomes. The older client may need additional caregivers in the home, since the spouse or significant other is most likely the same age. Older clients may need more time to learn the educational materials; however, once taught, they will have a good understanding and be able to adapt them to their lifestyle.

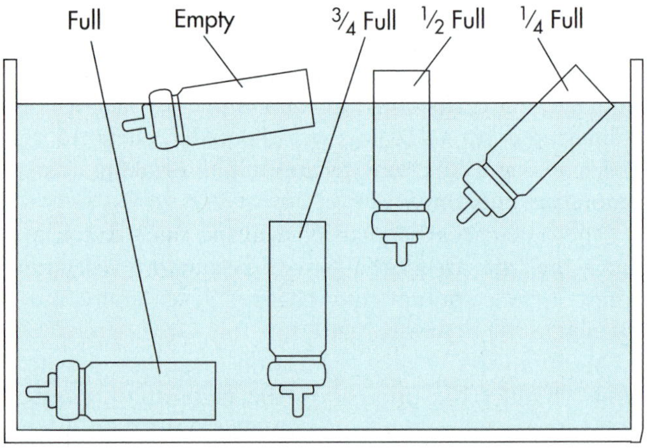

Fig. 22-10 Determining the amount of medication in the MDI. The amount of medication remaining in a metered-dose inhaler is assessed by dropping the canister into a bowl of water. The client should obtain a refill when the inhaler rises to the surface of the water and begins to tip over. (From Beare P, Myers J: *Principles and practice of adult health nursing,* ed 2, St Louis, 1994, Mosby.)

RESTRICTIVE PULMONARY DISEASE

Restrictive lung diseases result in loss of functioning alveoli, loss of lung volume and decreased chest wall compliance. Restrictive lung disease can be the result of extrapulmonary factors such as excessive weight and muscle mass, a chest splint, or restrictive dressing. Mechanisms of restrictive lung disease include pleural-based diseases, impaired lung expansion, impaired neuromuscular contraction, and thoracic deformities (Dettenmeier, 1992).

Bronchogenic Carcinoma

Lung cancer is the leading cause of cancer deaths in men, most often occurring at age 60 or 70. Tobacco smoking remains the leading cause of lung cancer with minor contributions by exposure to pollution and occupational risks. The increase in smoking by women has raised their death rate from lung cancer so that now it exceeds that of breast cancer (Morris, 1990).

The leading cell types of lung cancer include small or oat-cell carcinoma, nonsmall cell carcinoma, squamous cell, adenocarcinoma, alveolar-cell and large-cell carcinoma (Morris, 1990; Saltzman, 1992). The most common and lethal type of lung cancer is small or oat-cell carcinoma with a life expectancy of usually less than a year. Small-cell lung cancer is an aggressive cancer with metastasis to the central nervous system (CNS), bones, and liver.

MEDICAL MANAGEMENT

Bronchogenic Carcinoma

Diagnostic tests and procedures

Diagnosis is based on the clinical history and chest radiography. Sputum cytology is used to determine the cell type. The fiberoptic bronchoscope is used to obtain tissue confirmation of the diagnosis. Surgical diagnosis includes cervical mediastinoscopy, mediastinotomy, and thoracotomy (Matzdorff, Green, 1992). Pulmonary function testing is used to determine impairment in ventilation and help predict functionality if surgery is a consideration.

Treatment

Small-cell carcinoma is treated with chemotherapeutic regimens and radiation therapy. The older client may not be able to tolerate this medical regimen, especially if there is other organ involvement. Nonsmall-cell cancers are usually treated with surgical resection, followed with radiation and chemotherapy. If the older client has significant lung disease, resection of the lung or segmental resection may not be possible. The decision to perform a surgical resection is dependent on the amount of functional lung tissue that remains after the surgery.

Careful management of pain, symptoms of nausea and vomiting, and chemotherapy-related side effects are important in maintaining a level of comfort for the client and family.

Prognosis

Survival rates for clients with lung cancer is 10% at 5 years. Mortality for the older client undergoing surgical resection of the lung tumor is 10% to 14% (Burke, Walsh, 1992).

Clinical presentation of lung cancer can easily be mistaken for other chronic lung diseases such as chronic bronchitis. Many times there are no symptoms, or the symptoms are ignored or attributed to smoking or a preexisting lung disease. Common early signs include cough, chest pain, and hemoptysis (see Medical Management box, below).

NURSING MANAGEMENT

✤ ASSESSMENT

Assessment begins with a complete health history to identify risk factors for lung cancer. Common risk factors include smoking history, exposure to chemical pollutants, exposure to secondhand smoke and a familial history of lung cancer.

✤ DIAGNOSIS

Nursing diagnoses for bronchogenic carcinoma include, but are not limited to, (1) ineffective breathing pattern, (2) ineffective individual coping, (3) impaired gas exchange, (4) inability to sustain spontaneous ventilation, and (5) pain.

✤ PLANNING

Planning includes developing interventions and expected outcomes for the client that focus on improving gas exchange, promoting airway clearance and comfort. Expected outcomes include, but are not limited to, the following:

1. Client will be able to maintain arterial blood gas values at baseline.
2. Client will be able to sustain spontaneous respiration.
3. Client and family will be able to verbalize their feelings related to the diagnosis of bronchogenic carcinoma.
4. Client will be pain controlled.
5. Client will experience a decrease in the number of episodes of breathlessness.
6. Client will have lungs clear to auscultation.
7. Client will have a stable weight.
8. Client will report a decrease in feeling fatigued.
9. Client will have a realistic level of activity.

✤ INTERVENTION

Nursing care of the older client with bronchogenic carcinoma includes relief of pain, emotional support, and counseling and discussion of options and alternatives. The older client may have few friends and family for support, if losses through death have been many. The nurse needs to be sensitive to the values of the older client and how they view the diagnosis affecting their quality of life. Many older clients may be more concerned about immediate survival and quality of life issues than the 5-year postoperative survival (Morris, 1990).

✣ EVALUATION

Evaluation is based on the client's achievement of the expected outcomes.

Tuberculosis

Tuberculosis (TB) is caused by the *Mycobacterium tuberculosis* organism. It is most often seen in populations living in close quarters and those with little or no health care or preventive care. It is the number one fatal communicable disease in the United States (Morris, 1990).

MEDICAL MANAGEMENT

TB

Diagnostic tests and procedures

Diagnosis is based on chest X-ray, revealing a destructive process in the upper lobes and posterior segments. Sputum culture for AFB confirmed by culture is the definitive diagnosis. Any older client with a history of chronic cough or repeated bouts of pneumonitis should have a sputum for AFB (Lueckenotte, 1994).

Tuberculin skin testing in the older client is an unreliable indicator of tuberculosis. Older clients often display a false-negative skin test as a result of reduced immune system activity (Burke, Walsh, 1992; Morris, 1990). If skin testing is used, it is recommended that the standard 5-TU Mantoux technique test be given and then repeated to create a booster effect. The second test may be conducted with the 5-TU or the second strength 250-TU test (Morris, 1990).

Treatment

Treatment includes a combination of bactericidal drugs: 300 mg per day of Isoniazid, 600 mg per day Rifampin, and 1,500 mg per day Pyrazinamide for 2 months, then Isoniazid and Rifampin at the same daily dosage for 6 additional months. Monitoring of liver function on a monthly basis is recommended. Isoniazid can lead to toxic hepatitis and peripheral neuropathy, especially in the malnourished or diabetic older adult.

Prognosis

The prognosis for the older client with TB is good if the client follows the medical regimen and maintains good nutrition. The greater risk is the side effects of Isoniazid. These include hepatotoxicity, psychotic reactions, coordination difficulties, muscle twitching, memory impairment, loss of self control, dizziness, stupor, tinnitus, peripheral neuritis, agranulocytosis, aplastic anemia, hemolytic anemia, epigastric distress, dry mouth, nausea, vomiting, urinary retention, metabolic acidosis, and hyperglycemia (Karb et al, 1989).

TB is transmitted by inhalation of infected droplets aerosolized into the air from the cough or sneeze of an infected person (Kovach, Shore, 1991). TB is divided into primary and active TB. Primary TB occurs with the inhalation of the infected droplets and deposits into the upper lobes of the lung, since the organism is aerobic and the greatest ventilation is there. The body's immune system responds to the local inflammation by walling off the bacteria.

Active TB presents with symptoms. Inflammation of the airway leads to development of a lesion and necrosis of the tissue (Kovach, Shore, 1991). TB has the ability to remain inactive in the body for decades. In the older client, the presence of TB may be a reactivation of a dormat organism that has been present in the individual for some time. The older client's immune system changes increase the risk for developing reactivation of TB (see Chapter 14).

Signs and symptoms include sputum positive for acid-fast bacilli (AFB), fatigue, weight loss, weakness, night sweats, low-grade fever, and purulent sputum. If the disease has progressed the client may have hemoptysis, lung consolidation, crackles and wheezes on auscultation, upper-lobe patchy infiltrates, and cavitation on chest radiography. The older client may not present with all the classic symptoms and may only complain of weight loss, anorexia, and fever (see Medical Management box, at left).

NURSING MANAGEMENT

✣ ASSESSMENT

Assessment begins with a thorough health history. Since signs of TB are not classical in the older adult, suspect TB when the older client complains of weight loss and chronic cough.

✣ DIAGNOSIS

Nursing diagnoses for the older client with TB include, but are not limited to, (1) knowledge deficit (specify), (2) altered health maintenance, (3) infection or potential for infection (4) noncompliance related to prolonged therapy, and (5) social isolation.

✣ PLANNING

Planning for the older client with TB includes the client and family. If the client is a resident in a nursing home or extended care facility, the medical and nursing directors need to be included in planning. Expected outcomes for the client include, but are not limited to, the following:

1. Client will be able to demonstrate cough techniques.

2. Client/family will be able to verbalize the medication regimen.
3. Client/family will be able to verbalize the side effects of the antituberculosis medications.
4. Client will be able to verbalize the need for continued medication.
5. Client/family will be able to state how TB is transmitted.

✣ INTERVENTION

Nursing measures for the client with TB include education about TB and how it is transmitted. The client and family should be educated about the measures necessary to prevent further TB transmission, the importance of continued medication administration and good nutrition (Table 22-3).

✣ EVALUATION

Evaluation of the older client with TB is assessment of compliance with their medication regimen and public health measures. Evaluation includes monitoring of hepatic and renal function as well as repeated sputum cultures for AFB.

BRONCHOPULMONARY INFECTION

Influenza

Older clients are more prone to developing complications from the influenza virus, especially if they have underlying chronic illness. The normal aging process decreases the ability to clear secretions and to protect the

TABLE 22-3

Antituberculosis Medications

Medication	Dosage	Adverse reactions	Nursing considerations
Ethambutol hydrochloride (Etibi, Myambutol)	**Initial treatment:** PO-15 mg/kg daily **Retreatment:** PO-25 mg/kg daily × 60 days; decrease to 15 mg/kg daily	Reversible optic neuritis	Should not be used alone; second antitubercular drug is also given Monitor for decreased vision during drug therapy, weight, and serum uric acid levels Monitor hepatic, renal, and hemolytic parameters
Isoniazid (INH)	**Primary therapy:** PO-5 mg/kg daily up to 300 mg/day IM-same as PO	Anemia, hepatitis, hypersensitivity, peripheral neuritis, seizures, and systemic lupus erythematosus	Therapy lasts for 9 to 12 months and is used in conjunction with other antituberculosis medication Instruct the client to avoid alcohol
Rifampin (Rifaden, Rofact)	PO-600 mg daily	Decreased effectiveness of oral contraceptives, hemolysis, hepatic toxicity, increased metabolism of hepatically excreted drugs, induction of methadone withdrawal, renal failure, and thrombocytopenia	Give 1 hour before or 2 hours after meals Monitor hepatic function. (Urine may become red-orange colored) Instruct client to avoid alcoholic beverages Usually used with one other drug
Streptomycin sulfate	**Normal renal function:** Intramuscular (IM)-1 gm (or 15 mg/kg) daily for up to 3 weeks then 1 gm 2 to 3 times per week	Eighth cranial nerve damage, paresthesia, renal toxicity (rare), tinnitus, and vertigo	Given for 2 to 3 months, through deep IM injection Use upper outer quadrant of the buttocks Monitor renal function Use with at least one other antituberculosis drug
Pyrazinamide (PZA)	20 to 35 mg/kg daily up to 3 gm per day	Anorexia, arthralgia, gout (rare), hepatitis, hyperuricemia, nausea, renal failure (rare), and vomiting.	Monitor platelet count and complete blood cell count Have client take medication with meals or a snack to reduce gastric irritation Instruct client to report any problems with urination Monitor liver function tests Instruct client regarding signs of thrombocytopenia, such as unexplained bleeding or bruising, appearance of petechiae, and nosebleeds

MEDICAL MANAGEMENT

Influenza

Diagnostic tests and procedures

Diagnosis includes history of fever, chills, anorexia, and general malaise, which may be blunted or atypical in the older adult.

Treatment

Treatment includes rest, fluid, hydration, and careful monitoring for progression to a more serious illness. Antibiotics are often used to prevent a secondary bacterial infection, especially in older clients with underlying respiratory and cardiac disease.

Prognosis

Of influenza-related deaths, 80% to 90% occur in the older client.

airway. Older clients account for 80% to 90% of all influenza-related deaths (Ward, 1992).

Recognizing infection in the older client is difficult. The signs associated with infection may be subdued or absent (Schoemick et al, 1991). Changes in mental status, exacerbation of underlying chronic conditions, and subnormal temperature may signal an infection in the older client. Subnormal temperature accompanied by hypotension; rapid pulse; and cool, clammy skin are signs of sepsis in the older client (Schoemick et al, 1991) (see Medical Management box above).

Pneumonia

Pneumonia is an inflammation of the lung parenchyma, usually associated with filling of the alveoli with fluid (Kersten, 1989). Pneumonia can be viral, bacterial, or caused by aspiration, which is often found in the older adult. Pneumonia is a particularly serious illness in the older client, often resulting in death. The serious nature of the illness is related to the normal age-related deterioration of the immune system, underlying chronic illnesses, weakened cough reflex, and decreased mobility (Burke, Walsh, 1992). The diagnosis of pneumonia may be missed because symptoms are obscured by coexisting disease or masked by use of corticosteroids or antiinflammatory drugs (Gail, Lenfant, 1992) The client often requires hospitalization and may require admission to the intensive care unit (ICU) with subsequent intubation and mechanical ventilation. The incidence of pneumonia in older clients in chronic care institutions is two to three times higher than among the older client in the community (Gail, Lenfant, 1992). This is most likely a result of the fact that at any one time, almost 2% of the residents have a lower respiratory tract infection (Gail, Lenfant, 1992).

Bacterial Pneumonia

Older clients do not always have the classic symptoms of pneumonia seen in younger adults. Symptoms include dehydration, confusion, and increased respiratory rate greater than 26 breaths per minute (Brown, 1993). Fever and cough may be reduced or absent in the older client. Chest x-ray may show incomplete consolidation of the lung and multiple lobe pneumonia is common (Gail, Lenfant, 1992). Some older clients present dramatically, resembling septic shock or adult respiratory distress syndrome (ARDS) (Gleckman, 1992).

Streptococcus pneumoniae is the leading cause of community acquired pneumonia in the older client, accounting for approximately 25% of the cases (Brown, 1993; Gleckman, 1992). Five percent to 15% of the cases are caused by *Haemophilus influenzae, Moraxella (Branhamella) catarrhalis,* and *Legionella pneumophila.*

Nosocomial Pneumonia

Nosocomial pneumonia is most often caused by *Staphylococcus aureus, Klebsiella pneumoniae, Pseudomonas aeruginosa,* and *Escherichia coli.* Older clients have a three-fold higher incidence of developing nosocomial pneumonia than younger clients (Gail, Lenfant, 1992). Again, this is because of the normal age-related decline in the immune system and the coexisting underlying diseases.

Viral Pneumonia

Viral pneumonia in the older client is most often associated with a history of influenza A virus. The older client is especially susceptible to secondary bacterial infections such as *S. aureus* and *H. influenza.*

Aspiration Pneumonia

Aspiration pneumonia is commonly associated with clinical situations such as stupor, coma, cardiopulmonary resuscitation, alcohol or drug intoxication, neurological illnesses, nasogastric feeding tubes, and general anesthesia. Aspiration of gastric contents into the airway may result in obstruction, chemical pneumonitis, or infection (Morris, 1990). The older client is especially prone to aspiration as a result of the decreased cough and gag reflexes. In addition, positioning, feeding and the use of a feeding tube place the older client at increased risk for aspiration pneumonia. In the presence of narcotic medications, alcohol, and sedatives, the risk of aspiration is increased (see Medical Management box, p. 591).

MEDICAL MANAGEMENT

Pneumonia

Diagnostic tests and procedures

The diagnosis of pneumonia is made based on a history of colds and influenza and clinical presentation. Laboratory sampling includes total white blood cell count, blood cultures, and Gram stain and culture of sputum (Gleckman, 1992). Of older clients, 20% to 25% fail to demonstrate a leukocytosis and about one third are unable to produce a sputum sample. The chest PA and lateral radiograph is obtained to identify infiltrates and assess for complications such as effusions or lung abscess. If the client is dehydrated, infiltrates may not be evident even if they are present.

Treatment

Treatment consists of administration of the appropriate antibiotics, hydration, good nutrition and rest. Treatment with antibiotics can range from 1 to 3 weeks depending on the causative organism. There are no established guidelines for admission of the older client to the hospital. Recommendations for admission to the hospital include unstable vital signs, major concommitant illness, evidence of extrapulmonary involvement, leukopenia, hypoxemia, and $Pao_2 < 60$ mm Hg (Brown, 1993; Gleckman, 1992).

Prognosis

Pneumonia remains the most common cause of death in the older client because of an altered immune response as a result of aging, underlying chronic disease, and a diminished cough reflex.

NURSING MANAGEMENT

ASSESSMENT

Assessment begins with the older clients' history of fever, chills, and sputum color changes. Complete an assessment of the respiratory system, including a complete health history (see Box 22-8, p. 597).

DIAGNOSIS

The most often used nursing diagnoses for the older client with bronchopulmonary infection include, but are not limited to, (1) ineffective airway clearance, and (2) impaired gas exchange.

PLANNING

Expected outcomes for the older client with a bronchopulmonary infection include, but are not limited to, the following:

1. Client will maintain a patent airway.
2. Client will maintain an $Pao_2 > 55$ mm Hg.
3. Client will have a decrease in the complaints of fatigue.
4. Client will have lungs clear on auscultation.
5. Client will be able to effectively clear secretions.
6. Client will be able to sleep through the night without episodes of breathlessness.
7. Impaired mental status will be reduced or absent.

INTERVENTION

Nursing management of the older client with influenza or pneumonia includes maintenance of hydration, promotion of effective airway clearance, and proper positioning. Because of the ventilation perfusion imbalance in the lung, it is important to position the client with the "good lung down." This promotes drainage of secretions from the lung with the pneumonia and increases the perfusion of the good lung, resulting in improved oxygenation. The nursing challenge may be to keep the older client positioned on the appropriate side.

For both pneumonia and influenza, the key is early vaccination. It is recommended that influenza shots be obtained yearly between the middle of September and the end of October. To develop immunity requires about 6 weeks. Therefore the older client is at the peak of immunity during the influenza season, the end of November and December. The pneumococcal vaccine is recommended every 5 to 10 years after vaccination, because immunogenicity studies have shown declining antibody levels to certain pneumococcal vaccine antigens. The original pneumococcal vaccine, available in 1977, was a 14-valent vaccine. In 1983 a 23-valent vaccine replaced the original vaccine, accounting for 88% of the pneumococcal disease in the United States. It has been recommended that individuals vaccinated before 1983 need to be revaccinated with the 23-valent pneumococcal vaccine (Dettenmeier, 1992; USDHHS, 1991).

Nursing care to prevent aspiration focuses on careful assessment of residual volumes of feedings and proper positioning of the older client during and after eating.

EVALUATION

Evaluation includes achievement of the expected outcomes, return of sputum to preinfection color and consistency, and return to baseline respiratory status.

Other Respiratory Diseases

Pulmonary Edema and Noncardiogenic Pulmonary Edema

Pulmonary edema is an abnormal increase in the amount of extravascular fluid in the lungs and may be cardiogenic or noncardiogenic in origin (Kersten, 1989). The most common form of pulmonary edema is a result of left ventricular failure.

Cardiogenic pulmonary edema is the most common form of pulmonary edema caused by increased capillary hydrostatic pressure resulting from MI, mitral stenosis, decreased myocardial contractility, left ventricular failure, or fluid overload (Dettenmeier, 1992). Other factors that may predispose the client to pulmonary edema include congestive heart failure (CHF), infusion of excessive volumes of intravenous (IV) fluids, or an overly rapid infusion of IV fluids, impaired pulmonary lymphatic drainage from Hodgkin's disease or obliterative lymphangitis after radiation, inhalation of irritating gases, mitral stenosis, left atrial myxoma, pneumonia, and pulmonary veno-occlusive disease. A rise in the pulmonary capillary pressure occurs as a result of elevated left ventricular end-diastolic filling pressure, elevated left atrial pressure, and an elevated pulmonary venous pressure (Kersten, 1989).

Clinical presentation of acute cardiogenic pulmonary edema includes acute shortness of breath; orthopnea; frothy, blood-tinged sputum; cyanosis; diaphoresis; and tachycardia. Auscultation of the lungs reveals crackles in the bases, fremitus, and dullness to percussion (see Medical Management box below, left).

Noncardiogenic pulmonary edema is caused by a variety of noncardiac causes. Examples of noncardiogenic pulmonary edema include adult respiratory distress syndrome (ARDS), reexpansion pulmonary edema, and neurogenic pulmonary edema.

Clinical presentation of noncardiogenic pulmonary edema includes refractory hypoxemia, crackles on auscultation, hypotension, cyanosis, tachypnea, hyperventilation, and increased tracheobronchial secretions (see Medical Management box below, right).

MEDICAL MANAGEMENT

Pulmonary Edema

Diagnostic tests and procedures

Diagnosis is based on the clinical presentation. Arterial blood gas measurements are drawn to determine the arterial P_{O_2} level, arterial P_{O_2} saturation and the pH. Hemodynamic measurements reveal a decreased cardiac output, and increased pulmonary artery pressure and right heart pressure in biventricular failure (Dettenmaier, 1992). Because the older client has difficulty maintaining normal hemoglobin levels, it is important to take blood samples judiciously.

Treatment

Treatment includes improvement of gas exchange with supplemental oxygen, improvement of myocardial function by reduction of preload and afterload, and correction of the underlying process if possible. If the pulmonary edema is extensive, the older client may require transfer to the intensive care unit, initiation of mechanical ventilation and insertion of a pulmonary artery catheter.

Prognosis

The prognosis is good when symptoms are reversed easily and cardiac complications are controlled.

NURSING MANAGEMENT

✣ ASSESSMENT

Determine through the health history if the client has risk factors for the development of pulmonary edema. Assessment begins with evaluation of the respiratory and cardiac status. Observe the older client for the signs and symptoms of pulmonary edema.

✣ DIAGNOSIS

Nursing diagnoses for the older client with pulmonary edema include, but are not limited to, (1) ineffective breathing pattern, (2) impaired gas exchange, (3) inef-

MEDICAL MANAGEMENT

Noncardiogenic Pulmonary Edema (ARDS)

Diagnostic tests and procedures

The most commonly used test is the arterial blood gas to determine the degree of hypoxia. Other tests include the chest x-ray, complete blood count (CBC), and hemodynamic measurements. The older client may need intubation and mechanical ventilation. In addition, the placement of an arterial line and pulmonary artery catheter may be indicated to monitor oxygenation and cardiopulmonary hemodynamics.

Treatment

Treatment consists of supplemental oxygen therapy, support of ventilation, and maintenance of hemodynamics. Neuromuscular blocking agents, sedatives, and narcotics may be used to reduce anxiety, decrease the work of breathing, decrease O_2 consumption and increase O_2 delivery. Positive end expiratory pressure (PEEP) may be added to mechanical ventilation to improve oxygenation.

The pulmonary artery catheter is used to monitor the fluid volume status. Fluids and vasopressors may be indicated to maintain an adequate blood pressure. If a bacterial infection is evident, antibiotic therapy can be added. Corticosteroids are reserved for ARDS caused by a chemical injury or fatty emboli.

fective airway clearance, (4) decreased cardiac output, (5) fluid volume excess, (6) inability to sustain spontaneous ventilation, and (7) risk for infection.

✣ PLANNING

Planning includes developing interventions and expected outcomes for the older client. Expected outcomes include, but are not limited to, the following:

1. Client will maintain arterial blood gas values within normal limits.
2. Client will be able to maintain oxygenation within normal values.
3. Client will have a cardiac output within normal values.
4. Client will be able to verbalize feelings related to the illness.
5. Client will maintain a patent airway.
6. Client will maintain a balanced intake and output.
7. Client will have an alternative method of communication if on mechanical ventilation.
8. Client will maintain skin integrity.

✣ INTERVENTION

Interventions for pulmonary edema include positioning the client to improve ventilation by elevating the head of the bed 30 degrees. If the client is producing large amounts of frothy sputum, turn on the side to facilitate drainage. Provide reassurance for the client and family or significant other. If necessary, prepare for intubation and mechanical ventilation. This can be particularly frightening for the older client. Provide frequent suctioning to facilitate removal of secretions.

✣ EVALUATION

Evaluation is based on achievement of expected outcomes and reversal of the signs and symptoms.

NURSING MANAGEMENT

✣ ASSESSMENT

Assessment begins by identifying the older client at risk for development of noncardiogenic pulmonary edema. Predisposing factors include aspiration of gastric contents, pneumonia, thoracic injury, pulmonary contusion, smoke inhalation, multiple blood transfusions, uremia, cardiopulmonary bypass surgery, fracture of long bones, and sepsis.

✣ DIAGNOSIS

The nursing diagnoses for the client with ARDS include, but are not limited to, (1) impaired gas exchange, (2) ineffective airway clearance, (3) activity intolerance, (4) knowledge deficit (specify), and (5) inability to sustain spontaneous ventilation.

✣ PLANNING

Planning includes developing interventions and expected outcomes for the client. Expected outcomes include, but are not limited to, the following:

1. Client will be able to maintain arterial blood gases within normal values.
2. Client will maintain a patent airway.
3. Client will be able to sustain spontaneous ventilation without mechanical ventilation.
4. Client and family will be able to verbalize their feelings related to the illness.
5. Client will have stable hemodynamics.
6. Client will have balanced intake and output.
7. Client will maintain skin integrity.
8. Client will have an alternative method of communication if on mechanical ventilation.

An integral part of planning nursing care for the older client requiring intensive care is a discussion about the client's wishes with regard to high technology medical care. The client and family are asked if they have any advance medical directives (AMDs) and/or durable powers of attorney if the older client becomes unable to speak. If the client is unaware of AMDs and expresses an interest, a family conference including the physician, nurse, social worker, and pastoral caregiver is planned to help older clients express their wishes. If the older client has an AMD and/or a durable power of attorney, a copy should be placed in the medical record and reviewed with the older client, family, physicians, and other caregivers. It is important to understand and to respect the wishes of the older client and the family before initiation of high technology medical care. Swinburne et al. (1993) report that older adults requiring mechanical ventilation for short periods have as good a survival as younger clients (see Research box, p. 594).

✣ INTERVENTION

Interventions include supplemental oxygen, mechanical ventilation, and nursing measures to promote oxygen balance. Nursing care is planned to provide adequate rest periods. Monitoring of the PaO_2 saturation helps the nurse determine which activities deplete the O_2 saturation. Interventions such as suctioning, turning, and positioning have been well-documented as increasing O_2 consumption and decreasing arterial and mixed venous O_2 levels. The nurse plans care to decrease the number of interventions performed at one time. This helps minimize consumption and decrease the stress on the client.

It is very important to provide an alternative means of communication for the older client on mechanical venti-

RESEARCH

Swinburne AJ et al: Respiratory failure in the elderly, analysis of outcomes after treatment with mechanical ventilation, *Arch Intern Med* 153(14):1657-1662, 1993.

Sample, setting

1,860 individuals who were treated with mechanical ventilation for greater than 3 hours between 1974 and 1985; medical records were retrospectively reviewed; 282 clients aged greater than or equal to 80 years were compared with 1,578 clients less than 80 years of age.

Methodology

Clients were assigned to one of nine diagnostic groups and 10 premorbid chronic illnesses were recorded. Survival to discharge was determined for all clients. Survival after discharge was determined for clients greater than 80 years old.

Findings

Of the clients, 15% treated with mechanical ventilation were ≥ 80 years old. 30.9% of clients survived to discharge while 44% of clients < 80 years old survived. Clients ≥ 80 years old with preexisting renal disease, liver disease, chronic gastrointestinal disease with malnutrition, cancer or systemic illness had a 7% survival compared with 29% for younger clients. Older adults requiring greater than 15 days of mechanical ventilation had a 9% survival compared with 36% for younger clients.

Implications

The majority of older adults requiring short-term mechanical ventilation have nearly as good a survival as younger clients. A subgroup of clients ≥ 80 years old can be identified, whose chance of survival from respiratory failure is so poor that withholding or withdrawing treatment with mechanical ventilation may be appropriate.

lation. If the client has a hearing aide, it may be difficult for them to hear over the noise of the technology in the ICU setting.

The older client in the ICU often needs to be reoriented to time. The ICU does not acknowledge day and night. The older client is particularly sensitive to the continuous stimuli in the unit in the form of sounds, sights, smells, and touch and may become confused and combative. The nurse should try to establish a regular nighttime routine with the older client such as vital signs, assessment, oral care, and toileting. The lighting should then be reduced to a level as low as possible to promote rest and sleep while allowing for safe care. This helps the older client establish a routine or pattern they can count on as time to sleep.

EVALUATION

Evaluation is based on improvement in the clinical picture. This includes improving $Pa{O_2}$ and $Pa{CO_2}$ to baseline, stable hemodynamics (e.g., cardiac output, pulmonary artery pressure [PA], and pulmonary artery wedge pressure [PAWP]), blood pressure, heart rate, respiratory pattern, ability to sustain spontaneous ventilation, and achievement of expected outcomes.

Pulmonary Emboli

A pulmonary emboli, obstruction of the pulmonary artery bed by a thrombosis, is most often the result of a deep vein thrombosis in the older client. The thrombosis breaks loose, becoming an embolus, and travels to the lungs through the venous system, where it is trapped in a small vessel of the pulmonary circulation. If a large embolus occludes the lung, pulmonary infarction occurs causing necrosis of the lung tissue.

The embolus, composed of platelets, red blood cells, and white blood cells, releases vasoactive substances that cause bronchial constriction, ventilation perfusion mismatch, and hypoxia. The amount of dead space, ventilation in excess of perfusion, is increased leading to an increase in intrapulmonary shunt and hypoxia.

Risk factors for the development of pulmonary emboli include age greater than 40 years, immobility, history of vascular disease, COPD, heart disease, DM, and previous pulmonary emboli. Thromboembolism is more common in the older client who is naturally hypercoagulable (Mahler, 1993).

Clinical presentation includes coughing, dyspnea at rest, hypotension, hypoxia, hemoptysis, tachycardia, anginal or pleuritic chest pain, decreased $Pa{O_2}$, and S_3 gallop (see Medical Management box, p. 595).

NURSING MANAGEMENT

ASSESSMENT

Assessment begins with identification of risk factors for the development of pulmonary emboli. In the older adult, dehydration and immobility are the leading causes. If the older client has a history of recent fracture of a long bone, suspect a fat emboli. Clinical signs and symptoms include sudden dyspnea, chest pain, restlessness, weak, rapid pulse, tachypnea, and tachycardia.

DIAGNOSIS

Diagnoses for the older client with pulmonary emboli include, but are not limited to, (1) impaired gas exchange, (2) ineffective breathing pattern, (3) altered cardiopulmonary tissue perfusion, (4) risk for injury, and (5) inability to sustain spontaneous ventilation.

MEDICAL MANAGEMENT

Pulmonary Emboli

Diagnostic tests and procedures

Diagnosis is based on a ventilation-perfusion lung scan or pulmonary angiography. Arterial blood gases may reveal hypoxemia with an Pao_2 between 60 to 80 mm Hg (Mahler, 1993). An electrocardiogram (ECG) may show a right axis deviation, right bundle branch block, tall peaked P-waves, depressed ST segment, and supraventricular tachycardia if the emboli is extensive. Massive pulmonary emboli may result in electromechanical dissociation (EMD).

The chest x-ray may reveal an elevated hemidiaphragm, atelectasis and/or consolidation and the presence of a pleural effusion (Mahler, 1993).

Treatment

Heparin is the initial treatment of pulmonary emboli. Heparin is administered subcutaneously or intravenously to achieve a PT of 1.5 to 2.5 times control (Mahler, 1993). Thrombolytic therapy such as streptokinase, urokinase, or recombinant tissue plasminogen activator (TPA) is used in clients with extensive pulmonary emboli exhibiting shock to lyse the embolus. Clients with recurrent pulmonary emboli are candidates for Greenfield vena cava filters.

Prognosis

Prognosis for pulmonary emboli is guarded. Many times the diagnosis is made on postmortem examination.

✣ PLANNING

Planning includes developing interventions and expected outcomes for the client. Expected outcomes include, but are not limited to, the following:

1. Client will maintain arterial blood gases values within normal limits.
2. Client will be pain controlled.
3. Client will be able to sustain spontaneous ventilation without mechanical ventilation.
4. Client will maintain adequate oxygenation.
5. Client will have adequate pain control.

✣ INTERVENTION

Maintaining effective oxygenation and ventilation are paramount. Oxygen therapy is administered to improve oxygenation and decrease breathlessness. Heparin therapy is initiated to prevent formation of future clots. The older client needs reassurance and careful assessment and monitoring of vital signs. Sedation is used to relieve pain and anxiety and to reduce oxygen consumption. If the older client is dehydrated or hypotensive, IV fluids are administered. Vasopressors may be used if hypotension cannot be reversed with fluids.

The client needs to be monitored for complications of anticoagulant therapy. Observe the urine for color changes and check the stool for occult blood. Monitor the older client for complications of anticoagulant therapy: bruising, gastric bleeding, hemorrhage, and cerebral vascular accident.

Since immobility is a risk factor for the development of pulmonary emboli, it is important to get the older client mobile as soon as medically possible. Use antiembolic stockings and passive and active range-of-motion exercises during the acute phase. Encourage the older client to begin to move about as soon as medically feasible.

Education for the older client focuses on teaching the client and family the signs and symptoms of pulmonary emboli, the signs of anticoagulant therapy complications and the importance of exercise and mobility. An electric razor is recommended for male clients.

✣ EVALUATION

Evaluation is based on achievement of the expected outcomes.

RESPIRATORY ASSESSMENT

Health History

The health history begins with a series of questions directed to risk factors for respiratory illness. Table 22-4 lists questions used in the assessment of the respiratory system. Additional information includes a history of chest x-ray, tuberculosis testing, influenza vaccine, and Pneumovax (Kovach, Shore, 1991) (Box 22-8) (Table 22-4).

Lueckenotte (1994) recommends the following guidelines for physical examination of the older client:

- Be alert to the older client's energy level.
- Respect the client's modesty.
- Sequence the examination to keep position changes to a minimum.
- Develop an efficient sequence for examination that minimizes both nurse and client movement.
- Ensure comfort for the client.
- Explain each step in simple, clear terms.
- Share the findings with the client to reassure when possible.
- Encourage the client to ask questions.
- Project warmth, sincerity and interest in the client.
- Develop a standard format on which to note selected findings.

Physical Examination

When describing findings associated with the respiratory system, chest landmarks are used (Fig. 22-11). These

TABLE 22-4

Pulmonary History

Interview topics	Interview questions
Activity level	How would you desribe your activity level? Active? Sedentary? Are you able to do the activities you would like? Shopping? Walking? Housework? How far can you walk? Why do you stop? Has your activity changed recently? Can you climb stairs?
Breathlessness	Are you aware of your breathing? Has your breathing changed? When? How often do you have shortness of breath? Does a change in position relieve or increase the shortness of breath? Does your breathlessness interfere with things you want to do?
Cough	Do you cough frequently? Does anything seem to trigger the coughing? How would you describe your cough? Do you produce much sputum? How much? How often? What color? What consistency? What makes your cough better?
Smoking	Have you ever smoked? What do/did you smoke? How old were you when you started? Stopped? How many packs per day and how many years smoked?
Respiratory illness	Have you ever been told you have lung disease? What? When? Does your family have a history of tuberculosis, malignancy, emphysema, asthma, or chronic bronchitis? Have you ever had pneumonia? When? Have you ever taken steroids for your respiratory illness? What medications do you take?
Sleep patterns	How many hours do you sleep at night? Do you awaken frequently at night? Do you sleep during the day? Do you snore? How many pillows do you use at night? Do you wake up short of breath?
Oxygen therapy	Do you use oxygen at home? When? How much? How long have you been using oxygen? What type of system do you use?
Hospitalizations	When was your most recent hospitalization for respiratory illness? How many times were you admitted in the past year? Did you undergo intubation or mechanical ventilation? If so, what was the date and length of time?
Environmental factors	Have you ever been exposed to hazardous chemicals? What was the nature of your work? Are there environmental hazards? Possible allergens? Heating/air conditioning? Do you live in an urban or rural area?

From Weilitz PB: *Pocket guide to respiratory care,* St. Louis, 1991, Mosby.

landmarks help to locate and describe findings observed, palpated, or asucultated on the thorax.

Inspection

Inspection begins with overall evaluation of the older client's breathing pattern, body position, use of accessory muscles of respiration, chest wall configuration, and respiratory pattern. The anteroposterior diameter of the older client is increased and rounded, resembling the early stages of COPD (Kuhn, McGovern, 1992).

The respiratory pattern is observed for rate, depth, and inspiratory and expiratory cycles, noting the length of time in each phase (Table 22-5). Note whether the client is using pursed-lip breathing.

Observe the movement of the chest wall for symmetry of chest expansion. During inspiration, the chest wall should increase in lateral width and anteroposterior diameter. This may be a little more difficult in the older client with altered chest configuration. Unequal chest wall expansion suggests underventilation to the affected side.

BOX 22-8

Assessment of the Respiratory System

Subjective data
- Activity level
- Breathlessness
- Cough
- Smoking
- Respiratory illness
- Sleep patterns
- Oxygen therapy
- Hospitalizations
- Environmental factors

Objective data
- **Inspect:** Chest shape and symmetry; skin characteristics; respiratory rate and pattern; body position; use of accessory muscles of respiration; color, temperature, and appearance of extremities; and sputum color, consistency, amount and odor
- **Palpate:** Tracheal alignment, general chest wall characteristics, thoracic, and tactile fremitus
- **Percuss:** Posterior, lateral, and anterior chest wall; and diaphragmatic excursion
- **Auscultate:** Posterior, lateral, and anterior chest wall

Note the muscles of respiration the older client is using to breath. The sternocleidomastoid, trapezius, pectoral, and scalene muscles are less efficient than the diaphragm. These muscles are used when breathing becomes labored.

Observe the older client's extremities for color, temperature, and clubbing of the fingers (see Cultural Awareness box on p. 599). Color is the most unreliable indicator of adequate tissue oxygenation. The older client may also have diminished circulation to the periphery, further diminishing the reliability of color as an indicator of tissue oxygenation. The older client who continues to smoke has decreased peripheral vascular circulation as a result of the inhaled nicotine and its vasoconstrictive properties. Clubbing of the fingers is found in clients with chronic hypoxia, COPD, cystic fibrosis, and congenital heart disease (Fig. 22-12).

If the older client is able to produce sputum, inspect the sputum for color, consistency, amount, and odor.

Palpation

Palpation is used to assess any abnormalities suggested by the history or noted on inspection. The skin is palpated for temperature and tissue turgor, a measure of hydration (see Chapter 28).

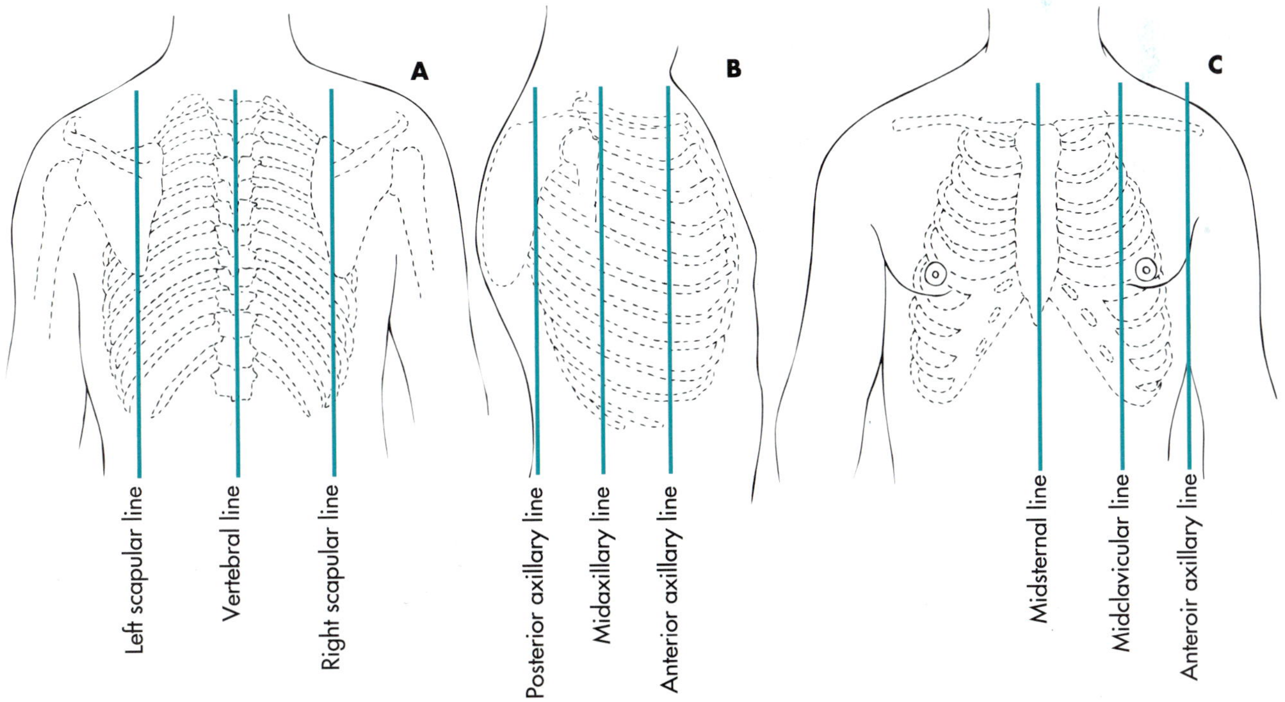

Fig. 22-11 **A** to **C** Anatomical chest wall landmarks. (From Potter AG, Perry PA: *Fundamentals of nursing,* ed 3, St Louis, 1993, Mosby.)

TABLE 22-5

Respiratory Pattern

Type/pattern	Rate (Breaths per minute)	Clinical significance
Eupnea 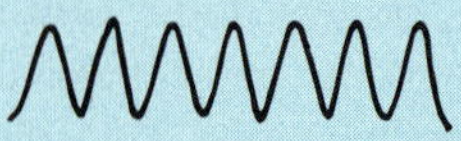	16-20	Normal
Tachypnea 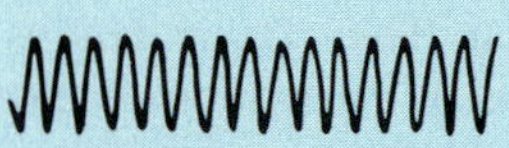	>35	Respiratory failure Response to fever Anxiety Shortness of breath Respiratory infection
Bradypnea 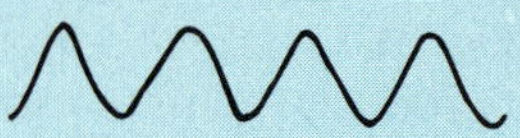	<10	Sleep Respiratory depression Drug overdose Central nervous system (CNS) lesion
Apnea 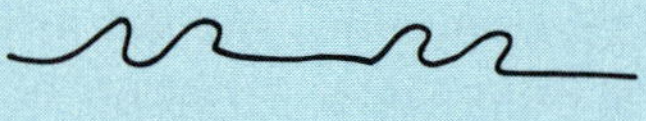	Periods of no respiration lasting >15 seconds	May be intermittent such as in sleep apnea Respiratory arrest
Hyperpnea 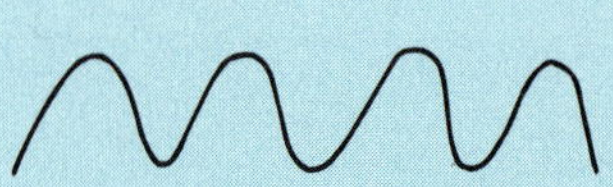	16-20	Can result from anxiety or response to pain Can cause marked respiratory alkalosis, parasthesia, tetany, confusion
Kussmaul's 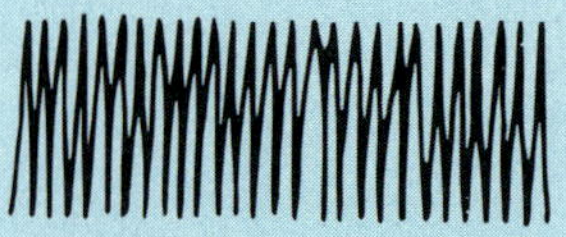	Usually >35, may be slow or normal	Tachypnea pattern associated with diabetic ketoacidosis, metabolic acidosis, or renal failure
Cheyne-Stokes 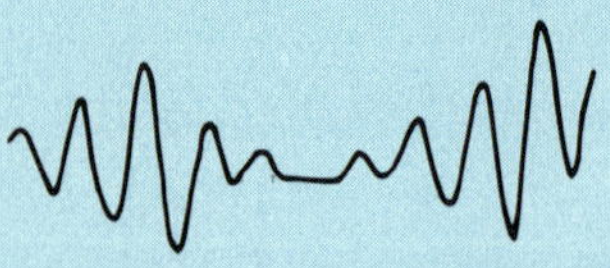	Variable	Crescendo-decrescendo pattern caused by alterations in acid base status. Underlying metabolic problem or neurocerebral insult
Biot's 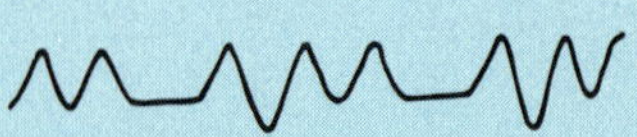	Variable	Periods of apnea and shallow breathing caused by CNS disorder; found in some healthy clients
Apneustic 	Increased	Increased inspiratory time with short grunting expiratory time; seen in CNS lesions of the respiratory center

From Weilitz PB: *Pocket guide to respiratory care,* St Louis, 1991, Mosby.

The thoracic skeleton and muscle mass are palpated for symmetry. Thoracic expansion is determined by placing the hands on the posterior chest wall with the thumbs along the spinal column. The client is asked to breath in and out normally while observing the movement of the thumbs to determine symmetry. Tactile fremitus is palpitation of vibrations felt through the chest wall as the client inspires and expires. Use the palmar base of the fingers or the ulnar aspect of the hand or fist.

CULTURAL AWARENESS

Assessment of Cyanosis in Darkly Pigmented Older Adults

1. Examine in favorable lighting conditions (e.g., use overbed light or natural sunlight).
2. Be attentive to factors that may mask cyanosis by causing vasoconstriction:
   A. Environmental conditions (e.g., air conditioning, mist tents)
   B. Client behaviors (e.g., smoking, medications causing vasoconstriction)
3. Be aware that the region around the mouth is often darker in people of Mediterranean descent.
4. Examine the usual places in which cyanosis is found:
   A. Lips
   B. Nail beds
   C. Circumoral region
   D. Cheek bones
   E. Earlobes

   However, be aware that the darker skin may mask the underlying cyanosis.
5. When cyanosis is questionable, apply light pressure to create pallor. In cyanosis the tissue color returns slowly by spreading from the periphery to the center. Normally the color returns in < 1 second, and it returns from below the pallid spot as well as from the periphery.
6. Observe for other clinical manifestations of decreased oxygenation of the brain:
   A. Changes in level of consciousness
   B. Increased respiratory rate
   C. Use of accessory muscles of respiration
   D. Nasal flaring
   E. Positional changes and other manifestations of respiratory distress.
7. Cyanosis of extremities: Cyanosis of an extremity may become more recognizable if the position of the extremity can be changed from elevated to dependent or vice versa.

Palpate the chest wall for subcutaneous emphysema or crepitation, or leakage of air into the subcutaneous tissues. Subcutaneous emphysema feels like popping small bubbles as you palpate across the chest. Subcutaneous emphysema can be caused by improperly placed tracheostomy tubes, chest trauma, and pleural or thoracic tears following an invasive procedure.

Percussion

Tapping an object to determine the amount of air, liquid or solid in the underlying tissue is percussion. It is accomplished by striking the middle finger of the nondominant hand with the middle finger of the dominant hand or with a percussion hammer. Sounds produced are flat, dull, resonant, or tympanic. The chest of the client with COPD is hyperresonant on percussion. Pneumonia, consolidation, and fluid in the lung percuss as flat and dull.

Auscultation

Auscultation is accomplished by listening to the chest through the diaphragm of the stethoscope. It is important to auscultate in an organized fashion, comparing one side of the thorax to the other (see nursing Care Plan, pp. 602-603; Fig. 22-13; and Table 22-6).

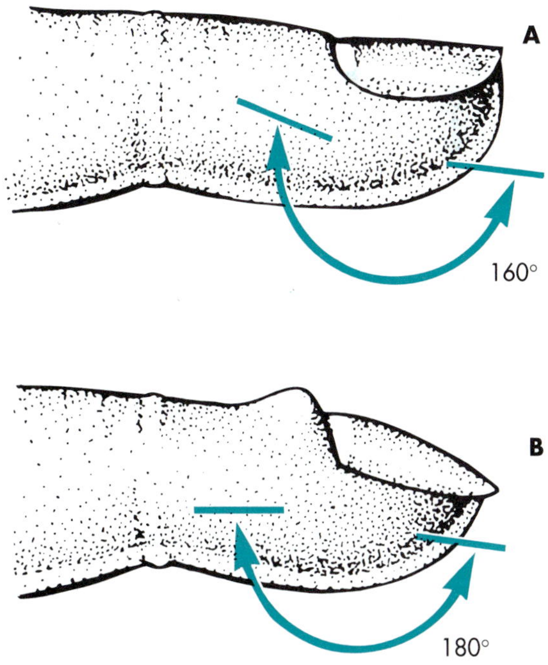

Fig. 22-12 Clubbing of the nail. A, Normal angle of the nail. B, Abnormal angle of the nail seen in late clubbing. (From Malasanos L: *Health assessment,* ed 4, St Louis, 1990, Mosby.

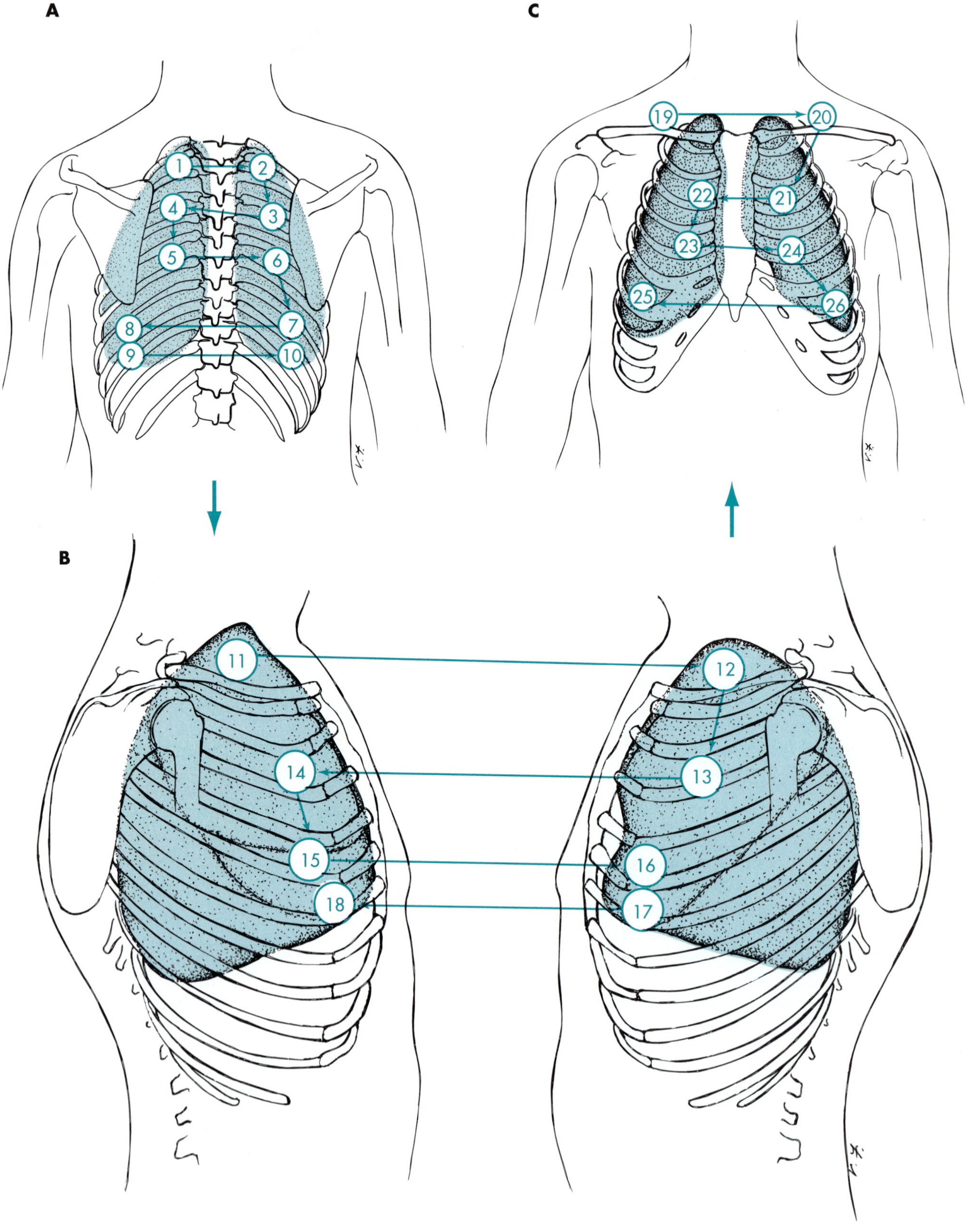

Fig. 22-13 **A** to **C**, The systematic pattern for auscultation. (From Potter AG, Perry PA: *Fundamentals of nursing,* ed 3, St Louis, 1993, Mosby.)

TABLE 22-6

Breath and Voice Sounds: Normal and Abnormal

Breath and voice sounds	Characteristics	Findings
Normal		
Vesicular	Heard over most of lung fields; low pitch; soft and short expirations	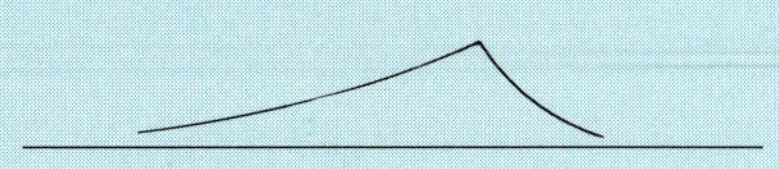 Low pitch, soft expirations
Bronchovesicular	Heard over main bronchus area and over upper right posterior lung field; medium pitch; expiration equals inspiration	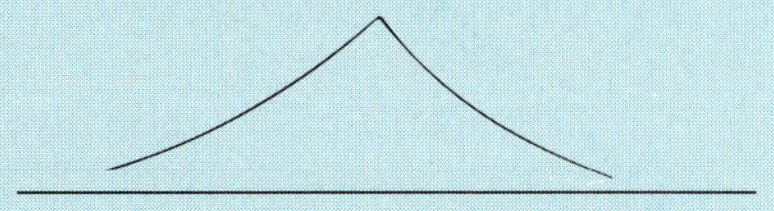
Bronchial	Heard only over trachea; high pitch; loud and long expirations	Medium pitch, medium expirations
Abnormal		
Bronchial when heard over peripheral lung fields	High pitch; loud and long expirations	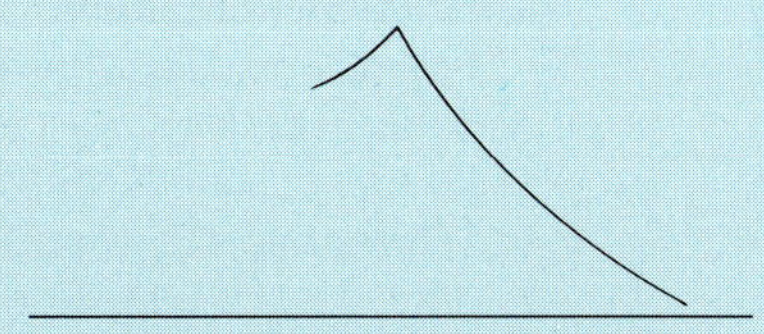
Bronchovesicular sounds when heard over peripheral lung fields	Medium pitch with inspirations equal to expirations	High pitch, loud expirations
Adventitious	*Crackles:* discrete, noncontinuous sounds *Fine crackles:* high-pitched, discrete, noncontinuous crackling sounds heard during end of inspiration (indicates inflammation or congestion)	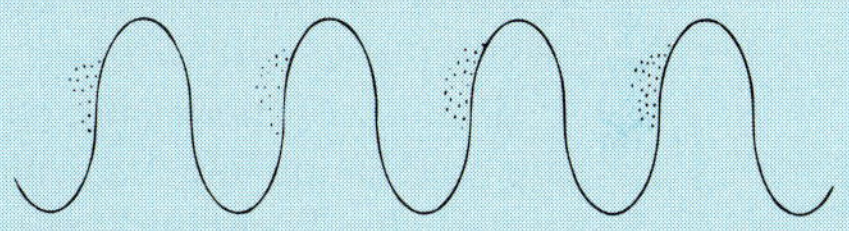
	Medium crackles: lower, moister sound heard during mid-stage of inspiration; not cleared by a cough	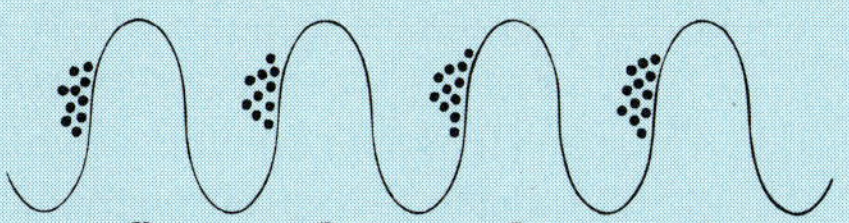
	Coarse crackles: loud, bubbly noise heard during inspiration; not cleared by a cough	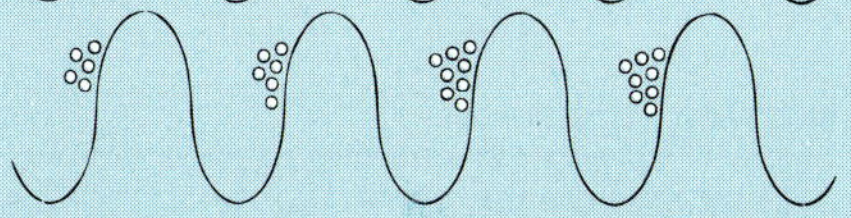
	Wheezes: continuous musical sounds; if low-pitched, may be called rhonchi *Sibilant wheeze:* musical noise sounding like a squeak; may be heard during inspiration or expiration; usually louder during expiration	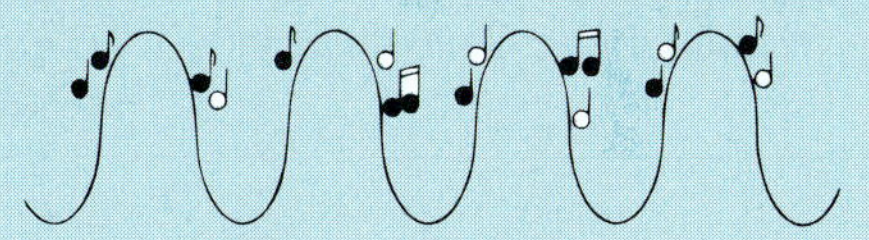
	Sonorous wheeze (rhonchi): loud, low, coarse sound like a snore heard at any point of inspiration or expiration; coughing may clear sound (usually means accumulation of mucus in trachea or large bronchi)	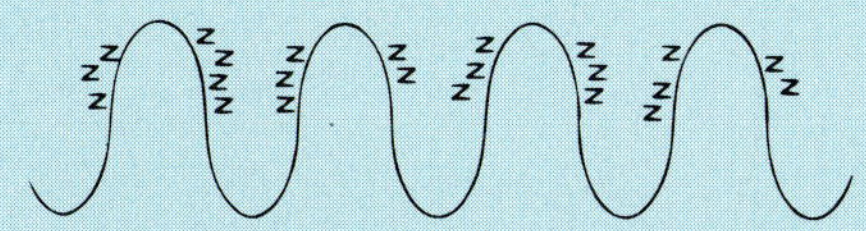
	Pleural friction rub: dry, rubbing, or grating sound, usually because of inflammation of pleural surfaces; heard during inspiration or expiration; loudest over lower lateral anterior surface	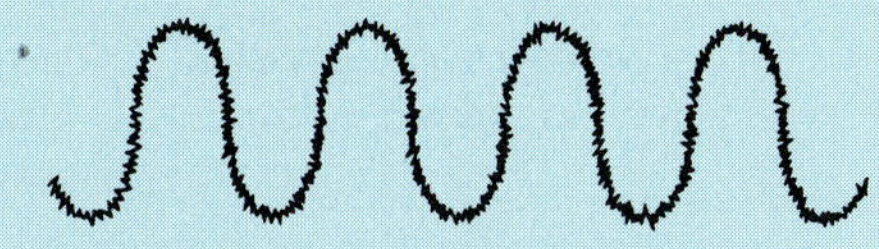
Resonance of spoken voice	*Bronchophony:* using diaphragm of stethoscope, listen to posterior chest as client says "ninety-nine"	*Negative response:* muffled "nin-nin" sound heard *Positive response:* clear, loud "ninety-nine" response heard because lung tissue is consolidated
	Whispered pectoriloquy: listen to posterior chest as client whispers "one, two, three"	*Negative response:* muffled sounds heard *Positive response:* clear "one, two, three" is heard because of lung consolidation
	Egophony: listen to posterior chest as the client says "e-e-e"	*Negative response:* muffled "e-e-e" sound heard *Positive response:* sound of "e" changes to "a-a-a" sound because of consolidation

From Thompson JM et al: *Mosby's clinical nursing,* ed 3, St. Louis, 1993, Mosby.

CARE PLAN

COPD

Clinical situation Mr. W is an 80-year-old retired truck driver admitted to the medical ICU for exacerbation of his COPD. He lives with his wife who is 78 years old. Mr. W continues to smoke 1 to 2 packs of cigarettes per day, as he has done since the age of 15.

Over the past week, Mrs. W has noticed a decrease in Mr. W's activity level and attention span. He has a productive cough of thick tenacious sputum, averaging 1 cup per day. Over the past week the sputum has become yellow in color. His appetite is decreased, and he is having difficulty sleeping at night, often awakening and gasping for breath. Mr. W is having increasing difficulty performing his self-care needs of bathing and dressing.

Physical examination reveals a thin man with weight of 138 lbs. He has a barrel chest and uses his accessory muscles of respiration to breath. Auscultation of the chest reveals diminished breath sounds with scattered coarse crackles bilaterally and no wheezes. Blood pressure is 138/68 mm Hg, a pulse of 92 beats per minute and a respiratory rate of 35 breaths per minute. An oral temperature is 38.3° C (101° F).

Laboratory tests reveal an ABG of pH 7.40, $Paco_2$ 41, Pao_2 55, Sao_2 90% , and HCO_3-28, and a white cell count of 12,000. Sputum cultures revealed *H. influenzae*. A diagnosis of *haemophilus pneumonaie* was made.

Because of increasing shortness of breath and decreasing oxygenation, he was intubated and placed on mechanical ventilation per the couple's wishes. IV antibiotic therapy was started, and bronchodilator therapy was initiated to reduce airway resistance and to promote pulmonary hygiene. Mr. W remained on mechanical ventilation for 6 days, when he was successfully weaned and transferred to the medical division.

He remained on the medical division for 10 additional days. Mr. W was sent home on home oxygen therapy, bronchodilators, and absolutely no smoking.

Nursing diagnoses	Outcomes	Interventions
Activity intolerance related to decreased strength and endurance	Client will be able to safely and comfortably perform activities of daily living (ADLs).	Provide active and passive range of motion to maintain mobility. Assess the need for supplemental oxygen to enhance activity tolerance. Arrange for physical therapy and occupational therapy consult. Pace activities to provide rest and to decrease episodes of breathlessness. Teach client to reduce activities that exacerbate fatigue. Provide suctioning as needed based on assessment findings.
Ineffective airway clearance related to retained secretions	Client will be able to effectively clear secretions with coughing or suctioning.	Provide chest physiotherapy to increase secretion removal and promote chest expansion as tolerated. Provide hydration to maintain fluid volume status and to decrease viscosity of secretions.
Impaired gas exchange related to alveolar hypoventilation	Client will maintain arterial blood gases at baseline as evidenced by ability to adhere to techniques and perform activities that maximize ventilation/perfusion matching.	Turn every 2 hours to promote ventilation and to help drain pulmonary secretions. Monitor arterial blood gases as ordered. Monitor pulse oximetry continously.
Inability to sustain spontaneous ventilation related to infection and decreased respiratory muscle endurance	Client will be able to maintain spontaneous ventilation without mechanical ventilation.	Provide mechanical ventilation during acute phase. Suction as needed based on assessment findings; maintain patent airway.

CARE PLAN

COPD—cont'd

Nursing diagnoses	Outcomes	Interventions
		Monitor peak airway pressure every 2 hours. Monitor ventilator settings every 2 hours. Provide an alternative means of communication. Provide reassurance for the client and family. Provide oral care every 2 hours. Provide rest periods. Schedule care activities based on client's energy level.
Impaired verbal communication related to endotracheal intubation.	Client will be able to effectively communicate with caregivers and his family.	Provide an alternative method of communication such as a picture board, talking board, or alphabet board. Be sure to speak in clear, short sentences and ask questions that only require a short response.
Knowledge deficit (home oxygen therapy, quit smoking) related to inexperience with concepts.	Client and family will be able to return demonstrate use of the home oxygen equipment Client and family will be able to verbalize oxygen safety measures. Client and family will be able to verbalize the need to quit smoking and techniques to achieve success.	Provide the client and family with information about home oxygen therapy, liter flow and equipment for home use. Provide instruction about oxygen safety. Instruct the client and family in smoking cessation techniques and how this relates to oxygen safety. Provide information about local smoking cessation programs.

Summary

Neural chemical control and the respiratory muscles conduct the process of respiration. The structures of the lungs include upper and lower airways, as well as extra- and intrapulmonary structures. Age-related changes in pulmonary structure and function include elastic recoil and musculoskeletal changes of the chest wall. There is also decreased compliance of the thorax. COPD, including asthma, chronic bronchitis, and emphysema is a common respiratory condition in the older adult. Restrictive lung disease and bronchopulmonary infection also affect older adults. Nursing management focuses on assessment, maximizing risk factors, managing treatment regimens, and most importantly, keeping the airway patent.

Key Points

- The changes in lung function that are associated with the aging process, in the absence of primary pulmonary disease, are not associated with a decrease in activity or increased breathlessness.
- Older adults with chronic lung disease can lead active lives with proper medical management.
- Breathing retraining (pursed-lip breathing, diaphragmatic breathing) can result in decreased breathlessness and increased oxygenation.
- It is important to include the family in care planning for the older adult with chronic lung disease.
- The older client with chronic lung disease may demonstrate unacceptable behavioral patterns because of loss of control experienced with chronic illness.
- Smoking cessation may not be achievable in the older client and interventions should focus on reducing the number of cigarettes smoked.
- Exercise plays an important part in overall lung function and has been shown to improve breathing in the older client.
- Care planning that includes the use of mechanical ventilation and other high technology should include the client and family to determine their AMDs.
- Primary nursing diagnoses for the older client with respiratory disease focus on increasing airway clear-

HOME CARE TIPS

- Encourage the homebound older adult client with repiratory disease to drink 8 to 10 glasses of water a day, if not contraindicated.
- Encourage the homebound older adult client with respiratory disease to exercise within their capacity to promote thoracic muscle conditioning.
- Monitor the homebound older adult client for smoking and exposure to second-hand smoke. Encourage family members to not smoke in the presence of the client.
- Encourage homebound older adult client to use pursed-lip-breathing to control breathlessness and improve oxygenation.
- Monitor pulse oximetry to assess oxygenation.
- Encourage frequent small meals to reduce breathlessness associated with eating.
- If the client is using home oxygen, assess the home environment for potential safety hazards, including possibility of client tripping over oxygen tubing.
- Assess client for confusion, occipital headaches and forgetfulness. This may be an indication of retaining carbon dioxide. Teach family caregivers these signs as well.

ance, decreasing breathlessness and improving oxygenation.

Critical Thinking Exercises

1. How might pulmonary hygiene measures be revised for the older, frail adult with a history of CHF?
2. You are caring for a 70-year-old man who has a 75 pack-per-year history of smoking. He has COPD but continues to smoke, stating it would be impossible to quit now and besides, "It's too late." How would you assist your client?
3. Think about your own personal views regarding advanced life-support measures in the older adult population. What are the ethical implications of placing (or not placing) an 80-year-old individual on mechanical ventilation for acute respiratory failure? How would you assist clients and family members faced with decisions of this nature?

REFERENCES

American Thoracic Society: Standards for the diagnosis and care of patients with chronic obstructive pulmonary disease (COPD) and asthma, *Am Rev Respir Dis* 136:225-243, 1987.

American Thoracic Society: Cigarette smoking and your health, *Am Rev Respir Dis* 132(5):1133-1138, 1985.

Bachman DL: Sleep disorders with aging: evaluation and treatment, *Geriatrics* 47(9):53-61, 1992.

Beare PG, Myers JL: *Principles and practice of adult health nursing,* ed 2, St. Louis, 1994, Mosby.

Bloom JW, Barreuther AD: Drug therapy of airways obstructive diseases. In Bressler R, Katz MD: *Geriatric pharmacology,* St. Louis, 1993, McGraw-Hill.

Brown RB: Community-acquired pneumonia: diagnosis and therapy of older adults, *Geriatrics* 48(2):43-50, 1993.

Burke MM, Walsh MB: *Gerontological nursing: care of the frail elderly,* St. Louis, 1992, Mosby.

Butler JC et al: Pneumoccal polysaccharide vaccine efficacy, *JAMA* 270(15):1826-1831, 1993.

Dettenmeier PA: *Pulmonary nursing care,* St. Louis, 1992, Mosby.

Foyt MM: Impaired gas exchange in the elderly, *Geriatr Nurs* 13(5):262-268, 1992.

Gail DB, Lenfant C: The ageing respiratory system. In Evans JG, Williams TF, editors: *Oxford textbook of geriatric medicine,* New York, 1992, Oxford University Press.

Gleckman RA: Pneumonia: update on diagnosis and treatment, *Geriatrics* 46(2):49-56, 1992.

Johnson PA et al: Applying nursing diagnosis and nursing process to activities of daily living and mobility, *Geriatr Nurs* 13(1):25-27, 1992.

Karb VB, Queener SF, Freeman JB: *Handbook of drugs for nursing practice.* St. Louis, 1989, Mosby.

Karper WB, Boschen MB: Effects of exercise on acute respiratory tract infection and related symptoms, *Geriatr Nurs* 14(1):15-18, 1993.

Kersten LD: *Comprehensive respiratory nursing,* Philadelphia, 1989, WB Saunders.

Kim MJ, McFarland GK, McLane AM: *Pocket guide to nursing diagnoses,* ed 3, St. Louis, 1993, Mosby.

King TE: Acute and chronic pulmonary disease. In Shrier RW, editor: *Geriatric medicine,* Philadelphia, 1990, WB Saunders.

Kinzel T: Managing lung disease in later life: a new approach, *Geriatrics* 46(1):54-59, 1991.

Kovach CR, Shore B: Managing a tuberculosis outbreak, *Geriatr Nurs* 12(1):29-30, 1991.

Kuhn JK, McGovern M: Respiratory assessment of the elderly *J Gertontolog Nurs* 18(5):40-43, 1992.

Listello D, Glauser F: COPD: primary care management with drug and oxygen therapies, *Geriatrics* 47(12):28-38, 1992.

Lueckenotte A: *Pocket guide to geriatric assessment,* ed 2, St. Louis, 1994, Mosby.

Mahler DA: *Pulmonary disease in the elderly patient,* New York, 1993, Marcel Dekker.

Matzdorff AC, Green D: Deep vein thrombosis and pulmonary embolism: prevention, diagnosis, and treatment, *Geriatrics* 47(8):47-63, 1992.

Morris JF: Pulmonary diseases. In Cassel CK, Riesenberg, Sorensen LB, Walsh JR: *Geriatric medicine,* ed 2, New York, 1990, Springer.

O'Donnell DE, Webb KA, McGuire MA: Older patients with COPD: benefits of exercise training, *Geriatrics* 48(1);59-66, 1993.

Overfield T: *Biologic variation in health and illness,* Menlo Park, Calif., 1985, Addison-Wesley.

Pierson DJ: Effects of aging on the respiratory system. In Pierson DJ, Kacmarek RM editors: *Foundations of respiratory care,* New York, 1992, Churchill Livingstone.

Poe RH, Utell MJ: Theophylline in asthma and COPD: changing perspectives and controversies, *Geriatrics* 46(4):55-65, 1991.

Saltzman AR: Pulmonary disorders. In Calkins E, Ford AB, Katz PR: *Practice of geriatrics,* ed 2, Philadelphia, 1992, WB Saunders.

Schoemick L, Katz P, Beam T: The many guises of infection, *Geriatric Nurs* 46(6):223-224, 1991.

Swinburne AJ et al: Respiratory failure in the elderly: analysis of outcomes after treatment with mechanical ventilation. *Arch Intern Med* 153(14):1657-1662, 1993.

Stein B: Adult vaccinations: protecting your patients from avoidable illness, *Geriatrics* 48(9):46-55, 1993.

Thompson JM et al: *Mosby's manual clinical nursing,* ed 3, St. Louis, 1993, Mosby.

US Department of Health and Human Services: *Guidelines for the diagnosis and management of asthma,* Pub No 91-3042, Bethesda, Md., 1991, National Heart, Lung and Blood Institute, National Institutes of Health.

Ward C: Influenza: the unwanted visitor, *Geriatr Nurs* 13(6):329-330, 1992.

Webster JR, Kadah H: Unique aspects of respiratory disease in the aged, *Geriatrics* 46(7):31-43, 1991.

Weilitz PB: *Pocket guide to respiratory care,* St. Louis, 1991, Mosby.

Yerg JE et al: Effect of endurance exercise training on ventilatory function in older individuals, *J Appl Physiol* 58(3):791-794, 1985.

BIBLIOGRAPHY

American College of Chest Physicians: Statement in spirometry: a report of the section on respiratory pathophysiology, *Chest* (83):547-550, 1983.

Brischetto MJ et al: Effect of aging on ventilatory response to exercise and CO_2, *J Appl Physiol* 56(5):1143-1150, 1984.

Chick TW, Cagle TG, Vega FA et al: The effect of aging on submaximal exercise performance and recovery, *J Gerontol* 46;B34-B38, 1991.

King TE, Schwartz MI: Pulmonary function and disease in the elderly. In Schrier RW, editor: *Clinical internal medicine in the aged,* Philadelphia, 1982, WB Saunders.

Matteson MA, McConnell ES: *Gerontological nursing concepts and practice,* Philadelphia, 1988, WB Saunders.

McFadden JP et al: Raised respiratory rate in elderly patients: a valuable physical sign, *BMJ* 284:626-627, 1982.

Murray JF: *The normal lung,* ed 2, Philadelphia, 1986, WB Saunders. Co.

Patrick JM, Bassey EJ, Fentem PH: The rising ventilatory cost of bicycle exercise in the seventh decade: a longitudinal study of nine healthy men, *Clin Sci* 65:521-526, 1983.

Petersen DD et al: Effects of aging on ventilatory and occlusion pressure responses to hypoxia and hypercapnia, *Am Rev Respir Dis* 124:387-391, 1981.

Rubin S, Tack M, Cherniak NS: Effect of aging on respiratory responses to CO_2 and inspiratory resistive loads, *J Gerontol* 37(3):306-312, 1982.

Ruppel G: *Manual of pulmonary function testing,* St. Louis, 1990, Mosby.

Shekleton ME: Coping with chronic respiratory difficulty, *Nurs Clin North Am* 22(3):569-579, 1987.

Taylor LD, Greenberg SD, Buffler PA: Health effects of indoor passive smoking, *Texas Med* 81(5), 1985.

Thompson JM et al: *Mosby's manual clinical nursing,* ed 3, St. Louis, 1994, Mosby.

Trulock E: Approaches to deep vein thrombosis and pulmonary embolism in aging, *Geriatrics* 43(2):101-106, 1988.

Wahba WM: Influence of aging on lung function-clinical significance of changes from age twenty, *Anesth Analg* 62:764-776, 1983.

West J: *Respiratory physiology: the essentials,* ed 3, Baltimore, 1985, Williams & Wilkins.

CHAPTER 23

Endocrine Function

LEARNING OBJECTIVES

On completion of this chapter, the reader will be able to:

1. Discuss the normal age-related changes that occur in endocrine system function.
2. Describe the two most common endocrine diseases in older adults: type II diabetes mellitus and hypothyroidism.
3. Apply the nursing process in caring for the older adult with Type II diabetes mellitus and hypothyroidism.

This chapter presents the normal endocrine system, general pathology of the endocrine system, and two specific disorders of the endocrine system: noninsulin-dependent diabetes mellitus (DM), or type II DM, and hypothyroidism. The chapter content focuses on the changes of aging to the endocrine system, as well as the nursing assessment and treatment of endocrine problems in the older adult. Two common endocrine diseases, hypothyroidism and type II DM, are the focus of a more detailed discussion.

INCIDENCE OF GENERAL PATHOLOGY OF THE ENDOCRINE SYSTEM IN OLDER ADULTS

The endocrine system is a chemical communication pathway system that maintains homeostasis through the release, transport, and interaction of hormones. Hormones produce effects through interaction with receptors, which in turn result in the activation of a multitude of cellular activities. Hormones, or chemical messengers, are secreted throughout life. In general, circulating levels of hormones remain in normal ranges from adolescence through adulthood. For example, baseline levels of hormones such as cortisol, glucagon, growth hormone, insulin, thyroxine, and testosterone are not altered by aging (Minnaker, 1990).

The endocrine system functions to support and to maintain growth, development, metabolism, energy production, and maintenance of body fluids, electrolytes, blood pressure and pulse, muscle, fat, bone, and reproduction. The endocrine system is regulated by feedback systems that often involve a chemical connection between structures of the brain (hypothalamus and anterior pituitary gland), peripheral glands (e.g., thyroid, pancreas), and hormones. Other regulatory mechanisms for the endocrine system include hormone interrelationships between cations, glucose, other hormones, and osmolarity of fluid volumes (Wilson, Foster, 1992).

The endocrine system displays rhythms that are hormone specific. Changing amounts of hormones over time can take the form of a circadian rhythm, as in the case of the hormone cortisol. Cortisol levels normally vary over a 24-hour period. The peaks and valleys seen with cortisol secretion may reflect responses to environmental stimuli such as light and darkness. The rhythms of hormone secretions continue into older adulthood. However, the aging endocrine system may show amplitude blunting or prolonged expansion in the circadian cycle. If hormone levels were represented on a graph along the *Y* axis and time was plotted over the *X* axis, amplitude blunting would be demonstrated by a shorter-than-normal peak of the level of cortisol. Aging is associated with a less-than-normal peak of hormone levels and also with a slower, flatter curve when compared with younger individuals.

NORMAL STRUCTURE OF THE ENDOCRINE SYSTEM

The endocrine system is a complex interrelated network comprised of many glands and hormones. Discrete glands of the body include the hypothalamus, anterior and posterior pituitary (one gland with two distinct physiologic parts), pineal, parathyroids, thyroid, thymus, pancreas, adrenals, ovaries, and testes. Each hormone has a specific target cell or tissue that is responsive to it (Table 23-1).

Hormones are chemical structures that are structurally related to either peptides/amino acids or steroids. Examples of peptide/amino acid hormones are thyroid hormones and insulin. Steroid hormones include testosterone, estrogen, and cortisol.

The endocrine system is based on a communication pathway between the hypothalamus gland, the anterior pituitary gland, peripheral glands, target tissues, and receptors through hormones. The communication pathway not only flows in one direction from the hypothalamus to the target tissues, but also returns to the hypothalamus.

The stepwise flow of hormones from the hypothalamus to the anterior pituitary gland to a peripheral gland is sometimes referred to as an axis. For example, the relationship of the hypothalamus to the anterior pituitary and adrenal gland is often called the HPA axis. Fig. 23-1 depicts the HPA axis: CRH is secreted from the hypothalamus, ACTH from the anterior pituitary gland, and cortisol from the adrenal gland. Again, the communication pathway not only flows from top to bottom but also from the adrenal gland back to the hypothalamus. Cortisol production is decreased when serum levels are high enough to feed back and suppress the production of CRH from the hypothalamus.

TABLE 23-1

Endocrine Glands, Hormones, and Abbreviations

Gland	Hormones and hormone abbreviations
Hypothalamus	Corticotropin-releasing hormone (CRH) Thyrotropin-releasing hormone (TRH) Growth hormone-releasing hormone (GHRH) Luteinizing hormone-releasing hormone (LHRH) Melanocyte-inhibiting factor (MIF) Prolactin-inhibiting factor (PIF) Somatostatin (SMS)
Anterior pituitary	Prolactin (PRL) Luteinizing hormone (LH) Follicle-stimulating hormone (FSH) Thyroid-stimulating hormone (TSH) Adrenocorticotropic hormone (ACTH) Growth hormone (GH)
Posterior pituitary	Vasopressin (or antidiuretic hormone) and oxytocin
Pineal	Melatonin
Parathyroids	Parathyroid hormone
Thyroid	Thyroxine (T4), triiodothyronine (T3), and calcitonin
Thymus	Thymin, thymopoietin, and thymosin
Pancreas	Glucagon, insulin, gastrin, and somatostatin
Adrenal cortex	Cortisol and aldosterone
Adrenal medulla	Epinephrine and norepinephrine
Testes	Testosterone and inhibin
Ovaries	Progesterone and estrogen

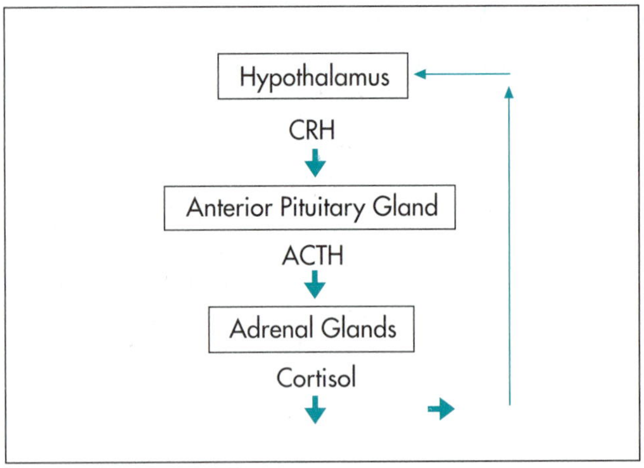

Fig. 23-1 The hypothalamus-pituitary-adrenal axis (HPA).

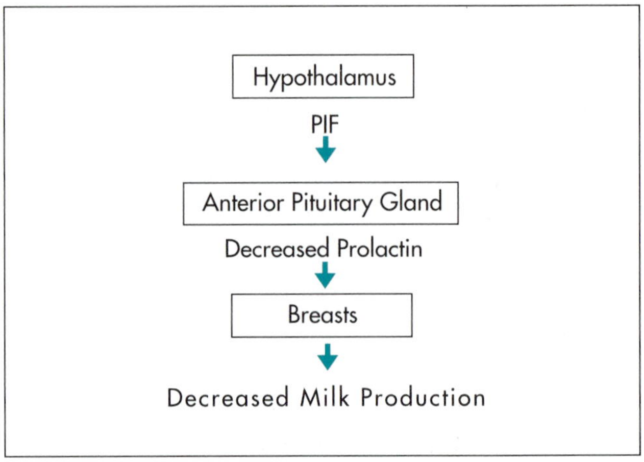

Fig. 23-2 Inhibitory hormones turning off the flow of hormones.

Thus an endocrine communication pathway is often described as a feedback loop. Feedback loops regulate hormone production. The human body relies on the ability of the endocrine system to regulate itself to help the body maintain homeostasis for functions such as electrolyte balance, metabolism, and energy use.

Two types of hormones produced by the hypothalamus are stimulating and inhibitory hormones. Stimulating or releasing hormones act on the anterior pituitary gland in such a way as to promote the secretion of its hormone. Inhibitory hormones or factors produced by the hypothalamus act on the anterior pituitary gland to turn off the production of its hormones.

One of the few examples of this inhibition system is found with the process of weaning an infant from breastfeeding. Successful weaning includes the desire to stop breastfeeding, coupled with the role of the hormone prolactin inhibiting factor (PIF). Fig. 23-2 depicts PIF from the hypothalamus acting on the anterior pituitary gland to block release of the hormone prolactin. When PIF inhibits prolactin production, the breast tissue responds with decreased milk production.

Hormones have specific target cells or tissues that are responsive to them. Hormones bind to structures located on the cell membrane or within the cell. Some hormones such as insulin have receptors in almost all cells of the body. In this case, a portion of the insulin receptor resides on the cell membrane surface (the alpha subunit) and extends into the interior of the cell (the beta subunit).

Once binding to receptors occurs, most hormones activate intracellular proteins and various chemical reactions.

General Endocrine Pathology

Proper functioning of the endocrine system relies on the appropriate functioning of all components of the system. For example, in normal thyroid hormone production and use, it is vital that the hypothalamus, anterior pituitary gland, thyroid gland, and target tissues and receptors be intact and functioning. Complex systems such as the endocrine system have many points where a problem can occur and subsequently alter the function of the entire system. For example, in type II DM, it is common for an individual to have insulin receptor defects that result in underuse or ineffective use of the hormone insulin. In addition, antibodies to insulin may be present, which destroy insulin once secreted and make it impossible to achieve normal blood glucose control. Some individuals with type II DM actually produce decreased or inadequate amounts of insulin. Thus three possible types of defects may be presented in type II DM: (1) abnormal receptors, (2) insulin antibodies, and (3) decreased insulin secretion. It is possible for disturbances at any level of a system to disrupt the entire system, resulting in metabolic upset.

Hypofunctioning States

An endocrine hypofunctioning state results from inadequate endocrine secretions. Hypothyroidism is a common example of an endocrine hypofunctioning state. Some causes of hypothyroidism include (1) a malfunctioning of the hypothalamus, as in the example of hypothalamus tumors; (2) a malfunctioning anterior pituitary gland, as in the case of hypopituitarism; (3) a malfunctioning of the thyroid gland, as occurs in traumatic destruction of thyroid tissue; and (4) decreased responsiveness of target tissues, as occurs in thyroid hormone **resistance**.

When an individual is hypothyroid, symptoms of weight gain, fatigue, and cold intolerance often result.

> ***Insight*** • *Apathy may be a general complaint from younger hypothyroid clients. The twist is that apathy is the most apparent symptom of hyperthyroidism in an older person.*

These symptoms occur whether the defect is at the hypothalamus, anterior pituitary, or thyroid gland level. When the defect involves a hypofunctioning peripheral gland like the thyroid, it is called *primary* hypothyroidism. If the hypothyroid state is a result of a nonfunctional anterior pituitary gland, the condition is called *secondary* hypothyroidism. *Tertiary* hypothyroidism results from a defect in the hypothalamus. As stated previously, hypofunctioning states may also result from defects in target tissues and receptors.

Hyperfunctioning States

An endocrine hyperfunctioning state results from excessive secretion of hormones. For example, in primary hyperthyroidism, there is hypersecretion of thyroid hormones, usually associated with an enlarged thyroid gland. Secondary hyperthyroidism can result from excess effects of TSH from the anterior pituitary gland. Tertiary hyperthyroidism can result from excessive production of TRH from the hypothalamus gland.

Common clinical symptoms of hyperthyroidism from any cause include nervousness, heat intolerance, and weight loss. These clinical symptoms clearly reflect the toxicity of excess thyroid hormones.

Resistance

Endocrine pathology may also be manifested in the form of hormone resistance, a condition in which tissue response to hormones is inadequate. Hormone resistance may be caused by a genetic defect, as in the case of thyroid hormone resistance, or acquired, as in the case of type II DM. The pathophysiology of these resistance states often involves defects in the cell membrane, receptors, or intracellular pathways. For example, in type II DM, an individual may have some defective insulin receptors on target tissues. Abnormally high levels of insulin and hyperglycemia result from the body's inability to use insulin effectively.

In hormone resistance states such as insulin resistance and thyroid hormone resistance, the individual blood levels of insulin and thyroid hormones may be increased respectively, yet the main symptoms are those of a hypofunctioning state. Resistance often results in the need for more than the usual hormone replacement.

NORMAL GLUCOSE METABOLISM

The pancreas is a pistol-shaped gland lying alongside the duodenum and behind the stomach. The pancreas produces digestive enzymes as well as hormones and therefore is said to be both an exocrine as well as an endocrine gland, respectively. Exocrine glands pass their secretions through tube-like structures. The pancreas sends its digestive enzymes to the small intestine through ducts. Endocrine secretions such as insulin are not carried along ducts. Instead, when insulin is secreted, it moves across the cell membrane into the capillary vessels around the pancreas and then into the circulation.

The endocrine tissue of the pancreas secretes the hormones glucagon and insulin, which normally control glucose levels. When a meal is consumed (the fed state), insulin production is stimulated to allow use of the glucose by the cells of the body. In the fed state, insulin levels are high, whereas glucagon levels are low. On the other hand, in the fasting state, glucagon levels rise when insulin levels decrease. Glucagon maintains normal levels of glucose required for the brain and other vital tissues in the fasting state by (1) stimulating the liver to use its stored glucose (glycogen) and (2) stimulating the production of glucose from nonglucose sources such as proteins and fats (gluconeogenesis). Insulin and glucagon are counterregulatory to each other, as seen from the comparison of the fed to the fasting state. Thus blood glucose levels are maintained in the normal range during both fasting and fed states.

The liver also plays an important role in glucose balance. Insulin exerts a powerful reaction in the liver by enhancing the rate of glucose metabolism. The liver stores glucose in the form of glycogen. These stores of energy allow maintenance of normal blood glucose levels between meals or in the fasting state. The liver is also able to convert energy from nonglucose sources by the process of gluconeogenesis under the influence of the hormone glucagon. This process involves converting amino acids derived from protein, and glycerol obtained from fat, into glucose to maintain blood glucose levels during fasting.

AGE-RELATED CHANGES IN GLUCOSE METABOLISM

Impaired glucose tolerance (IGT) is a state in which individuals have glucose levels that are abnormally high, but not at a diagnostic level consistent with DM. The prevalence of IGT increases with age. For example, 40% of people between the ages of 65 to 74 have IGT or DM. The prevalence of IGT and DM increases to 50% of individuals between ages 80 and 89. Type II DM is very common in the older population, with a prevalence range of

12% to 18%, depending on the study cited (Lun, Wing, 1993).

It is estimated that the fasting plasma glucose levels increase about 1 to 2 mg/100 ml for each decade past the age of 40 (Simon, Frishman, 1993). Thus, older people with normal fasting blood glucose values may exhibit elevated postprandial glucose levels.

Many studies have described an association between increased fasting blood glucose levels in older adults and an increased incidence of morbidity secondary to cardiovascular disease. In general, individuals with DM have a two-fold higher incidence of cardiovascular disease than those without DM, and they are more likely to develop strokes and atherosclerotic disease at an earlier age. Although DM does not cause atherosclerosis, the hyperglycemia associated with DM is believed to worsen this condition. Increased morbidity from myocardial infarction (MI), strokes, and hypertension has been reported in people with DM and cardiovascular disease when compared with those without DM. The incidence of hypertension is 26% to 34% in people with DM compared with 13% to 19% for people without DM (Simon, Frishman, 1993). Minnaker (1990) supported the association of DM with vascular complications when he stated that "diabetes accelerates the aging process or results in premature vascular events through effects on platelets, glycosylation of vascular tissues, cellular proliferative capacities, and the production of hypertension."

Recently reported research examining the relationship of tight blood glucose control and long-term complications of type I (insulin-dependent) DM demonstrated that these complications can be significantly reduced by keeping blood glucose levels close to normal (see Research box at left). Although the study was limited to individuals with type I DM, the findings are applicable to most individuals with type II DM. Research is planned to examine the effect of glucose control on long-term complications associated with type II DM.

RESEARCH

Shamoon H et al: Diabetes control and complications trial research group, *New Eng J Med* 329(14): 977-986, September 1993.

Sample, setting

This multidisciplinary research studied 1,441 clients with type 1 DM over a mean time of 6.5 years. Type 1 clients were randomized to receive intensive or conventional treatment. The effect of blood glucose control on the prevention and reduction of long-term complications of **retinopathy, neuropathy, nephropathy,** and cardiovascular disease was examined.

Methodology

This study was designed as a multicenter, randomized clinical trial. Conventional and intensive therapies were used in the groups. Multiple outcome variables were assessed, including retinopathy, neuropathy, nephropathy, cardiovascular disease, and quality of life.

Findings

The intensive therapy group demonstrated an average of 60% reduction in three long-term complications when compared with the conventional therapy group.

Implications

This well-designed study demonstrated that maintaining blood glucose values in a near-normal range helps prevent and delay the onset and severity of long-term complications. This information needs to be shared with clients who have DM. The nurse plays an essential role in teaching clients with DM the knowledge and skills they need to achieve **euglycemia.** Specifically, the nurse can teach clients accurate blood glucose monitoring, recognizing signs and symptoms of hypoglycemia, foot care, and when to contact the physician.

COMMON PROBLEMS AND CONDITIONS

Type II DM

Type II DM is a condition characterized by hyperglycemia. Although type I DM is a condition of absolute insulin deficiency, type II DM is considered to be a disorder of relative insulin deficiency.

Type I DM always requires **exogenously** administered insulin for blood glucose control, because insulin-producing cells of the pancreas have been destroyed to such an extent that the insulin-secreting ability of the gland is negligible or completely absent.

In type II DM, individuals may have defects of insulin secretion but many retain the ability to produce insulin in normal or supernormal levels. The central issue for most people with type II DM is that insulin produced is not effective in controlling the blood glucose levels without treatment (e.g., diet, exercise, or medications). Insulin, if prescribed, is not essential to life as in type I DM.

There are two main types of type II DM—obese and nonobese (National Diabetes Data Group, 1979). The majority of individuals with type II DM are obese or have been obese at the time of diagnosis. Of older people who have DM, over 90% have type II DM.

Although the cause of type II DM is unknown, it is believed that both genetics and the environment play important roles in the development of this condition. The most important variables associated with type II DM are obesity and insulin resistance. Insulin resistance is thought to be related to at least two factors—hyperglycemia and obesity. Obese type II clients have high levels of **endogenous** insulin or hyperinsulinemia, which in turn causes a reduction in the number of insulin receptors on target tissues. It is as if the body attempts to remedy the problem of glucose not entering the cell by increasing insulin production. Thus the basic pathophysiologic defects in type II DM are impaired insulin secretion and action. Insulin levels may be normal, elevated, or decreased in type II DM. Insulin resistance is a common factor but is often treatable.

Impaired insulin secretion and insulin resistance eventually lead to hyperglycemia in the individual with type II DM. As the condition progresses, the level of hyperglycemia can advance from a mild state (fasting blood glucose between 140 and 180 mg/100 ml) to more moderate or severe states (fasting blood glucose > 180 to 200 mg/100 ml). Thus a positive correlation exists between the degree of insulin resistance and the degree of hyperglycemia.

Approximately 38% of all individuals who have DM (both type I and type II) are over the age of 65 (Gambert, 1990). The condition is more common beyond the third decade and is sometimes called an age-prevalent disease.

MEDICAL MANAGEMENT

Type II DM

Diagnostic tests and procedures

Tests for DM can be divided into two categories—screening and diagnostic. Partially because of cost, screening tests are limited to select groups, especially in older adults. Individuals experiencing multiple infections or morbid obesity constitute two groups likely to be screened. Screening tests include a fasting blood glucose as measured in a laboratory.

Diagnostic testing for DM is indicated when (1) screening tests are positive, (2) classical symptoms of DM are present (e.g., polydipsia, polyuria, polyphagia, and weight loss), or (3) DM is suspected. Diagnosis of type II DM in older adults can be established with (1) a random laboratory blood glucose of ≥ 200 mg/100 ml with concurrent classical symptomatology, (2) a fasting laboratory blood glucose of ≥ 140 mg/100 ml on two separate occasions or (3) a fasting laboratory blood glucose of < 140 mg/100 ml and blood glucose ≥ 200 mg/100 ml 2 hours following ingestion of a 75 gm oral glucose load (oral glucose tolerance test [OGTT]). Generally speaking, the OGTT is not used often to diagnose type II DM, particularly in older adults. More commonly, the person has two fasting blood glucose tests with values greater than 140 mg/100 ml. Since this is diagnostic for DM, the client would not have to undergo the stress of a 3-hour glucose tolerance test with multiple sampling of blood.

Treatment

The primary treatment for type II DM includes diet, exercise, and medications (e.g., oral hypoglycemic agents, insulin, or both). Of these treatments, diet is of paramount importance. Dietary strategies are necessary to achieve euglycemia, maintain ideal body weight, and maximize nutritional status. Additional treatment for concurrent conditions such as hypertension, angina, and obesity is essential. These treatments may require modifications in the older adult population.

The physician may prescribe medications such as insulin, specifying species such as beef, pork, beef-pork combination, or human (biosynthetic or semisynthetic). The type of insulin is also specified, such as rapid-acting insulin (e.g., regular insulin) or intermediate-acting insulin (e.g., NPH insulin). The concentration of insulin is standardized in this country to U-100, or containing 100 units of insulin for every milliliter of solution. Individual schedules and doses of insulin are based on blood glucose test results.

Self-monitoring of blood glucose (SMBG) is essential to the successful use of insulin. Blood glucose testing must be done throughout the day and may include fasting (before breakfast) before meals, at bedtime, and at times when the individual is symptomatic for hypoglycemia or hyperglycemia. Testing of urine for ketones is usually reserved for days when hyperglycemia occurs (e.g., blood glucose levels > 250 mg/100 ml).

Prognosis

Individuals with DM who receive effective treatment with desired outcomes often have a good prognosis. Day to day management, however, is difficult for many. Compliance with dietary and exercise recommendations is a significant challenge for most individuals with type II DM.

The goals of diabetes management are to establish euglycemia and to prevent complications to nerves, blood vessels (particularly in the eyes), kidneys, and limbs. For example, it is recommended that individuals with DM have an assessment annually by an ophthalmologist and be examined routinely for hypertension by their physician. When euglycemia is reached the quality of life often improves, and mortality and morbidity decrease.

At the time of diagnosis, uncontrolled type II DM may be associated with symptoms of excessive thirst, hunger, and urination (i.e., **polydipsia, polyphagia**, and **polyuria,** respectively). Too often, however, the older individual with type II DM does not have classical symptomology. Clinical symptoms therefore range from being asymptomatic to coma.

Often, the newly diagnosed older individual will describe symptoms of fatigue, blurred vision, weight change (gain or loss), and infections. When questioned, both men and women attribute these changes to "aging." Individuals often have diabetes diagnosed with a concurrent infection such as a major foot or leg wound, vaginitis, or urinary tract infection. Other clients may have a major cardiovascular crisis such as stroke or MI. These people are often thought to have had DM for years. It is estimated that approximately 2.5% of DM cases in the United States are undetected (see Medical Management box on p. 611).

NURSING MANAGEMENT

ASSESSMENT

Comprehensive nursing assessment of the individual at risk for DM includes a thorough review of the past medical and family history, since type II DM very commonly crosses generations.

Ask the client about current medications, particularly diuretics, beta-blockers, antiseizure drugs, antihypertensives, and steroids. This review of medications is important because many of these drugs alter blood glucose (Table 23-2).

For clients already diagnosed with DM, assess medication name, type, dose, and schedule. If possible, try to observe medication administration. Assess self-care abilities or restrictions, self-monitoring of blood glucose, and any history of hypoglycemia or hyperglycemia.

The nutritional assessment includes a current weight and recent patterns of loss or gain, as well as usual dietary patterns and meal schedule. Because uncontrolled DM affects fluid and food balance, it is important to assess clients for signs and symptoms of nausea and vomiting, or hunger and thirst.

Assessment of elimination in the older adult with DM would include urinary incontinence, urinary frequency, nocturia, polyuria, impotence, and pain on urination. Evaluate for the presence of bowel incontinence, constipation, and diarrhea. When assessing elimination in the older adult, remember to obtain the past medical and surgical history, including problems with the prostate gland, urethra, or bladder. Stress incontinence is more common in older adults, for women as a result of childbearing, and for men as a result of enlargement of the prostate gland.

TABLE 23-2

Medications or Agents that Alter Glucose Control

Drugs that increase blood glucose	Drugs that decrease blood glucose
Corticosteroids	Insulin
Thiazides	Oral hypoglycemic agents (Sulfonylureas: Acetohexamide, Chlorpropamide, Glipizide, Glyburide, Tolazamide, and Tolbutamide)
Thyroid preparations	Alcohol
Phenytoin	Salicylates (high doses)
Epinephrine	Reserpine
Sugary preparations (many over the counter cold medications)	Clonidine
Estrogens	Phenylbutazone
Glucagon	Probenecid
Acetazolamide	Allopurinol
Caffeine	Pentamidine
Cyclophosphamide	Chloroquine
Ethacrynic acid	Dicumarol
Nicotine	Beta-blockers
Calcium-channel blockers	Clofibrate
Nonsteroidal anti-inflammatory drugs (NSAIDs)	Monoamine oxidase inhibitors (MAOIs)
Phenobarbitol	Anabolic steroids
Chloramphenicol	Potassium salts

Modified from Steil C: Prescription drugs and diabetes, *Diabetes Spectrum* 3(2):119-122, 1990.

The nurse also assesses current living conditions. Ask if the individual lives alone or with others, if the living arrangements afford the ability to prepare food, and if there are adequate financial resources for food and shelter. Determine if transportation to health care services is available to the client.

Evaluate the client's ability to learn before assessing the client's knowledge of DM and diabetes management. Learning styles vary, and it is important to know the client's preferred learning style to facilitate education. Some individuals prefer to learn by visual methods, others by listening, and others by experiencing the contact with a hands-on approach.

Methods the nurse can use to facilitate client learning include determining the client's prior knowledge of diabetes management, teaching practical information that the client identifies as important, projecting confidence in the client's ability to learn new information, involving the client actively in the learning, and giving the client feedback as progress is made in the learning. For example, the nurse learns that the physician wants the client with hyperglycemia to test blood glucose twice a day. The nurse needs to determine if the client has ever been taught these skills and if the client is ready to now begin the testing. The nurse could ask if the client prefers to read about SMBG or watch a video showing the procedure. The client can also watch a demonstration of the process by the nurse. The nurse should be flexible at meeting a client's request to skip the reading and jump into the demonstration. After demonstration of the techniques of using a lancet device and blood glucose meter, the nurse should ideally have several follow-up sessions to assist the client in the procedures. Feedback can be given for successful accomplishments, and assistance can be given for the parts of the procedure needing more practice. These are a few examples of techniques that may facilitate the client's learning. *A Core Curriculum For Health Professionals* provides additional principles of teaching and learning (Peragallo-Dittko et al, 1993).

Type II DM is associated with increased depression and memory problems in the older adult, compared with people without diabetes. These problems are often aggravated by uncontrolled diabetes or hyperglycemia. It is important for the nurse to evaluate the current and past blood glucose results. Assess the client's ability to remember simple facts, as well as mood and level of anxiety. For example, the nurse can ask the client to explain content that was just presented. When the client cannot recall content, the nurse needs to determine if there is a learning or memory problem. Memory testing can be accomplished simply by asking clients to repeat number sequences, or by making a short-term or long-term memory assessment. Ask the client about neurologic symptoms such as numbness, tingling, blurred vision, headaches, and inability to sense temperature, especially in the feet.

Assess the client's skin condition. Pay particular attention to the skin on the feet, legs, and elbows, since these areas are at greatest risk for skin breakdown because of pressure. Nursing assessment of the skin should include intactness, color, the presence of swelling, discharge, and odor, turgor, dryness, peeling, and lesions. Skin in the perianal area may provide information on current skin status and general hygiene practices. Clients with DM are prone to yeast or fungal infections in this area. Poor hygiene may predispose the individual to urinary or vaginal infections.

To assess circulation, take an apical pulse, noting rate and rhythm, and check pedal pulses bilaterally. Take blood pressure measurements in recumbent and sitting positions. Note any dizziness associated with change of position. Assess respiratory rate, depth, and chest sounds.

✣ DIAGNOSIS

Some common nursing diagnoses for the client with type II DM include, but are not limited to, altered nutrition: more than body requirement; altered nutrition: less than body requirements; pain; altered tissue perfusion; altered urinary elimination; sexual dysfunction; altered thought processes; and knowledge deficit: diabetes self-management and skills.

✣ PLANNING

Expected outcomes for the older adult with diabetes include, but are not limited to the following:

1. Client will understand the American Diabetes Association (ADA) diet, as evidenced by normal weight and hydration.
2. Client will understand insulin administration, as evidenced by demonstration of correct technique of drawing up and injecting insulin.
3. Client will maintain peripheral circulation, as evidenced by pink, warm extremities without lesions or ulcers.
4. Client will demonstrate daily foot care regimen of foot cleansing and inspection techniques.

The family or significant others also should be involved in the planning of care, since they so often provide the older adult with the support and reinforcement needed for long-term management of such a chronic condition.

✣ INTERVENTION

The nursing care of the client with type II DM is often complex. Since there are usually so many issues with which to deal, it is important to prioritize client problems. In general, emergent issues are at the top of the list. Examples of emergent or life-threatening crises include severe hyperglycemia, hypoglycemia, and sepsis. Once crises are resolved, the nurse can provide education to support the diabetes management. For example, once severe hyperglycemia is resolved, the issue of nutrition education can be addressed. Strategies to reach this goal include consultation with the registered dietician for a diet prescription. The diet is planned to achieve good nutrition, and to reach or to maintain ideal body weight, while decreasing the risk of hyperlipidemia, atherosclerosis, and hypertension. Once the diet plan is established, nursing interventions are then directed at supporting the recommendations of the dietician through assessment of the client's understanding of and adherence to the diet plan.

Client Education

It is estimated that the newly diagnosed individual with DM requires a minimum of 10 teaching hours to acquire survival level knowledge and skills (Sperling, 1988). The nurse provides or coordinates a variety of recommended diabetic teaching of content areas such as medications, pathophysiology of diabetes, monitoring of blood glucose and urine **ketones,** hypoglycemia and hyperglycemia, sick-day management, foot care, eye care,

BOX 23-1

Diabetic Aids for the Visually Impaired

Insulin syringe magnifiers
Use of smaller dosed syringes
Blood glucose meters that talk, display results in large type, and are easy to use
Syringe-filling devices with dose gauges
Needle and syringe holders

Modified from Beaser R et al: Buyer's guide to diabetes supplies, *Diabetes Fore* 46(10):48-88, October 1993.

complications, the diabetic diet, product supplies, and instructions on when to contact the health team. Teaching is facilitated when the client and significant others are actively involved in the learning, as in the instance of clients demonstrating SMBG to the nurse. Teaching aids such as booklets and handouts can enhance learning. Resources for client educational handouts may be obtained from the ADA, the National Diabetes Information Clearinghouse, and commercial sources.*

Medications Before beginning teaching of medications, obtain physician orders. The client should receive written instructions about the medication regimen. Whenever possible, enlist the aid of the client's significant other during teaching. Observe, if possible, the client identifying the correct medication. For example, when humulin insulin is prescribed, it is not equivalent to beef insulin. Injecting humulin insulin and then switching without a physician's order to beef or pork insulin alters the times of insulin action: initiation, peak insulin action, and duration of insulin action. Therefore it is important that the client can verbally state the type of insulin ordered and can identify the notations on the insulin bottles indicating the prescribed insulin type.

Observe the client and significant other preparing and administering the prescribed insulin dosages. Vision or manual dexterity problems, which may interfere with proper insulin delivery, can be identified through observation. Aids are available to assist visually impaired clients with insulin administration (Box 23-1).

Observe the client actually injecting insulin. Note if the client draws the accurate amount of insulin, injects into an appropriate site, and discards the sharp needle in a puncture-proof container.

Oral hypoglycemic agents (OHAs) are medications used to lower blood glucose concentrations in individuals with type II DM. The main mechanism of action of these drugs is to stimulate the secretion of the insulin-producing ability of the pancreas. Therefore these drugs are totally ineffective in the client with type I DM, since this client has lost the ability to have any insulin production. The OHAs also work by increasing the sensitivity of the body to the effects of insulin and decreasing the production of glucose from the liver. OHAs are more readily accepted by clients than insulin administration. More than 60% of all individuals with type II DM will, at least initially, be candidates for these agents.

OHA absorption from the gastrointestinal tract does not seem to be significantly affected in older people when compared with younger individuals. Distribution of OHAs in the older population may be decreased as a result of lower levels of serum albumin associated with aging. OHA metabolism and excretion are decreased in older people because of the changes of aging to liver and renal blood flow and decreased enzyme activity (Lun, Wing, 1993).

Table 23-3 lists currently prescribed first and second generation OHAs and includes information on onset and duration of action along with common dosages used for older adults. Note that the agents range in duration of action from as little as 6 to 12 hours for tolbutamide to 72 hours for chlorpropamide. Knowledge of the duration of drug actions such as OHAs becomes an important issue in situations where clients are asked not to eat or drink anything the night before hospital or outpatient procedures, but are asked to hold their OHAs. If the client stops taking chlorpropamide only the night before a procedure, the glucose-lowering effect of this drug lasts for 3 days, and a fasting client may develop the serious complication of hypoglycemia. The client on this drug should be advised to hold the drug for 72 hours in this type of fasting situation. Planning the care for clients on OHA requires an understanding of these drugs and their effects.

It is important for the nurse to teach clients who are taking OHAs the potential for drug interactions. All OHAs bind to serum proteins, but the first-generation OHAs compared with the second-generation OHAs have a higher incidence of interacting with other drugs that bind with albumin, such as anticoagulants, hydantoins, and salicylates. Because some over-the-counter (OTC) drugs negatively interact with OHAs, it is important for the client on OHAs to check with the physician before taking any new drugs. Older adults are more likely than younger adults to have many drugs ordered concurrently with an OHA.

Since hypoglycemia is the major complication of OHA therapy, clients should be instructed about this complication. OHAs are associated with other adverse effects such as rashes, itching, nausea, vomiting, liver damage, and increased urinary frequency and urgency. Routine medical visits for laboratory testing for complications is important. Alcohol ingestion may be contraindicated in

*American Diabetes Association (ADA): National Service Center; 1600 Duke Street; Alexandria, VA 22314, (800) ADA-DISC; National Diabetes Information Clearinghouse: Box NDIC; 9000 Rockville Pike; Bethesda, MD 20892, (301) 654-3327.

TABLE 23-3

Oral Hypoglycemia Agents

Drug	Onset of action	Duration of action	Dosages for older adults
First generation agents			
Acetohexamide (Dymelor)	1 hr	10 to 14 hrs	125 to 250 mg/day
Chlorpropamide (Diabinese)	1 hr	72 hrs	100 mg/day
Tolazamide (Tolinase)	4 to 6 hrs	10 to 14 hrs	100 mg/day
Tolbutamide (Orinase)	1 hr	6 to 12 hrs	500 mg QD-BID
Second generation agents			
Glipizide (Glucotrol)	1 hr	10 to 24 hrs	2.5 to 5 mg/day
Glyburide (Diabeta, Micronase)	1.5 hr	18 to 24 hrs	1.25 to 2.5 mg/day
Glyburide, micronized (Glynase Pres Tab)	1 hr	18 to 24 hrs	0.75 mg/day

Modified from Lun W, Wing S: Oral agents in the elderly, *Practic Diabetol* 12(4):10-13, December 1993.

TABLE 23-4

Levels of Hypoglycemia and Treatment

Hypoglycemia level	Symptoms	Treatment
Mild	Hunger, diaphoresis, nervousness, shakiness, tachycardia, and pale skin	15 grams of carbohydrate (4 oz. of juice, no sugar added)
Moderate	Headache, irritability, fatigue, blurred vision, and mood changes	15 grams of carbohydrate; may repeat
Severe	Unresponsiveness, confusion, coma, or convulsions	Glucagon, intravenous (IV) glucose

people receiving chlorpropamide therapy, since alcohol use can cause an "antabuse" effect, in which facial flushing, headaches, and dizziness occur.

Nursing interventions for clients on OHAs would include teaching clients to abstain from alcohol consumption and to be aware of the potential for side effects and complications such as hypoglycemia (Table 23-4).

Clients on medications that lower glucose levels should recognize the symptoms of mild hypoglycemia, should test their blood glucose, and if abnormal should ingest a source of rapid-acting carbohydrate, such as 4 ounces of orange juice. The early recognition and treatment of mild hypoglycemia prevent the more serious **neuroglycopenic** symptoms associated with moderate and severe hypoglycemia. Unrecognized and untreated hypoglycemia puts the individual with diabetes at risk for seizures and even death.

Emergency identification Another nursing intervention includes advising the client to carry medical emergency identification. In the event that the individual taking OHAs experiences a major complication such as severe hypoglycemia, medical emergency identification helps facilitate the treatment of the condition by health care workers or uninformed others.

Monitoring Monitoring of blood glucose is recommended for clients with type II DM, particularly those individuals on medications that lower blood glucose (e.g., oral hypoglycemic agents or insulin). Individuals with type II DM are also advised to perform urine testing for ketones when blood glucose levels exceed 250 mg/100 ml. Teaching clients or their significant others these skills is crucial to proper diabetes management. Constant reinforcement of these steps helps improve outcomes of accuracy in urine and glucose testing.

Exercise Exercise interventions require prior medical evaluation. Once the capabilities and limitations of the client are considered, the exercise program is personalized to the client. Teach the client the safety rules of exercising, which include wearing a medical-alert bracelet, checking blood glucose before exercise, identifying signs and symptoms of hypoglycemia, carrying a source of carbohydrate, avoiding exercise if the blood glucose is $\geq$ 250 mg/100 ml and avoiding dehydration.

Ability to exercise may decrease with aging, which may contribute to increasing weight patterns. Obesity is known to increase insulin resistance, which then leads to hyperglycemia. Exercise is a strategy for decreasing insulin resistance and decreasing hyperglycemia. It is known to be beneficial for older adults from physiologic and psychologic perspectives. However, exercise-related complications or injuries are more likely to occur in this population as a result of preexisting conditions such as cardiac, musculoskeletal, and ophthalmic diseases. Precautions and exercise modifications are indicated with older people to help prevent potential problems. Some examples of exercise modifications might include medical examination and assessment before initiating exercise programs and the gradual introduction of individualized exercises. The appropriate intensity level of exercises must be assessed as must the frequency of assessment of blood glucose levels before and after exercise. Modifications to exercising should be based on blood glucose results in the older adult (Graham, 1991). For example, individuals with blood glucose values > 250 mg/100 ml should not exercise, since blood glucose values may climb even higher. Exercising with blood glucose levels exceeding 250 mg/100 ml without the benefit of adequate amounts of insulin causes escalating hyperglycemia along with increased production of free fatty acids and ketones. Inadequate insulin levels also promote the release of glucose from the liver by gluconeogenesis and glycogenolysis. Exercise should be resumed only when blood glucose levels are in the normal range.

Lifestyle changes Lifestyle changes are required for individuals with DM. It is difficult to manage a chronic illness that affects diet, exercise, weight goals, medications, sexuality, and finances. Proper management of DM requires knowledge, skills, and organization of a team of experts with the client at the core of the team. Avoidance of smoking and alcohol consumption is believed to improve diabetes management.

Sick-day management Individuals with DM need to take special measures for "sick days." Sick days are usually defined as illness days for the individual with DM that necessitate alterations of typical treatment strategies, such as increasing medications (insulin doses), meals, and fluids; and initiation of medical interventions (antibiotics for infections). For example, when an individual with DM becomes ill with a "stomach flu," the stress of even this common type of illness may precipitate severe hyperglycemia. The individual may detect significant hyperglycemia during routine blood glucose testing and then should contact the physician for specific instructions on how to increase the insulin dosage. Sometimes the client is placed on a sliding scale of insulin. This system of insulin dosage indicates specific blood glucose ranges and doses of regular insulin. For example, the instructions to the client may be to give 4 units of regular insulin for blood glucose values ranging from 250 to 300 regular mg/100 ml. But for blood glucose values between 301 and 350 mg/100 ml, the client is instructed to give 6 units of regular insulin. Individuals with nausea and vomiting are instructed to

EMERGENCY TREATMENT

Sick-Day Management for the Individual With Diabetes

Definition of sick day

Sick days for individuals with diabetes are episodes of acute illnesses involving complications such as nausea, vomiting, and diarrhea. Illnesses trigger stress hormone production with resulting hyperglycemia. With the onset of gastrointestinal symptoms, individuals with diabetes become easily dehydrated. If the client's meal plan cannot be tolerated, easy-to-digest foods are taken instead. Examples of easy-to-digest foods include regular sodas, soups, popsicles, or crackers. This diet can be supplemented with noncaloric liquids like water or diet sodas to keep up with fluid loss from vomiting or diarrhea.

Individuals with DM must continue taking prescribed medications such as insulin or oral hypoglycemic agents, must ensure adequate hydration, and must test the urine and blood more often. Urine should be tested for ketones whenever the blood glucose is greater than 240 mg/100 ml. Other recommendations include taking temperature and weight, and recording all values and interventions. Clients with diabetes should contact their physicians whenever the treatment regimen is not working, which can be evidenced by worsening of fever; decreasing alertness or ability to think; vomiting more often than once; diarrhea persisting over 6 or more hours; blood glucose values > 250 mg/100 ml, despite additional insulin; moderate or large ketones in the urine; or if there are unanswered questions or concerns.

Sick-day management is important in the individual with type II DM, since illness left untreated may lead to a complication called **hyperglycemic hyperosmolar nonketotic coma (HHNC).**

This hyperglycemic condition is more common in older clients with type II DM, whereas the client with type I DM is more likely to experience **diabetic ketoacidosis.** HHNC is characterized by severe dehydration and hyperglycemia (blood glucose values > 600 mg/100 ml and hyperosmolarity of the blood > 340 mOsm/L of water). The treatment for this condition is insulin, IV fluids, discovery and treatment of the precipitating event (e.g., infection or cardiovascular problems) in an intensive care setting of a hospital.

take 8 ounces of fluids (nondiet beverages) hourly and increase monitoring of blood glucose and urine ketones. The instructions from the physician may indicate the levels of blood glucose and ketones that require an immediate call to the physician or visit to the emergency room (see Emergency Treatment box below).

Prevention of foot problems in individuals with DM Lower extremity amputations are a tragic yet preventable problem for individuals with DM. From 50% to 70% of all amputations of the feet are performed on individuals with DM.

Prevention of foot ulcers is the key to proper foot management in cases of DM. This is achieved through daily cleansing of the feet with nondrying agents, inspection of the feet, and prompt treatment of problems (see Client/Family Teaching box below).

Daily cleansing of the feet with nondrying agents is important to free the feet of potential infectious organisms. Lubrication of the feet (but not between the toes, where heat and lotions may be trapped and lead to infections) with nonscented lotions is often needed to help decrease skin dryness and cracking. Appliances such as corn pads and drying agents such as alcohol should be avoided, since they impair the integrity of the skin. New shoes need to be tested for good fit and gradually "broken in." Individuals or others should cut nails straight across to ensure that complications do not occur. Individuals with DM should seek care from the physician whenever wounds exhibit tenderness, swelling, or leakage of fluids. Individuals with diabetes with neuropathy of the feet, significant hyperglycemia (blood glucose values $>$ 250 mg/100 ml), or a past history of foot infections should seek medical care at the first sign of a foot infection.

✣ EVALUATION

The nurse evaluates the effectiveness of the care plan for the older client with DM by frequently measuring the achievement of established specific goals. For example, for nutritional goals the client is encouraged to select foods consistent with the meal plan. Achievement of weight change goals is measured over time with weight graphs. The client can log exercise accomplishments so that progress with activity is clearly displayed. Medication administration is observed and, when needed, critiqued by the nurse. When insulin is used, injection sites are checked for complications reflecting overuse of sites or local irritation. The client can log blood glucose values, and client values are compared with the laboratory results. Clients are examined to see if they are wearing or carrying medical-alert bracelets, or other emergency information. Clients can be asked to review their recent experiences with sick days and their management of fluids, nausea, vomiting, medications, and testing.

The nurse needs to reinforce the effective diabetes management strategies that the older client has used. For example, when the client improves in the technique for insulin injection, the nurse needs to recognize the client's skill. For DM measures not taken but needed, the nurse presents the information again and reassesses the problems. For example, if the client is not wearing medical emergency identification after being advised to do so, the nurse might bring this issue up for further discussion at the next contact period. It is important for the nurse to assess why the measures have not been followed so that adaptations can be made. A client may reveal that the reason an emergency identification is not being worn is because of the serpent design found on many of the bracelets or necklaces. Another brand of medical identification can then be obtained so that the individual will comply with wearing the identification.

A principle of diabetes management is having the client "take control" of the diabetes. Self-care activities such as daily inspection of the feet with basic diabetic foot care support this self-care approach. The nurse can help the client evaluate the effectiveness of self-care activities by direct examination and through interview techniques. The nurse can teach foot care and then physically inspect the client's feet.

Feet that are exposed to poor-fitting shoes reflect the problem of redness and swelling over contact points. By inspecting the feet of the client, the nurse demonstrates the importance of foot care, and shows cause and effect relationships with management strategies (i.e., poor-fitting shoes cause abnormalities of the feet).

CLIENT/FAMILY TEACHING

Prevention of Foot Ulcers in Individuals With Diabetes

The basic objectives for teaching foot care principles to the older client and family include the following:

Maintaining function and integrity through daily hygiene

Performing daily foot inspection

Seeking early interventions to problems

Preventing foot injuries by wearing proper-fitting shoes and not going barefoot

Wound Infections with Diabetes

Wound infections in older adults with DM are common and serious events requiring immediate attention. Symptoms can be virtually nonexistent or may consist of pain, swelling, and redness. Left untreated, the infection can spread from skin to fat, muscle, fascia, and bone. The rates of recovery from infections vary according to the time when treatment is initiated, forms of treatment, and the condition of the client.

CARE PLAN

DM WITH FOOT INFECTION

Clinical situation Mr. J noticed that his right foot ached slightly. Taking off his shoe, he could see that his foot was red and swollen with a small amount of purulent fluid draining from a lesion on the small toe. He could even see the indentations from his shoes on the skin of his feet. He was surprised that the foot looked this bad when he had no problems earlier. He made an appointment with his primary care physician. The appointment was 2 days after he first noticed the problem. During those 2 days Mr. J became increasingly tired. Despite nonstop drinking of fluids he was thirsty all the time. At the visit with his physician, Mr. J was found to have 3 + edema in the affected foot, a temperature of 101° F, and a blood glucose of 250 mg/100 ml. He was diagnosed with a diabetic foot infection. Mr. J first learned of his diagnosis of DM at the time of his foot infection.

The physician sent Mr. J to the local community hospital for inpatient admission. Hospitalization was necessary for two reasons—the treatment of his foot infection and treatment of his newly diagnosed DM.

Nursing diagnoses	Outcomes	Interventions
Impaired skin integrity related to altered metabolic state	Wound healing will occur, as demonstrated by decreasing size of wound and less purulent drainage, and by laboratory values for CBC with differential and electrolytes within normal limits. Circulation to affected area will be maintained, as evidenced by normal skin color and temperature, presence of pedal pulses, and no evidence of edema.	Assess wound with each dressing change for wound stage, epithelialization, color, edema, and discharge. Assess vital signs. Administer antibiotics as prescribed. Provide physician-ordered intravenous fluids, insulin, and medications. Notify physician for signs and symptoms of increased pain, swelling, drainage, or fever. Change linens as needed to maintain clean wound environment.
Pain related to treatments for foot ulcer (biopsy, curettage, and debridements)	Client will verbalize comfort during debridement procedures. Maintain stable vital signs before, during, and after procedure.	Provide pain control during debridements by premedicating before procedures. Assess client's vital signs and level of consciousness before administration of medications. Assess pain level, vital signs, and level of comfort and sedation post medication. Document client tolerance of procedure.
Knowledge deficit: newly diagnosed DM related to new experience	Client will verbalize and demonstrates understanding of diabetes and diabetes management as evidenced by client making appropriate diet selections, correctly and safely administering medications, and accurately testing blood glucose. Client will verbalize appropriate sick-day management regimen.	Assess client understanding of condition. Monitor readiness and determine best methods for teaching/learning. Provide diabetes teaching, including description of type II DM; ADA diet; exercise; medications; sick-day management; monitoring; lifestyle factors (e.g., smoking and alcohol); complications, especially hypoglycemia and hyperglycemia; and eye, kidney, nerve, foot, and vessel problems.
Knowledge deficit: foot care management related to new experience	Client will demonstrate daily foot care regimen of inspection, cleansing and using emollients.	Provide proper foot care teaching with demonstration, including daily inspection and cleansing, wearing shoes, avoidance of tape and drying chemicals, use of proper foot gear, applying emollients, keeping feet dry, and safe nail cutting. Have client return demonstration.
	Client will verbalize when to contact physician for complications.	Instruct on physician reportable signs and symptoms such as fever, pain, swelling, redness, and break in skin integrity.

CARE PLAN

DM WITH FOOT INFECTION—cont'd

Nursing diagnoses	Outcomes	Interventions
Impaired physical mobility related to foot wound	Client will achieve optimum level of physical mobility as evidenced by ability to safely meet self-care needs. Protects affected extremity as evidenced by ability to adhere to weight-bearing restriction.	Instruct client not to weight bear on infected foot. Set room up to maximize client independence with activities of daily living (ADLs).
Anxiety related to acute infection and recent diagnosis of DM	Client will verbalize reduced levels of anxiety with increasing knowledge and skill acquisition.	Assess client mood and coping mechanisms. Allow client to verbalize feelings about diagnosis of chronic disease of diabetes. Support client in self-care and management of diabetes by (1) encouraging involvement in self-care activities, (2) providing environment conducive to relaxation, and (3) reassuring when safely or accurately performs self-care skills and techniques.

Specific causal agents of diabetic foot infections include *Proteus, Klebsiella-Enterobacter, Pseudomonas, Escherichia coli, Staphylococcus, Streptococcus epidermis, Corynebacterium, Bacteroides fragilis,* and *Clostridia.* Polymicrobial wound infections are the rule in the older client with DM. Individual wounds may be infected with gram-positive cocci, gram-negative rods, and anaerobic bacteria.

Older individuals with DM are at a higher risk for complications to the feet than those without DM because of changes in nerves and blood vessels. Because of these commonly seen foot problems, the terminology "diabetic foot syndrome" has evolved to describe the vascular and neurologic pathology associated with DM. Inadequate blood flow to the feet, coupled with nerve damage, contributes to ulcer and infection development in older individuals with DM. Hyperglycemia also plays a contributory role in the process of foot problems, since blood glucose levels > 200 mg/100 ml are associated with an altered immune system leukocyte response.

Because of alterations in sensation related to peripheral neuropathy and vascular insufficiency, foot infections in older clients with DM may go undetected until they are at an advanced stage. Significant delays can occur before the physician is contacted and treatments are initiated, thus leading to prolonged recovery times. Other foot problems found with DM are loss of sweating leading to dry skin. Dry skin left untreated can progress to cracked skin, which allows for entry of organisms and subsequent infections.

The clinical symptoms of foot infections vary from no symptoms to fever, erythema, warmth, discharge with ulceration, and leukocytosis (Guthrie, 1988). The skin over and around the infection may appear to be white, pink, red, or in shades of blue. Blood vessels may be distended and pronounced over the infection site. Nail beds may be pale, and when pressed, show slower capillary refilling. (Normally when a nail bed is pressed, the color of the nailbed turns white, then immediately returns to the pinker color in 1 to 3 seconds.) The shape of the foot may be altered by infection as a result of significant soft tissue swelling. Sometimes, the foot takes a shape that resembles the bottom of a rocking chair. Lesions may drain or may be dry. Superficial inspection of the lesion may be deceptive, because what is often seen on the outside of the lesion does not reflect the extent of the problem beneath the skin surface. For example, when the older individual with DM has a grossly swollen, but nondraining, lesion on the sole of the foot, it is common for the infected fluids to be trapped below the lesion. If the foot looks swollen and red, despite the absence of discharge, it is likely that the infection is deeper. (see Medical Management box, p. 620 and nursing Care Plan, pp.618-619).

NORMAL THYROID ANATOMY AND FUNCTION

The thyroid gland has two lobes that affix to the trachea. The two lobes are connected by the isthmus. The thyroid gland is protected by the sternohyoid and sternothyroid muscles. The larger the muscle mass, the more

MEDICAL MANAGEMENT

Diabetic Foot Infection

Diagnostic tests and procedures

The medical management of a current diabetic foot infection includes determining the causative agent and condition of the foot. Cultures are taken, and because the infection may include more than one organism, the cultures may be taken from more than one site. If drainage exists, this would be one culture source. Culturing by **curettage** is recommended for some lesions. Sensitivy to determine choice of antibiotics.

The physician assesses vascular and neurologic function, and interventions begun as needed. Laboratory tests such as **glycosylated hemoglobin** (HgA1c), blood glucose, electrolytes, and complete blood count (CBC) with differential are commonly ordered. The HgA1c is used to assess the average blood glucose control over the previous 3 months. It is not used to diagnose DM but instead is used to reflect glycemic levels over the preceding 3-month period.

An x-ray may be ordered to determine if the bone is involved in the infection. Ultrasonography and magnetic resonance imaging (MRI) may be more sensitive than standard x-rays in detecting bone involvement (Yuh et al, 1991).

Treatment

Treatment with broad-spectrum antibiotics is initiated even before culture results are available. IV antibiotic therapy is used for diabetic foot infections that involve the bone or for clients with sepsis. Sometimes the antibiotics are changed based on the cultures and sensitivities. The physician decides if the foot can bear weight or if immobilization is required.

Surgical incision and drainage may be indicated. Surgical debridement of wound debris and dead tissues is crucial for resolution of extensive foot infections.

Local wound management approaches are varied, and are based on client conditions and the experiences of the physician. Soaking the wounds of clients with DM is usually *not* recommended, since hot soaks place the numb foot at risk for burns and metabolically stress the foot when arterial blood supply may be compromised. Topical solutions and dressings vary according to the wound stage and type. The wound care nurse specialist, collaborating with the physician, is often a tremendous resource for advice on products and strategies for wound management (see chapter 28).

Control of hyperglycemia is also part of the medical management of foot infections. Uncontrolled infection in the person with DM is often associated with escalating hyperglycemia. Management usually involves insulin therapy, often at higher-than-usual doses.

Pain may or may not be a problem for the older client with DM with a foot infection. Analgesics may be used on an "as needed" schedule. Acute pain management may involve narcotics during hospitalization.

Weight bearing on the neuropathic infected foot is avoided, because the pressure of weight bearing can damage newly forming cells that are repairing. Also, weight bearing makes the foot dependent and increases the potential for swelling, which slows healing. The elimination of weight bearing on an infected limb is achieved in several ways depending on the situation. For example, bedrest, crutches, walkers, wheelchair, contact casts, and special healing footgear may be used.

Prognosis

The prognosis for foot infections in the older client with diabetes varies, depending on the condition of the individual and the timing and appropriateness of the treatments. The risks for amputation and death are real and important enough to stress prevention for all individuals with DM.

difficult the thyroid is to palpate. It is one of the most vascular of the endocrine glands, having a large capillary system. The thyroid gland maintains more than 1 month's surplus store of thyroid hormone. The liver, kidney, and muscle store thyroid hormone outside of the thyroid gland.

Internally, the thyroid gland is composed of hollow spherical structures called follicles. Follicles surround a protein colloid sac; this colloid sac is the storage site for the prehormone thyroglobulin. The follicles are separated from one another by connective tissue containing parafollicular cells. The parafollicular cells produce thyrocalcitonin, a calcium-lowering hormone. Neighboring principal cells manufacture thyroxine (T_4), and triiodothyronine (T_3).

The hypothalamus, in response to inadequate serum thyroid hormones, secretes thyroid-releasing hormone (TRH). This stimulates the anterior pituitary gland to "release" thyroid-stimulating hormone (TSH).

TSH signals the thyroid gland to increase synthesis and release of thyroid hormones T_4 and T_3 into circulation; TSH levels peak during the late evening and early

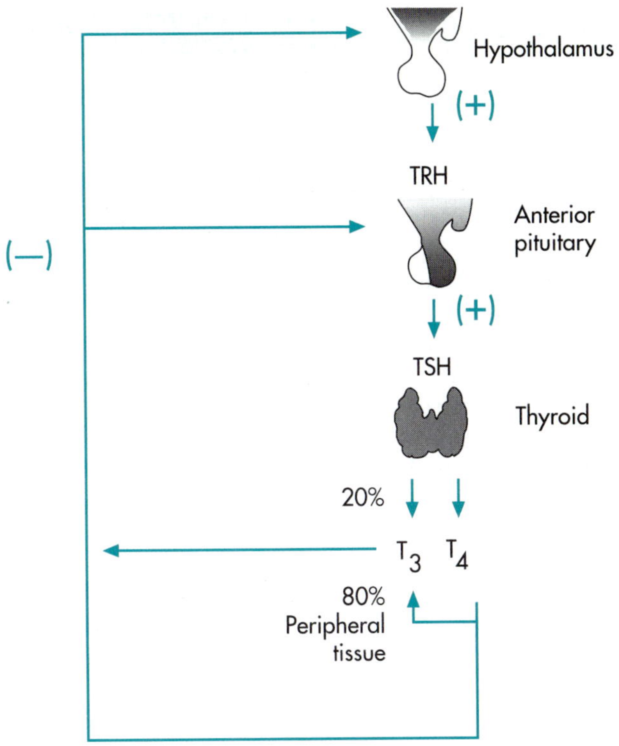

Fig. 23-3 Thyroid feedback.

morning hours. TSH secretion indicates decreased through a negative feedback loop when T_3 and T_4 levels are high. The negative feedback signal indicates that there is adequate levels of circulating thyroid hormone; TRH and TSH are not necessary at this time (Fig. 23-3).

Iodine is necessary to convert thyroglobulin to thyroxine. The follicular cells trap iodine from the plasma and through active transport; iodine then enters the thyroid cells and is oxidized. After attaching to the amino acid tyrosine, iodination occurs. The continued enzymatic coupling reaction produces T_4 and T_3; at this point, however, these hormones are still part of thyroglobulin. T_4 and T_3 are cleaved from thyroglobulin through an additional enzymatic reaction after stimulation of TSH. Thyroid hormones can then be released and can be stored in extracellular space and plasma. By specific deiodination in the peripheral tissue, 80% of T_4 is converted to T_3; T_3 is the form most often used for thyroid hormone function. T_4 and T_3 are bound to protein in the plasma; only a very small amount is unbound or free. The three proteins with a strong affinity to T_4 and T_3 are thyroid hormone-binding globulin, thyroxine-binding prealbumin, and albumin. Protein-bound thyroid hormone has no biologic activity, but keeps in equilibrium a constant level of free hormone by providing a reserve. Free T_3 and T_4 hormones (not bound to protein) act directly with the target tissue cell plasma membrane, mitochondria, and in the cell nucleus. All body cells are receptive to thyroid hormone.

Thyroid hormone primarily regulates catabolism for the expenditure of energy—"calorigenesis" at the cellular level. It increases the rate at which carbohydrates are burned and stimulates cells to break down proteins for fuel source. Thyroid hormone decreases the breakdown of fat and plays a role as an oxidative catalyst for activation of enzymes.

AGE-RELATED CHANGES IN THE THYROID

The normal aging thyroid consistently recognizes TSH and synthesizes thyroid hormone despite a decrease in thyroid follicle cell size. There is a decrease in size of the thyroid gland as a result of cellular atrophy, which is most notable in women over age 70. T_4 degradation is slower; the metabolic half-life of T_4 is several days longer than in younger adults. T_4 conversion to T_3 is diminished by 25% in older people. Thyroglobulin binding remains unchanged except with polypharmacy, since many drugs interfere with protein binding of T_4 and T_3.

Basal metabolic rate decreases by 30% when a person is in a hypothyroid state. However, when adjusted by body weight, less evidence of decline in basal metabolic rate occurs with aging.

Thyroid nodules are identified in 5% of people older than age 60, with 90% of nodules benign. Thyroid antibodies appear more often in women who are older than age 60 than in men or younger women. This condition of autoimmune thyroiditis can be triggered, for example, by a virus or treatment of Hodgkin's disease, which in turn manifests lymphocyte and plasma cell infiltrates, leading to the atrophy of thyroid tissue. Antithyroid antibodies can block the TSH receptors, yielding a thyroid deficient state (Box 23-2).

COMMON PROBLEMS AND CONDITIONS

Hypothyroidism

Autoimmune thyroiditis is the most common cause of primary **hypothyroidism** in older people; it is diagnosed in 5% of older women and 2% of men of the same age. Cases of mismanaged hyperthyroidism do occur where ablation of the thyroid gland with radioiodine or surgery has caused hypothyroidism. Drug-induced hypothyroidism can occur with lithium carbonate, amiodarone, and iodine. Another possible causative factor for hypothyroidism is posttreatment of head and neck cancer, such as radiation and surgery. Hypothalamic or pituitary problems are rarely the originating causes.

BOX 23-2

Normal Thyroid Values

T_4: 8 mcg/100 ml (TOTAL)
Free T_4: 2 ng/100 ml
T_3: 0.12 mcg/100 ml (TOTAL)
Free T_3: 0.28 ng/100 ml
TSH: less than 10 μ/l

Of the diagnoses of primary hypothyroidism, 90% are made during routine screening. The majority of cases are classified as subclinical hypothyroidism. Controversy currently exists over the cost and benefits of general thyroid screening and the efficacy of treating subclinical hypothyroidism.

The clinical symptoms of hypothyroidism in older people are atypical in comparison with hypothyroidism in younger people. The majority of cases (99%) of hypothyroidism in older adults are subclinical, inconspicuous, and have a slow progression toward thyroid failure. Since the condition is insidious, the symptoms are often attributed to "old age." Initially, nonspecific cognitive impairment, slow metabolism, and cardiovascular changes of accelerated macrovascular disease are apparent. Hypothyroidism may occur during a coexisting disease state. Depression is evident in half of the cases, along with underlying apathy and withdrawal.

The cause of the psychologic symptoms is unclear. Decreased appetite and weight loss are often overlooked. The decreased calorigenesis contributes to the symptom of cold intolerance. Hypercholesterolemia is also present as a metabolic change induced by limited thyroid hormone. Cardiovascular symptoms include bradycardia and angina pectoris, which occurs as often in women as in men. Dyspnea manifests as a result of congestive heart failure (CHF). Neuromuscular and neurosensory symptoms may not be linked to thyroid dysfunction when a client complains of muscle weakness, unsteady gait, hoarseness, or progressive deafness. A closer assessment may reveal a slow return phase of deep tendon reflexes, episodes of syncope, and rheumatic arthritis flares. Mild macrocytic anemia is commonly identified with hypothyroidism and occurs as a result of bone marrow hypoplasia of iron deficiency (Box 23-3) (see Medical Management box, p. 623).

BOX 23-3

Hypothyroidism in Older Adults

Signs and symptoms in order of precedence
Depression/lethargy
Mild anemia, constipation, weight loss or gain
Dyspnea
Muscle weakness/unsteady gait
Deafness, hoarseness
Chest pain/atrial fibrillation
Cold intolerance

Nursing Management

✣ ASSESSMENT

Subjective assessment of the older adult includes questioning about the following symptoms: constipation, lethargy, decreased tolerance to cold, generalized muscle weakness, and dry, atrophic skin. The client may answer questions in a slow and inappropriate manner as a result of the presence of emotional disturbances that are typically associated with hypothyroidism in older adults: depression, withdrawal, or dementia. The presence of cognitive slowing should be validated by previous documented history, or family or significant others.

The risk of overlooking hypothyroidism in older adults is high, because the symptoms of fatigue, altered cognitive function, and slowed physical movement are often attributed to "old age." The nurse should remember that the prevalence of hypothyroidism is high among older adults with cognitive impairment, and among women older than age 40 with such nonspecific complaints as fatigue (Goroll et al, 1995).

Objective assessment findings include dry skin and hair, hair loss, especially of the outer one third of the eyebrows; decreased hearing; slow, stiff movements; bradycardia; and dyspnea. In addition, review laboratory results for evidence of hyperlipidemia, anemia, and elevated blood glucose levels. Examine for the presence of infection. Physical examination should include careful palpation of the thyroid gland for size, consistency, and nodularity.

✣ DIAGNOSIS

Nursing diagnoses for the client with hypothyroidism include, but are not limited to: (1) constipation related to metabolic problems, (2) altered thought processes related to confusion as a result of altered thyroid function, (3) self-care deficit related to decreased strength and endurance and/or mental status changes as a result of altered thyroid function, and (4) fatigue related to decreased metabolic energy production.

✣ PLANNING

Expected outcomes for the older adult with hypothyroidism include but are not limited to the following: (1) client will establish a regular pattern of bowel movements, (2) client will experience fewer incidences of constipation, (3) client will return to baseline level of cognitive function, (4) client will perform self-care activities with minimum expenditure of energy and risk of injury, and (4) client will establish a satisfactory pattern of rest and activity that enables completion of everyday tasks. The family or significant others should be involved in the planning process, since their assistance may be needed with medication administration and monitoring the client's progress.

✥ INTERVENTION

The nursing plan of care should focus heavily on client and family education related to disease signs and symptoms, as well as medication therapy. Gradual replacement of thyroid hormone is essential. It is necessary for medication administration to be meticulously reviewed with the client and involved caregivers for their abilities to monitor the dosage accuracy and potential side effects.

> ***Insight*** • *Most myxedema coma clients are older than age 60. Coma may appear acutely after sedatives, cold weather, or infection. The mortality rate is 50%. Coma is reversible if recognized early and treated.*

Special precautions exist regarding proper dosing of levothyroxine sodium. Replacement therapy considerations include a history of heart disease, DM, hypertension, and decreased adrenal or pituitary function. It may take several weeks to notice a stabilization in symptoms of hypothyroidism. Double dosing and skip-

Thyroxin (on empty stomach)

MEDICAL MANAGEMENT

Hypothyroidism

Diagnostic tests and procedures

Laboratory screening for hypothyroidism typically indicates the presence of antithyroid antibodies, suppressed T_4, free T_4, a rise in TSH, and a normal T_3 level.

Treatment

Medical management of hypothyroidism consists of gradual, monitored replacement of thyroid hormone. The pattern of replacement is to initiate drug therapy with levothyroxine sodium at one third less dosage than is given to younger adults and to increase the dose at 4-week intervals. An average initial dose may be 25 to 50 mcg per day of levothyroxine sodium. Larger bolus doses of thyroxine may induce tachycardia and angina as a result of the increased myocardial oxygen demand. Likewise, thyroid hormone withdrawal should be slowly tapered over several months. Thyroid hormone panels are monitored during any adjustment of the hormone replacement and annually once the client is on a stable dose.

The TSH level is the best monitor for thyroid replacement. Continued elevation of TSH may indicate that the levothyroxine sodium dosage is too small or that the client is not consistently taking it. Suppressed TSH and elevated T_3 may be reflective of overmedication.

Investigation of potential underlying causes of hypothyroidism should be pursued, such as chronic illnesses or drugs that inhibit the function of thyroid hormones. It is paramount to review all the medications the client is taking to identify potential interactions with thyroid hormone. For example, a few drugs inhibit thyroxine absorption or effect by the progressive decrease in the metabolic clearance rate of T_4 in the liver. Drugs that accelerate T_4 breakdown are phenytoin, carbamazine, and rifampin. T_4 effect is elevated by estrogen and propanolol, and T_4 potentiates the effect of anticoagulants. As the client becomes euthyroid, other medications such as digoxin and insulin may need dose adjustments to accommodate the new metabolic state.

Prognosis

The prognosis for the older adult with hypothyroidism varies with the degree of the hypothyroid state and management of thyroid replacement therapy. Mild intellectual impairment from hypothyroidism is reversible, but treatment does not always return the mental status to the premorbid state, particularly in clients with more severe or prolonged hypothyroidism.

Prolonged hypothyroidism can lead to myxedema coma. The majority of clients who present with myxedema coma are older than age 60, and older individuals have a higher mortality. Epidemiologic studies indicate a strong correlation between the onset of myxedema coma with cold weather, infections, and sedative use. The coma results from reduced cerebral blood flow, hypoxia, hypercapnea, and hyponatremia. The myxedema client appears in a drowsy, often unconscious, or convulsive state. Hypothermia ($\leq$ 23.3°C, or 74°F), hypotension, periorbital edema, and nonpitting edema are also hallmark symptoms. Treatment at this critical period is aggressive IV boluses of thyroxine, correction of electrolyte abnormalities, and slow body core rewarming.

CARE PLAN

HYPOTHYROIDISM

Clinical situation Mrs. S is a 76-year-old who lives in a rural setting. She takes a bus to the senior center 3 days per week, where she participates in activities and enjoys a hot noon meal. Mrs. S has a past medical history of coronary heart disease. The staff has noticed she has withdrawn from the card table games, has complained of being tired and cold, and has had a poor appetite. Her apathetic affect is coupled with feelings of paranoia such as not being treated well at the center, but she is unable to articulate specific incidents.

The center has contacted the county community health nurse for further evaluation of Mrs. S. During the interview with the nurse, Mrs. S provides sketchy details of her problems. She describes that the duration of symptoms is about 4 months, occurring in a slow, delayed manner. She states that although it is summer, she uses an electric blanket, because she is so cold. Mrs. S is taking digoxin and cholestyramine. Signs of fatigue, weight loss, and hearing impairment are noted. Baseline blood values reveal that she is anemic, and has a deficient level of T_4 and an elevated of TSH. Mrs. S's daughter and neighbor are concerned about her physical deterioration and are alarmed by her paranoia. They are willing to be supportive of her care.

Nursing diagnoses	Outcomes	Interventions
Fatigue related to inability to restore energy secondary to effects of hypothyroidism	Client will verbalize overall improvement in energy as evidenced by verbalization of feeling rested and having energy to complete desired activities.	Determine physical limitations. Assess how much activity is required to build endurance. Monitor cardiorespiratory response to activity. Monitor sleep/rest and activity pattern; help client prioritize and identify alternate activities. Teach pacing techniques for performing ADLs. Assist the client in identifying which tasks friends and family can perform.
Altered thought process related to confusion as a result of hypothyroidism	Client will demonstrate improved cognitive functioning resulting in increased adaptive coping mechanisms.	Reassure that this condition is temporary. Keep directions concrete, simple, and specific. Encourage consistent daily routine. Identify potential dangers in the environment and make necessary adaptations to promote safety. Avoid unfamiliar situations for the client. Avoid situations that frustrate the client. Limit choices. Involve client and family in decision making.
Impaired home maintenance management related to altered cognitive functioning and fatigue	Client will adapt home environment to promote health and safety as evidenced by development of plan for keeping home clean and removing physical environmental hazards.	Arrange for assistance as needed (e.g., a homemaker or chore worker). Suggest safety aids for rental/purchase that promote independent self-care (e.g., bathtub rails, tub bench, and grab bars). Instruct to keep environment well-lit to enhance safe mobility. Assist family in developing realistic expectations of themselves in performing roles.
Lack of knowledge: medication therapy related to lack of previous experience	Client will demonstrate correct administration of levothyroxine regimen, including dose, time, and frequency. Receives a therapeutic level of thyroxine with minimal side effects.	Instruct client regarding drug name, purpose/action, correct self-administration, side effects, and precautions. Monitor for signs and symptoms of overtreatment, such as angina. Monitor for signs and symptoms of undertreatment, such as myxedema coma. Monitor for signs and symptoms of hypothermia, hypercapnia, hyponatremia, hypotension, and periorbital edema.

ping doses affect the therapeutic level of the drug, precipitating wide swings from the desired euthyroid state. Concomitant use of anticoagulants or cholestyramine interferes with drug absorption. Levothyroxine sodium overdose may manifest with severe chest pain, shortness of breath, and a fast, irregular heart rate. Symptoms of overtreatment may be identified in complaints of weight loss, difficulty sleeping, sweating, irritability, nervousness, leg cramps, fever, diarrhea, sensitivity to heat, or a headache. Hypothyroidism and hyperthyroidism often have opposing signs and symptoms. Understanding the symptoms of each reinforces knowledge of poor or precise control with regard to medication therapy. Blood levels of thyroid hormones are the best evaluation tool for monitoring treatment along with the client's perception of wellness (see nursing Care Plan, p. 624).

Insight • *The client should notify health care providers of any levothyroxine regimen before having dental work or surgery, since these procedures increase the metabolic demand on the body, as do other forms of severe stress.*

✣ EVALUATION

The nurse evaluates the client's achievement of the expected outcomes and return to a euthyroid state. Careful monitoring of signs and symptoms of hypothyroidism and hyperthyroidism is essential to monitoring the effects of replacement therapy.

HOME CARE TIPS

1. Regularly assess the homebound older adult diagnosed with an endocrine disorder for signs and symptoms indicating exacerbation or instability.
2. Instruct the caregiver and homebound older adult about reportable signs and symptoms related to the endocrine problem being monitored, and when to report these changes to the home care nurse or physician.
3. Instruct caregivers and homebound older adults on types, dosage of insulin, and technique of administering. Have caregiver and homebound older adult return demonstrate this skill. Ensure that they receive written instructions to assist them in the learning process.
4. Instruct caregivers and homebound older adults about laboratory indications used to evaluate endocrine disorders. Inform them of the results of the tests *after* the physician has been notified.
5. Instruct caregivers and homebound older adults on safety tips related to insulin injection. Injecting humulin insulin and then switching without a physician order to beef or pork insulin results in altering the times of insulin action, initiation, peak insulin action, and duration of insulin action.
6. Instruct caregivers and homebound older adults on diabetes management.
7. Instruct caregivers and homebound older adults on proper dosage of medications used to treat hormone imbalances associated with endocrine disorders.

Summary

The endocrine system is a complex chemical communication pathway system comprised of many glands and hormones that maintain homeostasis through the release, transport, and interaction of the various hormones. The system functions to support and to maintain growth, development, metabolism, energy production, and maintenance of bodily functions. Age-related changes in both the reception and production of hormones affect the function of the pituitary, parathyroid, thyroid, and adrenal glands, pancreas, ovaries, and testes. The common pathophysiologic changes that commonly occur in older people include type II DM and hypothyroidism. The nurse's role in caring for older clients with these disorders should emphasize maintenance of functional ability while promoting safe, effective management of medications aimed at producing stable organ function.

Key Points

- The endocrine system is regulated by feedback systems that involve a chemical connection between structures of the brain, peripheral glands, and hormones. The feedback loops regulate hormone production.
- Hormones secreted by the discrete glands of the body have specific target cells or tissues that are responsive to the hormone.
- An endocrine hypofunctioning state is one that results from inadequate endocrine secretions.
- An endocrine hyperfunctioning state is one that results from excessive secretion of hormones.
- Endocrine pathology may also be manifested in the form of hormone resistance, a condition in which there is an inadequate tissue response to hormones. Resistance can be caused by a genetic defect or acquired, as in the case of type II DM.
- Type II DM is very common in the older population, with a prevalence range of 12% to 18%, depending on the study cited.

- The most important variables associated with type II DM are obesity and insulin resistance.
- Older individuals with type II DM should strive for proper control of their blood glucose to reduce the risk for potential complications.
- A comprehensive nursing assessment of older clients with type II DM should include assessment of feet, knowledge of diabetes management (diet, desirable weight, exercise, medications, treatment of hypoglycemia and hyperglycemia), learning styles, and emergency identification.
- The optimum management of serious wounds in older clients with diabetes needs to involve a multidisciplinary health team.
- Primary hypothyroidism in older people may often be unnoticed or indiscernible. Symptoms of mild depression, apathy, decreased appetite, weight loss and weakness should be investigated.
- Thyroid hormone replacement should always be carefully monitored; follow-up appointments are essential for incremental dosing over several weeks.

Critical Thinking Exercises

1. Summarize the changes that occur in each of the endocrine glands with the aging process, and describe the consequences of those changes to the older adult client.
2. A 69-year-old man was recently diagnosed with diabetes. While teaching him to administer his own insulin, you note that he is unable to draw up the correct number of units of insulin. What further information do you need about your client before proceeding, and how can you best intervene?
3. Complications of diabetes, such as foot ulcers, are more serious when they occur in older adult clients. Explain why this is the case based on age-related physiologic changes.

REFERENCES

Beaser R et al: Buyer's guide to diabetes supplies, *Diabetes Forec* 10(46):48-88, October 1993.

Gambert S: Atypical presentation of diabetes in the elderly, *Clin Geriatr Med* 6(4):721-729, Nov. 1990.

Graham C: Exercise in the elderly patient with diabetes, *Practic Diabetol* 10(5):8-11 September/October 1991.

Guthrie D et al, editors: *Diabetes education: a core curriculum for health professionals,* 1988, American Association of Diabetes Educators.

Lun W, Wing S: Oral agents in the elderly, *Practic Diabetol* 12(4):10-13, December 1993.

Minnaker K: What diabetologist should know about elderly patients, *Diabetes Care* 13(suppl 2):34-45, February 1990.

National Diabetes Data Group: Classification and diagnosis of diabetes mellitus and other categories of glucose intolerance, *Diabetes* 28:1039-1057, 1979.

Peragallo-Dittko V, editor: *A core curriculum for diabetes education,* ed 2, Chicago, 1993, American Association of Diabetes Educators, AADE Education and Research Foundation.

Simon N, Frishman W: Diabetes mellitus in the elderly, *Practic Diabetol* 12(1):4-13, March 1993.

Sperling MA, editor: *Physician's guide to insulin dependent (Type I) diabetes diagnosis and treatment,* Alexandria, Va., 1988, ADA, Inc.

Wilson J, Foster D: Hormones and hormone action. In Wilson J, Foster D, editors: *Williams textbook of endocrinology,* Philadelphia, 1992, WB Saunders.

Yuh W et al: Osteomyelitis of the foot in diabetic patients: evaluation with plain film, 99m Tc-MDP bone scintigraphy, and MR imaging, *Diabetes Spectr* 4(2):80-86, March/April 1991.

BIBLIOGRAPHY

Ahroni J: Teaching foot care creatively and successfully, *Tool Chest Diabetes Educat* 19(4):320-325, July/August 1993.

Armbrecht H, Coe R, Wongsurawat IV: *Endocrine function and aging,* New York, 1990, Springer-Verlag.

Bardin C, editor: *Current therapy in endocrinology and metabolism,* ed 4, Philadelphia, 1992, BC Decker.

Cryer P: Glucose homeostasis and hypoglycemia. In Wilson J, Foster D, editors: *Williams textbook of endocrinology,* Philadelphia, 1992, WB Saunders.

Doenges M et al, editors: *Nursing care plans,* Philadelphia, 1985, FA Davis.

Franz M et al: *Goals for diabetes education,* American Diabetes Association Task Group for Diabetes Education, 1986, pp 10-12.

Fylling C: From research to practice conclusions, *Diabetes Spectr* 5(6):358-359, November/December 1992.

Goroll AH, May LA, Mulley AG: *Primary care medicine: office evaluation and management of the adult patient,* ed 3, Philadelphia, 1995, JB Lippincott.

Greenspan F: *Basic and clinical endocrinology,* Norwalk, Conn., 1991, Appleton & Lange.

Hall M, MacLennan W, Lye M: *Medical care of the elderly,* ed 3, New York, 1994, John Wiley & Sons.

Harris M et al: Prevalence of diabetes and impaired glucose tolerance and plasma glucose levels in the U.S. population aged 20-74 years, *Diabetes Spectr* 2(3):155-164, May/June 1989.

Hazlett J: The diabetes control and complications trial, *Diabetes Self Manag* 10(5):6-8, September/October 1993.

Hutchinson J, McGuckin M: Occlusive dressings: a microbiologic and clinical review 18(4):257-268, 1990.

Knighton D et al: Treating diabetic foot ulcers, *Diabetes Spectr* 3(1):51-56, January/February 1990.

Lebovitz H, editor: *Physician's guide to non-insulin dependent (type II) diabetes: diagnosis and treatment,* ed 2, Alexandria, Va., 1988, American Diabetes Association.

Levin M et al: *Neuropathic ulcers and the diabetic foot, treatment of chronic wounds number 1 in a series.* New York, June 1991, Curative Technologies, Inc., Wound Care Center.

Lipsky B et al: Foot ulceration and infections in elderly diabetics, *Clin Geriatr Med* 6(4):747-769, November 1990.

Lipsky B et al: Outpatient management of uncomplicated lower-extremity infections in diabetic patients, *Diabetes Spectr* 4(2):70, 1991.

Lloyd R: *Endocrine pathology,* New York, 1990, Springer-Verlag.
MacLennan W, Peden N: *Metabolic and endocrine problems in the elderly,* New York, 1989, Springer-Verlag.
Malone JM, Snyder M: Prevention of amputation by diabetic education, *Diabetes Spectr* 4(6):351, 1991.
McCloskey J, Bulechek G: *Nursing interventions classification,* Baltimore, 1992, Mosby.
McDougall I: *Thyroid disease in clinical practice,* New York, 1992, Oxford University Press.
McFarland G, McFarlane E: *Nursing diagnosis and intervention planning for patient care,* Baltimore, 1993, Mosby.
Mecklenburg R: Diabetes 1988 Sick Day Management, p. 15.
Mooradian A: Caring for the elderly nursing home patient with diabetes, *Diabetes Spectr* 5(6):318-320, 1992.
Morley J, Kaiser F: Unique aspects of diabetes mellitus in the elderly clinics, *Geriatr Med* 6(4):693-702, November 1990.
National Diabetes Data Group: Classification and diagnosis of diabetes mellitus and other categories of glucose intolerance, *Diabetes* 28:1039-1057, 1979.
Pecoraro R, Reiber G, Burgess E: Pathways to diabetic limb amputation: basis for prevention, *Diabetes Spectr* 5(6):329-334, November/December 1992.
Porte D, Kahn S: What geriatricians should know about diabetes mellitus, *Diabetes Care* 13(suppl 2):47-54, Feb. 1990.
Ruby K et al: The knowledge and practices of registered nurse, certified diabetes educators: teaching elderly clients about exercise, *Diabetes Educ* 19(4):299-306, July/August 1993.
Sapolsky R: Endocrine system. In Schneider, Rowe JW, editors: *Handbook of the biology of aging,* ed 3, San Diego, Calif., 1990, Academic Press.
Steil C: Prescription drugs and diabetes, *Diabetes Spectr* 3(2):119-122, 1990.
Unger R, Foster D: Diabetes mellitus. In Wilson J, Foster D, editors: *Williams textbook of endocrinology,* Philadelphia, 1992, WB Saunders.
Yarborough P, Goodman R: OTC products for diabetic foot care, *Practic Diabetol* 11(1):20-23, March 1992.
Yoshikawa T, Cobbs E, Brummel-Smith K: *Ambulatory geriatric care,* Baltimore, 1993, Mosby.

CHAPTER 24

Liver Function

LEARNING OBJECTIVES

On completion of this chapter, the reader will be able to:

1. Discuss the normal, age-related changes that occur in the liver.
2. Develop a nursing care plan for an older adult with primary biliary cirrhosis (PBC).
3. Discuss the nursing management of viral hepatitis C (HCV) in the older adult.
4. Apply the nursing process in the care of older clients with liver disorders.

Significant decrease of liver function is not an inevitable state of aging. Yet because the incidence of chronic diseases increases with age, liver disorders are more common. For example, the prevalence of gallstones increases with age. Therefore older people are more vulnerable to secondary biliary disorders and bacterial infections of the biliary system. Older individuals with viral hepatitis (A, B, C, and D) have a higher morbidity rate than younger people. Older clients with viral hepatitis also may have a greater incidence of secondary complications such as liver cancer. Systemic disease states such as heart failure also can precipitate abnormal changes in liver function.

Older people may show more overt signs and symptoms of autoimmune diseases of the liver. Older individuals with alcoholic liver disease often have more severe and protracted symptomology with their condition.

In general, liver pathology with aging is not a widespread problem. However, when it occurs, liver function tests are valid indicators of liver disease (Evans, 1992).

NORMAL STRUCTURE AND FUNCTION

The healthy liver is the largest organ in the body, weighing approximately 3.3 lbs. This wedge-shaped organ is situated in the upper right quadrant of the peritoneal cavity. The liver has two lobes that are encapsulated together, yet each has its own separate blood supply. The lobes are also divided into eight segments (Fig. 24-1).

The falciform ligaments attach and support the supe-

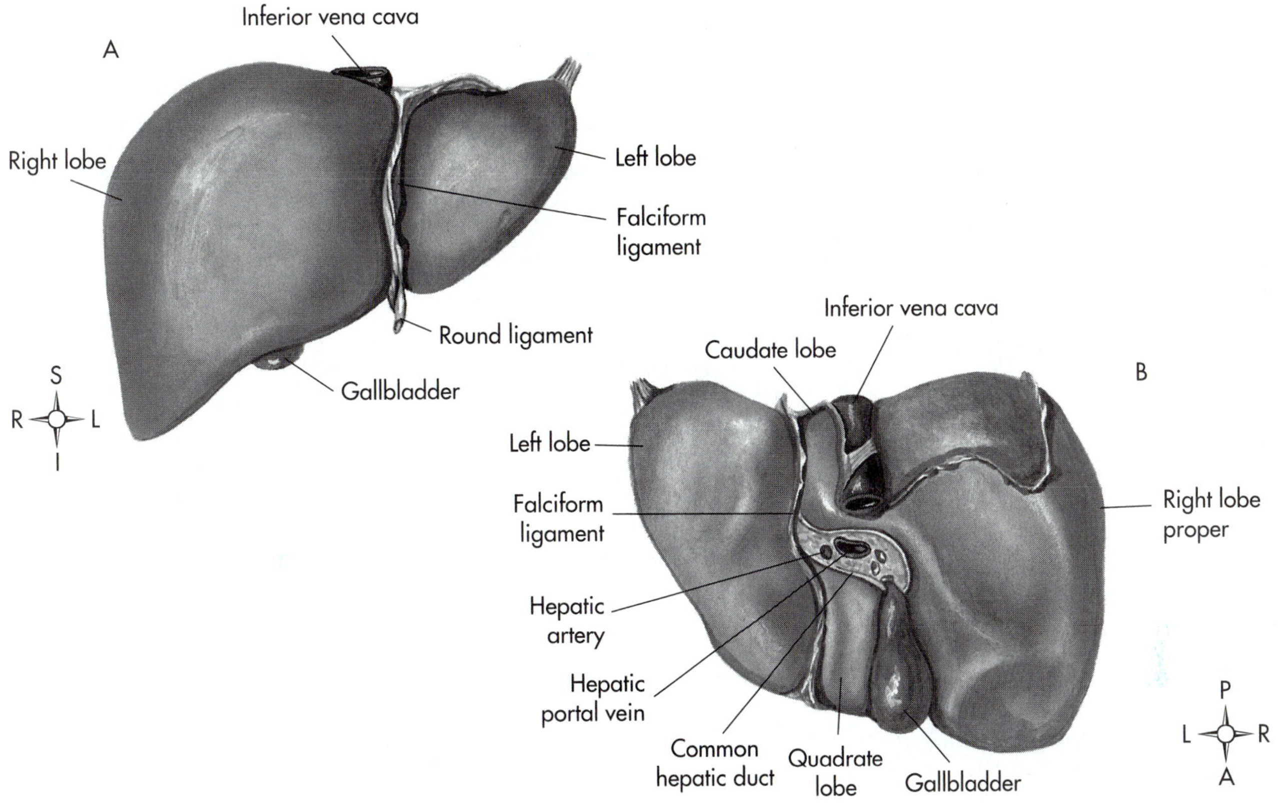

Fig. 24-1 Gross structure of the liver. **A,** Anterior view. **B,** Inferior view. (From Thibodeau GA, Patton KT: *Anthony's textbook of anatomy and physiology,* ed 14, St. Louis, 1994, Mosby.)

rior surface of the liver to the midline abdominal wall near the diaphragm. Posteriorly, the triangular ligaments support the structure, but the lateral aspect of the left liver is suspended freely. The triangular ligament becomes the lesser omentum, which is located between the stomach and the liver.

The sympathetic nerves enter from the thoracic segments. The parasympathetic nerve supply branches from the left and right vagus nerves.

The hepatic artery circulates 30% of the liver's oxygenated arterial blood flow from the abdominal artery. The portal vein carries 70% of the liver's nutrient-laden blood supply from the intestines and spleen, and it extends from the superior mesenteric vein. The liver receives about 1,000 to 1,400 ml/min of blood. The two main hepatic veins drain into the inferior vena cava.

The liver lymph nodes track along the ligaments of the inferior vena cava and the common bile duct. Deep lymphatic nodes lie alongside the portal vein and interface with the biliary and hepatic artery nodes.

The **hepatocyte** cells are the most important of the liver cells. Hepatocytes are part of the acinus structure, which consists of zones and portal blood tracks. The acinus component plays a role in the biochemical metabolic processes. Chains of hepatocytes surround the central vein and make up individual liver lobules.

Blood also flows from hepatic arteries and the portal vein into the sinusoids, which take the place of capillaries. The blood then flows from the sinusoids to the central vein. The venous sinusoids (vessels of endothelial cells) are lined with phagocytic **Kupffer's cells.** These Kupffer's cells are large macrophages that degrade old blood cells and bacteria. The sinusoids also store fat cells.

Hepatocytes are lined on one side by portal venous vessels (sinusoid) and on the other side by the **bile canaliculi** (Fig. 24-2). The **space of Disse** is an actual site located under the endothelial cells of the venous sinusoid. In this site, the plasma of the body circulates. Many plasma components such as proteins are exchanged within the liver in the space of Disse. Hepatocytes freely communicate with the intrahepatic bile duct system and the venous, arterial, and lymphatic vessels. It is easy to understand how the liver accomplishes its many functions,

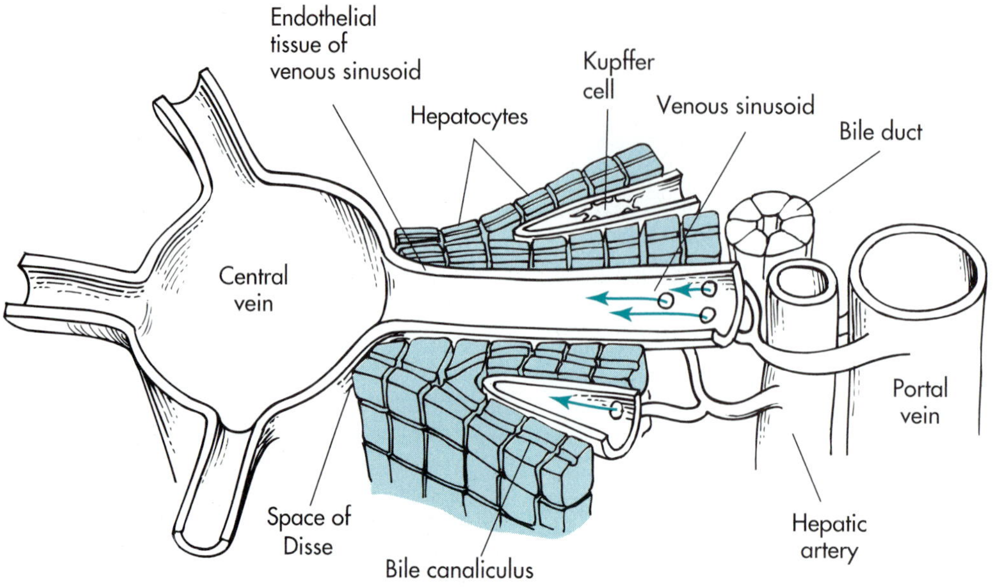

Fig. 24-2 Liver lobule unit.

since the hepatocyte communicates so freely with body fluids such as bile, blood, and lymph.

The liver surrounds the gallbladder, which contains concentrates and releases bile. The cystic duct attaches to the common hepatic duct, which in turn stems from the right and left hepatic ducts. The common hepatic duct then merges into the common **bile duct,** which travels through the pancreas and passes into the duodenal wall through the choledochal sphincter. The common bile duct ends by sharing a channel with the pancreatic duct at the Vater's ampulla.

The gallbladder contracts and empties in a sequential process. Ingested food stimulates cholecystokinin production, which causes the gallbladder to contract. Vagal stimulation also facilitates gallbladder contraction. The Oddi's sphincter relaxes with the stimuli of gallbladder contraction and bowel peristalsis. Lastly, bile discharges into the duodenum for direct action on small bowel contents.

Bile is an excretory product and a digestive secretion of the liver. It consists of water, electrolytes, bilirubin, cholesterol, phospholipids, and ions. Bile is stored in the gallbladder. The hormone cholecystokinin, which is produced by the small intestine, stimulates the release of bile.

Bile salts assist the body with the breakdown of fats into smaller molecules (emulsifying function), as well as the absorption of fats and fat-soluble vitamins.

Bilirubin excretion takes place through bile flow. Therefore, normal bilirubin excretion depends on an intact intra- and extrahepatic biliary system.

Four important functions of the liver are metabolism, detoxification, storage, and secretion. Metabolic functions are focused on conversion and storage of cellular fuel sources such as carbohydrates, proteins, and fats. The body has several mechanisms to maintain blood glucose levels. For example, the liver directly stores a 24-hour supply of simple sugars in the form of glycogen through the process of glucogenesis. Stored glycogen can be converted to glucose through glycogenolysis. Once glycogen stores are depleted, gluconeogenesis allows further glucose to be generated.

Protein metabolism involves the synthesis of albumin, globulins, and fibrinogen in the liver. The liver is the site where mast cells and proteins interact to produce anticoagulants such as heparin. Deamination of amino acids also occurs in the liver. In addition, ammonia, the harmful byproduct of protein, can be converted into urea in the liver and then excreted through the kidneys.

Fat can be stored in the liver and then used through catabolism, an oxidation process. Free fatty acids are converted into triglycerides and phospholipids. Cholesterol is also generated from lipid metabolism in the liver.

Detoxification of drugs and hormones is a unique function in the portal circulation of the liver. The Kupffer's cells phagocytize bacteria and viruses and are considered part of the immune defense system. Potential toxic substances such as hormones and drugs can be transformed into an inactive state and reconjugated for excretion into bile or urine.

The liver directly receives nutritional elements after digestion, then reconstructs, stores, and distributes these elements to other systems of the body. This is demonstrated with carbohydrates, which are stored in the form of glycogen, and with the conversion of amino acids into usable protein for peripheral tissue growth. The fat-soluable vitamins A, D, E, and K are stored in the liver, as are B_{12} and the elements copper and iron. Activation of the inert vitamin D occurs in the liver.

BOX 24-1

Normal Clinical Values of Liver Function Tests

1. Alkaline phosphatase (ALP)—20 to 90 U/L
2. Alanine aminotransferase (ALT), formerly called serum glutamic pyruvic transaminase (SGPT)—4 to 36 U/L
3. Aspartate aminotransferase (AST), formerly called serum glutamic oxaloacetic transaminase (SGOT)—Adult men: 8 to 46 U/L; adult women: 7 to 34 U/L
4. Billirubin—TOTAL: 0.3 to 1.2 mg/100 ml

Bile is produced by individual hepatocytes. The gallbladder is the reservoir for the storage and concentration of about 40 to 70 ml of bile. Each day the body releases about 1 l of bile per day for eventual emulsification effect in the small intestines. Plasma volume and homeostasis of electrolytes are also monitored by the liver, mainly water balance and sodium excretion.

A remarkable characteristic of the liver is its ability to regenerate tissue. Damaged liver tissue after assault by toxins, obstruction, or poor circulation can repair itself through the liver cell's cooperation with the immune system. Hepatocytes totally divide twice during a healthy lifetime (Box 24-1).

AGE-RELATED CHANGES IN STRUCTURE AND FUNCTION

The liver is a very sturdy organ and is resilient for most of its functions throughout the life span. However, there is a correlating decrease in overall liver mass (volume and weight), with progressive age, by approximately 37% (James, 1992). Although the hepatic lobe size remains the same over time, clearance studies have identified a 35% decline in blood flow with increased age (James, 1992). Hepatocytes and the spaces between them enlarge with age. In the absence of disease they continue to maintain their function. Most studies of alterations in hepatic function with aging have been limited to lower animals. Human studies have shown a decrease in enzyme activity along with a decrease in the synthesis of cholesterol and reduced bile storage with aging (James, 1992). Research on the metabolic actions of drug clearance shows a decreasing function with aging from 5% to 30%. There is some evidence to suggest that normal aging may adversely affect liver tissue regeneration. The mechanism of this effect is not fully known but may be a result of a generalized slowing of repair or an inadequate response to regeneration of liver tissue (Millward-Sadler et al 1992).

The increased vulnerability of older people to potential drug toxicity has implications for nursing (see Chapter 20). The nurse can be a proactive advocate by obtaining a detailed history of drug use, to include prescribed and over-the-counter (OTC) medications. Ask clients if they are being seen by several physicians, and obtain a history of smoking, alcohol, and caffeine intake. Explain the use and effect of all medications to the client and the family or significant other. Strongly encourage the client to discard all outdated, duplicate, and drugs that are not used. Ask the client to read the label to assess for clarity and type large enough to read. Assess for the need for a calendar or diary for tracking the medication schedule. Advocate to simplify the regimen as much as possible. The standard dose for a specific medication published in a formulary may still be too high for an older adult. Combination drug therapies can provide a beneficial effect in many cases, but stress with the client the need for continued monitoring by the primary care physician.

COMMON PROBLEMS AND CONDITIONS

Cirrhosis

Cirrhosis is a general term that refers to liver damage resulting from an inflammatory process. In cirrhosis, there is hepatic **parenchymal** damage and irreversible fibrosis.

About 80% of all cases of cirrhosis are because of alcohol abuse. Alcohol-induced cirrhosis is sometimes called Laennec's, portal, or micronodular cirrhosis. In this type of cirrhosis, the liver develops fatty infiltrates and enlarges in size, taking on a nodular appearance. The condition progresses with continued alcohol abuse until many hepatocytes die, replaced by scarring of the liver from deposition of connective and fibrotic tissues.

Insight • *Many health care providers assume that cirrhosis in the older person is almost always caused by alcohol abuse. In fact, this commonly held assumption has been challenged with the findings of today. Cirrhosis is not caused only by alcoholism. Nonalcohol-related diseases such as primary biliary cirrhosis, drug hepatotoxicity, and infectious and autoimmune hepatitis can also cause cirrhosis. Other conditions that can cause cirrhosis in older adults include some forms of heart disease (Levinson, Gordon, 1990).*

These changes cause obstruction and engorgement of the vascular or sinusoidal system of the liver, which then lead to portal hypertension. The serious complications of cirrhosis, **ascites,** encephalopathy, and esophageal **varices** are directly related to the severity of the portal hypertension (Maher, 1992).

Primary Biliary Cirrhosis

Primary biliary cirrhosis (PBC) is a rare chronic condition in which inflammation of the intrahepatic bile ductules leads to complications of **cholestasis** (blockage of bile flow), pruritus, jaundice, **hypercholesterolemia,** and malabsorption. The most significant feature of this condition is destructive **cholangitis,** destruction of the intrahepatic bile ducts. The term cholangitis refers to inflammation of the bile duct itself.

The cause of PBC is unknown, although an altered immune response has been theorized to be involved, since the condition is often seen with other autoimmune disorders such as thyroiditis. Supporting the autoimmunity association is the incidence of elevated **immune gamma globulin (IgG)** antibodies, which are found in 95% of individuals with PBC.

Sherlock (1991) describes four other possible causal variables besides the altered immune system, including "loss of tolerance to tissues displaying **human leukocyte antigen (HLA)** class antigens, immune-complex bile duct injury, mitochondrial antibodies cross reacting with gram-negative bacteria, and hepatic copper retention (found in all forms of cholestasis)."

The pathophysiologic process of cirrhosis is irreversible hepatic parenchymal damage and fibrosis. When this happens, the liver regenerates and forms nodules surrounded by concentric bands of fibrosis. Individual liver cells, or hepatocytes, necrose. As the damage progresses, parts of the liver architecture are destroyed, and connective tissue develops in the place of normal tissues. The vascular system of the liver is also adversely affected by these processes.

PBC involves pathology within the bile ducts. Analysis of bile ducts in PBC reveals lymphocytes and tissue damage that resembles the damage found in graft-versus-host disease. Unlike secondary biliary cirrhosis, where there is blockage of the bile ducts, in PBC there is usually no blockage or infection. Instead of blockage, in PBC the intrahepatic bile ducts actually disappear.

There are four stages of disease in PBC. Stage I, or chronic destructive cholangitis, manifests with destruction of both the small and medium bile ducts. Other parameters of stage II disease include acute and chronic inflammation, and bile stasis. Stage II is characterized by a reduction of the number of bile ducts, as well as proliferation of the ducts. In stage III, there is a continued downsizing in the number of ducts and hepatocytes, as well as an increase in fibrosis and scarring. The last stage of PBC is the point at which cirrhosis develops (Podolsky, Isselbacher, 1987).

The incidence of PBC increases with age and is most commonly found in women between the ages of 40 and 60. The average age of onset of PBC is 50. Although the condition usually begins in the fifth decade, the condition progresses well into the 6th and 7th decade of life for most clients, therefore it is a serious condition in the older adult population. Women are 10 times more likely to have PBC, and the condition is found throughout the world.

Initially, many individuals with PBC have no symptoms. The diagnosis of PBC is often made with treatment or screening for other problems. For example, the client may seek health care for thyroid disease or arthritis.

The chief early complaints are fatigue and pruritus. Later developing signs include jaundice, diarrhea, and slow weight loss. The weight loss of PBC is because of malabsorption resulting from an excessive loss of fat in the feces. Other symptoms or signs associated with PBC are bone pain, increased ease of bruising, and night blindness. These symptoms and signs appear as a result of malabsorption of vitamins and nutrients.

Skin changes include yellow plaque formations, as well as thickening and darkening of the skin. When itching is intense, development of skin lesions from scratching is common.

The pathophysiologic mechanism of why the client with PBC itches is not clearly known. Impaired secretion of bile associated with chronic liver disease leads to elevated serum levels of bilirubin, bile acids, and cholesterol. In the past, the cause of itching in PBC was thought to be a result of these agents exerting a pruritogenic effect on the nerves of the skin. Studies of the skin or serum did not show an association between itching and any particularly high concentration of a bile acid. Also, when itching ceases in end-stage liver failure, bile acids may be at the highest level. Therefore the theory that the high bile acids cause the itching is not supported with this evidence.

Recent research suggests other mechanisms may be involved in the pathology of the itching, such as a central neurogenic origin implicating opiate receptors. Treatments based on this theory have included the use of drugs such as narcan and nalmephene (see Research box, p. 633).

In advanced disease the ominous signs of ascites, bleeding from esophageal varices, and encephalopathy can occur. Esophageal varices are engorged and dilitated veins of the submucosa of the esophagus. Clients can have esophageal varices without pain. Esophageal varices can rupture and cause life-threatening hemorrhage. Older individuals who may already have some degree of anemia are at even greater risk from hemorrhaging.

RESEARCH

Bergasa NV et al: A controlled trial of naloxone infusions for the pruritus of chronic cholestasis. *Gastroenterol* 10(2): 544, 1992.

Sample, setting

Adult men and women participated in drug trials at the NIH in order to test the theory that the pruritus had a centrally mediated origin.

Methodology

Drugs were tested against placebos to assess the efficacy for reduction of itching in PBC.

Findings

Opiate antagonists were effective with some patients in reducing the pruritis found in PBC.

Implications

Individuals with PBC may have another alternative for treating their itching. The nurse should carefully assess patients for signs and symptoms of itching and contact the physician for appropriate medication orders. In addition, the nurse should monitor the effectiveness of any medication. Nursing measures, such as engaging the patient in diversional activities, should be implemented to augment the medication.

Esophageal varices are diagnosed by upper endoscopy procedures. Several procedures are used to treat bleeding esophageal varices, including injection of sclerosing agents into the varices, balloon tamponade, portal-systemic shunting, or **band ligation** during endoscopy, which is one of the more recently developed therapies. Esophageal variceal ligation involves applying rubber bands to the varices. During the endoscopic procedure, the varices are identified and suctioned into a section of the endoscope, then the rubber band is fastened around the varices. This procedure is repeated for each varix in the distal esophagus that is at risk for rupture.

Many of the procedures used to diagnose or to treat complications of cirrhosis (e.g., ERCP, endoscopy, and liver biopsy) may involve the use of conscious sedation. In **conscious sedation,** medications (usually intravenous [IV] drugs) are administered to relax the client and to reduce pain sensations during procedures. The intent is to maintain an awake and alert enough state so that the client can independently maintain an airway and respond to verbal commands. In the older adult, conscious sedation is indicated but dosages of medications and drug selection may be modified. Medications commonly used during conscious sedation include benzodiazepines such as Valium or Versed, as well as narcotics such as Demerol.

Older adults are more likely to have dentures or dental appliances that may interfere with procedures involving endoscopy. Aspiration, a risk of conscious sedation, may be slightly increased in this population. When giving verbal instructions to the older client under conscious sedation, it is important to know if the client has a hearing impairment. Individuals who are very old are at greater risk for environmental temperature variations, since their thermal control mechanisms may be less effective as a result of alterations of sweat gland function, vasomotor control, and basal metabolic rate (BMR) (McFarland, McFarlane, 1993). Therefore the temperature should be taken before procedures, and blankets should be available during and after procedures. Aging may adversely affect the ability to maintain the airway through effective coughing, particularly with conscious sedation. The risk of lung infection is greater in older adults because of their lower levels of immunoglobulin A, altered alveolar macrophage function, and decreased ciliary action (see Medical Management box, p. 634).

NURSING MANAGEMENT

The nursing management of the individual with PBC includes a comprehensive nursing care plan. Particular attention is given to the areas most likely to be affected by this condition, such as skin integrity, nutrition, coping, anxiety, and activity.

✣ ASSESSMENT

Clients should be asked for details about the typical signs and symptoms such as itching. Specific problem areas of the body may be identified by the client. The onset, intensity, frequency, and duration of itching should be documented. Previous treatments used and efficacy also assist in selection of therapies. The nurse should also inquire about overall skin condition, including integrity, sensations, thickening, coloring, and the presence of lesions.

Fatigue is often subjectively described in general ways such as "I don't have the energy I used to," or "I'm just not able to keep up all the things I used to be able to do." Clients can verbalize fatigue and activity changes more definitively by describing how many stairs they can climb or how long they can walk without stopping.

Mood can be assessed subjectively in a number of ways. Mood is a critical factor in this condition, since the complications of PBC can lead to serious depression and even suicide in some clients. Anxiety and coping can be evaluated in the interview by determining energy level, mood state, and self-care measures that are taken to effectively manage the condition. Inquire about the use of tranquilizers and sedatives. Allow time for clients to ver-

MEDICAL MANAGEMENT

PBC

Diagnostic tests and procedures

Liver biopsy is a procedure that may be used to diagnose PBC. Liver biopsy may identify the presence of intrahepatic duct cholestasis, but since it often does not include septal or interlobular bile ducts, it may not provide the needed information. Liver biopsies are carefully considered for the older individual, partly because of the risk of hemorrhage.

Other laboratory tests commonly conducted include serum bilirubin, alkaline phosphatase, alanine and aspartate transaminase, albumin, and antimitochondrial antibody (AMA). The results of these tests are usually increased in PBC. AMA is found in about 80% to 95% of clients with PBC and represents an important diagnostic test over another antibody, the bile canalicular antibody, which is only present in 20% to 40% of clients with PBC (Triger, Wright, 1992).

An endoscopic radiologic procedure called an **endoscopic retrograde cholangiopancreatography (ERCP)** is sometimes conducted to help visualize the duct system and rule out pathology such as bile duct stones or strictures. ERCPs are usually very well-tolerated in older adults, including frail older adults. Before these procedures were developed, some older individuals did not receive full treatment for disorders of the gastrointestinal or biliary system. **Endoscopy** procedures allow treatment and diagnosis without some of the more serious risks associated with surgical interventions (Hall, 1993).

Treatment

Treatment for PBC varies with whether the individual is asymptomatic, symptomatic (but not in end-stage liver disease), or in end-stage liver disease. No cure or proven therapy for PBC that is universally accepted for all clients exists. Drug therapies that have some efficacy include Colchicine, Ursodeoxycholic acid, D-penicillamine, Azathioprine, and Prednisolone, as well as immunosuppresive agents such as Chlorambucil, Cyclosporin A, and Methotrexate. Many of the drug therapies used in PBC have caused significant complications to bone, kidneys, and bone marrow.

The best treatment for PBC would be prevention of toxicity to the liver by the avoidance of possible harmful dietary and environmental assaults. Other treatments are based on the symptoms of the client. Cholestyramine is used to provide relief from pruritus. Some investigational agents recently used to relieve the severe pruritus of PBC include Narcan and Nalmephene (Bergasa et al, 1992). The client in the last stages of PBC may experience uncontrollable itching and severe jaundice. Intractable pruritus associated with neuropathy has been treated in the past with plasmapheresis with mixed results. The three types of drugs used in PBC include immunomodulators, antifibrotics, and anticholestatics. The first drug type is used in the early phase of the disease, whereas second and third types of drugs have been used to attempt to prevent cirrhosis and liver failure.

Diet therapy in PBC may include a low-fat diet prescription when **steatorrhea** is present. Supplementation with vitamins A, D, K, zinc, and calcium is prescribed for selected clients, depending on symptomology.

Liver transplantation is indicated in PBC when the liver has failed or when the client cannot tolerate the symptoms of the disease. In the past, older adults were not given full consideration for liver transplants as they are today. Levinson and Gordon (1991) stated, "Advanced age is no longer to be considered an absolute contraindication for liver transplantation." However, the issue remains controversial, as reflected in the statement from James (1992):

> In present circumstances, however, where resources are scarce, and particularly since prognosis following liver transplantation for whatever reason appears to be adversely affected by advanced age of the recipient, the author does not feel that liver transplantation is a viable option for treatment of individuals over 65 with terminal hepatic failure except in very unusual circumstances.

Prognosis

The results of studies determining life expectancy for individuals with symptomatic and asymptomatic PBC conflict (Levinson, Gordon, 1991). Medication regimens have shown variable lasting curative effects. When the condition occurs in conjunction with other factors such as high bilirubin levels, cirrhosis, portal hypertension, and decreased albumin levels, the prognosis is certainly less favorable.

Generally, the condition progresses slowly. Individuals have continued living with the condition for about 10 to 15 years after diagnosis. Once cirrhosis develops, however, the prognosis is more guarded, since cirrhosis is associated with life-threatening complications such as hemorrhage. About one half of the PBC clients with symptoms of liver pathology die if left untreated (i.e., do not undergo transplantation) within 5 years of diagnosis (James, 1992). Cause of death in these cases is a result of bleeding, ascites, encephalopathy, osteoporosis, and the risks of gallbladder disease. Gallstones occur more often in clients with PBC. For individuals who receive liver transplantation, the 5-year survival rate approaches 70%. It is one of the best options for clients with PBC who qualify.

balize their feelings about their condition and complications during the assessment.

Abdominal pain is a common complaint. Pain perceptions vary from person to person and the degree of complication from ascites and cirrhosis. Refer to Chapter 13 for specific pain assessment techniques.

Decreased appetite and weight loss are also common complaints. These reported problems are linked to changing elimination patterns resulting from malabsorption. Assess nutritional status by asking about weight gain and loss patterns.

Activity assessment should include information about current rest and activity patterns, ability to carry out activities of daily living (ADLs), and changes in these areas over time.

Assessment of scratching in a quantitative way can be difficult. Intermittent observations of clients may not indicate the actual amount of scratching over time. One research reference indicated that scratching activity, which is presumably linked with itching, maximized in the evening but diminished with sleep. Although scratching was most intense during the evening, daytime scratching was also intense (Talbot, 1991). In drug studies where the efficacy of one antipruritic agent is being compared with placebos or other agents, itching and scratching are quantitatively assessed through client questionnaires, logs, and nurse assessments.

Another methodology to assess efficacy of interventions for pruritus include looking at the condition of the skin before and after therapies such as Cholestyramine or Nalmephene. If itching is reduced, it is likely the number and severity of lesions resulting from scratching will decrease. Topical agents, relaxation techniques, gloving (particularly during sleep) and other interventions to relieve itching should be assessed from the client's perspective, as well as quantitatively through inspection of the skin.

✣ DIAGNOSIS

The most often used nursing diagnoses for the older client with PBC include, but are not limited to: (1) fatigue, (2) altered nutrition: less than body requirements, (3) impaired skin integrity, and (4) anxiety.

✣ PLANNING

Expected outcomes for the older client with PBC include, but are not limited to the following: (1) client will establish rest and activity patterns that enable meeting daily demands and participating in desired activities, (2) client will consume a well-balanced diet that promotes achievement of acceptable weight and provides energy for ADLs, (3) client will maintain intact skin, and (4) client will demonstrate effective coping mechanisms for management of anxiety or will experience reduced anxiety.

✣ INTERVENTION

Nursing management focuses on preventing complications from pruritus through teaching of prophylactic measures such as (1) compliance with antipruritic medications, (2) keeping nails trimmed short, (3) using topical agents to prevent dry, flaky skin, (4) wearing gloves during sleep, (5) using relaxation and distraction techniques, and (6) encouraging verbalization of feelings and frustrations related to management of the pruritus. The challenge for the nurse in managing the client's fatigue is to assist the client in identifying excessive demands and formulating options for decreasing them. Pacing, coupled with scheduling of activities that takes advantage of peak energy levels, enables the client to decrease the sense of fatigue.

The client's active participation in planning for nutritional health and well-being increases feelings of control over the situation. Use of a food diary to document oral intake and progress aids in early detection of inadequate intake. Identifying food preferences that enable the client to achieve nutritional requirements while avoiding or limiting foods with a high fat content is essential.

Assisting the client with identifying formerly useful coping skills and adding to that repertoire of skills is necessary for long-term management of this serious, chronic health problem. Communication, problem-solving, stress management, and maintaining social supports are all skills that may need to be developed to enhance effective coping. Encouraging verbalization of thoughts and feelings related to the disease and its effects on daily living is a critical nursing intervention. Assisting the client in seeking ways to channel those thoughts and feelings into positive action is a key challenge (see nursing Care Plan, pp. 636-637).

Insight • *Severe hypotension in older adults is associated with severe liver complications. Blood flow to the liver in general decreases with age. When preexisting conditions exist, such as right-sided heart failure, an older individual can experience shock liver with a severe hypotensive episode. In shock liver, the hepatic tissues become ischemic, liver enzymes rise, and overwhelming liver failure can occur. Lactic acid levels soar and clotting factors can decrease to dangerous levels. If the cause of the hypotensive event can be resolved, the liver may recover. If the hypoten-sive assault cannot be remedied, as in drug-induced hepatitis, the liver may not recover as rapidly (Levinson, Gordon, 1990).*

CARE PLAN

PBC

Clinical situation Mrs. L is a 65-year-old homemaker who has felt increasingly more fatigued over the last few years. She attributed the fatigue to her age and rheumatoid arthritis but was prompted to visit her health care provider's office because of the persistent and intense itching she has been experiencing for the last few months. The itching has been so severe that she has literally gouged herself in several places and, as a result, has a number of lesions over her arms and legs. She was examined in the office; a number of laboratory tests were conducted. On the first office visit, six different scratched lesions were identified and treated. The nurse practitioner is now seeing Mrs. L after receiving the laboratory test results. Mrs. L has elevated liver enzymes and a positive AMA.

Mrs. L is told that there is a strong suspicion that she has PBC. A liver biopsy is recommended, which Mrs. L agrees to have done. The results of the biopsy confirm the diagnosis of PBC.

Mrs. L is now being treated in the outpatient setting for recurring multiple skin lesions caused by intense scratching. Twelve distinct stage II lesions are identified on her arms and legs, measuring 0.5 cm in diameter. Some minor signs of infection are indicated by purulent discharge from half the lesions. Mrs. L is verbalizing distress from the itching.

Nursing diagnoses	Outcomes	Interventions
Fatigue related to lethargy secondary to cirrhosis	Client will establish a pattern of rest and activity that enables her to meet daily demands and participate in desired activities. Verbalizes improved rest and sleep.	Pace activities so that client does not tire. Assist in planning work so that strenuous activities are avoided. Use community and insurance resources for needed pharmacy, housekeeping, medical, and other services to reduce client exertion.
Altered nutrition: less than body requirements related to nausea of cirrhosis	Client wil consume a well-balanced diet that promotes achievement of acceptable weight and provides energy for ADLs.	Encourage client to eat low-fat diet as prescribed by physician. Teach the importance of taking vitamins and supplements (e.g., A, D, K, zinc, and calcium) as prescribed to prevent complications such as hemorrhage, bruising, bone pain, and diarrhea. Have client keep a log detailing weights, appetite, number of meals and snacks, and incidence of complications such as diarrhea, nausea and vomiting. Enlist support of family and friends for encouraging client to follow diet and to maintain ideal body weight and mass. Have family and friends assist client in obtaining diet and shopping for food.
Impaired skin integrity related to scratching from pruritus of cirrhosis	Client will not scratch or scratching decreases as evidenced by less itching; wound healing occurs, as demonstrated by smaller lesions.	Encourage compliance with prescribed medications (e.g., Colchine, Ursodeoxycholic acid, D-penicillamine, Azathioprine, Cyclosporin, Methotrexate, or Nalmephene). Provide client teaching regarding the avoidance of scratching. Use physician-recommended topical agents for relief of dry skin and itching. Have client assess for edema and notify physician for worsening of condition. Encourage the use of skin protective measures such as the use of special mattresses, avoidance of constrictive clothing that leaves marks on the skin, and wearing gloves when sleeping to reduce scratching.

CARE PLAN

PBC—cont'd

Nursing diagnoses	Outcomes	Interventions
		Have client change linens and clothes often, especially when wet. Encourage daily skin cleansing measures that do not cause drying.
Anxiety related to living with a chronic illness	Client will cope effectively with the stress of her condition.	Have client, family, and significant others observe for changes in mood, irritability, and anxiety. Help client identify effective coping strategies such as relaxation and distraction techniques to deal with stress from condition. Allow client to verbalize feelings with family, friends, and health care workers.

✤ EVALUATION

Evaluation is based on achievement of the expected outcomes. Participation of the family or significant other helps the client successfully manage this chronic disease (Box 24-2).

Insight* • *Standard functional assessment tools can reflect changes in self-care abilities and the person's perceptions of current quality of life. Functional assessment scores can then become a benchmark for monitoring the client's response to a treatment regimen (see Chapter 4).

Hepatitis C

Hepatitis is a general disease referring to inflammation of the liver. Hepatitis is caused by a variety of sources such as assault with chemicals, alcohol, and microorganisms, including viruses.

Viral hepatitis C represents one type of viral hepatitis in which the cause of the liver inflammation results from a specific viral systemic infection. It is now known that the majority of cases of posttransfusion non-A/non-B hepatitis are caused by the **hepatitis C virus (HCV).**

HCV is a single stranded ribonucleic acid (RNA) virus. This virus is the major causative agent associated with non-A/non-B hepatitis. There is now an assay to detect this antibody in the blood—**anti-HCV.**

BOX 24-2

Resources for Clients With Liver Disease

Comprehensive client teaching materials are available from the American Liver Foundation for clients with not only PBC but also other liver diseases. The Foundation's address is 998 Pompton Avenue, Cedar Grove, NJ 07009. Some of the materials available include the topic areas of liver transplantation, gallstones, cirrhosis, and alcohol-induced liver problems (McIntyre et al, 1991).

The pathophysiologic sequence of the liver damage resulting from viral hepatitis C may be simplified in the following description. First, the RNA virus surrounded by a protein coat enters the individual, as in the case of a client receiving blood contaminated by hepatitis C. Next, the virus enters the circulation and eventually reaches the liver where it has an affinity for infecting hepatocytes. HCV requires a host cell to reproduce and to spread infection. Not all hepatocytes become infected by the virus, but those that do develop subsequent changes to the integrity of the cell, including the cell membrane. Altered hepatocyte cells do not function properly and contribute to the clinical problems associated with hepatitis. An incubation period follows, and the immune system responds to the attack by the virus. The degree of response by the immune system is proportional to the degree of damage incurred in the liver. The damage to the liver from HCV includes, but is not limited to, infiltration of lymphocytes, individual hepatocyte death, hyperplasia of the Kupffer's cells, and in late stages, cholestasis.

HCV may be acute or chronic, and the type of hepatic pathology may vary accordingly. For example, pathologic manifestations are portal tract inflammation with lymphocytic aggregation and Kupffer's cell hyperplasia. Abnormal bile duct epithelium may be a marker for progressive disease and chronicity.

HCV is responsible for 80% to 95% of the non-A/non-B posttransfusion hepatitis cases. HCV is contracted predominantly through the parenteral route. The second highest incidence rate of HCV is among IV drug abusers sharing needles; it occurs in approximately 60% to 70% of these individuals. Acupuncture and tattoos are also considered needle vectors. The HCV prevalence with homosexuals is 4%, up to 8% in those who are also positive for human immunodeficiency virus (HIV). Hemodialysis clients are infected with HCV in 10% to 20% of cases. Hemophiliacs have a high rate of hepatitis C (approximately 70%). One study examined occupational exposures, citing a 4% transmission rate out of 100 needle sticks contaminated with HCV. Floreani et al. (1993) studied 315 institutionalized older adults and identified a 2.2% rate of HCV from previously acquired infections. The study concluded that institutionalization was not a risk factor itself, and that the 2.2% rate was the same incidence for all older individuals. The most challenging HCV cases derive from the 20% to 50% labeled as sporadic community-acquired because of the unknown mode of virus transmission. Thus the majority of older adults acquire HCV from blood transfusions or are undetermined sporadic community-acquired.

The incubation phase of hepatitis C is 2 to 16 weeks, with an average of 60 days. **Seroconversion,** the detectable presence of the antibody in serum, typically occurs after 20 to 22 weeks from clinical hepatitis exposure. The seroconversion rate is lower in self-limiting disease.

There are 150,000 new cases of HCV every year. Of acute HCV cases, 50% progress to chronic hepatitis. Cirrhosis develops in 20% of these chronic hepatitis cases within 1 to 2 decades after the acute illness phase. Primary hepatocellular carcinoma may also occur with increased risk, especially when hepatitis B coexists with HCV. Blood product testing in the United States has decreased the likelihood of blood transfusion as the mode of transmission, but caution should still be taken with the increasing rate of occupational exposure.

Of clients with HCV, 40% to 75% remain asymptomatic. Symptoms are usually mild and may include malaise, fatigue, lethargy, weight loss, and vague abdominal discomfort. Infection with HCV is usually identified by elevated ALTs during a general examination or a positive anti-HCV blood test before voluntary blood donation. Liver enzymes often fluctuate in the asymptomatic or mildly symptomatic phase from a minimum level to more than twice the normal values. Clinical symptoms may continue in chronic cases with increasing lethargy,

MEDICAL MANAGEMENT

HCV

Diagnostic tests and procedures

There are two serologic assays to detect anti-HCV. The most common is the Ortho HCV antibody enzyme-linked immunosorbent assay (ELISA) test system. The second is the Chiron RIBA HCV test system. The ELISA test is an enzyme-linked immunoassay, used to detect antibodies to this antigen, which has up to 50% false positive rate. With the prolonged interval between exposure to hepatitis and seroconversion of anti-HCV, detection may be difficult between a 6-month to 1-year time span. Diagnosis of acute versus chronic hepatitis C is not straightforward. Liver biopsy is necessary to document specific histologic changes.

Most HCV cases can be treated on an outpatient basis with a focus on rest and high calorie diet. Recombinant alpha-2b interferon (alpha-IFN) is an approved drug for treatment of chronic HCV. It inhibits viral RNA replication and alters the immune response to infection. Alpha-IFN therapy through subcutaneous injections three times per week over a 6-month period demonstrates up to a 50% response rate to HCV. Half of the clients who respond to alpha-IFN maintain normal liver function, whereas the other half relapse. Alpha-IFN does cause side effects in most clients. The most common acute effects are an influenza-like syndrome, which has symptoms such as fever, headache, and muscle aches. Other side effects of alpha-IFN are loss of appetite, fatigue, and decreased concentration. Deleterious effects such as bone marrow depression and acute psychologic manifestations such as clinical depression also occur. New research indicates that the drug can also cause occular changes and an increased propensity for secondary autoimmune diseases. Alpha-IFN is costly. The drug's effect on older people with HCV is undetermined. Although it is the drug of choice, researchers advocate cautious use of alpha-IFN in older clients by properly dosing the client and monitoring symptoms (Brocklehurst et al 1992, Levinson, Gordon, 1991).

Anti-HCV may disappear within 2 years if it is self-limited and spontaneously resolves. Clients who test positive for anti-HCV infection can also place others at risk. Hospitalization is necessary for acute cases of HCV involving changes in coagulation, dehydration, and ascites.

CARE PLAN

HEPATITIS C

Clinical situation Mr. T is an 82-year-old Vietnamese immigrant who resides with his son in a large urban area. His family is concerned about his weight loss and his inability to carry out his work in the family business. Through the interpreter the nurse case manager understands that he has experienced mild nausea, abdominal discomfort, and profound lack of energy for the past 6 months. Limitations were determined by his response that he is independent with his basic ADLs, although they take a greater amount of time to achieve. His meals are prepared by his family. Mr. T states that he had major surgery 10 years ago, during which he received blood transfusions; he has also had acupuncture on several occasions. He is stoic, but his family states that he has verbalized frustration with his decreased energy and is depressed that he cannot help support the family business.

The nurse case manager notes that Mr. T has a slow, steady gait and often needs to sit down. His abdominal girth is small, and there is no apparent sign of ascites. No indication of jaundice exists, and sclera, nail beds, mucosal, and skin color are normal. Mr. T's vital signs are normal with the exception of a mild febrile state of 37.7°C (99.86°F). His laboratory tests have confirmed positive anti-HCV and elevated levels of AST 70 U/L, ALT 80 U/L. These values are twice the normal range and indicate liver cell inflammation. The liver biopsy results indicate chronic active hepatitis. The physician has recommended a course of alpha-IFN injections of 3 million U, 3 times per week, to be administered over the next 6 months. Mr. T and his son have agreed to this and are willing to learn about the drug administration and side effects, and to come back for follow-up assessments (see Cultural Awareness box, p. 641).

Nursing diagnoses	Outcomes	Interventions
Activity intolerance related to general weakness from hepatitis infection	Client will develop a rest/activity pattern that allows client to meet daily demands and participate in desired activities.	Determine activity limitations by assessing changes in normal routine. Negotiate with client in prioritizing activities of importance that incorporate medical regimen, self-care needs and preferred leisure activities. Alternate rest and activity, set time frames, assess where modifications can be made (e.g., medication, or rest), and then allow to participate in sedentary parts of the family business (activity) to match capabilities. Rearrange home environment to save steps. Schedule the average rest period for approximately 1 hour. Suggest restful activities other than sleep, such as relaxation techniques, breathing exercises, reading, listening to music, or assembling a puzzle. During extended activities, encourage client to take short, frequent breaks (e.g., 20 minutes of movement, 5 to 10 minutes of rest, and 20 minutes of movement.) Use energy-conserving measures to save energy and to improve the distribution of energy to optimize functional abilities. Balance light and heavy activities or break down into smaller parts. Consider the time of day for planning activities when the client has energy. Suggest sitting while working or bathing, and using a wheeled cart to save steps conserves energy. Use adaptive equipment such as reachers or assistive devices. Teach that body position in energy conservation is based on good posture.

Continued.

HEPATITIS C—cont'd

Nursing diagnoses	Outcomes	Interventions
		Standing with shoulders shrugged, head forward, curved back are poor posture positions that drain energy.
Altered nutrition: less than body requirements related to weight loss and nausea from hepatitis	Client will maintain food intake to meet or exceed metabolic demands.	Assess weight weekly, set lower limit for which to contact health care providers. Monitor amount and type of food or fluids ingested; suggest maintaining a food diary. Instruct and negotiate with the client in selecting nutritious food items; times for eating small, frequent meals; and the use of high-calorie nutritional supplements. Include cultural preferences with client and family input. Explore if the client is taking a self-prescribed "special diet" as a naturalistic/folk remedy to restore his "balanced state." Monitor electrolyte values and albumin levels each monthly visit.
Knowledge deficit: new medication regimen related to lack of experience	Client will accurately receive alpha-IFN subcutaneous injections and does not exhibit medication side effects. Identifies significant and reportable side effects.	Appraise client level of knowledge of disease, clinical symptoms, and treatment regimen. Assess for sensory perceptual factors such as effective communication with interpretation of instructions in another language, as well as motor coordination abilities for self-injections. Explain the use of IFN, action, dosage, and subcutaneous injection site selection. Demonstrate how to draw up and administer alpha-IFN (available as a powder and requires reconstitution in 0.9% normal saline with preservative). Teach client and family regarding drug therapy. Once reconstituted, alpha-IFN is stable for 24 hours. Store in the refrigerator before and after reconstitution. Measure by using a tuberculosis or insulin syringe. Discard the drug if there is precipitate, it is not clear, or it is beyond 24 hours after reconstitution. Conduct subcutaneous injection teaching; review the client's adipose tissue for appropriate injection sites. Encourage verbalization of feelings related to self-injection. Provide rehearsal and return demonstration by the client and his son for correctly drawing up medication and administering it with proper technique and to the accurate site. Discuss special precautions, such as discarding needles and syringes in a hazardous waste container. Review alpha-IFN side effects such as influenza symptoms like fever, headache, myalgia; decreased granulocytes; decreased platelets; depression; alopecia; and thyroid function change.

CULTURAL AWARENESS

Cultural Sensitivity from Assessment to Implementation of the Nursing Care Plan

The interpretation of time may differ among cultures. Inquire about religious beliefs in health care and uses of folk medicine. Assess the involvement of family members in health care decisions. In reviewing functional ability of the individual at home and in the community, consider, for example, that managing money, completing housework, and preparing meals may be out of context from older people's normal routines in their own culture to begin with and are not a deviation from baseline.

Assess the individual's ability to read; people may also be illiterate in their native language, so bilingual material may not be appropriate. The Asian-American cornerstone in cultural style is respect in the form of titles and family, specifically, loyalty to parents. Moderation, caution, and knowledge are significant values. Emotions are minimally expressed, and privacy is important. The use of physical touch is limited in communication, so, in assessing the client, explain each time you touch the client. Direct eye contact may be uncomfortable for clients if they perceive a difference in education, social standing, and age; difference in gender may also limit direct eye contact. The word "yes" often indicates respect, not necessarily agreement. Clients of different cultures want the nurse to know that they are listening, so ensure validation of new knowledge through other means such as return demonstration.

anorexia, and nausea, and icterus may develop in 10% to 25% as the disease advances. Older people with chronic HCV often have advanced liver disease (Levinson, Gordon, 1991).

Chronic hepatitis is defined as a condition characterized by elevated transaminase levels for at least 6 months. In moderately severe HCV disease, clinical symptoms may progress to pronounced right upper quadrant pain with significantly increased liver enzymes. Pruritus may be a troublesome problem. As the disease progresses, pruritus and icterus escalate. Increasing liver failure usually manifests with ascites and renal changes. Cycling exacerbations of infection may occur in hepatitis C, but fulminant hepatitis is rare (see Medical Management box, p. 638).

NURSING MANAGEMENT

ASSESSMENT

HCV is often underreported by older people, as are other infectious diseases. The nursing assessment should begin with identifying a history of presumed exposure to the virus, such as confirmed blood transfusion. Question for changes in functional status. For example, ask if the client's level of activity and ability to perform ADLs have decreased from baseline levels. Review nutritional intake, and assess for anorexia. Question changes in the way clothes fit, and if family and friends have noticed weight loss in the older adult. Direct questions such as how groceries are obtained, how the house is cleaned, or how meals are prepared focus on areas of potential deficits and can set a benchmark for the person's "normal" level of activity. Assess the gastrointestinal system for changes such as abdominal pain and cholestasis. Evaluate the skin for the presence of jaundice and **spider angioma,** since these may reflect liver damage (Table 24-1).

TABLE 24-1

Assessment for HCV

Subjective	Objective
Weight loss	Anorexia
Abdominal pain	Icterus (jaundice)
Fatigue	Spider angioma
Nausea	Ascites (measure girth)
Malaise (discomfort)	Bleeding gums
Lethargy (indifference)	Elevated liver enzymes

Insight • *Standard functional assessment tools can reflect changes in self-care abilities and the person's perceptions of current quality of life. Functional assessment tools can then become a benchmark for monitoring the client's response to a treatment regimen (see Chapter 4).*

DIAGNOSIS

Nursing diagnoses are directly related to symptom management in supporting the client with HCV. Fatigue, which is determined by the client's identified limitations, requires monitoring activity and rest patterns. Altered nutrition: less than body requirements, confirmed by diet history and weight loss, requires negotiated interventions with the client.

PLANNING

Expected outcomes for the older client with HCV include, but are not limited to, the following: (1) client will experience decreased degree of fatigue or will return to baseline functional status level, and (2) client will maintain appropriate weight, fluid, and electrolyte balance.

INTERVENTION

Nursing interventions aimed at monitoring rest and activity levels, and then at instituting measures to assist the older adult in achieving a balance are key. Help the client identify daily demands, and assist with identifying options for decreasing those demands and the resultant energy losses. Pace activities to take advantage of peak energy levels. Monitor sleep pattern to assure sleep restores physical and mental energy. Small, frequent meals, supplements, and changes in food selection or preparation can all affect the older adult's lifestyle and require support to foster successful adjustment.

Client teaching to include the family or significant others encompasses sharing information about the virus itself and the impact of the various therapies on the client. Home health management of HCV includes consideration of safety issues, such as not sharing a toothbrush or razor with other family members. The client should be instructed to monitor for signs of progressive disease, such as bleeding gums, gastrointestinal bleeding, and development of ascites.

When alpha-IFN is used as a therapy, the client and family should become competent with subcutaneous drug administration and should be able to detect side effects. Normalization of liver function tests is a primary indicator of alpha interferon effectiveness.

EVALUATION

Evaluation includes achievement of the expected outcomes, coupled with the client's successful self-management of the disease (see nursing Care Plan, pp. 639-640).

Summary

The liver is a complex organ with the four important functions of metabolism (i.e., of fat, carbohydrate, and protein), detoxification, storage, and secretion. Essentially, the liver processes nearly every class of nutrients absorbed from the digestive tract. In addition, it plays a major role in regulating plasma cholesterol levels. Although resilient for most of its functions throughout the life span, there is a decrease in overall liver mass, blood flow, and enzyme activity with age. Cirrhosis is the most common hepatic disease associated with advancing age, but hepatitis C is responsible for 80% to 95% of the non-A/non-B posttransfusion hepatitis cases in adults. Nursing care of the older adult with cirrhosis is based on the causal factor, but generally, priorities of care are dictated by the acuity of the illness. Older adults with cirrhosis can be acutely ill and can even require critical nursing care. The nurse's role in caring for older people with hepatitis should focus on general supportive care that promotes rest, fluid balance, adequate nutritional intake, comfort, skin integrity, and overall functional ability.

HOME CARE TIPS

1. Regularly assess the homebound older adult diagnosed with a liver-related disorder or disease for signs and symptoms indicating exacerbation or instability.
2. Instruct caregivers and homebound older adults on reportable signs and symptoms related to the diagnosed liver problem and when to report these symptoms to the home care nurse or physician.
3. Instruct caregivers and homebound older adults about laboratory indications used to evaluate liver dysfunction (e.g., liver biopsy or serum bilirubin). Inform them of the results of any tests *after* the physician has been notified.
4. Use appropriate infection control measures for contagious liver diseases such as hepatitis. Instruct the client and family regarding these measures as well.

Key Points

- Significant decrease of liver function is not an inevitable outcome of aging, but because the incidence of chronic disease increases with advancing age, liver disorders are more common.
- The high correlation between polypharmacy, increased drug consumption, and age make the older person more prone to drug-induced liver disorders.
- The nursing management of older adults with cirrhosis includes assessment of nutritional status, skin, elimination, the respiratory system, anxiety, fatigue, and social issues.
- Hepatitis C is contracted chiefly through the parenteral route, yet 20% to 50% of cases are labeled sporadic community-acquired, because the mode of transmission is unknown.
- Nursing care of older adults with hepatitis is aimed at optimizing the client's quality of life through supportive interventions.

Critical Thinking Exercises

1. A 62-year-old man is admitted to the hospital with a diagnosis of cirrhosis of the liver. During the shift report, his primary care nurse states that he has been agitated and anxious but has not exhibited any manifestations of alcohol withdrawal. What assumptions did the nurse make? Are these assumptions valid? Explain.
2. Discuss how population trends and technologic advances may affect ethical issues related to liver transplantation in the older adult population.
3. Discuss how nursing care measures would be similar for an older adult client with cirrhosis and one with hepatitis.

REFERENCES

Bergasa NV: A controlled trial of naloxone infusions for the pruritus of chronic cholestasis, *Gastroenterol* 102(2):544-549, 1992.

Brocklehurst JC et al: The liver. In Tallis R and Fillet T: *Textbook of geriatric medicine and gerontology,* ed 4, New York, 1992, Churchill Livingstone.

Floreani A et al: Anti-hepatitis C virus in the elderly: a seroepidemiological study in a home for the aged, *Gerontology* 38:214-216, 1992.

Hall MR et al: *Medical care of the elderly,* New York, 1993, Wiley & Sons.

James OF: The liver. In Brocklehurst JC et al, editors: *Textbook of geriatric medicine and gerontology,* ed 4, New York, 1992, Churchill Livingstone.

Levinson JR, Gordon SC: Liver diseases in the elderly, *Clin Geriatr Med* 7(2):371-394, May 1991.

Maher JJ: Drug therapy for hepatic fibrosis, *Hosp Formul* 27:269-286, March 1992.

McFarland G, McFarlane E: *Nursing diagnosis and intervention,* ed 2, Baltimore, 1993, Mosby.

McIntyre N et al, editors: *Oxford textbook of clinical hepatology,* vol 2, New York, 1991, Oxford University Press.

Millward-Sadler G et al, editors: *Wright's liver and biliary disease: pathophysiology, diagnosis, and management,* ed 3, Philadelphia, 1991, WB Saunders.

Podolsky DK, Isselbacher KJ: Derangements of hepatic metabolism. In Branwald E et al, editors: *Harrison's principles of internal medicine,* ed 11, New York, 1991, McGraw-Hill.

Sherlock S: Primary biliary cirrhosis and vanishing bile ducts. In McIntyre N et al, editors: *Oxford textbook of clinical he patology,* Oxford, 1991, Oxford University Press.

Talbot TL et al: Application of piezo film technology for the quantitative assessment of pruritus. *Biomedical instrumentation and technology,* Philadelphia, 1991, Hanley and Belfus.

Triger DR, Wright R: Immunological aspects of liver disease. In Millward-Sadler GH et al, editors: *Wright's liver and biliary disease,* Philadelphia, 1992, WB Saunders.

BIBLIOGRAPHY

Bacon B: Managing chronic hepatitis recent advances in diagnosis and treatment, *Postgrad Med* 90(5):103-112, 1991.

Evans J, Williams T: *Oxford textbook of geriatric medicine,* New York, 1990, Oxford University Press.

Furst G, Gerber L, Smith C: *Rehabilitation through learning energy conservation and joint protection: a workbook for patients with arthritis,* NIH Pub No 85-2743, 1985, US Government Printing Office.

Giger J, Davidhizar R: *Transcultural nursing: assessment and intervention,* Baltimore, 1991, Mosby.

Hall MR et al: *Medical care of the elderly,* New York, 1993, Wiley & Sons.

Hegner B, Caldwell E: *Geriatrics,* ed 5, Albany, NY, 1991, Delmar.

Miller A, editor: *Gastroenterology nursing: a core curriculum,* ed 1, St Louis, 1993, Mosby.

Sherlock S, Dooley J: *Diseases of the liver and biliary system,* ed 9, London, 1993, Blackwell Scientific Publications.

Tang E: Hepatitis C virus: a review, *Western J Med* 155:164-168, 1991.

Yoshikawa T, Cobbs E, Brummel-Smith K: *Ambulatory geriatric care,* Baltimore, 1993, Mosby.

CHAPTER 25

Gastrointestinal Function

LEARNING OBJECTIVES

On completion of this chapter, the reader will be able to:

1. Delineate the functions of the gastrointestinal (GI) tract: motility, absorption, and secretion.
2. Describe the physiologic and functional changes in the GI system with advancing age.
3. Describe and differentiate among the cause, incidence, and pathophysiology of the various types of cancers of the GI tract: esophageal, stomach, pancreatic, and colon.
4. Compare and contrast the nature of gastric and duodenal ulcers, and describe appropriate nursing care.
5. Identify causes and complications of dysphagia and reflux, and the appropriate nursing interventions.
6. Explain primary and secondary preventive care related to the GI tract for the older client and the rationalizations for it.
7. Describe appropriate evaluation of older clients with symptoms such as abdominal pain, diarrhea, flatus, and constipation.
8. Perform a physical examination pertinent to the GI system.
9. Write an appropriate care plan for the older client with a GI disorder.

NORMAL STRUCTURE AND FUNCTION

The GI tract is also commonly referred to as the digestive system, the alimentary canal, and the gut, whereas the intestines are also called the bowel. It is important to understand normal structure, or anatomy, as well as function, or physiology, because an alteration in either disrupts the human body as a whole.

Anatomy of the GI Tract

The GI tract is a continuous hollow tube structure that begins with the oral cavity and terminates with the anal sphincter (Fig. 25-1). The GI tract includes the oral cavity, esophagus, stomach, and intestines. In addition, accessory organs include the liver (see Chapter 24), gallbladder, and pancreas.

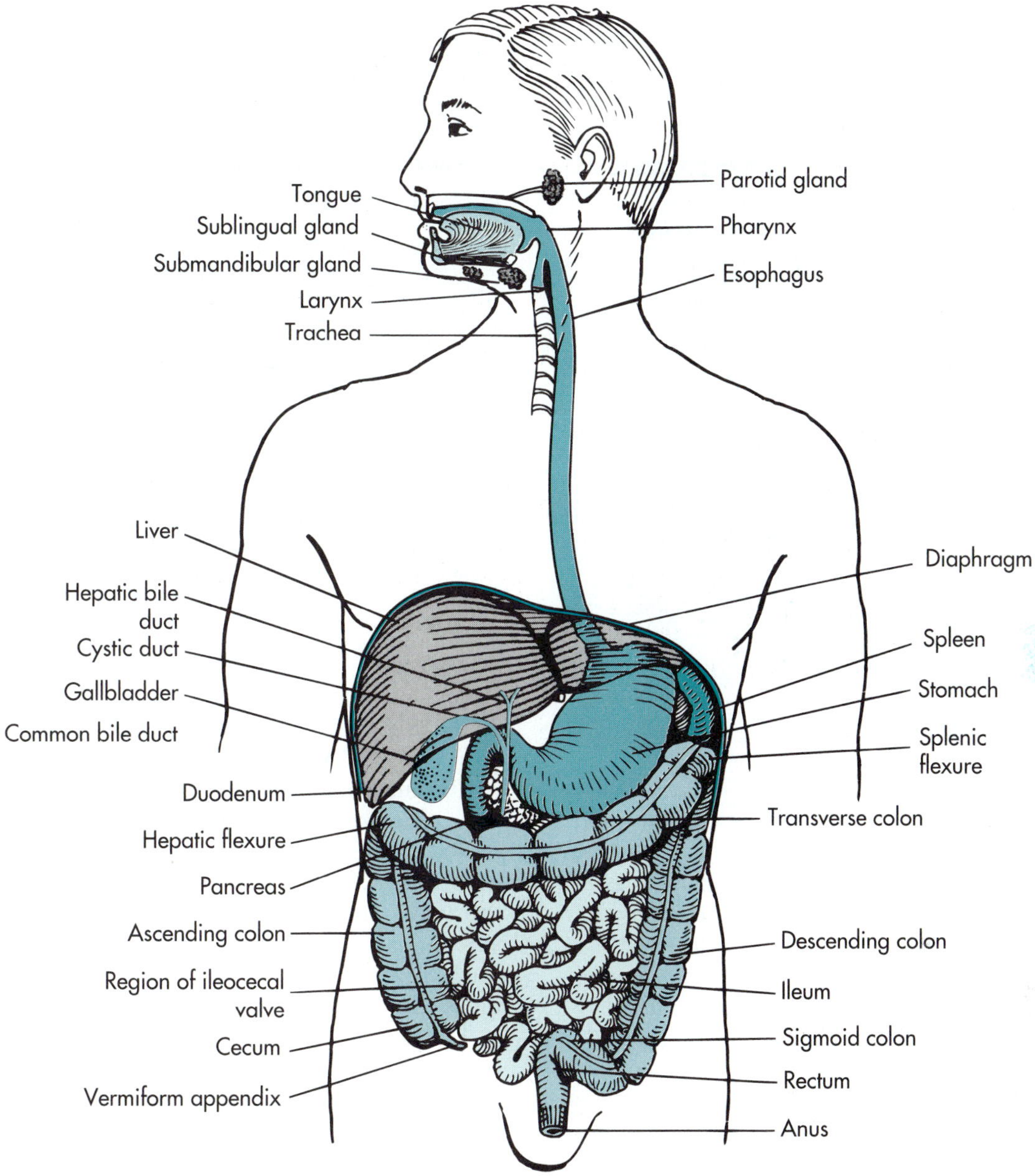

Fig. 25-1 The organs of the GI system and related structures. (From Phipps WJ, et al: *Medical-surgical nursing: concepts and clinical practice,* ed 5, St. Louis, 1995, Mosby.)

Oral Cavity/Pharynx

The oral cavity contains the lips, tongue and taste buds, cheeks, teeth, gums and salivary glands, and essentially prepares the food for eventual digestion and absorption. This includes reducing food particles to a manageable size, stimulating salivary glands to secrete saliva, and moving food toward swallowing (Collins, Bullock, 1992) (Table 25-1).

The salivary glands are comprised of the submaxillary, parotid, and sublingual glands, and continuously secrete saliva. Saliva is made of water, sodium, chloride, bicarbonate, urea, and ptyalin. Ptyalin is a salivary amylase, or an enzyme, that aids in the digestion of starch.

The pharynx is the structure responsible for swallowing and consists of the soft palate and epiglottis. It moves food into the esophagus, while at the same time, it closes off the trachea and nasal passages. Once the swallowing reflex is initiated by voluntary movement of food to the back of the mouth, swallowing continues as a reflex activity (Collins, Bullock, 1992).

TABLE 25-1

Participation of the Oral Structures in Digestion

Structure	Process
Teeth	Reduce food to sizes appropriate for swallowing; break down dense particles
Tongue	Places food in proper position for swallowing; mixes secretions to moisten food
Salivary glands	Moisten and lubricate foods in the mouth; add ptyalin enzyme for digestion of starches
Muscles of mastication or chewing	Provide movement for the grinding of food to smaller particles; provide more surface area for the digestive enzymes to act

TABLE 25-2

Sphincter Function

Sphincter	Function
Upper esophageal	Presents expulsion of food into posterior pharynx
Lower esophageal	Transports food bolus from esophagus to stomach and prevents gastric reflux into upper esophagus
Pyloric	Coordinates organized emptying of stomach and prevents reflux of duodenal contents
Ileocecal	Prevents retrograde expulsion of intestinal contents
Anal	Inhibits expulsion of colonic contents unless voluntary relaxation is established

From Bullock B, Rosendahl PP: *Pathophysiology: adaptation and alterations in function,* ed 3, Philadelphia, 1992, JB Lippincott.

Esophagus

The esophagus is a hollow muscular tube that allows the food from the pharynx to pass into the stomach. Glands along the esophagus secrete mucus to lubricate passing food and protect the mucosa, which is composed of squamous epithelium (Dworken, 1982).

Sphincter muscles are located in the pharynx and upper esophagus. An upper esophageal sphincter (UES) prevents food or fluid from moving into the posterior pharynx and trachea. Although no anatomic sphincter is located at the lower end of the esophagus, physiologic sphincter function is present in a narrowed area of muscle known as the cardiac or lower esophageal sphincter (LES). The cardiac sphincter normally remains constricted, then relaxes when a peristaltic wave passes through it, allowing food to pass into the stomach. This sphincter also prevents acid and gastric contents from refluxing into the esophagus (Table 25-2).

Stomach

The stomach is a curved, muscular, sac-like organ between the esophagus and small intestine (Fig. 25-1). Anatomically, the stomach consists of the cardia, fundus, body, antrum, and pylorus. The upper portion of the stomach is continuous with the esophagus, whereas the lower portion is continuous with the duodenum. These areas are not sharply demarcated anatomically. Histologically, the three distinct portions of the stomach include the cardia, the acid/pepsin-secreting area, and the pyloric gland area (Guyton, 1991). The stomach has a J-shaped curve at the bottom to slow the passage of food until it is of the right consistency to flow through the pylorus (O'Toole, 1992).

The interior lining of the stomach lies in mucosal folds called rugae (Collins, Bullock, 1992). Glands that produce and secrete gastric juices, which consist of mucous, enzymes, and hydrochloric acid, are located within the folds. These enzymes include pepsinogen, which aids in the digestion of proteins, and lipase, which helps break down fats. Hydrochloric acid helps break down foods, whereas the mucus acts as a lubricant.

The gastric secretions mix with the food entering the stomach. This combination of food and gastric secretions is now called **chyme,** which is then propelled into the small intestine through the pyloric sphincter by **peristalsis** (rhythmic muscular contractions) (Collins, Bullock, 1992).

Gallbladder

The gallbladder, a pear-shaped organ on the inferior surface of the liver, is part of the **biliary system.** The ducts within the biliary system provide a pathway for the bile that is transported to the gallbladder for storage or the intestine for use. The liver produces **bile,** which is then excreted into the hepatic ducts, where it then passes into the cystic duct and into the gallbladder for storage (Cassmeyer, Blevins, 1993). In addition to the storage of bile, the gallbladder also concentrates bile to a solution strength that is 5 to 10 times greater than that produced in the liver.

Bile contains water, cholesterol, bile salts, **bilirubin** and phospholipids, in addition to very small amounts of protein and electrolytes. Many drugs and hormones are excreted into the bile. The bile acids facilitate the digestion and absorption of fats, and activate the release of pancreatic enzymes.

Food, particularly lipids, causes the release of **cholecystokinin (CCK)** from the mucosa of the duodenum. The CCK is released into the blood and travels to the gallbladder. It stimulates the gallbladder to contract, and causes the Oddi's sphincter, which is at the end of the common bile duct, to relax, permitting the bile to enter the duodenum.

Most of the bile secreted into the duodenum is reabsorbed from the intestines, mainly from the terminal ileum. These bile salts are recirculated two to three times per meal. The reabsorption from the intestines is efficient so that only 15% to 25% of the bile salts are replaced each day (Cassmeyer, Blevins, 1993).

Pancreas

The pancreas is a long, flat, glandular organ that lies behind the stomach and is anatomically divided into three sections: head, body, and tail. The head lies in the curvature of the duodenum, and the tail rests against the spleen. The pancreas is composed of both exocrine and endocrine tissue. (See Chapter 23 for endocrine functions of the pancreas.) The exocrine (secretory) portion of the pancreas includes the acinar cells and the ducts. The acini secrete digestive enzymes, and the lining of the ducts from the acini secrete sodium bicarbonate. The combination of these is called pancreatic juice, which travels through the pancreatic duct, to the hepatic duct, and into the duodenum. This pancreatic juice contains enzymes for the breakdown of proteins, carbohydrates, and fats. The bicarbonate in the pancreatic juice helps neutralize the acidic chyme that is in the duodenum (O'Toole, 1992).

The regulation of the secretion of pancreatic juice is primarily hormonal, through the influence of the hormones secretin and cholecystokinin. The composition of the chyme in the duodenum influences the amount of each hormone that is released, and therefore the characteristic of the pancreatic juice is ever-changing (O'Toole, 1992).

Small Intestine

The small intestine begins at the pylorus and extends to the ileocecal valve. It is about 20 feet long in the average adult, and is divided into three sections: the duodenum, the jejunum, and the ileum (see Fig. 25-1). The duodenum is the widest part of the small intestine. The common bile duct empties into the duodenum, sending bile to break down fats, and the hepatic duct delivers pancreatic juice. Along the jejunum, the longest part of the small intestine, and the ileum, carbohydrates, proteins, and fats are broken down into sugar, fatty acids, amino acids, and glycerin. The lining of the small intestine absorbs these nutrients, and the bulky, unusable portions of the diet pass into the large intestine (O'Toole, 1992).

The wall of the small intestine is composed of four layers: mucosa, submucosa, muscularis, and serosa. The mucosa has multiple folds and finger-like protractions, called villi, which protrude into the lumen of the intestines and increase the surface area for absorption by about 600-fold. In between the villi are Lieberkühn's crypts, which are composed of cells that make the majority of the digestive secretions: absorptive cells and mucus-producing goblet cells (Collins, Bullock, 1992; Guyton, 1991).

Large Intestine

The large intestine begins at the ileocecal valve, which is the junction of the distal end of the ileum and the beginning of the cecum. Extending from the cecum is a small structure known as the vermiform appendix, which is essentially a nonfunctional pouch. The other portions of the large intestine are the colon, the rectum, and anal canal. The colon portion of the intestine is further divided into ascending, transverse, descending, and sigmoid colon. The rectum terminates in the anal canal (Collins, Bullock, 1992) (see Fig. 25-1, p. 645).

The mucus secreted in the large intestine aids in preventing trauma to the bowel by providing material that causes feces to form a mass, and it protects the bowel against bacteria. The large intestine is where most of the liquid and electrolytes are reabsorbed from the semiliquid material of the small intestine.

The proximal half of the large intestine is concerned with absorption, whereas the distal half is concerned with storage. The waste is formed into fairly solid feces and pushed down to the rectum for elimination. This process takes from 10 to 20 hours. Feces usually consist of three quarters water and one quarter solid matter, of which about 30% is dead bacteria. The normal brown color of feces is a result of the breakdown of bilirubin (Collins, Bullock, O'Toole, 1992).

Physiology

The main function of the GI tract is to provide the body with fluids, nutrients, and electrolytes, and dispose of waste products. This is accomplished through the overall processes of **motility, secretion, digestion,** and **absorption.**

Motility

Motility is the movement of food through the **alimentary track,** and occurs in each organ along the GI tract.

Initial ingestion of food requires chewing and swallowing. The ingested food bolus is broken down to smaller sizes by the teeth and put into proper alignment for swallowing by the tongue. Motility is begun by the process of swallowing.

Swallowing is important in digestion, because it increases esophageal peristaltic motion, decreases pressure in the lower esophagus, and initiates the gastroenteric reflex (Collins, Bullock, 1992). This, in turn, increases small bowel motility and aids in moving nutrients along the alimentary canal. Swallowing begins when the tongue moves a bolus of food to the pharynx. A primary peristaltic wave is initiated when the pharyngeal sphincter relaxes for less than a second. The bolus of food passes from the pharynx to the esophagus, while the respiratory passages close to prevent the aspiration of food.

Peristalsis, a sequential series of muscular movements, and pressure move the food down the esophagus. Secondary peristalsis continues until the food is in the stomach. As the food moves toward the lower esophageal sphincter, peristalsis causes the normally constricted area to relax, and food moves into the stomach.

Motor functions of the stomach consist of storage, mixing, and emptying. In storage, the muscular walls of the stomach expand. The thickness of the stomach is reduced, while the area is increased. When empty, the walls of the stomach are pressed together and have little storage capacity. The mixing is accomplished by peristalsis, whereby the partially digested food, along with stomach secretions, becomes the consistency of thick soup (chyme). The stomach then empties by contractions that gradually push the liquid into the small intestine (Collins, Bullock, 1992).

In the stomach, peristaltic motions become stronger and more frequent, about 3 per minute. Gastric motility occurs in phases. Phase 1 begins 1.5 to 2 hours after meals, when gastric contractions decrease to one every 4 to 5 minutes; phase 2 is a 30-minute period of irregular contractions; phase 3 consists of 15 minutes of sweeping contractions (Collins, Bullock, 1992). The stomach reaches its peak of activity about 2 hours after a meal, and may empty in 3-4 hours (O'Toole, 1992).

Motility of the small intestine can be divided into the mixing contractions and the propulsive contractions. When part of the small intestine becomes distended with chyme, the stretch of the intestinal wall elicits localized contractions spaced at intervals along the intestine. These contractions mix the chyme as often as 7 to 12 times a minute, allowing progressive mixing of solid food particles with the secretions of the small intestine (Collins, Bullock, 1992).

Chyme is propelled through the small intestine by peristaltic waves, which can occur in any part of the small intestine but usually move toward the anus. These propulsive movements are at a rate of 0.5 to 2 cm per second, and are much faster in the proximal intestine and much slower in the distal intestine. In the distal intestine, the propulsive movements are weaker and die out after a few centimeters, causing the movement of the chyme to become much slower. As a result, net movement of the chyme along the small intestine averages only 1 cm/min. This results in a 3- to 5-hour period for the passage of chyme from the pylorus to the ileocecal valve (Guyton, 1991).

The usual cause of peristalsis in the small intestine is distention. Therefore peristalsis of the small intestine is greatly increased after a meal. This is due in part to the entry of chyme into the duodenum but also by the distention of the stomach.

While the motility of the colon is normally sluggish, the movements have characteristics similar to those of the small intestine, and can be divided into mixing movements and propulsive movements (Collins, Bullock, 1992).

The mixing movements of the colon consist of a group of contractions of the smooth muscle that cause part of the large intestine to bulge outward into bag-like sacs, called **haustrations.** These cause the fecal matter to slowly roll over and move around so that all the fecal matter is exposed to the surface of the large intestine, and fluid is then progressively absorbed. Of the 750 ml daily load of chyme, only 20% is lost in the feces (Collins, Bullock, 1992).

Propulsion occurs by the combination of haustral contractions and mass movements of large amounts of feces. Mass movements occur only a few times each day, mostly for about 15 minutes during the first hour after eating breakfast. These movements can occur in any part of the colon, but most often occur in the transverse or descending colon. When feces are finally forced into the rectum, the desire for defecation is felt.

Motility of the GI tract is partially under the control of the nervous system, which controls the tone of the bowel, the rhythmic contractions, and the speed of movement through the gut. Therefore motility may be influenced by diseases and illnesses affecting the nervous system.

Secretion

In the GI tract, secretions provide a dual function of lubrication of intestinal contents and protection of the digestive tract. Several types of glands provide different types of secretions in the GI tract. Stimulation of the glands to secrete digestive juices are from either tactile stimulation, distention of the gut, or chemical stimulation. In the stomach and the intestines, several different types of GI hormonal mechanisms help regulate the volume and character of the secretions (Table 25-3).

Saliva, the main digestive secretion of the oral pharynx, is secreted primarily by the salivary glands. Saliva is made up primarily of ptyalin, which breaks down starches, but also contains water and mucus. The primary function of saliva is to lubricate the food to make swallowing easier. In addition, saliva helps prevent den-

TABLE 25-3

Digestive Enzymes

Enzyme	Source	Substrate	Products	Remarks
Ptyalin	Salivary glands	Starch	Smaller carbohydrates	
Pepsin	Chief cells of stomach mucosa	Protein (nonspecific)	Polypeptides	Activated by hydrochloric acid
Gastric lipase	Stomach mucosa	Triglycerides (lipids)	Glycerides and fatty acids	
Enterokinase	Duodenal mucosa	Trypsinogen	Trypsin	Activates or converts trypsinogen to trypsin; trypsinogen hydrolyzed to expose active site
Trypsin	Pancreas	Protein and polypeptides	Smaller polypeptides	Converts chymotrypsinogen to chymotrypsin
Chymotrypsin	Pancreas	Proteins and polypeptides (different specificity than trypsin)	Smaller polypeptides	
Nuclease	Pancreas	Nucleic acids	Nucleotides (base + sugar + PO_4)	
Carboxypeptidase	Pancreas	Polypeptides	Smaller polypeptides	Cleaves carboxy terminal end
Pancreatic lipase	Pancreas	Lipids, especially triglycerides	Glycerides, free fatty acids, glycerol	Very potent
Pancreatic amylase	Pancreas	Starch	2 disaccharide units = maltose	Very potent
Aminopeptidase	Intestinal glands	Polypeptides	Smaller peptides	
Dipeptidase	Intestine	Dipeptides	2 amino acids	
Maltase	Intestine	Maltose	2 glucose	
Lactase	Intestine	Lactose	1 glucose, 1 galactose	
Sucrase	Intestine	Sucrose	1 glucose, 1 fructose	
Nucelotidase	Intestine	Nucleotides	Nucleosides and phosphates (base + sugar)	
Nucleosidase	Intestine	Nucleosides	Base and sugar	
Intestinal lipase	Intestine	Fats	Glycerides, fatty acids, glycerol	

NOTE: Enzymes act on one another during and after digestion, but it is only after digestion (after their substrates are removed) that they have any marked effect on one another.

From Bullock B, Rosendahl PP: *Pathophysiology: adaptation and alterations in function,* ed 3, Philadelphia, 1992, JB Lippincott.

tal caries by destroying and washing away pathogenic oral bacteria. The salivary glands are controlled by the nervous system, producing saliva 2 to 3 seconds after stimulation by the sight, smell, or taste of food. They produce approximately 3 pints of saliva per day (O'Toole, 1992). Salivation can also occur in response to reflexes originating in the stomach and upper intestines. Saliva production and salivation are also affected by hydration status, as well as many drugs.

The stomach has mucus-secreting glands both on the surface of its lining and in the mucosa, where there are gastric and pyloric glands. The glands of the stomach secrete 1.5 to 3.0 L of gastric juice per day. The amount of secretion, however, varies with individual diets and exposure to other stimuli. Gastric secretion is cyclical, with the least amount secreted early in the morning (Fig. 25-2).

Gastric juice contains mucus, intrinsic factor, hydrochloric acid, pepsinogen, and electrolytes such as sodium, potassium, magnesium, chloride, and bicarbonate. The cells of the gastric glands secrete mucus, pepsinogen, and hydrochloric acid. Hydrochloric acid is secreted by the parietal cells in the fundus of the stomach. Pepsin, the main proteolytic enzyme of gastric juice, is secreted by cells of the gastric glands in the form of pepsinogen. Mucus is produced in the surface epithelium.

Gastric secretions and the mucosa are affected by a number of factors. Caffeine and nicotine increase the amount and acidity of gastric secretions. Alcohol only

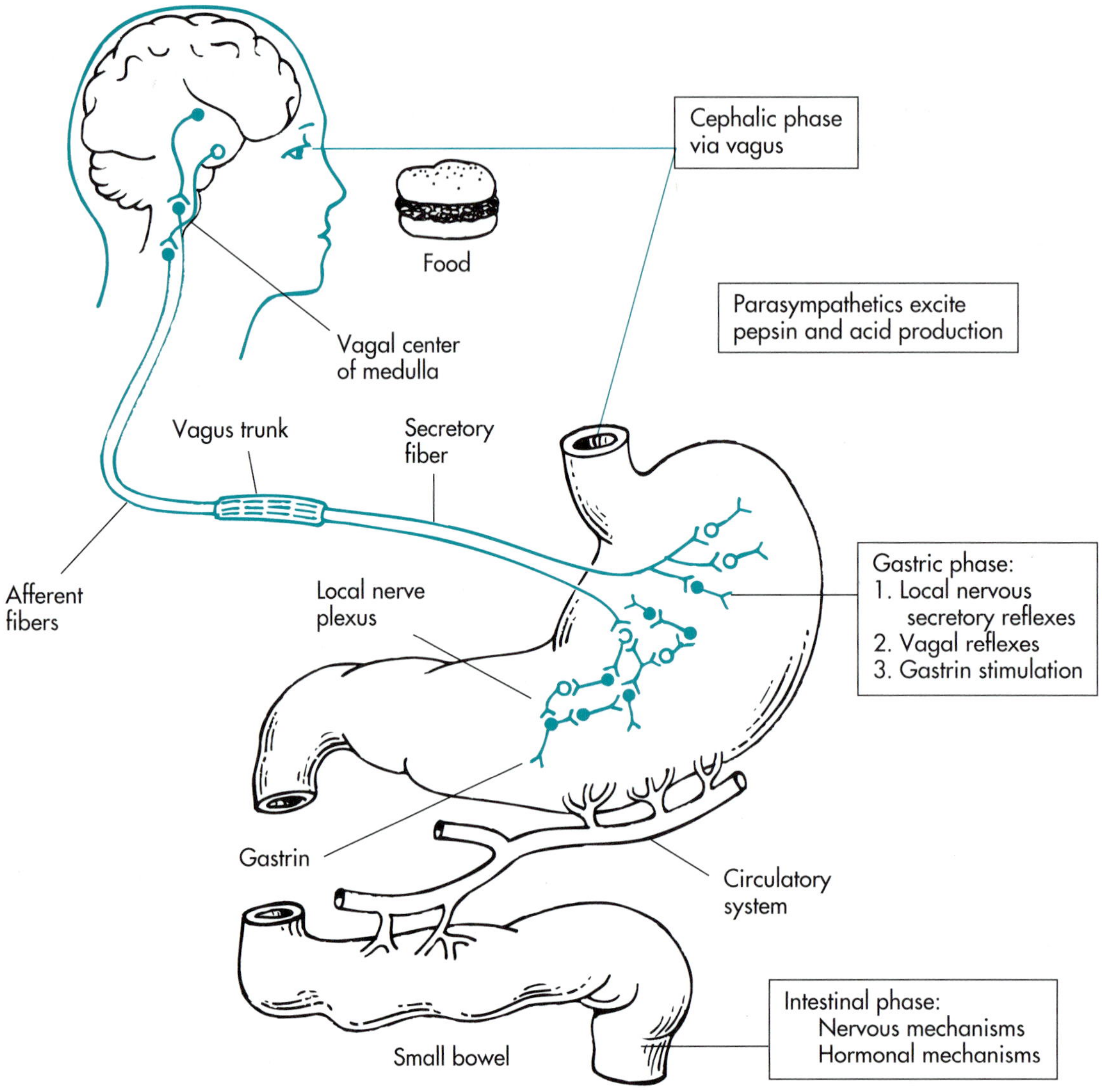

Fig. 25-2 The phases of gastric secretion and their regulation. (From Guyton AC: *Textbook of medical physiology,* ed 7, Philadelphia, 1986, WB Saunders.)

stimulates the amount of gastric secretion. Aspirin and nonsteroidal antiinflammatory drugs (NSAIDs) produce changes in the gastric mucosa and may decrease the total output of the mucus, which decreases its protective effect on the gastric mucosa. In addition, prolonged steroid use increases gastric secretion, which favors the development or recurrence of gastric ulcers.

The pancreas secretes digestive enzymes mainly in response to the presence of chyme in the small intestine. The pancreatic juice contains enzymes for the digestion of all three major types of food: protein, carbohydrates, and fats. Enzymes essential to the digestion of proteins include trypsin, chymotrypsin, carboxypeptidase, ribonuclease, and deoxyribonuclease. The enzyme for the digestion of carbohydrates is amylase. The main enzymes for the digestion of fats are lipase and cholesterol esterase. Pancreatic secretion, like gastric secretion, is regulated by both nervous and hormonal mechanisms.

Bile, secreted by the liver, contains no digestive enzyme, but is important for digestion because of the presence of bile salts. These bile salts help emulsify fat globules so that they can be further digested and can help transport the end-products of fat digestion to the intestinal villi where they can be absorbed. Most of the bile salts secreted in the bile are reabsorbed by the ileum and then resecreted by the liver. In the absence of bile in the intestines, as much as one half of dietary fat fails to be digested and absorbed. This results in fatty stools, or **steatorrhea** (Collins, Bullock, 1992).

The intestinal cells produce large quantities of secretions which contain enzymes that function to breakdown nutrients. An important secretion is CCK, which is secreted from the duodenal mucosa and absorbed into the bloodstream. The purpose of CCK is to stimulate the gallbladder and pancreas. CCK is secreted when chyme enters the small intestine and distends it. This CCK then stimulates the pancreas to release its enzymes into the duodenum. The stimulation from CCK also causes the gallbladder to contract and push bile into the small intestine to aid in the digestion of fats (Guyton, 1991).

Glands in the small intestine secrete mucus and other digestive juices. The majority of the digestive secretions are formed by crypts of Lieberkühn, located on the surface of the lumen of the small intestine.

The majority of the secretions in the large intestine consist of mucus. Whenever a portion of the large intestine becomes irritated, as occurs in a bacterial infection or enteritis, the mucosa secretes large quantities of water and electrolytes in addition to the normal mucus. This acts to dilute the irritating factors, and causes rapid movement of the feces toward the anus, resulting in diarrhea with a loss of large quantities of water and electrolytes.

Digestion

The food that we ingest can be classified as carbohydrates, proteins, or fats. These cannot be absorbed in their natural forms, and so are useless as nutrients without the process of digestion. All of the digestive enzymes and secretions work together to digest proteins, carbohydrates, and fats. Absorption depends on the breakdown of these nutrients by secretions to allow for movement from the intestinal lumen to the bloodstream.

Three major sources of carbohydrates are sucrose, lactose, and starches. The breakdown of carbohydrates begins in the mouth with the secretion of the enzyme ptyalin, which hydrolyzes starch into disaccharides of maltose and isomaltose. The action of ptyalin continues until the contents of the stomach are mixed with the stomach secretions, and the gastric secretions block the activity of the ptyalin. Immediately after the chyme empties from the stomach into the duodenum and mixes with the pancreatic juice, the remaining starches are broken down by amylase.

Most dietary fats consist of triglycerides. Essentially, all fat digestion occurs in the small intestine by emulsification by bile salts and pancreatic lipase.

The digestion of proteins begins in the stomach, with the enzyme pepsin. For this enzyme to work, the stomach must be acidic. Pepsin is capable of digesting all the different types of proteins in the diet. After proteins are initially broken down in the stomach by the pepsin, the pancreatic enzymes in the small intestine further break down proteins into amino acids.

TABLE 25-4

Principal Sites of Absorption

Nutrient	Absorptive site
Carbohydrates	Jejunum
Protein	Jejunum
Fat	Jejunum
Water	Jejunum; also, duodenum, ileum, and colon
Fat-soluble vitamins: A, D, E, K	Duodenum
Vitamin B_{12}	Terminal ileum
Other water-soluble vitamins	Duodenum
Iron	Duodenum
Calcium	Duodenum
Sodium	Jejunum by passive diffusion; ileum and colon by active transport
Potassium	Jejunum and ileum
Magnesium	Distal ileum

From Bullock B, Rosendahl PP: *Pathophysiology: adaptation and alterations in function,* ed 3, Philadelphia, 1992, JB Lippincott.

Absorption

The total quantity of fluid to be absorbed daily is equal to the amount ingested (about 1.5 l), in addition to the amount secreted in the various gastrointestinal secretions (about 7.5 l). About 8 to 8.5 l of the total 9 l are absorbed in the small intestine each day (Guyton, 1991).

The small intestine absorbs water, ions, and nutrients, whereas the large intestine absorbs water and ions but no nutrients (Collins, Bullock, 1992) (Table 25-4). The digestion of food is essentially completed in the small intestine.

AGE-RELATED CHANGES IN STRUCTURE AND FUNCTION

Many health-related complaints from the older adult pertain to the GI system, but the GI system is rarely responsible for death (Gioiella, Bevil, 1985). The nurse is often the first person to assess these complaints and to acknowledge the older client's situation. Knowledge of normal verses pathologic changes is essential, as is the ability to discern what is "normal" for each older client.

Little information is available on the effects of aging on the GI system, which may be because a decrease in normal function can occur without an effect on physiologic processes. More studies are needed to discern the effects of normal aging from the effects of disease, diet, habits, environmental factors, and medications (Gioiella, Bevil, 1985).

Many of the systemic changes in the functions of digestion and absorption of nutrients result from changes in the older client's cardiovascular and neurologic systems rather than from the GI system. For example, arteriosclerosis and other cardiovascular problems may cause a decrease in **splanchnic** and **mesenteric** blood flow, leading to a decrease in absorption in the small intestine. Since the motility of the entire GI system is affected by the nervous system, any change may cause a decrease in motility, reducing or increasing **transit time.** Other chronic illnesses, such as diabetes, which are associated with peripheral neuropathy that may affect the GI tract, predispose the older client to an increase in gastric reflux, **gastroparesis,** and fecal incontinence (Heitkemper, Carnevali, 1993).

Oral Cavity/Pharynx

Changes in the oral cavity have an effect not only on the older person's well-being, but may have a large impact on their overall nutrition and digestion. The most obvious change in the mouth is the loss of teeth. Most older clients over age 65 are edentulous (without teeth), and the teeth that are present are often diseased or decayed (Malasanos, Barkauskas, Stoltenberg-Allen et al, 1990). The two main causes of the loss of teeth are dental caries and periodontal disease (Storer, 1985). The teeth may also be mechanically worn down on the surface.

In addition to the teeth, the gingival tissues may recede, causing periodontal disease. The periodontal membrane weakens, making it more prone to infection (Miller, 1990). Many older adults have partial plates or dentures which may not fit properly, causing pain and discomfort. In addition, weaker jaw muscles and a shrinkage of the bony structure of the mouth may increase the work of chewing and result in increased fatigue with eating (Hogstel, 1994).

Taste buds may atrophy with age, resulting in an inability to discriminate between flavors, especially between salt and sweet (Linton, 1989). This may contribute to a decrease in the enjoyment of food, resulting in poor eating habits and nutritional deficiencies.

Although the amount of saliva produced may decrease slightly with age, this has not been shown to inhibit the breakdown of starches, and therefore has no detrimental effects on food digestion. The salivary glands secrete less ptyalin and amylase as age advances, and the saliva becomes more alkaline (Hogstel, 1994). Because of the decrease in saliva, the mucous membranes may become more dry, but with no change in the sensation of thirst (Birchenall, Streight, 1993).

Esophagus

Many of the age-related changes in the esophagus result in a decline in its motility. Degenerative changes in the smooth muscle lining the lower esophagus may contribute to a change in the amplitude of contractions, increased resting pressure, and increased numbers of disordered contractions. This decrease in intensity of propulsive waves and increase in frequency of nonperistaltic waves may result in a condition known as **presbyesophagus** (Miller, 1990). Whether this is truly a clinically significant problem is still under debate. Neurogenic, humeral, and vascular changes may also contribute to a decrease in esophageal motility (Heitkemper, Carnevali, 1993). These changes may lead to the complaint of **dysphagia,** heart burn, or vomiting of undigested foods. These symptoms may lead to poor nutrition, dehydration, and decreased food intake, as a result of a fear of the recurrence of symptoms.

In addition to motility changes, there may be a decrease in the resting pressure of the lower esophageal sphincter, resulting in symptoms of fullness, dysphagia, heartburn, and even sternal pain (Heitkemper, Carnavali, 1993).

Stomach

Age-related changes in the stomach include degeneration of the gastric mucosa, decreased secretion of gastric acids and digestive enzymes, and a decrease in motility. However, there is controversy over the clinical significance of age-related changes on gastric emptying. In addition, the cardiac sphincter may relax, leading to an increase in reflux and complaints of heartburn (Birchenall, Streight, 1993). However, because there is so little evidence of changes in the stomach as a result of aging, all gastric complaints warrant evaluation because they are likely to be genuine health problems (Heitkemper, Carnevali, 1993).

By age 60, gastric secretions decrease to 70% to 80% that of the average adult. A decrease in pepsin may hinder protein digestion, whereas a decrease in hydrochloric acid and intrinsic factor leads to malabsorption of iron, vitamin B_{12}, calcium, and folic acid. This, combined with atrophy of the mucosa and a decrease in protective juices, increases the incidence of pernicious anemia, peptic ulcer disease, and stomach cancer (Miller 1990).

Pernicious anemia is a condition most often seen in older adults. With a degeneration of the gastric mucosa, a loss and degeneration of parietal cells occurs, which in turn causes the production of intrinsic factor to decrease. This reduces the absorption of vitamin B_{12}, which causes an impairment in the production of red blood cells. This results in large, oval, fragile cells that have a life span of only a few weeks, as opposed to their normal life span of a few months (Linton, 1989). The resulting condition is known as pernicious anemia, and can only be treated with injections of vitamin B_{12}. Oral vitamin B_{12} cannot be absorbed and cannot be substituted for the injections, which must be continued throughout the life span.

These changes with age may affect the solubility and absorption of some drugs. For example, the decrease in stomach acidity can reduce the solubility of acidic drugs such as aspirin (Heitkemper, Carnevali, 1993). Changes in motility may cause some drugs to be absorbed more completely and others less effectively. When drug absorption problems occur, they are often as results of drug interactions that affect absorption. For example, the calcium, aluminum, and magnesium in antacids, and iron from iron supplements, interfere with the absorption of other medications that older adults may be concomitantly taking (Gioiella, Bevil, 1985).

Gallbladder

In men, gallbladder motility may increase with age, but it does not in postmenopausal women (Altman, 1990). In addition, the composition of bile may become more **lithogenic** with advancing age, possibly because of an increase in biliary cholesterol (Altman, 1990; Cassmeyer, Blevins, 1993). The bile salt pool also decreases as a result of a decrease in bile salt synthesis (Altman, 1990). Therefore the incidence of cholelithiasis and cholecystitis also increases in older adults (Cassmeyer, Blevins, 1993).

Pancreas

Anatomically, the pancreas shows changes with aging, such as the occurrence of ductal hyperplasia and fibrosis. However, these anatomic changes are not always associated with changes in physiologic function (Cassmeyer, Blevins, 1993). However, a decline in volume of pancreatic secretion occurs after the age of 40, and enzyme output diminishes with advancing age. This decrease in enzyme activity relates to the digestion of fats and may account for a vague intolerance to fatty foods in older adults. There is increased incidence of pancreatic cancer in older adults, as well as an increased incidence of pancreatitis.

Small Intestine

Age-related changes in the small intestine include atrophy of the mucosal surfaces, a decline in the weight of the small intestine, thinning of the villi, and a reduction in the number of lymphatic follicles (Miller, 1990). However, these do not seem to alter the functions of digestion and absorption of nutrients (Heitkemper, Carnevali, 1993).

Although there is a slight decrease in motility and absorption of the small intestine with advancing age, usually age-related changes are not enough to cause any significant impairment. Therefore any change in function reported by the older adult should be addressed seriously in search for underlying pathology of inflammation or infection.

Large Intestine

Age-related changes in the large intestine include a decrease in mucous secretion, decrease in elasticity of the rectal wall, but no documented changes in motility (Miller, 1990).

The tone of the internal anal sphincter decreases, which may lead to incontinence or incomplete emptying of the bowel. Nerve impulses, which usually indicate the need to defecate, may be dulled. This may account for

BOX 25-1

Primary Prevention Strategies for GI Problems in the Older Adult

Oral hygiene/preventive dental care
Daily flossing and brushing
Semiannual professional dental care
Properly fitting dentures

Nutrition
Foods that are low in fat, high in fiber
Small portions
Variety of textures, odors, and colors
Basic food groups (food guide pyramid)
Change in RDA for older adults:
- Decrease in calories
- Decrease in amount of B vitamins
- Decrease in iron for postmenopausal women
- Increase in calcium

Avoid spicy or irritating foods (e.g., hot pepper, coffee)
Maintain daily fluid intake of 2,000 ml (unless cardiac status contraindicates)

Habits
Avoid tobacco products (e.g., cigarettes, pipe or cigar smoking, and chewing tobacco)
Avoid large amounts of alcohol

Elimination
Maintain regular bowel routines
Do not avoid the urge to defecate
Avoid use of laxatives, suppositories, and enemas

Sleep/rest
Maintain activity level
Get adequate sleep

Compiled from Birchenall JM, Streight ME: *Care of the older adult,* ed 3, Philadelphia, 1993, JB Lippincott; Miller C: *Nursing care of older adults: theory and practice,* Glenview, Ill, 1990, Scott, Foresman.

the increased incidence of constipation (Birchenall, Streight, 1993). In addition, the incidence of development of diverticula increases, which may or may not cause symptoms.

PREVENTION

Although some changes in the GI system are associated with aging, some strategies for both primary and secondary prevention for problems are associated with the GI system (Boxes 25-1 and 25-2). Nurses caring for older clients should not only include instruction of these strategies in their care for older clients, but should also reinforce and should remind each client on an annual basis.

COMMON PROBLEMS AND CONDITIONS

No clear-cut GI diseases can be attributed directly to the aging process. However, many conditions show a higher incidence in older adults, and have a greater impact on the older client's physical and social well-being (Heitkemper, Carnevali, 1993).

Common complaints related to the GI system in the older adult include the following: (1) food does not taste the way it used to, (2) eating is not enjoyable any more, (3) indigestion and constipation occur more often, and (4) large meals cause bloating and discomfort (Birchenall, Streight, 1993). These complaints can be related to normal physiologic changes with aging, but must be distinguished from the pathologic problems that increase in frequency with older adults.

The following is an overview of common GI problems seen in the older client. See Box 25-3 for an explanation of diagnostic tests used in this section.

Gingivitis/Periodontis

The gingivae, or gums, are subject to localized and systemic diseases, problems caused by drug therapy, poor oral hygiene, and poor nutrition. Gingivitis, an inflammation of the gums surrounding the teeth, may result in pain, bleeding, and may lead to **periodontitis,** a spread of the inflammation to the underlying tissues, bones, or roots of the teeth (Collins, Bullock, 1992). This is the most common reason for tooth loss with advancing age. Gingivitis resulting from overgrowth of the gingiva, may occur in people taking phenytoin (Dilantin) on a long-term basis.

Candida albicans, or thrush, is an infection causing white lesions in the oral mucosa. It is often seen in persons with immune disorders such as acquired immunodeficiency syndrome (AIDS) or in those who have suppressed immune systems, such as individuals with transplants (see Medical Management box, p. 656, at left).

BOX 25-2

Secondary Prevention-Early Detection Strategies for GI Problems in the Older Adult

American Cancer Society recommendations for screening for colorectal cancer:

1. Digital rectal exam by health care provider every year after the age of 40.
2. Stool guaiac test by either the client or health care provider every year after the age of 50.
3. Sigmoidoscopy at age 50 and every 3 to 5 years after two negative tests. With a positive family history of colorectal cancer, however, initial screening should be 5 years before the age of the affected family member at diagnosis, or by age 40.

Other "red flags" requiring medical follow-up:

Mouth
Sore that does not heal
Any lump
A persistent red or white patch
Difficulty or painful chewing or swallowing

Stomach
Persistent indigestion or heartburn
Abdominal pain
Persistent nausea and/or vomiting

Elimination
Any change in bowel habits
Presence of any blood in stool

From Long BC, Roberts R: The patient with gastrointestinal problems. In Long BC, Phipps WJ, Cassmeyer VL, editors: *Medical-surgical nursing: a nursing process approach,* ed 3, St Louis, 1993, Mosby.

NURSING MANAGEMENT

ASSESSMENT

Assessment begins with a good history of dental care and dental hygiene practices. A complete health history, focusing on other illnesses and concomitant medications, as well as physical assessment of the mouth is necessary.

DIAGNOSIS

The most common nursing diagnoses used for the older client with gingivitis include, but are not limited to: (1) altered oral mucous membrane, (2) altered health maintenance, and (3) altered nutrition: less than body requirements, related to pain.

BOX 25-3

Radiologic and Diagnostic Tests and Procedures

Plain film of abdomen/kidneys, ureter, bladder (KUB)

A simple x-ray of the abdomen requiring no preparation; should include supine and erect views when an obstruction is suspected.

Upper GI/barium swallow

An x-ray using an opaque contrast medium (barium) to examine the structure and motility of the upper GI tract, including pharynx, esophagus, and stomach

May be extended (small bowel follow-through) to examine the duodenum and small bowel

Preparation is NPO after midnight the night before the test

Must increase fluids after examination to facilitate the evacuation of the barium, which colors stool white

Upper endoscopy

An endoscopic exam of the upper GI tract allowing for direct visualization through a lighted fiber optic tube that contains a lens, forceps, and brushes for biopsy

Preparation is similar to that of the upper GI.

Sedation is required.

The procedure is performed by the gastroenterologist in the procedure suite or at the bedside.

Barium enema

An x-ray using an opaque contrast medium to examine the lower GI tract

Preparation includes NPO after midnight the night before the procedure, as well as a bowel prep to clean out the large intestine before the procedure.

Ultrasound

A radiologic technique used to examine abdominal and other organs and tissues that does not use ionizing radiation

It cannot be used on organs that contain air, because the ultrasound waves cannot penetrate air.

Preparation depends on the organ being examined, and may require the client to be NPO up to 12 hours before the procedure.

Colonoscopy

An endoscopic examination of the colon with use of a colonoscope, which is inserted through the rectum

Preparation is similar to that of the barium enema. Sedation is required.

The procedure is conducted by the gastroenterologist in the GI procedure suite.

Flexible/sigmoidoscopy

An endoscopic examination of the interior of the sigmoid colon (does not examine as much of the colon as a colonoscopy)

Sedation is required.

The procedure is performed by the gastroenterologist in the GI procedure suite.

Preparation is similar to that of the barium enema.

Endoscopic retrograde cholangiopancreatography (ERCP)

A fluoroscopic upper endoscopic examination through the esophagus and duodenum into the common bile duct, used to examine structures in the biliary tree

Sedation is required.

The client must be NPO for 8 to 13 hours before the procedure, which is performed in the GI procedure suite by a gastroenterologist.

Nuclear medicine studies

Radionucleotide imaging using an injection of an isotope which concentrates at the site to be examined (e.g., HIDA scan, DISIDA scan, and liver scan)

No sedation is necessary.

Preparation is NPO after midnight the night before the test, which is performed in the nuclear medicine section of the radiology department.

Computerized tomography (CT) scan

A CT scan is used to produce pictures of internal organs of the body, and to allow visualization and identification of both normal and abnormal structures.

It may be performed with or without a contrast material.

Preparation varies from NPO 8 to 12 hours before the procedure to no preparation, depending on the type of CT scan ordered.

It is completed in the radiology department.

From Long BC, Roberts R: The patient with gastrointestinal problems. In Long BC, Phipps WJ, Cassmeyer VL, editors: *Medical-surgical nursing: a nursing process approach,* ed 3, St. Louis, 1993, Mosby.

✣ PLANNING

Expected outcomes for the older client with gingivitis or periodontitis include, but are not limited to, the following: (1) client will maintain a comfortable and functional oral cavity, (2) client will remain free of oral infections, (3) client will establish and maintain a mouth care routine, and (4) client will maintain regular professional dental care.

✣ INTERVENTION

Nursing management of the older client with gingivitis or periodontitis includes promotion of regular oral hygiene, regular preventive dental care, and maintenance

MEDICAL MANAGEMENT

Gingivitis/Periodontitis

Diagnostic tests and procedures

Diagnosis may initially be made by the client, but requires professional inspection and palpation. Although primary care providers can often diagnose gingivitis, a referral to a dentist is necessary for proper evaluation and treatment.

Treatment

Treatment consists of proper dental hygiene, including regular flossing and brushing. In addition, professional dental care on a semiannual basis, and as needed, is required for treatment and prevention of further complications.

Prognosis

Prognosis is good; however, clients need to remember that the key is prevention, which is through proper dental and mouth care.

of nutritional status. In addition, assessing the client's knowledge of the importance of oral hygiene and frequently reinforcing oral hygiene practices are important roles for the nurse. Oral hygiene includes regular flossing, brushing of teeth and dentures, and using saline mouth rinses as needed. Professional dental care should be sought routinely every 6 months and more often as needed. Proper fit of dentures at first and at all subsequent visits to both the dentist and primary health care provider also is encouraged. Pain relief to ensure adequate nutrition can be managed by non-narcotic pain medications (Tylenol or Aspirin), frequent mouth rinses, and a liquid or soft diet. The key to the treatment of gingivitis and periodontitis is prevention. Although good oral hygiene needs to begin early in life, it is never too late for the older client to begin routine dental care and oral hygiene.

✣ EVALUATION

Evaluation includes achievement of the expected outcomes, establishment and maintenance of regular dental care and oral hygiene practices, and prevention of infection.

Oral Cancer

Oral cancer commonly includes cancer of the salivary glands, floor of the mouth, tongue, and lips. Although not common (i.e., comprises 3% of all cancers), the presence of oral cancer can be devastating for the older adult, since appearance, speaking, and eating may be affected (Long, Roberts, 1993).

The causal factors have not been well-researched. However, risk factors focus on the exposure of **carcinogenic** agents, since the mouth is a conduit for air, food, fluids, and tobacco products. In the mouth, these carcinogenic agents include cigarettes, ethyl alcohol, snuff, chewing tobacco, betel nut, textile industries, and leather manufacturing. Other precipitating factors include nutritional deficiencies, such as vitamin B and riboflavin (Parzuchowski, 1991).

MEDICAL MANAGEMENT

Oral Cancer

Diagnostic tests and procedures

Diagnosis is by physical examination and biopsy of the lesion. Physical examination includes careful inspection under proper lighting and palpation.

Treatment

Stage I and II tumors may be treated by radiation and/or by surgery, stage III can be treated usually by both, and stage IV treatment is palliative. Surgery includes removal of the involved portion of the tongue, or hemiglossectomy. When there is metastasis to the surrounding tissue, a radical neck dissection may be done.

Prognosis

Prognosis depends on extent of the tumor's invasion. The mortality rate is higher for cancer of the tongue, because the lesion may go unnoticed. In contrast, the cure rate for cancer of the lip is high because of the visibility of the lesion (Long, Roberts, 1993).

The majority of oral cancers are squamous cell carcinomas. These tumors typically occur in clients between the ages of 40 and 70 years, and are more prevalent in men than women (Parzuchowski, 1991).

Cancer of the tongue, usually a squamous cell carcinoma, is more prevalent in men than women. The cancer begins as an ulceration, which may be precipitated by chronic irritations from tobacco, food, alcohol, occupational exposures, or malocclusion of the teeth. With growth of the tumor, the cancer metastasizes to the floor of the mouth and lymph nodes of the neck (Billings, Stokes, 1987). Unfortunately, metastases to the neck have occurred in more than 60% of people when the diagnosis is made. This is partly because of the great vascular and lymph drainage of the tongue and the location of the lesion, which may go unnoticed by the client.

Cancer of the lips usually results from squamous cells, but may also be caused by basal cell carcinoma. These cancers are usually a result of prolonged exposure to the sun (Smoller, Smoller, 1992).

Oral cancers are classified according to four stages. Stages I and II involve a local tumor only with no lymph node spread or metastases. In stage III, the tumor is > 4 cm, and there may be palpable lymph nodes. In stage IV, the tumor is invasive, with metastases to lungs or liver (Long, Roberts, 1993) (see Medical Management box, p. 656, at right).

Nursing Management

✣ ASSESSMENT

Assessment begins with a history of symptoms such as pain on lips, gums, floor or roof of mouth, or physically feeling or visualizing a lump or other abnormality. A history of previous experiences with cancer (either oral or other forms) and the older client's concomitant medical illnesses and medications is necessary. The physical examination includes a complete and thorough oral examination, focusing on palpating or visualizing any abnormalities, especially on the floor and roof of the mouth. Foul breath may be noted.

✣ DIAGNOSIS

Nursing diagnoses for the older client with oral cancer include, but are not limited to: (1) altered oral mucous membrane, (2) altered nutrition: less than body requirements, related to pain, and (3) body image disturbance.

✣ PLANNING

Expected outcomes for the older client with oral cancer include but are not limited to the following: (1) client's lesions and incisions will heal without infection, (2) client will maintain weight within acceptable range for height and age, (3) client will feed self, and (4) client will verbalize fears and concerns over body image changes.

✣ INTERVENTION

Nursing management for the older client with oral cancer includes maintenance of adequate nutrition, promotion of oral hygiene, provision of comfort, and facilitation of communication.

When part or all of the tongue is removed, the client may have difficulty swallowing and speaking. Referral to a speech therapist is useful for retraining in swallowing and speaking. Liquid diets and **gavage** feedings may be used to maintain adequate nutrition. Mouth care and oral hygiene are important to promote healing (Billings, Stokes, 1987).

Disfigurement and a poor prognosis may lead to coping difficulties that may require counseling. Encourage client to verbalize feelings and frustrations and to attend support groups that may facilitate adjustments.

✣ EVALUATION

Evaluation includes achievement of the expected outcomes, including maintenance of nutrition, prevention of infection, and resumption of activities.

Dysphagia and Achalasia

Dysphagia, or difficulty swallowing, is a symptom with many underlying causes. The origin depends on the cause, which includes stroke and other neurologic conditions, local trauma and tissue damage, achalasia, and tumors that obstruct the passage of food and liquids. Symptoms of dysphagia range from mild discomfort such as the feeling of a lump in the throat to a severe inability to swallow (O'Toole, 1992).

Achalasia is a common cause of dysphagia, nocturnal regurgitation, and noncardiac chest pain. It is the primary cause of the symptom of dysphagia (Saunderlin, 1993). Achalasia is an esophageal motility disorder that is characterized by a decrease in peristalsis of the body of the esophagus, increased resting pressure of the cardiac sphincter, and failure of the cardiac sphincter to fully relax during swallowing. These abnormalities cause food and liquids to accumulate in the distal end of the esophagus and may cause the esophagus to become greatly dilated (Aliberti, 1993; Collins, Bullock, 1992).

The cause of achalasia is poorly understood. Although it is a rare disorder, it is not uncommon. In the United States, between 1,000 and 1,500 cases of achalasia are diagnosed annually (Saunderlin, 1993).

MEDICAL MANAGEMENT

Dysphagia

Diagnostic tests and procedures

Diagnostic tests include a barium swallow, which can reveal a normally functioning pharynx and upper esophagus, but the lower esophagus will be a distended, nonemptying pouch (Collins, Bullock, 1992).

Treatment

Treatment of dysphagia depends on the cause. No cure exists for achalasia, so treatment is palliative and consists of restoring swallowing function as best as possible, primarily by pneumatic dilatation of the cardiac sphincter or through a surgical myotomy (splitting the muscle fibers of the sphincter) (Aliberti, 1993). Although drug therapy with calcium channel blockers or nitrates has been used, its therapeutic value has been disputed (Triadafilopoulus et al, 1991). Sometimes, surgery is required to decrease the amount of obstruction. Follow-up is required, because these clients have a higher frequency of developing esophageal carcinoma (Aliberti, 1993; Saunderlin, 1993).

Prognosis

Prognosis depends on the cause. Since achalasia is a chronic condition and has no cure, clients need to learn to live with their symptoms.

Symptoms of achalasia include progressive dysphagia, vomiting of food, nausea, and weight loss. The dysphagia progresses from solid foods to liquids. Pain occurs in only about one third of cases. Nocturnal aspiration can often occur, leading to infections of unusual organisms (mycobacteria) (Collins, Bullock, 1992). The onset of symptoms is insidious, and delay in diagnosis is common. However, severe, rapid weight loss indicates a secondary cause of achalasia, such as malignancy (see Medical Management box, p. 657).

Nursing Management

✣ ASSESSMENT

Assessment begins with an accurate and precise history that focuses on whether the dysphagia is with liquids, solids, or both, as well as the time frame for the progression of the dysphagia. Physical examination may be unremarkable.

✣ DIAGNOSIS

Nursing diagnoses for the older client with dysphagia include, but are not limited to: (1) altered nutrition: less than body requirements, (2) pain with swallowing, (3) fear related to diagnosis and prognosis, and (4) potential for aspiration.

✣ PLANNING

Expected outcomes for the older client with dysphagia include, but are not limited to, the following: (1) client will maintain weight, (2) client will remain free from aspiration, (3) client will learn techniques to swallow which minimize pain, and (4) client will be able to verbalize fears related to diagnosis and prognosis.

✣ INTERVENTION

Nursing management of the older client with dysphagia includes, but is not limited to, the following: maintenance of hydration and nutritional status, prevention of aspiration, provision of emotional support and information regarding diagnosis and prognosis, as well as support and reassurance with fear of eating because of the pain, difficulty in swallowing, and frequent regurgitation. Optimizing nutritional status and preventing weight loss are important, since fear of eating may lead to chronic weight loss. Instruction regarding eating habits and maintaining weight and nutrition is important. For example, small, frequent meals; pureed or soft diets; and high-protein, high-calorie foods are helpful. Instruct the client to elevate the head of the bed to prevent nocturnal aspiration (Aliberti, 1993; Saunderlin, 1993).

✣ EVALUATION

Evaluation includes achievement of the expected outcomes, prevention of aspiration, and maintenance of nutrition. Evaluation of coping with the diagnosis may be assessed through resumption of activities and ability to verbalize feelings.

Gastroesophageal Reflux/Esophagitis

Gastroesophageal reflux is the movement of gastric contents back up into the esophagus. Normally, pressure on the lower esophageal sphincter prevents backflow. But an incompetent lower esophageal sphincter is believed to be the primary cause of reflux esophagitis. Other causes include a hiatal hernia, prolonged gastric intubation (i.e., a feeding tube), ingestion of corrosive chemicals, medications, uremia, infections, mucosal alterations, and systemic diseases such as lupus. Gastroesophageal reflux is sometimes called gastroesophageal reflux disease (GERD), since it is often a chronic disease.

Esophagitis is simply an inflammation of the esophagus. Most often, this results from gastroesophageal reflux due to either prolonged vomiting or an incompetent lower esophageal sphincter. Amount of mucosal damage is related to the contact time between the esophageal mucosa and gastric contents, as well as the acidity and quantity of gastric secretions (Collins, Bullock, 1992).

Hydrochloric acid from the stomach alters the pH of the esophagus and allows mucosal protein to be denatured (Collins, Bullock, 1992). The pepsin in the gastric secretion has **proteolytic** properties that are enhanced when the pH is around 2.0. The combination of pepsin and hydrochloric acid increases the capability of damage. The reflux has been shown to cause an inflammation that penetrates to the muscularis layer, resulting in motor dysfunction and decreased esophageal clearance. The end results are increased esophageal contact time, more muscle damage, and increased amounts of reflux.

Symptoms include heartburn, retrosternal discomfort, and the regurgitation of sour, bitter material (Collins, Bullock, 1992). Symptoms are often precipitated by the ingestion of a large amount of fatty or spicy foods or alcohol. Interestingly, in a recent study, symptoms did not correlate with the amount and acidity of reflux but did correlate with stress and anxiety (Bradley et al, 1993). Strictures may develop that may make food passage difficult. Dysphagia for both liquids and solids increases when severe obstruction occurs. If regurgitation occurs often, substernal pain may result, occasionally mimicking a heart attack. Reflux may be aggravated by postural changes, such as lying supine when sleeping, but may occur in any position. Pulmonary **aspiration** as a result of reflux is common when the disease is severe, leading to pneumonia.

Hiatal Hernia

A hiatal hernia is a major cause of reflux and esophagitis, and occurs when part of the stomach protrudes through an opening of the diaphragm. The condition may be intermittent or continuous. The continuous type is least common, accounting for only about 10% of people with this condition. Either part or all of the stomach and even the intestines may herniate, causing **dyspepsia,** severe pain, and often agastric ulceration. The intermittent type, or sliding hernia, occurs with changes in position or with increased peristalsis. The stomach is forced through the opening of the diaphragm when prone, and moves back to its normal position when the person stands up. Most hiatal hernias are asymptomatic and require no treatment.

Symptoms, when they arise, include heartburn, gastric regurgitation, dysphagia, and indigestion. These symptoms are accentuated when in the supine position postprandially, and after overeating, physical exertion, or sudden change in posture (Collins, Bullock, 1992) (see Medical Management box below).

MEDICAL MANAGEMENT

GERD/ Esophagitis

Diagnostic tests and procedures

Diagnosis is based on clinical, radiographic, and endoscopic appearances. One of the most reliable tests for the diagnosis of esophagitis is the measurement of pH in the esophagus. In addition, biopsy of the esophagus to demonstrate inflammatory changes is also desirable. Nuclear medicine studies, such as scintiscans, which involve the swallowing of a radionucleotide, can demonstrate reflux by measuring the radioactivity of the esophagus in serial scans (Collins, Bullock, 1992).

Radiographs are necessary to diagnose and to document the presence of a hiatal hernia. If reflux is not determined by an upper GI series, then the hernia is considered to be of little clinical importance. Other causes of the symptoms must then be investigated. Hiatal hernias are found more often in the majority of upper GI series conducted, and the presence of one does not usually correlate with physical symptoms. Surgery is usually recommended for those with severe cases (i.e., those with the continuous type of hernia) and involves fixing the stomach to the abdominal wall by a fundoplication or gastropexy.

Treatment

Treatment for esophagitis is aimed at reducing the source of irritation. Antacids and a diet of bland foods to aid in neutralizing digestive juices are helpful, in addition to avoiding or eliminating smoking (Billing, Stokes, 1979). The preferred treatment for GERD consists of small, bland meals of easily digested foods, moderate exercise, sleeping with the upper part of the body elevated, and antacids, if necessary.

Prognosis

Prognosis is good. Frequent follow-up is necessary for the symptomatic older client to make sure peptic ulcers or gastric cancer do not develop.

NURSING MANAGEMENT

ASSESSMENT

Assessment begins with a history of symptoms and possible aggravating factors. The older client may use terms such as indigestion or heartburn, which need to be clearly defined. The older client may not use the term pain, and also may not be aware if regurgitation is present. Physical examination may be unremarkable.

DIAGNOSIS

Nursing diagnoses for the older client with gastroesophageal reflux include, but are not limited to: (1) high risk for aspiration, (2) altered nutrition: less than body requirements, and (3) knowledge deficit.

PLANNING

Expected outcomes for the older client with gastroesophageal reflux include, but are not limited to, the following: (1) client will maintain weight, (2) client will remain free from aspiration, and (3) client will verbalize understanding of disease process and treatment approaches.

INTERVENTION

Nursing management of the older client with gastroesophageal reflux includes maintenance of adequate nutrition, prevention of aspiration, and instructing client and family about the disease process and treatment approaches (see Client/Family Teaching box, p. 660).

EVALUATION

Evaluation includes achievement of expected outcomes, prevention of complications, and questioning the client regarding appropriate dietary and lifestyle changes.

Cancer of the Esophagus

In the United States, esophageal cancer accounts for approximately 10% of all GI tract cancers (Collins, Bullock, 1992; Savas, Zeroske, 1993). Unfortunately, these malignancies usually remain asymptomatic until they are surgically unresectable because of extension. In addition, many people with esophageal cancer attribute its signs and symptoms to some of the more common disorders that affect older adults (Frogge, 1990). Because of this fact, clients with esophageal cancer have probably the worst prognosis of all clients with malignancies of the GI tract (Savas, Zeroske, 1993).

Esophageal cancer is not common, since it contributes to 1% of all forms of cancer and is responsible for 2% of cancer deaths (Frogge, 1990). A significant difference in incidence rates exists according to geographic location. The highest incidence occurs in Turkey and eastern China at the rate of 20% to 25% (Collins, Bullock, 1992). This type of malignancy usually occurs after the age of 50, but in general develops at a younger age in black people compared with white. In addition, incidences are higher among men than women.

Although the cause of esophageal cancer is unknown, the relationship with geographic location suggests nutritional and environmental factors. While a strong correlation exists between heavy alcohol intake, cigarette smoking, and esophageal cancer, an even higher correlation exists in combination (Savas, Zeroske, 1993). Other predisposing factors include conditions of chronic irritation, untreated achalasia, environmental factors such as toxins, and vitamin deficiencies (Frogge, 1990; Savas, Zeroske, 1993).

Morphologically, the most common cancer is squamous cell, since it is the major cell type that lines the esophagus (Frogge, 1990). This malignancy may grow around the esophagus at the level of the diaphragm, impinging on the lumen of the tube, or it may cause a bulky, ulcerating tumor mass. Most tumors are found in the middle and lower one third of the esophagus (Collins, Bullock, 1992).

The tumor often spreads by invasion of the surrounding structures and can affect the mediastinum, trachea, lungs, bronchi, and major vessels (Frogge, 1990; Savas, Zeroske, 1993). In addition, it metastasizes by the lymph system, with flow either cephalad or caudad (Frogge, 1990). The tumor also metastasizes by hematogenous spread of tumor cells or tumor emboli. Distant metastases to lung, liver, adrenal glands, brain, bone, and kidney are common. The natural history of the disease includes swallowing difficulties, malnutrition, cachexia, pneumonia, and eventual death.

The earliest complaint is usually a mild dysphagia that becomes progressively worse, moving from dysphagia with solids only to dysphagia with liquids as well (Savas, Zeroske, 1993). Other symptoms include substernal pressure, fullness, and indigestion (Frogge, 1990). Eventually weight loss is a common complaint, as is general

CLIENT/FAMILY TEACHING

Heartburn, Hiatal Hernia, or Reflux

Nutrition/diet

Eat high-protein, low-fat foods
Avoid foods containing caffeine and chocolate
Eat small, frequent meals
Eat easily digestible foods
Achieve and maintain ideal body weight

Habits

Avoid smoking
Avoid alcohol

Activity/rest

Avoid lying down or bending over for 2 hours after meals
Avoid wearing tight belts or girdles during or after meals
Sleep with upper body elevated; use blocks, not pillows, under front legs of bed

From Long BC, Roberts R: The patient with gastrointestinal problems. In Long BC, Phipps WJ, Cassmeyer VL, editors: *Medical-surgical nursing: a nursing process approach,* ed 3, St. Louis, 1993, Mosby.

MEDICAL MANAGEMENT

Esophageal Cancer

Diagnostic tests and procedures

Diagnosis is best done through endoscopy so the tumor can be biopsied to identify the cell type (Savas, Zeroske, 1993). Other diagnostic tests include barium swallow, chest x-ray, and blood tests. Once diagnosed, endoscopic ultrasound can be used to stage the lesion, and CT scan can be used to identify any metastases (Savas, Zeroske, 1993).

Staging is important in treatment and prognosis, and is done with the TNM classification. Here, *T* represents depth of involvement of the esophageal wall, *N* is lymph node involvement, and *M* is evidence of metastases (Savas, Zeroske, 1993).

Treatment

Management of esophageal cancer may be curative or palliative, depending on the stage of the lesion. Surgery, radiation therapy, chemotherapy, or a combination may be used (Billings, Stokes, 1987; Frogge, 1990). Other treatments include esophageal dilatation, stenting, and laser photoablation and photodynamic therapy (Savas, Zeroske, 1993).

Prognosis

Because esophageal cancer grows rapidly, metastasizes early, and is diagnosed late, survival rates are poor (Frogge, 1990). Prognosis is very poor, with only about 6% surviving 5 years (Silverberg, Lubera, 1989).

CARE PLAN

ESOPHAGEAL CANCER

Clinical situation Mr. E is a 65-year-old retired factory worker and veteran who comes to the VA outpatient satellite clinic with the complaint of dysphagia. Within the last 4 months he has had pain and difficulty swallowing solid food, and therefore progressed to eating soft, then liquid foods. But within the last month this has progressed to problems with swallowing even liquids. He reports one episode of nocturnal regurgitation this last week. Other symptoms include 20-lb weight loss over the last 6 months, fatigue, and a dull back ache. Mr. E sheepishly admits that he still smokes, but has cut down from two packs to one pack per day. In addition, he admits to alcohol ingestion of beer and hard liquor, although he has cut down in amount and frequency over the last few years since the death of his wife.

His past medical history is unremarkable, except an amputation of two fingers on his right hand when he was in the service. He lives alone but near his daughter, whom he states convinced him to come to the clinic when he did not eat anything at her recent Thanksgiving dinner.

Physical examination reveals a thin but well-developed older man, with a weight of 140 lbs, temperature of 98° F (36. 6° C), pulse of 80 beats per minute, 18 respirations per minute, and blood pressure of 120/82 mm Hg. Inspection of his pharynx reveals no abnormalities except for poor dentition. Examination of his abdomen and rectal area are also unremarkable. Laboratory values reveal an iron deficiency anemia, but initial screening is otherwise unremarkable. He is scheduled for an endoscopy the next day. He returns to the clinic 1 week later to get his results, and his diagnosis is esophageal cancer. He is scheduled for radiation therapy and possibly surgery once the tumor has shrunk in size.

Nursing diagnoses	Outcomes	Interventions
Altered nutrition: less than body requirements, related to inadequate intake of nutrients secondary to dysphagia	Client will stabilize weight.	Encourage the use of small, frequent meals. Encourage the use of high-protein, high-calorie foods, and the use of supplements such as Ensure. Refer to dietician if necessary for specific recommendations. Discuss possibility of the use of tube feedings with client to supplement or as the sole means of delivering needed nutrients.
Impaired swallowing related to mechanical obstruction secondary to tumor	Client will swallow safely without gagging or aspirating. Client will maintain adequate nutrition/hydration.	Arrange for speech therapist consult to provide instruction regarding swallowing. Instruct client and family regarding need to have upright positioning during and after eating. Instruct client and family to rotate the client's head toward the affected side to facilitate swallowing. Provide rest periods before, during, and after feedings. With liquids, provide thick liquids first, adding thin liquids last; begin with cold and progress to hot. With foods, begin with pureed, progressing to soft, with small bites.
Fear related to uncertain prognosis, possible disfigurement, and loss of ability to eat	Client and family will identify sources of fears, and acquire knowledge to deal with the fears.	Encourage client and family to verbalize fears. Provide information to reduce distortions in perceptions. Encourage client and family to attend cancer support groups. Instruct client and family about impending treatments such as surgery and radiation therapy.

Continued.

CARE PLAN

ESOPHAGEAL CANCER—cont'd

Nursing diagnoses	Outcomes	Interventions
High risk for aspiration related to dysphagia	Client will not aspirate.	Assess client's ability to eat and drink. Assess respiratory status before, during, and after eating. Monitor for signs of aspiration: dyspnea, cough, wheezing, tachycardia, and elevated temperature. Observe and record color and character of sputum. Consult with speech therapist for techniques to improve swallowing. Instruct client and family to keep head elevated during and after eating/feedings.

malaise and anorexia. Postprandial regurgitation of undigested food may motivate the person to seek medical attention. Symptoms may be present for only weeks or months, yet the esophageal carcinoma can be advanced (Frogge, 1990). **Hematemesis** and guaiac positive stools are uncommon. Invasion of surrounding structures by the tumor may lead to back pain or respiratory distress (see Medical Management box, p. 660).

NURSING MANAGEMENT

ASSESSMENT

Assessment begins with an accurate history, focusing on risk factors for esophageal cancer. A review of systems may reveal symptoms of dysphagia, eating difficulties, or aspiration. Physical examination can probably reveal few findings definitive of the diagnosis. However, in advanced disease, the nurse may find palpable lymph nodes and perhaps organ enlargement resulting from metastasis. Other findings include significant and recent weight loss.

DIAGNOSIS

Nursing diagnoses for the older client with esophageal cancer include, but are not limited to: (1) altered nutrition: less than body requirements related to inadequate intake of nutrients in the diet because of dysphagia; (2) impaired swallowing; (3) fear related to uncertain prognosis, possible disfigurement, and loss of ability to eat; and (4) high risk for aspiration.

PLANNING

Expected outcomes for the older client with esophageal cancer include, but are not limited to, the following: (1) client will initially stabilize weight, and achieve a weight gain of 1 lb. every 3 weeks, depending on stage of disease; (2) client will consume a high-calorie diet; (3) client will remain free from aspiration; and (4) client will verbalize fears related to diagnosis and prognosis.

INTERVENTION

Nursing management of the older client with esophageal cancer includes maintenance of hydration and nutritional status, prevention of aspiration, maintenance of comfort, and provision of emotional support. Optimizing nutritional status and preventing further weight loss can be accomplished with small, frequent feedings; high-protein, high-calorie foods; supplements such as Ensure; and tube feedings if necessary. Nursing care to prevent aspiration focuses on assessment of respiratory status, assessment of difficulty with eating and drinking, and proper positioning during and after eating.

The nurse's role in the prevention and early detection of esophageal cancer may lead to early identification and perhaps improved prognosis for the older client. People with risk factors for esophageal cancer should be instructed to reduce or to eliminate them, and to be counseled regarding the need for frequent medical follow-up. Counseling on proper nutrition and elimination of smoking and alcohol are important for prevention (Frogge, 1990). Older clients with frequent upper GI complaints should be told to seek medical attention immediately.

✣ EVALUATION

Evaluation includes achievement of the expected outcomes, prevention of aspiration, and maintenance of adequate nutrition (see nursing Care Plan, pp. 661-662).

Gastritis

Gastritis refers to inflammation of the gastric mucosa, and occurs in acute or chronic forms. Although hydrochloric acid is present in gastritis, the amount of secretion does not have to be excessive.

Acute gastritis causes transient inflammation of the gastric mucosa, mucosal hemorrhages, and erosion into the mucosal lining. Although the cause is undetermined, it is frequently associated with alcoholism, aspirin or NSAID ingestion, smoking, and severely stressful conditions such as burns, trauma, central nervous system damage, chemotherapy, and radiation therapy (Collins, Bullock, 1992).

Chronic gastritis is an inflammation of the stomach lining that may occur repeatedly or continue over a period of time. Among its possible causes are ulcers, hiatal hernias, vitamin deficiencies, chronic alcohol use, gastric mucosal atrophy, **achlorhydria,** and peptic ulceration (Collins, Bullock, 1992; O'Toole, 1992). The continual loss of gastric mucosa eventually decreases gastric secretion and may lead to pernicious anemia, peptic ulcer disease, or gastric cancer (Long, Roberts, 1993).

The major symptom of gastritis is abdominal pain. Other symptoms include indigestion, distention, decreased appetite, nausea, and vomiting. Many clients with chronic gastritis are asymptomatic.

Stress ulcers, or erosions, may occur after a major insult to the body, such as burns, sepsis, or head trauma. Although an erosion is a form of gastritis, it is simply a superficial mucosal defect (erosion or ulceration) of the stomach that does not penetrate the muscularis layer.

Two mechanisms for producing stress ulcers have been proposed: (1) mucosal ischemia resulting from a lack of blood supply to the gastric mucosa during the poststress period, and (2) increased sensitivity of the gastric mucosa to hydrochloric acid and pepsin (Collins, Bullock, 1992).

The major clinical manifestation of gastric erosion is massive, painless, gastric bleeding with the onset 2 to 15 days after the initial insult. Signs include hematemesis and **melena,** and rarely include pain. Because of the danger of bleeding after acute stress, and the difficulty stopping it once it has started, preventive measures are routinely used to decrease hydrogen ion secretion and neutralize gastric acid. These include administration of antacids and H_2 blockers or sucralfate (see Medical Management box at left).

MEDICAL MANAGEMENT

Gastritis

Diagnostic tests and procedures

The diagnostic workup of gastritis includes an upper GI series or endoscopy. Laboratory values remain normal. Many times, diagnosis is based on symptoms and is a diagnosis of exclusion after other disorders are ruled out, including peptic ulcer disease and hiatal hernia.

Treatment

Treatment of gastritis includes the use of antacids, and possibly H_2 blockers, although the latter has been associated with mental status changes in the older adult. Also important is the avoidance of greasy, spicy foods. Meals of easily digested foods should be eaten at small, frequent intervals. In acute gastritis, intravenous (IV) therapy may be necessary to prevent fluid and electrolyte imbalances. After about 24 hours of IV fluids only, the older client is usually able to tolerate clear liquid feedings, slowly progressing to other foods that may be gradually introduced (Long, Roberts, 1993).

Prognosis

Prognosis is good when treated promptly. Occasionally, an acute erosion of the gastric mucosa can result in a massive GI hemorrhage. When this occurs, prompt medical intervention is imperative, with blood transfusions and the availability of life support if necessary.

NURSING MANAGEMENT

✣ ASSESSMENT

Assessment begins with a history and review of systems that may include complaints of indigestion, abdominal or epigastric discomfort, nausea, vomiting, or anorexia. Questioning clients about possible GI blood loss is also important (e.g., hematemesis and melena). With acute gastritis, signs of dehydration may be present (see Assessment of the GI System, pp. 688-690).

✣ DIAGNOSIS

Nursing diagnoses for the older client with gastritis include, but are not limited to (1) epigastric pain, (2) fluid volume deficit, and (3) knowledge deficit: disease and aggravating factors.

✣ PLANNING

Expected outcomes for the older client with gastritis include, but are not limited to, the following: (1) client will remain free of massive GI hemorrhage, (2) client will use measures to relieve pain, (3) client verbalizes understanding of disease and factors attributed to the disease, over which the client has control, and (4) client maintains adequate fluid and electrolyte balance.

✣ INTERVENTION

Nursing management of the older client with gastritis includes, but is not limited to, the following:

1. Delivery of medications to prevent upper GI bleeding as ordered
2. Antacids for discomfort
3. Small, frequent, easily digested meals
4. Maintenance of a calm environment to decrease effects of stress
5. Monitoring of fluid and electrolyte status
6. Teaching the older client about precipitating and contributory factors

Prevention and early diagnosis are important to prevent a catastrophic and potentially life-threatening GI hemorrhage, and is an area where the nurse plays an important role. Decreasing or eliminating alcohol and tobacco use, taking aspirin and other NSAIDs with food to prevent irritation on the gastric mucosa, and prompt medical attention to symptoms of indigestion and epigastric pain are necessary.

✣ EVALUATION

Evaluation includes achievement of the expected outcomes, decrease in symptoms, and lack of evidence of a GI hemorrhage or other complications.

Peptic Ulcer Disease

Peptic ulcer disease (PUD) is an ulcerative condition of the GI tract that results from an imbalance of gastric acid and pepsin. Ulcers occur in areas that are accessible to gastric secretions, like the lower esophagus, stomach, duodenum, and jejunum (Long, Roberts, 1993). Although the exact cause of peptic ulcers is unclear, they are thought to develop when the mucosal resistance to the gastric secretions is impaired, decreasing normal protective abilities. An increase in acid and pepsin from any cause may produce ulcerations if the protective mechanisms are not adequate.

Duodenal ulcers account for approximately 80% of all peptic ulcers, with the pyloric region of the duodenum being the most common site of all peptic ulcers (Fig. 25-3). Ulcers affect 10% to 15% of the general population (Collins, Bullock, 1992). However, although duodenal ulcers tend to occur in people 20 to 40 years of age, gastric ulcers occur more often in people over age 40 (Long, Roberts, 1993).

Both genetic and environmental theories have been proposed as the cause of peptic ulcers, as both gastric and duodenal ulcers tend to occur in families. Relatives

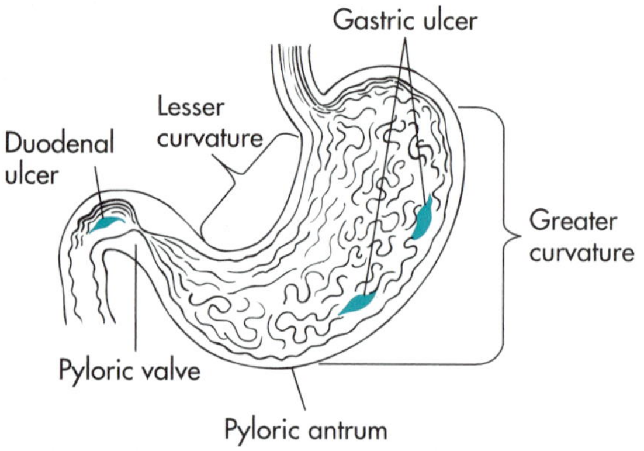

Fig. 25-3 Common locations of gastric and duodenal ulcers. (From Bullock B, Rosendahl PP: *Pathophysiology: adaptation and alterations in function,* ed 3, Philadelphia, 1992, JB Lippincott.)

of people with peptic ulcers have three times the expected number of ulcers (O'Toole, 1992). At present, no direct evidence exists that indicates dietary factors or occupation as causes of ulcer disease. In addition, psychologic factors such as anxiety or stress also play a role in the development of peptic ulcers, since these can alter gastric function. However, the evidence is inconclusive regarding the common belief that the person with the type A personality, striving for perfection, develops ulcers. Prolonged stress can produce a stress ulcer (see Gastritis, p. 663).

Gastric Ulcers

In gastric ulcers the level of hydrochloric acid secretion is usually normal or reduced. The problem lies in the increased rate of diffusion of gastric acid back into the tissue. This increased rate of diffusion leads to an inflammatory reaction in the tissue, leading to breakdown and bleeding of the mucosa (Long, Roberts, 1993). True achlorhydria, or lack of hydrochloric acid secretion, is rare with these ulcers and usually indicates a gastric carcinoma (Collins, Bullock, 1992).

Gastric ulcers are often associated with atrophy of the gastric glands. Gastritis always surrounds the ulcerated area. The classic ulcer has a sharply punched-out appearance with a smooth, clean base. Malignant gastric ulcers exhibit a shaggy, necrotic base, as opposed to the smooth base of nonmalignant ones. Benign ulcers are often found on the greater curvature of the stomach and are usually smaller than malignant ones. Clients with benign gastric ulcers should be encouraged to receive frequent follow-up, since these ulcers can often become malignant (Collins, Bullock, 1992).

The most common symptom with gastric ulcers is epigastric pain. Nausea, vomiting, and weight loss are common. Hemorrhage resulting from perforation occurs in 25% of these people and is often excessive. Perforation of the ulcer into the peritoneal cavity is less common than with a duodenal ulcer. Healing and recurrence are common. A lack of healing or failure to decrease in size suggests malignancy.

Zollinger-Ellison Syndrome

Zollinger-Ellison syndrome (ZES) is a triad of diseases comprising peptic ulcers, extreme gastric hyperacidity, and gastrin-secreting islet-cell tumors of the pancreas (a gastrinoma). Serum gastrin levels are markedly elevated and cause large amounts of hydrochloric acid to be produced. The tumors of ZES are malignant, and the increase in hydrochloric acid produces ulceration in any part of the stomach or duodenum. These ulcerations have a high probability of hemorrhage or rupture (Collins, Bullock, 1992).

Duodenal Ulcers

In contrast to gastric ulcers, people with duodenal ulcers (DUs) have a normal back diffusion of gastric acid but have an increased rate of gastric acid secretion (Long, Roberts, 1993). Although DUs occur in the presence of acid, hyperacidity is not always a significant precursor, since there may be an increase in secretion of gastrin or other substances from the duodenal wall (Collins, Bullock, 1992). If the increase in acid is not buffered in the stomach, the acid is propelled into the duodenum, leading to irritation of the duodenal mucosa (Long, Roberts, 1993).

Evidence that the disease has a strong family history and occurs among the Type O blood groups supports a genetic theory (Collins, Bullock, 1992; Long, Roberts, 1993). The genetic trait for hypersecretion of pepsinogen is autosomal dominant and may be a marker for predisposition to DU. Currently, an elevated serum pepsinogen level is under study as a significant indicator of predisposition to DU (Collins, Bullock, 1992).

Duodenal ulcers are usually deep, with a sharp line of demarcation from the normal tissue. Most of these ulcerations occur in the first part of the duodenum, close to the pylorus. A typical DU is an oval-shaped, indurated, funnel-shaped lesion that extends into the muscularis layer (Collins, Bullock, 1992).

Typically, the symptoms of DU are patterned to periods of exacerbations and remissions. Exacerbations are often triggered by stress and typically occur in the fall and spring. Symptoms follow a pain/food/relief pattern, with the pain beginning 90 minutes to 3 hours after eating. The pain is immediately relieved by food or antacids; is usually described as steady, burning, boring, aching or hunger-like; and is located in the midepigastrium, sometimes radiating to the back. The client rarely has a DU and does not complain of pain (Collins, Bullock, 1993).

Other GI symptoms include heartburn and regurgitation of sour/acid juice into the back of the throat. Anorexia is rare, because the client usually seeks food to relieve the pain. A DU may rupture because of erosion through the duodenal wall, and this leads to contamination of the peritoneal cavity **(peritonitis).** A slowly

MEDICAL MANAGEMENT

PUD

Diagnostic tests and procedures

Diagnosis of peptic ulcers relies much on the history and characteristics of the pain. An upper GI may demonstrate ulcer craters and outlet formations. Endoscopy is useful in revealing lesions too small to be seen on x-rays and in allowing tissue samples to be taken for biopsy. Gastric juice analysis may be helpful in people who do not have typical ulcer disease to determine the cycle of hydrochloric acid and pepsin secretion. Nocturnal levels of hydrochloric acid and pepsin are often higher in people with DU than in those with gastric ulcers.

Treatment

Treatment of peptic ulcers focuses on relieving the pain, promoting healing, and preventing complications. Assisting the client in identifying lifestyle factors that precipitate symptoms may enhance healing and may prevent recurrence of the disease. Medications to treat ulcers include antacids, histamine receptor antagonists, proton-pump inhibitors, and synthetic prostaglandins.

Prognosis

Prognosis is generally good, however, sometimes surgery, in the form of a partial or subtotal gastrectomy, is necessary to eliminate the ulcers that are resistant to treatment, are recurrent, or are premalignant. In addition, surgery may be necessary in the presence of complications or for those clients who are noncompliant with treatment.

Complications of duodenal ulcers include hemorrhage, perforation, and obstruction. Erosion of an artery or a vein at the base of the lesion may cause a hemorrhage. Hemorrhage occurs in 15% to 20% of cases of PUD. It may either be manifested through melena, guaiac-positive stools, or hematemesis and hemorrhagic shock. Ulcers located posteriorly are more likely to bleed than those in other locations. Perforations of active ulcers through the duodenal wall result in spilling of gastric contents into the peritoneum, leading to peritonitis. Scar formation may cause deformity, shortening, and stiffening of the duodenum, which may interfere with normal emptying of the stomach. Obstruction may result from stenosis, spasm, edema, and inflammation (see Emergency Treatment box, p. 666).

EMERGENCY TREATMENT

Acute Upper GI Bleeding

Definition

Vomiting of blood (hematemesis) or coffee-ground material usually signifies bleeding in the esophagus, stomach, or duodenum.

Cause

May be a result of esophageal varices or an erosion or rupture of a vessel within a peptic ulcer

Action

Start IV fluids, as ordered.

Monitor VS every 15 minutes initially, especially for postural changes. (Look for an increase in heart rate > 20 beats per minutes (BPM) and a drop in systolic blood pressure 10 mm Hg over baseline.)

Insert large-bore nasogastric (NG) tube for lavage and decompression.

Replace fluids by blood transfusion or volume expanders as ordered.

Obtain appropriate history from client or family concerning presence of ulcer or previous GI bleeds, medication use, and significant medical history.

bleeding ulcer may reveal guaiac positive stools. On physical examination, the only abnormality is possibly a tender epigastrium (see Medical Management box, p. 665).

NURSING MANAGEMENT

✣ ASSESSMENT

Assessment begins with evaluation of the client's complaint of abdominal or epigastric pain, the most common symptom of peptic ulcers. The pain should be assessed for presence, location, character, and alleviating and precipitating factors. Peptic ulcer pain is usually described as a gnawing, burning, or aching, usually in the epigastric area, and may radiate around to the back. The pain usually begins when the stomach is empty, and may disappear with the ingestion of food or antacid. Because of this, the pain often occurs at night when the stomach is empty (Long, Roberts, 1993).

The client may also exhibit signs of the complications of the peptic ulcer. Hemorrhage may be manifested as either melena or hematemesis (Long, Roberts, 1993). Perforation in the older client may not be manifested by a rigid abdomen, as it is so often with the younger client. Occasionally, the only sign of perforation in the older adult is abdominal pain, which may have a blunted presentation. An obstruction may be manifested by weight loss or projectile vomiting but may produce only subtle findings early in its course in the older adult.

✣ DIAGNOSIS

The most often used nursing diagnoses for the older client with peptic ulcer disease include, but are not limited to: (1) epigastric pain, (2) knowledge deficit, and (3) ineffective individual coping.

✣ PLANNING

Expected outcomes for the older client with peptic ulcer disease include, but are not limited to, the following: (1) client will report a decrease in abdominal or epigastric pain, (2) client will identify stressors and describe useful stress management techniques, and (3) client will acknowledge aggravating factors, such as smoking, alcohol use, or frequent use of aspirin or NSAIDs.

✣ INTERVENTION

Nursing management for the older client with peptic ulcer disease includes education of the client, focusing on lifestyle changes, dietary modifications, and medications that may be used in the treatment plan.

Lifestyle changes include cessation of smoking, cessation of alcohol consumption, and avoidance of other irritants such as aspirin-containing products and NSAIDs. In addition, stress reduction techniques such as exercise, relaxation training, biofeedback, or other appropriate outlets should be explored and individualized, depending on client needs and wishes. Dietary changes include avoiding foods that are irritating to the mucosa of the stomach, such as caffeine, alcohol, and spicy foods (Billings, Stokes, 1987) (see Client/Family Teaching box, p. 660).

Medications need to be taken as prescribed. The older client needs to be instructed that the only medication that can decrease the abdominal or epigastric pain are antacids. Other medications should be taken exactly as ordered but do not provide immediate relief of pain.

If surgery is performed, dietary modification may be necessary. Usually after a partial or subtotal gastrectomy, the client requires small, frequent meals because of the shrinkage of the stomach. Maintaining adequate nutrition and fluid and electrolyte balance is even more important for the older client.

✣ EVALUATION

Evaluation includes achievement of the expected outcomes, prevention of complications, elimination of symptoms, and an increased knowledge base regarding peptic ulcer disease.

Gastric Cancer

As with other forms of GI cancer, gastric cancer is insidious. Symptoms may be vague until the cancer has infiltrated and spread throughout the body, when the overt signs of cancer become evident (Long, Roberts, 1993). In addition, stomach cancer mimics other diseases such as ulcers and gastritis, so misdiagnosis and self-medication for chronic "stomach problems" are common and may delay the diagnosis and treatment of stomach cancer (Frogge, 1990).

Insight • *Recent research suggests that a bacteria,* Helicobacter pylori (H. pylori) *is linked to peptic ulcers and possibly to stomach cancer.* H. pylori *is common throughout the world, although prevalence is higher in developing countries and incidence increases with age. The evidence that suggested a link between* H. pylori *and ulcers stems from the significant differences in occurrence rates among those who were treated with antibiotics and those who were not. Because of these findings, it is becoming more common to treat both the ulcer and the* H. pylori. *Typical regimens are only 2 weeks in duration and consist of drug combinations of antibiotics (sometimes two), along with the typical antiulcer therapy (e.g., H_2 blockers). Research continues to search for those antibiotics (or a combination) that will be the most effective, will have the lowest incidence of side effects, and will be the most cost-effective.*

The incidence of gastric cancer is increasing in certain areas of the world, and decreasing in others, such as the United States. Gastric cancer usually occurs between the ages of 50 and 65 years of age, and strikes men twice as often as women (Collins, Bullock, 1992; Frogge, 1990). It occurs twice as often among black men and women as it does among white people, although the reason for this is unclear (Frogge, 1990).

The cause is unknown, although the incidence is higher when gastric acid is low (Long, Roberts, 1993). Environmental and genetic factors are associated with gastric cancer (Collins, Bullock, 1993; Frogge, 1990). These factors include diet (poor nutrition, food additives, vitamin A deficiency), low socioeconomic status, occupation, and urban residence. It also may be precipitated by polyps or degenerative changes in gastric ulcers, as well as achlorhydria (Collins, Bullock, 1992; Frogge, 1990).

Most gastric cancers are adenocarcinomas and occur in either polypoid, ulcerative, or infiltrative forms (Long, Roberts, 1993). The ulcerative form is the most common and produces symptoms similar to peptic ulcers. Most gastric cancers arise in the antrum, the lower third of the stomach (Frogge, 1990).

The tumor causes ulceration, obstruction, and hemorrhage. It may metastasize by extension and infiltration along the mucosa into the stomach wall and lymph vessels in three ways: by (1) lymphatic or vascular embolism to regional lymph nodes, (2) direct extension to adjacent organs, and (3) blood-borne spread (Frogge, 1990). The tumor may metastasize to the lung, bone, liver, spleen, pancreas, peritoneum, and esophagus (Collins, Bullock, 1992; Frogge, 1990).

Because of its elusive nature, gastric cancer is usually well-advanced when symptoms begin to appear. Symptoms of gastric cancer, when they occur, are vague and of variable duration. Because of this, people usually delay seeking medical attention for a few months after the initial onset of symptoms. Initially, the client may com-

MEDICAL MANAGEMENT

Gastric Cancer

Diagnostic tests and procedures

Gastric cancer is diagnosed by x-ray studies (an upper GI) and/or an endoscopy with a biopsy. CT scans are helpful in determining the diagnosis and extent of metastasis, as well as tumor extension (Collins, Bullock, 1992; Frogge, 1990). Laboratory tests include hematologic profiles that may reveal an anemia. Biopsies of the tumor are imperative, since it is often difficult to distinguish between gastric tumors and gastric ulcers.

Treatment

Treatment depends on the stage of disease. Staging is through the use of the TNM system (see Chapter 15). Localized gastric cancer is treated with surgery alone or in combination with chemotherapy and radiation therapy. Approximately 50% of clients are candidates for a curative resection, either a partial or total gastrectomy. Advanced tumors that are partially resectable, unresectable, or disseminated are treated with a combination of modalities, and may include palliative surgery, such as a jejunostomy tube (Frogge, 1990).

Prognosis

Survival rates are poor, with less than 5% to 15% surviving 5 years after diagnosis (Collins, Bullock, 1992; Frogge, 1990). Early diagnosis has improved mortality so that if a lesion is confined to the mucosa and submucosa, the 5-year survival rate improves to 60% to 90% (Collins, Bullock, 1992).

plain of a vague, uneasy sense of fullness, indigestion, and distention after meals, which may be passed off as stomach upset. As the disease progresses, anorexia, nausea, and vomiting may occur and lead to weight loss. Other symptoms include dysphagia, back pain, weakness, fatigue, hematemesis, and a change in bowel habits. Unfortunately, definitive clinical signs occur mostly with advanced disease and include weight loss, pain, vomiting, anorexia, dysphagia, and a palpable abdominal mass (Collins, Bullock, 1992; Frogge, 1990) (see Medical Management box p. 667).

Nursing Management

✣ ASSESSMENT

Assessment begins with a good history and review of symptoms pertaining to the GI system, particularly symptoms that the older client may not offer as a complaint unless asked. These include, but are not limited to, indigestion, discomfort after eating, nausea, anorexia, vomiting, or any chronic stomach "problem." In addition, questions regarding possible causes are helpful in the diagnosis. These include changes in dietary or bowel patterns and habits, prescription and over-the-counter (OTC) medications, and home remedies (Frogge, 1990). Physical examination may reveal no obvious abnormalities, except when advanced, the tumor may be palpable, especially through the thin skin and musculature of the older client's abdomen. In addition, lymph nodes may be palpable when metastases have occurred.

✣ DIAGNOSIS

The most often used nursing diagnoses for the older client with gastric cancer include, but are not limited to: (1) anticipatory grieving, (2) altered nutrition: less than body requirements, and (3) pain.

✣ PLANNING

Expected outcomes for the older client with gastric cancer include, but are not limited to, the following: (1) client will discuss thoughts and feelings related to diagnosis with appropriate people; (2) client will use appropriate resources; (3) client will maintain adequate nutrition, as evidenced by stabilization and maintenance of weight and consumption of a well-balanced, high-calorie diet; and (4) client will effectively manage pain.

✣ INTERVENTION

Nursing management of the older client with gastric cancer includes maintenance of hydration, nutrition, and fluid and electrolyte balance, as well as providing emotional support to the individual and family. Many clients and their families may feel guilty and negligent about the delay in seeking medical attention for the vague symptoms of gastric cancer. The nurse can support the client and family by dispelling misconceptions and offering a realistic sense of hope (Frogge, 1990).

Nursing care should also focus on the prevention and early diagnosis of gastric cancer, encouraging all older clients with GI symptoms, however trivial, to seek medical attention. In addition, identifying those at risk and encouraging them to seek medical care for evaluation on a regular basis is also important.

✣ EVALUATION

Evaluation includes achievement of the expected outcomes, prevention of malnutrition, maintenance of comfort, and continued family support.

Cholelithiasis/Cholecystitis

Cholelithiasis is the presence or formation of gallstones in the gallbladder. Gallstones are composed primarily of cholesterol, bile salts, bilirubin, calcium, and proteins (Cassmeyer, Blevins, 1990).

Cholecystitis is an inflammation of the gallbladder and is usually associated with cholelithiasis or obstruction of the bile ducts.

The incidence of gallstones varies among racial groups and countries, however, it is not known whether this is as a result of environmental or genetic factors (Schoenfield, 1988). The incidence of gallstones in women is three times higher than in men, and increases steadily with age (Dudley, Starin, 1991).

The formation of gallstones is primarily metabolic, and results from either increased cholesterol saturation (because of obesity, estrogen, or resection of the terminal ileum), increased levels of bilirubin (hemolytic anemias), or increased serum cholesterol (Cassmeyer, Blevins, 1993). In addition, slow emptying of the gallbladder may produce stasis and encourage the aggregation of cholesterol crystals, eventually leading to stone formation (Schoenfield, 1988). This is important in older adults because of the increased risk of gallstone formation from the use of hyperalimentation, and fasting states in acute illnesses. The majority of gallstones in western cultures are cholesterol stones, whereas other stones are classified as biliary pigment stones.

Gallstones may be present for many years without signs and symptoms. Much debate continues over whether these clients will eventually experience symptoms related to the gallstones, and therefore should be treated on diagnosis, regardless of symptoms. Of clients with gallstones, 20% to 50% are asymptomatic (Dudley, Starin, 1991; Cassmeyer, Blevins, 1993). Although many clients with gallstones complain of indigestion, the classic symptom, biliary pain, or colic, is typically a right-upper quadrant pain, ache, or pressure that may radiate to the right scapular area. The pain begins suddenly, often occurring directly after a meal. The pain can last from 15 minutes to 6 hours, and nausea and vomiting may be present. These attacks of pain can occur as infrequently as once every few years, or as often as every few days. Many times, these episodes are precipitated by the ingestion of fatty foods. The symptoms of biliary pain are due to an obstruction of the cystic or common bile duct, causing an increased pressure and distention of the gallbladder (Dudley, Starin, 1991). In most clients the initial symptom is biliary pain rather than acute cholecystitis or its complications.

When the stones lodge along the biliary tract, they obstruct the flow of bile. This results in **jaundice** because of the blockage of the flow of bilirubin. Calculous obstruction of the cystic duct may lead to cholecystitis. When the common bile duct becomes blocked, the bile cannot make it to the GI tract, so stools are clay-colored, since they lack the pigment. In addition, obstruction of the common bile duct may cause biliary pain, jaundice, pancreatitis, or cholangitis (an inflammation of the bile ducts) (Cassmeyer, Blevins, 1993; Dudley, Starin, 1991).

Cholecystitis may be acute or chronic, and is usually associated with gallstones or other obstructions of the biliary system. The inflammation in cholecystitis results in a thickening of the wall of the gallbladder, which can lead to ischemia, necrosis, gangrene, and possible perforation of the gallbladder itself, leading to peritonitis (Cassmeyer, Blevins, 1993). In chronic cholecystitis, the walls become thickened and inefficient at emptying. This is as a result of chronic chemical or mechanical irritation from stones exerting pressure on the mucosa or from biliary stasis (see Medical Management box below).

NURSING MANAGEMENT

ASSESSMENT

Assessment begins with a history of "attacks" of pain, identifying location, quality, and duration. Other symptoms include nausea, vomiting, and jaundice. Precipitating factors like large meals and alleviating factors (e.g., pain relievers or change of position) need to be documented. Physical examination may reveal a tender right upper quadrant and possibly jaundice.

MEDICAL MANAGEMENT

Cholelithiasis/Cholecystitis

Diagnostic tests and procedures

Diagnostic tests include ultrasound of the right upper quadrant to confirm the presence of the gallstones. An oral cholecystogram (OCG) may be done to determine whether the gallbladder is functioning, as well as the size and number of stones. For the OCG, iodine-based tablets are ingested for 2 consecutive days, with radiographs taken the morning of the third day. The iodine is taken up by the gallbladder, which then becomes radiopaque on x-ray. With chronic cholecystitis, the gallbladder cannot be seen because of fibrosis and thickening of its walls. In cases of suspected acute cholecystitis, nuclear medicine studies such as a hepatobiliary scan should be performed.

Treatment

Treatment options range from the conservative watch and wait approach, to medical/pharmacologic therapy, to surgery. Conservative treatment is appropriate for those clients with symptoms that might not be results of gallstones, or for the newly diagnosed client who has mild or infrequent symptoms or who is not willing or ready to opt for treatment (Dudley, Starin, 1991). Cholecystectomy (removal of the gallbladder) is the gold standard for the treatment of gallstones, since it is a cure for the disease. A newer surgery, laparoscopic cholecystectomy, has improved mortality and morbidity rates over the standard surgery but is not suitable for all clients. Laparoscopic cholecystectomy is conducted through a few small incisions in the abdominal wall, so recovery time is greatly reduced. Other less commonly used treatment options include lithotripsy and oral dissolution with bile salts. Both of these treatment modalities leave the gallbladder intact, and are popular for those who are poor surgical risks, or those with mild or infrequent symptoms. Their advantages and disadvantages need to be carefully reviewed for individual clients.

Prognosis

Prognosis for clients with cholelithiasis is good with few mortalities from the disease. The prognosis for clients with cholecystitis is primarily a result of surgical mortality and morbidity. In clients over age 65, the mortality rate of standard cholecystectomy is 6% and is higher in those with other preexisting illnesses (Margiotta et al, 1985). In addition, complication rates in the general population for emergency surgery are as high as 57%, compared with nonemergent rates of 18.7% (Sandler, Maule, Baltus, 1986).

✣ DIAGNOSIS

The most often used nursing diagnoses for the older client with cholelithiasis and/or cholecystitis include, but are not limited to: (1) pain, and (2) knowledge deficit regarding cause and treatment options.

✣ PLANNING

Expected outcomes for the older client with cholelithiasis and cholecystitis include, but are not limited to, the following: (1) client will feel relief and management of pain, (2) client will be knowledgeable of prevention of complications, and (3) client will have increased knowledge concerning disease process and treatment options available.

✣ INTERVENTION

Nursing management of the older client with cholelithiasis or cholecystitis includes providing pain relief, and instructing client and family about disease process, treatment options, and potential complications. The older client with cholelithiasis needs to know that foods high in fat may precipitate an attack of pain. They need to be aware of treatment options including types of surgery, medical dissolution, and lithotripsy, as well as the advantages and disadvantages of each. The client with cholecystitis may require hospitalization and may receive an IV and antibiotics. If managed at home, clients need to be on a clear liquid diet until pain is resolved, and then a slow advance to a regular diet, avoiding fatty foods. Signs and symptoms of complications need to be reviewed with both client and family.

✣ EVALUATION

Evaluation includes achievement of expected outcomes, prevention of complications, prevention of infection, and assessment of knowledge of disease process.

BOX 25-4

Etiologic Factors of Pancreatitis

Alcoholism
Biliary tract disease
Postoperative (abdominal, nonabdominal)
Postendoscopic retrograde cholangiopancreatography
Trauma (abdominal injury)
Metabolic (hyperlipidemia, uremia, renal failure, after renal transplantation, hypercalcemia, pregnancy, cystic fibrosis, kwashiorkor)
Vascular (shock, lupus erythematosus, thrombocytopenic purpura, polyarteritis, atheromatous embolism)
Drugs
- Association
  - Immunosuppressive—corticosteroids, L-asparaginase, azathioprine
  - Diuretics—thiazides, furosemide, ethacrynic acid
  - Estrogens, oral contraceptives
  - Antibiotics—tetracyclines, sulfonamides
- Possible association
  - Acetaminophen
  - Isoniazid, rifampin
  - Propoxyphene
  - Valproic acid, procainamide
  - Anticoagulants

Infections (mumps, viral hepatitis, coxsackievirus, echovirus, Ascaris, Mycoplasma)
Mechanical (ampulla of Vater tumor, Crohn's disease, diverticula, pancreas divisum)
Penetrating duodenal ulcer
Hereditary pancreatitis
Idiopathic

From Bullock B, Rosendahl PP: *Pathophysiology: adaptation and alterations in function,* ed 3, Philadelphia, 1992, JB Lippincott.

Pancreatitis

Pancreatitis is an inflammation of the pancreas and often has no known cause. The disorder may be acute or chronic, and the acute phase may become chronic after several acute attacks. In acute pancreatitis, the pancreas returns to normal after treatment. In chronic pancreatitis, permanent and progressive destruction of the pancreas occurs, whereby the normal tissue is replaced by fibrous tissue (Cassmeyer, Blevins, 1993).

Acute pancreatitis may be alcohol-induced or related to biliary tract disease. When it results from increased alcohol intake, the incidence is higher in younger men. The pancreatitis related to biliary tract disease is more likely to occur in women in their late 50s and 60s. Approximately 40% of pancreatitis is because of biliary disease, and another 40% results from alcoholism. Of the remaining, 5% is associated with other conditions, and the cause of the remainder is unknown (Heaman, 1992). In the United States, the primary cause of chronic pancreatitis is alcoholism (Cassmeyer, Blevins, 1993) (Box 25-4).

Pancreatitis is believed to be caused by activation of pancreatic enzymes, which may cause autodigestion of the pancreas (Burrell, 1992). The initiation of activation of the enzymes is thought to result from reflux of bile into the pancreatic duct, obstruction of the pancreatic duct, ischemia, anorexia, trauma, and toxins (Cassmeyer, Blevins, 1993).

Symptoms include severe abdominal pain in the epigastric to the right upper quadrant area, occasionally radiating through to the back. Pain is usually more intense when lying supine, and the client often remains in a flexed position to relieve pain (Cassmeyer, Blevins, 1993). Nausea, vomiting, abdominal distention, and fever are common (Heaman, 1992). In chronic pancreatitis, the pain may be continuous and accompanied by

MEDICAL MANAGEMENT

Pancreatitis

Diagnostic tests and procedures

There is no specific laboratory or radiologic test to diagnose pancreatitis. An elevation of serum amylase and lipase, as well as an occasional leukocytosis occurs. Ultrasound can be useful in the diagnosis of acute pancreatitis, assessing degree of inflammation and revealing a dilated common bile duct if the pancreatitis results from an obstruction from gallstones (Heaman, 1992).

Treatment

Treatment of acute pancreatitis is largely symptom management and is designed to rest the organ. This includes withholding food and fluids, necessitating IV hydration. Pain relief measures, including the use of narcotics, are often employed. Alcoholic pancreatitis responds well to elimination of alcohol; however, it does tend to recur. Surgical removal of the pancreas is only done in the severe form of the disease with life-threatening complications (O'Toole, 1992). The treatment for chronic pancreatitis is chiefly supportive. Pancreatic insufficiency can be treated with the administration of pancreatic enzymes with each meal. Pain relief is often a problem for these clients, and narcotics are often used (O'Toole, 1992).

Prognosis

Many complications can occur as a result of pancreatitis, and affect all organ systems. While the majority of clients with acute pancreatitis recover without any residual dysfunction, the mortality rate is 10% (Blake, 1988). There is no cure for chronic pancreatitis, and prognosis is not good (O'Toole, 1992).

weakness and jaundice (Hood, Dincher, 1992). In addition, in chronic pancreatitis, the stools often become bulky, fatty, and foul-smelling, and may accompany weight loss. Glucose intolerance is a late sign of chronic pancreatitis (O'Toole, 1992) (see Medical Management box above).

NURSING MANAGEMENT

✣ ASSESSMENT

Assessment begins with the older client's history of precipitating factors such as alcohol abuse or the presence of gallstones. Symptoms of abdominal pain, anorexia, nausea, and vomiting need to be assessed in detail. The client may be in tremendous pain and may be unable to answer, so reliance on a family member may be necessary. Depending on the amount of pain the client is experiencing at the time, physical examination may be difficult.

✣ DIAGNOSIS

The most often used nursing diagnoses for the older client with pancreatitis include, but are not limited to (1) fluid volume deficit related to vomiting, (2) pain, and (3) altered nutrition: less than body requirements.

✣ PLANNING

Expected outcomes for the older client with pancreatitis include, but are not limited to, the following: (1) client will maintain adequate fluid volume and electrolyte balance, (2) client will obtain pain relief, (3) client will stabilize weight, and (4) client will not experience complications.

✣ INTERVENTION

Nursing management of the older client with pancreatitis includes maintenance of fluid and electrolyte balance, providing pain relief measures, and preventing complications (Burrell, 1992). These include maintenance of IV therapy and monitoring intake and output, and obtaining specific gravity of urine, serum electrolytes, and weight. Pain is managed with both pharmacologic and nonpharmacologic relief measures.

An important consideration is the prevention of recurrence of acute pancreatitis through teaching. When pancreatitis results from alcohol abuse, teaching should center on the dangers of alcoholism and implications for the future. Referral and counseling may be needed (see Chapter 18). For the client with pancreatitis resulting from biliary tract disease, teaching about high lipid levels is important; providing information and emotional support is important for the client who may need to undergo surgery.

✣ EVALUATION

Evaluation includes achievement of expected outcomes, prevention of complications, prevention of recurrence (for acute pancreatitis), and maintenance of adequate nutrition.

Pancreatic Cancer

Cancer of the pancreas is the fourth and most common cause of death from cancer in men in the United States (Cassmeyer and Blevins, 1993; Frogge, 1990). It is seventh among all cancers in incidence, with a large increase occurring from a few years ago (Silverberg, Lubera, 1989). The disease usually affects older adults ages 60 to 70, and men more than women (Heaman, 1992; Frogge, 1990). It is believed that race and ethnicity may be factors in the development of pancreatic cancer.

Increased risk attributed to environmental factors has been suggested, since the incidence is higher in those exposed to industrial pollutants and those in urban areas. In addition, pancreatic cancer has been correlated with alcohol abuse, high fat diets, tobacco use, chronic pancreatitis, and lower socioeconomic status (Frogge, 1990).

Cancer of the pancreas is primarily an adenocarcinoma, and may involve the head, body, or tail of the pancreas (Heaman, 1992). Approximately 95% of pancreatic tumors arise from exocrine parenchyma (Frogge, 1990). The tumor is usually a hard, nodular, firm mass with a large amount of fibrosis (Frogge, 1990). Tumor commonly invades the entire pancreas and interrupts exocrine functions.

As tumor growth advances within the pancreas or on lymph nodes along the biliary tree, obstruction and compression of the common bile duct can result. Eventually, the carcinoma may infiltrate the duodenum, stomach, transverse colon, spleen, kidney, and surrounding blood vessels. Invasion by the celiac nerve plexus accounts for the severe pain associated with cancer of the body or tail of the pancreas.

Cancer of the pancreas grows rapidly so that at the time of diagnosis, the cancer has invaded locally or metastasized in 90% of individuals. Metastases occur through the blood stream and by peritoneal seeding, causing frequent metastases to the lung and bone.

Symptoms generally occur late in the course of the disease and are vague and insidious in onset. Although manifestations of the disease differ according to the location of the tumor in the pancreas (Frogge, 1990), in general the symptoms include anorexia, weight loss, nausea, and pain. Jaundice is a late sign (see Medical Management box below).

MEDICAL MANAGEMENT

Pancreatic Cancer

Diagnostic tests and procedures

The diagnosis is based on ultrasound, CT scan, nuclear imaging, angiography, and endoscopic retrograde cholangiopancreatography (ERCP). The ERCP is useful in diagnosis because biopsies and cytologies can be obtained. Physical examination may be unremarkable, and the use of laboratory tests for diagnosis is limited (Frogge, 1990).

Treatment

Palliative treatment may be offered, and includes surgery (the **Whipple procedure**) and/or chemotherapy (Billings, Stokes, 1987).

Prognosis

Usually at the time of the diagnosis the tumor is advanced and prognosis is poor (Heaman, 1992). Most clients live only 3 to 6 months after diagnosis (Cassmeyer, Blevins, 1993).

NURSING MANAGEMENT

✣ ASSESSMENT

Assessment begins with a history of symptoms and a review of possible precipitating causes of pancreatic cancer (such as environmental exposure to toxins or chronic alcohol ingestion/abuse). Physical examination may be unremarkable.

✣ DIAGNOSIS

Nursing diagnoses for the older client with pancreatic cancer include, but are not limited to: (1) pain and (2) ineffective family or individual coping related to terminal diagnosis.

✣ PLANNING

Expected outcomes for the older client with pancreatic cancer include, but are not limited to, the following: (1) client will remain free of pain, and (2) client and family will develop a broad base of support, and will verbalize feelings related to the diagnosis and prognosis.

✣ INTERVENTION

Nursing management for the older client with pancreatic cancer includes provision of pain relief and encouragement to verbalize feelings. Pain relief may require narcotics, and client and family members may require teaching concerning their prolonged use. Other nonpharmacologic measures of pain relief need to be offered, such as diversional activities, repositioning, and the use of meditation or massage. Client and family may benefit from attending a support group for cancer clients. However, due to poor prognosis, encouraging families to spend time with the older client is also important. Assisting client and family in dealing with an eminent death may also be necessary.

✣ EVALUATION

Evaluation includes achievement of expected outcomes, prevention of complications, and provision of a comfortable environment.

Enteritis

Enteritis, or gastroenteritis, is an inflammatory process of the stomach or small intestine. It may be caused by bacteria, viruses, medications, radiation, ingestion of irritating foods, or allergic reactions (Collins, Bullock, 1992). Bacterial enteritis is often caused by ingestion of food that is contaminated by bacteria containing toxins, and is commonly known as food poisoning (Long, Roberts, 1993). Examples of these bacteria include staphylococcus aureus, salmonella, and clostridium botulinum (Long, Roberts, 1993).

In addition, enteritis may result from parasitic infections such as amebiasis and trichinosis. In amebiasis, the cause is a protozoal parasite that primarily invades the large intestine. It is the inactive form, the cyst, which when ingested in fecally contaminated food or water, will pass into the intestines. Here, the active form is released and enters the intestinal wall, causing ulceration of the intestinal mucosa. Amebiasis is found primarily in tropical countries and where there is poor sanitation. Trichinosis, on the other hand, is transmitted through improperly cooked pork and is caused by the larvae of a roundworm that becomes imbedded into the striated muscles of animals that eat the infected pork. When the infected pork is eaten, the larvae live and develop in the host's intestine. The larvae are released and move toward the muscles of the host, where they can remain for many years (Long, Roberts, 1993).

Acute enteritis is a result of direct bacterial or viral infection or the effect of the toxins produced by the bacteria. This results in either an increased secretion of water into the intestinal lumen or an increase in motility, causing large amounts of food and fluid to be excreted (Long, Roberts, 1993). In general, enteritis causes inflammatory changes in the intestinal mucosa that return to normal when the offending agent is removed (Collins, Bullock, 1992).

The pathologic process has varying manifestations that result in symptoms of abdominal cramping, profuse diarrhea, and vomiting. With this profuse diarrhea, large amounts of fluid and electrolytes may be lost, leading to dehydration and electrolyte imbalances of hyponatremia, and hypokalemia (Long, Roberts, 1993). Older adults are particularly at risk for dehydration, and prompt treatment is required (see Medical Management box below).

MEDICAL MANAGEMENT

Enteritis

Diagnostic tests and procedures

Diagnostic tests include cultures and testing stool for ova and parasites. Blood tests include a CBC, which may reveal a leukocytosis, suggesting an infection. However, the diagnosis is often made on the basis of clinical findings only. Since it is a self-limiting condition, laboratory tests may be done only if improvement is not seen within a few days.

Treatment

Treatment is primarily supportive, aimed at preventing or correcting the fluid and electrolyte imbalance. IV hydration and nothing PO is routine hospital care, whereas the older client may be managed at home with clear liquids. Amebiasis and trichinosis are treated with appropriate medications, as is bacterial enteritis if symptoms persist or the clinical condition warrants it. Antidiarrheals are not often used, since the disease is self-limiting and use of antidiarrheals may prolong disease course.

Prognosis

Prognosis is good, but complications can occur if fluid and electrolyte imbalances are not treated promptly and aggressively.

NURSING MANAGEMENT

ASSESSMENT

Assessment begins with a history of nausea, vomiting, and diarrhea, including amount, duration, and frequency. Fever and abdominal discomfort may also be present. If food poisoning is suspected, question the client regarding possible sources of contamination. Physical examination includes inspection of mucous membranes, assessment of orthostatic blood pressures, and urine specific gravity which are helpful in assessing dehydration.

DIAGNOSIS

The most often used nursing diagnoses for the older client with enteritis include, but are not limited to: (1) fluid volume deficit related to vomiting and diarrhea and (2) diarrhea.

PLANNING

Expected outcomes for the older client with enteritis include, but are not limited to, the following: (1) client will maintain adequate fluid volume and electrolyte balance; and (2) client will have a continual decline in the number of bowel movements, until baseline is achieved.

INTERVENTION

Nursing management of the older client with enteritis includes maintenance of hydration and monitoring of fluid and electrolyte status. With severe vomiting and diarrhea, IV hydration will be necessary, and hospitalization is required. With milder forms of enteritis, clear liquids may be offered at home. In all cases, monitoring of signs and symptoms of dehydration is imperative. In addition, it is important for the nurse to determine if older clients have someone with them to monitor the status of a condition in case it worsens. Older clients need to be taught signs and symptoms of dehydration, as well as when to seek further medical care.

Prevention of bacterial and parasitic enteritis should also be discussed in stressing the need for good hand washing, especially before meals and food preparation.

✣ EVALUATION

Evaluation includes achievement of the expected outcomes, prevention of complications, and return to baseline status.

Ileus/Intestinal Obstruction

An ileus generally refers to a functional or organic obstruction of the bowel and is actually a failure of the bowel contents to move forward. It may occur in the small or large intestine, and is often further classified as physiologic, as a result of a mechanical bowel obstruction, or adynamic or paralytic, which results from an inhibition of bowel motility (O'Toole, 1992; Collins, Bullock, 1992).

An ileus may occur when peristalsis becomes diminished or absent because of a triggering of the inhibitory reflex by a noxious stimuli such as anesthesia, peritoneal injury, interruption of the nerve supply, abdominal injury or surgical manipulation, intestinal ischemia, and electrolyte imbalances.

An intestinal obstruction occurs when the lumen of the bowel is blocked by an actual mechanical obstruction. Common causes in older adults include volvulus, adhesions, hernias, infarction, and neoplasms.

After the blockage occurs, the bowel becomes distended by gas and air proximal to the area of blockage. If the process continues, gastric, biliary, and pancreatic secretions, along with water, electrolytes and serum proteins begin to accumulate in the area, causing an increase in intraluminal pressure. A third-space shift may occur when the circulating blood volume decreases as a result of the movement of water into the area, which may lead to dehydration, electrolyte imbalances, and hypovolemia (Collins, Bullock, 1992; O'Toole, 1992).

In an ileus, the lack of propulsive peristalsis makes the bowel unable to move contents downward, which leads to absence of bowel sounds and bowel distention with gas and fluid. The process is similar to that of bowel obstruction.

Clinical findings with an ileus include abdominal distention, decreased or absent bowel sounds, vomiting, and signs of dehydration and shock. Symptoms of an obstruction with perforation occur if the ileus is not treated by colonoscopic deflation (i.e., through an intestinal drainage tube) or surgery (Collins, Bullock, 1992).

Clinical manifestations of a bowel obstruction include the acute onset of severe cramping pain that correlates roughly to the area or level of obstruction. Pain may actually decrease in severity as the distention of the bowel increases. Increases in the rate and force of peristalsis cause **borborygmi,** loud and high-pitched bowel sounds, in the initial period, but these may progress to an absence of bowel sounds as the condition persists. Vomiting is almost always present, and may be bilious or feculent depending on the level of the obstruction. Diarrhea may occur if the obstruction is not complete (see Emergency Treatment, box p. 676).

Complications of intestinal obstructions include bowel ischemia, necrosis, perforation of the bowel, peritonitis, and hypovolemic shock. The affected bowel segment may become strangulated, causing necrosis, perforation, and loss of fluid and blood into the bowel. Impairment of blood supply leads to increased peristalsis and bacterial invasion of tissue, and finally causes necrosis and peritonitis when intestinal contents spill into the peritoneum. Infection and loss of fluid and electrolytes are a major problem (Collins, Bullock, 1992).

Hypovolemic shock may result when there is a shift of fluid greater than 10% of body weight. Septic shock may

MEDICAL MANAGEMENT

Ileus/Intestine Obstruction

Diagnostic tests and procedures

Diagnostic tests and procedures include an obstructive series of a plain abdominal x-ray, revealing distention of the bowel, along with air and fluid levels where the obstruction is located. Laboratory tests include a CBC, which may show leukocytosis, and a serum amylase, which may be elevated. Evaluation of electrolytes may reveal dehydration with a decrease in sodium and potassium, and an increase in bicarbonate, serum pH, and blood urea nitrogen (BUN). On physical examination, abdominal tenderness, rigidity, and fever usually indicate peritonitis.

Treatment

Treatment for abdominal distention includes decompression with an NG tube (such as a Miller-Abbot), which extends to the site of obstruction, and the use of constant suction (O'Toole, 1992). Fluid and electrolytes are provided intravenously. Surgery is necessary when the obstruction is complete, or when the bowel becomes gangrenous. The surgery performed is usually a resection of involved bowel, but depends on the condition of the bowel, and may include a permanent or temporary colostomy or ileostomy (O'Toole, 1992).

Prognosis

Prognosis depends on whether a complete obstruction or peritonitis has occurred. If the ileus is treated medically, prognosis is good.

CARE PLAN

ILEUS: OBSTRUCTION RESULTING FROM DIVERTICULITIS

Clinical situation Mrs. B is a 72-year-old retired seamstress who was recently admitted to the emergency room with abdominal pain. She was brought in by her daughter and son-in-law, with whom she lives. Her daughter reported that her mother had been complaining of abdominal pain for the past 24 hours, and since it did not subside, encouraged her to seek medical attention. Over the past 24 hours, Mrs. B reported left-sided lower abdominal pain, nausea, and more recently, vomiting. She was unsure whether she had a fever. Her daughter added that her mother had a lot of constipation recently, for which Mrs. B had taken various types of laxatives.

Her past medical history includes hypertension, for which she takes Procardia XL and hydrochlorothiazide; and hypercholesterolemia, for which she takes Mevacor on a daily basis. Her daughter also remembers her doctor telling her mother a few years ago that she had diverticulosis, which was diagnosed from an incidental finding on an x-ray. Her only past surgery was an uncomplicated cholecystectomy about 20 years ago for cholecystitis. Mrs. B stated that she was on no particular diet and has had few weight fluctuations over the past few years.

Physical examination reveals a thin woman, weighing 128 lbs, with temperature of 100.9° F (38.3° C) (orally), pulse of 98 beats per minute, 24 respirations per minute and blood pressure of 140/84 mm Hg. She is lying on the stretcher curled in a semifetal position. Her abdomen is not obviously distended, and her only scar is a midline incisional scar from her previous cholecystectomy. She has loud, high-pitched bowel sounds, but no audible bruits. Her abdomen is tender and a firm mass, possibly feces, is palpable in the left-lower quadrant. She has no elicitable rebound tenderness. She has tenderness on rectal examination and is thought to have stool high up in her rectal vault. However, her hemacult is guaiac negative.

Laboratory tests reveal a white blood cell count of 90,000 and a normal hemoglobin. A urinalysis is normal, as are serum electrolytes. Serum amylase is 500. A plain abdominal x-ray is ordered and reveals air-fluid levels, but no free air on the abdomen. She is given the diagnosis of ileus or obstruction resulting from diverticulitis.

Mrs. B was admitted to a general medical unit and had a surgical consultation. She was placed on IV fluids, restricted to have nothing PO, and had an NG tube placed to high intermittent gomco suction. IV antibiotic therapy was begun and continued for the remainder of her hospitalization. She was monitored closely and was managed medically. She was found to have an ileus only and never required surgery for a small bowel obstruction or perforation.

She was discharged to home on the eighth day after admission on her previous medications.

Nursing diagnoses	Outcomes	Interventions
Fluid volume deficit related to active loss of body fluid secondary to NG tube output	Client will maintain adequate fluid volume and electrolyte balance.	Monitor vital signs every 4 hours, or as ordered. Maintain IV therapy as ordered. Monitor intake and output hourly; skin moisture, color, and turgor; urine-specific gravity every 4 hours; serum electrolytes; and level of consciousness.
Altered nutrition: less than body requirements related to prolonged NPO status	Client will maintain preadmission weight.	Weigh client every day, or as ordered. Monitor serum albumin and protein. Administer IV hyperalimentation as ordered. When no longer NPO, encourage high-protein, high-calorie foods.
Constipation related to decreased mobility, daily ingestion of constipating medications, lack of dietary fiber	Client will establish a regular pattern of bowel movements.	Administer laxative medications, if ordered. When no longer NPO, encourage daily fluid intake of 2 L and high-fiber foods. Teach fiber-rich foods to include in diet. When able, encourage client to increase her activity level. Teach about constipating side effects of medications.

Continued.

CARE PLAN

ILEUS: OBSTRUCTION RESULTING FROM DIVERTICULITIS—cont'd

Nursing diagnoses	Outcomes	Interventions
Knowledge deficit: diverticular disease related to lack of exposure to knowledge about prevention and complications	Client and family will be able to verbalize dietary changes and be able to prevent constipation and further complications.	Provide client and family with written and verbal information concerning the importance of a high-fiber diet, the need to maintain an adequate fluid intake, and the need for light exercise. Provide client and family with written and verbal information concerning complications of diverticulosis, such as diverticulitis.
Pain (abdominal) related to reluctance to take pain medication	Client will obtain pain relief.	Assess and monitor degree of pain every 4 hours. Provide client with verbal and written instruction about analgesics. Provide other measures of pain relief, such as guided imagery, repositioning, and diversional activities. Provide encouragement by informing client that pain will decrease as the ileus improve.

also occur as a result of the contamination of the bloodstream in the peritoneum when the bowel ruptures or becomes gangrenous. Sepsis and hypovolemic shock are life-threatening and must be treated aggressively (see Medical Management box, p. 674).

NURSING MANAGEMENT

✣ ASSESSMENT

Assessment begins with a thorough history of the precipitating event, focusing on type and frequency of vomiting and diarrhea (profuse, fecal) and the location and character of pain (cramping, constant, diffuse). Physical examination should focus on presence and character of bowel sounds (loud, frequent, absent, or weak), presence of abdominal distention, vital signs, and urinary output (Long, Roberts, 1993).

EMERGENCY TREATMENT

The Acute Abdomen

Start IV fluids, as ordered
Place nasogastric (NG) tube for decompression
Monitor vital signs
Monitor intake and output
Assess for the following:
- Onset of pain
- Presence of vomiting or diarrhea
- Fever
- Past medical and surgical history

✣ DIAGNOSIS

Nursing diagnoses for the older client with an ileus or bowel obstruction include, but are not limited to: (1) fluid volume deficit related to loss of body fluids, and (2) abdominal pain.

✣ PLANNING

Expected outcomes for the older client with an ileus or intestinal obstruction include, but are not limited to, the following: (1) client will maintain adequate fluid volume and electrolyte balance and (2) client will verbalize comfort and pain relief after administration of analgesic.

✣ INTERVENTION

Nursing management of the older client with an ileus or intestinal obstruction includes maintenance of hydration and promotion of comfort. Dehydration can be prevented by providing IV fluids and electrolytes, as ordered. Monitoring intake and output, monitoring specific gravity, and monitoring for signs of fluid overload or dehydration are important. NG tubes are usually required for decompression, and maintenance of their patency and placement is imperative (see Research box, p. 677). Pain relief measures may require medications; however, narcotics are

RESEARCH

Metheny N et al: Effectiveness of pH measurements in predicting feeding tube placement: an update, *Nurs Res* 42(6):324-331, 1993.

Sample, setting

The sample consisted of 405 aspirates from small bore NG tubes and 389 aspirates from nasointestinal tubes, which were obtained from 605 subjects, ranging in age from 18 to 94 years (58% were over age 60) from patients in six acute care hospitals.

Methodology

Two thirds of the clients had feeding tubes placed "blind" at the bedside by personnel; others had tubes placed fluoroscopically by physicians. Data were collected in two phases: Phase I—within 5 minutes of abdominal x-ray (or 30 minutes within fluoroscopic insertions) for initially placed tubes and Phase II—when possible, after 1 or 2 days of tube feedings. Samples were tested immediately after collection with one of three types of pH paper and then with a pH meter.

Findings

Results supported the hypothesis that gastric placement was successfully distinguished from intestinal placement of the feeding tubes on the basis of pH meter readings and the presence/absence of acid inhibitors. In addition, acidic pH (<4) is a reasonable indicator of gastric (versus respiratory) placement, as a pH >6.0 is usually indicative of respiratory fluids.

Implications

Implications for perhaps modifying or changing traditional nursing practice are suggested for all nurses caring for clients with an NG tube, including older adults. Testing the pH of NG aspirates is a reliable method to confirm initial placement (when an x-ray is unavailable) and in establishing that the correct position has been maintained.

sometimes not allowed because of their effects on the bowel. Other comfort measures include repositioning, mouth care, skin care, and use of music or meditation. If surgery is required, preparation of client and family concerning what should be expected is also important.

✣ EVALUATION

Evaluation includes achievement of expected outcomes and prevention of complications (see nursing Care Plan, pp. 675-676).

Intestinal/Mesenteric Ischemia

In general, ischemia occurs when tissue demand for blood exceeds the supply, resulting in an accumulation of toxic

MEDICAL MANAGEMENT

Intestinal Ischemia

Diagnostic tests and procedures

Diagnosis is difficult, as there are no major laboratory or diagnostic tests. However, abdominal x-ray and arteriography are preferred. Laboratory tests such as a CBC would reveal a leukocytosis, and the serum amylase may be elevated.

Treatment

Treatment is primarily with surgery (resection or revascularization), although some clients respond to vasodilators. Antibiotics, IV therapy, volume replacement, and transfusions are common supportive therapies until diagnosis is certain and surgery is undertaken.

Prognosis

Prognosis depends on the correct diagnosis, and since there are few diagnostic tests or clinical criteria that help confirm the diagnosis, the mortality rate exceeds 70% to 90% (Hunter, Guernsey, 1988).

metabolites (Collins, Bullock, 1992). Intestinal ischemia can result from any condition that interferes with the blood supply to the mesentery, which is highly vascular. Prolonged ischemia results in death of the surface of the villi and epithelial cells, which in turn impairs the absorption of nutrients. In addition, the mucosal layer becomes necrotic and is shed into the stool as bloody diarrhea. This gangrene may lead to perforation of the intestine, leading to peritonitis and bacteremia.

Although intestinal or mesenteric ischemia is relatively rare, its high mortality rate and predominance in the older adult necessitates its importance to nurses taking care of older adults. Some degree of intestinal ischemia is present in all clients who have a history of other forms of ischemia, thrombosis, or infarction, or in clients who have chronic ischemia such as with atherosclerosis. The majority of these clients have a history of cerebrovascular, peripheral vascular, and/or coronary artery disease (Sinkinson, 1989).

Ischemic bowel disease comprises a spectrum of acute and chronic syndromes that usually affect older adults. The gut has an extensive collateral blood supply, and only when multiple diseased vessels are thrombosed or when a single artery is occluded do symptoms occur. The major syndromes of ischemic intestinal disease include acute embolic ischemia, acute thrombotic occlusion (ischemia colitis), nonocclusive ischemia, chronic intestinal ischemia (abdominal angina), and venous occlusive disease.

The clinical presentation initially is very nonspecific in all causes of mesenteric ischemia, and can mimic other, more common abdominal problems such as diverticulitis, appendicitis, and cholecystitis. Although the major symptom is abdominal pain, the clue to mesenteric ischemia is that the pain is out of proportion to what is elicited and found on physical examination (Sinkinson, 1989).

Symptoms of intestinal ischemia and infarction can be acute or chronic. Atherosclerotic ischemia may create an angina-like cramping abdominal pain, which becomes worse after meals and then dissipates. In colonic ischemia, the pain is worse in the left lower quadrant. Vasospasm and emboli produce an acute, severe abdominal pain with associated vomiting and diarrhea. Abdominal distention and tenderness are usually present. Bowel sounds may be loud and high-pitched (borborygmi) from an increased rate of peristalsis. Prompt diagnosis is imperative to prevent shock, peritonitis, or sepsis (see Medical Management box, p. 677).

Nursing Management

See nursing management of the older client with an ileus or intestinal obstruction, pp. 676-677.

Diverticula

Diverticula are sac-like protrusions of the mucosa along the GI tract (Collins, Bullock, 1992). A true diverticulum has all the layers of the bowels in its walls, whereas a false diverticulum occurs in a weak area of the muscularis layer of the bowel.

Diverticulosis is a disease of middle and old age, and the incidence increases with age. Approximately 20% of those over age 60 have diverticulosis, and the incidence is equal among men and women. It is the most common disease of the colon in the western world (Gioiella, Bevil, 1985).

These small sacs are formed by herniation of the mucous membrane outward through a separation in circular muscle fibers of the intestine. Diverticula develop as a result of increased intraluminal pressure, and can develop in any part of the digestive tract. They occur most often in the narrowest part of the colon on the left side, the descending and sigmoid colon. Colonic diverticula are usually multiple (Gioiella, Bevil, 1985).

The exact cause of diverticula is unknown, however. Because of the frequency of diverticula in older adults, it is thought that diverticula are related to the blood supply or nutrition of the bowel in older adults. Lack of dietary fiber or roughage, and decreased fecal bulk also have been correlated with this process (Collins, Bullock, 1992). With an increase in food bulk (as with dietary fiber) the pressure in the colon decreases. In contrast, when there is little waste in the colon, stronger muscle contractions are necessary to excrete it, and the pressure increases. This increase in pressure leads to muscle hypertrophy and the development of diverticula. It is in this manner that diverticula have also been linked to chronic constipation, and older adults who are obese. Atrophy of the musculature of the bowel wall may weaken the intestine and be a factor in the development of diverticula in older adults (Gioiella, Bevil, 1985).

The term diverticulosis refers to the presence of diverticula in the colon. Diverticulitis is an inflammation of or around a diverticular sac that results in retention of undigested food and bacteria in the sac. This hard mass is termed a fecalith (Collins, Bullock, 1992). In diverticulitis, the stasis in the sac leads to inflammation and/or infection. The mucous membranes may erode or perforate blood vessels, causing bleeding. Most frequently, however, diverticulitis is a consequence of localized perforation of a single diverticulum. Obstruction of the large intestine, fistulae, and abscesses may result. Rupture of the infected material into the peritoneal cavity may result in peritonitis. Approximately 15% of those with diverticulosis develop diverticulitis (Collins, Bullock, 1992; Gioiella, Bevil, 1985).

The majority of diverticula are asymptomatic and are often observed as incidental findings on x-ray or sigmoi-

MEDICAL MANAGEMENT

Diverticulitis/Diverticulosis

Diagnostic tests and procedures

Diagnosis of diverticular disease is through radiologic tests such as barium enema, flexible sigmoidoscopy, and colonscopy. With diverticulitis, laboratory tests such as a CBC may reveal leukocytosis and a slight anemia (if bleeding was present). The sedimentation rate may also be elevated (Gioiella, Bevil, 1985).

Treatment

Treatment of diverticulosis includes increasing fiber in the diet, and eliminating and preventing constipation. Diverticulitis is usually treated conservatively with bowel rest, IV fluids, and antibiotics. However, 20% of clients require a surgical resection for complications, including obstruction, perforation, hemorrhage, peritonitis, fistulae, or abscess (Gioiella, Bevil, 1985).

Prognosis

Prognosis for diverticulosis is good; however, clients must remember that it is a chronic illness, and prevention of complications is important. Prognosis with diverticulitis depends on the need for surgery and the presence of other complications.

doscopy. However, clinical manifestations of symptomatic diverticular disease include constipation or diarrhea, and left-sided lower abdominal pain. Over one half of clients with diverticulosis experience some change in bowel habits, and most complain of constipation (Gioiella, Bevil, 1985). Other symptoms include flatulence, nausea, or vomiting. In addition, signs of peritonitis, including abdominal pain, fever, abdominal rigidity, and rebound tenderness may appear if there is perforation. Surgery may be necessary if an obstruction or perforation is suspected (see Medical Management box, p. 678).

Nursing Management

✣ ASSESSMENT

Assessment begins with the older client's history of elimination patterns and changes to it, such as the client's frequency of defecation, stool characteristics (color, size, consistency), toileting habits, and course (improving or worsening, recurrent, or chronic changes in bowel habits). In addition, exercise patterns, presence of pain, bloating, nausea, vomiting, past medical history (hemorrhoids, bowel surgery), and family history of bowel problems such as polyps or colon cancer are also important. With diverticulitis, the client may have fever and chills. Physical examination may be unremarkable but may reveal a left lower quadrant tenderness or a guaiac-positive stool.

✣ DIAGNOSIS

The most used nursing diagnoses for the older client with diverticulosis or diverticulitis include, but are not limited to (1) constipation, (2) pain, and (3) knowledge deficit.

✣ PLANNING

Expected outcomes for the older client with diverticulosis and diverticulitis include, but are not limited to the following: (1) client will experience fewer episodes of constipation, (2) client will establish a regular pattern of bowel elimination, (3) client will obtain pain relief and remain free of abdominal pain, and (4) client will increase knowledge of self-care practices to minimize symptoms of diverticulosis and to prevent complications such as the development of diverticulitis.

✣ INTERVENTION

Nursing management of the older client with diverticulosis and diverticulitis includes the prevention and elimination of constipation, and the initiation of dietary changes. This includes teaching the client and family about the development of diverticulosis, and reinforcing that it is a chronic disease. In addition, review of high-fiber, high-roughage, high-residue foods, and the importance of achieving and maintaining adequate fluid status are necessary. Clients should be encouraged to consume up to 2,000 ml of fluids each day, unless contraindicated by cardiac status. Methods to relieve and to prevent constipation include an increase of fluids on a regular basis, light exercise on a regular basis, and a toileting program. The nurse can consult with the client's physician for mild analgesics and ointments for the control of pain, as necessary (Cox et al, 1989; Gioiella, Bevil, 1985).

The older client with diverticulitis needs pain management (either with antispasmotics, analgesics, or other measures such as a heating pad), bowel rest (IV fluids if NPO), and hospitalization if ill. The older client may be placed on a **low-residue diet,** slowly progressing to a regular diet. The nurse should teach self-care practices that promote bowel regularity and should administer stool softeners (such as Colace) as necessary. Again, encouragement of prevention of constipation is of the utmost importance.

✣ EVALUATION

Evaluation includes achievement of the expected outcomes, prevention of complications, and maintenance of regular bowel patterns and habits.

> ***Insight*** • *A guaiac-positive stool can be a result of a number of causes; however, in older adults this warrants additional evaluation to determine the exact cause. Some factors may yield a false guaiac-positive stool in any age group, including medications such as laxatives, iron supplements, cimetidine, anticoagulants, aspirin, and NSAIDs; foods such as red meat, uncooked vegetables, and fruits; and cooked vegetables such as broccoli, zucchini, green beans, carrots, cabbage, potatoes, and spinach. However, rectal bleeding can be a symptom of a GI problem such as hemorrhoids, rectal fissures, or cancer. In older adults, a guaiac-positive stool should be considered an indication of pathology until proven otherwise (Ruby, 1993).*

Hemorrhoids

Hemorrhoids are dilatations of the veins in the mucous membrane inside or outside the rectum (O'Toole, 1992). These dilatations are common and develop in susceptible people as a result of an increase in pressure in the hemorrhoidal venous plexus. Hemorrhoids are often related to the presence of varicose veins and are often

MEDICAL MANAGEMENT

Hemorrhoids

Diagnostic tests and procedures

Diagnosis is by visual inspection of the anal and rectal area, occasionally necessitating the use of an anoscope or proctoscope. Performing a hemacult test after the rectal examination is important to assess for the presence of blood.

Treatment

Treatment of external hemorrhoids is symptomatic and consists of applications of cold, astringent creams, anesthetic creams and ointments, use of sitz baths, and avoidance of constipation. Internal hemorrhoids may require sclerosis or cryosurgery if symptoms persist, and must be removed surgically by ligation or excision if complications such as strangulation or thrombosis occur.

Prognosis

Prognosis is good; however, it is a chronic condition, and recurrence of symptoms is common. It is best if the older client can prevent constipation.

called varicose veins of the rectum. Predisposition may result from constipation, pregnancy, liver disease, prolonged standing, and prostatic disease (Collins, Bullock, 1992; O'Toole, 1992).

Internal hemorrhoids may cause minor bleeding with defecation. The dilated venous sacs may protrude into the anal and rectal canals, where they become exposed, resulting in pain; thrombus, ulcerations, and bleeding then develop. External hemorrhoids produce varying degrees of pain, as well as pressure, itching, irritation, and a palpable mass. Bleeding occurs only if the external hemorrhoid is injured or ulcerated (O'Toole, 1992). Usually blood loss is insignificant, but chronic anemia may occur (see Medical Management box above).

NURSING MANAGEMENT

✣ ASSESSMENT

Assessment begins with the older client's history of constipation and symptoms of anal and rectal pain and/or blood on stool or toilet paper. In addition, past medical history and family history of bowel problems such as polyps or colon cancer are also important. Physical examination may be unremarkable except for a painful anus and rectum, to the point where thorough examination may be difficult, and guaiac-positive stool may occur.

✣ DIAGNOSIS

The most often used nursing diagnoses for the older client with hemorrhoids include, but are not limited to: (1) constipation, (2) anal/rectal pain, and (3) knowledge deficit regarding treatment and prevention.

✣ PLANNING

Expected outcomes for the older client with hemorrhoids include, but are not limited to, the following: (1) client will experience fewer episodes of constipation, (2) client will establish a regular pattern of bowel elimination, (3) client will obtain pain relief and remain free of anal/rectal pain, and (4) client will increase knowledge of self-care practices to minimize symptoms of hemorrhoids.

✣ INTERVENTION

Nursing management of the older client with hemorrhoids includes the prevention and elimination of constipation. This includes a review of high-fiber, high-roughage foods, and the importance of achieving and maintaining adequate fluid status. Older clients should be encouraged to consume up to 2,000 ml of fluids each day unless contraindicated. Nurses should encourage light exercise on a regular basis, and review the importance of a regular toileting routine. OTC anesthetic ointments and creams and sitz baths may be used for pain relief. Clients should be encouraged not to strain when defecating, since this may make hemorrhoids worse.

✣ EVALUATION

Evaluation includes achievement of the expected outcomes, prevention of complications, and maintenance of regular bowel patterns and habits.

Polyps

A polyp is any growth that protrudes from a mucous membrane, and in the GI tract it is often in the large intestine, where it protrudes into the lumen of the bowel. Polyps are usually an overgrowth of normal tissue, but sometimes, they are true tumors. Usually considered benign, they sometimes lead to complications or become malignant (Eastwood, Avunduk, 1988).

Although some people are born with polyps, they often occur in middle age. Multiple intestinal polyps may be a hereditary disorder (O'Toole, 1992; Eastwood, Avunduk, 1988).

The two most common types of colon polyps are adenomatous and hyperplastic. Adenomatous polyps are true neoplasms, and some are malignant. These growths begin in the mucosa deep within the crypts of the colonic mucosal glands. The polypoidal cells continue to divide and become hyperplastic growths. When reproductive control is lost throughout the mucosal crypt, a neoplasm results (Collins, Bullock, 1992). Polyps are generally very common and rarely exceed 5 mm in diameter. However, the risk of cancer developing from a polyp is directly related to its size (Eastwood, Avunduk, 1988). Cancer is more likely to occur in the villous adenomatous type of polyp. In addition, benign adenomatous polyps are believed to predispose to adenocarcinoma, in that some degenerate into cancerous lesions. In addition, adenomatous polyps also may coexist with adenocarcinoma elsewhere in the bowel. In general, the colon that produces polyps is at a higher risk of developing cancer (Eastwood, Avunduk, 1988).

Many clients with polyps are asymptomatic. These growths are often discovered incidentally by sigmoidoscopy or barium enema. Occasionally they may bleed, causing bright red blood in the feces. If the polyp is large enough, it may cause an obstruction (see Medical Management box below).

MEDICAL MANAGEMENT

Polyps

Diagnostic tests and procedures

Diagnosis of polyps in the colon consists of identification by barium enema, flexible sigmoidoscopy, or colonoscopy. If polyps are diagnosed on a barium enema, colonoscopy should be performed so that biopsy for cytology can be done.

Treatment

Treatment includes polypectomy during a complete colonoscopy. Since nonadenomatous polyps have little or no malignant potential, removal of these polyps is sufficient treatment. However, since adenomatous polyps may either predispose the client to the development of cancer or contain cancer themselves, all polyps should be biopsied to assess for adenocarcinoma.

Prognosis

Prognosis is good if adenomatous polyps are removed. However, the key to a good prognosis is adequate follow-up. Those clients with polyps found on a colonoscopy should have a colonoscopy once a year, until no polyps are found, and then return for a colonoscopy every 3 to 5 years. If polyps found were malignant, or if cancer is suspected, the client should have a colonoscopy every 3 to 6 months, depending on the involvement of the polyps (Eastwood, Avunduk, 1988). In addition to colonoscopies, clients should undergo annual tests for occult blood in the stool, as well as digital rectal examinations.

NURSING MANAGEMENT

ASSESSMENT

Assessment begins with a good history of any symptoms such as blood in or on the stool or toilet paper. A careful family history should be obtained, especially pertaining to a family history of polyps. Physical examination may be unremarkable; however, a guaiac-positive stool may be found on rectal examination.

DIAGNOSIS

The most often used nursing diagnoses include, but are not limited to: (1) knowledge deficit regarding importance of treatment and follow up and (2) fear.

PLANNING

Expected outcomes for the older client with polyps include, but are not limited to the following: (1) client will increase knowledge of disease process and potential outcomes, (2) client will obtain medical follow-up as suggested by the American Cancer Society or their own health care providers, and (3) client will not experience complications such as invasive colorectal cancer.

INTERVENTION

Nursing management of the older client with polyps includes education and reinforcement of suggested guidelines by the American Cancer Society to prevent the occurrence of colorectal cancer. In addition, the client who is to undergo a colonoscopy may need reinforcement of the importance of having the polyps removed. Reminders may need to be given to older clients as to when it is time to have another screening sigmoidoscopy, according to their health care provider and/or the American Cancer Society guidelines. Clients may need to be reminded also that although polyps are often asymptomatic, they may also bleed. However, the presence of any blood in the stool requires a repeat sigmoidoscopy.

EVALUATION

Evaluation includes achievement of the expected outcomes and prevention of complications, such as obstruction or invasive colorectal cancer.

Colorectal Carcinoma

Colorectal carcinoma is one of the most common cancers for both men and women in the United States. Cancer of the large intestine is second only to lung cancer for the greatest number of new cases and deaths (Collins, Bullock, 1992; Boarini, 1990). The incidence is second only to cancer of prostate and lung (in men), and second only to breast cancer (in women) (Boarini, 1990).

Colorectal cancer affects both genders equally. Although it can occur at any age, incidence increases in people over age 40, with a mean age at diagnosis occurring after 60 years of age (Boarini, 1990; Murphy, 1991). However, age is a significant risk factor for colorectal cancer, since risk increases rapidly above age 55 and doubles with each successive decade, reaching a peak at age 75. Prevalence is highest in northwest Europe and North America, and lowest in South America, Africa, and Asia (Collins, Bullock, 1992).

Although the cause of colorectal cancer is unknown, research has indicated that diet, environment, and genetics all play an important part in the development of the disease (Murphy, 1991). Most of the geographic distribution can be explained by dietary factors, although the action is unclear. It seems that dietary factors affect the exposure of the GI tract to carcinogens. Some dietary agents are thought to increase exposure to promoters of carcinogenesis, much like fats, and other dietary factors such as fiber and calcium are thought to reduce exposure (Boarini, 1990; Collins, Bullock, 1992).

Citizens of underdeveloped countries with a lower incidence of colorectal cancer generally eat diets high in fiber. In more westernized civilizations, fiber intake decreases, as the diet is composed of more refined foods. As a high-fiber diet reduces transit time, it appears to limit the time the colon is exposed to cancer promoters (Murphy, 1990). For example, an average white American has a transit time of 4 to 5 days, whereas that of a black African is only 30 to 35 hours. Colon cancer is more prevalent in the United States, probably because the American diet is much lower in fiber than the African diet (Collins, Bullock, 1992).

In addition to fiber, dietary fat has been linked to colorectal cancer. Current research proposes that a high-fat diet increases the amount of fecal bile acids, which may be mutagenic, and therefore promotes the development of colorectal cancer (Boarini, 1990).

In addition to diet, certain factors predispose a person to colorectal cancer. These include heredity, inflammatory bowel disease, anal intercourse, and colon polyps (Boarini, 1990; Collins, Bullock, 1992).

Adenocarcinoma accounts for 95% of the carcinomas of the colon (Boarini, 1990; Collins, Bullock, 1992; Murphy, 1991). The tumors tend to grow slowly and may remain asymptomatic for a long time.

About 60% to 70% of these carcinomas arise in the rectum, rectosigmoid area, or sigmoid colon (Collins, Bullock, 1992; Murphy, 1991). Cancer of the rectum is manifested as bright red bleeding through the rectum. Carcinomas in the sigmoid and descending colon tend to grow around the bowel, encircling it and leading to an obstruction. In these clients, a change in bowel habits is a common symptom. Cancer in the transverse colon is commonly manifested by a change in bowel habits and blood in the stool, and obstructions are common. On the right side, the tumors tend to be bulky, polypoid, fungating masses that tend to ulcerate. They tend to grow in, rather than around, the bowel. Either type may penetrate the bowel and cause abscesses, peritonitis, invasion of the surrounding organs, or bleeding. Tumor growth is by direct invasion and local extension; however, once it has invaded the lymph and vascular channels, metastases are likely. Metastases to the liver and lymphatic system are common, although other sites include brain, lung, bones, and adrenal glands (Collins, Bullock, 1992; Boarini, 1990).

Clinical manifestations depend on the location and extent of the tumor. Left-sided lesions often cause melena, diarrhea, and constipation. Right-sided tumors often cause weakness, malaise, and weight loss. Abdominal pain is rare with either type, and may result from obstructions or nerve involvement. An obstruction is often the first sign of the disease. Often, a mass is palpated on physical examination, or on a routine rectal examination, the stool is guaiac-positive. Although the duration of symptoms is not effective in predicting the degree of tu-

MEDICAL MANAGEMENT

Colorectal Cancer

Diagnostic tests and procedures

Diagnosis may be through barium enema, sigmoidoscopy, colonoscopy, and fecal occult blood screening. However, a biopsy is required for definitive diagnosis. Although 60% of polyps and cancers are visualized with the flexible sigmoidoscopy, a colonoscopy is necessary to detect cancer in the right colon. CT scans are useful in staging and evaluation of metastases.

Treatment

Treatment may include surgery, radiation therapy, chemotherapy, or a combination. Surgical procedures may include a bowel resection or a colonoscopy, and may be done for either palliative or curative means.

Prognosis

Prognosis depends on the extent of bowel involvement, the presence or absence of any spread, and the location of the lesion within the colon (Collins, Bullock, 1992). Despite recent advances, the overall 5-year survival rate nationally is 50% (Silverberg, Lubera, 1989). However, when colorectal cancer is detected and treated in the early stages, the 5-year survival rate is 80% to 90% (Collins, Bullock, 1992).

mor advancement, the diagnosis of cancer in asymptomatic people has been shown to be related to improved survival (Sugarbaker, Gunderson, Wittes et al, 1985).

The staging of colorectal tumors is through the Duke's classification system. This system classifies tumors into four major categories based on the degree and depth of tumor involvement, and the presence of lymph nodes (Murphy, 1991).

Colon cancers produce a wide variety of tumor antigens; the carcinoembryonic (CEA) is the most well-known. CEA levels are used to gauge the effectiveness of therapy and may be useful at the time of diagnosis for prognostic value. In addition, it is used to assess for recurrence. Its current use in mass screening and detection is limited (see Medical Management box, p. 682).

Nursing Management

✣ ASSESSMENT

Assessment begins with the older client's history of symptoms, such as diarrhea, constipation, abdominal pain, blood in stool, or melena. Generalized symptoms may have been overlooked by the older client, and include malaise, weight loss, weakness, and fatigue. Eliciting a family history of colorectal cancer, polyps and any history of previous bowel surgeries is also important. Physical examination may reveal a mass in the abdomen or a guaiac-positive stool, or it may be unremarkable.

✣ DIAGNOSIS

The most often used nursing diagnoses include, but are not limited to: (1) altered nutrition: less than body requirements, (2) pain, and (3) body image disturbance related to a colostomy.

✣ PLANNING

Expected outcomes for the older client with colorectal cancer include, but are not limited to the following: (1) client will maintain weight and adequate nutrition, (2) client will be able to manage pain, and (3) client will accept permanent or temporary body change from a colostomy.

✣ INTERVENTION

Nursing management of the older client with colorectal cancer depends on the stage of the disease and treatment modalities necessary. In general, older clients are at risk for weight loss and malnutrition, as a result of the cancer, and symptoms of vomiting or diarrhea. Encouragement of eating small, frequent, high-calorie, high-protein meals should be suggested. Allowing clients to eat some of their favorite foods on a regular basis may help maintain weight. The use of supplements such as Ensure, or tube feedings (at night) may be necessary to maintain adequate nutrition. Not every client with colorectal cancer complains of pain, but if present, the pain can be managed with both pharmacologic and nonpharmacologic relief measures. If the older client requires a colostomy either for treatment or as a palliative measure, the client should be encouraged to verbalize and express feelings on a regular basis. Referral to a support group or counseling may be necessary. Having the older client speak with or visit someone with a colostomy may help reduce anxiety, concerns, and fears associated with it. If the colorectal cancer is completely resected, reminding and encouraging the older client to have follow-up examinations and procedures to check for recurrence is of the utmost importance.

✣ EVALUATION

Evaluation includes achievement of the expected outcomes and prevention of complications.

Evaluation of Common GI Symptoms in the Older Client

The older adult may complain of a symptom related to the GI tract that has not yet been related to a diagnosis. Any symptom that an older client complains about needs to be thoroughly assessed, whether or not it has a known or probable cause. The following are a few of the common GI symptoms experienced by the older adult, including definition, assessment, nursing interventions, and self-care measures.

Nausea/Vomiting

Vomiting is controlled through a central vomiting center in the medulla. This center is close to the respiratory center and is also near the centers that control vestibular and vasomotor function. Occasionally stimuli from one center spills over to another, and symptoms may become mixed. No distinct nausea center exists; however, the symptom of nausea may result from early stimulation of the vomiting center (Haubrich, 1991) (Fig. 25-4).

Nausea may be difficult for clients to describe, since they may use the phrase, "I feel sick," to convey the symptom of nausea. It is important to keep in mind that although nausea usually precedes vomiting, it may also be a free-standing symptom. In general, nausea in the absence of vomiting is of central, rather than peripheral, origin. That is, the symptom is initiated centrally in the brain, rather than peripherally in the GI tract. Central nausea is usually a response to a metabolic disorder.

It is important to obtain a detailed description of events surrounding a complaint of nausea and vomiting. Was the vomiting preceded by nausea? Were the nausea and vomiting preceded by diarrhea or constipation? What was the estimated volume of vomiting? Were there

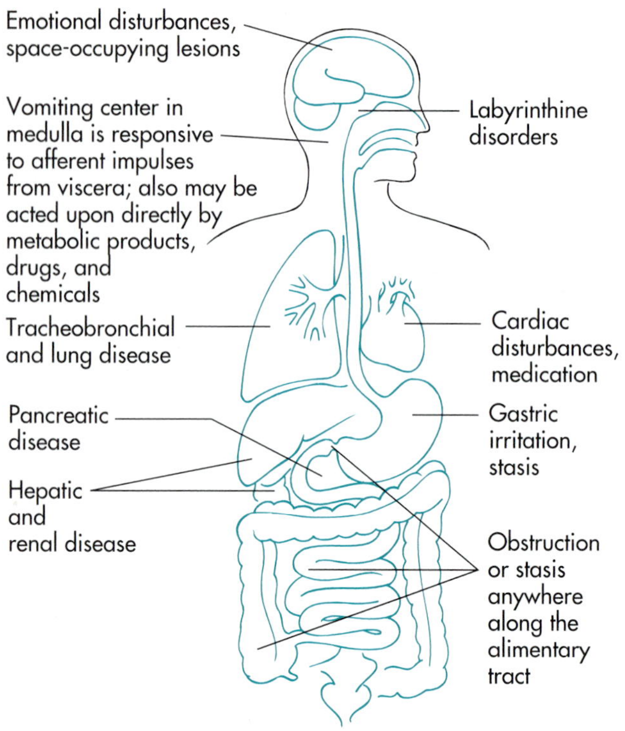

Fig. 25-4 Some of the many sources of nausea and vomiting. (From Berk JE, Haubrich WS, editors: *Gastrointestinal symptoms: clinical interpretation,* Philadelphia, 1991, BC Decker.)

recognizable food particles? Was it bilious? Was there blood present, and if so, was it bright red, dark brown, or black? Were the nausea and vomiting accompanied by other symptoms, such as fever, or sweating, pallor, and hypotension (a vasomotor response)? Was there pain of any sort? Were any drugs ingested? Does the client have any metabolic disorders, such as diabetes, hyperthyroidism, or renal insufficiency? Is coughing involved? What other factors surrounded the onset of the nausea and vomiting? What is the frequency; if frequent, are there signs of dehydration and electrolyte imbalance? Are there any precipitating and/or alleviating factors?

Nursing interventions include many self-help measures, including such dietary changes as bland foods, drinking liquids at a different time than eating solid foods, and small, frequent feedings. If vomiting occurs, fluid replacement should be a priority. Sips of soda every 15 minutes until more can be tolerated may decrease episodes of dehydration. In the older client, instruction concerning the signs and symptoms of dehydration and electrolyte imbalances as well as when to seek medical care are important. Any episodes of prolonged nausea and/or vomiting require careful evaluation by their health care providers.

Anorexia

Anorexia as a symptom should not be confused with anorexia nervosa, which is an eating disorder of psychiatric significance. The term anorexia literally means lack of appetite. Hunger and appetite are not synonymous. Hunger is related to the physiologic need for food.

It is important for the nurse to ascertain that decreased food intake is truly because of a loss of appetite. Once that is assured, questions regarding other symptoms must be asked, regarding weight loss, nausea, vomiting, abdominal pain, diarrhea, or constipation (Berk, 1991). In addition, psychosocial factors such as stress, grief, pain, or other concomitant illnesses may also need to be assessed.

Nursing interventions for the older client with anorexia include acknowledgement of the client's symptoms along with gentle encouragement to eat for nutritional purposes. Encouraging the older client to seek medical attention for anorexia is also important, since the client may not be aware that it is a problem.

Abdominal Pain

The symptom of abdominal pain is often difficult to assess fully, and in the older adult, it can become even more difficult to assess, even for the skilled clinician.

Although the assessment of pain is complicated, it is made easier by thinking in terms of the three pathways for pain impulses. The first is visceral pain pathways, which are activated by receptors in the wall of the abdominal viscera and develop from stretching or distending the abdominal wall, or from inflammation. This pain is often diffuse and poorly localized, and has a gnawing, burning, or cramping quality. The second is somatic or parietal pathways, which are activated by receptors in the parietal peritoneum and other supporting tissues. This type of pain is usually sharp, more intense, constant, and better localized than visceral pain. The third type of pathway is a referral pathway, which accounts for referred pain (i.e., pain is felt at a different site than the source of the pain, but shares the same dermatome). This pain is usually sharp and well-localized, and may resemble somatic pain (Eastwood, Avunduk, 1988; Haubrich, 1991).

In assessing any type of pain, important questions include for the exact duration, location, mode of onset, intensity, character, rhythmicity, relationship to food, alleviating and aggravating factors, and accompanying symptoms. For older clients, it is important for the nurse to keep in mind that they complain less of pain than do younger adults (Malasanos, Barkauskas, Stoltenberg-Allen, 1990).

Nurses may learn to distinguish features of various types of abdominal pain based on the client's symptoms, such as epigastric, small bowel (poorly localized mid abdominal or periumbilical), appendicitis, rectal/pelvic

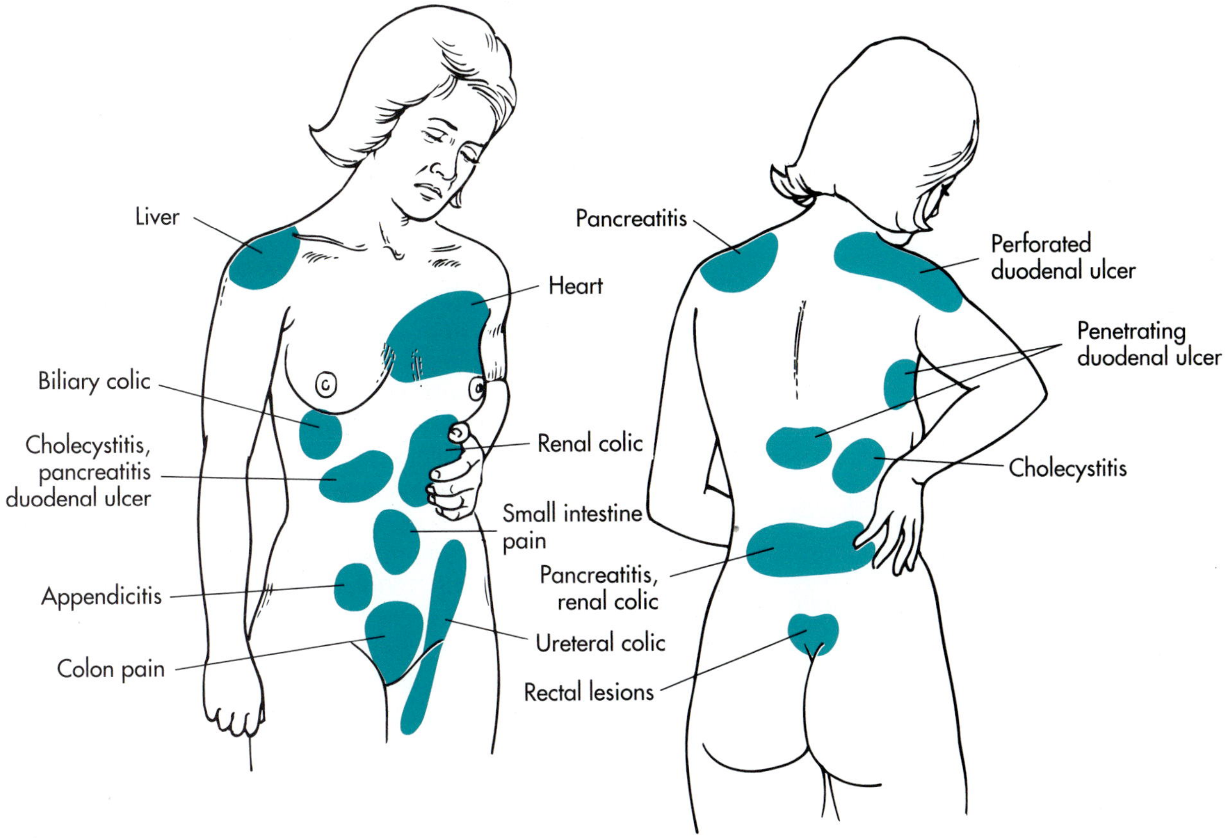

Fig. 25-5 Common sites of referred abdominal pain. Note that the pain's location may not be directly over or even near the site of the organ. (From Phipps WJ, et al: *Medical-surgical nursing: concepts and clinical practice,* ed 5, St. Louis, 1995, Mosby.)

pain, liver pain, biliary tract pain, and pancreatic pain (Fig. 25-5).

Nursing interventions include nursing measures to increase comfort and pain relief. Again, the nurse should encourage older clients to see their health care provider for a complete evaluation of the abdominal pain (see Emergency Treatment box, p. 676).

Gas

Unfortunately, flatulence has not been given the degree of concern that other GI symptoms have received. Complaints come in the form of belching, bloating or fullness, and flatus. About 99% of the gas present in the GI tract of adults is comprised of five gases: nitrogen, oxygen, hydrogen, carbon dioxide, and methane. The percentage of each depends on the source. These sources include swallowing, diffusion of gas from the bloodstream to the intestinal lumen, and food processing (Wick, 1993). All of these are odorless, and the unpleasant odor associated with flatus is probably a result of hydrogen sulfide that is metabolized from sulfur-containing foods (Berk, 1991). A frequency of 7 to 20 gas passages per day is considered normal (Wick, 1993).

Although belching primarily comes from the unconscious swallowing of air, it is important to assess the client further for other symptoms suggestive of gastritis or peptic ulcer disease (PUD). Many of the complaints of bloating and fullness are related to a motility disorder or malabsorption, but in older adults, it must be taken more seriously. It requires further assessment such as questioning about changes in bowel function, the presence of pain, or its accompaniment with other GI tract symptoms.

Although the expulsion of flatus is a normal event, excessive flatus may have several causes. Some clients may form more gas within the gut, some may swallow a lot of air, and others may have excessive flatus because of the nature of the foods consumed. Frequent offenders are air-containing foods such as whipped foods, carbonated beverages, certain fruits, gas-forming foods such as beans and legumes, and sulfur-containing foods such as eggs. In addition, clients who are **lactose** intolerant may

CULTURAL AWARENESS

Lactose Intolerance

Prevalence

Group	Percent
Asian Americans	94
American Indians	79
Blacks	75
Hispanics	50
Whites	17

Clinical manifestations after drinking milk

Flatus

Intestinal discomfort (cramping, abdominal pain)

Vomiting and diarrhea less frequently, (person may simply say, "Milk doesn't agree with me.")

Culture-specific nursing interventions

Suggest alternative calcium-rich foods such as the following:

Asian Americans

Leafy green vegetables, bok choy, tofu, fish with edible bones

Hispanics

Corn tortillas (if corn treated with lime); cheese, and cafe con leche (coffee with milk)

Usually able to tolerate fermented milk products such as yogurt, lactose-reduced milks, and sweet acidophilus milk

produce more gas (see Cultural Awareness box above). Careful questioning of the client may reveal one or a combination of these causes (Berk, 1991).

Nursing interventions focus on client education about the cause and nature of intestinal gas. The key to treatment is a change in dietary factors, focusing on eating more slowly and avoiding gas-producing foods.

Diarrhea

Diarrhea in a broad sense has come to mean increased frequency of the passage of loose stools. Diarrhea may be due to increased bowel motility or interferences in the normal absorption of water and nutrients in the bowel (Ruby, 1993). When an older client complains of diarrhea, it is important to ascertain exactly what is meant. In addition, the description of the complaint of diarrhea may be useless unless the client's normal bowel habits are known.

Questions to ask when assessing a client with the complaint of diarrhea include onset (recent or acute), precipitating events (travel out of the country or eating at a restaurant), timing (intermittent or continuous), presence of other associated factors (fever, weight loss, abdominal pain, vomiting, dietary or medication changes, or presence of any systemic diseases), characteristics of the diarrhea (frequency, consistency, volume, foul smell, presence of mucus or blood, incontinence, or awakening from sleep [e.g., nocturnal diarrhea usually points to an organic cause rather than a functional or infectious cause]). All of these questions help assess the diarrhea further to aid in consideration of the cause (McHardy et al, 1991).

Nursing care focuses on maintaining adequate hydration and nutrition, assessing for complications, as well as providing emotional support as necessary. Usual water loss in stools is 150 ml per day; severe diarrhea can account for up to 5 to 10 l of water loss daily. Therefore in the older client, assessing for signs and symptoms of dehydration and volume depletion is important. Client and family need to learn to report complications, such as increased thirst, weakness, dizziness, palpitation, or fatigue (Ruby, 1993). If fluid and electrolyte imbalances occur, either oral or parenteral treatment may be required, as diarrhea in older adults may be life-threatening. Nursing interventions should also be aimed at identifying and correcting the cause. Depending on the causative factor, antispasmodic and antidiarrheal medications may be used. Education of client and family should also include dietary changes such as avoiding gas-forming foods, vegetables, spices, and milk products for chronic diarrhea, and eating bland foods, such as the BRAT diet (bananas, rice, applesauce, toast) and clear liquids for acute diarrhea.

Constipation

Constipation has been broadly defined as an abnormally infrequent or difficult passage of hard, dry feces (Ruby, 1993). Failure to relieve the constipation may result in a fecal impaction. Constipation can be acute or chronic in onset, and either intermittent or constant in frequency.

Few data support the notion that constipation is more common among older clients (Wald, 1990). Contributing to this is the variability in definitions used in research and epidemiologic studies of the incidence and prevalence of constipation. Even in clinical practice, older clients often define constipation differently than their health care providers.

Although any acute change in bowel habits of the older adult warrants concern, many times the cause of constipation may be identified by careful questioning of the client. Common causes of constipation include diet (a decrease in fiber), medications (antacids, iron preparations, anticholinergics, or an overuse of laxatives),

Insight • *Although diarrhea in the older adult may be a result of medication side effects, lactose intolerance, fecal incontinence, or viral enteritis, another cause of diarrhea in the institutionalized older adult, and more often now, those at home, is tube feedings. Studies have shown that the incidence of diarrhea in a tube-fed client is 60% to 96% (Galindo-Ciocon, 1993). However, studies have shown that incidence rates can be lowered through changes in nursing practice that include concentration of formula, rate of feeding, and administration of the tube feeding. Findings from recent research include the following implications and practice guidelines:*

1. *When starting tube feedings, begin with a slower infusion rate with a lesser concentration. For example, begin with an infusion rate of a full strength isotonic formula at a slow rate (30 to 50 ml/hr), gradually increasing the rate over a few days until caloric needs are met. Hypertonic liquids should be diluted and begin at a slow rate, such as half strength at 50 ml/hr, and if tolerated, the concentration should be increased to three fourths strength, then full strength before the rate is increased (Martyn-Nemeth, Fitzgerald, 1992).*
2. *When using bolus or intermittent feedings, the rate should begin at less than 30 ml/min, and should never be faster than 300 ml/hour (Galindo-Ciocon, 1993; Martyn-Nemeth, Fitzgerald, 1992).*
3. *A wide range of temperatures can be tolerated if bolus feedings are administered over more than 30 minutes (Vines et al, 1992).*

metabolic abnormalities (diabetes, hypothyroidism), motility abnormalities, inflammation, mechanical obstruction (fecal impaction or cancer), environmental changes (inability to reach toilet, lack of privacy), depression, or misperception—belief that one bowel movement a day is necessary (Ruby, 1993; Sodeman, 1989; Wald, 1990).

Perhaps the most widespread cause of constipation in the older adult is diet. It is usually a lack of certain foods, rather than the addition of certain foods, that may lead to constipation. Many foods contain natural laxatives, such as fresh fruits and vegetables.

A second dietary cause of constipation is the lack of fiber or bulk and a decrease in fluid intake. In general, unrefined foods have more fiber than the refined foods, which are popular in American society and to which older adults may fall prey.

It is important to keep in mind that constipation can be a result of overuse or improper use of laxatives, or it may be a perceptual problem. Many older adults believe

CLIENT/FAMILY TEACHING

Bowel Training Program

Provide a private, stress-free atmosphere.
Include family and older client in all teaching.
Explain importance of responding to the urge to defecate.
Have client determine a specific time each day for bowel evacuation (e.g., after breakfast or dinner).
Have client sit on toilet or commode for evacuation.
Encourage high-fiber diet.
Encourage client to increase fluids to 2 L/day.
Avoid long-term or habitual use of laxatives; rather, use stool softeners, laxatives, suppositories or enemas only as needed.
Use psyllium seed bulking agents on a regular basis if dietary measures are not adequate.
Encourage light activity on a regular basis if possible.
If necessary, use digital stimulation to promote defecation, and massage left lower quadrant of the abdomen while on toilet.

From Long BC, Roberts R: The patient with gastrointestinal problems. In Long BC, Phipps WJ, Cassmeyer VL, editors: *Medical-surgical nursing: a nursing process approach,* ed 3, St. Louis, 1993, Mosby; Ruby PS: Constipation; diarrhea; fecal incontinence; rectal bleeding. In Loftis PA, Glover TL, editors: *Decision making in gerontologic nursing,* St. Louis, 1993, Mosby.

that one to two bowel movements a day are required for "normal" functioning. In this instance, the nurse can reinforce with the client and family that as long as the consistency is normal, and the bowel movements occur at regular intervals, there is no reason for concern. With an increase in age, there may be an increase in transit time through the bowel, causing a lengthening of the time between bowel movements.

Nursing interventions include methods to alleviate and to prevent further episodes of constipation. In teaching the older adult about dietary changes, it is important to remind them that fiber need not be a "medicine" but rather a "food." An increase in dietary fiber may result from an increase in bran in the diet, or the addition of psyllium preparations sold OTC.

Constipation is treated through dietary measures such as increasing fluid intake, increasing fiber and light exercise, and developing a regular toileting routine that includes responding to the urge to defecate. Medications can be laxatives and cathartics, which include bulking agents (bran, psyllium), emollients (mineral oil), stimulants (cascara, castor oil, bisacodyl), saline cathartics (milk of magnesia, citrate, sodium or potassium phosphate), osmotic agents (lactulose, sorbitol), and rectal agents—enemas and suppositories (bisacodyl, glycerin, soap suds) (see Client/Family Teaching box above and Research box, p. 688).

RESEARCH

Beverely, L. and Travis, I. (1992). Constipation: Proposed natural laxative mixtures. *J Gerontolog Nurs* October.

Sample, setting

The sample included 35 clients from a geropsychiatric unit who all had a primary diagnosis of Alzheimer's disease or senile dementia of Alzheimer's type. Of these clients, 23 were women and 12 were men; ages ranged from 58 to 95, with a mean age of 81.3.

Methodology

The frequency and consistency of bowel movements was recorded for each client for 1 month during the preintervention phase, while the patients received the routine bowel or lactulose protocol. A natural laxative mixture composed of dried fruit and prune juice was introduced to each client individually when a change in bowel habit was required. Once the research protocol was in effect, the stool softeners or laxatives were discontinued. Administration of the natural laxative mixture continued over a 3-month period, while frequency and consistency of stools, and ease of administration (by the nurses) was recorded. Per client costs were also recorded and analyzed for both pretreatment and intervention phases.

Findings

The actual number of stool frequencies were similar both in preintervention and intervention phases. However, based on the consistency of stools, the natural laxative mixture was found to be as effective as other methods in managing constipation in this group of clients. In addition, during the intervention phase, their cost was reduced over 50% from preintervention.

Implications

Although replication on a larger and perhaps more diverse population is necessary, results point out that a nonpharmacologic and nursing-managed bowel program can be both effective at managing constipation in older adults, as well as cost-effective.

Fecal Incontinence

Fecal incontinence, the involuntary passing of stool, may be acute or chronic, and demands evaluation. For the older adult, the loss of bowel control is devastating and may significantly alter the quality of life.

Fecal incontinence may be a result of colorectal lesions (perianal disease, proctitis, tumors), neurologic problems (neuropathy, spinal cord lesions), laxative abuse, impaction, chronic diarrhea, stress, medications, or general decline in muscle tone.

Nursing interventions focus on education concerning the prevention and treatment of incontinence in older adults. Examination of the cause of the incontinence is important for nurse, client, and family. Laxative abuse is completely preventable and treatable, simply with education and reassurance to the client that one to two bowel movements a day are not necessary to be "regular."

However, regardless of the cause, the older client who is aware of and distressed by the incontinence can usually be helped by a program of bowel control (see Client/Family Teaching box, p. 687). It is important to reassure the older client that control and retraining are achievable, since many older adults feel that fecal incontinence is the first step on the road to permanent institutionalization.

Other nursing interventions include methods to deal with the embarrassment of the incontinence, ways to decrease fecal odor, use of adult diapers, and skin care. Maintenance of skin integrity is important to prevent skin breakdown.

HEALTH HISTORY AND PHYSICAL EXAMINATION

Assessment of the GI System

See Box 25-5 for additional information on assessment of the GI system.

Subjective Data

Obtaining health histories from clients not only assists in assessing and diagnosing their health problems, but also is the main mechanism with which rapport is established between clients and health care providers. It may be necessary for the nurse to devote more time to get an adequate history from the older client because of hearing and sensory losses in both perception and reception (Malasanos, Barkauskas, Stoltenberg-Allen, 1990) in this age group.

As with any symptom, but especially with those surrounding the primary complaint, the nurse should obtain the symptom's location, quality, quantity, setting, associated phenomena, course since onset, and alleviating and aggravating factors (Malasanos, Barkauskas, Stoltenberg-Allen, 1990). In addition, negative information such as the lack of certain GI symptoms is also important.

Past medical history, including childhood illnesses, adult illnesses (both chronic and acute), hospitalizations, immunization status, allergies, and medications (prescription and OTC) are essential to the complete history. A family history is important to identify any illnesses of a genetic or familial nature, and in relation to the GI system, this includes cancer and polyps.

BOX 25-5

Health History and Physical Examination for the GI System

Subjective data

Dietary history
Bowel pattern
Stool consistency
Pain
Nausea
Vomiting
Tobacco use
Alcohol use
Concomitant illnesses
Medications (prescription and OTC)
Previous hospitalizations and/or surgeries
Occupational history
Cultural factors

Objective data

Inspection

The presence of lesions on lips, tongue, and oral cavity; quality and deficiencies of gums and teeth; shape and tone of abdomen; body position. Inspection of the abdomen reveals presence of any lesions or scars, as well as contour.

Auscultation

Bowel sounds in all four quadrants

Percussion

All four quadrants of abdomen

Palpation

Presence of organ enlargement, mass, hemorrhoids, and stool or mass in rectal vault, as well as quality of rectal tone; hemacult of stool for presence of blood

A social history should include habits of alcohol and tobacco use, past and present, and details such as type and amount. In addition, an occupational history to reveal potential exposure to carcinogens is important. Toileting habits and bowel patterns may be included here if not previously discussed. Questioning about diet and nutritional status such as "What foods did you eat yesterday?" may also be included here, if not previously discussed. An important part of the social history is questioning older clients about with whom they live and their financial status or arrangements.

Objective Data

In the physical examination of the GI system, one of the most important things to remember is that inspection is done first, followed by auscultation. This is because the movement or stimulation by pressure on the bowel because of palpation or percussion can alter the motility and heighten the sounds (Malasanos, Barkauskas, Stoltenberg-Allen, 1990).

Beginning with the first part of the GI system, the mouth, inspection includes assessment for lesions, growths, or abnormalities both on the lips and inside the mouth. Palpation with a gloved hand can be done to better assess the presence of any abnormality.

Moving on to the abdomen, inspection is best done supine, which for some older clients may be difficult or uncomfortable. Anatomic mapping of the abdomen is often done to further describe any abnormalities. One frequently used system divides the abdomen into four quadrants: right upper quadrant, right lower quadrant, left upper quadrant, and left lower quadrant. The abdomen can be examined visually for contour, presence of lesions, or scars (Malasanos, Barkauskas, Stoltenberg-Allen, 1990).

Auscultation is usually done next and begins with the use of the diaphragm of the stethoscope, which accentuates high-pitched sounds (Malasanos, Barkauskas, Stoltenberg-Allen, 1990). Motility of the bowel is assessed through listening to bowel sounds, which normally occur every 5 to 15 seconds. Auscultation for bruits is done with the bell of the stethoscope held lightly against the abdomen (Malasanos, Barkauskas, Stoltenberg-Allen, 1990).

Percussion is done to assess for fluid, distention, and masses, and for assessing the position and size of the liver and spleen (Malasanos, Barkauskas, Stoltenberg-Allen, 1990). General percussion of the entire abdomen reveals tympany in areas of the small and large intestine as a result of the presence of gas and dullness over the solid organs or masses. Percussion to determine the size of the liver is begun at the midclavicular line below the umbilicus and progresses up to the liver. The lower border of the liver is noted with the first dull percussion note after the previous tympanic sounds. This site should be marked on the abdomen. The upper border of the liver is ascertained by percussing in the midclavicular line from an area of lung resonance to the first dull percussion note (generally the fifth to seventh intercostal space). This point is also marked, and the distance between them is measured. The suggested normal range in the midclavicular line is 6 to 23 cm, with men having a larger value than women (Malasanos, Barkauskas, Stoltenberg-Allen, 1990).

Palpation is used to assess the shape, position, mobility, size, consistency, and tension of the organs in the abdomen. In the older client, the loss of connective tissue and muscle wasting may cause the abdominal wall to be thinner, allowing simpler and more accurate palpation of the abdomen (Malasanos, Barkauskas, Stoltenberg-Allen, 1990). The abdomen should be explored in all four quadrants with both light and deep palpation, but beginning with light palpation. In light palpation, the fingers are used to depress the abdominal wall approximately 1 cm. Moderate palpation is done with the side of the hand and is useful in assessing the liver and spleen. Deep palpation is done by pressing the distal half of the palmar surfaces of the fingers into the abdominal wall and may be done bimanually with the dominant hand placed lower (Malasanos, Barkauskas, Stoltenberg-Allen, 1990).

An enlarged tender gallbladder, indicative of cholecystitis, may be palpated below the liver margin. In addition, Murphy's sign is also useful in determining cholecystitis. During deep palpation, the examiner asks the client to take a deep breath. As the descending liver brings the gallbladder into contact with the examiner's hand, the older client with cholecystitis experiences pain and stops the normal inspiratory movement, indicating a positive Murphy's sign (Malasanos, Barkauskas, Stoltenberg-Allen, 1990).

The pancreas is not palpable; however, a mass, if present, may be felt as a vague sensation of fullness in the epigastrium by the older client (Malasanos, Barkauskas, Stoltenberg-Allen, 1990).

The presence of feces in the bowel is often palpable and may produce a sensation of a soft, boggy, round mass. In addition, a full bladder is sometimes mistaken for a mass and may be felt as a round, smooth, and tender mass (Malasanos, Barkauskas, Stoltenberg-Allen, 1990).

Completing the assessment of the GI system is assessment of the anus and rectum. This is best done with the older client in the left lateral position, with the knee flexed up to the chest. In examination of that part of the body, inspection is done first, looking for hemorrhoids, fissures, inflammation, or other lesions. The client is asked to bear down, as though defecating, so that rectal prolapse or internal hemorrhoids may be visualized (Malasanos, Barkauskas, Stoltenberg-Allen, 1990).

This is followed by palpation, which is conducted with the pad of the gloved, lubricated index finger. The examiner's finger is placed gently on the anus, and then pressure is applied until the sphincter relaxes, then the finger is inserted slowly. The older client should then be asked to tighten the sphincter around the examiner's finger, which will provide a measurement of muscle tone of the anal sphincter. The mucosa of the anal canal is then palpated for the presence of polyps or tumor. In men, the prostate gland can also be palpated at this time through the mucosa of the anterior wall of the rectum. On withdrawing the finger, the nurse should note the nature of the feces. A guaiac or hemacult test should be performed by wiping the gloved finger onto the appropriate paper slide (Malasanos, Barkauskas, Stoltenberg-Allen, 1990).

Laboratory tests may include blood tests such as a chemistry profile, CBC, amylase, lipase, liver enzymes, and stool studies. Other tests include biopsies, gastric analysis, and others, which are conducted during endoscopic procedures. In addition, radiologic tests and procedures are often necessary in any diagnostic GI workup (see Box 25-2, p. 654).

HOME CARE TIPS

1. Regularly monitor and assess the diagnosed GI disease or disorder for signs and symptoms indicating exacerbation or instability.
2. Weigh at regular intervals to assess nutritional status and absorption ability of the GI tract in the homebound older adult.
3. Teach the caregiver and homebound older adult appropriate dental hygiene practices.
4. Instruct the caregiver and homebound older adult on reportable signs and symptoms related any GI problem or disorder, and when to report these symptoms to the home care nurse or physician.
5. Instruct the caregiver and homebound older adult on the name, dose, frequency, side effects, and indications of both prescribed and OTC medications being used to treat the identified GI problem.
7. Instruct the caregiver and homebound older adult about laboratory indices used to evaluate GI disturbances. Inform them of the results of any tests *after* physician has been notified.
8. Assess and instruct on importance of maintaining hydration in the presence of GI disturbance.
9. Instruct the caregiver and homebound older adult on all aspects of any treatments used to provide nutritional support in the absence of a functioning GI system (e.g., enteral nutrition, total parenteral nutrition, formula supplements, etc.)

Summary

GI system-related symptoms and complaints are common with advancing age, and the nurse often is the first health care provider to identify and to acknowledge these. Therefore knowledge of normal, age-related changes in the GI system and appropriate management methods are essential. Since many of the older adult's concerns with this system are age-related and thus amenable to appropriate self-care practices, the nurse has the responsibility for teaching prevention and self-management strategies to the older adult with these concerns. However, the nurse must also teach the older adult that GI-related symptoms should not be dismissed as part of the normal aging process but should be reported, so an appropriate determination can be made.

Key Points

- A decline in the normal function in the GI tract may occur with aging, without an effect on physiologic processes.
- Any weight loss or complaint of dysphagia, indigestion, heartburn, vomiting, change in appetite, or change in stool in the older client warrants prompt evaluation by the health care provider.
- Primary and secondary prevention of problems in the GI tract should be part of the care for all older clients.
- Smoking, alcohol, and dietary factors are important risk factors for the development of GI cancers in the older client.
- Gastric ulcers have a higher incidence of becoming malignant in comparison with duodenal ulcers.
- Current research suggests that a bacteria may be a causal factor in the development of peptic ulcer disease, and perhaps even gastric cancer.
- Although treatment of asymptomatic gallstones is not currently recommended, the rise in new therapeutic treatment options for cholecystitis should lead to a decline in morbidity and mortality previously associated with cholecystectomies in older adults.
- While the incidence of pancreatic cancer is increasing in the United States, treatment remains palliative.
- Intestinal ischemia should be included in the differential diagnosis of the older client with a history of cardiovascular disease who complains of abdominal pain.
- A guaiac-positive stool in the older adult should be considered pathologic until proven otherwise.
- Intestinal polyps and a positive family history of polyps are the largest risk factors for the development of colorectal cancer.
- Although 60% of polyps and cancers are visualized with the flexible sigmoidoscopy; a colonoscopy is necessary to detect any suspected cancers in the right colon.

Critical Thinking Exercises

1. Your client, a 67-year-old male, has smoked at least a pack of cigarettes per day for the past 49 years. At present he is being treated for gastric ulcers. What relationship, if any, exists between his age, smoking history, and gastrointestinal disorder?
2. Explain the relationship between CVD and intestinal ischemia in the older adult.
3. Your 85-year-old grandfather confides in you that he recently has had bright red blood in his stools, but thinks it is because of hemorrhoids. He is reluctant to see his doctor because he does not want to go into the hospital. What advice should you give him? Why are bloody stools of particular importance in the older adult?

REFERENCES

Aliberti LC: Managing esophageal achalasia: medical and nursing implications, *Gastroenterol Nurs* 16(3):126-132, 1993.

Altman DF: Changes in gastrointestinal, pancreatic, biliary, and hepatic function with aging, *Gastroenterol Clin North Am* 19(2):227-233, 1990.

Berk JE: Anorexia; gaseousness. In Berk JE, Haubrich WS, editors: *Gastrointestinal symptoms: clinical interpretation,* Philadelphia, 1991, BC Decker.

Billings DM, Stokes LG: *Medical-surgical nursing: common health problems of adults and children across the lifespan,* ed 2, St. Louis, 1987, Mosby.

Birchenall JM, Streight ME: *Care of the older adult,* ed 3, Philadelphia, 1993, JB Lippincott.

Blake RL: Acute pancreatitis, *Prim Care,* 15(1):187-199, 1988.

Boarini J: Gastrointestinal cancer: colon, rectum, and anus. In Groenwald SL et al, editors: *Cancer nursing: principles and practice,* ed 2, Boston, 1990, Jones and Bartlett.

Bradley L et al: The relationship between stress and symptoms of gastroesophageal reflux: the influence of pyschological factors, *Am J Gastroenterol* 88(1):11-19, 1993.

Burrell LO, editor: *Adult nursing in hospital and community settings,* Norwalk, Conn., 1992, Appleton & Lange.

Cassmeyer VL, Blevins DB: The patient with biliary and pancreatic problems. In Long BC, Phipps WJ, Cassmeyer VL, editors: *Medical-surgical nursing: a nursing process approach,* ed 3, St. Louis, 1993, Mosby.

Collins A, Bullock BL: Normal functions of the gastrointestinal system, alterations in gastrointestinal function, and normal hepatobiliary and pancreatic exocrine function. In Bullock BL, Rosendahl PP, editors: *Pathophysiology: adaptations and alterations in function,* ed 3, Philadelphia, 1992, JB Lippincott.

Cox HC et al: *Clinical applications of nursing diagnosis,* Baltimore, 1989, Williams & Wilkins.

Dudley SL, Starin RB: Cholelithiasis: diagnosis and current therapeutic options, *Nurse Pract* 16(3):12-16, 1991.

Dworken HJ: *Gastroenterology: pathophysiology and clinical applications,* Boston, 1982, Butterworth.

Eastwood GL, Avunduk C: *Manual of gastroenterology: diagnosis and therapy,* Boston, 1988, Little, Brown.

Frogge MH: Gastrointestinal cancer: esophagus, stomach, liver, and pancreas. In Groenwald SL et al, editors: *Cancer nursing: principles and practice,* ed 2, Boston, 1990, Jones and Bartlett.

Galindo-Ciocon DJ: Tube feeding: complications among the elderly, *J Gerontol Nurs* 19(6):17-21, 1993.

Gioiella EC, Bevil CW: *Nursing care of the aging client: promoting healthy adaptation,* Norwalk, Conn., 1985, Appleton-Century-Crofts.

Guyton AC: *Textbook of medical physiology,* ed 8, Philadelphia, 1991, WB Saunders Co.

Haubrich WS: Abdominal pain, nausea and vomiting. In Berk JE, Haubrich WS, editors: *Gastrointestinal symptoms: clinical interpretation,* Philadelphia, 1991, BC Decker.

Heaman D: Normal and altered functions of the pancreas. In Bullock BL, Rosendahl PP, editors: *Pathophysiology: adaptations and alterations in function,* ed 3, Philadelphia, 1992, JB Lippincott.

Heitkemper M, Carnevali D: Gastrointestinal problems. In Carnevali DJ, Patrick M, editors: *Nursing management for the elderly,* ed 3, Philadelphia, 1993, JB Lippincott.

Hogstel MO: *Nursing care of the older adult,* ed 3, Albany, NY, 1994, Delmar.

Hood GH, Dincher JR: *Total patient care: foundations and practice of adult health history,* ed 8, St. Louis, 1992, Mosby.

Linton A: Gastrointestinal system. In Burggraf V, Stanley M, editors: *Nursing the elderly: a care plan approach,* Philadelphia, 1989, JB Lippincott.

Long BC, Roberts R: The patient with gastrointestinal problems. In Long BC, Phipps WJ, Cassmeyer VL, editors: *Medical-surgical nursing: a nursing process approach,* ed 3, St. Louis, 1993, Mosby.

McHardy GG, Haubrich WS, Berk JE: Diarrhea. In Berk JE, Haubrich WS, editors: *Gastrointestinal symptoms: clinical interpretations,* Philadelphia, 1991, BC Decker, Inc.

Malasanos L, Barkauskas V, Stoltenberg-Allen K: *Health assessment,* ed 4, St. Louis, 1990, Mosby.

Margiotta SJ, Willis IH, Wallack MK: Cholecystectomy in the elderly, *Am J Surg* 54(1):34-39, 1988.

Martyn-Nemeth P, Fitzgerald K: Clinical considerations: tube feeding in the elderly, *J Gerontol Nurs* 18(2):30-36, 1992.

Metheny N et al: Effectiveness of pH measurements in predicting feeding tube placement: an update, *Nurs Res* 42(6):324-331, 1993.

Miller C: *Nursing care of older adults: theory and practice,* Glenview, Ill., 1990, Scott, Foresman.

Murphy ME: Colorectal cancer. In Otto SE, editor: *Oncology nursing,* St. Louis, 1991, Mosby-Year Book.

O'Toole M editor: *Miller-Keane encyclopedia and dictionary of medicine, nursing, and allied health,* ed 5, Philadelphia, 1992, WB Saunders.

Parzuchowski J: Head and neck cancers. In Otto SE, editor: *Oncol Nurs,* St Louis, 1991, Mosby.

Ruby PS: Constipation; diarrhea; fecal incontinence; rectal bleeding. In Loftis PA, Glover TL, editors: *Decision making in gerontologic nursing,* St. Louis, 1993, Mosby.

Sandler RS, Maule WF, Baltus M: Factors associated with post operative complications in diabetics after biliary tract surgery, *Gastroenterol* 91(1):157-162A, 1986.

Saunderlin G: Esophageal achalasia, *Gastroenterol Nurs* 15(5):191-196, 1993.

Savas KM, Zeroske J: Nonresectable esophageal cancer, *Gastroenterol Nurs* 15(3):98-103, 1993.

Schoenfield L: Gallstones, *Clin Symp* 40(2):2-4, 1988.

Silverberg E, Lubera JA: Cancer statistics, *Cancer* 39(1):3-20, 1989.

Sinkinson CA, editor: How to diagnose mesenteric ischemia before it's too late, *Emerg Med Rep* 10(20):159-167, 1989.

Smoller J, Smoller BR: Skin malignancies in the elderly: diagnosable, treatable, and potentially curable, *J Gerontol Nurs* 18(5):19-23, 1992.

Sodeman W: Bowel habit. In Sodeman WA, Saladin TA, Boyd WP editors: *Geriatric gastroenterology,* Philadelphia, 1989, WB Saunders.

Storer R: The gastrointestinal system. In Brocklehurst JC, editor: *Textbook of geriatric medicine and gerontology,* Edinburgh, 1985, Churchill Livingstone.

Sugarbaker PH, Gunderson LL, Wittes RE: Colorectal cancer. In DeVita VT, Hellman S, Rosenberg SA, editors: *Cancer: principles and practice in oncology,* Philadelphia, 1985, JB Lippincott.

Triadafilopoulos G et al: Medical treatment of esophageal achalasia: double blind crossover study with oral nifedipine, verapamil, and placebo, *Dig Dis Sci* 36(3):260-267, 1991.

Vines SW et al: Research utilization: an evaluation of the research related to causes of diarrhea in tube-fed patients, *Appl Nurs Res* 5(4):164-173, 1992.

Wald A: Constipation and fecal incontinence in the elderly, *Gastrointest Clin North Am* 19(2):405-418, 1990.

Wick SB: Flatulence. In Loftis PA, Glover TL, editors: *Decision making in gerontologic nursing,* St. Louis, 1993, Mosby.

BIBLIOGRAPHY

Beverley L, Travis I: Constipation: proposed natural laxative mixtures, *J Gerontol Nurs* 18(10):5-12, 1992.

Gerlach MJM: Disorders of the stomach. In Burrell LO editor: *Adult nursing in hospital and community settings,* Norwalk, Conn., 1992, Appleton & Lange.

Hunter GC, Guernsey JM: Mesenteric ischemia, *Med Clin North Am* 72(5):1091-1115, 1988.

CHAPTER 26

Urinary Function

LEARNING OBJECTIVES

On completion of this chapter, the reader will be able to:

1. Describe how aging affects normal bladder function.
2. List four possible causes of acute incontinence.
3. List the types of persistent incontinence and their clinical characteristics.
4. List the components of the continence history.
5. Discuss the role of the functional and environmental assessment in the evaluation of urinary incontinence (UI).
6. Discuss how the nurse can use tests of provocation in making a nursing diagnosis in clients with UI.
7. Describe the behavioral interventions used to treat UI incontinence in cognitively intact clients.
8. Develop a client teaching plan for a client with urge incontinence.
9. Develop a caregiver teaching plan for a client with functional UI resulting from dementia.
10. Describe the effects of normal aging on renal function.
11. Identify the possible causes of acute and chronic renal failure.
12. Develop a nursing care plan for the client with renal failure.
13. Develop a nursing care plan for the client with a urinary tract infection.
14. Identify the treatment options for clients with bladder cancer.
15. List supportive services for the individual who has undergone a cystectomy.
16. Differentiate between benign prostatic hypertrophy and cancer of the prostate.
17. Develop a nursing care plan for the individual with benign prostatic hypertrophy.
18. Identify the treatment options for clients with prostate cancer.
19. Develop a nursing care plan for the individual with prostate cancer.

Urinary incontinence (UI), the involuntary loss of urine, is one of the most common health problems affecting older adults. It is a major clinical problem and a significant cause of disability and dependency. Physical health, psychologic well-being, social functioning, and health care costs can be adversely affected by incontinence. Individuals with UI are at increased risk for urinary tract infection, skin problems (e.g., rash, infections, and breakdown), and falls. Incontinence can cause psychologic distress and social isolation. It is a cause of caregiver burden and may be a factor in the decision to place older individuals in long-term care facilities. Economically, the cost of UI is staggering. In the community, more than $10 billion per year are spent on direct costs related to UI (Hu, 1990). Unfortunately, less than 0.5% of this money is spent on the evaluation and treatment of this problem. This is true despite the fact that in the majority of cases, incontinence can be cured or significantly improved through effective medical and nursing interventions (National Institutes of Health Consensus Development Conference, 1990).

NORMAL STRUCTURE AND FUNCTION OF THE LOWER URINARY TRACT

Continence is dependent on normal functioning of the lower urinary tract, along with adequate cognitive and physical functioning and an appropriate environment (Ouslander, 1990). The lower urinary tract allows storage of sufficient quantities of urine at low pressures and then, at an appropriate time and place, voluntary emptying of the bladder completely. The structures of the lower urinary tract are the bladder, urethra, and the periurethral striated muscle (the pubococcygeal muscle or **pelvic floor muscle**) (Fig. 26-1). The smooth muscle of the bladder wall (the detrusor muscle) normally relaxes during bladder filling and contracts to empty the bladder. Two sphincters, the internal and external sphincters, help maintain continence. The internal sphincter consists of smooth muscle in the bladder neck and proximal urethra. It is controlled by the autonomic (involuntary) nervous system. The external sphincter is formed by striated fibers of the pubococcygeal muscle of the pelvic floor and is controlled by the somatic (voluntary) nervous system.

Micturition, a complex process, is not completely understood (Ouslander, 1992). The most basic level of control is at the sacral micturition center. Urination is most easily understood as two relative discrete phases—one of bladder filling and urine storage and the other of bladder emptying. During filling, information on bladder volume is transmitted to the spinal cord. It, in turn, adjusts motor output. Sympathetic tone increases, relaxing the dome of the bladder and closing the internal sphincter. Parasympathetic tone decreases, inhibiting bladder contraction. At the same time, somatic innervation maintains tone in the external sphincter. During emptying, parasympathetic tone increases and sympathetic and somatic tone decrease. As a result, the bladder contracts and the sphincters relax.

Although the basic level of control is at the sacral spinal cord, lower urinary tract function is also influenced by higher centers, including the brainstem and the cerebral cortex. Although the neurophysiology of

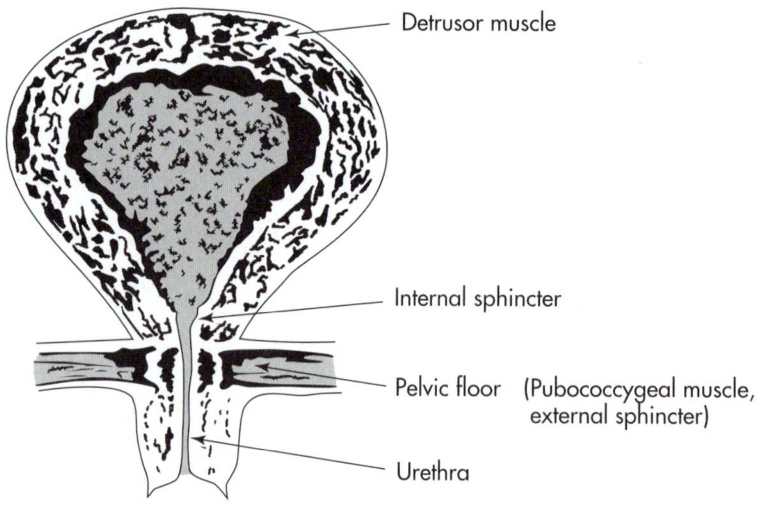

Fig. 26-1 The urinary bladder. (From Burke MM, Walsh MB: *Gerontologic nursing care of the frail elderly;* St. Louis, 1992, Mosby.)

micturition is not completely understood, it appears that the cerebral cortex exerts a predominately inhibitory influence, while the brainstem facilitates urination (Ouslander, 1990). Loss of cerebral cortex inhibitory influence over the lower urinary tract can occur in conditions such as dementia and strokes. As a result, the client may develop UI.

AGE-RELATED CHANGES IN STRUCTURE AND FUNCTION

Despite the beliefs of many older adults, and unfortunately, some health care providers, aging alone does not cause urinary incontinence. Aging does, however, affect the lower urinary tract. These age-related changes increase the older adult's susceptibility to other insults to the lower urinary tract. As a result, these insults (e.g., drug side effects, urinary tract infections, or conditions impairing mobility) are more likely to produce incontinence in an older client than in a younger one.

With age, bladder capacity decreases, the prevalence of involuntary bladder contractions increases, and more urine is produced at night. The reduction in bladder capacity and increase in involuntary bladder contractions can lead to urgency and frequency. Many older adults find that they have to empty their bladders more often than they did when they were younger. The increased urine formation at night leads to **nocturia.** Nocturia is very common with close to 70% of community-dwelling older adults getting up once per night to empty their bladders and 25% getting up twice (Ouslander, 1992).

In older women, age-related decreases in estrogen can affect the urethra (Brocklehurst, 1986; McDowell, Burgio, 1992; Ouslander, 1992). Thinning and increased friability of the urethral mucosa can contribute to urgency and frequency. A decrease in muscle tone and bulk can decrease urethral resistance.

Although not considered a normal change of aging, as men get older the prevalence of prostatic hypertrophy increases. Enlargement of the prostate can interfere with bladder emptying and can also precipitate involuntary bladder contractions.

Prevalence of UI

As many as one in three older adults living in the community have some degree of UI (Ouslander, 1992). Of these, one in four or five have severe incontinence (National Institutes of Health Consensus Development Conference, 1990). It is twice as prevalent among women as among men. Among homebound individuals, prevalence rates as high as 53% have been reported (Ouslander, 1992). UI is even more common among nursing home residents. At least half of the 1.5 million Americans in nursing homes suffer from urinary incontinence (National Institutes of Health Consensus Development Conference, 1990). It is estimated that 20% to 35% of older adults in acute care settings are incontinent (Ouslander, 1992).

Myths and Attitudes

Fewer than one half of the 10 million Americans with UI have had the problem evaluated or treated (National Institutes of Health Consensus Development Conference, 1990). Many people never report the problem to health care providers. This may be because of embarrassment or because they believe that it is not important enough to mention or that it cannot be treated.

In a number of research studies, investigators examined older adults' beliefs about UI and the reasons they had not sought treatment for this problem. In these studies, many participants thought that their incontinence was caused by aging (Gjorup et al, 1987; Goldstein et al, 1992; Jeter, Wagner, 1990; Jolleys, 1988; Mitteness, 1987). Women may also attribute their incontinence to being female (Brink, 1987; Goldstein et al, 1992; Jeter, Wagner, 1990; Jolleys, 1988). These beliefs may lead the older client, particularly older women, to think that incontinence is normal and not worth reporting to health care providers. Famous women advertising incontinent products without mentioning possible treatments helps to perpetuate this myth (McDowell, Burgio, 1990).

Although there is little systematic information about health care professionals' knowledge and attitudes about UI incontinence, there is evidence to suggest that many do not see incontinence as a treatable problem (Goldstein et al, 1992; Mitteness, 1990; National Institutes of Health Consensus Development Conference, 1990). Many health care providers do not ask clients about incontinence. Even when clients inform them about incontinence, many providers ignore the problem and do not provide adequate diagnosis and treatment.

COMMON PROBLEMS AND CONDITIONS

Acute Incontinence

UI is generally classified as either acute (transient) or chronic (persistent). **Acute incontinence** has a sudden onset, is generally associated with some medical or surgical condition, and generally resolves when the underlying cause is corrected (Ouslander, 1990) (Box 26-1). Medications are a common cause and should always be suspected as a potential cause of new incontinence.

Although the exact prevalence of acute incontinence is not known, any new onset of incontinence should be considered acute and possible precipitating causes should be ruled out. Addressing the cause has the potential to resolve the incontinence.

BOX 26-1

Causes of Acute UI

Restricted mobility
Fecal impaction
Delirium
Urinary tract infections

Endocrine disorders
Poorly controlled diabetes mellitus (DM)
Hypercalcemia

Medications
Anticholinergic medications
Beta-adrenergic medications
Alpha-adrenergic blockers
Alpha-adrenergic agonists
Calcium channel blockers
Diuretics
Psychotropics
Narcotics
Alcohol

Chronic Incontinence

Persistent incontinence is not related to an acute illness. It continues over time, often becoming worse. Major types of persistent incontinence include stress, urge, overflow, and functional incontinence (National Institutes of Health Consensus Development Conference, 1990). These types of incontinence can occur in combination, causing mixed incontinence. This is quite common in the geriatric population (Ouslander, 1992).

Stress Incontinence

Stress incontinence is commonly seen in older women. In this type of incontinence, involuntary loss of urine occurs as the result of a sudden increase in intraabdominal pressure. Stress incontinence is usually associated with weakening of the supporting tissues surrounding the bladder neck and urethra (Ouslander, 1992). This damage can be the result of pregnancy, vaginal deliveries, trauma during gynecologic or urologic surgery, obesity, or chronic coughing (McDowell, Burgio, 1992; Ouslander, 1992). Individuals with stress incontinence often leak urine with physical exertion such as coughing, sneezing, laughing, lifting, and exercise. Older women may report leaking when they change position, such as getting out of a chair, or if they lift a small child. These activities increase intraabdominal pressure, which increases bladder pressure. If the urethra, supporting tissues surrounding it, and bladder neck are abnormal, urethral resistance may be too low to withstand the increased pressure on the bladder, and involuntary urine loss occurs. Stress incontinence is uncommon in men, but can occur as a result of injury to the sphincters during prostate surgery or radiation therapy (Ouslander, 1992).

Urge Incontinence

Urge incontinence is also common in the older adult population. It is usually, but not always, associated with detrusor instability or hyperreflexia (Ouslander, 1990). The bladder escapes normal cerebral inhibition and contracts spontaneously (McDowell, Burgio, 1992). Common causes of urge incontinence include local genitourinary conditions such as cystitis, urethritis, tumors, stones, and diverticula, as well as central nervous system disorders such as strokes, dementia, and Parkinson's diseases (Ouslander, 1990). Individuals with urge incontinence typically give a history of involuntary urine loss following a sudden urge to void. Urgency and involuntary urine loss can be precipitated by the sound of running water, cold weather, or the sight of a toilet. Urinary accidents are sometimes large. A common scenario is that of arriving home, putting the key in the door, having a sudden urge to void, and leaking urine before reaching the bathroom (McDowell, Burgio, Candib, 1989). Urge incontinence is often accompanied by nocturia and complaints of frequency.

Overflow Incontinence

Overflow incontinence accounts for less than 10% of the incontinence seen in older adult clients (Ouslander, 1992). It occurs when a chronically full bladder increases bladder pressure to a level higher than urethral resistance, causing the involuntary loss of urine. Based on the history alone, overflow incontinence may be difficult to differentiate from stress or urge incontinence. Typically, individuals with overflow incontinence complain of the frequent loss of small volumes of urine. They may have both daytime and nighttime accidents. Additional complaints may include always being wet, frequency, a weak urine stream, hesitancy (difficulty starting to pass urine), interrupted voiding and/or a feeling of incomplete emptying (McDowell, Burgio, Candib, 1989). Overflow incontinence can occur as a result of an atonic bladder that does not contract adequately to empty (e.g., diabetic neuropathy, side effect of anticholinergic medications, or spinal cord injury); a mechanical obstruction to bladder emptying (e.g., prostatic hypertrophy, a large cystocele, or fecal impaction); or **dyssynergia,** a condition in which the sphincters contract during bladder contraction, preventing the bladder from emptying (e.g., multiple sclerosis) (McDowell, Burgio, 1992; Ouslander, 1992).

Functional Incontinence

In **functional incontinence,** involuntary urine loss occurs as a result of inability or unwillingness to toilet ap-

MEDICAL MANAGEMENT

UI

Diagnostic tests and procedures

The purpose of the diagnostic evaluation in urinary incontinence is threefold (Ouslander, 1992):

1. To identify potentially reversible factors that may be contributing to the incontinence
2. To identify clients who need more than the basic evaluation
3. To determine the type of incontinence so that appropriate treatment can be initiated

The basic evaluation for UI includes a history, physical examination, postvoid residual, urinalysis, and bladder diaries. This evaluation is indicated for all clients with incontinence and is often sufficient to diagnose the type of incontinence and to guide therapy (US Department of Health and Human Services, 1992).

Measure of postvoid residual (PVR) is recommended for all clients with UI. The client is asked to void and then PVR is measured either by catheterization or by pelvic ultrasound. A PVR over 100 ml may indicate inadequate bladder emptying.

A clean urine specimen should be collected for urinalysis as part of the basic evaluation for incontinence. It allows the clinician to detect associated or contributing problems such as hematuria, pyuria, bacteriuria, glycosuria, and proteinuria. It is often difficult to obtain a clean urine specimen from older incontinent women. For this reason, an in-and-out (straight) catheterization is often performed to obtain the specimen. In older incontinent men who have difficulty voiding spontaneously (e.g., the client with dementia), an adequate specimen can be obtained if the penis is cleansed with aseptic solution, and a clean condom catheter and collection bag are applied (Ouslander, 1992). The first voided specimen should be obtained and processed immediately. If there is a delay in processing a urine specimen, it should be refrigerated.

Additional diagnostic tests may be indicated if the diagnosis is unclear after the initial evaluation, if the findings on initial evaluation reveal select abnormalities (e.g., hematuria, pyruia, proteinuria, or glycosuria), or if the initial therapy is not successful. These tests include the following:

1. Additional laboratory tests to rule out contributing causes (urine culture, blood urea nitrogen, creatinine, serum calcium, blood glucose, and/or urine cytology)
2. Urodynamic tests to evaluate the anatomic and functional status of the lower urinary tract
3. Urethral pressure tests to measure resting and dynamic pressures in the urethra
4. Cystoscopy to provide direct visualization of the bladder and urethra
5. Imaging tests of the upper and/or lower urinary tract (US Department of Health and Human Services, 1992).

Treatment

Pharmacologic therapy

Although many cases of UI respond well to behavioral interventions and they are generally considered the safest initial therapy (National Institutes of Health Consensus Development Conference, 1990), in some cases pharmacologic treatment is indicated. The type of medications used depends on the type of incontinence. Drugs with anticholinergic or bladder smooth muscle relaxant properties can be used to treat urge incontinence. These include oxybutynin, propantheline, dicyclomine, flavoxate, and imipramine. All of these drugs can produce bothersome anticholinergic side effects (e.g., dry mouth and constipation) and can precipitate urinary retention in some clients (Ouslander, 1992).

Drugs that increase urethral resistance are sometimes used in the treatment of stress incontinence. The class of drugs used most often are the alpha-adrenergic agonists such as pseudoephedrine. Research findings on the effectiveness of these drugs are mixed with some studies reporting good results and some reporting only modest benefits (Wein, 1990). When drug therapy does work in stress incontinence, it may take months to realize the optimum benefits. Clients should be told not to expect a rapid, dramatic improvement in symptoms (Ouslander, 1992).

Although a cholinergic agonist (e.g., bethanechol) is sometimes used to stimulate bladder contraction or an alpha-adrenergic antagonist (e.g., prazosin) is sometimes used to relax the sphincter, drug therapy is usually of limited benefit in treating overflow incontinence. These drugs are generally used only for short-term therapy or in cases where other therapy such as surgery is contraindicated.

Surgical treatment

Surgical treatment is indicated when lower urinary tract pathology such as a bladder tumor, stone, or urethral diverticulum is contributing to incontinence. It is also indicated when an anatomic obstruction such as prostatic hypertrophy is causing UI (Ouslander, 1992).

Surgery is also used for some women with stress incontinence. Surgery may be considered in older women who have persistent stress incontinence after an adequate trial of nonsurgical therapy and for those with pelvic prolapse (Ouslander, 1992).

Prognosis

The majority of cases of incontinence can be cured or significantly improved with careful evaluation to identify treatable factors contributing to the incontinence, followed by implementation of appropriate medical and nursing interventions. Evaluation of the success of any efforts to restore urinary incontinence should be based on the older person's satisfaction and tolerance of the interventions and/or strategies to achieve the outcome.

propriately. It can be the result of physical, mental, psychologic, or environmental factors (McDowell, Burgio, 1992). Clients with physical disabilities affecting gait may have difficulty reaching the bathroom in a timely manner. Clients with cognitive impairment may not recognize their need to void or may have difficulty finding the toilet and preparing to void. Those with psychologic problems such as severe depression may lack the motivation to toilet appropriately. Environmental factors may play a role in causing incontinence, especially in acute and long-term care settings. Clients who are confined to beds or are restrained are dependent on caregiver assistance to the toilet. If that assistance is not available in a timely manner, the client is often incontinent. This is especially true if the client also has urgency. Functional incontinence should be a diagnosis of exclusion. Just because clients have dementia, are depressed, or have mobility problems does not necessarily mean they have functional incontinence. Careful evaluation often identifies treatable factors contributing to the incontinence (Ouslander, 1992) (see Medical Management box, p. 697).

NURSING MANAGEMENT

ASSESSMENT

The purpose of the nursing assessment in UI is to determine the type of incontinence and the factors contributing to it so that appropriate nursing interventions can be planned and implemented. In addition, the nursing assessment allows the nurse to identify those clients who need to be referred to a physician or advanced practice nurse for more complete evaluation. The assessment consists of a history, physical examination, functional assessment, environmental assessment, psychosocial assessment, and the evaluation of bladder habits.

History

During the history, information is collected about the client's UI and bladder habits; general health and functional status; medical problems; current medications; and past medical, surgical, and obstetric history. If clients are able to provide the history, they are the most accurate source of data. In situations such as cognitive impairment, however, the nurse may have to rely on secondary sources such as family caregivers or past medical records.

During the incontinence history, it is necessary to collect the following information:

1. The onset and clinical course of the incontinence
2. The frequency and volume of accidents
3. The circumstances that cause urine loss; ask clients specifically about leaking urine when they cough, sneeze, laugh, change positions, climb steps, exercise, have an urge to void, hear running water, are cold, and are sleeping. Also ask if caffeine, alcohol, or any medications cause involuntary urine loss. Ask if the client leaks urine without being aware that it occurred, has any postvoid dribbling, or leaks continuously.
4. Bladder habits including the frequency and volume of day and nighttime urination
5. Daily fluid intake
6. Self-management techniques the client uses to manage the incontinence (e.g., frequent voiding, restricting the volume or type of fluid, incontinent products, or urine collection devices)
7. Previous evaluation and treatment of the incontinence, including the client's perception of the effectiveness of previous treatment measures
8. Any other urinary tract symptoms, including urgency, burning, pain, hematuria, weakness of the urinary stream, intermittent stream, and difficulty emptying the bladder completely
9. Bowel habits, including constipation, laxative use, and fecal incontinence

Insight • *Most cases of urinary incontinence can be diagnosed and treated without urodynamic testing (Rose et al, 1990).*

In addition to the incontinence history, the nurse should also obtain a general health history. Inquire about current medical problems. Ask specifically about problems that can affect bladder function, including diabetes, congestive heart failure (CHF), bladder and kidney infections, strokes, Parkinson's disease, depression, memory problems, mobility problems, problems with coordination, and other neurologic problems or injuries. Ask about current medications and treatments, including the use of over-the-counter (OTC) medications. Inquire about previous surgeries, asking specifically about past urologic or gynecologic surgery. In men, ask specifically about prostate surgery and radiation. In women, obtain an obstetric history, including information about the number of pregnancies, type of deliveries, any complications during delivery, and birth weights of the infants. For postmenopausal women, inquire about estrogen replacement therapy.

Functional Assessment

Because function problems often contribute to urinary incontinence, the functional assessment is one of the most important parts of the evaluation. Information should be collected about the client's ability to perform normal physical activities of daily living (ADLs), including grooming, dressing, getting in and out of bed, and ambulating. Clients who have difficulties performing these ADLs often have difficulty toileting. Functional status can be assessed by unstructured questioning or by using a structured questionnaire such as the Older Americans Research and Service Center Instrument (OARS) (Duke University Center for the Study of Aging and Human Development, 1978) or the Katz Index of ADLs (Katz et al, 1963) (see Chapter 4).

Direct observation provides the most valuable information about the client's mobility and toileting ability. The following observational guide can be used in practice:

1. Place the client 15 feet from the toilet.
2. Ask the client to walk or propel the wheelchair to the toilet and to prepare and position for voiding.
3. Note how long it takes the client to reach the toilet and any difficulty getting undressed or positioning for voiding.
4. If the client is unable to toilet independently and a caregiver normally assists the client, observe the toileting procedure with the caregiver assisting.

Mental status should be assessed during the functional assessment. Cognitive ability can affect the client's ability to recognize the need to urinate, locate the toilet, and undress for toileting. In addition, knowledge of the client's cognitive status is essential in planning nursing interventions for incontinence. The most efficient way to assess cognitive status is to use a standardized instrument such as the Folstein Mini-Mental State Examination (Folstein, Folstein, McHugh, 1975) (see Chapter 4).

Environmental Assessment

Environmental barriers can contribute to UI. For example, the bathroom may be too far away or inaccessible to the client, the toilet may be too low or it may be difficult for the client to get on and off of it. The client may need human assistance in toileting and that may not be readily available. For these reasons, environmental assessment is an important component of the evaluation of urinary incontinence. It is necessary to note the following:

1. The distance to reach the toilet
2. Any barriers between the client's usual location and the toilet such as poor lighting, furniture or other objects; in the home, steps may present a barrier to toileting.
3. The size of the bathroom—is it large enough to accommodate the client and any assistive devices (wheelchair or walker) that must be used?
4. The toilet height—is it adequate?
5. The presence or absence of grab bars
6. The availability of caregiver or nursing staff assistance if needed to toilet
7. The availability of a call bell if needed

Psychosocial Assessment

Psychosocial assessment focuses on the impact of incontinence on the client's life and on the availability and quality of caregiver assistance in situations where it is needed. Ask the client how incontinence has affected social activities (e.g., visiting family and friends and attending social functions and church), self-esteem, mood, sexual activity, and family relationships. Also assess the client's desire and willingness to participate in a treatment program for incontinence. Effective nursing interventions for UI require active client involvement so motivation is an essential component in success. If the client does not want treatment for incontinence, the reasons should be explored. Is it, for example, a lack of knowledge, depression, or overwhelming physical, social, or psychologic problems?

If the client is dependent on another person to assist in toileting, caregiver assessment is an essential component of the psychosocial assessment. Is the caregiver (1) physically able to assist the client, (2) available on a consistent basis, and (3) willing to assist the client? What is the caregiver's attitude toward the client and toward incontinence? Does the caregiver have an adequate understanding of the problem and its management?

Physical Examination

The physical examination should include the following:

1. Inspection of gait and balance
2. Neurologic assessment to detect any weakness, paralysis, or sensory deficits in the lower extremities; these can affect the client's ability to toilet.
3. Abdominal examination to determine the presence or absence of bladder distention, suprapubic tenderness (seen in bladder infections), and costovertebral angle tenderness (seen in kidney infections)
4. Rectal examination to assess for fecal impaction; rectal sensation and tone; and, in men, the size, shape, and consistency of the prostate gland
5. Sitting and standing blood pressure to detect orthostatic hypotension and dizziness
6. A pelvic examination, including inspection of the vagina for the presence of atrophic changes, vaginitis, cystocele, rectocele, or uterine prolapse, any of which can contribute to urinary incontinence

Tests of Provocation

Additional useful information can often be gained by performing simple tests of provocation while the client has

NAME: ______________________________ DATE:

Instructions:

1. In the 1st column, mark the time every time you void.
2. In the 2nd or 3rd column, mark every time you accidently leaked urine.
3. In the 4th column, enter the event that caused the accident, or the circumstances of the accident.

URINATED IN TOILET	SMALL ACCIDENT	LARGE ACCIDENT	REASON FOR ACCIDENT

No. of Pads Used Today: __________ No. of Accidents: __________

Comments: ____

____

Fig. 26-2 Bladder diary. (Courtesy Benedum Geriatric Continence Program, Pittsburgh, Penn.)

a full bladder. The physician or advanced practice nurse generally performs these during urodynamic testing. They can, however, also be performed if the client has a full bladder from drinking fluids. A number of useful tests are listed below. During each maneuver, the nurse should observe for involuntary urine loss either by direct observation or by checking a previously applied dry absorbent pad. If the client leaks urine during any of the maneuvers, ask the client to try to stop the flow of urine. This allows the nurse to make some evaluation of pelvic floor muscle strength:

1. Ask the client to cough three or four times in a supine position.
2. Ask the client to stand; note any involuntary urine loss during the position change.
3. Ask the client to cough three or four times while standing.
4. If the client's physical condition permits, ask to bounce on heels three or four times.
5. Have the client listen to running water.
6. Ask the client to walk to the bathroom.
7. Have the client wash hands.

The first three and the sixth maneuvers are stress provocations, whereas the fifth and seventh are urge provocations.

Bladder Habits

One of the most effective ways to assess bladder habits is to ask the client or caregiver to keep a diary of the client's bladder habits, including the frequency of urination and any incontinent episodes, their relative volume, and the circumstances that precipitated their occurrence (e.g., coughing, sneezing, urgency, changing position, etc.). Fig. 26-2 shows a sample bladder diary used by the authors.

Bladder diaries can be used in the home, hospital, or nursing home and can be kept by the client or caregiver. They provide a more objective and accurate measure of the client's bladder habits than can be obtained by recall alone. If they are to be accurate, however, client's and caregivers need careful instructions on their completion.

Collecting bladder diaries during assessment helps to establish the type of UI and aids in planning nursing interventions. During treatment, diaries allow the nurse to assess progress and evaluate the effectiveness of interventions.

✣ DIAGNOSIS

The data collected during assessment along with the nurse's knowledge of UI will permit diagnosis of the type of incontinence the client is experiencing in most cases. There are times, however, when a more complex evaluation is needed to determine the cause of and most appropriate treatment for UI. In any new case of incontinence, acute and potentially reversible causes should be ruled out or treated. If acute incontinence is ruled out or treated and involuntary urine loss continues, a diagnosis of persistent or chronic incontinence must be considered.

The following nursing diagnoses are appropriate in clients with persistent incontinence:

1. Incontinence, stress
2. Incontinence, urge
3. Incontinence, overflow
4. Incontinence, functional
5. Incontinence, mixed

Incontinence, Stress

History Client reports leaking urine with activities that increase intraabdominal pressure (e.g., coughing, sneezing, laughing, lifting, position changes, walking, climbing steps, and/or exercise).

Objective observations Leaking urine with stress provocation; signs of pelvic floor relaxation (e.g., cystocele, rectocele, or uterine prolapse) may be observed on pelvic examination.

Bladder records Documentation of urine loss during physical activities that increase intraabdominal pressure.

Incontinence, Urge

History Client reports a sudden urge to void followed by involuntary urine loss; may also report that running water or cold weather precipitate involuntary urine loss.

Objective observations Leaking urine with urge provocation.

Bladder records Documentation of urine loss associated with urgency; urinary frequency and nocturia are also often documented.

Incontinence, Overflow

History The history is variable, but often reports frequent involuntary urine loss of small amounts. Urine loss may be associated with physical exertion. Other complaints may include decreased force of the urine stream, hesitancy, a feeling of incomplete bladder emptying, and/or frequent urination of small amounts of urine. Clients may also have risk factors for urinary retention such as diabetes or the use of anticholinergic medications.

Objective observations An elevated PVR (> 100 ml) is the hallmark of overflow incontinence. This should be part of the initial evaluation of clients with urinary incontinence. On abdominal examination, a distended bladder may be detected on percussion or palpation. In cases where overflow incontinence is related to prostatic hypertrophy, an enlarged prostate can be detected on rectal examination. In women, a large cystocele observed during pelvic examination may suggest the cause of overflow incontinence.

Bladder records Documentation of frequent small volume urinary accidents.

Incontinence, Functional

History Client or caregiver reports large volume urine loss in places other than the toilet, commode, bedpan, or urinal in the absence of symptoms of stress, urge, or overflow incontinence. The client may be unaware of the need to void or have significant mobility impairment.

Objective observations In pure functional incontinence, there is no leaking with stress or urge provocation and normal PVR. Mental status examination may reveal cognitive impairment. Functional assessment may reveal impaired mobility and toileting skills.

Bladder records Documentation of involuntary urine loss (often large accidents) without symptoms of urge or stress incontinence.

Incontinence, Mixed

Mixed incontinence indicates that the client has some combination of stress, urge, overflow, and/or functional incontinence. Among community-dwelling older adults, mixed urge and stress incontinence is very common. In clients with dementia or severe mobility problems, mixed urge and functional incontinence is common. In mixed incontinence, the history, objective observations, and bladder record findings vary depending on the types of incontinence present.

✣ PLANNING

Stress Incontinence

The long-term goal is that the client will reduce or will eliminate the number of stress accidents. Short-term goals include the following:

1. The client will master behavioral interventions (e.g., pelvic floor muscle exercises and stress strategies) designed to decrease the number of stress accidents.
2. The client will recognize the factors that precipitate stress accidents and will use the interventions to prevent accidents.

Urge Incontinence

The long-term goal is that the client will reduce or eliminate urge accidents. Short-term goals include:

1. The client will master the behavioral interventions designed to decrease urge accidents (e.g. pelvic floor muscle exercises, urge strategies, and bladder retraining).
2. The client will recognize those factors that precipitate urge accidents and use the interventions to prevent the accidents.

Overflow Incontinence

The long-term goal is that the client reduce or eliminate incontinence due to urinary retention and overflow. Short-term goals will vary with the underlying mechanism responsible for the incontinence but might include the following:

1. The client will seek urologic evaluation of the incontinence.
2. If the client has an acontractile bladder, client will master in-and-out self-catheterization.

Functional Incontinence

The long-term goal is that with caregiver assistance, the client will reduce or eliminate urinary accidents. Short-term goals might include the following:

1. The caregiver will master and implement behavioral interventions designed to reduce the number of urinary accidents.
2. The caregiver will remove environmental barriers to proper toileting.

✣ INTERVENTION

Nursing interventions for UI focus on **behavioral therapies.** The effectiveness of these interventions has been demonstrated in a number of research studies (Burgio et al, 1988; Burgio, Whitehead, Engel, 1985; Fantl et al, 1990, Smith et al, 1989). In 1988 the National Institutes of Health (NIH) held a consensus conference to review the current status of knowledge on UI. They stated, "As a general rule, the least invasive or dangerous procedures should be tried first. For many forms of incontinence, behavioral techniques meet this criterion" (National Institutes of Health Consensus Development Conference, 1990). Despite the effectiveness of these techniques, many nurses are not skilled at implementing them. The most appropriate behavioral intervention depends on the type of incontinence and the client's cognitive status.

> ***Insight* • *Behavior therapies are the only treatment for incontinence that do not have side effects. They are the initial treatment of choice for many forms of incontinence.***

Cognitively Intact

Two behavioral interventions useful in cognitively intact individuals are bladder retraining and pelvic floor muscle exercises. These interventions may be used alone or in combination, depending on the type of incontinence.

Bladder retraining In bladder retraining, the client is encouraged to adopt a gradually expanding voiding schedule. It is useful in correcting the habit of frequent toileting and in diminishing urgency. Clients are asked to postpone voiding until the scheduled time, voiding by the clock rather than each time they get an urge (McDowell, Burgio, 1992). This procedure is most useful for clients with urge incontinence and frequent urination. See the Research box below for the findings of a research study designed to examine the effectiveness of bladder retraining.

Pelvic floor muscle exercises Pelvic floor muscle exercises were first reported as a treatment for urinary incontinence by Kegel (1948). These exercises consist of alternating contraction and relaxation of the muscles of the pelvic floor. The muscles, including the pubococcygeal muscle surrounding the midportion of the urethra, contract as a unit. In older adults these muscles are often weakened from disuse atrophy. Many researchers have shown that diminished pelvic floor muscle strength is related to urinary incontinence (Walters, 1993). Correctly performed, pelvic floor muscle exercises strengthen the muscles, increasing urethral resistance and allowing the client to voluntarily use the muscles to prevent urinary accidents.

RESEARCH

Fantl JA et al: Efficacy of bladder training in older women with urinary incontinence, *JAMA* 265(5):609-613, 1991.

Sample, setting

The subjects included 123 cognitively intact, community-dwelling women age 55 to 90 with at least one episode of urinary incontinence per week.

Methodology

Participants were randomly assigned to the treatment or control group. Treatment subjects underwent a 6-week bladder-retraining protocol. Bladder diaries were used to assess the number of episodes of urinary incontinence pre- and posttreatment for both groups. The Incontinence Impact Questionnaire was used to assess quality of life.

Findings

The number of incontinent episodes decreased from 21 per week at baseline to 9 per week posttreatment for the treated group ($P < 0.0001$). Of the women, 12% had no incontinence episodes posttreatment, whereas 75% had a 50% or greater reduction in accidents. There was also a significant improvement in the quality of life for these participants ($P = 0.001$).

Implications

Bladder retraining can be an effective treatment for older women with urinary incontinence.

Insight • *Pelvic floor muscle exercises are potentially very effective in treating urinary incontinence. However, these exercises are often taught incorrectly.*

Clinicians often use verbal feedback during digital examination of the rectum or vagina to help clients identify their pelvic floor muscles. The nurse inserts two fingers into the vagina or one into the rectum and asks the client to contract the pelvic floor muscles. The client is given verbal feedback regarding the correctness of the procedure (McDowell, Burgio, 1992). Approximately one third of clients are correctly able to identify and to contract their pelvic floor muscles on digital examination. These clients can be given an exercise regimen to follow and often improve their pelvic floor muscle function with little or no additional intervention (Benzl, 1992). The majority of older clients, however, need additional help in identifying and learning to use their pelvic floor muscles. These clients often benefit from pelvic floor muscle biofeedback.

Biofeedback is not a treatment in itself, but if appropriately used, it can facilitate acquisition of the ability to contract and to use the pelvic floor muscles to prevent involuntary urine loss (Burgio, 1992). During biofeedback, the client is given immediate auditory and/or visual feedback of pelvic floor muscle contractions. By using this technique, the cognitively intact, motivated client can learn bladder inhibition and sphincter contraction by observing the results of attempts to control bladder and sphincter responses voluntarily (Burgio, Burgio, 1986).

A variety of techniques, including vaginal probes, rectal probes, and surface electromyographies (EMGs), have been used to provide biofeedback. Simultaneous feedback of pelvic floor and abdominal activity can assist the client in learning to selectively contract the pelvic floor muscles while keeping the abdominal muscles relaxed (McDowell, Burgio, 1992). The Research box on p. 704 summarizes the findings of a research study designed to examine the effectiveness of biofeedback-assisted pelvic floor muscle exercises in a sample of older adults.

After training with biofeedback or verbal feedback,

RESEARCH

McDowell BJ et al: An interdisciplinary approach to the assessment and behavioral treatment of urinary incontinence in geriatric outpatients, *JAGS*, 40:370-374, 1992.

Sample, setting

The sample included 29 community-dwelling older adults without dementia who were self- or physician-referred to the Continence Program of the University of Pittsburgh's Benedum Geriatric Center. Many had multiple medical problems (mean = 6.0). Individuals reporting stress and/or urge urinary incontinence for 3 months or longer were included in the study.

Methodology

During the study, 28 participants underwent biofeedback-assisted pelvic floor muscle training, while one was instructed with verbal feedback based on vaginal palpation. Treatment included home practice. Those voiding more than 8 times during their waking hours were also treated with bladder retraining to achieve a voiding schedule of every 3 hours.

Findings

Subjects recorded a mean of 16.9 accidents per week before treatment and 2.5 accidents per week posttreatment ($P < 0.01$). Individual reductions ranged from 30.8% to 100%. Ten clients had no accidents after treatment.

Implications

Older adults who are able and willing to participate in behavioral interventions for incontinence can benefit significantly even in the face of other health problems and disabilities.

the client must practice the pelvic floor muscle exercises at home. The client should be instructed to practice contracting and relaxing the pelvic floor muscles at least 45 times per day. The exercises should be done in three or four practice sessions per day. The client is asked to exercise lying down, sitting, and standing. This facilitates the client's ability to identify and use the muscles in any position. Remind the client to relax the abdominal muscles when exercising. You can ask clients to practice slowing or stopping the urine stream while voiding. This allows them to monitor their progress in using the correct muscles and in strengthening them (Box 26-2).

Once clients master the exercises, they should be taught strategies to prevent involuntary urine loss (stress and/or urge strategies). Clients with stress accidents should be instructed to contract their pelvic floor muscles before and during activities that precipitate leaking such as coughing, sneezing, lifting, or changing position.

BOX 26-2

Pelvic Floor Muscle Exercise Instructions

1. Do 45 pelvic floor muscle exercises *every* day.
2. Do the exercises in 3 sets: 15 at a time, 3 times a day.
   Do 15 lying down in the morning.
   Do 15 standing up in the afternoon.
   Do 15 sitting in the evening.
3. For each exercise:
   Squeeze for ____ seconds
   Relax for _____ seconds
4. Remember to *relax* all the muscles in abdomen and continue to breath normally when doing these exercises.

BOX 26-3

Urge Strategies

When client has an urge to void, instruct to:

- Stop and relax.
- Squeeze pelvic floor muscles 3 or 4 times quickly; do not hold.
- Wait for the urge to pass then walk slowly to the bathroom during the calm period.

Those with urge incontinence can be taught to contract their pelvic floor muscles to inhibit involuntary bladder contractions. The client is told to respond to an urge to void by relaxing and contracting the pelvic floor muscles three to four times quickly. When the urgency subsides, the client should walk to the toilet at a normal pace (Box 26-3).

Cognitively Impaired

The techniques described previously (bladder retraining, pelvic floor muscle exercises, and biofeedback) require active client involvement. Treating UI in individuals with cognitive impairment requires the use of other behavioral techniques that are caregiver-dependent rather than client-dependent. These include scheduled toileting, patterned urge response therapy, and prompted voiding. The success of these techniques is in large part dependent on the availability and motivation of the caregiver. They have been tested most often in long-term settings and researchers often report problems with consistent implementation of the treatment. For these behavioral techniques to be successful, nursing leadership must be committed to reducing the prevalence and severity of UI (McDowell, Burgio, 1992).

Scheduled toileting In scheduled toileting, the client is toileted on a regular, preset schedule. Family or

BOX 26-4

Prompted Voiding Instructions

- Approach the client at the scheduled times and ask if feeling wet or dry.
- Check to see if the client is wet or dry.
- If the client correctly identified present continent status, give positive feedback.
- Ask the client if it is preferable to use the toilet.
- If the response is yes, toilet the client; if it is no, encourage the client. *Never* force the client to toilet.
- Give positive feedback for appropriate toileting; do not give any negative feedback.

professional caregivers simply take the client to the toilet at the scheduled times, often every 2 hours.

Patterned urge response training Patterned urge response training (PURT) (Colling et al, 1992a) uses an individualized toileting schedule based on an intense baseline assessment of the client's normal voiding pattern. Once the client's normal voiding pattern is established, the client is toileted at these times. In her research on PURT, Colling used continuous electronic monitoring of voiding frequency to establish the precise voiding pattern of each subject (Colling et al, 1992b).

Prompted voiding Although still a caregiver-dependent therapy, in prompted voiding, there is more active client involvement. The goal is to increase client awareness of the need to toilet and, hopefully, to increase the frequency of self-initiated toileting. Clients are approached on a regular schedule, asked if wet or dry, and then prompted to toilet (Box 26-4). The client should never be forced to toilet or be reprimanded for failing to toilet appropriately. Do not discourage self-initiated toileting. Individuals who recognize the need to void and can do so successfully when given toileting assistance are probably the best candidates for prompted voiding (Schnelle, 1990).

It is not clear that the benefits of regularly toileting cognitively impaired individuals during the night outweigh the disruption that it causes in their sleep (Ouslander, 1992). Until further data are available, toileting protocols can be modified during the nighttime hours.

Other Nursing Interventions

Individuals with UI may decrease fluid intake as a way of trying to prevent accidents. This is not an effective method of managing incontinence. Adequate fluid intake is very important, especially for older adults who already have a decrease in total body water and are at increased risk for dehydration. In addition, inadequate fluid intake contributes to constipation, another problem commonly seen in the older adult population. Educate clients and caregivers about the importance of adequate fluid intake.

BOX 26-5

Management Suggestions for Nocturia

- Restrict fluids after dinner. It is important to drink enough fluids (usually 6 to 8 glasses per day), but drink the bulk of fluids during the day.
- Eliminate caffeine in the evening (i.e., caffeinated coffee, tea, cola beverages, and chocolate).
- Elevate legs in the afternoon so feet and ankles are not swollen when going to bed.

Insight • *Restricting oral fluids is not an effective method for decreasing UI.*

Individuals with incontinence, particularly those with urge accidents, should be advised to eliminate or to restrict their caffeine intake. This includes coffee, tea, caffeinated colas, and chocolate. In England, researchers found that caffeine increased detrusor irritability in a sample of women with detrusor instability (Creighton, 1990).

Some older adults, even those who are continent, complain of frequent nocturia that disrupts their sleep. Getting up once at night is probably a normal effect of aging. For clients who get up more often and feel that the quality of their sleep is disrupted, there are some measures that may be helpful. One is restricting fluid intake in the evening. Although it is important for the client to have adequate fluid intake, individuals with frequent nocturia should drink the bulk of this fluid before dinner. Also advise these individuals to eliminate caffeine in the evening. Going to bed with swollen ankles and feet increases nocturia. Clients with such swelling should be advised to elevate their legs for several hours during the afternoon to limit the amount of edema present at bedtime (Box 26-5).

Frail older adults are at increased risk for constipation and fecal impactions, which can cause acute incontinence and exacerbate persistent incontinence. Nurses should assess bowel habits regularly and institute preventive measures such as increased fiber intake, adequate fluids, and increased activity levels. UI increases the risk of skin rashes, infections, and breakdown. Changing incontinent pads often and scrupulous skin care provide the best protection against these complications.

For short-term use in conjunction with other treatment measures, pads or garments provide convenience and comfort. They are, however, expensive for long-term use and can be associated with skin rashes and breakdown if not changed often. They should not be used as a substitute for the evaluation and treatment of incontinence.

For men, external collection devices may be less expensive and time consuming than incontinent pads or garments. They are, however, associated with a number of complications including skin breakdown, urethral diverticula, and ischemic disease resulting from penile constriction (Warren, 1990). Practical external collection devices are generally not available for women.

If external collection devices are used, proper preparation of the skin is essential (Dickerson, 1990). The penis should be thoroughly washed and dried. It may be necessary to clip excessive hair from around the penile shaft. Apply an adhesive-enhancing skin preparation to the penile shaft, and allow it to dry before condom application. Self-adhesive condom catheters, although more expensive than regular condom catheters, eliminate the need for adhesive tape. Squeeze the penis gently with the condom in place until it adheres securely to the penis. If a regular condom catheter is used, apply two-sided tape around the shaft of the penis in a spiral fashion. Slowly unroll the condom catheter over the tape. Squeeze the penis gently until the condom adheres to the tape. For a more secure fit, apply a second strip of tape (again in a spiral fashion) on top of the condom. Always use stretchable adhesive tape. Never use plain adhesive, silk, or paper tape. The use of nonstretchable tape can result in tissue ischemia. The condom catheter should be removed daily, and the penis should be inspected for irritation or skin breakdown (US Department of Health and Human Services, 1992; Warren, 1986). The skin should be washed and dried before reapplication. If there is any evidence of trauma or infection, the condom should not be reapplied.

Individuals with overflow incontinence should be referred to a urologist to correct treatable causes. If the cause of incomplete bladder emptying is not correctable, measures such as crede maneuvers may help to empty the bladder. This can be done by telling the client to apply pressure over the suprapubic area to express additional urine after voiding has stopped (McDowell, Burgio, 1992). If this is ineffective in emptying the bladder, the treatment of choice is often intermittent in-and-out catheterization. This treatment has not been widely used in older adults and needs additional research to determine its safety and effectiveness (McDowell, Burgio, 1992).

Indwelling catheters (urethral or suprapubic) may be necessary for select clients with incontinence, but usage almost always results in bacteriuria (National Institutes of Health Consensus Development Conference, 1990). Because of the high risk of associated bladder infections and urinary sepsis, indwelling catheters should only be used to treat incontinence in very select circumstances (Ouslander, 1992) (Box 26-6).

BOX 26-6

Indications for the Use of Indwelling Catheters

- Urinary retention that cannot be corrected medically or surgically, cannot be managed practically by intermittent catheterization, *and* is causing persistent overflow incontinence, symptomatic urinary tract infections, and/or renal dysfunction
- Pressure sores or skin lesions that are being contaminated by incontinent urine
- To provide comfort for terminally ill or severely impaired clients

✣ EVALUATION

Evaluation is an integral and ongoing component of the management of UI. The client goals are the focal point for evaluation. The client's perception of the effectiveness of treatment and satisfaction with it should be assessed and documented. A variable number of older adults with incontinence may require more than one treatment modality to achieve a satisfactory reduction in incontinent episodes. As a result, the plan of care often evolves over time (see nursing Care Plans, pp. 707-708).

NORMAL RENAL STRUCTURE AND FUNCTION

The kidneys are paired organs located in the retroperitoneal space, level with the twelfth thoracic and the first through third lumbar vertebrae. Each kidney is about the size of a fist and weighs a quarter of a pound. The kidney is made up of two distinct areas—the cortex and the medulla. The cortex consists mainly of the nephrons, glomeruli, and the proximal and distal tubules. The medulla consists of the collecting ducts, loops of Henle, and vasta recta. The renal cortex is wrapped around the medulla; between each medullary papilla, the cortex thrusts deeply into the kidney and forms the columns Bertin. These columns form papillary tips and drain into branches of the collecting system, which then drain into the renal pelvis, and later empty into the ureter where active peristalsis carries the urine into the bladder for ex-

CARE PLAN

FUNCTIONAL INCONTINENCE

Clinical situation Mr. W is a 76-year-old retired steel worker who is to be discharged from the hospital following treatment for pneumonia. He will be going home in 2 days and has been referred to the visiting nursing agency for follow up care. Mr. W was diagnosed with dementia 4 years ago. He lives with his wife who is also his caregiver. They have 2 grown children who are supportive and one granddaughter who often stays with him when Mrs. W needs to go out. In addition to his dementia, Mr. W also has glaucoma. He is blind in his left eye and has markedly impaired vision in the right eye. He fractured his right hip 1 year ago. He walks with a cane and his gait is slow and unsteady. He fell and fractured his left shoulder 2 years ago. It healed, and he has fairly normal range of motion in that shoulder. During his hospitalization, he developed a pressure ulcer on his coccyx. It is healing and is now a stage 1 lesion. He has a moderate amount of ankle edema. His current medications include Timoptic eye drops, moisture barrier cream to his coccyx QID, and a multivitamin QD. Mr. W is able to get in and out of bed by himself but requires assistance with all other ADLs. He has been incontinent of urine for 3 years. According to Mrs. W, he generally knows that he needs to void but leaks urine before he gets to the bathroom. Mr. W wears incontinence undergarments. He also has enuresis and is usually wet in the morning. At home, he goes to bed at 9:30 PM and gets up about 7:30 AM. Mrs. W finds it very difficult to manage her husband's incontinence and states that it has increased the burden of caring for him.

Nursing diagnosis	Outcomes	Interventions
Incontinence, functional	Mrs. W will master behavioral therapies designed to treat incontinence in individuals with cognitive impairment. Mr. W will experience a decrease in the number of incontinent episodes.	Collect baseline bladder diaries to establish the frequency of urinary accidents and what precipitates them. Assess Mrs. W's willingness to participate in a behavioral program to treat her husband's incontinence. Teach Mrs. W how to implement a prompted voiding program. Assess her understanding by having her conduct a return demonstration of the technique. Visit weekly to assess implementation and success of the program. Have Mrs. W keep bladder diaries during treatment. Assess Mr. W's daily fluid intake. If daily fluid intake is less than 6 to 8 glasses of fluid per day, instruct Mrs. W to increase his fluid intake. Instruct her to restrict his fluids in the evening, providing the bulk of his fluids during the day. Instruct Mrs. W to restrict his caffeine intake with no caffeine in the evening. Tell Mrs. W to toilet him late in the evening, around 11:30 PM, and early in the AM, around 6:30 AM. Instruct Mrs. W to have Mr. W elevate his legs in the afternoon to reduce the amount of edema.

CARE PLAN

URINARY INCONTINENCE, MIXED

Clinical situation Mrs. N is a 71-year-old retired retailer whom the nurse is seeing following hospital discharge for the treatment of a diabetic foot ulcer. The nurse sees her two times per week to change the dressing and to assess wound healing. Mrs. N's medical problems include noninsulin-dependent diabetes mellitus (NIDDM) for 20 years, complicated by peripheral neuropathy. She also has coronary artery disease (CAD) with two myocardial infarctions (MIs) in the past, hypertension, hiatal hernia, diverticulitis, and osteoarthritis. She has had both hips replaced. She walks with a cane, and her gait is slow and sometimes unsteady. Her current medications include NPH insulin, ibuprofen, Cardizem CD, Dyazide, nitroglycerine, and oxybutynin. Her OTC medications include vitamins A, D, and E, Metamucil, and TUMS. She needs assistance with personal grooming and bathing.

She has had problems with constipation, but finds that daily Metamucil keeps her regular. Mrs. N has been incontinent for 5 years. She describes both stress and urge accidents and states that she has about 14 accidents per week. She denies nocturia. She drinks 3 to 4 cups of regular coffee or tea a day and drinks a considerable amount of ice tea in the summer. She has seen a urologist who put her on oxybutynin, which she has been taking for 2 years. Although it somewhat decreased her accidents, she does not think that it is very effective. She finds the incontinence disturbing and wishes that there was something more that she could do to treat it.

Nursing diagnosis	Outcomes	Interventions
Urinary incontinence, mixed	Mrs. N will master behavior techniques designed to treat mixed urge and stress incontinence. Mrs. N will experience a decrease in the number of urinary accidents.	Ask Mrs. N to keep baseline bladder diaries before treatment. Teach Mrs. N pelvic floor muscle exercises using verbal feedback of pelvic floor muscle contractions during rectal examination. Provide written instructions for practicing the exercises. Ask her to continue to keep bladder diaries during treatment. Review the diaries and assess her progress during weekly visits. Once she has mastered the exercises, teach urge and then stress strategies if indicated by the diaries. If Mrs. N is unable to identify her pelvic floor muscles using verbal feedback or is not making adequate progress, refer her to the continence nurse specialist for biofeedback. Advise Mrs. N to substitute decaffeinated coffee and tea for the regular coffee and tea she now drinks.

cretion. Renal function is dependent on a generous blood flow to the kidneys. Blood reaches the kidneys through the renal arteries. One fifth of the total cardiac output perfuses the kidney each minute (Brundage, 1992) (Fig. 26-3).

The renal system performs the following vital functions necessary for sustaining life: (1) filtration and elimination of waste products, (2) regulation of blood formulation and red blood cell production, (3) regulation of blood pressure, and (4) control of the body's chemical and fluid balance. This system is the regulator of the volume and composition of body fluids, selectively conserving fluids and electrolytes in times of shortage and excreting in times of oversupply (Smith, 1987).

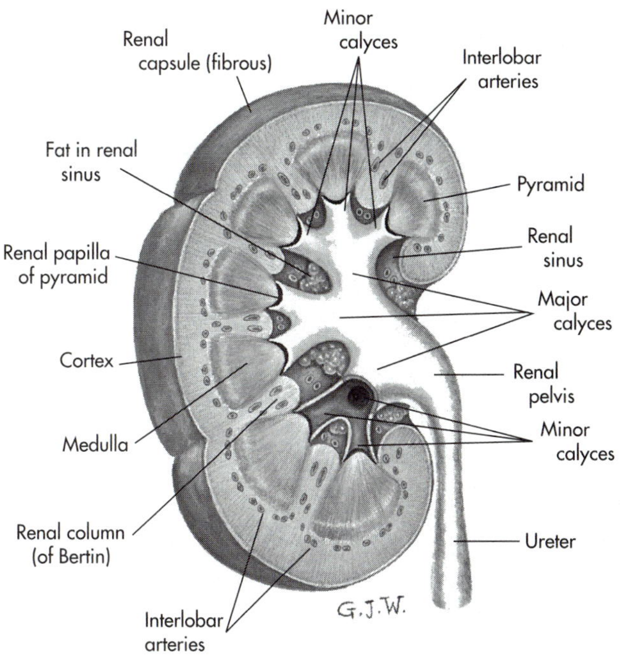

Fig. 26-3 Cross-section of the kidney showing basic structures. (From Brundage DJ: *Renal disorders,* St. Louis, 1992, Mosby.)

AGE-RELATED RENAL CHANGES

Age-related changes in renal function are the most dramatic of any human organ or system. In normal young adults, renal capacity far exceeds the ordinary demands. In the older adult, renal function, although diminished, still provides adequate regulation of body fluids under normal circumstances (Fillit, Rowe, 1992).

Age-induced changes in the kidneys are a reduction in weight and size, a decrease in the number of nephrons, increased interstitial tissue, a decrease in number of glomeruli, and a thickening of the glomerular and tubular membranes (Fillit, Rowe, 1992).

The physiologic changes within the kidney are a decrease in renal blood flow and a decline in glomerular filtration rate. These two changes are associated with an age-related decrease in cardiac output, renal mass, and filtration area. Vascular changes that occur with normal aging result in a decreased blood flow to the kidneys because of an increased tortuosity of blood vessels and tapering of blood vessel diameter (Rowe, 1986). Renal blood flow declines approximately 10% during each decade of life after young adulthood. By the ninth decade of life, the renal plasma flow is approximately 50% of its value in a 30-year-old person (Smith, 1987). The glomerular filtration rate decreases at an annual rate of approximately 0.8 ml/min/1.73 m^2. This decrease is observed in a decline in the creatinine clearance measurement. In longitudinal studies, creatinine clearance rates decreased from 140 ml/min/1.73 m^2 at age 25 to 34, to 97 ml/min/1.73 m^2 at age 75 to 84 (Rowe et al, 1976). Despite the decrease in creatinine clearance, serum creatinine remains stable, which is a result of a decreased muscle mass that maintains serum creatinine levels (Meyer, 1989).

With a decline in the glomerular filtration rate there are associated changes in tubular function. The development of diverticula and a decrease in the glomerular basement area results in a decline in the tubular's capacity to reabsorb and to excrete necessary electrolytes and waste. With these changes, an older adult has a diminished ability to filter, to concentrate, and to dilute urine in response to water, salt, excess, or diminished fluid (Lindeman, Tobin, Shock, 1985).

The net effect of these normal aging changes in the kidney is a decrease in the adaptive capacity of the kidneys. Under normal conditions, the aged kidney is able to effectively maintain fluid, electrolyte, and acid-base hemostasis. However, under the presence of stress, illness, changes in sodium and water intake, or administration of medications, the aged kidney is less likely to respond effectively to maintain homeostasis.

It has been shown that with decreased filtration rates, there is a prolonged half-life of medications primarily excreted through the kidney. Medications affected by decreases in glomerular filtration rates include digoxin, aminoglycoside antibiotics, tetracycline, vancomycin, chlorpropamide, procainamide, cimetidine, cephalosporin antibiotics, and nonsteroidal antiinflammatory drugs (NSAIDs) (Brundage, 1992).

NORMAL PROSTATE STRUCTURE AND FUNCTION

The prostate is a glandular, fibromuscular gland located just below the bladder, surrounding the male urethra (Fig. 26-4). In the normal adult male it weighs about 20 gm and is roughly the size and shape of a chestnut. There are four major areas of the prostate gland: (1) the peripheral zone, (2) the central zone, (3) the transition zone, and (4) the periureteral zone. The prostate is separated from the rectum by a layer of connective tissue, and its posterior surface is easily palpable on digital rectal examination. It normally feels smooth, symmetric, and somewhat rubbery (Freed, 1986).

Tubuloalveolar glands in the prostate secrete a colorless fluid containing enzymes, citric acid, spermine, potassium, calcium, and zinc into the urethra. The prostate gland is also perforated by the ejaculatory ducts that carry sperm and seminal vesicle secretions into the proximal urethra (Walsh, 1985).

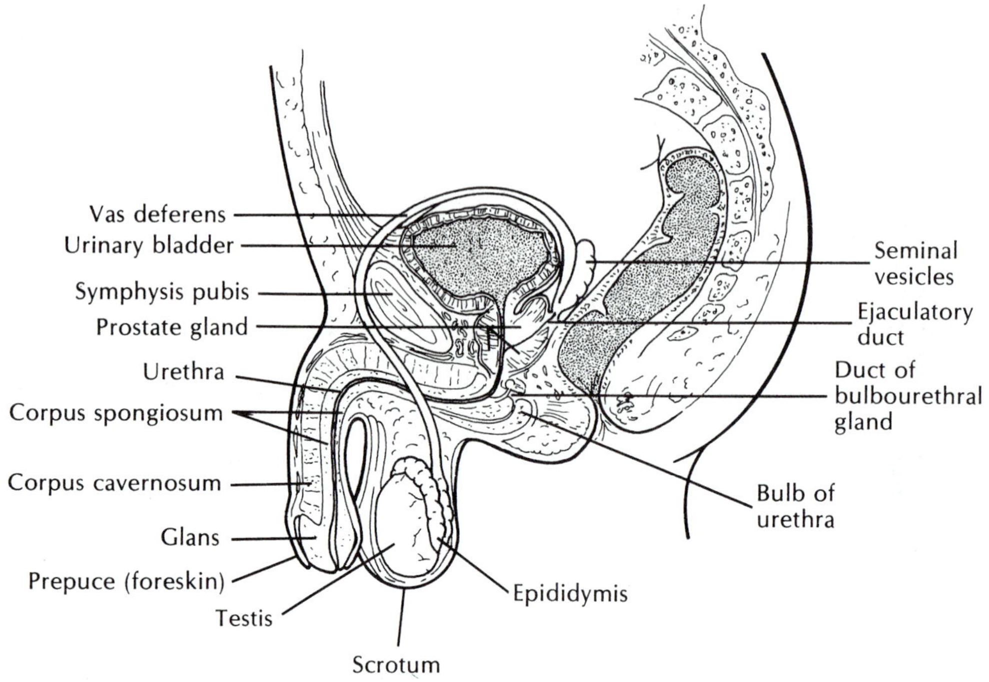

Fig. 26-4 Male pelvic organs. (From Anthony C, Thibodeau G: *Textbook of anatomy and physiology,* ed 12, St. Louis, 1987, Mosby.)

Age-Related Prostate Changes

The growth of the prostate gland is controlled by the testicular androgens, testosterone, dihydrotestosterone, and endogenous estrogens. The prostate gland enlarges slowly until puberty when rapid growth occurs. This rapid growth continues until the middle or the third decade of life. After age 45, the prostate gland and surrounding tissue undergo hyperplasia (Freed, 1986).

COMMON PROBLEMS AND CONDITIONS

Renal Diseases

Symptomatology of renal disease in older adults has not been clearly defined. Most older adults with renal insufficiencies may experience vague symptoms such as a decreased urine output, nausea, vomiting, and weakness. Most of the time, renal insufficiency is detected by laboratory evaluation (Fillit, Rowe, 1992).

The primary renal diseases occurring in older adults are those seen in younger adult clients. Moorthy and Zimmerman (1980) reviewed the diagnoses of 115 renal biopsy clients over age 60. Biopsies were performed for unexplained renal insufficiency, nephrotic syndrome, and hematuria. They found that 78 had primary glomerular disease, 27 had systemic disease with renal involvement, and 10 had renal disease from other causes, which included medication nephrotoxicity (Fillit, Rowe, 1992).

BOX 26-7

Causative Factors of ARF

Prerenal
Hemorrhage
Severe gastrointestinal (GI) losses
Burns
Renal trauma
Volume depletion
CHF
Hypoxia

Intrarenal (renal)
Thrombus
Stenosis
Hypertensive sclerosis
Glomerulonephritis
Pyelonephritis
Acute tubular necrosis
Diabetic sclerosis
Toxic damage

Postrenal
Obstructions (stenosis, calculi)
Prostatic disease
Tumors

From Brundage DJ: *Renal disorders,* St. Louis, 1992, Mosby.

Renal failure is not a normal consequence of aging. Renal failure is the inability of the kidneys to filter and excrete substances produced within the body. It is classified as either acute or chronic renal failure.

Acute Renal Failure

Acute renal failure (ARF) is the sudden and usually temporary decrease in glomerular filtration rate which results in the diminished ability of the kidney to filter and excrete metabolites (Talbott, 1992). Causes of acute renal failure may be described as prerenal, intrarenal, and postrenal. Prerenal causes are those that occur as a result of inadequate perfusion of a normal kidney. Intrarenal causes are those that develop related to intrinsic abnormalities within the kidney. Postrenal causes involve obstruction of the urinary tract, which results in a decreased flow of urine from the kidney (Brundage, 1992) (Box 26-7).

Acute renal failure can be divided into five stages: (1) onset: usually a short time from precipitating event to onset of **oliguria** and **anuria**; (2) **oliguria**-anuria stage: the period during which urinary output is less than 400 ml per 24 hours, with a duration of 8 to 15 days; (3) early diuretic stage: extends from the time daily output is greater than 400 ml per 24 hours to the time blood urea nitrogen (BUN) stops rising; (4) late diuretic stage: first day the BUN is stable; (5) convalescent stage: extends

CLIENT/FAMILY TEACHING

CRF

Your kidneys perform crucial functions that affect all parts of your body. Your kidneys, in fact, keep the rest of your body in balance and working properly. When chronic renal (kidney) disease causes the kidneys to fail, your whole body stops functioning correctly, and you can become extremely ill unless the condition is treated.

How do the kidneys function?

The kidneys are located at the bottom of the rib cage, one on each side of the spine. Each is about the size of a fist and contains about a million functioning units, called nephrons. The nephrons' job is to cleanse the blood of toxic wastes and excess fluid and to add needed chemicals such as hormones and vitamins. The cleansed blood is then returned to the bloodstream. About 200 quarts of fluid are filtered through the kidneys every 24 hours. Of this fluid, 2 quarts are eliminated as urine and the rest is retained in the body.

The kidneys are responsible for regulating the body's salt, potassium, and acid content. They also control the production of red blood cells and regulate blood pressure.

What causes chronic renal disease?

There are several different types and causes of chronic renal disease. *Glomerulonephritis,* which can arise from a number of immune disorders, is an inflammation of the kidney and can damage the nephrons. *High blood pressure,* whether a result of a kidney disorder or a cause of kidney disease, can hasten kidney failure. *Diabetes mellitus* may cause kidney disease. *Polycystic kidney disease* is an inherited disorder in which cysts form on kidney tissue and eventually destroy the healthy kidney tissue. *Congenital anomalies* can cause obstructions, which can lead to infection and destruction of kidney tissue. *Interstitial nephritis,* usually caused by drug use, is an inflammation of kidney tissue and leads to eventual destruction of the kidney. *Nephrotic syndrome* can occur with a variety of kidney problems, including glomerulonephritis, diabetes, and infections.

What are the signs of renal failure?

Because kidney failure sometimes gives no warning signs, it can go undiagnosed until it is well advanced. However, there are six warning signs of kidney disease that you should be aware of:

1. High blood pressure
2. Puffiness around the eyes and swelling in the hands and feet (edema)
3. Pain in the kidney area (the small of the back just below the ribs)
4. Difficulty urinating or burning during urination
5. More frequent urination and urinating during the night
6. Passage of bloody or cola-colored urine

How is renal failure treated?

When kidney failure is in its early stage, it may be slowed by special diets or medication or both. However, as the disease progresses and the kidneys no longer perform their duties of removing bodily wastes, other treatments must be used. The blood must be cleansed by using an artificial kidney (hemodialysis) or by introducing a cleansing solution into the abdomen (peritoneal dialysis). A kidney transplant, in which a healthy, donated kidney replaces the failed kidneys, can restore normal kidney function.

Outlook

There is no cure for chronic renal disease. Following the program your doctor prescribes for you is vitally important to helping you live with kidney failure. Thousands of people who have the disease are living active, productive lives.

From: DJ Brundage, *Renal disorders,* St. Louis, 1992, Mosby.

MEDICAL MANAGEMENT

ARF

Diagnostic tests and procedures

The diagnosis of ARF is made based on the development of a decline in urinary output, an elevation in BUN and potassium, and a decrease in creatinine clearance. Typical laboratory evaluation includes the following studies:

- Urinalysis
- Urine osmalality
- 24-hour urine:
  Creatinine clearance
  Protein excretion
- BUN
- Serum creatinine
- Electrolytes
- Hemoglobin and hematocrit
- Iron or ferritin
- Complete blood count (CBC)

Radiographic evaluation may include the following to evaluate for an obstruction:

- Renal ultrasound
- Intravenous pyelogram*
- Computed tomography (CT) scan*
- Magnetic resonance imaging (MRI)

Pathologic evaluation may include renal biopsy.

Treatment

Treatment consists of identification of older adults at risk and implementation of preventive interventions. Interventions may include prevention of dehydration, relief from obstruction, maximizing cardiac output to increase renal blood flow, and education regarding self-medication with OTC NSAIDs (Rodgers, Staniland, Lipkin, 1990).

The focus of subsequent treatment is control of uremic symptoms by dialysis, dietary protein and potassium restriction, maintenance of fluid, electrolyte, and acid-base balance, and control of possible infectious disease complications (Rodgers, Staniland, Lipkin, 1990).

Prognosis

The mortality of ARF in older adults is higher than in younger clients. Mortality rates are reported from 57% to 70% (Rodgers, Staniland, Lipkin, 1990).

*Assess creatinine clearance before use of contrast media; renal failure may be induced by contrast media.

Modified from Fillit H, Rowe J: The aging kidney. In Brocklehurst J, Tallis R, Fillit H, editors: *Textbook geriatric medicine and gerontology,* Edinburgh, UK, 1992, Churchill, Livingstone.

from the day BUN is stable to the day the client returns to normal activity and urine volume is normal—this may take several months (Brundage, 1992).

The older adult with acute renal failure usually has a sudden decline in urinary output (less than 400 ml per 24 hours) and an increase in blood urea nitrogen and creatinine levels. Additional symptomatology may include those listed in the Client/Family Teaching box, p. 711.

Older adults at risk for the development of ARF are those who have a predisposition to dehydration, are undergoing diagnostic evaluations using a contrast agent, or are receiving antibiotic therapy.

In most cases, when the source of the problem is eliminated, normal kidney function resumes (Brundage, 1992) (see Medical Management box, above).

Chronic Renal Failure

Chronic renal failure (CRF) is the permanent loss of kidney function (Box 26-8).

The symptomatology of CRF is dependent on the extent of the failure. The older adult with diminished renal reserve may be asymptomatic. As renal failure progresses, there is an increase in the retention of nitrogenous compounds, resulting in a decrease in creatinine clearance and an increase in BUN concentrations. A decrease in hemoglobin, hematocrit, calcium, and phosphorus may also occur. As the levels of nitrogenous wastes increase there is increased symptomatology. In the uremic stage the client has symptoms that include mental status changes, fatigue, neurologic disorders, anemia, **azotemia,** oliguria, hypertension, osteodystrophy,

nitrogen containing contents in blood

BOX 26-8

Causes of CRF

Age-dependent diseases

- Chronic glomerulonephritis
- Polycystic kidney disease
- Obstructive uropathy
- Diabetic nephropathy
- Hypertensive nephropathy
- Systemic lupus erythematosus (SLE)
- Gout

Modified from Rowe JW: Renal and lower urinary tract disease in the elderly. In Calkins E, Davis P, Ford A, editors: *The practice of geriatrics,* Philadelphia, 1986, JB Lippincott; Fillit H, Rowe J: The aging kidney. In Brocklehurst J, Tallis R, Fillit H, editors: *Textbook geriatric medicine and gerontology,* Edin-burgh, UK, 1992, Churchill, Livingstone.

MEDICAL MANAGEMENT

CRF

Diagnostic tests and procedures

The diagnosis of CRF is usually made based on a decrease in creatinine clearance, elevation of BUN level, and decrease in red blood cells. The remainder of the evaluation is identical to the client with ARF.

Treatment

Treatment of renal failure in the older adult is initially conservative. Conservative medical management consists of the following:

- Maintenance of fluid and electrolyte balance
- Correction of metabolic acidosis
- Blood pressure control
- Dietary management with a low protein, sodium, and potassium diet
- Correction of metabolic acidosis
- Maintenance of calcium and phosphorus balance; decreased phosphorus is treated with phosphate binding aluminum hydroxide or calcium carbonated antacids such as Amphojel, Basaljel, Alucap. Decreased calcium is treated with vitamin D and Calcitriol
- Correct anemia with iron supplements, packed red blood cells, and recombinant human erythropoietin
- Kidney replacement therapy within center or at home: hemodialysis, continuous ambulatory peritoneal dialysis; kidney transplantation if damage is severe.

Prognosis

Older adult clients with end stage renal disease (ESRD) generally have concomitant illnesses, such as DM, cardiac disease, or cancer in addition to their renal disease. Hence, their life expectancy is less than that of younger clients (Fillit, Rowe, 1992).

anorexia, nausea, vomiting, GI ulcerations, pruritus, and uremic frost (crystallized perspiration) (Talbott, 1992).

Older adults at risk for the development of CRF are those who have a history of DM, polycystic kidney disease, or atherosclerosis (see Medical management box, above).

NURSING MANAGEMENT

✣ ASSESSMENT

The assessment of the older adult with kidney disease should include a history and physical assessment. The history should focus on the potential risks an older adult may have for development of renal failure, as well as symptomatology of renal failure. Box 26-9 summarizes the nursing history and physical assessment to be obtained.

✣ DIAGNOSIS

Appropriate nursing diagnoses for the older adult client with renal disease can include the following: (1) fluid volume excess; (2) fluid volume deficit; (3) self-care deficit; (4) altered nutrition: less than body requirements; (5) altered tissue perfusion; (6) high risk for infection; (7) knowledge deficit; (8) altered urinary elimination; (9) potential for sexual dysfunction; and (10) ineffective coping.

✣ PLANNING

The development of a plan of care for the older adult with renal failure must include the client and family or significant others because of the potential for self-care deficits. Expected outcomes for the older client with renal failure include, but are not limited to, the following: (1) client will remain functional, (2) client will adhere to prescribed medication and diet regimen, (3) client will maintain blood pressure within acceptable limits, and (4) client will be able to perform ADLs satisfactorily.

✣ INTERVENTION

Interventions for the older adult with renal failure should focus on maintaining fluid and electrolyte balance; monitoring of nephrotic symptoms; educating about treatment regimens, diet management, and medication usage; and managing fatigue and low energy levels. Clients and significant others must be educated on the prescribed diet and fluid intake. The typically prescribed diet is a low-protein, low-sodium, and low-potassium diet. At times the diet is less than palatable, so with the normal age-related changes in the sense of taste and smell, adherence to a renal diet presents a challenge. The use of spices and seasonings to enhance taste has been found to be successful. For those individuals with renal failure who experience nausea resulting from uremic symptoms, it might be beneficial to administer a prescribed

BOX 26-9

Nursing Assessment of the Renal System

History

- Personal or family history of renal disease
- Recent surgery or illness (hypertension, gout, SLE, multiple myeloma, DM)
- Symptoms
  - Urine (frequency, amount, color, appearance)
  - Pain
  - Nausea or vomiting
  - Anorexia
  - Weight loss
  - Confusion
  - Fatigue
  - Pruritus
  - Edema
  - Thirst
  - Twitching
  - Bone pain
- Medications, especially antibiotics, antineoplastic agents, and nonsteroidal antiinflammatory medications
- Diet history
- Living situation
- Psychosocial supports

Physical assessment

- Inspect skin for hydration, uremic frost
- Cardiopulmonary status
- Neurologic status
- Musculoskeletal status
- Ophthalmoscopic examination and visual inspection (monthly if on dialysis)

Modified from Plawecki HM, Brewer S, Plawecki J: Chronic renal failure, *J Gerontolog Nurs* 13(12):14-17, 1987; Talbott L: Genitourinary system. In Hogstel MO, editor: *Clinical manual of gerontological nursing,* St. Louis, 1992, Mosby.

antiemetic before meals (see Box 26-8, p. 712, and Boxes 26-10 and 26-11, and Client/Family Teaching box, at right).

With the varied options of treatment available to the individual with renal failure it is important to educate the client and significant others about the prescribed modality. The American Kidney Foundation can provide individuals with educational information and in some areas assist with transportation to dialysis centers.*

✣ EVALUATION

Evaluation is an extremely important component in the care of the older adult with renal impairment. Subjective data can include the client's reported symptoms and quality of life (Talbott, 1992). Objective data would include improved renal function as evidenced by urine output and stable serum creatinine, an increase in creatinine clearance, and a decrease in BUN, serum potassium, and phosphorous.

Urinary Tract Infection

Urinary tract infection is second to respiratory infection as a cause of febrile illness in older adults (Melman,

*For more information contact the American Kidney Foundation; 30 East 33rd Avenue; New York, NY 10016; (800) 622-9010.

MEDICAL MANAGEMENT

Urinary Tract Infection

Diagnostic tests and procedures

Evaluation of a urinary tract infection includes a clean voided midstream urine for culture and sensitivity analysis. For suspected structural abnormalities an intravenous pyelogram (IVP) may be performed.

Treatment

After a specific organism is identified, specific antimicrobial therapy is started. If the urinary tract infection is a result of an obstruction, anatomic abnormalities or renal calculi, treatment is directed toward correcting the underlying cause.

Controversy exists regarding whether to initiate antimicrobial therapy in asymptomatic older adults because of the side effects and expense of antimicrobial therapy (Todd, 1990).

Prognosis

Older adults respond effectively to treatment of symptomatic urinary tract infection. Urinary tract infection has a poor prognosis in frail older adults because of the increased toxicity of antimicrobial therapy.

CLIENT/FAMILY TEACHING

Management of ARF

- Cause and episode of ARF.
- Prescribed diet and fluid regimen.
- Self-observational skills: measuring temperature, pulse, repirations, blood pressure, intake and output, daily weight.
- Personal hygiene
- Exercise and rest program
- Medication regimen (name of medication, purpose, dose, time interval, adverse reactions)
- Schedule of medical follow-up

Modified from Brundage DJ: *Renal disorders,* St. Louis, 1992, Mosby.

BOX 26-10

Renal Diet

Diet is very important for clients with renal (kidney) disorders. Because the kidneys cannot get rid of enough fluids and waste products, certain foods and liquids must be controlled. Controlling the amount of protein, calories, potassium, sodium, and fluids that you take in every day can help lessen your kidneys' workload, can make you feel less nauseated, and can boost your energy level.

Protein

Protein is important for building muscles and repairing tissues. People with kidney disorders, however, usually need to limit the amount of protein they consume, because the kidneys cannot rid the body of excess protein waste products.

There are two types of protein, *high-quality protein* and *low-quality protein.*

1. High-quality protein comes from animals and includes meat, chicken, fish, and eggs. You should eat high-quality protein at every meal.
2. Low-quality protein comes from plants and includes grains and vegetables. You need to limit how much low-quality protein you eat.

Calories

You need to consume enough calories every day to maintain your energy and prevent weight loss. Most of your calories should come from carbohydrates and unsaturated fats. If you need to increase your caloric intake, try adding margarine and oils that are low in cholesterol and jams, jellies, sugar, and honey to your diet.

Potassium

It is very important to control the amount of potassium in your diet. Too little potassium can cause muscle weakness, fatigue, and irregular heartbeats. Too much potassium can cause heart problems and even death.

Certain foods contain large amounts of potassium. These include dried beans, nuts, meat, fruits, vegetables, and milk. Salt substitutes also contain a large amount of potassium.

Sodium

Sodium can be found in a number of foods. Table salt and some prepared and packaged foods are very high in sodium.

Too much sodium will cause your body to retain fluid. Try using herbs and spices instead of salt to season your food.

Fluid

Fluid is anything you drink, of course, but it also includes things such as ice, gelatin, and ice cream—anything that is liquid at room temperature.

Too much fluid can cause a number of problems, including weight gain, swelling (edema), high blood pressure, shortness of breath, fluid in the lungs, and heart failure.

The amount of fluid you're allowed will depend on how much kidney function you have left.

Vitamins and minerals

The amount you get of some vitamins and minerals may also need to be controlled. These nutrients may include folic acid; vitamins A, B, C, and D; calcium; iron; zinc; aluminum; and phosphorus.

The renal diet your physician prescribes for you will depend on how much kidney function you have left. If you need to undergo peritoneal dialysis or hemodialysis, or if you have a kidney transplant, your diet will need to be adjusted.

Your dietitian will help you plan your diet. She can tell you where to buy special foods and how to read the labels on prepared foods. Follow your physician's instructions and your diet, and you will be doing the best thing for your body and helping yourself feel better.

From DJ Brundage: *Renal disorders,* St. Louis, 1992, Mosby.

1992). Urinary tract infection occurs in both older men and women. The causative factor in men is often related to prostatic enlargement, the result of benign prostatic hypertrophy (BPH) or carcinoma. In older women the causative factors include atrophic vaginitis, bladder descent, perivaginal contamination and estrogen deficiency (Melman, 1992). Additional causative factors include urinary stasis, institutionalization, DM, functional impairments, and bladder catheterization.

Urinary tract infection is characterized by a bacterial count greater than 100,000/ml of urine for a midstream clean catch specimen; 1,000/ml of urine for a urethral catheterized specimen, and any bacterial growth from a suprapubic catheter. The diagnosis of a urinary tract infection is difficult, since most older adults remain asymptomatic until a high bacterial count is present. In some older adults the symptoms may occur as a change in mental status, increased irritability, and frequent urination or incontinence. An older adult usually does not become febrile from a urinary tract infection until the presence of a high bacterial count (Brundage, 1992). At times bacteria is found on a routine examination, while the older adult remains asymptomatic. Controversy exists regarding the treatment of asymptomatic urinary tract infections because of the cost and possible renal and GI side effects of antimicrobial therapy, but for

BOX 26-11

What is Peritoneal Dialysis?

Peritoneal dialysis is one method of removing waste products and excess fluids from the blood when the kidneys stop functioning. Unlike hemodialysis, which is done with an artificial kidney machine, peritoneal dialysis is carried out in the client's own body.

How does peritoneal dialysis work?

Peritoneal dialysis takes place in your abdomen. A membrane, called the peritoneal membrane, surrounds your intestines and acts as a filtering membrane. A dialysate solution flows into the abdomen, where harmful toxins and excess fluids move from the blood to the dialysate. The solution is then drained out of the abdomen.

Before peritoneal dialysis can begin, a tube (catheter) will be inserted into the peritoneal cavity in your abdomen through a small incision. When the catheter is in place, you will have three types of peritoneal dialysis from which to choose: continuous ambulatory peritoneal dialysis, continuous cycling peritoneal dialysis, and intermittent peritoneal dialysis.

Continuous ambulatory peritoneal dialysis (CAPD) is done without the use of any machines. A bag of dialysate solution is warmed to body temperature. Then, while you sit or lie down, the solution flows into your abdomen through tubing that connects the catheter in your abdomen to the bag of dialysate. This takes about 10 minutes. The bag is hung on a stand so it is at a higher level than your abdomen.

After the solution is drained into your abdomen, you clamp the tubing, roll up the empty bag and tuck it into your clothing. Then you go about your normal daily activities. Four to 8 hours later, the dialysate solution must be drained out of your abdomen back into the bag. Again, sit or lie down while this occurs, but this time the bag must be lower than your abdomen. It takes about 10 to 20 minutes to drain out. A new bag of dialysate then flows into your abdomen, and the process begins anew. This process usually is repeated three to four times during the day and once at night.

Continuous cycling peritoneal dialysis (CCPD) takes place while you sleep, using a cycling machine. Before you go to sleep, you hook tubing from the machine to the catheter in your abdomen. Three to seven times during the night, the continuous cycling machine automatically drains dialysate solution into your abdomen and back out again. During the last run, the solution is left in your abdomen and will remain there during the day. It will be drained the following night. When you wake the next morning, you disconnect the tubing and go about your daily activities.

Intermittent peritoneal dialysis (IPD) is usually done in the hospital, three to five times a week. You will be dialyzed by a machine that takes 8 to 12 hours to complete a treatment. Treatment is usually carried out while you sleep.

Complications

Clients undergoing peritoneal dialysis are at some risk of developing an infection of the abdomen called *peritonitis.* If you experience abdominal pain or fever or notice that the dialysate solution that drains back into the bag or machine is cloudy, notify your doctor at once. Diarrhea, vomiting, and a swollen abdomen can also be signs of peritonitis and should be reported to your doctor.

Outlook

Peritoneal dialysis takes over the kidneys' function but does not cure kidney failure. You will need to undergo some form of dialysis for the rest of your life or until you receive a kidney transplant. Many clients lead near-to-normal lives despite peritoneal dialysis, except for the need to have the treatments and some restrictions on food and fluid intake.

From: DJ Brundage: *Renal disorders,* St. Louis, 1992, Mosby.

symptomatic older adults treatment is usually instituted (see Medical Management box, p. 714).

Nursing Management

✣ ASSESSMENT

Subjective assessment of urinary elimination patterns should be obtained. This assessment includes normal voiding patterns and alterations in those patterns, frequency, hesitancy, incontinence, nocturia, or urgency, and the characteristics of urine (i.e., color, odor, sediment). In addition, a mental status examination to detect changes in mood or thought processes may be indicated.

✣ DIAGNOSIS

Potential nursing diagnoses for the older client with a urinary tract infection include the following: altered urinary elimination and pain.

✣ PLANNING

Based on the diagnosis of a urinary tract infection, expected outcomes for the older client include, but are not limited to, the following: (1) client will have a urine bacterial count of < 100,000/ml of urine, (2) client will verbalize understanding and demonstrate use of appropriate perihygiene techniques, (3) client will drink at least 2,000 ml of fluid daily unless contraindicated, and (4) client will reestablish usual voiding pattern.

✣ INTERVENTION

Nursing management should focus on education of the older adult, including appropriate perihygiene measures such as front to back wiping techniques, adequate daily fluid intake, adherence to prescribed medication regimen, and reportable signs and symptoms of a recurring infection. Sterile technique should be used with urinary catheterization.

✣ EVALUATION

Evaluation includes achievement of the expected outcomes and prevention of symptomatic urinary tract infection.

Bladder Cancer

Bladder cancer accounts for 2% to 4% of diagnosed cancers. The incidence of bladder cancer is higher in men and increases with age. Bladder cancer may occur at any age but it is particularly common in the sixth decade of life (*Cancer Statistics,* 1990).

The cause of bladder cancer remains unclear. A variety of contributing factors has been identified. Smoking is clearly implicated in the promotion of 30% to 40% of bladder cancers (Richie, Shirley, Yogoda, 1985). Another one third of bladder cancer cases are thought to be related to industrial chemical exposure to aromatic amines found in dyes, leather tanning, and organic chemicals (Catalona, 1991).

Transitional cell carcinoma accounts for approximately 95% of all malignant bladder cancers. Characteristics of transitional cell tumors include growth into the bladder lumen, with the potential for local invasion into the bladder muscle, and regional spread into the surrounding lymph nodes, pelvis, or other pelvic structures. Hematologic dissemination of malignant cells results in lung, bone, and liver metastasis (*Cancer Statistics,* 1990).

The most common initial symptoms of bladder cancer are intermittent, painless gross, or microscopic hematuria and asymptomatic pyuria. Because symptoms are intermittent, there is a tendency to disregard their seriousness. Pain, frequency, and urgency from bladder irritation have often developed by the time clients seek treatment (*Cancer Statistics,* 1990) (see Medical Management box, p. 718).

NURSING MANAGEMENT

✣ ASSESSMENT

The purpose of the history and physical assessment is to determine the presence of any alterations in the individual's pattern of urinary elimination. Subjective assessment should focus on identifying the presence of pain, hematuria, dysuria, urgency, frequency, or voiding small volumes. Objective assessment findings include gross or microscopic hematuria. It is also important to assess the client's health beliefs related to the malignant process.

✣ DIAGNOSIS

From the data collected during the assessment and with the nurse's knowledge of bladder cancer and treatment methods, the nurse will be able to accurately establish nursing diagnoses for the client with bladder cancer.

The most common nursing diagnoses for clients with bladder cancer include (1) altered protection, (2) altered urinary elimination, (3) pain, (4) anxiety, (5) potential for sexual dysfunction, and (6) body image disturbance.

✣ PLANNING

Developing a plan of care involves the client and significant others. Expected outcomes include, but are not limited to, the following: (1) client will return to premorbid patterns of elimination or will establish new patterns of regular, complete urinary elimination; (2) client will verbalize comfort and/or pain relief; (3) client will reduce or resolve anxiety; (4) client will express satisfaction with sexuality; and (5) client will accept body change(s) and incorporation of same into self-concept.

✣ INTERVENTION

Nursing interventions for the client with bladder cancer focus on client education, psychosocial support, management of pain, and maintenance of adequate fluid and nutritional intake. The majority of clients with bladder cancer undergo a cystectomy and require education regarding the management of urinary diversion devices. To compound the fears and concerns a client has regarding a diagnosis of cancer, there is also a social stigma associated with the excretion of body fluids from an external device. Since clients may have difficulty coping, it is important that they are encouraged to verbalize fears and concerns, and referred to the appropriate supportive services if necessary.*

*Supportive services for individuals with bladder cancer include the American Cancer Society (contact local chapter) and the United Ostomy Association; 36 Executive Park, Suite 120; Irvine, CA 92714-6744; (800) 826-0826.

MEDICAL MANAGEMENT

Bladder Cancer

Diagnostic tests and procedures

Diagnosis of bladder cancer is made by cystoscopic examination with bladder biopsies. Additional diagnostic studies that may be performed include the following:

- Urine culture and sensitivity
- Urine cytology
- CBC
- BUN
- Creatinine
- Liver function studies
- Flow cytology
- IVP
- Renal ultrasound
- Bone scan
- Chest x-ray
- Cystoscopic retrograde
- Ureteropyelography

Treatment

Treatment decisions are made based upon the size and amount of local invasion of the tumor. Treatment options available to clients with bladder cancer include the following:

Noninvasive tumors
Transurethral resection
Laser fulguration
Intravesical chemotherapy
Resection of superficial tumors

Invasive tumors
Partial cystectomy
Radical cystectomy
Cystoprostatectomy
Total cystectomy with urinary diversion
Adjunct or palliative systemic chemotherapy
Adjunct or palliative radiotherapy (*Cancer statistics,* 1990)

Usually the entire bladder is resected. At times the tumors are so large and invasive that complete resection is not possible and residual disease persists after surgery. Residual disease is often amenable to treatment with radiation therapy, intravesical chemotherapy, and immunotherapy (Catalona, 1991).

Prognosis

Approximately 50% of clients with Stage C muscle invasion die within 5 years because of recurrence and metastatic disease. Individuals with superficial bladder cancers have an improved prognosis (Todd, 1990).

✣ EVALUATION

Evaluation of the interventions is based on the resolution of hematuria and a return of patterns of urinary elimination to premorbid parameters, or the establishment of a new pattern of regular, complete bladder evacuation (Gray, 1992).

Benign Prostatic Hypertrophy

Benign prostatic hypertrophy (BPH) is a benign enlargement of the prostate gland associated with the aging process. A synergistic effect between testosterone and endogenous estrogens, both of which are responsible for the proliferation of BPH, is reported to exist (Freed, 1986). It occurs in more than 80% of men over age 60 (Freed, 1986).

Initially BPH is asymptomatic. As hyperplasia increases, a man may begin to experience symptoms related to bladder outlet obstruction. These signs and symptoms include hesitancy initiating micturition, urgency, decreased force of urinary stream, incomplete bladder emptying, dribbling, frequency, and nocturia. With progressive hyperplasia the bladder wall loses elasticity and becomes thinner, resulting in increasing postvoid residuals, thus increasing the risk for bacteriuria and infection. If the condition is left untreated, the ureter and kidneys may be affected, increasing the risk of hydroureter, hydronephrosis, pyelonephritis, and renal impairment (Gray, 1992) (see Medical Management box p. 719).

NURSING MANAGEMENT

✣ ASSESSMENT

The purpose of the nursing assessment for the individual with BPH is to determine the extent of prostate enlargement and its effect on function so that appropriate nursing interventions can be planned and implemented. The assessment consists of a history, physical examination, and evaluation of voiding patterns (Box 26-12).

✣ DIAGNOSIS

The data collected during the history and physical assessment enables the nurse to identify appropriate nurs-

MEDICAL MANAGEMENT

BPH

Diagnostic tests and procedures

The purpose of the diagnostic evaluation of BPH is to evaluate the extent of obstruction and rule out a malignant process. Diagnostic evaluation includes a history, physical examination, digital rectal examination (DRE), prostatic ultrasound, serum creatinine, BUN, and urinary flow studies (Richie, Shirley, Yogoda, 1985).

Treatment

Treatment of BPH is conservative unless there are signs and symptoms of an obstruction. Surgical intervention with a transurethral prostatectomy (TURP) has traditionally been the treatment of choice. Noninvasive treatments such as hyperthermia, balloon dilation, and laser prostatectomy are being used with fewer risks (Gray, 1992).

Pharmacologic intervention

Two types of medications have been used to treat men with obstructive symptoms resulting from BPH: (1) alpha-adrenergic blockers that increase the tone of smooth muscle and increase the resistance at the outlet, resulting in relief of the signs and symptoms of obstruction (medications available include prazosin, phenoxybenzamine and terazosin); and (2) antiandrogen and testosterone blocking agents. Since it is known that BPH is stimulated by testosterone, these agents have been extremely effective in diminishing the size of the prostate gland. Medications available are flutamide (Eulexin), testosterone, leuprolide (Lupron), and finasteride (Proscar) (Gray, 1992; Miller, 1993).

Prognosis

Surgical and pharmacologic intervention eliminates the risk of subsequent obstructive symptoms (Gray, 1992; Miller, 1993).

ing diagnoses and develop a plan of care for the client experiencing BPH. In any suspected case of BPH the client must be referred for medical management and evaluation.

The following nursing diagnoses are appropriate in clients with BPH: (1) altered urinary elimination, (2) urinary retention (chronic or acute), (3) high risk for urinary tract infection, (4) potential for sexual dysfunction, (5) knowledge deficit, and (6) pain.

✜ PLANNING

Expected outcomes for the client with BPH include, but are not limited to, the following: (1) client's patterns of elimination will return to premorbid pattern, (2) client will show no evidence of urinary tract infection, (3) client will verbalize understanding of disease process and treatment regimen, (4) pain will have abated, and (5) sexual functioning will return to premorbid function.

BOX 26-12

Nursing Assessment for BPH

History

- Voiding habits
- Voiding patterns
- General health
- Functional status
- Past medical and surgical history
- Current medications
- Voiding habits and patterns
  - The initiation and caliber of the urinary stream
  - The presence of obstructive symptoms
    - Diurnal frequency
    - Nocturia
    - Hesitancy
    - Urgency
    - Urge incontinence
    - Incomplete bladder emptying
    - Postvoid dribbling
- Signs and symptoms of urinary tract infection
  - Dysuria
  - Frequency

Physical examination

The physical examination is usually conducted by the physician or an advanced practice nurse and includes a digital rectal examination of the prostate gland to evaluate the size, shape, and consistency of the prostate, and an abdominal examination to determine the presence or absence of bladder distention, suprapubic tenderness, or costovertebral angle tenderness.

✜ INTERVENTION

Nursing interventions for BPH focus on client education regarding the diagnosis and management of BPH. Education regarding the management of alterations in urinary elimination should include establishment of a frequent voiding schedule, and if prescribed, self-catheterization techniques. The educational plan should also include teaching the client regarding the sympathomimetic actions of decongestant medication and diet pills.

Nursing interventions must also take into account the type of treatment regimen used. For clients treated with nonsurgical methods, the interventions should focus on educating the client about signs and symptoms of progressive BPH. These include urgency, frequency, inadequate bladder emptying, reduced urinary stream, the

CLIENT/FAMILY TEACHING

BPH

Benign prostatic hyperplasia can alter your pattern of urinary elimination. If you notice any of the following changes, report them to your [physician]:

- Difficult to begin voiding
- Urine stream is weak
- Going to the bathroom more frequently
- Urine leakage
- The sensation of a full bladder after you have just gone to the bathroom
- Frequent voiding at night

From MO Hogstel: *Clinical manual of gerontological nursing,* St. Louis, 1992, Mosby.

prescribed medication regimen, and potential adverse reactions. For clients receiving surgical intervention, nursing interventions initially focus on immediate postoperative care. Most surgical procedures require general anesthesia and a few days of hospitalization. Interventions should focus on maintaining the client's level of function and prevention of iatrogenic effects associated with hospitalization, such as immobility, sensory deprivation, and social isolation. Posthospitalization clients require education related to prescribed temporary activity restrictions, signs and symptoms of urinary obstruction, and possible temporary incontinence. Surgical interventions may result in a temporary sexual dysfunction; the client should be given the opportunity to verbalize concerns and to be referred to appropriate supportive services, such as the urologist or a certified sex therapist (see Client/Family Teaching box, above).

✤ EVALUATION

Evaluation of the interventions is based on the return of urinary function to the premorbid state, client's relief of urinary symptoms, urinary tract infection that has been avoided or promptly managed, and client's continuation of satisfactory sexual relations (Gray, 1992).

Prostate Cancer

Prostate cancer is the most common cancer in men and constitutes about 28% of all new cancers. It is estimated that over 132,000 new cases of prostate cancer were diagnosed in 1992 and that more than 34,000 men died of the disease (Epstein, Hanks, 1992).

The incidence of prostate cancer increases with age. After the fourth decade of life, the risk of developing prostate cancer increases dramatically. Approximately 80% of all prostate cancers are diagnosed in men over age 65 (Walsh, Lepor, 1987). After the age of 85, the incidence of clinically evident disease is greater than 1,000 per 100,000 men. Cumulative data from an autopsy series suggest the true incidence of prostate cancer to be as high as 30% in men over age 50 and approaching 80% in men over age 80 (Blath, 1992).

The cause of prostate cancer is unclear. The following factors have all been implicated in the development of prostate cancer (Davis, 1991; Meikle, Smith, 1990):

1. Increasing age
2. African-American race
3. Hormonal influence (the presence of testosterone)
4. Environmental exposure to cadmium and zinc
5. Diet high in dietary fat
6. Diet low in beta carotene
7. Genetic predisposition
8. Infection with specific viruses (e.g., cytomegalovirus, herpes simplex 2, semen virus 40)
9. Sexual practices (multiple sexual partners)

Regardless of the unclear cause, two elements are necessary for the development of prostate cancer: the presence of testosterone and time.

Historically, the diagnosis of prostate cancer was made at an advanced stage in a symptomatic man reporting pain, weight loss, and varying degrees of alteration in urinary patterns. Presently, with improved screening tests and frequent examinations, clients with prostate cancer are diagnosed early (see Medical Management box, pp. 721-722).

NURSING MANAGEMENT

✤ ASSESSMENT

The assessment of the client with prostate cancer is the same as that for the client with benign prostatic hypertrophy (see Box 26-12, p. 719). It is also important for the nurse to assess the client's health beliefs and fears related to a malignant process.

✤ DIAGNOSIS

With the data collected from the assessment and the nurse's knowledge of prostate cancer and treatment modalities, the nurse can formulate appropriate nursing diagnoses. The following nursing diagnoses may be appropriate for clients with prostate cancer: (1) pain, (2) altered urinary elimination, (3) anxiety, (4) sexual dysfunction, (5) anticipatory grief, and (6) knowledge deficit.

✤ PLANNING

Expected outcomes for a client with prostate cancer include the following: (1) urinary elimination patterns will

MEDICAL MANAGEMENT

Prostate Cancer

Diagnostic tests and procedures

Screening for prostate cancer

Screening for prostate cancer is a hotly debated topic. Authorities disagree about the appropriate use of screening techniques for prostate cancer, since the natural history of the disease is variable and many histologic abnormalities are clinically insignificant. Widespread screening with effective techniques may indeed increase the rate of cancer detection, but it is not yet known whether increased detection will actually lead to improved quality of life or rates of survival (Brawler, Catalona, McConnell, 1992; Berger, 1993).

Screening methods include the following:

- Digital rectal examination (DRE)
- **Prostate-specific antigen (PSA)**
- Transrectal ultrasound (TRUS)

Despite the method of screening used, diagnosis of prostate cancer is definitive only after a biopsy is performed.

DRE

The DRE is the cornerstone of the physical examination for the detection of prostate cancer. During a rectal examination, the prostate gland is palpated for any changes in size, consistency, and contour. Any abnormalities in the prostate gland should prompt further investigation by transrectal ultrasound and biopsy (Berger, 1993).

The recommendation from the American Cancer Society is that men over age 50 have a DRE performed annually (Blath, 1992).

PSA

PSA is a glycoprotein secreted only by the prostate gland. PSA is produced by both normal and malignant cells. Elevations may occur in clients with carcinomas of the prostate, BPH, prostatitis, prostatic infection, urethritis, post-DRE, and in catheterized clients (Berger, 1993). It is important that a PSA level not be obtained after manipulation of the prostate gland, since this may result in a false elevation.

Results of the test are dependent on the assay that is used. The Hybitech Tandem R Assay is the most commonly used one; normal PSA levels range from 0 to 4 mg/ml (Osterling, 1991). An elevated PSA level is usually followed by a TRUS and a biopsy.

TRUS

TRUS is indicated only if the older adult male has an elevated PSA or an abnormal DRE. This ultrasonographic procedure identifies masses not found on DRE, evaluates the amount of tumor, estimates prostate size, and evaluates benign diseases of the prostate. Through this procedure, accurate biopsies of suspected tumors can be secured (Stevens, Miller, 1991).

After a biopsy confirms the diagnosis of prostate cancer, the following diagnostic studies may be performed to determine the presence and extent of disease (Gray, 1992):

- Serum alkaline phosphate
- BUN and creatinine
- IVP
- Radionuclide bone scan
- Chest x-ray
- Abdominal CT scan
- MRI

Staging of prostate cancer

Staging systems for prostate cancer are used to determine the options for care and the prognosis. The tumor (T), nodes (N), metastasis (M) system and a modified Jewett-Strong Marshall system are common classification systems for prostate cancer.

Treatment

Surgical intervention

Surgical intervention has historically been the primary therapy for prostate cancer. The specific type of intervention is dependent on the stage of clinical disease. For clients with disease confined to the prostate gland, radical prostatectomy is the most effective method for definitive treatment. Postoperative complications from this procedure include incontinence (2%), urethral stricture (8%), and impotence (94%) (Walsh, Lepor, 1987).

Other surgical interventions include a transurethral resection of the prostate may be performed to relieve bladder outlet obstruction and a bilateral orchiectomy to stop the release of testosterone in the management of metastatic disease (Walsh, Lepor, 1987).

Radiation therapy

External beam radiotherapy with or without interstitial radiation implantation has shown results comparable to those achieved by radical prostatectomy for men with disease confined to the prostate gland. Complications of curative radiation therapy include incontinence, urethral stricture, proctitis, and reported incidence of erectile dysfunction in 22% to 84% of men treated (Walsh, Lepor, 1987).

Hormonal and chemotherapy

Hormonal therapy has been effective in the management of advanced prostate cancer, without compromising the quality of life for most clients. Therapies may include a bilateral orchiectomy, estrogens or antiandrogen medications.

For advance stage metastatic disease chemotherapy may be used. Single regimen treatment with cyclophos-

Continued.

MEDICAL MANAGEMENT

Prostate Cancer—cont'd

phamide, 5-fluorouracil, adriamycin, methotrexate, and cisplatin has been associated with subjective responses and disease stabilization in 25% to 50% of clients (Davis, 1991).

Prognosis

In diseases confined to the prostate gland, complete response to therapy and achievement of a normal life span are reasonable expectations. More extensive disease can be managed effectively with results from complete response to partial remission. The treatment of individuals with advanced disease can result in a partial remission or stable disease for a gratifying period (Davis, 1991).

return to premorbid parameters, (2) expressions of anxiety about diagnosis and prognosis will be replaced by a realistic understanding of the likely prognosis, (3) client and his partner will have a mutually satisfying sexual relationship, (4) client will find comfort and/or pain resolution, (5) client and family will be able to express their grief and begin to prepare for the client's death (*Cancer Statistics,* 1990).

✣ INTERVENTION

The goals the nurse hopes to achieve with the client with prostate cancer are early detection and treatment of disease, restoration of urinary elimination and satisfactory sexual function, and maintenance of a desired quality of life.

Nursing interventions for the client with prostate cancer focus on education regarding early detection, the disease process, interventions, and effective management of symptoms related to the disease process and treatment regimens. Interventions may include referral to appropriate health care providers and supportive services. It is imperative that options be provided to clients and significant others regarding the management of impotence. These options may include referral to a urologist for consideration of injectable prostaglandin, vascular reconstructive surgery, or surgical implantation of a rigid or inflatable penile prosthetic or vacuum device (see nursing Care Plan, p. 723).

✣ EVALUATION

Evaluation of the interventions will be based on the client's relief of symptoms from the prostate obstruction and return of urinary elimination to premorbid parameter. Client will verbalize an understanding of tumor stage, treatment regimen and likely prognosis. Client will verbalize satisfying sexual expression (*Cancer Statistics,* 1990).

Summary

The changes in urinary function that occur with aging present some of the greatest nursing care challenges to nurses, older clients, and their family or significant others. The typical problems associated with altered urinary elimination are frustrating, embarassing, and disabling, and can seriously affect the older adults' functional ability. The role of the nurse includes advocacy for evaluation and treatment, providing emotional support and counseling, and developing individualized plans of care aimed at promoting self-care and functional ability.

Key Points

- Although the aging process does affect lower urinary tract function, aging alone does not cause UI.
- Medications, including a number of OTC drugs, can cause acute UI.
- Functional and environmental assessments are important components of the evaluation of UI.
- Bladder diaries provide a more objective measure of the severity and type of incontinence than recall alone and should be part of the evaluation of UI.
- Behavioral interventions are the initial treatment of choice for many clients with UI.
- Cognitively intact clients with urge and/or stress incontinence often respond well to properly taught pelvic floor muscle exercises.
- Once the client masters pelvic floor muscle exercises, the nurse can teach urge and/or stress strategies to prevent involuntary urine loss.
- Prompted voiding, habit training, and PURT can effectively reduce incontinence in clients with cognitive impairment, but their success is dependent on caregiver compliance.

CARE PLAN

PROSTATE CANCER

Clinical situation Mr. N is a 68-year-old retired attorney. He was enjoying his presumed good health and retirement of 2 years, playing golf four to five times a week. He was also enjoying time with his grandson, doing volunteer work at a homeless shelter once a week and serving on a number of community boards. At an annual physical examination he was found to have prostatic enlargement; serum prostate specific antigen showed a level of 30 ng/ml. He then underwent a transrectal prostatic ultrasound and was found to have a grossly enlarged prostate. A needle-guided biopsy was performed, which showed adenocarcinoma of the prostate gland. Because of the large size of the prostate mass, a metastatic evaluation consisting of a bone scan, chest x-ray, and MRI scan was performed. The metastatic evaluation failed to show any metastatic disease.

He then promptly sought the opinion of a well-respected urologist at a major medical center for the treatment of the prostate tumor. Another ultrasound biopsy was performed, and he was found to have stage C prostate cancer. The decision was made to treat the prostate tumor with Leuprolide to decrease testosterone excretion, and to maintain a low-fat diet.

Mr. N and his two sons are experiencing anxiety, fear, and anticipatory grief related to the diagnosis. Mr. N lost his wife 20 years ago to a protracted and difficult fight with breast cancer and has many bad memories of the effects of cancer.

Nursing diagnoses	Outcomes	Interventions
Anxiety related to diagnosis of cancer Knowledge deficit: current treatment modalities and prognosis related to lack of previous exposure.	Expressions of anxiety about diagnosis and prognosis will be replaced by a realistic understanding of the disease and the likely prognosis, as evidenced by satisfactory engagement in activities. Client and family will verbalize understanding of treatment regimen. Client and family will seek supportive services.	Reassure the client and family that prostate cancers are typically slow-growing and treatable. Reiterate explanation of diagnosis and treatment. Include family in teaching whenever possible. Refer to cancer support group services. Emphasize the importance in continuing present activities. Assist client to gain awareness of anxiety. Teach client relaxation techniques. Provide written information regarding prostate disease and treatment regimens. Encourage client and family members to attend educational and supportive services provided by the American Cancer Society.

- The aging process does alter kidney function, but renal failure is not a normal consequence of aging.
- Normal aging changes within the renal system require older adults to be monitored closely for adequate hydration and medication usage.
- Many older adults have asymptomatic urinary tract infections. At times, the only symptom may be an alteration in a person's mental status.
- Alterations in urinary elimination are common in men with benign prostatic hypertrophy.
- Cancer of the prostate is the most commonly diagnosed serious malignancy in older men. Many treatment options are available that maintain survival and quality of life.

HOME CARE TIPS

1. Regularly monitor and assess the homebound older adult for signs and symptoms of exacerbation of the diagnosed renal/urinary disease or disorder.
2. Instruct the caregiver and homebound older adult on reportable signs and symptoms related to the diagnosed renal/urinary system disorder and when to report these symptoms to the home care nurse or physician.
3. Instruct the caregiver and homebound older adult on the name, dose, frequency, and side effects of medications prescribed to treat the diagnosed renal/urinary system disease/disorder.
4. Assess functional and environmental factors that contribute to UI in the homebound older adult.
5. Instruct the caregiver and homebound older adult to keep a voiding diary to help the home care nurse establish the type of UI and plan nursing interventions.
6. Instruct the caregiver and homebound older adult on behavioral interventions (i.e., bladder retraining and pelvic floor exercises) to treat UI.
7. If the homebound older adult is cognitively impaired, the success of behavioral techniques (e.g., habit training, patterned urge response training, and prompted voiding) used to treat UI will be dependent on the availability and motivation of the caregiver.
8. Instruct the caregiver and homebound older adult on measures to reduce incontinence and to maintain comfort.
9. Use indwelling catheters as a last resort to treat UI.

Critical Thinking Exercises

1. Your 70-year-old female client complains that she has to get up once and sometimes twice each night to urinate. What additional information do you need to assess her urinary function?
2. A 73-year-old woman is admitted to your unit with complaints of weakness, dizziness, and feeling faint. The physician immediately orders a urine culture and sensitivity. Why does the physician suspect a urinary problem?
3. A 77-year-old man is scheduled to have a transurethral resection of the prostate (TURP) in the morning for prostate cancer. He is apprehensive and very concerned about the outcome of the surgery. As his nurse, how can you best address his needs at this time?

REFERENCES

Benzl JS: The pubococcygeus muscle. In Benson JT, editor: *Female pelvic floor disorders: investigation and management,* New York, 1992, WW Norton.

Berger NS: Prostate cancer: screening and early detection update, *Semin Oncol Nurs* 9:180-183, 1993.

Blath RA: Prostate cancer: new modalities aid in early detection, *Consultant* December 1992, 23-36.

Brawler MK, Catalona WJ, McConnell JD: Prostate cancer: is screening the answer?, *Patient Care* 10:55-68, 1992.

Brink CA: Absorbent pads, garments, and management strategies, *JAGS* 38:368-373, 1987.

Brocklehurst JC: The aging bladder, *Brit J Hosp Med,* 35(1):8-10, 1986.

Brundage DJ: *Renal disorders,* St. Louis, 1992, Mosby.

Burgio KL: Biofeedback therapy. In Benson JT, editor: *Female pelvic floor disorders: investigation and management,* N.Y., 1992, WW Norton.

Burgio KL, Burgio LD: Behavioral therapies for urinary incontinence in the elderly, *Clin Geriatr Med* 2:809-825, 1986.

Burgio KL, Whitehead WE, Engel BT: Urinary incontinence in the elderly: bladder-sphincter biofeedback and toileting skills in training, *Ann Intern Med* 103:507-515, 1985.

Burgio L et al: Behavioral treatment for urinary incontinence in elderly inpatients: initial attempts to modify prompted voiding and toileting procedures, *Behav Ther* 19:345-357, 1988.

Cancer Statistics: *Cancer* 40:9, 1990.

Catalona WJ: Bladder cancer. In Gillenwater JY, Howards SS, Duckett JW, editors: *Adult and pediatric urology,* Chicago, 1991, Mosby.

Colling J et al: Patterned urge response toileting for urinary incontinence: a clinical trial. In Tornquist E et al, editors: *Key aspect of elder care: managing falls, incontinence, and cognitive impairment,* N.Y., 1992a, Springer.

Colling J et al: The effect of patterned urge-response toileting (PURT) on urinary incontinence among nursing home residents, *JAGS* 40:135-141, 1992b.

Crieghton AM, Stanton SL: Caffeine: does it affect your bladder? *Brit J Urol* 66:613-614, 1990.

Davis M: Genital and urinary cancers. In Otto S, editor: *Oncology nursing,* St. Louis, 1991, Mosby.

Dickerson JL, Pidikiti RD: Problems with condom catheters, *JAMA* 263:3148-3149, 1990.

Duke University Center for the Study of Aging and Human Development: *Multidimensional functional assessment: The OARS methodology,* Durham, N.C., 1978, Duke University.

Epstein BE, Hanks GE: Prostate cancer: evaluation and radiotherapeutic management, *Cancer* 42(4):223-240, 1992.

Fantl JA et al: Efficacy of bladder training in older women with urinary incontinence, *JAMA* 265(5):609-613, 1991.

Fantl JA et al: Bladder training in the management of lower urinary tract dysfunction in women, *JAGS* 38:329-332, 1990.

Fillit H, Rowe J: The aging kidney. In Brocklehurst J, Tallis R, Fillit H, editors: Textbook geriatric medicine and gerontology, Edinburgh, 1992, Churchill Livingstone.

Folstein MF, Folstein SE, McHugh PR: "Mini-mental state": a practical method for grading cognitive state of patients for the clinician, *J Psychiatr Res* 1975.

Freed S: Genitourinary disease in the elderly. In Rossman I, editor: *Clinical geriatrics,* Philadelphia, 1986, JB Lippincott, 352-363.

Gjorup T et al: Is growing old a disease? A study of attitudes of elderly people to physical symptoms, *J Chron Dis* 40:1095-1098, 1987.

Goldstein M et al: Urinary incontinence: Why people do not seek help, *J Gerontolog Nurs* 18(4):12-20, 1992.

Gordon D: As ESRD population grows older difficult questions arise, *Dialysis and transplantation* 18:594-596, 1989.

Gray M: *Genitourinary disorders,* St. Louis, 1992, Mosby.

Hu T: Impact of urinary incontinence on health-care costs, *JAGS* 38:292-295, 1990.

Jeter KF, Wagner DB: Incontinence in the American home, *JAGS* 38:379-380, 1990.

Jolleys JV: Reported prevalence of urinary incontinence in women in a general practice, *Brit Med J* 296:1389-1392, 1988.

Katz S et al: Studies of illness in the aged. The index of ADL: a standardized measure of biological and psychosocial function, *J Am Med Assoc* 185:94ff, 1963.

Kegel AH: Progressive resistance exercise in the functional restoration of the perineal muscles, *Am J Obstet Gynecol* 52:242-245, 1948.

Lindeman RD, Tobin JD, Shock NW: Longitudinal studies on the rate of decline in renal function with age, *J Am Geriatr Soc* 33(4):278, 1985.

McDowell BJ, Burgio KL: Urinary elimination. In Burke MM, Walsh MB, editors: *Gerontologic nursing: care of the frail elderly,* Boston, 1992, Mosby.

McDowell BJ et al: An interdisciplinary approach to the assessment and behavioral treatment of urinary incontinence in geriatric outpatients. *JAGS* 40:370-374, 1992.

McDowell BJ, Burgio KL: Urinary incontinence. In Stasn AS, Lyles MF, editors: *Manual of geriatric nursing,* Glenview, Ill., 1990, Scott, Foresman/Little, Brown Higher Education.

McDowell BJ, Burgio KL, Candib D: Behavioral and pharmacologic treatment of persistent urinary incontinence, *J Am Acad Nurse Pract* 2:17-23, 1989.

Meikle WA, Smith JA: Epidemiology of prostate cancer, *Urol Clin North Am* 17:709-718, 1990.

Melman J: Asymptomatic urinary tract infection specific concerns in elderly patients, *Consultant* July:115-122, 1992.

Meyer R: Renal function in aging, *J Am Geriatr Soc* 37:791-798, 1989.

Miller CA: New medication for treatment of benign prostatic hyperplasia, *Geriatr Nurs* 2, 111-112, 1993.

Mitteness LS: Knowledge and beliefs about urinary incontinence in adulthood and old age, *JAGS* 38:374-378, 1990.

Mitteness LS: The management of urinary incontinence by community-living elderly, *Gerontologist* 25:185-193, 1987.

Moorthy AV, Zimmerman SW: Renal disease in the elderly: clinicopathologic analysis or renal disease in 115 elderly patients *Clin Nephrol* 14:223, 1980.

National Institutes of Health Consensus Development Conference: Urinary incontinence in adults, *JAGS* 38:265-272, 1990.

Osterling JE: Prostate specific antigen: a critical assessment of the most useful tumor marker for adenocarcinoma of the prostate, *J Urol* 145:907-923, 1991.

Ouslander JG: Geriatric urinary incontinence, *Dis Mon* 38(2):71-149, 1992.

Ouslander JG: Urinary incontinence. In Hazzard WR et al, editor: *Principles of geriatric medicine and gerontology,* Philadelphia, 1990, McGraw-Hill Information Services.

Richie J, Shirley WV, Yogoda A: Carcinoma of the bladder. In Devita VT,. Hellman S, Rosenberg SA, editors: *Cancer principles and practices of oncology,* Philadelphia, 1985, JB Lippincott.

Rodgers H, Staniland JR, Lipkin GW: Acute renal failure: a study of elderly patients, *Age Ageing,* 19(1):36-42, 1990.

Rose MA et al: Behavioral management of urinary incontinence in homebound older adults, *Home Health Care Nurse* 8(5):10-15, 1990.

Rowe J et al: The effect of age on creatinine clearance in men: cross-sectional and longitudinal study, *J Gerontol* 31(2):155-163, 1976.

Rowe JW: Renal and lower urinary tract disease in the elderly. In Calkins E, Davis P, Ford A, editors: *The practice of geriatrics,* Philadelphia, 1986, JB Lippincott.

Schnelle JF: Treatment of urinary incontinence in nursing home patients by prompted voiding, *JAGS* 38:356-360, 1990.

Smith EK: *Renal disease,* New York, 1987, Churchill Livingstone.

Smith JB et al: Managing urinary incontinence in community-residing elderly persons, *Gerontologist* 29:229-233, 1989.

Stevens JK, Miller JI: Transrectal ultrasound an aid to diagnosing prostate cancer, *AORN J* 53:1166-1178, 1991.

Talbott L: Genitourinary system. In Hogstel MO, editor: *Clinical manual of gerontological nursing,* St. Louis, 1992, Mosby.

Todd M: Treating UTIs: *Geriatr Nurs* 2:95-96, 1990.

US Department of Health and Human Services: *Clinical practice guidelines: urinary incontinence in adults,* (AAAHCPR Pub No 92-0039) Rockville, Md., 1992, US Department of Health and Human Services Public Health Service Agency for Health Policy and Research.

Walsh PC, Lepor H: The role of radical prostatectomy in the management of prostate cancer, *Cancer* 60:526-537, 1987.

Walsh PC: Diseases of the prostate. In Wyngarded JB, Smith LH, editors: *Cecil textbook of medicine,* Philadelphia, 1985, WB Saunders, 1248-1265.

Walters MD: Pelvic floor rehabilitation: the role of muscle training, *AUGS Quart Rep* 11(2):1993.

Warren JW: Urine-collection devices for use in adults with urinary incontinence, *JAGS* 38:364-367, 1990.

Warren JW: Catheters and catheter care, *Clin Geriatr Med* 2:857-858, 1986.

Watt R: Bladder cancer: etiology and pathophysiology, *Semin Oncol Nurs* 2, 256-259, 1986.

Wein AJ: Pharmacologic treatment of incontinence, *JAGS* 38:317-325, 1990.

BIBLIOGRAPHY

Blath RA: Prostate cancer: new modalities aid in early detection, *Consultant* December 1992, 23-36.

Chodak GW, Keller P, Schoenberg HW: Assessment of screening for prostate cancer using Digital Rectal Examination, *J Urol* 141(5):1136-1138, 1989.

Resnick NM: Initial evaluation of the incontinent patient, *JAGS* 38:311-316, 1990.

Rosansky SJ, Eggers PW: Trends in the U.S. end-stage renal disease population: 1973-1983, *Am J Kidney Dis* 9(2):91, 1987.

CHAPTER 27

Neurologic and Cognitive Function

LEARNING OBJECTIVES

On completion of this chapter, the reader will be able to:

1. Describe the major functions of the nervous system.
2. Identify structural changes of neurons, synapses, and composition that occur with aging.
3. Identify functional changes in sensorimotor and motor function, memory, cognition, sleep patterns, and proprioception that occur with aging.
4. Compare normal, age-related changes of the neurologic system to those associated with cognitive disorders.
5. Differentiate cognitive disorders that most often affect the older adult.
6. Identify DSM-IV criteria for depression, delirium, dementia, amnestic disorder, and other cognitive disorders.
7. Implement the nursing process when caring for clients with cognitive deficits.

STRUCTURE AND FUNCTION OF THE NERVOUS SYSTEM

Review of normal structure and function of the nervous system provides the basis for understanding disorders and related systemic changes affecting the older adult. The function of the nervous system is integrated with other body functions. This chapter can be supplemented by other references detailing the pathologic and physiologic function of the nervous system. Structures of the spinal cord and brain are reviewed in this chapter.

The nervous and endocrine systems accomplish the coordination and regulation of the body as a whole. The primary functions include communication, integration, and control of body functions. The spinal cord and brain constitute the central nervous system (CNS). The CNS is the center of the regulatory process. It integrates some incoming sensory information, evaluates this information, and initiates an outgoing response. The peripheral nervous system (PNS) extends from the CNS and is made up of ganglia, which contain neurons, and nerves consisting of billions of neuronal cell processes. The cranial and spinal nerves consist of fibers that form incoming and outgoing information pathways.

The spinal cord lies within the spinal cavity, extending from the foramen magnum to the lower border of the first lumbar vertebra. The cord does not completely fill the spinal cavity; it also contains meninges, spinal fluid, a cushion of adipose tissue and blood vessels. Two bundles of nerve fibers project from each side of the spinal cord: the dorsal nerve root and the ventral nerve root. They join to form the spinal nerve on each side of the spinal cord. The spinal cord is responsible for sensory and motor conduction pathways between peripheral nerves and the brain. It is also the composite of reflex centers for all spinal cord reflexes.

The brain is one of the largest adult organs. It weighs about 3 lbs. but is generally smaller in both women and older people (Thibodeaux, Patton, 1994). Neurons of the brain grow in size after postnatal life but do not increase in number. Six major divisions of the brain include the cerebral cortex (cerebrum), diencephalon (interbrain), cerebellum, medulla oblongata, pons, and mesencephalon (midbrain) (Fig. 27-1). The medulla oblongata, pons, and midbrain are often referred to collectively as the brainstem.

The cerebrum is separated into two hemispheres, with each hemisphere dividing into five lobes: frontal, parietal, temporal, occipital, and insula (island of Reil). The cerebrum is separated from the cerebellum by a transverse fissure. Three types of tracts lie inferior to the cerebral cortex and make up the cerebrum's internal white matter. These are projection, association, and commissural tracts. Basal ganglia, or islands of gray matter, are contained deep inside each cerebral hemisphere.

The diencephalon is the part of the brain located between the cerebrum and the midbrain. It consists of structures around the third ventricle: the thalamus, epithalamus, subthalamus, and hypothalamus. The diencephalon also includes the optic chiasma and pineal body.

The thalamus serves as the major relay station for sensory impulses (e.g., pain, temperature, touch, emotions, reflex) transmitted to the cerebral cortex. The hypothalamus links the nervous system and endocrine system, relaying messages that enable emotions to result in changes in bodily functions. It also plays an essential role in maintaining the waking state, regulating appetite, and maintaining normal body temperature.

The cerebellum is the second largest part of the brain, located below the posterior portion of the cerebrum. The cerebellum has two large lateral masses, the cerebellar hemispheres and a central section called vermis. The cerebellum is composed of some short and long tracts. The short tracts connect the cerebella cortex with nuclei located in the interior of the cerebellum. The longer tracts connect the cerebellum with other parts of the brain and spinal cord.

The medulla oblongata, pons, and midbrain make up the brain stem. The medulla attaches to the spinal cord. Nuclei in the medulla include respiratory and vasomotor centers. The reticular formation extends into the pons from the medulla with one important nucleus functioning in the control of respiration. The midbrain lies below the diencephalon and on the inferior surface of the cerebrum, above the pons. Fibers from the cerebellum and from the frontal lobe of the cerebral cortex end in this area, whereas fibers that extend into the rubrospinal tracts of the cord have cells of origin in the midbrain.

Each portion of the brain is responsible for select functions as described in Table 27-1, including those of sensation, voluntary movement, and mental functions (Fig. 27-2). The cerebral cortex performs all mental functions and many essential motor, sensory and visceral functions. The left and right hemispheres of the cerebrum each specialize in separate functions, but no part of the brain functions independently. The left hemisphere specializes in language function and dominates some nonverbal functions such as gesturing and hand movements. The right hemisphere functions to perceive auditory stimuli. This includes nonspeech sounds such as melodies, coughing, and laughing. Right hemisphere functions also include tactual perception and perceiving and visualizing spatial relationships. Cortical neurons are responsible for reception of sensory impulses and sending motor impulses. Conduction by cortical neurons may lead to visceral changes such as dilatation or constriction of blood vessels.

The limbic system forms a curving border on the medial surface of the cerebrum. The structures of the limbic system have primary connections with various other parts of the brain, notably the thalamus, fornix, septal nucleus, amygdaloid nucleus, and hypothalamus. The limbic system and supporting structures play a role in learning, memory, and emotions.

The cerebellum performs three general functions, all of which have to do with control of skeletal muscles. It acts with the cerebral cortex to produce skilled movement by coordinating activities of groups of muscles and controls skeletal muscles to maintain equilibrium and helps control posture.

Functions of the medulla include cardiac, vasomotor, and respiratory reflexes. The medulla also contains projection tracts between the cord and brain, providing many mechanisms for sensory motor function. The pons and midbrain serve as conduction pathways between the cord and other parts of the brain. The pons also functions as the reflex center for certain cranial nerve reflexes mediated by the third and fourth cranial nerves.

Two main types of cells compose the nervous system: neurons and neuroglia. Each performs the specific function of conducting impulses and thereby contributes to the general functions of communication and integration.

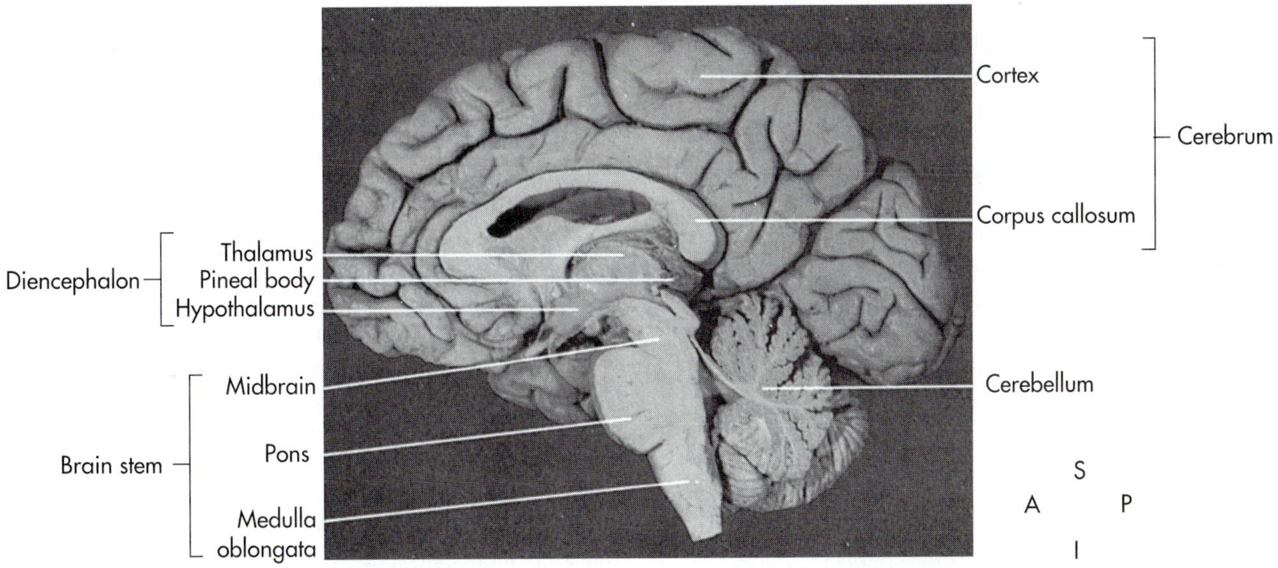

Figure 27-1 The CNS is divided into six main parts including (1) cerebrum, (2) diencephalon, (3) cerebellum, (4) pons, (5) medulla oblongata, and (6) midbrain (mesencephalon). (From Thibodeaux GA, Patton KT: *Anthony's textbook of anatomy and physiology,* ed 14, St. Louis, 1994, Mosby.)

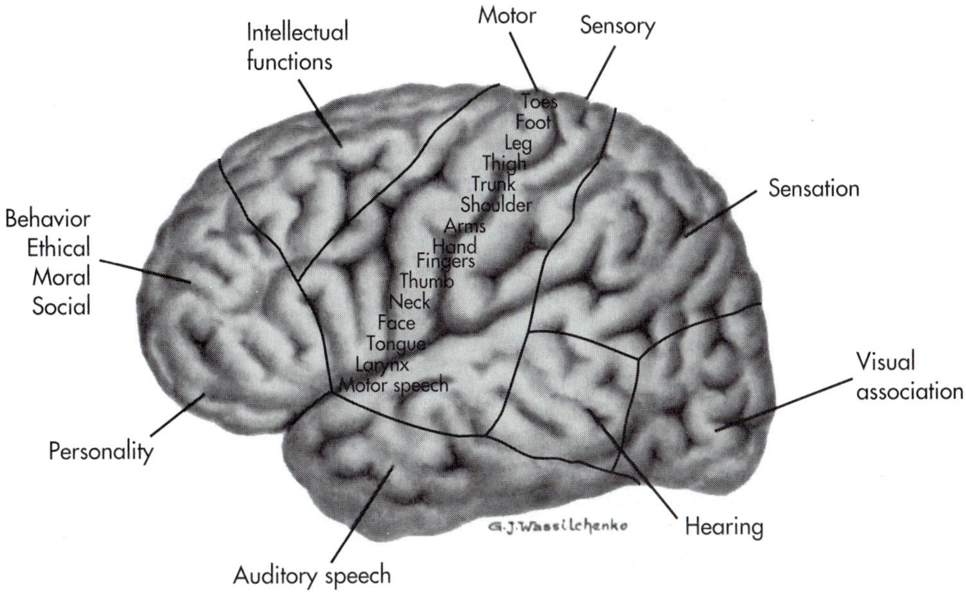

Figure 27-2 Lateral view of the cerebral hemisphere showing principal functional subdivisions of the cerebral hemisphere. (From Rudy EB: *Advanced neurological and neurosurgical nursing,* St. Louis, 1984, Mosby.)

TABLE 27-1

Functions of the Brain

Area	Function
Cerebrum	Conscious functions of analysis, integration, and interpretation of sensation; control of voluntary movement
Diencephalon	
Thalamus	Conscious recognition of crude sensation; involved in the emotional component of sensation, producing complex reflex movements and stimulus of the arousal or alerting mechanism
Hypothalamus	Control and integration of autonomic functions, control of anterior pituitary gland, mechanism for maintaining water balance; essential part of arousal or alerting mechanism, maintaining wakeful state; mechanism for regulating appetite or food intake; control of reproductive functions; and mechanism for maintaining body temperatures
Cerebellum	Synergetic control of muscle action to make movements smooth: postural reflexes and equilibrium
Medulla oblongata	Regulation of cardiac, vasomotor, and respiratory center; mediates reflex of coughing, vomiting, and sneezing; conducts impulses between the spinal cord and brain
Pons varolii	Contains tracts between the cord and various parts of the brain; center for cranial nerves 5 to 8; regulates respiration through the pneumotaxic centers
Midbrain	Contains projection tracts for functions of sensation and movement; centers for cranial nerves 3 to 4

Neurons specialize in impulse conduction, which makes all other nervous system functions possible. The neurons are classified according to the direction in which they conduct impulses and their structure (Fig. 27-3). The functional classifications are (1) afferent (sensory) neurons that transmit impulses to the spinal cord or brain, (2) efferent (motor) neurons that transmit away from the brain or spinal cord, and (3) interneurons for conducting impulses from afferent neurons toward or to the motor neurons. Interneurons are contained entirely within the CNS. Structural classification is determined by the number of processes. These are (1) multipolar neurons with only one axon and several dendrites, (2) bipolar neurons with only one axon and one dendrite, and (3) unipolar neurons that have a single process. The multipolar neurons predominate the nervous system.

Neurons are formed by a cell body and at least two processes: one axon and one or more dendrites (Fig. 27-4). The size, shape, orientation, and complexity of the dendrite affect the functions with other neurons. These processes are threadlike extensions from the cell body of the neuron. The elaborate branches of dendrites form circuits and networks within the nervous system. The axon of the neuron is a single process that extends from the cell body. The axon conducts impulses away from the cell body. Myelin is the lipid substance that forms the insulating covering of some axons, increasing the speed and efficiency of conduction among the neurons. Changes in myelin content of the nervous system may disrupt communication among the neurons.

Neuroglia perform the function of support and protection. Neuroglia provide structural support by anchoring the neuron to blood vessels. They provide physiologic support for neurons by producing myelin and eliminating nonfunctioning tissue (phagocytosis). Neuroglia are capable of cell division, giving them the ability to replace themselves. Clinically, they are the originating area of most tumors, since they are susceptible to abnormalities of cell division.

A synapse is the site of contact where transmission of the nerve impulse occurs between a neuron and another cell (Fig. 27-5). Transmission by the synapse may be neuron to neuron, neuron to muscle, or neuron to gland. Impulse transmission over a synapse is a chemical process that relies on release of a substance by the presynaptic neurons, although the resulting function is determined by the postsynaptic receptors, not by the neurotransmitter. More than 30 different compounds have been identified as having possible excitatory or inhibitory function. Examples of transmitter substances grouped into chemical classes include acetylcholine, amines, amino acids, and neuropeptides.

NORMAL AGE-RELATED CHANGES OF THE NEUROLOGIC SYSTEM

Structural and functional changes are intertwined and are dependent on variables, including the individual's genetic makeup and specific brain regions affected. Struc-

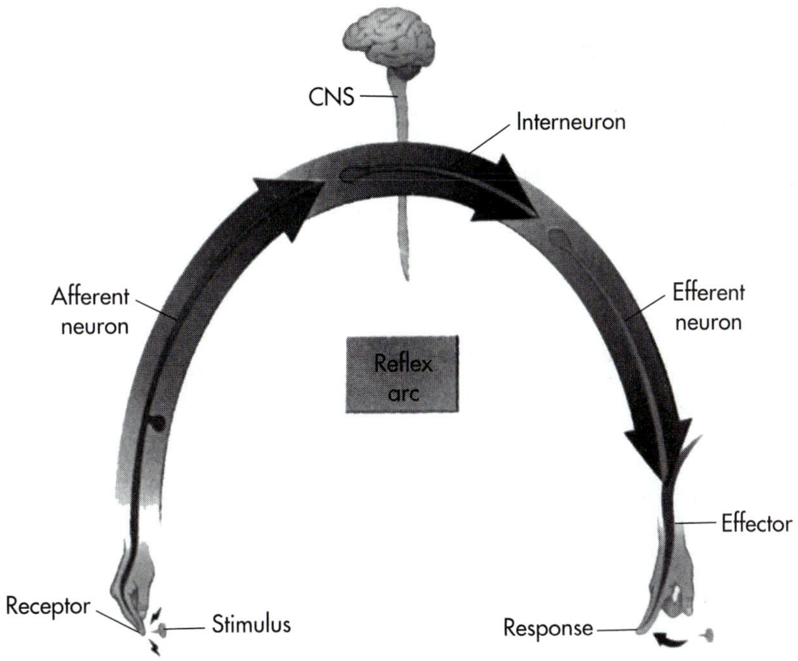

Figure 27-3 Neurons classified functionally according to the direction in which impulses are conducted. The typical pattern of impulse condition follows a pattern called the reflex arc. (From Thibodeaux G, Patton K: *Anthony's textbook of anatomy and physiology,* ed 14, St. Louis, 1994, Mosby.)

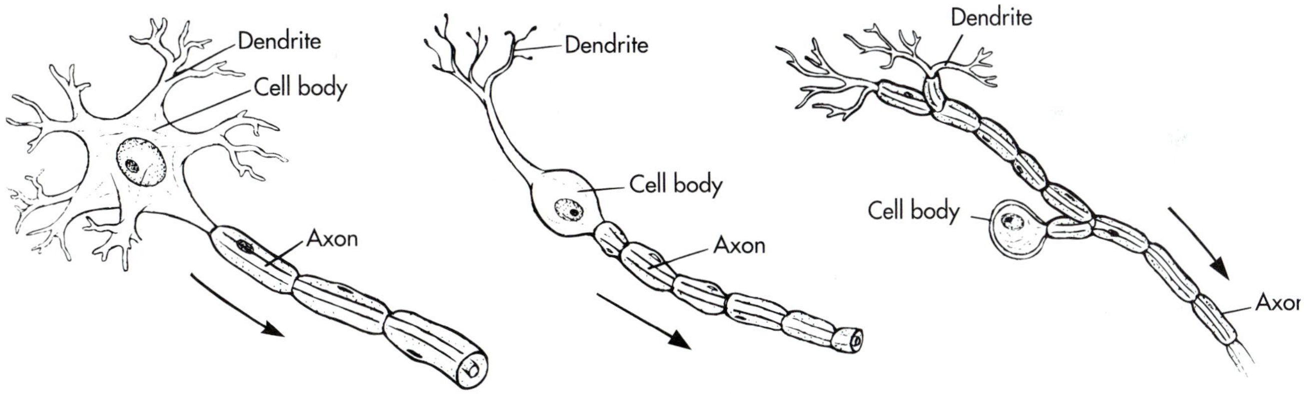

Figure 27-4 Structural classification of neurons. (1) Multipolar neuron, (2) bipolar neuron, and (3) unipolar neuron.(From Thibodeaux G, Patton K: *Anthony's textbook of anatomy and physiology,* ed 14, St. Louis, 1994, Mosby.)

tural and functional changes occur with aging, although specific causes of age-related changes remain unclear. Structural changes of the neuroanatomic features are not easily researched because of the interaction of experimental and environmental variables with biologic variables and the variance in life histories. A large percentage of older adults experience minor memory impairments, slower cognitive processing ability, changes in sleep patterns, vision, hearing, gait, and posture. In many cases, the neurologic diseases of aging present with clinical dysfunction that overlaps senescence. Anatomic structure changes include neuronal loss, synaptic changes, and changes in composition of brain and nerve cells.

The brain is sensitive to any changes in metabolism or oxygen supply. Impaired function caused by disease and adverse environmental changes may be accelerated as a result of changes in metabolism or oxygen supply. Changes may be caused by primary, age-related degeneration of neurons or may represent the cumulative effect

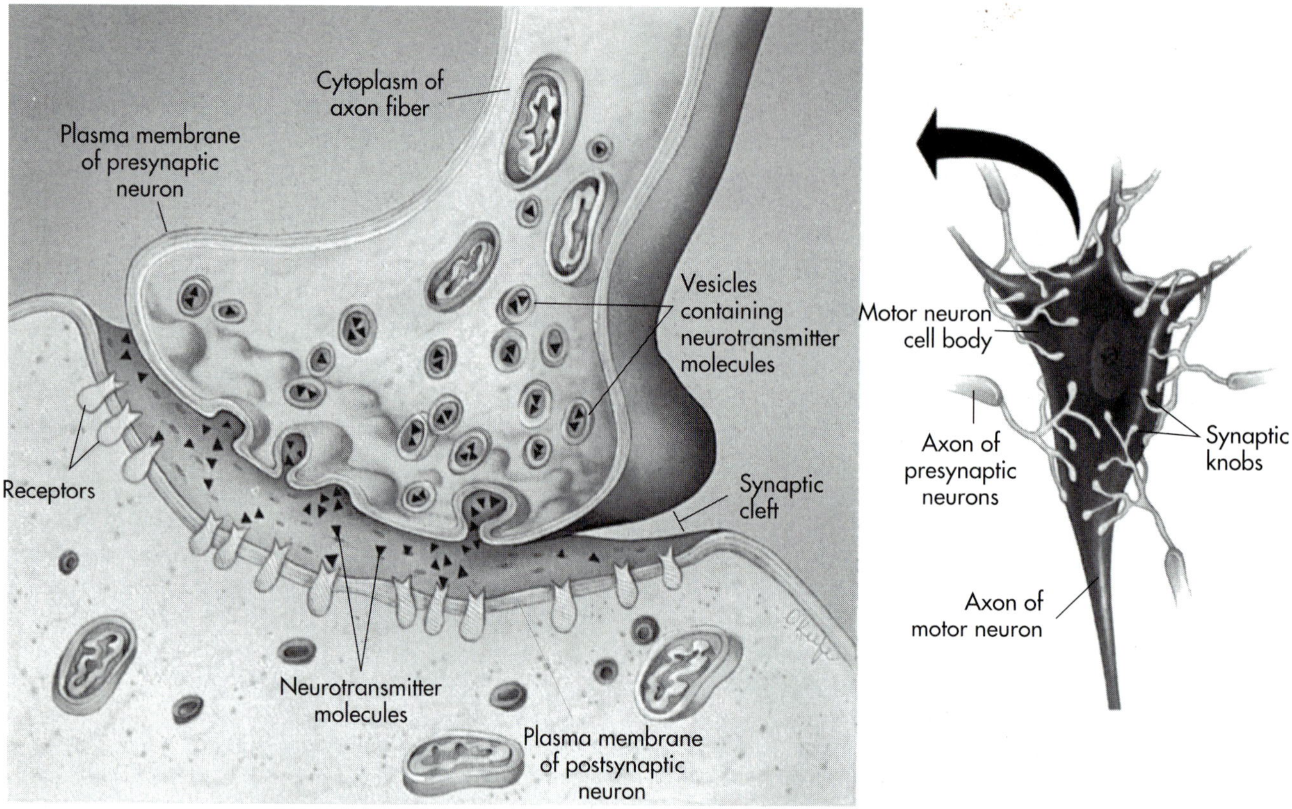

Figure 27-5 Structure of a synapse showing synaptic knob (or axon terminal of presynaptic neuron), the plasma membrane of a postsynaptic neuron and a synaptic cleft. On the arrival of an action potential at a synaptic knob, neurotransmitter molecules are released from vesicles in the knob into the synaptic cleft. Impulse conduction is initiated in the postsynaptic neuron by combining of neurotransmitter and receptor molecules in the plasma membrane of the postsynaptic neuron.

BOX 27-1

Age-Related Structural Changes in the Cerebrum

Decrease in brain weight
Reduction in number of functioning neurons
Increase in neuroglia
Increase in amount of senile plaque and neurofibrillary tangles
Accumulation of lipofuscin

of trauma, ischemia, and other pathologic conditions affecting the nervous system.

Structural Changes

Structural changes associated with aging include ventricular dilatation, brain atrophy, and increasing variability of brain size (Box 27-1). Cortical atrophy is greater in the frontal and temporal cortex. Gross morphologic changes show atrophy of ridges (gyri) and widening of the crevices (sulci). Enlargement of the ventricles may also be present. These changes can be validated with magnetic resonance imaging (MRI) and computerized tomography (CT) studies.

Neuronal Losses

Neuron loss is not a universal concomitant of aging, nor is it a straightforward loss. Neurons are postmiotic cells that do not duplicate themselves. A number of studies have measured cell size in the brains of young and old individuals, finding that neuron loss that occurs with aging affects the brain in varying parts and differing degrees. The loss of neurons to aging could have consequences with regard to the integrity of various brain regions and their ability to communicate with each other. Studies measuring neuron (cell body) size report that the function of aging may result in an increase, decrease, or unchanged size. It is estimated that approximately 100,000 neurons are lost daily and not replaced. This results in an approximate loss of 30% to 50% of the neurons from childhood to retirement (Willott, 1987). Actual brain weight changes have also been noted over a period of years, resulting in a 6% to 11% loss in brain weight in people over age 80 (Willott, 1987). The decrease in brain weight may be a result of the reduced neuron size rather than loss of neurons. A loss of neurons from some regions of the neocortex has been found to be common in the older adult. The neocortex forms the surface of the brain and is essential for most functions, from movement and perception to language, thinking, and "higher" functions. Change in neuron soma (cell body) size may indicate cellular pathology. The presence of a stable neuronal population does not guarantee that biochemical functions are intact. Unless pathology is present, the weight loss and atrophy bring few, if any, negative behavioral effects.

Theories on the loss or survival of neurons suggest that this is dependent on a number of variables, including species, specific brain region, and genetic makeup of the individual (Willott, 1987). Other theories suggest that wear and tear on the nervous system over the years causes death of the neuron. An example related to wear and tear is the accumulation of lipofuscins and neurofibrillary tangles on the inner structure of less active neurons (Katzman, Terry, 1983).

Synaptic Changes

Synaptic changes include a loss of dendrites and dendritic spines in some cells, and an increase in dendrites in other cells. These changes are believed to affect the release of chemical neurotransmitters and result in changes in neuronal communication. The changes in transmission and sensitivity of target cells to the neurotransmitters are inconclusive but may be caused by specific disorders. Norepinephrine and serotonin are believed to be underproduced in depressive disorders; dopamine is thought to be hypoactive in depression and inhibited in Parkinson's disease; and acetylcholine, responsible for cholinergic pathophysiology, has been implicated in movement disorders such as Parkinson's disease. Pathologic changes such as the degeneration of cholinergic neurons identified in Alzheimer's disease (AD) also affects synaptic responses.

Changes in Composition of the Brain and Nerve Cells

Accumulation of lipofuscin and neurofibrillary tangles are space-occupying lesions that occur in the older adult and affect nerve cell activity. Lipofuscins are yellow, insoluble granular pigments that are thought to be waste from partially broken-down membranes and other cell structures. These wastes are believed to fill up the cytoplasm and cause the cell to work less effectively. Accumulation of lipofuscins occur at differing rates in nerve cells; they are found more often in less active cells. Neurofibrillary tangles are abnormal neurofibers found in the cytoplasm of medium-size and large neurons. These neurofibers have been found only in humans and are less prevalent in the brains of healthy, active older adults.

Functional Changes

Functional changes in an older person do not consistently decline. Changes in sensorimotor and motor function, memory, cognition, sleep patterns, or proprioception occur at varying rates. Personality, or behaviors of the individual expressed by attitude and morale, remains generally more consistent during normal aging.

Sensorimotor Function

Decline in **sensorimotor function** is the most prevalent and notable change in the older person and may be the cause of other changes such as reaction time. The lens of the eye thickens and pupils appear smaller in older adults, so brighter light is used to compensate for visual loss. Presbyopia is caused by loss of elasticity of the lens, resulting in reduced ability to focus. Bifocal glasses or convex lenses are commonly used for correction. Presbycusis affects more than one third of the people over age 75 (Morris, McManus, 1991), resulting from neuronal loss in the inner ear. The common presenting complaint is difficulty understanding speech, caused by threshold loss at high frequencies. Consonants are also difficult to hear accurately.

Memory

Complaints common in the older adult include forgetting names, misplacing items, and poor recall of recent events or conversations. Short-term memory may decline with age, but long-term recall usually is maintained. Memory impairment as a sole symptom may be caused by an **amnesic syndrome** requiring continued monitoring. Although annoying, the difficulty remembering generally does not compromise everyday function. Strategies for adapting, such as making lists or posting reminder notes, can be incorporated to overcome the memory loss. Memory function in normal aging is preserved for relevant, well-learned material.

Cognition

Cognitive decline is modest in normal aging. Cognitive skills can be categorized as intellectual skills and speed-based psychomotor skills. Intellect is considered a collection of skills and achievements, described as crystallized intelligence (acquired knowledge), and fluid intelligence (ability to perceive spatial relationships, abstract reasoning) (Schaie, 1989). Crystallized intelligence is maintained throughout the lifetime, and skills may actually increase. Fluid intelligence peaks between ages 20 and 30 and declines in the years following (Jutagir, 1994).

Psychomotor skills also peak at age 20 but decline steadily thereafter. Age-related differences also become evident as the complexity of the task increases, which may be unrelated to the ability of the individual. In the absence of disease, some older people perform as well as younger, sedentary individuals. The prevalence of cognitive impairment was reported as 13% for moderate to severe ranges for people age 85 and older (Bachman et al, 1992). A combined clinical data and interview study reported prevalence of **dementia** of the Alzheimer's type (DAT) at 47% over age 85 (Evans et al, 1989). An investigation of longitudinal changes in cognitive functioning in a representative sample of people age 84 to 90 focused on the extent to which there is stability or decline in cognitive function during a 2-year period (Johansson, Zarit, Berg, 1992). The incidence of cognitive deficits ranged between 34% to 47%. This study indicated a pattern of high baseline rates of cognitive impairment, a relatively high incidence of individuals developing cognitive deficits over a 2-year period, and continuing stability of functioning for a majority of the respondents. Another longitudinal study examined the potential usefulness of objective psychologic tests to be used as predictors of follow-up cognitive status (Flicker, Ferris, Riesberg, 1991). Follow-up, using the Global Deterioration Scale (GDS) (Table 27-2) at 2 years showed that objective psychologic tests can be used to discriminate between mildly impaired older adults who are likely to undergo cognitive deterioration and those whose prognosis is benign.

TABLE 27-2

Global Deterioration Scale

Stage 1	No cognitive or functional decrements
Stage 2	Complaints of mild forgetfulness and some work difficulties
Stage 3	Mild cognitive impairment on cognitive battery, concentration problems, some difficulty at work and in traveling alone
Stage 4	Late confusional stage, increased problems in planning and handling finances, increased denial of symptoms, withdrawal
Stage 5	Poor recall of recent events, may need to be reminded about proper clothing and bathing
Stage 6	More advanced memory and orientation problems, needs assistance with activities of daily living (ADLs), more personality changes
Stage 7	Late dementia with loss of verbal abilities, incontinence, loss of ability to walk, may become comatose

Reprinted with permission from Reisberg B et al: The Global Deterioration Scale for assessment of primary degenerative dementia, *Am J Psychiatry* 139:1136-1139, 1982, American Psychiatric Association

Sleep Patterns

Change in sleep patterns is a consistent, age-related change. Older people exhibit a slight tendency for an increase in total daily sleep and experience an increased incidence of awakening after sleep onset. Electroencephalogram (EEG) studies of older adults often show reduced slow wave amplitude and more interrupted REM episodes during sleep. These changes in sleep patterns result in the older person feeling unrested (see Chapter 9).

Motor Function

A mild state of motor function change is common during aging, usually exhibited by a stooped, forward-flexed posture and a slow, somewhat shuffling gait. The gait abnormalities may be related to age-associated conditions such as arthritis of the hips, knees, or spine. Some loss of strength and slowing of motor reaction time is associated with normal aging and is not the cause of gait changes. Cutaneous sensory dysfunction, caused by loss of large myelinated fibers of the dorsal root ganglion, also may contribute to postural dysfunction and loss of Achilles tendon reflex. Mild muscular wasting may occur, particularly affecting grip strength. This may result in mild impairment of fine motor activities. Motor abnormalities, including akinesia, tremor, and rigidity, are believed to be directly related to abnormal output from the basal ganglia that results in disordered function in frontal cortical centers (Meara, 1994) and are not the result of normal aging.

Proprioception

Proprioception, or the ability to maintain an upright position without falling, depends on the ability to use balance, posture, and movement. Balance and postural stability are complex functions requiring multiple sensory input, motor output, and central integration of both components to accomplish balance and locomotion. Abnormalities of proprioception affecting "normal" older adults are results of changes in the nervous system and muscle. The difficulty with spacial orientation results in inability to avoid obstacles quickly, or respond with fast movement.

The normal gait requires balancing on a narrow base, using an intact neuromusculoskeletal frame and nervous system. The upper body and head movement tend to be used more by older adults to combat postural sway. Dynamic balance, or the ability to keep the body upright and poised during movement, also decreases with age. Older people take more steps to reposition their body mass over their feet than younger people. The decrease in postural stability with age affects women more than men. A 20% to 40% decline in the ability to stand on one leg with both eyes open and a 60% decline in the ability to complete the same task with the eyes closed occurs from ages 25 to 75 (Polvin, 1980).

Personality

Personality, described as the stable, distinctive patterns of behavior, thought, and emotion, remains stable during normal aging, although it may be influenced by an older adult's experiences. Signs of impaired emotional control, diminished initiative, withdrawal, or other changes should be considered an indicator of other problems. These symptoms may be an initial sign of brain dysfunction.

COMMON PROBLEMS AND CONDITIONS ASSOCIATED WITH ALTERED THOUGHT PROCESSES

Altered thought processes occur with cognitive decline or disturbances in **cognitive function.** Definitions of cognitive function may be interpreted differently, depending on the purpose (e.g., clinical assessment, research, or program evaluation). The term cognitive function includes several categories, including attention span, concentration, intelligence, judgment, learning ability, memory, orientation, perception, problem solving, psychomotor ability, reaction time, and social intactness (McDougall, 1990). The terms cognitive function and mental status are used interchangeably in the literature. The interdependent areas of affective and cognitive functioning are an overlap of mental status and should not be the sole determinant of the diagnosis.

Contributing Factors

Contributing factors associated with altered thought processes are believed to be neuroanatomic, caused by physiologic, environmental, or other factors. Reversible causes account for a significant percentage of clients who present with **delirium.** Causes include medication effects, depression, metabolic and nutritional deficiencies, increased intercranial pressure, or hydrocephalus.

All organs show an age-related decline with increased use of reserve capacity to maintain homeostasis. The aging brain, as with other organs, gradually loses its reserve capacity. It has been generally assumed that cognitive function declines in old age because of morphologic changes in cerebral tissue and decreases in circulatory capacity and neurotransmitters. Although these are considerations when determining the cause of changes in the cognitive function of the older adult, studies have challenged this thought.

> **Insight** • *Regeneration and rebuilding of the brain have been termed as plasticity and previously thought to be accomplished only by children and adolescents. It is believed there is also potential for increased plasticity in the older adult. Previously, it has been determined that because neurons are postmiotic, they are unable to replicate themselves and the brain stops growing during the postnatal period. Researchers have found that several axons can regenerate and that those repaired cells may be able to rebuild connections with other cells. The process has been reported as a regenerative process in Alzheimer's victims. Plasticity can continue if the older adult recognizes the need to maintain intellectual skills and participates in an active lifestyle.*

Mental Status Examinations

Mental status examinations are useful to quantify the level of dysfunction for purposes of planning and evaluating care. Cognitive function and mental states have overlapping characteristics, but are not the same. A basic neuropsychologic test battery evaluates memory, language, attention, conceptualization, attention, and visuospatial skills. Attention during the assessment should also be paid to hearing, gait, balance, distal deep tendon reflexes, plantar responses, primary sensory modalities in the lower extremities, and cerebrovascular integrity. The causes of behavioral disturbances in older clients with dementia are not always evident and many times, behavioral changes may signify additional pathologic processes.

Several screening questionnaires have been standardized for rating the mental status of clients. The Mental Status Questionnaire (MSQ) (Kahn et al, 1960), Mini-Mental State Examination (MMSE) (Folstein, Folstein, McHugh, 1975) (see Chapter 4), Functional Dimension Scale (FDS) (Moore, 1983), Information Memory Concentration Test (IMCT) (Blessed, Tomlinson, Roth, 1968), Short Blessed Test (SBT) (Katzman et al, 1983), and Short Portable Mental Status Questionnaire (SPMSQ) (Pfeiffer, 1975) (see Chapter 4) can be performed easily by most health care providers. These tests are used to screen clients for dementia and to quantify the degree of cognitive dysfunction for following the progress of the syndrome.

The MSQ is a 10-item list that asks the name and location of where the test is being taken; current date, month, and year; client age; and the name of the current U.S. president and predecessor. It is one of the shortest and most widely used instruments. The test is reliable in identifying clients with moderate to severe cognitive impairment. The MSQ is not beneficial for all client evaluations (Alexopoulos, 1991).

The IMCT (also called Blessed Dementia Scale) is used along with a scale of behavioral competence. The questions of orientation, recent and remote mem-

BOX 27-2

Short Blessed Test

"Now I would like to ask you some questions to check your memory and concentration. Some of them may be easy and some of them may be hard."

	Maximum error	Error score	Weight	Weighted score
1. What year is it now? ________	1	_____	×4 =	_______
2. What month is it now? ________	1	_____	×3 =	_______
Please repeat this phrase after me and remember it: John Brown, 42 Market Street, Chicago Number of trials to learning: ________				
3. About what time is it without looking at your watch (within 1 hour)? Response: ________ Actual Time: ________	1	_____	×3 =	_______
4. Count backwards from 20 to 1. (mark correctly sequenced numerals) 20 19 18 17 16 15 14 13 12 11 10 9 8 7 6 5 4 3 2 1	2	_____	×2 =	_______
5. Say the months of the year in reverse order. (mark correct months) D N O S A JL JN MY AP M F J	2	_____	×2 =	_______
6. Repeat the name and address I asked you to remember. John Brown, 42 Market Street, Chicago ___ _____ __ _____ _____ _______	5	_____	×2 =	_______
			TOTAL WEIGHTED SCORE	_______

Score ≥ 8 indicates impairment.

Katzman R et al: Validation of a short orientation-memory-concentration test of cognitive impairment, *Am J Psychiatry,* 140:734, 1983.

ory, and concentration have been a predictor of dementia or other cognitive disorders. Both aging and depression have an effect on IMCT performance (Jorm, Jacob, 1989). The Short Blessed Scale is a revised version consisting of six questions used by many disciplines (Box 27-2).

The Functional Dementia Scale (FDS) is designed for completion by caretakers of people with dementia to objectively monitor the disease course and to evaluate treatment. The items on the FDS were selected to assess the major problems associated with dementia such as emotional lability, wandering, agitation, incontinence, memory loss, and the need for supervision (Box 27-3). It is a brief scale capable of distinguishing varying degrees of functional limitation and is useful in establishing the level of impairment and assessing the impact of interventions over time.

The Mini-Mental State Examination (MMSE) is used to assess orientation, immediate and recent memory, attention, calculation, and language and motor skills. The Short Portable Mental Status Questionnaire (SPMSQ) is another brief scale used to detect the presence and degree of intellectual impairment. Items measured by this examination include orientation, memory, general knowledge, and subtraction. The MMSE and SPMSQ are discussed in detail in Chapter 4.

Psychiatric tests used for testing for dementia or disorders related to cognitive function include the Dementia Rating Scale (DRS) and the Wechsler Adult Intelligence Scale (WAIS). These are usually administered by a psychologist or psychiatrist. The DRS consists of five subscales with items arranged in order of difficulty. The DRS is more extensive than some other tests and may require 30 to 45 minutes to complete. The DRS is sensitive to clients with mild dementia but is most useful in assessing the functional capacity of individuals for whom

BOX 27-3

Functional Dementia Scale

Circle one rating for each item:
1. None or little of the time
2. Some of the time
3. Good part of the time
4. Most or all of the time

Patient ______________________
Observer ______________________
Position or relation to patient ______________________
Facility ______________ Date ____________

1	2	3	4	(01)	Has difficulty in completing simple tasks on own, e.g., dressing, bathing, doing arithmetic.
1	2	3	4	(02)	Spends time either sitting or in apparently purposeless activity.
1	2	3	4	(03)	Wanders at night or needs to be restrained to prevent wandering.
1	2	3	4	(04)	Hears things that are not there.
1	2	3	4	(05)	Requires supervision or assistance in eating.
1	2	3	4	(06)	Loses things.
1	2	3	4	(07)	Appearance is disorderly if left to own devices.
1	2	3	4	(08)	Moans.
1	2	3	4	(09)	Cannot control bowel function.
1	2	3	4	(10)	Threatens to harm others.
1	2	3	4	(11)	Cannot control bladder function.
1	2	3	4	(12)	Needs to be watched so doesn't injure self, e.g., by careless smoking, leaving the stove on, falling.
1	2	3	4	(13)	Destructive of materials around him, e.g., breaks furniture, throws food trays, tears up magazines.
1	2	3	4	(14)	Shouts or yells.
1	2	3	4	(15)	Accuses others of doing him bodily harm or stealing his possessions—when you are sure the accusations are not true.
1	2	3	4	(16)	Is unaware of limitations imposed by illness.
1	2	3	4	(17)	Becomes confused and does not know where he/she is.
1	2	3	4	(18)	Has trouble remembering.
1	2	3	4	(19)	Has sudden changes of mood, e.g., gets upset, angered, or cries easily.
1	2	3	4	(20)	If left alone, wanders aimlessly during the day or needs to be restrained to prevent wandering.

Reprinted with permission from Moore JT et al: A functional dementia scale, *J Fam Pract* 16:498, 1983. © Appleton and Lange, Inc.

the diagnosis of dementia has already been established. It may also be useful in assessing behavioral changes over time. The Wechsler Adult Intelligence Scale (WAIS) (Wechsler, 1981) is an intelligence test used by psychiatrists. The test is broadly divided into verbal and performance scales. The verbal subtests measure the general knowledge and vocabulary. The performance scales measure visual skills, including analysis of patterns and perceived relationships.

Numerous other diagnostic tools provide information regarding specific areas of cognitive decline (see Research box, p. 738). These tests can be used to determine if referral for further testing is necessary. In summary, key aspects of mental status assessments include the following:

1. Consideration of apparent and less obvious factors
2. Determining the nature of current difficulties
3. Obtaining a history of current and past related difficulties
4. Conducting a medical evaluation
5. Determining presence of psychiatric associated problems
6. Evaluation of the individual's ability to function on a day-to-day basis
7. Evaluation of the breadth and quality of social relationships and environmental resources

Cognitive Disorders Associated with Altered Thought Processes

Cognitive disorders associated with altered thought processes in the older person include disorders associated with dementia, delirium, depression, or amnestic or cognitive disorders of unspecified origin (Table 27-3). An accurate diagnosis of syndromes associated with altered thought processes is a challenge. Syndromes may go undiagnosed because of similarities in the presentation of cognitive dysfunction. Each has a distinct etiologic factor. Diagnosis of disease(s) underlying the cognitive syn-

RESEARCH

Baltes MM, Kuhl K, Sowarka D: Testing for limits of cognitive reserve capacity: A promising strategy for early diagnosis, *J Gerontol* 47:P165-167, 1992.

Sample, setting

Participants were selected from senior apartment buildings. The ages of the 81 participants ranged from 58 to 86. All participants were considered in satisfactory to good health, without visual or hearing impairments. A psychiatric assessment determined 25 of the participants were at risk for dementia.

Methodology

A psychiatric interview was conducted to differentiate healthy from at-risk older adults. A training program, Figural Relations, was conducted in five sessions with a pretest and posttest. Stepwise hierarchical analyses of regression were used to analyze the testing results.

Findings

Within the sample, pretraining scores did not permit prediction of at-risk status for dementia. Posttraining scores did accomplish this. It is believed that the healthy individuals were able to improve scores from pretest to posttest, providing the ability to determine those at-risk, whereas those that were premorbid did not improve scores.

Implications

The reserve capacity of a person allows a healthy person to maximize the cognitive system when needed. People demonstrating cognitive changes may benefit from training if the process is unrelated to dementia. The specific type of training that might be more beneficial for people with beginning symptoms of dementia is also significant and requires further studies. Nurses working with the older adult should recognize preventive measures for not only maintenance of the physical status, but of mental status. Degeneration of the neurologic system does occur, in spite of efforts to remain healthy, and measures can be taken by caregivers to determine preventive activities.

drome has implications, since appropriate treatment of many of the disease processes improves the cognitive status.

Depression

Depression is one of the most common disorders encountered in old age, and may present along with other disorders (Wragg, Jeste, 1989). Depression is an emotional disorder that can result in cognitive impairment. This is usually minimal, unless the depression is severe. Depression may occur concomitantly with early dementia because of the older adult's awareness of the loss of physical or intellectual functioning. Depressed older adults may neglect eating or caring for a chronic medical condition, resulting in a superimposed development of delirium.

Depression is likely to manifest itself through physical signs including fatigue, constipation, psychomotor retardation, repetitive mood cycles, changes in appetite, weight or sleep patterns. The clinical presentation of depression varies from person to person. Diagnosis of depression in older adults is difficult, resulting in an increased possibility of confusing the presenting symptoms with those of the physical and psychologic sequelae of normal aging or dementia. A significant relationship exists between depression and memory performance, slowing, and apathy, which creates difficulty in distinguishing depression from dementia. The depressed person may be cognitively oriented and able to perform satisfactorily on tests of memory, learning, and intelligence. Depending on the degree of depression, however, these people may respond to cognitive test questioning with, "I don't know." These people complain of memory loss, whereas those people who are organically impaired lack the insight into their cognitive loss to complain of its occurrence. Table 27-3 offers a comparison of selective features associated with dementia, delirium, and depression.

Estimates of depression among clients with dementia vary widely, from 15% to 57%, and depression may be 10 times higher among clients with AD than in the general older population (Alexopoulos, Abrams, Young, 1988). Major depressive disorder is associated with a high mortality rate (Rovner et al, 1992). Evidence suggests that death rates increase four times in individuals over age 55 (American Psychiatric Association [APA], 1994).

Pseudodementia is a label sometimes used for people with symptoms of depression who present with symptoms of dementia (Wells, 1989). Although there are some similarities in these disorders, the differences described in Table 27-4 can be used to differentiate the two disorders. Pseudodementia was once viewed as a benign entity; however, it now appears that many cases result in an irreversible disorder. The annual rate of dementia development in the general population is 2%, compared with 15% among clients who had initially recovered from pseudodementia (Kral, Emery, 1989). In some instances, the label refers to any disorder other than dementia that yields some cognitive disorder in older people and may be used as a synonym for depression or delirium.

Delirium

Delirium is referred to as a disturbance of consciousness that is accompanied by a change in cognition that cannot be better accounted for by a preexisting or evolving dementia (APA, 1994). It has a relatively rapid onset with

MEDICAL MANAGEM

Delirium

Diagnostic tests and proc

- Mental status exa
- EEG
- CT scan to hematom
- MRI to the

TABLE 27-3

Comparison of Symptoms Associated with Deme

	Dementia	Delirium
Orientation	Disoriented	Disorien sciousn awaren
Judgment	Focus on irrelevant concerns	Yes or n
Memory	Impaired for recent events, intact remote memory	Impaired events;
Behavior	Agitation or apathy, unable to perform self-care	Agitation able to
Onset	Gradual—months to years	Abrupt,
Mood/affect	Labile, inappropriate	Varies
Speech	Sparse, repetitive; does not complain of deficits; later does not attempt to conceal problems	May be fluent;
Prognosis	No return to predemented state	Resolves cause

TABLE 27-4

Comparison of Pseudodementia and Dementia

Pseudodementia	Dementia
Similarities	
Lack of self-care	Somatic complaints
Restlessness	Disorientation
Irritability	Memory and concentration difficulties
Loss of creativity	
Differences	
Onset quite abrupt	Onset insidious
Progression usually rapid	Progression usually slow
Client aware of deficits	Client not as aware
Complaint of memory loss	Client tries to hide loss (confabulation)
Global responses ("I don't know")	Near-miss answers
Client gives evidence of deficits	Client emphasizes accomplishments
Impairment not usually worse at night	Usually worse at night
Mood depressed	Client is typically "happy"
Vegetative symptoms (sleep disturbance, anorexia, fatigue, loss of sex drive)	Nonvegetative
History of psychiatric disturbance common	Not common
Suicide risk considerable	Suicide risk lower

a fluctuating and typically brief course. Symptoms include disturbances in the ability of the individual to concentrate or to maintain attention to external stimulus, and difficulty shifting from one topic to another. Disorganized thinking is evident in unfocused speech or difficulty understanding the individual. Other difficulties may include the following:

- Clouding of consciousness, fluctuation of awareness

ENT

dures
ninations

rule out brain tumor, subdural
a or hydrocephalus
reveal detailed structural changes in
brain
eurologic assessment
- Drug studies to identify drug toxicity as a cause
- Complete blood count (CBC) with differential to rule out septicemia
- Electrolyte studies to identify potassium and sodium deficits, or hypoglycemia, which can cause mental confusion
- Blood cultures
- Liver function studies
- Thyroid function studies
- Vitamin B and folate levels

Treatment

Determine and eliminate the causative factors or underlying conditions by conducting the following:

- Change medication therapy to eliminate medications that are unnecessary or contraindicated.
- Resume medication therapy if medications are not being taken properly
- Surgically correct structural causes (hematoma, tumor, hydrocephalus)
- Correct the medical disorder
- Administer antibiotic therapy for infectious disorders, and attain proper nutritional status

Prognosis

Delirium is a collection of cognitive deficits commonly associated with treatable conditions. The recovery will be determined by the cause of the condition and the rate with which it is reversed. Underlying diseases must be treated to prevent irreversible dementia.

- Misperceptions, illusions, or hallucinations
- Disoriented to place or time
- Memory problems
- Increase or decrease in physical activity
- Presence of strong emotional reactions

Causes of delirium are usually unrelated to changes of the nervous system (Table 27-5). The history, physical examination, and laboratory results may signify an organic cause, but until this is evident, a nonorganic cause must be considered a factor. Environmental factors such as rapid changes in location and sensory deprivation can precipitate delirium.

Delirium can be caused by multiple factors, including intoxication from prescribed drugs, interactions among drugs, metabolic disturbances with a disruption of complex physical and chemical processes that sustain life, cardiovascular problems, infection, fever, reaction to alcohol, pain, anemia, tumor, brain disorder, or chronic lung disease. The cause may also be related to disturbances in the sleep/wake cycle and physical or psychosocial stress. The disorder is given a specific diagnosis based on its cause (e.g., a general medical condition, substance intoxication or withdrawal, or a combination of these factors). In individuals over age 65 who are hospitalized for a general medical condition, approximately 10% are reported to exhibit delirium on admission. Another 10% to 15% may develop delirium while in the hospital (APA, 1994) (see Medical Management box above).

TABLE 27-5

Characteristics and Causes of Delirium

Characteristics	Causes
Rapid onset Reversible (treatable) Erratic lucidity and somnolence	Intoxicants (drugs and alcohol) Head injury Lack of sleep Tumor Hypoxia Malnutrition, nutritional deficiencies Small strokes (transient ischemic attack [TIA]) Hyperthermia or hypothermia Pain Stress Metabolic disorders Hyperthyroidism, hypothyroidism changes in blood glucose level hypoxia Postsurgical procedure

Dementia

Dementia is defined as a cognitive disorder characterized by multiple deficits of physiologic causes (APA, 1994). Dementia can be grouped into four categories, including primary degenerative dementia, vascular dementia, reversible or partially irreversible dementias, or other neurologic disorders. Reversible dementias may become irreversible without treatment of the causative factors. Dementia is characterized by loss of memory and at least one other disturbance of intellectual function (e.g., orientation, attention, calculation, language, and motor skills). Short- and long-term memory impairment occurs. The individual has difficulty with abstract thinking, such as being unable to define the differences among objects or words, or the inability to deal with life issues. Aphasia (the inability to understand words), agnosia (inability to recognize familiar objects), apraxia (problems manipulating things), and agraphia (difficulty writing and drawing) are all symptoms of dementia. Personality changes may become apparent.

Changes in neurologic status caused by a disease process result in dementia, which is generally a condition of later life. Specific causes have been linked to genetic factors, immunologic changes, and viral or environmental causes (Table 27-6). It is believed that if individuals reach the age of 80 without symptoms of dementia, they have an 80% probability of not developing dementia in later years. The disorder is prevalent in 13% to 20% of people over age 80. The more symptomatic dementias occur at earlier ages rather than later

TABLE 27-6

Characteristics and Causes Associated with Dementia

Characteristics	Causes
Slow, insidious onset	Degenerative disorders
Irreversible (nontreatable)	AD
Progressive	Pick's disease
	Huntington's chorea
	Vascular disorders
	Vascular dementia (multi-infarct dementia)
	Cerebrovascular accident (CVA)
	Aneurysm
	Infections
	Creutzfeldt-Jakob disease
	Human immunodeficiency virus (HIV)
	Syphilis
	Mechanical disorders
	Trauma
	Normal pressure hydrocephalus (NPH)
	Subdural hematoma
	Parkinson's disease
	Neoplastic disorders
	Glioma
	Meningitis

ages. Research of the problem has been difficult because of the lack of a standard definition of mild dementia, and difficulty in detecting symptoms of early dementia. Studies indicate that approximately 11% of older adults have mild dementia (Hinrichson, 1990); severe dementia is estimated to affect about 4% of people age 65 or older.

DAT AD is a progressive disorder, the cause of which is not fully understood. Research has focused on genetic, viral, environmental, immunologic and other theories. AD can only be accurately diagnosed with brain biopsy or autopsy, which shows accumulation of cortical neuritic (senile) plaques in the gray matter, neurofibrillary tangles in excess of those found in normal aging, amyloid angiopathy, and/or granulovascular degeneration of neurons in the pyramidal cell layer of the hippocampus. Without use of one of the methods of diagnosis, the diagnosis can only be *possible* AD. It is also known that people with AD have decreased amounts of choline acetyltransferase, a chemical in the brain that plays an important role in human learning and memory.

Probable AD is estimated to be diagnosed in approximately 4 million people in the United States. It is believed that by the year 2050 as many as 14 million Americans may be affected (National Institute of Aging [NIA], 1992). Approximately 60% of the dementia in people over age 65 is caused by AD.

AD is believed to be genetically transmitted in some instances but not an exclusively inherited disease. Researchers have reported the possible location of a gene associated with some kinds of AD, but this is only the first step in determining genetic transference. It has been found that AD is dominantly inherited in families with an early onset of dementia. The gene, chromosome 21, has also been associated with development of the disease. Evidence supports linkage to chromosome 21 in families with early onset disease and chromosome 19 in families with late onset disease. Chromosome 14 is also being linked to AD (Perrcak-Vance et al, 1991).

Viral residue from prior serious illness such as herpes zoster, herpes simplex, or viral encephalitis is believed to be a possible precursor for AD or primary degenerative dementia, although there is no direct evidence of a cause. Viral infection of the brain has become an important topic of study because of the association of dementia and acquired immunodeficiency syndrome (AIDS).

Researchers are studying the origin of the amyloid deposited in the senile plaques of brain cells of clients with AD. The amyloid precursor is considered to have an important role in myeloid deposition in AD. Amyloid fibrils in and around the cerebral blood vessels and amyloid-laden neuritic plaques replace the degenerating nerve endings.

Exposure to metals is considered a factor because of the fact that AD appears sporadically. Aluminum, mercury, cadmium, lead, and manganese have been studied.

The greatest attention has been paid to the presence of aluminum found in the core of neurofibrillary tangles. It has been suggested that clients with AD possess some genetic defect that produces a fault in the individual's ability to handle aluminum. Animals given large amounts of aluminum showed microscopic brain changes similar to those found in clients with AD; however, clients exposed to large amounts of aluminum (e.g., dialysis clients) do not consistently show changes. The belief that exposure to metals is the cause of AD remains a controversial issue.

Other factors being researched include environmental factors such as toxins or chemicals. Environmental factors that are associated with cognitive dysfunction include exposure to toxic substances or chemicals. A report by the Office of Technology Assessment (1990) focuses on industrial chemicals, pesticides, therapeutic drugs, food additives, or cosmetic ingredients. Chronic and excessive alcohol use is also associated with impaired cognitive functioning. The rate of decline in clients with AD varies, but those with long-term or recent history of alcohol abuse have been found to decline faster than nonabusers (Teri, Hughes, Larson, 1990). Reports suggest an association between AD and vitamin B_{12} deficiency. Lower levels of B_{12} have been seen in clients with AD than in clients with other dementia disorders (McCaddon, Kelly, 1994). Other theories to the cause of AD include abnormality in the immune system and the possibility of accumulated damages (insults) to the brain from various sources such as trauma.

Symptoms of AD are multifaceted (Table 27-7). Those afflicted demonstrate loss of intellectual abilities such as memory, judgment, abstract thought, and changes in personality and behavior. As the disease progresses, gait and motor disturbances increase. During the last stages, the individual becomes mute and bedridden. The average duration of illness is 8 to 10 years (APA, 1994).

Vascular dementia This type of dementia is the second most common type, accounting for 10% to 20% of the cases of dementia. It is also referred to as multi-infarct dementia (MID). Multiple medical problems may result in MID. These include arteriosclerotic plaques, blood dyscrasias, cardiac decompensation, primary hypertension, systemic emboli, or spasms of the blood vessels in segments of the brain (also referred to as transient ischemic attacks or TIAs). The progressive loss of brain tissue is a result of a series of small strokes (infarcts) caused by occlusions and blockages of the arteries to the brain. The onset may be gradual or abrupt. Gradual onset results in lack of awareness by the individual that an infarct is occurring. Abrupt onset results in immediate neurologic symptoms, including one-sided weakness or focal neurologic signs. Destruction of the brain tissue resulting from the small emboli or strokes may be localized or diffuse. Pathologically, asymmetric regions of cerebral softening and hemorrhage, with evidence of atherosclerotic disease, are diffuse and irregular. Factors contributing to the disease are arrhythmias, hypertension, myocardial infarction (MI), TIAs, peripheral vascular disease (PVD), diabetes mellitus (DM), obesity, and smoking. If there is a series of strokes, the pattern of decline in function increases. Some recovery of function occurs over the weeks to months that follow, but recovery often does not reach pre-stroke levels. As the damage from the infarct accumulates, the individual shows more widespread evidence of diminished mental ability. Symptoms depend on the location of the infarct. Symptoms that can suddenly begin include confusion and problems with recent memory, wandering, getting lost in familiar places, moving with rapid, shuffling steps, loss of bladder or bowel control, inappropriate display of emotions, or difficulty following instructions. Not all

TABLE 27-7

Symptoms of Normal Aging Versus Those Associated With AD

Symptoms	Normal aging	AD
Sensory loss	Gradual losses in vision, hearing, touch, smell, taste	Same losses as normal aging
Memory loss	Mild forgetfulness (able to use reminders, delayed recall); recall of long past events	Progressive memory loss (gradually unable to use reminders, eventually severe, no recall)
Thinking (cognitive impairment)	None or some impairment Problem-solving possibly less effective	Progressive losses in thinking skills (the ability to make decisions, to judge, to follow directions)
Paranoia, hallucinations	Some paranoia related to vision and hearing loss (may think others are talking about them)	Function of the illness, although symptoms vary among individuals
Self-care capacity	Usually able to perform all self-care tasks Increased reaction time	Progressively unable to care for themselves (eventually requires total care)

strokes result in intellectual impairment; some affect movement, vision, or other functions.

Pick's disease This rare, progressive, degenerative brain disorder involves atrophy of the frontal and temporal lobes of the cerebral cortex. This is accomplished by neuronal loss, gliosis, and the inclu-sion of the distinctive Pick bodies. Cells containing Pick bodies have large argyphilic intracytoplasmic filamentous inclusion bodies. Pick's disease is an uncommon type of progressive dementia with clinical features similar to AD; the disease is found in individuals between the ages of 40 and 60.

Parkinson's disease This neurologic disorder affects more than 25 million Americans, most of whom are older adults. It is most often seen between the ages of 40 and 60. Initial symptoms are changes in muscular movement such as physical rigidity, tremors, and difficulty walking. In later stages, memory problems and associated difficulties appear. At least one third of those afflicted develop a dementia syndrome. This disease is caused by a deficiency of the neurotransmitter dopamine. Physical symptoms can be treated fairly effectively in many clients during the early years of illness with L-dopa, but this does not improve the cognitive problems.

Other dementia-related diseases Dementia resulting from other diseases includes Huntington's disease (formerly called Huntington's chorea), Creutzfeldt-Jakob, and HIV. These are diseases that less commonly affect the older adult population. Huntington's disease is not widely associated with aging because of the broad variability in age at onset. The average life expectancy after diagnosis is 16 years, and the age range of diagnosis is 5 to 70 years. Huntington's disease is characterized by choreoathetoid movements (uncontrollable writhing). The disease begins with disturbances of gait and slurred speech. It is an autosomal dominant disorder with complete probability of inheritance of the defective gene. The cause is believed to be immunologic with serum immunoglobulins type G (IgG) antibodies directed against the human caudate nucleus. It has been suggested that the antineuronal antibody might reflect exposure to an agent such as a virus or to a common environmental factor.

Creutzfeldt-Jakob disease is a rare dementia with rapidly progressing qualities. It has been associated with a viral etiology, although a specific virus has not been isolated. Other theories are being investigated. The average onset is in the age range of 50 to 60 but has been diagnosed between ages 21 and 79. Clinical symptoms vary, but there are general symptoms of dizziness, irritability, or confusion, followed by dementia. Neurologic symptoms of visual difficulty, pyramidal, and extrapyramidal abnormalities and myoclonus often occur. The time span from the onset of symptoms until death is 6 to 12 months. There is no known cure or treatment for the disease.

HIV-associated dementia is a consequence of HIV. Dementia is characterized by forgetfulness, slowness, poor concentration, and difficulties in problem solving.

Clinical characteristics of organic diseases with symptoms of dementia are associated with behaviors, including mood disorders, psychosis, and agitation. Significant psychopathology occurs in individuals with AD or vascular dementia (Cohen et al, 1993). Reports of psychiatric problems vary considerably (see Research box, p. 744). A recent study reported that psychopathology is present in a significant proportion of clients with all levels of cognitive impairment (Eisdorfer, Cohen, Paveza, 1992). At least one psychiatric problem was present in 52% of the people with AD demonstrating mild cognitive impairment. Two or more psychiatric symptoms were displayed by 32% of the people. Of those with severe cognitive impairment, at least 80% had one psychiatric symptom and greater than 70% had two or more symptoms. Although AD and vascular dementia have different neuroanatomic and neurochemical changes, the psychiatric and behavioral changes are very similar. The interaction of diseases could reflect differences in duration of illness, cognitive impairment, the client's ability to express the symptoms, or the ability to detect the symptoms (Gorelick et al, 1993).

Memory loss is often described as the initial symptom of dementia, yet it is not always indicative until midway through progression of the disease. Personality alterations, especially increased paranoia and depression, are more likely to be demonstrated at the beginning phases of the disorder. Another early occurrence is mood change with a tendency toward depression or short-lived aggressive outbursts. Memory changes occur, especially for recent events, and attention deficits become more common. Disorientation to time and place occur, with clients typically becoming unaware of the location, season, or time of day. Verbal changes, including stereotypic speech and the tendency to repeat phrases or stories, are also exhibited.

Progression of the disease results in motor unrest, including wandering and the inability to sit still. Apathy, intellectual dullness, global failure of memory, and loss of self-awareness occur during the last phases of illness. During late stages, the ability to communicate in any meaningful fashion is lost, and finally, the ability to control bodily functions is lost.

Behaviors associated with dementia may be similar to those of depressive disorders. Cognitive impairment, disability in ADLs, an increased incidence of past psychiatric disorders, medical conditions, and more frequent treatment with psychotropic medications should be evaluated when considering a DSM-IV diagnosis for AD. Clients with dementia may have neurovegetative symp-

RESEARCH

Cohen D, et al: Psychopathology Associated with Alzheimer's disease and related disorders, *J Gerontol* 48:M255-M260, 1993.

Sample, setting

514 clients with AD, 135 clients with multi-infarct dementia, and 86 cases with mixed dementia from a group of community-residing participants were enrolled in an AD client registry.

Methodology

Occurrence of psychiatric signs and symptoms was measured from a psychiatric examination.

Findings

Clients with mixed dementia had more psychopathology than those with AD or multi-infarct disease alone. Two thirds of the clients with either AD or multi-infarct dementia had one or more psychiatric symptoms compared with approximately 75% of the mixed dementia group. One fifth of the mixed dementia group had five or more symptoms. Of the clients with AD or multi-infarct dementia, agitation was the most commonly observed symptom, followed by depression (24%), apathy (22%) and behavioral disorders (16% to 17%). Agitation occurred with the same frequency in the group with mixed dementia (28%), but other problems were more prevalent: behavior disorders (37%), depression (35%), and apathy (34%). The two most common psychiatric conditions in clients with AD or multi-infarct dementia, agitation, and depression, occurred in 11% with clients with AD, 7% multi-infarct clients, but 19% with both AD and multi-infarct dementia.

Implications

The symptoms of psychopathology can result in misleading implications for aging adults and their families. This research suggested that the occurrence of multiple psychiatric symptoms in community-residing clients with AD may be more extensive than previously believed. Improving knowledge about coexisting psychiatric symptoms and conditions may help facilitate the course of illness, assist families and health professionals in client care, and help evaluate treatment effects in future clinical trials. This information suggests the need for increased awareness when determining stages of the disease and providing assistance as decisions regarding care are determined. In addition, monitoring the outcome of the care provided is equally important.

toms such as psychomotor retardation, sleep difficulties, decreased appetite, loss of libido, social withdrawal, and decreased concentration in the absence of depression (Lazarus et al, 1987). Psychosis associated with dementia is estimated to occur in approximately 30% of clients with AD (Wragg, Jeste, 1989).

Clients with vascular dementia develop symptoms of psychosis less often (Ballard et al, 1991). Clients with dementia show symptoms of persecutory delusions, and simple auditory or visual hallucinations. Complex psychosis such as ideas of reference are not characteristic of the psychosis of dementia.

Agitation is characteristic of dementia; approximately 85% of the clients with dementia become agitated (Jeste, Krull, 1991). Agitation can be manifested as aggressive behavior, physical nonaggressive and verbal agitated behaviors (Gerdner, Buckwalter, 1994). It is a nonspecific disturbance and can also occur in the context of neurologic and psychiatric conditions (see Medical Management box, p. 745).

Amnestic Disorders

These disorders are characterized by a disturbance in memory that is either a result of the direct physiologic effects of a general medical condition or the persisting effects of a drug, medication, or toxin. The common symptom is memory impairment. Age and the course of the disorder may vary, depending on the pathologic process. Duration of the disturbance is a qualifier for the diagnosis. Transient disorders are those lasting less than one month; chronic disorders last more than one month.

Cognitive Disorders Not Otherwise Specified

This category of diagnosis is for those disorders characterized by cognitive dysfunction presumed to be a result of the physiologic effect of a medical condition but do not meet other criteria.

Diagnosis

History, behavioral observation, and functional and mental status examinations form the basis for a diagnosis of cognitive disorders. Medical screening is not conclusive for the evaluation of intellectual decline in an older adult, but it does provide valuable information to rule out treatable disorders. The only positive diagnosis for dementia-related disorders is brain tissue biopsy or autopsy of the brain. Screening for treatable, reversible causes is carried out and treatment initiated.

Diagnostic studies Laboratory tests may be used to assess the nervous system or rule out medical

MEDICAL MANAGEMENT

Dementia

Diagnostic tests and procedures
- Mental status examinations
- Chest x-ray
- ECG
- EEG
- CT scan to rule out brain tumor, subdural hematoma and hydrocephalus
- MRI to reveal detailed structural changes in the brain
- Neurological assessment
- Drug studies to identify drug toxicity as a cause; medications that can cause mental confusion include digoxin, theophylline, and phenytoin
- Thyroid function studies to rule out hypothyroidism, which can mimic early signs of dementia
- CBC with differential to rule out septicemia; dementia may be the only presenting symptom with septicemia
- Electrolyte studies to identify potassium and sodium deficits, as well as hypoglycemia, which can cause mental confusion
- Blood cultures
- Liver function tests
- Venereal disease research laboratory (VDRL)
- Vitamin B and folate to rule out deficiencies
- Urinalysis
- Lumbar puncture

Treatment
- Identify the highest level of functional capacity and initiate activities to maintain. Encourage physical and mental activity.
- Provide therapy (medication or other) to correct underlying medical conditions
- Minimize stressors in the environment
- Avoid use of medications with effects on the CNS.
- Emphasize and consult on nutritional needs.
- Manage behaviors.

Prognosis

Between 2% and 4% of the population over age 65 have DAT, resulting in a survival rate of approximately 8 to 10 years (APA, 1994). Other types of dementia are much less common in this age group. The prevalence of DAT and vascular dementia increases with age, particularly after age 75.

problems causing the disorder. The effect of aging must be considered when assessing the nervous system using laboratory tests and interpreting the values. CT scan, MRI, and EEG have been used for diagnosis of delirium or dementia. Pathologically, CT scan is useful in detecting space-occupying lesions (e.g., intracranial tumors, subdural hematoma, and hydrocephalus) that may lead to dementias. The pathologic changes seen with dementia can be identified, including ventricular enlargement, narrowing of the gyri, widening of the sulci, or brain atrophy. The diagnostic value of using CT to identify dementia has not been confirmed. Results of EEG may provide more specific information. Background frequency of the waking EEG can be correlated with the client's mental state. If the client is severely impaired and the EEG results are normal, the diagnosis may be pseudodementia. If the client has early or mild dementia, the EEG results may be abnormally slow, indicating a treatable diagnosis. Images obtained by MRI have a high resolution and may be useful in detection of multiple subcortical strokes and white matter disease. MRI could prove useful in diagnosis of vascular dementia. The disadvantage is that the testing requires laying motionless for a long period, which may be impossible for a client with dementia.

Positron emission tomography (PET) is a noninvasive technique that allows assessment of regional glucose use, oxygen consumption, and regional cerebral blood flow. This technique may be useful in differential diagnosis.

Cerebrospinal fluid (CSF) studies or electromyography (EMG) will not prove valuable if symptoms are caused by dementing disorders. CSF studies are part of the workup for identifying reversible causes. Laboratory screening tests to rule out treatable medical diagnoses that might be considered include CBC and electrolytes; chest x-ray; urinalysis; liver, kidney, and thyroid function tests; serum B_{12}; folate; syphilis serology; and drug studies.

Cerebral biopsy is considered the only definitive diagnosis to differentiate the type of dementia causing the symptoms, although this is not a routine test. The clinical profile, including laboratory tests and behavioral observations, has improved the classification of this disease.

DSM-IV criteria In 1952 the APA classified abnormal behaviors and provided an official manual of mental disorders with descriptions of diagnostic categories. The *Diagnostic and Statistical Manual of Mental Disorders* (DSM) is the most widely accepted system of classifying abnormal behaviors and is consistent in most respects with the World Health Organization (WHO) and the International Classification of Diseases (ICD).

The DSM-IV classification conceptualizes each of the disorders as a clinically significant behavioral or psychologic syndrome or pattern that can occur in a person and is associated with present distress and disability, an important loss of freedom, or with an increased risk of suffering death, pain, and disability. There is no assumption that each mental disorder is a discrete entity with sharp boundaries between it and other disorders. The disorders are classified for all age groups and are not specific to the older adult.

The DSM-IV disorders have been grouped into delirium, dementia, and amnestic and other cognitive disorders. The disorders are subdivided per cause:

Delirium
- Delirium resulting from a general medical condition (Box 27-4)
- Substance-induced delirium (as a result of a drug or medication, or toxin exposure)
- Delirium resulting from multiple causes
- Delirium not otherwise specified (if cause is indeterminate)

Dementia
- DAT (Box 27-5)
- Vascular dementia (Box 27-6)
- Dementia resulting from other general medical conditions (e.g., HIV, head trauma, Parkinson's disease, Huntington's disease)
- Substance-induced persisting dementia (resulting from drug abuse, a medication, or toxin exposure)
- Dementia resulting from multiple causes
- Dementia not otherwise specified (if the cause is indeterminate)

Amnestic disorder
- Amnestic disorder resulting from a general medical condition
- Substance-induced persisting amnestic disorder
- Amnestic disorder not otherwise specified

Cognitive disorder not otherwise specified
- Do not meet criteria for other disorders

Therapy

Cognitive disorders may be reversed if a causative factor can be identified and eliminated. Permanent dementia cannot be reversed using medical treatment, therefore

BOX 27-4

DSM-IV Diagnostic Criteria for Delirium Resulting From a General Medical

- Disturbance of consciousness (e.g., reduced clarity of awareness of the environment) with reduced ability to focus, to sustain, or to shift attention.
- A change in cognition (e.g., memory deficit, disorientation, language disturbance) or the development of a perceptual disturbance that is not better accounted for by a preexisting, established, or evolving dementia.
- The disturbance develops over a short period (usually hours to days) and tends to fluctuate during the course of the day.
- There is evidence from the history, physical examination, or laboratory findings that the disturbance is caused by the direct physiologic consequences of a general medical condition.

From: American Psychiatric Association: *Diagnostic and statistical manual of mental disorders,* ed 4, revised, Washington DC, 1994, The Association.

BOX 27-5

DSM-IV Diagnostic Criteria for DAT

A. The development of multiple cognitive deficits manifested by both
   1. Memory impairment (impaired ability to learn new information or to recall previously learned information)
   2. One (or more) of the following cognitive disturbances
      a. Aphasia (language disturbance)
      b. Apraxia (impaired ability to carry out motor activities despite intact motor function)
      c. Agnosia (failure to recognize or to identify objects despite intact sensory function)
      d. Disturbance in executive functioning (e.g., planning, organizing, sequencing, abstracting)

B. The cognitive deficits in Criteria A1 and A2 each cause significant impairment in social or occupational functioning and represent a significant decline from a previous level of functioning.

C. The course is characterized by gradual onset and continuing cognitive decline.

D. The cognitive deficits in Criteria A1 and A2 are not results of any of the following:
   1. Other CNS conditions that cause progressive deficits in memory and cognition (e.g., cerebrovascular disease [CVD], Parkinson's disease, Huntington's disease, subdural hematoma, normal-pressure hydrocephalus, brain tumor)
   2. Systemic conditions that are known to cause dementia (e.g., hypothyroidism; vitamin B_{12}, folic acid, or niacin deficiency; hypercalcemia; neurosyphilis; HIV infection)

E. The deficits do not occur exclusively during the course of a delirium.

F. The disturbance is not better accounted for by another Axis 1 disorder (e.g., major depressive disorder, schizophrenia).

From American Psychiatric Association: *Diagnostic and statistical manual of mental disorders,* ed 4, revised, Washington, D.C., 1994, The Association.

management of dementia consists of helping victims through progression of the disorder while allowing them as much dignity and independence as possible. The cognitive functions that are lost with most irreversible forms of dementia cannot be restored through psychotherapy. Interventions that may be of some value include memory retraining, therapy for social skills, communication skills, stress management skills, reminiscence therapy, and environmental modifications. Written schedules of activities, simplified routes from room to room, and written directions for cooking, bathing, and taking medications can aid people in finding their way around and prevent the frustration that results from getting lost or not recognizing once-familiar people and places (Box 27-7). It is important to maintain a regular schedule, to maintain an active status, and to prevent withdrawal from daily interactions.

BOX 27-6

DSM-IV Diagnostic Criteria for Vascular Dementia

A. The development of multiple cognitive deficits manifested by both
   1. Memory impairment (impaired ability to learn new information or to recall previously learned information)
   2. One (or more) of the following cognitive disturbances:
      a. Aphasia (language disturbance)
      b. Apraxia (impaired ability to carry out motor activities despite intact motor function)
      c. Agnosia (failure to recognize or identify objects despite intact sensory function)
      d. Disturbance in executive functioning (e.g., planning, organizing, sequencing, abstracting)

B. The cognitive deficits in Criteria A1 and A2 each cause significant impairment in social or occupational functioning and represent a significant decline from previous level of functioning.

C. Focal neurologic signs and symptoms (e.g., exaggeration of deep tendon reflexes, extensor plantar response, pseudobulbar palsy, gait abnormalities, weakness of an extremity) or laboratory evidence indicative of CVD (e.g., multiple infarctions involving cortex and underlying white matter) that are judged to be etiologically related to the disturbance.

D. The deficits do not occur exclusively during the course of a delirium.

From American Psychiatric Association: *Diagnostic and statistical manual of mental disorders,* ed 4, revised, Washington D.C., 1994, The Association.

Behavior therapies Art and music activities are being conducted as a measure to enhance interactions between clients and between clients and caregivers. A clinical project using art activities (using textures and shapes) by clients with AD (Sterrit, Pokorny, 1994) found recurring themes such as the following:

- Increased life review and reminiscence
- Increased interaction, expression of feelings, and exercise of abilities
- Ability to overcome limits and exercise choice
- Increased absorption and concern about others

Another investigation studying the effect of music sessions on AD residents in long-term care examined sensoroperceptual, expressive, and receptive abilities (Sambandham, Schirm, 1995). Observation periods occurred before, during, and after nursing intervention. Results were each significantly different among verbal responses of the residents. Patterns of alertness, energy, or activity levels were not predictable. It was determined that music sessions can enhance the long-term care environment. Humor has been identified as a communication

BOX 27-7

Nursing Management Strategies

Clients should be assessed for their orientation to improve their level of cognition. The following skills can be developed by identifying the motivation level of the participant and identifying the most important behaviors to change. Stability, consistency, self-identification and active participation are all important skills to be enhanced through the following programs:

- Memory retraining—Reality orientation to the surroundings and time (date, year)
- Social skill therapy—Reinforcing behaviors to be used when interacting with others
- Communication therapy—Improving speech patterns or words selected to complete a thought: minimizing sensory deprivation
- Stress management therapy—Identifying factors that minimize stress and using methods in management
- Reminiscence therapy—Using story telling and memory recall to identify with past experiences
- Behavior therapy—Maintaining consistency and stability to identify expectations in behaviors; recognizing environmental stressors and controlling; using written schedules and directions to assist with activities
- Pharmacotherapy—Use of medications to manage behaviors that are interfering with progress

strategy and stimulus that might be useful with older adults. Studies of specific groups are needed, but assessing for appropriate types of humor and using creative techniques such as a cartoon scrapbook, humor diary, humorous stories, and a humor bulletin board or posters might provide therapy for some cognitively impaired adults (Hulse, 1994).

The goal of using creative strategies to manage dementia is to slow the rate of deterioration and to prevent institutionalization as long as possible.

Pharmacotherapy Medications, especially major tranquilizers, tranquilizers with a shorter half-life (minor tranquilizers) and antidepressants, can be effective in managing some symptoms caused by dementia. Individual responses to medications can vary considerably, therefore these medications require close monitoring by health care workers and family members for action and side effects. Older people generally have a lower tolerance for these medications than younger people, and impairments (circulatory, metabolic) may interfere with the effectiveness of medication. Caregivers should be very familiar with dosages and side effects. Family members should have realistic expectations about changes they can expect and should be reminded to consult with the physician if there are questions. A response to the caregiver might be to increase dosage if the desired effect is not observed, which in turn could result in overdose or more side effects. Medication therapy is used to supplement care by treating symptoms. The family must continue to use skills rather than medications to manage behavior problems and caregiver stress. Medications cannot replace other therapeutic measures.

Major tranquilizers are commonly prescribed to manage symptoms of agitation, anxiety, suspiciousness, hostility, delusions, or hallucinations that sometimes occur with dementia. Resulting side effects listed in Box 27-8 must be monitored carefully and reported.

Minor tranquilizers may also be used to treat the symptoms of agitation and anxiety. These medications can build up in the body over time. Medications with a shorter half-life should be used to prevent this buildup, thus minimizing side effects (Box 27-9).

Antidepressants might be considered when depression coexists with a disease. These are given to decrease the aspects of a depressed mood, improve appetite and sleep habits, improve social habits and increase the level of energy. Some depression can be treated successfully, and the person's mental status can improve, although the cognitive disorder can remain unchanged if present. Most antidepressants take several weeks to months to reach a therapeutic level. Side effects are a concern and may compound existing deficits (Box 27-10). See Chapter 20 for a complete discussion of pharmacotherapy.

BOX 27-8

Side Effects Common With Major Tranquilizers

- Hypotension
- Extrapyramidal reactions
- Delirium or reversible dementia
- Acute, toxic confusional state
- Increased sensitivity to heat and cold
- Anticholinergic effects
  - Dry mouth
  - Blurred vision
  - Dilated pupils
  - Constipation
  - Urinary retention
  - Increased heart rate

NURSING MANAGEMENT

The goal when caring for older people that have symptoms of a cognitive disorder is to support existing sensory perception until the cognitive state returns to the previous level of function. The goal of caring for older people with dementing disorders should be directed toward maintaining good health and locomotor skills, with preservation of functional behaviors to minimize the loss of self-care. Although many abilities are lost, those retained skills are key factors in maintaining function and progress throughout the course of the disease. Dementia includes a variety of conditions that are caused by or associated with damage of brain tissue resulting in impaired cognitive function and, in more advanced stages, impaired behavior and personality. The care provided is similar in the beginning stages of cognitive disorders but becomes unique, depending on the type and progress of the disease. Philosophies about the care of the older adults with behavioral impairment have changed over

BOX 27-9

Side Effects of Tranquilizers With a Shorter Half-Life (Minor Tranquilizers)

- Oversedation
- Drowsiness and fatigue
- Nervousness
- Dizziness
- Irritability
- Depression
- Blurred vision

BOX 27-10

Side Effects of Antidepressants

- Drowsiness
- Dry mouth
- Urinary retention
- Nasal congestion
- Delirium
- Increased appetite for sweets
- Increased heart rate
- Blurred vision
- Dizziness, fainting
- Constipation
- Hypotension
- Arrhythmias
- Weight gain

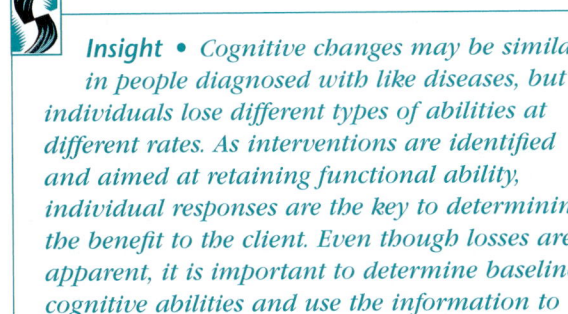

Insight • *Cognitive changes may be similar in people diagnosed with like diseases, but individuals lose different types of abilities at different rates. As interventions are identified and aimed at retaining functional ability, individual responses are the key to determining the benefit to the client. Even though losses are apparent, it is important to determine baseline cognitive abilities and use the information to individualize interventions that will facilitate independence. Family members are the best resource and asset in identifying interventions that are proving valuable in maintaining functional ability.*

the years. Public policy has shifted to encourage family members to care for the older adult in the home, thus decreasing health care costs and individualizing care to meet client needs. The nursing focus has shifted from being the caregiver to a role of coordinating care, teaching and assisting the family members with home care, providing supportive care and serving as a client advocate.

✣ ASSESSMENT

The older adult client with preexisting illness, sensory deficits, and a normal, age-related decreased response rate presents challenges when completing an assessment. Obtaining a baseline physical and mental status is imperative, since older people have a wide range of function and ability. Deficits and impairments may be inaccurately attributed to age or disease if accurate and complete baseline information is not available. Verbal and nonverbal responses from the client, family members, and significant others should be used to validate assessment data. The assessment process is ongoing to assure the accurate collection of information. The purpose of a comprehensive assessment is to determine problem areas as well as areas of strength of the client, family, and caregiver on which a plan of care, including education of families and caregivers, can be based.

Assessment data gathered at the time of an acute crisis, such as in a hospital setting, is critical for initial treatment. The special needs of an older adult with a cognitive disorder may require completing the assessment following treatment of the crisis to assure discreet symptoms are not overlooked and treatment is appropriate for the disorder.

Evaluation of the level of consciousness provides an indication of pathologic processes. Consciousness can be defined as the state of awareness of the self and the environment. The most widely used and universally accepted tool for measuring level of consciousness is the Glasgow Coma Scale. The scale measures eye-opening, verbal response, and motor response. This may be the appropriate tool to use for assessment of an older person in a critical state, whose neurologic status is undetermined or rapidly changing.

Older adults may experience traumatic injury, resulting in increased intracranial pressure. Classic symptoms of headache, vomiting, and papilledema do not always appear in an older person but could be more subtle (less obvious) because of normal, age-related changes caused by cerebral atrophy. These changes, including alterations in consciousness, cranial nerve deficits, and motor changes may mimic cognitive disorders.

Pupil changes can provide information about the condition of the brain and help identify the cause, responses, and location of pathology. Evaluation of pupil size and reaction to light may be difficult in the older adult. Pupils may appear smaller than normal and light reflex may be sluggish. Pupillary response is altered by presence of cataracts, retinal detachment, glaucoma, and sclerotic changes in the iris.

Neurologic disorders can cause a wide range of motor abnormalities. The extremities should be assessed for muscle strength and tone, and should be compared for symmetry. Many older people have normal age-related symmetrical weakness and muscular fatigue. Decreased vibratory sense in the feet, decreased Achilles reflexes, and decreased sensory perception may be caused by the normal loss of neurotransmitters or sensory receptors.

Mental status examinations for assessment of mental and cognitive function are necessary to identify impairments, which, for the older person, may have significant and permanent long-term effects. The type of cognitive assessment tool used varies, depending on the setting and results of the physical examination. An objective assessment may require more than obtaining orientation to person, place, and time, and should be considered before labeling a person "disoriented." It is important to thoroughly assess visual and hearing deficits and alter the environment to enhance a valid response from the client.

Problematic behaviors are commonly demonstrated by people with cognitive disorders. New behaviors should not be overlooked but should be viewed as a new symptom requiring assessment. The type and intensity of the behavior vary depending on the stage of disease, but each behavior exhibited requires a comprehensive, individualized assessment. Identifying the behavior and extenuating circumstances assists in ruling out treatment causes and determining the personal meaning associated with the behavior.

✣ DIAGNOSIS

Diagnoses are determined based on the assessment criteria. See Box 27-11 for a listing of the most commonly used nursing diagnoses for the older adult with cognitive impairment.

BOX 27-11

NANDA Nursing Diagnoses Appropriate for the Cognitively Impaired Older Adult

- Activity intolerance
- Altered family processes
- Altered nutrition: less than body requirements
- Altered role performance
- Altered thought processes
- Anxiety
- Bathing/hygiene self-care deficit
- Bowel incontinence
- Caregiver role strain
- Confusion/acute or chronic
- Dressing/grooming self-care deficit
- Fatigue
- Fear
- Feeding self-care deficit
- Functional incontinence
- High risk for injury
- Impaired physical mobility
- Impaired social interaction
- Ineffective family coping: compromised
- Ineffective family coping: disabling
- Knowledge deficit
- Noncompliance
- Self-esteem disturbance
- Spiritual distress

✣ PLANNING

Expected outcomes when caring for the older adult with cognitive changes differ for each diagnosis and include, but are not limited to, the following: (1) inappropriate behaviors such as agitation, combative behavior, or mood changes are eliminated or minimized; (2) socialization increases, as evidenced by voluntary participation in activities; (3) physical health is maintained; (4) family member(s) participate in activities and care.

✣ INTERVENTION

The cognitive losses experienced with depression, delirium, and dementia may be similar, but each person loses different abilities at different times, and each responds differently to interventions (Danner et al, 1993). The most effective interventions are individualized for each client. The focus on individuality includes determining past environmental and cultural influences that affect the person's response pattern. This can be accomplished by remaining attentive to needs as they are communicated, as well as to changes and responses in behavior, and using creativity in each situation. The best interventions are learned through trial and error, requiring commitment and communication from the family and caregiver. The efforts of health care personnel and caregivers result in determining the best strategies for managing care of the client with dementia. Identifying the stage of disease provides a starting point for management of care, but because each person's behavioral responses are based on an individual personal history and experiences, it requires persistence to determine the best time of day for activities and approaches that result in desired responses. The positive outcomes may be applicable for a period but may change as the disease progresses, resulting in the need to reevaluate strategies. General principles of care should be individualized when caring for people with dementia (Box 27-12).

Monitoring physical health and meeting basic needs is the cornerstone of care and preventive measures for the older adult with cognitive impairment. The limited ability to verbally communicate may prevent an older adult from relaying a problem or symptom. Nonverbal cues such as holding a body part or restlessness should be observed and considered indicative of a potential symptom requiring attention. Careful attention paid by the caregiver during the initial stages may eliminate problem-solving difficulties as the disease progresses by either minimizing the problem at an early stage or improving the ability to recognize signs conveyed by the client.

Behavior recognition is important for the care of the client and the caregiver. Behaviors exhibited by the client may become the primary method of communicating needs, therefore recognizing behaviors may be the first step to assure that appropriate care is provided. In

BOX 27-12

Principles for Implementation of Care for the Cognitively Impaired Older Adult

Monitor and maintain physical health
Recognize the meaning of behaviors
Adapt the environment (routines and setting)
Communicate in a simple, direct manner
Provide cues for reality orientation
Maintain social interaction and self-esteem

addition, stress created for the caregiver by the older adult demonstrating problematic behaviors may be eliminated if an awareness of the meaning of behaviors and methods of managing these are understood. Behaviors are a result of the disease, not a deliberate action. The caregiver must realize that the victim cannot control the behaviors and cannot be taught to change. The person demonstrating the symptoms may be unaware of their affect on others, while the family or other people involved may be more sensitive to the behaviors (see Research Box, p. 752). Use of physical or chemical restraints is not beneficial in controlling behaviors or managing the disease. Unless the behaviors are upsetting or dangerous, learning how to adjust when these occur will probably result in a less stressful environment.

Several studies and clinical observations have given initial support to the value of recognizing individual differences and behavioral patterns when designing effective nursing care approaches. The influence of past experiences of the perceived support may influence responses by the older adult. These experiences must be considered when creating a supportive environment. A study conducted by Burgener and Shimer (1993) identified varied ways older adults expressed their individuality and suggested nursing implications (Table 27-8). Supporting existing characteristics by nursing personnel and family may enhance the quality of the individual's living experience.

Environmental changes in routines or setting can improve adaptation by a person with a cognitive disorder. Consistency is a key factor when determining strategies for modifying the environment to create a sense of security, but routines should not be so rigid that changes won't be accepted. Mealtime, bath time, and activities should be predictable. Certain routines are comforting, such as sitting in the same chair or next to the same person during mealtime, and having the same caregiver. Changes in the routine should be introduced slowly and a stimulus provided to assure that feelings of comfort and security are not lost. Modifications in the environment for disorders such as AD may be required to pro-

TABLE 27-8

Individual Self-Concepts and Nursing Implications

Expressed self-concepts	Nursing implications
Retention of predominant skills	Focus on abilities rather than disabilities. Individualize activities, based on past skills, to increase success and meaning for older adults.
Spirituality	Assist in fulfilling the older adult's spiritual needs. Acknowledge important past practices.
Despair	Assess individual losses to assist in understanding behaviors. Design interventions to compensate for individual losses.
Loneliness	Recognize loneliness as a reality for the older adult. Allow older adult to express feelings of loneliness as therapeutic.
Connecting with others	Recognize and support methods that older adults use to connect with others. Assess individual responses on touch; design interventions based on response patterns.
Using social skills	Support existing social skills, adapting nursing care and the environment to allow for expression.
Humor	Assess positive responses to humor. Incorporate lighthearted, playful interactions into care, based on individual response patterns.
Sense of mastery	Assess individual abilities to perform tasks. Allow for as much self-care as possible within nursing care delivery.
Recognition of "logical expected behaviors"	Assess for individual meanings in behavioral responses. Recognize that distress may be a result of a lack of ability to perform behavior; adapt nursing approach.

From Burgener SC, Shimer R, Murrell L: Nursing care of cognitively impaired, institutionalized elderly, *J Gerontol Nurs* 17:37-43, 1993.

RESEARCH

Hinrichsen GA, Niederehe G: Dementia Management Strategies and adjustment of family members of older patients, *Gerontologist* 34:95-102, 1994.

Sample, setting

152 clients with a medical diagnosis of dementia and 152 family members providing their primary care were recruited from clinics and a social service program in the New York area.

Methodology

Methods chosen included measures that evaluated the extent to which dementia impaired the client's capacity to perform ADLs, the presence of memory and behavior problems, and the need for formal and informal supportive services. The management of dementia-related problems was measured using the Dementia Management Strategies Scale. This scale measures the frequency with which a family member employs specific strategies tied to behavioral problems.

Findings

Three Dementia Management Strategies were identified—criticism, encouragement, and active management. These were found to be associated with three indices of family members' emotional adjustment—burden, psychiatric symptoms, and desire to institutionalize the client. After controlling for the influence of family member and client background characteristics and family member coping, Dementia Management Strategies accounted for significant variance in family members' burden and desire to institutionalize the client. The use of active management and criticism was associated with greater burden, whereas use of encouragement was tied to less family member burden and less desire to institutionalize.

Implications

It is known that caregivers experience many problems when caring for the older adult with dementia. A variety of intervention programs have been developed to assist family members to deal with the behavioral changes of the relative with dementia. The adjustment of the caregiver and the method of managing varies for each individual, but this research suggests that common responses may be indicative of the caregiver's ability to manage care. Nurses play a role in counseling families regarding changes in behavior and making decisions about long-term care. These findings indicate that the three identified Dementia Management Strategies contribute to understanding of the determinants of adjustment in family members. Examination of specific family behaviors yields a better understanding of the interpersonal dynamics of dementia care, and should be evaluated by the nurse to determine appropriate recommendations for family members.

vide the security and safety necessary as the disease progresses. These modifications might include decreasing (but not eliminating) stimulus by using soft colors and limiting obstacles. Eliminating access to unsafe locations and unnecessary noises in the environment also may help in managing behaviors.

Relaying care and support through communication techniques is the most effective method with the person with dementia. Simple and direct communication is the most effective style, using both verbal and nonverbal behaviors. The older person is more inclined to respond to the nonverbal message in some situations. Like the environment, the tone for communication should be calm and relaxed. Using eye contact and touch when delivering a message helps to focus attention on the meaning. Simple words and short sentences along with simple gestures to demonstrate meaning are easiest to understand. Trust and security can be maintained through communication by assuring that actions are consistent with promises delivered. Distraction as a form of communication may be necessary to dissuade a person with memory impairments from engaging in undesirable activities. If the person refuses to do what is asked, a short time interval may be necessary before eliciting another response. Memory loss, aphasia, apraxia, agnosia, and disorientation make verbal communication less meaningful in later stages of dementia. This does not eliminate the need for speaking. Sound and voices may elicit a response, and may provide a calming effect and reality orientation.

Cues for reality orientation support failing memory in early stages of dementia and preserve independent function for a longer period. Printed signs and labels may become foreign, but many times, pictures evoke a response. People in all stages of the disease benefit from clocks, calendars, and mementos in the environment. As the disease progresses, orienting them to the caregiver and daily tasks improves their productivity and responses.

Maintaining social interaction and human contact in a variety of ways is beneficial to demonstrate caring for the older person. It also provides the much needed opportunity for participation in activities that is so important to prevent boredom and restlessness. The response from the older adult is positive if they are provided the opportunity to experience success and to contribute in a positive way. Independence should be encouraged and

RESEARCH

Browning JS, Schwirian PM: Spousal caregivers' burden: impact of care recipient health problems and mental status. *J Gerontol Nurs* 20(3):17-22, 1994.

Sample, setting

A convenience sample was obtained, consisting of 102 older men and women over age 60 who provided primary care for a spouse. The caregivers were mentally alert, competent and able to read English. The mean age of the caregiver was 73.2 years, and the mean age of the care receivers was 76.1 years. The mean years of education for caregivers was 11.9%, and 38.2% of the caregivers were men.

Methodology

An exploratory descriptive design was used to examine separately the effects of two kinds of impairment on caregiver burden. Caregiver burden was measured using a 22-item Burden Interview. Physical impairment was defined as the primary medical diagnosis for the dependent spouse. Mental impairment of the dependent older adult was measured by caregivers' responses to a modified 32-item memory and behavior problems checklist to determine how often the dependent older adult engaged in problem behavior.

Findings

A factor analysis of the burden interview resulted in three subscale components. The first subscale was related to the effect of caregiving on interpersonal relationships. The second contained items that reflected the caregiver's anxiety about the caregiving situation and uncertainty about the ability to continue in the role. The third subset related to the personal effect of the caregiver role on the spouse. The most common diagnoses reported for the caregiver were related to neurologic/mental dysfunction (63%), most commonly the sequelae of strokes. Problems related to cardiac function and circulation were found with 41% of the care receivers, and arthritis/degenerative joint disease was identified as a problem for 25% of the care receivers. Caregivers of spouses with diagnosis of stroke or arthritis reported higher care burdens, but the effect of mental impairment of the dependent older adult was greater than any physical problem.

Implications

Individuals with increasing levels of impairment are being cared for by the spouse or adult children because of earlier discharge from clinical settings. Nurses might consider these findings as they plan care of the cognitively impaired older adult. Nursing measures might include (1) increased sensitivity and understanding when assessing and planning for discharge, (2) seeking opportunities for communication and coordination between acute care-based and community-based nurses, and (3) an ongoing assessment of the caregiver.

self-esteem promoted by maintaining daily hygiene and grooming.

✣ EVALUATION

Evaluation is an ongoing process that takes place throughout the course of the dementia. Behaviors and activities require continual monitoring to determine variances from the baseline. Careful observation and recording of moods, behaviors, or memory provide clues to changes that are discreet. The observations should be communicated with other caregivers and family members to assure that consistency is maintained as changes occur (see nursing Care Plan, p. 754).

Client Care Challenges and Nursing Strategies

Cognitive loss creates challenges during all stages of the disease. Behavior problems and emotions that sometimes accompany dementia can increase the stress associated with care of an older adult. It is difficult to predict how individuals will manifest the behaviors. Changes may result in the need to attend to health and safety. The caregiver may also experience difficulties in coping with changes in behaviors as the disease progresses, since older people may no longer be able to care for themselves, participate in social activities, or remain in the home, placing a greater burden on the caretaker (see Research Box, above).

Behaviors Associated With Cognitive Disorders

Behaviors may be related to confusion or to an undetermined cause. General confusion may be a result of a change in environment or routine. Agitation is a result of mental and physical excitement exhibited by restless actions, repetitive movements or words, or discomfort shown by sighing, groaning, or crying. Agitation and restlessness may be indicative of underlying problems of boredom, fatigue, or hunger, or they may be symptoms of a physical illness such as hypoxia, delirium, urinary tract infection, or pain. Strategies for managing behaviors of confusion or agitation require individualization, since each person's response differs for various reasons. Communicating in a calm and caring method, assessing the environment and activities to assure a safe, therapeutic area, and monitoring positive responses might be a few of the strategies that should be emphasized when the confusion or agitation is exhibited.

The following behaviors and symptoms are associated

CARE PLAN

DELIRIUM

Clinical situation Mrs. T, a 72-year-old woman, is admitted to the surgical service of a community hospital with severe abdominal pain. She is a mild diabetic controlled on diet and had been in apparently good physical condition until 3 days before admission. She developed abdominal pain and complained of inability to move her bowels. Her husband says she had always complained of constipation and has been using laxatives for years.

Physical examination reveals that she is lethargic. Her pulse is 56 beats per minute and regular. Temperature is 36.2° C (97.2° F). Her abdomen is slightly distended and diffusely tender. Neurologic examination is normal except for depressed deep tendon reflexes. Her white blood count is 11,000 with a normal differential; blood glucose is 160 mg/100 ml.

Her husband claims that she has become increasingly more forgetful and unable to manage personal needs during the last month. Recently she has been incontinent of urine. For these reasons, the diagnosis of "delirium" was added to the initial diagnosis of acute abdomen.

A geriatrician was consulted for assessment. In addition to constipation, confusion, bradycardia, and fatigue, the geriatrician noted dry skin and a faint thyroidectomy scar on Mrs. T's neck. She was treated with hydration and enemas, resulting in resolution of abdominal symptoms. Her lethargy also diminished. Thyroid function tests were ordered, and Mrs. T was found to have hypothyroidism, which was treated.

Mr. T verbalizes considerable anxiety related to the aging process and often comments that his wife's condition is associated with getting old.

Nursing diagnoses	Outcomes	Interventions
Constipation related to inactivity and laxative dependence	Client will be relieved of immediate constipation as evidenced by passage of stool Client will also decrease the use of laxatives as evidenced by diet that includes fiber-rich foods Client will increase activity level as evidenced by walking independently with cane or walker and performing active range-of-motion exercises TID	Administer enemas as ordered. Discuss laxative use with Mrs. T; teach a schedule of activities consistent with functional ability. Teach dietary habits and modifications to increase bulk; recommend gradual increase in dietary bulk, 6-10 gm fiber per day. Teach range-of-motion exercises.
Altered thought processes related to memory loss and forgetfulness secondary to hypothyroidism	Client will demonstrate increased ability to function and perform personal care.	Teach Mr. and Mrs. T the disease process of hypothyroidism. Reassure them of the temporary effect on memory as a result of thyroid deficiency. Teach medication therapy and side effects. Teach husband how to cue wife as she performs self-care in bathing, dressing, toileting, and eating.

with AD: sundowning, wandering, paranoia, suspiciousness, hallucinations, catastrophic reactions, delusions, and hyperorality. These behaviors manifest in later stages of the disease and complicate management of the care. Each of these symptoms requires changes in nursing interventions to protect the client and to maintain comfort and security.

Sundown syndrome The term sundowning is applied to symptoms of agitation and restlessness that occur late in the day. The reason this occurs is unknown, but it is apparent there is an increased sensitivity to stress at this time of the day. It also appears that with less light, individuals lose the visual cues that help compensate for hearing and vision loss, leaving them more confused. Interventions may include the following:

- Schedule appointments and more demanding activities earlier in the day when the individual is more rested.
- Reduce stimulation in the environment as the day

progresses; seek activities that are calming such as playing soft music.

- Increase lighting levels and provide a night light at bedtime.
- Offer companionship and reassurance during the evening hours.
- Turn on room lights before dusk.

Wandering Wandering seems to be a continuation of a lifestyle pattern of the individual (very active people before the disease are more prone to wander). The behaviors may be goal directed, where the individual has a reason for "wandering," such as looking for the bathroom or another person. For others it appears to fulfill a need to help combat boredom or restlessness. Interventions might include the following:

- Assure that the environment is safe for wandering.
- Divert attention if the person needs to return to a specific area; fall in step with the walking pattern.
- Inform neighbors and police of this potential problem.
- Identify the individual with a medical alert bracelet.
- Observe for behaviors that might trigger the behavior and responses.
- Maintain a regular activity and exercise program.

Paranoia and suspiciousness Paranoid or suspicious behaviors exhibited by an individual may be reflective of a basic insecurity to memory and sensory loss. Each loss complicates others. For instance, individuals may misplace items. Because they cannot remember moving the item in the first place, they become suspicious of others and accuse them of stealing. In turn, paranoia sets in as individuals observe others talking, but cannot hear what is being said. They begin to fear that others are talking about them and cling to objects or hoard, fearing they will be stolen. Interventions for this type of behavior might include the following:

- Secure valuables and important items in locked locations or out of reach.
- Do not use confrontation or apply logic.
- Look in wastebaskets before emptying.
- Do not whisper or behave in a secretive manner.
- Keep extra items such as keys and glasses.

Catastrophic reaction Emotional outbursts or overreaction toward minor stresses have been coined catastrophic reaction. This may be precipitated by fatigue, overstimulation, inability to meet expectations, or misinterpretation of actions or words. The behaviors signal emotional overload and cannot be controlled by the client. The caregiver can recognize and respond to reactions if attentive to the individual. Reactions may be controlled by simplifying the environment or task and eliminating overstimulation that may cause a confusing feeling. The environment should be evaluated for "triggers" for the behavior. Signs of impending reaction might include restlessness or refusals. Withdrawing the individual from the environment where the reaction is occurring and providing a calming atmosphere may distract or divert the client. Explanations may not be understood, but a calm tone of voice, touch, and reassurance may alleviate the stressful situation. Following the incident, feelings related to the situation may linger and continue to cause distress. It may be necessary to temporarily separate the individual from the causative source.

Hallucinations Hallucinations are usually visual and auditory, with visual hallucinations being the most common type. The individual may see, hear, taste, touch, or smell something that has no external reality. If the problem persists, possible medical causes should be evaluated such as over- or under-medicating, toxicity, fever, infection, or a combination of causes. If the hallucination is disturbing, such as the feeling of bugs on the body when they are not there, offering protection and security may help to calm the client. Reasoning or logic is ineffective.

Delusions The individual may believe something to be true although it may be illogical or wrong. For instance, the individual may perceive a setting as being the workplace. Depending on the stage of the disease, reality orientation may be appropriate. If the disease has progressed, it may be best to go along with the individual's reality and to attempt to change behaviors that are disturbing about the situation.

Hyperorality Individuals may want to put everything within reach into their mouth. People with AD have a poor sense of judgment, therefore they cannot discriminate between harmful and safe items. Prevention is the best course of action. Remove small items and clutter from the environment and place locks on areas containing potentially harmful items.

Nutritional Needs

Nutrition becomes a problem when eating behaviors change. Feeding a client with dementia requires a developed sensitivity by the caregiver to subtle cues given by the client. Problems that occur during feeding include the following:

- Refusal to open mouth
- Opening and closing the mouth inappropriately
- Hoarding food in the mouth
- Refusal to swallow or coughing when swallowing
- Inability to taste food
- Lack of hunger

Strategies that may stimulate the client to eat include providing companionship during a meal without being distracting. Recognition of meal-related activity by others may entice the act of eating. It is also important to maximize the meal that seems to be most appealing to the client. Identify the time of day when food intake is increased and focus efforts on increasing the nutritional intake during this time. Frequent small meals and snacks may also be appealing. Physical health and oral health should be managed to assure the client feels good at meal time. In addition, constipation and diarrhea should be controlled (Chapman, Nelson, 1994).

People who demonstrate symptoms of moderate to severe cognitive impairment may also benefit from providing meals in the same place at the same time each day. Food choices should be limited and visualization of the food should be attained. This might require rotation of the plate during the meal. During later stages of dementia, the client may need to be reminded to open the mouth and chew. Serving one food at a time decreases confusion. Food should be soft and cut in small pieces. Thin liquids may prove difficult to swallow, therefore serving gelatins, pudding, or ice cream may decrease the problem with liquid intake (Minizak, 1994).

Difficulties feeding cannot be treated, but the caregiver can respond more effectively to the problems with sensitivity and an understanding of eating preferences.

Family Support

Cognitive disorders do not affect only one person, but become an extended disease. One of the most important considerations with dementias is to provide social and emotional support to the family, as well as to the client. Day-to-day problems such as finances, legal obligations, household chores, self-care needs, troublesome behaviors, and interpersonal conflicts are just some of the difficulties that must be managed.

The emotional aspects of caregiving are complex. Role changes and expectations are not always understood or planned. Loss of autonomy for the caregiver and older person causes varied reactions. The entire family is affected by changes in lifestyle, privacy, socialization, and plans when time and attention are diverted for purposes of caregiving. The encouragement and support of family members are critical to the motivation of the disabled older person. Strategies used for management of clients with dementia have been researched to determine how management of behavioral problems is associated with adjustment of family members.

Adjusting to the fact that a dementing disease is not reversible and often involves a lingering death places families in situations of dealing with grief over a long period. This adjustment can be associated with the grieving of death and dying. Every person advances through the stages at a different rate, and each uses individualized coping strategies. Some people waiver between stages and may never reach the stage of acceptance. If family members accept the idea that each person manages feelings in a certain way, the family can serve as a strong support through the adjustment process. Dr. Elizabeth Kübler-Ross (1969) described the adjustment to death, which has been compared to the adjustment for a fatal disease, in the following stages:

- Denial and isolation when shock and disbelief are expressed
- Anger and resentment resulting in feelings of persecution, bitterness toward others and self
- Bargaining with the intent of trying to heal the person and restore life by buying back with promises
- Depression and hopelessness
- Acceptance of the situation, with peace and final rest

Denial is the most common and frequently used defense, supporting the feeling that nothing is wrong. Beliefs about senility and old age lead the family to excuse the symptoms. The ability to deny that symptoms are occurring vary with the age of the person affected, the general health, emotional closeness to the individual, or preexisting family roles. Denial of the situation can be dangerous if treatment is not obtained or family conflict arises.

Once the family is able to move past denial, if a professional evaluation of the afflicted family member has not been obtained, this will be valuable in determining the disease process and actual degree of impairment. The period of evaluation may be lengthy because of the need for medical, psychiatric, and geriatric evaluation, followed by further evaluation to determine the course of therapy. This provides opportunities for the client to appear to have improved, often resulting in false hope. Families should be encouraged to make use of the "good days," and realize the stress they are placing on themselves by becoming hopeful. Family members should also be supported to face reality and made aware that "good days" decrease in number over time, while the number of days the family member demonstrates symptoms increases.

During the denial process, caregivers may become overinvolved in the care, leading to isolation and refusal of assistance or support. This may include an immediate spouse or the entire family. Overinvolvement can be healthy if learning and direction are accepted, and an opportunity could be provided to plan the care of the individual. It can also create barriers if the people fail to seek help when they should. Extreme overinvolvement leads to greater isolation and to the caregiver's sacrificing for the illness (see Client/Family Teaching box, p. 757).

The second stage, anger and resentment, results in family members displaying bitterness toward others or the outside world. During this stage, the family may attempt to counteract the illness and compensate for the relative's losses. Anger can stem from the added physical and emotional burden caused by the continued burden in the caregiving situation. It can also be caused by the isolation, which is interpreted as abandonment. The loss of control may precipitate feelings of guilt. Guilt develops out of the anger, and can arise for many reasons. In some situations, the stress may result in verbal or physical abuse of the loved one. It is not uncommon for family members to wish their loved one would die, and then feel guilty about that wish. Guilt may be triggered by angry acts and omissions, or because of the difficult decisions required in the care of the family member.

Bargaining may result when the family attempts to compensate for loss, resulting in an acceptable climate and creating a hopeful environment. Reality orientation by health care workers during initial contacts may help the family move through this stage, or the family may revert to previous stages if they are unable to come to terms with the disease process.

Depression may be defined as a mood of sadness that consists of feelings of helplessness and hopelessness. This may result from the inability to influence the outcome, and to see results from the "bargaining," isolation, or loneliness. The length of the stage of depression is dependent on the coping mechanisms and support systems available to the caregivers.

The final stage of acceptance is possible when the process of the disease and its effect on others is fully understood. It is easier once the family members have identified resources. These resources add to the strength and help with understanding the impact of the illness. New situations can precipitate return to previous stages of adjustment, creating the need to maintain coping strategies for prevention of a roadblock.

Financial arrangements can be a barrier to obtaining services that are needed. Public assistance programs for nursing home care, such as Medicaid, have financial requirements that must be fulfilled before the cost is covered by a mixture of state and federal funding. Family members caring for a relative usually can support long-term home care if they strategically use community resources, family, and friends.

The acceptance of a relative with dementia by a loved one depends on personal coping strategies, support and past experiences. Family adjustment can be enhanced by nursing personnel that integrate the family's care into the care planning process. As dementia progresses, spousal caregivers are faced daily with increasing levels of emotional, physical, and mental dysfunction. The main problems for caregivers were identified by Barnes and colleagues (1983) as (1) emotional stress during the diagnostic process, (2) inadequate understanding of the progressive nature of the disease, (3) denial of the illness and its ramifications and (4) a deep sense of loss and sadness as the disease progresses. Financial burdens and multiple role responsibilities also add to the burden experienced by the spouse or adult children. Problems must be recognized before they can be addressed with the caregiver. Caregivers are subject to loneliness, decreased social support, and depression. A comprehensive assessment of the caregiver and the caregiving situation may assist in identifying problems and planning ways of alleviating controllable factors.

Assessment of the caregiver's physical health, functional status, medication regimen, nutrition and exercise patterns may identify factors attributing to feelings of the caregiver. Caregivers need to be encouraged to take time out for relief from their task and participate in health promotion activities. Clinicians may also want to consider methods that expand the size and strengthen the social support system of the caregiver by identifying outside support groups and emphasizing the need to maintain relationships with family and friends.

CLIENT/FAMILY TEACHING

Coping With "Good Days" and "Bad Days"

The nature of a dementing illness and prognosis are important to the client and family when diagnosing, but it should also be emphasized that behavioral patterns may be inconsistent, resulting in the client having "good days" and "bad days." Symptoms may be exacerbated by stressors that are experienced, resulting in excess disability. Family members should be taught interventions that promote safety, comfort, function, and prevention of complications while diminishing stressors for the client. Disability can be caused by fatigue, changes in routine, high levels of stimulus or physical illness, discomfort, pain or medication reaction. Anticipating and teaching family members strategies to cope with common behavioral problems can be critical in affecting the outcome. The following suggestions can be recommended to family members:

1. Solve frustrating problems one at a time. Small changes make a difference in the results.
2. Seek opportunities for rest to maintain patience and tolerance.
3. Solve problems with common sense and imagination.
4. Maintain a sense of humor.
5. Establish an environment that provides the structure needed for safety and routine but allows some freedom of movement.
6. Provide activity, but prevent overstimulation and agitation.
7. Develop mechanisms of expressing personal frustration and anxiety.

Resources

In cases of clients with severe dementing disease, the caregiver has been described as the hidden victim of illness. Physical and mental strain placed on the caregiver can be significantly reduced if both family and community resources are sufficiently used. Family members may feel at first that they prefer to manage alone. Community resources become more important as the primary caregiver grows more isolated and overextended. The family should be encouraged to explore community resources and plan ahead before the need becomes critical (see Client/Family Teaching box, below).

Families may need guidance in determining sources to explore. These might include health professionals, community mental health centers, Area Agencies on Aging, medical information and referral programs, and resource centers or family support groups specific for the disease type. With the increased emphasis and public attention on AD, specific programs and resources have become available that are valuable when caring for any person with a dementing illness.

Community resources are meant to support, not replace, family involvement. In relying on community resources, families should be encouraged to use the following guidelines:

- Ask questions to clarify your understanding of the situation.
- Openly express needs and concerns.
- Use contact with individuals as an opportunity to increase understanding of other resources available.
- Seek guidance from resources when making difficult decisions.

CLIENT/FAMILY TEACHING

Maintaining the Caregiver's Mental Health

The family often becomes the primary target for providing noninstitutional care and is physically, emotionally, and financially burdened. The health of the caregiver is as important to establish as that of the older adult diagnosed with cognitive impairment. Caregivers are subject to increased levels of depression and depending on the amount of energy they exert in the care of their loved one, may ignore their own health needs. An assessment of physical health and functional status, medication regimen, nutrition, and exercise patterns is essential on an ongoing basis. Health promotion activities should be identified and maintained, in addition to emphasizing the need to expand and strengthen the support system available to the caregiver.

A significant growth of family support groups provides a network to help families faced with the impact of the disease. These groups aid members in coping with the inevitable losses faced by the victims of a dementing disease, such as forgetting where they are when they go for a walk in the neighborhood, not recognizing their own children, not being able to dress themselves, and in more advanced cases, needing assistance with eating, bathing, and toileting. These groups also provide caregivers with emotional support and respite.

Respite care is a type of service provided for family members requiring occasional relief from the pressures of continuous caregiving. Such relief can prevent premature institutionalization of the client as a result of the caregiver's physical and emotional stress. Respite programs offer services ranging from several hours to several weeks of relief.

Shared respite care is a program where a number of families may join together to provide caregiving on a rotating basis. Several family members may watch over a group of clients to allow others to have free time. By caring for the loved one in the company of others, caregivers find that social isolation is reduced.

Adult Day Centers help keep people with dementia in the community, promote remaining active and retaining learned skills, and provide respite for their family caregivers. Facilities are providing special units with services for cognitively impaired clients. These units provide a safe environment where clients can explore without getting lost and can participate in activities geared toward maintaining cognitive capacities. Some centers provide more specialized social work, nursing, or physical and occupational therapy services. These centers allow family members to remain employed, do errands, rest, and be involved in other important areas of their lives.

Home health care programs usually can provide nursing and personal care services to clients in their homes. Nursing care is usually not needed until the later stages of the illness, when coexisting medical problems occur. Many home health programs have nurse aides, homemakers, or care providers that can assist with personal needs. Home health personnel can help with direct care needs including meals and shopping, medications, cleaning, laundry, transportation, appraisal of the person's condition, and companionship.

Legal services are necessary when family members must consider questions related to the person's ability to handle finances and to make decisions. When some form of legal guardianship is being considered, the opinion of the treating physician and a mental health professional should be consulted.

Community mental health centers sometimes have specialized geriatric programs. These programs can provide a wide range of services, including comprehensive assessment, psychiatric evaluations, and individual, group, and family counseling. In addition, case-management services identify other community resources that can help to maintain the individual in the home. Mental health intervention may help in cases of lengthy periods of caregiving, a client with difficult behavior traits, or a difficult living environment.

Psychiatric hospitals offer assessment and behavior stabilization. They may be the last resort in cases of unmanageable behavior. The hospital staff can often assist the family with care planning and management (see nursing Care Plan, p. 760-761).

OTHER COMMON PROBLEMS AND CONDITIONS

Cerebrovascular Accident and TIA

A cerebrovascular accident (CVA) or stroke is a suddenly occurring condition in which the blood supply to the brain is reduced, resulting in an acute vascular brain lesion. The cessation of blood flow causes a disruption in oxygen supply to the affected portion(s) of the brain and causes neurons to cease functioning. Contributing factors to CVA include hypertension, diabetes, obesity, heavy smoking, heavy alcohol intake, anticoagulant medication therapy, high cholesterol levels, and sedentary lifestyle. Causes of CVA include hemorrhage, a ruptured or bleeding aneurysm, a thrombus, or an embolus. A TIA is a transient impairment of cerebral blood flow to a specific region of the brain as a result of arteriosclerotic involvement of the vessels supplying the brain. TIA is characterized by transient focal neurologic signs and symptoms of sudden onset, usually lasting for several minutes to 1 hour, with the absence of neurologic disturbances between attacks.

CVA may be the result of several pathologic changes. The formation of a thrombus resulting from arteriosclerosis can reduce blood flow to an area of the brain. Sclerotic plaque on the vessel walls promotes formation of thrombi and can result in a thrombotic stroke. Other changes that can lead to stroke may include an embolus that originates from a heart thrombus and lodges in a cerebral artery, causing brain infarction. Finally, a cerebral hemorrhage caused by hypertension or a ruptured intracerebral aneurysm can cause a stroke. Hypertension causes bleeding into the brain tissue, whereas a ruptured aneurysm bleeds into the subarachnoid space.

A CVA is generally defined by the motor area of the brain that is affected. A left CVA indicates there is a lesion on the left side of the brain, which results in right-sided weakness or paralysis. A right CVA indicates a lesion on the right side of the brain, resulting in weakness on the left.

TIA is a result of ischemia caused by occlusion or weakness of arterial walls, resulting in reduced blood

MEDICAL MANAGEMENT

CVA

Diagnostic tests and procedures

- Complete blood count (CBC) to determine the amount of blood loss from hemorrhage
- Blood glucose levels to identify diabetes or hypoglycemia, which can lead to other complications
- Prothrombin time (PT) and partial thromboplastin time (PTT) to determine baseline before anticoagulant therapy
- Computed tomography (CT) to differentiate infarction from hemorrhage and to reveal the extent of bleeding and brain compression
- Cerebral angiography to reveal the site of bleeding or blockage
- Skull and cervical spine x-ray to rule out fracture if associated with a fall

Treatment

Initial treatment of a CVA is maintenance of life support functions by preventing aspiration and reducing intracranial pressure. Treatment cannot reverse damage, but risk factors such as high blood pressure, high cholesterol, and diabetes are controlled. Surgical treatment may include carotid endarterectomy to remove blockage in the carotid artery. Aspirin has proven to be an effective antiplatelet agent in reducing the rate of strokes and may be combined with dipyridamole to reduce the occurrence. Anticoagulant therapy including heparin or coumadin may be initiated. Corticosteroids, anticonvulsants, analgesics, and antipyretics may be instituted.

TIA may easily be ignored because the symptoms resolve. Pharmacotherapy that may be initiated to inhibit platelet aggregation includes two tablets of buffered aspirin twice daily and dipyridamole (Persantine). Heparin or coumadin may be considered as therapy, although the outcome remains controversial.

Prognosis

Multiple reasons for a CVA account for the resulting differences in severity and symptomology. Recovery is affected by the severity of the CVA. If a stroke was severe, with maximum neurologic deficits at onset, the symptoms do not disappear. A high percentage of mortality occurs in the first month following a stroke. Recovery may take several months, depending on the extent of brain damage. Few stroke survivors survive 10 years (APA, 1994).

Return to normal function often occurs within a short period following a TIA. Although the symptoms may appear minor, a physician should be consulted for treatment to prevent CVA.

CARE PLAN

CAREGIVER STRAIN

Clinical situation Mrs. M, a 78-year-old woman, accompanied by her husband and daughter, was admitted to the hospital with symptoms of fever. Mrs. M lives with and is cared for by her husband, who insists he has been able to provide the necessary care.

The client has been in excellent health until approximately 6 years ago, when her family began to notice that she was becoming forgetful and occasionally confused. Over the years, her memory worsened. Her appearance became disheveled, her clothes stained, and she was unable to coordinate her clothing. Episodes of depression increased in frequency. She sometimes demonstrated paranoid behavior; she would walk to her female neighbors' homes and accuse them of having an affair with her husband, or accuse her husband of stealing from her.

Her intellect continued to decline. Words often failed her in spite of previously fluent speech patterns, until she was finally unable to communicate with words. Her husband provided constant care for her, stating that she behaved like "an infant." Her posture was stooped and she walked with a stilted gait. She became increasingly incontinent of urine and feces during the last five months. She was very uncooperative, resulting in difficulty encouraging mobility, and often refused to get out of bed.

Mr. M had been treating Mrs. M for a "cold" at home. She was congested with a temperature of 38.2° C (100.8° F) for approximately 3 days and had been responding inappropriately and lethargically. She was hospitalized; chest x-ray, CBC, and electrolyte studies were ordered. Intravenous (IV) antibiotic therapy was initiated.

Mr. M often visited the client. He grew increasingly despondent, and verbalized his feelings of inadequacy and inability to care for his wife. His daughter had been in contact with her parents during the last year by telephone, but because of her busy schedule, had not visited. Mr. M also commented on difficulties with his financial status.

Nursing diagnoses	Outcomes	Interventions
Caregiver role strain related to continued decline in health of wife and increased caregiving demands.	Client will have increased capacity to manage caregiving demands as evidenced by the following: • Increased ability to provide or assist with care • Increased familiarity with disease process • Maintenance of own physical and functional health • Appropriate support systems are identified • Participation in a support group • Obtaining daily assistance with personal care of wife • Mr. M will feel less isolated	Educate Mr. M and other family members on the irreversible condition of his wife. Develop a therapeutic relationship. Provide the opportunity for verbalization and listen to perceived feelings. Provide the opportunity to reminisce. Determine spouse's ability to deal with the grief process. Explore awareness of possible resources or agencies for emotional support or financial guidance; encourage use of respite services and make referrals. Include family and friends when teaching. Support Mr. M and the family in their decisions.
Impaired physical mobility related to change in mental status	Physical changes do not occur as evidenced by the following: • Intact skin • Increased activity level • Improved bowel and bladder continence	Relieve pressure on the skin by changing position or reducing pressure on bony prominences. Educate Mr. M on intervention strategies including: • Observation of skin for redness or broken areas; change position every 1 to 2 hours • Keep skin dry and clean • Provide possible range-of-motion exercises four times daily, gently and rhythmically; repeat each exercise three times. • Position in proper body alignment. • Involve client and family in exploring activi-

CARE PLAN

CAREGIVER STRAIN—cont'd

Nursing diagnoses	Outcome	Interventions
		ties of interest, and arrange for participation in these. • Monitor intake and output. • Establish and adhere to toileting routine.
Altered thought processes related to memory loss, confusion, and disorientation associated with dementia	Behaviors will be managed to maintain care of Mrs. M in the home as evidenced by the following: • Functional ability of Mrs. M increases • Family participation increases for care of Mrs. M • Environmental and routine modifications understood by Mr. M and implemented	Provide a structured, consistent, routine environment. Reorient Mrs. M only once per encounter. Divert attention by changing the subject as appropriate. Prevent barriers that do not cause harm (hoarding, wandering) as long as they are safe. Encourage regular physical activity and devise a schedule. Modify the environment to meet Mrs. M's needs (signage, familiar objects)
Impaired verbal communication related to the cognitive impairment	Effective verbal and nonverbal communication will be established as evidenced by the following: • Ability to communicate needs as dementia increases and verbal skills will decrease • Minimum frustration will be demonstrated by Mr. M	Approach Mrs. M using a relaxed manner and expression. Speak in a clear, low-pitched tone. Identify self to Mrs. M and use eye contact. Recognize nonverbal behaviors and determine their meaning (grimacing, restless). Minimize background noise when speaking to Mrs. M. Encourage reminiscence and story telling. Provide a therapeutic environment using music or art.
Functional incontinence related to cognitive deficit and loss of memory.	Bowel and bladder continence will be maintained as long as possible as evidenced by the following: • Less frequent episodes of incontinence • Fewer barriers to toileting	Maintain independence in toileting as long as possible. Manage episodes of incontinence; prevent secondary conditions by providing skin care and changing position. Determine changes in client needs related to toileting. Devise a toileting schedule. Teach Mr. M. to maintain accurate elimination records. Ensure fluid intake of six to eight glasses of water daily (before 6 P.M.).

flow to tissues. Thickening and calcification of the vessel caused by arteriosclerosis is the most common pathologic change.

Physical examination of the client with a stroke shows changes in the neurologic, respiratory, cardiovascular, and musculoskeletal systems. Findings may show weakness or paralysis on the opposite side of the brain lesion, poor proprioception, apraxia, dyslexia, impaired facial sensation with pain, ataxia, agnosia, decerebrate rigidity, aphasia, and impaired voluntary movement. Labored respirations, hyperventilation, or hypoventilation may be present. Cardiovascular changes appear as decreased or increased blood pressure, decreased pulse rate, dysrhythmias, or carotid bruits. Decreased muscle strength is also present on the affected side. Other symptoms include impaired spatial perception, inability to see objects on the affected side, nystagmus, tinnitus, or vertigo (see Medical Management box, p. 759).

Specific signs and symptoms of a TIA vary depending on which vessel is involved, the degree of obstruction of the vessel, and collateral blood supply. If the carotid system is involved, the person may experience blurred vision, gradual visual obstruction, flashes of light, and headaches. If the posterior system is involved, symptoms may include tinnitus, vertigo, bilateral sensory and motor symptoms, diplopia, facial weakness, and ataxia.

NURSING MANAGEMENT

ASSESSMENT

CVA symptoms reflect a fluctuating (gradual) or abrupt onset. The cause of the impairment results in variations in the presenting symptoms and an unpredictable disease course. Symptoms of TIA, which may be the initial indication of a cerebrovascular problem, may be reported by the client during a routine examination or associated with other medical problems. The client with symptoms of a TIA should be referred to a physician for further work-up to prevent occurrence of a CVA.

The client should be asked to describe usual activities and lifestyle. The nurse should query regarding a history of blackouts, dizziness, lightheadedness or headaches, faintness, weakness, or numbness. The nurse should also determine if vision, hearing, or speech deficits were present before the event; stability or trends in blood pressure over time; a history of hypertension or diabetes; and family or personal history of cerebrovascular or coronary artery disease (CAD), as well as family history of cerebrovascular accident. Ascertain typical daily nutritional intake, including alcohol intake and cigarette use. Identify if there has been any recent trauma to the head (Box 27-13).

BOX 27-13

Assessment of CVA

Subjective data

Sedentary lifestyle
History of blackouts, dizziness, lightheadedness, headaches, faintness, weakness, or numbness
History of vision, hearing, or speech deficits
History of hypertension, diabetes, or cerebrovascular or coronary artery disease
Obesity; history of diet high in fat and calories
Heavy alcohol or nicotine consumption
Family history of CVA
Recent head trauma

Objective data

Cardiovascular

Hypertension or hypotension
Carotid bruits

Gastrointestinal

Vomiting
Difficulty swallowing, gag reflex diminished
Incontinence

Neurologic

Loss of consciousness
Focal neurologic signs and symptoms
Abrupt onset of hemiplegia or impaired activity
One-sided weakness, numbness
Decreased attention span
Recent memory loss

Sensory

Aphasia
Inability to distinguish pain, heat, cold, and pressure
Inability to follow directions or understand questions
Speech difficulty (inability to form sentences, substitution of words)
Absent or diminished taste

DIAGNOSIS

Nursing diagnoses for the older adult client with a CVA include, but are not limited to: (1) altered cerebral tissue perfusion related to hemorrhage and/or increased intracranial pressure; (2) ineffective breathing pattern related to neuromuscular impairment; (3) high risk for aspiration related to neuromuscular weakness and dysphagia; (4) impaired physical mobility related to arm/leg weakness or paralysis; (5) impaired verbal communication related to aphasia and dysarthria from CVA; (6) high risk for injury related to seizures; (7) high risk for impaired skin integrity related to prolonged immobility; (8) altered patterns of urinary elimination related to immobility; (9) tactile and auditory sensory-perceptual alteration related to impaired proprioception and hearing loss; (10) eating, bathing, dressing, and toileting self-care deficit related to impairments secondary to CVA; and (11) knowledge deficit: medication use, rehabilitation, and long-term care for CVA related to lack of experience/exposure.

PLANNING

Nursing activities are planned to prevent potential complications of immobility, hyperthermia, constipation or fecal impaction, contractures, pneumonia, incontinence, urinary tract infection, dehydration, depression, or dependence on the caregiver. The plan of care may begin in the acute setting and be extended to home care throughout the course of the recovery. Outcomes include, but are not limited to, the following: (1) maintaining adequate cerebral tissue perfusion, (2) remaining free of pressure ulcers and contractures, (3) demonstrating an optimum level of mobility, (4) effectively using communication techniques to convey needs and desires and (5) successfully carrying out optimum self-care activities within imposed limitations.

✣ INTERVENTION

Initial care focuses on assessment and management of the airway and respiratory system to include auscultating lungs, suctioning the airway, and providing oxygen therapy as needed. A baseline neurologic assessment should be obtained and then carried out on a regular, ongoing basis. Positioning is critical to maintain the airway and to prevent complications related to vascular compromise. The ability to chew and to swallow is improved by sitting the client upright while eating and providing semisolid foods that are easy to swallow. Extremities with weakness or immobility are assessed for edema, and support is provided when moving or when out of bed. Passive range-of-motion exercises are initiated at least four times daily. Functional assessment of skills and activities of the client before the onset of the CVA should be determined as a guide to establishing rehabilitation goals.

Immediate attention to the family's needs should include teaching about the disease process and anticipated progress of the recovery and rehabilitation phases. Family and community resource people and services should be identified to assist with meeting the social or spiritual family needs. The family should be encouraged to communicate regularly with the client, recognizing that initially the client may be emotional and communication may be difficult, but that this response should improve over time. Excessive auditory and visual stimulation should be limited. In the event of emotional outbursts or crying, attention should be diverted from the task or topic. Commands should be delivered in a simple manner, such as one command at a time, with use of gestures and simple words, common phrases, or short sentences. Self-esteem should be maintained by focusing on the present improvements and assuring the client is commended for progress. Grooming should also be a priority, and the client is encouraged to become independent in these activities.

Throughout recovery, progress is measured against the baseline. Activity levels are increased, speech and occupational therapy is initiated, and transfer techniques are taught. Rehabilitation potential is assessed, and adaptive aids are provided when possible. Other therapies such as music, art, or pet therapy, as well as diversional activities, are included in daily routines. The client and family are taught about medication therapy, including type, dosage, and side effects. Home care activities, the physical layout of the home, lifestyle, and typical home management are identified. Measures are then taken to make the necessary changes to promote successful functioning at home.

Lifestyle changes should be discussed with the client and family to minimize the risk of another CVA. These changes may include weight control, smoking cessation, modifying dietary intake, controlling blood pressure, and reducing stress.

✣ EVALUATION

Clients' progress occurs in small increments, and interventions are modified to assist clients in meeting their goals. Evaluation criteria include the following:

- Maintenance of adequate cerebral tissue perfusion
- Freedom from pulmonary complications
- Elimination of aspiration from food, fluids, and secretions
- Prevention of contractures
- Freedom from edema in affected arm
- Maintenance of skin integrity
- Achievement of independence
- Pain minimization
- Increase in ability to communicate, to express feelings, and to understand others
- Prevention of incontinence
- Establishment of normal voiding pattern
- Compensation for sensory deficits, and physical and intellectual losses
- Participation by family members in rehabilitation process.

Summary

Many challenges face nurses caring for the older person. The older population is expected to continue to increase in number. By the year 2030 it is anticipated there will be 2.5 times as many older people as there were in 1980 (American Association of Retired Persons, 1991). It has been found that significant percentages of those people suffer some form of cognitive impairment, all of which could benefit from nursing care focusing on their special needs. Without radical changes in the way health care is allocated and delivered in this country, the issues of shrinking health care dollars, accessibility to care, increasing commercially managed care, and outright rationing of care will threaten care of older people. Those with cognitive impairment continue to be at high risk for limited access to appropriate and cost-effective care. This will become especially critical as more state hospitals are closed without adequate community-based treatment facilities in place. Cost-effective models for care should be developed and tested along the continuum of care from prevention of illness to management of acute illness, to restoration of function and finally, to maintenance at home or in the community. Also, older people are less active participants in their own care than others. They trust and accept physician's decisions and recommendations without question. This group needs extensive teaching to become informed consumers and partners in health care.

The practice of gerontologic nursing is collaborative and interdisciplinary in scope. This is necessitated by the vast complexity, diversity, and dissimilarity of older people in terms of their physical and mental conditions, health care needs, past life experiences, current lifestyles, culture, ethnicity, and resources. The family is an extremely important aspect of the practice, not only because the majority of older people live within a family setting, but because the family is becoming a primary provider of care. The most serious health problems occur in those more than 80 years old, and this group is likely to be cared for by relatives who are more than 65 years of age. The blend of medical-surgical, psychiatric, and community health nursing required to care for the older adult with cognitive impairment provides unique and unlimited opportunities and challenges in practice.

Key Points

- Cognitive impairment is not a result of the normal aging process. Physical health, medication therapy, personal and environmental stressors, or substance abuse may lead to cognitive impairment.
- Early diagnosis and treatment of a cognitive impairment may prevent an irreversible status.
- Mental status examinations are a useful tool for determining a diagnosis, but should be used in conjunction with reliable information from a history and physical assessment to assure the correct diagnosis.
- Dementia is essentially irreversible and may be the result of genetic influences, immunologic changes, or viral or environmental causes.
- Vascular dementia is preventable if the cause is determined early enough for treatment to be beneficial. Risk factors, including hypertension, diabetes, obesity, and smoking should be determined and eliminated to prevent the occurrence of vascular dementia.
- Numerous studies are conducted to determine the diagnosis of depression, delirium, or dementia. These studies may identify a physical problem resulting in the symptoms associated with cognitive impairment.
- Therapy for cognitive impairment includes nontraditional methodologies such as medication therapy. It relies on recognizing behavior patterns, identifying risk factors in the environment, and determining creative strategies for managing the client's care.
- The treatment goal when caring for people with symptoms of cognitive impairment is directed toward maintaining good health and locomotor skills, while preserving functional behaviors.
- Individualized strategies are the most effective interventions for managing clients with cognitive disorders.

HOME CARE TIPS

1. Assess sensorimotor function. A decline in this function is the most notable change in older adults and may be the cause of other changes such as reaction time.
2. Memory impairment may compromise teaching homebound clients, requiring the nurse to use alternative approaches, as well as rely on family and significant others involved in the caregiving.
3. Assess for signs of impaired emotional control, diminished initiative, withdrawal, or other changes, which may be initial signs of brain dysfunction.
4. Altered thought processes occur with cognitive decline or disturbances in cognitive function, both of which occur in homebound clients with dementia, depression, delirium, or amnestic disorders.
5. The effects of aging must be considered when interpreting laboratory tests and alerting physicians about abnormal results.
6. Instruct caregivers about dosages and side effects of medications, especially tranquilizers and antidepressants, that are used in managing symptoms caused by dementias.
7. Instruct caregivers on methods to manage behavior problems and caregiver stress.
8. Use social workers to assess community resources for caregivers and clients with dementia.
9. Assess the home environment of the older person with cognitive impairment for safety hazards, and provide caregivers with tips and strategies for reducing and eliminating the identified hazards.

- Consider the client's personality and lifestyle before the impairment when determining appropriate interventions.
- Evaluation is critical when caring for the cognitively impaired individual. Subtle changes in behavior may be indicative of a health problem, change in the stage of the disease, or potentially harmful problems.
- Families and friends are affected by the diagnosis of cognitive impairment of a loved one, and emotionally accept the information in a variety of ways. They may adjust to the information as one would prepare for death, and move through stages of acceptance at varying rates.
- Family members are often relied on as the initial caregivers during stages of the disease when impairment does not affect physical activity. The burden of caregiving is as important to determine as the disease, and family members require intervention to maintain their own health and emotional stability.
- The family should be aware of and involved in com-

munity resources as early as possible in the disease to promote their comfort in accessing outside assistance.

Critical Thinking Exercises

1. In assessing depression in the older adult, identify essential factors that help distinguish depression from dementia.
2. In what ways would you adjust your communication style for the older adult with any type of dementia?
3. A 62-year-old woman with AD in a long-term care facility is convinced that she is in someone else's home and often wanders in an attempt to find her own home. The family's attempts to reorient her have been futile. How can the family be assisted in coping with this problem?

REFERENCES

Alexopoulos GS, Abrams RC, Young RC: Cornell scale for depression in dementia, *Biol Psychiatry* 23:271-284, 1988.

Alexopoulos GS, Mattis S: Diagnosing cognitive dysfunction in the elderly: primary screening tests, *Geriatrics* 46:33-44, 1991.

American Association of Retired Persons: *A profile of older Americans,* Washington, D.C., 1991, The Association.

American Psychiatric Association: *Diagnostic and statistical manual of mental disorders,* ed 4, Washington, D.C., 1994, The Association.

Bachman DL et al: Prevalence of dementia and probable senile dementia of the Alzheimer's type in the Framingham study, *Neurology* 42:115-119, 1992.

Ballard CG et al: Paranoid features in the elderly with dementia, *Int J Geriatr Psychiatry* 6:155-157, 1991.

Barnes RF et al: Problems of families caring for Alzheimer's patients: use of a support group, *J Am Geriatr Soc* 29(2):80-85, 1983.

Blessed G, Tomlinson B, Roth M: The association between quantitative measures of dementia and senile change in cerebral grey matter of the elderly, *Br J Psychiatry* 114:797-811, 1968.

Burgener SC, Shimer M: Nursing care of cognitively impaired, institutionalized elderly, *J Gerontol Nurs* 17:37-43, 1991.

Chapman K, Nelson R: Loss of appetite: managing unwanted weight loss in the older patient, *Geriatrics* 49:54-59, 1994.

Cohen D et al: Psychopathology associated with Alzheimer's disease and related disorders, *J Gerontol* 48:M255-M260, 1993.

Danner C et al: Cognitively impaired elders: using research findings to improve nursing care, *J Gerontol Nurs* 4:5-11, 1993.

Eisdorfer C, Cohen D, Paveza G: An empirical evaluation of the global deterioration scale for staging Alzheimer's disease, *Am J Psychiatry* 149:190-194, 1992.

Evans DA et al: Prevalence of Alzheimer's disease in a community population of older persons, *J Am Med Assoc* 262:2551-2556, 1989.

Flicker C, Ferris SH, Riesberg B: Mild cognitive impairment in the elderly: predictors of dementia, *Neurology* 41:1006-1009, 1991.

Folstein MF, Folstein SE, McHugh PR: Mini-mental state: a practical method for grading the cognitive state of patients for the clinician, *J Psychiatr Res* 12:189-198, 1975.

Gorelick PB et al: Risk factors for dementia associated with multiple cerebral infarcts: a case-control analysis in predominantly African-American hospital-based patients, *Arch Neurol* 50:714-720, 1993.

Hulse JR: Humor: A nursing intervention for the elderly, *Geriatr Nurs* 15:88-90, 1994.

Jeste DV, Krull AJ: Behavioral problems associated with dementia: diagnosis and treatment, *Geriatrics* 46:28-34, 1991.

Johansson B, Zarit SH, Berg S: Changes in cognitive functioning of the oldest old, *J Gerontol* 47:P75-P80, 1992.

Jorm A, Jacob P: The informant questionnaire on cognitive decline in elderly (IQCODE): socio-demographic correlates, reliability, validity and norms, *Psychol Med* 19:1015-1022, 1989.

Jutagir R: Psychological aspects of aging: when does memory loss signal dementia? *Geriatrics* 49:45-51, 1994.

Kahn RL et al: Brief objective measures for the determination of mental status in the aged, *Am J Psychiatry* 117:326-328, 1960.

Katzman R et al: Validation of a short orientation-memory-concentration test of cognitive impairment, *Am J Psychiatry* 140:734, 1983.

Katzman R, Terry R: Normal aging of the nervous system. In Katzman R, Terry R, editors: *The neurology of aging,* Philadelphia, 1983, FA Davis.

Kral VA, Emery OB: Long-term follow-up of depressive pseudodementia of the aged, *Can J Psychiatry,* 34:445-446, 1989.

Kübler-Ross E: *On death and dying,* New York, 1969, Macmillan.

Lazarus LW et al: Frequency and presentation of depressive symptoms in patients with primary degenerative dementia, *Am J Psychiatry* 146:41-45, 1987.

McCaddon A, Kelly CL: Familial Alzheimer's disease and vitamin B_{12} deficiency, *Age Ageing* 23:334-337, 1994.

McDougall GJ: A review of screening instruments for assessing cognition and mental status in older adults, *Nurse Pract* 15:11, 1990.

Meara RJ: Review: the pathophysiology of the motor signs in Parkinson's disease, *Age Ageing* 23:342-346, 1994.

Moore JT: A functional dementia scale, *J Fam Pract* 16:499, 1983.

Morris JC, McManus DQ: The neurology of aging: normal versus pathologic change, *Geriatrics* 46:47-54, 1991.

National Institute of Aging: *Alzheimer's disease,* Pub No 85-1646, Bethesda, Md., 1985, The Institute.

Pfeiffer E: A short portable mental status questionnaire for assessment of organic brain deficit in elderly patients, *J Am Geriatr Soc* 23(10):433-441, 1975.

Polvin AR: Human neurologic function and the aging process, *J Am Geriatr Soci 28:1, 1980.*

Rovner BW et al: Depression and mortality in nursing homes, *JAMA* 265:993-996, 1992.

Sambandham M, Schirm V: Music as a nursing intervention for residents with AD in long term care, *Geriatr Nurs* 16:79-83, 1995.

Schaie KW: The hazards of cognitive aging, *Gerontologist* 29:484-493, 1989.

Sterritt PF, Pokorny ME: Art activities for patients with Alzheimer's and related disorders, *Geriatr Nurs* 15:155-159, 1994.

Teri L, Hughes J, Larson E: Cognitive deterioration in Alzheimer's disease: behavioral and health factors, *J Gerontol: Psychol Sci* 45:P58-P63, 1990.

Thibodeaux GA, Patton K: *Anthony's textbook of anatomy and physiology,* ed 14, St. Louis, 1994, Mosby.

Wechsler D: *Wechsler adult intelligence scale (revised),* New York, 1981, Harcourt Brace Jovanovich.

Wells CE: Pseudodementia, *Am J Psychiatry* 136:895-900, 1979.

Willott JF: Neurogerontology: the aging nervous system. In Ferraro KF, editor: *Gerontologist: perspectives and issues,* New York, 1987, Springer.

Wragg RE, Jeste DV: Overview of depression and psychosis in Alzheimer's disease, *Am J Psychiatry* 146:577-587, 1989.

BIBLIOGRAPHY

Abraham I et al: Multidisciplinary assessment of patients with Alzheimer's disease, *Nurs Clin North Am* 29:113-128, 1994.

Beck CK, Rawlins RP, Williams SR: *Mental health-psychiatric nursing: a holistic life cycle approach,* St. Louis, 1988, Mosby.

Ebersole P, Hess P: *Toward healthy aging: human needs and nursing response,* ed 4, St. Louis, 1994, Mosby.

Gatz M et al: Dementia: not just a search for the gene, *Gerontologist* 34:251-255, 1994.

Harper MS: *Management and care of the elderly: psychosocial perspectives,* Newbury Park, Calif., 1991, Sage Publications.

Hinrichsen GA: *Mental health problems and older adults,* Santa Barbara, Calif., 1990, ABC-CLIO.

Lange-Alberts ME, Shott S: Nutritional intake: Use of touch and verbal cueing, *J Gerontol Nurs* 20:36-40, 1994.

Lazare A: *Outpatient psychiatry: diagnosis and treatment,* ed 2, Baltimore, 1989, Williams & Wilkins.

Miziniak H: Persons with Alzheimer's: effects of nutrition and exercise, *J Gerontol Nurs* 20:27-32, 1994.

Pericak-Vance MA et al: Linkage studies in familial Alzheimer disease: evidence for chromosome 19 linkage, *Am J Hum Genet* 48:1034-1050, 1991.

Wallace M: Creutzfeldt-Jakob disease: assessment and management, *J Gerontol Nurs* 11:15-22, 1993.

CHAPTER 28

Integumentary System

LEARNING OBJECTIVES

On completion of this chapter, the reader will be able to:

1. Identify normal age-related skin changes.
2. Discuss three common skin problems and conditions experienced by older adults and the associated nursing implications.
3. Describe three types of skin cancers that affect older adults.
4. Differentiate between the three types of lower leg ulcers.
5. Describe the risk factors for pressure ulcer development.
6. Identify five pressure ulcer prevention strategies endorsed by the Agency for Health Care Policy and Research (AHCPR) clinical guidelines.
7. Discuss the components of a nutritional assessment and how the nurse can influence a client's nutritional status.
8. Discuss the healing trajectory and its influences on wound healing.
9. State three principles necessary for successful wound healing.
10. Conduct an assessment for a client with impaired skin integrity.
11. Determine when to appropriately use antiseptics.
12. Discuss five types of dressings including indications, contraindications, advantages, and drawbacks.

The integumentary system, or skin, is the largest organ of the body, weighing about 4 kilograms and covering approximately 2 miles^2 (Lookingbill, Marks, 1986). The primary function of the skin is to serve as a barrier against harmful bacteria and other threatening agents, making skin the first line of defense for the immune system. Other major functions of the integumentary system include preventing fluid loss and protecting the body from ultraviolet rays and other external environmental hazards. Thermal regulation of body temperature through radiation, conduction, convection, and evaporation is facilitated by nerve endings' sensory perceptions. Blood vessels assist in regulating blood pressure and reveal emotions such as anger, fear, or embarrassment through vasodilation, which causes redness. In the presence of sunlight the skin synthesizes vitamin D, which is then used by other parts of the body. Subcutaneous fat is the deepest layer of the integumentary system and provides insulation and caloric reservoir. Hair serves as body insulation and provides unique physical characteristics by virtue of its varying textures, shades, patterns, and colors. The nails allow grasping, may be used to enhance personal appearance, and are important in physical assessment, since appearance of the nails may indicate systemic conditions such as cyanosis or anemia, among others (Jakubovic, Ackerman, 1992; Wysocki, 1992).

One important function of the integumentary system, especially among older adults, is its aesthetic and cosmetic value. Nonverbal communication is conveyed through an almost endless array of facial expressions. The skin molds an individual's identity by reflecting a person's hereditary traits, race, and at times emotional state (Ebersole, Hess, 1994). Thus the integumentary system can greatly influence a person's self-esteem and self-concept.

It is always prudent and efficient to thoroughly assess the integumentary system. Skin assessment can help determine hydration status, potential for or actual infection, and other information about the individual, for example, sun exposure, attention to personal appearance, and scars. Inspection of the skin can alert the professional to allergic reactions, cancerous lesions, infectious diseases, cellulitis, toxic exposure, and pressure points. Palpation of the skin can identify tender areas, nodules, or masses (see Chapter 4).

The value of the integumentary system is demonstrated by the high morbidity and mortality rate associated with extensive burns when all functions of the skin are greatly compromised. The overall state of health is affected by physical or emotional insults to this system, such as loss of thermal regulation or fluid, impaired, barrier protection, and other catastrophic changes in physical appearance and functioning. It provides valuable information for comprehending its complexities.

NORMAL STRUCTURE AND FUNCTION

The integumentary system is one of the most complex body organs and is comprised of three major tissue layers and four appendages (Fig. 28-1). The three layers—epidermis, dermis, and subcutaneous fat—are stratified horizontally with various cell types and vertically with the appendages—eccrine sweat glands, apocrine sweat glands, hair follicles, and sebaceous glands, which produce various products (Jakubovic, Ackerman, 1992). A brief review of the integumentary system components follows, and can assist the nurse in comprehending age-related changes.

Epidermis

The epidermis is the outermost layer of the integumentary system and has four cellular layers. The stratum corneum, which is dead squamous cells containing protein keratin held tightly together with a lipid cement, forms a protective barrier and prevents fluid loss. The stratum granulosum, the second cellular layer, helps organize the keratin cells and is thought to aid in forming the lipid cement. The stratum spinosum, the third layer, contains keratinocytes, which produce the fibrous protein of keratin that eventually works its way up to the stratum corneum. The basal cell layer, which contains the stem cells that proliferate and migrate upward, also produces melanin, which gives the skin its pigmented color. Since the epidermis contains no vessels, it relies on the dermis for nutritional support (Jakubovic, Ackerman, 1992; Seidel et al, 1991; Wysocki, 1992).

The primary function of the epidermis is to provide protection from harmful agents and loss of fluids. It protects against invading microorganisms by creating a barrier and activating mast cells and macrophages in the dermis, which digest foreign material and summon other immune system members. The sebaceous glands secrete a heavy lipid, oily substance that maintains a low pH of 4 to 6.8 with a mean pH of 5.5. This acidic environment has natural antibacterial properties. Normal skin flora resides on the skin surface and are not pathologic unless the host's (client's) health becomes compromised. The following bacteria are usually found on human skin: *Staphylococcus* (primarily aureus and epidermis), *Streptococcus* (particularly Group A), *Acinetobacter, Corynebacterium, Propinomibacterium, Brevibacterioum, Peptococcus, Micrococcus,* and *Neisseria* (Lookingbill, Marks, 1986; Wysocki, 1992).

Protection against ultraviolet (UV) radiation is provided by the epidermis from synthesis of melanin (skin pigment). In addition, the skin also serves as a barrier against fluid and electrolyte loss. The value of this function is demonstrated when one considers that a burn victim with a 30% body burn will lose up to 4.1 l of fluid per day from the skin, compared with a normal daily fluid loss of 0.7 l (Wysocki, 1992).

Dermis

The dermis is the tough, elastic middle layer that contains protein structures, blood vessels, nerve endings, and appendages. The unmyelinated nerve endings of the dermis, regulated by the adrenergic fibers of the autonomic nervous system (ANS), provide the body with sensations of touch, pain, itching, and temperature control. The blood vessels provide nutrients and oxygen, and assist in temperature regulation through shunting or in-

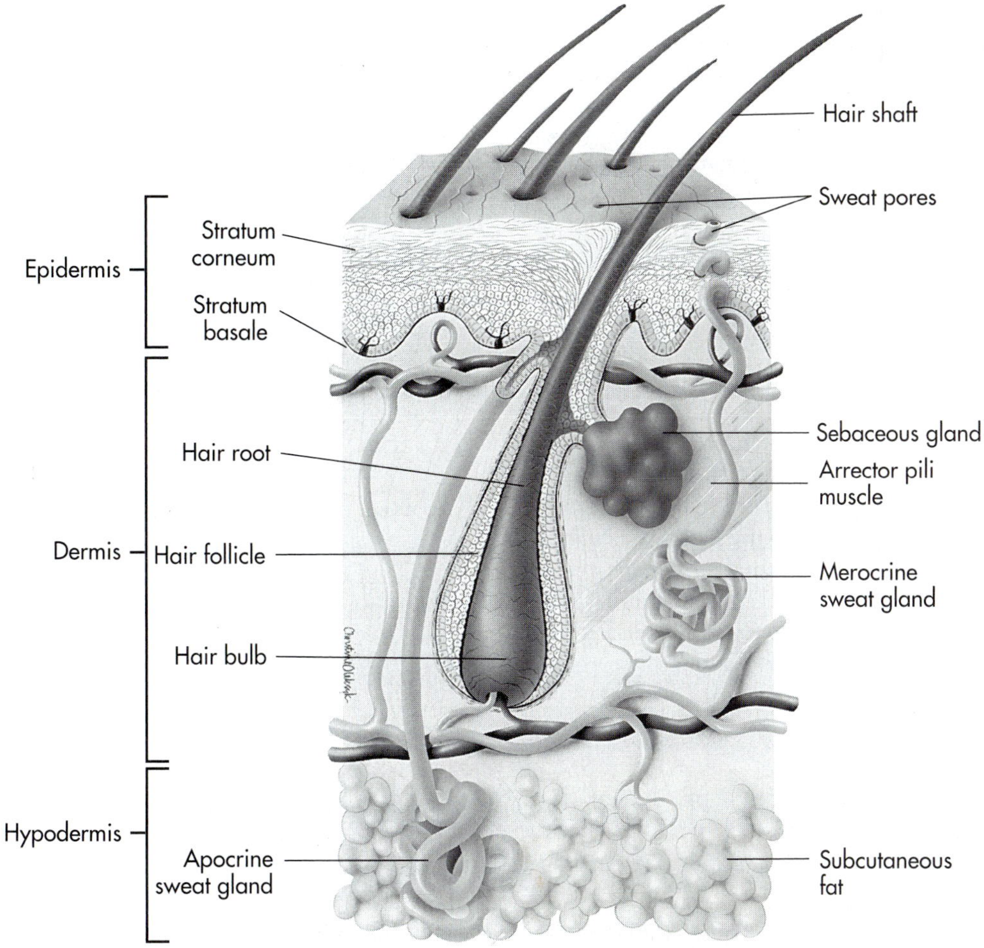

Fig. 28-1 Skin and hypodermis. (From Tate P, Seeley RR: *Understanding the human body,* St. Louis, 1994, Mosby.)

creasing blood supply (Jakubovic, Ackerman, 1992; Seidel et al, 1991; Wysocki, 1992). Mast cells, located around the vascular structures, manufacture and release histamine and heparin. Histocytes, which are essentially macrophages, accumulate melanin and debris created by infection (Habif, 1990). Collagen, the major protein structure of the dermis, gives the skin tensile strength. Elastin, a protein present in less quantity than collagen, provides the skin with elasticity and recoil (Wysocki, 1992).

Subcutaneous Fat

The subcutaneous fat layer lies between the dermis and underlying fascia and muscle. It provides insulation from cold, facilitates conductive heat loss, serves as a shock absorber from blunt trauma, and provides a food source for the body (Balin, 1990; Jakubovic, Ackerman, 1992; Parker, 1991). The layer is supplied with blood vessels and nerve endings. The amount of subcutaneous fat varies from individual to individual, and is directly correlated with an individual's weight.

Appendages

The skin appendages are the eccrine and apocrine sweat glands, hair follicles, sebaceous glands, and nails. All except the nails are vertically stratified in dermis and subcutaneous tissue layers. The eccrine sweat glands help regulate temperature by producing sweat (up to 10 l/day), which cools the body through evaporation. Apocrine sweat glands, found primarily in the axillae and genital areas, have no known function other than being responsible for body odor (Habif, 1990; Jakubovic, Ackerman, 1992; Parker, 1991; Seidel et al, 1991).

Hair consists of the root, hair shaft, and hair follicle (the root and its covering). The shaft contains melanocytes, giving hair its color. A capillary system at the base of the hair follicle supplies nourishment. Each hair goes through a growth, atrophy, and rest cycle. As this cycle is completed, hair is shed with the average person losing approximately 50 to 100 hairs per day. Sebaceous glands, located next to each hair follicle, keep the skin moist by secreting an oily substance known as sebum (Jakubovic, Ackerman, 1992; Seidel et al, 1991).

Nails are hard, keratin plates with an underlying vascular bed. The white crescent-shaped area at the proximal nail indicates the site of nail growth. Fingernails grow continuously at a rate of approximately 0.1 mm per day, with toenails growing at a slightly slower rate (Habif, 1990; Seidel et al, 1991). Nails provide pinching and grasping ability, and they can be a reflection of good grooming.

AGE-RELATED CHANGES IN SKIN STRUCTURE AND FUNCTION

The integumentary system reflects the normal aging process, which includes graying hair, increased number and depth of wrinkles, and thickening nails. Age changes are related primarily to environmental influences, particularly sunlight, and genetics (Dalziel, Bickers, 1992; Habif, 1990). Box 28-1 describes basic age-related skin changes and differentiates normal aging occurrences from pathologic changes.

BOX 28-1

Age-Related Skin Changes

- Loss of thickness, elasticity, vascularity, and strength which can delay healing process and increase risk of skin tears and bruising
- Increased lentigines (brown pigmented spots, or age spots)
- Loss of subcutaneous tissue causes wrinkling and sagging of skin, which can affect self-esteem, temperature control, and drug efficacy
- Loss of hair follicles along with thinning and graying
- Increased hair density in nose and ears, particularly men, which can clog external ear canals and impair hearing
- Thicker nails with longitudinal lines
- Decreased sebaceous and sweat gland activity, which affects thermoregulation and decreases sweating
- Higher incidence of benign and malignant skin growths

Epidermis

The turnover rate for the stratum corneum, the first layer of epidermis, declines by 50% as an individual grows older. This results in slower healing, reduced barrier protection, and delayed absorption of medications or chemicals placed on the skin. The area of contact between the epidermis and dermis decreases with age, resulting in easy separation of these layers. Therefore skin tears occur from harmless activities such as removing a bandage or pulling an individual up in the bed. Bruising occurs more easily as a result of these age-related skin changes. A thinner epidermis allows more moisture to escape and may compound previously existing skin problems. The number of melanocytes, which provide pigment and hair color, decreases with age, giving older adults less protection from UV rays, more pale skin color, and graying hair. Melanocytes also produce uneven pigmentation, causing the development of lentigines, also known as "age spots" or "liver spots." A direct correlation exists between sun exposure and the development of lentigines in the sixth decade of life, particularly on the dorsum of the hands and wrists (Balin, 1992; Dalziel, Bickers, 1992; Ebersole, Hess, 1994).

Dermis

The dermis decreases in thickness by approximately 20% with aging. The number of sweat glands, blood vessels, and nerve endings also decrease. These changes lead to diminished thermoregulatory function and inflammatory response, decreased tactile sensation, reduced pain perception, and development of wrinkles and sagging skin as a result of loss of underlying tissue. Collagen, a fibrous protein that provides tensile strength, stiffens and becomes less soluble. As a result of a loss of elastin and thicker elastin fibers, diminished skin elasticity occurs (Balin, 1992; Dalziel, Bickers, 1992; Ebersole, Hess, 1994).

Subcutaneous Fat

Aging results in a decreased amount of subcutaneous tissue and a redistribution of fat to the abdomen and thighs. Breast tissue also changes and becomes more granular and atrophic in appearance. As a result of a loss of padding supplied by subcutaneous tissues, there is a greater risk of hypothermia, skin shearing (see Pressure Ulcers, p. 790, for definition and negative results of shearing), and blunt trauma injury. The loss of this protective padding increases vulnerability of pressure points. Absorption of medications is also influenced by the decreased subcutaneous tissue and diminished vascular supply to the dermis (Balin, 1992; Ebersole, Hess, 1994).

Appendages

As an individual ages, fewer eccrine and apocrine sweat glands exist, resulting in decreased body odor and reduced evaporative heat loss because of decreased sweating. There is less need for antiperspirants and deodorants. However, older adults are at greater risk of heat stroke as a result of a compromised cooling mechanism. Older adults should avoid heat exposure over long periods and in areas of high humidity. Hats with wide brims

CULTURAL AWARENESS

Biocultural Variations in the Integumentary System During Health and Illness

Normal skin color ranges vary widely, and health care practitioners have made attempts to describe the variations seen by labeling observations with some of the following adjectives—copper, olive, tan, and various shades of brown (light, medium, dark). The term *ashen* is sometimes used to describe pallor.

Normal biocultural variations

Mongolian spots, irregular areas of deep blue pigmentation, are usually located in the sacral and gluteal areas but sometimes occur on the abdomen, thighs, shoulders, or arms. Mongolian spots are present in 90% of African Americans, 80% of Asian and Native Americans, and 9% of whites.

Vitiligo, a condition in which the melanocytes become nonfunctional in some areas of the skin, is characterized by unpigmented skin patches. Vitiligo affects more than 2 million Americans, primarily dark-skinned individuals. Older adults with vitiligo also have a statistically higher-than-normal chance of developing pernicious anemia, diabetes mellitus (DM), and hyperthyroidism.

Biocultural variations in illness

Cyanosis is the most difficult clinical sign to observe in darkly pigmented people. Because peripheral vasoconstriction can prevent cyanosis, environmental conditions such as air conditioning, mist tents, and other factors that may lower the room temperature should be noted. For the older adult to manifest clinical evidence of cyanosis, the blood must contain 5 gm of reduced hemoglobin in 1.5 gm of methemoglobin per 100 ml of blood.

Given that most conditions causing cyanosis also cause decreased oxygenation of the brain, other clinical symptoms, such as changes in level of consciousness, are evident. Cyanosis usually is accompanied by increased respiratory rate, use of accessory muscles of respiration, nasal flaring, and other manifestations of respiratory distress. When assessing people of Mediterranean descent, be aware that the circumoral region is normally dark blue.

Jaundice

In both light and dark-skinned clients, jaundice is best observed in the sclera. Many darkly pigmented people (e.g., African-American, Filipino-American, and others) have heavy deposits of subconjunctival fat that contain high levels of carotene in sufficient quantities to mimic jaundice. The fatty deposits become more dense as the distance from the cornea increases. The portion of the sclera that is revealed naturally by the palpebral fissure is the best place to accurately assess color. If the palate does not have heavy melanin pigmentation, jaundice can be detected there in the early stages (i.e., when serum bilirubin is 2 to 4 mg/100 ml). The absence of a yellowish tint of the palate when the sclera are yellow indicates carotene pigmentation of the sclera rather than jaundice. Light or clay-colored stools and dark golden urine often accompany jaundice in both light and dark-skinned clients.

Pallor

When assessing for pallor in darkly pigmented older adults, the nurse may experience difficulty because the underlying red tones that give brown or black skin its luster are absent. The brown-skinned individual manifests pallor with a more yellowish-brown color, and the black-skinned person appears ashen or gray. Generalized pallor can be observed in the mucous membranes, lips, and nail beds. The palpebral conjunctiva and nail beds are preferred sites for assessing the pallor of anemia. When inspecting the conjunctiva, the nurse should lower the lid sufficiently to visualize the conjunctiva near the outer canthus as well as the inner canthus. The coloration is often lighter near the inner canthus.

In addition to skin assessment, the pallor of impending shock is accompanied by other clinical manifestations such as increasing pulse rate, oliguria, apprehension, and restlessness. Anemias, particularly chronic iron deficiency anemia, may be apparent by the characteristic "spoon" nails, which have a concave shape. A lemon-yellow tint of the face and slightly yellow sclera accompany pernicious anemia, which is also manifested by neurologic deficits and a red, painful tongue. The nurse will also note the following symptoms in the presence of most severe anemias: fatigue, exertional dyspnea, rapid pulse, dizziness, and impaired mental function.

Erythema

Erythema (redness) is commonly associated with localized inflammation and is characterized by increased skin temperature. When assessing inflammation in dark-skinned clients, it is often necessary to palpate the skin for increased warmth, tautness or tightly pulled surfaces that may be indicative of edema, and hardening of deep tissues or blood vessels.

The erythema associated with rashes is not always accompanied by noticeable increases in skin temperature. Macular, papular, and vesicular skin lesions are identified by a combination of palpation and inspection, combined with the client's description of symptoms. For example, people with macular rashes usually complain of itching, and evidence of scratching will be apparent. When the skin is only moderately pigmented, a macular rash may become recognizable if the skin is gently stretched. Stretching the skin decreases the normal red tone, thus providing more contrast and making the macules appear brighter. In some skin disorders with generalized rash, the hard and soft palate are the locations where the rash is most readily visible.

The increased redness that accompanies carbon monox-

Continued.

CULTURAL AWARENESS

Biocultural Variations in the Integumentary System During Health and Illness—cont'd

ide poisoning and the blood disorders collectively known as the polycythemias can be observed in the lips of dark-skinned clients. Because lipstick masks the actual color of the lips, older adult women should be asked to remove it with a tissue.

Petechiae

In dark-skinned clients petechiae are best visualized in the areas of lighter melanization such as the abdomen, buttocks, and volar surface of the forearm. When the skin is black or very dark brown, petechiae cannot be seen. Most of the diseases that cause bleeding and microembolism formation, such as thrombocytopenia, subacute bacterial endocarditis, and other septicemias, are characterized by the presence of petechiae in the mucous membranes as well as the skin. Petechiae are most easily visualized in the mouth, particularly the buccal mucosa, and in the conjunctiva of the eye.

Ecchymotic lesions caused by systemic disorders are found in the same locations as petechiae, although their larger size makes them more apparent on dark-skinned individuals. When differentiating petechiae and ecchymosis from erythema in the mucous membrane, pressure on the tissue momentarily blanches erythema but not petechiae or ecchymosis.

and cool, light, breezy clothing should be worn when outdoors. It is important that older adults drink extra fluid (i.e., minimum of 2,000 ml per day, unless a medical condition contraindicates, such as in renal failure or congestive heart failure [CHF]) to maintain adequate hydration, particularly during the summer and in hot climates (Balin, 1992; Dalziel, Bickers, 1992; Ebersole, Hess, 1994).

Sebum oils the skin and provides an antimicrobial property. The sebaceous glands and pores become larger with aging; however, one study reports a 40% to 50% reduction in sebum production (Balin, 1990). In addition, another study reveals an increase in sebum production during later life (Franz, Kinney, 1986). Nevertheless, many older adults experience dry skin, which places them at a greater risk of infection as a result of an impaired immune response.

Hair thins, and growth declines. A progressive loss of melanin occurs, resulting in graying of the hair. Heredity influences when this graying process begins. Older women may have increased lip and chin hair while experiencing a thinning of hair on the head, axillae, and perineal area. Men lose scalp and beard hair, yet experience increased growth over eyebrows and in ears and nostrils. The increased hair in ears predisposes men to cerumen impaction, which leads to impaired hearing. Changes in patterns of hair growth and distribution as a person ages are thought to be hormone-related. Nails grow slower with age and become thicker, more brittle (may split or break easily), and dull; they also develop longitudinal striation with ridges (Balin, 1992; Ebersole, Hess, 1994; Fenske, Lober, 1992). These changes can affect a person's body image and self concept (see Cultural Awareness box, pp. 771-772).

COMMON PROBLEMS AND CONDITIONS

Benign Skin Growths

Cherry Angiomas

These growths are common, superficial vascular lesions that begin around age 30 and increase in number with age. They are red or deep purple dome-shaped papules. Although they are most commonly found on the trunk, they can be located anywhere on the body and vary in number (Balin, 1990; Caro, 1991; Young, Newcomer, 1993). As a testament to their prevalence, one study examined 163 people over 64 years of age and found that 75% of the participants had cherry angiomas (Balin, 1990). Since cherry angiomas are new growths, clients are often concerned they are malignant or indicative of a health problem. Provide reassurance that cherry angiomas are benign growths resulting from increased vascularity in the dermis and occur in most people (Caro, 1991; Habif, 1990). If scratched, the lesions will bleed but can be controlled easily with pressure.

Seborrheic Keratoses

These are benign, scaly growths that have a "stuck-on," crumbly appearance that varies in color from tan to brown to black. Characterized by slow growth, these lesions begin to appear later in life. The borders may be round and smooth or irregular and notched. To the untrained eye, these lesions can resemble a malignant melanoma, particularly when dark brown or black. They have a greasy feeling and often occur in sun-exposed areas (face, neck, and/or trunk) but can appear anywhere on the body. Diameters vary from 2 mm to 3 cm, and may be slightly or markedly elevated (Caro, 1991; Young,

Newcomer, 1993). A study of 163 older adult subjects found that 80% of the older adults had at least one seborrheic keratosis lesion (Balin, 1990). The growths are usually removed for cosmetic reasons or if irritated. If the lesion is "picked off," it will recur (Caro, 1991). Therefore it is best to have a dermatologist remove the growth if it is bothersome to a client. Reassure the client that the growths are benign and that most people have one or more. These lesions can affect self-esteem.

Skin Tags

These growths are common stalk-like, benign tumors often found on the neck, axillae, eyelids, and groin, although they can be located anywhere on the body. Beginning as early as age 20, these are tiny, flesh-colored or brown excrescences that develop into a long, narrow stalk (up to 1 cm). As they mature, easy removal with scissors, electrocautery, or liquid nitrogen can be done. Skin tags are usually excised only on request of the client (Balin, 1990; Caro, 1991). They occur in 64% of all older adults; however, they are rare in males (Balin, 1990).

Seborrheic Dermatitis

Seborrheic dermatitis is a chronic, inflammatory process affecting hairy areas of the body, particularly the scalp, eyebrows, face, and chest (Clark, Hopkins, 1992; Young, Newcomer, 1993). The cause is not known; however, there is a genetic predisposition in developing seborrheic dermatitis (Habif, 1990). Bed-bound clients, such as residents in nursing homes, and clients with Parkinson's disease are more prone to developing this condition. This is most likely a result of their compromised mobility. To differentiate between dandruff and seborrheic dermatitis, dandruff is scaling without inflammation, and seborrheic dermatitis is an inflammatory response sometimes associated with scaling. With inadequate care, dandruff can evolve into seborrheic dermatitis.

Seborrheic dermatitis appears as a white or yellow scale with a plaque-like appearance. An erythematous red base, indicating an inflammatory process, is *always* present. The usual pattern of distribution begins with the scalp and moves down toward the eyebrows, progressing to the chest with a bilateral, symmetrical presentation. Typical locations for seborrheic dermatitis are the scalp and scalp margins, eyebrows, base of the eyelashes, around the nose in a butterfly pattern, external ear canals, behind the ears, sternal area, and axillae. Minor itching can accompany the scaling and inflammation (Clark, Hopkins, 1992; Young, Newcomer, 1993) (see Medical Management box at left).

MEDICAL MANAGEMENT

Seborrheic Dermatitis

Diagnostic tests and procedures

Diagnosis is made based on clinical presentation with the hallmark symptom of erythemic, yellow-to-white scaly plaques that follow the pattern of starting at the scalp and moving downward in a bilateral, symmetrical manner.

Treatment

Shampoo containing selium should be applied for at least 10 minutes to the affected areas, *except face.* The face, eyebrows, nasal area, and ears can be cleansed with soap and water instead of the selium shampoo. Hydrocortisone 1% cream QD or BID can be applied to inflamed areas, including the face, until erythema resolves. Only group VI or VII steroid creams can be used on the face or scarring, skin atrophy, or acne can develop. To prevent recurrences, apply selium shampoo twice weekly, leaving on affected areas (except facial region) for 10 minutes, and use steroid cream QD PRN for erythema.

Prognosis

The dermatitis usually resolves in 2 to 3 weeks when treatment is delivered properly. Facial seborrhea dermatitis responds well to hydrocortisone 1% cream when kept on inflamed skin. Maintenance therapy must be delivered or there will be frequent recurrences, especially in bedbound clients.

NURSING MANAGEMENT

✣ ASSESSMENT

Nursing assessment consists of recognizing the inflammatory dermatitis and noting its location, degree of erythema, itching, and scaling. Examine the dermatitis for an erythematous base with yellow or white scales or plaques. The inflammatory process, with or without scales, begins at the scalp and moves downward to the eyebrows, nose, behind the ears, and eventually to the chest and axillae in a bilateral, symmetrical presentation. Inquire about itching, usual hygienic habits, and what the client has done to control the scaly, erythemic dermatitis. Bedbound individuals are more prone to develop seborrheic dermatitis; therefore targeting these clients to assess, in addition to thorough cleansing of scalp, hair, and skin, is a prevention strategy (Box 28-2).

✣ DIAGNOSIS

The nursing diagnosis for this skin condition is impaired skin integrity related to bedbound state and/or poor hygiene, which allows development of inflammatory process and plaques.

BOX 28-2

Seborrheic Dermatitis Assessment

Subjective data
Itching
Family history of seborrheic dermatitis
Usual hygienic habits
Use of home remedies or other self-care strategies

Objective data
Inspect: client's mobility; skin texture; color; temperature; and pattern and location of erythema, scales, and/or lesions
Palpate skin, noting induration, tenderness, or nodules

✣ PLANNING

The expected outcome is control of the inflammatory process with maintenance therapy using selium shampoo and/or hydrocortisone 1% cream. Following through with medical treatment increases client comfort; thus coordinate at least twice weekly shampooing and bathing, and if necessary (based on inflammation and location), application of steroid cream. Complete resolution of the inflammatory process may take several weeks. If maintenance therapy using dandruff shampoo is not continued, the inflammatory dermatitis will recur. Plan to teach client, staff, and family regarding the disorder and importance of maintenance therapy. One efficient strategy is to conduct teaching when delivering or directing care.

✣ INTERVENTION

One crucial aspect of nursing management is to ensure proper use of selenium shampoo by leaving on affected areas, *except face,* for 10 minutes. One successful strategy is to wet hair, chest, axillae, and affected areas, apply selenium shampoo, and then proceed with the rest of the bath or shower. After cleansing the affected areas, apply hydrocortisone 1% cream or other prescribed steroid cream, which decreases the inflammation and irritated red appearance of the skin. Note that steroid creams for the face must be low dose (group VI or VII), because scarring, skin atrophy, or acne can occur (Clark, Hopkins, 1992; Young, Newcomer, 1993). After inflammation and scaling have resolved, continue selenium shampoo on the scalp twice weekly as preventive maintenance therapy.

✣ EVALUATION

Nursing accountability and evaluation are supported through accurate, comprehensive charting that describes physical assessment and maintenance interventions. A weekly assessment of the lesions with a description of response to treatment, which includes maintenance therapy of selium shampoo, is recorded. In addition, address the response to teaching (i.e., verbalized understanding) as measured by client, family, or staff compliance with treatment.

Pruritus

Pruritus, or itching, is the most common dermatologic complaint of older adults (Balin, 1992). The mechanism of itching is not fully understood, but histamine is a known mediator of pruritus (Bernhard, 1992). It can be precipitated by heat, sudden temperature changes, sweating, clothing, associated cleaning products such as soap, fatigue, and emotional stress (Bernhard, 1992; Ebersole, Hess, 1994; Newman, Smith, 1991). Pruritus can be related either to a skin disorder or systemic disease; therefore the complaint should not be dismissed and warrants a complete assessment (Box 28-3). Often, pruritus is associated with dry skin, but can be associated with scabies, eczema, drug reaction, liver or renal disease, hyperglycemia, thyroid disease, prodromal symptoms of herpes zoster, venous stasis, or anemia (Balin, 1992; Bernhard, 1992; Fitzpatrick et al, 1992a) (see Medical Management box, p. 775).

NURSING MANAGEMENT

✣ ASSESSMENT

A full skin assessment is warranted when a client complains of pruritus. Interview the client to determine the location, intensity, and onset of itching. Inquire about any patterns of behavior that precipitate itching, that is, anxiety, environmental exposures, or friction (rubbing the skin with a towel). Obtain information about bathing practices and kinds of soaps, detergents, and skin products used. Look for rashes, vesicles, scaling, erythema—any of these suggest a skin disorder (Box 28-4).

✣ DIAGNOSIS

An appropriate nursing diagnosis is high risk for impaired skin integrity related to scratching. Other possible nursing diagnoses, which are dependent on the cause of the pruritus, are (1) pain related to persistent burning and itching, and (2) anxiety related to role strain, family crisis, or other sources of client's anxiety.

✣ PLANNING

The expected outcome is resolution of pruritus without injury from scratching. Plan time to teach the client and family regarding etiologic factors and the importance of not scratching.

BOX 28-3

Possible Sources of Pruritus

Skin disorders
Atopic eczema
Contact dermatitis
Urticaria/allergic reactions
Seborrheic dermatitis
Exfoliative dermatitis
Psoriasis
Bullous pemphigoid

Infestations
Scabies
Pediculosis
Fleas, bedbugs, mites

Infections
Herpes zoster
Candidiasis
Folliculitis
Impetigo

Miscellaneous
Liver disease/failure
Renal disease—uremia
Diabetes—hyperglycemia
Thyroid disease
Venous stasis
Xerosis (dry skin)
Abdominal cancer (visceral malignancies)
Central nervous system tumors (visceral malignancies)

Drugs that may cause pruritus
Opiates and derivatives
Phenothiazines
Tolbutamide
Erythromycin
Estrogen
Progestins
Testosterone
Aspirin
Quinidine
Vitamin B complex

Modified from Bernhard JD. In Moschella SL, Hurley HJ: *Dermatology*, ed 3, Philadelphia, 1992, WB Saunders; Ebersole P, Hess P: *Toward healthy aging: human needs and nursing response*, ed 4, St. Louis, 1994, Mosby.

✣ INTERVENTION

Nursing interventions are influenced by the cause of the pruritus. If dry, scaly skin (xerosis) is present with no lesions or erythema, the nurse should suggest the client apply emollients (e.g., Lubriderm, Moisturel, or Eucerin lotion), which have more lanolin or oily substances than many commercial lotions. Emollients need to be applied at least twice daily and immediately after bathing to trap moisture. Gently pat skin dry and avoid brisk drying with a towel. If the client is unable to apply lotion, instruct the caregiver in its use. Decrease the frequency of baths to a maximum of every other day (see Client/Family Teaching box, p. 776).

If itching persists, a lotion with ¼% menthol and 1% hydrocortisone (if no infectious process is present) may be prescribed. Antihistimanes may be needed to relieve itching and to prevent tissue breakdown from scratching. However, cautious use of these agents in older adults is warranted as a result of anticholinergic side effects that can cause confusion, urinary retention, and constipation (Davis, 1993; Ebersole, Hess, 1994; Newman, Smith, 1991). A diagnostic workup may be conducted to identify any systemic cause (e.g., cancer or diabetes) for persistent pruritus.

MEDICAL MANAGEMENT

Pruritus

Diagnostic tests and procedures

A comprehensive interview to identify an etiologic factor is vital to successful diagnosis and treatment (see Box 28-4 for a list of possible etiologic factors that can direct interview). Diagnostic tests may include a complete blood count (CBC), liver function tests, thyroid studies, blood glucose, blood urea nitrogen (BUN), creatinine, and electrolytes. A skin culture may be obtained if infection is suspected. Skin scrapings may be obtained to detect scabies.

Treatment

Treatment depends on the etiologic factor. Management of the disease process or skin disorder, such as diabetes, renal failure, candida, and scabies, often relieves the pruritus. Antihistamines may be prescribed to provide immediate relief; however, in older adults, constipation and urinary retention, and confusion may result from anticholinergic properties of the drug. Tricyclic antidepressants, which are H_1 and H_2 (histamine) blockers, may be an alternative drug, yet many have anticholinergic properties. Topical management includes lubricating lotions with ¼% menthol and 1% hydrocortisone, cold compresses of either cool water or Burow's solution (1:20 to 1:40 dilution), milk of magnesia, and steroid creams.

Prognosis

Pruritus is the most common dermatologic complaint; it also can be the result of a variety of sources. Successful management depends on the etiologic factor, client compliance with treatment, and the client's coping mechanisms if psychologic factors are involved.

BOX 28-4

Assessment of Pruritus

Subjective data

Itching—localized or generalized?
Onset
Pattern and frequency of itching
Allergy history
Change in soap, detergents, or skin products
Frequency of bathing
Medications, with a focus on the addition of any new medications
Anxiety

Objective data

Inspect the following: client's behavior (restlessness, scratching), clothing fit, skin texture, color, temperature, and pattern and location of erythema, hives, scales, vesicles, and/or lesions
Palpate the following: skin, noting induration, tenderness, or nodules

CLIENT/FAMILY TEACHING

Prevention and Treatment of Dry Skin (Xerosis)

Bathing/showering with warm water should not exceed every other day. Pat skin dry to avoid irritation. In the winter when the air is drier, one bath/shower a week is sufficient with a daily sponge bath to underarms, perineal area, and skin folds.
Bath oil can be used in a basin when sponge bathing, but not in tub or shower. To avoid risk of slipping in tub or shower, apply oil after bathing.
Avoid use of harsh soaps (e.g., Zest, Ivory, Dial); recommend a superfatted soap such as Dove, Basis, or Tone, or others in limited use with only one lathering.
Use heavy emollient lotions containing urea or lactic acid, such as Lubriderm, Nivea or Eucerin after bathing, when skin is moist. Mineral oil, petroleum jelly, or shortening are less expensive alternatives.
Never use alcohol or other drying rubs on skin, since these deplete natural skin oils.
Drink at least 1,500 to 2,500 ml of water per day to ensure adequate hydration (if not contraindicated by other medical conditions (e.g., CHF).
Avoid tight-fitting clothes that rub against skin.

Modified from Davis C: In Carnevali DL, Patrick M: *Nursing management for the elderly,* ed 3, Philadelphia, 1993, JB Lippincott; Ebersole P, Hess P: *Toward healthy aging: human needs and nursing response,* ed 4, St. Louis, 1994, Mosby; Newman DK, Smith DAJ: *Geriatric care plans,* Springhouse, Penn., 1991, Springhouse Corp.

Anxiety or stress may be the source of itching. If so, assess client's self-esteem and coping strategies, and identify any family or role strain or other factors that may lead to anxiety. Discuss stress management strategies, and assist client in determining effective strategies. A referral to a community agency or professional such as an advanced practice nurse, psychologist, or psychiatrist may be needed for continued support and guidance.

✣ EVALUATION

Evaluation can be supported with documentation of physical presentation, such as erythema, intact skin with no lesions, hives, or rash. In addition, document the response to client teaching, which includes concrete data such as verbalized understanding and applying emollients when itching rather than scratching.

Candidiasis

Candidiasis is an inflammatory process of the epidermis caused by a yeast-like fungus called *Candida albicans. C. albicans* is a normal flora in the mouth, vagina, and gut (moist habitat). Pregnancy, oral contraception, antibiotics, diabetes, topical and inhalant steroids, skin maceration, and immunocompromised conditions create an environment that fosters the development of yeast infections such as candidiasis. Moisture is crucial for development, therefore incontinent clients or individuals who sweat or have moisture (i.e., from not being dried well) accumulate in intertriginous areas (e.g., skin folds, between fingers or toes, under breasts, in folds of contracted extremities, or axillae) are ideal candidates for candidiasis infections (Fitzpatrick et al, 1992a; Habif, 1990). Candidiasis is most commonly seen in diaper-clad infants, incontinent clients, or bedbound individuals, although it can occur in anyone.

Candidiasis is characterized by erythematous, denuded, or raw skin usually surrounded by satellite papules or pustules. Satellite lesions are a helpful diagnostic clue. Red, erythematous areas on the buttocks, perineum, or intertriginous areas of incontinent clients also have diagnostic significance. Scaling may also be present, usually at the borders. Clients often complain of itching or burning in affected areas (Fitzpatrick et al, 1992a; Habif, 1990) (see Medical Management and Research boxes, p. 777).

NURSING MANAGEMENT

✣ ASSESSMENT

Nursing assessment includes inspection of skin, particularly under any fat folds where moisture will accumulate. A hallmark of candidiasis is a bright-red erythema with

MEDICAL MANAGEMENT

Candidiasis

Diagnostic tests and procedures

Diagnosis can be confirmed with a potassium hydroxide (KOH) wet prep, looking for septae hyphae and/or budding yeast. Clinical presentation is usually sufficient for diagnosis, especially if bright red erythema with satellite lesions within a moist environment are present.

Treatment

Topical management with nystatin or ketaconazole is the standard treatment, but note ketaconazole generates resistance sooner. A successful strategy is creating a 50/50 mixture of nystatin and desitin cream, which protects skin from moisture while treating the yeast infection. Hydrocortisone 1% may be added for more rapid relief of discomfort. Desitin has been accredited with resolving candidiasis alone in some cases. Powder is not recommended since it clumps and does not keep the skin dry over time. Maintaining dry skin and applying medicated cream is crucial for resolution. If raw, red areas persist even after above measures have been taken, another topical agent (e.g., ketaconazole) may need to be tried. Systemic management with oral agents is not effective since medications are not absorbed in the intestinal tract. In addition, inflammation is usually restricted to the epidermis; therefore topical management is more effective (Habif, 1990; Jones, 1991; Montes, 1992).

Prognosis

Candidiasis recurrence is frequent and can be chronic if skin is not kept dry. Treatment is most always successful if medicated barrier cream is diligently applied and skin kept dry. Powders commonly fail in controlling moisture, thus are not as successful in preventing and treating candidiasis.

satellite papules or pustules. Note any breaks in the skin, which place the client at a greater risk for infection or further breakdown. The client may be the one to alert the health care team of the infection. Conduct a medication assessment to identify any medications that may precipitate this fungal infection, such as antibiotics, oral contraceptives, or steroids. If the client has diabetes, hyperglycemia may be present; therefore conduct a diet assessment evaluating compliance, as well as checking blood sugar. For some individuals with type II diabetes, a candidiasis infection may be the first clinical presentation of hyperglycemia. Therefore a thorough health history is warranted when a candidiasis infection is present (Box 28-5).

RESEARCH

Frantz RA, Kinney CK: Variables associated with skin dryness in the elderly, *Nurs Res* 35(2):98-100, 1986.

Sample, setting

The sample included 76 older people age 65 to 97 (19 white men and 57 white women) residing in retirement centers or long-term care facilities.

Methodology

Subjects were interviewed using a 4-point Likert scale regarding sun exposure, hygiene habits, and use of lotion. A 5-point Likert scale was used to assess perceived skin dryness, supported with an examination by the investigator noting rough, scaly, and flaking skin. A 24-hour diet recall noting food and fluid intake was conducted. Using a standardized protocol, sebum secretion was measured.

Findings

Of the subjects, 59% showed evidence of dry skin, 41% did not. Statistical analysis revealed no significant association between severity of dry skin and sebum secretion rate, frequent bathing, adequate fluid intake, and use of lotion. A relationship between increased sun exposure and dry skin did exist.

Implications

Educate clients to wear wide brim hats, long sleeves, and other protection when out in the sun. Repeat studies and further research into the complexities of dry skin are necessary.

BOX 28-5

Assessment of Candidiasis

Subjective data

Itching
Burning, pain
Incontinence
Profuse sweating
Medications (antibiotics, oral contraceptives, steroids)
Diabetes

Objective data

Inspect the following: intertriginous areas, skin texture, color, temperature, pattern and location of erythema, lesions, and/or scales
Palpate the following: skin, noting induration, tenderness, or nodules

✣ DIAGNOSIS

Impaired skin integrity related to poor control of moisture (which fosters a *C. albicans* fungus infection) is a common diagnosis.

✣ PLANNING

The expected outcome is resolution of candidiasis and consequently increased client comfort. If incontinence or excessive moisture is the precipitating factor, the client, family, and staff need to be instructed about keeping the skin dry and promptly changing linens when wet so recurrence of this uncomfortable skin infection can be prevented. Plan time to assess client's or nursing staff's bathing technique, noting poor or improper drying.

✣ INTERVENTION

The main nursing intervention is keeping the skin dry, especially the intertriginous areas. A client's discomfort, costs, and nursing time could be minimized through preventive strategies such as drying skin well (particularly skin folds) after bathing or sweating episodes, and changing sheets as soon as possible after an incontinent episode. After changing linens, care should include cleansing and drying skin well, and applying Desitin cream to the buttocks and perineal area. Cornstarch or powder, whether medicated or scented, is not recommended as a result of clumping and resulting limited long-term skin protection. Creams are much more effective and efficient.

In the role of team leader and manager of client care, teach support staff and client to pat skin dry. Educate the staff and provide scientific rationale for changing linen, cleansing the affected area, and using a moisture barrier such as zinc oxide or Desitin. Stress the importance of prompt delivery of care following an incontinent event. It is important to keep topical antifungal agents on the infected area until healing is complete, which may take 2 to 3 weeks. If the yeast infection does not improve, inform the physician or advanced practice nurse so an alternative agent can be considered.

Management protocols can be developed and approved by the employee's institution, and medical and nursing staff with the intent of empowering the professional nurse to act immediately when candidiasis is present. This promotes quality care, client comfort, a sense of professional pride, and a team approach. Nursing management is key in resolving a candidiasis infection.

✣ EVALUATION

Ongoing evaluation of treatment efficacy is a major component of the nursing process; in addition, it assists in quality management activities. Document how the infection is responding to medical treatment as well as maintenance therapy of keeping skin dry and applying a moisture barrier. The effectiveness of client care can be supported with positive outcomes, compliance with preventive actions, and verbalized comprehension. If little improvement is seen in 2 weeks, ensure moisture control and application of antifungal cream are being maintained. Consultation with the physician or advanced practice nurse is needed when there is a poor response to therapy; another agent may be tried.

Herpes Zoster (Shingles)

Herpes zoster, also known as shingles, is caused by the reactivation of latent varicella zoster (chickenpox) virus. The virus remains in the dorsal nerve endings after an episode of chickenpox, which is usually experienced in childhood. The main reason for recurrence is an immune system deficiency. Conditions that may impair the immune system are advanced age, stress or emotional upset, fatigue, or radiation therapy. An immunocompromised state caused by disease (e.g., human immunodeficiency virus [HIV], lymphoma, leukemia, and other malignancies) or drugs (e.g., chemotherapy and steroids) can also activate the latent virus. Chickenpox is highly contagious, since it is an airborne virus. Herpes zoster is not as infectious, since it is related to reactivation of latent varicella-zoster. Therefore it is not necessary to isolate a client with herpes zoster. Cases of contracting shingles after personal exposure have been reported, but these have been in individuals who have not had chickenpox. Consequently, clients with herpes zoster should be cared for only by health care personnel who have had chickenpox or have positive serum varicella titers (Jarratt, 1991; Lamberg, 1991; Newman, Smith, 1991; Thiers, Sahn, 1992). As always, universal precautions should be exercised.

Approximately 50% of herpes zoster cases involve the thoracic region, 15% involve the cranial dermatomes, and 10% affect the cervical and lumbar regions. Ophthalmic herpes zoster is most serious, since it can cause blindness as a result of corneal scarring, and therefore always mandates referral to an ophthalmologist (Lamberg, 1991; Wade, 1993).

Herpes zoster often has prodromal symptoms of tingling, hyperesthesia, tenderness, and burning or itching pain along the affected **dermatome.** The prodromal symptoms are followed by vesicles with an erythematous base occurring within 3 to 5 days. A unilateral bandlike erythematous, maculopapular rash first occurs along the involved dermatome, and rarely crosses the midline of the body. The rash develops into clustered vesicles (usually on an erythematous base) that become purulent, rupture, and crust. These vesicles are vulnerable to secondary bacterial infections. Some lesions become necrotic and/or hemorrhagic. This occurs more often in older adults. It may take up to 1 month for the crusting lesions to heal, with mild cases resolving in 7 to 10 days.

The average duration for herpes zoster is 3 weeks (Thiers, Sahn, 1992). Scarring as well as permanent or temporary pigment discoloration may occur, especially in severe cases. Lymphadenopathy is not uncommon with an occasional temperature elevation (Jarratt, 1991; Lamberg, 1991; Thiers, Sahn, 1992). Post-infection paresthesias and meningoencephalitis may occur for 2 to 4 weeks when motor neurons and the central nervous system (CNS) are involved (Thiers, Sahn, 1992).

For individuals age 85 or older, there is a 50% probability of developing herpes zoster (Wade, 1993). Dissemination is often seen in older adults or immunosuppressed clients. Disseminated herpes zoster, which is rare and occurs in only 2% to 5% of the clients, is more serious because of its systemic nature. In disseminated herpes zoster, satellite lesions appear outside of the affected dermatome within 4 to 6 days after the initial eruption. Dissemination may be associated with fever, lymphadenopathy, headache, neck rigidity, and an increased risk of serious complications such as encephalitis, hepatitis, and pneumonitis (Lamberg, 1991; Thiers, Sahn, 1992; Wade, 1993). Disseminated herpes zoster has a mortality rate of 4% to 15% in immunocompromised clients (Balin, 1990).

One of the major complications from this acute viral infection is postherpetic neuralgia, pain that persists along the affected dermatome after resolution of vesicular lesions. Postherpetic neuralgia can last less than 1 year, but it may last a lifetime with little pain relief. It affects approximately 10% of the victims, who are primarily older adults and/or who have trigeminal or ophthalmic involvement (Lamberg, 1991; Thiers, Sahn, 1992; Wade, 1993) (see Medical Management box at right).

MEDICAL MANAGEMENT

Herpes Zoster

Diagnostic tests and procedures

Diagnosis can be made based on clinical presentation (vesicles with erythemic base along dermatome, itching, pain), yet a Tzanck smear from vesicle scrapings can confirm varicella zoster. A spinal tap may be done when disseminated herpes zoster is suspected.

Treatment

Acyclovir 800 mg PO 5 times daily for 7 to 10 days; intravenous (IV) therapy is initiated for severe cases or with trigeminal zoster. Acyclovir should be started within 72 hours of rash to decrease viral shedding, pain, and rash progression. Note that the acyclovir dosage must be reduced in clients with renal compromise. Topical acyclovir is not recommended, since systemic management is necessary to achieve an antiviral effect.

Corticosteroid therapy (both topical and systemic) may be initiated, in combination with acyclovir management, to decrease zoster pain; however, a recent study (n = 400) in which clients were monitored for 6 months revealed no difference in pain compared with clients who received only acyclovir (Wade, 1993). Thus steroid management may vary.

Analgesics for pain control as well as adjunctive therapies may be needed, for example, antidepressants and/or nonsteroidal antiinflammatory agents (NSAIDs). Topical management of open lesions using antibiotic ointment, especially in nursing homes and hospitals, are needed to prevent secondary bacterial infections (Fitzpatrick et al, 1992a; Thiers, Sahn, 1992; Wade, 1993).

Prognosis

Most acute cases resolve in 2 to 3 weeks, regardless of whether antiviral therapy is provided. Permanent or temporary discoloration and/or scarring may result. Of the clients with ophthalmic zoster, 50% experience ocular complications, the most severe consisting of corneal scarring and blindness. An increased risk of postherpetic neuralgia affects 10% of the clients with herpes zoster and with advanced age, cancer, and cranial nerve involvement. The pain from postherpetic neuralgia, which commonly is not controlled, may dissipate in 1 year or become chronic.

NURSING MANAGEMENT

✣ ASSESSMENT

Nursing assessment begins with interviewing the client to identify prodromal symptoms, such as burning, itching, or tingling along a dermatome prior to rash development. Obtain pertinent health history that addresses chickenpox history, medications, acquired immunodeficiency syndrome (AIDS), diabetes, cancer with recent chemotherapy, and other immunocompromised states. The nurse should also identify family members, friends, or staff who have not had chickenpox or the chickenpox vaccine since they may be at risk of infection. Inspect the area of discomfort looking for a unilateral, band-like erythemic, macular rash that evolves into clustered vesicles. Initially, the area may be a raised, erythemic rash before the vesicles appear. Eventually, the vesicles break and crust. Intense pain is often associated with the rash, particularly in older adults (Box 28-6).

✣ DIAGNOSIS

A common nursing diagnosis is pain related to inadequate relief from analgesics. Other nursing diagnoses in-

CARE PLAN

HERPES ZOSTER

Clinical situation Mr. H is a 78-year-old widower who resides in a nursing home because of his pulmonary handicap from COPD, which is compounded by right-sided heart failure and hypertension. He can ambulate short distances and needs some assistance with his activities of daily living (ADLs). He has a routine of getting out of bed for breakfast, afterward having his AM care, and then getting dressed for the day.

He uses two inhalants (bronchodilator and steroid), has been taking prednisone 10 mg PO QD for the past 5 years, and takes enalapril 10 mg PO BID and furosemide 80 mg PO QD for his CHF and hypertension.

Recently, he was complaining about burning pain on his right side; however, there was no clear cause. One day, Mr. H was so uncomfortable, he stayed in bed all day. No other complaints or changes occurred until approximately 3 days after the pain began, and some vesicles or clusters with red bases appeared only on the right lateral side and posterior back, following a dermatome. The nurse immediately recognized the situation and called the nurse practitioner who was managing Mr. H's care to inform of the above finding. Consequently, after confirming that his renal function was adequate, the nurse practitioner ordered acyclovir 800 mg 5 times daily for 7 days to decrease viral shedding, electrolytes, blood urea nitrogen (BUN) and creatinine laboratory tests 2 days after beginning acyclovir therapy to evaluate renal function, Tylox one cap PO Q 6 hours PRN pain, and topical antibiotic with telfa dressing BID when vesicles rupture and crust to prevent secondary infection.

Nursing diagnosis	Outcome	Interventions
High risk for infection related to herpes zoster and open lesions	Client will experience no secondary infection as evidenced by afebrile and other vital signs within normal limits (WNL), and client practices habits that decrease risk of infection.	Instruct client not to scratch or rub affected area in order not to break vesicles, which would increase risk of secondary infection. Assess vital signs, mental status, and skin lesions every shift to identify signs of infection (fever, tachycardia, erythema, tenderness, purulent discharge, confusion): If febrile, ensure adequate hydration since fever increases hydration needs. Tachycardia could precipitate congestive heart failure due to decreased cardiac output; monitor for SOB, rales, edema, and other signs of cardiovascular compromise. If vesicle lesions rupture, implement topical treatment, noting response. Ensure adequate nutrition to foster healing: Monitor food intake and ensure food preferences are being met Teach client and staff the need to eat 2,000 calories or more, and drink a minimum of 2,000 ml per day. Be alert for vesicles outside of involved dermatome, which could be indicative of disseminated herpes zoster; if occurs, contact physician or nurse practitioner immediately. Teach client, staff, and visitors the value of hand washing and proper disposal of dressing/treatment material as an infection control standard. Identify staff and visitors who have no known history of chickenpox or vaccine and inform them that they are not able to provide care for the client since they may not have an immunity to the varicella virus; isolation is not required; the infection control strategy is universal precautions.

BOX 28-6

Assessment of Herpes Zoster

Subjective

Itching (onset, precipitating factors, duration, and location)
Tingling (onset, precipitating factors, duration, and location)
Hyperesthesia (onset, duration, and location)
Burning, persistent pain
Chronic steroid use
Immunocompromised via drugs or disease
History of chickenpox

Objective

Inspect: skin characteristics, color, temperature, pattern of rash and/or lesions, configuration of rash/lesions, and appearance of lesions
Palpate: skin around lesions noting induration, tenderness, and/or pain

clude (1) high risk for infection related to vesicle rupture and crusting, and (2) impaired skin integrity related to itching, vesicles, and crusting.

✤ PLANNING

The expected outcome is prevention of secondary infection and pain relief during the acute phase. The nurse needs to allot time for daily skin assessment and especially administration of pain medication.

✤ INTERVENTION

Nursing interventions consist of notifying the physician or advance practice nurse when vesicles are identified, especially if they follow a dermatomal pattern. After a diagnosis is made, follow-through with medical and nursing management is paramount to client comfort. Lesions should be monitored closely for the development of secondary bacterial infections, evident by erythema, tenderness, or purulent discharge. If satellite lesions develop outside the dermatome, especially if the client is also experiencing headache, neck rigidity, or pulmonary congestion, the physician or advance practice nurse must be notified immediately, since this is indicative of disseminated herpes zoster. Stress the use of universal precautions and do not allow staff members who have not had chickenpox or a positive varicella titer to care for the client.

Teach clients, family members, and staff the cause of shingles so anxiety and misconceptions can be alleviated. Explain treatment to the client, family, and staff to increase compliance and involvement in care. Herpes zoster can be very painful, so prompt administration of pain medications is crucial for client comfort. For optimum pain control, instruct clients to inform you when they experience the initial onset of pain, before the pain becomes well-entrenched. Effective pain management is one area where nurses can have a positive impact on a client's quality of life (see Chapter 13).

✤ EVALUATION

Evaluation of nursing management focuses on pain control with documented results of medication administration and prevention of secondary infection by frequent monitoring of site. If pain is not relieved, consult the physician or advance practice nurse to obtain a different and hopefully more effective pain medication, or an addition of adjunctive therapy drugs such as NSAIDs or antidepressants. If evidence of cellulitis is noted, notify the physician or advance practice nurse to implement topical or oral antibiotic treatment. Documentation of assessment, client comprehension of teaching, and nursing interventions demonstrates nursing accountability (see nursing Care Plan, p. 780).

PREMALIGNANT SKIN GROWTHS

Actinic Keratosis

Actinic keratosis is a premalignant lesion of the epidermis that is caused by long-term exposure to UV rays. This precancerous lesion is more common in light-complexioned individuals and occurs most commonly on the dorsum of the hands, scalp, outer ears, face, and lower arms. Actinic keratosis may evolve into squamous cell carcinoma (SCC) if not treated, so it should receive prompt attention (Balin, 1992; Callen, 1991).

Actinic keratosis begins in vascular areas as a reddish macule or papule that has a rough, yellowish-brown scale that may itch or cause discomfort. During assessment, be attuned to the rough surface of the lesion and its location. Be particularly alert if a suspicious lesion is on a sun-exposed area. Accumulation of keratin can also lead to the formation of a cutaneous horn that tends to develop on the outer ear. Because of an abundant vascular supply, removal of the crust may cause bleeding. Induration, inflammation, or oozing may be indicative of malignancy and merits prompt referral (Balin, 1992; Callen, 1991; Koh, Bhawan, 1992) (see Medical Management box, p. 782).

NURSING MANAGEMENT

✤ ASSESSMENT

Interview the client to determine risk factors, such as frequency of activities with sun exposure and use of pre-

MEDICAL MANAGEMENT

Actinic Keratosis

Diagnostic tests and procedures

Diagnosis often is made based on clinical presentation; however, skin biopsy may be done.

Treatment

For facial lesions, topical treatment with 5-FU cream BID is more convenient and does not cause as much scarring as with liquid nitrogen. Cream or lotion should be massaged into the affected area until formation of crusting or eschar. Duration of treatment may be 3 to 8 weeks, but clients often are not able to tolerate treatment beyond 3 weeks because of the discomfort and uncomfortable appearance. Initially an inflammatory reaction causes a brilliant erythema and discomfort followed by erosion. After treatment, application of a topical steroid of hydrocortisone 1% BID can help speed healing and decrease inflammation.

Another option is to "burn off" the lesion with liquid nitrogen, which causes a blister and erosion. Topical antibiotic management may be required to prevent a secondary bacterial infection.

Prognosis

It is rare that actinic keratosis lesions evolve into SCC, especially if removed when first identified. Lesions usually do not recur unless prevention measures are not exercised and sun exposure continues. Clients should wear a hat and long sleeves, and should minimize exposure to sunlight to prevent recurrence.

ventive practices, for example, wearing a hat and long sleeves when working out in the yard. Inspect and palpate the skin, noting location and texture of any rough lesions. If hand lotion is often used, a roughness will not be present; therefore look for an erythemic macule or papule. The nurse should refer clients to their primary care provider whenever a suspicious lesion is found. Explain to the client the value of treating skin cancer early, which can also minimize scarring and disfigurement (Box 28-7).

✣ DIAGNOSIS

A common nursing diagnosis is impaired skin integrity related to removal of a lesion. Other nursing diagnoses are high risk for infection related to break in skin integrity, and body image disturbance related to disfigurement and scarring resulting from removal of lesion.

✣ PLANNING

The goal is removal of premalignant lesions without secondary infection and assisting in coping with any body image disturbance. Plan time for client education, stressing the need to use preventive practices. Allocate time to talk with the client and family to assess coping abilities with any body image changes.

BOX 28-7

Assessment of Actinic Keratosis

Subjective data

Sun exposure (e.g., gardening, farming, golfing, etc.)
Complaints of rough areas on skin associated with itching or discomfort
Use of sunscreens and other preventive practices

Objective data

Inspect the following: skin color, texture, and lesion's location, texture, color, shape, and size
Palpate the following: lesion, surrounding area, and lymph nodes

✣ INTERVENTION

Nursing management consists of reinforcing the treatment regimen with the client and family, monitoring the site with a focus on preventing a secondary infection, providing support, and teaching prevention strategies. To lower a client's anxiety and assist with body image changes, explain the treatment, stressing that erythema and crusting are temporary. The resulting body image trauma from treatment of many facial lesions can isolate an individual. The nurse may need to coordinate services such as grocery shopping to assist the client in coping with the disfigurement and meeting basic needs. Identify the client's fears and discuss them in an open, reassuring manner.

Wounds should be assessed for development of a bacterial infection, as seen by increased tenderness, purulent discharge, and possibly fever. Topical management with an antibiotic ointment may be implemented prophylactically.

Preventive strategies and education are necessary to prevent recurrence. Stress the need to wear hats with wide brims, long sleeves, and shirts to protect skin from sun exposure. If an individual is going to be in the sun, a sunscreen with a sun protection factor (SPF) of at least 15 should be applied; for dark-skinned individuals a sunscreen with an SPF of 8 is suggested.

✣ EVALUATION

Evaluation of nursing actions is supported with documentation addressing treatment progress, which includes physical description, client comprehension of educational information, and identification of and coping with any body image disturbances.

MALIGNANT SKIN GROWTHS

Basal Cell Carcinoma

Basal cell carcinoma (BCC) is the most common skin cancer and is more prevalent in fair-skinned, blond, or red-headed individuals with extensive previous sun exposure. BCC rarely occurs in African Americans. It occurs more often in men than women; however, this gender difference has decreased in recent years. BCC is most commonly found on the face and scalp, less often on the trunk, and rarely occurs on the hands. It may also arise from scars or burns, particularly in older adults who have experienced chronic sun damage. BCC usually does not metastasize, but if left untreated, it may metastasize to the bone, lungs, and brain (Balin, 1990; Caro, 1991; Lang, Maize, 1991).

Typically, BCC appears as a pearly papule with a depression in the center, giving the lesion a doughnut-like appearance with telangiectasia on or around the lesion. BCC can also appear as a blue-black pearly nodule (pigmented basal cell), or a red, scaly, or eczematous-appearing macule that is usually on the thoracic area (superficial spreading BCC). BCC can grow aggressively but follows the path of least resistance and usually does not infiltrate bone, cartilage, or muscle (Caro, 1991; Lang, Maize, 1991) (see Medical Management box at right).

MEDICAL MANAGEMENT

BCC

Diagnostic tests and procedures

Clinical presentation is often definitive, yet diagnosis of BCC is confirmed by biopsy.

Treatment

Treatment options depend on the extent of the lesion with removal by curettage and electrodesiccation, radiotherapy, liquid nitrogen, or topical 5-FU (for superficial lesions). Topical management with an antibiotic ointment after the lesion is removed may be used to prevent secondary infection.

Prognosis

After removal, recurrence is rare, with a "cure" rate of 90%. Clients should wear a hat and long sleeves, and should minimize exposure to sunlight to prevent future sun damage.

NURSING MANAGEMENT

ASSESSMENT

Nursing assessment begins with an interview focusing on length of time lesion has been present, presence of risk factors such as chronic sun exposure, and history of previous skin lesions. Conduct a skin assessment, being alert for pearly, doughnut-shaped lesions with telangiectasia. A magnifying glass may be useful to closely examine any lesion. Inspect and palpate the lesion, surrounding tissue, and lymph nodes (to identify possible metastasis). When a suspicious lesion is identified, refer the client to the primary care provider for prompt treatment. Explain to the client that early treatment lessens the extent of scarring and lowers risk of metastasis (Box 28-8).

BOX 28-8

Assessment of BCC

Subjective data

Sun exposure
Environmental/chemical exposures
History of previous skin lesions
History of current lesion
Use of sunscreens and other preventive practices

Objective data

Inspect the following: skin color, texture, and lesion's location, texture, shape, vascularity, color, and size
Palpate the following: lesion, surrounding area, and lymph nodes

DIAGNOSIS

A common nursing diagnosis is impaired skin integrity related to removal of a cancerous lesion. Other nursing diagnoses include (1) high risk for infection related to break in skin integrity and surgical wound, (2) body image disturbance related to disfigurement and scarring resulting from removal of cancerous lesion, and (3) fear of cancer, pain, or death related to having a cancerous skin lesion.

PLANNING

The goal of nursing management is to facilitate referral and treatment of suspicious lesions for removal without secondary infection. Plan time to discuss the client's and family's feelings about having a cancerous lesion to identify any need for a community referral or educational material. In addition, client education regarding prevention strategies needs to be included in the plan.

✣ INTERVENTION

Nursing management includes reinforcement of treatment regimen with monitoring wound for secondary infection (e.g., erythema, tenderness, and/or purulent discharge). Explain procedures, emphasizing that a wound or erosion can occur that may require a dressing. Teach the client and/or family dressing care and signs of infection. Removal can result in scarring, especially if the lesion was large; consequently, provide reassurance and address feelings related to having a cancerous lesion and associated body image changes. Focus on comfort, education, and emotional support.

Identify and discuss the client's feelings about having a cancerous lesion with referral to appropriate community resources if the client is having difficulty coping or has a high anxiety level. Explain that risk of metastasis is low and refer the client to the American Cancer Society (ACS) or local library for literature. Prevention strategies such as wearing long sleeves and hats with wide brims and using sunscreens should also be taught.

✣ EVALUATION

Evaluation of nursing management is supported by documenting nursing interventions that include dressing changes, monitoring for infection, pain control measures, comprehension of client education, and discussions related to body image changes and fear of cancer. If there is poor pain control or development of an infection, contact the physician or advance practice nurse for an alternative strategy.

Squamous Cell Carcinoma

SCC is skin cancer arising from the epidermis and is found most often on the scalp, outer ears, lower lip, and dorsum of the hands. SCC can also develop in chronic leg ulcers or open fractures with a 20% incidence of metastasis. SCC accounts for 90% of lip lesions. The etiologic factors of SCC can be UV rays, chemical carcinogens, and x-ray. SCC is more common in men and older adults, with the incidence increasing with geographic proximity to the equator. SCC usually remains localized, but can metastasize to lymph nodes (2%). This is particularly true of lip lesions. Therefore early detection and treatment are important (Balin, 1990; Dzubow, Grossman, 1991; Koh, Bhawan, 1992).

Symptoms of SCC usually include a thick, adherent scale with a soft, movable tumor that has well-defined borders. The center is often ulcerated or crusted. At first glance, SCC may even look like a wart. The base may be inflamed and red, and usually bleeds easily. SCC can arise from actinic keratosis, which supports early detection and removal of such lesions. If tumors are ignored or left unattended, they may enlarge, creating significant disfigurement after surgical excision (see Medical Management box above).

MEDICAL MANAGEMENT

SCC

Diagnostic tests and procedures

Clinical presentation is usually sufficient, yet diagnosis is supported with a biopsy specimen.

Treatment

Most common treatment is removal of the tumor by curettage and electrodesiccation. If the tumor is large or extensive, a scalpel excision is usually warranted. Topical management of the wound with antibiotic ointment may be needed to prevent secondary infection.

Prognosis

SCC usually remains localized with 2% metastasizing to surrounding lymph nodes. Lip lesions have a higher incidence of metastasis, therefore speedy removal is warranted.

NURSING MANAGEMENT

✣ ASSESSMENT

Interview the client, focusing on length of time lesion has been present, presence of risk factors such as chronic sun exposure, and history of previous skin lesions. Inspect and palpate lesion, surrounding tissue, and lymph nodes (to identify possible metastasis). A magnifying glass may be useful to closely examine any lesion. When a suspicious lesion is identified, especially if on or near the lip, refer the client to the primary care provider for prompt treatment. Explain to the client that early treatment lessens the extent of scarring and lowers the risk of metastasis (Box 28-9).

✣ DIAGNOSIS

A common nursing diagnosis is impaired skin integrity related to removal of a lesion. Other nursing diagnoses are high risk for infection related to break in skin integrity and surgical wound, and body image disturbance related to disfigurement and scarring resulting from removal of cancerous lesion. If the client has fear or anxiety related to having a cancerous lesion, an appropriate nursing diagnosis would be fear related to cancer, pain, and/or death.

✣ PLANNING

The goal of nursing management is to facilitate referral and treatment of suspicious lesions for removal without

BOX 28-9

Assessment of SCC

Subjective data
Sun exposure
Environmental/chemical exposures
History of previous skin lesions
History of current lesion
Lesion easily bleeds
Use of sunscreens and other preventive practices

Objective data
Inspect the following: skin color, texture, and lesion's location, texture, shape, vascularity, color, and size
Palpate the following: lesion, surrounding area, and lymph nodes

secondary infection. Plan time to discuss the client's and family's feelings about having a cancerous lesion to identify the need for a community referral or educational material. In addition, include prevention strategies in client education.

✣ INTERVENTION

Nursing management is the same as with BCC; however, more disfigurement may be present after removal. If the lesion is large and extensive, more intense emotional and social support may be needed. Identify and discuss the client's feelings about having a cancerous lesion with referral to appropriate community resources (e.g., a therapist or support group) if the client is having difficulty coping or is experiencing high levels of anxiety. Explain that the risk of metastasis is low, and refer the client to the ACS and local library for literature. The client may experience greater anxiety about long-term quality of life issues if metastasis is present. Focus on teaching the client and family how to care for the wound after removal of the lesion, signs of infection, prevention strategies, and appearance of questionable skin lesions that warrant examination by the primary care provider.

✣ EVALUATION

Evaluation, which is supported with documentation, focuses on preventing a wound infection, assisting the client to cope with changes in body image, and concrete client teaching outcomes such as verbalized understanding or return demonstration of a dressing change. If assessment reveals the development of an infection, the physician or advance practice nurse should be contacted so that therapy can be implemented. Return demonstrations of dressing changes assist in evaluating the client's comprehension and technique. In addition, obtain verbal understanding of teaching by asking the client to repeat prevention or list activities (e.g., ways of protecting skin from UV rays). This evaluation should be documented, as should the nursing assessment and interventions, which reflect nursing accountability.

Melanoma - most dangerous

Melanoma is a malignant neoplasm of pigment-forming cells that are capable of metastasizing to any organ of the body, even before the lesion is noted; therefore early detection is crucial. Melanoma represents 2% of all cancers, 1% of cancer-related deaths, and is the second most common cause of death in men ages 30 to 49. After excision, primary, "thin" ($<$ 76 mm thick) melanoma has a 5-year survival rate of approximately 98%. The survival rate for other stages is 83%. Melanoma incidence is rising. This is most likely a result of thinning of the ozone layer, combined with increased recreational sun exposure. A genetic predisposition to melanoma also exists, with 10% of clients having a parent and/or sibling with a history of melanoma. Individuals with a family history of melanoma should perform monthly skin self-examinations and have a professional skin evaluation at regular intervals (Fitzpatrick et al, 1992b; Koh, Bhawan, 1992; Lamberg, 1991).

Individuals at high risk are fair-skinned, have a tendency to sunburn rather than tan, have red or blond hair, have multiple nevi, and have a tendency to freckle. African Americans, Asians, and dark-skinned Caucasians are at less risk of developing melanoma. An individual with one melanoma is at risk for having another (Fitzpatrick et al, 1991b; Koh, Bhawan, 1992; Lamberg, 1991). The lifetime risk of a Caucasian for developing melanoma is 1:150 (Caro, 1991).

Melanoma's clinical hallmark is an irregularly shaped nevi (mole), papule, or plaque that has undergone a change, particularly in color. The lesion may itch or bleed; however, this is usually a later sign. Any mole or lesion that has irregularly shaped borders and has had a color change, usually of a darker color, should be examined by a dermatologist or family physician.

All melanomas grow both vertically and radially. During the radial (lateral) growth phase, metastasis occurs infrequently, which reinforces the need for early detection and seeking a professional examination (Caro, 1991; Fitzpatrick et al, 1992b; Koh, Bhawan, 1992) (Box 28-10).

There are four types of melanoma, the most common of which is the superficial spreading melanoma, which is slower growing. Superficial spreading melanoma accounts for 70% of all melanomas, occurring most commonly on the back in males and the extremities in females. The mean age of diagnosis is the mid-40's. Superficial melanoma is a flat, slightly elevated, pigmented papule or patch that has irregular borders and varied col-

BOX 28-10

Assessment of Melanoma

Subjective data
Sun exposure
Family history of melanoma
Tendency of sunburn rather than tan
Change in nevi appearance or color
Lesion in question bleeds easily

Objective data
Inspect the following: nevi or lentigo symmetry, borders, shape, color, size, location, and any bleeding
Palpate the following: nevi or lesion, surrounding area, and lymph nodes

ors within the lesion. Fortunately, superficial spreading melanoma usually enlarges slowly in a radial (lateral) fashion (Caro, 1991; Fitzpatrick et al, 1992b; Koh, Bhawan, 1992).

Nodular melanoma occurs in 15% to 30% of the clients with melanoma and has the worst prognosis, because it grows vertically at an early stage. Nodular melanoma is not often found on the head, neck, and trunk, and is more common in African-American or dark-skinned individuals. The mean age at diagnosis is the mid- to late-40s. Nodular melanoma is a hard, usually dark nodule arising from a preexisting mole (Caro, 1991; Fitzpatrick et al, 1992b; Koh, Bhawan, 1992).

Lentigo melanoma occurs in 5% to 10% of all melanoma clients and is more prevalent in females. Of these lesions, 30% to 50% arise in individuals with lentigo maligna. Therefore thorough skin assessment and instruction in self-examination is important in people with lentigo maligna. The mean age of occurrence is 70. Lentigo maligna melanoma is a brown-tannish macular lesion with varied pigmentation and highly irregular borders (Caro, 1991; Fitzpatrick et al, 1992b; Koh, Bhawan, 1992).

Acral lentiginous melanoma is less common (10% of all melanomas) and usually occurs on the palms, soles, fingers, and toes. It is more common in older adults with a mean age of 60 at the time of diagnosis. It is the most common melanoma found in African Americans; therefore inspection of the foot soles, palms, and hands is warranted when caring for African-American clients. Acral lentiginous melanoma resembles lentigo melanoma with its flat, irregular, discolored borders (Caro, 1991; Fitzpatrick et al, 1992b; Koh, Bhawan, 1992) (see Medical Management box above).

MEDICAL MANAGEMENT

Melanoma

Diagnostic tests and procedures
A biopsy of all suspicious lesions, based on clinical presentation, should be performed.

Treatment
Melanoma is excised completely using wide surgical margins. Skin grafts or flaps may be required. Decision to remove lymph nodes or limbs depends on location and presence of metastasis. All clients should have an annual physical examination, chest x-ray, and if necessary, computed tomograhy (CT) scan, or magnetic resonance imaging (MRI) to monitor for metastasis (Caro, 1991; Fitzpatrick et al, 1992b).

Prognosis
If not detected early enough, melamona can metastasize to the lymph system, which is associated with a poor prognosis. Lateral growth is usually slow, which can allow time for identification and removal before metastasis. Vertical growth is associated with a poor prognosis because metastasis occurs early.

NURSING MANAGEMENT

✣ ASSESSMENT

Nursing assessment begins with interviewing the client to determine how long the lesion has been present and identify risk factors such as chronic sun exposure and family history. Inspect and palpate the suspicious lesion, surrounding tissue, and lymph nodes (to identify possible metastasis). A magnifying glass may be useful to closely examine any lesion. When a suspicious lesion is identified, promptly refer the client to the primary care provider. Explain that early treatment lessens the extent of scarring and hopefully intervenes before metastasis. See Box 28-10 for a quick assessment guide. Since this is an aggressive cancerous lesion, discuss the client's feelings and fears about cancer.

✣ DIAGNOSIS

A common nursing diagnosis is impaired skin integrity related to removal of a cancerous lesion. Another major nursing diagnosis that may be applicable is fear of cancer, pain, and/or death related to having a cancerous skin lesion. Other nursing diagnoses include (1) high risk for infection related to break in skin integrity and surgical wound, and (2) body image disturbance related to disfigurement and scarring, resulting from removal of cancerous lesion.

✣ PLANNING

The goal of nursing management is to facilitate referral and treatment of suspicious lesions for removal without secondary infection and metastasis, and to address fears and feelings related to cancer with referral to community resources as indicated. Plan time to discuss the client's and family's feelings about having a cancerous lesion to identify the need for a community referral or educational material.

✣ INTERVENTION

Nursing management includes reinforcement of treatment regimen with monitoring wound for secondary infection (i.e., erythema, tenderness, and/or purulent discharge) and the caring component of nursing by discussing the client's and family's feelings related to cancer. Explain procedures and teach the client and/or family dressing care and signs of infection. Removal can result in scarring, especially if the lesion was large; consequently, provide reassurance and address feelings related to body image changes. Focus on comfort, education, and emotional support.

Identify and discuss the client's and family's feelings about having a cancerous lesion with referral to appropriate community resources if the client is having difficulty coping or has a high level of anxiety. Explain that there is a risk of metastasis and refer the client to the ACS or local library for literature. Prevention strategies such as wearing hats with wide brims, long sleeves, and using sunscreens should also be taught to both client and family. In addition, the client and family members should have annual skin assessments, since a hereditary tendency for occurrence exists.

✣ EVALUATION

Evaluation of nursing management is supported by documenting nursing interventions, which include dressing changes, monitoring for infection, pain control measures, comprehension of client education, and discussions related to body image changes and fears about cancer. If there is poor pain control or development of an infection, contact the physician or advance practice nurse for an alternative strategy.

Lower Extremity Ulcers

Chronic leg ulcers are a common problem in older adults, occurring primarily from three causes: arterial insufficiency, diabetic neuropathy, and venous hypertension (Table 28-1). A brief overview of each etiologic factor and treatment follows. Greater emphasis is placed on venous ulcers since these are more prevalent in older adults and more challenging as a result of their chronicity.

Arterial Ulcers

Arterial or ischemic ulcers result from arterial insufficiency and are not as prevalent as venous ulcers. Clients with arterial insufficiency, also referred to as peripheral vascular disease (PVD), have nine times the risk of amputation compared with those who only have venous disease (Reiber, Pecoraro, Koepsell, 1992). Arteriosclerosis—thickening and hardening of the arterial wall—is the primary cause for the decreased blood flow that results in ischemia and eventually tissue death. The term *arteriosclerosis obliterans* is used when atheromatous lesions develop in the lower extremities below the abdominal aorta. Smoking, diabetes, hyperlipoproteinemia, and hypertension are known risk factors for arteriosclerosis obliterans, which leads to arterial ulcer formation (McCulloch, Hovde, 1990; Reiber, Pecoraro, Koepsell, 1992; Zink, Rousseau, Holloway, 1992). It is established that 73% to 90% of the individuals with arterial insufficiency are smokers, 7% to 30% have diabetes, and 29% to 39% have hypertension (McCulloch, Hovde, 1990).

Pain with exercise, at night, or while resting is the most common sign of arterial insufficiency. Pain at rest indicates severely restricted arterial blood flow. The area proximal (above) to the painful area is usually the site of

TABLE 28-1

Leg Ulcer Differentiation

Type	Primary cause	Characteristics
Arterial	Arterial insufficiency; peripheral vascular disease	Located on toes, feet, or lower third of leg; irregular shape wound; thin, shiny, cool skin with cyanotic hue, loss of hair, thick toenails; pain with activity, rest, or at night
Diabetic neuropathy	Neuropathy	Located on plantar surface of foot; circular, often deep wounds; decreased or absent vibratory sensation, painful, paresthesia
Venous	Venous hypertension	Located on medial aspect of lower third of leg; irregular shape wound either flat or shallow crater; discoloration, varicosities, edema, exudate; pain relieved with activity

restricted blood flow. Pulses distal to the restriction may be present as a result of collateral circulation. The client may also complain of cramping, burning, or aching. As the disease advances, the extremity develops a cyanotic hue and becomes cool. The skin becomes thin, shiny, and dry, with an associated loss of hair and thickened toenails, all resulting from the diminished blood supply. Tissue anoxia leads to necrosis and poor healing. Arterial ulcers are usually located on the feet and toes. The causes must be corrected so that oxygen and other nutrients are available to promote healing of necrotic wounds. Consequently, treatment is usually surgical intervention with revascularization; if the disease is too advanced, amputation may be necessary (McCulloch, Hovde, 1990; Zink, Rousseau, Holloway, 1992).

Diabetic Neuropathy Ulcers

A Swedish study involving 742 people with diabetes found two thirds of the participants with diabetic neuropathy and 21% of the participants with a foot ulcer, infection, or gangrene (Kertesz, Chow, 1992). Risk factors for developing a diabetic foot ulcer are smoking, hypertension, lipoprotein abnormalities (particularly elevated low-density lipoprotein [LDL]), chronic hyperglycemia, absent vibratory sensation in the lower extremities, PVD, and poor outpatient diabetes education (McCulloch, Hovde, 1990; Reiber, Pecoraro, Koepsell, 1992). One independent risk factor for lower extremity amputation is loss of vibratory sense in the lateral malleus, medial malleus, and/or first dorsal metatarsal-tarsal joint. This sensory loss is associated with a 15.5% relative risk of amputation. Among the U.S. population, 5% have a lower extremity amputated and more than half of these individuals have diabetes (Reiber, Pecoraro, Koepsell, 1992). Therefore individuals with diabetes and neuropathy are at risk of developing lower leg ulcers, which may lead to an amputation.

Ulcers resulting from diabetic peripheral neuropathy tend to be bilateral, symmetrical, and located on the plantar surface of the foot. Clients usually complain of pain and paresthesias; however, they also have diminished or absent vibratory and temperature sensation of the affected extremities. Pain relieved by walking is one diagnostic sign of neuropathy. Neurotropic ulcers are usually well-perfused, yet the client with diabetes often has arterial insufficiency, which compromises healing abilities.

Treatment can vary, depending on the etiologic factors and wound condition. Client education regarding how to minimize the risk of chemical, thermal, and mechanical trauma is the first-line defense for diabetic foot ulcers. Stress to clients with diabetes, and particularly if PVD exists, any trauma to the lower leg, ankles, or feet can lead to an ulcer and possible amputation. Attention must be given to protect feet and lower legs with proper shoes and foot care. Orthotics (specially fitted shoes designed to prevent ulcers and to decrease callous formation by redistributing weight) may be helpful in preventing mechanical trauma. When an ulcer is pres-ent, a total contact casting may be applied to redistribute weight and to minimize trauma. Casting is contraindicated when cellulitis, sinus tracts, or excessive exudate are present (McCulloch, Hovde, 1990; Zink, Rousseau, Holloway, 1992). Some physicians use hyperbaric oxygenation in hopes of increasing oxygenation to the affected area; however, this treatment is controversial because of its questionable effectiveness in wounds that are circulatory compromised, such as in diabetic ulcers. The success of this strategy is dependent on the amount of circulation present in the affected area.

Venous Ulcer

Venous ulcer, or venous dermatitis, has been recognized for more than 2,000 years (Browse, Burnand, 1982). The etiology of this chronic, costly condition is not completely known, but has been attributed to chronic venous insufficiency. Venous ulcers affect 1% to 1.3% of the general population with a higher incidence (3.5%) in older adults. Chronic venous leg ulcers usually have an onset in early adulthood; however, peak prevalence is seen in people age 70 and older. Venous ulcers occur more often in women (3:1) than in men. The explanation for this significant difference is not clear, but is thought to be related to women's greater longevity (Baker et al, 1991; Goldman, Fronek, 1992; Zink, Rousseau, Holloway, 1992). Epidemiologic studies have revealed that 57% to 80% of all lower leg ulcers are related to venous insufficiency, with 10% to 25% having a combination of venous and arterial insufficiency (Goldman, Fronek, 1992).

Homans stated in 1917 that venous ulcers were related to venous stagnation, which led to anoxia and ulceration. Consequently, the term *venous stasis ulcer* or *dermatitis* was established. The concept of stasis was challenged in 1929 when research revealed higher oxygenation in limbs with venous ulcers. The correct term now is *venous ulcer* since the cause is not related to stasis. Browse and Burnand (1982) revealed the most current etiologic factor: an enlarged capillary bed from venous hypertension that causes leakage of fibrinogen into interstitial tissue, creating a fibrin cuff (Falanga, Eaglstein, 1986; McCulloch, Hovde, 1990; Zink, Roussaeu, Holloway, 1992). Falanga and Eaglstein (1993) are now proposing that the fibrin cuff facilitates the trapping of growth factors, which impedes healing.

Venous hypertension is the primary cause of venous ulcer. Valvular incompetence of the deep or perforating veins of the lower leg is present in the majority of venous ulcer cases. Venous hypertension leads to a tortuous capillary system, which causes an accumulation of fibrinogen, leukocytes, and erythrocytes. The accumulation of erythrocytes in the tissue produces a brownish skin discoloration caused by the release of hemoglobin (Zink, Rousseau, Holloway, 1992). Often, the discoloration and thickening of the skin (liposclerosis) is the first indication of venous hypertension. Capillary occlusion caused by trapping of white blood cells results in the release of proteolytic enzymes, which foster fibrinogen leakage. This excessive fibrinogen forms a fibrin cuff that impairs diffusion of oxygen, nutrients, and possibly growth factors (Falanga, Eaglstein, 1993; Zink, Rousseau, Holloway, 1993). The fibrinogen cuff creates a barrier that prevents or delays exchange of oxygen and other nutrients, resulting in cell death. Anoxia and trapping of growth factors are the primary causes of ulceration and poor healing. The fibrin cuff is irreversible, which sets the stage for frequent recurrence and makes venous ulcer a chronic disorder (see Medical Management box below).

The diagnosis of venous ulcer is commonly based on clinical presentation. Venous ulcers are usually on the medial aspect of the lower leg, with flat or shallow craters and irregular borders, accompanied by varicosities, liposclerosis (brown-ruddy color and thickened skin), and itching. Venous ulcers generate a large amount of exudate and are usually surrounded by erythema and edema. It is difficult at times to differentiate between cellulitis and typical venous ulcer presentation, since both have erythema, tenderness, and induration (Falanga, Eaglstein, 1986; Fitzpatrick, 1989; McCulloch, Hovde, 1990; Zink, Rousseau, Holloway, 1993).

It is well-recognized that venous ulcers heal with prolonged elevation of the affected extremity, however, compliance is difficult. Placement of 15 to 20 cm blocks at the foot of the client's bed can provide night elevation (Fitzpatrick, 1989; Partsch, 1991).

Research has demonstrated that compression therapy of at least 20 to 30 mm Hg at the ankle and distal lower leg decreases edema by compressing fluid through the fibrin cuff (Fitzpatrick, 1989; Goldman, Fronek, 1992; Mayberry et al, 1991; Partsch, 1991). In one study, 119 clients with venous ulcers were treated with only compression therapy; 97% of the clients' ulcers healed and 16% had recurrences. The most common cause of recurrence is noncompliance with compression therapy (Mayberry et al, 1991). Compression therapy is not a management option for arterial insufficiency; pain and cyanosis will occur from further impaired circulation.

MEDICAL MANAGEMENT

Venous Ulcers

Diagnostic tests and procedures

Diagnosis is usually made by clinical presentation of thickened, ruddy-brown discolored skin with flat, shallow ulcers containing a large amount of exudate, usually located on the medial aspect of the lower leg. Pruritus may be present. Doppler studies may be conducted to evaluate arterial blood flow to rule out arterial insufficiency.

Treatment

General treatment strategies are bed rest with legs elevated above the heart, compression therapy (with stockings, stiff bandages, or Unna boots), topical preparations (e.g., Silvadene), occlusive dressings, and venous valve surgery. Place 15 to 20 cm blocks under the food of the client's bed to provide night elevation and for edema management. Compression therapy is not a management option if arterial insufficiency also exists.

Prognosis

Venous ulcers are a chronic, recurring problem resulting from the permanent capillary fibrin cuff, which impedes circulation and fluid management.

NURSING MANAGEMENT

ASSESSMENT

Assess the location and characteristics of lower leg ulcers. Determine ulcer dimensions, depth, and amount of exudate. Palpate popliteal pulses at least every day if in acute care, and at every visit if in an ambulatory or home setting. Note any discoloration and degree of edema. Ascertain if the client experiences any pain or itching, and how it has been managed. Conduct a nutritional assessment, which includes weight, 24-hour diet recall, chewing abilities, and the client's food preparation abilities. Determine if shopping assistance is needed (Box 28-11).

DIAGNOSIS

The most common nursing diagnosis for this condition is impaired skin integrity related to altered circulation. Another possible nursing diagnosis is high risk for infection related to open, chronic wounds.

PLANNING

The overall nursing goal is to facilitate healing without infection by promoting treatment compliance and by providing client education regarding the disease process and treatment, stressing that venous ulcers are a chronic process. Time for client education will be needed.

INTERVENTION

Nursing management consists of keeping legs elevated above the heart, implementing compression therapy, ad-

BOX 28-11

Assessment of Lower Extremity Venous Ulcers

Subjective data
Complaints of itching
Large amount of discharge/exudate from ulcers
History of chronicity
Duration of symptoms
Leg pain relieved with activity

Objective data
Brownish discoloration
Skin thickening
Ulcer(s) on medial aspect of lower third of leg
Flat, shallow, crater-like ulcer with irregular borders
Large amount of exudate
Bilateral edema
Varicosities

ministering wound care, and conducting client education regarding venous ulcer cause and its chronic nature, the strategy of compression therapy, and specific wound care. Stress the need to maintain compression therapy to facilitate healing of ulcers and avoid further breakdown. Instruct the client to place 15 to 20 cm blocks at the foot of the bed at home for long-term edema management. Teach the client that venous ulcers generate a large amount of exudate and instruct how to change dressings. Infection is difficult to determine, since venous ulcers often have erythemic bases with induration; however, if the client develops a fever and tenderness surrounding the ulcer, contact the physician or advance practice nurse. Determine if any community services such as Meals-on-Wheels, grocery shopping assistance, and other support services are needed. Identify and discuss the client's feelings regarding chronicity and body image changes.

✣ EVALUATION

Evaluation focuses on prevention of further ulcer deterioration and infection, as well as the effectiveness of client education. Return demonstration of compression therapy application and wound care is a concrete evaluation and ensures client comprehension. Evaluation, which reflects nursing accountability, should be documented, as well as the nursing assessment and interventions.

PRESSURE ULCERS

Pressure ulcers (also known as bedsores, decubiti, or pressure sores) have plagued humans for centuries. The first documented case was around 2000 BC on an Egyptian mummy (Krasner, 1990). Hippocrates devised a debridement treatment with healing by secondary closure. Ambrose Pare, a sixteenth-century surgeon, published strategies for healing skin ulcers that challenged the existing practice of pouring hot oil on the wound. These included increased nutrition and mobility, debridement, and application of dressings (Levine, 1992).

It was not until the twentieth century that scientific research was begun to determine the etiology and appropriate management of pressure ulcers. Landis, in 1930, determined that the average capillary pressure before which ischemia occurs is below 32 mm Hg. In the 1950s, Kosiak found that pressure applied to rabbits' ears over 2 hours would result in ulceration. Thus the universal recommendation of turning every 2 hours was established. The first pressure ulcer risk assessment tool was designed and tested by Doreen Norton in the late 1950s, but not disseminated until 1962 when she presented study findings at a conference.

In 1962, researchers first demonstrated that moisture increases epithelialization (healing process) by using occlusive dressings (Krasner, 1991). In 1972 a plastic occlusive dressing was shown to decrease epithelialization time by half, which lead to film dressings, followed by hydrocolloidal dressings. The wound care market is now a multibillion dollar enterprise (Thompson-Bishop, Mottola, 1992).

This information explosion has resulted in varied terminology and beliefs. As a result, leading experts in pressure ulcer management and research formed the National Pressure Ulcer Advisory Panel (NPUAP) in 1987, with the intent of improving prevention and management through education, legislation, standardization of staging criteria, and identification of research needs. The NPUAP held consensus conferences beginning in May 1988, the outcome of which included standardized staging criteria that are endorsed by the International Association for Enterostomal Therapists (IAET) and the Agency for Health Care Policy and Research (AHCPR). Also, to standardize terms and to more accurately reflect the cause of pressure damage, the NPUAP decreed that pressure ulcer is the more appropriate term than pressure sores or decubitus. Therefore pressure ulcer is used throughout this discussion.

In December 1989 the Omnibus Budget Reconciliation Act (OBRA) established the AHCPR. Based on reviews of current research and practice, this agency is charged with developing clinical practice guidelines that appropriately and effectively prevent, diagnose, treat, and manage clinically relevant disorders and diseases (AHCPR, 1992). Pressure ulcer prevention and management was one of the first three areas reviewed by the AHCPR. As a result, *Pressure Ulcers in Adults: Prediction and Prevention* was published in May 1992, and *Treat-*

ment of Pressure Ulcers was published in February 1995. These comprehensive references are guides for the following discussion.*

Epidemiology of Pressure Ulcers

The epidemiology of pressure ulcers has been difficult to quantify and varies based on sample size, definition of terms, and type of facility. Although there have been methodologic limitations, incidence (new cases) and prevalence (over a specific time period) rates of pressure ulcers are sufficiently high to generate concern.

The incidence of pressure ulcers in hospitals ranges from 2.7% to as high as 60%. The prevalence rate in hospitals ranges from 3.5% to 29.5% (AHCPR, 1992). One large, nationwide study involving 148 hospitals revealed a prevalence rate of 9.2% (Meehan, 1990). Several studies have identified high-risk groups of hospitalized clients: quadriplegic clients, older clients with a hip fracture, orthopedic clients who are immobile, and critical care clients (AHCPR, 1992).

The prevalence rate of pressure ulcers in long-term care facilities ranges from 2.4% to 23%. It has been found that incidence rates vary among nursing care facilities due to the heterogeneous case-mix and staffing patterns. There is a need for better data to determine the degree of the problem in long-term care (AHCPR, 1992). It is believed that OBRA regulations have been instrumental in decreasing the incidence of pressure ulcers in nursing homes.

The prevalence of pressure ulcers in home-care clients is not well-known, but was reported in 1988 at 8.7%, with an incidence rate of 20%. A need definitely exists for more information related to incidence and prevalence rates among home-bound clients (ACHPR, 1992).

Etiology of Pressure Ulcers

Pressure on soft tissue over bony prominences or other hard surfaces is the primary causative factor in pressure ulcer formation. However, there are other contributing factors, which can explain why some individuals break down within 30 minutes, while others do not break down when lying in the same position for hours.

Pressure ulcers begin at the point of contact between soft tissue and a hard surface (i.e., bone). Consequently, an upside down, cone-shaped wound develops with the largest area of breakdown being near the bone. Common bony prominences susceptible to pressure ulcer development are the sacrum, ischial tuberosity (especially in a sitting position in a chair or upright in bed), lateral malleolus, trochanter, and heels. Yet, any pressure point

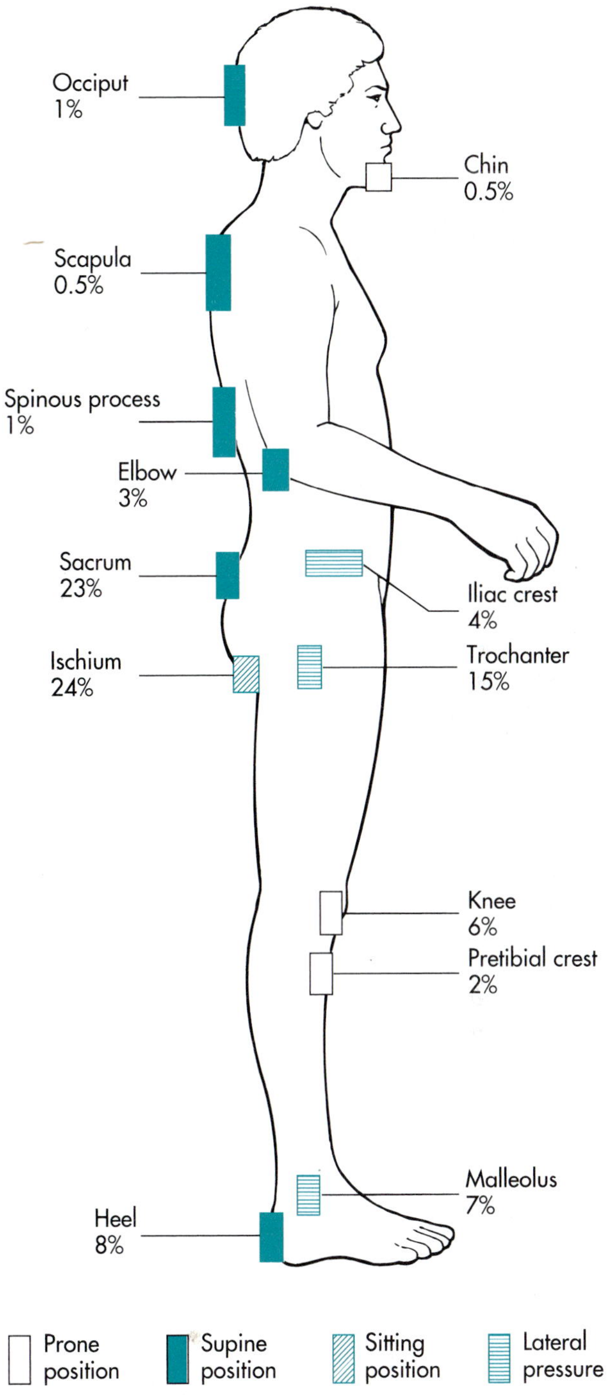

Fig. 28-2 Common sites for pressure ulcers and frequency of ulceration per site. (Data from Agris J, Spira M: *Clin Symp* 31(5):2 + , 1979.)

is a vulnerable area when pressure is intense and prolonged (Bryant et al, 1992; Maklebust, 1987; Rousseau, 1988; Sanders, 1992; Trelease, 1990) (Fig. 28-2).

The intensity of pressure that leads to capillary closure, compounded by the duration of pressure and tissue tolerance, lead to tissue anoxia, ischemia, edema, and eventually tissue necrosis. Immobility, decreased activity,

*To obtain educational material and guidelines on pressure ulcers contact the AHCPR Clearinghouse; P.O. Box 8547; Silver Spring, MD 20907; (800) 358-9295 or the National Pressure Ulcer Advisory Panel (NPUAP); State University of New York at Buffalo; Beck Hall; 3435 Main Street; Buffalo, NY 14214; (716) 881-3558.

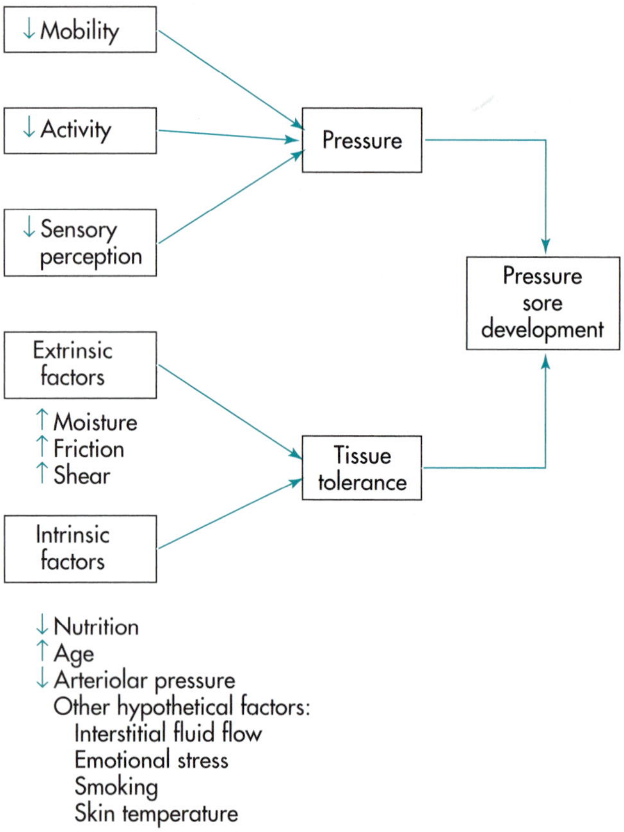

Fig. 28-3 Factors contributing to the development of pressure ulcers. (Reprinted with permission from Braden B, Bergstrom N: A conceptual schema for the study of the etiology of pressure sores, *Rehabil Nurs* 12(1):8, 1987. ©1987 Association of Rehabilitation Nurses.)

and decreased sensory perception place individuals at risk for unrelieved pressure that generates tissue ischemia and death. Tissue tolerance is influenced by extrinsic factors—moisture, friction, and shearing—and intrinsic factors—poor nutrition, advanced age, hypotension, emotional stress, smoking, and skin temperature (Bergstrom et al, 1987; Bryant et al, 1992; Sanders, 1992). The development of pressure ulcers is a complex, synergistic phenomena that makes prevention a challenge (Fig. 28-3).

Capillary pressure ensures the movement of blood through the capillary membrane, maintaining oxygenation and tissue nutrition. Exact capillary pressure is not known. Various studies have identified ranges from 10 to 14 mm Hg in the venous limb system, to 32 to 40 mm Hg in the arteriolar limb system (Bryant et al, 1992; Landis, 1930; Jester, Weaver, 1990). Capillary collapse can result from intense and prolonged pressure, which leads to tissue anoxia, ischemia, reactive hyperemia (erythema), leakage of plasma into interstitial tissue, and microvascular hemorrhage (observable) by nonblanchable erythema. If pressure persists, tissue death results. It is assumed that capillary pressure, which varies depending on location and individual, ranging from 10 to 32 mm Hg, must be exceeded to impair circulation.

Individuals with normal sensation regularly shift their weight, voluntarily and involuntarily, in response to the discomfort from capillary closure and resulting tissue anoxia (Bergstrom et al, 1987; Braden, Bergstrom, 1987; Sanders, 1992). People with sensory impairment (paralysis or sedation), however, do not have this normal protective reflex, which can explain the higher incidence of pressure ulcers among paralyzed individuals or in clients who undergo long surgical procedures. Clients with altered mental status as a consequence of disease (e.g., dementia) or medication may have decreased pain or tissue anoxia perception. These individuals are at risk for pressure ulcer development.

Tissue tolerance, another major contributing factor in the development of a pressure ulcer, is defined as the ability of the skin and supporting structures to endure the effects of pressure. The integumentary structures, blood vessels, interstitial fluid, and collagen, function as "springs" that transmit pressure load from the skin's surface to skeletal structures (Bergstrom et al, 1987; Braden, Bergstrom, 1987; Bryant et al, 1992). It is apparent, then, that poor tissue tolerance makes one more vulnerable to pressure intensity and duration, thus increasing the response to pressure. Shearing, friction, age-related changes in the integumentary system, low blood pressure, and nutritional status all influence the integrity of tissue tolerance.

Shearing, the sliding of parallel surfaces, causes stretching and occlusion of arterial supply, which is usually of the fascia and muscle. Shearing forces can decrease blood supply, leading to tissue ischemia and necrosis (Braden, Bergstrom, 1987; Bryant et al, 1992; Sanders, 1992). The most common position for shearing is when the head of the bed is elevated, causing the body to slide downward (Fig. 28-4). Resistance keeps the skin in place, while gravity pulls the body toward the foot of the bed. It is believed that shearing forces cause more damage than recognized, with as many as 40% of pressure ulcers resulting from shearing rather than pressure (Bryant et al, 1992).

Friction, the rubbing of skin against another surface, primarily affects the epidermal and dermal layers, causing a superficial abrasion (i.e., sheet burn) (Braden, Bergstrom, 1987; Maklebust, 1987; Sanders, 1992). Restless clients or those with persistent movements are at risk for friction injuries. However, when friction occurs concurrently with gravitational forces, shearing is the outcome.

Moisture from incontinence or profuse sweating can decrease tensile strength, alter skin resiliency to external forces, and exacerbate friction and shearing forces (Bryant et al, 1992; Braden, Bergstrom, 1987; Flam, 1990). Some experts believe friction and shearing forces

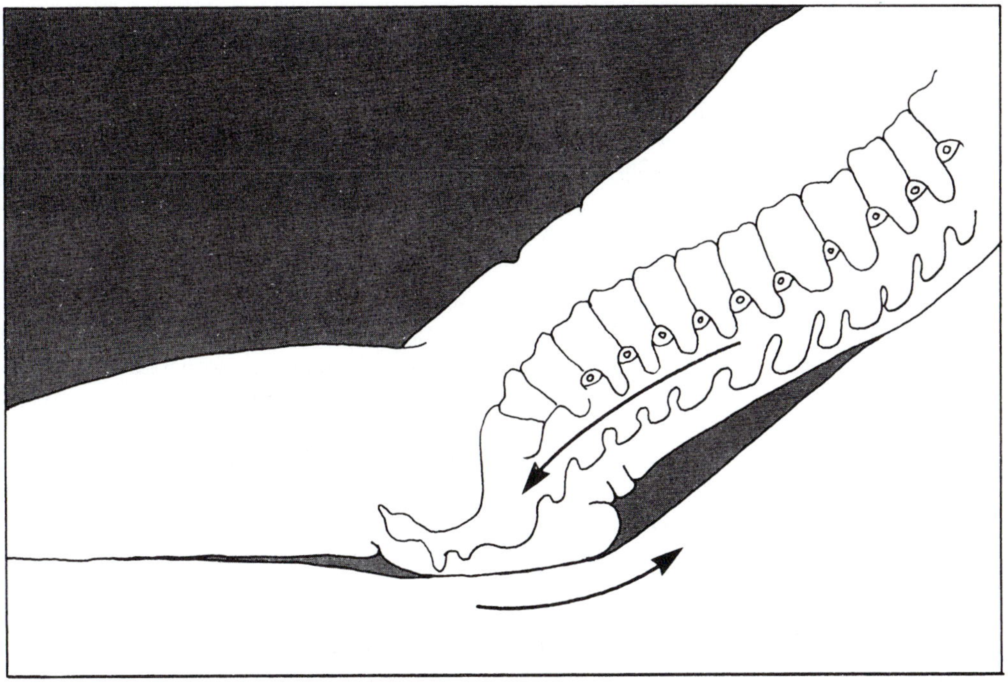

Fig. 28-4 Shearing force. (From Loeper JM et al: *Therapeutic positioning and skin care,* Minneapolis, 1986, Sister Kenny Institute.)

are increased in the presence of mild to moderate moisture and decreased in the presence of profuse moisture (Bryant et al, 1992). Therefore urinary incontinence (UI) may not be as significant in pressure ulcer development as once thought. Regardless, efforts should be made to keep skin dry.

As many studies have revealed, nutritional status greatly influences the development of pressure ulcers. Protein deficiency weakens tissue tolerance (i.e., the spring between skin surface and bony prominence), making soft tissue more susceptible to breakdown when pressure intensity is prolonged. Hypoproteinemia changes osmotic equilibrium, which leads to edema. Consequently, sluggish oxygenation and transportation create an environment for tissue breakdown and poor healing (Bobel, 1987; Bryant et al, 1992; Sanders, 1992). Serum albumin levels below 3.5 gm/100 ml have a correlation with pressure ulcer development and poor wound healing (Forse, Shizgal, 1980; Pinchcofsky-Devin, Kaminski, 1986; Ruberg, 1984; Stotts, Whitney, 1990). Proteins are also needed for collagen formation, granulation tissue formation, and immunologic response.

Individuals age 70 and older have a higher incidence of pressure ulcers (Allman, 1990; Maklebust, 1987; Meehan, 1990). With aging, the epidermis thins, elasticity decreases, and vessels degenerate, resulting in reduced blood flow. Collagen fibers stiffen and the immune response becomes sluggish (Balin, 1992; Dalziel, Bickers, 1992; Sanders, 1992). These age-related changes impair the early warning sign of erythema, delay crucial early immunologic responses, and impede the healing process, thereby making older adults at risk for pressure ulcer development.

Low blood pressure and dehydration can reduce circulation, especially in the microvasculature, which eventually leads to tissue ischemia (Bryant et al, 1992; Braden, Bryant, 1990; Braden, Bergstrom, 1987). Diastolic blood pressure below 60 mm Hg has been found to be a risk factor for pressure ulcer formation, presumably because of decreased peripheral circulation and subsequent ischemia (Bryant et al, 1992; Braden, Bryant, 1990; Gosnell, 1987).

Other intrinsic factors are stress, smoking, and elevated body temperature. Emotional stress with reduction in effective coping mechanisms leads to release of cortisol from the adrenal glands. The effects of cortisol are not completely understood but are believed to alter the skin's ability to absorb mechanical loads, such as pressure. In addition, cortisone may affect cellular metabolism between capillary beds and cells, making the skin vulnerable to breakdown and poor healing (Bryant et al, 1992; Braden, Bryant, 1990; Braden, Bergstrom, 1987). A relationship between cigarette smoking and pressure ulcer development is becoming evident, especially in spinal cord–injured clients. The reason is not clear but is thought to be related to vasoconstriction (Braden, Bryant, 1990; Bryant et al, 1992). Elevated temperature, especially in older adults, is associated with pressure ulcer formation, possibly caused by increased oxygen demands in anoxic tissue (Bryant et al, 1992).

The formation of a pressure ulcer is a complex process involving many variables within the nurse's control (e.g., pressure, shearing, moisture), as well as variables out of the nurse's control (e.g., smoking, malnutrition, low blood pressure, paralysis). The principal mechanism of injury is loss of microcirculation through pressure compressing the microvessels, or intrinsic factors causing soft tissue to become more vulnerable to lost blood supply.

Risk Assessment Tools

The success of pressure ulcer prevention depends on early identification of at-risk clients. As recommended by the AHCPR clinical guidelines, a valid, research-based assessment tool should be used. To establish consistency and accuracy, there should be written protocols specifying how the risk assessment tool should be used, when it should be used, and by which health care team members. A risk assessment should be conducted on all individuals who are bedbound, chairbound, incontinent, frail, disabled, nutritionally compromised, or have demonstrated altered mental status (AHCPR, 1992; Berstrom et al, 1987; Gosnell, 1987; Sanders, 1992). An assessment should be conducted on clients admitted to an acute care facility, rehabilitation hospital, nursing home, home care agency, or other health care facility (AHCPR, 1992). Identified high-risk individuals should be reassessed every 48 hours in acute care environments, weekly in skilled nursing facilities, and monthly in intermediate care settings (Braden, Bryant, 1990). If there is a change in the client's condition (e.g., decreased mobility, eating less, or a change in serum albumin), a risk assessment should be repeated.

Numerous instruments have been designed to identify clients at risk for pressure ulcer formation. Many tools, however, have not been subjected to vigorous evaluation of reliability and validity testing. The Braden and Norton risk assessment tools, according to AHCPR clinical guidelines, have undergone the most extensive evaluations.

The Norton Risk Assessment Scale was the first such tool designed for use in a study investigating geriatric nursing problems in hospitals. Consequently, it has set the stage for more comprehensive assessment tools. The study began in the late 1950s, but results were not disseminated until 1962 during a conference. At that time, it was believed pressure ulcers were the result of poor nursing care; however, additional research has revealed the problem to be much more complex. The Norton scale is simple to use and has only five assessment categories. Although the original research assessed nutritional status, it was not included in the scale because it was believed the client's general health was a reflection of nutritional status. Norton (1989) now believes that nutritional status, to include eating behaviors, would have been an important parameter to include. Clients with a score of 16 or lower on the Norton scale are considered to be at risk for pressure ulcer development (Norton, 1989) (Table 28-2).

The Braden Scale for Predicting Pressure Sore Risk was shown to be highly reliable when used by registered nurses and is the most rigorously tested risk assessment

TABLE 28-2

NORTON SCALE

NORTON RISK ASSESSMENT SCALE

		Physical Condition	Mental Condition	Activity	Mobility	Incontinent	TOTAL SCORE
		Good 4 Fair 3 Poor 2 Very Bad 1	Alert 4 Apathetic 3 Confused 2 Stupor 1	Ambulant 4 Walk/help 3 Chairbound 2 Bed 1	Full 4 Sl. limited 3 V. limited 2 Immobile 1	Not 4 Occasional 3 Usually/Urine 2 Doubly 1	
Name	Date						

Reprinted with permission, Norton D, McLaren R, and Exton-Smith AN: An investigation of geriatric nursing problems in hospital, 1962, reissue 1975, Churchill Livingstone, Edinburgh.

tool (AHCPR, 1992; Bergstrom et al, 1987). The Braden scale assesses sensory perception rather than mental status. Assessing sensory perception is thought to be a more precise at-risk indicator, since impaired sensation prevents an individual from sensing the need to change positions, which in turn decreases pressure intensity (Braden, Bergstrom, 1987; Sanders, 1992). As a general rule, a high-risk score on the Braden scale is 16 to 17 or lower. In nursing homes, it is 17 to 18 or lower (B. Braden, personal communication, Nov. 2, 1990) (Table 28-3) (see Research Box, p. 796).

Another tool discussed in the literature is Gosnell's Scale, designed in the mid-80s. Gosnell's Scale paralleled Norton's; however, it added nutritional and other medical variables such as medications, vital signs, and hydration status. Risk scoring has been revised from the original work, with higher scores reflecting greater risk (Gosnell, 1989). The tool requires more data collection but includes more in-depth assessment of intrinsic factors such as blood pressure and hydration. Although this tool has undergone some reliability and validity testing, AHCPR endorses the Braden and Norton scales, since these tools have been more extensively tested.

Prevention Strategies

Prevention is the first-line defense for pressure ulcers, which are costly health care problems that adversely affect a client's quality of life. The professional nurse has a responsibility to identify clients at risk for pressure ulcers and to implement research-based prevention strategies. Nurses as frontline providers and managers of care are key health care team members who can influence the prevalence of pressure ulcers and increase the client's quality of life. Nurses can mobilize the health care team when needs are identified by seeking a dietary consultation and alerting the physician or advance practice nurse when a client is not eating sufficiently or when a client develops nonblanchable erythema. Writ-

TABLE 28-3

BRADEN SCALE FOR PREDICTING PRESSURE SORE RISK

Patient's Name ____________ Evaluator's Name ____________ Date of Assessment

					Date of Assessment			
SENSORY PERCEPTION Ability to respond meaningfully to pressure-related discomfort	**1. Completely limited:** Unresponsive (does not moan, flinch, or grasp) to painful stimuli, due to diminished level of consciousness or sedation, OR limited ability to feel pain over most of body surface.	**2. Very Limited:** Responds only to painful stimuli. Cannot communicate discomfort except by moaning or restlessness, OR has a sensory impairment which limits the ability to feel pain or discomfort over 1/2 of body.	**3. Slightly Limited:** Responds to verbal commands but cannot always communicate discomfort or need to be turned, OR has some sensory impairment which limits ability to feel pain or discomfort in 1 or 2 extremities.	**4. No Impairment:** Responds to verbal commands. Has no sensory deficit which would limit ability to feel or voice pain or discomfort.				
MOISTURE Degree to which skin is exposed to moisture	**1. Constantly Moist:** Skin is kept moist almost constantly by perspiration, urine, etc. Dampness is detected every time patient is moved or turned.	**2. Moist:** Skin is often but not always moist. Linen must be changed at least once a shift.	**3. Occasionally Moist:** Skin is occasionally moist, requiring an extra linen change approximately once a day.	**4. Rarely Moist:** Skin is usually dry; linen requires changing only at routine intervals.				
ACTIVITY Degree of physical activity	**1. Bedfast:** Confined to bed	**2. Chairfast:** Ability to walk severely limited or nonexistent. Cannot bear own weight and/or must be assisted into chair or wheelchair.	**3. Walks Occasionally:** Walks occasionally during day but for very short distances, with or without assistance. Spends majority of each shift in bed or chair.	**4. Walks Frequently:** Walks outside the room at least twice a day and inside room at least once every 2 hours during waking hours.				
MOBILITY Ability to change and control body position	**1. Completely Immobile:** Does not make even slight changes in body or extremity position without assistance.	**2. Very Limited:** Makes occasional slight changes in body or extremity position but unable to make frequent or significant changes independently.	**3. Slightly Limited:** Makes frequent though slight changes in body or extremity position independently.	**4. No Limitations:** Makes major and frequent changes in position without assistance.				
NUTRITION Usual food intake pattern	**1. Very Poor:** Never eats a complete meal. Rarely eats more than 1/3 of any food offered. Eats 2 servings or less of protein (meat or dairy products) per day. Takes fluids poorly. Does not take a liquid dietary supplement, OR is NPO and/or maintained on clear liquids or IV's for more than 5 days.	**2. Probably Inadequate:** Rarely eats a complete meal and generally eats only about 1/2 of any food offered. Protein intake includes only 3 servings of meat or dairy products per day. Occasionally will take a dietary supplement, OR receives less than optimum amount of liquid diet or tube feeding.	**3. Adequate:** Eats over half of most meals. Eats a total of 4 servings of protein (meat, dairy products) each day. Occasionally will refuse a meal, but will usually take a supplement if offered, OR is on a tube feeding or TPN regimen, which probably meets most of nutritional needs.	**4. Excellent:** Eats most of every meal. Never refuses a meal. Usually eats a total of 4 or more servings of meat and dairy products. Occasionally eats between meals. Does not require supplementation.				
FRICTION AND SHEAR	**1. Problem:** Requires moderate to maximum assistance in moving. Complete lifting without sliding against sheets is impossible. Frequently slides down in bed or chair, requiring frequent repositioning with maximum assistance. Spasticity, contractures, or agitation leads to almost constant friction.	**2. Potential Problem:** Moves feebly or requires minimum assistance. During a move skin probably slides to some extent against sheets, chair, restraints, or other devices. Maintains relatively good position in chair or bed most of the time but occasionally slides down.	**3. No Apparent Problem:** Moves in bed and in chair independently and has sufficient muscle strength to lift up completely during move. Maintains good position in bed or chair at all times.					
				Total Score				

RESEARCH

Bergstrom et al: The Braden scale for predicting pressure sore risk, *Nurs Res* 36(4):205-210, 1987.

Sample, setting

Three different reliability studies were conducted on a rehabilitation unit, a cardiovascular and neurologic unit, and a skilled nursing facility. A total of 124 subjects, ranging in age from 37 to 100 were involved. Two different prospective validity studies were conducted on two 28-bed medical-surgical units in a large hospital. A total of 99 clients, ranging in age from 14 to 102 were involved.

Methodology

To determine interrater reliability when the tool was used by RNs, LPNs, and NAs, a graduate research nursing student directly observed the staff and conducted chart reviews over a period of weeks. Validity was tested by defining sensitivity and specificity of the scale. All clients who were free of skin breakdown when admitted to participating medical-surgical units were included in the prospective validity study. Staff were educated on use of the risk assessment tool, then used the tool to rate the client weekly and at time of discharge, death, or transfer.

Findings

The Braden scale was found to be highly reliable when used by RNs, primary nurses, and graduate students. There was nearly perfect agreement between raters and RNs. The interrater reliability between LPN and NA was satisfactory but not as good as the more educated health care team members.

Implications

RNs would be the best professionals to use the assessment tool. Institutional protocols establishing procedure for tool use will improve reliability of tool.

ten prevention protocols, endorsed by the health care team and institution, can empower the professional nurse to act independently and immediately when vulnerable clients are identified.

All at-risk individuals identified through use of a risk assessment tool should have a daily skin inspection with close attention to bony prominences, as recommended by AHCPR clinical guidelines. This routine assessment should be documented to demonstrate professional accountability and evaluate prevention strategy outcomes. Another skin-related activity recommended by AHCPR clinical guidelines is to cleanse skin with a mild, nonirritating cleanser using warm, not hot, water at the time of soiling to minimize irritation and dryness of the skin. Moisturizers, such as emollient lotions, should be used to keep the skin from drying and cracking. It is best to apply the lotion immediately after bathing to increase moisture absorbed by the skin. Skin should not be rubbed or massaged over bony prominences, because it may cause further deep tissue damage, especially if erythema is present (which already indicates injury) (AHCPR, 1992; Maklebust, 1987; Sanders, 1992).

Proper turning and placement reduces the effects of pressure, but not the intensity. It has been standard practice to turn clients a minimum of every 2 hours, and this continues to be endorsed in the AHCPR clinical guidelines. However, capillary closing pressure varies with each individual; therefore the ideal strategy is to determine the turning schedule based on development of erythema, which may precede ischemia (Bryant et al, 1992; Sanders, 1992; Seiler, Stahelin, 1989). For many reasons this ideal strategy may not be possible, but when staffing and client condition allows a turning schedule based on the clinical presentation of erythema, it should be done, particularly with frail, vulnerable clients.

Clients should be turned only at a 30-degree oblique angle, rather than a lateral, side-lying 90-degree angle, to decrease pressure intensity over the trochanter and lateral malleus prominences. It is also easier to turn a person at a 30-degree angle (Braden, Bryant, 1990; Bryant et al, 1992; Sanders, 1992; Seiler, Stehelin, 1989) (Fig. 28-5). To decrease pressure intensity on the heels, place a pillow(s) under the calves to lift the feet and heels off the bed. Heel protectors may be used if the support maintains a low interface pressure (Bryant et al, 1992). The pillow strategy is easier and more cost-efficient.

At-risk individuals should be placed on a pressure-reducing device in hopes of preventing development of a pressure ulcer by decreasing pressure intensity. Pressure-reducing support surfaces, such as mattress overlays, chair cushions or overlays, and specialized beds, redistribute weight over a larger area and reduce tissue-interface pressure. Tissue-interface pressure is the amount of pressure between the skin and resting surface (e.g., mattress). It has been thought that if the tissue-interface pressure is 32 mm Hg or lower, capillary closure will not occur (Bryant et al, 1992; Landis, 1930; Jester, Weaver, 1990). However, this logic may be questioned, since capillary closing pressures vary from one individual to another. Another practice is to compare, in percentage of tissue-interface pressure difference, a support surface tissue-interface pressure with a standard hospital mattress surface, that is, a bed with 50% less interface pressure than a regular hospital mattress versus a 35% difference (Bryant et al, 1992). As knowledge and technology in this area increase, a more accurate evaluation method for support surface selection will be developed.

Mattress overlays provide pressure reduction, are usually economic with a one-time charge, and are accessible in most environments. Overlays can be static (e.g., foam, gel, water, air-filled, or low-air loss) or dynamic (e.g., al-

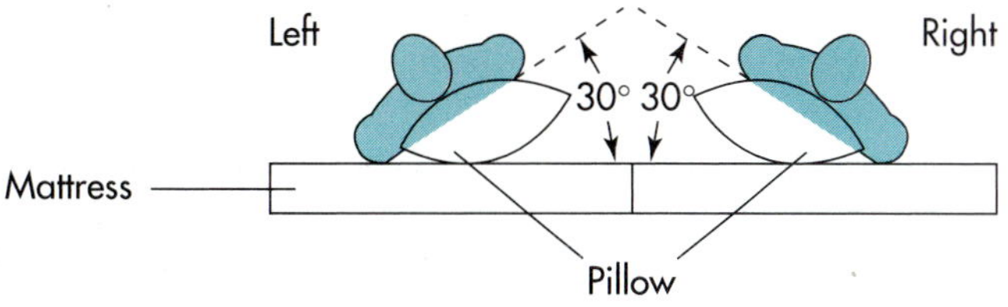

Right: ____ AM/PM ____ AM/PM ____ AM/PM ____ AM/PM ____ AM/PM ____ AM/PM

Left: ____ AM/PM ____ AM/PM ____ AM/PM ____ AM/PM ____ AM/PM ____ AM/PM

Flat*: ____ AM/PM ____ AM/PM ____ AM/PM ____ AM/PM ____ AM/PM ____ AM/PM

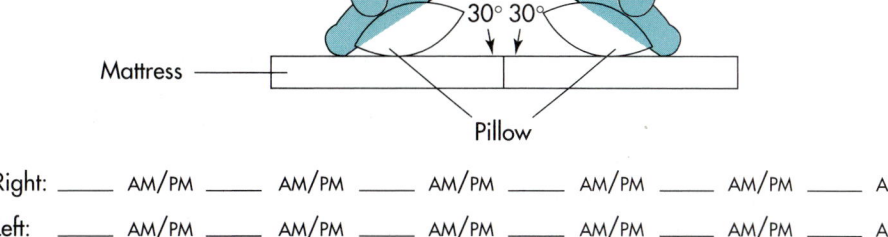

Fig. 28-5 Repositioning schedule. Begin with the person on his or her back. Reposition by placing pillows underneath the person's shoulder blades, buttocks, and thighs. Adjust the pillows so that the person is at a 30-degree angle to the mattress. Alternate the position from the right to the left. Elevating the head of the bed increases the risk for ulcer development and should be avoided. NOTE: Avoid placing people at high risk for ulcer development flat on their backs. (Modified from Seiler WO, Stahelin HB, *Geriatrics* 40:30, 1985. Reprinted with permission from *Fam Pract Recertifica,* 12:104, 1990.)

ternating air). Since the overlays are placed on top of a mattress, the height of the bed is increased, thus making it more difficult for clients to get in and out of the bed, which is a common client and nurse complaint. Some mattress overlays trap moisture and heat, which can be uncomfortable. Foam overlays should have a base height of at least 4 inches from the bottom to the *beginning* of the convolutions, not to the peak (AHCPR, 1992; Bryant et al, 1992; Jester, Weaver, 1990; Krouskop, Garber, Cullen, 1990), and a stiffness of 25% of indentation load deflection (ILD) (AHCPR, 1995). Foam overlays must also be examined regularly to assess for continued effectiveness (i.e., obvious sagging), since there is an associated limited lifetime use. Gel overlays are made of silicone or a silicone-like product, and thus are heavy and very expensive ($300 or more). Static air and water overlays must be checked regularly for proper inflation and cleaned periodically. Alternating air-filled overlays have less moisture buildup and maintain a more constant inflation; however, they can be noisy (Bryant et al, 1992; Krouskop, Garber, Cullen, 1990).

Specialty beds such as air-fluidized beds (Clintron) or low-air loss beds (Kin-Air or Flexicare) are generally used for individuals with multiple stage III and IV pressure ulcers or at high risk, that is, posterior grafts or flap procedures. The air-fluidized beds have antibactericidal properties as a result of temperature, alkalinity (pH of 10), and microorganisms getting trapped in the beads (Bryant et al, 1992). These beds can actually overheat a client and can elevate the body temperature if not adequately controlled. Specialty beds do not eliminate the need for meticulous nursing care. Clients still need to be repositioned, assessed, and kept clean and dry.

Skin moisture, whether the result of incontinence of urine or feces, perspiration, or wound exudate, should be kept at a minimum. If necessary, absorbent underpads or diapers can be used to maintain a dryer skin surface. Topical barriers, such as zinc oxide, can be applied after cleansing and gently drying the skin (AHCPR, 1992). Indwelling Foley catheters should only be used on a short-term basis and avoided if at all possible as a result of the risk of urinary tract infection (Sanders, 1992). Thought must be given as to the reason for a catheter and if the benefit of placement outweighs the risk of infection. With implementation of regular checks every 1 to 2 hours to keep skin clean and dry, and use of absorbent pads and topical barriers, catheter placement can be avoided, thus reducing client risk.

Skin injury from friction or shearing forces can be avoided by using proper turning techniques and proper placement. Friction injuries can be prevented by using proper transfer techniques and a drawsheet. Lubricants, topical barrier creams, film or hydrocolloid dressings, or protective padding can be used to reduce damage when skin moves across a coarse or hard surface. Shearing occurs when the body shifts and slides downward; therefore most shearing injuries can be eliminated with proper placement. For example, not elevating the head of the bed greater than 30 degrees and elevating knees slightly when the head is elevated prevent slipping down in bed. When sitting in a chair, placing the feet on a stool prevents sliding downward (AHCPR, 1992; Bryant et al, 1992; Sanders, 1992).

Nutritional status must be closely monitored by assessing caloric intake, weight, serum albumin, cholesterol, and total lymphocyte count. Accurate food intake should be monitored routinely to identify both the need for changes before a compromised state develops, and nutritionally at-risk clients. Hydration status is another important nutritional component to monitor since dehydration can contribute to development of a pressure ulcer. An older adult requires a minimum of 2,000 to 2,500 ml of water a day unless contraindicated such as in congestive heart failure or renal failure (Burnside, 1988). When the professional nurse recognizes a pattern of decreased food or water intake, a full assessment is warranted addressing food preferences, dentition, and swallowing difficulties. The client should also be evaluated for constipation or fecal impaction, which decreases appetite. A dietary consultation may be needed, as well as

BOX 28-12

Pressure Ulcer Prevention Points

I. Risk assessment

1. Consider all bed- or chair-bound persons, or those whose ability to reposition is impaired, to be at risk for pressure ulcers.
2. Select and use a method of risk assessment, such as the Norton scale or the Braden scale, that ensures systematic evaluation of individual risk factors.
3. Assess all at-risk patients at the time of admission to health care facilities and at regular intervals thereafter.
4. Identify all individual risk factors (decreased mental status, moisture, incontinence, nutritional deficits) to direct specific preventive treatments. Modify care according to the individual factors.

II. Skin care and early treatment

1. Inspect the skin at least daily, and document assessment results.
2. Individualize bathing frequency. Use a mild cleansing agent. Avoid hot water and excessive friction.
3. Assess and treat incontinence. When incontinence cannot be controlled, cleanse skin at time of soiling, use a topical moisture barrier, and select underpads or briefs that are absorbent and provide a quick drying surface to the skin.
4. Use moisturizers for dry skin. Minimize environmental factors leading to dry skin such as low humidity and cold air.
5. Avoid massage over bony prominences
6. Use proper positioning, transferring and turning techniques to minimize skin injury due to friction and shear forces.
7. Use dry lubricants (cornstarch) or protective coverings to reduce friction injury.
8. Identify and correct factors compromising protein/calorie intake and consider nutritional supplementation/support for nutritionally compromised persons.
9. Institute a rehabilitation program to maintain or improve mobility/activity status.
10. Monitor and document interventions and outcomes.

III. Mechanical loading and support surfaces

1. Reposition bed-bound persons at least every 2 hours, chair-bound persons every hour.
2. Use a written repositioning schedule.
3. Place at-risk persons on a pressure-reducing mattress/chair cushion. Do not use donut-type devices.
4. Consider postural alignment, distribution of weight, balance and stability, and pressure relief when positioning persons in chairs or wheelchairs.
5. Teach chair-bound persons, who are able, to shift weight every 15 minutes.
6. Use lifting devices (e.g., trapeze or bed linen) to move rather than drag persons during transfers and position changes.
7. Use pillows or foam wedges to keep boney prominences such as knees and ankles from direct contact with each other.
8. Use devices that totally relieve pressure on the heels (e.g., place pillows under the calf to raise the heels of the bed).
9. Avoid positioning directly on the trochanter when using the side-lying position (use the 30° lateral inclined position).
10. Elevate the head of the bed as little (maximum 30° angle) and for as short a time as possible.

IV. Education

1. Implement educational programs for the prevention of pressure ulcers that are structured, organized, comprehensive and directed at all levels of health care providers, patients, family and caregivers.
2. Include information on:
   a. Etiology of and risk factors for pressure ulcers
   b. Risk assessment tools and their application
   c. Skin assessment
   d. Selection/use of support surfaces
   e. Development/implementation of individualized programs of skin care
   f. Demonstration of positioning to decrease risk of tissue breakdown
   g. Accurate documentation of pertinent data
3. Include built-in mechanisms to evaluate program effectiveness in preventing pressure ulcers.

From National Pressure Ulcer Advisory Panel's Summary of the AHCPR Clinical Practice Guideline: *Pressure ulcers in adults: prediction and prevention,* AHCPR Pub No 92-0047, Rockville, Md., May 1992.

nutritional supplements. Weight changes slowly; therefore weighing the client monthly is sufficient and is needed more frequently only when assessing cardiovascular status. A weight loss of 5% to 10% is significant and a weight loss of one third of the ideal body weight (IBW) is an ominous sign (Lipkin, 1990; Morley, 1990).

A serum albumin of 3 gm/100 ml or lower is associated with protein malnutrition and increased morbidity and mortality (Bernard, Jacobs, Rombeau, 1986; Pinchcofsky-Devin 1990; Stotts, Whitney, 1990). Malnutrition is also correlated with a low total lymphocyte count (TLC), which is calculated by the following formula:

$$\text{TLC/ml} = \frac{\text{\% of lymphocytes} \times \text{WBC (white blood count)}}{100}$$

A TLC of 800 to 1,200 is indicative of moderate malnutrition and a count below 800 is classified as severely malnourished (Bernard et al, 1986; Pinchcofsky-Devin, 1990; Pinchcofsky-Devin, Kaminski, 1986). Pinchcofsky-Devin and Kaminski (1986) demonstrated a relationship between pressure ulcers and a TLC below 1,200. Serum protein and TLC are valid nutritional indicators for pressure ulcer development. Serum cholesterol is another nutritional parameter to monitor. Several studies have demonstrated a positive correlation between nursing home residents' and hospitalized clients' mortality and serum cholesterol below 120 to 150 mg/100 ml (Noel, Smith, Ettinger, 1991; Rudman, Feller, 1989). Therefore a serum cholesterol below 150 mg/100 ml warrants aggressive nutritional support.

Because of multiple risk factors and their synergistic effect on pressure ulcer development, prevention is a nursing challenge, offering an opportunity to demonstrate the impact of nursing by recognizing at-risk clients, immediately implementing prevention strategies, and preventing a costly health care problem. Most of all, prevention measures promote and provide quality client care, which is the primary goal of nursing care (Box 28-12).

Pressure Ulcer Management

Nurses play a key role in pressure ulcer management, since they are the professionals responsible for wound care and often the first team members to identify wound changes. In addition, the professional nurse, especially in long-term care, is perceived by physicians as an expert in pressure ulcer management. It is not uncommon for physicians to say, "Do whatever treatment you think is best." Often, the physician or advance practice nurse, when assessing medical management, asks the nurse to describe and to evaluate the treatment. Therefore it is important for the professional nurse to comprehend the healing process, to understand treatment strategies, and to maintain a current knowledge base. The following chapter discussion reviews the healing trajectory and treatment options, which include nutritional management. It is hoped the professional nurse will become empowered, will promote a positive image for nursing, and most importantly, be able to deliver more successful client care by comprehending the healing process physiology and the logic for treatment strategies.

Physiology of Wound Healing

An understanding of the healing process is necessary to critically analyze pressure ulcer care and determine the best management strategy. Pressure ulcer research has expanded our understanding of the etiology of pressure ulcers and the healing process. A brief overview of the healing trajectory follows.

There are three major stages of wound healing—inflammatory stage; proliferative, or granulation, stage; and maturation, or matrix formation stage. The inflammatory stage, characterized by redness, heat, pain, and swelling, lasts approximately 4 to 5 days. The inflammatory stage initiates the healing process by stabilizing the wound through platelet activity that stops bleeding and triggers the immune system. Neutrophils, monocytes, and macrophages arrive within 24 hours of the insult to control bacteria, to remove dead tissue, and to secrete angiogenesis factor (AGF) and other growth factors, which stimulate the development of granulation tissue. Bradykinin and histamine, released from injured cells, cause vasodilation, which leads to swelling. This creates the red, swollen, tender, clinical presentation often seen in wounds (Cooper, 1992; Cooper, 1990; Doughty, 1992; Wysocki, 1989). The inflammatory stage is crucial for successful healing, with a delayed or altered response possibly contributing to the development of chronic, stagnant wounds if appropriate growth factors and responses were not mobilized when first injured. Medications (i.e., steroids), decreased tissue oxygenation, poor nutritional status, and aging (i.e., decreased response of the immune system) can impair this stage.

The proliferative, or granulation, stage begins 24 hours after injury and continues up to 22 days. Three significant events occur—epithelialization, granulation, and collagen synthesis. Epithelialization, via a microscopic epithelial layer, seals and protects the wound from bacteria and fluid loss. This microscopic layer, which is fostered by a moist environment, is extremely fragile and can easily be washed away with aggressive wound irrigation or by harshly wiping the involved area. Granulation, also known as neovascularization, is the formation of new capillaries that generate and feed new tissue, creating a beefy-red tissue bed that bleeds easily. Collagen synthesis creates a support matrix that provides strength to the new tissue. Oxygen, iron, vitamin C, zinc, magnesium, and amino acids are necessary for collagen synthesis. Fibroblasts, stimulated in the first phase by AGF, are

BOX 28-13

Staging Criteria

Stage I

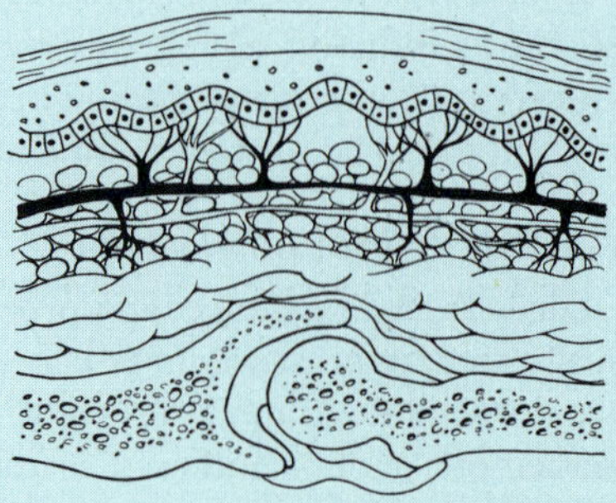

Nonblanchable erythema of intact skin; the heralding lesion of skin ulceration.

Stage II

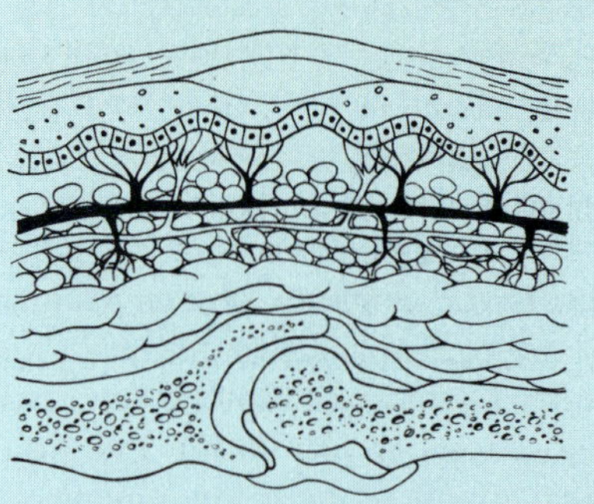

Partial thickness skin loss involving epidermis and/or dermis. The ulcer is superficial and presents clinically as an abrasion, blister, or shallow crater.

Stage III

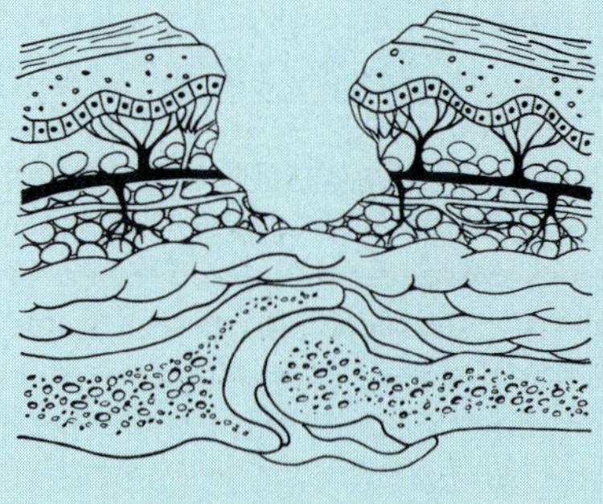

Full-thickness skin loss involving damage or necrosis of subcutaneous tissue, which may extend down to, but not through, underlying fascia. The ulcer presents clinically as a deep crater with or without undermining of adjacent tissue.

Stage IV

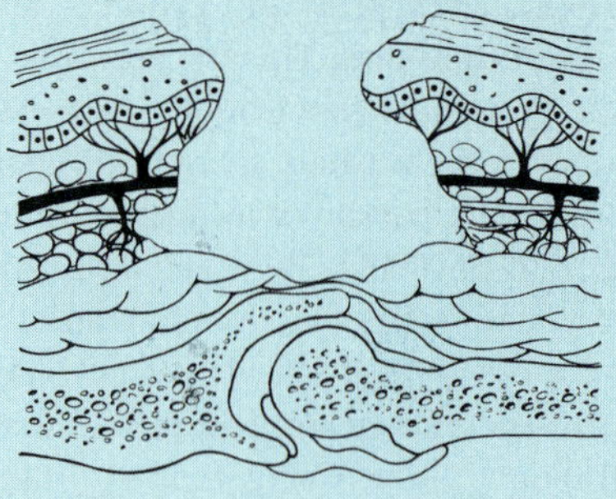

Full-thickness skin loss with extensive destruction, tissue necrosis, or damage to muscle, bone, or supporting structures (e.g., tendon, joint capsule, etc.) NOTE: undermining and sinus tracts may also be associated with stage IV pressure ulcers.

From Agency of Health Care Policy and Research: *Pressure ulcers in adults: prediction and prevention,* Clinical Practice Guideline, No. 3, Rockville, Md., 1992, US Department of Health and Human Services.

necessary for collagen production (Cooper, 1990; Doughty, 1992; Sieggreen, 1987; Wysocki, 1989). Therefore this phase rebuilds the injured area and can easily be influenced by the effectiveness of the inflammation stage and wound environment.

The maturation stage, also known as the differentiation or remodeling phase, is the final stage. It does not begin until 21 days after injury and can take up to 2 years to complete. During this stage maximum tensile strength is generated through collagen deposits that make the wound thicker, and more compact. These collagen deposits contract until closure is attained. Initially, the scarred area is a dark, scarlet-red color that fades over time to a silvery white color. Tensile strength only reaches 80% of preinjury capacity; therefore the "scarred" area is more vulnerable to breakdown or injury (Cooper, 1990; Sieggreen, 1987; Wysocki, 1989).

Definition of Terms and Staging Criteria

A pressure ulcer is "any lesion caused by unrelieved pressure resulting in damage of underlying tissue" and is usually over bony prominences (AHCPR, 1992).

The recommended staging criteria established by the National Pressure Ulcer Advisory Panel in 1989 has been adopted by AHCPR clinical practice guidelines (Box 28-13). If an ulcer is covered with eschar, a stage cannot be determined until the eschar is removed. See Box 28-14 for definitions of terms.

Basic Principles of Pressure Ulcer Management

Three basic principles guide successful pressure ulcer management:

1. Eliminate or minimize precipitating factors such as pressure, friction, shearing, and poor nutrition
2. Provide nutritional support and monitor nutritional status
3. Create and maintain a clean, moist wound environment with adequate circulation and oxygenation

The professional nurse is instrumental in ensuring the implementation of the above principles, which are necessary for successful healing.

Pressure ulcer prevention strategies must be implemented or wound care efforts are futile (see Box 28-12, p. 798). Through institutional policy and protocol, the professional nurse applies an appropriate mattress overlay without waiting for a physician's order. The professional nurse ensures proper technique is used by all staff when repositioning a client to minimize shearing and friction forces. As leader of the nursing team, the professional nurse is responsible for observing nursing aides

BOX 28-14

Definitions of Terms

Autolysis: Self-debridement of necrotic tissue by white blood cells, which is fostered by a dressing that retains moisture (e.g., transparent film); NOTE: A yellowish brown fluid is generated as a result of the white blood cells and breakdown of tissue

Debride: Removal of dead, damaged tissue

Epithelialization: Microscopic layer that covers an open wound, which creates a barrier that protects from fluid loss and bacterial assault; is very fragile and easily destroyed

Eschar: Thick, necrotic, devitalized tissue; often black in color, but can be yellowish.

Exudate: Wound discharge that can be serosanguinous, serous, or purulent

Friction: Rubbing of skin against another surface such as sheets, bed, chair, etc.

Granulation tissue: New capillary growth that creates a beefy-red color and tissue that bleeds easily (friable)

Interface pressure: Force exerted between body and support surface (e.g., mattress)

Pressure ulcer: Lesion caused by unrelieved pressure that causes tissue damage and death. Usually occurs over bony prominences or other pressure points (e.g., tubing, foreign material in bed, etc.).

Reactive hyperemia: Transient, blanching erythema from tissue anoxia, which generates a compensatory mechanism resulting in dilated vessels

Shearing force: Sliding of parallel surfaces when skeletal frame and deep fascia slide downward; the superficial fascia remains attached to the dermis, thus stretching or occluding arterial supply to fascia and muscle, which can lead to tissue anoxia and damage; most common position for this occurrence is when the head of the bed is elevated and the body slides downward

Sinus tract: Vertical tunnel connecting one anatomic compartment with another

Tissue tolerance: Skin's (i.e., blood vessels, interstitial fluid, collagen, and other structures) ability to endure effects of pressure without adverse consequences

Undermining: Separation of tissue under dermis creating a *horizontal* tunnel; can be measured by inserting cotton-tip applicator into tunnel, marking length on applicator, then placing next to tape measure to determine length of tunnel

Modified from Bryant RA et al: Pressure ulcers. In Bryant RA: *Acute and chronic wounds: nursing management,* St. Louis, 1992, Mosby; Agency of Health Care Policy and Research: *Pressure ulcers in adults: prediction and prevention,* Clinical Practice Guideline, No. 3, Rockville, Md., 1992, US Department of Health and Human Services; Sanders SL: *J Am Acad Nurse Pract* 4(3):101-106, 1992b.

or other support team members who deliver hands-on care to identify specific learning needs so pressure, shearing, and friction are minimized. Teaching the logic for such techniques can motivate staff to exercise more diligence in performing proper preventive actions. Teaching principles such as repetition of key information presented in a nonthreatening manner must be used. The professional nurse should reinforce appropriate activity with positive feedback. Prevention strategies then become a routine, which demonstrates and enhances the power of nursing.

Nutritional status should be followed with the physician or advance practice nurse monitoring serum albumin levels, weight, and food consumption so needs can be identified immediately. This also promotes a collaborative team effort among health care providers. When food intake is first noted to decrease, the professional nurse should identify reasons, such as not meeting food preferences, sore mouth, being rushed to eat, conflict with staff, depression, or pain.

For closure of the wound/ulcer, a clean, moist environment must be created and maintained. This principle, which has been scientifically established, is the key to successful healing and should guide the professional nurse and practitioner. Consequently, necrotic tissue must be removed and any infectious process (as seen by erythema, induration, and tenderness around the wound border; pus; or a pale wound bed) resolved to implement a dressing strategy that fosters rapid epithelialization and granulation.

It is important to know when to culture a wound because of the expense to the client and system. Also, inappropriate antibiotic use is decreased when wounds are cultured appropriately. All wounds are contaminated; therefore all cultures grow surface bacteria, and the true pathogen may not be identified. A culture is only warranted when cellulitis (i.e., erythema, induration, tenderness) or wound infection (evident by pale wound bed, pus, increased tenderness, persistent exudate, or no new growth) exists. To obtain an accurate culture, both anaerobic and aerobic cultures should be done (Alverez, Rozint, Wiseman, 1989; Baxter, Mertz, 1990; Doughty, 1992; Kertesz, Chow, 1992). The most accurate method, considered the gold standard for pressure ulcer cultures, is to obtain a tissue or needle aspiration biopsy (Kertesz, Chow, 1992). Per the AHCPR treatment guidelines, an ulcer is *not* to be cultured using a culturette, because colonized bacteria can be obtained, rather than the offending pathogen. An infected wound is either managed topically with antiseptics, or systemically, depending on the severity and risk of osteomyelitis.

Great controversy exists regarding the use of antiseptic solutions such as Betadine or acetic acid, because of their cytotoxic effects. Some authorities strongly believe that any solution that cannot be put in the eye should not be used, regardless of the wound condition, even if it is grossly infected. Antiseptic solutions should only be used when the wound is obviously infected, *never* on a healthy, granulating ulcer. Infection and associated stress on the wound are just as destructive, and maybe more so, as any antiseptic. The management goal must be kept in mind—to obtain a clean wound bed. If an antiseptic can facilitate the achievement of this wound environment, then it should be tried, especially if it means a client does not have to be admitted to a hospital or receive IV antibiotic therapy. The key to successful use of any antiseptic agent is discontinuing it when purulent discharge or signs of infection have resolved, so tissue destruction is minimal.

Antiseptic solutions are used with wet-to-dry dressings, which also provide some mechanical debridement. At times, a wound may be irrigated with the antiseptic; however, a rinse with normal saline should follow. The most common antiseptics are povidone-iodine, acetic acid, hydrogen peroxide, and sodium hypochlorite (also known as Dakin's or chloropactin). All four solutions are cytotoxic and destroy fragile epithelial tissue and fibroblasts. Povidone-iodine with *long-term* use or when *undiluted* can cause systemic iodine toxicity, which is evident by an unpleasant brassy taste, burning in the mouth or throat, sore gums and teeth, increased salivation, head and cold symptoms (rhinitis), gastric irritation, diarrhea, and occasional fever; it has been known to lead to death (Andrews, 1994; Goodman et al, 1990). The key to successful use of povidone-iodine is dilution; to use only a short term (3 to 5 days); and never to use on a healthy, granulating wound bed. Acetic acid is recommended for wounds infected with *Pseudomonas,* evident by a malodorous, green discharge, and/or positive culture. Hydrogen peroxide provides some debridement by effervescent action and is believed by many sources to cause gas embolism in tunneling wounds; however, this has not been supported with scientific data. It would be prudent not to use hydrogen peroxide in a sinus tract or deep, cavitous wound. A study involving antiseptics revealed hydrogen peroxide did not alter bacterial growth (Mertz et al, 1990). Sodium hypochlorite, which is essentially diluted Clorox, can affect clotting abilities and also burn intact healthy tissue not protected with zinc oxide. Second-degree burns have been witnessed from Dakin's solution that was inadvertently splashed on the skin surrounding a wound. Regardless of the solution, it should be used only during time of infection and wound stress. If the professional nurse notices antiseptic use has continued over 1 week, a reminder or question should be posed to the physician or advance practice nurse.

The first step in pressure ulcer management is to thoroughly assess the wound to determine the most effective strategy and dressing. The professional nurse is usually the first person to identify a need for change; therefore this assessment should be an ongoing process. Examine the wound noting its color, any discharge, bleeding, odor, degree of undermining, or presence of a sinus tract (can be measured using a cotton-tipped applicator), any necrotic tissue, pain or tenderness, and amount of erythema surrounding wound edges. Erythema around the wound is a normal phenomenon that signifies increased circulation to provide nutrients; however, if the erythema extends, infection or candidiasis should be suspected and the wound closely monitored. Ideally, the wound base should be a beefy-red color, which is indicative of granulation. However, some hydrogel and hydrocolloid dressings generate a pale pink wound bed, which usually means an "ill" wound bed. If the bed is pale pink and not associated with a purulent discharge or cellulitis, the wound environment is most likely clean and should just be observed. Note that granulation tissue has a rich capillary supply and bleeds easily and profusely when disturbed (e.g., when irrigated or dressing changed). Thus if a tunneling wound bleeds, it can be deduced that granulation tissue exists, although it is not visible as a result of the tunneling.

The wound assessment should be ongoing and supported with documentation. All new wounds should be described including color, discharge, tenderness, amount of necrotic tissue and/or undermining, dimensions, and stage. The wound measurements should include length, width, and depth. When measuring undermining, use a cotton-tipped applicator, marking depth on the applicator and placing next to a tape measure to obtain dimension and to note position (e.g., 4 cm at 2 O'CLOCK). It is not imperative all dimensions or locations of undermining be documented. Record only the greatest length since the wound cannot be deemed healed until closed. It is recommended that a written procedure stating how dimensions should be obtained and documented (e.g., length × width × depth × undermining) be developed to establish continuity and minimize confusion regarding the procedure.

Debridement For new, healthy tissue to develop, a clean, moist wound bed must be present. Infection decreases collagen synthesis and destroys epithelial tissue. Moist, necrotic tissue provides a perfect medium for bacteria and delays the inflammatory response, negatively affecting the healing trajectory (Doughty, 1992; Sanders, 1992). Therefore necrotic tissue must be debrided as soon as possible, and measures taken to resolve bacterial insults, such as Betadine wet-to-dry dressings, or topical antimicrobials until purulent discharge has dissipated. If necrotic tissue is not debrided, the nurse's efforts are futile and the client's comfort and quality of life are affected.

The removal of dry, hard eschar should be considered, since its presence slows the migration of epithelial cells and delays healing (Alvarez et al, 1989), except for stable heel ulcers, in which case dry eschar should be left intact (AHCPR, 1995). At times this dry eschar can serve as an efficient and comfortable dressing, but the area must be watched for development of infection. If the client has diabetes or has an ischemic wound with a dry, hard, intact eschar, it may be more prudent to leave the eschar in place. It serves as a barrier and does not place the client at risk for any possible problems from frequent dressing changes (e.g., infection, skin tears, candidiasis). The eschar must be monitored though. If it becomes soft and mushy, purulent discharge is most likely accumulating and will need to be removed. This is especially true if the wound is tender or has erythema indicating infection.

The three methods of debridement include mechanical, chemical, and surgical. Mechanical debridement (wet-to-dry dressings and/or whirlpool) is effective for removing slimy or stringy exudate that cannot be removed surgically or chemically (because of damage to viable tissue). If mechanical debridement using wet-to-dry dressings is employed, protect wound borders from maceration with zinc oxide or stoma adhesive. Whirlpool, either QD or BID, can mechanically debride and should be reserved for large, exudating wounds; it should be discontinued after the wound is clean or demonstrates stability. Mechanical debridement requires more nursing time, is more uncomfortable for the client, and destroys fragile epithelial cells. For these reasons, a more efficient method should be sought first.

Chemical debridement is costly ($20 to over $60 per tube) and time-consuming; however, it can be effective on small, necrotic areas or for removing yellow, tender eschar that is difficult to remove surgically. Chemical debridement is primarily used in the home setting or nursing home where appropriately educated or certified professionals are not readily accessible to surgically debride at the bedside. Chemical debridement may save the client from hospital admission. If used, the chemical enzyme *must not* be applied on healthy, viable tissue since the enzyme will destroy granulation tissue and epithelial cells. Be sure to read storage instructions for debriding enzymatics; some have to be refrigerated.

If the wound has a dry, rubbery eschar, surgical debridement is recommended over chemical debridement since chemical debridement takes much longer. The main principle that guides surgical debridement is to stop when bleeding occurs, indicating viable, healthy tissue has been reached. Since the wound is dirty, aseptic technique is appropriate. To prevent "showering" of bacteria from surgical debridement and to assist in cleaning up the wound, wet-to-dry dressings moistened with an antiseptic such as Betadine can be done every shift for 1 to 3 days, depending on the wound condition.

Hydrocolloid or hydrogel dressings can soften and facilitate removal of eschar if the wound is not infected.

TABLE 28-4

Type of Dressings

Advantages	Drawbacks	Contraindications
Gauze		
Allows for mechanical debridement via wet-to-dry dressing method Protects dry, healing wounds Serves as filler dressing for dead space Absorbs exudate Assists with cleaning up wound; manages exudate	Requires more frequent dressing changes Requires securing with tape or film Requires loose packing, or creates pressure and possibly enlarges the wound Destroys fragile epithelial cells and slows down healing, especially when gauze dries out	Use on a healthy, granulating wound unless moistened with saline or other noncytotoxic solution; even then fragile epithelial cells may be destroyed Use on dry, necrotic tissue, unless keeping eschar in place for protection (appropriate only when no signs of infection exist)
Nonadherent dressings or semipermeable polyurethane foam		
Decreases trauma to wound base and fragile epithelial cells, since does not adhere to tissue/wound base Protects dry, healing wound Has minimal to moderate absorption ability, particularly foam type, which can prevent or decrease maceration Insulates wound, particularly foam type (provides comfort)	Requires securing with tape or film Usually requires daily to Q shift dressing changes	Not appropriate for mechanical debridement, since does not adhere Use on a healthy, granulating wound unless a topical agent (i.e., bacitracin) is used Use on dry, necrotic tissue, unless keeping eschar in place for protection (appropriate only when no signs of infection exist)
Transparent film dressings		
Retains moisture, is semipermeable and comfortable Is water resistant, thus can seal and secure other dressings Allows easy inspection to monitor for complications Fosters autolysis as a result of moisture retention Minimizes friction injury when applied to vulnerable areas (e.g. elbows, coccyx, heels)	Can be difficult to apply Can leak	Use on infected or cellulitic wounds Use on thin, friable skin surrounding wound edges that cannot be protected with stoma adhesive (risk of creating other open wounds and/or skin tear) Use on exudative wounds
Hydrocolloidal dressings		
Retains moisture, which facilitates granulation and is comfortable Provides a water and bacteria barrier, which provides wound protection Requires less frequent dressing changes, which promotes efficient use of nursing time and comfort to the client Promotes removal of dry necrotic eschar when left in place for several days	Melt-out occurs, creating foul odor and possible leakage Unable to visibly monitor wound Can cause hypergranulation tissue (leafy, friable, beefy-red granulation tissue), which impedes healing and usually requires debridement/removal with sharp instrument or silver nitrate Is expensive, but requires fewer dressing changes	Use on infected or cellulitic wounds Use on thin, friable skin surrounding wound edges (more damage may be created when wafer removed) Use on heavy exudating wounds
Hydrogels		
Provides moisture, which facilitates granulation Facilitates some debridement for wounds with thin, stringy yellow eschar	Must use another product to keep in place and secure with tape or film	Use on heavy exudating wounds Use on cellulitic wound Use on wound with purulent discharge

TABLE 28-4

Type of Dressings—cont'd

Advantages	Drawbacks	Contraindications
Hydrogels—cont'd		
Promotes removal of dry necrotic eschar when dressing left in place for several days Nonadherent surface, which provides comfort to client Requires less frequent dressing changes, which promotes efficient use of nursing time and comfort to the client	Can cause hypergranulation tissue (leafy, friable, beefy-red granulation tissue), which impedes healing and usually requires debridement/removal with sharp instrument or silver nitrate Is expensive, but requires fewer dressing changes	

The body's own enzymes provide additional debriding and cleansing, which is known as autolysis (Alverez, Rozint, Wiseman, 1989; Doughty, 1992; Sanders, 1992). An occlusive dressing, such as a film or hydrocolloid dressing, facilitates autolysis (Alverez, Rozint, Wiseman, 1989). Note that autolysis creates a larger-appearing wound, since debris is being removed. Autolysis generates a brownish-yellow fluid that may have some pus in it as a result of dead cells and neutrophils. Do not become alarmed unless there is clinical evidence of infection (i.e., erythema, tenderness, heat, swelling).

Dressings: Care Principles and Types

The wound care market is a billion dollar business and has created many dressing options (Thompson-Bishop, Mottola, 1992). Therefore the professional nurse must have an understanding of the healing trajectory to select the best treatment option. The major goal is to create an environment that supports healing—a clean, moist, ulcer bed. The most efficient dressing strategy should be sought not only for time management purposes, but also for client comfort. If growth is neither visible nor evident in weekly measurements after 3 to 6 weeks, consideration should be given to changing the dressing strategy. A brief overview of the various dressing categories and general treatment principles is provided (Table 28-4).

With each dressing change, all open wounds should be *gently* irrigated with approximately 20 to 50 cc of normal saline using either a catheter tip syringe, a butterfly tubing with the needle cut off and connected to a Luer-lock syringe, or a syringe with a 19-gauge needle. However, if irrigation is too forceful, healing can be delayed because of the removal of fragile epithelial cells, which are the foundation for granulation tissue formation. After irrigation, the wound can be assessed.

It is prudent practice to always write the date and time of the dressing change on the outside of the dressing itself. This practice reflects professional accountability and assists in problem solving. For example, a wound having more discharge or a significant change may be related to the dressing not being changed soon enough or inadvertently not changed.

If the wound border has candidiasis, evident by a fire-red erythema usually with satellite lesions and denuded skin, a zinc oxide/nystatin (50/50) mixture can be applied on affected areas, then the dressing applied. Since candidiasis flourishes in a moist environment, a thoughtful assessment should be done to identify the reason for excess moisture. Is a moist dressing, such as gauze, overlapping on the wound edges? Is the film dressing generating so much fluid retention and maceration that candidiasis is occurring? If so, the zinc oxide/nystatin cream could be applied and the wound monitored. It may be that the dressing type needs to be changed. After the candidiasis has resolved, a stoma adhesive wafer can be placed around the wound to protect the skin from future problems. Stoma adhesive is recommended over a hydrocolloid dressing because tape and film dressings do not stick to the stoma adhesive barrier as they do to a hydrocolloid wafer. If no infection exists, another alternative that decreases maceration is to apply Vaseline or zinc oxide around the wound borders and to then apply the dressing.

Gauze dressings have been used for many years with success; however, there has been an explosion of scientific information regarding pressure ulcers and wound care since 1962, when moisture was first identified as a facilitator of healing. This discovery has generated many other effective and efficient options. Gauze disturbs the fragile epithelial layer, and so can impair or delay the healing process. Since there are so many effective, comfortable options available, gauze is primarily used for debriding and cleaning up a wound bed, except when used for protecting closed surgical wounds. However, when a wound has tunneling or undermining, saline-moistened gauze, *loosely* packed into the wound, can maintain a moist environment. Caution should be exercised not to pack tightly or have the moistened gauze touching the healing surface surrounding the ulcer to avoid additional damage and maceration. For large wounds/ulcers that require many 4 × 4s, a gauze roll (Kerlix) can be used, which decreases the risk of inadvertently leaving dressing material in the wound. If gauze is being used on a clean wound, the strategy should be wet-to-moist dressing to prevent drying of epithelial cells. Slightly moisten the gauze covering the wet gauze, touching the wound bed with normal saline. Place a dry gauze, or abdominal pad over the moist gauze and secure with tape. This should keep the wound moist at all times.

Some gauze is impregnated with material such as saline, povidone-iodine, or Vaseline. The hypertonic saline gauze (Mesalt) is an exudate absorber and assists in cleaning up wounds. After the exudate has diminished, a less harsh wound care product should be employed (e.g., a hydrogel). Gauze ribbons impregnated with povidone-iodine (Iodoform gauze) are effective for cleaning up a tunneling wound that has purulent or foul exudate. However, the povidone-iodine gauze should be stopped when the purulent foul exudate has resolved, so healthy tissue is not destroyed. It should not be used for a long period due to the risk of iodine toxicity and cytotoxic (destroys cells) properties. It is the practice of this author to not use Betadine on a wound for more than 3 to 5 days. Vaseline gauze is a good, inexpensive method for keeping a wound from drying out and protecting the wound and surrounding tissue. Vaseline gauze secured with Kerlix wrapped around the extremity, changed every 2 to 4 days and PRN is an effective strategy for healing skin tears. The Vaseline keeps the wound moist and provides protection from further insults.

Nonadherent dressings such as Telfa are used when the wound bed needs to be protected and epithelial cells not disturbed. Nonadherent dressings are suitable for skin tears, skin grafts, or other wounds that require minimal insult. Often, an antibiotic ointment is applied to the wound bed (which keeps it moist), then it is covered with a nonadherent dressing, and changed once or twice a day.

Foam dressings, which are nonadherent, absorbent dressings, protect an ulcer and assist in minimizing maceration of ulcer edges. In addition, foam dressings are comfortable. Foam dressings have also been used around tracheas; they are beneficial when candidiasis exists around tracheal stomas, acting to absorb moisture. Foam dressings are secured with tape or film and may be used in combination with hydrogels.

Transparent films are used for stage I or II pressure ulcers (superficial wounds), to secure dressings, to protect vulnerable areas from friction (i.e., elbows), and to facilitate autolysis. Transparent films, such as Opsite or Tegaderm, are semipermeable, thus allowing exchange of air. Film dressings can be left on for 3 to 7 days, but should be checked a minimum of once a day. When using film on fragile wounds such as skin tears, it is left in place till it comes off in order not to disturb or enlarge the wound. Film dressings facilitate autolysis, which causes fluid buildup, and consequently can lead to maceration of good tissue and dressing leakage. Vaseline or zinc oxide applied around the ulcer edges before placement of the film may prevent maceration.

Hydrocolloids such as DuoDERM are sticky, nonpermeable wafers containing a hydrocolloid material that eventually melts, combines with natural body fluids, and keeps the wound bed moist. The nonpermeable wafer also serves as a barrier and creates an hypoxic wound environment that stimulates granulation, as long as peripheral circulation provides enough oxygen (Alverez, Rozint, Wiseman, 1989; Doughty, 1992). Hydrocolloid wafers also protect high friction areas (e.g., elbows, coccyx, heels), thereby preventing further breakdown. When erythema is noted, especially in a vulnerable area or at pressure points, a hydrocolloid dressing can serve as a protective barrier; however, the progress of stage I ulcers is not easily monitored unless the wafer is removed. In addition, hydrocolloid dressings should not be used if candidiasis exists. Hydrocolloid wafers are usually changed every 3 to 7 days. It should be noted that a foul, sour odor is generated by hydrocolloid dressings, which is considered normal. Infection is present when erythema, warmth, tenderness or purulent discharge exists. After gently irrigating the wound base with normal saline, observe for purulent exudate and changes in the wound base. Hydrocolloid dressing should *never* be applied to ulcers that are infected, have purulent discharge, or when infection is suspected. The occlusive, moist environment provides a perfect medium for bacterial growth and worsens the infection.

Hydrogels are comprised primarily of water and are effective by maintaining a moist ulcer bed, which fosters healing. Hydrogels are also more comfortable for the client. Some hydrogels have debridement properties and are promoted as being safe on mildly infected wounds. However, caution should be exercised by close daily monitoring when using hydrogels on infected wounds. The moist, sealed environment can promote bacterial growth. After applying the gel with either a tongue blade (gently without disturbing fragile wound base) or with a 20- to 50-ml syringe filled with the gel, the site can be covered with gauze or a foam dressing such as Allevyn or LYOfoam, then secured with film (durable, moisture barrier yet not very permeable) or paper tape (more permeable but not as enduring). Foam dressings sealed with film cause minimal maceration. Because of reasons not completely understood, hypergranulation, evident by

PRESSURE ULCER

Clinical situation Mrs. P is an 82-year-old widowed homemaker who developed stage IV pressure ulcers on her coccyx and right ischium while recently hospitalized for congestive heart failure. Her decreased appetite and poor food intake, which resulted in a serum albumin level of 2.7 and cholesterol count of 128; her compromised cardiovascular state associated with a 12 lb weight gain; and initially not being placed on a mattress overlay led to the development of the pressure ulcers. The wounds were debrided and are beginning to granulate, her food intake and her stamina have increased, and her cardiovascular status has stabilized with resolution of the edema. Mrs. P was discharged home with home health care to monitor the wounds' progress and change the dressings.

Mrs. P has a strong desire to stay at home and maintain as much independence as possible. Currently Mrs. P has a home health aide coming into her home three times a week to assist her with bathing and personal care. Meals on Wheels is providing one meal, 5 days per week. The home health nurse is visiting every other day to do wound care and monitor her cardiovascular status. Mrs. P has three children, however, only one daughter, Mrs. V, lives locally. Mrs. V works full-time, and is an active parent of three children ages 11, 13, and 17. Mrs. V's husband is a busy professional who supports her involvement in her mother's care, yet is not able to assist her much with transporting their children to their activities or with her mother's care needs. The daughter is trying to support her mother's strong desire to stay at home.

The coccyx and ischial pressure ulcer are clean, are beginning to granulate, and are managed with a hydrogel, covered with a foam dressing to lessen maceration, and sealed with a transparent dressing that is changed every other day. It is estimated that complete healing will take 6 to 8 months, as long as nutritional status and other prevention strategies are maintained.

Nursing diagnosis	Outcome	Interventions
Impaired skin integrity related to alteration in nutritional state, altered circulation and immobilization	Mrs. P will have intact skin as evident by clean, healing wounds; circulation to skin maintained; laboratory values WNL	Implement pressure ulcer prevention strategies to create an environment that will foster healing and prevent further development of ulcers: Place mattress overlay on bed and obtain appropriate pressure relieving chair cushion to decrease ischial pressure. Teach client and family to lay out at 30-degree angle and support extremities with pillow when lying in bed to lessen trochanter pressure. Teach client, family, and nurses' aide to avoid hot baths and harsh soaps, use moisturizers for dry skin, not to massage over bony prominences, and drink a minimum of 2000 cc of water/fluids a day; monitor cardiovascular status for volume excess. Teach client not to sit at 45 to 90-degree angle when in bed or on couch to minimize shearing forces. Assess and treat incontinence by cleansing skin at the time of soiling, use a topical moisture barrier, and if necessary absorbent underpads or briefs to maintain a dry surface and decrease risk of additional skin breakdown. Inspect skin during home visit, observing for any pressure points, evident by erythema or skin breakdown. If stage I or II ulcer present, apply film or hydrocolloidal dressing to protect from further breakdown, if no infection of site is present.

Continued.

PRESSURE ULCER—cont'd

Nursing diagnosis	Outcome	Interventions
		Assess pressure ulcer when changing dressing, noting wound bed and border color, discharge, and general condition. Document each assessment and measure weekly. If wound bed is infected or cellulitic, as seen by erythema, tenderness, pale granulation tissue, or purulent discharge, change dressing to wet-to-dry with an antiseptic, only until wound is improved and not longer than 5 to 7 days to minimize damage to viable tissue. If wound is stagnate as documented with serial dimensions over 3 to 6 weeks, then consider changing to another dressing strategy. Monitor nutritional status, since it can influence skin integrity and healing process: Monthly weight monitoring gains or losses. 24-hour diet recall with each visit to assess eating habits and nutritional intake. Teach client and family the role nutrition plays with healing and general health status. Explain need of minimum fluid intake of 2000 cc/day; monitor carefully due to history of congestive heart failure. If weight loss is experienced, interview client to determine reason (i.e., food preferences not met, food cold or aesthetically unappealing, etc.). Examine oral cavity and if appropriate denture fit. As a result of hypoproteinemia, promote nutritional supplementation with high-caloric milk drink, such as 2 cal HN or Ensure Plus HN, or with ice cream milk shake with carnation drink mix to provide high level of carbohydrates and protein. Maintain a clean, moist wound environment to foster healing: If necrotic tissue present, facilitate debridement by arranging physician, nurse practitioner, or certified enterostomal therapist to perform bedside debridement. If only a small amount of necrotic tissue, chemical or mechanical debridement could be tried. Select most comfortable, economic, and efficient dressing, such as a hydrogel or hydrocolloidal dressing, with the intent of maintaining a moist wound environment, which fosters granulation, thus healing. Use clean technique for dressing care, sterile technique is not necessary since the wound is dirty. Gently irrigate wound with normal saline to clean wound, make appropriate assessment, and measure wound dimensions weekly. Teach client and family dressing care and changing technique to involve in care and to promote self-care.

TABLE 28-5

General Pressure Ulcer Care Guidelines

Stage	Actions	Dressing options
I	Implement prevention strategies (e.g., mattress overlay, nutritional assessment; reinforce value of turning, keeping dry, and minimizing friction)	Can protect with film or hydrocolloid
II and III	Implement prevention strategies, assess for infection, debride necrotic tissue, conduct nutritional assessment, and provide appropriate nutritional support	Can use film, if clean, depending on depth; hydrocolloid; hydrogel, wet-to-moist dressing; if infected, manage topically with antiseptic and wet-to-dry dressing until infection resolved and not > 5 days
IV	Same as above; specialized bed may be considered	If clean, hydrogel, hydrocolloid paste and wafer, or wet-to-moist dressing; if infected, manage topically with antiseptic and wet-to-dry dressing until infection is resolved and not > 5 days

development of red, leafy, friable tissue, can occur. The dressing strategy should be changed to one that does not maintain a hydrophilic state so hypergranulation tissue does not recur. Dressings using a hydrogel can be left in place for 1 day or up to 5 to 7 days, depending on the setting, product, and ulcer state (Table 28-5) (see nursing Care Plan pp. 807-808).

HOME CARE TIPS

1. Regularly assess for signs and symptoms of skin breakdown in the homebound older adult who is at high risk for the development of a pressure ulcer.
2. Assess for and instruct the caregiver and homebound older adult on factors that predispose to the development of a pressure ulcer.
3. Use the services of a wound care clinical nurse specialist in assessing, planning, and recommending appropriate wound care management techniques.
4. Prevention is the first line strategy for pressure ulcer care. Teach the caregiver of an at-risk homebound older adult the techniques for preventing a pressure ulcer—focusing on preventing moisture, avoiding friction and shear, changing position frequently, and assuring excellent nutritional intake.

Summary

Pressure ulcers are a costly health care problem, not only in terms of dollars, but also in nursing time and human lives. Prevention is the first-line defense for pressure ulcer development. Nursing has an opportunity to demonstrate the profession's power and accountability by implementing prevention strategies, and thereby having a positive impact on a client's quality of life, while preventing a costly health care problem. It is imperative the nurse conduct pressure ulcer risk assessments, use mattress overlays, teach support staff prevention and management techniques, monitor client's nutritional status, and serve as a role model by focusing on prevention. With expanded pressure ulcer knowledge and the publication of the AHCPR clinical guidelines, prevention measures are a nurse's responsibility.

Vital to successful healing is establishing a collaborative relationship with the physician and advance practice nurse, so collectively, the most efficient and effective strategies can be used. Collaboration develops trust and professional maturity, and is necessary for growth in our strained health care system.

Successful pressure ulcer management requires the application of the principles of healing, which should guide selection of treatment strategies. Frequent review of the healing trajectory, when reinforced with clinical examples, facilitates comprehension of this complex process. Pressure ulcer management is a science and an art that requires experience before the nurse feels competent.

Key Points

- As a result of normal, age-related changes in the skin, an older adult is more susceptible to skin tears and bruising caused by thinning of skin.
- An older adult is at greater risk for hypothermia, shearing, pressure damage, and blunt trauma as a result of decreased subcutaneous tissue.
- An older adult can experience altered medication absorption as a result of an age-related decrease in fatty tissue and dermis blood supply.
- An older adult is at increased risk of heat stroke as a re-

sult of the compromised cooling mechanism from decreased sweating.

- Typical locations for seborrheic dermatitis are the scalp margins progressing downward to eyebrows, base of eyelashes, around nose in a butterfly pattern, ears, and sternum.
- Pruritus warrants a full skin assessment, since it can be indicative of many diseases, drug reactions, and possibly cancer. Determine location, intensity, alleviating and aggravating events, onset, and what the client is doing to control it.
- Candidiasis, recognized by fire-red, denuded skin with satellite macules or pustules, develops in moist interiginous areas.
- Herpes zoster's prodromal is itching or burning along a dermatome, followed by a unilateral, band-like maculopapular rash and vesicles, which rarely crosses the midline.
- Notify physician or advance practice nurse if the following lesions are found on assessment of actinic keratosis: BCC, SCC, and melanoma.
- Venous hypertension leads to the formation of a capillary fibrin cuff, which causes chronic edema, decreased circulation, and recurring medial lower leg ulcers.
- Arterial ulcers are usually located on toes or feet and are associated with pain during activity, nighttime, and rest. The cause of decreased arterial blood flow must be corrected for ulcers to heal.
- Diabetic neuropathic ulcers are usually located on the plantar foot and heal if circulation is not impaired.
- Pressure ulcers are costly to humans, the health care system, and in nursing time. Prevention is the first line strategy for pressure ulcer care.
- Assess nutritional status of clients with pressure ulcers with monthly weight and laboratory parameters (serum albumin should not be checked more often than once every 6 weeks) and closely monitor food consumption.
- To minimize friction use sheets to pull the client up in bed and apply a film or hydrocolloid dressing to vulnerable areas such as elbows, coccyx, and heels.
- To minimize shearing forces, do not elevate head of the bed greater than 30 to 45 degrees and raise legs to keep the client from sliding down.
- Antiseptic solutions such as Betadine or acetic acid should be used only when the wound is infected; they should never be used on a clean, healthy wound since they are cytotoxic and destructive to tissue.
- Surface cultures have been shown to grow different organisms than what is in underlying tissues and blood cultures, thus routine wound cultures are not appropriate.

Critical Thinking Exercises

1. Outline major teaching points that would be beneficial to the integumentary health of older individuals.
2. A 69-year-old man has a history of basal cell carcinoma. After having a lesion removed from his scalp 2 years ago, he has been extremely anxious about other skin lesions and skin changes. What approach would you take to help your client reduce his anxiety and yet remain active in the prevention and early recognition of skin cancer?

REFERENCES

Agency of Health Care Policy and Research: *Treatment of pressure ulcers,* Clinical Practice Guideline, No. 3, Rockville, Md., 1994, US Department of Health and Human Services.

Agency of Health Care Policy and Research: *Pressure ulcers in adults: prediction and prevention,* Clinical Practice Guideline, No. 3, Rockville, Md., 1992, US Department of Health and Human Services.

Allman RM. In Hazzard WR et al, editors: *Principles of geriatric medicine and gerontology,* ed 2, New York, 1990, McGraw-Hill Information Services Co.

Alverez O, Rozint J, Wiseman D: Moist environment for healing: matching the dressing to the wound, *Wounds* 1(1):35-51, 1989.

Andrews LW: The perils of povidone-iodine use, *Ostomy/Wound Management* 23(1):68-72, 1994.

Baker SR et al: Epidemiology of chronic venous ulcers, *Br J Surg* 78:864-864, 1991.

Balin AK. In Evans JG, Williams TF, editors: *Oxford textbook of geriatric medicine,* New York, 1992, Oxford University Press.

Balin AK. In Hazzard WR et al, editors: *Principles of geriatric medicine and gerontology,* ed 2, New York, 1990, McGraw-Hill.

Baxter C, Mertz P: Local factors that affect wound healing. In Eaglstein W et al, editors: *New directions in wound healing,* Princeton, N.J., 1990, ER Squibb.

Bergstrom N et al: The Braden Scale for predicting pressure sore risk, *Nurs Res* 36(4):205-210, 1987.

Bobel LM: Nutritional implications in the patient with pressure sores, *Nurs Clin North Am* 22(2):379-389, 1987.

Braden BJ, Bergstrom N: Clinical utility of the Braden Scale for predicting pressure sore risk, *Decubitus* 2(3):44-51, 1987.

Braden BJ, Bryant RA: Innovations to prevent and treat pressure ulcers, *Geriatr Nurs* 11(4):182-186, 1990.

Browse NL, Burnand KG: The cause of venous ulceration, *Lancet* 2(8292):243-245, 1982.

Bryant RA et al, In Braynt RA, editor: *Acute and chronic wounds nursing management,* St. Louis, 1992, Mosby.

Burnside IM: *Nursing and the aged,* ed 3, New York, 1988, McGraw-Hill.

Callen JP. In Friedman RJ et al, editors: *Cancer of the skin,* Philadelphia, 1991, WB Saunders.

Caro WA. In Orkin M, Maibach HI, Dahl MV, editors: *Dermatology,* Norwalk, Conn, 1991, Appleton & Lange.

Clark RA, Hopkins TT. In Moschella SL, Hurley HJ, editors: *Dermatology,* ed 3, Philadelphia, 1992, WB Saunders.

Cooper DM. In Bryant RA editor: *Acute and chronic wounds,* St Louis, 1992, Mosby.

Cooper DM: Optimizing wound healing, *Nurs Clin North Am* 25(1):164-179, 1990.

Dalziel KL, Bickers DR. In Brocklehurst JC, Tallis RC, Fillit HM, et al: *Textbook of geriatric medicine and gerontology,* ed 4, New York, 1992, Churchill Livingstone.

Davis C. In Carnevali DL, Patrick M, editors: *Nursing management for the elderly,* ed 3, Philadelphia, 1993, JB Lippincott.

Doughty DB. In Bryant RA, editor: *Acute and chronic wounds,* St. Louis, 1992, Mosby.

Dzubow L, Grossman D. In Moschella SL, Hurley HJ, editors: *Dermatology,* ed 3, Philadelphia, 1992, WB Saunders.

Ebersole P, Hess P: *Toward healthy aging: human needs and nursing response,* ed 4, St. Louis, 1994, Mosby.

Falanga V, Eaglstein WH: Management of venous ulcers, *Am Fam Pract* 33(2):274-280, 1986.

Falanga V, Eaglstein WH: The "trap" hypothesis of venous ulceration, *Lancet* 341(8851):1006-1007, 1993.

Fenske NA, Lober CW. In Moschella SL, Hurley HJ, editors: *Dermatology* ed 3, Philadelphia, 1992, WB Saunders.

Fitzpatrick JE: Stasis ulcers: update on a common geriatric problem, *Geriatrics* 44(10):19-31, 1989.

Fitzpatrick TB et al: *Color atlas and synopsis of clinical dermatology,* ed 2, New York, 1992a, McGraw-Hill.

Fitzpatrick TB et al. In Balch CM et al, editors: *Cutaneous melanoma,* Philadelphia, 1992b, JB Lippincott.

Flam E: Skin maintenance in the bed-ridden patient, *Ostomy/Wound Management* 28:48-54, 1990.

Forse RA, Shizgal HM: Serum albumin and nutritional status, *J Parenter Enter Nutr* 4:450-454, 1980.

Goldman MP, Fronek A: Consensus paper on venous leg ulcer, *J Dermatol Surg Oncol* 18:592-602, 1992.

Gosnell DJ: Pressure sore risk assessment: a critic. I. The Gosnell scale, *Decubitus* 2(3):32-38, 1989.

Gosnell DJ: Assessment and evaluation of pressure sores, *Nurs Clin North Am* 22(2):399-415, 1987.

Habif TP: *Clinical dermatology: a color guide to diagnosis and therapy,* ed 2, St. Louis, 1990, Mosby.

Jakubovic HR, Ackerman AB. In Moschella SL, Hurley HJ, editors: *Dermatology* ed 3, Philadelphia, 1992, WB Saunders.

Jarratt ML. In Orkin M, Maibach HI, Dahl MV, editors: *Dermatology,* Norwalk, 1991, Appleton & Lange.

Jester J, Weaver V: A report of clinical investigation of various tissue support surfaces used for the prevention, early intervention and management of pressure ulcers, *Ostomy/Wound Management* 19(1):39-45, 1990.

Kertesz S, Chow AW: Infected pressure and diabetic ulcers, *Clin Geriatr Med* 8(4):835-851, 1992.

Koh HK, Bhawan J. In Moschella SL, Hurley HJ, editors: *Dermatology,* ed 3, Philadelphia, 1992, WB Saunders.

Kosiak M: Etiology and pathology of ischemic ulcers, *Arch Phys Med Rehabil* 40(2):62-69, 1958.

Krasner D: Resolving the dressing dilemma: selecting wound dressings by category, *Ostomy/Wound Manag* 35(4):62-70, 1991.

Krasner D, editor: *Chronic wound care,* King of Prussia, Pa., 1990, Health Management Publications.

Krouskop TA, Garber SL, Cullen BB. In Krasner D, editor: *Chronic wound care: a clinical source book for healthcare professional,* King of Prussia, Pa., 1990, Health Management Publications.

Landis EM: Micro-injection studies of capillary blood pressure in human skin, *Hear* 15(209), 1930.

Lamberg SL. In Barker LR, Burton JR, Zieve PD, editors: *Principles of ambulatory medicine,* Baltimore, 1991, Williams and Wilkins.

Lang PG, Maize JC. In Friedman RJ et al, editors: *Cancer of the skin,* Philadelphia, 1991, WB Saunders.

Levine JM: Historical notes on pressure ulcers: the cure of Ambrose Pare, *Decubitus* 5(2):23-26, 1992.

Lipkin EW. In Hazzard WR et al, editors: *Principles of geriatric medicine and gerontology,* ed 2, New York, 1990, McGraw-Hill Information Services Co.

Lookingbill DP, Marks JG: *Principles of dermatology,* Philadelphia, 1986, WB Saunders.

Maklebust J: Pressure ulcers: etiology and prevention, *Nurs Clin North Am* 22(2):359-377, 1987.

Mayberry JC et al: Fifteen-year results of ambulatory compression therapy for chronic venous ulcers, *Surgery* 109(5):575-581, 1991.

McCulloch JM, Hovde J. In Kloth LC, McCulloch JM, Feedar JA, editors: *Wound healing: alternatives in management,* Philadelphia, 1990, FA Davis.

Meehan M: Multisite pressure ulcer prevalence survey, *Decubitus* 3(2):14-17, 1990.

Mertz PM et al: The wound environment: implications from research studies for healing and infection. In Krasner D, editor: *Chronic wound care,* King of Prussia, Penn., 1990, Health Management Publications.

Montes LF. In Moschella SL, Hurley HJ, editors: *Dermatology,* ed 3, Philadelphia, 1992, WB Saunders.

Morley JE. In Hazzard WR et al: *Principles of geriatric medicine and gerontology,* ed 2, New York, 1990, McGraw-Hill.

Newman DK, Smith DAJ: *Geriatric care plans,* Springhouse Pa, 1991, Springhouse.

Noel MA, Smith TK, Ettinger WH: Characteristics and outcomes of hospitalized older patients who develop hypocholesterolemia, *J Am Geriatr Soc* 39(5):455-461, 1991.

Norton D: Calculation of the risk: reflections on the Norton Scale, *Decubitus* 2(3):24-31, 1989.

Parker F. In Orkin M, Maibach HI, Dahl MV, editors: *Dermatology,* Norwalk, 1991, Appleton & Lange.

Partsch H: Compression therapy of the legs, *J Dermatol Surg Oncol* 17:799-805, 1991.

Pinchcofsky-Devin GD. In Krasner D, editor: *Chronic wound care: a clinical source book for healthcare professionals,* King of Prussia, Pa., 1990, Health Management Publications.

Pinchcofsky-Devin GD, Kaminski MV: Correlation of pressure sores and nutritional status, *J Geriatr Soc* 34(6):435-440, 1986.

Reiber GE, Pecoraro RE, Keopsell TD: Risk factors for amputation in patients with diabetes mellitus, *Ann Intern Med* 117(2):97105, 1992.

Rousseau P: Pressure sores in the elderly I. *Geriatr Med Today* 7(2):28, 34-36, 1988.

Ruberg RL: Role of nutrition in wound healing, *Surg Clin North Am* 64(4):705-714, 1984.

Rudman D, Feller AG: Protein-calorie undernutrition in the nursing home, *J Am Geriatr Soc* 37(2):173-183, 1989.

Sanders SL: Pressure ulcers, part I: prevention strategies, *J Am Acad Nurse Pract* 4(2):63-70, 1992a.

Sanders SL: Pressure ulcers, part II: management strategies, *J Am Acad Nurs Pract* 4(3):101-106, 1992b.

Seidel HM et al: *Mosby's guide to physician examination,* ed 2, St Louis, 1991, Mosby.

Seiler WO, Stahelin MB: Decubitus ulceration in the elderly. In Katz PR, Calkins E, editors: *Principles and practice of nursing home care,* New York, 1989, Springer.

Sieggreen MY: Healing of physical wounds, *Nurs Clin North Am* 22(2):439-447, 1987.

Stotts NA, Whitney JD: Nutritional intake and status of clients in the home with open surgical wounds, *J Comm Health Nurs* 7:77-86, 1990.

Thiers BH, Sahn D. In Moschella SL, Hurley HJ, editors: *Dermatology,* ed 3, Philadelphia, 1992, WB Saunders.

Thomspon-Bishop JY, Mottola CM: Tissue interface pressure and estimated subcutaneous pressure of 11 different pressure-reducing support surfaces, *Decubitus* 5(2):42-48, 1992.

Trelease CC. In Krasner D, editor: *Chronic wound care a clinical source book for healthcare professionals,* King of Prussia, Pa, 1990, Health Management Publications.

Wade JC: *Present day management of varicella zoster.* Presented at Infectious Diseases in Everyday Medicine, Baltimore, April 19-20, 1993.

Wysocki AB: Surgical wound healing, *AORNJ* 49(2):502-518, 1989.

Wysocki AB. In Bryant RA, editor: *Acute and chronic wounds,* St Louis, 1992, Mosby.

Young EM, Newcomer VD: *Geriatric dermatology,* Philadelphia, 1993, Lea & Febiger.

Zink M, Rousseau P, Holloway GA. In Bryant RA, editor: *Acute and chronic wounds,* St. Louis, 1992, Mosby.

BIBLIOGRAPHY

Bernard JD: In Moschella SL, Hurley HJ, editors: *Dermatology,* ed 3, Philadelphia, 1992, WB Saunders.

Bobel LM: Nutritional implications in the patient with pressure sores, *Nurs Clin North Am* 22(2):379-389, 1987.

Burtis G, Martin S: *Applied nutrition and diet therapy,* Philadelphia, 1988, WB Saunders.

Frantz RA, Kinney CK: Variables associated with skin dryness in the elderly, *Nurs Res* 35(2):98-100, 1986.

Gilman AG et al: *The pharmacological basis of therapeutics,* New York, 1990, Pergamon Press.

CHAPTER 29

Sensory Function

LEARNING OBJECTIVES

On completion of this chapter, the reader will be able to:

1. Describe age-related changes in the senses.
2. Compare and contrast cataracts and glaucoma and the associated nursing interventions.
3. Compare and contrast retinal disorders and the medical and nursing management of each disorder.
4. Identify nursing interventions for the older person with low vision.
5. Describe the proper method for instilling eye medications.
6. Describe the proper method for removing impacted cerumen.
7. Identify safety measures for a client with vertigo.
8. Identify nursing interventions for a client with xerostomia.
9. Describe potential hazards for an older person with diminished senses of vision, hearing, and touch.
10. Conduct sensory system assessment and describe normal findings.
11. Describe aural rehabilitation methods to use with people who are hearing impaired.
12. Identify how activities of daily living (ADLs) are affected by sensory changes.

The senses provide a link with the outside world. They allow individuals to receive and interpret various stimuli, thus enabling interaction with the environment. Sensory changes can have a great impact on the quality of life for older adults. Visual and hearing impairments may interfere with communication, social interactions, and mobility, leading to social isolation. Olfactory, gustatory, and tactile deprivations can lead to nutritional problems and safety hazards. It is important to understand the sensory changes associated with aging to help older adults adapt and function as independently as possible.

The senses are the means by which the brain receives information about the surrounding world. In the past, five senses were recognized: sight, hearing, taste, smell, and touch. Today, additional senses are recognized and categorized into two major groups: general and special. General senses include the senses of touch, pressure, pain, temperature, vibration, and proprioception. General senses are further classified as somatic (those providing sensory information about the body and environment) or visceral (those providing information about internal organs). Special senses are produced by highly localized organs and specialized sensory cells. These include the sense of sight, hearing, taste, smell, and balance.

Sensation, or perception, is the conscious awareness and interpretation of sensory stimuli by sensory receptors. The brain receives stimuli from both inside and outside the body. Conscious sensation perception occurs via action potentials generated by receptors that reach the cerebral cortex.

VISION

Vision plays an integral part in a person's ability to function in the surrounding world. Visual acuity is imperative to the execution of daily activities; dressing, cooking, sewing, driving, and reading are all tasks that use eyesight. Much of the world around us is detected by the visual system, which includes the eyes, the accessory structures, and the optic nerves, tracts, and pathways. The accessory structures include the eyebrows, eyelids, eyelashes, and tear glands; together these function to help protect the eyes from direct sunlight and damaging materials. The eyes respond to light and initiate impulses that are transmitted to the brain by the optic nerves and tracts.

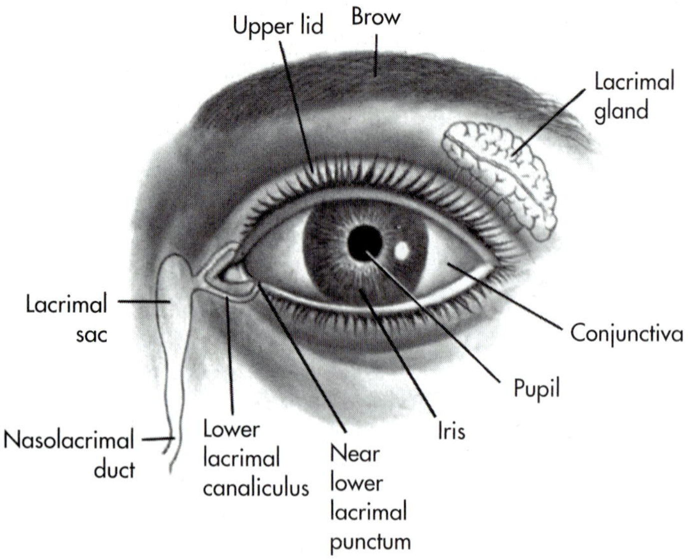

Fig. 29-1 The right eye and its accessory structures. (From Thompson JM et al.: *Mosby's clinical nursing,* ed 3, St. Louis, 1993, Mosby.)

NORMAL STRUCTURE

Accessory Structures

Accessory structures (the external eye) protect, lubricate, move, and aid in the function of the internal eye. The eyebrows, eyelids, conjunctiva, lacrimal apparatus, and extrinsic eye muscles make up the accessory structures (Fig. 29-1). The eyebrows protect the eyes by preventing perspiration and direct sunlight from entering. The eyelids and eyelashes protect the eyeballs from foreign objects by reflexively blinking. Blinking also helps lubricate the eyes by spreading tears over the surface of the eyes. The conjunctiva is a thin, transparent mucous membrane lining the surface of the eyelids. The lacrimal apparatus consists of the lacrimal gland and drainage system. The lacrimal gland produces tears to moisten, lubricate, and wash away foreign objects in the eye. Tears evaporate, and excess moisture drains out into the nasal cavity.

Movement of each eyeball is controlled by six extrinsic eye muscles: the superior, inferior, medial, and lateral rectus muscles, and the superior and inferior oblique muscles. The movements of the eye resemble the letter *H,* and both eyes move in the same direction because the muscle of one eye works with the corresponding muscle of the other. These muscles are innervated by three cranial nerves: the trochlear nerve (IV), the abducens nerve (VI), and the oculomotor nerve (III).

Internal Eye

The eye is constructed in three layers (Fig. 29-2). The outer layer consists of the sclera and the cornea; the middle layer is composed of the choroid, the ciliary body, and the iris; and the inner layer is the retina.

The sclera, or "white" of the eye, is a firm, opaque, white outer layer composed of elastic and collagen fibers. The sclera gives shape to the eye, protects the internal structures, and provides attachment for the extrinsic muscles. The anterior portion of the sclera continues to form the cornea. The cornea is avascular and transparent, thus allowing light to enter the lens of the eye. The cornea aids in focusing by bending or refracting entering light.

The middle layer of the eye is called the vascular tunic because it contains the most blood vessels of the eyeball. This layer has two portions. The posterior portion is a thin membrane called the choroid, and the anterior structures consist of the ciliary body and the iris. The ciliary body contains outer ciliary muscles, which change the shape of the lens, and inner structures, which produce aqueous humor.

The iris is the pigmented disk that is the colored part of the eye. The iris is surrounded by smooth muscle with an opening in the center called the pupil. It regulates the

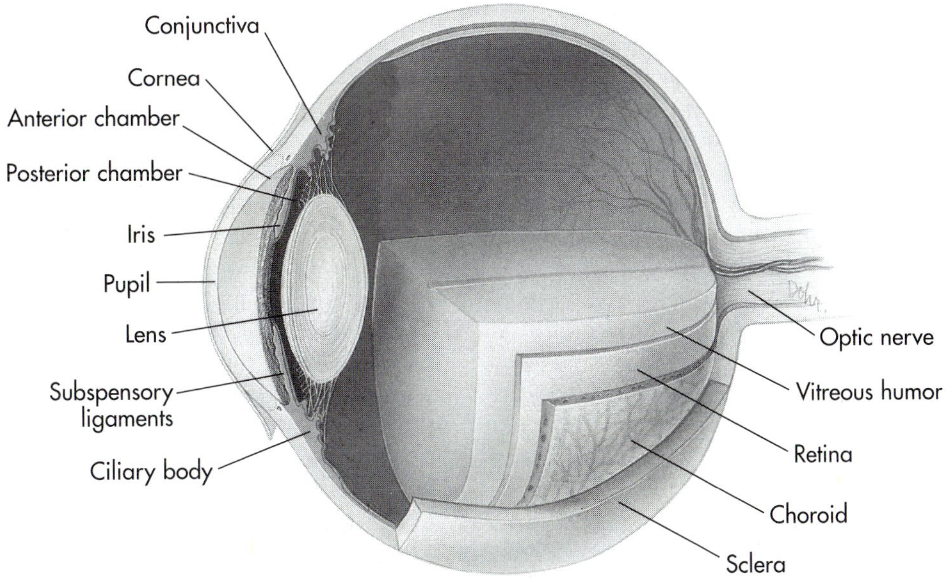

Fig. 29-2 Sagittal section of the eye demonstrating its layers. (From Seeley RR, Stephens TD, Tate P: *Anatomy and physiology,* ed 3, St. Louis, 1995, Mosby.)

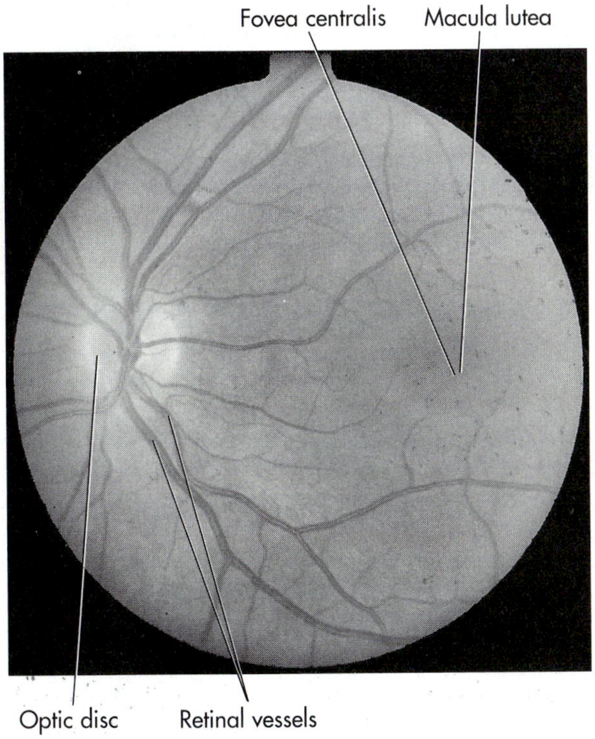

Fig. 29-3 Ophthalmoscopic view of the retina, showing the posterior wall of the retina as seen when looking through the pupil. Notice the vessels entering the eye through the optic disc (the optic nerve) and notice the macula lutea with the fovea (the part of the retina with the greatest visual acuity). (From Seeley RR, Stephens TD, Tate P: *Anatomy and physiology,* ed 3, St. Louis, 1995, Mosby.)

amount of light entering the eye by controlling the size of the pupil.

The retina is the innermost layer of the eye. It is formed by two layers: an inner sensory layer and an outer pigmented layer. The posterior region of the retina (the sensory portion) is the visual portion containing photoreceptor cells called rods and cones. Rods are involved in noncolor vision and vision under poor and changing lighting conditions. Cones are responsible for color vision and visual acuity. In an ophthalmoscopic examination, the following features of the retina can be examined: the macula, the portion of the retina with the greatest visual acuity (containing the greater number of cones and no rods); the optic disc; and the retinal blood vessels that emerge from the disc (Fig. 29-3).

Compartments of the Eye

Two major compartments are present in the eye: a smaller cavity anterior to the lens and a much larger cavity posterior to the lens. The lens separates the anterior compartment into two chambers: the anterior and posterior chambers. The anterior chamber lies in front of the iris and behind the cornea. The posterior chamber lies between the iris and the lens. Both chambers connect through the pupil and are filled with fluid called aqueous humor. This fluid helps maintain intraocular pressure, refract light, and provide nutrition for the inner eye structures. Aqueous humor is circulated in the eye, and if it is inhibited, glaucoma can result (see Glaucoma, p. 820).

The posterior cavity is much larger and is almost

completely surrounded by the retina. It is filled with a jellylike substance called vitreous humor. It maintains the shape of the eye and its internal structures and refracts light in the eye.

The lens is a transparent, biconvex structure lying behind the iris. The lens is suspended and moved by the muscles of the ciliary body. Changes in the shape (thickness) of the lens regulate the amount of light reaching the retina, which aids in focusing.

NORMAL FUNCTION

The eye acts like a camera. Light enters the eye through the iris. The cornea, lens, and fluids focus the light onto the retina. The retina then converts the light into impulses that are transmitted along the optic nerve and tract to the brain for interpretation (Seeley, Stephens, Tate, 1992).

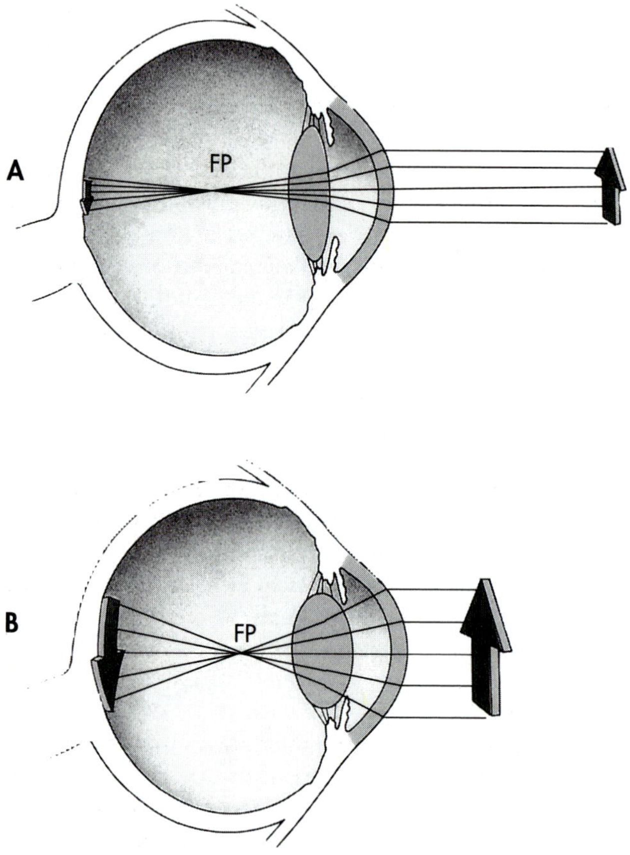

Fig. 29-4 Ability of the lens to focus images on the retina. The focal point (FP) is where light rays cross. **A,** Distant object: the lens is flattened, and the image is focused on the retina. **B,** Close object: the lens is more rounded and the image is focused on the retina. (From Seeley RR, Stephens TD, Tate P: *Anatomy and physiology,* ed 3, St. Louis, 1995, Mosby.)

The cornea, lens and aqueous fluids of the eye aid in focusing a clear image on the retina. Focusing in the eye is accomplished by changing the shape of the lens. When the ciliary muscles are relaxed, the choroid maintains tension on the lens, keeping it flat and allowing distant vision (Fig. 29-4A). When an object is brought closer than 20 feet to the eye, accommodation of the lens, constriction of the pupil, and convergence of the eyes bring the image into focus on the retina (Fig. 29-4B). The ciliary muscles contract and pull the choroid toward the lens, thus allowing the lens to assume a more spherical form. The convex lens then causes greater refraction of light, thereby completing the process of accommodation. Pupil constriction controls the depth of focus. A small pupillary opening allows a greater depth of focus. Pupillary diameter also regulates the amount of light entering the eye. Therefore more light is required when examining close objects. As an object moves closer, the eyes must rotate medially to keep the object in view in each eye. This process is called convergence. As light enters the eye, the focused image formed just past the focal point is inverted. However, the brain interprets the image as being right side up (Seeley, Stephens, Tate, 1992).

AGE-RELATED CHANGES IN STRUCTURE AND FUNCTION

Normal, age-related changes in the external and internal eye have been well documented. The eyeball sits in the ocular orbit, which is cushioned with fat that diminishes with aging and leads to drooping eyelids. Eyebrows may gray and become coarser in males, with outer thinning in both men and women. The conjunctiva thins and yellows in appearance. Additionally, this membrane may become dry because of diminished quantity and quality of tear production. The sclera may develop brown spots. The cornea yellows, and a noticeable surrounding ring (made up of fat deposits) called arcus senilis develops. The pupil decreases in size and loses its ability to constrict. Aging changes that decrease the size of the pupil and limit the amount of light entering the eye also occur in the iris. The lens increases in density and rigidity, affecting the ability of the eye to transmit and focus light. Ophthalmoscopic exam of the retina may reveal the following changes: blood vessels narrow and straighten, arteries may seem opaque and gray in color, and drusen, localized areas of hyaline degeneration, may be noted as gray or yellow spots near the macula (Lueckenotte, 1994).

Anatomic changes to the eye affect a person's visual ability, leading to potential problems in activities of daily living (ADLs). Light adaptation and visual fields are reduced. Therefore greater time is needed to adapt to changes in light intensities, and glare can cause pain and limit an individual's ability to identify objects. Peripheral vision is reduced, limiting the size of a visual field and adding to alterations in depth perception. The yellowing of the lens results in difficulty identifying certain colors, especially cool colors such as blue, green, and violet (Lueckenotte, 1994; Kart, Metress, Metress, 1992). These age-related changes in the older person's visual system lead to common complaints of increased glare, decreased visual acuity, and difficulty with light adaptation. Some of these complaints may indicate a more serious problem, such as cataract formation, and are discussed later in this chapter. Two common complaints of older adults, floaters and dry eyes, are discussed in the next section.

COMMON COMPLAINTS

Floaters and Flashers

Floaters appear as dots, wiggly lines, or clouds that a person may see moving in the field of vision. They become more pronounced when a person is looking at a plain background. Floaters occur more often after the age of 50 as tiny clumps of gel or cellular debris float in the vitreous humor in front of the retina. Floaters are caused by degeneration of the vitreous gel and are more common in older adults who have undergone cataract operations or yttrium aluminum garnet (YAG) laser surgery.

These floaters are normal and harmless, but they may be a warning sign of a more serious condition, especially if they increase in number and if there are changes in the type of floater, light flashes, or visual hallucinations. These symptoms may indicate a vitreous or retinal tear, which could lead to detachment. Additionally, visual hallucinations have been associated with a brain tumor or cortical ischemia. Therefore any of these symptoms warrant a complete eye examination by an ophthalmologist.

Flashers occur when the vitreous fluid inside the eye rubs or pulls on the retina and produces the illusion of flashing lights or lightning streaks. Flashers that appear as jagged lines, last 10 to 20 minutes, and are present in both eyes are likely to be caused by a spasm of blood vessels in the brain called a migraine. These flashers commonly occur with advancing age, but they warrant prompt medical attention if they increase in number, if a large number of new floaters appears, or if partial loss of side vision is noted (American Academy of Ophthalmology, 1992c).

The nurse should refer any client who experiences any of the above symptoms to an ophthalmologist for a comprehensive eye examination. If no cause is found for the floaters and flashers, then the nurse should teach the client about the condition and how to live with it. Clients should be taught to look up and down to get the floaters out of the field of vision. Additionally, the nurse should provide the client with the printed information instruction sheet, "Aging and Your Eyes," to learn more about floaters and flashers (Hogstel, 1992; Kollarits, 1992) (Box 29-1).

Dry Eyes

Dry eyes result as the quantity and quality of tear production diminish with aging. Stinging, burning, scratchiness, and stringy mucus are some of the symptoms. Surprisingly, increased tearing may be a symptom of dry eyes. If tear secretion is below normal, excess tears are produced by the lacrimal gland in response to irritation. If no foreign body is found, then it is called dry eye syndrome. Tear production decreases with age, and menopausal women are most often afflicted. Additionally, dry eyes can be associated with arthritis and certain medications. Treatment consists of tear replacement or conservation. Tears can be replaced by instilling an over-the-counter (OTC), artificial tear preparation to lubricate the eye and replace missing moisture. The tears may be used as often as necessary, especially before activities that require significant eye movement. Solid inserts that gradually release lubricants throughout the day are also available. An ophthalmologist can conserve the naturally produced tears by temporarily or permanently closing the lacrimal drainage system. Other methods of conservation include use of a humidifier when the heat is on, wrap-around glasses to reduce evaporation of eye moisture due to wind, and avoidance of smoke (American Academy of Ophthalmology, 1992b).

COMMON PROBLEMS AND CONDITIONS

Common problems related to the aging eye include presbyopia, ectropion and entropion, blepharitis, glaucoma, cataracts, retinal disorders, eye injuries, and visual impairment. Presbyopia is a normal change that occurs in the aging eye, but the remaining problems are eye diseases that are more prominent in older adults.

Presbyopia

The most common complaint of adults over the age of 40 is the diminished ability to focus clearly on close objects (arm's length), such as a newspaper. This is presbyopis, and it is not a disease but a degenerative change that occurs in the aging eye.

In **presbyopia** the lens loses its ability to focus on close objects. Accommodation is impaired as the lens thickens and loses its elasticity, and as the ciliary muscles weaken the lens' ability to contract is impaired. These changes in the lens lead to farsightedness, and therefore the affected older person holds objects at a distance to

BOX 29-1

Aging and Your Eyes

Poor eyesight is not inevitable with age. Some physical changes occur during the normal aging process that can cause a gradual decline in vision, but most older people maintain good eyesight into their 80s and beyond.

Older people generally need brighter light for such tasks as reading, cooking, or driving a car. In addition, incandescent light bulbs (regular household bulbs) are better than fluorescent lights (tubular overhead lights) for older eyes.

Certain eye disorders and diseases occur more frequently in old age, but a great deal can be done to prevent or correct these conditions. Here are some suggestions to help protect your eyes:

- Have regular health checkups to detect such treatable diseases as high blood pressure and diabetes, both of which may cause eye problems.
- Have a complete eye examination every 2 or 3 years since many eye diseases have no early noticeable symptoms. The examination should include a vision (and glasses) evaluation, eye muscle check, check for glaucoma, and thorough internal and external eye health exams.
- Seek more frequent eye health care if you have diabetes or a family history of eye disease. Make arrangements for care immediately if you experience signs such as loss or dimness in vision, eye pain, excessive discharge from the eye, double vision, or redness or swelling of the eye or eyelid.

Common eye complaints

Presbyopia (prez-bee-oh' pe-uh)—a gradual decline in the ability to focus on close objects or to see small print—is common after the age of 40. People with this condition often hold reading materials at arm's length, and some may have headaches or "tired eyes" while reading or doing other close work. There is no known prevention for presbyopia, but the focusing problem can be easily compensated for with glasses or contact lenses.

Floaters are tiny spots or specks that float across the field of vision. Most people notice them in well-lighted rooms or outdoors on a bright day. Although floaters are normal and are usually harmless, they may be a warning of certain eye problems, especially if associated with light flashes. If you notice a sudden change in the type or number of spots or flashes, call your doctor.

Dry eyes occur when the tear glands produce too few tears. The result is itching, burning, or even reduced vision. An eye specialist can prescribe special eyedrop solutions ("artificial tears") to correct the problem.

Excessive tears may be a sign of increased sensitivity to light, wind, or temperature changes. In these cases, protective measures (such as sunglasses) may solve the problem. Tearing may also indicate more serious problems, such as an eye infection or a blocked tear duct, both of which can be treated and corrected.

Eye diseases common in older adults

Cataracts are cloudy or opaque areas in part or all of the transparent lens located inside the eye. Normally, the lens is clear and allows light to pass through. When a cataract forms, light cannot easily pass through the lens, and this affects vision. Cataracts usually develop gradually, without pain, redness, or tearing in the eye. Some remain small and do not seriously affect vision. If a cataract becomes larger or denser, however, it can be surgically removed. Cataract surgery (in which the clouded lens is removed) is a safe procedure that is almost always successful. Cataract clients should discuss with their doctor the risks and benefits of this elective procedure. After surgery, vision is restored by using special eye-glasses or contact lenses or by having an intraocular lens implant (a plastic lens that is implanted in the eye during surgery).

Glaucoma occurs when there is too much fluid pressure in the eye, causing internal eye damage and gradually destroying vision. The underlying cause of glaucoma is often not known, but with early diagnosis and treatment it can usually be controlled and blindness prevented. Treatment consists of special eyedrops, oral medications, laser treatments, or in some cases surgery. Glaucoma seldom produces early symptoms and usually there is no pain from increased pressure. For these reasons, it is important for eye specialists to test for the disease during routine eye examinations in those over 35.

Retinal disorders are the leading cause of blindness in the United States. The retina is a thin lining on the back of the eye made up of nerves that receive visual images and pass them on to the brain. Retinal disorders include senile macular degeneration, diabetic retinopathy, and retinal detachment.

- Senile macular degeneration is a condition in which the macula (a specialized part of the retina responsible for sharp central and reading vision) loses its ability to function efficiently. The first signs may include blurring of reading matter, distortion or loss of central vision (for example, a dark spot in the center of the field of vision), and distortion in vertical lines. Early detection of macular degeneration is important since some cases may be treated successfully with laser treatments.
- Diabetic retinopathy, one of the possible complications of diabetes, occurs when small blood vessels that nourish the retina fail to do so properly. In the early stages of the condition, the blood vessels may leak fluid, which distorts vision. In the later stages, new vessels may grow and release blood

From U.S. Department of Health and Human Services: Aging and your eyes, *Age Page*, Public Health Service, 1983 National Institutes of Health.

BOX 29-1

Aging and Your Eyes—cont'd

into the center of the eye, resulting in serious loss of vision.

- Retinal detachment is a separation between the inner and outer layers of the retina. Detached retinas can usually be surgically reattached with good or partial restoration of vision. New surgical and laser treatments are being used today with increasing success.

Low-vision aids

Many people with visual impairments can be helped by using low-vision aids. These are special devices that provide more power than regular eyeglasses. Low-vision aids include telescopic glasses, light-filtering lenses, and magnifying glasses, along with a variety of electronic devices. Some are designed to be handheld; others rest directly on reading material. Partially sighted individuals often notice surprising improvements with the use of these aids.

For more information

The following organizations can send you more detailed information on eye care and eye disorders:

- Office of Scientific Reporting, National Eye Institute, Bldg 31, Rm 6A32, Bethesda, MD 20205. This institute, part of the federal government's National Institutes of Health, conducts and supports research on eye disease and the visual system. They can send you a list of free brochures on eye disorders.
- National Society to Prevent Blindness, 79 Madison Ave, New York, NY 10016. The Society has several free pamphlets on specific diseases affecting the eyes. To receive a free copy of their publication *The Aging Eye: Facts on Eye Care for Older Persons,* send them a self-addressed stamped envelope. They also have a *Home Eye Test for Adults* which is available for $1.00 (to cover the cost of postage and handling).
- American Foundation for the Blind, 15 West 16th St, New York, NY 10011. This organization can send you a list of their free publications on vision.
- Vision Foundation, 2 Mt Auburn St, Watertown, MA 02172. The Foundation has published a *Vision Inventory List,* which includes information on special products and services for visually impaired people. There is no charge for the *List.*
- Two professional societies gather, study, and publish eye care information: American Optometric Association, Communications Division, 243 North Lindbergh Blvd, St. Louis, MO 63141; and American Academy of Ophthalmology, 1833 Fillmore, PO Box 7424, San Francisco, CA 94120. Write to them for free information on eye care for older adults.

Publications

"Keeping an Eye on Glaucoma" is a reprint from the June 1979 issue of the *FDA Consumer.* It is available free from the Food and Drug Administration, 5600 Fishers Ln, Rockville, MD 20857. Please send your request on a postcard.

Cataracts: A Consumer's Guide to Choosing the Best Treatment is a large-print book available for $3.50 from the Public Citizen's Health Research Group, 2000 P St, NW, Suite 708, Washington, DC 20036.

clearly see them (Kart, Metress, Metress, 1992). Treatment involves wearing reading glasses or bifocals (two-part lenses that correct near and distant vision), and there is an excellent prognosis of corrected vision. Nursing care is aimed at encouraging the client to adjust to the glasses by wearing them and following up with a visit to the ophthalmologist every 2 years. Clients can be provided with an "Aging and Your Eyes" pamphlet for information about presbyopia.

Ectropion and Entropion

Ectropion and **entropion** are external eye conditions, specifically malpositions of the lower lid, that cause irritation to the eye. Ectropion (turning out) prevents normal closure and causes redness and tearing of the eyeball. Entropion (turning in) results in the eyelashes rubbing against the eye and causing corneal abrasion. Both conditions are caused by tissue laxity and scarring of the eyelids from infection.

Both can be treated by minor same-day outpatient surgery performed by an ophthalmologist. The prognosis for complete recovery and cessation of symptoms is excellent. Nurses need to assess older adults for these conditions, especially if they are complaining of dry, irritated eyes and excessive tearing (Lueckenotte, 1994; Hogstel, 1992).

Blepharitis

Blepharitis is a chronic inflammation of the eyelid margins that is more commonly found in older adults. Blepharitis can be caused by seborrhea (of the scalp, eyebrows, and eyelids) and infection, but both are usually found together. The use of antihistamines, anticholinergics, antidepressants, and diuretics can exacerbate this condition as a result of the drying effects of the medications. Additionally, the deficiency in tear production with aging can lead to infection. The symptoms include: red, swollen eyelids; matting and crusting along the base of the eyelash at margins; small ulcerations along lid margins; and complaints of irritation, itching, burning, tearing, and photophobia. Treatment is aimed at removing the bacteria and healing affected areas. Physicians may prescribe topical antibiotics or steroids. However, the nurse plays a large role in the treatment of this condition by teaching the client the following interventions. First, the client must be taught scrupulous eye hygiene, including good hand washing habits. Mild soap such as Ivory or Neutrogena should be used. Contact lens wearers must be taught proper cleaning and storage techniques to prevent contamination of the eye, lens, lens solution, and lens case. Since cosmetics are a common source of bacterial contamination, eye makeup products should be replaced every 3 to 6 months to avoid bacterial growth. It is also important that clients know to apply make-up with cotton balls and cotton-tipped applicators and to discard them after each use. Mascara should be water-resistant, free of lash-extending fibers, and not applied to the base of the lashes. Eyeliner should be a medium-hard pencil, and it should not be applied to the inner margin of the eyelid. Clients should avoid the use of aerosol hair sprays, since these can be irritating to the eyes. The inflammation and the client's comfort level will improve after a week of these hygienic practices. Blepharitis can be alleviated when nurses teach and reinforce the above procedures (Faherty, 1992).

Glaucoma

Glaucoma is the second leading cause of blindness in the United States and the first cause among African-Americans. The more common form has few if any symptoms and may cause partial visual loss before it is detected.

Glaucoma results from a blockage in the drainage of the fluid, the aqueous humor, in the anterior chamber of the eye (see Figure 29-2, p. 815). Normally this fluid drains through Schlemm's canal and is transported to the venous circulation system. If the fluid is formed faster than it can be eliminated, an increase in eye pressure results. Pressure is then transferred to the optic nerve where irreparable damage, possibly total blindness, can result. There are three types of glaucoma found in older adults: chronic open-angle glaucoma, angle-closure glaucoma, and secondary glaucoma.

Chronic Open-Angle Glaucoma

Chronic open-angle glaucoma, the most common type, (90% of all primary glaucoma) develops slowly. Degenerative changes in Schlemm's canal obstruct the escape of aqueous humor, resulting in increased intraocular pressure.

This type of glaucoma can damage vision so gradually and painlessly that a person is unaware of a problem until the optic nerve is badly damaged. Visual loss begins with deteriorating peripheral vision.

Angle-Closure Glaucoma

Angle-closure glaucoma is acute glaucoma that occurs suddenly as a result of complete blockage and requires

---

MEDICAL MANAGEMENT

Glaucoma

Diagnostic tests and procedures

People over 40 years of age should have yearly eye examinations that include the measurement of introcular pressure.

Subjective assessment, including family history (see Box 29-8, p. 829).

Tonometry to measure intraocular pressure.

Treatment

Open-angle glaucoma

Pharmacologic treatments are based on client's medical history and current condition.

- *Miotic drugs*—cause the pupil to contract and the iris to draw away from the cornea, allowing the fluid to drain. Examples: dipivefrin (Propine C Cap BID), pilocarpine, and physostigmine (eserine).
- *Carbonic anhydrase inhibitors*—decrease the production of aqueous humor.

  EXAMPLE: Acetazolamide (Diamox) and timolol (Timoptic).

  NOTE: Timolol should be used with caution in clients with congestive heart failure (CHF) and asthma.

The following types of surgery may be performed if medications are ineffective in controlling intraocular pressure: argon laser trabeculoplasty, trabeculectomy, cyclocryotherapy or sclerotomy. The two most common procedures, trabeculoplasty and trabeculectomy, are done with a laser. Trabeculoplasty involves the application of an argon laser on the trabecular meshwork. A nonpenetrating thermal burn that changes the meshwork configuration and leads to increased outflow of aqueous humor is produced. In trabeculectomy, an opening or fistula is made under a partial-thickness scleral flap.

Angle-closure glaucoma

Medications are given for emergency treatment, and if they are ineffective in lowering the intraocular pressure, laser iridotomy or iridectomy is necessary (Kollarits, 1990).

Prognosis

The prognosis is good if glaucoma is detected before vision loss occurs. Diagnosed clients have to follow a prescribed medication regimen daily for the rest of their lives. Once visual loss occurs, it is irreparable.

prompt medical attention to avoid severe vision loss or blindness.

The following symptoms of angle-closure glaucoma occur rapidly:

- Severe eye pain
- Redness in eye
- Clouded or blurred vision
- Nausea and vomiting
- Rainbow halos surrounding lights
- Pupil dilation
- Cornea appears steamy (Kart, Metress, Metress, 1992)

Secondary Glaucoma

Secondary glaucoma occurs when the drainage angle is damaged by eye injury or by other specific conditions, such as: injury, medication (such as steroids), tumors, inflammation, or abnormal blood vessels (American Academy of Ophthalmology, 1992d) (see Medical Management box, p. 820)

NURSING MANAGEMENT

ASSESSMENT

Clients with glaucoma may complain of dull eye pain, or they may experience no early symptoms. Visual field testing reveals loss of peripheral vision (tunnel vision) and an increased intraocular pressure on the ophthalmologic examination.

DIAGNOSIS

Potential nursing diagnoses for the client with glaucoma may include, but are not limited to (1) sensory perceptual alterations (visual) related to decreased peripheral vision; (2) knowledge deficit of glaucoma causes and treatments related to lack of exposure and inexperience; (3) pain related to increased intraocular pressure; (4) potential for infection related to eye drop instillation; and (5) dressing/grooming self care deficit related to visual impairment.

PLANNING

Expected outcomes for the client with glaucoma may include, but are not limited to, the following: (1) client will have no further loss of vision; (2) client will follow prescribed glaucoma care guidelines daily; (3) client will state that eye pain is decreased; (4) client will be free of eye infection; and (5) client will be able to perform ADLs safely and independently.

INTERVENTION

Nursing management is aimed at teaching the client that glaucoma is a chronic condition requiring continual lifelong medical treatment. Any current visual loss is permanent, and further loss can be prevented by following the care guidelines outlined in Boxes 29-2 and 29-3. If medication is unable to control rising intraocular pressure, then surgical intervention may be necessary.

Trabeculoplasty is usually performed on an outpatient basis and requires an intraocular pressure check 3 to 4 hours after surgery. A sudden rise in intraocular pressure can occur immediately after surgery. A 4-to-8 week wait is necessary to determine if the procedure was effective. However, continual use of glaucoma medications is necessary.

Trabeculectomy requires overnight hospitalization. Postoperative nursing care for the client who has had a trabeculectomy includes (1) routine postanesthesia care; (2) protection of the operative eye with an eye patch or a shield, proper positioning on the back or unoperative eye, and the use of a call light and siderails; (3) administration of pain medications and cold eye compress to maintain comfort; (4) monitoring the eye for increased intraocular pressure, bleeding, or infection; and (5) assistance and teaching of safe, independent performance of ADLs (Phipps, 1993b).

BOX 29-2

The Client With Glaucoma

1. Medical follow-up and eye medication will be required for the rest of life.
2. Eye drops *must* be continued as long as prescribed, even in the absence of symptoms.
   A. Blurred vision decreases with prolonged use.
   B. Avoid driving for 1 to 2 hours after administration of miotics.
3. To prevent complications:
   A. Press lacrimal duct for 1 minute after eye drop insertion to prevent rapid systemic absorption.
   B. Have a reserve bottle of eye drops at home.
   C. Carry eye drops on person (not in luggage) when traveling.
   D. Carry card or wear Medic-Alert bracelet identifying glaucoma and the eye drops solution prescribed.
4. Bright lights and darkness are not harmful.
5. There is no apparent relationship between vascular hypertension and ocular hypertension.
6. Report any reappearance of symptoms immediately to ophthalmologist.
7. If admitted to hospital for a different medical condition, alert staff of continued need to prescribed eye drops.
8. Avoid the use of mydriatic or cycloplegic drugs (for example, atropine) that dilate the pupils.

From Phipps WJ: The patient with eye problems. In Long BJ, Phipps WJ, Cassmeyer VS, editors: *Medical-surgical nursing: a nursing process approach,* ed 3, St. Louis, 1993, Mosby.

BOX 29-3

Method for Instilling Eye Drops

1. Wash hands before touching eye.
2. Cleanse eye if crusted or discharge present.
3. Tilt head back and look up.
4. Evert lower lid by pulling down gently on skin below eye.
5. Place drops on center of conjunctual sac or lower lid.
6. Avoid touching eye with top of dropper and squeezing eye shut.

Modified from Phipps WJ: The patient with eye problems. In Long BJ, Phipps WJ, Cassmeyer VS, editors: *Medical-surgical nursing: a nursing process approach,* ed 3, St. Louis, 1993, Mosby.

✣ EVALUATION

Evaluation includes achievement of the expected outcomes, no further visual loss, and the independent performance of ADLs.

Cataracts

Cataracts are the most common disorder found in the aging eye, and they occur in 65% of clients over age 50 and in 95% of clients over age 65 (Seeley, Stevens, Tate, 1992). The occurrence of cataracts with accompanying visual loss increases with advancing age.

A cataract is a clouding of the normally clear and transparent lens of the eye. The lens focuses light on the retina to produce a sharp image. When a cataract forms, the lens can become so opaque that light cannot be transmitted to the retina. Cataracts result from a change in the chemical composition of the lens; these changes can be caused by aging, eye injuries, certain diseases, and heredity. Additionally, there are different types of cataracts. The normal aging process may cause the lens to harden and turn cloudy. These cataracts are called senile cataracts and can occur as early as age 40. Eye injuries such as a hard blow, puncture, cut, or burn can damage the lens and result in a traumatic cataract. Secondary cataracts can be caused by certain infections, drugs, or diseases (such as diabetes).

The size and location of a cataract determine the amount of interference with clear sight. A cataract located near the center of the lens produces more noticeable symptoms, such as the following:

- Dimmed, blurred, or misty vision
- Brighter light to read
- Glare and light sensitivity
- Loss of color perception
- Recurrent eyeglass prescription changes (American Academy of Ophthalmology, 1992a)

MEDICAL MANAGEMENT

Cataracts

Diagnostic tests and procedures

Complete eye examination, including ophthalmoscopic examination

Treatment

The only corrective cataract treatment is surgery. Surgery is indicated when vision loss interferes with the normal daily activities of living, especially reading and driving. The ophthalmologist decides whether cataract surgery is necessary, basing the decision on the client's visual loss and other contributing intraocular diseases, such as optic nerve or retinal damage. Several types of surgery exist, but the most recent technique involves the use of ultrasound to break the lens into small fragments, which allows the lens to be removed through a much smaller incision. Once the lens is removed, the client needs a substitute lens to focus the eye. The various methods to restore vision include the intraocular lens (permanent lenses implanted inside the eye); hard, soft, or special extended-wear soft contact lenses; and cataract glasses. The ophthamologist helps clients decide which methods are best suited to their life-styles and health (American Academy of Ophthalmology, 1992a).

Prognosis

Cataract surgery is highly successful, and 95% of clients who undergo surgery regain useful vision. The client's prognosis is excellent with the use of a contact lens, cataracts glasses, or intraocular lens implant (Kollarits, 1992).

These symptoms develop slowly and at different rates in each eye (see Medical Management box above).

NURSING MANAGEMENT

✣ ASSESSMENT

Subjective complaints include having trouble reading and cleaning glasses often, thinking that dirty glasses are causing vision difficulties. Lens opacity may be visible on external or internal eye examination.

✣ DIAGNOSIS

The nursing diagnoses for the client with cataracts include but are not limited to the following: (1) sensory/perceptual alterations (visual) related to a hard and cloudy lens; (2) anxiety related to uncertain surgical outcome; (3) knowledge deficit: cataracts related to lack of exposure; (4) potential for injury related to changes in visual acuity; and (5) dressing/grooming self care deficit related to inability to see body and face clearly enough to maintain appearance of clothes and cosmetics.

✣ PLANNING

Expected outcomes include, but are not limited to, the following: (1) client will have cataract surgery when recommended by an ophthalmologist; (2) client will ask questions about pre-and postoperative care and report satisfaction with information; (3) client's affected eye will be free of increased intraocular pressure, stress on the suture line, hemorrhage, and infection; (4) client will verbalize appropriate home care activities to avoid and activities to do after cataract surgery; (5) client will demonstrate correct administration of eye drops; (6) client will avoid a fall, bumping into objects, or an automobile accident before or after surgery; and (7) client will dress and groom self when vision returns.

✣ INTERVENTION

Nursing management for a client with cataracts focuses mainly on preoperative and postoperative surgical care, since surgery is the only method for treating cataracts. However, because surgery is only indicated for advanced cataracts, older adults should not wait until vision loss is advanced to see an ophthalmologist. Delaying examination of the eye can lead to permanent vision loss if there is glaucoma present. Most cataract surgery is performed as outpatient surgery with the administration of a local anesthetic. This makes preoperative teaching difficult, since clients arrive just several hours before surgery. Many ambulatory centers conduct preoperative assessment and teaching by phone a week before surgery. Preoperative care involves administering eye drops and a sedative as ordered. Postoperative care requires teaching the client and family home care procedures for the period after cataract surgery (Client/Family Teaching Box at left) including the method for instilling eye drops (see Box 29-3, p. 822). The home care instructions need to include special precautions recommended by the ophthalmologist based on the type of surgery performed. If a lens implant has not been inserted, clients need to wear contact lenses or cataract glasses. Clients wearing cataract glasses experience loss of depth perception and distorted peripheral and color vision. They need to be taught that objects are magnified by 25% and appear larger and closer than they really are. This requires safety measures to be taken in the home, as well as the modification of dressing and cosmetic application after surgery (see nursing Care Plan, p. 824).

✣ EVALUATION

Evaluation includes achievement of the expected outcomes. Clients with successful cataract surgery will be free of complications with improved vision. Additionally, the clients will report performance of usual daily activities with the use of lens implant, contact lenses, or corrective glasses.

Retinal Disorders

Three common disorders that affect the retina of the older adult include **macular degeneration, diabetic retinopathy,** and **retinal detachment.** Each disorder is described in the following sections, and an overview of the associated medical and nursing management is included.

Macular Degeneration

Age-related macular degeneration (AMD) is the leading cause of blindness among older adults in the United

CLIENT/FAMILY TEACHING

Home Care After Cataract Surgery

Activities *not to do:*

Avoid rubbing or pressing on the eye.

Avoid bending at the waist or lifting heavy objects for at least a month:

- To pick objects up from the floor, kneel while keeping head erect.
- To put on stockings or to tie shoes, sit and raise foot to reach hand while keeping head erect.
- Use long pick-up "reachers" to pick up small objects from the floor.

Avoid straining with bowel movements (stool softener may be necessary).

Avoid showers and shampooing hair (soap may irritate eye) for specified time as instructed.

Limit reading (back and forth movement may loosen stitches).

Activities *to do:*

Sleep on back or unaffected side for prescribed time frame (3 to 4 weeks).

Apply metal eye shield at night or when napping to protect eye.

Wear glasses indoors (all day) and sunglasses with side shields outdoors.

Wash hands before instilling eye drops, and follow the correct procedure for eye drop instillation (Box 29-3, p. 822).

Follow steps for eyepad:

1. Wash hands before changing eyepad.
2. Use two oval eye pads.
3. Tape snugly and diagonally from above nose to lower cheek.

Modified from Phipps WJ: The patient with eye problems. In Long BJ, Phipps WJ, Cassmeyer VS, editors: *Medical-surgical nursing: a nursing process approach,* ed 3, St. Louis, 1993, Mosby.

CARE PLAN

CATARACTS

Clinical situation Mrs. S is a 75-year-old retired nurse who has been admitted to the skilled nursing unit of a local hospital for rehabilitation therapy following repair of a right hip fracture. She is accompanied by her daughter. Mrs. S has no significant medical history but a fall in her home precipitated the break in her in hip. She states she has been having trouble with her eyes and she tripped on the stairs. Since her admission to the hospital, a vision screening detected cataracts in both eyes and surgery was recommended once she recovers. Mrs. S is requiring assistance with all ADLs except eating. She is unable to bear weight on her right leg so assistance is needed to transfer to the toilet, chair or bed. She also needs help bathing and dressing the lower half of her body as she cannot reach her legs or feet. Mrs. S states her biggest concern is fear of falling again.

Nursing diagnoses	Outcomes	Interventions
Sensory, perceptual alteration (visual) related to hard and cloudy lens	Mrs S will have cataract surgery when appropriate.	Provide Mrs. S with printed information/instruction sheet "Aging and Your Eyes" (Box 29-1) and the client education sheet "Home Care After Cataract Surgery," (see Client/Family Teaching box, p. 823). Encourage Mrs. S and her daughter to speak with ophthalmologist about recommended surgery. Explain pre- and postoperative procedures related to recommended surgery.
Potential for injury related to altered visual acuity	Mrs. S will not fall.	Provide a safe environment—bed in low position, siderails as needed, call light and personal items in reach. Assist with transfers until Mrs. S demonstrates transfer safely unassisted. Assess home for factors that hinder or support vision changes.
Partial self-care deficit: bathing/hygiene, dressing/grooming, toileting related to immobility	Mrs. S will assist with self-care to fullest extent as evidenced by fulfilling needs for cleanliness, grooming and toileting.	Administer pain medication as needed before performing self-care. Encourage Mrs. S to perform as much of own care as possible to help restore independence. Provide assistance, supervision and teaching with the use of assistive devices as needed to perform self-care. Assess factors in home that support or hinder self-care.
Anxiety related to fear of falling	Mrs. S will report reduced anxiety, as evidenced by relaxed state and learning about cataract surgery.	Encourage expression of fears of falling. Use therapeutic communication to gain insight into Mrs. S's fears and give realistic feedback. Increase attention to Mrs. S when feeling anxious.

From McFarland GK, McFarlane EZ: *Nursing diagnosis and intervention*, ed 2, St. Louis, 1993, Mosby.

States. It does not cause total blindness but results in loss of close vision.

AMD is a poorly understood disease that causes damage to the macula, the key focusing area of the retina. As a result, there is a decline in central visual acuity that makes daily tasks requiring close vision nearly impossible. Peripheral vision is retained.

Types of AMD

"Dry" macular degeneration Also known as involutional macular degeneration, this type is caused by breakdown or thinning of macular tissue related to the aging process. Vision loss is gradual.

"Wet" macular degeneration Also known as exudative macular degeneration, this type results when

MEDICAL MANAGEMENT

Retinal Disorders

Diagnostic tests and procedures
Internal eye examination with ophthalmoscope
Color vision test
Grid test
Fluorescein angiography

Treatment

Macular degeneration and diabetic retinopathy

Laser therapy is proving beneficial in the treatment of wet macular degeneration and diabetic retinopathy. Argon laser photocoagulation seals or destroys the abnormal blood vessels. This procedure cannot cure macular degeneration or diabetic retinopathy, but it has been found to slow the rate of vision loss. Treatment of the dry form of macular degeneration and diabetic retinopathy that cannot be treated with laser surgery focuses on helping the client cope with visual impairment. The ophthalmologist can prescribe optical devices or refer clients to a low-vision specialist or center (see Box 29-4) (American Academy of Ophthalmology, 1992e).

Retinal detachment

Retinal detachment must be treated by surgery. The most recent method is called cryotherapy. Eighty-five percent to 90% of retinal detachments can be repaired by a combination of cryotherapy and scleral buckling. A probe with nitrous oxide or carbon dioxide is applied to the hole, causing scarring. Then, the sclera and choroid are buckled by placing a silicone band over the hole. The hole seals shut on the buckle and the subretinal fluid is reabsorbed (Kollarits, 1992).

Prognosis

Prognosis is excellent with surgery. About 90% of clients treated can be cured. However, sometimes a second operation is necessary, and the retinal detachment may occur in the other eye.

abnormal blood vessels form and hemorrhage on the retina. Vision loss may be rapid and severe.

Factors associated with the destruction of macular tissue include genetic inheritance and blue or medium pigmented eyes (Kart, Metress, Metress, 1992).

Symptoms of macular degeneration include the following:

- Difficulty performing tasks that require close central vision such as reading and sewing.
- Decreased color vision; colors look dim.
- Dark or empty area in the center of vision.
- Wavy appearance of straight lines on paper or in the environment (Hogstel, 1992).
- Words on a page look blurred (American Academy of Ophthalmology, 1992e).

Diabetic Retinopathy

Loss of visual function is one of the most common complications of diabetes. Altered circulation to the eye may result in retinal degeneration or detachment. The prevalence of diabetic retinopathy is 7% for those who have had diabetes for less than 10 years and 63% for those who have had diabetes for over 15 years (Stefanson, 1990).

This condition is a complication of diabetes that affects the capillaries and arterioles of the retina. Ballooning of these tiny vessels leads to hemorrhaging, scarring, and blindness. These vascular changes in and around the retina lead to macular edema, which causes the retina to swell. The retina loses its shape, and images are distorted. It is like having wrinkled film in a camera (Kart, Metress, Metress, 1992).

There are no symptoms of early retinal changes, and there may be no symptoms even when retinopathy is advanced. Early detection requires a complete ophthalmoscopic examination; therefore clients with diabetes should have a yearly examination by an ophthalmologist.

Retinal Detachment

Studies have shown that 6% of the population has small holes or tears in the retina. Aging tends to weaken these spots (Kollarits, 1992).

Retinal detachment occurs when the sensory layer of the retina separates from the pigmented layer. Tears or holes occur in the retina as a result of trauma, aging (degeneration), hemorrhage, or tumor. When a tear occurs, fluid seeps between the layers, causing detachment. The usual symptoms include the following:

- Light flashes
- "Swarms of gnats" in front of the eye (Kollarits, 1992)
- Loss of vision
- Curtain drawn before eyes (detachment has occurred quickly and is extensive) (Phipps, 1993b) (see Medical Management box at left).

NURSING MANAGEMENT

ASSESSMENT

There are no early symptoms of diabetic retinopathy and sometimes none with advanced retinopathy. Clients with macular degeneration may complain of inability to thread a needle or that the words on a page look blurred, making it difficult to read. Clients with retinal detachment notice flashes of light followed by floating spots before the eye and progressive loss of vision. The specific area of visual loss depends on where the detachment is located. When detachment occurs quickly and is extensive, the client may feel that a curtain has been drawn before the eyes. Ongoing nursing assessment involves monitoring the client's subjective statements about changes in vision and observing for signs of anxiety. All three retinal disorders are diagnosed by ophthalmoscopic examination.

✣ DIAGNOSIS

Nursing diagnoses are determined from analysis of the client assessment. Possible nursing diagnoses for a client with a retinal disorder may include, but are not limited to, the following: (1) sensory/perceptual alterations (visual) related to damaged macula or retina; (2) knowledge deficit of effect of diabetes on eyes caused by lack of exposure to accurate information; (3) knowledge deficit of retinal detachment condition, surgery, preoperative and postoperative care, and home care after surgery; and (4) anxiety related to fear of blindness.

✣ PLANNING

Expected client outcomes for an older person with a retinal disorder may include, but are not limited to, the following: (1) client will adjust successfully to vision loss by using low-vision aids; (2) client will state in own words the effect of diabetes on eyes; (3) client will see an ophthalmologist yearly; (4) client will ask questions about preoperative and postoperative retinal surgery care and report satisfaction with information; (5) client's affected eye will be free of further retinal detachment, infection, or hemorrhaging; (6) client will verbalize appropriate home care activities to follow after retinal surgery; (7) client will demonstrate correct administration of eye drops; and (8) client will report reduced anxiety.

✣ INTERVENTION

Clients with macular degeneration and diabetic retinopathy must learn to cope with chronic gradual vision loss. Clients must be taught how to obtain and use low-vision aids (Box 29-4). Teaching about the condition and encouraging yearly follow-up with an ophthalmologist helps clients understand the disease and how it affects their eyes (see Box 29-1, pp. 818-819). Clients with retinal detachment require the immediate care of bed rest in a proper position (retinal hole in most dependent position) and eye patches (one or both eyes may be prescribed) until surgery is performed. Safety precautions and means of communicating are essential for the client at this point. Postoperative care includes administration of eye medication, pain medication, antiemetics as needed, and cough medication as needed. Cold compresses are applied to reduce swelling and promote comfort. Clients must be instructed to avoid jerking movements of the head such as coughing, sneezing, and vomiting. If eyes are patched, safety precautions such as call lights, siderails, and necessary items within reach must be instituted. Finally, assistance is provided with ADLs and ambulation as needed to promote comfort and safety. Home care instructions to teach the client and family include the following: (1) report increases in floaters, flashes of light, decreased vision, drainage, or increased pain to an ophthalmologist; (2) administer eye drops (see Box 29-3, p. 822); (3) limit physical activity for 1 to 2 weeks, and resume active sports and heavy lifting as indicated by a physician; (4) make follow-up appointments with the ophthalmologist. Clients with any retinal disorder may experience anxiety about the loss of vision and possible blindness. The opportunity for clients to discuss their concerns needs to be provided. Nurses can reduce clients' anxiety by listening, answering questions honestly, and referring clients to available resources for further information (Phipps, 1993b).

BOX 29-4

Low-Vision Aids

- Magnifying devices
  - Glasses
  - Magnifying TV screen
- Large-print books, magazines, telephone pads, clocks, watches, playing cards
- Computers
- Reading machines
- Talking books, clocks and wrist watches
- Closed-circuit TV
- Special lighting—high-intensity reading lamps
- Special lenses
  - Telescopic for distance vision
  - Microscopic for close vision

From Redford JB: Assistive devices for the elderly. In Calkins E, Ford AB, Katz PR, editors: *Practice of geriatrics,* ed 2, Philadelphia, 1992, WB Saunders.

✣ EVALUATION

Evaluation includes achievement of the expected outcomes; clients with macular degeneration and diabetic retinopathy will describe the condition and report use of low vision aids. These clients will follow up yearly with an ophthalmologist. Clients who have had detachment surgery will experience no complications and gradual improvement in vision. Clients with any retinal disorder will report reduced anxiety as evidenced by their ability to learn and cope with their disease.

Visual Impairment

In the United States, 8 to 10 million people suffer from visual impairment that cannot be corrected by eyeglasses or contact lenses (US Department of Health and Human Services, 1990).

The visually impaired population includes those who are legally blind as well as those with vision over 20/200 (unable to see well enough to read a newspaper). Nearly 13% of people over the age of 65 have some form of visual impairment. Blindness in older people results from diabetic retinopathy, glaucoma, cataracts, and macular degeneration, and its incidence has increased as the number of people aged 65 and older grows (see Medical Management box at right).

MEDICAL MANAGEMENT

Visual Impairment

Sudden visual loss is considered a medical emergency and should be evaluated immediately. Sudden visual loss may be caused by retinal detachment or an eye injury (see Emergency Treatment box below).

The medical management of visual loss depends on the type, cause, and amount of visual loss experienced by the client. Any client with a visual handicap that cannot be improved by corrective lenses or surgery should be referrred to a low-vision specialist or center.

NURSING MANAGEMENT

ASSESSMENT

Nursing assessment of the client with impaired vision requires an understanding of the client's response to the visual loss. The older adult who becomes blind suddenly usually has a harder time adjusting to the handicap than a person who was born blind. Loss of vision may result in a self-esteem disturbance, leading to social isolation. A self-esteem disturbance leads to a decrease in self-confidence, which can affect interactions with others, the ability to carry out normal daily activities, job performance, and the desire to engage in familiar hobbies. Grief and mourning occur over the loss of vision and result in similar reactions to those experienced with death, such as denial, anger, guilt, hopelessness, and depression. The client's ability to cope with the loss depends on the type, amount, and duration of the visual loss, as well as the client's support system and coping style. Over time, people with visual losses are able to compensate by increasing sensitivity in the other senses of hearing, taste, touch, and balance. Objectively, the nurse should assess for signs and behaviors that indicate vision problems (Phipps, 1993b) (Box 29-5).

DIAGNOSIS

Potential nursing diagnoses for the client with visual impairment include, but are not limited to, the following: (1) self-esteem disturbance related to sudden loss of vision; (2) social isolation related to impaired communication; (3) ineffective individual coping related to sudden loss of vision; (4) feeding, bathing/hygiene, dressing/grooming, and toileting self-care deficits related to visual impairment; and (5) impaired physical mobility related to visual impairment.

PLANNING

Expected outcomes for a client with visual impairment include: (1) client will perceive self positively by making positive statements about self; (2) client will participate successfully in activities with others; (3) client will demonstrate increased objectivity and ability to solve problems, make decisions, and communicate needs; (4) client will safely provide self-care by using low-vision aids and environmental strategies; and (5) client will demonstrate the safe and correct use of adaptive devices to increase mobility (McFarland, McFarlane, 1993).

EMERGENCY TREATMENT

Eye Injuries

In the United States, there are 1.3 million eye injuries yearly, and more than 100,000 people are permanently disabled by these injuries (US Department of Health and Human Services, 1990).

Burns (chemical, flame)

1. Flush eye immediately with cool water or any available nontoxic liquid.
2. Seek medical assistance.

Foreign body (loose substance on conjunctiva such as dirt or an insect)

1. Pull upper lid down over lower lid to produce tearing and dislodge substance.
2. Irrigate eye with water if needed.
3. Do *NOT* rub eye.
4. Seek medical assistance if above interventions are unsuccessful.

Contact injury (hematoma, ecchymosis, laceration)

1. If no laceration is present, apply cold compresses.
2. If laceration is present, cover eye and seek medical assistance.

Penetrating objects

1. Do not remove object.
2. Place protective shield over eye (paper cup) and cover.
3. Seek medical assistance.

Modified from Phipps WJ: The patient with eye problems. In Long BJ, Phipps WJ, Cassmeyer VS, editors: *Medical-surgical nursing: a nursing process approach,* ed 3, St. Louis, 1993, Mosby.

BOX 29-5

Signs and Behaviors That May Indicate Vision Problems

Client may report
Pain in eyes
Difficulty seeing in darkened area
Double vision/distorted vision
Migraine headaches coupled with blurred vision
Flashes of light
Halos surrounding lights

Staff may notice
Getting lost
Bumping into objects
Straining to read/no reading
Spilling food on clothing
Social withdrawal
Less eye contact
Placid facial expressions
TV viewing at close range
Decreased sense of balance
Mismatching clothes

From McNeely E, Griffin-Shirley M, Hubbard A: Teaching caregivers to recognize diminished vision among nursing home residents, *Geriatr Nurs* 13 (6):332-335, 1992.

BOX 29-6

Suggestions for Communicating with and Caring for the Visually Impaired Nursing Home Resident

Always identify yourself clearly.
Always make it clear when you are leaving the room.
Make sure you have the resident's attention before you start to talk.
Try to minimize the number of distractions.
Whenever possible, choose bright clothes with bold contrasts.
Check to see that the best possible lighting is available.
Assess your position in relation to the resident. One eye or ear may be better than the other.
Try not to move items in resident's room.
Narrate your actions.
Try to keep the resident between you and the window, or you will appear as a dark shadow.
Use some means to identify residents who are known to be visually impaired.
Use the analogy of clock hands to help the resident locate objects.
Keep color and texture in mind when buying clothes.
Be careful about labeling residents as confused! They may be making mistakes because of poor vision.
Obtain and encourage use of low vision aids.

Modified from McNeeley E, Griffin-Shirley M, Hubbard A: Teaching caregivers to recognize diminished vision among nursing home residents, *Geriatr Nurs* 13(6):332-335, 1992.

RESEARCH

McNeely E, Griffin-Shirley N, Hubbard A: Teaching caregivers to recognize diminished vision among nursing home residents, *Geriatr Nurs* 13(6); 332-335, 1992.

Sample, setting

The sample included 87 employees from five long-term care (LTC) facilities in southwestern Atlanta. The employees were predominantly women between the ages of 20 to 60. Four were nurses with graduate degrees, and the rest were nursing assistants educated at the high school level. The mean employment time was 8.1 years.

Methodology

A videotape was designed to introduce or supplement an inservice program on the care of residents with visual impairments. The effectiveness of the videotape lesson was tested by two versions—one with and one without text overlay. The subjects were given a pretest and two posttests (one immediately after viewing the tape and another one 2 weeks later).

Findings

The test result scores revealed significant differences, with the greatest number of correct answers on the second posttest. The subjective comments made by the participants indicated a favorable response to the video.

Implications

LTC staff development programs need to include programs about characteristics and needs of people with visual impairments. Providing nursing staff, especially nursing assistants, with this type of education will assist them in delivering quality resident care.

✣ INTERVENTION

Counseling provides an opportunity for people who have become visually impaired to talk about feelings, concerns, and anxieties. Once these concerns and feelings have been identified, clients can be given assistance in identifying their strengths and resources. Problem solving can lead to alternative ways to complete the tasks of everyday living and recreation activities.

The nurse interacting with a client who is visually impaired must rely heavily on various techniques and methods when communicating with that person. See Box 29-6 for tips on communicating and caring for the visually impaired. Keep in mind that these tips can be used in any setting—home care, acute care or long-term care.

Strategies to increase adaptation to daily living include: (1) organizing the environment; (2) encouraging the use of the clock method of eating; and (3) using a sighted guide to assist in ambulation. Organizing the environment means placing items of clothing in specific drawers or closets to facilitate selection and placing furniture in specific locations to facilitate mobility. Additionally, the use of color contrast and coding schemes helps the client locate items; bright, sharply contrasting colors make furniture and personal items visually distinct. For example, a bright red toothbrush shows up well against a white sink. Coding schemes that facilitate independent living include applying fluorescent tape around light switches, thermostats, and keyholes. Coding with colored paper, textured paper such as sandpaper, or rubber bands can help the client differentiate medications. The clock method assists the client at meals, because the location of food on the plate is described in terms of a clock face. (For example, beans at the top of the plate are at the 12 o'clock position, and potatoes are at the 6 o'clock position at the bottom.) Additionally, a piece of bread or a roll can be used to push food onto the fork. Sighted guides, who lead people with visual impairments from place to place, help the client walk confidently (Box 29-7). The use of a cane or seeing-eye dog can also promote independence in mobility, especially when the client is in an unfamiliar environment.

The home health or community health nurse can assist with referral to a social worker who has the infor-

BOX 29-7

The Sighted Guide

1. Ask older adults if they would like to walk with a sighted guide.
2. If assistance is accepted, offer your elbow or arm. Older adults should grasp the guide's arm just above the elbow. If necessary, physically assist the older adult by guiding his or her hand to your arm or elbow.
3. The sighted guide will then go a half step ahead and slightly to the side of the older adult. The older adult's shoulder should be directly behind the guide's shoulder. (NOTE: If the older adult is frail, locate the hand on the guide's forearm. When this modified grasp is used, the older adult will be positioned laterally to the guide's body.)
4. The guide and older adult should be relaxed and walk at a comfortable pace. When approaching doorways or a narrow space, tell the older adult. The older adult then goes directly behind the guide. Some modifications may be needed for frail older adults. Be sure modifications are safe and comfortable.
5. Describe surroundings to the older adult as you walk to augment mobility and enrich experience.

Modified from McNeely E, Griffin-Shirley M, Hubbard A: Teaching caregivers to recognize diminished vision among nursing home residents, *Geriatr Nurs* 13(6):332-335, 1992.

BOX 29-8

Assessment of the Eyes

Subjective data

Review of related history

Employment: exposure to irritating chemicals or high-speed machinery
Allergies
Medications
Lenses—glasses or contact

Present

Difficulty with vision—one or both eyes
- Near or distant vision
- Central or peripheral
- Transient or prolonged
- Floaters
- Color vision
- Halos around lights
- Double vision

Pain
Secretions

Objective data

Assess visual acuity
- Distant vision using Snellen chart at a distance of 20 feet
- Near vision using Rosenbaum chart

Assess visual fields by confrontation
Assess extraocular muscle function
- Six cardinal fields of gaze

Assess for nystagmus with eye in extreme temporal-lateral position
Assess corneal light reflex
Assess accessory structures
- Inspect eyelids for position, color, closure and blinking
- Inspect eyebrow for quantity, condition and distribution of hair
- Inspect and palpate lacrimal apparatus for redness, edema, tenderness, discharge
- Inspect sclera and conjunctiva for color, lesions, edema
- Inspect cornea for transparency and test sensitivity
- Inspect anterior chamber for transparency
- Inspect iris for color, shape, depth
- Inspect pupil for size and shape
- Test reaction to light and accommodation
- Assess retinal structures with ophthalmoscope (Box 29-9)
  - Red reflex
  - Optic disc for size, shape, color
  - Retinal vessels
  - Retinal background
  - Macular area

From Lueckenotte AG: *Pocket guide to gerontologic assessment,* ed 2, St. Louis, 1994, Mosby.

BOX 29-9

Ophthalmoscopic Examination

1. Turn the diaphragm dial so that the small, round white light can be used. Turn on light to maximum brightness (old or defective batteries will reduce lighting).
2. Client should be comfortably seated. Either stand or be seated facing the client.
3. Client and examiner remove glasses. Removal of client's contact lenses is optional. It might help to reduce light reflection.
4. The room should be darkened.
5. Ask the client to hold both eyes open and to direct gaze slightly upward and straight ahead. Gaze should be fixed on some distant object and maintained even if the examiner's head gets in the way.
6. For examination of the client's right eye, hold the ophthalmoscope in your right hand, over your right eye. Stand slightly to the right, at about a 15 degree angle (temporally) from the client.
7. The ophthalmoscope is held with the index finger on the lens wheel. Rotate the lens wheel to 0 diopter setting (a lens that neither converges nor diverges light rays).
8. Place left hand over the client's right eye, with thumb on upper brow.
9. Hold the ophthalmoscope firmly against your head and approach to within 30 cm (12 inches) of the client. Direct ophthalmoscope light into the pupil. Continue approach, and red reflex will appear. Try to keep both eyes open.
10. Continue the approach until 3 to 5 cm (1 to 2 inches) from the client's eye. Retinal structures should come into view. Clear focus can be established by looking closely at a vessel to see if the borders are sharp. Wheel adjustments need to be made for refractive errors. The myopic client's eyeball may be longer than normal, requiring rotation of the lens wheel into the red (minus) numbers for clarity. The hyperopic or aphakic client will require lens wheel movement into the black (plus) numbers for clarity.
11. The examiner may not initially focus on the disc. It is helpful to follow vessel bifurcations that lead toward the disc.
12. After inspection of the disc, follow the vessels peripherally in each of four directions. Light must always be shown *through* the pupil as the examiner inspects in different directions. Beginning examiners often lose their view as they begin to scan the fundus. The client's pupil serves as a stable fulcrum while the examiner and ophthalmoscope move *as a unit* in viewing the retinal periphery.
13. Inspect the retinal background and the macula (2 DD temporal to the disc).

From Bowers AC, Thompson JM: *Clinical manual of health assessment,* ed 3, St. Louis, 1988, Mosby.

mation on local, state, and federal services available. Services to people with visual impairments include counseling, mobility training, vocational rehabilitation, self-care skills training, special education, and financial assistance. Low-vision aids such as "talking books," tapes, and tape players are available from public libraries, the Federation for the Blind, and the United States Library of Congress. Legal blindness entitles a person to some federal assistance. Financial assistance is based on need. However, blind people can report an additional tax deduction on federal income tax. The United States Department of Health and Human Services (Social and Rehabilitation Service) provides counseling and placement services (Phipps, 1993b; Kart, Metress, Metress, 1992).

Not surprisingly, Marx et al. (1992) found that nursing home residents with low vision are dependent for a significantly greater number of ADLs than residents with good vision. Their results imply that ADL dependency may place a greater burden on caregivers in any setting. Therefore it is imperative to provide routine screening for eye disorders, to treat reversible conditions whenever possible, and to institute low-vision training in the nursing home (see Research box, p. 828).

✣ EVALUATION

Evaluation includes achievement of the expected outcomes. See Boxes 29-8 and 29-9, pp. 829-830 for additional information on vision care in the older adult.

HEARING AND BALANCE

The organs of hearing and balance can be divided into three portions: the external ear, the middle ear, and the inner ear. The external and middle ears are only involved in hearing; the inner ear is involved in both hearing and balance. The external ear consists of the auricle and the external auditory canal, a passageway from the outside to the eardrum. The middle ear is an air-filled space that contains the tympanic membrane, the eardrum, and the auditory ossicles. The inner ear contains the sensory organs for hearing and balance. It is made up of interconnecting fluid-filled tunnels and

Insight • *More older people will be driving as those over age 65 grow in number. Motor vehicle crashes are the leading cause of death by unintentional injury for those age 65 to 74 and the second leading cause for those age 75 and older (Waller, 1985). The sensory information involved in driving is mostly visual. Age-related visual changes, as well as four of the major eye diseases (cataracts, macular degeneration, glaucoma, and diabetic retinopathy), have higher prevalence in those over age 75. The nurse is in a key position to assess the older person's ability to drive safely and to refer them to available resources. The American Association of Retired Persons (AARP) Mature Driver/55 Alive program helps older drivers improve their skills and prevent traffic accidents by covering age-related physical changes, declining perceptual skills, rules of the road, and local driving problems. Some auto insurance companies provide multiyear premium reductions to graduates of the Mature Driver/55 Alive program. Additionally, various occupational therapy departments provide behind-the-wheel assessment and assist in adaptive aids to facilitate driving (Reubin, 1992).*

chambers in the petrous portion of the temporal bone (Fig. 29-5).

AUDITORY STRUCTURES AND THEIR FUNCTIONS

External Ear

The auricle, or the pinna, is the fleshy part of the external ear and is composed of elastic cartilage covered with skin. The shape helps collect sound and guide the sound waves toward the external auditory canal. The S-shaped external auditory canal is about 2.5 cm in length and extends upward from the auricle to the tympanic membrane. The skin lining the canal contains hairs and sebaceous glands that produce cerumen, which is commonly called earwax. Their purpose is to protect foreign objects from reaching the eardrum.

Middle Ear

The middle ear is an air-filled chamber located in the temporal bone. The tympanic membrane, or eardrum, consists of a thin, concave, three-layered membrane that separates the middle ear from the external auditory canal. Its function is to increase the volume of sound. It contains simple epithelium on the inner and outer surfaces with a layer of connective tissue in between. The light reflex seen on a physical examination results from the middle ear's oblique position to the canal. The round and oval windows separate the middle ear from the in-

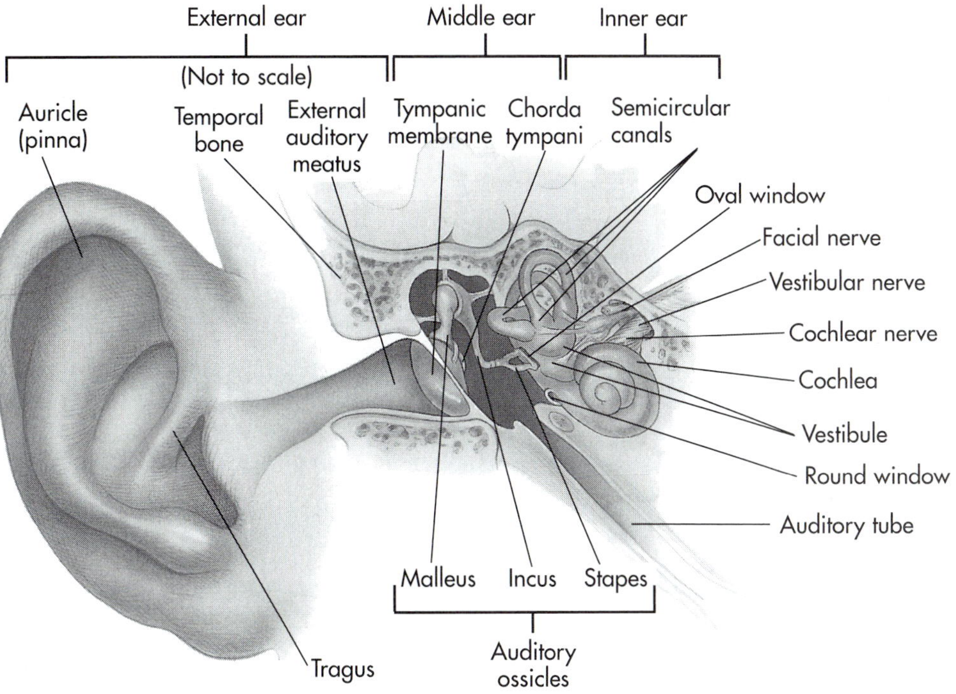

Fig. 29-5 External, middle, and inner ears. (From Seeley RR, Stephens TD, Tate P: *Anatomy and physiology,* ed 3, St. Louis, 1995, Mosby.)

ner ear. Two openings provide air passages from the middle ear. One passage opens into the mastoid process; the other, the auditory or eustachian tube, opens into the pharynx and allows the equalization of air pressure. Unequal pressure between the middle ear and the outside environment can distort the eardrum, dampen its vibrations, stimulate pain fibers, and make hearing difficult.

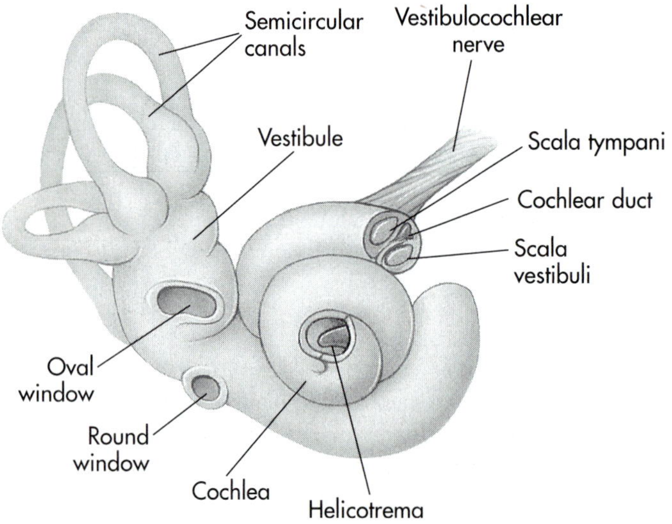

Fig. 29-6 Elements of the inner ear. (From Seeley RR, Stephens TD, Tate P: *Anatomy and physiology,* ed 2, St. Louis, 1992, Mosby.)

That is why when a person changes altitude, sounds may be distorted and the eardrum can become painful. These symptoms can be relieved by swallowing, yawning, and chewing, which allow air to pass through the auditory tube to equalize air pressure. This chamber contains three auditory ossicles, the malleus, the incus, and the stapes, that transfer vibrations from the tympanic membrane to the oval window. The handle of the malleus is attached to the inner surface of the tympanic membrane; vibrations of the membrane cause the malleus to vibrate as well. The head of the malleus is attached to the incus, which is attached to the stapes. The foot plate of the stapes fits into the oval window. Vibration of the window moves fluid within the inner ear and stimulates hearing receptors.

Inner Ear

The inner ear consists of two parts: outer bony tunnels called the bony labyrinth and inner smaller membranous tunnels called the membranous labyrinth. The membranous tunnels are filled with a fluid called endolymph, and the space between the two tunnels is filled with a fluid called perilymph. The bony labyrinth is divided into three regions: the vestibule, the semicircular canals, and the cochlea. The vestibule and semicircular canals contain receptors involved with balance. The cochlea contains the functional unit of hearing, the organ of Corti, which is located within the cochlear duct (Fig. 29-6).

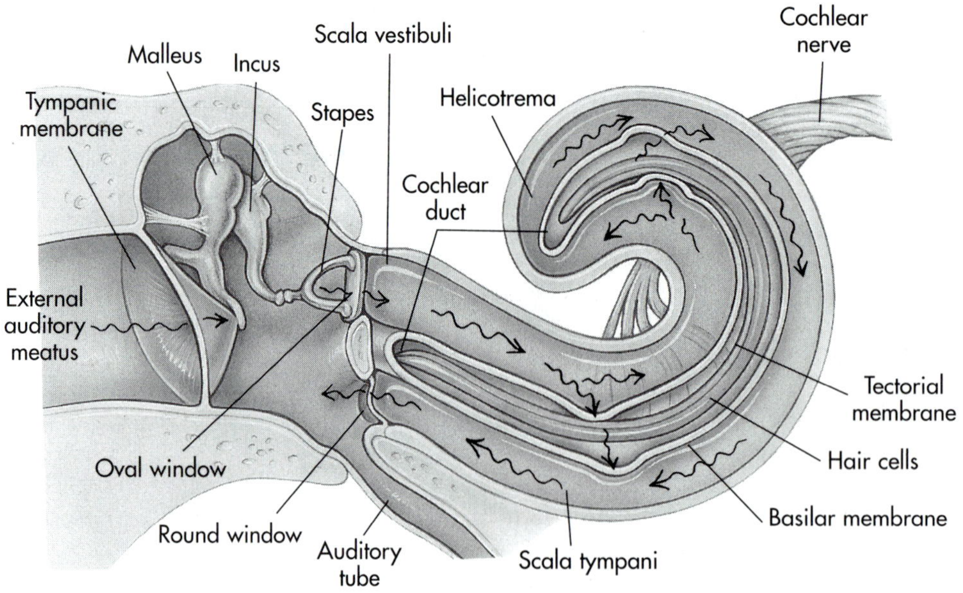

Fig. 29-7 Sound waves strike the tympanic membrane and cause it to vibrate. This vibration caused the three bones of the middle ear to vibrate, causing the footplate of the stapes to vibrate in the oval window. The vibration moves fluid within the cochlea and cochlear duct. Sound is detected in the hair cells of the Organ of Corti, which is transmitted to the central nervous system by the cochlear portion of the vestibulocochlear (CN VIII) nerve. (From Seeley RR, Stephens TD, Tate P: *Anatomy and physiology,* ed 2, St. Louis, 1992, Mosby.)

BOX 29-10

Steps Involved in Hearing

1. Sound waves are collected by the auricle and are conducted through the external auditory canal to the tympanic membrane, causing it to vibrate (Fig. 29-7).
2. The vibrating tympanic membrane causes the malleus, incus, and stapes to vibrate.
3. Vibration of the stapes causes the oval window to vibrate.
4. Vibration of the oval window moves fluid within the cochlea and cochlear duct.
5. The hair cells attached to the membrane of the cochlear duct become bent.
6. Bending of the hairlike projections causes depolarization, which induces action potentials.
7. The action potentials are conducted to the central nervous system (CNS).
8. The action potentials are interpreted in the cerebral cortex and are perceived as sound.

Modified from Seeley RR, Stephens TP, Tate P: The senses. In *Anatomy and physiology,* ed 2, St. Louis, 1992, Mosby.

The cell bodies are grouped into a cochlea, or spiral ganglion. These hairlike projections bend when sound waves enter the cochlea and convert sound waves into electrochemical impulses (Box 29-10).

BALANCE

The organs of balance are located within the inner ear and can be divided into two parts. The vestibule contains the static labyrinth, which consists of the utricle and saccule. This portion evaluates the position of the head relative to gravity or linear acceleration and deceleration. The second part is located in the semicircular canals and is called the kinetic labyrinth. This labyrinth evaluates movements of the head.

The utricle and saccule contain a patch of specialized epithelium called the macula. The macula consists of hair cells and resembles the organ of Corti. The hair cells are stimulated in response to movements, position, or acceleration of the head. The action potentials from the hair cells are translated to the brain. However, much of this information is not perceived consciously. Subconsciously the body responds by making subtle tone adjustments in muscles of the back and neck to restore the head to its proper neutral balanced position (Fig. 29-8).

The kinetic labyrinth (Fig. 29-9) consists of three semicircular canals placed at right angles to each other. The configuration of the semicircular canals allows a person to detect movement in all directions. The base of each semicircular canal expands into an ampulla. The ampulla contains specialized sensory epithelium, which forms an ampullar crest that is functionally and structurally similar to the macula. One portion of the ampullar crest is called the cupula and acts as a float that responds to fluid movements within the semicircular canals. Again, the movements of these hair cells initiate action potentials, which are transmitted to the CNS via the vestibular portion of the acoustic (VIII) nerve.

AGE-RELATED CHANGES IN STRUCTURE AND FUNCTION

Age-related changes in the external ear can be seen in the auricle, which appears larger because of continued cartilage formation and loss of skin elasticity. The lobule of the auricle becomes elongated with a wrinkled appearance. The periphery of the auricle becomes covered with coarse, wirelike hairs. Men have larger tragi that are laterally situated in the external canal. These tragi become larger and coarser. The auditory canal narrows as a result of inward collapsing. The hairs lining the canal become coarser and stiffer. Additionally cerumen glands atrophy, causing the cerumen to be much drier. In the middle ear, age-related changes to the tympanic membrane result in a dull, retracted, and gray appearance of the tympanic membrane. Degeneration of ossicular joints in the middle ear has also been noted. Finally, changes within the inner ear result in decreased vestibular sensitivity. Hearing loss is not a normal part of aging and should be evaluated further (Lueckenotte, 1994).

COMMON PROBLEMS AND CONDITIONS

Pruritus

Pruritus, itching within the external auditory canal, is related to age-related atrophic changes in the skin. Atrophy of the epithelium and epidermal sebaceous glands results in dryness. Often, chronic pruritus of the ear canal results from an itch-scratch-itch cycle initiated by the dry skin. The problem may be exacerbated by efforts to retard and remove dry earwax buildup. The canal may lose more moisture through the use of cotton-tipped applicators and alcohol-vinegar mixtures. Several drops of glycerine or mineral oil instilled in the ear canal daily decrease the dryness that alcohol drops tend to cause (Meyerhoff, Patt, 1992).

Cerumen Impactions

Cerumen impaction is a reversible, often overlooked cause of conductive hearing loss. Identification and removal of the impaction can restore hearing acuity and re-

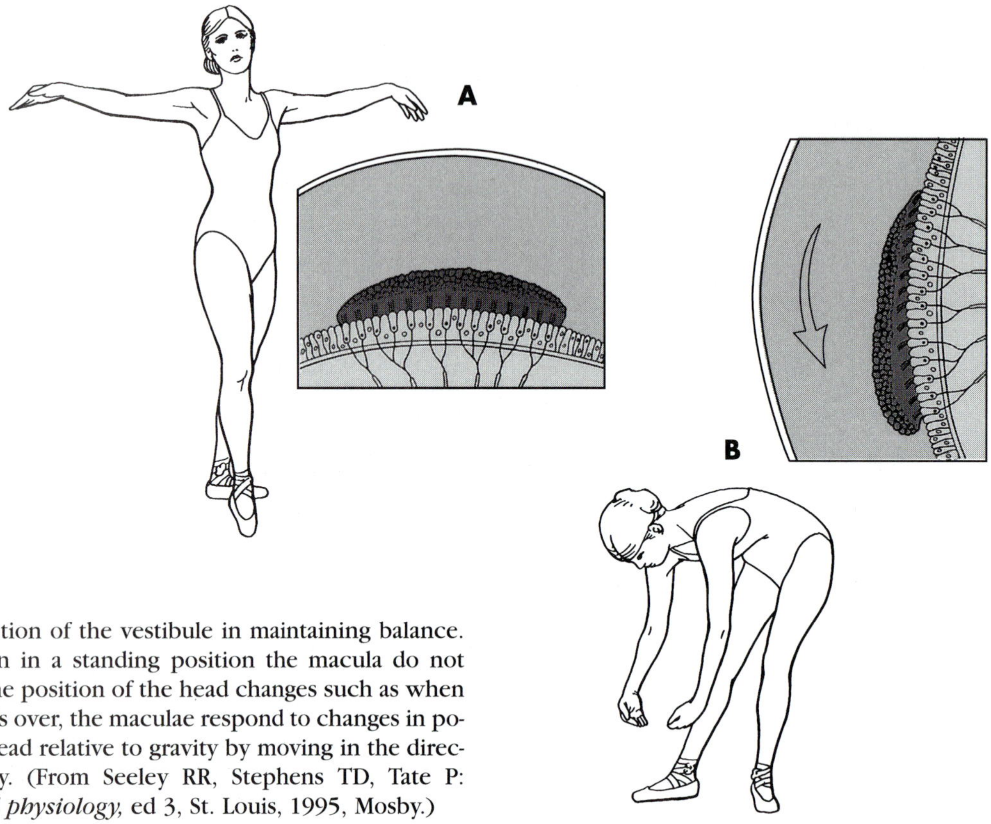

Fig 29-8 Function of the vestibule in maintaining balance. **A,** In a person in a standing position the macula do not move. **B,** As the position of the head changes such as when a person bends over, the maculae respond to changes in position of the head relative to gravity by moving in the direction of gravity. (From Seeley RR, Stephens TD, Tate P: *Anatomy and physiology,* ed 3, St. Louis, 1995, Mosby.)

lieve symptoms associated with impactions. Lewis-Cullinan and Janken (1990) found that removal of cerumen significantly improved hearing ability. The cerumen blockage may interfere with the passage of sound vibrations through the external auditory canal to the middle and inner ear, affecting a person's ability to hear and communicate. This impaired communication may then lead to social isolation and depression.

Cerumen is produced by the sebaceous and apocrine glands in the outer portion of the external auditory canal. Cerumen is eliminated from the ear by the action of the cilia and by the movements of chewing and talking. With increasing age, atropic changes in the sebaceous and apocrine glands lead to drier cerumen. These changes in the cerumen, coupled with a narrowed auditory canal and stiffer, coarser hairs lining the canal, lead to cerumen impaction.

Common symptoms of cerumen impactions include: hearing loss, feeling of fullness, itching, and tinnitus (ringing in the ears) (see Medical Management box, p. 836).

NURSING MANAGEMENT

ASSESSMENT

Clients with cerumen buildup may complain of ear fullness, itching, and difficulty hearing. An otoscopic examination shows that the external ear canal is obstructed by cerumen and that the tympanic membrane is not visible.

DIAGNOSIS

Potential nursing diagnoses for a client with the above assessment findings include: (1) sensory/perceptual alterations (auditory) related to cerumen impaction, and (2) social isolation related to difficulty communicating with family and friends.

PLANNING

Expected outcomes for a client with cerumen impaction include: (1) client will be free of cerumen impaction; (2)

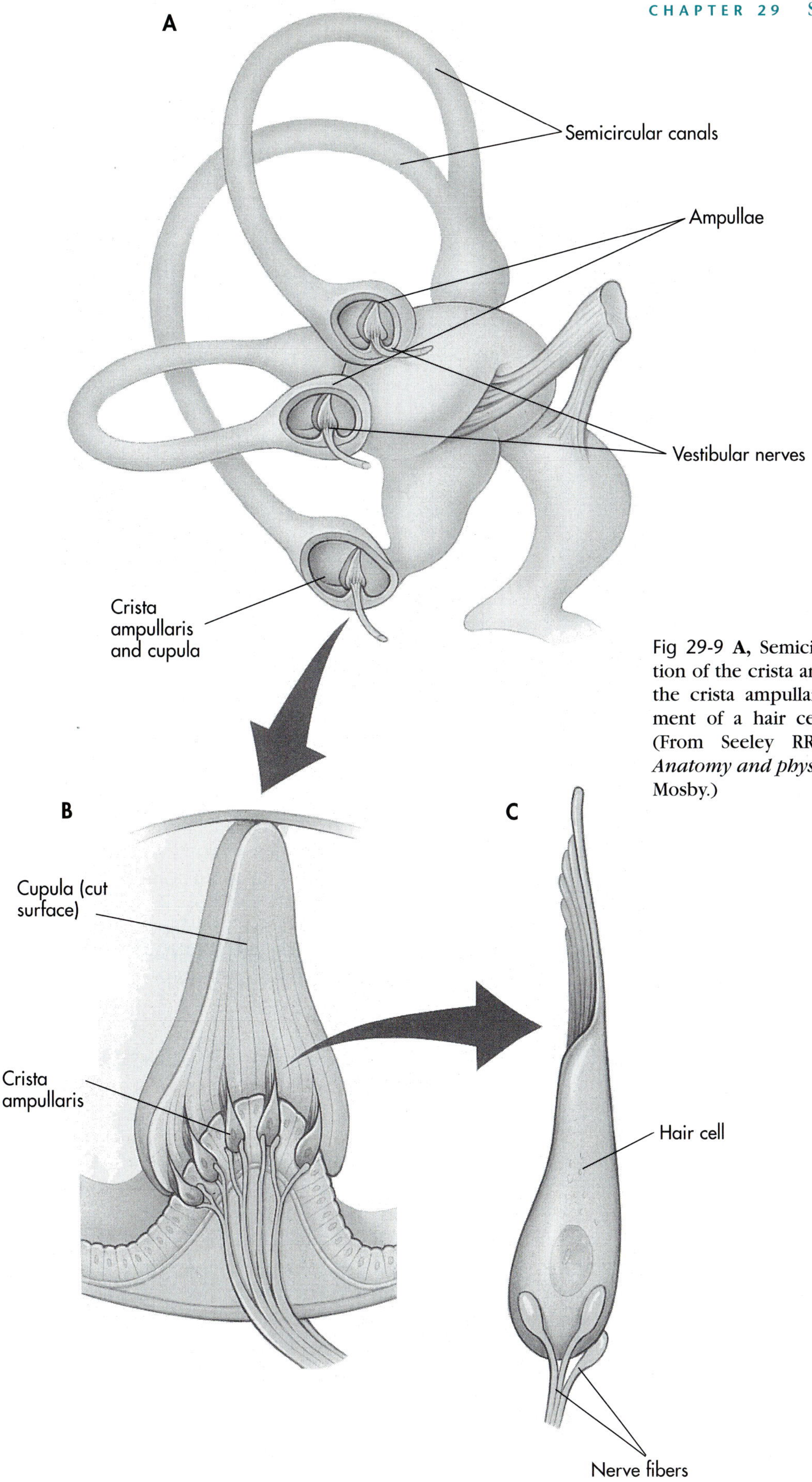

Fig 29-9 **A,** Semicircular canals showing location of the crista ampullaris. **B,** Enlargement of the crista ampullaris and cupula. **C,** Enlargement of a hair cell of the crista ampullaris. (From Seeley RR, Stephens TD, Tate P: *Anatomy and physiology,* ed 2, St. Louis, 1992, Mosby.)

MEDICAL MANAGEMENT

Cerumen Impaction

Diagnostic tests and procedures
Otoscopic examination

Treatment
Protocol for cerumen removal (Webber-Jones, 1992)
Clip and remove hairs in ear canal.
Instill a softening agent, mineral oil, or triethanolamine (Cerumenix) twice daily for several days until wax softens.
Irrigate the ear using a bulb syringe, a 2-to-4 ounce plastic syringe, or a Water Pik.
Use a solution of 3 ounces 3% hydrogen peroxide in one quart of water warmed to 98º to 100º F. If client is sensitive to hydrogen peroxide, use sterile normal saline solution.
Place towel around client's neck, tip head to side being drained with emesis basin under ear to catch drainage.
Do not inject air into client's ear or use high pressure when injecting fluid.
If cerumen is not washed out, begin the process again.
Firmly impacted cerumen must be manually extracted by a physician or advance practice nurse with an otoscope and a curette.

Prognosis
Cerumen impaction removal can restore hearing. Morley (1990) found that almost 50% of 40 hospitalized hearing-impaired clients with cerumen impaction had their hearing restored after cerumen removal.

client will follow proper instillation of softening agents, and (3) client will become involved in activities with family and friends.

✤ INTERVENTION

The nurse must assess clients for signs of hearing impairment that may indicate cerumen impaction such as: (1) difficulty understanding the spoken word—the client may ask why others are mumbling or deliberately excluding them from the conversation, (2) loud radio and TV volume, (3) withdrawal from social activities and accompanying depression, and (4) possible confusion and paranoia. Once an otoscopic examination reveals an impaction, the nurse should follow the protocol for cerumen removal. For clients living in the community, the client and family should be taught how to instill the softening agent. Mahoney (1993) found clients in a long-term care setting to have greater difficulty with detection and treatment of cerumen impaction and subsequently developed practice recommendations for long-term care nurses to follow when working with their clients (Box 29-11).

BOX 29-11

Practice Recommendations Related to Cerumen Impaction in the Long-Term Care Setting

Use a gerontological clinical nurse specialist/practitioner in the nursing home.
Conduct staff development program on hearing impairment and cerumen impaction.
Sensitize staff to the following:
- Ambient room noise;
- Hearing aid use; and
- Speech discrimination problems versus confusion.

Check for cerumen impaction on admission and then monthly.
Obtain an otoscope and train charge/treatment nurse in its use.
Evaluate present treatment practices.
Develop a standard protocol for cerumen impaction, prevention and treatment.

From Mahoney DF: Cerumen impaction: prevalence and detection in nursing homes, *Gerontol Nurs* 19(4):23-30,1993.

✤ EVALUATION

Client will achieve expected outcomes (Mahonney, 1993).

Tinnitus

Tinnitus is an annoying combination of both conductive and sensorineural hearing loss. It is a subjective sensation of noise in the ear defined as ringing, buzzing, or hissing. Individuals at any age may experience tinnitus but its prevalence increases with advancing age. For many older adults it is a chronic condition with which they must cope. For others it is an indication of permanent hearing loss or tumor.

The cochlear nerve contains hair cell receptors that convert sound waves into electric impulses. The most common causes of tinnitus are noise or toxin damage to the hair receptors of the cochlear nerve and age-related changes in the organs of hearing and balance. Tinnitus is not a disease but a symptom associated with many diseases, conditions, and medical treatments. Tinnitus can be classified as subjective or objective. Subjective tinnitus is audible only to the client and characterized as high-pitched, chronic, irreversible, and likely to be associated with hearing loss. Objective tinnitus, though rare, is audible both to the client and the examiner. It is more likely to be low-pitched and is often associated with an identifiable cause such as muscle spasms or vascular and musculoskeletal cranial disorders. An additional important classification of tinnitus is whether it is bilateral or unilateral. Unilateral tinnitus is associated with more serious diseases such as Meniere's disease, tumors, or vas-

MEDICAL MANAGEMENT

Tinnitus

Diagnostic tests and procedures

Health history (Box 29-12)
Laboratory tests
  Blood chemistries
  Complete blood count
  Thyroid profile
  Urinalysis
Chest X-Ray
Electrocardiogram
Physical Examination
  Hearing and balance testing (see Box 29-15, p. 841)
  Audiometric testing
Note: If unilateral or neurologic changes noted, otologic referral is necessary.

Treatment

If the diagnostic tests and procedures determine that the tinnitus is chronic and not a symptom of other diseases, then follow the interventions listed in Box 29-13, p. 839.

Prognosis

Tinnitus is seldom curable; however, with a systematic evaluation, people in whom it is a symptom of a more serious illness can be identified. House et al. (1987) reported a 10-year follow-up of 269 clients with chronic intractable tinnitus. Results revealed that 45% of the cases were controlled with complete relief or improved until clients were unaware of their tinnitus most of the time; 26% of the clients were not improved but accepted their tinnitus as no longer a problem; and 29% showed no change.

cular problems and requires an extensive work-up (see Medical Management box, above). Other causes for tinnitus are shown in Table 29-1.

BOX 29-12

Tinnitus Questionnaire

1. How long have you had "ringing" (or other sound) in your ears?
2. Describe as nearly as possible the sound you hear.
3. Is the sound in left, right, or both ears? Is it constant or occasional?
4. Does the sound change with exercise, climbing stairs, or fast walking?
5. Do you have a hearing problem?
6. Do you have ear pain, discharge, or an infection?
7. When is sound in ear(s) worse: daytime, evening, or night?
8. Does this sound interfere with sleep, television, radio, crowds, or conversation?
9. Do you grind your teeth or clench your jaws at times?
10. Have you recently had: Dental problems or treatments? Ear pain? Excessive ear wax? Ear discharge or infection? Cold or flu? Recent head or neck injury? Headaches? Dizziness? Balance difficulty? Visual problems? Swallowing problems? Speaking problems? Numbness or weakness anywhere?
11. Do you: Smoke? Drink coffee, tea, chocolate, cola or other carbonated drinks with caffeine; alcoholic or quinine water drinks?
12. What prescription medications do you take? What other medications do you take: aspirin, aspirin-containing medications, or ibuprofen (Advil) for headaches, joint pain or congestion; sleeping aids; or diet pills?
13. Do you experience considerable sudden or intense noise at work, home, or recreation that involves motor use or firearm use?
14. Have you or any family member had allergies? Arthritis? Anemia? Diabetes? High blood pressure? Thyroid problems?

From Ross V, Schevarria KH, Robinson B: Geriatric tinnitus: Causes, clinical treatment and prevention, *Gerontol Nurs* 17(10):6-11, 1991.

NURSING MANAGEMENT

ASSESSMENT

The Tinnitus Questionnaire should be used to gather necessary subjective data (see Box 29-12). Objectively, the client will have signs of subjective or objective unilateral or bilateral ringing in the ear.

DIAGNOSIS

Potential nursing diagnoses for the client with tinnitus include: (1) altered health maintenance related to lack of knowledge about tinnitus prevention practices; (2) sensory/perceptual alterations (auditory) related to ringing in ears; and (3) anxiety related to coping with chronic condition of ringing in ears.

PLANNING

Expected outcomes for the client with tinnitus include: (1) client will follow tinnitus prevention practices; (2) client will use home masking measures and a hearing aid or tinnitus masker to relieve tinnitus; and (3) client will cope with anxiety independently by using relaxation techniques.

INTERVENTION

Nursing interventions are outlined in Box 29-13. Clients should be taught prevention practices such as: (1) treating correctable problems (such as cerumen impaction

TABLE 29-1

Causes and Associated Factors of Tinnitus

Conditions that cause tinnitus	Drugs and other substances that aggravate or cause tinnitus	Recreational and job activities that cause noise-induced tinnitus
Aging	Caffeine	Power tool use (boat motors, lawnmowers, saws)
Noise-induced damage	Aspirin and combined drugs	Motorcycle and racetrack riding
Ototoxicity	Antimicrobials	Firearm use (hunting, target practice)
Stress	Atropine sulfate	Headphone abuse
Hypertension	Chloroquine (Aralen)	
Hyperthyroidism	Quinidine sulfate	
Vascular abnormalities	Quinine sulfate	
Familial hyperlipidemia	Antidepressants: Nortriptyline (Aventyl, Pamelor)	
Hypercholesterolemia	Nicotine	
Hypertriglyceridemia	Antihistamines and combinations	
Meniere's disease	Nonsteroidal antiinflammatory drugs (NSAIDS)	
Acoustic neuroma	Antihypertensives	
Temporomandibular joint dysfunction	Cyclobenzaprine HCl (Flexeril)	
	Ergot and ergotamine derivatives	
	Mechlorethamine HCl (Mustargen)	

From Ross V, Echevarria KH, Robinson B: Geriatric tinnitus: causes, clinical treatment and prevention, *Gerontol Nurs* 17(10):6-11, 1991.

and ear infection) that cause tinnitus, (2) softening loud sounds with improved acoustics, (3) using noise-protective ear plugs, and (4) avoiding ototoxic substances in foods, drinks, and drugs. Teach clients about the following home masking measures that produce a variety of distracting sounds: (1) portable radio tuned between stations, (2) loud ticking clock, (3) soft pleasant music, (4) electric fan, and (5) sleeping with head elevated on two pillows. Recommend that clients be evaluated for aids or a specially designed masker to improve tinnitus. Coping strategies to relieve anxiety and stress, such as relaxation training, biofeedback, and counseling, should be taught.

✣ EVALUATION

Achievement of the expected outcomes is evidenced by clients following recommended tinnitus interventions and strategies to cope with the chronic ringing in their ears.

HEARING LOSS

It is estimated that there are 7 to 10 million adults age 65 and older in the United States suffering from some type of hearing impairment. Hearing loss is not a normal part of the aging process and should be further evaluated for proper treatment.

Hearing impairment is classified as conductive, senorineural, or mixed. Conductive hearing loss results from interruption of the transmission of sound through the external auditory canal and middle ear. Conditions that may result in conductive hearing loss are cerumen impaction, otitis media, and otosclerosis (fixation of auditory ossicles).

Sensorineural hearing loss results from damage to the inner ear, the auditory nerve, or the brain so that sound waves are not interpreted correctly. Mixed hearing loss is a conductive hearing loss superimposed on a sensorineural hearing loss.

Presbycusis

Presbycusis, a sensorineural hearing loss, is the most common form of hearing loss in older adults. Typically, the hearing loss is bilateral, resulting in difficulty hearing high-pitched tones and conversational speech. It affects men more than women.

The cause of presbycusis remains unclear. Studies linking a direct cause have proven no clear correlation. Therefore, it remains a diagnosis of exclusion, in which other causes of hearing loss are ruled out. Other causes include the following (Kart, Metress, Metress, 1992):

- Noise-induced hearing loss (prolonged exposure to loud noise)
- Infection
- Head injury
- Diabetes
- Stroke
- Heart disease
- Hereditary factors

Symptoms experienced by the client are as follows:

- Increased volume on TV or radio
- Tilting head towards person speaking

BOX 29-13

Chronic Tinnitus Interventions

Correct physical problems:
Remove ear wax or foreign bodies, itching, or inflammation
Evaluate hypertension
Improve acoustics to promote healthy hearing
Wear noise-protective ear plugs
Check dental and temporomandibular joint problems

Avoid ototoxic substances in foods, drinks, and drugs:
Delete quinine, aspirin, and antiinflammatory drug compounds
Delete caffeine, chocolate, tea, and alcohol
Reassure older adult that tinnitus is not life-threatening

Teach simple home masking measures to relieve tinnitus:
Radio tuned between stations
Clocks that tick
Soft, pleasant, distracting music
Semi-elevated head position to sleep
Recommend evaluation for properly fitted hearing aid; may relieve tinnitus even if hearing loss is mild
More sophisticated, commercial tinnitus maskers and instruments (sold by Sears Roebuck and JC Penney) are matched to individualized pitch of one's tinnitus
Teach relaxation training to cope with stress and promote sleep; combined with biofeedback, this has been proved to be beneficial for long-term tinnitus sufferers
Contact local self-help tinnitus support groups (for information, contact the American Tinnitus Association, PO Box 5, Portland, OR 97207)

From Ross V, Schevarria KH, Robinson B: Geriatric tinnitus: Causes, clinical treatment and prevention, *Gerontol Nurs* 17(10):6-11,1991.

- Cupping hand around one ear
- Watching speaker's lips
- Speaking loudly
- Not responding when spoken to (Hogstel, 1992) (see Medical Management box at right)

Nursing Management

✣ ASSESSMENT

Subjective data that should be obtained from a client suffering from hearing loss should include the following: (1) onset, type, and progression of hearing loss, including differences in either ear; (2) family history of hearing loss; (3) presence of other symptoms: pressure or pain in ears, ringing in ear, or dizziness; (4) history of head injury or noise exposure; and (5) current medications with known ototoxic effects (see Table 29-1). Objectively, the client may display some behavioral symptoms of hearing loss (Box 29-14).

A complete hearing evaluation should be conducted (Box 29-15). See the Research box on p. 840 for recommended hearing screening.

✣ DIAGNOSIS

Nursing diagnoses based on analysis of the client's hearing loss include (1) sensory/perceptual alterations (auditory) related to sensorineural hearing loss, (2) social isolation related to hearing loss, and (3) self-esteem disturbance related to hearing loss.

✣ PLANNING

Expected outcomes for a client with a hearing loss include (1) client will effectively use aural rehabilitative techniques, (2) client will maintain satisfactory social contacts and activities with others, and (3) client will perceive self positively as evidenced by positive self-talk and behaviors.

✣ INTERVENTION

Interventions for the client with a hearing impairment focus on aural rehabilitation and facilitating communication. Clients often deny their hearing loss and need much encouragement and support to explore the various methods to improve hearing. Provide clients with a printed information sheet on hearing loss (Box 29-16). Aural rehabilitation includes auditory training, speech reading training, and hearing aids. Auditory training helps

MEDICAL MANAGEMENT

Presbycusis: Hearing Impaired

Diagnostic tests and procedures
External and internal (otoscopic) ear examination
Hearing tests including audiometric evaluation

Treatment
Surgically placed cochlear implants
Hearing Devices
Auditory rehabilitation

Prognosis
Hearing loss associated with presbycusis is gradual, and most older adults adjust over time. Mild and moderate hearing loss can be effectively treated with hearing aids; however, not all older people adjust and use these devices effectively. Therefore, hearing aid users and their families need to participate in teaching and counseling sessions.

BOX 29-14

Behavioral Clues Indicating Difficulty Hearing

Any adult who:

Is irritable, hostile, hypersensitive in interpersonal relations
Has difficulty in hearing upper frequency consonants
Complaints about people mumbling
Turns up the volume on television
Asks for frequent repetition and answers questions inappropriately
Loses sense of humor; becomes grim
Leans forward to hear better; face serious and strained
Shuns large- and small-group audience situations
May appear aloof and "stuck-up"
Complains of ringing in the ears
Has an unusually soft or loud voice
Repeatedly states, "What did you say?"

From Phipps WJ: The patient with ear problems. In Long BC, Phipps WJ, Cassmeyer VS, editors: *Medical-surgical nursing: a nursing process approach* ed 3, St Louis, 1993, Mosby.

the person with a hearing impairment listen to a speaker by differentiating between gross sounds. Speech reading training includes lip reading and speech skills. Lip reading requires understanding of verbal communication by integrating lip movements, facial expressions, gestures, and environmental clues. This process is extremely difficult without auditory clues. Speech skills must be conserved with the reduced auditory feedback experienced by the client with impaired hearing. People who have hearing impairments must learn to work intelligently with inefficient communication and decreased speech. Hearing aids amplify sound but do not improve the ability to hear. Clients and their families should be instructed on the basics of hearing aid use and care (see Client/Family Teaching box, p. 845). All nurses and nursing assistants should have a basic understanding of how to work with a hearing aid to assist the client who is unable to care for the aid. Clients and their families should be taught where to obtain and how to use assisted listening devices (see Client/Family Teaching box, p. 844, at left). Finally, families and caregivers who work with a hearing impaired client should be taught strategies to improve communication (see Client/Family Teaching box, p. 844, at right).

Services for the hearing impaired are available to give information and include the following (Phipps, 1993a):

1. American Academy of Otolaryngology—Head and Neck Surgeons, 1 Prince St., Alexandria, VA 20005; a professional society for physicians specializing in diseases of the ear and related areas, it can provide information on hearing and balance disorders.
2. American Annals of the Deaf, 5034 Wisconsin Ave., NW, Washington, DC 20016. Every year the April issue lists a directory of programs and services for the deaf available by state and includes information about the type of facilities.
3. American Federation of the Physically Handicapped, Inc., 1370 National Press Building, Washington, DC 20004; provides counseling and information.
4. American Speech-Language-Hearing Association, 10801 Rockville Pike, Dept AP, Rockville, MD 20852. This association can answer questions or mail information on hearing aids or hearing loss

Text continued on p. 845.

RESEARCH

O'Rourke C et al: Effectiveness of a hearing screening protocol for the elderly, *Geriatr Nurs* 14(2): 66-69, 1993.

Sample, setting

The sample included 60 older adults age 56 to 90 (mean age was 76.7) who attended hearing screenings sponsored by a local university speech and hearing clinic.

Methodology

Hearing screening protocol incorporated four tests: case history, visual inspection, pure-tone screening, and the Hearing Handicap Inventory for the Elderly-Screening Version (HHIE-S).

Findings

The abbreviated case history and the visual inspection were quick to administer. They helped indentify four subjects in need of medical referral who had previously not been identified with other screening tools. Both pure-tone screening and the HHIE-S have been suggested as effective screening tools. When the HHIE-S was used in combination with the case history and the visual inspection only, 13 of the 15 subjects (22%) would not have been identified as needing additional evaluation, when in fact they did. However, when the pure-tone screening was used in combination with the case history and visual inspection, only three subjects (5%) would not have been identified as needing additional evaluation, when in fact they did.

Implications

Nurses in any setting, but especially those in long term and extended care facilities, can initiate hearing screening of older adults. Given the time constraints in a screening protocol, the most efficient hearing screening protocol for the older adult is pure-tone screening used in conjunction with a case history and a visual inspection.

BOX 29-15

Assessment of Hearing and Balance

The acoustic nerve (cranial nerve VIII) is tested by evaluating hearing. Subjective assessment of auditory function begins when the client responds to your questions and directions. This should occur without excessive repetition. Speech should be clear with a proper tone; monotonous tone and erratic volume may indicate hearing loss.

Hearing evaluation

Whispered voice test

1. Occlude opposite ear and stand 1 to 2 feet from the ear being tested.
2. Softly whisper numbers and ask client to repeat the words heard.
3. Gradually increase loudness of whisper until the client responds accurately.
4. Repeat the procedure with the other ear.

The client should be able to hear softly whispered words with 50% accuracy.

Watch tick test

1. Occlude opposite ear and place ticking watch 5 inches from ear being tested.
2. Slowly move watch toward the ear.
3. Ask client to indicate when ticking is heard.
4. Repeat procedure with the other ear.

The client should be able to hear ticking watch at a distance of 1 to 2 inches.

Tuning fork tests

The tuning fork is used to compare hearing by bone conduction with that by air conduction. Hold the base of the tuning fork and set in vibration by tapping the tines gently.

Weber test

1. Place vibrating tuning fork on client's forehead.
2. Ask client if sound is heard equally in both ears or better in one ear (laterilization of sound).

The client should hear the sound equally in both ears.

Rinne test

1. Place the base of the vibrating tuning fork against the client's mastoid bone.
2. Ask the client to indicate when sound is no longer heard and note the time elapsed in seconds (*bone conduction).*
3. Quickly move the still vibrating tines 1 inch from the auditory canal.
4. Ask the client to tell you when the sound is no longer heard and note time elapsed in seconds (*air conduction).*
5. Compare the number of seconds sound is heard by bone conduction versus air conduction.

Air-conducted sound should be heard twice as long as bone-conducted sound.

Balance testing

Romberg test

1. Ask client to stand, feet together and arms at sides, with eyes open, then closed.
2. NOTE: Stand close and be prepared to catch client if he/she falls. Slight swaying of the body is expected but not to the point of falling. If the client is unable to perform the Romberg test, do not perform other balance tests.
3. May also ask client to stand on one foot with eyes closed and arms at sides.
4. Repeat test on other foot.

Balance on each foot should be maintained for 5 seconds with slight swaying.

Gait

1. Observe the barefooted client walk a short distance with eyes open and then turn and walk with eyes closed.
2. Note gait pattern, arm movements and stability.
3. If any abnormal gait patterns are noted, have the client walk in a tandem (heel-toe) fashion.
4. Have the client walk in a straight line with eyes open and arms at the sides.

Note any extension of the arms for balance; instability noted by lateral staggering or falling. Slight swaying is expected.

Coordination and proprioception testing

Rapid alternating rhythmic movements

1. Instruct client to pat knees with palms and back of hands rapidly.
2. As an alternative, have the client rapidly touch the thumb to each finger on the same hand, in sequence from the index finger to the pinky and back.

Finger-to-nose test

1. With eyes closed, have the client touch the nose with the index finger of one hand.
2. Alternate hands and increase speed.

Finger-to-finger test

1. With eyes open, have the client touch his/her nose with their index finger and then touch your index finger.
2. The examiner should hold index finger 18″ from the client and move the position of the finger during testing.

Heel-to-shin test

1. Have the client sit and run the heel of one foot up and down the shin (from the ankle to the foot) of the opposite leg.
2. Repeat the procedure with the other heel.

During above testing, all movement should be rapid, smooth, rhythmic and accurate.

From Lueckenotte AG: *Pocket guide to gerontological assessment,* ed 2, St. Louis, 1994, Mosby.

BOX 29-16

Hearing and Older Adults

It is easy to take good hearing for granted. In the world of the hearing impaired, words in a conversation may be misunderstood, musical notes might be missed, and a ringing doorbell may go unanswered. Hearing impairment ranges from difficulty understanding words or hearing certain sounds to total deafness.

Because of fear, misinformation, or vanity, some people will not admit to themselves or anyone else that they have a hearing problem. It has been estimated, however, that approximately 30% of adults age 65 through 74 and about 50% of those age 75 through 79 suffer some degree of hearing loss. In the United States alone, more than 10 million older people are hearing impaired.

If ignored and untreated, hearing problems can grow worse, hindering communication with others, limiting social activities, and reducing constructive use of leisure time. People with hearing impairments often withdraw socially to avoid the frustration and embarrassment of not being able to understand what is being said. In addition, hearing-impaired people may become suspicious of relatives and friends who "mumble" or "don't speak up."

Hearing loss may cause an older hearing-impaired person to be wrongly labeled as "confused," "unresponsive," or "uncooperative." At times, the feelings of powerlessness and frustration experienced by older individuals trying to communicate with others result in depression and withdrawal.

While older people today are, in general, demanding greater satisfaction from life, those with hearing impairments often find the quality of their lives diminished. Fortunately, help is available, in the form of surgery, treatment with medicines, special training, a hearing aid, or an alternate listening device.

Some common signs of hearing impairment

Words are difficult to understand.
Sounds such as the dripping of a faucet or the high notes of a violin cannot be heard.
A hissing or ringing background noise is heard continually.
Another person's speech sounds slurred or mumbled.
Television programs, concerts, and social gatherings are less enjoyable because much goes unheard.

Diagnoses of hearing problems

If you are having trouble hearing, see your doctor for treatment or referral to a hearing specialist. By ignoring the problem, you may be overlooking a serious medical condition. Hearing impairments may be caused by exposure to excessively loud noises over a long period of time, viral infections, vascular incidents (such as heart conditions or stroke), head injuries, certain drugs, tumors, excessive ear wax, heredity, or age-related changes in the ear mechanisms. In view of the importance of good hearing, seeking medical help is certainly worthwhile.

In some cases, the diagnosis and treatment of a hearing problem may take place in the family doctor's office. More complicated cases may require the help of specialists known as *otologists* or *otolaryngologists*. These specialists are doctors of medicine or doctors of osteopathy with extensive training in ear problems. They will conduct a thorough examination, take a medical history, ask about hearing problems affecting other family members, and order any other necessary laboratory tests. Many times they will then refer the client to an *audiologist*. Audiologists specialize in the identification, prevention, and management of hearing problems and in the rehabilitation of people with hearing loss. They do not prescribe drugs or perform surgery, but they can recommend and sometimes dispense hearing aids. To test hearing, the audiologist uses an audiometer, a device which electronically generates sounds of different pitches and loudness. The testing is painless and within a short time the degree of hearing impairment can be determined and a course of treatment recommended.

Types of hearing loss

Presbycusis (pronounced prez-bee-ku' sis) is a common type of hearing loss in older people. Changes in the delicate workings of the inner ear lead to difficulties understanding speech, and possibly an intolerance for loud sounds, but not total deafness. Thus, "don't shout-I'm not deaf!" is frequently heard from older people with this type of hearing impairment.

Every year after age 50 we lose some of our hearing ability. The decline is gradual and progressive so that by age 60 or 70 as many as 25% of older adults are noticeably hearing impaired. Just as the graying of hair occurs at different rates, presbycusis develops differently from person to person.

Although presbycusis is usually attributed to aging, it does not affect everyone and some researchers view it as a disease. Environmental noise, certain drugs, improper diet, and genetic makeup may contribute to this disorder. Although the condition is permanent, there is much a person can do to function well despite the impairment.

Conduction deafness is another form of hearing loss sometimes experienced by older adults. It involves blockage or impairment of the mechanical movement in the outer or middle ear so that sound waves are not able to travel properly through the ear. This may be caused by packed ear wax, extra fluid, abnormal bone growth in the ear, or infection. People with this problem often find that voices and other sounds seem muffled, but their own voices sound louder than normal. As a result, they often speak softly. Depending on the cause, flushing of the ear, medicines, or surgery will prove successful in most cases

Central deafness is a third type of hearing loss that oc-

From US Department of Health and Human Services, Public Health Service, 1983, National Institutes of Health.

BOX 29-16

Hearing and Older Adults—cont'd

curs in older adults, although it is quite rare even in this age group. It is caused by damage to the nerve centers within the brain. Sound levels are not affected, but understanding of language usually is. The causes include extended illness with a high fever, lengthy exposure to loud noises, use of certain drugs, head injuries, vascular problems, or tumors. Central deafness cannot be treated medically or surgically, but for some, special training by an audiologist or speech therapist can be beneficial.

Treatment

Examination and test results from the family doctor, ear specialist, and/or audiologist will determine the most effective treatment for a specific hearing problem. In some cases, medical treatment such as flushing the ear canal to remove packed ear wax or surgery may restore some or all of hearing ability.

At other times, a hearing aid may be recommended. A hearing aid is a small device designed to amplify sounds. Although hearing aids are not recommended for all hearing difficulties, some people can benefit from a properly used device. Before you can buy a hearing aid, you must either obtain a written statement from your doctor (stating that your hearing impairment has been medically evaluated and that you might benefit from a hearing aid) or sign a waiver stating that you do not desire a medical evaluation.

Should a hearing aid be the recommended form of treatment for you, there are several things you should know about buying one. As an informed consumer you should shop for a hearing aid just as for any other product. There are many models on the market, offering different kinds of help for different kinds of problems. Hearing tests can determine the nature of the hearing problem, but only you can judge the comfort, convenience, and quality of sound of an aid. Remember, too, that you are not only buying a product, but a set of services which include any necessary adjustments, counseling in the use of the aid, maintenance, and repairs throughout the warranty period. Before deciding where to buy your aid, consider the quality of service as well as the quality of the merchandise.

When buying a hearing aid keep in mind that the most expensive hearing aid may not be the best for you. You may find one that sells for less and offers you more satisfaction. Buy an aid with only those features you need. Also, be aware that the controls for many of the special features are tiny and may be difficult to adjust. Choose an aid you can operate easily. Many hearing aid dealers (usually called "dispensers") offer a free trial period of up to 30 days so that you may wear the aid before making a decision. It is a good idea to take advantage of the trial period since it often takes at least a month to become comfortable with the new hearing aid. Your dispenser should have the patience and skill to help you through the adjustment period.

At times, people with certain types of hearing impairments may need special training. One form, speech-reading, trains a person to receive visual cues from lip movements as well as facial expressions, body posture and gestures, and the environment. Auditory training may include hearing aid orientation, but it is also designed to help hearing-impaired people identify their specific communication problems and to better handle them. Although neither speech-reading nor auditory training can improve damaged hearing, they can reduce the handicapping effects of hearing impairment by making the best use of the hearing ability that remains. If needed, counseling is also available so that hearing-impaired older people are able to maintain a positive self-image while understanding their communication abilities and limitations.

Cost

Because hearing impairments have so many causes, it is important to be examined by your doctor as soon as you suspect a problem with your hearing. Too often, people with hearing problems fail to get medical attention until the condition is beyond help. Unfortunately, the high cost of hearing health care contributes to this neglect. Medicare will pay for the diagnosis and evaluation of hearing loss if requested by a physician, but it will often not pay for the means to correct it. In some states Medicaid covers some costs of a hearing aid. Before buying an aid you may want to contact one of the organizations listed in this box. Many local chapters are able to provide information concerning Medicaid coverage of hearing aids.

If you have problems hearing

See your doctor to determine the cause of your hearing problem. Ask if you should see a specialist.

Do not hesitate to ask people to repeat what they have just said.

Try to limit background noise (stereo, television, etc.).

Do not hesitate to tell people that you have a hearing problem and what they can do to make communication easier.

If you know someone with a hearing problem

Speak slightly louder than normal. However, shouting will not make the message any clearer, and may sometimes distort it. Speak at your normal rate, but not too rapidly. Do not overarticulate. This distorts the sounds of speech and makes use of visual clues more difficult.

Speak to the person at a distance of 3 to 6 feet. Position yourself near good light so that your lip movements, facial expressions, and gestures may be seen clearly. Wait until you are visible to the hearing-impaired person before speaking. Avoid chewing, eating, or covering your mouth when speaking.

Never speak directly into the person's ear. This prohibits

Continued.

BOX 29-16

Hearing and Older Adults—cont'd

the listener from making use of visual clues.

If the listener does not understand what was said, rephrase the idea in short, simple sentences.

Arrange living rooms or meeting rooms so that no one is more than 6 feet apart and all are completely visible. In meetings or group activities where there is a speaker presenting information, ask the speaker to use the public address system.

Treat the hearing-impaired person with respect. Include the person in all discussions about him or her. This helps alleviate the feelings of isolation common in hearing-impaired people.

For your reference

If you would like further information about hearing problems, you may contact the organizations listed below. Please be sure to state clearly what type information you would like to receive.

American Academy of Otolaryngology—Head and Neck Surgeons, 1 Prince St., Alexandria, VA 20005. The Academy is a professional society of medical doctors specializing in diseases of the ear and related areas. They can provide information on hearing and balance disorders.

American Speech-Language-Hearing Association, 10801 Rockville Pike, Dept AP, Rockville, MD 20852 (or call 1-[800]-638-8255 for the National Association for Hearing and Speech Action). Either organization can answer questions or mail information on hearing aids or hearing loss and communication problems in the elderly. They can also provide a list of certified audiologists in each state.

Office of Scientific and Health Reports, National Institute of Neurological and Communicative Disorders and Stroke, Bldg 31, Rm 8A06, Bethesda, MD 20205. The Institute is the focal point within the Federal government for research on hearing loss and other communication disorders. Ask for the Institute's pamphlet *Hearing Loss: Hope Through Research.*

Self Help for Hard of Hearing People (*Shhh*), 4848 Battery Lane, Dept E, Bethesda, MD 20814. *Shhh* is a nationwide organization for the hard of hearing. Their national office publishes a bimonthly journal reporting the experiences of those with hearing impairments as well as new developments in the field of hearing loss. A number of publications and reprints are available for the hard of hearing.

CLIENT/FAMILY TEACHING

Assisted Listening Devices

These are devices designed to amplify sound or transform sound into tactile or visual signals. These systems allow a hearing impaired person to communicate more effectively and function more independently.

Amplifiers for the telephone, TV, or radio
Close-captioned television
Teletypewriters
Doorbell and telephone that light as well as ring
Flashing smoke detectors and alarm clocks
Burglar alarms that light up as well as sound

Modified from Hogstel MO: *Clinical manual of gerontological nursing,* St. Louis, 1992, Mosby.

CLIENT/FAMILY TEACHING

Strategies to Improve Communication When There is Hearing Loss

Provide good visual contact with clients. Hearing-impaired individuals need to supplement hearing with lipreading. They need to be able to see the speaker's face and lips. Avoid situations where there is glare or shadows on the client's field of vision.

Reduce or eliminate background noise.

Speak at a normal rate and volume. Do not over-articulate or shout. Keep hands away from mouth when talking.

Use shorter sentences and pause at the end of each sentence.

Use gestures, such as pointing, when appropriate.

Inform clients of topics to be discussed and of changes in topics.

To monitor their understanding, have clients repeat important information.

Avoid the appearance of frustration.

From Taylor KS: Geriatric hearing loss: management strategies for nurses, *Geriatr Nurs* 14(2):76,1993.

CLIENT/FAMILY TEACHING

Hearing Aid Assessment Tool for Cleaning, Inserting, and Troubleshooting

Component	Look	Listen
Earmold or in-the-ear aid	Opening clear? Cracks, rough areas? Check fit.	Use sounds (a/u/c/s)
Battery	Using battery tester, check voltage (replace at 1.1 or below). Compartment clean? Battery contacts clean? Battery inserted properly (match + on battery to + on battery compartment)? Is battery compartment shut all the way?	
Case	Cracks? Separating?	Press case gently Interruption in amplification?
Microphone	Clean? Visible damage?	
Dials	Clean? Easily rotated?	Rotate-Reasonable gain variation? Static?
Switches	Clean? Easy to move?	Turn on and off Static?
Cord (body aid)	Cracked? Frayed? Connection plugs clean?	Run fingers down cord-Clean? Interruption in amplification? Connections tight?
Tubing (behind-ear aid)	Cracks? Good connection to earmold and aid? Moisture? Debris?	Cover opening of ear mold and turn to maximum gain Feedback? Distortion? Static?
Receiver (body aid)	Cracks? Firmly attached to earmold snap?	Reduced gain? Substitute spare receiver and recheck
Volume control	Smooth, gradual increase	Five speech sounds clearly amplified?
Distortion		Clear quality?
Feedback	Recheck receiver snap, tubing, and earmold	Turn to maximum gain to check External feedback? Internal?

From Palumbo MV: Hearing access 2000: increasing awareness of the hearing impaired, *Gerontol Nurs* 16(9):26-31, 1990.

and communication problems in the older adults, and provide a list of certified audiologists in each state.

5. Gallaudet College, 7th and Florida Ave., Washington, DC 20002; the only liberal arts college for the deaf in the world.
6. National Association of Hearing and Speech Agencies, 919 18th St. NW, Washington DC 20006; provides counseling and information.
7. Office of Scientific and Health Reports, National Institute of Neurological and Communicative Disorders and Stroke, Bldg 31, Rm 8A06, Bethesda, MD 20205; a focal point for research on hearing loss and other communication disorders. (Pamphlet: *Hearing loss: hope through research*).
8. Self-Help for Hard-of-Hearing People (Shhh), 4848 Battery Lane, Dept E, Bethesda, MD 20814. This nationwide organization for the hard-of-hearing publishes a bimonthly magazine that includes experiences of the hard-of-hearing and new developments in the field of hearing loss; publications and reprints are available.
9. Society of Otorhinolaryngology and Head-Neck Nurses, Inc., 439 N Causeway, New Smyrna Beach, FL 32069. This professional nursing society for nurses who specialize in caring for clients with problems of the ear, nose, and throat can provide information on hearing and balance disorders.
10. State Office of Vocational Rehabilitation (in each

state); provides vocational training and placement services.

11. Veterans Administration; provides audiology clinics and rehabilitation services for veterans.

✣ EVALUATION

Evaluation is based on achievement of expected client outcomes as evidenced by the client using aural rehabilitation techniques and devices to enhance communication.

BALANCE—COMMON PROBLEMS AND CONDITIONS

Dizziness and disequilibrium

Dizziness and disequilibrium are common complaints of older adults. An estimated 12.5 million older people in the United States are affected by these conditions. Although there is a general decrease in vestibular sensitivity with aging, the symptoms of dizziness or imbalance should not be considered a normal part of aging. Balance disorders contribute to deficits in ambulation that may interfere with an older person's ability to carry out normal ADLs. The five age-related conditions of disequilibrium that have been documented in older adults are:

1. **Benign positional vertigo**—severe episodes of vertigo precipitated by placing one's head in a particular position.
2. **Ampillary disequilibrium**—vertigo of disequilibrium caused when the head is turned quickly to the right or left, or by extension or flexion.
3. **Macular disequilibrium**—vertigo precipitated by a change of head position in relation to the direction of gravitational force (e.g., severe dizziness when rising from bed).
4. **Vestibular ataxia of aging**—constant feeling of imbalance with ambulation (Meyerhoff, Patt, 1992).
5. **Meniere's disease**—a disease that is not very common but is seen more often in older women. The most significant symptom is sudden dizziness, and thus this disease poses safety issues related to a potential fall.

MEDICAL MANAGEMENT

Vertigo and Meniere's Disease

Diagnostic tests and procedures

Vertigo

Vestibular function tests (see Box 29-15)
Quantitative testing
- Caloric stimulation (warm and cool water irrigations in ear)
- Rotational and posturography (body positioning with visual and proprioceptive cues)

Meniere's disease

Vestibular function tests
Quantitative testing
Audiogram
Electronystagmography
Radiograph of the internal auditory canal (Phipps, 1993a)

Treatment

Vertigo

Pharmacologic
- Meclizine (Antivert)

Vestibular rehabilitation
- Vestibular exercise program (Phipps, 2993a)

Meniere's disease

Decreased fluid intake
Low-sodium diet
Pharmacologic
- Diuretic
- Antihistamine
- Meclizine (Antivert)

Surgical
- Decompressions of endolymphatic sac
- Labyrinthectomy (Phipps, 1993a)

Prognosis

Vertigo

Treatment can often ease the symptoms of vertigo, but a large percentage of clients continue to experience dizziness and imbalance. Treatment is then aimed at adaptation to maintain optimum safe daily functioning (Meyerhoff, Patt, 1992).

Meniere's disease

There is no cure for Meniere's Disease, so medications are given simply to relieve symptoms during an acute attack. The client must learn to live with the disease; however, as the attacks reoccur, surgery may be necessary. The major complication is total loss of hearing.

Balance is regulated by inner ear vestibular function, vision, and impulses from skeletal muscles. Although the vestibular system of the inner ear is the most common source of dizziness and balance disorders, the following causes must also be considered:

- Visual disturbances
- Musculoskeletal disorders
- Neurologic dysfunctions
- Metabolic abnormalities
- Cardiovascular disease
- Medications (Meyerhoff, Patt, 1992)

Signs and symptoms vary for each disorder but may include any of the following:

- Whirling dizziness when the head is moved in a certain position
- Dizziness or imbalance when moving the head quickly to the right, left, up, or down
- Constant feeling of imbalance when walking

Meniere's Disease

Meniere's disease is caused by pressure within the labyrinth of the inner ear, which is a result of excess endolymph that causes swelling in the cochlea. It is unclear what causes the excess fluid. The three major characteristics are vertigo, tinnitus, and hearing loss. Other associated symptoms include loss of balance, nausea and vomiting, and spasmodic eye movement (see Medical Management box, p. 846).

NURSING MANAGEMENT

✣ ASSESSMENT

Subjective data include a description of vertigo episodes (frequency, duration); accompanying symptoms such as nausea and vomiting, hearing loss, or tinnitus; history of balance problems; and drug history. Objective data include a complete assessment of hearing and balance (see Box 29-15, p. 841). Table 29-2 provides information on interpretation of tuning fork tests.

✣ DIAGNOSIS

Potential nursing diagnoses for the client with vertigo and Meniere's disease include: (1) sensory/perceptual alterations (kinesthetic) related to vertigo and imbalance; (2) potential for injury related to acute onset of vertigo; (3) knowledge deficit of cause of vertigo and its treatment related to lack of exposure and inexperience; (4) knowledge deficit of preoperative and postoperative surgical care for Meniere's disease related to lack of exposure; and (5) anxiety related to uncertainty of future vertigo attacks.

TABLE 29-2

Interpretation of Tuning Fork Tests

Test	Conductive hearing loss	Sensorineural hearing loss
Weber	Laterilization of sound to deaf ear.	Laterilization of sound to better ear.
Rinne	Bone conduction heard as long as or longer than air conduction.	Air conduction heard longer than bone conduction (>2x).

From Bullock B, Rosendahl PP: *Pathophysiology: adaptation and alterations in function,* ed 3, Philadelphia, 1992, JB Lippincott.

✣ PLANNING

Expected outcomes for the client include: (1) client will accurately follow prescribed medication regimen and exercise protocol; (2) client will safely follow measures to reduce dizziness and prevent falls; (3) client will state the causes and treatment of vertigo; (4) client will ask questions about surgical care for Meniere's disease; and (5) client will meet own self-care needs as evidenced by reports of normal appetite, sleep, and activity.

✣ INTERVENTION

Pharmacologic treatment includes antivertiginous drugs such as meclizine (Antivert) or diphenhydramine (Benadryl). Meclizine may cause drowsiness; clients should be instructed to avoid alcoholic beverages while taking this drug. Clients with a history of asthma, glaucoma, or enlargement of the prostate gland must be monitored carefully while taking meclizine because of its anticholinergic action. Diphenhydramine, an antihistamine, is likely to cause dizziness, sedation, and hypotension in older clients. A diuretic such as hydrochlorothiazide (HydroDIURIL) and a low-sodium diet help remove excess endolymph fluid. Clients on diuretic therapy need to be monitored for evidence of fluid or electrolyte imbalance. Vestibular exercises are aimed at improving visual following when the head is stationary, gaze stability during head movements, balance in standing and during ambulation (Meyerhoff, Patt, 1992). Surgery may be performed for Meniere's disease to prevent further damage and sensorineural hearing loss. A client undergoing ear surgery is given a local anesthetic. Preoperative care includes giving instructions for postoperative care and sedating the client. Postoperative care includes the following: (1) positioning the operative ear up for 4 hours after surgery; (2) medicating for pain and vertigo; (3) following safety precautions—siderails up, call light in reach, assistance with ambulation; (4) monitoring the client for changes in hearing or vertigo, for neurologic symptoms such as headache, or for facial paralysis; (5) instructing the client to keep mouth open when sneezing or coughing. There is no complete cure for vertigo. Therefore clients must be taught the following measures to reduce dizziness: (1) move slowly; (2) avoid bright, glaring lights—a quiet, darkened room is best; (3) if vertigo occurs during ambulation then lie down immediately and hold the head still. The client with vertigo must be taught the causes of vertigo, pharmacologic treatment and vestibular exercises, and measures to reduce vertigo and promote safety during an acute attack.

✣ EVALUATION

Evaluation includes achievement of the expected outcomes.

TASTE AND SMELL

The senses of taste and smell detect the safety of the environment as well as its pleasantness or unpleasantness. There is some evidence that the senses of smell and taste diminish with aging. A decreased sensitivity to odors may at times be dangerous for the older person; for example, a person may fail to detect the odor of smoke or leaking gas. Loss of smell and taste can affect an older person's appetite, which may lead to nutritional problems.

NORMAL STRUCTURE AND FUNCTION

The senses of taste and smell work closely with one another. They are, however, very distinct anatomically. Olfaction, the sense of smell, occurs in response to odors that enter the olfactory recess, which lies in the superior part of the nasal cavity (Fig. 29-10). The olfactory recess is comprised of specialized nasal epithelium called the olfactory epithelium. Smell is the least understood sense. This results from the difficulty in studying the olfactory epithelium because of its location and from the subjective nature of the sense itself. However, most physiologists believe that the wide variety of detectable smells are actually combinations of a smaller number of primary odors. The following seven primary classes of odors have been identified: (1) camphoraceous, (2) musky, (3) floral, (4) pepperminty, (5) ethereal, (6) pungent, and (7) putrid.

Taste is mainly a function of the taste buds in the mouth, but one's sense of smell also contributes strongly to taste perception. Taste is important because it allows people to select foods they desire and foods with specific nutritive substances to supply the body's tissues.

The taste buds are the sensory structures that detect taste stimuli. The taste buds are found on three of four different types of papillae of the tongue (Fig. 29-11). Circumvallate (surrounded by a groove or valley) papillae

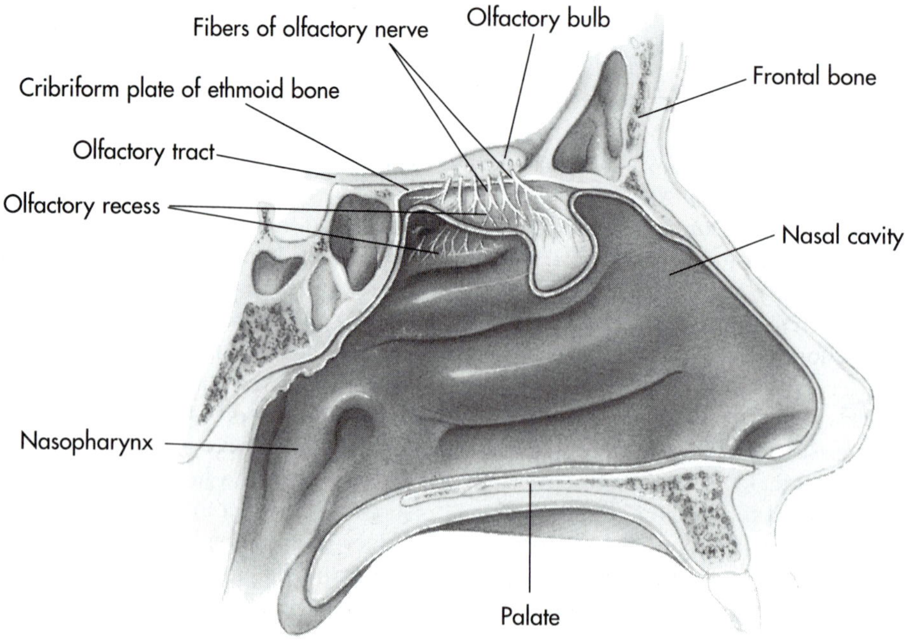

Fig 29-10 Lateral wall of the nasal cavity (cut in sagittal section) showing the olfactory recess and olfactory bulb. (From Seeley RR, Stephens TD, Tate P: *Anatomy and physiology,* ed 3, St. Louis, 1995, Mosby.)

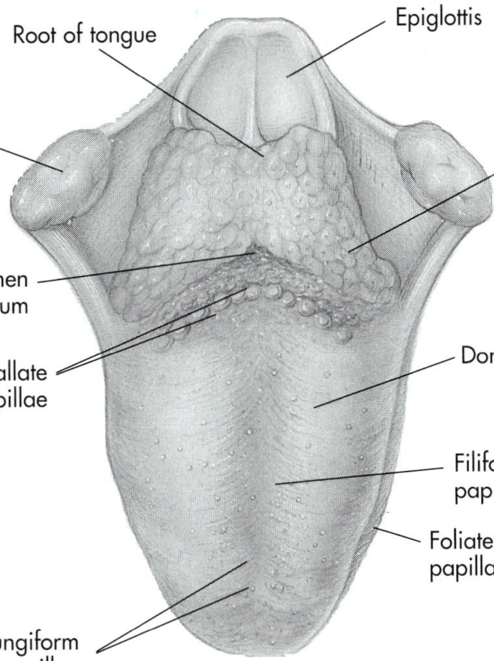

Fig. 29-11 Papillae and taste buds. (From Seeley RR, Stephens TD, Tate P: *Anatomy and physiology,* ed 3, St. Louis, 1995, Mosby.)

are the largest but least numerous of the papillae. Eight to twelve of these form a V-shaped row along the anterior and posterior borders of the tongue. Fungiform (mushroom-shaped) papillae are scattered irregularly over the front surface of the tongue. They appear as small red dots and are interspersed among the filiform (filament-shaped) papillae which contain no taste buds. Finally, foliate (leaf-shaped) papillae are located on the sides of the tongue. Additional taste buds are located on the palate, tonsillar pillars, and nasopharynx. Adults have approximately 10,000 taste buds that rapidly degenerate after the age of 45. Dr. Schiffman (1983) reports that the average 75-year-old has about half as many taste buds and olfactory neurons as the average 20-year-old.

The basic tastes detected by the taste buds can be divided into four types: sour, salty, sweet, and bitter. Thresholds vary for the four primary tastes. Sensitivity for bitter substances is the highest; sensitivities for sweet and salty are the lowest. Although all taste buds are able to detect all four of the basic tastes, each taste bud is usually most sensitive to one. The stimulus type to which each taste bud responds most strongly is associated with its location on the tongue. The sweet and salty tastes are located primarily on the tip of the tongue, the sour taste is on the lateral sides of the tongue, and the bitter taste is on the back of the tongue. However, the hundreds of different types of tastes that we experience result from varying degrees of stimulation of the four primary sensations of taste, as well as from the simultaneous stimulation of smell in the nose and from tactile and pain nerve endings in the mouth.

AGE-RELATED CHANGES

Age-related changes in the sense of smell and taste are related to changes in the oral mucosa, tongue, and pathologic state of the nasal cavity. Changes in smell occur as the olfactory and gustatory nuclei in the brain decline. It is thought that the basal cells may not continue to replace olfactory neurons as aging occurs. Additionally, olfactory receptors in the roof of the mouth regress, resulting in reduced sensitivity of the olfactory nerves. Weiffenbach and Bartoshuk (1992) reviewed studies from various smell and taste clinics that noted the primary causes of olfactory loss as upper respiratory infection (URI), head trauma, and nasal symptoms. Olfactory loss means the person is unable to perceive odors such as garlic, onion, or fried chicken. The majority of studies indicate a dramatic decline with age to sensitivity of airborne chemical stimuli. Additionally, recognition of odors declines dramatically with age. This has been well documented in cross-sectional age studies, but some older people have shown adequate and improved olfactory function. However, without longitudinal studies it is impossible to tell whether these people have maintained their function over the years or if they have experienced a decline from previous higher levels of functioning.

The dimming of taste results from changes within the papillae and associated taste buds. Schiffman and Pasternak (1979) report that the number of nerve endings, the number of papillae, and the number of taste buds per papillae all decline with age. Taste bud renewal is slowed in older adults and more pronounced with estrogen, zinc, and protein deficiencies. Weiffenbach and Bartoshuk (1992) reviewed and summarized previous and recent taste studies. They noted the important result that the sensory function of taste remains strong with advancing age. The findings indicate a strong taste nervous system. Earlier and modern studies have demonstrated a decline in taste sensitivity; however, the age differences are limited. Additionally, these differences are likely to affect a limited area or single aspect of functioning and do not apply to all older adults. These studies provide no conclusive evidence that normal aging involves a predictable loss of taste sensation. Therefore loss-of-taste complaints from older adults deserve a complete assessment, since they may be related to a pathologic condition of the nervous system.

MEDICAL MANAGEMENT

Xerostomia

Diagnostic tests and procedures

Diagnosis is determined by the following:
- Interview including thorough health history
- Oral examination of mouth and oropharynx
- Taste testing (see Box 29-17, including local anesthetics)

For further definitive testing, referral to a dentist, neurologist or multidisciplinary taste and smell center may be necessary.

Treatment

If dry mouth is a result of decreased saliva production, one of the following measures may be prescribed:
- Artificial saliva
- Mouth rinses
- Hard candy or gum
- Pharmacologic Sialogogues, drugs that stimulate the flow of saliva
- Pilocarpine HC1 10 gtts of a 10% solution after meals. (However, these drugs have negative side effects, so they are seldom used.)

Prognosis

The prognosis is good but unfortunately in many cases no effective treatment is available. Clients may need counseling in appetite nutrition and coping strategies.

From Winkler S: Oral aspects of aging. In Calkins E, Ford AB, Katz PR editors: *Practice of geriatrics,* ed 2, Philadelphia, 1992, WB Saunders.

COMMON PROBLEMS AND CONDITIONS

Xerostomia

Xerostomia, the one common age-related condition affecting taste, involves a decrease in salivary production that leads to thicker mucus and a dry mouth. This decrease in salivary production leads to changes in the mouth and oropharynx that interfere with an older person's ability to eat, perhaps leading to appetite and nutritional problems.

There is a decrease in the flow and quality of saliva as a result of regressive changes in the salivary glands. As the ptyalin content of saliva decreases and the mucin content increases, the saliva becomes thick. This leads to bacterial and plaque formation in the oral cavity and its related structures.

Factors leading to a decrease in salivary flow include the following:

- Disease states
  - Diabetes mellitus (DM)
  - Nephritis
  - Pernicious anemia
- Conditions
  - Menopause
  - X-ray radiation
  - Mouth—breathing
  - Dehydration
  - Vitamin deficiencies
  - Oral infection
- Administration of certain medications
  - Phenothiazine
  - Chlorpromazine
  - Belladonna
  - Atropine (Winkler, 1992)

Complaints of abnormal taste sensations, burning of the oral tissues and tongue, and cracking of the lips are common. The oral mucosa is dry, thin, and smooth, and the tongue may have a thick, white, foul-smelling coating. The decrease in salivary flow interferes with chewing and swallowing. Clients with dentures may complain of sore gums and tissues, as well as denture slippage from the loss of saliva flow, which forms a mechanical barrier (see Medical Management box above).

BOX 29-17

Assessment of Olfaction and Taste

It is imperative when interviewing clients with complaints of taste loss to differentiate if there is a true taste loss or if an olfactory loss is presenting as a taste loss. The client most likely has an olfactory loss rather than a taste loss if salt, sugar, sourness of lemon juice, or bitterness of medicines can be tasted. Clients who say these substances taste weak are likely demonstrating a true taste loss. In addition some clients may complain of unusual or phantom sensations. Have the client describe the quality of the sensation. Clients will describe taste phantoms (involving salty, sweet, sour, bitter, or metallic) as continuous but on questioning it is noted to change with eating and drinking. Smell phantoms are usually unpleasant and are described in terms of odors—garlic, gasoline.

The assessment of olfactory and taste function involves the assessment of cranial nerves.

CN I—Olfactory function

Two vials of aromatic odors (coffee, peppermint)
Instruct client to close eyes and occlude one naris.
Hold open vial under nose. Have client breathe deeply through open nare and identify odor.
Repeat with other side.
After brief rest period, repeat procedure with second odor.

CN VII facial and CN IX glossopharyngeal—taste functions

Salty, sweet, bitter and sour solutions.
Apply one solution at a time to the lateral side of the following areas of the tongue:
Salty—anterior third
Sweet—tip
Bitter—posterior third
Sour—middle
Have client protrude tongue and identify taste.
Have client rinse mouth with water between solutions.
Test both sides of the tongue.

From Lueckenotte AG: *Pocket guide to gerontological assessment,* ed 2, St. Louis, 1994, Mosby.

NURSING MANAGEMENT

✣ ASSESSMENT

Subjective assessment should include a health history of factors leading to a decrease in salivary flow and the client's oral complaints. Objectively, the lips on a client with xerostomia appear red, inflamed, cracked, dry, and possibly bleeding. The tongue has red areas, a coated base, and appears thicker with prominent lingual groove and papillae. The mucous membranes of the palate and the lining of the mouth and gums appear dry, red, and edematous. The saliva is scant, ropy, and viscid. The amount of moisture in the oral cavity can be assessed by running a gloved finger over the oral mucosa to evaluate stickiness, indicating dry mucous membranes. The client's voice may be dry and raspy, and the client may complain of difficulty articulating words. Taste testing is performed to evaluate taste sensation, which may be diminished (Box 29-17).

✣ DIAGNOSIS

Potential nursing diagnoses for the client with xerostomia include the following: (1) sensory/perceptual alterations (gustatory) related to decrease in salivary flow; and (2) altered oral mucous membrane related to changes induced by xerostomia.

✣ PLANNING

Expected outcomes for the client with xerostomia include the following: (1) client will verbalize an increase in taste sensation; (2) client will exhibit unimpaired oral mucosa tissue integrity as evidenced by moist, pink, smooth mucosal surfaces; (3) client will verbalize no oral discomfort; (4) client will state contributing factors, symptoms, and treatment of xerostomia; and (5) client will demonstrate correct oral hygiene regimen.

✣ INTERVENTION

Nursing interventions for the client with xerostomia focus on attaining an intact oral mucosa tissue integrity. Teaching clients about the factors leading to a decrease in salivary flow, as well as associated symptoms, is key to the prevention and treatment of xerostomia. The treatment regimen focuses on increasing salivary flow. Clients need to be taught basic oral hygiene of brushing twice daily with a soft toothbrush and nonabrasive fluoride toothpaste, as well as daily flossing. Fluid balance is vital to maintain moisture in the oral cavity. Clients need to take in 2 to 3 l of fluid per day, unless contraindicated. Additionally, foods prepared with gravy or sauces contain moisture and should be included in the diet (if not contraindicated). Additional methods to teach clients to increase salivary flow include the use of artificial saliva, sugar-free hard candy, and gum.

✣ EVALUATION

Evaluation of the interventions is based on the appearance of the oral mucous membranes, the client's relief of symptoms, and an increased level of comfort by following effective daily treatment practices (McFarland, McFarlane, 1993).

TOUCH

At birth, the sense of touch is the most developed sense. Touch involves tactile information on pressure, vibration, and temperature. Though touch, pressure, and vibration are commonly classified as separate sensations, they are detected by the same types of receptors. The only difference among these three are: (1) touch sensation usually results from stimulation of receptors in the skin or in tissues immediately beneath the skin, (2) pressure sensation generally results from deformation of deeper tissues, and (3) vibration sensation results from rapidly repetitive sensory signals.

There are at least six entirely different types of tactile receptors known: true nerve endings, hair follicle receptors, pacinian corpuscles, Merkel's disks, Meissner's corpuscles, and Ruffini's organs. Free nerve endings are found everywhere in the skin and in many other tissues. They are responsible for pain, temperature, itch, and movements. The temperature receptors in the skin and other tissues consist of three types of free nerve endings. One type, the warm receptor, increases its action potential rate as the skin temperature increases. Finally, pain receptors are stimulated only by extreme degrees of cold or heat.

It is difficult to determine whether losses in tactile sensitivity can be attributed to aging itself or to disease states that occur more often in older adults. There are few studies related to aging and tactile senses, and they have questionable methodologies and contain small sample sizes. The most recent study conducted by Stevens (1992) found that spatial acuity in the fingertip deteriorated with age when assessed by 2-point thresholds measured with a forced-choice method. Over half of the variance in the 2-point threshold was attributable to age. Similarly, Thornbury and Mistretta (1981) found increases in tactile thresholds of the pads of index fingers with aging; however, they noted wide variation in touch sensitivity.

Two studies examining sensation of the ventral forearm both noted slightly higher thresholds in the older subjects. However, Stevens (1992) found this elevated 2-point discrimination threshold minor as compared to the fingertip. Additionally, Harkins, Price, and Martelli (1986) reported greater similarities among the age groups than differences in estimation of painful heat to the forearm.

The most common disorders affecting tactile information include cerebrovascular accident (CVA), peripheral vascular disease (PVD) and diabetic neuropathy. All three conditions involve changes in the vascular system that result in decreased blood flow to various parts of the body. Signs and symptoms of a CVA are dependent on the cerebral artery affected and the portion of the brain supplied by that artery (see Chapter 27). In PVD and diabetic neuropathy, the impaired blood flow manifests as a loss of sensation most commonly noted in the lower extremities. Box 29-18 provides an overview of the sensory portion of

BOX 29-18

Assessment of Touch, Pressure, Vibration, and Proprioception

The sensory system portion of the neurologic examination includes tests for tactile sensation, pressure, vibration and proprioception (kinesthetic sense). The testing is conducted with the client's eyes closed. The examination consists of organized testing of opposite corresponding arms, trunk, and legs, beginning distally and moving up the body part. The examiner should compare the sensations on one side with those on the other. Only slight differences should be noted. If definite differences are noted, the abnormal area should be defined for further testing.

Physical examination

Primary sensory function

Light touch-indicate when and where touch is felt when lightly touched with wisp of cotton.

Pain-differentiate sharp and dull sensations when point and hub of a sterile needle are applied to symmetrical areas of the body.

Temperature-identify hot and cold sensations when a part of the body is submerged in hot and cold water (or hot and cold water in test tube).

Vibration-indicate when a buzz starts and stops when the handle of a vibrating tuning fork is held against a bony prominence.

Discriminatory sensory function

Two-point discrimination-distinguish two points when simultaneously touched with two sharp objects.

Position-identify the direction when the lateral surface of the distal phalanx of the thumb, index finger or great toe is moved up or down.

Stereognosis-identify familiar objects when placed in one's hand.

Graphesthesia-recognize numbers or letters drawn on the palm of the hand.

From Lueckenotte AG: *Pocket guide to gerontological assessment,* ed 2, St. Louis, 1994, Mosby.

CARE PLAN

DIABETES MELLITUS

Clinical situation Mr. J is a 75-year-old retired engineer who has been admitted to your long-term care facility from his home. At the time of his admission, he is accompanied by his son. Twenty-five years ago, he was diagnosed with noninsulin-dependent diabetes mellitus. He has been taking insulin injections for the last 10 years. Mr. J currently suffers from diabetic retinopathy in both eyes and neuropathy in his lower extremities. In the past he has had several toes on both feet amputated. However, in the last 6 months he has become progressively weaker and less mobile after the removal of all the toes on his right foot.

Mr. J is able to eat, dress, and ambulate short distances (approximately 50 feet) with a walker unassisted. He has had increasing difficulty grooming, ambulating, and bathing because of his low vision and poor sensation in his lower extremities.

When he was at home, he was receiving services from home health, but with his increasing weakness, he and his son decided he needed 24-hour assistance.

Nursing diagnoses	Outcome	Interventions
Sensory/perceptual alterations (visual) related to complication of diabetes mellitus manifested as diabetic retinopathy	Mr. J will successfully use methods designed for the individual with visual impairment.	Teach Mr. J and his son about the use of low-vision aids. Encourage and support his use of chosen aids (see Box 29-4). Teach Mr. J and his son how to organize his new room to facilitate his mobility and locations of items. Teach Mr. J to use the clock method to identify food items at mealtimes. Provide Mr. J with a sighted guide until he becomes familiar with new environment (see Box 29-7, p. 829).
Sensory/perceptual alterations (tactile) related to complications of diabetes mellitus manifested as diabetic neuropathy	Mr. J's lower extremities will remain free of trauma.	Examine skin, legs, and feet for any breakdown, lesions, or reddened areas. Evaluate neurovascular status of the legs and feet daily, noting any loss of sensation. Teach Mr. J skin, leg, and foot care (Box 29-19).
Bathing/hygiene self-care deficit related to visual impairment and decreased sensation in both lower extremities (BLE)	Client will complete bath, hygiene care, and grooming with assistance.	Provide type of bath at a time Mr. J prefers. Provide supervision and assistance as necessary to afford maximum privacy and active participation. Monitor grooming activity and assist as necessary to ensure client's appearance is neat and clean.

the neurologic examination to be performed when gathering objective data about tactile information.

The common thread among the previously described disorders is the alteration of peripheral tissue perfusion. Nursing interventions are directed toward preventing accidental trauma and injury in the affected limbs. Client education focusing on skin, leg, and foot care is summarized in the Client/Family Teaching box on p. 854. The effectiveness of nursing interventions is determined by the absence of trauma, especially in the lower extremities (see nursing Care Plan above).

Insight • *The problem of falling is common and serious, especially in the frail older adult. In 1991, the National Safety Council reported falls as the second leading cause of accidental death in the United States. Among persons age 75 and older, falls were the leading cause of accidental death (National Safety Council, 1992). Research has well documented the occurrence of falls in the older adult in every setting. Nursing studies have focused on assessment of fall risk factors that provide the foundation for a fall-prevention program. However, nursing research related to falls in a long-term care setting is lacking. As increasing numbers of older adults spend time in this setting, whether for short-term rehabilitation or an extended stay, this type of research will be imperative to provide quality nursing care. Researchers must analyze the key factors affecting falls: the financial constraints (staffing ratios), increasing resident acuity, and federal regulations concerning physical and chemical restraint use. Therefore future research aimed at injury prevention programs may be the key to quality care in a long-term care environment.*

CLIENT/FAMILY TEACHING

Skin, Leg, and Foot Care

Foot care

Do not use tobacco.
Inspect your feet daily for blisters, cuts, and scratches.
Use a mirror to see the bottom of the feet. Always check between the toes for dryness, redness, tenderness, and localized areas that rub (hot spots).
Inspect the inside of your shoes daily for foreign objects, nail points, torn linings, and rough areas.
Wash feet daily. Dry carefully, especially between the toes.
Avoid temperature extremes. Test water with elbow before bathing.
Soak feet only if specifically prescribed by your health care provider. For dry feet, use a very thin coat of lubrication cream or oil. Apply this after bathing and drying feet. Do not put the oil or cream between the toes.
If feet are cold at night, wear socks to bed. Do not apply hot water bottles or heating pads or soak feet in hot water.
Cut nails in contour with the toes. Do not cut deep down the sides or corners.
Do not use chemical agents for the removal of corns and calluses. Do not use corn plasters.
Do not cut corns and calluses. These should be treated regularly by an experienced health care provider.
Do not use adhesive tape on your feet.
If your vision is impaired, have a family member or friend inspect your feet and shoes daily or assist with foot care.

Footwear

Avoid walking barefoot or in thongs or sandals if your feet are insensitive.
Avoid wearing open-toed shoes or sandals unless specifically prescribed by a health care provider.

Preventive care instructions

Never walk barefoot on surfaces such as hot sandy beaches or on the cement or asphalt around swimming pools that are often hot; you may not be able to feel the increased temperature.
Wear clean and properly fitting socks or stockings at all times with your shoes.
Avoid wearing mended socks or stockings with seams.
Avoid wearing garters, elastic bands on socks, and/or rolling hose.
Avoid crossing your legs; this can cause pressure on nerves and blood vessels. Shoes should be properly measured and should fit at the time of purchase. Shoes should be made of material that breathes, such as leather.
Avoid pointed toes or high-heeled shoes.
If your feet have decreased sensation, rotate your shoes three to four times/day. Before putting on your shoes, check the insides of the shoes by hand to ensure that there are no rough surfaces (e.g., nail heads) and no small objects (e.g., pebbles, coins) in your shoes.
Wear appropriate shoes for the weather. In winter, take special precautions such as wearing wool socks and protective foot gear, e.g., fleece-lined boots.

Stay in contact with your health care provider

See your physician or podiatrist regularly and be sure that your feet are examined at each visit.
Notify your health care provider at once if you develop a blister, sore, or crack in the skin of your feet.
Have your physician check any injury to your legs, feet or toes.

From Haire-Joshu P: *Management of diabetes mellitus: perspectives of care across the lifespan,* St. Louis, 1992, Mosby.

Summary

Older adults' senses are the key to their interaction with the environment. As these senses decline because of normal age-related changes or pathologic conditions, nurses in every setting must adapt intervention to maintain the highest independent level of functioning.

The focus of gerontologic nursing care can be found in Lillian Morrison's poem (1987), *Body.*

BODY

Lillian Morrison

I have lived with it for years,
this big cat, developed an
affection for it. Though it is
aging now, I cannot abandon it
nor do I want to. I would love
to throw it about in play but
must be careful. It cannot summon
that agile grace of old. Yet
it's really pleasant to be with,
familiar, faithful, complaining
a little, continually going
about its business, loving to lie down.

Key Points

- Studies have documented age-related changes in the senses of vision and hearing.
- Age-related changes remain questionable in the senses of taste and smell.
- A cataract is an opacity of the lens and requires surgery for successful treatment.
- Glaucoma is increased intraocular pressure (IOP) and requires life-long treatment with medications to lower the IOP.
- Retinal detachment requires immediate medical attention, and can only be repaired by surgical intervention.
- Macular degeneration and diabetic retinopathy have few successful treatments and require low-vision interventions.
- Organizing the environment, using the clock method of eating, and assisting ambulation with a sighted guide help a person who is visually impaired maintain independence.
- Hearing loss affects an older person's ability to communicate and can lead to depression, social isolation, and loss of self-esteem.
- Cerumen impaction prevention and treatment is an important nursing function in the care of the older adult, especially the LTC setting.
- Vertigo can be a chronic, annoying condition, but use of proper safety measures and measures to reduce dizziness can facilitate daily functioning.
- Xerostomia can cause pain in the oral mucosa, gums, and tongue, leading to alterations in taste. Treatment includes a daily oral care regimen and methods to increase salivary production.
- Older people with a diminished sense of touch are at risk for injury especially in the affected limb(s).

HOME CARE TIPS

1. Sensory changes can lead to social isolation in the homebound older adult (e.g.,not being able to interact effectively with family members as a result of visual or hearing deficits).
2. Sensory changes increase safety hazards (such as burning or falling) in the homebound older adult.
3. Instruct the caregiver and homebound older adult on signs and symptoms of age-related sensory changes. Instruct them to report to their physician or home care nurse any signs and symptoms that interfere with independent function or present a safety hazard.
4. Instruct the caregiver and homebound older adult about prescribed treatments or surgical procedures (e.g., preoperative and postoperative care of cataract surgery, eye drops, ear drops, and antibiotics).
5. Assist the caregiver and homebound older adult in organizing the environment to accommodate any decreased sensory function (e.g., use of color contrast, bold print books, or hearing aid on the telephone).

Critical Thinking Exercises

1. A 68-year-old woman with diabetic retinopathy is blind in the right eye and has limited vision in the left eye. Her daughter is concerned about her mother living alone, but her mother insists that she is still able to care for herself. She admits that the major problem is meal preparation. What strategies could you suggest for assisting her in adapting meal preparation, keeping safety in mind?
2. Discuss how you would communicate with an older adult who is hearing impaired without addressing the person as though she or he were deaf?

REFERENCES

American Academy of Ophthalmology: *Cataract: clouding the lens of sight,* 1992a.

American Academy of Ophthalmology: *Dry eye: understanding your condition,* 1992b.

American Academy of Ophthalmology: *Floaters and flashes: should you be concerned?* 1992c.

American Academy of Ophthalmology: *Glaucoma: early detection can save your life,* 1992d.

American Academy of Ophthalmology: *Macular degeneration: major cause of central vision loss,* 1992e.

Faherty B: Chronic blepharitis: easy clinical interventions for a common problem, *Gerontol Nurs* 18(3):24-27,1992

Harkins SW, Price DD, Martelli M: Effects of age on pain perception: thermonociception, *Gerontol* 41(1):58-63, 1986.

Hogstel MO: Vision and hearing: In Hogstel MO editor: *Clinical manual of gerontological nursing,* St. Louis, 1992, Mosby.

House J et al: Help for the patient with tinnitus, *Patient Care*15: 89-103, 153,1987.

Kart CS, Metress EK, Metress SP: *Human aging and chronic disease.* Boston, 1992, Jones & Bartlett.

Kollarits CR: The aging eye. In Calkins E, Ford AB, Katz PR editors: *Practice of geriatrics,* ed 2, Philadelphia, 1992, WB Saunders.

Lewis-Cullinan C, Janken JK: Effect of cerumen removal on the hearing ability of geriatric patients *Adv Nurs* 15(5): 597,1990.

Lueckenotte AG: *Pocket guide to gerontologic assessment,* ed 2, St. Louis, 1994, Mosby.

Mahoney DF: Cerumen impaction: prevalence and detection in nursing homes, *Gerontol Nurs* 19(4) 23-30, 1993.

Marx MS et al: The relationship between low vision and performance of activities of daily living in nursing home residents, *Am Geriatr Soc* 40(10): 1018-1020, 1992.

McFarland GK, McFarlane EZ: *Nursing diagnosis and intervention,* ed 2, St. Louis, 1993, Mosby.

Meyerhoff W, Patt BS: Otologic disorders. In Calkins E, Ford AB, Katz PR editors: *Practice of geriatrics,* ed 2, Philadelphia, 1992, WB Saunders.

Morrison L: Body. In Martz S, editor: *When I Am An OLD WOMAN I Shall Wear Purple,* ed 2, Watsonville, Calif., 1987, Papier-Mache Press.

National Safety Council: Accident facts, *National Safety Council,* Chicago, 1992.

Phipps WJ: The patient with ear problems. In Long BC, Phipps WJ, Cassmeyer VS, editors: *Medical-surgical nursing: a nursing process approach,* ed 3, St. Louis, 1993a, Mosby.

Phipps WJ: The patient with eye problems. In Long BC, Phipps WJ, Cassmeyer VS, editors: *Medical-surgical nursing: a nursing process approach,* ed 3, St. Louis, 1993b, Mosby.

Reuben DB: The physician and the aging driver. In Calkins E, Ford AB, Katz PR, editors: *Practice of geriatrics,* ed 2, Philadelphia, 1992, WB Saunders.

Schiffman SS: Taste and smell in disease I and II, *N Engl J Med* 308(21,22): 1275-1279, 1337-1343, 1983.

Schiffman SS, Pasternak M: Decreased discrimination of food odors in the elderly, *J Gerontol* 34(1): 73-79, 1979.

Seeley RR, Stephens TP, Tate P: The senses. In *Anatomy of Physiology* ed 2, St. Louis, 1992, Mosby.

Stefansson E: The eye. In Hazzard W et al, editors: *Principles of geriatric medicine and gerontology,* New York, 1990, McGraw-Hill.

Stevens JC: Aging and spatial acuity of touch, *J Gerontol* 47(1): 35-40,1992.

Thornbury JM, Mistretta CM: Tactile sensitivity as a function of age, *J Gerontol* 36(1): 34-39, 1981.

US Department of Health and Human Services: *Healthy People 2000 National Health Promotion and Disease Prevention Objectives,* Washington D.C., 1990, Public Health Services.

Waller PF: Preventing injury to the elderly. In Phelps HT, Gaylord SA, editors: *Aging and public health,* New York, 1985, Springer.

Webber-Jones J: Doomed to deafness, *Am J Nurs* 92(11): 37-40, 1992.

Weiffenbach JM, Bartoshuk LM: Taste and smell, *Clinic Geriatr Med* 8(3): 543-555, 1992.

Winkler S: Oral aspects of aging. In Calkins E, Ford AB, Katz PR, editors: *Practice of geriatrics,* ed 2, Philadelphia, 1992, WB Saunders.

BIBLIOGRAPHY

Bowers AC, Thompson JM: *Clinical manual of health assessment,* ed 3, St. Louis, 1988, Mosby.

Haire-Joshu P: *Management of diabetes mellitus: perspectives of care across the lifespan,* St. Louis, 1992, Mosby.

McNeely E, Griffin-Shirley M, Hubbard A: Teaching caregivers to recognize diminished vision among nursing home residents, *Geriatr Nurs* 13(6): 332-335, 1992.

Morley JE, Kahl MJ, Peak M: Hearing impairment in the nursing home, *Gerontologist,* 30(296), 1990.

O'Rourke C et al: Effectiveness of a hearing screening protocol for the elderly, *Geriatr Nurs* 14(2): 66-69, 1993.

Palumbo MV: Hearing access 2000: increasing awareness of the hearing impaired, *J Gerontol Nurs* 16(9): 26-31, 1990.

Redford JB: Assistive devices for the elderly. In Calkins E, Ford AB, Katz PR, editors: *Practice of geriatrics,* ed 2, Philadelphia, 199, WB Saunders.

Ross V, Echevarria KH, Robinson B: Geriatric tinnitus: causes, clinical treatment and prevention, *J Gerontol Nurs* 17(10): 6-11, 1991.

Seidel HM et al: *Mosby's guide to physical examination,* ed 3, St. Louis, 1994, Mosby.

Taylor KS: Geriatric hearing loss: management strategies for nurses, *Geriatr Nurs,* 14(2): 74-76, 1993.

Thornbury JM, Mistretta CM: Tactile sensitivity as a function of age, *J Gerontol* 36(1): 34-39, 1981.

US Department of Health and Human Services: Aging and your eyes, *Age Page,* Public Health Services, Bethesda, Md., 1983, National Institutes of Health.

US Department of Health and Human Services: *Hearing and the elderly,* Public Health Services, Bethesda, Md., 1983, National Institutes of Health

Waldzak M et al: Elder hearing aids: infrared listening device in a geriatric day center, *J Gerontol Nurs* 19(8): 5-9, 1993.

Chapter 30

Musculoskeletal Function

LEARNING OBJECTIVES

On completion of this chapter, the reader will be able to:

1. Describe the normal structure and function of the musculoskeletal system.
2. Discuss the age-related changes in the musculoskeletal system.
3. Discuss the nursing management of clients with fractures of the hip, wrist, clavicle, and vertebrae.
4. Differentiate between the etiologic factors, pathophysiology, clinical presentation, and treatment of osteoarthritis, rheumatoid arthritis, gout, and polymyalgia rheumatica.
5. Identify the nursing interventions associated with rheumatoid arthritis, osteoarthritis, gout, and polymyalgia rheumatica.
6. Discuss the pathophysiology, treatment, and nursing management of osteoporosis.
7. Describe the indications and nursing management for clients with amputations.
8. Discuss the causes and management of common foot problems in older adults.
9. Conduct a physical assessment of the musculoskeletal system.

Musculoskeletal problems are of major concern to older adults. Of older adults living in the community, 40% have arthritis and 17% report having other chronic problems of the musculoskeletal system (*A Profile of Older Americans, 1992*). Complaints in this system are common, because normal aging predisposes to the development of diseases such as osteoarthritis and osteoporosis. Diseases of the musculoskeletal system are generally not fatal but do cause chronic pain and disability (Calkins, 1992). Chronic conditions of the musculoskeletal system may contribute to impaired function and disability in older adults in the areas of self-care and mobility. The ability to perform activities of daily living (ADLs) such as bathing, dressing, and eating may be impaired. Instrumental activities of daily living (IADLs), the ability to perform tasks such as managing finances, preparing food, managing transportation, and keeping house, may also be affected. These functional impairments can be devastat-

CULTURAL AWARENESS

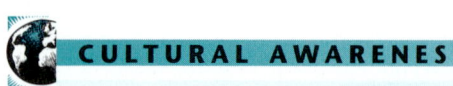

Biocultural Variations in the Musculoskeletal System

Bone	Remarks
Frontal	Thicker in African-American men than white men
Parietal/ Occipital	Thicker in white men than in African-American men; occipital protuberance palpable in Eskimos
Palate	Tori (protuberances) along the suture line of the hard palate, which is problematic for denture wearers Incidence: African Americans 0% Whites 24% Asian Americans Up to 50% American Indians Up to 50%
Mandible	Tori (protuberances) on the lingual surface of the mandible near the canine and premolar teeth, which is problematic for denture wearers Most common in Asian Americans and American Indians; exceeds 50% in some Eskimo groups
Humerus	Torsion or rotation of proximal end with muscle pull Whites > African Americans Torsion in African Americans is symmetrical; torsion in whites tends to be greater on right than left side
Radius/Ulna	Length at the wrist variable Ulna or radius may be longer Equal length Swedish 61% Chinese 16% Ulna longer than radius Swedish 16% Chinese 48% Radius longer than ulna Swedish 23% Chinese 10%
Vertebrae	24 vertebrae are found in 85% to 93% of all people. Racial and gender differences reveal 23 or 25 vertebrae in select groups

Vertebrae	Population
23	11% of African American women
25	12% of Eskimo and American Indian men

Related to lower back pain and lordosis

Bone	Remarks
Pelvis	Hip width is 1.6 cm (0.6 in) smaller in African-American women than white women; Asian women have significantly smaller pelvises
Femur	Convex anterior: Native Americans Straight: African American Intermediate: White
Second tarsal	Second toe longer than the great toe Incidence: Whites 8% to 34% African Americans 8% to 12% Vietnamese 31% Melanesians 21% to 57%
Height	Clinical significance for joggers and athletes White men are 1.27 cm (0.5 in) taller than African-American men and 7.6 cm (2.9 in) taller than Asian-American men White women = African-American women Asian women are 4.14 cm (1.6 in) shorter than white or African-American women
Composition of long bones	Longer, narrower, and denser in African Americans than whites; bone density in whites greater than Chinese, Japanese, and Eskimos Osteoporosis lowest in African-American men; highest in white women

Muscle	Remarks
Peroneus tertius	Responsible for dorsiflexion of foot Muscle absent: Asians, Native Americans, and Whites 3% to 10% African Americans, Berbers 10% to 15% (Sahara desert) 24% No clinical significance because the tibialis anterior also dorsiflexes the foot
Palmaris longus	Responsible for wrist flexion Muscle absent: Whites 12% to 20% Native Americans 2% to 12% African Americans 5% Asians 3% No clinical significance because three other muscles are also responsible for flexion

Data from Overfield T: *Biologic variation in health and illness: race, age, and sex differences.* Menlo Park, Calif., 1985, Addison-Wesley.

ing to older adults who desire to maintain independence. When dependence occurs, it can result in loss of self-esteem, the perception of decreased quality of life and depression (see Cultural Awareness box, p. 858).

NORMAL STRUCTURE AND FUNCTION

The skeletal system provides a framework for the body, protects vital organs, stores mineral and marrow elements for forming new blood cells, and provides levers for the skeletal muscles (Fig. 30-1). Muscles of the skeleton function to move the bones. At the microscopic level, bones are composed of the haversian system and bone cells. The haversian system contains blood vessels and lymphatics. This system provides nutrients to the bone cells. The bone cells are composed of osteoblasts, osteocytes, and osteoclasts. Osteoblasts are the cells that form new bone and the bone matrix. Osteocytes, or mature bone cells, function to maintain bone. Osteoclasts reabsorb bone tissue.

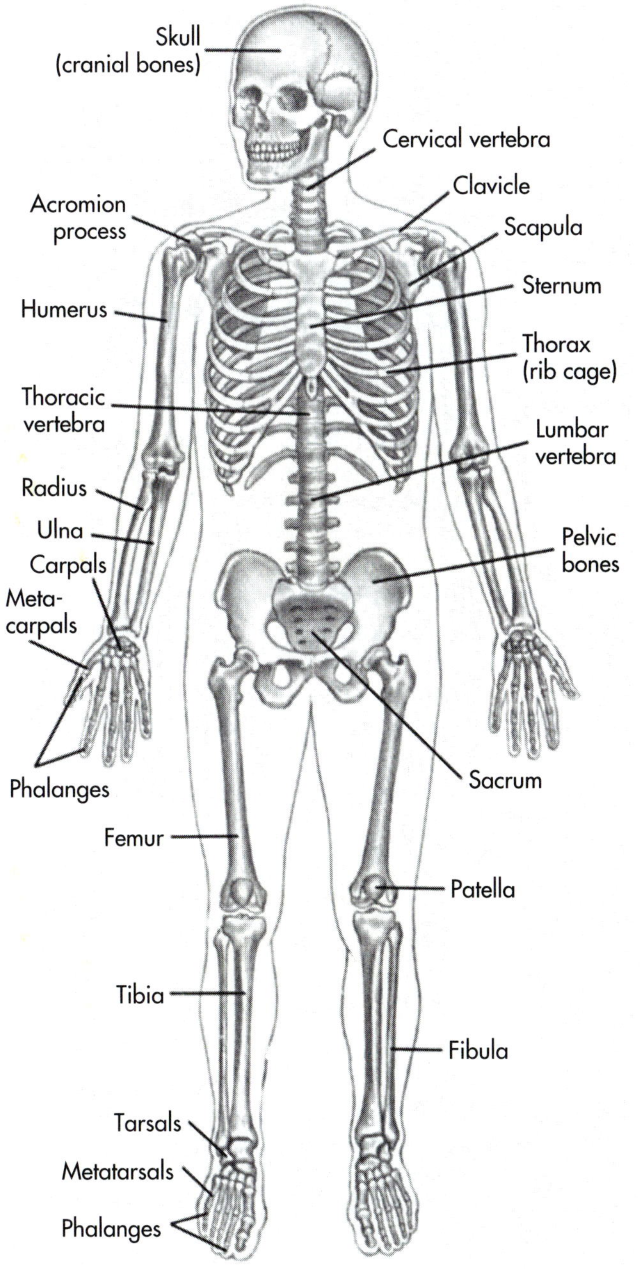

Fig. 30-1 Bones that make up axial and appendicular skeletons. (From Thompson JM et al: *Mosby's clinical nursing*, ed 3, St. Louis, 1993, Mosby.)

Bone tissue is comprised of collagen, organic materials, and the inorganic compounds calcium and phosphate. Bone tissue is in a continuous state of growth and remodeling. The two classifications of bone are cortical and cancellous, also called trabecula. Cortical bone is compact, or dense. It forms the outer layer of all bones and the shaft of the long bones. Cancellous bone is light and porous, or spongy. It has a rich blood supply and is found at the ends of bones.

Joints, the area where two bones are articulated, are important structures in the musculoskeletal system. The purpose of these articulations is to connect bones. The action of joints allows bones to move and change position. Joints consist of a fibrous capsule that forms a cavity where two bones are joined. The capsule is lined with a vascular connective tissue, the synovial membrane. This membrane lubricates and nourishes the articular cartilage. The ends of the bones are covered by cartilage, an avascular, nerveless, rigid tissue.

Skeletal muscles are the structures that allow for movement of the body. Bundles of muscle cells or muscle fibers are bound together to form the individual muscles. When the nerve cells of the skeletal muscles secrete acetylcholine, a neurotransmitter, the muscle cells contract, which results in movement.

Tendons and ligaments are dense, fibrous, connective tissue in the musculoskeletal system that allows body movements while providing stability. Bones are connected to bones by ligaments, whereas tendons attach muscles to bones.

AGE-RELATED CHANGES IN STRUCTURE AND FUNCTION

The musculoskeletal system is affected in numerous ways by the aging process. Changes in muscle include a pronounced decrease in muscle mass and muscle strength that occurs gradually over time. The actual number of muscle cells decreases, replaced by fibrous connective tissue. As a result, muscle mass, tone, and strength decrease. The elasticity of ligaments, tendons, and cartilage decrease, as does bone mass, which results in weaker bones. The intervertebral discs lose water, causing a narrowing of the vertebral space. This shrinkage may result in a loss of 1½ to 3 inches of height. The lordotic or convex curve of the back flattens and both flexion and extension of the lower back are decreased. Posture and gait change. Posture, as a result of the changes in the spine, assumes a position of flexion. Changes in posture result in a shift in the center of gravity. In men, the gait becomes small-stepped with a wider based stance. Women become bow-legged, with a narrow standing base, and walk with a waddling gait.

The articular cartilage erodes in older adults. This has not been proven to be either a direct result of the aging process or the result of wear and tear on the joint.

All of the changes mentioned may cause the problems of pain, impaired mobility, self-care deficit and increased risk of falls for older adults. Approximately one third of those age 65 and older have falls each year. About 2% of this group are hospitalized as a result of injuries incurred during the fall. It has been estimated that one half of the residents in nursing homes have falls each year. Falls are the most common cause of accidental death in older adults (see Chapter 11) (Rubenstein et al, 1978). When falls result in injury and hospitalization, the risk of iatrogenic illness and immobility can start a downward trajectory, which ultimately results in death. Falls may also cause a cycle of disuse. This pattern of disuse usually occurs after the individual has experienced repeated falls. The fall experience causes a fear of falling. To avoid falls, the individual decreases mobility; with decreased mobility, muscle strength decreases, joints become stiff, and pain develops, resulting in disability, loss of independence, and frailty.

Current research has documented that some of the diseases and decline in the musculoskeletal system can be decreased or prevented through the use of regular programs of active exercise and resistive muscle strengthening.

EMERGENCY TREATMENT

Fractures

If a fracture is suspected, assess injured area for the following:
Movement
Pain
Color
Temperature
Pulse
Sensation

If fracture is open and bleeding is present:
Apply pressure
Apply sterile dressing

Immobilize the fracture site

Insight • *If you don't use it you lose it! Hospitalization with bed rest and inactivity very quickly results in shortened muscles, changes in joint structure and may contribute to decreased range of motion and contracture. Changes occur most rapidly in the lower extremities (Creditor, 1993). These changes occur by the second day of hospitalization. To prevent this from happening, hospitalized older adults should not be on bed rest. They should be out of bed and ambulating daily unless medical condition prohibits. If bed rest is necessary, exercises of the lower extremity should be planned.*

COMMON PROBLEMS AND CONDITIONS OF THE MUSCULOSKELETAL SYSTEM

Fractures

Fractures are serious problems for older adults that often result in some loss of functional ability. A fracture is a break or disruption in the continuity of the bone (Ruda, 1992). Fractures may occur because of trauma to a bone or joint, or they may be the result of pathologic processes such as osteoporosis or neoplasms. When bones are subjected to more stress than can be withstood, a fracture occurs. Stresses on bones may be from major trauma such as automobile accidents or falls. Falls are the most common cause of fractures in older adults. The most frequently occurring fractures in this population are hip or fractures of the proximal femur, colles (wrist), vertebral and clavicular. Fractures are classified as open or closed, by the location and type of fracture (Fig. 30-2).

The completed process of bone healing is called union. After fractures occur, regenerative cells, fibroblasts, and osteoblasts move to the fracture site and lay down a fibrous matrix of collagen—the callus. This process usually occurs within 7 days after injury. As the healing process takes place the callus bridges the fracture site and the distance between the bone fragments decreases. In the final stage of bone healing, remodeling or absorption of excess cells and calcification occurs.

The history given by the client with a fracture includes trauma followed by immediate local pain. Tenderness, swelling, muscle spasm, deformity, bleeding and loss of function are also seen with fractures (see Emergency Treatment box at left).

The specific presentation depends on the location and the type of fracture. Treatment depends on the site

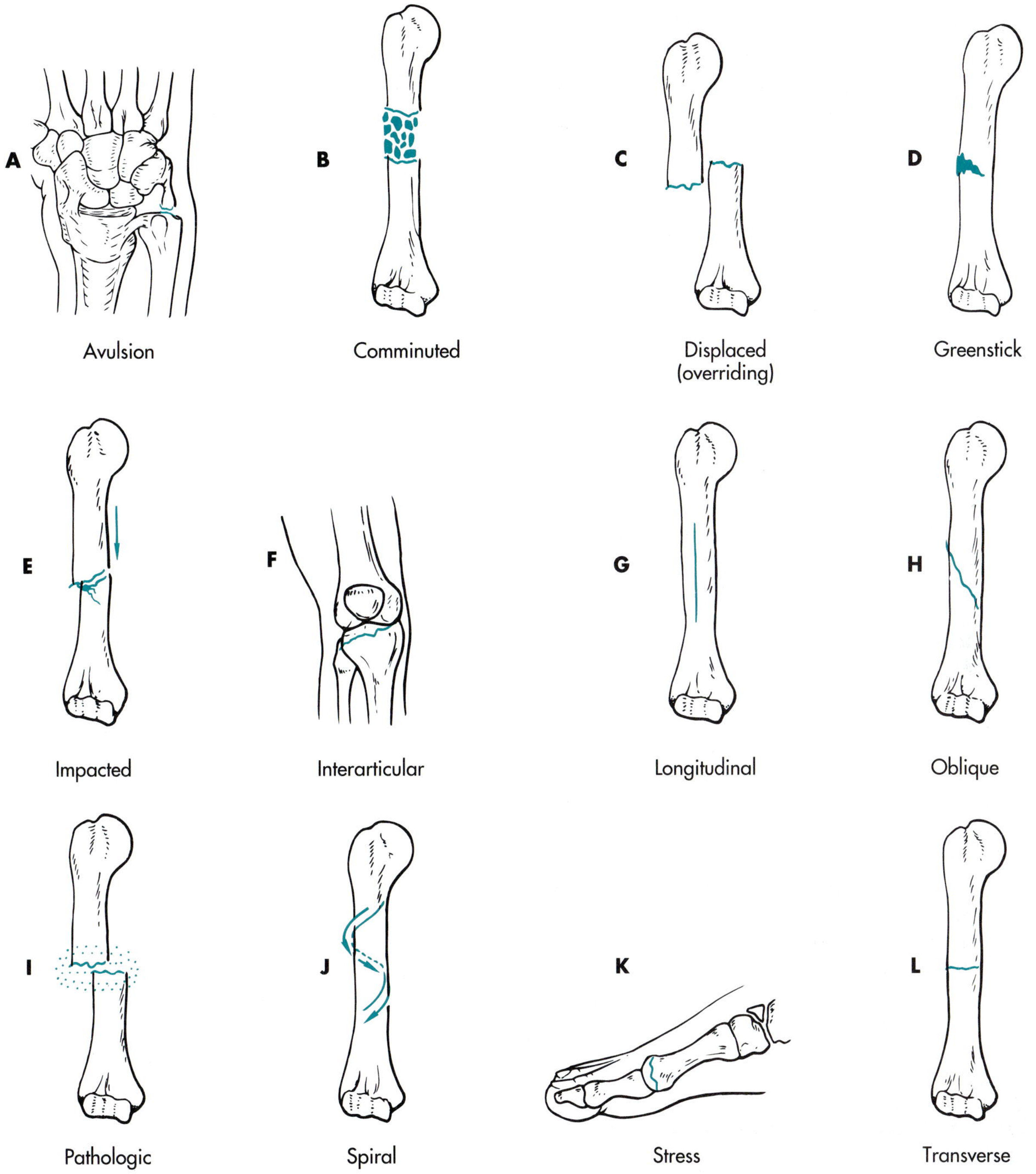

Fig. 30-2 Types of fractures. **A,** An avulsion is a fracture of bone resulting from the strong pulling effect of tendons or ligaments at the bone attachment. **B,** A comminuted fracture is a fracture with more than two fragments. The smaller fragments appear to be floating. **C,** A displaced (overriding) fracture involves a displaced fracture fragment that is overriding the other bone fragment. The periosteum is disrupted on both sides. **D,** A greenstick fracture is an incomplete fracture with one side splintered and the other side bent. The periosteum is not torn away from the bone. **E,** An impacted fracture is a comminuted fracture in which more than two fragments are driven into each other. **F,** An interarticular fracture is a fracture extending to the articular surface of the bone. **G,** A longitudinal fracture is an incomplete fracture in which the fracture line runs along the axis of the bone. The periosteum is not torn away from the bone. **H,** An oblique fracture is a fracture in which the line of the fracture extends in an oblique direction. **I,** A pathologic fracture is a spontaneous fracture at the site of a bone disease. **J,** A spiral fracture is a fracture in which the line of the fracture extends in a spiral direction along the shaft of the bone. **K,** A stress fracture is a fracture occurring at the site of a muscle attachment. It is caused by a sudden, violent force or repeated, prolonged stress. **L,** A transverse fracture is a fracture is which the line of the fracture extends across the bone shaft at a right angle to the longitudinal axis. (From Lewis SM, Collier IC: *Medical-surgical nursing: assessment and management of clinical problems,* ed 3, St. Louis, 1992, Mosby.)

MEDICAL MANAGEMENT

Fractures

Diagnostic tests and procedures
History and physical examination
X-ray examination
Computed tomography (CT) scan
Magnetic Resonance Image (MRI)

Treatment
Fracture reduction
Manipulation
Closed reduction
Open reduction
Traction
Fracture immobilization

Prognosis
Prognosis is excellent, unless nonunion or other complications occur.

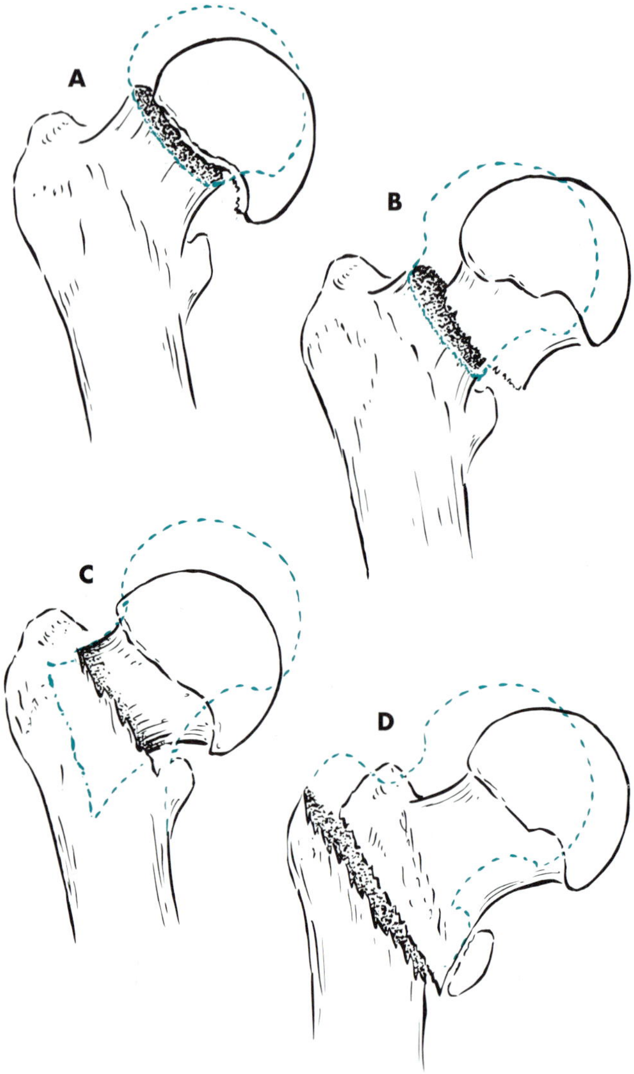

Fig. 30-3 Fractures of the hip. **A,** Subcapital fracture. **B,** Transcervical fracture. **C,** Impacted fracture of base of neck. **D,** Intertrochanteric fracture. (From Phipps WJ et al: *Medical-surgical nursing: concepts and clinical practice,* ed 5, St. Louis, 1995, Mosby.)

and type of the fracture. The goals of fracture management include realignment of the fracture fragments, maintaining realignment, and restoring function of the injured part (see Medical Management box above).

Hip Fractures

Hip fractures are the most disabling type of fracture for older adults (Fig. 30-3). They usually are caused by falls with direct trauma to the hip. Approximately 15% to 20% of clients with hip fractures die as a result of complications from the fracture. The complications of hip fracture are generally related to immobility. They include pneumonia, sepsis from urinary tract infection, and pressure ulcers. With the aging of the population, especially in the numbers over age 75, it is expected that the incidence of hip fractures increases. Hip fractures are classified by their location. Intracapsular fractures occur within the capsule. Extracapsular fractures occur below the capsule. Fractures are further subdivided into intertrochanteric and subtrochanteric. Intertrochanteric fractures occur between the greater and lesser trochanter. Subtrochanteric fractures occur below the trochanter (Russell, 1992).

After the fall or other injury that results in the fractured hip, the client has an affected extremity that is externally rotated and shortened. Tenderness and severe pain at the fracture site may be present.

Immediately after the injury the joint should be immobilized. Buck's (Fig. 30-4) or Russell's traction is used until the client is stabilized. After the client is stabilized, surgical repair, the preferred treatment, is performed. The type of surgical repair depends on the location and type of fracture and can include internal fixation with pins, plates, and screws, or prosthetic replacement of the femoral head (Fig. 30-5).

NURSING MANAGEMENT

✣ ASSESSMENT

Hip fractures are most often related to falls. After a fall or other injury that causes hip trauma the nurse assesses the site for evidence of fracture. This includes inspecting the site for direct evidence of injury, shortening and/or

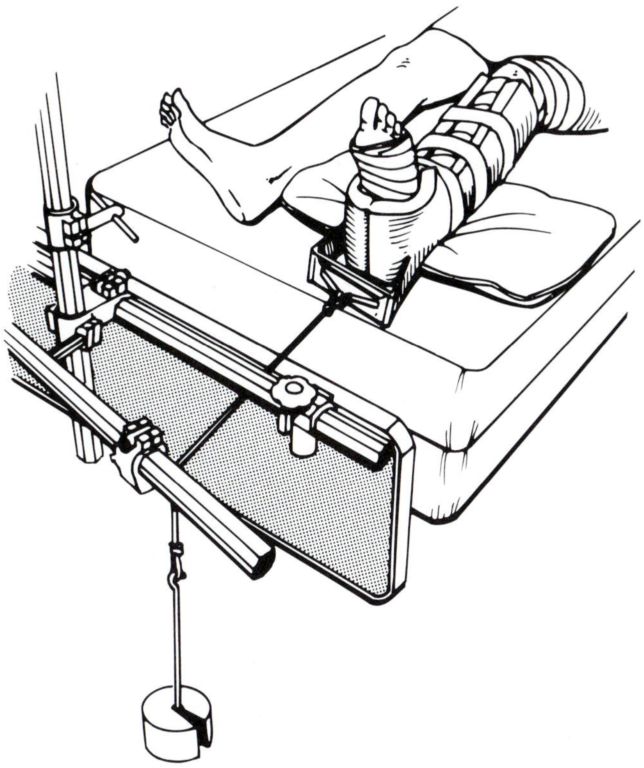

Fig. 30-4 Buck's extension. Heel is supported off bed to prevent pressure on heel, weight hangs free of bed, and foot is well away from footboard of bed. The limb should lie parallel to the bed unless prevented, as in this case, by a slight knee flexion contracture. (From Phipps WJ et al: *Medical-surgical nursing: concepts and clinical practice,* ed 5, St. Louis, 1995, Mosby.)

external rotation. The presence of pain or tenderness at the site of injury is assessed.

✣ DIAGNOSIS

Nursing diagnoses for the client with hip fracture may include pain, impaired physical mobility, high risk of wound infection, self-care deficit, impaired home maintenance management, and high risk for impaired skin integrity.

✣ PLANNING

Expected outcomes for the older client with a hip fracture include but are not limited to, the following: (1) client reports comfort and relief of pain after administration of analgesic, (2) client follows exercise/rehabilitation regimen prescribed by physical therapist for regaining function of affected joint, (3) client's surgical wound remains clean and intact without evidence of inflammation or drainage, (4) client safely performs self-care activities within activity and energy expenditure limitations, (5) client implements prescribed hip precautions into ADLs, and (6) client's skin remains intact during hospital stay.

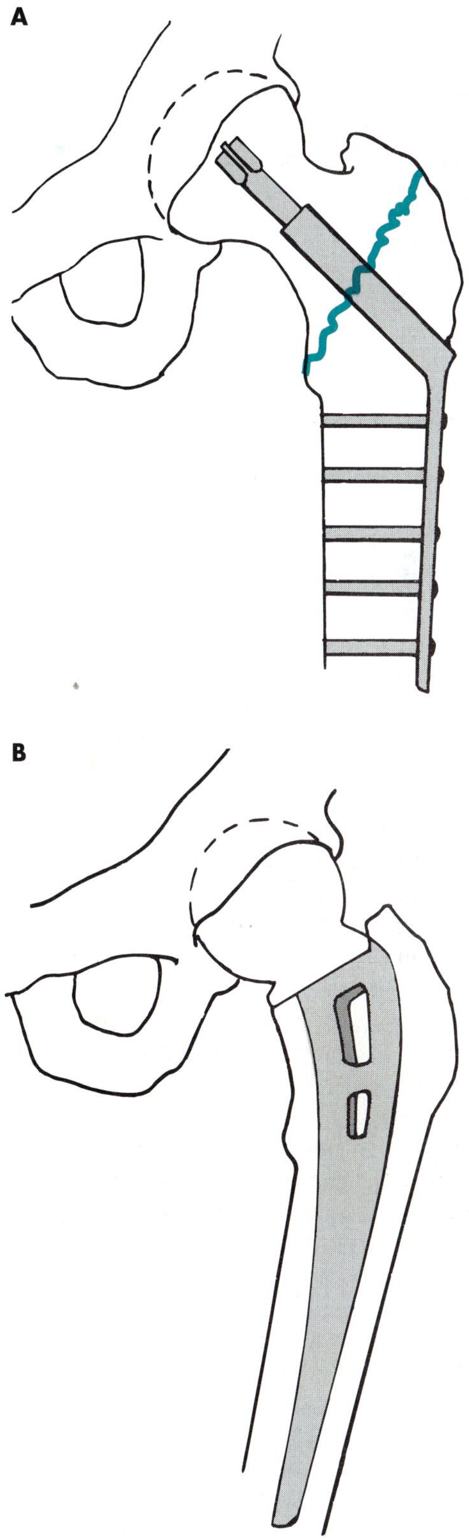

Fig. 30-5 **A,** Nail used to repair a hip fracture. **B,** Prosthesis to repair a hip fracture. (From Long BC et al: *Medical-surgical nursing: a nursing process approach,* ed 3, St. Louis, 1993, Mosby.)

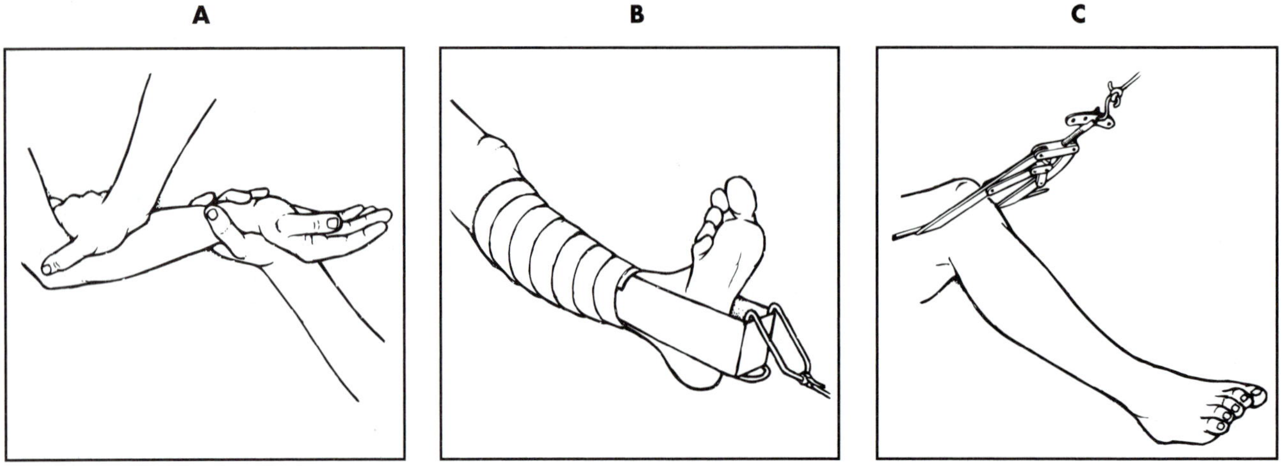

Fig. 30-6 Traction techniques including **A,** manual, **B,** skin, and **C,** skeletal. (Courtesy Zimmer Traction Handbook, 1994, Zimmer.)

✣ INTERVENTION

Before surgery, the client's medical condition is stabilized. In the preoperative period, severe muscle spasms can cause intense pain. Pain medication, positioning and traction are used to manage pain (Fig. 30-6).

The immediate postoperative period requires monitoring of vital signs and intake and output. Turning, deep breathing, and coughing are used to prevent respiratory complications. The operative site is monitored for signs of infection and bleeding. Movement, circulation, and sensation of the extremity are assessed to determine impaired circulation. Mental status is assessed as delirium is a common complication of hip fractures (see Chapter 27) (see Research box, p. 865). Pain is managed through careful administration of pain medication. Because of the normal physiologic aging changes that affect pharmacokinetics and pharmacodynamics, older adults are at risk for developing sedation, changes in mental status and respiratory depression with the use of narcotic analgesics (see Chapter 20). To prevent these problems, lower initial doses of narcotics than those used with younger adults may be used. The individual's response to the pain medication and the pain are closely monitored. If low doses are tolerated, the dose may be carefully increased. Keeping the affected extremity in alignment during turning also decreases pain. This is done using pillows between the knees or an abduction splint. Walkers and canes are prescribed by the physical therapist. The nurse needs to ensure that the client uses safe technique with either device (see Client/Family Teaching box, p. 865) (Fig. 30-7).

Clients who have their fractures repaired with femoral head prostheses are at risk for dislocation. The nurse should give the client and family instructions on preventing dislocation. Dislocation may occur when the joint is abducted and internally rotated. Activities to be avoided are crossing the legs and feet while seated, sitting on low seats, and abducting the legs when lying on the side. The client is instructed not to put on socks or shoes without the aide of assistive devices, not to cross legs, not to lie on the affected side, to use a raised toilet seat and a shower chair, and to use a pillow between the legs while in bed. Activities that can cause dislocation should be avoided for six weeks until muscles surrounding the joint are healed and stabilization at the joint is present. Symptoms of dislocation are severe pain of sudden onset and external rotation of the leg.

Following the devastating events of hip fracture and surgery, comprehensive multidisciplinary rehabilitation focuses on the goal of returning the client to the prior level of function and preventing disability. Specific areas of treatment are gait and transfer training, muscle strengthening through active assistive exercises, teaching the use of adaptive techniques for dressing and teaching about the correct use of assistive devices. These

Insight • *After older adults undergo periods of hospitalization and disuse, with resultant loss of muscle strength, intensive programs of physical therapy should be recommended. Muscle strength, size and functional mobility can be regained with intensive programs of resistance training (Fiatarone et al, 1990). By improving strength, gait is improved and the risk of falls that cause fractures and functional dependency is decreased, even in the oldest old.*

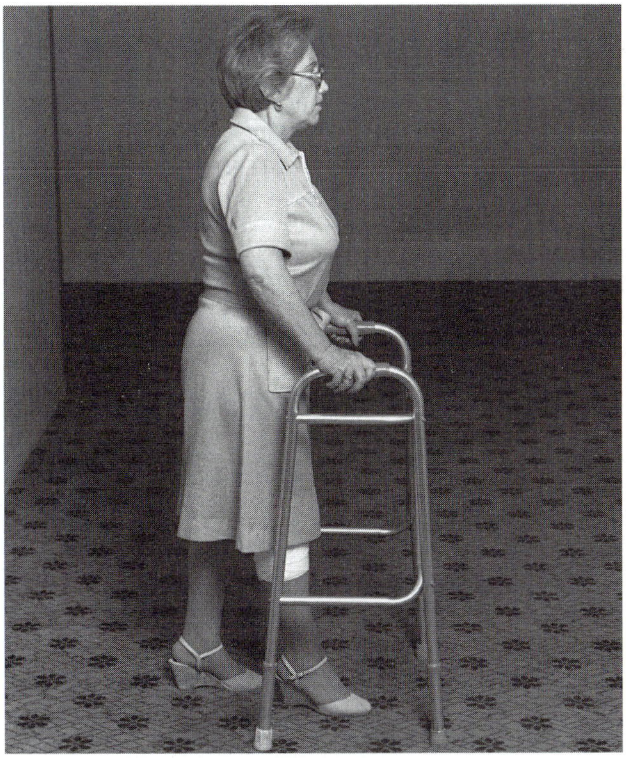

Fig. 30-7 Walking with a walker. The walker is moved about 6 inches in front of the resident. Both feet are moved up to the walker. (From Potter PA, Perry AG: *Fundamentals of nursing: concepts, process, and practice,* ed 2, St. Louis, 1985, Mosby.)

CLIENT/FAMILY TEACHING

Correct Use of Walkers

A walker should always rest on all four legs, not two.
Correct body position should be maintained:
- Posture erect
- Elbows slightly bent
- Wrists extended
- Shoulders relaxed

Sturdy, comfortable, hard-soled shoes should be worn.
Walker and affected leg should be moved together.
Be alert for hazards such as uneven surfaces or wet floors.

programs are directed by physical and occupational therapists. The loss of independence and decreased functional ability also must be addressed. These losses can lead to depression (see Chapter 12). The nurse's role is to identify the client's strengths, give positive feedback and reinforcement for progress in achieving goals. Discharge planning focuses on using family and social support networks, and ongoing physical therapy programs.

RESEARCH

O'Brien L et al: Hospitalized elders risk of confusion with hip fractures, *J Gerontolog Nurs* 19(2):25-31, 1993.

Sample, setting

101 African-American and Caucasian women age 45 years or older with the diagnosis of hip fracture were admitted to 10 participating hospitals in New York City and 20 participating hospitals in Philadelphia from September 1987 through July 1989.

Methodology

Cognitive function was measured using the Kahn Goldfarb Mental Status Questionnaire. An extensive chart review was conducted to describe demographic and clinical characteristics hypothesized to be associated with confusion. These included demographics, number of chronic illnesses, mental status at admission, history of psychiatric illnesses, admission hemoglobin, use of anxiolytic drugs, use of physical restraints, type of surgical anesthesia, descriptive behaviors, renal failure, heart failure, urinary tract infection, sepsis, pressure sores, and status at the time of discharge.

Findings

Clients with hip fractures and severe or moderate confusion were significantly more likely to be over age 75. Those with severe confusion were more likely to have a preexisting diagnosis of psychiatric illness and were significantly more likely to experience medical complications during the illness. This group was more likely to be discharged to nursing homes. The use of physical restraints was most common in those with severe confusion.

Implications

It is crucial to accurately assess the baseline mental status of clients with hip fractures and to monitor changes throughout the course of hospitalization. Factors that put this group at risk for developing transient acute confusion should be identified. Interventions to avoid or ameliorate this problem should be planned. These include taking comprehensive medication histories, monitoring medications, restricting the use of medications with anticholinergic effects, reducing urinary tract infections by limiting the length of time urinary catheters are used. Environmental risk factors should be reduced by systematically reorienting clients; providing calendars, clocks, and current newspapers; and maintaining easy access to glasses and hearing aids.

EVALUATION

The client who sustains a fracture will have minimal pain at the fracture site. Circulation to the affected extremity is maintained. If necessary, physical and occupational therapies will be utilized so that the client will maintain muscle

CARE PLAN

FRACTURED HIP

Clinical situation Ms. W is an 88-year-old executive secretary who is admitted to the skilled nursing unit of the local hospital for restorative care following surgical repair of a fractured left hip. The hip was repaired with a femoral head prosthesis. Ms. W fell when getting on the city bus. Before this incident, Ms. W worked 3 days per week. Her general health status is good. She lives alone on the second floor of a two-story building. Her only family is a niece who lives 60 miles away.

On admission, Ms. W is a thin, slender woman who looks younger than her stated age. She is in no acute pain. The left hip incision is clean and dry with the staples intact. Ms. W transfers with the moderate assistance of two people. During the transfer she becomes tense and tells the nurses that she is afraid of falling and that she has to get on her feet so that she can get back to work. Because the surgical procedure has caused decreased range of motion and weakness in her left leg, Ms. W requires assistance with bathing and dressing her lower extremities.

Nursing diagnoses	Outcome	Interventions
Impaired physical mobility related to alteration in musculoskeletal function as a result of fracture and surgical repair	Client will ambulate 50 feet with a pickup walker.	Consult with physical therapy for program of muscle strengthening, transfer training, and gait training. Reinforce physical therapy training. Give positive feedback for gains made. Instruct to take deep breaths and relax before transfers. Assist with transfers. Give specific instructions before transfers. Instruct on hip precautions. Teach use of walker. Give pain medication 30 to 60 minutes before physical therapy.
Self-care deficit: bathing, dressing lower extremities related to alteration in musculoskeletal function as a result of fracture and surgical repair	Client will bathe and dress lower extremities with the use of assistive devices.	Consult with occupational therapy for specific assistive devices. Teach use of assistive devices. Allow adequate time for bathing and dressing. Give positive feedback for gains made.
Knowledge deficit: home care program related to limited exposure	Client will verbalize knowledge of home care program. Client will verbalize satisfaction with discharge plans.	Assess support systems and need for home services. Assess home safety, instruct on wound care, home exercise program. Plan for discharge with client and team members. Use community services, visiting nurse, physical therapy, and niece.

strength, joint mobility, and the ability to perform ADLs with assistive devices (see nursing Care Plan above).

Colles Fracture

A **Colles fracture** is a fracture of the distal radius that is usually a result of reaching out with an open hand to break the fall. This fracture is seen most often in older women with osteoporosis. The client with a Colles fracture has pain at the site of the fracture that begins immediately after the traumatic episode; local edema, swelling, and a visible deformity from the displacement of the distal bone fragment are also present.

Treatment of a Colles fracture is usually closed reduction and immobilization with a forearm splint or cast. Nursing measures include elevating the extremity to decrease edema and neurovascular assessment to monitor for complications. The client is instructed to actively move the thumb and fingers to improve venous return and decrease edema and to prevent stiffness of the shoulder by actively moving the joint.

Clavicle Fracture

Clavicle fractures, like Colles fractures, occur after a fall on an outstretched hand or a fall on the shoulder. The majority of these fractures occur in the middle one third of the clavicle. The client with a fractured clavicle has point tenderness, local edema, and crepitus. The shoulder is noticeably deformed, dropping downward, forward, and inward. Treatment of clavicular fracture includes reduction of the fracture. The joint is immobilized either with a sling or a cast. Nursing measures include monitoring for neurovascular complications such as compartment syndrome, elevating the extremity, and active movement of the hand and fingers.

Casts and cast care Casts are devices that immobilize, maintain, support and protect realigned bones (Salmund, Mooney, Verdisco, 1991). They promote healing of fractured bones and allow early weight bearing. Casts are made of plaster of paris or synthetic materials such as fiberglass.

After the cast is applied, the extremity is elevated to the level of the heart to decrease edema. The plaster cast is left open to the air for 48 to 72 hours to dry. The client is told that the cast will feel warm during the drying process. To prevent indentations in the cast during the drying period, the nurse should support the cast by the palms of the hands rather than by fingers. The client can bear weight when the cast is dry. The client is instructed to keep the cast dry. Plaster casts can be covered with plastic to keep them dry during showering or bathing. Clients with fiberglass casts are allowed to bathe. The client is instructed to maintain movement of the extremity to prevent muscle atrophy (see Client/Family Teaching box above).

CLIENT/FAMILY TEACHING

Cast Care

- Keep casted extremity elevated for the first 24 hours.
- When cast is wet, lift with palms of hands.
- Observe the extremity for swelling, color changes, movement, and sensation.
- If any changes occur, contact health care provider.
- Do not put anything inside the cast.
- Do not get plaster cast wet; cover with plastic for bathing.

The nurse's role is to monitor for and prevent cast complications. The skin around the cast is protected by petaling with tape. The skin around the cast should be inspected for signs of breakdown or irritation. Neurovascular checks are performed to determine if there is excessive constriction caused by the cast that could result in compartment syndrome, a compression of the structures within the fascial walls. The compression causes destruction of venous circulation and arterial occlusion, leading to ischemia and tissue destruction. Any change in capillary refill, skin color, skin temperature, or excessive pain should be reported immediately to the physician.

Falls in Older Adults

Falls are a common cause of fractures and injury that result in disability and institutionalization, and may even lead to death for older adults. It has been estimated that one third of older adults fall each year (Edwards, Cere, Leblond, 1993). Falls in this population usually have multiple causes. Assessment of risk factors and specific client interventions are keys to preventing falls (Hogue, 1992).

Falls or unintentional changes in position occur as the result of complex interrelated factors. The factors are divided into intrinsic and extrinsic factors. Intrinsic factors are those internal to the client, such as age-related physiologic changes and disease processes. Extrinsic factors are caused by conditions in the environment. It is important for the nurse to have knowledge of these factors to prevent falls.

Intrinsic Factors

Age-related changes in vision that contribute to falls are decreased visual acuity, and changes in depth perception. These changes predispose an individual to tripping or falling because they are unable to adequately see hazards in the environment. Increased postural sway, changes in gait, decreased muscle mass, strength and coordination are also intrinsic factors. Pathologic conditions that cause changes in gait, alteration in balance, or hypotension may result in falls. Such conditions include Alzheimer's disease (AD), Parkinson's disease, diabetic neuropathies, cardiac arrhythmias, syncope, transient ischemic attacks, arthritis, and foot problems. Medications that cause hypotension or decrease the individual's awareness of the environment are considered intrinsic factors. The categories of these medications are sedatives and hypnotics, tranquilizers, tricyclic antidepressants, antihypertensives, and diuretics.

Extrinsic Factors

Environmental problems include inadequate lighting, loose rugs or stair treads, wet or slippery floors, clutter, uneven surfaces, and electrical cords. The environment outdoors also presents hazards such as uneven, slippery walkways and poor lighting at night. Hazards that are found in hospitals and long-term care facilities include clutter, assistive devices such as wheelchairs, walkers, overbed tables with wheels, glare, inadequate lighting, highly polished floors, bedrails, restraints, and call lights that are out of the client's reach (Stone, Chenitz, 1991).

Preventing Falls

Preventing falls requires a multidimensional program that focuses on modifying the extrinsic factors, correcting intrinsic factors, and educating the client and family. The nurse in the community setting can perform an environmental assessment and make recommendations for eliminating environmental risks. During the home assessment the client's ability to safely manage ambulation in the environment should be observed. Box 30-1 summarizes fall prevention strategies in the different health care settings.

BOX 30-1

Fall Prevention

Community setting

Environmental assessment
Recommend environmental modifications
Recommend exercise programs to improve gait, strength, and endurance

Hospital/long-term care setting

Environmental assessment
Environmental modifications
Improve lighting
Lower beds
Improve client call systems
Individual risk assessment
History of falls
Mental status
Sensory deficits
Medications
Mobility and self-care status
Incontinence or urgency
Dizziness or postural hypotension

NURSING MANAGEMENT

ASSESSMENT

On admission to the hospital or long-term care facility, older adults should be assessed for fall risk factors. The assessment is ongoing throughout the client's length of stay. Formal assessment tools may be used for the assessment (Table 30-1).

DIAGNOSIS

The most common nursing diagnosis for the client who is at risk for falling is high risk for injury, as evidenced by the presence of the intrinsic and/or extrinsic factors identified above.

PLANNING

Planning care for the older adult at risk of falling focuses on reducing or eliminating the identified risk factors, which includes appropriate nursing management of any of the physical, psychosocial, or environmental intrinsic and extrinsic factors. The client and family should be included in the planning process, with the overall goal of preserving dignity and maintaining independence. Expected outcomes include but are not limited to, the following: (1) client remains free of personal injury, (2) client incorporates personal safety tips into daily routine aimed at preventing falls, (3) client recognizes factors that may increase risk of injury from falls. The risk factors identified in any client situation are highly individual and guide selection of specific outcomes.

INTERVENTION

After risk is assessed, individualized nursing interventions to prevent falls are implemented. The client and family are educated on methods used to prevent falls. Written instructions that focus on increasing the safety of the home environment are given to clients and families (see Client/Family Teaching box, p. 869). In the hospital or long-term care setting, interventions focus on manipulating the environment, educating the client and family, implementing rehabilitation programs to improve functional abilities in ADLs, and careful monitoring of medication side effects. Specific measures to use include scheduled toileting, bedside commodes, placing call lights and belongings within easy reach, and educating the client in transfer techniques. The client is also instructed to call for help if not independent in transfers, and to sit on the side of the bed for 1 minute before standing. Environmental interventions include keeping beds in the lowest position with brakes on, grab bars in the bathroom, night lights, and nonskid wax on floors. In some cases, fall monitoring devices that sound an alarm when the client starts to get out of bed may be helpful.

Restraint Use

Using restraints does not prevent falls. Clients who fall while restrained have been shown to have more serious injuries (Tinetti et al, 1991). In some cases, restraints have been implicated as the cause of death. Under OBRA, the Omnibus Budget Reconciliation Act of 1987, regulations state that clients in nursing homes and hospital-based skilled nursing units have the right to be free from physical restraints. Restraints should be used only as a last resort after other interventions have failed. If restraints must be used, the least restrictive devices should be used, employing the FDA guidelines described in Box 30-2.

TABLE 30-1

Fall Assessment Tool

	Initial score	Reassessed score
Client factors	15	15
History of falls	15	15
Confusion	5	5
Age (over 65)	5	5
Impaired judgment	5	5
Sensory deficit	5	5
Unable to ambulate independently	5	5
Decreased level of cooperation	5	5
Increased anxiety/emotional liability	5	5
Incontinence/urgency	5	5
Cardiovascular/respiratory disease affecting perfusion and oxygenation	5	5
Medications affecting blood pressure or level of consciousness	5	5
Postural hypotension with dizziness	5	5
Environmental factors		
First week on unit	5	5
Attached equipment (e.g., IV pole, chest tubes, appliances, oxygen tubing, etc.)	5	5
	_______	_______
TOTAL POINTS	_______	_______

Implement fall precautions for score of 15 or greater.

Modified from Hollinger L, Patterson R: A fall prevention program for the acute care setting. In Funk SO et al, editors: *Key aspects of elder care: Managing falls, incontinence and cognitive impairment.* New York, 1992, Springer.

Insight • *Restraints do not prevent falls, although nurses use restraints to prevent falls and injury. Clients who are restrained continue to fall and may suffer more serious injuries if they fall while restrained. In a study conducted in a nursing home (Tinetti, et al, 1991), falls and injuries increased in frequency as restraint use increased. Nurses must continue to test and to implement alternative interventions to maintain client safety.*

✣ EVALUATION

Evaluation includes achievement of the expected outcomes while assuring the dignity and independence of the client. This is one of the most challenging tasks faced by the gerontologic nurse caring for an older adult—to preserve self-esteem while protecting from harm. In addition, the nurse may need to frequently reassess the

CLIENT/FAMILY TEACHING

Preventing Falls

Home safety

Remove scatter rugs; other rugs should be free from tears and tacked down.
Do not polish floors.
Keep electrical and extension cords at the periphery of rooms.
Avoid clutter.
Install grab rails in the bathroom.
Use nonskid mats in showers and bathtubs.
Use stable chairs with arms.
Use adequate nonglare lighting, especially around stairs and in bathrooms and kitchens.
Use night lights in bedroom and bathrooms.
Install securely fastened handrails on both sides of stairs.
Keep stairs in good repair.

Other tips

Always wear properly fitting shoes with non-skid soles.
Use assistive devices, i.e., canes, walkers, as instructed (Fig. 30-8).
Change positions slowly, sit on the side of the bed for 1 to 2 minutes before standing.
Do not rush to reach the telephone. Use portable telephones.

BOX 30-2

Guidelines for Restraint Use

1. Assess the cause for which the restraint is being used, develop alternatives to restraint use, and implement alternatives before applying restraints.
2. Use restraints only for a strictly defined period of time.
3. Follow institutional policy on the use of restraints.
4. Obtain informed consent from the client or guardian before use. Explain the reason for the device to the client/guardian.
5. Use the type of restraint that is appropriate to the client's condition.
6. Use the correct size.
7. Never secure restraints to the bed rails.
8. Tie restraints with quick release hitches.
9. Observe clients in restraints often.
10. Remove the restraints at least every 2 hours to allow for positioning and ADLs.

Modified from the Department of Health and Human Services, Food and Drug Administration: *FDA Safety Alert: potential hazards with restraint devices,* July 15, 1992.

A B C

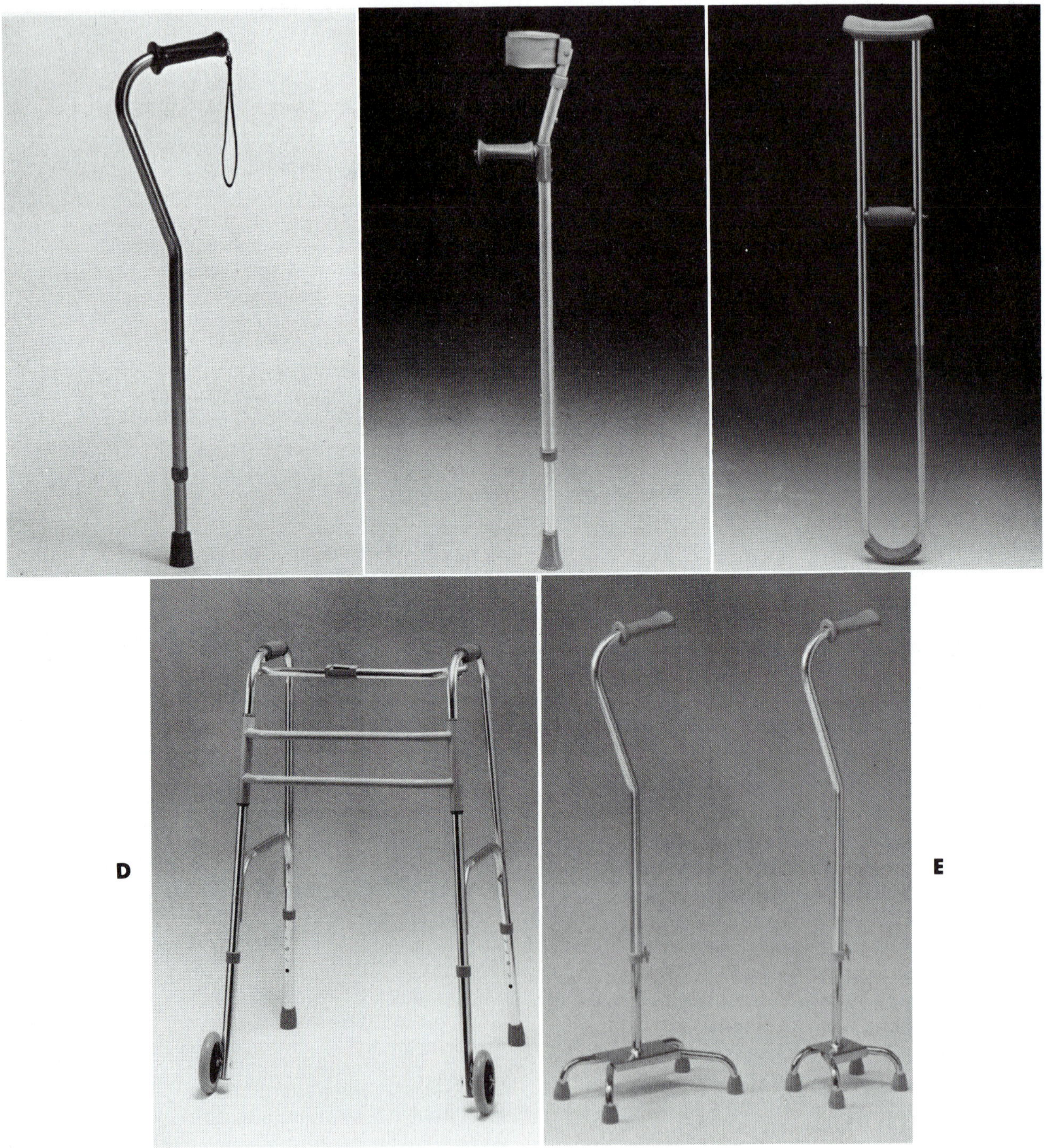

D E

Fig. 30-8 Assistive devices. **A,** Ortho cane with wrist strap. **B,** A forearm crutch stabilizes your elbow while you walk. **C,** New "rolling crutch" provides smoother contact with the ground. **D,** Walker with front wheels allows constant contact with the ground. **E,** Quad cane offers more support than a single-stem walker. (Courtesy Lumex, Inc., New York.)

client's risk based on any further changes in the client's condition.

Osteoarthritis

Osteoarthritis, also known as degenerative joint disease, is a noninflammatory disease of weight-bearing joints that is characterized by progressive articular cartilage deterioration with the formation of new bone in the joint space (Salmund, Mooney, Verdisco, 1991). This is the most common type of arthritis seen in older adults.

The exact cause of osteoarthritis is not well understood. The degeneration of the joint is not caused by aging alone. Age, trauma, lifestyle, obesity, and genetics have been cited as predisposing factors in the development of osteoarthritis.

In osteoarthritis the articular cartilage thins and is lost, particularly in areas of increased stress. As the cartilage deteriorates, there is a proliferation of bone at the margins of the joints. When the joint cartilage is lost, the two bone surfaces come into contact with each other. This results in joint pain. The distal interphalangeals, proximal interphalangeals, knees, spine, and hips are the joints most commonly affected by osteoarthritis (Hochberg, 1991).

The most common symptom is a gradual onset of aching joint pain. The pain occurs with activity and is relieved with rest. Stiffness after periods of inactivity that resolves with activity is also seen in osteoarthritis. Crepitus, a grating sound and sensation, may be heard and felt in affected joints on range of motion. The affected joints have a decreased range of motion. The degeneration of the joint structure may result in muscle spasm, gait changes, and disuse of the joint. Bony enlargement, or Heberden's nodes, may be seen on the distal interphalangeals (see Medical Management box at right).

Nursing Management

✣ ASSESSMENT

Nursing assessment of the client with osteoarthritis begins with a thorough history of the problem. Data gathered include information about the onset, location, quality, and duration of the joint pain. Questions about precipitating factors, medications used, and impact on functional abilities should be asked. Affected joints should be inspected for pain, tenderness, swelling, redness, crepitation, and range of motion.

✣ DIAGNOSIS

Nursing diagnoses for older adults with osteoarthritis include pain, impaired physical mobility, and self-care deficits.

✣ PLANNING

The focus of the nursing plan is on protecting the joint and maintaining function. The specifics of the plan are individualized to the client and joints affected.

✣ INTERVENTION

Instructions on joint protection and energy conservation are given. For clients with mild pain, an exercise program

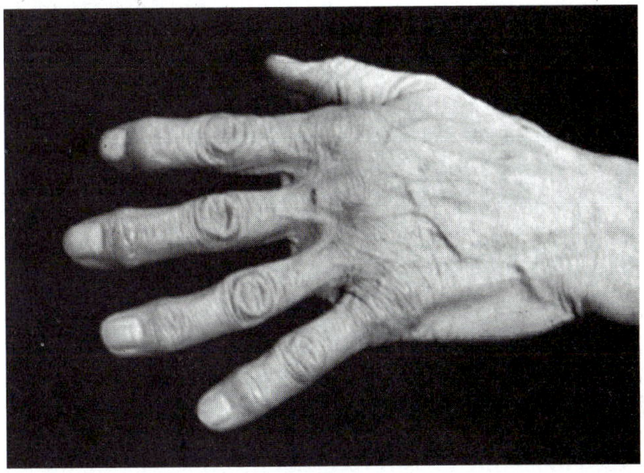

Fig. 30-9 Left hand of a 71-year-old woman with OA and Heberden's nodes. (From Lewis SM, Cox IC: *Medical-surgical nursing: assessment and management of clinical problems,* ed 3, St. Louis, 1992, Mosby.)

MEDICAL MANAGEMENT

Osteoarthritis

Diagnostic tests and procedures

History—Includes gradual onset of joint pain with activity, relieved with rest, stiffness after periods of inactivity; condition may be aggravated by changes in barometric pressure

Physical examination—Findings include: asymmetrical joint involvement, Heberdens nodes (Fig. 30-9)

Laboratory findings—Negative rheumatoid factor, synovial fluid will be increased

X-ray findings—Joint space narrowing, spur formation, and bony sclerosis.

Treatment

Medications—Mild analgesics: Aspirin, nonsteroidal antiinflammatory drugs (NSAIDs)

Rest and joint protection

Heat or cold therapy

Surgery—Joint replacement

Prognosis

Disability may be caused, but with treatment, function can be maintained that increases range of motion is used. Rest periods between activities are recommended. Heat and/or cold treatments to the joint may decrease pain.

Other interventions to relieve pain may be used (see Chapter 13). Relaxation techniques, biofeedback, hypnosis, and therapeutic massage are useful techniques in managing osteoarthritic pain. The nurse instructs the client in these techniques and supports the client's use of them.

✣ EVALUATION

The client with osteoarthritis reports minimum pain along with the ability to perform ADLs with minimum joint discomfort. Self-care practices that include a program of regular exercise, the use of adaptive devices, and adherence to a prescribed medication regimen are followed.

Joint replacement

Surgical procedures, including joint replacement when the chronic pain is not controlled and when the decreased range of motion in the affected joint interferes with the older adult's ability to function at an optimum level, are used to treat osteoarthritis. The surgical procedures most often performed are arthroplasty, or joint reconstruction or replacement. The goals of surgery are to relieve pain and to prevent disability by improving joint function.

In the preoperative period the focus of nursing care is on educating the client about the surgical procedure and the postoperative course. After total hip and total knee arthroplasty, goals of the postoperative period are preventing complications, relieving pain, and restoring function. Major complications are joint infection and thromboembolism. Infection control measures are vigilantly maintained. To prevent infection, urinary catheters are avoided. Anticoagulants are used prophylactically to prevent thromboembolism. In the first 48 hours postoperative, narcotic analgesics should be administered on a regular schedule. This is often done with patient-controlled analgesia (PCA). With PCA, the client self-administers a predetermined dose of intravenous analgesic through an infusion pump. Rehabilitation begins in the first 24 to 48 hours postoperatively. The physical therapy program includes muscle strengthening and range-of-motion exercises, as well as gait training.

Clients who have total hip arthroplasties are at risk for hip dislocation. The hip is maintained in a position of abduction and neutral rotation. To maintain abduction while in bed, abduction splints or pillows are placed between the client's legs. The client is given instructions on hip precautions as described in Client/Family Teaching box above.

CLIENT/FAMILY TEACHING

Hip Precautions

Do sit with your hips at a 90-degree or greater angle.
Do not bend forward more than 90 degrees.
Do not lift your knee on the operated side higher than your hip.
Do not cross legs at knees or ankles.
Do keep pillows between your legs when lying on your side or your back.
Do not bend to put on shoes; use a long shoe horn.
Do not bend down to reach items on the floor.
Do not sit in low chairs.

Following total knee arthroplasty the goals are to prevent complications and to restore knee function to 90 degrees of flexion. Continuous passive motion (CPM) machines are devices that are used as an aid in achieving joint motion. CPM is an electrically driven device that continuously moves the knee through a preset range of flexion and extension.

With diagnosis-related groups and shorter hospital stays, older clients who have been deconditioned before surgery may need to have continued rehabilitation programs. This can be accomplished through a home therapy program or by a brief stay in a long-term care unit that provides rehabilitation services (see Research box, p. 873).

Infected arthroplasty Infection of the joint is a serious complication of joint replacement. The incidence of deep infections of joint replacements is 1% to 2% (Salmund, Mooney, Verdisco, 1991). The infection may be a result of contamination during surgery, draining hematomas, delayed healing or distant sites of infection, particularly urinary tract infections. The most common contaminants are staphylococci and gram-positive aerobic streptococci. The new joint is a foreign body and if pathogens are introduced, they persist on the surface of the prosthesis.

Bacterial infection may also be enhanced by the cement used in the procedure. Clients with rheumatoid arthritis, diabetes mellitus (DM), poor nutritional status, and those on long-term corticosteroid therapy are at risk for developing infection. The infection is treated with long-term intravenous (IV) antibiotic therapy, usually for 6 weeks. In some cases the infected prosthesis may be replaced. Joint infections may lead to disability and lengthen the rehabilitative process. The long-term antibiotic therapy and extended restorative period may require a short stay in a long-term care facility or the administration of IV antibiotics at home. Clients who are discharged with IV antibiotics require teaching about the medications and follow-up by a home health nurse.

TABLE 30-2

Differentiating Rheumatoid Arthritis from Osteoarthritis

	Rheumatoid arthritis	Osteoarthritis
Age at onset	Third and fourth decades	Fifth and sixth decades
Onset	Gradual	Gradual
Disease course	Exacerbations and remissions	Variable, progressive
Duration of stiffness	1 to 24 hours	30 minutes or less
Joint pain	Worse in morning	Worse after activity
Joints involved	Proximal interphalangeal	Distal interphalangeal
	Metacarpophalangeal	Knees, hips
	Metatarsophalangeal	Lumbar, cervical
	Knees, hips, wrists	Spine
Symmetric pattern	Almost always present	Occasionally
Constitutional manifestations	Present	Absent
Synovial fluid	Increased cells	Few cells
	Decreased viscosity	Normal viscosity
X-ray findings	Abnormalities present	Abnormalities present
Eosinophil sedimentation rate	Almost always elevated	Occasionally elevated
Positive rheumatoid factor	Almost always	Never

RESEARCH

Kelly H: Patient perceptions of pain and disability after joint arthroplasty, *J Orthoped Nurs* 10(6):43-50, 1992.

Sample, setting

The sample included 29 clients with rheumatoid or osteoarthritis who had either total hip or total knee arthroplasty performed by one orthopedic surgeon in the Midwest.

Methodology

Health status was measured with the Health Assessment Questionnaire. Impact of the disease was measured with the Arthritis Impact Measure (AIMS). Pain was assessed before surgery, 6 weeks and 6 months postoperatively with the McGill Pain Questionnaire.

Findings

Clients reported significant decrease in pain at 6 weeks and 6 months postoperatively. Physical activity, measured by the AIMs, improved significantly.

Implications

Nurses can provide clients who are contemplating arthroplastic surgery with this information to help them make decisions concerning surgery and to give them positive feedback after their postoperative course.

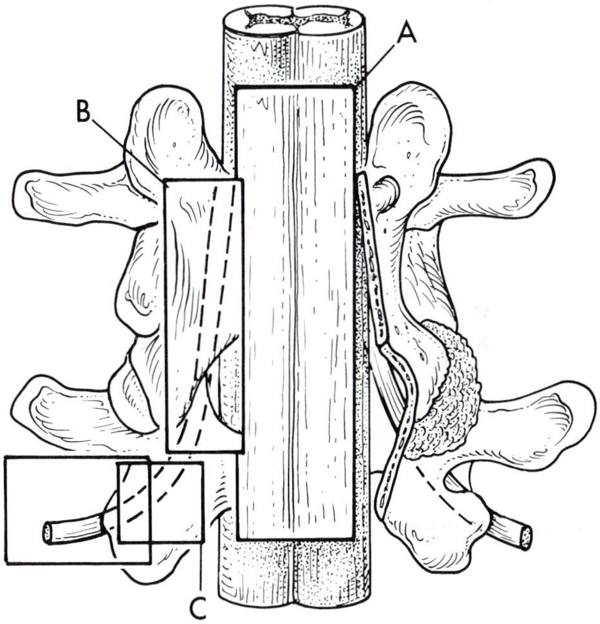

Fig. 30-10 Three dimensional illustration of segmental stenoses. **A,** Anatomic. **B,** Segmental. **C,** Pathologic. (Redrawn from Ciric I et al: *J Neurosurg* 53:433, 1980.)

Spinal Stenosis

Osteoarthritis also affects the facet joints of the spine and can lead to spinal stenosis. Spinal stenosis is caused by a bony overgrowth that produces a narrowing of the neural foramen (Chase, 1991). This results in back pain and loss of function in the innervated muscles. Although spinal stenosis can occur at any level, the most frequent site of spinal stenosis is at L4 and L3 (Fig. 30-10).

Goals of nursing interventions for spinal stenosis include controlling pain and maintaining physical functioning. If interventions are not successful in managing pain and the pain causes disability, surgical decompression and fusion are done.

Rheumatoid Arthritis

Rheumatoid arthritis is a chronic, systemic, inflammatory disease that causes joint destruction and deformity and results in disability. The onset of the disease most commonly occurs in the third or fourth decade. However, rheumatoid arthritis can also develop in older adults. When present in older adults the disease is usually a chronic problem.

The cause of rheumatoid arthritis is not known. The most commonly accepted theory is that it is an autoimmune disease that causes inflammation most often in joints but also affects other connective tissue. Joint involvement most often starts with the proximal interphalangeals, metacarpophalangeals, and wrists, and in later stages of the disease, knees and hips are affected.

In the initial phase of rheumatoid arthritis, the synovial membrane becomes inflamed and thickens, associated with an increased production of synovial fluid. The change is called pannus. As the pannus tissue develops it causes erosion and destruction of the joint capsule and subchondral bone. These processes result in decreased joint motion, deformity, and finally ankylosis or joint immobilization.

The course of rheumatoid arthritis is variable. Generally the onset is gradual and the course is one of remissions and exacerbations (Nesher, Moore, Zuckner, 1991). The symptoms are painful stiff joints, decreased range of motion in the joints, joint swelling, and deformity (Fig. 30-11). The joint stiffness is present in the morning and lasts from 30 minutes to 6 hours. On examination, the affected joints are warm and swollen. Deformities of the joints include ulnar deviation of the wrists, boutonniere deformity caused by contractures of the distal interphalangeal joints and proximal interphalangeal joints, and swan-neck deformity caused by contractures of the distal interphalangeal joint (Fig. 30-12). Systemic symptoms that are present include fatigue, anorexia, weight loss, and anemia. Rheumatoid arthritis in older adults may appear atypically. That is, large joints are affected more often and the onset may be sudden. Fatigue, weakness, and fever may be present (Table 30-2) (see Medical Management box at right).

Nursing Management

✣ ASSESSMENT

A careful nursing history is taken. Questions are asked about family history and constitutional symptoms, including fever, anorexia, weight loss, fatigue, and duration of joint stiffness. On physical examination, the affected joints are inspected for symmetrical involvement, pain, tenderness, swelling, heat, erythema, and deformity.

✣ DIAGNOSIS

Nursing diagnoses for the older adult with rheumatoid arthritis include pain, impaired mobility, fatigue, altered nutrition: less than body requirements, self-care deficits, and body image disturbance.

✣ PLANNING

Goals for the client with rheumatoid arthritis include the following: (1) client will prevent excessive disability, (2) client will control pain, and (3) client will promote optimum functional status. Clients and families need extensive education to cope effectively with the chronic disease of rheumatoid arthritis. Areas for teaching include pain management, drug therapy, self-care, mobility, environmental adaptation, and management of fatigue and depression.

MEDICAL MANAGEMENT

Rheumatoid Arthritis

Diagnostic tests and procedures

History—Morning stiffness, pain, tenderness, erythema, swelling over the affected joint, fatigue, weakness, and weight loss.

Physical examination—Subcutaneous nodules over bony prominences, enlarged lymph nodes and joint deformities, that is, swan-neck, boutonniere, and ulnar deviation.

Laboratory findings—Positive rheumatoid factor, elevated erythrocyte sedimentation rate, decreased red blood cell count, increased white blood cell count, increased C-reactive protein. Serum electrophoresis shows increased alpha- and Y-globulins, and decreased albumin; volume of synovial fluid is increased, and viscosity decreased.

X-ray findings—May show cartilage erosion and subluxations.

Treatment

Medications—NSAIDs, penicillamine, hydroxychloroquine, adrenocorticosteroids and immunosuppressives (Table 30-3, pp. 876-877).

Rest

Joint protection

Exercise program

Surgery, including joint replacement

Prognosis

The prognosis varies depending on the disease. Rheumatoid arthritis is a chronic and progressive disease, which is likely to result in disability and decreased functional status.

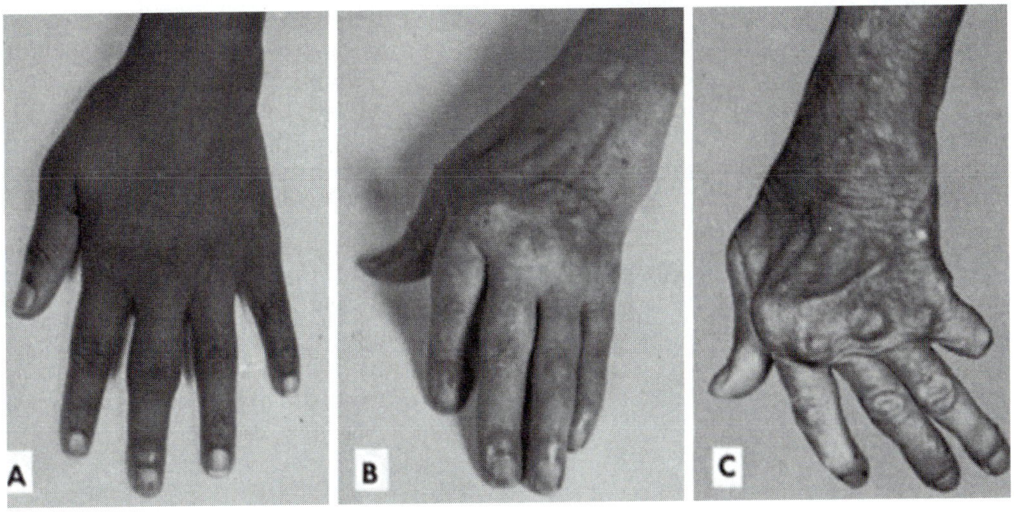

Fig. 30-11 Rheumatoid arthritis of the hand. **A,** Early stage. **B,** Moderate involvement. **C,** Advanced stage. (From Brashear H, Raney R: *Handbook of orthopaedic surgery,* ed 10, St Louis, 1986, Mosby.)

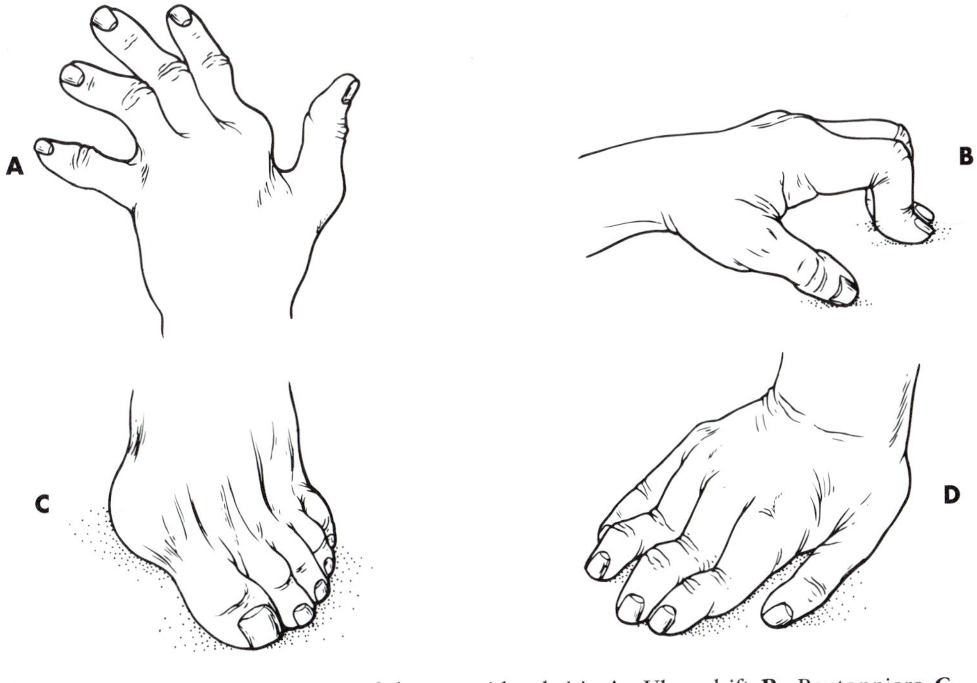

Fig. 30-12 Typical deformities of rheumatoid arthritis. **A,** Ulnar drift. **B,** Boutonniere. **C,** Hallux valgus. **D,** Swan-neck deformity. (From Lewis SM, Collier IC: *Medical-surgical nursing: assessment and management of clinical problems,* ed 3, St. Louis, 1992, Mosby.)

TABLE 30-3

Drug Use, Side Effects, and Nursing Implications

Drug	Rationale for use	Side effects	Nursing implications
Salicylates: Aspirin	Used in early disease phase; analgesic, antipyretic, and antiinflammatory	Gastrointestinal (GI) irritation; slight elevation of liver enzymes; tinnitus (reversible)	Administer with milk or food. Teach use of enteric coated tablets. Evaluate for GI pain or bleeding, tinnitus.
NSAIDs Long-term: Diclofenac, Fenoprofen, Ibuprofen, Indomethacin, Ketoprofen, Mefanamic acid, Naproxen, Salsalate, Sulindac, Tolmetin	Used when salicylates are ineffective; analgesic, antipyretic, and antiinflammatory actions; generally inhibit prostaglandin synthesis	GI irritation; diarrhea; fluid retention, edema; interstitial nephritis; nephrotic syndrome; dizziness, tachycardia, blurred vision, headaches; cholestatic hepatitis; bone marrow depression	Must be administered 1 to 2 weeks before therapeutic response is seen. Administer with food or antacids Assess for GI pain, occult bleeding. Teach to avoid alcohol. Evaluate renal and hepatic function regularly.
Short-term: Phenylbutazone	Specific for adjunctive use	Same as above	Same as above; a 1-week trial is suggested. Evaluate complete blood count (CBC). Use with caution in older adults.
Oxyphenbutazone	Effective for articular symptoms in some clients	Same as above	Same as above; use under close medical supervision.
Antimalarials: Hydroxychloroquine sulfate, Hydroxychloroquine phosphate	Used for severe destructive disease; 3 to 6 months needed to reach therapeutic levels.	GI irritation; skin rash and changes; retinal changes; bone marrow depression	Advise ophthalmologic examination every 4 to 6 weeks. Allow 6 to 8 weeks for therapeutic effects to begin. Evaluate CBC regularly. Assess for GI effects, headaches, dizziness, hearing effects, hepatotoxicity. Evaluate for water and sodium retention.
Auranofin	Effects cumulative, slow onset of effects (8 to 14 weeks); dosage may be gradually decreased after remission	Proteinuria; interstitial fibrosis; metallic taste	Teach skin care. Evaluate GI discomfort. Check urine for blood and protein.
Penicillamine	As effective as gold, but more toxic; unknown mechanism of action; effects seen in 2 months.	GI irritation; taste alterations; blood dyscrasias; skin rash; stomatitis; nephrotic syndrome, glomerulonephritis; autoimmune syndrome; proteinuria	Evaluate CBC, liver, and renal function weekly for 2 months, then monthly. Teach to report sore throat or fever.
Antirheumatics: Gold sodium thiomalate, Aurothioglucose	Used when salicylates and NSAIDs fail; remission-inducing action suppresses inflammation.	Skin rashes, pruritus; stomatitis; diarrhea; blood dyscrasias; hepatitis	Give with NSAIDs until efficacy is reached. Assess CBC, as well as renal and liver function often.
Steroids: Systemic, Prednisone, Prednisolone, Hydrocortisone	For use with incapacitating disease; used cautiously and preferably short-term	Multiple toxic effects including osteoporosis, gastric ulcers, risk of infection susceptibility, hirsutism, acne,	Teach client not to stop medication abruptly. Administer for short time periods, taper dose slowly.

Modified from Moore KA: Arthritic disorders. In Salmond SW, Mooney NE, Verdisco LA, editors: *Core curriculum for orthopaedic nursing,* ed 2, Pitman, N.J., 1991, National Association of Orthopaedic Nurses.

TABLE 30-3

Drug Use, Side Effects, and Nursing Implications—cont'd

Drug	Rationale for use	Side effects	Nursing implications
		emotional lability, menstrual irregularities, edema, moon facies, hypokalemia, cataracts, glaucoma	Monitor for side effects, including hypertension and hyperglycemia.
Intraarticular	Used when only one or two joints are involved; used for pain relief, to increase function; benefits last 2 weeks to several months; joints most amenable are ankles knees, hips, shoulders, hands	Same as above	Teach client that effects may be short-lived. Advise that administration limited to two to four infections per year per joint.
Immunosuppressive: Azathioprine Methotrexate Cyclophosphamide	Used with advanced disease; affect immune system to decrease inflammation; teratogenic potential	Hepatitis, cirrhosis; GI ulcers; infection susceptibility; bone marrow suppression; alopecia; skin rash	Evaluate CBC, liver and renal function weekly. Assess older adults closely for signs of toxicity.

INTERVENTION

Education on managing pain includes information on medication, the effects of stress and anxiety on pain, stress management techniques, the use of heat and cold, and other interventions to decrease pain. Stress and anxiety can cause muscle tension and worsen joint pain. Progressive relaxation and guided imagery (see Chapter 13) are taught to decrease anxiety and stress. Application of heat and cold to the affected joints decreases cutaneous nerve stimulation. Ice packs are applied to inflamed joints after the acute inflammation. Moist heat is useful in relaxing muscles and increasing joint mobility.

The role of the nurse in medication management is to teach the client about the action, side effects, and special precautions related to the specific medications (see Table 30-3, p. 876-877). Older adults are especially prone to drug reactions and must be monitored closely for the occurrence of this problem.

Insight • *Older adults who take NSAIDs are at risk for developing peptic ulcers and GI hemorrhage, which can lead to death. The nurse should be aware of and monitor for this potential side effect. Risk factors for these side effects include dose, length of time used, treatment with combinations of NSAIDs and a history of gastric ulcers.*

Decreased mobility of joints of the upper extremities and fatigue contribute to self-care deficits. Occupational therapists work with clients to improve joint function and prevent disability. The modalities used include exercises, splints, teaching methods to protect joints, and teaching about the use of assistive devices. Splints are used to protect joints, maintain joint function, and to decrease pain. The nurse reinforces the use of these devices, and monitors for correct use.

Limitations of mobility because of pain and joint stiffness can lead to disuse and greater disability. To prevent excessive disability, the client is taught body mechanics and proper body alignment, and given recommendations for an exercise program. Using good body mechanics and keeping the body in a position of optimum alignment decrease joint stress and fatigue. Physical therapists prescribe individualized therapeutic exercise programs, which include strengthening and stretching exercises, range of motion, and endurance training.

Fatigue is a common constitutional symptom of rheumatoid arthritis. Fatigue can interfere with the older adult's achievement of optimum functional independence. Methods used to decrease fatigue include balancing rest with activity, scheduled short rest periods (1-2 hours), practicing relaxation techniques, and adapting the environment to simplify work.

Coping with chronic illness, the pain, the deformity, and alterations in body image can predispose to depression. If clinical depression occurs, medical evaluation and treatment are indicated.

The joint deformities and alteration in self-concept can lead to alteration in sexual functioning. The nurse needs to be aware of this and openly discuss issues of sexuality and give advice on methods to maintain physical intimacy. Suggestions include the use of analgesics before sexual activity, planning for sexual activity after periods of rest, alternative positions to coitus and encouraging use of alternative methods for maintaining physical intimacy (see Chapter 10).

Adults with rheumatoid arthritis, a chronic disease that causes pain, leads to deformity, and in some cases, results in disability, require many supports to cope with the disease. The nurse's role is to provide the older adult with information about supports that are available so that optimum levels of functioning can be reached. A good resource is the Arthritis Foundation, which publishes written educational materials that address exercise programs, work simplification, and information about the disease process.* Support groups and self-help classes in 6-week sessions are conducted by local chapters. Content of the classes includes self-efficacy, exercise, pain management, depression, stress management, and nontraditional therapies.

✣ EVALUATION

The client with rheumatoid arthritis will experience minimum discomfort and be able to perform ADLs with assistive devices. Individuals who are coping effectively with the disease process will adhere to the prescribed medical regimen, participate in a regular exercise program, will verbalize acceptance of the physical changes, and will feel in control over their bodies.

Gouty Arthritis

Gout is a disease in which acute attacks of arthritis occur as a result of elevated levels of serum uric acid. During acute gout attacks, joint inflammation is caused by sodium urate crystals in the joint.

Gout is classified as primary or acquired. Primary gout is an inborn disease of purine metabolism. Acquired gout is caused by medications that affect excretion of uric acid. These medications include thiazide diuretics. Gout usually occurs in the middle years and is more prevalent in men than women.

In gout, there may be an excessive production and/or a decreased urinary excretion of uric acid. The excess monosodium urate salts are deposited in joints and surrounding connective tissue. The deposits of the uric acid crystals are called tophi.

Gout can present as an acute or chronic condition. The onset of gout is sudden and is manifested by an acute attack of joint pain in one or up to four joints. The most commonly affected joint is the great toe. Other joints affected by gout include the ankle, knee, wrist, and elbow (Fig. 30-13). The affected joint becomes hot, reddened, and tender. The pain can be severe and interferes with mobility, self-care, and functional abilities. Chills and fever may also be present. Acute attacks of gout usually subside in 7 days regardless of treatment. In chronic gout the uric acid crystals cause bone destruction and deformity. Crystals of uric acid can also be deposited in the kidney and cause nephrolithiasis (see Medical Management box below).

*For more information, contact the Arthritis Foundation, 1314 Spring Street, NW, Atlanta, GA 20309, (800)283-7800.

NURSING MANAGEMENT

✣ ASSESSMENT

Client's lifestyle and risk factors that contribute to the development of gout are assessed. Pain and its impact on the client are also assessed.

✣ DIAGNOSIS

Nursing diagnoses for clients with gout include pain, impaired physical mobility, activity intolerance, and altered health maintenance.

MEDICAL MANAGEMENT

Gout

Diagnostic tests and procedures

History—Family history

Physical examination—Painful, inflamed affected joints; tophi may be present

Laboratory findings—Elevated serum uric acid, elevated white blood cell count, and elevated erythrocyte sedimentation rate may be seen in the acute state; presence of sodium urate crystals in synovial fluid

X-ray examination—May show tophi and/or bone destruction

Treatment

Pharmacotherapeutic—Colchicine (antiinflammatory, controls pain); probenecid (decreases level of uric acid by enhancing renal secretion); allopurinol (decreases synthesis of uric acid); analgesics, corticosteroids (interarticular).

Prognosis

Prognosis is good; proper treatment quickly terminates the attack; intervals between attacks vary, but remissions often become shorter if the disease progresses.

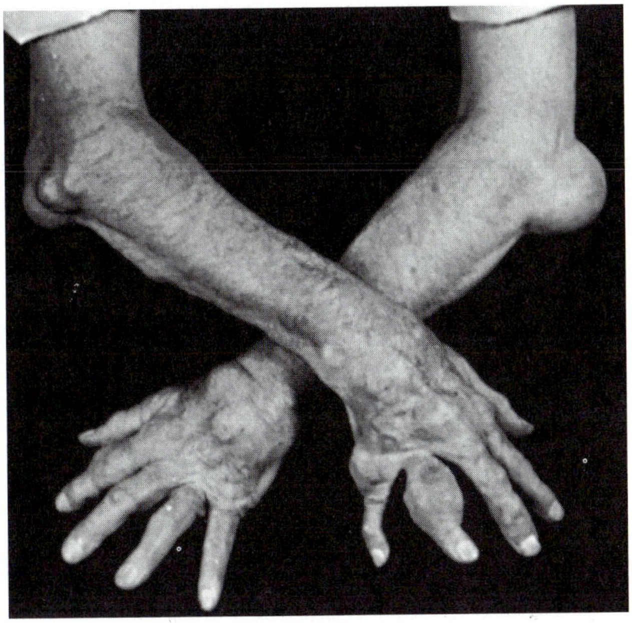

Fig. 30-13 Tophaceous gout. (From Lewis SM, Cox IC: *Medical-surgical nursing: assessment and management of clinical problems,* ed 3, St. Louis, 1992, Mosby.)

✣ PLANNING

The overall management goal is to alleviate the symptoms without placing the older adult at further risk because of pharmacologic treatment. Expected outcomes for the older adult with gout include but are not limited to the following: (1) client will verbalize comfort and pain relief with use of analgesics, (2) client will safely perform self-care activities within limits of existing mobility limitations, (3) client modifies activity/rest pattern based on limitations imposed by acute attack, and (4) client will incorporate health practices aimed at reducing recurrent attacks.

✣ INTERVENTION

In the acute phase, the goal of nursing management is to relieve pain. During an acute attack of gout, the pain may be so severe that the client is unable to bear weight or to tolerate clothing or blankets on the affected joint. Pain medication, including narcotic analgesics, may need to be used to gain adequate pain control. Colchicine is also used in the acute phase; it usually results in relief of pain in 1 to 2 days. The affected joints are immobilized. Heat or ice packs are applied to the joint to provide local relief.

Nursing interventions promote renal function and prevent the formation of stones. Fluid intake of 3 L/day is recommended unless cardiac condition is compromised.

Preventing recurrent attacks of gout is also a goal. This is accomplished through client education. Since obesity and diets high in proteins have been linked to gout, information about the role of diet in gout is provided. Foods that are high in purines, such as shellfish and organ meats, should be avoided. Alcoholic beverages should be avoided. For overweight clients, weight reduction diets are recommended to decrease the stress on affected joints. The dietician is consulted to assist in diet modification.

✣ EVALUATION

Clients with gout will have pain relieved during acute attacks. To prevent future attacks the medication regimen and diet will be followed.

Osteoporosis

Osteoporosis is a common metabolic bone disorder of older adults, characterized by a gradual decrease in bone mass. The incidence of osteoporosis in older adults is 20 million (Craven, Dietsch, 1993). Osteoporosis is most prevalent in older women.

The process of maintaining bone is constant. Old bone cells are removed by osteoclasts and new bone cells are laid down by osteoblasts. The complete process of bone formation takes 4 to 5 months. With osteoporosis, an alteration in this process occurs, and the rate of bone resorption exceeds the rate of bone formation. This loss of minerals and proteins results in decreased bone mass and brittle bones.

Osteoporosis is classified as primary and secondary osteoporosis. The cause of primary osteoporosis is not clearly understood. Secondary osteoporosis, seen in 15% of the cases, is the result of diseases such as hyperthyroidism, hyperparathyroidism, GI disorders, neoplasms, and alcoholism. In women, early oophorectomy is a cause of secondary osteoporosis. Long-term use of corticosteroid therapy, methotrexate, aluminum-containing antacids, phenytoin, and heparin can result in secondary osteoporosis. Prolonged immobility which causes calcium excretion is also a cause of secondary osteoporosis.

Primary osteoporosis is further classified into Type I and Type II. Type I osteoporosis is related to menopausal estrogen deficiency and is seen in women between the ages of 51 to 75. In Type I osteoporosis, trabecular bone in the vertebral column, hips, and wrists is lost. Because Type I osteoporosis is related to estrogen deficiency, it is seen six times more often in women than in men.

Type II osteoporosis occurs in both men and women over the age of 75. A gradual loss of cortical bone, the bone that provides support, is a predisposing factor to hip fracture. Age-related changes in vitamin C synthesis that result in decreased calcium absorption are thought to be the etiology of Type II osteoporosis.

Certain risk factors for the development of osteoporosis have been identified (Box 30-3). Those risk factors that can be modified with lifestyle changes include

BOX 30-3

Risk Factors for Development of Osteoporosis

Female gender
Increasing age
White race
Thin body frame
History of bilateral oophorectomy
Alcoholism
Cigarette smoking
Calcium intake below daily requirements

calcium intake, cigarette smoking and consumption of alcoholic beverages. Age, gender, race, and body frame are risk factors that cannot be changed. The nurse can educate the client about these risk factors and make suggestions to modify lifestyle and nutrition before the age of risk (McMahon, Peterson, Schilke, 1992).

Osteoporosis is called a "silent killer" because there are frequently no clinical symptoms until fractures occur. The initial complaint may be back pain or fatigue. The fatigue results from the increased demand on muscles to keep the body in an upright position with a decreased bone mass. Osteoporotic fractures are most commonly seen in the vertebrae of the thoracic spine, the femoral neck, and the wrist. Fractures may occur with routine activities such as bending, lifting, and coughing. Osteoporosis of the spinal vertebrae causes a loss of height of 1 to 2½ inches. Also seen is the "dowager's hump," or kyphosis, which results from the vertebrae sliding on top of each other (Fig. 30-14).

X-rays and bone densitometry are used in the diagnosis. Because x-rays cannot detect osteoporosis until 25% to 40% of the bone is lost, they are not used until the later stages of the disease. For early detection of the disease, bone densitometry is used. In this procedure, either single or dual photons are used. In a single dose, one photon is passed through the bone being measured, whereas in dual photon, the photons are of two different energies. Laboratory studies are conducted to distinguish the osteoporosis from other diseases that can cause bone loss. CBCs, serum calcium, serum phosphorous, alkaline phosphatase and urinary calcium are all normal in osteoporosis.

The key to managing osteoporosis is prevention. The goal of prevention is to stop bone loss in people with decreasing bone density (McMahon, Peterson, Schilke, 1992). Reducing risk factors, calcium and estrogen replacement therapy, as well as exercise, are strategies used to prevent osteoporosis (see Medical Management box at right).

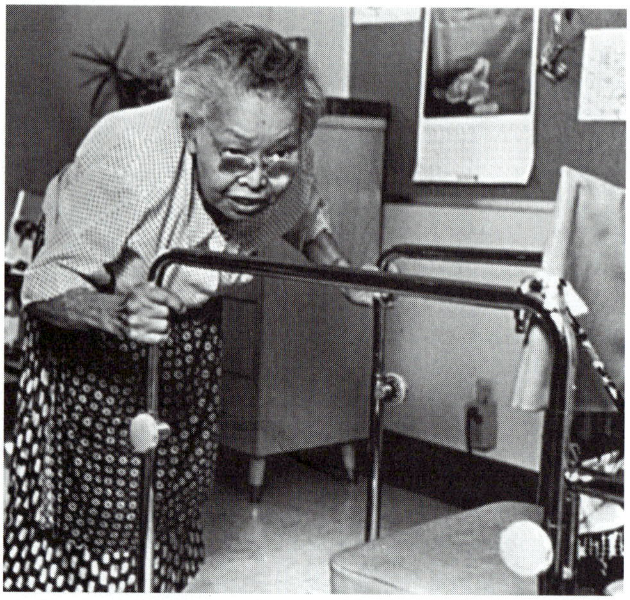

Fig. 30-14 Kyphosis has caused this elderly woman to stoop very low. This reduction of chest cavity size makes oxygen exchange difficult. (Courtesy Ken Yamaguchi. In Castillo HM: *The nurse assistant in long-term care: a rehabilitative approach,* St. Louis, 1992, Mosby.)

MEDICAL MANAGEMENT

Osteoporosis

Diagnostic tests and procedures
History—Family history, smoking, alcohol and calcium intake
Physical examination—Kyphosis, pain
Bone densitometry—Rather than routine radiographs which do not show osteoporosis until 25% to 40% of the bone is lost
Laboratory findings—CBC, serum calcium, serum alkaline phosphatase, and urine calcium will be normal but are studied to distinguish other diseases that can result in bone loss

Treatment
Prevention
Exercise
Supplemental calcium
Supplemental vitamin D
Estrogen replacement therapy (ERT)
Ethidionate disodium (Didronel)

Prognosis
Prognosis is good if fractures do not occur. Fractures can lead to permanent disability and a downward trajectory, which may result in death.

Adequate nutritional intake of calcium should be instituted in early childhood and continued throughout the life span. The current recommendation for daily calcium intake is 1,000 mg for premenopausal women and 1,500 mg for postmenopausal women (Table 30-4). Milk, either low-fat or nonfat, is a very good source of calcium and vitamin D. Vitamin D intake is essential for the synthesis of calcium. For individuals unable to consume adequate calcium, intake supplements are recommended. Various forms of supplements are available. Calcium carbonate is thought to be the best supplement because it contains 40% elemental calcium, is least expensive, and requires taking the least number of tablets. Calcium supplements should be taken with meals and followed by at least 10 ounces of water to promote absorption (Sardana, 1992).

Exercise programs that include weight bearing have been shown to prevent bone loss. Beneficial exercises for older adults include walking, low impact aerobics, and racquet sports. Exercises should be done three times per week for 30 to 60 minutes. Moderation in the exercise program is recommended.

Use of estrogen replacement therapy (ERT), who should take it, and how long it should be taken is controversial. Estrogen acts by decreasing bone resorption. The risks of ERT include an increased incidence of breast and uterine cancer. ERT is started as early as possible in the postmenopausal period. The benefits of ERT in decreasing the incidence of hip fracture outweigh the risks. ERT is contraindicated for those who have a history of breast cancer, or of thromboembolic disease. Low-dose estrogen (0.625 mg of conjugated estrogens) is prescribed in ERT. Individuals on ERT should perform breast self-examination monthly and have mammography annually. If abnormal vaginal bleeding occurs, medical evaluation is indicated.

Increasing bone mass is the focus of treating established osteoporosis. The treatment of choice at this time is an antiresorption agent, ethidionate disodium (Didronel), which acts by inhibiting osteoclasts. Ethidionate has been shown to slow bone loss to prevent compression fractures of the vertebrae when administered in a cyclic fashion of 400 mg daily for 2 weeks every 3 months.

TABLE 30-4

Dietary Sources of Calcium

Food	Serving	Calcium content
Milk		
Skim	8 oz.	302
2% fat	8 oz.	297
Whole	8 oz.	291
Cheeses		
Swiss	1 oz.	272
Processed American	1 oz.	174
mozzarella	1 oz.	207
Cottage cheese	1 oz.	135
Other dairy products		
Yogurt, lowfat	8 oz.	415
Ice cream, vanilla	1 cup	176
Ice milk, vanilla	1 cup	274
Seafood		
Oysters	1 cup	226
Pink salmon, canned with bones	3 oz.	167
Vegetables		
Collards, frozen or fresh	1 cup	357
Broccoli, fresh	1 cup	177
Broccoli, frozen	1 cup	94
Mustard greens	1 cup	104
Dried beans (cooked and drained)		
Navy beans	1 cup	90
Pinto beans	1 cup	86
Red kidney beans, canned	1 cup	74
Other foods		
Blackstrap molasses	2 tblsp.	274
Tofu	4 oz.	108

Modified from: US Department of Agriculture: Human nutrition information servings, *Home Garden bullet* No. 72, 1985.

NURSING MANAGEMENT

✣ ASSESSMENT

A careful history that includes questions about life-long intake of calcium, pain, fatigue, and fractures is obtained. History also focuses on the presence of risk factors, family history, age of onset of menopause, ERT, smoking, exercise patterns, and caffeine intake. Physical examination includes inspection to determine if kyphosis is present.

✣ DIAGNOSIS

Nursing diagnoses for clients with osteoporosis include body image disturbance, fatigue, altered health maintenance, knowledge deficit, impaired physical mobility, pain, self-care deficit, and high risk for trauma.

✣ PLANNING

Expected outcomes for the older adult with osteoporosis include, but are not limited to, the following: (1) client will establish an activity/rest pattern that supports ability to maintain desired lifestyle and to meet everyday demands, (2) client will verbalize comfort and pain relief with use of analgesics, (3) client will safely perform self-care activities, (4) client will maintain regular exercise program, (5) client will make environmental adaptations to reduce fall risk, and (6) client will have adequate daily intake of calcium and vitamin D.

✜ INTERVENTION

The nurse's role focuses on education, pain management, and promoting optimum function. Teaching emphasizes the identification and minimization of controllable risk factors. These include cigarette smoking and excessive use of alcohol and caffeine. Exercise programs are recommended. Exercises that place stress on the bone and thus strengthen the bone are the most beneficial. Such programs include walking to strengthen lower extremities and lifting light weights to strengthen the upper extremities and vertebrae. Provide information about dietary intake of calcium and techniques to prevent falls and improve home safety.

Compression fractures of the vertebrae can cause pain that interferes with function. Control of pain is achieved through the use of analgesics, relaxation techniques, and transcutaneous electrical nerve stimulation (TENS). TENS is a device made up of cutaneous electrodes that are connected to low voltage battery packs. The mechanism of action of TENS is not clearly understood. It is thought the TENS activates large nerve fibers that inhibit response of relay neurons in the dorsal horn to incoming injury signals. When the levels of stimulation are intense, the brain stem descending inhibitory system is activated. This process results in a decreased pain threshold in the cells of the dorsal horn (see Chapter 13).

✜ EVALUATION

The client with osteoporosis will take measures at home to maintain safety and to prevent injury, including fractures. A well-balanced diet and medication program will be followed, as well as participation in a regular exercise program (see Research box at right and nursing Care Plan, pp. 883-884).

RESEARCH

Nagia A, Bennett S: Postmenopausal women factors in osteoporosis preventive behaviors, *J Gerontol Nurs* 18(2):23-32:1992.

Sample, setting

Subjects included 91 postmenopausal women ages 54 to 83 who reside in a large senior citizen residential apartment complex and volunteer at a large Midwestern hospital.

Methodology

Knowledge of osteoporosis was measured using a multiple choice test developed by the authors. Perceptions of barriers and benefits to milk intake were measured using the Milk Barriers/Benefits Scale. Health promoting behaviors were measured by the Health Promotion Lifestyle Profile. Osteoporosis preventive measures were measured by a questionnaire developed by the researchers.

Findings

The mean daily calcium intake was 374 mg. Of the subjects, 19% took calcium supplements. Negative correlation existed with age and knowledge of osteoporosis. Osteoporosis preventive behaviors were positively and significantly correlated with calcium intake from milk, knowledge of osteoporosis prevention, and the Health Promotion Lifestyle Profile. Calcium intake from milk was significantly and positively correlated with knowledge of osteoporosis preventive behaviors and the Health Promotion Lifestyle Profile.

Implications

Nurses need to give older women information about osteoporosis and how to prevent it. They also need to be certain that women understand and follow preventive behaviors.

Paget's Disease

Paget's disease is an inflammatory disease of the bone in which both osteoclasts and osteoblasts proliferate. The processes of bone formation and bone resorption do not always proceed at the same rate.

The cause of Paget's disease is not known. Recent evidence supports the theory that a viral infection of the osteoclasts causes the disease. There is a familial predisposition to Paget's disease, occurring most often in men over 40.

Increased activity of osteoclasts leads to increased bone resorption. Bone formation is increased to compensate. This abnormal remodeling causes deformed and enlarged bones. Vascularity in the abnormal bones is increased, which results in excessive warmth over the bones involved. Bones affected by the disease are structurally weak and prone to pathologic fractures.

The onset of Paget's disease is insidious. The first symptom is bone pain, which is not relieved with rest and movement. The intensity of the pain varies from mild to severe; quality can be stabbing or dull. If bones of the skull are involved, headache and conductive hearing loss may occur. Barreling of the chest, kyphosis, skull enlargement, and bowing of the tibia and femur are commonly seen bone deformities. The bowing of legs and kyphosis cause a reduction of height. Bones most often involved are the pelvis, femur, skull, tibia, and the spine.

The prognosis for clients with Paget's disease is not favorable because of the complications that may develop. They include pathologic fracture and loss of hearing related to changes in the temporal bone. The overgrowth of the spinal vertebrae can cause cord compression and paralysis (see Medical Management box, p. 884).

CARE PLAN

OSTEOPOROSIS WITH FRACTURED THORACIC VERTEBRAE

Clinical situation Mrs. R is a 79-year-old widow who has severe osteoporosis and who has recently fractured T4 and T5 vertebrae. After the fracture she complained of severe pain, which limited her daily activity and caused her to spend most of the day in bed. The period of bed rest has caused her to be weak. Before the fracture she was independent in mobility and self-care. She drove and participated in activities with her friends on a regular basis. She is referred to the home care agency for pain management and physical therapy to upgrade her ADL skills and endurance.

Mrs. R has no other health problems. She lives alone in a two-story house. The bathroom is on the second floor. Since the fracture, Mrs. R has stayed on the second floor all day except for one trip to the kitchen on the first floor to fix a meal. Mrs. R's major support is her daughter who lives in another state. She has several close friends, but they are unable to help her because of their health problems.

On the admission visit, the nurse finds Mrs. R's house to be in an unsafe condition. The rooms and stairs are cluttered with papers, boxes, and other objects. Mrs. R tells the nurse that her pain is somewhat improved, but it still limits her ability to take care of herself and her home. She also tells the nurse, "I don't understand this osteoporosis; how did *that* cause my fractures?"

Nursing diagnoses	Outcomes	Interventions
High risk for injury related to unsafe environment	Client will remain free from fracture or other injuries and will verbalize unsafe features of home and a plan to correct.	Discuss outcomes of unsafe environment: risks of falling and fracture as a result of cluttered environment. Use homemaker and friends to reduce clutter. Teach safe transfer and ambulation techniques, to wear sturdy supportive footwear, to avoid lifting heavy objects, and to bend from the knees when lifting.
Knowledge deficit: osteoporosis related to lack of exposure	Client will verbalize basic information about disease process, outcomes and treatment.	Provide information and instruction on osteoporosis, including pathophysiology of the disease, treatment regimen, and information about medication schedule, doses, and side effects. Stress importance of dietary intake of calcium and provide information on foods that are high in calcium.
Impaired physical mobility related to pain and musculoskeletal impairment	Client will safely ambulate 100 feet using pick-up walker and will participate in a daily exercise program.	Consult with physical therapy for a program of muscle strengthening, endurance development, stair training, and regular exercise. Reinforce physical therapy training. Give positive feedback for gains made. Instruct to make limited trips up and down stairs until strength is improved. Instruct on taking pain medication before exercise program, and the need for regular rest periods throughout the day.
Pain related to inadequate knowledge of pain management	Client will verbalize that pain is tolerable. Pain will not interfere with ability to participate in daily activities.	Assess pain and effectiveness of prescribed medication. Instruct to take pain medication before activities and on a regular basis until pain diminishes. Instruct on the use of diversional activities and relaxation techniques.
Self-care deficit: bathing and dressing lower extremities, related to pain and prolonged immobility	Client will bathe and dress lower extremities with the use of assistive devices.	Assist client in setting short-term, realistic goals. Consult with occupational therapy for specific assistive devices.

Continued.

CARE PLAN

OSTEOPOROSIS WITH FRACTURED THORACIC VERTEBRAE—cont'd

Nursing diagnoses	Outcomes	Interventions
		Instruct on use of assistive devices. Provide assistance, supervision, and teaching as needed to promote self-care. Give positive feedback for gains made.

Nursing Management

Alteration in comfort caused by the pain of Paget's disease can be severe. Interventions to control pain include pharmacologic and nonpharmacologic methods. Aspects of pain management discussed in relation to osteoporosis are applicable here (see pp. 879-882).

~~Osteomyelitis~~

Osteomyelitis is an infection of the bone which can be either acute or chronic. Acute osteomyelitis resolves in 4 weeks when treated with antibiotics. Chronic osteomyelitis lasts longer than 4 weeks and does not respond to initial treatment with antibiotics.

Invasion of the bone by microorganisms is the cause of osteomyelitis. Microorganisms enter the bone directly through an open fracture or stage IV pressure ulcer. Blood-borne bacteria from distant sources such as urinary tract infections can indirectly inoculate the bone.

Staphylococcus aureus is the most common bacteria seen in osteomyelitis. Other gram-negative bacteria such as *Escherichia coli* and *pseudomonas* are causative agents of osteomyelitis. Osteomyelitis is seen most often in older adults as a complication of stage IV pressure ulcers.

Bacteria enter the bone through the blood supply and lodge in an area of the bone where sluggish circulation occurs. The bacteria multiply, resulting in an inflammatory response. Pus and vascular congestion develop, causing increased pressure in the bone, which leads to ischemia and vascular compromise. The necrotic bone separates from living bone. The devitalized areas are called sequestra.

In the older adult with osteomyelitis related to a bone injury, the presenting signs are localized pain, tenderness on palpation, redness, warmth to touch, and edema. In osteomyelitis related to infected pressure ulcers, the symptoms may be subtle changes in mental status, low-grade temperature, and increased purulent wound drainage. These signs and symptoms may go unnoticed until sepsis occurs.

MEDICAL MANAGEMENT

Paget's Disease

Diagnostic tests and procedures

History—Sudden onset of bone pain, headache, hearing loss

Physical examination—Kyphosis, bowed legs, barrel chest

X-ray findings—Areas of decreased bone density; affected bones are enlarged, opaque, radiolucent, with widening of the cortex

Laboratory findings—Elevated serum alkaline phosphatase, serum acid phosphatase, and urinary hydroxyproline

Treatment

Pain control—Salicylates and NSAIDs

Calcitonin—For decreasing serum alkaline phosphatase and urinary hydroxyproline

Cytotoxic agents—Mithracin (Mythramycin), dactinomycin (Actinomycin), etidionate disodium (didronel)

Prognosis

Prognosis is not favorable because of complications.

If treated early, the prognosis of osteomyelitis is good. The older adult may not have classic signs of infection. Often, the first sign of the osteomyelitis may be sepsis; in these cases, the prognosis is poor (see Medical Management box, p. 885).

Nursing Management

✚ ASSESSMENT

The nurse caring for the older adult with the risk for developing osteomyelitis must be aware of the subtlety of the presenting signs and symptoms of infection.

DIAGNOSIS

Nursing diagnoses include pain, impaired physical mobility, impaired skin integrity, and ineffective coping.

PLANNING

Expected outcomes for the older adult with osteomyelitis include, but are not limited to, the following: (1) client will report pain relief with use of analgesics; (2) client will understand antibiotic therapy, including purpose, action, and side effects; (3) client will correctly self-administer antibiotic therapy treatment; and (4) client will use effective coping strategies in adapting to changes in health status. Because of the long-term nature of the problem, the family and significant others of clients with chronic osteomyelitis need to be involved in the planning process.

INTERVENTION

Prevention of the development of osteomyelitis includes using sterile technique during dressing changes and following strict wound precautions. The client with infected pressure ulcers will most likely be functionally impaired and will return to a long-term care setting for completion of IV antibiotic treatment. Clients with osteomyelitis as a result of other causes will be discharged on oral antibiotics. Discharge planning will involve teaching about the importance of completing the course of oral antibiotics, methods to prevent infection, and specific techniques of wound management. An alternate treatment is a medication pump which is surgically implanted to deliver continuous antibiotic to the site of infection.

The long-term treatment of chronic osteomyelitis creates psychologic coping issues. Lengthy hospitalizations, immobility, and dependence can lead to feelings of anger and decreased self-worth. To help clients cope more effectively, the nurse allows the client to make informed decisions about care and consults with therapeutic recreation specialists for diversional activities. The prolonged immobility can lead to the complications of immobility and self-care deficit. To prevent these problems, physical and occupational therapy are consulted. They provide individualized exercise programs that promote optimum function and prevent disability.

EVALUATION

Clients with osteomyelitis will participate in decision making regarding treatment and will adhere to the prescribed medical regimen, including an exercise program.

MEDICAL MANAGEMENT

Osteomyelitis

Diagnostic tests and procedures
History—Recent trauma or surgery
Physical examination—Tenderness or pain
Positive bone biopsy
X-ray findings—Positive radionuclide (gallium and indium) scans
Laboratory findings—Elevated white blood cell count and eosinophil sedimentation rate

Treatment
Broad-spectrum IV antibiotics
Surgical debridement may be done

Prognosis
Prognosis is good with early treatment; if the first sign is sepsis, the prognosis is poor.

Amputation

Amputation of the lower extremity is a common surgical procedure in older clients. The level of amputation depends on the extent of the disease process. Peripheral vascular disease (PVD), infection, neoplasm, and traumatic injury may all lead to lower extremity amputation, with PVD being the most common cause. In PVD caused by atherosclerosis and diabetes, circulation is inadequate to maintain cellular function.

Atherosclerosis and diabetes are predisposing factors in the development of foot or extremity ulcers. The ulcers can be chronically infected. Osteomyelitis with bone destruction results in amputation of the extremity.

In PVD, the chronic obstruction of the arteries results in inadequate circulation that causes tissue hypoxia. When the tissues are inadequately perfused for prolonged periods, atrophy of the underlying tissue occurs. This decreased circulation leads to delayed healing of injured feet and/or lower extremities. When ischemic ulcers do not heal, infection and necrosis or gangrene develop.

Gangrene manifests as a blackened area. The temperature in the affected area is lower than that of the nonaffected area, and pain may be present. In the chronically infected extremity ulcer, the ulcer persists despite treatment with antibiotics (see Medical Management box, p. 886).

NURSING MANAGEMENT

ASSESSMENT

Before the surgical procedure, a complete nursing assessment is done to determine how other diseases affect function. The focus of this assessment is on mobility and self-care ability. How does the client ambulate? Are assistive devices required? What is the extent of self-care abilities? Assessment of the affected limb includes peripheral pulses, temperature, sensation, and movement. The specific characteristics of the ulcer or gangrenous area are noted, including location, size, and color. The individual's perception of the surgery is ascertained. Clients are asked how they feel about the impending surgical procedure and how they see the impact of the amputation on their health and lifestyle.

✣ DIAGNOSIS

Nursing diagnoses may include body image disturbance, potential for impaired skin integrity, pain, impaired physical mobility, activity intolerance, and ineffective coping.

✣ PLANNING

Expected outcomes for the older client who has had an amputation include, but are not limited to, the following: (1) client will report pain relief with administration of analgesics, (2) client will demonstrate acceptance of body image change, as evidenced by expression of positive statements regarding body and active involvement (looking or touching) with treatment of stump, (3) client's incisional area(s) remains clean, without evidence of infection, and (4) client will safely perform self-care activities within activity and energy expenditure limitations.

✣ INTERVENTION

Client education is an important nursing role in preventing amputation. Since the majority of amputations are a result of PVD, clients need knowledge of how to control illnesses that can lead to amputation. Clients with diabetes and PVD are taught how to inspect and how to care for their feet and lower extremities (refer to Chapter 23). Instructions include information on promptly notifying a health care provider if there are changes in temperature, sensation, and color. If a sore develops, prompt treatment must be sought. Methods to protect the lower extremity from injury are included in the teaching plan.

Preoperative Care

Amputation is a major threat to an individual's body image and has the potential to lead to ineffective coping. To assist with adjustment in the postoperative phase, the client requires intensive information about the surgical procedure. Client teaching includes information about the purpose of the amputation, the potential use of a prosthesis, and the rehabilitation program. To assist in the rehabilitation phase, exercises to strengthen upper extremities are taught. Postoperative care, including information about positioning, turning, compression bandaging, and pain control is discussed. Clients require information about phantom sensation and limb pain. Phantom limb sensation is the feeling of tingling, itching, or aching in the limb. Phantom limb pain is a painful sensation that occurs immediately after the amputation.

MEDICAL MANAGEMENT

Amputation

Diagnostic tests and procedures

If infection is present, the white blood count may be elevated. Arteriography is done to determine circulatory status of the affected extremity. In osteomyelitis, bone scans and MRI are used to determine the extent of the disease.

Treatment

Amputation is either above the knee (AKA) or below the knee (BKA). The type of procedure done depends on the nature of the damage to the extremity. Below the knee is the most commonly performed type of amputation. The aim of the amputation is to preserve extremity length and function for prosthetic fitting. To achieve this, efforts are made to salvage as much of the limb as possible.

Prognosis

Prognosis depends on the client's general health status. Some clients adjust well to functioning with a prosthesis and others function well but do not adapt to using a prosthesis.

Postoperative Care

Routine postoperative care is provided in the immediate postop period. Clients are monitored carefully for complications that may be a result of preoperative health problems. Complications include hemorrhage and infection. The postoperative dressing depends on the type of prosthesis that will be used. Prostheses are either immediate prosthetic fitting or delayed prosthetic fitting. Since older adults may be debilitated from multiple chronic illnesses and the chronic condition that caused the amputation, there will likely be a delayed prosthetic fitting. Dressings are either rigid or soft in delayed prosthetic fitting. The rigid dressing may be made from either plastic or plaster of paris. The advantage of this type of dressing is that it decreases edema. Soft dressings consist of Kerlix, covered with an elastic wrap that acts as a compression dressing. The compression dressing is used to support the tissues, to decrease pain and edema, and to promote shrinking of the stump. The soft dressing is changed daily, using sterile technique. The wound is assessed for signs and symptoms of infection. A dry dressing is applied directly to the suture site.

Pain Management

In the immediate postoperative period (48 to 72 hours), pain medication is given on a regular schedule. Because of age-related changes in pharmacokinetics and pharma-

BOX 30-4

Guidelines for Postoperative Pain Management

Give the lowest possible effective dose.
Increase intervals between doses.
Combine narcotics with non-narcotic analgesics.
Closely monitor effectiveness and response.

codynamics, clients receiving narcotic analgesics should be monitored closely for response and side effects. The effect of narcotics may last longer and may also result in excessive sedation, confusion, or respiratory depression. Initial doses may be lower than those used for younger adults. Based on the individual's pain relief and tolerance, doses may be increased. Morphine sulfate is the medication used most often in this phase of care. See Box 30-4 for guidelines on pain management.

Rehabilitative Care

The rehabilitative phase starts immediately after surgery with the application of the dressing. The dressing is important for prosthesis fitting, because it shapes the stump for the prosthesis. The compression dressing is worn continuously and removed at least two times per day. Care is taken to properly apply the dressing. It should be wrapped snugly and securely, but not so tightly that it impairs circulation. A stump shrinker, a continuous tube of elasticized fabric that is closed at one end, may be used instead of the wrap.

When the client's condition is stable, physical therapy is begun. Nursing goals for this phase include preventing complications and assisting the client to reach an optimum level of functioning. The physical therapy program includes active range of motion, upper extremity strengthening, and gait training. For ambulation, walkers are used with older adults rather than crutches, because crutches require greater upper extremity strength and endurance. The nurse reinforces the exercise program and assists the client in learning safe transfer techniques.

Prosthetic Fitting

Not all older adults are candidates for prostheses. Multiple chronic illnesses may result in a state of debilitation in which the client will not have the strength and reserve to complete a program of intense prosthetic training. These clients are taught transfer techniques and wheelchair mobility.

Delayed prosthetic fitting takes place when the stump is healed and well-molded. The fitting is done by a prosthetist who makes a mold of the stump. As the stump shrinks, adjustments in the prosthesis are made. The client is instructed to assess the stump daily for signs of irritation from an ill-fitting prosthesis.

The physical therapist and prosthetist instruct the client in the use of the prosthesis. The physical therapist also works on gait training. The nurse reinforces the teaching and provides the amputee with reinforcement on performance. For different types of prosthesis, see Fig. 30-15.

The individual who has an amputation experiences a loss and a major threat to body image. The normal response to loss is grief. The grieving process and the adjustment to the loss is an individualized response that is characterized by vacillations in the recognized stages of grief: denial, isolation, anger, bargaining, depression, and acceptance (Fraley, 1992).

Body image is an individual's subjective perception of the body. Gradual changes in body image are easier to adapt to than those that have an abrupt onset, such as the change experienced by an amputee. The adaptation to the change in body image does not always reflect the extent of the injury, but is related to that individual's feelings toward self as a total person (Fraley, 1992).

The role of the nurse in helping amputees adjust to changes in body image is to help them discover a new self. Traumatic change in body image, such as experienced by the amputee, may be characterized by revulsion in viewing the amputation. Viewing the amputation and looking in the mirror at the total self picture may be difficult. Accepting the body changes is a gradual process. The nurse allows the client time to work through this process. Broad, open-ended questions are asked about the body changes. Examples of questions to ask include "How do you see yourself?" or "How do you think others see you?" (Ebersole, Hess, 1994). Talking with other amputees one-on-one and in support groups are interventions that are helpful in adapting to change in body image. The nurse should give positive and realistic feedback about the individual's progress made in functional abilities, such as "Your transfers are improving, because your balance is better" (see nursing Care Plan, p. 889-890).

✜ EVALUATION

Evaluation is based on achievement of expected outcomes, as evidenced by the client exhibiting a positive outlook about the body image change, performing self-care and other activities safely and adequately, and experiencing adequate pain relief over time, with eventually no need for analgesics.

Polymyalgia Rheumatica

Polymyalgia rheumatica is a chronic inflammatory condition that is characterized by sudden onset of muscle stiffness and aching (myalgia) in the neck, shoulders, and hip girdle.

The disease occurs after 50 years, most often in those 65 years and over. Women are affected more than men.

MEDICAL MANAGEMENT

Polymyalgia Rheumatica

Diagnostic tests and procedures
History—Muscle stiffness, aching pain, constitutional symptoms of fever, malaise, and anorexia
Physical examination—Muscle tenderness
Laboratory findings—Elevated eosinophil rate (usually but not always), normochromic, normocytic anemia, elevated plasma viscosity and C-reactive protein.
X-ray findings—Normal

Treatment
NSAIDs
Corticosteroids

Prognosis
Prognosis is good

The cause of polymyalgia rheumatica is not known. Infection with altered immune response has been suggested but not proven as the cause. Likewise, a genetic predisposition is suggested, but not confirmed. The pathophysiology of polymyalgia rheumatica is not clearly understood.

The clinical presentation of polymyalgia rheumatica is similar to that of rheumatoid arthritis and osteoarthritis. Symptoms include muscle stiffness and aching in the neck, shoulders, and hip girdle. The muscle stiffness is present in the morning and lasts more than 1 hour. Constitutional symptoms such as fever, malaise, anorexia, and weight loss may be present. Initially, the pain may be limited to one area but generally develops in a symmetrical fashion. Objective signs of muscle weakness are not present on physical exam. Joint swelling is usually absent, and there are no limitations in range of motion. The symptoms last at least 4 weeks without treatment (see Medical Management box, above).

Polymyalgia rheumatica is treated with NSAIDs and steroids (see Table 30-3, pp. 876-877). If the disease is polymyalgia rheumatica, there is generally a marked improvement in symptoms 1 to 2 days after the beginning of the treatment with steroids. This marked improvement so soon after initiation of treatment is not seen in rheumatoid arthritis or osteoarthritis.

NURSING MANAGEMENT

ASSESSMENT

History, physical examination, and functional assessment are important in determining the impact of the disease on functional abilities.

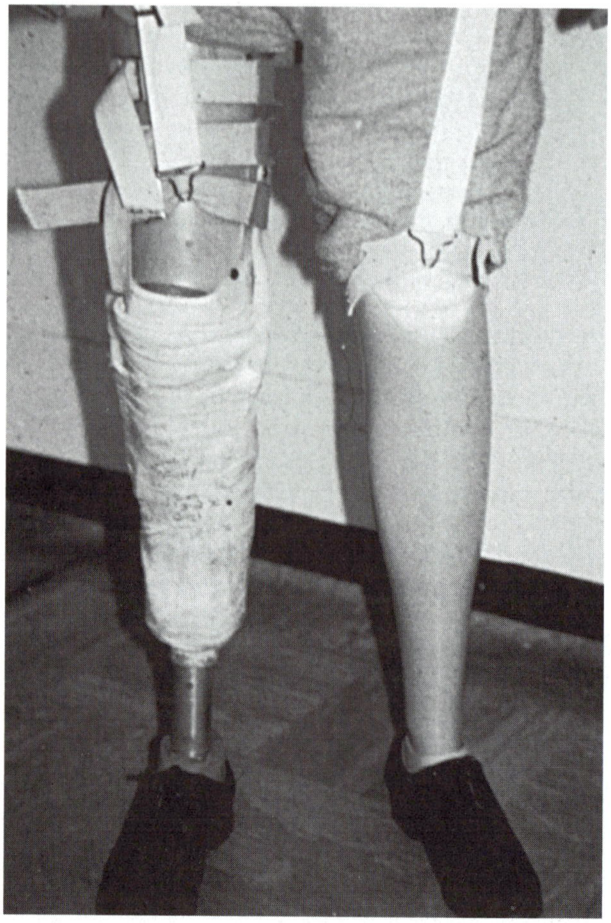

Fig. 30-15 Two types of prosthesis. Patellar tendon-bearing type, below-the-knee prosthesis with cuff suspension *(left)*. Early fitting below-the-knee rigid plaster dressing with pylon *(right)*. (From Lewis SM, Cox IC: *Medical-surgical nursing: assessment and management of clinical problems,* ed 3, St. Louis, 1992, Mosby.)

DIAGNOSIS

Nursing diagnoses for clients with polymyalgia include: pain, altered mobility, fatigue, self-care deficit, and ineffective coping.

PLANNING

Expected outcomes for the older client with polymyalgia include, but are not limited to, the following: (1) client will report pain relief with initiation of treatment; (2) client will verbalize understanding of pharmacologic therapy, including purpose, action, and side effects of prescribed drugs; (3) client will establish an activity/rest pattern based on limitations imposed by disease; (4) client will incorporate effective coping strategies in adapting to the changes imposed by the acute attack; and (5) client will verbalize understanding of the treatment and prognosis.

CARE PLAN

AMPUTATION

Clinical situation Mr. C is a 75-year-old, retired truck driver with the medical history of insulin-dependent diabetes mellitus (IDDM), PVD, and a chronic right foot ulcer. Since the foot ulcer did not respond to conservative treatment, he underwent a right BKA. Before this surgical procedure, Mr. C had been hospitalized for 3 weeks for treatment of the foot ulcer. During the hospitalization, he became weak and deconditioned. He now requires assistance with eating, ADLs, and maximum assistance for transfers. Mr. C complains of phantom limb pain and requires pain medication every 4 to 6 hours.

The prolonged illness, hospitalization, and amputation have caused Mr. C to feel hopeless. He has told the nurses that he is tired of being in the hospital, sick, and in pain. Mr. C has also verbalized feelings about not being the man he once was. He does not initiate any self-care and needs encouragement to complete self-care. Mr. C has a supportive wife and family. His wife has rheumatoid arthritis and feels that it will be difficult for her to care for her husband unless he participates in his care and is rehabilitated with a prosthesis. Mr. C is stable 4 days postoperatively and is beginning physical therapy for preprosthetic training.

Nursing diagnoses	Outcomes	Interventions
Body image disturbance related to amputation, impaired mobility, and prolonged hospitalization	Client will verbalize feelings of acceptance of change in body image.	Allow verbalization of feelings, actively listen to feelings. Give positive feedback for progress made in self-care and mobility and for aspects of general appearance. Encourage normal activities such as dressing in street clothes. Encourage participation in support groups.
Pain related to surgical procedure, and phantom limb sensation	Client will verbalize that pain is tolerable. Pain will not interfere with ability to participate in ADLs.	Assess pain and effectiveness of medications. Administer pain medications as ordered. Provide diversional activities and alternative treatments such as relaxation techniques.
Potential for alteration in skin integrity related to disease process, surgical procedure, age-related changes, and immobility	Incision will heal without signs or symptoms of infection. Skin will remain free from pressure ulcers.	Assess incision and pressure areas (use a risk assessment scale) daily for signs of infection or pressure ulcers. Change surgical dressing with aseptic technique. Reposition every 2 hours; position to keep pressure off bony prominences. Teach client how to change positions. Provide adequate caloric, protein, and fluid intake. Wrap stump with compression dressing, or stump shrinker.
Impaired physical mobility related to below the knee amputation, and prolonged immobility	Transfers independently and ambulates 10 feet with a pick-up walker. Range of motion remains within normal limits. Flexion contracture does not develop.	Consult with physical therapy for a program of muscle strengthening, transfer training and gait training. Reinforce physical therapy training. Give positive feedback for gains made. Teach transfer techniques; assist with transfers. Teach safe use of walker. Give pain medications 30 to 60 minutes before therapy. Do not elevate stump on pillows. Keep stump in good alignment. Reinforce use of active range of motion exercises. Encourage lying on the abdomen for 30 minutes two times per day.
Activity tolerance related to prolonged immobility, decondition-	Client will attend and participate in daily therapy program with	Encourage participation in therapy program. Gradually increase activity.

Continued.

CARE PLAN

AMPUTATION—cont'd

Nursing diagnoses	Outcomes	Interventions
ing, and disease processes	normal physiologic response.	Allow at least 60 minutes of rest after therapy. Monitor vital signs before, during, and after therapy.
Ineffective individual coping related to amputation	Client will use effective coping strategies and will participate in rehabilitation program.	Assist client in identifying previously successful coping skills. Suggest and describe effective coping skills. Encourage activities that enhance self-esteem. Encourage use of support systems. Encourage participation in amputation support group. Include family, especially spouse, in support group.
Potential for ineffective family coping related to spouse's chronic illness, and disability	Family will use effective coping strategies and support client's participation in the rehabilitation process.	Encourage verbalization of feelings when client not present. Suggest and describe effective coping skills. Suggest to take time to care for self. Discuss with client and spouse after individual counseling.

✣ INTERVENTION

The medical diagnosis of polymyalgia rheumatica is difficult to make, and since symptoms are similar to those of rheumatoid arthritis and osteoarthritis, is often misdiagnosed. The client who has been to many physicians in the attempt to receive the correct diagnosis and proper treatment may be frustrated, angry, and worn-out. The nurse needs to listen to the client's concerns and give information about the disease and treatment plan. This includes information about treatment with and side effects of corticosteroids. The nurse monitors for the development of side effects. The client is reassured that the dose of medication will be tapered and eventually the disease will subside.

✣ EVALUATION

The client verbalizes understanding of the medical regimen including side effects of medications and that the disease will eventually subside.

yes

Foot Problems

The foot is often overlooked in assessment and care of older adults. Foot problems, especially pain, are common in older adults. The incidence and severity of foot problems increase with age. After age 65, 75% of the population complains of foot problems. More than 80% of those over age 55 demonstrate arthritic changes on x-ray. Foot problems may cause an unsteady gait and result in falls.

The foot is a complex structure composed of 26 bones, 33 joints, and numerous ligaments, tendons, and muscles. The foot is necessary for ambulation. During standing and ambulation, the foot provides body support and absorbs shock. Painful feet can be the result of congenital deformities, weak structure, injuries, and diseases such as DM, rheumatoid arthritis, or osteoarthritis. Shoes that are ill-fitting result in foot pain by crowding the toes and impeding normal movement (*Harvard Health Letter,* 1993).

As people age, feet show signs of wear and tear. The cushioning layer of fat on the soles of the feet become thin. Years of walking cause the metatarsal bones to spread and the ligaments to stretch which results in wider feet (Gudas, 1992).

Specific Problems

Corns Corns are thickened and hardened dead or hyperkeratotic tissue that develops over bony protuberances. Corns often cause localized pain. Corns are caused by ill-fitting or loose shoes that constantly place pressure on bony prominences. Soft corns are produced by the bony prominence of one toe rubbing against the adjacent toe in the web space between the toes. Soft corns are macerated because of moisture in the web space (Fig. 30-16).

Warm water soaks are used to soften corns before gentle rubbing with a pumice stone or callus file. Another treatment is gentle debridement by a podiatrist. To relieve pain and to prevent the development of corns, moleskin or cotton pads are placed over areas of rubbing and pressure. Wider and softer shoes are recommended.

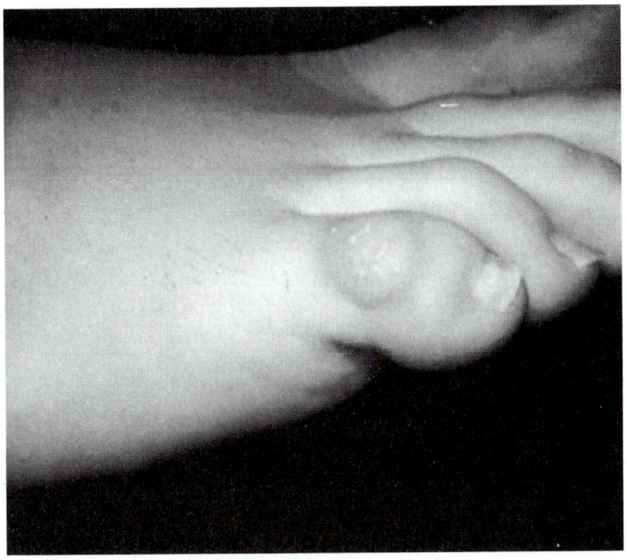

Fig. 30-16 Hard corn on lateral aspect of fifth toe over prominent condyles of proximal phalanx. (Reprinted with permission from Coughlin MJ: *Postgrad Med* 75:191-198, 1984.)

Topical applications of salicylic acid should be avoided in older adults, because they may cause irritation, burns, or infection, especially in those with DM and impaired circulation.

Calluses Calluses or plantar keratoses are dead tissue found on the plantar surfaces of the feet. They form under the metatarsal heads, most commonly the second and third head. About half of the population over 65 years of age have some degree of plantar calluses (Gudas, 1992). The aging changes of decreased toe function and decreased fat padding contribute to their development. Soft-soled shoes with the addition of insoles are recommended. Treatment is the same as for corns.

Bunions **Bunions,** or hallux valgus, have the greatest prevalence in those over 50 years of age, with women experiencing them four times more often than men. This is as a result of the fact that women wear narrow, pointed, high-heeled shoes. Arthritis and related age changes such as ligament and tendon atrophy predispose older adults to bunions.

Bunions appear as bony protuberances on the side of the great toe (Fig. 30-17). In bunions, the large toe angles laterally toward the second toe. As the great toe rubs against the shoe, the bursa becomes inflamed, resulting in bursitis and pain. Initial treatment of bunion is with soft leather shoes that are flat, wide, and lace-up. Walking or running shoes with a wide toe box prevent rubbing on the bunion. Moleskin "bunion" pads can be used to protect the bony protrusion. NSAIDs are prescribed to decrease foot pain. Surgical interventions are used after conservative treatment has failed. The surgical procedure includes removal of the bursa sac and correction of the bony deformity.

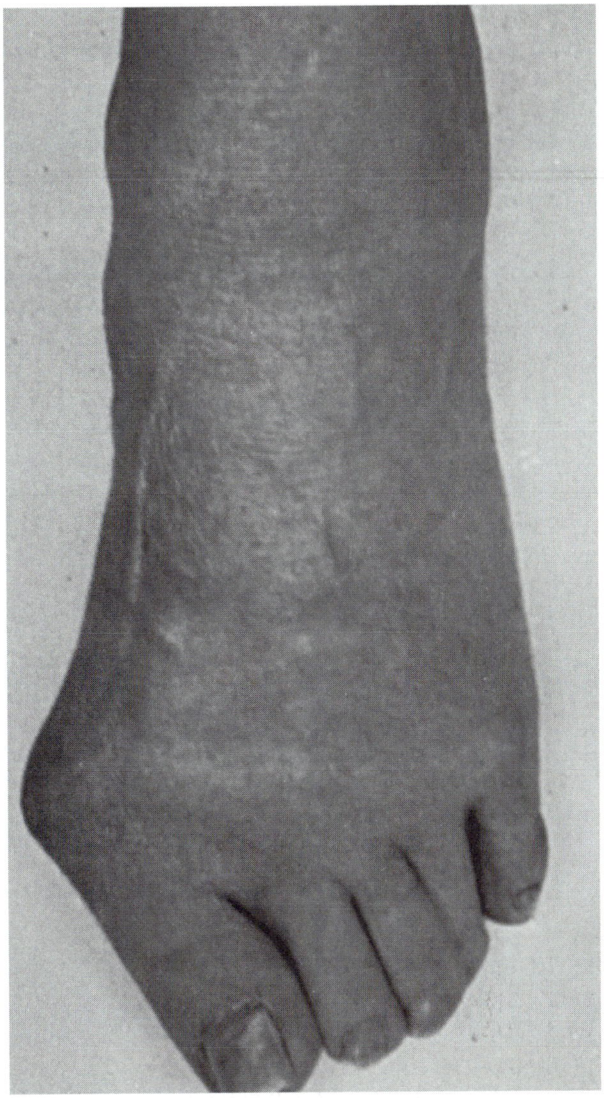

Fig. 30-17 Hallux valgus angulation of first three toes, overlapping of middle toe on fourth toe, and wide, flat metatarsus. (From Mann RA, Coughlin MJ: *Surgery of the foot and ankle,* ed 6, vol 1, St. Louis, 1993, Mosby.)

Hammertoe **Hammertoes** are a deformity of the second toe. In this deformity, the metatarsophalangeal joint is dorsiflexed; the proximal interphalangeal joint is plantar flexed, and there is callus formation on the dorsum of the proximal interphalangeal joint and the end of the affected toe. The result is a toe that is in a clawlike position (Fig. 30-18). Improperly fitted shoes, muscle weakness, or arthritis cause hammertoe. Symptoms include pain and burning on the bottom of the foot and problems walking in shoes. Initially, pain may be relieved with a moleskin toe pad. Other treatments for hammertoe include metatarsal arch support, orthotics, splints, and passive manual stretching of the proximal interphalangeal joint. Surgical correction is done if the conservative treatment is ineffective.

Nail disorders Toenail problems are common in older adults. **Onychauxis** are hypertrophic nails with the nail borders curving into the soft tissue of the toe. This disorder can cause nail bed ulcers, infection, and pain. Older adults with problems of the nails should be referred to a podiatrist.

Client education The nurse has an important role in educating clients about proper foot care and footwear. Essential to the prevention of foot problems are shoes that fit well. The shoe should not crowd the toes and should be of the correct length and width. Shoes that are too short or narrow can force the great toe into a position of hallux valgus (bunion). Shoes should be wide enough to allow bending of the toes and movement of the foot muscles. Adequate arch support should be provided. Women should avoid high heels.

Clients should be taught that foot care includes daily hygiene and changing socks daily. Socks or stockings should be loose enough to avoid the development of pressure ulcers. Toenails should be trimmed with nail clippers. Clients with impaired vision, mobility, or self-care deficit may require assistance to perform this task safely. To prevent the development of ingrown toenails and infections, the nails should be trimmed straight across. If persistent foot problems develop, a podiatrist should be consulted.

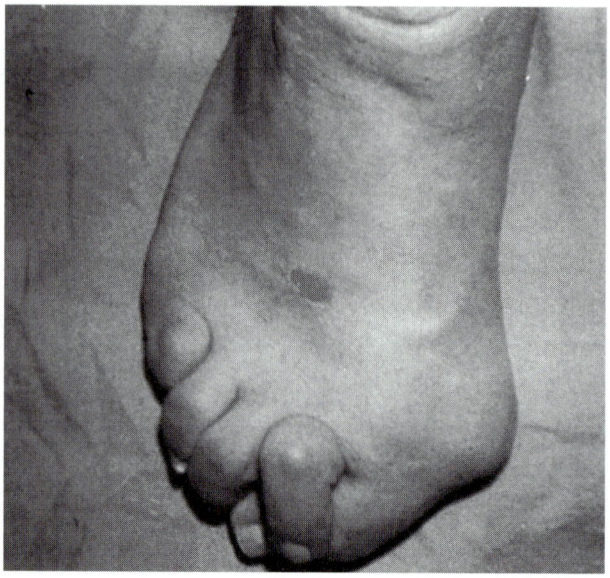

Fig. 30-18 Hammertoe associated with hallux valgus. (From Crenshaw AH, editor: *Campbell's operative orthopaedics,* ed 8, St. Louis, 1992, Mosby.)

ASSESSMENT OF THE MUSCULOSKELETAL SYSTEM

Musculoskeletal disorders are the most common chronic condition occurring in older people. These diseases are not generally fatal, but do cause pain and discomfort. Such disorders, along with the normal age-related changes of the system, predispose the older person to deconditioning, disability, and dependency. Careful assessment of the musculoskeletal system is essential for the nurse in assisting older people to reach an optimum level of functioning (Box 30-5).

History

Correct diagnosis depends on an accurate history that includes past health, family and social history. Several disorders directly or indirectly affect the musculoskeletal system. Questions about history of DM, tuberculosis, poliomyelitis, osteomyelitis, osteoarthritis, rheumatoid arthritis, gout, or neuromuscular injuries should be asked. Information gathered about musculoskeletal injuries include history of fractures, sprains, strains or dislocations, as well as treatment and interference with optimal functioning. The client should be asked about hospitalizations for musculoskeletal problems. The date and reason for hospitalization and specifics about the treatment are obtained.

Medication history is an important component of the history. Questions should be asked about OTC and prescription medications including the name, the reason for taking the medication, the dose, the frequency, length of time taken, and the effectiveness of the medication. Particular attention should be paid so medication used to treat musculoskeletal problems and those that adversely affect the system, including anticonvulsants (osteomalacia), steroids (osteoporosis, muscle weakness), and those that cause gait disturbances (psychotropics, antiparkinsonism agents) can be identified. Women are asked about estrogen replacement therapy.

Information about diet is obtained. This includes data about the average daily diet intake. It is important to assess for adequate intake of protein, calcium, and vitamins C and D. Weight history is important, since weighing more than the ideal body weight puts stress on the joints and predisposes to unstable ligaments.

The family history includes questions about musculoskeletal diseases that have a family predisposition. These disorders include rheumatoid arthritis, osteoarthritis, and gout.

Questions about the client's lifestyle are asked. Occupational history is important, because some jobs can cause damage to the musculoskeletal structure. Information about occupational injuries is obtained. Questions are asked about the specifics of exercise programs. The client is asked to describe any limitations that may cause problems in maintaining exercise programs, such as decreased range of motion, joint pains, or fatigue.

BOX 30-5

Musculoskeletal Assessment

Health history

Past—Fractures, injuries, surgeries, illnesses, including diabetes, tuberculosis, poliomyelitis, osteomyelitis, rheumatoid arthritis, gout, osteoarthritis.

Family—Gout, rheumatoid arthritis, osteoarthritis, osteoporosis.

Social and personal—Occupation, exercise patterns, safety practices, diet.

Medications—Prescription and over-the-counter (OTC) preparations.

Review of systems—Muscle pain, spasms or weakness, joint pain, swelling, erythema, crepitus, range of motion, backache, gait changes.

Physical examination

Inspection—Symmetry, posture, gait, general body build, muscle size, limb-length discrepancy, and gross deformities.

Palpation—Joints and muscles for temperature, swelling, pain, tenderness, or crepitation.

Muscle strength—Graded on a scale of 0 to 5.

Movement—Evaluate passive and active range of motion using the following principles:

1. Symmetry is the key.
2. Develop and use a consistent approach.
3. Consider the effect of findings on the client's functional ability.
4. Observe facial expression for indication of pain or discomfort.
5. Maneuvers can be carried out in a variety of positions; select position based on client comfort and safety, with minimal changes required.
6. Demonstrate maneuvers while instructing client.
7. Be watchful of client for sudden loss of balance as maneuvers are performed; be prepared to provide support.
8. Passive range of motion testing may be required if client is partially or fully immobilized.
9. Use a goniometer only if gross joint motion reduction is suspected. Measure angles of greatest flexion and extension, and compare measurements with expected norms.

From: Lueckenotte AG: *Pocket guide to gerontologic assessment,* ed 2, St. Louis, Mosby, 1994.

Functional assessment is completed to determine the impact of musculoskeletal disorders on the individual's ability to achieve optimum levels of functioning in ADLs. Areas assessed include bathing, dressing, toileting, transfers, ambulation, and eating (see Chapter 4).

Review of Systems

The review of systems is completed to determine the presence of musculoskeletal problems that were not elicited in the general history. Questions are asked to determine the presence of muscle pain, spasms or weakness, joint pain, swelling, erythema, crepitus, limitation of movement, backache, and gait changes. If there are positive answers, data about the onset, duration, and psychologic effect are gathered. Questions to ask about identified problems include the following:

- When did the symptoms begin?
- Are the symptoms continuous or intermittent?
- Are there precipitating factors?
- Does anything help the symptoms?
- Does anything worsen the problem?
- Are any home remedies used?
- How does the problem affect ability to function?

The in-depth history provides the nurse with specific areas to focus on during the physical examination.

Physical Examination

Before the start of the examination, measures should be instituted that provide privacy for the client. The initial stage of the examination is inspection. The client is observed for overall body symmetry, posture, general body build, muscle size, limb-length discrepancy, and gross deformities. If the person is able to ambulate, gait should be assessed for any abnormalities.

Areas that appear abnormal on inspection or that have been described as part of a physical complaint in the history are palpated. During palpation, the bones, joints, and muscles are assessed for localized temperature changes, swelling, localized pain or tenderness, and crepitation. Joints are assessed for active and passive range of motion. Active range of motion is assessed before passive. During assessment of range-of-motion, symmetry is observed, as well as the client's facial expression for signs of discomfort or pain. Strength of muscles is tested with range of motion. Muscle strength is graded on a scale of 5 to 0:

5 Normal
4 Good
3 Fair
2 Poor
1 Trace (slight contractibility)
0 Absent (Salmund, Mooney, Verdisco, 1991)

To determine the impact of musculoskeletal conditions on the individual's ability to function in daily life, functional assessments may be used. Examples of functional assessment tools include the *PULSES Profile* (Granger, Albrecht, Hamilton, 1979), the Barthel Index (Granger, Albrecht, Hamilton, 1979), and the Katz (Katz et al, 1963) Index of ADLs (see Chapter 4).

Summary

Problems of the musculoskeletal system can have great impact on the day-to-day life of older adults. Conditions such as osteoarthritis, rheumatoid arthritis, osteoporosis and fractures can result in functional disability, chronic pain, and decreased quality of life.

The role of the nurse working with clients with musculoskeletal disorders is to promote safe, optimum function in mobility and self-care. Interventions to promote comfort and to relieve pain are critical in the maintenance of function. To prevent serious disability, it is essential that clients resume activity as soon as possible after episodes of acute illness. A key nursing role is to educate clients about the importance of musculoskeletal activity in maintaining function.

Key Points

- A high incidence of musculoskeletal disorders exists in older adults.
- Musculoskeletal disorders are a major cause of functional impairments in older adults.
- The most common sites for fractures in older adults are hip, wrist (Colles), and vertebrae.
- Osteoporosis is more prevalent in older women than in older men.
- Demographic factors associated with osteoporosis include female gender, age, and white race.
- Lower extremity amputations in older adults most often are the result of PVD and DM.
- Symptoms of osteoarthritis, rheumatoid arthritis, gouty arthritis, and polymyalgia rheumatica are similar.
- Age-related changes in a variety of body systems predispose older adults to falls.
- Assessment of the musculoskeletal system includes examination of bones, muscles, and joints.
- Physical activity and exercise is key to preventing disability from musculoskeletal disorders in older adults.

Critical Thinking Exercises

1. A 78-year-old woman has suffered a musculoskeletal injury that requires a period of bedrest and limited mobility. How will her age affect her ability to tolerate a period of decreased mobility? Explain.
2. You are caring for two clients: a 71-year-old man with gouty arthritis and a 69-year-old woman with rheumatoid arthritis. What aspects of their care will be similar? Different?
3. A 72-year-old man has lived a fairly sedentary lifestyle as an accountant. Now that he is retired, he recognizes the need to be active to maintain his health as long as possible. He is concerned, however, that it is too late for him to start exercising, since he has never indulged in such activities. What encouragement, if any, can you give to him, and what suggestions can you make for an exercise program?

HOME CARE TIPS

1. Assessment of the musculoskeletal system includes examination of bones, muscles, and joints in the homebound older adult.
2. Instruct the caregiver and homebound older adult about reportable signs and symptoms related to the musculoskeletal system disease/disorder being treated, and when to report these changes to the homecare nurse or physician.
3. Instruct the caregiver and homebound older adult on the name, dose, frequency, side effects, and indications of both the prescribed and OTC medications being used to treat the identified musculoskeletal problem.
4. Musculoskeletal problems increase safety hazards (e.g., falls) in the homebound older adult.
5. Assess for functional impairments, such as inability to provide self-care and perform IADLs. If necessary, have social worker identify community resources for additional assistance with identified impairments, such as transportation and food preparation.
6. Assess the activity tolerance level that may be affected by musculoskeletal problems.
7. Instruct the caregiver and homebound older adult about the diagnosed musculoskeletal disease or disorder; focusing on self-care measures that maintain or promote independence.
8. Have physical therapist and occupational therapist evaluate and teach the caregiver and homebound older adult how to adapt the environment based on the specific musculoskeletal problem (e.g., gait walking, use of hand-held devices to assist with eating, splints, prosthesis, etc.)
9. Instruct the caregiver and homebound older woman on the necessity of calcium supplements and exercise to maintain proper skeletal function.

REFERENCES

American Association of Retired Persons and the Administration on Aging, US Department of Health and Human Services: *A profile of older Americans: 1992,* Washington, D.C., 1993, The Association and The Administration.

Calkins E: Musculoskeletal diseases in the elderly. In Calkins E, Ford A, Kate P, editors: *Practice of geriatrics,* Philadelphia, 1992, WB Saunders.

Chase J: Spinal stenosis: when arthritis is more than arthritis, *Nurs Clin North Am* 29(4):53-64, 1991.

Craven R, Dietsch K: Musculoskeletal problems. In Carnevali DL, Patrick M, editors: *Nursing management for the elderly,* Philadelphia, 1993, JB Lippincott.

Creditor M: Hazards of hospitalization of the elderly, *Ann Intern Med* 118(3):219-223, 1993.

Ebersole P, Hess P: *Towards healthy aging: human needs and nursing response,* ed 4, St. Louis, 1994, Mosby .

Edwards N, Cere M, Leblond D: A community based intervention to prevent falls at home, *Commun Health* 15(4):51-65, 1993.

Fiatarone MA et al: High-intensity strength training in nonagenarians, *JAMA* 263(20):3029-3034, 1990.

Fraley AM: *Nursing and the disabled across the life span,* Boston, 1992, Jones and Bartlett.

Granger CV, Albrecht GL, Hamilton BB: Outcomes of comprehensive medical rehabilitation: measures of PULSES profile and Barthel index, *Arch Phys Med Rehab* 60:145-154, 1979.

Gudas J: Foot problems. In Calkins E, Ford B, Katz R, editors: *Practice of geriatrics,* Philadelphia, 1992, WB Saunders.

Harvard Health Letter, Dogged by pain, February 1993:4-6.

Hochberg MC: Epidemiology of osteoarthritis: current concepts and new insights, *J Rheumatol* 18(Suppl. 27):46, 1991.

Hogue C: Managing falls: the current basis for practice. In Funk SG et al, editors: *Key aspects of elder care: managing falls, incontinence, and cognitive impairment,* New York, 1992, Springer.

Katz S, Ford AB, Moskowitz RW et al: Studies of the illness of the aged. The Index of ADL: a standardized measure of biological and pyschosocial function, *JAMA* 185:94-98, 1963.

McMahon MA, Peterson C, Schilke J: Osteoporosis: identifying high-risk persons, *J Gerontol Nurs* 18(10):19-26, 1992.

Nesher G, Moore TL, Zuckner J: Rheumatoid arthritis in the elderly, *J Am Geriatr Soc* 39(3):284-294, 1991.

Rubenstein LZ et al: Falls and instability in the elderly, *J Am Geriatr Soc* 36:266-278, 1978.

Ruda S: Nursing assessment: musculoskeletal system. In Lewis SM, Collier IC, editors: *Medical-surgical nursing,* St. Louis, 1992, Mosby.

Russell TA: Fractures of hip and pelvis. In Crenshaw, editor: *Campbell's operative orthopedics,* St. Louis, 1992, Mosby.

Salmund SW, Mooney NE, Verdisco LA, editors: *Core curriculum for orthopedic nursing,* New Jersey, 1991, Pitman. Published for the National Association of Orthopedic Nursing by Antony J. Janetti.

Sardana R: Nutritional management of osteoporosis, *Geriatr Nurs* 18(6):315-319, 1992.

Stone JT, Chenitz WC: The problem of falls. In Chenitz WC, Stone JT, Salisbury S, editors, *Clinical gerontological nursing: a guide to advanced practice,* Philadelphia, 1991, WB Saunders.

Tinetti ME et al: Mechanical restraint use among residents of skilled nursing facilities, *JAMA* 265(4):468-471, 1991.

BIBLIOGRAPHY

Brady R et al: Geriatric falls: prevention strategies for the staff, *J Gerontol Nurs* 19(9):26-32, 1993.

Calkins E: Arthritis in the elderly, *Bull Rheum Dis* 40(3):1-9, 1991.

Gates SJ, Cuckler JM: Degenerative disorders. In Maher AB, Salmund SW, Pellino TA, editors: *Orthopedic nursing,* Philadelphia, 1994, WB Saunders.

Geier K: Metabolic conditions. In Maher AB, Salmund DW, Pellino TA, editors: *Orthopedic nursing,* Philadelphia, 1994, WB Saunders, pp 463-475, 487-497.

Goodwin JS: Progress in gerontology: polymyalgia rheumatica and temporal arteritis, *J Am Geriatr Soc* 40:515-525, 1992.

Griffin M, Piper JM, Daugherty JR: Non-steroidal drug use and increased risk for peptic ulcer disease in elderly persons, *Ann Intern Med* 114:257-263, 1991.

Hammerman D: Aging and osteoarthritis: basic mechanisms, *J Am Geriatr Soc* 41:760-770, 1993.

Hay EK: That old hip, *Nurs Clin North Am* 26(1):44-51, 1991.

Hogstel M, Taylor-Martof M: Perioperative care. In Hogstel M, editor: *Nursing care of the older adult,* Albany, N.Y., 1992, Delmar.

Hogue C: Managing falls: the current basis for practice.

Hollinger L, Patterson P: A fall precaution program for the acute care setting. In Funk SG et al, editors: *Key aspects of elder care: managing falls, incontinence and cognitive impairment,* New York, 1992, Springer.

Kirkpatrick MK, Edwards MK, Finch N: Assessment and prevention of osteoporosis through use of a client self-reporting tool, *Nurs Pract* 16(7):16-26, 1991.

Lamb K, Miller J, Hernandez M: Falls in the elderly: causes and prevention, *Orthop Nurs* 6(2):45-49, 1987.

Liscum B: Osteoporosis: the silent disease, *Orthop Nurs* 11(4):21-24, 1992.

Lueckenotte A: *A pocket guide to gerontologic assessment,* ed 2, St. Louis, 1994, Mosby.

Maher AB, Addams S, Shatbaie J: Amputation and replantation. In Maher AB, Salmund SW, Pelinno TA, editors: *Orthopedic nursing,* Philadelphia, 1994, WB Saunders.

McCourt AE, editor: *The specialty practice of rehabilitation nursing: a core curriculum,* Skokie, Ill., 1993, The Rehabilitation Nursing Foundation of the Association of Rehabilitation Nurses.

O'Brien LA, Grisso JA, Maislin G et al: Hospitalized elders: risk of confusion with hip fracture, *J Gerontol Nurs* 19(2):25-31, 1993.

Sattin RW et al: The incidence of fall injury events among the elderly in a defined population, *Am J Epidemiol* 131:1028-1037, 1990.

Snyder P: Fractures. In Maher AB, Salmund SW, Pellino TA, editors: *Orthopedic nursing,* Philadelphia, 1994, WB Saunders.

Stone JT, Chenitz WC: The problem of falls. In Chenitz WC, Stone JT, Salisbury S, editors: *Clinical gerontological nursing: a guide to advanced practice,* Philadelphia, 1991, WB Saunders.

Part Seven

Special Care Settings

CHAPTER 31

Acute Care

LEARNING OBJECTIVES

On completion of this chapter, the reader will be able to:

1. Describe acute care hospital use patterns in the older adult population.
2. Describe a functional model of care.
3. Identify ways to modify the physical and social environment of care for the hospitalized older adult.
4. Discuss the importance of advocacy within an interdisciplinary framework.
5. Describe one case management strategy.
6. List adaptations that can be made to support and facilitate learning in the older adult.
7. Describe common causes of iatrogenic illness.
8. Discuss ethical and legal issues that commonly occur in the treatment of the hospitalized older adult.
9. List three presentation differences that may occur in the older adult client.
10. Describe two nursing interventions for each of the three conditions that make up the geriatric triad.

Older adults are a diverse, heterogeneous group in terms of age, life experiences, the aging process, health habits, attitude, and response to illnesses. Over 90% of the health care needs of older people and their caregivers fall within the domain of nursing practice (Fulmer, Walker, 1990). Virtually all nurses will care for the vulnerable, often high-risk, older adult in the acute care setting at some time (Phillips, 1990); the unique knowledge and skills of caring for this subset of the older adult population are essential.

CHARACTERISTICS OF THE OLDER ADULT

Adults over age 50 consume nearly 65% of hospital services (Kane, 1993). Those over age 65 make up 37% of the total hospital admissions and constitute 47% of patient days, with an average length of stay of 8.3 days (American Hospital Association [AHA], 1992). The over-85 group is the fastest growing segment of the U.S. population. The major causes of death in those over 65 are heart disease, cancer, stroke, chronic obstructive pulmonary disease (COPD), pneumonia, and influenza (US Department of Health and Human Services, 1992c); these diseases invariably require hospitalization and extensive nursing care.

More than 80% of those over age 65 have a chronic illness or functional disability (Phillips, 1990); those over age 75 have three or four chronic illnesses. The exacerbation of a chronic illness or the complication of one profoundly affects the progress of the hospitalized client. People over age 65 typically spend three times as many days in the hospital as younger people. This age group is increasingly influencing the nature of acute care facilities and required professional caretaker skills.

ACUTE CARE ENVIRONMENT

Caregivers are challenged to attend to the individual needs of those admitted to the acute care setting. The older adult is not likely to be admitted to the hospital until a very high level of acuity or complexity exists. The intensity of care required for the typically emergent condition for which the older adult was admitted, compounded by the normal aging process, chronic illness, and impaired functional status, requires astute care planning and case management on the part of the health care team.

Hospitalization is a major risk for older people; for many, hospitalization is followed by an irreversible decline in functional status and a change in the quality and style of life (Hoenig, Rubenstein, 1991). A positive environment can facilitate a client's optimum level of progress. However, a negative environment can create stress, discomfort, and confusion, as well as limit mobility. As a person becomes more impaired, whether physically or psychologically, there is a greater dependency on the physical and social environment and an increased sensitivity to environmental changes (Schainer, 1991). Older adults' concerns with the acute care environment include insensitivity of caregivers; feelings of abandonment; lack of personal attention and dignity; lack of safety, control, and comfort; and lack of communication and information (Kane, 1993).

The rapidly rising costs of care foster a climate in which the quality and multiple aspects of acute care are questioned. The value and efficacy of hospitalization have come under increasing scrutiny. The technologic and mechanistic orientation toward care has tended to obscure those activities aimed at improving functioning of the chronically, physically, and mentally disabled. Effective caregiving practices can enable older people to improve their independence and to live in their preferred setting. However, in the hospital setting health professionals can become so involved in delivering services in the most cost-effective way that they may neglect the importance of "caring for people." The hospital is a highly technologic system that sometimes fails to meet many human needs; a focus on the promotion and preservation of health is needed. High technology ("high-tech") is a common and prominent orientation for acute care settings. The high value placed on technology

RESEARCH

Taylor HA: Geriatric nurses and models of help orientation, *Geriatr Nurs* 13:197-200, July/Aug, 1992.

Sample, setting

Sixty-eight female aides, LPNs, and RNs, ranging in age from 21 to 70, from black, white, and Hispanic origins with educational backgrounds varying from less than high school to a master's degree. Subjects were from nursing homes and home health care.

Methodology

The Help Orientation Test (HOT) indicates subjects' orientation to four different help orientation models.

Findings

The help orientation model rated highest by subjects was the medical model, which says that people have little responsibility for causing and/or finding solutions for their problems. People are seen as unable to rely on themselves, and others should identify and solve these problems, as well as evaluate outcomes.

The models rated lowest by subjects were the moral and compensatory models. The moral model sees people as having high responsibility for both problems and solutions. People are seen as capable and are expected to solve their own problems. Helping actions involved are through motivational methods only.

The compensatory model sees people as having little responsibility for causing their problems but high responsibility for solving them. People are seen as victims of circumstance, but also as having the potential for self-direction. Help is given through provision of temporary goods, information, or opportunities only.

Implications

Because the needs of older people for autonomy, growth, and competence are often not recognized by professional caregivers, the chosen medical helping orientation model may reinforce dependency, facilitating the lessening of competence and associated life satisfaction the older adult may experience. This may be more detrimental than helpful. Since recipients of help based on the moral or competency models are more likely to become more competent and have higher life satisfaction, a greater sense of health, well-being, and quality of life, as well as greater coping abilities, it would seem that nurses need to be aware of their own help orientation.

nurtures a task orientation that may detract from the holistic focus required for the care of older adults. A balance between "high-tech" and "high-touch" is required to ensure effective care and a high level of functional status for the older adult client.

The biomedical model practiced in the hospital needs to be expanded to become a social model in which health or cure may not be the highest goal, but rather the promotion of self-reliance as an expression of human dignity and development, and the recognition that there is more than one form of curing or healing. Major health problems are closely linked to social values and economic interests; social integration and social support are central to health and well-being (Kickbusch, 1981; Kovner, 1990; Ryder, 1992) (see Research box, p. 900).

Acute care centers have traditionally provided care within a medical model with the focus on diagnosis and treatment, rather than on a functional model, which integrates all aspects of care. The older adult, however, is usually hospitalized because of an exacerbation of a chronic illness or complications, rather than an isolated episode of acute illness. Focusing on a functional model ensures a discharge from the facility with the concerns related to both medical and functional stability being considered.

Quality control of the environment, personnel, and services is ensured by professional organizations, regulatory agencies, and third-party payers. The American Nurses Association (ANA) (1987) is one organization that provides standards for professional practice; it also provides certification for specific areas of practice, such as gerontologic nursing. The standards of regulatory agencies provide some parameters and expectations for care of the older adult. The Joint Commission for Accreditation of Healthcare Organizations (JCAHO) is a voluntary agency that accredits hospitals (JCAHO, 1995). Some of the issues the agency addresses in relation to the older adult include nutritional status assessment, competence of nursing staff, assessment of client functional status, medication administration, use of restraints, and family and client involvement in care. Another agency is the Centers for Disease Control and Prevention; reporting mechanisms and policies regarding influenza vaccine, pneumococcal vaccine, levels of physical activity for older people, and occupational safety are addressed. Various outside agencies do have influence on the care of the older adult in the hospital and provide further assurance of quality control.

Physical Environment

Older adults have a decreased ability to adapt to an unfamiliar environment; they have less reserve to draw on and less efficient homeostasis. In addition, many are alone and without family support. Multiple stimuli, such as contact with many departments, many personnel, and multiple room changes, can prompt confusion and exhaustion, as well as a loss of crucial personal items, such as hearing aids, prostheses, dentures, and eyeglasses. Modifying the environment for older adult clients can be done in many ways (Box 31-1). Some modifications require additional resources, but many can be changed as a result of observations and minimal creativity on the part of the nursing staff.

BOX 31-1

Environmental Modifications

- "Blue" fluorescent lighting
- Night-lights
- Extra lighting in bathrooms
- Lighting intensity consistent throughout
- Light switches that glow
- Solid-color designs for floors (avoidance of patterns)
- Nonskid, nonglare floor wax
- Carpeting with uncut, low pile and padding underneath
- Contrasting color to identify boundaries between floor and wall
- Nonglossy wall surfaces
- Polarized window glass to decrease glare
- Nonglare glass over pictures (avoidance of abstract designs)
- Rounded handrails for easy grasp in all areas where ambulation occurs (use of high-contrast colors)
- Levers versus knobs for doors and dressers
- Large-numbered, white-on-black (or black-on-white) clocks with nonglare glass
- Large-print calendars within client's line of vision
- Telephones with large numbers available
- Glasses cases and prosthesis cases attached to bedside within reach
- Amplified and hearing aid–compatible phones available
- Beds that lower to height that, when client is sitting on edge, both of client's feet are on the floor
- Chairs with armrests
- Portable elevated toilet seats available
- Grab bars in shower and around toilet

Modified from Morath J, Fulton J: Acute care of elders. In Burnside I: *Nursing and the aged,* ed 3, New York, 1988, McGraw-Hill; Tideiksaar R: Environmental modifications. In *Falls in older persons: prevention and management in hospitals and nursing homes,* Boulder, Colo., 1993, Tactilitics.

Professional Staff

Professional staff must play the role of advocate for the older hospitalized adult. The care in the acute care environment requires an interdisciplinary approach. Positive and reality-based professional attitudes regarding aging and human development are imperative. Care given to older adult clients by professionals with limited knowledge or with conflicting health discipline approaches can lead to a client's irreversible functional decline and to unnecessary side effects and complications. The rights of older adults require that care options be presented and explored; they and their family need empowerment to be actively involved in the decision making about their care. Advocates also must be politically astute and able to identify and develop strategies for meeting unique needs. Advocates also are aggressive in seeking information regarding the resources and in identifying the *rights* of the older adult (Becker, 1986).

The nurse, knowing the changes associated with aging, should also be an advocate for appropriate care and treatment from all disciplines. For example, both physical therapy and occupational therapy are often needed to maintain or restore function, yet are often neglected. Confusion is often labeled as Alzheimer's disease (AD) without adequate assessment data. Medications are often given without being closely monitored for efficacy and side effects. Nurses have many opportunities to suggest to all disciplines care options that are more appropriate for older adults.

The nurse's role in caring for the older adult who requires acute, episodic care is probably central to the client's progress. Nurses are at the forefront of providing nursing care of older adults often assuming the leadership role in **interdisciplinary care** (Carty, Day, 1993). Caring for the older adult in an acute care setting presents a unique challenge. Many complex issues, such as **ageism,** continuity of care, and iatrogenic illnesses must be resolved. It is the unique role of the nurse to take charge, to be an **advocate,** to empower older adults and their families, and by being with older adult clients, to facilitate their own understanding of life's momentary meaning (Phillips, 1990).

A lack of clinical role models is available for those who wish to become specialists as gerontologic nursing. As of June 1995, approximately 600 nurses are certified as gerontologic clinical nurse specialists in the United States (American Nurses' Credentialing Center: personal communication, 1995). However, older adults' needs are complex; they rarely have a single diagnosis, and they account for 20% to 40% of those hospitalized (Phillips, 1990). Nurses in acute care focus more of their care on older adults than on any other age group. The nurse must be an advocate and must work with the individual and family to meet the specific needs of this heterogeneous group. The nurse must also be a **social agent** to develop and to participate in social change at a broader level to ensure optimum care of this age group (Guse, Degner, 1990).

Case Management

Acute care settings are increasingly moving toward managed care. This is occurring in the interest of more efficient, quality care for the client, as well as in the interest of cost containment. Care requirements are specifically mapped out with identified time lines to ensure optimum progress during the hospital stay. **Case management** also involves a higher level of discharge planning to ensure ongoing care after discharge and to decrease the incidence of **recidivism;** older adults are at high risk for readmission (Holloway, Pokorny, 1994; Newman, Lamb, Michaels, 1991).

Case management requires interdisciplinary teamwork in all aspects of client care: physical, functional, psychosocial, spiritual, cognitive, and economic. Professional teamwork and collaboration enhance communication, optimize care and goal achievement, decrease fragmentation, and make the care more cost and time efficient. The benefits of multiple health care disciplines working together provide a broader scope to the problem-solving process in acute care (Dugan, Mosel, 1992). All of these efforts are aimed at achieving a higher level of client outcomes, satisfaction with the hospitalization, and appropriate planning for postdischarge activities.

Hospitals are also expanding their corporate structures to include other settings along the continuum for the older person, including day care, home care, and skilled care facilities. The challenge in developing a continuum of care includes effective communication systems to ensure the integration of all services. The nurse is most often responsible for this continuity, reducing the fragmentation of care that often occurs.

CLIENT CARE ISSUES

The health care team is responsible for a number of client care issues in the acute care environment: learning needs, decision making and self-care, iatrogenic illness, and ethical-legal concerns.

Learning Needs

Recognition of the importance of supporting and facilitating self-care behaviors for clients and their families is a responsibility of the health care team but is most often implemented and coordinated by the nurse. Adaptations can be made to support and facilitate learning in the older adult via the sensory, motor, and cognitive systems (Box 31-2). Assessment of sensory and cognitive status is the first step in determining if adaptations are needed. Sensory and cognitive changes require a multisensory approach. Teaching strategies should be individualized and need to include multiple sensory stimuli: seeing, hearing, touching, and smelling. Also important may be the presence of family members or other home caregivers during the teaching-learning process to allow for information needs to be reinforced by significant others once the client is home.

Motivation and rewards are specific to each individual to enhance learning and compliance with needed self-

BOX 31-2

Adaptations for the Older Learner

General tips

Ensure that the person is free of pain, hunger, thirst, and cold, and has voided; attend to physical needs.
Assess sensory and cognitive functions.
Physically offer fluids during session.
Provide for toileting breaks.
Set mutual long-term goals and short-term goals to reach these.
Encourage family participation.
Break down psychomotor skills step by step.
Problem solve any barriers that present themselves.
Provide variety; use diverse teaching methods.

Tips to accommodate visual changes

Make certain the client's eyeglasses are clean and on.
Use 14- to 16-point type on all reading materials.
Use Serif lettering.
Use double or triple space between lines.
Use nonglossy, off-white paper with black letters for high contrast.
Avoid blues, greens, or violets to differentiate print, or pictures from print.
Use sheer curtains or polarized glass to minimize window glare.
To minimize glare, avoid placing client facing a sunny window.
Use halogen lights; focus light directly on object to be viewed from behind the person.
Use contrasting colors to help differentiate depth.

Tips to accommodate hearing changes

Minimize all background noise (i.e., turn off radio or TV; close door).
If person has hearing aids, make sure they are on and working.
Sit face-to-face to facilitate lipreading.
Speak normally, or lower the pitch of your voice.
Use pictures, models, or written key words to reinforce verbal teaching.
Select videos or slide or tape presentations that use speakers with deeper voices.
Demonstrate tasks.

Tips to accommodate cognitive changes

Slow pace and allow extra time for person to respond.
Provide short sessions, presenting one topic at a time.
Give only relevant information.
Use examples or analogies related to life experiences.
Give concrete, rather than abstract, information.
Repeat key words often.
Reinforce with printed materials.
Whenever possible, use materials that the person can feel, touch, and manipulate.

Modified from Weinrich SP, Boyd M, Nussbaum J: Continuing education: adapting strategies to teach the elderly, *J Gerontol Nurs* 15(11):17-21, 1989; Weinrich SP, Boyd M: Education in the elderly, adapting and evaluating teaching tools, *J Gerontol Nurs* 18(1):15-20, 1992.

care. Compliance with new health care regimens can be promoted by clearly identifying benefits of behaviors that are of value to the client, reinforcing information through support systems, and involving significant others in the learning process. The older adult is much more capable of using previous experiences to problem solve than the young person. The nurse should teach what is *immediately applicable* to the life of the older adult. Decreasing the risk of a heart attack may not be nearly as important as increasing function so that the older adult can go to church or spend time with the family. The content of teaching should address not only the care of the disease but also the maintenance of functional status. The nurse should also document teaching and referrals, as well as prepare the client for possible setbacks (Dellasega et al, 1994).

Acute care centers are often hostile to the family caregiver, the technology is frightening, and the family member feels powerless. Even assertive visitors may hesitate to interrupt busy professionals with questions or requests. This is unfortunate, since the family members responsible for giving care once the client returns home miss the best opportunity to learn needed skills under supervision until a level of comfort, if not expertise, is acquired. The family members may also miss the chance to learn about normal aging and how to promote independence. Active participation of family members or other postdischarge caregivers should be encouraged (Schirm, Collier, 1992); they have a wealth of information about the client's past behaviors, home environment, and future needs.

Knowledge is only one aspect of client performance or behavior. Other barriers to compliance need to be assessed as well. What is the home environment like? Are there limited finances or other resources? Does the client have *access* to adequate food, housing, and medications? What are the client's health beliefs? How will the treatment benefit or alter lifestyle? What is the cost/benefit of follow-through on any regimen? Have the opportunity and resources been identified for later questions and information? Is the client comfortable with using available resources?

Participative Decision Making and Self-Care

Many older adults have the expectation of being physically cared for by family members when they are ill. This may not be consistent with the caregiver's goal for the client to increase physical and mental independence. Studies conducted in acute care geriatric units have shown that older adults encouraged to care for themselves retain higher levels of function and mental status compared with older adults who were not encouraged to do self-care (Huber, Kennard, 1991; Meissner et al, 1989). One major barrier in assisting the client in developing self-care is the shorter length of hospital stay; clients are often sent home still requiring physical care or other assistance. Teaching and encouraging self-care are imperative and crucial points to be addressed throughout the hospital stay.

Iatrogenic Illness

Iatrogenic illness, medical treatment meant to be therapeutic that instead causes additional problems, is common in older adults. If the illness or abnormal state is induced by inadvertent or erroneous nursing interventions, it has been referred to as **nursigenic illness** (Miller, 1975). The individual's increased exposure to the health care system increases risks for iatrogenic illness. Common problems include infection, malnutrition, incontinence, sleep disturbance, and immobility. The greater the client's and family's participation and collaboration with the nurse, the more likely it is that iatrogenic problems can be ameliorated or prevented (Kenny, 1990).

Problems can start before admission; caregivers or emergency medical system (EMS) providers may not consider the need for modified techniques or drug doses in clients with arthritis or renal or liver dysfunction (Butcher, 1990). Treatments that result in immobility, such as bed rest or restraints, often result in functional disability in older adults. These clients are often vulnerable to rapid loss of muscle strength, urinary incontinence (UI) or retention, fecal impaction or constipation, respiratory depression, falls, confusion, depression, lack of appetite, and many other complications. It is not unusual for these symptoms to occur in clients immobilized for periods as short as 24 to 48 hours (Creditor, 1993). The occurrence of iatrogenic illnesses often represents a vicious circle, with one treatment or lack of treatment causing another symptom (Buckwalter, Stolley, 1991).

Polypharmacy (taking five or more drugs) is a common cause of iatrogenic illness (Kroenke, Penholt, 1990; Stolley et al, 1991). The effects are often similar to those seen with immobility. Different physicians focusing individually on a particular disease process with insufficient coordination of treatment contribute to the polypharmacy seen in older adults. Incorrect diagnoses, multiple conditions, changes in nutritional status, fluid and electrolyte imbalance, poor communication, and the vagueness of presenting symptoms all contribute to polypharmacy or inappropriate medications. In addition, polypharmacy may occur without the awareness of health care personnel, because clients may be taking a number of over-the-counter (OTC) medications, which could interfere with the pharmacologic action of other, prescribed medications. The risk of adverse reactions may be exacerbated by the physiologic changes associated with aging; risks can be reduced by careful review of medication usage and client counseling (US Department of Health and Human Services, 1992a). Nursing care requires careful attention to drug histories and an awareness of potential drug-induced symptoms.

Ethical-Legal Issues

Older adults are a vulnerable population; all caregivers in the acute care environment must be knowledgeable and aware of the numerous ethical-legal issues surrounding their hospitalization (Bahr, 1991). Some issues that are specific to the environment include advance directives, competency, restraints, prolongation of life with technology, and abuse.

Nurses in the acute care setting often work with clients at the end of life; advance medical directives (AMDs) are a critical consideration. Clients, families, and clinicians continue to struggle with ethical decision making (Zimbelman, 1994). Although the Patient Self-Determination Act (PSDA) for AMDs is a step in the direction of greater knowledge and choice for end-of-life issues, its current actual application has a long way to go. Older adults and their families should begin the process before serious illness occurs. However, many older hospitalized adults have no AMDs, nor have they discussed them with family or health care providers. Additional education and communication regarding AMDs are major needs to be considered by the case management team; decisions regarding content and strategy are most often implemented by the nursing staff (see Chapter 3).

Competency of individuals who are incapacitated during the acute phase of an illness and unable to make their own decisions for health care is often an issue. If the person is being asked to sign a consent form, the physician and hospital are accepting competency. A competent person always has the right to refuse, as well as consent to treatment. If the client is incompetent and has a Durable Power of Attorney for health care, the designated decision maker must consent to treatment. The client may also have a living will specifying desires (see Chapter 3).

Restraints are often used with older adult clients; the prevalence of physical restraints is difficult to determine; Frengley and Mion (1986) report that clients over age 70 had a 20.3% incidence. The form of restraint can be either physical or pharmacologic, and it is typically used to protect from injury, prevent interference with treatment, or control disruptive behavior (Strumpf, Evans, Schwartz, 1991). The acuity level of the clients, coupled with major physiologic changes and the increased use of medications, may prompt caregivers in hospitals to consider the use of restraints. In all decisions regarding restraints, the rights of the older adult must be balanced with the caregiver's accurate identification of the need for restraints. Restraints cannot be used for purposes of discipline or staff convenience (Burke, Walsh, 1992; Papougenis, 1991). The application of restraints imposes an overwhelming powerlessness on an older adult, prompting loss of control over the environment. The Health Care Financing Administration (HCFA) proposed a rule that, since October 1989, has been a condition for Medicare program participation in the long-term care setting: "The resident has a right to be free from unnecessary drugs and physical restraints and is provided treatment to reduce dependency on drugs and physical restraints" (US Department of Health and Human Services, 1989).

The prolongation of life in the acute care environment by means of advanced technology, such as feeding tubes and ventilators, is another ethical consideration for the older adult. As least 50 courts in 16 states have considered issues surrounding the prolongation of life. Nearly all support the client's right to privacy and limit the power of government to control treatment (Meehan, 1989). The prolongation of life issue that is often most troubling is the termination of hydration and nutrition. Many medical centers across the country have developed guidelines for nutritional support in treatment of the terminally ill. These guidelines help caregivers weigh the benefits and difficulties of such treatment while protecting the dignity of the client and the family.

It is also important that nurses who work with older adults know the signs of older adult abuse and neglect. Most states have mandatory reporting laws; all suspected cases of abuse or neglect must be reported to protection agencies or law enforcement. An admission to an acute care facility is often the circumstance that brings abuse (e.g., physical, psychologic, financial) and neglect to the attention of professionals who can intervene. Without such intervention, abuse almost always continues and often escalates.

NURSING CARE

The attitude of the nurse and other health professionals in caring for the older adult is crucial to the delivery of effective care in the acute care setting. Attitudes can reflect the decremental model in which aging is an undesirable event characterized by personal decline, or the **negentropic** model, in which aging is normal from the time of conception and is the thread that provides coherence and meaning to life (Phillips, 1990).

Older adults admitted to the acute care setting face caregivers' preconceived ideas about their basic characteristics and needs. Ageism is systematic stereotyping and discrimination against individuals because they are old (Butler, 1990; Pohl, Boyd, 1993). The victims of the prejudice tend to adopt the same negative definitions about themselves and perpetuate the stereotypes; the end result is a self-fulfilling prophecy (Miller, 1990). The nurse's and the client's expectations for self-care in the acute care environment may be limited. The need for independence is negated almost at the time of admission. The cumulative effect of the stereotyping and low expectations for activity may result in dysfunctional behaviors on the part of the older adult client. The crisis orientation and task focus of acute care is also a deterrent

BOX 31-3

Case Study

An 86-year-old man has just been admitted with dehydration. He is not a good historian because of acute confusion. However, his family indicates that he is an active, independent man who recently participated in the Senior Olympics. The nurse instructs him not to get out of bed by himself, since he is old and frail. He has to void and calls for the nurse, but he cannot wait, so he walks to the bathroom and falls. To protect him from further falls, he is put in a vest restraint. He already has a reddened area over his sacrum. He then needs to void again but cannot, so he wets the bed. The client is now restrained and has an incontinent brief in place. Symptoms of depression and loss of appetite soon become evident. A feeding tube is inserted. The confusion gradually becomes more apparent; the client pulls at his various tubes, prompting the nurse to apply wrist restraints. The client's whole life space has become a hospital bed. The cognitive impairments and the ever-changing environment prompt yelling out (fear or anger). A chemical restraint is then applied in the form of a medication to reduce the agitation.

Questions

1. At what point in this case could the nurse have applied different interventions?
2. What alternative interventions could have been attempted?
3. What possible outcomes could have been achieved with these alternate interventions?
4. Did the client display nursigenic or iatrogenic responses to the interventions identified in the case study? Explain.

> **Insight** • *"Heroes doggedly persist in finding the cause of a problem when others are eager to dismiss it as a normal complication in an old, sick patient. Heroes recognize a budding problem before it blooms into disaster—like the nurse who recognized an elder's sudden confusion as a sign of infection before his temperature rose" (Huey, 1991).*

to holistic care (Dugan and Mosel, 1992). Older people are often users of hospital services and experience longer lengths of stay; optimum care delivery can decrease the costs of care and complications (Box 31-3).

Assessment

A priority at the beginning of every hospitalization is the assessment of the older adult's baseline functional status in order to develop an individual plan of care within the acute care environment (Calvani, Douris, 1991) (Box 31-4). The uniqueness of assessment in the acute care setting includes recognition that older adults are in an unfamiliar environment, which is not conducive to facilitating function at a time when reserves and homeostatic needs are compromised by acute illness. Many common activities of daily living (ADLs) and mental status assessment tools include areas that may not be easily assessed at the time of admission, or may not be as significant at this time (i.e., orientation when a calendar is not present in the room and when daily routines are disrupted). The primary goal of the acute care nurse providing care to the hospitalized older adult is to maximize the client's independence by enhancing function. Functional strengths and weaknesses need to be identified; the plan of care must identify interventions that build on the strengths, as well as facilitate overcoming the weaknesses. Function integrates all aspects of the client's condition; any change in functional status should be interpreted as a classic sign of illness or as a complication in an older adult. By knowing the older client's baseline function, the nurse can assess new-onset signs or symptoms before they trigger a downward spiral of dependency and permanent impairment.

Care of the older adult is made increasingly complex because manifestations of acute illness are less predictable, the causes are more variable, and the possible consequences are more far-reaching than in other age groups (Miller, 1990). Older adults are less likely to maintain and regain a homeostatic state when presented with physiologic stressors. The differences in presentation of signs and symptoms in the aged are related to changes in sensation, autonomic nervous function, and the immune system. The expression of those changes may also be different from expressions of the same incident in another age group.

Warshaw (1985) provided some examples to illustrate these differences. Children have high fevers and pain; adults have fever, pain, and tachycardia. Alternatively,

BOX 31-4

Functional Assessment Tools

Barthel index
(Granger, Albrecht, Hamilton, 1979)
Measures 15 self-care and mobility functions; used commonly in rehabilitation; range is 100 (maximum independence) to 0 (total dependence); a score of 40 or less indicates severe level of dependence

Functional Assessment Inventory (FAI)
(Pfeiffer, 1982)
Is a shortened form of the Older Americans Resources and Services-Multidimensional Functional Assessment Questionnaire (OARS-MFAQ) and measures 5 areas, including physical health, ADLs, mental health, social resources, and financial resources

Instrumental Activities of Daily Living (IADLs)
(Lawton, Brody, 1969)
Measures more complex activities, such as home management skills, management of finances, and transportation

Katz index for ADL
(Katz et al, 1963)
Measures 6 different ADL functions and is scored by performance versus ability; 1 point is given for each dependent task and 1 for each independent task

PULSES profile
(Granger, Albrecht, Hamilton, 1979)
Used commonly in rehabilitation settings; measures functional performance in mobility, self-care, medical status, and psychosocial functions; items are scored on a 4-point scale from independent to dependent; scores range from 6 (most independent) to 24 (most dependent)

Rapid Disability Scale-2
(Linn, Linn, 1982)
Measures 18 areas incorporating ADLs, IADLs, degree of disabilities, and degree of special problems (e.g., depression, confusion)

Insight • *Of critical importance in the care of hospitalized older adults is the need to know their baseline level of function, because that baseline represents the standard against which any change will be measured. The nurse should never attribute a decrement or decline in function to "normal" aging. Functionally oriented nursing care emphasizes and builds on the strengths and abilities of the older adult client to minimize disability and maximize independence.*

the older adult may indicate "I just don't feel right." Symptoms may not match the classic textbook presentation. The older client may not express any symptoms, even though a disease process or a change in functional status is evident to others. Symptoms of an infection include shortness of breath and confusion, rather than fever, chills, and a high white blood cell count. Subtle signs of a catastrophic illness may not be picked up until the client is in crisis. Symptoms may result from the treatment (iatrogenesis), not the disease process.

Insight • *Any alteration in the older adult client's health status, no matter how slight, warrants further investigation. Events such as falls are often viewed as routine or expected occurrences in the acute care setting. However, a fall in the older adult client is often a prodromal sign of impending illness that requires a complete and thorough investigation to identify the subtle change in health status that may be occurring.*

The Geriatric Triad

The **geriatric triad** includes falls, changes in cognitive status, and incontinence (Wells, 1992). These three conditions need special attention during hospitalization. Falls are common throughout life. Of significance in the older adult is the fact that falls can be a classic sign of illness; the older adult in the acute care setting is often at high risk for falls and consequent injuries. The strange environment, confusion, medications, immobility, urinary urgency, and age-related sensory changes all contribute to this increased risk. Falls resulting in injury can be minimized by gait training and strengthening exercises, appropriate nutrition, careful monitoring of medications, toileting, environmental modifications, proper footwear, and control of orthostatic hypotension (Brady et al, 1993). Bed alarms and leg alarms are being tried in many institutions to provide warning and thereby minimize falls (see Chapter 11 and Emergency Treatment box above).

EMERGENCY TREATMENT

Falls

- Reassure client and family.
- Examine for presence of injury.
- Call attending physician to assess physical injury.
- Advocate for adequate assessment to include methods designed to identify covert or symptomless consequences of the fall (e.g., computed tomography [CT] scan and radiograph).
- Explore with physician the cause of the fall by review of the client history, including any history of falls and any intrinsic or extrinsic factors that may be related to the fall.
- Document the incident and precipitating factors, along with a plan to prevent future falls.
- Implement a fall prevention program.

There are three commonly occurring changes in cognitive status in the older adult: **delirium, depression**, and **dementia.** There are many screening tools available to help the nurse accurately identify cognitive impairment. Delirium, or an acute confusional state, is the most common cause of confusion in the acute care setting. It is characterized by an abrupt onset and an acute, reversible disturbance in global cognitive abilities and information processing.

The incidence among older adults may range from 20% to 80% (Foreman, 1990; O'Brien, 1992). There are multiple contributing factors, such as dehydration, electrolyte imbalance, pain, fecal impaction, sensory deprivation or overload, medications, infections, and nutritional disturbances. Potential causes must be addressed and treated rather than attributing behavioral changes to "old age" or dementia. An inappropriate assessment may place the client at great risk for increased mortality, increased length of stay, and lessened functional recovery

Insight • *Nursing interventions aimed at treating the cause of the acute confusional state (delirium) can dramatically reverse the condition. There are scores of possible causes, all of which can be classified into the following three categories: physiologic, psychologic, and environmental (Foreman, 1986). It is not uncommon for the causes to be multiple in nature, requiring skill and creativity in designing appropriate interventions for a quick reversal.*

(Neelon and Champagne, 1992). Therefore it is crucial to obtain a history of the client's baseline status from those who know the client well or live with the client. In addition, knowledge of valid indicators of delirium (i.e., problems with attention and concentration versus disorientation and agitation) (Foreman, 1990) is critical, or the delirium may well be missed.

Interventions for delirium specific to the acute care environment include identifying and treating the cause, attention to the environment, enhancing vision and hearing, controlling pain, providing opportunities for frequent toileting, avoiding control issues, and using distraction. Whenever possible, familiar objects should be included in the room, and the existence of technology should be reduced. Consistent caregivers and a consistent routine also help. Using slow, calm movements and listening to feeling tones enable the caregiver to better prevent agitation. Family caregivers may also suggest beneficial interventions that have proved to be successful and more closely reflect the home environment.

Depression is a reversible mood disorder associated with chronic or acute reaction to stressors, various chronic illnesses, medications, or biochemical causes. Acute illnesses or the onset of chronic conditions may exacerbate the potential for depression. Men between the ages of 65 and 74 have the highest suicide rate in the United States (US Department of Health and Human Services, 1992c). It is important to recognize depression and refer the older adult client to appropriate mental health personnel. Listening to the person in a nonjudgmental manner, validating feelings, and pointing out small successes can also help the older person cope (see Chapter 12).

Dementia is a chronic irreversible change in structure and function of the brain; it is often progressive and is distinguished by its insidious onset (Travis, Moore, 1991) (see Chapter 27). AD is the most common type of dementia in older adults. Care should be used when labeling clients as having dementia, since the cause of behavioral changes may actually be delirium or depression. In acute care, the dementia client with superimposed delirium is often seen. These clients are at particular risk of having health care providers totally miss the delirium, since it is often assumed that the change in cognitive status is a worsening of the dementia. The prevalence of dementia is 5% to 10% in people over age 65 and 20% to 40% in those who reach age 80 (US Department of Health and Human Services, 1992c). Approaches to maximize and to support the client's level of cognitive functioning are determined by astute observation of behaviors and responses, as well as review of the client's history and interaction with family caregivers. Older adults with irreversible dementia do express individualization, but since the presentation may be foreign to the nurse, it is often just overlooked in the acute care institution. Expressions of selfness may include retention of predominant past skills, spirituality, despair, loneliness, connecting with others, social skills, humor, task mastery, and responding with "expected" behaviors (Burgener, Shimer, Murrell, 1992). These expressions must be addressed in plans of care so that all care providers are familiar with the client's unique expressions (Table 31-1).

An acute care admission may be the ideal time to discover and treat the problem of incontinence. Little was known about the nature of incontinence or potential nursing interventions to improve or cure it until the early 1980s, when researchers began studying and then publishing protocols. An excellent reference reflects the extent of these studies: *Clinical Practice Guidelines for Urinary Incontinence in Adults* (US Department of Health and Human Services, 1992b). Urinary and fecal incontinence are common problems for older adults, which are often made worse because of hospitalization and the belief of many caregivers that incontinence is a normal consequence of aging or a normal result of hospitalization (Fruendl, Dugan, 1992). The older adult with or without a history of incontinence is at high risk for an exacerbation of symptoms. Hospital treatments or diagnostic studies often require nothing by mouth or an increase in fluid intake, as frequently happens with intravenous (IV) medications. Sedation can also interfere with bladder and bowel control in an older adult, although it may cause no problems in younger clients. Physician or nursing orders for bed rest, urinary catheters, restraints, or medications can commonly affect bladder and bowel control. Pain and confusion resulting from acute disease conditions or changes in environment also interfere with continence (Lincoln, Roberts, 1989). Any incidence of incontinence while the client is in the acute care environment needs to be evaluated and treated; surgical and medical interventions, as well as behavioral management on the part of nursing, often cure or significantly improve incontinence. Client and family education is essential in the treatment and control of incontinence.

In addition to the geriatric triad, several other nursing care issues that are of a critical nature for this population must be considered in the acute care environment; these include skin integrity, hydration, physical activity, and self-care. The geriatric triad of confusion, falls, and incontinence can and often does lead to another major problem in acute care: skin integrity impairment. The Agency for Health Care Policy and Research (AHCPR) has developed clinical practice guidelines for the prevention and treatment of pressure ulcers, which should be implemented in the acute care environment (US Department of Health and Human Services, 1992a). Risk assessment must be done on admission and at regular, consistent intervals given the potential for rapid change in the older client's physical status (see Chapter 28).

TABLE 31-1

Changes in Cognitive Status

	Delirium	Dementia	Depression
Onset	Sudden and acute	Insidious, subtle, gradual; difficult to pinpoint	Can be sudden or gradual, depending on course; can pinpoint date
Duration	Brief; often clears within 1 month or when underlying disorder is resolved	2 to 20 years	Weeks to years; variable
Awareness	Clouded state of consciousness, disoriented	Alert and aware	Directed inward; self-absorbed
Mood/behavior	Easily distracted; incoherent speech; difficulty with attention and concentration; hallucinations and illusions; disturbed sleep/wake cycle; increased or decreased psychomotor activity; fluctuation of symptoms: lucid at times, often worse at night	Personality changes; emotionally labile; may become easily agitated—catastrophic reactions	Often aware of cognitive problems; apathetic, feelings of hopelessness, worthlessness; vague somatic complaints
Task performance	Often unable to carry out tasks; difficulty following directions	Tries hard to carry out activities; gradual loss of abilities	Although able, little effort
Mental function	Disorganized thinking; fluctuating impairments in memory, coherence, orientation, and perceptions	Impairments in memory, abstract thinking, judgment, language; loss of common knowledge	Selective memory loss: "I don't know" answers on cognitive tests

Older adults commonly have a decreased sense of thirst. Unless fluids are readily accessible (rather than verbally offered) and placed within vision and reach, the older adult client may not maintain an adequate fluid intake. NPO status or fluid restriction places the older adult at even greater risk for dehydration, which has a significant rate of morbidity and mortality among older people. Those with cognitive impairments who are not aware of the need to drink or who do not have the sensation of thirst are at greatest risk. Also, older adults with incontinence may intentionally restrict their fluid intake to reduce the incidence of incontinent episodes. Water is the best fluid, but variety should also be a consideration when attempting to increase the fluid intake of an older client. Caffeinated beverages should be avoided because of their diuretic effect. Careful monitoring of the client's intake and output is essential to ensuring an optimum fluid intake.

Older adults often eat two smaller meals per day and are not hungry at other times. The large portions served three times a day in the hospital setting are often overwhelming to the client. By obtaining a nutritional history at the time of admission, which includes food and fluid likes and dislikes, the nurse can work with the dietitian to accommodate these as much as possible. In some hospitals, bland foods are served on white plates, with white utensils and trays, on white overbed tables. Taking the plates off the tray, placing a colorful mat on the table, and dressing up the service may help accommodate visual deficits to enhance appetite and improve intake. An additional strategy is to introduce older adults to each other and to facilitate socialization during meals.

A key ingredient to healthy aging is physical activity (US Department of Health and Human Services, 1992c). The functional capacity of adults is increased by physical activity; the need for exercise does not change with age (Schilke, 1991). The hazards of hospitalization for older adults are dominated by functional decline; many instances of decline in acute care are attributable more to enforced immobility than to disease progression. The problem can be reduced by ambulation, reality orientation, increased sensory stimulation, and attention to functional or organizational changes (discharge planning, case management, family-oriented care). The physiologic constraints for each client need to be identified; the valid reasons for total bed rest are very few. The use of physical restraints should be limited, if not avoided altogether; in addition to the powerlessness and other adverse responses, restraints severely limit self-care and physical activity. Older adults who lie in bed for a week may age 10 years (Rappaport, 1992). Older adults retain higher levels of function and mental status when they are encouraged to care for themselves and be active, as compared with older adults who do not actively participate in self-care (Huber, Kennard, 1991; Meissner et al, 1989).

Sensitivity to the older client's needs after discharge must be attended to throughout the hospitalization. The health team's success at determining and facilitating the older adult's ability to function effectively outside the hospital may keep the client from experiencing functional decline and from being readmitted (Holloway, Pokorny, 1994). There is a compelling need to identify ways to promote and support the caregiving efforts of families (Collier, Schirm, 1992). Social isolation for older adults is a risk factor for disease processes and decreased functional independence; it is of critical importance that functional status not decline during the hospitalization and then prompt more problems after discharge.

FUTURE TRENDS AND RESEARCH

Nurses working with the older adult in the acute care environment will increasingly be challenged by the role. The growing number of older adults in this setting, the increased complexity of their conditions and their care, and the generation of new knowledge, skills, and technology will all add to the excitement of caring for the older adult.

Broader models of case management will better ensure continuity of care. Capitation will increase; facilities will be reimbursed higher dollar amounts for keeping older adults out of the acute care environment. Two models that are developing these trends include the Program for All-inclusive Care for the Elderly (PACE) in San Francisco (Krane, Illston, Miller, 1992) and Carondelet St. Mary's Professional Nurse Case Management in Tuscon, Arizona (Ethridge, 1991; Michaels, 1991).

Nurses will increasingly be obligated to become social agents in gerontology. State-of-the-art practice, the allocation of resources, and public policy issues require that the professional nurse be actively involved in advocacy for this age group. The ethical and legal considerations will continue to escalate with longer life spans, increasing numbers of frail older people, improved technology, and limited resources.

The need for expertise, manpower, and education of nurses in this area requires more attention to faculty expertise and curriculum development (Nelson, 1992; Yurchuck and Brower, 1990). Only 50% of nurse faculty now have formal gerontology preparation (Malliarakis and Heine, 1990). This has important consequences for both students and clients (Johnson, 1990). Additional attention to gerontology must be provided in staff development and continuing education programs.

The need for more research specific to acute care of the older adult cannot be overstated. There is a need to update current data in the area of gerontologic nursing; descriptive research could provide a stronger base for planning in the acute care environment. Assessment tools, as well as tools for managing and measuring status for this age group, need to be developed or refined; many of the tools that are available were developed for the middle-age adult. Development of assessment tools that evaluate domains of cognitive functioning also is needed. Research to ascertain techniques that assist in maintenance and enhancement of functional ability of the aged is imperative (Danner et al, 1993).

Summary

Virtually all nurses working in the medical-surgical acute care setting will care for older adults at some time. Older adults constitute a heterogeneous group of clients whose needs challenge the skills of the professional caregiver. The rapid changes in the acute care environment need to accommodate the biopsychosocial and spiritual needs of this group of clients.

Specific client care issues in the acute care environment include learning needs, decision making and self-care, iatrogenic illness, ethical-legal concerns, and the critical care issues of the traditional geriatric triad: falls, changes in cognitive status, and continence. There are specific acute care–oriented accommodations that need to take into account the complexity and diversity of characteristics existing in older adults. Nursing care overall must reflect a positive attitude toward the aging process.

Care of the older adult in the future acute care environment will increasingly be a challenging role for the nurse. The numbers and complexity of conditions presented will be balanced by new knowledge, skills, research opportunities, and technology—this is an exciting time to be a health care provider for the older adult population.

Key Points

- Adults over age 50 use nearly 65% of hospital services, and 80% of those over the age of 65 have a chronic illness or functional disability.
- Using a functional model of care along with a medical model ensures a discharge from the acute care facility with the concerns of both medical and functional stability being met.
- The physical and social environment in which care occurs must be modified to facilitate maintenance of function and reduce the incidence of iatrogenic complications.
- The nurse, knowing the changes associated with aging, should be an advocate for appropriate care and treatment from all disciplines.

- The challenge in developing a continuum of care includes developing effective communication systems to ensure integration of all services within the acute care center and the community.
- Adaptations can be made to support and facilitate learning in the older adult via the sensory, motor, and cognitive systems. However, the nurse must be aware that knowledge is only one aspect of client behavior. Other barriers to compliance must be assessed as well.
- Older adults are vulnerable to the consequences of iatrogenic immobility and polypharmacy, which precipitate a vicious circle, with one treatment or lack of treatment causing another symptom.
- Ethical and legal guidelines help caregivers weigh the benefits and difficulties of treatment while protecting the dignity of the client and family.
- Knowledge of specialized geriatric assessment components, as well as an awareness of presentation differences, is needed for accurate assessment and the prevention of emergent, sometimes fatal, complications in this client population.
- Three conditions that require special attention during the hospitalization of older adults are falls, changes in cognitive status, and incontinence.

Critical Thinking Exercises

1. You have just admitted a 93-year-old woman to your nursing unit. In what ways will you have to modify the hospital physical and social environment to accommodate the needs of this client? Why are such modifications necessary?
2. An 86-year-old man is being treated for a cardiac disorder. He is alert and interested in his care, but has a hearing deficit. On teaching him about his cardiac medications, he often gets confused about the dosing schedules, and the names and side effects of each medication. Offer several strategies to assist him to remain independent and to maintain accurate medication schedules and monitoring.
3. A 78-year-old woman has been admitted to your unit for urosepsis and dehydration. She has been transferred to the acute care setting from a long-term care facility. She has no relatives in the immediate area. At times, she has difficulty making decisions about her care. As her nurse, what is your responsibility to this client other than providing for her physical needs?

REFERENCES

American Hospital Association: *National hospital panel survey report,* Chicago, 1992, The Association.

American Nurses' Association: *Standards and scope of gerontological nursing practice,* Chicago, 1987, The Association.

Bahr RT: Selected ethical and legal issues in aging. In Baines EM: *Perspectives on gerontological nursing,* Newbury Park, Calif., 1991, Sage.

Becker PH: Advocacy in nursing: perils and possibilities, *Holistic Nurs Pract* 1:54-63, 1986.

Brady R et al: Geriatric falls: prevention strategies for the staff, *J Gerontol Nurs* 19(9):26-32, 1993.

Buckwalter KC, Stolley JM: Iatrogenesis in the elderly, *J Gerontol Nurs* 17(9):3, 1991.

Burgener S, Shimer R, Murrell L: Expressions of individuality in cognitively impaired elders, *J Gerontol Nurs* 19(4):13-22, 1992.

Burke MM, Walsh MB: *Gerontological nursing,* St. Louis, 1992, Mosby.

Butcher T: Caring for the elderly, *J Emerg Med Serv* 15(12):56-74, Dec 1990.

Butler R: A disease called ageism, *J Am Geriatr Soc* 38:178-180, 1990.

Calvani D, Douris K: Functional assessment: a holistic approach to rehabilitation of the geriatric client, *Rehabil Nurs* 16(6):330-335, 1991.

Carty GES, Day SS: Interdisciplinary care: effect in acute hospital setting, *J Gerontol Nurs* 19(3):22-32, 1993.

Collier JAH, Schirm V: Family-focused nursing care of hospitalized elderly, *Int J Nurs Stud* 29(1):49-57, 1992.

Creditor M: Hazards of hospitalization of the elderly, *Ann Intern Med* 118(3):219-223, 1993.

Danner C et al: Cognitively impaired elderly: using research findings to improve nursing care, *J Gerontol Nurs* 19(4): 5-11, 1993.

Dellasega C et al: Nursing process: teaching elderly clients, *J Gerontol Nurs* 20(1):31-38, 1994.

Dugan J, Mosel L: Patients in acute care settings: which health care services are provided? *J Gerontol Nurs* 18(7):31-36, 1992.

Ethridge P: A nursing HMO: Carondelet St. Mary's experience, *Nurs Manage* 22(7):22-27, 1991.

Foreman M: Acute confusional states in hospitalized elderly: a research dilemma, *Nurs Res* 35:34-37, 1986.

Foreman M: Complexities of acute confusion, *Geriatr Nurs,* 11(3):136-139, May-June, 1990.

Frengley J, Mion L: Incidence of physical restraints on acute general medical wards, *J Am Geriatr Soc* 348:565-568, 1986.

Freundl M, Dugan J: Urinary incontinence in the elderly: knowledge and attitude of long-term care staff, *Geriatr Nurs* 13(2):70-75, 1992.

Fulmer TT, Walker MK: Lessons from the elderly boom in ICU, *Geriatr Nurs* 11(3):120-121, 1990.

Granger CV, Albrecht GL, Hamilton BB: Outcome of comprehensive medical rehabilitation: measures of PULSES profile and Barthel index, *Arch Phys Med Rehabil* 60:145-154, 1979.

Guse L, Degner L: Nurses as advocates and social agents. In Corr D, Corr C: *Nursing care in an aging society,* New York, 1990, Springer.

Hoenig HM, Rubenstein LZ: Hospital associated deconditioning and dysfunction, *J Am Geriatr Soc* 39:220-222, 1991.

Holloway CM, Pokorny ME: Early hospital discharge and independence: what happens to the elderly? *Geriatr Nurs* 15(1):24-27, 1994.

Huber M, Kennard A: Functional and mental status outcomes of clients discharged from acute gerontological versus medical/surgical units, *J Gerontol Nurs* 17(7):20-24, 1991.

Huey F: Everyday heroes, *Geriatr Nurs,* 12(3):107, May/June 1991.

Johnson MA, Connelly JR: *Nursing and gerontology status report,* Washington, DC, 1990, Association for Gerontology and Higher Education.

Joint Commission for Accreditation of Healthcare Organizations, *Accreditation manual for hospitals,* Oakbrook Terrace, Ill., 1995, The Commission.

Kane R, Illston L, Miller N: Qualitative analysis of the Program of All-inclusive Care for the Elderly (PACE), *Gerontologist* 32(6):771-780, 1992.

Kane VL: Listening to older patients, *Health Manage Q,* pp 11-15, Third quarter, 1993.

Katz S et al: Studies of illness in the aged: the index for ADL: a standardized measure of biological and psychosocial function, *JAMA* 185:914-919, 1963.

Kenny T: Erosion of individuality in care of elderly people in hospital: an alternative approach, *J Adv Nurs* 15:571-576, 1990.

Kickbusch I: Involvement in health: a social concept of health education, *Int J Health Educ* 24:3, 1981.

Kovner AR: *Health care delivery in the United States,* ed 4, New York, 1990, Springer Publishing.

Kroenke K, Penholt E: Reducing polypharmacy in the elderly, *J Am Geriatr Soc* 38(1):31-36, 1990.

Lawton HP, Brody EM: Assessment of older people, self maintaining and instrumental activities of daily living, *Gerontologist* 9:179, 1969.

Lincoln R, Roberts R: Continence issues in acute care, *Nurs Clin North Am* 24(3):741-754, 1989.

Linn MW, Linn BS: The rapid disability rating scales: 2, *J Am Geriatr Soc* 30(6):378-382, 1982.

Malliarakis DR, Heine C: Is gerontological nursing included in baccalaureate nursing programs? *J Gerontol Nurs* 16(6):4-7, 1990.

Meehan J: ANA files brief in right to refuse treatment case, *Am Nurse* 10:3, 1989.

Meissner P et al: Maximizing the functional status of geriatric patients in an acute community hospital setting, *Gerontologist* 29(4):524-528, 1989.

Michaels C: A nursing HMO—10 months with Carondelet St. Mary's hospital based nurse case management, *Aspen's Advisor Nurse Exec* 6(11):1-4, 1991.

Miller C: *Nursing care of older adults: theory and practice,* Glenview, Ill., 1990, Scott Foresman.

Miller MB: Iatrogenic and nursigenic effects of prolonged immobilization of the ill aged, *J Am Geriatr Soc* 23:360-369, 1975.

Mion L et al: A further exploration of the use of physical restraints in hospital patients, *J Am Geriatr Soc* 37:949-956, 1989.

Neelon V, Champagne M: Managing cognitive impairment: the current bases for practice. In Funk SG et al, editors: *Key aspects of elder care,* New York, 1992, Springer Publishing.

Nelson M: Geriatric nursing in the baccalaureate curriculum, *J Gerontol Nurs* 18(7):26-30, 1992.

Newman M, Lamb G, Michaels C: Nurse case management, *Nurs Health Care* 12(8):404-408, 1991.

O'Brien M: Dealing with delirium, *Postgrad Med* 91(4):463-470, 1992.

Papougenis D: Restraint alternatives for common challenges—parts 1 to 3, *Untie Elderly Newslett* 3:3, 1991.

Pfeiffer E: *Functional Assessment Inventory,* Tampa, Fla., 1982, University of South Florida College of Medicine.

Phillips L: The elderly, the nurse, and the challenge. In Corr D, Corr C: *Nursing care in an aging society,* New York, 1990, Springer Publishing.

Pohl JM, Boyd CJ: Ageism within feminism, *Image* 25(3):199-203, 1993.

Rappaport S (speaker): Treatment of infections in the elderly, *Seventeenth annual VAMC geriatric medicine seminar,* Dayton, Ohio, 1992.

Ryder RL: End of life issues—a practice perspective, *J Prof Nurs* 8(4):199, 1992.

Schainer JS: Environments for nursing care of the older client, In Chenity WC, Stone JT, Salisbury SA: *Clinical gerontological nursing,* Philadelphia, 1991, WB Saunders.

Schilke JM: Slowing the aging process with physical activity, *J Gerontol Nurs* 17(6):4-8, 1991.

Schirm V, Collier JH: Nurses' involvement of families in care of hospitalized elders, *J Nurs Care Qual* Special Report:36-43, 1992.

Stolley J et al: Iatrogenesis in the elderly: drug related problems, *J Gerontol Nurs* 17(9):12-17, 1991.

Strumpf NE, Evans LK, Schwartz D: Physical restraint of the elderly. In Chenitz WC, Stone JT, Salisbury, SA: *Clinical gerontological nursing,* Philadelphia, 1991.

Travis S, More S: Nursing and medical care of primary dementia patients in a community hospital setting, *Appl Nurs Res* 4(1):14-18, 1991.

US Department of Health and Human Services: Interpretive guidelines for February 2, 1989. In *Health Care Financing Administration Medicaid state operations manual,* Rockville, Md., 1988, The Department.

US Department of Health and Human Services: *Clinical practice guideline: skin care in adults,* 1992a, Rockville, Md., Agency for Health Care Policy and Research.

US Department of Health and Human Services: *Clinical practice guideline: urinary incontinence in adults,* 1992b, Rockville, Md., Agency for Health Care Policy and Research.

US Department of Health and Human Services: *Healthy people 2000: national health promotion and disease prevention objectives,* Boston, 1992c, Jones & Bartlett.

Warshaw G (guest lecture): *Medical assessment in the geriatric client,* course material, University of Cincinnati, Cincinnati, Ohio, 1985.

Wells T: Managing falls, incontinence, and cognitive impairment: nursing research. In Funk SG et al, editors: *Key aspects of elder care,* New York, 1992, Springer Publishing.

Yurchuck ER, Brower HT: Faculty preparation for gerontological nursing, *J Gerontol Nurs* 20(1):17-24, 1990.

Zimbelman J: Good life, good death, and the right to die: ethical considerations for decisions at the end of life, *J Prof Nurs* 10(1):22-37, 1994.

CHAPTER 32

Home Care

LEARNING OBJECTIVES

On completion of this chapter, the reader will be able to:

1. Discuss why care of older adults in their homes or in a community setting is a timely and important option.
2. Describe a profile of the "typical" noninstitutionalized older adult including common diagnoses and functional limitations.
3. Discuss community-based long-term care, including the need, funding mechanisms, profile of services and housing options.
4. Analyze the role of informal caregivers, their characteristics, the demographics of caregiving, the tasks involved, trends influencing caregiving, and the impact of caregiving.
5. Distinguish the categories and types of home care organizations in existence.
6. Explain the benefits of home care compared with hospitals or nursing homes.
7. Describe the process to follow for continuity of care from hospital to home care.
8. Discuss the role of various disciplines on the home care team.
9. Identify the three ways home care agencies are regulated.
10. Discuss ways in which quality is assured in home care.

This chapter focuses on care of the older adult in home and community settings. Topics to be covered include health care needs of community-living older people, community-based services, the role of family members and friends in providing informal care, and the role of home care agencies and home health nurses in community-based care for this population.

THE OLDER POPULATION

Age Distribution

The United States is an aging society. The older population is growing at a rate that surpasses all other age groups, and this trend is expected to continue into the next century. Of the total U.S. population of 252.7 mil-

TABLE 32-1

Age Distribution of the Population Over 65 (1991)

Age range	Number (in thousands)	Percent of population over age 65	Percent of U.S. population
65 to 74	18,280	57.6	7.2
75 to 84	10,314	32.5	4.1
85 or >	3,160	9.9	1.3
TOTAL	31,754	100	12.6

From the US Bureau of the Census: *Statistical abstracts of the United States,* ed 12, 1992, The Bureau.

lion, 31.8 million people (12.6%) are over the age of 65 (US Bureau of the Census, 1992). This reflects an increase in the over-65 population of almost 59% since 1970 and 24% since 1980, compared with an increase of 9% for the population under age 65. In fact, since 1900 the *percent* of Americans age 65 and older has tripled (from 4.1% to 12.6%) and the *number* has increased over 10 times (from 3.1 million to 31.8 million) (American Association of Retired Persons [AARP], 1992). See Table 32-1 for age distribution of the population over 65 as of 1991.

Not only are there more Americans over the age of 65, but the age composition of this group has changed dramatically. Compared with 1900, the older population is made up of more individuals over the age of 85, and in fact, this segment of the population (sometimes referred to as "frail" older adults) is the fastest growing segment of the entire U.S. population. The older population will continue to grow in the future, although the rate of growth will diminish. Fig. 32-1 illustrates the projected growth of the U.S. population over the age of 65. By the year 2050, there will be about 79 million older people, two and one half times the number in 1991, representing almost 21% of the U.S. population (AARP, 1992).

Living Arrangements

Only 5% of the population over age 65 resides in institutional settings, but this percent increases with age from 1% of people age 65 to 74 years, to 5% of people 74 to 84 years, and to 25% of people 85 years and older (*A profile of older Americans,* 1992). Because this chapter is focused on care of older people in home and community settings, all of the data presented is for the *noninstitutionalized* portion of the older population.

Among those age 65 and older, 67% live in a family setting, either with a spouse or with other relatives. However, there are significant differences in living arrangements by gender. Of men, 82% live in family settings compared with only 56% of women. As seen in Table 32-2, more women than men live alone and the majority of men live with spouses (US Bureau of the Census, 1992). At older age strata, the proportion of those living with other relatives and nonrelatives remains stable for both

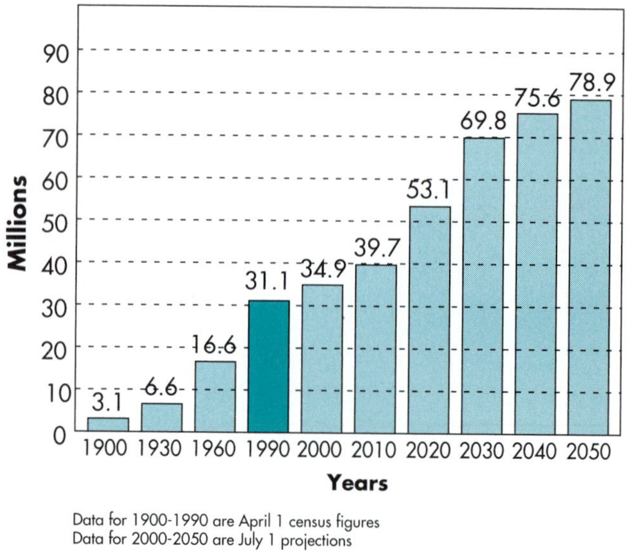

Fig. 32-1 Projected growth of U.S. population 65 and older. (US Bureau of the Census: *Statistical abstracts of the United States,* ed 112, Lanham, Md., 1992, Bernan Press; US Bureau of the Census: *Population projections of the United States by age, sex, race, and Hispanic origin: 1992 to 2050,* Washington, D.C., 1992, US Government Printing Office.

men and women. However, among women, there is a significant increase in the proportion of individuals living alone versus with a spouse. This increase is much smaller for men.

Gender and Marital Status

Of the older population, 60% is female and 40% is male. Women outnumber men in every age category, but the discrepancy increases with increasing age. In the 85-and-older category, there are nearly three times the number of women as men, reflecting the fact that, on average, women live longer than men. As a result of the greater female to male ratio, there are gender differences in marital status among older adults (Table 32-3). Men are almost twice as likely as women to be married, and women are more than three times as likely as men to be widowed. In actual numbers, there are 4.7 times as many widowed women as men (8.5 million versus 1.8 million) (US Bureau of the Census, 1992).

Among those 65 and older, there is an almost equal distribution between women who are married and those who are widowed; the majority of men are married. At older age strata, however, there is a significant increase in the proportion of women who are widowed and a significant decrease in the proportion of women who are married. These changes are much smaller for men.

Racial Composition

Eighty-nine percent of the older population is white. Eight percent are black, whereas other races, including

TABLE 32-2

Living Arrangements of the Population Over 65 (1991)

Living situation	Women Number in thousands (%)	Men Number in thousands (%)
Living alone	7,370 (42%)	2,008 (16%)
With spouse	7,018 (40%)	9,410 (75%)
With other relatives	2,807 (16%)	878 (7%)
With nonrelatives	351 (2%)	251 (2%)
TOTAL	17,546 (100%)	12,547 (100%)

From US Bureau of the Census: *Statistical abstracts of the United States,* ed 12, 1992, The Bureau.

TABLE 32-3

Marital Status of the Population Over 65 (1991)

Marital status	Women Number in thousands (%)	Men Number in thousands (%)
Single	900 (5%)	542 (4%)
Married	7,255 (42%)	9,591 (76%)
Widowed	8,464 (48%)	1,841 (15%)
Divorced	925 (5%)	572 (5%)
TOTAL	17,544 (100%)	12,546 (100%)

From US Bureau of the Census: *Statistical abstracts of the United States,* ed 12, 1992, The Bureau.

American Indians, Eskimos, Aleuts, and Asians/Pacific Islanders represent 3%. Hispanics *of any race* constitute 4% of the population over age 65 (US Bureau of the Census, 1992; AARP, 1992).

QUALITY OF LIFE

Quality of life is a term that describes the intricate relationship between physical health, emotional well-being, life satisfaction, and social and family connections. As life expectancy increases, the quality of later life has become more important. A major determinant of quality of life for older adults is place of residence (Fogel, 1992; Colsher, Wallace, 1990).

Place of Residence

The majority of older people prefer to live independently in their own homes rather than in institutional settings or with children or other relatives (AARP, 1990). In addition to the financial benefits of home ownership, living in one's own home means maintaining ties with familiar community services, religious organizations, informal support networks, and health care providers. Houses are not merely assets but objects of emotional attachment and a source of meaning, because they are the site of significant life events and memories (Fogel, 1992). Even for those older adults who are not home owners, living independently in an apartment or other dwelling means maintaining privacy and control over one's life, and may provide an adaptive function as older people experience accumulated losses (Rowles, 1993).

This emphasis on independent living has produced a new gerontologic concept—**aging in place.** Aging in place refers to growing older within a specific environmental setting. Aging is a dynamic process, and as people age, their needs for supportive assistance become greater. In the past, there was a tendency to fit the *person* to the *environment.* That is, as older individuals' dependency needs increased, they were relocated from less restrictive to more restrictive environments, for example, from living alone to living with family to assisted living to nursing home care. Aging in place means that older individuals remain "in place" and the environment is modified to meet their changing needs.

This environmental modification includes both structural home modifications as well as provision of informal and formal supports. Indeed, aging in place depends on family support, community services, and adequate financial resources. When an older individual is frail or disabled, aging in place is a function of a family's willingness and ability to provide personal and instrumental care, as well as the availability of appropriate community services. As Morris and Morris (1992) note, "For those who remain in the community despite functional deficits, impaired cognition, and marginal health status, the web of support services must be both complex and continuing." Nurses play a vital role in this "web" of support services, particularly nurses who work in such settings as home care, outpatient clinics, and adult day care.

HEALTH CARE NEEDS OF NONINSTITUTIONALIZED OLDER ADULTS

Common Diagnoses

Noninstitutionalized older adults experience both acute and chronic illnesses, but health problems in the older population are predominantly related to chronic conditions that restrict independent functioning. More than 80% of people over the age of 65 have at least one chronic illness, and multiple illnesses are common among those over age 75. The most common chronic conditions for older adults in 1990 included arthritis (47%), hypertension (37%), hearing impairments (32%), heart disease (29%), orthopedic impairments (17%), cataracts and sinusitis (15% each), and diabetes and tin-

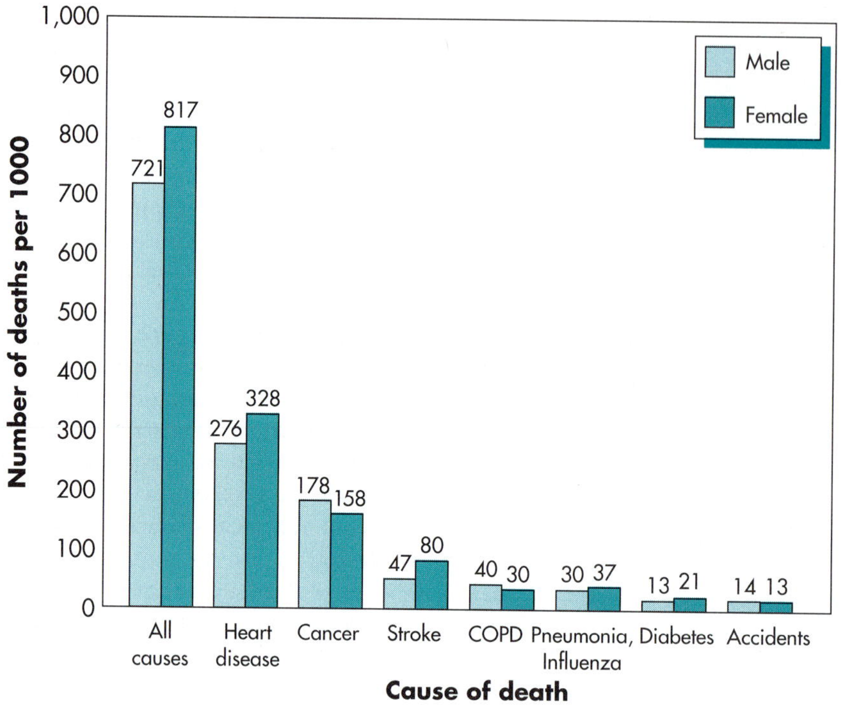

Fig. 32-2 Leading causes of death for people 65 and older. (From US Bureau of the Census: *Statistical abstracts of the United States,* ed 112, Lanham, Md., 1992, The Bureau/Bernan Press.)

nitus (9% each) (US Bureau of the Census, 1992; AARP, 1992). Respiratory infections and injuries were the most prevalent acute conditions among older adults (US Bureau of the Census, 1992).

Major reasons for hospitalizations among older adults are heart disease, cancer, stroke, pneumonia, hyperplasia of the prostate (men), and fractures (women) (National Center for Health Statistics, 1992). The leading causes of death among older adults are heart disease, cancer, stroke, chronic obstructive pulmonary disease (COPD), pneumonia and influenza, diabetes, and accidents (US Bureau of the Census, 1992) (Fig. 32-2).

Although they make up only 12.6% of the U.S. population, older people use a significantly greater proportion of all health care resources. They account for 34% of all hospital stays, 36% of total health care expenditures, and have the highest per capita need for acute and long-term health care (AARP, 1992). Benefits from government programs such as Medicare and Medicaid cover about two thirds of these health care expenditures and the remaining one third is covered by other third-party payors and out-of-pocket payments (US Bureau of the Census, 1992).

Functional Status

Functional status is a term used to describe the ability of an individual to perform the normal, expected, or required activities. In reference to older adults, it refers to the capacity to perform the self-care activities necessary to live independently. Although there is a relationship between acute and chronic disease as well as functional status, disease status does not always predict an older person's level of independent functioning. Functional status is a facet of physical health that must be assessed separately from acute and chronic disease and from physical impairments such as hearing loss or hip fracture.

A variety of measurement tools is available to assess functional status. Some of these tools are more appropriate for research purposes and some are more useful in a clinical setting (see Chapter 4). In general, all of the tools measure either (1) activities of daily living (ADLs), which are essential for personal care such as bathing, grooming, dressing, eating, toileting, walking, and transferring; (2) instrumental activities of daily living (IADLs), which assess one's ability to perform more complex personal, household, and social tasks (e.g., taking medications appropriately, meal preparation, house cleaning/light housework, laundry, handling money, shopping, traveling in the community, using the telephone); or (3) a combination of both ADLs and IADLs.

For the older adult population, adapting to functional limitations is a crucial issue in maintaining independence and is perhaps the most important task of old age. In fact, functional limitations rather than disease status are more predictive of service use, including length of hospital stay, nursing home placement, home health care, and use of supportive community services

(Leon, Lair, 1990). In general, functional measures are much more useful in describing the service needs of older adults living in the community than measures of acute and chronic illness. Because of their ability to predict service needs, functional measures are used to determine eligibility for many state and federally funded community-based, long-term care programs. For example, most federally funded programs dictate that an individual requires supervision or assistance in two out of seven categories of ADLs and/or IADLs to be eligible for benefits.

Cognitive impairment, which often affects an individual's functional status, may be another type of eligibility criterion used by various community programs. Although cognitive impairment alone does not meet the criteria for most home health care services covered by Medicare, many states provide services for individuals with Alzheimer's disease (AD) and related dementias through Medicaid and Medicare waiver programs.

Functional Limitations of Noninstitutionalized Older Adults

Several population-based studies have generated national estimates of functional impairments among those 65 years of age and older.* In general, approximately 21% (5.9 million) of noninstitutionalized older adults experience impairments in ADLs and/or IADLs and for the majority, these impairments are chronic (i.e., have persisted 3 months or more) as opposed to temporary in nature. More older people experience problems with IADLs (18%) than with ADLs (13%), but there is a great deal of overlap between the two types of impairments (Leon, Lair, 1990). In particular, those who experience ADL impairments such as bathing or dressing almost always have difficulty in one or more IADLs. This is because IADLs are tasks that require higher levels of physical and cognitive skills than ADLs. If an older individual is having difficulty with a relatively simple task such as bathing, the person will almost certainly have difficulty with more complex tasks such as shopping or doing laundry.

In addition, the majority of older adults who experience either ADL or IADL impairments have difficulty with more than one task. Of those with ADL problems, 46% have only one problem, 33% have two or three problems, and 21% have four or more problems. Of those with IADL problems, 28% have only one problem, 33% have two or three problems, and 39% have four or more problems (Leon, Lair, 1990). The most common ADL problems are bathing, walking, and transferring; feeding is the least common problem. The most common IADL problems are getting around in the community and shopping, followed by housework and meal preparation; using the telephone is the least common problem.

Age and gender are associated with increased functional dependence. Of people age 65 to 69, 10% are functionally impaired, compared with 57% of those 85 and older (Leon, Lair, 1990). In every age category, higher proportions of women than men have functional limitations. In addition, functional limitations are more common among the black population and those who live alone or with other relatives, and are on Medicaid. To a great extent, these differences reflect age and gender differences in functional status.

Although not specifically assessed in national surveys, cognitive impairments are also associated with functional limitations. For example, individuals with deficits in memory, language, abstract thinking, and judgment have great difficulty executing ADLs or IADLs (shopping, paying bills, preparing meals, and even personal care tasks) even though they may have no *physical* impairments or disabilities. Cognitively impaired individuals often need supervision and cuing, rather than physical assistance, to perform ADLs and IADLs.

The key facts summarized in Box 32-1 suggest that to be effective, informal and formal support services must be ongoing, must be directed toward both instrumental as well as personal care needs, and must target the oldest old and those in lower income levels. IADLs are distinct from ADLs and require very different types of supportive services. IADLs must be attended to consistently, but not necessarily, on a daily basis. They also do not require special training or sophisticated skills. In contrast, ADLs must be attended to daily and the person providing the assistance may require special training, for example, in transferring or toileting techniques. The majority of individuals who only require assistance with IADLs get their needs met exclusively through formal services. However, almost no one who requires assistance with three or more ADLs can remain in the community with formal services alone; they must rely on informal care

BOX 32-1

Key Facts About Functional Status in Older Adults

- Functional impairments are chronic as opposed to time-limited problems.
- Most older people experience impairments in *both* ADLs and IADLs.
- Most older people experience impairments in more than one area of ADL or IADL activity.
- Functional impairments are associated with increasing age, poverty, female gender, and cognitive deficits.

*Such population-based studies include the following: National Health Interview surveys, National Health and Nutrition Examination surveys, National Long-Term Care surveys, National Medical Expenditure surveys, and National Nursing Home surveys.

BOX 32-2

Services for Older Individuals

Access services
Case management
Information and referral
Transportation

Community-based services
Adult day care
Congregate nutrition programs
Elder abuse/protective services
Health screening/wellness promotion services
Housing services
Institutional respite care
Legal assistance
Multipurpose senior centers
Psychologic counseling
Retirement planning

In-home services
Home-delivered meals
Home health services
Home hospice care
Homemaker services
Home maintenance and repair/chore services
In-home respite care
Personal emergency response systems
Telephone monitoring and friendly visitors

provided by family and friends (Guralnik, Simonsick, 1993). What is not yet clear is the cost effectiveness of providing increasing amounts of formal and informal services to maintain older adults in the community.

COMMUNITY-BASED LONG-TERM CARE

Overview of Long-Term Care

Long-term care refers to medical and nonmedical services provided over extended periods of time to chronically, functionally impaired people, most of whom are old. These services enable individuals to live in the community for as long as possible. The goal of long-term care is not to cure but to promote rehabilitation, restoration, maintenance of function, and minimization of decline. Long-term care for older adults consists of three major types of services: (1) *formal institutional* services, primarily nursing home care; (2) *formal noninstitutional* services, primarily community and home-based services; and (3) *informal noninstitutional* services provided by family and friends. The focus of this chapter is on formal and informal noninstitutional services provided in home and community settings (Box 32-2).

Noninstitutional long-term care encompasses a broad range of services from "high-" to "low-tech," delivered in a variety of community settings, addressing health-related and social needs, and using both formal and informal providers. Because our health care system does not have an integrated structure of community services, there is a great deal of geographic variability in the types of community services available, eligibility criteria, and reimbursement mechanisms. This variability or fragmentation of services means that there are situations in which services overlap as well as gaps in service delivery.

Because of this fragmentation, noninstitutional long-term care depends on coordination of efforts between informal and formal care providers. In some instances, families function as case managers, assuring that resources and services are provided appropriately. In other situations, case management services are provided by formal organizations such as home health care agencies or managed care agencies. Nurses who work in community and home health settings play a key role in coordination of formal and informal services. These nurses must be familiar with community resources and should assist older individuals and their families to access these resources. Home health nurses have a particular responsibility to evaluate the need for additional services, to identify appropriate community resources, and to initiate the referral process.

Funding Mechanisms for Long-Term Care

Of all of expenditures for long-term care, 80% are for institutional services and only 20% are for noninstitutional community and home-based services (Short, Leon, 1990). Medicare is designed primarily to cover hospital care for acute illness and its home care benefit is targeted at people who have short-term skilled care needs. Medicaid provides greater coverage for long-term, nonskilled and custodial care, but the emphasis is on institutional (nursing home) settings. In 1993 only 36% of federal and state long-term care expenditures were for home care, the majority of which was for Medicare postacute benefits (Weiner, Illston, Hanley, 1994). There is growing awareness, however, that institutional settings are not the ideal or preferred settings for older people, and there is a trend toward the provision of more noninstitutional long-term care services. The diagnosis related groups (DRGs) emphasis on early hospital discharge, increased appreciation of quality of life issues, and the desire to age in place have stimulated development of community and home-based services to meet the needs of older individuals. In addition, there has been a steady increase in federal funding of formal noninstitutional services through social services block grants (Title XX), the Older Americans Act of 1965, and the Department of Veterans Affairs (Short, Leon, 1990).

This trend toward formal, noninstitutional long-term care services is reflected in proposals for national health care reform. Advocates of health care reform acknowledge the need for a long-term care program that is responsive to the needs of people with functional impairments, cognitive deficits, and chronic illnesses as well as acute illnesses. Long-term care benefits are being defined more broadly to include a variety of community and home-based services necessary for noninstitutional living (American Medical Association [AMA], 1993; Weiner, Illston, 1994). These include nonmedical services such as personal care and homemaker/chore services, as well as ongoing skilled nursing care and case monitoring for high-risk individuals. Although many of these services already exist, they are not covered benefits under current private and public funding mechanisms.

Profile of Community- and Home-Based Services

Area Agencies on Aging

The major goal of the Older Americans Act (OAA) of 1965 was to remove barriers to independent living for older individuals and to ensure the availability of appropriate services for those in need. The act established a national network of federal, state, and Area Agencies on Aging (AAAs), which are responsible for providing a range of community services for older adults. The OAA requires that each AAA designate community "focal points" as places where anyone in the community can receive information, services, and access to all of a community's resources for older people. Multipurpose senior centers often serve as these "focal points" but community centers, churches, hospitals, and town halls may also be designated as "focal points." The types of services provided through the OAA and AAAs include information and referral for medical and legal advice; psychological counseling; pre- and postretirement planning; programs to prevent abuse, neglect, exploitation; programs to enrich life through educational and social activities; health screening and wellness promotion services; and nutrition services (*Community-based services under the OAA and other programs,* 1993).

Multipurpose Senior Centers

Senior centers are community facilities that provide a broad range of services to older adults in the community. These services include health screening; health promotion and wellness programs; social, educational, and recreational activities; congregate meals; and information and referral services for older individuals and their families. Senior centers are used primarily by relatively active and independent older adults. Nursing care and custodial care services are not provided by senior centers. Older adults who require these types of services would benefit from attending an adult day care program. Funding for senior centers is provided primarily through the OAA and agencies such as the United Way.

Adult Day Care

Adult day care programs provide a variety of health and social services to older adults who live alone or with family in the community. Most people who use adult day care are physically frail and/or cognitively impaired and require supervision or assistance with ADLs. Day care programs help delay institutionalization for older people who require some supervision but do not need continuous care. This allows family members to maintain their lifestyles and employment and still provide home care for their older relative. Most adult day care programs operate 5 days per week during typical business hours, and usually charge on a per diem basis. Key services include transportation to and from the facility, assistance with personal care, nursing and therapeutic services, meals, and recreational activities. Adult day care programs vary considerably in terms of eligibility criteria and the types of services they provide.

Adult day care programs are not federally regulated but may be licensed and/or certified by the state. Certification is required to receive federal funding such as Medicaid, Veterans Administration (VA), and OAA funding. Medicaid is a major funding source for most of these programs; however, participants usually pay some part of the fee. Private sources of funding include foundations, religious organizations, businesses, and the United Way.

Respite Care

Respite care provides short-term relief or time off for people providing home care to an ill, disabled, or frail older adult. Adult day care programs are a form of respite on a regular basis. Respite is also provided at home and in institutional settings such as specially designated hospital or nursing home units. Respite staff include both health professionals and trained volunteers. In-home and institutional respite may be provided on a regular schedule, for example, 4 hours per week or for longer time intervals such as a week or a weekend on an intermittent basis.

Hospice Care

Hospice care offers comprehensive programs of health care in home or institutional settings for the terminally ill and their families and is usually available 24 hours a day, 7 days per week. Most hospice providers are Medicare-certified and are affiliated with a home-health care organization.

Home Health Care

Home health care is one of the oldest and most familiar community-based services used by older adults. It consists primarily of skilled nursing and medical services, as well as personal care services such as bathing and feeding provided by home health aides. Most older adult home health care services are funded through the Medicare program, which targets its services to people with short-term, medically-oriented needs, usually following a hospitalization. For a more detailed discussion on hospice care, home health care, and Medicare criteria, see Home Care, pp. 929-931.

Homemaker Services

Homemaker services include such things as housecleaning, laundry, food shopping, meal preparation, and running errands. Fees vary according to the types and frequency of services provided and are usually not covered by Medicare or Medicaid. Reduced-rate or free programs may be offered through local AAAs.

Home Maintenance and Repair/Chore Services

These are services for maintaining the physical and structural environment of the home and they are most useful for older individuals or couples who live alone. These types of services can make the difference between continuing to live independently in one's own home (i.e., "age in place") or moving into more sheltered housing. Services include major and minor household maintenance and repairs; lawn care and yard work; snow removal; and home renovation to make it safer, or more handicap-accessible (e.g., enlarging doorways, lowering counters and cabinets, installing grab bars, handrails, and nonskid tread on floors). Reduced-rate or free programs may be offered through local AAAs.

Nutrition Services

Nutrition services provide older adults with inexpensive, nutritious meals at home or in group settings. Home-delivered meals or Meals-on-Wheels programs deliver hot meals at home once or twice a day, 5 days per week, and can accommodate special diets. Congregate meal sites provide meals in group settings such as senior centers, churches, synagogues, schools, or senior housing. The advantage of congregate meal sites is that they provide opportunities for socialization for those older people who are otherwise socially isolated. Most nutrition programs are free or charge a minimal fee. Nurses need to be aware, however, that some older people view nutrition services as a "handout" and may refuse to participate in these programs.

Transportation Services

Many communities provide transportation services for disabled older adults, either through public or private agencies. Transportation may be by volunteer drivers, bus, taxi, train, or public van equipped to accommodate wheelchairs. The fee for such transportation services is usually minimal and is often based on a sliding scale. In addition, many facilities that serve older adults have their own transportation services (e.g., adult day care, senior centers, and health facilities).

Telephone Monitoring and Friendly Visitors

Telephone monitoring programs provide regular phone contact, usually daily, to older people who live alone or who are alone during the day. The phone calls provide social contact, as well as a check, for those who are concerned about their health and safety. Friendly visitors provide home visits for the purpose of companionship, assisting with correspondence, and assessing needs. Telephone monitoring staff and friendly visitors are volunteers who work through local community organizations such as churches, synagogues, senior centers, and social service agencies. Even if older adults live in areas where these formal services are not available, nurses can encourage informal telephone monitoring and visiting by family members, friends, and neighbors.

Personal Emergency Response Systems

Personal Emergency Response Systems (PERSs) are home monitoring systems that allow an older person to obtain immediate assistance in emergent situations, such as a fall or life-threatening symptoms. A PERS consists of a small device worn on the body which, when triggered, will send an alarm to a central monitoring station. The central monitoring station then contacts predesignated people or the police who respond to the emergency. A PERS can be purchased or leased, and there is usually a monthly monitoring fee. Because these devices are relatively expensive, they are not a practical alternative for older adults in lower-income brackets.

Housing Options for Older Adults

Although most older people prefer to live independently, financial status, functional status, and physical health may dictate consideration of alternative housing options which provide a more protective and supportive environment. Table 32-4 describes the most common housing options for older adults. Each option has its advantages and disadvantages. The decision about which option is most appropriate must consider such factors as the amount and type of assistance the older person requires, financial resources, geographic mobility, preferences for privacy and social contact, and the types of housing available. The American Association of Retired Persons (AARP) has several publications that describe each of these options in greater detail, including issues to consider when evaluating each of the options.

Use of Community and Home-Based Services by Older Adults

Of the 5.9 million noninstitutionalized people age 65 and older who experience functional impairments in

TABLE 32-4

Housing Options for Older Adults

Type of housing	Description of housing
Accessory apartments	An accessory apartment is a self-contained apartment unit within a house that allows an individual to live independently without living alone. It generates additional income for older homeowners, and it allows older renters to live near relatives or friends and to remain in a familiar community.
Board and care homes (also called assisted-living facilities, personal care homes, sheltered care, residential care or domiciliary care facilities)	A rental housing arrangement that provides a room, meals, utilities, as well as laundry and housekeeping services for a group of residents. These facilities offer a homelike atmosphere in which residents share meals and have opportunities to interact with each other. What distinguishes these facilities from simple boarding homes is the fact that they provide protective oversight and regular contact with staff members. Some facilities offer additional services such as nonmedical personal care (bathing and grooming), and social and recreational activities. In many states, these facilities operate without specific regulation or licensure, so the quality of service may vary a great deal.
Congregate housing	Congregate housing was authorized in 1970 by the Housing and Urban Development Act. It is a group-living arrangement, usually an apartment complex, that provides tenants with private living units (including kitchen facilities), housekeeping services, and meals served in a central dining room. It is different from Board and Care facilities, because it provides professional staff such as social workers, nutritionists, and activity therapists who organize social services and activities.
Elder Cottage Housing Opportunity (ECHO)	These are small, self-contained portable units that can be placed in the back or side yard of a single family dwelling. The idea was developed in Australia (called "granny flats") to allow older adults to live near family and friends, but still retain privacy and independence. ECHO units are distinct from mobile homes in that they are barrier-free and energy efficient units specifically designed for older or disabled people.
Foster home care	Foster care for adults is similar in concept to foster care for children. It is a social service administered by the state that places an older person who needs some protective oversight and/or assistance with personal care into a family environment. Foster families receive a stipend to provide board and care, and older clients have a chance to participate in family and community activities. Adult foster care is appropriate for older adults who cannot live independently but who do not want or need institutional care.
Homesharing	Homesharing involves two or more unrelated people living together in a house or apartment. Homesharing takes many forms. For example, it may involve an older and younger person living together or it may involve two or more older people living together. It may involve sharing all living expenses, sharing rent only, or exchanging services for rent. For the older homeowner, renting out a bedroom generates revenue that may make it possible to afford taxes and home expenses. Homesharing is viewed by many older people as a practical alternative to moving in with adult children. Some communities provide house-matching programs, usually sponsored by local senior centers or AAAs.
Life Care or Continuing Care Retirement Communities (CCRCs)	These facilities are designed to support the concept of "aging in place." That is, they provide a continuum of living arrangements and care, from assistance with household chores to nursing home care, all within a single retirement community. Residents live independently in apartments or houses and contract with the community for specified health and social services as needed. If a resident's need for health and nursing care prohibits independent living, the individual can move from a residential unit to the community's health care unit or nursing home facility. In addition to providing shelter, meals, and health care, CCRCs provide a variety of services and activities such as religious services, adult education classes, a library, trips, and recreational and social programs. The key attribute of CCRCs is that they guarantee a lifetime commitment to take care of an individual as long as they remain in the retirement community. The major disadvantage of CCRCs is that they can be quite expensive; most CCRCs require a nonrefundable entrance fee and charge a monthly assessment, which may increase.

Modified from AARP: *Tomorrow's choices,* Washington, D.C., 1988, The Association; *Your home, your choice,* Washington, D.C., 1984, The Association; *Staying at home: a guide to long-term care and housing,* Washington, D.C., 1992, The Association.

CULTURAL AWARENESS

Community-Based Long-Term Care for Hispanic Older Adults

The number of Latinos older than 65 is projected to increase by 500% by the year 2030. In a national survey of 2,299 Latinos (of any Hispanic ancestry, but predominantly Mexican-American and Puerto Rican-American) age 65 and older, Wallace and Lew-Ting (1992) found that Latinos have higher rates of disability than their white counterparts and a higher need for community-based long-term care.

Two major factors influence the interest and ability of Latino families to seek formal long-term care: cultural and structural.

Cultural influences include the belief systems and preferences that cause certain patterns of health care use. Because long-term care often involves nontechnical assistance that can be provided by family members, Latino older adults tend to use nursing homes less often as family members make sacrifices to help older relatives. More acculturated families provide lower levels of care and less informal support for older adults than less acculturated ones.

Structural influences include the way the health care system and other social institutions are organized and operated. They may present both incentives and barriers to the use of health services. Given the importance of income and insurance in determining long-term care use, there is a major gap in the health insurance status of Latino older adults. In the general population, one third of Latinos are uninsured, compared with 13% of whites or 19% of African Americans. This is largely because Latinos are concentrated in industries such as personal services and construction that do not offer insurance and because they live in states—Texas and Florida—with stringent Medicaid eligibility criteria. As a result, serious illness in the family is considered a financial problem almost twice as often among Latinos as other whites (39% versus 19%).

Research reveals that the need for in-home health services for older Latinos is substantial. Mexican-American older adults are less likely than the average Latino to use in-home health services despite similar levels of need. Nurses should not assume that Latino families are taking care of their disabled older members simply because of a cultural preference. Nurses should provide information and advice on the use of in-home health services when an older Latino client is physically disabled.

Wallace SP, Lew-Ting C: Getting by at home: community-based term care of Latino elders, *West J Med* 157:337-344, 1992.

CULTURAL AWARENESS

Cultural Self-Efficacy in Caring for Older Adults in Community Settings

Bernal and Froman (1987; 1993) developed the Cultural Self-Efficacy Scale to measure the perceived sense of self-efficacy of community health nurses caring for clients from culturally diverse backgrounds (Black, Latino, and Southeast Asian). In administering the scale to a nationwide sample of community health nurses, the researchers found a rather low level of confidence in the ability of the nurses to care for the three culturally distinct population groups. The highest average responses were for blacks. Each respondent had the most complete history of cultural or ethnic interaction within his or her own cultural group. Diversity of case load also correlated positively, that is, as community health nurses carry more varied client loads, they become exposed to more cultures and have the opportunity to experience success working with those clients in their cultural milieu. The researchers concluded that community health nurses need exposure to the culturally diverse groups that make up their case loads and their communities. The scale could easily be adapted to elicit responses about subgroups, for example, by changing the cultural categories from Latinos to Puerto Ricans, Cubans, Mexican Americans, and so forth. The Cultural Self-Efficacy Scale could be useful in determining the confidence with which nurses care for older adults from various cultural backgrounds in community-based settings.

Bernal H, Froman R: Influences on the cultural self-efficacy of community health nurses, *J Transcult Nurs* 4(2):24-31, 1993; Bernal H, Froman R: The confidence of community health nurses in caring for ethnically diverse populations. *Image: J Nurs Scholarship* 19(4):201-203, 1987.

ADLs and/or IADLs, only 2.1 million (35.5%) receive any formal community-based services. Another 2.1 million people (35.5%) receive only informal care from family and friends, and 1.7 million people (29%) do not receive any services at all. Only 16% of those people who require care receive both formal and informal services (Short, Leon, 1990).

The most recent national data (Short, Leon, 1990) found that the formal service used most routinely was home care, which includes home health care, personal care, and homemaking services. Smaller percentages of older adults used such services as senior centers, nutrition services, transportation services, or telephone monitoring services (Fig. 32-3). Less than 1% of older adults used adult day care. The majority of service users received these services exclusively at home (home care, home-delivered meals, telephone monitoring); about one quarter received services exclusively in the community (senior centers, congregate meals, transportation,

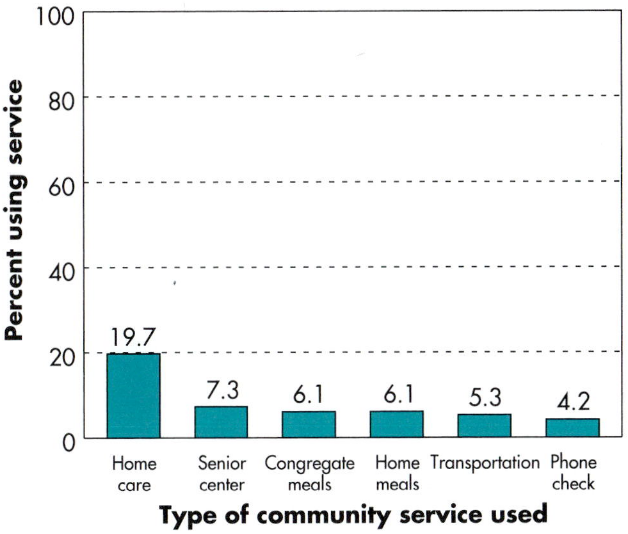

Fig. 32-3 Use of community-based services by functionally impaired people 65 and older (From Agency for Health Care Policy and Research: *National medical expenditure survey* Department of Health and Human Services Pub No [PHS] 90-3466, 1990.)

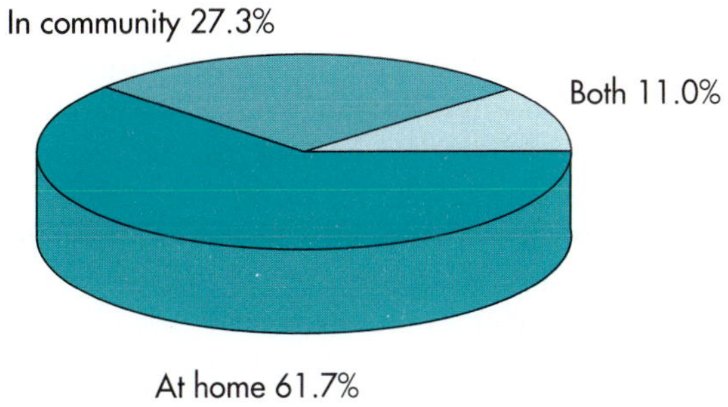

Fig. 32-4 Site of services used by people 65 and older (From Agency for Health Care Policy and Research: *National medical expenditure survey* Department of Health and Human Services Pub No [PHS] 90-3466, 1990.)

and adult day care); and a minority received services in both home and community settings (Fig. 32-4) (see Cultural Awareness boxes, p. 922).

INFORMAL NONINSTITUTIONAL CARE

Reduction in hospital lengths of stay because of implementation of the Medicare Prospective Payment System in 1983, coupled with the sheer increased number of older individuals, has resulted in a population of community-living older people who are more impaired and who have more health care needs than ever before. Older individuals are discharged from hospitals much sooner and much sicker than in the past. Data from the most recent national surveys (Bensen, 1991) indicate that 77.5% of people age 65 and older are discharged directly to home from the hospital, but only 9.4% of these people are referred to home care programs. For people 75 and older, the figure is 12.3%. These are relatively small percentages and reflect the reliance on informal care provided by family and friends and possibly inadequate referral to home health services.

Optimum continuity of care from hospital to home depends on formal linkages between institutional and community systems and between formal and **informal caregivers.** Nurses play a pivotal role in coordinating care between institutional and home settings and in monitoring care delivery in the home setting. This is particularly true for older clients with chronic illnesses whose trajectories are unpredictable or involve acute episodes that result in hospitalization, for example, chronic obstructive pulmonary disease (COPD) or cancer. Although there has been a tremendous growth in home care over the past few years, this growth could not have occurred without reliance on the informal care provided by family and friends. Indeed, Schirm (1990) uses the term "shared caregiving" to describe the interdependence between family members and nurses in caring for chronically ill older people. Schirm notes, however, that shared caregiving is constrained by a health care system that reimburses only skilled care services and by policies that do not support the complementary roles of formal and informal care providers. A study of 295 Medicare home health beneficiaries (Benjamin, Fox, Swan, 1993) revealed that 85% of study participants discharged from home health care had continuing needs related to medical care or functional status. Study participants relied on informal care or non-Medicare formal services to meet these needs (Box 32-3).

BOX 32-3

Definition of an Informal Caregiver

Informal caregivers provide *unpaid* assistance to another person who has some degree of physical, mental, emotional, or economic impairment that limits independence and necessitates ongoing assistance. Caregivers *provide* and/or *coordinate* services and resources that are needed by the impaired person to remain in the home and community.

Profile of the Informal Caregiver

Most caregivers for older individuals are close relatives. Indeed, one of the functions of a family is to care for and nurture its members. Within a family, the exchange of care is a common occurrence. Yet caring for an ill, frail, or disabled family member shifts the "ordinary exchange of care" into what has been labeled "extraordinary care" (Kingson, Hirshorn, Cornman, 1986). This extraordinary exchange of care refers to situations that are more demanding than the response to everyday needs. Like ordinary exchanges of care, it includes both tangible support and emotional support, but the nature of the support is much different and involves a whole new set of tasks. For example, tangible support now means such things as assisting with ADLs, monitoring and managing symptoms, giving medications, and implementing medical treatments and regimens. It also might involve instrumental tasks to help the person maintain independent living such as shopping, paying bills, preparing food or making telephone calls. Emotional support, which is an important aspect of family care, is extended to include helping the person cope with loss, pain, disability, or chronic illness, and helping other family members cope with the altered situation. These kinds of situations tend to disrupt the family system by (1) disturbing normal patterns of interaction and lifestyle, (2) forcing reassignment of tasks and roles among family members, (3) introducing new tasks and roles depending on the illness or disability; and (4) altering the relationships of family members to the person who is ill and to each other.

Caring for a family member who has a chronic illness or disability requires a significant expenditure of time and energy over long periods, involves tasks that may be new, unpleasant, or uncomfortable, and is often a role that has not been anticipated or chosen (Biegel, Sales, Schulz, 1991). Despite this, families shoulder an enormous amount of the long-term care burden and in fact, have been termed "the first line of defense against institutionalization" (Soldo, Myllyluoma, 1983). Studies of institutionalization among older adults have consistently shown that nursing home placement occurs not because of the severity of impairment or disability of the client, but because the client has no family support system or because of changes in the family support system resulting from death, divorce, and relocation. Given equivalent levels of disability, the most significant predictors of institutionalization are being a widow, living alone, being childless or having fewer children, and having fewer social supports (Foley et al, 1992; Newman et al, 1990; Pearlman, Crown, 1992; Salive et al, 1993) (see Cultural Awareness box above).

CULTURAL AWARENESS

Family Care for Older Adults

Care of older adults by family members in various cultures may be supported for several reasons as:
- A substitute for formal services
- A more affordable alternative
- A caring option consistent with cultural values and preferences
- A means of overcoming language barriers that often are problematic in health care

McKenna MA: Transcultural perspectives in the nursing care of the elderly. In Andrews MM, and Boyle JS, editors: *Transcultural concepts in nursing care*, Philadelphia, 1995, JB Lippincott.

Demographics of Caregiving

National data provide a picture of who the informal caregivers are and what they do (AARP and the Travelers Companies Foundation, 1988; Stone, Cafferata, Sangl, 1987; US Select Committee on Aging, House of Representatives, 1987). Seven million households or almost 8% of all U.S. households contain a caregiver. Although caregiving occurs within the family context, the major responsibility for care usually falls to one person. Even when there are other family members who assist with the care, the *primary* caregiver continues to make most of the decisions and to monitor the care. Only in rare instances do families establish a shared caregiving arrangement.

The racial composition of caregivers closely parallels the racial composition of the general population—80% of white and 20% of other races. Approximately 72% of caregivers are women, primarily wives and daughters, and 28% of caregivers are husbands, sons, and other men. Almost all informal caregivers are related to the care recipient; 36% of caregivers are spouses, 37% are adult children, and 27% are other relatives as well as a small proportion of unpaid, nonrelated helpers. The average age of caregivers is 57, but 36% are age 65 or older. This group of older caregivers is comprised primarily of spouses and children caring for even older parents. In fact, 10% of the caregivers in national studies are individuals age 75 and older caring for spouses or surviving parents. As more people live to very old ages, we will see an increase in this phenomenon of the "young old" caring for the "old old."

Most caregivers have other competing demands on their time. For example, 70% of caregivers are married and a significant proportion have dependent children. In addition, 31% of all caregivers are employed outside the home and this figure increases to 50% when considering adult children caring for older parents. Of course, this is the group (often referred to as the "sandwich generation") most likely to have child care responsibilities as well. Although not addressed in national studies, it is quite likely that adult child caregivers may be caring for more than one older parent simultaneously.

Caregiving Tasks

Caregivers perform a wide range of activities and tasks that are reflective of the impaired person's needs. These activities or tasks can be divided into two broad types: (1) the actual provision of personal, instrumental, and health-related care; and (2) managing the care given by informal and formal providers. National data (Stone, Cafferata, Sangl, 1987; US Select Committee on Aging, House of Representatives, 1987) reveal that the most commonly cited type of assistance was related to household tasks (e.g., meal preparation, laundry, housecleaning), shopping, and transportation. Other tasks often performed by caregivers were assistance with personal care (e.g., feeding, bathing, dressing, and toileting) and indoor mobility. More than half of the caregivers administered medications and injections and provided wound care.

Family members make a long-term commitment to care for their older relatives. The majority of caregivers in national studies had been providing care between 1 and 4 years, whereas 20% had been caregivers 5 years or longer. Eighty percent of caregivers provide care seven days a week and spend an average of 4 hours per day on caregiving tasks. Of interest is the fact that less than 10% of caregivers used formal services. Those who did were caring for the most severely impaired older people and had slightly higher incomes than those caregivers who did not use formal services.

Current Trends That Influence Caregiving

The term "caregiving" has appeared in health care literature only in the past 10 to 15 years. Although family caregiving is not a *new* phenomena, the experience of caregiving is becoming more common, or as Brody (1985) has noted, it is becoming a *normative* experience. Because of a decrease in the death rate, life expectancy has increased significantly, but the age of onset of chronic illness has not been delayed. As a result, there is an increase in the number of older individuals living with chronic illnesses and functional impairments and a consequent increase in demand for family care. Families are providing greater amounts and more complex types of care over longer periods than ever before. At the same time, a number of social trends have decreased the availability of female caregivers who make up the majority of the caregiver population (Himes, 1992). These trends include the following:

1. Changing family structures
   - Women are marrying later in life and are delaying childbearing until later ages, so there is an increased likelihood of overlap between child care and older adult care responsibilities.
   - An increase in divorce rates, a decrease in remarriage rates, and an increase in the number of unwed mothers means that increasing numbers of women are the sole support of families and cannot assume a full-time caregiver role.
   - Lower birthrates and an increase in the number of childless couples will reduce the pool of family caregivers.
2. Increased labor force participation by women and especially by women with children
3. Increased geographic mobility that leads to long-distance caregiving.

Impact of Caregiving

Caregiving is, or will be, a reality for most Americans. It affects families, workplaces, and communities. Caregiving can be considered a "job," and for those who work outside the home, it is like taking on a second job. Becoming a caregiver is an event that usually requires learning new skills, accepting new roles, and readjusting one's lifestyle. Caregiving can be conceptualized as a chronic stressor, an array of demands and hassles that confront the caregiver on a daily basis. Although there are some caregiving situations that stabilize over time and become "routine," most caregiving situations are not stable. The client's condition often becomes progressively worse. With Alzheimer's disease (AD) and other dementias, this progression is slow and unpredictable. As the client's condition deteriorates, the caregiver must continually readjust to the new situation. In this sense, caregiving requires ongoing coping efforts to maintain homeostasis. Caregiving becomes a way of life, and the role of caregiver must be integrated with the individual's many other roles.

Research over the past 10 years has demonstrated that caring for a family member over a long period can produce a number of negative consequences, including psychologic, physical, and financial strains; job conflict; and family disruption.

Psychologic/Emotional Strain

The feelings caregivers experience are in many ways similar to the feelings experienced by the person with the chronic illness or disability. Faced with competing demands, caregivers relinquish opportunities for socialization and recreation. They report feelings of social isolation because of constriction of their social activities and feelings of emotional isolation because others do not understand what they are going through. Caregivers also report feelings of anxiety about the care they are providing, potential problems, financial concerns, concerns about their own health, and concerns about the future. Many caregivers also express guilt that they are not doing enough or that they are not as patient and caring as they should be. Sadness, grief, anger, and decreased life satisfaction are also common among caregivers, especially as they come to terms with changes in their relationships to the clients and changes in their lifestyles.

The most consistent and significant finding among the many studies of caregivers is an increased prevalence of depression or depressive symptomatology compared with the general population. Cross-sectional and longitudinal data document that 30% to 50% of caregivers exhibit depressive symptoms, evidenced by sleep disturbances, fatigue, irritability, mood swings, somatic complaints, decreased appetite, inability to concentrate, and feelings of loss of control (Baumgarten et al, 1994; Schulz, Vistainer, Williamson, 1990; Schulz, Williamson, 1991; Tennstedt, Cafferata, Sullivan, 1992). Some studies have shown a greater use of antidepressants, tranquilizers, sleeping pills, and pain medications among caregivers than among the general population (Clipp, George, 1990).

Dolores, 71, whose husband died of cancer after a long and debilitating illness, provides a classic example of the psychologic effects of caregiving:

> The last few months of his life he was given Dilaudid, which caused him to have hallucinations. His sleeplessness caused my sleeplessness, because he constantly called to me in his drug-laden state. My lack of sleep made deep inroads on my sense of reality. I have several gaps in my memory of that terrible time, probably because I was carrying on as I have been programmed to do, operating at full speed with vastly reduced amounts of energy (Sommers, Shields, 1987).

Physical Strain

Caregiving can be physically stressful, especially for older caregivers or for those whose caregiving tasks include frequent bending, lifting, and moving. In addition, psychologic stress can contribute to stress-related physical problems. For example, some studies have shown a relationship between chronic stress and suppression of the immune system in caregivers of people with dementia (Kiecolt-Glaser et al, 1991; McCann, 1991). Research shows that caregivers have a higher prevalence of self-reported physical symptoms and medication use, and poorer self-rated health than the general population (Baumgarten et al, 1994; Baumgarten et al, 1992; McCann, 1991; Schulz, Vistainer, Williamson, 1990). Physical health problems are even more common among those caregivers who feel less supported by family and friends; who feel more socially isolated; and who are caring for people with cognitive impairments, mood disturbances (e.g., depression, anxiety), and behavior problems (e.g., agitation, aggression, combativeness, wandering) (Clipp, George, 1993; Draper et al, 1992; Silliman, 1993).

For some individuals and in some circumstances, caregiving may precipitate or exacerbate physical illness. Many caregivers report that they do not see a physician on a regular basis and delay seeking treatment for their own health problems. Chronic stress may lead to appetite and sleep disturbances, or inappropriate use of alcohol, tobacco, or drugs. Finally, changes in physical health may occur, because caregivers lack the time or energy to engage in health-promoting behaviors such as exercise, weight control, stress management, or self-examination.

Financial Strain

Caregiving results in many "out of pocket" costs. Of caregivers in one national study (AARP and the Travelers Companies Foundation, 1988), 42% reported incurring additional expenses related to caregiving such as travel, telephone bills, special diets and medications, physician fees, medical equipment, hospital care, in-home nursing care, and other support services. A study of costs of care for people with AD living in the community found that 65% of services provided to clients were paid out-of-pocket by clients and/or their family members (Rice et al, 1993).

Medicare, Medicaid, and most private health insurance companies do not provide the type of home care benefits needed by people with chronic illness or disability. Often, the needs include custodial care of the client and services to support the caregiver, such as respite care, adult day care, and homemaker services. Because these services are not covered benefits, families either pay out-of-pocket or forego using these services. Some insurers are beginning to develop long-term care policies, but their adequacy is yet to be proved.

In the United States, policy makers have begun to explore strategies to encourage and to support family care. These strategies include (1) expanding federal tax incentives for family caregiving, (2) family leave and wage replacement for family caregivers, and (3) direct payments to family caregivers or care recipients (Gerald, 1993). For example, 13 states currently have obtained waivers to allow Medicaid to directly compensate family caregivers, and in 1993, President Bill Clinton signed into law the Family and Medical Leave Act. For businesses with more than 50 employees, this act grants each employee 12 weeks of unpaid leave per year for family or medical reasons while maintaining job benefits and seniority. Small businesses with 50 or fewer employees are exempt.

Job Conflict

Studies of employed caregivers (Creedon, Tiven, 1989; Scharlach, 1994; Stone, Short, 1990) show that they report more job-family conflict and more frequent job stress than noncaregivers. Findings also demonstrate that caregivers use the telephone excessively, make more mistakes, and have higher accident rates, tardiness, and absenteeism than noncaregivers. Employed caregivers use such strategies as unpaid time off, rearranging work schedules, and decreasing their work hours to meet caregiving responsibilities. In addition, the prospect of making work accommodations discourages some caregivers from working at all. This has implications for present and future financial status, because caregivers who reduce their work hours or quit their jobs lose not only current salary but also employment-related benefits and future earnings in the form of pension and social security income.

Some companies have implemented programs and policies to support employed caregivers, but this is not a widespread practice. These employer-sponsored initiatives include (1) policies that support caregiving, such as flex time, family leave, and benefits for part-time workers; (2) financial benefits such as subsidies for respite and adult day care, and dependent care assistance programs that allow employees to place pretax dollars in special accounts to be used for caregiving expenses; (3) caregiving seminars, support groups, and information and referral services offered on-site; and (4) employer-sponsored adult day care and respite services.

Family Disruption

Caregiving occurs within the context of individual and family history, values, and patterns of interaction. The need for caregiving often creates a situational crisis that may reactivate old family patterns of conflict, sibling rivalry, and issues of control and decision making. Even well-integrated and highly functional families can be torn apart when confronted with the demands of caregiving because caregiving necessitates family reorganization. Fifty to 75% of caregivers report making lifestyle changes as a result of caregiving, such as taking fewer vacations and spending less time with family and friends (AARP and the Travelers Companies Foundation, 1988; Stone, Cafferata, Sangl, 1987; US Select Committee on Aging, House of Representatives, 1987). There are more demands on the caregiver's time and possibly on space within the family home, because in the majority of caregiving situations, the care-recipient lives with the caregiver.

In situations where an older person lives far away, family members must arrange long-distance caregiving. If the older person has a well-established social network, the family member may be able to organize this network to provide the needed assistance. If an informal network is not available or is not sufficient to provide the necessary care, formal services need to be identified. A growing number of professionals are offering "long-distance" case management services designed to help family members locate and coordinate social and health care services in another city or state. These types of services support the concept of aging in place; they allow the older person to continue living in their preferred residence and they provide peace of mind to far-away family members. Information about long-distance caregiving is available from AARP and from independently published reference books.

Positive Aspects of Caregiving

Although caregiving can be very stressful, most caregivers also say that they get a sense of satisfaction, pride, gratification, and meaning from their role (Farran et al, 1991; Lawton et al, 1992; Lawton et al, 1991). These positive factors contribute to a sense of caregiver well-being but do not necessarily diminish the stressful aspects of the role. Research has demonstrated that caregiving is a universally stressful experience, even for those people who derive satisfaction and meaning from the caregiver role. Feelings of stress and satisfaction do not represent two ends of a continuum but are feelings that coexist and independently affect the caregiver's physical and psychologic health.

Ethnic Issues in Caregiving

Most caregiving research has been conducted in samples of predominantly white people, so there is little understanding about the dynamics of caregiving in other racial and ethnic groups. Studies of black caregivers have demonstrated that they experience fewer negative consequences related to caregiving; seem to tolerate behavior problems better; use more informal support systems such as friends, neighbors, and church associates; provide home care for longer periods; and use nursing homes less often than white caregivers (Miller et al, 1995; Lawton et al, 1992; McGadney, 1993; Salive et al, 1993; Wolinsky et al, 1994). However, much more research is needed to determine the validity of these preliminary findings.

Caregiver's Needs

Informal caregivers have two basic types of needs of which nurses must be aware: (1) needs related to the care they are providing and (2) personal needs.

Needs Related to the Provision of Care

The first need families may have is in making a decision about home care versus institutional care. If the nurse is working with a family who is facing chronic illness and disability as a *new* situation, the nurse should ask many questions about the home situation and what plans the family has for providing care. Planning is very important *before* assuming the caregiving role. Informal caregivers may have the desire to provide care, but they may not have the resources or capacity to do so. Nurses must help families evaluate the factors that might influence their decision (Box 32-4).

Informal caregivers often receive little or no preparation for home care. The caregiving situation may occur suddenly after a health crisis, leaving little time to plan or prepare. Caregivers want education for their caregiving roles and they expect nurses in hospital and home care settings to provide it (McCann, 1988; Matthis, 1991). This education should begin in the hospital but it

RESEARCH

Matthis EJ: Family caregivers want education for their caregiving roles, *Home Health Care Nurse,* 10(4):19-22, 1992.

Sample, setting

The sample included 441 members of 47 women's clubs randomly selected from 1609 Nebraska Cooperative Extension Women's Clubs. Of these 441 members, 86 (19.5%) were currently providing care to an ill or disabled adult relative and 161 (36.5%) anticipated doing so in the future. Noncaregivers (n = 194; 44% of the sample) were those who were not currently providing care and did not anticipate doing so in the future.

Methodology

All participants completed a questionnaire regarding their needs for education in relation to 45 caregiving tasks in four broad categories: (1) assisting disabled adults, (2) maintaining own well-being, (3) maintaining family well-being, and (4) health and human resources. Participants rated the importance of learning about each of these 45 caregiving tasks on a scale from 1 (no importance) to 5 (high importance). Mean importance scores were calculated for each caregiving task for the total sample and for subgroups of current caregivers, future caregivers, and noncaregivers.

Findings

Noncaregivers did not rate any task item higher than 3. Current caregivers gave 13 items mean importance scores of 4 or greater and future caregivers gave 26 items mean importance scores of 4 or greater. Mean importance scores were computed for each caregiver subgroup on the four categories of caregiving tasks. Analysis of variance revealed no significant differences between current and future caregivers in any of the categories.

Implications

Both current and future caregivers assign great importance to learning about caregiving tasks. Future caregivers had twice as many ratings of 4 as current caregivers, perhaps reflecting the fact that current caregivers have already mastered many caregiving tasks. However, both current and future caregivers had similar topical interests, indicating that it may be appropriate to combine groups for some caregiving educational programs. Home health care agencies need to take a more active role in preparing future caregivers for the caregiver role and in educating them about home health resources and services.

BOX 32-4

Planning for Informal Caregiving

- What is the anticipated illness trajectory?
- Who will be the primary caregiver?
- What sources of informal support are available?
- What skills and limitations does the caregiver have? These limitations might be physical, emotional, financial, or social.
- Will the caregiving role be one primarily of care provider or care manager?
- What does this mean in terms of changes in lifestyle?
- Will the caregiver have to move, quit working, or restrict his or her social life?
- What dynamic factors need to be considered, such as the quality of the relationship between caregiver and client?

is often difficult to anticipate all the problems that may arise in the home setting. Therefore referrals to home health care agencies should be made whenever possible. Caregivers need to know how to give physical care correctly and safely, how to monitor the client for changes in status, and when to seek professional guidance. Potential caregivers should be encouraged to care for clients while they are still in the hospital setting so that they can practice their skills in a supportive environment (Shively, Djupe, Lester, 1993) (see Research box at left).

When working with caregivers and clients with chronic illnesses or disabilities, the nurse must remember that the family is the client. The role of the nurse is to provide services that maximize the family's ability to manage the chronic illness at home, and minimize undue dependency. The nurse must also realize that compromise is necessary. The most appropriate plan for managing the chronic illness may not be the most ideal in terms of the family unit. The goal should be optimum care for the client at the least physical, emotional, and social cost to the family.

Caregivers also have a need for information and assistance in obtaining services necessary to support their caregiving roles (Vinton, 1991). Caregivers often function as case managers, but they have no formal training for this role. Caregivers may not use available services either, because they do not know about them or because they are misinformed about the nature of the service. In addition, the U.S. health care system is characterized by fragmented services and barriers to accessing services for which people are eligible, so caregivers need help in dealing with the complex network of providers, payors, and regulators. Home care nurses often provide case management services for caregivers and their clients.

Caregivers also report that they need positive feedback, reassurance, and appreciation for doing a good job. This support may come from a variety of sources such as the client, other family members, and health professionals. Discharge from home health care is stressful for some caregivers, because it means the loss of an important source of verbal feedback and encouragement. Caregivers need to know that someone else is monitoring the client's care and that they may sometimes feel abandoned after being discharged from home care. This need for support and reassurance is especially important for those caregivers who are providing custodial care over long periods. Unfortunately, the current system of care does not allow for meeting the needs of caregivers and clients on a long-term basis. When the home care is purely custodial, there are no provisions for periodic monitoring to determine if needs have changed, to assist the family with planning for the future, or to provide ongoing education, support, and health monitoring for client and caregiver. To address this issue, Medicare has authorized some home health care agencies to keep selected high risk or potentially unstable cases open to monitor client status and the provision of informal care, and to provide skilled services as needed (Benjamin, Fox, Swan, 1993).

Caregivers' Personal Needs

Nurses need to talk with caregivers about ways to maintain their own physical health and mental well-being. This involves helping caregivers set realistic expectations, ask for help from others, make time for personal needs, identify sources of emotional support, and engage in health promoting behaviors.

Caregivers often set unrealistic expectations of themselves and the care they provide. Some caregivers want to be perfect and may need help identifying at what point things are "good enough." Nurses can help caregivers identify realistic expectations and set limits so that they can conserve time and energy for themselves and other family members. Setting limits may involve making compromises, letting go of some things, family reorganization, and asking others for help. Nurses can help caregivers be creative in problem-solving and can actively enlist the support of other family and friends in the caregiving process. Some caregivers have great difficulty allowing others to participate in the care because of pride, because they want things done in a particular way or because they worry that the client will object. Nurses must assist caregivers to see the benefits of involving others in the care process, perhaps by reinforcing the idea that "caring" encompasses both direct care *and* assuring that care is given by others. Some caregivers want help from others but do not know how to ask for it. Remind caregivers that they must be specific in their requests; family and friends cannot help if they do not know what is needed.

Nurses may also need to talk with caregivers about the importance of personal time each day, even if this is just a 10-minute soak in the tub or a phone call to a friend. Mental breaks can be as important as physical breaks. Caregivers need periodic respite—time away from caregiving without feeling guilty and time that is devoted to personal needs and pleasure rather than household errands or business. This respite may involve having a family member or friend stay with the client, or it may involve using formal in-home or institutional respite care. If the caregiver is not able to sleep undisturbed through the night on a regular basis, the nurse needs to help the caregiver identify solutions such as hiring someone to sit with the client at night. Chronic sleep deprivation can lead to irritability, depression, loss of concentration and judgment, and magnification of feelings such as discouragement and anxiety.

Caregivers may need advice about exercise, nutrition, health care, and managing stress. Home health nurses should take the time to talk with caregivers about how they are feeling, perhaps checking blood pressure or weight, inquiring about their medications, and giving them an opportunity to talk about problems and concerns. Assessing caregivers for symptoms of stress is also important. These symptoms may include the following:

- *Physical:* Headaches, muscle aches, fatigue, loss of appetite, hypertension, frequent colds or influenza
- *Emotional:* Extremes of anger, sadness, anxiety, guilt, loneliness, hopelessness, inability to feel pleasure or joy
- *Mental:* Forgetfulness, difficulty making decisions, inability to concentrate
- *Interpersonal:* Withdrawal, blaming others, impatience, feeling sensitive to criticism
- *Spiritual:* Feelings of alienation, lack of purpose and meaning in life

Caregivers need someone who listens, who lets them talk about their feelings without being judgmental or giving unwanted advice. Nurses are in a good position to do this, because they are usually much more objective than a family member or friend. It may be helpful to discuss with caregivers ways in which they can increase the positive aspects of their situation, such as helping caregivers find pleasure, a challenge, or some sense of meaning or purpose in what they are doing.

HOME CARE

Home care consists of multiple health and social services that are delivered to recovering, chronically ill or disabled individuals of all ages in their place of residence. There are three main categories of home care agencies: home health agencies, home care aide organizations, and hospices. In combination, these three kinds of agencies numbered 13,951 in the United States as of February, 1993 (National Association of Home Care [NAHC], 1993).

Home Health Agency

The predominant and most familiar provider of home care is the home health agency. Home health agencies have as their primary function the treatment or rehabilitation of clients through the intervention of skilled nurses or therapists. Clients admitted to a home health agency must be under the supervision of a physician, and services are provided in accordance with a physician's signed order.

Although a home health agency can provide as little as skilled nursing and one other service, most home health agency services include skilled nursing, physical therapy, speech therapy, occupational therapy, medical social work, and home health care. In addition, many agencies offer nutritional services on a limited basis. Agencies also provide disposable medical supplies as appropriate to the diagnosis and treatment plan for the client.

In a home health agency the unit of service is the visit. The plan of treatment for a client is based on the diagnosis, functional ability, disciplines needed and a proposed number of visits. Box 32-5 provides a typical 62-day certification of a plan of treatment for a client referred because of progressive symptoms associated with Parkinson's disease.

Agencies are most often described and compared on the basis of visits, that is, an agency may be described making 10,000 visits a year. This agency might then be compared in size with another agency making 100,000 visits a year. Fees are established for a visit and usually vary by discipline. Billing to a third party payor or to the client is on the basis of a visit and usually done once per month.

To date, most home health benefits, regardless of payor, have been fashioned after the Medicare home care benefit. As a result, to be eligible for reimbursed services the following criteria must be present:

> . . . the client is *homebound,* meaning that the client leaves his or her home infrequently and only for medically necessary services; the client's condition requires *skilled, intermittent care* to treat the qualifying condition; and the referring *physician approves* the plan of treatment, in writing, and *certifies* that the client is homebound and has a skilled need (JCAHO, 1993).

Home Care Aide Organizations

This category of organization is designed to provide paraprofessional, personal care and support to functionally impaired individuals needing assistance with ADLs. Although assistance with all ADLs is available, the most common services provided are assistance with bathing, meal preparation and housework. There are several categories of paraprofessionals available: home health aides, homemakers, chore housekeepers, and companions or sitters.

Most often, these organizations provide long-term care that is considered neither skilled nor intermittent and therefore not eligible for payment under the Medicare program. Services may be purchased hourly, by the shift, or when a "live-in" is needed, by the day or month. Individuals pay on a fee-for-service basis or, in some cases, the state or other organization contracts with a home care aide organization to provide service by the hour.

BOX 32-5

Certification of Treatment Plan (62 Days)

Skilled nursing

3 to 4 times per week for 2 weeks; 2 to 3 times per week for 2 weeks; 1 to 2 times per week for 4 weeks

Skilled nursing provides skilled observation and assessment of vital signs, urinary and bowel function, ADLs, response to medications and nutritional status, as well as teaching and training for medication management and nutritional compliance.

Physical therapy

2 to 3 times per week for 4 weeks; 1 to 3 times per week for 4 weeks

Physical therapy provides evaluation, therapeutic exercises, transfer training, and home safety evaluation and plan.

Occupational therapy

2 to 3 times per week for 4 weeks; 1 to 2 times per week for 4 weeks

Occupational therapy provides evaluation for adaptive equipment or devices, and ADL training.

Home health aide

3 to 4 times per week for 8 weeks

Home health aide provides assistance with personal care and ambulation, reinforcement of exercises, and occupational therapy plan.

Medical social work

2 to 3 visits total

Medical social work provides counseling for long-range planning and decision making, as well as community resource planning, and evaluates for adult day care.

Insight • *In the almost 30 years since the enactment of the Medicare benefit, home care managers and staff have adopted the Medicare Paradigm. A paradigm is a model, a pattern, or a "set of rules and regulations that define boundaries and tell us how to be successful within those boundaries. Paradigms also act as filters through which we view the world" (Barker, 1989). Applying this concept to home care, managers and staff act as though the only way of delivering home care services is the Medicare way. This Paradigm Effect (Barker, 1989) prevents home care personnel from visualizing other models that could be used to provide home care services, and therefore limits creative solutions to clinical and reimbursement challenges. To read more about paradigms and their influence on the way we view the world, conduct a library search looking under* paradigm *or watch the video tape: Barker JA;* Discovering the future: the business of paradigms, *ed 2, Burnsville, Mn., 1989, Charthouse.*

There is less descriptive information about the type and number of home care aide organizations, since they are not licensed in most states nor are they Medicare-certified. The National Home Caring Council and the JCAHO does accredit home care aide organizations but only at the request of the agency. The National Home Caring Council is working to define and to standardize the training for nonprofessional providers of care in the home. Three categories of workers are being proposed—from an individual providing only supportive services and no personal care, to one who is able to provide complete personal care. Because there is still no consistent standard of training except for home health aides provided by state licensed, Medicare-certified or JCAHO accredited organizations, consumers must be careful who they hire to provide assistance in their homes. Even though there is a "let the buyer beware" caveat, this type of service is essential for many individuals or couples to live independently and for family caregivers who work or are in need or respite.

Hospice

Hospice is a special component of home care for clients in the final stages (usually the last 6 months) of a terminal illness. Medical, social, psychologic and spiritual care services are provided by a team of nurses, social workers, physicians, pastoral care counselors, and volunteers. Other services such as home health aide, nutrition support and therapy are added as the need is demonstrated by the client and family. In a hospice program, only palliative care associated with comfort, pain control and symptoms associated with the terminal illness is provided, although a great deal of psychologic and social support is available to the client and family before, during and after the death.

Home hospice services were included as a Medicare benefit under the Omnibus Budget Reconciliation Act of 1984 (OBRA '84). Since that time, home hospice programs have grown to approximately 1,700 in the United States. By allowing the client to stay home, hospice has become a more humane way to support the dying client and family.

Other Services Provided in the Home

Additional home-based services are growing rapidly. Physician, dentist and podiatric house calls, portable laboratory services, mobile x-ray and other diagnostic testing, monitoring of heart arrhythmias and sleep apnea, as well as home beauty and barber services are all now available.

Although components of the spectrum of home based services, home medical equipment (HME), home oxygen and home infusion supply companies are considered to be vendors of products and not services. When a service such as respiratory therapy is used to monitor home oxygen equipment, it is usually treated as an overhead expense and not billed as a separate visit.

PROFILE OF HOME HEALTH AGENCIES

Proprietary Agencies

A proprietary or for-profit home care agency is designed to make money for its owners. Until 1982, proprietary home care agencies were not allowed to participate in the Medicare program. This was changed in response to a concern that there were not enough home care services available to meet the demand. As a result, OBRA '82 allowed proprietary home care agencies to become Medicare certified, but they were not allowed to make a profit on the Medicare portion of their business. Owners of a for-profit entity are stock holders in the corporation.

Facility-based Agencies

A facility-based home care agency is defined as being a department or component part of an organization. A few facility-based home care agencies are parts of skilled nursing facilities or rehabilitation centers, but in the vast majority of cases, home care agencies are hospital-based, meaning they function as a department of the hospital. They may or may not share clinical, financial, or management services with the hospital. What determines a facility-based home care agency from the Medicare program's point of view is if it receives an allocation of the institution's corporate overhead. A facility-based home care agency, according to JCAHO, shows evidence of an organizational and functional relationship between the home care agency and the facility, or public representation of the home care agency as a service of the facility.

The first hospital-based home care agency was established in 1946. Hospital-based home care agencies were few in number until the enactment of Medicare reform (OBRA '82) when hospitals began to be paid for clients on Medicare on the basis of DRGs. With shorter lengths of stays, hospitals established home care agencies or affiliated with existing home care agencies to provide options for clients who were going home with existing health care needs.

Governmental Agencies

Governmental home care agencies are those operated by a health department or any other governmental organization. In some states, a large proportion of the home care services are provided by health departments. In other states, health departments provide traditional public health services in the home but give little, if any, care to recovering, disabled, or chronically ill individuals.

Visiting Nurse Associations

A visiting nurse association (VNA) or community nursing service (CNS) is a community-based home care agency with a governing board made up of community representatives. Because of the commitment to provide home care services to a defined community and a not-for-profit status, VNAs are often recipients of United Way or Community Givers funds.

Private, Not-for-Profit

A private, not-for-profit, or free-standing home care agency is a corporate entity, owned and operated by an individual or group. The owners of a not-for-profit entity are members of the corporation rather than shareholders. Table 32-5 illustrates the differences in number and percent of each category of agency type. The greatest growth has come as hospitals have established their own home care agency and as proprietary agencies have become Medicare-certified.

Since 1967, the first full year of the Medicare program, the number of Medicare-certified home care agencies has grown by nearly 400%. There were 6,902 Medicare-certified home care agencies, as of August 1993. The number of non-Medicare home care agencies, including home care aide organizations, was estimated to be 6,231, based on a 1993 NAHC survey. Table 32-6 depicts the growth in certified and noncertified agencies from 1967 to 1993.

TABLE 32-5

Number of Medicare-Certified Home Care Agencies by Category

Category	Number	Percent
Proprietary	2,440	35.3
Facility-based*	2,049	29.7
Governmental/public	1,176	17.0
Visiting nurse association	598	8.7
Private, not-for-profit	551	8.0
Other	88	1.3
TOTAL	6,902	100

*Includes hospital, rehabilitation, and skilled nursing facility–based agencies
From NAHC: *Basic statistics about home care,* Washington, D.C., 1993, The Association.

TABLE 32-6

Number of Certified Home Health Agencies, Hospice Programs, and Other Noncertified Agencies* from 1967 to 1993

	Certified		Noncertified
Year	HHA	Hospice	Other
1967	1,753	DNA†	DNA
1977	2,496	DNA	DNA
1987	5,785	DNA	DNA
1988	5,794	DNA	DNA
1989	5,676	597	4,824
1990	5,695	774	5,296
1991	5,780	898	5,755
1992	6,004	1,039	5,454
1993	6,497	1,223	6,231

*Includes home health agencies, home care aide organizations, and hospices that do not participate in the Medicare program
†Data not available
From NAHC: *Basic statistics about home care,* Washington, D.C., 1993, The Association.

Benefits of Home Care

In survey after survey, older Americans chose home as their treatment place of choice. Because of changes in technology, equipment is smaller, easier to manage and less expensive. As a result, individuals who at one time could only be treated in the hospital can now be managed at home. Family, friends, and even clients themselves can be taught to manage enteral and parenteral feedings, central lines, pain control, antibiotic therapy, and urinary catheters with a minimum of assistance.

Among those older adults who can benefit from home care services are people with the following circumstances:

- Have chronic medical conditions such as congestive heart failure (CHF), COPD, brittle diabetes, kidney and liver disease with subsequent transplantation, AD, sequela from strokes
- Have chronic mental illnesses such as depression, schizophrenia, and other psychoses
- Need additional assistance to live alone because of age, illness, disability, short-term memory deficit or confusion
- Need continued treatment after discharge from a hospital or nursing home
- Require short-term assistance at home after same-day or outpatient surgery, are terminally ill and want to die, or their family wants them to die with dignity and in the comfort of their own home

Home care is less expensive than hospitalization in most cases. For example, considerable savings can be achieved through the use of home care services with infusion therapy vendor support.

Although home care services are being used for the financial considerations, there are also sound medical and humane reasons for treatment to take place in a person's home. There is evidence that people recover faster at home than in institutions and nosocomial infections from exposure to multiple infectious processes are minimized in a person's home.

CONTINUITY OF CARE

Enhancement of the **continuum of care** from hospital to home is a goal shared by both hospital and home care personnel. According to Evashwick and Weiss (1987), continuum of care can be defined as "an integrated, client-oriented system of care composed of both services and integrating mechanisms that guides and tracks clients over time through a comprehensive array of health, mental health and social services spanning all levels of intensity of care." To assure that a continuum of care exists from hospital to home, the "Plan, Do, Check, Act Cycle" in Box 32-6 should be followed.

Box 32-7 contains a listing of client characteristics that should suggest further evaluation for a home care referral. Whether this assessment is done as a prehospitalization screening, at the time of admission to the hospital, after a client's condition has changed or as the client is being discharged is not the issue. What really matters is that the assessment for home care needs is done by someone before the client leaves the hospital (Box 32-7).

Ideally a client is screened for home care needs at the time of admission to a hospital to ensure adequate time to plan for continuity of care. In most cases, unless a client is already known to a home care agency, discharge planning occurs late in the hospital stay. As hospital lengths of stay are becoming shorter and shorter, the time available to adequately plan for a client's postdischarge care is limited. Home care agencies and hospital discharge planners or utilization managers need to develop a good working relationship to assure that client's going home have a plan that picks up where the hospital plan left off. To ensure a smooth transition from hospital to home, all disciplines—nurses, physicians, physical therapists, social workers, etc.—who were providing care to the client in the hospital should provide qualitative and quantitative information about the client's disposition at discharge. In addition to demographics, examples of necessary information are as follows:

- Identification of the physician who will be signing the home care orders
- A description of the client's knowledge about the disease and the treatment
- A summary of the client's independence with certain skills
- Quantitative measures of range of motion and client response to treatment modalities
- Identification of known social situations that could complicate or could hinder the home treatment plan

BOX 32-6

Plan, Do, Check, Act Cycle

Plan

Gather data on admission
Identify goals for discharge
Identify specific functional problems
Validate that a problem exists
Structure problems by delineating components

Do

Gather information about resources
Select all possible options
Identify measurable objectives in terms of the client's functional problems
Analyze each option for capacity to fulfill objectives
Identify advantages and disadvantages

Check

Compare alternatives for probability of fulfilling discharge objectives
Project results of alternatives
Explore alternatives with the client and family
Choose among alternatives

Act

Develop the discharge plan
Implement the plan
Evaluate and follow-up on the plan
Revise the plan as indicated
Update the resource file

BOX 32-7

High-Risk Client Indicators for Home Care Services

Inadequate social and financial support system
Lack of family and significant others
Verbal or physical abuse by family or significant others
History of neglect—self-neglect or caregiver unable or unwilling to provide care
Mismanagement of finances
Family requiring substantial teaching and assurance
Home safety concerns
Potential future placement needs
Unexpected readmission to the hospital within 15 to 30 days
Frequent readmissions

Alteration of health care problem or management
Change in mental status
Frequent readmissions
Noncompliant behavior before or during hospitalization
Comatose states, AD, stroke, syncope, dementia, etc.
Rapidly failing eyesight
Increased anxiety
Postsuicide attempt
History of substance abuse
Terminal or preterminal condition

Inability to perform self-care activities
Bedridden status
Wheelchair-bound
Seen in the hospital by physical, occupational, or speech therapy
Postamputation
Post-hip or knee replacement
New assistive devices
Foley, ileoconduit, suprapubic catheter, incontinence
Do Not Resuscitate (DNR) or Do Not Intubate (DNI) orders

Complex health management regimen
Enteral or parenteral feedings
Ostomies or tubes of any kind
Draining wounds
Postwound debridement or irrigation and debridement for decubiti
Pain management
Intravenous (IV) antibiotics
Hickman, peripherally inserted central catheter (PICC) Landmark insertion
IV chemotherapy
Lab acquisition and monitoring
Multiple medications or major medication change
Ventilator dependent
Oxygen dependent
Hemodialysis or peritoneal dialysis
Sepsis
Low-air loss bed or other complex medical equipment

- A list of supplies and/or medications sent home with the client
- Identification of expectations for rehospitalizations or follow-up clinic visits.

Anything that would enhance a timely and efficient response from a home care agency would be valuable information.

Role of the Home Care Agency

Occasionally there is a need for the home care agency to visit the client while still in the hospital or while a client is visiting the physician's office. In these cases, home care agencies usually make a predischarge visit to assess client needs, learn a new treatment or technique, or reassure the client and family about the postdischarge plan.

Admission to the home care agency begins with referral intake. Referrals are most often called to the agency. After the referral information has been received, the agency confirms home care benefits, schedules the admission visit consistent with the expectation of the discharge planner, physician, or client, and communicates the referral information to the nurse who will be admitting the client into service. The most common way to assign clients to nurses is by geographic area. In some cases, assignments are based on the special needs of a client and assigned to specialty groups. Examples of specialty groups include infusion therapy teams, psychiatric teams, orthopedic or rehabilitation teams, and hospice or terminal care teams.

Home Care Admission

At the time of admission to the home care agency, assessment information is obtained to establish the plan of care, and certain information is provided to the client and family. Although a nurse usually conducts the initial assessment and establishes the plan of treatment, each professional discipline also conducts an assessment for their treatment plan. The initial assessment varies from agency to agency, but the usual components consist of demographic information, chief complaint, history of present illness and past medical history, known allergies, family and household history, review of systems, life system profile to include ADLs and IADLs, and home and neighborhood safety, formal and informal support systems to include a caregiver assessment, economic and financial factors, spiritual/religious beliefs, and identification of client/family concerns and/or questions.

A statement of client rights and responsibilities is explained and left in the home. Information about the agency hours, how to reach the agency, and the various providers of care during working hours and after hours is given to the client and caregivers. In some states a "hot line" number is available should a client have a problem that cannot be resolved by the agency. Clients are also given information and counseled about advance directives. Examples of advance medical directives (AMDs) that a client may have specified include a living will; durable power of attorney for health care; and DNR and DNI orders (see Chapter 3).

Insurance Coverage

Nearly all clients over age 65 are covered by Medicare. To be eligible for Medicare home care benefit, the client must meet certain criteria. Clients must be *homebound*, which means they have physical (i.e., they are bedridden, wheelchair-bound or reliant on assistive devices) or medical conditions that limit the ability to leave home (and when they do so it is only for medical care). The client's condition must warrant a *skilled, intermittent service*, which is defined by Medicare as skilled nursing, physical therapy or speech therapy. If there is a "skilled need," the client is eligible for the other reimbursable services such as occupational therapy, medical social service, and home health services. Intermittent services are defined as "more than one," unless the provider intended to make additional visits and, because of a client-specific reason, could not. The client must also have a *physician's written plan of treatment* for the service, frequency and duration of care provided. Although these criteria are specific to the Medicare benefit, many other payors such as Medicaid, Blue Cross/Blue Shield, and other commercial plans have designed their home care coverage after the Medicare plan. The future of home care coverage under redesigned health care plans is being debated. What is certain is that there will be home care coverage, but probably not without a strategy to limit the use.

IMPLEMENTING THE PLAN OF TREATMENT

Role of the Physician

According to a recent AMA publication (1992), the physician's role as a member of the home care team is to prescribe the home care plan of treatment. The document further specifies that the physician's role includes the following:

- Management of medical problems
- Identification of the client's home care needs
- Establishment/approval of a plan of treatment with identification of both short- and long-term goals
- Evaluation of new, acute, or emergent medical problems based on information supplied by other team members
- Provision for continuity of care to and from all settings (e.g., institution, home, and community)
- Communication with the client's team members and with physician consultants
- Support for other team members
- Participation, as needed, in home care/family conferences
- Reassessments of care plan, outcomes of care
- Evaluation of quality of care
- Documentation in appropriate medical records
- Provision for 24-hour, on-call coverage by the physician (AMA, 1992)

Role of the Nurse

The registered nurse (RN), in most cases, conducts the initial evaluation visit after a client has been referred for home care. During the initial visit and appropriate subsequent visits, the nurse assesses the physical, functional, emotional, socioeconomic, and environmental well-being of the client. Nurses initiate the plan of care and make revisions as appropriate and necessary throughout the length of stay in home care.

Other activities requiring the specialized skill of registered nurses include the following:

- Health and self-care teaching
- Coordination and case management of complex care needs
- Medication administration and teaching
- Wound and decubitus care
- Urinary catheter care and teaching
- Ostomy care and teaching
- Laboratory services
- Pre- and postsurgical care
- Care of the terminal client

Additional activities provided by some home care nurses include the following:

- Case management
- Intravenous (IV) therapy, enteral and parenteral nutrition, and chemotherapy
- Psychiatric nursing care
- Case management (see Research box, p. 936).

Characteristics of a Home Care Nurse

Nurses who work in home care are required to have a diverse set of skills and abilities. Many say that home care nurses must be generalists, that is, they must know a lit-

RESEARCH

Martin KS, Scheet NJ, Stegman MR: Home health clients: characteristics, outcomes of care, and nursing interventions, *Am J Pub Health,* 83(12):1730-1734, 1993.

Sample, setting

This study examined 2403 clients served by four home health agencies in Nebraska, New Jersey, and Wisconsin (two large urban agencies and two small rural agencies). Clients were predominantly older women (average age of 68.6 years), married or widowed, and 85% Caucasian.

Methodology

Over a 2-year period, the Omaha System was used to provide descriptive data about the characteristics of home health clients, the nursing services they receive, and the outcomes of care. The Omaha System is a comprehensive documentation scheme composed of three parts: (1) *Problem Classification Scheme* - a client-focused taxonomy of nursing diagnoses classified into four global domains (physiologic, psychosocial, environmental, and health-related behaviors); (2) *Problem Rating Scale* - for each health problem identified, clients receive a numeric rating from 1 to 5 on three subscales that measure their knowledge, behavior, and current status; (3) *Intervention Scheme* - a hierarchical organization of problem-specific nursing plans and interventions in four categories (surveillance; health teaching, guidance, and counseling; treatment and procedures; and case management).

Findings

Of the clients, 60% were partially or totally dependent and required a spouse or adult child to serve as primary caregiver. Mean length of service was 35 days, and clients experienced an average of four problems. The most common problems were in the physiologic (71%) and health-related behaviors (23%) domains. The most common interventions used were surveillance (59%) and health teaching, guidance, and counseling (26%). In all four home health agencies, mean ratings for knowledge, behavior, and status increased significantly from admission to discharge.

Implications

Study results support the feasibility of using the Omaha System to describe and quantify nursing practice in a home health setting. Results also establish a relationship between nursing services and client outcomes and suggest that home health services positively affect client outcomes.

tle about a lot of things. Although the majority of clients in a home care nurse's caseload are 65 or older with multiple chronic diseases, the rest of the caseload is likely to be diverse. The home care nurse must be able to apply all aspects of the nursing process to meet the needs of an often diverse older adult caseload. Home care referrals for this population might include the following: acute or chronic medical condition management, multiproblem families, pre- and postoperative surgeries, infectious disease, terminal illness, and problems of a serious psychiatric nature. The home care nurse must coordinate care with all disciplines involved with the case and must report findings, changes, and recommendations to the primary physician. The home care nurse must also work cooperatively with community resources and governmental agencies if a situation warrants. The nurse, often the sole health care provider visiting a client's home, knows that observations made must be acted on immediately and the instruction provided must last until the next visit. If emergency hospitalization is required, the nurse will coordinate it with the family, the physician, the hospital and the emergency services. In some cases, nurses must not only look out for the client's safety but for their own as well. Some neighborhoods are dangerous. Some clients are combative. Some homes do not meet minimal hygienic standards. Sometimes visits are needed in the evening or night. The home care nurse must be self-reliant, self-assured and comfortable providing care in the client's locale. Not all nurses are comfortable in the home and community but those who believe it to be the best way to practice nursing.

Role of the Physical Therapist

The physical therapist (PT) evaluates and treats clients by providing the following services:

- Teaching and assisting with gait, transfers, stair climbing, wheelchairs, and all other mobility needs
- Assessing for needed assistive devices and arranging for the necessary equipment
- Providing therapy exercises for range of motion, strength, and endurance
- Providing pain management using physical modalities and agents such as ultrasound and transcutaneous electric nerve stimulation (TENS)
- Providing caregivers with lifting and handling techniques
- Conducting a presurgical evaluation of function and environment
- Providing special exercise programs designed for cardiac clients
- Providing pulmonary physical therapy

PTs can provide other services as appropriate for clients with special needs or order from physicians who have special requirements for the client's plan of treatment.

Role of the Occupational Therapist

The occupational therapist (OT) works with clients to improve, regain or retain their ADLs and IADLs:

- Feeding
- Toilet transfers and toileting
- Dressing
- Tub transfers and bathing
- Meal preparation
- Doing housework
- Money management
- Shopping

The OT provides home programs to maximize ADLs and IADLs and teaches ways caregivers can reduce stress and injury. The OT also attends to adaptive methods such as the following:

- Adaptive device training
- Home safety
- Energy conservation
- Joint protection methods
- Splinting and designing orthotics
- Developing techniques for the visually impaired

Sometimes clients require the services of a psychiatric OT. Among other services, the psychiatric OT plans, implements, and evaluates therapeutic activities designed to improve a homebound psychiatric client's level of functioning.

Role of the Speech Pathologist

The speech pathologist provides the following services for home care clients:

- Swallowing evaluations
- Instructing client/family in compensation techniques
- Providing language evaluation and treatment
- Providing cognitive-linguistic evaluation and treatment
- Assisting with augmentive communication for clients with a tracheotomy or on a ventilator

Role of the Medical Social Worker

The social worker in home care provides the following services:

- Psychosocial assessment of a client and family situation
- Counseling for a client or family
- Referrals to community resources such as homemakers, Meals on Wheels, and financial resources
- Nursing home placement
- Assistance with a guardianship process
- Assistance with referrals for housing
- Assistance with referrals for adult day care programs
- Assistance with long-term planning
- Assistance with AMDs

Role of the Home Health Aide

The home health aide is a nonprofessional caregiver who has completed a course of study and has been certified. In addition, a home health aide is required to complete at least 12 hours of inservice training each year of employment. According to the U.S. Department of Labor Bureau of Statistics (1993), the job of the home health aide is the fastest growing occupation today and that growth is expected into the next decade. Under the direction of an RN, home health aides assist clients with intermittent personal care services such as ADLs and hygiene, take vital signs, perform simple duties such as nonsterile dressing changes or Foley catheter care, provide assistance with medications that are normally self-administered and report changes in the client's condition or needs. Home health aides must be supervised by an RN at least every 2 weeks.

Role of the Dietitian

At times, it is necessary to provide additional nutritional assessment and evaluation when a client's condition warrants. Although this is an infrequently used service, and not reimbursable under the Medicare benefit, home care agencies usually have a dietitian available to consult with the nurse or with the client and family.

HOME CARE MANAGEMENT AND SUPPORT

Governing Body

Home care agencies that are Medicare-certified, state licensed or accredited are required to have a governing body. The governing body has the legal authority and responsibility for the operation of the agency. Federal, state, or accreditation standards require only that there must be a governing body but do not state how that body is constituted. A governing body can, therefore, consist of a single person or numerous representatives. A proprietary agency may have as its governing body the officers of the corporation. A VNA may have a large community-based board as its governing body representing consumers and community. A hospital-based agency, as a department of the hospital, is governed by the hospital's board of trustees. Under regulation, the governing body has several specified tasks: it oversees the management and fiscal affairs of the home care agency, it appoints a qualified administrator, it appoints and receives reports from a professional advisory board or otherwise arranges for professional advice, and it adopts and reviews written bylaws or the equivalent. The governing body is responsible for assuring the quality of the agency, its people, and services.

Advisory and Evaluation Function

Medicare regulation, some state licensure rules, and accreditation organizations require that professional advice be available to the governing body and agency management. In most agencies, a professional advisory board is appointed by the governing body. This group is often comprised of professionals representing the various disciplinary services provided by the agency. A typical professional advisory board is made up of nurses, physicians, therapists, one or more social workers, and one or more consumer representatives. Consumer representation is essential for an agency to be advised on how care is delivered and what services are needed. Often, the consumer representation comes from current or former recipients of care—a client, a spouse, other relative, or friend of a client.

Policy and Procedure

Home care agencies are required to comply with accepted professional practice standards and principles of safe and appropriate client care. To this end, an agency must have a system for assuring that all professional agency personnel are currently licensed or certified, meet the appropriate health standards, and follow agency clinical policies and procedures that are consistent with state law and accepted standards of care. An agency must also have standards for recording clinical findings and interventions in the client's clinical record and a process for assuring the confidentiality of that record. Agencies must also have policies and procedures that address personnel issues, billing and financial activities, and general business practices.

Regulation

There are three kinds of regulation that can affect how a home care agency functions: certification, licensure, and accreditation.

Medicare Certification

To participate in the Medicare programs and be reimbursed for providing services, a home care agency must be Medicare-certified. The certification process occurs at the time an agency makes application to participate in the Medicare program and at least yearly thereafter. The rules and regulations are clearly specified in a Medicare manual (HIM-11), and the criteria for the yearly recertification process and procedure are also available to the agency. Recertification is done on-site at the agency. Surveyors assess the structure, process, and outcome of service delivery by reviewing key agency documents, making home visits, interviewing staff and clients and reviewing client records. If deficiencies of concern are noted, the surveyors may schedule return visits throughout the year or may even deny or may revoke an agency's participation in the Medicare program.

State Licensure

Some states require home care agencies to be licensed. The rules and regulations for licensure in most states closely follow the Medicare requirements and often the state licensure and the Medicare certification process occur at the same time by the same surveyors. States have the option to adopt regulations that differ or are more stringent than the Medicare guidelines. In a case where the state has more exacting regulations, the agency is required to meet the state requirements.

Accreditation

The two organizations accrediting home care agencies include (1) the JCAHO and (2) the Community Health Accreditation Program (CHAP) through the National League for Nursing (NLN).

Consumers and purchasers of home care services are demanding validation that care and services are of the highest quality. By establishing standards or "statements of expectation that define the structures and processes that must be substantially in place in an organization to enhance the quality of care" (JCAHO, 1993), and requiring regular on-site evaluation based on the standards, the accrediting body can provide minimum assurance that an agency is providing a quality service. Accreditation is currently an elective process for most home care agencies. The exception is for a facility-based agency whose facility is accredited by the JCAHO. In that instance, the home care agency is required to become accredited.

QUALITY ASSESSMENT AND IMPROVEMENT

A major emphasis within most home care agencies and the focus of public concern is the assurance that the home care products and services are of consistently high quality. In addition to regulation and accreditation, agencies have elected to monitor their quality in several ways.

Utilization Review

The purpose of utilization review activities is to verify the appropriateness of services delivered to clients. Both the quality and quantity of services are monitored as open and discharged charts are reviewed by a team of professionals. Utilization review activities are usually conducted on a quarterly basis but special reviews can be done at any time. Focused reviews such as a review of all clients with human immunodeficiency virus (HIV), acquired immunodeficiency syndrome (AIDS), or all hip fracture referrals can be conducted as a check of a special program or a specific diagnosis. Unless a focused review is being conducted, client charts are selected at random and the care, as documented, is compared with selected criteria. Reports of the findings are reviewed by management, the professional advisory board, and the governing body. Adverse findings are addressed through a correction plan.

Quality Monitoring

Quality assurance activities may be approached in many different ways as long as the purpose is to set standards and monitor care delivery against those standards. Each agency identifies the standards that are of interest and concern. Indicators of quality are established and the monitoring processes are set into place. As health care has begun to know and to understand the need for continuous quality improvement, the principles of quality management are being used.

Home care is made up of multiple systems which are dependent on one another to function well. The process of admitting a client to home care, for example, is dependent on a timely and accurate referral from hospital discharge planning, scheduling the admission visit, relaying accurate information to the admission nurse, informing the client or family of the date and time of the visit, having the appropriate assessment tools and forms at the time of the visit, conducting a thorough and accurate assessment, verifying financial information, developing the plan of treatment and timing of the next visits, documenting that visit, submitting the paperwork in a timely manner, informing the physician and additional home care personnel of the findings, and sending for physician orders. If any of these steps are not done on time or not done at all, the system could fail. Present quality assurance activities are aimed at improving systems by improving team functioning, using objective measures of system success or failure, and understanding that customer satisfaction is the ultimate gauge of a quality organization.

Because customer satisfaction is so important to home care agencies, a great deal of emphasis is placed on determining what the customer needs and wants. Client and other customer satisfaction surveys are one common way to measure satisfaction. Quality can also be assessed through the use of customer focus groups, periodic telephoning of customers to allow them to comment on their care (clients) or the care of their clients (physicians), discussions with staff about how to improve care, and benchmarking other agencies that have a good reputation or are known for doing certain things well.

Insight • *Cost, quality, and access are the goals of health care reform. The challenge for home care is to provide a high-quality and accessible service at an affordable price. To meet this challenge, home care agencies must continuously look for new ways to package, price, and evaluate their services. Development of critical pathways alone or with a hospital is one approach being used by home care agencies. The pathway provides a predetermined and consistent approach to care delivery that can be more easily evaluated, analyzed for its cost and marketed to third-party payors. To read more about critical pathways conduct a library search looking under: critical pathways; case management tools; CareTracs; or Care Maps™*

Summary

The majority of the noninstitutionalized population over age 65 is made up of white women who are either married and living with spouses or widowed and living alone. At older age strata, there is a significant increase in the number of women who are widowed and living alone. As the U.S. population continues to age, the health care system will be challenged to meet the diverse and changing needs of older individuals in home and community settings.

The health care needs of a growing, noninstitutionalized older adult population, coupled with rapid, evolving change in today's health care delivery system, demand continued exploration of alternative services and delivery mechanisms that support the care of older people in home and community settings. This chapter explored the current health care needs of community-living older people, community-based services, the role of family members and friends in providing informal care, and the role of home care agencies and home health nurses in community-based care for this population.

The need for programs and services aimed at supporting older people and their caregivers in the community setting will continue to grow. Options for care must expand, and nontraditional alternatives must be developed for the use of various health care personnel. The reimbursement structure is currently, and will clearly continue to be, challenged to accommodate these developments.

This is an exciting and challenging time for the community-based gerontologic nurse. Meeting the diverse and complex needs of the community-residing older adult clearly requires self-direction and self-reliance, but

BOX 32-8

Case Study

The following situation depicts how a team of home care providers coupled with client determination can accomplish more than any one discipline working independently.

Situation

Mrs. K is a 66-year-old Polish housewife who suffered a left cerebrovascular accident (CVA) on February 25. Her hospitalization consisted of a stay in acute care followed by an extensive stay in rehabilitation. She was discharged to home with a referral to home care on May 1. On admission to home care, the nurse's assessment indicated Mrs. K had right hemiparesis and aphasia. She had bowel and urinary incontinence (UI) with an indwelling Foley catheter. Her blood pressure was 150/92, apical pulse 76, respiration 18, and temperature 98.0° F (36.6° C). These vital sign findings remained consistent throughout the initial stages of her home care program. She also complained of gastrointestinal (GI) pain. Her behavior was described as labile with periods of agitation, tearfulness, hyperventilation and impulsivity. She required 24-hour supportive care with maximum assistance with ADLs. She wore a right short leg brace and a sling to prevent subluxation of her right arm. A wheelchair, hospital bed, and commode were ordered by the hospital discharge planner to aid Mrs. K's care. She was given prescriptions for the following nine medications:

- Folic acid 1 mg, PO, QD
- Colace 240 mg PO, QD
- Dulcolax suppository ½ to 1 PR, Q AM PRN
- Pepcid 40 mg, PO, QHS, PRN
- Chloral hydrate 500 mg, PO, QHS, PRN
- Enteric-coated ASA 325 mg, PO QD
- Metamucil 1 tbsp., PO, QD, PRN
- Milk of Magnesia 2 tbsp., PO, PRN
- Norvasc 5 mg, PO, QHS

Although Mrs. K had the support of two sons and her sister, the primary caregiver was her 69-year-old retired husband. Mr. K wanted his wife at home but had no experience or desire to assist with caregiving. This attitude made it more difficult for the home care team to develop and to implement the plan of care.

Because of the severe sequela of the stroke, the following services were ordered:

- **Nursing:** One to three times per week to observe vital signs, to assure medication compliance, to assess bowel and bladder function, to change Foley catheter, and to begin bowel training program
- **Physical therapy:** Two to three times per week to decrease spasticity, to increase range of motion, and to increase endurance
- **Speech pathology:** Two times per week to improve communication abilities
- **Occupational therapy:** Two to three times per week to assess and to reinforce ADLs
- **Medical social work:** Two to four times per month to assist with community resources and possible placement in a nursing home
- **Home health aide service:** Three to four times per week to assist with personal care

Early in the home care program, it was determined that Mrs. K's labile behavior was interfering with her home rehabilitation program. She cried easily, became agitated, and would hyperventilate when frustrated. When transferring or walking she would anticipate the next move before it was time to move, thereby increasing her risk for falls and injury. The hyperventilation interfered with therapy, so whatever treatment being conducted would have to stop until she became calm and ready to continue. After some discussion of this problematic behavior, the team determined that teaching Mrs. K to breathe slowly, deeply, and through pursed lips would diminish the hyperventilation. This technique was successful to the point that Mrs. K was able to independently recognize when she was beginning to hyperventilate and would then stop herself. A psychiatric OT was able to provide additional assistance to Mrs. K and the team to minimize the additional labile behaviors. During this time, the primary nurse was able to assist Mrs. K with a bowel and bladder program and was able to successfully remove the Foley catheter. Bowel control was achieved through dietary changes and consistent use of the commode. Mrs. K's blood pressure was also under control and her GI upset was diminished by consistently eating breakfast.

The home health aide worked with physical and occupational therapy to reinforce the exercises and safe transfer techniques. Since the aide was assisting with personal care, she was able to reinforce physical and occupational therapy exercises while assisting with transfers, walking, and bathing. The aide reported that Mrs. K wanted to use the bathtub and recommended that placement of the commode in the tub could allow Mrs. K to safely transfer to the commode and then into the tub. This observation and recommendation from the home health aide greatly enhanced Mrs. K's progression with self-care activities.

Although team members worked on their individual treatment plans, they also shared observations and planned combined goals with Mrs. K. Her husband, however, would distance himself from the planning and indicated that he wanted to be only minimally involved with her treatment. He did, however, reiterate his commitment to have her at home and "try to make it work."

With the active involvement of all the team members, Mrs. K made significant progress toward independence. She had progressed from using only the wheelchair to a hemi-walker, and was ready to begin training with a four-prong cane when her husband died suddenly, October

BOX 32-8

Case Study—cont'd

10, having recently been diagnosed with pancreatic cancer. This unexpected event caused Mrs. K to become depressed and to regress in her progress. The team requested the involvement of a psychiatric nurse to work with Mrs. K on the grieving process and to conduct a suicide risk assessment. Mrs. K had made suicidal statements that alarmed several of the team members. Although it is usually necessary to have a psychiatrist involved when a psychiatric nurse makes visits, in this case, the psychiatric nurse visited in place of the primary nurse and also provided medical/surgical nursing services. The psychiatric nurse made three visits, working with Mrs. K on the grief process, planning for the upcoming holidays, and dealing with issues of altered body image brought on by the stroke. Mrs. K shared her concern that her grandchildren were afraid of her because of her stroke. At this point, Mrs. K indicated that she was ready to continue her treatment and that there was no further allusion to suicide.

Since Mrs. K was now alone and the temporary assistance from her adult children was not a permanent solution, a referral was made to social work to help Mrs. K plan for her future living arrangements. A 24-hour, live-in homemaker was hired as a temporary measure until Mrs. K could decide if she wanted to move to a retirement community. In some respects, the presence of the homemaker in the home encouraged Mrs. K to make greater accomplishments, since she refused to allow the homemaker to do certain things in the kitchen and would not allow her to assist with personal care. Mrs. K also tackled stair climbing so that she could get outside for walks.

At this time Mrs. K continues with her home exercise program. She has not made a decision about moving, so her live-in homemaker is still with her. She is completely independent with dressing, bathing, meal preparation, and ambulation. The team of home care personnel have conducted several case conferences regarding Mrs. K and her progress. Her progress is the result of the dedication of a diverse team of home care workers and the desire of an individual to work hard and to set her sights on goals no one thought she could attain.

the most successful gerontologic nurse in this setting practices in a coordinated and collaborative manner with the other interdisciplinary team members (Box 32-8). The shifting scene in health care of older adults is emphasizing health maintenance, promotion, and prevention for this population. Gerontologic nurses must be ready to take on the role of advocate for older adults and their caregivers who reside in the community, demanding quality services and programs that address the increasingly complex needs of this group.

Key Points

- The ability of older people to "age in place" as they become more functionally impaired depends on the availability of family support, community-based social and health care services, and adequate financial resources.
- The OAA of 1965 established a national network of federal, state, and AAAs that are responsible for providing a range of community services for older adults. However, there is a great deal of geographic variability in the types of community services available, eligibility criteria, and reimbursement mechanisms.
- Increasing numbers of older people are discharged from hospitals with significant needs related to medical care and functional impairments, so home health care for older adults is becoming more common and more complex.
- The experience of caring for an older family member is becoming more common (a "normative" experience) among people age 45 and older. In fact, families are providing greater amounts and more complex types of care over longer periods than ever before.
- To be eligible for the Medicare home care benefit, an individual must be homebound; have a condition that requires skilled, intermittent care; and have a referring physician who approves the plan of treatment in writing and certifies that the client is homebound and has a skilled need.
- The National Association for Home Care (NAHC), 519 C Street, NE, Washington, D.C., 20002-5809, represents the interests of Americans who need home care and the caregivers who provide them with in-home health and supportive services. NAHC is a trade association that serves the nation's home care agencies, hospices, and home care aide organizations.
- Home care is often chosen as a preferred treatment site because people want to be home and because it is usually less expensive than hospitalization. In addition, technology has evolved to support complex treatments in the home and to minimize exposure to multiple infectious processes.
- Assessment for home care should be done early in a client's hospital stay. Hospital discharge planners and home care managers must work together closely to assure the continuity of care necessary for a timely and

effective discharge.

- The home care nurse assesses the physical, functional, emotional, socioeconomic, and environmental well-being of the client. The nurse works in collaboration with all other members of the home care team as their services are needed to address the home care plan of treatment.
- The governing body of a home care organization has the legal authority and responsibility for the operation of the agency.
- Quality assessment and improvement activities are designed to assess and to improve the quality of client care. The leaders of the home care organization must support this quality focus and be committed to continual monitoring and evaluation of the quality of activities.

Critical Thinking Exercises

1. Outline your approach in lobbying with your state legislature regarding funding for noninstitutional community and home-based services for the older adult population. Do you have personal experiences that would serve as testimony of the need?
2. A 90-year-old woman has been living with her 68-year-old daughter for 5 years. The daughter is suffering from complications of long-term diabetes and feels she is no longer able to care for her mother. No other family members are willing to take their mother into their home. How would you go about determining the options available for the mother?

REFERENCES

American Association of Retired Persons: *A profile of older Americans,* Washington, D.C., 1992, The Association.

American Association of Retired Persons: *Understanding senior housing for the 1990's: an AARP survey of consumer preferences, concerns, and needs,* Washington, D.C., 1990, The Association.

American Association of Retired Persons and The Travelers Companies Foundation: *National survey of caregivers: summary of findings,* Washington, D.C., 1988, The Association.

American Medical Association: *Physicians and home care guidelines for the medical management of the home care patient,* Chicago, Ill., 1992, The Association.

American Medical Association: *Synopsis of Clinton health system proposal,* Chicago, September 13, 1993, The Association.

Barker JA: *Discovering the future: the business of paradigms,* ed 2, (videotape) Burnsville, Minn., 1989, Charthouse Learning Corporation.

Baumgarten M et al: The psychological and physical health of family members caring for an elderly person with dementia, *J Clin Epidemiol* 45(1):61-70, 1992.

Baumgarten M et al: Health of family members caring for elderly persons with dementia, *Ann Intern Med* 120(2):126-132, 1994.

Benjamin AE, Fox PJ, Swan JH: The posthospital experience of elderly medicare home health users, *Home Healthc Serv Qu* 14(2/3):19-35, 1993.

Bensen PM: *AHCPR monograph-tracing the elderly through the health care system: an update,* Pub. No. AHCPR 91-11, Rockville, Md., 1991, Department of Health and Human Services, Public Health Service, Agency for Health Care Policy and Research.

Biegel DE, Sales S, Schulz R: *Family caregiving in chronic illness,* Newbury Park, Calif., 1991, Sage.

Brody EM: Parent care as a normative family stress, *Gerontologist* 25:19-29, 1985.

Clipp EC, George LK: Dementia and cancer: a comparison of spouse caregivers, *Gerontologist* 33(4):534-541, 1993.

Clipp EC, George LK: Psychotropic drug use among caregivers of patients with dementia. *J Am Geriatr Soc* 38(3):227-235, 1990.

Colsher PL, Wallace RB: Health and social antecedents of relocation in rural elderly persons, *J Gerontol Soc Sci* 45(1):S32-38, 1990.

Creedon MA, Tiven M: *Eldercare in the workplace,* Washington, D.C., 1989, National Council on the Aging and National Association of State Units on Aging.

Draper BM et al: A comparison of caregivers for elderly stroke and dementia victims, *J Am Geriatr Soc* 40(9):896-901, 1992.

Evashwick CJ, Definition of continuum of care, In Evashwick CJ, Weiss LJ, editors: *Managing the continuum of care,* Rockville, Md., 1987, Aspen.

Farran CJ et al: Finding meaning: an alternative paradigm for Alzheimer's disease family caregivers, *Gerontologist* 31(4):483-489, 1991.

Farran CJ et al: Finding meaning as a moderator of caregiver distress: a comparison of African American and white caregivers of persons with dementia, (under review).

Fogel BS: Psychological aspects of staying at home, *Generations* 16(2):15-19, 1992.

Foley DJ et al: The risk of nursing home admission in three communities, *J Aging Health* 4(2):155-173, 1992.

Gerald LB: Paid family caregiving: a review of progress and policies, *J Aging Soc Pol* 5(1/2):73-89, 1993.

Guralnik JM, Simonsick EM: Physical disability in older Americans, *J Gerontol* 48(special issue):3-10, 1993.

Himes CL: Future caregivers: projected family structures of older persons, *J Gerontol Soc Sci* 47(1):S17-26, 1992.

Joint Commission on the Accreditation of Health Care Organizations: *Accreditation manual for home care, Volume I standards,* Oakbrook Terrace, Ill., 1993, The Commission.

Kiecolt-Glaser J et al: Spousal caregivers of dementia victims: longitudinal changes in immunity and health, *Psychosom Med* 53:345-362, 1991.

Kingson ER, Hirshorn BA, Cornman JM: *Ties that bind: the interdependence of generations,* Washington, D.C., 1986, Seven Locks Press.

Lawton MP et al: A two-factor model of caregiving appraisal and psychological well-being, *J Gerontol Psychol Sci* 46(4):P181-189, 1991.

Lawton MP et al: The dynamics of caregiving for a demented elder among black and white females, *J Gerontol Soc Sci* 47(4):S156-164, 1992.

Leon J, Lair T: *Functional status of the noninstitutionalized elderly: estimates of ADL and IADL difficulties,* Pub. No. 90-3462, National Medical Expenditure Survey Research Findings 4, Rockville, Md., 1990, Department of Health and Human Services, Public Health Service, Agency for Health Care Policy and Research.

Matthis EJ: Top twenty educational wants of current family caregivers of disabled adults, *Home Health Nurse* 9(3):23-25, 1991.

McCann J: *Effects of stress on spouse caregivers' psychological health and cellular immunity,* Ann Arbor, Mich., 1991, Dissertation Abstracts International, DAI-B 52/08, University Microfilms.

McCann J: Long term home care for the elderly: perceptions of nurses, physicians, and primary caregivers, *Q Rev Bull* 14(3):66-74, 1988.

McGadney BF: Stressors and social supports as predictors of burden for black and white caregivers of elders with dementia, *Gerontologist Prog Abstr* 33(special issue):70, 1993.

Miller B et al: Gender and race in care of the cognitively impaired, *Final Report* Grant No. RO1#AG09416, Washington, D.C., 1995, National Institute of Aging.

Morris JN, Morris SA: Aging in place: the role of formal human services, *Generations* 16(2):41-48, 1992.

National Association for Health Care: *Basic statistics about home care,* Washington, D.C., 1993, The Association.

National Center for Health Statistics: *Health data on older Americans, United States,* Series 3, No. 27, Washington, D.C., 1992, The Center.

National Council on Aging Community-based services under the OAA and other programs, *Perspective on Aging, NCOA Public Policy Agenda 1993-1994* 22(1):20-25 1993.

Newman SJ et al: Overwhelming odds: caregiving and the risk of institutionalization, *J Gerontol Soc Sci* 45(5):S173-183, 1990.

Pearlman DN, Crown WH: Alternative sources of social support and their impacts on institutional risk, *Gerontologist* 32(4):527-535, 1992.

Rice DP et al: The economic burden of Alzheimer's disease care, *Health Aff* Summer:164-176, 1993.

Rowles GD: Evolving images of place in aging and "aging in place," *Generations,* 17(2):65-70, 1993.

Salive ME et al: Predictors of nursing home admission in a biracial population, *Am J Pub Health* 83(12):1765-1767, 1993.

Scharlach AE: Caregiving and employment: competing or complementary roles? *Gerontologist,* 34(3):378-385, 1994.

Schirm V: Shared caregiving responsibilities for chronically ill elders, *Holistic Nurs Pract* 5(1):54-61, 1990.

Schulz R, Vistainer P, Williamson GM: Psychiatric and physical morbidity effects of caregiving, *J Gerontol Psychol Sci* 45(5):P181-191, 1990.

Schulz R, Williamson G: A 2-year longitudinal study of depression among Alzheimer's caregivers, *Psychol Aging* 6(4):569-578, 1991.

Shivley S, Djupe AM, Lester P: Lessons in caring: a "Care by Caregiver" program, *Geriatr Nurs* Nov/Dec:304-306, 1993.

Short P, Leon J: *Use of home and community services by persons ages 65 and older with functional difficulties,* Pub. No. 90-3466, National Medical Expenditure Survey Research Findings 5, Rockville, Md., 1990, Department of Health and Human Services, Public Health Service, Agency for Health Care Policy and Research.

Silliman RA: Predictors of family caregivers' physical and psychological health following hospitalization of their elders, *J Am Geriatr Soc* 41(10):1039-1046, 1993.

Soldo B, Myllyluoma J: Caregivers who live with dependent elderly, *Gerontologist* 23:605-611, 1983.

Sommers T, Shields L: *Women take care: the consequences of caregiving in today's society,* Gainesville, Fla., 1987, Triad.

Stone R, Cafferata GL, Sangl J: Caregivers of the frail elderly: a national profile, *Gerontologist* 27(5):616-626, 1987.

Stone R, Short PF: The competing demands of employment and informal caregiving to disabled elders, *Med Care* 28(6):513-526, 1990.

Tennstedt S, Cafferata GL, Sullivan L: Depression among caregivers of impaired elders, *J Aging Health* 4(1):58-76, 1992.

United States Select Committee on Aging, House of Representatives: *Exploding the myths: caregiving in America,* Comm. Pub. No. 99-611, Washington, D.C., 1987, US Government Printing Office.

US Bureau of the Census: *Statistical abstracts of the United States, 112th edition, Bureau of the Census,* Lanham, Md., 1992, Bernan Press.

US Labor Department, Bureau of Statistics: *Monthly labor review* 116(11), 1993.

Vinton L: Health care connections: linking hospital and community-based care for the elderly and their caregivers, *Gerontol Geriatr Educ* 11(3):57-66, 1991.

Weiner JM, Illston LH: Health care reform in the 1990's: where does long-term care fit in? *Gerontologist* 4(3):402-408, 1994.

Weiner JM, Illston LH, Hanley RJ: *Sharing the burden: strategies for public and private long-term care insurance,* Washington, D.C., 1994, The Brookings Institution.

Wolinsky FD et al: Changes in functional status and the risks of subsequent nursing home placement and death, *J Gerontol Soc Sci* 48(3):S94-101, 1994.

BIBLIOGRAPHY

Harris MD: *Handbook of Home Health Care Administration,* Gaithersburg, Md., 1994, Aspen.

Mundinger MO: *Home care controversy: too little, too late, too costly,* Rockville, Md., 1983, Aspen Systems Corp.

CHAPTER 33

Long-Term Care

LEARNING OBJECTIVES

On completion of this chapter, the reader will be able to:

1. Describe demographic characteristics of residents living in nursing facilities.
2. List five common risk factors for institutionalization.
3. Identify differences between the medical and psychosocial models of care for institutional long-term care.
4. Summarize key aspects of resident rights as they relate to the nursing facility.
5. List assessment components included in the Minimum Data Set of the Resident Assessment Instrument.
6. Describe common clinical management programs existing in the nursing facility for skin problems, incontinence, nutritional problems, infection control, and mental health.
7. Differentiate types of nursing care delivery systems found in the nursing facility.
8. Describe assisted living, special care units, and subacute care units as specialty care settings of the nursing facility.
9. Identify two ways in which nurses can enhance the involvement of family members in the care of residents in nursing facilities.
10. Explain recent innovations in the practice setting of nursing facilities.

OVERVIEW OF LONG-TERM CARE

Definition

Long-term care has several meanings in the gerontologic nursing literature. The phrase is most accurately used to describe a collection of health, personal, and social services provided over a prolonged period to people who have lost or never acquired functional capacity (Kane and Kane, 1987). Recipients of long-term care services typically include older adults but may also include developmentally disabled people, people permanently impaired from traumatic injuries, and chronically ill younger people. These settings can be categorized on a continuum according to their restrictiveness. Settings are more restrictive to less restrictive as one moves from

TABLE 33-1

Continuum of Settings in Which Long-Term Care is Provided

Institutional	Community	In home
Nursing facility	Hospice	Home health nursing
Group home	Adult day care center	Home health rehabilitative services
Board and care facility	Senior center	Homemaker
Continuing care retirement communities	Congregate meal programs	Home-delivered meals
		Adaptive devices to home environment

the institutional setting, to the community at large, to the home. Table 33-1 illustrates this continuum of settings in which long-term care services may be provided.

The nursing home is the dominant setting in which long-term care is provided. Before 1987 the nursing home was commonly referred to as either a skilled nursing facility or an intermediate care facility. These facilities described different resident populations depending on the state in which the facility was located. In some states, the more functionally impaired residents lived in intermediate care facilities, whereas in other states, the more impaired residents lived in skilled nursing facilities.

With the passage of the **Omnibus Budget Reconciliation Act of 1987 (OBRA '87),** distinctions between a skilled nursing facility and an intermediate care facility were no longer meaningful. The term **nursing facility** replaced both of these terms. For the purposes of this chapter, long-term care refers to the nursing facility.

History

In Western civilization, the origins of the modern nursing facility can be traced to descriptions of specialized hospitals for the aged that existed during the fourth century (Shore, 1993). During medieval times, groups of religious women cared for the sick and the poor.

Early English law provided the foundation on which local government activities in America developed to provide services to the poor. Among other things, the parlimentary statute of 1597 to 1598 authorized the raising of funds to assist the destitute, including any older people who were unable to care for themselves.

In America during the 1600s and 1700s, almshouses were places where dependent, destitute, and older people lived. These communal facilities were financially supported by private rather than by government organizations. During the nineteenth and early twentieth centuries, various church-related, ethnic, and voluntary groups converted private homes into communal settings where the aged and the destitute could live (Shore, 1993).

Government involvement in nursing facilities is a relatively recent phenomenon. With the passage of the Social Security Act of 1935, a federal-state public assistance program for older people called Old Age Assistance (OAA) was established. The act prohibited the payment of OAA funds to public institutions providing care to poor older adults. Consequently, voluntary and proprietary nursing homes flourished.

In 1950 the Social Security Act was amended, enabling public institutions to receive payments for care of beneficiaries of OAA. States having such public institutions were required to establish programs for licensing nursing homes, although standards for licensing and regulation were not specified (Institute of Medicine [IOM], 1986).

Since the 1950s, federal government participation in nursing homes has grown. See Table 33-2 for a summary of federal government involvement in the nursing home industry from 1954 to 1993. Both financial and regulatory programs were developed during this period, illustrating the relationship between public policy and the nursing facility.

Demographics of Nursing Facilities and Residents

In the United States, there are nearly 19,000 nursing facilities and between 1.5 and 2 million nursing facility beds (Ouslander, Osterweil, and Morley, 1991). Facilities are owned by the government, by for-profit organizations, and by not-for-profit organizations. Nursing facilities may be freestanding, located in a hospital setting, or on the campus of a retirement community that has multiple levels of care. Facilities may be owned and operated in a variety of ways, including a family or person owning and operating one facility, a local or regional small chain of facilities, or a national chain of nursing homes. Increasingly, large corporations are expected to dominate the nursing facility market (Kane, 1993).

The number of people living in nursing facilities at any one time was over 15 million in 1990 (Rubenstein and Wieland, 1993). Residents can be categorized into two groupings, depending on their length of stay. Short-term residents are those who leave the facility in 3 to 6 months. They tend to be younger, have more physical problems, and are admitted from a hospital. The growth in subacute and managed care in nursing facility settings has increased the percentage of short-term residents. The ratio of long-term residents to short-term ones is currently nine to one and is expected to decrease in those facilities that develop subacute programs.

Long-term residents are the more traditional users of the nursing facility. These include people staying at the

TABLE 33-2

History of the Federal Government and the Nursing Home Industry (1954-1993)

1954: Hill-Burton Act amended, providing funds to nonprofit organizations for construction of skilled nursing facilities meeting hospital-like building codes.
1956: Social Security Act amended to increase OAA payments for nursing home services.
1958-1959: Legislation passed, enabling Small Business and Federal Housing Administration to provide aid to proprietary nursing home construction and operation.
1959: Special Senate Subcommittee on Problems of the Aged and Aging established, reporting on quality problems in nursing homes.
1963-1974: Moss Committee (Senate Special Committee on Aging) held hearings and investigated reports of quality problems in nursing homes.
1965: Medicare and Medicaid programs were enacted, expanding federal funding of nursing home services. U.S. Department of Health, Education, and Welfare (HEW) was given authority to set standards for nursing homes choosing to participate in these programs.
1974: Federal nursing home certification regulations were revised. HEW established federal regional offices for long-term care standards enforcement.
1974: Office of Nursing Home Affairs (ONHA) began a study of quality in nursing homes.
1980: Health Care Financing Administration (HCFA) published a proposed certification process called Patient Appraisal and Care Evaluation (PACE).
1981: Proposed PACE certification process was rescinded by the Reagan administration.
1983: HCFA and Congress agreed to postpone all regulatory changes in nursing homes until a committee appointed by the IOM made recommendations for changes.
1985: A modified survey instrument called the Patient Care and Services (PaCS) was selectively used in every state.
1987: Major nursing home reform legislation was passed in the Omnibus Budget Reconciliation Act (OBRA).
1989: OBRA '89 pushed the OBRA '87 implementation date to October 1990.
1994: HCFA released the final OBRA '87 survey, as well as certification and enforcement regulations.

facility for 6 months or more and remaining there until they die. Long-term residents tend to be older and have more cognitive and functional impairments (Millsap, 1995).

Risk Factors of Institutionalization

As life expectancy increases and the size of the older adult population grows, the risk of a person entering a nursing facility at some point increases. Almost a third of men and just over half of women who turned 65 in 1990 are expected to live in a nursing facility before they die (Jette et al, 1992).

Personal risk factors for institutionalization include advanced age, physical disability, mental impairment, Caucasian race, living without a spouse, and the presence of chronic medical conditions, such as heart disease, arthritis, hypertension, and diabetes (Jette et al, 1992; Millsap, 1995). (see Cultural Awareness box, at right). Factors contributing to the need for institutionalization can be categorized according to characteristics of the person, characteristics of the person's support system, and community resources available to the person (Table 33-3).

People needing help with activities of daily living (ADLs) or instrumental activities of daily living (IADLs) live both in the community and in nursing facilities. Fig. 33-1 illustrates that people with greater levels of functional impairment live in nursing facilities. The level of disability or limitations in ADLs and IADLs increases greatly with age. For the old-old, or people age 85 and older, nearly one in two dependent women and one in three dependent men live in a nursing facility rather than in the community (Guralnik and Simonsick, 1993).

CULTURAL AWARENESS

Cultural Diversity in Nursing Homes

Historically, a higher percentage of older adults from culturally diverse backgrounds have been cared for in home environments than have those who are white. Among the 85 + age group residing in nursing homes, 23% are white, 10% are Hispanic, and 10% are Asian/Pacific Islander in heritage.

Wray LA: Health policy and ethnic diversity in older Americans: dissonance or harmony: *West J Med* 157(special ed):357-361, 1992.
Yeatts DE, Crow T, Folts E: Service use among low-income minority elderly: strategies for overcoming barriers, *Gerontologist* 32(1):24-32, 1992.

Issues of Quality and Cost

Before the late 1960s, institutional long-term care was an unregulated industry. It is widely reported that the quality of care existing in many facilities was low (Freeman, 1990; IOM, 1986). Internal quality controls that were supposed to provide for services that were safe, that met certain standards of adequacy, and that were as advertised were lacking (Kane, Kane, 1989).

In the past 40 years, numerous laws have been passed

TABLE 33-3

Factors Affecting the Need for Nursing Home Admission

Characteristics of the individual
Age, sex, race
Marital status
Living arrangements
Degree of mobility
Ability to perform basic and instrumental activities of daily living
Urinary incontinence
Behavior problems
Mental status
Memory impairment
Mood disturbance
Tendency for falls
Clinical prognosis
Income
Payment eligibility
Need for special services
Characteristics of the support system
Family capability
Age of spouse (if married)
Presence of responsible relative (usually adult child)
Family structure of responsible relative
Employment status of responsible relative
Physician availability
Amount of care currently received from family and others
Community resources
Formal community resources
Informal support systems
Presence of long-term care institutions
Characteristics of long-term care institutions

From Ouslander J, Osterweil D, Morley J: *Medical care in the nursing home,* New York, 1991, McGraw-Hill.

that affect the quality and cost of institutional long-term care. See Table 33-2 for a summary of such legislation. Issues regarding quality have been addressed by strengthening the external quality control mechanism through health care regulation. The existence of internal quality control programs has been mandated. Programs may take the form of the traditional quality assurance program or the total quality improvement model promoted by the Joint Commission on Accreditation of Healthcare Organizations (JCAHO).

Donabedian's framework (1980) for defining quality health services includes the dimensions of structure, process, and outcome. This framework has been widely used to define and measure the quality of nursing facilities (Davis, 1991). Before the passage of OBRA '87, structural and process criteria regarding quality were emphasized, with minimum attention given to outcome

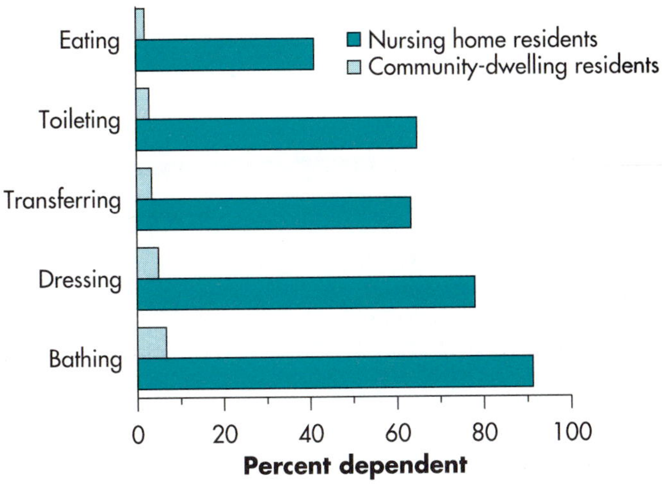

Fig. 33-1 Ability to perform basic ADLs among nursing home residents versus community-dwelling older adults. (From Ouslander J, Osterweil D, Morley J: *Medical care in the nursing home,* St. Louis, 1991, McGraw-Hill.)

measures (Aaronson, Zinn, Rosko, 1995). Structure refersto fixed program characteristics, including system, provider, and consumer characteristics. Process refers to actions or operations of a technical and interpersonal nature. Outcome refers to end results for consumers.

Outcome measures of quality are being focused on as the most important dimension of quality. In the nursing facility, these include clinical end points such as laboratory values and measures of functional status, or outcomes from the consumer's perspective, such as general well-being, life satisfaction, or perceived autonomy (Mitty, 1992).

The cost of institutional long-term care is a growing concern to older adults and baby boomers. Financing of nursing facility care comes from private payments by individuals or families and from public payments by Medicaid (Fig. 33-2). For many Americans, the cost of care in a nursing facility is excessive. The purchase of private long-term care insurance is becoming an increasingly popular option. In 1990 about 2% of long-term care expenditures were covered by insurance; by the year 2020, financing of long-term care by private insurance will increase to 6.6% (*Aging America,* 1991).

Medical and Psychosocial Models of Care

Nursing facilities evolved from the acute care hospital system and the medical model (Lidz, Arnold, 1995). Like hospitals, nursing facilities were designed around departments and professions rather than the consumers who they served (Strasen, 1991). The organization of nursing facilities tends to be hierarchic and bureaucratic (Brannon, 1992).

The medical model has sustained a role for residents

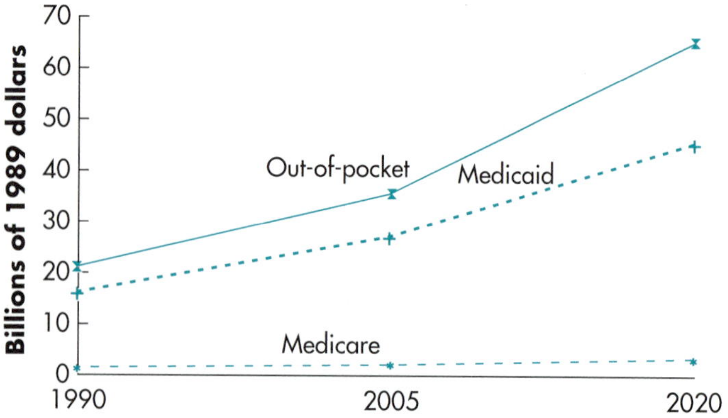

Fig. 33-2 Projected nursing home expenditures for people age 65 and older, by source of payment: 1990 to 2020. (From US Department of Health and Human Services: *Aging America: trends and projections,* 1991, The Department.)

that emphasizes them as being sick and in need of physician-directed help. Compliance with the medical regimen is emphasized. Care instructions are described as "orders." Residents are expected to comply with staff and medical decisions rather than actively participate in determining them (Lidz and Arnold, 1995).

One of the broad changes mandated by the passage of OBRA '87 is an emphasis on the social and psychologic outcomes of institutional long-term care, in addition to the traditional medical outcomes. Psychosocial outcomes are supported by a psychosocial model of care—one that emphasizes the life experience of residents (Agich, 1993). Residents' subjective evaluations of their quality of life in the nursing facility are meaningful and valuable. Resident decision making, exercise of basic civil rights, and experience of personal choice and control are emphasized. The current exploration of strategies to enhance resident perception of autonomy and the growth of alternative care systems, such as assisted living, are consequences of this emphasis on residents' rights (Gamroth, Semradek, Tornquist, 1995).

CLINICAL ASPECTS OF THE NURSING FACILITY

Regulatory Framework

Regulation is one of the most powerful forces that drives clinical practice in the nursing facility. The nursing home industry is believed to be second only to the nuclear power industry in the degree of regulation that guides its operations (Kane, 1995). Although other health care settings are controlled by state and federal regulations, the depth and scope of nursing facility regulation create a unique regulatory burden for the nurse practicing in this setting.

Society uses state nurse practice acts, and state and federal laws to ensure that consumers are protected when they receive health care services from nursing personnel in a nursing facility. State and federal laws are also used to ensure industry accountability among those providers who participate in the Medicare and Medicaid programs. Providers who fail to achieve certain standards of quality in their services cannot continue to be paid with state and federal reimbursement through the Medicare and Medicaid programs.

Table 33-2, p. 946, summarizes the history of federal involvement in regulating the nursing home industry in an attempt to raise the standard of services provided. OBRA '87 is the current regulatory framework used to protect vulnerable consumers, to ensure that nursing home residents receive adequate and safe care, and to protect their civil rights (IOM, 1986).

Every clinical program and clinical intervention that the nurse participates in needs to be understood in the context of this regulatory framework. Box 33-1 summarizes the topics covered by the 15 major regulatory requirements defined by OBRA '87.

BOX 33-1

The Major Regulatory Level A Requirements Defined by OBRA '87

- Resident rights
- Admission, transfer, and discharge rights
- Resident behavior and facility practices
- Quality of life
- Resident assessment
- Quality of care
- Nursing services
- Dietary services
- Physician services
- Specialized rehabilitative services
- Dental services
- Pharmacy services
- Infection control
- Physical environment
- Administration

Resident Rights

One of the accomplishments of the IOM's 1986 Committee on Nursing Home Regulation report was to lay the foundation for greater regulatory support of resident rights in the nursing facility. Emphasis on resident rights was directly related to a revised view of residents as active participants and decision makers in their care and life in the institutional setting. The ethical principle of autonomy was viewed as a primary force in guiding clinical and management interventions in this setting. Kane and Caplan's book (1990), *Everyday Ethics: Resolving Dilemmas in Nursing Home Life,* was a seminal work describing the complexities of promoting resident autonomy and resident rights in the ordinary life events of frail older residents.

Resident rights that are unique to the nursing facility setting are promoted in several practical ways. These include the establishment and maintenance of a resident council, the public display of posters listing resident rights in the facility, the public display of local ombudsman program information, the public display of annual state inspection results, an aggressive attempt to provide opportunities for residents to exercise their right to vote during public elections and to provide the opportunity to self-administer medications by competent residents, and an informed consent process for the use of side rails and chemical and physical restraints, in addition to informed consent for withdrawal or withholding of life-sustaining treatments (Gamroth, Semradek, and Tornquist, 1995).

Strategies directed at the delivery of nursing care include active participation of residents and certified nursing assistants in care planning (Ryden, 1990), the provision of opportunities for residents to make meaningful choices in their daily lives and to participate in meaningful activities (Nick, 1992), and the promotion of resident and family roles that include active participation and responsibility in the life of the nursing facility (Semradek and Gamroth, 1995).

Resident Assessment

Interdisciplinary functional assessment of the resident is the cornerstone of clinical practice in this setting. OBRA '87 prescribed the method of resident assessment and care plan development in an instrument known as the **Resident Assessment Instrument (RAI)** Version 2.0. The RAI consists of three parts: the **Minimum Data Set (MDS), Resident Assessment Protocols (RAPs),** and the utilization guidelines specified in the State Operations Manual transmittal no. 272 (HCFA, 1995).

The MDS is a tool that includes a comprehensive assessment of the resident. Tool categories include resident background information; cognitive, communication/hearing, and vision patterns; physical functioning and structural problems; mood, behavior, and activity pursuit patterns; psychosocial well-being; bowel and bladder continence; health conditions; disease diagnoses; oral/nutritional and dental status; skin condition; medication use; and special treatments and procedures.

Deadlines for completion of each tool section, as well as care-planning decisions emanating from the assessment process, are prescribed by regulation. Box 33-2 lists the 18 problem areas that need to be addressed in the care-planning process. The outcome of the interdisciplinary team's clinical decision making related to the 18 problem areas as it relates to care plan development is explicitly described in the RAP summary.

BOX 33-2

The 18 RAP Problem Areas of the Resident Assessment Protocol Summary

Delirium
Cognitive loss/dementia
Visual function
Communication
ADL functional/rehabilitation potential
Urinary incontinence and indwelling catheter
Psychosocial well-being
Mood state
Behavior problem
Activities
Falls
Nutritional status
Feeding tubes
Dehydration/fluid maintenance
Dental care
Pressure ulcers
Psychotropic drug use
Physical restraints

The specific method used to complete the RAI varies from facility to facility. Some facilities assign one nurse to complete all documentation related to the RAI; others distribute this responsibility among all the nurses. The RAI is completed on each resident annually, when a significant change of condition occurs (as defined by the HCFA manual), on admission, and quarterly, using a one-page abbreviated version of the RAI.

Both licensed vocational/practical nurses and registered nurses may contribute to the RAI. However, only a registered nurse can sign the document and function as the RN assessment coordinator (RAC). The RAC signs and certifies the completion of the assessment, not the accuracy of the assessment data (HCFA, 1995). Contributions to the RAI are also made by the dietary supervisor, social worker, recreational therapist, medical records clerk, and physical and occupational therapist.

The overall goal of the RAI is to provide an ongoing, comprehensive assessment of the resident, emphasizing functional ability and both a physical and a psychosocial profile of the resident. It is also a key component in the development of a national data base for long-term care. By 1997, the revised version of the MDS, MDS Version 2.0, will be required by all providers and states participating in the Medicaid and Medicare programs (Foltz, 1994).

Skin Care

Skin care programs in the nursing facility are focused on prevention and treatment of skin problems. Preventive strategies include prevention of pressure sores, skin tears, and dry skin or xerosis. Although the true incidence of pressure ulcers in nursing facilities is not known, the development of pressure ulcers during a stay in a nursing facility is considered an indicator of poor quality of care (Ouslander, Osterweil, Morley, 1991) (see Chapter 28).

Other skin-related problems commonly occurring in this setting and treated include dry skin, dermatitis and eczema, herpes zoster, scabies, pediculosis, bullous pemphigoid, and skin tumors. Common skin tumors seen in an older adult nursing facility population include basal cell carcinoma, squamous cell carcinoma, malignant melanoma, superficial spreading melanoma, and Kaposi's sarcoma (Ouslander, Osterweil, Morley, 1991).

Most nursing facilities have a structured skin program that is coordinated by a licensed vocational/practical nurse or a registered nurse and that is participated in by all nursing department staff. On admission, the resident's skin is thoroughly assessed. Individual risk for developing pressure ulcers is established, and preventive interventions are initiated as appropriate. These may include some type of supplemental bed mattress, heel protectors, the initiation of vitamin and nutritional supplements, and a schedule for turning bed-bound residents. The certified nursing assistant plays a key role in providing effective, preventive skin care by assisting the resident in routine bathing, toileting, and maintenance of schedules for turning and repositioning.

Based on the physical examination, as well as RAI data, a care plan is initiated. Individual states have varying regulations concerning the required frequency of the nurse's clinical staging and routine assessment of pressure ulcers. For example, in California the nurse needs to measure, stage, and evaluate the efficacy of the skin treatment weekly.

The director of nursing may work with the medical director or individual physicians practicing in the facility to coordinate and standardize treatments for various stages of pressure ulcers. Another alternative is to intervene in skin problems on a case-by-case basis according to the preference of the resident's attending physician.

Facilities may have sustained relationships with companies that manufacture specialized beds for residents with stage 3 or stage 4 pressure ulcers. Often the company may provide a nurse consultant as a clinical resource to the facility. The nurse functioning as the skin program coordinator might meet routinely with the consultant. The two nurses often work collaboratively, along with the dietician, to treat skin problems.

Incontinence

A 1989 National Institutes of Health Consensus Conference on incontinence characterized urinary incontinence as "epidemic" in nursing facilities (Ouslander and Schnelle, 1993). Approximately 41% to 55% of nursing facility residents have some degree of urinary incontinence. This common health problem has financial, physical, and psychosocial consequences.

The cost of managing urinary incontinence in the nursing facility, including cost related to labor, supplies, and laundry, has been estimated at between $0.5 and $3 billion annually (in 1984 dollars) (Ouslander, Schnelle, 1993). Physical consequences of incontinence include skin breakdown, urinary tract infection, and an increased risk of falling and consequent hip fracture (Case-Gamble, 1995). Urinary incontinence is one of the most psychologically distressing health problems faced by older adults. It may lead to depression, decreased self-esteem, and social isolation (Case-Gamble, 1995).

One of the features of OBRA '87 was the inclusion of specific standards and recommendations for the assessment and treatment of urinary incontinence. Clinical programs in nursing facilities are directed at prevention, treatment, and management of the incontinence.

Prevention is aimed at reducing the risk of developing urinary incontinence among residents of nursing facilities who are at risk. Preventive measures include assessment of individual patterns of elimination so that anticipatory assistance with toileting may be provided, aggressive staff response to residents' requests for assistance in toileting, and arrangement of the physical environment to minimize the physical effort involved in getting to the bathroom.

Treatment programs are resident oriented and are focused on creating changes in the function of the lower urinary tract. Interventions include surgery, pharmacologic interventions, bladder training, pelvic muscle exercises, and biofeedback procedures (Ouslander and Schnelle, 1993).

Management programs for urinary incontinence are the dominant form of intervention in the nursing facility. These are caregiver oriented and are focused on changing the behaviors of caregivers to minimize the amount of incontinence experienced by the resident. Interventions include scheduled toileting, habit training, prompted voiding, the use of pads, protective undergarments, chronic indwelling catheterization, and intermittent catheterization. Effective management of urinary incontinence involves a well-coordinated and sustained effort between licensed nursing staff and certified nursing assistants (see Chapter 26).

Nutrition

Nutritional deficiencies contribute to adverse clinical outcomes in nursing facility residents. Protein-calorie undernutrition results from two broad categories of factors: those causing inadequate intake and those causing increased nutritional requirements (Abbasi et al, 1993).

Inadequate intake results from eating functions altered by the normal aging process of the gastrointestinal tract, as described in Chapter 25. Other contributing factors include the loss of manual dexterity, the effects of dementing illnesses, ingestion of anorexigenic drugs, chronic medical disorders, and any institutional aspects of the environment that are not conducive in a physical or psychologic way to eating (Abbasi et al, 1993).

Increased nutritional requirements may be a consequence of hyperactivity in some people with dementing illnesses. Infectious illnesses, periods of recovery following surgical interventions that require tissue healing, and recovery from pressure ulcers place additional nutritional requirements on nursing facility residents.

Various clinical interventions are directed at the nutritional support of residents, including programs focused on maintaining adequate caloric intake and programs focused on effective identification of residents requiring supplemental nutritional support.

Enhancement of the dining experience through improved esthetics, improved dining room service, attractive food preparation, and increased sensitivity to the social nature of mealtimes is focused on maintenance of adequate caloric intake. Other strategies related to this goal include increasing the amount of staff assistance available to residents who need various types of assistance with eating and improvement in staff techniques in providing eating assistance. Sensitivity to dental needs and provision of the proper textures of foods most easily consumed by each resident are additional strategies.

In nursing facilities, the most common program directed at prompt identification of residents requiring supplemental nutritional support consists of routine weighing programs for residents. Weights are taken daily, weekly, biweekly, or monthly, depending on the analysis of the severity of weight loss or gain experienced by the resident. Interdisciplinary team members, including the nurse, restorative nursing assistant, dietician, and speech therapist, may meet routinely to review weight changes and develop interventions directed at supplemental nutritional support. In addition to strategies already described, changes in therapeutic diets, the use of nutritional products such as Ensure, vitamin supplements, enteral nutrition products, or laboratory work may be considered.

Compliance with OBRA '87 requires aggressive monitoring of the parameters of nutritional status, with attention focused on quarterly weight losses characterized as significant or severe. The functional implications of reduced caloric intake are to be considered. As with urinary incontinence, undernutrition in nursing facilities is preventable to a significant degree through prevention, early intervention, and treatment (Abbasi et al, 1993).

Medications

One of the basic services provided in the nursing facility is the administration of medications through the oral, intravenous, intramuscular, subcutaneous, or enteral route. The federal Medicare Part A program provides reimbursement for a prescribed period related to the daily administration of medications, with the exception of orally or rectally administered medications, by a licensed nurse (Millsap, 1995).

In the nursing facility, the licensed nurse is often responsible for the administration, documentation, storage, ordering, medication cart stocking, and destruction of many medications. Because many nursing facilities do not have an on-site pharmacy, the nursing staff is responsible for medication-related functions that are handled by the pharmacy staff in an acute care hospital setting.

Monitoring for the clinical manifestations of polypharmacy, the occurrence of adverse drug reactions, and the overuse of PRN drug orders has increasingly been emphasized since the passage of OBRA '87. The pharmacist contributes to this monitoring effort in a monthly drug review of residents at each facility. The nurse has numerous structured opportunities to monitor for these clinical problems. These opportunities include routine interactions with residents while administering medications, as well as assessment at quarterly care-planning conferences, during monthly review of psychotropic drug regimens, and when completing the long form of the Minimum Data Set (Williams, Thompson, and Brummel-Smith, 1993).

The routine use of certain drugs, including long-acting benzodiazepine drugs, hypnotics, sedatives, anxiolytics, and antipsychotic medications, has been curtailed since the passage of OBRA '87. Recommended drug dosages and indications for use of such medications are given to federal and state regulators to assist them in the survey and inspection process of each nursing facility (HCFA, 1994).

The emphasis on client rights is well illustrated with medication administration. The resident or this person's legal representative needs to sign an informed consent before the administration of a psychotropic medication. Nurses must document their ongoing instruction to the resident or the legal representative regarding the initiation of new drug therapy and changes in the dosage of medication. If a resident is cognitively intact, the opportunity to self-administer medications is to be provided (HCFA, 1994).

Rehabilitation

The provision of rehabilitation programs in the nursing facility setting has increased over the past 10 years. Factors contributing to this growth in rehabilitation include the OBRA '87–related regulatory mandate that facilities provide services directed at achieving the highest practicable level of physical, mental, and psychosocial well-being for residents; the growth of the subacute level of care, including nursing facility participation in managed care programs; and sustained political will to control the growth of health care expenditures (Gill, Howells, and Hoffman, 1993).

Rehabilitation teams in nursing facilities consist of occupational and physical therapists, speech/language pathologists, and the facility interdisciplinary team members, including the nurse and social worker. Occasionally a physiatrist, a physician specializing in physical medicine and rehabilitation, may coordinate the team (Drew-Cates, 1995).

For facilities participating in the Medicare or health maintenance organization (HMO) rehabilitation programs, weekly rehabilitation meetings are held and clinical cases are reviewed. Residents and family members participate in these meetings to promote communication, effective discharge planning, and client/family education.

Rehabilitation programs can be categorized into two groups. The more intensive rehabilitation programs are reimbursed through the Medicare Part A program or an HMO rehabilitation benefit. These include daily or twice-daily therapy sessions directed ideally toward returning the resident to a prior level of function and to residence in the community. Reconditioning, ADL training, treatment of dysphagia, cognitive retraining, and treatment of aphasia are therapeutic components of these programs.

The less intensive rehabilitation programs that exist in nursing facilities are reimbursed through the Medicare Part B program or private payments, or they are part of the basic services offered by the nursing facility. These services include restorative nursing programs involving ambulation, ADLs, self-feeding, and range of motion. Such programs are provided by specially trained certified nursing assistants who are supervised by the physical and occupational therapists and the speech/language pathologist. Program goals are focused on the maintenance of functional gains achieved during the more intensive rehabilitation program or on regaining a level of function lost because of a short-term illness.

Infection Control

Infections commonly occurring in residents of nursing facilities include lower respiratory tract, urinary tract, and skin and soft tissue infections. Other significant infectious processes in this setting include respiratory illnesses, gastrointestinal illnesses, ectoparasite infections, and colonization and infection with multidrug-resistant bacteria (Toledo et al, 1993).

Reasons why older adults are at increased risk for infection are described in Chapter 14. The institutionalized status of nursing facility residents further increases their risk. Nursing facilities are mandated to have an infection control program focused on prevention and treatment as a means of protecting residents from infectious illnesses.

Preventive programs consist of education in staff orientation programs and ongoing inservice programs about the benefits of routine handwashing. Universal precautions or body substance isolation practices are enforced in nursing facilities. Many of the same preventive clinical practices that one associates with an acute care setting related to infection control are found in the nursing facility.

An infection control committee consisting of staff members representing each department meets either monthly or quarterly to review data describing prevalence and incidence rates of infection. Any new or proposed revisions in policies and procedures are discussed by this committee. Typically, one nurse is designated as the infection control nurse and is responsible for coordinating surveillance, data-collecting activities, and ongoing educational sessions for the facility (Culley and Courtney, 1993).

When a resident develops an infection, the nurse relies heavily on the observational skills of the certified nursing assistants to notice subtle differences in the mood, eating habits, and overall functional status of the resident. Such changes may be the harbingers of an infectious illness (Toledo et al, 1993).

In the nursing facility, the effectiveness of infection control programs is hampered by the limited amount of licensed nursing time available to coordinate programs, as compared with the resources available in acute care settings for infection control activities, the variability in surveillance techniques used from setting to setting, and the inconsistency in reporting prevalence rates versus incidence rates of infection (Toledo et al, 1993).

Mental Health

General topics related to mental health and aging are described in Chapter 12. Among the aged and institutionalized population, mental health issues of particular concern include a variety of behavioral problems and manifestations of depression. Behavioral problems can be categorized into four groups: aggressive behaviors, such as hitting or kicking; physically nonaggressive behaviors, such as wandering; verbally agitated behaviors; and hiding and hoarding (Cohen-Mansfield et al, 1993).

Since the passage of OBRA '87 and its emphasis on quality of life, resident rights, and minimization of the use of chemical and physical restraints, understanding how to effectively manage behavioral problems and their impact on the community of residents has become increasingly important. Because the residents are living in a community setting, behavioral problems are not just an issue for the affected resident. The aberrant behavior of one resident has an impact on other residents, who may be a roommate, dining companion, or participant in a group activity involving the disturbed resident.

Residents manifesting behavioral problems commonly have dementing illnesses. More than 60% of nursing facility residents have some degree of cognitive deficits. Interventions used to control behavioral problems include the use of psychotropic medications, with drug effectiveness and the occurrence of side effects regularly monitored; changing the environment to accommodate the aberrant behavior, such as adding a door alarm for wandering residents in some cases; and using stimulation such as exercise, music, and touch to decrease the incidence of the aberrant behaviors (Cohen-Mansfield et al, 1993).

Since psychologists are now able to receive Medicare reimbursement for psychologic services provided to residents of nursing facilities, they are used to assist residents in coping with depression. Standard pharmacologic approaches are also used to treat the depressed nursing facility resident.

MANAGEMENT ASPECTS OF THE NURSING FACILITY

Interdisciplinary Practice

Coordinated interdisciplinary clinical practice focused on the provision of comprehensive assessment and care planning to achieve desired resident outcomes is a goal of OBRA '87. Aspects of the structure and process of interdisciplinary clinical practice are mandated by regulation. For example, in the Health Care Finance Administration Resident Assessment Instrument Manual, the forms to be used and the timetable for interdisciplinary assessment and care planning are defined. The process is described in the RAPs. These are educational tools and facilitate clinical decision making (HCFA, 1995).

In general, the director of nursing or other members of the nursing department tend to function as the coordinator of the interdisciplinary team. This occurs for a couple of practical reasons. A registered nurse is responsible for signing the completed MDS, a portion of which is completed by each interdisciplinary team member. Compliance with many regulatory requirements is documented, in part, through the use of the RAI. Nursing practice in the nursing facility is broad in its scope and relates to numerous regulatory requirements. For example, resident rights, quality of life, resident assessment, quality of care, and infection control are directly related to nursing practice.

Organizational Aspects of the Nursing Facility

The typical nursing facility has a hierarchic and bureaucratic organizational design (Brannon, 1992; Culley and Courtney, 1993). The administrator is the head of the organization. Departments include nursing, food service management or dietary, activities, social services, medical records, laundry, maintenance, central supply, housekeeping, business office, and clerical staff. Each facility has a medical director, who may or may not have residents living at the facility. Consultant arrangements are usually made for the provision of many services, including pharmacy, laboratory and x-ray, rehabilitation, psychology, audiology, dentistry, ophthalmology, and podiatry (Pozgar, 1992).

The Department of Nursing in the Nursing Facility

In 1992 nursing and personal care facilities employed 1.5 million employees (Hollander Feldman, 1994). These include both professional and paraprofessional staff members. Paraprofessional staff provide the majority of direct services to residents.

The nursing department is the largest department in the nursing facility. It consists of registered nurses, most of whom are associate degree nurse (ADN) graduates, licensed vocational nurses, certified nursing assistants, and, occasionally, geriatric nurse practitioners. Examples of job descriptions for nursing staff in a nursing facility are provided by Culley and Courtney (1993).

Eight percent of the registered nurse work force work in long-term care facilities (Culley and Courtney, 1993). Certified nursing assistants are the largest employee group in the nursing department and the facility as a whole, making up 66% of the work force in the nursing home (Schnelle et al, 1993).

Working in the nursing facility presents rewards and problems for employees. Rewards include the opportunity to establish long-term relationships with residents and family members and an opportunity to work in a setting that has a holistic orientation toward resident care. For example, in the course of their regular work day, staff members may participate in parties and special events involving the residents.

Sources of difficulty in the setting include low wages and poor benefits, demanding work both physically and emotionally, and limited opportunities for advancement. Average turnover among certified nursing assistants ranges from 44% to 48%, although other estimates are higher than this (Hollander Feldman, 1994).

Nursing Care Delivery Systems

Several nursing care delivery systems are found in the nursing facility. One is functional nursing, in which the jobs of licensed nurses and certified nursing assistants are determined according to work tasks. For example, in a functional care delivery system there is an MDS nurse, an admission nurse, a medication nurse, a treatment nurse, a skin nurse, a restorative nursing assistant, and a feeding assistant. Certified nursing assistants may take groupings of rooms as an assignment for a variable period. A charge nurse functions as the first-line manager.

One reason why this care delivery system is so widely used is its inherent efficiency, which is desirable in an environment where staffing is kept at the minimum level required by regulation (Sullivan and Decker, 1992).

A team nursing approach is a more integrated care delivery system than functional nursing. The licensed nurse, working with a group of residents numbering from 15 to 50, provides medications and treatments to residents, functions as the charge nurse or first-line supervisor to the certified nursing assistants working on the shift, communicates with physicians, and maintains the required documentation for the residents. The licensed nurse may change the resident group on a scheduled basis, ranging from every week to every month. Certified nursing assistant assignments may change every week or every month.

A third care delivery system is case management, which incorporates the features of team nursing. However, care assignments are permanent for the nursing department staff. Licensed nurses and certified nursing assistants are given authority and accountability for the broad achievement of care outcomes with the group of residents with whom they work. This system is most feasible in an environment where staffing is maintained at a level well beyond the regulatory requirement (Culley and Courtney, 1993).

Regardless of the care delivery system used, the registered nurse practicing in the nursing facility is challenged to work effectively with licensed practical or vocational nurses and certified nursing assistants, incorporating them into a professional practice model of nursing. It is essential that the registered nurse practicing in this setting have excellent supervisory and management skills. The leadership positions in the department of nursing are held by the registered nurse. These positions include the director of nursing services and, increasingly, the director of staff development. Although registered nurses earn an average of 35% less in nursing facilities than in hospitals (Wilging, 1992), they have the opportunity to significantly affect the quality of care and the quality of life of many residents (see Research box at right).

RESEARCH

Kolanowski A et al: Contextual factors associated with disturbing behaviors in institutionalized elders, *Nurs Res* 43(2):73-78, 1995.

Sample, setting

The sample consisted of 586 people age 60 and older from three Philadelphia-area large, nonprofit, religious-affiliated nursing homes.

Methodology

Disturbing behaviors were determined from a behavior subscale of the Psychogeriatric Dependency Rating Scale. Physical characteristics of the environment were measured using room type and physical restraint intensity. Organizational climate was measured using staff mix. The psychosocial milieu was measured using nursing staff burnout scores, staff members' perception of the importance of restraints in care of older people, and the number of alternatives to restraints that staff members could list. Cognitive status was measured using the Folstein Mini-Mental State Examination. Mood was measured using the Cornell Scale for Depression.

Findings

Scores for agitated psychomotor behavior accounted for most of the explained variance in disturbing behaviors. There were significant relationships between the occurrence of agitated psychomotor behavior and greater functional dependency of residents, lower mental status scores, and greater use of psychotropic drugs. There were significant relationships between agitated psychomotor behavior and restraint use, and a staff mix with fewer licensed personnel.

Implications

When staffing ratios are developed, a higher ratio of licensed personnel may reduce the incidence of disturbing behaviors. Residents with disturbing behaviors require a broad base of professional skill and expertise that is best provided by professional-level nursing staff.

Total Quality Management

The essence of **total quality management (TQM)** is the promotion of an intense focus on the customer and customer satisfaction (Raimondo, 1993). The notion of the resident being a customer has been supported by OBRA's emphasis on quality of life, quality of care, and resident autonomy. The institutional long-term care industry has embraced the principles of total quality management as a means of analyzing faulty organizational processes that impede the achievement of desired resident or customer outcomes.

This focus on process is desirable in a setting where interdisciplinary assessment and services must be highly coordinated among departments to achieve quality outcomes. For example, a successful dining program involves coordination among nursing, social services, food services, and housekeeping staff.

For registered nurses in the nursing facility to embrace the principles of TQM, they need to be committed to quality, to view residents as customers, to listen and communicate effectively with staff members, and to aggressively promote team work. Barriers to implementation of TQM include misunderstanding TQM as a program that can be overlaid on traditional management practices rather than recognizing the transformational nature of TQM in the life of the organization. The high number of paraprofessionals, employees having English

CULTURAL AWARENESS

Research on Attitudes Toward Nursing Home Residents Among Aides of Three Cultural Groups

In a study by Robinson (1994), the attitudes toward older adult nursing home clients of 255 nursing home aides from three cultural groups (African Americans, English-speaking Caribbeans, and Haitians) were assessed. The sample was drawn from five nursing homes in the metropolitan New York area. Aides from all three groups had positive attitudes toward the older adults in their care, with the English-speaking Caribbean group expressing the most positive attitudes. Results were interpreted as reflecting the cultural norms of the three groups, which included the infrequent placement of older persons in nursing homes. While the aides believed older adults were valuable and stated that they enjoyed their interactions with residents, they regarded the act of placing an older relative in a nursing home as negative. The researchers concluded that findings suggest a need for inservice workshops in cultural diversity for aides who serve clients from different cultures.

Robinson A: Attitudes toward nursing home residents among aides of three cultural groups, *J Cult Divers* 1(1):16-18, 1994.

as a second language, and the relatively low educational level of employees pose additional barriers. The registered nurse needs to design creative approaches to training employees in the principles of TQM (Raimondo, 1993) (see Cultural Awareness box, above).

SPECIALTY CARE SETTINGS

Assisted Living Programs

Assisting living is one of the fastest growing industries in the United States. Studies estimate that 1.2 million residents in the United States live in 40,000 to 65,000 assisted living facilities. It is an increasingly attractive long-term care setting, placed between home care and the nursing facility in the continuum of long-term care settings (Dewey, 1994). Because assisted living is still developing and is largely unregulated, there is great diversity in the types of service delivery models used and in the types of services offered.

Assisted living settings are homelike and offer an array of services, including meals, assistance with bathing and dressing, social and recreational programs, personal laundry and housekeeping services, transportation, 24-hour security, an emergency call system, health checks, medication administration, and minor medical treatments (Kane, Wilson, 1993).

The nursing contribution to the assisted living setting and resident has been conceptualized as nursing practice being dependent on medicine and as a part of the medical model. Consequently, the nurse is viewed in a functional capacity, as the person to pour medications and provide minor medical treatment.

If nurses were viewed by the assisted living facility as professional nurses view themselves, the nursing contribution could include a much broader and more holistic array of services. The professional nurse could incorporate a wellness and illness model into the assisted living program and help to coordinate the services provided by various departments, such as social services, activities, physical and occupational therapy, housekeeping, and resident relations. This burgeoning long-term care setting provides much opportunity for professional nurses to define their contributions and enhance the services offered to frail older adults living in assisted living facilities.

Special Care Units

Since the late 1980s the popularity of specialized units for demented clients has expanded. A **special care unit** (SCU) is the designation given to freestanding or attached units that specialize in the care of people with Alzheimer's disease and other types of dementing illnesses. Behavioral manifestations of dementia are managed in the environment without the use of chemical or physical restraints whenever possible (Sand, Yeaworth, and McCabe, 1992). As the number of these units have expanded, the National Institute on Aging (NIA) has awarded $2.25 million to nine research teams throughout the United States to explore issues such as the standardization of a definition of SCUs and the impact of the unit programs on residents and others (NIA, 1991).

SCUs have physical environment features that are thought to control stimuli and maximize safety, yet minimize environmental barriers to freedom of movement. Specific admission and discharge policies help to maintain a relatively homogeneous client population. Program features emphasize nutrition, structured daily activities, family involvement, and special staff training in behavioral manifestations of dementia and communication skills with residents (Sand, Yeaworth, McCabe, 1992). An interdisciplinary team coordinates services and care, similar to their participation with residents in the traditional nursing facility.

Employment opportunities for the nurse in the SCU are similar to those of the traditional nursing facility. The SCU is a desirable work setting if the nurse has a particular interest in the health care needs of people with Alzheimer's disease and other dementing illnesses that have behavioral manifestations. Some assisted living settings specialize in serving the cognitively impaired resident. Nurses working with these special resident populations are in a position to provide valuable consultation regarding people with Alzheimer's disease to nurses

RESEARCH

Nystrom A, Segesten K: On sources of powerlessness in nursing home life, *J Adv Nurs* 19:124-133, 1994.

Sample, setting

The sample consisted of 24 clients, age 65 or older, from a Swedish nursing home.

Methodology

Observations of the daily life of clients were made during a period of 6 months, recorded using observational note taking and taped interviews.

Findings

Affection and caring between clients and nursing home personnel were displayed; however, patients often used expressions of powerlessness and hopelessness. The powerlessness experienced by the clients was categorized as being existentially or environmentally derived.

Implications

Providing opportunities for more privacy, physical space for personal belongings, and greater control over resources, time schedules, and choice of personnel are recommended. The nurse is in a key position in the nursing facility to actively promote and advocate for such opportunities.

practicing in other settings, including the hospital, home, and nursing facilities.

Subacute Care

Subacute care, a $1 billion business annually, has become an increasingly popular level of care (Burk, 1994). Its growth has been spurred on by the belief that up to 40% of clients in acute medical or rehabilitation hospital units could be treated as effectively in less costly settings. With increased political awareness of the rising costs of the Medicare and Medicaid programs, the prospect of significant savings provided by subacute care is an attractive one.

Subacute care is an industry category rather than a reimbursement or regulatory category. Currently, there are no licensure or regulatory requirements for subacute care. Professional organizations have developed guidelines for the clinical and business development of this level of care. Care may be reimbursed through the Medicare program, HMO benefits, private payments, or the Medicaid program.

Clients in a subacute unit are stable and no longer acutely ill. They may require services such as rehabilitation, intravenous medication therapy, parenteral nutrition, complex respiratory care, and wound management.

Insight • *The nursing facility has not traditionally been considered a setting in which aggressive rehabilitative services or acute care types of treatments, such as ventilator care and intravenous infusion therapy, are provided. Subacute care is a growing industry in which services such as these are offered to older clients. The development of managed care, HMOs, and the desire to reduce health care expenditures have contributed to the growth of this industry.*

To care for such clients, the nursing staff requires a level of clinical skill beyond what is typically needed in the nursing facility. Staffing levels, particularly related to licensed nurses, are higher in response to the increased client acuity (Gill, Balsano, 1994).

A RESIDENT'S PERSPECTIVE OF LIFE IN A NURSING FACILITY

Rosalie Kane (1990) has characterized nursing facility life as being limited by routine, regulation, and restricted opportunity. G. Janet Tulloch (1995) has described institutional life from a firsthand perspective. She has lived in the Washington Home since 1965, when she was 42. Tulloch has written about the ways in which residents' rights and autonomy, or a sense of control over daily life, may be curtailed and enhanced. Since the registered nurse functions as a leader of the nursing department in the nursing facility, it is worthwhile to listen to the voice of an actual resident, one whose life is directly affected by the actions of nurses and certified nursing assistants.

Tulloch suggests that caregivers not be so quick to judge the behaviors of residents. She suggests avoiding superficial analyses of what may appear to be negative behaviors. Rigid enforcement of residents' rights is recommended.

Tulloch recommends creating an entire environment promoting choice and autonomy. Promoting resident involvement in meaningful relationships and activities is one way to achieve this. Deeply respecting each resident's individuality is another. She cautions against overly professionalizing resident-nurse relationships, so that little room is left for a genuine and mutually beneficial dynamic occurring between these two people. These are important aspects for the registered nurse to keep in mind and work to integrate into clinical and management practice.

Even though the nursing facility often does not look or feel particularly homelike, it is, in fact, the resident's home. Anything that can be done to individualize the resident's living environment and increase opportunities for choice, individual preference, and privacy will benefit the resident (see Research box, p. 956).

FAMILY INVOLVEMENT IN THE NURSING FACILITY

Families can play an essential role in the life of an institutionalized older person, much as they did when the resident was living in the community. Family members provide a social network that connects residents with their former life and with the community at large (Millsap, 1995).

Caregivers need to view the family member as an important contributor to the life of the resident and to the facility. Family members can help staff members interpret resident behaviors in the context of the resident's life history. Better understanding of what it means to be a supportive family member of a resident needs to be pursued (Hofland, 1995). Developing ways to promote communication and a sense of connectedness between a resident and an out-of-town family member is important. A thoughtful nurse can create opportunities for long-distance family relationships to flourish by using the mail and the telephone as a means of staying in touch with one another.

Family members and nursing staff can collaborate effectively with demented residents. Valuable information that otherwise would not be known about a demented resident may be learned through a family member (Anderson et al, 1992).

INNOVATIONS IN THE NURSING FACILITY

Several exciting, innovative programs have developed in nursing facilities over the past 10 years, including the Community College–Nursing Home Partnership, the Teaching Nursing Home Program, the use of geriatric nurse practitioners in the nursing facility, and the Lazarus Project.

The Community College–Nursing Home Partnership

In 1986 a proposal was funded by the W.K. Kellogg Foundation to improve care in nursing facilities through affiliation with nursing students, and to alter the associate degree curriculum to enable graduates to prepare for roles in both long-term and acute care (Sherman and Waters, 1994). Six demonstration sites were developed, which then assisted other ADN programs in making similar curriculum changes. Consequently, 300 second-generation ADN programs have incorporated the teaching of gerontologic nursing and clinical laboratory experience in a nursing facility during the second year of the program. In 1990 the National League for Nursing Council of Associate Degree Programs issued a document identifying the competencies and practice patterns of associate degree nurses, incorporating data from the Community College–Nursing Home Partnership (Sherman, Waters, 1994).

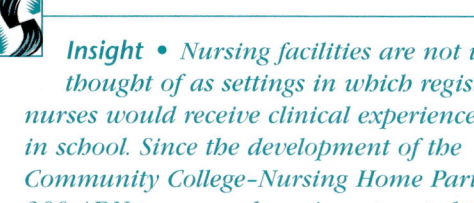

> ***Insight*** • *Nursing facilities are not usually thought of as settings in which registered nurses would receive clinical experience while in school. Since the development of the Community College–Nursing Home Partnership, 300 ADN programs have incorporated the teaching of gerontologic nursing and a clinical rotation in a nursing facility during the second year of the ADN program.*

The Teaching Nursing Home Program

The Robert Wood Johnson Foundation initiated the Teaching Nursing Home Program, which was begun in 1981 and concluded in 1987. The program was intended to serve as a catalyst to improve care in nursing homes by involving nursing schools and highly skilled nurses in the setting (Mezey, Lynaugh, Cartier, 1989). Program staff from the University of Pennsylvania assisted the 11 schools of nursing and 12 nursing homes throughout the United States that participated in the program. Key components of program participation included a shared mission statement, faculty appointment with clinical responsibilities at the nursing facility, opportunities for graduate education, commitment to interdisciplinary care of residents, and fiscal acknowledgment of the affiliation's mission. The book *Nursing Homes and Nursing Care: Lessons from the Teaching Nursing Homes,* written by Mathy, Mezey, Joan Lynaugh, and Mary Cartier in 1989, provides an excellent account of the program.

Geriatric Nurse Practitioners in the Nursing Facility

Over the past 19 years, six studies have been conducted to evaluate the impact of the nurse practitioner (NP) on older adult residents of nursing facilities. Residents under the care of an NP have a lower hospitalization rate compared with comparable groups of residents without an NP. The impact of NPs on quality of care was examined by considering resident functional status, medication use, and the reduction in disruptive behaviors. These variables did not show consistent improvements with the use of an NP. However, overall the NP working with physician backup provides care as good as, if not better than, that provided by the physician working alone (Kane et al, 1989).

The Lazarus Project

In 1989 at the Augustana Home of Minneapolis, a public-community model of governance was adopted by nursing facility residents as a means of promoting autonomy. The broadest purpose of the project was to create a link between citizenship and health care for the older adult that could involve those individuals who were institutionalized. The Lazarus Project was based on the democratic ideal of shared governance. Access to information, emphasis on negotiation, an acceptance of conflict, diversity, and power as part of a vibrant public-spirited environment was promoted (Kari, Hayle, Michels, 1995).

THE FUTURE OF THE NURSING FACILITY

The future of the nursing facility is complicated and uncertain. Its destiny is intimately linked to public policy regarding health care reform, long-term care, and mechanisms of reimbursement. Certain aspects of this service setting are flourishing, including subacute care and SCUs for the cognitively impaired. Some industry analysts believe that the rapidly developing market of assisted living programs will radically change the face of the nursing facility over the next 10 years. It is speculated that the nursing facility will exist to provide care for severely cognitively and physically impaired residents.

Whatever happens, it is essential that the professional nurse play a dominant role in improving and transforming this practice setting. Nurses can better prepare themselves to play this role by becoming better educated in gerontologic nursing, nursing administration, health care regulation, and public policy related to long-term care.

Nurses need to be leaders in helping to transform the traditional nursing home from the rigid and opportunity-restricted institution that it has become to one that promotes resident autonomy and deeply values the individuality of the resident. Professional nurses who conceptualize their practice as including care for the whole person, principles of health promotion and disease prevention, and creative use of the organizational and social environment to achieve health outcomes will make a valuable contribution to society. Through such efforts, and those of other like-minded professionals committed to achieving excellence, the nursing facility will be transformed to a place where people truly can live out their days with dignity, integrity, and a sense of personal autonomy.

Summary

This chapter has presented a variety of issues relevant to long-term care of older people. Care of this type has existed for centuries, evolving into the specialty care settings discussed. Clearly, the entire long-term care industry is not only one of the greatest challenges to society at large, but to all health care professionals.

Recent attempts at regulating nursing facilities for the benefit of the resident's overall health and well-being are an important yet modest step toward reform. The role of professional nurses in continuing reform within this setting must continue to be one of caring and innovative leadership, a difficult and formidable task in view of the tremendous challenges described. Building on the existing innovations that have already been initiated in this unique setting can be a stimulating experience for the committed gerontologic nursing leader who is not intimidated by or apprehensive about the complicated and uncertain future of the nursing facility.

Key Points

- Residents in nursing facilities can be categorized according to their length of stay as short-term residents or long-term residents.
- Risk factors for institutionalization include advanced age, physical disability, mental impairment, Caucasian race, living without a spouse, and the presence of chronic medical conditions.
- The medical model of care emphasizes client compliance, whereas the psychosocial model of care emphasizes resident participation and exercise of choice.
- Resident rights are promoted by the resident council, distribution of consumer information, and the process of informed consent.
- The Minimum Data Set includes a comprehensive and interdisciplinary assessment of the resident.
- The registered nurse plays a key role in all clinical programs, including programs for skin, incontinence, nutrition, infection control, and the promotion of mental health.
- Nursing care delivery systems in nursing facilities vary from functional nursing, to team nursing, to case management.
- Assisted living programs, special care units for dementia, and subacute care units provide unique opportunities for registered nurses wishing to specialize in one aspect of care provided in an institutional setting.
- Family members can be involved in the resident's life by being included in care conferences.
- Recent innovations in the nursing facility involve self-governance programs for residents, nursing education programs, and the use of geriatric nurse practitioners.

Critical Thinking Exercises

1. What is OBRA, and what positive impact is it designed to make on the care of older adults residing in long-term care facilities?
2. A 90-year-old man has fractured his hip and his recovery has been very slow. He has suffered occasional complications, but he is progressing. Why might long-term care be advantageous to him during his recovery process?
3. While talking with several students in your class about future job possibilities, one states, "I'll work anywhere except a long-term care facility. I can't see wasting my education on people who are just waiting to die." What information can you provide that may positively influence the perception of long-term care?

REFERENCES

Aaronson W, Zinn J, Rosko M: Do for-profit and not-for-profit nursing homes behave differently? *Gerontologist* 34:775-786, 1995.

Abbasi A et al: Nutritional problems in the nursing home population: opportunities for clinical interventions. In Rubenstein S, Wieland D, editors: *Improving care in the nursing home: comprehensive reviews of clinical research,* Newbury, Park, Calif., 1993, Sage.

Agich G: *Autonomy and long-term care,* New York, 1993, Oxford University Press.

Anderson K et al: *Patients with dementia: involving families to maximize nursing care,* 18(7):19-25, 1992.

Brannon D: Toward second-generation nursing home research, *Gerontologist* 32(3):293-294, 1992.

Burk S: Defining the challenge: subacute care, *Provider* 2:37-50, 1994.

Case-Gamble A: Urinary incontinence in the elderly. In Stanley M, Gauntlett Beare P, editors: *Gerontological nursing,* Philadelphia, 1995, FA Davis.

Cohen-Mansfield J et al: Assessment and management of behavior problems in the nursing home. In Rubenstein L, Wieland D, editors: *Improving care in the nursing home: comprehensive reviews of clinical research,* Newbury Park, Calif., 1993, Sage.

Culley J, Courtney J: Nursing in the long-term care facility. In Goldsmith S, editor: *Long-term care administration handbook,* Gaithersburg, Md., 1993, Aspen.

Davis M: On nursing home quality: a review and analysis, *Med Care Rev* 48:129-166, 1991.

Dewey J: The shaping of an industry: will the assisted living boom lead to new regulation? *Provider* 20(11):39-42, Nov 1994.

Donabedian A: *The definition of quality and approaches to its assessment,* Ann Arbor, Mich., 1980, Health Administration Press.

Drew-Cates J: Rehabilitation nursing in gerontology. In Stanley M, Gauntlett Beare P, editors: *Gerontological nursing,* Philadelphia, 1995, FA Davis.

Foltz D: Long-term care national database, *Med Rec Newslett* Nov 1994.

Freeman I: Developing systems that promote autonomy: policy considerations. In Kane R, Caplan A, editors: *Everyday ethics: resolving dilemmas in nursing home life,* New York, 1990, Springer.

Gamroth L, Semradek J, Tornquist E: *Enhancing autonomy in long-term care: concepts and strategies,* New York, 1995, Springer.

Gill H, Balsano A: The move toward subacute care, *Nurs Homes* 43(4):7-11, 1994.

Gill C, Howells J, Hoffman E: Rehabilitation in the nursing facility. In Rubenstein L, Wieland D, editors: *Improving care in the nursing home: comprehensive reviews of clinical research,* Newbury Park, Calif., 1993, Sage.

Guralnik J, Simonsick E: Physical disability in older Americans, *J Gerontol* 48(special issue), 1993.

Health Care Finance Administration: *Resident assessment instrument training manual and resource guide,* Baltimore, 1995, The Administration.

Health Care Finance Administration: *Survey, certification and enforcement procedures,* Baltimore, 1994, The Administration.

Hofland B: Resident autonomy in long-term care: paradoxes and challenges. In Gamroth L, Semradek J, Tornquist E, editors: *Enhancing autonomy in long-term care: concepts and strategies,* New York, 1995, Springer.

Hollander Feldman P: Introduction: "dead end" work or motivating job? Prospects for frontline paraprofessional workers in long-term care, *Generations* 28(3):7-12, 1994.

Institute of Medicine: *Improving the quality of care in nursing homes,* Washington, D.C., 1986, National Academy Press.

Jette A et al: High-risk profiles for nursing home admissions, *Gerontologist* 32(5):634-640, 1992.

Kane R: Everyday life in nursing homes: "the way things are." In Kane R, Caplan A, editors: *Everyday ethics: resolving dilemmas in nursing home life,* New York, 1990, Springer.

Kane R: Policy development and quality of care, *J Long-Term Care Admin,* 21(3):29-35, fall 1993.

Kane R: Autonomy and regulation in long-term care: an odd couple, an ambiguous relationship. In Gamroth L, Semradek J, Tornquist E, editors: *Enhancing autonomy in long-term care: concepts and strategies,* New York, 1995, Springer.

Kane R, Caplan A: *Everyday ethics: resolving dilemmas in nursing home life,* New York, 1990, Springer.

Kane R, Kane R: *Long-term care: principles, programs, and policies,* New York, 1987, Springer.

Kane R, Kane R: Reflections on quality control, *Generations,* 13(1):63-69, winter 1989.

Kane R et al, Assessing the effectiveness of geriatric nurse practitioners. In Mezey M, Lynaugh J, Cartier M, editors: *Nursing homes and nursing care: lessons from the teaching nursing homes,* New York, 1989, Springer.

Kane R, Wilson K: *Assisted living in the United States: a new paradigm for residential care for frail older persons?* Washington, D.C., 1993, American Association of Retired Persons.

Kari N, Hayle P, Michels P: The politics of autonomy: lessons from the Lazarus Project. In Gamroth L, Semradek J, Tornquist E, editors: *Enhancing autonomy in long-term care: concepts and strategies,* New York, 1995, Springer.

Lidz C, Arnold R: The medical model and its effect on autonomy: a comparison of two long-term care settings. In Gamroth L, Semradek J, Tornquist E, editors: *Enhancing autonomy in long-term care: concepts and strategies,* New York, 1995, Springer.

Mezey M, Lynaugh J, Cartier M: *Nursing homes and nursing care: lessons from the teaching nursing homes,* New York, 1989, Springer.

Millsap P: Nurses' role with the elderly in the long-term care setting. In Stanley M, Gauntlett Beare P, editors: *Gerontological nursing,* Philadelphia, 1995, FA Davis.

Mitty E: *Quality imperatives in long-term care: the elusive agenda,* New York, 1992, National League for Nursing Press.

National Institute of Aging, *press release,* 1991.

Nick S: Long-term care: choices for geriatric residents, *J Gerontol Nurs* 18(7):11-18, 1992.

Ouslander J, Osterweil D, Morley J: *Medical care in the nursing home,* New York, 1991, McGraw-Hill.

Ouslander J, Schnelle J: Assessment, treatment, and management of urinary incontinence in the nursing home. In Rubenstein L, Wieland D, editors: *Improving care in the nursing home: comprehensive reviews of clinical research,* Newbury Park, Calif., 1993, Sage.

Pozgar G: *Long-term care and the law: a legal guide for health care professionals,* Gaithersburg, Md., 1992, Aspen.

Raimondo: Total quality management. In Goldsmith S, editor: *Long-term care administration handbook,* Gaithersburg, Md., 1993, Aspen.

Rubenstein L, Wieland D: *Improving care in the nursing home: comprehensive reviews of clinical research,* Newbury Park, Calif., 1993, Sage.

Ryden M: Response to personal control and other determinants of psychological well-being in nursing home elders, *Scholar Inq Nurs Pract* 4(2):103-108, 1990.

Sand B, Yeaworth R, McCabe B: Alzheimer's disease: special care units in long-term care facilities, *J Gerontol Nurs,* 18(3):28-34, March 1992.

Schnelle J et al: Managing nurse aides to promote quality of care in the nursing home. In Rubenstein L, Wieland D, editors: *Improving care in the nursing home: comprehensive reviews of clinical research,* Newbury Park, Calif., 1993, Sage.

Semradek J, Gamroth L: Prologue to the future. In Gamroth L, Semradek J, Tornquist E, editors: *Enhancing autonomy in long-term care: concepts and strategies,* New York, 1995, Springer.

Sherman S, Waters V: Community college–nursing home partnerships. In McCloskey J, Grace H, editors: *Current issues in nursing,* ed 4, St. Louis 1994, Mosby.

Shore H: History of long-term care. In Goldsmith S, editor: *Long-term care administration handbook,* Gaithersburg, Md., 1993, Aspen.

Strasen L: Redesigning hospitals around patients and technology, *Nurs Econ* 9:233-238, 1991.

Sullivan E, Decker P: *Effective management in nursing,* ed 3, Redwood City, Calif., 1992, Addison-Wesley.

Toledo S et al: Infections and infection control. In Rubenstein L, Wieland D, editors: *Improving care in the nursing home: comprehensive reviews of clinical research,* Newbury Park, Calif., 1993, Sage.

Tulloch G: A resident's view of autonomy. In Gamroth L, Semradek J, Tornquist E, editors: *Enhancing autonomy in long-term care: concepts and strategies,* New York, 1995, Springer.

US Department of Health and Human Services: *Aging America: trends and projections,* 1991, The Department.

Wilging P: A strategy for quality assurance in long-term care. In Mitty E, editor: *Quality imperative in long-term care: the elusive agenda,* New York, 1991, National League for Nursing Press.

Williams B, Thompson J, Brummel-Smith K: Improving medication use in the nursing home. In Rubenstein L, Wieland D, editors: *Improving care in the nursing home: comprehensive reviews of clinical research,* Newbury Park, Calif., 1993, Sage.

Appendix A

Organizations Providing Resources and Information For and About Older Adults

Administration on Aging
330 Independence Avenue S.W.
Washington, DC 20201
(202) 619-0556

Adult Development and Aging
Gerontology Center
University of Georgia
100 Chandler Hall
Athens, GA 30602
(404) 542-3954

Age and Ageing
Bailliere Tindall
7-8 Henrietta Street
Covent Garden
London, England WCZE 8QE

Alzheimer's Association
919 North Michigan Avenue, Suite 1000
Chicago, IL 60611-1676
(800) 272-3900

Alzheimer's Disease Education and Referral Center
P.O. Box 8250
Silver Spring, MD 20907-8250

American Academy of Home Care Physicians
10480 Little Patuxeny Parkway,
Suite 760A
Columbia, MD 21044
(410) 730-1623

American Academy of Physical Medicine and Rehabilitation
122 S. Michigan Avenue, Suite 1300
Chicago, IL 60603-6107
(312) 922-9366

American Association for Continuity of Care
1730 N. Lynn Street, Suite 520
Arlington, VA 22209
(703) 525-1191

American Association for Geriatric Psychiatry
P.O. Box 376-A
Greenbelt, MD 20768
(301) 220-0952

American Association for International Aging
1133 20th Street N.W., Suite 333
Washington, DC 20036
(202) 822-8893

American Association of Homes and Services for the Aging
901 E Street N.W., Suite 500
Washington, DC 20004-2037

American Association of Homes for the Aging
1129 20th Street N.W., Suite 400
Washington, DC 20036-3489

American Association of Public Health Dentistry (AAPHD)
10619 Jousting Lane
Richmond, VA 23235-3838
(804) 272-8344

American Association of Retired Persons (AARP)
601 E Street N.W.
Washington, DC 20049
(202) 434-2277

American Bar Association Commission on Legal Problems of the Elderly
1800 M Street N.W.
Washington, DC 20036
(202) 331-2297

American Cancer Society National Office
1599 Clifton Road N.E.
Atlanta, GA 30329
(404) 320-3333

American College of General Practitioners
330 East Algonquin Road
Arlington Heights, IL 60005
(800) 323-0794

American College of Healthcare Administrators
325 S. Patrick Street
Alexandria, VA 22314
(703) 549-5822

American College of Nursing Home Administrators
4650 East-West Freeway
Washington, DC 20014

American College of Osteopathic Internists (ACOI)
300 5th Street N.W.
Washington, DC 20002
(202) 546-0095

American College of Physicians
6th Street and Race
Philadelphia, PA 19106
(800) 523-1546 or (215) 351-2400

American Congress of Rehabilitation Medicine
5700 Old Orchard Road
Skokie, IL 60077
(708) 966-0095

American Council of the Blind
1155 15th Street N.W., Suite 720
Washington, DC 20005
(202) 467-5081

American Dental Association
211 East Chicago Avenue
Chicago, IL 60611-2678
(312) 440-2500

American Diabetes Association
Diabetes Information Service Center
1660 Duke Street
Alexandria, VA 22314
(800) ADA-DISC

American Dietetic Association
216 W. Jackson Boulevard, Suite 800
Chicago, IL 60605-6995
(312) 899-0040

American Federation for Aging Research (AFAR)
1414 Avenue of the Americas,
18th Floor
New York, NY 10019
(212) 752-AFAR
(212) 832-2298 (FAX)

American Foundation for the Blind, Inc.
National Office
15th West 16th Street
New York, NY 10011
(212) 620-2000

American Geriatrics Society
770 Lexington Avenue, Suite 300
New York, NY 10021
(212) 308-1414

American Health Care Association
1201 L Street N.W.
Washington, DC 20005-4014
(202) 842-4444

American Heart Association
7320 Greenville Avenue
Dallas, TX 75231
(214) 373-6300

American Hospital Association (AHA)
840 Lakeshore Drive
Chicago, IL 60611
(312) 280-6357

American Lung Association
1740 Broadway
New York, NY 10019-4373
(212) 315-8700

American Medical Association (AMA)
515 N. State Street
Chicago, IL 60610
(312) 464-5000

American Medical Directors Association (AMDA)
10480 Little Patuxeny Parkway,
Suite 760
Columbia, MD 21044
(800) 876-2632

American Nursing Home Association
(see American Health Care Association)

American Occupational Therapy Association
1383 Piccard Drive
P.O. Box 1725
Rockville, MD 20849-1725
(301) 948-9626

American Optometric Association
1505 Prince Street, Suite 300
Alexandria, VA 22314
(703) 739-9200

American Osteopathic Association
142 East Ontario Street
Chicago, IL 60611-2864
(312) 280-5800
(800) 621-1773

American Parkinson's Disease Association
60 Bay Street, Suite 401
Staten Island, NY 10301
(800) 825-2732

American Psychiatric Association
1400 K Street N.W.
Washington, DC 20005
(202) 682-6000
(202) 682-6114 (FAX)

American Psychiatric Nurses' Association
6900 Grove Road
Thorofare, NJ 08086

American Psychological Association
Division of Adult Development
750 First Street N.E.
Washington, DC 20002-4242
(202) 336-5500

American Public Health Association
1015 15th Street N.W.
Washington, DC 20005
(202) 789-5600

American Public Welfare Association
810 1st Street N.E., Suite 500
Washington, DC 20002-4267
(202) 682-0100

American Red Cross
National Headquarters
430 17th Street N.W.
Washington, DC 20006
(202) 737-8300

American Society for Geriatric Dentistry
211 East Chicago Avenue, 17th Floor
Chicago, IL 60611
(312) 440-2500 x 2660

American Society for Parenteral and Enteral Nutrition
8630 Fenton Street, Suite 412
Silver Spring, MD 20910-3805
(301) 587-6315

American Society of Consultant Pharmacists
1321 Duke Street
Alexandria, VA 22314-3563
(703) 739-1300
(703) 739-1321 (FAX)

American Society on Aging
833 Market Street, Suite 512
San Francisco, CA 94103-1824
(415) 882-2910

American Speech-Language-Hearing Association
10801 Rockville Pike
Rockville, MD 20852
(301) 897-5700
(800) 638-8255

ANA Council on Gerontological Nursing
600 Maryland Avenue S.W., Suite 100W
Washington, DC 20024-2571

Arthritis Foundation
1314 Spring Street N.W.
Atlanta, GA 30309

Association of Hospital-Based Nursing Facilities
3500 Masons Mill Business Park, Suite 501A
Huntington Valley, PA 19006
(215) 657-9992

Association of Humanistic Gerontology
1711 Solano Avenue
Berkeley, CA 94707

Association of University Programs in Health Administration Office of Long-term Care and Aging
1911 North Fort Meyer Drive, Suite 503
Arlington, VA 22209
(703) 524-5500

Association for Gerontology in Higher Education (AGHE)
1001 Connecticut Avenue N.W., Suite 410
Washington, DC 20036-5504
(202) 429-9277

Beverly Foundation
70 South Lake Avenue, Suite 750
Pasadena, CA 91101

Catholic Charities USA
1731 King Street
Alexandria, VA 22314
(703) 549-1390

Catholic Health Association of the United States
4455 Woodson
St. Louis, MO 63134-3797
(314) 427-2500

Children of Aging Parents
1609 Woodbourne Road, Suite 302-A
Levittown, PA 19057
(215) 945-6900

Combined Federal Campaign
21 M Street N.W.
Lower Lobby 14
Washington, DC 20037
(202) 488-2087

Commission on Legal Problems of the Elderly
1800 M Street N.W.
Washington, DC 20036
(202) 331-2297

Concern in Care of the Aging
(see American Association of Homes for the Aging)

Consultant Dietitians in Healthcare Facilities
P.O. Box 60
Armada, MI 48005
(313) 784-9766

Consumer Nutrition Hotline
(800) 366-1655

Council of Nursing Home Nurses
600 Maryland Avenue S.W., Suite 100W
Washington, DC 20024-2571

Department of Veterans Affairs
Veterans Health Administration
Nursing Service Programs (118c)
810 Vermont Avenue N.W.
Washington, DC 20420
(202) 299-4000

Design for Aging/Architecture for Health
American Institute of Architects
1735 New York Avenue N.W.
Washington, DC 20006
(202) 626-7361

Dietary Managers Association
One Pierce Place, Suite 1220W
Itasca, IL 60143-3111
(708) 775-9200

Dietitians and Health Care Facilities Consultant
P.O. Box 2067
Pensacola, FL 32513
(414) 432-9224

Elder Health Program
University of Maryland
School of Pharmacy
20 North Pine Street
Baltimore, MD 21201
(410) 328-3243

Family Caregiver Alliance
425 Bush Street, Suite 500
San Francisco, CA 94108

Federal Council on Aging
330 Independence Avenue S.W.,
Room 4280 HHS-N
Washington, DC 20201

Federation of American Health Systems
1111 19th Street N.W., Suite 402
Washington, DC 20036
(202) 833-3090

Food and Drug Administration (FDA)
Professional and Consumer Programs
5600 Fishers Lane, Suite 1685
Parklawn Building
Rockville, MD 20857
(301) 443-5006

Foundation for Hospice and Home Care
519 C Street N.E.
Washington, DC 20002
(202) 547-6586

Geriatric Research and Training Center (GRTC)
350 Masons Mill Road, Suite 501B
Huntington Valley, PA 19006
(215) 657-9993
(215) 657-9547 (FAX)

Gerontological Nutritionists
4103 44th Street
Sacramento, CA 95820
(916) 451-7149

Gerontological Society of America
1275 K Street N.W., Suite 350
Washington, DC 20005-4006
(202) 842-1275

Gray Panthers
1424 16th Street N.W., Suite 602
Washington, DC 20036
(202) 387-3111

Health Care Organization
Division of Long-Term Care
Room 2F5 Oak Meadows Building
Baltimore, MD 21207
(410) 966-6049

Health Resources and Services Administration
Room 1405 HRSA
5600 Fisher Lane
Rockville, MD 20857
(301) 443-2216

Healthcare Financial Management Association
1050 17th Street N.W., Suite 700
Washington, DC 20036
(202) 296-2920

Healthcare Financing Administration
200 Independence Avenue S.W.,
Suite 314G
HHH Building
Washington, DC 20201
(202) 690-6113

Hillhaven Foundation
1148 Broadway Plaza
P.O. Box 2264
Tacoma, WA 98401-2264
(206) 756-4755

House Select Committee on Aging
House Office Building
Annex 1, Room 712
Washington, DC 20515

Institute for Retired Professionals
New School of Social Research
60 W. 12 Street
New York, NY 10011

Institute on Aging
The Medical Center of Central Massachusetts
119 Belmont Street
Worchester, MA 01605
(508) 793-6166
(508) 793-6906 (FAX)

International Federation on Aging
Secretariat - Canada
380 St. Antoine Street W., Suite 3200
Montreal, Quebec H24 3X7
Canada
(514) 987-8191
(514) 987-1948 (FAX)

International Federation on Aging
c/o AARP
601 E Street N.W.
Washington, DC 20006

International Senior Citizens Association, Inc.
537 S. Commonwealth Avenue, Suite 4
Los Angeles, CA 90020
(213) 380-0135

Joint Commission on Accreditation of Healthcare Organizations (JCAHO)
1 Renaissance Boulevard
Oakbrook Terrace, IL 60181
(708) 916-5600

Mental Disorders of the Aging
Research Branch DCR
Room 11 C-03
5600 Fishers Lane
Rockville, MD 20857

Mountain States (Human Services Organization)
950 North Cole Road
P.O. Box 6756
Boise, ID 83704
(208) 322-4880

National Alliance of Senior Citizens
2525 Wilson Boulevard
Arlington, VA 22201

National Arthritis Foundation
P.O. Box 19000
Atlanta, GA 30326
(800) 283-7800

National Asian-Pacific Center on Aging
Melbourne Tower
1511 Third Avenue, Suite 914
Seattle, WA 98101
(206) 624-1221

National Association for Hispanic Elderly
3325 Wilshire Boulevard, Suite 800
Los Angeles, CA 90010-1724
(213) 487-1922

National Association for Home Care
519 C Street N.W.
Washington, DC 20002-5809
(202) 547-7424

National Association for Senior Living Industries
184 Duke of Gloucester Street
Annapolis, MD 21401-2523
(410) 263-0991

National Association of Area Agencies on Aging
1112 16th Street N.W., Suite 100
Washington, DC 20036
(202) 296-8130

National Association of Directors of Nursing Administration in Long-term Care (NADONA-LTC)
10999 Reed Hartman Highway,
Suite 229
Cincinnati, OH 45242
(800) 222-0539

National Association of Home Care
519 C Street N.E.
Washington, DC 20002-5809
(202) 547-7424

National Association of Medical Equipment Suppliers (NAMES)
625 Slaters Lane, Suite 200
Alexandria, VA 22314
(703) 836-6263

National Association of Nutrition and Aging Services Programs
2675 44th Street S.W., Suite 305
Grand Rapids, MI 49509
(616) 531-9909
(800) 999-6262

National Association of Psychiatric Health Systems
1319 F Street N.W., Suite 1000
Washington, DC 20004
(202) 393-6700

National Association of Rehabilitation Facilities
1730 N. Lynn Street, Suite 502
Arlington, VA 22209
(703) 525-1191

National Association of Social Workers
750 First Street N.E.
Washington, DC 20002
(202) 408-8600

National Association of Spanish Speaking Elderly
2025 I Street N.W., Suite 219
Washington, DC 20006

National Association of State Units on Aging
2033 K Street N.W., Suite 304
Washington, DC 20006
(202) 785-0707

National Association of the Deaf
814 Thayer Avenue
Silver Spring, MD 20910-4500
(301) 587-1788
(301) 587-1789 (TTY)

National Bar Association
1225 11th Street N.W.
Washington, DC 20001
(202) 842-3900

National Cancer Institute
Office of Communications
Room 10A24
9000 Rockville Pike
Rockville, MD 20892
(800) 4-CANCER

National Caucus and Center on the Black Aged, Inc.
1424 K Street N.W., Suite 500
Washington, DC 20005
(202) 637-8400

National Center for Nutrition and Dietetics
(see American Dietetic Association)

National Citizens Coalition for Nursing Home Reform
1224 M Street N.W., Suite 301
Washington, DC 20005
(202) 393-2018

National Clearinghouse on Technology and Aging
College of Health and Human Services
Ohio University
Athens, OH 45701
(614) 593-2133
(614) 593-0555 (FAX)

National Committee for Prevention of Elder Abuse
(see Institute on Aging)

National Conference on Geriatric Nurse Practitioners
P.O. Box 270101
Fort Collins, CO 80527-0101
(303) 493-7793

National Consumers League
815 15th Street N.W., Suite 928
Washington, DC 20005
(202) 639-8140

National Council of Senior Citizens, Inc.
1331 F Street N.W.
Washington, DC 20004-1171
(202) 347-8800
(202) 624-9595 (FAX)

National Council on the Aging
(includes National Institute of Senior Citizens and National Institute on Adult Day Care)
409 3rd Street S.W., Suite 200
Washington, DC 20024
(202) 479-1200

National Gerontological Nursing Association
c/o Mosby-Year Book, Inc.
7250 Parkway Drive, Suite 510
Hanover, MD 21076
(800) 723-0560

National Hospice Organization (NHO)
1901 North Moore Street, Suite 901
Arlington, VA 22202
(703) 243-5900

National Indian Council on Aging
6400 Uptown Boulevard N.E.,
Suite 510W
Albuquerque, NM 87110
(505) 242-9505

National Institute of Mental Health Public Inquiries Office
Room 15C-05
5600 Fishers Lane
Rockville, MD 20857
(301) 443-4513

National Institute on Aging
Public Information Office
Federal Building
Room 5C27, Building 31
9000 Rockville Pike
Bethesda, MD 20892

National Interfaith Coalition on Aging
(*see* National Council on the Aging)

National League for Nursing
350 Hudson Street
New York, NY 10014
(212) 989-9393

National Meals on Wheels Foundation
1133 20th Street N.W., Suite 321
Washington, DC 20036
(202) 463-6039

National Mental Health Association
1021 Prince Street
Alexandria, VA 22314-2971

National Osteoporosis Foundation
1150 17th Street N.W., Suite 500
Washington, DC 20036
(202) 223-2226

National Pharmaceutical Council
1894 Preston White Drive
Reston, VA 22091
(703) 620-6390

National Policy Center on Housing and Living Arrangements for the Older Americans
University of Michigan
2000 Bonisteel Boulevard
Ann Arbor, MI 48109

National Rehabilitation Association
633 S. Washington Street
Alexandria, VA 22314
(703) 836-0850

National Senior Citizens Law Center
1815 H Street N.W., Suite 700
Washington, DC 20006
(202) 887-5280

National Stroke Association
8480 East Orchard Road, Suite 1000
Englewood, CO 80111-5015
(303) 771-1700

National Student Nurses Association
555 W. 57th Street, Suite 137
New York, NY 10019
(212) 581-2211

Non-Prescription Drug Manufacturer Association
1150 Connecticut Avenue N.W.
Washington, DC 20036
(202) 429-9260

Occupational Safety and Health Administration
Information and Consumer Affairs
200 Constitution Avenue N.W.
Washington, DC 20210
(202) 523-8151

Older Women's League (OWL)
666 11th Street N.W., Suite 700
Washington, DC 20001
(202) 783-6686

Oncology Nursing Society
501 Holiday Drive
Pittsburgh, PA 15220-2749
(412) 921-7373

Pharmaceutical Manufacturers Association
1100 15th Street N.W.
Washington, DC 20005
(202) 835-3400

Public Health Service
Room 721H
200 Independence Avenue S.W.
Washington, DC 20201
(202) 245-6867

Senate Special Committee on Aging
Dirksen Senate Office Building
Room 623
Washington, DC 20510

Senior Care Centers of America, Inc.
26 E. Second Street A-1
Moorestown, NJ 08057
(609) 778-0624

Social Security Administration
6401 Security Boulevard
Baltimore, MD 21235

Society for Ambulatory Care Professionals (SACP)
(see American Hospital Association)

The Center for Social Gerontology
2307 Shelby Avenue
Ann Arbor, MI 48103-3895
(313) 665-1126

U.S. Department of Health and Human Services
Superintendent of Documents
P.O. Box 371954
Pittsburgh, PA 15250-7954

United States Pharmacopeial Convention, Inc.
12601 Twinbrook Parkway
Rockville, MD 20852
(301) 881-0666

United Way Headquarters
95 M Street S.W.
Washington, DC 20024
(202) 488-2000

Veterans Administration
(see Department of Veterans Affairs)

Video Respite™
Innovative Caregiving Resources
P.O. Box 17332
Salt Lake City, Utah 84117
(801) 272-9446

Appendix B

Journals on Aging

AARP News Bulletin
AARP Fulfillment
AARP Publications
3200 East Carson Street
Lakewood, CA 90712

AARP News Bulletin
American Association of Retired Persons
601 E Street N.W.
Richmond, VA 23235-3838

Age and Ageing
Bailliere Tindall
7-8 Henrietta Street
Covent Garden
London, England WCZE 8QE

Age Page
National Institute on Aging
U.S. Department of Health and Human Services
U.S. Government Printing Office
Washington, DC 20402

Aging
Raven Press
1185 Avenue of the Americas
New York, NY 10036

Aging International
International Federation on Aging
380 St. Antoine Street W., Suite 3200
Montreal, Quebec H24 3X7

American Journal of Alzheimer's Care and Related Disorders and Research
Prime National Publishing Corporation
470 Boston Post Road
Weston, MA 02193

Clinical Gerontologist
Haworth Press
10 Alice Street
Binghamton, NY 13904-1580

Educational Gerontology
Hemisphere Publishing Corporation
1900 Frost Road, Suite 101
Briston, PA 19007

Experimental Aging Research
Taylor and Francis Publishing
1900 Frost Road, Suite 101
Bristol, PA 19007-1598

Experimental Gerontology
Pergamon Press, Inc.
660 White Plains Road
Tarrytown, NY 10591

Generations
American Society on Aging
833 Market Street, Suite 511
San Francisco, CA 94103-1824

Geriatric Nursing
Mosby-Year Book, Inc.
11830 Westline Industrial Drive
St. Louis, MO 63146

Geriatrics
Avanstar Communications, Inc.
7500 Old Oak Boulevard
Cleveland, OH 44130

Gerontologist
Gerontological Society of America
1275 K Street N.W., Suite 350
Washington, DC 20005-4006

Gerontology and Geriatrics Education
Haworth Press, Inc.
10 Alice Street
Binghamton, NY 13904

Gray Panther Network
Gray Panthers
1424 18th Street N.W.
Washington, DC 20036

International Journal of Aging and Human Development
Baywood Publishing Co., Inc.
26 Austin Avenue, Box 337
Amityville, NY 11701

Journal of Aging and Health
Sage Publications
2455 Telber Road
Newsbury Park, CA 91320

Journal of Aging and Social Policy
Haworth Press, Inc.
10 Alice Street
Binghamton, NY 13904

Journal of the American Geriatrics Society
Williams & Wilkins
428 East Preston Street
Baltimore, MD 21202-3993

Journal of Geriatric Psychiatry
International Universities Press, Inc.
59 Boston Road
Madison, CT 06443-1542

Journal of Gerontological Nursing
Slack, Inc.
6900 Grove Road
Thorofare, NJ 08086-9447

Journal of Long Term Care Administration
American College of Health Care Administrators
325 S. Patrick Avenue
Alexandria, VA 22314

Journal of Nutrition for the Elderly
Haworth Press, Inc.
10 Alice Street
Binghamton, NY 13904

Modern Maturity
American Association of Retired Persons (Long Beach)
3200 E. Carson Street
Lakewood, CA 90712

Nurse Practitioner
Vernon Publications, Inc.
3000 Northup Way, Suite 200
Bellevue, WA 98004

Perspective on Aging
National Council on the Aging
409 3rd Street S.W.
Washington, DC 20024

Senior Citizens News
National Council of Senior Citizens
1311 F Street N.W.
Washington, DC 20004-1171

APPENDIX C

NANDA Accepted Nursing Diagnoses

Activity intolerance
Activity intolerance, risk for
Adaptive capacity, decreased: intracranial*
Adjustment, impaired
Airway clearance, ineffective
Anxiety
Aspiration, risk for
Body image disturbance
Body temperature, altered, risk for
Bowel incontinence
Breastfeeding, effective
Breastfeeding, ineffective
Breastfeeding, interrupted
Breathing pattern, ineffective
Cardiac output, decreased
Caregiver role strain
Caregiver role strain, risk for
Communication, impaired verbal
Community coping, potential for enhanced*
Community coping, ineffective*
Confusion, acute*
Confusion, chronic*
Constipation
Constipation, colonic
Constipation, perceived
Coping, defensive
Coping, family: potential for growth
Coping, ineffective family: compromised
Coping, ineffective family: disabling
Coping, ineffective individual
Decisional conflict (specify)
Denial, ineffective
Diarrhea
Disuse syndrome, risk for
Diversional activity deficit
Dysreflexia
Energy field disturbance*
Environmental interpretation syndrome: impaired*
Family processes, altered: Alcoholism*
Family processes, altered
Fatigue
Fear
Fluid volume deficit
Fluid volume deficit, risk for
Fluid volume excess
Gas exchange, impaired
Grieving, anticipatory

*1994 changes

Grieving, dysfunctional
Growth and development, altered
Health maintenance, altered
Health-seeking behaviors (specify)
Home maintenance management, impaired
Hopelessness
Hyperthermia
Hypothermia
Incontinence, functional
Incontinence, reflex
Incontinence, stress
Incontinence, total
Incontinence, urge
Infant behavior, disorganized*
Infant behavior, disorganized: risk for*
Infant behavior, organized: potential for enhanced*
Infant feeding pattern, ineffective
Infection, risk for
Injury, perioperative positioning: risk for*
Injury, risk for
Knowledge deficit (specify)
Loneliness, risk for*
Management of therapeutic regimen, community: ineffective*
Management of therapeutic regimen, families: ineffective*
Management of therapeutic regimen, individual: effective*
Management of therapeutic regimen, individuals: ineffective
Memory, impaired*
Mobility, impaired physical
Noncompliance (specify)
Nutrition, altered: less than body requirements
Nutrition, altered: more than body requirements
Nutrition, altered: risk for more than body requirements
Oral mucous membrane, altered
Pain
Pain, chronic
Parent/infant/child attachment, altered: risk for*
Parental role conflict
Parenting, altered
Parenting, altered, risk for
Peripheral neurovascular dysfunction, risk for
Personal identity disturbance
Poisoning, risk for
Posttrauma response
Powerlessness
Protection, altered
Rape-trauma syndrome
Rape-trauma syndrome: compound reaction
Rape-trauma syndrome: silent reaction
Relocation stress syndrome
Role performance, altered
Self-care deficit, bathing/hygiene
Self-care deficit, dressing/grooming
Self-care deficit, feeding
Self-care deficit, toileting
Self-esteem disturbance
Self-esteem, chronic low
Self-esteem, situational low
Self-mutilation, risk for
Sensory/perceptual alterations (specify) (visual, auditory, kinesthetic, gustatory, tactile, olfactory)
Sexual dysfunction
Sexuality patterns, altered
Skin integrity, impaired
Skin integrity, impaired, risk for
Sleep pattern disturbance
Social interaction, impaired
Social isolation
Spiritual distress (distress of the human spirit)
Spiritual well-being, potential for enhanced*
Suffocation, risk for
Swallowing, impaired
Thermoregulation, ineffective
Thought processes, altered
Tissue integrity, impaired
Tissue perfusion, altered (specify type) (renal, cerebral, cardiopulmonary, gastrointestinal, peripheral)
Trauma, risk for
Unilateral neglect
Urinary elimination, altered
Urinary retention
Ventilation, inability to sustain spontaneous
Ventilatory weaning process, dysfunctional (DVWR)
Violence, risk for: self-directed or directed at others

Glossary

absorption The act of taking up or in, specifically, the passage of the end products of digestion from the gastrointestinal tract into the blood and lymph vessels and cells of the tissues

abuse An act or omission that results in harm or threatened harm to the welfare of an older adult

accident mitigation An action taken after an accident to prevent further occurrence

acculturation A process of cultural change in individuals that leads them to adopt elements from one or more cultural groups distinct from their own

achlorhydria Absence of hydrochloric acid in the gastric secretions

activities of daily living (ADLs) Activities required for independent living, such as eating, toileting, bathing, transferring, walking, and going outside

acute incontinence Incontinence of sudden onset that is generally associated with some medical or surgical condition and that has the potential to resolve when the underlying condition is treated

acute renal failure (ARF) The sudden and usually temporary decrease in glomerular filtration rate, which results in the diminished ability of the kidney to filter and excrete metabolites

adjuvant drugs A medication without intrinsic analgesic properties but is helpful in treating certain types of chronic pain

adult day care A community-based group program that provides structured activities, meals, personal care, health services, and social services during the day to older adults who are physically frail and/or cognitively impaired and who require supervision or assistance with ADLs and IADLs

advance directives (advance medical directives, AMDs) Documents that permit a person to set forth, in writing, wishes regarding health care that are to be used to make such decisions at a time when they are unable to speak for themselves

advocacy The act of supporting a group, an idea, or a cause; professional staff aggressively support and assure quality care for the older adult, and staff members also influence policy making and the development/acquisition of resources that are in the best interest of this age group

afterload The amount of tension created by the ventricles during contraction to eject blood against pressure in the aortic valve and in the pulmonic and circulatory systems

ageism A systematic stereotyping and discrimination against individuals because they are old

aging in place Growing older within a specific environmental setting of choice; as people age and become more independent, they remain "in place" and the environment is modified to meet their changing needs; this environmental modification includes both structural home modifications as well as the provision of informal and formal support services

akathesia A subjective state of motor restlessness in which the person is unable to stay still

alimentary tract or alimentary canal All organs making up the route food takes as it passes through the body from mouth to anus; the digestive tract

alveolar-arterial oxygen gradient Difference between the oxygen level in the alveoli and the level in the blood; the wider the gradient, the less efficient the gas exchange

alveolar macrophage Defense cells of the lung; responsible for engulfing and digesting foreign material in the lung

alveoli Gas-exchanging units at terminal bronchioles

amnesic syndrome Memory impairment in the absence of other cognitive impairments

ampillary disequilibrium Vertigo of disequilibrium caused when the head is turned quickly to the right or left, or by extension or flexion

anaplasia A change in a cell's structure characterized by a loss of differentiation; a characteristic of malignant cells

anemia A reduction in the number of red blood cells or a decrease in quality or quantity of hemoglobin

angiotensin-converting enzyme inhibitors (ACEIs) A drug used to treat hypertension that acts by inhibiting ACEs, which reduces the formation of the pressor substance angiotensin II, and decreases the angiotensin-mediated secretion of aldosterone from the adrenal cortex

angle-closure glaucoma Acute increased intraocular pressure as a result of complete blockage of the flow of aqueous humor

anticholinergic A property of a drug, which exerts side effects including dry mouth, blurred vision, constipation, urinary retention, and acute confusion in older adults

antihepatitis C (anti-HCV) Antibody to the hepatitis C antigen

antihistamine A class of drugs that causes drowsiness, nervousness, restlessness, and changes in mental status or insomnia

antisoporific A drug that inhibits sleep

anuria Diminution of urine secretion to 100 ml or less per 24 hours

anxiolytic A class of drugs considered to be a "minor tranquilizer," which has antianxiety properties, the benzodiazepines are anxiolytic drugs

arteriosclerosis obliterans A gradual narrowing of the arteries with degeneration of the intima and thrombosis

ascites Serious fluid accumulation in the peritoneal cavity

aspiration The inspiration of foreign material (vomitus, mucus) into the airway and respiratory tract

assimilation The disappearance of outward behavior traits that distinguish a minority population or an individual from the host culture; the disappearance of exclusive and discriminatory behavior on the part of the members of the host culture, which permits the minority group or individual to join the host society

asylee An alien in the United States or any port of entry unable or unwilling to return to own country of nationality, or to seek protection of that country because of persecution or well-founded fear of persecution

automaticity The ability to spontaneously initiate impulses

azotemia The presence of nitrogen-containing compounds in the blood

backward heart failure Failure resulting when the ventricle (left or right) fails to eject its contents, resulting in the accumulation of blood in the atria, pulmonary and venous systems, vital organs, and the entire systemic circulation

bacteriuria Presence of bacteria in the urine

band ligation Type of treatment for esophageal varices that uses a rubber band device applied over varices to prevent bleeding

basal energy expenditure (BEE) A formula used to mathematically calculate an individual's estimation of energy needs

behavioral therapies A group of treatments that reduce incontinence through systematic changes in patient behaviors and environmental conditions

benign or rational suicide Suicide by people who perceive that life has no remaining quality; usually takes the form of exhibiting some form of control over the death experience, such as by stopping eating

benign positional vertigo Severe episodes of vertigo precipitated by placing head in a particular position

benign prostatic hypertrophy (BPH) A benign enlargement of the prostate gland

bereavement The state of having experienced a significant loss

beta-blocker A drug used to treat hypertension, ventricular dysrhythmias, and prophylaxis angina; acts by competitively blocking stimulation at beta adrenergic receptor sites, resulting in a decrease in heart rate, force of contraction, and plasma renin, slowed AV conduction, and lowered blood pressure

bibliotherapy A form of behavioral treatment that includes the use of a variety of media materials such as books, pamphlets, audiotapes, and videotapes, which are used by clients in a variety of settings as an adjunct to other treatment modalities

bile Clear yellow/orange liquid produced by the liver and concentrated and stored in the gallbladder

bile canaliculi Vessels found in the liver that carry bile secretions

bile duct Vessel larger than a bile canaliculus that carries bile secretions

biliary system or biliary tract The organs, ducts, etc. that participate in secretion (the liver), storage (gallbladder) and delivery (hepatic and bile ducts) of bile into the duodenum

bilirubin A water-soluble orange bile pigment produced by the breakdown of heme in the bloodstream, taken up by the liver, conjugated, and excreted in the bile; an elevated bilirubin level leads to jaundice

biofeedback A behavioral training technique that (1) detects and measures a physiologic response, (2) amplifies and processes the measured response, and (3) immediately feeds back a form of the response to the client

blepharitis Chronic inflammation of the eyelid margins that is more commonly found in older adults

borborygmi Loud, high-pitched bowel sounds caused by propulsion of gas through the intestines or from increased peristalsis

bronchiole Small airway of the respiratory system; there are two types of bronchioles, terminal and respiratory

bunion A bony deformity of the great toe that appears as a bony protuberance on the side of the toe

caffeine A naturally occurring substance that has central nervous system stimulant properties, including sleeplessness, nervousness, insomnia, tremors, increase in heart rate, and relaxation of bronchial smooth muscles

calcium channel antagonist A drug used to treat hypertension, chronic stable angina, dysrhythmias, and unstable angina that acts by inhibiting influx of extra cellular calcium ions into cardiac muscle and vascular smooth muscle cells; this action results in relaxation of coronary vascular smooth muscle, dilation of coronary and peripheral arteries, and slowed SA/AV node conduction

carcinogenic The ability or tendency to produce or cause cancer

carcinoma A malignant tumor of epithelial cells

caregiver stress/burden The strain or tension associated with the caregiving experience

care manager Health care professional who provides assistance to older people and their families with locating and coordinating services. Care managers can evaluate an older person's situation and needs, establish an interface with health care providers, arrange for needed services, monitor the older person's status and compliance with established treatment plans, provide on-the-spot crisis management, and keep the family informed about progress and changes in the older person's condition and situation

case law (common law) Principles and rules of action that derive their authority from judgments and decrees of the court

case management Providing efficiency in care delivery by developing protocols, mapping out identified time lines for care, assuring appropriate discharge planning, and determining acceptable client outcomes

cataracts Cloudy or opaque areas in part or all of the transparent lens located inside the eye

cerumen impaction Earwax blocking the ear canal

chemotaxis A positive or negative response to a chemical stimulus; in the immune system, neutrophils are attracted toward the bacterial products, damaged tissue and activated components of complement, (a positive response) resulting in the digestion of the bacterium or antigen

chemotherapy A cancer treatment modality that involves the use of drugs to destroy cancer cells with minimum toxicity to healthy cells

cholangitis Inflammation of the bile duct

cholecystokinin (CCK) A hormone secreted in the small intestine that stimulates the gallbladder to contract and the pancreas to secrete enzymes

cholestasis Blockage of bile flow

chordae tendinae The strands of tendon that anchor the cusps of the mitral and the tricuspid valves to the papillary muscles of the ventricles of the heart, preventing prolapse of the valves into the atria during ventricular contraction

chromatin Material within a cell nucleus from which the chromosomes are formed; many of the nuclei of malignant cells contain unusually large amounts of chromatin

chronic illness Impairment lasting at least 3 months with ongoing psychosocial and economic complications requiring health care for support and maintenance of the client's self-care capacity

chronic open-angle glaucoma Increased intraocular pressure from slow degenerative changes in the Schlemm's canal that obstruct the escape of aqueous humor

chronic renal failure (CRF) The permanent loss of kidney function in which the symptomatology is dependent on the extent of failure

chyme A combination of food and gastric secretions formed in the stomach

cilia Hair-like projections responsible for cleaning the lung

circadian rhythm The normal physiologic sleep-wake cycle occurring roughly over a 24-hour period; numerous events may influence the circadian rhythm including travel, time perception, season, light perception, stress, illness, medications and possibly gender

codification The process of collecting and arranging the laws of a country or state into a code or system of law promulgated by legislative authority

cognitive function The combined actions of the cognitive domains, including attention span, concentration, intelligence, judgment, learning ability, memory, orientation, perception, problem solving, psychomotor ability, reaction time or social intactness; a decline in any of the domains can interfere with independent functioning

cohort A group of people who share life experiences such as a particular event or period in history

Colles fracture A fracture of the distal radius

common law *See* case law

competency To be capable of doing a certain thing and/or having the capacity to understand and act reasonably

complement One of 11 enzymatic proteins in blood plasma that act with specific antibodies to destroy corresponding antigens; complement acts by causing lysis of bacteria or foreign proteins

compliance A change in behavior to follow medical or health-related instructions; measure of the distensibility of the lung volume; change in volume/change in pressure

conductivity The ability to transmit an electrical impulse along cell membranes

conscious sedation Type of sedation that uses medications (usually intravenous) to provide relaxation and reduction of pain sensations during medical procedures such as endoscopy

conservator (guardian) A person lawfully invested with the power of taking care of the person and/or managing the property and rights of another person, who, for a reason of age, understanding, or self-control, is considered incapable of managing their own affairs

continuum of care An integrated, client-oriented system of care composed of both services and integrating mechanisms that guides and tracks clients over time through a comprehensive array of health, mental health, and social services, spanning all levels of intensity of care

contractility The ability of cardiac cells to respond to an impulse by contracting

CT scan (computed tomography) An x-ray technique that produces a film representing a detailed cross section of tissue structure

cultural adaptation The process by which a cultural or subcultural group learns to adjust, to cope, or to struggle with modes of behavior and attributes of other cultures to meet cultural expectations, live by desired norms, and/or to survive

cultural blindness Viewing all cultures as the same

cultural conflict Anxiety experienced when people interact with individuals who have different beliefs, values, customs, languages, and ways of life other than their own

cultural ideals The behaviors members of society believe should occur; cultures make allowances for behaviors that differ from the ideal

cultural imposition Imposing personal values, beliefs, and practices on another individual or group

cultural manifest The behaviors, beliefs, and feelings of a group that outsiders can readily observe

cultural negotiation Modifying the health care system to include folk health care practices in the plan of care

cultural relativism Knowledge based on the idea that a client's behaviors or actions within a cultural system have merit and are valid

cultural sensitivity Recognizing, acknowledging, and valuing that behavior patterns vary between and within ethnic groups

cultural shock A state of disorientation, confusion, frustration, and a feeling of helplessness produced by being in a culture markedly different from a person's own

cultural stumbling blocks Negative responses individuals and groups display when they encounter people from other ethnic groups; these responses include cultural blindness, cultural shock, cultural conflict, cultural imposition, ethnocentrism, discrimination, prejudice, racism, and stereotyping

culture Learned and transmitted knowledge about a particular culture, with its values, beliefs, rules of behavior, and lifestyle practices, that guides a designated group in their thinking and actions in patterned ways

curettage The excision of materials from the body with the use of an instrument called a curet

delirium Disturbance of consciousness and a transient change in cognition that develop over a short period; may be associated with a physical change such as illness or medication use; results in difficulty maintaining attention to external stimuli and disorganized thinking; an acute confusional state; reversible disturbance in global cognitive abilities and information processing

delirium tremens (DTs) A severe sign of withdrawal manifested by frightening visual hallucinations, diaphoresis, and seizures; can be fatal

dementia Loss of intellectual abilities including memory, judgment, abstract thought, and changes in behavior and personality of sufficient severity to interfere with functioning; a chronic irreversible change in structure and function of the brain; Alzheimer's Disease is the most common type of dementia in adults

dementia special care unit (DSCU) (or Alzheimer's unit [AU]) A specially designed environment, usually in a nursing facility, that provides individualized care for residents with DAT; these units usually provide specially prepared staff, a safe, secure, comfortable environment, and special programs that provide the appropriate amount of exercise, stimulation, and rest

depression A reversible mood disorder associated with chronic or acute reaction to stressors, various chronic illnesses, medications, or biochemical causes

dermatome Area of the skin innervated by a single posterior spinal nerve

diabetic ketoacidosis A hyperglycemic emergency usually associated with type I diabetes mellitus and characterized by the presence of ketones in the blood and urine

diabetic retinopathy A complication of diabetes that results in the ballooning of the capillaries and arterioles of the retina, that leads to hemorrhaging, scarring, and blindness

diagnosis related group (DRG) A means of categorizing clients to reflect relative intensity of services

diaphragm Major dome-shaped muscle of respiration that separates the thoracic and abdominal cavities

digestion The act or process of the break down of food into chemical substances that can be absorbed into the blood and used by the body tissues

disability Failure to function at an expected level

discrimination The differential treatment of individuals because they belong to a specific racial, ethnic, religious, or social group, the result of which is inequitable experiences and opportunities for the disadvantaged group, and advantages for the perpetrator

disposable income Personal income less personal tax and non-tax payments; the income available for spending and saving

Do Not Resuscitate order (DNR) A specific order from a physician and entered on the physician order sheet that instructs health care providers not to use or to order specific methods of therapy

"dry" macular degeneration (involutional macular degeneration) Break down or thinning of macular tissue related to the aging process; *see also* "wet" macular degeneration

durable power of attorney (for health care decisions) A legal instrument by which a person can designate someone else to make health care decisions at a time in the future when the person may be rendered incompetent; the person delegating the power is called the principal, and the person to whom the power is granted is called the agent

duty Obligatory conduct owed by a person to another person, such as the duty of care owed to a client by the nurse

dysfunctional grieving A grief process that progresses in an unhealthy way and does not move toward resolution

dyspareunia Painful intercourse in a woman

dyspepsia Epigastric discomfort after meals; heartburn; may be associated with reflux

dysphagia Difficulty in swallowing

dyspnea The perception of breathlessness; shortness of breath or difficulty breathing

dyssynergia A condition in which the sphincters contract during bladder contraction, preventing the bladder from emptying

dystonia A movement disorder that is characterized by intense muscle spasms and results in abnormal body posture and movements

ectropion Turning out of the eyelids that prevents normal closure and causes redness and tearing of the eyeball

ejaculation Ejection of the seminal fluid from the male urethra

Elderly Protective Services The range of laws and regulations enacted to protect older adults from and help deal with abusive situations

enculturation The process of acquiring knowledge, and internalizing values and ways of thinking and acting as transmitted by previous generations, to become a competent adult in the select culture of community

endogenous A substance produced by the body, as in the production of insulin from the pancreas

endoscopic retrograde cholangiopancreatography (ERCP) A radiologic test used to visualize the bile and pancreatic duct system

endoscopy Procedure in which a scope is passed to visualize gastrointestinal tissues

entitlement Rights conferred on a person who qualifies by age, disability, income level, etc., such as food stamps

entropion Turning in of the eyelids that results in the eyelashes rubbing against the eye and causing corneal abrasion

ethnic identity The willingness of an individual to identify and embrace the rules, customs, values, history, and perceptions of the group

ethnicity A social differentiation of people based on group membership, shared history, common place of origin, shared values, perceptions, feelings, assumptions, and physical characteristics

ethnocentrism The emotional attitude that a person's own culture or ethnic group has greatest priority, superiority, and worth

euglycemia A normal level of blood glucose

euthanasia Putting to death people with incurable and distressing diseases as an act of mercy; euthanasia is illegal in every state

excitability The ability to respond to a stimulus by generating a cardiac impulse along cell membranes

exogenous Development of a substance from a source outside the body as in the delivery of insulin by injection

extrapyramidal symptoms (EPS) Responses to treatment or drug (e.g., a neuroleptic agent) that mimic the signs of extrapyramidal disease, that is, muscle rigidity, eyes fixed in a deviated position, arched posture, akathisia, akinesia, and perioral tremor

family dynamics The ways and methods family members interact with each other, including the communication patterns, family alliances, and symbiotic relationships

flashers Flashes of light or lightning streaks that appear in the field of vision

flat affect No fluctuations in expression of feeling tones

floaters Tiny spots or specks that float across the field of vision

follicular depletion The emptying of the small sacs that secrete various female sex hormones

forward heart failure Failure resulting when low cardiac ejection in the arterial system leads to poor perfusion and congestion of vital organs, evidenced by mental confusion and muscle weakness; renal, mesenteric, or hepatic insufficiency and shock

functional incontinence Involuntary urine loss resulting from inability or unwillingness to toilet appropriately

functional status The ability of an individual to perform normal, expected, or required activities; in reference to older adults, it is the capacity to perform the self-care activities necessary to live independently such as personal care tasks (ADLs) and complex personal, household, and social tasks (IADLs)

gastroparesis Paralysis of the stomach; the inability of the stomach to empty normally

gavage Feeding through a tube passed into the stomach; tube feeding

geriatric psychiatrist A physician trained as a psychiatrist with special education and experience in diagnosing and treating mental and behavioral disorders in older people

geriatric triad Includes 3 primary concerns with the older adult in the institutional setting: cognitive status, falls, and incontinence

glaucoma An increased intraocular pressure in the eye that results from a blockage in the drainage of the fluid (aqueous humor) in the anterior chamber of the eye

glycosylated hemoglobin A test of blood indicating glucose control levels over the previous 3 to 4 month period

glycosuria Presence of glucose in the urine

gout An arthritic disease in which attacks of arthritis occur as a result of elevated levels of serum uric acid

grab bars Wooden, metal, or plastic supports used in bathrooms to assist a person in using the toilet, tub, and shower; grab bars must be located so they are convenient and should support a 250-pound load; they may be wall-mounted or attached to the toilet or tub

grief The acute reaction to one's perception of loss, incorporating physical, psychological, social and spiritual aspects

guardian *See* conservator

half-life The time it takes for the opioid to decrease to half its initial plasma concentration

hammertoe A deformity in which the second toe has a clawlike position

handicap Follows impairment and is a burden the person must overcome to maintain functional ability

H_2 antagonist A drug that acts by inhibiting histamine (H_2) at the H_2 receptor site in parietal cells, which inhibits gastric acid secretion; used for short-term treatment of ulcers; gastroesophageal reflux disease

haustration The formation of a bag-like sac or pouch of the colon

HbA_{1c} A measurement of glycosylated hemoglobin that reflects the stability of glucose levels in the body for 100 to 120 days before test date

health care agent A trusted person designated to express a person's wishes regarding the withholding or withdrawal of life support

healthy death The culmination of the dying process in which the dying person's physical comfort, psychosocial, and spiritual needs are met

hematemesis The vomiting of blood; its appearance depends on the length of time blood has been in the stomach. Since the gastric acids change bright red blood to a brownish or coffee-ground color, bright red blood in the vomitus indicates a fresh hemorrhage and little contact of the blood with gastric juices

hematocrit Percentage of total blood volume represented by erythrocytes

hepatitis C virus The causative RNA viral agent resulting in hepatitis C infection

hepatocyte A parenchymal cell of the liver

home care Multiple health and social services that are delivered to recovering, chronically ill or disabled individuals, of all ages, in their places of residence; most older adult home health care services are funded through the Medicare program, which targets its services to people with short-term, medically oriented needs, usually following a hospitalization

hospice care Hospice offers comprehensive programs of health care in home or institutional settings for people in the final stages (usually the last 6 months) of a terminal illness; hospice is usually available 24 hours a day, 7 days per week and provides palliative care (e.g., pain control, symptom management, and comfort measures) to enhance the quality of remaining life, as well as social, psychologic, and spiritual care services for the client and family

human leukocyte antigens (HLA) Histocompatibility antigens found on the surface of nucleated cells

hypercapnia Abnormal elevation of carbon dioxide in the blood

hypercholesterolemia Abnormally high levels of cholesterol

hyperosmolar hyperglycemic nonketotic coma (HHNC) A syndrome of severe hyperglycemia and dehydration most commonly associated with type II diabetes mellitus

hypnotic A drug that produces drowsiness and facilitates the onset or maintenance of sleep

hypopnea Shallow or slow breathing

hypothyroidism A clinical state of thyroid hormone deficiency

hypoxemia Abnormally low oxygen level in the blood

iatrogenic illness Illness or complications that result not from the initial disease process, but rather from the medical treatments that were meant to be therapeutic

immune gamma globulin (IgG) One class of immunoglobulins that is primarily involved in the recall immune response

impairment Pathophysiologic condition that does not always result in a secondary disability

impotence Inability of the male to achieve and maintain erection

informal caregiver Provides *unpaid* assistance to another person who has some degree of physical, mental, emotional, or economic impairment that limits independence and necessitates ongoing assistance; caregivers *provide* and/or *coordinate* services and resources that are needed by the impaired person to remain in the home and community

informed consent The process by which a competent individual is provided with information enabling them to make a reasoned decision about any treatment or intervention that is to be done to them

interdisciplinary care Care provided by a diverse team of professionals from several disciplines who collaborate to optimize care and decrease fragmentation of professional services

jaundice Yellowness of skin, sclerae, mucous membranes and secretions as a result of elevated bilirubin in the bloodstream; also called icterus; it is not a disease but a symptom

ketones/ketone bodies The substances acetone, acetoacetic acid, and β-hydroxybutyric acid produced from lipid metabolism

Kupffer's cells Phagocytic cells lining the venous sinusoids of the liver

lactose A sugar derived from milk; many people are lactose intolerant as a result of a hereditary lactase deficiency, whereby they lack the enzyme in the mucosa of the small intestine needed to break down lactose

lithogenic Stone forming

living will An instrument intended to provide written expression of a client's wishes regarding the use of medical treatment in the event of a terminal illness or condition

locus of control The idea of being in charge of one's life; significant to neutralizing loss of identity and ego strength

long-term care A collection of health, personal, and social services provided over a prolonged period to people who have lost or never acquired functional capacity; long-term care for older adults consists of three major types of services: (1) *formal institutional* services, primarily nursing home care; (2) *formal noninstitutional* services such as home health care, adult day care, hospice, respite, and nutrition services; and (3) *informal noninstitutional* services provided by family and friends

low-residue diet A diet low in fiber

macular degeneration Damage to the macula, the key focusing area of the retina with a resulting decline in central visual acuity

macular disequilibrium Vertigo precipitated by a change of head position in relation to the direction of gravitational force (e.g., severe dizziness when rising from bed)

Medicaid A joint federal-state program (configured differently from state to state) to provide funds to the deserving poor: those people whose income and assets fall below certain levels and who are aged, blind, disabled, or members of families with dependent children

Medicare A health insurance program available to social security and railroad retirement recipients who are over the age of 65 or disabled; administered by the Health Care Financing Administration of the Department of Health and Human Services

melena Dark stools/feces as a result of blood pigments; it indicates bleeding somewhere in the gastrointestinal tract

Meniere's disease Pressure in the labyrinth of the inner ear caused by excess endolymph that causes swelling in the cochlea

mesenteric Pertaining to the membranous fold attaching various organs to the body wall, specifically referring to the membrane which connects the small intestine to the abdomen

metastasis The process by which tumor cells are spread to distant parts of the body

minimum data set A component of the resident assessment instrument; it is a tool that includes a comprehensive assessment of the resident, including both physical and psychosocial assessment

monoamine oxide inhibitors (MAOIs) A class of antidepressants that have a profound effect on sleep by suppressing REM sleep

motility The movement of food/chyme through the digestive tract

mourning A long-term process of resolving acute grief reactions

negentropy A process in open systems which leads to increasing order and complexity in the system

negligence The omission to do something that a reasonable person, guided on those considerations that ordinarily regulate the conduct of human affairs, would do, or the omission to do something that a prudent and reasonable person would not do; a breach of duty

nephropathy Complication of diabetes mellitus characterized by proteinuria, hypertension, edema, and renal insufficiency

neuroglycopenic Moderate to severe symptoms of hypoglycemia including somnolence, slurred speech, agitation, confusion, and coma

neuroleptic Another term for an antipsychotic medication; mechanism of action is blocking the action of dopamine, a sympathomimetic catecholamine involved in nerve impulse transmission in extrapyramidal motor system pathways

neuroleptic malignant syndrome (NMS) A rare but serious side effect of high-potency antipsychotics that may lead to death; initial symptoms include a decreased temperature, the development of EPS, and delirium; if untreated, it progresses to hyperthermia, stupor, severe EPS, and coma

neuropathy Complication of diabetes mellitus involving nerve damage to myelinated nerve fibers

nocturia Awakening at night to avoid

non-REM The first stage of sleep characterized by slow wave sleep; following the normal awake state, the stages of sleep include stage I: descending sleep; stage II; unequivocal sleep; stage III: deep wave sleep, and stage IV: cerebral sleep

nonsteroidal antiinflammatory drug (NSAID) A drug that decreases prostaglandin synthesis by inhibiting an enzyme needed for biosynthesis; used to treat mild to moderate pain

normative aging Usual or functional aging

nursigenic illness Illness or abnormal state induced by inadvertent or erroneous nursing interventions

nursing facility Commonly described as a nursing home; the terms *skilled nursing facility* and *intermediate care facility* have been replaced by this term

obstructive lung disease Respiratory disease characterized by decreased airway size, decreased airflow, and increased airway secretions

Older Americans Act Legislation passed by congress and signed into law by President Lyndon Johnson on July 14, 1965. The act provides services for older people through programs and grants for social services, research and demonstration projects, and personnel training; it also established the Administration on Aging in the Department of Health, Education, and Welfare

oliguria Diminution of urinary secretion to between 100 ml and 400 ml in 24 hours

ombudsman An official advocate for a certain group of people; usually investigates complaints

Omnibus Budget Reconciliation Act of 1987 (OBRA '87) Landmark federal legislation affecting nursing facilities which imposes standards governing the care of older adults in U.S. nursing facilities

oncogene A potential cancer-inducing gene

onychauxis Hypertrophic toenails in which the nail borders curve into the soft tissue of the toe

opioid-naivé A client who had not had prior exposure to opioids

opsonization A process in which antibodies and complement coat the surface of antigens, making them more vulnerable to phagocytosis

oral hypoglycemic agents Medications used in type II diabetes mellitus to help obtain and maintain euglycemia

osteoarthritis (degenerative joint disease) A noninflammatory disease of weight-bearing joints that is characterized by progressive deterioration of articular cartilage

osteomyelitis An infection of the bone

osteoporosis A metabolic bone disease that is characterized by a gradual decrease in bone mass

overflow incontinence Involuntary urine loss from a chronically full bladder

over-the-counter (OTC) medication A drug that can be purchased without a physician's prescription

Paget's disease An inflammatory disease of the bone in which both osteoblast and osteoclast proliferate, resulting in bony deformities

pain distress A measurement of the extent to which pain affects a client

pain intensity A measurement of the amount of pain that a client is experiencing

paranoid personality disorder A psychiatric disorder characterized by extreme suspiciousness and distrust; client is withdrawn, reserved, fearful, and secretive, and exhibits isolated behavior; factors thought to play a role in its development in older people include medications, sensory impairment, powerlessness, helplessness, and increased dependence

paraphrenia A late-onset delusion of persecution that usually occurs more often in women; cause is unknown, but sensory impairments are believed to play a role

parenchyme The cells of an organ that are supported by a connective tissue system

pelvic floor muscles A group of muscles, including the pubococcygeal muscle, that surround the rectum, the vagina in women, and the urethra; these muscles support pelvic floor structures and provide external sphincter control for the urethra

pension A regular payment made to a person who has fulfilled certain conditions such as retirement after a certain number of years of service

periodontitis Inflammation of the gums and tissues supporting the teeth

peristalsis Rhythmic, wave-like, muscular contractions or movements by which the digestive tract propels its contents

peritonitis Inflammation of the peritoneum from inflammation of abdominal organs, perforation, or rupture of a cyst or organ

persistent incontinence Incontinence that is not related to an acute illness and is persistent over time

PET scan (positron emission topography) A computerized radiographic technique that examines the metabolic activity of various body structures

pharmacokinetics The process by which drugs are absorbed, distributed, metabolized, and excreted

photo-oncogene A genetically transmitted precursor to an oncogene; when cancer develops, the photo-oncogene has been altered or damaged to allow expression of the oncogene

physiologic dead space Area in the lung that does not participate in gas exchange; includes the anatomical dead space and the portion of the alveoli that does not exchange oxygen and carbon dioxide

placebo Any medical treatment or nursing care that produces an effect in a client because of its implicit or explicit intent and not because of its specific nature or therapeutic properties

polydispia Excessive thirst

polymyalgia rheumatica A chronic inflammatory condition that is characterized by sudden onset of stiffness and aching in the neck, shoulder, and hip girdle

polyphagia Increased ingestion of food

polypharmacy The prescription, use, or administration of more medications than indicated clinically; this combined use of drugs may have untoward effects on the client

polyuria Excessive secretion of urine

poverty level The poverty index in the United States is based on monetary income and the department of Agriculture's 1961 Economy Food Plan; it reflects the different consumption requirements of families based on their size and consumption; poverty thresholds are updated every year to reflect changes in the consumer Price Index

poverty of speech Decreased amount and quality of verbal communication

powerlessness Feeling or thought that one has no choice over events; perception that stressors are unalterable

prejudice A hostile attitude toward individuals simply because they belong to a particular group assumed to have objectionable qualities

preload The stretch of myocardial fiber at end diastole

presbycusis Bilateral sensorineural hearing loss, resulting in hearing high-pitched tones and conversational speech

presbyesophagus Impaired esophageal function as a result of aging

presbyopia Diminished ability to focus on close objects or to see small print; common after age 40

primary biliary cirrhosis (PBC) A chronic inflammatory condition of the liver leading to blockage of bile flow

pro-drug A drug that is not active until it is metabolized by the liver to an active chemical compound

proprioception The ability to maintain an upright position without falling, using posture, balance, and movement

Prospective Payment System (PPS) The program to pay for care prospectively with per case payments based primarily on client diagnosis

prostate-specific antigen (PSA) A glycoprotein secreted by the prostate gland; elevations may occur in men with prostate cancer

proteinuria Presence of protein in the urine

proteolytic Characterized by or promoting the break down of proteins

pseudohyponatremia A condition of low sodium levels in the presence of normal osmolarity

psychological autopsy Processing the events and behaviors surrounding a client's suicide

psychotropic agent A drug that is psychoactive, exerting effects on brain function, behavior, or experience, as well as modifying mental activity; generally includes anxiolytics, antipsychotics, antidepressants, and sedative/hypnotic agents

quality of life A multidimensional concept that includes physical well-being, psychological well-being, social well-being, and spiritual well-being; the quality of life model provides a means for assessing the impact of disease and treatment on the client

race A division of the species that differs from other divisions by the frequency with which certain hereditary traits appear among its members

racism The belief that a race is by nature superior to another; it is the combination of the hostile attitude of prejudice and the differential treatment and behavior of discrimination directed at a specific ethnic or minority group

radiation A cancer treatment modality used for its curative effects and to control the growth of cancer cells when a cure is considered impossible

recidivism A tendency to relapse, indicated by a hospital readmission within a short period for the same diagnosis as a result of lack of progress or deterioration in condition

refractory period The brief period of relaxation of muscle during which excitability is depressed; if stimulated, it will respond, but a stronger stimulus is required, and response is less

regulations Rules of action and conduct often developed to explain and interpret statutes and to prescribe methods for carrying out statutory mandates

rehabilitation Restoration of a person with a disability to the fullest potential of which he is capable

REM A stage of sleep characterized by rapid eye movements, body movements increasing, and a generalized state of stressfulness with increases in respiration, heart rate and blood pressure; the REM cycle follows the non-REM stage

resident assessment instrument An interdisciplinary method of resident assessment and care plan development used by all nursing facilities participating in the Medicare and Medicaid programs

resident assessment protocol A component of the resident assessment instrument; it is a tool to assist in the identification of resident problems and the development of the plan of care

resistance A condition in which tissue response to hormones is inadequate, as in insulin resistance or thyroid hormone resistance

respite Respite provides short-term relief or time off for people providing home care to an ill, disabled, or frail older adult; may be provided at home or in institutional settings; respite staff includes both health professionals and trained volunteers

restless leg syndrome A form of periodic leg movement in which a person subjectively experiences restlessness of the legs and difficulty keeping the legs still. This may be from diseases of the spine, degenerative joint disease of the disks, or peripheral vascular disease among others

restrictive lung disease Respiratory disease characterized by decreased expansion of the lungs and/or thorax resulting in decreased lung volumes and capacities

retinal detachment The sensory layer of the retina separates from the pigmented layer

retinopathy An ocular complication of type II diabetes mellitus associated with changes to blood vessels, hemorrhage, and detachment of the retina

rheumatoid arthritis A chronic, systemic, inflammatory disease that causes joint destruction and deformity

sanctions A penalty or punishment provided as a means of enforcing a law or regulation

sarcoma A malignant tumor of connective tissue cells

schizophrenia A thought disorder characterized by an altered perception of reality, alterations in thought processes (both content and form), and a decline in performance of activities of daily living, as well as occupational and social functioning

secondary glaucoma Increased intraocular pressure when the drainage angle is damaged by eye injury, medications, or specific conditions such as tumors, inflammation, or abnormal blood vessels

secretion The process of synthesis and release of a substance

sedative A drug that decreases activity and has a calming effect

selective serotonin reuptake inhibitor (SSRI) A class of anti-depressants which may affect sleep by causing insomnia, somnolence, agitation or nervousness

self monitoring of blood glucose (SMBG) The testing of blood glucose values by the client with diabetes mellitus, utilizing visual or meter systems

sensorimotor function Ability to use the senses of vision, hearing, smell and touch independently and in a combined manner to perceive within the environment and adapt in the event of loss

septicemia A condition in the blood caused by bacterial or fungal infections

seroconversion Antibody development after exposure to infection or immunization

serum albumin An indicator of protein nutrition; in older adults, low albumin levels can increase the risk of mortality

sex hormone A substance originating in an organ, gland, or part, that is conveyed through the blood to another part of the body, stimulating it by chemical action to increased functional activity of the sexual system or to increase secretion of another hormone (e.g., testosterone, estrogen, and progesterone)

sexual deviance Sexual behavior that is considered abnormal or socially unacceptable

sexual dysfunction State in which an individual's sexual health or function is viewed as unsatisfying, unrewarding, or inadequate

sexual orgasm A state of physical and emotional excitement that occurs at the climax of sexual activity

sleep A physiologic state in which the person is achieving rest for the body and mind; sleep is natural and reoccurring

sleep apnea Cessation of breathing during sleep that may vary from mild to severe forms in which depression, cardiac arrhythmias, or hypertension may develop

social agent An individual who participates in social change, particularly in public policy making, to ensure optimum decisions regarding a certain issue or population, such as decisions regarding older adults

soporific A drug that promotes sleep

space of Disse Site located under the endothelial cells of the venous sinusoid of the liver

special care unit A specialized unit that is adapted both physically and operationally to the unique needs of the demented older person

spider angioma Vascular and purpuric lesion of the skin characterized by red and sometimes raised discolorations resembling fine spidery marks

splanchnic Pertaining to the viscera; any large organ in the abdomen

standard A measure against which conduct is compared to ascertain conformity to an accepted or established level of performance

static balance The ability to stand in place without assistance

statutes Laws created by legislation that can be enacted at the federal and state level

steatorrhea Fatty stools

stereotype A rigid, preconceived idea, opinion, attitude, or belief about a cultural group that is applied indiscriminately to all of its members

stomatitis Inflammation of the mucous membranes of the oral cavity

stress incontinence Involuntary urine loss occurring as a result of a sudden increase in intraabdominal pressure

subculture A fairly large aggregation of people who are members of a larger cultural group, and who have shared characteristics that are not common to all members of the culture, enabling them to be thought of as a distinguishable subgroup

substance abuse A maladaptive pattern of substance use manifested by recurrent and significant adverse consequences related to the repeated use of substances

substance dependence A cluster of cognitive, behavioral, and physiologic symptoms indicating that the individual continues use of the substance despite significant substance-related problems

successful aging A more efficient state of wellness that is free of chronic disease

sundowning A behavior that has been observed among individuals with dementia to occur as the sun goes down; it is characterized by worsening confusion, agitation, and motor restlessness such as wandering or pacing

supplemental security income (SSI) A federal program conducted by the Social Security Administration that pays monthly checks to people who are aged, disabled, or blind and who do not have many resources or much income

supplementation Dietary addition that differentiates between intensified malnutrition and possible resulting illness, and nutrition adequacy

tardive dyskinesia (TD) A potential permanent, neurologic side effect of neuroleptic medications characterized by involuntary movements especially of the face, lips, and tongue; the trunk and extremities may also be involved; it is most likely to develop in clients who have used neuroleptics for more than 2 years; no effective treatment exists

tinnitus Subjective sensation of noise in the ear defined as ringing, buzzing, or hissing

total quality management (TQM) A management approach that emphasizes an intense focus on the customer and customer satisfaction with the delivery of a service

transcultural nursing The subfield of nursing that focuses on a comparative study and analysis of different cultures and subcultures in the world with respect to their caring behavior, nursing care, health-illness values, beliefs, and patterns of behavior with the goal of developing a scientific and humanistic body of knowledge in order to provide culture-specific and culture-universal nursing care practices

transit time The time taken for food to pass through the small and large intestines; a longer or increased transit time slows the passage of food/chyme/feces through the intestines, whereas in a shorter or decreased transit time, food/chyme/feces transits quicker

translocation Displacing or dislocating a person from familiar surroundings

tricyclic antidepressant A class of antidepressants that may exert some degree of sedation, ranging from mild to moderate to strong, depending on the chemical structure

urge incontinence Involuntary urine loss associated with a sudden urge to void

urinary incontinence (UI) Involuntary loss of urine

vaginismus Painful spasm of the vagina from contraction of the surrounding muscles

values A standard or criterion for guiding action, developing and maintaining attitudes toward relevant objects and situations, justifying one's own and others' actions and attitudes, morally judging self and others, and comparing self with others

values history An instrument that asks questions related to quality versus length of life that a person sees as important to maintain during terminal care; as an adjunct to the end-of-life decision-making process, it can be used to offer insight into a person's own values or underlying beliefs regarding the preparation and explanation of their advance medical directives

varices Engorged blood vessels often found in the esophagus

vestibular ataxia of aging Constant feeling of imbalance with ambulation

visual feedback training Using visual cues to perform nursing interventions with hearing-impaired older adults

wellness Dynamic series of processes perceived as an active state of becoming and continually working to create harmony among spiritual, affective, physiologic, psychologic, and social well-being

"wet" macular degeneration (exudative macular degeneration) Abnormal blood vessels form and hemorrhage on the retina; *see also* "dry" macular degeneration

Whipple procedure The surgical removal of the distal one third of the stomach, the entire duodenum and the head of the pancreas (a pacreatoduodenectomy), requiring three subsequent anastamoses: gastrojejunostomy, choledochojejunostomy, and pancreatic jejunostomy, often done for pancreatic cancer

xerostomia Common age-related condition affecting taste that involves a decrease in salivary production that leads to thicker mucus and a dry mouth

Index

T

S

Q

R

N

E

D

C

U

V

W

X

Y

Z